MW01077897

The Oxford Handbook of Stress and Mental Health

OXFORD LIBRARY OF PSYCHOLOGY

The Oxford Handbook of Stress and Mental Health

Edited by

Kate L. Harkness

Elizabeth P. Hayden

OXFORD
UNIVERSITY PRESS

2020

OXFORD
UNIVERSITY PRESS

Oxford University Press is a department of the University of Oxford.
It furthers the University's objective of excellence in research, scholarship,
and education by publishing worldwide. Oxford is a registered trade mark of
Oxford University Press in the UK and certain other countries.

Published in the United States of America by Oxford University Press
198 Madison Avenue, New York, NY 10016, United States of America.

Library of Congress Cataloging-in-Publication Data
Names: Harkness, Kate L., editor. | Hayden, Elizabeth P., editor
Title: The Oxford handbook of stress and mental health / edited by
Kate L. Harkness, Elizabeth P. Hayden.
Description: New York, NY : Oxford University Press, [2020] |
Series: Oxford library of psychology | Includes bibliographical references and index.
Identifiers: LCCN 2019026861 (print) | LCCN 2019026862 (ebook) |
ISBN 9780190681777 (hardback) | ISBN 9780190681784 | ISBN 9780190681791 (epub)
Subjects: LCSH: Stress management—Handbooks, manuals, etc. |
Stress (Psychology)—Treatment. | Mental illness—Treatment.
Classification: LCC RA785 .O937 2020 (print) | LCC RA785 (ebook) | DDC 155.9/042—dc23
LC record available at https://lccn.loc.gov/2019026861
LC ebook record available at https://lccn.loc.gov/2019026862

9 8 7 6 5 4 3 2 1

Hardback printed by Marquis, Canada

ACKNOWLEDGMENTS

I (Kate Harkness) would like to sincerely thank my dear friend and partner in this project, Elizabeth Hayden. Working with Elizabeth is always fun and intellectually engaging, and this volume is greatly enriched by her deep thinking and keen insights. We would both like to thank our Editor at Oxford University Press, Sarah Harrington, for her tireless and enthusiastic support of this project from its very earliest stage through to production. I would also like to thank my close colleague and mentor, Scott Monroe, for his unflagging encouragement and friendship, and for instilling in me a love of stress research. I would also like to acknowledge the many gifted and committed students at Queen's University who have enriched my thinking about stress and made my job fun, especially Margaret Lumley, Jeremy Stewart, Raegan Mazurka, Cherie Larocque, and Simone Cunningham. Finally, my deepest gratitude goes to my partner in all things, Mark Sabbagh, and our children, Pablo and Ruby. I would not be the scientist or person I am without their encouragement, support, and love.

I (Elizabeth Hayden) would like to express my gratitude to my very close friend and colleague, Kate Harkness, for inviting me to work with her on this volume. This project has been an exceptionally rewarding experience, and as always, my own scholarship has been enriched through collaboration with Kate. I would also like to thank Dan Klein, Emily Durbin, Ted Beauchaine, Thomas Olino, and Lea Dougherty for their long-standing support and friendship. In particular, not just my career but my life overall would be much less rewarding and interesting without Dan's unflagging mentorship. I would also like to thank the tremendously talented and dedicated young psychological scientists with whom I have had the pleasure to work, especially Yuliya, Pan, Matt, Ola, Andrew, and Lindsay, given their dedication to the lab while this book has been in production. Finally, I would like to thank my husband, Jeremy Hake, who has tirelessly encouraged me to pursue my career goals. I wish all female academics and scientists had such supportive partners.

CONTENTS

ABOUT THE EDITORS

Kate L. Harkness is a Professor in the Departments of Psychology and Psychiatry at Queen's University. Her research programme is focused on understanding how stress exposures throughout the lifespan lead to critical changes in biological and psychological mechanisms that cause and maintain depression. She is an associate editor for *Journal of Abnormal Psychology*. Her research has been funded by the Canadian Biomarker Integration Network for Depression, the Canadian Institutes of Health Research, the Ontario Mental Health Foundation, the Social Sciences and Humanities Research Council of Canada, and the Sick Kids Foundation.

Elizabeth P. Hayden is a Professor in Psychology at the University of Western Ontario and the Brain and Mind Institute. Her research interests include understanding the developmental processes that lead to mental health problems across the lifespan, as well as developing novel assessment and measurement approaches to improve early identification of vulnerability to psychopathology. She is an associate editor for *Psychological Assessment*. Her research has been funded by the Canadian Institutes of Health Research, the Natural Sciences and Engineering Research Council of Canada, the Social Sciences and Humanities Research Council of Canada, and the National Institute of Mental Health.

CONTRIBUTORS

Lauren B. Alloy
Department of Psychology
Temple University

Elizabeth N. Aslinger
Department of Psychology
University of Pittsburgh

Gordon J. G. Asmundson
Department of Psychology
University of Regina

Deanna M. Barch
Departments of Psychological & Brain
Sciences, Psychiatry, and Radiology
Washington University in St. Louis

Corinne P. Bart
Department of Psychology
Temple University

J. Gayle Beck
Department of Psychology
University of Memphis

Blessy Bellamy
Department of Psychology
University of Pittsburgh

George Bonanno
Department of Counseling and Clinical
Psychology
Columbia University

Dante Cicchetti
Institute of Child Development
University of Minnesota

Bruce E. Compas
Department of Psychology
Vanderbilt University

Elisabeth Conradt
Department of Psychology
University of Utah

Christopher C. Conway
Department of Psychology
Fordham University

Gail Corneau
Department of Psychology
University of North Carolina, Greensboro

Alexandra F. Corning
Department of Psychology
University of Notre Dame

Joanna Crawford
St. Vincent's Urban Mental Health
and Wellbeing Centre
St. Vincent's Hospital

BreAnne A. Danzi
Department of Psychology
University of Miami

Terrence Deak
Department of Psychology
Binghamton University-State University
of New York

Samantha Denefrio
The Graduate Center
The City University of New York

Tracy A. Dennis-Tiwary
Hunter College
The City University of New York

Philip A. Desormeau
Department of Psychology
University of Toronto Scarborough

Maria Ditcheva
Department of Psychology
University of North Carolina, Greensboro

Thomas S. Dodson
Department of Psychology
University of Memphis

Jenalee R. Doom
Department of Pediatrics
University of Michigan

Elizabeth A. Edershile
Department of Psychology
University of Pittsburgh

Reneé El-Gabalawy
Department of Psychology
University of Manitoba

Bruce J. Ellis
Department of Psychology
University of Utah

Roberto España
Department of Psychology
Emory University

Katrina Goines
Department of Psychology
Emory University

Sherryl H. Goodman
Department of Psychology
Emory University

Bryan Grant
Department of Psychology
Western University

Megan R. Gunnar
Institute of Child Development
University of Minnesota

Meeka S. Halperin
Department of Psychology
Emory University

Constance Hammen
Department of Psychology
University of California,
Los Angeles

Benjamin L. Hankin
Department of Psychology
University of Illinois, Urbana-Champaign

Kate L. Harkness
Department of Psychology
Queen's University

Elizabeth P. Hayden
Department of Psychology, Brain and
Mind Institute
Western University

Lauren Henry
Department of Psychology
Vanderbilt University

George F. Koob
Neurobiology of Addiction Section
National Institute on Drug Abuse
National Institutes of Health

Annette M. La Greca
Department of Psychology
University of Miami

Keira B. Leneman
Institute of Child Development
University of Minnesota

Alexandra J. Lipinski
Department of Psychology
University of Memphis

Kan Long
Department of Counseling and Clinical
Psychology
Columbia University

Nestor L. Lopez-Duran
Department of Psychology
University of Michigan

Allison LoPilato
Department of Psychology
Emory University

Dennis F. Lovelock
Department of Psychology
Binghamton University–State University
of New York

Ashley N. Marchante-Hoffman
Department of Psychology
University of Miami

Katie A. McLaughlin
Department of Psychology
Harvard University

Rebekah J. Mennies
Department of Psychology
Temple University

Valerie J. Micol
Department of Psychology
University of Michigan

Jamie E. Mondello
Department of Psychology
Binghamton University–State University
of New York

Scott M. Monroe
Department of Psychology
University of Notre Dame

Sarah Myruski
The Graduate Center
The City University of New York

Richard W. J. Neufeld
Department of Psychology
Western University

Tommy H. Ng
Department of Psychology
Temple University

Derek Novacek
Department of Psychology
Emory University

Thomas M. Olino
Department of Psychology
Temple University

Thomas F. Oltmanns
Department of Psychological
and Brain Sciences
Washington University in St. Louis

David Pagliaccio
Department of Psychiatry
Columbia University

Jenny E. Pak
Department of Psychology
Binghamton University–State University
of New York

Allison M. Pickover
Department of Psychology
University of Memphis

Jens C. Pruessner
Department of Psychology
University of Constance

Andrea Roberts
Department of Psychology
University of Michigan

Tina H. Schweizer
Department of Psychology
University of Illinois, Urbana-Champaign

Zindel V. Segal
Department of Psychology
University of Toronto Scarborough

Nila Shakiba
Department of Psychology
University of Utah

George M. Slavich
Cousins Center for
Psychoneuroimmunology
University of California, Los Angeles

Catherine B. Stroud
Department of Psychology
Williams College

Naomi Tarlow
Department of Psychology
University of Miami

Madison K. Titone
Department of Psychology
Temple University

Han N. Tran
Department of Psychology
University of Memphis

Rudolf Uher
Department of Psychiatry
Dalhousie University

Leandro F. Vendruscolo
Neurobiology of Addiction Section
National Institute on Drug Abuse
National Institutes of Health

Isabella M. Viducich
Department of Psychology
University of Notre Dame

Kelsey D. Vig
Department of Psychology
University of Regina

Allison Vreeland
Department of Psychology
Vanderbilt University

Suzanne Vrshek-Schallhorn
Department of Psychology
University of North Carolina, Greensboro

Elaine Walker
Department of Psychology
Emory University

Kathleen M. Walsh
Department of Psychology
University of Toronto Scarborough

Christina Noel White
Department of Psychological
and Brain Sciences
Washington University in St. Louis

Kay Wilhelm
St. Vincent's Urban Mental Health
and Wellbeing Centre
St. Vincent's Hospital

Zuzanna K. Wojcieszak
Department of Psychology
Temple University

William C. Woods
Department of Psychology
University of Pittsburgh

Aidan G. C. Wright
Department of Psychology
University of Pittsburgh

Ellen Zakreski
Department of Psychology
McGill University

Introduction

Kate L. Harkness *and* Elizabeth P. Hayden

Abstract

In this introductory chapter, we provide an overview of *The Handbook of Stress and Mental Health*. We begin by introducing the scope of the issue and critically operationally defining the construct of stress. We then provide a description of the chapters included in the volume. The contributors represent international leaders in the field of stress and provide authoritative and integrative review and analysis of the evidence base in this crucial area of study.

Keywords: stress, mental health, development, assessment, etiology, treatment

Exposure to stress is a ubiquitous feature of the human condition and has been throughout our evolution. Physical anthropologists have provided extensive skeletal evidence of stress in prehistoric populations that has been linked to environmental pressures, including nutritional deprivation, economic transition, and intergroup conflict (Goodman, Thomas, Swedlund, & Armegalos, 1988). The sophist Gorgias' (483–376 BC) *Encomium of Helen* is credited as providing the earliest account in the West of psychological symptoms resulting from exposure to stress. Gorgias' detailed descriptions of Greek soldiers returning from combat invoke symptoms consistent with the current diagnostic criteria for posttraumatic stress disorder: "the sight inscribes in the mind images of objects seen. And the terrifying images often remain, and what remains corresponds to words spoken" (cited in Ustinova & Cardeña, 2014). The Roman philosopher and statesman Cicero (106–43 BC) also attributed his recurrent episodes of depression and suicidality to stressful events, such as his exile from Rome and the death of his daughter Tullia.

In the present day, stress has been implicated as an etiological factor in every psychiatric disorder in current nosological systems. This extends from posttraumatic stress disorder, for which exposure to traumatic stress is an explicit diagnostic criterion, to other disorders long understood to involve stress-related etiologies, such as the anxiety and depressive disorders, to disorders that have traditionally been associated more strongly with neurobiological factors, such as bipolar disorder and the schizophrenia spectrum. The extensive literature on stress and mental health merits an in-depth analysis of the role of stress in psychopathology as well as the diverse mechanisms that mediate and/or moderate the effect of stress exposure. The current handbook, written by an international group of renowned experts in the field of stress, provides a scholarly, comprehensive volume that takes a multidisciplinary perspective on stress and specifically integrates issues of stress assessment, mechanisms, and treatment around the central theme of mental health.

Stress Defined

The term *stress* has two meanings, which are often conflated in the literature on the role of stress in mental health. The first involves the events or challenges in the environment to which individuals are exposed (i.e., stress *exposure*; e.g., Dohrenwend & Dohrenwend, 1974). These exposures can be acute (e.g., getting fired from a job) or chronic (e.g., ongoing arguments with a spouse), range from minor (e.g., getting a speeding ticket) to severe (e.g., being diagnosed with a life-threatening disease) to traumatic (e.g., sexual assault), and can occur throughout the life span. What defines the construct of stress exposure is that it comprises objectively observable external pressures on the individual. This meaning is distinguished from the second, which focuses on the individual's response to these external environmental exposures (i.e., stress *response*; e.g., Selye, 1955). These responses involve the internal perturbations and/or manifestations of stressful exposures, which can be measured at multiple levels of analysis (e.g., psychological states of fear, anxiety, or depression; sympathetic nervous system and hypothalamic-pituitary adrenal cortical activation).

Stress exposures are typically and reliably associated with a stress response. However, the association is not perfect, and measurement of the stress response cannot be taken as a proxy for the exposure (or vice versa). Importantly, the response to any given stress exposure is influenced by a wide variety of individual difference factors, including personality and temperament, cognitive style, previous and concurrent stress exposure, genetic vulnerability, and so on (see Harkness & Monroe, 2016). Given the multidetermined nature of stress responses, there is pronounced variation in responses to the same objectively defined stress exposures both across individuals as well as within individuals over time (e.g., Ellis, Boyce, Belsky, Bakermans-Kranenburg, & van IJzendoorn, 2011).

Both exposure to stressful life events and the psychological and physiological responses to such environmental exposures are highly relevant to mental health. As noted earlier, stress exposures, independently and objectively defined, contribute strongly to the etiology of mental disorders. Additionally, individuals with mental disorders, and those prone to disorder, evidence stronger psychological, physiological, and neurobiological responses to stress exposures, as well as higher levels of symptoms and signs indicative of psychological stress, than healthy individuals. As we summarize next, the chapters in this volume provide a comprehensive and authoritative review of the types of stress exposures most strongly associated with each mental disorder. And, in separate analysis, they characterize in detail the nature of the stress

responses at multiple levels of analysis that are associated with disorder in the face of exposure.

Structure of the Handbook

This volume contains a total of 33 chapters. The first three chapters address the definition and assessment of the main classes of stress exposures—major life events and chronic difficulties (Chapter 1, Monroe & Slavich), daily stressors and hassles (Chapter 2, Wright, Aslinger, Bellamy, Eckershile, & Woods), and the broad category of adverse childhood experiences (Chapter 3, McLaughlin). All three of these chapters address the crucial importance of distinguishing between stress exposure and the stress response both conceptually and in measurement. They also each provide a critical review of the most methodologically rigorous tools in the field for assessing stress exposures across several dimensions (e.g., chronicity, severity, and developmental timing). Finally, in Chapter 4, Neufeld and Grant provide a comprehensive analysis of strategies to model the relations of stress exposure, stress response (e.g., coping), and mental health. The authors in these first four chapters, then, provide a critical foundation in terms of the operationalization of stress that can be used to evaluate the theoretical and empirical evidence provided in the subsequent chapters linking stress to mental health.

The next 10 chapters focus on the association of stress exposure to the etiology and course of several mental disorders. Each chapter focuses on a different disorder and, consistent with the introductory material, reviews literature bearing on several dimensions of stress. Emphasis is placed on a review of studies using methodologically rigorous methods that clearly measure the stress exposure unconfounded by the stress response. Issues unique to each mental health condition are also highlighted.

Specifically, in Chapter 5, Vrshek-Schallhorn, Ditcheva, and Corneau highlight the unique role of life events involving themes of interpersonal loss, humiliation, and entrapment in triggering episodes of major depressive disorder, as well as the very recent research on targeted rejection events as specific risk exposures for depression. In their chapter on bipolar disorder, Alloy, Titone, Ng, and Bart (Chapter 6) expand upon the distinction between the types of life events just mentioned that trigger episodes of depression and those that trigger manic episodes. Specifically, consistent with the behavioral activation/reward hypersensitivity and circadian dysregulation theories of bipolar disorder,

Alloy and colleagues review evidence for the unique role of events involving reward and those involving the disruption of social rhythms in triggering mania. In Chapter 7, Goines, LoPilato, Novacek, Epana, and Walker review evidence for the role of early and proximal stress exposures in precipitating schizophrenia in those at clinical high risk, and for the role of ongoing exposure to proximal life events in the exacerbation of psychotic symptoms. These authors provide a comprehensive and rigorous account of the neurobiological mechanisms that mediate the relation of stress exposure and psychosis, providing a rich integration of stress exposure and the stress response in the etiology of this spectrum.

The personality disorders are covered in Chapter 8 by White, Conway, and Oltmanns. Here the authors focus on the specific role of adverse childhood exposures, including abuse and neglect, in the etiology of the personality disorders, and in the development of maladaptive personality traits. A particularly unique contribution of this chapter is the authors' discussion of how to disentangle environmental and genetic influences in the research on adverse childhood events in personality pathology. In Chapter 9, using a neurobiological model of alcohol addiction as their foundation, Vendruscolo and Koob provide a compelling understanding of the effect of alcohol on the body's stress response system—the hypothalamic-pituitary-adrenal (HPA) axis—thereby intriguingly positing alcohol as the stress exposure that initiates a stress response cascade that maintains that exposure and leads to addiction. In Chapter 10, Corning and Viducich integrate the most common stress antecedents of the eating disorders and obesity, including childhood trauma, and particularly sexual trauma, and traumatic illness, with prevailing etiological models of eating disorders (sociocultural drive for thinness; negative appearance-related feedback). In so doing, they put forth the novel proposal that negative affect may act as a specific mediator of the relation between stress and eating disorders.

While the aforementioned disorders can all be linked to stressful life events to varying degrees, posttraumatic stress disorder is unique as the only mental disorder that explicitly includes the etiological role of a traumatic stress exposure as a diagnostic criterion. While stress exposure is linked to posttraumatic stress disorder by definition, LaGreca, Danzi, Marchante-Hoffman, and Tarlow (Chapter 11) provide a deep and exhaustive exploration into the wide variability of traumatic exposures—from large-scale natural disasters to personal assaults—and the differential implications of this variability for the development of posttraumatic stress disorder and acute stress disorder across the life span. Finally, using posttraumatic stress disorder as an anchor, Vig, El-Gabalawy, and Asmundson (Chapter 14) review in fascinating detail an integrative psychobiobehavioral model for the comorbidity of trauma-related psychopathology and medical conditions ranging from cardiovascular disease and diabetes to respiratory and musculoskeletal diseases.

A developmental perspective lays the foundation for a richer and deeper understanding of the processes by which stress exposure relates to (mal) adaption. Stress exposure in early life is covered in Chapters 12 and 13, as well as in Chapters 20 and 24. Doom and Cicchetti (Chapter 12) provide a definitive characterization of the field of developmental psychopathology, as well as a comprehensive review of stress in a developmental psychopathology framework. A particularly important contribution of this chapter is the integration of the moderating and mediating influences of genetic, neuroendocrine, and other individual difference factors in the relation of stress to psychopathology in children, thereby presaging discussion of these factors in future chapters, but again through the unique lens of development. Complementing Doom and Cicchetti's analysis is the authoritative contribution of Leneman and Gunnar (Chapter 25) in which they review in exquisite detail the state of the current evidence on brain development and the effects on the brain of stress exposure during specific developmental periods, from exposure prenatally through to adolescence. Pagliaccio and Barch (Chapter 20) hone in specifically on the neuroimaging literature to provide a deep analysis of the effects of early life stress on brain structure and function. Finally, Goodman and Halperin (Chapter 13) explore maternal perinatal depression as a unique stress exposure on the developing fetus and infant that has significant implications for development and future psychopathology in these offspring. Important issues of timing of exposure are covered, as well as outcomes across several domains.

The volume then provides a detailed review of the prevailing theories and mechanisms that have been proposed to account for the etiological relation of stress to mental disorder. The mechanisms, while reviewed separately, are by no means mutually exclusive and instead likely work together to drive the onset and course of mental disorders. For example, a history of depression is associated with both the generation of (Chapter 15, Hammen), and sensitization to (Chapter 16, Stroud), stressful life events, and these two mechanisms working together have been proposed to drive a recurrent course in the disorder (e.g., Hammen, 2006). Olino, Wojcieszak, and Mennies (Chapter 18) provide an integrative analysis explicitly when they discuss models by which particular personality traits may be linked to psychopathology through the mechanism of stress generation (Chapter 15). On the neurobiological side, Slavich (Chapter 23) provides direct evidence for a mechanistic link between the hypothalamic-pituitary-adrenal (HPA) axis (Chapter 21, Lopez, Roberts, Foster, & Mayer) and the immune system. Specifically, he explains that prolonged release of the stress hormone cortisol as a result of chronic stress exposure can make immune cells less sensitive to the anti-inflammatory effects of glucocorticoids, resulting in HPA-axis-related increases in inflammation that have been associated with a variety of mental and physical health disorders. Similarly, Pruessner's (Chapter 22) detailed and comprehensive review provides the psychophysiological level of analysis of the major neurobiological stress response systems to complement the neurohormonal and neuroinflammatory mechanisms discussed in Chapters 21 and 23.

We also emphasize that the distinction between psychological and neurobiological explanatory mechanisms is a false dichotomy, and it is widely understood that the effects of stress can be observed at multiple levels of analysis simultaneously. Lopez-Duran and colleagues (Chapter 21) explicitly provide this integration when they review the role of the HPA axis, and the stress hormone cortisol specifically, in regulating attentional vigilance to threat (Chapter 17, Hankin & Schweizer), as well as emotional regulation (Chapter 19, Dennis-Tiwary, Denefrio, & Myruski) and interpersonal behavioral responsivity (Chapter 15, Hammen) in the face of stress. Similarly, Uher (Chapter 24) discusses in detail the role of genetic factors in predisposing to particular temperaments and personality traits (Chapter 18), as well as cognitive processes such as attentional bias to threat (Chapter 17), that heighten sensitivity to the stressful life event exposures that trigger mental disorder. Uher also reviews the fascinating evidence implicating genes in the generation of stress (i.e., gene–environment correlation). That is, individuals with at-risk genetic predispositions may select themselves into environments that are associated with heightened exposure to stress. Further, Shakiba, Conradt, and Ellis (Chapter 27) integrate across genetic, neuroendocrine, cognitive,

and personality levels of analysis to present their comprehensive biological sensitivity to context model of susceptibility to mental health disorders as a result of early life stress. Finally, it is important to note that the list of mechanisms included here is not exhaustive. There are several mechanisms and theoretical perspectives that we have not included because of space constraints (e.g., evolutionary and sociocultural theories, the role of neurotransmitters such as dopamine and serotonin).

The final chapters examine factors that mitigate the effects of stress, including internal psychological factors such as coping and resilience, as well as treatments for stress-related disorders. The terms "coping" and "resilience" have been defined and operationalized in many different ways, leading to inconsistencies and confusion in the literature linking these constructs to mental health outcomes. The chapters in this volume provide much-needed and authoritative clarity. In Chapter 26, Compas, Vreeland, and Henry review in detail the structure of coping and emphasize the importance of conceptualizing coping as a strategy that can adapt flexibly to changing environmental demands. It is this coping flexibility, according to the authors, that may most strongly predict psychological adjustment. Long and Bonanno take up this same theme in presenting their unified framework of resilience (Chapter 28). Specifically, they too assert that resilience should be conceptualized not as a static personality trait but as a process that unfolds dynamically and flexibly over time.

Ideally, both theoretical models and descriptive work characterizing linkages between stressors and outcomes contribute to the development of prevention and intervention efforts. Using depression as their prototypical stress-related disorder, Mondello, Pak, Lovelock, and Deak (Chapter 29) review evidence for exciting new drug development targets in the inflammatory (Chapter 23) and HPA axis (Chapter 21) systems. Taking cognitive-behavioral (CB) theories of stress-related disorder as their foundation, Beck, Pickover, Lipinski, Tran, and Dodson (Chapter 30) review psychological treatments for acute stress disorder and posttraumatic stress disorder, with a particular focus on comparing and contrasting cognitive processing therapy (CPT) and prolonged exposure (PE). Desormeau, Walsh, and Segal (Chapter 31) integrate CB therapy with the practice of mindfulness, defined by Jon Kabat-Zinn (2003) as "the awareness that emerges through paying attention on purpose, in the present moment, and nonjudgmentally to the unfolding of experience moment to moment" (p. 145). They provide compelling evidence that mindfulness reduces the ruminative and elaborative cognitive processes (e.g., Chapter 17) that underlie and maintain stress-related disorders. Finally, Wilhelm and Crawford (Chapter 32) explore the fascinating effect that writing about stress and trauma has on physical and mental health outcomes. Importantly, they provide evidence for situations in which expressive writing is *not* an effective stress-reduction strategy and may even be harmful. In the final chapter of the volume (Chapter 33, Hayden and Harkness), we provide an integrative discussion of the common and unique themes presented, with a particular eye to guiding future research in this exciting and evolving field.

Over 1 billion people worldwide suffer from a mental or substance use disorder, and these disorders are the leading worldwide cause of disability (Institute for Health Metrics and Evaluation, 2018). As should be clear by the breadth of coverage in this volume, stressful environments, and individual differences in responses to these environments, are key to understanding the etiology and course of all mental disorders. Further, stress mechanisms provide a robust theoretical and empirical framework upon which to focus prevention, intervention, and novel treatment development priorities. Our goal in preparing this volume was to provide in one authoritative work an overview of the most important and timely theory and research regarding the role of stress in mental health. To the extent that we were successful in achieving this goal, it is because of the authors who contributed their deep and broad knowledge of the field to create expertly written chapters. We extend our deepest gratitude to all of these contributors. We genuinely appreciate the time and commitment that they have made to providing integrative summaries and, in many cases, major updates of their previous work. We are also grateful to Oxford University Press, and in particular Sarah Harrington, for providing a vision for this volume and supporting this work from its inception through to publication.

References

Dohrenwend, B. S., & Dohrenwend, B. P. (1974). *Stressful life events: Their nature and effects.* Oxford, UK: John Wiley & Sons.

Ellis, B. J., Boyce, W. T., Belsky, J., Bakermans-Kranenburg, M. J., & van IJzendoorn, M. H. (2011). Differential susceptibility to the environment: An evolutionary-neurodevelopmental theory. *Development and Psychopathology, 23*(1), 7–28. doi:10.1017/S0954579410000611

Goodman, A. H., Thomas, R. B., Swedlund, A. C., & Armegalos, G. J. (1988). Biocultural perspectives on stress in prehistoric, historical, and contemporary population research. *Yearbook of Physical Anthropology, 31*, 169–202.

Hammen C. (2006). Stress generation in depression: Reflections on origins, research, and future directions. *Journal of Clinical Psychology, 62*, 1065–1082.

Harkness, K. L., & Monroe, S. M. (2016). The assessment and measurement of human life stress: Basic premises, operational principles, and design requirements. *Journal of Abnormal Psychology, 125*, 727–745.

Institute for Health Metrics and Evaluation (IHME). (2018). *Findings from the Global Burden of Disease Study 2017.* Seattle, WA: IHME.

Kabat-Zinn, J. (2003). Mindfulness-based interventions in context: past, present, and future. *Clinical Psychology: Science and Practice, 10*, 144–156.

Selye, H. (1955). Stress and disease. *Science, 122*, 625–631.

Ustinova, Y., & Cardeña, E. (2014). Combat stress disorders and their treatment in ancient Greece. *Psychological Trauma: Theory, Research, Practice, and Policy, 6*(6), 739–748. doi:10.1037/a0036461

Major Life Events

A Review of Conceptual, Definitional, Measurement Issues, and Practices

Scott M. Monroe *and* George M. Slavich

Abstract

The purpose of the present chapter is to provide an overview of key issues involving the definition and assessment of major life events for researchers interested in the effects of life stress on a wide range of disorders. General conceptual and definitional issues are addressed initially, and a conceptual heuristic is proposed for guiding inquiry on major life stress and human disorder. This heuristic is drawn upon to develop principled practices for assessing, operationalizing, and finally quantifying major life events. Throughout the chapter, contemporary approaches for research on major life events are evaluated, their relative merits and shortcomings discussed, and their psychometric credentials formally compared. In closing, we consider future directions for research on major life events and their implications for health and disease.

Keywords: life stress, stressful life events, assessment, human disorder, health, disease

> Central to the concept of natural selection (Darwin, 1859)—the struggle for existence—is the idea that the dynamic physical and social environments are full of obstacles, dangers, challenges, and threats. They must be met with appropriate, discriminated, integrated (organismic) responses that protect the organism. They must be overcome so that the organism survives to reproduce.
>
> —*Herbert Weiner* (1992, p. 2)

The purpose of the present chapter is to provide an overview of key issues involving the definition and assessment of major life events, which we consider to be the "obstacles, dangers, challenges, and threats" that are imposed by the dynamic physical and social environments people must overcome throughout their lives. Although there are many types of circumstances that are more or less stressful, we focus on major life events given that they typically impose substantial acute, adaptive demands upon the individual and can have significant implications for mental and physical health. Other forms of life stress, such as early life stress during infancy or childhood, chronic stress, and daily or minor

stressors, are covered elsewhere in the volume (see Chapters 2–4, this volume).

We first address general conceptual and definitional issues with which investigators must grapple, and we propose a conceptual heuristic for guiding inquiry on major life stress and human disorder. We then draw upon this heuristic to develop principled practices for assessing, operationalizing, and finally quantifying major life events. Informed by this analysis, throughout the chapter we evaluate common approaches for understanding major life events in contemporary research, discuss their relative merits and shortcomings, and formally compare their psychometric credentials. In closing, we consider future directions for research on major life events and their implications for health and disease. Our intent is to provide an overview of the topic that is useful to researchers interested in the effects of life stress for a wide range of disorders, and who seek to conduct their studies using conceptually informed and methodologically sound procedures.

General Conceptual and Definitional Issues
Historical and Contemporary Considerations

> The present state of knowledge, as I understand it, suggests that if one wishes to study the relation between a social variable and a health variable, one should begin with the hypothesis that both kinds of variables are often loosely and variously defined...and that the results of any investigation may be dependent upon the definitions and methods of measurement that are used....It follows that one should first make as precise, as complete, and as concrete a definition and measurement of the social variable as one can.
>
> —*Hinkle* (1974, p. 335)

"Stress" is an extraordinarily popular term, a "social variable" relevant in scientific circles and in common everyday parlance. Many studies have documented a variety of psychological and medical conditions associated with stress (e.g., Cohen, Janicki-Deverts, & Miller, 2007; Slavich, 2016). These sources of evidence, however, are based upon a plethora of assessment and measurement practices. These diverse approaches differ substantially in the procedures adopted, and in turn they yield varying degrees of scientific evidence. It is probably safe to say that not a day goes by when a person does not hear or use the term "stress" or "stressful" at least once. Indeed, stress is readily invoked in the absence of reliable research evidence, to casually explain away mysterious disorders—an etiological "placeholder" for conditions of unknown or poorly understood origins (Monroe, 2008). Unfortunately, the sheer popularity of the idea of stress in scientific, clinical, and social circles has become an impediment to understanding what stress might "be" and how it may confer susceptibility to disorder and disease (Monroe & Slavich, 2016).

Current research on life stress continues be such that, in the past words quoted earlier, both the social and health variables are "loosely and variously defined," and much of the existing corpus of evidence is "dependent upon the definitions and methods of measurement that are used." Perhaps most critically, progress has not been made in making "as precise, as complete, and as concrete a definition and measurement of the social variable as one can" (Hinkle, 1974, p. 355). These are humbling observations—first penned nearly a half-century ago—which point to ongoing conundrums regarding "stress."

On Defining Stress

Since its infusion into the modern research culture by Hans Selye, the term "stress" has defied "precise," "complete," and "concrete definitions." Selye himself apparently struggled with the term over his life and lamented, "Everybody knows what stress is, and nobody knows what it is" (Selye, 1973). Indeed, one early critic of Selye's work in the 1950s quipped, "Stress, in addition to being itself, was also the cause of itself, and the result of itself"' (Humphrey, 2005).

One enduring obstacle has been that "stress" often refers to different and distinct components of a sequential process. For example, some theorists and researchers have used "stress" to describe exposures to the external environment—specifically the changing objective circumstances to which the organism or individual is subjected (e.g., relationship loss, job termination, natural disaster, etc.; Dohrenwend & Dohrenwend, 1974). Alternatively, others have focused on the psychological and physiological responses to environmental exposures (e.g., subjective distress, cortisol levels, emotion circuitry of the brain, and so on). Finally, yet others have enlarged the temporal scope encapsulating ongoing sequential iterations between exposures and responses over time, wherein exposures are "coped with" through responses, altering the environmental circumstances and changing the nature of the subsequent adaptive demands requiring further responses (e.g., transactional and whole organism models of stress; Lazarus & Folkman, 1984; Weiner, 1992).

As a result of blurring these related theoretical pieces that represent components of a sequential and progressive process, the concept of stress continues to be unacceptably vague and indistinct. Every decade or so there are renewed clarion calls to terminate the confusion, to abandon or replace the term "stress," along with the cacophony of associated connotations. (For a recent series of such interchanges, see Kagan, 2016, and responses by Cohen, Gianaros, & Manuck, 2016; McEwen & McEwen, 2016.) These dire requests to end the terminology of stress, however, may be premature or too sweeping in scope. As discussed next, a more productive approach can build upon past work and begin to provide a more secure and productive pathway forward.

The Missing Environment

Recently, Hammen observed, "Ironically, environmental stress has often been a silent player in human studies of stress processes" (Hammen, 2016, p. 335). This eminent life stress investigator noted that the environmental conditions to which individuals are exposed frequently are omitted from the investigative agenda. In its place, many researchers *presume* stress to predominantly represent not "what is going on in the person's world," but rather "what is going on in their minds about their world" (Hammen, 2016, p. 336). In other words, Hammen (2016) contends that stress responses have been accepted as consequences of different physical and social environmental exposures, but without a research agenda explicitly taking into account the nature of the environmental exposures involved. She emphasized that "stress experiences and exposure have been conceptually or empirically neglected or inadequately conceived, or measured poorly, or measured narrowly in psychopathology research" (Hammen, 2016, p. 336).

Relatedly, Harkness and Monroe (2016) recently brought attention to the underappreciated importance of precise and independent specification of the environmental conditions to which individuals are exposed. They complement Hammen's (2016) insights and argue that without explicitly taking the environment into account, information about stress responses is severely compromised and is perhaps rendered meaningless or misleading. We address this paradoxical situation next, outline a conceptual heuristic for prioritizing information about the environmental exposures, and illustrate how such advances could significantly enhance research on life stress.

PRIORITIZING AND INTEGRATING THE ENVIRONMENT INTO STRESS RESEARCH

Theoretical models of stress–disorder relations begin with the assumption that environmental challenges and demands elicit responses that are intended to be adaptive for addressing acute, pressing needs. Over more prolonged periods of activation, however, these responses can become detrimental for psychological and physical health (e.g., McEwen & Gianaros, 2011; Shields & Slavich, 2017). From this standpoint, stress exposures *precede* and *precipitate* stress

responses, which in turn, eventually result in potential pathogenic processes. Figure 1.1 provides a schematic illustration of this serial course and the types of factors involved. Several key implications follow from this straightforward characterization of the fundamentally sequential nature regarding the temporal dynamics of the stress process (see Harkness & Monroe, 2016).

First and most apparent, without an initial environmental challenge there is no stress response. But without explicitly taking the environment into account, this matter simply cannot be determined, which leads to serious problems. As indicated in Figure 1.1, environmental exposures are only one of many factors that influence the ongoing and/or "downstream" psychobiological status of the person. Even under tranquil environmental circumstances some individuals will have perturbations in mind or body resulting from influences unrelated to stress, yet still will give rise to an *appearance* of stress activation (i.e., due to the multitude of factors unrelated to stress affecting the person's psychobiological state). For instance, some people will have elevated cortisol or heightened psychological distress for reasons other than a recent stressful exposure. Ironically, by not directly assessing environmental exposures, researchers place themselves in the awkward and ultimately unproductive position of studying people who evidence stress "responses," but who have no discernable stressful exposures.

The multidetermined nature of psychological and biological states that are correlated with stress response indicators places significant constraints on what can be inferred from much of the existing research on life stress. By not incorporating measures of stress exposures and instead relying only on measures of stress responses, it is not possible to evaluate to what degree a particular individual's stress responses is attributable to prior environmental demands versus individual differences in other psychological or biological attributes (see Figure 1.1). This also means that responses to stressful environmental exposures are easily obscured or masked owing to the diluting effects of the myriad other factors affecting the state of the person. In summary, to be able to reliably detect any stress response, a strong effect of the stress exposure is required—well above and beyond the cumulative effects of the multitude of other influences involved. The attenuation of effects attributable to environmental exposures by the influences of the other factors involving stress response systems could explain

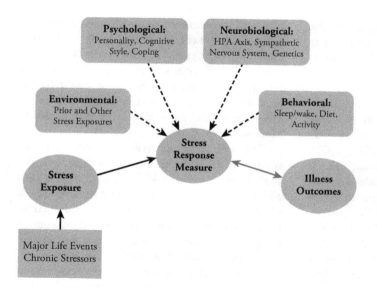

Figure 1.1 Stress exposure and the multidetermined measures of stress responses (adapted from Harkness & Monroe, 2016).

the tenuous effects often reported in research on stress responses, and the lack of replicability of findings across studies.

Even more scientifically worrisome, researchers are not always able to ensure that the psychological and biological status of the person is independent of the pathological processes attributable to the disorder under study. Indeed, in many instances the psychobiological condition of the individual may be contaminated by, or confounded with, the early antecedents, correlates, or consequences of the psychological or physical disorder in question (see Figure 1.1). For instance, elevated cortisol levels commonly follow exposure to stressful circumstances (e.g., Dickerson & Kemeny, 2004). However, elevated cortisol levels also are very common in depressed people (e.g., Jarcho, Slavich, Tylova-Stein, Wolkowitz, & Burke, 2013; Stetler & Miller, 2011). If the investigator relies solely upon stress responses (i.e., cortisol as an indicator of stress), he or she cannot determine if the heightened cortisol is a con-sequence of stressful exposure(s) or an artifact of—and therefore confounded with—the incipient psy-chobiology of major depression. Concerns such as these are too frequent, yet severely limit the causal inferences that can be drawn from studies examining links between stress response and disease (Harkness & Monroe, 2016).

Second, stress response systems evolved over time to enhance adaptation to a wide range of envi-ronmental exposures and threatening demands (Weiner, 1992). As a result, stress responses possess little if any inherent meaning independent of stress exposures; rather, they are consequent to, and

thereby a function of, the types and degrees of environmental challenges faced by organism. This means that stress responses become meaningful only when understood in the context of the eliciting circumstances or adaptive demands that a person is confronting. Phrased differently, stress responses can only be understood in light of their precipitating social or physical circumstances (Monroe & Roberts, 1990). It is the *interaction* between stress exposures and stress responses that lies at the conceptual heart of stress research (e.g., Hankin, Abramson, Miller, & Haeffel, 2004; Harkness & Monroe, 2016; Monroe & Simons, 1991; Moore & Depue, 2016).

Third, a prerequisite for research on stress responses is the preliminary yet foundational demonstration of a functional relationship between stress exposures and pathological outcomes. Otherwise, research on stress responses has no effects of environmental exposures to explain. If associations are detected with "stress responses" without taking exposures into account, once again such effects can be more parsimoniously explained by other influential factors (e.g., neuroticism) or by confounding factors (e.g., attributable to effects of the disorder) (see Figure 1.1). As psychologist Ray Hyman once dryly commented, "Don't try to explain how something works until you find out that it works" (Hall, 2014, p. 23).

Lastly, the nature of the environmental exposures faced by the person necessarily delimits and informs the kinds of responses available to address the par-ticular types of challenges imposed. Stress exposures provide very useful theoretical clues about which kinds of stress responses should be considered and assessed. In a sense, conducting research on stress responses without attention to their hypothetical origins can be seen as placing the empirical cart before the theoretical horse (Harkness & Monroe, 2016).

Overall, stress research could benefit greatly from investigating stress responses within the theoretical context of their environmental origins. For present purposes, we focus on major life events as one class of environmental exposures that can be studied to better understand the implications of stress processes for health and well-being. Along these lines, we now turn to some of the theoretical and methodological considerations for conducting research on major life events.

ASSESSING, OPERATIONALIZING, AND QUANTIFYING MAJOR LIFE EVENTS: PRINCIPLES AND PRACTICES

At a general level, major life events can be defined as "environmental changes that have a definable beginning point in time and that would be expected to be associated with at least some degree of psychological threat, unpleasantness, or behavioral demands" (Harkness & Monroe, 2016, p. 729). Examples include beginning or ending an important personal relationship, starting or terminating employment, incurring a serious illness, changing residence, and so on. An ongoing challenge for stress researchers has been how to translate theoretical examples of life events such as these into scientifically sound operational definitions of the environmental exposures—namely major life events.

One obstacle is that "life events" often have an illusory simplicity about them—a seemingly intuitive obviousness and face validity—that often undermines methodologically credible measurement practices. Marriages, divorces, births, and deaths all have a familiar "ring" to them; all seem to be pretty obvious kinds of experiences to which everyone can readily recognize and relate. But such appearances often are deceiving. For example, when is a life event not a life event? Or perhaps more properly stated, when is an environmental exposure, or change in a person's life circumstances, not sufficiently severe or impactful so as to qualify as a "major life event"? This is a core matter around which opinions vary, over which research traditions have clashed in the past, and indeed about which little resolution has been achieved to this day. The disagreements stem from opposing—and perhaps irreconcilable—assumptions about how the fundamental task of measurement should be undertaken (Brown, 1974, 1989; Monroe, 2008).

A goal for research, therefore, is to provide a standardized system for operationalizing people's recent life experiences as the presence or absence major life events believed to confer susceptibility to disorder. Such a system should be reliable over time and replicable across investigators. To comply with these basic standards, investigators need to adopt sensitive procedures for gathering extensive initial information about people's lives (i.e., assessment), employ reliable decision rules for determining which exposures qualify (or not) as major life events and rate these exposures along theoretically-relevant dimensions (i.e., operationalization), and implement consistent procedures for representing the processed information as a summary index (i.e., quantification) (McQuaid et al., 1992). We adopt these serial phases as a convenient way to represent the overarching measurement process, and we portray the general objectives and specific tasks for each phase in Figure 1.2.

Figure 1.2 Phases of the measurement process for major life events.

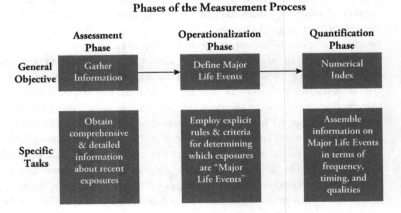

Phases of the Measurement Process

	Assessment Phase	Operationalization Phase	Quantification Phase
General Objective	Gather Information	Define Major Life Events	Numerical Index
Specific Tasks	Obtain comprehensive & detailed information about recent exposures	Employ explicit rules & criteria for determining which exposures are "Major Life Events"	Assemble information on Major Life Events in terms of frequency, timing, and qualities

The Assessment of Major Life Events

A guiding principle in the assessment phase of life stress is theoretical: What is it about the social or physical environment that is potentially important for understanding the origins of psychopathology or disease (Harkness & Monroe, 2016; Monroe, 2008)? By focusing on major life events, we assume that large-scale life changes represent reasonable conceptual candidates; consequently, we restrict theoretical attention to environmental changes of sufficient magnitude "that would be expected to be associated with at least some degree of psychological threat, unpleasantness, or behavioral demands" (Harkness & Monroe, 2016, p. 729).[1] Since the focus is on *major* environmental exposures, sufficient information must be gathered about all possible exposures to provide a basis for subsequently determining what constitutes "major" and what does not. The initial assessment phase, then, refers to the means via which this "front-end" all-inclusive information is obtained about a person's recent life circumstances. This initial stage in turn becomes the foundation upon which the next two stages depend. As next explained, there are two primary approaches for assessing someone's recent life circumstances (see Figure 1.2).

MAJOR LIFE EVENT ASSESSMENT ALTERNATIVES

One general approach utilizes structured or semistructured interview protocols (Monroe, Slavich, & Georgiades, 2014). Trained interviewers cover a broad and open-ended range of possible exposures, providing multiple openings to help respondents recall and talk about their recent experiences. A calendar commonly is used to assist with recall, help with accurate dating, and thereby ensure ascertained exposures predate the onset of the disorder under study. By design, the interview procures detailed information about a broad range of environmental exposures and situations occurring over the recent past (e.g., 3 months to a year). This is because sufficient information about all exposures will be needed to make judgments about which events qualify as a "major life event." The interviewer is responsible for gathering all of this foundational information, which he or she does by encouraging an open dialogue with the respondent to develop a common understanding regarding the basic meaning, or "spirit," of any particular life event (e.g., "collaborative cognition" through discussion to clarify that reports of recent exposures are consistent with the a priori definition of the major life

events the researcher intends to assess; Belli, 1998; Monroe, 2008; Schwarz, 2007).

During a life stress interview, for example, an individual might respond affirmatively to a query about a recent "break-up of an important relationship." Upon further probing, however, the interviewer might learn that the event happened to another person (e.g., sibling, child, friend) or that it was not major (e.g., after a date or two, the couple agreed to only be friends). Most important, this example conveys a critical point: any exposure or change is not automatically a "major life event." Indeed, as we discuss later, many exposures reported by study participants do not meet the formal operational requirements to qualify as a major life event (McQuaid et al., 1992; McQuaid et al., 2000; Monroe, 2008).

An alternative approach for assessing the initial information about a person's recent life circumstances utilizes self-report checklists. These contain a variety of commonly experienced life events (e.g., the SRE, Holmes & Rahe, 1967; the Life Experiences Survey, Sarason, Johnson, & Siegel, 1978). This highly popular and convenient approach requires study participants to decide which life events have been recently encountered, thereby eliminating the need for a "middle person" (i.e., interviewer). Life events are typically listed as brief stem descriptors of different exposures (e.g., "change in health of family member," "personal injury or illness," "change in financial status"; Holmes & Rahe, 1967). Since only a finite number of possible exposures can be included (e.g., roughly 40 to over 100 life events), different self-report life event checklists have been developed to assess environmental exposures for specific populations (e.g., adolescents are unlikely to be taking out mortgages; midlife adults are unlikely to be failing important exams at school; etc.; Dohrenwend, 1974). Study participants are instructed to report all of the life events that they have encountered in the recent past (e.g., ranging from the past month through the past year).

EVALUATIVE COMMENTS

The objective of the assessment phase is to gather extensive information about people's lives for making determinations about which exposures qualify as a major life event. With this objective in mind, two distinctions between these alternative research practices can be made. First, in terms of practicality, self-report checklists are without question far less costly in research time and expense. Large numbers of people can be assessed relatively quickly and economically. Second, with respect to the primary objective of the assessment phase, interview-based procedures are without question better able to gather more comprehensive information. Interview-based procedures also are superior in terms of coverage of potential exposures (i.e., checklists only contain a subset of the range of possible exposures), as well as in terms of supplying richly detailed information about the exposures and more broadly about the respondent's general life circumstances.

Pivotal questions concern whether or not the practical conveniences afforded in the assessment phase with self-report checklists are worth the loss of detailed information about participants' lives, or they are worth the potential scientific compromises entailed. These questions, however, can only be fully evaluated within a consideration of the subsequent two phases of the measurement process. We address the operationalization phase next.

The Operationalization of Major Life Events

The objective of this second phase in the measurement process is to cull from the general information about the ongoing ebb and flow of a person's life and to define the kinds of environmental exposures that qualify as "major life events" (see Figure 1.2). When any particular environmental exposure constitutes a major life event, though, is not as intuitively obvious as it might seem, and it can be a surprisingly challenging task. In the following, we first present the basic principles confronting researchers for operationalizing major life events. Throughout we draw upon concrete examples to help illustrate requirements for this definitive phase. We then present the two major approaches—namely, interviews and self-report checklist approaches—and evaluate them in light of these standards.

BASIC PRINCIPLES: DEFINING AND DIFFERENTIATING MAJOR LIFE EVENTS

Deciding upon what does and does not constitute a major life event lies at the heart of the research enterprise. In theory and practice, however, there are many ways "major life events" can be defined and operationalized. For research to progress and provide cumulative knowledge, basic research principles dictate that the procedures are standardized and replicable.

Information about environmental exposures gathered from the initial assessment needs to be leveraged in a systematic manner to inform decisions about which recent life changes do or do not constitute a major life event. There are two parts to

this task. First are threshold considerations: What determines if an exposure is of a sufficient magnitude to be declared a major life event? Distinctions must be made between what counts as "major," "minor," and "no" events. This is because, as described previously, not all exposures are necessarily major life events (e.g., break-up of an "important relationship" that happens to involve a casual friend, or which occurs after 1–2 dates). To make such decisions reliably, operational criteria and decision rules are used. This increases confidence that different researchers will handle information in similar ways (e.g., requiring that the event directly involves the study participant or a significant other; including only "break-ups" that meet specified criteria, such as duration, intent to marry, etc.).

Second, and less immediately apparent, life events often are not isolated or independent occurrences. They frequently are the causes, consequences, or correlates of other life events or circumstances. On the one hand, apparently different life events may simply represent the same experiences (i.e., two life events reflect the same exposure, and are redundant). For instance, a participant might respond affirmatively both to questions about a "traffic accident" and about "troubles with the law." However, both events could reflect the identical environmental circumstance. For example, an individual was involved in a traffic accident and received a ticket for a driving infraction that resulted in the accident. Investigators must thus avoid the potential trap of erroneously inflating the stress measure due to inclusion of simple redundancies in the processed information.

On the other hand, different kinds of associations between life events frequently are even less apparent and thus more methodologically challenging. One common situation pertains to how some exposures increase the likelihood of other exposures happening (e.g., serially related events). For instance, a close friend or relative may become seriously ill, a week later he or she is hospitalized, and 2 weeks later he or she dies. Does such a scenario count as one, two, or three major life events? There are many variations on this same theme that arise in people's lives that need to be handled in a consistent manner. For example, some life "calamities" incorporate a number of intrinsic facets that, on the surface, might appear to be several different major life events (e.g., one very major event and its rippling out into additional exposures). A marital break-up may or may not involve serious arguments with one's spouse, changes of residence, loss of income, infidelity, reconciliation, loss of friends, and so on. Should these changes in someone's recent life circumstances be defined by one overarching major life event or by several major life events that are causally intertwined components or consequences of the overarching event?

Another type of association between major life events and people's life circumstances involves chronic stressors. Chronic stressors are distinct from acute life events with regard to their recurring and/or enduring nature, and they have different effects than acute life events (Muscatell, Slavich, Monroe, & Gotlib, 2009). Examples include prolonged marital strife, chronic illness, persistent financial difficulties, and unemployment (Hammen, 2005; Harkness & Monroe, 2016). Many exposures can appear superficially to be acute major life events. However, as one learns more about the person's life situation, it becomes apparent that there is an enduring environmental problem that occurs repeatedly or unendingly over time. For instance, "troubles at work" or "arguments with spouse" may reflect single, acute major life events; however, they may also be indicators of something more enduringly troublesome, persistent, or chronic in a person's employment or marital life.

Conceptually, acute and chronic stressors have distinct theoretical implications with respect to the psychobiology of stress and potential susceptibility to illness (e.g., Hammen, Kim, Eberhart, & Brennan, 2009; Monroe, Slavich, Torres, & Gotlib, 2007). Consequently, acute and chronic environmental exposure should be assessed and evaluated independently. Measurement practices need to avoid confounding acute life events and chronic stressors, which could inadvertently inflate either category. Standard practices are required for determining when to collapse repeated exposures into one overarching chronic stressor (e.g., marital disputes occurring on a regular basis become part of the rating of chronic stress and are not each rated also as separate acute life events). Measurement practices, though, still need to provide guidance for determining when acute life events, even if associated with a chronic stressor, represent a substantial acute change in the chronic stressor exposure and thereby merit an independent rating (e.g., physical violence for the first time within an ongoing marital difficulty) (Harkness & Monroe, 2016).

A different form of interconnectedness that is important to take into account pertains to major life events that are concomitants or consequences of illness. As pointed out many years ago (Hudgens,

1974), major life events can reflect the presence (e.g., changes in eating, sleeping, or social habits) or the consequences (e.g., problems at work or with relationships) of disorder. Another methodological imperative is to establish that such confounding does not spuriously inflate the number and kinds of major life events, and speciously account for associations between major life events and illness.

INTERVIEW-BASED APPROACHES

Interview-based approaches can be divided into two common practices for operationalizing major life events: interviewer-scored and investigator-based systems (Brown, 1989; Harkness & Monroe, 2016). In the interviewer-scored systems, interviewers decide which exposures qualify as a major life event. Typically, at least some prespecified operational rules, decision criteria, or guidelines are provided to assist the interviewer with, and promote standardization of, the operational system. Examples of interviewer-scored systems include the Kendler Life Stress Interview (LSI; Kendler et al., 1995), the Brief Life Event List (ISEL; Paykel, 1997), and the Structured Life Events Inventory (SLI; Wethington, Kessler, & Brown, 1993)

Investigator-based systems differ from interviewer-scored systems in that the stress exposure information gathered is subsequently presented to a panel of independent trained raters. The presenter, who is typically the person who conducted the interview, withholds information about participants' reactions to the exposures, as well as their clinical status (i.e., whether or not he or she developed the disorder under study). The purpose of this intermediate step is to ensure that decisions about defining exposures are kept separate from knowledge about a participant's subjective responses or subsequent morbid status (see Figure 1.1). Indeed, if raters are aware that a person was upset by a particular exposure, or that he or she has or has not become ill, then they could be biased in their ratings (e.g., elevating a minor event to a major event). Without such methodological precautions, it cannot be assured that confounding biases, and not the exposures, account for any associations between the stress measures and adverse outcomes.

Investigator-based approaches also differ from interviewer-scored approaches with respect to how decisions concerning recent exposures are made. In general, investigator-based systems provide raters with opportunities to consult written materials, as well as time to discuss and clarify decisions before final consensus judgments are rendered. As in the case of the interviewer-scored systems, typically there are at least minimal operational rules, criteria, and guidelines that are prespecified to standardize ratings (see later). Examples of such systems include the Life Events and Difficulties Schedule (LEDS; Brown & Harris, 1978), the UCLA Episodic Life Event Interview (Hammen, 1991), and the Standardized Event Rating System (Dohrenwend, Raphael, Schwartz, Stueve, & Skodol, 1993).

As indicated, both interviewer-scored and investigator-based systems typically incorporate manuals that provide a priori guidelines, criteria, and examples for deciding when an exposure counts as a major life event. Probably the most elaborate and widely known system is the Life Events and Difficulties Schedule (LEDS), developed by George Brown and Tirril Harris (Brown & Harris 1978). The LEDS includes an extensive manual that provides explicit decision rules and operational criteria for (1) defining and rating acute and chronic life stress, (2) distinguishing between complex constellations of acute and chronic forms of stress, and (3) rating the severity of major life events and chronic difficulties using a comprehensive, 500-page manual that includes approximately 5,000 case exemplars to help raters anchor and standardize their assessment decisions. Some examples help to illustrate how such procedures are implemented.

With respect to defining and distinguishing major life events, a number of guidelines have been established within the LEDS system. For instance, one issue concerns the person who was the primary "focus" of the event (i.e., who was mainly affected by the exposure?). As noted previously, respondents often are very inclusive in reporting recent exposures and bring up life events that mainly happened to others in their social sphere (e.g., friends, family members). The LEDS distinguishes between self- and other-focused events, setting higher criteria for inclusion of the latter (with case exemplars provided to assist with such decisions). Another issue concerns how associated exposures are addressed in the measurement system (e.g., event sequences and "overarching" complex events that have many other associated events, as explained earlier). For instance, how might the example of an illness followed by a hospitalization be handled? Is this one event or two?

More generally, elaborate determinations involving sequences of exposures, multifaceted or compound exposures, and associations between acute major life events and chronic stressors are processed with the application of similarly designed prespecified

rules and guidelines (see Brown & Harris, 1978). These operational guidelines are based on rationale assumptions about the types and severity of the exposures, but they are inevitably arbitrary to some extent. For example, with regard to major depression, substantial evidence indicates that only major life events that include the respondent as a "focus" of the event are critical for onset, and not major life events that primarily impact other individuals within the respondent's social field (see Brown & Harris, 1978). The virtue is that any arbitrary element is treated in a standardized manner, which can allow for further research to evaluate the validity of the presumption. Overall, these procedures guide decisions and enhance the standardization of operationalizing major life events.

The LEDS and related interview-based systems take the measurement of major life events one step further by incorporating procedures to make the objective ratings more personally sensitive to the unique characteristics of the individual's life situation (Brown & Harris, 1989; Hammen, 2005). Drawing upon the wealth of information from the interview, raters can use both the "big picture" and the personal details of the respondent's biographical circumstances to operationalize a major life event and to adapt and fine-tune the scoring of each life event. These "contextual ratings" serve to place the exposure in the broader life circumstances for each individual, thus increasing the likelihood that the personal meaning and impact of the life event will be represented in the final ratings.

The rating of a woman's pregnancy provides an example of how contextual ratings work. This event has a standard base value in the LEDS manual, but it can be modified depending upon the particulars of the respondent's life situation. For example, if the woman is in a stable relationship, the pregnancy was planned, and there are adequate financial resources, then the event "pregnancy" typically will be rated in a standard manner. However, the event would be rated more severely for a woman with an unplanned pregnancy, without a partner, without financial resources, and with four other children. In essence, raters draw upon the wealth of information from the interview to infer the meaning and impact of the exposure for the average person in a similar life situation, but without compromising the independence of measurement for exposures and responses.

Lastly, the LEDS and similar systems provide a foundation of information on major life events, which can serve as the basis for enlarging inquiry into other methodological and theoretical topics.

Major life events possess many characteristics and qualities that may be conceptually meaningful. Distinctions between these theoretical characteristics can be very useful for expanding knowledge about different types of stress–disorder relations. For example, some life events are "fateful," occurring entirely independently of the respondent's actions or control. Distinctions between "fateful" and "nonfateful" events can be important for enhancing prediction of disorder onset (e.g., for depression, see Shrout et al., 1989), as well as methodologically for ensuring that relations between major life events and adverse outcomes are not artifacts of confounding associations (e.g., personality or pre-existing disorder generating the life events and causing the adverse outcome; Brown & Harris, 1978; Kendler, Karkowski, & Prescott, 1999). (See Figure 1.1.)

Interestingly, this extended capability of interview-based systems means that they can provide a foundation for research on specific social or psychological dimensions of major life events that may be more etiologically relevant for different forms of pathology. Rating schemes for these more specific and refined dimensions of potential adaptive demands and personal consequences can be developed. For instance, the likelihood of depression onset increases substantially as more refined dimensions are evaluated for specific types, severities, and qualities of stressful exposures (e.g., see Brown & Harris, 1989), with effects being strongest for severe life events involving attributes such as interpersonal loss, social rejection, and humiliation (Kendler, Hettema, Butera, Gardner, & Prescott, 2003; Slavich, Thornton, Torres, Monroe, & Gotlib, 2009). Qualities of "loss" versus "danger" also may be illuminating for distinguishing the onset of depressive versus anxiety-related conditions (e.g., fired versus threatened with job loss; Finlay-Jones & Brown, 1981; Monroe, 1990).

SELF-REPORT LIFE EVENT CHECKLISTS

As described previously, self-report life event checklists have study participants respond to brief descriptors of life events that they may have encountered in the recent past. The assessment of the general information about a person's life circumstances, and any decisions about the criteria for defining life events, are not separate or independent phases in the measurement process. Consequently, the assessment of the general information about the person's life is synonymous—simultaneously fused—with the actual operational definition. Each study participant performs both measurement tasks simultaneously—

that is, participants (a) assess their exposures and (b) decide whether each exposure qualifies as a "life event." This approach, therefore, directly violates the methodological mandate to ensure independence in assessing and defining major life events, and individuals' responses to such stressors (see Figure 1.1).

More specifically, each study participant is charged with interpreting what each very brief life event description means (e.g., what the exposure "is"), whether he or she recently experienced such a situation, and (if deciding affirmatively) whether the exposure was "major." Furthermore, study participants are responsible for deciding if apparently different descriptors of life events reflect the same exposure (i.e., event redundancies), if sequential events should be counted as one or more events, or how multifaceted events should be handled. The respondent is the sole and decisive arbiter of, and authority over, what ultimately counts as a major life event and what does not. Ultimately, therefore, the utility of self-report checklists depends upon how research participants make critical definitional and operational decisions, a task for which they have received no training.

EVALUATIVE COMMENTS

A primary objective of the operational phase is to provide a reliable means for determining which recent experiences in a person's life qualify as major life events and which do not. Ideally, this phase provides sufficient structure and guidance for condensing the wealth of information about someone's life, and for handling the tangled interconnections between various experiences, into the presence or absence of discrete major life events. A primary *requirement* of the operational phase is to ensure independence in measurement of exposures and responses. Importantly, the procedures for defining which exposures do or do not qualify as a major life event, as well as rating qualities of the exposures, cannot be subject to influence by confounding information regarding the person's psychological or biological responses to the exposure (see Figure 1.1).

Interview-based procedures typically incorporate operational criteria, rules, and guidelines for making determinations about which types of exposures qualify as major life events. These practices are prespecified, typically codified in written manuals, and implemented by trained raters. In contrast, self-report life event checklists present only brief descriptors of a variety of major life events for each study participant to evaluate. These practices depend upon their ability to determine (1) if an experience counts as a life event (or not); (2) when an endorsed life event actually occurred; (3) if sequentially related events count as one or more separate events; and (4) if complex events count as one or more separate events. On common-sense grounds, the interview-based methods rest upon firmer methodological grounds as compared to self-report checklists for reliably determining which recent experiences in a person's life qualify as major life events.[2]

Regarding the primary requirement to ensure independence in measurement of exposures and responses, the research approach must control for influences that could spuriously explain associations between major life events and illness. In this regard, the distinction drawn within the interview-based methods becomes important to recognize. With investigator-based systems, raters are blind to both the participant's response to major life events and to whether the participant developed any pathological outcomes. However, with interview-based systems, the rater is not necessarily blinded to either possible source of influences.[3] Raters' awareness of participants' responses or clinical outcomes could inadvertently bias their exposure ratings and thereby confound them. Strictly speaking, the researcher has no basis for refuting these alternative explanations for any association found between major life events and the adverse outcome.

Self-report life event checklist measures have similar, but even more glaring methodological limitations and sources of potential bias. Study participants obviously are aware of their responses to the exposures they have faced. They also generally know their health status and potential risk for adverse health outcomes. A serious concern, therefore, is that minor or trivial life events can become imbued with special meaning by the respondent and be idiosyncratically elevated to the definitional status of major life events.[4] A related concern is that, even if the exposure would qualify as a major life event, the participant's ratings of the severity or other qualities of the exposure are equally likely to be influenced by his or her perceptions or knowledge about the matter.[5] In both instances, the potential for confounding between exposures and responses is very high and cannot be ruled out. Under these methodological circumstances, associations between major life events and disorder may be readily affirmed, but only because of confounding in measurement.

Another problem for self-report checklists is that they introduce considerable error variance into the definition and operationalization of major life events (Dohrenwend, 2006). When left to their own devices, for example, study participants inevitably differ in their interpretations of the life event descriptors and, consequently, in their definition and operationalization of major life events. Much of this "intracategory variation" problem can be attributed simply and directly to the naivety of study participants in deciding which of their recent life experiences match the life event descriptors on the checklist (Dohrenwend, 2006). For example, two persons may report a "lost driver's license" (Dohrenwend, Askenasy, Krasnoff, & Dohrenwend, 1978); one of these individuals may have been convicted of drunk driving (the intended exposure), whereas another simply may have misplaced the item. Consequently, there is no assurance that a major life event reported by one person corresponds to that reported by another; moreover, either or neither may match the type of life event that the researcher had in mind. More generally, this means that within any particular life event category (1) participants commonly endorse a variety of qualitatively distinct exposures, and (2) many of these endorsed exposures differ significantly from the type of exposure intended by the investigator (see also Monroe, 2008).

Lastly, we note consequences of the idiosyncratic motivations of study participants as they complete self-report checklists. Respondents may stretch definitions of major life events to satisfy the perceived needs of the researcher (e.g., they want to be "good subjects" and provide useful information) or to avoid embarrassment (e.g., they don't want investigators to think their lives are uneventful or boring). The extent of a mismatch between the information sought by the investigator and the interpretation by the respondent can be bewildering. Indeed, in prior research we inquired about events that may have happened but were not listed on a life event checklist. One participant, for instance, noted that her husband recently had a heart attack. When asked why she didn't report a "Serious illness in close family member," she said the event wasn't stressful. As a result of his heart attack, her husband had quit smoking, become more patient, and was easier to get along with (also see Monroe, 2008). Valid associations between major life events and disorder become very difficult to detect with extraneous "noise" contaminating measurement practices.

The Quantification of Major Life Events

The purpose of this culminating phase is to abstract the attributes and qualities of major life events that hypothetically confer vulnerability and to quantify the information into a final numerical index. Simply stated, how is the extensive material processed and parsed to develop a decisive integrative index? What goes into the resultant indicator? Curiously, this phase has received little (if any) critical attention. Yet, since the utility of all prior information depends on the integrity of this final phase in the measurement process, and since alternative quantification procedures can yield very different final indices, it is a topic overdue for analysis. The basic task is how to combine the wealth of information about major life events in a principled and powerful manner (see Figure 1.2).

To begin with, a monolithic or singular approach to quantifying major life events is unlikely to be universally useful for all pathological outcomes. Not all disorders are necessarily related to life stress, and those that may be are unlikely to be a consequence of generic life stress. Rather, different kinds of stress will likely prove to be more or less influential for different kinds of pathological outcomes. Consequently, the quantification phase should target the types of exposures and the suspected impacts that are most theoretically consistent with the particular disorder of interest under investigation (McQuaid et al., 1992).

In what follows, we first outline theoretical and temporal distinctions that need to be drawn, and next we confront combinatorial challenges researchers face for assembling the final summary index. These matters involve basic decisions investigators make, explicitly or implicitly, about what kinds of life events are to be included, or excluded, from all of the information gathered, and how to optimally represent such information. In principle, these decisions are similar across the major measurement systems (e.g., interview procedures or self-report checklists). However, in practice, differences from the assessment and operationalization phases carry through into the quantification phase, resulting in characteristic differences across the systems, which we then discuss and evaluate.

MAJOR LIFE EVENTS AND DISORDERS: THEORETICAL AND TEMPORAL QUALITIES

Major life events commonly differ with regard to the kinds of adaptive demands entailed. The death of a close friend has different meanings and personal consequences than the dissolution of a marriage; each of these "losses" has qualitatively distinct implications relative to "additions" of the birth of a child or getting married (both of which also differ considerably in their personal consequences); and moving to a new city, being fired from work, or winning the lottery also point to contrasting social, psychological, and biological ramifications. Even

the same life event (e.g., divorce) can have very different meaning and implications depending on an individual's specific role in the event (e.g., as the initiator of a divorce vs. the target of the rejection; Slavich, O'Donovan, Epel, & Kemeny, 2010). What is it about major life events that might predispose someone to pathology? More specifically, what is it about particular *kinds* of major life events that predispose to a range of and/or specific *types* of disorders?

Viewed in this manner, it can be appreciated that many conceptual alternatives exist for processing the information from the prior measurement phases and finally quantifying life stress. Whereas the operational phase of measurement supplies a broad landscape of opportunities for rating a range of theoretical qualities associated with major life events, the quantification phase selectively draws from and implements these theoretical distinctions to fine-tune and tailor the measurement process for the final summary index for the particular disorder in question. For instance, different types of major life stress have been found to predict the onset of diverse pathological conditions, such as anxiety disorders (e.g., Finlay-Jones & Brown, 1981), coronary heart disease (e.g., Neilson, Brown, & Marmot, 1989; Schneiderman, Ironson, & Siegel, 2005), appendectomy (e.g., Creed, 1989), and even bipolar disorder (Johnson, 2005) and psychosis generally (e.g., Mansueto & Faravelli, 2017). Such a system for operationalizing major life events provides a flexible and powerful system for investigating the environmental origins of a wide variety of psychological and physical disorders (Brown & Harris, 1989).

Another key theoretical dimension is that of *time*. This topic touches upon several considerations. First are questions about the duration of heightened susceptibility. Major life events can have a significant immediate impact, but they also can have longer term consequences. For instance, losing a job often has a profound and prolonged impact, whereas incurring a brief period of being laid-off typically would be less likely to have significant enduring effects. The impact also is likely to change over time as the person recovers and adapts. For example, the loss of a significant relationship is likely to be more acute and painful immediately after it happens, and typically less, or much less, a year later. Further, the impact and its duration may be moderated by subsequent major life events. For example, losing a job and being hired into a new position shortly thereafter usually has less enduring pernicious consequences than becoming permanently unemployed.

Assessing the precise timing of life event exposures is critical for two additional reasons. First and most important, it enables investigators to ensure that the life events that are included in the final stress exposure indices occurred before, and not after, the outcome(s) being studied. Second, it allows researchers to study whether life events occurring during certain times or periods of life are more or less influential.

Overall, generic measures of environmental exposures will be insensitive for quantifying effects of causal relevance for physical and psychological disorders. What these points and examples make clear is that major life events (1) differ theoretically with regard to the kinds of adverse consequences they initiate, which may be more or less associated with different disorders; (2) vary with regard to the duration of adverse consequences they propagate over time; and (3) interact with other major life events in moderating the adverse consequences over time. These theoretical and temporal distinctions have direct implications for developing the final summary index. Specifically, how is such variation in the adverse effects of major life events best represented for probing stress–disorder relations?

A VARIETY OF CALCULI FOR QUANTIFYING MAJOR LIFE EVENTS

Innumerable approaches exist for the final quantification of major life events. At one end of the spectrum, investigators have simply summed all events occurring in the recent past (e.g., last month or past year) (Holmes & Rahe, 1967). At the other end of the spectrum, researchers have designated one type of life event occurring within a specific interval (e.g., e.g., severe life events within 3 months of depression onset; Brown & Harris, 1989). Between these two practices, much methodological creativity and inconsistency are evident, with many opportunities for questionable decisions at best, and shameless *p*-hacking at worst, resulting in methodological chaos and inconsistent results.

At the heart of the matter is the question of how optimally to assemble varied and diverse characteristics of major life events that are hypothetically linked to pathogenic processes. A common operating procedure has been "additivity": that major life events can be summated to represent the cumulative adverse effects. As explained previously, however, not all major life events are theoretically comparable or similar with respect to their pathogenic potential;

rather, they vary by kind, recency, interactions with other major life events, and the type of disorder under investigation. These points raise grave concerns about the common practice of simply adding up all recent major life events.[6]

Methodologically, too, an additivity assumption is challenging. Without guidelines for standardizing the interrelations between sets of complex events (e.g., event sequences, superordinate events, etc.; see earlier discussion), final summary indices for theoretically similar circumstances vary tremendously across studies. For example, one investigator may subsume a number of affiliated events constituting a marital break-up as one exposure, whereas another may rate each of the affiliated events as separate exposures (e.g., arguments, move, separation, divorce, changes in friendship, altered economic circumstances, etc.). Overall, the summation of all major events, without attention to these distinctions, results in an insensitive final indicator at best and a misleading one at worst.

All of these points raise a combinatorial conundrum for stress research regarding how to optimize the aggregation of information about major life events in terms of qualities, time, and outcomes. Ironically, this culminating endpoint is perhaps the most imperfectly understood and most variably implemented component of the measurement process. Decisions about these matters should be grounded in an understanding of the disorder under study, particularly with regard to the types of exposures of theoretical interest, as well as to the temporal dynamics of exposure impact over time. With greater awareness of these issues, we hope that the field can move toward more theoretically coherent and standardized procedures.

EVALUATIVE COMMENTS

Interview- and investigator-based approaches supply a rich array of information facilitating selection of the kinds of exposures and their timing in relation to the onset of the disorder under study. Concerns over "intracategory" variation are minimized, handling of complex exposures and event sequences is standardized, and timing of life events and disorder onset is established. Based upon the disorder under study, theory or past precedent can guide researchers to optimize the final index. Overall, the requisite ingredients are available to provide a flexible and reliable final index for the particular disorder of interest. However, to be methodologically pristine, the final index should be constructed a priori, or at least independent of the researcher's knowledge of the participant's reactions and disorder status.

Turning to self-report checklist measures, constraints and concerns from the prior phases become ever more apparent and magnified. Problems in assessing and operationalizing major life events from the prior two phases remain, as potential biases and extraneous noise are carried through. But these problems can also be exacerbated as they are aggregated into the final index. First, the final index across study participants represents an unknown amalgamation of major and minor life events, major and minor life event sequences, and major and minor life event complexes. Second, the final index is confounded with the respondent's reactions to the exposure, as well as awareness of his or her clinical status. Third, the timing of exposures and the timing of disorder onset are not reliably established (Harkness & Monroe, 2016). Finally, in deciding which exposures to include or not, for methodological purity the researcher should not be aware of the respondent's reactions to exposures or clinical status. Overall, it is difficult to escape the conclusion that, with self-report checklists, the investigator has lost control over the core operational responsibilities in the research enterprise, raising grave doubts about the utility of the final summary index.

Empirical Evidence: Reliability and Validity Studies

In the early days of research, much discussion focused prematurely upon advanced theoretical issues involving stressful life events, with "only relatively scant attention to the foundation issue of the dependability of the data being reported" (Jenkins, Hurst, & Rose, 1979, p. 382). A tendency remains for the mundane but fundamental matters of reliability and validity to be overshadowed by impulsive excitement about theoretical possibilities. Yet the differences we have pointed out in the principles and procedures for measuring major life events strongly point to the likelihood of differences in their psychometric qualifications. Although in theory questions about reliability and validity are relatively straightforward, the answers too often have been littered with partial truths and selective reporting. The "foundation issue of the dependability of the data being reported" merits much greater scientific respect (Jenkins et al., 1979, p. 382).

In the following, we initially clarify the information needed to inform psychometric decisions for research on major life events. We next discuss the psychometric properties of self-reports checklists and interview-derived procedures separately, and finally directly compare the different approaches.

PSYCHOMETRIC PROPERTIES: RELIABILITY AND VALIDITY

With regard to test-retest reliability, early psychometric research on self-report life event checklists documented that, as the period of recall increases (e.g., beyond 7–14 days), "reliability drops precipitously for both total scores and individual events" and is "particularly poor when the checklist is self-administered" (Dohrenwend, 2006, p. 481; e.g., .30–.60, Neugebauer, 1984; see also Paykel, 1983; Rabkin & Struening, 1976). Low reliability has been found, too, when participants report repeatedly over short longitudinal intervals (e.g., monthly), and then report on life events for the entire retrospective time period. For example, there was agreement on only 25% of the events using such a method, with many more events reported in the monthly assessments (Raphael, Cloitre, & Dohrenwend, 1991; see also Monroe, 1982). Finally, very low co-informant agreement has been found (e.g., 33% for the SRRS; Yager, Grant, Sweetwood, & Gerst, 1981; Neugebauer, 1983) (see also Harkness & Monroe, 2016; Monroe, 2008).[7] There are few recent reports addressing these psychometric topics, yet since the basic format of these measures has not changed, there is no reason for optimism about the matter (see Dohrenwend, 2006).[8] In summary, the available evidence strongly indicates that respondents do not provide reliable information about their recent life events when using self-report life event checklists.

Given problematic psychometric underpinnings for self-report life event checklists, many articles address these core issues in oblique and misleading ways. "Cosmetic psychometrics" sidestep disclosure of basic psychometric information and thereby elude criticism (Harkness & Monroe, 2016). For example, a common practice in large-scale epidemiological studies is simply to omit psychometric information altogether, relying solely on the face validity or on a long-standing tradition of using checklists such as the SRRS (e.g., Kalmbach et al., 2016; Määttänen et al., 2015; Tamers et al., 2015). Another strategy is to claim "good reliability and validity," either with no evidentiary basis provided or by referring to studies that, when examined, do not furnish the implied psychometric support (e.g., Kindt, Kleinjan, Janssens, & Scholte, 2015). Some recent reports are even bold enough to proclaim the SRRS to be the "gold standard" for stress assessment (e.g., Marchetto et al., 2016).

In contrast, interview-based procedures are more successful in documenting acceptable levels of reliability.[9] For example, early research on the LEDS indicated 81% agreement for any life event between patients with schizophrenia and relatives, and 79% agreement between depressed patients and relatives (Brown & Harris, 1978, p. 71). Early work with the UCLA Episodic Life Events Interview found interjudge correlations of .77 for objective threat ratings and .85 for independence ratings (Hammen, 1991). For ratings of the same severe life events occurring in the past year, Brown, Sklair, Harris, and Birley (1973) reported 91% rater agreement, and Monroe et al. (2007) indicated high interrater agreement for severe events corrected for chance (e.g., for pairwise comparisons of 2–4 raters ranged from 0.72 to 0.79, mean = 0.76; Cohen's k, corrected for differences in the number of raters per event; Uebersax, 1982). Examining the "falloff" or diminishing frequency of life events over progressively longer retrospective intervals (presuming the diminishing frequency is due to forgetting or underreporting), there is evidence that severe events are reported reliably for at least 1 year, whereas events of a lesser degree of severity may begin falloff slightly after 5 or more months (Brown, 1989, p. 37).

Finally, studies directly comparing checklist and interview methods are most central and revealing. Comparisons between respondent- and investigator-defined major life events indicate very low concordance between the two (e.g., perhaps less than 40% of the time; Gorman, 1993; Lewinsohn, Rohde, & Gau, 2003; McQuaid et al., 1992; Monroe, 2008). McQuaid et al. (1992) found that only 38.5% of life events reported with a self-report checklist were the same as life events defined by the LEDS (Brown & Harris 1978). Further, Lewinsohn et al. (2003) made similar comparisons between self-report and interview-based methods. For life events primarily involving the study participants, they found that 67.5% of events reported on the checklist met the criteria for their stress interview. Yet for life events primarily involving other individuals, the concordance rate was only 19.7%. Because life events primarily involving other people were reported about twice as often as those involving the participant, the overall percentage of life events based on the interview criterion that matched the self-report measure was well below 50%. It is noteworthy that this lack of agreement between methods is also found when restricting reporting to highly significant life events. For instance, Duggal et al. (2000) found that only 32% of severe life events occurring prior to the onset of major depression were endorsed on a self-report checklist (see also Harkness & Monroe, 2016; Monroe, 2008; Simons, Angell, Monroe, & Thase, 1993). Finally, with regard to falloff of event reporting over time, Neilson et al. (1989, p. 322) estimated a rate of 5% per year with the LEDS in their 10-year study, compared to a rate of 5% per *month* for retrospective reporting with life events checklists.

The situation is more complex with respect to predictive validity. Given that self-report procedures have a high error rate for identifying major life events (e.g., exceeding 50%, as noted earlier), the utility of comparative validity studies is questionable (Monroe, 2008). Nonetheless, a handful of studies provide relevant data. On the one hand, interview-based methods have been found to be superior in studies of life stress and depression (e.g., predicting greater depressive symptoms or lower probability of remission, McQuaid et al., 2000; detecting severe events typically found to precede depression onset, Duggal et al., 2000). On the other hand, self-report measures of life events sometimes have yielded similar or different associations when compared with interview-based measures (e.g., McQuaid et al., 2000; see also Wagner, Abela, & Brozina, 2006).

As Dohrenwend (2006) observed, studies suggesting comparable ability for the two approaches to discriminate between disordered and nondisordered groups occur despite the two approaches often identifying different major life events (Costello & Devins, 1988; Duggal et al., 2000; Katschnig, 1986; Raphael et al., 1991). How might such seemingly discrepant findings be reconciled with respect to validity considerations? It must be recalled that investigator-based approaches methodologically ensure that exposures, responses, and outcomes are not confounded. In contrast, self-report life event measures do not provide such methodological safeguards. Consequently, a parsimonious interpretation is that such findings reflect different underlying associations for the two measurement approaches and outcomes: one valid, one confounded.

SUMMARY AND CONCLUSIONS
Comparisons of psychometric characteristics for interview-based and self-report checklists differ substantially. Comparative research conclusively favors the scientific credibility of interview-derived procedures and points to unacceptably poor performance

for self-report checklists. Reports favoring the latter typically supply only superficial or "a la carte" psychometric information and overlook or ignore the well-documented psychometric limitations. In recognition these matters, Harkness and Monroe (2016) recently averred, "To be very clear about this matter, based on all available evidence we cannot envision any circumstances under which self-report checklists of life events, in good scientific conscience, can be recommended or justified" (p. 737).

Future Directions

Looking forward, several broad issues could be addressed to improve research on life events and health. First, despite recognition that life events can occur in several life domains (e.g., romantic relationships, financial, education, work, crime, etc.) and involve different social-psychological characteristics (e.g., interpersonal loss, physical danger, humiliation, entrapment, etc.), very few studies to date have investigated the effects of different life event types. This has occurred even though the few studies that examined such effects have found notable differences in associations between specific types of life events and psychological, biological, and behavioral outcomes (e.g., Brown, Harris, & Hepworth, 1995; Keller, Neale, & Kendler, 2007; Keller & Nesse, 2006; Kendler et al., 2003; Murphy, Slavich, Chen, & Miller, 2015). Because such *stressor characteristic* studies are rare, however, the current empirical literature on life events largely obscures potential stressor-specific effects, leaving the impression that life stress is a singular, unitary construct. To address this issue, more studies are needed that characterize different types of life events and, in turn, examine their effects. Such research will help identify when and for what outcomes different life events exert the same versus different effects, which will ultimately help advance theoretical formulations of stress.

Because identifying different types of life events requires quality measurement systems that obtain contextual details, the second issue we raise has to do with the usability and scalability of existing gold standard systems for assessing life events. Presently, there is an inherent and rather dramatic trade-off between usability versus reliability and validity in life event instruments. Whereas self-report measures that produce relatively low-quality data are inexpensive, easy to administer, and therefore simple to integrate into studies of stress and health, investigator- and interview based-systems that produce high-quality data require extensive training and

expertise, and substantial financial support to implement. Therefore, we should not be too surprised that more investigators choose the former over the latter, especially when research funding is limited and other expensive procedures (e.g., fMRI, GWAS, etc.) are often involved. Valuable goals, therefore, would be to (1) improve the usability and scalability of high-quality life event instruments so they can be used more widely and by investigators who want to assess life events well, but who are not stress assessment experts, and (2) encourage collaborative relations between investigators interested in stress, but without expertise in measuring life stress, with investigators possessing such expertise (Harkness & Monroe, 2016).

Finally, attention should be paid to a growing mismatch between contemporary theories of stress and health, and the instruments that are most commonly used to assess life events. More specifically, whereas numerous theories have recently proposed that cumulative life stress occurring over the entire life span plays a role in shaping many aspects of mental and physical health (e.g., Graham, Christian, & Kiecolt-Glaser, 2006; Lupien, McEwen, Gunnar, & Heim, 2009; McEwen, 1998; Slavich & Cole, 2013), the instruments most commonly used for assessing life events typically only capture exposures occurring over the past few weeks or 1–2 years maximum, leaving the rest of the person's life unexamined. As a result, while it is easy to find theoretical articles on how life events might accumulate over time to shape human health and behavior, the empirical basis for such conjecture is almost nonexistent since only a few studies have actually assessed lifetime stress exposure.

The development of the Stress and Adversity Inventory (STRAIN) has been impactful in this regard as it provides investigators with a tool for quickly assessing individuals' exposure to a variety of acute life events and chronic difficulties that are known to impact health (Slavich & Shields, 2018). The system has been found to predict a number of health-related outcomes, including sleep difficulties, memory, cognitive function, metabolic activity, fatigue, depression, and mental and physical health (Cuneo et al., 2017; Dooley, Slavich, Moreno, & Bower, 2017; Goldfarb, Shields, Daw, Slavich, & Phelps, 2017; Kurtzman et al., 2012; Shields et al., 2017; Toussaint, Shields, Dorn, & Slavich, 2016). The system shows good immunity from factors that are known to bias self-reporting (e.g., social desirability, personality), and it also demonstrates excellent concurrent validity, discriminate validity, and test-retest reliability over 2–4 weeks (rs = .90–.92 for the main stress indices; see Slavich & Shields, 2018). To maximize efficiency, though, the STRAIN does not generate independent stress exposure ratings, meaning there still is room for achieving the ultimate goal of simultaneously maximizing both instrument scalability *and* objectivity.

Conclusions

Although life stress is accorded a central role in many contemporary models of psychopathology and physical health, the conceptualization and assessment of a key form of stress exposure—namely, major life events—remains in practice too frequently unstandardized and crude. Put simply, major life events are defined and assessed in a multitude of different ways, and measurement error (e.g., due to poor reliability, confounding of predictor with outcome, etc.) is all too common. A few gold-standard instruments exist for obtaining high-quality reports of individuals' major life event exposure, but these systems are used infrequently, with a majority of studies instead using instruments that suffer from critical limitations. These measurement concerns can produce findings that are confounded or difficult to replicate, or, in the worst cases, ethnically questionable. Looking forward, we believe the field can benefit from additional clarity around the conceptual and definitional issues we have discussed, as well as from the more frequent implementation of stress assessment systems that yield high-quality life event information. For while there is no question that major life events can play a key role in shaping human health and behavior, opportunities for enhancing definitional and conceptual clarity, and improving measurement, abound.

Notes

1. Note that this is a "first-pass" attempt to distinguish a class of major life events (as opposed to more minor kinds of exposures). As we will see, further distinctions can be made in the operationalization phase with respect to more specific dimensions associated with major life events that may be especially relevant for understanding different psychological or physical health conditions. For example, major life events involving loss may be especially important for the development of major depression, whereas major life events entailing "danger" may be more relevant for anxiety-related conditions (Monroe, 1990).

2. We will, however, review herein the research with regard to reliability considerations and direct comparisons of the two approaches.

3. With regard to independence in rating exposures and responses, it is not possible for the interviewer to be aware of, and potentially influenced by, the respondent's reactions to the life event as the respondent recounts the story. With regard to the independence for rating exposures and outcomes, confounding is a major concern with cross-sectional research designs, but with appropriate precautions it may be less of a concern for prospective designs.

4. Note a companion concern that major life events may be "downgraded" and dismissed as being inconsequential from the perspective of the participant (see Monroe, 2008).

5. Such a tendency to inflate (or to underestimate) exposures could be an interesting response characteristic that moderates the stressful consequences of exposures (see Monroe & Kelley, 1995). But as we have emphasized, a cardinal methodological requirement is that the measurement of exposures and responses be performed separately and independently.

6. One strategy to crudely address such concerns has been to provide subjective or personal ratings of major life events. However, as indicted in Figure 1.1 and discussed previously, without the use of blinded scoring this strategy compromises the research in terms of the likelihood of confounding exposures, responses, and outcomes.

7. Some articles report Cohen's kappa reliability statistics, reflecting internal consistency of the measure. But as pointed out by several critics, this form of reliability is not appropriate for life event measures, as there is no a priori rationale for why different life events should co-occur (Cleary, 1981; Monroe, 1982). Stress is the product or *consequence* of event exposures, not a common latent variable that "creates" the event exposures.

8. An advocate for life event self-report checklist methods might cite the List of Threatening Experiences (LTE) as counterexample to our argument, representing an abbreviated measure with acceptable psychometric properties (Brugha & Cragg, 1990). The reported test-retest and interrater reliability were indeed very good, but these statistics were based upon a test-retest interval of 1-day for the 12-item measure. As indicated previously, test-retest reliability for self-administered life events checklists "drops precipitously for both total scores and individual events" as the period of recall increases (e.g., beyond 7–14 days) (Dohrenwend, 2006, p. 481). Further, there is no protection against "double-reporting" (e.g., "You became unemployed…," "You were sacked from your job," and "You had a major financial crisis"; see Brugha & Cragg, 1990, p. 78). And, of course, the participant's determination of what constitutes a major event can be influenced by his or her response and/or health status.

9. Given the lengthy time requirements for interview-based procedures (e.g., 1–2 hours for the interview alone, and additional time for ratings), test-retest reliability studies are essentially nonexistent for these measures. Psychometric information for these measures is based predominately upon agreement across informants and interrater reliability.

References

Belli, R. F. (1998). The structure of autobiographical memory and the event history calendar: Potential improvements in the quality of retrospective reports in surveys. *Memory, 6*(4), 383–406. doi:10.1080/741942610

Brown, G. W. (1974). Meaning, measurement, and stress of life events. In B. S. Dohrenwend & B. P. Dohrenwend (Eds.), *Stressful life events: Their nature and effects* (pp. 217–243). New York, NY: Wiley.

Brown, G. W. (1989). Life events and measurement. In G. W. Brown & T. O. Harris (Eds.), *Life events and illness* (pp. 3–45). New York, NY: Guilford Press.

Brown, G. W., & Harris, T. O. (1978). *Social origins of depression: A study of psychiatric disorders in women*. New York, NY: Free Press.

Brown, G. W., & Harris, T. O. (1989). *Life events and illness*. New York, NY: Guilford Press.

Brown, G. W., Harris, T. O., & Hepworth, C. (1995). Loss, humiliation and entrapment among women developing depression: A patient and non-patient comparison. *Psychological Medicine, 25*, 7–21.

Brown, G. W., Sklair, F., Harris, T. O., & Birley, J. L. T. (1973). Life vents and psychiatric disorders: 1. Some methodological issues. *Psychological Medicine, 3*, 74–78.

Brugha T. S., & Cragg D. (1990). The List of Threatening Experiences: The reliability and validity of a brief life events questionnaire. *Acta Psychiatrica Scandanavica, 82*, 77–81.

Cleary, P. J. (1981). Problems of internal consistency and scaling in life event schedules. *Journal of Psychosomatic Research, 25*, 309–320.

Cohen, S., Gianaros, P. J., & Manuck, S. B. (2016). A stage model of stress and disease. *Perspectives on Psychological Science, 11*(4), 456–463. http://doi.org/10.1177/1745691616646305

Cohen, S., Janicki-Deverts, D., & Miller, G. (2007). Psychological stress and disease. *Journal of the American Medical Association, 298*(14), 1685–1687. doi:10.1001/jama.298.14.1685

Costello, C. G., & Devins, G. M. (1988). Two-staged screening for stressful events and chronic difficulties. *Canadian Journal of Behavioural Science, 20*, 85–92.

Creed, F. (1989). Appendectomy. In G. W. Brown & T. O. Harris (Eds.), *Life events and illness* (pp. 213–231). New York, NY: Guilford Press.

Cuneo, M. G., Schrepf, A., Slavich, G. M., Thaker, P. H., Goodheart, M., Bender, D.,…Lutgendorf, S. K. (2017). Diurnal cortisol rhythms, fatigue and psychosocial factors in five-year survivors of ovarian cancer. *Psychoneuroendocrinology, 84*, 139–142.

Darwin, C. (1859). *On the origin of species by means of natural selection, or, the perseveration of favored races in the struggle for life*. London, UK: John Murray.

Dickerson, S. S., & Kemeny, M. E. (2004). Acute stressors and cortisol responses: A theoretical integration and synthesis of laboratory research. *Psychological Bulletin, 130*, 355–391.

Dohrenwend, B. P. (1974). Problems in defining and sampling the relevant population of stressful life events. In B. S. Dohrenwend & B. P. Dohrenwend (Eds.), *Stressful life events: Their nature and effects* (pp. 275–310). New York, NY: Wiley.

Dohrenwend, B. P. (2006). Inventorying stressful life events as risk factors for psychopathology: Toward resolution of the problem of intracategory variability. *Psychological Bulletin, 132*(3), 477–495. doi:10.1037/0033-2909.132.3.477

Dohrenwend, B. S., Askenasy, A. R., Krasnoff, L., & Dohrenwend, B. P. (1978). Exemplification of a method for scaling life events: The PERI Life Events Scale. *Journal of Health and Social Behavior, 19*(2), 205–229.

Dohrenwend, B. P., Raphael, K. G., Schwartz, S., Stueve, A., & Skodol, A. (1993) The structured probe and narrative rating method for measuring stressful life events. In B. S. Dohrenwend (Ed.), *Handbook of stress: Theoretical and clinical aspects* (2nd ed., p. 174–199). New York, NY: Free Press.

Dohrenwend, B. S., & Dohrenwend, B. P. (1974) *Stressful life events: Their nature and effects*. Oxford, UK: John Wiley & Sons.

Dooley, L. N., Slavich, G. M., Moreno, P. I., & Bower, J. E. (2017). Strength through adversity: Moderate lifetime stress exposure is associated with psychological resilience in breast cancer survivors. *Stress and Health, 33*, 549–557.

Duggal, S., Malkoff-Schwartz, S., Birmaher, B., Anderson, B. P., Matty, M. K., Houck, P. R.,…Frank, E. (2000). Assessment of life stress in adolescents: Self-report versus interview methods. *Journal of the American Academy of Child and Adolescent Psychiatry, 39*(4), 445–452. doi:10.1097/00004583-200004000-00013

Finlay-Jones, R., & Brown, G. W. (1981). Types of stressful life event and the onset of anxiety and depressive disorders. *Psychological Medicine, 11*, 803–815.

Goldfarb, E. V., Shields, G. S., Daw, N. D., Slavich, G. M., & Phelps, E. A. (2017). Low lifetime stress exposure is associated with reduced stimulus-response memory. *Learning and Memory, 24*, 162–168.

Gorman, D. M. (1993). A review of studies comparing checklist and interview methods of data collection in life event research. *Behavioral Medicine, 19*, 66–73.

Graham, J. E., Christian, L. M., & Kiecolt-Glaser, J. K. (2006). Stress, age, and immune function: Toward a lifespan approach. *Journal of Behavioral Medicine, 29*, 389–400.

Hall, H. (2014). On miracles. *Skeptic Magazine, 19*, 17–23.

Hammen, C. (1991). Generation of stress in the course of unipolar depression. *Journal of Abnormal Psychology, 100*(4), 555–561. doi:10.1037//0021-843X.100.4.555

Hammen, C. (2005). Stress and depression. *Annual Review of Clinical Psychology, 1*(1), 293–319. doi.org/10.1146/annurev.clinpsy.1.102803.143938

Hammen, C. (2016). Depression and stressful environments: Identifying gaps in conceptualization and measurement. *Anxiety, Stress, & Coping, 29*(4), 335–351. doi.org/10.1080/10615806.2015.1134788

Hammen, C., Kim, E. Y., Eberhart, N. K., & Brennan, P. A. (2009). Chronic and acute stress and the prediction of major depression in women. *Depression and Anxiety, 26*, 718–723. http://dx.doi.org/10.1002/da.20571

Hankin, B. L., Abramson, L. Y., Miller, N., & Haeffel, G. J. (2004). Cognitive vulnerability-stress theories of depression: Examining affective specificity in the prediction of depression versus anxiety in three prospective studies. *Therapy, 28*(3), 309–345.

Harkness, K. L., & Monroe, S. M. (2016). The assessment and measurement of adult life stress: Basic premises, operational principles, and design requirements. *Journal of Abnormal Psychology, 125*(5), 727–745. http://doi.org/10.1037/abn0000178

Hinkle, L. E., Jr. (1974). The concept of "stress" in the biological and social sciences. *The International Journal of Psychiatry in Medicine, 5*(4), 335–357. http://doi.org/10.2190/91DK-NKAD-1XP0-Y4RG

Holmes, T. H., & Rahe, R. H. (1967). The social readjustment rating scale. *Journal of Psychosomatic Research, 11*(2), 213–221.

Hudgens, R. W. (1974). Personal catastrophe and depression: A consideration of the subject with respect to medically ill adolescents, and a requiem for retrospective life-event studies. In B. S. Dohrenwend & B. P. Dohrenwend (Eds.), *Stressful life events: Their nature and effects* (pp. 119–149). New York, NY: John Wiley & Sons.

Humphrey, J. H. (2005). *Anthology of stress revisited: Selected works of James H. Foreword by Paul J. Rosch*. New York, NY: Nova Science Publishers.

Jarcho, M. R., Slavich, G. M., Tylova-Stein, H., Wolkowitz, O. M., & Burke, H. M. (2013). Dysregulated diurnal cortisol pattern is associated with glucocorticoid resistance in women with major depressive disorder. *Biological Psychology, 93*, 150–158.

Jenkins, C. D., Hurst, M. W., & Rose. R. (1979). Life changes. Do people really remember? *Archives of General Psychiatry, 36*, 379–384.

Johnson, S. L. (2005). Mania and dysregulation in goal pursuit: A review. *Clinical Psychology Review, 25*, 241–262.

Kagan, J. (2016). An overly permissive extension. *Perspectives on Psychological Science, 11*(4), 442–450. http://doi.org/10.1177/1745691616635593

Kalmbach, D. A., Pillai, V., Arnedt, J. T., Anderson, J. R., & Drake, C. L. (2016). Sleep system sensation: Evidence for changing roles of etiological factors in insomnia. *Sleep Medicine, 21*, 63–69.

Katschnig, H. (1986). Measuring life stress—a comparison of the checklist and the panel technique. In H. Katschnig (Ed.), *Life events and psychiatric disorders* (pp. 74–106). New York, NY: Cambridge University Press.

Keller, M. C., Neale, M. C., & Kendler, K. S. (2007). Association of different adverse life events with distinct patterns of depressive symptoms. *American Journal of Psychiatry, 164*, 1521–1529.

Keller, M. C., & Nesse, R. M. (2006). The evolutionary significance of depressive symptoms: Different adverse situations lead to different depressive symptom patterns. *Journal of Personality and Social Psychology, 91*, 316–330.

Kendler, K. S., Hettema, J. M., Butera, F., Gardner, C. O., & Prescott, C. A. (2003). Life event dimensions of loss, humiliation, entrapment, and danger in the prediction of onsets of major depression and generalized anxiety. *Archives of General Psychiatry, 60*(8), 789. http://doi.org/10.1001/archpsyc.60.8.789

Kendler, K. S., Karkowski, L. M., & Prescott, C. A. (1999). Causal relationship between stressful life events and the onset of major depression. *American Journal of Psychiatry, 156*(6), 837–841.

Kendler, K. S., Kessler, R. C., Walters, E. E., MacLean, C., Neale, M. C., Heath, A. C., & Eaves, L. J. (1995). Stressful life events, genetic liability, and onset of an episode of major depression in women. *American Journal of Psychiatry, 152*(6), 833–842.

Kindt, K. C. M., Kleinjan, M., Janssens, J. M. A. M., & Scholte, R. H. J. (2015). Cross-lagged associations between adolescents' depressive symptoms and negative cognitive style: The role of negative life events. *Journal of Youth and Adolescence, 44*, 2141–2153.

Kurtzman, L., O'Donovan, A., Koslov, K., Arenander, J., Epel, E. S., & Slavich, G. M. (2012). Sweating the big stuff: Dispositional pessimism exacerbates the deleterious effects of life stress on metabolic health. *European Journal of Psychotraumatology, 3*.

Lazarus, R. S., & Folkman, S. (1984). *Stress, appraisal, and coping.* New York, NY: Springer.

Lewinsohn, P. M., Rohde, P., & Gau, J. M. (2003). Comparability of self-report checklist and interview data in the assessment of stressful life events in young adults. *Psychological Reports, 93*, 459–471.

Lupien, S. J., McEwen, B. S., Gunnar, M. R., & Heim, C. (2009) Effects of stress throughout the lifespan on the brain, behaviour and cognition. *Nature Reviews Neuroscience, 10*, 434–445.

Määttänen, I., Jokela, M., Pulkki-Råback, Keltikangas-Järvinen, L., Swan, H., Toivonen, L., Merjonen, P., & Hintsa, T. (2015). Brief report: Emotional distress and recent stressful life events in long QT syndrome mutation carriers. *Journal of Health Psychology, 20*(11), 1445–1450.

Mansueto, G., & Faravelli, C. (2017). Recent life events and psychosis: The role of childhood adversities. *Psychiatry Research, 256*, 111–117. http://doi.org/10.1016/j.psychres.2017.06.042

Marchetto, N., Glynn, R., Ferry, M. L., Ostojic, M., Wolff, S. M., Yao, R., & Haussmann, M. F. (2016). Prenatal stress and newborn telomere length. *American Journal of Obstetrics and Gynecology, 215*(1), 94.e1–e8. http://doi.org/10.1016/j.ajog.2014.10.255

McEwen, B. S. (1998). Stress, adaptation, and disease: Allostasis and allostatic load. *Annals of the New York Academy of Sciences, 840*, 33–44.

McEwen, B. S., & Gianaros, P., 2011. (2011). Stress-and allostasis-induced brain plasticity. *Annual Review of Medicine, 62*(1), 431–445. http://doi.org/10.1146/annurev-med-052209-100430

McEwen, B. S., McEwen, C., 2016. (2016). Response to Jerome Kagan's essay on stress (2016). *Perspectives on Psychological Science, 11*(4), 451–455. http://doi.org/10.1177/1745691616646635

McQuaid, J. R., Monroe, S. M., Roberts, J. R., Johnson, S. L., Garamoni, G. L., Kupfer, D. J., & Frank, E. (1992). Toward the standardization of life stress assessment: Definitional discrepancies and inconsistencies in methods. *Stress Medicine, 8*, 47–56. doi: 10.1002/smi.2460080107

McQuaid, J. R., Monroe, S. M., Roberts, J. E., Kupfer, D. J., & Frank, E. (2000). A comparison of two life stress assessment approaches: Prospective prediction of treatment outcome in recurrent depression. *Journal of Abnormal Psychology, 109*(4), 787–791. doi:10.1037/0021-843X.109.4.787

Monroe, S. M. (1982). Assessment of life events: Retrospective vs concurrent strategies. *Archives of General Psychiatry, 39*, 606–610.

Monroe, S. M. (1990). Psychosocial factors in anxiety and depression. In J. D. Maser & C. R. Cloninger (Eds.), *Comorbidity of mood and anxiety disorders* (pp. 463–497). Washington, D.C.: American Psychiatric Press.

Monroe, S. M. (2008). Modern approaches to conceptualizing and measuring human life stress. *Annual Review of Clinical Psychology, 4*, 33–52.

Monroe, S. M., & Kelley, J. M. (1995). Stress appraisal. In S. Cohen, R. Kessler, & L. U. Gordon (Eds.), *Measuring stress: A guide for health and social scientists* (pp. 122–147). New York, NY: Oxford University Press.

Monroe, S. M., & Roberts, J. E. (1990). Conceptualizing and measuring life stress: Problems, principles, procedures, progress. *Stress Medicine, 6*(3), 209–216.

Monroe, S. M., & Simons, A. D. (1991). Diathesis-stress theories in the context of life stress research: Implications for the depressive disorders. *Psychological Bulletin, 110*, 406–425.

Monroe, S. M., & Slavich, G. M. (2016). Psychological stressors: Overview. In George Fink (Ed.), *Stress concepts and cognition, emotion, and behavior (Vol. 1), Handbook of stress series* (pp. 109–115). Burlington, VT: Academic Press.

Monroe, S. M., Slavich, G. M., & Georgiades, K. (2014). The social environment and depression: The roles of life stress. In I. H. Gotlib & C. L. Hammen (Eds.), *Handbook of depression* (3rd ed., pp. 296–314). New York, NY: The Guilford Press.

Monroe, S. M., Slavich, G. M., Torres, L. D., & Gotlib, I. H. (2007). Major life events and major chronic difficulties are differentially associated with history of major depressive episodes. *Journal of Abnormal Psychology*, *116*(1), 116–124. http://doi.org/10.1037/0021-843X.116.1.116

Moore, S. R., & Depue, R. A. (2016). Neurobehavioral foundation of environmental reactivity. *Psychological Bulletin*, *142*, 107–164.

Murphy, M. L. M., Slavich, G. M., Chen, E., & Miller, G. E. (2015). Targeted rejection predicts decreased anti-inflammatory gene expression and increased symptom severity in youth with asthma. *Psychological Science*, *26*, 111–121.

Muscatell, K. A., Slavich, G. M., Monroe, S. M., & Gotlib, I. H. (2009). Stressful life events, chronic difficulties, and the symptoms of clinical depression. *Journal of Nervous and Mental Disease*, *197*, 154–160.

Neilson, E., Brown, G. W., & Marmot, M. (1989). Myocardial infarction. In G. W. Brown & T. O. Harris (Eds.), *Life events and illness* (pp. 313–342). New York, NY: Guilford Press.

Neugebauer, R. (1983). Reliability of life-event interviews with outpatient schizophrenics. *Archives of General Psychiatry*, *40*(4), 378–383. doi:10.1001/archpsyc. 1983.01790040032005.

Neugebauer, R. (1984). The reliability of life-events reports. In B. S. Dohrenwend & B. P. Dohrenwend (Eds.), *Stressful life events and their contexts* (pp. 85–107). New Brunswick, NJ: Rutgers University Press.

Paykel, E. S. (1983). Methodological aspects of life events research. *Journal of Psychosomatic Research*, *27*(5), 341–352. doi:10.1016/0022-3999(83)90065-X

Paykel, E. S. (1997). The interview for recent life events. *Psychological Medicine*, *27*(2), 301–310. doi:10.1017/S0033291796004424

Rabkin, J. G., & Struening, E. L. (1976). Life events, stress, and illness. *Science*, *194*(4269), 1013–1020.

Raphael, K. G., Cloitre, M., & Dohrenwend, B. P. (1991). Problems of recall and misclassification with checklist methods of measuring stressful life events. *Health Psychology*, *10*, 62–74.

Sarason, I. G., Johnson, J. H., & Siegel, J. M. (1978). Assessing the impact of life changes: Development of the Life Experiences Survey. *Journal of Consulting and Clinical Psychology*, *46*, 932–946.

Selye, H. (1973). The evolution of the stress concept. *American Scientist*, *61*, 692–699.

Schneiderman, N., Ironson, G., & Siegel, S. D. (2005). Stress and health: Psychological, behavioral, and biological determinants. *Annual Review of Clinical Psychology*, *1*, 607–628.

Schwarz, N. (2007). Cognitive aspects of survey methodology. *Applied Cognitive Psychology*, *21*(2), 277–287. doi:10.1002/acp.1340

Shields, G. S., Doty, D., Shields, R. H., Gower, G., Slavich, G. M., & Yonelinas, A. P. (2017). Recent life stress exposure is associated with poorer long-term memory, working memory, and self-reported memory. *Stress*, *20*, 598–607.

Shields, G. S., & Slavich, G. M. (2017). Lifetime stress exposure and health: A review of contemporary assessment methods and biological mechanisms. *Social and Personality Psychology Compass*, *11*(8), e12335.

Shrout, P. E., Link, B. G., Dohrenwend, B. P., Skodol, A. E., Stueve, A., & Mirotznik, J. (1989). Characterizing life events as risk factors in depression: The role of fateful loss events. *Journal of Abnormal Psychology*, *98*, 460–467.

Simons, A. D., Angell, K. L., Monroe, S. M., & Thase, M. E. (1993). Cognition and life stress in depression: Cognitive factors and the definition, rating, and generation of negative life events. *Journal of Abnormal Psychology*, *102*(4), 584–591. doi:10.1037/0021-843X.102.4.584

Slavich, G. M. (2016). Life stress and health: A review of conceptual issues and recent findings. *Teaching of Psychology*, *43*, 346–355.

Slavich, G. M., & Cole, S. W. (2013). The emerging field of human social genomics. *Clinical Psychological Science*, *1*, 331–348.

Slavich, G. M., O'Donovan, A., Epel, E. S., & Kemeny, M. E. (2010). Black sheep get the blues: A psychobiological model of social rejection and depression. *Neuroscience and Biobehavioral Reviews*, *35*, 39–45.

Slavich, G. M., & Shields, G. S. (2018). Assessing lifetime stress exposure using the Stress and Adversity Inventory for Adults (Adult STRAIN): An overview and initial validation. *Psychosomatic Medicine*, *80*, 17–27.

Slavich, G. M., Thornton, T., Torres, L. D., Monroe, S. M., & Gotlib, I. H. (2009). Targeted rejection predicts hastened onset of major depression. *Journal of Social and Clinical Psychology*, *28*, 223–243.

Stetler, C., & Miller, G. E. (2011). Depression and hypothalamic-pituitary-adrenal activation: A quantitative summary of four decades of research. *Psychosomatic Medicine*, *73*(2), 114–126. http://doi.org/10.1097/PSY.0b013e31820ad12b

Tamers, S. L., Okechukwu, C., Marino, M., Guéguen, A., Goldberg, M., & Zins, M. (2015). Effect of stressful life events on changes in smoking among the French: Longitudinal findings from GAZEL. *European Journal of Public Health*, *25*, 711–715.

Toussaint, L., Shields, G. S., Dorn, G., & Slavich, G. M. (2016). Effects of lifetime stress exposure on mental and physical health in young adulthood: How stress degrades and forgiveness protects health. *Journal of Health Psychology*, *21*, 1004–1014.

Uebersax, J. S. (1982). A generalized kappa coefficient. *Educational & Psychological Measurement*, *42*, 181–183.

Wagner, C., Abela, J. R. Z., & Brozina, K. (2006). A comparison of stress measures in children and adolescents: A self-reported checklist versus an objectively rated interview. *Journal of Psychopathology and Behavioral Assessment*, *28*, 251–261.

Weiner, H. (1992). *Perturbing the organism*. Chicago: University of Chicago Press.

Wethington, E., Kessler, R. C., & Brown, G. W. (1993). *Training manual and technical report for the Structured Life Events Inventory*. Ithaca, NY: Life Course Institute, Cornell University.

Yager, J., Grant, I., Sweetwood, H. L., & Gerst, M. (1981). Life event reports by psychiatric patients, non-patients, and their partners. *Archives of General Psychiatry*, *38*, 343–347. doi:10.1001/archpsyc.1981.01780280111013.

Daily Stress and Hassles

Aidan G. C. Wright, Elizabeth N. Aslinger, Blessy Bellamy,
Elizabeth A. Edershile, *and* William C. Woods

Abstract

Daily stress and hassles refers to quotidian adversity and the friction of moving through life. They have proved to be strongly associated with mental health, and serve as a proximal catalyst and outcome of symptomatology. Despite their intuitive and accessible nature, the constructs of daily hassles and stress pose several significant challenges in their conceptualization and measurement. This chapter reviews historical and contemporary approaches to measuring and assessing daily stress and hassles. Conceptual and definitional issues are covered, followed by three generations of daily stress assessment: cross-sectional, ambulatory assessment, and passive sensing. A selective summary is provided of research on daily stress as it relates to mental health.

Keywords: daily stress, daily hassles, assessment, measurement, ambulatory assessment

How was your day? Did you make it out of the house on time? Was traffic a breeze? Slow day at the office? Deadline looming? Boss acknowledge all your hard work? Did you get along with everyone, or did you have any disagreements? Did your kid get in trouble at school? Did your spouse complain about your habits? How's your sex life? Now, are you feeling stressed? The study of daily stress and hassles occupies itself with the answers to these questions. In short, "daily stress and hassles" refers to quotidian adversity and the friction of moving through life. This emphasis on minor or micro-stressors was brought to the fore in the 1970s by several investigators with concerns about the exclusive focus on major life events in the stress research of the time. Perhaps no other individual or group was as influential as Dr. Richard Lazarus and his colleagues working on the Berkeley Stress and Coping Project. This work led to a series of seminal papers in the early 1980s that included the first effort to develop a catalogue and measure of daily hassles (Kanner, Coyne, Schaefer, & Lazarus, 1981). Since then, the study of daily stress, both separate from and as a supplement to major life events, has

blossomed. Major findings in this area have relevance to both physical and mental health.

Here we consider how daily stress and hassles are conceptualized and operationalized across three generations of their measurement. The first generation borrowed its methodology from the life events literature, employing cross-sectional checklists and severity ratings of experienced stressors. The second generation involves the use of ambulatory assessment techniques, encompassing daily diaries, ecological momentary assessment, experience sampling, and ambulatory psychophysiology, to intensively and repeatedly assess stress in an individual's natural environment. Now cresting over the horizon is the third generation, in which passive sensing devices are being used in conjunction with machine learning to facilitate the automated capture of stress in daily life.

In much of the daily hassles and stress literature there is a parallel focus on coping. Depending on one's perspective, coping may be viewed as a necessary component of the dynamic process of stress. Transactional views of stress notwithstanding, we will not cover the concept or measurement of coping in much detail here, and instead we remain primarily focused on the definition and measure of daily stress and the hassles that drive it.

Definitional and Conceptual Foundations

Defining daily hassles, stressors, and stress would almost seem unnecessary for anyone likely to read this chapter. By virtue of being a human adult, the reader undoubtedly has more direct and informative experience with daily hassles and stress than any text can provide. Nevertheless, that with which we are most familiar often poses the greatest challenge for assessment and measurement in the behavioral sciences. Daily hassles and stress appear to be no different. As described by Lazarus and Delongis (1983), hassles are the "irritating, frustrating, distressing demands and troubled relationships that plague us day in and day out" (p. 247). Examples of hassles (or stressors) include quotidian events such as inclement weather, traffic, work demands, arguments with one's spouse, financial concerns, and disciplining a child, and many others. Beyond this basic description, articulating the essence and outlining the boundary conditions of the construct prove more difficult, especially in the context of studying their relationship to mental disorder (Dohrenwend, Dohrenwend, Dodson, & Shrout, 1984).

The motivation for measuring and studying daily hassles emerged from both practical and conceptual concerns with the study of stress up through the 1970s (DeLongis et al., 1982; Kanner et al., 1981; Lazarus, 1984; Lazarus & DeLongis, 1983). In part, the modest association between major life events (e.g., divorce, job loss, heart attack, death of a loved one) and health outcomes, a major early focus of the stress literature, was a catalyzing frustration (Kanner et al., 1981). More important was the fact that the assessment of major life events, often in cross-section, provided little access to the processes or mechanisms by which they conduced to ill health. This aligned with a growing emphasis on viewing stress as a contextualized and transactional process (Coyne & Lazarus, 1980; Lazarus & Launier, 1978). From this perspective, an event is stressful when it is appraised as having relevance for the individual, it is harmful or threatening, and it outstrips the individual's capacity to cope or manage. The implication is that not all events will be equally stressful for all individuals under all circumstances. Embedded in this conceptualization of stress is a process that unfolds and exerts its effects across time.

Indeed, a consensual definition of stress has long eluded the field. It is not our goal to resolve these issues, and instead we adopt an ecumenical perspective which views stress, generically, as a process. As such, "stress" can be broken down into constituent components, which in turn have measurement implications. Specifically, a key distinction to be made is between external events or stimuli (i.e., stressors) and internal responses to those events (e.g., perceived stress). As Monroe (2008) summarizes, different perspectives exist on which components should be emphasized as a function of differing definitions of stress (see also Monroe and Slavich, this volume). Different theorists and researchers have adopted views of stress as stimulus driven, response defined (either consensually or idiosyncratically), reflected in change or the potential thereof, in terms of biological or psychological processes, and so forth (Dougall & Baum, 2011). In our view, all of these approaches have relevance and validity, and it is incumbent on the researcher to clearly define and support their selected focus and measurement approach. These are likely to vary with study aims and feasibility.

As a general rule, however, when studying daily hassles and stress, we recommend making attempts to assess both stimuli and responses, because these will allow the most rich and textured mapping of the stress landscape. In the context of daily hassles and stress, environmental events or stimuli may include such examples as social conflicts, insufficient time at work, or lack of money. In terms of the measurement of daily stress, Kamarck, Shiffman, and Wethington, (2011) further distinguished between affective- and appraisal-based approaches to capturing responses to stimuli. Common affective responses to stress might include anxiety, sadness, or anger, whereas appraisal-based measures might emphasize cognitive evaluation of demands and available resources to deal with stressors. A clear implication is that, to the degree possible, measurement approaches should attempt to avoid confounding events and responses (Harkness & Monroe, 2016). For instance, asking whether a traffic jam occurred as an initial prompt, and then asking how stressful that particular event was. Although this would seem to be straightforward, this distinction often requires thoughtful consideration. To illustrate, in a relevant early debate, Dohrenwend and Shrout (1985) noted that although Kanner and colleagues' (1981) seminal measure of daily hassles included both a list of events and a rating of severity, the rating of severity began at *somewhat severe* and ranged to *extremely severe*. Thus, there was no way to endorse events as having occurred, but that the participant was unbothered by them. In effect, event and response were confounded, even if there was the ability to measure severity to some degree.

A related issue that has long plagued the stress literature is the importance and challenge of differentiating between *objective* and *subjective measures* of stressful events (see Monroe, 2008 for a review). At first glance, it may seem that measures of environmental stimuli would be objective, whereas measures of responses would be subjective. However, this is not necessarily the case. On the one hand, it is the case that the stress response, whether affective or appraisal based, will be subjective by definition. The interest is in how an individual perceives, evaluates, and responds to any given event. On the other hand, in practice, environmental event measures vary in the degree of their objectivity. The issue is that there may be disagreement between subjects and researchers about which events qualify as stressors. For instance, does the flu count as a major medical event? What about an argument with a spouse—is that a major family conflict? Variability in the interpretation of life event categories such as medical event, conflict, or even death of a close friend can result in a highly heterogeneous, and therefore unreliable and potentially invalid assessment of events (Dohrenwend, 2006). Without exhaustive lists of life stressors, the ability to objectively evaluate experienced stress is eroded. Further, the conclusion reached is that certain measurement approaches, namely checklists of broad and ambiguous categories without a great deal of further instruction or probing, result in poorer stress assessment as compared to detailed interviews (Dohrenwend, 2006; Harkness & Monroe, 2016; Monroe, 2008). Yet these limitations of checklist measures can be mitigated to some degree with additional modification (e.g., category descriptions/exemplars and severity ratings; Dohrenwend, 2006).

This issue has largely played out in the measure of major life events, not daily hassles and stress. Nevertheless, there has been some consideration of the issue in this context, as we review next (see Almeida, Stawski, & Cichy, 2011). Our intuition, although we have found little relevant discussion by other researchers, is that the measurement of categories of daily hassles and stress is less susceptible to impact of intracategory variability. One reason may be that many of the events that are the focus of daily hassles and stress measurement are so minor as to defy ambiguity or confusion. Harkness and Monroe (2016) raised this possibility as well. Another possibility is that, depending on assessment method, many daily hassles are events more proximal to the appraisal and response process than major life events, thereby allowing clearer categorization. Or perhaps it is just expected that categorization of daily hassles will be infused with more subjectivity, given the origins of the construct and their measurement. Regardless of why objectivity has received less attention in this context, the lessons learned in the assessment of life events likely have similar implications for assessing daily hassles and stress: Researchers should strive to disambiguate event and response. We discuss these issues herein, pointing out concerns and offering suggestions, across the three generations of daily stress measurement.

Building on this distinction between (a potential) stressor as an environmental event and stress as the subjective response, a further challenge is delineating the boundary of daily hassles and stress and symptoms of poor mental health. Indeed, almost from the outset, concerns were raised about measurement confounding of daily stress and psychiatric symptomatology (Dohrenwend et al., 1984; Kohn & Macdonald, 1992; Marziali & Pilkonis, 1986). For instance, concerning examples from the original Hassles Scale (Kanner et al., 1981) included the following: "troubling thoughts about your future," "thoughts about death," "fear of rejection," "not getting enough sleep," "regrets over past decisions," "not enough personal energy," "nightmares," "use of alcohol," and "personal use of drugs." All but the last two describe cardinal symptoms of the internalizing spectrum (e.g., depression, worry, social anxiety; see, e.g., Kotov et al., 2017 for a review), whereas the final two might be considered hallmarks of the externalizing spectrum (e.g., substance use and antisocial behavior). Alternatively, alcohol or drug use might be understood in some contexts as maladaptive coping strategies, whereas nightmares are often used as markers for a severe traumatic stress reaction. If we take this to be confounding, then the concern is that associations with psychopathology would be artificially inflated, leading to overvaluing daily stress as a potential causal factor and possibly pathologizing normative experiences. This concern has been addressed somewhat on empirical grounds, in studies that have shown associations between stress inventories and key outcomes above and beyond some forms of symptomatology (e.g., Cohen & Williamson, 1988). Others have sought to devise inventories "uncontaminated" by outcomes, including psychiatric symptomatology (e.g., Kohn & Macdonald, 1992).

At the same time, each of the earlier listed items from the Hassles Scale is likely to be normatively stressful to some degree. There are many others that could fit in there as well. In other words, all fall well within the bounds of normal adult experiences, we all experience them to some degree or another from time to time, and most might feel at least a twinge of passing stress, if not more, at their occurrence. That those who experience them more frequently, acutely, and for longer duration are considered to be of poorer mental health might only serve to further reinforce the point that the boundaries between normality and psychopathology are illusory. As Sullivan (1954) so eloquently put it, "We all show everything that any mental patient shows, except for the pattern, the accents, and so on" (p. 183). Indeed, some contemporary perspectives on the manifestation of classic psychiatric syndromes argue these types of mundane but stressful experiences operate as potential catalysts that can spread in activation to a network of other maladaptive behavior (Borsboom, 2017). However, who is vulnerable to these processes, when, and under what conditions is all a matter of future investigation. The key point is that the boundary between stressor, response, and feature of psychopathology is quite blurry. Although it remains a significant challenge in measurement, we do not view the overlap between daily hassles and stress as a fatal issue, but rather one that requires thoughtful attention from the investigator. The items one includes or excludes for a particular investigation or analysis may differ depending on the population or phenomena of interest, the context in which they are being studied, and the temporal resolution of sampling.

These boundary definitions highlight that the areas of mental health and daily hassles/stress is a natural, if not necessary, pairing. Many of the key concepts that have emerged in stress research, such as reactivity or sensitivity to stress and maladaptive coping strategies (e.g., vicious cycles), suggest that stress processes or, more precisely, maladaptation in these stress processes is the core of many mental disorders. Take, for example, the first criterion of borderline personality disorder as articulated in the *Diagnostic and Statistical Manual of Mental Disorders* (*DSM*), "frantic efforts to avoid real or imagined abandonment" (American Psychiatric Association, 2013). This describes, or at the very least implies, the outlines of a specific stress process, which includes *event→intermediary→response* (c.f. Wright, 2014). In this example, perceptions of abandonment (whether it is real or imagined is beside the point for this illustration) lead to catastrophic appraisals, ultimately triggering frantic efforts (e.g., threats, violence, suicide attempts). Many more such examples can be enlisted from throughout the *DSM*. As will be discussed later, a great deal of research has examined aspects of psychopathology that might be understood through the generic lens of daily stress processes, even if often framed within disorder specific terminology and assessments. Other concepts, such as stress generation, have emerged from the study of stress as it is relevant for psychiatric disorders (Hammen, 1991, 2006; Liu & Alloy, 2010). Although most often studied in the context of major life events, many of the specific manifestations of disorders (e.g., interpersonal dysfunction in depression) may lead to stress generation in daily hassles and stress, and possibly serve as the catalyst for certain types of major life events (e.g., "dependent" events like divorce or being fired for cause; Hammen, 2006).

This brings us to a final relevant consideration related to daily hassles and stress, which is that although they may be the main factor of interest in their own right, they may also be the mechanism by which major life events and chronic stressors exert their effects. For instance, a loss of job, death of a spouse, or a major medical illness may be inherently stressful to some degree, but this may be partly or even wholly explained by the impact they have on daily routine and one's ability to deal with life's challenges. In the case of these three examples, it is not difficult to imagine how they might result in a loss of financial, social, and physical resources necessary to meet everyday needs and challenges. In times of gainful employment, a trip to the grocery is a mundane occurrence. When unemployed, however, the same trip can serve as a poignant reminder of the struggle to make ends meet and activate any number of concerns about finances, health, and family. Early research found that daily hassles and stress accounted for the association between major life events and health outcomes, as well as maintained an independent predictive effect (Eckenrode, 1984; Kanner et al., 1981; Wagner, Compas, & Howell, 1988). Interpreted in a mediational framework, these findings suggest that daily hassles and stress are how major life events lead to important outcomes.

To the extent that psychopathology often involves maladaptation in the normative management of daily stressors in various ways (e.g., sensitivity, reactivity, maladaptive coping strategies), then it is reasonable to conclude that those experiencing or vulnerable to psychopathology will be more likely to be impacted by a major life event. Events may even create sensitization effects that manifest via these pathways (e.g., Monroe & Harkness, 2005). These possible mechanisms are worth considering, in large part because daily hassles and stress processes are much easier to intervene upon than major life events, which may have no direct remedy (e.g., loss of a spouse). More research is needed in this area, especially as it relates to psychopathology.

In summary, daily hassles and stress refer to the often mundane and minor stressors most of us experience daily or with some regularity—the friction of moving through daily life. The study of daily hassles and stress emerged as somewhat of a counterpoint to the study of major life events. Despite this, there are many shared considerations in their conceptualization and measurement, including the focus on stress as a process, differentiating between events and responses, and understanding that there are likely to be individual and time/context-specific variability in the links between events and responses. Daily hassles and stress have a very blurry boundary with symptoms of psychopathology, which is important to attend to when considering research linking the two. Because of this, though, the study of daily stress and psychopathology is a natural pairing, and stress processes may serve as a generic and flexible model for understanding maladaptation in mental and behavioral functioning. We now turn to the specifics of measuring daily hassles and stress.

Three Generations of Daily Hassles and Stress Assessment

We have parsed the assessment and measurement of daily hassles and stress into three broad "generations" of techniques. These are intended to organize the available methodology, not to suggest that the techniques contained in each are mutually exclusive or conceptually incompatible. They do, however, roughly correspond to early techniques, contemporary state-of-the-art, and emerging directions in the measurement of daily stress.

First Generation—Cross-Sectional Inventories

As noted in the previous section, the early measure of daily hassles and stress followed from the assessment of life events. Accordingly, similar techniques were adopted and the first available measures were checklists. The major benefit of this approach is its facility and economy of administration. Cross-sectional self-report measures are cheap and easy to administer, require no special training of staff or participants, and can be quickly and easily scored by computer.

Measures in this category generally use a retrospective cross-sectional format, asking participants to report on their frequency, degree, or severity of stressors, responses, or appraisals in the recent past. Thus, by "cross-sectional" we do not mean to imply that the participant is only responding about his or her current state, but rather is usually being asked to aggregate over a period of time. One month (or 30 days) is a common time frame (Cohen, Kamarck, & Mermelstein, 1983; Kanner et al., 1981). Inventories of this type can and have been administered frequently in repeated waves to prospectively study the effect of stress over time (e.g., Delongis et al., 1982).

Quite a few checklist measures are available for assessing daily hassles. The original checklist measure, the Daily Hassles Scale (Kanner et al., 1981),[1] was fashioned after similar inventories measuring life events. It includes a list of 117 statements that are "a number of ways in which a person can feel hassled" (p. 24), plus an "other" response option. Participants are asked to circle those hassles that have happened within the last month and then rate those that have occurred on the level of perceived severity using a scale of *somewhat severe, moderately severe*, and *extremely severe*. Scoring has included both frequency (count of endorsed hassles) and intensity (mean severity score of all items checked). The Daily Hassles Scale enjoyed early widespread use after its publication over three decades ago, and a large number of scales have been based on it, have modified it to create neutral wording (Delongis, Folkman, & Lazarus, 1988), expanded it to include interpersonal events (Maybery & Graham, 2001), or altered it for special populations like adolescents (e.g., Compas et al., 1987; Kohn & Milrose, 1993) and college students (e.g., Blankstein, Flett, & Koledin, 1991; Kohn, Lafreniere, & Gurevich, 1990). As such, it serves as a good exemplar for this category of measures, although researchers interested in using this type of instrument may wish to audition several for match to their specific study (e.g., special population, age range, number of items).

The Perceived Stress Scale (Cohen, Kamarck, & Mermelstein, 1983) has taken a different tack to the measure of stress, focusing not on events, but largely on the appraisal. As such, it represents an unambiguous measure of the stress response, but not events. Similar to the Daily Hassles Scale, the referenced time frame is the past month, and participants are asked to endorse how frequently they have experienced various responses to stress (both appraisal and affective) on a scale ranging from *never* (0) to *very often* (4). Example items include "In the past month, how often have you felt you could not cope with all the things that you had to do?" and "In the past month, how often have you been angered because things were outside of your control?" The original measure included 14 items, but 4- and 10-item short forms have been developed, and Cohen and Williamson (1988) recommend the 10-item version due to the preferred psychometrics. The Perceived Stress Scale has been very widely used, and the 10-item version has been included in the National Institutes of Health Toolbox (http://www.healthmeasures.net).

Despite their widespread use, major concerns have been raised about checklist measures because they often confound event and response. As discussed earlier, much more has been written about this in the life events literature, although others have noted the issue applies to daily hassles and stress as well (Harkness & Monroe, 2016). We agree that the available measures do little to disambiguate events from response, making it difficult to uncritically recommend their use. However, inventories do differ in their design features in ways that mitigate the concerns somewhat. For instance, in the original Daily Hassles Scale, endorsing an event required also endorsing it as stressful to some degree (i.e., there was no "not stressful" response option), yet the revised form and other measures do allow endorsing that an event occurred, but that it was not experienced as stressful (Delongis et al., 1988). Additional concerns have been raised about overlap with symptomatology (e.g., fear of rejection, thoughts about death; Dohrenwend et al., 1984), and there have been efforts to make revised scales that remove items that might also be considered symptoms (e.g., Mayberry & Graham, 2001). Different scoring algorithms also raise concerns about capitalizing on chance. For instance, authors have suggested checklists might be scored for "frequency" (count of items endorsed) or "severity" (e.g., Delongis et al., 1982). Unless theory is sufficiently precise about which aspect of daily stress is presumed to be in operation, then considering both predictors moves a study from confirmatory to exploratory and should therefore be treated as such in the statistical inferences and conclusions. This is especially the case when there are otherwise concerns about confounding. A final concern is that it is very challenging to retrospectively recall relatively minor daily events with much accuracy over long periods of time, further muddying the interpretation of these checklists.

The study of life events has dealt with many of the problems with self-report checklists through the use of detailed interviews (see Harkness & Monroe, 2016; Monroe, 2008 for reviews). Although interviews serve to address many of the concerns about intracategory variability and confounding described earlier, it is not clear that a similar approach would be successful at mitigating this same concern in the assessment of daily hassles and stress. This is in part because the nature and number of the events differ substantially. In the case of life events, these are generally major and rarely occurring events that are likely to stand out with some prominence. In the case of daily hassles, the mundane nature of the targets is likely to undermine the utility of a long-term (e.g., 1-month) retrospective interview about myriad daily events. As such, the added time/cost of an interview is unlikely to be worth it, because it is not clear that it would lead to improved data quality given the nature of what is being recalled. For instance, other research areas have adopted interviews for assessing daily events, namely the alcohol and substance abuse literature, with limited success. Termed the time-line follow-back approach (Sobell & Sobell, 1992), an interviewer reviews a recent period asking participants to recall, for example, whether and how much a participant drank. Standard techniques, such as anchoring to holidays and the participants' schedule, are used to increase the fidelity of the responses. However, this approach has performed unevenly when compared to daily diaries, suggesting it does poorly at capturing the exact patterning of use and may even underestimate use (Carney, Tennen, Affleck, Del Boca, & Kranzler, 1998). This raises questions about its ultimate utility and incremental validity over retrospective generalizations captured by the much less cumbersome self-report questionnaires. Further, adding multiple, possibly many, categories of events would likely make the approach cumbersome. Therefore, the differences between daily hassles and stress and life events motivate construct-specific solutions. However, as we discuss in the next section, an interview approach may prove beneficial in daily diary approaches to stress assessment in a manner similar to life events assessment.

As discussed throughout, thoughtful selection of items that take care not to confound event and response (e.g., neutral wording) and separate assessment of severity that gives an option for nonstressful response is important. Nevertheless, for some, this may not adequately address concerns about confounding when using checklist measures. An alternative approach is to forego attempts to measure the events, and instead just focus on subjective or perceived stress. If this is acceptable given the study aims (i.e., the emphasis is on perceived stress or response to stressors, not the events themselves), then this would be the most economical and "clean" approach. The 10-item Perceived Stress Scale would provide a well-validated measure for this purpose, and we would recommend this approach.

Second Generation—Ambulatory Assessment

Up to now we have considered cross-sectional measures of daily hassles and stress. But many of the most interesting questions about daily hassles and stress as they relate to mental health require a shift to dynamic assessments (Wright & Hopwood, 2016). As Chassan (1959) put it:

> The clinician knows he [sic] is dealing with process. He [sic] cannot help but remain unimpressed with statistical procedures and results which are applied to observations made at comparatively isolated points in time, and which do not tell him [sic] something of what has been happening along the way.
> (p. 397)

In other words, if we are interested in understanding stress as a process, then it should be measured as such. Earlier we emphasized the importance of measuring both events and response, here we discuss approaches that are designed to measure the components of the stress process on a relevant timescale. By definition, daily hassles are intended to be those events whose effects are acute in nature, and the peak impact is likely to be transient. But how frequently an event occurs, how delayed is the peak of the response, how long lasting is the response, and what then does the response predict (e.g., maladaptive coping) are all questions of stress dynamics. Moreover, daily stress is likely contextualized, with its triggers and responses varying according to place and circumstance. To answer these questions, dynamic data are needed.

Traditionally, dynamic assessment of daily hassles and stress was difficult. However, over the past 25 years there has been a revolution in the availability and affordability of the tools needed for capturing and analyzing ambulatory assessment data. Ambulatory assessment encompasses a range of techniques (e.g., ecological momentary assessment, experience sampling methodology, ambulatory psychophysiology, daily diaries) to assess behavior, physiology, and settings in an individual's lived environment, and it has experienced a dramatic rise in use in recent years

(Hamaker & Wichers, 2017). Several excellent reviews have extensively covered ambulatory assessment in psychological research (e.g., Moskowitz, Russell, Sadikaj, & Sutton, 2009; Shiffman, Stone, & Hufford, 2008; Trull & Ebner-Priemer, 2013; Wrzus & Mehl, 2015), and so we will not provide an in-depth review here. We will, however, highlight several notable features as they relate to the assessment of daily stress.

Regardless of the specific instantiation (e.g., daily diary, ecological momentary assessment), ambulatory assessment is designed to sample people's behavior intensively and repeatedly in their natural environment. As such, ambulatory assessment offers two major benefits to the daily hassles and stress researcher. First, as we alluded to earlier, by sampling individuals many times, the goal is to capture different points along a dynamic process. For instance, if one is interested in the affective response to stressors, by giving participants surveys about the occurrence of stressful events and affect several times a day, one could determine the effect of a stressful event on one's affect in the moment relative to times when there were no stressors. Individual differences in this effect could be evaluated. More complex questions, such as lead–lag relationships, duration of response, and mitigating factors (e.g., interpersonal support) could be examined. Second, by asking about an individual's current or very recent (e.g., past 2 hours) experiences, biases of retrospection are greatly reduced (Ebner-Priemer & Trull, 2009). Retrospective biases have been shown to affect ratings of events, and by asking immediately (or shortly; Himmelstein, Woods, & Wright, in press) after, these biases can be mitigated (see Shiffman et al., 2008 for a review). In the current context, this feature of ambulatory assessment is likely to be critical, because many of the targets of assessment are likely to be mundane and easily forgotten or selectively remembered upon later recall. For instance, it may be that individuals relatively frequently experience events that have the potential to be stressful (e.g., traffic jams, work demands), but only retrospectively recollect those instances that are highlighted in memory by actually being stressful. This would be consistent with literature that has found overestimates of symptom intensity and frequency (see e.g., Van Den Brink et al., 2001 for a review). By assessing potentially stressful events in situ shortly after they happened, both those that lead to a strong response and those that do not will be captured, therefore allowing for more valid estimates of the effect of events per se as opposed to responses.

A major consideration for ambulatory assessment of stress is the sampling frame. For some questions, total amount of events or stress over a period of time may be the focus, but other designs will want to target specific events to understand their effects. Common sense dictates that assessment schedules should match the occurrence and timing of the phenomena of interest. In practice this can be challenging. In part this is because there is infrequently detailed information on the timing and frequency of relevant events. For instance, one might be interested in studying whether self-mutilation is used as a strategy to reduce negative affect or in response to stress. The question that immediately follows is does the mutilation occur immediately when stress is experienced, after some sustained period of time, or threshold of severity (Nock & Prinstein, 2004)? Even if these types of processes were well articulated by theory, real-world considerations, such as burden, fatigue, and rarity of events, impinge upon the assessment enterprise. For one, events and behavior of interest may not occur on the same timescale. Nightly sleep, often studied as both an outcome and predictor of daily stress, occurs once per day, whereas stressful events and their evoked response can happen many times within a day. Some high-value events may be quite rare (e.g., interpersonal conflict, self-mutilation), such that even with frequent sampling an assessment is unlikely to capture many instances. One might be tempted to reduce the frequency of sampling (e.g., once daily), but sample for a longer period of time (e.g., 100 days; Wright & Simms, 2016). But this may blur the specific processes leading up to the target behavior if they occur on a briefer timescale. Selecting a sampling frame often involves trade-offs between frequency and fidelity. Being able to make reliable inferences requires some minimum of observations of an event, whereas making inferences at the right level of granularity requires the correct timing. Both are important, but they may be at odds with each other in many scenarios. Thus, rules that require sampling more or less frequently than an event can be expected to occur are generally misguided, and instead the exact timing schedule should be selected based on substantive and methodological concerns (both practical and quantitative).

Three general categories of sampling frames have been developed: event-contingent, fixed, and random interval. Event-contingent recording is tied to the occurrence of some event, a situation, or internal state. This approach is often used for rare or unpredictable events, as might be the case in meaningful interpersonal interactions (Moskowitz & Zuroff, 2004) or binge-eating episodes (Smyth et al., 2007). The target of the assessment is instructed to complete a survey or begin recording at the start of or soon after an event has occurred. A long-standing challenge associated with this approach is the difficulty determining whether all relevant events have been reported. Assuming they all were captured would be overly optimistic, and realistically some degree of missing data is expected. It is difficult to get a sense of the amount and nature of the missing data, and one must hope that the observed cases are representative of the total set of cases (i.e., missing is completely at random). A recent study that experimentally varied the sampling frame suggests that event-contingent recordings result in the same basic descriptive features (means and variances) and associations (between- and within-person) as random sampling (Himmelstein et al., 2018), although more work in the stress domain would be valuable. Further, passive sensing of behavior or ambient context could be leveraged to safeguard against missed events by detecting them and prompting the participant to respond. Alternatively, one sensor could be used to trigger other sensors (e.g., Bluetooth contact between smartphones in proximity could engage the microphone to capture an interpersonal interaction). Assessing daily hassles or stressors using an event-contingent design may prove challenging if the goal is to broadly sample hassles, because there may be too many "events" for a subject to keep track of. Yet event-contingent recording has been frequently used for specific types of events. For instance, theoretical models of personality disorders emphasize interpersonal situations as being triggering events for symptoms, which can be understood in a stress-response model (Hopwood et al., 2013; Miskiewicz et al., 2015). Focusing assessments on circumscribed domain, such as interpersonal situations specifically, works well in an event-contingent design.

An alternative approach is to adopt a fixed or random interval of assessment. Daily diaries commonly use a fixed interval approach. The assessment target is asked to complete a survey each evening. Less common, although also feasible, is an hourly or subhourly interval. For example, Kamarck and colleagues (1998) examined the associations among stressors (social conflict and task strain), emotional activation, and cardiovascular activity in daily life by sampling individuals every 45 minutes over several days. Naturally, the narrower the interval, the more participant burden; therefore, brief fixed intervals generally require stronger justification. Fixed intervals need not be symmetrical, and building in some asymmetry to more densely sample important parts of a process is conceivable (e.g., few samples during the day but frequent assessments on nights when substance use occurs; Piasecki et al., 2011). A noted problem with fixed-interval recording is that the assessment target may learn to anticipate the prompts and as a result change their behavior in anticipation (i.e., reactivity). Continuous sampling, as is the case with most passive sensors, would be considered on a fixed schedule, albeit with very high sampling rate (e.g., every minute or second).

Random or pseudo-random prompts have been used to get around these concerns. A typical approach might be to sample 6–8 times per day, but at random times or at random within a time block (e.g., 2 hours) to avoid large periods without sampling. A limitation of truly random prompts arises when one wants to use statistical models that examine auto-regressive effects (i.e., time-series models), which have traditionally relied on an assumption of equal sampling interval. New methods are being developed that circumvent or account for unequal intervals. Alternatively, random assessments within defined blocks might be assumed to be equidistant on average, and estimated effects interpreted accordingly. Pseudo-random sampling schedules appear to be the most frequently used in contemporary mental health research, although fixed-time and event-contingent sampling are well represented.

It should also be noted that these various sampling approaches are not mutually exclusive, such that they can be combined with good effect. For instance, one might combine event-contingent sampling with random prompt sampling in order to decouple assessments of events and affect (e.g., Greeno, Wing, & Shiffman, 2000). This approach, although more burdensome, allows for examining antecedents and consequents of events.

Some of the measurement considerations associated with intensive longitudinal daily hassles and stress assessment are similar to those discussed in the preceding section on cross-sectional methods (i.e., First Generation). For instance, accurately categorizing events and differentiating event from response remain formidable challenges. However, the structural aspects of ambulatory assessment raise specific considerations that must be addressed. First, participant burden is a much larger concern. The most obvious and direct way this manifests is in the need for briefer assessments at each time point. Long lists of very specific events are inadvisable, and shorter but more general assessments are preferred.

For instance, using something like the revised Daily Hassles Checklist (DeLongis et al., 1988), which contains over 50 items, would likely overburden participants if given daily or more than once per day, and further it would be grossly inefficient, given that any particular event is likely to be rare. Furthermore, long inventories of specific events would come with the opportunity cost of not being able to ask detailed questions about antecedents, context, and outcomes. Brevity is at a premium.

Among the available ways to assess stressors, events, or stimuli, Kamarck et al. (2011) have distinguished between close-ended and open-ended approaches. Close-ended approaches directly ask about stressors, either generally (e.g., *Has a problem occurred in the last 30 min?* Marco & Suls, 1993) or specifically (e.g., *In the past 10 minutes, did your activity require working hard?* Kamarck et al., 1998), and participants are asked to respond with either a binary (yes vs. no) or ordinal (e.g., YES|yes|no|NO) scale. In contrast, an open-ended approach would provide a prompt (e.g., *Did anything go wrong today in the house, with the children, or others in the household, at work, or elsewhere?*) and solicit a free-response report of the event that could then be coded later (e.g., Caspi, Bolger, & Eckenrode, 1987). Kamarck and colleagues (2011) concluded that the "closed-ended data appear to be sufficient, in the sense that these are associated with concurrent measures of negative affect and salivary cortisol" (pp. 601–602). However, these different approaches do have potentially important implications. Close-ended approaches are more vulnerable to subjectivity, but they are less burdensome for the participant and researcher. High burden for participants may introduce concerns about data quality and bias. It is worth noting that in a typical ambulatory assessment study, each participant might complete 50–100 records. If even a minority of those (e.g., 30%; Kamarck et al., 2011) report on problems, this will mean 15–30 codings per participant. Closed- and open-ended approaches to measurement are useful distinctions, but they should not be considered mutually exclusive, and combinations have been employed as well (e.g., Almeida et al., 2002).

We next consider several specific implementations of these approaches. In line with the cross-sectional assessments, the first measures created for intensive repeated measurement were checklists, largely intended for once-daily assessments (i.e., daily diary designs). Examples include the Daily Stress Inventory (Brantley, Waggoner, Jones, & Rappaport, 1987) and the Assessment of Daily Events Checklist

(Stone & Neale, 1984). These measures are very similar in structure and content to traditional cross-sectional checklists, although the items are geared more to a daily assessment routine. For instance, the Daily Stress Inventory includes items like "unable to complete a task" and "had car trouble," which are then checked if they occurred and rated on a scale from "not stressful" to "caused me to panic." As we noted earlier, issues related to objectivity in the assessment of the stimuli have been less commonly debated in this context (cf. Harkness & Monroe, 2016), but even a cursory review of this class of measures raises this concern. The same can be said of construct creep, wherein a subset of items clearly straddles the boundary between traditional conceptualizations of stress and symptoms of mental disorders. Some inventories (e.g., Daily Experiences Survey; Hokanson, Stader, Flynn, & Tate, 1992) even borrow directly from common measures of depression in their item construction. Thus, our admonitions from the introductory section remain relevant for some measures in this space. Investigators using this approach should consider whether responses are best interpreted from an environmental or perceived stress perspective.

Others have adopted a less detailed approach, more in line with the needs of studies that employ multiple assessments per day. For instance, from Suls and his colleagues, a single item was used to measure stress (Has a problem occurred in the last 30 min?), often paired with a second question related to whether it is a new or ongoing stressor (e.g., Suls & Martin, 2005). Economy is prioritized over comprehensiveness and detail. This approach might work very well if the assessment of daily hassles and stress is part of a larger bouquet of constructs that need to be assessed at each time point, but it is probably best interpreted as perceived stress, not a strict objective measure of environmental events. Others have taken a similarly concise approach but leveraged open-ended responding to elicit detail that can be coded and used to distinguish between events and nonevents, or exclude symptoms of mental disorders to avoid confounding (e.g., Bolger & Zuckerman, 1995; Caspi et al., 1987; Eckenrode, 1984). The open-ended approach always affords the investigator with the option of treating the data as a binary close-ended marker or subjecting the responses to the more detailed and effortful coding.

Readers familiar with the assessment of major life events (Monroe & Slavich, this volume; Monroe, 2008) may note the lack of interview measures in the assessment of daily life stress. In large part this is because the demands of collecting intensive longitudinal data preclude repeated interviewing. There are some exceptions, such as the Daily Diary Interview (Walker, Smith, Garber, Van Slyke, & Claar, 2001). However, this measure largely used the interview format to ultimately administer a checklist. The measure that stands apart from others is the Daily Inventory of Stressful Events (DISE; Almeida, Wethington, & Kessler, 2002), which was designed to include the benefits of both the interview and the checklists approaches. Designed to be administered as a semistructured end-of-day phone interview, the DISE uses seven stem questions to probe daily stressor occurrence, including questions about arguments or disagreements, avoided arguments or disagreements, events at work or school, events at home, experiences with discrimination, events that occurred to a relative or close friend, and finally a catch-all "other" question. In response to these, the interviewer solicits an open-ended narrative description of the event, which is recorded. Follow-up probes are used to ensure enough detail about the objective features of the event to later rate several components. Participants are also asked for a severity rating of each event using a 4-point scale (1 = not at all stressful; 2 = a little, 3 = somewhat, 4 = very stressful). For those events scored as somewhat or very stressful on this scale, further questions probe primary appraisal of what was perceived to have been at risk in the situation (e.g., finances, health and safety; Lazarus & Folkman, 1984). Almeida and colleagues (2002; see also Alemida, Stawski, & Cichy, 2011) provide additional detail about measurement development.

What distinguishes the DISE from similar inventories is the use of an investigator rating method, wherein the recorded answers are transcribed and rated by trained research staff using standardized criteria. In this way, the DISE gets around the thorny issue of subjective and objective ratings of events. Almeida and colleagues (2002; 2011) report high interrater reliability of the DISE features, which can be used to generate three broad classifications of events: interpersonal tensions, overloads, and network (e.g., something happens to close friend or relative) events. A full accounting of the criteria used and the resulting scores are beyond the scope of this chapter, but some notable implications bear mentioning. First, one might wonder whether objective ratings result in many fewer participant reported events being recognized as *true* events according to the DISE's criteria. It appears that this is not a major issue, as only 5% of participant reported events in the National Study of Daily Events did not meet this threshold. However, it should be noted that the DISE appears to estimate a lower prevalence of daily events than checklist measures (Almeida et al., 2011). A second question is whether participant endorsement of stem questions results in a different classification of events than do staff ratings. There appears to be a larger discrepancy about the content, such that "nearly 14%" of events' content differed across self- and expert ratings. A final issue is whether and how much this impacts substantive questions that might be posed in the data. It would seem that these discrepancies do not have a major impact, as event-level associations with key outcomes like physical health symptoms are similar to checklist style inventories, and the DISE is often administered in self-report form (e.g., Neupert, Almeida, Mroczek, & Spiro, 2006; Wright, Hopwood, & Simms, 2015) or only the self-report responses from the interview are used in analyses (e.g., Chiang, Turiano, Mroczek, & Miller, 2018). Thus, it would seem reasonable to question whether the intensive and costly nature of the interview-based administration of the DISE is, in fact, necessary and worth any incremental gain in objectivity. Nevertheless, the DISE is one of the few measures that offers this potential added value.

This section has largely focused on traditional general assessments of daily hassles and stress that seek to broadly if not comprehensively cover daily stressors. At the same time, as it pertains to mental disorders, there may be specific hypothesized pathways or triggers of negative affect (response) or symptoms (e.g., maladaptive coping). When, due to theory or some other rationale, the focus is on a particular environmental event(s), alternative approaches are available. For instance, Smyth and colleagues (2007) used a greatly reduced subset of the Daily Stressors Inventory items rated as relevant for bulimia nervosa patients to investigate stress as a trigger for binge and purge episodes. This type of design selectively uses items from existing stress inventories. An alternative approach is to leverage general assessments of the environment, behavior, or cognition as specific antecedents in an unfolding stress process. Basic measures of affect could then be used to measure the response (e.g., Kamarck et al., 2011). The momentary assessment of interpersonal behavior in situations (Moskowitz, 1994; Moskowitz & Zuroff, 2005) has been profitably used in this way to study interpersonal triggers of negative affect in social phobia (Sadikaj et al., 2015), borderline personality disorder (Sadikaj et al., 2013), and narcissistic personality pathology (Wright et al., 2017). In each of these examples a general model of interpersonal behavior (the interpersonal circumplex) was used to examine the types of behaviors from interaction partners that lead to amplifications of negative affect among those with certain forms of psychopathology (e.g., those with social anxiety are sensitive to withdrawal from others, whereas those high in pathological narcissism respond negatively when others are dominant or assertive). By using a general model that covers all relevant behavior, the specificity of the pattern can be established (e.g., negative affect is linked with withdrawal, but not submissiveness). In principle, this approach could be expanded to other domains of interest for specific forms of psychopathology.

A final consideration for the intensive repeated measurement of daily hassles and stress is statistical modeling issues. The resulting data can be used to answer straightforward questions using only basic analytic approaches (e.g., mean number of days people diagnosed with major depression experience interpersonal stress). However, some of the more exciting questions related to dynamic processes go beyond average levels, by definition. These might include questions related to instability in affect over time, establishing lead–lag relationships (e.g., stress generation), within-person coupling of stress and affect (i.e., stress sensitivity/reactivity), individual differences in these dynamic features, or even personalized (i.e., idiographic) models of stress processes (e.g., Wright et al., 2019). A full discussion of these issues extends well beyond the current chapter; therefore, we recommend several accessible resources such as Walls and Schafer (2006) and Bolger and Laurenceau (2013).

Examples From Clinical Literature

In the prior two sections, we reviewed what we have termed the first and second generations of daily hassle and stress measurement. Prior to pointing to future directions in the next section (i.e., the third generation), we pause to review some of the ways these approaches have been implemented in clinical research, primarily focusing on depression supplemented by some additional examples from other forms of psychopathology.

Early research of the association between daily stress and major depressive disorder (MDD) relied typically on cross-sectional designs consisting of retrospective reports gathered at one or, rarely, two data collection sessions. Despite the advent of more sophisticated ambulatory assessment techniques that can capture dynamic processes, first-generation designs are still used in contemporary research. Measures of daily stress in this literature often list a number of potential stressors from a broad host of domains such as home life, work/school, finances, social life, romantic life, and general hassles (D'Angelo & Wierzbicki, 2003; Frison & Eggermont, 2015; Jung & Khalsa, 1989). Specialized measures of stress have been used with special populations, such as minority groups (Safdar & Lay, 2003) and expecting mothers (Field et al., 2006). Cross-sectional studies of daily stress and depression have varied in their approaches assessing extent of experience (Anderson, Goddard, & Powell, 2010; Barker, 2007; Mcintosh, Gillanders, & Rodgers, 2010; Sim, 2000), intensity (Bouteyre, Maurel, & Bernaud, 2007; Jung & Khalsa, 1989), or stressfulness (Frison & Eggermont, 2015). Cross-sectional research of this kind has routinely implicated daily hassles in the maintenance of depressive symptoms (Barker, 2007; Bouteyre et al., 2007; D'Angelo & Wierzbicki, 2003; Jung & Khalsa, 1989; Mcintosh et al., 2010; Safdar & Lay, 2003; Sim, 2000). Studies assessing daily stress across multiple domains have found that some domains pull for more depressive symptoms than others (D'Angelo & Wierzbicki, 2003; Safdar & Lay, 2003; Sim, 2000), although the exact domains vary across studies. Some research with two collection sessions have also linked depression at baseline to greater daily hassles at follow-up (Barker, 2007), although this finding has been contradicted by in-the-moment studies of daily stress and depressive symptoms (Peeters, Nicolson, Berkhof, Delespaul, & deVries, 2003). More conclusive research is needed on daily or momentary stress generation processes.

Researchers interested in the longitudinal association between daily stress and MDD have often used daily diary designs to assess participants over time. As we noted earlier, one benefit of adopting this research strategy is the ability to assess within-person, dynamic processes in stress and depression (Almeida, Neupert, Banks, & Serido, 2005; Cohen, Gunthert, Butler, O'Neill, & Tolpin, 2005). As with cross-sectional daily stress research, researchers using daily diary designs often rely on measures that assess multiple domains, such as home, work, social network, and finances (Butler, Hokanson, & Flynn, 1994; Sliwinski, Almeida, Smyth, & Stawski, 2010). In one such study, the authors compared the affective reactivity of depressed patients to interpersonal and noninterpersonal stressors, finding that the former was more strongly linked with depressive symptoms (Gunthert, Cohen, Butler, & Beck, 2007).

As with cross-sectional studies, measures of daily stress have varied in how they capture stress, assessing undesirability (Gunthert, Cohen, Butler, & Beck, 2005; Gunthert et al., 2007; O'Neill, Cohen, Tolpin, & Gunthert, 2004), unpleasantness (Dunkley et al., 2017), severity (Sliwinski et al., 2010), or stressfulness (Bell & D'Zurilla, 2009; O'Neill et al., 2004). Measures used in daily diary studies have been in both checklist (Butler et al., 1994; Cohen et al., 2008) and Likert (Bell & D'Zurilla, 2009; Dunkley et al., 2017; Gunthert et al., 2005, 2007; O'Neill et al., 2004; Sliwinski et al., 2010) formats. Daily diary studies have replicated the association of hassles and depression reported in cross-sectional studies (Bell & D'Zurilla, 2009; Dunkley et al., 2017; Gunthert et al., 2007; O'Neill et al., 2004). Some studies have measured the role of daily stress in the treatment of depression, finding that patients with more negative perceptions of stressors typically have poorer treatment response (Cohen et al., 2008; Gunthert et al., 2005). A common interest for daily diary researchers is affective reactivity to daily stressors, defined as the association between stress and later affect (Cohen et al., 2008; Dunkley et al., 2017; O'Neill et al., 2004; Sliwinski et al., 2010). Often researchers calculate participants' unique associations between momentary stress and later affect as a measure of affective reactivity (e.g., Wichers et al., 2010). A recent review of ambulatory assessment studies of MDD found that much of this literature focused on understanding how the disorder influences momentary links between stress and affect (Aan het Rot, Hogenelst, & Schoevers, 2012). Cumulatively, these studies have found that daily stress and affective reactivity to stress both exacerbate MDD symptoms (Booij et al., 2018; Bylsma et al., 2011; Myin-Germeys et al., 2003b; Peeters et al., 2010, 2003; van Winkel et al., 2015; Wichers et al., 2010). The ability of ambulatory assessment designs to study the dynamic relationship between daily stress, affective reactivity, and MDD has led to both psychological (Wichers, 2014) and biopsychosocial (Sher, 2004) theories of the disorder as well as complex quantitative models (Dunkley et al., 2017).

Although daily stress has most often been studied in terms of its associations with depression, it is likely to have implications to psychopathology writ large. Although there are notable studies in other domains of psychopathology, such as thought disorders (Collip et al., 2013; Compton et al., 2008; Myin-Germeys et al., 2003a; Tessner et al., 2011), personality disorders (Coifman et al., 2012; Glaser et al., 2008; Lariviere et al., 2016; Tolpin et al.,

2003; Wright et al., 2015), and general maladaptive behaviors like aggression (Sprague, Verona, Kalkhoff, & Kilmer, 2011), to name a few, this remains an area ripe for more programmatic inquiry. We encourage researchers focused on other domains of psychopathology to consider adapting the lens of stress processes in their programs of research as has been fruitfully done in depression. It would be important to understand which of these processes are unique to depression, general to psychopathology, or differ in their manifestation across domains.

Third Generation—Future Directions With Passive Sensing

We end this chapter with a discussion of passive sensing, which represents an exciting and promising future direction for stress research. Due to the highly technical nature of this area, we provide a conceptual overview and point to extant and emerging issues. Although ambulatory assessment measures of daily hassles and stress represent the state of the science, and we believe they should be the method to turn to for those interested in understanding daily stress processes, they are not without limitations. For one, they are burdensome, and the burden places an upper limit on the frequency and amount of assessment. This could erode data quality by leading to participant fatigue, and it leaves many potentially interesting events or responses not sampled. As we noted earlier, in most cases the sampled events can be assumed to be representative of the full population of events, and this should mitigate major concerns. Nevertheless, in some scenarios this might be a major problem. For instance, when seeking to statistically model the antecedents and consequences of events and responses, assuming exact temporal ordering might be a problem. Second, most ambulatory assessment studies rely on self-reported events and responses. An individual's subjective experience may very well be the most important psychological feature of stress, but it is unarguably an incomplete picture. The long-standing issue of objective measurement of stress resurfaces here, and presumably non-self-report measurement would be advantageous for addressing lingering concerns about biases. Largely due to these reasons, a number of researchers have turned to passive sensing in order to detect daily stress in the moment.

Passive sensing encompasses a large number of specific techniques and procedures, but all generally involve the continuous collection of data from sensors that are either worn by an individual (e.g., respiration coil) or embedded in his or her mobile devices (e.g., smartphone). The use of standard medical sensors (e.g., blood pressure cuffs) in ambulatory assessment has been around for quite some time (see, e.g., Fahrenberg, 1996 for a review), but leveraging the impressive sensor array embedded in our phones (e.g., ubiquitous computing) is more novel. Indeed, the modern smartphone really only gained prominence in the past decade following the release of Apple's iPhone in 2007. Today's smartphone is likely to include (there are some differences across models) sensors for movement (e.g., accelerometer, gyroscope), location (GPS, Wifi), temperature, moisture, altitude, noise (microphone), light, and proximity with other devices (e.g., Bluetooth). As Mohr and colleagues (2017) recently pointed out in a review of passive sensing as it relates to mental health, these individual sensors directly generate low-level data. Which is to say, they likely are not immediately useful for measuring complex constructs like stress, but rather require several levels of aggregation or transformation. We will return to this issue shortly, but for now the key point to take away is that devices that seem as mundane as those we carry everywhere in our pockets generate highly diverse and continuous streams of data. These can be augmented with sophisticated psychophysiological sensors in specialized arrays or as part of other common devices (e.g., smartwatches and step counters) that also continuously record across several channels of sensors. Additional data on device usage can be recorded, such as screen on/off, call logs, texting, application usage, and even keystroke recording.

Some of these streams of data have obvious utility for extracting higher level features that are easily interpretable. For instance, GPS coordinates can be used to inform types of location, such as work, home, gym, bar, and so forth. Others, such as light sensors might seem less clearly relevant, unless one considers that it might be a strong marker for something like a sleep-wake cycle. A relatively complex behavior like sleep-wake cycle will not rest entirely on a sensor like ambient light, but instead would be informed by several others (e.g., ambient noise captured from the microphone, screen activation, accelerometer). This brings us to the challenge of fruitfully using the data from passive sensing. Moving up along the conceptual hierarchy, from basic sensor-level data to mid-level feature and on to higher level features (Mohr et al., 2017), is unlikely to be a linear affair. Many of the informative streams of data for identifying complex states are likely to be unintuitive; one would not be able to divine the important variables a priori. To make these abstractions, one is likely to need some form of machine learning. Machine learning may sound highly technical, and in some forms it can be, but on its surface it is just some form of supervised or unsupervised learning algorithm. Arguably, step-wise regression, which most readers will remember as being discouraged in basic graduate statistics, is a basic form of machine learning. Predictors are auditioned for a regression model, and only those that are statistically significant at some criterion (e.g., $p < .05$) are retained in the final model. The basic logic is that the data drive the decisions of which variables to retain as informative. When coupled with something like logistic regression, machine learning can be used to develop a probability model for classifying some outcome (e.g., stressful event).

So, how are passive sensing and machine learning leading to the future of daily stress assessment? The basic logic is that the array of potential sensors alluded to earlier can be used to predict when an individual is experiencing "stress." In order to develop a model for predicting stress, it would require instances of both stress and nonstress to differentiate between. With sufficient instances to work with, the model would be able to "learn" which features from the passive sensors predict stressful experiences with high fidelity. Once the algorithm has "learned" when an individual is experiencing stress, the participant would not be required to respond to report on stress. Therein lies the very exciting aspect of this methodology. It takes the recording of stress out of the participant's hands, making it truly continuous, putatively objective, and nonburdensome. Beyond just assessing daily stress in research, this sort of approach could also be used to facilitate just-in-time interventions to disrupt stress processes.

Work in this area is still in its infancy, but it is progressing rapidly. One aspect of this area that is simultaneously exciting and challenging is the potential to develop personalized models of stress. That is, algorithms would be employed to develop a model for each individual that would be tailored to his or her own stress profile. Similar to prior sections, in passive sensing the challenge remains of what to use as "ground truth" in defining stress, and arguably it is an even larger issue. If one uses self-reports as the target, then the model will be a model of perceived stress. We highlight one study by Plarre and colleagues (2011) that illustrates how some of these issues are being dealt with in passively sensing stress. Participants ($N = 21$) underwent several standard stress induction procedures in the laboratory while undergoing psychophysiological recording (Plarre

et al., 2011). Stressors included public speaking, mental arithmetic, and cold-pressor. Throughout the procedure participants rated their stress. The psychophysiological data were used to classify stressful states from the in-lab self-reports (i.e., "physiological classifier"). It achieved >90% accuracy. These algorithms were then tested in real life using an ambulatory assessment procedure, by comparing the algorithm's stress predictions based on worn ambulatory sensors to self-reported stress in the moment (i.e., a "perceived stress model"). The model achieved a median correlation of .72, although the value ranged across participants from ~.2 to 1.0 for individual participants.

This is just one example, and other investigators have adopted alternative procedures, for instance sampling vocal frequency from smartphone microphones (Adams et al., 2014). There are pros and cons to different systems (e.g., psychophysiological sensors can be obtrusive, microphones may not be reliable when in a purse), and significant challenges remain (e.g., accounting for other potential influences on sensors). Much work remains to be done in the passive sensing of stress. In particular, studies require much larger samples before they can be considered confidence inspiring. Indeed, it is not uncommon for studies to report single-digit or low double-digit sample sizes. Thus, the field really remains at the "proof of concept" stage and remains to be scaled to the point where results might be considered reliable. Nevertheless, the potential benefits of taking the measurement of stress out of the hands of participants and patients and offloading that to a perpetually vigilant mobile device is very appealing.

Conclusion

The measurement of daily hassles and stress would seem to be a mundane affair. Indeed, if the interest is in a basic assessment of perceived stress, it can be straightforward and easily implemented. But there are also many compelling research questions about the links between daily hassles and stress and mental health that require considerably greater thought and care if they are to be convincingly addressed. Major issues that plague the entire stress measurement enterprise, such as distinguishing between event and response, between subjective and objective assessment of events, and between stressors and symptoms are just as important for daily hassles and stress as they are for any other area. This has not always received detailed attention. Some aspects of the phenomenon (i.e., events are quotidian by definition) make differentiating these issues challenging, although not impossible. There is also much to be gained by contemporary approaches that assess individuals intensively and repeatedly in their natural environment in order to faithfully represent dynamic stress processes. We reiterate that one's research goals may not be best served by using stress measures per se; instead, it is preferable to assess specific contextual features that might serve as specific triggers for certain forms of psychopathology. Finally, we look forward to advances in the areas of passive sensing that are likely to lead to new insights as methods improve and sample sizes increase.

Acknowledgments

Aidan Wright's effort on this project was supported by the National Institute of Mental Health (L30 MH101760). The opinions expressed are solely those of the authors and not those of the funding source. After AGCW, authorship was determined alphabetically; second authorship is shared.

Note

1. Note that the Daily Hassles Scale was originally presented alongside a checklist of uplifts, which are quotidian positive events. However, the addition of uplifts to hassles/stress has rarely incremented the prediction of important outcomes, and therefore they have received much less attention in the literature.

References

Aan het Rot, M., Hogenelst, K., & Schoevers, R. A. (2012). Mood disorders in everyday life: A systematic review of experience sampling and ecological momentary assessment studies. *Clinical Psychology Review, 32*(6), 510–523.

Adams, P., Rabbi, M., Rahman, T., Matthews, M., Voida, A., Gay, G., . . . & Voida, S. (2014, May). Towards personal stress informatics: Comparing minimally invasive techniques for measuring daily stress in the wild. In *Proceedings of the 8th International Conference on Pervasive Computing Technologies for Healthcare* (pp. 72–79). Oldenberg, Germany: ICST (Institute for Computer Sciences, Social-Informatics and Telecommunications Engineering).

Almeida, D. M., Neupert, S. D., Banks, S. R., & Serido, J. (2005). Do daily stress processes account for socioeconomic health disparities? *The Journals of Gerontology: Psychological Sciences and Social Sciences, 60B*(II), 34–39.

Almeida, D. M., Stawski, R. S., & Cichy, K. E. (2011). Combining checklist and interview approaches for assessing daily stressors: The Daily Inventory of Stressful Events. In R. J. Contrada & A. Baum (Eds.), *The handbook of stress science: Biology, psychology, and health* (pp. 583–595). New York, NY: Springer.

Almeida, D. M., Wethington, E., & Kessler, R. C. (2002). The Daily Inventory of Stressful Events (DISE): An interview based approach for measuring daily stressors. *Assessment, 9*, 41–55.

American Psychiatric Association. (2013). *Diagnostic and statistical manual of mental disorders* (5th ed.). Washington, DC: Author.

Anderson, R. J., Goddard, L., & Powell, J. H. (2010). Reduced specificity of autobiographical memory as a moderator of the relationship between daily hassles and depression. *Cognition and Emotion, 24*(4), 702–709.

Barker, D. B. (2007). Antecedents of stressful experiences: Depressive symptoms, self-esteem, gender, and coping. *International Journal of Stress Management, 14*(4), 333–349.

Bell, A. C., & D'Zurilla, T. J. (2009). The influence of social problem-solving ability on the relationship between daily stress and adjustment. *Cognitive Therapy and Research, 33*(5), 439–448.

Blankstein, K. R., Flett, G. L., & Koledin, S. (1991). The Brief College Student Hassles Scale: Development, validation, and relation with pessimism. *Journal of College Student Development, 32*(3), 258–264.

Bolger, N., & Laurenceau, J. P. (2013). *Intensive longitudinal methods: An introduction to diary and experience sampling research*. New York, NY: Guilford Press.

Bolger, N., & Zuckerman, A. (1995). A framework for studying personality in the stress process. *Journal of Personality and Social Psychology, 69*(5), 890–902.

Booij, S. H., Snippe, E., Jeronimus, B. F., Wichers, M., & Wigman, J. T. W. (2018). Affective reactivity to daily life stress: Relationship to positive psychotic and depressive symptoms in a general population sample. *Journal of Affective Disorders, 225*, 474–481.

Borsboom, D. (2017). A network theory of mental disorders. *World Psychiatry, 16*(1), 5–13.

Bouteyre, E., Maurel, M., & Bernaud, J. L. (2007). Daily hassles and depressive symptoms among first year psychology students in France: The role of coping and social support. *Stress and Health, 23*(2), 93–99.

Brantley, P. J., Waggoner, C. D., Jones, G. N., & Rappaport, N. B. (1987). A daily stress inventory: Development, reliability, and validity. *Journal of Behavioral Medicine, 10*(1), 61–74.

Butler, A. C., Hokanson, J. E., & Flynn, H. A. (1994). A comparison of self-esteem lability and low trait self-esteem as vulnerability factors for depression. *Journal of Personality and Social Psychology, 66*(1), 166–177.

Bylsma, L. M., Taylor-Clift, A., & Rottenberg, J. (2011). Emotional reactivity to daily events in major and minor depression. *Journal of Abnormal Psychology, 120*(1), 155–167.

Carney, M. A., Tennen, H., Affleck, G., Del Boca, F. K., & Kranzler, H. R. (1998). Levels and patterns of alcohol consumption using timeline follow-back, daily diaries and real-time "electronic interviews." *Journal of Studies on Alcohol, 59*(4), 447–454.

Caspi, A., Bolger, N., & Eckernode, J. (1987). Linking person and context in the daily stress process. *Journal of Personality and Social Psychology, 52*(1), 184–195.

Chassan, J. B. (1959). On the development of clinical statistical systems for psychiatry. *Biometrics, 15*(3), 396–404.

Chiang, J. J., Turiano, N. A., Mroczek, D. K., & Miller, G. E. (2018). Affective reactivity to daily stress and 20-year mortality risk in adults with chronic illness: Findings from the National Study of Daily Experiences. *Health Psychology, 37*(2), 170–178.

Cohen, L. H., Gunthert, K. C., Butler, A. C., O'Neill, S. C., & Tolpin, L. H. (2005). Daily reactivity as a prospective predictor of depressive symptoms. *Journal of Personality, 73*(6), 1687–1714.

Cohen, L. H., Gunthert, K. C., Butler, A. C., Parrish, B. P., Wenze, S. J., & Beck, J. S. (2008). Negative affective spillover from daily events predicts early response to cognitive therapy for depression. *Journal of Consulting and Clinical Psychology, 76*(6), 955–965.

Cohen, S., Kamarck, T., & Mermelstein, R. (1983). A global measure of perceived stress. *Journal of Health and Social Behavior, 24*(4), 385–396.

Cohen, S., & Williamson, G. M. (1988). Perceived stress in a probability sample of the United States. In S. Spacapan & S. Oskamp (Eds.), *The social psychology of health* (pp. 31–67). Newbury Park, CA: Sage.

Coifman, K. G., Berenson, K. R., Rafaeli, E., & Downey, G. (2012). From negative to positive and back again: Polarized affective and relational experience in borderline personality disorder. *Journal of Abnormal Psychology, 121*(3), 668–679.

Collip, D., Wigman, J. T. W., Myin-Germeys, I., Jacobs, N., Derom, C., Thiery, E., & van Os, J. (2013). From epidemiology to daily life: Linking daily life stress reactivity to persistence of psychotic experiences in a longitudinal general population study. *PLoS ONE, 8*(4): e62688.

Compas, B. E., Davis, G. E., Forsythe, C. J., & Wagner, B. M. (1987). Assessment of major and daily stressful events during adolescence: The Adolescent Perceived Events Scale. *Journal of Consulting and Clinical Psychology, 55*(4), 534–541.

Compton, M. T., Carter, T., Kryda, A., Goulding, S. M., & Kaslow, N. J. (2008). The impact of psychoticism on perceived hassles, depression, hostility, and hoplessness in non-psychiatric African Americans. *Psychiatry Research, 159*, 215–225.

Coyne, J. C., & Lazarus, R. S. (1980). Cognitive style, stress perception, and coping. In I.L Kutash & L.B. Schlesinger (Eds.), *Handbook on stress and anxiety* (pp. 144–158). San Francisco: Jossey-Bass.

D'Angelo, B., & Wierzbicki, M. (2003). Relations of daily hassles with both anxious and depressed mood in students. *Psychological Reports, 92*, 416–418.

DeLongis, A., Coyne, J. C., Dakof, G., Folkman, S., & Lazarus, R. S. (1982). Relationship of daily hassles, uplifts, and major life events to health status. *Health Psychology, 1*(2), 119–136.

DeLongis, A., Folkman, S., & Lazarus, R. S. (1988). The impact of daily stress on health and mood: Psychological and social resources as mediators. *Journal of Personality and Social Psychology, 54*(3), 486–495.

Dohrenwend, B. P. (2006). Inventorying stressful life events as risk factors for psychopathology: Toward resolution of the problem of intracategory variability. *Psychological Bulletin, 132*, 477–495.

Dohrenwend, B. P., & Shrout, P. E. (1985). "Hassles" in the conceptualization and measurement of life stress variables. *American Psychologist, 40*(7), 780–785.

Dohrenwend, B. S., Dohrenwend, B. P., Dodson, M., & Shrout, P. E. (1984). Symptoms, hassles, social supports, and life events: Problem of confounded measures. *Journal of Abnormal Psychology, 93*(2), 222–230.

Dougall, A. L., & Baum, A. (2011). Stress, health, and illness. In A. Baum, T.A. Revenson, & J. Singer (Ed.), *Handbook of health psychology* (pp. 321–337). Routledge: New York, NY.

Dunkley, D. M., Lewkowski, M., Lee, I. A., Preacher, K. J., Zuroff, D. C., Berg, J. L.,...Westreich, R. (2017). Daily stress, coping, and negative and positive affect in depression: Complex trigger and maintenance patterns. *Behavior Therapy, 48*(3), 349–365.

Ebner-priemer, U. W., & Trull, T. J. (2009). Ecological Momentary Assessment of Mood Disorders and Mood Dysregulation. *Psychological Assessment, 21*(4), 463–475.

Eckenrode, J. (1984). Impact of chronic and acute stressors on daily reports of mood. *Journal of Personality and Social Psychology. 46*(4), 907–918.

Fahrenberg, J. (1996). Ambulatory assessment: Issues and perspectives. In J. Fahrenberg & M. Myrtek (Eds.), *Ambulatory assessment: Computer-assisted psychological and psychophysiological methods in monitoring and field studies* (pp. x3–20). Seattle, WA: Hogrefe and Huber.

Field, T., Diego, M., Hernandez-Reif, M., Figueiredo, B., Deeds, O., Contogeorgoes, J., & Ascencio, A. (2006). Prenatal paternal depression. *Infant Behavior and Development, 29*(4), 579–583.

Frison, E., & Eggermont, S. (2015). The impact of daily stress on adolescents' depressed mood: The role of social support seeking through Facebook. *Computers in Human Behavior, 44*, 315–325.

Glaser, J. P., Os, J. Van, Mengelers, R., & Myin-Germeys, I. (2008). A momentary assessment study of the reputed emotional phenotype associated with borderline personality disorder. *Psychological Medicine, 38*(9), 1231–1239.

Greeno, C. G., Wing, R., & Shiffman, S. (2000). Binge antecedents in obese women with and without binge eating disorder. *Journal of Consulting and Clinical Psychology, 68*, 95–102.

Gunthert, K. C., Cohen, L. H., Butler, A. C., & Beck, J. S. (2005). Predictive role of daily coping and affective reactivity in cognitive therapy outcome. *Behavior Therapy, 36*, 77–88.

Gunthert, K. C., Cohen, L. H., Butler, A. C., & Beck, J. S. (2007). Depression and next-day spillover of negative mood and depressive cognitions following interpersonal stress. *Cognitive Therapy and Research, 31*(4), 521–532.

Hamaker, E. L., & Wichers, M. (2017). No time like the present: Discovering the hidden dynamics in intensive longitudinal data. *Current Directions in Psychological Science, 26*(1), 10–15.

Hammen, C. (1991). Generation of stress in the course of unipolar depression. *Journal of Abnormal Psychology, 100*(4), 555–561.

Hammen, C. (2006). Stress generation in depression: Reflections on origins, research, and future directions. *Journal of Clinical Psychology, 62*(9), 1065–1082.

Harkness, K. L., & Monroe, S. M. (2016). The assessment and measurement of adult life stress: Basic premises, operational principles, and design requirements. *Journal of Abnormal Psychology, 125*(5), 727–745.

Himmelstein, P. H., Woods, W. C., & Wright, A. G. C. (in press). A comparison of signal- and event-contingent recording methodologies for social situations in ambulatory assessment. *Psychological Assessment.*

Hokanson, J. E., Stader, S. R., Flynn, H. A., & Tate, R. L. (1992). The daily experiences survey: An instrument for daily recordings of multiple variables associated with psychopathology. Unpublished manuscript, Florida State University.

Hopwood, C. J., Wright, A. G. C., Ansell, E. B., & Pincus, A. L. (2013). The interpersonal core of personality pathology. *Journal of Personality Disorders, 27*(3), 271–295.

Jung, J., & Khalsa, H. K. (1989). The relationship of daily hassles, social support, and coping to depression in black and white students. *Journal of General Psychology, 116*(4), 407–417.

Kamarck, T. W., Shiffman, S. M., Smithline, L., Goodie, J. L., Paty, J. A., Gnys, M., & Jong, J. Y. K. (1998). Effects of task strain, social conflict, and emotional activation on ambulatory cardiovascular activity. *Health Psychology, 17*(1), 17–29.

Kamarck, T. W., Shiffman, S., & Wethington, E. (2011). Measuring psychosocial stress using ecological momentary assessment methods. In R. J. Contrada & A. Baum (Eds.), *The handbook of stress science: Biology, psychology, and health* (pp. 597–617). New York, NY: Springer.

Kanner, A. D., Coyne, J. C., Schaefer, C., & Lazarus, R. S. (1981). Comparison of two modes of stress measurement: Daily hassles and uplifts versus major life events. *Journal of Behavioral Medicine, 4*(1), 1–39.

Kohn, P. M., & Macdonald, J. E. (1992). The Survey of Recent Life Experiences: A decontaminated hassles scale for adults. *Journal of Behavioral Medicine, 15*(2), 221–236.

Kohn, P. M., & Milrose, J. A. (1993). The inventory of high-school students' recent life experiences: A decontaminated measure of adolescents' hassles. *Journal of Youth and Adolescence, 22*(1), 43–55.

Kohn, P. M., Lafreniere, K., & Gurevich, M. (1990). The inventory of college students' recent life experiences: A decontaminated hassles scale for a special population. *Journal of Behavioral Medicine, 13*(6), 619–630.

Kotov, R., Krueger, R. F., Watson, D., Achenbach, T. M., Althoff, R. R., Bagby, R. M., . . . Eaton, N. R. (2017). The Hierarchical Taxonomy of Psychopathology (HiTOP): A dimensional alternative to traditional nosologies. *Journal of Abnormal Psychology, 126*(4), 454–477.

Larivière, N., Denis, C., Payeur, A., Ferron, A., Levesque, S., & Rivard, G. (2016). Comparison of objective and subjective life balance between women with and without a personality disorder. *Psychiatric Quarterly, 87*(4), 663–673.

Lazarus, R. S. (1984). Puzzles in the study of daily hassles. *Journal of Behavioral Medicine, 7*(4), 375–389.

Lazarus, R. S., & DeLongis, A. (1983). Psychological stress and coping in aging. *American Psychologist, 38*(3), 245–254.

Lazarus, R. S., & Folkman, S. (1984). *Stress, appraisal, and coping*. New York, NY: Springer.

Lazarus, R. S., & Launier, R. (1978). Stress-related transactions between person and environment. In L.A. Pervin & M. Lewis (Eds.), *Perspectives in interactional psychology* (pp. 287–327). Boston, MA: Springer.

Liu, R. T., & Alloy, L. B. (2010). Stress generation in depression: A systematic review of the empirical literature and recommendations for future study. *Clinical Psychology Review, 30*(5), 582–593.

Marco, C.A., & Suls, J. (1993). Daily stress and the trajectory of mood: spillover, response assimilation, contrast, and chronic negative affectivity. *Journal of Personality and Social Psychology, 64*(6), 1053–1063.

Marziali, E. A., & Pilkonis, P. A. (1986). The measurement of subjective response to stressful life events. *Journal of Human Stress, 12*(1), 5–12.

Maybery, D. J., & Graham, D. (2001). Hassles and uplifts: Including interpersonal events. *Stress and Health, 17*(2), 91–104.

Mcintosh, E., Gillanders, D., & Rodgers, S. (2010). Rumination, goal linking, daily hassles and life events in major depression. *Clinical Psychology and Psychotherapy, 17*(1), 33–43.

Miskewicz, K., Fleesons, W., Arnold, E.M., Law, M. K., Mneimne, M., & Furr, R. M. (2015). A contingency-oriented approach to understanding borderline personality disorder: situational triggers and symptoms. *Journal of Personality Disorders, 29*(4), 486–502.

Mohr, D. C., Zhang, M., & Schueller, S. M. (2017). Personal sensing: Understanding mental health using ubiquitous sensors and machine learning. *Annual Review of Clinical Psychology, 13*, 23–47.

Monroe, S. M. (2008). Modern approaches to conceptualizing and measuring human life stress. *Annual Review of Clinical Psychology, 4*, 33–52.

Monroe, S. M., & Harkness, K. L. (2005). Life stress, the "kindling" hypothesis, and the recurrence of depression: Considerations from a life stress perspective. *Psychological Review, 112*(2), 417–445.

Moskowitz, D. S. (1994). Cross-situational generality and the interpersonal circumplex. *Journal of Personality and Social Psychology, 66*(5), 921–933.

Moskowitz, D. S., Russell, J. J., Sadikaj, G., & Sutton, R. (2009). Measuring people intensively. *Canadian Psychology/Psychologie Canadienne, 50*(3), 131–140.

Moskowitz, D. S., & Zuroff, D.C. (2004). Flux, pulse, and spin: Dynamic additions to the personality lexicon. *Journal of Personality and Social Psychology, 86*(6), 880–893.

Moskowitz, D. S., & Zuroff, D. C. (2005). Assessing interpersonal perceptions using the interpersonal grid. *Psychological Assessment, 17*(2), 218–230.

Myin-Germeys, I., Krabbendam, L., Delespaul, P. A. E. G., & Van Os, J. (2003a). Do life events have their effect on psychosis by influencing the emotional reactivity to daily life stress? *Psychological Medicine, 33*(2), 327–333.

Myin-Germeys, I., Peeters, F., Havermans, R., Nicolson, N. A., deVries, M. W., Delespaul, P., & van Os, J. (2003b). Emotional reactivity to daily life stress in psychosis and affective disorder: An experience sampling study. *Acta Psychiatrica Scandinavica, 107*(2), 124–131.

Neupert, S. D., Almeida, D. M., Mroczek, D. K., & Spiro III, A. (2006). Daily stressors and memory failures in a naturalistic setting: Findings from the va normative aging study. *Psychology and Aging, 21*(2), 424–429.

Nock, M. K., & Prinstein, M. J. (2004). A functional approach to the assessment of self-mutilative behavior. *Journal of Consulting and Clinical Psychology, 72*(5), 885–890.

O'Neill, S. C., Cohen, L. H., Tolpin, L. H., & Gunthert, K. C. (2004). Affective reactivity to daily interpersonal stressors as a prospective predictor of depressive symptoms. *Journal of Social and Clinical Psychology, 23*(2), 172–194.

Peeters, F., Berkhof, J., Rottenberg, J., & Nicolson, N. A. (2010). Ambulatory emotional reactivity to negative daily life events predicts remission from major depressive disorder. *Behaviour Research and Therapy, 48*(8), 754–760.

Peeters, F., Nicolson, N. A., Berkhof, J., Delespaul, P., & deVries, M. (2003). Effects of daily events on mood states in major depressive disorder. *Journal of Abnormal Psychology, 112*(2), 203–211.

Piasecki, T. M., Jahn, S., Wood, P. K., Robertson, B. M., Epler, A. J., Cronk, N. J., . . . Sher, K. J. (2011). The subjective effects of alcohol-tobacco co-use: An ecological momentary assessment investigation. *Journal of Abnormal Psychology, 120*(3), 557–571.

Plarre, K., Raij, A., Hossain, S. M., Ali, A. A., Nakajima, M., Al'Absi, M., . . . Siewiorek, D. (2011, April). Continuous inference of psychological stress from sensory measurements collected in the natural environment. In *Information Processing in Sensor Networks (IPSN), 10th International Conference* (pp. 97–108). Chicago, IL: IEEE.

Sadikaj, G., Moskowitz, D. S., Russell, J. J., & Zuroff, D. C. (2015). Submissiveness in social anxiety disorder: The role of interpersonal perception and embarrassment. *Journal of Social and Clinical Psychology*, *34*(1), 1–27.

Sadikaj, G., Moskowitz, D. S., Russell, J. J., Zuroff, D. C., & Paris, J. (2013). Quarrelsome behavior in borderline personality disorder: Influence of behavioral and affective reactivity to perceptions of others. *Journal of Abnormal Psychology*, *122*(1), 195–207.

Safdar, S., & Lay, C. H. (2003). The relations of immigrant-specific and immigrant- nonspecific daily hassles to distress controlling for psychological adjustment and cultural competence. *Journal of Applied Social Psychology*, *33*(2), 299–320.

Sher, L. (2004). Daily hassles, cortisol, and the pathogenesis of depression. *Medical Hypotheses*, *62*, 198–202.

Shiffman, S., Stone, A. A., & Hufford, M. R. (2008). Ecological momentary assessment. *Annual Review of Clinical Psychology*, *4*, 1–32.

Sim, H. (2000). Relationship of daily hassles and social support to depression and antisocial behavior among early adolescents. *Journal of Youth and Adolescence*, *29*(6), 647–659.

Sliwinski, M. J., Almeida, D. M., Smyth, J., & Stawski, R. S. (2010). Intraindividual change and variability in daily stress processes: Findings from two measurement-burst diary studies. *Psychology of Aging*, *24*(4), 828–840.

Smyth, J. M., Wonderlich, S. A., Heron, K. E., Sliwinski, M. J., Crosby, R. D., Mitchell, J. E., & Engel, S. G. (2007). Daily and momentary mood and stress are associated with binge eating and vomiting in bulimia nervosa patients in the natural environment. *Journal of Consulting and Clinical Psychology*, *75*(4), 629–638.

Sobell, L. C., & Sobell, M. B. (1992). Timeline follow-back. In R.Z. Litten & J.P Allen (Eds.), *Measuring alcohol consumption* (pp. 41–72). Totowa, NJ: Humana Press.

Sprague, J., Verona, E., Kalkhoff, W., & Kilmer, A. (2011). Moderators and mediators of the stress-aggression relationship: executive function and state anger. *Emotion*, *11*(1), 61–73.

Stone, A. A., & Neale, J. M. (1984). New measure of daily coping: Development and preliminary results. *Journal of Personality and Social Psychology*, *46*(4), 892–906.

Sullivan, H. S. (1954). *The psychiatric interview*. New York, NY: W.W. Norton.

Suls, J., & Martin, R. (2005). The daily life of the garden-variety neurotic: Reactivity, stressor exposure, mood spillover, and maladaptive coping. *Journal of Personality*, *73*(6), 1485–1509.

Tessner, K. D., Mittal, V., & Walker, E. F. (2011). Longitudinal study of stressful life events and daily stressors among adolescents at high risk for psychotic disorders. *Schizophrenia Bulletin*, *37*(2), 432–441.

Tolpin, L. H., Gunthert, K. C., Cohen, L. H., & O'Neill, S. C. (2003). Borderline personality features and instability of negative affect and self-esteem. *Journal of Personality*, *72*, 111–138.

Trull, T. J., & Ebner-Priemer, U. (2013). Ambulatory assessment. *Annual Review of Clinical Psychology*, *9*, 151–176.

Van Den Brink, M., Bandell-Hoekstra, E., & Abu-Sadd, H. (2001). The occurrence of recall bias in pediatric headache: A comparison of questionnaire and diary data. *Headache*, *41*, 11–20.

van Winkel, M., Nicolson, N. A., Wichers, M., Viechtbauer, W., Myin-Germeys, I., & Peeters, F. (2015). Daily life stress reactivity in remitted versus non-remitted depressed individuals. *European Psychiatry*, *30*(4), 441–447.

Wagner, B. M., Compas, B. E., & Howell, D. C. (1988). Daily and major life events: A test of an integrative model of psychosocial stress. *American Journal of Community Psychology*. *16*, 189–205.

Walker, L. S., Smith, C. A., Garber, J., Van Slyke, D. A., & Claar, R. (2001). The relation of daily stressors to somatic and emotional symptoms in children with recurrent abdominal pain. *Journal of Consulting and Clinical Psychology*, *69*, 85–91.

Walls, T. A., & Schafer, J. L. (Eds.). (2006). *Models for intensive longitudinal data*. New York, NY: Oxford University Press.

Wichers, M. (2014). The dynamic nature of depression: A new micro-level perspective of mental disorder that meets current challenges. *Psychological Medicine*, *44*(7), 1349–1360.

Wichers, M., Peeters, F., Geschwind, N., Jacobs, N., Simons, C. J. P., Derom, C.,...van Os, J. (2010). Unveiling patterns of affective responses in daily life may improve outcome prediction in depression: A momentary assessment study. *Journal of Affective Disorders*, *124*(1–2), 191–195.

Wright, A. G. C. (2014). Integrating trait and process based conceptualizations of pathological narcissism in the DSM-5 era. In A. Besser (Ed.), *Handbook of psychology of narcissism: Diverse perspectives* (pp. 153–174). Hauppauge, NY: Nova Science Publishers.

Wright, A. G. C., Gates, K. M., Arizmendi, C., Lane, S., Woods, W. C., & Edershile, E. A. (2019). Focusing personality assessment on the person: Modeling general, shared, and person specific processes in personality and psychopathology. *Psychological Assessment*, *31*(4), 502–515.

Wright, A. G. C., & Hopwood, C. J. (2016). Advancing the assessment of dynamic psychological processes. *Assessment*, *23*(4), 399–403.

Wright, A. G. C., Hopwood, C. J., & Simms, L. J. (2015). Daily interpersonal and affective dynamics in personality disorder. *Journal of Personality Disorders*, *29*(4), 503–525.

Wright, A. G. C., & Simms, L. J. (2016). Stability and fluctuation of personality disorder features in daily life. *Journal of Abnormal Psychology*, *125*(5), 641–656.

Wright, A. G. C., Stepp, S. D., Scott, L. N., Hallquist, M. N., Beeney, J. E., Lazarus, S. A., & Pilkonis, P. A. (2017). The effect of pathological narcissism on interpersonal and affective processes in social interactions. *Journal of Abnormal Psychology*, *126*, 898–910.

Wrzus, C., & Mehl, M. R. (2015). Lab and/or field? Measuring personality processes and their social consequences. *European Journal of Personality*, *29*(2), 250–271.

Early Life Stress and Psychopathology

Katie A. McLaughlin

Abstract

Exposure to chronic or severe stressful life events during childhood and adolescence—frequently referred to as early life stress (ELS) or childhood adversity—has powerful and lasting associations with psychopathology across the life course. This chapter reviews the growing body of research on ELS and psychopathology across the life course, with a particular focus on the mechanisms that explain the strong associations between ELS and psychopathology. To address these questions, I review evidence on the links between ELS and psychopathology and highlight divergent conceptual models of ELS that advocate different approaches to uncovering these mechanisms. I end by addressing different approaches to the measurement and analysis of ELS that have emerged from these conceptual frameworks.

Keywords: stress, early life stress, childhood adversity, adverse childhood experience, development, psychopathology

Exposure to stressful life events has long been recognized as a risk factor for the onset of psychopathology. Over the past two decades, however, evidence from diverse scientific disciplines has demonstrated that certain types of stressful life events that occur during childhood and adolescence have particularly powerful and lasting associations with psychopathology across the life course (Afifi et al., 2008; Edwards, Holden, Felitti, & Anda, 2003; Green et al., 2010; MacMillan et al., 2001; McLaughlin et al., 2012). These experiences are frequently referred to as early life stress (ELS) or childhood adversity. This chapter reviews the growing body of research on ELS and its associations with psychopathology. What is ELS and how does it differ from normative experiences of stress? How is ELS related to psychopathology and, critically, what are the mechanisms that explain these associations? To address these questions, I review evidence on the links between ELS and psychopathology and highlight divergent conceptual models of ELS that advocate different approaches to uncovering these mechanisms. I end by

addressing different approaches to the measurement and analysis of ELS that have emerged from these conceptual frameworks.

Defining Early Life Stress

Despite the burgeoning interest in the links between ELS and psychopathology, there has been a surprising lack of consistency in the literature with regard to the definition and measurement of the construct. Until very recently, ELS was a construct in search of a definition. Even the terminology used to refer to ELS varies widely across studies. Some of the most commonly used terms other than ELS include childhood adversity, adverse childhood experiences, and household dysfunction. But to what does the construct of ELS or childhood adversity actually refer, and is it different from other types of childhood stressors? As I have noted elsewhere (McLaughlin, 2016), a definition of ELS has remained elusive because the construct is both difficult to define concretely but fairly obvious to most observers, making it an example of the classic standard of *you know it when you see it*. Recent efforts to define ELS and distinguish it from other types of stressors—particularly more normative forms of stress exposure—grew out of two related lines of inquiry.

First, extensive research had been conducted on normative stressors occurring during childhood and adolescence. Stress has been defined by Monroe (2008) as reflecting the ongoing adaptation required by environmental conditions that change over time. Within this broad perspective, stress is comprised of three components that interact with one another: (1) environmental conditions that require adaptation (i.e., stressors); (2) the psychological and neurobiological response of an organism to these changes in environmental conditions (i.e., the stress response); and (3) the ongoing transaction between an organism and the environment that unfolds across time (i.e., adaptation to stress) (Monroe, 2008). The environmental component of stress aligns most closely with the concept of ELS. Even in early studies of environmental stressors, it was recognized that stressful experiences occurring in childhood might have particular significance for mental health (Bifulco, Brown, & Adler, 1991; Bifulco, Brown, & Harris, 1987). Indeed, extensive research documents associations between exposure to stressors in childhood and adolescence and the subsequent onset of psychopathology (Grant et al., 2003, 2006; Grant, Compas, Thurm, & McMahon, 2004; Hammen, 2008). Within this literature, a variety of distinctions among different types of stressors have been utilized based on (a) temporal characteristics of the stressor (i.e., differentiating chronic stressors such as marital conflict from acute life events like a car accident) (Adrian & Hammen, 1993); (b) stressor severity, such that major stressors like parental divorce are distinguished from more minor events and hassles like failing a test (Grant, 2003); (c) the role of the child in contributing to the occurrence of the stressor, with independent events (i.e., those that the child played no role in generating, like a car accident) considered separately from dependent events that a child contributed to in some way, such as peer conflict (Rudolph & Hammen, 1999); and (d) the source of stress. With regard to sources of stress, a variety of distinctions have been made, with interpersonal stressors frequently differentiated from those occurring in the academic domain or from other noninterpersonal forms of stress (Rudolph et al., 2000). Studies of childhood stress exposure and psychopathology typically assess a wide range of stressors, some of which would be considered to be forms of ELS (e.g., exposure to violence) and many of which would not (e.g., peer-related stressors; academic stressors; daily hassles). This body of work has informed recent attempts to define ELS and to distinguish experiences of adversity that reflect ELS from the wide range of stressors that have been studied in relation to developmental psychopathology.

A second body of work informing modern conceptualization of ELS emerged from the seminal Adverse Childhood Experiences (ACE) study (Anda et al., 2006; Felitti et al., 1998), which examined ELS as a determinant of adult physical and mental health. In many ways, the genesis of the modern construct of ELS began with this study. Before the ACE study, most work on ELS focused on specific, individual types of adverse experiences, such as parental divorce, death of a parent, sexual abuse, or poverty (Amato & Keith, 1991; Duncan, Brooks-Gunn, & Kato Klebanov, 1994; Molnar, Buka, & Kessler, 2001). Research on specific forms of ELS had evolved as relatively independent lines of inquiry until the ACE study, which considered numerous types of adversity—including abuse, neglect, parental psychopathology and substance use, parental loss, domestic violence, and parental criminal behavior—to be indicators of the same underlying construct, termed "adverse childhood experiences" or "household dysfunction" (Dube et al., 2001; Felitti et al., 1998). The study documented high levels of co-occurrence among these multiple forms of ELS and strong associations between ELS exposure and adult health (Dong et al., 2004; Edwards et al., 2003; Felitti et al., 1998). Although the findings of the ACE study provided the impetus for many recent studies of ELS, a concrete definition of "adverse childhood experience" or "household dysfunction" was never provided. According to the Centers for Disease Control and Prevention (CDC) website for the ACE study, the ACE score—a count of the total number of adversities experienced, is designed to assess "the total amount of stress experienced during childhood."

I have recently proposed a definition of childhood adversity (or ELS) that builds on definitions of life stress (Monroe, 2008) and models of experience-expectant brain development (Baumrind, 1993; Fox, Levitt, & Nelson, 2010). Specifically, adversity (or ELS) refers to *environmental circumstances that are either serious (i.e., severe) or ongoing over time (i.e., chronic); are likely to require significant adaptation by an average child; and represent a deviation from the expectable environment* (McLaughlin, 2016). The expectable environment refers to a wide range of environmental inputs that the human brain expects to encounter in order to develop normally. Expected environmental inputs range from sensory and perceptual experiences (e.g., variation in patterned light information that is required for normal development of the visual system) to social experiences, such as the presence of a sensitive and responsive caregiver and exposure to language (Fox et al., 2010). Deviations from the expectable environment often take two primary forms: an absence of expected inputs (e.g., the absence of a primary caregiver or limited exposure to complex language) or the presence of unexpected inputs that represent significant threats to the physical integrity or well-being of the child (e.g., exposure to violence) (Farah et al., 2008; Humphreys & Zeanah, 2015; McLaughlin & Sheridan, 2016; McLaughlin, Sheridan, & Lambert, 2014; Sheridan & McLaughlin, 2014). These deviations reflecting either deprivation or threat can be chronic (e.g., prolonged neglect) or involve single events that are severe enough to represent a deviation from the expectable environment (e.g., sexual abuse). This provides a reasonable working definition of ELS: exposure during childhood or adolescence to environmental circumstances that are likely to require significant psychological, social, or neurobiological adaptation by an average child and that represent a deviation from the expectable environment.

This definition provides some clear boundary conditions about the types of stressful experiences that are and are not reflective of ELS. The most obvious boundary condition involves the developmental timing of exposure—ELS must occur early in development. Most research on ELS has taken a fairly broad definition of what constitutes early life and includes events occurring during either childhood or adolescence. An additional boundary condition centers on the specific component of stress to which ELS refers. In the proposed definition, ELS refers to a specific event or ongoing conditions *in the environment*. ELS thus refers to environmental circumstances or events and not a child's response to those events or adaptation over time. Perhaps the most meaningful boundary condition involves the types of environmental circumstances that qualify as ELS. The proposed definition restricts ELS to environmental conditions that are likely to require significant adaptation by an average child—this means that not all childhood stressors qualify as ELS. Transient events or minor hassles should not qualify, but neither should major life events that do not represent a deviation from the expectable

environment such as the death of a grandparent, enrolling in a new school, or experiencing the end of a close friendship. These are all examples of events that would qualify as meaningful stressors and could certainly influence mental health, but they are not examples of ELS. This boundary condition provides the clearest distinction between ELS and more broad definitions of stressors that occur during childhood or adolescence (Grant et al., 2003, 2004; Rudolph & Hammen, 1999; Rudolph et al., 2000). At the same time, this condition is the most difficult to define clearly, as there is no absolute rule or formula that can be used to distinguish circumstances requiring significant adaptation from those that are less severe or impactful. Nevertheless, a guiding principle is that ELS should only include events that are likely to have a meaningful and lasting impact on developmental processes for most children who experience them. More specifically, only environmental experiences that are likely to alter fundamental aspects of emotional, cognitive, social, or neurobiological development should qualify as ELS.

An unresolved issue for the field is whether the definition of ELS should be narrow or broad. For example, many population-based studies have included parental psychopathology and parental divorce as forms of ELS (Felitti et al., 1998; Green et al., 2010). Because psychopathology and divorce are common, consideration of any form of parental psychopathology or any type of divorce as a form of ELS results in a fairly broad definition. A more useful approach might be to consider only those cases of parental psychopathology or divorce that result in parenting behavior that deviates from the expectable environment (i.e., consistent unavailability, unresponsiveness, or insensitive care) or that produce adverse situations that would require adaptation by most children (e.g., economic adversity, emotional abuse) as meeting the threshold for ELS. Despite some unresolved questions regarding the scope of stressors that qualify as ELS, the field has reached a general consensus about the types of experiences that *do* reflect ELS. Although not exhaustive, the following experiences are frequently examined as indicators of ELS: physical, sexual, and emotional abuse; physical and emotional neglect; exposure to domestic violence; other forms of interpersonal violence exposure (e.g., in the community); separation or abandonment from caregivers (e.g., early institutional rearing, parental death, other loss of a parent); and chronic or extreme poverty and other indicators of economic adversity and material deprivation (e.g., food insecurity). For the remainder of this review, I focus specifically on these forms of ELS and do not review other forms of stress occurring in childhood and adolescence. I use the terms "ELS" and "adversity" interchangeably in this review.

Early Life Stress and Psychopathology

The link between ELS and psychopathology has been investigated extensively. Hundreds of studies have examined associations between ELS exposure and risk for psychopathology, and the evidence is consistent and clear. Exposure to ELS is associated with an increased risk for experiencing many commonly occurring forms of psychopathology (Evans, Li, & Whipple, 2013; McLaughlin, 2016). Here, I briefly review this evidence, focusing specifically on findings from epidemiological studies designed to allow inferences to be drawn at the population level and longitudinal studies that examine the onset of psychopathology after the occurrence of ELS.

Population-based and longitudinal studies have documented five general patterns with regard to ELS and the distribution of mental disorders in the population. First, epidemiological studies that are designed to estimate population prevalence have consistently found that exposure to ELS is common. In the original ACE study, about two thirds of US adults (67.3%) reported exposure to at least one major form of ELS (Dong et al., 2004). The ACE study focused on adults who were members of the Kaiser Health Plan in San Diego, California, but it did not use probability sampling or weighting, key features of epidemiological studies that allow inferences to be made at the population level. In epidemiological surveys of the US population that use probability sampling and weighting, the prevalence of exposure to ELS is estimated at about 50% (Green et al., 2010; Kessler, Davis, & Kendler, 1997; McLaughlin, Conron, Koenen, & Gilman, 2010; McLaughlin et al., 2012), although the prevalence of specific types of ELS (e.g., physical abuse) varies across studies. Similar prevalence estimates have been reported in other high-income countries as well as in low- and middle-income countries worldwide (Benjet et al., 2009; Kessler et al., 2010; Rosenman & Rodgers, 2004). Population-based studies indicate clearly that children throughout the world frequently experience ELS.

A second general finding is that individuals who have experienced ELS are at elevated risk for developing a lifetime mental disorder compared to those without such exposure (Edwards et al., 2003; Green et al., 2010; Kessler, 1997, 2010; MacMillan,

et al., 2001; McLaughlin, Conron, et al., 2010; McLaughlin et al., 2012). In epidemiological studies, the magnitude of this risk scales with the degree of exposure to ELS, such that the odds of developing a lifetime mental disorder increase as the degree of exposure to ELS increases (Edwards et al., 2003; Green et al., 2010; Kessler et al., 1997, 2010; McLaughlin, Conron, et al., 2010; McLaughlin et al., 2012). Greater risk for lifetime psychopathology among those with a history of ELS has also been observed in numerous longitudinal studies (Caspi et al., 2014; Cohen, Brown, & Smailes, 2001; Fergusson, Horwood, & Lynskey, 1996; Fergusson & Lynskey, 1996; Weich, Patterson, Shaw, & Stewart-Brown, 2009), and the magnitude of that risk also increases with greater exposure to ELS. Few consistent individual differences have been documented with regard to the association of ELS with lifetime psychopathology, including differences based on sex and race/ethnicity (Ahern, Karasek, Luedtke, Bruckner, & van der Laan, 2016; McLaughlin, Conron, et al., 2010; McLaughlin et al., 2012). For example, in a nationally representative sample of over 10,000 US adolescents, the associations of 10 forms of ELS with lifetime disorders—including mood, fear, behavioral, and substance disorders—did not vary across White, Black, and Hispanic/Latino adolescents (Ahern et al., 2016). In a population-based study of US adults, the associations between violence exposure and onset of mental disorders by adolescence did not vary for males and females (Dunn, Gilman, Willett, Slopen, & Molnar, 2012), although stronger associations between child abuse and some mental disorders were reported in a population-based sample of adults in Ontario, Canada (MacMillan et al., 2001). Cross-national variation in the association of ELS with lifetime psychopathology is also minimal; in a study of over 50,000 respondents from 21 countries worldwide, the association of ELS exposure with lifetime mental disorders exhibited little meaningful variation across countries (Kessler et al., 2010).

Third, exposure to ELS is associated with virtually all commonly occurring forms of psychopathology, and the associations of ELS with mental disorders are largely nonspecific. Individuals who have experienced ELS are more likely to develop mood, anxiety, substance use, and disruptive behavior disorders than those with no history of ELS exposure, with little meaningful variation in the strength of associations across disorder classes in epidemiological studies (Chapman et al., 2004; Dube et al., 2003; Green et al., 2010; Kessler et al., 1997, 2010;

McLaughlin et al., 2012). Exposure to ELS is also associated with psychotic experiences (Janssen et al., 2004; McGrath et al., 2017) and suicidal ideation and attempts (Afifi et al., 2008; Bruffaerts et al., 2010; Dube et al., 2001; Molnar, Berkman, & Buka, 2001) in population-based studies, with the magnitude of association in the same range as for other forms of psychopathology. Multiple epidemiological studies have shown that associations between child maltreatment and lifetime psychopathology operate entirely through a latent liability to experience internalizing and externalizing psychopathology, with no direct effects on specific mental disorders that are not explained by this latent liability (Caspi et al., 2014; Keyes et al., 2012). Evidence from longitudinal studies is consistent with these general patterns (Cohen et al., 2001; Fergusson et al., 1996; Weich et al., 2009). Exposure to ELS is associated with elevated risk of depression, anxiety, behavior problems, substance abuse, suicidal behavior, and psychotic experiences at later points in development (Cohen et al., 2001; Enns et al., 2006; Fergusson et al., 1996; Fergusson & Lynskey, 1996; Jaffee, Caspi, Moffit, Polo-Tomás, & Taylor, 2007; Johnson et al., 2002; Kelleher et al., 2013; Phillips, Hammen, Brennan, Najman, & Bor, 2005; Varese et al., 2012; Widom, DuMont, & Czaja, 2007).

Fourth, exposure to ELS is associated with heightened vulnerability to psychopathology that persists across the life course. In epidemiological studies, ELS exposure is associated not only with risk of developing a mental disorder in childhood and adolescence (McLaughlin et al., 2012) but also in adulthood (Benjet, Borges, & Medina-Mora, 2010; Green et al., 2010; Kessler et al., 1997, 2010; McLaughlin, Conron et al., 2010). Greater odds of mental disorder onset in adulthood are observed among those with a history of ELS even after adjusting for the presence of psychopathology at earlier points in development (Chapman et al., 2004; Green et al., 2010; Kessler et al., 2010). Prospective studies confirm these patterns. For example, in a 45-year longitudinal study, exposure to ELS was associated with elevated risk for depression and anxiety disorders in adolescence, early adulthood, and middle adulthood, with no meaningful reduction in the magnitude of associations with increasing age (Clark, Caldwell, Power, & Stansfeld, 2010). Associations between ELS and psychopathology in middle adulthood remained even after accounting for earlier onset mental disorders. Similar findings have emerged from other long-term prospective studies, indicating that the risk for psychopathology associated with exposure to ELS persists well into adulthood (Collishaw et al., 2007; Koenen, Moffit, Poulin, Martin, & Caspi, 2007; McLaughlin et al., 2010; Weich et al., 2009).

Finally, exposure to ELS explains a substantial proportion of mental disorder onsets in the population, both in the United States and cross-nationally (Afifi et al., 2008; Green et al., 2010; Kessler et al., 2010; McLaughlin et al., 2012). Approximately 30% of lifetime mental disorders in the population are attributable to exposure to ELS. This reflects both the high prevalence of exposure to ELS and the strong associations of ELS with the onset of psychopathology. Together, findings from epidemiological and longitudinal studies indicate clearly that exposure to ELS powerfully shapes risk for psychopathology in the population.

Common Approaches to Conceptualizing Early Life Stress
Discrete Stressors
Prior to the ACE study, most research on ELS focused on specific types of individual stressors. This approach continues in some lines of research even today. Common types of ELS that, until recently, had been studied in relative isolation from one another included physical abuse (Springer, Sheridan, Kuo, & Carnes, 2007; Sugaya et al., 2012), sexual abuse (Molnar, Buka, et al., 2001; Mullen, Martin, Anderson, Romans, & Herbison, 1993; Trickett, Noll, & Putnam, 2011), neglect (Dubowitz, Papas, Black, & Starr, 2002), parental death (Fristad, Jedel, Weller, & Weller, 1993), parental divorce (Chase-Lansdale, Cherlin, & Kiernan, 1995), and poverty (Duncan et al., 1994; McLeod & Shanahan, 1993; McLoyd, 1998).

The ACE study was the first to consider each of these distinct types of stressors as reflecting indicators of the same underlying construct: adverse childhood experiences or ELS. Each of the forms of ELS described earlier—along with several others, including parental psychopathology and substance abuse, parental criminal behavior, and emotional abuse—were assessed in the ACE study. One of the key findings from the ACE study was that most people who have experienced one form of ELS have also experienced multiple other adverse experiences (Dong et al., 2004). This finding has been replicated in population-based studies of children (Finkelhor, Ormrod, & Turner, 2007; McLaughlin et al., 2012) and adults (Green et al., 2010; Kessler et al., 2010). These findings raise serious concerns about approaches to studying ELS that focus on individual types of adversity and fail to account for the co-occurrence between different forms of ELS. This is a major limitation in studies focusing on a single type of ELS, as it is impossible to determine whether any observed associations between a particular form of ELS (e.g., physical abuse) and outcome (e.g., depression) represent true consequences of the focal adversity in question or the downstream effects of other co-occurring experiences (e.g., poverty) that may have different developmental consequences. Without measuring and controlling for co-occurring forms of ELS, the strong possibility of confounding by other forms of adversity cannot be ruled out. An additional limitation when considering discrete forms of ELS individually is an inherent assumption that the mechanisms linking each of these types of experiences with downstream developmental outcomes, including psychopathology, are completely distinct. In other words, this approach implicitly assumes that the mechanisms linking, for example, sexual abuse with depression are distinct from those linking physical abuse or domestic violence with depression. While there is certainly some variability in core underlying developmental mechanisms across different forms of adversity, it is also quite likely that at least some mechanisms are shared across multiple types of ELS.

Recognition of the high co-occurrence of different forms of ELS led to a shift in the way that ELS is conceptualized, with many recent studies examining multiple forms of ELS jointly. These approaches are described in the next section on "Cumulative Risk." However, examination of discrete individual forms of ELS remains common for some types of adversity. For example, institutional rearing is often studied as a discrete exposure, separate from other forms of ELS (Gunnar, van Dulmen, & The International Adoption Project Team, 2007; McLaughlin, Sheridan et al., 2014; Rutter et al., 2010; Tottenham et al., 2011). This reflects the fact that many children who participate in research following institutional rearing have been adopted into families who have a strong desire to be parents, are relatively well-off financially, and generally have low levels of co-occurring adversity, as well as the fact that institutional rearing is a well-defined exposure with a clear onset and offset but for which co-occurring adversities occurring in the institutional environment are typically not assessed systematically.

Cumulative Risk

The prevailing approach to assessing and conceptualizing ELS over the past decade has been the cumulative risk approach. This approach tallies the number of distinct forms of ELS experienced to create a risk score without regard to the type, chronicity, or severity of the experience and uses this risk score as a predictor of outcomes (Dube et al., 2001; Evans et al., 2013; Felitti et al., 1998). For example, a child who experienced physical abuse, sexual abuse, and domestic violence would have a risk score of three; a child who experienced poverty, neglect, and maternal depression would also have a risk score of three. Cumulative risk thus focuses on the *number* of distinct types of ELS a child has experienced rather than the severity of those experiences or type of adversity. A critical assumption in the cumulative risk approach is that discrete forms of ELS have additive effects on downstream developmental outcomes (Evans et al., 2013). That assumption implies that each additional form of ELS a child experiences will have statistically similar effects on developmental outcomes, regardless of the number of co-occurring adverse experiences the child has had.

A cumulative risk approach involves a variety of benefits as compared to studying discrete forms of ELS in isolation. The first concerns the co-occurrence of different forms of ELS; this issue was described in the previous section on discrete stressors. A second is that multiple risk exposures have consistently been shown to have more robust effects on developmental outcomes than single exposures (Evans et al., 2013). Indeed, this is a well-replicated and fairly intuitive finding (Dube et al., 2001; Dube et al., 2003; Green et al., 2010; Jaffee et al., 2007; McLaughlin et al., 2012). In addition, the cumulative risk approach can identify children that would benefit from intervention, as children with high degrees of exposure to multiple forms of ELS are clearly in greatest need of intervention (Evans et al., 2013). Finally, some have argued that a cumulative risk score confers statistical advantages over other strategies for measuring and modeling ELS because they are parsimonious (i.e., they use one value for ELS rather than multiple metrics); they are unweighted (i.e., they consider all forms of ELS to be equal in their developmental effects); they are not sensitive to collinearity among predictors (i.e., multiple forms of ELS can be tallied and summed without introducing collinearity into a statistical model); they are more stable statistically than individual stressors; and they are easily understandable to policymakers and other relevant stakeholders outside the scientific community (Evans et al., 2013). The argument regarding parsimony and ease of understanding cumulative risk scores is borne out by recent trends. The cumulative risk approach has been widely adopted following the ACE study and has generated considerable interest in understanding the long-term consequences of ELS and preventing those effects. The importance of ELS has been acknowledged in policy briefs by major medical organizations, including the American Academy of Pediatrics and the American Heart Association. Risk scores can also be used as a screening tool to identify those children in greatest need of intervention; indeed, some medical clinics have begun to screen for ELS as a routine part of clinical practice (Burke, Hellman, Scott, Weems, & Carrion, 2011). Thus, the cumulative risk approach has broad appeal, particularly for clinicians and policymakers.

However, some of the assumptions used to justify the cumulative risk approach are not borne out in empirical data. In particular, existing evidence indicates that the effects of multiple ELS exposures on mental health outcomes are not additive. Instead, the associations of multiple forms of adversity with psychopathology have been shown to be subadditive in several population-based studies (Green et al., 2010; Kessler et al., 2010; McLaughlin et al., 2012), such that as the number of ELS exposures increases, the odds of developing a mental disorder also increase, but at a *decreasing rate*. Thus, the incremental effect of having a sixth ELS exposure on risk for psychopathology (compared to having five) is lower than the incremental effect of experiencing a second type of ELS relative to having one (Green et al., 2010; Kessler et al., 2010; McLaughlin et al., 2012). Advocates for a cumulative risk approach acknowledge that evidence for the assumption of additivity is highly mixed (Evans et al., 2013).

Several other limitations of the cumulative risk approach are worth noting. First, the use of dichotomous (1,0) indicators for each ELS experience means that only high-severity ELS experiences are counted in risk scores (Evans et al., 2013). While it is fairly obvious that extreme exposures (e.g., repeated, chronic physical abuse) will likely have larger developmental impacts than less severe experiences (e.g., occasional violence within the family), it is also clear that even low levels of exposure to ELS can have profound impacts on child development. Moreover, considering only extreme cases makes it impossible to evaluate how the severity or chronicity of exposure to ELS influences outcomes of interest. Second, as I have argued elsewhere (McLaughlin & Sheridan, 2016), the cumulative risk approach also has significant limitations when

used to identify mechanisms linking ELS with developmental outcomes, including psychopathology. Most notably, risk scores fail to distinguish between distinct types of environmental experience and assume that all forms of ELS will have similar effects on developmental processes. The assumption is that the wide range of experiences encompassed in the ELS construct—including abuse, domestic violence, poverty, neglect, institutional rearing, parental loss, and many others—will all have *identical* effects on child development. Implicit in this assumption is the notion that all forms of ELS influence development through the same underlying mechanisms that are largely universal or shared across many types of adverse experiences. In other words, risk scores assume that experiencing physical abuse, sexual abuse, and domestic violence (risk score of 3) will influence a child's development in exactly the same way as experiencing poverty, neglect, and maternal depression (also a risk score of 3). As I review next in the section on "Dimensions of Experience," this assumption is highly tenuous. Thus, cumulative risk models have serious limitations when used to identify mechanisms through which ELS increases risk for psychopathology.

Dimensions of Experience

My colleague Margaret Sheridan and I have developed an alternative to the cumulative risk model that conceptualizes ELS as a multidimensional construct and articulates specific developmental mechanisms linking particular dimensions of adverse environmental experience with psychopathology (McLaughlin & Sheridan, 2016; McLaughlin, Sheridan, & Lambert, 2014; Sheridan & McLaughlin, 2014). Rather than counting the total number of adversities, our approach attempts to distill complex adverse experiences into core underlying dimensions that cut across multiple forms of ELS. The model posits that many forms of ELS can be aligned along dimensions, and that similar developmental mechanisms will be observed for experiences that align along the same dimension. This model is based on two principles. First, it is possible to extract core underlying dimensions of environmental experience that occur in numerous types of adversity that share common features. Two initial dimensions proposed in our model are *threat*, which encompasses experiences involving harm or threat of harm to the child, and *deprivation*, which involves an absence of expected inputs from the environment during development, such as cognitive and social stimulation (e.g., complex language directed at the child).

Conceptually, these dimensions cut across numerous experiences that reflect the core feature of threat or deprivation to varying degrees. For example, threat of harm to the child is a key component of many forms of ELS, including physical and sexual abuse, witnessing domestic violence, and exposure to other forms of interpersonal violence (e.g., in the school or community). The degree of threat involved in chronic physical abuse is higher than the degree of threat involved in occasional exposure to violence occurring in one's community, but both experiences share a core feature of threat to the child. In contrast, deprivation involving low levels of cognitive stimulation is a core feature of neglect, institutional rearing, other forms of parental absence, and occurs more often in families living in poverty or with low levels of parental education, though not universally (Bradley & Corwyn, 2002; Bradley, Corwyn, McAdoo, & Coll, 2001; Hart & Risley, 1995). Our conceptualization of threat and deprivation as key dimensions of ELS aligns with other recent work arguing for distinctions between forms of adversity that represent the presence of harmful versus inadequate environmental input (e.g., abuse vs. neglect) (Humphreys & Zeanah, 2015). Critically, although threat and deprivation are dimensions that are reflected in many common forms of ELS, other dimensions also clearly exist. For example, environmental predictability is a dimension that has relevance for many forms of ELS. Thus, a two-dimensional model is simply a starting point for conceptualizing adverse environmental experiences based on underlying dimensions.

The second principle on which the model is based is that different dimensions of ELS have distinct influences on children's development. Specifically, our model argues that different dimensions of adversity have unique influences on emotional, cognitive, and neurobiological development, and that understanding these distinct developmental pathways is critical for identifying mechanisms linking ELS with psychopathology (McLaughlin, 2016; McLaughlin & Sheridan, 2016; McLaughlin, Sheridan, & Lambert, 2014; Sheridan & McLaughlin, 2014). In other words, a key assumption in the dimensional model is that the mechanisms linking different forms of ELS with psychopathology are not universal. This idea is not novel. Early conceptual models of child maltreatment argued for the importance of considering distinct types of maltreatment as reflecting different dimensions of experience with unique developmental consequences (Manly, Cicchetti, & Barnett, 1994; Manly, Kim, Rogosch, &

Cicchetti, 2001). Seth Pollak's seminal work on behavioral and neural differences in emotion perception and recognition among children who were abused versus neglected demonstrates clearly that distinct forms of ELS have different effects on developmental processes (Pollak, Cicchetti, Hornung, & Reed, 2000; Pollak & Sinha, 2002; Pollak & Tolley-Schell, 2003). More recently, other groups have also articulated similar ideas regarding distinctions between different types of ELS (Farah et al., 2008; Humphreys & Zeanah, 2015). Both principles of our model—that ELS can be distilled into core underlying dimensions that cut across multiple forms of adversity and that the mechanisms linking distinct dimensions of adversity to the onset of psychopathology vary across different ELS dimensions—are conceptually similar to ideas that have long been articulated in the field but are often ignored in current approaches involving cumulative risk.

Finally, a key element of this model is not just that ELS can be distilled into core underlying features that can be conceptualized as dimensions, but that in order to identify these mechanisms it is essential to control for co-occurring types of exposures when examining the effects of a particular dimensions of ELS (McLaughlin, Sheridan, & Lambert, 2014; Sheridan & McLaughlin, 2014, 2016; Sheridan, Peverill, & McLaughlin, 2017). This is essential, as many forms of ELS co-occur, as reviewed earlier in this chapter. The goal is not to identify children who have only experienced one particular form of ELS in isolation—that would obviously be a fool's errand. The goal is to demonstrate that despite the co-occurrence of ELS experiences, there is at least some specificity in the mechanisms that link particular forms of ELS with downstream outcomes. Such an approach is critical for isolating whether developmental processes that are impacted by adversity globally or are specific to particular forms of ELS. Moreover, it is essential to control for co-occurring exposures because if one demonstrates, for example, an association between violence exposure and working memory without controlling for co-occurring forms of ELS known to be associated with working memory (e.g., poverty, neglect) (Finn et al., 2016; Leonard, Mackey, Finn, & Gabrieli, 2015; Noble, McCandliss, & Farah, 2007), it would be easy to find a spurious association with violence exposure that is in fact explained by co-occurring adversity. Understanding how particular developmental processes are influenced by ELS and whether these effects are specific or general is of critical importance for developing targeted and effective preventive interventions.

How do the assumptions and justification for a dimensional model diverge from those associated with cumulative risk? Both cumulative risk and the dimensional model share the assumption that multiple ELS exposures will have stronger effects on developmental outcomes than single exposures and that experiences that are more chronic or severe are also more likely to influence development (Evans et al., 2013; McLaughlin & Sheridan, 2016; McLaughlin, Sheridan, & Lambert, 2014), but the approach for addressing these issues differs. Cumulative risk advocates dichotomizing each exposure and creating one risk score; the dimensional model argues for assessing ELS across multiple dimensions and including separate variables for those dimensions in the same model. Dimensions can be modeled in a variety of ways, and the specific approach for representing a particular dimension (e.g., threat) is not prescribed. For example, a variable could be created to represent the frequency of exposure to threat (i.e., the frequency of exposure to multiple forms of violence); a variety score could also be used (i.e., reflecting the number of distinct types of threat a child has experienced). The specific approach can vary based on the assessments available in a given study; the key is to create a composite that represents a *dimension* of threat exposure, ranging from an absence of that experience to a high level of exposure and to control for co-occurring exposures along other dimensions (e.g., deprivation). The primary distinction between these approaches lies in the assumption that all forms of ELS are equal in their developmental effects—a core tenet of the cumulative risk model that justifies using an unweighted count of adversities (Evans et al., 2013). As reviewed in the sections that follow, accumulating evidence suggests that the developmental processes influenced by different dimensions of ELS are at least partially distinct (Busso, McLaughlin, & Sheridan, 2017; Everaerd et al., 2016; Lambert, King, Monahan, & McLaughlin, 2017; Lawson et al., 2017; Sheridan et al., 2017). This raises questions about the assumption of universal ELS effects on which the cumulative risk model is based with regard to understanding mechanisms linking ELS with psychopathology.

The dimensional model also diverges from cumulative risk with regard to assumptions regarding the statistical modeling of ELS. Cumulative risk scores provide a more parsimonious modeling strategy (i.e., a single variable) than using multiple composites reflecting different ELS dimensions. In contrast, the dimensional model advocates for the importance of including multiple indicators of distinct ELS dimensions in the same statistical model; an approach that cumulative risk assumes will introduce problematic collinearity into the statistical model. However, it is clear from population-based data that while different forms of ELS co-occur, that co-occurrence is not sufficiently high to introduce problematic collinearity. Table 3.1 presents polychoric correlations among 10 distinct forms of ELS assessed in the National Comorbidity Survey—Replication Adolescent Supplement (NCS-A), a nationally representative study of over 10,000 US adolescents. Several patterns are notable. First, although most

Table 3.1. Polychoric correlations among domains of early-life stress in the National Comorbidity Survey Replication—Adolescent Supplement (NCS-A)

	1	2	3	4	5	6	7	8	9	10
1. Physical abuse	—									
2. Domestic violence	.58	—								
3. Sexual abuse	.30	.37	—							
4. Violent victimization	.28	.33	.87	—						
5. Witnessing violence	.20	.23	.21	.33	—					
6. Emotional abuse	.45	.39	.30	.32	.22	—				
7. Poverty	.20	.16	.01	.00	.11	.12	—			
8. Financial hardship	.32	.34	.23	.25	.21	.25	.29	—		
9. Food insecurity	.23	.21	.15	.15	.13	.17	.24	.30	—	
10. Neglect	.46	.48	.45	.44	.17	.59	.16	.34	.18	—

Note: Polychoric correlations were calculated after applying sample weights to adjust for non-response and differential selection probabilities as well as to make the sample socio-demographic distributions representative of the U.S.; indicators of threat are in rows 1–6 and indicators of deprivation are in rows 7–10.

forms of ELS are correlated, the associations are mostly in the small to moderate range ($r = 0.1–0.6$). The strongest correlations are among experiences of maltreatment, including abuse and neglect, and domestic violence ($r = 0.4–0.6$), and most of the strongest associations are among indicators reflecting the same underlying dimension (i.e., physical, sexual, and emotional abuse and domestic violence are all indicators of threat, and thus would be reflected in a single threat composite). Cross-dimension associations between neglect and threat indicators are also moderate ($r = 0.4–0.6$), but not sufficiently high that they would be problematic when included in the same statistical model. Other indictors of deprivation, such as poverty and food insecurity, exhibit correlations of small magnitude with indicators of threat ($r = 0.1–0.3$). Prior work with the NCS-A demonstrates that collinearity is not a problem even in a model that includes separate variables for more than 10 distinct types of ELS in predicting psychopathology (McLaughlin et al., 2012). Thus, the co-occurrence of different forms of ELS in the population is meaningful, but not so dramatic that it is not possible to tease apart distinct associations between particular experiences and relevant developmental outcomes.

Mechanisms Linking Early Life Stress With Psychopathology

Identifying developmental mechanisms that underlie the strong associations between ELS and psychopathology is a major goal of ongoing research. Determining how experiences of ELS influence development in emotional, social, cognitive, and neurobiological domains and how disruptions in specific developmental processes, in turn, confer greater risk for psychopathology is a pressing research priority (McLaughlin, 2016). As noted earlier, ELS exhibits strong patterns of multifinality, predicting elevated risk for the onset of virtually all commonly occurring mental disorders (Green et al., 2010; Kessler et al., 2010; McLaughlin et al., 2012). However, the mechanisms that explain how ELS influences this liability to psychopathology are only beginning to be understood. Greater understanding of these mechanisms is needed to inform the development of interventions to prevent the onset of mental health problems in children who have experienced ELS. In order to intervene effectively, it is necessary to understand the developmental processes that are altered by experiences of ELS and how they ultimately contribute to the etiology of mental disorders. Many of the later chapters in this volume

are concerned explicitly with mechanisms linking stress to the onset of psychopathology. Here, I focus on two broad approaches for conceptualizing and studying these mechanisms that have emerged from prevailing models of ELS: cumulative risk and dimensions of adversity. Each model articulates a different perspective on the mechanisms linking ELS with psychopathology and whether those mechanisms are general or specific to particular types of ELS.

General/Universal Mechanisms

One of the key assumptions of the cumulative risk model is that different forms of ELS have largely similar effects on developmental outcomes (Evans & Kim, 2007; Evans et al., 2013). As noted earlier, this assumption implies that a child who has experienced physical abuse, sexual abuse, and domestic violence (and thus has a risk score of 3) will have similar developmental outcomes as a child who has experienced poverty, maternal depression, and neglect (and thus also has a risk score of 3). It is assumed that not only are the effects of these vastly different social and environmental experiences *qualitatively* similar but also *quantitatively* similar, such that each distinct type of ELS will have an effect of equal magnitude on any developmental process in question (Evans et al., 2013). This assumption of equivalence is fundamental to the cumulative risk score approach.

Is it possible that all forms of ELS influence development through the same underlying mechanisms? Around the same time that findings from the ACE study emerged, the concept of allostatic load was introduced as a comprehensive neurobiological model of the effects of stress (McEwen, 1998, 2000). Allostatic load provides a framework for explaining the neurobiological mechanisms linking multiple forms of ELS—as well as other forms of stress experienced later in life—to downstream health outcomes. Advocates of cumulative risk argue that allostatic load, and the associated disruptions in the regulation of stress response systems and other regulatory systems, represents a common mechanism that explains how numerous forms of seemingly disparate adverse experiences influence the wide range of developmental outcomes associated with ELS (Evans & Kim, 2007; Evans et al., 2013).

The concept of allostatic load and the links between stress exposure and allostatic load have been reviewed extensively elsewhere (Danese & McEwen, 2012; McEwen, 1998, 2012; McEwen & Gianaros, 2010; McEwen & Seeman, 1999). Briefly, the process of allostasis allows an organism to adapt to changing environmental demands through changes in regulatory systems, including the hypothalamic-pituitary-adrenal (HPA) axis and the autonomic nervous system (ANS) (McEwen, 1998, 2000). These regulatory systems work to maintain homeostasis and promote recovery following environmental stressors (McEwen, 2000). These adaptations to stressors produce physiological changes that are adaptive in the short term but maladaptive in the long term (McEwen, 2000). For example, glucocorticoid release following a stressor produces rapid improvements in immunity, but chronic glucocorticoid release leads to maladaptive long-term changes in brain regions with high concentrations of glucocorticoid receptors, including the hippocampus, amygdala, and prefrontal cortex (PFC) (McEwen, 2000, 2012). This long-term wear-and-tear on the body's regulatory systems resulting from chronic adaptation to stress is referred to as allostatic load (McEwen, 2000; McEwen & Seeman, 1999). Extensive evidence suggests that exposure to ELS disrupts stress response system functioning, including the ANS and HPA axis (Frodl & O'Keane, 2013; Gunnar & Quevedo, 2007; McCrory, De Brito, & Viding, 2010; Wilkinson & Goodyer, 2011), the primary regulatory systems that govern allostatic responses (McEwen, 2000). Indeed, greater cumulative risk has been linked to higher levels of allostatic load, even in children (Evans, 2003; Evans, Kim, Ting, Tesher, & Shannis, 2007). These disruptions are the central mechanism explaining downstream consequences of ELS in the cumulative risk model.

Dysregulation in stress response systems and allostatic load represents a plausible pathway linking ELS with mental health. ELS has been associated consistently with alterations in stress response systems, including changes in diurnal regulation of the HPA axis (Alink, Cicchetti, Kim, & Rogosch, 2012; Doom, Cicchetti, & Rogosch, 2014; Doom, Cicchetti, Rogosch, & Dackis, 2013; Gunnar, Morison, Chisolm, & Schuder, 2001; van der Vegt, van der Ende, Kirschbaum, Verhulst, & Tiemeier, 2009; Zalewski, Lengua, Thompson, & Kiff, 2016) and reactivity of the HPA axis and ANS to laboratory stressors (Gunnar, Frenn, Wewerka, & Van Ryzin, 2009; Harkness, Stewart, & Wynne-Edwards, 2011; MacMillan et al., 2009; McLaughlin, Sheridan, Alves, & Mendes, 2014; McLaughlin et al., 2015). Similarly, disruptions in the regulation and reactivity of the HPA axis and ANS have also been linked with psychopathology in cross-sectional studies,

and they have occasionally been shown to predict the subsequent onset of psychopathology, particularly depression (Adam et al., 2010; Wilkinson & Goodyer, 2011).

But are these stress pathways a universal mechanism that explains all—or even most—of the elevations in psychopathology that are associated with exposure to ELS? There are several problems with this assumption. First, the specific pattern of altered stress response system functioning associated with ELS varies across studies. The most commonly observed pattern involves blunted reactivity to laboratory stressors and globally reduced output (e.g., a flat diurnal rhythm) (Gunnar & Vazquez, 2001; MacMillan et al., 2009; McLaughlin, Sheridan, et al., 2015); this pattern has been observed in meta-analyses of chronic stress and HPA axis function (Miller, Chen, & Zhou, 2007). However, numerous studies document the opposite pattern—elevated reactivity to stressors or globally increased HPA axis output (Fries, Shirtcliff, & Pollak, 2008; Gunnar et al., 2001), and effects frequently vary by sex (Doom et al., 2013). This is true even for studies examining the same type of ELS exposure (e.g., institutional rearing). Thus, even when considering the effects of ELS on a relatively circumscribed set of neurobiological processes, there is wide variability across studies in the nature of these relationships.

Second, although disruptions in stress response systems and allostatic load have been consistently linked to the onset of physical health problems, such as cardiovascular disease (Heim, Ehlert, & Helhammer, 2000; Seeman, Singer, Rowe, Horwitz, & McEwen, 1997), evidence for their role in the etiology of mental disorders is less clear. The literature on stress response system disruption and psychopathology has produced widely variable findings. For example, depression and posttraumatic stress disorder (PTSD) are two mental disorders that have been frequently studied in relation to cortisol regulation and reactivity. Meta-analysis indicates an absence of a meaningful relationship between diurnal cortisol and depression (Knorr, Vinberg, Kessing, & Wetterslev, 2010), and that adults with depression have similar cortisol response to laboratory stress paradigms as those without depression, but delayed recovery of the cortisol response; particularly among older adults and those with more severe depression (Burke, Davis, Otte, & Mohr, 2005). For PTSD, two meta-analyses have produced conflicting results, with one demonstrating an absence of an association between PTSD and HPA axis function (Klaassens, Giltay, Cuijpers, van Veen, & Zitman,

2012) and the other indicating moderately lower daily cortisol output among those with PTSD than trauma-exposed controls (Morris, Compas, & Garber, 2012). Prospective studies have also produced conflicting findings, with some demonstrating associations between cortisol awakening response and later onset of a depressive episode (Adam et al., 2010) and others failing to replicate this effect (Carnegie et al., 2014; Nederhof et al., 2015). Moreover, disruptions in stress response system functioning are clearly an insufficient mechanism to explain the wide range of other developmental outcomes that are commonly observed among children who experience ELS. For example, children exposed to neglect and poverty often exhibit difficulties in the domain of expressive and receptive language (Farah et al., 2006; Hildyard & Wolfe, 2002). There is no obvious link between stress response system functioning and language ability, which indicates that other mechanisms are involved.

Finally, allostatic load and disruptions in stress response system functioning provide little in the way of intervention targets for preventing the onset of psychopathology in children exposed to ELS. Aside from attempting to prevent exposure to ELS in the first place, how might we intervene to prevent the downstream consequences of ELS based on the allostatic load model? Few effective intervention approaches for children exposed to ELS have been developed as a result of cumulative risk models or stress dysregulation mechanisms. Although psychosocial interventions can influence cortisol regulation, the nature of these intervention effects varies widely across studies (Slopen, McLaughlin, & Shonkoff, 2014). Thus, although cumulative risk models are useful for screening and identifying children in need of intervention because of high levels of ELS exposure, they provide little guidance about *how* to intervene.

Specific Mechanisms

One of the guiding principles of the dimensional model of ELS is that unique emotional, social, cognitive, and neurobiological pathways underlie the links between different dimensions of adverse early experience and developmental outcomes, including psychopathology (McLaughlin, 2016; McLaughlin & Sheridan, 2016; McLaughlin, Sheridan, & Lambert, 2014; Sheridan & McLaughlin, 2014). Specifically, the model argues that the mechanisms linking experiences of threat with psychopathology are at least partially distinct from those underlying the association between deprivation and psychopathology.

Here, I briefly review predictions about the neurodevelopmental mechanisms that underlie the associations of threat and deprivation with psychopathology and existing evidence for these predictions.

With regard to threat, the dimensional model predicts that threatening experiences during childhood alter emotional development in ways that facilitate the rapid identification of potential threats in the environment (McLaughlin & Lambert, 2016; McLaughlin, Sheridan, & Lambert, 2014; Sheridan & McLaughlin, 2014). This is an adaptive response to being raised in an environment characterized by danger. Specifically, children whose early environment involves a high degree of threat should exhibit changes in emotion perception and recognition, attention and memory for emotional stimuli, emotional learning, emotional reactivity, and emotion regulation; these changes in social and emotional processing should be most pronounced for negative stimuli (e.g., angry or fearful faces) that could predict the presence of threat in the environment (McLaughlin & Lambert, 2016). Existing evidence supports these predictions. Enhanced processing of threatening social and emotional information has been consistently observed in children who have experienced physical or sexual abuse—environments characterized by a high degree of threat. For example, children exposed to these types of threatening environments exhibit attention biases toward threatening stimuli, including faster attentional engagement and slower attentional disengagement from anger, and are more likely to perceive neutral facial expressions as threatening (Gibb, Schofield, & Coles, 2008; Pollak et al., 2000; Pollak & Sinha, 2002; Pollak & Tolley-Schell, 2003). Social information processing biases involving preferential attention to threatening cues and attributions of hostility in ambiguous situations are also common among children who have experienced abuse (Dodge, Bates, & Pettit, 1990; Dodge, Petit, Bates, & Valente, 1995).

With regard to emotional learning, emerging evidence indicates altered patterns of threat-safety learning in children who have experienced threat. Specifically, children exposed to violence exhibit skin conductance response of equal magnitude to both threat and safety cues in a fear conditioning paradigm (McLaughlin et al., 2016), which may reflect generalization of fear from the cue that predicts threat to the cue that predicts safety. Elevated emotional reactivity to threat following childhood threat exposure has been observed using a variety of metrics of emotional reactivity, including self-reported emotional responses (Heleniak, Jenness, Van der Stoep, McCauley, & McLaughlin, 2016; Heleniak, King, Monahan, & McLaughlin, 2018; Hennessy, Rabideau, Cicchetti, & Cummings, 1994), negative emotional reactions to daily stressors (Glaser, van Os, Portegijs, & Myin-Germeys, 2006; Wichers et al., 2009), amygdala activation to negative emotional cues (McCrory et al., 2011, 2013; McLaughlin, Peverill, Gold, Alves, & Sheridan, 2015), and threat-related autonomic nervous system reactivity (Heleniak, McLaughlin, Ormel, & Riese, 2016; McLaughlin, Sheridan, Alves, et al., 2014). Emotion regulation difficulties are also well documented among children who have been exposed to violence, including in tasks assessing implicit and explicit forms of emotion regulation (Lambert et al., 2017; Marusak, Martin, Etkin, & Thomason, 2015; Powers, Etkin, Gyurak, Bradley, & Jovanovic, 2015) as well as adult reports of children's emotion regulation abilities (Kim & Cicchetti, 2010; Kim-Spoon, Cicchetti, & Rogosch, 2013). In addition to behavioral indicators, atypical function in amygdala-prefrontal circuitry that supports these emotion regulation processes has also been observed consistently in children who have experienced abuse and other forms of interpersonal violence (Herringa et al., 2013; Marusak, Etkin, & Thomason, 2015; Marusak, Martin et al., 2015; McLaughlin, Peverill, Gold, Alves, & Sheridan, 2015).

The disruptions in social and emotional processing that have been observed in children raised in threatening environments have been linked to multiple forms of psychopathology (see McLaughlin & Lambert, 2016, for a review). Briefly, enhanced perceptual salience and attention toward threatening stimuli, as well as social information processing biases (e.g., hostile attribution bias), have been associated with anxiety (Briggs-Gowan et al., 2015; Shackman, Shackman, & Pollak, 2007), PTSD (Briggs-Gowan et al., 2017), and conduct problems (Shackman & Pollak, 2014). Difficulty discriminating between threat and safety cues in fear conditioning paradigms is associated with externalizing psychopathology (Fairchild, van Goozen, Stollery, & Goodyer, 2008; McLaughlin et al., 2016). Heightened emotional reactivity to negative stimuli has been linked to internalizing and externalizing problems in cross-sectional studies (Heleniak, McLaughlin, et al., 2016; McLaughlin, Sheridan, Alves, et al., 2014) and predicts the future onset of psychopathology (Heleniak, Jenness, et al., 2016; McLaughlin, Kubzansky, et al., 2010). Elevated amygdala response to negative stimuli assessed

prior to trauma exposure predicts the onset of PTSD symptoms following a traumatic stressor (McLaughlin, Busso, et al., 2014) as well as increases in internalizing symptoms following exposure to stressful life events (Swartz, Knodt, Radtke, & Hariri, 2015). Finally, difficulties with emotion regulation observed in children exposed to violence are associated with the onset of both internalizing and externalizing psychopathology (McLaughlin, Hatzenbuehler, Mennin, & Nolen-Hoeksema, 2011; Michl, McLaughlin, Shepherd, & Nolen-Hoeksema, 2013; Nolen-Hoeksema, Stice, Wade, & Bohon, 2007), as well as onset of PTSD symptoms following a traumatic event (Jenness et al., 2016). Multiple longitudinal studies demonstrate that emotion regulation difficulties are a mechanism linking childhood exposure to threat to the onset of internalizing and externalizing problems (Heleniak, Jenness, et al., 2016; Kim & Cicchetti, 2010).

In contrast to these social and emotional processing mechanisms in children exposed to threat, the dimensional model posits that deprivation influences development through a set of mechanisms that are at least somewhat distinct. Deprivation refers to an absence of social and cognitive stimulation and constrained opportunities for learning among children whose interactions with supportive caregivers are limited. This kind of deprivation has frequently been observed among children who experience neglect and institutional rearing. For example, children who are neglected experience low levels of sensitive, responsive, and stable caregiving, as do children raised in institutions whose interactions with caregivers are infrequent and lacking in sensitive and contingent responding (Bousha & Twentyman, 1984; Gaudin, Polansky, Kilpatrick, & Shilton, 1996; Kaufman Kantor et al., 2004; Smyke et al., 2007). Because most types of early learning occur in the context of interactions with caregivers, learning opportunities are constrained among children who experience less frequent and stable caregiving. The absence of consistent interactions with a caregiver deprives children of sensory, motoric, linguistic, and social experiences that caregivers provide that provide fodder for early learning. Children who are neglected or raised in institutional settings experience meaningful reductions in cognitive stimulation, learning opportunities, supervision by adults, and interactions with caregivers (Bousha & Twentyman, 1984; Hines, Kaufman Kantor, & Holt, 2006; Kaufman Kantor, et al., 2004; Nelson, Furtado, Fox, & Zeanah, 2009; Smyke et al., 2007; Zeanah et al., 2003). Although low socioeconomic status

(SES) is not inherently associated with this type of cognitive and social deprivation, many studies suggest that children being raised in poverty or by parents with low levels of education experience, on average, lower levels of cognitive stimulation, fewer learning opportunities at home and school, and less exposure to complex language than children raised in higher SES families (Bradley & Corwyn, 2002; Bradley et al., 2001; Crosnoe et al., 2010; Garrett, Ng'andu, & Ferron, 1994; Hart & Risley, 1995; Linver, Brooks-Gunn, & Kohen, 2002; Sheridan, Sarsour, Jutte, D'Esposito, & Boyce, 2012).

This type of early deprivation in cognitive and social stimulation can have pronounced effects on children's cognitive development, particularly in the domains of language and executive functioning (McLaughlin, 2016; Sheridan & McLaughlin, 2016). Indeed, poor performance on tasks of expressive and receptive language and executive functioning has been consistently observed among children who experience deprivation related to neglect (Allen & Oliver, 1982; Culp et al., 1991; Spratt et al., 2012), institutional rearing (Albers, Johnson, Hostetter, Iverson, & Miller, 1997; Bos, Fox, Zeanah, & Nelson, 2009; Colvert et al., 2008; Hostinar, Stellern, Schaefer, Carlson, & Gunnar, 2012; Loman et al., 2013; McDermott et al., 2013; Pollak et al., 2010; Rakhlin et al., 2015; Tibu et al., 2016; Windsor et al., 2011), and low SES (Blair, 2002; Farah et al., 2006; Fernald, Marchman, & Weisleder, 2013; Noble et al., 2007; Noble, Norman, & Farah, 2005; Raver, Blair, Willoughby, & The Family life Project Key Investigators, 2013; Weisleder & Fernald, 2013). SES-related differences in language and executive functioning are observable as early as infancy (Clearfield & Niman, 2012; Fernald et al., 2013). Deprivation-related adversity involving neglect is more strongly associated with these cognitive outcomes than experiences of threat, such as physical and sexual abuse (Hildyard & Wolfe, 2002). In addition to these behavioral differences, altered function in the neural networks that support language and executive functioning—particularly the lateral prefrontal cortex—have been observed in children who have experienced deprived early environments, including institutional rearing (Mueller et al., 2010) and low SES (Kishiyama, Boyce, Jimenez, Perry, & Knight, 2009; Raizada, Richards, Meltzoff, & Kuhl, 2008; Sheridan et al., 2012). Critically, these neural differences are not present at birth (Brito, Fifer, Myers, Elliott, & Noble, 2016), suggesting that they are the result of environmental experience.

This variability in language and executive functioning is likely shaped by early learning opportunities and environmental stimulation. For example, the degree of stimulation in the home as well as the amount and quality of maternal language predicts children's language skills (Farah et al., 2008; Hoff, 2003). Direct links have also been demonstrated between the degree of enrichment and stimulation in the early caregiving environment and children's cognitive outcomes, including executive functioning and school achievement (Crosnoe et al., 2010; Duncan, 2003; Sarsour et al., 2011). SES-related differences in both language ability and executive functioning are mediated by the complexity of language spoken at home and the degree of enrichment in the home environment (Hoff, 2003; Sarsour et al., 2011; Sheridan et al., 2012). Interventions that increase children's access to learning opportunities and provide more consistent and structured interactions with adults have consistently been shown to improve cognitive development among children growing up in low-SES families in both experimental (Campbell, Pungello, Miller-Johnson, Burchinal, & Ramey, 2001; Schweinhart, Berrueta-Clement, Barnett, Epstein, & Weikart, 1985) and observational studies (Anderson et al., 2003; Gormley, Gayer, Phillips, & Dawson, 2005), providing additional support for the role of cognitive and social stimulation in shaping children's cognitive development.

Together, these disruptions in cognitive development are associated with later risk for externalizing psychopathology. With regard to language ability, meta-analysis indicates that language difficulties prospectively predict the onset of externalizing behavior (Chow & Wehby, 2016). Prospective studies also suggest that children with low language ability are at elevated risk for internalizing problems (Bornstein, Hahn, & Suwalsky, 2013; Salmon, O'Kearney, Reese, & Fortune, 2016). Poor executive functioning is a core feature of attention-deficit/hyperactivity disorder (ADHD; Martinussen, Hayden, Hogg-Johnson, & Tannock, 2005; Sergeant, Geurts, & Oosterlaan, 2002; Willcutt, Doyle, Nigg, Faraone, & Pennington, 2005), and it has been shown to mediate the association between deprivation-related ELS and the onset of ADHD (Tibu et al., 2016). Some studies have observed executive functioning difficulties in children with other forms of externalizing psychopathology, including conduct disorder and oppositional defiant disorder (Clark, Prior, & Kinsella, 2002; Hobson, Scott, & Rubia, 2011), while others have found that poor executive functioning is specific to ADHD (Oosterlaan, Scheres, & Sergeant, 2005). However, poor executive functioning prospectively predicts the onset of substance use problems and other types of risky behavior (Crews & Boettiger, 2009; Patrick, Blair, & Maggs, 2008), including criminal behavior (Moffitt et al., 2011) and the likelihood of becoming incarcerated (Yechiam et al., 2008). Executive functioning is a less well-established risk factor for internalizing problems, but difficulties with inhibition and cognitive flexibility that emerge in the context of emotional processing have been linked to risk for depression (Goeleven, De Raedt, Baert, & Koster, 2006; Joorman & Gotlib, 2010), potentially by increasing rumination (Joorman, 2006).

Altogether, substantial progress has been made in delineating the mechanisms that underlie the associations of ELS with psychopathology. While some general mechanisms have been identified that are common across many forms of ELS (e.g., disruptions in physiological stress response systems), many of these mechanisms appear to differ as a function of the specific type of ELS experienced. Exposure to trauma and forms of ELS involving threat have clear associations with emotional and social information processing and emotion regulation, whereas exposure to forms of ELS involving deprivation have much stronger associations with cognitive processes, including language and executive functioning. These emerging findings highlight mechanisms that are unique to particular forms of ELS but can also explain underlie the transdiagnostic associations of ELS with psychopathology.

Measurement and Modeling of Early Life Stress

In this last section, I discuss issues that arise in the measurement of ELS and approaches for modeling the associations of ELS with psychopathology and intermediate mechanisms. I end with a brief review of assessment tools that are commonly used to measure ELS.

Assessment of Early Life Stress

A general issue to consider with regard to the assessment of ELS concerns reliability and validity, particularly for retrospective assessments of ELS in adulthood. These issues have been reviewed in depth elsewhere (Hardt & Rutter, 2004; Widom, Raphael, & DuMont, 2004), so I address them here briefly. Methodological studies have generally concluded that ELS exposures can be assessed with reasonable reliability and validity, that prospective assessment in childhood is generally preferable to retrospective assessment in adulthood, and that the

primary bias involved in ELS assessments is underreporting of exposure (Hardt & Rutter, 2004; Widom, Raphael, & DuMont, 2004). With regard to reliability, prospective studies have documented high reliability of reports of some ELS experiences (e.g., parental death) but modest reliability for most forms of ELS, including child maltreatment; this moderate reliability is largely driven by high rates of underreporting (i.e., false negatives) (Fergusson, Horwood, & Woodward, 2000; Finlay-Jones, Scott, Duncan-Jones, Byrne, & Henderson, 1981; Widom & Morris, 1997; Widom & Shepard, 1996). Across studies, little evidence has been found for false positives, or false reports of ELS. Underreporting of ELS exposure is relatively unsurprising, and there are numerous reasons why research participants decline to endorse ELS that they have experienced, ranging from a desire for privacy to concerns about protecting caregivers or other people involved. Other factors that contribute to low reliability of ELS reports include memory biases (e.g., forgetting, mood-congruent recall, and poor memory for events in very early childhood) and lack of knowledge of certain forms of ELS even at the time they occurred (e.g., parental SES) (Hardt & Rutter, 2004). The validity of ELS reports is more challenging to evaluate because there is no gold standard assessment to confirm or deny the presence of ELS. Reports of ELS exposure have often been compared to sibling or parent reports and to documented reports of child maltreatment (e.g., by child protective services). Although concordance of self-reports with those of other informants or documented records provides good evidence for the presence of exposure, a lack of concordance does not suggest an absence of exposure. Parent and sibling reports involve the same types of biases present in self-reports of ELS exposure, and only a minority of ELS cases come to the attention of authorities (Brown, Cohen, Johnson, & Salzinger, 1998). Thus, neither of these methods provides a definitive test of validity of ELS reports. On the whole, there is general agreement that ELS reports—particularly when focused on the presence or absence of certain experiences—have sufficient reliability and validity, even when assessed retrospectively in adulthood (Hardt & Rutter, 2004).

ELS can be assessed using numerous methodological approaches, each of which involves relative strengths and weaknesses. The first issue to consider involves the informant. By far, self-report is the most common method for assessing ELS, followed by caregiver report. Self-reports are generally the preferred approach as many ELS experiences may be known only to the respondent. Moreover, caregivers may be motivated to underreport certain types of ELS experiences (e.g., abuse, harsh discipline). However, caregiver reports may be the preferred approach in some situations, particularly when participants are young children or when there is a possibility that ELS exposure occurred early in development. In studies of children, a combination of both child and caregiver report is advisable, with an "or" rule to combine across informants. Such an approach is the best way to mitigate underreporting on the part of either the child or caregiver. Substantiated records can also be used to assess certain types of ELS, particularly those that fall under the purview of child protective services—including physical and sexual abuse, neglect, and domestic violence. A benefit of this approach is that ELS reports are substantiated, reducing the risk of false positives. A downside is that documented cases of maltreatment reflect only a small proportion of actual cases, many of which never come to the attention of authorities, and reflect only the most severe or frequent exposures. When using documented cases of maltreatment, there is also substantial risk of false negatives in the control group. For example, a seminal longitudinal study of maltreatment defined cases by court-documented maltreatment and required that the control group have no court-documented maltreatment; maltreated children were matched to controls on sociodemographic factors. When maltreatment was assessed in this cohort in adulthood, 49% of the control group reported some form of maltreatment (Widom, Weiler, & Cottler, 1999). Thus, underreporting and false negatives are major concerns when only documented maltreatment is used to define exposure.

A second issue to consider is method of assessment. ELS can be assessed using self-report and caregiver-report surveys and interviews as well as official records from child protective services. Self-report and caregiver report questionnaires are typically either checklists (i.e., yes/no questions about whether the respondent experienced a particular exposure) or Likert-scale assessments of the frequency or severity of particular types of ELS. Checklists have the same inherent limitations as checklist assessments of more general types of stress, including lack of contextual detail and wide variability in the types of experiences that produce a positive endorsement (e.g., a respondent whose parent abstained from alcohol during her entire childhood due to alcohol abuse prior to the

respondent's birth and a respondent whose parent drank heavily throughout his entire childhood may each endorse having a parent with a drinking problem on a checklist) (Dohrenwend, 2006). On the other hand, there is general agreement that assessments about the presence or absence of ELS exposures are more valid than assessments of the timing, frequency, or severity of those experiences when the recall interval is long (Hardt & Rutter, 2004), suggesting that checklist-type assessments may be preferable for retrospective assessment of ELS in adulthood. Questionnaires designed to assess the frequency or severity of ELS exposure are generally preferable to checklists for assessment in childhood as they constrain the degree of intracategory variability common in checklist methods, and they are better suited for designs utilizing a dimensional approach to conceptualizing ELS. ELS can also be assessed using interview-based assessments, which allow for greater details to be collected about the specific experiences being endorsed. Some of the limitations of ELS checklists can be mitigated by administering them in an interview format that allows for follow-up questions to probe the specific nature of experiences participants endorse. Contextual threat interviews can be adapted to assess ELS, although these interviews were generally not designed to assess ELS specifically. Contextual threat interviews have the advantage of more objective coding of the severity of ELS exposures (Rudolph & Hammen, 1999), but they are limited in the sense that maltreatment and other more severe types of ELS are not typically probed directly, which is likely to magnify underreporting. Contextual threat interviews also tend to focus on circumscribed periods of time (e.g., the past 6–12 months), limiting their utility if the goal is to assess exposures across a longer time interval.

Overall, many methods are available for assessing ELS, and the choice of a measure needs to be determined by the specific research question with attention to balancing the strengths and limitations of different approaches. I advocate the use of both questionnaires and interviews. We routinely encounter children in my lab who are reluctant to report ELS on a questionnaire but are more forthcoming in an interview, as well as children who will not disclose the details of ELS experiences to an unfamiliar interviewer but are willing to endorse items on a questionnaire. Inclusion of multiple assessment methods and multiple reporters typically reduces the likelihood of false negatives to the greatest degree possible.

Early Life Stress Measures

Numerous measures have been developed to measure ELS. Here I highlight the most widely used and psychometrically sound measurement tools for assessing this construct. Specifically, Table 3.2 summarizes commonly used and validated measures of ELS. This is provided as a reference for those interested in incorporating measures of ELS into their research. The table reviews the domains of ELS assessed by the measure, method of administration (i.e., questionnaire vs. interview), and informant (i.e., self-report or caregiver report) and provides citations for existing psychometric evidence. Additionally, I note how the measure can be used to model cumulative risk and/or dimensions of adversity. Many of the measures used to assess dimensions of adversity could also be utilized within a cumulative risk approach. To do so simply requires selecting a threshold to turn a dimensional measure into a dichotomous indicator of exposure (e.g., determining the threshold of emotional abuse that qualifies as exposure). In general, however, I would caution against study-specific or ad hoc determinations of what qualifies as the presence or absence of exposure—a key limitation with cumulative risk models (Evans et al., 2013).

Statistical Analysis of Early Life Stress

Most existing work on ELS and psychopathology has used a between-person approach to study these associations. In other words, ELS is assessed, and some type of ELS score is generated for each subject. That score is entered into a statistical model—typically, some type of regression model—to examine whether the level of ELS exposure is associated with psychopathology or some other outcome. This type of between-person approach can reveal whether participants who have higher levels of ELS exposure are also more likely to exhibit psychopathology. This basic approach is widely used in studies of both the cumulative risk and dimensional model of ELS. The primary distinction is in how the ELS variable is constructed. As reviewed earlier in the chapter, the ELS variable used in studies of cumulative risk represents a count of the number of distinct types of ELS a participant has experienced. To create this count, ELS exposure is dichotomized into present versus absent (i.e., 1 vs. 0) across multiple distinct forms of ELS, and the number of exposures that are classified as present are summed to create the risk score (see Evans et al., 2013). The resulting count score is then entered as a predictor into the regression model. Within a dimensional approach, continuous

variables for ELS are constructed within each dimension being examined (e.g., threat, deprivation). These variables can be created either from a single measure of adversity or by standardizing composite scores taken from multiple measures of adversity and averaging or summing the standardized scores. This variable would be entered into a regression model, first independently (i.e., without variables for other dimensions of ELS) and then in a model that also includes a continuous variable representing another dimension of adversity (e.g., deprivation). This approach allows one to evaluate the associations of each dimension with psychopathology or other outcomes when examined in isolation (i.e., not controlling for co-occurring exposures) and after adjustment for co-occurring forms of ELS, the latter of which allows inferences to be made about developmental outcomes that are specifically associated with a particular dimension of adversity over and above other co-occurring types of ELS.

Person-level approaches have also been utilized in studies of ELS and psychopathology, typically latent class analysis or some other type of cluster-based modeling (Ford, Elhai, Connor, & Frueh, 2010; McChesney, Adamson, & Shevlin, 2015). The goal of these types of person-level approaches is to identify how different forms of ELS cluster within children and to identify meaningful groups of children who have experienced the same types of adversity. When applied to experiences of ELS, latent class models typically generate a handful of groups (or classes) that differ both in terms of the types and severity of ELS experiences. One must then evaluate and describe how the clusters differ from one another. For example, a latent class analysis of trauma exposure in a nationally representative sample of US adolescents revealed four classes that were described as low risk (i.e., relative absence of trauma exposure), sexual assault, nonsexual trauma, and high risk (i.e., exposure to multiple traumatic events) (McChesney et al., 2015). Class membership can then be associated with mental health or developmental outcomes. Person-level approaches are considerably less common than regression-based between-person models. They can be useful for determining how different types of ELS cluster within children in a particular sample, but the solutions are inherently study specific and generally do not replicate in other samples. Clustering is often based on multiple ELS characteristics, and thus clusters can reflect combinations of the type of ELS experienced and the frequency and severity of exposure simultaneously. This can create challenges for studying the links

Table 3.2. Commonly used measures of early-life stress/childhood adversity

Measure	Informant	Type of Assessment	ELS Exposures Assessed	ELS Variable Types	Alignment with Cumulative Risk and Dimensional Models	Key Citations and Psychometric Evaluations
Childhood Trauma Questionnaire (CTQ)	• Child Report	• Questionnaire • Likert-scale assessment of frequency of exposure	• Physical abuse • Sexual abuse • Emotional abuse • Physical neglect • Emotional neglect	• Continuous variable representing frequency of exposure to each ELS domain • Validated cut-offs exist for generating dichotomous indicators for each domain (Walker et al., 1999)	• Dimensional – assessment of both threat (abuse sub-scales) and deprivation (physical neglect sub-scale); emotional neglect sub-scale does not reflect either dimension • Cumulative risk – each sub-scale can be dichotomized based on validated thresholds	• Bernstein, et al. (1994). Initial reliability and validity of a new retrospective measure of child abuse and neglect. *American Journal of Psychiatry, 151,* 1132–1136. • Bernstein et al. (1997). Validity of the Childhood Trauma Questionnaire in an adolescent psychiatric population. *Journal of the American Academy of Child & Adolescent Psychiatry, 36,* 340–348.
Juvenile Victimization Questionnaire (JVQ)	• Child Report • Parent Report	• Questionnaire • Checklist	• Conventional crime (e.g., theft) • Physical abuse • Sexual abuse/assault • Emotional abuse • Neglect • Indirect victimization/ witnessing violence (including domestic violence) • Peer and sibling victimization	• Dichotomous variable representing exposure to each ELS domain • Dichotomous exposure variables are summed to create variety scores (i.e., number of exposures) in different domains (e.g., child maltreatment, direct and indirect violence exposure)	• Dimensional – assessment of both threat (abuse sub-scales) and deprivation (physical neglect sub-scale); emotional neglect sub-scale does not reflect either dimension • Cumulative risk – each sub-scale can be dichotomized based on validated thresholds	• Finkelhor, D., Ormrod, R., Turner, H., & Hamby, S. L. (2005). The victimization of children and youth: A comprehensive, national survey. *Child Maltreatment, 10,* 5–25. • Hamby, S. L., & Finkelhor, D. (2004). The Comprehensive Juvenile Victimization Questionnaire. Durham, NH: University of New Hampshire.

Measure	Format	Domains	Scoring	References
Adverse Childhood Experiences (ACES) Questionnaire	• Self-Report (designed for adult reporting) • Questionnaire • Checklist	• Physical abuse • Sexual abuse • Emotional abuse • Neglect • Parental divorce • Domestic violence • Parental psychopathology and substance abuse • Parental criminal behavior	• Dichotomous variable representing exposure to each ELS domain • Dichotomous exposure variables are summed to create cumulative ACE score • Cumulative risk – a cumulative risk score reflecting a count of the number of ELS domains experienced	Anda, R. F., Felitti, V. J., Bremner, J. D., Walker, J. D., Whitfield, C. L., Perry, B. D., . . . Giles, W. H. (2006). The enduring effect of abuse and related adverse experiences in childhood: A convergence of evidence from neurobiology and epidemiology. *European Archives of Psychiatry and Clinical Neuroscience, 256*, 174–186. Felitti, V. J., Anda, R. F., Nordenberg, D., Williamson, D. F., Spitz, A. M., Edwards, V., . . . Marks, J. S. (1998). Relationship of childhood abuse and household dysfunction to many of the leading causes of death in adults: The Adverse Childhood Experiences (ACE) Study. *American Journal of Preventive Medicine, 14*, 245–258.
Childhood Experiences of Care and Abuse Interview or Questionnaire	• Child Report • Interview • Assesses presence of exposure as well as frequency and severity	• Physical abuse • Sexual abuse • Emotional abuse • Neglect • Parental loss or separation • Domestic violence** The original measure does not assess domestic violence, but items have been added to the interview and are available upon request by the author of this chapter	• Dichotomous variable representing exposure to each ELS domain • Continuous variable for frequency of emotional abuse and neglect • Continuous variable for severity of physical and sexual abuse • Dimensional – assessment of both threat (abuse sub-scales) and deprivation (neglect sub-scale) • Cumulative risk – each ELS domain can be dichotomized based on validated thresholds (see www.ceca.interview.com for scoring details)	Bifulco, A., Brown, G. W., & Harris, T. O. (1994). Childhood Experiences of Care and Abuse (CECA): a retrospective interview measure. *Journal of Child Psychology and Psychiatry, 35*, 1419–1435. Bifulco, A., Bernazzani, O., Moran, P. M., & Jacobs, C. (2005). The childhood experience of care and abuse questionnaire (CECA.Q): Validation in a community series. *British Journal of Clinical Psychology, 44*, 563–581.

(continued)

Table 3.2. Continued

Measure	Informant	Type of Assessment	ELS Exposures Assessed	ELS Variable Types	Alignment with Cumulative Risk and Dimensional Models	Key Citations and Psychometric Evaluations
Traumatic Events Screening Inventory (TESI)	• Child Report • Parent Report	• Questionnaire or Interview • Checklist followed by severity assessment	• Physical abuse • Sexual abuse • Domestic violence • Community violence • Accidents • Injuries and hospitalizations	• Dichotomous variable representing exposure to each ELS domain	• Dimensional – assessment of threat • Cumulative risk –a count of the number of ELS domains experienced	• Ippen, C. G., Ford, J., Racusin, R., Acker, M., Bosquet, M., Rogers, K.,…Edwards, J. (2002). Traumatic Events Screening Inventory - Parent Report Revised. • Ribbe D. Psychometric review of Traumatic Event Screening Instrument for Children (TESI-C) In: Stamm BH, editor. Measurement of stress, trauma, and adaptation. Lutherville, MD: Sidran Press; 1996. pp. 386–387. https://www.ptsd.va.gov/professional /assessment/child/tesi.asp
Conflict Tactics Scale (Parent-Child version)	• Parent report (parent-child version)	• Questionnaire • Likert-scale assessment of frequency of exposure	• Physical abuse • Sexual abuse • Emotional abuse/ verbal aggression • Corporal punishment • Neglect	• Continuous variable for frequency of exposure to each ELS domain	• Dimensional – assessment of both threat (abuse sub-scales) and deprivation (neglect sub-scale)	• Straus, M. A., Hamby, S. L., Finkelhor, D., Moore, D. W., & Runyan, D. (1998). Identification of child maltreatment with the Parent-Child Conflict Tactics Scales: Development and psychometric data for a national sample of American parents. Child abuse & neglect, 22(4), 249–270. • Bennett DS, Sullivan MW, Lewis M. Relations of parental report and observation of parenting to maltreatment history. Child Maltreatment. 2006; 11:63–75.

Instrument	Report	Method	Domains	Variable	Dimensional/Categorical	References
Traumatic Experiences Checklist (TEC)	• Child Report	• Questionnaire • Checklist	• Physical abuse • Sexual abuse • Emotional abuse • Emotional neglect • Parental loss or separation (including divorce) • Parental psychopathology • Injuries and accidents	• Dichotomous variable representing exposure to each ELS domain • Continuous severity scores	• Dimensional – assessment of threat dimension • Cumulative risk – count of the number of ELS domains experienced	• Nijenhuis, E. R., Van der Hart, O., & Kruger, K. (2002). The psychometric characteristics of the Traumatic Experiences Checklist (TEC): First findings among psychiatric outpatients. Clinical Psychology & Psychotherapy, 9(3), 200–210.
Violence Exposure Scale for Children - Revised	• Child Report • Parent Report	• Interview • Likert-scale assessment of frequency of exposure	• Direct violence exposure/victimization • Indirect violence exposure/witnessing	• Continuous variable for frequency of exposure to each ELS domain	• Dimensional – assessment of threat dimension	• Raviv, A., Erel, O., Fox, N. A., Leavitt, L., Raviv, A., Dar, I.,…Greenbaum, C. W. (2001). Individual measurement of exposure to everyday violence among elementary schoolchildren across various settings. Journal of Community Psychology 29, 117–140. • Raviv, A., Raviv, A., Shimoni, H., Fox, N. A., & Leavitt, L. A. (1999). Children's self-report of exposure to violence and its relation to emotional distress. Journal of Applied Developmental Psychology 20, 337–353.
Screen for Adolescent Violence Exposure (SAVE) KID-SAVE (for children 3rd–7th grade)	• Child Report	• Questionnaire • Likert-scale assessment of frequency of exposure	• Direct violence exposure/victimization • Indirect violence exposure/witnessing • Physical abuse • Emotional/verbal abuse	• Continuous variable for frequency of exposure to each ELS domain	• Dimensional – assessment of threat dimension	• Hastings, T. L., & Kelley, M. (1997). Development and validation of the Screen for Adolescent Violence Exposure (SAVE). Journal of Abnormal Child Psychology, 25(6), 511–520. • Flowers, A. L., Hastings, T. L., & Kelley, M. L. (2000). Development of a screening instrument for exposure to violence in children: The KID-SAVE. Journal of Psychopathology and Behavioral Assessment, 22(1), 91–104.

between clusters and developmental mechanisms. In general, person-level modeling is useful for understanding the within-person clustering of ELS but is a less useful strategy for examining associations between ELS experiences and downstream outcomes, including psychopathology.

An emerging analytic approach that has not yet appeared in published studies of ELS and psychopathology but is being pursued in several research groups is network analysis. Network analysis methods are used in a wide range of scientific disciplines (Barabasi, 2011) and have increasingly been applied to the study of psychopathology (Borsboom & Cramer, 2013; McNally, 2016). These methods allow relationships to be quantified within complex systems. Although detailed description of network analysis is beyond the scope of this chapter, at core a network is a set of elements—referred to as nodes—that are related to one another through connections, referred to as edges. As applied to psychopathology, nodes are typically specific types of symptoms and the associations among these symptoms (i.e., edges) can be modeled in a variety of ways to understand the relationships among symptoms in the network (Borsboom & Cramer, 2013; McNally, 2016). Network analysis relies on an association matrix of the nodes in a network and provides numerous tools for understanding that underlying set of associations. Such an approach provides a tool for examining some of the predictions of a dimensional model of ELS, which posits that certain dimensions of ELS will be associated with particular developmental processes, but not others (McLaughlin, Sheridan, & Lambert, 2014; Sheridan & McLaughlin, 2014). These questions can be examined by treating ELS exposures and the developmental mechanisms of interest as nodes of the same network. Community detection algorithms can be used to determine whether the predicted associations of particular dimensions of ELS with specific developmental outcomes are observable within the network, while simultaneously adjusting for co-occurring dimensions of ELS and other mechanisms. Such an approach has the potential to generate innovative new directions in understanding the developmental mechanisms linking ELS with psychopathology outcomes.

Conclusion

Early life stress is among the most potent risk factors for the onset of psychopathology. Children who experience ELS are more likely to develop virtually all commonly occurring forms of psychopathology than children who have never been exposed to ELS. Identifying the developmental mechanisms that underlie the strong links between ELS and mental health outcomes is an active area of research within the ELS literature. Recent advances in the conceptualization and modeling of ELS are poised to facilitate improved understanding of these developmental pathways. Greater knowledge of these mechanisms is required in order to develop more effective interventions to prevent the onset of psychopathology in children who have experienced ELS, a pressing issue for the field.

References

Adam, E. K., Doane, L. D., Zinbarg, R. E., Mineka, S., Craske, M. G., & Griffith, J. W. (2010). Prospective prediction of major depressive disorder from cortisol awakening responses in adolescence. *Psychoneuroendocrinology, 35*, 921–931.

Adrian, C., & Hammen, C. (1993). Stress exposure and stress generation in children of depressed mothers. *Journal of Consulting and Clinical Psychology, 61*, 354–359.

Afifi, T. O., Enns, M. W., Cox, B. J., Asmundson, G. J. G., Stein, M. B., & Sareen, J. (2008). Population attributable risk fractions of psychiatric disorders and suicide ideation and attempts associated with adverse childhood experiences. *American Journal of Public Health, 98*, 946–952.

Ahern, J., Karasek, D., Luedtke, A. R., Bruckner, T. A., & van der Laan, M. J. (2016). Racial/ethnic differences in the role of childhood adversities for mental disorders among a nationally representative sample of adolescents. *Epidemiology, 27*, 697–704.

Albers, L. H., Johnson, D. E., Hostetter, M. K., Iverson, S., & Miller, L. C. (1997). Health of children adopted from the former Soviet Union and Eastern Europe. Comparison with preadoptive medical records. *JAMA: The Journal of the American Medical Association, 278*(11), 922–924.

Alink, L. R., Cicchetti, D., Kim, J., & Rogosch, F. A. (2012). Longitudinal associations among child maltreatment, social functioning, and cortisol regulation. *Developmental Psychology, 48*, 224–236.

Allen, R. E., & Oliver, J. M. (1982). The effects of child maltreatment on language development. *Child Abuse and Neglect, 6*, 299–305.

Amato, P. R., & Keith, B. (1991). Parental divorce and adult well-being: A meta-analysis. *Journal of Marriage and the Family, 53*, 43–58.

Anda, R. F., Felitti, V. J., Bremmer, J. D., Walker, J. D., Whitfield, C. L., Perry, B. D., . . . Giles, W. H. (2006). The enduring effect of abuse and related adverse experiences in childhood: A convergence of evidence from neurobiology and epidemiology. *European Archives of Psychiatry and Clinical Neuroscience, 256*, 174–186.

Anderson, L. M., Shinn, C., Fullilove, M. T., Scrimshaw, S. C., Fielding, J. E., Normand, J., . . . Task Force on Community Preventive Services. (2003). The effectiveness of early childhood development programs: A systematic review. *American Journal of Preventive Medicine, 24*, 32–46.

Barabasi, A. L. (2011). The network takeover. *Nature Physics, 8*, 14–16.

Baumrind, D. (1993). The average expectable environment is not good enough: A response to Scarr. *Child Development, 64*, 1299–1317.

Benjet, C., Borges, G., & Medina-Mora, M. E. (2010). Chronic childhood adversity and onset of psychopathology during three life stages: Childhood, adolescence and adulthood. *Journal of Psychiatric Research, 44*(11), 732–740. doi:10.1016/j.jpsychires.2010.01.004

Benjet, C., Borges, G., Medina-Mora, M. E., Zambrano, J., Cruz, C., & Méndez, E. (2009). Descriptive epidemiology of chronic childhood adversity in Mexican adolescents. *The Journal of Adolescent Health: Official Publication of the Society for Adolescent Medicine, 45*(5), 483–489. doi:10.1016/j.jadohealth.2009.03.002

Bifulco, A., Brown, G. W., & Adler, Z. (1991). Early sexual abuse and clinical depression in adult life. *British Journal of Psychiatry, 159*, 115–122.

Bifulco, A., Brown, G. W., & Harris, T. O. (1987). Childhood loss of parent, lack of adequate parental care and adult depression: a replication. *Journal of Affective Disorders, 12*, 115–128.

Blair, C. (2002). School readiness. Integrating cognition and emotion in a neurobiological conceptualization of children's functioning at school entry. *The American Psychologist, 57*(2), 111–127.

Bornstein, M. H., Hahn, C. S., & Suwalsky, J. T. (2013). Language and internalizing and externalizing behavioral adjustment: Developmental pathways from childhood to adolescence. *Development and Psychopathology, 25*, 857–878.

Borsboom, D., & Cramer, A. O. (2013). Network analysis: An integrative approach to the structure of psychopathology. *Annual Review of Clinical Psychology, 9*, 91–121.

Bos, K. J., Fox, N. A., Zeanah, C. H., & Nelson, C. A. (2009). Effects of early psychosocial deprivation on the development of memory and executive function. *Frontiers in Behavioral Neuroscience, 3*, 16.

Bousha, D. M., & Twentyman, C. T. (1984). Mother–child interactional style in abuse, neglect, and control groups: Naturalistic observations in the home. *Journal of Abnormal Psychology, 93*, 106–114.

Bradley, R. H., & Corwyn, R. F. (2002). Socioeconomic status and child development. *Annual Review of Psychology, 53*(1), 371–399. doi:10.1146/annurev.psych.53.100901.135233

Bradley, R. H., Corwyn, R. F., McAdoo, H. P., & Coll, C. G. (2001). The home environments of children in the United States part I: Variations by age, ethnicity, and poverty status. *Child Development, 72*(6), 1844–1867.

Briggs-Gowan, M. J., Grasso, D., Bar-Haim, Y., Voss, J., McCarthy, K. J., Pine, D. S., & Wakschlag, L. S. (2017). Attention bias in the developmental unfolding of posttraumatic stress symptoms in young children at risk. *Journal of Child Psychology and Psychiatry, 57*, 1083–1091.

Briggs-Gowan, M. J., Pollak, S. D., Grasso, D., Voss, J., Mian, N. D., Zobel, E.,...Pine, D. S. (2015). Attention bias and anxiety in young children exposed to family violence. *Journal of Child Psychology and Psychiatry, 56*, 1194–1201.

Brito, N. H., Fifer, W. P., Myers, M. M., Elliott, A. J., & Noble, K. G. (2016). Associations among family socioeconomic status, EEG power at birth, and cognitive skills during infancy. *Developmental Cognitive Neuroscience, 19*, 144–151.

Brown, J., Cohen, P., Johnson, J. G., & Salzinger, S. (1998). A longitudinal analysis of risk factors for child maltreatment: Findings of a 17-year prospective study of officially recorded and self-reported child abuse and neglect.

Bruffaerts, R., Demyttenaere, K., Borges, G., Haro, J. M., Chiu, W. T., Hwang, I.,...Nock, M. K. (2010). Childhood adversities as risk factors for onset and persistence of suicidal behavior. *British Journal of Psychiatry, 197*, 20–27.

Burke, H. M., Davis, M. C., Otte, C., & Mohr, D. C. (2005). Depression and cortisol responses to psychological stress: A meta-analysis. *Psychoneuroendocrinology, 30*, 846–856.

Burke, N. J., Hellman, J. L., Scott, B. G., Weems, C. F., & Carrion, V. G. (2011). The impact of adverse childhood experiences on an urban pediatric population. *Child Abuse and Neglect, 35*, 408–413.

Busso, D. S., McLaughlin, K. A., & Sheridan, M. A. (2017). Dimensions of adversity, physiological reactivity, and externalizing psychopathology in adolescence: Deprivation and threat. *Psychosomatic Medicine, 79*, 162–171.

Campbell, F. A., Pungello, E. P., Miller-Johnson, S., Burchinal, M., & Ramey, C. T. (2001). The development of cognitive and academic abilities: Growth curves from an early childhood educational experiment. *Developmental Psychology, 37*, 231–242.

Carnegie, R., Araya, R., Ben-Shlomo, Y., Glover, V., O'Connor, T. G., O'Donnell, K. J.,...Lewis, G. (2014). Cortisol awakening response and subsequent depression: Prospective longitudinal study. *British Journal of Psychiatry, 204*, 137–143.

Caspi, A., Houts, R. M., Belsky, D. W., Goldman-Mellor, S. J., Harrington, H., Israel, S.,...Moffit, T. E. (2014). The p factor: One general psychopathology factor in the structure of psychiatric disorders? *Clinical Psychological Science, 2*, 119–137.

Chapman, D. P., Whitfield, C. L., Felitti, V. J., Dube, S. R., Edwards, V. J., & Anda, R. F. (2004). Adverse childhood experiences and the risk of depressive disorders in adulthood. *Journal of Affective Disorders, 82*, 217–225.

Chase-Lansdale, P. L., Cherlin, A. J., & Kiernan, K. E. (1995). The long-term effects of parental divorce on the mental health of young adults: A developmental perspective. *Child Development, 66*, 1614–1634.

Chow, J. C., & Wehby, J. H. (2016). Associations between language and problem behavior: A systematic review and correlational meta-analysis. *Educational Psychology Review*, 1–22.

Clark, C., Caldwell, T., Power, C., & Stansfeld, S. (2010). Does the influence of childhood adversity on psychopathology persist across the lifecourse? A 45-year prospective epidemiologic study. *Annals of Epidemiology, 20*, 385–394.

Clark, C., Prior, M., & Kinsella, G. (2002). The relationship between executive function abilities, adaptive behaviour, and academic achievement in children with externalising behaviour problems. *Journal of Child Psychology and Psychiatry, 43*, 785–796.

Clearfield, M. W., & Niman, L. C. (2012). SES affects infant cognitive flexibility. *Infant Behavior and Development, 35*, 29–35.

Cohen, P., Brown, J., & Smailes, E. (2001). Child abuse and neglect and the development of mental disorders in the general population. *Development and Psychopathology, 13*, 981–999.

Collishaw, S., Pickles, A., Messer, J., Rutter, M., Shearer, C., & Maughan, B. (2007). Resilience to adult psychopathology following childhood maltreatment: Evidence from a community sample. *Child Abuse and Neglect, 31*, 211–229.

Colvert, E., Rutter, M., Kreppner, J. M., Beckett, C., Castle, J., & Groothues, C. (2008). Do theory of mind and executive functioning deficits underlie the adverse outcomes associated with profound early deprivation? Findings from the English and Romanian adoptees study. *Journal of Abnormal Child Psychology, 36*, 1057–1068.

Crews, F. T., & Boettiger, C. A. (2009). Impulsivity, frontal lobes and risk for addiction. *Pharmacology, Biochemistry, and Behavior, 93*(3), 237–247. doi:10.1016/j.pbb.2009.04.018

Crosnoe, R., Leventhal, T., Wirth, R. J., Pierce, K. M., Pianta, R., & The NICHD Child Care Research Network. (2010). Family socioeconomic status and consistent environmental stimulation in early childhood. *Child Development, 81*, 972–987.

Culp, R. E., Watkins, R. V., Lawrence, H., Letts, D., Kelly, D. J., & Rice, M. L. (1991). Maltreated children's language and speech development: Abused, neglected, and abused and neglected. *First Language, 11*, 377–389.

Danese, A., & McEwen, B. S. (2012). Adverse childhood experiences, allostasis, allostatic load, and age-related disease. *Physiological and Behavior, 106*, 29–39.

Dodge, K. A., Bates, J. E., & Pettit, G. S. (1990). Mechanisms in the cycle of violence. *Science, 250*, 1678–1683.

Dodge, K. A., Petit, G. S., Bates, J. E., & Valente, E. (1995). Social information-processing patterns partially mediate the effect of early physical abuse on later conduct problems. *Journal of Abnormal Psychology, 104*, 632–643.

Dohrenwend, B. P. (2006). Inventorying stressful life events as risk factors for psychopathology: Toward resolution of the problem of intracategory variability. *Psychological Bulletin, 132*, 477–495.

Dong, M., Anda, R. F., Felitti, V. J., Dube, S. R., Williamson, D. F., Thompson, T. J.,...Giles, W. H. (2004). The interrelatedness of multiple forms of childhood abuse, neglect, and household dysfunction. *Child Abuse and Neglect, 28*, 771–784.

Doom, J. R., Cicchetti, D., & Rogosch, F. A. (2014). Longitudinal patterns of cortisol regulation differ in maltreated and nonmaltreated children. *Journal of the American Academy of Child & Adolescent Psychiatry, 53*, 1206–1215.

Doom, J. R., Cicchetti, D., Rogosch, F. A., & Dackis, M. N. (2013). Child maltreatment and gender interactions as predictors of differential neuroendocrine profiles. *Psychoneuroendocrinology, 38*, 1442–1454.

Dube, S. R., Anda, R. F., Felitti, V. J., Chapman, D. P., Williamson, D. F., & Giles, W. H. (2001). Childhood abuse, household dysfunction, and the risk of attempted suicide throughout the life span: Findings from the Adverse Childhood Experiences Study. *JAMA: Journal of the American Medical Association, 286*, 3089–3096.

Dube, S. R., Felitti, V. J., Dong, M., Chapman, D. P., Giles, W. H., & Anda, R. F. (2003). Childhood abuse, neglect, and household dysfunction and the risk of illicit drug use: the adverse childhood experiences study. *Pediatrics, 111*, 564–572.

Dubowitz, H., Papas, M. A., Black, M. M., & Starr, R. H., Jr. (2002). Child neglect: Outcomes in high-risk urban preschoolers. *Pediatrics, 109*, 1100–1107.

Duncan, G. J. (2003). Modeling the impacts of child care quality on children's preschool cognitive development. *Child Development, 74*, 1454–1475.

Duncan, G. J., Brooks-Gunn, J., & Kato Klebanov, P. (1994). Economic deprivation and early childhood development. *Child Development, 65*, 296–318.

Dunn, E. C., Gilman, S. E., Willett, J. B., Slopen, N., & Molnar, B. E. (2012). The impact of exposure to interpersonal violence on gender differences in adolescent-onset major depression: results from the National Comorbidity survey replication (NCS-R). *Depression and Anxiety, 29*, 392–399.

Edwards, V. J., Holden, G. W., Felitti, V. J., & Anda, R. F. (2003). Relationship between multiple forms of childhood maltreatment and adult mental health in community respondents: Results from the adverse childhood experiences study. *American Journal of Psychiatry, 160*, 1453–1460.

Enns, M. W., Cox, B. J., Afifi, T. O., De Graaf, R., Ten Have, M., & Sareen, J. (2006). Childhood adversities and risk for suicidal ideation and attempts: A longitudinal population-based study. *Psychological Medicine, 36*, 1769–1778.

Evans, G. W. (2003). A multimethodological analysis of cumulative risk and allostatic load among rural children. *Developmental Psychology, 39*, 924–933.

Evans, G. W., & Kim, P. (2007). Childhood poverty and health: Cumulative risk exposure and stress dysregulation. *Psychological Science, 18*, 953–957.

Evans, G. W., Kim, P., Ting, A. H., Tesher, H. B., & Shannis, D. (2007). Cumulative risk, maternal responsiveness, and allostatic load among young adolescents. *Developmental Psychology, 43*, 341–351.

Evans, G. W., Li, D., & Whipple, S. S. (2013). Cumulative risk and child development. *Psychological Bulletin, 139*, 1342–1396.

Everaerd, D., Klumpers, F., Zweirs, M., Guadalupe, T., Franke, B., van Oostrom, I.,...Tendolkar, I. (2016). Childhood abuse and deprivation are associated with distinct sex-dependent differences in brain morphology. *Neuropsychopharmacology, 41*, 1716–1723.

Fairchild, G., van Goozen, S. H. M., Stollery, S. J., & Goodyer, I. M. (2008). Fear conditioning and affective modulation of the startle reflex in male adolescents with early-onset or adolescence-onset conduct disorder and healthy control subjects. *Biological Psychiatry, 63*, 279–285.

Farah, M. J., Betancourt, L., Shera, D. M., Savage, J. H., Giannetta, J. M., Brodsky, N. L.,...Hurt, H. (2008). Environmental stimulation, parental nurturance and cognitive development in humans. *Developmental Science, 11*(5), 793–801.

Farah, M. J., Shera, D. M., Savage, J. H., Betancourt, L., Gianetta, J. M., Brodsky, N. L.,...Hurt, H. (2006). Childhood poverty: Specific associations with neurocognitive development. *Brain Research, 1110*, 166–174.

Felitti, V. J., Anda, R. F., Nordenberg, D., Williamson, D. F., Spitz, A. M., Edwards, V.,...Marks, J. S. (1998). Relationship of childhood abuse and household dysfunction to many of the leading causes of death in adults: The Adverse Childhood Experiences (ACE) study. *American Journal of Preventive Medicine, 14*, 245–258.

Fergusson, D. M., Horwood, L. J., & Lynskey, M. T. (1996). Childhood sexual abuse and psychiatric disorder in young adulthood: II. Psychiatric outcomes of childhood sexual abuse. *Journal of the American Academy of Child & Adolescent Psychiatry, 35*, 1365–1374.

Fergusson, D. M., Horwood, L. J., & Woodward, L. J. (2000). The stability of child abuse reports: A longitudinal study of the reporting behaviour of young adults. *Psychological Medicine, 30*, 529–544.

Fergusson, D. M., & Lynskey, M. T. (1996). Adolescent resiliency to family adversity. *Journal of Child Psychology and Psychiatry, 37*, 281–292.

Fernald, A., Marchman, V. A., & Weisleder, A. (2013). SES differences in language processing skill and vocabulary are evident at 18 months. *Developmental Science*, *16*(2), 234–248. doi:10.1111/desc.12019

Finkelhor, D., Ormrod, R., & Turner, H. (2007). Polyvictimization and trauma in a national longitudinal cohort. *Development and Psychopathology*, *19*, 149–166.

Finlay-Jones, R., Scott, R. A., Duncan-Jones, P., Byrne, D., & Henderson, S. (1981). The reliability of reports of early separations. *Australian and New Zealand Journal of Psychiatry*, *15*, 27–31.

Finn, A. S., Minas, J. E., Leonard, J. A., Mackey, A. P., Salvatore, J., Goetz, C.,…Gabrieli, J. D. (2016). Functional brain organization of working memory in adolescents varies in relation to family income and academic achievement. *Developmental Science*, *20*(5). doi:10.1111/desc.12450

Ford, J. D., Elhai, J. D., Connor, D. F., & Frueh, B. C. (2010). Poly-victimization and risk of posttraumatic, depressive, and substance use disorders and involvement in delinquency in a national sample of adolescents. *Journal of Adolescent Health*, *46*, 545–552.

Fox, S. E., Levitt, P., & Nelson, C. A. (2010). How the timing and quality of early experiences influence the development of brain architecture. *Child Development*, *81*(1), 28–40. doi:10.1111/j.1467–8624.2009.01380.x

Fries, A. B. W., Shirtcliff, E. A., & Pollak, S. D. (2008). Neuroendocrine dysregulation following early social deprivation in children. *Developmental Psychobiology*, *50*, 588–599.

Fristad, M. A., Jedel, R., Weller, R. A., & Weller, E. B. (1993). Psychosocial functioning in children after the death of a parent. *American Journal of Psychiatry*, *150*, 511–513.

Frodl, T., & O'Keane, V. (2013). How does the brain deal with cumulative stress? A review with focus on developmental stress, HPA axis function and hippocampal structure in humans. *Neurobiology of Disease*, *52*, 24–37.

Garrett, P., Ng'andu, N., & Ferron, J. (1994). Poverty experiences of young children and the quality of their home environments. *Child Development*, *65*, 331–345.

Gaudin, J. M., Polansky, N. A., Kilpatrick, A. C., & Shilton, P. (1996). Family functioning in neglectful families. *Child Abuse and Neglect*, *20*, 363–377.

Gibb, B. E., Schofield, C. A., & Coles, M. E. (2008). Reported history of childhood abuse and young adults' information processing biases for facial displays of emotion. *Child Maltreatment*, *14*, 148–156.

Glaser, J. P., van Os, J., Portegijs, P. J., & Myin-Germeys, I. (2006). Childhood trauma and emotional reactivity to daily life stress in adult frequent attenders of general practitioners. *Journal of Psychosomatic Research*, *61*, 229–236.

Goeleven, E., De Raedt, R., Baert, S., & Koster, E. H. W. (2006). Deficient inhibition of emotional information in depression. *Journal of Affective Disorders*, *93*, 149–157.

Gormley, W. T., Gayer, T., Phillips, D., & Dawson, B. (2005). The effects of universal pre-K on cognitive development. *Developmental Psychology*, *41*, 872–884.

Grant, K. E., Compas, B. E., Stuhlmacher, A. F., Thurm, A. E., McMahon, S. D., & Halpert, J. A. (2003). Stressors and child and adolescent psychopathology: Moving from markers to mechanisms of risk. *Psychological Bulletin*, *129*, 447–466.

Grant, K. E., Compas, B. E., Thurm, A. E., & McMahon, S. D. (2004). Stressors and child and adolescent psychopathology:

Measurement issues and prospective effects. *Journal of Clinical Child and Adolescent Psychology*, *33*, 412–425.

Grant, K. E., Compas, B. E., Thurm, A. E., McMahon, S. D., Gipson, P. Y., Campbell, A. J.,…Westerholm, R. I. (2006). Stressors and child and adolescent psychopathology: Evidence of moderating and mediating effects. *Clinical Psychology Review*, *26*, 257–283.

Green, J. G., McLaughlin, K. A., Berglund, P., Gruber, M. J., Sampson, N. A., Zaslavsky, A. M., & Kessler, R. C. (2010). Childhood adversities and adult psychopathology in the National Comorbidity Survey Replication (NCS-R) I: Associations with first onset of DSM-IV disorders. *Archives of General Psychiatry*, *62*, 113–123.

Gunnar, M. R., Frenn, K., Wewerka, S., & Van Ryzin, M. J. (2009). Moderate versus severe early life stress: Associations with stress reactivity and regulation in 10–12 year-old children. *Psychoneuroendocrinology*, *34*, 62–75.

Gunnar, M. R., Morison, S. J., Chisolm, K., & Schuder, M. (2001). Salivary cortisol levels in children adopted from Romanian orphanages. *Development and Psychopathology*, *13*, 611–628.

Gunnar, M. R., & Quevedo, K. (2007). The neurobiology of stress and development. *Annual Review of Psychology*, *58*, 145–173.

Gunnar, M. R., van Dulmen, M. H. M., & The International Adoption Project Team. (2007). Behavior problems in postinstitutionalized internationally adopted children. *Development and Psychopathology*, *19*, 129–148.

Gunnar, M. R., & Vazquez, D. M. (2001). Low cortisol and a flattening of expected daytime rhythm: Potential indices of risk in human development. *Development and Psychopathology*, *13*(3), 515–538.

Hammen, C. (2008). Stress exposure and stress generation in adolescent depression. In S. Nolen-Hoeksema & L. M. Hilt (Eds.), *Handbook of depression in adolescents* (pp. 305–344). New York, NY: Routledge.

Hardt, J., & Rutter, M. (2004). Validity of adult retrospective reports of adverse childhood experiences: review of the evidence. *Journal of Child Psychology and Psychiatry*, *45*, 260–273.

Harkness, K. L., Stewart, J. G., & Wynne-Edwards, K. E. (2011). Cortisol reactivity to social stress in adolescents: Role of depression severity and child maltreatment. *Psychoneuroendocrinology*, *36*, 173–181.

Hart, B., & Risley, T. R. (1995). *Meaningful differences in the everyday experiences of young American children*. Baltimore, MD: Paul H. Brooks.

Heim, C., Ehlert, U., & Helhammer, D. H. (2000). The potential role of hypocortisolism in the pathophysiology of stress-related bodily disorders. *Psychoneuroendocrinology*, *25*, 1–35.

Heleniak, C., Jenness, J., Van der Stoep, A., McCauley, E., & McLaughlin, K. A. (2016). Childhood maltreatment exposure and disruptions in emotion regulation: A transdiagnostic pathway to adolescent internalizing and externalizing psychopathology. *Cognitive Therapy and Research*, *40*, 394–415.

Heleniak, C., King, K. M., Monahan, K. C., & McLaughlin, K. A. (2018). Disruptions in emotion regulation as a mechanism linking community violence exposure to adolescent internalizing problems. *Journal of Research on Adolescence*, *28*(1), 229–244.

Heleniak, C., McLaughlin, K. A., Ormel, J., & Riese, H. (2016). Autonomic nervous system reactivity as a mechanism linking child trauma to adolescent psychopathology. *Biological Psychology*, *120*, 108–119.

Hennessy, K. D., Rabideau, G. J., Cicchetti, D., & Cummings, E. M. (1994). Responses of physically abused and nonabused children to different forms of interadult anger. *Child Development*, 65, 815–828.

Herringa, R. J., Birn, R. M., Ruttle, P. L., Stodola, D. E., Davidson, R. J., & Essex, M. J. (2013). Childhood maltreatment is associated with altered fear circuitry and increased internalizing symptoms by late adolescence *Proceedings of the National Academy of Sciences*, 110, 19119–19124.

Hildyard, K. L., & Wolfe, D. A. (2002). Child neglect: Developmental issues and outcomes. *Child Abuse and Neglect*, 26, 679–695.

Hines, D. A., Kaufman Kantor, G., & Holt, M. K. (2006). Similarities in siblings' experiences of neglectful parenting behaviors. *Child Abuse and Neglect*, 30, 619–637.

Hobson, C. W., Scott, S., & Rubia, K. (2011). Investigation of cool and hot executive function in ODD/CD independently of ADHD. *Journal of Child Psychology and Psychiatry*, 52, 1035–1043.

Hoff, E. (2003). The specificity of environmental influence: Socioeconomic status affects early vocabulary development via maternal speech. *Child Development*, 74(5), 1368–1378.

Hostinar, C. E., Stellern, S. A., Schaefer, C., Carlson, S. M., & Gunnar, M. R. (2012). Associations between early life adversity and executive function in children adopted internationally from orphanages. *Proceedings of the National Academy of Sciences*, 109, 17208–17212.

Humphreys, K. L., & Zeanah, C. H. (2015). Deviations from the expectable environment in early childhood and emerging psychopathology. *Neuropsychopharmacology*, 40, 154–170.

Jaffee, S. R., Caspi, A., Moffit, T. E., Polo-Tomás, M., & Taylor, A. (2007). Individual, family, and neighborhood factors distinguish resilient from non-resilient maltreated children: A cumulative stressors model. *Child Abuse and Neglect*, 31, 231–253.

Janssen, I., Krabbendam, L., Bak, M., Hanssen, M., Vollebergh, W., de Graaf, R. D., & van Os, J. (2004). Childhood abuse as a risk factor for psychotic experiences. *Acta Psychiatrica Scandinavica*, 109, 38–45.

Jenness, J., Jager-Hyman, S., Heleniak, C., Beck, A. T., Sheridan, M. A., & McLaughlin, K. A. (2016). Catastrophizing, rumination, and reappraisal prospectively predict adolescent PTSD symptom onset following a terrorist attack. *Depression and Anxiety, epub ahead of print.* doi:10.1002/da.22548

Johnson, J. G., Cohen, P., Gould, M. S., Kasen, S., Brown, J., & Brook, J. S. (2002). Childhood adversities, interpersonal difficulties, and risk for suicide attempts during late adolescence and early adulthood. *Archives of General Psychiatry*, 59, 741–749.

Joorman, J. (2006). Differential effects of rumination and dysphoria on the inhibition of irrelevant emotional material: Evidence from a negative priming task. *Cognitive Therapy and Research*, 30, 149–160.

Joorman, J., & Gotlib, I. H. (2010). Emotion regulation in depression: Relation to cognitive inhibition. *Cognition and Emotion*, 24, 281–298.

Kaufman Kantor, G., Holt, M. K., Mebert, C. J., Straus, M. A., Drach, K. M., Ricci, L. R.,...Brown, W. (2004). Development and preliminary psychometric properties of the Multidimensional Neglectful Behavior Scale—Child Report. *Child Maltreatment*, 9, 409–428.

Kelleher, I., Keeley, H., Corcoran, P., Ramsay, H., Wasserman, C., Carli, V.,...Cannon, M. (2013). Childhood trauma and psychosis in a prospective cohort study: Cause, effect, and directionality. *American Journal of Psychiatry*, 170, 734–741.

Kessler, R. C., Davis, C. G., & Kendler, K. S. (1997). Childhood adversity and adult psychiatric disorder in the US National Comorbidity Survey. *Psychological Medicine*, 27(5), 1101–1119.

Kessler, R. C., McLaughlin, K. A., Green, J. G., Gruber, M. J., Sampson, N. A., Zaslavsky, A. M.,...Williams, D. R. (2010). Childhood adversities and adult psychopathology in the WHO World Mental Health Surveys. *British Journal of Psychiatry*, 197, 378–385.

Keyes, K. M., Eaton, N. R., Krueger, R. F., McLaughlin, K. A., Wall, M. M., Grant, B. F., & Hasin, D. S. (2012). Childhood maltreatment and the structure of common psychiatric disorders. *British Journal of Psychiatry*, 200, 107–115.

Kim, J., & Cicchetti, D. (2010). Longitudinal pathways linking child maltreatment, emotion regulation, peer relations, and psychopathology. *Journal of Child Psychology and Psychiatry*, 51, 706–716.

Kim-Spoon, J., Cicchetti, D., & Rogosch, F. A. (2013). A longitudinal study of emotion regulation, emotion lability-negativity, and internalizing symptomatology in maltreated and nonmaltreated children. *Child Development*, 84, 512–527.

Kishiyama, M. M., Boyce, W. T., Jimenez, A. M., Perry, L. M., & Knight, R. T. (2009). Socioeconomic disparities affect prefrontal function in children. *Journal of Cognitive Neuroscience*, 21(6), 1106–1115. doi:10.1162/jocn.2009.21101

Klaassens, E. R., Giltay, E. J., Cuijpers, P., van Veen, T., & Zitman, F. G. (2012). Adulthood trauma and HPA-axis functioning in healthy subjects and PTSD patients: A meta-analysis. *Psychoneuroendocrinology*, 37, 317–331.

Knorr, U., Vinberg, M., Kessing, L. V., & Wetterslev, J. (2010). Salivary cortisol in depressed patients versus control persons: A systematic review and meta-analysis. *Psychoneuroendocrinology*, 35, 1275–1286.

Koenen, K. C., Moffit, T. E., Poulin, R., Martin, J., & Caspi, A. (2007). Early childhood factors associated with the development of post-traumatic stress disorder: Results from a longitudinal birth cohort. *Psychological Medicine*, 37, 181–192.

Lambert, H. K., King, K. M., Monahan, K. C., & McLaughlin, K. A. (2017). Differential associations of threat and deprivation with emotion regulation and cognitive control in adolescence. *Development and Psychopathology*, 29, 929–940.

Lawson, G. M., Camins, J. S., Wisse, L., Wu, J., Duda, J. T., Cook, P. A.,...Farah, M. J. (2017). Childhood socioeconomic status and childhood maltreatment: Distinct associations with brain structure. *PLoS One*, 12, e0175690.

Leonard, J. A., Mackey, A. P., Finn, A. S., & Gabrieli, J. D. (2015). Differential effects of socioeconomic status on working and procedural memory systems. *Frontiers in Human Neuroscience*, 9, 554.

Linver, M. R., Brooks-Gunn, J., & Kohen, D. E. (2002). Family processes as pathways from income to young children's development. *Developmental Psychology*, 38(5), 719–734.

Loman, M. M., Johnson, A. E., Westerlund, A., Pollak, S. D., Nelson, C. A., & Gunnar, M. (2013). The effect of early deprivation on executive attention in middle childhood. *Journal of Child Psychology and Psychiatry*, 54, 37–45.

MacMillan, H. L., Fleming, J. E., Streiner, D. L., Lin, E., Boyle, M. H., Jamieson, E.,...Beardslee, W. (2001). Childhood abuse and lifetime psychopathology in a community sample. *American Journal of Psychiatry*, 158, 1878–1883.

MacMillan, H. L., Georgiades, K., Duku, E. K., Shea, A., Steiner, M., Niec, A.,...Schmidt, L. A. (2009). Cortisol response to stress in female youths exposed to childhood maltreatment: Results of the Youth Mood Project. *Biological Psychiatry, 66*, 62–68.

Manly, J. T., Cicchetti, D., & Barnett, D. (1994). The impact of subtype, frequency, chronicity, and severity of child maltreatment on social competence and behavior problems. *Development and Psychopathology, 6*, 121–143.

Manly, J. T., Kim, J. E., Rogosch, F. A., & Cicchetti, D. (2001). Dimensions of child maltreatment and children's adjustment: Contributions of developmental timing and subtype. *Development and Psychopathology, 13*, 759–782.

Martinussen, R., Hayden, J., Hogg-Johnson, S., & Tannock, R. (2005). A meta-analysis of working memory impairments in children with attention-deficit/hyperactivity disorder. *Journal of the American Academy of Child & Adolescent Psychiatry, 44*, 377–384.

Marusak, H. A., Etkin, A., & Thomason, M. E. (2015). Disrupted insula-based neural circuit organization and conflict interference in trauma-exposed youth. *Neuroimage: Clinical, 8*, 516–525.

Marusak, H. A., Martin, K. R., Etkin, A., & Thomason, M. E. (2015). Childhood trauma exposure disrupts the automatic regulation of emotional processing. *Neuropsychopharmacology, 40*, 1250–1258.

McChesney, G. C., Adamson, G., & Shevlin, M. (2015). A latent class analysis of trauma based on a nationally representative sample of US adolescents. *Social Psychiatry and Psychiatric Epidemiology, 50*, 1207–1217.

McCrory, E. J., De Brito, S. A., Kelly, P. A., Bird, G., Sebastian, C. L., Mechelli, A.,...Viding, E. (2013). Amygdala activation in maltreated children during pre-attentive emotional processing. *British Journal of Psychiatry, 202*, 269–276.

McCrory, E. J., De Brito, S. A., Sebastian, C. L., Mechelli, A., Bird, G., Kelly, P. A., & Viding, E. (2011). Heightened neural reactivity to threat in child victims of family violence. *Current Biology, 21*, R947–R948.

McCrory, E., De Brito, S. A., & Viding, E. (2010). Research review: The neurobiology and genetics of maltreatment and adversity. *Journal of Child Psychology and Psychiatry, 51*, 1079–1095.

McDermott, J. M., Troller-Renfree, S., Vanderwert, R., Nelson, C. A., Zeanah, C. H., & Fox, N. A. (2013). Psychosocial deprivation, executive functions and the emergence of socio-emotional behavior problems. *Frontiers in Human Neuroscience, 7*, 167.

McEwen, B. S. (1998). Protective and damaging effects of stress mediators. *New England Journal of Medicine, 338*, 171–179.

McEwen, B. S. (2000). Allostasis and allostatic load: Implications for neuropsychopharmacology. *Neuropsychopharmacology, 22*, 108–124.

McEwen, B. S. (2012). Brain on stress: How the social environment gets under the skin. *Proceedings of the National Academy of Sciences, 109*, 17180–17185.

McEwen, B. S., & Gianaros, P. J. (2010). Central role of the brain in stress and adaptation: links to socioeconomic status, health, and disease. *Annals of the New York Academy of Sciences, 1186*, 190–222. doi:10.1111/j.1749–6632.2009.05331.x

McEwen, B. S., & Seeman, T. E. (1999). Protective and damaging effects of mediators of stress: Elaborating and testing the concepts of allostatsis and allostatic load. *Annals of the New York Academy of Sciences, 896*, 30–47.

McGrath, J. J., McLaughlin, K. A., Saha, S., Aguilar-Gaxiola, S., Al-Hamzawi, A., Alonso, J.,...Kessler, R. C. (2017). The association between childhood adversities and subsequent first onset of psychotic experiences: A cross-national analysis of 23 998 respondents from 17 countries. *Psychological Medicine, 47*, 1230–1245.

McLaughlin, K. A. (2016). Future directions in childhood adversity and youth psychopathology. *Journal of Clinical Child & Adolescent Psychology, 45*, 361–382.

McLaughlin, K. A., Busso, D. S., Duys, A., Green, J. G., Alves, S., Way, M., & Sheridan, M. A. (2014). Amygdala response to negative stimuli predicts PTSD symptom onset following a terrorist attack. *Depression and Anxiety, 10*, 834–842.

McLaughlin, K. A., Conron, K. J., Koenen, K. C., & Gilman, S. E. (2010). Childhood adversity, adult stressful life events, and risk of past-year psychiatric disorder: A test of the stress sensitization hypothesis in a population-based sample of adults. *Psychological Medicine, 40*, 1647–1658.

McLaughlin, K. A., Green, J. G., Gruber, M. J., Sampson, N. A., Zaslavsky, A., & Kessler, R. C. (2012). Childhood adversities and first onset of psychiatric disorders in a national sample of adolescents. *Archives of General Psychiatry, 69*, 1151–1160.

McLaughlin, K. A., Hatzenbuehler, M. L., Mennin, D. S., & Nolen-Hoeksema, S. (2011). Emotion regulation and adolescent psychopathology: A prospective study. *Behaviour Research and Therapy, 49*, 544–554.

McLaughlin, K. A., Kubzansky, L. D., Dunn, E. C., Waldinger, R. J., Vaillant, G. E., & Koenen, K. C. (2010). Childhood social environment, emotional reactivity to stress, and mood and anxiety disorders across the life course. *Depression and Anxiety, 27*, 1087–1094.

McLaughlin, K. A., & Lambert, H. K. (2016). Child trauma exposure and psychopathology: mechanisms of risk and resilience. *Current Opinion in Psychology, 14*, 29–34.

McLaughlin, K. A., Peverill, M., Gold, A. L., Alves, S., & Sheridan, M. A. (2015). Child maltreatment and neural systems underlying emotion regulation. *Journal of the American Academy of Child & Adolescent Psychiatry, 54*, 753–762.

McLaughlin, K. A., & Sheridan, M. A. (2016). Beyond cumulative risk: A dimensional approach to childhood adversity. *Current Directions in Psychological Science, 25*, 239–245.

McLaughlin, K. A., Sheridan, M. A., Alves, S., & Mendes, W. B. (2014). Child maltreatment and autonomic nervous system reactivity: Identifying dysregulated stress reactivity patterns using the biopsychosocial model of challenge and threat. *Psychosomatic Medicine, 76*, 538–546.

McLaughlin, K. A., Sheridan, M. A., Gold, A. L., Lambert, H. K., Heleniak, C., Duys, A.,...Pine, D. S. (2016). Maltreatment exposure, brain structure, and fear conditioning in children. *Neuropsychopharmacology, 41*, 1956–1964.

McLaughlin, K. A., Sheridan, M. A., & Lambert, H. K. (2014). Childhood adversity and neural development: Deprivation and threat as distinct dimensions of early experience. *Neuroscience and Biobehavioral Reviews, 47*, 578–591.

McLaughlin, K. A., Sheridan, M. A., Tibu, F., Fox, N. A., Zeanah, C. H., & Nelson, C. A. (2015). Causal effects of the early caregiving environment on stress response system development in children. *Proceedings of the National Academy of Sciences, 112*, 5637–5642.

McLaughlin, K. A., Sheridan, M. A., Winter, W., Fox, N. A., Zeanah, C. H., & Nelson, C. A. (2014). Widespread reductions in cortical thickness following severe early-life deprivation: A neurodevelopmental pathway to ADHD. *Biological Psychiatry, 76*, 629–638.

McLeod, J. D., & Shanahan, M. J. (1993). Poverty, parenting, and children's mental health. *American Sociological Review, 58*, 351–366.

McLoyd, V. C. (1998). Socioeconomic disadvantage and child development. *American Psychologist, 53*, 185–204.

McNally, R. J. (2016). Can network analysis transform psychopathology? *Behaviour Research and Therapy, 86*, 95–104.

Michl, L. C., McLaughlin, K. A., Shepherd, K., & Nolen-Hoeksema, S. (2013). Rumination as a mechanism linking stressful life events to symptoms of depression and anxiety: Longitudinal evidence in early adolescents and adults. *Journal of Abnormal Psychology, 122*, 339–352.

Miller, G. E., Chen, E., & Zhou, E. S. (2007). If it goes up, must it come down? Chronic stress and the hypothalamic-pituitary-adrenocortical axis in humans. *Psychological Bulletin, 133*, 25–45.

Moffitt, T. E., Arseneault, L., Belsky, J., Dickson, N., Hancox, R. J., Harrington, H.,...Caspi, A. (2011). A gradient of childhood self-control predicts health, wealth, and public safety. *Proceedings of the National Academy of Sciences, 108*, 2693–2698.

Molnar, B. E., Berkman, L. F., & Buka, S. L. (2001). Psychopathology, childhood sexual abuse and other childhood adversities: relative links to subsequent suicidal behaviour in the US. *Psychological Medicine, 31*, 965–977.

Molnar, B. E., Buka, L., & Kessler, R. C. (2001). Child sexual abuse and subsequent psychopathology: Results from the National Comorbidity Survey. *American Journal of Public Health, 91*, 753–760.

Monroe, S. M. (2008). Modern approaches to conceptualizing and measuring human life stress. *Annual Review of Clinical Psychology, 4*, 33–52.

Morris, M. C., Compas, B. E., & Garber, J. (2012). Relations among posttraumatic stress disorder, comorbid major depression, and HPA function: A systematic review and meta-analysis. *Clinical Psychology Review, 322*, 301–315.

Mueller, S. C., Maheu, F. S., Dozier, M., Peloso, E., Mandell, D., Leibenluft, E.,...Ernst, M. (2010). Early-life stress is associated with impairment in cognitive control in adolescence: an fMRI study. *Neuropsychologia, 48*, 3037–3044.

Mullen, P. E., Martin, J. M., Anderson, J., Romans, S. E., & Herbison, G. P. (1993). Childhood sexual abuse and mental health in adult life. *British Journal of Psychiatry, 163*, 721–732.

Nederhof, E., van Oort, F. V. A., Bouma, E. M. C., Laceulle, O. M., Oldehinkel, A. J., & Ormel, J. (2015). Predicting mental disorders from hypothalamic-pituitary-adrenal axis functioning: A 3-year follow-up in the TRAILS study. *Psychological Medicine, 45*, 2403–2412.

Nelson, C. A., Furtado, E. A., Fox, N. A., & Zeanah, C. H. (2009). The deprived human brain. *American Scientist, 97*, 222.

Noble, K. G., McCandliss, B. D., & Farah, M. J. (2007). Socioeconomic gradients predict individual differences in neurocognitive abilities. *Developmental Science, 10*, 464–480.

Noble, K. G., Norman, M. F., & Farah, M. J. (2005). Neurocognitive correlates of socioeconomic status in kindergarten children. *Developmental Science, 8*, 74–87.

Nolen-Hoeksema, S., Stice, E., Wade, E., & Bohon, C. (2007). Reciprocal relations between rumination and bulimic, substance abuse, and depressive symptoms in female adolescents. *Journal of Abnormal Psychology, 116*(1), 198–207.

Oosterlaan, J., Scheres, A., & Sergeant, J. A. (2005). Which executive functioning deficits are associated with AD/HD, ODD/CD and comorbid AD/HD+ ODD/CD? *Journal of Abnormal Child Psychology, 33*, 69–85.

Patrick, M. E., Blair, C., & Maggs, J. L. (2008). Executive function, approach sensitivity, and emotional decision making as influences on risk behaviors in young adults. *Journal of Clinical and Experimental Neuropsychology, 30*(4), 449–462.

Phillips, N. K., Hammen, C., Brennan, P. A., Najman, J. M., & Bor, W. (2005). Early adversity and the prospective prediction of depressive and anxiety disorders in adolescents. *Journal of Abnormal Child Psychology, 33*, 13–24.

Pollak, S. D., Cicchetti, D., Hornung, K., & Reed, A. (2000). Recognizing emotion in faces: Developmental effects of child abuse and neglect. *Developmental Psychology, 36*, 679–688.

Pollak, S. D., Nelson, C. A., Schlaak, M. F., Roeber, B. J., Wewerka, S., Wiik, K. L.,...Gunnar, M. R. (2010). Neurodevelopmental effects of early deprivation in postinstitutionalized children. *Child Development, 81*, 224–236.

Pollak, S. D., & Sinha, P. (2002). Effects of early experience on children's recognition of facial displays of emotion. *Development and Psychopathology, 38*, 784–791.

Pollak, S. D., & Tolley-Schell, S. A. (2003). Selective attention to facial emotion in physically abused children. *Journal of Abnormal Psychology, 112*(3), 323–338.

Powers, A., Etkin, A., Gyurak, A., Bradley, B., & Jovanovic, T. (2015). Associations between childhood abuse, posttraumatic stress disorder, and implicit emotion regulation deficits: Evidence from a low-income, inner-city population. *Psychiatry, 78*, 251–264.

Raizada, R. D. S., Richards, T. L., Meltzoff, A., & Kuhl, P. K. (2008). Socioeconomic status predicts hemispheric specialisation of the left inferior frontal gyrus in young children. *NeuroImage, 40*(3), 1392–1401. doi:10.1016/j.neuroimage.2008.01.021

Rakhlin, N., Hein, S., Doyle, N., Hart, L., Macomber, D., Ruchkin, V.,...Grigorenko, E. L. (2015). Language development of internationally adopted children: Adverse early experiences outweigh the age of acquisition effect. *Journal of Communication Disorders, 57*, 66–80.

Raver, C. C., Blair, C., Willoughby, M., & The Family life Project Key Investigators. (2013). Poverty as a predictor of 4-year-olds' executive function: New perspectives on models of differential susceptibility. *Developmental Psychology, 49*, 292–304.

Rosenman, S., & Rodgers, B. (2004). Childhood adversity in an Australian population. *Social Psychiatry and Psychiatric Epidemiology, 39*, 695–702.

Rudolph, K. D., & Hammen, C. (1999). Age and gender as determinants of stress exposure, generation, and reactions in youngsters: A transactional perspective. *Child Development, 70*, 660–677.

Rudolph, K. D., Hammen, C., Burge, D., Lindberg, N., Herzberg, D. S., & Daley, S. E. (2000). Toward an interpersonal life-stress model of depression: The developmental context of stress generation. *Development and Psychopathology, 12*, 215–234.

Rutter, M., Sonuga-Barke, E. J. S., Beckett, C., Bell, C. A., Castle, J., Kreppner, J. M.,...Stevens, S. E. (2010). Deprivation-specific psychological patterns: Effects of institutional deprivation by the English and Romanian Adoptee Study Team. *Monographs of the Society for Research in Child Development, 75*(1), Article 295.

Salmon, K., O'Kearney, R., Reese, E., & Fortune, C. A. (2016). The role of language skill in child psychopathology: Implications for intervention in the early years. *Clinical Child and Family Psychology Review*, 19, 352–367.

Sarsour, K., Sheridan, M. A., Jutte, D., Nuru-Jeter, A., Hinshaw, S. P., & Boyce, W. T. (2011). Family socioeconomic status and child executive functions: The roles of language, home environment, and single parenthood. *Journal of the International Neuropsychological Society*, 17(1), 120–132. doi:10.1017/S1355617710001335

Schweinhart, L. J., Berrueta-Clement, J. R., Barnett, W. S., Epstein, A. S., & Weikart, D. P. (1985). Effects of the Perry Preschool program on youths through age 19: A summary. *Topics in Early Childhood Special Education*, 5, 26–35.

Seeman, T. E., Singer, B. H., Rowe, J. W., Horwitz, R. I., & McEwen, B. S. (1997). Price of adaptation: allostatic load and its health consequences. MacArthur studies of successful aging. *Archives of Internal Medicine*, 157, 2259–2268.

Sergeant, J. A., Geurts, H., & Oosterlaan, J. (2002). How specific is a deficit of executive functioning for attention-deficit/hyperactivity disorder? *Behavioural Brain Research*, 130, 3–28.

Shackman, J. E., & Pollak, S. D. (2014). Impact of physical maltreatment on the regulation of negative affect and aggression. *Development and Psychopathology*, 26, 1021–1033.

Shackman, J. E., Shackman, A. J., & Pollak, S. D. (2007). Physical abuse amplifies attention to threat and increases anxiety in children. *Emotion*, 7, 838–842.

Sheridan, M. A., & McLaughlin, K. A. (2014). Dimensions of early experience and neural development: Deprivation and threat. *Trends in Cognitive Sciences*, 18, 580–585.

Sheridan, M. A., & McLaughlin, K. A. (2016). Neurobiological models of the impact of adversity on education. *Current Opinion in Behavioral Sciences*, 10, 108–113.

Sheridan, M. A., Peverill, M., & McLaughlin, K. A. (2017). Deprivation, but not trauma, influences prefrontal recruitment during a working memory filtering task. *Development and Psychopathology*, 29, 1777–1794.

Sheridan, M. A., Sarsour, K., Jutte, D., D'Esposito, M., & Boyce, W. T. (2012). The impact of social disparity on prefrontal function in childhood. *PloS One*, 7(4), e35744.

Slopen, N., McLaughlin, K. A., & Shonkoff, J. P. (2014). Interventions to improve cortisol regulation in children: A systematic review. *Pediatrics*, 133, 312–326.

Smyke, A. T., Koga, S., Johnson, D. E., Fox, N. A., Marshall, P. J., Nelson, C. A.,...the BEIP Core Group. (2007). The caregiving context in institution-reared and family-reared infants and toddlers in Romania. *Journal of Child Psychology and Psychiatry*, 48, 210–218.

Spratt, E. G., Friedenberg, S. L., Swenson, C. C., Larosa, A., De Bellis, M. D., Macias, M. M.,...Brady, K. T. (2012). The effects of early neglect on cognitive, language, and behavioral functioning in childhood. *Psychology*, 3(2), 175–182. doi:10.4236/psych.2012.32026

Springer, K. W., Sheridan, J., Kuo, D., & Carnes, M. (2007). Long-term physical and mental health consequences of childhood physical abuse: Results from a population-based sample of men and women. *Child Abuse and Neglect*, 31, 517–530.

Sugaya, L., Hasin, D. S., Olfson, M., Lin, K. H., Grant, B. F., & Blanco, C. (2012). Child physical abuse and adult mental health: A national study. *Journal of Traumatic Stress*, 25, 384–392.

Swartz, J. R., Knodt, A. R., Radtke, S. R., & Hariri, A. R. (2015). A neural biomarker of psychological vulnerability to future life stress. *Neuron*, 85, 505–511.

Tibu, F., Sheridan, M. A., McLaughlin, K. A., Fox, N. A., Zeanah, C. H., & Nelson, C. A. (2016). Disruptions of working memory and inhibition mediate the association between exposure to institutionalization and symptoms of attention-deficit/hyperactivity disorder. *Psychological Medicine*, 46, 529–541.

Tottenham, N., Hare, T., Millner, A., Gilhooly, T., Zevin, J. D., & Casey, B. J. (2011). Elevated amygdala response to faces following early deprivation. *Developmental Science*, 14, 190–204.

Trickett, P. K., Noll, J. G., & Putnam, F. W. (2011). The impact of sexual abuse on female development: Lessons from a multigenerational, longitudinal research study. *Development and Psychopathology*, 23, 453–476.

van der Vegt, E. J. M., van der Ende, J., Kirschbaum, C., Verhulst, F. C., & Tiemeier, H. (2009). Early neglect and abuse predict diurnal cortisol patterns in adults: A study of international adoptees. *Psychoneuroendocrinology*, 34, 660–669.

Varese, F., Smeets, F., Drukker, M., Lieverse, R., Lataster, T., Viechtbauer, W.,...Bentall, R. P. (2012). Childhood adversities increase the risk of psychosis: A meta-analysis of patient-control, prospective-and cross-sectional cohort studies. *Schizophrenia Bulletin*, 38, 661–671.

Weich, S., Patterson, J., Shaw, R., & Stewart-Brown, S. (2009). Family relationships in childhood and common psychiatric disorders in later life: Systematic review of prospective studies. *British Journal of Psychiatry*, 194, 392–398.

Weisleder, A., & Fernald, A. (2013). Talking to children matters: early language experience strengthens processing and builds vocabulary. *Psychological Science*, 24(11), 2143–2152. doi:10.1177/0956797613488145

Wichers, M., Schrijvers, D., Geschwind, N., Jacobs, N., Myin-Germeys, I., Thiery, E.,...van Os, J. (2009). Mechanisms of gene-environment interactions in depression: Evidence that genes potentiate multiple sources of adversity. *Psychological Medicine*, 39, 1077–1086.

Widom, C. S., DuMont, K., & Czaja, S. J. (2007). A prospective investigation of major depressive disorder and comorbidity in abused and neglected children grown up. *Archives of General Psychiatry*, 64, 49–56.

Widom, C. S., & Morris, S. (1997). Accuracy of adult recollections of childhood victimization: Part 2. Childhood sexual abuse. *Psychological Assessment*, 9, 34–46.

Widom, C. S., Raphael, B., & DuMont, K. (2004). The case for prospective longitudinal studies in child maltreatment research: Commentary on Dube, Williamson, Thompson, Felitti and Anda 2004. *Child Abuse and Neglect*, 28, 715–722.

Widom, C. S., & Shepard, R. L. (1996). Accuracy of adult recollections of childhood victimization: Part 1. Childhood physical abuse. *Psychological Assessment*, 8, 412–421.

Widom, C. S., Weiler, B. L., & Cottler, L. B. (1999). Childhood victimization and drug abuse: A comparison of prospective and retrospective findings. *Journal of Consulting and Clinical Psychology*, 67, 867–880.

Wilkinson, P. O., & Goodyer, I. M. (2011). Childhood adversity and allostatic overload of the hypothalamic–pituitary–adrenal axis: A vulnerability model for depressive disorders. *Development and Psychopathology*, 23, 1017–1037.

Willcutt, E. G., Doyle, A. E., Nigg, J. T., Faraone, S. V., & Pennington, B. F. (2005). Validity of the executive function theory of attention-deficit/hyperactivity disorder: A meta-analytic review. *Biological Psychiatry, 57*, 1336–1346.

Windsor, J., Benigno, J. P., Wing, C. A., Carroll, P. J., Koga, S. F., Nelson, C. A.,...Zeanah, C. H. (2011). Effect of foster care on young children's language learning. *Child Development, 82*(4), 1040–1046. doi:10.1111/j.1467–8624.2011.01604.x

Yechiam, E., Kanz, J. E., Bechara, A., Stout, J. C., Busemeyer, J. R., Altmaier, E. M., & Paulsen, J. S. (2008). Neurocognitive deficits related to poor decision making in people behind bars. *Psychonomic Bulletin & Review, 15*(1), 44–51.

Zalewski, M., Lengua, L. J., Thompson, S. F., & Kiff, C. J. (2016). Income, cumulative risk, and longitudinal profiles of hypothalamic–pituitary–adrenal axis activity in preschool-age children. *Development and Psychopathology, 28*, 341–353.

Zeanah, C. H., Nelson, C. B., Fox, N. A., Smyke, A. T., Marshall, P. J., Parker, S. W., & Koga, S. (2003). Designing research to study the effects of institutionalization on brain and behavioral development: The Bucharest Early Intervention Project. *Development and Psychopathology, 15*, 885–907.

Quantitative Modeling of Stress and Coping

Richard W. J. Neufeld *and* Bryan Grant

Abstract

Forms of modeling in the field are described in nontechnical terms. Included are analytical (mathematical), computational (computer simulation, mainly of connectionist networks), and statistical (generic, transcontent data theory, and methods) modeling. Distinctions among modeling forms are stipulated, and each is exposited through the method of illustration, with exemplary prototypes. Potential avenues of integration among complementing types of analytical modeling are identified. Emphasized throughout is the demonstrable need to invoke formal modeling to rigorously address the long-held dynamical nature of the topic domain. It is noted that analytical modeling can disclose otherwise intractable information, including that with implications for stress-related intervention; it can also prescribe its own empirical tests and measures, resembling theory-assessment technology found in longer established scientific disciplines.

Keywords: stress and coping, formal modeling, nonlinear system dynamics, stress and affect, mixture models, dynamical systems, clinical stress, coping, stress measurement

Everything should be made as simple as possible, but no simpler.
—*Albert Einstein*, quoted by *Roger Sessions*, New York Times, January 8, 1950

This chapter is devoted to the exposition of quantitative modeling in stress and coping. Attention is given to models of normal, healthy functioning that arguably are poised to lend insight into deviations associated with psychopathology (e.g., Maher, 1966). Of late, the discipline of psychology has seen an accelerated pace of activity in quantitative theory and testing, including that incorporating clinical disorders. Clinical-science developments, however, have focused largely on cognitive abnormalities and deficits. Despite the importance of the topic, much less by way of decidedly quantitative theory and testing is available on relations between stress and psychopathology. It is hoped that the present exposition will contribute to redressing this gap. We begin with some general considerations, followed by a categorization of available quantitative modeling.

Earlier writers on the topic called for a transactional, interactive approach to stress, coping, and related variables (Lazarus & Folkman, 1984; Lazarus & Launier, 1978; cf. Lazarus, 1999). Responding to such a challenge mandated a level of theoretical rigor equipped for the complexity of the phenomena being addressed (Staddon, 1984). Investigators have risen to the challenge with quantitative developments and applications, including modeling involving linear and nonlinear dynamical system, stochastic analytical modeling, and statistical data modeling. Such developments arguably provide stress-coping information that has significant implications for stress-related psychopathology, uniquely conveyed by formal modeling applications. They also speak directly to methodological impasses in research design and measurement. We begin with some essential considerations and distinctions, including the description of an epistemic strategy in clinical psychological modeling, followed by relevant categories of stress and categories of modeling.

Epistemic Strategy in Clinical Psychological Modeling

The currently adopted epistemic strategy of formal modeling in clinical psychological science has been applied mainly in the domain of cognitive psychopathology (Neufeld, 2015). Its basic tenets, however, are general; quantitative models of normal functioning are adjusted to accommodate deviations associated with clinical disturbance (see Figure 4.1). Those parts of the model that do not require adjustment to capture maladaptation are thought to capture functioning spared by the disorder, whereas others reflect system functioning that has been affected by the disorder.

Note, in turn, that accommodation of clinical deviations by the appropriated model structure speaks to the validity of the structure itself. Successful accommodation of psychopathology-related variations of empirical data becomes a source of construct validity of any model. This aspect of formal model evaluation, an instance of "model-generalization testing" (Busemeyer & Wang, 2000), is one in which clinical science arguably plays an important, broader role.

Types of Stressors Addressed by Quantitative Modeling

Two main categories of stressors, traumatic life events (e.g., death of a spouse, divorce, residential or occupational relocation) and daily hassles (Holmes & Rahe, 1967; Lazarus & Folkman, 1984), have been examined in research on stress and psychopathology. The distinction between these two event types continues to permeate empirical research and integrative reviews on relations between stress and psychopathology (e.g., Monroe & Harkness, 2005). The concept of allostasis, referring to the daily negotiation of environmental demands, self-maintenance activities, and other essentially routine occurrences involved in sustaining a state of equilibrium, captures efforts aimed at managing daily-hassle stressors.

Certain modeling developments from the field of affect science, for example, have been brought to bear on the attainment and maintenance of equilibrium, with respect to affect valence and intensity. Implicated has been stress specifically in terms negative affect (Lazarus, 1999; Lazarus & Launier, 1978). Also addressed has been the repositioning of affect, following daily drift or other dislodgement away from an average or baseline location. Examples of clinical disorders addressed with model developments from affect science have included borderline personality disorder (Ebner-Priemer, Houben, Santangelo, et al., 2015) and depression (Lodewyckx, Turelinckx, Kuppens, et al., 2011).

Types of Modeling
Normative and Descriptive Modeling

A normative model of stress and coping transactions depicts the objectively optimal operation of the system involved (analogous to models of rational preference and choice in economics; see Table 4.1 for a summary of types of modeling). Such operation most often is expressed mathematically, as in

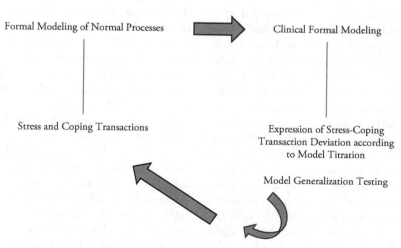

Formal Modeling of Normal Processes

Clinical Formal Modeling

Stress and Coping Transactions

Expression of Stress-Coping Transaction Deviation according to Model Titration

Model Generalization Testing

Figure 4.1 Relations between clinical and formal modeling.

Table 4.1. Types of Modeling Available to Psychological Clinical Scientists

Analytical, Mathematical Modeling		Computational	Statistical
		High-dimensional network models, leaning mainly on computer simulation	Modelling of data covariance structures, including those incorporating observational time trajectories
Stochastic		Deterministic Mainly low-dimensional nonlinear dynamial systems	
Classical Frequentist Including maximum-likelihood parameter estimation	Bayesian Prior (probability-mixing) distribution(s) of model properties (e.g., parameters)		

statistical maximization of performance speed and/or accuracy, given a presenting task and system resources. To take an example from the highly modeled domain of cognitive performance, the task may comprise the intake of a stimulus array, such as a visual scene, in order to detect a key piece of information, like a face, or object (target). Appearance of the target may occur in various segments of the display, but with differing probabilities (as with a computer screen containing certain program-relevant information). Given a fixed amount of attentional resources (processing capacity), it can be shown that visual attention can be apportioned to the respective segments so as to maximize the likelihood of target detection within the display's time duration (e.g., Neufeld, Townsend, & Jette, 2007). This mathematically computed optimal allocation is a normative model of attention deployment, showing what an organism ideally ought to do. The normative model, however, may not represent typical human activity, such as that occurring among stress-susceptible individuals in stressful contexts (Neufeld, Townsend, & Jette, 2007). Portraying what individuals actually do, in this case by way of (suboptimal) processing-resource allocation, comprises a descriptive model of performance (see, e.g., Edwards, 1998). Similar observations apply to idealized and actual stress-coping transactions.

A normative model may be constructed, along with a descriptive model for healthy controls. A comparison of the two would indicate where the descriptive model departs from the normative ideal. A descriptive model associated with clinical disorder would comprise a variation on the healthy-control descriptive model and potentially reveal points of further departure from the normative-model ideal. Both normative and descriptive models have been implemented in studying stress, coping, and clinical disturbance. The distinction is instantiated in the case of decisional control, a form of coping implementing predictive judgments concerning coping options, described in detail later in this chapter.

Analytical Modeling, High-Dimensional Network Computational Modeling, Low-Dimensional Nonlinear Dynamical System Modeling, and Statistical Modeling

There are different categories of quantitative modeling. It is important to distinguish them from each other, because they differ in purpose, their main quantitative tools, and also in elegance of their formal developments. These distinctions extend to modeling of stress and coping with respect to psychopathology. Here we review the main divisions of modeling, earmarking uses in the current substantive domain.

Analytical Modeling

Note that to a large degree, analytic modeling in clinical and other psychological science is dynamic, as follows: the independent variable is time; the observed dependent or output variable is a response of interest, as in a stimulus detection, a choice or decision, or an episode of negative affect; and production of the output is modeled as a function of time. Analytic modeling of stress and coping includes both normative and descriptive varieties, and it requires that progression of theoretical statements be governed by precise rules of successive statement transitions. The language of analytic modeling can take the form of computer syntax, symbolic logic, and mathematics. Most prominent, and dominating the historical landscape of science, is the language of mathematics.

Stochastic and Deterministic Analytical Modeling

In most clinical science applications, analytical modeling is stochastic, which means it provides for an intrinsic indeterminacy of a modeled phenomenon. Doob (1953) has described a stochastic model as a "mathematical abstraction of an empirical process whose development is governed by probabilistic laws" (p. v). Essentially, a quantitative summary of nature's perturbation of the output of some process from one observation to the next (e.g., experimental trials, or epochs of stressor encounters) is built into the structure of stochastic models. Predictions concern features of *distributions*, or the relative frequencies of observations, across values of an independent variable (e.g., frequency of responses to an experimental task across time). Targets of model predictions thus become empirical-distribution properties, ranging from summary statistics (e.g., means and variances) to fine-tuned distribution features, such as proportions of responses falling into demarcated segments of the independent variable (e.g., time intervals), or even the continuous contour of relative frequencies (probability-density function) over the range of independent-variable values (e.g., Evans, Hastings, & Peacock, 2000; Townsend & Ashby, 1983; Van Zandt, 2000).[1] Variability of output values is woven into model predictions; for example, variance across the independent variable, computed on empirical observations, is at least partly stipulated in terms of model structure and parameters, rather than being categorized in toto as model-extraneous noise (e.g., Neufeld, 1998).

Analytic modeling also can be deterministic. Unlike stochastic analytical modeling, randomness now is not an intrinsic feature of the output-generating system, but rather is tagged as model-exogenous noise. Like psychometric measurement error, any empirical departure from deterministic model predictions is designated as random noise. With respect to stress, coping, and psychopathology, deterministic analytical models are used mainly in theoretical low-dimensional nonlinear dynamical systems (NDS), a form of modeling expanded upon later.

An important feature of analytical modeling is that it extends analytical developments from the data analysis enterprise to that of theoretical reasoning.

Verbally articulated theories combined with data analysis (e.g., analysis of variance and its multivariate extensions) represents a "mixed deductive system" (Braithwaite, 1968). In such a system, the research question of interest may be constructed according to conjectural reasoning, possibly aided, for example, by flow diagrams. In contrast, the extension of mathematical formulations to theory and hypothesis generation, through "theorem-proof continuity" and "closed-form derivations," makes for a pure deductive scientific system. This kind of scientific system, comprising "strong theory," is characteristic of more established scientific disciplines such as physics. The distinguishing feature of a pure deductive scientific system is that its specification, testing, measurement, and vindication or falsification are conducted in a uniform language with unambiguous terms and clearly defined operations (cf. Meehl, 1978). These assets are proprietary to formal (usually mathematical) specification (contemporarily writ large, for example, in detection of the Higgs Boson, through the Large Hadron Collider at CERN, Switzerland). It should not go unnoticed that in the history of science, laws of nature (e.g., Newton's universal law of gravitation) are stated mathematically.

INDIVIDUAL-DIFFERENCE EXTENSIONS OF STOCHASTIC ANALYTICAL MODELING

Analytical modeling extensions, with potentially important measurement implications, include provision for individual differences in properties of the operative process model (base model) of observed output, through the introduction of hierarchical model structures (e.g., Oravecz, Turelinckx, & Vandekerchkhove, 2011; Lodewyckx et al., 2011, see later). Hierarchical structures allow for base model properties (typically base model parameters) to be considered as randomly distributed across individuals (statistical random effects). The distributions of model parameters are random mixing distributions, or Bayesian priors. The parameters governing such mixing distributions, or "hyperparameters," can themselves be randomly distributed via additional mixing distributions, which in turn are governed by "meta parameters," and so on. Visualization of such hierarchical stacking of stochastic distributions is facilitated through the use of "directed acyclic graphs" (see, e.g., Busemeyer & Diederich, 2010).

Individualization of the operative base model, anchored in the more comprehensive hierarchical framework, is availed through Bayesian methodology. By exploiting the status of mixing distributions as "Bayesian priors," Bayes's theorem can be applied.

Recall that Bayes's theorem is $Pr(A|B) = Pr(A)$ $Pr(B|A)/Pr(B)$ in which A currently is a candidate parameter value (or some other model property, such as model architecture), and B is a data specimen from an individual. The individualized parameter estimate can be extracted as the mean of the personalized posterior distribution, which visually comprises $Pr(A|B)$ on the Y axis, as set against A on the X axis (a statistical property of this form of estimation being known as "Bayes"). Note that iterative updating of the prior also is available by letting the current posterior distribution stand as the new prior (mixing distribution) upon a subsequent cycle of data input, and so on ("Bayesian updating").

An important asset of Bayesian applications in clinical science is the stabilization of individual parameter estimates though the anchoring influence of the Bayesian prior. The resulting diminished variation in parameter estimates across data sets is known as "Bayesian shrinkage." This asset seems especially valuable in the context of clinical science. Here, practical constraints on the size of individual data acquisition may seriously compromise the stability of parameter estimation, as obtained through classical frequentist, non-Bayesian procedures (e.g., maximum likelihood estimation), that rest exclusively on the immediate data set. Bayesian stabilizing influences on parameter estimation has been illustrated in the exposition of mathematical tools for the clinical study of memory and other processes (Batchelder, 1998) and in the study of schizophrenia cognitive abnormality (Neufeld, Vollick, Carter, et al., 2007). Altogether, Bayesian methodology simultaneously facilitates both nomothetic (group-level) and idiographic (person-specific) inferences about the modeled subject matter.

Examples of mixture models in clinical research, and their merits over and against classical, frequentist (Fisherian) approaches are becoming increasingly available in the clinical science literature (e.g., Batchelder, 1998; Carter, Neufeld, & Benn, 1998; Matzke, Hughes, Badcock, et al., 2017; Neufeld, Carter, Boksman, et al., 2002; Neufeld, 2007a, 2007b, 2015; Neufeld et al., 2010; Neufeld & Williamson, 1996; Riefer, Knapp, Batchelder, et al., 2002; see also contributions in Neufeld, 2007b and Neufeld & Townsend, 2010).

LOW-DIMENSIONAL NONLINEAR DYNAMICAL SYSTEM MODELING

Although less prominent than stochastic modeling in the formal modeling literature, low-dimensional NDS modeling presents itself as the form of modeling in some ways most relevant to stress-coping phenomena. It uniquely implements continuous interaction among theoretically prescribed variables, such as environmental stressors, coping activity, experienced stress activation, and cognitive coping resources (including psychopathology-related deficits). It can be said that NDS modeling presents itself as equal to the task of methodologically coming to grips with long-standing conjectures about the dynamical nature of psychological stress (reviewed in Neufeld, 1999).

Model structure entails interconnected variables ("coupled system dimensions"), but in clinical science the variables are drastically fewer in number (and more macroscopic) than usually is the case with computational network modeling (see later). These differences make for the common distinction between "high-dimensional networks" and "low-dimensional NDS networks." Continuous interactions of the system variables over time are expressed specifically as differential equations. The differential equations stipulate the momentary change of each dimension at immediate time t, as determined by the extant values of other system dimensions, potentially including that of the dimension whose momentary change is being specified (e.g., Fukano & Gunji, 2012). The nonlinear status of the system can arise from the differential equations' cross-product terms, conveying continuous system-dimension interactions, or nonlinear functions of individual system dimensions, such as raising the terms expressing extant momentary status to a power other than 1.0. The status of system variables at time t is available via solution to the defining set of differential equations. Because of the complexity endowed by nonlinearity, solutions virtually always are computed through numerical simulation, rather than being solved analytically.

System dimensions are endowed with their substantive meaning according to the theoretical content being modeled (e.g., dimensions of subjective fear, and physical symptoms, in dynamical modeling of panic disorder; Fukano & Gunji, 2012). That is, analogous to electrons, the nature of the system dimensions is inferred according to the dimensions' operation in the formal deductive system in which they operate (see, e.g., Flanagan, 1991).

Note that a variation on the aforementioned description comprises the progression of changes in system dimensions over discrete trials (e.g., successive husband–wife interchanges; Gottman, Murray, Swanson, et al., 2002). Such sequential transitions are implemented through discrete trial difference-equations, which now take the place of continuous-time differential equations.

Model-predicted trajectories can be tested against trajectories of empirical observations, as obtained, for example, through experience-sampling methodology (e.g., Qualtrics; Bolger, Davis, & Rafaeli, 2008). In addition, empirical data can be evaluated for the presence of dynamical signatures (distinctive time-series patterns, or "numerical diagnostics") generated by computer simulation of system functioning. It is possible, moreover, to search empirical data for time-series numerical diagnostics that characterize complex dynamical interactions in general. This latter endeavor, however, has been criticized when undertaken more or less as a blind search, rather than one guided by a proposed differential-equation NDS model—such a more informed, productive undertaking being historically exemplified in physics (Wagenmakers, van der Maas, & Farrell, 2012). Extended exposition of NDS model development, from a clinical science perspective, has been presented in Gottman et al. (2002), Levy, Yao, McGuire, et al. (2012), and Neufeld (1999) (elaborated upon later).

High-Dimensional Network Computational Modeling

High-dimensional computational modeling expresses recurrent adjustments typically among a relatively large number of activated and activating units (sometimes called "neurodes," meaning neurons, or assemblies of neurons in the case of neuro-connectionist modeling) that have been organized into a network architecture. The interplay of the units is implemented through computer syntax (see, e.g., Farrell & Lewandowsky, 2010). Some of its proponents have advanced this form of modeling as a method uniquely equipped to address the computational capacity of the brain and, as such, have viewed the workings of a connectionist network as a brain metaphor (addressing so-called deep-structure cognitive architecture). Strengths of connections among the network units vary iteratively over the course of the network's generation of target output values. Variation in network architecture (essentially paths and densities of interunit connections), and/or connection activation, present themselves as potential expressions of cognitive abnormalities. High-dimensional computational modeling may be quite close to the procedures in analytical modeling but tend to emphasize incorporation of major assumptions into computer algorithms, rather than through the construction of explicit equations for use in theorem and prediction development.

Moreover, mathematical and computational models may be mutually informative as to the mechanisms at play in a particular clinical process or set of processes (Marr, 1982). The construction of the unit network, the strength of unit connections, and the unit-activation algorithm are nevertheless not by and large themselves specifically of mathematical derivation or theorem-proof construction. It might be said that though many such models can be crafted to generate predictive efficacy, they are not explicitly mathematical in that they are typically constructed with "black box," algorithm-based techniques rather than being designed with interpretable components by a human mind.

High-dimensional computational modeling may hold some promise as a platform for further development of clinical stressology. For example, laboratory stress induction has led to reduced functional magnetic resonance imaging (fMRI)-assessed activation of the dorsolateral prefrontal cortex, with an associated impairment of its functions (Qin, Hermans, van Marle, et al., 2009). At the cognitive-behavioral level, stochastic analytical modeling has shown psychological stress to impinge on several aspects of cognition (Neufeld, 2016; Neufeld & McCarty, 1994; Neufeld, Townsend, & Jette, 2007), in turn with implications for clinical symptomatology (e.g., schizophrenia thought-content disorder; Neufeld, Boksman, Vollick, et al., 2010), and notably when coping with stress is cognition contingent. High-dimensional computational modeling thus may represent a currently underused investigative platform of stress–psychopathology relations.

Statistical Modeling

Statistical modeling addresses data organization, transcending content domains. It involves generic data theory, such as the modeling of observed-variable covariance structures. This is in contrast to analytical modeling, which is inspired by the content domain of focal interest and is unique thereto. To illustrate content specificity in the case of stress and coping, a goal may be to develop a normative model of stress negotiation addressing environmental contingencies for reducing the probability of an adverse event. The modeler may do so by expressing quantitatively the identified main variables, such as amount of situational coping optionality; requisite predictions and decision making, and their cognitive-energy demands; and consequent reduction in threat (likelihood) of adverse-event occurrence. Quantification may involve translating key variables into parameters of mathematical combinatorics, allowing computation of threat-reducing contingencies; or differential equations representing continuously interacting variables of an NDS (illustrated with reference to decisional control and specific NDS models later). Construction of the model is content specific, with analytical developments driven by the substantive issue of principal interest. Moreover, measurement and model-testing implications are embedded in the constructed model itself.

Statistical modeling concerns itself with theory of data structure (e.g., that of an intervariable covariance matrix) for purposes of partitioning and analysis, and its quantitative foundations are not dependent on the research context. That is, the subject matter under scrutiny does not typically affect the analysis technique selected, beyond the selection of a well-known statistical test that suits the research design—rather than the research topic per se. Because hypotheses to which it is applied, by and large, are nonformal (e.g., conjectured paths of influence in structural equation modeling (SEM), moderation–mediation analysis, or hierarchical, multilevel analysis), statistical modeling is part of a mixed deductive scientific system (a combination of verbal description coupled with a standard test of significance, or Bayesian statistical alternative). As with any statistical analysis, focus is on treatment of the presenting empirical data. In contrast, the focus in mathematical modelling is on theoretical mechanisms held as responsible for bringing the data about in a direct fashion.

More specifically, statistical modeling (see, e.g., Rodgers, 2010), such as SEM, including confirmatory factor analysis, multilevel modeling (MLM), mixture growth modeling, and taxometric analysis ("discrete finite mixture-model testing for staggered, or quasi-staggered latent distributions of clinical and control groups") supplies a platform for data organization and inferences about its resulting structure. To be sure, parameters such as path weights and factor loadings are estimated using methods shared with formal analytical modeling, Contra analytical modeling, however, the format of the proposed model structure (again, typically one of univariate variance, or multivariate variance-covariance) and computational methods are transcontent. In the case of analytical formal modeling, it might be said that measurement models and empirical-testing methods are part and parcel of process models of observed responses and data production. Extended treatment of formal-model distinctives and assets in clinical science is available elsewhere (e.g., Neufeld, 2007a, 2015; Shanahan, Townsend, & Neufeld, 2015; see

also Ahn & Busemeyer, 2016, regarding special clinical-setting considerations of model application).

Comment: Selected Points of Common Origin of Statistical and Analytical Modeling

Note that certain statistical modeling approaches used in psychology and clinical science, such as SEM and its variants, have precedents in the physical and mathematical-statistical sciences (McCallum & Ashby, 1986; Van Montfort & Bijeveld, 2004). These precedents have included linear dynamical systems state-space modeling, and random-walk and Wiener-process modeling (expanded upon later in this chapter). The latter have evolved into the Orenstein-Uhlenbeck stochastic differential equation, from earlier work on Brownian motion, by Einstein and by Wiener (as described in Oravecz et al., 2011). Such earlier formulations have been directly adapted and extended to the study of stress specifically as a negative emotion (e.g., Lazarus, 1999; Lazarus & Launier, 1978), and emotion dysregulation, conjoint with borderline personality disorder (Ebner-Priemer, Houben, Santangelo et al., 2015; Oravecz et al., 2011). Because dynamical models such as Orenstein-Uhlenbeck, and linear-dynamical-systems models, have been devoted to specific content areas, they are demarcated here as examples specifically of analytical modeling.

Application of Analytical Modeling to Stress, Coping, and Mental Health

We begin this section by describing models of stress-and-coping dynamics, from affect science. Emphasis is on psychological stress and psychopathology involving intersections among heightened negative affect, emotion dysregulation, borderline personality disorder, and depression. Note, however, that the described modeling strategies themselves are general and can be implemented in other forms of psychopathology where affect dynamics come into play.

Following this is consideration of a cognition-intensive form of coping known as "decisional control." Decisional control (DC) entails positioning oneself in a multifaceted stressing situation, so as to minimize the probability of an adverse event. Doing so requires the formulation of predictive judgments for navigating the situation in terms of options and potential outcomes. Failure to implement DC, for example, may result in elevated levels of environmental stressors that are outside the influence of symptomatology (e.g., economic or climactic upheavals; Rnic, Dozois, Machado, et al., in preparation).

Because coping-related cognition is done in the company of stress, the effects of stress on cognitive functioning itself are relevant. Stress may compromise its own resolution and such compromise may exacerbate, and be exacerbated by, cognitive deficits found in many forms of psychopathology. The intersection of stress effects on cognition, and of cognitive deficit, is formally expressed with special reference to thought-content disorder in schizophrenia, which is discussed later in this chapter.

Stress-Relevant Modeling From Affect Science, With Illustrative Applications to Psychopathology

AN INDIVIDUAL-DIFFERENCE LATENT STOCHASTIC DYNAMICAL DIFFERENTIAL-EQUATION MODEL AND BORDERLINE PERSONALITY DISORDER

Described herein is an adaptation to the present content domain, and hierarchical extension (accommodating individual differences in model operation), of a model from the physical sciences, originally motivated by observations of Brownian motion (the random movement of a particle suspended in a liquid; Oravecz et al., 2011). The model contains three parameters related to the dynamics of reinstating what the authors call a "home base," or average level of affect tone cum affect intensity or activation (dynamic-system equilibrium), following dislodgement therefrom.

One parameter is the home-base "dynamical-system attractor" itself. It expresses the characteristic, or trait-like level, of affect tone and activation. A second parameter, β, conveys attractor strength, or the pull-back to the asymptotic status following some relocation that may occur, for instance, through spontaneous drift, or episodic displacement by some environmental incident. Speed of return is affected by current proximity to the attractor state, current increase in proximity to the state, and current change in the increase (deceleration with nearness to the attractor state). A third parameter potentially bearing on psychological disturbance is the degree of affect variability across time.

Hierarchical mixing-distribution properties are appropriated to the individual, via a Bayesian analytical platform. Each parameter of the model is assumed to be normally distributed across individuals, collectively forming a multivariate normal distribution. Person-specific electronic diary data mediate parameter estimates to the individual through elaboration of Bayesian posterior computation, $P(A|B)$, discussed earlier.

At the nomothetic, group level, the following profile of hierarchical, Orenstein-Uhlenbeck mixture-model parameters was found for individuals with borderline personality disorder (Ebner-Priemer et al., 2015). The modeled affect attractor of individuals with borderline personality disorder was found to be comparatively more negative and variable. Although less consistent across the investigators' three data sets (and analysis formats—hierarchical Orenstein-Uhlenbeck versus multilevel statistical modeling; see later), the attractor strength β, or speed of return to the "baseline value," was lower as compared to controls. This reduced attractor strength also was associated with greater across-time, affect-dimension auto-correlation (coalescence of adjacent observations). Considering the architecture of the hierarchical mixture model, the individual-difference multivariate mixing distribution of the earlier dynamical affect properties, in the case of borderline personality disorder, in effect was shifted away from that of controls, in the directions indicated.

As described earlier, an important asset of the hierarchical model architecture comprises the availability of parameter estimates applicable to the base affect model at the individual level of operation. Covariates whose own values can change person-wise over time or can remain time invariant (as in the case of relatively stable individual personality traits) can also be integrated. In the initial testing of the model (Oravecz et al., 2011), the five dimensions of the Five-Factor model of personality were included as time-invariant covariates. Bidimensional affect (activation and tone) were sampled among 80 university students, again via electronic experience sampling technology. Importantly, the best fitting predictions to the empirical data (model empirical fit) emanated from a full model, with individualized parameters β, bidimensional affect equilibrium, and variability, along with the individual covariate predictors of individual base-model properties. This mixture model, providing for personalized expression, and personality correlates thereof, obviously was more complex than less comprehensive, reduced models, which served for comparison. Superior empirical fit of the full hierarchical model nevertheless stood up to adjustment for its level of model complexity (penalization for model parameter set size).

Customization to the individual participant, of results from the hierarchical modeling application, is available by implementing the participant-wise longitudinal electronic sampling of affect state, into the hierarchical model structure. It should not go unnoticed that given the assumptions of this structure, the distribution of individualized Bayesian posterior estimates (individual "Bayes estimates," earlier), and their Bayesian-prior parameter-mixing distribution, should cohere. Individualized Bayesian posterior estimates, however, allow the implementation of covariates, by linking them to person-specific parameter values.

CODA

Note that the Orenstein-Uhlenbeck model, of which that of Oravecz et al. (2011) is a hierarchical extension, is considered as part of the family known as random walk models (Cox & Miller, 1965). Such models have a rich history in mathematical psychology (e.g., Busemeyer & Townsend, 1993; Link & Heath, 1975; Ratcliff, 1978). Base models comprising extensions of random-walk models have been called diffusion models (see also Ebner-Priemer et al., 2015). Random-walk/diffusion models in turn fall into the category of Wiener-process models. By way of further contextualization, the Wiener-process models can be mimicked by "sequential sampling" and "race models" (Khodadadi & Townsend, 2015), which themselves have been a notable part of theoretical advances in psychology. Here, responses and their latencies are viewed as resulting from the accumulation of a requisite amount of task-relevant information, or activating stimulus properties (see, e.g., Busemeyer & Townsend, 1993; Townsend & Nozawa, 1997).

The hierarchical Orenstein-Uhlenbeck model concentrates on a return to a home base, or typical level of affect state, following a natural drift (e.g., associated with diurnal variation), or episode of dislodgement. Home base, or average level of affect itself, can be thought of as dynamical, in that it results from offsetting forces ("stasis"), rather than simply being an inert state. Modeled reinstatement of affect-system equilibria, following momentary dislodgement, is shared by low-dimensional NDS models (earlier). The latter system also can go beyond dynamical equilibria, or "fixed point attractors," to producing other interesting behaviors. Depending on values of its controlling parameters, an NDS can be set into perpetual motion, settling into a cyclical pattern, with associated amplitude and period ("limit cycle"; for stress-coping behavioral significance, see later). It also can produce a chaotic attractor, which is quasi-periodic, never repeating the same values; is sensitive to starting values ("butterfly effect"); and can appear random, although mathematically subject to a set of governing differential equations.

Other NDS properties of potential interest come to the fore, including stability of the fixed-point and limit cycle attractors, meaning their relative (in)vulnerability to perturbation from outside sources.

AN INDIVIDUAL-DIFFERENCE LINEAR DYNAMICAL-SYSTEMS MODEL AND CARDIOVASCULAR PSYCHOPHYSIOLOGY OF DEPRESSION

Another noteworthy analytical modeling format from affect science, with its birthplace in the physical sciences, is linear-systems modeling of state–space relations (Lodewyckx et al., 2011). Given a certain degree of overlap with the differential-equation model of Oravecz et al. (2011), the present model is described more briefly.

Linear-systems modeling mediates input (system-influencing) and output (observed) variables through quantitatively specified momentary latent states. It overlaps somewhat with statistical modeling, such as SEM, MLM, and canonical correlation of time series (Akaike, 1976; MacCallum & Ashby, 1996; Van Montfort & Bijleveld, 2004). As with the hierarchical Orenstein-Uhlenbeck model, a notable extension of Linear-systems modeling in affect science involves the addition of mixing distributions of model properties, once again integrating expression of model functioning at the group-collective level, with that at the level of the individual group member. This model has been applied by Lodewyckx et al. (2011) to the study of cardiovascular psychophysiological responses, occurring among depressed adolescents during stressing interchanges with parents.

A Simple First-Order Linear Differential Equation Model for Coping Propensity

We describe an analytical model that once more illustrates the potential value of formally implementing theoretical propositions about clinically significant aspects of stress and coping. Although simple in structure, this model nevertheless potentially conveys theoretically poignant features of propensity to appropriate available coping options (coping propensity). Certain clinical symptomatology may be seen as extremes of coping propensity. Obsessive-compulsive symptomatology, for example, may be considered excessive engagement in "coping activity," with little or no "objective environmental consequence." Selected behavioral deficits associated with depression, on the other hand, may be considered as a marked abstinence from potentially efficacious "stimulus-directed," or "problem-focused coping" (Neufeld, 1982).

The formulation represents an effort to place relations between coping propensity, and cognitive appraisal of coping efficacy, on a quantitative footing (Neufeld, 1987, 1989, 1999). It assumes that the propensity to engage in available coping activity increases with appraised efficacy of the presenting coping option(s). Cognitive appraisal of coping efficacy, in turn, is put into decision-theoretic terms. Predicted efficacy increases as the subjective probability of stressor-event occurrence given coping engagement, is exceeded by that given abstinence form engagement. Coping propensity, quantified as relative frequency, or probability of coping occurrence, across episodes of opportunity for such occurrence (possibly related also to latency of instigation, and intensity, or resistance to obstruction), is considered to vary with discrepancy in the earlier probabilities (Lees & Neufeld, 1999).

Within this formulation, coping propensity is predicted according to the expression e^{-mn}, where e is the base of the natural logarithm; m is the *vulnerability* of coping-incentive cues (e.g., cues conveying coping-success among peers) to cue-detracting stimulation, or "noise" (e.g., distracting, incentive-undermining events); and n is the current level of such noise. Vulnerability of coping-incentive cues may comprise, for example, variables offsetting the cues' initial attentional registration, such as lack of prominence or salience in the attentional field. Vulnerability m also increases with organismic resistance to cue-efficacy incentive properties (Mothersill & Neufeld, 1985; Neufeld & Herzog, 1983).

For $m > 0$, values of e^{-mn} are decreasing and positively accelerating as n increases. More coping disincentive at the appraisal level, as detracting influences come into play (e.g., occurrence of antiefficacy information, or discouraging social influences), results in faster dissipation of coping propensity—but according to a specific trajectory over n. The parameter m increases as robustness in the strength of incentive properties decreases (see Figure 4.2).

Like many analytical models, the present one superficially may appear simple. Such may be part and parcel of its formal apparatus. Constraints on precision expose boundaries of applicability. Model composition, moreover, is trimmed to address the interplay of core variables, with mathematical tractability figuring into the developments. What can be hoped for nevertheless is verisimilitude with the goings on of the targeted phenomenon.

Potential payoff from such endeavors are proprietary to quantification. These may include measurement, and even intervention implications. Meeting the challenge of empirically operationalizing model properties (coping propensity; parameters m and n) is rewarded by their embeddedness in a formal deductive system. In the current instance, coping propensity is quantitatively linked to cognitively appraised coping efficacy, which is defined in explicitly decision-theoretic terms.

Assessment implications come to the fore. Value of the parameter m in principle is estimable as the reciprocal of the observed average level of coping propensity. An estimate of the extant level of n is

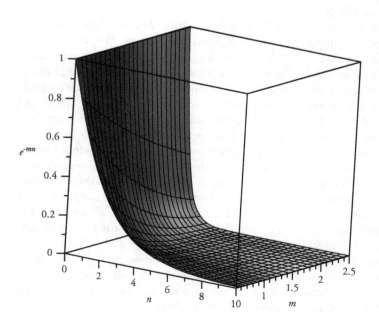

Figure 4.2 Trajectory of e^{-mn} illustrated for values of m ranging from 0 to 2.5.

available as $-ln$(current level of coping propensity)$/m$. Model-predicted level of coping propensity for the any value of n then is available as e^{-mn}. Extant rate of change (slope of e^{-mn}) with a slight increase in n is $-me^{-mn}$, the change in the change (acceleration) being m^2e^{-mn}. The slope and acceleration of e^{-mn} may be valuable in estimating, for example, when the relative toll taken by n on coping propensity is higher or lower, and in ascertaining opportune regions of n for appreciable returns on "n-reducing" therapeutic interventions.

Relevance of the first-order linear differential equation to psychological stress and coping research has been rediscovered, as the "dissipation component" of the "reservoir model of perceived stress" (Bergeman & DeBoeck, 2014). In this model, momentary change in perceived stress is defined as a linear combination of current stress input and present level of carried-forward, nondissipated stress. Isolating on the dissipation component, the "noise" variable n, of e^{-mn} becomes time t, and the other part of the exponent, $-m$, becomes their rate of stress dissipation β, where β < 0.

Analytic Modeling of Cognition-Intensive Coping and Compromised Cognitive Deficit in Psychopathology: A Game-Theoretic Approach to Decisional Stress Control

Decisional control (DC; Averill, 1973; Thompson, 1981) is a form of coping with stressors, consisting of positioning oneself in a multifaceted stressing situation so as to minimize the probability of an adverse social or physical event (Lees & Neufeld, 1999; Morrison, Neufeld, & Lefebvre, 1988; Movellan & McClelland, 2001). In that way, DC is "preventative," or "prophylactic" (for a taxonomy of coping as related to impending adverse events, see Neufeld, 1990). This form of coping is cognition intensive, inasmuch as it entails predictive judgments of threat (adverse-event probability) associated with presenting options, necessary for safety maximizing choices (e.g., a low-risk task in an occupational setting).

DC can be compromised by any cognitive deficit that impairs information processing necessary to form predictive judgments. Because the necessary information processing takes place in the context of stress, moreover, a potentially exacerbating factor is the toll taken by stress itself on cognitive functioning (Neufeld, 2016; Neufeld & McCarty, 1994; Neufeld, Townsend, & Jette, 2007). DC has been viewed in game-theoretic terms (Morrison et al., 1988; Shanahan & Neufeld, 2010), meaning that the individual is "playing a game against the environment," the goal being to minimize threat of an adverse social or physical incident. In other words, the individual is seen as navigating the stressful situation using selection and choice options for maximal returns by way of threat reduction.

Within this framework, analytical modeling can quantify the properties of situations that determine the degree to which DC is available, cognitive demands (predictive judgments) necessary to realize its threat-reducing potential, and the amount of threat reduction (diminished adverse-event probability) attending DC implementation. These DC-prescribed properties have been translated into specific formulae enabling numerical predictions (technically, through combinatoric equations). Quantification has addressed, for example, the undermining effects on choice, of uncertainty regarding outcomes attending available DC selections.

A Stochastic-Model Interpretation of Stress-Effected Symptomatology

Of concern in the study of stress–psychopathology relations is the empirical establishment of stress as a causal agent of disorder occurrence or as a precipitant (as opposed to consequent) of symptom episodes (returned to later). A parallel concern is the identification of explanatory mechanisms allowing stress to assume these roles. An example, relating stress activation and schizophrenia thought-content disorder (delusions and thematic hallucinations), is as follows: Cognitive neuroscience studies of schizophrenia have educed deficits in stimulus encoding (cognitively preparing and transforming presenting stimulation for involvement in other operations, such as those in so-called working memory) as a central debility in schizophrenia cognition (Neufeld, 2007c; Yates, 1966; see also Cutler & Neufeld, 2017). Stochastic analytical modeling has charted its composition, disclosing possible symptom significance, and what further may happen with the impingement of stress.

To elaborate, encoding operations often are subjected to limited time windows. For example, two fellow employees may be conversing quietly beside a water cooler. In passing by this scene, only a fraction of its details may be encoded (e.g., the quiet conversation), with attentionally peripheral information potentially excluded. In the present example, the quiet conversation may involve the planning of a recreational outing. A set of hunting or fishing regulations and a topographical map may comprise an inconspicuous part of the scene. The latter items may be lost to the encoding process during its limited interval, more so with encoding impairment.

These items, however, defensibly are key to endowing that which is more central (notably the quiet conversation) with its objective significance. Without being escorted by contextualizing cues, the fragment that has been absorbed may be construed as being personally significant, even conspiratorial (Maher, 1988). Apropos of the negative bent on false beliefs, a defensive interpretation may be understood as protective; that is, falsely inferring malice may be less jeopardous than falsely inferring benevolence.

The earlier conjecture on development of false beliefs has been quantitatively uploaded onto a stochastic modeling platform (Neufeld et al., 2010). Stress effects then have been introduced to this modeling platform. Specifically, stress defensibly is considered to reduce the speed of encoding, independent of health or deficit. The formalized stress effects then are shown to intersect with pre-existing encoding deficit, so as to exacerbate the risk of missing atttentionally peripheral, but potentially reality-grounding, cues.

Figure 4.3 visually illustrates the proposed stochastic model of stress–symptom relations. The three-dimensional response surface presents the computed probability of successfully completing an encoding process (within a time window *t* of 3 arbitrary units). Certain stimuli may be less salient (e.g., more peripheral in the visual field), but nevertheless vital to veridical inferences about an encountered scenario

(as exemplified earlier). Figure 4.3 quantitatively depicts the intersection of stress (transduced into parameter *r*) and formalized schizophrenia encoding deficit (parameter *m*), in affecting the probability of encoding success. A plane corresponding to a probability value of .80 intersects the response surface. This plane conveys an imposed minimal probability (minimum relative frequency) of completing the encoding process, required for veridical inferences.

Lower values of *m*, conveying healthy encoding, are seen to protect against subcritical probabilities, regardless of *r*. Similarly, the toll taken by higher values of *m* is mitigated with reduction in *r*. Conversely, the response surface dips below the critical amount more quickly with increased *r*, when *m* is higher, and likewise for increased *m*, when *r* is higher (mathematical and related specifics are provided in Neufeld et al., 2010; see also Taylor, Theberge, Williamson et al., 2016, 2017).[2]

All told, a defensible mathematical angle on stress–symptom relations is yielded by such modeling, potentially rendering unique insights into the nuances of the path taken by stress in promoting symptomatology. Modeling results also provide a formal aspect to the prominent conjecture of "context deficit" in schizophrenia (Dobson & Neufeld, 1982; George & Neufeld, 1985), one evidently maintaining heuristic currency in the field (e.g., Cohen,

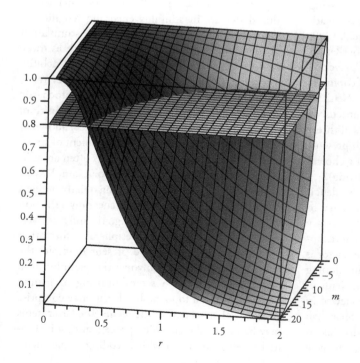

Figure 4.3 Probability of registering attentionally peripheral information. Higher values of parameter *r* are aligned with reduced speed of encoding reality-grounding stimuli, on the periphery of the attentional field, exacerbated by stress activation. Higher values of parameter *m* are aligned with formally identified schizophrenia encoding deficit. The .80 intersecting plane conveys an arbitrary critical value, below which incomplete information fosters false beliefs. Computations are for a time window *t* of 3 arbitrary units. (See text for further details.)

Barch, Carter, & Servan Schreiber, 1999; Kerns & Berenbaum, 2003).

Stress May Not Always Be Detrimental: A Race Model of Negative Thought Content in Depression

Within a formal modeling context, the clinical scientist can play with model properties to explore the interactions of model-identified vulnerability factors with other significant variables, such as psychological stress. For example, some depressive disorders may be understood in terms of automatic negative thoughts, it being postulated that psychological stress enhances such characteristic patterns of cognition in individuals at risk for depression (Hartlage, Alloy, Vasquez, & Dykman, 1993). Translating these contentions into terms established in mainstream quantitative cognitive science, however, shows that psychological stress instead *reduces* the ascendancy of well-practiced negative thoughts in clinically depressed individuals, at least within this defensible assumptive framework (Neufeld, 1996; Townsend & Neufeld, 2004).

The quantitative translation begins with expressing the dominance of well-practiced (so-called automatic) negative versus less practiced (so-called effortful) nonnegative thought content, as higher average occurrence rates for the former. With these rate properties in tow, the well-practiced and less-practiced thought content then enter a formally modeled "horse race," where the faster rates for negative-thought generation evince higher winning probabilities, for all race durations. Note that although these derivations result from basic computations in integral calculus, they nevertheless yield precise predictions and lay bare their associated assumptions.

Differentiating the earlier horse-race expression of the probability of "negative-thought" victory, with respect to a parameter conveying the effects of stress on processing capacity ("r," see earlier; see also Figure 4.3) leads to a negative derivative.[3] Formalized in this way, then, the result shows psychological stress to actually handicap the negative thought contender.

It is conceivable that reduction in the ascendancy of well-practiced negative thoughts in the face of stressing environmental demands and pressures, in favor of less-practiced, but more adaptive cognitive processes, conveys a certain protective function. In all events, this example illustrates the hazards of depending on unaided verbal reasoning in attempting to deal with complex intervariable relations (including stress effects on psychopathology) and

exemplifies the disclosure through available formal modeling, of subtleties that are both plausible and clinically significant—if initially counterintuitive (Staddon, 1984; Townsend, 1984).

Stress–Symptomatology Interaction as a Low-Dimensional Nonlinear Dynamical System

A challenge in assessing the tenability of stress as a causal agent of symptomatology is that of creating a clean independent variable. Symptomatology, and its social and other consequences, may be a source of stress increase, rather than the other way around, and each may progressively change the other ("reciprocal determinism"). In addition, both stress and symptomatology may stem from a distinct third variable, such as "generalized distress." Classical statistical methods, such as cross-correlation, lagged cross-correlation, and other lag time-series analyses (e.g., Harris, 1963; see cross-correlation suggestion of Corcoran, Walker, Hout, et al., 2003, on the study of stress–schizophrenia relations, and Norman & Malla's [1994], much earlier application thereof), as well as elaborations on these methods (e.g., Granger causality; time-series structural equation modeling), aim to address these complex issues. Linear association of symptomatology at a current time t with stress at $t - l$ (where l is a designated time lag) may be statistically adjusted for (again, usually linear) relations with symptom level at time $t - l$. Doing so represents an effort statistically to throw into relief, through partial-correlation computations, the hypothesized unique role of stress as a symptom-altering antecedent. Synchronous associations, such as that between stress and symptomatology at time t also may be partialed out. Additional variations on statistical estimation, such as mediation and moderation analysis, and extensions thereof, may come into play (see also later section on "Statistical Modeling in Stress and Psychopathology").

In the absence of experimental control, such computational methods may be seen as the only methodological option available for addressing stress–psychopathology relations of interest. It has been well established, however (since Cochran, 1957) that nuisance effects may be over- or underremoved using partialing or covariance adjustments. In addition, variables are residualized according to their linear association with the partialed-out variables. This means that their psychometric structure likely is changed from that of their original format, compromising their substantive interpretation and their established validity and reliability (Gardner &

Neufeld, in submission; Neufeld, 1989; Neufeld & Gardner, 1990; issues reviewed in Lees & Neufeld, 1994). One attempted antidote to these problems has been to isolate stressors that are clearly independent of symptoms (e.g., Spring, 1981; Spring & Coons, 1982). Such stressors include economic recessions or natural disasters, for example.

Arguably lost with methods enumerated thus far is the so-called richness of the phenomenon, in terms of the variables' (system dimensions') operation in their in situ, ecologically valid state (over and against, notably, change in measure structure through statistical residualization). Low-dimensional NDS models, on the other hand, allow for theoretical intervariable dynamical interactions to remain intact. Indeed, in the history of stressology, it has been contended that such dynamics are the sine qua non of psychological stress itself (verbal postulates to this effect reviewed in Neufeld, 1999). Within this modeling infrastructure, the role of each system variable can be isolated, and tautological inferences avoided, if the modeled reciprocal influences are distinct for each variable and nonlinear in structure.

An Illustrative Unidimensional Nonlinear Dynamical Model

A simple example of an NDS that nevertheless possesses selected nontrivial stress-related properties is one that expresses the possible compounding effects of one's current stress state on one's ensuing state. As applied to stress and selected symptoms of psychopathology, stress may exacerbate reactivity to ensuing stressors, thus producing progressively greater vulnerability. Higher existing vulnerability elevates

subsequent vulnerability, relative to more resilience (see e.g., Monroe & Harkness, 2005, and Post, 1992, on the kindling of life stress in depression). This succession of events can be translated into an explicit, if simple formal theory. Doing so raises what otherwise might remain a flow diagram to the status of a scientific model, thus formalizing the structure, ushering in quantitative prediction, and disclosing theoretical and measurement information inaccessible to nonformal theory. To illustrate, changes of an organismic state at time t [in standard notation, $dY(t)/dt$] can be defined as a function of its existing state, for example $Y(t)^2$, where $Y(t)$ is the state at time t. In addition to the definition of momentary change, we need a defined or estimated initial condition, or value of $Y(t)$ at $t = 0$. Stipulating this value as $1/c$, where c is a constant, the state of the organism $Y(t)$ at any time t, or its "initial value solution" is $1/(c - t)$. Inspection shows a division by 0 when t reaches c. Unbounded or infinite values of $Y(t)$ occur at this point (a mathematical singularity is encountered), taken to imply unsustainable stress, and system breakdown. The system now collapses under its own weight.

Higher values of c are deemed to signify lower vulnerability, or more resilience. Trajectories of $Y(t)$, for two values of c are presented in Figure 4.4. A value of $c = 2$ results in $Y(t)$ being lower at $t = 0$ and remaining bounded twice as long as with $c = 1$. Observe the location of $Y(t)$ for $c = 2$, when that for $c = 1$ escapes bounded values.

Note that there is a qualitative change in system behavior when values of c cross into negative territory, and positive outcomes occur; the system

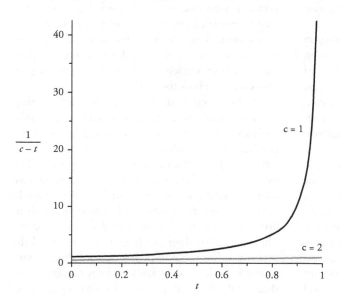

Figure 4.4 Behavior of a nonlinear unidimensional differential equation, with differing initial conditions $1/c$, $c > 0$.

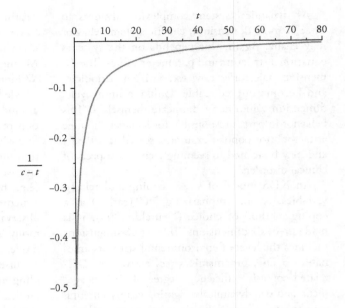

Figure 4.5 Behavior of a unidimensional nonlinear differential equation, with $c < 0$.

$$\frac{1}{c-t}$$

transmogrifies, to never generate unbounded values. An example, where $c = -2$, is shown in Figure 4.5. The emergence of $Y(t)$ containment, antipodal to the case where $c > 0$, illustrates what is known as a bifurcation; a sudden shift in system output occurs to a gradual change in its controlling parameter(s) (c continuously decreasing until it crosses the 0 boundary). The parameter c now retains its interpretation as a stress-tolerance agent, but an increase in its absolute value indicates less average distance from asymptotic stability.

Altogether, this is potentially useful clinical information. Measurement implications are forthcoming, regarding $Y(t)$, the trajectory of stress vulnerability, and c, an individual-difference parameter possibly having psychometrically measurable (e.g., personality) correlates. Predictions are quantitative (e.g., as with those described for a first-order linear differential equation, see earlier [Figure 4.2]), except for model-prescribed discontinuities in $Y(t)$, which nevertheless have a quantitative basis. Model testing also is forthcoming (see earlier section "Low-Dimensional Nonlinear Dynamical System Modeling").

Multi (Low)-Dimensional Nonlinear Dynamical System Models

Moving beyond a single-dimension system, more of the claimed dynamical richness and substantive implications of continuous interactions among variables from the present domain become available. Consider, for example, the normal waxing and

waning of stress and coping. An increase in stress may activate an increase in coping activity. Elevation in coping may then diminish perceived stress to a point where coping efforts are relaxed. As coping subsides, unresolved stressors accumulate, reactivating coping, which in turn subdues the level of prevailing stressors, and so on. Such a pattern of temporally staggered oscillations (in this case, a "two-dimensional limit cycle") can occur in nonlinear dynamical systems when a steady, equilibrium state ("fixed-point attractor") becomes unstable. Fixed-point instability can occur to certain changes in system parameters, such as raising the degree to which the individual's environment is conducive to high levels of stress (e.g., the classical case of family "emotional expressiveness," in the case of schizophrenia; Goldstein, 1987; Nicholson & Neufeld, 1992).

Turning to stress-generating symptomatology, sustained kinesis again may occur, as follows. Increased symptomatology (e.g., bizarre, inappropriate behavior) may lead to elevation in interpersonal and other stress, whose punishing properties may suppress the associated symptomatology. The resulting decline in symptom-generated stress may then give way to increased symptom expression, once again instigating more stress, and so on (Neufeld & Nicholson, 1992; Nicholson & Neufeld, 1992). Note in passing that modeling of such rises and falls of interacting variables has its historical roots in the theory of predator–prey relations, contributed to nonlinear science by mathematical ecology (e.g., Roughgarden, 1979).

As dynamical system complexity advances to three or more dimensions, chaotic system behavior may ensue. Again, this depends on the system's equational structure and parameter values. The dimension trajectories now escape from periodicity and become unpredictable. Unlike a limit cycle, dimension values never duplicate themselves. This behavior in part is responsible for its label, "strange attractor" (for popular examples, see Gleick, 1987), and may be related to seemingly chaotic aspects of clinical disorders.

An NDS model of stress, coping and related variables, is one emphasizing DC (earlier) as a coping method of choice (Neufeld, 1999). It is made up of six dimensions. This set of dimensions includes the level of environmental stressors amenable to DC, organismic stress activation, DC-related cognitive efficiency, degree of DC engagement, and two dynamical weighting factors, entering into the nonlinear definitions of the second and fourth dimensions (see earlier), and whose own changes over time are nonlinear functions of other system dimensions.

The third dimension, DC-related cognitive efficiency, is partly a function of stress activation (second dimension) and makes provision for stress-susceptibility associated with psychopathology. Such stress susceptibility notably takes the form of disorder-related deficit in DC-related information processing. Note that construction of this formal theory has been spawned by substantive subject matter from the addressed content domain. Analysis of the system has disclosed interesting, emergent mathematical properties, which are detailed in Levy et al. (2012).

Observe that NDS modeling allows for individual differences in model operation. For example, mention was made of the present six-dimensional model's provision for stress susceptibility associated with psychopathology. Other system parameters ("controlling parameters"), and their combinations, can vary with personality and other individual-difference covariates (see, e.g., Levy et al., 2012).

Methods of Model Selection

A word is in order regarding selection from among competing models. The topic of model selection is important for a variety of reasons, including conceptualization of thmodeled topic, empirical research design, and scientific and potentially applied measurement technology. Modeling a phenomenon of interest may involve model construction more or less from scratch or selecting or adapting one from existing candidates. Model selection methodology has received extensive study in psychology and elsewhere (e.g., special journal issues edited by Myung, Forster, & Browne, 2000; Wagenmakers & Waldorp, 2006).

Methods of model selection typically are organized around two requirements: empirical fit and economy of explanation. These requirements come to the fore whether one is dealing with analytical or statistical modeling (see later). An aim is to optimize fit against parsimony; as model complexity increases (e.g., by adding parameters or expanding model structure), predictions may come closer to a set of observations, but they do so at the expense of parsimony. Additionally, certain parts of an expansive model may be unreliable across empirical studies, because they are influenced by study-specific sampling and measurement error. Generally, simpler models that nevertheless show predictive efficacy generalize better to new studies. Fortunately, the technology of model selection offers indexes of model efficiency that integrate goodness of empirical fit with penalization for model complexity.

Statistical Modeling in Stress and Psychopathology

Statistical modeling typically refers to the broad grouping of models used in inferential statistics which are based upon the general linear model (GLM). Typically relying on least-squares or maximum-likelihood estimation of model parameters (although hierarchical Bayesian mixture-model extensions [described earlier under the section "Individual-Difference Extensions of Stochastic Analytical Modeling"], are available), the purpose of these methods is to either derive a function which best approximates given data or separates out one or more groups based on means or latent constructs. Emphasized heavily in graduate-level statistical courses in psychology, these methods nonexhaustively include canonical correlation, regression, t-test models, analysis of variance models (ANOVA), SEM, and MLM. It is expected that this form of modeling is one with which readers are at least somewhat familiar. Extensiveness of this section has been curtailed accordingly and addresses what may be less well known. Examples of stress research using a path model, and a repeated-measures design ANOVA, are available in Falk, Norris, and Quinn (2014), and Monroe, Harkness, Simons, and Thase (2001). An overview of the use of SEM in psychological research is presented by MacCallum and Austin (2000).

As mentioned in the section "Statistical Modeling" earlier, statistical model construction is typically guided by nonformal hypotheses, and the research design, or the format of empirical data on hand. As stress is considered to be transactional in nature, some provision is needed for dynamical properties of the subject matter in one's research design. Research designs, therefore, often use more than one time point to gather information, in an effort to explore change. In recent years, there has been an increase in models incorporating temporal sequencing, taking on multiwave longitudinal design formats. Interactional research on stress–psychopathology relations thus more effectively may explore hypothesized immediate and delayed intervariable relations. These models can help inform directionality: whether increased stressful life events precede increased symptoms of psychopathology, whether worsening symptoms are followed by an increase in experienced stressful events, and whether there exist time-delayed relationships among variables. (Corcoran et al. [2003] review how such time series analyses may inform the study of stress and schizophrenia [see also Norman & Malla, 1994].)

More recently, Shapero, Hankin, and Barrocas (2013) used a multiwave MLM to estimate possible reciprocal influences between interpersonal and achievement-related stressors, and depressive symptomatology, among adolescents. Using a lagged design allowed the authors to statistically control for each individual's $t-1$ stressor scores prior to examining how the respective variables were predictive of each other at subsequent time points. Similarly, a study by Hankin (2008) used a lagged design MLM approach to investigate the association between hypothesized etiological factors for depression and experienced life stressors. The use of such designs has indicated that symptomatology may be linked to later elevation in stressor levels, even for environmental stressors seemingly impervious to symptomatology per se.[4]

Assets of time-lagged measurement within an MLM approach are twofold: The approach allows for the estimation of changes in individual variability in measured variables, over time, as well as individual differences in such changes. Also availed is improved estimation of model properties at the level of the individual, through Bayesian stabilization ("Bayesian shrinkage"); see earlier section on "Individual-Difference Extensions of Stochastic Analytical Modeling"). Although often focusing on analyzing linear trends in repeated-measures data, more advanced forms of MLM and SEM accommodate nonlinear trends, including those comprising piecewise or local linearity. Growth curve models (GCMs) are an alternative to ANOVA models, in which later time points are not subtracted from earlier time points to create difference scores. Rather, later time points are regressed onto earlier time points and residuals of the resulting function are subjected to analysis.

This approach is similar to that of autoregressive cross-lagged designs. GCM differs, however, in terms of its focus on individuals across time points rather than on pooled group data at specific time points. Instead of data-smoothing techniques common in GLM models, designed to create a function representing group changes over time points, GCMs creates a function for each individual (individual growth curves). As well, predictor variables can be added to describe individual differences in starting points or trajectories. These predictor variables can be time-invariant covariates (stable over time; for example, gender or personality traits) or time-variant covariates, influenced by incidents at different time points (for example, stressful life occurrences or changes in an individual's environment). As such, GCMs can provide information both at the individual level (random effects) and group level (fixed-effects summaries of group-aggregated individual effects).

GCMs are sometimes referred to as latent GCMs. Measured variables (MVs) are believed to be fallible indicators of latent-variable constructs (LVs). In GCM, MVs across time points are used to infer individual growth curves in underlying LVs. As might be expected, GCMs can be analyzed using SEM and MLM approaches; however, some methods of nonlinear GCMs typically rely on SEM approaches which allow the time parameter to vary ("unequal intervals"). Alternatively, piecewise models simplify nonlinear trends by breaking time points into hypothethized or content-informed groupings, possibly corresponding with developmental milestones. In piecewise models, linear functions are created across a range of time points and connected at their joints to other, adjacent linear functions (connecting intervals of "local linearity," but yielding global nonlinearity see, e.g., Seiffge-Krenke, Aunola Nurmi, 2009, & Felt, Depaoli, & Tiemensma, 2017)

Lastly, GCMs can become more elaborate to accommodate ways in which multiple constructs may co-vary dynamically. For example, multivariate GCMs can be created to investigate how factors related to stress generation will co-vary with those of symptomatology over time. An application of nonlinear latent GCM for multivariate data has been presented by Blozis, Conger, and Harring (2007).

Future Directions

The field of stress, coping, and psychopathology is ripe for benefits of formal theory construction and testing. Compared to other domains of psychological science, relatively few examples are available on the combined intersection of stress, coping, and psychopathology. Rigorous applications relevant to the intersection of stress and coping, however, can be drawn from affect science, as described in this chapter.

Instances of formal modeling in the general area of psychological stress and coping, such as those using game-theoretic and low-dimensional NDS approaches, also are rare. Modeling from these domains nevertheless has been used to infer implications of clinical abnormalities for stress-related transactions. Of principal interest is the conjunction of model-stipulated cognitive-behavioral demands and cognitive-behavioral debilities associated with psychopathology. For instance, documented cognitive deficits stand to compromise necessary predictive judgments, as expressed in formal theory of DC. Stress sensitivity, moreover, is a specific dimension ("organismic stress activation") in the six-dimensional nonlinear-dynamical-system model of stress and coping, described under the earlier section "Multi(Low-) Dimensional Nonlinear Dynamical Systems Models."

We have reviewed modeling options that arguably are poised for application in the field. An effort has been made to present available methods in sufficient detail to unveil potential compatibility of modeling strategies with problem areas. Technical developments, required for scrupulous implementation, and references to supporting computer software are available in cited sources. Knowledge of specialized quantitative methods may be called for; tutorial and other treatments of relevant background material are contained in the cited resources (e.g., Neufeld, 1998, 2007b). In some cases, collaborations with technically oriented colleagues may be helpful. As with nonformal theorizing conjoint with research design and statistics, however (e.g., Kirk, 1982), knowledge of one's substantive problem domain, in lockstep with awareness of modeling options, is ideal for recognizing occurrences of natural fit between subject matter and modeling methods. However, there are many benefits to applying these quantitative methods, such as the application of Bayesian methods, mediating group-level analyses of processes related to stress, coping, and associated abnormalities.

Note that deficit in processes involved in stress-related transactions, and negotiation of environmental demands, termed "critical deficit" (Neufeld, 2015; see Neufeld & Broga, 1981, for a quantitative portrayal of "critical deficit" [versus experimental psychopathology's more conventional "differential" deficit]),[5] stand to be of important ecological significance when it comes to executing daily self-maintenance routines. The interface of model derivations in cognition and affect mechanisms, with formalized stress-coping exigencies, constitutes fallow ground for future directions.

Modeling developments within the confines of stress, coping, and psychopathology themselves stand to be productively integrated. For example, hierarchical Orenstein-Uhlenbeck and hierarchical linear dynamical state-space models address dynamics of a system's return to an equilibrium state, following dislodgement from the state. Formally stipulated candidate sources of potential dislodgement, such as an imposed period of waiting (see note 1, and related text) can be integrated into models emphasizing the dynamics of equilibrium reattainment; additional insights arguably await such quantitative integration.

Note as well that interpretation of model parameters often is an exercise in construct validity. Does the parameter behave in accordance with its imputed meaning? Is it selectively sensitive to variation in observed variables to which it supposedly pertains? For example, does a parameter expressing speed of transacting a cognitive or affective process selectively vary with the physical intensity of relevant stimulation? Is a parameter conveying the number of constituent operations (subprocesses) of a modeled process sensitive to variation in task complexity?

A parameter also should affect model predictions in line with our understanding of what the parameter represents. Certain parameters may relate to sheer success or accuracy of process completion and should affect associated model predictions. Other parameters may be assigned to speed of successful completions, and still other parameters may predict confidence in response selection, among other possibilities. This form of construct validity for model parameters—derived from their operation within a formal deductive system (Braithwaite, 1968)—is known as "analytical construct validity" (elaborated upon in Neufeld, 2007a; see also Pitt, Kim Navarro et al., 2006). As with construct validity generally, ascertaining the substantive significance of model parameters is an important ongoing challenge.

It is possible to regress process-model properties onto other variables, such as psychometric measures of personality, ability, or psychopathology. This procedure has been used to advantage in the case of item response theory parameters and elsewhere (e.g., Baghaei & Hohensinn, 2017; the Orenstein-Uhlenbeck model, discussed earlier). The structure of the predictive linear combination speaks to construct validity of the predicted parameter values.

Neuroimaging may increasingly make its way into investigations of stress, coping, and mental health, given its widespread application to clinical science, and this method can be integrated into formal cognitive-behavioral models. Functional neuroimaging with respect to cognitive processes associated with "cognition-intensive coping" (e.g., DC-related predictive judgments) comes to the fore. Formal modeling of cognitive processes defensibly is fundamental to rigorous treatment of the functional aspect of functional neuroimaging, such as fMRI (Taylor et al., 2016), and functional magnetic resonance spectroscopy (for descriptions, see Taylor, Neufeld, Schaefer et al., 2015; Taylor et al., 2017).

Finally, but arguably of considerable importance, tools of analytical modeling can be used for secondary data analyses. Such application can release otherwise untapped information lodged in (often expensive) past studies (Novotney, 2009). The upshot is a substantively informed meta-analysis; existing data are subjected to model predictions, rather than actuarial tabulation of generic effect-size estimates (see also Introduction in Neufeld, 2007b, 2016; Townsend, 1984).

Concluding Comments

In the history of science, quantitative modeling has propelled advances in the disciplines to which it has been applied. The lesson arguably holds in clinical science, including the study of stress, coping, mental health, and psychopathology. Provided are measurement models, avenues of testing, and information that otherwise would remain invisible.

A desired property of theory in longer established disciplines is "aesthetic appeal" (e.g., succinctness of theoretical propositions, making for simplicity pending the unwrapping of their manifold implications). Aesthetic appeal arguably is proprietary to formal theory, notably of an analytical nature. Precision, moreover, fosters falsifiability, considered indispensable to scientific progress. Consequently, and again, considering the history of older disciplines, it is anticipated that clinical science, including its domain of stressology, will become increasingly reliant on quantitative modeling and that such will be reflected in the scientific literature and in educational curricula.

Acknowledgments
Manuscript preparation was supported by the Social Sciences and Humanities Research Council of Canada in the form of an Insight Grant to the first author and a Joseph-Armand Bombardier Canada Graduate Scholarship to the second author.

Notes

1. See, for example, the elegant mathematical research on the psychological cost of waiting by Osuna (1985), Gzyl and Osuna, (2013), Suck and Holling (1997), Denuit and Genest (2001), and Kocas (2015).
2. Cognitive- and statistical-science principled, Bayesian measurement methods, for monitoring symptom-significant cognitive functioning, and for monitoring cognitive aspects of treatment-regimen efficacy, all generated from the present modeling infrastructure, also are presented in Neufeld et al. (2010).
3. The same result can be shown with a simple algebraic operation.
4. Formal theoretical reasons for this association are tendered in Rnic, Dozois, Machado, et al. (in preparation).
5. The essential concept of "critical deficit" subsequently has resurfaced—if in nonquantitative terms—under the label "functionally significant deficit" (e.g., Green, Horan, & Sugar, 2013).

References

Ahn, W-Y., & Busemeyer, J. (2016) Challenges and promises or translating computational tools into clinical practice. *Current Opinion in Behavioral Sciences, 11*, 1–7.

Akaike, H. (1976). Canonical correlation analysis of time series and the use of information criterion. *Mathematics in Science and Engineering, 126*, 27–96.

Averill, J. R. (1973). Personal control over aversive stimuli and its relationship to stress. *Psychological Bulletin, 80*, 286–303.

Baghaei, P., & Hohensinn, C. (2017). A method of Q-matrix validation for the linear logistic test model. *Frontiers in Quantitative Psychology and Measurement, 8*, 1–7. doi:10.3389/fpsyg.2017.00897

Batchelder, W. H. (1998). Multinomial processing tree models and psychological assessment. *Psychological Assessment, 10*, 331–344.

Bergeman, C. S., & Deboeck, P. R. (2014). Trait stress resistance and dynamic stress dissipation on health and well-being: The reservoir model. *Research in Human Development, 11*, 108–125.

Blozis, S. A., Conger, K. J., & Harring, J. R. (2007). Nonlinear latent curve models for multivariate longitudinal data. *International Journal of Behavioral Development, 31*(4), 340–346.

Bolger, N., Davis, A., & Rafaeli, E. (2008) Diary methods: Capturing life as it is lived. *Annual Review of Psychology, 54*, 579–616.

Braithwaite, R. B. (1968). *Scientific explanation: A study of the function of theory, probability and law in science.* New York, NY: Cambridge University Press.

Busemeyer, J.R., & Diedrich, A. (2010) *Cognitive modeling.* Thousand Oaks, CA: Sage.

Busemeyer, J. R., & Townsend, J. T. (1993). Decision field theory: A dynamic-cognitive approach to decision making in an uncertain environment. *Psychological Review, 100*, 432–459.

Busemeyer, J. R., & Wang, Y. (2000). Model comparisons and model selections based on generalization test methodology. *Journal of Mathematical Psychology, 44*(1), 171–189.

Cochran, W. G. (1957). Analysis of covariance: Its nature and uses. *Biometrics, 13,* 261–281.

Carter, J. R., Neufeld, R. W. J., & Benn, K. D. (1998). Application of process models in assessment psychology: Potential assets and challenges. *Psychological Assessment, 10,* 379–395.

Cohen, J. D, Barch, D. M, Carter, C. S, & Servan-Schreiber, D. (1999). Schizophrenic deficits in the processing of context: Converging evidence from three theoretically motivated cognitive tasks. *Journal of Abnormal Psychology, 108,* 120–133.

Corcoran, Walker, Hout, R., Mittal, V., Tessner, K., Kestler, L., & Malaspina, D. (2003). The stress cascade and schizophrenia: Etiology and onset. *Schizophrenia Bulletin, 29*(4), 671–679.

Cox, D. R., & Miller, H. D. (1965). *The theory of stochastic processes.* London, UK: Methuen.

Cutler, C. D., & Neufeld, R. W. J. (2017) Addressing very short stimulus encoding times in modeling schizophrenia cognitive deficit. *Journal of Mathematical Psychology, 79,* 53–63.

Denuit, M., & Genest, C. (2001). An extension of Osuna's model for stress caused by waiting. *Journal of Mathematical Psychology, 45,* 115–130.

Dobson, D., & Neufeld, R.W.J. (1982). Paranoid-nonparanoid schizophrenic distinctions in the implementation of external conceptual constraints. *Journal of Nervous and Mental Disease, 170,* 614–621.

Doob, J. L. (1953). *Stochastic processes.* New York, NY: John Wiley & Sons.

Ebner-Priemer, U. W., Houben, M., Santangelo, P., Kleindienst, N., Turelinckx, F., Oravecz, Z.,…Bohus, M. (2015). Unraveling affective dysregulation in borderline personality disorder: A theoretical model and empirical evidence. *Journal of Abnormal Psychology, 124,* 186–198.

Edwards, W. (1998). Tools for and experiences with Bayesian normative modeling. American Psychologist, 53, 416–428.

Evans, M., Hastings, N., & Peacock, B. (2000). *Statistical distributions* (3rd ed.). New York, NY: Wiley & Sons.

Falk, N. H., Norris, K., & Quinn, M. G. (2014). The factors predicting stress, anxiety and depression in the parents of children with autism. *Journal of Autism and Developmental Disorders, 44*(12), 3185–3203.

Farrell, S., & Lewandowsky, S. (2010). Computational models as aids to better reasoning in psychology. *Current Directions in Psychological Science, 19,* 329–335.

Felt, J. M., Depaoli, S., & Tiemensma, J. (2017). Latent growth curve models for biomarkers of the stress response. *Frontiers in Neuroscience, 11,* 315.

Flanagan, O. (1991). *Science of the mind* (2nd ed.). Cambridge, MA: MIT Press.

Fukano, T., & Gunji, Y. P. (2012). Mathematical models of panic disorder. *Nonlinear Dynamics, Psychology and Life Sciences, 16,* 457–470.

Gardner, R. C., & Neufeld, R. W. J. (in submission). Beware of the regression coefficient with which you are not intimately familiar.

George, L., & Neufeld, R. W. J. (1985). Cognition and symptomatology in schizophrenia. *Schizophrenia Bulletin, 11,* 264–285.

Gleick, J. (1987). *Chaos.* New York, NY: Viking.

Goldstein, M. J. (1987). Psychosocial issues. *Schizophrenia Bulletin, 13,* 157–171.

Gottman, J. M., Murray, J. D., Swanson, C. C., Tyson, R., & Swanson, K. R. (2002). *The mathematics of marriage: Dynamic nonlinear models.* Cambridge, MA: The MIT Press.

Green, M. F., Horan, W. P., & Sugar, C. A. (2013). Has the generalized deficit become the generalized criticism? *Schizophrenia Bulletin, 39,* 257–262.

Gzyl, H., & Osuna, E. E. (2013). A further extension of Osuna's model for psychological stress. *Journal of Contemporary Mathematical Sciences, 8,* 801–814.

Hankin, B. L. (2008). Cognitive vulnerability–stress model of depression during adolescence: Investigating depressive symptom specificity in a multi-wave prospective study. *Journal of Abnormal Child Psychology, 36*(7), 999–1014.

Harris, C. (Ed.) (1963). *Problems in measuring change.* Madison: University of Wisconsin Press.

Hartlage, S., Alloy, L. B., Vázquez, C., & Dykman, B. (1993). Automatic and effortful processing in depression. *Psychological Bulletin, 113*(2), 247–278.

Holmes, T. H., & Rahe, R. H. (1967). The social readjustment rating scale. *Journal of Psychosomatic Research, 11,* 213–218.

Kerns, J. G., & Berenbaum, H. (2003). The relationship between formal thought disorder and executive functioning component processes. *Journal of Abnormal Psychology, 112,* 339–352.

Kirk, R. E. (1982). *Experimental design: Procedures for the behavioral sciences.* Belmont, CA: Brooks Cole.

Khodadadi, A., & Townsend, J. T. (2015). On mimicry among sequential sampling models. *Journal of Mathematical Psychology, 68–69,* 37–48.

Kocas, C. (2015). An extension of Osuna's model to observable queues. *Journal of Mathematical Psychology, 66,* 53–58.

Lazarus, R. S. (1999). *Stress and emotion: A new synthesis.* New York, NY: Springer.

Lazarus, R. S., & Folkman, S. (1984). *Stress, appraisal and coping.* New York, NY: Springer.

Lazarus R. S., & Launier, R. (1978). Stress-related transactions between person and environment. In L. A. Pervin & M. Lewis (Eds.), *Perspectives in interactional psychology* (pp. 287–327). New York, NY: Plenum.

Lees, M., & Neufeld, R. W. J. (1994). Matching the limits of clinical inference to the limits of quantitative methods: A formal appeal to practice what we consistently preach. *Canadian Psychology, 35,* 268–282.

Lees, M. C., & Neufeld, R. W. J. (1999). Decision-theoretic aspects of stress arousal and coping propensity. *Journal of Personality and Social Psychology, 77,* 185–208.

Levy, L. R., Yao, W., McGuire, G., Vollick, D. N., Jetté, J., Shanahan, M. J., Hay, J., & Neufeld, R. W. J. (2012). Nonlinear bifurcations of psychological stress negotiation: New properties of a formal dynamic model. *Nonlinear Dynamics, Psychology and Life Sciences, 16,* 429–456.

Link, S. W., & Heath, R. A. (1975). A sequential theory of psychological discrimination. *Psychometrika, 40,* 77–105.

Lodewyckx, T., Turelinckx, F., Kuppens, F., Allen, N., & Sheeber, L. (2011). A hierarchical state space approach to affective dynamics. *Journal of Mathematical Psychology, 55,* 68–83.

Maccallum, R. C., & Austin, J. T. (2000). Applications of structural equation modeling in psychological research. *Annual Review Psychology, 51,* 201–226.

Maher, B. (1966). *Principles of psychopathology: An experimental approach.* New York, NY: McGraw Hill.

Maher, B. (1988). Delusions as the product of normal cognitions. In T. F. Oltmanns & B. A. Maher (Eds.), *Delusional beliefs* (pp. 333–336). New York, NY: John Wiley & Sons.

Marr, D. (1982). *Vision*. San Francisco, CA: Freeman.

Matzke, D., Hughes, M., Badcock, J. C., Michie, P., & Heathcote, A. (2017). Failures of cognitive control or attention? The case of stop-signal deficits in schizophrenia. *Attention, Perception and Psychophysics, 79*, 1078–1086.

McCallum, R., & Ashby, F. G. (1986). Relationships between linear systems theory and covariance structure modeling. *Journal of Mathematical Psychology, 30*, 1–27.

Meehl, P. E. (1978). Theoretical risks and tabular asterisks: Sir Karl, Sir Ronald, and the slow progress of soft psychology. *Journal of Consulting and Clinical Psychology, 46*(4), 806–843.

Monroe, S. M. & Harkness, K. L. (2005). Life stress, the "Kindling" hypothesis, and the recurrence of depression: Considerations from a life stress perspective. *Psychological Review, 112*, 417–445.

Monroe, S. M., Harkness, K., Simons, A. D., & Thase, M. E. (2001). Life stress and the symptoms of major depression. *The Journal of Nervous and Mental Disease, 189*(3), 168–175.

Morrison, M. S., Neufeld, R. W. J., & Lefebvre, L. A. (1988). The economy of probabilistic stress: Interplay of controlling activity and threat reduction. *British Journal of Mathematical and Statistical Psychology, 41*, 155–177.

Mothersill, K. J., & Neufeld, R. W. J. (1985). Probability learning and coping in dysphoria and obsessive-compulsive tendencies. *Journal of Research in Personality, 19*, 152–165.

Movellan, J., & McClelland, J. L. (2001). The Morton–Massaro law of information integration: Implications for models of perception. *Psychological Review, 108*, 113–148.

Myung, I. J., Forster, M. R., & Browne, M. (Eds.). (2000). Model selection. [Special issue]. *Journal of Mathematical Psychology, 44*(1), 1–232.

Neufeld, R. W. J. (1982). On decisional processes instigated by threat: Some possible implications for stress-related deviance. In R. W. J. Neufeld (Ed.), *Psychological stress and psychopathology* (pp. 240–270). New York, NY: McGraw-Hill.

Neufeld, R. W. J. (1987). Mathematical note on propensity to engage in counter-stress activity. *Perceptual and Motor Skills, 65*, 493–494.

Neufeld, R. W. J. (1989). Methodological aspects of laboratory studies of stress. In R. W. J. Neufeld (Ed.), *Advances in the investigation of psychological stress* (pp. 71–132). New York, NY: John Wiley & Sons.

Neufeld, R. W. J. (1990). Coping with stress, coping without stress, and stress with coping: On inter-construct redundancies. *Stress Medicine, 6*, 117–125.

Neufeld, R. W. J. (1996). *Stochastic models of information processing under stress. Research Bulletin No. 734*, London, ON: Department of Psychology, University of Western Ontario.

Neufeld, R. W. J. (1998). Introduction to special section on process models in psychological assessment. *Psychological Assessment, 10*, 307–315.

Neufeld, R. W. J. (1999). Dynamic differentials of stress and coping. *Psychological Review, 106*, 385–397.

Neufeld, R. W. J. (2007a). Composition and uses of formal clinical cognitive science In B. Shuart, W. Spaulding & J. Poland (Eds.), *Modeling complex systems: Nebraska Symposium on Motivation* (Vol. 52, pp. 1–83). Lincoln: University of Nebraska Press.

Neufeld, R. W. J. (2007b). *Advances in clinical cognitive science: Formal modeling and assessment of processes and symptoms.* Washington, DC: American Psychological Association.

Neufeld, R. W. J. (2007c). On the centrality and significance of encoding deficit in schizophrenia. *Schizophrenia Bulletin, 33*, 982–993.

Neufeld, R. W. J. (2015). Mathematical modeling applications in clinical psychology. In J. R. Busemeyer, J. T. Townsend, Z. Wang, & A. Eidels (Eds.), *Oxford handbook of computational and mathematical psychology* (pp. 341–368). Oxford, UK: Oxford University Press.

Neufeld, R. W. J. (2016). Modeling stress effects on coping-related cognition. In J. Houpt & L. Blaha (Eds.), *Mathematical modeling of perception and cognition: Essays in honor of James T. Townsend* (pp. 172–195). New York, NY: Taylor & Francis.

Neufeld, R. W. J., Boksman, K., Vollick, D., George, L., & Carter, J. (2010). Stochastic dynamics of stimulus encoding in schizophrenia: Theory, testing, and application. *Journal of Mathematical Psychology, 54*, 90–108.

Neufeld, R. W. J., & Broga, M. I. (1981). Evaluation of information-sequential aspects of schizophrenic performance, II: Methodological considerations. *Journal of Nervous and Mental Disease, 169*, 569–579.

Neufeld, R. W. J., Carter, J. R., Boksman, K., Jetté, J., & Vollick, D. (2002). Application of stochastic modelling to group and individual differences in cognitive functioning. *Psychological Assessment, 14*, 279–298.

Neufeld, R. W. J., & Gardner, R. C. (1990). Data aggregation in evaluating psychological constructs: Multivariate and logical-deductive considerations. *Journal of Mathematical Psychology, 34*, 276–296.

Neufeld, R. W. J., & Herzog, H. (1983). Acquisition of probabilities in anticipatory appraisals of stress. *Personality and Individual Differences, 4*, 1–7.

Neufeld, R. W. J., & McCarty, T. (1994). A formal analysis of stressor and stress-proneness effects on basic information processing. *British Journal of Mathematical and Statistical Psychology, 47*, 193–226.

Neufeld, R. W. J., & Nicholson, I. R. (1992). *Differential and other equations essential to a servocybernetic [systems] approach to stress-schizophrenia relations*. Research Bulletin #698, Department of Psychology, University of Western Ontario.

Neufeld, R. W. J., & Townsend, J. T., eds. (2010). Special issue: Contributions of mathematical psychology to clinical science and assessment. *Journal of Mathematical Psychology, 54*(1), 2–214.

Neufeld, R. W. J., Townsend, J. T., & Jetté, J. (2007). Quantitative response time technology for measuring cognitive-processing capacity in clinical studies. In R. W. J. Neufeld (Ed.), *Advances in clinical cognitive science: Formal modeling and assessment of processes and symptoms* (pp. 207–238). Washington, DC: American Psychological Association.

Neufeld, R. W. J., Vollick, D., Carter, J. R., Boksman, K., Levy, L., George, L., & Jetté, J. (2007). A mathematical process account of group and individual differences in memory-search facilitative stimulus encoding, with application to schizophrenia. In R. W. J. Neufeld (Ed.), *Advances in clinical cognitive science: Formal modeling and assessment of processes and symptoms* (pp. 147–177). Washington, DC: American Psychological Association

Neufeld, R. W. J., & Williamson, P. (1996). Neuropsychological correlates of positive symptoms: Delusions and hallucinations. In C. Pantelis, H. E. Nelson, & T. R. E. Barnes (Eds.), *Schizophrenia: A neuropsychological perspective* (pp. 205–235). London, UK: John Wiley & Sons.

Nicholson, I. R., & Neufeld, R. W. J. (1992). A dynamic vulnerability perspective on stress and schizophrenia. *American Journal of Orthopsychiatry, 62*, 117–130.

Norman, R. M., & Malla, A. K. (1994). A prospective study of daily stressors and symptomatology in schizophrenic patients. *Social Psychiatry and Epidemiology, 29*, 244–249.

Novotney, A. (2009). Science on a shoestring. *Monitor on Psychology, 40*(1), 42–44.

Oravecz, Z., Tuerlinckx, F., & Vandekerckhove, J. (2011). A hierarchical latent stochastic differential equation model for affective dynamics. *Psychological Methods, 16*, 468–490.

Osuna, E. E. (1985). The psychological cost of waiting. *Journal of Mathematical Psychology, 29*, 82–105.

Pitt, M. A., Kim, W., Navarro, J., & Myung, J. I. (2006). Global model analysis by parameter space partitioning. *Psychololgical Review, 113*, 57–83.

Post, R. M. (1992). Transduction of psychosocial stress into the neurobiology of recurrent affective disorder. *American Journal of Psychiatry, 149*, 999–1010.

Qin, H., van Marle, H. J. F., Luo, J., & Fernandez, G. (2009). Acute psychological stress reduces working memory-related activity in the dorsolateral prefrontal cortex. *Biological Psychiatry, 66*, 25–32.

Ratcliff, R. (1978). A theory of memory retrieval. *Psychological Review, 85*, 59–108.

Riefer, D.M., Knapp, B. R., Batchelder, W. H., Bamber, D., & Manifold, V. (2002). Cognitive psychometrics: Assessing storage and retrieval deficits in special populations with multinomial processing tree models. *Psychological Assessment, 14*, 184–201.

Rnic, K., Dozois, D. J. A., Machado, D. A., & Neufeld (in preparation). Stress generation: A comprehensive meta-analytic review and reconceptualization.

Rodgers, J. L. (2010) The epistemology of mathematical and statistical modeling: A quiet methodological revolution. *American Psychologist, 65*(1), 1–12.

Roughgarden, J. (1979). *Theory of population genetics and evolutionary ecology: An introduction.* New York, NY: MacMillan.

Seiffge-Krenke, I., Aunola, K., & Nurmi, J.-E. (2009). Changes in stress perception and coping during adolescence: The role of situational and personal factors. *Child Development, 80*(1), 259–279.

Shanahan, M. J., & Neufeld, R. W. J. (2010). Coping with stress through decisional control: Quantification of negotiating the environment. *British Journal of Mathematical and Statistical Psychology, 63*, 575–601.

Shanahan, M. J., Townsend, J. T., & Neufeld, R. W. J. (2015). Mathematical models in clinical psychology. In R. Cautin & S. Lilienfield (Eds.), *Encyclopedia of clinical psychology* (1st ed., 594–603). London, UK: John Wiley & Sons.

Shapero, B. G., Hankin, B. L., & Barrocas, A. L. (2013). Stress generation and exposure in a multi-wave study of adolescents: Transactional processes and sex differences. *Journal of Social and Clinical Psychology, 32*(9), 989–1012.

Spring, B. (1981). Stress and schizophrenia: Some definition issues. *Schizophrenia Bulletin, 112*, 24–33.

Spring, B., & Coons, H. (1982). Stress as a precursor of schizophrenia. In R. W. J. Neufeld (Ed.), *Psychological stress and psychopathology* (pp. 13–54). New York, NY: McGraw-Hill.

Staddon, J. E. R. (1984). Social learning theory and the dynamics of interaction. *Psychological Review, 91*, 502–507.

Suck, R., & Holling, H. (1997). Stress caused by waiting: A theoretical evaluation of a mathematical model. *Journal of Mathematical Psychology, 41*, 280–286.

Taylor, R., Neufeld, R. W. J., Schaefer, B., Densmore, M., Osuch, E. A., Rajakumar, N., Williamson, P. C., & Théberge, J. (2015). Functional magnetic resonance spectroscopy of glutamate and glutamine in schizophrenia and major depressive disorder—Anterior cingulate activity during a color-word Stroop task. *Nature Partner Journals: Schizophrenia, 15028*, 1–8.

Taylor, R., Théberge, J., Williamson, P., Densmore, M. & Neufeld, R. W. J. (2016). ACC neuro-over-connectivity is associated with mathematically modeled additional encoding operations of Schizophrenia Stroop-Task performance. *Frontiers in Quantitative Psychology and Measurement.* doi:10.3389/fpsyg.2016.01295.

Taylor, R., Theberge, J., Williamson, P., Densmore, M., & Neufeld, R. W. J. (2017). Systems-factorial technology-disclosed stochastic dynamics of Stroop processing in the cognitive neuroscience of schizophrenia. In M. Fific, N. Altieri, & D. Little (Eds.), *Systems factorial technology: A theory-driven methodology for the identification of perceptual and cognitive mechanisms* (pp. 351–380). New York, NY: Taylor & Francis.

Thompson, S. (1981). Will it hurt less if I can control it? A complex answer to a simple question. *Psychological Bulletin, 90*, 89–101.

Townsend, J. T. (1984). Uncovering mental processes with factorial experiments. *Journal of Mathematical Psychology, 28*, 363–400.

Townsend, J. T., & Ashby, F. G. (1983). *Stochastic modelling of elementary psychological processes.* Cambridge, UK: Cambridge University Press.

Townsend, J. T., & Neufeld, R. W. J. (2004). Mathematical theory-driven methodology and experimentation in the emerging quantitative clinical cognitive science: Toward general laws of individual differences. Paper presented at the Association for Psychological Science–sponsored symposium on Translation Psychological Science in Honor of Richard M. McFall, Chicago, IL, May 2004.

Townsend, J. T., & Nozawa, G. (1997). Serial exhaustive models can violate the Race Model Inequality: Implications for architecture and capacity. *Psychological Review, 104*, 595–602.

Van Montfort, K., & Bijleveld, C. (2004). Dynamic analysis of multivariate panel data with non-linear transformations. *Journal of Mathematical Psychology, 48*, 322–333.

Van Zandt, T. (2000). How to fit a response time distribution. *Psychonomic Bulletin and Review, 7*, 424–465.

Wagenmakers, E.-J., van der Maas, H. L. J., & Farrell, S. (2012). Abstract concepts require concrete models: Why cognitive scientists have not yet embraced nonlinearly-coupled, dynamical, self-organized critical, synergistic, scale-free, exquisitely context-sensitive, interaction-dominant, multifractal, interdependent brain-body-niche systems. *TopiCS, 4*, 87–93.

Wagenmakers, E. J., & Waldorp, L. (2006). Special issue on model selection. *Journal of Mathematical Psychology, 50*(2), 99–213.

Yates, A., (1966). Psychological deficit. *Annual Review of Psychology, 17*, 111–144.

Stress in Depression

Suzanne Vrshek-Schallhorn, Maria Ditcheva, *and* Gail Corneau

Abstract

That life stress precipitates depression is one of the most replicated findings in psychiatric research, but prior to Brown and Harris's seminal contributions, insufficiently rigorous methods led to underestimates of the effects of stress and threatened the field. This chapter provides a methodological and historical overview, followed by a review of evidence that recent stress predicts depression across the life span. It also examines demographic vulnerability factors and research on early adversity and depression, closing with future directions. Two themes manifest throughout. First, stress assessment that uses investigator-rated severity, accounts for severity, establishes temporal precedence, and isolates the few months prior to depression onset remains critical to progress. Second, identifying the most potent forms of stress for depression is a key question that will facilitate both preventive/intervention efforts and more powerful tests in mechanistic research. Although evidence points to interpersonal forms of stress, few studies provide the necessary direct tests.

Keywords: life stress, early adversity, stressful life events, chronic stress, major difficulties, adults, adolescents, children, depression

Few findings in psychiatric research are as consistent and well documented as the conclusion that validly assessed life stress causes unipolar major depressive disorder. And yet, this seemingly well-explored topic persists in captivating researchers, mental health practitioners, and lay people alike. The topic's continued draw likely reflects two truths. First, depression is a paramount public health concern—among the most common and costly of illnesses (Ferrari et al., 2013; Greenberg et al., 2003). Thus, understanding the mechanisms by which it emerges and endures is very likely to lead to interventions that reduce both suffering and economic cost to society. Second, evidence from behavioral genetic studies indicates that environmental factors unique to the individual, perhaps chiefly life stress, contribute a majority of the variance in risk for depression (a meta-analytic point estimate of 63%; Sullivan, Neale, & Kendler, 2000). Thus, efforts to understand the stress-depression link are likely to be valuable to society.

What is critical to appreciate about the contemporary understanding of the robust, causal association between life stress and depression is that, for a time, this conclusion was very much in doubt—and the reasons for the reversal of this opinion over time are relevant to current research. Four critical methodological factors led to stronger, more persuasive data: using contextual investigator-rated assessment interviews, ascertaining the temporal precedence of stressors before depression onsets, accounting for stressor severity in one of several ways, and isolating a relatively brief window of time prior to disorder onsets. We will argue that for stress and depression research to advance in an age of brief measures and "big data," it will not only be necessary to continue to adhere to those four methodological advances but also to hone in on which forms of stress are most potent with greater methodological care.

In this chapter, we examine evidence for the relationship between stress and depression. Following key definitions of stress, we first provide a brief introduction to methodological issues critical to evaluating the stress and depression literature, which we elaborate on as relevant throughout the chapter. We then divide our review by the timing of stress—examining recent stress for the majority of the chapter, followed by early life adversity in a shorter section. Within our review of recent stress, following a historical overview, we structure our review by developmental period in reverse chronological order from adulthood to adolescence to childhood, with more discussion devoted to findings in adults and about stressful life events, reflecting the relative balance of the literature. Throughout the chapter, we consider what forms of stress are most potent and the methodological reasons that existing work struggles to definitively answer this question. We conclude the discussion of recent stress by highlighting demographic differences in stress exposure and sensitivity. Although models of the action of stress on depression emphasize the role of pre-existing risk factors or diatheses, these are reviewed in other chapters on cognitive (see Hankin & Schweizer, this volume), personality (see Olino, Wojcieszak, & Mennies, this volume), and genetic (see Uher, this volume) vulnerabilities. In addition to highlighting future directions in review subsections throughout the chapter, we close with overarching future directions and emphasize the importance of delineating the most potent forms of stress in the onset of depression.

Key Definitions

Researchers have focused primarily on three broad forms of stress in the pathway to depression—stressful life events, chronic stress, and early adversity (for examples of each, refer to Table 5.1). Stressful life events refer to acute occurrences that confer relatively long-term (> 1 week) negative impact or threat on any aspect of the individual's life; we describe various dimensions of events later. Although chronic stress, also known as chronic difficulties, has been operationalized in different ways, it consistently captures more long-standing challenges than do acute events. By contrast, early adversity—which often encompasses childhood and adolescent adversity—typically represents an amalgam of events and chronic stress rather than distinguishing between them. It is instead defined by the early developmental stage (i.e., prior to adulthood) in which it occurred. Depending on the measure used in assessment, early adversity may capture maltreatment by a caregiver as well as adversity that is out of the control of the caregiver (e.g., death of a parent).

Methodological Considerations in Life Stress and Depression Research

Several methodological points inform our approach in this chapter and merit brief discussion prior to the literature review. First, here we use the term "stress" to refer to objective, negative life circumstances (such as the forms defined earlier), based on a conceptualization of stress as the environmental pressure exerted on an individual (e.g., Dohrenwend & Dohrenwend, 1969). This conceptualization contrasts with one in which stress captures the individual's physiological or emotional *response* to that environmental pressure or his or her *perception* of stress (referred to as "biologic stress;" e.g., Selye, 2013). This distinction is critical for reasons we describe later in the historical overview of stressful event methodology. Second, our emphasis on objective stress necessitates a focus on forms of assessment that ensure objective stress, and not perceptions or responses to stress, are captured. Thus, we have primarily cited evidence utilizing objective interview-based measures in which investigators make judgments based on the full context of events—not self-report questionnaires or checklists, due to known validity problems (e.g., Harkness & Monroe, 2016; McQuaid et al., 1992). In cases where we felt it was necessary to mention questionnaire-based studies, we have noted the methodological approach for readers.

Third, although there is a well-characterized *bidirectional* relationship between objective stress and depression (see Hammen, this volume), here we focus on evidence that stress causally precipitates depression. The critical methodological ingredient for ensuring potential causality is establishing *temporal precedence* of stress before depression. Temporal precedence refers to stressful circumstances occurring prior to depression onset (e.g., job termination leading to depression onset), and not vice versa (e.g., difficulty getting out of bed when depressed, causing tardiness to work, leading to job termination). Because depression is known to generate stress for individuals, to prevent overestimating the causal impact of stress on depression, it is critical to use only instances in which the stressor occurred first. The need for temporal precedence requires that studies examine stress and depressive episodes longitudinally, rather than examining cross-sectional relationships between recent stress and current depression. Even longitudinal research on stress,

Table 5.1. Examples of Types of Life Stress

Form of Stress	Example(s)
Major event	Although severity is assigned by rating teams based on the full context of events, the sudden, unexpected death of a very close loved one such as a partner, best friend, or child would typically be rated as a major event.
Minor event	Although severity depends upon the full context of the event, an argument among a group of friends that lasts for 5 days but lacks long-term impacts (> 1 week) to the friend group and other aggravating features would often be rated as a minor event.
Interpersonal event	Loss of a loved one; romantic breakup; argument with friend, partner, or family member; separation from a close other.
Noninterpersonal event	Failing a course, job loss, acute illness or injury to oneself, acute financial problems
Dependent event	Argument with a friend, partner, or family member, failing a course, a car accident where one is at fault
Independent event	Being the victim of a crime, death of a loved one, being diagnosed with an illness
Interpersonal chronic stress or major difficulty	Examples vary across assessment tools, but an elevation in LSI chronic stress consistent with a LEDS major difficulty would be frequent conflict and lack of emotional support for over 2 years in a romantic relationship
Noninterpersonal chronic stress or difficulty	Examples vary across assessment tools, but an elevation in LSI chronic stress consistent with an LEDS major difficulty would be employment for 2 years or more
Early adversity, including maltreatment	For example, any of the following occurring to an individual below the age of 18; often divided into childhood adversity and adolescent adversity: • Separation or loss: a parent leaving the family or being imprisoned • Physical neglect: inappropriate, insufficient levels of supervision for the developmental stage (being left alone overnight at age 5) • Emotional abuse: name-calling, blaming the minor for things for which he or she is not responsible; • Sexual abuse: molestation, incest, being shown pornographic materials • Physical abuse: hitting, physical punishments, being locked out of the home in the cold as punishment

Note: Event types are not mutually exclusive; that is, an event can be major, interpersonal, and dependent, for example. The examples provided are intended to be illustrative rather than comprehensive. LSI = Life Stress Interview (Hammen et al., 1987); LEDS = Life Events and Difficulties Schedule (Bifulco et al., 1989).

however, is not usually truly prospective (i.e., assessing stress at one timepoint and depression at another). In most cases, recent stress and depression are retrospectively assessed simultaneously, and careful dating is used to establish temporal precedence. Cross-sectional research that cannot establish temporal precedence is less authoritative than longitudinal research additionally because, in community samples, this approach is likely to overlook episodes triggered by stress in the recent past and thereby underestimate the effects of stress. We have therefore de-emphasized work that relies on cross-sectional analyses and have pointed to this methods choice when we did choose to cite such work.

Recent Stress Impacts Depression in Adults
Historical Overview
A large body of research has established that recent stress precipitates depression during adulthood; we

begin by providing some historical context, which is vital for understanding how life stress research should proceed.

HOLMES AND RAHE'S PROBLEMATIC QUESTIONNAIRE MEASURES
Some of the first and most widely cited systematic evidence to link life experiences to the onset of several types of physical illness (Rahe, Meyer, Smith, Kjaer, & Holmes, 1964) stimulated later work on stress and depression and used the Schedule of Recent Events (SRE; Hawkins, Davies, & Holmes, 1957). As reviewed by Rahe (1978), the SRE was developed in the 1950s and used a checklist format to inquire whether and when 42 events had occurred within the past 10 years. It was later expanded to add 13 experiences and was renamed as the Recent Life Changes Questionnaire (Rahe, 1975). Similar work attempting to account not only for

occurrence of events but also their relative severity relied on the Social Readjustment Rating Scale (SRRS), which used severity "weights" derived from studies using the Social Readjustment Rating Questionnaire (SRRQ; Holmes & Rahe, 1967). To develop the SRRS, Holmes and Rahe selected healthy participants (to prevent bias introduced by ill individuals) and surveyed them using the SRRQ about how intense and lengthy they felt that adjustment to 43 experiences would be for the average person—ignoring the desirability of each experience. These resulted in average weights assigned to each type of experience (e.g., death of a spouse = 100, marriage = 50, beginning or ending school = 26, vacation = 13). In the SRRS, these average weights were multiplied by event frequency in the past year to derive a total score. The extension of these questionnaire-based approaches from physical illnesses to mood disturbances followed in epidemiological samples that relied on cross-sectional self-reports and utilized correlational analyses. For example, Rahe (1974) applied this approach in two samples of thousands of US and Norwegian sailors who provided questionnaire reports of depression symptoms and their changes in life circumstances, resulting in correlations of $r = .22$ and $.36$, respectively (also see Myers, Lindenthal, & Pepper, 1971; Rahe, 1979).

The many methodological flaws of this approach and its resulting small effect sizes, however, ultimately led to doubt about the effects of events on illness. For example, in a review of studies relying on Holmes and Rahe's SRE, Tausig (1982, p. 52) later concluded that "attempts to observe stress have generally yielded low to modest estimates of the contribution of stressful events to the appearance of some order of disturbance," including depression. Although these problems led one reviewer to conclude that the checklist approach had been abandoned (Mazure, 1998), it has since resurged in at least one research area seeking rapid, inexpensive measures of stress (for a discussion, see Monroe & Reid, 2008).

BROWN AND HARRIS INTRODUCE
CONTEXTUAL THREAT METHODS

Prompted by this emerging pessimistic view of the effect of events and by the methodological flaws inherent in checklist and average-weight assessment approaches, Brown and Harris and colleagues published seminal contributions that have fundamentally shaped the conceptualization and measurement of life stress in psychopathology. In an often overlooked commentary, Brown, Sklair, Harris, and

Birley (1973) first outlined three critical and timeless sources of potential bias in the assessment of life events that point to the importance of interviewer ratings of stressor context and to the sheer implausibility of stressor checklist validity. First, they point to "effort after meaning," the attempt to provide a post hoc explanation for an undesired outcome, citing evidence that mothers of babies with certain serious birth defects report more negative events during pregnancy, whereas later work showed that chromosomal abnormalities were to blame. Second, they note that individuals experiencing a depression onset may experience events as more severe than they ordinarily would—confounding the measure of stress exposure with vulnerability, perceived stress, and stress *response*. The implication of these first two potential sources of bias is that the investigator should determine whether to include a reported event and what severity rating to assign it.

Third, they identified that it was critical to develop conventions for what qualified as an event (a minimum threshold) across interviewers to apply common standards. To address these issues, the authors introduced the important methodological advancement of an investigator-rated severity scale. The interviewer (though in these same researchers' later approaches, blind raters) judged the level of "threat or difficulty implied by the event once the more immediate effects were over...about one week after its occurrence" (G. Brown et al., 1973, p. 77) for a typical person in all the same circumstances, taking no account of the participant's report of severity, from 1 to 4 (none, little, moderate, or marked).

Soon after, Brown and Harris (1978) debuted their watershed *Social Origins of Depression* text describing the Camberwell studies of life stress and depression in working-class British women ages 18–65, which formed the basis for the Life Events and Difficulties Schedule (LEDS; Bifulco et al., 1989). Participants for the primary analyses were 114 psychiatric inpatients and outpatients (73 and 41, respectively) with a primary depression diagnosis and no comorbid alcohol dependence or psychotic disorder, a comparison group of 382 women from the same community without psychiatric diagnoses, plus 37 community women discovered to have had past-year depressive episode onsets on interview, but who had not sought treatment. In this study, unlike their previous one, interviewers collected detailed information about each event's context from the participant and presented this information to a rating team blind to the participant's diagnosis and emotional response to the event.

The primary conclusions of this seminal study were that, from an array of 28 event characteristics examined, *long-term* contextual threat (i.e., threat 1 week after the event occurred) appeared most critical in precipitating an episode of depression. "Severe" events (those with moderate to marked long-term contextual threat level—the top 2 points of the 4-point scale—which we also refer to as "major events" throughout) were present among 61% of patients and 68% of women with untreated onsets, versus 20% of controls in the 38 weeks prior to a depression onset among patients compared to the same period prior to interview among controls. Similarly, Brown and Harris investigated the relative frequency of all "difficulties" (more long-standing challenges lasting at least 4 weeks and not arising due to an event), blindly rated on a 6-point severity scale. They reported that only those difficulties of 2 years or longer in duration, rated in the highest 3 points of the scale, and not involving health problems—which they then coined *major difficulties*—were linked with depression. Specifically, 47% of patients and 49% of women with untreated onsets, versus 17% of controls, experienced at least one major difficulty in the 38 weeks prior to illness onset or interview.

ADDITIONAL EARLY FINDINGS FOR RECENT STRESS

These findings implicating severe events and major difficulties echoed Brown and Harris's earlier work predicting "psychiatric disturbances" broadly—much of which was depression—in 114 adult women patients seeking treatment and 220 randomly selected community women (G. Brown, Bhrolchain, & Harris, 1975). Findings were also consistent with evidence of their contemporaries who used similar interview-based measures, evaluated severity, and established temporal precedence. For example, severe recent events were more common prior to depression onset than in a comparable period of time in controls (Paykel, 1976) and severe recent events predicted postpartum depression among women assessed 6 weeks after delivery (Paykel, Emms, Fletcher, & Rassaby, 1980). Their 1978 findings were also mostly consistent with work that emerged soon after their report, which addressed any concern about the treatment-seeking nature of the original sample. Brown and Harris (1989) summarized the findings of 10 samples of women from the general population studied using the LEDS published between 1978 and 1986. This revealed that 84% of women (218 of 261) with a major depressive episode

onset experienced at least one severe event or major difficulty prior to onset (ranging from 3 months to 1 year) compared to only 32% of nondepressed control women (558 of 1,745) who experienced either form of stress in a comparable timeframe (G. Brown & Harris, 1989). The percentage of affected individuals experiencing a severe event ranged from 42% to 93% (68% in aggregate), while the percentage experiencing a major difficulty ranged from 15% to 55% (38% in aggregate), leading Brown and Harris to conclude that the results for chronic stress were "somewhat less consistent than those for events" (p. 58).

Thus, the work of Brown and Harris and their like-minded contemporaries provided evidence for the value of contextual investigator-rated assessment of life stress and set the standard for four subsequent decades of stress and depression research, which we now review. In the review of recent stress in adults, we first discuss stressful life events, second chronic stress, and last, demographic predictors of stress exposure and sensitivity.

Stressful Life Events

To probe the relationship between stressful life events and depression, we examine evidence for (1) the role of event severity, (2) whether multiple events increase risk, (3) duration of event potency, (4) which event types appear to be the most important, and (5) the extent to which events are causally related to depression.

SEVERITY OF EVENTS

One of the most consistent findings within event and depression research is that major severity events significantly increase risk for depression onsets, while lesser severity minor events generally do not (see Table 5.1 for event examples). Evidence for this emerged from some of the earliest interview-based studies (G. Brown & Harris, 1978; Paykel et al., 1980; Shrout et al., 1989; Surtees et al., 1986) as well as in the years that followed (e.g., Kendler, Karkowski, & Prescott, 1998; Vrshek-Schallhorn et al., 2015). However, the early literature focused so rapidly on severe events that, in many cases, minor event effect sizes are not included (e.g., Costello, 1982), and others have summed the severity scores of all events (Hammen, Kim, Eberhart, & Brennan, 2009). Despite the implication that severity is dichotomous, when examined in one very large study (albeit one in which interviewers and not blind raters assigned severity), the best-fitting models indicated a linear dimensional effect of severity (Kendler et al., 1998).

When minor events uncharacteristically do appear to precipitate depression, stress sensitization by prior depression may have increased the person's vulnerability (for a more detailed review, see Stroud, this volume), based on Post's (1992) "kindling" hypothesis that recurrences of depression occur in response to progressively less severe events. In one 5-year longitudinal study of older adolescent women, interview-assessed minor events significantly grew in their impact (i.e., risk of depression onset given the presence of a recent event) for recurrences compared to first onsets, whereas major events did not significantly change in impact between first onsets versus recurrences, remaining a significant predictor of both (Stroud, Davila, Hammen, & Vrshek-Schallhorn, 2011). This finding expanded on other work showing associations of minor events with recurrences of depression (Lenze, Cyranowski, Thompson, Anderson, & Frank, 2008; Monroe, Roberts, Kupfer, & Frank, 1996; Monroe et al., 2006; Ormel, Oldehinkel, & Brilman, 2001; Rudolph & Flynn, 2007).

NUMBER OF EVENTS

Next, a number of studies—but not all—support that multiple events increase risk for depression onset beyond the effect of a single event. In an analysis combining all severities of interview-assessed events, an increasing number of events robustly increased risk for depression onset, with risk following an exponential growth pattern (Kendler et al., 1998). Importantly, however, when investigators have not accounted for events' severity as in this case, an alternative explanation is that as the number of events increased, so did the probability of experiencing one major event (which then increased the likelihood for depression). Yet two other studies did account for event severity and indicate that multiple events increase risk regardless of severity. First, statistical models examining how the impact of interview-assessed events declines as time passes (i.e., decay models) better predicted depression onset when *all* events experienced were included in an additive fashion, rather than when models were simplified to represent the presence of at least one severe event (Surtees, 1989). This suggested that multiple events behaved in a cumulative and dimensional fashion to raise risk, such that major events increased risk more and for longer duration than did minor ones, which had a very short-lived impact. Second, among a small sample (*N* = 52) of people with highly recurrent depression (median of 4 lifetime episodes) whose most recent episode was preceded by at least one

severe interview-assessed event in the prior 6 months, those who experienced at least one additional event—whether severe or minor—had an episode onset sooner following the severe event than those who did not (Frank et al., 1996). Contrasting other evidence, in the Camberwell Studies, experiencing multiple severe events was only associated with increased risk for depression when the severe events were *unrelated* to each other—and even then, the increase in risk due to having a second or third event was relatively small (G. Brown & Harris, 1978). Thus, despite some inconsistency in these findings, the balance of evidence appears to indicate that multiple events increase risk for depression onset.

DURATION OF STRESSOR IMPACT

Several types of evidence suggest that the effects of stressful experiences for increased depression risk fade relatively quickly after stress exposure ends, and that using an appropriate timeframe in analyses is critical to maximizing effects. Several studies have used fine-grained, month-to-month approaches, but one twin study with repeated assessments used a latent variable approach in a sample of women in middle adulthood to first isolate the unique environmental contribution to depression risk, and second to tease apart the relative contribution of the past-year environment versus that prior. Of the unique environmental variance, past-year factors accounted for 70%, while experiences occurring prior to the past year accounted for only 13% and diagnostic error accounted for 17% (Kendler & Gardner, 2017). This supports a relatively larger contribution of past-year stressors than earlier life stressors, at least in this sample's age range.

Converging evidence using a more fine-grained approach also suggests that stressful life events confer significant risk for depression for a relatively brief amount of time not longer than several months. Investigations using interview methods showed that (1) events precipitated depression most often within 3 weeks and almost always within 9 weeks of the event (G. Brown & Harris, 1978), (2) events significantly predicted depression for 1 month, but not later (Kendler et al., 1995), and (3) decay models approximating the declining impact of events over time indicated events are significantly impactful for depression onset no longer than 13 weeks (Surtees & Wainwright, 1999). In one study that suggested somewhat greater heterogeneity in duration of event impact on risk, this appears to be due to combining acute events with more long-standing problems similar to Brown and

Harris's (1978) chronic difficulties (Kendler et al., 1998). In sum, most evidence indicates that stressful events exert their risk-increasing effects for depression onset within the first month and not beyond 3 months after event occurrence. Based on this evidence, most recent research on stressful events examines the past 1 to 3 months to predict episode onsets; using longer periods of time dilutes estimates of the effects of events for depression.

EVENT TYPE

Research has examined several characteristics of stress thought to contribute to potency in hopes of elucidating how stress precipitates depression; the two earliest identified event characteristics implicated were independence, which we discuss first, and loss, which we discuss second. A major methodological weakness of most of this research is that investigators most often "compare" the effects of different types of events by testing whether each, separately, is a statistically significant predictor of depression and concluding that the significant predictor is more important than the nonsignificant one. We highlight rare examples when investigators test the difference between effect sizes—a step needed to support the inference that one form of stress is more potent than another.

Event Dependence-Independence

Terminology related to independence differs somewhat across methodologies, with one capturing *illness* independence and other independence from the participant's *behavior*. This distinction was initially of interest to researchers because it was reasoned that a link between independent events and depression onsets would strengthen confidence about the causal role of stress in illness onset (G. Brown & Harris, 1978). Brown and Harris (1978) thus classified events as "independent" (chance or fateful events such as an employer closing down that could not have been evoked by illness), "possibly independent" (events such as marital separation, when it appeared that illness followed rather than preceded the event, but the event was not a chance or fateful occurrence), and "illness-related" events that clearly occurred after depressive onset. Brown and Harris (1978) excluded this latter category of events from analyses due to their lack of temporal precedence. They reasoned a link between independent events and illness would rule out the possibility that subclinical symptoms caused events and then grew into clinically significant illness manifestations (pp. 73–74). In a different life events

interview loosely inspired by the LEDS, however, Hammen categorized events as "probably independent *of the subject*, probably dependent *on the subject*, or ambiguous (possibly both dependent and independent)" (emphasis added; Hammen, Marks, Mayol, & DeMayo, 1985, p. 312). Importantly, in research that has followed using Hammen's approach, ambiguous events (including many interpersonal events such as marital separation, defined as "possibly independent" by Brown and Harris) have been classified with *dependent* events because they are thought to be at least partly caused by the individual's behavior or characteristics. This distinction later took on new meaning as investigators began to seek potent events to maximize the stress-depression effect size (Surtees et al., 1986).

It is evident from the research that followed that independent events (at least major ones) usually predict depression onset, but the case that either independent or dependent events are more potent is flawed. A strong theoretical case for either is lacking in the literature, and overall, evidence for dependence and independence has been equivocal: Studies that initially appear to implicate either independent or dependent events rarely in fact do so when examined more closely. Two initially appear to implicate independent events as more potent. First, in a community sample of 449 women including 38 depression onsets, events which were "possibly independent"—those that might *or* might not have been caused partly by the woman's behavior—had a "particularly strong" association with depression (as opposed to fully independent events), but the authors neither directly tested whether these events were more potent, nor delineated which events were dependent on the participant's behavior (Costello, 1982). Second, in a sample of 96 depressed patients and 404 nondepressed controls, although interview-assessed severe independent events discriminated patients from controls, when examined separately, it was event severity and not event independence that discriminated depressed patients from controls (Shrout et al., 1989).

Conversely, two studies initially appear to implicate dependent events as more potent. First, in a comparison of 35 women with recent onsets of depression with 485 nondepressed women, both recent event severity and event dependence alone significantly discriminated between the two groups (Surtees et al., 1986), but our confidence in these findings is reduced because of the small sample of depressed women, coupled with the possibility that dependent events may have also been more severe.

Second, in a large twin study sample, direct tests showed dependent events to be significantly more likely to precipitate depression than independent events (Kendler, Karkowski, & Prescott, 1999). However, this test was conducted for an aim other than identifying the most potent type of event, and likely for this reason, other potentially confounding event dimensions, including severity and interpersonal status (defined later), were not accounted for. Consistent with this explanation, in two samples of emerging adults, once interview-rated event severity and interpersonal status were accounted for, dependence did not further refine which stressors uniquely predicted depression onsets (Vrshek-Schallhorn et al., 2015). Taken together, the evidence reflects that event independence versus dependence is not critical for determining the likelihood of precipitating depression on average, particularly once other dimensions are accounted for.

Loss and Related Dimensions

Loss was defined broadly by Brown and Harris (1978) to include real or threatened separations from loved ones, including deaths, negative revelations about a close other (i.e., loss of one's positive conceptualization of the relationship), life-threatening illness of a close other, real or threatened material loss or disappointment, real or threatened forced change in housing, and a miscellaneous loss category including job elimination. Brown and Harris (1978) noted that in the Camberwell Studies, upward of 70% of severe events regardless of the study group (patients, community onsets, or non-depressed controls) involved some element of loss. They interpreted this to mean that loss is critical to the etiology of depression, but provided little inferential statistical support for this assertion. In this same work, they suggested that danger (severe threat without the element of loss) was linked with mixed depression and anxiety manifestations, but again based this conclusion on their impressions of the data. Subsequent work, however, statistically supported a role for loss in depression and a role for danger in anxiety cases. Among 164 patients with depression, anxiety, or both, plus healthy controls, recent interview-assessed major loss events were more common prior to depression onset than they were in controls in a comparable timeframe. By contrast, recent major danger events were reported more commonly by anxiety patients than controls, and both forms of major events were implicated in combined depression and anxiety onsets (Finlay-Jones & Brown, 1981). Critically, however, this did

not establish that either type of event was more potent than other events.

Potentially Critical Aspects of Loss: Tests of Humiliation, Entrapment, and Bereavement

Brown's research group later advanced the idea that certain kinds of loss events—those with high potential for evoking feelings of humiliation or of being trapped ("entrapment")—may be the most potent. In 353 community mothers of children completing LEDS interviews spanning 2 years, severe humiliation and entrapment events (a combined category) preceded depression onsets significantly more often than did losses without those elements. This difference was demonstrated by a chi-squared test followed by orthogonal contrast post hoc tests. In addition, though not predicted, bereavement events were also significantly more potent than non-death losses (G. Brown, Harris, & Hepworth, 1995). In a replication, among 172 randomly selected suburban Zimbabwean women, severe humiliation, entrapment, or bereavement events in the LEDS were significantly more likely to precede depression than were other severe loss or danger events (Broadhead & Abas, 1998).

These initial tests of the primacy of humiliation and entrapment had three important limitations. First, they did not permit generalizations to men. Second, humiliation and entrapment were included in a single category for inferential statistics on event potency, which begged the question of whether both types were in fact similarly potent. Third, the hierarchical and dichotomous rating approach applied only evaluated whether events were losses or danger events if they were not first rated as humiliations or entrapments. This approach prohibited tests of multiple event attributes simultaneously and obscured that many humiliations and entrapments were also losses. A third study addressed each of these issues.

Kendler et al. (2003) used investigator ratings of dimensional likelihood of humiliation, loss, danger, and entrapment for all severe events of 7,322 male and female adult members of twin pairs. In separate analyses, the loss and humiliation dimensions were significantly related to onsets of pure depression or depression combined with generalized anxiety within the month following event occurrence. Danger and entrapment were not significantly related at any point to pure depression, although each predicted the combined depression and anxiety syndrome a month after the event. Further, the effect of these dimensions did not vary by gender in interaction tests, extending results for humiliation and loss to males. Importantly, in a model containing both humiliation and loss dimensions to account for their correlation, both continued to significantly and uniquely predict depression onsets (Kendler, Hettema, Butera, Gardner, & Prescott, 2003). However, there were no explicit tests of the difference of effect sizes of these types of events, so although the loss dimension had a descriptively larger effect size than humiliation, it cannot be said that the loss dimension is more potent than humiliation. Similarly, bereavement was not assessed as its own dimension, and effect sizes for bereavement losses were similar in magnitude (with overlapping confidence intervals) to nonbereavement losses.

What can be concluded about humiliation, entrapment, danger, loss, and bereavement? There is clearly not good evidence that danger alone is particularly important for depression, and entrapment was either combined with humiliation in tests or was not a critical predictor when tested alone, suggesting this evidence is weak. Loss, humiliation, and to a lesser extent bereavement, however, have stronger, if imperfect, evidence bases.

Recent Investigations Examine Targeted Rejection and Broad Interpersonal Status

More recently, loss, humiliation, and bereavement have received less attention, as investigators have examined related but different dimensions. One such dimension, targeted rejection, refers to an intentional severing of a social relationship with an individual. For example, a one-sided romantic breakup represents a targeted rejection of one person, whereas a mutually agreed-upon romantic breakup does not. Among people with a recent depressive episode onset following a stressful event, those with a targeted rejection event became depressed an average of 30.4 days after the event, significantly faster than those who experienced a different type of event, who had onsets an average of 107.5 days later, suggesting that targeted rejection might be particularly potent (Slavich, Thornton, Torres, Monroe, & Gotlib, 2009). A second such dimension examines a theme common to loss, humiliation, bereavement, and targeted rejection: All are interpersonal in nature.

Beyond evidence from the dimensions of loss, humiliation, and bereavement, theory has implicated the broader dimension of interpersonal stress (that which primarily impacts the quality or quantity of relationships with other people) as central to depression risk (e.g., Joiner & Timmons, 2009; Whisman, 2001).

Providing evidence for interpersonal stress, one study using two independent samples of emerging adults examined multiple forms of stress simultaneously in a single model per sample to account for correlations among forms of stress. Interpersonal forms of stress (both major events and chronic stress) consistently predicted depressive episode onset over and above other forms of stress in the model (i.e., statistically unique prediction). By contrast, noninterpersonal major events emerged as statistically unique predictors in very limited instances (Vrshek-Schallhorn et al., 2015). Further, in this study, both interpersonal chronic and episodic stress contributed significantly greater unique variance to depression onset than did their noninterpersonal counterparts—a rare direct test of the difference in magnitude of effect size. Taken together with prior evidence for the potential importance of humiliation, loss, and bereavement, all of which have strongly interpersonal themes, there is collectively a relatively strong body of evidence for the importance of various forms of interpersonal stress in depression.

FUTURE DIRECTIONS FOR ACUTE LIFE EVENTS AND DEPRESSION RESEARCH

In the preceding section, we have reviewed evidence that (1) event severity is critical in the stress-depression pathway, (2) multiple events increase depression risk beyond the occurrence of a single event, (3) the effects of stressful events on increased depression risk fade within 3 months, and (4) there is good evidence that events with interpersonal elements (including humiliations, losses, bereavements, and targeted rejections) are particularly potent for depression, whereas there is not good evidence that the dependence-independence distinction matters much. Extant research, however, has not yet considered a number of potentially important questions.

First, when evaluating whether the occurrence of multiple events heightens risk for depression compared to single event occurrence, the extant studies do not account for event independence versus dependence. Although we concluded that this distinction is not critical for event potency, the patterns of event clusters might be meaningful in another way. Successive dependent events might indicate that declining functioning and stress generation were involved in a downward spiral following an initial event, rather than supporting an exclusively causal pathway of multiple events to depression—and this would have meaningful implications for depression prevention. Thus, in the future, studies should characterize the independence of multiple events occurring prior to depression onset.

Second, the use of retrospective measures of stressful events has marked value for some questions. For mechanistic questions, however, retrospective measures preclude "real-time" collection of multimodal variables during the peak risk window following an event. Existing efforts to examine unfolding stress utilize individuals who have recently received life-altering medical diagnoses (e.g., stroke; Ramasubbu, Tobias, Buchan, & Bech-Hansen, 2006), experienced a natural disaster (Kilpatrick et al., 2007), or begun a stressful training program such as medical internship (Sen et al., 2010) or military basic training (Joiner & Schmidt, 1998). Another approach assesses individuals only after an event without a pre-event baseline for comparison (e.g., job losses; Howe et al., 2016), but this presents interpretive problems. It is challenging to examine stressful events as they unfold in part because it is difficult to predict when such rare events—especially major, negative events—will occur. One approach may be to enroll a very large sample that completes baseline measures and frequently (e.g., weekly) responds to event screenings, but only completes more intensive measures once study staff conclude a major event has occurred. Such an approach may be readily possible using automated screening tools available to researchers.

Third, the relationship of event severity, type, and number to the clinical *characteristics* of depressive episodes has been insufficiently examined. One effort using the LEDS in 100 individuals diagnosed with current depression showed that experiencing a severe event prior to depression onset (versus no severe event) was associated with greater episode severity, heightened cognitive and somatic symptoms, and greater life impairment (Muscatell, Slavich, Monroe, & Gotlib, 2009). Additionally, a large-scale effort examined participants who had experienced depression symptom episodes across four interview assessments (Keller, Neale, & Kendler, 2007). This study assessed symptoms of depression and self-indicated "causes" of the symptoms (including whether the symptoms began "out of the blue") which were then coded by interviewers, a drawback that might have introduced bias. A between-person analysis of 3,137 individuals experiencing only one symptom episode and an independent within-person analysis of 1,719 individuals with multiple symptom episodes came to remarkably similar conclusions. Relationship losses predicted sadness, anhedonia, and appetite loss, while failure events

and chronic stressors predicted hypersomnia and fatigue, and episodes emerging "out of the blue" predicted increased appetite, fatigue, and self-harm ideation. These efforts suggest this is a promising future direction that has been insufficiently explored. In particular, it may be useful to examine the influence of various types of stress on empirically supported symptom clusters or dimensions, consistent with recent efforts to inform dimensional outcomes such as impaired positive valence functioning that are relevant to depression but also cut across diagnoses (e.g., Cuthbert & Insel, 2013). Such an approach to stress and depression research may be likely to illuminate mechanistic pathways. Next, we turn to chronic stress.

Evidence for the Influence of Recent Chronic Stress in Adulthood

We first examine the historical underpinnings of objective chronic stress assessment, then methodological challenges, followed by a review of evidence, and last, future directions for this area. We hold that assessing chronic stress presents perhaps even more methodological challenges than assessing events, and that historical methodological heterogeneity and limitations have led—with unclear scientific merit—to diminished enthusiasm for studying chronic stress.

HISTORICAL OVERVIEW

Early chronic stress measurement was marked by pronounced heterogeneity and methodological limitations, which have likely led to widely varying estimates of chronic stress potency for depression. As noted earlier, Brown and Harris (1978) linked chronic difficulties to depression onset, but based on their impressions of the data, they concluded that the link between major difficulties and depression did not appear to be as robust in their original study (1978) nor as consistent across a series of later LEDS investigations (1989) as the link between severe events and depression. Consistent with their interpretation, at least one LEDS investigation failed to link major chronic difficulties with depression onset in the absence of a severe event (G. Brown et al., 1995). In contrast to the LEDS approach to conceptualizing major difficulties (i.e., present or absence of a problem lasting 2 or more years, rated in the more severe half of a 6-point scale, and not involving health problems), another approach, Hammen's UCLA Life Stress Interview (LSI; Hammen et al., 1987), conceptualized chronic stress dimensionally as a range from the best possible quality of life to the poorest quality of life assessed in 8 to 10 domains (e.g., close friend relationship, family relationships, finances). In the LSI, the interviewer assigns a single chronic stress score for each domain for the entire period assessed, often the most recent 6 or 12 months. The LSI has been used to show that chronic stress predicts symptom worsening among already depressed individuals (Hammen, Davila, Brown, Ellicott, & Gitlin, 1992), and that chronic stress also predicts depression in a younger at-risk sample (Hammen, Shih, & Brennan, 2004). Still other research has operationalized chronic stress as the presence or absence of a single risk factor without accounting for contextual factors that make stressor severity differ between individuals. This approach may have contributed to disparate results; for example, while poverty (yes/no) predicted first onsets of depression (Bruce & Hoff, 1994), having a disabled child (yes/no) was not associated with lifetime or current rates of depression (N. Breslau & Davis, 1986).

METHODOLOGICAL CHALLENGES IN CHRONIC STRESS RESEARCH

Beyond measure heterogeneity, there are several specific methodological challenges facing chronic stress assessment that may have hampered progress in establishing it as an important contributor to depression. First, failing to assess chronic stress over a wide array of areas (in contrast to the LEDS and LSI) is likely to underestimate its impact (Mazure, 1998). Second, we suggest that the dichotomization of even major chronic stress as present or absent, as opposed to using a dimensional severity scale, reduces power (Cohen, 1983; MacCallum, Zhang, Preacher, & Rucker, 20022), which may have contributed to the inconsistent effects Brown and Harris (1989) and others (N. Breslau & Davis, 1986) have observed. We acknowledge, however, that dichotomization does not appear to lead to inconsistent results for recent major events, suggesting the problem for chronic stress might be due to a combination of dichotomization and weaker true effect sizes. Third, when dimensional indicators such as those in the UCLA LSI are used ranging from best to worst possible quality of life, despite their likely advantage for power, results do not indicate whether good conditions are protective or bad conditions are hazardous (or both in a truly dimensional manner) without follow-up analyses.

Fourth, the LEDS classifies major difficulties as independent, possibly independent, or dependent—akin to the LEDS classification for events—although

all forms of major difficulties significantly discriminated those with depression onsets and those without onsets, with similar relative risk scores in one analysis (Surtees et al., 1986). We suggest, however, that because of the challenge of ruling out that a person's behavior (potentially years ago) did not contribute to their chronic stress level, all forms of chronic stress should be conceptualized as *potentially* dependent—inextricably intertwined with the individual's characteristics, abilities, behaviors, and level of functioning. For example, chronic severe marital difficulties depend on the interpersonal interactions of two individuals. Indeed, some have observed that overlap of chronic stress and functioning level is particularly evident in the LSI partly because it captures the full range of quality of life (Harkness & Monroe, 2016), but we speculate that this is true of all chronic stress measures.

Fifth, it is important to note that the temporal precedence of chronic stress to depression onset cannot be ascertained in some studies that simultaneously assess recent chronic stress and depression. For example, the LSI yields a single score per life domain for the time period covered in the interview (e.g., past year) and would overlap temporally with depression diagnosed within that same interview window, regardless of how carefully the depressive episode is dated. Thus, in multiwave studies, an LSI from a prior wave can be used to establish temporal precedence (e.g., Hazel, Hammen, Brennan, & Najman, 2008). By contrast, because the LEDS treats chronic stressors as dichotomous constructs with discrete beginnings and endings, establishing temporal precedence is more readily accomplished.

POTENCY OF CHRONIC STRESS FOR DEPRESSION

Given the inconsistent early evidence and heterogeneous methods, perhaps it is not surprising that chronic stress has received less attention than major stressful life events in depression etiology research. This relative lack of research appears to have persisted despite reviews over an extended period of time arguing that the lack of focus on chronic stress is mistaken (Kessler, 1997) and calling for greater attention (Hammen, 2005). This lack of attention to chronic stress might suggest to readers that chronic stress's contributions to depression are significantly weaker than those of stressful events, but this is in fact unclear. This question remains inadequately tested.

Indeed, some evidence suggests that chronic stress may be as important as events; such results emerged from one large epidemiological study with more than 1,700 participants defining chronic stress as stressors beginning 12 months or more prior to the interview (McGonagle & Kessler, 1990). However, one limitation of this study's findings is the method of event ratings, which was not based on contextual threat. Rather, events were included if the event type was "typically" rated as high moderate to severe in its impact based on other research, similar to the approach used by Holmes and Rahe in their SRRS. It is likely this procedure led to the inclusion of a number of minor events, which have little impact, as well as the exclusion of some major events, thereby underestimating the true influence of events. Therefore, this particular approach may have *overestimated* the relative contribution of chronic stress. Furthermore, the use of self-reported depressive symptoms as the outcome also precludes establishing temporal precedence and hampers causal interpretation.

However, evidence for the importance of chronic stress has also emerged from limited studies using the LEDS and the LSI, both of which rate events contextually. Major difficulties (in this case, those in the upper *four* points of the LEDS 6-point scale) appeared to be as important for depressive episode onset as did acute events in a clinical sample of 50 Spanish individuals with depression and 50 controls (Rojo-Moreno, Livianos-Aldana, Cervera-Martinez, Dominguez-Carabantes, & Reig-Cebrian, 2002). It should be noted, however, that this outcome may in part be due to the authors excluding dependent events from analyses in an effort to heighten causal certainty. Similarly, dimensionally rated interpersonal LSI chronic stress was a significant unique predictor of depressive episode onset over and above several other forms of stress (including major interpersonal events, which were also a significant unique predictor) in two samples of emerging adults studied using the LSI (Vrshek-Schallhorn et al., 2015). Critically, however, neither of the former two studies aimed to test the difference in effect sizes between chronic stress and major events for predicting major depression. Thus, it is not possible to make statistical inferences about their relative contributions, but it is clear from Vrshek-Schallhorn et al. (2015) that interpersonal chronic stress contributed significantly to depression prediction even after accounting for major interpersonal events. Future efforts examining how multiple forms of stress predict depression should expand on this evidence. Thus, while it is apparent from both smaller samples using gold-standard stress assessment methods and from large epidemiological samples that chronic stress is an important contributor to depression, its precise relative contribution as compared to events remains an unresolved empirical question.

Chronic stress may also be important for its action through pathways other than a direct, independent path to depression; it may moderate other vulnerabilities and it appears to predict depression course. One study showed an interaction that approached significance in which chronic stress amplified the impact of interview-assessed events (Hammen et al., 2009). Chronic stress also appears to be associated with a more recurrent course of depression. In a diverse sample of 96 adults with current depression, the presence of major difficulties was associated with a greater number of prior depressive episodes (Monroe, Slavich, Torres, & Gotlib, 2007). Similarly, chronic stress has been shown to predict increased symptom growth over time in already depressed individuals (Hammen et al., 1992).

Interim Summary and Future Directions for Chronic Stress

We continue to advocate for greater attention to chronic stress, particularly through studies specifically designed to test the influence of chronic stress across a range of life domains on depression, ideally using repeated measures or other approaches to establish temporal precedence. Such "purpose-built" studies will avoid interpretive challenges of some large-scale epidemiological research using less intensive measures. Even *if* the impact of chronic stress is somewhat less robust than that of major events, as might be implied by the relative lack of research conducted on it, existing work does suggest that chronic stress represents an important factor in depression's etiology for many individuals. Given how common and costly depression is, chronic stress is an important public health variable worthy of increased attention. Moreover, it is not necessarily true that chronic stress contributes less robustly than events to depression's etiology. Testing the difference in the variance each contributes—particularly in large, generalizable samples using dimensional measures—is an important future direction for life stress research. Next, we turn to evidence for the stress–depression relationship in younger populations, covering more evidence on events, consistent with the literature.

Recent Stress Impacts Depression in Adolescents

The occurrence of depression among youth increases significantly during adolescence, particularly at age 14 onward (assessed as the 12 months prior to age 15; Hankin et al., 1998), rendering this period critical for etiological investigation. In an early study extending stress and depression work in adults to adolescents, Goodyer and colleagues (1985) found that adolescents in all diagnostic categories—including those diagnosed with depression—had experienced more interview-assessed recent, severe events prior to disorder onset compared to a matched period of time in controls. Over the past three decades, subsequent empirical investigations have further characterized the stress–depression relationship in adolescents, focusing more on events than chronic stress like the adult literature, with the goals of identifying the potentially causal and maintaining roles of stress in depression, as well as characterizing the specific forms of stress that exert an especially potent influence. Much of the work in this area also characterizes the contributions of various forms of interpersonal stress, although as is true for the adult literature, few papers test the difference in effects between multiple forms of stress.

Several interview-based studies provided additional support for stress in depression without attempting to establish particularly potent forms of stress. One such study, a 5-year longitudinal investigation employing the LSI that followed women during the transition from late adolescence into emerging adulthood, established both recent episodic and chronic stress as significant predictors of prospective depression (Daley, Hammen, & Rao, 2000). In this study, heightened levels of episodic stress measured across various life domains over the preceding 3 months increased risk for depression onset. Additionally, elevated chronic stress in the same 3-month period increased the likelihood of first onsets but not recurrences of depression. Similarly, work using an interview-based stress measure further supported that adolescents with depression experienced heightened levels of recent, acute stress prior to onset compared to controls (Williamson et al., 1998).

Attention to Interpersonal Stressors in Adolescents

Interpersonal theories of depression and empirical findings highlight that interpersonal stress is a potent predictor of depression among youth (for a review, see Rudolph et al., 2000). While few studies directly test the relative strengths of interpersonal and noninterpersonal stressors as predictors or correlates of depression, one such cross-sectional interview-based study did so. It revealed that among an outpatient clinical sample of youth (ages 8–18), dependent, interpersonal episodic events and chronic stressors were significantly more strongly associated with current depression symptom severity than their respective noninterpersonal counterparts in tests of dependent correlations (Rudolph et al., 2000).

Several studies establishing temporal precedence provide evidence for the potency of interpersonal stress in depression, although again without testing the difference between interpersonal and noninterpersonal stress. First, interview-assessed major disappointments (including such events as romantic breakups and academic failures) and interpersonal losses (deaths and permanent separations) in the prior month (but not events capturing danger to oneself or close others) predicted major depressive episode onsets in 12 to 16 year olds (Goodyer, Tamplin, Herbert, & Altham, 2000). Second, in a sample of emerging adults (ages 18–21) with a history of depression, those experiencing greater interview-assessed recent chronic interpersonal stress were at heightened risk for prospective depression recurrence, while noninterpersonal chronic stress did not predict recurrence (Sheets & Craighead, 2014).

Third, in a study following youth over 3 years, maladaptive response styles (i.e., greater endorsement of nonvolitional reactions, such as rumination, and lesser use of higher order, approach-oriented coping strategies, such as problem solving, assessed by questionnaire) to interview-assessed interpersonal stressors at baseline predicted greater stress generation—specifically heightened dependent, interpersonal events—over the subsequent 2 years. In turn, this generated dependent, interpersonal stress was associated with greater past-month depression symptom severity at a 3-year follow-up (Flynn & Rudolph, 2011). Notably, interpersonal stress, but not noninterpersonal stress, mediated the relationship between maladaptive baseline stress responses and later depressive symptoms. Fourth, elevated chronic family stress—one form of interpersonal stress—at baseline among older adolescent women predicted greater likelihood of experiencing a first onset of depression over the subsequent 2-year period (Eberhart & Hammen, 2006). Fifth, in a 6-year interview-based study of adolescents (the overall goal of which was to evaluate certain diathesis-stress interactions), both interview-assessed interpersonal and noninterpersonal achievement-related events separately predicted the first onset of a major depressive episode (Carter & Garber, 2011); however, this study neither simultaneously tested the stressors nor compared their effect sizes. From these five studies, it is clear that interpersonal stressors significantly and prospectively predict depression onset, although it is not possible to conclude from the available literature that the forms of interpersonal stress tested are significantly more potent than their noninterpersonal counterparts.

Within the domain of interpersonal stressors, romantic attachment-related stress has emerged as particularly salient for adolescent populations. In exploratory analyses of two samples beginning in late adolescence, the romantic stress domain of interview-assessed chronic stress was the only statistically unique predictor of the onset of major depressive episodes when simultaneously tested with other interpersonal domains of chronic stress in both samples (Vrshek-Schallhorn et al., 2015). Though exploratory, this finding complements previous work examining relationship status and depressive symptoms in adolescents. Among those in romantic relationships, those with a more preoccupied relational style—a form of insecure attachment marked by low trust, high dependence, and difficulty regulating emotions—experienced increased severity of depression symptoms (Davila, Steinberg, Kachadourian, Cobb, & Fincham, 2004). Furthermore, questionnaire-assessed romantic breakup events appeared to play a role in initial depression onset—but not significantly in recurrences—among high schoolers (Monroe, Rohde, Seeley, & Lewinsohn, 1999). Critically, these breakups contributed significant unique variance to risk for a major depressive episode over and above other questionnaire-assessed life events and daily hassles.

Taken together, there is good evidence from studies able to ascertain temporal precedence that stress precipitates depression in adolescents. Although research has focused on interpersonal stress, sometimes specifically romantic stress, future research should work to show that these forms of stress are significantly more potent than other forms of stress.

Recent Stress Impacts Depression in Childhood

The study of depression in childhood represents a relatively young field compared to parallel efforts in adolescent and adult populations. Extant research suggests that exposure to stress predicts various maladaptive outcomes, including depression, in children. Moreover, diverse forms of recent stress, including events and chronic stress in a variety of life domains, have been associated with childhood depressive symptoms and diagnoses. Notably, studies of the effects of stress on childhood depression often examine depression symptom severity rather than depression diagnoses, given greater assessment challenges and lower rates of diagnoses in children as compared to adolescents or adults.

Focus on Events

Evidence for the role of recent episodic stress in depression among children comes from a number of studies representing samples at different stages of child development, but across all of these studies, longer timeframes following events are used than the comparable adult and adolescent literatures. In an investigation of risk factors for psychiatric disorders among daughters (ages 9 to 14 at baseline) of depressed and healthy mothers, daughters of depressed mothers were more likely to develop a disorder—in most cases, major depression—over the subsequent 30 months. Importantly, the children of depressed mothers who developed psychopathology including depression in this study reported heightened interview-assessed *dependent* events, but not *independent* events over the study period (Gershon et al., 2011). Several studies also suggest associations between stressful life events and depression in samples as young as preschool age. In the first prospective longitudinal study investigating the onset of depression in this age group, both early and recent episodic stressors reported through interviews by primary caregivers significantly predicted depression diagnosis at age 6 (Bufferd et al., 2014). Further, heightened questionnaire-based mother reports of child exposure to events in the year prior to baseline predicted greater severity of preschoolers' depression symptoms 6 months after baseline (Luby, Belden, & Spitznagel, 2006), and heightened past-year exposure to interview-assessed stressful events predicted prospective increases in an internalizing scale which includes depression symptoms (Kushner, Barrios, Smith, & Dougherty, 2016).

Interpersonal Stressors

Additional research on the stress–depression relationship in childhood focuses on individual interpersonal domains, such as family and peer functioning, which are known to influence development. As in the adult and adolescent literatures, however, studies have not tested the difference in potency between targeted forms of stress and other forms. For example, in the context of a gene–environment interaction study, baseline levels of interview-assessed chronic family stress did not act independently but interacted with a certain potential genetic risk factor for depression under stress, the serotonin transporter polymorphism, to predict depressive symptoms at a 6-month follow-up (Jenness, Hankin, Abela, Young, & Smolen, 2011). Of note, although this sample included a combined sample of children and adolescents (ages 7–16), the effect of chronic family stress in conjunction with genotype held for both developmental periods. Providing additional evidence for the role of family functioning in childhood psychopathology, a longitudinal investigation following caregivers and their children from 7 months to 3 years of age found that questionnaire-assessed self-reported harsh parenting and maternal stress at baseline significantly predicted both internalizing and externalizing symptoms in offspring (Bayer, Hiscock, Ukoumunne, Price, & Wake, 2008).

Interpersonal stress in the peer domain has been a focus of research for children and adolescents. A longitudinal investigation with youth ages 7 to 16 demonstrated that, among younger participants, greater interview-assessed chronic stress in peer relationships over the 3-year study period heightened risk for the onset of major depression or a significant subclinical manifestation (Hankin et al., 2015). Additionally, extensive research not reviewed in detail here has considered the role of a particular form of peer stress—peer victimization—in depression, with evidence to support a significant association between such experiences and depressive symptoms among children (for a review and meta-analysis of cross-sectional studies predominantly using questionnaires, see Hawker & Boulton, 2000).

Collectively, this work suggests a predictive role for various forms of stress in both childhood and adolescent depression. In particular, interpersonal stressors—including those experienced in relationships with family members and peers—have been a focus of research, although direct tests of greater potency are lacking. Moreover, when considered with findings in older samples, interpersonal stress confers risk for depression across the life span.

Interim Summary of Recent Stressors Across the Life Span

Taken together, there is strong evidence that recent, stressful life events prospectively predict depression symptoms and diagnoses across the life span. The contextual threat assessment approach of Brown and Harris (1978) rescued life events and depression research from the pessimistic conclusions generated by Holmes and Rahe's questionnaire methodology, and thus should be a continued focus of current work. There is a smaller body of evidence implicating interview-assessed chronic stress in depression

symptoms and diagnoses across the life span, and this literature has been hampered by methodological heterogeneity and other limitations which should be addressed in future research. As we have alluded to throughout the section on recent stress, a theme cutting across stressors that researchers have suggested might be particularly potent (humiliation, loss, bereavement, targeted rejection) is their interpersonal nature. Direct tests of differential potency are limited, but those available support that interpersonal stress is significantly more potent than noninterpersonal stress. Thus, as discussed in detail later, a critical future direction for stress research will be to test the difference between the effects of stressors thought to be more potent against theoretically less potent stressors. Next, we review evidence for how demographic factors influence stress exposure and stress vulnerability to depression.

Who Is Most Impacted by Recent Stress? Demographic Variables in the Stress–Depression Relationship

Most models of how stress contributes to depression acknowledge that people differ in their vulnerability to stress due to pre-existing factors (diatheses), and researchers have devoted considerable attention to these diathesis-stress or vulnerability-stress models. Other chapters in this text consider cognitive, personality, and genetic vulnerabilities. Here we consider whether demographic factors—gender, race and ethnicity, and socioeconomic status—influence the stress–depression relationship. In each of these areas, research has examined differences in stress exposure and stress vulnerability.

Gender and Stress in Depression

Research has reliably indicated that females are at approximately double the risk of developing depression compared to males (Nolen-Hoeksema, 2001). This gender difference emerges during the transition to mid-puberty (Angold, Costello, & Worthman, 1998) and is maintained throughout much of the adult life course (for a review, see Kuehner, 2003). Given the role of stressful experiences in precipitating depression, several theories propose that gender influences the stress–depression relationship through gender differences in exposure and vulnerability to stress.

STRESS EXPOSURE AND GENDER

The transition to adolescence is marked by physiological, hormonal, and social role changes (Cyranowski, Frank, Young, & Shear, 2000), and interview-based assessments document an accompanying increase in stressful experiences for both sexes (Rudolph & Hammen, 1999). The stress exposure theory posits that females experience more frequent stressors during this transitional period. Support for this theory comes from findings that while both genders report increases in stress during the transition to adolescence, females experience greater increases in stressful life events compared to males, whether stress is assessed with questionnaire (Ge, Lorenz, Conger, Elder, & Simons, 1994) or with interviews (Rudolph & Hammen, 1999), the latter of which also demonstrated that substantial increases in interpersonal, dependent stressors among girls accounted for the emerging gender difference in stress exposure. This domain-specific finding of increased interpersonal, dependent stressors in females has been replicated in a separate sample of adolescent females and shown to partially mediate the gender–depression relationship (Shih, Eberhart, Hammen, & Brennan, 2006). In a further study, significantly more females than males reported interview-assessed stressors focused on people in their social networks, a form of interpersonal stress, prior to depression onset in three age groups spanning adolescence to middle age, but not among those 50 years or older (Harkness et al., 2010). Taken together, evidence supports the importance of interpersonal stressors for females across adolescence and much of the adult life span.

STRESS VULNERABILITY AND GENDER

In addition to evidence for differences in stress exposure, stress vulnerability theories posit that females have more depressogenic *responses* to stressors—possibly chiefly interpersonal stressors—and that this at least partly accounts for the gender gap in rates of depression. This view is empirically supported by studies showing that females experienced more distress (Rudolph, 2002) and depressive symptoms in response to interview-assessed interpersonal events (Shih et al., 2006), and more depressive symptoms in response to interview-assessed interpersonal conflict stress (Rudolph & Hammen, 1999) than did males. Moreover, higher levels of interview-assessed familial early adversity predicted greater depression symptoms after *mild* recent interpersonal stressors in pubertal females and prepubertal boys, but not in pubertal males (Rudolph & Flynn, 2007).

Influence of Race and Ethnicity in the Stress and Depression Relationship

The prevalence of major depression also varies across racial and ethnic groups, prompting investigations into the roles of race and ethnicity—mainly in

Black and White groups—in the stress–depression relationship. A full review of epidemiological studies is beyond the scope of this chapter, but we highlight a conundrum for depression researchers. Evidence reviewed next suggests greater stress exposure among Black compared to White groups, but lower prevalence of depression is found among African American, Caribbean Black, and non-Hispanic Black groups compared to non-Hispanic White groups (J. Breslau et al., 2005; Riolo, Nguyen, Greden, & King, 2005; Williams et al., 2007), although some studies report the opposite as well (Rodriquez et al., 2018).

Two main hypotheses provide a framework for investigating a possible moderating role of race and ethnicity in the relationship between stress and depression (George & Lynch, 2003). The first contends that stress exposure varies by social status, which is influenced in part by race and ethnicity (for evidence from questionnaire-based stress measures, see R. J. Turner & Avison, 2003; R. J. Turner, Wheaton, & Lloyd, 1995), while the second proposes that—assuming stress exposure is held constant—social groups differ in risk for maladaptive responses to stress due to their levels of certain vulnerability factors (Kessler, 1979).

Both hypotheses have garnered some empirical support, although we caution that this evidence base is exclusively cross-sectional and assesses stress with questionnaires. Supporting a stress exposure model, in a sample of African Americans and non-Hispanic Whites, race was no longer a significant correlate of current depressive symptoms (which, in this sample, were higher in the African American subsample than the non-Hispanic White subsample prior to covarying other factors) when questionnaire measures of traumatic events, recent episodic stressors, and chronic stressors were incorporated into the regression model. Each of these stressors was a significant correlate of depression, suggesting that depression symptoms are associated with heightened exposure to stress among both groups (Taylor & Turner, 2002). Additionally, regarding differential stress exposure, a potentially potent form of stress in the context of race and ethnicity is discrimination at both individual and institutional levels (Grote, Bledsoe, Wellman, & Brown, 2007). Evidence points to a noxious role for discrimination in depression: Heightened exposure increases both depressive symptoms (Hunter, Case, Joseph, Mekawi, & Bokhari, 2017) and the risk of experiencing a lifetime major depressive episode (Budhwani, Hearld, & Chavez-Yenter, 2015).

Finally, research also provides partial support for a role for differential stress vulnerability when exposure level is held constant. Among a national sample of groups identifying as Black (including African American and Caribbean Black) or non-Hispanic White, exposure to stressful life events and race interacted when gender-specific models were considered (Assari & Lankarani, 2016). Black men exposed to stress were at significantly *lower* odds of a major depressive episode compared to White men exposed to stress; no such evidence was found among women, however. Lower maladaptive stress reactivity may in part account for the apparent paradox of higher levels of stress yet lower rates of depression in Black individuals, but a lack of evidence in women suggests other factors play a role.

Potential additional reasons for the contrast between higher stress exposure but lower depression rates among Black individuals may include group differences in socialization and beliefs about low mood, including mental health stigmas. Indeed, one meta-analysis indicated that mental health–related stigma was negatively associated with treatment seeking, and this was disproportionately true for ethnic minorities, including Black individuals (Clement et al., 2015). A recent commentary concluded that despite substantial efforts, empirically supported explanations for lower depression rates among Black individuals remain elusive (Breland-Noble & Griffith, 2017). Thus, this remains an area for future examination.

Although less research has examined other racial groups, the limited available evidence suggests that major depression also appears to be less prevalent among Asian Americans compared to Whites (Budhwani et al., 2015). Prevalence differences, however, are not clear between Latino and White groups. Though a meta-analysis found no significant difference between the two groups (Mendelson, Rehkopf, & Kubzansky, 2008), the summary odds ratio (0.89) suggested a slightly but not significantly lower prevalence of major depression among Latinos. Furthermore, findings from a large-scale study published after the meta-analysis demonstrated significantly lower depression prevalence among Latinos compared to non-Latino Whites (Alegría et al., 2008).

Although more empirical work has focused on gender than race and ethnicity in stress and depression, similar themes of stress exposure and vulnerability have emerged (Assari & Lankarani, 2016; George & Lynch, 2003). Research from the race, ethnicity, and health disparities literature lends support to two apparent "paradoxes" related to stress exposure and physical health outcomes (but not yet mental health outcomes). For example, among older Mexican Americans, those living in neighborhoods with a higher percentage of Mexican Americans experienced lower prevalence of several medical conditions, including stroke and cancer, as well as lower mortality rates, despite exposure to greater poverty (Eschbach, Ostir, Patel, Markides, & Goodwin, 2004). This effect, known as the *barrio advantage*, suggests that protective factors related to social support mitigate the negative effects of poverty-related stress on health outcomes. These findings align with a larger body of research on the *Hispanic paradox*, which suggests similar or lower mortality rates among Latino groups compared to White groups despite greater exposure to environmental stressors related to lower socioeconomic status (for a review, see Franzini, Ribble, & Keddie, 2001).

Future research should investigate the relationship between differential exposure and vulnerability among more diverse samples and take racial and cultural socialization into account. Although evidence suggests a lower prevalence of major depression among racial and ethnic minority groups when compared to White groups, these findings should also be interpreted with the knowledge that prevalence of major depression varies by ethnic subgroup, nativity status, and age (Alegría et al., 2008; Budhwani et al., 2015; González, Tarraf, Whitfield, & Vega, 2010; Szaflarski et al., 2016).

Socioeconomic Status in the Stress–Depression Relationship

Evidence linking socioeconomic status (SES) and depression risk has been inconsistent. One meta-analysis identified no significant association between SES and depression symptoms in over 60,000 children completing the Children's Depression Inventory (Twenge & Nolen-Hoeksema, 2002), but a meta-analysis examining adults (> age 16) indicated that there is a modest yet significant effect of lower SES on increased risk for depression (Lorant et al., 2003). Further, a more recent estimate relying on over 43,000 in-person interviews significantly linked low SES with depression risk (Hasin, Goodwin, Stinson, & Grant, 2005).

Findings, however, are relatively consistent in linking lower SES with more frequent stressful events and higher chronic stress. One study using five self-report survey samples of approximately 700 to 2,000 people each found relatively consistent evidence that low SES is weakly but significantly correlated with greater likelihood of self-reported negative life events across all aspects of life (McLeod & Kessler, 1990). Other findings indicate that low SES is associated with fewer interview-assessed coping resources, including having fewer close confidants (G. Brown & Harris, 1978). Further, evidence indicates that which *types* of stressors are most potent may vary across the SES spectrum. In an emerging adult sample, a significant interaction of interview-assessed noninterpersonal major events and SES indicated that this form of stress was relatively more potent for individuals of lower SES than those of higher SES. Further, interpersonal chronic stress was more impactful among higher SES individuals, while noninterpersonal chronic stress was more potent among lower SES individuals (Vrshek-Schallhorn et al., 2015). Major interpersonal events, however, remained potent precipitants of depression regardless of SES. Taken together, lower SES appears to modestly but significantly enhance risk for depression, and it appears to do so through modestly increased stress exposure and nuanced differences in vulnerability.

In summary, there is relatively consistent evidence for greater stress exposure among women, racial and ethnic minority groups, and lower SES populations, and this appears to account at least in part for the gender difference in depression. However, a puzzle remains for future research to reconcile evidence of lower rates of depression among some minority groups with evidence of greater stress exposure and even stress sensitivity. Next, we turn our attention to the early adversity and depression literature.

Early Adversity Has Both Proximal and Distal Effects

"Early adversity" has been used to capture a heterogeneous group of negative and uncontrollable experiences of children and adolescents (<18 years old), ranging from more traditional examples such as exposure to maltreatment (including physical, sexual, and emotional abuse and neglect), death of a parent, and separation from a parent (see Table 5.1 for additional examples) to more broadly defined indicators such as parental psychopathology. Here we focus on more traditional forms of adversity and not parental psychopathology. This review first examines methodological factors that should be considered in evaluating the literature, then describes evidence for both proximal and distal effects of early adversity, explores evidence that certain forms of adversity are more potent than others, and discusses several

pathways that may reconcile how early experiences can confer long-term impact.

Methodological Challenges for Early Adversity Research

There are three primary salient methodological issues in early adversity and depression research. First, many studies rely on designs in which adversity and depression history are simultaneously self-reported, which does not allow establishment of temporal precedence to ensure that stress precedes and therefore potentially causes depression. This challenge is salient for child and adolescent samples, in which the stress–depression association is more proximal, but in adults, this is not a concern when it is established that the first onset of depression occurred *after* the adversity.

Second, many studies understandably use retrospective reports of early adversity, partly because of mandatory reporting to social services when mental health researchers learn of the ongoing abuse of a minor, and partly because of logistic and funding challenges of conducting extended longitudinal research. Retrospective reports may be subject to forgetting or biased recall, perhaps particularly in clinical samples. However, some have argued that retrospective reports *under-* rather than overestimate adversity's occurrence, suggesting that retrospective reports actually provide a relatively conservative adversity measure (for a review, see Hardt & Rutter, 2004). Similarly, evidence suggests that psychopathology does not bias reporting (for a review, see Brewin, Andrews, & Gotlib, 1993).

Third, the quality of assessment varies widely. As in the recent stress literature, interview-based contextual assessment of adversity offers substantial advantages over self-report checklist measures of adversity. Of the available interview tools (for a review, see Roy & Perry, 2004), the Childhood Experiences of Care and Abuse (CECA; Bifulco, Brown, & Harris, 1994) interview, a counterpart of the LEDS, has the advantage of yielding ratings of severity blind to the participant's response. One alternative to retrospective self-reports is to rely on substantiated or documented cases of abuse using official records (e.g., social service agency records). However, this approach also poses challenges to generalizability because these reports likely represent the most severe cases of adversity. Moderate severity adversity (severe enough to cause harm, but unlikely to be discovered and reported to authorities) may be overlooked. Such omissions would contribute to underestimating the impact of the full spectrum of adversity severity. Considering each of these concerns, it seems that there is no one approach that is completely without drawbacks. Scientists then do well to prioritize longitudinal research with interview measures and to pursue replication across methods.

Proximal Effects of Child Maltreatment

Maltreatment is associated with a range of near-term negative outcomes in youth (for reviews of this expansive area, see Springer, Sheridan, Kuo, & Carnes, 2003; Staudt, 2001), and several studies using documented abuse provide evidence for a significant relationship between recent maltreatment in children and depression. First, in a study comparing individuals in middle childhood with a history of prior maltreatment (abuse and neglect documented in official records) to those without such history, experiences of physical abuse and physical neglect predicted higher self-reported depressive symptoms at baseline (Kim & Cicchetti, 2006). Second, a large-scale study conducted in Australia examined the effects of childhood sexual abuse using all records of reported sexual childhood abuse cases and subsequent contacts of the 2,759 victims with the public mental health system over a 31-year period, as compared to those of age- and gender-matched (but otherwise randomly selected) controls drawn from the electoral database. Diagnostic records showed that individuals with a history of childhood sexual abuse were at significantly elevated risk for a range of psychiatric disorders, including depression, both in youth (prior to age 18) and in adulthood, compared to controls (Cutajar et al., 2010).

Childhood Adversity Also Has Distal Effects on Depression During Adolescence and Adulthood

Consistent evidence for the etiological role of early adversity in later depression comes from three decades of research in (1) large epidemiological studies using primarily questionnaire measures (Felitti et al., 1998; Kessler, Davis, & Kendler, 1997), (2) twin studies using questionnaire assessment of sexual abuse (Kendler et al., 2000), and (3) large birth cohort studies utilizing a combination of interviews and questionnaires (Jaffee et al., 2002), among other evidence. Aggregating this work, three separate meta-analyses concluded that exposure to significant early adversity (e.g., physical abuse, sexual abuse, or neglect) significantly increases the risk for depression in adulthood, with pooled odds ratios ranging from 1.49 to 3.06 across various forms of adversity in the three meta-analyses (Li, D'Arcy, & Meng, 2016;

Lindert et al., 2014; Norman et al., 2012). Li et al. (2016) is particularly noteworthy for its exclusion of studies that relied on retrospective self-reports of maltreatment, and seven of eight studies included used reviews of official records.

Early adversity's association with increased risk for later depression also spans both adolescence and adulthood. The most robust causal evidence that adversity during childhood leads to later depression comes from prospective research. For example, in a large ($N = 639$) 17–year prospective study of official records-based cases of physical abuse and neglect and retrospectively self-reported sexual abuse, maltreated individuals exhibited an increased risk of developing depression during adolescence and early adulthood compared to nonmaltreated individuals (J. Brown, Cohen, Johnson, & Smailes, 1999). Further, in a prospective birth cohort study ($N = 998$), higher childhood adversity exposure (e.g., parental criminality, loss/separation, or psychopathology) assessed through a combination of questionnaires and interviews was associated with juvenile-onset depression (10–14 years), although not significantly with first onsets of depression in emerging adulthood (17–25 years of age), which could be consistent with declining impact as time passes after the adversity (Jaffee et al., 2002). Contrasting this latter finding, in other prospective research, early adversity has been linked to depression during adulthood. In one prospective cohort study, over 600 individuals with documented cases of early adversity (physical abuse, sexual abuse, or neglect) were at increased risk for current and lifetime depression diagnoses compared to over 500 demographically matched nonabused controls, although effects fluctuated somewhat by type of adversity (Widom, DuMont, & Czaja, 2007).

Early Adversity Influences Depression Course

Early adversity not only impacts depression occurrence but also influences the clinical course of the disorder, including the frequency of recurrences, age of onset, and duration of episodes. A meta-analysis examining frequency of episode occurrence showed that, in 16 epidemiological samples with more than 23,000 combined participants, childhood maltreatment was associated with recurrent or persistent depression with a 2.27 combined odds ratio (Nanni, Uher, & Danese, 2012). One study is particularly compelling for its use of the CECA interview among a sample of sister pairs, in which parental maltreatment was associated with greater rates of chronic depression. In the sister pairs that were discordant on maltreatment, the maltreated siblings experienced a greater increase in risk for chronic depression compared to their nonmaltreated siblings (G. Brown, Craig, Harris, Handley, & Harvey, 2007). Further, a history of childhood sexual abuse, physical abuse, and neglect has been shown to predict significantly earlier age of depression onset in studies with questionnaire measures (Bernet & Stein, 1999) and those based on official records (Widom et al., 2007). Additionally, interview-assessed early adversity was associated with longer episodes (Zlotnick, Mattia, & Zimmerman, 2001).

Childhood adversity has also been linked to poorer depression treatment outcomes. In a meta-analysis using 10 clinical trials comprising more than 3,000 combined participants, childhood maltreatment history was associated with poorer treatment response to both psychotherapy and medication compared to those without such history, with a 1.43 combined odds ratio (Nanni et al., 2012). In one study that examined the relative effectiveness of several treatments for those who had experienced prior maltreatment (ascertained by questionnaire), psychotherapy was significantly more effective at treating depression than medication alone, and adding medication to psychotherapy did not provide significant benefits beyond psychotherapy alone (Nemeroff et al., 2003). Taken together, this evidence supports that not only is childhood adversity associated with greater rates of depression, it also impacts important clinical outcomes of persistence, recurrence, and treatment response.

Content of Adversity During Early Development

There has been considerable discussion regarding which types of adversity might be most noxious in the etiology of depression. One hypothesis is that emotional abuse such as verbal aggression and emotional neglect may increase risk for depression more than other types of adversity by directly providing negative content to a child (e.g., "You are worthless"), contributing to the development of negative self-schemas (Rose & Abramson, 1992), as supported by one quantitative review using a combination of self-reports and official records (Gibb, 2002). Evidence for the potency of emotional abuse comes from studies examining different forms of early adversity, which have found that emotional abuse was significantly more strongly associated with depression compared to other types of maltreatment when

assessed by questionnaire (Gibb, Chelminski, & Zimmerman, 2007) and when assessed by interview (Lumley & Harkness, 2007; Spinhoven et al., 2010). Similarly, neglect is hypothesized to activate loss-related schemas, as supported by a study using the CECA interview (Lumley & Harkness, 2007), and to sensitize individuals to later dependent stress, assessed with a questionnaire in one supportive study (Shapero et al., 2014). A meta-analysis of 12 CECA studies provides some support for these hypotheses, such that psychological abuse had the largest descriptive effect size (defined as coercive control; Cohen's $d = .93$), followed by physical and emotional neglect ($d = .81$). Further, these effects did not overlap the 95% confidence intervals of several other forms of abuse, including sexual abuse ($d = .50$) and antipathy (coldness, hostility; $d = .51$), supporting greater potency for psychological abuse and neglect in depression (Infurna et al., 2016).

There is also evidence that the effects of different types of early adversity vary by gender. A large ($N = 34,653$) representative sample of the US population was assessed using retrospective questionnaires of early abuse and neglect and lifetime diagnostic interviews for internalizing (anxiety, depression) and externalizing disorders (addiction, antisocial personality). A latent variable analysis demonstrated that, among both genders, emotional abuse was significantly more strongly related to latent internalizing than to externalizing. Further, among women, physical abuse was significantly more strongly related to internalizing than to externalizing, while among men, physical abuse was more strongly related to externalizing that to internalizing—the latter a particularly sharp contrast with results for women (Keyes et al., 2012). Similarly, among men, sexual abuse was more strongly related to internalizing, whereas among women, it was related significantly to both internalizing and externalizing, but the strength of the two paths did not significantly differ.

Impact of Adversity Timing During Childhood and Adolescence

In addition to discussion of the most potent forms of early adversity, there has been discussion regarding whether earlier childhood adversity is more potent than later childhood or adolescent adversity for the etiology of depression, but this evidence base is somewhat inconsistent and usually does not test the difference in effects between developmental periods. The hypothesis that earlier adversity is more potent than later adversity reasons that earlier adversity interferes with the successful development of emotion regulation and attachment style (for reviews, see Baer & Martinez, 2006; Cicchetti & Toth, 1995), cognitive processes (for a review, see Beck, 2008), and biological systems (for a review, see Heim, Newport, Mletzko, Miller, & Nemeroff, 2008) required for later adaptive psychological functioning. Evidence consistent with that view comes from a study using baseline physical harm interviews and annual follow-up questionnaires predicting internalizing symptoms in eighth grade (Keiley, Howe, Dodge, Bates, & Pettit, 2001) as well as from a study examining official records (Manly, Kim, Rogosch, & Cicchetti, 2001). Additional support comes from a prospective study of abuse and neglect in official records, which demonstrated that adversity during earlier developmental periods (i.e., infancy through preschool age; 0–5 years) was more strongly associated with increased depressive symptoms in adulthood than was adversity experienced later in childhood (6–11 years; Kaplow & Widom, 2007). Last, in a large (N = 907) longitudinal study of maltreatment documented through official records, although adversity limited to childhood (0–11 years) showed overall fewer significant associations with a range of negative outcomes than adolescent adversity, adversity limited to childhood predicted questionnaire-based current depression symptoms in early adulthood, while adolescent adversity did not (Thornberry, Henry, Ireland, & Smith, 2010).

Not all evidence, however, supports that early adversity is more potent than later adversity. For example, in a study utilizing official records to document maltreatment and interviewing victims within 8 weeks of discovery, age at discovery of sexual abuse predicted depression symptoms, such that adolescents had greater depression symptoms, which may be due to the surge in depression symptoms observed in adolescents or to adolescents' more advanced cognitive development (Feiring, Taska, & Lewis, 1998). Indeed, in this study, feelings of shame and cognitive attributional style partly accounted for the observed association between age and depression. A further study utilizing retrospective interviews of early adversity found that, when including both childhood (age 0–9) and preadolescent to adolescent (age 9–16) interview-based adversity as predictors, only later adversity contributed significant unique variance in the prediction of first depression onsets during late adolescence and early adulthood, potentially due to the attenuation of the effects of earlier adversity over time (Vrshek-Schallhorn, Wolitzky-Taylor, et al., 2014).

What Might Account for the Paradoxical Long Action of Early Adversity?

Although there is broad evidence for the association between early adversity and depression in adulthood, many studies examining this relationship do not assess or simultaneously report on *recent* life stress, which would permit examination of whether early adversity contributed statistically unique effects above and beyond recent stress. Some scholars have proposed a stress-recency model (Shanahan, Copeland, Costello, & Angold, 2011), which posits that stressors pose a time-limited risk, such that they are most potent shortly after occurrence and decline in potency as time passes, consistent with the adult event literature. In line with this, interview-assessed childhood adversity predicted childhood-onset depression more strongly than it did adult-onset depression, while adult-onset depression was most strongly associated with adversity in adulthood (Shanahan et al., 2011).

This stress-recency model poses an intriguing question: If the effects of stressful events for depression are most noxious shortly after event occurrence and abate soon thereafter, how can this be reconciled with evidence that adversity persistently increases risk for depression occurrence years, even decades later? One possibility is that early stress may make individuals more vulnerable to later stress even in milder forms (stress sensitization theory; Monroe & Harkness, 2005). The implication is that even when early adversity does not quickly provoke depressive onsets, such experiences leave individuals more vulnerable to the effects of later—possibly less severe—stressors. In support, individuals with a history of interview-assessed maltreatment have been shown to be more likely to report *less severe life stress* prior to depression onset compared to those without such history (Harkness, Bruce, & Lumley, 2006). Additionally, pubertal girls and prepubertal boys (but not prepubertal girls and pubertal boys) who experienced questionnaire-assessed family disruption or loss exhibited more depressive symptoms in response to later interview-assessed interpersonal stressors compared to controls (Rudolph & Flynn, 2007), and individuals who experienced interview-assessed early parental loss demonstrated greater sensitivity to later interview-assessed interpersonal losses (Slavich, Monroe, & Gotlib, 2011), suggesting that early stress not only sensitizes to later stress but also may do so in a congruent stressor-specific fashion. Finally, Hammen and colleagues (2000) demonstrated a significant stress sensitization interaction between early adversity and recent events in a sample of young women, such that those with a history of questionnaire-assessed early adversity were significantly more prone to depression in early adulthood under *lower* levels of interview-assessed recent episodic stress than their counterparts without early adversity. Under higher levels of recent event stress, early adversity did not further discriminate risk.

A second possibility is that early adversity leads to higher levels of chronic and acute stress later, a stress continuation or stress generation model. Some scholars have speculated that early adversity contributes to higher levels of later and ongoing stressors; thus, childhood adversity could be in part conceptualized as a risk for stress continuation. Support for this view comes from four studies showing that early adversity's relationship with later depression is mediated by more proximal stress. In a large epidemiological survey, the relationship between interview-assessed childhood family violence and recurrent depression was mediated by recent, adult chronic interpersonal stress (Kessler & Magee, 1994). Similarly, a study of over 600 participants using questionnaire measures found that recent stress mediated the association between childhood adversity and adult depression symptoms (H. A. Turner & Butler, 2003). These findings were replicated and extended by a study that showed the effects of early adversity on depression diagnoses were mediated by a composite score of recent interview-assessed events and chronic stress (Hazel et al., 2008). Finally, a fourth study showed that only recent interpersonal—not noninterpersonal—interview-assessed chronic stress mediated the relationship between childhood adversity and later depression (Vrshek-Schallhorn et al., 2015).

In summary, the evidence shows that early adversity prospectively predicts depression, and it is associated with earlier onset, more frequent episodes, and poorer treatment responses. Although there is good support that emotional abuse has significantly greater effects on depression than other forms of abuse, there is mixed evidence regarding whether early childhood adversity is more likely to lead to depression than adversity occurring later in childhood or in adolescence. Finally, there is evidence that the relatively long action of early adversity might be due to stress sensitization effects or stress continuation effects, in which early adversity breeds adversity during adulthood. Key future directions include

expanding upon these latter two possibilities and investigating how to interrupt stress continuation.

Future Directions

In addition to future directions we have identified throughout the chapter, here we discuss four overarching future directions for stress and depression research.

Assessment Quality Remains as Relevant as Ever Before

As we reviewed, prior to Brown and Harris's and their contemporaries' contributions to stress assessment, early efforts to characterize the stress–depression relationship produced unconvincing effect sizes and used assessment approaches that confounded vulnerability, symptoms, and objective exposure, among other issues. The critical methodological advancements (best practices) that resolved confounds and isolated etiologically potent stress were using (ideally blinded) investigators' rather than participants' judgments of event thresholds and severity, accounting for severity, establishing temporal precedence, and using time-sensitive approaches that isolate 1–3 months prior to depression onset. Unfortunately, the assessment approaches that include these advancements tend to require a great deal of investigator resources (training, personnel, supervision, and participant time) even to produce several hundred interviews. In an age of "big data" with datasets of 10,000 or more participants, and high demands for investigator productivity, we argue that life stress and depression research—including diathesis-stress interaction mechanistic research—will not progress further without continued use of these best practices. Nowhere has this been clearer than in gene–environment interaction research, where more robust interaction effects emerged for interview and other objective measures of stress than for questionnaire measures of stress (Karg, Burmeister, Shedden, & Sen, 2011). One potential solution is for life stress researchers to join together to use consensus best practice interviews to generate larger datasets.

Isolating the Most Potent Forms of Stress Will Aid Intervention and Basic Research Efforts

Just as learning that only major and not minor events significantly predicted depression led to progress in Brown and Harris's era, isolating the most potent forms of stress will lead to progress today. This is useful for at least two reasons: (1) knowing what forms of stress to target in preventive interventions and (2) minimizing multiple testing, boosting consistency across studies, and focusing resources wisely in mechanistic research such as diathesis-stress research and biological research on stress. Genetic research, for example, is particularly concerned with minimizing multiple testing due to the large number of genetic variants measured in some studies, an issue compounded by testing multiple forms of stress in interactions with genetic variants. There is also evidence that certain biological systems are preferentially sensitive to certain forms of stress (Dickerson & Kemeny, 2004; Vrshek-Schallhorn, Mineka, et al., 2014), and identifying the most potent forms of stress for depression is likely to produce larger effect sizes when biological predictors of stress response or biological stress response outcomes are studied.

To identify the most potent forms, studies will first need to account for positive correlations between forms of stress, which can obscure which form is contributing statistically unique effects; this can be accomplished by including multiple forms of stress in the same statistical model. Studies will also need to test the difference in effect sizes between forms of stress predicting depression, for example through deviance tests, facilitated by modern statistical software platforms. In some cases, it may also be useful to characterize and validate new approaches to data reduction that account for total stress burden (e.g., Hazel et al., 2008), perhaps aggregating across relevant stressors (e.g., interpersonal chronic and episodic stress). These efforts should acknowledge that potent forms of stress may vary across development and demographic factors, given evidence that the potency of noninterpersonal stress varied as a function of SES (Vrshek-Schallhorn et al., 2015).

Life Stress and Depression Researchers Should Contribute to Depression Prevention and Intervention Efforts

Stress and depression researchers should increasingly turn their attention to translational efforts aimed at applying what has been learned from the past 40 years of research. First, they have the opportunity to offer a unique perspective. Too often, in popular culture and even in psychological science, stress is conceptualized as only the emotional *response* to circumstances, which suggests emotion regulation skill interventions for stress-related disorders. Stress and depression researchers can make the case that stress can also be conceptualized as objective experiences—the negative events and more chronic circumstances

individuals face—which suggests the addition of problem-solving skills in interventions to modify the environment when objective stress is elevated. Second, stress researchers can also use evidence to point to the most noxious forms of stress as targets for intervention during treatment or in public health depression prevention efforts.

Third, stress researchers also can help pursue research on the effectiveness of interventions to interrupt stress continuation effects between childhood and early adulthood. Evidence that early adversity's influence on depression in adulthood is mediated by recent stress suggests that early adversity disrupts the formation of healthy life skills, including those vital to interpersonal functioning, which help keep later stress at bay. For example, the same adult caregiver who perpetrates emotional abuse on a child is likely to frequently model ineffectual and stress-generating interactions with other people. Thus, the same child who is victimized by emotional abuse may also be likely to approach adulthood with poorly developed interpersonal skills. Indeed, a study conducted exclusively among lower SES children in a Head Start preschool program indeed found evidence that maltreated children had poorer social skills than their nonmaltreated peers (Darwish, Esquivel, Houtz, & Alfonso, 2001). One potentially fruitful preventive intervention (or even treatment, post diagnosis) for individuals previously exposed to prior early adversity could be an adaptation of the interpersonal skills module used in Dialectical Behavior Therapy. At least one effort has augmented traditional exposure therapy with emotion regulation and interpersonal skills training to treat child abuse–related posttraumatic stress disorder with clear benefits (Cloitre, Koenen, Cohen, & Han, 2002), but similar efforts could be applied more broadly.

Greater Study of Race, Ethnicity, and Culture in Stress–Depression Research

Finally, although many of the samples in the studies we reviewed were diverse, objective stress and depression research has paid insufficient attention to race, ethnicity, and culture in the stress-depression pathway. Objective stress research should examine the contrast we observed (evidence of greater stress exposure but also lower rates of depression in Black compared to White individuals) as well as the influence of cultural factors in stress exposure and responding. Future research should also examine a wider array of minority groups, for example to understand acculturative stress in immigrant communities.

Conclusion

Taken together, evidence linking an array of forms and timings of life stress with depression is robust. The evidence for this relationship extends across the life span, with recent stress predicting depression symptoms and onsets at every age, and distal stress from childhood enhancing risk and worsening depression course years later in adulthood. Evidence for the relationship also extends across multiple forms of stress, but more research has focused on stressful life events than on chronic stress. We argue that this lack of attention to chronic stress is mistaken because there is evidence that chronic stress predicts depression even after stressful events are accounted for. The literature also provides early evidence consistent with a conclusion that several manifestations of interpersonal stress are more potent than other forms of stress, but studies have rarely carried out the decisive tests of effect size magnitude necessary to firmly draw this conclusion. Moving forward, stress and depression researchers should redouble their efforts to use best practice assessment techniques, work to isolate the most potent forms of stress, contribute to intervention and prevention efforts, and pay greater attentions to issues of race, ethnicity, and culture.

References

Alegría, M., Canino, G., Shrout, P. E., Woo, M., Duan, N., Vila, D., . . . Meng, X. (2008). Prevalence of mental illness in immigrant and non-immigrant U.S. Latino groups. *The American journal of psychiatry, 165*(3), 359–369.

Angold, A., Costello, E. J., & Worthman, C. M. (1998). Puberty and depression: The roles of age, pubertal status and pubertal timing. *Psychological Medicine, 28*(1), 51–61.

Assari, S., & Lankarani, M. M. (2016). Association between stressful life events and depression: Intersection of race and gender. *Journal of Racial and Ethnic Health Disparities, 3*(2), 349–356. doi:10.1007/s40615-015-0160-5

Baer, J. C., & Martinez, C. D. (2006). Child maltreatment and insecure attachment: a meta-analysis. *Journal of Reproductive and Infant Psychology, 24*(3), 187–197. doi:10.1080/02646830600821231

Bayer, J. K., Hiscock, H., Ukoumunne, O. C., Price, A., & Wake, M. (2008). Early childhood aetiology of mental health problems: A longitudinal population-based study. *Journal of Child Psychology and Psychiatry, 49*(11):1166–1174. doi:10.1111/j.1469-7610.2008.01943.x

Beck, A. T. (2008). The evolution of the cognitive model of depression and its neurobiological correlates. *American Journal of Psychiatry, 165*(8), 969–977.

Bernet, C. Z., & Stein, M. B. (1999). Relationship of childhood maltreatment to the onset and course of major depression in adulthood. *Depression and Anxiety, 9*(4), 169–174. doi:10.1002/(SICI)1520-6394(1999)9:4<169::AID-DA4>3.0.CO;2-2

Bifulco, A., Brown, G., Edwards, A., Harris, T., Neilson, E., Richards, C., & Robinson, R. (1989). *Life events and difficulties schedule (LEDS-2) Vol. 1: Life events manual.* London, England: Royal Holloway and Bedford New College, University of London.

Bifulco, A., Brown, G. W., & Harris, T. O. (1994). Childhood Experience of Care and Abuse (CECA): A retrospective interview measure. *Journal of Child Psychology and Psychiatry, 35*(8), 1419–1435.

Breland-Noble, A. M., & Griffith, D. M. (2017). Introduction to the Special Issue on Health Disparities and Diversity. *Journal of Clinical Psychology in Medical Settings, 24*(3–4), 179–181.

Breslau, J., Aguilar-Gaxiola, S., Kendler, K. S., Su, M., Williams, D., & Kessler, R. C. (2005). Specifying race-ethnic differences in risk for psychiatric disorder in a USA national sample. *Psychological Medicine, 36*(1), 57–68. doi:10.1017/S0033291705006161

Breslau, N., & Davis, G. (1986). Chronic stress and major depression. *Archives of General Psychiatry, 43*(4), 309–314.

Brewin, C. R., Andrews, B., & Gotlib, I. H. (1993). Psychopathology and early experience: A reappraisal of retrospective reports. *Psychological Bulletin, 113*(1), 82–98.

Broadhead, J. C., & Abas, M. A. (1998). Life events, difficulties and depression among women in an urban setting in Zimbabwe. *Psychological Medicine, 28*(1), 29–38.

Brown, G., Bhrolchain, M. N., & Harris, T. (1975). Social class and psychiatric disturbance among women in an urban population. *Sociology, 9*(2), 225–254.

Brown, G., Craig, T. K. J., Harris, T. O., Handley, R. V., & Harvey, A. L. (2007). Development of a retrospective interview measure of parental maltreatment using the Childhood Experience of Care and Abuse (CECA) instrument—A life-course study of adult chronic depression—1. *Journal of Affective Disorders, 103*(1), 205–215.

Brown, G., & Harris, T. (1978). *Social origins of depression: A study of psychiatric disorder in women.* Oxfordshire, UK: Tavistock.

Brown, G., & Harris, T. (1989). *Life events and illness.* New York, NY: The Guilford Press.

Brown, G., Harris, T. O., & Hepworth, C. (1995). Loss, humiliation and entrapment among women developing depression: A patient and non-patient comparison. *Psychological Medicine, 25*(1), 7–21.

Brown, G., Sklair, F., Harris, T. O., & Birley, J. L. (1973). Life-events and psychiatric disorders Part 1: some methodological issues. *Psychological Medicine, 3*(1), 74–87.

Brown, J., Cohen, P., Johnson, J. G., & Smailes, E. M. (1999). Childhood abuse and neglect: Specificity of effects on adolescent and young adult depression and suicidality. *Journal of the American Academy of Child & Adolescent Psychiatry, 38*(12), 1490–1496. doi:10.1097/00004583-199912000-00009

Bruce, M. L., & Hoff, R. A. (1994). Social and physical health risk factors for first-onset major depressive disorder in a community sample. *Social Psychiatry and Psychiatric Epidemiology, 29*(4), 165–171.

Budhwani, H., Hearld, K. R., & Chavez-Yenter, D. (2015). Depression in racial and ethnic minorities: The impact of nativity and discrimination. *Journal of Racial and Ethnic Health Disparities, 2*(1), 34–42. doi:10.1007/s40615-014-0045-z

Bufferd, S. J., Dougherty, L. R., Olino, T. M., Dyson, M. W., Laptook, R. S., Carlson, G. A., & Klein, D. N. (2014). Predictors of the onset of depression in young children: A multi-method, multi-informant longitudinal study from ages 3 to 6. *Journal of Child Psychology and Psychiatry, 55*(11), 1279–1287. doi:10.1111/jcpp.12252

Carter, J. S., & Garber, J. (2011). Predictors of the first onset of a major depressive episode and changes in depressive symptoms across adolescence: Stress and negative cognitions. *Journal of Abnormal Psychology, 120*(4), 779–796. doi:10.1037/a0025441

Cicchetti, D., & Toth, S. L. (1995). A developmental psychopathology perspective on child abuse and neglect. *Journal of the American Academy of Child & Adolescent Psychiatry, 34*(5), 541–565. doi:10.1097/00004583-199505000-00008

Clement, S., Schauman, O., Graham, T., Maggioni, F., Evans-Lacko, S., Bezborodovs, N., ... Thornicroft, G. (2015). What is the impact of mental health-related stigma on help-seeking? A systematic review of quantitative and qualitative studies. *Psychological Medicine, 45*(1), 11–27.

Cloitre, M., Koenen, K. C., Cohen, L. R., & Han, H. (2002). Skills training in affective and interpersonal regulation followed by exposure: A phase-based treatment for PTSD related to childhood abuse. *Journal of Consulting and Clinical Psychology, 70*(5), 1067.

Cohen, J. (1983). The cost of dichotomization. *Applied Psychological Measurement, 7*(3), 249–253.

Costello, C. G. (1982). Social factors associated with depression: A retrospective community study. *Psychological Medicine, 12*(2), 329–339.

Cutajar, M. C., Mullen, P. E., Ogloff, J. R. P., Thomas, S. D., Wells, D. L., & Spataro, J. (2010). Psychopathology in a large cohort of sexually abused children followed up to 43 years. *Child Abuse & Neglect, 34*(11), 813–822. doi:10.1016/j.chiabu.2010.04.004

Cuthbert, B. N., & Insel, T. R. (2013). Toward the future of psychiatric diagnosis: The seven pillars of RDoC. *BMC Medicine, 11*(1), 126.

Cyranowski, J. M., Frank, E., Young, E., & Shear, M. K. (2000). Adolescent onset of the gender difference in lifetime rates of major depression: A theoretical model. *Archives of General Psychiatry, 57*(1), 21–27. doi:10.1001/archpsyc.57.1.21

Daley, S. E., Hammen, C., & Rao, U. (2000). Predictors of first onset and recurrence of major depression in young women during the 5 years following high school graduation. *Journal of Abnormal Psychology, 109*(3), 525–533.

Darwish, D., Esquivel, G. B., Houtz, J. C., & Alfonso, V. C. (2001). Play and social skills in maltreated and non-maltreated preschoolers during peer interactions. *Child Abuse & Neglect, 25*(1), 13–31.

Davila, J., Steinberg, S. J., Kachadourian, L., Cobb, R., & Fincham, F. (2004). Romantic involvement and depressive symptoms in early and late adolescence: The role of a preoccupied relational style. *Personal Relationships, 11*(2), 161–178.

Dickerson, S. S., & Kemeny, M. E. (2004). Acute stressors and cortisol responses: A theoretical integration and synthesis of laboratory research. *Psychological Bulletin, 130*(3), 355–391.

Dohrenwend, B., & Dohrenwend, B. (1969). *Social status and psychological disorder: A causal inquiry.* New York, NY: Wiley-Interscience.

Eberhart, N. K., & Hammen, C. L. (2006). Interpersonal predictors of onset of depression during the transition to adulthood. *Personal Relationships, 13*(2), 195–206. doi:10.1111/j.1475-6811.2006.00113.x

Eschbach, K., Ostir, G. V., Patel, K. V., Markides, K. S., & Goodwin, J. S. (2004). Neighborhood context and mortality

among older Mexican Americans: Is there a barrio advantage? *American Journal of Public Health, 94*(10), 1807–1812.

Feiring, C., Taska, L., & Lewis, M. (1998). The role of shame and attributional style in children's and adolescents' adaptation to sexual abuse. *Child Maltreatment, 3*(2), 129–142. doi:10.1177/1077559598003002007

Felitti, V. J., Anda, R. F., Nordenberg, D., Williamson, D. F., Spitz, A. M., Edwards, V., ... Marks, J. S. (1998). Relationship of childhood abuse and household dysfunction to many of the leading causes of death in adults: The Adverse Childhood Experiences (ACE) Study. *American Journal of Preventive Medicine, 14*(4), 245–258.

Ferrari, A. J., Charlson, F. J., Norman, R. E., Patten, S. B., Freedman, G., Murray, C. J., ... Whiteford, H. A. (2013). Burden of depressive disorders by country, sex, age, and year: Findings from the global burden of disease study 2010. *PLoS Medicine, 10*(11), e1001547.

Finlay-Jones, R., & Brown, G. W. (1981). Types of stressful life event and the onset of anxiety and depressive disorders. *Psychological Medicine, 11*(4), 803–815.

Flynn, M., & Rudolph, K. D. (2011). Stress generation and adolescent depression: Contribution of interpersonal stress responses. *Journal of Abnormal Child Psychology, 39*(8), 1187–1198. doi:10.1007/s10802-011-9527-1

Frank, E., Tu, X. M., Anderson, B., Reynolds, C. F., 3rd, Karp, J. F., Mayo, A., ... Kupfer, D. J. (1996). Effects of positive and negative life events on time to depression onset: an analysis of additivity and timing. *Psychological Medicine, 26*(3), 613–624.

Franzini, L., Ribble, J., & Keddie, A. (2001). Understanding the Hispanic paradox. *Ethnicity & Disease, 11*(3), 496–518.

Ge, X., Lorenz, F. O., Conger, R. D., Elder, G. H., & Simons, R. L. (1994). Trajectories of stressful life events and depressive symptoms during adolescence. *Developmental Psychology, 30*(4), 467.

George, L. K., & Lynch, S. M. (2003). Race differences in depressive symptoms: A dynamic perspective on stress exposure and vulnerability. *Journal of Health and Social Behavior, 44*(3), 353. doi:10.2307/1519784

Gershon, A., Hayward, C., Schraedley-Desmond, P., Rudolph, K. D., Booster, G. D., & Gotlib, I. H. (2011). Life stress and first onset of psychiatric disorders in daughters of depressed mothers. *Journal of Psychiatric Research, 45*(7), 855–862. doi:10.1016/j.jpsychires.2011.03.016

Gibb, B. E. (2002). Childhood maltreatment and negative cognitive styles: A quantitative and qualitative review. *Clinical Psychology Review, 22*(2), 223–246.

Gibb, B. E., Chelminski, I., & Zimmerman, M. (2007). Childhood emotional, physical, and sexual abuse, and diagnoses of depressive and anxiety disorders in adult psychiatric outpatients. *Depression and Anxiety, 24*(4), 256–263. doi:10.1002/da.20238

González, H. M., Tarraf, W., Whitfield, K. E., & Vega, W. A. (2010). The epidemiology of major depression and ethnicity in the United States. *Journal of Psychiatric Research, 44*(15), 1043–1051. doi:10.1016/j.jpsychires.2010.03.017

Goodyer, I., Kolvin, I., & Gatzanis, S. (1985). Recent undesirable life events and psychiatric disorder in childhood and adolescence. *The British Journal of Psychiatry, 147*(5), 517–523. doi:10.1192/bjp.147.5.517

Goodyer, I., Tamplin, A., Herbert, J., & Altham, P. (2000). Recent life events, cortisol, dehydroepiandrosterone and the onset of major depression in high-risk adolescents. *The British Journal of Psychiatry, 177*(6), 499–504.

Greenberg, P., Kessler, R., Birnbaum, H., Leong, S., Lowe, S., Berglund, P., & Corey-Lisle, P. (2003). The economic burden of depression in the United States: How did it change between 1990 and 2000? *Journal of Clinical Psychiatry, 64*(12), 1465–1475.

Grote, N. K., Bledsoe, S. E., Wellman, J., & Brown, C. (2007). Depression in African American and white women with low incomes: The role of chronic stress. *Social Work in Public Health, 23*(2–3), 59–88.

Hammen, C. (2005). Stress and depression. *Annual Review of Clinical Psychology, 1*, 293–319.

Hammen, C., Adrian, C., Gordon, D., Burge, D., Jaenicke, C., & Hiroto, D. (1987). Children of depressed mothers: Maternal strain and symptom predictors of dysfunction. *Journal of Abnormal Psychology, 96*(3), 190–198.

Hammen, C., Davila, J., Brown, G., Ellicott, A., & Gitlin, M. (1992). Psychiatric history and stress: Predictors of severity of unipolar depression. *Journal of Abnormal Psychology, 101*(1), 45–52.

Hammen, C., Henry, R., & Daley, S. (2000). Depression and sensitization to stressors among young women as a function of childhood adversity. *Journal of Consulting and Clinical Psychology, 68*(5), 782–787.

Hammen, C., Kim, E., Eberhart, N., & Brennan, P. (2009). Chronic and acute stress and the prediction of major depression in women. *Depression and Anxiety, 26*(8), 718–723.

Hammen, C., Marks, T., Mayol, A., & DeMayo, R. (1985). Depressive self-schemas, life stress, and vulnerability to depression. *Journal of Abnormal Psychology, 94*(3), 308–319.

Hammen, C., Shih, J. H., & Brennan, P. A. (2004). Intergenerational transmission of depression: Test of an interpersonal stress model in a community sample. *Journal of Consulting and Clinical Psychology, 72*(3), 511–522.

Hankin, B., Abramson, L. Y., Moffitt, T. E., Silva, P. A., McGee, R., & Angell, K. E. (1998). Development of depression from preadolescence to young adulthood: Emerging gender differences in a 10-year longitudinal study. *Journal of Abnormal Psychology, 107*(1), 128–140.

Hankin, B., Young, J. F., Abela, J. R. Z., Smolen, A., Jenness, J. L., Gulley, L. D.,…Oppenheimer, C. W. (2015). Depression from childhood into late adolescence: Influence of gender, development, genetic susceptibility, and peer stress. *Journal of Abnormal Psychology, 124*(4), 803–816. doi:10.1037/abn0000089

Hardt, J., & Rutter, M. (2004). Validity of adult retrospective reports of adverse childhood experiences: Review of the evidence. *Journal of Child Psychology and Psychiatry, 45*(2), 260–273.

Harkness, K., Alavi, N., Monroe, S. M., Slavich, G. M., Gotlib, I. H., & Bagby, R. M. (2010). Gender differences in life events prior to onset of major depressive disorder: The moderating effect of age. *Journal of Abnormal Psychology, 119*(4), 791–803. doi:10.1037/a0020629

Harkness, K., Bruce, A. E., & Lumley, M. N. (2006). The role of childhood abuse and neglect in the sensitization to stressful life events in adolescent depression. *Journal of Abnormal Psychology, 115*(4), 730–741. doi:10.1037/0021-843X.115.4.730

Harkness, K., & Monroe, S. (2016). The assessment and measurement of adult life stress: Basic premises, operational principles, and design requirements. *Journal of Abnormal Psychology, 125*(5), 727–745.

Hasin, D. S., Goodwin, R. D., Stinson, F. S., & Grant, B. F. (2005). Epidemiology of major depressive disorder: Results from the National Epidemiologic Survey on Alcoholism and Related Conditions. *Archives of General Psychiatry, 62*(10), 1097–1106.

Hawker, D. S. J., & Boulton, M. J. (2000). Twenty years' research on peer victimization and psychosocial maladjustment: A meta-analytic review of cross-sectional studies. *Journal of Child Psychology and Psychiatry, 41*(4), 441–455.

Hawkins, N., Davies, R., & Holmes, T. (1957). Evidence of psychosocial factors in the development of pulmonary tuberculosis. *American Review of Tuberculosis and Pulmonary Disease, 75*(5), 768–779.

Hazel, N., Hammen, C., Brennan, P., & Najman, J. (2008). Early childhood adversity and adolescent depression: The mediating role of continued stress. *Psychological Medicine, 38*(4), 581–589.

Heim, C., Newport, D. J., Mletzko, T., Miller, A. H., & Nemeroff, C. B. (2008). The link between childhood trauma and depression: Insights from HPA axis studies in humans. *Psychoneuroendocrinology, 33*(6), 693–710. doi:10.1016/j.psyneuen.2008.03.008

Holmes, T. H., & Rahe, R. H. (1967). The social readjustment rating scale. *Journal of Psychosomatic Research, 11*(2), 213–218.

Howe, G. W., Cimporescu, M., Seltzer, R., Neiderhiser, J. M., Moreno, F., & Weihs, K. (2016). Combining stress exposure and stress generation: Does neuroticism alter the dynamic interplay of stress, depression, and anxiety following job loss? *Journal of Personality, 85*(4), 553–564.

Hunter, C. D., Case, A. D., Joseph, N., Mekawi, Y., & Bokhari, E. (2017). The roles of shared racial fate and a sense of belonging with African Americans in Black immigrants' race-related stress and depression. *Journal of Black Psychology, 43*(2), 135–158.

Infurna, M. R., Reichl, C., Parzer, P., Schimmenti, A., Bifulco, A., & Kaess, M. (2016). Associations between depression and specific childhood experiences of abuse and neglect: A meta-analysis. *Journal of Affective Disorders, 190*, 47–55. doi:10.1016/j.jad.2015.09.006

Jaffee, S. R., Moffitt, T. E., Caspi, A., Fombonne, E., Poulton, R., & Martin, J. (2002). Differences in early childhood risk factors for juvenile-onset and adult-onset depression. *Archives of General Psychiatry, 59*(3), 215–222. doi:10.1001/archpsyc.59.3.215

Jenness, J. L., Hankin, B. L., Abela, J. R. Z., Young, J. F., & Smolen, A. (2011). Chronic family stress interacts with 5-HTTLPR to predict prospective depressive symptoms among youth. *Depression and Anxiety, 28*(12), 1074–1080. doi:10.1002/da.20904

Joiner, T., & Schmidt, N. B. (1998). Excessive reassurance-seeking predicts depressive but not anxious reactions to acute stress. *Journal of Abnormal Psychology, 107*(3), 533–537.

Joiner, T., & Timmons, K. A. (2009). Depression in its interpersonal context. In I. H. Gotlib & C. Hammen (Eds.), *Handbook of depression* (2nd ed., pp. 322–339). New York, NY: The Guilford Press.

Kaplow, J. B., & Widom, C. S. (2007). Age of onset of child maltreatment predicts long-term mental health outcomes. *Journal of Abnormal Psychology, 116*(1), 176–187. doi:10.1037/0021-843X.116.1.176

Karg, K., Burmeister, M., Shedden, K., & Sen, S. (2011). The serotonin transporter promoter variant (5-HTTLPR), stress, and depression meta-analysis revisited: Evidence of genetic moderation. *Archives of General Psychiatry, 68*(5), 444–454.

Keiley, M. K., Howe, T. R., Dodge, K. A., Bates, J. E., & Pettit, G. S. (2001). The timing of child physical maltreatment: A cross-domain growth analysis of impact on adolescent externalizing and internalizing problems. *Development and Psychopathology, 13*(4), 891–912.

Keller, M. C., Neale, M. C., & Kendler, K. S. (2007). Association of different adverse life events with distinct patterns of depressive symptoms. *American Journal of Psychiatry, 164*(10), 1521–1529.

Kendler, K., Bulik, C. M., Silberg, J., Hettema, J. M., Myers, J., & Prescott, C. A. (2000). Childhood sexual abuse and adult psychiatric and substance use disorders in women: An epidemiological and cotwin control analysis. *Archives of General Psychiatry, 57*(10), 953–959. doi:10.1001/archpsyc.57.10.953

Kendler, K., & Gardner, C. (2017). Genetic and environmental influences on last-year major depression in adulthood: A highly heritable stable liability but strong environmental effects on 1-year prevalence. *Psychological Medicine, 47*(10), 1816–1824. doi:10.1017/S0033291717000277

Kendler, K., Hettema, J. M., Butera, F., Gardner, C. O., & Prescott, C. A. (2003). Life event dimensions of loss, humiliation, entrapment, and danger in the prediction of onsets of major depression and generalized anxiety. *Archives of General Psychiatry, 60*(8), 789–796.

Kendler, K., Karkowski, L., & Prescott, C. (1998). Stressful life events and major depression: Risk period, long-term contextual threat, and diagnostic specificity. *Journal of Nervous and Mental Disease, 186*(11), 661–669.

Kendler, K., Karkowski, L., & Prescott, C. (1999). Causal relationship between stressful life events and the onset of major depression. *American Journal of Psychiatry, 156*(6), 837–841.

Kendler, K., Kessler, R., Walters, E., MacLean, C., Neale, M., Heath, A., & Eaves, L. (1995). Stressful life events, genetic liability, and onset of an episode of major depression in women. *American Journal of Psychiatry, 152*(6), 833–842.

Kessler, R. (1979). A strategy for studying differential vulnerability to the psychological consequences of stress. *Journal of Health and Social Behavior, 20*(2), 100–108. doi:10.2307/2136432

Kessler, R. (1997). The effects of stressful life events on depression. *Annual Review of Psychology, 48,* 191–214. doi:10.1146/annurev.psych.48.1.191

Kessler, R., Davis, C. G., & Kendler, K. S. (1997). Childhood adversity and adult psychiatric disorder in the US National Comorbidity Survey. *Psychological Medicine, 27*(5), 1101–1119.

Kessler, R., & Magee, W. (1994). Childhood family violence and adult recurrent depression. *Journal of Health and Social Behavior, 35*(1), 13–27.

Keyes, K. M., Eaton, N. R., Krueger, R. F., McLaughlin, K. A., Wall, M. M., Grant, B. F., & Hasin, D. S. (2012). Childhood maltreatment and the structure of common psychiatric disorders. *The British Journal of Psychiatry, 200*(2), 107–115.

Kilpatrick, D. G., Koenen, K. C., Ruggiero, K. J., Acierno, R., Galea, S., Resnick, H. S.,...Gelernter, J. (2007). The serotonin transporter genotype and social support and moderation of posttraumatic stress disorder and depression in hurricane-exposed adults. *American Journal of Psychiatry, 164*(11), 1693–1699.

Kim, J., & Cicchetti, D. (2006). Longitudinal trajectories of self-system processes and depressive symptoms among maltreated and nonmaltreated children. *Child Development, 77*(3), 624–639.

Kuehner, C. (2003). Gender differences in unipolar depression: An update of epidemiological findings and possible explanations. *Acta Psychiatrica Scandinavica, 108*(3), 163–174.

Kushner, M. R., Barrios, C., Smith, V. C., & Dougherty, L. R. (2016). Physiological and behavioral vulnerability markers increase risk to early life stress in preschool-aged children. *Journal of Abnormal Child Psychology, 44*(5), 859–870. doi:10.1007/s10802-015-0087-7

Lenze, S., Cyranowski, J. M., Thompson, W. K., Anderson, B., & Frank, E. (2008). The cumulative impact of nonsevere life events predicts depression recurrence during maintenance treatment with interpersonal psychotherapy. *Journal of Consulting and Clinical Psychology, 76*(6), 979–987.

Li, M., D'Arcy, C., & Meng, X. (2016). Maltreatment in childhood substantially increases the risk of adult depression and anxiety in prospective cohort studies: systematic review, meta-analysis, and proportional attributable fractions. *Psychological Medicine, 46*(4), 717–730. doi:10.1017/S0033291715002743

Lindert, J., von Ehrenstein, O. S., Grashow, R., Gal, G., Braehler, E., & Weisskopf, M. G. (2014). Sexual and physical abuse in childhood is associated with depression and anxiety over the life course: Systematic review and meta-analysis. *International Journal of Public Health, 59*(2), 359–372. doi:10.1007/s00038-013-0519-5

Lorant, V., Deliège, D., Eaton, W., Robert, A., Philippot, P., & Ansseau, M. (2003). Socioeconomic inequalities in depression: A meta-analysis. *American Journal of Epidemiology, 157*(2), 98–112.

Luby, J. L., Belden, A. C., & Spitznagel, E. (2006). Risk factors for preschool depression: The mediating role of early stressful life events. *Journal of Child Psychology and Psychiatry, 47*(12), 1292–1298. doi:10.1111/j.1469-7610.2006.01672.x

Lumley, M. N., & Harkness, K. L. (2007). Specificity in the relations among childhood adversity, early maladaptive schemas, and symptom profiles in adolescent depression. *Cognitive Therapy and Research, 31*(5), 639–657. doi:10.1007/s10608-006-9100-3

MacCallum, R. C., Zhang, S., Preacher, K. J., & Rucker, D. D. (2002). On the practice of dichotomization of quantitative variables. *Psychological Methods, 7*(1), 19–40.

Manly, J. T., Kim, J. E., Rogosch, F. A., & Cicchetti, D. (2001). Dimensions of child maltreatment and children's adjustment: Contributions of developmental timing and subtype. *Development and Psychopathology, 13*(4), 759–782.

Mazure, C. M. (1998). Life stressors as risk factors in depression. *Clinical Psychology: Science and Practice, 5*(3), 291–313.

McGonagle, K. A., & Kessler, R. C. (1990). Chronic stress, acute stress, and depressive symptoms. *American Journal of Community Psychology, 18*(5), 681–706.

McLeod, J. D., & Kessler, R. C. (1990). Socioeconomic status differences in vulnerability to undesirable life events. *Journal of Health and Social Behavior, 31,* 162–172.

McQuaid, J. R., Monroe, S. M., Roberts, J. R., Johnson, S. L., Garamoni, G. L., Kupfer, D. J., & Frank, E. (1992). Toward the standardization of life stress assessment: Definitional discrepancies and inconsistencies in methods. *Stress Medicine, 8*(1), 47–56.

Mendelson, T., Rehkopf, D. H., & Kubzansky, L. D. (2008). Depression among Latinos in the United States: A meta-analytic review. *Journal of Consulting and Clinical Psychology, 76*(3), 355–366.

Monroe, S., & Harkness, K. (2005). Life stress, the "kindling" hypothesis, and the recurrence of depression: Considerations from a life stress perspective. *Psychological Review, 112*(2), 417–444.

Monroe, S., & Reid, M. (2008). Gene-environment interactions in depression research: Genetic polymorphisms and life-stress polyprocedures. *Psychological Science, 19*(10), 947–956.

Monroe, S., Roberts, J. E., Kupfer, D. J., & Frank, E. (1996). Life stress and treatment course of recurrent depression: II. Postrecovery associations with attrition, symptom course, and recurrence over 3 years. *Journal of Abnormal Psychology, 105*(3), 313–328.

Monroe, S., Rohde, P., Seeley, J. R., & Lewinsohn, P. M. (1999). Life events and depression in adolescence: Relationship loss as a prospective risk factor for first onset of major depressive disorder. *Journal of Abnormal Psychology, 108*(4), 606–614. doi:10.1037//0021-843X.108.4.606

Monroe, S., Slavich, G., Torres, L., & Gotlib, I. (2007). Major life events and major chronic difficulties are differentially associated with history of major depressive episodes. *Journal of Abnormal Psychology, 116*(1), 116–124.

Monroe, S., Torres, L., Guillaumot, J., Harkness, K., Roberts, J., Frank, E., & Kupfer, D. (2006). Life stress and the long-term treatment course of recurrent depression: III. Nonsevere life events predict recurrence for medicated patients over 3 years. *Journal of Consulting and Clinical Psychology, 74*(1), 112–120.

Muscatell, K. A., Slavich, G. M., Monroe, S. M., & Gotlib, I. H. (2009). Stressful life events, chronic difficulties, and the symptoms of clinical depression. *The Journal of Nervous and Mental Disease, 197*(3), 154–160.

Myers, J. K., Lindenthal, J. J., & Pepper, M. P. (1971). Life events and psychiatric impairment. *Journal of Nervous and Mental Disease, 152*(3), 149–157.

Nanni, V., Uher, R., & Danese, A. (2012). Childhood maltreatment predicts unfavorable course of illness and treatment outcome in depression: A meta-analysis. *American Journal of Psychiatry, 169*(2), 141–151.

Nemeroff, C. B., Heim, C. M., Thase, M. E., Klein, D. N., Rush, A. J., Schatzberg, A. F., ...Keller, M. B. (2003). Differential responses to psychotherapy versus pharmacotherapy in patients with chronic forms of major depression and childhood trauma. *Proceedings of the National Academy of Sciences, 100*(24), 14293–14296.

Nolen-Hoeksema, S. (2001). Gender differences in depression. *Current Directions in Psychological Science, 10*(5), 173–176.

Norman, R. E., Byambaa, M., De, R., Butchart, A., Scott, J., & Vos, T. (2012). The Long-term health consequences of child physical abuse, emotional abuse, and neglect: A systematic review and meta-analysis. *PLoS Medicine, 9*(11), e1001349. doi:10.1371/journal.pmed.1001349

Ormel, J., Oldehinkel, A. J., & Brilman, E. I. (2001). The interplay and etiological continuity of neuroticism, difficulties, and life events in the etiology of major and subsyndromal, first and recurrent depressive episodes in later life. *American Journal of Psychiatry, 158*(6), 885–891.

Paykel, E. S. (1976). Life stress, depression and attempted suicide. *Journal of Human Stress, 2*(3), 3–12.

Paykel, E. S., Emms, E., Fletcher, J., & Rassaby, E. (1980). Life events and social support in puerperal depression. *The British Journal of Psychiatry, 136*(4), 339–346.

Post, R. (1992). Transduction of psychosocial stress into the neurobiology of recurrent affective disorder. *American Journal of Psychiatry, 149*(8), 999.

Rahe, R. H. (1974). The pathway between subjects' recent life changes and their near-future illness reports: Representative results and methodological issues. In B. Dohrenwend & B. Dohrenwend (Eds.), *Stressful life events: Their nature and effects*. Oxford, England: John Wiley & Sons.

Rahe, R. H. (1975). Epidemiological studies of life change and illness. *The International Journal of Psychiatry in Medicine, 6*(1–2), 133–146.

Rahe, R. H. (1978). Life change measurement clarification. *Psychosomatic Medicine, 40*(2), 95–98.

Rahe, R. H. (1979). Life change events and mental illness: an overview. *Journal of Human Stress, 5*(3), 2–10.

Rahe, R. H., Meyer, M., Smith, M., Kjaer, G., & Holmes, T. H. (1964). Social stress and illness onset. *Journal of Psychosomatic Research, 8*(1), 35–44.

Ramasubbu, R., Tobias, R., Buchan, A. M., & Bech-Hansen, N. T. (2006). Serotonin transporter gene promoter region polymorphism associated with poststroke major depression. *The Journal of Neuropsychiatry and Clinical Neurosciences, 18*(1), 96–99.

Riolo, S., Nguyen, T. A., Greden, J. F., & King, C. A. (2005). Prevalence of depression by race/ethnicity: Findings from the National Health and Nutrition Examination Survey III. *American Journal of Public Health, 95*(6), 998–1000.

Rodriquez, E. J., Livaudais-Toman, J., Gregorich, S. E., Jackson, J. S., Nápoles, A. M., & Pérez-Stable, E. J. (2018). Relationships between allostatic load, unhealthy behaviors, and depressive disorder in US adults, 2005–2012 NHANES. *Preventive Medicine, 110*, 9–15.

Rojo-Moreno, L., Livianos-Aldana, L., Cervera-Martinez, G., Dominguez-Carabantes, J., & Reig-Cebrian, M. (2002). The role of stress in the onset of depressive disorders. *Social Psychiatry and Psychiatric Epidemiology, 37*(12), 592–598.

Rose, D. T., & Abramson, L. (1992). Developmental predictors of depressive cognitive style: Research and theory. In D. Cicchetti & S. L. Toth (Eds.), *Developmental perspectives on depression* (Vol. 4, pp. 323–349). University of Rochester Press: Rochester, NY.

Roy, C. A., & Perry, J. C. (2004). Instruments for the assessment of childhood trauma in adults. *The Journal of Nervous and Mental Disease, 192*(5), 343.

Rudolph, K. (2002). Gender differences in emotional responses to interpersonal stress during adolescence. *Journal of Adolescent Health, 30*(4), 3–13.

Rudolph, K., & Flynn, M. (2007). Childhood adversity and youth depression: Influence of gender and pubertal status. *Development and Psychopathology, 19*(2). doi:10.1017/S0954579407070241

Rudolph, K., & Hammen, C. (1999). Age and gender as determinants of stress exposure, generation, and reactions in youngsters: A transactional perspective. *Child Development, 70*(3), 660–677.

Rudolph, K., Hammen, C., Burge, D., Lindberg, N., Herzberg, D., & Daley, S. E. (2000). Toward an interpersonal life-stress model of depression: The developmental context of stress generation. *Development and Psychopathology, 12*(2), 215–234.

Selye, H. (2013). *Stress in health and disease*. Boston, MA: Butterworths.

Sen, S., Kranzler, H. R., Krystal, J. H., Speller, H., Chan, G., Gelernter, J., & Guille, C. (2010). A prospective cohort study investigating factors associated with depression during medical internship. *Archives of General Psychiatry, 67*(6), 557–565.

Shanahan, L., Copeland, W. E., Costello, E. J., & Angold, A. (2011). Child-, adolescent- and young adult-onset depressions: Differential risk factors in development? *Psychological Medicine, 41*(11), 2265–2274. doi:10.1017/S0033291711000675

Shapero, B. G., Black, S. K., Liu, R. T., Klugman, J., Bender, R. E., Abramson, L. Y., & Alloy, L. B. (2014). Stressful life events and depression symptoms: The effect of childhood emotional abuse on stress reactivity: Child emotional abuse and stress sensitization. *Journal of Clinical Psychology, 70*(3), 209–223. doi:10.1002/jclp.22011

Sheets, E., & Craighead, W. (2014). Comparing chronic interpersonal and noninterpersonal stress domains as predictors of depression recurrence in emerging adults. *Behaviour Research and Therapy, 63*, 36–42.

Shih, J. H., Eberhart, N. K., Hammen, C. L., & Brennan, P. A. (2006). Differential exposure and reactivity to interpersonal stress predict sex differences in adolescent depression. *Journal of Clinical Child & Adolescent Psychology, 35*(1), 103–115. doi:10.1207/s15374424jccp3501_9

Shrout, P. E., Link, B. G., Dohrenwend, B. P., Skodol, A. E., Stueve, A., & Mirotznik, J. (1989). Characterizing life events as risk factors for depression: The role of fateful loss events. *Journal of Abnormal Psychology, 98*(4), 460.

Slavich, G., Monroe, S. M., & Gotlib, I. H. (2011). Early parental loss and depression history: Associations with recent life stress in major depressive disorder. *Journal of Psychiatric Research, 45*(9), 1146–1152. doi:10.1016/j.jpsychires.2011.03.004

Slavich, G., Thornton, T., Torres, L. D., Monroe, S., & Gotlib, I. (2009). Targeted rejection predicts hastened onset of major depression. *Journal of Social and Clinical Psychology, 28*(2), 223–243.

Spinhoven, P., Elzinga, B. M., Hovens, J. G. F. M., Roelofs, K., Zitman, F. G., van Oppen, P., & Penninx, B. W. J. H. (2010). The specificity of childhood adversities and negative life events across the life span to anxiety and depressive disorders. *Journal of Affective Disorders, 126*(1–2), 103–112. doi:10.1016/j.jad.2010.02.132

Springer, K. W., Sheridan, J., Kuo, D., & Carnes, M. (2003). The long-term health outcomes of childhood abuse. *Journal of General Internal Medicine, 18*(10), 864–870.

Staudt, M. M. (2001). Psychopathology, peer relations, and school functioning of maltreated children: A literature review. *Children & Schools, 23*(2), 85–100.

Stroud, C. B., Davila, J., Hammen, C., & Vrshek-Schallhorn, S. (2011). Severe and nonsevere events in first onsets versus recurrences of depression: Evidence for stress sensitization. *Journal of Abnormal Psychology, 120*(1), 142–154.

Sullivan, P., Neale, M., & Kendler, K. (2000). Genetic epidemiology of major depression: Review and meta-analysis. *American Journal of Psychiatry, 157*(10), 1552–1562.

Surtees, P. (1989). Adversity and psychiatric disorder: A decay model. In G. W. Brown & T. O. Harris (Eds.), *Life events and illness* (pp. 161–195). New York, NY: The Guilford Press.

Surtees, P., Miller, P. M., Ingham, J., Kreitman, N., Rennie, D., & Sashidharan, S. (1986). Life events and the onset of affective disorder: a longitudinal general population study. *Journal of Affective Disorders, 10*(1), 37–50.

Surtees, P., & Wainwright, N. (1999). Surviving adversity: Event decay, vulnerability and the onset of anxiety and depressive disorder. *European Archives of Psychiatry and Clinical Neuroscience, 249*(2), 86–95.

Szaflarski, M., Cubbins, L. A., Bauldry, S., Meganathan, K., Klepinger, D. H., & Somoza, E. (2016). Major depressive disorder and dysthymia at the intersection of nativity and racial–ethnic origins. *Journal of Immigrant and Minority Health, 18*(4), 749–763. doi:10.1007/s10903-015-0293-y

Tausig, M. (1982). Measuring life events. *Journal of Health and Social Behavior, 23*(March), 52–64.

Taylor, J., & Turner, R. J. (2002). Perceived discrimination, social stress, and depression in the transition to adulthood: Racial contrasts. *Social Psychology Quarterly, 65*(3), 213–225. doi:10.2307/3090120

Thornberry, T. P., Henry, K. L., Ireland, T. O., & Smith, C. A. (2010). The causal impact of childhood-limited maltreatment and adolescent maltreatment on early adult adjustment. *Journal of Adolescent Health, 46*(4), 359–365. doi:10.1016/j.jadohealth.2009.09.011

Turner, H. A., & Butler, M. J. (2003). Direct and indirect effects of childhood adversity on depressive symptoms in young adults. *Journal of Youth and Adolescence, 32*(2), 89–103. doi:10.1023/A:1021853600645

Turner, R. J., & Avison, W. R. (2003). Status variations in stress exposure: Implications for the interpretation of research on race, socioeconomic status, and gender. *Journal of Health and Social Behavior, 44*(4), 488–505. doi:10.2307/1519795

Turner, R. J., Wheaton, B., & Lloyd, D. A. (1995). The epidemiology of social stress. *American Sociological Review, 60*(1), 104–125. doi:10.2307/2096348

Twenge, J. M., & Nolen-Hoeksema, S. (2002). Age, gender, race, socioeconomic status, and birth cohort difference on the children's depression inventory: A meta-analysis. *Journal of Abnormal Psychology, 111*(4), 578–588.

Vrshek-Schallhorn, S., Mineka, S., Zinbarg, R., Craske, M., Griffith, J., Sutton, J.,…Adam, E. K. (2014). Refining the candidate environment: Interpersonal stress, the serotonin transporter polymorphism, and gene-environment interactions in major depression. *Clinical Psychological Science, 2*(3), 235–248.

Vrshek-Schallhorn, S., Stroud, C. B., Mineka, S., Hammen, C., Zinbarg, R. E., Wolitzky-Taylor, K., & Craske, M. G. (2015). Chronic and episodic interpersonal stress as statistically unique predictors of depression in two samples of emerging adults. *Journal of Abnormal Psychology, 124*(4), 776–790.

Vrshek-Schallhorn, S., Wolitzky-Taylor, K., Doane, L. D., Epstein, A., Sumner, J. A., Mineka, S.,…Adam, E. K. (2014). Validating new summary indices for the Childhood Trauma Interview: Associations with first onsets of major depressive disorder and anxiety disorders. *Psychological Assessment, 26*(3), 730–740. doi:10.1037/a0036842

Whisman, M. A. (2001). The association between marital dissatisfaction and depression. In S. Beach (Ed.), *Marital and family processes in depression: A scientific foundation for clinical practice* (pp. 3–24). Washington, DC: American Psychological Association.

Widom, C. S., DuMont, K., & Czaja, S. J. (2007). A prospective investigation of major depressive disorder and comorbidity in abused and neglected children grown up. *Archives of General Psychiatry, 64*(1), 49–56.

Williams, D. R., González, H. M., Neighbors, H., Nesse, R., Abelson, J. M., Sweetman, J., & Jackson, J. S. (2007). Prevalence and distribution of major depressive disorder in African Americans, Caribbean Blacks, and non-Hispanic Whites: Results from the National Survey of American Life. *Archives of General Psychiatry, 64*(3), 305–315.

Williamson, D. E., Birmaher, B., Frank, E., Anderson, B. P., Matty, M. K., & Kupfer, D. J. (1998). Nature of life events and difficulties in depression adolescents. *Journal of the American Academy of Child and Adolescent Psychiatry, 37*(10), 1049–1057.

Zlotnick, C., Mattia, J., & Zimmerman, M. (2001). Clinical features of survivors of sexual abuse with major depression. *Child Abuse & Neglect, 25*(3), 357–367. doi:10.1016/S0145-2134(00)00251-9

Stress in Bipolar Disorder

Lauren B. Alloy, Madison K. Titone, Tommy H. Ng, *and* Corinne P. Bart

Abstract

Environmental experiences play an important part in the development and maintenance of bipolar spectrum disorders (BSDs). Consequently, in this chapter, we review evidence on the role of life stress in the onset and course of BSDs. We begin with methodological issues relevant to demonstrating life stress's role in the development and course of BSDs. We consider the effects of exposure both to recent life events and childhood stressors, as well as whether the influence of stressor exposure changes over the course of BSDs. We also address whether the effects of different types of life event exposure depend on mood episode polarity (hypomanic/manic versus depressive episodes) and whether there are specific theoretically relevant types of life events that are particularly likely to trigger bipolar episodes or symptoms. We end with suggestions for future research that may lead to a more complete understanding of the bipolar disorder–stress association.

Keywords: bipolar spectrum disorders, life stress, childhood stressors, mood episode polarity, onset, course

Bipolar disorders are characterized by extreme contrasts in mood (euphoria or irritability versus sadness), motivation (excessive goal pursuit versus withdrawal and anhedonia), cognition (grandiosity and racing thoughts versus worthlessness), and behavior (supercharged energy, decreased need for sleep, and increased talkativeness versus fatigue, psychomotor retardation, and lethargy) that occur within the same individual. They occur on a continuum or spectrum of severity from the milder cyclothymic disorder (involving brief periods of hypomania and depression), to bipolar II disorder (involving at least one hypomanic episode and at least one major depressive episode), to full-blown bipolar I disorder (involving at least one manic episode) at the most severe end of the continuum (e.g., Akiskal, Djenderedjian, Rosenthal, & Khani, 1977; Alloy et al., 2012; Birmaher et al., 2006; 2009; Cassano et al., 1999; Goodwin & Jamison, 2007). Moreover, milder forms of bipolar disorder sometimes progress to the more severe forms (e.g., Akiskal et al., 1977;

Alloy et al., 2012; Birmaher et al., 2006, 2009; Kochman et al., 2005). Approximately 4.4% of the US population exhibits a disorder in the bipolar spectrum (Merikangas et al., 2007), and these disorders are among the leading causes of functional disability worldwide (e.g., Miklowitz & Johnson, 2006), often involving severe personal, social, and economic costs. For example, individuals with bipolar spectrum disorders (BSDs) experience divorce, substance abuse, suicide, and impairment in academic and occupational functioning at high rates (e.g., Boland, Stange, Adams, et al., 2016; Conway, Compton, Stinson, & Grant, 2006; Judd et al., 2008; Nusslock, Alloy, Abramson, Harmon-Jones, & Hogan, 2008), although they also exhibit high creativity and significant achievement (Johnson, Murray, et al., 2012).

Although a variety of neurobiological mechanisms have been proposed to explain the pathophysiology of BSDs, and these disorders exhibit a strong genetic predisposition (Craddock & Sklar,

2013), the importance of environmental experiences in the development and maintenance of BSDs has gained increasing recognition over the past quarter century (e.g., Alloy et al., 2005). Consequently, in this chapter, we review evidence on the role of life stress in the onset and course of BSDs. We consider the effects of exposure to both recent life events and childhood stressors, as well as whether the influence of life stress exposure changes over the course of BSDs. In addition, we address whether the effects of different types of life event exposure depend on mood episode polarity (hypomanic/manic versus depressive episodes) and whether there are specific types of life events relevant to hypothesized theoretical models of vulnerability to BSDs that are particularly likely to trigger bipolar mood episodes or symptoms. However, we begin with a discussion of methodological issues relevant to demonstrating a role of life stress in the onset and course of BSDs and the special challenges posed by BSDs for this endeavor.

Methodological Issues in Life Stress Research and Challenges Posed by Bipolar Disorders

In general, to demonstrate that life stress is a risk factor for BSD onset or worsening course or a precipitant of bipolar mood symptoms or episodes, one must show (1) that the life events temporally precede mood episode or symptom onsets/exacerbations, and (2) that the life events are not solely a consequence of bipolar symptoms (Alloy et al., 2005; i.e., that event reports are not biased by the presence of mood symptoms or that the occurrence of the events is not caused by stress generation processes [Hammen, 1991], that is, generated by symptoms or behaviors characteristic of individuals with BSDs). Thus, cross-sectional or retrospective studies that compare bipolar individuals to healthy controls or to individuals with another disorder (e.g., unipolar depression) on concurrent or past life stress can suggest a potential precipitating role for life events, but they are inadequate for establishing temporal precedence of the stressors relative to bipolar symptoms. Indeed, in retrospective studies especially, there is a risk of bipolar individuals exhibiting "effort after meaning" bias (Brown & Harris, 1978), in which they may recall information about life stress prior to bipolar episodes in such a way as to justify the occurrence of their mood symptoms. Studies that compare remitted or euthymic bipolar individuals to healthy controls on life stress or that longitudinally compare bipolar individuals in depressed, hy-

pomanic or manic (hereafter referred to as hypo/manic), and euthymic states are an improvement over cross-sectional or retrospective studies because they can demonstrate life stress even in the absence of symptoms of the disorder. However, such "remitted designs" cannot distinguish between the alternatives that the life events are causes or consequences of BSDs (see Just, Abramson, & Alloy, 2001; Lewinsohn, Steinmetz, Larson, & Franklin, 1981). Thus, prospective, longitudinal designs in which life stress is assessed prior to the occurrence of bipolar mood episodes are best suited to establishing both the stressors' temporal precedence and independence from symptoms (Alloy et al., 2005). Consequently, in our review of the role of life stress in BSDs, the methodologically stronger longitudinal and prospective studies should be given more weight in conclusions about life stress–BSD relationships.

However, even prospective longitudinal studies cannot establish that life stress is a causal risk factor for or precipitant of BSDs on their own (Kraemer et al., 1997). To do this, one must rule out plausible third variable explanations and show that manipulations of life stress lead to changes in the likelihood of mood episodes or symptoms. For example, genetic predisposition is a plausible third variable important to rule out in the case of stress–BSD associations. Genetic vulnerability as expressed in temperament or other behavioral substrates may be associated with a greater likelihood of exposure to life stressors (i.e., "genotype–environment correlation"; Plomin & Crabbe, 2000). Few studies in the literature attempt to rule out genetic predisposition, but those that try do so by controlling for family history of bipolar disorder and, thus, control for family environment associated with having a bipolar relative in addition to genetic predisposition to bipolarity. We note any studies that control for family history of bipolarity.

Given that manipulating life stress to induce bipolar symptoms would be ethically questionable, treatment studies that attempt to reduce the effects of life events are relevant to demonstrating the causal significance of life stress for bipolar mood episodes. However, few intervention studies actually examine whether reduction in stressors is the mechanism of any observed change in bipolar symptoms or course. Thus, we do not include a review of treatment studies that target life stress in their interventions in this chapter (but see Alloy et al., 2005).

There are additional methodological issues relevant to understanding the relationship between life stress and BSDs. First, some studies do not include a healthy control group to allow for conclusions about whether the life stress encountered by BSD individuals differs from that of controls. Second, the way in which life stress is assessed may be problematic in some research. Studies that use self-report of life events on questionnaires may be open to individual differences in subjective interpretations of what experiences count as an instance of various life event categories (Harkness & Monroe, 2016). Thus, greater weight should be given to studies that use well-validated life events interviews with clear event category criteria (see Monroe & Slavich chapter, this volume). Third, there is considerable variability across studies in the time intervals (e.g., <3 months, 6 months, 1 year, >1 year) used to assess exposure to life events. Given that events that precede bipolar symptoms/episodes by shorter time intervals may be likely to have greater causal relevance, studies that employ long time intervals for assessing events (either retrospective recall periods or prospective follow-up periods) may not capture the most etiologically relevant events. Fourth, many studies do not separately examine the role of life stress in hypo/manic versus depressive episodes of BSD. Fifth, some studies use hospital admission or beginning of treatment as the time of episode onset, which may not correspond well with the actual time of episode onset, making it more difficult to establish temporal precedence for life stress. Sixth, many studies identify mood episodes and then examine life stress during an interval prior to these episodes. But this approach can lead to Type 1 errors because it ignores instances in which events occurred and did not lead to mood episode onsets. Seventh, sample selection also may influence observed stress–BSD associations. Small samples may be underpowered to detect existing life event–mood episode/symptom associations and severe, patient samples may lead to detection of stress–mood episode/symptom associations that are biased by the effects of medication or psychotherapy exposure.

Moreover, BSDs pose additional challenging methodological issues for demonstrating that life stress is a risk factor for mood episodes and symptoms. First, as a consequence of multiple mood swings and interepisode symptoms, many bipolar individuals lead chaotic lives. This, in turn, may increase the likelihood that they contribute to the occurrence of stressful events through impulsivity, extreme goal striving, and other symptoms (Hammen, 1991). Indeed, researchers (e.g., Hammen, 1991) make a distinction between dependent events that are likely to be at least partly caused by an individual's symptoms or behaviors (e.g., fight with a spouse, failing an exam) versus independent events (e.g., death of a loved one, losing one's house in a tornado) that are fateful and uncontrollable. Individuals with BSDs are likely to experience many dependent events as a result of their many mood swings and symptoms occurring even between episodes. Although dependent events may precipitate bipolar symptoms and episodes, the fact that their occurrence can also be a consequence of bipolar individuals' behavior makes it more difficult to clearly establish their causal role in BSDs. In contrast, because individuals cannot readily contribute to the occurrence of independent events, a causal role for independent events that precede bipolar symptoms or episodes may be inferred more readily. Second, because BSDs are highly recurrent with significant interepisode symptoms and functional impairment, it can be difficult to assess stressors at a time when the individual is asymptomatic in order to establish independence of these events from bipolar symptoms. Residual symptoms may bias the assessment of life stress; thus, studies of the role of stressors in BSDs need to control for current mood and symptoms. With these methodological caveats in mind, we turn first to a review of the role of recent life stressors in BSDs.

Recent Life Stress and Bipolar Spectrum Disorders

Prior reviews of the literature on life stress and BSDs have concluded that individuals with BSDs experience increased life events prior to first onsets and recurrences of mood episodes (Alloy et al., 2005, 2009; Alloy, Abramson, Smith, Gibb, & Neeren, 2006; Alloy, Abramson, Walshaw, Keyser, & Gerstein, 2006; Johnson, 2005; Johnson & Kizer, 2002). Indeed, a recent meta-analysis (Lex, Bazner, & Meyer, 2017) of 42 studies including 4,562 participants with BSDs, 4,020 with unipolar depression, 464 with schizophrenia, 123 with physical illnesses, and 31,962 healthy controls found that BSD individuals experienced more life events relative to physically ill and healthy controls, but not more than individuals with unipolar depression or schizophrenia. Participants with BSD also reported more life events prior to mood episodes than during euthymic phases. In addition, the specific event of childbirth affected individuals with BSD more than those with unipolar depression. Most of the studies included in this meta-analysis were retrospective and the meta-analysis did not separate the role of life events in depressive versus hypo/manic episodes of bipolar disorder. However, the evidence suggests that whereas negative life events may contribute to depressive episodes, both negative and positive life events may be important in precipitating hypo/mania.

Cross-Sectional and Retrospective Studies

As reflected in the Lex et al. (2017) meta-analysis, most published studies of the role of recent life stress in BSDs have been cross-sectional or retrospective, and thus, are suggestive but not as informative as the smaller number of longitudinal or prospective studies (see Table 6.1 for the cross-sectional and retrospective studies). Some earlier retrospective studies used nonoptimal measures of life stress, namely medical chart reviews, in bipolar I patient samples (Ambelas, 1979, 1987; Clancy, Crowe, Winokur, & Morrison, 1973; Leff, Fischer, & Bertelsen, 1976). However, on the positive side, these researchers did rate the degree of independence of the stressors on the patients' behavior. These studies found that the bipolar patients experienced a higher rate of independent stressors in the 1–3 months prior to onset of a mood episode than controls, with 20%–66% of the bipolar patients experiencing at least one independent stressor during this pre-episode period.

Another group of cross-sectional or retrospective studies improved upon the stress assessments by administering life events questionnaires to assess past stressors to individuals with BSDs (Beyer, Kuchibhatla, Cassidy, & Krishnan, 2008; Bidzinska, 1984; Dunner, Patrick, & Fieve, 1979; Horesh & Iancu, 2010; Hosang et al., 2010; 2012; Kulhara, Basu, Mattoo, Sharan, & Chopra, 1999; Neria et al., 2008; Rucklidge, 2006). The earlier three of these studies found that stressful events preceded both the first episode (Bidzinska, 1984; Dunner et al., 1979) and episode relapses (Bidzinska, 1984; Kulhara et al., 1999) of bipolar disorder; however the Bidzinska and Dunner et al. studies did not include a comparison control group. Another three of these studies specifically compared bipolar to unipolar patients as well as to healthy controls on life events checklists. Horesh and Iancu (2010) used an 86-item life events questionnaire, and all patient participants were taking lithium and were in remission. From medical chart review, the authors determined the dates of the patients' first and last episode onsets and then examined events from the questionnaire occurring in the year prior to each episode onset. They found that the unipolar and bipolar groups did not differ from each other in terms of

their scores on the questionnaire, and both reported more total life events in the year before their first and last episodes than did the controls during a similar time period. Specifically, both the unipolar and bipolar groups had more negative and loss events, the unipolar group had more positive and achievement events, and the bipolar group had more uncontrollable events. Hosang et al. (2010, 2012) used an 11-item checklist of major stressors occurring in the 6 months prior to worst mood episode in very large samples of bipolar I and II and unipolar depressed patients and controls recruited from genetic studies. They found that bipolar and unipolar participants did not differ and both were more likely to report at least one event, and more events, in the 6 months prior to their worst episode than healthy controls in the 6 months prior to the study. Moreover, in the bipolar group, there was a significant association between interpersonal, financial, and job loss events preceding both manic and depressive episodes, and dependent stressors were associated with episodes, whereas independent events were not. In addition, bipolar episodes were more associated with financial crisis, whereas unipolar episodes were more related to death of a spouse and illness in a close relative.

Beyer et al. (2008) compared older (49+) and younger (18–49) bipolar patients to age-matched healthy controls on a self-report events checklist. They found that stressors were equally as common in the older as the younger bipolar patients, and both groups reported more events than the age-matched controls. In a cross-sectional design, Rucklidge (2006) compared a small group of adolescents with BSDs with healthy controls on a life events checklist. The BSD group reported more negative life events than the controls as well as a greater history of traumatic events (50% vs. 10%). Finally, Neria and colleagues (2008) specifically examined exposure to traumatic life events in a large primary care patient sample. Compared to patients without BSD ($n = 881$), those with BSD ($n = 96$) were 2.6 times more likely to report physical or sexual assault and 2.9 times as likely to have current posttraumatic stress disorder (PTSD).

Four retrospective studies improved further on life stress assessments by including life events interviews (such as the Paykel interview [Paykel, 1980] or the Life Events and Difficulties Schedule [LEDS; Brown & Harris, 1978]) and a determination of whether the events were independent or dependent on the participants' behavior (Aronson & Shukla, 1987; Davenport & Adland, 1982; El Kissi et al.,

Table 6.1. Retrospective and Cross-Sectional Studies of Life Events and Bipolar Disorder

Study	Sample	Life Events Measures	Bipolar Disorder and Other Psychopathology Measures	Results
Ambelas (1979)	67 bipolar manic 60 surgical control patients	Review of medical charts	Clinical diagnosis	More manic patients than controls (28% vs. 6%) had independent stressful event in 4 weeks prior to hospital admission ($d = .98$)
Ambelas (1987)	90 bipolar manic age-matched surgical control patients	Review of medical charts	Clinical diagnosis	4 weeks prior to hospital admission, 66% of first episode manic and 20% of recurrent episode manic patients vs. 8% of controls had independent stressful event in (d's = 1.81, 1.25)
Aronson & Shukla (1987)	30 bipolar I patients	Occurrence of major hurricane	Clinical diagnosis–DSM-III	Increase in relapses in 2 weeks after hurricane than in 1 month before hurricane ($d = .75$)
Bebbington et al. (1993)	31 manic, 14 psychotic depressed, 52 schizophrenic, 207 control patients	Structured interview–LEDS	Clinical diagnosis	Manic patients experienced more independent, severe events 3 months before relapse than controls ($d = 1.26$)
Beyer et al. (2008)	146 bipolar patients (88 ages 18–49; 58 ages >49); 101 age-matched controls	Questionnaire DDSI	Diagnostic interview –SCID	Both younger and older bipolar patients had more negative events in past year than controls (ORs = 4.72, 4.91); however, no significant difference in number of negative events between bipolar groups
Bidzinska (1984)	50 bipolar patients, 47 unipolar patients, 100 controls	Questionnaire Life Events Questionnaire	Clinical diagnosis	Bipolar and unipolar patients had more life events in 3 months prior to first onset episodes ($d = .51$) and relapses ($d = .44$) than controls
Chakraborty et al. (2007)	18 ATPD, 20 manic	Structured interview–PLES	Clinical diagnosis–ICD-10	Bipolar I manic patients had fewer undesirable and impersonal events in 6 months prior to current episode than those with acute/transient psychosis
Chung et al. (1986)	14 hypomanic, 15 schizophrenic, 9 schizophreniform, 30 control patients	Structured interview–LEDS	Clinical diagnosis–DSM-III	Hypomanic patients had twice as many independent, long-term threat events than controls, but this effect was not significant ($d = .40$)
Clancy et al. (1973)	100 bipolar patients, 225 unipolar patients, 200 schizophrenic patients	Review of medical charts	Clinical diagnosis based on chart review	39% of unipolar, 27% of bipolar, and 11% of schizophrenic patients had stressful event in 3 months prior to disorder onset (d's = .33 –.62)
Davenport & Adland (1982)	40 bipolar men	Occurrence of wife's pregnancy	Clinical diagnosis based on chart review	50% onset rate of mood episodes during or after wife's pregnancy

(continued)

Table 6.1. Continued

Study	Sample	Life Events Measures	Bipolar Disorder and Other Psychopathology Measures	Results
Dunner et al. (1979)	79 bipolar I patients	Questionnaire	Clinical diagnosis	50% of bipolar patients had a life event within 3 months preonset; work and interpersonal stressors were associated with onset of manic vs. depressive episode ($d = .75$)
El Kissi et al. (2013)	60 bipolar I/II patients, 60 unaffected siblings, 60 stomatology outpatient controls	Structured interview–Paykel's interview for Recent life events	Clinical diagnosis	Bipolar patients and their siblings had more total life events than controls, but the three groups did not differ on life events with objective negative impact
Hillegers et al. (2004)	140 adolescent offspring of bipolar parents	Structured interview–LEDS	Diagnostic interview–K–SADS	Offspring had 10% increased risk of mood disorder per unit increase in life events
Horesh & Iancu (2010)	30 bipolar I patients, 30 unipolar patients, 60 controls	Questionnaire - ALEQ, CLEL	Diagnostic interview–SCID	Unipolar and bipolar patients had significantly more total, negative, and general loss events than controls in year before first depressive episode, while bipolar patients had significantly more total and ambiguous events in year before first manic episode than controls
Hosang et al.	512 bipolar I and II, 1,447 unipolar, 1,346 controls	Questionnaire -LITE-Q	Diagnostic interview–SCAN	Patients reported more adverse events prior to affective episodes compared to controls (62.8% – 71.9% vs. 48.4%)
Hosang et al. (2012)	512 bipolar I & II LTE-Q, 1,448 unipolar, 1,291 controls	Structured Interview – SCAN	Diagnostic Interview	Whereas dependent events were equally important before affective episodes in both unipolar and bipolar, independent events were only significantly associated with worst depressive episode in unipolar patients (OR = 1.71)
Joffe et al. (1989)	28 bipolar patients, 14 with recent mania and 14 with no recent mania	Structured interview–PERI-LEI	Diagnostic interview–SADS	Bipolar patients with recent mania had more independent events in 3 months prior to onset than corresponding 3-month period for bipolar patients without recent mania ($d = .75$)
Kennedy et al. (1983)	20 manic patients, 20 orthopedic controls	Structured interview–Recent Life Events Interview	Diagnostic interview–Renard Diagnostic Interview	Manic patients had more independent events 4 months prior to hospital admission than controls ($d = .79$) or than 4 months after admission ($d = .74$)
Kulhara et al. (1999)	118 bipolar patients Presumptive Stressful Life Events Scale	Questionnaire based on chart review	Clinical diagnosis – ICD-9	Number of life events predicted frequency of episode relapses over 11-year follow-up ($d = .22$)
Leff et al. (1976)	55 manic inpatients	Review of medical charts	Clinical diagnosis and diagnostic interview–PSE	35% of bipolar patients had independent stressful event in 1 month prior to disorder onset

Study	Sample	Measure	Diagnostic	Findings
Neria et al. (2008)	96 bipolar patients, 881 control patients	Questionnaire—LES	Clinical diagnosis based on chart review and Questionnaire – MDQ	Bipolar patients were 2.6 times more likely to report physical/sexual assault and 2.9 times more likely to have current PTSD than nonbipolar patients
Ostiguy et al. (2009)	70 youth (ages 13–26), 37 with bipolar parent, 33 with unaffected parents	Structured interview—UCLA-LSI	Diagnostic Interview –SCID & K-SADS	Offspring of bipolar parents had more episodic stress in past year and more chronic family, financial, and health stress in past 6 months compared to controls; groups did not differ on number of dependent events
Perris (1984)	16 bipolar, 58 unipolar, 81 neurotic affective patients	Structured interview	Clinical diagnosis	Bipolar patients had more independent events in year prior to episode onset than unipolar patients (d = .45), but nonsignificant fewer than neurotic patients (d = –.29)
Petti et al. (2004)	50 youth (ages 6–17) of bipolar families; 23 with bipolar parent and 27 with unaffected parents	Questionnaire – LEC completed by youth and parents	Diagnostic interview– DICA	Youth with bipolar or unipolar disorder had more negative life events in past year than youth without mood disorder based on parent report; no effect based on youth report
Rucklidge (2006)	63 youth (ages 13–17); 24 with bipolar and 39 controls	Questionnaire – LEC	Diagnostic interview – K-SADS	Bipolar patients had more negative life events (d = .81), and greater history or traumatic events (50 vs. 10%) compared to controls
Sclare & Creed (1990)	30 bipolar patients	Structured interview– PSE	Diagnostic interview–PSE	More bipolar patients had an independent event prior to hospital admission than postdischarge (d = .70)
Wals et al. (2005)	132 offspring of bipolar parents	Structured interview–LEDS	Diagnostic interview–LEDS	Dependent life events associated with increased risk of mood episode in offspring with affected parents (OR = 5.4), but was not significant when controlling for prior anxiety/depression

LEDS = Life Events and Difficulties Schedule; PERI-LEI = Psychiatric Epidemiology Research Interview-Life Events Interview; LEC = Life Events Checklist; SLE = Schedule for Life Events; *DSM = Diagnostic and Statistical Manual of Mental Disorders*; ICD = International Classification of Diseases; K-SADS = Kiddie Schedule for Affective Disorders and Schizophrenia; SADS = Schedule for Affective Disorders and Schizophrenia; PSE = Present State Examination; DICA = Diagnostic Interview for Children and Adolescents; ALEQ = Adult Life Events Questionnaire; CLEL = Childhood Life Events List; SCID = Structured Diagnostic Interview for *DSM-IV*; LTE-Q = List of Threatening Events Questionnaire; SCAN = Schedule for Clinical Assessments in Neuropsychiatry; DDSI = Duke Social Support Index; PLES = Presumptive Stressful Life Events Scale; MDQ = Mood Disorders Questionnaire; LES = Life Events Scale; UCLA-LSI = UCLA Life Stress Interview.

2013; Perris, 1984). Of these four studies, two obtained findings consistent with a precipitating role for independent stressors and two did not. Aronson and Shukla (1987) found an increase in relapses in the 2 weeks following a hurricane than in the 1 month prior to the hurricane for bipolar I patients. Similarly, Davenport and Adland (1982) found a 50% onset rate of mood episodes in bipolar men during or after their wives' pregnancies. Neither of these studies included a comparison control group. In contrast, Perris (1984) found that bipolar patients reported more life events in the 1 year prior to episode onset than unipolar depressed patients, but nonsignificantly fewer events than neurotic patients. And El-Kissi et al. (2013) reported that bipolar I and II patients and their siblings had higher global life events scores, and specifically, more work, socio-family, and health stressors than age- and sex-matched controls. The bipolar group also reported more desirable events than their siblings or the controls. However, the siblings had higher scores on uncontrollable (i.e., independent) events than the bipolar patients or controls.

Six retrospective studies examined whether independent stressors were associated with manic episodes specifically (Bebbington et al., 1993; Chakraborty, Chatterjee, Choudhary, Singh, & Chakraborty, 2007; Chung, Langeluddecke, & Tennant, 1986; Joffe, MacDonald, & Kutcher, 1989; Kennedy, Thompson, Stancer, Roy, & Persad, 1983; Sclare & Creed, 1990). In four of these studies, the manic patients reported significantly more independent negative events in the period prior to manic episode onset than controls (Bebbington et al., 1993; Kennedy et al., 1983) or than in the period after onset (Joffe et al., 1989; Kennedy et al., 1983; Sclare & Creed, 1990). In contrast, Chung et al. (1986) found that 14 manic patients' rate of independent threatening events on a life events interview in the 26 weeks prior to onset did not significantly differ from controls' rate; however, the rate for the manic patients was twice as high as controls, suggesting that issues with statistical power may have played a role in the lack of significance. Finally, Chakraborty et al. (2007) observed that bipolar I manic patients reported *fewer* undesirable and independent events on a questionnaire for the 6-month period prior to the current episode than patients with acute and transient psychosis; however, this study did not include a nonpatient comparison group.

Of special interest are four cross-sectional or retrospective studies of recent stressors in the offspring of bipolar parents compared to the offspring of parents without mood disorders (Hillegers et al., 2004; Ostiguy et al., 2009; Petti et al., 2004; Wals et al., 2005). In a cross-sectional study, Ostiguy et al. (2009) reported that the offspring of bipolar parents experienced both more episodic stressors over the past 12 months and more chronic stress in family relationships, finances, and health over the past 6 months than the offspring of control parents. The other three retrospective studies of the adolescent offspring of bipolar parents all found that offspring who developed a bipolar disorder themselves experienced significantly more negative life events than did unaffected offspring. However, in the case of the Wals et al. (2005) study, only dependent life events were related to increased risk of a mood episode in the offspring of the bipolar parents, but this was no longer significant when prior anxiety and depressive symptoms of the offspring were controlled.

In summary, cross-sectional and retrospective studies suggest that individuals with BSDs and their offspring experience more stressful life events prior to onsets and recurrences of mood episodes than do healthy controls and their offspring, or than they experience during periods of euthymia. Some of these studies also suggest that the increased stressors prior to mood episodes are independent of the bipolar individuals' behaviors and characteristics. However, the cross-sectional and retrospective studies cannot establish temporal precedence of the stressors relative to bipolar symptoms or episodes, and thus, do not provide a strong basis for inferring a causal role for stressful events in BSDs. Prospective studies are needed to more confidently conclude that stressful events precede and precipitate bipolar mood episodes and symptoms.

Prospective Studies

Although fewer in number, the prospective studies of life stress and BSD provide a stronger basis on which to draw conclusions about the role of life events in triggering bipolar mood episodes or symptoms (see Table 6.2 for the prospective studies). Four prospective studies used questionnaire assessments of life events in bipolar patients, but they did not distinguish between events that were independent or dependent on participants' behavior (Christensen et al., 2003; Hall, Dunner, Zeller, & Fieve, 1977; Gilman et al., 2015; Koenders et al., 2014). In addition, they did not include comparison groups of healthy controls. In the earliest of these studies, Hall et al. (1977) assessed life events monthly for 10 months and reported that bipolar patients who experienced a relapse of hypomania

Table 6.2. Prospective Studies of Life Events and Bipolar Disorder

Study	Sample	Life Events Measures	Bipolar Disorder and Other Psychopathology Measures	Results
Christensen et al. (2003)	56 bipolar patients	Questionnaire–Paykel LES	Chart review and ICD-10	Bipolar women, but not men, had more events in 3 months prior to a depression onset than a control period
Ellicott et al. (1990)	61 bipolar outpatients	Structured interview– LEDS	Diagnostic interview–DSM-III-R	Bipolar patients who had high levels of negative life events had 4.53 times higher risk of relapse than those with low levels of stress
Gershon, Johnson, & Miller (2013)	131 bipolar I patients	Structured interview–LEDS	Diagnostic interview–SCID, DSM-IV	Interpersonal chronic stress severity predicted depression but not mania over follow-up
Gilman et al. (2015)	34,653 nationally representative participants	Questionnaire–checklist of life events interview	Fully structured DSM-IV criteria	Personal losses, interpersonal problems, and economic difficulties were associated with increased risk of first onset and recurrent manic episodes. Economic difficulties and financial/interpersonal instability were associated with prospective depressive episodes
Hall et al. (1977)	38 bipolar I patients	Questionnaire –SLE	Clinical diagnosis	No difference in number of events in 1 mo. prior to onset for patients who relapsed vs. those who did not (d = .77); hypomanic relapsers had more work-related events than nonrelapsers
Hammen & Gitlin (1997)	52 bipolar outpatients	Structured interview– LEDS	Diagnostic interview–DSM-III-R	Patients who relapsed had more negative life events in 3 months and 6 months preonset than those who did not relapse (ds = .52, .56)
Hunt et al. (1992)	63 bipolar I patients	Structured interview– Paykel interview	Diagnostic interview–SADS	Patients who relapsed were more likely to have a preonset severe event than those who did not relapse (d = .76)
Johnson & Miller (1997)	67 bipolar I patients	Structured interview– LEDS	Diagnostic interview SCID	Patients who had a severe, independent event during index episode took 3 times longer to recover than those with no event (d = –.92)
Kim et al. (2007)	38 bipolar I/II/NOS adolescents aged 13–17	UCLA Life Stress Interview	Diagnostic interview–KSADS	High chronic stress assoc. with less improvement in mood symptoms over 1 year. High chronic stress in peer relations associated with less improvement in manic symptoms over 1 year
Koenders et al. (2014)	173 bipolar I/II outpatients	Paykel's self-report questionnaire	Diagnostic interview, Dutch versions of MINI-PLUS	Negative life events associated with increases in depression and manic symptoms at follow-up, whereas positive life events associations with manic symptom severity at follow-up
McPherson et al. (1993)	58 bipolar I patients	Structured interview–SADS	Diagnostic interview–SADS	No difference in number of severe, independent events in months preceding relapse compared with control periods (ds = 1.0)
Pardoen et al. (1996)	27 bipolar patients, 24 unipolar patients	Structured interview–Paykel interview, 26 normal controls	Diagnostic interview–SADS	Bipolar and unipolar patients who relapsed did not differ from non-relapsers on life events in prior 2 months; bipolar patients with manic or hypomanic relapse had more marital stressors than nonrelapsers

LEDS = Life Events and Difficulties Schedule; PERI-LEI = Psychiatric Epidemiology Research Interview-Life Events Interview; LEC = Life Events Checklist; SLE = Schedule for Life Events; DSM = Diagnostic and Statistical Manual of Mental Disorders; ICD = International Classification of Diseases; K-SADS = Kiddie Schedule for Affective Disorders and Schizophrenia; SADS = Schedule for Affective Disorders and Schizophrenia; SCID = Structured Clinical Interview; MINI-PLUS = MINI-International Neuropsychiatric Interview; PSE = Present State Examination; DICA = Diagnostic Interview for Children and Adolescents; ESM = Experience Sampling Method.

had a greater number of work-related events than nonrelapsers, although relapsers and nonrelapsers did not differ in the overall number of events they experienced. Christensen et al. (2003) administered life events questionnaires every 3 months for 3 years to bipolar patients and found a greater number of events in the 3 months prior to a depressive episode than a control period for bipolar women, but not men. Koenders and colleagues (2014) assessed life events and mood symptoms with questionnaires every 3 months for 2 years in a sample of outpatients with a range of BSDs. Controlling for time to follow-up, gender, education, and medication, negative life events were associated with increases in both depressive and manic symptoms at follow-up, as well as more functional impairment. In addition, positive life events were associated with subsequent manic symptom severity and functional impairment, but not with depressive symptoms. Gilman et al. (2015) used a life events checklist administered at Wave 1 of the National Epidemiologic Survey on Alcohol and Related Conditions (NESARC, *n* = 34,653) inquiring about events in the past year to predict onsets of manic and depressive episodes over a 3-year follow-up (Wave 2). They found that personal losses, interpersonal problems, and economic difficulties were associated with increased risk of first onset and recurrent manic episodes over the follow-up (ORs = 1.5–3.0). Depressive episodes over follow-up also were associated with economic difficulties and financial/interpersonal instability.

An additional eight prospective studies used gold-standard interview assessments of life events, but only one of these studies included a control group (Pardoen et al., 1996). Pardoen et al. (1996) administered life events interviews and symptom assessments to remitted bipolar patients, unipolar depressed patients, and healthy controls every 2 months for 1 year. They found no difference in numbers of life events for both bipolar and unipolar patients who relapsed versus those who did not relapse. However, bipolar patients who had a hypo/manic relapse experienced more marital stressors prior to the relapse compared to other bipolar patients. In a bipolar outpatient sample, Ellicott, Hammen, Gitlin, Brown, and Jamison (1990) found that those with high numbers of stressful events had a 4.5-fold increase in relapse rate over 2-year follow-up than those with a lower number of stressors. In substantially the same sample, Hammen and Gitlin (1997) also found that the bipolar patients who relapsed over 2 years experienced more severe (i.e., major) events and more total stress in the 6 months prior to

relapse than did those who did not relapse. Hunt, Bruce-Jones, and Silverstone (1992) reported that although manic and depressive relapses did not differ in their rates of severe events in the previous month, overall 19% of 52 relapses among the bipolar patients were preceded by a severe event in the prior month compared to 5% of patients with a severe event at other times.

In contrast, McPherson, Herbison, and Romans (1993) did not obtain a significant difference in moderately severe, independent events in the month prior to relapse compared to control periods among bipolar patients. However, this study was limited by a high attrition rate and the absence of a required well period before study entry. Johnson and Miller (1997) examined negative events monthly as a predictor of time to recovery from a mood episode among bipolar inpatients. They found that controlling for medication compliance, those who experienced a severe, independent event during the index episode took three times longer to recover than those who did not experience such an event. Kim, Miklowitz, Biuckians, and Mullen (2007) examined chronic and episodic stressors via interview at 3-month intervals in a small sample (*n* = 38) of adolescents with BSDs who were participating in a trial of family-focused psychoeducation therapy. They found that controlling for time, sex, treatment condition, and specific bipolar diagnosis, high chronic stress was associated with less improvement in any type of mood symptoms over 1-year follow-up, and that high chronic stress in peer relationships, in particular, predicted less improvement in manic symptoms. There also was a trend (*p* < .06) for exposure to severe, independent events to exacerbate manic symptoms. A similar role for chronic stress exposure was obtained in the study by Gershon, Johnson, and Miller (2013). They conducted monthly life events interviews and diagnostic assessments over 2 years in a large bipolar I sample. Controlling for gender and medication, they found that exposure to traumatic events was correlated with more severe interpersonal chronic stress, and that chronic stress severity, particularly interpersonal chronic stress severity, in turn, predicted greater depression but not mania over follow-up.

In summary, although somewhat more mixed in their findings than the cross-sectional and retrospective studies, the prospective studies provide more convincing evidence that stressful life events, including independent stressors, predict onsets and recurrences of bipolar mood episodes and longer time to recovery from mood episodes. There is also some evidence that exposure to chronic stress, particularly of an interpersonal nature, is predictive of greater symptom severity and less improvement over follow-up. Moreover, as discussed further later, the evidence from both the retrospective and prospective studies suggests that negative life events predict both depressive and hypo/manic symptoms and episodes, whereas positive life events only appear to trigger hypo/manic symptoms/episodes (see also Alloy et al., 2005, 2006). However, in the next section, we address whether particular types of negative and positive events featured in recent theoretical models of bipolar disorder are especially likely to precipitate bipolar mood episodes.

Life Events in Bipolar Depression Versus Hypo/mania

Although many of the studies reviewed earlier do not separately examine the role of life stress in hypo/manic versus depressive episodes of BSD, those that do provide information about whether life event triggers differ based on episode polarity. A few studies reviewed earlier only examined life events in relation to manic episodes. Of these studies, Chung et al. (1986) did not find an increase in independent negative life events prior to manic episode onsets; however, the other four of these studies (Bebbington et al., 1993; Joffe et al., 1989; Kennedy et al., 1983; Sclare & Creed, 1990) did obtain an association between independent negative life events and manic episodes. No clear conclusion regarding episode polarity may be drawn from three cross-sectional or retrospective studies. Whereas Hosang et al. (2010) reported that adverse life events and Hosang et al. (2012) found that interpersonal, financial, and job loss events predicted mania and depression equally, Beyer et al. (2008) observed that negative life events predicted depressive episodes more strongly than manic ones.

The prospective studies tend to be somewhat more consistent in finding that negative life events predict manic as well as depressive episodes (Gilman et al., 2015; Hunt et al., 1992; Kim et al., 2007; Koenders et al., 2014), but Christensen et al. (2003) and Johnson et al. (2008) found that negative life events only predicted depression, and Gershon et al. (2013) reported that chronic stress only predicted depression. On the other hand, Pardoen et al. (1996) found that marital stressors only predicted mania and Koenders et al. (2014) reported that positive life events also only predicted manic episodes. As discussed in more detail in the next section, studies of reward relevant events have yielded much more

consistent evidence that reward system-activating events, such as goal-striving, goal-attainment, work-related, and anger-inducing events precipitate hypo/manic symptoms and episodes specifically and not depression (Boland, Stange, LaBelle et al., 2016; Carver, 2004; Francis-Raniere et al., 2006; Hall et al., 1977; Harmon-Jones et al., 2002; Johnson et al., 2000; 2008; Nusslock et al., 2007, whereas reward system–deactivating events such as failures and losses trigger depressive symptoms and episodes but not hypo/mania (Boland, Stange, LaBelle et al., 2016; Francis-Raniere et al., 2006).

Specific Theoretically Based Life Events as Precipitants of Bipolar Mood Episodes

Aside from sometimes distinguishing between independent and dependent life events and episodic versus chronic stress, almost all retrospective and prospective studies of the association between life events and BSDs reviewed earlier have not tested theoretically driven hypotheses about types of life events that may precipitate bipolar mood symptoms or episodes. Yet there are several theoretical models of BSDs that do make explicit predictions about specific categories of life events that should contribute to occurrences of hypo/mania and depression among individuals with or at risk for BSDs. In this section, we consider two well-supported psychobiological theories of BSDs, the Behavioral Approach System (BAS)/reward hypersensitivity theory and the social and circadian rhythm dysregulation theory, and the evidence for their predictions that goal or reward-relevant life events or social rhythm disrupting events, respectively, will precipitate bipolar symptoms/episodes.

According to the BAS/reward hypersensitivity theory of BSDs (e.g., Alloy & Abramson, 2010; Alloy, Abramson, Urošević, Bender, & Wagner, 2009; Alloy, Nusslock, & Boland, 2015; Alloy, Olino, Freed, & Nusslock, 2016; Depue & Iacono, 1989; Johnson, Edge, Holmes, & Carver, 2012; Nusslock & Alloy, 2017; Urošević, Abramson, Harmon-Jones, & Alloy, 2008), vulnerability to BSDs is reflected in an overly sensitive reward system that is hyperreactive to goal- and reward-relevant cues. In response to BAS-activation life events involving rewards or goal striving and attainment, this hypersensitivity leads to excessive activation of the reward system and, in turn, hypo/manic symptoms. In response to BAS-deactivation life events involving nonattainment of goals or rewards (i.e., definite failures and irreconcilable losses), reward hypersensitivity leads to excessive deactivation or down-regulation of the reward system and bipolar depressive symptoms. Much evidence supports the reward hypersensitivity theory of BSDs (see Alloy, Nusslock, et al., 2015; Alloy, Olino, et al., 2016; Nusslock & Alloy, 2017, for recent comprehensive reviews), including that reward hypersensitivity is a mood-independent trait associated with BSDs, as well as a vulnerability factor for the first onset and recurrence of mood episodes and a worse course of BSD.

Five prospective studies have examined specifically the hypothesis that the occurrence of BAS or reward-relevant events will predict bipolar symptoms and episodes. In bipolar I samples, Johnson and colleagues (2000, 2008) administered the LEDS monthly along with bipolar symptom measures over an average of 27 months. Consistent with the BAS/reward hypersensitivity model, they found that goal attainment events (BAS-activating), but not positive events in general, predicted increases in manic symptoms, but not depressive symptoms over follow-up. In contrast, severe negative events predicted increases in depressive, but not manic, symptoms over follow-up (Johnson et al., 2008). Similarly, Nusslock, Abramson, Harmon-Jones, Alloy, and Hogan (2007) reported that independent of treatment and medication status, undergraduate students with BSDs were more likely to have an onset of a new hypomanic episode, but not a depressive episode, following exposure to BAS-activating goal-striving life events (studying for and taking final exams) than were other, nonstudent BSD individuals who did not experience the goal-striving events (43% vs. 4%). Francis-Raniere, Alloy, and Abramson (2006) examined the combination of BAS-relevant cognitive/personality characteristics and BAS-relevant life events assessed with a LEDS-like interview in predicting hypo/manic and depressive symptoms over a 4-month follow-up in a large sample of individuals with BSDs. Controlling for baseline mood symptoms and total number of events experienced, they found that the interaction of a BAS-relevant perfectionistic and self-critical cognitive style with BAS-relevant positive events predicted increases in hypo/manic symptoms, whereas this cognitive style in interaction with BAS-relevant negative life events predicted increases in depressive symptoms. Finally, in a sample of adolescents at high versus low risk for BSDs based on exhibiting high versus moderate levels of BAS/reward sensitivity and using LEDS-like life event interviews, Boland, Stange, LaBelle et al. (2016) found that BAS-activating events predicted increases in hypo/manic symptoms over an average of 8 months of follow-up, whereas

BAS-deactivating events predicted increases in depressive symptoms over the follow-up, and these effects were stronger for the high BAS than the moderate BAS participants (BAS × Events interactions).

Additionally, although not designed to specifically test the BAS/reward hypersensitivity model of BSDs, other evidence is relevant to the model's prediction that BAS-activation and deactivation events predict hypo/mania and depression, respectively. For example, anger-provocation events, which have been theorized to also activate the BAS/reward system, have been found to predict hypomanic symptoms (e.g., Carver, 2004; Harmon-Jones et al., 2002). In contrast, events involving failures or losses (BAS-deactivating events) have been found to precipitate depressive episodes (see Alloy et al., 2005, 2009, for a review). Thus, the evidence to date suggests that BAS/reward system–activating and –deactivating events may specifically contribute to hypo/manic and depressive symptoms and episodes of BSDs, respectively.

Another major theoretical model of BSDs, the social and circadian rhythm dysregulation model, suggests that disruption of circadian rhythms is a central mechanism in the neurobiological vulnerability to BSDs (see Alloy, Nusslock, et al., 2015; Alloy, Ng, Titone, & Boland, 2017, for reviews). Circadian rhythm dysregulation may arise either from stable, trait-like abnormalities of the suprachiasmatic nucleus's (SCN) pacemaking control over bodily functions or from dysfunction in the entrainment of the SCN by external cues or zeitgebers (German for "timegivers") (Grandin, Alloy, & Abramson, 2006). According to the social zeitgeber theory of BSDs (Ehlers, Frank, & Kupfer, 1988; Grandin et al., 2006), when individuals with or vulnerable to BSDs experience life events that disrupt their daily zeitgebers or social rhythms/activity schedules (e.g., bedtime, wake time, mealtimes, start of work), these schedule changes disturb their circadian rhythms and precipitate somatic symptoms, eventually culminating in bipolar mood episodes. Thus, this theory predicts that social rhythm disruption (SRD) events should precipitate bipolar mood episodes and symptoms. The social/circadian rhythm model of BSDs is well supported (see Alloy, Nusslock, et al., 2015; Alloy, Ng., et al., 2017, for recent reviews), including evidence that individuals with BSDs exhibit circadian phase delay (particularly in the depressive phase), have irregular social rhythms, sleep/wake, and activity patterns as stable trait markers, and that such social/circadian rhythm dysregulation may provide vulnerability to BSD.

Moreover, consistent with the social/circadian rhythm dysregulation model, Boland et al. (2012) demonstrated that individuals with BSDs exhibited greater sensitivity to SRD than demographically (sex, race, age) matched controls following the occurrence of multiple types of life events. Life events were assessed with a LEDS-type interview and SRD following exposure to the various events was interviewer rated. Boland et al. (2012) found that BSD individuals experienced significantly more interviewer-rated SRD and sleep loss than the healthy controls following all classes of life events of similar intensity and valence (major positive, major negative, minor positive, and minor negative).

Several studies have examined whether SRD events predict onsets of mood episodes in individuals with or at risk for BSDs. Although they did not include a control group or even directly assess SRD, Kadri, Mouchtaq, Hakkou, and Moussaoui (2000) found that 45% of 20 bipolar patients relapsed during the month of Ramadan, the Muslim fasting period involving significant changes in social rhythms (i.e., no meals); 71.4% of the relapses were manic episodes. Four studies directly tested whether SRD events predict bipolar mood symptoms or episodes. In two retrospective studies employing life events interviews, Malkoff-Schwartz et al. (1998, 2000) found that bipolar I patients experienced more interviewer-rated SRD events in the 8- and 20-week periods prior to onset of manic, but not depressive, episodes than during a matched control period not preceding an episode. In contrast, in a prospective study using a LEDS-type interview to assess life events and a diagnostic interview every 4 months for a year, Sylvia et al. (2009) reported that individuals with BSDs experienced more SRD events in the 8-week periods prior to onsets of *depressive*, but not hypomanic, episodes than in matched 8-week control periods. In addition, in between-subjects analyses, BSD participants with a depressive episode onset experienced more SRD events in the 8 weeks before the episode than did demographically matched (sex, race, age) BSD participants with no episode onset during the same 8-week period. There was no effect for hypomanic episodes. Finally, Boland, Stange, LaBelle et al. (2016) found that SRD events predicted increases in *both* hypo/manic and depressive symptoms in a prospective study of high and moderate BAS/reward sensitivity adolescents that also employed LEDS-type interviews. Specifically, Boland, Stange, LaBelle et al. (2016) found that high BAS/reward-sensitive adolescents experienced significantly more interviewer-rated SRD than did

moderate BAS/reward-sensitive adolescents following the occurrence of both BAS-activating and deactivating life events. This increased SRD from BAS-activating and deactivating events, in turn, predicted increases in hypo/manic and depressive symptoms, respectively (i.e., SRD mediated the predictive associations between occurrence of the reward-relevant events and symptom increases) that were stronger for the high than the moderate reward-sensitive adolescents. In sum, the evidence to date indicates that events that specifically disrupt daily social rhythms (and, hypothetically, circadian rhythms) may be particularly likely to lead to bipolar mood symptoms and episodes. Moreover, whether SRD is more strongly predictive of hypo/manic or depressive episodes may depend on whether the events that disrupt social rhythms (and, presumably, circadian rhythms) are BAS activating or BAS deactivating. Future research should attempt to clarify the conditions under which SRD events trigger hypo/manic versus depressive symptoms and episodes.

Kindling and Stress Sensitization

Some research on the life events–BSD association has specifically addressed whether the nature of this association changes over the course of bipolar disorder (see Stroud chapter, this volume). According to Post's (1992) kindling hypothesis, unipolar and bipolar mood episodes may become more autonomous with each recurrence such that life events are more likely to trigger earlier than later episodes in the course of these disorders. Monroe and Harkness (2005) specified two alternative interpretations or models of the kindling effect: "stress sensitization" and "stress autonomy." Both of these perspectives suggest that major life events play an important role in triggering initial mood episodes and that successive recurrences are increasingly likely to occur in the absence of severe events. According to the stress sensitization model, the declining association between major events and episodes occurs because of progressive sensitization to more minor stressors. That is, minor events that were incapable of initiating a first onset develop the ability to precipitate recurrences. Over repeated mood episodes, although major events retain the ability to trigger episodes, they are no longer necessary, and minor events (which may fall below the threshold of severity of events captured on most life events measures) become the more probable precipitant. Thus, although the impact of major events should increase with each episode as the individual becomes sensitized to stress, the frequency of major events should decrease over time, as episode recurrences are increasingly precipitated by the more commonly occurring minor events. The impact and frequency of minor events become stronger with episode recurrences. Alternatively, the stress autonomy model suggests that progressive stress insensitivity occurs with recurrences. That is, recurrences become increasingly less dependent on life events in general. Thus, the impact and frequency of both major and minor life events should decrease with each successive episode recurrence.

Bender and Alloy (2011) recently provided a comprehensive review of the literature examining the kindling hypothesis in BSDs. Their review included cross-sectional and retrospective studies of rates of life events prior to first versus later episodes (Ambelas, 1979; 1987; Bidzinska, 1984; Dunner et al., 1979; Ehnvall & Agren, 2002; Glassner & Haldipur, 1983; Glassner, Haldipur, & Dessauersmith, 1979; Johnson, Andersson-Lundman, Aberg-Wistedt, & Mathe, 2000: Kennedy et al., 1983; Perris, 1984), a study examining whether the number of previous episodes moderates the association between recent life events and an index episode (Hlastala et al., 2000), and three prospective studies of the kindling effect (Dienes, Hammen, Henry, Cohen, & Daley, 2006; Hammen & Gitlin, 1997; Swendsen, Hammen, Heller, & Gitlin, 1995). Bender and Alloy (2011) concluded that support for the kindling effect in bipolar disorder was quite inconsistent. Only eight of the 14 studies included in their review obtained a kindling effect, and two of these studies only obtained evidence of kindling within specific subgroups of bipolar patients (those with six or more episodes, Bidzinska, 1984; or with decreasing well intervals, Ehnvall & Agren, 2002). None of the four methodologically strongest studies supported the kindling hypothesis, and one of these obtained findings opposite of kindling (Hammen & Gitlin, 1997). Moreover, the studies reviewed did not examine the impact and frequency of major and minor life events separately and, thus, could not distinguish between stress sensitization and autonomy models of kindling. Nor did they examine whether any kindling effects are episode polarity specific or event valence specific.

However, four newer studies of kindling in BSDs have been published since the Bender and Alloy (2011) review was conducted. In their retrospective study of remitted unipolar and bipolar patients on lithium and healthy controls, Horesh and Iancu (2010) ascertained first and most recent mood episode dates from medical chart review and asked participants to retrospectively complete a life events questionnaire including the year in which each event they endorsed occurred. Consistent with kindling and stress sensitization in particular, they found that more severe events appeared to precede the first than the most recent mood episode. Kemner, van Haren, et al. (2015) and Kemner, Mesman, Nolen, Eijckemans, and Hillegers (2015) conducted two studies of kindling, one in offspring of bipolar parents (Kemner, Mesman, et al., 2015) and the other in a twin sample with bipolar I or II disorder (Kemner, van Haren, et al., 2015). The bipolar offspring study was prospective and assessed life events with the LEDS interview. Although Kemner, van Haren, et al. (2015) did not obtain an interaction between the number of previous mood episodes and recent life events in predicting mood episodes, the impact of severe life events decreased with recurring episodes. The bipolar twin study also used the LEDS to assess events, but it was retrospective and used first and subsequent hospital admissions. The authors found that more severe life stress (taking into account both the frequency and severity of life events) was associated with both first and recurrent hospitalizations. However, there was some suggestion of a stronger effect of life events on the first than recurrent admissions (Kemner, van Haren, et al., 2015). Finally, Weiss et al. (2015) conducted a prospective study of kindling in a large sample of participants with BSDs (bipolar II and cyclothymia) using a LEDS-type life event interview and prospectively ascertained mood episodes. Moreover, they examined both the impact and frequency of major and minor, positive and negative life events in order to compare the stress sensitization and autonomy models of kindling and mood episode polarity. Their findings were partially consistent with the stress sensitization model and inconsistent with the stress autonomy model. Specifically, they found that BSD individuals with more prior mood episodes had an increased frequency of negative minor, but not major, events preceding depressive episodes and of positive minor, but not major, events preceding hypo/manic episodes. However, the number of past mood episodes did not moderate the association between life events and time to prospective onsets of depression or hypo/mania.

Another group of studies have extended the kindling hypothesis regarding the impact of recurrent mood episodes to the effects of exposure to childhood life stress. That is, these studies have tested a form of the stress sensitization model and asked whether exposure to childhood stress or adversity increases the likelihood that recent life events will precipitate mood episodes among individuals with BSDs. The logic is that because early child adversity has been found to increase stress reactivity across the lifespan (e.g., Harkness, Bruce, & Lumley, 2006; Heim, Newport, Mletzko, Miller, & Nemeroff, 2008), proximal life events may be more likely to precipitate bipolar mood episodes for individuals with more versus less childhood stress exposure.

Three partially prospective studies have tested this childhood stress sensitization hypothesis for BSDs. The studies were partially prospective in that although childhood stress was assessed retrospectively, the relationship between recent life events and subsequent mood episodes was examined prospectively. Dienes et al. (2006) assessed childhood adversity and recent life events via structured interview in 58 adults with bipolar I disorder. They found an interaction between the severity of early adversity and recent stressors, such that bipolar I patients with early adversity reported lower levels of stressors prior to a recurrent episode than did those without early adversity, consistent with stress sensitization. Dienes et al. did not distinguish between recurrences of manic versus depressive episodes. In an epidemiological study of 34,653 adults, Gilman et al. (2015) used life events checklists administered at Wave 1 to assess events in the past year and at Wave 2 (3 years later) to assess childhood adversity to predict onsets of manic and depressive episodes at Wave 2. Partially supporting stress sensitization, they obtained a significant interaction between greater childhood adversity and past-year stressors in predicting to first onset, but not recurrent, manic episodes, such that past-year stressors were more likely to predict a first-onset manic episode if there was a history of childhood abuse and neglect. This effect did not occur for depressive episodes. Finally, Shapero et al. (2017) used a LEDS-type interview and diagnostic interviews to assess recent life events and mood episodes, respectively, every 4 months and a questionnaire to assess past childhood adversity in a sample of young adults with BSDs (mostly bipolar II) followed for over 3 years. They tested the hypothesis that as the number of childhood stressors increased, the number of recent life events preceding a mood episode would decrease in number but increase in impact separately for recent positive and negative events and hypo/manic and depressive

episodes. Shapero et al. obtained partial support for a sensitization effect of childhood adversity that was specific to negative events and depressive episodes. Consistent with the sensitization hypothesis, controlling for number of prior mood episodes, individuals with greater early adversity had fewer negative events prior to a depressive episode, but this did not hold for positive events prior to a hypo/manic episode. In addition, the number of early adverse events did not interact with any type of proximal events to predict time to onset of prospective depressive or hypo/manic episodes, counter to the impact component of the childhood stress sensitization hypothesis. In summary, based on the few studies to date, there is some, but by no means complete, support for a sensitization effect of early childhood adversity in the course of BSDs.

Stress Generation

So far, our review has focused on stress exposure models of BSDs in which recent life events act as potential precipitants of bipolar symptoms and episodes. However, the association between BSDs and life stress may occur in the opposite causal direction as well. That is, individuals with BSDs may not just be passive recipients of environmental stressors but, instead, may contribute in direct or indirect ways through their symptoms, characteristics, and behaviors to the occurrence of life events via stress generation processes (Hammen, 1991, 2006; Liu & Alloy, 2010; see Hammen chapter, this volume). To demonstrate stress generation, the distinction between independent and dependent life events is relevant. Bipolar episodes or symptoms should only contribute to events that are at least partially dependent on individuals' behavior, not to independent events that are fateful or uncontrollable.

Although an extensive literature has demonstrated stress generation in individuals with unipolar depression or at risk for depression (see Liu & Alloy, 2010; Liu, 2013, for reviews), only a few studies have examined stress generation processes in BSDs. Two studies (Kemner, Mesman, et al., 2015a; Ostiguy et al., 2009) of the offspring of bipolar parents did not find evidence of stress generation. In a cross-sectional study using a LEDS-type interview to assess life events, Ostiguy et al. (2009) found that offspring of bipolar parents did not differ from the offspring of control parents on the average number of life events rated as dependent. Likewise, Kemner, Mesman, et al. (2015) did not obtain a difference in the association between dependent versus independent events and mood episodes in a large sample of offspring of bipolar parents.

In contrast, five other studies of individuals with BSDs have obtained greater evidence for stress generation. Koenders et al. (2014) did not distinguish between dependent and independent events in their prospective study of outpatients with BSDs assessed with a life events questionnaire; however, they did find that manic symptom severity predicted an increased occurrence of subsequent positive life events. Depressive symptoms did not predict subsequent negative events. In their retrospective study of a large sample of bipolar I and II individuals drawn from genetic studies and assessed with a life events checklist, Hosang and colleagues (2012) found that only dependent events were associated with mood episodes among the bipolar group. In a short-term longitudinal study employing a LEDS-type interview of life events in a sample of individuals with BSDs and demographically matched (sex, race, age) healthy controls, Bender, Alloy, Sylvia, Urošević, and Abramson (2010) found the BSD group experienced higher rates of subsequent total dependent events over 4 months of follow-up than did the healthy controls. In addition, over follow-up, baseline hypomanic symptoms predicted increases in positive and negative achievement events and negative interpersonal events, whereas baseline depressive symptoms predicted decreases in positive interpersonal events. These findings held when controlling for the occurrence of diagnosable hypo/manic and depressive episodes during the follow-up period. Finally, two studies specifically tested whether individuals with BSDs or vulnerable to BSDs generate BAS/reward-relevant events. In a longitudinal study of individuals with BSDs and demographically matched (sex, race, age) healthy controls using a LEDS-type interview, Urošević et al. (2010) found that compared to the controls, the BSD group experienced increased rates of both dependent BAS-activating and BAS-deactivating events over follow-up. Similarly, Boland, Stange, LaBelle et al. (2016) also observed that adolescents at risk for BSD based on exhibiting high BAS/reward sensitivity experienced increased rates of both dependent BAS-activating and BAS-deactivating events (assessed with a LEDS-type interview) over 8 months of follow-up compared to moderate BAS/reward sensitivity adolescents. These latter two findings suggest that individuals with or at risk for BSDs based on reward hypersensitivity may be at double jeopardy for BSD mood episodes because they both experience more reward-relevant events through stress generation processes and then react to the occurrence of these events with greater mood symptoms.

Childhood Stress and Bipolar Spectrum Disorders

All but three studies of the role of childhood adversity in BSDs employ cross-sectional or retrospective designs in which youths or adults with BSDs are asked to recall their childhood histories. The three other studies also assess childhood adversity retrospectively, but they follow participants prospectively. Even within the cross-sectional or retrospective studies, very few have attempted to ascertain whether the childhood stressors preceded the onset of BSD. And most of these studies do not control for participants' mood states at the time of recall of their childhood experiences, increasing the chance of mood-dependent reporting biases, nor do they obtain other informants' perspectives or corroborating evidence of the childhood experiences. In addition, the vast majority of studies of childhood stress and BSDs have focused on childhood maltreatment (physical and sexual abuse, and sometimes emotional abuse and neglect), with very few studies including a broader array of childhood adversities. Moreover, the childhood maltreatment studies vary as to whether they assess maltreatment with well-established measures or measures of questionable reliability and validity (e.g., single items). Finally, in the maltreatment studies, the different forms of abuse may not be examined in the same study with statistical controls for their overlap; thus, which forms of abuse are most relevant to the course of BSDs is often unclear (Alloy, Abramson, Smith, et al., 2006). Table 6.3 displays the studies of childhood stress and BSDs.

Childhood Maltreatment

In a recent meta-analysis of 30 studies of childhood maltreatment (sexual, physical, or emotional abuse, neglect, or family conflict) prior to age 18 and negative outcomes in patients with bipolar disorder, Agnew-Blais and Danese (2016) found that bipolar patients with a history of childhood maltreatment had greater mania, depression, and psychosis severity, a greater number of both manic and depressive episodes, an earlier age of bipolar disorder onset, higher risk of suicide attempt and rapid cycling, and a higher risk of comorbidity with anxiety disorders, PTSD, and alcohol and drug use disorders than bipolar patients with no child abuse history. Maniglio (2013) also completed a recent qualitative review of the association between childhood sexual abuse

Table 6.3. Studies of Childhood Stress and Bipolar Spectrum Disorders

Study	BD Sample	BD Diagnostic Methods	Stress Measures	Results
Agnew-Blais & Danese (2016)	N/A	N/A	N/A	Patients with BD and history of childhood maltreatment had greater mania, depression, and psychosis severities, greater risk of suicide attempt, rapid cycling and comorbidity with PTSD, anxiety disorders, substance misuse disorders, alcohol misuse disorder, greater number of manic and depressive episodes, and earlier age of onset, relative to those with BD but without childhood maltreatment.
Alvarez et al. (2011)	102 BD, schizophrenia, or schizoaffective disorder	Unclear	Traumatic Life Events Questionnaire	History of psychological abuse and domestic violence witness were associated with higher number of admissions.
Bergink et al. (2016)	980,554 people born in Denmark from January 1, 1980, to December 31, 1998, to parents born in Denmark	Register review	Register review	Exposure to most of the early life stresses was associated with increased risk for BD, with the strongest risk factor being parental psychopathology.
Brown et al. (2005)	330 BD I or II	SCID	Clinical interview	History of any childhood abuse was associated with increased rates of involuntary hospitalizations, disability pension, PTSD, panic disorder, and alcohol use disorder.
Carballo et al. (2008)	168 BD	SCID	Clinical interview	History of childhood abuse and family history of suicidality was associated with suicidality, impulsivity, history of aggression, early onset of BD and hospitalization, and comorbidity with substance use disorder and borderline personality disorder.
Conus et al. (2010)	118 BD I with psychotic mania	Clinical interview	Chart review	Exposure to sexual and/or physical abuse was associated with poorer premorbid functioning, higher rates of forensic history, decreased likelihood of living with family during treatment period, and increased likelihood of treatment disengagement.
De Pradier et al. (2010)	137 BD	Diagnostic Interview for Genetic Studies	THQ	Childhood sexual abuse was associated with cannabis abuse or dependence, an association more important in patients carrying the short allele of the 5-HTTLPR of the 5-HTT gene.
Dienes et al. (2006)	64 BD I	SCID	Clinical interview	Early life stress was associated with a greater effect of recent stressful events on recurrence and earlier onset of BD.
Du Rocher Schudlich et al. (2015)	152 BD I, II, NOS, or cyclothymia	K-SADS	Clinical interview and review of charts and Department of Child and Family Services records	Physical abuse was associated with a worse global family environment, more severe depressive and manic symptoms, a greater number of subthreshold manic/ hypomanic symptoms, increased likelihood of suicidality and PTSD diagnosis, and more self-reported alcohol or drug use. Sexual abuse was associated with a worse global family environment, more severe manic symptoms, a greater number of episodes, past hospitalizations, current and past comorbid Axis I diagnoses, and subthreshold manic/hypomanic symptoms, and greater mood swings.

(continued)

Table 6.3. Continued

Study	BD Sample	BD Diagnostic Methods	Stress Measures	Results
Eren et al. (2014)	116 BD I	Clinical interview	Childhood Abuse and Neglect Questionnaire	Childhood trauma was associated with greater number of depressive episodes, total episodes, and attempted suicide.
Etain et al. (2017)	270 BD I or II	Diagnostic Interview for Genetic Studies	CTQ	Emotional abuse and physical abuse were associated with increased delusional beliefs.
Etain et al. (2013)	587 BD I, II, or NOS	SCID/Diagnostic Interview for Genetic Studies	CTQ	Childhood trauma was associated with earlier age of BD onset, suicide attempts, rapid cycling, and an increased number of depressive episodes.
Gao et al. (2009)	561 rapid cycling BD I or II	MINI	Own measure	Physical abuse was associated with increased number of suicide attempts.
Gao et al. (2010)	564 rapid cycling BD I or II	MINI	Own measure	Physical abuse was associated with increased risk for substance use disorders.
Garno et al. (2008)	100 BD I or II	SCID	CTQ	Childhood emotional abuse, emotional neglect, and physical abuse, but not sexual abuse and physical neglect, were associated with trait aggression.
Garno et al. (2005)	100 BD I or II	SCID	CTQ	History of severe childhood abuse was associated with more manic/hypomanic symptoms and depressive symptoms and episodes and an earlier age of onset. Sexual abuse was associated with lifetime suicide attempts.
Goldberg & Garno (2005)	100 BD I or II	SCID	CTQ	History of childhood abuse was associated with increased rates of PTSD.
Goldstein et al. (2008)	249 BD I, II, or NOS	K-SADS	Clinical interview	Sexual abuse and physical abuse were associated with substance use disorder.
Grandin et al. (2007)	155 BD II, NOS, or cyclothymia	SADS-L	Childrens Life Events Scale	History of childhood maltreatment was associated with greater depressive symptoms. Total, independent, and dependent events were associated with earlier age of onset of BD episodes.
Leverich et al. (2003)	648 BD I or II	SCID	Clinical interview	Early physical abuse and sexual abuse were associated with suicide attempts.
Leverich et al. (2002)	631 BD I or II	SCID	Clinical interview	History of physical or sexual abuse was associated with earlier age of onset, increased cycling and lifetime Axis I disorders, increased severity of mania, increased rates of suicide attempts and negative psychosocial stressors occurring before the first and most recent mood episodes, and longer duration of time ill until the entry to treatment.

Study	Sample	Diagnostic method	Trauma measure	Findings
Li et al. (2014)	132 BD	SCID	CTQ—Short Form, Childhood Experience of Care and Abuse Questionnaire	Childhood trauma was associated with earlier age of onset and more severe PTSD and anxiety symptoms.
Maguire et al. (2008)	60 BD I or II	Clinical interview	CTQ and THQ	Trauma was associated with frequency of hospital admissions, quality of life, and inter-episode depressive symptoms.
Maniglio (2013)	N/A	N/A	N/A	Child sexual abuse was associated with PTSD, suicide attempts, substance/alcohol use disorders, psychotic symptoms, and an early age of onset.
Marchand et al. (2005)	66 BD I, II, NOS, or cyclothymia	Chart review	Chart review	History of sexual abuse and neglect were associated with decreased response to treatment. History of physical abuse was associated with more hospitalization, delay of diagnosis, and decreased response to treatment.
McIntyre et al. (2008)	381 BD I, II, NOS, or cyclothymia	Chart review	Chart review	History of childhood abuse was associated with lifetime suicidality; comorbid psychiatric disorders, and medication usage.
Miller et al. (2013)	80 BD I, II, or NOS	Modified SCID, MINI	CTQ	BDNF met allele carriers with childhood sexual abuse had higher severity of illness and earlier age of onset, compared to those without childhood sexual abuse.
Mowlds et al. (2010)	52 BD I or II	Clinical interview	CTQ, THQ	Childhood trauma was associated with current interepisode depressive severity, but not BD severity or autobiographical memory specificity.
Neria et al. (2005)	109 BD	SCID	Composite International Diagnostic Interview, SCID, and chart review	Childhood trauma was associated with higher general distress and less happiness.
Nolen et al. (2004)	285 BD or schizoaffective disorder	SCID	Own measure	History of childhood abuse was associated with mania severity and the total number of overall illness episodes.
Perich et al. (2014)	157 BD I or II	SCID	Own measure	Physical or sexual abuse was associated with more self-harm or suicidal behaviors and higher stress.
Post et al. (2016)	968 BD I or II	SCID	Own measure	Family loading for psychiatric illness and childhood adversity combine to have a large effect on age of onset of BD.
Post et al. (2015)	634 BD I or II	SCID	Own measure	History of verbal abuse was associated with earlier age of onset, anxiety and substance abuse comorbidity, rapid cycling, and increasing frequency or severity of mania and depression.
Post et al. (2013)	968 BD I or II	SCID	Own measure	Childhood stressors were associated with greater rates of negative life events, lifetime anxiety disorders, and parental mood disorders.

(continued)

Table 6.3. Continued

Study	BD Sample	BD Diagnostic Methods	Stress Measures	Results
Romero et al. (2009)	446 BD I, II, or NOS	K-SADS	K-SADS	History of any abuse was associated with living with a nonintact family, PTSD, psychosis, conduct disorder, and first-degree family history of mood disorder.
Sala et al. (2014)	1600 BD I or II	Alcohol Use Disorder and Associated Disabilities Interview Schedule	Own measure	A dose–response relationship between number of childhood maltreatment instances and severity of BD in clinical characteristics, probability of treatment, lifetime prevalence of psychiatric comorbidity, incidence of anxiety disorders, substance use disorder, and nicotine dependence, and level of psychosocial functioning.
Watson et al. (2014)	60 BD I or II	SCID	CTQ	Controlling for age and sex, emotional neglect was the only significant CTQ subscale associated with BD. CTQ subscale scores were higher in those with rapid cycling BD.

BD = bipolar disorder; CTQ = Childhood Trauma Questionnaire; IQ = Intelligence Quotient; K-SADS = Schedule for Affective Disorders and Schizophrenia for Children and Adolescents; MINI = Mini-International Neuropsychiatric Interview; N/A = not applicable; NOS = not otherwise specified; PTSD = posttraumatic stress disorder; SCID = Structured Clinical Interview for *DSM-IV*; THQ = Trauma History Questionnaire.

specifically and characteristics of BSD in 18 studies of 2,996 bipolar adults and youths. Maniglio concluded that childhood sexual abuse was related strongly to comorbid PTSD, and less strongly, but also significantly, to suicide attempts, psychotic symptoms, comorbid alcohol and drug use disorder, and an early age of bipolar disorder onset.

Multiple studies have examined whether a history of childhood maltreatment is associated with various indicators of severity of BSDs. Three studies assessed child abuse history via a medical chart review and found that a history of childhood physical (CPA) and sexual abuse (CSA) was associated with worse treatment outcome among bipolar outpatients (Marchand, Wirth, & Simon, 2005), poorer premorbid functioning in a bipolar I sample (Conus et al., 2010), and lifetime suicidality in bipolar outpatients (McIntyre et al., 2008). However, CPA and CSA were not associated with other indicators of severity, such as rapid cycling, recurrent mood episodes, or hospitalizations in the McIntyre et al. (2008) study.

Another 13 studies assessed childhood abuse history with reliable and valid questionnaires (De Pradier, Gorwood, Beaufils, Adès, & Dubertret, 2010; Erten et al., 2014; Etain et al., 2013; 2017; Garno, Goldberg, Ramirez, & Ritzler, 2005; Miller et al., 2013; Mowlds et al., 2010; Watson et al., 2014), such as the Childhood Trauma Questionnaire (Bernstein et al., 2003) or Trauma History Questionnaire (Hooper, Stockton, Krupnick, & Green, 2011), or with their own single item (Gao et al., 2009) or questionnaire measures of child abuse (Nolen et al., 2004; Perich et al., 2014; Post et al., 2013; Sala, Goldstein, Wang, & Blanco, 2014). These studies found that a history of abuse in general or of CPA or CSA was associated with greater mood symptom severity (Miller et al., 2013; Nolen et al., 2004; Sala et al., 2014; but Mowlds et al. (2010) did not obtain an association between child abuse and symptom severity and in the Nolen et al. study, the relationship was no longer significant when other illness variables were controlled), a larger number of mood episodes (Erten et al., 2014; Etain et al., 2013; Garno et al., 2005), greater delusions (Etain et al., 2017, but De Pradier et al. (2010) found no association between CSA and psychosis), more suicide attempts (Erten et al., 2014; Etain et al., 2013; Gao et al., 2009; Garno et al., 2005; Perich et al., 2014), and greater likelihood of rapid cycling (Etain et al., 2013; Garno et al., 2005; Post et al., 2013; Watson et al., 2014) among bipolar patients. Of particular interest, Miller et al. (2013) found that it was only the

combination of CSA and brain-derived neurotrophic factor met allele genotype that predicted greater severity of bipolar disorder. Only two studies have examined the association between childhood emotional abuse (CEA) and the severity of bipolar course (Alvarez et al., 2011; Post et al., 2015). In a sample of bipolar outpatients, Alvarez et al. (2011) observed that hospital admissions were twice as high in those with CEA than those without CEA, assessed retrospectively via questionnaire. Using their own questionnaire measure of childhood abuse in a large sample of bipolar outpatients, Post et al. (2015) found that CEA was related to greater frequency or severity of mania and depression and rapid cycling.

Seven studies assessed childhood maltreatment with clinical interviews or semistructured diagnostic interviews. These studies found that CPA and CSA histories were associated with greater depressive and manic symptom severity (Du Rocher Schudlich et al., 2015; Neria, Bromet, Carlson, & Naz, 2005), more major depressive episodes (Brown et al., 2005), longer illness duration (Romero et al., 2009), less likelihood of remission (Neria et al., 2005), more suicide attempts (Brown et al., 2005; Carballo et al., 2008; Du Rocher Schudlich et al., 2015; Leverich et al., 2002, 2003), and greater rapid cycling (Brown et al., 2005).

A large number of studies of the association between childhood maltreatment and BSDs specifically have examined whether child abuse is related to the age of onset of the bipolar disorder. These studies are particularly relevant because an association between a history of child abuse and earlier onset age could suggest that the abuse contributed to the development of the BSD. However, because these studies are almost all cross-sectional or retrospective and the studies do not establish the onset date of the abuse, it is also possible that an earlier onset of BSD led the individual to be more likely to be maltreated. Nonetheless, with the exception of the studies by McIntyre et al. (2008) and Romero et al. (2009), 10 studies (Carballo et al., 2008; Dienes et al., 2006; Etain et al., 2013; Garno et al., 2005; Leverich et al., 2002; Li et al., 2014; Miller et al., 2013; Post et al., 2013, 2015, 2016) employing chart review, questionnaire, or interview assessments of abuse history all find that greater CEA (Etain et al., 2013; Post et al., 2015), CPA, and CSA are associated with an earlier age of onset of BSD across a wide range of youth and adult samples.

Finally, many studies have investigated whether a history of childhood maltreatment in individuals with BSDs is related to comorbid diagnoses. These studies have routinely found that individuals with BSD who have a history of childhood abuse are more likely to have at least one comorbid disorder than BSD individuals without an abuse history. Specifically, a maltreatment history has been found to increase the rate of comorbid PTSD (Brown et al., 2005; Du Rocher Schudlich et al., 2015; Goldberg & Garno, 2005; Li et al., 2014; Romero et al., 2009; but see Maguire, McCusker, Meenagh, Mulholland, & Shannon, 2008, for an exception), anxiety disorders in general (Brown et al., 2005; Li et al., 2014; Post et al., 2013, 2015; Sala et al., 2014), alcohol and substance use disorders (Brown et al., 2005; Carballo et al., 2008; De Pradier et al., 2010; Gao et al., 2010; Garno et al., 2005; Goldstein et al., 2008; Leverich et al., 2002; Post et al., 2015; Romero et al., 2009; Sala et al., 2014), and personality disorders (Carballo et al., 2008; Leverich et al., 2002).

Childhood Adversity

Only three retrospective studies have investigated types of childhood adversity other than or in addition to childhood maltreatment in relation to BSDs. Maguire et al. (2008) examined the association between childhood trauma exposure (including maltreatment) assessed by questionnaires and the severity of bipolar disorder in 60 outpatients with BSDs. They found that trauma exposure predicted interepisode depressive symptoms and the number of hospital admissions. Despite being retrospective, the other two studies assessed the timing of exposure to the childhood stressors and the timing of BSD onset in order to better determine whether childhood adversity might contribute to BSD onset. Grandin, Alloy, and Abramson (2007) assessed a wide range of moderate to severe childhood stressors (including maltreatment) and their dates of occurrence with a questionnaire in a large nonpatient sample of individuals with BSDs and demographically matched (age, sex, race) healthy controls. They found that the total number of childhood stressors, and particularly, stressors rated as independent of one's behavior, that occurred prior to bipolar individuals' age of BSD onset (using the same cutoff age for the matched healthy controls) were associated with bipolar versus control status. Also, total number and number of independent childhood events predicted an earlier age of onset of BSD. In addition, in contrast to the stress generation hypothesis, Grandin et al. (2007) found that BSD status did not predict the number of childhood stressors, particularly events rated as dependent on one's behavior, that occurred after the bipolar individuals' age of onset. In a

population cohort study of 980,554 individuals born in Denmark between 1980 and 1998, Bergink et al. (2016) examined the following eight forms of childhood adversity occurring before age 15 assessed by population registers as predictors of a diagnosis of BSD after age 15: familial disruption, parental medical illness, any parental psychopathology, parental labor market exclusion, parental imprisonment, placement in foster care, and parental natural and unnatural death. Bergink et al. found that by far the strongest risk factor for BSD onset was any mental disorder in a parent (hazard ratio of 3.53) and the additional effects of any of the other childhood events for bipolar risk were minimal. However, among the people without any parental psychopathology, exposure to any of these childhood adversities increased risk for a BSD diagnosis.

Overall, the literature on childhood stress and BSD is consistent with the idea that exposure to greater childhood adversity, and maltreatment in particular, is associated with an earlier age of onset, a more severe course, and greater psychiatric comorbidity of bipolar disorder. However, because the vast majority of studies investigating the role of childhood stress exposure are either cross-sectional or retrospective and, with a few exceptions, do not attempt to assess the timing of childhood stress exposure relative to BSD onset, the hypothesis that childhood adversity exposure contributes causally to BSD onset remains speculative. In addition, an important potential confound in understanding whether childhood stress exposure is causally related to BSDs is genetic and familial factors. This is especially problematic when the childhood adversity being studied involves exposure to parental psychopathology (in which parents also pass on susceptibility genes for BSD to their children) or stressors that primarily happen to a parent (e.g., incarceration). But it also is relevant in studies examining the effect of childhood maltreatment, given that parents with psychopathology (who share genetic risk with their children) are more likely to perpetrate abuse than parents without mental illness. Thus, future studies that examine the childhood adversity exposure–BSD association also need to control for genetic and familial confounds.

Summary and Future Directions for Research on Stress and Bipolar Disorders

Our conclusions regarding the role of recent and childhood stressors in the onset and course of BSDs must still be somewhat tentative pending further studies that address the methodological limitations of much of the existing literature on the stress–bipolar disorder association. More prospective, longitudinal studies are needed with adequate bipolar sample sizes, healthy control groups, controls for mood state or symptoms at the time of stress assessment, standardized, state-of-the-art life events interviews, shorter time intervals for assessing events likely to be of causal relevance, and separate examination of events that may predict depressive versus hypo/manic episodes and symptoms in order to draw more confident conclusions.

However, given these caveats, our review suggests that exposure to recent life stressors predicts more severe mood symptoms, recurrences of mood episodes, and longer time to recovery from episodes and may be a causal factor in bipolar symptomatology. In addition, exposure to childhood adversity, particularly maltreatment, is associated with a worse course of BSD, including more severe symptoms, earlier age of onset, increased suicidality, and greater comorbidity. Moreover, positive life events appear to be uniquely predictive of hypo/manic symptoms and episodes, whereas negative life events trigger both depression and hypo/mania. But a growing body of evidence suggests that particular stressors featured in successful theoretical models of BSDs, namely goal- and reward-relevant events and social rhythm-disrupting events, are especially likely to precipitate bipolar symptoms and episodes, and may even work in an integrated fashion to trigger mood symptoms/episodes (Alloy, Boland, Ng, Whitehouse, & Abramson, 2015; Boland, Stange, LaBelle et al., 2016). Our review also suggests that the evidence for a changing association between recent stressors and bipolar mood episodes over the course of bipolar disorder (i.e., kindling) is mixed. However, on balance, the evidence is more strongly supportive of a stress sensitization effect of exposure to recurrent mood episodes or childhood adversity on the recent events–mood episode association, in which more minor stressors gain the capacity to trigger mood episodes, than it is of a stress autonomy effect, in which mood episodes simply become autonomous from stressful events. Finally, our review suggests that the association between recent stress and BSD is bidirectional. Not only are individuals with BSDs likely to be exposed to greater stress prior to mood episodes, but they also appear to contribute to the occurrence of the very stressors (via stress generation processes) to which they then react with mood symptoms, placing them at double risk for mood pathology.

Based on our review, we believe there are several important directions for future research in the stress and bipolar disorder area beyond the obvious need for more prospective studies with adequate methodological controls. First, future studies on stress and bipolar disorder need to routinely examine polarity-specific associations so that a better understanding of the specific types of events that trigger or are generated by depression and hypo/mania may be obtained. Second, the growing body of evidence supporting a role for reward-relevant and social rhythm-disrupting events in the onset and course of bipolar mood episodes suggests that further research on these categories of events is warranted as well as on other types of events derived from other successful mechanistic theories of the pathophysiology of BSDs. Prospective tests of theory-driven events as triggers of bipolar mood episodes are likely to advance our understanding of environmental contributors to BSD faster than continued atheoretical tests of stress–bipolar associations. Third, future studies should examine moderators of the stress–BSD association. Most models of psychopathology in general, and bipolar disorder in particular, are based on vulnerability–stress perspectives in which specific genetic, behavioral, or neurobiological characteristics lead some individuals to react to specific stressors with bipolar symptoms. Thus, additional studies are needed that examine the interaction between hypothesized vulnerabilities for BSD and stressors relevant to those vulnerabilities as predictors of bipolar mood episodes (see Alloy et al., 2005, 2006 for studies that test cognitive vulnerability–stress interactions in BSDs). For example, given the evidence for reward-relevant and social rhythm disruption events as triggers of bipolar mood episodes, studies that test whether such events are particularly likely to precipitate episodes in individuals who are hypersensitive to rewards or exhibit greater social or circadian rhythm irregularity, respectively, would be particularly important. Likewise, studies that examine whether exposure to childhood maltreatment or other forms of childhood adversity moderate the association between parental psychopathology and offspring development of BSDs would be very valuable. Fourth, studies that investigate mediators of the stress–BSD association are also needed in order to understand the mechanisms by which recent events and childhood adversity contribute to bipolar disorder (see the chapters in Section 3 of this volume for possible stress mechanisms). Finally, given the ethical and practical problems associated with conducting true randomized experiments that manipulate exposure to stress, future treatment studies involving randomized assignment to therapy conditions that target reductions in stressors versus control conditions could be very helpful in more clearly elucidating the causal role of stressful events in BSDs.

In recent years, there have been great strides in understanding the psychological and neurobiological processes involved in BSDs. However, these processes are likely triggered by exposure to relevant environmental circumstances. Thus, exciting research that takes off in some of the directions we suggest from the existing literature on stress and bipolar disorder reviewed herein holds great promise for a true understanding of the causes of bipolar spectrum disorders and, thus, the development of more efficacious interventions that target these causes.

Acknowledgments

Preparation of this chapter was supported by National Institute of Mental Health grants MH077908 and MH102310 to Lauren B. Alloy.

References

Agnew-Blais, J., & Danese, A. (2016). Childhood maltreatment and unfavourable clinical outcomes in bipolar disorder: A systematic review and meta-analysis. *The Lancet Psychiatry, 3*, 342–349.

Akiskal, H. S., Djenderedjian, A. H., Rosenthal, R. H., & Khani, M. K. (1977). Cyclothymic disorder: Validating criteria for inclusion in the bipolar affective group. *The American Journal of Psychiatry, 134*, 1227–1233.

Alloy, L. B., & Abramson, L. Y. (2010). The role of the Behavioral Approach System (BAS) in bipolar spectrum disorders. *Current Directions in Psychological Science, 19*, 189–194.

Alloy, L. B., Abramson, L. Y., Smith, J. M., Gibb, B. E., & Neeren, A. M. (2006). Role of parenting and maltreatment histories in unipolar and bipolar mood disorders: Mediation by cognitive vulnerability to depression. *Clinical Child and Family Psychology Review, 9*, 23–64.

Alloy, L. B., Abramson, L. Y., Urošević, S., Bender, R. E., & Wagner, C. A. (2009). Longitudinal predictors of bipolar spectrum disorders: A behavioral approach system perspective. *Clinical Psychology: Science and Practice, 16*, 206–226.

Alloy, L. B., Abramson, L. Y., Urošević, S., Walshaw, P. D., Nusslock, R., & Neeren, A. M. (2005). The psychosocial context of bipolar disorder: Environmental, cognitive, and developmental risk factors. *Clinical Psychology Review, 25*, 1043–1075.

Alloy, L. B., Abramson, L. Y., Walshaw, P. D., Keyser, J., & Gerstein, R. K. (2006). A cognitive vulnerability-stress perspective on bipolar spectrum disorders in a normative adolescent brain, cognitive, and emotional development context. *Developmental Psychopathology, 18*, 1055–1103.

Alloy, L. B., Boland, E. M., Ng, T. H., Whitehouse, W. G., & Abramson, L. Y. (2015). Low social rhythm regularity predicts first onset of bipolar spectrum disorders among at risk individuals with reward hypersensitivity. *Journal of Abnormal Psychology, 124*, 944–952.

Alloy, L. B., Ng, T. H., Titone, M. K., & Boland, E. M. (2017). Circadian rhythm dysregulation in bipolar spectrum disorders. *Current Psychiatry Reports, 19*(21), 1–10.

Alloy, L. B., Nusslock, R., & Boland, E. M. (2015). The development and course of bipolar spectrum disorders: An integrated reward and circadian rhythm dysregulation model. *Annual Review of Clinical Psychology, 11*, 213–250.

Alloy, L. B., Olino, T. M., Freed, R. D., & Nusslock, R. (2016). Role of reward sensitivity and processing in major depressive and bipolar spectrum disorders. *Behavior Therapy, 47*, 600–621.

Alloy, L. B., Urošević, S., Abramson, L. Y., Jager-Hyman, S., Nusslock, R., Whitehouse, W. G., & Hogan, M. (2012). Progression along the bipolar spectrum: A longitudinal study of predictors of conversion from bipolar spectrum conditions to bipolar I and II disorders. *Journal of Abnormal Psychology, 121*, 16–27.

Alvarez, M.-J., Roura, P., Osés, A., Foguet, Q., Solà, J., & Arrufat, F.-X. (2011). Prevalence and clinical impact of childhood trauma in patients with severe mental disorders. *The Journal of Nervous and Mental Disease, 199*, 156–161.

Ambelas, A. (1979). Psychologically stressful events in the precipitation of manic episodes. *The British Journal of Psychiatry, 135*, 15–21.

Ambelas, A. (1987). Life events and mania. A special relationship? *The British Journal of Psychiatry, 150*, 235–240.

Aronson, T. A., & Shukla, S. (1987). Life events and relapse in bipolar disorder: The impact of a catastrophic event. *Acta Psychiatrica Scandinavica, 75*, 571–576.

Bebbington, P., Wilkins, S., Jones, P., Foerster, A., Murray, R., Toone, B., & Lewis, S. (1993). Life events and psychosis. Initial results from the Camberwell Collaborative Psychosis Study. *The British Journal of Psychiatry, 162*, 72–79.

Bender, R. E., & Alloy, L. B. (2011). Life stress and kindling in bipolar disorder: Review of the evidence and integration with emerging biopsychosocial theories. *Clinical Psychology Review, 31*, 383–398.

Bender, R. E., Alloy, L. B., Sylvia, L. G., Urošević, S., & Abramson, L. Y. (2010). Generation of life events in bipolar spectrum disorders: A re-examination and extension of the stress generation theory. *Journal of Clinical Psychology, 66*, 907–926.

Bergink, V., Larsen, J. T., Hillegers, M. H. J., Dahl, S. K., Stevens, H., Mortensen, P. B.,... Munk-Olsen, T. (2016). Childhood adverse life events and parental psychopathology as risk factors for bipolar disorder. *Translational Psychiatry, 6*, e929.

Bernstein, D. P., Stein, J. A., Newcomb, M. D., Walker, E., Pogge, D., Ahluvalia, T.,... Zule, W. (2003). Development and validation of a brief screening version of the Childhood Trauma Questionnaire. *Child Abuse & Neglect, 27*, 169–190.

Beyer, J. L., Kuchibhatla, M., Cassidy, F., & Krishnan, K. R. (2008). Stressful life events in older bipolar patients. *International Journal of Geriatric Psychiatry, 23*, 1271–1275.

Bidzinska, E. J. (1984). Stress factors in affective diseases. *The British Journal of Psychiatry, 144*, 161–166.

Birmaher, B., Axelson, D., Strober, M., Gill, M. K., Valeri, S., Chiappetta, L.,... Keller, M. (2006). Clinical course of children and adolescents with bipolar spectrum disorders. *Archives of General Psychiatry, 63*, 175–183.

Birmaher, B., Axelson, D., Monk, K., Kalas, C., Goldstein, B., Hickey, M. B.,... Brent, D. (2009). Lifetime psychiatric disorders in school-aged offspring of parents with bipolar disorder: The Pittsburgh Bipolar Offspring study. *Archives of General Psychiatry, 66*, 287–296.

Boland, E. M., Bender, R. E., Alloy, L. B., Conner, B. T., Labelle, D. R., & Abramson, L. Y. (2012). Life events and social rhythms in bipolar spectrum disorders: An examination of social rhythm sensitivity. *Journal of Affective Disorders, 139*, 264–272.

Boland, E. M., Stange, J. P., Adams, A. M., LaBelle, D. R., Ong, M. L., Hamilton, J. L.,... Alloy, L. B. (2016). Associations between cognitive functioning, sleep disturbance, and work disability in bipolar disorder. *Psychiatry Research, 230*, 567–574.

Boland, E. M., Stange, J. P., LaBelle, D. R., Shapero, B. G., Weiss, R. B., Abramson, L. Y., & Alloy, L. B. (2016). Affective disruption from social rhythm and Behavioral Approach System (BAS) sensitivities: A test of the integration of the social zeitgeber and BAS theories of bipolar disorder. *Clinical Psychological Science, 4*, 418–432.

Brown, G. R., McBride, L., Bauer, M. S., & Williford, W. O. (2005). Impact of childhood abuse on the course of bipolar disorder: a replication study in U.S. veterans. *Journal of Affective Disorders, 89*, 57–67.

Brown, G. W., & Harris, T. (1978). *Social origins of depression: A study of psychiatric disorder in women.* New York, NY: Free Press.

Carballo, J. J., Harkavy-Friedman, J., Burke, A. K., Sher, L., Baca-Garcia, E., Sullivan, G. M.,... Oquendo, M. A. (2008). Family history of suicidal behavior and early traumatic experiences: additive effect on suicidality and course of bipolar illness? *Journal of Affective Disorders, 109*, 57–63.

Carver, C. S. (2004). Negative affects deriving from the Behavioral Approach System. *Emotion, 4*, 3–22.

Cassano, G. B., Dell'Osso, L., Frank, E., Miniati, M., Fagiolini, A., Shear, K.,... Maser, J. (1999). The bipolar spectrum: a clinical reality in search of diagnostic criteria and an assessment methodology. *Journal of Affective Disorders, 54*, 319–328.

Chakraborty, R., Chatterjee, A., Choudhary, S., Singh, A. R., & Chakraborty, P. (2007). Life events in acute and transient psychosis—a comparison with mania. *The German Journal of Psychiatry, 10*, 36–40.

Christensen, E. M., Gjerris, A., Larsen, J. K., Bendtsen, B. B., Larsen, B. H., Rolff, H.,... Schaumburg, E. (2003). Life events and onset of a new phase in bipolar affective disorder. *Bipolar Disorders, 5*, 356–361.

Chung, R. K., Langeluddecke, P., & Tennant, C. (1986). Threatening life events in the onset of schizophrenia, schizophreniform psychosis and hypomania. *The British Journal of Psychiatry, 148*, 680–685.

Clancy, J., Crowe, R., Winokur, G., & Morrison, J. (1973). The Iowa 500: Precipitating factors in schizophrenia and primary affective disorder. *Comprehensive Psychiatry, 14*, 197–202.

Conus, P., Cotton, S., Schimmelmann, B. G., Berk, M., Daglas, R., McGorry, P. D., & Lambert, M. (2010). Pretreatment and outcome correlates of past sexual and physical trauma in 118 bipolar I disorder patients with a first episode of psychotic mania. *Bipolar Disorders, 12*, 244–252.

Conway, K. P., Compton, W., Stinson, F. S., & Grant, B. F. (2006). Lifetime comorbidity of DSM-IV mood and anxiety disorders and specific drug use disorders: Results from the National Epidemiologic Survey on Alcohol and Related Conditions. *The Journal of Clinical Psychiatry, 67*, 247–257.

Craddock, N., & Sklar, P. (2013). Genetics of bipolar disorder. *The Lancet, 381*(9878), 1654–1662.

Davenport, Y. B., & Adland, M. L. (1982). Postpartum psychoses in female and male bipolar manic-depressive patients. *American Journal of Orthopsychiatry, 52*, 288–297.

De Pradier, M., Gorwood, P., Beaufils, B., Adès, J., & Dubertret, C. (2010). Influence of the serotonin transporter gene polymorphism, cannabis and childhood sexual abuse on phenotype of bipolar disorder: A preliminary study. *European Psychiatry, 25*, 323–327.

Depue, R. A., & Iacono, W. G. (1989). Neurobehavioral aspects of affective disorders. *Annual Review of Psychology, 40*, 457–492.

Dienes, K. A., Hammen, C., Henry, R. M., Cohen, A. N., & Daley, S. E. (2006). The stress sensitization hypothesis: Understanding the course of bipolar disorder. *Journal of Affective Disorders, 95*, 43–49.

Du Rocher Schudlich, T., Youngstrom, E. A., Martinez, M., Kogosyoungstrom, J., Scovil, K., Ross, J.,... Findling, R. L. (2015). Physical and sexual abuse and early-onset bipolar disorder in youths receiving outpatient services: Frequent, but not specific. *Journal of Abnormal Child Psychology; New York, 43*, 453–463.

Dunner, D. L., Patrick, V., & Fieve, R. R. (1979). Life events at the onset of bipolar affective illness. *The American Journal of Psychiatry, 136*, 508–511.

Ehlers, C. L., Frank, E., & Kupfer, D. J. (1988). Social zeitgebers and biological rhythms: A unified approach to understanding the etiology of depression. *Archives of General Psychiatry, 45*, 948–952.

Ehnvall, A., & Agren, H. (2002). Patterns of sensitisation in the course of affective illness. A life-charting study of treatment-refractory depressed patients. *Journal of Affective Disorders, 70*, 67–75.

El Kissi, Y., Krir, M. W., Nasr, S. B., Hamadou, R., El Hedda, R., Bannour, S., & Ali, B. B. H. (2013). Life events in bipolar patients: a comparative study with siblings and healthy controls. *Journal of Affective Disorders, 151*, 378–383.

Ellicott, A., Hammen, C., Gitlin, M., Brown, G., & Jamison, K. (1990). Life events and the course of bipolar disorder. *American Journal of Psychiatry, 147*, 1194–1198.

Erten, E., Funda Uney, A., Saatçioğlu, Ö., Özdemir, A., Fıstıkçı, N., & Çakmak, D. (2014). Effects of childhood trauma and clinical features on determining quality of life in patients with bipolar I disorder. *Journal of Affective Disorders, 162*, 107–113.

Etain, B., Aas, M., Andreassen, O. A., Lorentzen, S., Dieset, I., Gard, S.,... Melle, I. (2013). Childhood trauma is associated with severe clinical characteristics of bipolar disorders. *The Journal of Clinical Psychiatry, 74*, 991–998.

Etain, B., Lajnef, M., Bellivier, F., Henry, C., M'bailara, K., Kahn, J. P.,... Fisher, H. L. (2017). Revisiting the association between childhood trauma and psychosis in bipolar disorder: A quasi-dimensional path-analysis. *Journal of Psychiatric Research, 84*, 73–79.

Francis-Raniere, E. L., Alloy, L. B., & Abramson, L. Y. (2006). Depressive personality styles and bipolar spectrum disorders: Prospective tests of the event congruency hypothesis. *Bipolar Disorders, 8*, 382–399.

Gao, K., Chan, P. K., Verduin, M. L., Kemp, D. E., Tolliver, B. K., Ganocy, S. J.,... Calabrese, J. R. (2010). Independent predictors for lifetime and recent substance use disorders in patients with rapid-cycling bipolar disorder: Focus on anxiety disorders. *American Journal on Addictions, 19*, 440–449.

Gao, K., Tolliver, B. K., Kemp, D. E., Ganocy, S. J., Bilali, S., Brady, K. L.,... Calabrese, J. R. (2009). Correlates of historical suicide attempt in rapid-cycling bipolar disorder: A cross-sectional assessment. *The Journal of Clinical Psychiatry, 70*, 1032–1040.

Garno, J. L., Goldberg, J. F., Ramirez, P. M., & Ritzler, B. A. (2005). Impact of childhood abuse on the clinical course of bipolar disorder. *The British Journal of Psychiatry: The Journal of Mental Science, 186*, 121–125.

Garno, J. L., Gunawardane, N., & Goldberg, J. F. (2008). Predictors of trait aggression in bipolar disorder. *Bipolar Disorders, 10*, 285–292.

Gershon, A., Johnson, S. L., & Miller, I. (2013). Chronic stressors and trauma: prospective influences on the course of bipolar disorder. *Psychological Medicine, 43*, 2583–2592.

Gilman, S. E., Ni, M. Y., Dunn, E. C., Breslau, J., McLaughlin, K. A., Smoller, J. W., . . . Perlis, R. H. (2015). Contributions of the social environment to first-onset and recurrent mania. *Moleecular Psychiatry, 20(3)*, 329–336.

Glassner, B., & Haldipur, C. V. (1983). Life events and early and late onset of bipolar disorder. *The American Journal of Psychiatry, 140*, 215–217.

Glassner, B., Haldipur, C. V., & Dessauersmith, J. (1979). Role loss and working-class manic depression. *The Journal of Nervous and Mental Disease, 167*, 530–541.

Goldberg, J. F., & Garno, J. L. (2005). Development of posttraumatic stress disorder in adult bipolar patients with histories of severe childhood abuse. *Journal of Psychiatric Research, 39*, 595–601.

Goldstein, B. I., Strober, M. A., Birmaher, B., Axelson, D. A., Esposito-Smythers, C., Goldstein, T. R., . . . Keller, M. B. (2008). Substance use disorders among adolescents with bipolar spectrum disorders. *Bipolar Disorders, 10*, 469–478.

Goodwin, F. K., & Jamison, K. R. (2007). *Manic-depressive illness: Bipolar disorders and recurrent depression* (Vol. 1). New York, NY: Oxford University Press.

Grandin, L. D., Alloy, L. B., & Abramson, L. Y. (2006). The social zeitgeber theory, circadian rhythms, and mood disorders: review and evaluation. *Clinical Psychology Review, 26*, 679–694.

Grandin, L. D., Alloy, L. B., & Abramson, L. Y. (2007). Childhood stressful life events and bipolar spectrum disorders. *Journal of Social and Clinical Psychology, 26*, 460–478.

Hall, K. S., Dunner, D. L., Zeller, G., & Fieve, R. R. (1977). Bipolar illness: A prospective study of life events. *Comprehensive Psychiatry, 18*, 497–502.

Hammen, C. (1991). Generation of stress in the course of unipolar depression. *Journal of Abnormal Psychology, 100*, 555–561.

Hammen, C. (2006). Stress generation in depression: Reflections on origins, research, and future directions. *Journal of Clinical Psychology, 62*, 1065–1082.

Hammen, C., & Gitlin, M. (1997). Stress reactivity in bipolar patients and its relation to prior history of depression. *American Journal of Psychiatry, 154*, 856–857.

Harkness, K. L., Bruce, A. E., & Lumley, M. N. (2006). The role of childhood abuse and neglect in the sensitization to stressful life events in adolescent depression. *Journal of Abnormal Psychology, 115*, 730–741.

Harkness, K. L., & Monroe, S. M. (2016). The assessment and measurement of adult life stress: Basic premises, operational principles, and design requirements. *Journal of Abnormal Psychology, 125*, 727–745.

Harmon-Jones, E., Abramson, L. Y., Sigelman, J., Bohlig, A., Hogan, M. E., & Harmon-Jones, C. (2002). Proneness to hypomania/mania symptoms or depression symptoms and asymmetrical frontal cortical responses to an anger-evoking event. *Journal of Personality and Social Psychology, 82*, 610–618.

Heim, C., Newport, D. J., Mletzko, T., Miller, A. H., & Nemeroff, C. B. (2008). The link between childhood trauma and depression: Insights from HPA axis studies in humans. *Psychoneuroendocrinology, 33*, 693–710.

Hillegers, M. H., Burger, H., Wals, M., Reichart, C. G., Verhulst, F. C., Nolen, W. A., & Ormel, J. (2004). Impact of stressful life events, familial loading and their interaction on the onset of mood disorders. *The British Journal of Psychiatry, 185*, 97–101.

Hlastala, S. A., Frank, E., Kowalski, J., Sherrill, J. T., Tu, X. M., Anderson, B., & Kupfer, D. J. (2000). Stressful life events, bipolar disorder, and the "kindling model." *Journal of Abnormal Psychology, 109*, 777–786.

Hooper, L. M., Stockton, P., Krupnick, J. L., & Green, B. L. (2011). Development, use, and psychometric properties of the Trauma History Questionnaire. *Journal of Loss and Trauma, 16*, 258–283.

Horesh, N., & Iancu, I. (2010). A comparison of life events in patients with unipolar disorder or bipolar disorder and controls. *Comprehensive Psychiatry, 51*, 157–164.

Hosang, G. M., Korszun, A., Jones, L., Jones, I., Gray, J. M., Gunasinghe, C. M., . . . Farmer, A. E. (2010). Adverse life event reporting and worst illness episodes in unipolar and bipolar affective disorders: Measuring environmental risk for genetic research. *Psychological Medicine, 40*, 1829–1837.

Hosang, G. M., Korszun, A., Jones, L, Jones, I., McGuffin, P., & Farmer, A. E. (2012). Life-event specificity: Bipolar disorder compared with unipolar depression. *The British Journal of Psychiatry, 201*, 458–465.

Hunt, N., Bruce-Jones, W., & Silverstone, T. (1992). Life events and relapse in bipolar affective disorder. *Journal of Affective Disorders, 25*, 13–20.

Joffe, R. T., MacDonald, C., & Kutcher, S. P. (1989). Live events and mania: A case- controlled study. *Psychiatry Research, 30*, 213–216.

Johnson, S. L. (2005). Life events in bipolar disorder: towards more specific models. *Clinical Psychology Review, 25*, 1008–1027.

Johnson, L., Andersson-Lundman, G., Aberg-Wistedt, A., & Mathé, A. A. (2000). Age of onset in affective disorder: Its correlation with hereditary and psychosocial factors. *Journal of Affective Disorders, 59*, 139–148.

Johnson, S. L., Cueller, A. K., Ruggero, C., Winett-Perlman, C., Goodnick, P., White, R., & Miller, I. (2008). Life events as predictors of mania and depression in bipolar I disorder. *Journal of Abnormal Psychology, 117*, 268–277.

Johnson, S. L., Edge, M. D., Holmes, M. K., & Carver, C. S. (2012). The behavioral activation system and mania. *Annual Review of Clinical Psychology, 8*, 243–267.

Johnson, S. L., & Kizer, A. (2002). Bipolar and unipolar depression: A comparison of clinical phenomenology and psychosocial predictors. In I. H. Gotlib & C. L. Hammen (Eds.), *Handbook of depression* (pp. 141–165). New York, NY: Guilford Press.

Johnson, S. L., & Miller, I. (1997). Negative life events and time to recovery from episodes of bipolar disorder. *Journal of Abnormal Psychology, 106*, 449–457.

Johnson, S. L., Murray, G., Fredrickson, B., Youngstrom, E. A., Hinshaw, S., Bass, J. M., . . . Salloum, I. (2012). Creativity and bipolar disorder: Touched by fire or burning with questions? *Clinical Psychology Review, 32*, 1–12.

Johnson, S. L., Sandrow, D., Meyer, B., Winters, R., Miller, I., Solomon, D., & Keitner, G. (2000). Increases in manic symptoms after life events involving goal attainment. *Journal of Abnormal Psychology, 109,* 721–727.

Judd, L. L., Schettler, P. J., Solomon, D. A., Maser, J. D., Coryell, W., Endicott, J., & Akiskal, H. S. (2008). Psychosocial disability and work role function compared across the long-term course of bipolar I, bipolar II and unipolar major depressive disorders. *Journal of Affective Disorders, 108,* 49–58.

Just, N., Abramson, L. Y., & Alloy, L. B. (2001). Remitted depression studies as tests of the cognitive vulnerability hypotheses of depression onset: A critique and conceptual analysis. *Clinical Psychology Review, 21,* 63–83.

Kadri, N., Mouchtaq, N., Hakkou, F., & Moussaoui, D. (2000). Relapses in bipolar patients: Changes in social rhythm? *International Journal of Neuropsychopharmacology, 3,* 45–49.

Kemner, S. M., Mesman, E., Nolen, W. A., Eijckemans, M. J. C., & Hillegers, M. H. J. (2015). The role of life events and psychological factors in the onset of first and recurrent mood episodes in bipolar offspring: Results from the Dutch Bipolar Offspring Study. *Psychological Medicine, 45,* 2571–2581.

Kemner, S. M., van Haren, N. E., Bootsman, F., Eijkemans, M. J., Vonk, R., van der Schot, A. C., . . . Hillegers, M. H. (2015). The influence of life events on first and recurrent admissions in bipolar disorder. *International Journal of Bipolar Disorders, 3,* 1–8.

Kennedy, S., Thompson, R., Stancer, H. C., Roy, A., & Persad, E. (1983). Life events precipitating mania. *The British Journal of Psychiatry, 142,* 398–403.

Kim, E. Y., Miklowitz, D. J., Biuckians, A., & Mullen, K. (2007). Life stress and the course of early onset bipolar disorder. *Journal of Affective Disorders, 99,* 37–44.

Kochman, F. J., Hantouche, E. G., Ferrari, P., Lancrenon, S., Bayart, D., & Akiskal, H. S. (2005). Cyclothymic temperament as a prospective predictor of bipolarity and suicidality in children and adolescents with major depressive disorder. *Journal of Affective Disorders, 85,* 181–189.

Koenders, M. A., Giltay, E. J., Spijker, A. T., Hoencamp, E., Spinhoven, P., & Elzinga, B. M. (2014). Stressful life events in bipolar I and II disorder: Cause or consequence of mood symptoms? *Journal of Affective Disorders, 161,* 55–64.

Kraemer, H. C., Kazdin, A. E., Offord, D. R., Kessler, R. C., Jensen, P. S., & Kupfer, D. J. (1997). Coming to terms with the terms of risk. *Archives of General Psychiatry, 54,* 337–343.

Kulhara, P., Basu, D., Mattoo, S. K., Sharan, P., & Chopra, R. (1999). Lithium prophylaxis of recurrent bipolar affective disorder: Long-term outcome and its psychosocial correlates. *Journal of Affective Disorders, 54,* 87–96.

Leff, J. P., Fischer, M., & Bertelsen, A. (1976). A cross-national epidemiological study of mania. *The British Journal of Psychiatry, 129,* 428–442.

Leverich, G. S., Altshuler, L. L., Frye, M. A., Suppes, T., Keck, P. E., McElroy, S. L., . . . Post, R. M. (2003). Factors associated with suicide attempts in 648 patients with bipolar disorder in the Stanley Foundation Bipolar Network. *The Journal of Clinical Psychiatry, 64,* 506–515.

Leverich, G. S., McElroy, S. L., Suppes, T., Keck, P. E., Denicoff, K. D., Nolen, W. A., . . . Post, R. M. (2002). Early physical and sexual abuse associated with an adverse course of bipolar illness. *Biological Psychiatry, 51,* 288–297.

Lewinsohn, P. M., Steinmetz, J. L., Larson, D. W., & Franklin, J. (1981). Depression- related cognitions: Antecedent or consequence? *Journal of Abnormal Psychology, 90,* 213–219.

Lex, C., Bazner, E., & Meyer, T. D. (2017). Does stress play a significant role in bipolar disorder? A meta-analysis. *Journal of Affective Disorders, 208,* 298–308.

Li, X.-B., Liu, J.-T., Zhu, X.-Z., Zhang, L., Tang, Y.-L., & Wang, C.-Y. (2014). Childhood trauma associates with clinical features of bipolar disorder in a sample of Chinese patients. *Journal of Affective Disorders, 168,* 58–63.

Liu, R. T. (2013). Stress generation: Future directions and clinical implications. *Clinical Psychology Review, 33,* 406–416.

Liu, R. T., & Alloy, L. B. (2010). Stress generation in depression: A systematic review of the empirical literature and recommendations for future study. *Clinical Psychology Review, 30,* 582–593.

Maguire, C., McCusker, C. G., Meenagh, C., Mulholland, C., & Shannon, C. (2008). Effects of trauma on bipolar disorder: The mediational role of interpersonal difficulties and alcohol dependence. *Bipolar Disorders, 10,* 293–302.

Malkoff-Schwartz, S., Frank, E., Anderson, B. P., Hlastala, S. A., Luther, J. F., Sherrill, J. T., Houck, P. R., & Kupfer, D. J. (2000). Social rhythm disruption and stressful life events in the onset of bipolar and unipolar episodes. *Psychological Medicine, 30,* 1005–1010.

Malkoff-Schwartz, S., Frank, E., Anderson, B. P., Sherrill, J. T., Siegel, L., Patterson, D., & Kupfer, D. J. (1998). Stressful life events and social rhythm disruption in the onset of manic and depressive bipolar episodes: A preliminary investigation. *Archives of General Psychiatry, 55,* 702–707.

Maniglio, R. (2013). Prevalence of child sexual abuse among adults and youths with bipolar disorder: A systematic review. *Clinical Psychology Review, 33,* 561–573.

Marchand, W. R., Wirth, L., & Simon, C. (2005). Adverse life events and pediatric bipolar disorder in a community mental health setting. *Community Mental Health Journal, 41,* 67–75.

McIntyre, R. S., Soczynska, J. K., Mancini, D., Lam, C., Woldeyohannes, H. O., Moon, S., . . . Kennedy, S. H. (2008). The relationship between childhood abuse and suicidality in adult bipolar disorder. *Violence and Victims, 23,* 361–372.

McPherson, H., Herbison, P., & Romans, S. (1993). Life events and relapse in established bipolar affective disorder. *British Journal of Psychiatry, 163,* 381–385.

Merikangas, K. R., Akiskal, H. S., Angst, J., Greenberg, P. E., Hirschfeld, R. M., Petukhova, M., & Kessler, R. C. (2007). Lifetime and 12-month prevalence of bipolar spectrum disorder in the National Comorbidity Survey replication. *Archives of General Psychiatry, 64,* 543–552.

Miklowitz, D. J., & Johnson, S. L. (2006). The psychopathology and treatment of bipolar disorder. *Annual Review of Clinical Psychology, 2,* 199–235.

Miller, S., Hallmayer, J., Wang, P. W., Hill, S. J., Johnson, S. L., & Ketter, T. A. (2013). Brain-derived neurotrophic factor val66met genotype and early life stress effects upon bipolar course. *Journal of Psychiatric Research, 47,* 252–258.

Monroe, S. M., & Harkness, K. L. (2005). Life stress, the "kindling" hypothesis, and the recurrence of depression: Considerations from a life stress perspective. *Psychological Review, 112,* 417–445.

Mowlds, W., Shannon, C., McCusker, C. G., Meenagh, C., Robinson, D., Wilson, A., & Mulholland, C. (2010). Autobiographical memory specificity, depression, and trauma in bipolar disorder. *British Journal of Clinical Psychology, 49,* 217–233.

Neria, Y., Bromet, E. J., Carlson, G. A., & Naz, B. (2005). Assaultive trauma and illness course in psychotic bipolar disorder: Findings from the Suffolk County mental health project. *Acta Psychiatrica Scandinavica, 111,* 380–383.

Neria, Y., Olfson, M., Gameroff, M. J., Wickramaratne, P., Pilowsky, D., Verdeli, H.,...Shea, S. (2008). Trauma exposure and posttraumatic stress disorder among primary care patients with bipolar spectrum disorder. *Bipolar Disorders, 10,* 503–510.

Nolen, W. A., Luckenbaugh, D. A., Altshuler, L. L., Suppes, T., McElroy, S. L., Frye, M. A.,...Post, R. M. (2004). Correlates of 1-year prospective outcome in bipolar disorder: Results from the Stanley Foundation Bipolar Network. *American Journal of Psychiatry, 161,* 1447–1454.

Nusslock, R., Abramson, L. Y., Harmon-Jones, E., Alloy, L. B., & Hogan, M. E. (2007). A goal-striving life event and the onset of hypomanic and depressive episodes and symptoms: Perspective from the behavioral approach system (BAS) dysregulation theory. *Journal of Abnormal Psychology, 116,* 105–115.

Nusslock, R., & Alloy, L. B. (2017). Reward processing and mood disorder symptoms: An RDoC and translational neuroscience perspective. *Journal of Affective Disorders, 216,* 3–16.

Nusslock, R., Alloy, L. B., Abramson, L. Y., Harmon-Jones, E., & Hogan, M. E. (2008). Impairment in the achievement domain in bipolar spectrum disorders: Role of behavioral approach system hypersensitivity and impulsivity. *Minerva Pediatrica, 60,* 41–50.

Ostiguy, C. S., Ellenbogen, M. A., Linnen, A. M., Walker, E. F., Hammen, C., & Hodgins, S. (2009). Chronic stress and stressful life events in the offspring of parents with bipolar disorder. *Journal of Affective Disorders, 114,* 74–84.

Pardoen, D., Bauwens, F., Dramaix, M., Tracy, A., Genevrois, C., Staner, L.,...Mendlewicz, J. (1996). Life events and primary affective disorders: A one year prospective study. *British Journal of Psychiatry, 169,* 160–166.

Paykel, E. S. (1980). Recall and reporting of life events. *Archives of General Psychiatry, 37,* 485.

Perich, T., Mitchell, P. B., Loo, C., Hadzi-Pavlovic, D., Roberts, G., Green, M.,...Corry, J. (2014). Cognitive styles and clinical correlates of childhood abuse in bipolar disorder. *Bipolar Disorders, 16,* 600–607.

Perris, H. (1984). Life events and depression: Part 2. Results in diagnostic subgroups, and in relation to the recurrence of depression. *Journal of Affective Disorders, 7,* 25–36.

Petti, T., Reich, W., Todd, R. D., Joshi, P., Galvin, M., Reich, T.,...Nurnberger, J. (2004). Psychosocial variables in children and teens of extended families identified through bipolar affective disorder probands. *Bipolar Disorders, 6,* 106–114.

Plomin, R., & Crabbe, J. (2000). DNA. *Psychological Bulletin, 126,* 806–828.

Post, R. M. (1992). Transduction of psychosocial stress into the neurobiology of recurrent affective disorder. *The American Journal of Psychiatry, 149,* 999–1010.

Post, R. M., Altshuler, L. L., Kupka, R., McElroy, S. L., Frye, M. A., Rowe, M.,...Nolen, W. A. (2015). Verbal abuse, like physical and sexual abuse, in childhood is associated with an earlier onset and more difficult course of bipolar disorder. *Bipolar Disorders, 17,* 323–330.

Post, R. M., Altshuler, L. L., Kupka, R., McElroy, S. L., Frye, M. A., Rowe, M.,...Nolen, W. A. (2016). Age of onset of bipolar disorder: Combined effect of childhood adversity and familial loading of psychiatric disorders. *Journal of Psychiatric Research, 81,* 63–70.

Post, R. M., Altshuler, L., Leverich, G., Nolen, W., Kupka, R., Grunze, H.,...Rowe, M. (2013). More stressors prior to and during the course of bipolar illness in patients from the United States compared with the Netherlands and Germany. *Psychiatry Research, 210,* 880–886.

Romero, S., Birmaher, B., Axelson, D., Goldstein, T., Goldstein, B. I., Gill, M. K.,...Keller, M. (2009). Prevalence and correlates of physical and sexual abuse in children and adolescents with bipolar disorder. *Journal of Affective Disorders, 112,* 144–150.

Rucklidge, J. J. (2006). Psychosocial functioning of adolescents with and without paediatric bipolar disorder. *Journal of Affective Disorders, 91,* 181–188.

Sala, R., Goldstein, B. I., Wang, S., & Blanco, C. (2014). Childhood maltreatment and the course of bipolar disorders among adults: Epidemiologic evidence of dose-response effects. *Journal of Affective Disorders, 165,* 74–80.

Sclare, P., & Creed, F. (1990). Life events and the onset of mania. *The British Journal of Psychiatry, 156,* 508–514.

Shapero, B. G., Weiss, R. B., Burke, T. A., Boland, E. M., Abramson, L. Y., & Alloy, L. B. (2017). Kindling of life stress in bipolar disorder: Effects of early adversity. *Behavior Therapy, 48,* 322–334.

Swendsen, J., Hammen, C., Heller, T., & Gitlin, M. (1995). Correlates of stress reactivity in patients with bipolar disorder. *The American Journal of Psychiatry, 152,* 795–797.

Sylvia, L. G., Alloy, L. B., Hafner, J. A., Gauger, M. C., Verdon, K., & Abramson, L. Y. (2009). Life events and social rhythms in bipolar spectrum disorders: A prospective study. *Behavior Therapy, 40,* 131–141.

Urošević, S., Abramson, L. Y., Alloy, L. B., Nusslock, R., Harmon-Jones, E., Bender, R., & Hogan, M. E. (2010). Increased rates of events that activate or deactivate the Behavioral Approach System, but not events related to goal attainment, in bipolar spectrum disorders. *Journal of Abnormal Psychology, 119,* 610–615.

Urošević, S., Abramson, L. Y., Harmon-Jones, E., & Alloy, L. B. (2008). Dysregulation of the Behavioral Approach System (BAS) in bipolar spectrum disorders: Review of theory and evidence. *Clinical Psychology Review, 28,* 1188–1205.

Wals, M., Hillegers, M. H., Reichart, C. G., Verhulst, F. C., Nolen, W. A., & Ormel, J. (2005). Stressful life events and onset of mood disorders in children of bipolar parents during 14-month follow-up. *Journal of Affective Disorders, 87,* 253–263.

Watson, S., Gallagher, P., Dougall, D., Porter, R., Moncrieff, J., Ferrier, I. N., & Young, A. H. (2014). Childhood trauma in bipolar disorder. *The Australian and New Zealand Journal of Psychiatry, 48,* 564–570.

Weiss, R. B., Stange, J. P., Boland, E. M., Black, S. K., LaBelle, D. R., Abramson, L. Y., & Alloy, L. B. (2015). Kindling of life stress in bipolar disorder: Comparison of sensitization and autonomy models. *Journal of Abnormal Psychology, 124,* 4–16.

Stress in Schizophrenia

Katrina Goines, Allison LoPilato, Derek Novacek, Roberto España, *and* Elaine Walker

Abstract

This chapter contains a review and discussion of evidence linking various types of psychosocial stress with the onset and course of schizophrenia and other psychotic disorders. Stress has long been considered an important factor in the etiology of psychosis and psychotic disorders. Specifically, stress is thought to interact with pre-existing biological vulnerabilities to trigger psychosis through complex changes to various biological processes (e.g., changes to HPA axis, neurotransmitter activity, and inflammatory processes). This chapter includes discussion of a wide variety of stress experiences, including daily hassles, life events, trauma, childhood adversity, and minority stress, and explores the scientific evidence linking these stressors with psychosis and psychotic disorders. Biological processes and biomarkers associated with both stress and psychosis are also discussed. Finally, important questions relating to the future study of stress and psychosis are considered.

Keywords: schizophrenia, psychosis, stress, trauma, childhood adversity, minority stress, HPA axis

Introduction

Psychotic disorders are considered to be the most serious mental illnesses because, by definition, they compromise the individual's capacity to comprehend reality. Moreover, the modal age range for the clinical onset of schizophrenia and other psychoses is in late adolescence and early adulthood. As a result, these disorders can derail the individual's attainment of adult developmental milestones, including the achievement of educational, social, and occupational goals.

The defining symptoms of psychosis, typically referred to as "positive" symptoms, include hallucinations, delusions, and thought disorder. In addition, the patient may manifest one or more "negative" symptoms that entail a decrease in functional capacity. Negative symptoms range from blunted affect and anhedonia (i.e., decreases in the expression and experience of emotion) to deficits in motivation and alogia (reduced speech).

Though etiologic theories of schizophrenia and other psychotic disorders have evolved with scientific advances in neuroscience and genetics,

environmental stress has remained an enduring factor in models of the disorder. The neural diathesis-stress model of schizophrenia (Walker & Diforio, 1997; Walker, Mittal, & Tessner, 2008) is currently the dominant framework for understanding how environmental stressors interact with pre-existing biological vulnerabilities to precipitate the onset of schizophrenia. According to this model, psychosocial stressors act upon pre-existing latent vulnerabilities to trigger the onset of psychosis through a cascade of complex neurodevelopmental, inflammatory, and neurochemical (e.g., dopaminergic, glutamatergic) changes (Pruessner, Cullen, Aas, & Walker, 2017). In addition to triggering the onset of the disorder, there is also evidence that environmental stress leads to fluctuations in psychotic symptom severity over the course of illness (Myin-Germeys, Marcelis, Krabbendam, Delespaul, & van Os, 2005).

Consistent with this, there is a large literature documenting the relationship between environmental stressors and risk for schizophrenia and other psychotic disorders (Aiello, Horowitz, Hepgul,

Pariante, & Mondelli, 2012; Holtzman et al., 2013; Mizrahi, 2016; Pruessner et al., 2017). Environmental stress in these studies ranges from experiences of early life stress and childhood adversity (Holtzman et al., 2013; McGrath et al., 2017; Varese et al., 2012), to stress triggered by psychosocial events and contexts (e g., urban versus rural settings, immigrant status) across the life span (Phillips, Francey, Edwards, & McMurray, 2007), social-evaluative threats and defeat (Oh, Yang, Anglin, & DeVylder, 2014; Selten, van der Ven, Rutten, & Cantor-Graae, 2013), minority status (Veling, 2013), and low socioeconomic status (SES; Agerbo et al., 2015). While the mechanisms underlying these associations remain an area of active investigation, they are thought to involve stress-mediated changes to brain structure and/or function, including inflammatory processes, neurotransmitter activity, gene expression, and regulation of the hypothalamic-pituitary-adrenal (HPA) axis. Many of these mechanisms are reviewed in later chapters and will not be explicitly discussed in detail here.

In the following sections, we review the cumulative evidence linking various types of stress with the onset and course of schizophrenia and other psychotic disorders. We broaden our focus to include "other" psychotic disorders because of increasing evidence that current diagnostic distinctions among subtypes of psychosis (e g., schizophrenia, schizoaffective, mood disorder with psychotic features) do not align with distinct biological vulnerabilities or etiologic pathways (Buka & Fan, 1999; Craddock, O'Donovan, & Owen, 2009; Moore et al., 2007). The present review also includes growing evidence from research on the "psychosis prodrome," which has received considerable attention in the past decade. The prodrome is the period of functional decline and gradual emergence of symptoms that typically precedes the clinical onset of psychotic disorders (Yung & McGorry, 1996a, 1996b). Utilizing data from retrospective studies, investigators have identified the nature of the subclinical, or "attenuated," symptoms that usually precede schizophrenia and other psychoses. Based on these findings, structured diagnostic interviews have been developed to identify individuals who are at increased clinical high risk (CHR) for psychosis (Addington & Heinssen, 2012). By following these CHR individuals longitudinally, investigators are able to shed light on the preonset behavioral course as well as factors associated with a transition to clinical psychosis. This longitudinal approach offers unique opportunities for elucidating the role of stress in psychotic

disorders. Thus, in this review, longitudinal studies that provide support for causal effects of stress on risk will be highlighted. Factors that may act as moderators, particularly sex, will also be addressed. It should be noted that while the prenatal environment is implicated in both stress and psychosis risk (Markham & Koenig, 2011), the discussion in this review will be limited to postnatal stress.

Research on psychotic experiences in healthy or nonclinical samples will also be included in this review. Psychotic experiences are relatively common outside of clinical psychotic disorders or CHR syndromes (Van Os, Linscott, Myin-Germeys, Delespaul, & Krabbendam, 2009). Additionally, when psychotic experiences occur in otherwise healthy, nonclinical individuals, these experiences are typically transient (Van Os et al., 2009) and may be triggered by stress (Collip et al., 2013). The link between these nonclinical psychotic experiences and clinical psychotic disorders is a current topic of debate in the field (Murray & Jones, 2012), although it is likely that the etiology of psychotic symptoms in these different contexts varies considerably. However, similarities in risk factors for psychotic symptoms within and outside of clinical disorder suggest that these experiences have relevance to the study of psychosis (Kelleher & Cannon, 2011). Further, the transient, stress-reactive characteristics of some nonclinical psychotic experiences suggest that studies of such experiences may be especially useful for understanding the role of acute stress in the emergence of positive psychotic symptoms (Collip et al., 2013).

Finally, it is important to note that the adverse effects of stress exposure are not assumed to be specific to psychotic disorders; there are large bodies of research documenting the potential for stress to heighten risk for a range of mental as well as physical disorders. Thus, the nature of the psychiatric symptoms triggered by stress is assumed to vary as a function of pre-existing individual differences in vulnerability. Additionally, many of the stress-related biomarkers and processes discussed in this chapter are also associated with many nonpsychotic disorders. This may partially explain the high degree of diagnostic comorbidity found in psychotic samples. Further, there is increasing evidence of etiologic heterogeneity in schizophrenia and other psychoses, and it is likely that etiologic subtypes vary in stress sensitivity. For example, some schizophrenia patients may not be particularly stress-sensitive, and those who are may be genetically predisposed to be more biologically sensitive to psychosocial stress, or they may experience heightened stress sensitivity conferred by early childhood trauma or other adverse experiences.

Stress and Psychosis

Before reviewing the literature, it is important to briefly clarify the term "stress" used throughout this chapter. There are inherent difficulties in conceptualizing stress and capturing its breadth and complexity (Monroe, 2008). In exploring the causal relationship between stress and schizophrenia in this chapter, we find it important to distinguish among three related components of stress: (1) the stressful event or experience; (2) the subjective perception and appraisal of the event/experience; and (3) the biological stress response. Additionally, there are also individual differences in vulnerability to stress that operate across each of these components.

To examine the causal relationship between stress and psychosis, it is important to consider the evidence for each of these components. In the following sections, we review the current literature linking each of these components to psychosis and psychotic symptoms. While these components will be discussed separately for the sake of clarity, it is understood that they are transactional processes. For example, appraising an event as very stressful may result in a stronger biological stress response, and additionally, experiencing a stronger biological stress response to an event may result in the individual rating the event as more stressful. Finally, after establishing the evidence for the relationship between stress and psychosis more broadly, we will explore associations between psychosis and two specific domains of stress that have received increasing attention in the psychosis literature, namely childhood adversity and stress determined by minority status.

Stressful Events and Experiences

The first component of stress involves the stressful event or circumstance itself. In the literature, this can range from major life events (e.g., loss of a family member, serious illness, birth of a child) to daily hassles (e.g., arguments, being late for an appointment, transportation problems). These are often rated by retrospective self-report, although real-time recording methodologies also exist (e.g., experience sampling methodology). A review of the literature suggests that stressful events (1) precede the onset of schizophrenia, (2) may occur at higher rates in psychosis-prone individuals, and (3) exacerbate psychotic symptoms.

There is emerging evidence that stressful life events may precede and precipitate the onset of schizophrenia. Recent work with CHR youth have found that those who went on to develop a psychotic disorder reported a higher number of stressful life events at baseline relative to both controls and CHR individuals who later remitted (Trotman et al., 2014). Retrospective studies also show that psychotic patients report more stressful life events in the year preceding psychotic illness than did controls (Chakraborty, Chatterjee, Choudhary, Singh, & Chakraborty, 2007; Faravelli, Catena, Scarpato, & Ricca, 2007; Raune, Kuipers, & Bebbington, 2009), although this effect was not present in all studies (see Phillips et al., 2007, for review). The difference between patients and controls may be especially apparent for certain types of stressful events, such as those that are considered threatening/intrusive (e.g., physical assault) (Raune et al., 2009). Together, these findings suggest that stressful events, especially those that are threatening, may trigger psychosis in some individuals. However, it is also important to consider other potential reasons for the association between stressful life events, or other measures of subjective stress, and psychotic outcomes. For example, it is likely that those with psychotic symptoms elicit more stress in their environment than those without psychotic symptoms. Additionally, as we describe in more detail later, there is evidence that psychotic individuals and those at high risk perceive their experiences as more stressful than controls. In fact, both of these explanations may contribute to the generally greater stress experienced by individuals with psychosis, which may then put them at further risk of psychotic symptoms exacerbation.

Indeed, there is evidence that stressful experiences may also exacerbate psychotic symptoms. One of the early landmark studies on stress and schizophrenia found that increases in the number of life stressors (e.g., loss of a family member, serious illness, birth of a child) were associated with subsequent increases in psychotic symptoms (Browen & Birley, 1968). This finding has been replicated in a number of studies (Day et al., 1987; Nuechterlein et al., 1992; Pallanti, Quercioli, & Pazzagli, 1997), and it suggests the stressful events may be causally related to severity of psychotic symptoms. Notably, these findings hold even when stressful life events are restricted to "independent" events—that is, events which are presumably outside of the patient's control and unrelated to his or her clinical state (Bebbington et al., 1993), thus reducing the likelihood of evocative processes.

While there is evidence linking stressful events to schizophrenia onset and psychotic symptoms, it is not yet clear to what extent the nature, intensity, and duration of these stressful experiences drive the observed relationships (Phillips et al., 2007). For example, there is some evidence of a threshold effect, whereby symptom exacerbation or onset is only precipitated after some number of stressful events have been experienced (e.g., 10 or more) (Lataster, Myin-Germeys, Lieb, Wittchen, & van Os, 2012). Further, it has also been suggested that frequency of daily hassles (i.e., everyday stressors that most people experience) may have an even stronger effect on psychotic symptoms than isolated stressful events (Malla & Norman 1992; Phillips et al., 2007). Indeed, a longitudinal study of youth at high risk for psychosis found that while a greater total number of stressful life events was experienced by the high-risk group as opposed to controls, it was the number of daily hassles (minor stressors that occurred within 24 hours of the interview) that predicted worsening of symptoms 1 year later (Tessner, Mittal, & Walker, 2009). More work is clearly needed to better understand the nature of the relationships observed between stressful experiences and psychosis.

Perceptions of Stress

Stress perception is also associated with psychotic disorders. The growing recognition that an individual's subjective appraisals of stress will likely impact on his or her physiological and psychological response to it has led to an increase in studies looking at perceived stress. This emerging literature has found that (1) psychotic patients report greater subjective stress, (2) increases in subjective stress are associated with fluctuations in psychotic symptom intensity, and (3) increased stress perception may be associated with psychosis proneness more broadly.

Compared with healthy controls, psychotic patients report greater subjective distress in relation to both stressful events in experimental studies (Dinzeo, Cohen, Nienow, & Docherty, 2004, 2008; Veling, Pot-Kolder, Counotte, van Os, & van der Gaag, 2016) as well as in relation to daily hassles by self-report (Myin-Germeys, van Os, Schwartz, Stone, & Delespaul, 2001). Individuals with psychosis also report life events to be less controllable compared to those without psychosis (Horan et al., 2005). Interestingly, this pattern is also observed among CHR individuals (Trotman et al., 2014), with some evidence that this group actually exceeds first-episode psychosis patients in terms of perceived stress (Palmier-Claus, Dunn, & Lewis, 2012; Pruessner, Iyer, Faridi, Joober, & Malla, 2011). Experience

sampling method (ESM) studies have provided important clues about the temporal association between daily stressors and psychotic symptoms. For example, Myin-Germeys and colleagues (2005) found that increased subjective stress (associated with daily stressors) was positively associated with fluctuations in psychosis intensity in psychotic patients. This close temporal relationship provides strong evidence for a direct link between stress and psychotic symptoms.

Further studies have shown that stress sensitivity, or emotional reactivity to minor stressors, may be linked to psychosis proneness not just in psychotic individuals but across the continuum of psychosis severity. For example, stress sensitivity is associated with more severe positive subthreshold psychotic symptoms and affective symptoms in those at risk for developing psychosis (Corcoran et al., 2012). Interestingly, relatives of those with psychosis show greater stress sensitivity in reaction to daily life stressors in a way that cosegregates with severity of positive symptoms in the proband with psychosis (Lataster, Collip, Lardinois, Van Os, & Myin-Germeys, 2010), suggesting that reactivity to stressors may be associated with familial risk for psychosis. Finally, this relationship appears to exist even in the general nonpsychiatric population with healthy individuals who experience more subthreshold psychotic experiences reporting greater stress sensitivity (Collip et al., 2013). The findings on heightened stress perception and sensitivity have even prompted some researchers to propose a stress sensitivity "pathway to psychosis" in which sensitivity, or emotional reactivity, to stress can be considered both a marker of liability for psychosis and a factor that actively contributes to psychotic illness progression (Myin-Germeys & van Os, 2007).

Biological Responses to Stress

There are a number of psychobiological levels that participate in the stress response process. Although this chapter does not focus on stress mechanisms in detail, there are a number of stress response factors that show specific associations with schizophrenia pathology and warrant attention. These include (1) HPA dysfunction, (2) dopamine, (3) inflammation, and (4) epigenetic regulation of neurotrophic factors.

Stress and HPA Axis Activity

There is substantial evidence linking HPA axis dysregulation to psychosis, and several lines of investigation point to an association between increased cortisol secretion and psychosis. HPA reactivity and baseline cortisol levels show a normative increase during adolescence/young adulthood (Gunnar, Wewerka, Frenn, Long, & Griggs, 2009), the same developmental period when individuals are at highest risk of developing psychosis. In studies focusing on psychotic symptoms specifically, hypercortisolemia caused by administration of exogenous corticosteroids can cause psychotic symptoms (Buchman, 2001; Warrington & Bostwick, 2006). Further, in those with disorders characterized by hypercortisolemia (e.g., Cushing's disease), psychotic symptoms have been shown to remit in conjunction with reduced cortisol levels in response to certain medications (Chan et al., 2011; Chu et al., 2001). Research has also shown that antipsychotic medications have the effect of reducing cortisol and that patients with the strongest cortisol reduction are among the best responders (Holtzman et al., 2013; Walker et al., 2008). Taken together, these lines of investigation suggest that increased cortisol may directly impact psychosis.

In addition to studies looking at cortisol, there are also indirect lines of investigation that point to compromised regulation of the HPA axis. For example, known risk factors for schizophrenia (e.g., prenatal maternal stress) have been found to impact the development and regulation of the HPA axis (Maccari et al., 2003). Additionally, volumetric reductions of the hippocampus are well documented in psychotic patients. Given the role of the hippocampus in modulating HPA activation, and reports of an inverse correlation between cortisol levels and hippocampal volume in psychotic patients (Mondelli, Pariante et al., 2010), these findings have been interpreted as another indicator of HPA dysregulation in psychosis. Finally, glucocorticoid receptors are reduced in those with psychosis, suggesting problems with negative feedback mechanisms on the HPA axis (Perlman, Webster, Kleinman, & Weickert, 2004; Webster, Knable, O'grady, Orthmann, & Weikert, 2002). These findings lend further support to theories that compromised HPA function is linked with psychosis.

Despite this compelling evidence, the relation between cortisol and psychosis has been inconsistent and varies based on what indices of cortisol are examined. Before reviewing the evidence, it is important to note several methodological challenges in this area of investigation that should be taken into consideration when interpreting the findings (summarized from Pruessner et al., 2017). First, many of the psychotropic medications prescribed

to CHR and psychotic patients, especially the antipsychotics, alter HPA activity. In particular, antipsychotics and antidepressants dampen cortisol secretion and may, thereby, reduce stress sensitivity. The resulting reductions in cortisol and stress sensitivity may even be one of the mechanisms of action of these drugs. Thus, HPA-related differences between controls and psychotic/high-risk participants may be obscured when studying groups of participants who take antipsychotic and other psychiatric medications. Additionally, this effect may not be of comparable impact across all psychotic/high-risk participants, as symptom severity is also linked with likelihood of being prescribed a psychiatric medication, such that those with more severe symptoms are more likely to be on medication and taking a higher dosage (Woods et al., 2013). Thus, when studying medicated patients, the underlying relations between stressor, stress response, and psychotic symptoms may be obscured and/or biased.

Second, CHR and psychotic patient samples are diagnosed on the basis of manifesting positive symptoms that exceed a predetermined threshold. Thus, the variance in positive symptom severity is constrained in these samples. For example, the commonly used Structured Interview for Prodromal Syndromes (SIPS) (Miller et al., 2003) and Comprehensive Assessment of At-Risk Mental States (CAARMS) (Yung et al., 2002) both have lower and higher severity cut-off scores to designate risk status. Individuals scoring between 3 and 5 on a 6-point severity scale of psychotic-like symptoms may meet criteria for an "at-risk" designation, but those scoring lower than 3 (i.e., normal-range severity) and higher than 5 (i.e., psychotic-level severity), are be excluded from this group. Other symptoms (e.g., negative psychotic symptoms) are allowed to vary naturally without cut-offs. A similar issue is present when using samples of psychotic patients who have to meet diagnostic criteria based on positive symptoms, but not other psychotic symptoms. Thus, when studying psychotic and high-risk samples, there is a restriction of range on positive psychotic symptoms that results in a reduced likelihood that psychotic symptoms will correlate with other measures (e.g., biological stress measures).

On a related note, the biological "law of initial values" indicates that baseline levels of a biomarker of stress reactivity, such as cortisol, are associated with the responsivity of that marker to stress. This is presumably due to homeostatic mechanisms in the body, which work to keep levels of hormones within certain absolute limits. Thus, the most chronically highly stressed individuals (potentially those with more severe psychotic symptoms) may not show an increase in cortisol in response to stress challenge in experimental studies. This adds complexity to the interpretation of findings from paradigms assessing cortisol reactivity to tasks.

Finally, there are a multitude of practical methodological factors that can greatly influence measurement of cortisol. For example, cortisol levels are strongly influenced by circadian rhythms, so the time of day of sampling can have big impacts on results. Additionally, variations in cortisol sampling methods (e.g., serum versus saliva collection) and assay procedures should be kept in mind when comparing results across studies.

In what follows we will briefly review the findings on basal cortisol levels, cortisol awakening response (CAR), cortisol reactivity, and hair cortisol concentration (HCC). For a more extensive review of this topic, see Pruessner et al. (2017).

BASAL CORTISOL LEVELS

Several reviews have now concluded that first-episode psychosis is characterized by elevated salivary and/or blood cortisol (Borges, Gayer-Anderson, & Mondelli, 2013; Bulut, Bulut, & Guriz, 2016; Carol & Mittal, 2015; Karanikas, Antoniadis, & Garyfallos, 2014; Pruessner et al., 2017) and in CHR patients (Aiello et al., 2012; Carol & Mittal, 2015; Karanikas & Garyfallos, 2015; Pruessner et al., 2017). Notably, in the largest longitudinal study to date, Walker and colleagues (2013) found that youth who transitioned to psychosis had higher baseline salivary cortisol than either controls or CHR subjects whose symptoms remitted. However, there have been inconsistencies in this pattern, some of which may be due to the cortisol dampening effects of antipsychotic medication (Mondelli, Dazzan, et al., 2010). Findings on the association between cortisol and psychotic symptom severity are also mixed. A systematic review found that most of the cross-sectional evidence did not support an association between cortisol and psychotic symptom severity in those at risk for psychosis (Karanikas & Garryfallos, 2015). However, the authors noted that, despite this pattern, two studies with larger cohorts employing strong design (multiple saliva samples) did find a positive association between psychotic symptoms and elevated cortisol (Collip et al., 2011; Walker et al., 2013).

CORTISOL AWAKENING RESPONSE

The cortisol awakening response (CAR)—the sharp normative increase in cortisol that occurs between 15 and 40 minutes after wakening (Pruessner et al., 1997)—has also received attention in the psychosis literature. Findings on group differences have been mixed, with some finding attenuated CAR in psychotic patients (Mondelli, Dazzan, et al., 2010) and CHR patients (Day et al., 2014), while others finding no group differences (Girshkin et al., 2016; Hempel et al., 2010; Pruessner, Vracotas, Joober, Pruessner, & Malla, 2013) or even an increase in CHR participants who converted to psychosis versus those who did not (Labad et al., 2015). A recent review of available evidence concluded that CAR is attenuated in those with a psychotic disorder, but it may not be attenuated in those at risk (Berger et al., 2016). The number of studies in this area is still limited and inconsistencies may be due to sex differences (Carol, Spencer, & Mittal, 2016; Pruessner et al., 2017) and methodological issues in measuring CAR (Berger et al., 2016; Pruessner et al., 2017).

CORTISOL REACTIVITY TO STRESS TASKS

A limited number of studies have examined cortisol response to a psychosocial stressor, producing mixed findings. A meta-analysis investigating HPA axis responses to a social stress (i.e., Trier Social Stress test) found that those with schizophrenia showed reduced cortisol before and after social stress compared to healthy controls (Ciufolini, Dazzan, Kempton, Pariante, & Mondelli, 2014). Relatively reduced cortisol reaction to stress has also been observed in CHR participants who are naïve to antipsychotic medication (Pruessner et al., 2013), but not consistently across all studies (Mizrahi et al., 2012). Methodological issues in cortisol collection (e.g., time-of-day influences) may be a factor in the mixed findings across studies. An additional issue relevant to this type of method is that, as noted previously, measurement of cortisol is impacted by baseline levels. Thus, due to homeostatic mechanisms, those with higher baseline levels of cortisol will exhibit lower reactivity.

HAIR CORTISOL CONCENTRATION

Studies of hair cortisol concentration (HCC) enable researchers to measure systemic exposure to cortisol on a month-by-month basis, providing a new way of examining cortisol levels and change in cortisol over time. Two recent studies have employed this methodology in psychotic samples, and findings suggest that cortisol is higher in nonmedicated first-episode psychosis in comparison to healthy controls, and cortisol abnormalities may begin before onset of psychosis (Andrade et al., 2016) and may differentiate inpatients from outpatients with severe mental illness (Streit et al., 2016). The HCC methodology may be especially helpful as it bypasses some of the limitations of cross-sectional work on HPA activity. However, more work using this methodology is needed to confidently understand normal versus abnormal HCC patterns over time, especially given the effect of various confounds, including smoking and frequency of hair washing.

In summary, there are several lines of evidence to support the role of HPA axis dysfunction in psychotic disorders. However, there is not a clear pattern to the exact nature of this dysfunction, and methodological issues likely contribute to much of the variability in this literature. Overall, it seems that psychotic and CHR patients tend to show elevated basal cortisol and may show attenuated CAR and cortisol responses to stress. Cross-sectional studies have provided inconsistent findings regarding the association between psychotic symptom severity and cortisol, whereas longitudinal studies find that elevated cortisol is associated with risk for conversion to psychotic disorder, as well as worsening of symptoms in an established psychotic disorder. Taken together, this area of research provides evidence for the role of stress in psychosis and suggests biological mechanisms that may act as mediators.

Stress and Dopamine

The synergistic relationship between HPA and dopamine (DA) warrants attention here in light of the prominent role DA plays in the etiology of schizophrenia and psychotic symptoms. Predominant theories of schizophrenia posit that increased DA activity in the striatum is the biological abnormality underpinning positive symptoms of psychosis (Howes & Kapur, 2009). Subcortical hyperdopaminergic activity may also be associated with hypodopaminergic activity in prefrontal areas, the latter of which may be associated with some of the cognitive symptoms of psychosis (Howes & Kapur, 2009). One important downstream effect of HPA axis dysfunction is altered DA activity, providing a critical link between stress, HPA axis functioning, and DA dysregulation.

However, there is also evidence that stress is directly related to altered DA regulation. For example, several investigations utilizing positive emission tomography (PET) in healthy volunteers have found that psychosocial stress produces modest increases in striatal DA release (Booij et al., 2016; Mizrahi et al., 2012; Pruessner, Champagne, Meaney, &

Dagher, 2004; Soliman et al., 2008; but not Montgomery, Mehta, & Grasby, 2006). With respect to PET studies of clinical samples, Soliman and colleagues (2008) found that a psychosocial stress challenge was associated with increased striatal DA release in schizotypal participants. They also found indirect evidence for a negative association between striatal DA activity and frontal lobe function. Meanwhile, a study by Mizrahi and colleagues (2012) looking at three groups (antipsychotic-naïve patients with schizophrenia, CHR individuals, and healthy volunteers) found significant stress-induced increases in striatal DA in schizophrenia patients compared to the healthy volunteers, with an intermediate effect found for CHR participants. This study also tested for stress-induced changes in salivary cortisol levels and found that schizophrenia patients exhibited the largest cortisol response to stress, followed by the CHR group. Cortisol and DA response to stress were correlated in this study, supporting a link between the two.

In summary, studies of healthy subjects indicate a relation between stress and augmentation of subcortical DA activity which may be mediated by cortisol secretion. Findings from research exploring striatal DA in response to stress in clinical samples suggest that stress-induced striatal DA activity and cortisol may be heightened in psychotic disorders and those at risk of psychosis. Thus, while limited, the available evidence suggests that stress augments DA activity, one of the neural mechanisms thought to contribute to psychotic symptoms.

Stress and Inflammation

The role of inflammation in psychosis (Bergink, Gibney, & Drexhage, 2014; Carter, Bullmore, & Harrison, 2014), and the possibility that stress may underlie and precipitate relevant inflammatory processes, has been investigated in recent years. Schizophrenia patients show elevations in inflammatory markers compared to controls (Miller, Buckley, Seabolt, Mellor, & Kirkpatrick, 2011), and postmortem studies show that brains of those with schizophrenia reveal elevated inflammation and other stress markers (Fillman, Sinclair, Fung, Webster, & Weickert, 2014). A recent study with CHR youth found that elevations in inflammatory markers at baseline were associated with later conversion to psychosis (Focking et al., 2016). This all adds to the growing evidence that inflammation is implicated in psychotic disorders.

There is also strong evidence that social stress influences the immune response (see Kiecolt-Glaser,

McGuire, Robles, & Glaser, 2002, for review). For example, glucocorticoids (e.g., cortisol), which are released during stress, are known to have strong anti-inflammatory effects (Vinson, 2009). However, acute and chronic stress have differing impacts on the immune system, with chronic stress resulting in more maladaptive changes to the immune system (Segerstrom & Miller, 2004). Chronic stress is also known to be detrimental to many cognitive abilities, and there is evidence that this association may be mediated by stress-related increases in inflammation (Mondelli et al., 2011). Animal models of maternal immune activation have generated interesting and enlightening findings with regard to how stress interacts with the immune system to promote risk for psychosis. For example, one preclinical study found that prenatal immune activation and peripubertal stress acted synergistically in the development of sensorimotor gating deficiencies that are considered viable animal models of schizophrenia (Giovanoli et al., 2013). Interestingly, adult exposure to stress did not result in the same alterations, suggesting that stress exposure at certain developmental stages may lead to psychotic symptoms through activating immune-related biological vulnerabilities. Overall, while there is strong evidence for both an association between inflammation and psychosis, and between inflammation and stress, there is limited research addressing associations between stress, inflammation, *and* psychosis. More research is needed to clarify exactly how stress and inflammation interact to produce risk for psychosis.

Genetic Vulnerability to Stress Sensitivity and Psychosis Risk

Of course, while most people are exposed to stressful experiences, the incidence of psychotic disorders in the population is below 3%, implicating genetic and other individual differences in susceptibility to the negative effects of stress. Although a review of this literature is beyond the scope of this chapter, genes that may be implicated in vulnerability to stress have been identified, including catechol-O-methyltransferase (COMT), brain-derived neurotrophic factor (BDNF), and the DA D2 receptor (DRD2) genes. The COMT gene is a particularly promising candidate as it has been linked to both stress sensitivity and psychosis (Montag et al., 2008; Wonodi, Stine, Mitchell, Buchanan, & Thaker, 2003). COMT is an enzyme that is important for degrading DA, particularly in the human prefrontal cortex (PFC). A functional polymorphism of the gene entails a switch from valine (*val*) to methionine

(*met*) (COMT Val158Met). Both the *val* and the *met* variants are common in the population, but the *met* variant is associated with lower enzymatic activity (i.e., less degradation of DA in brain, especially the PFC, which likely results in generally higher levels of available DA in the PFC compared to the *val* variant).

General population studies have found that the *met* variant may be associated with anxiety (Olsson et al., 2005; Stein et al., 2005) and stronger reactions to psychosocial stress (Drabant et al., 2006; Smolka et al., 2005). Consistent with this, a PET study of healthy controls and relatives of those with psychosis showed that *met* hetero- and homozygotes in both groups showed reduced DA release in the PFC in response to stress, and also higher subjective ratings of stress in comparison to *val* homozygotes (*val/val* genotype) (Hernaus et al., 2013). Research in psychotic samples has also found that patients with the *met/met* genotype experience the highest levels of psychotic reactivity to stressors in comparison with other genotypes (Collip et al., 2010; van Winkel et al., 2008). In CHR youth, Walder and colleagues (2010) found that the *met/met* genotype was associated with higher cortisol levels at 1-year follow-up (in comparison to *val/met* and *val/val* genotypes), and *met* carriers showed increased cortisol levels throughout the 1-year study period. This suggests that the COMT genotype may moderate stress sensitivity via modulation of HPA axis function. There is also evidence that the *val* variant is associated with risk for psychosis, although it is believed to moderate vulnerability through different routes than the *met* allele. For example, the *val* variant may be associated with cognitive impairment (Tunbridge, Harrison, & Weinberger, 2006) and vulnerability to psychotogenic effects of marijuana (Caspi et al., 2005; Nieman et al., 2016). Thus, while COMT may be involved in vulnerability to psychosis through various paths, evidence suggests that the *met* variant is associated with psychosis risk through a general liability for heightened stress sensitivity.

Sex Differences

Among the most well-established aspects of psychotic disorders are the sex differences in onset and course. Compared to females, males with schizophrenia and other psychoses tend to have an earlier age at onset, and poorer premorbid social and cognitive functioning, postonset social and occupational functioning, treatment compliance, and long-term prognosis (Ochoa et al., 2012). There is also evidence that the overall incidence may be higher in males than females, although epidemiological studies find no sex differences in terms of prevalence of schizophrenia. This is in contrast to affective disorders, where it is well established that stress-related disorders, such as depression, anxiety, and posttraumatic stress disorder (PTSD) are lower in males (Bangasser & Valentino, 2014). Given the demonstrated association between stress and psychosis, these sex differences raise the question of whether there are sexual dimorphisms in stress exposure or the stress response that are unique to risk for psychosis, resulting in higher rates and poorer prognosis in males.

Sex differences in psychiatric disorders have been the impetus for research on sexual dimorphisms in the neurobiological systems that mediate the stress response. To date, there is no consistent trend in the findings to suggest that the HPA axis is more active in healthy females than males; baseline and stress-induced cortisol responses do not show consistent sex differences (Bangasser & Valentino, 2014), although a recent review suggests that females may show a larger cortisol response in childhood, with a shift in adulthood to a greater response in males (Hollanders, van der Voorn, Rotteveel, & Finken, 2017). While these sex differences are not pronounced, the developmental changes are likely associated with maturational changes in gonadal hormones. There appear to be more consistent normative sex differences in the neural circuitry involved in emotional response. A meta-analysis revealed that a key region for emotion processing, the amygdala, showed valence-dependent sex differences in activation (Stevens & Hamann, 2012); adult males show more pronounced amygdala activation in response to positive emotional stimuli, whereas females show a greater amygdala response to negative emotion, consistent with evidence that females respond more strongly to negative events than males (Hamilton, Stange, Abramson, & Alloy, 2015).

To date, there is little evidence that there are sex differences in HPA function in CHR or psychotic patients. A recent review of the literature on psychotic patients indicates that there is no consistent evidence of differences between males and females in baseline cortisol, the CAR, or stress-induced HPA function (Pruessner et al., 2017). This also holds for studies of CHR samples. Nonetheless, there are relatively few studies of sex differences in HPA function in psychosis, and male patients do tend to be more heavily medicated than females, a factor that could mask sex differences in HPA activity.

Sex differences in the neurobiological response to stress have recently been documented in a recent magnetic resonance imaging (MRI) study of patients with psychosis (Goldstein et al., 2015). In response to a visual stress challenge, both male and female patients showed a stronger cortisol response than healthy controls. However, there were sex differences in the fMRI response to the stress task, with male patients showing fMRI hyperactivity compared to same-sex controls in the hypothalamus, parahippocampal gyrus, amygdala, and anterior cingulate. In contrast, female patients showed hyperactivity relative to controls in anterior hippocampus and amygdala, and hypoactivity in orbital and medial prefrontal cortices. Compared to all groups, female patients with psychosis showed lower activity in the prefrontal and orbitofrontal cortices. These findings suggest that sex differences in the response to stress may involve cortical regions governing inhibitory control of arousal. Brain function in response to stress and stress hormones is an area deserving further investigation in psychosis research.

There is evidence from studies of nonclinical samples that females report greater subjective distress in response to stressful events (Hyde, Mezulis, & Abramson, 2008). This difference may be more pronounced in CHR samples. In response to daily stressors, female CHR patients report higher subjective stress than males (Moskow et al., 2016; Trotman et al., 2014). Similarly, using the Experience Sampling Method, it has been shown that female patients with psychosis report significantly greater emotional reactivity, both increased negative and decreased positive affect, to daily stress when compared with males (Myin-Germeys et al., 2004).

In summary, there is limited evidence of sex differences in biological aspects of the stress response in psychosis, although a recent study using fMRI suggests that brain functional responses to stress may show sex differences. However, several reports indicate that CHR females experience more subjective distress than males in response to daily stressors. Further research is needed to explore the relation of self-reported subjective distress with neurobiological responses to stress. As described later, however, in studies of psychotic and at-risk samples, there is evidence that exposure to childhood adversity not only elicits a greater distress in women but also may be more common among women than men with psychotic disorders (Myin-Germeys et al., 2004). It is as yet unclear why women, who by most accounts report greater stress, also show better prognosis when diagnosed with a psychotic disorder. However, some researchers have suggested that there may be two partially distinct pathways to developing psychotic disorders, and women may be more represented in the affective/stress-sensitive pathway that tends to have a more episodic course of illness and better overall prognosis, whereas men may be more represented in the cognitive impairment/neurodevelopmental pathway that is characterized by more chronic negative and cognitive symptoms and poorer prognosis (Myin-Germeys & Van Os, 2007). This is a new and interesting avenue of research and more work is needed to clarify the apparent discrepancy between female experience of stress and psychotic outcomes.

Summary

In sum, there is substantial evidence that stressful experiences and increased stress sensitivity/perceptions of stress are associated with increased risk for psychosis, and that a number of stress-related biological processes are associated with psychosis. In addition, there are notable sex differences in subjective responses to stress. Drawing on this evidence, we now turn to a specific stressor, childhood adversity, that has received significant attention in the psychosis literature. Childhood adversity, which includes trauma occurring in childhood, is a known risk factor for psychotic symptoms and may play an important role in the development of sensitivity to later stressors. Additionally, studying adversity/stress exposure prior to illness onset helps to avoid some of the confounds present when studying stress and psychotic symptoms concurrently.

Childhood Adversity and Psychosis

Childhood adversity is a broad term that encompasses a range of adverse and stressful experience, such as family violence, physical and sexual abuse, and neglect, that occur during childhood. Examining the relationship between childhood adversity and psychosis offers a unique opportunity to help tease apart the direction of the stress–psychosis relationship. As reviewed by previous researchers, assumptions about the nature and direction of the relationship between stress and psychosis with respect to causality should be made cautiously. More specifically, it is possible that the factors that make individuals vulnerable for psychosis (e.g., cognitive impairment, social skills deficits) may also put them at risk for exposure to more life stress (Phillips et al., 2007). Thus, instead of stress leading to psychosis, it may be that psychosis-risk leads to and generates greater stress. Although it is certainly true that those manifesting signs of a severe mental illness are indeed at higher risk for various adverse experiences (e.g.,

homelessness, relationship instability, poverty), including victimization (Goodman et al., 2001), childhood adversity presents a unique opportunity to examine stress prior to the clinical manifestation of vulnerability.

In line with this argument, Alemany and colleagues' (2013) monozygotic twin study suggests that *genetically inherited* vulnerability to psychosis is not a significant confound in studies of childhood adversity and psychosis risk. More specifically, they found that within-pair (MZ twin) differences in exposure to childhood adversity were significantly associated with differences in subthreshold psychotic symptom severity (i.e., the twin who experienced more childhood adversity also experienced more severe subthreshold psychotic symptoms). Since the twins were monozygotic, the differences in subthreshold psychotic symptoms are attributable to environmental factors (e.g., childhood adversity). This design enabled researchers to rule out some gene–environment correlations (e.g., the environmental exposures were not selected by the individuals based on particular heritable factors), and the findings add to evidence that childhood adversity plays a role in engendering or exacerbating risk for psychotic disorder

Recent empirical studies and reviews have explored links between psychosis and childhood adversity in detail (see Holtzman et al., 2013; Misiak et al., 2017; Morgan & Gayer-Anderson, 2016, for reviews). These studies range from investigations of the association between childhood adversity and current psychotic symptoms in clinical samples (e.g., CHR and psychotic sample) to psychotic-like symptoms in nonclinical and general population samples. Additionally, a number of studies have also provided evidence linking childhood adversity to stress sensitivity, as well as a number of the biological stress response processes reviewed earlier (e.g., HPA, immune factors).

Childhood Adversity and Psychotic Symptoms

There is ample evidence that childhood adversity is associated with a higher likelihood of later psychotic experiences (Fisher et al., 2010; Trotta, Murray, & Fisher, 2015; Varese et al., 2012). A meta-analysis by Varese and colleagues (2012) found that patients with a psychotic disorder were 2.72 times more likely to have experienced childhood adversity than healthy controls and that there was a population attributable risk (PAR) of 33%. This means that, assuming causality, the elimination of adverse childhood experiences would reduce the number of people with psychosis by 33%. Although several studies included in this meta-analysis relied on self-report, the association between childhood adversity and psychotic disorder was also observed in those studies utilizing other methods. Additionally, the authors pointed out that self-reported retrospective assessment of childhood traumas tends to underestimate rather than overestimate occurrence of trauma (Hardt & Rutter, 2004).

Childhood adversity is associated with psychotic-like experiences, such as low-grade delusion ideation, isolated auditory hallucinations, and perceptual aberrations even among individuals who do not have a psychotic disorder (Janssen et al., 2004; Kelleher et al., 2008; Sommer et al., 2008). A large multinational study (n = 23,998) of the association of childhood adversity and psychosis found that those exposed to childhood adversity had an increased probability of later psychotic experiences (OR = 2.3; McGrath et al., 2017). Consistent with previous work, the study estimated that the overall population attributable risk proportion (PARP) for psychotic experiences associated with childhood adversity was 30.9%. The researchers also found evidence of differential effects of type of adversity. For example, adversities related to maladaptive family functioning (e.g., parental mental illness, family violence, abuse and neglect) had the strongest associations and accounted for 24% of the attributable risk proportion. Meanwhile, sexual abuse was strongly and uniquely associated with childhood-onset psychotic experiences (OR = 8.5), whereas other types of adversity were associated with adolescent-onset psychotic experiences.

It should be noted that the aforementioned studies examined psychotic experiences within a general population, but they did not directly investigate the role of childhood adversity on psychotic disorders per se. However, there is evidence that nonclinical psychotic experiences are associated with higher risk of developing a psychotic disorder in life (Van Os, Linscott, Myin-Germeys, Delespaul, & Krabbendam, 2009) Further, a recent systematic review and meta-analysis of 20 prospective studies tentatively concluded that childhood adversity is associated with not just the onset of subthreshold psychotic experiences but also with the persistence of psychotic experiences (Trotta et al., 2015). Methodological limitations of the studies under review made comparisons between studies difficult, and the conclusions are tentative. However, the preliminary evidence suggests that the experience of

childhood adversity may play a causal role in the progression from subthreshold psychotic symptoms to full-blown psychotic disorder. Additional evidence for this comes from studies of individuals at risk of developing psychosis, which show that the experience of childhood adversity is a significant predictor of who will continue on to develop a psychotic disorder (Thompson et al., 2013; Yung et al., 2015). Further, in patients with psychosis, childhood adversity has been associated with more severe psychotic symptoms compared to patients who did not experience childhood adversity (Faravelli et al., 2017).

Childhood Adversity and Stress Sensitivity

There is also evidence that childhood adversity may sensitize the stress system and mediate the association between stressful events and subthreshold psychotic symptoms in both healthy (Gibson et al., 2014; Laloyaux et al., 2016; Rossler et al., 2016) and psychosis-spectrum patient populations (Lardinois, Lataster, Mengelers, Van Os, & Myin-Germeys, 2011). In fact, experiences with adversity in childhood are likely to influence both cognitive and biological processes that shape future subjective perceptions of stress. For example, childhood adversity may shape the development of locus of control, coping strategies, and schemas that may lower an individual's tolerance to subsequent stressors (Chorpita & Barlow, 1998). Additionally, early experiences with adversity may calibrate the developing corticolimbic circuit, such that it becomes more attuned, and responsive, to detecting potential stressors and threats (Chen & Baram, 2016).

In a prospective longitudinal study of healthy adolescents and young adults, Lataster and colleagues (2012) found that severe, recent stressors were associated with a higher risk of psychosis only among individuals with a history of childhood adversity. Rossler and colleagues (2016) also explored the relationships between childhood adversity, stress sensitivity, and psychotic-like experiences in a large community sample and found that there was indirect effect of childhood trauma on subclinical psychotic symptoms, and the effect was through stress sensitivity. Similarly, Laloyaux and colleagues (2016) found that stress sensitivity partially mediated the association between previous adverse life events and current psychotic experiences in a community sample, although there is some evidence that this effect is specific to females (Gibson et al., 2014).

Studies using both at-risk and psychotic samples have also provided support for the mediating role of stress sensitivity. A virtual reality study using a sample with high psychosis liability (i.e., 55 individuals had a recent onset psychotic disorder and 20 additional participants were designated as at high risk for developing psychosis) showed that a history of childhood trauma was associated with more severe psychotic symptoms and also with more subjective distress in response to the virtual social stress exposures (Veling et al., 2016). Another study employed an experience sampling method (ESM) approach to investigate the everyday stress reactivity of 50 patients with psychosis (Lardinois et al., 2011). The authors found that psychotic patients with a history of childhood trauma showed both increased stress sensitivity to everyday stressors, as well as momentary elevations of psychotic symptom intensity that were temporally related to the everyday stressful events (Lardinois et al., 2011). Together these findings suggest that the effect of childhood adversity on psychotic symptoms may at least be partially mediated by increases in stress sensitivity in everyday life.

Childhood Adversity, HPA Axis, and Psychosis

Alterations in the HPA axis are considered a key mechanism underlying the association between childhood adversity and psychosis. The traumagenic neurodevelopmental model hypothesizes that exposure to early stressors results in a sensitized or overactive HPA axis that responds to stressors with elevated releases of cortisol (Read, Perry, Moskowitz, & Connolly, 2001). In addition, acute and chronic stressors may result in compromised hippocampal-regulated negative feedback on the HPA axis (Barker, Gumley, Schwannauer, & Lawrie, 2015). The resulting increases in cortisol have augmenting effects on striatal dopamine, thereby increasing risk for psychosis and psychotic symptoms (Read et al., 2001). However, findings related to cortisol in childhood adversity vary widely across studies (Gunnar & Quevedo, 2007; Lupien, McEwen, Gunnar, & Heim, 2009; Repetti, Robles, & Reynolds, 2011; Tyrka et al., 2008), and both patterns of elevated and relatively low basal cortisol levels and reactivity are reported in individuals exposed to a wide range of childhood adversities (see Hunter, Minnis, & Wilson, 2011, for review).

These inconsistencies likely stem from multiple factors. For example, it is likely that HPA axis regulation changes as a function of stage of psychotic illness. As a result, HPA dysfunction may differ when comparing healthy samples to risk samples for psychosis (Pruessner et al., 2017). As previously discussed, antipsychotics and other medications are

known to have effects on the HPA axis and may further confound results. Additionally, the impact of trauma, abuse, and/or neglect may also vary according to type (Essex et al., 2011), length, severity, and developmental timing of the exposure (Bosch et al., 2012). For example, a study of internationally adopted children found that the effects of abuse and neglect differed according to severity (van der Vegt et al., 2009). Individuals who had experienced the most severe neglect were observed to have the flattest diurnal cortisol slopes, whereas those who experienced moderately severe abuse had steeper diurnal cortisol slopes and generally higher cortisol levels (van der Vegt et al., 2009). This may help explain mixed findings in the literature about the direction of the effect of childhood adversity on HPA axis function.

Childhood Adversity, Inflammation, and Psychosis

Childhood adversity is also associated with inflammatory and immune processes (Coelho, Viola, Walss-Bass, Brietzke, & Grassi-Oliveira, 2014), which, as previously discussed, may be implicated in psychosis. A recent meta-analysis found that childhood trauma is associated with a pro-inflammatory state in adulthood, and it is specifically associated with increased levels of CRP, IL-6, and TNF-alpha (Baumeister, Akhtar, Ciufolini, Pariante, & Mondelli, 2016). This meta-analysis also found differential effects of various types of childhood adversity, such that physical and sexual abuse appeared to be associated with higher TNF-alpha and IL-6 levels in adulthood, whereas parental absence was associated with higher CRP levels in adulthood (Baumeister et al., 2016). Additionally, certain individual characteristics (e.g., depression, a history of early stress) may make males particularly susceptible to increased inflammatory responses to acute stressors in adulthood (Pace et al., 2006).

Inflammatory factors are also elevated in those with psychosis (see Feigenson et al., 2014; Kirkpatrick & Miller, 2013, for reviews); for example, individuals experiencing their first episode of psychosis showed elevated serum levels of IL-1alpha, IL-1beta, IL-8, and TNF-alpha compared to controls (Di Nicola et al., 2013). Moreover, this study revealed that the pro-inflammatory state was associated with both childhood adversity and current stressors, such that those with psychosis who had experienced childhood trauma had even higher serum TNF-alpha levels compared to psychotic patients without a trauma history, and those reporting more recent stressful events had higher TNF-alpha mRNA levels in their leukocytes (Di Nicola et al., 2013). Another study of schizophrenic patients found that peripheral levels of IL-6 and TNF-alpha were higher only in those patients who had a history of childhood trauma, and TNF-alpha levels were increased in correlation with the number of traumatic events experienced (Dennison et al., 2012). These findings suggest that the relationship between inflammation and psychosis may be a consequence of both previous childhood adversity and more recent stress exposures.

Genetic Vulnerability to Childhood Adversity and Psychosis Risk

Exposure to childhood adversity is unfortunately quite common, with a large-scale study finding that 37.9% of respondents from the general population experienced adversity before 18 years of age (McGrath et al., 2017). Of course, the majority of people exposed to childhood adversity do not go on to develop a psychotic disorder. Researchers have turned to genetics studies and looked to gene–environment interactions to better understand the differential risk for psychosis following childhood adversity. As mentioned in the previous section on "Genetic Vulnerability to Stress Sensitivity and Psychosis Risk," there are a number of candidate genes that are implicated in stress and vulnerability to psychosis. The COMT gene, while most frequently discussed in relation to sensitivity to general life stressors, is of course also implicated in vulnerability to childhood adversity and psychosis risk (Green et al., 2014). However, in this section, we will limit our discussion to the BDNF gene, which has specifically received a lot of attention in the childhood adversity literature.

Brain-derived neurotrophic factor (BDNF) is important for neuron growth and survival in response to stress, as well as synaptic plasticity. Low BDNF serum levels have been found in individuals who have experienced childhood adversity (Theleritis et al., 2014), as well as schizophrenia patients (Fernandes et al., 2014; Green, Matheson, Shepherd, Weickert, & Carr, 2011). In FEP patients, childhood adversity has been associated with lower blood BDNF levels, suggesting an important role for BDNF in the association between psychosis onset and a history of childhood adversity (Theleritis et al., 2014). In another study of FEP youth, serum BDNF fully mediated the association between the number of previous traumas and current psychotic symptomatology (Fawzi et al., 2013).

A single nucleotide polymorphism (SNP) in the BDNF gene that results in a valine (*val*) to methionine (*met*) switch (Val66Met) is associated with reduced activity-dependent BDNF secretion, and it has been studied extensively in relation to risk for psychiatric disorders, especially psychosis (see Notaras, Hill, & van den Buuse 2015 for review). At the level of BDNF protein expression, which is believed to be abnormally reduced in schizophrenia, high levels of childhood adversity combined with the presence of the *met* polymorphism have additive effects that lead to reduced BDNF mRNA expression (Aas et al., 2014), suggesting that the detrimental impact of the *met* variant may be exacerbated by the presence of childhood adversity. Interestingly, there is evidence that at the symptom level, the BDNF Val66Met genotype moderates the effect of childhood abuse on psychotic-like experiences even among nonclinical samples. Alemany and colleagues (2011) found that in a sample of healthy college students, the *met* carriers reported more psychotic-like experiences than the *val* carriers in the presence of childhood abuse exposure (Alemany, 2011). Although these findings have not been replicated in all samples (Ramsay et al., 2013) and inconsistences still exist in the literature, they provide compelling evidence for a gene–environment interaction and may help to explain how stressors such as childhood adversity increase risk for psychosis, likely via compromised neural development and plasticity.

In addition to genetic differences, increasing evidence suggests that patients with psychotic disorders may have altered patterns of gene expression. Specifically, studies have shown that that psychosis patients have differential methylation patterns in genes associated with stress response pathways such as glucocorticoid receptor (Auta et al., 2013), BDNF (Auta et al., 2013; Dong et al., 2015), and immune/inflammation associated genes (Frydecka et al., 2014). Studies of those exposed to childhood adversity also show altered DNA methylation of genes implicated in stress response, such as the glucocorticoid receptor (McGowan et al., 2009; Perroud et al., 2011; Radtke et al., 2015), FKBP5 (Klengel et al., 2013; Tyrka et al., 2015), and BDNF (Perroud et al., 2013; Thaler et al., 2014). More studies will be needed to address the potential links between childhood adversity, epigenetic changes, and psychosis. This may prove to be an important and fruitful area of inquiry, especially if future investigations are able to improve upon current methodological issues (e.g., lack of longitudinal studies, heterogeneity in methodology and type of tissue studied) while taking into account complexities such as type of stress exposure and developmental timing of exposure (see Fiori & Turecki, 2016; Vinkers et al., 2015, for reviews).

Sex Differences in Responses to Childhood Adversity in Psychosis Risk

A review of the literature on childhood adversity and psychosis reveals the presence of sex differences in various domains (e.g., stress sensitivity, and genetic and neurobiological vulnerabilities). A large case-control study of sex differences in childhood adversity and psychosis found that females with a psychotic disorder were twice as likely to report childhood adversity than their male counterparts (Fisher et al., 2009). Further, they found that women in the control group who had a history of childhood physical abuse were 3 times as likely to report psychotic-like symptoms than women without a trauma history. This study found no such pattern for males in either the psychotic group or the control group (Fisher et al., 2009).

It is still unclear whether these findings are due to females reporting, and perhaps experiencing, higher numbers of traumatic events than males, or due to females being more stress-sensitive and vulnerable to negative effects of environmental stressors. Both may be true; however, there is growing evidence for sex differences in stress sensitivity as it relates to psychosis. For example, in a study on a nonclinical, college-aged sample, Gibson and colleagues (2014) found that stress sensitivity mediates the relationship between childhood adversity and later psychotic experiences in females only. This echoes previously described work by Myin-Germeys and colleagues, who have suggested that the "stress-sensitive pathway" to psychosis is more closely associated with the female sex, whereas males who develop psychosis are more likely to follow a "cognitive impairment/neurodevelopmental pathway" characterized by relatively reduced stress sensitivity and a more chronic and deteriorating course of illness.

However, there is also evidence of a sex-specific association with certain "vulnerability" alleles of the COMT and BDNF genes that suggests *males* are more vulnerable to the deleterious effects of childhood adversity on psychotic symptoms (de Castro-Catala et al., 2015; Castro-Catala et al., 2016), perhaps due to interactions with sex hormones (e.g., testosterone increases COMT activity). Additionally, it has been found that childhood adversity is associated with reduced hippocampal volume in males, but not females (Samplin et al., 2013), although

individuals of both sexes experienced increased symptoms of psychopathology in response to a history of childhood adversity. This suggests that while females may be more resilient to the neurobiological impacts of childhood adversity, they are not necessarily more resilient to the psychological effects. Far more research is necessary to better understand the sex-specific effects of childhood adversity and their relation to psychosis.

Summary

There is ample evidence linking childhood adversity with psychosis, and growing evidence that this link is causal, acting through mediators such as stress sensitivity. Large-scale studies have indicated that eliminating childhood adversity could reduce the occurrence of psychosis in the population by approximately a third. There is strong evidence for the involvement of various biological mediators, including HPA dysregulation and inflammation, as well as important individual differences in vulnerability to childhood adversity (e.g., BDNF genotype). However, more work is needed to clarify the effects of childhood trauma on these biological processes, especially with regard to HPA axis dysregulation, where the data are mixed on the specific direction of the impacts (e.g., hyposecretion vs. hypersecretion of cortisol). Additional work is also needed to better understand how adversity type, timing, and severity impact risk for psychosis. Consistent with this, a growing body of evidence has begun to highlight the unique effects of different types of adversity on psychotic symptoms (e.g., Essex et al., 2011; Fisher et al., 2010). Finally, there is some evidence of sex differences with regard to the association between childhood adversity and psychosis, with females expressing more stress sensitivity and reporting more exposure to childhood traumas, while males may be more susceptible to gene–environment influences and deleterious impacts on brain development.

Minority Stress and Psychosis

Other related areas of research that are currently receiving increasing attention in the literature on stress and psychosis are the topics of racial/ethnic discrimination and stress related to migration and refugee status. For this review, we have summarized these literatures, as well as a small literature on sexual minority status and psychosis, under the broad umbrella term of "minority stress." We acknowledge that, in doing so, we have combined several very different, diverse groups that each have their own specific risk and resiliency factors associated with them; however, a review of the literature quickly shows that the proposed mechanisms at play in higher psychosis risk for these groups are very similar and center on the idea of minority or "outsider" status being a unique and important type of stressor that enhances risk for psychosis.

Despite decades of epidemiological evidence indicating that racial/ethnic minorities and migrants are at higher risk of developing psychosis, research investigating a causal association between minority status and psychosis has only recently begun. As a result, the empirical literature is much smaller than that reviewed in the previous two sections. In addition, studies of mediation focus largely on psychological mediators such as perceived discrimination and social defeat, and there have been no tests of biological mediators to our knowledge. Thus, we will break with the structure from the previous two sections and instead review the available literature on the association of minority stress and psychosis based on minority group (i.e., racial/ethnic minorities, migrants and refugees, and sexual minorities).

Racial/Ethnic Minority Status and Psychosis

Evidence indicates that risk of psychotic disorders is increased in those with ethnic minority status in several countries around the world (Veling, 2013). Individuals of African and Caribbean descent have been found to experience psychosis at a rate of 2–3 times higher in the United States (Bresnahan et al., 2007) and 4–5 times higher in the United Kingdom (Kirkbride, Jones, Ullrich, & Coid, 2012; Kirkbride et al., 2017). Moreover, a recent study of youth with psychosis-risk syndromes revealed that Black/African American participants were at about 2.5 times greater risk for conversion to psychosis relative to Caucasian participants (Brucato et al., 2017), which adds further supports to evidence of heightened psychosis risk among racial/ethnic minority groups.

Several reasons for this effect may exist, including diagnostic bias related to minority status (Gara et al., 2012; Veling et al., 2013). For example, as reviewed by Baker and Bell (1999), clinicians tend to overvalue psychotic symptoms and undervalue affective symptoms when making a diagnosis in African Americans. However, studies in which clinicians were blinded to patient ethnicity still showed higher rates of psychosis in minority groups (Veling et al., 2007), suggesting that there are other mechanisms at play. Further, studies of subthreshold psychotic experiences in the general population

(which are self-reported and do not rely on clinician diagnosis) also show higher levels of psychotic experiences for racial/ethnic minorities (Cohen & Marino, 2013; DeVylder, Oh, Corcoran, & Lukens, 2014; Morgan et al., 2008; Paksarian, Merikangas, Calkins, & Gur, 2016). Many have suggested that some of this elevated risk may stem from stress associated with minority status; specifically, lower SES and associated environmental factors such as reduced access to resources, poorer nutrition, and increased exposure to toxins (e.g., lead). However, there is also evidence that SES cannot fully explain the additional psychosis risk present in racial/ethnic minorities. For example, studies have found that psychosis risk is still higher in Blacks compared to Whites living in the same neighborhood (Faris & Dunham, 1939) or when SES is statistically controlled for (Arnold, 2004; Kirkbride et al., 2008). And in the example of immigrants, ethnic density studies have found that those living in the most socioeconomically deprived neighborhoods actually show lower risk of psychotic disorder than immigrants living in more affluent neighborhoods, when compared to nonimmigrant populations in those neighborhoods (Boydell et al., 2001; Veling et al., 2008). Thus, SES cannot fully explain differential patterns of psychosis risk.

Other popular theories focus largely on chronic social stressors as the central mechanism through which ethnic and racial minorities are put at higher risk of psychosis. These theories include the social defeat hypothesis (Selten et al., 2013; Selten & Cantor-Graae, 2005, 2007), the sociodevelopmental model (Morgan, Charalambides, Hutchinson, & Murray, 2010), and the minority stress model (Meyer, 1995, 2003). These theories focus on stress related to ethnic density (Shaw et al., 2012) and perceived discrimination (Berg et al., 2011) as potential explanations for disparities. There is also evidence that higher levels of childhood trauma in ethnic minorities may mediate the relationship between ethnic minority status and psychotic symptoms (Berg et al., 2015). Of these proposed mediators, perceived discrimination has received the strongest support.

Perceived Discrimination and Psychosis

The experience of discrimination is known to be associated with numerous adverse physical and mental health outcomes (see Lewis, Cogburn, & Williams, 2015, for review). There is now increasing evidence that it is also implicated in the etiology of psychotic disorders, likely through stress-related augmenting effects of the HPA axis on the dopamine system. In a large sample of the Dutch population, perceived discrimination or the self-reported experience of discrimination was predictive of the onset of psychotic symptoms in a dose-response fashion (Janssen et al., 2003). A similar study was conducted using a large nonclinical sample of ethnic minorities in the Netherlands, where it was found that those who experienced higher levels of perceived discrimination were significantly more likely to endorse subthreshold psychotic experiences, and there was a linear relationship between degree of perceived discrimination reported and odds of reporting the psychotic experience (Oh et al., 2014). Specifically, in comparison to those ethnic minorities who experienced no perceived discrimination, those who experienced the highest amount of perceived discrimination were 3.8 times more likely to endorse auditory hallucinations, almost 3 times more likely to endorse visual hallucinations, and about 4 times more likely to report delusions. This analysis was performed while controlling for important variables such as income-to-poverty ratio, immigration status, and substance use (Oh et al., 2014).

Perceived discrimination has also been found to be associated with attenuated psychotic symptoms in youth experiencing psychosis-risk syndromes (Shaikh et al., 2016; Stowkowy et al., 2016). Findings from the North American Prodrome Longitudinal Study suggest that youth at clinical high risk for psychosis experience more perceived discrimination than controls (Saleem et al., 2014). Moreover, perceived discrimination was also found to be predictive of later conversion to psychosis (Stowkowy et al., 2016). One virtual reality (VR) study explored the relationship between perceived discrimination and paranoia in a sample of youth at risk for psychosis (Shaikh et al., 2016). The VR situation involved an underground train ride with avatars (computer-simulated people) who displayed ambiguous behavior (e.g., smiling, talking). The authors found that higher levels of perceived discrimination were associated with greater paranoia in the VR experience, suggesting a route through which a general sense of perceived discrimination can interact with everyday events to foster psychotic symptoms such as paranoia.

Together these findings suggest that perceived discrimination may be implicated in the etiology of psychotic disorders and is postulated to partially explain the increased rates of psychosis among Blacks and immigrant groups. However, it should be noted that existing study designs have not clarified the direction of the association between psychotic symptoms and perceived discrimination. For example, it is possible that those with more severe psychotic symptoms, especially paranoia, also experience more perceived discrimination. Further empirical research is warranted to address this confound and test this and other theories of enhanced psychosis risk among racial/ethnic minorities. For example, studies that assess the effect of discrimination measured more objectively (i.e., not just the *perception* of discrimination) would help to address this confound and would be an important addition to this area of research.

Migrants, Refugees, and Psychosis

Many studies have found that immigrants have higher rates of psychotic disorders than nonimmigrants (Coid et al., 2008; Fearon et al., 2006; Veling et al., 2006). A meta-analysis on this topic estimated that first-generation immigrants (i.e., those born in their origin country and travelled to their new country) and second-generation immigrants (i.e., first-generation immigrants' children who are born in their new country) have relative risk ratios of 2.7 and 4.5, respectively, when compared to nonimmigrants in the new country (Cantor-Graae & Selten, 2005). A thorough review of the literature on psychosis in immigrants (Veling & Susser, 2011) revealed that higher risk of psychosis in immigrants is found in most, but not all immigrant groups in different countries, and risk rates vary considerably based on ethnic group and country examined. For example, incidence rate ratios were highest for African-Caribbean and Black African immigrant groups in comparison to White populations in England, and Asian immigrants had a more moderate increase in incidence (Fearon et al., 2006).

Several initial explanations have been suggested for the higher risk of psychosis in immigrants, including increased risk in the country of origin, selective migration (Selten et al., 2007), and diagnostic bias, which have been found to be unsatisfactory (see Veling & Susser, 2011, for more on this). More recently, research has begun to focus on potential causal relationships between immigrants' environment and development of psychosis. Among others, the concepts of acculturative stress, ethnic density, social defeat, and perceived discrimination have featured in this discussion, and there is some evidence suggesting that these types of stress may mediate the association between immigrant status and higher psychosis risk. Veling and Susser (2011) point out that a causative relationship between immigration and psychosis is likely acting on many levels, including the neighborhood of the immigrants, the ethnic group they belong to, and at the individual level. Understanding how stress plays a role at each of these levels is important to understanding the potentially causal role of stress in psychosis for this population.

At the level of the neighborhood, ethnic density (i.e., the proportion of people in the neighborhood belonging to one's own ethnic group) has been found to be associated with risk for severe mental illness. A study from the Netherlands showed that immigrants had higher rates of schizophrenia only when they were from areas of lower ethnic density—that is, when there were fewer people in their area with their same ethnic background (Veling et al., 2008). Immigrants from areas high in ethnic density, in which there were more people of their same ethnic background, showed no statistically significant increase in incidence compared with native Dutch (Veling et al., 2008). Another study performed in London found a "dose-response" relationship whereby incidences of schizophrenia in minorities increased when ethnic density of the areas decreased (Boydell et al., 2001). These studies echo seminal work in the field from the 1930s that revealed higher incidences of schizophrenia in African Americans who lived in predominantly White neighborhoods (Faris & Dunham, 1939). Together, they show that SES differences cannot explain differences in incidence in these cases. In these cases, it is likely that ethnic density serves as a proxy for some other stress-related constructs such as perceived discrimination, positive ethnic identity/acculturation, and/or neighborhood cohesion.

At the level of the ethnic group, there is (limited) evidence of a dose-response effect for acculturative stress in immigrants. A study of Asian and Latino first-generation immigrants to the United States found that acculturative stress showed a dose-response effect with psychotic experiences in immigrants, such that higher levels of acculturative stress were associated with higher risk for psychotic experiences (DeVylder et al., 2013). There were also differences in symptom types depending on ethnic group (Latino vs. Asian), which brings up the issue of how certain groups may experience more acculturative stress than others based on ease of assimilation and/or differential experiences of discrimination. This may depend on variables such as speaking the same language and skin color differences. Indeed, Kirkbride and colleagues (2017) found that visible minority immigrants to the United Kingdom (e.g.,

Black people of African and Caribbean heritage, and people of Pakistani origin) were at increased risk of psychosis, whereas White immigrants showed no increase in psychosis risk compared to nonimmigrants. Another study performed in The Hague in the Netherlands found that different ethnic groups (e.g., those from Morocco, Suriname, Turkey, or Westernized countries) were subject to different rates of schizophrenia and psychosis in a way that correlated with the amount of discrimination experienced by the particular group (i.e., the groups experiencing the greatest discrimination also had the highest incidence rate ratios of psychotic disorder, and groups experiencing less discrimination had lower rates of psychotic disorders) (Veling, Selten, Susser, Laan, & Hoek, 2007). A strength of this particular study was that it included both self-report-based measures of perceived discrimination as well as more objective measures of discrimination by ethnic group (i.e., based on official reports of discrimination collected by the Anti-Discrimination Bureau). The authors reported that results from both measures were surprisingly concordant, suggesting that amount of perceived discrimination and number of objective discriminatory events are closely linked (Veling et al., 2007).

At the level of the individual, it appears that age at immigration may have a significant effect on risk for psychosis. Specifically, it appears that most, but not all (Cantor-Graae et al., 2003) studies show that *younger age* at the time of immigration is associated with *increased* risk (De Vylder et al., 2013). Two studies have directly investigated this in large immigrant samples and found that those who migrated as children showed the highest risk of psychosis, with risk decreasing with older age of migration (Kirkbride et al., 2017; Veling, Hoek, Selten, & Susser, 2011). Some studies have also found that second-generation immigrants are at higher risk of psychosis than their first-generation counterparts (Coid et al., 2008; Veling et al., 2006), but this may vary based on ethnic group and host country (Bourque et al., 2011; Kirkbride et al., 2017). This provides additional support for the idea that the amount of time spent in the new country of residence, and by extension, the amount of exposure to minority stress, may play a role in effect of immigration on psychosis. However, confounds related to typical age of psychosis onset should also be considered (i.e., older immigrants may have less risk due to having already passed the typical age of onset for psychosis).

These aforementioned factors likely have an impact on individuals who immigrate for various reasons, although additional stressors exist for specific groups of immigrants such as refugees (i.e., people forced to leave their country or place of origin in order to escape persecution, war, or natural disaster), who have often endured chaotic lives and traumatic experiences prior to settling in their new country of residence. In keeping with a stress-diathesis model of psychosis, we would expect refugees to experience a higher risk for psychosis in comparison to those who immigrate for other reasons (e.g., economic migrants). Indeed, a recent study out of Sweden comparing incidence rates of psychosis in immigrant and refugee populations with each other and with native-born Swedes found that refugees were 66% more likely to develop a psychotic disorder compared to nonrefugee immigrants (Hollander et al., 2016). Refugees were also found to be 3.6 times more likely to develop a psychotic illness compared to the general Swedish population (Hollander et al., 2016). The authors suggest that the higher psychosis risk in refugees is directly related to higher likelihood of having experienced adversities such as conflict, persecution, and violence (Hollander et al., 2016).

Sexual Minorities and Psychosis

If stress related to minority status is the mediating link between racial/ethnic minority status and higher psychosis risk, such an association may be found in other minority groups as well. Emerging evidence from several studies investigating lesbian, gay, bisexual, and transgender (LGBT) specific risk for psychosis provides support for this. Two population-based studies, one in the United Kingdom (Chakraborty et al., 2011) and one in the United States (Bolton & Sareen, 2011), both indicate that nonheterosexual status is associated with 3–4 times increased risk of probable psychosis. A subsequent study out of the Netherlands using the large NEMESIS datasets (NEMESIS-1, $n = 5,927$; NEMESIS-2, $n = 5308$) similarly found that being lesbian, gay, or bisexual was associated with a 2.5 times increased odds of reporting psychotic symptoms as compared to those identifying as heterosexual (Gevonden et al., 2014). This study went further to test possible mediators of the association and found that perceived discrimination occurring in the past year mediated a large portion of the effect (i.e., 34%). A history of being bullied in school, childhood trauma, and illicit drug use each mediated smaller portions of the effect. The overall finding that LGB status was associated with higher risk of psychotic symptoms remained robust when

tested in each sample independently (NEMESIS-1, OR = 2.56; NEMESIS-2, OR = 2.30), when statistically controlling for additional variables (i.e., urbanicity, foreign-born parents, and illicit drug use), and when using different definitions of sexual minority status. Thus, the available evidence suggests that sexual minorities are at higher risk for psychosis, and exposure to minority-related stressors (e.g., perceived discrimination, bullying) may represent an important route through which these minorities experience enhanced psychosis risk.

There are indications in the literature that transgender individuals may also be at heightened risk for psychosis (e.g., à Campo, Nijman, Merckelbach, & Evers, 2003). However, to date there are no empirical studies that have specifically investigated this, possibly due to the complexities involved in gathering a large enough sample of transgender individuals as well as confounds such as hormone therapy.

Sex Differences in Minority Stress and Psychosis

The limited number of studies that have examined sex differences specific to minority stress and psychosis have produced mixed findings. However, where there was an effect of gender, it was males who were found to be at higher risk of psychotic illness (Binbay et al., 2012; Hollander et al., 2016; Selten et al., 2012; van der Ven et al., 2016; Veling et al., 2006). In fact, the first systematic review of sex differences in psychosis risk in migrant populations revealed a dramatic gender gap for Moroccan-Dutch immigrants, such that a meta-analysis of incidence studies found a male-to-female ratio of 5.1 for migrants from North Africa (van der Ven et al., 2016). This was in comparison to a male-to-female incidence ratio of 1.8 for nonmigrant Europeans. One explanation offered for this sex-specific effect is an "achievement-expectation mismatch" in which North African males experience a lowering of expected social status upon migrating to the Netherlands, whereas for North African females, the change in social status may be smaller or even in a positive direction. Additionally, Moroccan-Dutch males in the Netherlands experience severe social marginalization, stigma, and frequent contact with police, with statistics indicating that a majority of Moroccan-Dutch males have been charged for a crime before the age of 23 (Gijsberts, Huijnk, & Dagevos, 2012). In this particular study, the gender gap described in Moroccan-Dutch immigrants was not observed in migrant groups from other areas (e.g., Asia, Central and South American, and other

Western countries). However, other groups have also found a higher risk for male versus female migrants in Turkish populations and in both migrants and refugees to Sweden from various origin countries (Binbay et al., 2012; Hollander et al., 2016). One recent neuroimaging study of migrants in the Netherlands showed that the expected finding of reduced pACC gray matter volume, thought to be implicated in altered neural stress processing (Diorio et al., 1993), was present only in male migrants (Akdeniz et al., 2017), providing a preliminary neurobiological explanation for the sex differences described earlier. It is important to note that all sex differences reviewed here come from studies of migrants and refugees, and no such studies have yet been conducted on nonimmigrant racial minorities such as African Americans.

Summary

Current estimates show markedly increased prevalence of psychotic disorders in various minority groups, even when controlling for relevant confounds. As reviewed earlier, "minority stress" encompasses multiple factors at the level of the individual (prior traumatic experiences), ethnic/minority group (visibility/ease in ability to assimilate), neighborhood (ethnic density), and the larger population (structural discrimination). Each of these levels involves a significant opportunity for exposure to stress, which likely underlies the increased risk for psychosis among minority groups. This topic warrants additional research aimed at testing theories and mediators of the association between minority status and psychosis.

Discussion

In the research literature on mental illness, stress has most often been explored as an etiological factor in mood and anxiety disorders. But the focus has broadened over the past few decades, and the role of stress in triggering or exacerbating psychotic disorders has now been well documented. Further, stress is now more broadly conceptualized to include early trauma and adversity, life events, daily stressors, and the impact of sociocultural factors, such as urbanicity, discrimination, and immigrant status.

As discussed in other chapters in this volume, stress entails a threat to the organism's homeostasis. In the case of psychosis, it is clear that these threats can emanate from both the distal and proximal environments. The distal factors include aspects of the sociocultural and physical milieu that threaten the individual's well-being. In the sociocultural

realm, discrimination and the challenges immigrant families face in negotiating an unfamiliar cultural context appear to add to the risk for later onset of psychosis. More proximally, in the context of the family, the individual's exposure to abuse, neglect, and poverty can add another layer of adversity that disturbs homeostasis. Then, as the vulnerable individual's developmental trajectory unfolds, cumulative life event and daily stressors may exceed the threshold for triggering the onset of a psychotic disorder.

Of course, the effects of stress exposure are moderated by individual differences. Notable among these are individual differences in the perception of how stressful a given event is. To date, research findings indicate that events and experiences that are perceived as more stressful are more strongly associated with psychotic symptoms in the general population, as well as in clinical CHR and diagnosed psychotic patients. Thus, the subjective response matters, and one component of vulnerability to psychosis may be stress sensitivity, or the propensity to experience more distress in response to adverse events.

There is evidence that individual differences in stress sensitivity are determined by a variety of factors. Genetic vulnerabilities appear to be one source of the congenital vulnerability to stress. Early in the life course, exposure to trauma and adversity may also confer vulnerability and influence the individual's subsequent biobehavioral response to stress exposure and, thereby, increase risk for psychosis (Read et al., 2014). The accumulating findings on the relation of immigrant status and discrimination with risk for psychotic disorders lend support to a broader conceptualization of stress.

The biological systems and mechanisms associated with the response to stress are described in other chapters in this volume. In this chapter, we have addressed the relevance of genetic factors, inflammation, and the HPA axis in mediating the effects of stress on risk for psychosis. The cumulative research findings indicate that the HPA axis is dysregulated in some CHR and psychotic patients, and there may be a subgroup of patients who are more sensitive than others to the psychotomimetic effects of cortisol. Indeed, research has shown that corticosteroid treatment for anti-inflammatory/immunosuppressant purposes can induce serious mental illness, including psychosis, in 16%–20% of individuals (Judd et al., 2014). Thus, psychosis can be triggered in a sizable subgroup of mentally healthy individuals by the administration of synthetic cortisol. The neurobiological factors that confer risk for steroid-induced psychosis in this subgroup may be similar to those that underlay stress sensitivity in those at risk for psychosis. Identifying psychological and biological markers of stress sensitivity is among the important issues to be addressed in future research.

Future Directions

There are four general areas that should be given priority in future research on the role of stress in the etiology of psychosis. The first involves increasing our understanding of neurobiological mechanisms, or how distal and proximal environmental factors get "under the skin" to influence brain function. While we have strong evidence that stress exposure is associated with psychosis and psychotic symptoms, it is less clear what processes underlie these associations. This research should be grounded on the assumption that there is no single biological process; the mediating mechanisms may involve neuroimmune function in some individuals and neurodegenerative processes in others. Further, it should not be assumed that all patients suffering from psychotic disorders are sensitive to stress; instead, we should assume that psychosis is characterized by etiological heterogeneity, meaning that individual differences in neurobiological processes should be a focus of this research.

Second, we also need to examine whether the type and nature of stressful experiences have common or unique effects. As described earlier, we know that the threats to physical safety inherent in childhood trauma can set the stage for future vulnerability to psychotic and other mental disorders. But many of the life-event stressors that have been linked with psychosis do not involve threats to physical safety, but rather challenges to self-esteem and/or the psychological ability to cope. Do these two general classes of stressors function through the same general pathways to heighten risk for disorder? Or do different classes or types of stress have distinct effects on underlying mechanisms (see McLaughlin, Sheridan, & Lambert 2014)?

Third, several lines of evidence from animal and human studies suggest there are sensitive periods, in which the effects of stress are amplified and more permanent. Thus, it will be important to examine stress-related risk for psychosis in relation to developmental timing and sensitive periods. It appears that early childhood events can elevate risk for psychosis, yet it is clear that the modal age at onset of psychosis is during the period of late adolescence and early adulthood. This raises several questions. Is the adolescent period one that is inherently associated with stress sensitivity, independent of earlier experiences? How might earlier events, in conjunction with congenital vulnerability, "sensitize" the system to later stressors? Given the different developmental trajectories of various brain regions, as well as the different demands and opportunities inherent in each developmental period, how might the specific timing of stressors influence risk for psychosis? We will need to better understand how stress interacts with developmental processes and how that timing alters biological and psychological systems related to psychosis risk.

Finally, there are critical questions about prevention and intervention. For example, is stress sensitivity modifiable? Can the adverse effects of stress be ameliorated by interventions aimed at enhancing cognitive coping with past exposures or psychological inoculation against future stress sensitivity? Developing experimental interventions with these objectives will benefit from a greater understanding of the protective factors that buffer or mitigate the association between stress and the emergence of psychosis. Given that many of the environmental stressors linked with psychosis are not easily preventable (childhood adversity, minority status, SES, unpredictable life events), a focus on interventions that augment coping and other protective factors is needed.

References

à Campo, J., Nijman, H., Merckelbach, H., & Evers, C. (2003). Psychiatric comorbidity of gender identity disorders: A survey among Dutch psychiatrists. *American Journal of Psychiatry, 160*(7), 1332–1336.

Aas, M., Haukvik, U. K., Djurovic, S., Tesli, M., Athanasiu, L., Bjella, T., . . . Melle, I. (2014). Interplay between childhood trauma and BDNF val66met variants on blood BDNF mRNA levels and on hippocampus subfields volumes in schizophrenia spectrum and bipolar disorders. *Journal of Psychiatric Research, 59*, 14–21.

Addington, J., & Heinssen, R. (2012). Prediction and prevention of psychosis in youth at clinical high risk. *Annual Review of Clinical Psychology, 8*, 269–289.

Agerbo, E., Sullivan, P. F., Vilhjálmsson, B. J., Pedersen, C. B., Mors, O., Børglum, A. D., . . . Ripke, S. (2015). Polygenic risk score, parental socioeconomic status, family history of psychiatric disorders, and the risk for schizophrenia: A Danish population-based study and meta-analysis. *JAMA Psychiatry, 72*(7), 635–641.

Aiello, G., Horowitz, M., Hepgul, N., Pariante, C. M., & Mondelli, V. (2012). Stress abnormalities in individuals at risk for psychosis: A review of studies in subjects with familial risk or with "at risk" mental state. *Psychoneuroendocrinology, 37*(10), 1600–1613.

Akdeniz, C., Schäfer, A., Streit, F., Haller, L., Wüst, S., Kirsch, P., . . . Meyer-Lindenberg, A. (2017). Sex-dependent association of perigenual anterior cingulate cortex volume and migration background, an environmental risk factor for schizophrenia. *Schizophrenia Bulletin, 43*(4), 925–934.

Alemany, S., Arias, B., Aguilera, M., Villa, H., Moya, J., Ibáñez, M. I., ... Fañanás, L. (2011). Childhood abuse, the BDNF-Val66Met polymorphism and adult psychotic-like experiences. *The British Journal of Psychiatry, 199*(1), 38–42.

Alemany, S., Goldberg, X., van Winkel, R., Gastó, C., Peralta, V., & Fañanás, L. (2013). Childhood adversity and psychosis: Examining whether the association is due to genetic confounding using a monozygotic twin differences approach. *European Psychiatry, 28*(4), 207–212.

Andrade, E. H., Rizzo, L. B., Noto, C., Ota, V. K., Gadelha, A., Daruy-Filho, L., ... Bressan, R. A. (2016). Hair cortisol in drug-naïve first-episode individuals with psychosis. *Revista Brasileira de Psiquiatria, 38*(1), 11–16.

Arnold, L. M., Keck, P. E., Collins, J., Wilson, R., Fleck, D. E., Corey, K. B., ... Strakowski, S. M. (2004). Ethnicity and first-rank symptoms in patients with psychosis. *Schizophrenia Research, 67*(2–3), 207–212. doi:10.1016/S0920-9964(02)00497-8

Auta, J., Smith, R. C., Dong, E., Tueting, P., Sershen, H., Boules, S., ... Guidotti, A. (2013). DNA-methylation gene network dysregulation in peripheral blood lymphocytes of schizophrenia patients. *Schizophrenia Research, 150*(1), 312–318.

Baker, F. M., & Bell, C. C. (1999). Issues in the psychiatric treatment of African Americans. *Psychiatric Services, 50*(3), 362–368.

Bangasser, D. A., & Valentino, R. J. (2014). Sex differences in stress-related psychiatric disorders: Neurobiological perspectives. *Frontiers in Neuroendocrinology, 35*(3), 303–319.

Barker, V., Gumley, A., Schwannauer, M., & Lawrie, S. M. (2015). An integrated biopsychosocial model of childhood maltreatment and psychosis. *The British Journal of Psychiatry, 206*(3), 177–180.

Baumeister, D., Akhtar, R., Ciufolini, S., Pariante, C. M., & Mondelli, V. (2016). Childhood trauma and adulthood inflammation: A meta-analysis of peripheral C-reactive protein, interleukin-6 and tumour necrosis factor-α. *Molecular Psychiatry, 21*(5), 642.

Bebbington, P., Wilkins, S., Jones, P., Foerster, A., Murray, R., Toone, B., & Lewis, S. (1993). Life events and psychosis. Initial results from the Camberwell Collaborative Psychosis Study. *The British Journal of Psychiatry, 162*(1), 72–79.

Berg, A. O., Aas, M., Larsson, S., Nerhus, M., Hauff, E., Andreassen, O. A., & Melle, I. (2015). Childhood trauma mediates the association between ethnic minority status and more severe hallucinations in psychotic disorder. *Psychological Medicine, 45*(1), 133–142. http://doi.org/10.1017/S0033291714001135

Berg, A. O., Melle, I., Rossberg, J. I., Romm, K. L., Larsson, S., Lagerberg, T. V., ... Hauff, E. (2011). Perceived discrimination is associated with severity of positive and depression/anxiety symptoms in immigrants with psychosis: A cross-sectional study. *BMC Psychiatry, 11*(1), 77.

Berger, M., Kraeuter, A. K., Romanik, D., Malouf, P., Amminger, G. P., & Sarnyai, Z. (2016). Cortisol awakening response in patients with psychosis: Systematic review and meta-analysis. *Neuroscience & Biobehavioral Reviews, 68*, 157–166.

Bergink, V., Gibney, S. M., & Drexhage, H. A. (2014). Autoimmunity, inflammation, and psychosis: a search for peripheral markers. *Biological Psychiatry, 75*(4), 324–331.

Binbay, T., Alptekin, K., Hayriye, E., Zağlı, K., Druker, M., Tanık, F. A., ... van Os, J. (2012). Lifetime prevalence and correlates of schizophrenia and disorders with psychotic symptoms in the general population of Izmir, Turkey. *Turk Psikiyatri Dergisi, 23*(3), 149–160.

Bolton, S. L., & Sareen, J. (2011). Sexual orientation and its relation to mental disorders and suicide attempts: Findings from a nationally representative sample. *The Canadian Journal of Psychiatry, 56*(1), 35–43.

Booij, L., Welfeld, K., Leyton, M., Dagher, A., Boileau, I., Sibon, I., ... Cawley-Fiset, E. (2016). Dopamine cross-sensitization between psychostimulant drugs and stress in healthy male volunteers. *Translational Psychiatry, 6*(2), e740.

Borges, S., Gayer-Anderson, C., & Mondelli, V. (2013). A systematic review of the activity of the hypothalamic–pituitary–adrenal axis in first episode psychosis. *Psychoneuroendocrinology, 38*(5), 603–611.

Bosch, N. M., Riese, H., Reijneveld, S. A., Bakker, M. P., Verhulst, F. C., Ormel, J., & Oldehinkel, A. J. (2012). Timing matters: long term effects of adversities from prenatal period up to adolescence on adolescents' cortisol stress response. The TRAILS study. *Psychoneuroendocrinology, 37*(9), 1439–1447.

Bourque, F., van der Ven, E., & Malla, A. (2011). A meta-analysis of the risk for psychotic disorders among first-and second-generation immigrants. *Psychological Medicine, 41*(5), 897–910.

Boydell, J., Van Os, J., McKenzie, K., Allardyce, J., Goel, R., McCreadie, R. G., & Murray, R. M. (2001). Incidence of schizophrenia in ethnic minorities in London: Ecological study into interactions with environment. *British Medical Journal, 323*(7325), 1336–1338.

Bresnahan, M., Begg, M. D., Brown, A., Schaefer, C., Sohler, N., Insel, B., ... Susser, E. (2007). Race and risk of schizophrenia in a US birth cohort: Another example of health disparity? *International Journal of Epidemiology, 36*(4), 751–758.

Brown, G. W., & Birley, J. L. (1968). Crises and life changes and the onset of schizophrenia. *Journal of Health and Social Behavior, 9*(3), 203–214.

Brucato, G., Masucci, M. D., Arndt, L. Y., Ben-David, S., Colibazzi, T., Corcoran, C. M., ... Lister, A. (2017). Baseline demographics, clinical features and predictors of conversion among 200 individuals in a longitudinal prospective psychosis-risk cohort. *Psychological Medicine, 4*(11), 1–13. http://doi.org/10.1017/S0033291717000319

Buchman, A. L. (2001). Side effects of corticosteroid therapy. *Journal of Clinical Gastroenterology, 33*(4), 289–294.

Buka, S. L., & Fan, A. P. (1999). Association of prenatal and perinatal complications with subsequent bipolar disorder and schizophrenia. *Schizophrenia Research, 39*(2), 113–119.

Bulut, S. D., Bulut, S., & Güriz, O. (2016). The relationship between sex hormone profiles and symptoms of schizophrenia in men. *Comprehensive Psychiatry, 69*, 186–192.

Cantor-Graae, E., Pedersen, C. B., Mcneil, T. F., & Mortensen, P. B. (2003). Migration as a risk factor for schizophrenia: a Danish population-based cohort study. *The British Journal of Psychiatry, 182*(2), 117–122.

Cantor-Graae, E., & Selten, J. P. (2005). Schizophrenia and migration: A meta-analysis and review. *American Journal of Psychiatry, 162*(1), 12–24.

Carol, E. E., & Mittal, V. A. (2015). Resting cortisol level, self-concept, and putative familial environment in adolescents at ultra high-risk for psychotic disorders. *Psychoneuroendocrinology, 57*, 26–36.

Carol, E. E., Spencer, R. L., & Mittal, V. A. (2016). Sex differences in morning cortisol in youth at ultra-high-risk for psychosis. *Psychoneuroendocrinology, 72*, 87–93.

Carter, C. S., Bullmore, E. T., & Harrison, P. (2014). Is there a flame in the brain in psychosis? *Biological Psychiatry, 75*(4), 258–259.

Caspi, A., Moffitt, T. E., Cannon, M., McClay, J., Murray, R., Harrington, H.,...Poulton, R. (2005). Moderation of the effect of adolescent-onset cannabis use on adult psychosis by a functional polymorphism in the catechol-O-methyltransferase gene: longitudinal evidence of a gene X environment interaction. *Biological Psychiatry, 57*(10), 1117–1127.

Chakraborty, R., Chatterjee, A., Choudhary, S., Singh, A. R., & Chakraborty, P. (2007). Life events in acute and transient psychosis—a comparison with mania. *Geriatric Journal of Psychiatry, 10*, 36–40.

Chakraborty, A., McManus, S., Brugha, T. S., Bebbington, P., & King, M. (2011). Mental health of the non-heterosexual population of England. *British Journal of Psychiatry, 198*(2), 143–148.

Chan, L. F., Vaidya, M., Westphal, B., Allgrove, J., Martin, L., Afshar, F.,...Storr, H. L. (2011). Use of intravenous etomidate to control acute psychosis induced by the hypercortisolaemia in severe paediatric Cushing's disease. *Hormone Research in Paediatrics, 75*(6), 441–446.

Chen, Y., & Baram, T. Z. (2016). Toward understanding how early-life stress reprograms cognitive and emotional brain networks. *Neuropsychopharmacology, 41*(1), 197–206.

Chorpita, B. F., & Barlow, D. H. (1998). The development of anxiety: the role of control in the early environment. *Psychological Bulletin, 124*(1), 3.

Chu, J. W., Matthias, D. F., Belanoff, J., Schatzberg, A., Hoffman, A. R., & Feldman, D. (2001). Successful long-term treatment of refractory Cushing's disease with high-dose mifepristone (RU 486). *Journal of Clinical Endocrinology & Metabolism, 86*(8), 3568–3573.

Ciufolini, S., Dazzan, P., Kempton, M. J., Pariante, C., & Mondelli, V. (2014). HPA axis response to social stress is attenuated in schizophrenia but normal in depression: Evidence from a meta-analysis of existing studies. *Neuroscience & Biobehavioral Reviews, 47*, 359–368.

Coelho, R., Viola, T. W., Walss-Bass, C., Brietzke, E., & Grassi-Oliveira, R. (2014). Childhood maltreatment and inflammatory markers: A systematic review. *Acta Psychiatrica Scandinavica, 129*(3), 180–192.

Cohen, C. I., & Marino, L. (2013). Racial and ethnic differences in the prevalence of psychotic symptoms in the general population. *Psychiatric Services, 64*(11), 1103–1109. http://doi.org/10.1176/appi.ps.201200348

Coid, J. W., Kirkbride, J. B., Barker, D., Cowden, F., Stamps, R., Yang, M., & Jones, P. B. (2008). Raised incidence rates of all psychoses among migrant groups: Findings from the East London first episode psychosis study. *Archives of General Psychiatry, 65*(11), 1250–1258. http://doi.org/10.1001/archpsyc.65.11.1250

Collip, D., Nicolson, N. A., Lardinois, M., Lataster, T., Van Os, J., & Myin-Germeys, I. (2011). Daily cortisol, stress reactivity and psychotic experiences in individuals at above average genetic risk for psychosis. *Psychological Medicine, 41*(11), 2305–2315.

Collip, D., van Winkel, R., Peerbooms, O., Lataster, T., Thewissen, V., Lardinois, M.,...Myin-Germeys, I. (2010). COMT Val158Met–stress interaction in psychosis: Role of background psychosis risk. *CNS Neuroscience & Therapeutics, 17*(6), 612–619.

Collip, D., Wigman, J. T., Myin-Germeys, I., Jacobs, N., Derom, C., Thiery, E.,...van Os, J. (2013). From epidemiology to daily life: Linking daily life stress reactivity to persistence of psychotic experiences in a longitudinal general population study. *PLoS One, 8*(4), e62688.

Corcoran, C. M., Smith, C., McLaughlin, D., Auther, A., Malaspina, D., & Cornblatt, B. (2012). HPA axis function and symptoms in adolescents at clinical high risk for schizophrenia. *Schizophrenia Research, 135*(1), 170–174.

Craddock, N., O'Donovan, M. C., & Owen, M. J. (2009). Psychosis genetics: Modeling the relationship between schizophrenia, bipolar disorder, and mixed (or "schizoaffective") psychoses. *Schizophrenia Bulletin, 35*(3), 482–490.

Day, R., Nielsen, J. A., Korten, A., Ernberg, G., Dube, K. C., Gebhart, J.,...Sartorius, N. (1987). Stressful life events preceding the acute onset of schizophrenia: A cross-national study from the World Health Organization. *Culture, Medicine and psychiatry, 11*(2), 123–205.

Day, F. L., Valmaggia, L. R., Mondelli, V., Papadopoulos, A., Papadopoulos, I., Pariante, C. M., & McGuire, P. (2014). Blunted cortisol awakening response in people at ultra high risk of developing psychosis. *Schizophrenia research, 158*(1), 25–31.

de Castro-Catala, M., Barrantes-Vidal, N., Sheinbaum, T., Moreno-Fortuny, A., Kwapil, T. R., & Rosa, A. (2015). COMT-by-sex interaction effect on psychosis proneness. *BioMed research international, 2015.*

de Castro-Catala, M., van Nierop, M., Barrantes-Vidal, N., Cristóbal-Narváez, P., Sheinbaum, T., Kwapil, T. R.,...Rosa, A. (2016). Childhood trauma, BDNF Val66Met and subclinical psychotic experiences. Attempt at replication in two independent samples. *Journal of Psychiatric Research, 83*, 121–129.

Dennison, U., McKernan, D., Cryan, J., & Dinan, T. (2012). Schizophrenia patients with a history of childhood trauma have a pro-inflammatory phenotype. *Psychological Medicine, 42*(9), 1865–1871.

DeVylder, J. E., Oh, H. Y., Corcoran, C. M., & Lukens, E. P. (2014). Treatment seeking and unmet need for care among persons reporting psychosis-like experiences. *Psychiatric Services, 65*(6), 774–780.

DeVylder, J. E., Oh, H. Y., Yang, L. H., Cabassa, L. J., Chen, F. P., & Lukens, E. P. (2013). Acculturative stress and psychotic-like experiences among Asian and Latino immigrants to the United States. *Schizophrenia Research, 150*(1), 223–228.

Di Nicola, M., Cattaneo, A., Hepgul, N., Di Forti, M., Aitchison, K. J., Janiri, L.,...Mondelli, V. (2013). Serum and gene expression profile of cytokines in first-episode psychosis. *Brain, Behavior, and Immunity, 31*, 90–95.

Dinzeo, T. J., Cohen, A. S., Nienow, T. M., & Docherty, N. M. (2004). Stress and arousability in schizophrenia. *Schizophrenia Research, 71*(1), 127–135.

Dinzeo, T. J., Cohen, A. S., Nienow, T. M., & Docherty, N. M. (2008). Arousability in schizophrenia: relationship to emotional and physiological reactivity and symptom severity. *Acta Psychiatrica Scandinavica, 117*(6), 432–439.

Diorio, D., Viau, V., & Meaney, M. J. (1993). The role of the medial prefrontal cortex (cingulate gyrus) in the regulation of hypothalamic-pituitary-adrenal responses to stress. *Journal of Neuroscience, 13*(9), 3839–3847.

Dong, E., Ruzicka, W. B., Grayson, D. R., & Guidotti, A. (2015). DNA-methyltransferase1 (DNMT1) binding to CpG rich GABAergic and BDNF promoters is increased in the brain of schizophrenia and bipolar disorder patients. *Schizophrenia Research, 167*(1), 35–41.

Drabant, E. M., Hariri, A. R., Meyer-Lindenberg, A., Munoz, K. E., Mattay, V. S., Kolachana, B. S.,...Weinberger, D. R. (2006). Catechol O-methyltransferase val158met genotype and neural mechanisms related to affective arousal and regulation. *Archives of General Psychiatry, 63*(12), 1396–1406.

Essex, M. J., Shirtcliff, E. A., Burk, L. R., Ruttle, P. L., Klein, M. H., Slattery, M. J.,...Armstrong, J. M. (2011). Influence of early life stress on later hypothalamic–pituitary–adrenal axis functioning and its covariation with mental health symptoms: A study of the allostatic process from childhood into adolescence. *Development and Psychopathology, 23*(4), 1039–1058.

Faravelli, C., Catena, M., Scarpato, A., & Ricca, V. (2007). Epidemiology of life events: Life events and psychiatric disorders in the Sesto Fiorentino study. *Psychotherapy and Psychosomatics, 76*(6), 361–368.

Faravelli, C., Mansueto, G., Palmieri, S., Sauro, C. L., Rotella, F., Pietrini, F., & Fioravanti, G. (2017). Childhood adversity, cortisol levels, and psychosis: A retrospective investigation. *Journal of Nervous and Mental Disease, 205*(7), 574–579.

Faris, R. E. L., & Dunham, H. W. (1939). Mental disorders in urban areas: An ecological study of schizophrenia and other psychoses. Oxford, England: Univ. Chicago Press.

Fawzi, M. H., Kira, I. A., Fawzi, M. M., Jr., Mohamed, H. E., & Fawzi, M. M. (2013). Trauma profile in Egyptian adolescents with first-episode schizophrenia: Relation to psychopathology and plasma brain-derived neurotrophic factor. *Journal of Nervous and Mental Disease, 201*(1), 23–29.

Fearon, P., Kirkbride, J. B., Morgan, C., Dazzan, P., Morgan, K., Lloyd, T.,...Mallett, R. (2006). Incidence of schizophrenia and other psychoses in ethnic minority groups: Results from the MRC AESOP Study. *Psychological Medicine, 36*(11), 1541–1550. http://doi.org/10.1017/S0033291706008774

Feigenson, K. A., Kusnecov, A. W., & Silverstein, S. M. (2014). Inflammation and the two-hit hypothesis of schizophrenia. *Neuroscience & Biobehavioral Reviews, 38*, 72–93.

Fernandes, B. S., Berk, M., Turck, C. W., Steiner, J., & Goncalves, C. A. (2014). Decreased peripheral brain-derived neurotrophic factor levels are a biomarker of disease activity in major psychiatric disorders: A comparative meta-analysis. *Molecular Psychiatry, 19*(7), 750.

Fillman, S. G., Sinclair, D., Fung, S. J., Webster, M. J., & Weickert, C. S. (2014). Markers of inflammation and stress distinguish subsets of individuals with schizophrenia and bipolar disorder. *Translational Psychiatry, 4*(2), e365.

Fiori, L. M., & Turecki, G. (2016). Investigating epigenetic consequences of early-life adversity: Some methodological considerations. *European Journal of Psychotraumatology, 7*(1). https://doi.org/10.3402/ejpt.v7.31593

Fisher, H., Morgan, C., Dazzan, P., Craig, T. K., Morgan, K., Hutchinson, G.,...Murray, R. M. (2009). Gender differences in the association between childhood abuse and psychosis. *British Journal of Psychiatry, 194*(4), 319–325.

Fisher, H. L., Jones, P. B., Fearon, P., Craig, T. K., Dazzan, P., Morgan, K.,...Murray, R. M. (2010). The varying impact of type, timing and frequency of exposure to childhood adversity on its association with adult psychotic disorder. *Psychological Medicine, 40*(12), 1967–1978.

Föcking, M., Dicker, P., Lopez, L. M., Cannon, M., Schäfer, M. R., McGorry, P. D.,...Amminger, G. P. (2016). Differential expression of the inflammation marker IL12p40 in the at-risk mental state for psychosis: A predictor of transition to psychotic disorder? *BMC Psychiatry, 16*(1), 326.

Frydecka, D., Karpiński, P., & Misiak, B. (2014). Unravelling immune alterations in schizophrenia: Can DNA methylation provide clues? *Epigenomics, 6*(3), 245–247.

Gara, M. A., Vega, W. A., Arndt, S., Escamilla, M., Fleck, D. E., Lawson, W. B.,...Strakowski, S. M. (2012). Influence of patient race and ethnicity on clinical assessment in patients with affective disorders. *Archives of General Psychiatry, 69*(6), 593–600. http://doi.org/10.1001/archgenpsychiatry.2011.2040

Gevonden, M. J., Selten, J. P., Myin-Germeys, I., de Graaf, R., Ten Have, M., Van Dorsselaer, S.,...Veling, W. (2014). Sexual minority status and psychotic symptoms: Findings from the Netherlands Mental Health Survey and Incidence Studies (NEMESIS). *Psychological Medicine, 44*(2), 421–433. http://doi.org/10.1017/S0033291713000718

Gibson, L. E., Anglin, D. M., Klugman, J. T., Reeves, L. E., Fineberg, A. M., Maxwell, S. D.,...Ellman, L. M. (2014). Stress sensitivity mediates the relationship between traumatic life events and attenuated positive psychotic symptoms differentially by gender in a college population sample. *Journal of Psychiatric Research, 53*, 111–118.

Gijsberts, M., Huijnk, W., & Dagevos, J. (2012). Jaarrapport integratie 2011. Den Haag: Sociaal en Cultureel Planbureau, 101, 100.

Giovanoli, S., Engler, H., Engler, A., Richetto, J., Voget, M., Willi, R.,...Schedlowski, M. (2013). Stress in puberty unmasks latent neuropathological consequences of prenatal immune activation in mice. *Science, 339*(6123), 1095–1099.

Girshkin, L., O'Reilly, N., Quidé, Y., Teroganova, N., Rowland, J. E., Schofield, P. R., & Green, M. J. (2016). Diurnal cortisol variation and cortisol response to an MRI stressor in schizophrenia and bipolar disorder. *Psychoneuroendocrinology, 67*, 61–69.

Goldstein, J. M., Lancaster, K., Longenecker, J. M., Abbs, B., Holsen, L. M., Cherkerzian, S.,...Seidman, L. J. (2015). Sex differences, hormones, and fMRI stress response circuitry deficits in psychoses. *Psychiatry Research: Neuroimaging, 232*(3), 226–236.

Goodman, L. A., Salyers, M. P., Mueser, K. T., Rosenberg, S. D., Swartz, M., Essock, S. M.,...Swanson, J. (2001). Recent victimization in women and men with severe mental illness: prevalence and correlates. *Journal of Traumatic Stress, 14*(4), 615–632.

Green, M. J., Chia, T. Y., Cairns, M. J., Wu, J., Tooney, P. A., Scott, R. J.,...Bank, A. S. R. (2014). Catechol-O-methyltransferase (COMT) genotype moderates the effects of childhood trauma on cognition and symptoms in schizophrenia. *Journal of Psychiatric Research, 49*, 43–50.

Green, M. J., Matheson, S. L., Shepherd, A., Weickert, C. S., & Carr, V. J. (2011). Brain-derived neurotrophic factor levels in schizophrenia: A systematic review with meta-analysis. *Molecular Psychiatry, 16*(9), 960.

Gunnar, M., & Quevedo, K. (2007). The neurobiology of stress and development. *Annual Reviews in Psychology, 58*, 145–173.

Gunnar, M. R., Wewerka, S., Frenn, K., Long, J. D., & Griggs, C. (2009). Developmental changes in hypothalamus–pituitary–adrenal activity over the transition to adolescence: Normative changes and associations with puberty. *Development and Psychopathology, 21*(1), 69–85.

Hamilton, J. L., Stange, J. P., Abramson, L. Y., & Alloy, L. B. (2015). Stress and the development of cognitive vulnerabilities to depression explain sex differences in depressive symptoms during adolescence. *Clinical Psychological Science, 3*(5), 702–714.

Hardt, J., & Rutter, M. (2004). Validity of adult retrospective reports of adverse childhood experiences: Review of the evidence. *Journal of Child Psychology and Psychiatry*, *45*(2), 260–273.

Hempel, R. J., Tulen, J. H., Van Beveren, N. J., Röder, C. H., De Jong, F. H., & Hengeveld, M. W. (2010). Diurnal cortisol patterns of young male patients with schizophrenia. *Psychiatry and Clinical Neurosciences*, *64*(5), 548–554.

Hernaus, D., Collip, D., Lataster, J., Ceccarini, J., Kenis, G., Booij, L.,...Myin-Germeys, I. (2013). COMT Val158Met genotype selectively alters prefrontal [18F] fallypride displacement and subjective feelings of stress in response to a psychosocial stress challenge. *PLoS One*, *8*(6), e65662.

Hollander, A.-C., Dal, H., Lewis, G., Magnusson, C., Kirkbride, J. B., & Dalman, C. (2016). Refugee migration and risk of schizophrenia and other non-affective psychoses: Cohort study of 1.3 million people in Sweden. *British Medical Journal*, *352*, 1–8. http://doi.org/10.1136/bmj.i1030

Hollanders, J. J., van der Voorn, B., Rotteveel, J., & Finken, M. J. (2017). Is HPA axis reactivity in childhood gender-specific? A systematic review. *Biology of Sex Differences*, *8*(1), 23.

Holtzman, C. W., Trotman, H. D., Goulding, S. M., Ryan, A. T., Macdonald, A. N., Shapiro, D. I.,...Walker, E. F. (2013). Stress and neurodevelopmental processes in the emergence of psychosis. *Neuroscience*, *249*, 172–191.

Horan, W. P., Ventura, J., Nuechterlein, K. H., Subotnik, K. L., Hwang, S. S., & Mintz, J. (2005). Stressful life events in recent-onset schizophrenia: Reduced frequencies and altered subjective appraisals. *Schizophrenia Research*, *75*(2), 363–374.

Howes, O. D., & Kapur, S. (2009). The dopamine hypothesis of schizophrenia: Version III—the final common pathway. *Schizophrenia Bulletin*, *35*(3), 549–562.

Hunter, A. L., Minnis, H., & Wilson, P. (2011). Altered stress responses in children exposed to early adversity: a systematic review of salivary cortisol studies. *Stress*, *14*(6), 614–626.

Hyde, J. S., Mezulis, A. H., & Abramson, L. Y. (2008). The ABCs of depression: Integrating affective, biological, and cognitive models to explain the emergence of the gender difference in depression. *Psychological Review*, *115*(2), 291.

Janssen, I., Hanssen, M., Bak, M., Bijl, R. V., De Graaf, R., Vollebergh, W.,...Van Os, J. (2003). Discrimination and delusional ideation. *British Journal of Psychiatry*, *182*(1), 71–76.

Janssen, I., Krabbendam, L., Bak, M., Hanssen, M., Vollebergh, W., Graaf, R. D., & Os, J. V. (2004). Childhood abuse as a risk factor for psychotic experiences. *Acta Psychiatrica Scandinavica*, *109*(1), 38–45.

Judd, L. L., Schettler, P. J., Brown, E. S., Wolkowitz, O. M., Sternberg, E. M., Bender, B. G.,...Joëls, M. (2014). Adverse consequences of glucocorticoid medication: Psychological, cognitive, and behavioral effects. *American Journal of Psychiatry*, *171*(10), 1045–1051.

Karanikas, E., Antoniadis, D., & Garyfallos, G. D. (2014). The role of cortisol in first episode of psychosis: a systematic review. *Current Psychiatry Reports*, *16*(11), 503.

Karanikas, E., & Garyfallos, G. (2015). Role of cortisol in patients at risk for psychosis mental state and psychopathological correlates: A systematic review. *Psychiatry and Clinical Neurosciences*, *69*(5), 268–282.

Kelleher, I., & Cannon, M. (2011). Psychotic-like experiences in the general population: characterizing a high-risk group for psychosis. *Psychological Medicine*, *41*(1), 1–6.

Kelleher, I., Harley, M., Lynch, F., Arseneault, L., Fitzpatrick, C., & Cannon, M. (2008). Associations between childhood trauma, bullying and psychotic symptoms among a school-based adolescent sample. *British Journal of Psychiatry*, *193*(5), 378–382.

Kiecolt-Glaser, J. K., McGuire, L., Robles, T. F., & Glaser, R. (2002). Emotions, morbidity, and mortality: New perspectives from psychoneuroimmunology. *Annual Review of Psychology*, *53*(1), 83–107.

Kirkbride, J. B., Barker, D., Cowden, F., Stamps, R., Yang, M., Jones, P. B., & Coid, J. W. (2008). Psychoses, ethnicity and socio-economic status. *British Journal of Psychiatry*, *193*(1), 18–24.

Kirkbride, J. B., Jones, P. B., Ullrich, S., & Coid, J. W. (2012). Social deprivation, inequality, and the neighborhood-level incidence of psychotic syndromes in East London. *Schizophrenia Bulletin*, *40*(1), 169–180.

Kirkbride, J. B., Hameed, Y., Ioannidis, K., Ankireddypalli, G., Crane, C. M., Nasir, M.,...Spyridi, S. (2017). Ethnic minority status, age-at-immigration and psychosis risk in rural environments: Evidence from the SEPEA Study. *Schizophrenia Bulletin*, *43*(6), 1251–1261.

Kirkpatrick, B., & Miller, B. J. (2013). Inflammation and schizophrenia. *Schizophrenia Bulletin*, *39*(6), 1174–1179.

Klengel, T., Mehta, D., Anacker, C., Rex-Haffner, M., Pruessner, J. C., Pariante, C. M.,...Nemeroff, C. B. (2013). Allele-specific FKBP5 DNA demethylation mediates gene-childhood trauma interactions. *Nature Neuroscience*, *16*(1), 33–41.

Labad, J., Stojanovic-Pérez, A., Montalvo, I., Solé, M., Cabezas, Á., Ortega, L.,...Gutiérrez-Zotes, A. (2015). Stress biomarkers as predictors of transition to psychosis in at-risk mental states: Roles for cortisol, prolactin and albumin. *Journal of Psychiatric Research*, *60*, 163–169.

Laloyaux, J., Dessart, G., Van der Linden, M., Lemaire, M., & Larøi, F. (2016). Maladaptive emotion regulation strategies and stress sensitivity mediate the relation between adverse life events and attenuated positive psychotic symptoms. *Cognitive Neuropsychiatry*, *21*(2), 116–129.

Lardinois, M., Lataster, T., Mengelers, R., Van Os, J., & Myin-Germeys, I. (2011). Childhood trauma and increased stress sensitivity in psychosis. *Acta Psychiatrica Scandinavica*, *123*(1), 28–35.

Lataster, T., Collip, D., Lardinois, M., Van Os, J., & Myin-Germeys, I. (2010). Evidence for a familial correlation between increased reactivity to stress and positive psychotic symptoms. *Acta Psychiatrica Scandinavica*, *122*(5), 395–404.

Lataster, J., Myin-Germeys, I., Lieb, R., Wittchen, H. U., & van Os, J. (2012). Adversity and psychosis: a 10-year prospective study investigating synergism between early and recent adversity in psychosis. *Acta Psychiatrica Scandinavica*, *125*(5), 388–399.

Lewis, T. T., Cogburn, C. D., & Williams, D. R. (2015). Self-reported experiences of discrimination and health: Scientific advances, ongoing controversies, and emerging issues. *Annual Review of Clinical Psychology*, *11*, 407–440.

Lupien, S. J., McEwen, B. S., Gunnar, M. R., & Heim, C. (2009). Effects of stress throughout the lifespan on the brain, behaviour and cognition. *Nature Reviews Neuroscience*, *10*(6), 434.

Maccari, S., Darnaudery, M., Morley-Fletcher, S., Zuena, A. R., Cinque, C., & Van Reeth, O. (2003). Prenatal stress and long-term consequences: Implications of glucocorticoid hormones. *Neuroscience & Biobehavioral Reviews*, *27*(1), 119–127.

Malla, A. K., & Norman, R. M. (1992). Relationship of major life events and daily stressors to symptomatology in schizophrenia. *Journal of Nervous and Mental Disease*, 180(10), 664–667.

Markham, J. A., & Koenig, J. I. (2011). Prenatal stress: Role in psychotic and depressive diseases. *Psychopharmacology*, 214(1), 89–106.

McGowan, P. O., Sasaki, A., D'alessio, A. C., Dymov, S., Labonté, B., Szyf, M.,...Meaney, M. J. (2009). Epigenetic regulation of the glucocorticoid receptor in human brain associates with childhood abuse. *Nature Neuroscience*, 12(3), 342–348.

McGrath, J. J., McLaughlin, K. A., Saha, S., Aguilar-Gaxiola, S., Al-Hamzawi, A., Alonso, J.,...Florescu, S. (2017). The association between childhood adversities and subsequent first onset of psychotic experiences: A cross-national analysis of 23,998 respondents from 17 countries. *Psychological Medicine*, 47(7), 1230–1245.

McLaughlin, K. A., Sheridan, M. A., & Lambert, H. K. (2014). Childhood adversity and neural development: Deprivation and threat as distinct dimensions of early experience. *Neuroscience & Biobehavioral Reviews*, 47, 578–591.

Meyer, I. H. (1995). Minority stress and mental health in gay men. *Journal of Health and Social Behavior*, 36(1), 38–56.

Meyer, I. H. (2003). Prejudice, social stress, and mental health in lesbian, gay, and bisexual populations: Conceptual issues and research evidence. *Psychological Bulletin*, 129(5), 674.

Miller, B. J., Buckley, P., Seabolt, W., Mellor, A., & Kirkpatrick, B. (2011). Meta-analysis of cytokine alterations in schizophrenia: Clinical status and antipsychotic effects. *Biological Psychiatry*, 70(7), 663–671.

Miller, T. J., McGlashan, T. H., Rosen, J. L., Cadenhead, K., Ventura, J., McFarlane, W.,...Woods, S. W. (2003). Prodromal assessment with the structured interview for prodromal syndromes and the scale of prodromal symptoms: predictive validity, interrater reliability, and training to reliability. *Schizophrenia Bulletin*, 29(4), 703.

Misiak, B., Krefft, M., Bielawski, T., Moustafa, A. A., Sąsiadek, M. M., & Frydecka, D. (2017). Toward a unified theory of childhood trauma and psychosis: A comprehensive review of epidemiological, clinical, neuropsychological and biological findings. *Neuroscience & Biobehavioral Reviews*, 75, 393–406.

Mizrahi, R. (2016). Social stress and psychosis risk: common neurochemical substrates? *Neuropsychopharmacology: Official publication of the American College of Neuropsychopharmacology*, 41(3), 666–674.

Mizrahi, R., Addington, J., Rusjan, P. M., Suridjan, I., Ng, A., Boileau, I.,...Wilson, A. A. (2012). Increased stress-induced dopamine release in psychosis. *Biological Psychiatry*, 71(6), 561–567.

Mondelli, V., Cattaneo, A., Murri, M. B., Di Forti, M., Handley, R., Hepgul, N.,...Morgan, C. (2011). Stress and inflammation reduce BDNF expression in first-episode psychosis: A pathway to smaller hippocampal volume. *Journal of Clinical Psychiatry*, 72(12), 1677.

Mondelli, V., Dazzan, P., Hepgul, N., Di Forti, M., Aas, M., D'Albenzio, A.,...Morgan, C. (2010). Abnormal cortisol levels during the day and cortisol awakening response in first-episode psychosis: The role of stress and of antipsychotic treatment. *Schizophrenia Research*, 116(2), 234–242.

Mondelli, V., Pariante, C. M., Navari, S., Aas, M., D'Albenzio, A., Di Forti, M.,...Papadopoulos, A. S. (2010). Higher cortisol levels are associated with smaller left hippocampal volume in first-episode psychosis. *Schizophrenia Research*, 119(1), 75–78.

Monroe, S. M. (2008). Modern approaches to conceptualizing and measuring human life stress. *Annual Review of Clinical Psychology*, 4, 33–52.

Montag, C., Buckholtz, J. W., Hartmann, P., Merz, M., Burk, C., Hennig, J., & Reuter, M. (2008). COMT genetic variation affects fear processing: Psychophysiological evidence. *Behavioral Neuroscience*, 122(4), 901.

Montgomery, A. J., Mehta, M. A., & Grasby, P. M. (2006). Is psychological stress in man associated with increased striatal dopamine levels?: A [11C] raclopride PET study. *Synapse*, 60(2), 124–131.

Moore, T. H., Zammit, S., Lingford-Hughes, A., Barnes, T. R., Jones, P. B., Burke, M., & Lewis, G. (2007). Cannabis use and risk of psychotic or affective mental health outcomes: A systematic review. *The Lancet*, 370(9584), 319–328.

Morgan, C., Charalambides, M., Hutchinson, G., & Murray, R. M. (2010). Migration, ethnicity, and psychosis: toward a sociodevelopmental model. *Schizophrenia Bulletin*, 36(4), 655–664.

Morgan, C., & Gayer-Anderson, C. (2016). Childhood adversities and psychosis: Evidence, challenges, implications. *World Psychiatry*, 15(2), 93–102.

Morgan, C., Kirkbride, J., Hutchinson, G., Craig, T., Morgan, K., Dazzan, P.,...Leff, J. (2008). Cumulative social disadvantage, ethnicity and first-episode psychosis: A case-control study. *Psychological Medicine*, 38(12), 1701–1715.

Moskow, D. M., Addington, J., Bearden, C. E., Cadenhead, K. S., Cornblatt, B. A., Heinssen, R.,...Tsuang, M. T. (2016). The relations of age and pubertal development with cortisol and daily stress in youth at clinical risk for psychosis. *Schizophrenia Research*, 172(1), 29–34.

Murray, G. K., & Jones, P. B. (2012). Psychotic symptoms in young people without psychotic illness: mechanisms and meaning. *The British Journal of Psychiatry*, 201(1), 4–6.

Myin-Germeys, I., Krabbendam, L., Delespaul, P. A., & Van Os, J. (2004). Sex differences in emotional reactivity to daily life stress in psychosis. *Journal of Clinical Psychiatry*, 65(6), 805–809.

Myin-Germeys, I., Marcelis, M., Krabbendam, L., Delespaul, P., & van Os, J. (2005). Subtle fluctuations in psychotic phenomena as functional states of abnormal dopamine reactivity in individuals at risk. *Biological Psychiatry*, 58(2), 105–110.

Myin-Germeys, I., & van Os, J. (2007). Stress-reactivity in psychosis: Evidence for an affective pathway to psychosis. *Clinical Psychology Review*, 27(4), 409–424.

Myin-Germeys, I., van Os, J., Schwartz, J. E., Stone, A. A., & Delespaul, P. A. (2001). Emotional reactivity to daily life stress in psychosis. *Archives of General Psychiatry*, 58(12), 1137–1144.

Nieman, D. H., Dragt, S., van Duin, E. D., Denneman, N., Overbeek, J. M., de Haan, L.,...Wunderink, L. (2016). COMT Val 158 Met genotype and cannabis use in people with an at risk mental state for psychosis: Exploring gene x environment interactions. *Schizophrenia Research*, 174(1), 24–28.

Notaras, M., Hill, R., & van den Buuse, M. (2015). The BDNF gene Val66Met polymorphism as a modifier of psychiatric disorder susceptibility: Progress and controversy. *Molecular Psychiatry*, 20(8), 916–930.

Nuechterlein, K. H., Dawson, M. E., Gitlin, M., Ventura, J., Goldstein, M. J., Snyder, K. S.,...Mintz, J. (1992). Developmental processes in schizophrenic disorders:

Longitudinal studies of vulnerability and stress. *Schizophrenia Bulletin, 18*(3), 387–425.

Ochoa, S., Usall, J., Cobo, J., Labad, X., & Kulkarni, J. (2012). Gender differences in schizophrenia and first-episode psychosis: A comprehensive literature review. *Schizophrenia Research and Treatment, 2012*, 916198. doi:10.1155/2012/916198

Oh, H., Yang, L. H., Anglin, D. M., & DeVylder, J. E. (2014). Perceived discrimination and psychotic experiences across multiple ethnic groups in the United States. *Schizophrenia Research, 157*(1), 259–265.

Olsson, C. A., Anney, R. J., Lotfi-Miri, M., Byrnes, G. B., Williamson, R., & Patton, G. C. (2005). Association between the COMT Val158Met polymorphism and propensity to anxiety in an Australian population-based longitudinal study of adolescent health. *Psychiatric Genetics, 15*(2), 109–115.

Pace, T. W., Mletzko, T. C., Alagbe, O., Musselman, D. L., Nemeroff, C. B., Miller, A. H., & Heim, C. M. (2006). Increased stress-induced inflammatory responses in male patients with major depression and increased early life stress. *American Journal of Psychiatry, 163*(9), 1630–1633.

Paksarian, D., Merikangas, K. R., Calkins, M. E., & Gur, R. E. (2016). Racial-ethnic disparities in empirically-derived subtypes of subclinical psychosis among a US sample of youths. *Schizophrenia Research, 170*(1), 205–210.

Pallanti, S., Quercioli, L., & Pazzagli, A. (1997). Relapse in young paranoid schizophrenic patients: A prospective study of stressful life events, P300 measures, and coping. *American Journal of Psychiatry, 154*(6), 792–798.

Palmier-Claus, J. E., Dunn, G., & Lewis, S. W. (2012). Emotional and symptomatic reactivity to stress in individuals at ultra-high risk of developing psychosis. *Psychological Medicine, 42*(5), 1003–1012.

Perlman, W. R., Webster, M. J., Kleinman, J. E., & Weickert, C. S. (2004). Reduced glucocorticoid and estrogen receptor alpha messenger ribonucleic acid levels in the amygdala of patients with major mental illness. *Biological Psychiatry, 56*(11), 844–852.

Perroud, N., Paoloni-Giacobino, A., Prada, P., Olié, E., Salzmann, A., Nicastro, R., ... Huguelet, P. (2011). Increased methylation of glucocorticoid receptor gene (NR3C1) in adults with a history of childhood maltreatment: A link with the severity and type of trauma. *Translational Psychiatry, 1*(12), e59.

Perroud, N., Salzmann, A., Prada, P., Nicastro, R., Hoeppli, M. E., Furrer, S., ... Malafosse, A. (2013). Response to psychotherapy in borderline personality disorder and methylation status of the BDNF gene. *Translational Psychiatry, 3*(1), e207.

Phillips, L. J., Francey, S. M., Edwards, J., & McMurray, N. (2007). Stress and psychosis: Towards the development of new models of investigation. *Clinical Psychology Review, 27*(3), 307–317.

Pruessner, J. C., Champagne, F., Meaney, M. J., & Dagher, A. (2004). Dopamine release in response to a psychological stress in humans and its relationship to early life maternal care: A positron emission tomography study using [11C] raclopride. *Journal of Neuroscience, 24*(11), 2825–2831.

Pruessner, M., Cullen, A. E., Aas, M., & Walker, E. F. (2017). The neural diathesis-stress model of schizophrenia revisited: An update on recent findings considering illness stage and neurobiological and methodological complexities. *Neuroscience and Biobehavioral Reviews, 73*, 191–218.

Pruessner, M., Iyer, S. N., Faridi, K., Joober, R., & Malla, A. K. (2011). Stress and protective factors in individuals at ultra-high risk for psychosis, first episode psychosis and healthy controls. *Schizophrenia Research, 129*(1), 29–35.

Pruessner, M., Vracotas, N., Joober, R., Pruessner, J. C., & Malla, A. K. (2013). Blunted cortisol awakening response in men with first episode psychosis: Relationship to parental bonding. *Psychoneuroendocrinology, 38*(2), 229–240.

Pruessner, J. C., Wolf, O. T., Hellhammer, D. H., Buske-Kirschbaum, A., Von Auer, K., Jobst, S., ... Kirschbaum, C. (1997). Free cortisol levels after awakening: A reliable biological marker for the assessment of adrenocortical activity. *Life Sciences, 61*(26), 2539–2549.

Radtke, K. M., Schauer, M., Gunter, H. M., Ruf-Leuschner, M., Sill, J., Meyer, A., & Elbert, T. (2015). Epigenetic modifications of the glucocorticoid receptor gene are associated with the vulnerability to psychopathology in childhood maltreatment. *Translational Psychiatry, 5*(5), e571.

Ramsay, H., Kelleher, I., Flannery, P., Clarke, M. C., Lynch, F., Harley, M., ... Cannon, M. (2013). Relationship between the COMT-Val158Met and BDNF-Val66Met polymorphisms, childhood trauma and psychotic experiences in an adolescent general population sample. *PLoS One, 8*(11), e79741.

Raune, D., Kuipers, E., & Bebbington, P. (2009). Stressful and intrusive life events preceding first episode psychosis. *Epidemiology and Psychiatric Sciences, 18*(3), 221–228.

Read, J., Fosse, R., Moskowitz, A., & Perry, B. (2014). The traumagenic neurodevelopmental model of psychosis revisited. *Neuropsychiatry, 4*(1), 65.

Read, J., Perry, B. D., Moskowitz, A., & Connolly, J. (2001). The contribution of early traumatic events to schizophrenia in some patients: A traumagenic neurodevelopmental model. *Psychiatry: Interpersonal and Biological Processes, 64*(4), 319–345.

Repetti, R. L., Robles, T. F., & Reynolds, B. (2011). Allostatic processes in the family. *Development and Psychopathology, 23*(3), 921–938.

Rössler, W., Ajdacic-Gross, V., Rodgers, S., Haker, H., & Müller, M. (2016). Childhood trauma as a risk factor for the onset of subclinical psychotic experiences: Exploring the mediating effect of stress sensitivity in a cross-sectional epidemiological community study. *Schizophrenia Research, 172*(1), 46–53.

Saleem, M. M., Stowkowy, J., Cadenhead, K. S., Cannon, T. D., Cornblatt, B. A., McGlashan, T. H., ... Woods, S. W. (2014). Perceived discrimination in those at clinical high risk for psychosis. *Early Intervention in Psychiatry, 8*(1), 77–81.

Samplin, E., Ikuta, T., Malhotra, A. K., Szeszko, P. R., & DeRosse, P. (2013). Sex differences in resilience to childhood maltreatment: Effects of trauma history on hippocampal volume, general cognition and subclinical psychosis in healthy adults. *Journal of Psychiatric Research, 47*(9), 1174–1179.

Segerstrom, S. C., & Miller, G. E. (2004). Psychological stress and the human immune system: A meta-analytic study of 30 years of inquiry. *Psychological Bulletin, 130*(4), 601.

Selten, J. P., & Cantor-Graae, E. (2005). Social defeat: risk factor for schizophrenia?. *British Journal of Psychiatry, 187*(2), 101–102.

Selten, J. P., & Cantor-Graae, E. (2007). Hypothesis: Social defeat is a risk factor for schizophrenia? *The British Journal of Psychiatry, 191*(S51), s9–s12.

Selten, J. P., Laan, W., Kupka, R., Smeets, H. M., & Van Os, J. (2012). Risk of psychiatric treatment for mood disorders and psychotic disorders among migrants and Dutch nationals in

Utrecht, The Netherlands. *Social psychiatry and psychiatric epidemiology*, *47*(2), 271–278.

Selten, J. P., van der Ven, E., Rutten, B. P., & Cantor-Graae, E. (2013). The social defeat hypothesis of schizophrenia: An update. *Schizophrenia Bulletin*, *39*(6), 1180–1186.

Shaikh, M., Ellett, L., Dutt, A., Day, F., Laing, J., Kroll, J., ... Valmaggia, L. R. (2016). Perceived ethnic discrimination and persecutory paranoia in individuals at ultra-high risk for psychosis. *Psychiatry Research*, *241*, 309–314.

Shaw, R. J., Atkin, K., Bécares, L., Albor, C. B., Stafford, M., Kiernan, K. E., ... Pickett, K. E. (2012). Impact of ethnic density on adult mental disorders: Narrative review. *British Journal of Psychiatry*, *201*(1), 11–19.

Smolka, M. N., Schumann, G., Wrase, J., Grüsser, S. M., Flor, H., Mann, K., ... Heinz, A. (2005). Catechol-O-methyltransferase val158met genotype affects processing of emotional stimuli in the amygdala and prefrontal cortex. *Journal of Neuroscience*, *25*(4), 836–842.

Soliman, A., O'driscoll, G. A., Pruessner, J., Anne-lise, V. H., Boileau, I., Gagnon, D., & Dagher, A. (2008). Stress-induced dopamine release in humans at risk of psychosis: A [11C] raclopride PET study. *Neuropsychopharmacology*, *33*(8), 2033.

Sommer, I. E., Daalman, K., Rietkerk, T., Diederen, K. M., Bakker, S., Wijkstra, J., & Boks, M. P. (2008). Healthy individuals with auditory verbal hallucinations; who are they? Psychiatric assessments of a selected sample of 103 subjects. *Schizophrenia Bulletin*, *36*(3), 633–641.

Stein, M. B., Fallin, M. D., Schork, N. J., & Gelernter, J. (2005). COMT polymorphisms and anxiety-related personality traits. *Neuropsychopharmacology*, *30*(11), 2092.

Stevens J., Hamann S. (2012). Sex differences in brain activation to emotional stimuli: A meta-analysis of neuroimaging studies. *Neuropsychologia*, *50*, 1578–1593.

Stowkowy, J., Liu, L., Cadenhead, K. S., Cannon, T. D., Cornblatt, B. A., McGlashan, T. H., ... Woods, S. W. (2016). Early traumatic experiences, perceived discrimination and conversion to psychosis in those at clinical high risk for psychosis. *Social Psychiatry and Psychiatric Epidemiology*, *51*(4), 497–503.

Streit, F., Memic, A., Hasandedić, L., Rietschel, L., Frank, J., Lang, M., ... Nöthen, M. M. (2016). Perceived stress and hair cortisol: Differences in bipolar disorder and schizophrenia. *Psychoneuroendocrinology*, *69*, 26–34.

Tessner, K. D., Mittal, V., & Walker, E. F. (2009). Longitudinal study of stressful life events and daily stressors among adolescents at high risk for psychotic disorders. *Schizophrenia Bulletin*, *37*(2), 432–441.

Thaler, L., Gauvin, L., Joober, R., Groleau, P., de Guzman, R., Ambalavanan, A., ... Steiger, H. (2014). Methylation of BDNF in women with bulimic eating syndromes: Associations with childhood abuse and borderline personality disorder. *Progress in Neuro-Psychopharmacology and Biological Psychiatry*, *54*, 43–49.

Theleritis, C., Fisher, H. L., Shäfer, I., Winters, L., Stahl, D., Morgan, C., ... Russo, M. (2014). Brain derived neurotropic factor (BDNF) is associated with childhood abuse but not cognitive domains in first episode psychosis. *Schizophrenia Research*, *159*(1), 56–61.

Thompson, A. D., Nelson, B., Yuen, H. P., Lin, A., Amminger, G. P., McGorry, P. D., ... Yung, A. R. (2013). Sexual trauma increases the risk of developing psychosis in an ultra high-risk "prodromal" population. *Schizophrenia Bulletin*, *40*(3), 697–706.

Trotman, H. D., Holtzman, C. W., Walker, E. F., Addington, J. M., Bearden, C. E., Cadenhead, K. S., ... Tsuang, M. T. (2014). Stress exposure and sensitivity in the clinical high-risk syndrome: Initial findings from the North American Prodrome Longitudinal Study (NAPLS). *Schizophrenia Research*, *160*(1), 104–109.

Trotta, A., Murray, R. M., & Fisher, H. L. (2015). The impact of childhood adversity on the persistence of psychotic symptoms: A systematic review and meta-analysis. *Psychological Medicine*, *45*(12), 2481–2498.

Tunbridge, E. M., Harrison, P. J., & Weinberger, D. R. (2006). Catechol-o-methyltransferase, cognition, and psychosis: Val 158 Met and beyond. *Biological Psychiatry*, *60*(2), 141–151.

Tyrka, A. R., Ridout, K. K., Parade, S. H., Paquette, A., Marsit, C. J., & Seifer, R. (2015). Childhood maltreatment and methylation of FK506 binding protein 5 gene (FKBP5). *Development and Psychopathology*, *27*(4pt2), 1637–1645.

Tyrka, A. R., Wier, L., Price, L. H., Ross, N., Anderson, G. M., Wilkinson, C. W., & Carpenter, L. L. (2008). Childhood parental loss and adult hypothalamic-pituitary-adrenal function. *Biological Psychiatry*, *63*(12), 1147–1154.

van der Vegt, E. J., Van Der Ende, J., Kirschbaum, C., Verhulst, F. C., & Tiemeier, H. (2009). Early neglect and abuse predict diurnal cortisol patterns in adults: A study of international adoptees. *Psychoneuroendocrinology*, *34*(5), 660–669.

van der Ven, E., Veling, W., Tortelli, A., Tarricone, I., Berardi, D., Bourque, F., & Selten, J. P. (2016). Evidence of an excessive gender gap in the risk of psychotic disorder among North African immigrants in Europe: A systematic review and meta-analysis. *Social Psychiatry and Psychiatric Epidemiology*, *51*(12), 1603–1613. doi:10.1007/s00127-016-1261-0

Van Os, J., Linscott, R. J., Myin-Germeys, I., Delespaul, P., & Krabbendam, L. (2009). A systematic review and meta-analysis of the psychosis continuum: Evidence for a psychosis proneness–persistence–impairment model of psychotic disorder. *Psychological Medicine*, *39*(2), 179–195.

van Winkel, R., Henquet, C., Rosa, A., Papiol, S., Fañanás, L., De Hert, M., ... Myin-Germeys, I. (2008). Evidence that the COMTVal158Met polymorphism moderates sensitivity to stress in psychosis: An experience-sampling study. *American Journal of Medical Genetics Part B: Neuropsychiatric Genetics*, *147*(1), 10–17.

Varese, F., Smeets, F., Drukker, M., Lieverse, R., Lataster, T., Viechtbauer, W., ... Bentall, R. P. (2012). Childhood adversities increase the risk of psychosis: A meta-analysis of patient-control, prospective-and cross-sectional cohort studies. *Schizophrenia Bulletin*, *38*(4), 661–671.

Veling, W. (2013). Ethnic minority position and risk for psychotic disorders. *Current Opinion in Psychiatry*, *26*(2), 166–171.

Veling, W., Pot-Kolder, R., Counotte, J., van Os, J., & van der Gaag, M. (2016). Environmental social stress, paranoia and psychosis liability: A virtual reality study. *Schizophrenia Bulletin*, *42*(6), 1363–1371.

Veling, W., Selten, J. P., Susser, E., Laan, W., Mackenbach, J. P., & Hoek, H. W. (2007). Discrimination and the incidence of psychotic disorders among ethnic minorities in The Netherlands. *International Journal of Epidemiology*, *36*(4), 761–768.

Veling, W., Selten, J. P., Veen, N., Laan, W., Blom, J. D., & Hoek, H. W. (2006). Incidence of schizophrenia among ethnic minorities in the Netherlands: A four-year first-contact study. *Schizophrenia Research*, *86*(1–3), 189–193. http://doi.org/10.1016/j.schres.2006.06.010

Veling, W., & Susser, E. (2011). Migration and psychotic disorders. *Expert Review of Neurotherapeutics, 11*(1), 65–76.

Veling, W., Susser, E., Van Os, J., Mackenbach, J. P., Selten, J. P., & Hoek, H. W. (2008). Ethnic density of neighborhoods and incidence of psychotic disorders among immigrants. *American Journal of Psychiatry, 165*(1), 66–73. http://doi.org/10.1176/appi.ajp.2007.07030423

Vinkers, C. H., Kalafateli, A. L., Rutten, B. P., Kas, M. J., Kaminsky, Z., Turner, J. D., & Boks, M. P. (2015). Traumatic stress and human DNA methylation: A critical review. *Epigenomics, 7*(4), 593–608.

Vinson, G. P. (2009). The adrenal cortex and life. *Molecular and Cellular Endocrinology, 300*(1), 2–6.

Walder, D. J., Trotman, H. D., Cubells, J. F., Brasfield, J., Tang, Y., & Walker, E. F. (2010). Catechol-O-Methyltransferase (COMT) modulation of cortisol secretion in psychiatrically at-risk and healthy adolescents. *Psychiatric Genetics, 20*(4), 166.

Walker, E., Mittal, V., & Tessner, K. (2008). Stress and the hypothalamic pituitary adrenal axis in the developmental course of schizophrenia. *Annual Review of Clinical Psychology, 4*, 189–216.

Walker, E. F., & Diforio, D. (1997). Schizophrenia: A neural diathesis-stress model. *Psychological Review, 104*(4), 667.

Walker, E. F., Trotman, H. D., Pearce, B. D., Addington, J., Cadenhead, K. S., Cornblatt, B. A., . . . Tsuang, M. T. (2013). Cortisol levels and risk for psychosis: Initial findings from the North American prodrome longitudinal study. *Biological Psychiatry, 74*(6), 410–417.

Warrington, T. P., & Bostwick, J. M. (2006). Psychiatric adverse effects of corticosteroids. *Mayo Clinic Proceedings, 81*(10) 1361–1367.

Webster, M. J., Knable, M. B., O'grady, J., Orthmann, J., & Weickert, C. S. (2002). Regional specificity of brain glucocorticoid receptor mRNA alterations in subjects with schizophrenia and mood disorders. *Molecular Psychiatry, 7*(9), 985.

Wonodi, I., Stine, O. C., Mitchell, B. D., Buchanan, R. W., & Thaker, G. K. (2003). Association between Val108/158 Met polymorphism of the COMT gene and schizophrenia. *American Journal of Medical Genetics Part B: Neuropsychiatric Genetics, 120*(1), 47–50.

Woods, S. W., Addington, J., Bearden, C. E., Cadenhead, K. S., Cannon, T. D., Cornblatt, B. A., . . . Walker, E. F. (2013). Psychotropic medication use in youth at high risk for psychosis: Comparison of baseline data from two research cohorts 1998–2005 and 2008–2011. *Schizophrenia Research, 148*(1), 99–104.

Yung, A. R., Cotter, J., Wood, S. J., McGorry, P., Thompson, A. D., Nelson, B., & Lin, A. (2015). Childhood maltreatment and transition to psychotic disorder independently predict long-term functioning in young people at ultra-high risk for psychosis. *Psychological Medicine, 45*(16), 3453–3465.

Yung, A. R., & McGorry, P. D. (1996a). The initial prodrome in psychosis: Descriptive and qualitative aspects. *Australian and New Zealand Journal of Psychiatry, 30*(5), 587–599.

Yung, A. R., & McGorry, P. D. (1996b). The prodromal phase of first-episode psychosis: Past and current conceptualizations. *Schizophrenia Bulletin, 22*(2), 353–370.

Yung, A., Phillips, L., McGorry, P., Ward, J., Donovan, K., & Thompson, K. (2002). Comprehensive assessment of at-risk mental states (CAARMS). Melbourne, Australia: University of Melbourne, Department of Psychiatry, Personal Assessment and Crisis Evaluation Clinic.

Stress and Personality Disorders

Christina Noel White, Christopher C. Conway, *and* Thomas F. Oltmanns

Abstract

This chapter reviews literature investigating the complex relationships between stress and personality disorders. Various forms of early life adversity, particularly experiences of abuse and neglect, portend the development of personality disorders and maladaptive personality traits later in life. Much of this association appears to be causal (i.e., independent of genetic risk). A comparatively much smaller literature suggests that acute stressful events later in development show complex interrelations with personality disorders. These connections appear to be bidirectional, such that not only does stress influence the development of personality, but personality also influences stress exposure. Additionally, personality traits influence the way in which individuals respond to stressors, both psychologically and physiologically. Our review concludes by underlining enduring methodological problems and conceptual issues that await resolution in future empirical work.

Keywords: stress, personality, personality disorders, stress generation, stress reactivity

Stress and personality disorders (PDs) are intimately intertwined. Early observations linked childhood maltreatment to borderline, antisocial, and other PDs, and this connection has been substantiated by more recent work. This research area has evolved in the past few decades to cover the link between other forms of stress—spanning the entire life course—that affect the development, maintenance, and treatment of PD. For instance, independent of childhood maltreatment, acute stressors occurring in adolescence and early adulthood are thought to trigger the onset of PD, and minor hassles—minor stressors that unfold over hours or days—have been shown to predict a poorer temporal course of PD symptoms (e.g., Stepp et al., 2013; Wright & Simms, 2016). Just as researchers originally predicted that childhood trauma was the preeminent cause of PD, they also presumed that the association between stress and PD was unidirectional. However, scholars have recently begun to examine the possibility that not only does stress portend disorder, but that PDs can set the stage for continued stress

exposure. This "stress generation" model, originally developed in the context of depression (Hammen, 1991), has expanded theoretical accounts of the time course and progression of PD.

Previous studies have demonstrated repeatedly that personality and stress are related, to the extent that individual differences in personality influence stress exposure, reactivity, and recovery (see Williams et al., 2011). Because altered stress processes are related to poor health outcomes (e.g., Reuben et al., 2016; Shields & Slavich, 2017), stressful life events and adverse life experiences represent potential mechanisms through which personality and its disorders may impact health (e.g., Gale et al., 2017; Iacovino et al., 2016; Smith et al., 2012; Timoney et al., 2017). This chapter will review existing research investigating how both "normal" personality traits and maladaptive personality traits or disorders are related to stress.

First, we acknowledge that conceptualizations and classification of maladaptive personality have been subject to close scrutiny and reevaluation in recent years. Traditional diagnostic categories have focused on specific types of PD (e.g., borderline PD) that are distinct from normative aspects of personality. Many experts now feel strongly, however, that dimensional systems focused primarily on basic personality traits, such as neuroticism (negative affectivity), conscientiousness (disinhibition), and agreeableness (antagonism), show superior construct validity for understanding both normative and pathological aspects of personality (e.g., Widiger & Mullins-Sweatt, 2010; Widiger & Trull, 2007); furthermore, many clinicians seem to favor this approach. The official diagnostic manual (*DSM-5*) now includes an alternative dimensional model in a section designated for disorders that require further study. Similarly, the next version of *The International Classification of Diseases* (*ICD-11*) will include a dimensional definition of PDs. In this chapter, we will consider evidence based on traditional diagnostic categories as well as data based on the use of basic personality traits that lie at the heart of personality pathology.

Disentangling Genetic and Environmental Influences

Many of the environmental circumstances that are theoretically implicated in the onset or exacerbation of personality pathology are partly under genetic control. Such gene–environment correlation (see Scarr & McCartney, 1983) creates the potential for interpretative problems in studies examining the pathogenic effects of life stress on risk for PD. If the same genetic liabilities that set the stage for stressful life events (e.g., mugging, divorce, contentious relationships with coworkers) also predispose to PD, then life stress and personality pathology will be non–causally related, at least to some extent. Stated differently, genetic factors potentially can serve as the primary causal factor underlying both PD and life events.

Studies of genetically related individuals are able to parse the genetic versus environmental influences on some phenotype. Such behavioral genetic investigations have conclusively shown that PDs are moderately heritable, meaning that a substantial minority of individual differences in PD risk in a sample is attributable to genetic variation (South et al., 2012). More relevant to our discussion, they are also capable of dissecting the genetic and environmental factors driving the *correlation* between phenotypes. This research design therefore has the potential to detect causal effects, if they exist, of life stress on PD. Due to the added difficulty of recruiting

genetically related people (e.g., twins), the vast majority of life stress research does not account for the potential of genetic confounding. This is as true in the PD field as it is for other psychiatric problems. Therefore, there are comparatively few studies that isolate the environmentally mediated effects of life stress on personality pathology. We review several of the most prominent behavioral genetic studies—all using twin samples—to dissect the genetic and environmental foundations of the stress–PD relationship.

Distel and coworkers examined self-reported borderline personality disorder (BPD) features in a combined sample from the Netherlands Twin Registry and the East Flanders Prospective Twin Survey. Initial studies from this dataset pointed to the possibility of life stress influences on BPD pathology, as 58% of disorder variation was accounted for by unique environmental influences (i.e., experiences that are not shared across twins, such as marriage or medical illness), whereas the remaining 42% of variance was explained by genetic factors (Distel et al., 2008). These investigators also found evidence of gene–environment correlation that linked the genetic substrate of BPD to increased likelihood of exposure to divorce, violent assault, sexual assault, and job loss (Distel et al., 2010). Nevertheless, their analyses indicated that genetic influences could not fully explain the phenotypic (i.e., observed) correlation between life stress and BPD. That is, there was evidence of causal (i.e., environmentally mediated) effects of divorce, accidents, sexual (but not violent) assault, and job loss on disorder risk (Distel et al., 2010).

In the Norwegian Twin Registry, investigators assessed PD symptoms with structured interview and monitored the occurrence of childhood traumatic events that qualified from *DSM-IV* posttraumatic stress disorder criterion A1 (i.e., an event that involved actual or threatened death or serious injury, or a threat to the physical integrity of self or others) (Berenz et al., 2013). Approximately 17% of the sample of 2,780 twins reported experiencing such a childhood stressor. In the general sample, when researchers did not adjust for genetic effects, childhood trauma significantly predicted all PDs, albeit to a very modest degree (approximately 1% of the variance across disorders). In a follow-up analysis, familial factors (e.g., shared genes, common family environment) were controlled by concentrating on a subsample of twin pairs that were discordant for trauma exposure. In the discordant twin sample, childhood trauma was significantly related only to BPD and antisocial PD symptom severity. Even for these disorders, the effect sizes were surprisingly small (less than 1% of variance explained). These findings indicate that genetic factors play a critical role in the development of PDs and require further research.

A similar discordant co-twin analysis was performed in the Minnesota Twin Family Study (Bornovalova et al., 2013). These authors used a multimodal assessment across several measurement occasions in this longitudinal study to ascertain whether participants had been exposed to physical, sexual, or emotional abuse in childhood. BPD severity was evaluated via self-report at age 24. In preliminary analyses, the research team found that exposure to all of these forms of abuse predicted greater levels of BPD features in early adulthood (r range: .12 to .24). However, paralleling results from the Norwegian Twin Registry, Bornovalova et al. (2013) found that after adjusting for common genetic influences on abuse exposure and PD, there was virtually no direct (i.e., causal) effect of childhood abuse on rates of BPD pathology.

The specter of genetic confounding threatens to undercut the validity of life stress research across psychological science. We conclude from this small, but growing, literature that genetic confounding can explain some of the observed covariation between life stress and PD. At the same time, there is solid evidence—in the PD literature and for other stress-liked disorders (e.g., Kendler, Karkowski, & Prescott, 1999)—that part of the stress–PD association is causal. We advise that more genetically informative research is needed to resolve the true size of the causal effect of life stress—in childhood and throughout the life span—on PD risk. Further, in typical correlational designs, investigators can raise awareness for the possibility of confounding by acknowledging the inferential limitations of standard observational studies on life stress.

Childhood Adversity and the Development of Personality Disorders

Twin studies have demonstrated conclusively that nongenetic factors do have an impact on the development of personality, although it is still unclear to what extent. For example, much of the variance in trait neuroticism measured in identical twins is explained by life experiences that they did not share (Keller et al., 2005; Lake et al., 2000), suggesting that life experiences, including exposure to stressful life events, shape the way in which personality develops. Both interpersonal and attachment perspectives

have generated significant research in this area, guiding empirical work on the consequences of early childhood adversity and its impact on personality pathology. Many researchers have hypothesized that the development of PDs is largely the result of childhood adversity and maladaptive early attachment to caregivers, as well as experiences of childhood abuse and neglect (Bowlby, 1969; Levy, 2005; Skodol et al., 2005). Exposure to poverty, parental conflict, low closeness to parents, punishments characterized by guilt or aggression, and parental death and illness during childhood and adolescence have also been found to be predictive of the development of PD symptoms later in life (Cohen et al., 2005; Crawford et al., 2009), particularly BPD and antisocial PD (e.g., Afifi et al., 2011; Battle et al. 2004). Childhood adversity may lead to the development of insecure attachment styles, which may lay the groundwork for the development of the maladaptive emotion regulation abilities and coping behaviors that characterize many PDs (Bateman & Fonagy, 2010; Levy et al., 2005; Shaver & Mikulincer, 2008).

Studies concerned with the influence of stressful childhood experiences and the development of PDs have focused largely on BPD (see Zanarini, 2000, for review). BPD is typically a chronic mental disorder characterized by instability in identity, interpersonal relationships, and affective responses. Individuals diagnosed with BPD exhibit impulsive behaviors, often in the form of high-risk behaviors including self-injury, angry outbursts, substance abuse, and suicidal behavior. They may experience impaired functioning in multiple domains of life such as health and occupational functioning (American Psychiatric Association, 2013). BPD patients report significantly greater childhood adversity, particularly abuse (Soloff, Lynch, & Kelly, 2002) and neglect (Johnson et al., 2000), more so than individuals with other PDs (Battle et al., 2004; Skodol et al., 2005; Zanarini et al., 1989), suggesting that stressful life experiences in childhood may place an individual at a greater risk of developing BPD compared to other PDs. The McLean Study of Adult Development (MSAD), a longitudinal investigation of individuals diagnosed with BPD, found that over 90% of their sample reported experiences of abuse and/or neglect before the age of 18 years (Zanarini et al., 2005). In particular, BPD patients tend to report a high rate of childhood sexual abuse, with some studies reporting rates as high as 50%–70% (Paris, 2001), and these traumas tend to be more severe and occur at an earlier age for individuals who later develop BPD compared to other PDs (Skodol et al., 2005). In addition, BPD patients often report abuse and neglect being perpetrated by both of their parents (Zanarini et al., 2005).

The findings regarding childhood adversity and BPD should be interpreted with caution, of course, because this area of research faces a number of methodological challenges. For example, most studies must depend on retrospective recall for the measurement of exposure to childhood abuse and neglect. These reports provide useful information, but they also may underestimate the frequency of childhood adversity (e.g., Widom & Shepard, 1996), possibly reducing power to detect associations with personality and other adult outcomes. Another challenge involves the need to account for the influence of potential third variables. Their constant presence makes it difficult to determine if a specific form of trauma leads to the development of personality pathology, or if the cumulative effect of other forms of adversity and disadvantage may be to blame. Because child abuse is usually accompanied by a wide variety of dysfunctional family dynamics (e.g., Herrenkohl et al., 2008; Nash et al., 1993), it is difficult to determine which stressors are most harmful. Thus, even though research has found a relationship between BPD and childhood abuse, the specific role of abuse in the development of BPD remains unclear.

Although many studies have reported an association between childhood adversity and personality pathology, stressful experiences in childhood do not lead invariably to the development of PDs or maladaptive traits (see Paris, 2001, for review). Furthermore, childhood adversity may increase a person's risk of developing psychopathology in general rather than personality pathology in particular; similar experiences of abuse or neglect increase risk for many different types of adjustment problems (Tyrka et al., 2009). For example, in studies utilizing clinical populations, patients diagnosed with a wide variety of mental illnesses tend to report significantly more adverse experiences during childhood compared to healthy controls (e.g., Rutter & Maughan, 1997). When community samples are examined, however, only a small minority of individuals with similar experiences of childhood adversity goes on to develop mental disorders, including various PDs (e.g., DuMont et al., 2007; Garmezy & Masten, 1994). These findings suggest that individuals who do develop personality pathology following childhood adversity may have a more specific (or a multifaceted) form of vulnerability that contributed

to this specific phenotype. Determining the specific nature of these vulnerabilities will obviously be an important direction for future research.

Some investigators have suggested that the distinction between individuals who achieve positive adaptation in the face of childhood adversity and those who later develop mental disorders is rooted in factors such as biological temperament and intelligence. That is, compensatory adaptive traits or greater intelligence can serve to reduce the negative impact of childhood adversity on mental health (Afifi & MacMillan, 2011; Paris, 2001). There are also sex differences in responses to childhood trauma. One study suggested that females show lower vulnerability than males in terms of the onset of future mental disorders (DuMont et al., 2007), but another found that females abused as children may be at greater risk of developing BPD compared to males (e.g., Tyrka et al., 2009). Psychosocial buffers may also account for differences in responses to stressful childhood experiences. For example, research suggests that the more time a child spends with healthy caregivers, the more likely he or she will achieve adaptive outcomes after experiencing trauma (e.g., Afifi & MacMillan, 2011; Anthony & Cohler, 1987; Ludy-Dobson & Perry, 2010). This finding suggests that positive social influences may serve to buffer the effects of childhood stress on the development of psychopathology. Future studies investigating positive outcomes in the context of childhood adversity may help ascertain how these variables serve to shield an individual from subsequent disorder.

The main conclusion that can be drawn from the existing literature regarding the effect of childhood adversity on the development of personality pathology is that childhood adversity does not seem to have a specific relationship to mental disorders, including personality pathology (Paris, 1999; Rutter, 1989). Many mental illnesses, including PDs, are related to similar experiences of childhood stress, suggesting that other factors influence the progression of disorder. Future studies may shed light on the nature of these inherent susceptibilities, as well as psychosocial and biological mechanisms that lead to differential outcomes among individuals who experience similar stressors.

Personality Disorders and Stress Generation

Historically, it has been presumed that the association between life stress and psychopathology is unidirectional, such that stressors trigger new onsets of disorder and contribute to the progression or recurrence of existing syndromes. Although this perspective has been supported by decades of systematic observation, recent work consistently demonstrates that people partially control their own environmental circumstances. In turn, certain maladaptive traits—including those in the PD domain—predispose some to encounter more than their fair share of stressful events.

Stress generation theory (Hammen, 1991) proposes that psychopathological states and traits, particularly depression, cause people to evoke or select into stressful environments. Similarly, the observation of gene–environment correlation (e.g., Scarr & McCartney, 1983) demonstrates that inherited genetic vulnerabilities—possibly mediated through temperament and personality characteristics—can shape our environments. This leads to the paradoxical result that many "environmental" variables are moderately heritable (Kendler & Baker, 2007). Similar theories in personality psychology, such as person-environment fit (Roberts & Pomerantz, 2004) and the correspondence principle (Caspi et al., 2005), also dictate that preexisting personality styles can have a major influence on environmental exposures. These personal characteristics lead us to select into particular social, educational, and occupational niches, which often in turn amplify those salient characteristics (e.g., an extraverted adolescent seeking out gregarious peers, who in turn influence the adolescent to be even more outgoing).

Hammen (1991, 2006) applied these ideas to understand the stressful environments of depressed women. Her initial findings showed that women with a history of depression encountered substantially more stressful life events than nondepressed and medically ill counterparts. This was true for a particular class of stressor called dependent stress, which refers to events that are under personal control, at least to some extent, such as a romantic breakup or job loss due to poor performance. The stress generation effect was especially pronounced for dependent stressors that were interpersonal in nature, such as conflicts with close friends and relatives, as opposed to noninterpersonal events like a car accident or disappointing report card. In contrast, as one might expect, depressed women were no more likely than others to encounter so-called independent events that were entirely fateful (e.g., natural disaster, death of close relative). Subsequent studies support the stress generation theory in depression, documenting the stress generation effect in children (Rudolph & Hammen, 1999), adolescents

(Hammen & Brennan, 2001; Patton et al., 2003), and adults (Chun, Cronkite, & Moos, 2004). Furthermore, results suggested that the effect operated even when patients were not in the midst of a depressive episode, indicating that some state-independent vulnerability factor related to depression might be driving the process of stress generation.

Although research is in its early stages, there is evidence to suggest that the stress generation effect also applies to PDs, not just major depression. One line of studies reported robust stress generation effects for Cluster B PDs (i.e., antisocial, BPD, histrionic, narcissistic), such that these were prospectively related to elevated rates of interpersonal dependent stressors in young women (e.g., Daley et al., 1998; Iacoviello, Alloy, Abramson, Whitehouse, & Hogan, 2007; Ilardi, Craighead, & Evans, 1997). For instance, over 4 years of follow-up, high school students with greater BPD symptoms were more prone to experience romantic conflict, partner abuse, and unwanted pregnancy (Daley, Burge, & Hammen, 2000). These associations were observed across all Cluster B conditions and major depressive disorder, but effect sizes may be greatest for BPD because the salience of interpersonal disruptions (e.g., abandonment fears, tumultuous relationships) is most prominent in that disorder. A wealth of clinical research on BPD and other PDs does strongly suggest that these conditions set the stage for interpersonal dysfunction (for a meta-analysis, see Wilson, Stroud, & Durbin, 2017).

Stress generation research indicates that even subclinical symptoms of PDs can influence the generation of subsequent stressful life events. In recent years, researchers are increasingly adopting a dimensional approach to PD phenotypes. Not only are they treating the symptoms of any diagnostic category as a continuous index of disorder severity, they are also focusing on the normal- and abnormal-range personality traits that form the scaffolding of PD categories (e.g., Widiger & Trull, 2007). Neuroticism, a risk factor for most, if not all, PDs, has been perhaps most heavily examined as a predictor of stressful events. In one of the best tests of the reciprocal associations between person and environment, Jeronimus and colleagues (2014) showed in a 16-year study of personality and life experiences that not only did negative life events predict fluctuations in neuroticism, but trait elevations were in turn associated with greater exposure to negative life events. Several other studies have documented this same phenomenon, finding neuroticism to be longitudinally associated with more daily hassles, acute stressors, and ongoing strains (e.g., Gunthert, Cohen, & Armeli, 1999; Kercher et al., 2009).

To a lesser extent, other traits underpinning PDs have been investigated as part of the stress generation process. Impulsivity, which combines with neuroticism to form the substrate of most Cluster B syndromes, is a likely candidate to provoke stressful events. At least one study has detected stress-generating effects of trait impulsivity (Liu & Kleiman, 2012). Other research teams have reported that disinhibition, arguably the temperamental foundation of antisocial behavior disorders such as antisocial PD, prospectively predicts elevated rates of chronic and acute stressful events in high-risk adolescents and adults (Conway, Hammen, & Brennan, 2012; Snyder, Young, & Hankin, 2017). Other trait vulnerability markers for PDs—such as avoidant and anxious attachment, dependency, and reassurance-seeking—appear to set the stage for life stress as well (e.g., Hankin et al., 2005; Shahar et al., 2004; Shih et al., 2009).

Our own prospective study of older adults, called the St. Louis Personality and Aging Network (SPAN), integrates these developing literatures on personality traits and disorders as instigators of stressful life events. We recruited a representative sample of 1,630 community residents who were between the ages of 55 and 64 at the time of baseline assessment (for sampling details see Oltmanns, Rodrigues, Weinstein, & Gleason, 2014). Participants completed a comprehensive assessment focused on normal-range personality traits as well as PDs. Informant reports of these same traits (in the identified participant) were also gathered. We assessed stressful life events in a two-stage process. First, participants indicated via questionnaire which (if any) in a list of 15 threatening events they had experienced in the past 6 months (or since their last study contact). Then, investigators telephoned participants who had endorsed serious stressors to probe the timing and circumstances of each event in order to ensure that they were indeed major negative life events (as opposed to daily hassles, positive events, or life events that caused insufficient disruption during the specified timeframe). Finally, we measured a range of health, social, and occupational outcomes that we hypothesized to be related to PDs. All the aforementioned assessments were repeated at various follow-up occasions.

Our first report from SPAN examined interviewer-rated symptoms of all 10 *DSM-IV* PDs and neuroticism as predictors of stressful life events over the first 6 months of follow-up (Gleason, Powers, &

Oltmanns, 2012). Only BPD symptoms ($r = .23$) and neuroticism ($r = .17$) exhibited statistically significant zero-order associations with the rate of stressful life event exposure over the follow-up interval. As expected, neuroticism was moderately correlated with BPD features as well ($r = .40$). Nonetheless, in multivariate analyses, both constructs retained significant associations with stress exposure. Further, avoidant and paranoid PD symptoms emerged as protective factors against stressful events, despite a small, positive zero-order correlation between these variables. We speculated that social isolation, although arguably itself a chronically stressful experience, puts a ceiling on the chances of experiencing interpersonal and occupational conflict among people at risk for these conditions.

We extended this finding by examining the prospective influence of PDs on stress exposure across a longer timeframe in a subsequent study (Powers, Gleason, & Oltmanns, 2013). In this investigation, we also analyzed the content of life stressors in more detail. Specifically, consistent with Hammen's (1991) original taxonomy, we distinguished between events potentially under participants' control (i.e., dependent stressors) versus fateful events (i.e., independent stressors). Our results showed that BPD and histrionic PD were related to elevated dependent stress over 6-, 12-, and 18-month follow-up occasions. When we isolated interpersonal dependent events, BPD was the only remaining significant predictor.

These two reports clearly indicated that BPD pathology accounted for much of the connection between the PD domain and future exposure to dependent stress. We then extended this line of work by concentrating on the dynamic associations between stress exposure and BPD over 5 years in SPAN (Conway, Boudreaux, & Oltmanns, in press). Not only was this the longest follow-up period yet investigated in the literature on life stress and BPD, but we also engineered a multimodal assessment of BPD personality features. That is, we created a latent variable reflecting the shared variance among the Structured Interview for DSM-IV Personality, Multi-source Assessment of Personality Pathology, and NEO Personality Inventory–Revised. These measures, along with our typical interview assessment of life stress, were administered on three occasions, each separated by approximately 2.5 years.

Figure 8.1 presents the results from our autoregressive cross-lagged model. We found strong, but imperfect, stability among the BPD pathology factor scores across assessment waves ($rs > .90$). After adjusting for this continuity in BPD pathology, life

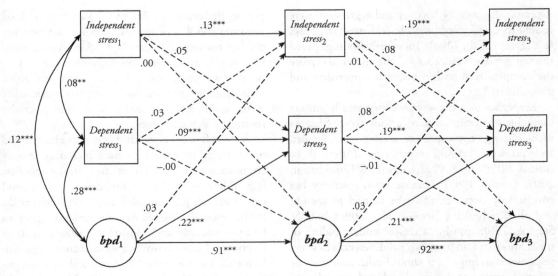

Figure 8.1 Autoregressive cross-lagged model of borderline pathology and life stress over 5 years. Dashed lines denote statistically nonsignificant effects. (see Conway, Boudreaux, and Oltmanns, 2018 for more complete information).

stress had virtually no prospective influence on BPD personality features. In contrast, BPD pathology predicted increases in subsequent dependent events (i.e., stressors to which individuals may have contributed), but not independent events (i.e., fateful stressors), exposure over time. This pattern of associations is consistent with a stress generation effect. Thus, the SPAN dataset did not provide support for a dynamic view of PD and environmental stress mutually reinforcing one another over time, although the absence of a "stress exposure" effect was possibly related to the inertia of BPD pathology which seems to emerge among older adults.

Collectively, the available evidence signals that PD and its constituent traits can be influential stress-generating mechanisms. This conclusion probably comes as no surprise to clinicians, who observe first-hand the dependent stressors that characterize this population. Further, not all traits are equally potent vulnerability factors; BPD and other Cluster B syndromes appear to create the most havoc. Again, this result is consistent with clinical experience with BPD patients, who have the reputation among practitioners of leading somewhat chaotic lives, especially with respect to social relationships (Lieb, Zanarini, Schmahl, Linehan, & Bohus, 2004). It remains to be seen which exact trait components of BPD pathology (e.g., negative affect, impulsivity, antagonism)—and, possibly, interactions thereof—are driving the connection with life stress.

We propose that the next phase of research on stress generation should examine causal models that test whether increased exposure to dependent stress

acts as a maintenance factor for personality disorder and comorbid health outcomes. Stated differently, we should evaluate whether heightened exposure to romantic conflict in the context of, say, BPD in fact sets the stage for worsening BPD symptoms. Such meditational tests of course require longitudinal studies with intensive follow-up data structures. Finally, it is well established that PDs—especially BPD—are often accompanied by enduring psychosocial impairment, even during periods of remission (e.g., Gunderson et al., 2011). Future research is needed to test whether stress generation might explain this long-term dysfunction, such that acutely symptomatic periods provoke major, long-term stressors (e.g., job loss, medical illness) that limit social, occupational, and leisure functioning for years to come, even after symptoms have abated.

Personality Disorders as Moderators of Stress Reactivity

Maladaptive personality characteristics can also affect ways in which people respond to stressors, both psychologically and physiologically (e.g., Cohen & Edwards, 1989; Nater et al., 2010). Interest in the connection between personality and response to stress can be traced back to early work on stress reactivity and Type A personality, which was characterized by ambition, aggression, and anxiety. In comparison, Type B personality was characterized by a more tolerant and relaxed demeanor. Studies investigating Type A personality and stress responses were largely inconclusive (Carroll, 1992), but they did provide evidence that particular facets of Type

A personality, namely hostility and aggression, were related to exaggerated physiological stress responses (e.g., Smith et al., 2004). These early findings paved the way for later work that has continued to explore the complex relationship between personality and stress reactivity.

Responses to acute stressors vary greatly among individuals and depend upon a wide array of factors including cognitive appraisals, coping styles, gender, and previous stressful experiences (Alsentali & Anshel, 2015; Carroll, 1992; Kudielka & Kirschbaum, 2005; Lovallo, 1997). Because stress reactivity has consistently been found to be related to mental and physical health (Carroll et al., 2009; Chida & Steptoe, 2010), gaining a clearer understanding of the factors that lead to individual differences in stress responses is an important public health concern. For example, exaggerated cortisol and cardiovascular reactivity to stress have been linked to coronary artery calcification, depression, and inflammatory diseases (Hamer et al., 2010; Holsboer, 2000; Mason, 1991). Blunted physiological stress responses are also linked to a variety of negative health outcomes, including obesity, substance dependence, and lower self-reported health (Carroll et al., 2008; Lovallo, 2007; Phillips et al., 2012). It has been suggested that abnormal stress responses are indicative of dysregulation in motivational brain circuitry, leading to poor health behaviors (Lovallo, 2011). Thus, understanding how personality traits are related to stress reactivity may lead to important advances in public health.

Personality Traits and Response to Laboratory Stressors

Studies of reactivity to laboratory stressors have found that personality accounts for ample psychological and physiological variability in stress responses. For instance, Childs and colleagues (2014) studied self-reported personality traits in relation to reactions to the Trier Social Stress Test (TSST), a laboratory stressor designed to elicit stress responses in both the sympatho-adrenomedullary (SAM) and hypothalamic-pituitary-adrenal (HPA) axes. These researchers measured participants' salivary cortisol as an index of HPA axis reactivity, heart rate, and blood pressure (SAM axis measures), as well as emotional responses to the TSST. Their results indicated that personality accounted for 11% of the variance in participant emotional responses. Specifically, those individuals who scored higher on a measure of emotional negativity, a construct similar to neuroticism, exhibited significantly greater aversive mood during recovery from the stressor. In addition,

personality explained 8% of the variance in blood pressure, and 4% of the variance in heart rate and cortisol responses. Interestingly, the proportion of variance in stress responses accounted for by personality was comparable to demographic variables, including race and sex, indicating that personality is just as important to consider in stress reactivity research as demographics.

Although many personality traits have been found to be related to stress responses, including conscientiousness (e.g., Childs et al., 2014), openness (e.g., Bibbey et al., 2013; Schneider et al., 2011), and extraversion (e.g., Schneider, 2004; Schneider et al., 2011), research suggests that neuroticism tends to be most strongly and consistently related to stress responses. Neuroticism is a well-documented risk factor for various mental and physical illnesses, including depression (Forbes, 2009; Mezulis et al., 2010; Morris et al., 2010; Siegrist, 2008) and cardiovascular disease (Lahey, 2009). The link between neuroticism and poor health outcomes may be largely due to altered stress responses. An abundance of research has found that neuroticism is significantly related to abnormal stress responses, even after controlling for potential confounding variables such as sex, age, socioeconomic status, smoking, and body mass index (e.g., Bibbey et al., 2013). However, the influence of neuroticism on stress responses appears to be different for psychological versus physiological stress responses. Research consistently finds that individuals higher in neuroticism tend to have greater negative emotions, perceptions, and thoughts when introduced to a stressor compared to those lower in neuroticism (e.g., Childs et al., 2014; Schneider 2004). Indeed, neuroticism and negative psychological responses to stress are overlapping constructs. On the other hand, the relationship between physiological stress responses and neuroticism seems to be more complicated. Many studies have found that higher neuroticism is related to blunted cortisol responses (e.g., Kirschbaum et al., 1993; Oswald et al., 2006; Phillips et al., 2005), whereas other studies have found the opposite relationship or no relationship at all between cortisol and neuroticism (e.g., Kirschbaum et al., 1995; Schommer et al., 1999; Wirtz et al., 2007). Cardiovascular measures of stress reactivity tend to yield more consistent results in relation to neuroticism. Specifically, a meta-analysis of 71 studies indicated that high neuroticism is associated with blunted cardiovascular reactivity (Chida & Hamer, 2008).

The discordant cortisol findings in relation to neuroticism may be due to several factors. For instance, many studies suffer from a lack of statistical power, making it less likely that an effect will be found (e.g., Kirschbaum et al., 1995). In addition, arbitrary categorization of neuroticism scores (Hutchinson & Ruiz, 2011), a lack of variability in neuroticism scores, and insufficient laboratory stressors are common methodological issues plaguing research on neuroticism and stress (e.g., Williams et al., 2009). Because the HPA axis is notoriously difficult to activate in laboratory settings, future research on neuroticism and stress should utilize stressors that have been shown to elicit the largest cortisol responses, such as the TSST (see Dickerson & Kemeny, 2004). Additionally, sex differences in HPA reactivity to laboratory stressors have been observed in many studies (Kudielka & Kirschbaum, 2005), suggesting that it may be beneficial to further research the role of sex in the relationship between personality and stress reactivity. Lastly, although stress responses change over the course of the life span (e.g., Kudielka et al., 2009), most studies investigating neuroticism and stress have employed college-aged participants (Verschoor & Markus, 2011). High cortisol responses to stressors initiate a negative feedback process that gradually down-regulates the HPA axis (McEwen, 1998, 1999). Thus, individuals with high cortisol responses in youth may eventually show blunted cortisol responses later in life. In line with this hypothesis, research involving older participants does tend to show that highly neurotic individuals exhibit blunted cortisol responses (e.g., Bibbey et al., 2013), while studies involving younger participants tend to show no association between neuroticism and cortisol reactivity (e.g., Kirschbaum et al., 1992; Williams et al., 2009). Future research should consider developmental changes in stress responses (and personality, for that matter) when investigating neuroticism and stress.

Future research should attempt to determine the relationship between stress reactivity and personality traits such as conscientiousness, extraversion, agreeableness, and openness. It would undoubtedly prove beneficial to dissect these traits into facets and determine if these facets are uniquely related to stress physiology of both the HPA and SAM axes, as well as affective and cognitive responses to stressors. Perhaps only certain facets of these traits are related to certain aspects of stress reactivity. Additionally, future research will benefit from comparing the physiological effects of different types of acute stressors on individuals to determine if these traits are uniquely related to stress reactivity but only for specific types of stressors. For instance, extraverted individuals may not be reactive to stress induced by negative social evaluation, as in the TSST, but they may be responsive to stress induced by other factors such as physical exertion. Comparing stress reactivity across different types of stressors may show that these traits are related to stress reactivity but only in specific contexts.

Another important direction for future research is to determine the mechanisms by which personality influences stress. Although personality is thought to affect stress responses in multiple ways, past work has focused largely on the relationship between personality and appraisals of stress. Stress responses are heavily influenced by cognitive appraisals of both the stressor and one's own ability to cope with a stressor (see Lazarus, 1999). If an individual interprets a stressor as being beyond their ability to cope, it is said that they have appraised the stressor as being a threat. On the other hand, if an individual interprets a stressor as being manageable in relation to his or her ability to cope, it is said the individual has appraised the stressor as being a challenge (Lazarus, 1999). Threat appraisals, compared to challenge appraisals, tend to result in exaggerated physiological stress responses (e.g., Schneider, 2004; Tomaka, Blascovich, Kelsey, & Leitten, 1993). Given evidence that personality can affect how an individual interprets a stressor (e.g., Kaplan, 1996; Magnus et al., 1993; Schneider et al., 2011), appraisals may be one mechanism by which personality influences stress responses.

Previous studies have supported this notion, showing that specific personality traits are related to differential appraisals of laboratory stressors. For instance, high trait assertiveness is related to greater challenge appraisals compared to threat appraisals of an impending stressor (Tomaka et al., 1999). Neuroticism may be particularly influential with regard to stressor appraisals. Schneider found that neuroticism was related to more threat appraisals compared to challenge appraisals (Schneider, 2004; Schneider et al., 2011). Theoretically, neuroticism may cause an individual to allocate more attention to negative aspects of stressors and potential negative consequences, which in turn may lead to an increase in threat appraisals. Some studies have found that extraversion is related to significantly greater confidence in one's ability to cope with stressors (e.g., Penley & Tomaka, 2002), while others have found no significant relationship between challenge appraisals and extraversion (e.g., Schneider, 2004). Dissecting broad personality traits like neuroticism and extraversion into their facets may help to explain what aspects of personality are affecting stress appraisals.

Personality Pathology and Response to Laboratory Stressors

Stress response in BPD has been the topic of many research studies. Individuals with BPD tend to be more susceptible to negative emotional responses to social threats or rejection (Domes et al., 2009), reporting greater shame in response to negative evaluations (Gratz et al., 2010), suggesting their responses to social stressors may be unique compared to other types of stressors. It has been suggested that individuals with BPD are more susceptible to social stress because their emotional regulation mechanisms are inadequate, causing their physiological stress response to be exaggerated or blunted. This idea is supported by studies indicating that many individuals with BPD exhibit reduced negative feedback of the HPA axis (i.e., the biological process by which the HPA axis returns to normal functioning after a stressor has passed). Reduced feedback may result in an excess of cortisol for some people with BPD (Zimmerman & Choi-Kain, 2009), while other BPD patients exhibit blunted cortisol responses to stressors (for a review, see Zimmerman & Choi-Kain, 2009). Individuals with BPD also tend to show slower physiological recovery from stressors (Walter et al., 2008), which further supports the notion that HPA axis negative feedback processes are compromised in this population. Imaging studies have indicated that individuals with BPD, particularly women with BPD, exhibit diminished hippocampal gray matter as well as increased hypothalamic volume compared to healthy controls, and these structural differences are related to trauma history (Kuhlmann et al., 2013), suggesting potential neurobiological mechanisms by which BPD may lead to abnormal stress responses. The specific nature and intensity of HPA dysregulation in individuals with BPD appears to be related to the severity of their symptoms, the nature of their traumatic history, and comorbid diagnoses including depression and posttraumatic stress disorder (Zimmerman & Choi-Kain, 2009). Further research is clearly required to fully understand what factors are leading to either increases or decreases in cortisol reactivity among BPD patients.

Social cognition research has found that individuals with BPD exhibit deficits in social cognitive processes, such as facial affect recognition, but primarily while under stress (Daros et al., 2013). Thus, the social maladjustment that characterizes BPD may be due in part to the fact that individuals with BPD exhibit exaggerated stress responses, particularly to social stressors, and this exaggerated response can interfere with their social cognitive abilities, which then contributes to further social difficulties. Future research is still required as other studies have found no evidence of altered physiological stress responses or social cognition in BPD samples (e.g., Deckers et al., 2015). Deckers and colleagues (2015) suggest that mixed results regarding BPD and stress reactivity may be due to the effects of comorbid depression. In the future, incorporating a depression measure may help determine if depressive symptoms are driving the potential relationship between BPD and stress reactivity.

The unique relationship between BPD and stress may also be related, at least in part, to increased impulsivity (e.g., Gagnon et al., 2013), a defining characteristic of BPD. In laboratory settings, tasks developed to measure impulsive decision making have indicated greater impulsivity among individuals diagnosed with BPD (e.g., Svaldi et al., 2012). Impulsivity is particularly heightened in individuals with BPD who are confronted with social stressors, including perceived rejection or abandonment (Berenson et al., 2011; Brodsky et al., 2006; Coifman et al., 2012; Welch & Linehan, 2002; Yen et al., 2005). For example, images depicting negative social experiences elicit greater emotional and physiological stress reactivity in individuals with BPD compared to control participants (Limberg et al., 2011; Sauer et al., 2014). Increased rejection sensitivity and greater stress responses to social stimuli suggest that individuals with BPD tend to be uniquely sensitive to social stressors. It is important to keep in mind, however, that individuals with BPD also show an exaggerated stress response to noninterpersonal stressors, suggesting that their problems with emotional regulation may result in a general tendency to overreact to all stressors (Berenson et al., 2016). Thus, impulsivity, a hallmark of BPD, may cause individuals with BPD to exhibit exaggerated stress responses which could lead to the development of stress-related disorders. Consistent with this idea, BPD has been linked to an increased risk of stress-related health outcomes such as obesity, diabetes, and hypertension (Frankenburg & Zanarini, 2004). Interventions targeting impulsivity in BPD, particularly in interpersonal contexts, may be useful in helping individuals with BPD prevent or delay the onset of stress-related diseases.

Conclusions

The relationship between stress and PDs is complex and bidirectional. Research suggests that personality pathology can develop, at least in part, as a result of stressful or traumatic life events, particularly childhood experiences of abuse and neglect. Although the effects of early childhood adversity are clearly nonspecific, portending a wide array of psychopathologies, they are undeniably important in the genesis of personality disorders and therefore feature prominently in most PD etiological traditions. Future research should attempt to determine the factors influencing susceptibility to the development of (as well as resistance to) specific forms of personality pathology. Where possible, we note also that genetically informative research designs will be valuable in trying to identify ways in which genetic factors work in combination with stressful experiences in promoting the development of personality pathology.

Considering the effects of personality on future stress, certain personality characteristics and disorders have been found to be associated with an increase in the probability of experiencing both future major stressful experiences and daily hassles. According to the stress generation theory, personality characteristics can cause individuals to place themselves in situations that lead to stressful life experiences. In particular, research indicates that BPD symptoms play a significant role in the generation of stressful life events. In the future, research should examine which exact trait components, or combination of components, of BPD pathology (e.g., neuroticism, impulsivity, antagonism) are contributing to the generation of stress. Also, we propose that future stress generation research should investigate causal models testing whether increased exposure to dependent stress serves to reinforce or maintain mental disorder and comorbid health outcomes.

Previous research has also consistently demonstrated that individual differences in personality influence stress reactivity and recovery. Because altered stress processes, both psychological and physiological, are related to poor health outcomes, stressful life events may serve as an important mechanism by which personality and personality pathology impact both physical and mental health. Neuroticism seems to be a particularly significant predictor of stress reactivity, suggesting that this trait may play a critical role in the development of stress-related health problems. Dissecting personality traits, particularly neuroticism, into facets to determine their potentially uniquely relationship to psychological and physiological stress reactivity is an important direction for future research. Additionally, this line of research should investigate the effects of personality on reactivity to different types of stressors. By comparing stress reactivity across different types of stressors, we may find that certain traits are related to stress reactivity but only in certain contexts. Lastly, subsequent studies should attempt to discern the specific processes by which personality influences stress reactivity.

References

Afifi, T. O., & MacMillan, H. L. (2011). Resilience following child maltreatment: A review of protective factors. *The Canadian Journal of Psychiatry, 56*(5), 266–272.

Afifi, T. O., Mather, A., Boman, J., Fleisher, W., Enns, M. W., MacMillian, H., & Sareen, J. (2011). Childhood adversity and personality disorders: Results from a nationally representative population-based study. *Journal of Psychiatric Research, 45*, 814–822. doi:10.1016/j.jpsychires.2010.11.008

Alsentali, A. M., & Anshel, M. H. (2015). Relationship between internal and external acute stressors and coping style. *Journal of Sport Behavior, 38*(4), 357–375.

American Psychiatric Association. (2013). *Diagnostic and statistical manual of mental disorders* (5th ed.). Arlington, VA: Author.

Anthony, E. J., & Cohler, B. J. (Eds.). (1987). *The invulnerable child*. New York, NY: Guilford Press.

Bateman, A., & Fonagy, P. (2010). Mentalization based treatment for borderline personality disorder. *World Psychiatry, 9*(1), 11–15.

Battle, C. L., Shea, M. T., Johnson, D. M., Yen, S., Zlotnick, C., Zanarini, M. C.,...Morey, L. C. (2004). Childhood maltreatment associated with adult personality disorders: Findings from the Collaborative Longitudinal Personality Disorders Study. *Journal of Personality Disorders, 18*(2), 193–211.

Berenson, K. R., Downey, G., Rafaeli, E., Coifman, K. G., & Leventhal Paquin, N. (2011). The rejection-rage contingency in borderline personality disorder. *Journal of Abnormal Psychology, 120*, 681–690.

Berenson, K. R., Gregory, W. E., Glaser, E., Romirowsky, A., Rafaeli, E., Yang, X., & Downey, G. (2016). Impulsivity, rejection sensitivity, and reactions to stressors in borderline personality disorder. *Cognitive Therapy and Research, 40*, 510–521.

Berenz, E. C., Amstadter, A. B., Aggen, S. H., Knudsen, G. P., Reichborn-Kjennerud, T., Gardner, C. O., & Kendler, K. S. (2013). Childhood trauma and personality disorder criterion counts: A co-twin control analysis. *Journal of Abnormal Psychology, 122*(4), 1070–1076. http://doi.org/10.1037/a0034238

Bibbey, A., Carroll, D., Roseboom, T. J., Phillips, A. C., & de Rooij, S. R. (2013). Personality and physiological reactions to acute psychological stress. *International Journal of Psychophysiology, 90*, 28–36. doi:/10.1016/j.ijpsycho.2012.10.018

Bornovalova, M. A., Huibregtse, B. M., Hicks, B. M., Keyes, M., McGue, M., & Iacono, W. (2013). Tests of a direct effect of childhood abuse on adult borderline personality disorder traits: A longitudinal discordant twin design. *Journal of Abnormal Psychology, 122*(1), 180–194. http://doi.org/10.1037/a0028328

Bowlby, J. (1969). *Attachment and loss, Vol. 1: Attachment*. New York, NY: Basic Books.

Brodsky, B. S., Groves, S. A., Oquendo, M. A., Mann, J., & Stanley, B. (2006). Interpersonal precipitants and suicide attempts in borderline personality disorder. *Suicide and Life-Threatening Behavior, 36*(3), 313–322.

Carroll, D. (1992). *Health psychology: Stress, behaviour and disease.* Bristol, PA: The Falmer Press.

Carroll, D., Phillips, A. C., & Der, G. (2008). Body mass index, abdominal adiposity, obesity, and cardiovascular reactions to psychological stress in a large community sample. *Psychosomatic Medicine, 70*(6), 653–660. doi:10.1097/PSY.0b013e31817b9382

Carroll, D., Lovallo, W. R., & Phillips, A. C. (2009). Are large physiological reactions to acute psychological stress always bad for health? *Social and Personality Psychology Compass, 3,* 725–743. doi:10.1111/j.1751-9004.2009.00205.x

Caspi, A., Roberts, B. W., & Shiner, R. L. (2005). Personality development: Stability and change. *Annual Review of Psychology, 56,* 453–484. doi:10.1146/annurev.psych.55.090902.141913

Chida, Y., & Hamer, M. (2008). Chronic psychosocial factors and acute physiological responses to laboratory-induced stress in healthy populations: A quantitative review of 30 years of investigations. *Psychological Bulletin, 134,* 829–885.

Chida, Y., & Steptoe, A. (2010). Greater cardiovascular responses to laboratory mental stress are associated with poor subsequent cardiovascular risk status: A meta-analysis of prospective evidence. *Hypertension, 55,* 1026–1032. doi:10.1161/HYPERTENSIONAHA.109.146621

Childs, E., White, T., & de Wit, H. (2014). Personality traits modulate emotional and physiological responses to stress. *Behavioral Pharmacology, 25,* 493–502. doi:10.1097/FBP.0000000000000064.

Chun, C., Cronkite, R. C., & Moos, R. H. (2004). Stress generation in depressed patients and community controls. *Journal of Social and Clinical Psychology, 23*(3), 390–412.

Cohen, S., Crawford, T. N., Johnson, J. G., & Kasen, S. (2005). The children in the community study of developmental course of personality disorder. *Journal of Personality Disorder, 19*(5), 466–486.

Cohen, S., & Edwards, J. R. (1989). Personality characteristics as moderators of the relationship between stress and disorder. In R. W. J. Neufeld (Ed.), *Wiley series on health psychology/behavioral medicine. Advances in the investigation of psychological stress* (pp. 235–283). Oxford, UK: John Wiley.

Coifman, K. G., Berenson, K. R., Rafaeli, E., & Downey, G. (2012). From negative to positive and back again: Polarized affective and relational experience in borderline personality disorder. *Journal of Abnormal Psychology, 121,* 668–679.

Conway, C., Boudreaux, M., & Oltmanns, T. F. (in press). Dynamic associations between borderline personality disorder and stressful life events over five years in older adults. *Personality Disorders: Theory, Research, and Treatment.*

Conway, C. C., Hammen, C., & Brennan, P. A. (2012). Expanding stress generation theory: Test of a transdiagnostic model. *Journal of Abnormal Psychology, 121*(3), 754–766. doi:10.1037/a0027457

Crawford, T.N., Cohen, P.B., Chen, H., Anglin, D.M., & Ehrensaft, M. (2009). Early maternal separation and the trajectory of borderline personality disorder symptoms. *Development and Psychopathology, 21,* 1013–1030.

Daley, S. E., Burge, D., & Hammen, C. (2000). Borderline personality disorder symptoms as predictors of 4-year romantic relationship dysfunction in young women: Addressing issues of specificity. *Journal of Abnormal Psychology, 109,* 451–460.

Daley, S. E., Hammen, C., Davila, J., & Burge, D. (1998). Axis II symptomatology, depression, and life stress during the transition from adolescence to adulthood. *Journal of Consulting and Clinical Psychology, 66,* 595–603.

Daros, A. R., Zakzanis, K. K., & Ruocco, A. C. (2013). Facial emotion recognition in borderline personality disorder. *Psychological Medicine, 43,* 1953–1963.

Deckers, J. W. M., Lobbestael, J., van Wingen, G. A., Kessels, R. P. C., Arntz, A., & Egger, J. I. M. (2015). The influence of stress on social cognition in patients with borderline personality disorder. *Psychoneuroendocrinology, 52,* 119–129. doi:10.1016/j.psyneuen.2014.11.003

Dickerson, S. S., & Kemeny, M. E. (2004). Acute stressors and cortisol responses: A theoretical integration and synthesis of laboratory research. *Psychological Bulletin, 130*(3), 355–391.

Distel, M. A., Trull, T. J., Derom, C. A., Thiery, E. W., Grimmer, M. A., Martin, N. G., ... Boomsma, D. I. (2008). Heritability of borderline personality disorder features is similar across three countries. *Psychological Medicine 38*(9), 1219–1229.

Distel, M. A., Willemsen, G., Ligthart, L., Derom, C. A., Martin, N. G., Neale, M. C., ... Boomsma, D. I. (2010). Genetic covariance structure of the four main features of borderline personality disorder. *Journal of Personality Disorders 24*(4), 427–444.

Domes, G., Schulze, L., & Herpertz, S. C. (2009). Emotion recognition in Borderline Personality Disorder- A review of the literature. *Journal of Personality Disorders, 23*(1), 6–19. doi:10.1521/pedi.2009.23.1.6

DuMont, K. A., Widom, C. S., & Czaja, S. J. (2007). Predictors of resilience in abused and neglected children grown-up: The role of individual and neighborhood characteristics. *Child Abuse & Neglect, 31*(3), 255–274.

Forbes, E. E. (2009). Where's the fun in that? Broadening the focus on reward function in depression. *Biological Psychiatry, 66*(3), 199–200. doi:10.1016/j.biopsych.2009.05.001

Frankenburg, F. R., & Zanarini, M. C. (2004). The association between borderline personality disorder and chronic medical illnesses, poor health-related lifestyle choices, and costly forms of health care utilization. *The Journal of Clinical Psychiatry, 65*(12), 1660–1665.

Gagnon, J., Daelman, S., & McDuff, P. (2013). Correlations of impulsivity with dysfunctional beliefs associated with borderline personality. *North American Journal of Psychology, 15,* 167–178.

Gale, C. R., Cukic, I., Batty, G. D., McIntosh, A. M., Weiss, A., & Deary, I. J. (2017). When is higher neuroticism protective against death? Findings from UK Biobank. *Psychological Science, 28,* 1345–1357.

Garmezy, N., & Masten, A. S. (1994). Chronic adversities. In M. Rutter & L. Hersov (Eds.), *Child and adolescent psychiatry: Modern approaches* (3rd ed., pp. 191–208). London, UK: Blackwell.

Gleason, M. E. J., Powers, A. D., & Oltmanns, T. F. (2012). The enduring impact of borderline personality pathology: Risk for threatening life events in later middle-age. *Journal of Abnormal Psychology, 121*(2), 447–457. doi:10.1037/a0025564

Gratz, K. L., Rosenthal, M. Z., Tull, M. T., Lejuez, C. W., & Gunderson, J. G. (2010). An experimental investigation of emotional reactivity and delayed emotional recovery in borderline personality disorder: The role of shame. *Comprehensive Psychiatry, 51*(3), 275–285. doi:10.1016/j.comppsych.2009.08.005

Gunderson, J. G., Stout, R. L., McGlashan, T. H., Shea, M. T., Morey, L. C., Grilo, C. M., ... Skodol, A. E. (2011). Ten-year course of borderline personality disorder: Psychopathology and function from the Collaborative Longitudinal Personality Disorders study. *Archives of General Psychiatry*, *68*(8), 827–837.

Gunthert, K. C., Cohen, L. H., & Armeli, S. (1999). The role of neuroticism in daily stress and coping. *Journal of Personality and Social Psychology*, *77*(5), 1087–1100. doi:10.1037/0022-3514.77.5.1087

Hamer, M., O'Donnell, K., Lahiri, A., & Steptoe, A. (2010). Salivary cortisol responses to mental stress are associated with coronary artery calcification in healthy men and women. *European Heart Journal*, *31*(4), 424–429. doi:10.1093/eurheartj/ehp386

Hammen, C. (1991). Generation of stress in the course of unipolar depression. *Journal of Abnormal Psychology*, *100*(4), 555–561. doi:10.1037/0021-843X.100.4.555

Hammen, C. (2006). Stress generation in depression: Reflections on origins, research, and future directions. *Journal of Clinical Psychology*, *62*, 1065–1082. doi:10.1002/jclp.20293

Hammen, C., & Brennan, P. A. (2001). Depressed adolescents of depressed and nondepressed mothers: Tests of an Interpersonal Impairment Hypothesis. *Journal of Consulting and Clinical Psychology*, *69*(2), 284–294.

Hankin, B. L., Kassel, J. D., & Abela, J. R. Z. (2005). Adult attachment dimensions and specificity of emotional distress symptoms: Prospective investigations of cognitive risk and interpersonal stress generation as mediating mechanisms. *Personality and Social Psychology Bulletin*, *31*(1), 136–151.

Herrenkohl, T. I., Sousa, C., Tajima, E. A., Herrenkohl, R. C., & Moylan, C. A. (2008). Intersection of child abuse and children's exposure to domestic violence. *Trauma, Violence, & Abuse*, *9*(2), 84–99.

Holsboer, F. (2000). The corticosteroid receptor hypothesis of depression. *Neuropsychopharmacology*, *23*(5), 477–501. doi:10.1016/S0893-133X(00)00159-7

Hutchinson, J. G., & Ruiz, J. M. (2011). Neuroticism and cardiovascular response in women: Evidence of effects on blood pressure recovery. *Journal of Personality*, *79*, 277–302.

Iacoviello, B. M., Alloy, L. B., Abramson, L. Y., Whitehouse, W. G., & Hogan, M. E. (2007). The role of cluster B and C personality disturbance in the course of depression: A prospective study. *Journal of Personality Disorders*, *21*(4), 371–383.

Iacovino, J. M., Bogdan, R., & Oltmanns, T.F. (2016). Personality predicts health declines through stressful life events during late mid-life. *Journal of Personality*, *84*, 536–546.

Ilardi, S. S., Craighead, W. E., & Evans, D. D. (1997). Modeling relapse in unipolar depression: The effects of dysfunctional cognitions and personality disorders. *Journal of Consulting and Clinical Psychology*, *65*(3), 381–391.

Jeronimus, B. F., Riese, H., Sanderman, R., & Ormel, J. (2014). Mutual reinforcement between neuroticism and life experiences: A five-wave, 16-year study to test reciprocal causation. *Journal of Personality and Social Psychology*, *107*(4), 751–764.

Johnson, J. G., Smailes, E. M., Cohen, P., Brown, J., & Bernstein, D. P. (2000). Associations between four types of childhood neglect and personality disorder symptoms during adolescence and early adulthood: Findings of a community-based longitudinal study. *Journal of Personality Disorders*, *14*(2), 171–187.

Kaplan, H. B. (1996). Psychosocial stress from the perspective of self-theory. In H. B. Kaplan (Ed.), *Psychosocial stress: Perspective on structure, theory, life-course, and methods* (pp. 175–244). San Diego, CA: Academic Press.

Keller, M. C., Coventry, W. L., Heath, A. C., & Martin, N. G. (2005). Widespread evidence for non-additive genetic variation in Cloninger's and Eysenck's personality dimensions using a twin plus sibling design. *Behavior Genetics*, *35*(6), 707–721.

Kendler, K. S., & Baker, J. H. (2007). Genetic influence on measures of the environment: A systematic review. *Psychological Medicine*, *37*(5), 615–626.

Kendler K. S., Karkowski, L. M., & Prescott, C. A. (1999). Causal relationship between stressful life events and the onset of major depression. *American Journal of Psychiatry*, *156*, 837–841.

Kercher, A. J., Rapee, R. M., & Schniering, C. A. (2009). Neuroticism, life events and negative thoughts in the development of depression in adolescent girls. *Journal of Abnormal Child Psychology*, *37*(7), 903–915.

Kirschbaum, C., Bartussek, D., & Strasburger, C. J. (1992). Cortisol responses to psychological stress and correlations with personality traits. *Personality and Individual Differences*, *13*, 1353–1357.

Kirschbaum, C., Pirke, K. M., Hellhammer, D. H. (1993). The Trier Social Stress test—a tool for investigating psychobiological stress responses in a laboratory setting. *Neuropsychobiology*, *28*, 76–81.

Kirschbaum, C., Prussner, J. C., Stone, A. A., Federenko, I., Gaab, J., Lintz, D., Schommer, N., Hellhammer, D. H. (1995). Persistent high cortisol responses to repeated psychological stress in a subpopulation of healthy men. *Psychosomatic Medicine*, *57*, 468–474.

Kudielka, B. M., Hellhammer, D. H., & Wust, S. (2009). Why do we respond so differently? Reviewing determinants of human salivary cortisol responses to challenge. *Psychoneuroendocrinology*, *34*, 2–18.

Kudielka, B. M., & Kirschbaum, C. (2005). Sex differences in HPA axis responses to stress: A review. *Biological Psychology*, *69*, 113–132.

Kuhlmann, A., Bertsch, K., Schmidinger, I., Thomann, P. A., & Herpertz, S. C. (2013). Morphometric differences in central stress-regulating structures between women with and without borderline personality disorder. *Journal of Psychiatry & Neuroscience* *38*(2), 129–137.

Lahey, B. B. (2009). Public health significance of neuroticism. *American Psychologist*, *64*(4), 241.

Lake, R. I., Eaves, L. J., Maes, H. H., Heath, A. C., & Martin, N. G. (2000). Further evidence against the environmental transmission of individual differences in neuroticism from a collaborative study of 45,850 twins and relatives on two continents. *Behavior Genetics*, *30*, 223–233. doi:10.1023/A:1001918408984

Lazarus, R. S. (1999). *Stress and emotion: A new synthesis*. New York, NY: Springer.

Levy, K. N. (2005). The implications of attachment theory and research for understanding borderline personality disorder. *Development and Psychopathology*, *17*, 959–986. doi:10.10170S0954579405050455

Lieb, K., Zanarini, M. C., Schmahl, C., Linehan, M. M., & Bohus, M. (2004). Borderline personality disorder. *Lancet*, *364*(9432), 453–461.

Limberg, A., Barnow, A., Freyberger, H. J., & Hamm, A. O. (2011). Emotional vulnerability in borderline personality disorder is cue specific and modulated by traumatization. *Biological Psychiatry, 69,* 574–582.

Liu, R. T., & Kleiman, E. M. (2012). Impulsivity and the generation of negative life events: The role of negative urgency. *Personality and Individual Differences, 53,* 609–612.

Lovallo, W. R. (1997). *Stress & health: Biological and psychological interactions.* Thousand Oaks, CA: Sage.

Lovallo, W. R. (2007). Individual differences in response to stress and risk for addiction. In M. Al'Absi (Ed.), *Stress and addiction: Biological and psychological mechanisms* (pp. 227–248). Burlington, MA: Elsevier.

Lovallo, W. R. (2011). Do low levels of stress reactivity signal poor states of health? *Biological Psychology, 86*(2), 121–128.

Ludy-Dobson, C. R., & Perry, B. D. (2010). The role of healthy relational interactions in buffering the impact of childhood trauma. In E. Gil (Ed.), *Working with children to heal interpersonal trauma: The power of play* (pp. 26–43). New York, NY: Guilford Press.

Magnus, K., Diener, E., Fujita, F., & Pavot, W. (1993). Extraversion and neuroticism as predictors of objective life events: A longitudinal analysis. *Journal of Personality and Social Psychology, 65,* 1046–1053.

Mason, D. (1991). Genetic variation in the stress response: susceptibility to experimental allergic encephalomyelitis and implications for human inflammatory disease. *Immunology Today, 12*(2), 57–60.

McEwen, B. S. (1998). Protective and damaging effects of stress mediators. *The New England Journal of Medicine, 338,* 171–179.

McEwen, B. S. (1999). Stress and hippocampal plasticity. *Annual Review of Neuroscience, 22,* 105–122.

Mezulis, A. H., Funasaki, K. S., Charbonneau, A. M., & Hyde, J. S. (2010). Gender differences in the cognitive vulnerability-stress model of depression in the transition to adolescence. *Cognitive Therapy and Research, 34*(6), 501–513. doi:10.1007/s10608-009-9281-7

Morris, M. C., Ciesla, J. A., & Garber, J. (2010). A prospective study of stress autonomy versus stress sensitization in adolescents at varied risk for depression. *Journal of Abnormal Psychology, 119*(2), 341–354. http://doi.org/10.1037/a0019036

Nash, M. R., Hulsey, T. L., Sexton, M. C., Harralson, T. L., & Lambert, W. (1993). Long-term effects of childhood sexual abuse: Perceived family environment, psychopathology, and dissociation. *Journal of Consulting Clinical Psychology, 61,* 276–283.

Nater, U. M., Bohus, M., Abbruzzese, E., Ditzen, B., Gaab, J., Kleindienst, N., ... Ehlert, U. (2010). Increased psychological and attenuated cortisol and alpha-amylase responses to acute psychosocial stress in female patients with borderline personality disorder. *Psychoneuroendocrinology, 35*(10), 1565–1572.

Oltmanns, T. F., Rodrigues, M. M., Weinstein, Y., & Gleason, M. E. J. (2014). Prevalence of personality disorders at midlife in a community sample: Disorders and symptoms reflected in interview, self, and informant reports. *Journal of Psychopathology and Behavioral Assessment 36*(2), 177–188. doi:10.1007/s10862-013-9389-7

Oswald, L. M., Zandi, P., Nestadt, G., Potash, J. B., Kalaydjian, A. E., Wand, G. S. (2006). Relationship between cortisol responses to stress and personality. *Neuropsychopharmacology, 31,* 1583–1591.

Paris, J. (1999). *Nature and nurture in psychiatry: A predisposition-stress model of mental disorders.* Washington, DC: American Psychiatric Press.

Paris, J. (2001). Psychosocial adversity. In W. J. Livesley (Ed.), *Handbook of personality disorders: Theory, research, and treatment* (pp. 231–241). New York, NY: The Guilford Press.

Patton, G. C., Coffey, C., Posterino, M., Carlin, J. B., & Bowes, G. (2003). Life events and early onset depression: Cause or consequence? *Psychological Medicine, 33,* 1203–1210.

Penley, J. A., & Tomaka, J. (2002). Associations among the Big Five, emotional responses, and coping with acute stress. *Personality and Individual Differences, 32,* 1215–1228.

Phillips, A. C., Carroll, D., Burns, V. E., Drayson, M. (2005). Neuroticism, cortisol reactivity, and antibody response to vaccination. *Psychophysiology, 42,* 232–238

Phillips, A. C., Roseboom, T. J., Carroll, D., & de Rooij, S. R. (2012). Cardiovascular and cortisol reactions to acute psychological stress and adiposity: Cross-sectional and prospective associations in the Dutch Famine Birth Cohort Study. *Psychosomatic Medicine, 74,* 699–710. doi:10.1097/PSY.0b013e31825e3b91

Powers, A. D., Gleason, M. E. J., & Oltmanns, T. F. (2013). Symptoms of borderline personality disorder predict interpersonal (but not independent) stressful life events in a community sample of older adults. *Journal of Abnormal Psychology, 122*(2), 469–474. doi:10.1037/a0032363

Reuben, A., Moffitt, T. E., Caspi, A., Belsky, D. W., Harrington, H., Schroeder, F., ... Danese, A. (2016). Lest we forget: Comparing retrospective and prospective assessments of adverse childhood experiences in the prediction of adult health. *Journal of Child Psychology and Psychiatry, 57,* 1103–1112.

Roberts, B. W., & Pomerantz, E. M. (2004). On traits, situations, and their integration: A developmental perspective. *Personality and Social Psychology Review, 8*(4), 402–416.

Rudolph, K. D., & Hammen, C. (1999). Age and gender as determinants of stress exposure, generation, and reactions in youngsters: A transactional perspective. *Child Development, 70,* 660–677. doi:10.1111/1467

Rutter, M. (1989). Pathways from childhood to adult life. *Journal of Child Psychology and Psychiatry, 30,* 23–51.

Rutter, M., & Maughan, B. (1997). Psychosocial adversities in psychopathology. *Journal of Personality Disorders, 11,* 4–18.

Sauer, C., Arens, E. A., Stopsack, M., Spitzer, C., & Barnow, S. (2014). Emotional hyper-reactivity in borderline personality disorder is related to trauma and interpersonal themes. *Psychiatry Research, 220,* 468–478.

Scarr, S., & McCartney, K. (1983). How people make their own environments: A theory of genotype -> environment effects. *Child Development, 54*(2), 424–435.

Schneider, T. R. (2004). The role of neuroticism on psychological and physiological stress responses. *Journal of Experimental Social Psychology, 40,* 795–804.

Schneider, T. R., Rench, T. A., Lyons, J. B., & Riffle, R. R. (2011). The influence of neuroticism, extraversion and openness on stress responses. *Stress and Health, 28,* 102–110.

Schommer, N. C., Kudielka, B. M., Hellhammer, D. H., & Kirschbaum, C. (1999). No evidence for a close relationship between personality traits and circadian cortisol rhythm or a single cortisol stress response. *Psychological Reports, 84,* 840–842.

Shahar, G., Joiner, T. E., Zuroff, D. C., & Blatt, S. J. (2004). Personality, interpersonal behavior, and depression: Co-existence of stress-specific moderating and mediating effects. *Personality and Individual Differences, 36*(7), 1583–1596.

Shaver, P. R., & Mikulincer, M. (2008). Adult attachment and cognitive and affective reactions to positive and negative events. *Social and Personality Psychology Compass, 2*, 1844–1865. doi:10.1111/j.1751-9004.2008.00146.x

Shields, G.S., & Slavich, G.M. (2017). Lifetime stress exposure and health: A review of contemporary assessment methods and biological mechanisms. *Social and Personality Psychology Compas, 11*, 17–27.

Shih, J. H., Abela, J. R. Z., & Starrs, C. (2009). Cognitive and interpersonal predictors of stress generation in children of affectively ill parents. *Journal of Abnormal Child Psychology, 37*, 195–208.

Siegrist, J. (2008). Chronic psychosocial stress at work and risk of depression: Evidence from prospective studies. *European Archives of Psychiatry and Clinical Neuroscience, 258*. doi:10.1007/s00406-008-5024-0

Skodol, A. E., Gunderson, J. G., Shea, M. T., McGlashan, T. H., Morey, L. C., Sanislow, C. A.,...Stout, R. L. (2005). The Collaborative Longitudinal Personality Disorders Study (CLPS): Overview and implications. *Journal of Personality Disorders, 19*, 487–504.

Smith, T. W., Gallo, L. C., Shivpuri, S., & Brewer, A. L. (2012). Personality and health: Current issues and emerging perspectives. In A. Baum, T. Bevenson, & J. Singer (Eds.), *Handbook of health psychology* (pp. 375–404). New York: Psychology Press.

Smith, T. W., Glazer, K., Ruiz, J. M., & Gallo, L. C. (2004). Hostility, anger, aggressiveness and coronary heart disease: An interpersonal perspective on personality, emotion and health. *Journal of Personality, 72*, 1217–1270.

Snyder, H. R., Young, J. F., & Hankin, B. L. (2017). Chronic stress exposure and generation are related to the p-factor and externalizing specific psychopathology in youth. *Journal of Clinical Child and Adolescent Psychology, 25*, 1–10.

Soloff, P. H., Lynch, K. G., Kelly, T. M. (2002). Childhood abuse as a risk factor for suicidal behavior in borderline personality disorder. *Journal of Personality Disorders, 16*(3), 201–214. doi:10.1521/pedi.16.3.201.22542

South, S., Reichborn-Kjennerud, T., Eaton, N., & Krueger, R. (2012). Behavior and molecular genetics of personality disorders. In Thomas A. Widiger (Ed.), *The Oxford handbook of personality disorders* (pp. 143–166). New York: Oxford University Press.

Stepp, S. D., Olino, T. M., Klein, D. N., Seeley, J. R., & Lewinsohn, P. M. (2013). Unique influences of adolescent antecedents on adult borderline personality disorder features. *Personality Disorders: Theory, Research, and Treatment, 4*(3). doi:10.1037/per0000015.

Svaldi, J., Philipsen, A., & Matthies, S. (2012). Risky decision making in borderline personality disorder. *Psychiatry Research, 197*, 112–118.

Timoney, L. R., Walsh, Z., Shea, M. T., Yen, S., Ansell, E. B., Grilo, C. M.,...Gunderson, J. G. (2017). Personality and life events in a personality disorder sample. *Personality Disorders: Theory, Research, and Treatment, 8*, 376–382.

Tomaka, J., Blascovich, J., Kelsey, R. M., & Leitten, C. L. (1993). Subjective, physiological and behavioral effects of threat and challenge appraisal. *Journal of Personality and Social Psychology, 66*, 248–260.

Tomaka, J., Palacios, R., Schneider, K. T., Colotla, M., Concha, J. B., & Herrald, M. M. (1999). Assertiveness predicts threat and challenge reactions to potential stress among women. *Journal of Personality and Social Psychology, 76*, 1008–1021.

Tyrka, A. R., Wyche, M. C., Kelly, M. M., Price, L. H., & Carpenter, L. L. (2009). Childhood maltreatment and adult personality disorder symptoms: Influence of maltreatment type. *Psychiatry Research, 3*(28), 281–287.

Verschoor, E., & Markus, C. R. (2011). Affective and neuroendocrine stress reactivity to an academic examination: Influence of the 5-HTTLPR genotype and trait neuroticism. *Biological Psychology, 87*, 439–449.

Walter, M., Bureau, J. F., Holmes, B. M., Bertha, E. A., Hollander, M., Wheelis, J., Brooks, N. H., & Lyons-Ruth, K. (2008). Cortisol response to interpersonal stress in young adults with borderline personality disorder: A pilot study. *European Psychiatry, 23*, 201–204.

Welch, S., & Linehan, M. M. (2002). High-risk situations associated with parasuicide and drug use in borderline personality disorder. *Journal of Personality Disorders, 16*, 561–569.

Widiger, T. A., & Mullins-Sweatt, S. N. (2010). Clinical utility of a dimensional model of personality disorder. *Professional Psychology: Research and Practice, 41*(6), 488.

Widiger, T. A., & Trull, T. J. (2007). Plate tectonics in the classification of personality disorder: Shifting to a dimensional model. *The American Psychologist, 62*(2), 71–83.

Widom, C. S., & Shepard, R. L. (1996). Accuracy of adult recollections of childhood victimization: Part 1. Childhood physical abuse. *Psychological Assessment, 8*, 412–421.

Wirtz, P. H., Elsenbruch, S., Emini, L., Rudisuli, K., Groessbauer, S., & Ehlert, U. (2007). Perfectionism and the cortisol response to psychosocial stress in men. *Psychosomatic Medicine, 69*, 249–255.

Williams, P. G., Rau, H. K., Cribbet, M. R., & Gunn, H. E. (2009). Openness to experience and stress regulation. *Journal of Research in Personality, 43*, 777–784.

Williams, P. G., Smith, T. W., Gunn, H. E., & Uchino, B. N. (2011). Personality and stress: Individual differences in exposure, reactivity, recovery, and restoration. In R. J. Contrada & A. Baum (Eds.), *The handbook of stress science: Biology, psychology, and health* (pp. 231–245). New York, NY: Springer.

Wilson, S., Stroud, C. B., & Durbin, C. E. (2017). Interpersonal dysfunction in personality disorders: A meta-analytic review. *Psychological Bulletin, 143*(7), 677–734.

Wright, A. G., & Simms, L. J. (2016). Stability and fluctuation of personality disorder features in daily life. *Journal of Abnormal Psychology, 125*(5), 641.

Yen, S., Pagano, M., Shea, M. T., Grilo, C., Gunderson, J., Skodol, A.,...Zanarini, M. C. (2005). Recent life events preceding suicide attempts in a personality disorder sample: Findings from the collaborative longitudinal personality disorders study. *Journal of Consulting and Clinical Psychology, 73*, 99–105.

Zanarini, M. C. (2000). Childhood experiences associated with the development of borderline personality disorder. *Psychiatric Clinics, 23*(1), 89–101.

Zanarini, M. C., Frankenburg, F. R., Reich, D. B., Hennen, J., & Silk, K. R. (2005). Adult experiences of abuse reported by borderline patients and axis II comparison subjects over six years of prospective follow-up. *Journal of Nervous and Mental Disease, 193*, 412–416.

Zanarini, M. C., Gunderson, J. G., Marino, M. F., Schwartz, E. O., & Frankenburg, F. R. (1989). Childhood experiences of borderline patients. *Comprehensive Psychiatry, 30*, 18–25.

Zimmerman, D. J., & Choi-Kain, L. W. (2009). The hypothalamic–pituitary–adrenal axis in borderline personality disorder: A review. *Harvard Review of Psychiatry, 17*, 167–183.

Alcohol Dependence Conceptualized as a Stress Disorder

Leandro F. Vendruscolo *and* George F. Koob

Abstract

Alcohol use disorder is a chronically relapsing disorder that involves (1) compulsivity to seek and take alcohol, (2) difficulty in limiting alcohol intake, and (3) emergence of a negative emotional state (e.g., dysphoria, anxiety, irritability) in the absence of alcohol. Alcohol addiction encompasses a three-stage cycle that becomes more intense as alcohol use progresses: *binge/intoxication, withdrawal/negative affect,* and *preoccupation/anticipation*. These stages engage neuroadaptations in brain circuits that involve the basal ganglia (reward hypofunction), extended amygdala (stress sensitization), and prefrontal cortex (executive function disorder). This chapter discusses key neuroadaptations in the hypothalamic and extrahypothalamic stress systems and the critical role of glucocorticoid receptors. These neuroadaptations contribute to negative emotional states that powerfully drive compulsive alcohol drinking and seeking. These changes in association with a disruption of prefrontal cortex function that lead to cognitive deficits and poor decision making contribute to the chronic relapsing nature of alcohol dependence.

Keywords: addiction, alcohol dependence, stress, glucocorticoids, extended amygdala

Alcohol use disorder, also known as alcohol addiction, is a broad term for any alcohol drinking pattern that leads to mental or physical health problems. Six percent of the world's population suffers from mortality and morbidity that are associated with alcohol dependence (World Health Organization, 2014). Behavioral approaches are effective (PsycNET Record Display) and three medications (e.g., disulfiram, acamprosate, and naltrexone) are approved by the United States Food and Drug Administration for the treatment of alcohol use disorder (Koob & Mason, 2016). Behavioral therapy and medications are modestly effective, but a lack of knowledge and availability in medical practice limit their use. As in the treatment of mental illness in general, more effective, practical, and acceptable treatments would alleviate much suffering.

Alcohol is initially consumed for its pleasurable effects (e.g., euphoria) via positive reinforcement processes. Positive reinforcement is defined as the process by which a usually pleasant stimulus (e.g.,

alcohol's euphorigenic effect) increases the frequency of a particular behavior (e.g., drinking). Alcohol addiction involves compulsive alcohol seeking and drinking, difficulty limiting alcohol intake, and the emergence of a negative emotional state (e.g., dysphoria, anxiety, and irritability) during alcohol abstinence. The latter reflects a motivational withdrawal syndrome that can persist long after alcohol abstinence and helps perpetuate compulsive alcohol drinking and seeking via negative reinforcement. Negative reinforcement is defined as the process by which the removal of an aversive state increases the probability of a response (e.g., alcohol is consumed to alleviate anxiety, pain, and dysphoria). Negative reinforcement is conceptually distinct from punishment, which involves the presentation of an aversive stimulus that suppresses behavior.

Alcohol addiction encompasses a three-stage cycle (Koob & Le Moal, 1997; Koob et al., 2014): *binge/intoxication* (heavy alcohol drinking), *withdrawal/negative affect* (anxiety, dysphoria, irritability,

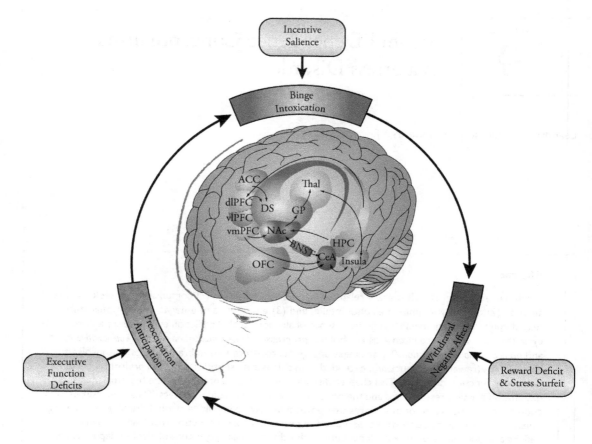

Figure 9.1 Three stages of the addiction cycle—*binge/intoxication, withdrawal/negative affect*, and *preoccupation/anticipation*—from the perspective of functional neurocircuitry deficits that correspond to each stage, respectively: incentive salience, reward deficit disorder/stress surfeit disorder, and executive function disorder. Modified from Koob, Everitt, and Robbins (2008) with permission.

pain), and *preoccupation/anticipation* (craving). The stages are interconnected and become more intense as alcohol use progresses (Figure 9.1). These three stages involve neuroplasticity in numerous brain circuits, including the basal ganglia (incentive salience/pathological habit formation), extended amygdala (reward deficit/stress surfeit), and prefrontal cortex (executive function disorder).

The multifaceted nature of the neurobiology of alcohol addiction involves a complex interaction between alterations in brain reward and stress systems and executive function that engage multiple neurocircuits and neurotransmitter systems (for a comprehensive review, see Koob & Volkow, 2016). Much work has focused on incentive salience and pathological habit formation that are associated with the *binge/intoxication* stage (Berridge, 2012; Everitt et al., 2008). Alcohol intoxication and withdrawal produce neuroadaptations in the stress system that in turn drive further excessive and compulsive drinking associated with the *withdrawal/negative affect*

stage. Additionally, chronic alcohol use generates a physiological stress response and impairs the individual's capacity to effectively respond to external stressful stimuli, which is also a crucial aspect of the interplay between alcohol use and stress. As such, stress has an important effect on initially driving alcohol drinking and precipitating craving and relapse in later phases of alcohol dependence (Koob & Mason, 2016).

Animal models of alcohol dependence have provided critical information about the biological factors that underlie alcohol dependence. The use of experimental animals, particularly nonhuman primates and rodents (Jimenez & Grant, 2017; Vendruscolo & Roberts, 2014), in preclinical alcohol research gives the experimenter control over several factors, such as the animal's genetic background, the environment, and exposure to alcohol, which are more difficult to control in humans. Although no animal model fully recapitulates alcohol dependence in humans, experimental animals exhibit behaviors (e.g., alcohol drinking, excessive alcohol drinking, compulsive-like alcohol drinking, motivational withdrawal, hyperalgesia, etc.) and neurochemical changes (e.g., increase in γ-aminobutyric acid [GABA] transmission in the brain) that are similar to humans and respond to treatments that affect drinking similarly to humans (Koob, Kenneth Lloyd, & Mason, 2009; Tunstall, Carmack, Koob, & Vendruscolo, 2017; Vendruscolo et al., 2015).

Using mainly rodent models as a framework, we argue that repeated, intense cycles of alcohol intoxication and withdrawal trigger neuroadaptations first at the level of the hypothalamic-pituitary-adrenal (HPA) axis, a primary neuroendocrine stress system, and subsequently in extrahypothalamic brain regions (i.e., basal ganglia, extended amygdala, and prefrontal cortex). Activation of the HPA axis by alcohol via corticotropin-releasing factor (CRF) and the consequent release of glucocorticoids (cortisol in nonhuman primates and humans, corticosterone in rats, hereafter termed CORT) in the bloodstream can facilitate alcohol reward during initial drug taking. However, repeated and intense activation of the HPA axis by alcohol and alcohol withdrawal disrupts the HPA axis (endocrine tolerance). Alcohol not only drives the HPA stress response and extrahypothalamic CRF stress response but also drives other brain stress systems in the extended amygdala that interact with or parallel the actions of CRF. These neuroadaptations lead to hypofunctional brain reward systems (hypohedonia), stress surfeit (anxiety, irritability, pain), and executive dysfunction (cognitive deficits, poor decision making, and poor judgment) and are associated with advanced or more severe alcohol use disorder, defined previously as substance dependence on alcohol. These neuroadaptations are further postulated to mediate the transition from controlled, recreational alcohol drinking to the loss of control and compulsive alcohol drinking via negative reinforcement (i.e., removal of anxiety, pain, and dysphoria by alcohol increases the probability of drinking alcohol), which is the focus of this chapter.

Animal Models of Alcohol Dependence

Different patterns of alcohol drinking (e.g., recreational drinking, binge drinking, and dependence-induced drinking) can be modeled using rodent models. Continuous access to alcohol (e.g., via two-bottle choice in the home cage) often produces low and stable levels of alcohol drinking. Biological sex, the genetic makeup of the animals, and the environment greatly influence the amount of alcohol that is consumed in this model (Crabbe, Wahlsten, & Dudek, 1999; Vendruscolo et al., 2006, 2008). Binge drinking, defined by the National Institute on Alcohol Abuse and Alcoholism as an excessive pattern of alcohol drinking that produces blood alcohol levels >0.08 g/dl within a 2 hr period, roughly five or more drinks on an occasion for men and four or more for women, can be modeled using sweeteners to make alcohol solutions more palatable (Ji, Gilpin, Richardson, Rivier, & Koob, 2008) or by restricting intake to specific periods of the dark cycle (e.g., drinking-in-the-dark model; Holgate, Shariff, Mu, & Bartlett, 2017; Rhodes, Best, Belknap, Finn, & Crabbe, 2005; Thiele & Navarro, 2014). Intermittent 24 hr access to alcohol (e.g., on Mondays, Wednesdays, and Fridays) has been shown to produce an escalation of alcohol drinking over time (Fredriksson et al., 2017; Simms et al., 2008; Wise, 1973) and can also be used to model binge drinking. Furthermore, after prolonged voluntary drinking and a period of abstinence, rats typically exhibit an "alcohol deprivation effect," whereby alcohol drinking significantly increases (Sinclair, 1979; Sinclair & Senter, 1968; Vengeliene, Bilbao, & Spanagel, 2014). These models of voluntary drinking are typically conducted in the animal's home cage with the presentation of one (or more) bottles with alcohol and water in a free-choice paradigm. These models are mostly used to study the *binge/intoxication* stage of alcohol addiction.

Binge drinking is a common and harmful pattern of alcohol drinking, particularly in teenagers and young adults, that may or may not be associated with dependence. Binge drinking has been associated with health consequences (e.g., impaired immune system, emergency room visits), behavioral consequences (e.g., motor vehicle fatalities, unsafe sex), social consequences (e.g., campus vandalism, violent behavior), and academic consequences (e.g., poor academic performance, dropouts; Hingson, Zha, & White, 2017). Emerging issues include extreme binge drinking (Hingson & White, 2013), which corresponds to two or more times the binge drinking thresholds, and binge drinking in people who are 65 years of age and older (Breslow, Castle, Chen, & Graubard, 2017). Exposure to environmental stressors increases the occurrence of binge drinking.

Alcohol drinking in free-choice models captures consummatory aspects because minimal effort is required by the animals to obtain alcohol. In contrast, operant self-administration models, in which the animal is required to produce an operant response (e.g., press a lever) to gain access to alcohol, are used to model different aspects of alcohol drinking and seeking. Different from the free-choice bottle models, operant models of alcohol self-administration involve training the animals to perform a response, typically press a lever or nosepoke, to obtain a dose of alcohol. To motivate rodents to perform an operant response to obtain alcohol, an early sucrose-fading training procedure was developed (for review, see Samson, 1986). Because rats avidly drink sucrose (more than alcohol), adding sucrose to the alcohol solution greatly facilitates the training of rats to perform an operant response to obtain the alcohol solution. Once stable responding is achieved, the sucrose (or another sweetener) is progressively faded from the solution while the alcohol concentration progressively increases. By removing the sweetener from the alcohol solution, the experimenter can investigate the neurobiology of alcohol drinking without additional confounding factors, such as the biological factors that underlie the consumption of sweet solutions. Other training procedures that do not use a sweetener for the acquisition of operant behavior to obtain alcohol are also commonly used (e.g., Priddy et al., 2017).

In operant models, both appetitive/motivational aspects (e.g., press a lever to receive a dose of alcohol) and consummatory aspects (e.g., drinking alcohol) of alcohol can be evaluated (Cunningham, Fidler, & Hill, 2000; Tabakoff & Hoffman, 2000). These procedures are used to study alcohol seeking and alcohol drinking (*binge/intoxication and preoccupation/anticipation* stages) that initiate and perpetuate alcohol addiction. Reinforcement contingencies can be adjusted to examine the animals' motivation to obtain alcohol. For example, a fixed-ratio 1 (FR1) schedule of reinforcement requires the animal to perform a single operant response (i.e., press the lever once) to obtain alcohol, reflecting a low workload. In progressive-ratio schedules of reinforcement, the animal is required to respond progressively more to obtain alcohol, reflecting a high workload. Progressive-ratio schedules are used as an index of reward efficacy or compulsive-like behavior (Hodos, 1961). In second-order schedules of reinforcement (Lamb, Pinkston, & Ginsburg, 2015), the animal is required to perform a certain number of operant responses at one operandum (e.g., a lever) to gain access to another operandum (e.g., a different lever) that leads to alcohol delivery. Models of the reinstatement of alcohol seeking typically utilize exposure to cues that are associated with alcohol availability, stress, or alcohol itself following absti-

nence and are used to model relapse-like behavior (Mantsch et al., 2016).

Although these models are useful for understanding some aspects of alcohol drinking, none of them fully recapitulate all aspects of alcohol dependence. A major obstacle in the development of valid models of alcohol dependence is that rodents typically do not voluntarily drink sufficient alcohol to produce somatic signs of dependence (e.g., tail stiffness, abnormal gait/posture, and vocalization upon touch) or motivational signs of dependence (e.g., higher anxiety-like behavior, hypohedonia, hyperalgesia, compulsive-like responding, and escalated alcohol drinking and seeking). Exceptions to this rule involve the induction of dependence on alcohol by free-choice drinking in alcohol-preferring rats and very prolonged (6–9 months) voluntary self-administration in Wistar rats (Hölter et al., 1998; Waller, McBride, Lumeng, & Li, 1982; Wolffgramm & Heyne, 1995). However, the rapid induction of alcohol dependence can be produced with passive exposure to large amounts of alcohol (exceeding 150–200 mg/dl) via alcohol vapor inhalation (for review, see Vendruscolo & Roberts, 2014), intragastric alcohol infusion (Fidler, Oberlin, Struthers, & Cunningham, 2009; De Guglielmo, Martin-Fardon, Teshima, Ciccocioppo, & Weiss, 2015), or an alcohol liquid diet (Gilpin et al., 2009; Lieber & De Carli, 1973). These methods are frequently combined with voluntary drinking or operant alcohol self-administration to assess alcohol drinking and seeking in alcohol-dependent animals during abstinence.

Once dependent on alcohol via passive intragastric infusion, rats and mice self-administer high doses of alcohol (0.12 mg/dl in 30 min; Fidler, Clews, & Cunningham, 2006; Fidler et al., 2011), indicating a dependence-induced increase in alcohol intake. In an alcohol liquid diet procedure, a nutritionally complete diet (Lieber & De Carli, 1973) that typically contains 5%–12% (v/v) alcohol is often offered as the sole source of calories that is available to the animals. Using this method, rodents ingest sufficient amounts of the liquid diet to produce dependence and exhibit escalated alcohol drinking during abstinence (Gilpin et al., 2009). Chronic, intermittent exposure to alcohol vapors also reliably produces an escalation of alcohol drinking during withdrawal. Passive daily cycles of alcohol intoxication (e.g., 14 h of vapor ON) and withdrawal (e.g., 10 h of vapor OFF) are typically controlled by the experimenter to maintain blood alcohol levels around 150–250 mg/dl during the intoxication phase (Gilpin et al.,

2009; Vendruscolo & Roberts, 2014). Rats have also been shown to self-administer alcohol vapor to the point of dependence (De Guglielmo, Kallupi, Cole, & George, 2017), indicating that alcohol vapor itself is reinforcing to the animals. Additionally, alcohol vapor exposure has been successfully used to produce dependence in mice (Finn et al., 2007; Lopez, Miles, Williams, & Becker, 2017). These models of alcohol dependence are useful for studying the *withdrawal/negative affect* stage of alcohol addiction, in which humans drink to relieve a negative emotional state (Heinz et al., 2003). Such negative emotional states reflect a lower ability to feel pleasure concomitantly with higher pain sensation, anxiety, and depression symptoms in the absence of alcohol. External stressful stimuli and internal malaise may accentuate these negative emotional states. These long-lasting changes perpetuate compulsive alcohol drinking and contribute to craving and relapse to alcohol seeking and use following abstinence.

Validation of the vapor exposure model showed that alcohol-dependent rats that were passively exposed to alcohol vapor and tested during acute withdrawal (i.e., 6–8 hr after removal from alcohol vapor) self-administered more alcohol than nondependent rats under an FR1 schedule of reinforcement. Dependent rats also exhibited greater motivation to obtain alcohol compared with nondependent rats in a progressive-ratio test and were more persistent in maintaining alcohol drinking despite punishment (i.e., when a bitter substance, quinine, was added to the alcohol solution), indicating compulsive-like alcohol consumption (Vendruscolo et al., 2012). Fixed-ratio, progressive-ratio, and quinine adulteration tests are useful for assessing the consummatory and appetitive aspects of alcohol drinking (Aoun et al., 2017; Barbier et al., 2015).

Disruption of the Hypothalamic-Pituitary-Adrenal Axis in Alcohol Dependence

The endocrinologist Hans Selye first described a key role for the HPA axis and glucocorticoids in stress responses. Selye conceptualized stress and HPA axis function as adaptive responses to environmental challenges, termed "general adaptive syndrome" (Selye, 1950). These discoveries motivated the search for releasing factors in the hypothalamus (Guillemin, 1978) and the discovery of CRF (Vale et al., 1981). The HPA axis is a primary neuroendocrine system that mediates physiological responses to environmental stimuli (McEwen, 2007; McEwen et al., 2015; Myers et al., 2014). In response to environmental

stimuli, the paraventricular nucleus (PVN) of the hypothalamus stimulates the anterior pituitary to release adrenocorticotropic hormone (ACTH) into the bloodstream via CRF that is released into the portal system. Adrenocorticotropic hormone activates melanocortin receptor 2 (an ACTH receptor) in the cortex of the adrenal glands, thus causing the rapid production and release of CORT into the blood circulation. Circulating CORT exerts actions on many tissues to produce many physiological (Garabedian, Harris, & Jeanneteau, 2017; Kadmiel & Cidlowski, 2013) and behavioral (Packard, Egan, & Ulrich-Lai, 2016) changes. Negative feedback mechanisms along the HPA axis, including the PVN and pituitary, prevent further CORT release.

In the brain, CORT binds to two types of receptors: mineralocorticoid receptors (type I) and glucocorticoid receptors (type II). Mineralocorticoid receptors have high affinity for CORT, whereas glucocorticoid receptors have lower affinity for CORT so that high circulating CORT levels are necessary to activate these receptors (McEwen, 2007). Activation of the HPA axis is adaptive and critical for survival. However, intense and sustained HPA axis activation may lead to Cushing's disease in humans and long-lasting detrimental neuroadaptations that contribute to the development of mental disorders (Koob & Kreek, 2007; Packard et al., 2016; Sinha et al., 2011; Stephens & Wand, 2012), which is mitigated in chronic stress in normal mammals by the negative feedback of CORT to hypothalamic and pituitary CRF.

Acute exposure to alcohol activates the HPA axis in humans (Mendelson & Stein, 1966; Figure 9.2), nonhuman primates (Jimenez & Grant, 2017), and rodents (Ellis, 1966; Ogilvie, Lee, Weiss, & Rivier, 1998; Richardson, Lee, O'Dell, Koob, & Rivier, 2008). In nondependent rats, adrenalectomy decreased alcohol drinking, which was restored by CORT replacement. Glucocorticoid receptor antagonism also blocked alcohol reward, reflected by conditioned place preference, in mice (Rotter et al., 2012). These findings indicate that CORT may contribute to alcohol's acute rewarding/reinforcing effects (Fahlke, Hård, Eriksson, Engel, & Hansen, 1995) in a nondependent state and, by extrapolation, contribute to incentive salience and pathological habit formation (Marinelli & Piazza, 2002). The effects of CORT on alcohol's rewarding effects may involve the release of dopamine in the mesolimbic system (Juarez et al., 2017). In rats that were subjected to adrenalectomy to suppress endogenous glucocorticoids, extracellular dopamine levels decreased in

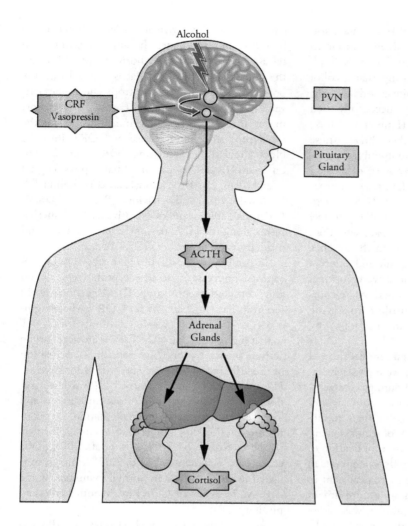

Alcohol

CRF
Vasopressin

PVN

Pituitary
Gland

ACTH

Adrenal
Glands

Cortisol

Figure 9.2 Alcohol-induced HPA axis activation. In response to alcohol intoxication, the paraventricular nucleus (PVN) of the hypothalamus releases corticotropin-releasing factor (CRF), which then causes the release of adrenocorticotropic hormone (ACTH) by the anterior pituitary. Following transit through the bloodstream, ACTH stimulates the release of glucocorticoids by the adrenal gland.

the shell portion of the nucleus accumbens (Barrot et al., 2000). Thus, CORT, via interactions with the dopamine system, appears to be required for reward function in response to alcohol.

However, excessive activation of the HPA axis by repeated alcohol exposure and withdrawal leads to the dysregulation of HPA axis activity (Adinoff, Ruether, Krebaum, Iranmanesh, & Williams, 2003; Rasmussen et al., 2000; Richardson, Lee, et al., 2008; Sinha et al., 2011). Alcohol-induced activation of the HPA axis has been shown to be blunted (i.e., neuroendocrine tolerance) in alcohol dependence in both humans and animal models (Richardson, Lee, et al., 2008; Stephens & Wand, 2012), similar to the neuroendocrine tolerance of chronic stress described earlier. For example, an intravenous infusion of 1 g/kg alcohol significantly increased blood ACTH and CORT levels in nondependent rats but not in alcohol-dependent rats, despite these two groups having similar levels of alcohol in the blood.

This blunted HPA axis response to alcohol may contribute to the decrease in alcohol-induced rewarding effects in alcohol dependence. Critically, dysregulation of the HPA axis in alcohol dependence has been associated with alcohol craving and relapse (O'Malley, Krishnan-Sarin, Farren, Sinha, & Kreek, 2002). Importantly, the opioid receptor antagonist naltrexone has been shown to both have anti-craving effects and activate the HPA axis (O'Malley et al., 2002). The anti-craving effect of naltrexone is likely attributable to the blockade of μ-opioid receptors in limbic brain regions. Activation of the HPA axis may be a consequence of (1) naltrexone physiologically blocking the tonic inhibitory effect that endogenous opioids (e.g., endorphins; Stephens & Wand, 2012) have on the PVN and modulatory stress-related regions (e.g., locus coeruleus) and (2) naltrexone causing a direct aversive/stressful response in rats and humans that consume high levels of alcohol (Mitchell et al., 2009).

Furthermore, alcohol-associated cues have been reported to stimulate CORT release in abstinent alcoholics (Fox, Bergquist, Hong, & Sinha, 2007) and produce craving, suggesting that CORT may also contribute to a conditioned, appetitive response to promote relapse.

The blunted HPA axis function in alcohol dependence that was described earlier may be attributable to CRF downregulation in the PVN (Makino, Gold, & Schulkin, 1994; Richardson, Lee, et al., 2008; Swanson & Simmons, 1989). However, concomitant with the downregulation of CRF in the PVN, CRF levels in extrahypothalamic brain regions (e.g., central nucleus of the amygdala and dorsolateral bed nucleus of the stria terminalis) are upregulated following chronic exposure to either CORT or alcohol (Makino et al., 1994; Roberto et al., 2010; Shepard, Barron, & Myers, 2000; Sommer et al., 2008). This bidirectional regulation of CRF has been hypothesized to depend on glucocorticoid receptors and mediated by interactions between glucocorticoid receptors and various steroid-related co-regulators (Edwards et al., 2015). Functionally, the downregulation of CRF in the PVN and upregulation of CRF in the extended amygdala have been implicated in hypohedonia and stress sensitization in alcohol dependence (see later).

Using pharmacological compounds, the blockade of CRF1 receptors or vasopressin (a co-regulator of the HPA axis that potentiates CRF's effects) V1b receptors reduces compulsive-like alcohol drinking and seeking in rodents (Edwards, Guerrero, Ghoneim, Roberts, & Koob, 2012; Funk, O'Dell, Crawford, & Koob, 2006; Marinelli et al., 2007; Richardson, Zhao, et al., 2008; Roberto et al., 2010; Sommer et al., 2008; Valdez et al., 2002). The blockade of CRF1 receptors (systemic or intracentral nucleus of the amygdala) also decreases anxiety- and depression-like behavior (Baldwin, Rassnick, Rivier, Koob, & Britton, 1991; Breese, Knapp, & Overstreet, 2004; Knapp, Overstreet, Moy, & Breese, 2004; Overstreet, Knapp, & Breese, 2004; Rassnick, Heinrichs, Britton, & Koob, 1993; Valdez, Sabino, & Koob, 2004) and attenuates allodynia (i.e., an exacerbated tactile response) in alcohol dependence (Edwards, Vendruscolo, et al., 2012). Both anxiety and pain are hypothesized to contribute to compulsive alcohol drinking (Aoun et al., 2017; Egli, Koob, & Edwards, 2012) in the *withdrawal/negative affect* stage.

In summary, the aforementioned literature suggests that repeated alcohol exposure, similar to excessive stress exposure (e.g., life adversities), may cause

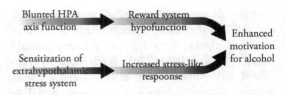

Figure 9.3 Alcohol dependence is associated with decreased HPA axis function that contributes to reward hypofunction. Concomitantly, extrahypothalamic stress systems become sensitized, which contributes to greater stress-like responses. From Tunstall et al. (2017) with permission.

a condition of a hypofunctional HPA axis and stress surfeit in vulnerable individuals (Figure 9.3). This dysregulated stress response is argued to contribute to negative emotional states that drive compulsive alcohol drinking and seeking via negative reinforcement, which is reflected by compulsive alcohol seeking and drinking from a self-medication perspective. These same neuroadaptations may underlie the vulnerability to reward- and stress-related mental disorders, such as anxiety, depression, and pain, which are highly comorbid with alcohol use disorder.

Alterations of Glucocorticoid Receptor Activity in Alcohol Dependence

Alcohol dependence has been reported to be associated with CORT-dependent plasticity in brain reward and stress regions. Acute alcohol withdrawal (i.e., 6–24 hr into withdrawal) was accompanied by the downregulation of glucocorticoid receptor mRNA in the prefrontal cortex, nucleus accumbens, and bed nucleus of the stria terminalis, a putative compensatory effect of receptor overactivation that is possibly attributable to an increase in HPA axis activity in acute alcohol withdrawal (Rasmussen et al., 2000). Perhaps more important, glucocorticoid receptor signaling in the central nucleus of the amygdala, indexed by higher levels of phosphorylated glucocorticoid receptors, was found to be upregulated in dependent rats compared with nondependent rats (Vendruscolo et al., 2015). Notably, the neurophysiology and regulation of glucocorticoids are complex. Plasma levels of CORT have been reported to not necessarily reflect brain levels. In a comparative study of plasma and brain levels of CORT in mice, Little et al. (2008) reported that CORT levels increased in several brain regions in alcohol-dependent mice compared with nondependent mice, although both dependent and nondependent mice had equal levels of CORT in blood. These results support the hypothesis of greater activation of glucocorticoid receptors during acute alcohol withdrawal. One contribution of higher levels of CORT in the brain to alcohol dependence may involve changes in the activity of 11β-hydroxysteroid dehydrogenase 1 (11β-HSD1), which is usually colocalized with glucocorticoid receptors and converts inactive glucocorticoids (e.g., cortisone and 11β-dehydrocorticosterone) into active glucocorticoids (e.g., cortisol and corticosterone).

The functional role of glucocorticoid receptors in the alcohol dependence-induced escalation of drinking during acute withdrawal was evaluated using both acute and chronic glucocorticoid receptor antagonism with mifepristone (also called RU-38486 or RU-486). Chronic mifepristone administration via subcutaneous mifepristone pellets for controlled drug delivery blocked the escalation of alcohol drinking and compulsive-like alcohol seeking in alcohol-dependent rats, without affecting behavior in nondependent rats (Vendruscolo et al., 2012). Once escalated levels of alcohol drinking were established via repeated cycles of alcohol intoxication and withdrawal, acute treatment with mifepristone or the selective glucocorticoid receptor antagonist CORT113176 significantly decreased alcohol drinking in dependent but not nondependent rats (Vendruscolo et al., 2015). The inhibition of 11β-HSD with carbenoxolone was also found to reduce escalated alcohol drinking in both rats and mice (Sanna et al., 2016). Additionally, intracentral nucleus of the amygdala mifepristone infusions significantly decreased alcohol drinking in dependent rats during acute withdrawal (Vendruscolo et al., 2015).

During protracted alcohol abstinence (i.e., several weeks of abstinence from alcohol), glucocorticoid receptor mRNA expression levels were upregulated in the nucleus accumbens, bed nucleus of the stria terminalis, and central nucleus of the amygdala in dependent rats compared with nondependent rats (Vendruscolo et al., 2012) as opposed to glucocorticoid receptor downregulation in acute withdrawal. These findings suggest that HPA axis activity may be at least temporarily reduced during protracted abstinence (Rasmussen et al., 2000) and indicate that the expression of glucocorticoid receptors is dynamically regulated in an alcohol-dependent versus postdependent state. These dynamic changes suggest that glucocorticoid receptor dysregulation contributes not only to dysregulated reward and stress function early in alcohol withdrawal but also to the long-lasting symptoms that persist into protracted abstinence.

Studies that used a systems-biology approach (i.e., based on the assembly and interrogation of gene regulatory networks to investigate genome-wide gene activity in protracted alcohol abstinence) converge with the aforementioned literature on glucocorticoids. The gene that encodes glucocorticoid receptors, NR3C1, was found to be a master regulator in multiple brain regions, including the medial prefrontal cortex, nucleus accumbens, central nucleus of the amygdala, and ventral tegmental area in alcohol dependence (Repunte-Canonigo et al., 2015). During protracted abstinence, chronic, systemic administration of mifepristone (Vendruscolo et al., 2012) and mifepristone infusions in the nucleus accumbens and ventral tegmental area (Repunte-Canonigo et al., 2015) also decreased compulsive-like alcohol drinking specifically in vapor-exposed rats with a history of alcohol dependence. These results, together with findings that indicate that hypersensitivity to stress-related behaviors (e.g., anxiety- and depression-like behavior; Valdez et al., 2004; Walker et al., 2010) persist long into protracted abstinence, suggest that the dysregulation of glucocorticoid receptor function is a mechanism by which negative emotional states persist into protracted abstinence in the *preoccupation/anticipation* stage. In humans, stress and stressors have also been associated with relapse and vulnerability to relapse (Marlatt & Gordon, 1980), and individuals with addiction were hypersensitive to pain during withdrawal, particularly in the face of negative affect (Jochum, Boettger, Burkhardt, Juckel, & Bär, 2012). Indeed, the leading precipitant of relapse in a large-scale replication of Marlatt's taxonomy analysis was negative affect (Lowman, Allen, Stout, and the The Relapse Research Group, 2002), and others found that negative emotion, including elements of anger, frustration, sadness, anxiety, and guilt, was a key factor in relapse (Zywiak, Connors, Maisto, & Westerberg, 2002).

Glucocorticoid receptors and CORT have been implicated in other alcohol-related behaviors. During alcohol withdrawal, CORT levels were positively correlated with the severity of cognitive deficits in individuals with alcohol dependence (Errico, King, Lovallo, & Parsons, 2002). Similarly, in rodents, CORT has been shown to contribute to alcohol withdrawal-induced brain neurotoxicity via the activation of glucocorticoid receptors (Cippitelli et al., 2014; Jacquot et al., 2008; Mulholland et al., 2005; Sharrett-Field, Butler, Berry, Reynolds, & Prendergast, 2013). Treatment with mifepristone during acute withdrawal attenuated memory deficits in mice during protracted alcohol abstinence (Jacquot et al., 2008). The dentate gyrus of the hippocampus exhibits robust neurogenesis and is affected by alcohol dependence (Mandyam, 2013), and mifepristone exerted a neuroprotective effect in this brain region in rats that were exposed to binge-like alcohol (Cippitelli et al., 2014). Furthermore, mifepristone has been reported to decrease alcohol drinking and seeking in rodents under stressful experimental conditions (Koenig & Olive, 2004; O'Callaghan, Croft, Jacquot, & Little, 2005; Simms et al., 2012). Mifepristone also attenuated motor cross-sensitization between stress and alcohol in mice (Roberts, Lessov, & Phillips, 1995) and reduced somatic signs of alcohol withdrawal (Jacquot et al., 2008; Sharrett-Field et al., 2013), indicating that the decrease in glucocorticoid receptor function via receptor antagonism normalized several signs of enhanced stress and alcohol dependence. Systemic and intracentral nucleus of the amygdala (but not intrabasolateral amygdala) administration of mifepristone suppressed the stress-induced reinstatement of alcohol seeking (Simms et al., 2012). Furthermore, rats that were chronically exposed to alcohol drinking and dependence exhibited robust cue/context-induced reinstatement of alcohol seeking during protracted abstinence, an effect that was correlated with higher glucocorticoid receptor activity in the medial prefrontal cortex (Somkuwar et al., 2017). For a thorough review of the interaction of stress hormones, the prefrontal cortex, and alcohol dependence, see Lu and Richardson (2014). These findings suggest that the reinstatement of alcohol seeking may involve a contribution from the dysregulation of glucocorticoid receptor activity in the central nucleus of the amygdala, ventral striatum, and prefrontal cortex, which may have implications for the contribution of stress to relapse in the *preoccupation/anticipation* stage of alcohol addiction. More parsimoniously, prefrontal cortical driving of the extended amygdala and ventral striatum provides the "go signal," whereas the prefrontal cortex provides the "stop signal." An imbalance between these two systems drives craving and relapse to alcohol seeking and use (Koob & Volkow, 2016).

Translational Evidence of Alterations of Glucocorticoid Receptor Activity and Corticotropin-Releasing Factor in Alcohol Dependence

In light of the involvement of glucocorticoid receptors in animal models, a recent double-blind, randomized, placebo-controlled, human laboratory study included 56 non-treatment-seeking individuals who met the diagnostic criteria for alcohol use disorder and tested the effects of mifepristone on alcohol drinking and seeking (Figure 9.4; Vendruscolo et al., 2015). Mifepristone-treated subjects (600 mg daily, orally, for 1 week) exhibited lower craving for alcohol compared with placebo-treated subjects. Craving was precipitated by the presentation of cues that were associated with the individual's preferred alcoholic beverage in the laboratory. Mifepristone-treated subjects also reported a reduction of alcohol

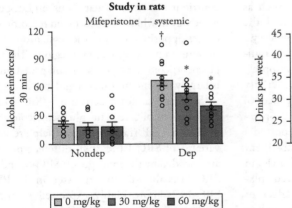
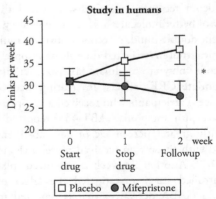

Figure 9.4 (*A*) Higher glucocorticoid receptor function mediates compulsive-like alcohol self-administration in alcohol-dependent rats. The blockade of glucocorticoid receptors with systemic mifepristone injections dose-dependently reduced alcohol intake, specifically in dependent rats. The data are expressed as the mean ± SEM number of lever presses in 30-min operant self-administration sessions. Every lever press (FR1 schedule of reinforcement) resulted in the delivery of 0.1 ml of alcohol (10%, w/v) or water. Dotplots indicate individual observations for each condition. (*B*) In a clinical study in alcohol-dependent individuals, mifepristone reduced alcohol cue-induced craving and drinking and improved liver function. The data are expressed as the total number of alcoholic drinks consumed per week (estimated marginal mean ± SEM). *$p < 0.05$, mifepristone versus placebo. From Vendruscolo et al. (2015) with permission.

drinking during pharmacological treatment and at least for 1 week after treatment cessation. Importantly, few adverse effects were reported by mifepristone-treated individuals, and liver function appeared to improve in this group of subjects. These effects are possibly attributable to an indirect glucocorticoid receptor-mediated decrease in CRF neurotransmission. A larger study is ongoing to confirm the potential of mifepristone for the treatment of alcohol dependence. A genetic alteration (i.e., single-nucleotide polymorphism) of the FK506-binding protein, a negative regulator of glucocorticoid receptors, was associated with problematic drinking in humans (Nylander et al., 2017), providing additional support for dysregulation of the glucocorticoid receptor system in alcohol dependence.

Two double-blind, randomized, placebo-controlled, human laboratory studies with treatment-seeking subjects with alcohol use disorder failed to support the efficacy of CRF1 receptor antagonists in reducing craving for alcohol (Kwako et al., 2015; Schwandt et al., 2016). However, it is still premature to conclude that compounds that target CRF neurotransmission are ineffective for the treatment of alcohol dependence. Numerous reasons may explain the prior lack of efficacy of anti-CRF compounds in humans (for review, see Schreiber & Gilpin, 2018; Spierling & Zorrilla, 2017), such as poor pharmacokinetic profiles of the drugs, inadequate experimental populations, and the temporal window of alcohol withdrawal symptoms, but the overall target of CRF still remains viable. Additional well-designed studies with novel anti-CRF compounds and indirect modulators of CRF activity, such as glucocorticoid receptor antagonists, may aid the discovery of better molecules with clinical efficacy.

A recent double-blind, placebo-controlled, multisite clinical trial investigated the role of vasopressin, which is known to modulate HPA axis activity and potentiate CRF's effects, in treating alcohol dependence. Participants who received a vasopressin V1B receptor antagonist (ABT-436) reported a significantly greater percentage of days abstinent compared with those who received placebo (Ryan et al., 2017). Another 24-week randomized, placebo-controlled study investigated the effect of baclofen, a GABA derivative that is reported to decrease craving for alcohol in humans (Farokhnia et al., 2017; Reynaud et al., 2017), on HPA axis function. Alcohol-dependent patients exhibited higher ACTH levels compared with healthy controls. In the alcohol-dependent group, a high dose of baclofen significantly decreased cortisol levels

compared with placebo-treated patients (Geisel, Schlemm, Hellweg, Wiedemann, & Müller, 2018). Furthermore, higher basal cortisol:ACTH or stress-induced cortisol:ACTH ratios have been reported to be strongly associated with drinks per drinking days in alcohol-dependent men following treatment discharge (Adinoff et al., 2017). Altogether, these findings illustrate the potential of medications that modulate HPA axis function for the treatment of alcohol use disorder.

Sensitization of Brain Stress Systems by Alcohol

Glucocorticoid receptors produce genomic and non-genomic effects (Gray, Kogan, Marrocco, & McEwen, 2017; Kadmiel & Cidlowski, 2013). Nongenomic effects will not be discussed herein. The glucocorticoid receptor is a transcription factor that belongs to the nuclear receptor superfamily. When activated by CORT, glucocorticoid receptors translocate from the cytoplasm to the nucleus. The process of intracellular glucocorticoid receptor trafficking is regulated by a host of chaperones. In the nucleus, glucocorticoid receptors bind directly to glucocorticoid response elements in the DNA or indirectly by tethering to other transcription factors to cause the activation or repression of gene expression (Grbesa & Hakim, 2017; Kadmiel & Cidlowski, 2013). As discussed earlier, chronic alcohol exposure and withdrawal or chronic stress and CORT exposure downregulate CRF in the PVN (i.e., HPA axis tolerance that contributes to reward deficits). CRF upregulation in extrahypothalamic regions (e.g., extended amygdala) contributes to stress surfeit. Thus, an intriguing issue is the way in which glucocorticoid receptor activation causes opposite effects in the regulation of CRF expression in two distinct brain regions. The valence of glucocorticoid receptor actions on gene transcription is largely dependent on co-regulators.

Steroid receptor coactivator 1 (SRC-1) has been critically implicated in glucocorticoid receptor-mediated CRF transcription. There are two splice variants of SRC-1 (i.e., two different proteins that are encoded by the same gene): SRC-1a and SRC-1e. SRC-1a is abundantly expressed in the PVN, and SRC-1e is more highly expressed in the central nucleus of the amygdala (Meijer et al., 2000). Importantly, SRC-1e has been reported to repress CRF transcription. However, SRC-1e has been shown to lack repressive function (Zalachoras et al., 2016). The overexpression of SRC-1a in cells that contain glucocorticoid receptors increased both the efficacy and potency of glucocorticoid receptor-dependent

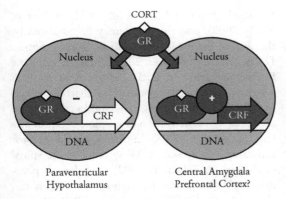

CORT

Nucleus

Nucleus

GR

CRF

DNA

GR

CRF

DNA

Paraventricular
Hypothalamus

Central Amygdala
Prefrontal Cortex?

Figure 9.5 Glucocorticoid receptors exert distinct regulatory actions on the expression of corticotropin-releasing factor (CRF) in the paraventricular nucleus (PVN) and central nucleus of the amygdala. Steroid receptor co-activator 1 (SRC-1) has divergent effects on the expression of CRF within these two stress-regulatory regions. CRF is downregulated in the PVN, whereas CRF is upregulated in the central nucleus of the amygdala and potentially in the prefrontal cortex. These neuroadaptations are hypothesized to contribute to brain reward hypofunction and stress sensitization that characterize the transition from recreational alcohol drinking to compulsive drinking. From Edwards et al. (2015) with permission.

repression of CRF expression, whereas SRC-1e significantly reduced glucocorticoid receptor-dependent repression of the CRF promoter (Van der Laan, Lachize, Vreugdenhil, de Kloet, & Meijer, 2008).

Thus, the divergent actions of SRC-1a and SRC-1e and different distributions in the brain may at least partially explain the opposite effects of CORT/glucocorticoid receptors on the expression of CRF in the PVN and central nucleus of the amygdala and potentially prefrontal cortex (Figure 9.5). Recently, Zalachoras et al. (2016) used antisense oligonucleotides, which are synthetic single-stranded strings of nucleic acids that interfere with gene expression by binding to RNA, to manipulate SRC-1 splice variants in vivo. Antisense oligonucleotides are synthetic single-stranded strings of nucleic acids that bind to RNA and thereby alter or reduce the expression of target RNA. In this approach, antisense oligonucleotide infusion in the central nucleus of the amygdala favored the action of SCR-1a over SRC-1e (i.e., repressed CRF expression) and decreased anxiety/fear-like behavior in mice (Zalachoras et al., 2016). The effect of manipulating SRC-1 splice variants in compulsive drinking remains to be determined. This is an exciting new therapeutic opportunity, given that antisense oligonucleotides have already been successfully used in humans for the treatment of neurodegenerative disorders (Evers, Toonen, & van Roon-Mom, 2015).

Interim Summary

Similar to chronic stress, alcohol misuse and alcohol withdrawal alter reward and stress systems in the brain. These changes led to blunted reward function and stress sensitization that contributes to negative emotional states that drive compulsive alcohol seeking and drinking. Additionally, in alcohol dependence, the impact of stressors is exacerbated, which further drives the dysregulations described earlier. Because these brain changes are long lasting, and negative emotional states persist long into protracted abstinence, individuals with a history of alcohol dependence are particularly vulnerable to stress-induced alcohol craving and relapse. More specifically, the preclinical and clinical findings that are discussed herein provide compelling evidence of a role for corticosterone-dependent plasticity and alterations of glucocorticoid receptor neurotransmission in hypothalamic and extrahypothalamic brain regions in all three stages of the alcohol addiction cycle. Glucocorticoid receptor antagonism combined with behavioral treatments to cope with stress, such as cognitive-behavioral therapy (Longabaugh & Morgenstern, 1999), may be potentially effective in normalizing negative feedback along the HPA axis and reversing the sensitization of extrahypothalamic stress systems and disruption of executive function.

Brain Stress Systems: Beyond Glucocorticoids and Corticotropin-Releasing Factor

The central role of glucocorticoids and CRF in the brain in behavioral responses to stressors and, more important for the present review, in the *withdrawal/negative affect* stage of the alcohol addiction cycle does not exclude other parallel brain stress systems, some of which interact with CRF directly, others perhaps indirectly (Koob, 2015). Norepinephrine systems in the extended amygdala play a role in the negative motivational state and increased self-administration associated with dependence and alcohol dependence in particular. In animals and humans, central noradrenergic systems are activated during acute withdrawal from alcohol. In humans, alcohol withdrawal is associated with the activation of noradrenergic function, and the signs and symptoms of alcohol withdrawal in humans are blocked by postsynaptic β-adrenergic receptor blockade (Romach & Sellers, 1991). Alcohol withdrawal signs are also blocked in animals by α1-adrenergic receptor antagonists and β-adrenergic receptor antagonists and the selective blockade of norepinephrine synthesis (Trzaskowska & Kostowski, 1983). Using the alcohol vapor model, the α1-adrenergic receptor antagonist prazosin and β-adrenergic receptor antagonists selectively blocked the increase in drinking that was associated with acute withdrawal (Gilpin & Koob, 2010; Walker, Rasmussen, Raskind, & Koob, 2008). Thus, converging data suggest that noradrenergic neurotransmission is enhanced during alcohol withdrawal and that noradrenergic functional antagonists can block aspects of alcohol withdrawal.

The dynamic nature of the brain's stress system responses to challenge is illustrated by the pronounced interaction between central nervous system CRF systems and central nervous system norepinephrine systems. Conceptualized as a feed-forward system at multiple levels of the pons and basal forebrain, CRF activates norepinephrine, and norepinephrine in turn activates CRF (Koob, 1999). Much pharmacological, physiological, and anatomical evidence supports an important role for a CRF-norepinephrine interaction in the region of the locus coeruleus in response to stressors (Valentino, Page, & Curtis, 1991; Van Bockstaele et al., 1998). However, norepinephrine also stimulates CRF release in the PVN (Alonso, Szafarczyk, Balmefrézol, & Assenmacher, 1986), bed nucleus of the stria terminalis, and central nucleus of the amygdala. Such feed-forward systems were further hypothesized to have powerful functional significance for mobilizing an organism's response to environmental challenge, but such a mechanism may be particularly vulnerable to pathology (Koob, 1999). For example, these results are consistent with the hypothesis that noradrenergic brainstem systems can drive forebrain CRF systems and vice versa in a stress-activating loop that can possibly kindle brain stress responsivity once engaged (Koob, 1999).

Dynorphin is an opioid peptide that binds to κ-opioid receptors. The activation of κ-opioid receptors produces aversive effects in animals and humans (Mucha & Herz, 1985; Pfeiffer, Brantl, Herz, & Emrich, 1986). Chronic administration of psychostimulants and opioids has long been hypothesized to activate cyclic adenosine monophosphate response element binding protein (CREB), which in turn activates dynorphin in medium spiny neurons that in turn feedback and decrease the activity of ventral tegmental dopamine neurons (Carlezon, Nestler, & Neve, 2000; Nestler, 2001). Although κ-opioid receptor agonists suppress nondependent drinking, presumably via aversive stimulus effects (Wee & Koob, 2010), κ-opioid antagonists block the excessive drinking associated with alcohol withdrawal and dependence (Hölter, Henniger, Lipkowski, &

Spanagel, 2000; Schank et al., 2012; Walker & Koob, 2008), and this effect may be mediated by the shell of the nucleus accumbens (Nealey, Smith, Davis, Smith, & Walker, 2011). There are dynamic interactions between CRF and κ-opioid receptor systems. Some have hypothesized that the effects of CRF in producing negative emotional states are mediated by the activation of κ-opioid receptor systems (Land et al., 2008). In turn, κ-opioid receptor activation can activate CRF systems in the spinal cord (Song & Takemori, 1992), and there is pharmacological evidence that dynorphin systems can also activate the CRF system. A CRF1 receptor antagonist blocked the κ-opioid receptor agonist-induced reinstatement of cocaine seeking in squirrel monkeys (Valdez, Platt, Rowlett, Rüedi-Bettschen, & Spealman, 2007).

Other neurotransmitter/neuromodulatory systems that comprise the brain stress system in the extended amygdala include vasopressin, hypocretin (orexin), substance P, and neuroimmune factors (Figure 9.6). In addition to CRF and dynorphin, there is evidence that norepinephrine, vasopressin, substance P, and hypocretin (orexin) may all contribute to negative emotional states of drug withdrawal, particularly alcohol withdrawal (Koob, 2008). For example, using the compulsive-like alcohol seeking model of excessive drinking during withdrawal in dependent rats, a β-adrenergic receptor antagonist and vasopressin V1b receptor antagonist blocked excessive drinking (Edwards, Guerrero, et al., 2012; Gilpin & Koob, 2010; Walker et al., 2008). Knockout of the neurokinin-1 receptor blocked drinking in mice, and a substance P receptor antagonist blocked craving in humans with alcohol use disorder (George et al., 2008). A hypocretin-1 receptor antagonist selectively decreased drinking in dependent mice (Lopez, Moorman, Aston-Jones, & Becker, 2016). A likely target for these actions is the extended amygdala, suggesting that multiple distributed systems from the brainstem and hypothalamus converge in the extended amygdala to contribute to negative emotional states (Figure 9.6). Thus, activation of this pro-stress, pro-negative emotional state system is multidetermined and comprises the neurochemical bases for hedonic opponent processes (Koob, 2015). However, one may hypothesize that there is a multidetermined anti-stress buffer neurocircuitry that may help return the organism to homeostasis if activated. Thus, vulnerability to alcohol use disorder may involve not only a sensitized stress system but also a hypoactive stress buffer, so that behavioral and pharmacological

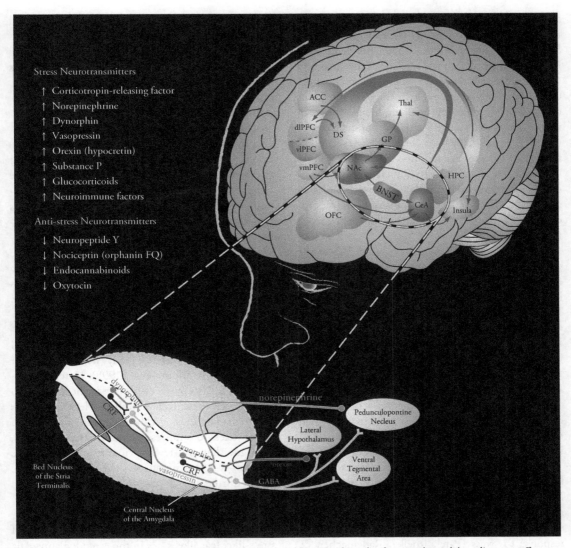

Figure 9.6 Neural circuitry associated with the three stages of the addiction cycle, with a focus on the *withdrawal/negative affect* stage and the extended amygdala. The targets that are identified in this review that are relevant to the *withdrawal/negative affect* stage are listed in the left-hand corner. In the right-hand corner is the neurocircuitry of the pathophysiology of addiction. The negative emotional state of withdrawal engages activation of the extended amygdala. The extended amygdala is composed of several basal forebrain structures, including the bed nucleus of the stria terminalis, central nucleus of the amygdala, and possibly the medial portion (or shell) of the nucleus accumbens. Stress neurotransmitters: neurotransmitter systems that are engaged in the neurocircuitry of the extended amygdala that convey negative emotional states. Anti-stress neurotransmitters: neurotransmitter systems that may buffer negative emotional states. The lower diagram illustrates the extended amygdala in detail. A major neurotransmitter in the extended amygdala is corticotropin-releasing factor (CRF), projecting to the brainstem where noradrenergic neurons provide a major projection reciprocally to the extended amygdala. Acb, nucleus accumbens; BLA, basolateral amygdala; VTA, ventral tegmental area; SNc, substantia nigra pars compacta; VGP, ventral globus pallidus; DGP, dorsal globus pallidus; BNST, bed nucleus of the stria terminalis; CeA, central nucleus of the amygdala; NE, norepinephrine. Modified from Koob (2015) and Koob and Volkow (2010) with permission.

interventions that block pro-stress and stimulate anti-stress systems may be particularly interesting targets for the treatment of alcohol use disorder.

Brain Anti-Stress Systems

Neuropeptide Y has been hypothesized to have effects that are opposite to CRF in the negative

motivational state of withdrawal from drugs of abuse (Heilig & Koob, 2007). NPY is a neuropeptide with dramatic anxiolytic-like properties. It is localized to the amygdala, and evidence suggests that the activation of NPY in the central nucleus of the amygdala can selectively block dependence-induced drinking. Intracerebroventricular NPY administration blocked the increase in drug intake that was associated with alcohol dependence (Thorsell, Slawecki, & Ehlers, 2005a, 2005b). An injection of NPY directly in the central nucleus of the amygdala (Gilpin, Misra, & Koob, 2008) and the viral vector-enhanced expression of NPY in the central nucleus of the amygdala also blocked the increase in drug intake that was associated with alcohol dependence (Thorsell et al., 2007). At the cellular level, NPY, like CRF1 receptor antagonists, blocks the increase in GABA release in the central nucleus of the amygdala that is produced by alcohol. When administered chronically, NPY blocks the transition to excessive drinking with the development of dependence (Gilpin et al., 2011).

Nociceptin (also known as orphanin FQ) is the endogenous ligand for the nociceptin opioid (NOP) receptor (formerly referred to as opioid receptor-like-1; Meunier et al., 1995; Reinscheid et al., 1995). Nociceptin generally attenuates stress-like responses and has a broad anxiolytic-like profile in animals. Nociceptin and synthetic NOP receptor agonists blocked alcohol consumption in rats, decreased the reinstatement of drug-seeking behavior (De Guglielmo et al., 2015; Economidou et al., 2008), and had effects on GABA synaptic activity in the central nucleus of the amygdala, similar to NPY. High numbers of nociceptin-containing neurons are found in the extended amygdala, cortex, and midbrain.

Cannabinoid agonists can have both anxiogenic-like and anxiolytic-like effects in rodents (Viveros, Marco, & File, 2005), but the effects of endocannabinoids are more consistent. Several studies indicate that endocannabinoid production increases in response to stress (Patel, Roelke, Rademacher, & Hillard, 2005). The elevation of interstitial endocannabinoid levels through the inhibition of endocannabinoid clearance mechanisms produces anxiolytic-like effects in various animal models of anxiety, particularly under stressful or aversive conditions, and a reduction of CB1 receptor signaling produces anxiogenic-like behavioral effects (Serrano & Parsons, 2011). Additionally, the disruption of CB1 receptor signaling impairs the extinction of aversive memories, which may have similarities to deficits that are associated with stress pathophysiology, such as post-traumatic stress disorder (Serrano & Parsons, 2011). Supporting this hypothesis, there is evidence that excessive alcohol-seeking behavior can be blocked by endocannabinoid clearance inhibition (Zhou et al., 2017). Thus, the dysregulation of endocannabinoid function may be hypothesized to contribute to the negative affective disturbances that are

associated with drug dependence and protracted withdrawal, or one could speculate that endocannabinoids play a protective role in preventing drug dependence by buffering the stress activation that is associated with withdrawal.

Allostatic Stress System Changes in Addiction: A Neurocircuitry Perspective

Our hypothesis is that as dependence on alcohol develops, reward systems are compromised, and brain stress systems, such as CRF and dynorphin, are recruited in the extended amygdala. We further hypothesize that these brain stress neurotransmitters that are known to be activated during the development of excessive drug taking comprise a between-system opponent process, and this activation is manifest when the drug in removed, producing anxiety, hyperkatifeia, and irritability symptoms associated with acute and protracted abstinence. Between-system neuroadaptations can also impact within-system neuroadaptations to further exacerbate negative emotional states by suppressing reward function, which was originally hypothesized for dynorphin by Carlezon et al., 1998). Here, the activation of CREB by excessive dopamine and opioid peptide receptor activation in the nucleus accumbens is hypothesized to trigger the induction of dynorphin to feedback to suppress dopamine release. Thus, we argue that anti-reward circuits are recruited as between-system neuroadaptations (Koob & Bloom, 1988) during the development of addiction and produce aversive or stress-like states (Aston-Jones, Delfs, Druhan, & Zhu, 1999; Koob, 2003; Nestler, 2001) via two mechanisms: direct activation of stress-like, fear-like states in the extended amygdala (CRF) and indirect activation of a depression-like state by suppressing dopamine (dynorphin and possibly CRF).

The hypothesized allostatic, sensitized stress state and dysregulated reward state produce the motivational symptoms of acute withdrawal and protracted abstinence and provide the basis by which drug priming, drug cues, and acute stressors acquire even more power to elicit drug-seeking behavior (Koob, 2015; Vendruscolo et al., 2012). Notably, multiple detoxifications and reinstatement to dependence in humans can "kindle" withdrawal and produce less responsiveness to treatments (Malcolm, Roberts, Wang, Myrick, & Anton, 2000). Blockade of the brain stress systems, however, can block the development of "kindling" anxiety-like responses in animal models, lending support to the key role of brain stress systems in kindling phenomena (Breese,

Overstreet, Knapp, & Navarro, 2005). Thus, the combination of decreases in reward system function and recruitment of anti-reward systems provides a powerful source of negative reinforcement that contributes to compulsive drug-seeking behavior and addiction.

Summary

The complex nature of the brain stress system involves multiple neurotransmitter systems that mediate stress sensitization, dysphoria, hypohedonia, and executive dysfunction. The present chapter focused on the role of the HPA axis and extrahypothalamic stress systems in alcohol dependence. We discussed evidence that indicates that chronic exposure to alcohol leads to neuroadaptations that underlie incentive sensitization/pathological habit formation, reward hypofunction/stress sensitization, and impairments in executive function. These neuroadaptations contribute to the development of negative emotional states that powerfully drive compulsive alcohol drinking and seeking in moderate to severe alcohol use disorder. Activation of the HPA axis is involved in glucocorticoid-dependent alcohol reinforcement during the initial phase of alcohol use in the *binge/intoxication* stage of addiction. As drinking intensifies, the HPA axis becomes compromised (neuroendocrine tolerance), and extrahypothalamic stress systems (e.g., extended amygdala) become concomitantly sensitized. These neuroadaptations lead to reward hypofunction and stress surfeit that underlie the negative emotional states (i.e., anxiety, dysphoria, pain, irritability) that are characteristic of the *withdrawal/negative affect* stage. These changes are accompanied by prefrontal cortex dysfunction, thus compromising executive function (i.e., cognitive deficits and poor decision making) that may contribute to craving and relapse in the *preoccupation/anticipation* stage.

Acknowledgments

The authors thank Michael Arends for assistance with manuscript preparation and editing. The National Institute on Drug Abuse Intramural Research Program supported this work.

References

Adinoff, B., Leonard, D., Price, J., Javors, M. A., Walker, R., Brown, E. S.,...Rao, U. (2017). Adrenocortical sensitivity, moderated by ongoing stress, predicts drinking intensity in alcohol-dependent men. *Psychoneuroendocrinology, 76*, 67–76.

Adinoff, B., Ruether, K., Krebaum, S., Iranmanesh, A., & Williams, M. J. (2003). Increased salivary cortisol concentrations during chronic alcohol intoxication in a naturalistic clinical sample of men. *Alcoholism: Clinical and Experimental Research, 27*, 1420–1427.

Alonso, G., Szafarczyk, A., Balmefrézol, M., & Assenmacher, I (1986). Immunocytochemical evidence for stimulatory control by the ventral noradrenergic bundle of parvocellular neurons of the paraventricular nucleus secreting corticotropin releasing hormone and vasopressin in rats. *Brain Research 397*, 297–307.

Aoun, E. G., Jimenez, V. A., Vendruscolo, L. F., Walter, N. R., Barbier, E., Ferrulli, A.,...Leggio, L. (2017). A relationship between the aldosterone-mineralocorticoid receptor pathway and alcohol drinking: Preliminary translational findings across rats, monkeys and humans. *Molecular Psychiatry*. doi:10.1038/mp.2017.97.

Aston-Jones, G., Delfs, J. M., Druhan, J., & Zhu, Y. (1999). The bed nucleus of the stria terminalis. A target site for noradrenergic actions in opiate withdrawal. *Annals of the NY Academy of Sciences, 877*, 486–498.

Baldwin, H. A., Rassnick, S., Rivier, J., Koob, G. F., & Britton, K. T. (1991). CRF antagonist reverses the "anxiogenic" response to ethanol withdrawal in the rat. *Psychopharmacology (Berlin), 103*, 227–232.

Barbier, E., Tapocik, J. D., Juergens, N., Pitcairn, C., Borich, A., Schank, J. R.,...Heiling, M. (2015). DNA methylation in the medial prefrontal cortex regulates alcohol-induced behavior and plasticity. *Journal of Neuroscience, 35*, 6153–6164.

Barrot, M., Marinelli, M., Abrous, D. N., Rougé-Pont, F., Le Moal, M., & Piazza, P. V. (2000). The dopaminergic hyper-responsiveness of the shell of the nucleus accumbens is hormone-dependent. *European Journal of Neuroscience, 12*, 973–979.

Berridge, K. C. (2012). From prediction error to incentive salience: Mesolimbic computation of reward motivation. *European Journal of Neuroscience, 35*, 1124–1143.

Breese, G. R., Knapp, D. J., & Overstreet, D. H. (2004). Stress sensitization of ethanol withdrawal-induced reduction in social interaction: Inhibition by CRF-1 and benzodiazepine receptor antagonists and a 5-HT1A-receptor agonist. *Neuropsychopharmacology, 29*, 470–482.

Breese, G. R., Overstreet, D. H., Knapp, D. J., & Navarro, M. (2005). Prior multiple ethanol withdrawals enhance stress-induced anxiety-like behavior: Inhibition by CRF1- and benzodiazepine-receptor antagonists and a 5-HT1a-receptor agonist. *Neuropsychopharmacology, 30*, 1662–1669.

Breslow, R. A., Castle, I.-J. P., Chen, C. M., & Graubard, B. I. (2017). Trends in alcohol consumption among older Americans: National Health Interview Surveys, 1997 to 2014. *Alcoholism: Clinical and Experimental Research, 41*, 976–986.

Carlezon, W. A., Nestler, E. J., & Neve, R. L. (2000). Herpes simplex virus-mediated gene transfer as a tool for neuropsychiatric research. *Critical Reviews in Neurobiology, 14*, 47–67.

Carlezon, W. A., Thome, J., Olson, V. G., Lane-Ladd, S. B., Brodkin, E. S., Hiroi, N.,...Nestler, E. J. (1998). Regulation of cocaine reward by CREB. *Science, 282*, 2272–2275.

Cippitelli, A., Damadzic, R., Hamelink, C., Brunnquell, M., Thorsell, A., Heilig, M.,...Eskay, R. L. (2014). Binge-like ethanol consumption increases corticosterone levels and neurodegneration whereas occupancy of type II glucocorticoid receptors with mifepristone is neuroprotective. *Addiction Biology, 19*, 27–36.

Crabbe, J. C., Wahlsten, D., & Dudek, B. C. (1999). Genetics of mouse behavior: Interactions with laboratory environment. *Science, 284*, 1670–1672.

Cunningham, C. L., Fidler, T. L., & Hill, K. G. (2000). Animal models of alcohol's motivational effects. *Alcohol Research & Health*, *24*, 85–92.

Economidou, D., Hansson, A. C., Weiss, F., Terasmaa, A., Sommer, W. H., Cippitelli, A.,...Heilig, M. (2008). Dysregulation of nociceptin/orphanin FQ activity in the amygdala is linked to excessive alcohol drinking in the rat. *Biological Psychiatry*, *64*, 211–218.

Edwards, S., Guerrero, M., Ghoneim, O. M., Roberts, E., & Koob, G. F. (2012). Evidence that vasopressin V1b receptors mediate the transition to excessive drinking in ethanol-dependent rats. *Addiction Biology*, *17*, 76–85.

Edwards, S., Little, H. J., Richardson, H. N., &Vendruscolo, L. F. (2015). Divergent regulation of distinct glucocorticoid systems in alcohol dependence. *Alcohol*, *49*, 811–816.

Edwards, S., Vendruscolo, L. F., Schlosburg, J. E., Misra, K. K., Wee, S. Park, P. E.,...Koob, G. F. (2012). Development of mechanical hypersensitivity in rats during heroin and ethanol dependence: Alleviation by CRF₁ receptor antagonism. *Neuropharmacology*, *62*, 1142–1151.

Egli, M., Koob, G. F., & Edwards, S. (2012). Alcohol dependence as a chronic pain disorder. *Neuroscience & Biobehavioral Reviews*, *36*, 2179–2192.

Ellis, F. W. (1966). Effect of ethanol on plasma corticosterone levels. *Journal of Pharmacology and Experimental Therapeutics*, *153*, 121–127.

Errico, A. L., King, A. C., Lovallo, W. R., & Parsons, O. A. (2002). Cortisol dysregulation and cognitive impairment in abstinent male alcoholics. *Alcoholism: Clinical and Experimental Research*, *26*, 1198–1204.

Everitt, B. J., Belin, D., Economidou, D., Pelloux, Y., Dalley, J. W., & Robbins, T. W. (2008). Review. Neural mechanisms underlying the vulnerability to develop compulsive drug-seeking habits and addiction. *Philosophical Transactions of the Royal Society of London*, *363*, 3125–3135.

Evers, M. M., Toonen, L. J. A., & van Roon-Mom, W. M. C. (2015). Antisense oligonucleotides in therapy for neurodegenerative disorders. *Advanced Drug Delivery Reviews*, *87*, 90–103.

Fahlke, C., Hård, E., Eriksson, C. J., Engel, J. A., & Hansen, S. (1995). Consequence of long-term exposure to corticosterone or dexamethasone on ethanol consumption in the adrenalectomized rat, and the effect of type I and type II corticosteroid receptor antagonists. *Psychopharmacology (Berlin)*, *117*, 216–224.

Farokhnia, M., Schwandt, M. L., Lee, M. R., Bollinger, J. W., Farinelli, L. A., Amodio J. P.,...Leggio, L. (2017). Biobehavioral effects of baclofen in anxious alcohol-dependent individuals: A randomized, double-blind, placebo-controlled, laboratory study. *Translational Psychiatry*, *7*, e1108.

Fidler, T. L., Clews, T. W., & Cunningham, C. L. (2006). Reestablishing an intragastric ethanol self-infusion model in rats. *Alcoholism: Clinical and Experimental Research*, *30*, 414–428.

Fidler, T. L., Dion, A. M., Powers, M. S., Ramirez, J. J., Mulgrew, J. A., Smitasin, P. J.,...Cunningham, C. L. (2011). Intragastric self-infusion of ethanol in high and low drinking mouse genotypes after passive ethanol exposure. *Genes, Brain, and Behavior*, *10*, 264–275.

Fidler, T. L., Oberlin, B. G., Struthers, A. M., & Cunningham, C. L. (2009). Schedule of passive ethanol exposure affects subsequent intragastric ethanol self-infusion. *Alcoholism: Clinical and Experimental Research*, *33*, 1909–1923.

Finn, D. A., Snelling, C., Fretwell, A. M., Tanchuck, M. A., Underwood, L., Cole, M.,...Roberts, A. J. (2007). Increased drinking during withdrawal from intermittent ethanol exposure is blocked by the CRF receptor antagonist D-Phe-CRF(12-41). *A Alcoholism: Clinical and Experimental Research*, *31*, 939–949.

Fox, H. C., Bergquist, K. L., Hong, K-I., & Sinha, R. (2007). Stress-induced and alcohol cue-induced craving in recently abstinent alcohol-dependent individuals. *Alcoholism: Clinical and Experimental Research*, *31*, 395–403.

Fredriksson, I., Adhikary, S., Steensland, P., Vendruscolo, L. F., Bonci, A., Shaham, Y.,...Bossert, J. M. (2017). Prior exposure to alcohol has no effect on cocaine self-administration and relapse in rats: Evidence from a rat model that does not support the gateway hypothesis. *Neuropsychopharmacology*, *42*, 1001–1011.

Funk, C. K., O'Dell, L. E., Crawford, E. F., & Koob, G. F. (2006). Corticotropin-releasing factor within the central nucleus of the amygdala mediates enhanced ethanol self-administration in withdrawn, ethanol-dependent rats. *Journal of Neuroscience*, *26*, 11324–11332.

Garabedian, M. J., Harris, C. A., & Jeanneteau, F. (2017). Glucocorticoid receptor action in metabolic and neuronal function. *F1000Research*, *6*, 1208.

Geisel, O., Schlemm, L., Hellweg, R., Wiedemann, K., & Müller, C. A. (2018). Hypothalamic-pituitary-adrenocortical axis activity in alcohol-dependent patients during treatment with high-dose baclofen. *Pharmacopsychiatry*, doi:10.1055/s-0043-124189.

George, D. T., Gilman, J., Hersh, J., Thorsell, A., Herion, D., Geyer, C.,...Heilig, M. (2008). Neurokinin 1 receptor antagonism as a possible therapy for alcoholism. *Science*, *319*, 1536–1539.

Gilpin, N. W., & Koob, G. F. (2010). Effects of β-adrenoceptor antagonists on alcohol drinking by alcohol-dependent rats. *Psychopharmacology (Berlin)*, *212*, 431–439.

Gilpin, N. W., Misra, K., Herman, M. A., Cruz, M. T., Koob, G. F., & Roberto, M. (2011). Neuropeptide Y opposes alcohol effects on gamma-aminobutyric acid release in amygdala and blocks the transition to alcohol dependence. *Biological Psychiatry*, *69*, 1091–1099.

Gilpin, N. W., Misra, K. , & Koob, G. F. (2008). Neuropeptide Y in the central nucleus of the amygdala suppresses dependence-induced increases in alcohol drinking. *Pharmacology, Biochemistry, and Behavior*, *90*, 475–480.

Gilpin, N. W., Smith, A. D., Cole, M., Weiss, F., Koob, G. F., & Richardson, H. N. (2009). Operant behavior and alcohol levels in blood and brain of alcohol-dependent rats. *Alcoholism: Clinical and Experimental Research*, *33*, 2113–2123.

Gray, J. D., Kogan, J. F., Marrocco, J., & McEwen, B. S. (2017). Genomic and epigenomic mechanisms of glucocorticoids in the brain. *Nature Reviews Endocrinology*, *13*, 661–673.

Grbesa, I., & Hakim, O. (2017). Genomic effects of glucocorticoids. *Protoplasma*, *254*, 1175–1185.

De Guglielmo, G., Kallupi, M., Cole, M. D., & George, O. (2017). Voluntary induction and maintenance of alcohol dependence in rats using alcohol vapor self-administration. *Psychopharmacology (Berlin)*, *234*, 2009–2018.

De Guglielmo, G., Martin-Fardon, R., Teshima, K., Ciccocioppo, R., & Weiss, F. (2015). MT-7716, a potent NOP receptor agonist, preferentially reduces ethanol seeking and reinforcement in post-dependent rats. *Addiction Biology*, *20*, 643–651.

Guillemin, R. (1978). Peptides in the brain: The new endocrinology of the neuron. *Science, 202*, 390–402.

Heilig, M., & Koob, G. F. (2007). A key role for corticotropin-releasing factor in alcohol dependence. *Trends in Neuroscience, 30*, 399–406.

Heinz, A., Löber, S., Georgi, A., Wrase, J., Hermann, D., Rey, E.-R.,...Mann, K. (2003). Reward craving and withdrawal relief craving: Assessment of different motivational pathways to alcohol intake. *Alcohol and Alcoholism, 38*, 35–39.

Hingson, R. W., & White, A. (2013). Trends in extreme binge drinking among US high school seniors. *JAMA Pediatrics, 167*, 996–998.

Hingson, R. W., Zha, W., & White, A. M. (2017). Drinking beyond the binge threshold: Predictors, consequences, and changes in the U.S. *American Journal of Preventive Medicine, 52*, 717–727.

Hodos, W. (1961). Progressive ratio as a measure of reward strength. *Science, 134*, 943–944.

Holgate, J. Y., Shariff, M., Mu, E. W. H., & Bartlett, S. (2017). A rat drinking in the dark model for studying ethanol and sucrose consumption. *Frontiers in Behavioral Neuroscience, 11*, 29.

Hölter, S. M., Engelmann, M., Kirschke, C., Liebsch, G., Landgraf, R., & Spanagel, R. (1998). Long-term ethanol self-administration with repeated ethanol deprivation episodes changes ethanol drinking pattern and increases anxiety-related behaviour during ethanol deprivation in rats. *Behavioral Pharmacology, 9*, 41–48.

Hölter, S. M., Henniger, M. S., Lipkowski, A. W., & Spanagel, R. (2000). Kappa-opioid receptors and relapse-like drinking in long-term ethanol-experienced rats. *Psychopharmacology (Berlin), 153*, 93–102.

Jacquot, C., Croft, A. P., Prendergast, M. A., Mulholland, P., Shaw, S. G., & Little, H. J. (2008). Effects of the glucocorticoid antagonist, mifepristone, on the consequences of withdrawal from long term alcohol consumption. *Alcoholism: Clinical and Experimental Research, 32*, 2107–2116.

Ji, D., Gilpin, N. W., Richardson, H. N., Rivier, C. L., & Koob, G. F. (2008). Effects of naltrexone, duloxetine, and a corticotropin-releasing factor type 1 receptor antagonist on binge-like alcohol drinking in rats. *Behavioral Pharmacology, 19*, 1–12.

Jimenez, V. A., & Grant, K. A. (2017). Studies using macaque monkeys to address excessive alcohol drinking and stress interactions. *Neuropharmacology, 122*, 127–135.

Jochum, T., Boettger, M. K., Burkhardt, C., Juckel, G., & Bär, K.-J. (2012). Increased pain sensitivity in alcohol withdrawal syndrome. *European Journal of Pain, 14*, 713–718.

Juarez, B., Morel, C., Ku, S.M., Liu, Y., Zhang, H., Montgomery, S.,...Han, M. H. (2017). Midbrain circuit regulation of individual alcohol drinking behaviors in mice. *Nature Communication 8*(1), 2220. doi:10.1038/s41467-017-02365-8. Erratum in: *Nature Communication* 2018 *9*(1), 653.

Kadmiel, M., & Cidlowski, J. A. (2013). Glucocorticoid receptor signaling in health and disease. *Trends in Pharmacology Science, 34*, 518–530.

Knapp, D. J., Overstreet, D. H., Moy, S. S., & Breese, G. R. (2004). SB242084, flumazenil, and CRA1000 block ethanol withdrawal-induced anxiety in rats. *Alcohol, 32*, 101–111.

Koenig, H. N., & Olive, M. F. (2004). The glucocorticoid receptor antagonist mifepristone reduces ethanol intake in rats under limited access conditions. *Psychoneuroendocrinology, 29*, 999–1003.

Koob, G., & Kreek, M. J. (2007). Stress, dysregulation of drug reward pathways, and the transition to drug dependence. *American Journal of Psychiatry, 164*, 1149–1159.

Koob, G. F. (1999). Corticotropin-releasing factor, norepinephrine, and stress. *Biological Psychiatry, 46*, 1167–1180.

Koob, G. F. (2003). Alcoholism: Allostasis and beyond. *Alcoholism: Clinical and Experimental Research, 27*, 232–243.

Koob, G. F. (2015). The dark side of emotion: The addiction perspective. *European Journal of Pharmacology, 753*, 73–87.

Koob, G. F., & Bloom, F. E. (1988). Cellular and molecular mechanisms of drug dependence. *Science, 242*, 715–723.

Koob, G. F., Buck, C. L., Cohen, A., Edwards, S., Park, P. E., Schlosburg, J. E., Schmeichel, B.,..., George, O. (2014). Addiction as a stress surfeit disorder. *Neuropharmacology, 76*(Pt B), 370–382. doi:10.1016/j.neuropharm.2013.05.024.

Koob, G. F., Everitt, B. J., & Robbins, T. W. (2008). Reward, motivation, and addiction. In L. G. Squire et al. (Eds.), *Fundamental neuroscience* (3rd ed., pp. 987–1016). Amsterdam, the Netherlands: Academic Press.

Koob, G. F., Kenneth Lloyd, G., & Mason, B. J. (2009). Development of pharmacotherapies for drug addiction: A Rosetta stone approach. *Nature Reviews Drug Discovery, 8*, 500–515.

Koob, G. F., & Le Moal, M. (1997). Drug abuse: Hedonic homeostatic dysregulation. *Science, 278*, 52–58.

Koob, G. F., & Mason, B. J. (2016). Existing and future drugs for the treatment of the dark side of addiction. *Annual Reviews in Pharmacology and Toxicology, 56*, 299–322.

Koob, G. F., & Volkow, N. D. (2010). Neurocircuitry of addiction. *Neuropsychopharmacology, 35*, 217–238.

Koob, G. F., & Volkow, N. D. (2016). Neurobiology of addiction: A neurocircuitry analysis. *Lancet Psychiatry, 3*, 760–773.

Kwako, L. E., Spagnolo, P. A., Schwandt, M. L., Thorsell, A., George, D. T., Momenan, R.,...Heilig, M. (2015). The corticotropin releasing hormone-1 (CRH1) receptor antagonist pexacerfont in alcohol dependence: A randomized controlled experimental medicine study. *Neuropsychopharmacology, 40*, 1053–1063.

Lamb, R. J., Pinkston, J. W., & Ginsburg, B. C. (2015). Ethanol self-administration in mice under a second-order schedule. *Alcohol, 49*, 561–570.

Land, B. B., Bruchas, M. R., Lemos, J. C., Xu, M., Melief, E. J., & Chavkin, C. (2008). The dysphoric component of stress is encoded by activation of the dynorphin kappa-opioid system. *Journal of Neuroscience, 28*, 407–414.

Lieber, C. S., & De Carli, L. M. (1973). Ethanol dependence and tolerance: A nutritionally controlled experimental model in the rat. *Research Communications in Chemical Pathology and Pharmacology, 6*, 983–991.

Little, H. J., Croft, A. P., O'Callaghan, M. J., Brooks, S. P., Wang, G., & Shaw, S. G. (2008). Selective increases in regional brain glucocorticoid: A novel effect of chronic alcohol. *Neuroscience, 156*, 1017–1027.

Longabaug, R., & Morgenstern, J. (1999). Cognitive-behavioral coping-skills therapy for alcohol dependence: Current status and future directions. *Alcohol Research Amp Health*.

Lopez, M. F., Miles, M. F., Williams, R. W., & Becker, H. C. (2017). Variable effects of chronic intermittent ethanol exposure on ethanol drinking in a genetically diverse mouse cohort. *Alcohol, 58*, 73–82.

Lopez, M. F., Moorman, D. E., Aston-Jones, G., & Becker, H. C. (2016). The highly selective orexin/hypocretin 1 receptor antagonist GSK1059865 potently reduces ethanol drinking in ethanol dependent mice. *Brain Research, 1636,* 74–80.

Lowman, C., Allen, J., Stout, R. L., and The Relapse Research Group. (2002). Replication and extension of Marlatt's taxonomy of relapse precipitants: Overview of procedures and results. *Addiction, 91,* 51–72.

Lu, Y.-L., & Richardson, H. N. (2014). Alcohol, stress hormones, and the prefrontal cortex: A proposed pathway to the dark side of addiction. *Neuroscience, 277,* 139–151.

Makino, S., Gold, P. W., & Schulkin, J. (1994). Corticosterone effects on corticotropin-releasing hormone mRNA in the central nucleus of the amygdala and the parvocellular region of the paraventricular nucleus of the hypothalamus. *Brain Research, 640,* 105–112.

Malcolm, R., Roberts, J. S., Wang, W., Myrick, H. & Anton, R. F. (2000). Multiple previous detoxifications are associated with less responsive treatment and heavier drinking during an index outpatient detoxification. *Alcohol, 22,* 159–164.

Mandyam, C. D. (2013). The interplay between the hippocampus and amygdala in regulating aberrant hippocampal neurogenesis during protracted abstinence from alcohol dependence. *Frontiers in Psychiatry, 4,* 61.

Mantsch, J. R., Baker, D. A., Funk, D., Lê, A. D., & Shaham, Y. (2016). Stress-induced reinstatement of drug seeking: 20 years of progress. *Neuropsychopharmacology, 41,* 335–356.

Marinelli, M., & Piazza, P. V. (2002). Interaction between glucocorticoid hormones, stress and psychostimulant drugs. *European Journal of Neuroscience,16,* 387–394.

Marinelli, P. W., Funk, D., Juzytsch, W., Harding, S., Rice, K. C., Shaham, Y.,... Le, A. D. (2007). The CRF1 receptor antagonist antalarmin attenuates yohimbine-induced increases in operant alcohol self-administration and reinstatement of alcohol seeking in rats. *Psychopharmacology (Berlin), 195,* 345–355.

Marlatt, A., & Gordon, J. (1980). Determinants of relapse: Implications for the maintenance of behavior change. Paper presented at Behav Med Chang Health Lifestyles NY EUA BrunnerMazel. P. O. Davidson & D. M. Davidson, organizers.

McEwen, B. S. (2007). Physiology and neurobiology of stress and adaptation: Central role of the brain. *Physiology Review, 87,* 873–904.

McEwen, B. S., Gray, J. D., & Nasca, C. (2015). 60 years of neuroendocrinology: Redefining neuroendocrinology: Stress, sex and cognitive and emotional regulation. *Journal of Endocrinology, 226,* T67–83.

Meijer, O. C., Steenbergen, P. J., & De Kloet, E. R. (2000). Differential expression and regional distribution of steroid receptor coactivators SRC-1 and SRC-2 in brain and pituitary. *Endocrinology, 141,* 2192–2199.

Mendelson, J. H., & Stein, S. (1966). Serum cortisol levels in alcoholic and nonalcoholic subjects during experimentally induced ethanol intoxication. *Psychosomatic Medicine, 28,* 616–626.

Meunier, J. C., Mollereau, C., Toll, L., Suaudeau, C., Moisand, C., Alvinerie, P.,... Monsarrat, B. (1995). Isolation and structure of the endogenous agonist of opioid receptor-like ORL1 receptor. *Nature, 377,* 532–535.

Mitchell, J. M., Bergren, L. J., Chen, K. S., Rowbotham, M. C., & Fields, H. L. (2009). Naltrexone aversion and treatment efficacy are greatest in humans and rats that actively consume high levels of alcohol. *Neurobiology of Disease, 33,* 72–80.

Mucha, R. F., & Herz, A. (1985). Motivational properties of kappa and mu opioid receptor agonists studied with place

and taste preference conditioning. *Psychopharmacology (Berlin), 86,* 274–280.

Mulholland, P. J., Self, R. L., Harris, B. R., Little, H. J., Littleton, J. M., & Prendergast, M. A. (2005). Corticosterone increases damage and cytosolic calcium accumulation associated with ethanol withdrawal in rat hippocampal slice cultures. *Alcoholism: Clinical and Experimental Research, 29,* 871–881.

Myers, B., McKlveen, J. M., & Herman, J. P. (2014). Glucocorticoid actions on synapses, circuits, and behavior: Implications for the energetics of stress. *Frontiers in Neuroendocrinology, 35,* 180–196.

Nealey, K. A., Smith, A. W., Davis, S. M., Smith, D. G., & Walker, B. M. (2011). κ-opioid receptors are implicated in the increased potency of intra-accumbens nalmefene in ethanol-dependent rats. *Neuropharmacology. 61,* 35–42.

Nestler, E. J. (2001). Molecular basis of long-term plasticity underlying addiction. *Nature Reviews in Neuroscience, 2,* 119–128.

Nylander, I., Todkar, A., Granholm, L., Vrettou, M., Bendre, M., Boon, W.,... Comasco, E. (2017). Evidence for a link between Fkbp5/FKBP5, early life social relations and alcohol drinking in young adult rats and humans. *Molecular Neurobiology, 54,* 6225–6234.

O'Callaghan, M. J., Croft, A. P., Jacquot, C., & Little, H. J. (2005). The hypothalamopituitary-adrenal axis and alcohol preference. *Brain Research Bulletin, 68,* 171–178.

Ogilvie, K., Lee, S., Weiss, B., & Rivier, C. (1998). Mechanisms mediating the influence of alcohol on the hypothalamic-pituitary-adrenal axis responses to immune and nonimmune signals. *Alcoholism: Clinical and Experimental Research, 22,* 243S–247S.

O'Malley, S. S., Krishnan-Sarin, S., Farren, C., Sinha, R., & Kreek, M. J. (2002). Naltrexone decreases craving and alcohol self-administration in alcohol-dependent subjects and activates the hypothalamo-pituitary-adrenocortical axis. *Psychopharmacology (Berlin), 160,* 19–29.

Overstreet, D. H., Knapp, D. J., & Breese, G. R. (2004). Modulation of multiple ethanol withdrawal-induced anxiety-like behavior by CRF and CRF1 receptors. *Pharmacology, Biochemistry, and Behavior, 77,* 405–413.

Packard, A. E. B., Egan, A. E., & Ulrich-Lai, Y. M. (2016). HPA axis interactions with behavioral systems. *Comprehensive Physiology, 6,* 1897–1934.

Patel, S., Roelke, C. T., Rademacher, D. J., & Hillard, C. J. (2005). Inhibition of restraint stress-induced neural and behavioural activation by endogenous cannabinoid signalling. *European Journal of Neuroscience, 21,* 1057–1069.

Pfeiffer, A., Brantl, V., Herz, A., & Emrich, H. M. (1986). Psychotomimesis mediated by kappa opiate receptors. *Science, 233,* 774–776.

Priddy, B. M., Carmack, S. A., Thomas, L. C., Vendruscolo, J. C. M., Koob, G. F., & Vendruscolo, L. F. (2017). Sex, strain, and estrous cycle influences on alcohol drinking in rats. *Pharmacology, Biochemistry, and Behavior, 152,* 61–67.

Rasmussen, D. D., Boldt, B. M., Bryant, C. A., Mitton, D. R., Larsen, S. A., & Wilkinson, C. W. (2000). Chronic daily ethanol and withdrawal: 1. Long-term changes in the hypothalamo-pituitary-adrenal axis. *Alcoholism: Clinical and Experimental Research, 24,* 1836–1849.

Rassnick, S., Heinrichs, S. C., Britton, K. T., & Koob, G. F. (1993). Microinjection of a corticotropin-releasing factor antagonist into the central nucleus of the amygdala reverses anxiogenic-like effects of ethanol withdrawal. *Brain Research, 605,* 25–32.

Reinscheid, R. K., Nothacker, H. P., Bourson, A., Ardati, A., Henningsen, R. A., Bunzow, J. R., ... Civelli, O. (1995). Orphanin FQ: A neuropeptide that activates an opioidlike G protein-coupled receptor. *Science, 270*, 792–794.

Repunte-Canonigo, V., Shin, W., Vendruscolo, L. F., Lefebvre, C., van der Stap, L. Kawamura, T., ... Sanna, P. P. (2015). Identifying candidate drivers of alcohol dependence-induced excessive drinking by assembly and interrogation of brain-specific regulatory networks. *Genome Biology, 16*, 68.

Reynaud, M., Aubin, H.-J., Trinquet, F., Zakine, B., Dano, C., Dematteis, M., ... Detilleux, M. (2017). A randomized, placebo-controlled study of high-dose baclofen in alcohol-dependent patients—The ALPADIR Study. *Alcohol and Alcoholism, 52*, 439–446.

Rhodes, J. S., Best, K., Belknap, J. K., Finn, D. A., & Crabbe, J. C. (2005). Evaluation of a simple model of ethanol drinking to intoxication in C57BL/6J mice. *Physiology and Behavior, 84*, 53–63.

Richardson, H. N., Lee, S. Y., O'Dell, L. E., Koob, G. F., & Rivier, C. L. (2008). Alcohol self-administration acutely stimulates the hypothalamic-pituitary-adrenal axis, but alcohol dependence leads to a dampened neuroendocrine state. *European Journal of Neuroscience, 28*, 1641–1653.

Richardson, H. N., Zhao, Y., Fekete, E. M., Funk, C. K., Wirsching, P., Janda, K. D., ... Koob, G. F. (2008). MPZP: A novel small molecule corticotropin-releasing factor type 1 receptor (CRF1) antagonist. *Pharmacology, Biochemistry, and Behavior, 88*, 497–510.

Roberto, M., Cruz, M. T., Gilpin, N. W., Sabino, V., Schweitzer, P., Bajo, M., ... Parsons, L. H. (2010). Corticotropin releasing factor-induced amygdala gamma-aminobutyric acid release plays a key role in alcohol dependence. *Biological Psychiatry, 67*, 831–839.

Roberts, A. J., Lessov, C. N., & Phillips, T. J. (1995). Critical role for glucocorticoid receptors in stress- and ethanol-induced locomotor sensitization. *Journal of Pharmacology and Experimental Therapy, 275*, 790–797.

Romach, M. K., & Sellers, E. M. (1991). Management of the alcohol withdrawal syndrome. *Annual Review of Medicine, 42*, 323–340.

Rotter, A., Biermann, T., Amato, D., Schumann, G., Desrivieres, S., Kornhuber, J., ... Muller, C. P. (2012). Glucocorticoid receptor antagonism blocks ethanol-induced place preference learning in mice and attenuates dopamine D2 receptor adaptation in the frontal cortex. *Brain Research Bulletin, 88*, 519–524.

Ryan, M. L., Falk, D. E., Fertig, J. B., Rendenbach-Mueller, B., Katz, D. A., Tracy, K. A., ... Litten, R. Z. (2017). A phase 2, double-blind, placebo-controlled randomized trial assessing the efficacy of ABT-436, a novel V1b receptor antagonist, for alcohol dependence. *Neuropsychopharmacology, 42*, 1012–1023.

Samson, H. H. (1986). Initiation of ethanol reinforcement using a sucrose-substitution procedure in food- and water-sated rats. *Alcoholism: Clinical and Experimental Research, 10*, 436–442.

Sanna, P. P., Kawamura, T., Chen, J., Koob, G. F., Roberts, A. J., Vendruscolo, L. F., ... Repunte-Canonigo, V. (2016). 11β-hydroxysteroid dehydrogenase inhibition as a new potential therapeutic target for alcohol abuse. *Translational Psychiatry, 6*, e760.

Schank, J. R., Goldstein, A. L., Rowe, K. E., King, C. E., Marusich, J. A., Wiley, J. L., ... Heilig, M. (2012). The kappa opioid receptor antagonist JDTic attenuates alcohol seeking and withdrawal anxiety. *Addiction Biology, 17*, 634–647.

Schreiber, A. L., & Gilpin, N. W. (2018). Corticotropin-releasing factor (CRF) neurocircuitry and neuropharmacology in alcohol drinking. *Handbook of Experimental Pharmacology.* doi:10.1007/164_2017_86.

Schwandt, M. L., Cortes, C. R., Kwako, L. E., George, D. T., Momenan, R., Sinha, R., ... Heilig, M. (2016). The CRF1 antagonist verucerfont in anxious alcohol-dependent women: Translation of neuroendocrine, but not of anti-craving effects. *Neuropsychopharmacology, 41*, 2818–2829.

Selye, H. (1950). Stress and the general adaptation syndrome. *British Medical Journal, 1*, 1383–1392.

Serrano, A., & Parsons, L. H. (2011). Endocannabinoid influence in drug reinforcement, dependence and addiction-related behaviors. *Pharmacology Therapy, 132*, 215–241.

Sharrett-Field, L., Butler, T. R., Berry, J. N., Reynolds, A. R., & Prendergast, M. A. (2013). Mifepristone pretreatment reduces ethanol withdrawal severity in vivo. *Alcoholism: Clinical and Experimental Research, 37*, 1417–1423.

Shepard, J. D., Barron, K. W., & Myers, D. A. (2000). Corticosterone delivery to the amygdala increases corticotropin-releasing factor mRNA in the central amygdaloid nucleus and anxiety-like behavior. *Brain Research, 861*, 288–295.

Simms, J. A., Haass-Koffler, C. L., Bito-Onon, J., Li, R., & Bartlett, S. E. (2012). Mifepristone in the central nucleus of the amygdala reduces yohimbine stress-induced reinstatement of ethanol-seeking. *Neuropsychopharmacology, 37*, 906–918.

Simms, J. A., Steensland, P., Medina, B., Abernathy, K. E., Chandler, L. J., Wise, R., ... Bartlett, S. E. (2008). Intermittent access to 20% ethanol induces high ethanol consumption in Long-Evans and Wistar rats. *Alcoholism: Clinical and Experimental Research, 32*, 1816–1823.

Sinclair, J. D. (1979). Alcohol-deprivation effect in rats genetically selected for their ethanol preference. *Pharmacology, Biochemistry, and Behavior, 10*, 597–602.

Sinclair, J. D., & Senter, R. J. (1968). Development of an alcohol-deprivation effect in rats. *Quarterly Journal of Studies in Alcohol, 29*, 863–867.

Sinha, R., Fox, H. C., Hong, K.-I. A., Hansen, J., Tuit, K., & Kreek, M. J. (2011). Effects of adrenal sensitivity, stress- and cue-induced craving, and anxiety on subsequent alcohol relapse and treatment outcomes. *Archives in General Psychiatry, 68*, 942–952.

Somkuwar, S. S., Vendruscolo, L. F., Fannon, M. J., Schmeichel, B. E., Nguyen, T. B., Guevara, J., ... Mandyam, C. D. (2017). Abstinence from prolonged ethanol exposure affects plasma corticosterone, glucocorticoid receptor signaling and stress-related behaviors. *Psychoneuroendocrinology, 84*, 17–31.

Sommer, W. H., Rimondini, R., Hansson, A. C., Hipkind, P. A., Gehlert, D. R., Barr, C. S., ... Heilig, M. E. (2008). Upregulation of voluntary alcohol intake, behavioral sensitivity to stress, and amygdala crhr1 expression following a history of dependence. *Biological Psychiatry, 63*, 139–145.

Song, Z. H., & Takemori, A. E. (1992). Stimulation by corticotropin-releasing factor of the release of immunoreactive dynorphin A from mouse spinal cords in vitro. *European Journal of Pharmacology, 222*, 27–32.

Spierling, S. R., & Zorrilla, E. P. (2017). Don't stress about CRF: Assessing the translational failures of CRF1 antagonists. *Psychopharmacology (Berlin), 234*, 1467–1481.

Stephens, M. A. C., & Wand, G. (2012). Stress and the HPA axis: Role of glucocorticoids in alcohol dependence. *Alcohol Research Current Review, 34*, 468–483.

Swanson, L. W., & Simmons, D. M. (1989). Differential steroid hormone and neural influences on peptide mRNA levels in CRH cells of the paraventricular nucleus: A hybridization histochemical study in the rat. *Journal of Comparative Neurology, 285*, 413–435.

Tabakoff, B., & Hoffman, P. L. (2000). Animal models in alcohol research. *Alcohol Research, 24*, 77–84.

Thiele, T. E., & Navarro, M. (2014). "Drinking in the dark" (DID) procedures: A model of binge-like ethanol drinking in non-dependent mice. *Alcohol, 48*, 235–241.

Thorsell, A., Repunte-Canonigo, V., O'Dell, L. E., Chen, S. A., King, A. R., Lekic, D.,...Sanna, P. P. (2007). Viral vector-induced amygdala NPY overexpression reverses increased alcohol intake caused by repeated deprivations in Wistar rats. *Brain Journal of Neurology, 130*, 1330–1337.

Thorsell, A., Slawecki, C. J., & Ehlers, C. L. (2005a). Effects of neuropeptide Y and corticotropin-releasing factor on ethanol intake in Wistar rats: Interaction with chronic ethanol exposure. *Behavioral Brain Research, 161*, 133–140.

Thorsell, A., Slawecki, C. J., & Ehlers, C. L. (2005b). Effects of neuropeptide Y on appetitive and consummatory behaviors associated with alcohol drinking in wistar rats with a history of ethanol exposure. *Alcoholism: Clinical and Experimental Research, 29*, 584–590.

Trzaskowska, E., & Kostowski, W. (1983). Further studies on the role of noradrenergic mechanisms in ethanol withdrawal syndrome in rats. *Polish Journal of Pharmacology, 35*, 351–358.

Tunstall, B. J., Carmack, S. A., Koob, G. F., & Vendruscolo, L. F. (2017). Dysregulation of brain stress system mediates compulsive alcohol drinking. *Current Opinion in Behavioral Science, 13*, 85–90.

Valdez, G. R., Platt, D. M., Rowlett, J. K., Rüedi-Bettschen, D., & Spealman, R. D. (2007). Kappa agonist-induced reinstatement of cocaine seeking in squirrel monkeys: A role for opioid and stress-related mechanisms. *Journal of Pharmacology and Experimental Therapy, 323*, 525–533.

Valdez, G. R., Roberts, A. J., Chan, K., Davis, H., Brennan, M., Zorrilla, E. P.,...Koob, G. F. (2002). Increased ethanol self-administration and anxiety-like behavior during acute ethanol withdrawal and protracted abstinence: Regulation by corticotropin-releasing factor. *Alcoholism: Clinical and Experimental Research, 26*, 1494–1501.

Valdez, G. R., Sabino, V., & Koob, G. F. (2004). Increased anxiety-like behavior and ethanol self-administration in dependent rats: Reversal via corticotropin-releasing factor-2 receptor activation. *Alcoholism: Clinical and Experimental Research, 28*, 865–872.

Vale, W., Spiess, J., Rivier, C., & Rivier, J. (1981). Characterization of a 41-residue ovine hypothalamic peptide that stimulates secretion of corticotropin and beta-endorphin. *Science, 213*, 1394–1397.

Valentino, R. J., Page, M. E., & Curtis, A. L. (1991). Activation of noradrenergic locus coeruleus neurons by hemodynamic stress is due to local release of corticotropin-releasing factor. *Brain Research, 555*, 25–34.

Van Bockstaele, E. J., Colago, E. E., &Valentino, R. J. (1998). Amygdaloid corticotropin-releasing factor targets locus coeruleus dendrites: Substrate for the co-ordination of emotional and cognitive limbs of the stress response. *Journal of Neuroendocrinology, 10*, 743–757.

Van der Laan, S. Lachize, S. B., Vreugdenhil, E., de Kloet, E. R., & Meijer, O. C. (2008). Nuclear receptor coregulators differentially modulate induction and glucocorticoid receptor-mediated repression of the corticotropin-releasing hormone gene. *Endocrinology, 149*, 725–732.

Vendruscolo, L. F., Barbier, E., Schlosburg, J. E., Misra, K. K., Whitfield, T. W., Logrip, M. L.,...Koob, G. F. (2012). Corticosteroid-dependent plasticity mediates compulsive alcohol drinking in rats. *Journal of Neuroscience, 32*, 7563–7571.

Vendruscolo, L. F., Estey, D., Goodell, V., Macshane, L. G., Logrip, M. L., Schlosburg, J. E.,...Mason, B. J. (2015). Glucocorticoid receptor antagonism decreases alcohol seeking in alcohol-dependent individuals. *Journal of Clinical Investigation, 125*, 3193–3197.

Vendruscolo, L. F., Izídio, G. S., Takahashi, R. N., & Ramos, A. (2008). Chronic methylphenidate treatment during adolescence increases anxiety-related behaviors and ethanol drinking in adult spontaneously hypertensive rats. *Behavioral Pharmacology, 19*, 21–27.

Vendruscolo, L. F., & Roberts, A. J. (2014). Operant alcohol self-administration in dependent rats: Focus on the vapor model. *Alcohol, 48*, 277–286.

Vendruscolo, L. F., Terenina-Rigaldie, E., Raba, F., Ramos, A., Takahashi, R. N., & Mormède, P. (2006). Evidence for a female-specific effect of a chromosome 4 locus on anxiety-related behaviors and ethanol drinking in rats. *Genes, Brain and Behavior, 5*, 441–450.

Vengeliene, V., Bilbao, A., & Spanagel, R. (2014). The alcohol deprivation effect model for studying relapse behavior: A comparison between rats and mice. *Alcohol, 48*, 313–320.

Viveros, M. P., Marco, E. M., & File, S. E. (2005). Endocannabinoid system and stress and anxiety responses. *Pharmacology, Biochemistry, and Behavior, 81*, 331–342.

Walker, B. M., Drimmer, D. A., Walker, J. L., Liu, T., Mathé, A. A., & Ehlers, C. L. (2010). Effects of prolonged ethanol vapor exposure on forced swim behavior, and neuropeptide Y and corticotropin-releasing factor levels in rat brains. *Alcohol, 44*, 487–493.

Walker, B. M., & Koob, G. F. (2008). Pharmacological evidence for a motivational role of kappa-opioid systems in ethanol dependence. *Neuropsychopharmacology, 33*, 643–652.

Walker, B. M., Rasmussen, D. D., Raskind, M. A., & Koob, G. F. (2008). Alpha1-noradrenergic receptor antagonism blocks dependence-induced increases in responding for ethanol. *Alcohol, 42*, 91–97.

Waller, M. B., McBride, W. J., Lumeng, L., & Li, T. K. (1982). Induction of dependence on ethanol by free-choice drinking in alcohol-preferring rats. *Pharmacology, Biochemistry, and Behavior, 16*, 501–507.

Wee, S., & Koob, G. F. (2010). The role of the dynorphin-kappa opioid system in the reinforcing effects of drugs of abuse. *Psychopharmacology (Berlin), 210*, 121–135.

Wise, R. A. (1973). Voluntary ethanol intake in rats following exposure to ethanol on various schedules. *Psychopharmacologia, 29*, 203–210.

Wolffgramm, J., & Heyne, A. (1995). From controlled drug intake to loss of control: The irreversible development of drug addiction in the rat. *Behav Brain Research, 70*, 77–94.

World Health Organization. (2014). Global status report on alcohol and health. https://www.who.int/substance_abuse/publications/alcohol_2014/en/

Zalachoras, I., Verhoeve, S. L., Toonen, L. J., Weert, L. T. C. M., van Vlodrop, A. M., Mol, I. M.,...Meijer, O. C. (2016). Isoform switching of steroid receptor co-activator-1 attenuates glucocorticoid-induced anxiogenic amygdala CRH expression. *Molecular Psychiatry, 21*, 1733–1739.

Zhou, Y., Schwartz, B. I., Giza, J., Gross, S. S., Lee, F. S., & Kreek, M. J. (2017). Blockade of alcohol escalation and "relapse" drinking by pharmacological FAAH inhibition in male and female C57BL/6J mice. *Psychopharmacology (Berlin), 234*, 2955–2970.

Zywiak, W. H., Connors, G. J., Maisto, S. A., & Westerberg, V. S. (2002). Relapse research and the reasons for Drinking Questionnaire: A factor analysis of Marlatt's relapse taxonomy. *Addiction, 91*, 121–130.

Stress in Eating Disorders and Obesity

Alexandra F. Corning *and* Isabella M. Viducich

Abstract

Stress has long been implicated in the development and maintenance of both eating disorders and obesity. In this chapter, evidence for the most commonly implicated putative stressors, as culled from cross-sectional and longitudinal studies, is reviewed within the framework of the diathesis-stress model. These stressors include childhood maltreatment and sexual violation; military combat and military sexual violation; traumatic stress, injury, and illness; occupational stress; sociocultural pressure to be thin; and negative appearance-related feedback. Constructs that may mediate or moderate pathways from stressors to problematic eating are identified within the framework of the maladaptive coping model, wherein stress initiates a cascade of events potentially leading to disordered eating. Methodological challenges are identified and new directions based on recent analytic advances are proposed.

Keywords: eating disorder, obesity, stress, diathesis-stress model, maladaptive coping model

What is the relationship between stress and eating disorders and obesity? Does stress cause, or otherwise compel, normative eating behavior to become disordered? Does stress lead to overeating and obesity? Does either the experience of having an eating disorder or being obese increase the likelihood of incurring more frequent or severe life stressors? Alternately, is the relationship dynamic, such that the relation between eating behaviors and stress reciprocally influence one another over time? In this chapter, we examine the literature pertaining to these questions, acknowledging the methodological limitations that make definitive answers sometimes elusive, and offer suggestions for future research and practice.

Eating Disorders and Obesity Defined

The current diagnostic conceptualizations of eating disorders, per the *Diagnostic and Statistical Manual of Mental Disorders*, 5th edition (*DSM-5*; American Psychiatric Association [APA], 2013), are considered generally improved due primarily to *DSM-5*'s greater reliance on empirical data to define diagnostic criteria. However, for many in the field, substantial, unresolved issues remain, including the concern that diagnostic criteria remain overly prototyped, the preponderance of individuals in the miscellaneous diagnostic category, the questionable validity of various diagnostic criteria, and the frequent migration of patients across diagnostic boundaries (Fairburn & Cooper, 2007; Wonderlich, Joiner, Keel, Williamson, & Crosby, 2007). With these caveats in mind, we nevertheless next provide foundational descriptions of the most well-studied eating disorders affecting adolescents and adults, namely anorexia nervosa (AN), bulimia nervosa (BN), binge eating disorder (BED), and other specified feeding or eating disorder (OSFED).

AN, often viewed as the prototypical eating disorder, is actually the least common, with a 12-month prevalence rate ranging from just 0.12% to 0.40% (APA, 2013; Ghaderi & Scott, 2001). It is characterized by persistent caloric restriction leading to a significantly low weight, an intense fear of gaining weight manifested in restriction or compensation through purging, and perception of one's body as overweight or one's self-evaluation being unduly influenced by one's body shape or weight (APA, 2013). The amenorrhea criterion was removed with *DSM-5*, thus permitting the diagnosis of AN in premenstrual girls, postmenopausal women, boys, and men. Disorders commonly comorbid with AN include depression, bipolar disorder, anxiety, obsessive-compulsive disorder (OCD), and substance abuse (APA, 2013).

BN has a 12-month prevalence rate of 1.0%–1.5% (APA, 2013; Ghaderi & Scott, 2001). It is characterized by engagement in a cycle of binging followed by purging at least once a week for 3 months and that one's self-evaluation is unduly influenced by one's body shape or weight (APA, 2013). A *binge* is the consumption of an amount of food substantially greater than most individuals would eat in a similar period and under similar circumstances, accompanied by a feeling of lack of control over the consumption. *Purging* is the willful attempt to rid one's body of the calories consumed, and it includes behaviors such as self-induced vomiting, abuse of diuretics and laxatives, and excessive exercise. The most common BN comorbidities are bipolar, depression, anxiety, substance abuse, and disordered personality features (APA, 2013).

BED has a 12-month prevalence rate similar to, or exceeding that, of BN, with estimates ranging from 0.73% to 1.46% (Ghaderi & Scott, 2001; Hudson, Hiripi, Pope, & Kessler, 2007; Micali et al., 2017). It is characterized by recurrent binge eating (defined earlier), not followed by purging, that occurs at least once a week for at least three months and is accompanied by marked distress (APA, 2013). Commonly comorbid disorders are bipolar, depression, anxiety, and substance abuse.

Finally, for disorders of eating not meeting criteria for AN, BN, or BED, a diagnosis of OSFED may apply. OSFED replaces the not otherwise specified (NOS) label employed for over 30 years (*DSM-III-R*; APA, 1987). Although intended to provide diagnostic acknowledgment of atypical, and hence, unusual, presentations of eating disorders, OSFED instead accounts for 50.3% to 70.5% of all eating disorder diagnoses (Fairburn et al., 2007; Ricca et al., 2001; Turner & Bryant-Waugh, 2004). Common comorbidities are depression, OCD, posttraumatic stress disorder symptoms, and phobias (Mustelin, Lehtokari, & Keski-Rahkonen, 2016). OSFED is not less severe: Persons with this diagnosis have levels of psychopathology not significantly different from those with AN and BED and have significantly poorer physical health than individuals with BN (Thomas, Vartanian, & Brownell, 2009).

Obesity, on the other hand, is not an eating disorder. Rather, obesity is an outcome of caloric imbalance in the direction of accumulated adiposity, and it reflects overweight resulting from heterogeneous and complex etiology. Furthermore, obesity is not considered a mental illness, nor does obesity imply the presence of psychopathology (Marcus & Wildes, 2009). Obesity, rather, is an end state resulting most often from a confluence of factors and may occur in either the presence or absence of psychopathology (e.g., BED vs. a leptin imbalance). Body mass index (BMI) is the most common means of assessing weight status (i.e., overall body fat), and hence obesity, likely because it is inexpensive and easy to obtain and calculate.

Worldwide, overweight and obesity rates are soaring. In Canada, over half of all adults (56%) are overweight or obese (Institute for Health Metrics and Evaluation [IHME], 2014); in the United Kingdom, 62% are overweight or obese (IHME, 2014), and in the United States, the rate exceeds two out of every three adults (Flegal, Carroll, Kit, & Ogden, 2012). Obesity is problematic because it is associated with dangerous physical and mental health risks, such as high blood pressure, heart disease, stroke, diabetes, osteoarthritis, liver disease, and some cancers (Bedogni et al., 2005; Colditz, Willett, Rotnitzky, & Manson, 1995; Folsom, Kaye, Potter, & Prineas, 1989; Lee & Paffenbarger, 1992; Manson et al., 1992; Rexrode et al., 1997; Rimm et al., 1995; Sellers et al., 1992; Tanamas et al., 2013; Willett et al., 1995; Witteman et al., 1989). It also is strongly associated with depression and various anxiety disorders (Gariepy, Nitka, & Schmitz, 2010; Luppino et al., 2010).

The Theorized Roles of Stress in Eating Disorders and Obesity

Stress has long been implicated in the development and maintenance of both eating disorders (e.g., Beumont, Abraham, Argall, George, & Glaun, 1978; Degortes et al., 2014; Miller, 1988; Pike et al., 2006; Rosen, Compas, & Tacy, 1993) and obesity (Faulkner & Duecker, 1989; Koch, Sepa, & Ludvigsson, 2008; Rowland & Antelman, 1976; Suliman et al., 2016; Wamala, Wolk, & Orth-Gomér, 1997). What, however, is the nature of the relation of stress to eating disorders and stress to obesity?

Both disordered eating and obesity likely arise from a complex interplay of genetic, interpersonal, and cultural conditions. Indeed, the well-known *diathesis-stress model* (Gottesman, 1991), which predominates contemporary conceptualizations of eating disorder pathogenesis as well as many examinations of obesity (e.g., Carr et al., 2013; Kuijer, Boyce, & Marshall, 2015), organizes these conditions predictively. In brief, this model positions biological and genetic conditions, temperament, and childhood and adolescent experiences as predispositional vulnerabilities. Stressful life events (be they daily hassles, acute traumas, or chronic stressors) interact with such vulnerabilities to increase an individual's likelihood of developing psychopathology. For example, an individual dispositionally prone to perfectionistic self-expectations may be particularly negatively affected by weight-related teasing, responding by engaging in highly restrained eating, which escalates into AN.

The diatheses most commonly cited as contributors to disordered eating include genetics, particularly as they intersect with puberty onset (e.g., Becker, Keel, Anderson-Fye, & Thomas, 2004; Culbert, Burt, McGue, Iacono, & Klump, 2009); deficits in interoceptive awareness (i.e., poor recognition of internal physical and emotional states) (e.g., Leon, Fulkerson, Perry, & Cudeck, 1993); low self-esteem (e.g., Ghaderi, 2001); elevated perfectionism (e.g., Joiner, Heatherton, Rudd, & Schmidt, 1997); repeated exposure to the thin ideal and internalization of thin ideal (e.g., Becker et al., 2004); weight-related teasing (e.g., Becker, et al., 2004); body dissatisfaction (e.g., Leon et al., 1993); problematic family functioning (e.g., enhanced criticality, enmeshment, poor attachment, overvaluation of thinness) (e.g., Wold, 1987); and overall poor coping skills, such as avoidant coping and coping inefficacy (e.g., MacNeil, Esposito-Smythers, Mehlenbeck, & Weismoore, 2012).

Importantly, however, contemporary diathesis-stress models acknowledge the likelihood of interactions between multiple vulnerabilities and stressors, as well as disorders, iteratively or recursively, over the course of development. In the *maladaptive coping model*, for example, pathology is viewed not as a reflexive response to the stressor itself, but an ineffective, or maladaptive, means of coping with the negative emotional state evoked by the stressor. Specifically, stressors evoke subjective, emotional reactions (e.g., loneliness, fear, meaninglessness) that become intolerable, leading the individual to engage in primitive coping behaviors aimed largely at escape-avoidance (e.g., binge eating). Such attempts to self-soothe usually provide short-term relief, but become maladaptive when relied upon regularly

(e.g., binge-eating disorder). In this conceptualization, factors commonly comorbid with the pathology under study (e.g., depression, anxiety) may play mediational or moderational roles or both, in the trajectory of the stress-pathology relation. Finally, such models acknowledge that stressors and outcomes may be bidirectional and transactional; as such, problematic eating- and body-related cognitions and behaviors may, themselves, serve as stressors. For example, proponents of family-based therapy for AN (i.e., Maudsley family therapy) recognize that an adolescent ED patient's refusal to eat family meals escalates both personal and familial stress (Le Grange & Loeb, 2014), consistent with findings from stress-generation theory (Hammen, 1991).

Additionally, contemporary models recognize that a well-handled stressor may prevent subsequent pathology, and the resulting absence of pathology may then contribute to the individual's ability to positively cope with subsequent stressors; conversely, a poorly handled stressor may be succeeded by pathology and increased encounters with subsequent stressors, accompanied by poor coping and greater likelihood of pathology (Masten, 2014). For example, competent parenting that promotes boundary fidelity and self-esteem, such that respect from authority figures is expected, may help prevent pathology in an otherwise dispositionally vulnerable adolescent, and it may also assist her in averting future sources of interpersonal stress.

Methodological Challenges Facing Stress, Eating Disorder, and Obesity Researchers

Stress, eating disorder, and obesity researchers face numerous methodological challenges that place limitations on the internal and external validity of their results. In this section, we present those challenges most germane to the intersection of these constructs and which deserve consideration in the critical analysis of this literature.

Methodological Challenges to Stress Research

Challenges stress researchers in the fields of disordered eating and obesity face include sampling issues, choice of assessment techniques, the conceptualization and operationalization of stress, and design limitations (Ball & Lee, 2000; Liu, 2015). First, eating disorder samples employed in stress studies often are not representative of the broader population of those with eating disorders. Therefore, making sound inferences to the general population about both the antecedents and consequences of stress often is challenging. In most stress research pertaining to eating disorders and obesity, recruitment of community-based samples (which tend to be more representative) is infrequent relative to university and hospitalized patient samples. Both samples contain a degree of homogeneity (e.g., socioeconomic status and valuing of higher education in the former case and clinical severity in the latter) that does not extend to the larger population. As Ball and Lee (2000) have noted, persons hospitalized for an eating disorder are most likely in the later stages of the disorder, may face greater stress related to hospitalization (e.g., restricted freedom, forced feeding, close monitoring), and findings based on this population are not necessarily applicable to those who, for example, are subclinical or in the earlier stages of severity.

Second, the variety of methods available to assess stress and stressors complicates synthesis of the literature focused on eating disorders. Ball and Lee's (2000) evaluation of the stress and disordered eating literature revealed that very few studies use the same measure to assess stressors. In some studies, standardized assessment instruments are employed; in others, stressful life events are identified from patients' case histories or interviews. In some studies, the recency of the event is queried, whereas, in others, only its personal impact is assessed. Often timeframes for reporting life stressors are imposed upon participants (e.g., within the past month), and they vary widely across studies. Other times, participants are asked to reflect on a particular period preceding the onset of disordered eating and indicate life stressors that occurred during that period. These divergent approaches to measuring stress are problematic not only because they create the possibility that individuals could have forgotten about, omitted, or overestimated the salience of given stressful life events, but because it is difficult to make comparisons across studies.

Third, how life stressors are conceptualized has implications for the stress and eating disorder and obesity literatures. Due primarily to their economy, much of the stress literature uses circumscribed checklists (Dohrenwend, 2006), especially the widely used Schedule of Recent Experiences (SRE; Holmes & Rahe, 1967). This checklist includes life events such as "death of family member," "trouble with in-laws," and "retirement from work." Dohrenwend (2006) suggests that more apt descriptors for these items than life events are "lists of topics" or "categories of events" (p. 479, Dohrenwend, 2006) due to the infinite ways by which individuals may come to

endorse them. For example, "major personal injury or illness" may be endorsed positively both by those who recently broke an arm and those surviving lung cancer. Predetermined event lists sidestep the importance of subjectivity in the evaluation of life events. If a potentially stressful event is not represented on a checklist, its impact cannot be assessed. Both eating disorders and obesity are associated, for example, with histories of sexual assault, a violation so grave it increases the odds of posttraumatic stress disorder (PTSD) four-fold (e.g., Walsh, Koenen, Aiello, Uddin, & Galea, 2014), yet this life event is absent from the SRE.

Fourth, there is the problem of the pathological behavior itself serving as a stressor—that is, stressors may be confounded with outcomes. For example, the extent to which individuals may go to avoid family meals or execute a binge episode may be highly stressful, particularly as the individual believes engagement in these behaviors is largely necessary or unavoidable. This confounding of stressor and health outcome occurs even within assessments; for example, the SRE includes among its potential stressors "major change in eating habits."

Finally, one of the most significant methodological issues that plague stress research with human populations is the general lack of prospective designs and thus the inability to draw conclusions about temporal precedence. Cross-sectional studies assist in identifying significant correlates but are limited in their ability to speak to causal processes; nevertheless, such designs represent the majority of work in this field for several reasons (e.g., lower cost, some events [e.g., physical and sexual violation] are nonamenable to experimental analogues), as opposed to longitudinal and experimental designs. Additionally, cross-sectional studies often rely on self-report of current or past stressors or pathology, and therefore are prone to reporting and memory bias. Although prospective studies of the relationship between stressful life events and eating disorders or obesity exist (e.g., Carroll, Phillips, & Der, 2008; Copeland et al., 2015; Roberts, Deleger, Strawbridge, & Kaplan, 2003; Rosen et al., 1993; Rosengren et al., 2015; Siahpush et al., 2014), they are the minority.

Methodological Challenges in Eating Disorder and Obesity Research

Challenges eating disorder researchers face include the low base rate of eating disorders, restrictive diagnostic criteria, the secrecy and shame that characterized eating disorders, and the frequent and sometimes unavoidable need to use retrospective reports. First, the lifetime prevalence rates for eating disorders, especially for AN (Hudson et al., 2007; Stice, Marti, & Rohde, 2013) and BN (Hudson et al., 2007; Stice et al., 2013), are quite low (c.f., the lifetime depression prevalence rate is 16.6%; Kessler, Petukhova, Sampson, Zaslavsky, & Wittchen, 2012). BED prevalence rates are low as well at 3.0%–3.5% (Hudson et al., 2007; Stice et al., 2013). Although many people suffer from *disordered eating*, the diagnostic criteria used to operationalize *eating disorder* are stringent, perhaps overly so (see e.g., Dazzi & Di Leone, 2014; Fairburn & Cooper, 2007; Wonderlich, Joiner, Keel, Williamson, & Crosby, 2007, for a discussion of this issue). Far more individuals exhibit subthreshold symptoms, although they do not differ significantly from diagnosed persons in terms of impairment. Researchers have found, for example, no differences in comorbid psychopathology (i.e., anxiety and depression) between those who binge and purge twice a week (as was required for BN diagnosis by *DSM-IV*) versus once a week (revised under *DSM-5*) (MacDonald, McFarlane, & Olmsted, 2014). Whereas the loosening of this criterion in *DSM-5* more accurately situates the boundary between eating disorder and disordered eating, data are not yet available to indicate whether the revised criterion of once per week is overly restrictive. Indeed, for several symptoms, debates regarding accurate placement of the boundary between diagnosis and normality are vigorous and ongoing (e.g., Fairburn et al., 2007; Grilo, 2013; McDonald et al., 2014; Vannucci et al., 2013).

Second, because patients with eating disorders are often highly secretive regarding their eating behaviors and symptoms, this population is challenging to recruit for research participation. Specifically, most people struggling with eating disorders go to great lengths to keep the behaviors in which they engage private because of associated shame they experience. For example, a college student who secretly binges may live alone to avoid the interpersonal stress of having to hide binging behavior from roommates. Such individuals are highly unlikely to volunteer for eating disorder studies. In the case of AN, highly restrained eating and the pursuit of weight loss are congruent with the individual's values, goals, and sense of self (i.e., the symptoms are *ego-syntonic*). As such, the individual actively avoids impediments to caloric restriction, including the attention of mental health professionals and researchers, who may seek to reduce eating pathology.

Finally, in terms of delineating onset, retrospective patient reports are often used, but they are subject to problems associated with memory bias. Whereas an individual may report lucidly recalling a specific comment from a coach, parent, or peer that purportedly caused her or his disordered eating, it is possible that the respondent was already in the early stages of problematic eating and related behaviors. Retrospective self-report may erroneously identify a landmark along the evolution of an eating disorder as the point of initiation simply because that point (e.g., a negative comment) was particularly memorable. In addition, in the case of persons with severe AN, cognitive processes, including memory for specific events (e.g., recall of stressors and their estimated onset), are often impaired (Nikendei et al., 2011). Obtaining accurate estimates of time of onset is difficult and probably is best estimated via longitudinal, multiwave, prospective studies employing frequent assessment points. Due to the difficulty and cost of multiwave studies, particularly in samples of patients with a low base rate disorder, researchers most often rely on retrospective self-reports.

Because of these aforementioned methodological challenges, the majority of studies in the field of eating disorders use dimensional measures of disordered eating (i.e., lists of symptoms rated for severity or frequency) rather than focusing on those with diagnosable eating disorders. As such, most study results are most appropriately generalizable to those with disordered eating and not necessarily to those with diagnosable eating disorders.

Although obesity researchers are not faced with the same diagnostic, sample size, and recruitment issues, they confront other challenges, including the pitfalls borne of the simplicity of BMI, reverse causality, and the validity of particular cut points across ethnic groups. First, BMI alone frequently is used to establish obesity status (i.e., BMI > 30), although in actuality obesity is etiologically heterogeneous (e.g., due to genetic mutation, hormonal and other medical conditions, medication side effects, binge eating), the context surrounding the BMI (e.g., high muscle mass in an athlete that contributes to a high BMI), or the implications of dichotomizing a continuous measure (i.e., a person with a BMI of 29.99 is technically not obese, although such a person is likely not appreciably different from an obese individual in terms of behavior, etiology, etc.). Second, cross-sectional studies cannot disentangle causality from reverse causality, wherein weight gain is the result, not cause, of a particular health problem. Finally, there is evidence that body fat differences across ethnic and other population groups may warrant the application of different cut points for different groups (Wang, 2004), but this observation generally has not influenced how obesity is assessed in empirical studies.

Stressful Life Events Antecedent to Disordered Eating

Under the general rubric of the diathesis-stress model, *risk factors* for eating disorders and obesity have been identified, some of which are dispositional vulnerabilities (e.g., genetic variations, hormonal differences) and others environmental or situational stressors (e.g., sexual abuse, chronic weight teasing) (e.g., Danese & Tan, 2014; Hilbert et al., 2014; Robinson, 2012). Although the universe of potential environmental and situational stressors is infinite, researchers are guided in their pursuit by a knowledge of between-group differences (e.g., sex, age, race, sexual orientation) that promote differential exposure or reactivity to stressors, an understanding of individual differences (e.g., personality factors, subjective appraisals of life events), the accumulated scientific literature, and themes culled across patient narratives. In this section, we review findings associated with the sources of stress most commonly implicated in theoretical models and assessed in empirical studies. These include childhood maltreatment and sexual violation; military combat and military sexual violation; traumatic stress, injury, and illness; occupational stress; sociocultural pressure to be thin; and negative appearance-related feedback.

Traumatic Events

Traumatic events are negative events that occur abruptly and are experienced as shocking and overwhelming, typically involving threatened or actual serious injury, physical violation, or death. In this section, we review the disordered eating literature pertaining to childhood maltreatment and sexual violation, military combat and military sexual violation, and traumatic injury and illness.

CHILDHOOD MALTREATMENT AND SEXUAL VIOLATION

Childhood maltreatment (i.e., abuse and neglect) has long been theorized to be associated with the development of obesity and eating disorders. Conclusively assessing these associations, however, is resource intensive and otherwise difficult for numerous reasons, including that maltreatment often remains hidden, irrespective of inviting prompts, minors can participate in research only upon custodial consent, and memories (e.g., perpetrators, timeframes) may be influenced by recall bias. As such,

cross-sectional, retrospective data predominate, and prospective designs, which minimize such biases, are far fewer. Finally, of the prospective studies, those focusing on obesity far outnumber eating disorder studies (e.g., Bentley & Widom, 2009; Boynton-Jarrett, Rosenberg, Palmer, Boggs, & Wise, 2012; Richardson, Dietz, & Gordon-Larsen, 2014), likely due to the higher base rate of obesity. Additionally, its assessment is straightforward, as it requires measurement of but two variables, height and weight, which easily can be included in large, survey-style prospective studies.

Earlier work was inconsistent in terms of establishing whether childhood maltreatment was associated with obesity. However, a recent meta-analysis of 41 studies totaling nearly 200,000 participants (Danese & Tan, 2014) showed that, regardless of how maltreatment was conceptualized (i.e., sexual, emotional, or physical abuse or physical neglect), the methodology used (i.e., retrospective or prospective; questionnaire, interview, or recorded measures of abuse), or how obesity was assessed (e.g., self-report, third-party; categorically or continuously), childhood maltreatment predicted an increased odds of obesity (odds ratio = 1.36, 95% confidence interval = 1.26–1.47) over the life course. The only exception to this was emotional neglect, which showed no association with obesity (odds ratio = 1.21; 95% CI = 0.92–1.60).

Several studies have found similar associations between childhood maltreatment, particularly childhood sexual abuse, and eating disorders. O'Brien and Sher (2013) concluded that childhood sexual abuse is indeed associated with higher rates of lifetime eating disorders based on their literature review of studies conducted over the past two decades. For example, Claes and Vandereycken (2007) found that almost half (48%) of all patients (N = 77) receiving treatment in an eating disorder inpatient unit for either AN or BN reported childhood sexual abuse, and, of these, BN patients reported significantly more childhood sexual abuse. Additionally, in a study of 145 outpatients meeting *DSM* criteria for BED (APA, 1994), 30% reported experiencing childhood sexual abuse (Grilo & Masheb, 2001).

Smolak and Murnen (2002) conducted a formal meta-analysis of 53 studies assessing the relation between childhood sexual abuse and disordered eating. Whereas their overall results indicated an effect of small size (r = .10), they cautioned that there was significant variability in effect size based on how disordered eating was operationalized and assessed in different studies, which ranged from formal clinical diagnoses to screening devices (e.g., the EAT, EDI; Garner, Olmsted, Bohr, & Garfinkel, 1982; Garner, Olmsted, & Polivy, 1983) to scales assessing engagement in specific (usually bulimic) behaviors. Smolak and Murnen found that the more restricted the definition (e.g., a focus solely on bulimic behaviors), the smaller the relation between childhood sexual abuse and eating pathology. As they point out, until researchers have gained a better understanding of the numerous mechanisms by which individuals may come to engage in disordered eating in the aftermath of childhood sexual violation and why, assessment of disordered eating behaviors should be broad.

The means by which childhood sexual abuse serves as a risk factor for later obesity and disordered eating are numerous. Some of the more prominent notions include that the experience leads to a sense of lack of control, spurring (a) the individual to exert any means of control over the body possible, taking the form of overcontrol of food intake (consistent with restrained eating by persons with AN); (b) adoption of a dissociative coping style (e.g., consistent with many persons' experience of bingeing wherein there is little memory of the binging episode); (c) maturity fears (via striving to obtain or maintain a very low weight and, prior to *DSM-5*, cessation of menses as seen in AN); (d) body shame or body hatred (taking the form of body dissatisfaction, a well-established prerequisite for both AN and BN); (e) the accumulation of fat in an attempt to shield oneself against future abuse (e.g., as in the case, at times, of obesity); and (f) resultant negative mood states, such as depression and anxiety, or low self-esteem, especially in the context of emotional dysregulation, which may prompt engagement in poor (usually avoidant) coping mechanisms (e.g., overeating as seen in binge eating and obesity) (e.g., Becker & Grilo, 2011; Charatan, 2015; Shafran, Fairburn, Nelson, & Robinson, 2003; and, for an overview, see Williamson, White, York-Crowe, & Stewart, 2004). Importantly, conditions comorbid with both eating disorders and obesity also are found in significantly greater proportions in sexually violated individuals. For example, whereas only 32% of Felitti's (1991) nonviolated sample reported depression, a full 83% of the sexually violated individuals reported depression. Depression, as just one instance of a comorbid condition, may mediate the path between sexual violation and overeating, such that individuals falling to depression may attempt to cope with their negative mood, decreased motivation, and low self-worth through undereating or overeating.

MILITARY COMBAT AND MILITARY SEXUAL VIOLATION

It is well understood that military men and women deployed to warzones and exposed to combat-related violence experience a host of mental and physical health problems (Kintzle et al., 2015). In a large (*N* = 48,378), 3-year, prospective study assessing the effects of combat exposure on various health outcomes, women exposed to military combat were 1.78 times more likely to develop a new episode of disordered eating and 2.35 times more likely to lose at least 10% of their body weight than their deployed peers not exposed to combat (Jacobson et al., 2009).

Women in the military also experience additional, in-service sexual violation by both their superiors and peers, referred to as military sexual trauma (i.e., violation ranging from sexual harassment to sexual assault). Prevalence estimates of sexual trauma incurred by women in the military vary broadly across studies, depending on how it is assessed (see O'Brien & Sher, 2013). Recent estimates from veterans of Operation Iraqi Freedom and Operation Enduring Freedom in Afghanistan indicate that over 15% of women veterans reported incurring military sexual trauma compared to 0.7% of their male peers (Mattocks et al., 2012). (Whereas this estimate likely underestimates both men's and women's experiences of military sexual trauma for both unique and overlapping reasons [see Kintzle et al., 2015], just as with civilian sexual violation, the sex disparity remains great nonetheless.)

The double jeopardy for women in the military puts them at compounded risk for both obesity and eating disorders. In large, national samples of women veterans using US VA services, those who reported experiencing military sexual trauma were significantly more likely than those not reporting such trauma to be obese (Frayne, Skinner, Sullivan, & Freund, 2003; Skinner, 2000). Furthermore, of those who had experienced military sexual trauma, 27% had eating disorders (Skinner, 2000).

TRAUMATIC STRESS, INJURY, AND ILLNESS

Traumatic stress, injury, and illness long have been theorized to antecede both obesity and eating disorders, yet the presence of any relation, much less its directionality, has not yet been made clear. Suliman and colleagues (2016) conducted a meta-analysis aimed at better understanding the relation between PTSD and BMI. Their eligibility criteria (e.g., at least 16 years old, representative sample, meaningful non-PTSD comparison sample, BMI measured anthropometrically, PTSD assessed based on *DSM* criteria) resulted in inclusion of 30 studies, of which cross-sectional designs predominated. While their meta-analysis revealed a positive association between PTSD and BMI, with effect sizes ranging from small to large, sex moderated these results; perhaps surprisingly, men with PTSD had elevated BMIs relative to their peers, whereas women with PTSD did not. Because most of the studies were cross-sectional, however, it is not clear whether men's PTSD contributes to increased odds of elevated BMI or vice versa. Importantly, the few prospective studies in this area show that PTSD and elevated BMIs are related in women as well and, moreover, provide support for PTSD as antecedent to elevated BMI. Whereas cross-sectional results often point to areas of needed longitudinal attention, the disparity revealed by design differences here underscores the potential to overlook important group differences. Particularly for women, intervening variables, such as comorbidities or cascades of subsequent stressors, may show their effects on BMI only with the passage of time.

It has been theorized that obesity may increase the odds of incurring particular stressors, such as traumatic injury or illness, which, in turn, have their own stress-inducing, negative sequelae. In an investigation of workplace traumatic injury, Pollack and Cheskin (2007) reviewed the literature to discern whether obesity increases the odds of such injury. Their search of the psychological, medical, and occupational literatures yielded 12 studies published between 1985 and 2005 meeting their inclusion criteria. Of these, only three yielded clear evidence of a positive association between obesity and traumatic workplace injury. Possibly contributing to this result is researchers' employment of varying BMI cutoffs and definitions of injury, reliance on self-report rather than objective data (e.g., company medical records), and uneven attention to confounding factors. Moreover, none of the 12 studies were prospective. Finally, as paltry the evidence for this relation, it may have been inflated by the *file-drawer problem* (Rosenthal, 1979), wherein studies showing no association are far less likely to be published, resulting in a literature biased toward the appearance of positive effects. Therefore, we cannot yet draw meaningful conclusions about the relations between these variables, at least in regard to traumatic workplace injury.

The experience of acute physical illness, too, long has been assumed to be a stressor that precedes eating disorder onset, with various psychological and physiological pathways hypothesized to play causal roles; however, the amassed data do not yet provide clear evidence of such a relation. In one study, for example, researchers examining early-onset eating disorders in children (ages 7–19) categorized cases ($N = 90$) into early-onset AN or "other eating disorders," and culled data regarding prior physical illnesses from the patients' medical charts (Watkins, Sutton, & Lask, 2001). Lacking a healthy comparison group, the researchers compared rates of physical illness in their sample to those of adult normal controls reported in a separate study. Their results showed greater number of prior physical illnesses in the eating disorder patients compared to the healthy controls, and significantly more serious illnesses in the anorexic group. Whereas these results suggest physical illnesses is a significant antecedent to eating disorder onset, they were based on retrospective data, physical illness was not defined, bulimic patients were excluded, children were compared to adults, and the referral sources were tertiary (specialist-level) centers, implying greater symptom severity in the eating disorders sample. It seems clear that serious physical illness may affect appetite and mobility, in addition to promoting comorbidities (e.g., depression), resulting in disordered eating in some individuals. As it stands, however, serious illness does not seem to be a common pathway to disordered eating.

Chronic Stressors

Chronic stressors are any perceived threat that represents a "continuous assault on homeostasis" (p. 57, Michopoulos, 2016). In this section, we review the literature pertaining to those that have received the most attention in the obesity and eating disordered literatures, which are ongoing occupational stress, sociocultural pressure to be thin and valuation of thinness, and negative appearance-related feedback.

OCCUPATIONAL STRESS

Adults spend approximately 8 hours per day at work; thus, the correlates and effects of occupational stress on eating-related problems warrant empirical attention. This literature is predominated by studies positioning weight-related outcomes such as overweight and obesity (vs. eating disorders) as the outcome variable, perhaps due to the relative ease of assessing overweight and obesity, and because onset, at least for AN and BN, typically precedes matriculation into the workforce. Occupational stress is a heterogeneous construct, referring to structural factors such as prolonged work hours, low pay, and sedentary restrictions as well as to psychosocial stressors such as conflict of opinions, high job demands, inadequate autonomy, and sexual harassment.

Some cross-sectional studies show support for a relation between workplace stress and obesity. In a study of male workers in Japan (N = 208; ages 19-60), age-adjusted analyses showed a positive, cross-sectional relation between self-reported tension and anxiety and obesity (Nishitani & Sakakibara, 2006), and at least one prospective study supports an association as well. In a 14-year study of 10,308 civil service employees in London, chronic occupational stress predicted the development of metabolic syndrome, which is a risk factor for type 2 diabetes, heart diseases, and stroke (Chandola, Brunner, & Marmot, 2006). A component of metabolic syndrome is obesity. Chandola et al. excluded obese persons at baseline and statistically controlled for metabolic syndrome confounds (i.e., smoking, alcohol consumption, poor diet, low physical activity). Results indicated that employees with more incidents of chronic stress (i.e., reporting markers at three of four time points) had double the odds of developing metabolic syndrome over the 14-year study, and that those at the lowest pay grades had double the odds of those at the highest pay grades. However, in a review of 39 studies assessing the relation of psychosocial stress at work and various weight-related outcomes (e.g., BMI, waist-to-hip ratio, waist circumference, weight change, status as overweight or obese), out of 220 associations tested, only 24% revealed a positive relation (Solovieva, Lallukka, Virtanen, & Viikari-Juntura, 2013). The authors concluded that there is little evidence for a consistent relation between psychosocial workplace stress and weight-related outcomes, and called for prospective studies of nonobese persons at baseline, and for the use of analytical tools designed to test models of causation.

SOCIOCULTURAL PRESSURE TO BE THIN AND VALUATION OF THINNESS

Body dissatisfaction, or displeasure with weight or shape, is so prevalent that over 30 years ago, Rodin and colleagues characterized it as a source of "normative discontent" for girls and women (Rodin, Silberstein, & Striegel-Moore, 1984, p. 267), and current research estimates that in the United States alone it affects over 50 to 100 million adults (Frederick, Jafary, Gruys, & Daniels, 2012).

Adolescence and young adulthood are risk periods for increases in body dissatisfaction, especially for girls and women. Girls followed from eighth grade through the sophomore year in high school experience a significant increase in body dissatisfaction across this transition, whereas their male counterparts, though they express body dissatisfaction, show no similar increase across this transition: By tenth grade, 44% of girls, compared to 16% of boys, report moderate to extreme body dissatisfaction (Bearman, Presnell, Martinez, & Stice, 2006). Undergraduate women report high rates of body dissatisfaction, with estimates ranging from 82.6% to 94% (Corning, Krumm, & Smitham, 2006; Laus, Costa, & Almeida, 2015; Monteath & McCabe, 1997). Body dissatisfaction among men is growing, however, with estimates at 83.4% for adolescent boys and 72.2% for college-aged males (Laus et al., 2015; Ricciardelli & McCabe, 2001).

These rates are particularly concerning given that body dissatisfaction is a prerequisite to, and well-established risk factor for, AN and BN (e.g., Stice & Shaw, 2002). Whereas body dissatisfaction can be focused on a specific body part or one's shape, it generally centers on perceiving oneself as not adequately thin. *Valuation of thinness* refers to confounding one's degree of thinness with one's overall self-evaluation. The *DSM-5* criteria for both AN and BN purposefully more broadly frame this as undue influence of body shape and weight on one's self-evaluation likely because valuation of thinness is explicit in AN but may not be present in all cases of BN. While this raises the question of whether body dissatisfaction can rightly be regarded as a distinct stressor that precipitates disorder versus an early manifestation of eating pathology, it seems likely that some aspects of body dissatisfaction and valuation of thinness can be interpreted as culturally based sources of stress, as discussed later in this section.

The various media to which children, adolescents, and adults are exposed is a significant source of sociocultural pressure to be thin. A recent meta-analysis of 90 effects from both correlational and experimental studies revealed a clear, inverse association between media exposure and body satisfaction (Mean $d = -.28$) (Grabe, Ward, & Hyde, 2008). This is unsurprising considering the heightened exposure of youth to media images and their accompanying messages. According to a recent representative, self-report survey of media consumption by 8- to 18-year-olds (N = 2,002), young people spend an average of 7 hours and 38 minutes per day consuming media content, a figure that rises when simultaneous media use (e.g., social networking while movie watching) is considered (Rideout, Foehr, & Roberts, 2011). Moreover, 92% of youth report the content they watch contains at least some sexual imagery and activity (Ybarra, Strasburger, & Mitchell, 2014), suggesting that exposure to bodies that are typically thin and fit is especially high. More specifically, depictions of women—both sexual (e.g., in sex scenes) and nonsexual (e.g., in situation comedies, in commercials)—are representative of the *thin ideal*, or a feminine physique that, excepting the breasts, is ultra-slim and has virtually no body fat. It is a contrived body type that is unattainable via natural means for the vast majority of girls and women and achievable only through digital altering or surgery.

The mechanism by which the thin ideal spurs body dissatisfaction is a process and outcome termed *thin-ideal internalization* (Thompson, Heinberg, Altabe, & Tantleff-Dunn, 1999). Thin-ideal internalization refers to adoption of the media's message (reinforced by peers and family via modeling, criticism, teasing, and shaming) that the thin-ideal body type, given adequate commitment, is indeed attainable, and, moreover, obtaining it will bring success (e.g., social, financial, and romantic). Body dissatisfaction results from making repeated, upward comparisons to the onslaught of thin-ideal depictions with which girls and women are faced daily, repeatedly being reminded of the discrepancy between one's appearance and that of the thin ideal, and concluding that one's appearance is inadequate. Such dissatisfaction serves as a form of cognitive and/or affective chronic stress from which relief is infrequent given the ubiquity of the thin ideal, the ongoing effort put forth to embody it, and the failures that inevitably result.

The media are reliant on the mass insecurity engendered by the thin ideal and employ it strategically and reliably to promote purchasing. Individuals, nonetheless, vary in the extent to which they buy into the thin ideal, and there is some evidence of group differences as well. African American college women and men, for example, show significantly less internalization of media and societal standards of thinness and attractiveness ideals than do their European American peers (Dye, 2016). However, for those who have internalized the thin ideal, not only is body dissatisfaction higher, but they express greater frequency of problematic eating attitudes and behavior (Stice, Mazotti, Krebs, & Martin, 1998; Stice, Schupak-Neuberg, Shaw, & Stein, 1994). Subsequent, prospective designs have confirmed that these are indeed outcomes of, and not merely concomitant with, internalization of the thin ideal. Thin-ideal internalization prospectively predicts subsequent rises in body dissatisfaction

(Stice & Whitenton, 2002) and binging and purging (Stice & Agras, 1998). It also sets off a mediational chain wherein thin-ideal internalization prospectively predicts in girls (*M* age at baseline = 14.9) body dissatisfaction which, in turn, prospectively predicts both negative affect and dieting, two known precursors to engagement in bulimic behaviors over the course of 2.5 years of high school (Stice, 2001).

NEGATIVE APPEARANCE-RELATED FEEDBACK

Appearance-related feedback is as any verbal or nonverbal exchange in which an individual receives information regarding another's opinion about her or his weight, shape, body, or overall appearance (Menzel et al., 2010). When such feedback is negative, it can take the form of weight- or shape-related teasing, critical comments about weight or shape, and body shaming. Negative appearance-related feedback, particularly when chronic, serves as a stressor leading to marked distress and impairment (Gray, Kahhan, & Janicke, 2009). Across studies, 27%–45% of children report being teased about their weight (Lampard, MacLehose, Eisenberg, Neumark-Sztainer, & Davison, 2014; Quick, McWilliams, & Byrd-Bredbenner, 2013). Among overweight children, up to 78% have been teased or criticized about some aspect of their appearance, and almost 90% of this teasing was weight related (Hayden-Wade et al., 2005). Such victimization comes from multiple sources. In a sample of middle-schoolers (*N* = 4,746), among very overweight children (i.e., BMIs >95th percentile), 63% of girls and 58% of boys reported being teased by their peers, and 47% of girls and 34% of boys also reported being teased by family members (Neumark-Sztainer et al., 2002).

Investigations of negative appearance-related feedback differ in focus across the obesity and eating disorder fields. Obesity researchers generally have assessed the negative effects that the stress of weight teasing, for example, have on children who are already obese (Krukowski et al., 2009; Libbey, Story, Neumark-Sztainer, & Boutelle, 2008; Madowitz, Knatz, Maginot, Crow, & Boutelle, 2012). Body image and eating disorder researchers generally have conceptualized negative appearance-related feedback as a putative, antecedent stressor to such outcomes as body dissatisfaction, disordered eating, and diagnosable-level eating disorders (Fairburn et al., 1998; Gonçalves, Machado, Martins, & Machado, 2014; Loth, Mac Lehose, Bucchianeri, Crow, & Neumark-Sztainer, 2014; Machado, Gonçalves, Martins, Hoek, & Machado, 2014; Menzel et al., 2010; Pike et al., 2006, 2008).

Weight-related teasing of obese children has been associated with a number of negative outcomes, including significant impairments in emotional state, health behavior, and academic performance (Krukowski et al., 2009; Libbey et al., 2008; Madowitz et al., 2012). Madowitz et al.'s (2012) cross-sectional, self-report study of 80 obese children found significantly higher rates of depression in those weight teased by their peers. Additionally, these children were five times more likely to engage in unhealthy weight control behaviors such as fasting, vomiting, excessive exercise, and use of diet pills, diuretics, and laxatives. Libbey et al. (2008) found similar results in their cross-sectional study of 130 adolescents (ages 12–20) at or above the 85th weight percentile. The self-reported experience of frequent weight teasing by family members and peers was associated with higher levels of depression, anxiety, and anger, lower self-esteem, and greater engagement in disordered eating thoughts and behaviors.

Finally, based on data from an annual, cross-sectional telephone survey of randomly selected parents of Arkansas public school children, Krukowski et al. (2009) presented evidence for the mediating effect of weight-based teasing on the well-established relation between overweight status and poor academic achievement in children and adolescents ages 4–13. As predicted, overweight status (BMI > 85th percentile for age and sex) predicted poorer school performance. Experiencing weight-based teasing from peers mediated this relation, such that being overweight was associated with incurring more weight-based teasing, which, in turn, was associated with poorer academic performance. Importantly, however, mediational analyses of cross-sectional data may over- or underestimate mediated effects (Maxwell & Cole, 2007) and, thus, mediational inferences can be made confidently only when data are collected longitudinally. Generally speaking, due to the preponderance of cross-sectional studies in this area, caution should be taken in making inferences about causation.

As stated earlier, negative appearance-related feedback is positioned as a putative stressor accounting for variance in disordered eating attitudes and behaviors. Numerous studies, for example, suggest a link between exposure to appearance- or weight-based teasing and body dissatisfaction, especially in overweight individuals. A meta-analysis of cross-sectional and longitudinal studies evaluating the relation of appearance-related teasing and weight-related teasing to body dissatisfaction revealed medium effect sizes in both cases ($r = .32$, $r = .39$, respectively) (Menzel et al., 2010). For example, Kostanski and Gullone (2007) asked 431 children (ages 7–10) to complete a measure of weight teasing by friends and parents and assessed their body dissatisfaction via the Figure Rating Scale (Collins, 1991), which presents children with seven preadolescent figure drawings from which to choose their actual and ideal body figures. Being a recipient of weight teasing was associated with poorer body dissatisfaction, and this relationship was more pronounced for overweight children. Similarly, Neumark-Sztainer et al.'s (2010) cross-sectional study of 356 high school girls revealed a significant relation between self-reported, family-based weight teasing and body dissatisfaction. Such teasing may in fact be antecedent to body dissatisfaction, which is a well-established risk factor for the development to eating disorder symptoms.

It is not clear, however, whether weight teasing exerts an influence on body dissatisfaction over time. On the one hand, results of a 5-year prospective study of 440 adolescent girls and 366 adolescent boys, in which body dissatisfaction and weight teasing were assessed at baseline and 5 years later, indicated that weight teasing predicted subsequent body dissatisfaction (Paxton, Eisenberg, & Neumark-Sztainer, 2006). On the other hand, results of a 1-year prospective study of 496 adolescent girls (ages 11–15 at baseline), in which body dissatisfaction and weight teasing were assessed at baseline and 1 year later, showed no effect of weight teasing on increases in body dissatisfaction (Stice & Whitenton, 2002). Thus, whereas there is cross-sectional evidence of a relation between these constructs, particularly for overweight children, longitudinal evidence of the effects of weight-based teasing on body dissatisfaction is varied and inconclusive.

The association between negative appearance-related feedback and disordered eating behaviors also is not clear. Whereas a meta-analysis (Menzel et al., 2010) of cross-sectional and longitudinal studies evaluating the effects of weight teasing on disordered eating behaviors (i.e., dietary restraint, binging and purging) indicated medium effect sizes between weight teasing and dietary restraint and between weight teasing and bulimic behaviors ($r = .35$, $r = .36$, respectively), cross-sectional studies virtually carried these results because so few longitudinal effects were available for inclusion. Longitudinal studies generally do not appear to support such relations. Results from a 10-year-follow-up study from Project EAT found no long-term effect of antecedent experience of weight teasing on dieting behavior or disordered eating (Loth et al., 2014). Adolescents (ages 11–18) were asked how frequently they were teased about their weight. Ten years later, in early adulthood, weight-related teasing assessed at baseline was not predictive of either dieting behavior or disordered eating. It may be that weight-related teasing has more immediate, proximal effects on, for example, risk factors such as negative affect and self-worth. For example, in Loth et al.'s prospective analyses of the Project EAT data, among young men, both self-esteem and depression at baseline were significant predictors of persistent dieting 10 years later. Among young women, baseline body dissatisfaction was a significant predictor of both persistent dieting and the initiation of dieting 10 years later.

Toward assessing whether critical comments about one's weight or shape serve as stressors that promote eating disorder diagnoses, researchers most frequently have employed retrospective, case-controlled studies (e.g., Fairburn et al., 1998; Gonçalves et al., 2014; Machado et al., 2014; Pike et al., 2006, 2008). Researchers in this area typically retrospectively assess for the presence of antecedent life events (including negative appearance-related feedback) in three groups: individuals with one or more eating disorders (AN, BN, or BED as confirmed via the *Structured Clinical Interview for DSM-IV* or the Eating Disorder Evaluation; Fairburn & Cooper, 1993; First, Spitzer, Williams, & Gibbon, 1995); individuals with a current, non-eating-disorder psychiatric condition; and healthy controls having no current psychiatric condition. Many studies use the original or an adapted version of Fairburn et al. (1998)'s Oxford Risk Factor Interview (RFI) that asks participants to retrospectively report on the occurrence (usually over the past year) of a broad range of stressful life events.

Pike et al. (2008) employed the aforementioned design in their three-group, retrospective, case-control study of women with AN, which used the RFI to assess for the presence of stressful antecedent events. Of all the stressful events reported to have occurred in the previous year, only the experience of critical comments about weight, shape, or eating emerged as an antecedent life event specific to AN. Whereas other stressful events, such as physical abuse, were associated with AN, such events were reported at similar rates in the non-eating-disorder psychiatric condition. Similar results using essentially the same design have been reported by Fairburn et al. (1998), Gonçalves et al. (2014), and Pike et al. (2006): Exposure to critical comments

about weight or shape is an antecedent life event specific to clinically significant eating disorders, rather than psychopathology in general. A study by Machado et al. (2014), however, indicated no significant difference in the number of critical comments surrounding body weight or shape reported by women with AN ($n = 86$) compared to psychiatric controls ($n = 68$), suggesting negative feedback may serve as an antecedent to general psychopathology.

Establishing negative appearance-related feedback as a causative stressor leading to the development of eating disorders requires that temporal precedence be clearly established. As stated earlier, the case-controlled studies in this area have relied on retrospective recall. Thus, whereas their results point to a possible causal relation between negative appearance-related feedback and the later development of eating disorders, prospective designs are needed to establish negative appearance-related feedback as an unequivocal antecedent. Most certainly, it is possible that this variable works through other variables over time (e.g., prompts negative affect), which in turn promotes unhealthy eating—and body-related behaviors characteristic of eating disorders.

Negative Affect as a Mediator of the Stressor–Eating Disorder and Obesity Relation

Herein we have presented numerous antecedents to pathological eating behavior. Researchers and clinicians understand, however, that causal models must account for why these stressors are associated with disordered eating, rather than other psychiatric outcomes, in some individuals. Thus, when stressors precede problematic eating behavior, the relation between stress and disordered eating specifically is mediated by other etiologically important factors. In addition, at any node along this causal chain, the presence of moderating factors will influence the expression and intensity of the nodal events and, ultimately, the outcome. For example, an individual who develops depression as a result of stress may attempt to cope with this negative mood state by overeating. In this chain, the stressor prompted a depressive reaction, which, in turn, stimulated overeating in an attempt to reduce the negative affect. This same individual may be part of a social group characterized by support or, alternately, may receive little to no social support, thus moderating the depressive symptoms, which in turn influences eating to cope. Indeed, the overarching, predominating theoretical perspective on the etiology of disordered eating (which may or may not lead to obesity) held by researchers and clinicians is the *maladaptive coping model* wherein the experience of stress initiates a cascade of events that can, through various means, eventuate in disordered eating. The primary mediating mechanism by which they are purported to do so is the negative affect occurring in reaction to the perceived stress, particularly depression and anxiety.

Numerous studies—cross-sectional and longitudinal, biological and psychological—support aspects of this model. First, there is abundant evidence that both depression and anxiety are highly comorbid with eating disorders and obesity (APA, 2013; Gariepy et al., 2010; Hudson et al., 2007; Luppino et al., 2010; O'Brien, & Vincent, 2003). As just one example, in a sample of obese and nonobese persons (each group n = 293), logistic regression predicted obesity and overweight status from two variables: being a "housewife" (the only predictive sociodemographic variable) and having a history of psychopathology, including depression, anxiety, and eating disorders. Moreover, individuals with a diagnosis of such disorders had a 2.7 times greater likelihood of being obese than their healthy counterparts (Pinna et al., 2016).

Second, evidence from both cross-sectional and longitudinal designs is consistent with the maladaptive coping model. For example, in a cross-sectional study of the relation of stress and disordered eating among Chinese policewomen (N = 245), perceived stress had no direct effect on disordered eating behavior, yet there was clear evidence of the indirect effects of perceived stress on disordered eating through both depression and anxiety (Chen et al., 2012). In another cross-sectional study, undergraduate women (N = 147) completed measures of stress, coping style, and binge-eating behavior (Sulkowski, Dempsey, & Dempsey, 2011). The only of four coping styles found to mediate the relation between stress and binge eating was emotional coping—an unproductive means of coping that comprises numerous depressive reactions, including ceasing hobbies and self-isolating. Moreover, longitudinal evidence of the mediating role of negative affect comes from numerous tests of the dual-pathway model, which predicts bulimic symptoms (e.g., Stice, 2001). In this model, stressors such as thin-ideal internalization promote downstream stress in the form of body dissatisfaction. Body dissatisfaction, in turn, spurs both negative affect and engagement in dieting, each of which predicts engagement in binging and purging behaviors.

Additionally, recursive, dynamic relations likely characterize the mediational chain. In a sample of adolescent girls (N = 496) solicited from middle schools (ages 11–15) and assessed for 8 years, annually, into early adulthood (19–23), depression predicted subsequent bulimic symptoms, and bulimic symptoms predicted subsequent depression levels (Presnell, Stice, Seidel, & Madeley, 2009). In fact, a meta-analysis of 30 longitudinal studies revealed that eating disorder symptoms predicted subsequent depression, and depressive symptoms predicted subsequent eating disorder symptomatology (Puccio, Fuller-Tyszkiewicz, Ong, & Krug, 2016).

It should be noted that in some (most often longitudinal) studies, these directional paths are not found, and, in fact, evidence for reversed paths emerges. Rosen and colleagues (1993), for example, assessed life event stress in adolescent girls (M age = 15.92; N = 143) from three college preparatory boarding schools in the northeastern United States using the Adolescent Perceived Events Scale (Compas, Davis, Forsythe, & Wagner, 1987) and their levels of eating pathology via the EAT. Stress did not predict disordered eating four months later, but disordered eating predicted stress levels. It is possible some studies do not capture the stressor-as-antecedent effect due to poor assessment of stress or because the initial, evocative stressor assessed at baseline has lost its potency and been eclipsed by more proximal factors. Certainly eating pathology and obesity can serve as sources of stress; in a 5-year prospective study of 2,123 adults age 50 and over from Alameda County, California, major depressive disorder did not predict obesity 5 years later, but obesity was predictive of major depressive disorder across this time period (Roberts et al., 2003).

Implications and Conclusions

The diathesis-stress model serves as the primary organizing framework for understanding the pathogenesis of disordered eating, including behaviors that result in obesity. According to this model, unique, constitutional vulnerabilities, in combination with life stressors, increase the risk of pathological eating attitudes and behaviors. The most convincing evidence for both the identification of antecedent stressors that contribute to pathological eating as well as their roles along causal chains comes from longitudinal, prospective designs and laboratory experiments. However, the former are highly resource intensive and the latter generally must employ simulations of stressors (e.g., peer rejection) and outcomes that may not map onto the phenomenology of disorder (e.g., experimentally induced body dissatisfaction, which is presumably transient).

The empirical literature is dominated by cross-sectional studies, most of which rely on self-report, and many of which assess life events retrospectively. Whereas such studies are prone to recall and other biases and cannot demonstrate temporal precedence or causation, the associations they identify provide direction for more resource-intensive investigations. At the same time, sole reliance on cross-sectional findings to inform longitudinal inquiry can cause researchers to overlook potentially important predictors. Specifically, cross-sectional examinations may not capture relations that unfold over time, as we have seen in cross-sectional studies that fail to find associations between PTSD and BMI among women, a relation that emerges in longitudinal examinations. Furthermore, mediational tests conducted with cross-sectional data may over- and underestimate true mediational effects present in longitudinal data (Maxwell & Cole, 2007). Finally, some putative stressors identified via cross-sectional investigations, especially recurrent stressors, may be virtually impossible to effectively study prospectively or experimentally (e.g., childhood sexual abuse). Nevertheless, these stressors should not be dismissed because their complexity currently eludes full validation.

Advances being made in methods and data-analytic strategies will further illuminate our understanding of eating pathology. The validity of cross-sectional designs already can be enhanced, for example, via techniques such as ecological momentary assessment (EMA). This naturalistic method avoids the bias inherent in retrospective recall while providing more ecologically valid data regarding antecedents and consequences of stressors. Goldschmidt et al. (2012), for instance, used EMA to disentangle the relation between premeal and postmeal negative affect and loss of control while eating (a core feature of binge eating) in obese persons with and without BED. Similarly, functional magnetic resonance imaging (fMRI), used for clinical brain mapping, has the potential to observe appetite-related brain activation in response to specific stimuli in real time. Wagner and colleagues (2015), for example, via fMRI found differential, higher order brain response to sucrose in women recovered from AN versus BN. These groups' taste-related brain regions showed significantly different activity in response to repeated presentation of sucrose, with the AN group showing decreased sensitization and the BN group showing increased sensitization. Finally, data-analytic strategies, such as time-series analysis, will increasingly be used to analyze fluctuations over

time within a given individual (e.g., affective responsivity to food presentations) and to draw comparisons across symptomatic and asymptomatic individuals (see Hamaker, Grasman, & Kamphuis, 2016). Through situating events accurately in time, each of these techniques has the potential to inform our understanding of causality.

Ultimately, researchers work to elucidate stressors and the pathways through which they influence pathological eating to inform prevention and treatment efforts. In some cases, specific stressors, once identified, can be targeted for reduction or elimination altogether. For example, weight-based teasing can be minimized through parenting and school-based programs. Similarly, sexual violation of women as well as men in the military by their commanders and peers can be drastically reduced via programming, monitoring, and the application of appropriate sanctions.

Stressors, however, also can be countered by *resilience*. Resilience refers to a learned process of adaptation in the face of negative life events and is characterized by "good outcomes in spite of serious threats to adaptation or development" (p. 228; Masten, 2001). A well-known hallmark of resilience is *positive self-feelings* (Masten, 2001), a self-concept characterized by high self-esteem and self-worth, as well as a view of the self as generally efficacious and competent. Notably, those suffering from disordered eating consistently demonstrate significantly lower self-esteem (and related self-feelings) than their symptom-free peers (Cervera et al., 2003; Ghaderi & Scott, 2001; Kendler et al., 1991). Survey studies indicate large, inverse relations ($r = -.61$) between self-esteem and eating pathology in undergraduate women (Mayhew & Edelmann, 1989), and self-esteem distinguished undergraduate women with eating disorder symptoms from their asymptomatic peers ($d = 59$) (Corning et al., 2006). Among overweight and obese women, those who binge eat have significantly lower self-esteem (Cohen's $d = .69$) (Herbozo, Schaefer, & Thompson, 2015), and cross-sectional data from 2,163 pairs of female twins (ages 17–55) demonstrate that low self-esteem predicts bulimic pathology (Kendler et al., 1991).

The nature of the temporal ordering of self-esteem and eating pathology has been examined in numerous prospective studies, and the preponderance of data shows that low self-esteem seems to set the stage for maladaptive eating, and that low self-esteem and the severity of eating pathology as well as obesity are closely associated in a linear manner (Cervera et al., 2003; Ghaderi & Scott, 2001;

Hesketh, Wake, & Waters, 2004). Disordered eating usually begins in mid- to late adolescence (e.g., Stice, Marti, Shaw, & Jaconis, 2009)—the same period wherein adolescents face the task of identity exploration toward the goal of positive identity development and a coherent sense of self. Over the course of adolescence, identity and self-esteem mutually reinforce one another (Luyckx et al., 2013), working in tandem to propel an either upward or downward trajectory. For the adolescent whose sense of self is ill formed, dispersed, or weak, maladaptive coping behaviors (such as binging or caloric restriction) may be adopted in response to stressful life events. Given the downward trajectory and weaker identity formation associated with lowered self-esteem, such maladaptive coping mechanisms can become intertwined with the developing self, and ultimately eclipse normative identity development.

As we have contended elsewhere (Corning & Heibel, 2016), disordered eating prevention efforts should be aimed at healthy adolescent identity development and resilience building. Such prevention efforts to date, however, have not made the promotion of healthy identity development a priority. The content of current prevention programs ranges from behavioral (e.g., nutrition and dietary training) to educational (e.g., media literacy) to psychological (e.g., dissonance based). Of these, only about half have been shown effective at reducing risk factors and even fewer reduce actual eating pathology; in addition, their effectiveness wanes substantially with time (Stice, Shaw, & Marti, 2007). Interventions that promote self-esteem through competence—and relationship building, such as youth organization programs (e.g., Girl Scouts, 4-H, Girls on the Run) and self-affirmation interventions adopted from social psychology that promote identity-bolstering (see Armitage, 2012; Bucchianeri & Corning, 2012; Harris et al., 2014; Logel & Cohen, 2012; Powell, Simpson, & Overton, 2015) should be tested further for their efficacy in reducing eating disorder and obesity risk.

The etiologies of both eating disorders and obesity are multifactorial. The diathesis-stress model, which positions stressors as antecedent to pathology, continues to predominate etiological conceptualizations. And although the universe of potential stressors is infinite, we have reviewed those most commonly garnering theoretical and empirical attention. Across the stressors assessed, cross-sectional designs frequently yield predicted associations that vary in the extent to which they bear out in longitudinal examinations. Burgeoning methodological and design developments are converging to both increase the internal validity in this area of research and provide insight into the brain processes associated with the experience of stressful life events. Prevention efforts continue to be aimed at the identification of causal stressors and their amelioration through programming efforts. Given the identity issues so often characterizing those who suffer from eating disorders and obesity, we call for the development of empirically supported program efforts aimed at fostering positive identity development and resilience during adolescence.

References

American Psychiatric Association. (1987). *Diagnostic and statistical manual of mental disorders* (3rd ed., revised). Washington, DC: Author.

American Psychiatric Association. (1994). *Diagnostic and statistical manual of mental disorders* (4th ed.). Washington, DC: Author.

American Psychiatric Association. (2013). *Diagnostic and statistical manual of mental disorders* (5th ed.). Washington, DC: Author.

Armitage, C. J. (2012). Evidence that self-affirmation reduces body dissatisfaction by basing self-esteem on domains other than body weight and shape. *Journal of Child Psychology and Psychiatry, 53*, 81–88.

Ball, K., & Lee, C. (2000). Relationship between psychological stress, coping and disordered eating: A review. *Psychology & Health, 14*(6), 1007–1035.

Bearman, S. K., Presnell, K., Martinez, E., & Stice, E. (2006). The skinny on body dissatisfaction: A longitudinal study of adolescent girls and boys. *Journal of Youth and Adolescence, 35*(2), 229–241.

Becker, D. F., & Grilo, C. M. (2011). Childhood maltreatment in women with binge-eating disorder: Associations with psychiatric comorbidity, psychological functioning, and eating pathology. *Eating and Weight Disorders, 16*(2), e113–e120.

Becker, A. E., Keel, P., Anderson-Fye, E., & Thomas, J. J. (2004). Genes and/or jeans?: Genetic and socio-cultural contributions to risk for eating disorders. *Journal of Addictive Diseases, 23*(3), 81–103.

Bedogni, G., Miglioli, L., Masutti, F., Tiribelli, C., Marchesini, G., & Bellentani, S. (2005). Prevalence of and risk factors for nonalcoholic fatty liver disease: The Dionysos nutrition and liver study. *Hepatology, 42*(1), 44–52.

Bentley, T., & Widom, C. S. (2009). A 30-year follow-up of the effects of child abuse and neglect on obesity in adulthood. *Obesity, 17*(10), 1900–1905.

Beumont, P. J. V., Abraham, S. F., Argall, W. J., George, G. C. W., & Glaun, D. E. (1978). The onset of anorexia nervosa. *Australian and New Zealand Journal of Psychiatry, 12*(3), 145–149.

Boynton-Jarrett, R., Rosenberg, L., Palmer, J. R., Boggs, D. A., & Wise, L. A. (2012). Child and adolescent abuse in relation to obesity in adulthood: The Black women's health study. *Pediatrics, 130*, 245–253.

Bucchianeri, M. M., & Corning, A. F. (2012). An experimental test of women's body dissatisfaction reduction through self-affirmation. *Applied Psychology: Health and Well-Being, 4*, 188–201.

Carr, K. A., Lin, H., Fletcher, K. D., Sucheston, L., Singh, P. K., Salis, R. J.,...Epstein, L. H. (2013). Two functional serotonin polymorphisms moderate the effect of food reinforcement on BMI. *Behavioral Neuroscience, 127*(3), 387–399.

Carroll, D., Phillips, A. C., & Der, G. (2008). Body mass index, abdominal adiposity, obesity, and cardiovascular reactions to psychological stress in a large community sample. *Psychosomatic Medicine, 70*(6), 653–660.

Cervera, S., Lahortiga, F., Martínez-González, M. A., Gual, P., Irala-Estévez, J. d., & Alonso, Y. (2003). Neuroticism and low self-esteem as risk factors for incident eating disorders in a prospective cohort study. *International Journal of Eating Disorders, 33*(3), 271–280.

Chandola, T., Brunner, E., & Marmot, M. (2006). Chronic stress at work and the metabolic syndrome: Prospective study. *British Medical Journal, 332*(7540), 521–524.

Charatan, D. L. (2015). "I won't grow up, never grow up, not me!": Anorexia nervosa and maturity fears revisited. In J. Petrucelli (Ed.), *Body-states: Interpersonal and relational perspectives on the treatment of eating disorders* (pp. 120–132). New York, NY: Routledge/Taylor & Francis.

Chen, J., Wang, Z., Guo, B., Arcelus, J., Zhang, H., Jia, X.,...Yang, M. (2012). Negative affect mediates effects of psychological stress on disordered eating in young Chinese women. *PLoS ONE, 7*(10), 5.

Claes, L., & Vandereycken, W. (2007). Is there a link between traumatic experiences and self-injurious behaviors in eating-disordered patients? *Eating Disorders: The Journal of Treatment & Prevention, 15*(4), 305–315.

Colditz, G. A., Willett, W. C., Rotnitzky, A., & Manson, J. E. (1995). Weight gain as a risk factor for clinical diabetes mellitus in women. *Annals of Internal Medicine, 122*(7), 481–486.

Collins, M. E. (1991). Body figure perceptions and preferences among preadolescent children. *International Journal of Eating Disorders, 10*(2), 199–208.

Compas, B. E., Davis, G. E., Forsythe, C. J., & Wagner, B. M. (1987). Assessment of major and daily stressful events during adolescence: The adolescent perceived events scale. *Journal of Consulting and Clinical Psychology, 55*(4), 534–541.

Copeland, W. E., Bulik, C. M., Zucker, N., Wolke, D., Lereya, S. T., & Costello, E. J. (2015). Does childhood bullying predict eating disorder symptoms? A prospective, longitudinal analysis. *International Journal of Eating Disorders, 48*(8), 1141–1149.

Corning, A. F., & Heibel, H. D. (2016). Re-thinking eating disorder prevention: The case for prioritizing the promotion of healthy identity development. *Eating Disorders: The Journal of Treatment & Prevention, 24*(1), 106–113.

Corning, A. F., Krumm, A. J., & Smitham, L. A. (2006). Differential social comparison processes in women with and without eating disorder symptoms. *Journal of Counseling Psychology, 53*(3), 338–349.

Culbert, K. M., Burt, S. A., McGue, M., Iacono, W. G., & Klump, K. L. (2009). Puberty and the genetic diathesis of disordered eating attitudes and behaviors. *Journal of Abnormal Psychology, 118*(4), 788–796.

Danese, A., & Tan, M. (2014). Childhood maltreatment and obesity: Systematic review and meta-analysis. *Molecular Psychiatry, 19*(5), 544–554.

Dazzi, F., & Di Leone, F. G. (2014). The diagnostic classification of eating disorders: Current situation, possible alternatives and future perspectives. *Eating and Weight Disorders, 19*(1), 11–19.

Degortes, D., Santonastaso, P., Zanetti, T., Tenconi, E., Veronese, A., & Favaro, A. (2014). Stressful life events and binge eating disorder. *European Eating Disorders Review, 22*(5), 378–382.

Dohrenwend, B. P. (2006). Inventorying stressful life events as risk factors for psychopathology: Toward resolution of the problem of intracategory variability. *Psychological Bulletin, 132*(3), 477–495.

Dye, H. (2016). Are there differences in gender, race, and age regarding body dissatisfaction? *Journal of Human Behavior in the Social Environment, 26*(6), 499–508.

Fairburn, C. G., & Cooper, Z. (1993). The Eating Disorder Examination (12th edition). In C. G. Fairburn & G. T. Wilson (Eds.), *Binge eating: Nature, assessment, and treatment* (pp. 317–360). New York, NY: Guilford Press.

Fairburn, C. G., & Cooper, Z. (2007). Thinking afresh about the classification of eating disorders. *International Journal of Eating Disorders, 40*, S107–S110.

Fairburn, C. G., Cooper, Z., Bohn, K., O'Connor, M. E., Doll, H. A., & Palmer, R. L. (2007). The severity and status of eating disorder NOS: Implications for *DSM-V*. *Behaviour Research and Therapy, 45*(8), 1705–1715.

Fairburn, C. G., Doll, H. A., Welch, S. L., Hay, P. J., Davies, B. A., & O'Connor, M. E. (1998). Risk factors for binge eating disorder: A community-based, case-control study. *Archives of General Psychiatry, 55*(5), 425–432.

Faulkner, K. K., & Duecker, S. J. (1989). Stress, time distortion, and failure to recover among obese individuals: Implications for weight gain and dieting. *International Journal of Eating Disorders, 8*(2), 247–250.

Felitti, V. J. (1991). Long-term medical consequences of incest, rape, and molestation. *Southern Medical Journal, 84*(3), 328–331.

First, M. B., Spitzer, R. L., Williams, J. B. W., & Gibbon, M. (1995). *Structured clinical interview for DSM-IV (SCID-I) (User's guide and interview). Research Version.* New York, NY: Biometrics Research Department, New York Psychiatric Institute.

Flegal, K. M., Carroll, M. D., Kit, B. K., & Ogden, C. L. (2012). Prevalence of obesity and trends in the distribution of body mass index among US adults, 1999–2010. *Journal of the American Medical Association, 307*(5), 491–497.

Folsom, A. R., Kaye, S. A., Potter, J. D., & Prineas, R. J. (1989). Association of incident carcinoma of the endometrium with body weight and fat distribution in older women: early findings of the Iowa Women's Health Study. *Cancer Research, 49*(23), 6828–6831.

Frayne, S. M., Skinner, K. M., Sullivan, L. M., & Freund, K. M. (2003). Sexual assault while in the military: Violence as a predictor of cardiac risk? *Violence and Victims, 18*(2), 219–225.

Frederick, D. A., Jafary, A. M., Gruys, K., & Daniels, E. A. (2012). *Surveys and the epidemiology of body image dissatisfaction* (pp. 766–774). Chapter in Cash T. F. (Ed.), *Encyclopedia of body image and human appearance.* San Diego, CA: Elsevier Academic Press.

Gariepy, G., Nitka, D., & Schmitz, N. (2010). The association between obesity and anxiety disorders in the population: A systematic review and meta-analysis. *International Journal of Obesity, 34*(3), 407–419.

Garner, D. M., Olmsted, M. P., Bohr, Y., & Garfinkel, P. E. (1982). The Eating Attitudes Test: Psychometric features and clinical correlates. *Psychological Medicine, 12*(4), 871–878.

Garner, D. M., Olmsted, M. P., & Polivy, J. (1983). Development and validation of a multidimensional eating disorder inventory for anorexia nervosa and bulimia. *International Journal of Eating Disorders, 2*(2), 15–34.

Ghaderi, A. (2001). Review of risk factors for eating disorders: Implications for primary prevention and cognitive behavioural therapy. *Scandinavian Journal of Behaviour Therapy, 30*(2), 57–74.

Ghaderi, A., & Scott, B. (2001). Prevalence, incidence and prospective risk factors for eating disorders. *Acta Psychiatrica Scandinavica, 104*, 122–130.

Goldschmidt, A. B., Engel, S. G., Wonderlich, S. A., Crosby, R. D., Peterson, C. B., Le Grange, D.,... Mitchell, J. E. (2012). Momentary affect surrounding loss of control and overeating in obese adults with and without binge eating disorder. *Obesity, 20*(6), 1206–1211.

Gonçalves, S. F., Machado, B., Martins, C., & Machado, P. P. (2014). Eating and weight/shape criticism as a specific life-event related to bulimia nervosa: A case control study. *The Journal of Psychology: Interdisciplinary and Applied, 148*(1), 61–72.

Gottesman, I. I. (1991). *Schizophrenia genesis: The origins of madness.* San Francisco, CA: Freeman.

Grabe, S., Ward, L. M., & Hyde, J. S. (2008). The role of the media in body image concerns among women: A meta-analysis of experimental and correlational studies. *Psychological Bulletin, 134*(3), 460–476.

Gray, W. N., Kahhan, N. A., & Janicke, D. M. (2009). Peer victimization and pediatric obesity: A review of the literature. *Psychology in the Schools, 46*(8), 720–727.

Grilo, C. M. (2013). Why no cognitive body image feature such as overvaluation of shape/weight in the binge eating disorder diagnosis? *International Journal of Eating Disorders, 46*, 208–211.

Grilo, C. M., & Masheb, R. M. (2001). Childhood psychological, physical, and sexual maltreatment in outpatients with binge eating disorder: Frequency and associations with gender, obesity, and eating-related psychopathology. *Obesity Research, 9*(5), 320–325.

Hamaker, E. L., Grasman, R. P. P. P., & Kamphuis, J. H. (2016). Modeling bas dysregulation in bipolar disorder: Illustrating the potential of time series analysis. *Assessment, 23*(4), 436–446.

Hammen, C. (1991). Generation of stress in the course of unipolar depression. *Journal of Abnormal Psychology, 100*(4), 555–561.

Harris, P. R., Brearley, I., Sheeran, P., Barker, M., Klein, W. M. P., Creswell, J. D.,... Bond, R. (2014). Combining self-affirmation with implementation intentions to promote fruit and vegetable consumption. *Health Psychology, 33*, 729–736.

Hayden-Wade, H., Stein, R. I., Ghaderi, A., Saelens, B. E., Zabinski, M. F., & Wilfley, D. E. (2005). Prevalence, characteristics, and correlates of teasing experiences among overweight children vs. non-overweight peers. *Obesity Research, 13*(8), 1381–1392.

Herbozo, S., Schaefer, L. M., & Thompson, J. K. (2015). A comparison of eating disorder psychopathology, appearance satisfaction, and self-esteem in overweight and obese women with and without binge eating. *Eating Behaviors, 17*, 86–89.

Hesketh, K., Wake, M., & Waters, E. (2004). Body mass index and parent-reported self-esteem in elementary school children: Evidence for a causal relationship. *International Journal of Obesity, 28*(10), 1233–1237.

Hilbert, A., Pike, K. M., Goldschmidt, A. B., Wilfley, D. E., Fairburn, C. G., Dohm, F.,... Striegel Weissman, R. (2014). Risk factors across the eating disorders. *Psychiatry Research, 220*(1–2), 500–506.

Holmes, T. H., & Rahe, R. H. (1967). The Social Readjustment Rating Scale. *Journal of Psychosomatic Research, 11*(2), 213–218.

Hudson, J. I., Hiripi, E., Pope, H. G., Jr., & Kessler, R. C. (2007). The prevalence and correlates of eating disorders in the National Comorbidity Survey Replication. *Biological Psychiatry, 61*(3), 348–358.

Institute for Health Metrics and Evaluation. (2014). *Overweight and obesity viz.* Seattle, WA: IHME, University of Washington. Available from http://vizhub.healthdata.org/obesity.

Jacobson, I. G., Smith, T. C., Smith, B., Keel, P. K., Amoroso, P. J., Wells, T. S.,... Millennium Cohort Study Team. (2009). Disordered eating and weight changes after deployment: Longitudinal assessment of a large US military cohort. *American Journal of Epidemiology, 169*(4), 415–427.

Joiner, T. E., Jr., Heatherton, T. F., Rudd, M. D., & Schmidt, N. B. (1997). Perfectionism, perceived weight status, and bulimic symptoms: Two studies testing a diathesis-stress model. *Journal of Abnormal Psychology, 106*(1), 145–153.

Kendler, K. S., MacLean, C., Neale, M., Kessler, R. C., Heath, A., & Eaves, L. (1991). The genetic epidemiology of bulimia nervosa. *The American Journal of Psychiatry, 148*(12), 1627–1637.

Kessler, R. C., Petukhova, M., Sampson, N. A., Zaslavsky, A. M., & Wittchen, H. (2012). Twelve-month and lifetime prevalence and lifetime morbid risk of anxiety and mood disorders in the United States. *International Journal of Methods in Psychiatric Research, 21*(3), 169–184.

Kintzle, S., Schuyler, A. C., Ray-Letourneau, D., Ozuna, S. M., Munch, C., Xintarianos, E.,... Castro, C. A. (2015). Sexual trauma in the military: Exploring PTSD and mental health care utilization in female veterans. *Psychological Services, 12*(4), 394–401.

Koch, F., Sepa, A., & Ludvigsson, J. (2008). Psychological stress and obesity. *The Journal of Pediatrics, 153*(6), 839–844.

Kostanski, M., & Gullone, E. (2007). The impact of teasing on children's body image. *Journal of Child and Family Studies, 16*(3), 307–319.

Krukowski, R. A., West, D. S., Perez, A. P., Bursac, Z., Phillips, M. M., & Raczynski, J. M. (2009). Overweight children, weight-based teasing and academic performance. *International Journal of Pediatric Obesity, 4*(4), 274–280.

Kuijer, R. G., Boyce, J. A., & Marshall, E. M. (2015). Associating a prototypical forbidden food item with guilt or celebration: Relationships with indicators of (un)healthy eating and the moderating role of stress and depressive symptoms. *Psychology & Health, 30*(2), 203–217.

Lampard, A. M., MacLehose, R. F., Eisenberg, M. E., Neumark-Sztainer, D., & Davison, K. K. (2014). Weight-related teasing in the school environment: Associations with psychosocial health and weight control practices among adolescent boys and girls. *Journal of Youth and Adolescence, 43*(10), 1770–1780.

Laus, M. F., Costa, T. M. B., & Almeida, S. S. (2015). Gender differences in body image and preferences for an ideal silhouette among Brazilian undergraduates. *Eating Behaviors, 19*, 159–162.

Le Grange, D., & Loeb, K. L. (2014). Family-based treatment for adolescent eating disorders. In J. Ehrenreich-May & B. C. Chu (Eds.), *Transdiagnostic treatments for children and adolescents: Principles and practice* (pp. 363–384). New York, NY: Guilford Press.

Lee, I. M., & Paffenbarger, R. S., Jr. (1992). Quetelet's index and risk of colon cancer in college alumni. *Journal of the National Cancer Institute*, *84*(17), 1326–1331.

Leon, G. R., Fulkerson, J. A., Perry, C. L., & Cudeck, R. (1993). Personality and behavioral vulnerabilities associated with risk status for eating disorders in adolescent girls. *Journal of Abnormal Psychology*, *102*(3), 438–444.

Libbey, H. P., Story, M. T., Neumark-Sztainer, D., & Boutelle, K. N. (2008). Teasing, disordered eating behaviors, and psychological morbidities among overweight adolescents. *Obesity*, *16*, S24–S29.

Liu, R. T. (2015). A developmentally informed perspective on the relation between stress and psychopathology: When the problem with stress is that there is not enough. *Journal of Abnormal Psychology*, *124*(1), 80–92.

Logel, C., & Cohen, G. L. (2012). The role of the self in physical health: Testing the effect of a values-affirmation intervention on weight loss. *Psychological Science*, *23*, 53–55.

Loth, K. A., MacLehose, R., Bucchianeri, M., Crow, S., & Neumark-Sztainer, D. (2014). Predictors of dieting and disordered eating behaviors from adolescence to young adulthood. *Journal of Adolescent Health*, *55*(5), 705–712.

Luppino, F. S., de Wit, L. M., Bouvy, P. F., Stijnen, T., Cuijpers, P., Penninx, B. W. J. H., & Zitman, F. G. (2010). Overweight, obesity, and depression: A systematic review and meta-analysis of longitudinal studies. *Archives of General Psychiatry*, *67*(3), 220–229.

Luyckx, K., Klimstra, T. A., Duriez, B., Van Petegem, S., Beyers, W., Teppers, E., & Goossens, L. (2013). Personal identity processes and self-esteem: Temporal sequences in high school and college students. *Journal of Research in Personality*, *47*, 159–170.

MacDonald, D. E., McFarlane, T. L., & Olmsted, M. P. (2014). "Diagnostic shift" from eating disorder not otherwise specified to bulimia nervosa using *DSM-5* criteria: A clinical comparison with *DSM-IV* bulimia. *Eating Behaviors*, *15*(1), 60–62.

MacNeil, L., Esposito-Smythers, C., Mehlenbeck, R., & Weismoore, J. (2012). The effects of avoidance coping and coping self-efficacy on eating disorder attitudes and behaviors: A stress-diathesis model. *Eating Behaviors*, *13*(4), 293–296.

Machado, B., Gonçalves, S. F., Martins, C., Hoek, H. W., & Machado, P. P. (2014). Risk factors and antecedent life events in the development of anorexia nervosa: A Portuguese case-control study. *European Eating Disorders Review*, *22*(4), 243–251.

Madowitz, J., Knatz, S., Maginot, T., Crow, S. J., & Boutelle, K. N. (2012). Teasing, depression and unhealthy weight control behaviour in obese children. *Pediatric Obesity*, *7*(6), 446–452.

Manson, J. E., Nathan, D. M., Krolewski, A. S., Stampfer, M. J., Willett, W. C., & Hennekens, C. H. (1992). A prospective study of exercise and incidence of diabetes among US male physicians. *Journal of the American Medical Association*, *268*(1), 63–67.

Marcus, M. D., & Wildes, J. E. (2009). Obesity: Is it a mental disorder? *International Journal of Eating Disorders*, *42*(8), 739–753.

Masten, A. S. (2001). Ordinary magic: Resilience processes in development. *American Psychologist*, *56*(3), 227–238.

Masten, A. S. (2014). *Ordinary magic: Resilience in development*. New York, NY: Guilford Press.

Mattocks, K. M., Haskell, S. G., Krebs, E. E., Justice, A. C., Yano, E. M., & Brandt, C. (2012). Women at war: Understanding how women veterans cope with combat and military sexual trauma. *Social Science & Medicine*, *74*(4), 537–545.

Maxwell, S. E., & Cole, D. A. (2007). Bias in cross-sectional analyses of longitudinal mediation. *Psychological Methods*, *12*(1), 23–44.

Mayhew, R., & Edelmann, R. J. (1989). Self-esteem, irrational beliefs and coping strategies in relation to eating problems in a non-clinical population. *Personality and Individual Differences*, *10*(5), 581–584.

Menzel, J. E., Schaefer, L. M., Burke, N. L., Mayhew, L. L., Brannick, M. T., & Thompson, J. K. (2010). Appearance-related teasing, body dissatisfaction, and disordered eating: A meta-analysis. *Body Image*, *7*(4), 261–270.

Micali, N., Martini, M. G., Thomas, J. J., Eddy, K. T., Kothari, R., Russell, E., . . . Treasure, J. (2017). Lifetime and 12–month prevalence of eating disorders amongst women in mid-life: A population-based study of diagnoses and risk factors. *BMC Medicine*, *15*, 12. http://doi.org/10.1186/s12916–016–0766–4

Michopoulos, V. (2016). Stress-induced alterations in estradiol sensitivity increase risk for obesity in women. *Physiology & Behavior*, *166*, 56–64.

Miller, T. W. (1988). Advances in understanding the impact of stressful life events on health. *Hospital & Community Psychiatry*, *39*(6), 615–622.

Monteath, S. A., & McCabe, M. P. (1997). The influence of societal factors on female body image. *Journal of Social Psychology*, *137*(6), 708–727.

Mustelin, L., Lehtokari, V., & Keski-Rahkonen, A. (2016). Other specified and unspecified feeding or eating disorders among women in the community. *International Journal of Eating Disorders*, *49*, 1010–1017.

Neumark-Sztainer, D., Bauer, K. W., Friend, S., Hannan, P. J., Story, M., & Berge, J. M. (2010). Family weight talk and dieting: How much do they matter for body dissatisfaction and disordered eating behaviors in adolescent girls? *Journal of Adolescent Health*, *47*(3), 270–276.

Neumark-Sztainer, D., Falkner, N., Story, M., Perry, C., Hannan, P. J., & Mulert, S. (2002). Weight-teasing among adolescents: Correlations with weight status and disordered eating behaviors. *International Journal of Obesity*, *26*(1), 123–131.

Nikendei, C., Funiok, C., Pfüller, U., Zastrow, A., Aschenbrenner, S., Weisbrod, M., . . . Friederich, H. (2011). Memory performance in acute and weight-restored Anorexia Nervosa patients. *Psychological Medicine*, *41*(4), 829–838.

Nishitani, N., & Sakakibara, H. (2006). Relationship of obesity to job stress and eating behavior in male Japanese workers. *International Journal of Obesity*, *30*(3), 528–533.

O'Brien, B. S., & Sher, L. (2013). Child sexual abuse and the pathophysiology of suicide in adolescents and adults. *International Journal of Adolescent Medicine and Health*, *25*(3), 201–205.

O'Brien, K. M., & Vincent, N. K. (2003). Psychiatric comorbidity in anorexia and bulimia nervosa: Nature, prevalence and causal relationships. *Clinical Psychology Review*, *23*(1), 57–74.

Paxton, S. J., Eisenberg, M. E., & Neumark-Sztainer, D. (2006). Prospective predictors of body dissatisfaction in adolescent girls and boys: A five-year longitudinal study. *Developmental Psychology*, *42*(5), 888–899.

Pike, K. M., Hilbert, A., Wilfley, D. E., Fairburn, C. G., Dohm, F. A., Walsh, B. T., & Striegel-Moore, R. (2008). Toward an understanding of risk factors for anorexia nervosa: A case-control study. *Psychological Medicine, 38*(10), 1443–1453.

Pike, K. M., Wilfley, D., Hilbert, A., Fairburn, C. G., Dohm, F., & Striegel-Moore, R. (2006). Antecedent life events of binge-eating disorder. *Psychiatry Research, 142*(1), 19–29.

Pinna, F., Sardu, C., Orrù, W., Velluzzi, F., Loviselli, A., Contu, P., & Carpiniello, B. (2016). Psychopathology, psychosocial factors and obesity. *Rivista Di Psichiatria, 51*(1), 30–36.

Pollack, K. M., & Cheskin, L. J. (2007). Obesity and workplace traumatic injury: Does the science support the link? *Injury Prevention, 13*(5), 297–302.

Powell, P. A., Simpson, J., & Overton, P. G. (2015). Self-affirming trait kindness regulates disgust towards one's physical appearance. *Body Image, 12*, 98–107.

Presnell, K., Stice, E., Seidel, A., & Madeley, M. C. (2009). Depression and eating pathology: Prospective reciprocal relations in adolescents. *Clinical Psychology & Psychotherapy, 16*(4), 357–365.

Puccio, F., Fuller-tyszkiewicz, M., Ong, D., & Krug, I. (2016). A systematic review and meta-analysis on the longitudinal relationship between eating pathology and depression. *International Journal of Eating Disorders 49*(5), 439–454.

Quick, V. M., McWilliams, R., & Byrd-Bredbenner, C. (2013). Fatty, fatty, two-by-four: Weight-teasing history and disturbed eating in young adult women. *American Journal of Public Health, 103*(3), 508–515.

Rexrode, K. M., Hennekens, C. H., Willett, W. C., Colditz, G. A., Stampfer, M. J., Rich-Edwards, J. W.,...Manson, J. E. (1997). A prospective study of body mass index, weight change, and risk of stroke in women. *Journal of the American Medical Association, 277*(19), 1539–1545.

Ricca, V., Mannucci, E., Mezzani, B., Di Bernardo, M., Zucchi, T., Paionni, A.,...Faravelli, C. (2001). Psychopathological and clinical features of outpatients with an eating disorder not otherwise specified. *Eating and Weight Disorders, 6*(3), 157–165.

Ricciardelli, L. A., & McCabe, M. P. (2001). Dietary restraint and negative affect as mediators of body dissatisfaction and bulimic behavior in adolescent girls and boys. *Behaviour Research and Therapy, 39*(11), 1317–1328.

Richardson, A. S., Dietz, W. H., & Gordon-Larsen, P. (2014). The association between childhood sexual and physical abuse with incident adult severe obesity across 13 years of the National Longitudinal Study of Adolescent Health. *Pediatric Obesity, 9*, 351–361.

Rideout, V. J., Foehr, U. G., & Roberts, D. F. (2011). *Generation M2: Media in the lives of 8– to 18–year-olds*. Retrieved from The Kaiser Family Foundation website: http://kff.org/other/report/generation-m2-media-in-the-lives-of-8-to18-year-olds/

Rimm, E. B., Stampfer, M. J., Giovannucci, E., Ascherio, A., Spiegelman, D., Colditz, G. A., & Willett, W. C. (1995). Body size and fat distribution as predictors of coronary heart disease among middle-aged and older US men. *American Journal of Epidemiology, 141*(12), 1117–1127.

Roberts, R. E., Deleger, S., Strawbridge, W. J., & Kaplan, G. A. (2003). Prospective association between obesity and depression: Evidence from the Alameda County study. *International Journal of Obesity, 27*(4), 514–521.

Robinson, W. R. (2012). Gender-specific effects of early nutritional restriction on adult obesity risk: Evidence from quasi-experimental studies. *Obesity, 20*(12), 2464–2466.

Rodin, J., Silberstein, L., & Striegel-Moore, R. (1984). Women and weight: A normative discontent. *Nebraska Symposium on Motivation, 32*, 267–307.

Rosen, J. C., Compas, B. E., & Tacy, B. (1993). The relation among stress, psychological symptoms, and eating disorder symptoms: A prospective analysis. *International Journal of Eating Disorders, 14*(2), 153–162.

Rosengren, A., Teo, K., Rangarajan, S., Kabali, C., Khumalo, I., Kutty, V. R.,...Yusuf, S. (2015). Psychosocial factors and obesity in 17 high-, middle- and low-income countries: The prospective urban rural epidemiologic study. *International Journal of Obesity, 39*(8), 1217–1223.

Rosenthal, R. (1979). File drawer problem and tolerance for null results. *Psychological Bulletin, 86*, 638–641.

Rowland, N. E., & Antelman, S. M. (1976). Stress-induced hyperphagia and obesity in rats: A possible model for understanding human obesity. *Science, 191*(4224), 310–312.

Sellers, T. A., Kushi, L. H., Potter, J. D., Kaye, S. A., Nelson, C. L., McGovern, P. G., & Folsom, A. R. (1992). Effect of family history, body-fat distribution, and reproductive factors on the risk of postmenopausal breast cancer. *New England Journal of Medicine, 326*(20), 1323–1329.

Shafran, R., Fairburn, C. G., Nelson, L., & Robinson, P. H. (2003). The interpretation of symptoms of severe dietary restraint. *Behaviour Research and Therapy, 41*(8), 887–894.

Siahpush, M., Huang, T. T., Sikora, A., Tibbits, M., Shaikh, R. A., & Singh, G. K. (2014). Prolonged financial stress predicts subsequent obesity: Results from a prospective study of an Australian national sample. *Obesity, 22*(2), 616–621.

Skinner, K. M. (2000). *Quality of life in women veterans using VA ambulatory health care: Final report*. Bedford, MA: Health Services Research and Development Service, Center for Health Quality, Outcomes, and Economic Research.

Smolak, L., & Murnen, S. K. (2002). A meta-analytic examination of the relationship between child sexual abuse and eating disorders. *International Journal of Eating Disorders, 31*, 136–150.

Solovieva, S., Lallukka, T., Virtanen, M., & Viikari-Juntura, E. (2013). Psychosocial factors at work, long work hours, and obesity: A systematic review. *Scandinavian Journal of Work, Environment & Health, 39*(3), 241–258.

Stice, E. (2001). A prospective test of the dual-pathway model of bulimic pathology: Mediating effects of dieting and negative affect. *Journal of Abnormal Psychology, 110*(1), 124–135.

Stice, E., & Agras, W. S. (1998). Predicting onset and cessation bulimic behaviors during adolescence: A longitudinal grouping analysis. *Behavior Therapy, 29*(2), 257–276.

Stice, E., Marti, C. N., & Rohde, P. (2013). Prevalence, incidence, impairment, and course of the proposed *DSM-5* eating disorder diagnoses in an 8-year prospective community study of young women. *Journal of Abnormal Psychology, 122*(2), 445–457.

Stice, E., Marti, C. N., Shaw, H., & Jaconis, M. (2009). An 8-year longitudinal study of the natural history of threshold, subthreshold, and partial eating disorders from a community sample of adolescents. *Journal of Abnormal Psychology, 118*(3), 587–597.

Stice, E., Mazotti, L., Krebs, M., & Martin, S. (1998). Predictors of adolescent dieting behaviors: A longitudinal study. *Psychology of Addictive Behaviors, 12*(3), 195–205.

Stice, E., Schupak-Neuberg, E., Shaw, H. E., & Stein, R. I. (1994). Relation of media exposure to eating disorder symptomatology: An examination of mediating mechanisms. *Journal of Abnormal Psychology, 103*(4), 836–840.

Stice, E., & Shaw, H. E. (2002). Role of body dissatisfaction in the onset and maintenance of eating pathology: A synthesis of research findings. *Journal of Psychosomatic Research, 53*(5), 985–993.

Stice, E., Shaw, H., & Marti, C. N. (2007). A meta-analytic review of eating disorder prevention programs: Encouraging findings. *Annual Review of Clinical Psychology, 3*, 207–231.

Stice, E., & Whitenton, K. (2002). Risk factors for body dissatisfaction in adolescent girls: A longitudinal investigation. *Developmental Psychology, 38*(5), 669–678.

Suliman, S., Anthonissen, L., Carr, J., du Plessis, S., Emsley, R., Hemmings, S. M. J., ... Seedat, S. (2016). Posttraumatic stress disorder, overweight, and obesity: A systematic review and meta-analysis. *Harvard Review of Psychiatry, 24*(4), 271–293.

Sulkowski, M. L., Dempsey, J., & Dempsey, A. G. (2011). Effects of stress and coping on binge eating in female college students. *Eating Behaviors, 12*(3), 188–191.

Tanamas, S. K., Wluka, A. E., Davies-Tuck, M., Wang, Y., Strauss, B. J., Proietto, J., ... Cicuttini, F. M. (2013). Association of weight gain with incident knee pain, stiffness, and functional difficulties: A longitudinal study. *Arthritis Care & Research, 65*(1), 34–43.

Thomas, J. J., Vartanian, L. R., & Brownell, K. D. (2009). The relationship between eating disorder not otherwise specified (EDNOS) and officially recognized eating disorders: Meta-analysis and implications for *DSM. Psychological Bulletin, 135*(3), 407–433.

Thompson, J. K., Heinberg, L. J., Altabe, M., & Tantleff-Dunn, S. (1999). *Exacting beauty: Theory, assessment, and treatment of body image disturbance.* Washington, DC: American Psychological Association.

Turner, H., & Bryant-Waugh, R. (2004). Eating disorder not otherwise specified (EDNOS): Profiles of clients presenting at a community eating disorder service. *European Eating Disorders Review, 12*(1), 18–26.

Vannucci, A., Theim, K. R., Kass, A. E., Trockel, M., Genkin, B., Rizk, M., ... Taylor, C. B. (2013). What constitutes clinically significant binge eating? Association between binge features and clinical validators in college-age women. *International Journal of Eating Disorders, 46*(3), 226–232.

Wagner, A., Simmons, A. N., Oberndorfer, T. A., Frank, G. K. W., McCurdy-McKinnon, D., Fudge, J. L., ... Kaye, W. H. (2015). Altered sensitization patterns to sweet food stimuli in patients recovered from anorexia and bulimia nervosa. *Psychiatry Research: Neuroimaging, 234*(3), 305–313.

Walsh, K., Koenen, K. C., Aiello, A. E., Uddin, M., & Galea, S. (2014). Prevalence of sexual violence and posttraumatic stress disorder in an urban African-American population. *Journal of Immigrant and Minority Health, 16*(6), 1307–1310.

Wamala, S. P., Wolk, A., & Orth-Gomér, K. (1997). Determinants of obesity in relation to socioeconomic status among middle-aged Swedish women. *Preventive Medicine: An International Journal Devoted to Practice and Theory, 26*(5), 734–744.

Wang, Y. (2004). Epidemiology of childhood obesity—Methodological aspects and guidelines: What is new? *International Journal of Obesity, 28*, S21–S28.

Watkins, B., Sutton, V., & Lask, B. (2001). Is physical illness a risk factor for eating disorders in children and adolescents? A preliminary investigation. *Eating Behaviors, 2*(3), 209–214.

Willett, W. C., Manson, J. E., Stampfer, M. J., Colditz, G. A., Rosner, B., Speizer, F. E., & Hennekens, C. H. (1995). Weight, weight change, and coronary heart disease in women. Risk within the "normal" weight range. *Journal of the American Medical Association, 273*(6), 461–465.

Williamson, D. A., White, M. A., York-Crowe, E., & Stewart, T. M. (2004). Cognitive-behavioral theories of eating disorders. *Behavior Modification, 28*(6), 711–738.

Witteman, J. C., Willett, W. C., Stampfer, M. J., Colditz, G. A., Sacks, F. M., Speizer, F. E., ... Hennekens, C. H. (1989). A prospective study of nutritional factors and hypertension among US women. *Circulation, 80*(5), 1320–1327.

Wold, P. N. (1987). Characterization of the affective diathesis as it relates to bulimia. *Psychiatric Journal of the University of Ottawa, 12*(4), 234–238.

Wonderlich, S. A., Joiner, T. E., Jr., Keel, P. K., Williamson, D. A., & Crosby, R. D. (2007). Eating disorder diagnoses: Empirical approaches to classification. *American Psychologist, 62*(3), 167–180.

Ybarra, M. L., Strasburger, V. C., & Mitchell, K. J. (2014). Sexual media exposure, sexual behavior, and sexual violence victimization in adolescence. *Clinical Pediatrics, 53*, 1239–1247.

CHAPTER 11

Trauma Exposure in Posttraumatic Stress and Acute Stress Disorders

Annette M. La Greca, BreAnne A. Danzi, Ashley N. Marchante-Hoffman, *and* Naomi Tarlow

Abstract

This chapter reviews the literature on the association between traumatic stress exposure and rates of both posttraumatic stress disorder (PTSD) and acute stress disorder (ASD) among children and adults. It begins by reviewing current definitions of PTSD and ASD, which vary substantially across diagnostic systems. The chapter highlights research linking large-scale events, such as natural disasters and acts of terrorism, with the emergence of PTSD and ASD, as well as the literature on the impact of individual traumatic events, such as sexual assault, child sexual abuse, and medical trauma. The chapter concludes by noting several important directions for future research in the area of trauma exposure and traumatic stress.

Keywords: PTSD, acute stress disorder, trauma exposure, natural disasters, terrorism, sexual assault, child sexual abuse, medical trauma, children, adults

Exposure to potentially traumatic events is a common occurrence for individuals of all ages. Epidemiological studies reveal that, by age 16, about two thirds of youth experience at least one potentially traumatic event (PTE) (Copeland, Keeler, Angold, & Costello, 2007; Costello, Erkanli, Fairbank, & Angold, 2002; McLaughlin et al., 2013). Other studies find that 84% of college students report having experienced at least one PTE, with about a third reporting four or more PTEs (e.g., Vrana & Lauterbach, 1994). Moreover, data from a nationally representative sample of US adults revealed that about 90% reported PTE exposure; in fact, exposure to multiple traumatic events was the norm (Kilpatrick et al., 2013).

Traumatic experiences typically involve *real or perceived threat to one's life and safety*, or to that of loved ones. These experiences may include exposure to devastating natural disasters, acts of violence (such as war, sexual assault, maltreatment/abuse, and terrorism), motor vehicle accidents, and physical injuries, as well as life-threatening illnesses (e.g., Bonanno, Brewin, Kaniasty, & La Greca, 2010;

Price, Kassam-Adams, Alderfer, Christofferson, & Kazak, 2016). Although exposure to PTEs already is high, it appears that the occurrence of several traumatic events, such as mass shootings (i.e., an incident with three or more homicide victims) and climate-related disasters, are on the rise in the United States (Cohen, Azrael, & Miller, 2014; Dodgen et al., 2016) and worldwide (e.g., United Nations Office for Disaster Risk Reduction, 2017). Thus, one might anticipate that PTE exposure also will be on the rise over the next few decades.

Fortunately, exposure to PTEs typically does not result in psychological disorder (Copeland et al., 2007; Furr et al., 2010). Nevertheless, a significant minority of youth and adults (typically 20%–30% or less) may develop posttraumatic stress disorder (PTSD) or significant, persistent, posttraumatic stress symptoms (PTSS) (Bonanno et al., 2010).

Rates of PTSD vary widely depending on factors such as trauma type, severity, duration, and timing of the PTSD assessment (La Greca, Taylor, & Herge, 2012). Moreover, PTSD prevalence rates will likely change depending on the diagnostic criteria for PTSD being implemented. For example, the definition of PTSD in the latest version of the *Diagnostic and Statistical Manual*, fifth edition (i.e., *DSM-5*; American Psychiatric Association, 2013) differs substantially from that in the soon-to-be-released update of the *International Classification of Diseases*, 11th edition (i.e., *ICD-11*; World Health Organization, 2017).

This chapter focuses primarily on the link between trauma exposure and PTSD (or significant PTSS) in youth and adults. It also touches on acute stress disorders, which have not been as well studied as PTSD. Specifically, the first section reviews existing and emerging definitions of PTSD and acute stress. The next sections discuss various types of trauma exposure (large-scale disasters, other traumatic events) and the evidence linking trauma exposure to PTSD. The final section discusses the existing evidence base and highlights important areas for further research.

Definitions of Posttraumatic Stress Disorder and Acute Stress Disorder
Posttraumatic Stress Disorder
Posttraumatic stress disorder (PTSD) is unique among psychological disorders in that it is precipitated by an external event. Defined for the first time in 1980 by the *Diagnostic and Statistical Manual of Mental Disorders*, third edition (*DSM-III*; American Psychiatric Association, 1980), the definition of PTSD has changed substantially in subsequent editions, and debate over the conceptualization of the disorder is still ongoing. Currently, very different diagnostic models of PTSD have been proposed by *DSM-5* (American Psychiatric Association, 2013) and *ICD-11* (World Health Organization, 2017).

DSM-IV
Most research on PTSD has been conducted using the definition provided by the fourth edition of the *Diagnostic and Statistical Manual of Mental Disorders* (*DSM-IV*; American Psychiatric Association, 1994). In *DSM-IV*, PTSD contains 17 symptoms across three symptom clusters: re-experiencing, avoidance, and arousal. Re-experiencing may take the form of intrusive memories, nightmares, flashbacks, or physiological or psychological distress when reminded of the trauma. The avoidance cluster includes avoidance of external or internal reminders of the trauma as well as symptoms of emotional numbing, such as anhedonia, detachment, restricted range of affect, or a sense of a foreshortened future. The arousal cluster encompasses symptoms such as

irritability, insomnia, hypervigilance, startle response, and concentration problems. A minimum of six symptoms across the three clusters is required for a diagnosis. Symptoms must be present for at least 1 month after trauma exposure.

DSM-5
In 2013, the criteria for PTSD in *DSM-5* were expanded to include 20 symptoms across four symptom clusters (re-experiencing, avoidance, arousal, and a new cognitions/mood cluster). These changes reflect a "broad approach" to conceptualizing PTSD by incorporating symptoms that reflect the many diverse clinical presentations of the disorder, with the goal of allowing clinicians flexibility in diagnosing PTSD (Friedman, 2013). However, the broad approach results in PTSD being a highly heterogeneous disorder encompassing a large number of different clinical presentations, with over 600,000 possible symptom combinations (Galatzer-Levy & Bryant, 2013).

In *DSM-5*, the re-experiencing and arousal clusters remained essentially the same as in *DSM-IV*; however, the avoidance cluster was refined to require active avoidance of internal or external cues reminiscent of the trauma. The new cognitions/mood cluster consists of symptoms such as negative beliefs, negative emotions, anhedonia, and distorted cognitions about blame. A minimum of six symptoms across the four clusters is required for a diagnosis, and symptoms must be present for at least 1 month after trauma exposure.

DSM-5 "PRESCHOOL CRITERIA"
The *DSM-5* definition of PTSD was based on research with adults and, to some extent, with adolescents (Friedman, Resick, Bryant, & Brewin, 2011); the criteria were assumed to apply to preadolescents (ages 7–12 years). However, *DSM-5* also introduced separate criteria for diagnosing PTSD in children ages 6 years and younger (American Psychiatric Association, 2013), due to concerns about the developmental insensitivity of the adult-based criteria. This decision was based on multiple studies showing that alternative algorithms designed to be developmentally sensitive (i.e., that included behaviorally anchored symptoms and reduced cognitive symptoms) identified substantially more trauma-exposed preschool youth with PTSD than did the *DSM-IV* criteria (Scheeringa, Zeanah, & Cohen, 2011). Consequently, *DSM-5* developed PTSD criteria for children 6 years and younger that eliminated certain cognitively advanced symptoms (e.g., negative beliefs, distorted cognitions) and included a behavioral item

reflecting social withdrawal (to reflect feeling emotionally estranged). This model of PTSD contains 16 symptoms across three clusters (re-experiencing, arousal, and a cluster containing both avoidance and cognitions/mood symptoms). However, at present, no studies of the utility of these criteria with preschool-aged children could be found.

ICD-11

ICD-11 takes a narrow approach to conceptualizing PTSD by only including symptoms considered "core" to PTSD. The rationale for this approach is to improve clinical utility, reduce assessment burden, and reduce overlap with other disorders (Maercker et al., 2013). Specifically, the *ICD-11* definition has symptom clusters for re-experiencing, avoidance, and arousal. Notably, re-experiencing means to experience the trauma *as if it were happening in the present*, which can take the form of vivid memories, nightmares, or flashbacks. Similar to *DSM-5*, the avoidance cluster refers to active avoidance of internal or external cues associated with the trauma. The arousal cluster reflects an ongoing sense of threat, in the form of hypervigilance or exaggerated startle response. A minimum of three symptoms, one from each symptom cluster, is required, and symptoms must be present for at least several weeks.

COMPLEX POSTTRAUMATIC STRESS DISORDER

ICD-11 also will propose diagnostic criteria for complex PTSD, which is believed to emerge after prolonged and repeated trauma (from which escape is not possible), such as slavery, torture, or child abuse. Complex PTSD includes all the diagnostic requirements for *ICD-11* PTSD as well as additional symptoms that reflect disturbances in self-organization (Karatzias et al., 2016, 2017), such as problems with negative self-concept, affect dysregulation, and interpersonal problems (Brewin et al., 2017). Individuals with complex PTSD may view themselves as worthless and struggle with feelings of failure or guilt following a traumatic experience. Complex PTSD is also characterized by difficulty feeling close to other people and problems in maintaining important personal relationships (World Health Organization, 2017).

Acute Stress Disorder/Acute Stress Reaction

Acute stress disorder (ASD) was introduced by *DSM-IV* to describe acute stress responses during the first month following trauma exposure, with the goal of identifying people likely to develop PTSD and facilitating early access to health care. However, subsequent research found that ASD had very limited success in accurately predicting PTSD in adults (Bryant, Friedman, Spiegel, Ursano, & Strain, 2011) or children (Rosenberg et al., 2015; Zhou, Zhang, Wei, Liu, & Hannak, 2016).

DSM-5

ASD was revised in *DSM-5* to capture trauma reactions that would benefit from treatment during the first month post trauma, as it may be challenging to receive health care in the United States without a diagnosis (Bryant, 2017). Specifically, *DSM-5* reduced the emphasis on dissociative symptoms (e.g., detachment, unawareness of surroundings, derealization, depersonalization) that were a central component of ASD in *DSM-IV*, and instead it focused on severe reactions to trauma exposure. Individuals must present with at least nine symptoms that reflect any of the following: intrusion (e.g., nightmares, memories, flashbacks), negative mood (e.g., inability to experience position emotions), dissociation (e.g., being in a daze, amnesia), avoidance (e.g., avoidance of internal or external cues), or arousal (e.g., insomnia, hypervigilance). Symptoms must be present for 3 to 30 days for a diagnosis (American Psychiatric Association, 2013).

ICD-11

ICD-11 takes a different approach, by characterizing acute stress as neither pathological nor a disorder, but rather as a normative response to a terrifying or traumatic event (Maercker et al., 2013). Thus, ASD is relabeled "acute stress reaction" and categorized in a section containing reasons for clinical encounters that are not disorders. Acute stress reaction is characterized by emotional, cognitive, somatic, or behavioral symptoms that occur shortly after a terrifying or traumatic event, and which may include physiological signs of anxiety (e.g., tachycardia), as well as confusion, anxiety, sadness, anger, social withdrawal, or stupor (Maercker et al., 2013; World Health Organization, 2017). However, because the individual's reactions are transient and often begin to subside within a week or so (or when the individual is removed from the threatening situation), these reactions are considered to be within the normal range of response to a traumatic stressor.

Current Issues in the Conceptualization of Posttraumatic Stress Disorder and Acute Stress Disorder

Current conceptualizations of PTSD diverge widely, presenting an opportunity for research comparing alternative approaches, but also posing challenges for identifying individuals with PTSD. A few key points are worth noting here. First, there is low agreement between the diagnostic models for *DSM-5* and *ICD-11*. Findings reveal that there is only about a 30%–40% overlap in cases for youth (Danzi & La Greca, 2016; La Greca, Danzi, & Chan, 2017) and adults (e.g., Stein et al., 2014). Thus, additional research is warranted to reconcile the diverging conceptualizations of PTSD proposed by *DSM-5* and *ICD-11*. Future studies that incorporate and evaluate both conceptualizations are needed to determine which perspective has the strongest concurrent and predictive validity for identifying distressed individuals after traumatic events and over time. Moreover, the large body of literature that examined risk and vulnerability for PTSD (based on *DSM-IV*) warrants replication to verify that the same risk and vulnerability factors are relevant to the *DSM-5* and *ICD-11* conceptualizations.

Second, both *DSM-5* and *ICD-11* approaches to PTSD and ASD were based on adult research (Friedman et al., 2011), with limited attention to whether the diagnostic criteria fit children's trauma responses. In fact, some symptoms added to *DSM-5* PTSD, such as cognitively oriented symptoms, may be inappropriate for children (Danzi & La Greca, 2016; La Greca et al., 2017; Scheeringa, Zeanah, & Cohen, 2011). Other evidence suggests that the current symptom thresholds in *DSM-5* for ASD may be too stringent for children (McKinnon et al., 2016). Future research is needed to evaluate and improve PTSD and ASD diagnostic criteria for children of different developmental levels.

Finally, with respect to ASD, the distinction between a pathological versus normative response to experiencing a fundamentally abnormal and horrific traumatic event is an ongoing debate in the mental health field (Frances, 2013). The different approaches to this issue are reflected in the *DSM-5* versus *ICD-11* characterizations of ASD versus acute stress response, respectively, even though both the *DSM* and *ICD* workgroups share the same goal of identifying clinically distressed individuals and improving clinical services. In general, most individuals recover following a traumatic experience (Bonanno et al., 2010; La Greca et al., 2013b); however, identifying the subset of individuals who remain chronically distressed over time is important for delivering targeted interventions. The clinical and research utility of ASD as a diagnosis would benefit from improving its predictive relationship with PTSD.

Types of Trauma Exposure Leading to Posttraumatic Stress Reactions

Individuals may be exposed to a range of potentially traumatic events (PTEs) throughout the life span, with 3% to 60% of individuals reportedly developing PTSD following a PTE (Neria, Nandi, & Galea, 2008). Traumatic stressors vary on dimensions that may affect the extent to which the PTE is associated with negative mental health outcomes and with challenges in delivering clinical services. First, PTEs may be either large-scale events, such as natural disasters, terrorism, and war, or traumatic events that affect a few individuals at a time, such as maltreatment, rape, and medical trauma. The large-scale events, often generically referred to as disasters (e.g., Bonanno et al., 2010), differ from other traumatic events as they affect entire communities or large segments of the population; as such, they may cause widespread distress and present logistical challenges for identifying and treating trauma-exposed individuals. Second, PTEs may be acute (i.e., only occur one time) or chronic experiences. Typically, greater chronicity is associated with higher risk for negative mental health consequences (Danese & McEwen, 2012; Karam et al., 2014) and may be associated with more complex forms of PTSD (Brewin et al., 2017). Third, proximity to the event can greatly affect outcomes. There is strong evidence indicating that individuals most directly affected by a PTE (e.g., actual victims of a terrorist attack or sexual assault) are more likely to develop posttraumatic stress reactions compared to those who are witnesses or otherwise less directly affected (Bonanno et al., 2010).

Disasters and Other Large-Scale Events

Large-scale traumatic events (a.k.a. disasters) include natural disasters (e.g., earthquakes, fires, hurricanes), intentional human-made disasters (e.g., war, terrorism), and unintentional human-made disasters (e.g., plane crash, oil spill, power plant explosions). Large-scale disasters are unpredictable, destructive, and occur frequently worldwide (Bonanno et al., 2010; Warsini et al., 2014). They have the potential to greatly affect both individuals and communities instantaneously, making it critical to understand the mental health effects of such events and how best to intervene in a timely manner. Many researchers have assessed the mental health consequences of disasters for youth and adults, finding that they can lead to negative mental health outcomes, including anxiety, depression, substance abuse, stress-related health problems, and PTSD (see Bonanno et al., 2010). Of these, posttraumatic stress reactions (PTSD and ASD) are the most widely studied and are the focus of this section.

Due to the unpredictability of disasters, their varying magnitude and destructiveness, the different postdisaster timing of assessments, and the different measurement strategies that have been used across studies, prevalence rates for the impact of disasters on mental health vary widely. Nevertheless, methodologically strong studies indicate that rates of PTSD are low (5%–10%) within community samples exposed to disasters (Bonanno et al., 2010; Copeland, Keeler, Angold, & Costello, 2007), suggesting that most individuals can adapt successfully to such events. The negative impact of these events is concentrated in those directly exposed to the disaster, first responders (who may experience secondary traumatic stress via exposure to the suffering of others), and vulnerable populations, such as children and ethnic/racial groups that are both culturally in the minority and of lower socioeconomic status (Bonanno et al., 2010; Neria et al., 2008).

Key Role of Exposure to the Traumatic Event

Across large-scale disasters, and also other types of traumatic events, direct exposure to the traumatic event typically shows a "dose-response" association with poor psychological adjustment (Bonanno et al., 2010). A key element of exposure is *life threat*. That is, the event either poses immediate physical danger to the individual or involves witnessing others' death or serious injury. Typically, the experience of life threat is captured through the occurrence of *objective life-threatening events* (e.g., doors or windows breaking in the place one stays in during a hurricane; being inside a building that is under a direct sniper or terrorist attack) or through *individuals' perceptions of life threat*; these aspects of life threat are interrelated (e.g., La Greca et al., 1996, 2010; Yelland et al., 2010). In general, however, perceived life threat is one of the strongest predictors of posttrauma PTSS in youth and adults (Bonanno et al., 2010; La Greca et al., 2010; Lai, La Greca, Auslander, & Short, 2013; Norris, Kaniasty, Conrad, Inman, & Murphy, 2002; Ozer, Best, Lipsey, & Weiss, 2003), consistent with the notion that individuals' subjective appraisals of threat are more important than objective trauma severity (Bonanno et al., 2010; Halligan, Michael, Clark, & Ehlers, 2003).

A second and often related element of exposure has to do with *loss and life disruption* that can ensue in the aftermath of a traumatic event. For example, loss of one's home due to a natural disaster, or loss of a family member due to an act of violence, may lead to a series of stressful and disruptive life events that challenge children's and adults' ability to cope and recover. These events are also predictive of PTSD and PTSS (e.g., Bonanno et al., 2010; La Greca et al., 2010; Vernberg et al., 1996).

Although exposure to the traumatic event is believed to be critical for the emergence of symptoms of PTSD, other pre- and posttrauma variables also are important risk factors for the occurrence and persistence of PTSD. With respect to *pretrauma characteristics*, demographic variables such as age, gender, ethnicity, and socioeconomic status may play a role. With respect to age, Norris and colleagues (2002) conducted a comprehensive review of the disaster literature (1981 to 2000), finding that children were more likely than adults to exhibit extreme impairment post disaster. Other studies indicate that younger children may be more vulnerable to developing PTSD post disaster than older youth (e.g., Weems et al., 2010; Yelland et al., 2010). With respect to gender differences,[1] females appear to be at higher risk than males for PTSD following disasters and acts of terrorism (e.g., Hoven et al., 2005; Norris et al., 2002; Weems et al, 2010), although the magnitude of such gender differences is often modest. Pretrauma biological variables, such as the presence of certain genetic markers, may also confer a higher risk for PTSD in trauma exposed youth and adults (e.g., Kilpatrick et al., 2007; La Greca, Lai, Joormann, Auslander, & Short, 2013a). However, the mechanisms linking these risk factors to PTSD and stress-related outcomes are not well understood and are currently under investigation (e.g., Uddin, Amstadter, Nugent, & Koenen, 2012; Yehuda, Pratchett, & Pelcovitz, 2012).

With respect to the *posttrauma recovery period*, factors such as the availability of social support and the occurrence of other life stressors (e.g., loss of job, death in the family) during the recovery period have been found to either mitigate or exacerbate disasters' impact (e.g., Kaniasty & Norris, 2008; La Greca et al., 1996, 2010, 2013b). For detailed discussions of pre- and posttrauma risk factors for PTSD in adults and youth, the reader is referred to several sources (Bonanno et al., 2010; Breslau, 2012; La Greca et al., 2012). Similar risk factors have been implicated in the development of acute stress disorders (see Biggs et al., 2012).

Natural Disasters

Natural disasters are extremely common and largely unavoidable. In particular, natural disasters that are related to extreme weather events (e.g., hurricanes, tornadoes, floods, fires caused by extreme heat) are on the rise due to climate change (Crimmins et al., 2016; Save the Children, 2008; United Nations Office for Disaster Risk Reduction, 2014). Natural disasters are unpredictable and have widespread impact, yet they affect individuals to varying degrees with respect to PTSD. For example, according to a review conducted by Warsini et al. (2014), some studies found rates of PTSD between 34% and 63% following a major earthquake (e.g., Chan et al., 2011; Wang, Zhang, Shi, & Wang, 2009), whereas others found rates lower than 23% following other earthquakes (e.g., Cao, McFarlane, & Klimidis 2003) and hurricanes (e.g., DeSalvo et al., 2007). Compared to intentional human-made disasters (such as terrorist attacks and bombings, which are violent acts), natural disasters appear to be associated with lower rates of PTSD (Galea, Nandi, & Vlahov, 2005; Neria et al., 2008).

As indicated earlier, actual or perceived life threat and greater loss and destruction after a disaster have been strongly linked with higher risk for PTSD (Bonanno et al., 2010; Neria et al., 2008; Soldatos et al., 2006; Warsini et al., 2014). In this regard, disaster-related loss of a loved one is an especially potent predictor of PTSD, as it incorporates strong elements of perceived life threat and major life disruption and loss (e.g., Furr, Comer, Edmunds, & Kendall, 2010; Galea et al., 2005). Accordingly, Chan et al. (2011) found that 50.2% of individuals who lost a family member due to an earthquake in China met criteria for PTSD, which is almost twice the percentage of those who did not lose a family member (27.1%). In addition, although methodological inconsistencies across studies have resulted in a wide range of PTSD prevalence rates, studies consistently show that a significant proportion of youth experience elevated PTSS during the first several months post disaster (Furr et al., 2010). It is believed that disaster-related life disruption adversely affects children's functioning through missed school, reduced academic functioning, missed social opportunities, and increased exposure to major life stressors (Silverman & La Greca, 2002).

Fortunately, for most individuals, PTSD symptoms appear to decrease significantly during the first year after disaster exposure (Furr et al., 2010; La Greca et al., 1996, 2010). For example, La Greca et al. (1996) examined PTSD symptoms in elementary school children 3, 7, and 10 months after Hurricane Andrew, a Category 5 hurricane with sustained winds exceeding 160 miles per hour, making it one of the most destructive hurricanes to strike the United States. The high rates of "probable" PTSD in children (38%) at 3 months post disaster were reduced to 18% 7 months later. The majority of children who endorsed significant PTSD symptoms at 10 months post disaster had reported severe or very severe PTSD levels at 3 months, such that more severe symptoms shortly after the disaster predicted chronicity of symptoms.

Intentional, Human-Made Disasters: War and Terrorism

Intentional, human-made disasters primarily refer to war and terrorism. According to a systematic review (Neria et al., 2008), researchers generally have found the highest rates of PTSD in directly exposed victims of these kinds of intentional disasters (which are violent in nature), followed by first responders (i.e., disaster workers, firefighters, police officers), and then general community members. Traumatic events like war and terrorist attacks often result in mass casualties, thus contributing to the perception that one's life and the lives of loved ones are in danger. Thus, it is not surprising to see strong linkages between these events and PTSD in children and adults.

War and Political Unrest

Children and adults exposed to violence resulting from political unrest (e.g., Israeli-Palestinian conflict; political violence in Central and South America) are at high risk for ASD and PTSD (Ayer et al., 2015; Eisenman, Gelberg, Liu, & Shapiro; 2003; Slone, Lavi, Ozer, & Pollak, 2017). In particular, military personnel, and especially those deployed for combat duty, are at elevated risk for PTSD (e.g., Hoge et al., 2004). In fact, a recent meta-analysis revealed that military groups in Iraq (vs. Afghanistan) who were combat deployed had much higher prevalence rates of PTSD than other military personnel.

In general, the psychological functioning of military veterans is a well-studied area of the PTSD and ASD literature. There are over 21 million veterans in the United States (Department of Veterans Affairs, 2016). US veterans have rates of PTSD that are two to four times as high as US civilians, depending on the research methodology used (Richardson, Frueh, & Acierno, 2010). Among US veteran samples, rates of PTSD ranged from 2.2% to 15.2% following the Vietnam War and 1.9% to 13.2% following the Gulf War. In the more recent conflicts in the Middle

East (i.e., Iraq, Afghanistan), rates of PTSD are estimated to range from 4% to 17.1% in US veterans. Interestingly, rates of PTSD in UK veterans following the Iraq War were only 3% to 6%. This difference between US and UK veterans might be due to US veterans' greater war exposure, such as via greater combat intensity, but it also may be due to other factors such as military training or sociopolitical issues (Richardson et al., 2010).

Gender is an important issue to consider in regard to combat exposure and PTSD. Although the military has historically been male dominated, the number of females in the military has increased over the past decades, and at present, female veterans comprise about 10% of the total veteran population in the United States (Department of Veterans Affairs, 2016). Like their male counterparts, women in the military experience combat, but also may face additional stressors such as lower social support and being a victim of sexual assault (Carlson, Stromwall, & Lietz, 2013). Consequently, women are 1.6 to 3 times more likely to receive a mental health diagnosis post deployment compared to men (Wojcik, Akhtar, & Hassell, 2009). Additionally, higher rates of PTSD have been found among younger, less educated veterans, as well as veterans who are Black or Hispanic (Dohrenwend, Turner, Turse, Lewis-Fernandez, & Yager, 2008; Richardson et al., 2010; Xue et al., 2015). Other risk factors for PTSD include longer deployment, nonofficer ranks, prior trauma exposure, intensity of combat experience, and lack of postdeployment support (Xue et al., 2015). With respect to long-term effects, war-related PTSD is associated with lower rates of rapid recovery relative to all other trauma types (Kessler et al., 2017). The median duration for PTSD in those who experienced war-related traumas is 5 years (Kessler et al., 2017).

Terrorism

Acts of terrorism also have been associated with PTSD in children and adults. Starting with the 1995 bombing of the Federal Building in Oklahoma City (e.g., Pfefferbaum et al., 1999; Tucker, Pfefferbaum, Nixon, & Dickson, 2000) and continuing through more recent events such as the Boston Marathon Bombing (Comer et al., 2014), elevated levels of PTSS have been found among the youth and adults most directly exposed to these violent events.

The most studied terrorist event in the United States is the attacks of September 11, 2001. A systematic review of this literature (Neria, DiGrande, & Adams, 2011) revealed that the prevalence of PTSD among persons with high exposure to the attacks was substantial. Demographic factors, including Hispanic ethnicity, female gender, and younger age were associated with higher likelihood of developing PTSD. Consistent with data on natural disasters, this review found that rates of PTSD dropped over the course of the year after the attack (from 5% at 12 months to 3.8% at 24 months post attack).

Aside from those directly exposed to terrorism, first responders appear to be an especially vulnerable population following mass-violence events, although most research focuses on the victims, rather than the helpers. Reviews have found that first-responder rates of PTSD following terrorist and mass-violence events range from 1.3% to 23% (Neria et al., 2008; Wilson, 2015). For example, 22.5% of the 9/11 terrorist attack first responders (i.e., disaster workers, firefighters, police officers) met criteria for PTSD 2 weeks after the event; 20% continued to meet criteria for PTSD 10 to 15 months later (Fullerton, Ursano, Reeves, Shigemura, & Grieger, 2006). Fullerton, Ursano, & Wang (2004) also found increased rates of ASD for first responders (25.6%) post-9/11; those who met criteria for ASD were 7.33 times more likely to meet criteria for PTSD after 13 months.

In addition to direct victims and first responders, certain subgroups may be particularly vulnerable to developing adverse PTSS reactions to mass violence and terrorism. In that regard, ethnic and gender minorities, low-income individuals, clinical samples, and children/youth appear most at risk. For example, a review by Neria and colleagues (2008) revealed that rates of PTSD in children ranged from 28.4% at 1 month following the 1984 sniper attack in Los Angeles (Pynoos, Nader, Frederick, Gonda, & Stuber, 1987) to 18.4% at 6 months after the 9/11 terrorist attacks (Hoven et al., 2005); these rates are high compared to adults who experienced similar events. Some possible reasons why children represent a vulnerable population after mass violence include that they are still developing their perceptions of safety and security and must rely on caregivers (who have likely experienced the same event) to help them cope; in turn, modeling calm behavior might be difficult for a caregiver who is also distressed. Other studies have found that ethnic minority groups also are at higher risk for PTSD. For example, Galea et al. (2002) found higher rates of PTSD in Hispanic individuals compared to other ethnic groups following the 9/11 terrorist attack. Galea et al. (2002) also found that PTSD rates decreased from 7.5% to 0.6% at 6 months following the 9/11 terrorist attack; however, after 1 year, the prevalence of PTSD remained relatively high for low-income minorities (10.2%). Although reasons for elevated rates of PTSD among minorities is unclear, lower socioeconomic status, lower levels of educational attainment, and lower rates of treatment-seeking likely contribute to the elevated levels of PTSS among minorities compared to Whites (Roberts, Gilman, Breslau, Breslau, & Koenen, 2011).

Despite variations in the severity of PTSS reactions across various groups, the consensus across most studies is that symptoms of PTSD decrease over the first year after exposure to mass violence (Neria et al., 2008), and most individuals (about 80%) are resilient or recover from their levels of initial distress (Bonanno et al., 2010). These findings are promising and speak to the high degree of resilience most youth and adults display in the face of adversity.

Technological Disasters: Oil Spills, Nuclear Explosions, and Water Contamination

Unintentional, human-made disasters include technological malfunctions, such as plane crashes, oil spills, and chemical or nuclear plant explosions. Overall, researchers have found wide-ranging rates of PTSD in direct victims and first responders immediately following technological disasters (15%–75%; Neria et al., 2008). Technological disasters differ from other types of disasters because *they often pose less immediate physical threat*; however, the short- and long-term threats to the community (and those living in the community) can be substantial and uncertain. For example, the Exxon Valdez oil spill, which occurred near a rural town in Alaska, did not cause any human deaths but damaged the local fishing business, a major source of revenue within the community. Palinkas et al. (1993) showed that PTSS levels were elevated among individuals most exposed to the negative impact of the oil spill. Among those exposed, women were particularly vulnerable to PTSS and other signs of psychological distress (Palinkas, Petterson, Russell, & Downs, 1993). Moreover, the oil spill was associated with substantial uncertainty and worries about the detrimental health effects that might emerge over time; not surprisingly, parents reported elevated levels of PTSS, anxiety, and depression relative to adults without children, especially if the parents observed changes in their children since the disaster (Palinkas, 2012).

More recently, researchers have begun to (and continue to) examine the impact of the Flint water crisis that adversely affected the entire city of Flint, Michigan. This event triggered a federal state of emergency as thousands of children and families were exposed to contaminated water (Durando, 2016). Many Flint children had abnormally high levels of lead in their systems, which could have serious long-term cognitive consequences for the developing brain. Recent findings showed that individuals who reported the lowest water quality also reported higher PTSD symptoms than those with better water quality (Kruger, Kodjebacheva, & Cupal, 2017). In particular (and similar to oil spill studies), many families reported increases in stress and anxiety (Cuthbertson, Newkirk, Ilardo, Loveridge, & Skidmore, 2016) related to the anticipation of potential negative outcomes for their children (in this case, later cognitive decline due to lead exposure). Thus, it appears that long-term anxiety may be a common response to disasters that lead to considerable uncertainty about negative long-term health outcomes, especially in parents of young children.

Other technological disasters have resulted in both direct physical threat and long-term community impact. For example, the Chernobyl nuclear power plant explosion in 1986, which released at least 5% of the radioactive reactor core into the atmosphere, exposed many individuals to radiation and led to substantial community resettlement. This disaster resulted in first-responder deaths and increased childhood health problems among those directly exposed to contamination (Bromet, Havenaar, & Guey, 2011). In terms of long-term outcomes, a 25-year review of research related to this technological accident showed that first responders and clean-up workers continued to report elevated PTSD symptoms two decades after the event. Furthermore, mothers of children exposed to radiation were twice as likely to meet criteria for PTSD 19 years after the disaster than mothers whose children were not exposed (Adams, Guey, Gluzman, & Bromet, 2011; Bromet et al., 2011). These elevated levels of PTSD were largely explained by the mothers' continued concerns about the accident-related health risks for their children and were not due to any differences in age, education, SES, or occurrence of other recent life stressors (Adams et al., 2011). Similar to research on natural disasters, those most directly affected by the accident (and who presumably had strong perceptions of life threat or fear of harm to loved ones) experienced the most lasting adverse mental health effects. Nevertheless, in general, symptoms of

PTSD also decreased over time for survivors and first responders of technological disasters (Neria et al., 2008).

Large-Scale Community Violence Events
Mass Shootings

Unfortunately, there has been a rise in mass shootings in the United States over the past 15 years (see Schmidt, 2014). Many mass shootings occur in the United States, although these events also occur in European countries with low firearm homicide rates (Shultz et al., 2014). In the United States, the most prominent and lethal of the school shooting "rampages" include Columbine High School, Virginia Tech University, and Sandy Hook Elementary School (Shultz, Cohen, Muschert, & Flores de Apodaca, 2013) as well as the recent, devastating mass shooting at Marjory Stoneman Douglas High School in Parkland, Florida (Burch & Mazzei, 2018). Notably, in the 5 years since Sandy Hook, there have been more than 200 school shootings in the United States, which have claimed over 400 victims and led to 138 deaths (Patel, 2018).

Research has examined the impact of mass shootings, especially those occurring in schools, on PTSD symptoms. For example, after the Virginia Tech shootings (April 2007), 16.4% of the 1,145 students at the school met cutoffs for elevated PTSD symptoms; in particular, females were more likely to develop high PTSD symptoms. In addition, there was a significant relationship between PTSD symptoms at 3–4 months and reckless behavior at 1 year, which is notable given that reckless behavior since has been added to the *DSM-5* criteria for PTSD (Blevins, Wusik, Sullivan, Jones, & Hughes, 2016). More recently, Shultz and colleagues (2014) conducted a comprehensive review of studies on the mental health impact of mass shootings. Their findings revealed that symptoms of PTSD, anxiety, and depression all were significantly elevated for those in physical proximity (e.g., hearing gunfire, seeing the gunman fire on someone) or social proximity (i.e., loss of someone close, inability to confirm the safety of friends) to the shootings; acute stress reactions were also common among those exposed to the shooting.

The long-term effects of mass shootings are still unclear, although one study has shown that PTSD rates decline substantially over the first year after a mass shooting. Specifically, rates of PTSD in college women exposed to a mass shooting at Northern Illinois University declined from 48% about 1 month after the event to 12% about 8 months after

the shooting (Littleton, Kumpula, & Orcutt, 2011; Shultz et al., 2014).

Riots and Civil Disturbance

Another example of shared community violence with mental health repercussions concerns riots and civil unrest. Perhaps the most remarkable of such events was the Los Angeles civil disturbance that occurred in the spring of 1992 following the acquittal of four police officers for the use of excessive force in the arrest and beating of an African American man, Rodney King (https://en.wikipedia.org/wiki/1992_Los_Angeles_riots). The unrest occurred over several days and included widespread rioting, looting, arson, and assault, leading to more than 50 deaths and over $1 billion in property damages (https://www.cnn.com/2013/09/18/us/los-angeles-riots-fast-facts/index.html). Research on the mental health impact of these events is scant, although a study of 202 Korean American victims who sustained financial loss or physical injury found that the majority reported severe distress and symptoms of PTSD (Kim-Goh, Suh, Blake, & Hiley-Young, 1995).

More recently, the August 2014 protests in Ferguson, Missouri, in response to a White police officer's fatal shooting of a young Black man, offers another example of shared community violence. Galovski et al. (2016) found that proximity to the Ferguson riots was associated with posttraumatic reactions in adult community members as well as police officers, and that community members were more likely to exceed clinical cutoffs for PTSD relative to police officers. In addition, Black community members had higher PTSS than White community members. Fear in reaction to one's exposure to the riots, the amount of media exposure, and one's reactions to the media (e.g., amount of negative emotion) all directly contributed to elevated PTSS. In White participants (and not in Blacks), life interruptions (due to the riots) also contributed to elevations in PTSD scores.

Other Community Violence

Individuals can also be exposed to violence in the community when they are the target of an assault or crime. Although not necessarily a community-wide event, these types of trauma exposure bear many similarities to community-wide violence events, and thus are discussed here.

The Bureau of Justice Statistics, which surveys US households annually and asks whether individuals ages 12 and older have been victims of crimes, reports that violent crime has declined over the period from 1993 to 2016. According to their statistics, in 2016, 21.1 people per 1,000 (.02%) reported being the victim of violent crime, which translates to 5.7 million violent victimizations in persons age 12 or older (Gramlich, 2018). Violent crime events have been associated with PTSD and PTSS in the victims. Specifically, among adults, population-based studies indicate that crime events, such as aggravated assault, are associated with high rates of PTSD in victims (Breslau et al, 1991; Resnick et al., 1993; Resnick & Kilpatrick, 1994). Many community violence studies include a broad spectrum of violence exposure, such as assaultive violence, injury, shocking experience, learning about traumas to loved ones, sudden unexpected death of a close friend or relative, and other stressful situations. In a study of university students (Khan et al., 2016), the overall rate of probable PTSD was 25.6% among the 299 subjects exposed to a traumatic event. Assaultive violence, endorsed by 169 subjects, was the community violence type most associated with PTSD, with 35% of assaultive violence victims screening positive for probable PTSD.

Numerous studies have focused on the impact of exposure to community violence among youth. In particular, youth living in inner cities are both victims and witnesses of an alarming number of violent incidents (e.g., seeing someone beaten up, shot, or killed; Luthar & Goldstein 2004), although youth living in rural areas are not immune to such violence exposure (Sullivan, Kung, & Farrell, 2004). Among children and adolescents, exposure to violence in the community or school is associated with increased risk for PTSD. A meta-analysis by Fowler, Tompsett, Braciszewski, Jacques-Tiura, and Baltes (2009) reviewed 114 studies of community violence exposure in youth, finding that total exposure to community violence predicted negative mental health symptoms, with the strongest effects found for PTSD. Other important findings were that recent exposure was associated more strongly with PTSD symptoms than lifetime exposure, and that victimization was more predictive of youths' internalizing problems than was witnessing or hearing about community violence. Generally, Fowler et al. (2009) observed stronger findings for older youth, suggesting that exposure to community violence has a greater impact on adolescents compared to children. In terms of gender, all-female samples demonstrated stronger effects for the association between community violence exposure and PTSD, relative to mixed-gender samples. However, these gender-related findings are difficult to interpret because of the diverse sampling methodologies used across the studies (e.g., residents of homeless shelters, adjudicated youth, college samples, children with behavior problems). Other research suggests that boys report more frequent exposure to violence than girls, although boys and girls did not differ in self-reported PTSD (Cross et al., 2018).

Community violence also has been related to ASD in youth. For example, Hamrin, Jonker, and Scahill (2004) reported that, when compared to demographically similar youth with chronic medical conditions, youth with gunshot injuries endorsed significantly higher rates of ASD symptoms (75% vs. 14%).

With respect to long-term effects of community violence, Denson and colleagues (2007) report that rates of PTSD remain somewhat consistent across the first year after exposure. According to Kessler et al. (2017), the mean duration of PTSD after physical assault is 22.7 months, while the mean durations after mugging and kidnapping are 115.0 and 115.9 months, respectively. The long-term effects of community violence on PTSD rates in youth remain unclear, as there is little longitudinal research in this area (Fowler et al., 2009).

Effects of Individual Traumatic Events on Posttraumatic Stress Disorder and Acute Stress Disorder

Disasters are large-scale events that are community-wide (Neria et al., 2008; Norris et al., 2002). However, other traumatic and potentially life-threatening events (e.g., motor vehicle accidents, rape, child abuse) are frequent occurrences and also contribute to PTSD and other stress reactions among those affected. To this point, recent data from the WHO Mental Health Surveys (Kessler et al., 2017), which assessed over 68,000 adults from 24 countries, found that 70.4% of the respondents experienced lifetime traumas, and most of these traumas were due to traumatic experiences other than disasters. Overall, the highest level of PTSD risk was evident among those who experienced interpersonal violence (and especially intimate partner sexual violence), such as rape or other sexual assault. Notably, among children and adolescents, child sexual abuse also has been associated with higher rates of PTSD compared to other traumatic events (Deblinger, Mannarino, Cohen, Runyon, & Steer, 2011; Mclean, Morris, Conklin, Jayawickreme, & Foa, 2015). Kessler et al. (2017) reported that other types of physical violence, such as child physical abuse, or being physically assaulted, also conferred elevated risk for PTSD, and that medically related traumas, such as being involved in a life-threatening accident or having a life-threatening illness, also conferred increased risk. Next some highlights from these areas of trauma exposure are reviewed.

Intimate Partner Violence and Sexual Abuse
Rape and Sexual Assault
According to the WHO World Mental Health Survey, lifetime prevalence rates of any type of intimate partner or sexual violence are approximately 22.8%, with rates of rape and other sexual assault at 3.2% and 5.8%, respectively. In that survey, the odds of being exposed to intimate partner or sexual violence were over twice as high in women compared to men (Benjet et al., 2016). There is a robust literature linking rape and sexual assault to PTSD and ASD in adults; among adults, experiencing sexual violence confers high risk for developing PTSD, with rape conferring the highest risk (19.0%), although other types of sexual assault are associated with heightened risk as well (10.5%; Kessler et al., 2017). ASD rates are also high in rape victims as well as those who experienced other forms of sexual assault. In one sample of sexual assault and rape victims, 59% of participants met criteria for ASD and an additional 7% met subclinical criteria (Elklit & Christiansen, 2010).

Due to lower rates of rape reported in men, many studies of PTSD and ASD among rape victims include only females (Elklit & Christiansen, 2010; Mgoqi-Mbalo, Zhang, & Ntuli, 2017; Tiihonen Möller, Bäckström, Söndergaard, & Helström, 2014). Factors specific to the sexual assault have predicted PTSD, such as perceived life threat, sexual assault by a group, being subjected to several sexual acts, and injury (Tiihonen Möller et al., 2014). Other factors associated with developing PTSD after sexual assault include severe depression within one month of the assault, history of two or more traumatic events, and psychiatric treatment history (Tiihonen Möller et al., 2014). In addition, being sexually assaulted by an intimate partner is associated with a longer duration of PTSD symptoms (Kessler et al., 2017). Support from an intimate partner after experiencing sexual violence may be an important protective factor against developing PTSD, as not being married or in a cohabiting relationship is one factor associated with developing PTSD after rape (Mgoqi-Mbalo et al., 2017). However, studies have shown that more general social support does not protect against PTSD after rape (Armour, Shevlin, Elklit, & Mroczek, 2012; Mgoqi-Mbalo et al., 2017)

Importantly, the category of intimate partner or sexual violence is associated with a longer duration of PTSD symptoms relative to most other trauma types, with the exception of physical violence and war-related trauma (which account for similar or longer duration of symptoms, respectively). Intimate partner or sexual violence accounts for 42.7% of person-years with PTSD in the population (Kessler et al., 2017). These findings highlight the tremendous need for treatment of trauma symptoms in this population.

Childhood Sexual Abuse
Substantial research has focused on the effects of childhood sexual abuse (CSA) on children and adults (e.g., Mclean et al., 2015; Norman et al., 2012). Overall, this type of abuse differentially affects males and females, with rates for CSA at about 27% for females and 5% for males in the United States (Finkelhor, Shattuck, Turner, & Hamby, 2014). According to a meta-analysis on the effects of CSA on children and adults, there is a 143% increase in likelihood of developing PTSD after experiencing CSA (Paolucci et al., 2001).

In children, Kaplow, Dodge, Amaya-Jackson, and Saxe (2005) found that younger age at onset of CSA and dissociative symptoms immediately after the abuse were associated with PTSS. Studies of CSA have not found gender differences in PTSD symptoms or diagnosis, however (Carey, Walker, Rossouw, Seedat, & Stein, 2008; Kaplow et al., 2005). Many studies focus on the long-term impact of CSA, which can be gleaned from studies of adults that examined the association between retrospectively reported CSA and adult psychiatric problems, including PTSD. For example, Jonas et al. (2011) found that adult PTSD was strongly associated with CSA, especially if nonconsensual sexual intercourse was involved. Further, among the adults who experienced CSA, the odds of developing PTSD were doubled for those who also experienced sexual assault in adulthood (i.e., revictimization).

In adults, several elements of CSA (e.g., age of abuse; repeated abuse vs. single-instance abuse; abuse by touching or sexual intercourse) have been examined as predictors of ASD and PTSD (e.g., Jonas et al., 2011; Kaltman et al., 2005). With respect to age, one study of college women (Kaltman et al., 2005) found higher rates of PTSD and ASD among those who retrospectively reported experiencing sexual assault in adolescence versus during childhood; this may reflect the fact that a larger percentage of those assaulted in adolescence experienced complete rape (66%) than did younger victims (20%). In contrast, Kaplow et al. (2005) found that younger age at onset of CSA was associated with greater PTSS. Younger age of CSA (prior to 14 years) also has been associated with symptoms consistent with Complex PTSD (Brewin et al., 2017), such as difficulties with anger modulation, self-destructiveness, suicidal behavior, dissociative symptoms, and somatization, compared to those experiencing CSA after age 14 (Roth et al., 1997). Gender is another important demographic risk factor for PTSD among CSA victims; for victims aged 16 and above, the odds of developing PTSD were substantially higher in women than in men (Jonas et al., 2011).

Taken together, recent research demonstrates the "dose response" effect of CSA and other types of sexual assault on developing ASD and PTSD symptoms, such that experiencing repeated sexual trauma or being exposed to different types of sexual assault increases the likelihood of these symptoms. Further, both CSA and sexual assault are associated with long-term impacts on mental health.

Medical Trauma: Life-Threatening Injuries and Illnesses

Medical trauma, including diagnosis of a life-threatening illness or other potentially life-threatening medical events (e.g., motor vehicle accidents, injury), also confers risk for ASD and PTSD in children and adults. Both types of medical trauma are discussed next.

Motor Vehicle Accidents and Injuries

Trauma symptoms are commonly studied in the aftermath of motor vehicle accidents (MVAs; Meiser-Stedman, Dalgleish, Glucksman, Yule, & Smith, 2009; Nickerson, Aderka, Bryant, & Hofmann, 2013). In fact, MVAs are one of the most common types of trauma, with the Kessler et al. (2017) epidemiological survey finding that 14% of respondents had experienced a life-threatening automobile accident. MVAs can be life-threatening and thus contribute to perceptions of physical danger and life threat. Not surprisingly, MVAs have been associated with PTSD and ASD in both youth and adults. Among adults, for example, many studies have examined PTSD prevalence in MVA victims over the course of a year post event. A systematic review (Heron-Delaney, Kenardy, Charlton, & Matsuoka, 2013) found that rates of PTSD ranged from 8% to 45% at 1 month, 8% to 30% at 3 months, 6% to 28% at 6 months, and 7% to 26% at 12 months post accident.

There have been many studies of ASD following MVAs, as individuals involved in MVAs are often seen soon after the potentially traumatic event for medical evaluation (Bryant, Friedman, Spiegel, Ursano, & Strain, 2011). In studies of MVA admissions at trauma hospitals, prevalence of ASD has varied, ranging from 13% to 41% (Harvey & Bryant, 1998; Yaşan, Güzel, Tamam, & Ozkan, 2009). Importantly, many MVA victims meet criteria for ASD, except for the dissociative symptoms cluster (Yaşan et al., 2009). Harvey and Bryant (1998) also demonstrated that ASD rates were high in MVA victims, and that when dissociative symptoms were excluded from the criteria (which is the case now in *DSM-5*), ASD rates increased further.

When assessing PTSD risk in MVA victims, it is important to consider injury type and severity. In a study of predominantly MVA victims (86%) admitted to an emergency department (Roitman, Gilad, Ankri, & Shalev, 2008), loss of consciousness and head injury were associated with a higher chance of developing PTSD relative to those that did not experience head injury; however, whiplash was not associated with a higher occurrence of PTSD symptoms. In particular, the group that lost consciousness endorsed more PTSD symptoms than other groups and was slower to recover from PTSD symptoms. Loss of consciousness may be a specific predictor of PTSD symptoms, distinct from injury severity, as Ehlers, Mayou and Bryant (1998) found that loss of consciousness but not injury severity was associated with a higher rate of PTSD. Another variable associated with ASD or PTSD is the fatality of the accident (Harvey & Bryant, 1998).

Gender is also an important consideration. Bryant and Harvey (2003) found that diagnoses of ASD were more predictive of subsequent PTSD in females than in males (perhaps because females were more likely to endorse the dissociative symptoms required for a diagnosis of ASD). Loss and life disruption, which predicts PTSD in those who experience a disaster or violent event (Comer et al., 2010; La Greca et al., 2010), also predicts PTSD symptoms in individuals experiencing MVAs. For example, persistent financial problems and involvement in the legal system (i.e., planning or initiating compensation claims) have been associated with meeting criteria for PTSD and having more severe symptoms (Ehlers, Mayou, & Bryant, 1998).

MVAs also have implications for ASD and PTSD in children. Using a developmentally sensitive algorithm for PTSD for children aged 2 to 6 years, children's rates of parent-reported PTSD symptoms were 6.5% at 2–4 weeks after an accident and 10.0% at 6 months post accident (Meiser-Stedman, Smith, Glucksman, Yule, & Dalgleish, 2008). Using these same PTSD criteria in children aged 7 to 10 years, combined child- and parent-reported PTSD rates were 50.0% after 2–4 weeks and 40.0% after 6 months (Meiser-Stedman et al., 2008). When children were reassessed 3 years later, a significant percentage still met criteria for PTSD (7.0% based on *DSM-IV* criteria, 16.9% based on developmentally sensitive criteria; Meiser-Stedman, Smith, Glucksman, & Dalgleish, 2017). Meiser-Stedman and colleagues (2017) further found that risk factors for PTSD in children involved in MVAs included parents' PTSS and persistent injury in the month after the event, although by 3 years post accident, persistent injury no longer predicted PTSS. Further, findings regarding injury severity as a predictor of PTSD or ASD symptoms are inconsistent, with the possible exception of burns where the greater percentage of total body area burned predicts a greater likelihood of developing ASD (Brosbe, Hoefling, & Faust, 2011). Also, for the most part, injury type has not been associated with PTSS (Brosbe et al., 2011), with the exception of complex fractures and burns; children experiencing such injuries have a higher likelihood of reporting chronic distress (Le Brocque et al., 2010). Finally, demographic characteristics also play a role in the development of children's PTSS after an injury. Some studies indicate that lower age confers greater risk for immediate PTSS but not persistent PTSS (Price et al., 2016). In addition, some studies found that female gender predicts symptoms of PTSD after an injury, although findings regarding gender are inconsistent (Brosbe et al., 2011).

Parents also report symptoms of PTSD or ASD following medical injury to their child. For example, in parents of children with traffic-related injuries, 25% met partial ASD criteria, and 12% met full criteria (Kassam-Adams, Fleisher, & Winston, 2009). Predictors of parents meeting criteria for ASD included direct (vs. indirect) exposure to the incident and parent appraisals of child pain. However, stress reactions abated over time; 6 months after the injury, 7% of parents met partial PTSD criteria, while 8% met full criteria. Although ASD and PTSD levels were associated with each other, ASD status was not a sensitive predictor of parents' PTSD (Kassam-Adams et al., 2009).

In terms of the long-range impact of child injury, both child and parent traumatic stress tends to decline over time, with rates declining substantially from 1 to 6 months and also from 6 to 10 or more months post injury (Price et al., 2016). Overall, then, the literature in youth and adults demonstrates that rates of ASD and PTSD after motor vehicle accidents are high. Nevertheless, rates of PTSD decrease substantially over time and rarely exceed 20%–30% after 1 year (Heron-Delaney et al., 2013; Meiser-Stedman et al., 2017).

Life-Threatening Medical Illness

The effects of potentially life-threatening illness on the development of ASD and PTSD have been studied in several patient populations, especially those with some form of cancer. Among adults, for example, a study of 200 patients with acute leukemia found that 14% met criteria for ASD (based on *DSM-IV*), while 18% met criteria for subsyndromal ASD (Rodin et al., 2013). Meeting criteria for ASD was associated with greater physical distress, poorer communication with health care providers, less perceived social support, lower self-esteem and spiritual well-being, and higher attachment anxiety (Rodin et al., 2013).

In adult patients with head/neck or lung cancer, Kangas, Henry, and Bryant (2005) found the rate of ASD was 28% in the month after diagnosis, with an additional 32% endorsing subsyndromal ASD. At 6 months post diagnosis, 53% of those who met criteria for ASD met criteria for PTSD, with lower rates for those with subsyndromal (17%) or no ASD (4%). At 12 months post diagnosis, rates of PTSD decreased even further, so that only 14% of the patients were diagnosed with PTSD; this group was comprised only of those who had previously met criteria for ASD (40%) or subsyndromal ASD (14%).

In a study of breast cancer patients after diagnosis and prior to cancer treatment, 2.4% met criteria for ASD and 1.2% met criteria for PTSD. At 7.5 months post diagnosis, and again at 1 year post diagnosis, 1.8% met PTSD criteria. In the overall sample, the number of patients endorsing any PTSD symptoms decreased over time, from approximately 82% prior to treatment to 57% 1 year later. Notably, patients who received chemotherapy or mastectomy did not differ significantly from patients who did not receive such treatments (Voigt et al., 2017).

In addition to life-threatening illnesses, the experience of pain has been an element of illness and injury that is strongly associated with PTSD symptoms. A review by Roy-Byrne and colleagues (2008) examined PTSD in patients of varying illness types. Among chronic pain patients, rates of PTSD ranged from 7.3% to 10.7%, higher than the rate for the general population. Among patients with a severe physical injury, greater quality and intensity of peri-traumatic pain increased the odds of being diagnosed with PTSD at 4 and 8 months post injury, perhaps because the presence of pain may be a signal for "life threat."

Among children, life-threatening illnesses and their treatments have been associated with PTSD and ASD in youth and in their parents. The National Child Traumatic Stress Network has termed the psychological and physiological response of children and their families to such trauma as "pediatric medical traumatic stress" (PMTS). PMTS encompasses PTSD symptoms, such as re-experiencing, avoidance of reminders of the event, and hyper-arousal; it includes PTSD, ASD, and subclinical presentations and is most studied with regard to pediatric cancer and injuries (Price et al., 2016).

Among children newly diagnosed with cancer, 7% reported clinically significant PTSS (Landolt, Yström, Sennhauser, Gnehm, & Vollrath, 2012). However, PTSS is primarily studied in child survivors of cancer, rather than those who are newly diagnosed. Rates of PTSS in child cancer survivors range from 8% to 75%, and predictors of PTSS in children with cancer include longer length of hospital stay and poorer disease outcome (Price et al., 2016).

After a diagnosis of pediatric cancer (in their child), parental rates of traumatic stress decline from initially high rates of 40% to 83% (1 month post diagnosis), but then plateau throughout the rest of the year (Price et al., 2016). High rates of ASD also have been found in parents of children with life-threatening illnesses. Mortensen and colleagues (2015) found that 17% of mothers of children in a Pediatric Intensive Care Unit met criteria for ASD, with an additional 17% displaying sub-clinical symptoms; in contrast, 6.8% of the fathers met criteria for ASD and 22.7% endorsed subclinical symptoms. Younger age of child was related to higher ASD in mothers, while high illness severity score was associated with high ASD in fathers.

As with other types of traumas, factors predicting pediatric traumatic stress in youth include greater perceptions of life threat and history of psychological factors, as well as genetic factors and elevated cortisol levels. In addition, parents' symptoms of PTSD are predictive of PTSD symptoms in their children (Price et al., 2016). In contrast, findings are limited regarding demographic characteristics (e.g., age, gender) in the development of pediatric PTSS; in youth with cancer, no age or gender differences

were found with regard to PTSS both in those recently diagnosed and also in longer term survivors (Phipps, Larson, Long, & Rai, 2005).

Overall, rates of PTSD and ASD symptoms due to life-threatening illness or injury are high in the immediate aftermath of an injury or diagnosis but decline substantially over time. Because illnesses and injuries differ in course and nature, more research on specific medical populations, particularly in areas beyond injury or cancer, would help delineate risk factors specific to illness type.

Summary and Future Research Directions

Over the past few decades, tremendous strides have been made in our understanding of how traumatic events lead to PTSD in youth and adults. Although most individuals are resilient in the face of traumatic events, a significant minority develops symptoms consistent with ASD or PTSD, which are associated with significant functional impairment. The text that follows highlights several important directions for future research, and also notes several research limitations.

Conceptualization of Posttraumatic Stress Disorder

As noted earlier, current conceptualizations of post-traumatic stress are very divergent and require further study. At present, there is no consensus on what constitutes the "best" approach to defining and identifying PTSD or ASD. (Is it *DSM-5*? Is it *ICD-11*?) Consequently, until the conceptualization of PTSD is resolved, researchers would be wise to evaluate symptoms that reflect both *DSM-5* and *ICD-11* conceptualizations. Shifting focus away from targeting the "presence or absence of a diagnosis" to an approach that examines the various PTSD symptoms clusters (e.g., re-experiencing, avoidance, arousal, cognition/mood) may be illuminating and help to refine our understanding of PTSD. For example, recent work on genetic markers associated with vulnerability to PTSD in children reveals that the Met allele for the COMT gene is associated PTSD as defined by *ICD-11* but not by *DSM-5* (Danzi & La Greca, 2018). By evaluating symptom clusters more directly, a clearer picture of PTSD risk can emerge.

The PTSD diagnostic dilemma is especially acute for children and adolescents, as the vast majority of relevant studies have focused on adults. Moving forward, more research is needed on the conceptualization of PTSD and ASD in youth at different developmental levels, especially preschool and preadolescent youth. Notably, no studies of the "fit" or validity of the *DSM-5* or *ICD-11* conceptualizations of PTSD for children under 6 years of age could be found, despite the 2013 publication of *DSM-5* criteria for this age group (American Psychiatric Association, 2013). Further study of preadolescent youth (7–12 years) is also warranted. While both the *DSM-5* and *ICD-11* diagnostic criteria for PTSD appear to fit preadolescent children's trauma responses (Danzi & La Greca, 2016; La Greca et al., 2017), the diagnostic overlap is poor. Interestingly, evidence suggests that the less restrictive *DSM-5* criteria for young children also fit preadolescent children's responses and identifies more distressed children than the adult-based criteria (Danzi & La Greca, 2017). Thus, developmental issues in the conceptualization of PTSD and ASD require further attention.

Finally, at present, there is a growing body of research on the conceptualization of complex PTSD. Most studies focus on adults (Brewin et al., 2017; Karatzias et al., 2016, 2017), although complex PTSD has begun to receive attention in children and adolescents as well (Sachser, Keller, & Goldbeck, 2016). Because childhood experiences of physical or sexual abuse appear to be strongly associated with complex PTSD in adults (Brewin et al., 2017), studies of the relevance of complex PTSD for children and adolescents who experience physical or sexual abuse would be especially desirable.

Traumatic Exposure
SECOND-HAND EXPOSURE
As noted, disasters have the potential to elicit PTSD in children and adults. Given advances in technology, and the nearly ubiquitous use of smartphones and social media platforms among youth and adults (Pew Research Institute, 2017a, 2017b), the impact of *second-hand exposure to traumatic events* is a growing area of concern. With increased access to news worldwide, and through mobile technologies that can facilitate news access 24/7, individuals can hear about disasters within minutes of the event. In addition, information provided on network and cable news, social media, and other communication tools (e.g., Twitter, Instagram) often is accompanied by graphic images and sometimes gory details. This potentially traumatic disclosure of the details of disasters has the potential to increase individuals' perceptions of threat and vulnerability. Not surprisingly, then, children's and adults' media exposure to disasters and other potentially traumatic events has been linked with higher risk for acute stress reactions

and symptoms of PTSD following events such as the 9/11 terrorist attacks, the Oklahoma City bombing, and the Boston Marathon bombing (e.g., Busso, McLaughlin, & Sheridan, 2014; Comer, Bry, Poznanski, & Golik, 2016; Garfin, Holman, & Silver, 2015; Pfefferbaum et al., 2003; Schuster et al., 2001; Tucker, Pfefferbaum, Nixon, & Dickson, 2000), even among individuals who live remotely from the actual disaster (Fallahi & Lesik, 2009; Yeung et al., 2016). Youth with high stress reactivity, a history of psychopathology, or prior exposure to violence are at particularly high risk for experiencing PTSD symptoms from media coverage (Busso et al., 2014; Garfin et al., 2015).

Understanding the impact of second-hand exposure is an area of high research need. As discussed by (Comer et al., 2016), it is unclear whether the individual's interaction with media (i.e., passively reading news articles versus sharing on social media or searching for graphic information) might have a differential impact on stress reactions. Further, with high rates of smartphone and technology use among 12- to 18-year-olds (Lenhart, 2015), it has become increasingly difficult for parents to monitor their youth's media and Internet usage, and thus their potential for disaster exposure. In view of the continued increase in access to world news via many different platforms, it is critical to understand the influence of media coverage on PTSS in both directly and indirectly trauma-exposed individuals.

FAMILY TRANSMISSION
Another important aspect of exposure that warrants further attention is the potential *transmission of exposure through family members*. As noted previously, parents of children with life-threatening illness or injuries are at risk for elevated symptoms of PTSD and ASD (e.g., Price et al., 2016). Similarly, it would be important to know whether youth whose parents experience life-threatening events or illnesses are also at greater risk for ASD or PTSD. Some research suggests this is the case as, for example, Duarte and colleagues (2006) found that children of emergency medical technicians had a high prevalence of probable PTSD (18.9%) 6 months after the World Trade Center attacks.

IMMIGRATION-RELATED STRESSORS
Future studies that focus on *immigration-related trauma* would also be useful, especially in today's sociopolitical world where there is substantial violent conflict. Based on the 2010 Census, about 37 million migrant adults and 3 million migrant youth (under

18 years of age) reside in the United States (US Census, 2010). Recent evidence suggests that this population is at high risk for PTSD. As an illustration, Perreira and Ornelas (2013) found that 29% of foreign-born Latino adolescents and 34% of foreign-born Latino parents experienced trauma during the process of migrating to the United States (e.g., arrest or murder of a family member, serious illness or injury). Among those who exposed to migration-related trauma, 9% of the adolescents and 21% of their parents were at risk for PTSD.

GENDER ISSUES

Finally, greater attention to gender- and sex-related issues in trauma-exposure is needed. In particular, further research on the *impact of sexual assault on men* would be desirable. To date, most of the sexual assault literature has focused on women, who generally are at higher risk than men for this type of trauma exposure. However, recent awareness of extensive sexual abuse of males by Catholic priests (Terry & Freilich, 2012) and by powerful celebrities (https://www.buzzfeed.com/claudiarosenbaum/hollywood-sex-abuse-scandal-male-victims?utm_term=.ck3lZvn12#.brAZ0mR3o) has brought attention to the extensive trauma inflicted on males by sexual abuse. By the same token, further research on the *impact of trauma exposure on women in the military* is needed; as noted earlier, women who serve in the military are often exposed to multiple traumatic stressors (e.g., combat, sexual assault) and have higher rates of PTSD than men in the military (Carlson et al., 2013; Wojcik et al., 2009).

Long-Term Effects of Trauma Exposure

For many types of trauma exposure, the long-term psychological impact is unknown. In some cases, the long-term impact of traumatic events has been studied via adults' retrospective accounts of childhood traumatic experiences. However, prospective and longitudinal studies of the impact of trauma exposure are relatively rare (Bonanno et al., 2010). An important advancement in our understanding of the long-term impact of trauma is that investigators have begun to examine patterns of outcome following exposure to traumatic events, such as disasters (Bonanno, Rennicke & Dekel, 2005; La Greca et al., 2013b; Norris, Tracy, & Galea, 2009) or life-threatening medical procedures (Lam et al., 2010). This literature highlights different trajectories of distress (such as PTSD) that individuals may follow after trauma. These trajectories may include resilient (no or low distress over time), recovering (initial

distress that abates over time), chronic (initial distress that does not remit), and delayed (low to moderate initial distress that increases over time). This person-centered approach to understanding the impact of traumatic events highlights the fact that most individuals are resilient in the face of trauma exposure (Bonanno et al., 2010). Further, studying predictors of the different posttrauma trajectories can facilitate a better understanding of who will recover and who will remain chronically distressed; such information has important implications for when and how to intervene (La Greca et al., 2013b). Such an approach can also facilitate understanding the patterns of risk and recovery among differentially vulnerable groups (i.e., directly vs. indirectly exposed individuals, minority groups, children, parents, first responders). Finally, the trajectory approach can provide a better understanding of how trauma unfolds over time and identify critical periods for intervention, after which recovery is more tenuous.

Mechanisms Linking Trauma Exposure and Stress Reactions

Although multiple risk and resilience factors for PTSD and ASD following trauma exposure have been examined (e.g., Biggs et al., 2012; Breslau, 2012; Bonanno et al., 2010; La Greca et al., 2012), less attention has been devoted to understanding the underlying mechanisms that link these factors to the onset or maintenance of a stress-related disorder. This is likely due, at least in part, to the relative dearth of prospective and longitudinal studies of the impact of trauma exposure and to the absence of information regarding individuals' pretrauma functioning (Bonanno et al., 2010), which might affect vulnerability. In addition, mechanisms might vary across different types of traumatic events (Breslau, 2012). Readers are referred to several sources for details on a range of mechanisms (e.g., genetic, biological, cognitive, family) that might underlie the association between trauma exposure and PTSD (Ehlers, Ehring, & Kleim, 2012; Monson, Fredman, Dekel, & Macdonald, 2012; Uddin et al., 2012; Yehuda et al., 2012). Here a few issues pertinent to understanding mechanisms are highlighted.

For example, investigators have attempted to evaluate mechanisms that might explain why female gender is a risk factor for PTSD following trauma exposure, even though males are more likely to experience trauma than females (Breslau, 2012; Furr et al., 2010; Gurwitch et al., 2002; Hoven et al., 2005; Norris et al., 2002). Several explanations for these gender differences have been ruled out, including that females experience more sexual assault than males (which is associated with high rates of ASD and PTSD), have a greater history of prior trauma exposure or pre-existing depression, or are simply more likely to report distress symptoms (Breslau, 2012). Accordingly, others have speculated that females might experience greater perceived life threat during a traumatic event than males (Bonanno et al., 2010), thus contributing to their higher rates of PTSD. Supporting this notion, Goenjian and colleagues (2001) found that adolescent girls exposed to a devastating hurricane reported more PTSS than boys, but this gender difference no longer held when perceived life threat was statistically controlled. Further research that examines mechanisms that contribute to girls' and women's greater vulnerability to PTSD following traumatic events would be desirable.

Cognitive vulnerabilities also have been a major area of interest in understanding factors that contribute to PTSD in trauma-exposed individuals. In this regard, anxiety sensitivity (i.e., the fear of one's own anxiety reaction) is believed to contribute to PTSD and to accentuate adverse responses to a traumatic stressor; available research supports this notion (e.g., Marshall, Miles, & Stewart, 2010). Another line of research has examined attentional bias to trauma-related cues and other cognitive vulnerabilities that contribute to PTSD (see Ehlers et al., 2012, for a review). Further efforts to understand these and other mechanisms will be important to advance our understanding of PTSD and how best to approach its treatment.

Finally, a clearer understanding of the reasons or mechanisms underlying the common comorbidity between PTSD and other psychological dysfunction would be useful. In addition to PTSD, trauma exposure has been associated with symptoms of grief, depression, anxiety, stress-related health problems, and increased substance use, all of which are commonly comorbid with PTSD (see Bonanno et al., 2010). For example, in a large national sample of adolescents, Kilpatrick and colleagues (2003) found that nearly 75% of the youth who met criteria for PTSD displayed comorbid diagnoses of depression or substance use. High levels of comorbidity between PTSD and depression also have been found in youth affected by natural disasters (e.g., Goenjian et al., 1995, 2005), youth residing in refugee camps during war conflict (Thabet, Abed, & Vostanis, 2004), and adolescent survivors of physical abuse (Malmquist, 1986; Pelcovitz et al., 1994). Thus, efforts to understand transdiagnostic mechanisms

that could underlie both PTSD and other commonly co-occurring disorders would be extremely valuable.

Methodological Issues

Despite the wealth of research examining the contributions of trauma exposure to the development of PTSD and ASD, several limitations to this body of research warrant attention in the future. Two methodological issues that will help strengthen trauma-related research going forward are highlighted next. (See Norris, Galea, Friedman, & Watson, 2006 for more extensive details on methodological issues in disaster research.)

First, many trauma studies include convenience samples of individuals who are either interested in participating or potentially most affected by the traumatic event (Bonanno et al., 2010; Neria et al., 2008). This may result in skewed estimates of trauma-related psychopathology and contribute to the wide range of PTSD rates that are apparent across studies. As a result, it is difficult to determine the actual severity of a particular trauma's impact. Studies that emphasize population-based sampling methods (e.g., Bromet & Havenaar, 2007; Schlenger & Silver, 2006) will be important and useful to address this concern.

Second, standardized, well-validated measures of PTSD and ASD, and of trauma exposure, should be used across studies. This will aid in drawing more consistent conclusions about the nature and course of trauma exposure and PTSD. Given the current dilemma regarding the discrepancies between DSM-5 and ICD-11 definitions of PTSD, the use of measures that capture both sets of relevant symptoms are needed (e.g., Elhai et al., 2013; Karatzias et al., 2016). With respect to trauma exposure, a number of well-validated measures are available; in particular, the website for the National Center for PTSD lists measures that may facilitate the assessment of trauma exposure (https://www.ptsd.va.gov/professional/assessment/te-measures/index.asp).

Conclusion

In conclusion, there are a wide range of potentially traumatic events that lead to PTSD or acute stress reactions in children and adults. Given the relatively high rates of trauma exposure that individuals experience, and the potential for psychological distress that can be impairing, the impact of trauma on youth and adults should remain a critical research area in the future. Overall, the most pressing issues for further investigation include the following: clarifying the conceptualization and definition of PTSD and ASD in children and adults; examining the impact of second-hand exposure to trauma and the contributions of modern technology in heightening individuals' trauma responses; understanding the long-term impact of trauma exposure as well as factors that predict patterns of risk and recovery after traumatic events; and gaining a better understanding of underlying mechanisms that link trauma exposure to posttraumatic stress reactions in children and adults.

Note

1. For the most part, investigators have used "gender" and "sex" interchangeably when referring to differences between males and females. However, there are important distinctions between "gender" (a social construct) and "sex" (a biological construct), which are valuable considerations in biomedical research (Krieger, 2003), and merit attention in future research on individuals' vulnerability to traumatic stress (see Krieger, 2003).

References

Adams, R. E., Guey, L. T., Gluzman, S. F., & Bromet, E. J. (2011). Psychological well-being and risk perceptions of mothers in Kyiv, Ukraine, 19 years after the Chornobyl disaster. *International Journal of Social Psychiatry, 57*(6), 637–645.

American Psychiatric Association. (1980). *Diagnostic and statistical manual of mental disorders* (3rd ed.). Washington, DC: Author.

American Psychiatric Association. (1994). *Diagnostic and statistical manual of mental disorders* (4th ed.). Washington, DC: Author.

American Psychiatric Association. (2013). *Diagnostic and statistical manual of mental disorders* (5th ed.). Washington, DC: Author.

Armour, C., Shevlin, M., Elklit, A., & Mroczek, D. (2012). A latent growth mixture modeling approach to PTSD symptoms in rape victims. *Traumatology, 18*(1), 20–28.

Ayer, L., Venkatesh, B., Stewart, R., Mandel, D., Stein, B., & Schoenbaum, M. (2015). Psychological aspects of the Israeli–Palestinian conflict: A systematic review. *Trauma, Violence, & Abuse, 18*(3), 332–338.

Benjet, C., Bromet, E., Karam, E. G., Kessler, R. C., McLaughlin, K. A., Ruscio, A. M.,...Descartes, P. (2016). The epidemiology of traumatic event exposure worldwide: Results from the World Mental Health Survey Consortium. *Psychological Medicine, 46*(2), 327–343.

Biggs, Q. M., Guimond, J. M., Fullerton, C. S., Ursano, R. J., Gray, C., Goldenberg, M.,...& Tyler, M. P. (2012). The epidemiology of acute stress disorder and other early responses to trauma in adults. In J.G. Beck & D.M. Sloan (Eds.), *The Oxford handbook of traumatic stress disorders* (pp. 69–83). New York, NY: Oxford University Press.

Blevins, C. E., Wusik, M. F., Sullivan, C. P., Jones, R. T., & Hughes, M. (2016). Do negative changes in worldview mediate links between mass trauma and reckless behavior? A longitudinal exploratory study. *Community Mental Health Journal, 52*(1), 10–17.

Bonanno, G. A., Brewin, C. R., Kaniasty, K., & La Greca, A. M. (2010). Weighing the costs of disaster: Consequences, risks, and resilience in individuals, families, and communities. *Psychological Science in the Public Interest, 11*(1), 1–49.

Bonanno, G., Rennicke, C., & Dekel, S. (2005). Self-enhancement among high-exposure survivors of the September 11th terrorist attack: Resilience or social maladjustment? *Journal of Personality and Social Psychology, 88*(6), 984–998.

Breslau, N. (2012). Epidemiology of posttraumatic stress disorder in adults. In Beck, J. G. & Sloan, D. M. (Eds.), *The Oxford handbook of traumatic stress disorders* (pp. 84–97). New York, NY: Oxford University Press.

Breslau, N., Davis, G. C., Andreski, P., & Peterson, E. (1991). Traumatic events and posttraumatic stress disorder in an urban population of young adults. *Archives of General Psychiatry, 48*(3), 216–222.

Brewin, C.R., Cloitre, M., Hyland, P., Shevlin, M., Maercker, A., Bryant, R.A.,...Reed, G.M. (2017). A review of current evidence regarding the ICD-11 proposals for diagnosing PTSD and complex PTSD. *Clinical Psychology Review, 58*, 1–15.

Bromet, E. J., Havenaar, J. M., & Guey, L. T. (2011). A 25 year retrospective review of the psychological consequences of the Chernobyl accident. *Clinical Oncology, 23*(4), 297–305.

Bromet, E. J. & Havenaar, J. M. (2007). Basic epidemiological approaches to disaster research: Value of face-to-face procedures. In F. H. Norris, S. Galea, M. J. Friedman, and P. J. Watson (Eds.) *Methods for disaster mental health research* (pp. 95–110). New York, NY: Guilford Press.

Brosbe, M. S., Hoefling, K., & Faust, J. (2011). Predicting posttraumatic stress following pediatric injury: A systematic review. *Journal of Pediatric Psychology, 36*(6), 718–729.

Bryant, R.A. (2017). Acute stress disorder. *Current Opinion in Psychology, 14*, 127–131.

Bryant, R.A., Friedman, M.J., Spiegel, D., Ursano, R., & Strain, J. (2011). A review of acute stress disorder in DSM-5. *Depression and Anxiety, 28*, 802–817.

Bryant, R. A., & Harvey, A. G. (2003). Gender differences in the relationship between acute stress disorder and posttraumatic stress disorder following motor vehicle accidents. *Australian and New Zealand Journal of Psychiatry, 37*(2), 226–229.

Burch, A. D. S., & Mazzei, P. (2018) Death toll is at 17 and could rise in Florida school shooting. *New Your Times*, February 14, 2018. Available at https://www.nytimes.com/2018/02/14/us/parkland-school-shooting.html.

Busso, D. S., McLaughlin, K. A., & Sheridan, M. A. (2014). Media exposure and sympathetic nervous system reactivity predict PTSD symptoms after the Boston Marathon bombings. *Depression and Anxiety, 31*(7), 551–558.

Cao, H., McFarlane, A. C., & Klimidis, S. (2003). Prevalence of psychiatric disorder following the 1988 Yun Nan (China) earthquake. *Social Psychiatry and Psychiatric Epidemiology, 38*(4), 204–212.

Carey, P. D., Walker, J. L., Rossouw, W., Seedat, S., & Stein, D. J. (2008). Risk indicators and psychopathology in traumatised children and adolescents with a history of sexual abuse. *European Child and Adolescent Psychiatry, 17*(2), 93–98.

Carlson, B. E., Stromwall, L. K., & Lietz, C. A. (2013). Mental health issues in recently returning women veterans: Implications for practice. *Social Work, 58*(2), 105–114.

Chan, C. L. W., Wang, C. W., Qu, Z., Lu, B. Q., Ran, M. S., Ho, A. H. Y.,...Zhang, X. (2011). Posttraumatic stress disorder symptoms among adult survivors of the 2008 Sichuan earthquake in China. *Journal of Traumatic Stress, 24*(3), 295–302.

Cohen, A. P., Azrael, D., & Miller, M. (2014). Rate of mass shootings has tripled since 2011, Harvard research shows. *Mother Jones*, 15. Retrieved from https://www.motherjones.com/politics/2014/10/mass-shootings-increasing-harvard-research/

Comer, J. S., Bry, L. J., Poznanski, B., & Golik, A. M. (2016). Children's mental health in the context of terrorist attacks, ongoing threats, and possibilities of future terrorism. *Current Psychiatry Reports*, 18(9), 1–8.

Comer, J.S., Dantowitz, A., Chou, T., Edson, A.L., Elkins, R.M., Kerns, C., Brown, B., Green, J.G. (2014). Adjustment among area youth after the Boston Marathon bombing and subsequent manhunt. *Pediatrics*, 134(1), 7–14.

Comer, J. S., Fan, B., Duarte, C. S., Wu, P., Musa, G. J., Mandell, D. J., ... Hoven, C. W. (2010). Attack-related life disruption and child psychopathology in New York City public school children 6-months post-9/11. *Journal of Clinical Child and Adolescent Psychology*, 39(4), 460–469.

Copeland, W. E., Keeler, G., Angold, A., & Costello, E. J. (2007). Traumatic events and posttraumatic stress in childhood. *Archives of General Psychiatry*, 64(5), 577–584.

Costello, E. J., Erkanli, A., Fairbank, J. A., & Angold, A. (2002). The prevalence of potentially traumatic events in childhood and adolescence. *Journal of Traumatic Stress*, 15(2), 99–112.

Crimmins, A., Balbus, J. L., Gamble, C. B....and Ziska, L. (2016). *The impacts of climate change on human health in the United States: A scientific assessment*. Retrieved from https://health2016.globalchange.gov

Cross, D., Vance, L. A., Kim, Y. J., Ruchard, A. L., Fox, N., Jovanovic, T., & Bradley, B. (2018). Trauma exposure, PTSD, and parenting in a community sample of low-income, predominantly African American mothers and children. *Psychological Trauma: Theory, Research, Practice and Policy*, 10(3), 327–335.

Cuthbertson, C. A., Newkirk, C., Ilardo, J., Loveridge, S., & Skidmore, M. (2016). Angry, scared, and unsure: Mental health consequences of contaminated water in Flint, Michigan. *Journal of Urban Health*, 93(6), 899–908.

Danese, A., & McEwen, B. S. (2012). Adverse childhood experiences, allostasis, allostatic load, and age-related disease. *Physiology and Behavior*, 106(1), 29–39.

Danzi, B. A., & La Greca, A. M. (2016). DSM-IV, DSM-5, and ICD-11: Identifying children with posttraumatic stress disorder after disasters. *Journal of Child Psychology and Psychiatry*, 57(12), 1444–1452.

Danzi, B. A., & La Greca, A. M. (2017). Optimizing clinical thresholds for PTSD: Extending the DSM-5 preschool criteria to school-aged children. *International Journal of Clinical and Health Psychology*, 17, 234–241.

Danzi, B. A., & La Greca, A. M. (2018). Genetic pathways to posttraumatic stress disorder and depression in children: Investigation of catechol-O-methyltransferase (COMT) Val158Met using different PTSD diagnostic models. *Journal of Psychiatric Research*, 102, 81–86. doi:10.1016/j.jpsychires.2018.03.014

Deblinger, E., Mannarino, A. P., Cohen, J. A., Runyon, M. K., & Steer, R. A. (2011). Trauma-focused cognitive behavioral therapy for children: Impact of the trauma narrative and treatment length. *Depression and Anxiety*, 28(1), 67–75.

Denson, T. F., Marshall, G. N., Schell, T. L., & Jaycox, L. H. (2007). Predictors of posttraumatic distress 1 year after exposure to community violence: The importance of acute symptom severity. *Journal of Consulting and Clinical Psychology*, 75(5), 683–692.

Department of Veterans Affairs (2016). Women Veterans Population [Table 6L]. *VetPop2014*. Retrieved from http://www.va.gov/vetdata]http://www.va.gov/vetdata.

DeSalvo, K. B., Hyre, A. D., Ompad, D. C., Menke, A., Tynes, L. L., & Muntner, P. (2007). Symptoms of posttraumatic stress disorder in a New Orleans workforce following Hurricane Katrina. *Journal of Urban Health*, 84(2), 142–152.

Dodgen, D., Donato, D., Kelly, N., La Greca, A. M., Morganstein, J., Dutta, T., ... Ursano, R. xxx (2016). Mental health and well-being. *Interagency Special Report on the Impacts of Climate Change on Human Health in the United States*. Retrieved from https://health2016.globalchange.gov.

Dohrenwend, B.P., Turner, J.B., Turse, N.A., Lewis-Fernandez, R., & Yager, T.J. (2008). War-related posttraumatic stress disorder in black, Hispanic, and majority white Vietnam veterans: The roles of exposure and vulnerability. *Journal of Traumatic Stress*, 21, 133–141.

Duarte, C.S., Hoven, C.W., Wu, P., Bin, F., Cotel, S., Mandell, D.J., ... & Markenson, D. (2006). Posttraumatic stress in children with first responders in their families. *Journal of Traumatic Stress*, 19, 301–306.

Durando, J. (2016) "How water crisis in Flint became federal state of emergency." USA Today Network, January 20, 2016, Retrieved from https://www.usatoday.com/story/news/nation-now/2016/01/19/michigan-flint-water-contamination/78996052/.

Ehlers, A., Ehring, T., & Kleim, B. (2012). Information processing in posttraumatic stress disorder. In J. G. Beck & D. M. Sloan (Eds.), *The Oxford handbook of traumatic stress disorders* (pp. 191–218). New York, NY: Oxford University Press.

Ehlers, A., Mayou, R. A., & Bryant, B. (1998). Psychological predictors of chronic posttraumatic stress disorder after motor vehicle accidents. *Journal of Abnormal Psychology*, 107, 508–519.

Eisenman, D. P., Gelberg, L., Liu, H., & Shapiro, M.F. (2003). Mental health and health-related quality of life among adult Latino primary care patients living in the United States with previous exposure to political violence. *JAMA*, 290(5), 627–634.

Elhai, J. D., Layne, C. M., Steinberg, A. S., Vrymer, M. J., Briggs, E. C., Ostrowski, S. A., Pynoos, R. S. (2013). Psychometric properties of the UCLA PTSD Reaction Index. Part 2: Investigating factor structure findings in a national clinic-referred youth sample. *Journal of Traumatic Stress*, 26, 10–18.

Elklit, A., & Christiansen, D. M. (2010). ASD and PTSD in rape victims. *Journal of Interpersonal Violence*, 25(8), 1470–1488.

Fallahi, C. R., & Lesik, S. A. (2009). The effects of vicarious exposure to the recent massacre at Virginia Tech. *Psychological Trauma: Theory, Research, Practice and Policy*, 1, 220–230.

Finkelhor, D., Shattuck, A., Turner, H. A., & Hamby, S. L. (2014). The lifetime prevalence of child sexual abuse and sexual assault assessed in late adolescence. *Journal of Adolescent Health*, 55(3), 329–333.

Fowler, P. J., Tompsett, C. J., Braciszewski, J. M., Jacques-Tiura, A. J., & Baltes, B. B. (2009). Community violence: A meta-analysis on the effect of exposure and mental health outcomes of children and adolescents. *Development and Psychopathology*, 21(1), 227–259.

Frances, A. (2013). *Saving normal: An insider's revolt against out-of-control psychiatric diagnosis, DSM-5, Big Pharma, and the medicalization of ordinary life.* New York, NY: William Morrow & Co.

Friedman, M. J. (2013). Finalizing PTSD in DSM-5: Getting here from there and where to go next. *Journal of Traumatic Stress, 26*(5), 548–556.

Friedman, M. J., Resick, P. A., Bryant, R. A., & Brewin, C. R. (2011). Considering PTSD for DSM-5. *Depression and Anxiety, 28*(9), 750–769.

Fullerton, C. S., Ursano, R. J., Reeves, J., Shigemura, J., & Grieger, T. (2006). Perceived safety in disaster workers following 9/11. *The Journal of Nervous and Mental Disease, 194,* 61–63.

Fullerton, C. S., Ursano, R. J., & Wang, L. (2004). Acute stress disorder, posttraumatic stress disorder, and depression in disaster or rescue workers. *American Journal of Psychiatry, 161*(8), 1370–1376.

Furr, J. M., Comer, J. S., Edmunds, J. M., & Kendall, P. C. (2010). Disasters and youth: A meta-analytic examination of posttraumatic stress. *Journal of Consulting and Clinical, 78*(6), 765–780.

Galatzer-Levy, I. R., & Bryant, R. A. (2013). 636,120 ways to have posttraumatic stress disorder. *Perspectives on Psychological Science, 8*(6), 651–662.

Galea, S., Ahern, J., Resnick, H., Kilpatrick, D., Bucuvalas, M., Gold, J., & Vlahov, D. (2002). Psychological sequelae of the September 11 terrorist attacks in New York City. *New England Journal of Medicine, 346*(13), 982–987.

Galea, S., Nandi, A., & Vlahov, D. (2005). The epidemiology of post-traumatic stress disorder after disasters. *Epidemiologic Reviews, 27*(1), 78–91.

Galovski, T. E., Peterson, Z. D., Beagley, M. C., Strasshofer, D. R., Held, P., & Fletcher, T. D. (2016). Exposure to violence during Ferguson protests: Mental health effects for law enforcement and community members. *Journal of Traumatic Stress, 29*(4), 283–292.

Garfin, D. R., Holman, E. A., & Silver, R. C. (2015). Cumulative exposure to prior collective trauma and acute stress responses to the Boston Marathon bombings. *Psychological Science, 26*(6), 675–683.

Goenjian, A. K., Molina, L., Steinberg, A. M., Fairbanks, L. A., Alvarez, M. L, Goenjian, H. A., & Pynoos, R. S. (2001). Posttraumatic stress and depressive reactions among Nicaraguan adolescents after Hurricane Mitch. *American Journal of Psychiatry, 158*(5), 788–794.

Goenjian, A. K., Pynoos, R. S., Steinberg, A. M., Najarian, L. M., Asarnow, J. R., Karayan, I., Ghurabi, M., Fairbanks, L. A. (1995). Psychiatric comorbidity in children after the 1988 earthquake in Armenia. *Journal of the American Academy of Child and Adolescent Psychiatry, 34*(9), 1174–1184.

Goenjian, A. K., Walling, D., Steinberg, A. M., Karayan, I., Najarian, L. M., Pynoos, R. (2005). A prospective study of posttraumatic stress and depression reactions among treated and untreated adolescents 5 years after a catastrophic disaster. *American Journal of Psychiatry, 162*(12), 2302–2308.

Gramlich, J. (2018). Five facts about crime in the U.S. Pew Research Center. Retrieved from http://www.pewresearch.org/fact-tank/2018/01/30/5-facts-about-crime-in-the-u-s/.

Gurwitch, R. H., Sitterle, K. A., Young, B. H., & Pfefferbaum, B. (2002). The aftermath of terrorism. In A. M. La Greca, W. K. Silverman, E. M. Vernberg, & M. C. Roberts (Eds.)

Helping children cope with disasters and terrorism. Washington, DC: American Psychological Association.

Halligan, S. L., Michael, T., Clark, D. M., & Ehlers, A. (2003). Posttraumatic stress disorder following assault: The role of cognitive processing, trauma memory, and appraisals. *Journal of Consulting and Clinical Psychology, 71,* 419–431.

Hamrin, V., Jonker, B., & Scahill, L. (2004). Acute stress disorder symptoms in gunshot-injured youth. *Journal of Child and Adolescent Psychiatric Nursing, 17*(4), 161–172.

Harvey, A. G., & Bryant, R. A. (1998). The relationship between acute stress disorder and posttraumatic stress disorder: A prospective evaluation of motor vehicle accident survivors. *Journal of Consulting and Clinical Psychology, 66*(3), 507–512.

Heron-Delaney, M., Kenardy, J., Charlton, E., & Matsuoka, Y. (2013). A systematic review of predictors of posttraumatic stress disorder (PTSD) for adult road traffic crash survivors. *Injury, 44*(11), 1413–1422.

Hoge, C. W., Castro, C. A., Messer, S. C., McGurk, D., Cotting, D. I., & Koffman, R. L. (2004). Combat duty in Iraq and Afghanistan, mental health problems, and barriers to care. *New England Journal of Medicine, 351*(1), 13–22.

Hoven, C. W., Duarte, C. S., Lucas, C. P., Wu, P., Mandell, D. J., Goodwin, R. D.,...& Musa, G. J. (2005). Psychopathology among New York City public school children 6 months after September 11. *Archives of General Psychiatry, 62*(5), 545–551.

Jonas, S., Bebbington, P., Mcmanus, S., Meltzer, H., Jenkins, R., Kuipers, E.,...Brugha, T. (2011). Sexual abuse and psychiatric disorder in England: Results from the 2007 Adult Psychiatric Morbidity Survey. *Psychological Medicine, 41*(4), 709–719.

Kaltman, S., Krupnick, J., Stockton, P., Hooper, L., & Green, B. L. (2005). Psychological impact of types of sexual trauma among college women. *Journal of Traumatic Stress, 18,* 547–555.

Kangas, M., Henry, J. L., & Bryant, R. A. (2005). The course of psychological disorders in the 1st year after cancer diagnosis. *Journal of Consulting and Clinical Psychology, 73,* 763–768.

Kaniasty, K., & Norris, F. H. (2008). Longitudinal linkages between perceived social support and posttraumatic stress symptoms: Sequential roles of social causation and social selection. *Journal of Traumatic Stress, 21*(3), 274–281.

Kaplow, J. B., Dodge, K. A., Amaya-Jackson, L., & Saxe, G. N. (2005). Pathways to PTSD, part II: Sexually abused children. *American Journal of Psychiatry, 162*(7), 1305–1310.

Karam, E. G., Friedman, M. J., Hill, E. D., Kessler, R. C., McLaughlin, K. A., Petukhova, M.,...& Girolamo, G. (2014). Cumulative traumas and risk thresholds: 12-month PTSD in the World Mental Health (WMH) surveys. *Depression and Anxiety, 31*(2), 130–142.

Karatzias, T., Shevlin, M., Fyvie, C., Hyland, P., Efthymiadou, E., Wilson, D.,...Cloitre, M. (2017). Evidence of distinct profiles of Posttraumatic Stress Disorder (PTSD) and Complex Posttraumatic Stress Disorder (CPTSD) based on the new ICD-11 Trauma Questionnaire (ICD-TQ). *Journal of Affective Disorders, 207,* 181–187.

Karatzias, T., Shevlin, M., Fyvie, C., Hyland, P., Efthymiadou, E., Wilson, D.,...Cloitre, M. (2016). An initial psychometric assessment of an ICD-11 based measure of PTSD and complex PTSD (ICD-TQ): Evidence of construct validity. *Journal of Anxiety Disorders, 44,* 73–79.

Kassam-Adams, N., Fleisher, C. L., & Winston, F. K. (2009). Acute stress disorder and posttraumatic stress disorder in parents of injured children. *Journal of Traumatic Stress*, 22(4), 294–302.

Kessler, R. C., Aguilar-Gaxiola, S., Alonso, J., Benjet, C., Bromet, E. J., Cardoso, G., ... Koenen, K. C. (2017). Trauma and PTSD in the WHO World Mental Health Surveys. *European Journal of Psychotraumatology*, 8(sup5), 1353383.

Khan, A. A., Haider, G., Sheikh, M. R., Ali, A. F., Khalid, Z., Tahir, M. M., ... Saleem, S. (2016). Prevalence of post-traumatic stress disorder due to community violence among university students in the world's most dangerous megacity: A cross-sectional study from Pakistan. *Journal of Interpersonal Violence*, 31(13), 2302–2315.

Kilpatrick, D., Koenen, K., Ruggiero, K., Acierno, R., Galea, S., Resnick, H., Roitzsch, J., Boyle, J., & Gelernter, J. (2007). The serotonin transporter genotype and social support and moderation of posttraumatic stress disorder and depression in hurricane-exposed adults. *American Journal of Psychiatry*, 164(11),1693–1699.

Kilpatrick, D. G., Resnick, H. S., Milanak, M. E., Miller, M. W., Keyes, K. M., & Friedman, M. J. (2013). National estimates of exposure to traumatic events and PTSD prevalence using *DSM-IV* and *DSM-5* criteria. *Journal of Traumatic Stress*, 26(5), 537–547.

Kilpatrick, D. G., Ruggiero, K. J., Acierno, R., Saunders, B. E., Resnick, H. S., & Best, C. L. (2003). Violence and risk of PTSD, major depression, substance abuse/dependence, and comorbidity: Results from the National Survey of Adolescents. *Journal of Consulting and Clinical Psychology*, 71(4), 692–700.

Kim-Goh, M., Suh, C., Blake, D. D., Hiley-Young, B. (1995). Psychological impact of the Los Angeles riots on Korean-American victims: Implications for treatment. *American Journal of Orthopsychiatry*, 65(1), 138–146.

Krieger, N. (2003). Genders, sexes, and health: What are the connections—and why does it matter? *International Journal of Epidemiolgoy*, 32, 652–657.

Kruger, D. J., Kodjebacheva, G. D., & Cupal, S. (2017). Poor tap water quality experiences and poor sleep quality during the Flint, Michigan Municipal Water Crisis. *Sleep Health*, 3(4), 241–243.

La Greca, A. M., Danzi, B. A., & Chan, S. F. (2017). DSM-5 and ICD-11 as competing models of PTSD in preadolescent children exposed to a natural disaster: Assessing validity and co-occurring symptomatology. *European Journal of Psychotraumatology*, 8(1), 1310591.

La Greca, A. M., Lai, B., Joormann, J., Auslander, B., & Short, M. (2013a). Children's risk and resilience following a natural disaster: Genetic vulnerability, posttraumatic stress, and depression. *Journal of Affective Disorders*, 151, 860–867.

La Greca, A. M., Lai, B. S., Llabre, M. M., Silverman, W. K., Vernberg, E. M., & Prinstein, M. J. (2013b). Children's postdisaster trajectories of PTS symptoms: Predicting chronic distress. *Child Youth Care Forum*, 42, 351–369.

La Greca, A. M., Silverman, W. K., Lai, B., & Jaccard, J. (2010). Hurricane-related exposure experiences and stressors, other life events, and social support: Concurrent and prospective impact on children's persistent posttraumatic stress symptoms. *Journal of Consulting and Clinical Psychology*, 78(6), 794–805.

La Greca, A. M., Silverman, W. K., Vernberg, E. M., & Prinstein, M. J. (1996). Symptoms of posttraumatic stress in children after Hurricane Andrew: A prospective study. *Journal of Consulting and Clinical Psychology*, 64(4), 712.

La Greca, A. M., Taylor, C. J., & Herge, W. M. (2012). Traumatic stress disorders in children and adolescents. In J. G. Beck & D. M. Sloan (Eds.), *The Oxford handbook of traumatic stress disorders* (pp. 98–118). New York, NY: Oxford University Press.

Lai, B. S., La Greca, A. M., Auslander, B. A., & Short, M. B. (2013). Children's symptoms of posttraumatic stress and depression after a natural disaster: Comorbidity and risk factors. *Journal of Affective Disorders*, 146(1), 71–78.

Lam, W. W. T., Bonanno, G. A., Mancini, A. D., Hol, S., Chan, M., Hung, W. K., Or, A., & Fielding, R. (2010). Trajectories of psychological distress among Chinese women diagnosed with breast cancer. *Psycho-Oncology*, 19(10), 1044–1051.

Landolt, M. A., Ystrøm, E., Sennhauser, F. H., Gnehm, H. E., & Vollrath, M. E. (2012). The mutual prospective influence of child and parental post-traumatic stress symptoms in pediatric patients. *Journal of Child Psychology and Psychiatry*, 53(7), 767–774.

Le Brocque, R. M., Hendrikz, J., Kenardy, J. A. (2010). The course of posttraumatic stress in children: Examination of recovery trajectories following traumatic injury. *Journal of Pediatric Psychology*, 35(6), 637–645.

Lenhart, A. (2015). Teens, social media and technology overview 2015. *Pew Research Center*. Retrieved from http://www.pewinternet.org/2015/04/09/teens-social-media-technology-2015/.

Littleton, H., Kumpula, M., & Orcutt, H. (2011). Posttraumatic symptoms following a campus shooting: The role of psycho-social resource loss. *Violence and Victims*, 26(4), 461–476.

Luthar, S., & Goldstein, A. (2004). Children's exposure to community violence: Implications for understanding risk and resilience. *Journal of Clinical Child and Adolescent Psychology*, 33(3), 499–505.

Maercker, A., Brewin, C. R., Bryant, R. A., Cloitre, M., Reed, G. M., van Ommeren, M., ... & Rousseau, C. (2013). Proposals for mental disorders specifically associated with stress in the International Classification of Diseases-11. *The Lancet*, 381(9878), 1683–1685.

Malmquist, C. P. (1986). Children who witness parental murder: Posttraumatic aspects. *Journal of the American Academy of Child & Adolescent Psychiatry*, 25(3), 320–325.

Marshall, G. N., Miles, J. N., & Stewart, S. H. (2010). Anxiety sensitivity and PTSD symptom severity are reciprocally related: Evidence from a longitudinal study of physical trauma survivors. *Journal of Abnormal Psychology*, 119(1), 143–150.

McKinnon, A., Meiser-Stedman, R., Watson, P., Dixon, C., Kassam-Adams, N., Ehlers, A., ... Dalgleish, T. (2016). The latent structure of Acute Stress Disorder symptoms in trauma-exposed children and adolescents. *Journal of Child Psychology and Psychiatry*, 57(11), 1308–1316.

McLaughlin, K. A., Koenen, K. C., Hill, E. D., Petukhova, M., Sampson, N. A., Zaslavsky, A. M., & Kessler, R. C. (2013). Trauma exposure and posttraumatic stress disorder in a national sample of adolescents. *Journal of the American Academy of Child and Adolescent Psychiatry*, 52(8), 815–830.

McLean, C. P., Morris, S. H., Conklin, P., Jayawickreme, N., & Foa, E. B. (2015). Trauma characteristics and posttraumatic stress disorder among adolescent survivors of childhood sexual abuse. *Journal of Family Violence*, 29(5), 559–566.

Meiser-Stedman, R., Dalgleish, T., Glucksman, E., Yule, W., & Smith, P. (2009). Maladaptive cognitive appraisals mediate the evolution of posttraumatic stress reactions: A 6-month follow-up of child and adolescent assault and motor vehicle accident survivors. *Journal of Abnormal Psychology*, *118*(4), 778–787.

Meiser-Stedman, R., Smith, P., Glucksman, E., & Dalgleish, T. (2017). Posttraumatic stress disorder in young children three years post-trauma: Prevalence and longitudinal predictors, *Journal of Clinical Psychiatry*, *78*(3), 334–339.

Meiser-Stedman, R., Smith, P., Glucksman, E., Yule, W., & Dalgleish, T. (2008). The posttraumatic stress disorder diagnosis in preschool- and elementary school-age children exposed to motor vehicle accidents. *The American Journal of Psychiatry*, *165*, 1326–1337.

Mgoqi-Mbalo, N., Zhang, M., & Ntuli, S. (2017). Risk factors for PTSD and depression in female survivors of rape. *Psychological Trauma: Theory, Research, Practice, and Policy*, *9*(3), 301–308.

Monson, C. M., Fredman, S. J., Dekel, R., & Macdonald, A. (2012). Family models of posttraumatic stress disorder. In J. G. Beck & D. M. Sloan (Eds.), *The Oxford handbook of traumatic stress disorders* (pp. 219–234). New York, NY: Oxford University Press.

Mortensen, J., Olesen Simonson, B., Eriksen, S. B., Skovby, P., Dall, R., & Elklit, A. (2015). Family-centered care and traumatic symptoms in parents of children admitted to PICU. *Scandinavian Journal of Caring Sciences*, *29*(3), 495–500.

Neria, Y., DiGrande, L., & Adams, B. G. (2011). Posttraumatic stress disorder following the September 11, 2001, terrorist attacks: A review of the literature among highly exposed populations. *The American Psychologist*, *66*(6), 429–446.

Neria, Y., Nandi, A., & Galea, S. (2008). Post-traumatic stress disorder following disasters: A systematic review. *Psychological Medicine*, *38*(4), 467–480.

Nickerson, A., Aderka, I. M., Bryant, R. A., & Hofmann, S. G. (2013). The role of attribution of trauma responsibility in posttraumatic stress disorder following motor vehicle accidents. *Depression and Anxiety*, *30*(5), 483–488.

Norman, R. E., Byambaa, M., De, R., Butchart, A., Scott, J., & Vos, T. (2012). The long-term health consequences of child physical abuse, emotional abuse, and neglect: A systematic review and meta-analysis. *PLoS Medicine*, *9*(11), e1001349.

Norris, F. H., Friedman, M. J., Watson, P. J., Byrne, C. M., Diaz, E., & Kaniasty, K. (2002). 60,000 disaster victims speak: Part I. An empirical review of the empirical literature, 1981–2001. *Psychiatry: Interpersonal and Biological Processes*, *65*(3), 207–239.

Norris, F. H., Galea, S., Friedman, M. J., & Watson, P. J. (2006). *Methods for disaster mental health research*. New York, NY: Guilford Press.

Norris, F. H., Kaniasty, K., Conrad, M. L., Inman, G. L., & Murphy, A. D. (2002). Placing age differences in cultural context: a comparison of the effects of age on PTSD after disasters in the United States, Mexico, and Poland. *Journal of Clinical Geropsychology*, *8*(3), 153–173.

Norris, F. H., Tracy, M., & Galea, S. (2009). Looking for resilience: understanding the longitudinal trajectories of responses to stress. *Social Science Medicine*, *68*, 2190–2198.

Ozer, E. J., Best, S. R., Lipsey, T. L., & Weiss, D. S. (2003). Predictors of posttraumatic stress disorder and symptoms in adults: A meta-analysis. *Psychological Bulletin*, *129*(1), 52–73.

Palinkas, L. A. (2012). A conceptual framework for understanding the mental health impacts of oil spills: lessons from the Exxon Valdez oil spill. *Psychiatry: Interpersonal & Biological Processes*, *75*(3), 203–222.

Palinkas, L. A., Petterson, J. S., Russell, J., & Downs, M. A. (1993). Community patterns of psychiatric disorders after the Exxon Valdez oil spill. *The American Journal of Psychiatry*, *150*(10), 1517.

Paolucci, E. O., Genuis, Mark. L., & Violato, C. (2001). A meta-analysis of the published research on the effects of child sexual abuse. *The Journal of Psychology*, *135*(1), 17–36.

Patel, J. K. (2018). After Sandy Hook, more than 400 people have been shot in over 200 school shootings. *The New York Times*. Retrieved from https://www.nytimes.com/interactive/2018/02/15/us/school-shootings-sandy-hook-parkland.html.

Pelcovitz, D., Kaplan, S., Goldenberg, B., Mandel, F., Lehane, J., & Guarrera, J. (1994). Posttraumatic stress disorder in physically abused adolescents. *Journal of the American Academy of Child and Adolescent Psychiatry*, *33*(3), 305–312.

Perreira, K. M., & Ornelas, I. (2013). Painful passages: Traumatic experiences and post-traumatic stress among U.S. immigrant Latino adolescents and their primary caregivers. *International Migration Review*, *47*(4), 976–1005.

Pew Research Institute. (2017a). *Social Media Fact Sheet*. Retrieved from http://www.pewinternet.org/fact-sheet/social-media/

Pew Research Institute (2017b). *Mobile Fact Sheet*. Retrieved from http://www.pewinternet.org/fact-sheet/mobile/

Pfefferbaum, B., Nixon, S. J., Tucker, P. M., Tivis, R. D., Moore, V. L., Gurwitch, R. H., Pynoos, R. S., Geis, H. K. (1999). Posttraumatic stress responses in bereaved children after the Oklahoma City bombing. *Journal of the American Academy of Child and Adolescent Psychiatry*, *38*(11), 1372–1379.

Pfefferbaum, B., Sconzo, G. M., Flynn, B. W., Kearns, L. J., Doughty, D. E., Gurwitch, R. H., ... Nawaz, S. (2003). Case finding and mental health services for children in the aftermath of the Oklahoma City bombing. *The Journal of Behavioral Health Services and Research*, *30*(2), 215–227.

Phipps, S., Larson, S., Long, A., & Rai, S. N. (2005). Adaptive style and symptoms of posttraumatic stress in children with cancer and their parents. *Journal of Pediatric Psychology*, *31*(3), 298–309.

Price, J., Kassam-Adams, N., Alderfer, M. A., Christofferson, J., & Kazak, A. E. (2016). Systematic review: A reevaluation and update of the integrative (trajectory) model of pediatric medical traumatic stress. *Journal of Pediatric Psychology*, *41*(1), 86–97.

Pynoos, R. S., Nader, K., Frederick, C., Gonda, L., & Stuber, M. (1987). Grief reactions in school age children following a sniper attack at school. *Israel Journal of Psychiatry and Related Sciences*, *24*(1–2), 53–63.

Resnick, H. S., Kilpatrick, D. G., Dansky, B. S., Saunders, B. E., & Best, C. L. (1993). Prevalence of civilian trauma and posttraumatic stress disorder in a representative national sample of women. *Journal of Consulting and Clinical Psychology*, *61*, 984–991.

Resnick, H. S., & Kilpatrick, D. G. (1994). Crime-related PTSD: Emphasis on adult general population samples. *PTSD Research Quarterly*, *5*(3), 1–3.

Richardson, L., Frueh, B., & Acierno, R. (2010). Prevalence estimates of combat-related post-traumatic stress disorder: Critical review. *Australian and New Zealand Journal of Psychiatry*, *44*(1), 4–19.

Roberts, A. L., Gilman, S. E., Breslau, J., Breslau, N., & Koenen, K. C. (2011). Race/ethnic differences in exposure to traumatic events, development of posttraumatic stress disorder, and treatment-seeking for post-traumatic stress disorder in the United States. *Psychological Medicine*, *41*(1), 71–83.

Rodin, G., Yuen, D., Mischitelle, A., Minden, M. D., Brandwein, J., ... Zimmermann, C. (2013). Traumatic stress in acute leukemia. *Psycho-Oncology*, *22*(2), 299–307.

Roitman, P., Gilad, M., Ankri, Y. L. E., & Shalev, A. Y. (2008). PTSD symptom clusters associated with physical health and health care utilization in rural primary care patients exposed to natural disaster. *Journal of Traumatic Stress, 21*(1), 75–82.

Rosenberg, L., Rosenberg, M., Robert, R., Richardson, L., Sharp, S., Holzer, C. E., Thomas, C. & Myer, W. J. (2015). Does acute stress disorder predict subsequent posttraumatic stress disorder in pediatric burn survivors? *Journal of Clinical Psychiatry, 76*(11), 1564–1568.

Roth, S., Newman, E., Pelcovitz, D., van der Kolk, B., & Mandel, F. S. (1997). Complex PTSD in victims exposed to sexual and physical abuse: Results from the DSM-IV field trial for posttraumatic stress disorder. *Journal of Traumatic Stress, 10*(4), 539–555.

Roy-Byrne, P. P., Davidson, K. W., Kessler, R. C., Asmundson, G. J. G., Goodwin, R. D., Kubzansky, L., . . . Stein, M. B. (2008). Anxiety disorders and comorbid medical illness. *General Hospital Psychiatry, 30*(3), 208–225.

Sachser, C., Keller, F., & Goldbeck, L. (2016). Complex PTSD as proposed for ICD-11: Validation of a new disorder in children and adolescents and their response to trauma-focused cognitive behavioral therapy. *Journal of Child Psychology and Psychiatry, 58*, 160–168. http://dx.doi.org/10.1111/jcpp.12640.

Save the Children. (2008). *Protecting children in a time of crisis*. Annual report, 2008. Retrieved from http://www.savethechildren.org/atf/cf/%7B9def2ebe-10ae-432c-9bd0-df91d2eba74a%7D/Final-Annual-Report-Complete-pdf-2-3-09-2.pdf

Scheeringa, M. S., Zeanah, C. H., & Cohen, J. A. (2011). PTSD in children and adolescents: Toward an empirically based algorithm. *Depression and Anxiety, 28*(9), 770–782.

Schlenger, W., & Silver, R. (2006). Web-based methods in terrorism and disaster research. *Journal of Traumatic Stress, 19*(2), 185–193.

Schmidt, M. S. (2014). F.B.I. confirms a sharp rise in mass shootings since 2000. *The New York Times*. Retrieved from https://www.nytimes.com/2014/09/25/us/25shooters.html?_r=0.

Schuster, M. A., Stein, B. D., Jaycox, L. H., Collins, R. L., Marshall, G. N., Elliott, M. N., . . . Berry, S. H. (2001). A national survey of stress reactions after the September 11, 2001 terrorist attacks. *New England Journal Medicine, 345*, 1507–1512.

Shultz, J. M., Cohen, A. M., Muschert, G. W., & Flores de Apodaca, R. (2013). Fatal school shootings and the epidemiological context of firearm mortality in the United States. *Disaster Health, 1*(2), 84–101.

Shultz, J. M., Thoresen, S., Flynn, B. W., Muschert, G. W., Shaw, J. A., Espinel, Z., . . . Cohen, A. M. (2014). Multiple vantage points on the mental health effects of mass shootings. *Current Psychiatry Reports, 16*(9), 469.

Silverman, W. K., & La Greca, A. M. (2002). Children experiencing disasters: Definitions, reactions, and predictors of outcomes. In A. M. La Greca, W. K. Silverman, E. M. Vernberg, & M. C. Roberts (Eds.), *Helping children cope with disasters and terrorism* (pp. 11–34). Washington, DC: American Psychological Association.

Slone, M., Lavi, I., Ozer, E. J., & Pollak, A. (2017). The Israeli-Palestinian conflict: Meta-analysis of exposure and outcome relations for children of the region. *Children and Youth Services Review, 74*, 50–61.

Soldatos, C. R., Paparrigopoulos, T. J., Pappa, D. A., & Christodoulou, G. N. (2006). Early post-traumatic stress disorder in relation to acute stress reaction: An ICD-10 study among help seekers following an earthquake. *Psychiatry Research, 143*(2), 245–253.

Stein, D. J., McLaughlin, K. A., Koenen, K. C., Atwoli, L., Friedman, M. J., Hill, E. D., . . . Kessler, R. C. (2014). DSM-5 and ICD-11 definitions of posttraumatic stress disorder: Investigating "narrow" and "broad" approaches. *Depression and Anxiety, 31*(6), 494–505.

Sullivan, T. N., Kung, E. M., & Farrell, A. D. (2004). Relation between witnessing violence and drug use initiation among rural adolescents: Parental monitoring and family support as protective factors. *Journal of Clinical Child and Adolescent Psychology, 33*(3), 488–498.

Terry, K. L., & Freilich, J. D. (2012). Understanding child sexual abuse by Catholic priests from a situational perspective. *Journal of Child Sexual Abuse, 21*, 437–455.

Thabet, A. A., Abed, Y., & Vostanis, P. (2004). Comorbidity of PTSD and depression among refugee children during war conflict. *Journal of Child Psychology and Psychiatry, 45*(3), 533–542.

Tiihonen Möller, A., Bäckström, T., Söndergaard, H. P., & Helström, L. (2014). Identifying risk factors for PTSD in women seeking medical help after rape. *PLoS One, 9*(10), e111136.

Tucker, P., Pfefferbaum, B., Nixon, S., & Dickson, W. (2000). Predictors of post-traumatic stress symptoms in Oklahoma City: Exposure, social support, peri-traumatic response. *Journal of Behavioral Health Services and Research, 27*, 406–416.

Uddin, M., Amstadter, A.B., Nugent, N. R., & Koenen, K. C. (2012). Genetics and genomics of posttraumatic stress disorder. In J. G. Beck & D. M. Sloan (Eds.), *The Oxford handbook of traumatic stress disorders* (pp. 143–158). New York, NY: Oxford University Press.

United Nations Office for Disaster Risk Reduction. (2014). *Annual Report, 2014*. Retrieved from http://www.unisdr.org/files/42667_unisdrannualreport2014.pdf

United Nations Office for Disaster Risk Reduction. (2017). Disaster statistics. Retrieved on July 28, 2017 from: https://www.unisdrorg/we/inform/disaster-statistics.

US Census (2010). US Census 2010 statistics. Retrieved from https://www.census.gov/2010census/

Voigt, V., Neufeld, F., Kaste, J., Bühner, M., Sckopke, P., Wuerstlein, R., . . . Hermelink, K. (2017). Clinically assessed posttraumatic stress in patients with breast cancer during the first year after diagnosis in the prospective, longitudinal, controlled COGNICARES study. *Psycho-Oncology, 26*(1), 74–80.

Vernberg, E. M., La Greca, A. M., Silverman, W. K., & Prinstein, M. J. (1996). Prediction of posttraumatic stress symptoms in children after Hurricane Andrew. *Journal of Abnormal Psychology, 105*(2), 237.

Vrana, S., & Lauterbach, D. (1994), Prevalence of traumatic events and post-traumatic psychological symptoms in a nonclinical sample of college students. *Journal of Traumatic Stress, 7*, 289–302.

Wang, L., Zhang, Y., Shi, Z., & Wang, W. (2009). Symptoms of posttraumatic stress disorder among adult survivors two months after the Wenchuan Earthquake. *Psychological Reports, 105*(3), 879–885.

Warsini, S., West, C., Ed, G. D., Res Meth, G. C., Mills, J., & Usher, K. (2014). The psychosocial impact of natural disasters among adult survivors: An integrative review. *Issues in Mental Health Nursing, 35*(6), 420–436.

Weems, C. F., Taylor, L. K., Cannon, M. F., Marino, R. C., Romano, D. M.,...Triplett, V. (2010). Posttraumatic stress, context, and the lingering effects of the Hurricane Katrina disaster among ethnic minority youth. *Journal of Abnormal Child Psychology, 38*, 49–56.

Wilson, L. C. (2015). A systematic review of probable posttraumatic stress disorder in first responders following man-made mass violence. *Psychiatry Research, 229*(1), 21–26.

Wojcik, B. E., Akhtar, F. Z., & Hassell, H. L. (2009). Hospital admissions related to mental disorders in U.S. Army soldiers in Iraq and Afghanistan. *Military Medicine, 174*, 1010–1018.

World Health Organization. (2017). ICD-11 Beta draft. Retrieved from http://apps.who.int/classifications/icd11/browse/l-m/en

Xue, C., Ge, Y., Tang, B., Liu, Y., Kang, P., Wang, M., & Zhang, L. (2015). A meta-analysis of risk factors for combat related PTSD among military personnel and veterans. *PLoS ONE, 10*(3), 1–21.

Yaşan, A., Güzel, A., Tamam, Y., & Ozkan, M. (2009). Predictive factors for acute stress disorder and posttraumatic stress disorder after motor vehicle accidents. *Psychopathology, 42*(4), 236–241.

Yehuda, R., Pratchett, L., & Pelcovitz, M. (2012). Biological contributions to PTSD: Differentiating normative from pathological response. In J. G. Beck & D. M. Sloan (Eds.), *The Oxford handbook of traumatic stress disorders* (pp. 159–174). New York, NY: Oxford University Press.

Yelland, C., Robinson, P., La Greca, A. M., Lock, C., Kokegei, B, Ridgway, V. & Lai, B. (2010). Bushfire impact on youth. *Journal of Traumatic Stress, 23*, 274–277.

Yeung, N. C., Lau, J. T., Xiaonan Yu, N., Zhang, J., Xu, Z., Chow Choi, K.,...Yeung, C. (2016). Media exposure related to the 2008 Sichuan earthquake predicted probable PTSD among Chinese adolescents in Kunming, China: A longitudinal study. *Psychological Trauma: Theory, Research, Practice, and Policy.* https://doi.org/10.1037/tra0000121

Zhou, P., Zhang, Y., Wei, C., Liu, Z. & Hannak, W. (2016). Acute stress disorder as a predictor of posttraumatic stress: A longitudinal study of Chinese children exposed to the Lushan earthquake. *Psychology Journal, 5*(3), 206–214.

The Developmental Psychopathology of Stress Exposure in Childhood

Jenalee R. Doom *and* Dante Cicchetti

Abstract

This chapter reviews how the field of developmental psychopathology has shaped research on risk and resilience processes in the context of childhood stress. The central tenets of developmental psychopathology, including its transdisciplinary and multilevel nature, equifinality and multifinality, developmental cascades, and the interaction of risk and protective factors across development, guide research aiming to understand individual differences in response to stressors during childhood. Various stressors that children experience, including maltreatment, poverty, institutional care, malnutrition, and environmental exposures, can lead to different effects on biology and behavior depending on the type, timing, chronicity, and severity of the stressor. Genetics, psychobiology, and neurophysiology have been incorporated into this research to enhance our understanding of individual differences in functioning following childhood stress. Future directions include more fully incorporating sex differences into studies of childhood stress and utilizing research in this area to create effective interventions for children experiencing severe stress.

Keywords: developmental psychopathology, stress, childhood, resilience, genetics, psychobiology, transdisciplinary, multilevel, individual differences

Chronic, severe stress in childhood is associated with greater risk of cognitive, emotional, behavioral, and health problems, and an increased risk of psychopathology throughout the life span (Lupien, McEwen, Gunnar, & Heim, 2009; Shonkoff, Boyce, & McEwen, 2009); see December 2017 special issue of *Development and Psychopathology* entitled "Biological and Behavioral Effects of Early Adversity on Multiple Levels of Development"). However, there are significant individual differences in outcomes following chronic stress. Some individuals start on trajectories toward emotional or behavior problems while some do remarkably well despite a harsh early environment (Masten & Cicchetti, 2016). Researchers have made a great deal of progress in the past few decades documenting how stress affects development, understanding the mechanisms by which stress affects development, and describing factors that foster resilience in the face of stress.

This progress has largely been guided within the framework of developmental psychopathology. Despite this progress, there are many remaining questions that we need to answer in order to fully understand processes of risk and resilience (Masten & Cicchetti, 2016).

This chapter is not a comprehensive review of research on the effects of stress on development and risk for psychopathology. However, we will provide an overview of the developmental psychopathology framework and major research areas addressing childhood stress exposure that have been guided by the framework. First, we will briefly review the tenets of developmental psychopathology and a few theories and models that have informed or been informed by developmental psychopathology. Then, we will outline different types of childhood stress that have profound impacts on development, viewed from a developmental psychopathology perspective. The influence of genetics in relation to childhood stress will then be discussed. The timing and chronicity of early stress will be considered in relation to the specific effects of these stressors, as well as the concept of resilience in the context of stress. Finally, we will consider sex differences in response to childhood stress and focus on unanswered questions and important future directions for research in order to improve the lives of children, adolescents, and adults who have experienced early stress.

Tenets of Developmental Psychopathology

The developmental psychopathology framework guides research and intervention work that aims to elucidate the developmental mechanisms that underlie normal and abnormal development to prevent and treat psychopathology (Cicchetti, 2016a, 2016b, 2016c, 2016d). This framework sets forth main tenets that guide the field, including the transdisciplinary and multilevel nature of developmental psychopathology, equifinality and multifinality, cascading effects across development, the interaction of risk and protective factors, and the consideration of context in determining adaptation versus maladaptation.

First, developmental psychopathology is inherently transdisciplinary. It is impossible to fully understand an individual's functioning and developmental trajectory by an analysis from one discipline. Psychology alone is not equipped to answer questions about changes in molecular biology that may affect current and future functioning; likewise, molecular biologists cannot assess current psychosocial functioning and pathways to adaptive or maladaptive psychological functioning solely through analysis at the micro level. However, contributions of these and other disciplines are needed to assemble the pieces of the puzzle that is human development. As individual disciplines accumulate more knowledge about normal and abnormal development, the field has grown increasingly interdisciplinary and collaborative in nature in order to create models that more accurately characterize pathways from early stress to later functioning. Likewise, interdisciplinary work informs prevention and intervention efforts by broadly and deeply assessing individual functioning and considering the multitude of individual and environmental factors that may influence intervention effectiveness.

Developmental psychopathology broadly transcends a multitude of disciplines while also approaching development from multiple levels. The multilevel nature of developmental psychopathology is particularly important for addressing how early stress affects development because effects can occur on multiple levels, including, but not limited to, genetics/epigenetics, stress physiology, immune functioning, neural activity, cognition, emotion, behavior, social networks (e.g., family, peers, teachers), community, culture, and even at national and international levels in the form of public and global policy. An important aspect of the multilevel nature of developmental psychopathology is the recognition that bidirectional and transactional processes occur between each of these different levels (Cicchetti & Dawson, 2002), such that social networks can influence neural activity and emotion just as neural activity and emotion can influence our social behavior and networks. Functioning at each of these levels does not operate in isolation, and it is vital to recognize how operations at each of these levels may be interacting at different points in time and development to shape observable phenotypes.

Another important consideration in the developmental psychopathology framework is the heterogeneity in developmental outcomes despite similar early experiences. For example, two children may have similar maltreatment experiences during early childhood, yet one of them is struggling with psychopathology as an adult while one is adapting well despite his or her early experience. These vastly different adult phenotypes resulting from the same early experience are examples of multifinality, with different pathways leading to different end states despite a shared initial early state (Cicchetti & Rogosch, 1996). On the other hand, two adults with vastly different childhood circumstances might both develop depression, although their developmental pathways to the disorder are dissimilar. This is an example of equifinality, the concept that different initial states and processes can lead to the same end state (Cicchetti & Rogosch, 1996). Multifinality and equifinality are particularly important to consider when creating and delivering interventions for those who are suffering adverse consequences following the experience of childhood stress, as children who have experienced maltreatment can respond to the stressor or an intervention in distinct ways that will likely have implications for their risk for future psychopathology. Likewise, pathways to outcomes such as depression and behavior problems are diverse, and as a result, prevention and intervention efforts may be more effective if these diverse pathways are taken into account.

The developmental psychopathology framework is helpful for understanding phenomena such as developmental cascades, which refer to effects that spread across multiple levels (micro to macro), across multiple domains (e.g., peer vs. family functioning), or across systems (e.g., within an individual, in a family system, in a community; Masten & Cicchetti, 2010). An example of a developmental cascade that has been widely replicated is the cascade from early conduct problems to later internalizing and externalizing problems, health risk, and poorer school performance (Herrenkohl et al., 2010; Masten et al., 2005). Thus, problems in one domain can cascade to multiple domains, suggesting that an early risk factor may initially influence a single domain but alters the course of development more broadly over time. Developmental cascades may explain why early problems following childhood stress can cascade to problems at multiple levels and across domains in adolescence and adulthood. Cascading effects can be direct or indirect through a number of pathways, and they may be either adaptive or maladaptive. However, it is important to note that cascades are not deterministic; not all early problems spread to other domains, and there is great variability between individuals in the characteristics of cascades. Developmental cascades are particularly important for creating interventions, as well-timed interventions directed at specific targets may halt maladaptive cascades or promote adaptive cascades (Masten & Cicchetti, 2010). Interventions that attempt to disrupt maladaptive cascades are central to developmental psychopathology, as interventions that change mediators between a stressor and a negative outcome and successfully disrupt a pathway to the negative outcome inform our understanding of developmental processes. For example, toddler–parent psychotherapy has been shown to reorganize attachment between mothers with depression and their toddlers (Toth, Rogosch, Manly, & Cicchetti, 2006), which could disrupt known developmental cascades between attachment insecurity and internalizing and externalizing problems (Fearon, Bakermans-Kranenburg, Van IJzendoorn, Lapsley, & Roisman, 2010; Groh, Roisman, van IJzendoorn, Bakermans-Kranenburg, & Fearon, 2012).

The study of developmental psychopathology is enhanced by examining normal and abnormal development together. Conceptualizing psychopathology as a developmental deviation allows us to both outline the principles of normal development and to understand where normative processes can go awry (Sroufe, 1990). Certainly, in the context of stress exposure in childhood, these early processes that lead certain individuals to proceed in an adaptive manner versus deviating to developing psychopathology are vitally important. Abnormal developmental processes during stages of rapid neurodevelopment shed a light on how normal development should proceed during early sensitive periods and what processes are absolutely necessary for normal development. Likewise, investigations of both risk and resilience must be studied together, because it is likely that certain processes that increase risk for certain disorders are occurring at the same time as processes that are protective. In addition, identifying risk factors may help us to determine protective factors, and vice versa. For example, the knowledge that unpredictability in the early environment is a risk factor for later psychopathology points researchers to investigate whether early environmental stability serves as a protective factor that may be incorporated into interventions (Doom, VanZomeren-Dohm, & Simpson, 2016; Simpson, Griskevicius, Kuo, Sung, & Collins, 2012).

It is necessary to consider the complexity of development because individuals are rarely faced with only risk or protective factors. Indeed, there is an ongoing interplay between risk and protective factors in each individual that can change the probability of adaptation versus maladaptation in individual domains following early stress. Genetic, physiological, social, environmental, nutritional, and cultural processes, among others, may interact with each other over time to push the system toward maladaptation or adaptation. For example, an individual may have a genetic propensity toward schizophrenia and have grown up in poverty, which would confer risk for the onset of schizophrenia, yet also have a supportive social network and stable employment, which serve as protective factors. No individual factor determines whether this individual will develop schizophrenia, but these factors are likely to interact with each other and other contextual factors over time to shape his or her risk for psychopathology. Thus, the complexity of understanding multiple risk and resilience pathways is a central theme of the developmental psychopathology perspective.

Importantly, developmental psychopathology is sensitive to context, with the recognition that what is adaptive in one context may be maladaptive in another. For example, childhood stress has been associated with perturbations in threat-related attention biases (Pine et al., 2005). Altered attention to threat has been associated with anxiety symptoms and disorders and is thus maladaptive (Mogg & Bradley, 1998), particularly if one lives in a low-threat context. However, changes in vigilance in a highly threatening environment might be adaptive, particularly if vigilance is increased, as the ability to detect threats may allow one to act quickly in a way that could preserve one's life or safety. Thus, it is essential to consider adaptations to early stress relative to the current context, as intervening to change a behavior that is adaptive for the current context may lead to negative outcomes for the individuals. An understanding of the immediate social and structural environment, culture, and global environment may be important for creating interventions that promote adaptive behaviors within specific contexts.

Central to developmental psychopathology is the principle of developmental plasticity, which is the ability of the brain and other physiological systems to reorganize and adapt to ongoing experiences throughout the life course. Plasticity is essential to adapt to current environments and to prepare for future environments. According to evolutionary theories, current experiences change functioning on multiple levels, which guides the path of development to expect a future environment that is similar to the current or past environment. Thus, any changes made to adapt to the environment are theoretically beneficial as long as the future environment matches the current or past environment. However, development may become abnormal if these processes go awry. Plasticity is necessary in order to shape development by responding to ongoing experiences and challenges. Neural plasticity from the molecular to the systemic level is essential for normal development and also contributes to aberrations in development (Cicchetti & Walker, 2003; Cowell, Cicchetti, Rogosch, & Toth, 2015; Van Praag, Kempermann, & Gage, 2000). Biological factors impact psychosocial processes, just as psychosocial experiences affect gene expression and subsequent brain development and functioning (Cicchetti & Tucker, 1994; Kandel, 1998; Kolb & Whishaw, 1998). Importantly, neural plasticity does not remain stable throughout the life span, as experiences that occur during rapid periods of neurodevelopment are more likely to have lasting effects on functioning (Knudsen, 2004). The prenatal and early postnatal years in humans are associated with the greatest neuroplasticity, and thus, stressful experiences that occur early in life are thought to be particularly important for shaping neurodevelopment (Shonkoff et al., 2012; Teicher et al., 2003).

Theories and Models Informing the Role of Stress in Developmental Psychopathology

To describe research on how childhood stress shapes later adaptation, it is important to highlight a few theories and models that have guided research in the field or have utilized the developmental psychopathology framework. Thus, we will briefly discuss the organizational-developmental perspective, developmental systems theory, the allostatic load model, and the adaptive calibration model in relation to developmental psychopathology.

The organizational perspective of development argues that developmental outcomes are shaped by interactions between biological, genetic, psychological, and sociological variables within specific environmental contexts (Cicchetti & Schneider-Rosen, 1986; Egeland, Carlson, & Sroufe, 1993; Sroufe, 1979). Any of these variables may serve as risk or protective factors, and these variables interact in transactional processes over time. The individual is an active participant in development, whereby his or her feelings, expectations, and attitudes guide interpretations of new experiences, such as a stressful event, and organize future behavior based on these interpretations. Patterns of behavior are not static in the context of stress and may change over time. Thus, competence at one particular time point does not ensure later competence, but rather prepares an individual for competence in the next developmental stage. Severe stressors during childhood can negatively influence competence, which may or may not impact competence at later developmental stages depending on risk and resilience processes unfolding over time. The organizational perspective is essential for informing developmental psychopathology's focus on multiple levels of functioning across development and understanding how risk and protective factors interact over time.

Developmental systems theory examines how individuals carry out transactions with their environments and how these transactions affect biology, genetics, behavior, and the environment of the individual across development (Ford & Lerner, 1992). Thus, development is the result of many interacting systems that must be understood within one's ecological context, or as a dynamic cascade of many of these transactional processes happening over time (Cox, Mills-Koonce, Propper, & Gariépy, 2010). Over time, these processes lead to behavior patterns through self-organization that emerges from the interactions of these systems. Developmental systems theory informs developmental psychopathology through delineating the transactional nature of multilevel interactions between the individual, biology, and the environment across time.

The allostatic load model (McEwen, 1998; McEwen & Seeman, 1999) revolves around the concept of allostasis, which refers to an organism maintaining stability by constantly adapting to changes in the environment. Allostatic load refers to wear and tear on the body due to repeated cycles of allostasis, particularly if biological systems have difficulty with efficient activation or cessation following environmental challenges (McEwen & Seeman, 1999). For example, repeated activation of cardiovascular, neuroendocrine, immune, or metabolic systems in response to challenge may lead to damage resulting from these mediators that have negative implications for mental and physical health (Juster, McEwen, & Lupien, 2010). The allostatic load model takes into account perceived stress, physiological and behavioral responses to stress, and individual differences in responses, which are important determinants of allostasis and allostatic load (McEwen & Seeman, 1999). The allostatic load model is informative for considering how adaptations made in response to stress could lead to negative consequences for multiple biological systems and behavior.

The adaptive calibration model is an evolutionary-developmental theory on the origin of individuals differences in stress response systems (Del Giudice, Ellis, & Shirtcliff, 2011), which is an extension of the biological sensitivity to context theory (Boyce & Ellis, 2005). Unlike the allostatic load model, the adaptive calibration model frames adaptations to the environment as part of an organism's life history strategy, which biologically organizes one's developmental trajectory and how resources are allocated in order to improve evolutionary fitness via activities such as mating and parenting. The adaptive calibration model also argues that there are differences in sensitivity to the environment and experiences that can lead to individual differences in responses to certain environments. For example, an individual who is more biologically sensitive to the environment may gain greater benefits from a positive environment and suffer greater harm from a negative environment than someone who is less biologically sensitive to the environment. Across the life span, information about the environment is encoded in order to feed back onto the stress system's calibration. The evolutionary nature of this theory is particularly apparent when arguing that organisms have evolved to be able to modify their developmental trajectory to match the current environment in order to

enhance the chances of successful adaptation. This model is important for developmental psychopathology in understanding multilevel effects of childhood stress across development while also providing a framework for understanding possible reasons behind the phenomena of multifinality and equifinality.

Types of Stress Exposure Within the Developmental Psychopathology Framework

Childhood stress is often broadly construed, ranging from social stressors such as maltreatment or harsh parenting, to environmental stressors like living in poverty or a dangerous neighborhood, to physical stressors such as poor nutrition, health problems, or toxin exposure. These stressors may be acute, such as the death of a parent, or chronic, such as living in an institution or foster care for long periods of time. In addition, stressors can range from mild to toxic in severity, with the toxic stressors associated with the highest risk for mental and physical health problems across development, even though there is variability in which stressors may be toxic for certain individuals (Shonkoff et al., 2012). Measuring and conceptualizing childhood stress for the purposes of integrating it in research and interventions poses several challenges. First, young children may not always be reliable reporters of stressful experiences, and children may not be aware of family-level stressors that nevertheless impact the child through changes in caregiving or in the environment. Retrospective reporting of childhood stress is also subject to problems with accurate recall (Hardt & Rutter, 2004; Maughan & Rutter, 1997). Second, there is a long-standing debate regarding whether to measure objective stressors or one's subjective response to the stressor. Third, some researchers argue that it is best to measure stress as a composite of all negative experiences in childhood, while others argue that specific stressors may have unique effects on development and should be studied separately. Similarly, there is a problem with nonindependence of stressors, meaning that individuals who experience a stressor like poverty will be more likely to experience other types of stressors, like malnutrition, maltreatment, and neighborhood violence. Thus, it is challenging to identify unique effects of specific stressors. Although we will not resolve these issues in this chapter, we believe it is important to remember these points while considering the effects of different stressful experiences in childhood on development. We now review a nonexhaustive list of childhood stressors that have been examined through a developmental psychopathology lens and discuss how these stressors heighten risk for maladaptive development.

Maltreatment

A large body of literature has documented the impacts of child maltreatment, such as neglect, emotional abuse, physical abuse, and/or sexual abuse, on neurobiological, socioemotional, cognitive, and behavioral functioning across the life span (Cicchetti & Valentino, 2006). Extensive research shows that child maltreatment increases the likelihood of disruptions in developmental processes and downward effects on multiple levels of functioning, including neurobiology, cognition, emotion, behavior, and social functioning (Cicchetti & Toth, 1995; De Bellis, 2001; Masten & Cicchetti, 2010). Specifically, alterations in physiological responsiveness, emotion understanding, attachment, social information processing, academic achievement, peer and romantic relationships, attention, and neural processes have been related to the experience of child maltreatment (Cicchetti & Valentino, 2006; De Bellis, 2001). These alterations place children who have experienced maltreatment at significant risk for problems such as substance abuse and psychopathology throughout the life span (Cicchetti & Valentino, 2006). Adding to the stress of maltreatment, children who have been maltreated are more often from homes characterized by low socioeconomic status (Sedlak et al., 2010), and they have therefore typically been exposed to stressors associated with poverty in addition to maltreatment.

However, not every child who has been maltreated is doomed to a future of psychopathology or poor functioning on multiple levels. Many maltreated children do remarkably well despite this traumatic early experience, and researchers have focused on these children to understand what factors promote positive adaptation, or resilience, following maltreatment (Cicchetti, 2013; Masten, 2001). Resilience is an ongoing process influenced by multiple individual, social, environmental, and cultural factors, so adaptations made in several domains can be adaptive at one time point and maladaptive later, or vice versa. Overall, there is evidence that ego resiliency, positive self-esteem, active coping, quality friendships, and a consistent supportive relationship with at least one adult are protective factors related to a higher likelihood of adaptive functioning (Cicchetti, 2013). Genetic, neurobiological, and physiological factors also play a role in resilience processes (Cicchetti, 2013). We can use these in-

sights to create interventions that promote resilient functioning in children who have experienced maltreatment.

Institutional Deprivation

A significant literature on neglect focuses on children's experience of early social deprivation due to institutional (e.g., orphanage) care. Though the quality of institutional settings varies widely, these are typically marked by some degree of social and stimulus deprivation for infants and children. This involves fewer social interactions with caregivers, instability of caregivers, and less quality interaction with the environment. Children who have experienced significant periods of institutional care, even after placement in stable families, show aberrant interpersonal behavior, including indiscriminate friendliness and a higher likelihood for insecure attachment (Bruce, Tarullo, & Gunnar, 2009; Chisholm, 1998), and they are more likely to have emotional difficulties and internalizing and externalizing problems (Colvert et al., 2008; Zeanah et al., 2009). Recent research suggests that early alterations in cognitive control and visual attentional biases may cascade to predict later psychiatric symptoms (Troller-Renfree, Zeanah, Nelson, & Fox, 2017). In addition, early alterations in emotion recognition may precede psychiatric problems as well (Fries & Pollak, 2004). Overall, for many domains, the longer the child spends in institutional care, the more severe the alterations in functioning tend to be, but there is typically a great deal of recovery for children who are adopted out of these environments into homes with stable, supportive caregivers (Doom & Gunnar, 2016).

Harsh Parenting

Harsh parenting, or care that is aversive to the child but less so than maltreatment, refers to a punitive parenting style characterized by spanking, being overly negative, and threatening or yelling at the child. Harsh parenting has been associated with increased risk for behavior problems that can have lasting effects on multiple domains, particularly child aggression (L. Chang, Schwartz, Dodge, & McBride-Chang, 2003). One study demonstrated that child emotion regulation mediates the association between harsh parenting and child aggression, indicating potential emotional and cognitive effects that are more proximal in timing to the exposure to harsh parenting (L. Chang et al., 2003). Interestingly, harsh parenting from mothers was more associated with impaired child emotion regulation, whereas harsh parenting from fathers was more strongly associated with child aggression, suggesting that the impact of harsh parenting differs depending on the parent (L. Chang et al., 2003).

Poverty

Children growing up in poverty have higher rates of anxiety and attention problems, depression, and conduct disorders (Hackman, Farah, & Meaney, 2010). These children are more likely to have subclinical levels of internalizing and externalizing problems, lower intelligence, and poorer academic achievement, with a greater duration of poverty linked to greater risk for negative outcomes (Hackman et al., 2010). Of course, poverty is complex. It does not solely indicate low education or income, but it can also encompass a wide range of stressors that are more commonly experienced by children living in poverty, including household stress and chaos, neighborhood violence, parental psychopathology, disruptions in parenting and relationships, fewer community supports, poor nutrition, and environmental contaminants, among others (Evans & English, 2002). It is difficult to empirically determine what aspects of poverty provide the greatest risk to children, but it is likely that many of these poverty-associated factors interact over time to influence risk and resilience processes.

Research on the effects of child poverty on lifespan development and the positive effects of early intervention have repeatedly stated that investments in high-quality interventions early in life have the greatest impact on lifetime outcomes and the highest return on investment (Heckman, 2006). Thus, any interventions to reduce poverty or the effects of poverty on development will be the most effective during sensitive early periods of development in order to promote positive developmental cascades of outcomes across multiple levels.

Family and Community Violence

Witnessing violence in the home can have a profound effect on children's socioemotional development, behavior, and risk for psychopathology. A meta-analysis indicated that exposure to domestic violence was associated with greater child emotional and behavioral problems; witnessing domestic violence increased problems in children who had suffered abuse themselves (Wolfe, Crooks, Lee, McIntyre-Smith, & Jaffe, 2003). A separate meta-analysis indicated that being exposed to multiple forms of violence was more highly associated with behavior problems in childhood than one form of violence and that risk was similar for those who

witnessed interparental violence and those who were victims of violence themselves (Sternberg, Baradaran, Abbott, Lamb, & Guterman, 2006).

Witnessing violence in the neighborhood or community also increases risk for psychopathology. Children witnessing violence in the community or seeing a gun or drugs at home report higher levels of distress (Martinez & Richters, 1993), and youth who witness community violence have higher rates of posttraumatic stress disorder (PTSD), depression, aggression, and externalizing behaviors (Buka, Stichick, Birdthistle, & Earls, 2001). African American and Latino boys living in disadvantaged neighborhoods who were exposed to community violence experienced greater increases in aggression over 1 year (Gorman–Smith & Tolan, 1998). Positive family functioning—even in the context of high levels of community violence—has been shown to be a protective factor against youth perpetrating violence (Gorman-Smith, Henry, & Tolan, 2004).

Natural and Humanmade Disasters

Children who have experienced the trauma of a disaster, such as hurricanes, tsunamis, earthquakes, and large fires, are at an increased risk for developing posttraumatic stress disorder (PTSD), depression, anxiety disorders, and other types of acute stress reactions and adjustment problems (Kar, 2009). Children may be less equipped to cope with the stress of a disaster than adults, which could partially explain children's increased vulnerability to psychopathology and other impairments post disaster (Goldmann & Galea, 2014). It is difficult to predict children's responses to disasters, but on average, risk for adjustment problems rises with the frequency, number, or intensity of exposure (Masten & Narayan, 2012). However, there is a great deal of variation, with some individuals showing positive adaptation, or resilience, in response to a disaster while others show greater maladaptation than would be expected given their exposure, indicating vulnerability (Masten & Narayan, 2012). Most effects of disaster exposure are short term, although these can have lasting effects. Children who experience the loss or injury of a loved one typically have greater negative effects than those who only sustained material losses (Masten & Narayan, 2012). Of course, protective factors moderate outcomes following disasters. One of the most consistent findings in the disaster literature is the buffering effect of being close in proximity to parents and other attachment figures when disaster strikes (Masten & Narayan, 2012). Other protective factors include self-efficacy, self-regulation, belief that there is meaning in life, religious beliefs, intelligence, and community supports (Masten, 2001; Masten & Narayan, 2012). Developmental cascades of positive or negative adaptation should be tracked following the onset of a disaster, with attention to the multiple levels of functioning that can be affected by an acute stressor.

Chaos and Unpredictability

In addition to major negative life events, there has been increased focus on the role that chronic unpredictability plays in shaping neurodevelopment and lifetime risk for psychiatric disorders. Forms of chaos examined in the field include a lack of structure and routine, background noise and crowding, frequent moves and substandard housing, and a frenetic pace of life (Evans, Gonnella, Marcynyszyn, Gentile, & Salpekar, 2005). Chaos is more common in low-income families, and there is evidence that chaos mediates at least some of the association between poverty and disruptions in socioemotional development (Evans et al., 2005). Studies of unpredictability and chaos in childhood have demonstrated that in households with higher levels of chaos, children are more likely to have problems behaviors, particularly combined with low-quality parenting (Coldwell, Pike, & Dunn, 2006). Further, another group found that household chaos during the first years of life predicted greater child conduct problems and callous-unemotional behaviors, mediated by parenting behavior (Mills-Koonce et al., 2016). Early unpredictability has even shown associations with adolescent and adult outcomes. For example, greater unpredictability (e.g., changes in residence, cohabitation, and parental occupation) before 5 years has been associated with greater externalizing behaviors and substance use in adolescence, and greater externalizing/criminal behaviors and more sexual partners in adulthood (Doom et al., 2016; Simpson et al., 2012). However, later unpredictability (between 6–16 years) was not as powerful a predictor of these later behaviors as early unpredictability, indicating a possible sensitive period for the experience of unpredictability (Doom et al., 2016; Simpson et al., 2012). Early unpredictability and chaos may interfere with the child's belief that he or she is an effective agent with control over the environment, alter the development of self-regulation, and lead to interruptions while the child is engaging with his or her environment (Evans et al., 2005). Disruptions in these processes may not be advantageous for shaping adaptive functioning in more stable environments, but they may set up neural systems that are more able to function in chaotic future environments.

Racial Discrimination

There are many forms of discrimination that may have negative psychological consequences; we will focus on the racial discrimination literature. Experiences of racial discrimination have repeatedly been associated with poorer mental health in children (Priest et al., 2013). Racial discrimination may impact children directly or indirectly, such as through a caregiver's experience that increases stress on that individual, which then affects his or her health or behavior. One study of African American families demonstrated that mothers with greater perceptions of racial discrimination experienced a stronger cascade from poorer maternal psychological functioning to negative parenting behaviors (Murry, Brown, Brody, Cutrona, & Simons, 2001). Thus, racial discrimination likely impacts children even without their direct or conscious experience of it.

Racial discrimination may be even more distressing for individuals who experience immigration-related stress, which has further implications for family stability and safety. Future research is needed to better measure perceived discrimination in younger children and to conduct these studies across more racial/ethnic groups (Pachter & Garcia Coll, 2009). Interventions that aim to reduce racial discrimination or the impact of racial discrimination on health should be sensitive to culture and context in order to achieve the best outcomes for minority youth (Spencer, Noll, Stoltzfus, & Harpalani, 2001).

Nutritional Deficiencies

Stressors not often considered in the stress and developmental psychopathology literatures are macronutrient and micronutrient deficiencies, which is unfortunate because psychosocial stressors can interfere with nutrient absorption and trafficking (Monk, Georgieff, & Osterholm, 2013), leading to nutritional deficiencies. Thus, a nutritional deficiency may be an extra "hit" to development in the context of psychosocial or environmental stress or a potential mediating pathway by which stress influences development. Low energy intake and macronutrient deficiencies, such as low protein or fat intake, in childhood have been associated with altered brain development. Linear growth stunting, low weight-for-height in young children, and signs of macronutrient deficiencies have been related to less play and positive affect, and also to a lower likelihood of secure attachment compared to typically growing children (Gardner, Walker, Powell, & Grantham-McGregor, 2003; Graves, 1978). These early issues can lead to conduct and attention problems and poorer quality relationships (S. Chang, Walker, Grantham-McGregor, & Powell, 2002; Galler & Ramsey, 1989; Richardson, Birch, Grabie, & Yoder, 1972). Childhood growth stunting has also been associated with greater depression and anxiety symptoms, lower self-esteem, and increased hyperactivity (Walker, Chang, Powell, Simonoff, & Grantham-McGregor, 2007).

Childhood micronutrient deficiencies have also been associated with alterations in neurodevelopment. For example, iron deficiency during infancy has been associated with poorer cognitive functioning, emotional difficulties, and behavior problems, with some impairments from this early deficiency apparent into adulthood (Lozoff et al., 2006). Recent work on iron deficiency has examined developmental cascades and pathways from early nutrition to later functioning. Adults who experienced chronic iron deficiency in infancy reported greater negative emotions and dissociation/detachment than adults who were iron sufficient in infancy, with behavior problems during adolescence mediating this pathway (Lozoff et al., 2013). In addition, early iron deficiency predicted poorer emotion regulation in childhood, which was then associated with more risky sexual behavior and alcohol use in adolescence (East et al., 2017). These literatures are important for researchers studying early stress and psychopathology to consider.

Environmental Toxins

Although rarely studied in the stress and developmental psychopathology literatures, environmental toxins may negatively impact neurodevelopment and have lasting effects on mental health. Lead is one of the best-understood toxins in relation to child brain development (Grigg, 2004). Children are especially sensitive to lead exposure because they absorb greater amounts of lead through the gastrointestinal tract and more lead gets into the brain (Grigg, 2004). In addition, sensitive periods of brain development early in life put children at risk for greater damage to rapidly developing neural systems. Greater lead levels in children have been associated with lower IQ and less adaptive classroom behavior (Needleman et al., 1979), which could promote developmental cascades to psychopathology and maladaptation across development. Interactions between psychosocial stressors and environmental toxins should be considered when studying pathways of risk and resilience across development. More efforts

must also be implemented to reduce risk of preventable lead exposure (e.g., the Flint Michigan water crisis; Hanna-Attisha, LaChance, Sadler, & Champney Schnepp, 2016) to improve mental health and adaptive functioning in children.

Genetics, Stress, and Developmental Psychopathology

Advancements in genetic and epigenetic methods and an increased interest in integrating genetic methods into psychopathology research have resulted in an explosion of research attempting to understand the relative contributions of genetics versus the environment, how genes interact with the environment, and how the environment can affect the epigenome. We know through twin and adoption studies that many types of psychopathology associated with childhood stress exposure are partly heritable (Rhee & Waldman, 2002; Sullivan, Neale, & Kendler, 2000). We also know that there are independent effects of genotype and environment, suggesting both genetics and the environment predict risk for psychopathology, and the interaction of genotype and environment (G x E interaction) may confer further risk. There is a great deal of research on stable genetic variation among individuals that impact developmental outcomes, including single-nucleotide polymorphisms (SNPs), which are sites on DNA where a single nucleotide may differ between individuals. Such genetic variation has been targeted as a moderator of experiences and may lead to multifinality in outcomes for individuals experiencing the same type of childhood stressor. The first report on gene–environment interactions for psychiatric outcomes found that individuals with the low-activity MAOA allele who also experienced maltreatment were at an increased risk for antisocial behavior (Caspi et al., 2002). Investigations into many different gene candidates have followed, including FKBP5, a gene that regulates glucocorticoid receptor sensitivity, which in the context of childhood maltreatment has been associated with greater risk for PTSD in adulthood (Binder, Bradley, Liu, et al., 2008). However, there have been concerns about the replicability of many G x E candidate gene studies.

Researchers have also considered how different genotypes might interact with each other and the environment to predict further risk (e.g., G x G x E interaction; (Cicchetti, Rogosch, & Oshri, 2011). Others have utilized previous data on "risk alleles," or alleles that confer risk in interaction with stressful environments, to create polygenic risk scores that combine these alleles into a composite that indexes overall risk across genes. One study utilizing polygenic risk scores reported independent effects of both the polygenic risk score and childhood trauma on risk for adult depression, as well as an interaction indicating that polygenic risk score was a stronger predictor of depression in the context of child trauma (Peyrot et al., 2014). Understanding the interactions of genes with each other and the environment is a complex task, however, and the exact downstream mechanisms for the effects of the genome on multilevel functioning are not understood, but such work holds promise for identifying targets for understanding pathways from environmental risk to disorder.

With advancements in methodology and statistics, researchers have been able to capture the effects of not just one or a handful of SNPs, but the potential contributions across the entire genome. Genome-wide association studies (GWASs) have incorporated studies of the whole genome to identify potential genetic loci that are associated with observed traits, which capture genetic influences rather than G x E interactions. This data-driven approach has been used to identify novel genes that reach the threshold of significance that may play unexpected yet important roles in conferring risk for disorders in the face of childhood stress (Bogdan, Hyde, & Hariri, 2013). Perhaps with improving statistical tools, it will be possible to understand how genome-wide patterns may interact with the environment, and childhood stress specifically, to affect risk and resilience across development.

More recently, epigenetic processes (changes to the genome that are functionally relevant but do not alter the nucleotide sequence, such as chemical modifications that change gene transcription; Zhang & Meaney, 2010) have become of interest to researchers of early stress and developmental psychopathology. Modifications such as DNA methylation or histone modification can alter the accessibility of DNA and the structure of chromatin, which then change gene expression. These changes have been targeted as a pathway by which childhood stress is embedded to confer risk for disorder (see 2016 *Development and Psychopathology* special section, vol. 28[4 part 2]). There is optimism that by understanding potential "rules" that govern epigenetics and gene expression, researchers can develop interventions that change gene expression and activity of downstream mediators of risk and resilience to lead to more favorable outcomes (Szyf & Bick, 2013).

A seminal study in the effect of early experience on the epigenome in rodents reported that pups of low-licking and low-grooming mothers had greater methylation of the glucocorticoid receptor promoter than pups of high-licking and high-grooming mothers, and these alterations lasted into adulthood (Weaver et al., 2004). Parallel findings have also been reported in humans. A study of children exposed to physical maltreatment showed that these children had greater methylation of exon 1 of the *NR3C1* glucocorticoid receptor promoter region than nonmaltreated children (Romens, McDonald, Svaren, & Pollak, 2015). This gene is the same gene that was found to be hypermethylated in the hippocampi of adult suicide victims that had experienced child abuse (McGowan et al., 2009). These suicide victims who had experienced child abuse also demonstrated decreased levels of glucocorticoid receptor mRNA, signaling a possible downstream mediator of hypermethylation on psychiatric risk (McGowan et al., 2009). However, there is difficulty with establishing causality due to the long period of time since the abuse in childhood. Changes in epigenetic patterns have also been reported in response to maternal deprivation (Massart et al., 2016), institutional care (Esposito et al., 2016; Naumova et al., 2012), and maternal depression (Cicchetti, Hetzel, Rogosch, Handley, & Toth, 2016). Further, epigenetic changes have repeatedly associated with psychiatric disorders such as depression, addiction, and schizophrenia (Tsankova, Renthal, Kumar, & Nestler, 2007). There is evidence that these alterations are potentially reversible (Roth & Sweatt, 2011; Weaver et al., 2004), suggesting that the epigenome remains plastic in postmitotic cells.

Another area of recent interest has been in the transgenerational inheritance of the effects of early stress, including effects on the epigenome or on parental behavior that could impact the next generation even if they never directly experienced the stressor. Altered *BDNF* DNA methylation has been reported in the offspring of females exposed to maltreatment in early life (Roth, Lubin, Funk, & Sweatt, 2009), suggesting an epigenetic mechanism of transmitting risk across generations or preparing offspring for a harsh environment. It is unclear whether demethylation of targeted DNA molecules as a result of an intervention may result in this change in the offspring, potentially decreasing risk for later disorder.

Timing of Early Stress and Implications for Developmental Psychopathology

Childhood stressors may lead to different effects on brain development and behavior depending on the developmental timing of the stressor. Depending on the neurobiological development of the individual experiencing the stressor, his or her sociocultural and environmental context, genetics, personal history with stress, among other factors, the timing of a stressor may produce vastly different outcomes. For example, seminal work by Hubel and Wiesel demonstrated that restricting visual input during an early sensitive period had long-lasting effects on vision that are not apparent if visual input is restricted after the system's early development (Hubel & Wiesel, 1962). Although the visual system has a relatively short sensitive period early in life, many of the neural systems in humans have more protracted periods of development (Stiles & Jernigan, 2010), leaving the brain vulnerable to insults but also open to experiences that enhance development. Likewise, these brain regions and neural circuits each have unique sensitive periods of development that may help to explain the effects of early stress on functioning (Teicher, Tomoda, & Andersen, 2006). Interestingly, the duration of sensitive periods has been shown to vary between individuals based on environmental inputs (Knudsen, 2004), such that there are individual differences with respect to when sensitive periods begin and end. In this section, we will discuss examples of the differential effects of stressor timing on development. Although this chapter is focused on childhood stress, we want to emphasize that stressors outside of this period, such as during prenatal development or during adolescence and beyond, have specific effects that must be considered when endeavoring to understand developmental psychopathology across the life span (see 2015 *Development and Psychopathology* special issue on sensitive periods, vol. 27, issue 2).

The adoption literature has shed light on early sensitive periods due to the well-defined removal from a sometimes depriving environment and placement in a typically well-resourced family that is highly committed to the child. Depending on the timing of adoption and time spent in an institution or other care arrangements, researchers have been able to determine which periods of development are associated with the greatest risk for later cognitive, social, emotional, and behavior problems. Overall, children adopted before 12 months of age have better outcomes than those adopted after 12 months (Juffer & van IJzendoorn, 2009). One meta-analysis reported that children adopted before 12 months were just as likely to be securely attached as children who were living in their birth families (Van den Dries, Juffer, van IJzendoorn, & Bakermans-Kranenburg, 2009), suggesting that the sensitive period for attachment may not end during the first year of life. However, children adopted after 12 months were less likely to be securely attached than their nonadopted peers (Van den Dries et al., 2009), indicating that there does appear to be a sensitive period for attachment and that it closes sometime after 12 months of age. Interestingly, growing evidence indicates that for most, but not all, domains of functioning, as long as institutional care is limited to the first 4–6 months of life, there is no significant increase in long-term adverse effects (Zeanah, Gunnar, McCall, Kreppner, & Fox, 2011). Thus, for many domains of functioning, the sensitive period lasts beyond 4–6 months of age.

Researchers are still trying to understand whether the effects of adversity during specific sensitive periods can be reversed or whether there are sensitive periods at different points in development that make reversal of effects more likely. At this point, there is evidence in the epigenetics literature that some of these effects of early stress can be reversed (Roth & Sweatt, 2011; Weaver et al., 2004). While there is mounting evidence that early stressors such as caregiver abuse and separation from a caregiver are associated with stable alterations in DNA methylation and gene expression in the animal literature (discussed earlier in section on "Genetics, Stress, and Developmental Psychopathology"), there is also evidence that at least some of these effects may be modifiable following these early experiences (Roth & Sweatt, 2011), which is an exciting prospect for future interventions seeking modifiable targets that may influence functioning.

The hypothalamic-pituitary-adrenal (HPA) axis, which assists with the coordination of the brain and body's response to stress, and epigenetic regulation of the HPA axis have shown sensitivity to stressor timing. A 3-hour daily separation of infant mice from caregivers during a sensitive period of development in infancy has been shown to trigger epigenetic modifications that change HPA activity (Murgatroyd et al., 2009). Specifically, this early stressor induced HPA hyperactivity in basal and stress-related conditions and altered memory and coping behavior (Murgatroyd et al., 2009). Similar timing effects on the HPA axis have been reported in humans. An examination of adolescents followed longitudinally in the TRAILS cohort showed that while adversities between ages 0 and 5 years were not associated with cortisol reactivity to social stress, adversities between ages 6 and 11 years were associated with heightened reactivity, particularly for those who had experienced pre- or postnatal adversity (Bosch et al., 2012).

Conversely, adolescents who had experienced adversity between 12 and 13 or 14 and 15 years demonstrated cortisol hyporeactivity to stress (Bosch et al., 2012). It is unclear whether puberty may play a role in transitions from hyper- to hyporeactivity in response to stress.

Volumetric magnetic resonance imaging (MRI) and functional MRI (fMRI) studies have revealed timing differences in the effects of early stress on the brain, which is in line with work on typical brain development showing major developmental differences in the brain and neural circuitry from prenatal life to adulthood. Preliminary evidence suggests that adult women who experienced repeated episodes of sexual abuse in childhood had reduced hippocampal volume compared to healthy control women if the episodes occurred at preschool age (3–5 years) or early adolescence (11–13 years; (Andersen et al., 2008). If the episodes of abuse occurred during middle childhood (9–10 years), corpus callosum volume was reduced, and the frontal cortex was reduced for those with sexual abuse experienced between 14 and 16 years compared to controls (Andersen et al., 2008). Although these timing effects need to be replicated in a larger sample, and preferably a sample with objective reports of maltreatment, they provide important data concerning effects of maltreatment timing on the developing brain. A prospective longitudinal study demonstrated that at age 24, adults from families with lower income at age 9 showed reduced dorsolateral and ventrolateral cortex activity and failed to inhibit amygdala activation during a task requiring regulation of negative emotion (Kim et al., 2013). In this study, concurrent adult income was not associated with neural activation during the task, suggesting that the middle childhood environment had stronger programming effects than the current environment. Additionally, experiencing chronic stress across childhood and adolescence (at 9, 13, and 17 years) mediated the association between age 9 income and dorsolateral and ventrolateral cortex activity at 24 (Kim et al., 2013), suggesting that chronic stress exposure starting in childhood may be a mechanism by which these stressful experiences are programmed in the brain.

It is also unknown whether certain systems exhibit greater plasticity than others (Cicchetti, 2015), responding more to both positive inputs, such as stable, sensitive relationships, and negative inputs, such as chronic stress. Although we are gathering more data about the duration of sensitive periods across different systems, we have many questions to

answer about the potential beginnings and endings of sensitive periods, the peak of plasticity during sensitive periods, and potential reemergence of sensitive periods at key points in development. These questions are especially difficult to answer when considering sensitive periods for complex behaviors and skills, such as executive function and social behavior, and phenotypes such as depression, schizophrenia, or conduct disorder. Such insights will be particularly important when creating evidence-based, developmentally sensitive interventions.

Another consideration relevant to timing is the possibility for childhood stress exposure to lead to sleeper effects months or years later. Sleeper effects are not immediately observed but may emerge at a later point. These are likely due to underlying vulnerabilities as a result of the stressor that may worsen and become more apparent across development when relevant systems are challenged. An example from the adoption literature is that children adopted from the less severely depriving orphanages did not show clinical- or borderline-level problems until around 12 years of age or older (Merz & McCall, 2010). These reports suggest that the effects of institutional care are not solely due to immediate behaviors that help children adapt to orphanage care but are maladaptive in a family setting (Zeanah et al., 2011). Institutional care may disrupt more basic processes that become more apparent when relevant tasks emerge later in development, such as during adolescence (Zeanah et al., 2011). Thus, the timing of potential downstream effects must be considered in addition to the timing of the stressor.

The question of timing is particularly important in the intervention literature, as interventions that occur during a period of high plasticity for the intervention target are more likely to have effects. Much of the literature on childhood poverty and other stressors highlights the importance of intervening as early as possible while the brain is experiencing rapid development (Doyle, Harmon, Heckman, & Tremblay, 2009). Programs intended to ameliorate the effects of early poverty and stress that occur during childhood are more likely to have a positive impact on developmental outcomes than interventions that occur during adolescence and adulthood because the brain has greater plasticity during the early years (Doyle et al., 2009). Interventions that begin even earlier, such as in infancy or even prenatally, might have even greater potential for positive developmental cascades. It is important to note that even though early interventions are often considered to be the most effective for producing change, interventions that are appropriately timed to intervene during a sensitive period of development may be even more effective than an earlier time point that is not a sensitive period. For example, an intervention to improve peer relationships or reduce delinquency and substance use may be better suited for late childhood or early adolescence than infancy. Questions of timing should always be considered in light of the developmental science literature. Likewise, the developmental literature must be informed by the timing of interventions that successfully change the behavior or outcome of interest, because this change could signal that there is malleability in that trait at the time the intervention was delivered. One example is the Bucharest Early Intervention Project in which children living in an orphanage were placed into foster care at various points in early development. A follow-up of these children at age 8 years demonstrated that children who were placed into foster care before 2 years of age had similar brain electrical activity to a never-institutionalized group, but those who were placed into foster care after 24 months showed significant differences in electrical activity compared to both of these groups, suggesting a sensitive period for early intervention in this domain (Vanderwert, Marshall, Nelson III, Zeanah, & Fox, 2010). Basic and intervention scientists must embrace cross-talk between the literatures to advance both basic science and interventions.

Stress, Adaptation, and Maladaptation

Children's responses to stress must be considered in context to assess adaptation versus maladaptation. A child who develops behavior problems following maltreatment may struggle in a classroom where disruptive behaviors are not tolerated; thus, these behaviors would be maladaptive for functioning in the classroom. These same behaviors may serve a protective role in that other children may be weary of getting into fights with this child, which protects the child from certain peer conflicts. These behaviors may also help the child get attention and social interaction from teachers and other adults that he or she is not getting at home, which may be an adaptive response to a pathological environment. Thus, when considering negative behaviors or other outcomes following severe childhood stress, it is paramount to consider how this behavior might be functioning to help the child adapt, even if it is not adaptive in all contexts. The importance of considering both adaptations and the environment in research on developmental psychopathology and

interventions for children who have experienced early stress cannot be overstated.

Researchers often think about the stress literature using a deficit model, which only highlights negative effects of stress. While acknowledging the significant deficits that often result for many children, it is important to consider the unique strengths and abilities that children who have experienced chronic stress may have that can help them adapt in certain contexts (Ellis, Bianchi, Griskevicius, & Frankenhuis, 2017). Recent work has supported *specialization and sensitization hypotheses* (Ellis et al., 2017), which, within the evolutionary-developmental framework, argues that harsh, unpredictable environments enhance certain cognitive abilities in order to solve problems in these same environments (Frankenhuis & de Weerth, 2013). One example is that the ability to shift attention in harsh, unpredictable environments may enhance adaptation to take advantage of fleeting opportunities, even though sustained attention abilities may be impaired (Mittal, Griskevicius, Simpson, Sung, & Young, 2015). The sensitization hypothesis argues relatedly that these enhanced cognitive capabilities will be specific to conditions of stress and uncertainty rather than in nonthreatening circumstances (Mittal et al., 2015). A better understanding of these enhanced abilities will be necessary for designing interventions that take advantage of these abilities to increase intervention effectiveness and improve functioning in a variety of settings.

An example of this effect of early experience comes from a study comparing youth who had a history of previous institutionalization to those who did not. In an experimental paradigm designed to test exploration versus exploitation strategies, formerly institutionalized youth were less likely to explore and more likely to exploit immediate rewards (Humphreys et al., 2015). The exploitation strategy was associated with greater success in a restricted task condition compared to a generous task condition. Thus, this history of early stress was associated with a strategy that favored a greater likelihood of success only in a condition of restriction, which likely matches an early environment where there is little control over future rewards. This behavior may be adaptive in unpredictable environments but maladaptive in stable, predictable environments.

Similarly, environmental mismatch (Nederhof & Schmidt, 2012) refers to maladaptive outcomes that may occur when the current environment does not match the environment for which one has been behaviorally and biologically prepared. For example, if an individual's behavior and physiology has been programmed to be successful in a harsh early environment, the individual may experience difficulties if he or she ultimately lives in an environment of stability with many resources in adulthood. The individual may have been programmed to be vigilant to threat in early life, but this may not be adaptive in a low-risk environment and may lead to issues with attention or anxiety. It is possible that some individuals are more sensitive to the effects of early experience and thus have more difficulty adjusting to a change in the environment than others who were less sensitive to the environment (Nederhof & Schmidt, 2012). A better understanding of sensitivity to the environment and environmental mismatch may help us to understand resilience and successful versus unsuccessful adaptations to different environments following early stress. The environmental mismatch hypothesis is particularly interesting for individuals in the development psychopathology field because this hypothesis considers the timing of exposures, developmental processes, and individual differences that may affect multiple levels of functioning. Thinking about environmental mismatch leads us to the question of whether interventions designed to promote behaviors that are more likely in children from low-risk backgrounds would be adaptive for children from high-risk backgrounds, particularly in contexts with the greatest levels of risk (e.g., in a dangerous neighborhood or with a maltreating caregiver). We must also ask whether such interventions designed to promote resilience work with or work against the adaptations children have already made to their high-risk environments (Ellis et al., 2017). We must strive to promote positive outcomes without taking away the certain skills necessary to survive in that environment.

The concept of resilience is essential to discuss when considering positive outcomes despite the experience of childhood stress. Although childhood stress has been associated with a greater likelihood of cognitive, socioemotional, and behavior problems, some who experience such adversity later excel in multiple domains. Resilience is a process that includes positive adaptation in the context of significant stress (Luthar, Cicchetti, & Becker, 2000). Resilience is a dynamic developmental process, which indicates that it has the capacity to change over time in response to the environment and is greatly influenced by individual factors (Egeland et al., 1993; Luthar et al., 2000). Researchers have identified many factors that promote resilience processes, including individual factors such as intelligence and self-control, relationship factors such as sensitive, reliable parenting, and systems-level factors such as community support and effective schools (Masten, 2001, 2014). These factors support basic processes that allow individuals to flexibly adapt to their environment while supporting the development of psychological and physiological systems that are needed for successful adaptation to future environments. These factors, and others that support resilience processes, have been referred to as "ordinary magic" because they utilize normal human resources in children, families, and communities but have powerful effects on promoting resilience (Masten, 2001). A limitation of this literature is that it is difficult to differentiate between factors that decrease risk versus factors that promote resilience. A better understanding of the incremental contribution of resilience factors will be important for interventions that seek to promote specific resilience factors in addition to decreasing risk factors. It is important to remember, though, that some factors associated with resilience may not be adaptive in every context. Coping, a process that is often discussed in the resilience and developmental psychopathology literatures, can be adaptive or maladaptive depending on the type of coping used, the environmental context, and the characteristics of the individual (Compas, Orosan, & Grant, 1993; Zeidner & Saklofske, 1996). It is important to recognize that adaptive coping can occur even in the context of psychopathology (Cicchetti, 2010; Masten, 2014), so there is a great deal of variation in risk and protective factors interacting at a particular time. As a result, there is a need to understand both adaptive and maladaptive processes and recognize that these processes may be occurring at the same time in an individual.

Sex Differences

Sex differences in psychopathology, mechanisms that lead to psychopathology, vulnerability to stress, and resilience processes have been a growing focus in the developmental psychopathology literature. Simultaneously, the National Institutes of Health have required researchers to include participants of both sexes to be able to examine biological sex as a variable that might moderate the processes we are studying. Although sex differences in the prevalence of disorders may be well studied, there is less of a focus on sex differences in vulnerability to stress at different time points, how moderators impact risk for disorders, and the mechanisms that contribute to risk and resilience. We will attempt to highlight examples of research that incorporates sex differences in the study of childhood stress and developmental psychopathology.

One of the most prominent sex differences in the developmental psychopathology literature is that for depression. Depression is twice as likely to afflict females versus males (Nolen-Hoeksema, 2001), and this sex difference appears around the time of puberty. Careful developmental work has elucidated that sex differences in the prevalence of depression begin to emerge at 13–15 years of age, but the peak rate of divergence between the sexes is between 15 and 18 years (Hankin et al., 1998). Thus, this period during late adolescence may be a crucial point to intervene to reduce depression, particularly for females. Biological, socioemotional, cognitive, and behavioral differences between males and females during this period should also be targeted to understand what causes this substantial sex difference in depression. Interventions that reduce sex differences in depression during this period will help us to understand causality by experimentally determining which targets the intervention successfully altered to reduce depressive symptoms.

Sex differences in response to stress have been observed in several domains, and these sex differences could contribute to known disparities in certain health problems, such as depression, conduct disorder, autoimmune disorders, and cardiovascular disease. For example, boys with more pervasive maltreatment (i.e., chronic, severe, multiple types of maltreatment) demonstrated greater diurnal cortisol levels in middle childhood than girls with similar maltreatment experiences (Doom, Cicchetti, Rogosch, & Dackis, 2013). Similarly, girls with early but not recent maltreatment experiences and girls with more pervasive maltreatment experiences showed diurnal cortisol production consistent with down-regulation across development (Doom et al., 2013). These patterns may predispose males and females to different disorders as early as childhood, and these early differences suggest that biological sex is a critically important variable to consider even before the onset of puberty.

Genetic variants may also differentially operate to increase vulnerability or protection from the effects of trauma for boys versus girls. The corticotropin-releasing hormone receptor 1 (CRHR1) A-allele appears to protect males who experienced childhood trauma—but not females—from developing depression in adulthood, and this variant also predicts differential response to the dexamethasone/

corticotropin-releasing hormone (CRH) test for males only (Heim et al., 2009). This test has been associated with HPA dysregulation and risk for depression. Sex differences in protection from the effects of trauma by genotype are an important avenue for researchers to explore to continue to elucidate disparities in psychopathology by sex.

Extensive research shows that children who experienced maltreatment are at an increased risk for affective disorders, and for females, trauma during the rapid period of brain development in early childhood is the highest predictor for lifetime risk of affective disorders (Bale & Epperson, 2015). There are numerous differences in brain architecture and hormonal milieu by sex during typical development, and traumatic early experiences have been shown to alter brain development in a sex-specific manner (De Bellis & Keshavan, 2003; Teicher et al., 2003). These divergences at baseline and in response to childhood stress must be more closely studied in order to understand risk for maladaptation.

In response to witnessing or being the victim of violence, studies have reported that girls have more serious symptomatology, such as anger, anxiety, depression, and posttraumatic stress, than boys (Gorman-Smith & Tolan, 2003). Girls may display more psychological distress in response to violence exposure while boys may display more risky behaviors (Gorman-Smith & Tolan, 2003). The disaster literature has documented similar sex differences in response to stress, with girls showing greater anxiety symptoms and boys displaying more "belligerence" (Masten & Narayan, 2012). One of the most consistent sex differences in response to stress is that females who are exposed to disasters, terrorism, or war in childhood or adolescence report greater posttraumatic stress symptoms than males (Masten & Narayan, 2012). Males have been shown to be more susceptible to substance use disorders than females following trauma (Goldmann & Galea, 2014). However, it is difficult to disentangle biological sex from differences in males and females' exposure to stress, interpretations of stress, and self-report of the stressors and psychological/behavioral symptoms (Masten & Narayan, 2012). Future work must consider these potential contributors to sex differences in response to trauma in order to create more fine-grained interventions following childhood stress.

Future work must consider how pathways to mental and physical health problems following early stress may differ by sex. Data from the Midlife Development in the United States (MIDUS) survey suggested that childhood trauma was associated with an increased risk for metabolic syndrome in adulthood for both men and women, partially mediated by the pathway of poor-quality sleep (Lee, Tsenkova, & Carr, 2014). For women only, stress-induced eating partially mediated this pathway, suggesting that this target may be specific to interventions in females (Lee et al., 2014). In addition, intervention effectiveness must be tested by sex to ensure that both males and females derive benefits from interventions. If only one sex benefits from an intervention, in-depth analysis is needed to understand why.

Future Directions in Developmental Psychopathology

Although much progress has been made in the understanding of developmental pathways between childhood stress, psychopathology, and resilience, there are still many questions that must be answered. First, we need to better understand how the timing, type, and severity of stress during development affect outcomes. There is a great deal of heterogeneity in functioning between individuals. In addition, individuals may have adaptive functioning in some domains, such as social behavior and cognitive functioning, but not other domains, such as emotion regulation and stress system functioning. More careful phenotyping and gathering both objective and subjective measures of the environment and individuals' stress histories, if possible, will yield greater understanding into individual differences in functioning at multiple levels. Similarly, we need to understand what these individual differences mean for personalized interventions. There is an urgent need to adapt interventions for individuals based on type of stress, timing and chronicity of stressor, and age at the time of intervention in order to enhance prevention and intervention effectiveness. In light of processes related to environmental mismatch and adaptations made to stressful environments, it will be important for prevention and intervention scientists to consider how responses to stress may be adaptive to the current environment, and whether altering these responses may in turn decrease one's ability to function in a threatening environment. Although highly difficult to conduct, individualized interventions may be the most effective when paired with changes in the environment that complement cognitive, behavioral, socioemotional, and biological alterations targeted by the intervention. Interventions should also capitalize on unique strengths of children who have experienced early stress, such as enhancements in specific types of

memory formation, heightened attention to different types of information, or performance on certain risk-taking tasks, in order to increase adherence and effectiveness (Ellis et al., 2017).

We have extensive evidence that childhood stress alters neurobiological systems, cognition, emotion, and behavior, but we still have much more to understand about specific neurobiological mechanisms that link early stress to these later outcomes. The best evidence for causal models and neurobiological pathways is in animal models. For example, researchers have documented epigenetic changes in response to maltreatment in mice, which are then linked to alterations in the HPA axis, cognition, and behavior (Murgatroyd et al., 2009). Although we cannot causally test these pathways or have highly controlled environments in humans, we should continue to assess multiple levels of functioning across time to test whether these pathways likely operate in humans. Because there are likely pathways operating at multiple levels that lead to biological and behavioral embedding of early experiences, we should investigate how these pathways interact over time to alter functioning. Genetics and epigenetics, neural activity and neurotransmitter systems, the autonomic nervous and immune systems, the HPA axis, the microbiome, and the environment, among a host of other factors interact over time to produce complex phenotypes. A greater understanding of these pathways and interactions will provide valuable targets for interventions that seek to promote adaptive functioning at multiple levels. In addition, future work in the G x E, childhood stress, and psychopathology literatures is needed to understand the interaction between genetics and environmental contributions to risk and resilience. For example, passive gene–environment correlations (rGE; e.g., parent and child share genes and parent also shapes environment for the child), active correlations (genetically influenced traits lead one to seek out particular environments), and evocative correlations (genetically influenced traits evoke environmental responses) may make stressful environments more likely for certain individuals. Thus, childhood stress may be partially due to both genetics and the environment, which is important to remember for prevention and intervention.

In the future, we must keep working on creating truly developmental theories that integrate psychological, genetic, physiological, environmental, and cultural processes that guide normal and abnormal development. There is a great need for research that integrates cultural development into developmental psychopathology, including the ways in which culture affects biology, incorporating assessment of individual- and society-level cultural processes, and the best ways to integrate culture into interventions (Causadias, 2013). We must continue to refine our measures, study designs, and statistical approaches to analyze complex longitudinal data at multiple levels. We have made a great deal of progress in the past three decades on integrating biological measures into psychology research, and we should keep trying to mechanistically understand how psychological and biological processes interact across development. This effort includes implementing both psychological *and* biological measures pre and post intervention in order to understand the potential biological mechanisms that may significantly mediate intervention effectiveness. Finally, we must use interventions as a way to study causality of psychopathology in the face of stress. Although randomizing children to stressful conditions is not possible, we can randomize children to interventions. If children respond to these multilevel interventions, this provides evidence that these targeted systems are sensitive to the environment at that point in development (Cicchetti, 2013). Randomization to preventive interventions serves the same function for testing theories and pathways from stress to psychopathology (Howe, Reiss, & Yuh, 2002). Such investigations will allow us to understand what is a causal agent in a disorder versus a byproduct of that disorder. These investigations will also inform us about the developmental periods when interventions are maximally effective. Effective interventions can also help us to identify targets for future interventions in order to make sure that each portion of an intervention contributes to adaptive functioning.

Conclusion

The field of developmental psychopathology has made extensive progress in incorporating biology and multiple levels of functioning, documenting developmental cascades, and creating interventions that interrupt maladaptive cascades following early stress. However, there is still a great deal that we must learn to understand the progression of typical and atypical development, which will require a better integration of genetics, biology, behavior, emotion, cognition, context, and culture longitudinally. We also must develop, implement, and test interventions that consider individual differences and the environment across development in order to learn more about the nature of development and to support children who have experienced early stress.

Acknowledgments

F32HD088029 to Jenalee Doom and a Klaus J. Jacobs Research Prize to Dante Cicchetti.

References

Andersen, S. L., Tomada, A., Vincow, E. S., Valente, E., Polcari, A., & Teicher, M. H. (2008). Preliminary evidence for sensitive periods in the effect of childhood sexual abuse on regional brain development. *The Journal of Neuropsychiatry and Clinical Neurosciences, 20*(3), 292–301. doi:10.1176/appi.neuropsych.20.3.292

Bale, T. L., & Epperson, C. N. (2015). Sex differences and stress across the lifespan. *Nature Neuroscience, 18*(10), 1413.

Binder, E. B., Bradley, R. G., Liu, W., Epstein, M.P., Deveau, T. C., Mercer, K. B.,...Ressler, K. J. (2008). Association of fkbp5 polymorphisms and childhood abuse with risk of posttraumatic stress disorder symptoms in adults. *Journal of the American Medical Association, 299*(11), 1291–1305. doi:10.1001/jama.299.11.1291

Bogdan, R., Hyde, L., & Hariri, A. (2013). A neurogenetics approach to understanding individual differences in brain, behavior, and risk for psychopathology. *Molecular Psychiatry, 18*(3), 288–299.

Bosch, N. M., Riese, H., Reijneveld, S. A., Bakker, M. P., Verhulst, F. C., Ormel, J., & Oldehinkel, A. J. (2012). Timing matters: Long term effects of adversities from prenatal period up to adolescence on adolescents' cortisol stress response. The TRAILS study. *Psychoneuroendocrinology, 37*(9), 1439–1447. doi:10.1016/j.psyneuen.2012.01.013

Boyce, W. T., & Ellis, B. J. (2005). Biological sensitivity to context: I. An evolutionary–developmental theory of the origins and functions of stress reactivity. *Development and Psychopathology, 17*(2), 271–301.

Bruce, J., Tarullo, A. R., & Gunnar, M. R. (2009). Disinhibited social behavior among internationally adopted children. *Development and Psychopathology, 21*(1), 157–171.

Buka, S. L., Stichick, T. L., Birdthistle, I., & Earls, F. J. (2001). Youth exposure to violence: prevalence, risks, and consequences. *American Journal of Orthopsychiatry, 71*(3), 298.

Caspi, A., McClay, J., Moffitt, T. E., Mill, J., Martin, J., Craig, I. W.,...Poulton, R. (2002). Role of genotype in the cycle of violence in maltreated children. *Science, 297*(5582), 851–854. doi:10.1126/science.1072290

Causadias, J. M. (2013). A roadmap for the integration of culture into developmental psychopathology. *Development and Psychopathology, 25*(4pt2), 1375–1398.

Chang, L., Schwartz, D., Dodge, K. A., & McBride-Chang, C. (2003). Harsh parenting in relation to child emotion regulation and aggression. *Journal of Family Psychology, 17*(4), 598.

Chang, S., Walker, S., Grantham-McGregor, S., & Powell, C. (2002). Early childhood stunting and later behaviour and school achievement. *Journal of Child Psychology and Psychiatry, 43*(6), 775–783.

Chisholm, K. (1998). A three year follow-up of attachment and indiscriminate friendliness in children adopted from Romanian orphanages. *Child Development, 69*(4), 1092–1106.

Cicchetti, D. (2010). Resilience under conditions of extreme stress: A multilevel perspective. *World Psychiatry, 9*(3), 145–154.

Cicchetti, D. (2013). Annual research review: Resilient functioning in maltreated children—past, present, and future perspectives. *Journal of Child Psychology and Psychiatry, 54*(4), 402–422.

Cicchetti, D. (2015). Neural plasticity, sensitive periods, and psychopathology. *Development and Psychopathology, 27*(2), 319.

Cicchetti, D. (Ed.) (2016a). *Developmental Psychopathology* (Vol. 1, Theory and Method, 3rd ed.). New York: Wiley.

Cicchetti, D. (Ed.) (2016b). *Developmental Psychopathology* (Vol. 2, Developmental Neuroscience, 3rd ed.). New York: Wiley.

Cicchetti, D. (Ed.) (2016c). *Developmental Psychopathology* (Vol. 3, Maladaptation and Psychopathology, 3rd ed.). New York: Wiley.

Cicchetti, D. (Ed.) (2016d). *Developmental Psychopathology* (Vol. 4, Risk, Resilience, and Intervention, 3rd ed.). New York: Wiley.

Cicchetti, D., & Dawson, G. (2002). Multiple levels of analysis. *Development and Psychopathology, 14*(3), 417–420.

Cicchetti, D., Hetzel, S., Rogosch, F. A., Handley, E. D., & Toth, S. L. (2016). Genome-wide DNA methylation in 1-year-old infants of mothers with major depressive disorder. *Development and Psychopathology, 28*(4pt2), 1413–1419. doi:10.1017/S0954579416000912

Cicchetti, D., & Rogosch, F. A. (1996). Equifinality and multifinality in developmental psychopathology. *Development and Psychopathology, 8*(4), 597–600. doi:10.1017/S0954579400007318

Cicchetti, D., Rogosch, F. A., & Oshri, A. (2011). Interactive effects of CRHR1, 5-HTTLPR, and child maltreatment on diurnal cortisol regulation and internalizing symptomatology. *Development and Psychopathology, 23*(4), 1125–1138. doi:10.1017/S0954579411000599

Cicchetti, D., & Schneider-Rosen, K. (1986). An organizational approach to childhood depression. In *Depression in young people: Developmental and clinical perspectives* (pp. 71–134). New York, NY: Guilford Press.

Cicchetti, D., & Toth, S. L. (1995). A developmental psychopathology perspective on child abuse and neglect. *Journal of the American Academy of Child & Adolescent Psychiatry, 34*(5), 541–565.

Cicchetti, D., & Tucker, D. (1994). Development and self-regulatory structures of the mind. *Development and Psychopathology, 6*(4), 533–549.

Cicchetti, D., & Valentino, K. (2006). An ecological-transactional perspective on child maltreatment: Failure of the average expectable environment and its influence on child development. In *Developmental psychopathology (2nd ed.)* (pp. 129–201). New York, NY.

Cicchetti, D., & Walker, E. F. (2003). *Neurodevelopmental mechanisms in psychopathology.* New York, NY: Cambridge University Press.

Coldwell, J., Pike, A., & Dunn, J. (2006). Household chaos—links with parenting and child behaviour. *Journal of Child Psychology and Psychiatry, 47*(11), 1116–1122.

Colvert, E., Rutter, M., Beckett, C., Castle, J., Groothues, C., Hawkins, A.,...Sonuga-Barke, E. J. (2008). Emotional difficulties in early adolescence following severe early deprivation: Findings from the English and Romanian adoptees study. *Development and Psychopathology, 20*(2), 547–567.

Compas, B. E., Orosan, P. G., & Grant, K. E. (1993). Adolescent stress and coping: Implications for psychopathology during adolescence. *Journal of Adolescence, 16*(3), 331–349.

Cowell, R. A., Cicchetti, D., Rogosch, F. A., & Toth, S. L. (2015). Childhood maltreatment and its effect on neurocognitive functioning: Timing and chronicity matter. *Development and Psychopathology, 27*(2), 521–533.

Cox, M. J., Mills-Koonce, R., Propper, C., & Gariépy, J.-L. (2010). Systems theory and cascades in developmental psychopathology. *Development and Psychopathology, 22*(3), 497–506.

De Bellis, M. D. (2001). Developmental traumatology: The psychobiological development of maltreated children and its implications for research, treatment, and policy. *Development and Psychopathology, 13*(3), 539–564.

De Bellis, M. D., & Keshavan, M. S. (2003). Sex differences in brain maturation in maltreatment-related pediatric posttraumatic stress disorder. *Neuroscience & Biobehavioral Reviews, 27*(1), 103–117.

Del Giudice, M., Ellis, B. J., & Shirtcliff, E. A. (2011). The adaptive calibration model of stress responsivity. *Neuroscience & Biobehavioral Reviews, 35*(7), 1562–1592.

Doom, J. R., Cicchetti, D., Rogosch, F. A., & Dackis, M. N. (2013). Child maltreatment and gender interactions as predictors of differential neuroendocrine profiles. *Psychoneuroendocrinology, 38*(8), 1442–1454. doi:10.1016/j.psyneuen.2012.12.019

Doom, J. R., & Gunnar, M. R. (2016). Institutional deprivation and neurobehavioral development in infancy. In *Environmental experience and plasticity of the developing brain* (pp. 185–214). New York, NY: Wiley.

Doom, J. R., VanZomeren-Dohm, A. A., & Simpson, J. A. (2016). Early unpredictability predicts increased adolescent externalizing behaviors and substance use: A life history perspective. *Development and Psychopathology, 28*(4pt2), 1505–1516.

Doyle, O., Harmon, C. P., Heckman, J. J., & Tremblay, R. E. (2009). Investing in early human development: Timing and economic efficiency. *Economics and Human Biology, 7*(1), 1–6. doi:10.1016/j.ehb.2009.01.002

East, P., Delker, E., Lozoff, B., Delva, J., Castillo, M., & Gahagan, S. (2017). Associations among infant iron deficiency, childhood emotion and attention regulation, and adolescent problem behaviors. *Child Development.* doi:10.1111/cdev.12765

Egeland, B., Carlson, E., & Sroufe, L. A. (1993). Resilience as process. *Development and Psychopathology, 5*(4), 517–528.

Ellis, B. J., Bianchi, J., Griskevicius, V., & Frankenhuis, W. E. (2017). Beyond risk and protective factors: An adaptation-based approach to resilience. *Perspectives on Psychological Science, 12*(4), 561–587.

Esposito, E. A., Jones, M. J., Doom, J. R., MacIsaac, J. L., Gunnar, M. R., & Kobor, M. S. (2016). Differential DNA methylation in peripheral blood mononuclear cells in adolescents exposed to significant early but not later childhood adversity. *Development and Psychopathology, 28*(4pt2), 1385–1399. doi:10.1017/S0954579416000055

Evans, G. W., & English, K. (2002). The environment of poverty: Multiple stressor exposure, psychophysiological stress, and socioemotional adjustment. *Child Development, 73*(4), 1238–1248.

Evans, G. W., Gonnella, C., Marcynyszyn, L. A., Gentile, L., & Salpekar, N. (2005). The role of chaos in poverty and children's socioemotional adjustment. *Psychological Science, 16*(7), 560–565.

Fearon, R., Bakermans-Kranenburg, M. J., Van IJzendoorn, M. H., Lapsley, A. M., & Roisman, G. I. (2010). The significance of insecure attachment and disorganization in the development of children's externalizing behavior: A meta-analytic study. *Child Development, 81*(2), 435–456.

Ford, D. H., & Lerner, R. M. (1992). *Developmental systems theory: An integrative approach*. Thousand Oaks, CA: Sage.

Frankenhuis, W. E., & de Weerth, C. (2013). Does early-life exposure to stress shape or impair cognition? *Current Directions in Psychological Science, 22*(5), 407–412.

Fries, A. B. W., & Pollak, S. D. (2004). Emotion understanding in postinstitutionalized Eastern European children. *Development and Psychopathology, 16*(2), 355–369. doi:10.1017/S0954579404044554

Galler, J. R., & Ramsey, F. (1989). A follow-up study of the influence of early malnutrition on development: Behavior at home and at school. *Journal of the American Academy of Child & Adolescent Psychiatry, 28*(2), 254–261.

Gardner, J. M., Walker, S. P., Powell, C. A., & Grantham-McGregor, S. (2003). A randomized controlled trial of a home-visiting intervention on cognition and behavior in term low birth weight infants. *The Journal of Pediatrics, 143*(5), 634–639.

Goldmann, E., & Galea, S. (2014). Mental health consequences of disasters. *Annual Review of Public Health, 35*, 169–183.

Gorman-Smith, D., Henry, D. B., & Tolan, P. H. (2004). Exposure to community violence and violence perpetration: The protective effects of family functioning. *Journal of Clinical Child and Adolescent Psychology, 33*(3), 439–449.

Gorman-Smith, D., & Tolan, P. H. (2003). Positive adaptation among youth exposed to community violence. In *Resilience and vulnerability: Adaptation in the context of childhood adversities* (pp. 392–413). New York, NY: Cambridge University Press.

Gorman–Smith, D., & Tolan, P. (1998). The role of exposure to community violence and developmental problems among inner-city youth. *Development and Psychopathology, 10*(1), 101–116.

Graves, P. (1978). Nutrition and infant behavior: A replication study in the Katmandu Valley, Nepal. *The American Journal of Clinical Nutrition, 31*(3), 541–551.

Grigg, J. (2004). Environmental toxins; their impact on children's health. *Archives of Disease in Childhood, 89*(3), 244–250. doi:10.1136/adc.2002.022202

Groh, A. M., Roisman, G. I., van IJzendoorn, M. H., Bakermans-Kranenburg, M. J., & Fearon, R. P. (2012). The significance of insecure and disorganized attachment for children's internalizing symptoms: A meta-analytic study. *Child Development, 83*(2), 591–610.

Hackman, D. A., Farah, M. J., & Meaney, M. J. (2010). Socioeconomic status and the brain: Mechanistic insights from human and animal research. *Nature Reviews. Neuroscience, 11*(9), 651.

Hankin, B. L., Abramson, L. Y., Moffitt, T. E., Silva, P. A., McGee, R., & Angell, K. E. (1998). Development of depression from preadolescence to young adulthood: Emerging gender differences in a 10-year longitudinal study. *Journal of Abnormal Psychology, 107*(1), 128.

Hanna-Attisha, M., LaChance, J., Sadler, R. C., & Champney Schnepp, A. (2016). Elevated blood lead levels in children associated with the Flint drinking water crisis: A spatial analysis of risk and public health response. *American Journal of Public Health, 106*(2), 283–290.

Hardt, J., & Rutter, M. (2004). Validity of adult retrospective reports of adverse childhood experiences: Review of the evidence. *Journal of Child Psychology and Psychiatry, 45*(2), 260–273.

Heckman, J. J. (2006). Skill formation and the economics of investing in disadvantaged children. *Science, 312*(5782), 1900–1902.

Heim, C., Bradley, B., Mletzko, T. C., Deveau, T. C., Musselman, D. L., Nemeroff, C. B., . . . Binder, E. B. (2009). Effect of childhood trauma on adult depression and neuroendocrine function: Sex-specific moderation by CRH Receptor 1 Gene. *Frontiers in Behavioral Neuroscience, 3*, 41. doi:10.3389/neuro.08.041.2009

Herrenkohl, T. I., Kosterman, R., Mason, W. A., Hawkins, J. D., McCarty, C. A., & McCauley, E. (2010). Effects of childhood conduct problems and family adversity on health, health behaviors, and service use in early adulthood: Tests of developmental pathways involving adolescent risk taking and depression. *Development and Psychopathology, 22*(3), 655–665. doi:10.1017/S0954579410000349

Howe, G. W., Reiss, D., & Yuh, J. (2002). Can prevention trials test theories of etiology? *Development and Psychopathology, 14*(4), 673–694.

Hubel, D. H., & Wiesel, T. N. (1962). Receptive fields, binocular interaction and functional architecture in the cat's visual cortex. *The Journal of Physiology, 160*(1), 106–154.

Humphreys, K. L., Lee, S. S., Telzer, E. H., Gabard-Durnam, L. J., Goff, B., Flannery, J., & Tottenham, N. (2015). Exploration-exploitation strategy is dependent on early experience. *Developmental Psychobiology, 57*(3), 313–321.

Juffer, F., & van IJzendoorn, M. H. (2009). International adoption comes of age: Development of international adoptees from a longitudinal and meta-analytical perspective. In *International advances in adoption research for practice* (pp. 169–192). Wiley-Blackwell: West Sussex, UK.

Juster, R.-P., McEwen, B. S., & Lupien, S. J. (2010). Allostatic load biomarkers of chronic stress and impact on health and cognition. *Neuroscience & Biobehavioral Reviews, 35*(1), 2–16. doi:https://doi.org/10.1016/j.neubiorev.2009.10.002

Kandel, E. R. (1998). A new intellectual framework for psychiatry. *American Journal of Psychiatry, 155*(4), 457–469.

Kar, N. (2009). Psychological impact of disasters on children: Review of assessment and interventions. *World Journal of Pediatrics, 5*(1), 5–11.

Kim, P., Evans, G. W., Angstadt, M., Ho, S. S., Sripada, C. S., Swain, J. E., . . . Phan, K. L. (2013). Effects of childhood poverty and chronic stress on emotion regulatory brain function in adulthood. *Proceedings of the National Academy of Sciences, 110*(46), 18442–18447.

Knudsen, E. I. (2004). Sensitive periods in the development of the brain and behavior. *Journal of Cognitive Neuroscience, 16*(8), 1412–1425.

Kolb, B., & Whishaw, I. Q. (1998). Brain plasticity and behavior. *Annual Review of Psychology, 49*(1), 43–64.

Lee, C., Tsenkova, V., & Carr, D. (2014). Childhood trauma and metabolic syndrome in men and women. *Social Science & Medicine (1982), 105*, 122–130. doi:10.1016/j.socscimed.2014.01.017

Lozoff, B., Beard, J., Connor, J., Felt, B., Georgieff, M., & Schallert, T. (2006). Long-lasting neural and behavioral effects of iron deficiency in infancy. *Nutrition Reviews, 64*, S34–S43. doi:10.1111/j.1753-4887.2006.tb00243.x

Lozoff, B., Smith, J. B., Kaciroti, N., Clark, K. M., Guevara, S., & Jimenez, E. (2013). Functional significance of early-life iron deficiency: Outcomes at 25 years. *Journal of Pediatrics, 163*(5), 1260–1266. doi:10.1016/j.jpeds.2013.05.015

Lupien, S. J., McEwen, B. S., Gunnar, M. R., & Heim, C. (2009). Effects of stress throughout the lifespan on the brain, behaviour and cognition. *Nature Reviews Neuroscience, 10*(6), 434–445.

Luthar, S. S., Cicchetti, D., & Becker, B. (2000). The construct of resilience: A critical evaluation and guidelines for future work. *Child Development, 71*(3), 543–562.

Martinez, P., & Richters, J. E. (1993). The NIMH community violence project: II. Children's distress symptoms associated with violence exposure. *Psychiatry, 56*(1), 22–35.

Massart, R., Nemoda, Z., Suderman, M. J., Sutti, S., Ruggiero, A. M., Dettmer, A. M.,... Szyf, M. (2016). Early life adversity alters normal sex-dependent developmental dynamics of DNA methylation. *Development and Psychopathology, 28*(4pt2), 1259–1272. doi:10.1017/S0954579416000833

Masten, A. S. (2001). Ordinary magic: Resilience processes in development. *American Psychologist, 56*(3), 227.

Masten, A. S. (2014). Global perspectives on resilience in children and youth. *Child Development, 85*(1), 6–20.

Masten, A. S., & Cicchetti, D. (2010). Developmental cascades. *Development and Psychopathology, 22*(3), 491.

Masten, A. S., & Cicchetti, D. (2016). Resilience in development: Progress and transformation. In *Developmental psychopathology* (pp. 271–333). Hoboken, NJ: John Wiley & Sons, Inc.

Masten, A. S., & Narayan, A. J. (2012). Child development in the context of disaster, war, and terrorism: Pathways of risk and resilience. *Annual Review of Psychology, 63*.

Masten, A. S., Roisman, G. I., Long, J. D., Burt, K. B., Obradović, J., Riley, J. R.,... Tellegen, A. (2005). Developmental cascades: Linking academic achievement and externalizing and internalizing symptoms over 20 years. *Developmental Psychology, 41*(5), 733. doi:10.1037/0012-1649.41.5.733

Maughan, B., & Rutter, M. (1997). Retrospective reporting of childhood adversity: issues in assessing long-term recall. *Journal of Personality Disorders, 11*(1), 19–33.

McEwen, B. S. (1998). Stress, adaptation, and disease: Allostasis and allostatic load. *Annals of the New York Academy of Sciences, 840*(1), 33–44. doi:10.1111/j.1749-6632.1998.tb09546.x

McEwen, B. S., & Seeman, T. (1999). Protective and damaging effects of mediators of stress: Elaborating and testing the concepts of allostasis and allostatic load. *Annals of the New York Academy of Sciences, 896*(1), 30–47.

McGowan, P. O., Sasaki, A., D'Alessio, A. C., Dymov, S., Labonté, B., Szyf, M.,... Meaney, M. J. (2009). Epigenetic regulation of the glucocorticoid receptor in human brain associates with childhood abuse. *Nature Neuroscience, 12*(3), 342–348. doi:10.1038/nn.2270

Merz, E. C., & McCall, R. B. (2010). Behavior problems in children adopted from psychosocially depriving institutions. *Journal of Abnormal Child Psychology, 38*(4), 459–470. doi:10.1007/s10802-009-9383-4

Mills-Koonce, W. R., Willoughby, M. T., Garrett-Peters, P., Wagner, N., Vernon-Feagans, L., & Investigators, F. L. P. K. (2016). The interplay among socioeconomic status, household chaos, and parenting in the prediction of child conduct problems and callous–unemotional behaviors. *Development and Psychopathology, 28*(3), 757–771.

Mittal, C., Griskevicius, V., Simpson, J. A., Sung, S., & Young, E. S. (2015). Cognitive adaptations to stressful environments: When childhood adversity enhances adult executive function. *Journal of Personality and Social Psychology, 109*(4), 604–621.

Mogg, K., & Bradley, B. P. (1998). A cognitive-motivational analysis of anxiety. *Behaviour Research and Therapy, 36*(9), 809–848.

Monk, C., Georgieff, M. K., & Osterholm, E. A. (2013). Research review: Maternal prenatal distress and poor nutrition—mutually influencing risk factors affecting infant neurocognitive development. *Journal of Child Psychology and Psychiatry, 54*(2), 115–130. doi:10.1111/jcpp.12000

Murgatroyd, C., Patchev, A. V., Wu, Y., Micale, V., Bockmühl, Y., Fischer, D.,... Spengler, D. (2009). Dynamic DNA methylation programs persistent adverse effects of early-life stress. *Nature Neuroscience, 12*(12), 1559–1566.

Murry, V. M., Brown, P. A., Brody, G. H., Cutrona, C. E., & Simons, R. L. (2001). Racial discrimination as a moderator of the links among stress, maternal psychological functioning, and family relationships. *Journal of Marriage and Family, 63*(4), 915–926.

Naumova, O. Y., Lee, M., Koposov, R., Szyf, M., Dozier, M., & Grigorenko, E. L. (2012). Differential patterns of whole-genome DNA methylation in institutionalized children and children raised by their biological parents. *Development and Psychopathology, 24*(1), 143–155.

Nederhof, E., & Schmidt, M. V. (2012). Mismatch or cumulative stress: Toward an integrated hypothesis of programming effects. *Physiology & Behavior, 106*(5), 691–700.

Needleman, H. L., Gunnoe, C., Leviton, A., Reed, R., Peresie, H., Maher, C., & Barrett, P. (1979). Deficits in psychologic and classroom performance of children with elevated dentine lead levels. *New England Journal of Medicine, 300*(13), 689–695.

Nolen-Hoeksema, S. (2001). Gender differences in depression. *Current Directions in Psychological Science, 10*(5), 173–176.

Pachter, L. M., & Garcia Coll, C. (2009). Racism and child health: A review of the literature and future directions. *Journal of Developmental and Behavioral Pediatrics: JDBP, 30*(3), 255–263. doi:10.1097/DBP.0b013e3181a7ed5a

Peyrot, W. J., Milaneschi, Y., Abdellaoui, A., Sullivan, P. F., Hottenga, J. J., Boomsma, D. I., & Penninx, B. W. (2014). Effect of polygenic risk scores on depression in childhood trauma. *The British Journal of Psychiatry, 205*(2), 113–119.

Pine, D. S., Mogg, K., Bradley, B. P., Montgomery, L., Monk, C. S., McClure, E.,... Kaufman, J. (2005). Attention bias to threat in maltreated children: Implications for vulnerability to stress-related psychopathology. *American Journal of Psychiatry, 162*(2), 291–296.

Priest, N., Paradies, Y., Trenerry, B., Truong, M., Karlsen, S., & Kelly, Y. (2013). A systematic review of studies examining the relationship between reported racism and health and wellbeing for children and young people. *Social Science & Medicine, 95*, 115–127.

Rhee, S. H., & Waldman, I. D. (2002). Genetic and environmental influences on antisocial behavior: A meta-analysis of twin and adoption studies. *Psychological Bulletin, 128*(3), 490.

Richardson, S., Birch, H., Grabie, E., & Yoder, K. (1972). The behavior of children in school who were severely malnourished in the first two years of life. *Journal of Health and Social Behavior, 13*(3), 276–284.

Romens, S. E., McDonald, J., Svaren, J., & Pollak, S. D. (2015). Associations between early life stress and gene methylation in children. *Child Development, 86*(1), 303–309.

Roth, T. L., Lubin, F. D., Funk, A. J., & Sweatt, J. D. (2009). Lasting epigenetic influence of early-life adversity on the BDNF gene. *Biological Psychiatry, 65*(9), 760–769. doi:10.1016/j.biopsych.2008.11.028

Roth, T. L., & Sweatt, J. D. (2011). Epigenetic mechanisms and environmental shaping of the brain during sensitive periods of development. *Journal of Child Psychology and Psychiatry, and Allied Disciplines, 52*(4), 398–408. doi:10.1111/j.1469-7610.2010.02282.x

Sedlak, A. J., Mettenburg, J., Basena, M., Peta, I., McPherson, K., & Greene, A. (2010). *Fourth national incidence study of child abuse and neglect (NIS-4). Washington, DC: US Department of Health and Human Services.*

Shonkoff, J. P., Boyce, W. T., & McEwen, B. S. (2009). Neuroscience, molecular biology, and the childhood roots of health disparities: Building a new framework for health promotion and disease prevention. *Journal of the American Medical Association, 301*(21), 2252–2259. doi:10.1001/jama.2009.754

Shonkoff, J. P., Garner, A. S., Siegel, B. S., Dobbins, M. I., Earls, M. F., McGuinn, L.,...Care, D. (2012). The lifelong effects of early childhood adversity and toxic stress. *Pediatrics, 129*(1), e232–e246. doi:10.1542/peds.2011-2663

Simpson, J. A., Griskevicius, V., Kuo, S. I., Sung, S., & Collins, W. A. (2012). Evolution, stress, and sensitive periods: The influence of unpredictability in early versus late childhood on sex and risky behavior. *Developmental Psychology, 48*(3), 674.

Spencer, M. B., Noll, E., Stoltzfus, J., & Harpalani, V. (2001). Identity and school adjustment: Revisiting the "acting White" assumption. *Educational Psychologist, 36*(1), 21–30.

Sroufe, L. A. (1979). The coherence of individual development: Early care, attachment, and subsequent developmental issues. *American Psychologist, 34*(10), 834.

Sroufe, L. A. (1990). Considering normal and abnormal together: The essence of developmental psychopathology. *Development and Psychopathology, 2*(4), 335–347.

Sternberg, K. J., Baradaran, L. P., Abbott, C. B., Lamb, M. E., & Guterman, E. (2006). Type of violence, age, and gender differences in the effects of family violence on children's behavior problems: A mega-analysis. *Developmental Review, 26*(1), 89–112.

Stiles, J., & Jernigan, T. L. (2010). The basics of brain development. *Neuropsychology Review, 20*(4), 327–348.

Sullivan, P. F., Neale, M. C., & Kendler, K. S. (2000). Genetic epidemiology of major depression: Review and meta-analysis. *American Journal of Psychiatry, 157*(10), 1552–1562.

Szyf, M., & Bick, J. (2013). DNA methylation: A mechanism for embedding early life experiences in the genome. *Child Development, 84*(1), 49–57. doi:10.1111/j.1467-8624.2012.01793.x

Teicher, M. H., Andersen, S. L., Polcari, A., Anderson, C. M., Navalta, C. P., & Kim, D. M. (2003). The neurobiological consequences of early stress and childhood maltreatment. *Neuroscience & Biobehavioral Reviews, 27*(1), 33–44.

Teicher, M. H., Tomoda, A., & Andersen, S. L. (2006). Neurobiological consequences of early stress and childhood maltreatment: Are results from human and animal studies comparable? *Annals of the New York Academy of Sciences, 1071*(1), 313–323.

Toth, S. L., Rogosch, F. A., Manly, J. T., & Cicchetti, D. (2006). The efficacy of toddler-parent psychotherapy to reorganize attachment in the young offspring of mothers with major depressive disorder: A randomized preventive trial. *Journal of Consulting and Clinical Psychology, 74*(6), 1006.

Troller-Renfree, S., Zeanah, C. H., Nelson, C. A., & Fox, N. A. (2017). Neural and cognitive factors influencing the emergence of psychopathology: Insights from the Bucharest Early Intervention Project. *Child Development Perspectives, 12*(1), 28–33.

Tsankova, N., Renthal, W., Kumar, A., & Nestler, E. J. (2007). Epigenetic regulation in psychiatric disorders. *Nature Reviews Neuroscience, 8*(5), 355–367.

Van den Dries, L., Juffer, F., van IJzendoorn, M. H., & Bakermans-Kranenburg, M. J. (2009). Fostering security? A meta-analysis of attachment in adopted children. *Children and Youth Services Review, 31*(3), 410–421.

Van Praag, H., Kempermann, G., & Gage, F. H. (2000). Neural consequences of environmental enrichment. *Nature Reviews Neuroscience, 1*(3), 191.

Vanderwert, R. E., Marshall, P. J., Nelson, C. A. III, Zeanah, C. H., & Fox, N. A. (2010). Timing of intervention affects brain electrical activity in children exposed to severe psychosocial neglect. *PLoS One, 5*(7), e11415.

Walker, S. P., Chang, S. M., Powell, C. A., Simonoff, E., & Grantham-McGregor, S. M. (2007). Early childhood stunting is associated with poor psychological functioning in late adolescence and effects are reduced by psychosocial stimulation. *Journal of Nutrition, 137*(11), 2464–2469.

Weaver, I. C., Cervoni, N., Champagne, F. A., D'Alessio, A. C., Sharma, S., Seckl, J. R.,...Meaney, M. J. (2004). Epigenetic programming by maternal behavior. *Nature Neuroscience, 7*(8), 847–854. doi:10.1038/nn1276

Wolfe, D. A., Crooks, C. V., Lee, V., McIntyre-Smith, A., & Jaffe, P. G. (2003). The effects of children's exposure to domestic violence: A meta-analysis and critique. *Clinical Child and Family Psychology Review, 6*(3), 171–187.

Zeanah, C., Egger, H. L., Smyke, A. T., Nelson, C. A., Fox, N. A., Marshall, P. J., & Guthrie, D. (2009). Institutional rearing and psychiatric disorders in Romanian preschool children. *American Journal of Psychiatry, 166*(7), 777–785.

Zeanah, C., Gunnar, M. R., McCall, R. B., Kreppner, J. M., & Fox, N. A. (2011). Sensitive Periods. *Monographs of the Society for Research in Child Development, 76*(4), 147–162. doi:10.1111/j.1540-5834.2011.00631.x

Zeidner, M., & Saklofske, D. (1996). Adaptive and maladaptive coping. In M. Zeidner & N. S. Endler (Eds.), *Handbook of coping: Theory, research, applications* (pp. 505–531). Oxford, England: John Wiley & Sons.

Zhang, T.Y., & Meaney, M. J. (2010). Epigenetics and the environmental regulation of the genome and its function. *Annual Review of Psychology, 61*, 439–466.

Perinatal Depression as an Early Stress

Risk for the Development of Psychopathology in Children

Sherryl H. Goodman *and* Meeka S. Halperin

Abstract

This chapter provides a review of research and a description of the central issues regarding the stressor of depression in mothers during pregnancy and the postpartum periods in relation to risk for the development of psychopathology in offspring. Where evidence allows, causal relations are emphasized; otherwise, limitations are noted, especially those regarding being able to draw causal conclusions from the correlational approaches typically taken in this area of study. Evidence for mechanisms in the transmission of risk is also described, given the potential for understanding causal relations. With the developmental psychopathology perspective of depression as a stressor for offspring, the focus is on vulnerabilities to and early signs of disorder as well as mental health outcomes per se. The chapter concludes with suggested critical issues in the field and recommendations for future directions for research.

Keywords: depression, stress, pregnancy, postpartum period, developmental psychopathology, risk, vulnerabilities, mechanisms

From a developmental perspective, women's experiences during pregnancy and the postpartum periods are early opportunities for stress to play a role in risk for the development of psychopathology in offspring. In this chapter, we review research and describe the central issues regarding the stressor of maternal depression, along with its comorbidities and other correlates, and their effects on the fetus and infant as well as later child functioning. By "depression" we refer not only to the symptoms, duration, and impairment required to meet *DSM-5* criteria for major depressive disorder (MDD) (American Psychiatric Association, 2013) but also to clinically significant levels of depressive symptoms. With regard to the latter, although some may dismiss this group as being of less concern than women with MDD, large-scale studies have revealed that, of women who screen positive for depression in the postpartum period based on established cut scores for depression symptom scales, nearly 70% meet diagnostic criteria for unipolar depressive disorders,

typically MDD (Wisner et al., 2013). Moreover, we have found few differences in correlates of depression between pregnant women with elevated symptom levels that did not meet criteria for major depressive episode (MDE) and those with MDE (Goodman & Tully, 2009).

We focus on associations between the stressor of perinatal depression in women and vulnerabilities to, or early signs or symptoms of, disorder in offspring. Where evidence allows, we emphasize causal relations; otherwise, we note limitations in being able to draw causal conclusions from the correlational approaches typically taken in this area of study. Although Section 3 of this volume explicates models for the transmission of risk, we also describe evidence for mechanisms in the transmission of risk, given the potential for understanding causal relations. Because we take a developmental psychopathology perspective on depression as a stressor for offspring, we focus on vulnerabilities to, and early signs of, disorder as well as mental health outcomes per se. Further, we suggest critical issues in the field and recommend future directions for research.

Depression in Mothers During Pregnancy and the Postpartum Period: Why Women?

The lifetime rate of MDD is about 21% of adult women in the United States (Kessler et al., 1994) (about 15% in Canada), a rate that is consistently two to three times higher than for men (Akhtar-Danesh & Landeen, 2007; M. M. Weissman et al., 1996). The differentially higher prevalence of depression in women than men begins in early adolescence (Hankin & Abramson, 1999), and the mean age of onset of MDD is about 25 years (M. M. Weissman et al., 1996), which is in the midst of childbearing years (i.e., ages 15–49). That is, two reasons to be concerned about depression in women relative to men are its higher prevalence and the coinciding of its typical age of onset with conception, pregnancy, and early parenting. A third reason is that depression in mothers is more strongly associated with risk for the development of psychopathology than is depression in fathers, especially during infancy and toddlerhood (Connell & Goodman, 2002; Natsuaki et al., 2014). In this chapter, we focus on women, while emphasizing the role of men as partners and co-parents, where the literature allows.

Depression During Pregnancy

Contrary to commonly presented media depictions of beaming pregnant women, rates of depression during pregnancy are high and pregnant women are at an elevated risk for depression. Based on a meta-analytic review, as many as 18.4% of pregnant women are depressed (major or minor depression) at some point during pregnancy, with 12.7% experiencing an episode of MDD (Gavin et al., 2005). These rates refer to period prevalence, which is the percentage of the population with depression over the specified period of time—in this case, between conception and delivery. In terms of elevated symptoms, large surveys of pregnant women seeking prenatal care reveal that 20% of pregnant women exceed the established cutoff for clinically significant levels of depressive symptoms (Marcus, Flynn, Blow, & Barry, 2003). It is important to note that these rates are based on US or Canadian women; rates of perinatal depression are typically higher in low- and middle-income countries (Husain et al., 2012).

Depression During the Postnatal Period

We refer to the period of approximately the first year following delivery as the postnatal period. Based on a meta-analytic review, as many as 19.2% of mothers with newborns (in the first 3 months after delivery) have major or minor depression, including 7.1% with an episode of MDD, with rates declining somewhat toward the end of the first year postpartum (Gavin et al., 2005). As with prenatal depression, low- to middle-income countries have higher rates, with estimates ranging from 13% to 50%, relative to high-income countries (Parsons, Young, Rochat, Kringelbach, & Stein, 2012).

Depression Across the Perinatal Period

By "the perinatal period," we refer to both the pregnancy and, approximately, the first year postpartum. One of the major reasons for concern about depression during pregnancy is that it is a risk factor for postnatal depression (Norhayati, Hazlina, Asrenee, & Emilin, 2015). Analyses of trajectories of symptoms from third trimester through 12 months postpartum in a large cohort of women pregnant with their first child revealed that depression during pregnancy tends to persist through the first year postpartum, with small reductions in symptoms found in a subset of women (McCall-Hosenfeld, Phiri, Schaefer, Zhu, & Kjerulff, 2016). In another large study of women who screened positive for postnatal depression at 4 to 6 weeks postpartum, about a third of them had an episode onset during pregnancy (and another 26% had onset before pregnancy) (Wisner et al., 2013). Nonetheless, it is also important to consider that some women who were not depressed in the third trimester became depressed by 6 months postpartum and those symptom levels increased at 12 months postpartum (McCall-Hosenfeld et al., 2016). In terms of diagnoses, between one third and one half of women with postnatal depression are experiencing their first episode of depression (Räisänen et al., 2014).

There are several important implications of these findings. First, there may be important differences among women who are depressed during both pregnancy and the postpartum period, relative to during only one of those periods. Second, similarly, there may be important differences among infants who are exposed to their mothers' depression during both pregnancy and the postpartum period, relative to during only one of those periods. Third, for women whose postnatal depression had its onset during pregnancy, infant functioning attributed to the mother's postnatal depression may be at least partially attributable to prenatal depression; for this reason, researchers are encouraged to begin studies of perinatal depression during pregnancy to better differentiate the impact of depression during one period versus the other. Although infants exposed during only one of these developmental periods may seem to be less at risk than those exposed during both periods, this may not always be the case. For example, prenatal programming suggests that infants are born prepared for an environment similar to their fetal environment (D. J. P. Barker, 1998; Glover, O'Connor, & O'Donnell, 2010). In this case, infants whose fetal experiences or exposures prepare them for a depriving postnatal environment, thus potentially conferring benefit by helping them to anticipate qualities of the postnatal environment, might be disadvantaged by a mismatch between the pre- and postnatal environments.

The Role of Anxiety

Anxiety is also highly prevalent in women during pregnancy and the postpartum period, although a recent review revealed a wide range of estimated rates (Leach, Poyser, & Fairweather-Schmidt, 2015). During pregnancy, anxiety is not only highly correlated with depression (Goodman & Tully, 2009); it is also one of the main risk factors for depression during pregnancy, along with history of depression and other factors (Lancaster et al., 2010; Verreault et al., 2014). Further, there is increasing understanding of pregnancy-specific anxiety (i.e., fear of childbirth or health of the child), which is somewhat distinct from generalized anxiety, with peaks in both early and late pregnancy (Huizink, Mulder, Robles de Medina, Visser, & Buitelaar, 2004). In terms of the postpartum period, among a large sample of early postpartum women who screened positive for depression, 90.8% had a primary diagnosis of MDD and almost two thirds of those had comorbid disorders, with 82.9% of the comorbid disorders being anxiety disorders (Wisner et al., 2013). Thus, any model linking perinatal depression to child functioning must also take into consideration the anxiety that is often secondary to depression.

Given the high level of comorbidity between depression and anxiety, both prenatally and postnatally, it has been challenging to sort out differential effects of one versus the other on children. When either one alone is studied, such designs leave unanswered the extent to which the other may have explained the findings. When both are studied, statistical controls for each other are problematic given the high level of correlation between the two (Miller & Chapman, 2001). Perhaps a more important question, rather than the differential effects of depression, relative to anxiety, is how each may be associated with later child functioning via different developmental pathways. Researchers are encouraged to pursue this topic.

The Role of Stress Experienced by Women During Pregnancy and the Postpartum Periods

Similarly, depression in women is often accompanied by a set of comorbid conditions or correlates that fall under the broad construct of stress and, as such, may mark the presence of other biological and environmental risks to the fetus and infant. Prenatal stress has been a particular focus given the understanding that depression during pregnancy may be a stressor for the fetus. In terms of stress per se, higher levels of stress during pregnancy are associated with adverse outcomes in infants and toddlers, including birth outcomes (e.g., lower birthweight; neurodevelopment of newborns), greater temperamental negative affectivity and fearfulness, more sleep problems, and lower cognitive-intellectual functioning (for a review, see Glover, 2014). Remarkably, prenatal stress also prospectively predicts child anxiety and depression, attention-deficit/hyperactivity (ADHD), and conduct problems in school-aged and adolescent offspring (Glover, 2014). Yet in interpreting this set of findings, it is important to consider a caveat: that mild stress, in contrast to severe stress, may have beneficial associations with infant outcomes (DiPietro, Novak, Costigan, Atella, & Reusing, 2006; Liu, 2017).

Maternal Perinatal Depression and Child Functioning: Evidence for Associations

The impact of perinatal depression on youth, like depression that occurs in mothers at other times in children's development, is characterized by multifinality (Cicchetti & Rogosch, 1996). That is, mothers' perinatal depression has been theorized and tested for its association with a broad range of offspring outcomes, including emotional, cognitive, and behavioral outcomes. The following section reviews findings on associations between perinatal depression and infant and child outcomes.

Prenatal Influences

In the Goodman and Gotlib (1999) model, one of the four mechanisms proposed to link depression in mothers with the development of psychopathology in offspring was the prenatal environment. Since then, a substantial number of studies report that mothers' depression during pregnancy is associated with adverse outcomes in offspring, and a smaller number of studies have addressed potential mechanisms for those associations. We review both here.

Prenatal Depression and Birth Outcomes

Beginning with the earliest outcomes that can be measured in newborns, prenatal maternal depression is associated with infants' preterm birth and lower birth weight, as reported in a meta-analytic review (Grote et al., 2010), while higher maternal self-rated positive affect during the third trimester of pregnancy has been associated with decreased risk of delivering a preterm child (odds ratio 0.8-fold for each standard deviation of higher positive affect) (Pesonen et al., 2016). Such associations are of concern since preterm birth is correlated with the later development of attention difficulties (Galéra, Côté, Bouvard, & et al., 2011; Talge et al., 2010), communication delays and difficulties with social interactions (Mahoney, Minter, Burch, & Stapel-Wax, 2013), internalizing behavior (Talge et al., 2010), and depressive disorder during adolescence (Patton, Coffey, Carlin, Olsson, & Morley, 2004). Prenatal maternal depression has also been linked to several other infant vulnerabilities to psychopathology and child outcomes, which will be discussed.

Prenatal Depression and Infant Attachment and Temperament

Maternal depression during pregnancy has been associated with later-emerging infant vulnerabilities, including disorganized attachment (Hayes, Goodman, & Carlson, 2013) and "difficult" temperamental characteristics. When controlling for postpartum psychological state, maternal prenatal depression, anxiety, and stress are all associated with heightened temperamental fearfulness in response to novelty (Davis et al., 2004, 2007) and infants' greater temperamental negative affectivity (Rouse & Goodman, 2014). Individual differences in infant temperament are important because they are stable over time (Putnam, Rothbart, & Gartstein, 2008), predict childhood temperament (Komsi et al., 2006, 2008), have been associated with later social, emotional, and personality development (Kagan, 1998; Rothbart & Sheese, 2007), and the development of psychopathology (Putnam & Stifter, 2005). Thus, the infants' temperament characteristics that have been found to be associated with prenatal exposure to maternal depression are likely key indices of infants' vulnerability to the development of psychopathology.

Prenatal Depression and Child Behavioral and Emotional Functioning

Several prospective studies have provided evidence of associations between maternal depression and anxiety during pregnancy and offspring outcomes that occur later in development, that is, beyond infancy. Prenatal depression is associated with child internalizing and externalizing behavior (Velders et al., 2011) and attention problems (Batenburg-Eddes et al., 2013) at 3 years of age. In a review, mothers' prenatal distress (depression, anxiety, and/or stress) was associated with school-age children's global development, socioemotional development, and behavior with small to medium effect sizes (Kingston & Tough, 2013). In children 6–9 years old, higher maternal depression and state anxiety were associated with lower visuospatial working memory performance, but associations between depression and visuospatial working memory performance were better explained by pregnancy-specific anxiety (Buss, Davis, Hobel, & Sandman, 2011). At 8 years of age, prenatal depression has been associated with child externalizing behavior (E. D. Barker, Jaffee, Uher, & Maughan, 2011) and child internalizing behavior with prenatal anxiety (E. D. Barker et al., 2011). In adolescence, prenatal depression has been associated with greater risk for developing depression (Pawlby, Hay, Sharp, Waters, & O'Keane, 2009; Pearson et al., 2013), low social competence (Korhonen, Luoma, Salmelin, & Tamminen, 2012), and antisocial behavior (Hay, Pawlby, Waters, Perra, & Sharp, 2010). Further, prenatal maternal prenatal depression, anxiety, and stress predicted internalizing, externalizing, and depressive symptoms when offspring were 21 years of age (Betts, Williams, Najman, & Alati, 2014). Generally, this set of findings is interpreted as suggesting that prenatal depression may have long-lasting effects on children. An important caution, however, is that without controlling for depression in mothers at other periods of time, the findings could also be interpreted as support for familiality of depression (see Hannigan, McAdams, Neiderhiser, & Eley, 2017 for related findings on this point).

Relatedly, it is important to keep in mind that these findings are correlational, and thus do not warrant conclusions of causality. Thapar and Rutter (2009) remind us that there are many confounding factors in these relationships, including those that are possible mechanisms that could explain the ties between depression in mothers and child functioning, such as placental functioning, maternal cortisol, environmental toxins, and effects of programming, to name a few. Further, it is important to better understand what clinical characteristics of depression might matter most for infants. For example, compared to mothers with prenatal MDD, mothers who had prenatal dysthymia had higher cortisol levels during pregnancy, and their fetuses had lower weight, shorter abdominal circumference, and shorter femur length (Field & Diego, 2008). Thus, it is important for future studies to consider variability within depression in relating prenatal depression to child outcome.

Prenatal Depression and Child Autonomic Functioning

Several studies have related mothers' prenatal depression to their infants' autonomic functioning. An index of autonomic functioning, cardiac activity, specifically indices of the parasympathetic nervous system (PNS), has been routinely studied as a physiological indicator of emotion regulation. The PNS slows the autonomic nervous system (ANS) and regulates its "resting state." The vagal system, a central component of the PNS, is involved in emotional expression, experience, and regulation (Porges, 2011), and vagal tone maintains internal homeostasis and response to environmental demands (Porges, Doussard-Roosevelt, & Maiti, 1994). As such, vagal tone may index vulnerability to the development of psychopathology (Porges, Doussard-Roosevelt, Portales, & Greenspan, 1996). Vagal tone is measured via the amplitude of respiratory sinus arrhythmia (RSA), the heart rate variability over the respiratory cycle (Beauchaine, 2012; Porges, 2007). Among infants, individual differences in vagal tone are reliable (Porges et al., 1996). Evidence for criterion validity includes correlations with infant negative reactivity and stress regulation capacity (Bazhenova, Plonskaia, & Porges, 2001; Porges et al., 1994, 1996; Stifter & Fox, 1990). Evidence for predictive validity includes 9-month-old infants' lower RSA suppression (change from baseline to a demanding task) being associated with more depressive and social withdrawal symptoms at 3 years of age (Porges et al., 1996) and higher vagal tone predicting lower behavioral reactivity and less temperament difficulty at 3 years of age (Porges et al., 1994).

To our knowledge, only two studies have related mothers' prenatal depression to their offspring's autonomic functioning. In both studies, mothers with elevated prenatal depression symptom levels, compared to those with low depressive symptom levels, had neonates with lower vagal tone; in the more recent of the two studies, mothers' prenatal cortisol was also a predictor, although a model testing mediation by prenatal cortisol was not supported (Field et al., 2004; Jones et al., 1998). These findings, from ethnically diverse lower-middle socioeconomic status samples, suggest that newborns of prenatally depressed women differ in their physiology within the first week after delivery.

Prenatal Depression and Child Brain Functioning

Asymmetry in frontal electroencephalogram (EEG) activation during a resting state is well established as an index of individual differences in emotion regulation, beginning in infancy. Greater left, relative to right, activation in the frontal brain region (relative right-side EEG asymmetry or negative asymmetry values) has been linked with lower emotion regulation (Fox, 1994) and greater vulnerability to the development of both depression and anxiety (Thibodeau, Jorgensen, & Kim, 2006). In the only two published studies we found on this, women with elevated prenatal depression symptom levels, compared to those with low symptom levels, had neonates with greater relative right frontal EEG activity (Field et al., 2004; Jones et al., 1998). Later, we review findings on postnatal depression and infants' right frontal EEG asymmetry.

Structural magnetic resonance imaging (MRI) and resting-state functional MRI (fMRI) have also been used to index brain functioning in the infant offspring of depressed mothers. Using these indices, prenatal maternal depression has been associated with infants' greater functional connectivity of the amygdala in several brain regions, including the left temporal cortex and insula, the bilateral anterior cingulate, and the ventromedial prefrontal and medial orbitofrontal cortices (Qiu et al., 2015). These connectivity patterns are consistent with those found in adults and adolescents MDD (Ramasubbu et al., 2014; Tahmasian et al., 2013; Zeng et al., 2012). Although these findings suggest that maternal depression during pregnancy may have lasting effects by possibly altering brain connectivity during fetal development, longitudinal studies beginning in pregnancy are needed to test this mechanism of effect.

Prenatal Depression and Child Neuroendocrine Functioning

The hypothalamic-pituitary-adrenal (HPA) axis is the central part of the neuroendocrine system.

The HPA axis is responsible for the regulation of stress responses, as well as mood and emotions, with cortisol, the main "stress" hormone produced by the HPA system, used as an index of the HPA axis stress response. Alterations of the HPA axis may be a potential mechanism underlying the association between maternal depression and offspring risk for the development of psychopathology (Goodman & Gotlib, 1999). Children may have a greater predisposition to dysregulated stress response systems from being exposed to stressors during the prenatal or postpartum period (Gunnar, Porter, Wolf, & Rigatuso, 1995). Further, stressors during the prenatal or postpartum period may work through epigenetic processes to change HPA axis functioning (Booij, Wang, Levesque, Tremblay, & Szyf, 2013). Both models suggest ways in which the HPA system may play a role in the development of psychopathology.

Consistent with these theoretical models, pregnant women's cortisol levels (from a single urine sample obtained mid-morning) have been found to be associated with a range of indices of fetal, newborn, and infant functioning. Infants exposed prenatally to elevated maternal cortisol levels have been found to have restricted fetal growth, low birth weight, and preterm birth (Diego et al., 2009; Diego, Jones, et al., 2006; Field, Hernandez-Reif, et al., 2006), and exposure to elevated maternal cortisol levels (saliva collected upon awakening) in late pregnancy predicted infants' greater negative temperament from birth through 5 months of age (de Weerth, van Hees, & Buitelaar, 2003). Further, exposure to higher maternal cortisol levels early in pregnancy, a decrease in cortisol across gestation, and lower cortisol in late pregnancy (saliva collected in early afternoon) predicted infants' slower rate of cognitive development over the first postnatal year and poorer cognitive functioning at 12 months of age (Davis & Sandman, 2010). In the same sample followed over time, lower maternal cortisol in late pregnancy predicted 6- to 9-year-old children's reduced cortical thickness in frontal regions and lower child cognitive performance (Davis, Head, Buss, & Sandman, 2017).

Turning from mothers' to infants' cortisol, researchers have also found associations between prenatal maternal depression and children's elevated cortisol levels (findings on postpartum depression and children's cortisol levels will be reviewed later in this chapter). Newborns of depressed mothers have been found to have elevated cortisol levels, as do their mothers (Lundy et al., 1999). Prospectively, prenatal exposure to maternal depressed and anxious mood was associated with infants' greater cortisol stress response at 3 months of age (Oberlander et al., 2008).

Sex Differences in Offspring Outcomes Associated With Prenatal Depression

In regard to potential sex differences in offspring vulnerability, researchers have drawn contradictory conclusions. In one review of the literature, researchers concluded that female fetuses, relative to male, may be more susceptible to programming vulnerability, especially of the hypothalamic-pituitary-adrenal axis (HPA), with important implications for stress reactivity specifically and vulnerability for the later development of psychopathology, more broadly (Carpenter, Grecian, & Reynolds, 2017). Yet in a study of mice, researchers drew the opposite conclusion: Prenatal stress was more strongly and most consistently associated with a range of depressive-like phenotypes in males, relative to females, including greater HPA axis responsivity (Mueller & Bale, 2008). Thus, more research is needed to understand male relative to female vulnerability to early life programming.

Postnatal Influences
Postnatal Depression and Child Behavioral and Emotional Functioning

Several researchers prospectively examined associations between maternal depression during the postnatal period and later child functioning. Postnatal depression is associated with several outcomes in 4- to 5-year-old children, including conduct and emotional problems (Hanington, Heron, Stein, & Ramchandani, 2012), lower ego resiliency and social competence, with associations stronger for girls than for boys (Kersten-Alvarez et al., 2012), and physical aggression and inattention (Letourneau, Tramonte, & Willms, 2013). Postnatal depression has also been associated with internalizing and externalizing symptoms in 6- to 8-year-old children (Fihrer, McMahon, & Taylor, 2009) and internalizing symptoms in children between 10 and 15 years of age (Verbeek et al., 2012). Postnatal depression has been associated with increased risk of depression (Murray et al., 2011) and low social competence in 16- to 17-year-old boys, but not girls (Korhonen et al., 2012). In terms of interacting predictors, among 3-year-old children, maternal depression predicted greater risk for adjustment difficulties in those who were high in negative emotionality during infancy, compared to those low in negative emotionality as infants (Dix & Yan, 2014).

Postnatal Depression and Child Autonomic Functioning

In contrast to having found only two studies of mothers' prenatal depression in relation to their offspring's autonomic functioning, we found several studies that related mothers' postpartum depression to their infants' autonomic functioning. In a study comparing 3-month-old infants of postnatally depressed mothers to nondepressed mothers, infants of depressed mothers failed to show associations between RSA amplitude and observed facial affective expressions of joy and interest that were seen in infants of nondepressed mothers (Pickens & Field, 1995). Further, in infants aged 3–6 months, those of depressed mothers had lower vagal tone when interacting with their mothers, compared to those with nondepressed mothers (Field et al., 1988). However, in another study comparing infants of depressed mothers to those of nondepressed mothers, the two groups did not differ in vagal tone at 3 months, but at 6 months of age, infants of depressed mothers had lower vagal tone than infants of nondepressed mothers (Field, Pickens, Fox, Nawrocki, & Gonzalez, 1995). Across this series of studies, findings are consistent with the idea that maternal depression influences infants' systems involved in physiological markers of emotion regulation, evidence for which may emerge between 3 and 6 months of age.

In a few studies, researchers tested infants' autonomic functioning as a potential moderator of the association between postpartum depression and infant emotional or behavioral functioning. One found that 3- and 6-month-old infants' baseline (resting) RSA moderated the association between mothers' concurrent depressive symptoms and infants' sleep problems 1 year later (Gueron-Sela et al., 2017); specifically, infants who had higher baseline RSA, which may indicate a predisposition for greater physiological reactivity, who also had mothers with more depressive symptoms were more likely to have sleep problems at 18 months of age. Also in infants of mothers with greater depressive symptoms, lower average RSA withdrawal at 3 and 6 months (RSA during still-face subtracted from baseline RSA) was associated with more sleep problems at 18 months. In another study testing moderators of the association between postpartum depression and infant function, RSA was treated as the outcome, with attachment status as the moderator. With a prospective design, infants of mothers who had high postpartum depressive symptoms at 2 months had lower resting RSA at 14 months if they had disorganized attachment, compared to those with nondisorganized attachment (Tharner et al., 2013).

Postnatal Depression and Child Brain Functioning

Like prenatal depression, maternal postnatal depression is related to newborns' greater relative right frontal EEG activity. For example, in infants between 3 and 6 months of age, those whose mothers were depressed concurrently had greater relative right frontal EEG activity compared to infants of nondepressed mothers (Field, Fox, Pickens, & Nawrocki, 1995). Also in the same age group, infants of mothers who were depressed and withdrawn displayed greater relative right frontal EEG activity than infants of mothers who were depressed and intrusive (Diego, Field, Jones, & Hernandez-Reif, 2006). The 10-month-old infants of depressed mothers also displayed greater relative right frontal EEG activity while being shown happy face stimuli and during a mother–infant play interaction, compared to infants of nondepressed mothers (Jones, Field, Fox, Davalos, & Gomez, 2001). Among 13- to 15-month-old infants, those with depressed mothers displayed lower left frontal EEG activity compared to infants of nondepressed mothers. Further, compared to infants of mothers with subthreshold depression, infants whose mothers had MDD displayed lower left frontal EEG activity (Dawson, Frey, Panagiotides, Osterling, & Hessl, 1997). Thus, patterns of frontal EEG activity thought to reflect lower emotion regulation are found in children of mothers with postpartum depression. Further, newborns of mothers with both prenatal and postpartum (postdelivery) depression displayed greater relative right frontal EEG activity compared to infants of mothers with only prenatal or postnatal depression, and relative to infants of nondepressed mothers (Diego et al., 2004).

Postnatal Depression and Child Neuroendocrine Functioning

Like prenatal depression, maternal postnatal depression is related to children's elevated cortisol levels. Early maternal depression (beginning in infancy) was a strong predictor of children's cortisol at 4.5 years of age (Essex, Klein, Cho, & Kalin, 2002). Further, newborns of mothers with both pre- and postnatal (1-week postbirth) depression had elevated cortisol levels when compared to infants of mothers with only prenatal depression, only postpartum depression, and infants of nondepressed mothers (Diego et al., 2004). It has been suggested that the lower emotional availability of postnatally depressed mothers may be a key factor in contributing to negative changes in cortisol levels of their infants (Field, 1994), perhaps particularly so for those with prenatal exposure. Longitudinal studies are needed to test prenatal depression and postnatal emotional availability or other qualities of mother–infant interaction as potential mediators or moderators of the relationship between maternal perinatal depression and child neuroendocrine functioning.

Mechanisms of Action in Prenatal and Postpartum Depression

Although the focus of our chapter is on evidence for causal relations between perinatal depression and child functioning, referring readers to Section 3 of this volume for a focus on mechanisms, we touch on perinatal-specific models of transmission of risk from mothers to offspring. The aim of this section is to lay a foundation for interpreting the evidence linking pre- or postnatal depression to child functioning. As is clear from the literature just reviewed, tests of association between depression in mothers and functioning in the children have often used correlational designs, and thus, are not able to address causality. An understanding of potential mechanisms for those associations, hand in hand with an overview of the correlational findings, enables evaluation of conceptual models for causal relations, that is, how it is that perinatal depression may be associated with the development of psychopathology in children. While Goodman and Gotlib (1999) noted the limited number of studies designed to explicitly test mediational models of transmission of risk, more recent tests of mediation models have increased our understanding of mechanisms.

Biological Mechanisms

The notion of fetal programming, although most often studied with regard to fetal growth and risk for the later development of diseases (D. J. P. Barker, 1998), is increasingly applied to the understanding of how the in utero environment associated with depression in mothers might increase offspring risk for psychopathology (Janssen et al., 2016). In terms of prenatal biological mechanisms associated with depression, researchers have focused on altered placental functioning, such as downregulation of 11b-HSD2 (the enzyme that metabolizes cortisol) or upregulation of the expression of the placental glucocorticoid receptor, fetal exposure to mothers' elevated cortisol (potentially programming the fetal HPA axis) (Glover et al., 2010; Glover, O'Donnell, O'Connor,

Ramchandani, & Capron, 2015; Kane, Schetter, Glynn, Hobel, & Sandman, 2014), and pregnant and postpartum women's lower brain-derived neurotrophic factor (BDNF) and immune system dysregulation (Christian, 2015; Christian, Mitchell, Gillespie, & Palettas, 2016). Of this work, exposure to maternal cortisol has received the most research attention, with higher prenatal maternal cortisol predicting infants' elevated cortisol and a range of other outcomes, including greater fearful reactivity to novelty and fussiness during infancy and greater anxiety symptoms in children between 6 and 9 years of age (Davis et al., 2004, 2007; Davis & Sandman, 2012; de Weerth et al., 2003; Karlén, Frostell, Theodorsson, Faresjö, & Ludvigsson, 2013; Zijlmans, Riksen-Walraven, & de Weerth, 2015). Thus, in utero exposure to elevated maternal cortisol may precipitate heightened reactivity in offspring, which might in turn influence maladaptive offspring stress responding later in development. This model warrants further testing.

Biological mechanisms most likely also play a role in the effects of postnatal depression on child functioning. Although it is now well accepted that brain development continues after birth, recent findings point to specific influences of mothers' perinatal depression on offspring brain development that continue beyond the prenatal period into the postnatal period (Wen et al., 2017). Thus, the stressors (e.g., in the caregiving environment) that infants may experience due to having a mother with depression (Hammen, 2002) may interfere with the development of stress-regulating neural circuits, which increase infants' risk for psychopathology. Similarly, the HPA axis continues to develop postnatally, and stressors associated with inadequate caregiving, which often accompanies depression in mothers (Lovejoy, Graczyk, O'Hare, & Neuman, 2000), may alter the course of HPA axis development (Apter-Levi et al., 2016).

Genetics

Genetic mechanisms may also play an important role. Depression runs in families. A meta-analytic review revealed an odds ratio of 3.98—a nearly fourfold increase in risk of MDD in the offspring of depressed parents—relative to those with no psychopathology in their parents (Rice, Harold, & Thapar, 2002). Moreover, heritability of perinatal depression is higher than for nonperinatal depression; specifically, in a sample of female twins and a separate population-based cohort of sisters, heritability estimates were 54% and 44% for perinatal depression in the two samples, respectively, relative to 32% in nonperinatal depression (Viktorin et al., 2016).

Prenatal exposures may also be associated with later child functioning through epigenetic changes in the offspring's DNA. As an example, pregnant mothers' experience of intimate partner violence was associated with the methylation status of the glucocorticoid receptor (GR) gene of their adolescent offspring (Radtke et al., 2011). Findings emerging from studies of children conceived through in vitro fertilization may also be reflective of epigenetic processes. For example, prenatal stress has been found to be associated with child externalizing behavior problems even in the absence of a genetic relationship between the fetus and mother (Rice et al., 2010). Animal studies, using cross-fostering designs, have been able to take even further steps than in studies of humans in teasing apart the impact of pre- and postnatal stress exposure. That is, researchers are able to assign offspring to mothers at birth, thereby separating pre- and postnatal effects. As an example of findings from this design, prenatal stress was found to influence offspring behavior indirectly via changes in the quality of the postnatal rearing environment (Champagne & Meaney, 2006).

Antidepressant Medication

Any consideration of biological mechanisms should take into account use of antidepressant medication (ADM), whether in pregnancy, when medicine may be directly transmitted to the fetus via the placenta, or in the postpartum period, when it may be transmitted via breast milk. The consideration of ADM is especially important given estimates that at least 75% of pregnant women who are identified as being depressed are referred for pharmacotherapy (Dietz et al., 2007). Further, at least in the United States, around one half of pregnancies are unintended (Finer & Kost, 2011), and many women of childbearing age use antidepressants (Pratt, Brody, & Gu, 2011); thus, some women taking antidepressants may be unaware of their pregnancy, leading their babies to be exposed to medication in utero.

The literature on effects of ADM during pregnancy has been extensively reviewed (e.g., Oberlander & Vigod, 2016; Pearlstein, 2015). Prenatal exposure to antidepressants is associated with concurrent fetal brain blood flow and neurobehavior (Hanley, Hookenson, Rurak, & Oberlander, 2016) and also related to birth weight and gestational age, though the reported effect sizes are small (Ross et al., 2013). There is also a small elevated risk

for transient (self-limiting) neonatal discontinuation syndrome, such as mild respiratory distress (Oberlander, Misri et al., 2004). A recent study reported links between ADM exposure and newborn brain function, as revealed by scalp EEG (Videman et al., 2017). Specifically, ADM-exposed newborns, relative to controls, showed reduced interhemispheric connectivity, lower cross-frequency integration, and reduced frontal activity at low-frequency oscillations; these group differences were not explained by maternal depression or anxiety.

Later in development, prenatal ADM exposure has been associated with children's risk for disorders such as autism (Viktorin, Uher, Reichenberg, Levine, & Sandin, 2017), intellectual disability (Viktorin, Uher, Kolevzon, et al., 2017), and ADHD (Man et al., 2017); however, with all three outcomes, the causal link was with severity of the depression per se and confounders such as maternal age, and not ADM. In contrast, prenatal ADM exposure was associated with higher internalizing (but not externalizing) behavior in children at ages 3 and 6 years, such that children exposed to ADM were more likely to exceed clinical cut-offs for internalizing behavior problems (15.9 vs. 1.5% at age 3 years; 13.6 and 3% at age 6 years) compared to children not exposed to antidepressants during fetal development, even after controlling for mothers' depressive symptom levels throughout the pregnancy, at 6 months postpartum, and concurrent to child outcomes (Hanley, Brain, & Oberlander, 2015). That is, with the exception of children's internalizing behaviors, pregnant women's personal characteristics associated with the likelihood of taking antidepressants, including being more severely depressed, are often more strongly associated with child outcomes than ADM usage during pregnancy. However, it is noteworthy that internalizing problems specifically were associated with prenatal ADM exposure even after accounting for severity of depression. ADMs (SRIs in particular) are consistently associated with changes in central serotonin signaling, which, in turn may account for links between ADM and internalizing symptoms, whereas different biological mechanisms may account for increases in externalizing behaviors or attention problems (Hanley et al., 2015).

In the postpartum period, infant exposure to mothers' ADMs can occur through breast milk. This is compelling given that more than two thirds of mothers in the United States at least initiate breastfeeding (Li, Darling, Maurice, Barker, & Grummer-Strawn, 2005) and prenatal depression is not a significant predictor of breastfeeding initiation or duration (Amiel Castro, Glover, Ehlert, & O'Connor, 2017). A pooled analysis of data across 57 studies revealed that maternal ADM dosage did not predict infant plasma levels of some antidepressants, was weakly correlated with plasma levels of others (citalopram and fluoxetine), and significantly correlated with plasma levels of one (i.e., fluoxetine) (A. M. Weissman et al., 2004). Important next steps in this line of research will examine how these exposures might be related to infant development and later risks for the development of psychopathology.

Animal models indicate that male and female offspring are differentially affected by maternal ADM; male rat pups exposed via maternal breast milk to fluoxetine had greater anxiety-like behavior and more impaired HPA axis negative feedback when they became adults (Gobinath, Workman, Chow, Lieblich, & Galea, 2016); this same effect was not found for female rats. However, Hanley et al. (2016) found that fetal exposure to SRIs was associated with higher internalizing behavior (but not externalizing behavior) in 3-year-olds regardless of the sex of the child; moreover, this association persisted through 6 years of age. It will be important for researchers to design studies to resolve these discrepant findings across species.

Behavioral Mechanisms

In addition to biological mechanisms, behavioral mechanisms are purported to play a role in linking both prenatal and postnatal depression to children's development of psychopathology. Before delving into these, it is important to note that, while all behavioral phenomena have biological correlates, the level of analysis at which the phenomenon may be best understood (and treated) may not be biological. More specifically, mechanisms that we denote as behavioral here (e.g., mothers' prenatal health behaviors) undoubtedly have a biological level of analysis, although that does not imply that a biological level of study is superior (cf. Miller, Rockstroh, Hamilton, & Yee, 2016). One important implication of this complexity is the resulting challenge to interpreting potential mechanisms of effect that might serve as targets of prevention or early intervention.

Prenatal Health Behaviors

In pregnancy, women's depression is associated with inadequate nutrition, exercise, and sleep (Zuckerman, Amorao, Bauchner, & Cabral, 1989), greater use of alcohol, drugs, and cigarettes (Marcus, 2009; Prevatt, Desmarais, & Janssen, 2016; Smedberg, Lupattelli,

Mardby, Overland, & Nordeng, 2015), and later initiation and decreased usage of prenatal care (Redshaw & Henderson, 2013). For each of these behaviors, there are extensive literatures linking them to adverse offspring outcomes. For example, large, population-level data reveal that mothers' smoking during pregnancy is associated with significantly higher rates of severe mental illness in offspring (Quinn, Rickert, Weibull, & et al., 2017). Moreover, as noted, the nature of these behavioral mechanisms clearly has implications for biological mechanisms in terms of the exposures of the fetus to substances and challenges to growth and development. This is just one example of an important future direction—to jointly consider biological and behavioral mechanisms in integrative models, consistent with transdisciplinary approaches.

Parenting

In the postpartum period, most of the attention to behavioral mechanisms has focused on parenting. Maternal depression throughout pregnancy is highly predictive of postnatal depression (Robertson, Grace, Wallington, & Stewart, 2004), and postpartum depression is a strong predictor of parenting quality (Belsky, 1984). Relative to women who experience depression for the first time, those women who experience a recurrence of depression during the postnatal period are at a greater risk of experiencing cognitive and/or biological vulnerabilities that may negatively influence parenting quality (Phillips, Sharpe, Matthey, & Charles, 2010). In women with histories of depression prior to pregnancy, we found that women's recurrence of clinically significant depressive symptoms during pregnancy or the postpartum period was associated with less sensitive parenting with their 12-month-old infants (Goodman, Bakeman, McCallum, Rouse, & Thompson, 2017). Thus, many children who are exposed to their mothers' postnatal depression will experience at least two risk mechanisms: exposure during prenatal development and exposure to poor parenting quality.

Building on the evidence of prenatal influences of infant and child vulnerabilities and outcomes, in studies of postnatal depression, parenting may serve as a mechanism in the transmission of risk from depression in mothers to the development of psychopathology in children in at least two ways: (1) depressed mothers' modeling, for example, of less positive and more negative behaviors and affect, as well as less modeling of appropriate emotion regulation skills, and (2) depressed mothers' providing less support for their infants' developing emotion regulation skills, for example, being less sensitive and responsive and more harsh and lax.

Postnatal maternal depression has been related to more negative and less positive parenting of infants, more disengagement, and more observed negative and decreased positive affect (Lovejoy et al., 2000). Moreover, the association was no stronger for current depression relative to history of depression. That is, associations between depression history and parenting are found even when women are between episodes, suggesting the potential influence of subclinical symptoms or other vulnerabilities to depression (e.g., temperamental emotionality) on parenting. Elevated maternal depression symptoms are also associated with decreased accuracy in mothers' interpretation of their infants' emotional expressions, especially those that are positive (Broth, Goodman, Hall, & Raynor, 2004). Each of these aspects of parenting has been found to be associated with important aspects of children's development. For example, mothers being physically or emotionally absent and, more broadly, their responsiveness have been associated with infants' and children's development of emotion regulation (Calkins, 1994; Field, 1994).

In terms of parenting as a mediator of associations between perinatal depression and offspring outcomes, support is mixed and nuanced. For example, in the NICHD Study of Early Child Care, Campbell and colleagues failed to find that mothers' sensitivity, measured as an average of ratings from observations of mothers' interactions with their offspring spanning from 6 months through 7 years of age, mediated the association between mothers' severity and chronicity of perinatal depressive symptoms and children's psychopathology symptoms or social competence at age 7 years (Campbell, Matestic, von Stauffenberg, Mohan, & Kirchner, 2007). On the other hand, mothers' hostile, critical responses to their children's oppositional behavior mediated the association between maternal depression when the child was 2–4 months of age and the child's quality of attachment to the mother at 16–18 months; this same mediating effect was not found for child internalizing or externalizing behavior problems at 34–37 months (Caughy, Huang, & Lima, 2009). Another study found support for mediation by negative parenting in the association between mothers' depressive symptoms and social, emotional, and behavioral outcomes in 36-month-old children; moreover, for one of the outcomes, separation distress, the association was stronger for children who had been high in negative emotionality

at 6 months of age (Dix & Yan, 2014). Dix and Yan also found that negative parenting was more common among children who were high, rather than low, in negative emotionality as infants. This is consistent with our finding that 3- month-olds emotionality or affectivity predicted mothers' sensitivity during 12-month face-to-face interactions (Goodman et al., 2017)

Overall, support for mothers' quality of parenting as a mediator of the association between her depression and children's outcomes is mixed and requires further consideration. Researchers might consider designing studies to enable stringent tests of mediation. In particular, studies designed to test potential mediation of an association between a predictor (independent variable; presumed causal variable) and a dependent variable (presumed outcome) minimize biases when they are studied longitudinally, with multiple waves of cross-lagged data, which allows for an independent variable to have an effect on the presumed mediator and for the presumed mediator to have an effect on the dependent variable (Maxwell & Cole, 2007). Preventive interventions accomplish the same goals and meet the same criteria. There are some promising findings from such studies; for example, an intervention to enhance mothers' sensitive responsiveness to their 6-month-old infants, selected to be high on irritability, was associated with the infant increases in sociability, soothability, and exploratory behavior at posttest and stronger attachment 3 months later, relative to a control group (van den Boom, 1994). Further, although prenatal depression predicts postnatal depression and parenting stress (Misri et al., 2010), many studies that relate maternal depression to sensitive parenting do not include measures of prenatal depression (Heron, O'Connor, Evans, Golding, & Glover, 2004), which points to the need for prospective studies that address chronicity and timing of depression (c.f. Goodman et al., 2017).

It is important to keep in mind that the relationship between parenting and child characteristics is bidirectional, in that child factors elicit particular parenting qualities. Perhaps most relevant is infant temperament, which is associated with depression in mothers (Britton, 2011; Field, Diego, et al., 2006). We found early infant temperament to be a significant predictor of sensitive parenting with 12-month-old infants among mothers with histories of depression (Goodman et al., 2017). Moreover, among mothers who are at risk for the development of postpartum depression, irritability and "difficult" temperament in offspring predict postpartum depression (Murray, Stanley, Hooper, King, & Fiori-Cowley, 1996).

Stressful Environments

In addition to parenting, stressful environments may also account for the offspring vulnerability associated with maternal depression. That is, depression in mothers is understood to be stress generating (Hammen, 1991), and stress has been found to at least partially explain associations between depression in mothers and the development of psychopathology in children (Compas, Connor-Smith, Saltzman, Thomsen, & Wadsworth, 2001; Grant et al., 2003; Hammen, 2002). However, much of that literature is limited to studies of children and adolescents of depressed mothers. Thus, more studies are needed on the role of stress generation as a mechanism for associations between perinatal depression in mothers' and children's development of psychopathology.

Moderators of Associations Between Mothers' Perinatal Depression and Children's Psychopathology Contextual Moderators

In addition to mechanisms, a model of the association between perinatal depression and children's development of psychopathology would be incomplete without consideration of potential moderators, as proposed by Goodman and Gotlib (1999). That is, it is critical to address for whom or under what circumstances might the association between maternal depression and child outcomes differ. This focus on moderators is consistent with an extensive literature establishing two key points: (1) perinatal depression's links to problems in children are often moderate or small in effect size, suggesting that perinatal depression is not deterministic; and (2) perinatal depression often co-occurs with other contextual risk factors. Rather, in addition to comorbid anxiety, perinatal depression also frequently co-occurs with marital/partner relationship issues (including intimate partner violence) (Biaggi, Conroy, Pawlby, & Pariante, 2016), poverty (Mukherjee, Coxe, Fennie, Madhivanan, & Trepka, 2016), and other stressors. Each of these alone, regardless of the co-occurring depression, is associated with the development of psychopathology in offspring (e.g. Davies & Cummings, 1994). Thus, there is strong support for the important role of moderators of the association between perinatal depression and child functioning.

Parents' Relationship Quality

A depressed mother's quality of relationship with her husband or partner is a good example of a condition under which depression's effects on the children could be exacerbated, if relationship quality is poor or if interparental conflict is present, or mitigated, if the relationship quality is strong. Yet despite knowledge that perinatal depression co-occurs with marital/partner relationship issues (including intimate partner violence) (Biaggi et al., 2016; Whisman, Davila, & Goodman, 2011), we found no studies of the potential moderating role of relationship issues in associations between perinatal depression in mothers and children's development of psychopathology (although see Letourneau, Duffett-Leger, & Salmani, 2009). In one study, perinatal depression in fathers, rather than mothers, was associated with greater disharmony in the partner relationship, but there was no evidence that relationship quality moderated the association between depression in fathers and infant temperament (e.g., distress, soothability) (Ramchandani et al., 2011).

Some support for the moderating role of parents' relationship comes from studies of older children. For example, in children ranging from 9 to 15 years of age who had a parent (mother or father) with a history of MDD, the relation between parent depressive symptoms and youth internalizing problems was specific to youth in high interparental conflict families (Breslend et al., 2016). Moreover, the model was consistent for boys and girls. There was no moderation by interparental conflict for the association between parents' depression and youth externalizing problems. In a related finding, mothers' melancholic depression increased risk for depression in children aged 8 to 12 years old regardless of fathers' antisocial behavior (Shannon, Beauchaine, Brenner, Neuhaus, & Gatzke-Kopp, 2007).

Given the strong conceptual basis for parents' relationship quality as a moderator of the association between mothers' depression and child functioning, and the supportive evidence with older children, an important future direction is for research on relations between perinatal depression, marital conflict, and child outcomes. A related topic also needing study is the potential moderating role of paternal depression and paternal involvement in the relationship between perinatal maternal depression and child outcomes.

Household Income

A similar moderating role might be played by household income. That is, higher income may afford families the additional resources, such as quality child care, that could protect infants against the negative effects of mothers' depression. In contrast, poverty may exacerbate the effects, whether due to fewer resources to assist with childcare or poverty's often associated stressful life events and hassles. Consistent with that idea, Mukherjee and colleagues, using data from the US Pregnancy Risk Assessment Monitoring System (PRAMS), found that stressors were more strongly associated with elevated postpartum depressive symptoms among women living in states with lower socioeconomic status on average (Mukherjee et al., 2016). More specifically, using data from a large US national survey, maternal depression (albeit not specific to perinatal) was more strongly associated with young children's cognitive development in the context of poverty, whereas affluence reduced the strength of association (Petterson & Albers, 2001). In a large cohort study in the United Kingdom, mothers' depression and poverty during their child's infancy independently predicted children's externalizing and internalizing behavior problems at age 3 years (Kiernan & Huerta, 2008). Rather than testing moderation, however, these researchers tested mediation and found that about a third of poverty's influence on children's behavior problems was mediated by mothers' postnatal depression. In another study of postpartum depression, family income moderated the effects of mothers' postpartum depression on parenting qualities (NICHD Early Child Care Research Network, 1999). Specifically, among families with higher income-to-needs ratio, chronic symptoms of depression were associated with greater maternal sensitivity, whereas among those with lower incomes, postpartum depression was associated with decreased sensitivity. However, poverty did not moderate associations between women's postpartum depression and child outcomes at 36 months. An important future direction for this line of studies is an examination of the potential of poverty-relief programs or experimental interventions to enhance sensitive parenting, particularly among women with postnatal depression, and to examine potential benefits to the children, both during infancy and later in development.

Predictors of Perinatal Depression

Another perspective on the question of context is to consider that women are not randomly assigned to become depressed during pregnancy or the postpartum period. In this regard, it is helpful to examine predictors of which women become depressed during the perinatal period. Recent reviews of this literature, albeit qualitative and not quantitative, reveal some predictors that are unique to the perinatal period and others that also predict depression at other periods of women's lives. Specifically, women are more likely to become depressed during pregnancy if they have a personal history of anxiety or depression (although recall Raisanen et al.'s 2014 finding that half of women depressed during pregnancy had not been previously depressed), absence of a partner or other social support, unplanned or unwanted pregnancy, a history of adverse life events, past alcohol use and cigarette smoking, and low income (Biaggi et al., 2016). Thus, in interpreting associations between perinatal depression and children's development of psychopathology, it is essential to acknowledge the likely influence of these additional variables. Given knowledge of the role of these constructs in enhancing the likelihood of perinatal depression, future research would benefit from testing their potential role in explaining associations between perinatal depression and children's development of psychopathology. At minimum, it seems wise to treat these constructs as being of direct interest rather than as confounding variables.

Depression in Fathers

Similarly, knowledge of assortative mating among individuals with psychiatric disorders reminds us that nonrandom factors are also involved in the selection of mates (Nordsletten et al., 2016). Specifically, individuals with depression are more likely to marry others with depression than would be expected by chance (see Mathews & Reus, 2001, for a review), and the fathers of babies born to women with perinatal depression are more likely to have depression than fathers of babies born to nondepressed mothers (K.R. Merikangas, Weissman, Prusoff, & John, 1988). Findings from a large nationally representative sample in the United Kingdom support this in that mothers' depressive symptoms were a significant predictor of fathers' depressive symptoms at infant age 9 months (Nath et al., 2016). There are several reasons to be concerned about this in terms of child outcomes: (1) children inherit genes from both parents and thus have two parents from whom they might inherit alleles associated with depression; (2) couples concordant for depression are more likely than other couples to divorce, exposing the children to these additional stressors (K.R. Merikangas, 1984); (3) fathers with depression may be less able or less inclined to provide the support that pregnant and postpartum mothers need, to serve as healthy role models for children, and to actively contribute to parenting. This information is relevant in interpreting research on fathers as moderators of associations between perinatal depression and children's development of psychopathology.

Paternal Involvement

In order to consider paternal factors as moderators of associations between perinatal depression and children's development of psychopathology, it is essential to first understand how mothers' perinatal depression is associated with fathers' involvement. That is, do fathers become more involved with their infant offspring when mothers are depressed, perhaps to compensate for the mother? Or do fathers become less involved, perhaps as a reaction to maternal depression? We addressed these questions in a longitudinal study of women at risk for perinatal depression, with risk defined by past depression, measuring paternal involvement with both a questionnaire (administered to mothers and fathers) and a time diary interview with the fathers, when infants were 3, 6, and 12 months of age (Goodman, Lusby, Thompson, Newport, & Stowe, 2014). When mothers were depressed in the first 6 months postpartum, fathers were more involved with their infants, supporting the compensatory/buffering model; however, when mothers' depressive symptoms persisted into the second half of the infants' first year, fathers were less involved with their infants, consistent with the idea of spillover from maternal depressive symptoms.

The next question in this line of studies is the extent to which fathers' compensatory role moderates the negative association between mothers' perinatal depression and children's functioning. In an explicit test of fathering as a moderator of the effects of maternal depression, albeit on family process rather than child functioning per se, fathers were less sensitive and more intrusive when mothers were depressed; further, fathers' interactive qualities (i.e., sensitivity and intrusiveness) with their 6-year-old children moderated the effect of mothers' concurrent depression on family cohesion, particularly when mothers were depressed in the first 9 months postpartum (Vakrat, Apter-Levy, & Feldman, 2018). That is, when fathers' sensitivity was high, mothers' depression was not associated with family cohesion; however, when fathers' sensitivity was low, maternal depression was significantly associated with lower family cohesion. Similarly, the association between mothers' depression and family cohesion was specific to fathers' engagement with the children being low rather than high. Longitudinal studies of how mothers' and fathers' qualities of parenting unfold over time in relation to each other are clearly needed to clarify whether fathers engage with their children in ways that help the children by compensating for the otherwise negative correlate of mothers' depression. Intervention studies might test models of supports or education to fathers that might enable them to overcome the challenges of parenting well when mothers are depressed. Such studies have the opportunity to inform practice and policy as well as experiments to test causal models (see Gage, Munafò, & Davey Smith, 2016 for a broader discussion of this issue).

Maternal and Child Characteristics as Moderators

In this section, we continue the focus on maternal and child characteristics that might moderate links between perinatal depression in mothers and functioning in children, such as timing and chronicity of maternal perinatal depression and parenting qualities, as well as child temperament and sex.

Timing and Chronicity of Mothers' Perinatal Depression

A better understanding of the role of timing of children's exposure to perinatal depression will inform models of the development of psychopathology in children and may have implications for the design of preventive interventions. Of particular interest is the question of whether children are particularly sensitive to maternal depression during pregnancy relative to the postpartum period, or whether maternal depression that is persistent through both time periods is most harmful. In one long-term follow-up study, 10- to 12-year-old children's cortisol awakening response (CAR) varied in relation to timing of mothers' perinatal psychological distress (Vänskä et al., 2015); when mothers had been depressed prenatally, children's CAR was intensified—a relatively steep increase in cortisol from awakening to 1 hour later. In contrast, when mothers first became depressed in the postpartum period, children's CAR was reduced. In terms of depression that is persistent from pregnancy through the postpartum period, it is also important to consider the chronicity of the mother's depression more broadly, that is, before the pregnancy, which also likely marks children's heightened risk for adverse outcomes.

Rates of depression vary somewhat by trimester (Bennett, Einarson, Taddio, Koren, & Einerson, 2004; Gavin et al., 2005), which may also be an important factor to consider in predicting child outcomes. Glover (2009) has suggested that depression during the second trimester per se may be most harmful to the fetus, based on the potential mediating role of maternal cortisol. Consistent with that idea, we found that, controlling for depression symptom levels in other trimesters, only second-trimester depression symptoms predicted infant temperament negative affectivity (Rouse & Goodman, 2014). Further, we found that when postpartum depression symptom levels were in the model, only antenatal depression symptoms predicted infant negative affectivity. Laurent, Ablow, and Measelle (2011) reported that mothers' prenatal depressive symptoms, in interaction with their 18-month postnatal symptoms, predicted infants' HPA response to a stressor, as well as infants' coordination of their HPA and sympathetic nervous systems and infant–mother HPA attunement. Specifically, the findings implicated change in mothers' perinatal depression, even reductions in symptoms, in negative child stress response profiles.

Overall, these findings show that the timing of mothers' depression has long-term implications for children's stress regulation. However, before firm conclusions can be drawn, a comprehensive review of this literature is needed to identify patterns in how timing of perinatal depression relates to concurrent and subsequent child functioning. For example, in my own lab (Goodman), we found that prenatal depression predicted 3-month-olds' temperamental negative affectivity (Rouse & Goodman, 2014) and 12-month-olds' disorganized attachment, regardless of postnatal depression levels (although the latter effect on attachment was specific to those with less optimal early parenting) (Hayes et al., 2013). Prenatal depression also predicted 3- and 6-month-olds' greater relative right frontal EEG activity only when postnatal depression was also high (Lusby, Goodman, Bell, & Newport, 2014). We interpret these findings as suggesting that different associations between timing and specific outcomes may reveal developmental mechanisms that are specific to particular outcomes. Experimental designs may play an important role here in that interventions timed to improve mothers' depressive symptoms at different points across the perinatal period can be used to test hypotheses about differential effects of timing on infants' functioning.

More broadly, it is essential to again remember that these studies are correlational and thus cannot be used to infer causality. Experimental work using lab-induced stressors and, conversely, lab-induced relaxation is useful in addressing this gap. For example, Monk and colleagues found that stress induced in pregnant women at 36–38 weeks gestational age was associated with elevated fetal heart rate, albeit only in mothers who were depressed and/or anxious (Monk et al., 2011). Conversely, DiPietro and colleagues induced relaxation in women during pregnancy (32 weeks gestation) and, relative to rest alone, observed decreased fetal heart rate, increased fetal heart rate variability, suppressed fetal movement, and increased coupling of fetal movement with fetal heart rate (DiPietro, Costigan, Nelson, Gurewitsch, & Laudenslager, 2008).

Further, although we focused on timing here, it is increasingly understood that perinatal depression is diverse in multiple ways, including etiology, clinical characteristics such as severity and timing of onset or symptom profiles, comorbidities, correlates, and so on. Efforts to characterize and understand that diversity (e.g., Apter, Devouche, Gratier, Valente, & Nestour, 2012; Postpartum Depression: Action towards Causes and Treatment [PACT] Consortium, 2015) may inform our understanding of factors that exacerbate or reduce associations of perinatal depression with children's development of psychopathology.

Mothers' Parenting

Although earlier in this chapter we argued that mothers' negative parenting may mediate ties between mothers' perinatal depression and children's development of psychopathology, it is also essential to consider the potential compensating (moderating) role of higher quality maternal care. An impressive animal research literature (studies of rat mothers and pups) has identified aspects of positive maternal care (i.e., maternal licking and grooming of rat pups) that have been found to counteract both behavioral and physiological effects of prenatal stress (Champagne, Francis, Mar, & Meaney, 2003; Del Cerro et al., 2010). Translating this work to humans, Meaney and colleagues also found that mothers' reported frequency of stroking their infants moderated the effect of prenatal depression on infant's subsequent vagal reactivity to a stressor and mother-reported infant anger proneness and fear (see Sharp et al., 2012 for a broader discussion of this issue). Similarly, the quality of parent–child attachment has been found to moderate the association between mothers' prenatal stress and child outcomes such as fearfulness (Bergman, Sarkar, Glover, & O'Connor, 2008).

Also consistent with this idea is a finding from the large Early Child Care study in the United States, which followed mothers and their children from birth through 36 months of age (NICHD Early Child Care Research Network, 1999). They found that, among children of depressed mothers, those whose mothers were rated as more sensitive (from observations over 36 months) had better outcomes relative to children with less sensitive mothers. This moderated model was supported for 36-month-olds' expressive language skills and mother-reported cooperative behavior, but not school readiness, verbal comprehension, observed compliance, and behavior problems. That is, maternal sensitivity acted as a buffer of the potential negative effects of mothers' postnatal depression on a subset of outcomes. Important next steps in this line of research are to better understand the personal and contextual qualities that may be associated with postpartum depressed mothers being able to parent sensitively. Intervention studies could play a role in answering that question by identifying moderators of the effectiveness of interventions designed to improve sensitive parenting in women with depression during the postpartum period. Subsequent studies could then be designed to address those moderators, potentially enabling more women with postpartum depression to engage in sensitive parenting even if depression persists.

Child Temperament

Children's individual difference qualities such as temperament—emotion regulation, in particular—may reduce or exacerbate associations between perinatal depression and children's development of psychopathology (Rothbart & Posner, 2006). That is, children, including infants, with less reactivity and better developed early emotion regulation skills might (1) be better able to cope with a mother's depression in the postpartum period and (2) be easier to care for (e.g., more easily soothed), which might be especially important for a mother with depression.

We found a few direct tests of this model. In one, infants' negative emotionality (measured at 3 and 12 months) moderated the association between mothers' and toddlers' depression-like symptoms when the infants were 18 months old: When mothers' depression symptom levels were high, toddlers' depressive-like symptoms were also high, regardless of their negative emotionality in infancy; however, when mothers' depressive symptoms were low, toddlers' depression-like symptoms were high only among those with high negative affectivity in infancy (Gartstein & Bateman, 2008). In another direct test of this model, although not specific to perinatal depression, among children whose mothers had a lifetime history of depression, children's higher temperament positive affectivity (but not negative affectivity) at age 3 predicted their lower morning cortisol (but not evening cortisol) at age 6; there was no significant association between child PA at age 3 and morning cortisol at age 6 for children of mothers with no history of depression (Dougherty et al., 2013). Further, the model was specific to depression, and not anxiety, in the mothers. In a third direct test with 5-year-olds, mothers' depressive symptoms were more strongly associated with their children's behavior problems only among children who were high, relative to low, on surgency and negative affect, two of the three factor analytically derived factors of child temperament (Jessee, Mangelsdorf, Shigeto, & Wong, 2012).

When considering child temperament as a potential moderator of relations between perinatal maternal depression and children's own psychopathology, it is also important to consider that child temperament may interact with other vulnerabilities, at the same or different levels of analyses, in ways that illuminate when perinatal depression might be more strongly associated with adverse child outcomes. In preliminary tests of this model, we found that, when mothers' prenatal depressive symptoms were low, infant negative affectivity and frontal EEG asymmetry were not significantly associated at 3, 6, or 12 months of age (Lusby, Goodman, Yeung, Bell, & Stowe, 2016). In contrast, among infants of mothers with higher prenatal depressive symptoms, infant temperamental negative affectivity and frontal EEG asymmetry were negatively associated at 3 months of age and positively associated by 12 months of age. Further, postnatal depression predicted shifts in the association between negative affectivity and frontal EEG asymmetry. The latter finding is suggestive of the importance of considering transactional models. Consistent with a transactional model, Pesonen and colleagues (Pesonen et al., 2008) found that higher maternal stress predicted an increase in children's temperamental negative emotionality and a decrease in their positive affectivity from infancy through the subsequent 5 years; weak support was found for the opposite direction—that higher temperament negative emotionality and lower positive affectivity in infants contributed to an increase in maternal stress from the time her child was an infant through the subsequent 5-year period. Also consistent with transactional models is consideration of traits (temperament) not only in infants but also in mothers, and how they may interrelate over time. Although not a study of depression in mothers, Gratz et al. found support for an important role of the confluence of trait vulnerabilities in *both* mothers and infants in the intergenerational transmission of infants' early expressions of those trait vulnerabilities (Gratz et al., 2015).

Sex of Child

The sex of the child may play a moderating role in associations between perinatal depression and offspring outcomes. Findings on prenatal stress in rodents are informative. For the most part, prenatal stress in rats is differentially associated with female and male offspring functioning, predicting fear and depression-like behaviors in female offspring, and problems in learning and memory in male offspring (Weinstock, 2007). A study of mice revealed a role of timing of stress in relation to sex moderation. Specifically, only male pups whose mothers experienced stress early in pregnancy showed greater behavioral and HPA axis stress responsivity and more anhedonia (Mueller & Bale, 2008).

In humans, child sex has typically not been found to play a significant moderating role of ties between maternal depression and child psychopathology until adolescence, perhaps because socialization of emotion may play an especially critical role for girls during this developmental transition (Sheeber, Davis, & Hops, 2002) when rates of depression begin to diverge between boys and girls (Hankin & Abramson, 1999). Somewhat contradictory to this notion, in a meta-analytic review, when all ages of children were considered, we found that child gender moderated the association between depression in mothers and child internalizing, but not externalizing, problems, with larger effect sizes for girls relative to boys (Goodman et al., 2011). We were unable to test the association for child negative or positive affect or behavior, the constructs often measured in infants in relation to perinatal

depression, since too few studies reported results separately by child gender. Thus questions remain unanswered about the potential moderating role of gender in relations between perinatal depression and child psychopathology.

Empirical Approaches and Challenges: Research Design Considerations

There are several challenges in considering evidence for causal relations between the stressors that we focus on here (perinatal depression and its correlates) and child functioning (vulnerabilities to, or early signs or symptoms of, disorder). Among the most concerning challenges is the reliance on drawing causal conclusions from correlational, nonexperimental data. As noted by Kendler, "There is no question more fundamental for observational epidemiology than that of causal inference" (Kendler, 2017). Among the many concerns with correlational approaches is the typical reliance on testing linear relationships. An important direction for future research is to consider nonlinear relationships between risk and child outcomes. In particular, we encourage continued exploration of the possibility of optimal outcomes for children exposed to moderate stress, relative to especially low or high stress, as has been found with prenatal stress (DiPietro et al., 2006; Liu, 2017).

Longitudinal Designs

Perhaps most obvious is the need for longitudinal, rather than cross-sectional designs. To address important questions regarding the long-term child outcomes associated with perinatal depression, it is crucial to begin studies during pregnancy and follow children throughout the postpartum period and beyond. Many studies that consider the effects of maternal depression begin after the birth of the child, but it is important to examine depression chronicity, severity, timing, and recurrence throughout the entire perinatal period to develop a better understanding of maternal mental health and child functioning over time.

Experimental Designs

Experimental designs may also prove useful in elucidating causal mechanisms. Importantly, this includes the consideration of interventions, whether prevention or treatment, as experimental tests of causal models. This has long been a tenet of a developmental psychopathology perspective. Experiments or quasi-experiments and intervention studies are necessary to provide information regarding mechanisms, both behavioral and biological, that are involved in these associations, and to reveal causality in the possible pathways that relate maternal depression with child outcomes (Donofrio, Class, Lahey, & Larsson, 2014). Understanding these mechanisms may lead to the design and implementation of effective preventative and treatment interventions. In terms of the effect of mothers' perinatal depression on children, our conceptual models offer opportunities not only to intervene prenatally but also postnatally, with the latter potentially providing tests of the potential of postnatal environments to mitigate effects of the prenatal exposures (Huizink & Bögels, 2013). Ideas for experimental designs have been mentioned at various points in this chapter.

Interventions also have the potential to generate knowledge of mechanisms that are purported to explain associations between the risk and the outcome. Future longitudinal studies are needed that assess the effects of interventions that target reduction of maternal depression, anxiety, and/or stress beginning in the first trimester of pregnancy on long-term child outcomes (Glover, 2014). As we have noted in this review, such knowledge is accumulating, although additional research is needed.

Developmental and Contextual Implications for Measurement
Approaches to Measuring Depression in Mothers

Are associations between perinatal depression and children's development of psychopathology different depending on whether depression in mothers was measured with a diagnostic interview or a self-report symptom questionnaire? In a meta-analytic review of this literature, although not limited to perinatal depression, measurement type did not moderate the association between depression in mothers and children's positive or negative affect or behavior, which is the outcome most often measured in infants and young children and, thus, most relevant to the topic of this chapter (Goodman et al., 2011). Nonetheless, the issue remains that reliance on diagnoses, relative to dimensional approaches, interferes with tests of linear relationships between mothers' depression and child outcomes.

Approaches to Assessing Child Functioning

Approaches to the measurement of child functioning in relation to mothers' perinatal depression include questionnaire-based assessments (mother-, child-, teacher-, or other-reported), observations, and biological measures. Each of these has its own considerations in terms of challenges to reliability and validity. In our meta-analytic review of this literature, mentioned in the previous paragraph, we addressed concerns that the degree of association between depression in mothers and child functioning might vary based on the source of data on the child, with a particular concern about mothers' reports (Goodman et al., 2011). We found that, for both internalizing and externalizing problems, mothers' reports were associated with significantly larger effect sizes than studies that obtained data from teachers or other adults or from children (e.g., for internalizing: weighted means r of .25 relative to .15 or .17 for mother, teacher, and child, respectively). This pattern of findings might be explained by mothers with depression being more sensitive to emotional or behavioral problems in their children than other informants, including the children themselves, or that mothers with depression are negatively biased in their perceptions of their children. Although this topic has received much attention (e.g., Richters, 1992), more research is needed to sort out the sources of these differences in degree of association. At minimum, it is important to acknowledge that any tendency of depressed mothers to overreport their children's problems likely represents a small, yet significant, contribution to the findings (Goodman et al., 2011).

Sampling Issues

In terms of sampling strategies, researchers are encouraged to give serious consideration to potential confounds. One option is to consider confounds within the approach to sampling. For example, if there is reason (theoretical or empirical) to be concerned about antidepressant medication use as a confound in a hypothesized association between mothers' perinatal depression and a particular aspect of child functioning, one might select women all of whom have taken the concerning medication, none of whom have taken the medication, and half of whom have taken the medication (noting implications for statistical power). In all cases, a careful approach to measurement of medication use is required.

Final Remarks
Toward Dynamic Conceptual Models

A clear and strong conclusion from this review is the importance of recognizing that much of the field has replaced main effect and linear patterns of association and causation with dynamic conceptual models. This is especially true with regard to causal models but also an important consideration in regard to "outcomes." That is, a single vulnerability or sign of disorder is most likely an inadequate model of processes linking maternal depression and child functioning. Essentially, risk factors are complex, vulnerabilities are numerous and co-occurring, protective factors are likely present (Cicchetti & Schneider-Rosen, 1986), and longitudinal developmental mediational pathways may vary across individuals (e.g., Koukounari, Stringaris, & Maughan, 2017). In a previous review, we delved into the potential of several such models, including diathesis-stress models, transactional models of risk or vulnerability, and differential susceptibility models (see Goodman, 2015, for a review).

Clinical Significance

The extensive reliance on observational, correlational designs, even if longitudinal, and the small effect sizes found for perinatal depression on child outcomes may raise concerns about clinical meaningfulness of this phenomenon. We conclude that the findings reviewed here are, indeed, clinically meaningful based on the range of outcomes associated with mothers' perinatal depression, the long-term implications of the child outcomes, the support for causal associations that comes from animal studies, the emerging literature from experiments and interventions, and the need to increase our understanding of mechanisms (biological and behavioral; prenatal and postnatal).

A few efforts have been made to provide context for interpreting the effect sizes. For example, although this review focused on anxiety, Glover (2014) summarized the findings from a large population-based study in the United Kingdom, noting that children of mothers who scored in the top 15% of the distribution for anxiety had children who were at double the risk of emotional or behavioral problems between the ages of 4 and 7 years, even after controlling for a wide range of possible confounders, including postnatal depression in the mothers. More broadly, this raised the risk for children's psychopathology from 5% in the general population to about 10% in the children whose mothers were in the high anxiety group. Although not specific to perinatal depression, in our meta-analytic review, the overall weighted mean effect size of .22 for the association between depression in mothers and children's internalizing problems indicates that about 68% of children of depressed mothers, whether meeting diagnostic criteria or high symptom levels, are worse off than the average child of a nondepressed mother (Goodman et al., 2011).

What to Do

Although much more work needs to be done to determine best approaches to clinical intervention, whether prevention or treatment, we close with recommendations. In particular, interventions for mothers who are depressed or at risk for depression need to be started early, that is, in pregnancy if not before. Several evidence-based approaches are available, including antidepressant medications. Moreover, interpersonal therapy, behavioral activation, cognitive-behavioral therapy, and mindfulness-based cognitive therapy have been modified for the prevention or treatment of depression in pregnancy or the postpartum period (Glover, 2014; Goodman & Garber, 2017). Goodman and Garber advocate for integrated approaches that address the two purported mechanisms of risk: the depression in the mothers and her qualities of parenting, with additional consideration of dealing with barriers to enrollment, retention, and maintenance. It is also essential for the silos of "adult" and "child" treatment to be broken down so that clinicians treating mothers with depression consider their opportunities and responsibilities to attend to parenting and children's risk for psychopathology and vice versa (Zalewski, Goodman, Cole, & McLaughlin, 2017). Overall, we encourage continued work on the understanding and treatment of risk for the development of psychopathology in children of mothers with depression during the perinatal period.

References

Akhtar-Danesh, N., & Landeen, J. (2007). Relation between depression and sociodemographic factors. *International Journal of Mental Health Systems, 1*(1), 4. doi:10.1186/1752-4458-1-4

American Psychiatric Association. (2013). *Diagnostic and statistical manual of mental disorders* (DSM-5). Washington, DC: Author.

Amiel Castro, R. T., Glover, V., Ehlert, U., & O'Connor, T. G. (2017). Antenatal psychological and socioeconomic predictors of breastfeeding in a large community sample. *Early Human Development, 110*, 50–56. doi:10.1016/j.earlhumdev.2017.04.010

Apter-Levi, Y., Pratt, M., Vakart, A., Feldman, M., Zagoory-Sharon, O., & Feldman, R. (2016). Maternal depression across the first years of life compromises child psychosocial adjustment; relations to child HPA-axis functioning. *Psychoneuroendocrinology, 64*, 47–68.

Apter, G., Devouche, E., Gratier, M., Valente, M., & Nestour, A. L. (2012). What lies behind postnatal depression: is it only a mood disorder? *Journal of Personality Disorders, 26*(3), 357–367. doi:10.1521/pedi.2012.26.3.357

Barker, D. J. P. (1998). In Utero programming of chronic disease. *Clinical Science*, 95, 115–128.

Barker, E. D., Jaffee, S. R., Uher, R., & Maughan, B. (2011). The contribution of prenatal and postnatal maternal anxiety and depression to child maladjustment. *Depression and Anxiety*, 28(8), 696–702.

Batenburg-Eddes, V., Brion, M., Henrichs, J., Jaddoe, V., Hofman, A., Verhulst, F.,...Tiemeier, H. (2013). Parental depressive and anxiety symptoms during pregnancy and attention problems in children: A cross-cohort consistency study. *Journal of Child Psychology and Psychiatry*, 54(5), 591–600.

Bazhenova, O. V., Plonskaia, O., & Porges, S. W. (2001). Vagal reactivity and affective adjustment in infants during interaction challenges. *Child Development*, 72(5), 1314–1326. doi:10.1111/1467-8624.00350

Beauchaine, T. P. (2012). Physiological markers of emotion and emotion dysregulation in externalizing psychopathology. *Monographs of the Society for Research in Child Development*, 77(2), 79–86. doi:10.1111/j.1540-5834.2011.00665.x

Belsky, J. (1984). The determinants of parenting: A process model. *Child Development*, 55(1), 83–96.

Bennett, H. A., Einarson, A., Taddio, A., Koren, G., & Einerson, T. R. (2004). Prevalence of depression during pregnancy: A systematic review. *Obstetrics and Gynecology*, 103(4), 698–709.

Bergman, K., Sarkar, P., Glover, V., & O'Connor, T. (2008). Quality of child-parent attachment moderates the impact of antenatal stress on child fearfulness. *Journal of Child Psychology and Psychiatry*, 49(10), 1089–1098.

Betts, K. S., Williams, G. M., Najman, J. M., & Alati, R. (2014). The relationship between maternal depressive, anxious, and stress symptomsl during pregnancy and adult offspring behavioral and emotional problems. *Depression and Anxiety*. doi:10.1002/da.22272

Biaggi, A., Conroy, S., Pawlby, S., & Pariante, C. M. (2016). Identifying the women at risk of antenatal anxiety and depression: a systematic review. *Journal of Affective Disorders*, 191, 62–77.

Booij, L., Wang, D. S., Levesque, M. L., Tremblay, R. E., & Szyf, M. (2013). Looking beyond the DNA sequence: The relevance of DNA methylation processes for the stress-diathesis model of depression. *Philosophical Transactions of the Royal Society B-Biological Sciences*, 368(1615). doi:10.1098/rstb.2012.0251

Breslend, N. L., Parent, J., Forehand, R., Compas, B. E., Thigpen, J. C., & Hardcastle, E. (2016). Parental depressive symptoms and youth internalizing and externalizing problems: The moderating role of interparental conflict. *Journal of Family Violence*, 1–9. doi:10.1007/s10896-016-9817-z

Britton, J. R. (2011). Infant temperament and maternal anxiety and depressed mood in the early postpartum period. *Women & Health*, 51(1), 55–71. doi:10.1080/03630242.2011.540741

Broth, M. R., Goodman, S. H., Hall, C., & Raynor, L. C. (2004). Depressed and well mothers' emotion interpretation accuracy and the quality of mother–infant interaction. *Infancy*, 6(1), 37–55.

Buss, C., Davis, E. P., Hobel, C., & Sandman, C. (2011). Maternal pregnancy-specific anxiety is associated with child executive function at 6–9 years age. *Stress*, 14(6), 665–676.

Calkins, S. D. (1994). Origins and outcomes of individual differences in emotion regulation. *Monographs of the Society for Research in Child Development*, 59(2–3), 53–72.

Campbell, S. B., Matestic, P., von Stauffenberg, C., Mohan, R., & Kirchner, T. (2007). Trajectories of maternal depressive symptoms, maternal sensitivity, and children's functioning at school entry. *Developmental Psychology*, 43(5), 1202–1215. doi:10.1037/0012-1649.43.5.1202

Carpenter, T., Grecian, S. M., & Reynolds, R. M. (2017). Sex differences in early-life programming of the hypothalamic–pituitary–adrenal axis in humans suggest increased vulnerability in females: a systematic review. *Journal of Developmental Origins ofÂ HealthÂ and Disease*, 8(2), 244–255. doi:10.1017/S204017441600074X

Caughy, M. O. B., Huang, K.-Y., & Lima, J. (2009). Patterns of conflict interaction in mother–toddler dyads: Differences between depressed and non-depressed mothers. *Journal of Child and Family Studies*, 18(1), 10–20.

Champagne, F. A., Francis, D. D., Mar, A., & Meaney, M. J. (2003). Variations in maternal care in the rat as a mediating influence for the effects of environment on development. *Physiology and Behavior*, 79(3), 359–371.

Champagne, F. A., & Meaney, M. J. (2006). Stress during gestation alters postpartum maternal care and the development of the offspring in a rodent model. *Biological Psychiatry*, 59(12), 1227–1235.

Christian, L. M. (2015). Stress and immune function during pregnancy: An emerging focus in mind-body medicine. *Current Directions in Psychological Science*, 24(1), 3–9. doi:10.1177/0963721414550704

Christian, L. M., Mitchell, A. M., Gillespie, S. L., & Palettas, M. (2016). Serum brain-derived neurotrophic factor (BDNF) across pregnancy and postpartum: Associations with race, depressive symptoms, and low birth weight. *Psychoneuroendocrinology*, 74, 69–76.

Cicchetti, D., & Rogosch, F. A. (1996). Equifinality and multifinality in developmental psychopathology. *Development & Psychopathology*, 8, 597–600.

Cicchetti, D., & Schneider-Rosen, K. (1986). An organizational approach to childhood depression. In M. Rutter, C. E. Izard, & P. B. Read (Eds.), *Depression in young people: Developmental and clinical perspectives* (pp. 71–134). New York, NY: Guilford Press.

Compas, B. E., Connor-Smith, J. K., Saltzman, H., Thomsen, A. H., & Wadsworth, M. E. (2001). Coping with stress during childhood and adolescence: Problems, progress, and potential in theory and research. *Psychological Bulletin*, 127(1), 87–127.

Connell, A. M., & Goodman, S. H. (2002). The association between psychopathology in fathers versus mothers and children's internalizing and externalizing behavior problems: A meta-analysis. *Psychological Bulletin*, 128, 746–773.

Davies, P. T., & Cummings, E. M. (1994). Marital conflict and child adjustment: An emotional security hypothesis. *Psychological Bulletin*, 116(387–411).

Davis, E. P., Glynn, L. M., Schetter, C. D., Hobel, C., Chicz-Demet, A., & Sandman, C. A. (2007). Prenatal exposure to maternal depression and cortisol influences infant temperament. *Journal of the American Academy of Child & Adolescent Psychiatry*, 46(6), 737–746.

Davis, E. P., Head, K., Buss, C., & Sandman, C. A. (2017). Prenatal maternal cortisol concentrations predict neurodevelopment in middle childhood. *Psychoneuroendocrinology*, 75, 56–63.

Davis, E. P., & Sandman, C. A. (2010). The timing of prenatal exposure to maternal cortisol and psychosocial stress is associated with human infant cognitive development. *Child Development*, 81(1), 131–148.

Davis, E. P., & Sandman, C. A. (2012). Prenatal psychobiological predictors of anxiety risk in preadolescent children. *Psychoneuroendocrinology*, 37(8), 1224–1233. doi:10.1016/j.psyneuen.2011.12.016

Davis, E. P., Snidman, N., Wadhwa, P. D., Glynn, L. M., Schetter, C. D., & Sandman, C. A. (2004). Prenatal maternal anxiety and depression predict negative behavioral reactivity in infancy. *Infancy*, 6(3), 319–331.

Dawson, G., Frey, K., Panagiotides, H., Osterling, J., & Hessl, D. (1997). Infants of depressed mothers exhibit atypical frontal brain activity: A replication and extension of previous findings. *Journal of Child Psychology and Psychiatry*, 38(2), 179–186.

de Weerth, C., van Hees, Y., & Buitelaar, J. K. (2003). Prenatal maternal cortisol levels and infant behavior during the first 5 months. *Early Human Development*, 74(2), 139–151.

Del Cerro, M., Perez-Laso, C., Ortega, E., Martín, J., Gomez, F., Perez-Izquierdo, M., & Segovia, S. (2010). Maternal care counteracts behavioral effects of prenatal environmental stress in female rats. *Behavioural Brain Research*, 208(2), 593–602.

Diego, M. A., Field, T., Hernandez-Reif, M., Cullen, C., Schanberg, S., & Kuhn, C. (2004). Prepartum, postpartum, and chronic depression effects on newborns. *Psychiatry: Interpersonal and Biological Processes*, 67(1), 63–80.

Diego, M. A., Field, T., Hernandez-Reif, M., Schanberg, S., Kuhn, C., & Gonzalez-Quintero, V. H. (2009). Prenatal depression restricts fetal growth. *Early Human Development*, 85(1), 65–70.

Diego, M. A., Field, T., Jones, N. A., & Hernandez-Reif, M. (2006). Withdrawn and intrusive maternal interaction style and infant frontal EEG asymmetry shifts in infants of depressed and non-depressed mothers. *Infant Behavior & Development*, 29(2), 220–229.

Diego, M. A., Jones, N. A., Field, T., Hernandez-Reif, M., Schanberg, S., Kuhn, C., & Gonzalez-Garcia, A. (2006). Maternal psychological distress, prenatal cortisol, and fetal weight. *Psychosomatic Medicine*, 68(5), 747–753.

Dietz, P. M., Williams, S. B., Callaghan, W. M., Bachman, D. J., Whitlock, E. P., & Hornbrook, M. C. (2007). Clinically identified maternal depression before, during, and after pregnancies ending in live births. *American Journal of Psychiatry*, 164(10), 1515–1520. doi:10.1176/appi.ajp.2007.06111893

DiPietro, J. A., Costigan, K. A., Nelson, P., Gurewitsch, E. D., & Laudenslager, M. L. (2008). Fetal responses to induced maternal relaxation during pregnancy. *Biological Psychology*, 77(1), 11–19. doi:http://dx.doi.org/10.1016/j.biopsycho.2007.08.008

DiPietro, J. A., Novak, M. F. S. X., Costigan, K. A., Atella, L. D., & Reusing, S. P. (2006). Maternal psychological distress during pregnancy in relation to child development at age two. *Child Development*, 77(3), 573–587.

Dix, T., & Yan, N. (2014). Mothers' depressive symptoms and infant negative emotionality in the prediction of child adjustment at age 3: Testing the maternal reactivity and child vulnerability hypotheses. *Development and Psychopathology*, 26(01), 111–124.

Donofrio, B., Class, Q., Lahey, B., & Larsson, H. (2014). Testing the developmental origins of health and disease hypothesis for psychopathology using family-based, quasi-experimental designs. *Child Development Perspectives*, doi:10.1111/cdep.12078

Dougherty, L. R., Smith, V. C., Olino, T. M., Dyson, M. W., Bufferd, S. J., Rose, S. A., & Klein, D. N. (2013). Maternal psychopathology and early child temperament predict young children's salivary cortisol 3 years later. *Journal of Abnormal Child Psychology*, 41(4), 531–542.

Essex, M. J., Klein, M. H., Cho, E., & Kalin, N. H. (2002). Maternal stress beginning in infancy may sensitize children to later stress exposure: Effects on cortisol and behavior. *Biological Psychiatry*, 52, 776–784.

Field, T. (1994). The effects of mother's physical and emotional unavailability on emotion regulation. *Monographs of the Society for Research in Child Development*, 59(2–3), 250–283.

Field, T., & Diego, M. A. (2008). Prenatal dysthymia versus major depression effects on the neonate. *Infant Behavior & Development*, 31(2), 190–193. doi:10.1016/j.infbeh.2007.10.004

Field, T., Diego, M. A., Dieter, J., Hernandez-Reif, M., Schanberg, S., Kuhn, C.,…Bendell, D. (2004). Prenatal depression effects on the fetus and the newborn. *Infant Behavior & Development*, 27(2), 216–229.

Field, T., Diego, M. A., Hernandez-Reif, M., Figueiredo, B., Deeds, O., Contogeorgos, J., & Ascencio, A. (2006). Prenatal paternal depression. *Infant Behavior and Development*, 29(4), 579–583.

Field, T., Fox, N. A., Pickens, J., & Nawrocki, T. (1995). Relative right frontal EEG activation in 3-to 6-month-old infants of "depressed" mothers. *Developmental Psychology*, 31, 358–363.

Field, T., Healy, B., Goldstein, S., Perry, S., Bendell, D., Schanberg, S.,…Kuhn, C. (1988). Infants of depressed mothers show "depressed" behavior even with nondepressed adults. *Child Development*, 59(6), 1569–1579.

Field, T., Hernandez-Reif, M., Diego, M. A., Figueiredo, B., Schanberg, S., & Kuhn, C. (2006). Prenatal cortisol, prematurity and low birthweight. *Infant Behavior & Development*, 29(2), 268–275.

Field, T., Pickens, J., Fox, N. A., Nawrocki, T., & Gonzalez, J. (1995). Vagal tone in infants of depressed mothers. *Development and Psychopathology*, 7, 227–231.

Fihrer, I., McMahon, C. A., & Taylor, A. J. (2009). The impact of postnatal and concurrent maternal depression on child behaviour during the early school years. *Journal of Affective Disorders*, 119(1–3), 116–123.

Finer, L. B., & Kost, K. (2011). Unintended pregnancy rates at the state level. *Perspectives on Sexual and Reproductive Health*, 43(2), 78–87.

Fox, N. A. (1994). The development of emotion regulation: Biological and behavioral considerations. *Monographs of the Society for Research in Child Development*, 59.

Gage, S. H., Munafò, M. R., & Davey Smith, G. (2016). Causal inference in developmental origins of health and disease (DOHaD) research. *Annual Review of Psychology*, 67, 567–585.

Galéra, C., Côté, S. M., Bouvard, M. P., & et al. (2011). Early risk factors for hyperactivity-impulsivity and inattention trajectories from age 17 months to 8 years. *Archives of General Psychiatry*, 68(12), 1267–1275. doi:10.1001/archgenpsychiatry.2011.138

Gartstein, M. A., & Bateman, A. E. (2008). Early manifestations of childhood depression: influences of infant temperament and parental depressive symptoms. *Infant & Child Development*, 17(3), 223–248. doi:10.1002/icd.549

Gavin, N. I., Gaynes, B. N., Lohr, K. N., Meltzer-Brody, S., Gartlehner, G., & Swinson, T. (2005). Perinatal depression:

A systematic review of prevalence and incidence. *Obstetrics and Gynecology*, *106*(5), 1071–1083. doi:10.1097/01. AOG.0000183597.31630.db

Glover, V. (2009). Antenatal stress and anxiety, effects on behavioural and cognitive outcomes for the child, and the role of the HPA axis. *European Psychiatry*, *24*(S63–02), S302.

Glover, V. (2014). Maternal depression, anxiety and stress during pregnancy and child outcome; what needs to be done. *Best Practice & Research Clinical Obstetrics & Gynaecology*, *28*(1), 25–35. doi:http://dx.doi.org/10.1016/j.bpobgyn.2013.08.017

Glover, V., O'Connor, T. G., & O'Donnell, K. (2010). Prenatal stress and the programming of the HPA axis. *Neuroscience & Biobehavioral Reviews*, *35*(1), 17–22. doi:10.1016/j. neubiorev.2009.11.008

Glover, V., O'Donnell, K., O'Connor, T., Ramchandani, P., & Capron, L. (2015). Prenatal anxiety and depression, fetal programming and placental function. *Psychoneuroendocrinology*, *61*, 3–4.

Gobinath, A. R., Workman, J. L., Chow, C., Lieblich, S. E., & Galea, L. A. M. (2016). Maternal postpartum corticosterone and fluoxetine differentially affect adult male and female offspring on anxiety-like behavior, stress reactivity, and hippocampal neurogenesis. *Neuropharmacology*, *101*, 165–178. doi:10.1016/j.neuropharm.2015.09.001

Goodman, S. H. (2015). Infant vulnerability to psychopathology. In S. D. Calkins (Ed.), *Handbook of infant biopsychosocial development* (pp. 392–424). New York, NY: Guilford Press.

Goodman, S. H., Bakeman, R., McCallum, M., Rouse, M. H., & Thompson, S. F. (2017). Extending models of sensitive parenting of infants to women at risk for perinatal depression. *Parenting*, *17*(1), 30–50. doi:10.1080/15295192.2017.1262181

Goodman, S. H., & Garber, J. (2017). Evidence-based interventions for depressed mothers and their young children. *Child Development*, doi:10.1111/cdev.12732

Goodman, S. H., & Gotlib, I. H. (1999). Risk for psychopathology in the children of depressed mothers: A developmental model for understanding mechanisms of transmission. *Psychological Review*, *106*, 458–490.

Goodman, S. H., Lusby, C. M., Thompson, K., Newport, D. J., & Stowe, Z. N. (2014). Maternal depression in association with fathers' involvement with their infants: spillover or compensation/buffering? *Infant Mental Health Journal*, *35*(5), 495–508. doi:10.1002/imhj.21469

Goodman, S. H., Rouse, M. H., Connell, A., Broth, M., Hall, C., & Heyward, D. (2011). Maternal depression and child psychopathology: A meta-analytic review. *Clinical Child and Family Psychology Review*, *14*, 1–27. doi:10.1007/s10567-010-0080-1

Goodman, S. H., & Tully, E. C. (2009). Recurrence of depression during pregnancy: Psychosocial and personal functioning correlates. *Depression and Anxiety*, *26*(6), 557–567.

Grant, K. E., Compas, B. E., Stuhlmacher, A. F., Thurm, A. E., McMahon, S. D., & Halpert, J. A. (2003). Stressors and child and adolescent psychopathology: Moving from markers to mechanisms of risk. *Psychological Bulletin*, *129*, 447–466.

Gratz, K. L., Kiel, E. J., Latzman, R. D., Moore, S. A., Elkin, T. D., Megason, G. C., & Tull, M. T. (2015). Complex interrelations of trait vulnerabilities in mothers and their infants. *Infancy*, *20*(3), 306–338.

Grote, N. K., Bridge, J. A., Gavin, A. R., Melville, J. L., Iyengar, S., & Katon, W. J. (2010). A meta-analysis of depression during pregnancy and the risk of preterm birth, low birth weight, and intrauterine growth restriction. *Archives of General Psychiatry*, *67*(10), 1012–1024. doi:10.1001/archgenpsychiatry.2010.111

Gueron-Sela, N., Propper, C. B., Wagner, N. J., Camerota, M., Tully, K. P., & Moore, G. A. (2017). Infant respiratory sinus arrhythmia and maternal depressive symptoms predict toddler sleep problems. *Developmental Psychobiology*, *59*(2), 261–267.

Gunnar, M. R., Porter, F. L., Wolf, C. M., & Rigatuso, J. (1995). Neonatal stress reactivity: Predictions to later emotional temperament. *Child Development*, *66*, 1–13.

Hammen, C. (1991). Generation of stress in the course of unipolar depression. *Journal of Abnormal Psychology*, *100*, 555–561.

Hammen, C. (2002). Context of stress in families of children with depressed parents. In S. H.Goodman & I. H. Gotlib (Eds.), *Children of depressed parents: Mechanisms of risk and implications for treatment* (pp. 175–202). Washington, DC: American Psychological Association.

Hanington, L., Heron, J., Stein, A., & Ramchandani, P. (2012). Parental depression and child outcomes—is marital conflict the missing link? *Child: Care, Health and Development*, *38*(4), 520–529. doi:10.1111/j.1365-2214.2011.01270.x

Hankin, B. L., & Abramson, L. Y. (1999). Development of gender differences in depression: Description of possible explanations. *Annals of Medicine*, *31*, 372–379.

Hanley, G. E., Brain, U., & Oberlander, T. F. (2015). Prenatal exposure to serotonin reuptake inhibitor antidepressants and childhood behavior. *Pediatric Research*, *78*(2), 174–180. doi:10.1038/pr.2015.77

Hanley, G. E., Hookenson, K., Rurak, D., & Oberlander, T. F. (2016). Fetal effects of in utero serotonin reuptake inhibitor (SRI) antidepressant exposure. In *Fetal development* (pp. 365–381). New York, NY: Springer.

Hannigan, L., McAdams, T., Neiderhiser, J., & Eley, T. (2017). Shared genetic influences do not explain the association between parent-child relationship quality and offspring internalizing symptoms: results from a children-of-twins study. *Psychological Medicine*, *46*(6), 786–786. doi:10.1017/S0033291717001908

Hay, D. F., Pawlby, S., Waters, C. S., Perra, O., & Sharp, D. (2010). Mothers' antenatal depression and their children's antisocial outcomes. *Child Development*, *81*(1), 149–165.

Hayes, L. J., Goodman, S. H., & Carlson, E. (2013). Maternal antenatal depression and infant disorganized attachment at 12 months. *Attachment and Human Development*, *15*(2), 133–153. doi:10.1080/14616734.2013.743256

Heron, J., O'Connor, T. G., Evans, J., Golding, J., & Glover, V. (2004). The course of anxiety and depression through pregnancy and the postpartum in a community sample. *Journal of Affective Disorders*, *80*(1), 65–73.

Huizink, A. C., & Bögels, S. M. (2013). Moving beyond the longitudinal approach to understand prenatal mechanisms. *Australian Psychologist*, *48*(4), 246–248. doi:10.1111/ap.12023

Huizink, A. C., Mulder, E. J. H., Robles de Medina, P. G., Visser, G. H. A., & Buitelaar, J. K. (2004). Is pregnancy anxiety a distinctive syndrome? *Early Human Development*, *79*(81–91).

Husain, N., Cruickshank, K., Husain, M., Khan, S., Tomenson, B., & Rahman, A. (2012). Social stress and depression during pregnancy and in the postnatal period in British Pakistani mothers: A cohort study. *Journal of Affective Disorders*, *140*(3), 268–276.

Janssen, A. B., Kertes, D. A., McNamara, G. I., Braithwaite, E. C., Creeth, H. D., Glover, V. I., & John, R. M. (2016). A role for the placenta in programming maternal mood and childhood behavioural disorders. *Journal of Neuroendocrinology*, 28, 1–6.

Jessee, A., Mangelsdorf, S. C., Shigeto, A., & Wong, M. S. (2012). Temperament as a moderator of the effects of parental depressive symptoms on child behavior problems. *Social Development*, 21(3), 610–627.

Jones, N. A., Field, T., Fox, N. A., Davalos, M., & Gomez, C. (2001). EEG during different emotions in 10-month-old infants of depressed mothers. *Journal of Reproductive and Infant Psychology*, 19(4), 295–312.

Jones, N. A., Field, T., Fox, N. A., Davalos, M., Lundy, B., & Hart, S. (1998). Newborns of mothers with depressive symptoms are physiologically less developed. *Infant Behavior & Development*, 21(3), 537–541.

Kagan, J. (1998). Biology and the child. In W. Damon and N. Eisenberg (Eds.), *Handbook of child psychology: Social, emotional, and personality development* (pp. 77–235). Hoboken, NJ: John Wiley & Sons Inc.

Kane, H. S., Schetter, C. D., Glynn, L. M., Hobel, C. J., & Sandman, C. A. (2014). Pregnancy anxiety and prenatal cortisol trajectories. *Biological Psychology*, doi:10.1016/j.biopsycho.2014.04.003

Karlén, J., Frostell, A., Theodorsson, E., Faresjö, T., & Ludvigsson, J. (2013). Maternal influence on child HPA axis: A prospective study of cortisol levels in hair. *Pediatrics*, 132(5), e1333–e1340. doi:10.1542/peds.2013–1178

Kendler, K. S. (2017). Causal inference in psychiatric epidemiology. *JAMA Psychiatry*. doi:10.1001/jamapsychiatry.2017.0502

Kersten-Alvarez, L., Hosman, C., Riksen-Walraven, J., van Doesum, K., Smeekens, S., & Hoefnagels, C. (2012). Early school outcomes for children of postpartum depressed mothers: Comparison with a community sample. *Child Psychiatry & Human Development*, 43(2), 201–218. doi:10.1007/s10578-011-0257-y

Kessler, R. C., McGonagle, K. A., Zhao, S., Nelson, C. B., Hughes, M., Eshleman, S., ... Kendler, K. S. (1994). Lifetime and 12-month prevalence of DSM-III-R psychiatric disorders in the United States: Results from the National Comorbidity Survey. *Archives of General Psychiatry*, 51, 8–19.

Kiernan, K. E., & Huerta, M. C. (2008). Economic deprivation, maternal depression, parenting and children's cognitive and emotional development in early childhood1. *The British Journal of Sociology*, 59(4), 783–806. doi:10.1111/j.1468-4446.2008.00219.x

Kingston, D., & Tough, S. (2013). Prenatal and postnatal maternal mental health and school-age child development: A systematic review. *Maternal and Child Health Journal*, doi:10.1007/s10995-013-1418-3

Komsi, N., Raikkonen, K., Heinonen, K., Pesonen, A.-K., Keskivaara, P., Jarvenpaa, A. L., & Strandberg, T. E. (2008). Continuity of father-rated temperament from infancy to middle childhood. *Infant Behavior and Development*, 31(2), 239–254. doi:10.1016/j.infbeh.2007.10.002

Komsi, N., Raikkonen, K., Pesonen, A.-K., Heinonen, K., Keskivaara, P., Jarvenpaa, A.-L., & Strandberg, T. E. (2006). Continuity of temperament from infancy to middle childhood. *Infant Behavior and Development*, 29(4), 494–508.

Korhonen, M., Luoma, I., Salmelin, R., & Tamminen, T. (2012). A longitudinal study of maternal prenatal, postnatal and concurrent depressive symptoms and adolescent well-being. *Journal of Affective Disorders*, 136(3), 680–692.

Koukounari, A., Stringaris, A., & Maughan, B. (2017). Pathways from maternal depression to young adult offspring depression: an exploratory longitudinal mediation analysis. *International Journal of Methods in Psychiatric Research*, 26(2). doi:10.1002/mpr.1520

Lancaster, C. A., Gold, K. J., Flynn, H. A., Yoo, H., Marcus, S. M., & Davis, M. M. (2010). Risk factors for depressive symptoms during pregnancy: A systematic review. *American Journal of Obstetrics & Gynecology* (January), 5–14.

Laurent, H. K., Ablow, J. C., & Measelle, J. (2011). Risky shifts: How the timing and course of mothers' depressive symptoms across the perinatal period shape their own and infant's stress response profiles. *Development and Psychopathology*, 23(2), 521–538. doi:10.1017/s0954579411000083

Leach, L. S., Poyser, C., & Fairweather-Schmidt, K. (2015). Maternal perinatal anxiety: A review of prevalence and correlates. *Clinical Psychologist*, 21, 4–19.

Letourneau, N., Duffett-Leger, L., & Salmani, M. (2009). The role of paternal support in the behavioural development of children exposed to postpartum depression. *The Canadian Journal of Nursing Research*, 41(3), 86.

Letourneau, N., Tramonte, L., & Willms, J. D. (2013). Maternal depression, family functioning and children's longitudinal development. *Journal of Pediatric Nursing*, 28(3), 223–234.

Li, R., Darling, N., Maurice, E., Barker, L., & Grummer-Strawn, L. M. (2005). Breastfeeding rates in the United States by characteristics of the child, mother, or family: The 2002 National Immunization Survey. *Pediatrics*, 115(1), e31–e37. doi:10.1542/peds.2004-0481

Liu, R. T. (2017). Childhood adversities and depression in adulthood: Current findings and future directions. *Clinical Psychology: Science and Practice*, doi:10.1111/cpsp.12190

Lovejoy, M. C., Graczyk, P. A., O'Hare, E., & Neuman, G. (2000). Maternal depression and parenting behavior: A meta-analytic review. *Clinical Psychology Review*, 20(5), 561–592.

Lundy, B., Jones, N. A., Field, T., Pietro, P., Nearing, G., Davalos, M., ... Kuhn, C. (1999). Prenatal depression effects on neonates. *Infant Behavior and Development*, 22, 119–129.

Lusby, C. M., Goodman, S. H., Bell, M. A., & Newport, D. J. (2014). Electroencephalogram patterns in infants of depressed mothers. *Developmental Psychobiology*, 56(3), 459–473. doi:10.1002/dev.21112

Lusby, C. M., Goodman, S. H., Yeung, E. W., Bell, M. A., & Stowe, Z. N. (2016). Infant EEG and temperament negative affectivity: Coherence of vulnerabilities to mothers' perinatal depression. *Development and Psychopathology*, 28(4pt1), 895–911. doi:10.1017/S0954579416000614

Mahoney, A. D., Minter, B., Burch, K., & Stapel-Wax, J. (2013). Autism spectrum disorders and prematurity: A review across gestational age subgroups. *Advances in Neonatal Care*, 13(4), 247–251.

Man, K. K. C., Chan, E. W., Ip, P., Coghill, D., Simonoff, E., Chan, P. K. L., ... Wong, I. C. K. (2017). Prenatal antidepressant use and risk of attention-deficit/hyperactivity disorder in offspring: Population based cohort study. *BMJ*, 357, j2350. doi:10.1136/bmj.j2350

Marcus, S. M. (2009). Depression during pregnancy: rates, risks and consequences. *Canadian Journal of Clinical Pharmacology*, 16(1), 15–22.

Marcus, S. M., Flynn, H. A., Blow, F. C., & Barry, K. L. (2003). Depressive symptoms among pregnant women screened in obstetrics settings. *Journal of Women's Health*, 12(4), 373–380.

Mathews, C. A., & Reus, V. I. (2001). Assortative mating in the affective disorders: A systematic review and meta-analysis. *Comprehensive Psychiatry, 42*(4), 257–262. doi:https://doi.org/10.1053/comp.2001.24575

Maxwell, S. E., & Cole, D. A. (2007). Bias in cross-sectional analyses of longitudinal mediation. *Psychological Methods, 12*(1), 23–44.

McCall-Hosenfeld, J. S., Phiri, K., Schaefer, E., Zhu, J., & Kjerulff, K. (2016). Trajectories of depressive symptoms throughout the peri- and postpartum period: Results from the first baby study. *Journal of Women's Health.* doi:10.1089/jwh.2015.5310

Merikangas, K. R. (1984). Divorce and assortative mating among depressed patients. *American Journal of Psychiatry, 141*(1), 74–76.

Merikangas, K. R., Weissman, M. M., Prusoff, B. A., & John, K. (1988). Assortative mating and affective disorders: Psychopathology in offspring. *Psychiatry, 51*, 48–57.

Miller, G. A., & Chapman, J. P. (2001). Misunderstanding analysis of covariance. *Journal of Abnormal Psychology, 110*(1), 40–48. doi:10.1037/0021-843X.110.1.40

Miller, G. A., Rockstroh, B. S., Hamilton, H. K., & Yee, C. M. (2016). Psychophysiology as a core strategy in RDoC. *Psychophysiology, 53*(3), 410–414. doi:10.1111/psyp.12581

Misri, S., Kendrick, K., Oberlander, T. F., Norris, S., Tomfohr, L., Zhang, H. B., & Grunau, R. E. (2010). Antenatal depression and anxiety affect postpartum parenting stress: A longitudinal, prospective study. *Canadian Journal of Psychiatry-Revue Canadienne De Psychiatrie, 55*(4), 222–228.

Monk, C., Fifer, W. P., Myers, M. M., Bagiella, E., Duong, J. K., Chen, I. S.,…Altincatal, A. (2011). Effects of maternal breathing rate, psychiatric status, and cortisol on fetal heart rate. *Developmental Psychobiology, 53*(3), 221–233.

Mueller, B. R., & Bale, T. L. (2008). Sex-specific programming of offspring emotionality after stress early in pregnancy. *Journal of Neuroscience, 28*(36), 9055–9065. doi:10.1523/Jneurosci.1424-08.2008

Mukherjee, S., Coxe, S., Fennie, K., Madhivanan, P., & Trepka, M. J. (2016). Antenatal stressful life events and postpartum depressive symptoms in the United States: The role of women's socioeconomic status indices at the state level. *Journal of Women's Health, 26*(3), 276–285. doi:10.1089/jwh.2016.5872

Murray, L., Arteche, A., Fearon, P., Halligan, S., Goodyer, I., & Cooper, P. (2011). Maternal postnatal depression and the development of depression in offspring up to 16 years of age. *Journal of the American Academy of Child and Adolescent Psychiatry, 50*(5), 460–470. doi:10.1016/j.jaac.2011.02.001

Murray, L., Stanley, C., Hooper, R., King, F., & Fiori-Cowley, A. (1996). The role of infant factors in postnatal depression and mother-infant interactions. *Developmental Medicine & Child Neurology, 38*(2), 109–119.

Nath, S., Psychogiou, L., Kuyken, W., Ford, T., Ryan, E., & Russell, G. (2016). The prevalence of depressive symptoms among fathers and associated risk factors during the first seven years of their child's life: Findings from the Millennium Cohort Study. *BMC Public Health, 16*(1), 509. doi:10.1186/s12889-016-3168-9

Natsuaki, M. N., Shaw, D. S., Neiderhiser, J. M., Ganiban, J. M., Harold, G. T., Reiss, D., & Leve, L. D. (2014). Raised by depressed parents: Is it an environmental risk? *Clinical Child and Family Psychology Review*, 1–11. doi:10.1007/s10567-014-0169-z

NICHD Early Child Care Research Network. (1999). Chronicity of maternal depressive symptoms, maternal sensitivity, and child functioning at 36 months. *Developmental Psychology, 35*(5), 1297–1310.

Nordsletten, A. E., Larsson, H., Crowley, J. J., Almqvist, C., Lichtenstein, P., & Mataix-Cols, D. (2016). Patterns of nonrandom mating within and across 11 major psychiatric disorders. *JAMA Psychiatry, 73*(4), 354–361.

Norhayati, M., Hazlina, N. N., Asrenee, A., & Emilin, W. W. (2015). Magnitude and risk factors for postpartum symptoms: a literature review. *Journal of Affective Disorders, 175*, 34–52.

Oberlander, T. F., Misri, S., Fitzgerald, C.E., Kostaras, X., Rurak, D., & Riggs, W. (2004). Pharmacologic factors associated with transient neonatal symptoms following prenatal psychotropic medication exposure. *Journal of Clinical Psychiatry 65*, 230–237.

Oberlander, T. F., Grunau, R., Mayes, L., Riggs, W., Rurak, D., Papsdorf, M.,…Weinberg, J. (2008). Hypothalamic-pituitary-adrenal (HPA) axis function in 3-month old infants with prenatal selective serotonin reuptake inhibitor (SSRI) antidepressant exposure. *Early Human Development, 84*(10), 689–697. doi: 10.1016/j.earlhumdev.2008.06.008

Oberlander, T. F., & Vigod, S. N. (2016). Developmental effects of prenatal selective serotonin reuptake inhibitor exposure in perspective: Are we comparing apples to apples? *Journal of the American Academy of Child & Adolescent Psychiatry, 55*(5), 351–352. doi:http://dx.doi.org/10.1016/j.jaac.2016.02.012

Parsons, C. E., Young, K. S., Rochat, T. J., Kringelbach, M. L., & Stein, A. (2012). Postnatal depression and its effects on child development: A review of evidence from low- and middle-income countries. *British Medical Bulletin, 101*. doi:10.1093/bmb/ldr047

Patton, G. C., Coffey, C., Carlin, J. B., Olsson, C. A., & Morley, R. (2004). Prematurity at birth and adolescent depressive disorder. *British Journal of Psychiatry, 184*(5), 446–447.

Pawlby, S., Hay, D. F., Sharp, D., Waters, C. S., & O'Keane, V. (2009). Antenatal depression predicts depression in adolescent offspring: Prospective longitudinal community-based study. *Journal of Affective Disorders, 113*(3), 236–243. doi:http://dx.doi.org/10.1016/j.jad.2008.05.018

Pearlstein, T. (2015). Depression during Pregnancy. *Best Practice & Research Clinical Obstetrics & Gynaecology.* doi:10.1016/j.bpobgyn.2015.04.004

Pearson, R. M., Evans, J., Kounali, D., Lewis, G., Heron, J., Ramchandani, P. G.,…Stein, A. (2013). Maternal depression during pregnancy and the postnatal period: Risks and possible mechanisms for offspring depression at age 18 years. *JAMA Psychiatry*, doi:10.1001/jamapsychiatry.2013.2163

Pesonen, A.-K., Lahti, M., Kuusinen, T., Tuovinen, S., Villa, P., Hämäläinen, E.,…Räikkönen, K. (2016). Maternal prenatal positive affect, depressive and anxiety symptoms and birth outcomes: The PREDO study. *PLoS ONE, 11*(2).

Pesonen, A.-K., Räikkönen, K., Heinonen, K., Komsi, N., Järvenpää, A. L., & Strandberg, T. (2008). A transactional model of temperamental development: Evidence of a relationship between child temperament and maternal stress over five years. *Social Development, 17*(2), 326–340.

Petterson, S. M., & Albers, A. B. (2001). Effects of poverty and maternal depression on early child development. *Child Development, 72*(6), 1794–1813. doi:10.1111/1467-8624.00379

Phillips, J., Sharpe, L., Matthey, S., & Charles, M. (2010). Subtypes of postnatal depression? A comparison of women with recurrent and de novo postnatal depression. *Joournal of*

Affective Disorders, *120*(1–3), 67–75. doi:10.1016/j.jad.2009.04.011

Pickens, J. N., & Field, T. (1995). Facial expressions and vagal tone of infants of depressed and non-depressed mothers. *Infant and Child Development*, *4*(2), 83–89.

Porges, S. W. (2007). The polyvagal perspective. *Biological Psychology*, *74*(2), 116–143.

Porges, S. W. (2011). *The polyvagal theory: Neurophysiological foundations of emotions, attachment, communication, and self-regulation*. New York, NY: Norton.

Porges, S. W., Doussard-Roosevelt, J. A., & Maiti, A. K. (1994). Vagal tone and the physiological regulation of emotion. *Monographs of the Society for Research in Child Development*, *59*(2–3, Serial Np. 240), 167–186.

Porges, S. W., Doussard-Roosevelt, J. A., Portales, A. L., & Greenspan, S. I. (1996). Infant regulation of the vagal "brake" predicts child behavior problems: A psychobiological model of social behavior. *Developmental Psychobiology*, *29*, 697–712.

Postpartum depression: Action towards causes and treatment (PACT) consortium. (2015). Heterogeneity of postpartum depression: A latent class analysis. *The Lancet Psychiatry*, *2*(1), 59–67. doi:10.1016/S2215-0366(14)00055-8

Pratt, L. A., Brody, D. J., & Gu, Q. (2011). Antidepressant use in persons aged 12 and over: United States, 2005–2008.

Prevatt, B. S., Desmarais, S. L., & Janssen, P. A. (2016). Lifetime substance use as a predictor of postpartum mental health. *Archives in Womens Mental Health*. doi:10.1007/s00737-016-0694-5

Putnam, S. P., Rothbart, M. K., & Gartstein, M. A. (2008). Homotypicl and heterotypic continuity of find-grained temperament during infancy, toddlerhood, and early childhood. *Infant and Child Development*, *17*, 387–405.

Putnam, S. P., & Stifter, C. A. (2005). Behavioral approach-inhibition in toddlers: Prediction from infancy, positive and negative affect components, and relations with behavior problems. *Child Development*, *76*, 212–226.

Qiu, A., Anh, T. T., Li, Y., Chen, H., Rifkin-Graboi, A., Broekman, B. F.,...Meaney, M. J. (2015). Prenatal maternal depression alters amygdala functional connectivity in 6-month-old infants. *Transl Psychiatry*, *5*, e508. doi:10.1038/tp.2015.3

Quinn, P. D., Rickert, M. E., Weibull, C. E., & et al. (2017). Association between maternal smoking during pregnancy and severe mental illness in offspring. *JAMA Psychiatry*. doi:10.1001/jamapsychiatry.2017.0456

Radtke, K. M., Ruf, M., Gunter, H. M., Dohrmann, K., Schauer, M., Meyer, A., & Elbert, T. (2011). Transgenerational impact of intimate partner violence on methylation in the promoter of the glucocorticoid receptor. *Translational Psychiatry*, *1*(7), e21.

Räisänen, S., Lehto, S. M., Nielsen, H. S., Gissler, M., Kramer, M. R., & Heinonen, S. (2014). Risk factors for and perinatal outcomes of major depression during pregnancy: A population-based analysis during 2002–2010 in Finland. *BMJ Open*, *4*(11), e004883.

Ramasubbu, R., Konduru, N., Cortese, F., Bray, S., Gaxiola-Valdez, I., & Goodyear, B. (2014). Reduced intrinsic connectivity of amygdala in adults with major depressive disorder. *Frontiers in Psychiatry*, *5*.

Ramchandani, P. G., Psychogiou, L., Vlachos, H., Iles, J., Sethna, V., Netsi, E., & Lodder, A. (2011). Paternal depression: an examination of its links with father, child and family

functioning in the postnatal period. *Depression and Anxiety*, *28*(6), 471–477.

Redshaw, M., & Henderson, J. (2013). From antenatal to postnatal depression: Associated factors and mitigating influences. *Journal of Women's Health*, *22*(6), 518–525. doi:10.1089/jwh.2012.4152

Rice, F., Harold, G. T., Boivin, J., van den Bree, M., Hay, D. F., & Thapar, A. (2010). The links between prenatal stress and offspring development and psychopathology: disentangling environmental and inherited influences. *Psychological Medicine* *40*(2), 335–345.

Rice, F., Harold, G. T., & Thapar, A. (2002). The genetic aetiology of childhood depression: A review. *Journal of Child Psychology and Psychiatry and Allied Disciplines*, *43*, 65–79.

Richters, J. E. (1992). Depressed mothers as informants about their children: A critical review of the evidence for distortion. *Psychological Bulletin*, *112*(3), 485–499.

Robertson, E., Grace, S., Wallington, T., & Stewart, D. E. (2004). Antenatal risk factors for postpartum depression: A synthesis of recent literature. *General Hospital Psychiatry*, *26*(4), 289–295.

Ross, L. E., Grigoriadis, S., Mamisashvili, L., Vonderporten, E. H., Roerecke, M., Rehm, J.,...Cheung, A. (2013). Selected pregnancy and delivery outcomes after exposure to antidepressant medication: A systematic review and meta-analysis. *JAMA Psychiatry*, 1–8. doi:10.1001/jamapsychiatry.2013.684

Rothbart, M. K., & Posner, M. I. (2006). Temperament, attention, and developmental psychopathology. *Developmental Psychpathology*, *2*, 465–501.

Rothbart, M. K., & Sheese, B. E. (2007). *Temperament and emotion regulation*. New York, NY: Guilford Press.

Rouse, M. H., & Goodman, S. H. (2014). Perinatal depression influences on negative affectivity: Timing, severity, and co-morbid anxiety. *Infant Behavior & Development*, *37*(4), 739–751.

Shannon, K. E., Beauchaine, T. P., Brenner, S. L., Neuhaus, E., & Gatzke-Kopp, L. (2007). Familial and temperamental predictors of resilience in children at risk for conduct disorder and depression. *Development & Psychopathology*, *19*(3), 701–727.

Sharp, H., Pickles, A., Meaney, M., Marshall, K., Tibu, F., & Hill, J. (2012). Frequency of infant stroking reported by mothers moderates the effect of prenatal depression on infant behavioural and physiological outcomes. *PLoS ONE*, *7*(10). doi:10.1371

Sheeber, L., Davis, B., & Hops, H. (2002). Gender-specific vulnerability to depression in children of depressed mothers. In S. H.Goodman & I. H. Gotlib (Eds.), *Children of depressed parents: Mechanisms of risk and implications for treatment* (pp. 253–274). Washington, DC: American Psychological Association.

Smedberg, J., Lupattelli, A., Mardby, A. C., Overland, S., & Nordeng, H. (2015). The relationship between maternal depression and smoking cessation during pregnancy—a cross-sectional study of pregnant women from 15 European countries. *Archives in Womens Mental Health*, *18*, 73–84.

Stifter, C. A., & Fox, N. A. (1990). Infant reactivity: Physiological correlates of newborn and 5-month temperament. *Developmental Psychology*, *26*(4), 582.

Tahmasian, M., Knight, D. C., Manoliu, A., Schwerthöffer, D., Scherr, M., Meng, C.,...Khazaie, H. (2013). Aberrant intrinsic connectivity of hippocampus and amygdala overlap in the fronto-insular and dorsomedial-prefrontal cortex in major depressive disorder. *Frontiers in Human Neuroscience, 7*, 1–10.

Talge, N. M., Holzman, C., Wang, J., Lucia, V., Gardiner, J., & Breslau, N. (2010). Late-preterm birth and its association with cognitive and socioemotional outcomes at 6 years ofaAge. *Pediatrics, 126*(6), 1124–1131.

Thapar, A., & Rutter, M. (2009). Do prenatal risk factors cause psychiatric disorder? Be wary of causal claims. *British Journal of Psychiatry, 195*, 100–101.

Tharner, A., Dierckx, B., Luijk, M. P. C. M., van Ijzendoorn, M. H., Bakermans-Kranenburg, M. J., van Ginkel, J. R.,... Tiemeier, H. (2013). Attachment disorganization moderates the effect of maternal postnatal depressive symptoms on infant autonomic functioning. *Psychophysiology, 50*(2), 195–203. doi:10.1111/psyp.12003

Thibodeau, R., Jorgensen, R. S., & Kim, S. (2006). Depression, anxiety, and resting frontal EEG asymmetry: A meta-analytic review. *Journal of Abnormal Psychology, 115*(4), 7150729.

Vakrat, A., Apter-Levy, Y., & Feldman, R. (2018). Fathering moderates the effects of maternal depression on the family process. *Development and Psychopathology, 30*(1), 27–38.

van den Boom, D. C. (1994). The influence of temperament and mothering on attachment and exploration: An experimental manipulation of sensitive responsiveness among lower-class mothers with irritable infants. *Child Development, 65*, 1457–1477.

Vänskä, M., Punamäki, R. L., Lindblom, J. K., Tolvanen, A., Flykt, M., Unkila-Kallio, L.,... Tiitinen, A. (2015). Timing of early maternal mental health and child cortisol regulation. *Infant and Child Development*. doi:10.1002/icd.1948

Velders, F., Dieleman, G., Henrichs, J., Jaddoe, V. V., Hofman, A., Verhulst, F.,... Tiemeier, H. (2011). Prenatal and postnatal psychological symptoms of parents and family functioning: The impact on child emotional and behavioural problems. *European Child & Adolescent Psychiatry, 20*(7), 341–350. doi:10.1007/s00787-011-0178-0

Verbeek, T., Bockting, C. L. H., van Pampus, M. G., Ormel, J., Meijer, J. L., Hartman, C. A., & Burger, H. (2012). Postpartum depression predicts offspring mental health problems in adolescence independently of parental lifetime psychopathology. *Journal of Affective Disorders*. doi:10.1016/j.jad.2011.08.035

Verreault, N., Da Costa, D., Marchand, A., Ireland, K., Dritsa, M., & Khalifé, S. (2014). Rates and risk factors associated with depressive symptoms during pregnancy and with postpartum onset. *Journal of Psychosomatic Obstetrics & Gynecology, 35*(3), 84–91.

Videman, M., Tokariev, A., Saikkonen, H., Stjerna, S., Heiskala, H., Mantere, O., & Vanhatalo, S. (2017). Newborn brain function is affected by fetal exposure to maternal serotonin reuptake inhibitors. *Cerebral Cortex, 27*(6), 3208–3216.

Viktorin, A., Meltzer-Brody, S., Kuja-Halkola, R., Sullivan, P. F., Landén, M., Lichtenstein, P., & Magnusson, P. K. E. (2016). Heritability of perinatal depression and genetic overlap with nonperinatal depression. *American Journal of Psychiatry, 173*(2), 158–165. doi:10.1176/appi.ajp.2015.15010085

Viktorin, A., Uher, R., Kolevzon, A., Reichenberg, A., Levine, S. Z., & Sandin, S. (2017). Association of antidepressant medication use during pregnancy with intellectual disability in offspring. *JAMA Psychiatry*. doi:10.1001/jamapsychiatry.2017.1727

Viktorin, A., Uher, R., Reichenberg, A., Levine, S. Z., & Sandin, S. (2017). Autism risk following antidepressant medication during pregnancy. *Psychological Medicine, 47*(16), 2787–2796.

Weinstock, M. (2007). Gender differences in the effects of prenatal stress on brain development and behaviour. *Neurochemical Research, 32*(10), 1730–1740.

Weissman, A. M., Levy, B. T., Hartz, A. J., Bentler, S., Donohue, M., Ellingrod, V. L., & Wisner, K. L. (2004). Pooled analysis of antidepressant levels in lactating mothers, breast milk, and nursing infants. *American Journal of Psychiatry, 161*(6), 1066–1078.

Weissman, M. M., Bland, R. C., Canino, G. J., Faravelli, C., Greenwald, S., Hwu, H.-G.,... Yeh, E.-K. (1996). Cross-national epidemiology of major depression and bipolar disorder. *JAMA, 276*(4), 293–299. doi:10.1001/jama.1996.03540040037030

Wen, D., Poh, J., Ni, S., Chong, Y., Chen, H., Kwek, K.,... Meaney, M. (2017). Influences of prenatal and postnatal maternal depression on amygdala volume and microstructure in young children. *Translational Psychiatry, 7*(4), e1103.

Whisman, M. A., Davila, J., & Goodman, S. H. (2011). Relationship adjustment, depression, and anxiety during pregnancy and the postpartum peirod. *Journal of Family Psychology, 25*(3), 375–383.

Wisner, K. L., Sit, D. Y., McShea, M. C., Rizzo, D. M., Zoretich, R. A., Hughes, C. L.,... Hamusa, B. H. (2013). Onset timing, thoughts of self-harm, and diagnoses in postpartum women with screen-positive depression findings. *JAMA Psychiatry, 70*(5), 490–498. doi:10.1001/jamapsychiatry.2013.87

Zalewski, M., Goodman, S. H., Cole, P. M., & McLaughlin, K. A. (2017). Clinical considerations when treating adults who are parents *Clinical Psychology: Science and Practice, 24*(4), 370–388.

Zeng, L.-L., Shen, H., Liu, L., Wang, L., Li, B., Fang, P.,... Hu, D. (2012). Identifying major depression using whole-brain functional connectivity: a multivariate pattern analysis. *Brain, 135*(5), 1498–1507.

Zijlmans, M. A., Riksen-Walraven, J. M., & de Weerth, C. (2015). Associations between maternal prenatal cortisol concentrations and child outcomes: A systematic review. *Neuroscience & Biobehavioral Reviews, 53*, 1–24.

Zuckerman, B., Amorao, H., Bauchner, H., & Cabral, H. (1989). Depressive symptoms during pregnancy: Relationships to poor health behaviors. *American Journal of Obstetrics and Gynecology, 160*, 1107–1111.

Stress and Comorbidity of Physical and Mental Health

Kelsey D. Vig, Renée El-Gabalawy, *and* Gordon J. G. Asmundson

Abstract

This chapter discusses the complex relationship between stress and physical health, with a focus on comorbid posttraumatic stress disorder (PTSD) and physical health conditions. There is a great deal of evidence that stress and mental health conditions, such as PTSD, often co-occur with physical health conditions. This chapter reviews this evidence, describes potential mechanisms underlying the comorbidity, and outlines theoretical frameworks for understanding the relationship between stress and physical health. It considers the ways in which stress leads to poor physical health, how physical health conditions can lead to stress, and how other factors may both increase stress and worsen physical health. Clinical implications of comorbid mental and physical health conditions and suggestions for future research in the area are also discussed.

Keywords: stress, physical health, mental health, comorbidity, posttraumatic stress disorder

Stress and compromised mental health have been long recognized for their adverse effects on physical health, from increasing the risk of a common cold to being associated with life-threatening health conditions (McEwen, 1998). The body of literature focusing on the negative impact of mental disorders on physical health has grown dramatically in the past few decades, providing compelling evidence to support the intricate comorbid relationship and positing a number of different pathways to account for the relationship. Mood and anxiety disorders (including trauma-related disorders), in particular, have been shown to have a number of negative physical health sequelae. Further, comorbid mental and physical health conditions reciprocally exacerbate the severity of both conditions, resulting in more complex clinical presentations. Historically, a large proportion of the literature has focused on the impact of mood disorders on physical health; but, more recently, anxiety disorders have also garnered significant attention.

In this chapter, we provide a brief and general overview of the body of literature focusing on stress and physical illness. The term "stress" can be conceptualized as anything that disrupts homeostasis (Selye, 1956). At the extreme, major stressors and chronic stress can both elicit and characterize mental disorders. Although several mental disorders have been associated with comorbid physical health conditions (for review, see Roy-Byrne et al., 2008), we focus this chapter on posttraumatic stress disorder (PTSD) in particular. PTSD is a severe and debilitating mental disorder included in the *Diagnostic and Statistical Manual of Mental Disorders* (fifth edition; *DSM-5*) that is characterized by a constellation of symptoms that develop and persist following exposure to a major stressor or traumatic event (e.g., physical assault, sexual violence, natural disaster, military combat; American Psychiatric Association, 2013). Primary symptoms include hyperarousal, avoidance, re-experiencing, and negative changes in cognition and mood that cause clinically significant distress or impairment in functioning.

Many cross-sectional and some longitudinal studies have reported associations between PTSD and a large range of physical health conditions, and both trauma exposure and PTSD symptoms have been implicated in comorbidities. We review the evidence demonstrating relationships between PTSD and various medical conditions and highlight potential mechanisms underlying the relationships. We discuss theoretical frameworks for understanding the direction of causality and the potential role of third variables in these comorbid relationships. We end the chapter by considering the clinical implications of comorbid mental and physical health conditions and providing insights into future areas of research.

Historical Overview

Philosophers and researchers have long recognized the influence of psychological states and stress on the body. Indeed, Hippocrates indicated, "It is more important to know what sort of person has a disease than to know what sort of disease a person has," alluding to the importance of understanding psychological well-being in the context of illness (Abrahams & Silver, 2010). In the 20th century, Cannon (1929a, 1929b, 1939) observed that threats to an organism's homeostasis elicited physiological responses designed to optimize the ability to "fight or flight," and that different types of threats (e.g., psychosocial, physical) could all elicit similar physiological responses. Selye (1956) further developed Cannon's theories and introduced the concept of a "General Adaptation Syndrome" to describe the body's nonspecific response to stress. The General Adaptation Syndrome has three stages: an "alarm reaction," which is similar to Cannon's concept of a "fight-or-flight" response and includes the immediate physiological responses to stress; a stage of resistance, where the organism adapts to the stressor; and a stage of exhaustion, where the organism's capacity to adapt to the stressor is exceeded. Selye suggested that while the body's physiological response to stress may be adaptive in the short term, continued or repeated activation of the stress response could result in mental and physical health problems.

In the 1970s, there was even greater recognition of the relationship between mental and physical health. Researchers proposed models that incorporated psychological factors as contributors to physical illness and disease, which challenged traditional medical models that focused solely on biological aspects of health. Notably, the Biopsychosocial Model of Health (Engel, 1980) attributed disease to factors relating to biology, psychology, and social influences. The introduction of the Biopsychosocial Model of Health contributed to a greater focus in the scientific literature on the impact of psychological processes

on physical illness. Today, it is well recognized that stress negatively impacts mental and physical health (Goldstein & Kopin, 2007).

Scope of the Problem

In 1988, DeLongis, Folkman, and Lazarus noted significant relationships between daily stress and general health complaints such as flu-like symptoms, headaches, and sore throat. Researchers now recognize that stress and anxiety are associated with more serious physical health conditions that pose an even greater threat to the individual. There is substantial evidence that anxiety disorders are associated with increased prevalence for many physical health conditions, including gastrointestinal (GI) conditions, chronic pain, and cardiovascular diseases (Andreski, Chilcoat, & Breslau, 1998; Roy-Byrne et al., 2008; Scott et al., 2007). Comorbid anxiety disorders and physical health conditions are associated with greater disability (Sareen, Cox, Clara, & Asmundson, 2005) and worse health-related quality of life (Sareen et al., 2006). Furthermore, comorbid anxiety disorders and physical health conditions can create challenges for practitioners, including difficulties with accurate identification and effective treatment, and highlight the greater need for collaborative care (Aquin, El-Gabalawy, Sala, & Sareen, 2017).

Results from the US National Comorbidity Survey suggest that the relationship between anxiety disorders and physical health conditions is not specific to a particular type of physical health condition (e.g., neurological, vascular, respiratory; Sareen et al., 2005). Adjusted odds ratios (AORs) for past-year physical health conditions and anxiety disorders ranged from 1.66 (for respiratory conditions) to 2.28 (for bone or joint conditions), and the associations remained statistically significant even after controlling for potential confounding variables such as mood disorders, substance use disorders, and sociodemographic variables. However, associations with physical health conditions are not uniform across all anxiety disorders. PTSD, in particular, has been linked to a greater variety of physical conditions than other anxiety disorders, with AORs ranging from 1.88 for vascular conditions to 3.32 for metabolic and autoimmune conditions (Sareen et al., 2005). A recent meta-analysis supported these findings, showing that PTSD was associated with greater severity and frequency of GI, cardio-respiratory, pain, and other physical health symptoms compared to other anxiety disorders (Pacella, Hruska, & Delahanty, 2013). Furthermore, individuals with PTSD report a greater number of physical health complaints overall when compared to those without PTSD (Fetzner, McMillan, & Asmundson, 2012; O'Toole & Catts, 2008; Ouimette et al., 2004). Although the incidence of PTSD is greater in women, and women and men tend to be exposed to different types of traumas (Kessler, Sonnega, Bromet, Hughes, & Nelson, 1995), sex does not appear to moderate the relationship between PTSD and most physical health outcomes (Pacella et al., 2013; Pietrzak et al., 2012); however, there are a few exceptions that will be highlighted in subsequent sections.

Current State of Evidence

PTSD has been linked to specific medical conditions, such as cardiovascular disease (CVD) and diabetes, as well as general indicators of poor physical health that are risk factors for a variety of medical conditions, such as hypertension and obesity (Coughlin, 2011). At the extreme, PTSD may also be implicated in accelerated aging (Lohr et al., 2015) and increased risk of mortality (Ahmadi et al., 2011). Before providing a comprehensive review of the evidence of the comorbidity of physical health conditions with PTSD, we will discuss the role of trauma in the relationship between PTSD and physical health.

Trauma Exposure

Physical health conditions have been associated not only with full PTSD but also with subsyndromal PTSD and trauma exposure without PTSD (Fetzner et al., 2012; Husarewycz, El-Gabalawy, Logsetty, & Sareen, 2014). When comparing individuals with subthreshold PTSD to those with full PTSD, full PTSD appears to be associated with the largest number of medical conditions. For example, PTSD in US veterans has been shown to be associated with a greater number of comorbid physical conditions and greater effect sizes than subthreshold PTSD (El-Gabalawy, Blaney, Tsai, Sumner, & Pietrzak, 2018). These trends have also been corroborated in general population-based studies of adults and older adults (Pietrzak, Goldstein, Southwick, & Grant, 2011; 2012).

PTSD is more consistently associated with an increased incidence of physical health conditions than trauma exposure alone (O'Toole & Catts, 2008). For example, PTSD has been linked to increased body mass index (BMI) when compared to both healthy controls and trauma-exposed controls (Suliman et al., 2016). PTSD has also been associated with an increased incidence of type 2 diabetes (Lukaschek et al., 2013) and metabolic syndrome (MetS; Weiss et al., 2011), which is a constellation of risk factors for cardiovascular diseases (central obesity, hypertension, hyperglycemia, and dyslipidemia). These relationships were not observed when examining trauma-exposed individuals without PTSD. Individuals with PTSD were also more likely to experience angina, tachycardia, hypertension, stomach ulcers, gastritis, and arthritis compared to trauma-exposed individuals without PTSD; but the incidence of diabetes did not differ between groups (Pietrzak et al., 2012).

Other researchers have observed a relationship between trauma exposure and physical health conditions after controlling for PTSD or when comparing traumatized individuals who did and did not develop PTSD. After controlling for PTSD and other potential confounding factors in a nationally representative sample of American adults, trauma exposure was associated with CVD, arteriosclerosis/hypertension, GI disease, diabetes, arthritis, and obesity (Husarewycz et al., 2014). Relationships between trauma exposure and physical health conditions differed according to the type of traumatic event; specifically, individuals with injurious traumas (e.g., accidents, sexual/physical assault) and witnessing traumas had increased odds of all physical health conditions; those with psychological traumas (e.g., neglect, stalking) had increased odds of CVD, GI disease, diabetes, and arthritis; and combat-related traumas were not positively associated with any of the physical health conditions. A representative study of the German elderly population found that trauma exposure was associated with an increased prevalence of all physical health conditions evaluated, whereas PTSD was only associated with an increased prevalence for half the physical health conditions assessed (Glaesmer, Brähler, Gündel, & Riedel-Heller, 2011). Similarly, results from a population-based survey in Germany suggested that conditions such as stroke, renal disease, and arthritis were related to trauma exposure, but not PTSD; yet liver disease and peripheral arterial disease were associated with PTSD, but not trauma exposure (Spitzer et al., 2009). Mediation analyses indicated that respiratory and cardiovascular conditions were related to both PTSD and trauma exposure, and PTSD only partially mediated the relationship between trauma exposure and each physical health condition. Another study noted that PTSD generally did not mediate the relationship between trauma exposure and physical health conditions (Norman et al., 2006). Finally, emerging research suggests that the absence of lifetime trauma, compared to those who are trauma exposed, may be protective for various physical health states, including hypercholesterolemia and cancer (El-Gabalawy et al., 2018).

It may be possible to reconcile some of the inconsistent findings for trauma exposure, PTSD, and physical health conditions by considering trauma burden, instead of viewing trauma exposure as a dichotomous entity. This view is in line with theories of allostatic load discussed later in this chapter. Experiencing a greater number of traumatic events has been associated with increased odds of having CVD, arteriosclerosis/hypertension, GI diseases, diabetes, arthritis, and chronic pain (Husarewycz et al., 2014). A longitudinal study of US military veterans noted that the total number of lifetime traumas had an indirect effect on future MetS severity through initial PTSD severity (Wolf et al., 2016). Another study found that, after controlling for total lifetime trauma, the relationship between PTSD and chronic physical health conditions disappeared (Sledjeski, Speisman, & Dierker, 2008). Further research is still needed to better understand the associations between trauma burden, PTSD, and physical health conditions; however, these findings and others support a stress-diathesis conceptualization of PTSD and physical health conditions, where greater levels of stress characterized by PTSD symptoms may be associated with greater risk of medical conditions.

Comorbid Medical Conditions

CARDIOVASCULAR CONDITIONS

The association between PTSD and cardiovascular symptoms is well established. PTSD has been associated with an increased incidence of CVD and risk factors for CVD, including hypertension, hyperlipidemia, and atherosclerosis (Abouzeid, Kelsall, Forbes, Sim, & Creamer, 2012; Edmondson, Kronish, Shaffer, Falzon, & Burg, 2013; Kang, Bullman, & Taylor, 2006; Kibler, Joshi, & Ma, 2009; Sareen et al., 2007). Individuals with PTSD are also significantly more likely to have MetS (Bartoli, Carrà, Crocamo, Carretta, & Clerici, 2013; Heppner et al., 2009; Rosenbaum et al., 2015; Weiss et al., 2011). A 2-year longitudinal study of veterans found that PTSD severity at study onset predicted future MetS severity; however, MetS severity at study onset did not predict future PTSD severity, suggesting that the effect of PTSD on MetS is unidirectional (Wolf et al., 2016). Further supporting the association between PTSD and cardiovascular outcomes, one prospective co-twin study found that twins with PTSD were more than twice as likely to develop coronary heart disease (Vaccarino et al., 2013). This association was only slightly reduced when comparing PTSD-discordant twins, suggesting that familial and early environmental factors account for some, but not all, of the association between PTSD and cardiovascular outcomes. In contrast, a cross-sectional co-twin study found that the relationship between PTSD and increased carotid artery intima-media thickness, a measure of subclinical atherosclerosis, disappeared when examining PTSD-discordant twins (Goetz et al., 2014). This suggests that familial and early environmental factors confound the relationship between cardiovascular outcomes; however, the study was limited by a cross-sectional design and the use of lifetime as opposed to current PTSD.

Multiple longitudinal studies have demonstrated that PTSD leads to an increased risk of developing CVD (Jordan, Miller-Archie, Cone, Morabia, & Stellman, 2011; Kubzansky, Koenen, Jones, & Eaton, 2009; Kubzansky, Koenen, Spiro, Vokonas, & Sparrow, 2007; Roy, Foraker, Girton, & Mansfield, 2015; Scherrer et al., 2010). A meta-analytic study estimated that PTSD is associated with a 27% increase in risk for coronary heart disease or cardiac-specific mortality (Edmondson et al., 2013). Few studies have reported no association between cardiovascular conditions and PTSD (e.g., Weisberg et al., 2002); therefore, this association with PTSD is generally seen as the most robust of all the physical health conditions.

GASTROINTESTINAL CONDITIONS

PTSD has been associated with GI conditions in general (Fetzner et al., 2012; Wolfe, Schnurr, Brown, & Furey, 1994) and with specific GI conditions, including stomach/gallbladder problems (Lauterbach, Vora, & Rakow, 2005), Crohn's disease, ulcers/ulcerative colitis (Sareen et al., 2007), dyspepsia (Maguen, Madden, Cohen, Bertenthal, & Seal, 2014), and irritable bowel syndrome (IBS; Irwin, Falsetti, Lydiard, & Ballenger, 1996). However, some studies have failed to replicate the association between PTSD and GI conditions (e.g., Cohen et al., 2006; McFarlane, Atchison, Rafalowicz, & Papay, 1994; Ouimette et al., 2004), including one prospective study of disaster survivors (Dirkzwager, Van der Velden, Grievink, & Yzermans, 2007). Inconsistences across studies may be the result of examining GI conditions as a collective, instead of individually; however, in a nationwide prospective cohort study, there was an overall increased incidence of GI conditions in PTSD, and most of the GI conditions were individually associated with increased incidence in PTSD (Gradus et al., 2017). In terms of sex differences, a longitudinal study noted that male veterans with PTSD were at a greater risk of developing IBS compared to female veterans with PTSD (Maguen et al., 2014), although female veterans with PTSD were still more likely to have IBS than female veterans without PTSD (Savas et al., 2009).

Obesity and Type 2 Diabetes Mellitus

PTSD severity positively correlates with BMI, fat mass, and fasting blood glucose levels, which are risk factors for obesity, cardiometabolic disease, and diabetes (Farr et al., 2015). These associations were maintained at follow-up 2.5 years later. In a nationally representative sample, individuals with current PTSD were more likely to have a BMI classified as "obese" (Pagoto et al., 2012), which is consistent with the findings from an earlier study of primary care patients (Weisberg et al., 2002). One study noted that only current PTSD was associated with obesity (Pagoto et al., 2012), while another found that both lifetime and current PTSD were associated with an increased risk for obesity (Smith, Tyzik, Neylan, & Cohen, 2015). A meta-analysis comparing BMI in individuals with and without PTSD noted that PTSD was associated with significantly higher BMI for males, but not for females (Suliman et al., 2016).

Studies have obtained conflicting results regarding the association between PTSD and an increased incidence of type 2 diabetes mellitus (Agyemang, Goosen, Anujuo, & Ogedegbe, 2012; Glaesmer et al., 2011; Goodwin & Davidson, 2005; Lukaschek et al., 2013; Sareen et al., 2007; Sledjeski et al., 2008; Spitzer et al., 2009). In a population-based sample of US veterans, subthreshold PTSD, but not full PTSD, was associated with increased odds of diabetes (El-Gabalawy et al., 2018). Similar to differential findings observed in the literature examining GI conditions, these conflicting findings may relate to a failure to distinguish between typologies of diabetes (i.e., type 1 and type 2 diabetes) when reporting results. Indeed, prior research has indicated differential findings for type 1 and type 2 diabetes on PTSD (Tsai & Shen, 2017). Perhaps most convincing are longitudinal studies indicating that individuals with PTSD are more likely to develop type 2 diabetes (Boyko et al., 2010; Miller-Archie et al., 2014; Roberts et al., 2015; Vaccarino et al., 2014). The reverse does not seem to be true; that is, individuals with type 2 diabetes are not more likely to develop PTSD (Roberts et al., 2015).

Musculoskeletal and Chronic Pain Conditions

Individuals with PTSD are more likely to have a musculoskeletal diagnosis (Barrett et al., 2002; Fetzner et al., 2012; McFarlane et al., 1994; O'Toole & Catts, 2008; Ouimette et al., 2004) and report more pain (Ouimette et al., 2004; Pacella et al., 2013; Weisberg et al., 2002). Studies have consistently observed a relationship between PTSD and arthritis (Lauterbach et al., 2005; Pietrzak et al., 2012; Sareen et al., 2007; Sledjeski et al., 2008; Weisberg et al., 2002), and PTSD and chronic pain in general (Beckham et al., 1997; Bryant et al., 1999; Shipherd et al., 2007). One twin study noted that PTSD symptom severity is positively associated with the prevalence of rheumatoid arthritis and that this relationship is independent of genetic factors (Boscarino, Forsberg, & Goldberg, 2010). There is also evidence of an increased risk of fibromyalgia, back problems, headaches, migraines, and other chronic pain conditions (Amir et al., 1997; Peterlin, Tietjen, Meng, Lidicker, & Bigal, 2008; Sareen et al., 2007; Sledjeski et al., 2008). This literature, and related shared vulnerability (i.e., PTSD and chronic pain conditions share similar predisposing biopsychosocial factors) and mutual maintenance (i.e., PTSD and chronic pain conditions are maintained by similar psychological factors) models, are reviewed in detail elsewhere (for reviews, see Asmundson, Coons, Taylor, & Katz, 2002; Asmundson & Katz, 2009).

Respiratory Conditions

Compared to other physical health conditions, limited research has examined the association between PTSD and respiratory conditions. One study did not observe a relationship between respiratory conditions and PTSD (Sareen et al., 2005), while other studies have noted that PTSD is associated with an increased prevalence of respiratory conditions (Barrett et al., 2002; El-Gabalawy et al., 2018; McFarlane et al., 1994). Of the respiratory conditions typically examined, PTSD has most consistently been linked to asthma (Lauterbach et al., 2005; O'Toole & Catts, 2008; Sareen et al., 2007; Weisberg et al., 2002) and bronchitis (Lauterbach et al., 2005; Sareen et al., 2007).

Mortality

Some studies have noted that veterans with PTSD have an increased risk of death (Ahmadi et al., 2011; Boscarino 2006a, 2006b; Schlenger et al., 2015); however, other studies have failed to replicate this effect (Abrams, Vaughan-Sarrazin, & Vander Weg, 2011; Chwastiak, Rosenheck, Desai, & Kasis, 2010; O'Toole, Catts, Outram, Pierse, & Cockburn, 2010). Results regarding specific causes of death have been equally inconsistent. Veterans with PTSD who served in the Vietnam War had increased rates of mortality due to cardiovascular events and cancer compared to veterans without PTSD (Boscarino, 2006b), and the risk of death following coronary artery bypass grafting surgery for coronary artery disease is greater for patients with PTSD relative to those without (Dao et al., 2010). Another group of researchers noted increased rates of cancer mortality; but they found that PTSD was associated with decreased mortality from CVD, which may have occurred because of a failure to account for competing causes of death in the statistical models (Schlenger et al., 2015).

Other Health Conditions

Many researchers have included other health conditions such as sensory conditions (e.g., blindness, deafness), venereal and infectious diseases (e.g., HIV/AIDS, yeast infections), and various neurological conditions (e.g., epilepsy, stroke, multiple sclerosis) when evaluating associations between PTSD and physical health conditions. Associations between PTSD and physical health conditions beyond those discussed earlier have limited evidence at present and, therefore, are not discussed in detail. One potential reason for this lack of evidence is that many of these conditions are relatively uncommon and either could not be included in statistical analyses at all or had to be grouped with related conditions in order to be analyzed, making it difficult to discern whether associations truly exist. For example, cancer, epilepsy, and stroke are often grouped with other conditions for analysis, and evidence of associations with PTSD is inconsistent. Three studies included cancer in separate analyses; two reported associations between cancer and PTSD (Sareen et al., 2007; Sledjeski et al., 2008), and one did not (Weisberg et al., 2002). Two additional studies included cancer with other conditions such as allergies, acne, and aplastic anemia. In this case, one study reported an association with PTSD (Fetzner et al., 2012), while the other did not (Barrett et al., 2002). Evidence for associations of stroke and epilepsy with PTSD follows much the same pattern (e.g., Lauterbach et al., 2005; Pietrzak et al., 2012; Sareen et al., 2007). Future research focusing more specifically on these conditions is needed to clarify potential associations with PTSD.

Theoretical Frameworks

There are three possible explanations for the association between exposure to traumatic stress, subsequent PTSD, and physical health conditions. First, stress/PTSD may cause or exacerbate physical health conditions. Second, it is possible that physical health conditions cause or exacerbate stress/PTSD. Finally, a third factor (e.g., a genetic predisposition) might cause both stress/PTSD and physical health conditions. Most of the literature has focused on the first explanation, and results from longitudinal studies suggest that PTSD is a predisposing factor for physical health conditions (e.g., El-Gabalawy, Mackenzie, Pietrzak, & Sareen, 2014; Roy et al., 2015; Wolf et al., 2016). Researchers have now begun investigating the mechanisms by which stress/PTSD lead to physical health conditions. There is also considerable evidence that physical health conditions can elicit PTSD (Parker et al., 2015); however, revisions to the *DSM-5* now limit the types of medical incidents that can be considered traumatic events (APA, 2013; Pai, Suris, & North, 2017). Finally, some evidence points to genetic predispositions or shared vulnerabilities as factors underlying both PTSD and physical health conditions (e.g., Asmundson, Coons, et al., 2002; Asmundson & Katz, 2009; Stein et al., 2016).

Stress and Posttraumatic Stress Disorder Lead to Physical Health Conditions

The model of allostasis and allostatic load developed by McEwen and Stellar (1993) provides a valuable framework for understanding how stress and mental health problems can lead to physical health conditions. Allostasis is the active process of adaptation whereby the body works to maintain homeostasis through physiological changes in the body's stress response systems (McEwen, 2008). The two major neuroendocrine systems that are activated in response to stress are the hypothalamic-pituitary-adrenocortical (HPA) axis and the locus coeruleus/norepinephrine-sympathetic (LC/NE) system (Friedman & McEwen, 2004). Allostasis can lead to imbalances in the HPA axis and the LC/NE system, which increases allostatic load, a concept similar to Selye's General Adaptation Syndrome (Friedman & McEwen, 2004). Allostatic load is the cost to the body that is incurred by the body's physiological response to stress (McEwen, 1998). It occurs as a result of chronic increases or dysregulation in allostasis, such as failing to stop bodily responses to stress when they are no longer needed, failing to initiate stress responses when they are needed, or failing to

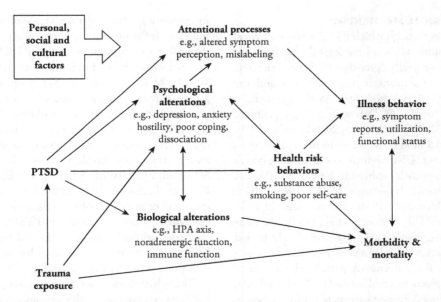

Figure 14.1 Schnurr and Green's model connecting trauma exposure, posttraumatic stress disorder (PTSD), and physical health. From Schnurr, 2015.

habituate to repeated exposures to the same stressor. Allostatic load and the associated physiological dysfunctions are thought to account for why individuals who are chronically stressed, exposed to trauma, or experiencing a mental illness are at a greater risk of developing physical illnesses (Glover, Stuber, & Poland, 2006; McEwen, 2003).

Schnurr and Green (2004) expanded on a model originally proposed by Schnurr and Jankowski (1999) connecting trauma exposure, PTSD, and physical health using the concept of allostasis (Figure 14.1). According to Schnurr and Green's model, PTSD and other psychological alterations lead to physical health conditions directly through physiological mechanisms (e.g., increased blood pressure, suppressed immune system) and indirectly through behavioral mechanisms (e.g., substance use, poor diet, lack of exercise). Other factors such as attentional processes (e.g., altered symptom perception, mislabeling symptoms) and illness behaviors (e.g., symptom reports, functional status) further influence these direct and indirect pathways to physical illness (Schnurr & Green, 2004). Schnurr and Green's model is supported by empirical research finding that PTSD mediates the relationship between trauma exposure and poor physical health outcomes (Campbell, Greeson, Bybee, & Raja, 2008; Kimerling, Clum, & Wolfe, 2000; Schnurr & Spiro, 1999; Schuster-Wachen et al., 2013; Tansill, Edwards, Kearns, Gidycz, & Calhoun, 2012); however, a number of studies have observed only partial mediation, suggesting that PTSD does not entirely account for the association between trauma exposure and physical health conditions (Norman et al., 2006; Schnurr, Spiro, & Paris, 2000; Taft, Stern, King, & King, 1999; Wolfe et al., 1994). To reconcile these findings, Schnurr and Green's model also includes other psychological alterations (e.g., depression, anxiety, hostility) as potential pathways connecting trauma exposure and physical health conditions.

There are two important features of Schnurr and Green's model that are worth highlighting. First, trauma exposure only leads to physical conditions when (1) injury or illness occurs during the traumatic event, or (2) there is a significant distress reaction to the traumatic event (i.e., PTSD or other psychological alterations; Schnurr & Green, 2004). In other words, the psychological response to a stressor is a key element of the connection between stress and physical illness. Second, Schnurr and Green emphasize the cumulative and interactive effects of the components of the model. Individual physiological or behavioral alterations may not be sufficient to cause a physical illness; but multiple alterations could increase allostatic load and lead to a physical illness. Other factors like age, sex, race/ethnicity, perceived predictability and controllability of a stressor, personality factors (e.g., optimism, pessimism, the desire to control one's experiences), and social support may further influence these pathways (Dougall & Baum, 2004; Schnurr & Green, 2004).

PHYSIOLOGICAL MECHANISMS

One pathway through which PTSD leads to physical health conditions is physiological mechanisms. Researchers generally agree that PTSD is characterized by dysregulations in the HPA axis and the sympathetic-adrenal-medullary (SAM) system, a component of the LC/NE system (e.g., Heim & Nemeroff, 2009; Pace & Heim, 2011; Yehuda, 2009). Cerebrospinal fluid concentrations of corticotropin-releasing factor (CRF), which coordinates the body's response to stress by initiating both the HPA and LC/NE systems (Friedman & McEwen, 2004; Owens & Nemeroff, 1991), are increased in individuals with PTSD (Bremner et al., 1997). The association between increased CRF and PTSD-related dysregulations in the HPA axis is complex, as research consistently finds decreased peripheral concentrations of the glucocorticoid cortisol in PTSD (Yehuda, 2006). Finding decreased cortisol is unexpected given that CRF stimulates the release of adrenocorticotropin (ACTH) and ACTH stimulates the release of cortisol. Enhanced glucocorticoid sensitivity may account for these paradoxical findings; however, results have been inconsistent and further research is still needed (Pace & Heim, 2011).

Elevated concentrations of norepinephrine in individuals with PTSD provide evidence of altered SAM system functioning (Pace & Heim, 2011). Furthermore, PTSD is associated with increases in basal cardiovascular activity (i.e., heart rate and blood pressure), as well as excessive sympathetic nervous system reactivity in response to stimuli related to the traumatic event (Buckley, Holohan, Greif, Bedard, & Suvak, 2004; Buckley & Kaloupek, 2001; Keane et al., 1998; Pole, 2007; Rabe, Dörfel, Zöllner, Maercker, & Karl, 2006). Research has found elevated heart rate in response to loud noises in a group of combat veterans with PTSD, but no difference in their monozygotic twins or a group of combat veterans without PTSD, suggesting that cardiovascular hyperarousal is a consequence of the disorder rather than a predisposing factor (Orr et al., 2003).

Stress/PTSD also influence(s) the immune system (Pace & Heim, 2011). Researchers have exposed participants to a rhinovirus and then quarantined them to prevent exposure to other viruses. Participants who reported more stressful life events, more chronic stressful life events, and greater levels of perceived stress were more likely to develop cold symptoms, indicating that stress has immunosuppressive effects (Cohen et al., 1991, 1998). Trauma exposure has been associated with an increase in proinflammatory cytokines, which the body releases in response to physical or psychological threat to increase inflammation (Kendall-Tackett, 2009). According to a systematic review, PTSD is also associated with increased inflammation (Gill, Saligan, Woods, & Page, 2009). PTSD symptom severity has been positively correlated with concentrations of the proinflammatory cytokines interleukin (IL)-1β, IL-6, and tumor necrosis factor α, and negatively correlated with concentrations of the anti-inflammatory cytokine IL-4 (Tucker, Jeon-Slaughter, Pfefferbaum, Khan, & Davis, 2009; von Känel et al., 2007, 2010). Veterans with PTSD have greater concentrations of proinflammatory markers compared to veterans without PTSD, suggesting that associations between PTSD and increased inflammation cannot be explained by trauma exposure alone (Lindqvist et al., 2017).

The physiological alterations discussed earlier have all been associated with various physical health conditions. Cortisol has an immunosuppressive function (Denson et al., 2009) and has been implicated in various physical conditions, including MetS (Brunner et al., 2002), diabetes (Shamoon, Hendler, & Sherwin, 1980), and chronic pain (Vachon-Presseau et al., 2013). Sympathetic system hyperactivity is associated with hypertension and other cardiovascular conditions (Adameova, Abdellatif, & Dhalla, 2009; Julius & Gudbrandsson, 1992). Abnormally high concentrations of proinflammatory cytokines result in excessive inflammation and the individual becomes more vulnerable to physical illness (Kendall-Tackett, 2009). Inflammation is adaptive in response to acute stress because it facilitates wound healing and fights infection; however, chronic inflammation contributes to the pathogenesis and progression of autoimmune diseases (e.g., rheumatoid arthritis) and CVD (Kemeny, 2003; Kendall-Tackett, 2009).

The precise sequence of physiological changes connecting stress/PTSD and physical health conditions remains unknown. For inflammatory bowel disease alone, there are eight main pathways that have been proposed to account for the association with stress (Bernstein, 2017). The interdependence of the nervous, immune, and endocrine systems makes it difficult to identify the specific physiological changes mediating the associations between PTSD and physical health conditions. Different systems in the body all interact with one another, resulting in a cascade of physiological effects (Dougall & Baum, 2004). For example, both low cortisol and enhanced SAM system activity increase inflammation (Pace & Heim, 2011). Additional research is still needed to clarify how exactly PTSD-related physiological changes translate to physical health conditions. One possibility is that these physiological changes lead to accelerated aging, which results in increased mortality and earlier onset of medical conditions associated with normal aging (e.g., CVD, MetS, type 2 diabetes). Studies examining senescence-related biomarkers (e.g., leukocyte telomere length, pro-inflammatory markers) indicate that PTSD may be associated with a phenotype of accelerated aging (Lohr et al., 2015).

BEHAVIORAL MECHANISMS

The second pathway through which PTSD leads to physical health conditions is behavioral mechanisms. Maladaptive health behaviors such as an unhealthy diet, a lack of physical activity, and substance use predict morbidity and mortality from multiple causes, including hypertension, hyperlipidemia, CVD, diabetes, and obesity (Gehi, Ali, Na, & Whooley, 2007; Haskell, 2003; Lichtenstein et al., 2006; World Health Organization, 2003). Stress has been associated with a higher fat diet, lower levels of physical activity, and increases in smoking (Ng & Jeffery, 2003), behaviors which influence the body's physiological response to stress and exacerbate allostatic load (McEwen, 1998; Schnurr & Jankowski, 1999). Similarly, researchers suggest that individuals with PTSD exhibit more maladaptive health behaviors and fewer positive health behaviors compared to healthy and trauma-exposed controls (Dedert, Calhoun, Watkins, Sherwood, & Beckham 2010; Edmondson & Cohen, 2013; Godfrey, Lindamer, Mostoufi, & Afari, 2013). Compared to those without PTSD, individuals with PTSD consume more fast food and sugary drinks, engage in more unhealthy dieting behaviors (Hirth, Rahman, & Berenson, 2011), are more likely to smoke (Jacobsen, Southwick, & Kosten, 2001; Zen, Zhao, Whooley, & Cohen, 2012), have increased cannabis use (Cougle, Bonn-Miller, Vujanovic, Zvolensky, & Hawkins, 2011), are more likely to meet criteria for a substance use disorder (Jacobsen et al., 2001), report more medication nonadherence (Kronish, Edmondson, Li, & Cohen, 2012; Zen et al., 2012), have more sleep problems (Hulme, 2000), and engage in less physical activity (Zen et al., 2012).

Behaviors such as substance use and unhealthy eating may be used as a means of coping with the distress, intrusions, and hyperarousal that are characteristic of PTSD (Rheingold, Acierno, & Resnick, 2004), while other behaviors like poor sleep may be a consequence of PTSD symptoms (Kendall-Tackett, 2009). Studies evaluating whether maladaptive health behaviors mediate the relationship between PTSD and physical illness have had mixed results (e.g., Asmundson, Stein, & McCreary, 2002; Crawford, Drescher, & Rosen, 2009; Del Gaizo, Elhai, & Weaver, 2011; Flood, McDevitt-Murphy, Weathers, Eakin, & Benson, 2009; Vasterling et al., 2008). In line with Schnurr and Green's (2004) model, some studies have controlled for maladaptive health behaviors and still found a robust association between PTSD and physical health conditions (e.g., Farr et al., 2015; Roberts et al., 2015), indicating that maladaptive health behaviors explain some, but not all, of the association with physical illnesses.

One concern with Schnurr and Green's model is the failure to account for the possibility that poor physical health could be an artifact of increased exposure to the health care system. Individuals with PTSD have more contact with the health care system (Elhai, North, & Frueh, 2005); therefore, it is possible that an individual with PTSD is more likely to have his or her physical health condition recognized and treated. One study accounted for this possibility and still found associations between PTSD and physical health conditions (Roberts et al., 2015), while another found that physical health conditions mediated the association between PTSD and increased health service utilization (Deykin et al., 2001). Nonetheless, most of the studies discussed in this chapter did not control for increased contact with the health care system when examining comorbid PTSD and physical health conditions.

Physical Health Conditions Lead to Stress/Posttraumatic Stress Disorder

The association between stress or poor mental health and physical health conditions is not unidirectional, particularly in the case of PTSD. A prospective study of a military cohort noted that individuals who reported worse physical health at baseline were more likely to develop combat-related PTSD (LeardMann, Smith, Smith, Wells, & Ryan, 2009). Poor physical health has also been identified as a risk factor for persistent PTSD (Armenta et al., 2018). The exact mechanisms underlying this relationship have yet to be fully elucidated. One possibility is that some physical health conditions, such as neurological conditions, influence cognitive processing and impair an individual's ability to cope with exposure to a traumatic event, thereby increasing the risk of developing PTSD. This possibility has yet to be empirically tested, and much more research is needed to clarify the role of poor physical health as a risk factor for PTSD.

Physical health conditions negatively impacting mental health is perhaps most clearly illustrated by the inclusion of serious medical conditions as potential traumatic events in the diagnostic criteria for PTSD; however, the *DSM-5* included substantial changes to these criteria (APA, 2013). One such change was the revision of Criterion A, which was previously criticized for being too inclusive (Spitzer, First, & Wakefield, 2007). The revision aimed to narrow the definition of what could be considered a traumatic event by requiring that the event include "actual or threatened death, serious injury, or sexual violence" (APA, 2013, p. 271). Furthermore, the criteria now specify that medical incidents are only considered traumatic if they include sudden, catastrophic events; in short, medical conditions due to natural causes, such as a diabetes or cancer, do not qualify as traumatic. As such, most of the physical health conditions described in this chapter would not be considered traumatic and would not be sufficient to obtain a PTSD diagnosis. These changes to the diagnostic criteria have been associated with reduced PTSD prevalence rates (Kilpatrick et al., 2013).

DSM-5 changes notwithstanding, a significant body of literature suggests that medical conditions, particularly those that are acute and considered life threatening, can induce posttraumatic stress reactions. Prevalence rates from empirical studies vary; but a recent meta-analysis noted that one fifth of critical illness survivors develop clinically significant PTSD symptoms in the first year after discharge (Parker et al., 2015). A systematic review identified perceived severity of the disease, as opposed to objective severity, as the most consistent risk factor for the development of cardiac-disease-induced PTSD (Vilchinsky, Ginzburg, Fait, & Foa, 2017).

Illness-induced PTSD has been associated with a number of negative consequences. In a sample of patients who experienced a myocardial infarction, posttraumatic symptoms related to the incident were positively correlated with the risk of another cardiovascular event (von Känel et al., 2011). Similarly, a review of responses to acute coronary syndromes found that those who developed PTSD had an increased risk of mortality and future cardiac events (Edmondson et al., 2012). Illness-induced PTSD has been associated with greater disability and worse quality of life compared to illnesses without subsequent PTSD (Cordova, Riba, & Spiegel, 2017; Goldfinger et al., 2014).

Due to differences between the traditional PTSD framework and illness-induced PTSD, Edmondson

(2014) proposed the Enduring Somatic Threat (EST) model of PTSD to better capture the psychological and behavioral consequences of life-threatening medical illnesses. The EST model focuses specifically on the psychological and behavioral consequences that differ from traditional PTSD symptoms, including whether the event is perceived as ongoing or occurring in the past, whether the trauma resides within or outside the individual, and the nature and consequences of avoidance behaviors. The EST model also highlights a key commonality between traditional and illness-induced PTSD; specifically, traumatic events provoke an awareness of mortality, which is the underlying source of distress. At present, empirical evidence for the EST model is only beginning to emerge and it is unclear how valuable the model will be for furthering the current understanding of illness-induced PTSD.

A Third Factor Causes Stress, Posttraumatic Stress Disorder, and Physical Health Conditions

The final potential explanation for the association between stress, PTSD, and physical health conditions is that a third factor, such as a genetic predisposition or shared vulnerability, exacerbates or causes each condition. Although this possibility has received less attention than either of the unidirectional associations between stress/PTSD and physical health conditions, it is not without merit. A genome-wide association study investigating genetic risk factors for PTSD in military samples found preliminary evidence for an association between *ANKRD55*, a gene that has been implicated in inflammatory and immune disorders, and PTSD in African American participants (Stein et al., 2016). The authors also observed significant pleiotropy between PTSD and rheumatoid arthritis in European American participants, further highlighting the potential genetic link between PTSD and inflammation.

As discussed earlier, PTSD is associated with a variety of neuroendocrine and inflammatory dysregulations that have also been implicated in physical health conditions; however, it is unclear whether these dysregulations are a result of PTSD or whether they are a risk factor for the disorder. One study found evidence that concentrations of proinflammatory cytokines in individuals with PTSD revert to levels comparable to those of nontraumatized controls following recovery from PTSD (Gill, Saligan, Lee, Rotolo, & Szanton, 2013). The authors suggested that biological functions may normalize following recovery from PTSD, but they also noted that due to the cross-sectional design they could not determine whether inflammatory alterations were a direct consequence of PTSD. For example, some individuals may also be genetically predisposed to develop inflammation in response to all injuries, whether physical or psychological. Furthermore, although concentrations of proinflammatory cytokines in individuals with PTSD decreased, this does not necessarily mean these concentrations were not already elevated prior to developing PTSD.

In contrast, prospective studies and studies examining individuals at greater risk for PTSD suggest that inflammatory alterations are a risk factor for PTSD (Yehuda, 2009). Twins with PTSD had elevated levels of inflammatory biomarkers; but most of the associations were no longer statistically significant when comparing within discordant pairs (Plantinga et al., 2013). There was no evidence that zygosity influenced the relationship between inflammatory markers and PTSD, suggesting that shared familial factors, but not genetics, may be confounding the association. Additional longitudinal research is needed to determine whether neuroendocrine and inflammatory dysregulations are the pathway through which PTSD leads to physical health conditions, or whether such dysregulations are an underlying causal factor for both PTSD and particular physical health conditions.

Also relevant to the possibility that some third factor causes stress/PTSD and physical health conditions is the shared vulnerability model proposed by Asmundson and colleagues (Asmundson, Coons, et al., 2002; Asmundson & Katz, 2009) to explain the common co-occurrence of anxiety disorders, including PTSD, and chronic pain. While these models differ in degree of focus on risk (i.e., vulnerability) versus maintaining factors and on specific paths of association, all draw on tenets of evidence-based cognitive-behavioral models of PTSD and chronic pain. The shared vulnerability model holds that individual difference factors (e.g., fear of feeling anxious, selective attention for threat, sense of uncontrollability, lower threshold for sympathetic nervous system activation) predispose people to develop PTSD and chronic pain when exposed to certain environmental conditions (e.g., traumatic incident, injury). The model also predicts that co-occurring PTSD and disabling pain are most likely to develop when vulnerable people are exposed to an event that is both traumatic and painful, since such experiences facilitate associations between the traumatic event and pain. As a result, reminders of the event (e.g., intrusive thoughts) and pain sensations trigger additional anxiety and pain and, thereby, maintain symptoms and associated functional limitations. Several recent comprehensive reviews (Asmundson & Katz, 2009; Beck & Clapp, 2011; Liedl & Knaevelsrud, 2008) have shown that the postulates of the shared vulnerability models have garnered considerable empirical support to date. It remains to be determined whether the postulates of the shared vulnerability model explain the comorbidity between anxiety disorders other than PTSD and physical health condition and, likewise, whether similar postulates might apply to significant but non-trauma-related stress.

Clinical Applications

Comorbid PTSD and physical health conditions are common and can result in poorer health outcomes than either condition alone; as such, the comorbidity magnifies personal suffering and adds burden to the health care systems (Asmundson & Katz, 2009; Knight & Sayegh, 2011). It is essential to understand temporal relationships between PTSD and physical health conditions to develop both intervention and prevention initiatives that will reduce the individual and societal burden of comorbidities. More generally, the same reasoning applies to stress and physical health conditions. From a prevention perspective, understanding mechanisms of association will provide the means to develop prevention targets, such as behavior modification and promotion of health behaviors. From an intervention perspective, research suggests that improving mental health in the context of illness improves disease-related outcomes. To facilitate appropriate interventions in this context, it is important for health care professionals to adequately identify comorbidities. Adequate identification can be challenging when, for example, patients tend to focus on physical health as opposed to mental health, and health professionals may generally have greater difficulty identifying a mental disorder in the context of a severe and debilitating medical illness.

More broadly, the growing body of research that has confirmed the intricate relationship between physical and mental health has resulted in a number of health care practice changes over the past few decades. Collaborative care models that incorporate mental health care into general medical practice are garnering significant attention (Bluestein & Cubic, 2009; Horgan et al., 2009; Patel et al. 2013). The term "behavioral medicine," first coined by Birk (1973), has developed into a subspecialty multidisciplinary practice that accounts for biological, psychological, and social factors implicated in illness. Further, psychologically based interventions are becoming common practice in specialty health settings (Astin et al., 2003). One example is the opioid epidemic in chronic pain sufferers, which has highlighted the shortcomings of strictly relying on a biomedical model of care focused on pharmacological solutions. There is now growing support for psychologically based interventions, such as cognitive-behavioral therapies, for the treatment of chronic pain (Gatchel, Peng, Peters, Fuchs, & Turk, 2007). These health care changes provide examples of the growing recognition of the relationship between mental and physical health, and the importance of targeting all aspects of health when treating individuals with physical health conditions.

Conclusion

Historical and contemporary researchers have acknowledged the intricate relationship between physical and mental health. A large body of literature provides compelling evidence of a link between PTSD, arguably the most extreme manifestation of stress, and various physical health conditions. This relationship is not unidirectional; stress/PTSD can worsen physical health, poor physical health can lead to stress/PTSD, and other variables, such as a genetic predisposition or shared vulnerability, can simultaneously lead to stress/PTSD and physical health conditions. Biological, psychological, and sociological factors further influence the pathways between PTSD and physical health conditions. Given that comorbid PTSD and physical health conditions have been associated with worse health outcomes, it is critical that clinicians identify and consider all aspects of health when developing treatment plans for patients. Future directions for research, many of which were mentioned throughout the chapter, include clarifying sex differences in comorbidities, a greater focus on lesser studied physical conditions such as cancer and stroke in comorbid relationships, and controlling for increased exposure to the health care system when examining comorbidities. Longitudinal research investigating proposed mechanisms and pathways connecting PTSD and physical health is imperative. Addressing these issues may aid in advancing our understanding of the associations between stress/PTSD and physical health conditions, as well as state-of-the-art preventative, assessment, and treatment efforts.

References

Abouzeid, M., Kelsall, H. L., Forbes, A. B., Sim, M. R., & Creamer, M. C. (2012). Posttraumatic stress disorder and hypertension in Australian veterans of the 1991 Gulf War. *Journal of Psychosomatic Research, 72*, 33–38. doi:10.1016/j.jpsychores.2011.08.002

Abrahams, E., & Silver, M. (2010). The history of personalized medicine. In E. Gordon & S. Koslow (Eds.), *Integrative neuroscience and personalized medicine* (pp. 3–16). New York, NY: Oxford University Press.

Abrams, T. E., Vaughan-Sarrazin, M., & Vander Weg, M. W. (2011). Acute exacerbations of chronic obstructive pulmonary disease and the effect of existing psychiatric comorbidity on subsequent mortality. *Psychosomatics, 52,* 441–449. doi:10.1016/j.psym.2011.03.005

Adameova, A., Abdellatif, Y., & Dhalla, N. S. (2009). Role of the excessive amounts of circulating catecholamines and glucocorticoids in stress-induced heart disease. *Canadian Journal of Physiology and Pharmacology, 87,* 493–514. doi:10.1682/JRRD.2007.05.0077

Agyemang, C., Goosen, S., Anujuo, K., & Ogedegbe, G. (2012). Relationship between post-traumatic stress disorder and diabetes among 105,180 asylum seekers in the Netherlands. *The European Journal of Public Health, 22,* 658–662. doi:10.1093/eurpub/ckr138

Ahmadi, N., Hajsadeghi, F., Mirshkarlo, H. B., Budoff, M., Yehuda, R., & Ebrahimi, R. (2011). Post-traumatic stress disorder, coronary atherosclerosis, and mortality. *The American Journal of Cardiology, 108,* 29–33. doi:10.1016/j.amjcard.2011.02.340

American Psychiatric Association. (2013). *Diagnostic and statistical manual of mental disorders: DSM-V.* (5th ed.). Washington, DC: Author.

Amir, M., Kaplan, Z., Neumann, L., Sharabani, R., Shani, N., & Buskila, D. (1997). Posttraumatic stress disorder, tenderness and fibromyalgia. *Journal of Psychosomatic Research, 42,* 607–613. doi:10.1016/S0022-3999(97)00009-3

Andreski, P., Chilcoat, H., & Breslau, N. (1998). Post-traumatic stress disorder and somatization symptoms: A prospective study. *Psychiatry Research, 79,* 131–138. doi:10.1016/S0165-1781(98)00026-2

Aquin, J. P., El-Gabalawy, R., Sala, T., & Sareen, J. (2017). Anxiety disorders and general medical conditions: Current research and future directions. *Focus, 15,* 173–181. doi:10.1176/appi.focus.20160044

Armenta, R. F., Rush, T., LeardMann, C. A., Millegan, J., Cooper, A., & Hoge, C. W. (2018). Factors associated with persistent posttraumatic stress disorder among US military service members and veterans. *BMC Psychiatry, 18,* 48. doi:10.1186/s12888-018-1590-5

Asmundson, G. J. G., Coons, M. J., Taylor, S., & Katz, J. (2002). PTSD and the experience of pain: Research and clinical implications of shared vulnerability and mutual maintenance models. *The Canadian Journal of Psychiatry, 47,* 930–937. doi:10.1177/070674370204701004

Asmundson, G. J. G., & Katz, J. (2009). Understanding the co-occurrence of anxiety disorders and chronic musculoskeletal pain: The state-of-the-art. *Depression and Anxiety, 26,* 888–901.

Asmundson, G. J., Stein, M. B., & McCreary, D. R. (2002). Posttraumatic stress disorder symptoms influence health status of deployed peacekeepers and nondeployed military personnel. *The Journal of Nervous and Mental Disease, 190,* 807–815. doi:10.1097/00005053-200212000-00002

Astin, J. A., Shapiro, S. L., Eisenberg, D. M., & Forys, K. L. (2003). Mind-body medicine: State of the science, implications for practice. *The Journal of the American Board of Family Practice, 16*, 131–147. doi:10.3122/jabfm.16.2.131

Barrett, D. H., Doebbeling, C. C., Schwartz, D. A., Voelker, M. D., Falter, K. H., Woolson, R. F., & Doebbeling, B. N. (2002). Posttraumatic stress disorder and self-reported physical health status among U.S. Military personnel serving during the Gulf War period: A population-based study. *Psychosomatics, 43*, 195–205. doi: 10.1176/appi.psy.43.3.195

Bartoli, F., Carrà, G., Crocamo, C., Carretta, D., & Clerici, M. (2013). Metabolic syndrome in people suffering from posttraumatic stress disorder: A systematic review and meta-analysis. *Metabolic Syndrome and Related Disorders, 11*, 301–308. doi:10.1089/met.2013.0010

Beck, J. G., & Clapp, J. D. (2011). A different kind of comorbidity: Understanding posttraumatic stress disorder and chronic pain. *Psychological Trauma, 3*, 101–108.

Beckham, J. C., Crawford, A. L., Feldman, M. E., Kirby, A. C., Hertzberg, M. A., Davidson, J. R. T., & Moore, S. D. (1997). Chronic posttraumatic stress disorder and chronic pain in Vietnam combat veterans. *Journal of Psychosomatic Research, 43*, 379–389. doi:0.1016/S0022-3999(97)00129-3

Bernstein, C. N. (2017). The brain-gut axis and stress in inflammatory bowel disease. *Gastroenterology Clinics, 46*, 839–846. doi:10.1016/j.gtc.2017.08.006

Birk, L. (1973). Biofeedback: Behavioral medicine. New York, NY: Grune & Stratton.

Bluestein, D., & Cubic, B. A. (2009). Psychologists and primary care physicians: A training model for creating collaborative relationships. *Journal of Clinical Psychology in Medical Settings, 16*, 101–112. doi:10.1007/s10880-009-9156-9

Boscarino, J. A. (2006a). External-cause mortality after psychologic trauma: The effects of stress exposure and predisposition. *Comprehensive Psychiatry, 47*, 503–514. doi:10.1016/j.comppsych.2006.02.006

Boscarino, J. A. (2006b). Posttraumatic stress disorder and mortality among U.S. army veterans 30 years after military service. *Annals of Epidemiology, 16*, 248–256. doi:10.1016/j.annepidem.2005.03.009

Boscarino, J. A., Forsberg, C. W., & Goldberg, J. (2010). A twin study of the association between PTSD symptoms and rheumatoid arthritis. *Psychosomatic Medicine, 72*, 481–486. doi:10.1097/PSY.0b013e3181d9a80c

Boyko, E. J., Jacobson, I. G., Smith, B., Ryan, M. A., Hooper, T. I., Amoroso, P. J., . . . & Millennium Cohort Study Team. (2010). Risk of diabetes in US military service members in relation to combat deployment and mental health. *Diabetes Care, 33*, 1771–1777. doi:10.2337/dc10-0296

Bremner, J. D., Licinio, J., Darnell, A., Krystal, J. H., Owens, M. J., Southwick, S. M., . . ., & Charney, D. S. (1997). Elevated CSF corticotropin-releasing factor concentrations in posttraumatic stress disorder. *American Journal of Psychiatry, 154*, 624–629. doi:10.1176/ajp.154.5.624

Brunner, E. J., Hemingway, H., Walker, B. R., Page, M., Clarke, P., Juneja, M., . . ., & Papadopoulos, A. (2002). Adrenocortical, autonomic, and inflammatory causes of the metabolic syndrome. *Circulation, 106*, 2659–2665. doi:10.1682/JRRD.2007.05.0077

Bryant, R. A., Marosszeky, J. E., Crooks, J., Baguley, I. J., & Gurka, J. A. (1999). Interaction of posttraumatic stress disorder and chronic pain following traumatic brain injury.

The Journal of Head Trauma Rehabilitation, 14, 588–594. doi:10.1097/00001199-199912000-00007

Buckley, T. C., Holohan, D., Greif, J. L., Bedard, M., & Suvak, M. (2004). Twenty-four-hour ambulatory assessment of heart rate and blood pressure in chronic PTSD and non-PTSD veterans. *Journal of Traumatic Stress, 17*, 163–171. doi:10.1023/B:JOTS.0000022623.01190.f0

Buckley, T. C., & Kaloupek, D. G. (2001). A meta-analytic examination of basal cardiovascular activity in posttraumatic stress disorder. *Psychosomatic Medicine, 63*, 585–594. doi:10.1097/00006842-200107000-00011

Campbell, R., Greeson, M. R., Bybee, D., & Raja, S. (2008). The co-occurrence of childhood sexual abuse, adult sexual assault, intimate partner violence, and sexual harassment: A mediational model of posttraumatic stress disorder and physical health outcomes. *Journal of Consulting and Clinical Psychology, 76*, 194–207.

Cannon, W. B. (1929a). *Bodily changes in pain, hunger, fear and rage*. New York, NY: D. Appleton & Co.

Cannon, W. B. (1929b). Organization for physiological homeostasis. *Physiological Reviews, 9*, 399–431. Retrieved from http://physrev.physiology.org/

Cannon, W. B. (1939). *The wisdom of the body*. New York, NY: W.W. Norton.

Chwastiak, L. A., Rosenheck, R. A., Desai, R., & Kasis, L. E. (2010). Association of psychiatric illness and all-cause mortality in the national Department of Veterans Affairs health care system. *Psychosomatic Medicine, 72*, 817–822. doi:10.1097/PSY.0b013e3181eb33e9

Cohen, S., Frank, E., Doyle, W. J., Skoner, D. P., Rabin, B. S., & Gwaltney, J. M. Jr (1998). Types of stressors that increase susceptibility to the common cold in healthy adults. *Health Psychology, 17*, 214–223. doi:10.1037/0278-6133.17.3.214

Cohen, H., Jotkowitz, A., Buskila, D., Pelles-Avraham, S., Kaplan, Z., Neumann, L., & Sperber, A. D. (2006). Post-traumatic stress disorder and other co-morbidities in a sample population of patients with irritable bowel syndrome. *European Journal of Internal Medicine, 17*, 567–571. doi:10.1016/j.ejim.2006.07.011

Cohen, S., Tyrrell, D. A., & Smith, A. P. (1991). Psychological stress and susceptibility to the common cold. *New England Journal of Medicine, 325*, 606–612. doi:10.1056/NEJM199108293250903

Cordova, M. J., Riba, M. B., & Spiegel, D. (2017). Post-traumatic stress disorder and cancer. *Lancet Psychiatry, 4*, 330–338. doi:10.1016/S2215-0366(17)30014-7

Coughlin, S. S. (2011). Post-traumatic stress disorder and cardiovascular disease. *The Open Cardiovascular Medicine Journal, 5*, 164–170. doi:10.2105/9780875530161ch07

Cougle, J. R., Bonn-Miller, M. O., Vujanovic, A. A., Zvolensky, M. J., & Hawkins, K. A. (2011). Posttraumatic stress disorder and cannabis use in a nationally representative sample. *Psychology of Addictive Behaviors, 25*, 554–558. doi:10.1037/a0023076

Crawford, E. F., Drescher, K. D., & Rosen, C. S. (2009). Predicting mortality in veterans with posttraumatic stress disorder thirty years after Vietnam. *Journal of Nervous and Mental Disease, 197*, 260–265. doi:10.1097/NMD.0b013e31819dbfce

Dao, T. K., Chu, D., Springer, J., Gopaldas, R. R., Menefee, D. S., Anderson, T., . . ., Nguyen, Q. (2010). Clinical depression, posttraumatic stress disorder, and comorbid depression and posttraumatic stress disorder as risk factors for in-hospital mortality after coronary artery bypass grafting surgery. *Journal of Thoracic and Cardiovascular Surgery, 140,* 606–610. doi:10.1016/j.jtcvs.2009.10.046

Dedert, E. A., Calhoun, P. S., Watkins, L. L., Sherwood, A., & Beckham, J. C. (2010). Posttraumatic stress disorder, cardiovascular, and metabolic disease: A review of the evidence. *Annals of Behavioral Medicine, 39,* 61–78. doi:10.1007/s12160-010-9165-9

Del Gaizo, A. L., Elhai, J. D., & Weaver, T. L. (2011). Posttraumatic stress disorder, poor physical health, and substance use behaviors in a national trauma-exposure sample. *Psychiatry Research, 188,* 390–395. doi:10.1016/j.psychres.2011.03.016

DeLongis, A., Folkman, S., & Lazarus, R. S. (1988). The impact of daily stress on health and mood: Psychological and social resources as mediators. *Journal of Personality and Social Psychology, 54,* 486–495. doi:10.1037/0022-3514.54.3.486

Denson, T. F., Spanovic, M., & Miller, N. (2009). Cognitive appraisals and emotions predict cortisol and immune responses: A meta-analysis of acute laboratory social stressors and emotion inductions. *Psychological Bulletin, 135,* 823–853. doi:10.1037/a0016909

Deykin, E. Y., Keane, T. M., Kaloupek, D., Fincke, G., Rothendler, J., Siegfried, M., & Creamer, K. (2001). Posttraumatic stress disorder and the use of health services. *Psychosomatic Medicine, 63,* 835–841. doi:10.1097/00006842-200109000-00018

Dirkzwager, A. J., Van der Velden, P. G., Grievink, L., & Yzermans, C. J. (2007). Disaster-related posttraumatic stress disorder and physical health. *Psychosomatic Medicine, 69,* 435–440. doi:10.1097/PSY.0b013e318052e20a

Dougall, A. L., & Baum, A. (2004). Psychoneuroimmunology and trauma. In P. P. Schnurr & B. L. Green (Eds.), *Trauma and health: Physical health consequences of exposure to extreme stress* (pp. 129–155). Washington, DC: American Psychological Association.

Edmondson, D. (2014). An enduring somatic threat model of posttraumatic stress disorder due to acute life-threatening medical events. *Social and Personality Psychology Compass, 8,* 118–134. doi:10.1111/spc3.12089

Edmondson, D., & Cohen, B. E. (2013). Posttraumatic stress disorder and cardiovascular disease. *Progress in Cardiovascular Diseases, 55,* 548–556. doi:10.1016/j.pcad.2013.03.004

Edmondson, D., Kronish, I. M., Shaffer, J. A., Falzon, L., & Burg, M. M. (2013). Posttraumatic stress disorder and risk for coronary heart disease: A meta-analytic review. *American Heart Journal, 166,* 806–814. doi:10.1016/j.ahj.2013.07.031

Edmondson, D., Richardson, S., Falzon, L., Davidson, K. W., Mills, M. A., & Neria, Y. (2012). Posttraumatic stress disorder prevalence and risk of recurrence in acute coronary syndrome patients: A meta-analytic review. *PloS ONE, 7*(6), e38915. doi:10.1371/journal.pone.0038915

El-Gabalawy, R., Blaney, C., Tsai, J., Sumner, J. A., & Pietrzak, R. H. (2018). Physical health conditions associated with full and subthreshold PTSD in U.S. military veterans: Results from the National Health and Resilience in Veterans Study. *Journal of Affective Disorders.227,* 849–853. doi:10.1016/j.jad.2017.11.058

El-Gabalawy, R., Mackenzie, C., Pietrzak, R., & Sareen, J. (2014). A longitudinal examination of anxiety disorders and physical health conditions in a nationally representative sample of U.S. older adults. *Experimental Gerontology, 60,* 46–56. doi:10.1016/j.exger.2014.09.012

Elhai, J. D., North, T. C., & Frueh, B. C. (2005). Health service use predictors among trauma survivors: A critical review. *Psychological Services, 2,* 3–19. doi:10.1037/1541-1559.2.1.3

Engel, G. L. (1980). The clinical application of the biopsychosocial model. *American Journal of Psychiatry, 137,* 535–544. doi:10.1176/ajp.137.5.535

Farr, O. M., Ko, B. J., Joung, K. E., Zaichenko, L., Usher, N., Tsoukas, M.,..., & Mantzoros, C. S. (2015). Posttraumatic stress disorder, alone or additively with early life adversity, is associated with obesity and cardiometabolic risk. *Nutrition, Metabolism and Cardiovascular Diseases, 25,* 479–488. doi:10.1016/j.numecd.2015.01.007

Fetzner, M. G., McMillan, K. A., & Asmundson, G. J. G. (2012). Similarities in specific physical health disorder prevalence among formerly deployed Canadian forces veterans with full and subsyndromal PTSD. *Depression and Anxiety, 29,* 958–965. doi:10.1002/da.21976

Flood, A. M., McDevitt-Murphy, M. E., Weathers, F. W., Eakin, D. E., & Benson, T. A. (2009). Substance use behaviors as a mediator between posttraumatic stress disorder and physical health in trauma-exposed college students. *Journal of Behavioral Medicine, 32,* 234–243. doi:10.1007/s10865-008-9195-y

Friedman, M. J., & McEwen, B. S. (2004). Posttraumatic stress disorder, allostatic load, and medical illness. In P. P. Schnurr & B. L. Green (Eds.), *Trauma and health: Physical health consequences of exposure to extreme stress* (pp. 157–188). Washington, DC: American Psychological Association

Gatchel, R. J., Peng, Y. B., Peters, M. L., Fuchs, P. N., & Turk, D. C. (2007). The biopsychosocial approach to chronic pain: Scientific advances and future directions. *Psychological Bulletin, 133,* 581–624. doi:10.1037/0033-2909.133.4.581

Gehi, A. K., Ali, S., Na, B., & Whooley, M. A. (2007). Self-reported medication adherence and cardiovascular events in patients with stable coronary heart disease: The heart and soul study. *Archives of Internal Medicine, 167,* 1798–1803. doi:10.1001/archinte.167.16.1798

Gill, J. M., Saligan, L., Lee, H., Rotolo, S., & Szanton, S. (2013). Women in recovery from PTSD have similar inflammation and quality of life as non-traumatized controls. *Journal of Psychosomatic Research, 74,* 301–306. doi:10.1016/j.jpsychores.2012.10.013

Gill, J. M., Saligan, L., Woods, S., & Page, G. (2009). PTSD is associated with an excess of inflammatory immune activities. *Perspectives in Psychiatric Care, 45,* 262–277. doi:10.1111/j.1744-6163.2009.00229.x

Glaesmer, H., Brähler, E., Gündel, H., & Riedel-Heller, S. G. (2011). The association of traumatic experiences and posttraumatic stress disorder with physical morbidity in old age: A German population-based study. *Psychosomatic Medicine, 73,* 401–406. doi:10.1097/PSY.0b013e31821b47e8

Glover, D. A., Stuber, M., & Poland, R. E. (2006). Allostatic load in women with and without PTSD symptoms. *Psychiatry: Interpersonal and Biological Processes, 69,* 191–203. doi:10.1521/psyc.2006.69.3.191

Godfrey, K. M., Lindamer, L. A., Mostoufi, S., & Afari, N. (2013). Posttraumatic stress disorder and health: A preliminary study of group differences in health and health behaviors. *Annals of General Psychiatry, 12*(30), 1–8. doi:10.1186/1744-859X-12-30

Goetz, M., Shah, A., Goldberg, J., Cheema, F., Shallenberger, L., Murrah, N. V.,...Vaccarino, V. (2014). Posttraumatic stress disorder, combat exposure, and carotid intima-media thickness in male twins. *American journal of epidemiology*, *180*(10), 989–996. doi: 10.1093/aje/kwu225

Goldfinger, J. Z., Edmondson, D., Kronish, I. M., Fei, K., Balakrishnan, R., Tuhrim, S., & Horowitz, C. R. (2014). Correlates of post-traumatic stress disorder in stroke survivors. *Journal of Stroke and Cerebrovascular Diseases, 23*, 1099–1105. doi:10.1016/j.jstrokecerebrovasdis.2013.09.019

Goldstein, D. S., & Kopin, I. J. (2007). Evolution of concepts of stress. *Stress, 10*, 109–120. doi:10.1080/10253890701288935

Goodwin, R. D., & Davidson, J. R. (2005). Self-reported diabetes and posttraumatic stress disorder among adults in the community. *Preventive Medicine, 40*, 570–574. doi:10.1016/j.ypmed.2004.07.013

Gradus, J. L., Farkas, D. K., Svensson, E., Ehrenstein, V., Lash, T. L., & Sørensen, H. T. (2017). Posttraumatic stress disorder and gastrointestinal disorders in the Danish population. *Epidemiology, 28*, 354–360. doi:10.1097/EDE.0000000000000622

Haskell, W. L. (2003). Cardiovascular disease prevention and lifestyle interventions: Effectiveness and efficacy. *Journal of Cardiovascular Nursing, 18*, 245–255. doi:10.1097/00005082-200309000-00003

Heim, C., & Nemeroff, C. B. (2009). Neurobiology of posttraumatic stress disorder. *CNS Spectrums, 14*, 13–24. doi:10.1016/S0959-4388(00)00080-5

Heppner, P. S., Crawford, E. F., Haji, U. A., Afari, N., Hauger, R. L., Dashevsky, B. A., ... & Baker, D. G. (2009). The association of posttraumatic stress disorder and metabolic syndrome: A study of increased health risk in veterans. *BMC Medicine, 7*, 1–8. doi:10.1186/1741-7015-7-1

Hirth, J. M., Rahman, M., & Berenson, A. B. (2011). The association of posttraumatic stress disorder with fast food and soda consumption and unhealthy weight loss behaviors among young women. *Journal of Women's Health, 20*, 1141–1149. doi:10.1089/jwh.2010.2675

Horgan, S., LeClair, K., Donnelly, M., Hinton, G., MacCourt, P., & Krieger-Frost, S. (2009). Developing a national consensus on the accessibility needs of older adults with concurrent and chronic, mental and physical health issues: A preliminary framework informing collaborative mental health care planning. *Canadian Journal on Aging/La Revue Canadienne du Vieillissement, 28*, 97–105. doi:10.1017/S0714980809090175

Hulme, P. A. (2000). Symptomatology and health care utilization of women primary care patients who experienced childhood sexual abuse. *Child Abuse & Neglect, 24*, 1471–1484. doi:10.1016/S0145-2134(00)00200-3

Husarewycz, M. N., El-Gabalawy, R., Logsetty, S., & Sareen, J. (2014). The association between number and type of traumatic life experiences and physical conditions in a nationally representative sample. *General Hospital Psychiatry, 36*, 26–32. doi:10.1016/j.genhosppsych.2013.06.003

Irwin, C., Falsetti, S. A., Lydiard, R. B., & Ballenger, J. C. (1996). Comorbidity of posttraumatic stress disorder and irritable bowel syndrome. *The Journal of Clinical Psychiatry, 57*, 576–578. doi:10.4088/JCP.v57n1204

Jacobsen, L. K., Southwick, S. M., & Kosten, T. R. (2001). Substance use disorders in patients with posttraumatic stress disorder: A review of the literature. *American Journal of Psychiatry, 158*, 1184–1190. doi:10.1176/appi.ajp.158.8.1184

Jordan, H. T., Miller-Archie, S. A., Cone, J. E., Morabia, A., & Stellman, S. D. (2011). Heart disease among adults exposed to the September 11, 2001 World Trade Center disaster: Results from the World Trade Center Health Registry. *Preventive Medicine, 53*, 370–376. doi:10.1016/j.ypmed.2011.10.014

Julius, S., & Gudbrandsson, T. (1992). Early association of sympathetic overactivity, hypertension, insulin resistance, and coronary risk. *Journal of Cardiovascular Pharmacology, 20*, S40–S48. Retrieved from http://journals.lww.com

Kang, H. K., Bullman, T. A., & Taylor, J. W. (2006). Risk of selected cardiovascular diseases and posttraumatic stress disorder among former World War II prisoners of war. *Annals of Epidemiology, 16*, 381–386. doi:10.1016/j.annepidem.2005.03.004

Keane, T. M., Kolb, L. C., Kaloupek, D. G., Orr, S. P., Blanchard, E. B., Thomas, R. G., ... & Lavori, P. W. (1998). Utility of psychophysiology measurement in the diagnosis of posttraumatic stress disorder: Results from a department of Veteran's Affairs cooperative study. *Journal of Consulting and Clinical Psychology, 66*, 914–923. doi:10.1037/0022-006X.66.6.914

Kemeny, M. E. (2003). The psychobiology of stress. *Current Directions in Psychological Science, 12*, 124–129. doi:10.1111/1467-8721.01246

Kendall-Tackett, K. (2009). Psychological trauma and physical health: A psychoneuroimmunology approach to etiology of negative health effects and possible interventions. *Psychological Trauma: Theory, Research, Practice, and Policy, 1*, 35–48. doi:10.1037/a0015128

Kessler, R. C., Sonnega, A., Bromet, E., Hughes, M., & Nelson, C. B. (1995). Posttraumatic stress disorder in the National Comorbidity Survey. *Archives of General Psychiatry, 52*, 1048–1060. doi:10.1001/archpsyc.1995.03950240066012

Kibler, J. L., Joshi, K., & Ma, M. (2009). Hypertension in relation to posttraumatic stress disorder and depression in the US National Comorbidity Survey. *Behavioral Medicine, 34*, 125–132. doi:10.3200/BMED.34.4.125-132

Kilpatrick, D. G., Resnick, H. S., Milanak, M. E., Miller, M. W., Keyes, K. M., & Friedman, M. J. (2013). National estimates of exposure to traumatic events and PTSD prevalence using DSM-IV and DSM-5 criteria. *Journal of Traumatic Stress, 26*, 537–547. doi:10.1002/jts.21848

Kimerling, R., Clum, G. A., & Wolfe, J. (2000). Relationships among trauma exposure, chronic posttraumatic stress disorder symptoms, and self-reported health in women: Replication and extension. *Journal of Traumatic Stress, 13*, 115–128. doi:10.1023/A:1007729116133

Knight, B. G., & Sayegh, P. (2011). Mental health and aging in the 21st century. *Journal of Aging & Social Policy, 23*, 228–243. doi: 10.1080/08959420.2011.579494

Kronish, I. M., Edmondson, D., Li, Y., & Cohen, B. E. (2012). Post-traumatic stress disorder and medication adherence: Results from the Mind Your Heart study. *Journal of Psychiatric Research, 46*, 1595–1599. doi:10.1016/j.jpsychires.2012.06.011

Kubzansky, L. D., Koenen, K. C., Jones, C., & Eaton, W. W. (2009). A prospective study of posttraumatic stress disorder symptoms and coronary heart disease in women. *Health Psychology, 28*, 125–130. doi:10.1037/0278-6133.28.1.125

Kubzansky, L. D., Koenen, K. C., Spiro, A., Vokonas, P. S., & Sparrow, D. (2007). Prospective study of posttraumatic stress disorder symptoms and coronary heart disease in the Normative Aging Study. *Archives of General Psychiatry, 64*, 109–116. doi:10.1001/archpsyc.64.1.109

Lauterbach, D., Vora, R., & Rakow, M. (2005). The relationship between posttraumatic stress disorder and self-reported health problems. *Psychosomatic Medicine, 67,* 939–947. doi:10.1097/01.psy.0000188572.91553.a5

LeardMann, C. A., Smith, T. C., Smith, B., Wells, T. S., & Ryan, M. A. (2009). Baseline self reported functional health and vulnerability to post-traumatic stress disorder after combat deployment: Prospective US military cohort study. *British Medical Journal, 338,* b1273. doi:10.1136/bmj.b1273

Lichtenstein, A. H., Appel, L. J., Brands, M., Carnethon, M., Daniels, S., Franch, H. A.,…& Karanja, N. (2006). Diet and lifestyle recommendations revision 2006. *Circulation, 114,* 82–96. doi:10.1161/CIRCULATIONAHA.106.176158

Liedl, A., & Knaevelsrud, C. (2008). Chronic pain and PTSD: The perpetual avoidance model and its treatment implications. *Torture, 18,* 69–76.

Lindqvist, D., Dhabhar, F. S., Mellon, S. H., Yehuda, R., Grenon, S. M., Flory, J. D.,…Reus, V. I. (2017). Increased pro-inflammatory milieu in combat related PTSD—A new cohort replication study. *Brain, Bhehavior, and Immunity, 59,* 260–264. doi:10.1016/j.bbi.2016.09.012

Lohr, J. B., Palmer, B. W., Eidt, C. A., Aailaboyina, S., Mausbach, B. T., Wolkowitz, O. M.,…Jeste, D. V. (2015). Is posttraumatic stress disorder associated with premature senescence? A review of the literature. *The American Journal of Geriatric Psychiatry, 23,* 709–725. doi:10.1016/j.jagp.2015.04.001

Lukaschek, K., Baumert, J., Kruse, J., Emeny, R. T., Lacruz, M. E., Huth, C.,…Ladwig, K. H. (2013). Relationship between posttraumatic stress disorder and type 2 diabetes in a population-based cross-sectional study with 2970 participants. *Journal of Psychosomatic Research, 74,* 340–345. doi:0.1016/j.jpsychores.2012.12.011

Maguen, S., Madden, E., Cohen, B., Bertenthal, D., & Seal, K. (2014). Association of mental health problems with gastrointestinal disorders in Iraq and Afghanistan veterans. *Depression and Anxiety, 31,* 160–165. doi:10.1002/da.22072

McEwen, B. S. (1998). Protective and damaging effects of stress mediators. *New England Journal of Medicine, 338,* 171–179. doi:10.1056/NEJM199801153380307

McEwen, B. S. (2003). Mood disorders and allostatic load. *Biological Psychiatry, 54,* 200–207. doi:10.1016/S0006-3223(03)00177-X

McEwen, B. S. (2008). Central effects of stress hormones in health and disease: Understanding the protective and damaging effects of stress and stress mediators. *European Journal of Pharmacology, 583,* 174–185. doi:10.1016/j.ejphar.2007.11.071

McEwen, B. S., & Stellar, E. (1993). Stress and the individual: Mechanisms leading to disease. *Archives of Internal Medicine, 153,* 2093–2101. doi:10.1001/archinte.1993.00410180039004

McFarlane, A. C., Atchison, M., Rafalowicz, E., & Papay, P. (1994). Physical symptoms in post-traumatic stress disorder. *Journal of Psychosomatic Research, 38,* 715–726. doi:10.1016/0022-3999(94)90024-8

Miller-Archie, S. A., Jordan, H. T., Ruff, R. R., Chamany, S., Cone, J. E., Brackbill, R. M.,…Stellman, S. D. (2014). Posttraumatic stress disorder and new-onset diabetes among adult survivors of the World Trade Center disaster. *Preventive Medicine, 66,* 34–38. doi:10.1016/j.ypmed.2014.05.016

Ng, D. M., & Jeffery, R. W. (2003). Relationships between perceived stress and health behaviors in a sample of working adults. *Health Psychology, 22,* 638–642. doi:10.1037/0278-6133.22.6.638

Norman, S. B., Means-Christensen, A. J., Craske, M. G., Sherbourne, C. D., Roy-Byrne, P. P., & Stein, M. B. (2006). Associations between psychological trauma and physical illness in primary care. *Journal of Traumatic Stress, 19,* 461–470. doi:10.1002/jts.20129

Orr, S. P., Metzger, L. J., Lasko, N. B., Macklin, M. L., Hu, F. B., Shalev, A. Y., & Pitman, R. K. (2003). Physiologic responses to sudden, loud tones in monozygotic twins discordant for combat exposure: Association with posttraumatic stress disorder. *Archives of General Psychiatry, 60,* 283–288. doi:10.1001/archpsyc.60.3.283

O'Toole, B. I., & Catts, S. V. (2008). Trauma, PTSD, and physical health: An epidemiological study of Australian Vietnam veterans. *Journal of Psychosomatic Research, 64,* 33–40. doi:10.1016/j.jpsychores.2007.07.006

O'Toole, B. I., Catts, S. V., Outram, S., Pierse, K. R., & Cockburn, J. (2010). Factors associated with civilian mortality in Australian Vietnam veterans three decades after the war. *Military Medicine, 175,* 88–95. doi:10.1093/aje/kwp146

Ouimette, P., Cronkite, R., Henson, B. R., Prins, A., Gima, K., & Moos, R. H. (2004). Posttraumatic stress disorder and health status among female and male medical patients. *Journal of Traumatic Stress, 17,* 1–9. doi:10.1023/B:JOTS.0000014670.68240.38

Owens, M. J., & Nemeroff, C. B. (1991). Physiology and pharmacology of corticotropin-releasing factor. *Pharmacological Reviews, 43,* 425–473. Retrieved from http://pharmrev.aspetjournals.org/

Pace, T. W., & Heim, C. M. (2011). A short review on the psychoneuroimmunology of posttraumatic stress disorder: From risk factors to medical comorbidities. *Brain, Behavior, and Immunity, 25,* 6–13. doi:10.1016/j.bbi.2010.10.003

Pacella, M. L., Hruska, B., & Delahanty, D. L. (2013). The physical health consequences of PTSD and PTSD symptoms: A meta-analytic review. *Journal of Anxiety Disorders, 27,* 33–46. doi:10.1016/j.janxdis.2012.08.004

Pagoto, S. L., Schneider, K. L., Bodenlos, J. S., Appelhans, B. M., Whited, M. C., Ma, Y., & Lemon, S. C. (2012). Association of post-traumatic stress disorder and obesity in a nationally representative sample. *Obesity, 20,* 200–205. doi:10.1038/oby.2011.318

Pai, A., Suris, A. M., & North, C. S. (2017). Posttraumatic stress disorder in the DSM-5: Controversy, change, and conceptual considerations. *Behavioral Sciences, 7,* 1–7. doi: 10.3390/bs7010007

Parker, A. M., Sricharoenchai, T., Raparla, S., Schneck, K. W., Bienvenu, O. J., & Needham, D. M. (2015). Posttraumatic stress disorder in critical illness survivors: A metaanalysis. *Critical Care Medicine, 43,* 1121–1129. doi:10.1097/CCM.000000000000088

Patel, V., Belkin, G.S., Chockalingam, A., Cooper, J., Saxena, S., & Unutzer, J. (2013). Grand challenges: Integrating mental health services into priority health care platforms. *PLoS Medicine, 10,* e1001448. doi:10.1371/journal.pmed.1001448

Peterlin, B. L., Tietjen, G., Meng, S., Lidicker, J., & Bigal, M. (2008). Post-traumatic stress disorder in episodic and chronic migraine. *Headache: The Journal of Head and Face Pain, 48,* 517–522. doi:10.1111/j.1526-4610.2008.00917.x

Pietrzak, R. H., Goldstein, R. B., Southwick, S. M., & Grant, B. F. (2011). Medical comorbidity of full and partial posttraumatic stress disorder in United States adults: Results from wave 2 of the National Epidemiologic Survey on Alcohol and Related Conditions. *Psychosomatic Medicine, 73,* 697–707. doi:10.1097/PSY.0b013e3182303775

Pietrzak, R. H., Goldstein, R. B., Southwick, S. M., & Grant, B. F. (2012). Physical health conditions associated with posttraumatic stress disorder in US older adults: Results from wave 2 of the National Epidemiologic Survey on Alcohol and Related Conditions. *Journal of the American Geriatrics Society, 60*, 296–303. doi:10.1111/j.1532-5415.2011.03788.x

Plantinga, L., Bremner, J. D., Miller, A. H., Jones, D. P., Veledar, E., Goldberg, J., & Vaccarino, V. (2013). Association between posttraumatic stress disorder and inflammation: A twin study. *Brain, Behavior, and Immunity, 30*, 125–132. doi:10.1016/j.bbi.2013.01.081

Pole, N. (2007). The psychophysiology of posttraumatic stress disorder: A meta-analysis. *Psychological Bulletin, 133*, 725–746. doi:10.1037/0033-2909.133.5.725

Rabe, S., Dörfel, D., Zöllner, T., Maercker, A., & Karl, A. (2006). Cardiovascular correlates of motor vehicle accident related posttraumatic stress disorder and its successful treatment. *Applied Psychophysiology and Biofeedback, 31*, 315–330. doi:10.1007/s10484-006-9027-1

Rheingold, A. A., Acierno, R., & Resnick, H. S. (2004). Trauma, posttraumatic stress disorder, and heath risk behaviours. In P. P. Schnurr & B. L. Green (Eds.), *Trauma and health: Physical health consequences of exposure to extreme stress* (pp. 217–243). Washington, DC: American Psychological Association.

Roberts, A. L., Agnew-Blais, J. C., Spiegelman, D., Kubzansky, L. D., Mason, S. M., Galea, S.,...Koenen, K. C. (2015). Posttraumatic stress disorder and incidence of type 2 diabetes mellitus in a sample of women: A 22-year longitudinal study. *JAMA Psychiatry, 72*, 203–210. doi:10.1001/jamapsychiatry.2014.2632

Rosenbaum, S., Stubbs, B., Ward, P. B., Steel, Z., Lederman, O., & Vancampfort, D. (2015). The prevalence and risk of metabolic syndrome and its components among people with posttraumatic stress disorder: A systematic review and meta-analysis. *Metabolism, 64*, 926–933. doi:10.1016/j.metabol.2015.04.009

Roy, S. S., Foraker, R. E., Girton, R. A., & Mansfield, A. J. (2015). Posttraumatic stress disorder and incident heart failure among a community-based sample of US veterans. *American Journal of Public Health, 105*, 757–763. doi:10.2105/AJPH.2014.302342

Roy-Byrne, P. P., Davidson, K. W., Kessler, R. C., Asmundson, G. J. G., Goodwin, R. D., Kubzansky, L.,...Stein, M. B. (2008). Anxiety disorders and comorbid medical illness. *General Hospital Psychiatry, 30*, 208–225. doi:10.1016/j.genhosppsych.2007.12.006

Sareen, J., Cox, B. J., Clara, I., & Asmundson, G. J. G. (2005). The relationship between anxiety disorders and physical disorders in the US National Comorbidity Survey. *Depression and Anxiety, 21*, 193–202. doi:10.1002/da.20072

Sareen, J., Cox, B. J., Stein, M. B., Afifi, T. O., Fleet, C., & Asmundson, G. J. G (2007). Physical and mental comorbidity, disability, and suicidal behavior associated with posttraumatic stress disorder in a large community sample. *Psychosomatic Medicine, 69*, 242–248. doi:10.1097/PSY.0b013e31803146d8

Sareen, J., Jacobi, F., Cox, B. J., Belik, S. L., Clara, I., & Stein, M. B. (2006). Disability and poor quality of life associated with comorbid anxiety disorders and physical conditions. *Archives of Internal Medicine, 166*, 2109–2116. doi:10.1001/archinte.166.19.2109

Savas, L. S., White, D. L., Wieman, M., Daci, K., Fitzgerald, S., Laday Smith, S.,...El-Serag, H. B. (2009). Irritable bowel syndrome and dyspepsia among women veterans: Prevalence and association with psychological distress. *Alimentary Pharmacology & Therapeutics, 29*, 115–125. doi:10.1111/j.1365-2036.2008.03847.x

Scherrer, J. F., Chrusciel, T., Zeringue, A., Garfield, L. D., Hauptman, P. J., Lustman, P. J.,...True, W. R. (2010). Anxiety disorders increase risk for incident myocardial infarction in depressed and nondepressed Veterans Administration patients. *American Heart Journal, 159*, 772–779. doi:10.1016/j.ahj.2010.02.033

Schlenger, W. E., Corry, N. H., Williams, C. S., Kulka, R. A., Mulvaney-Day, N., DeBakey, S.,...Marmar, C. R. (2015). A prospective study of mortality and trauma-related risk factors among a nationally representative sample of Vietnam veterans. *American Journal of Epidemiology, 182*, 980–990. doi:10.1093/aje/kwv217

Schnurr, P. P. (2015). Understanding pathways from traumatic exposure to physical health. In U. Schnyder & M. Cloitre (Eds.), *Evidence based treatments for trauma-related psychological disorders: A practical guide for clinicians* (pp. 87–103). doi:10.1007/978-3-319-07109-1_5

Schnurr, P. P., & Green, B. L. (2004). Understanding relationships among trauma, posttraumatic stress disorder, and health outcomes. In P. P. Schnurr & B. L. Green (Eds.), *Trauma and health: Physical health consequences of exposure to extreme stress* (pp. 247–275). Washington, DC: American Psychological Association.

Schnurr, P. P., & Jankowski, M. K. (1999). Physical health and post-traumatic stress disorder: Review and synthesis. *Seminars in Clinical Neuropsychiatry, 4*, 295–304. doi:10.153/SCNP00400295

Schnurr, P. P., & Spiro, A. (1999). Combat exposure, posttraumatic stress disorder symptoms, and health behaviors as predictors of self-reported physical health in older veterans. *Journal of Nervous and Mental Disease, 187*, 353–359. doi:10.1097/00005053-199906000-00004

Schnurr, P. P., Spiro, A., & Paris, A. H. (2000). Physician-diagnosed medical disorders in relation to PTSD symptoms in older male military veterans. *Health Psychology, 19*, 91–97. doi:10.1037/0278-6133.19.1.91

Schuster-Wachen, J., Shipherd, J. C., Suvak, M., Vogt, D., King, L. A., & King, D. W. (2013). Posttraumatic stress symptomatology as a mediator of the relationship between warzone exposure and physical health symptoms in men and women. *Journal of Traumatic Stress, 26*, 319–328. doi:10.1002/jts.21818

Scott, K. M., Bruffaerts, R., Tsang, A., Ormel, J., Alonso, J., Angermeyer, M. C.,...Gasquet, I. (2007). Depression-anxiety relationships with chronic physical conditions: Results from the World Mental Health Surveys. *Journal of Affective Disorders, 103*, 113–120. doi:10.1016/j.jad.2007.01.015

Selye, H. (1956). *The stress of life*. New York, NY: McGraw-Hill.

Shamoon, H., Hendler, R., & Sherwin, R. S. (1980). Altered responsiveness to cortisol, epinephrine, and glucagon in insulin-infused juvenile-onset diabetics: A mechanism for diabetic instability. *Diabetes, 29*, 284–291. doi:10.2337/diab.29.4.284

Shipherd, J. C., Keyes, M., Jovanovic, T., Ready, D. J., Baltzell, D., Worley, V.,...Duncan, E. (2007). Veterans seeking treatment for posttraumatic stress disorder: What about comorbid chronic pain? *Journal of Rehabilitation Research and Development, 44*, 153–166. doi:10.1682/jrrd.2006.06.0065

Sledjeski, E. M., Speisman, B., & Dierker, L. C. (2008). Does number of lifetime traumas explain the relationship between PTSD and chronic medical conditions? Answers from the National Comorbidity Survey-Replication (NCS-R). *Journal of Behavioral Medicine, 31*, 341–349. doi:10.1007/s10865-008-9158-3

Smith, B. N., Tyzik, A. L., Neylan, T. C., & Cohen, B. E. (2015). PTSD and obesity in younger and older veterans: Results from the mind your heart study. *Psychiatry Research, 229*, 895–900. doi:10.1016/j.psychres.2015.07.044

Spitzer, C., Barnow, S., Völzke, H., John, U., Freyberger, H. J., & Grabe, H. J. (2009). Trauma, posttraumatic stress disorder, and physical illness: Findings from the general population. *Psychosomatic Medicine, 71*, 1012–1017. doi:10.1097/PSY.0b013e3181bc76b5

Spitzer, R. L., First, M. B., & Wakefield, J. C. (2007). Saving PTSD from itself in DSM-V. *Journal of Anxiety Disorders, 21*, 233–241. doi:10.1016/j.janxdis.2006.09.006

Stein, M. B., Chen, C. Y., Ursano, R. J., Cai, T., Gelernter, J., Heeringa, S. G.,...Nievergelt, C. M. (2016). Genome-wide association studies of posttraumatic stress disorder in 2 cohorts of US Army soldiers. *JAMA Psychiatry, 73*, 695–704. doi:10.1001/jamapsychiatry.2016.0350

Suliman, S., Anthonissen, L., Carr, J., du Plessis, S., Emsley, R., Hemmings, S. M.,...Seedat, S. (2016). Posttraumatic stress disorder, overweight, and obesity: A systematic review and meta-analysis. *Harvard Review of Psychiatry, 24*, 271–293. doi:10.1097/HRP.0000000000000106

Taft, C. T., Stern, A. S., King, L. A., & King, D. W. (1999). Modeling physical health and functional health status: The role of combat exposure, posttraumatic stress disorder, and personal resource attributes. *Journal of Traumatic Stress, 12*, 3–23. doi:10.1023/A:1024786030358

Tansill, E. C., Edwards, K. M., Kearns, M. C., Gidycz, C. A., & Calhoun, K. S. (2012). The mediating role of trauma-related symptoms in the relationship between sexual victimization and physical health symptomatology in undergraduate women. *Journal of Traumatic Stress, 25*, 79–85. doi:10.1002/jts.21666

Tsai, J., & Shen, J. (2017). Exploring the link between posttraumatic stress disorder and inflammation-related medical conditions: An epidemiological examination. *Psychiatric Quarterly, 88*, 909–916. doi:10.1007/s11126-017-9508-9

Tucker, P., Jeon-Slaughter, H., Pfefferbaum, B., Khan, Q., & Davis, N. J. (2009). Emotional and biological stress measures in Katrina survivors relocated to Oklahoma. *American Journal of Disaster Medicine, 5*, 113–125.

Vaccarino, V., Goldberg, J., Magruder, K. M., Forsberg, C. W., Friedman, M. J., Litz, B. T.,...Smith, N. L. (2014). Posttraumatic stress disorder and incidence of type-2 diabetes: A prospective twin study. *Journal of Psychiatric Research, 56*, 158–164. doi:10.1016/j.jpsychires.2014.05.019

Vaccarino, V., Goldberg, J., Rooks, C., Shah, A. J., Veledar, E., Faber, T. L.,...Bremner, J. D. (2013). Post-traumatic stress disorder and incidence of coronary heart disease: A twin study. *Journal of the American College of Cardiology, 62*, 970–978. doi:10.1016/j.jacc.2013.04.085

Vachon-Presseau, E., Roy, M., Martel, M. O., Caron, E., Marin, M. F., Chen, J.,...Rainville, P. (2013). The stress model of chronic pain: Evidence from basal cortisol and hippocampal structure and function in humans. *Brain, 136*, 815–827. doi:10.1093/brain/aws371

Vasterling, J. J., Schumm, J., Proctor, S. P., Gentry, E., King, D. W., & King, L. A. (2008). Posttraumatic stress disorder and health functioning in a non-treatment-seeking sample of Iraq war veterans: A prospective analysis. *Journal of Rehabilitation Research and Development, 45*, 347–358. doi:10.1682/JRRD.2007.05.0077

Vilchinsky, N., Ginzburg, K., Fait, K., & Foa, E. B. (2017). Cardiac-disease-induced PTSD (CDI-PTSD): A systematic review. *Clinical Psychology Review, 55*, 92–106. doi:10.1016/j.cpr.2017.04.009

von Känel, R., Begré, S., Abbas, C. C., Saner, H., Gander, M. L., & Schmid, J. P. (2010). Inflammatory biomarkers in patients with posttraumatic stress disorder caused by myocardial infarction and the role of depressive symptoms. *Neuroimmunomodulation, 17*, 39–46. doi:10.1159/000243084

von Känel, R., Hari, R., Schmid, J. P., Wiedemar, L., Guler, E., Barth, J.,...Begré, S. (2011). Non-fatal cardiovascular outcome in patients with posttraumatic stress symptoms caused by myocardial infarction. *Journal of Cardiology, 58*, 61–68. doi:10.1016/j.jjcc.2011.02.007

von Känel, R., Hepp, U., Kraemer, B., Traber, R., Keel, M., Mica, L., & Schnyder, U. (2007). Evidence for low-grade systemic proinflammatory activity in patients with posttraumatic stress disorder. *Journal of Psychiatric Research, 41*, 744–752. doi:10.1016/j.jpsychires.2006.06.009

Weisberg, R. B., Bruce, S. E., Machan, J. T., Kessler, R. C., Culpepper, L., & Keller, M. B. (2002). Nonpsychiatric illness among primary care patients with trauma histories and posttraumatic stress disorder. *Psychiatric Services, 53*, 848–854. doi:10.1176/appi.ps.53.7.848

Weiss, T., Skelton, K., Phifer, J., Jovanovic, T., Gillespie, C. F., Smith, A.,...Ressler, K. J. (2011). Posttraumatic stress disorder is a risk factor for metabolic syndrome in an impoverished urban population. *General Hospital Psychiatry, 33*, 135–142. doi:10.1016/j.genhosppsych.2011.01.002

Wolf, E. J., Bovin, M. J., Green, J. D., Mitchell, K. S., Stoop, T. B., Barretto, K. M.,...Rosen, R. C. (2016). Longitudinal associations between post-traumatic stress disorder and metabolic syndrome severity. *Psychological Medicine, 46*, 2215–2226. doi:10.1017/S0033291716000817

Wolfe, J., Schnurr, P. P., Brown, P. J., & Furey, J. (1994). Posttraumatic stress disorder and war-zone exposure as correlates of perceived health in female Vietnam War veterans. *Journal of Consulting and Clinical Psychology, 62*, 1235–1240. doi:10.1037/0022-006X.62.6.1235

World Health Organization. (2003). *Diet, nutrition and the prevention of chronic diseases* (WHO Technical Report No. 916). Retrieved from http://www.who.int/dietphysicalactivity/publications/trs916/en/

Yehuda, R. (2006). Advances in understanding neuroendocrine alterations in PTSD and their therapeutic implications. *Annals of the New York Academy of Sciences, 1071*, 137–166. doi:10.1196/annals.1364.012

Yehuda, R. (2009). Status of glucocorticoid alterations in post-traumatic stress disorder. *Annals of the New York Academy of Sciences, 1179*, 56–69. doi:10.1111/j.1749-6632.2009.04979.x

Zen, A. L., Zhao, S., Whooley, M. A., & Cohen, B. E. (2012). Post-traumatic stress disorder is associated with poor health behaviors: Findings from the heart and soul study. *Health Psychology, 31*, 194–201. doi:10.1037/a002598

Stress Generation and Depression

Constance Hammen

Abstract

This chapter defines stress generation, noting evidence of the bidirectional effects of stress and depression on each other, contributing to recurrence and chronicity of depression and continuing stressors. Studies have documented elevated levels of acute negative life events as well as enduring stressful life circumstances, especially stressful interpersonal situations. Besides depression, predictors of stress generation include maladaptive cognitions and individual traits and experiences that lead to dysfunctional emotional and behavioral reactions, as well as dysfunctional coping styles and resources. Although stress generation may occur in many forms of psychopathology, there appears to be a unique link between major depression and the occurrence of interpersonal dependent stressors. Patterns of vulnerability–stress–depression relationships support an emphasis on the importance of interpersonal and interactional themes in many forms of depression, perhaps especially for women. Stress generation perspectives highlight environmental contributors to and consequences of depression. Goals for future research and clinical implications/applications are noted.

Keywords: stress generation, recurrent depression, interpersonal stressors, interpersonal dysfunction, stress predictors

The concept of stress generation arose directly from observations during life stress interviews of individuals participating in longitudinal studies of risk for depression. Conceptually it stemmed indirectly from the mix of ideas about human agency, the views of individuals not as passive recipients or responders to stimuli but as active contributors, responding to environments as perceived. These ideas are elaborated in Hammen (2006) and included Bandura's reciprocal determinism, Walter Mischel's emphasis on situational factors as sometimes more reliable predictors of behavior than traits, and the cognitive constructivist ideas of Michael Mahoney (Bandura, 1982, 1986; Mahoney, 1974; Mischel, 1968, 1973; Mischel & Shoda, 1995). These thinkers were early powerful critics of classical behaviorism and personality models of

human behavior, but a good many other intellectual threads also influenced thinking about why some people get depressed and others do not, and these have been relevant to the focus on stress in the lives of depressed people.

This chapter addresses several questions: What is stress generation and why is it important? What is the relevant empirical work on the bidirectional interplay of stress and depression? Can the concept of stress generation be expanded beyond application to acute life events? What are the interpersonal aspects and consequences of stress generation? Is depression unique in aspects of stress generation? What are the origins and predictors of stress generation? Finally, what are the unresolved conceptual, empirical, and methodological issues and implications for treatment and intervention?

What Is Stress Generation and Why Is It Important?

In interviewing research participants multiple times over years (observations also confirmed in clinical work with depressed patients), their descriptions of the context of recent negative events often suggested that some individuals were reporting circumstances in which their characteristics and behaviors contributed to the occurrence of negative events. Subjecting this observation to empirical evaluation, Hammen (1991a) compared total 12-month acute life event impact across four groups of women (all mothers of children aged 12–18): bipolar, unipolar depressed, medically ill, or well women. Women with a previous diagnosis of major depressive disorder (unipolar) had the most stress overall, but when the stressors were subdivided by content categories, the groups did not differ in independent events (fateful, outside the person's control). However, depressed women had more "dependent" stress (caused at least in part by their own behaviors and characteristics). The effect was particularly strong for events with interpersonal/relational content, and notably, the largest subcategory of interpersonal events had conflict content, and the unipolar depressed women reported remarkably more conflict event impact than all the other groups. Thus, it appears that stress generation in depression is largely about interpersonal stress to which the person has contributed. Significantly also, when the temporal association between depressive episodes and stress occurrence was systematically examined, the majority of the life events did not occur during the episode—some preceded and many followed recovery from the episode. It appeared that depressive mood states were not the sole driver of life difficulties, raising further questions to probe.

There are three key implications of the stress generation phenomenon in depression. If stress triggers depression in the vulnerable, then stress generation experiences likely portend a recurrent or chronic course of depression. Second, continuing patterns of stress and depression predict continuity of stress over many years, and such accumulated stress burden, also called allostatic load (McEwen, 1998), may have additional negative health consequences over time. Third, elevated levels of stress, especially interpersonal stress, likely have a negative impact on others in the life space of a depressed person, and thereby may contribute to distress in family members and friends—including the intergenerational transmission of depression.

These implications, plus treatment implications, will be elaborated further next.

Research on Stress Generation and Depression
Depression History Predicts Dependent Stress

There have been several reviews of the empirical findings on stress generation (e.g., Hammen, 2005, 2006; Hammen & Shih, 2008; Liu, 2013; Liu & Alloy, 2010). As Liu (2013) noted, accounts of stress generation should be limited to studies with stress assessment procedures such as interviews that provide an objective basis for determining the crucial issue of whether an event is "dependent" or "independent" on the person, as the latter life events are not hypothesized to be part of stress generation. A good many studies are therefore not noted because they are based on checklists that obscure the context in which events occurred. Further, the meaning of the same item (their contribution to the event) across different people cannot be determined without further probes (but see more comprehensive reviews by Hammen & Shih, 2008 and Liu & Alloy, 2010 that include diverse stress measures). Also, it is important to emphasize the role of interpersonal life events, based on the original Hammen (1991a) findings, and some studies that did not make distinctions in content are not noted. In a later section, the unique role of interpersonal content and its implications is highlighted. Similarly, many studies have other methodological shortcomings, such as cross-sectional designs, which make it more difficult to determine the temporal order of depression and stress. Additionally, it is important to select and test samples based on their history of depression, rather than current symptomatology, since stress generation does not specify that events occur only or mostly because of depressive symptomatology.

Overall, longitudinal studies of samples with ascertained depression histories have demonstrated stress generation (dependent interpersonal events) in adults (e.g, Chun, Cronkite, & Moos, 2004; Cui & Vaillant, 1997; Daley et al., 1997; Hammen, 1991a; see also Hammen & Brennan, 2002) and children and adolescents (e.g., Hammen, Hazel, Brennan, & Najman, 2012; Harkness, Lumley, & Truss, 2008; Harkness & Stewart, 2009; Rudolph, 2008; Rudolph et al., 2000; Rudolph, Flynn, Abaied, Groot, & Thompson, 2009). As the field has moved more recently toward studies of specificity and predictors of stress generation, additional studies are cited in the following sections.

Depression as a Consequence of Stress Generation

Not only does depression history predict interpersonal dependent stress but also an important corollary is the prediction that stress generation leads to further depression. Most studies have not specifically collected and reported on depression following evidence of stress generation. To some extent this is an omission due to the clear empirical evidence of depression following stress exposure in the literature, but it also reflects a relative dearth of longitudinal studies. However, several longitudinal studies demonstrated that dependent interpersonal events predicted further depression during follow-ups (e.g., Davila, Hammen, Burge, Paley, & Daley, 1995; Hammen, Hazel, Brennan, & Najman, 2012; Hammen, Shih, & Brennan, 2004; Rudolph et al., 2009; Shapero, Hankin, & Barrocas, 2013).

Continuity of Stress Occurrence

A further implication of stress generation is that stress occurrence is likely to be fairly continuous over long periods of time, thus predicting high rates of interpersonal stress among those depressed individuals who show initial stress generation. For instance, our group has shown stress continuity over periods of 15 years, 20 years, and recently 30 years, beginning with exposure to adverse environments in the earliest years of life. Hazel, Hammen, Brennan, and Najman (2008) found significant stability of stress burden for youth exposed to high levels of family financial hardship, parental marital dissatisfaction, elevated levels of maternal life events, and maternal diagnoses between birth and 5 years and at age 15. Hammen et al. (2012) also found significant stability between youth early adversity exposure and elevated levels of stress generation at ages 15 and 20—and predicted and found bidirectional associations between depressive disorders and stress over the 20-year period. Similarly, when a subset of the same sample was followed up by questionnaires at age 30, similar long-term patterns of bidirectional associations were observed between depression and stress, including childhood adversity, and stress and depression by 15 and 20 predicting stress and depression at age 30 (Hammen & Brennan, 2016).

Uliaszek et al. (2012), noting the stability of stress exposure over time, posited that stress genera-tion might operate through a stress continuation model (essentially a statistical artifact) rather than a stress causation model. That is, stress might be elevated following depression due to high levels of pre-existing stress. They tested the competing models by controlling for initial levels of stress and found support for the stress causation model when stress was measured by moderate to severe events (see also Harkness & Stewart, 2009; Rudolph et al., 2009). Thus, stress generation predicts continuing new stressors.

The continuity of stress over many years raises additional considerations. One is that the relationship between stress and depression may alter. The notions of "kindling" and stress sensitization have been investigated in longitudinal studies, and they generally confirm the increasing likelihood that less stress is needed to trigger depressive episodes (see Stroud chapter, this volume). Second, continuity of stress has implications not only for the course of depression. We might speculate that a long-term stress burden perhaps exacerbated by stress generation has the potential for contributing to other adverse conditions besides depression, most particularly if exposure to adversity occurs in the developmentally critical periods of early life. McEwen and others, for example, have written extensively on allostatic load, the detrimental physiological consequences of overload of the allostatic system, the complex interactions between the nervous, endocrine, and immune systems to adapt to environmental challenges and maintain homeostasis (e.g., McEwen, 1998; McEwen & Morrison, 2013). Considerable research has been devoted to understanding how "toxic" stress "gets under the skin" to promote maladaptive psychological and physical health. Danese and McEwen (2012), for example, detail the considerable implications of maladaptive stress responses for cognitive development, mental health, and immune dysregulation promoting long-term risk for various health conditions (see also Slavich chapter, this volume).

Expanding Stress Generation: Selection Into Difficult Circumstances

As a general observation, too little research on stress and depression has focused on chronic, ongoing conditions of individuals' lives, encompassing functioning in typical roles, such as financial, marital and family, and health difficulties. This is a problem, in my view, because in studying diathesis-stress models, depressive episodes and experiences are typically attributed to acute negative life events but commonly neglect the potential impact of unmeasured ongoing, chronic stressors. Hammen and colleagues developed the UCLA Life Stress Interview to include assessment of both acute and chronic stress in adults, which was also expanded and modified for use with child and adolescent samples (e.g., Hammen, Adrian, et al., 1987; Hammen, Gordon, et al., 1987; Hammen, Marks, Mayol, & deMayo, 1985; Rudolph et al., 2000).

Assessing ongoing conditions in each of several typical roles, for example, promoted the observation that individuals make choices and select into certain circumstances that have long-range implications. Adolescent choices are among the most developmentally significant experiences, especially those involving establishment of long-term romantic and family, educational, and occupational decisions and commitments.

The notion of selection into certain environments has a distinguished history in conceptualization of gene–environment interplay (e.g., Kendler, Karkowski, & Prescott, 1999; Plomin, DeFries, & Loehlin, 1977; Scarr & McCartney, 1983), as well as in personality and social psychology (e.g., Buss, 1987). These investigators challenged the notion of humans as passive in the face of genetic predispositions, and instead they characterized the role of choices and how certain actions and behavioral styles influence how genetic tendencies are played out.

Depression may be relevant to such life choices, decisions, and behaviors in the same way that it predicts generation of dependent interpersonal life events. For example, time and again our interviews in longitudinal studies provided anecdotal support for the observation that individuals with histories of depression often made choices or decisions that had long-term consequences of entrapping them in difficult relationships and creating environments with a high likelihood of continuing challenges and stressors (e.g., Hammen, Rudolph, Weisz, Rao, & Burge, 1999). Commonly, we and others had observed "assortative mating" such as depressed women marrying men with psychopathology (e.g., Brennan, Hammen, Katz, & Le Brocque, 2002; Hammen, 1991b; Hammen et al., 1999). We applied the concept of "selection" to our data in several specific ways. In our study of youth at risk for depression due to maternal depression, we studied adolescents' selection into abusive relationships between ages 15 and 20, finding reports of severe physical abuse in 16% of the sample overall, especially women; importantly, youth depressive disorder by

age 15 was a significant predictor of being a victim of severe intimate partner violence (Keenan-Miller, Hammen, & Brennan, 2007; see also Capaldi, Knoble, Shortt, & Kim, 2012; Rao, Hammen, & Daley, 1999 relating to associations between youth depression and physical violence in romantic relationships). Notably also, depressed youth have been shown to have committed romantic relationships or marriage with low levels of satisfaction (Gotlib, Lewinsohn, & Seeley, 1998). Therefore, in data from our sample of youth at risk for depression, we examined relationship functioning in late adolescence and early adulthood. Katz, Hammen, and Brennan (2013) found that high risk due to maternal depression predicted offspring having a committed romantic relationship at age 20 with lower reported relationship satisfaction (and their partners also reported lower satisfaction; see also Daley & Hammen, 2002). Also, Raposa, Hammen, and Brennan (2015) found evidence that youth with depression or risk for depression, and who also experienced childhood adversity, tended to report close friendships at age 20 with young adults with elevated levels of psychopathology; having best friends with internalizing and personality pathology was a predictor of youths' own further depression several years later.

In addition to mate and friendship choices of depressed individuals that are potentially predictive of long-term interpersonal stress, another life choice portending enduring challenges is the decision to bear children during the teenage years. Young women who were depressed by age 15 were at greater risk for childbearing before age 20 in our high-risk sample (Hammen, Brennan, & Le Brocque, 2011). Many such women in the sample were not currently involved with the father of their babies and often had low educational attainment and lacked financial independence. Interpersonal dysfunction at age 15 was a significant mediator of the link between young women's prior depression and early childbearing. Notably also, prior depression tended to predict further depression during young motherhood and poorer functioning in the maternal role (Hammen et al., 2011).

Finally, "extended" stress generation is often an outcome for depressed parents because they tend to have offspring with elevated rates of disorder (discussed later). A depressed mother may not only generate stressors in her own life, but she is embedded in an ongoing parental role with children whose behaviors are problematic. Raposa, Hammen, and Brennan (2011) hypothesized that offspring with diagnoses of disorders are likely to contribute to the stress of the mother, eventuating in further maternal depression beyond her prior depression. Specifically, Raposa et al. (2011) found that youth disorders by age 15 predicted mothers' depressive episodes over the subsequent 5 years. In particular, the investigators focused on stressors experienced by the mothers that involved their child, examining both acute stressors and chronic strain in the mother–child relationship. The link between youth psychopathology and subsequent maternal depression over the next 5 years was mediated by both acute and chronic child-related stress in the mothers' lives.

In sum, stress generation in depressed individuals may be extended to include selection into and creation of relationships with others who themselves have psychopathology, into maladaptive or less satisfying close relationships with romantic partners and close friends, and into childbearing roles in which the depressed person is ill-equipped or lacking support to function effectively in the maternal role. It should be emphasized that while stress generation may result from decisions and behaviors of the depressed person, in addition individuals also may be entrapped in situations mostly not under their control. Examples might include impaired family networks in which parents or siblings have disorders or dysfunctions that create problems and stressors for others. Financial and work circumstances may be limited due to low educational and socioeconomic conditions and opportunities, or individuals may be encumbered by chronic medical illnesses or dangerous and impoverished neighborhoods where alternatives are not easily available. In short, choices may beget challenging conditions, but depriving environments also beget stressful environments. Clearly a broad "stress generation" perspective has clinical implications requiring a comprehensive view of treatments and interventions for depression that go beyond altering individual symptoms with relatively simple solutions. This topic is addressed further in a later section.

Interpersonal Aspects of Stress Generation
Stress With Interpersonal Content
Stress generation has been defined as events at least partly dependent on the person, determined by use of interviews that examine the context in which a negative event occurs. Over time, evidence has emerged that depression-related stress generation should be understood in the context of a broad interpersonal perspective on depression vulnerability and its consequences. In the original Hammen

(1991a) study, it was the subcategory of interpersonal content events that was especially associated with history of major depression. Subsequent studies that have examined and analyzed event content have generally reported similar patterns (e.g., Chun et al., 2004; Rudolph et al., 2000; Shih & Eberhart, 2010). Importantly, Conway, Hammen, and Brennan (2012) explored the specificity of the link between disorders and stress generation by use of latent variable modeling to examine the unique contributions of transdiagnostic internalizing and externalizing factors and specific syndromes. Conway et al. (2012) found that once variance due to the internalizing factor was partialled out, only diagnoses of unipolar depression contributed incrementally to the generation of *interpersonal* dependent stress (but not noninterpersonal dependent stress); the externalizing dimension was unrelated to interpersonal stress.

Throughout our research on risk factors for depression we have found a common theme of dysfunction and high levels of chronic stress in interpersonal roles—family relations, romantic relations, and peer and social difficulties. Review of this extensive body of research is beyond the scope of this chapter (but see Hames, Hagan, & Joiner, 2013; Hammen & Shih, 2014). Clearly such interpersonal difficulties of depressive individuals are at the heart of stress generation, and a later section deals more explicitly with the characteristics of individuals that are predictive of stress generation.

Impact of Interpersonal Stress on Others
Liu (2013) noted that among the implications of (interpersonal) stress generation is the negative impact on others in the life space of a depressed person. Thus, going beyond the depressive consequences of stress generation for the individual, stress generation appears to have pernicious consequences by exposing others to the effects of stressors. Interpersonal dependent stress may contribute to distress in family members and friends—including the intergenerational transmission of depression.

Coyne (1976a) was one of the first to specifically focus on the impact of depression on other people, finding that it could elicit rejection in strangers because the symptoms may be aversive to others, and even induce negative moods in others, a phenomenon that came to be called "contagion" affecting strangers, roommates, and friends (e.g., Joiner & Katz, 1999). Moreover, Coyne and colleagues observed that partners/significant others of a depressed person (or with another disorder) may become engaged in a mutually aversive process in which they attempt to offer help and support but often find that the recipient does not get better or declines to accept advice, leading to frustration and eventually disengagement, which the depressed or ill person experiences as rejection (Coyne, 1976b). In one study spouses of patients with depression were troubled and their lives burdened by a number of the patients' symptoms and consequences of symptoms, to the point that they became significantly distressed themselves (Coyne et al., 1987). Not surprisingly, depression is often associated with marital difficulties, disruption, and dissatisfaction (e.g., reviewed in Davila, Stroud, & Starr, 2014). In one epidemiological survey, for example, Zlotnick, Kohn, Keitner, and Della Grotta (2000) found significantly more marital dissatisfaction among depressed patients than in individuals with nondepressive disorders. Hammen and Brennan (2002) showed that while marital dissatisfaction is highest among couples with a currently depressed spouse, such dissatisfaction is relatively high even when not in a depressive episode compared to never-depressed couples. Although not directly tested in these studies, it is presumed that at least part of the contribution to distress is conflicts, as well as other problematic behaviors contributed by the depressed person.

Perhaps the most dramatic example of stress generation effects on others is intergenerational transmission of depression and elevated risk to offspring for other disorders and impaired functioning in relevant roles (meta-analysis in Goodman et al., 2011; reviewed in Hammen, 2017). Impaired parenting is likely the most critical mediator of the effects of parental depression on children (reviewed in Goodman, 2007; Stein et al., 2014). However, maternal depression is also commonly correlated with high levels of maternal (generated) stress, to which the child is exposed (Hammen, Brennan, & Shih, 2004; Hammen et al., 1987; Hammen, Hazel, et al., 2012; Hammen, Shih, & Brennan, 2004). Similarly, as noted, marital discord rates are high among depressed individuals, and interparental conflicts are stressful and have a negative impact on children's emotional and behavioral development (e.g., reviewed in Cummings & Davies, 2002). For example, Hanington, Heron, Stein, and Ramchandani (2012) examined the contributions of parental depression and marital discord, and found that marital discord partially mediated the association between parental depression and child outcomes defined as emotional and conduct problems.

Gender Differences in Interpersonal Stress Generation

A second implication of the role of interpersonal life events is the likelihood of gender differences in stress generation and in depressive reactions to relational life events. A good many stress generation studies were conducted on female-only samples, or they did not examine gender differences or controlled for gender. However, the Liu and Alloy (2010) review suggests a trend toward finding stronger evidence of the pattern among females. Rudolph et al. (2000) found that adolescent girls in a clinical sample reported more interpersonal stress than boys did. Similarly, Shih, Eberhart, Hammen, and Brennan (2006) found that adolescent girls in a maternal depression high-risk sample reported more dependent interpersonal events than boys did. Clearly further studies are needed to address the issue in adult samples.

To the degree that females are generally socialized and predisposed to nurture and emphasize bonds among family and friends, the quality of such ties to others is a high priority for maintaining personal well-being and thus a source of vulnerability when interpersonal conflicts, rejections, and exits occur. Women who are vulnerable to depression might not only be susceptible to depression in the face of relational difficulties, but also their cognitions and behaviors relevant to evaluating and maintaining the quality of their bonds may result in maladaptive responses that actually impair ties with others. Such maladaptive relational styles might be especially likely to occur in those who have been exposed in early life to harsh or neglectful parenting and were also unable to acquire adequate interpersonal problem-solving skills, a topic which is addressed further in a later section.

Is Stress Generation Specific to Depression?

To a considerable extent, all forms of psychopathology are intertwined with stressors and stressful circumstances: Chronic and episodic psychological disorders invariably have the potential to disrupt performance in expected roles, and diagnostic criteria typically require such evidence. Symptomatology clearly contributes to the occurrence of acute major life events, such as legal violations, car accidents, relationship failures, school expulsion, and serious debt or bankruptcy, as well as impaired functioning in one or more key roles—marital and parental relationships, social functioning, finances, and work. Stressors and stressful conditions are likely to exacerbate the severity and duration of symptomatology, and influence the timing of relapses and recurrence over the course of disorder. Unfortunately, however, despite increasing numbers of research articles linking course of disorders and stress, few studies have examined stress generation and bidirectional associations between stress and disorders, or used contextual interview measures to ascertain details of event occurrence, dependence/independence, and objective ratings of magnitude of stress in longitudinal designs.

Apart from depression, studies of stress generation with suitable methodologies have been more common for anxiety disorders and have found evidence of increased levels of *dependent* stress among those with anxiety disorders or comorbid anxiety and depression disorders (Connolly, Eberhart, Hammen, & Brennan, 2010; Daley et al., 1997; Harkness & Luther, 2001; Phillips, Carroll, & Der, 2015; Uliaszek et al., 2012). Axis II pathology was found to be associated with stress generation in a study by Daley, Hammen, Davila, and Burge (1998). Controlling for prior depression status, Cluster B symptoms were incremental predictors of dependent and conflict stressors over the subsequent 2 years. In a separate sample of high school women, Daley, Rizzo, and Gunderson (2006) found that the link between borderline personality disorder symptoms and subsequent depression was mediated by interpersonal stress. Powers, Gleason, and Oltmanns (2013) also found that borderline personality disorder symptoms predicted more interpersonal life events in a community sample of men and women, aged 55–64.

Few studies have explicitly examined the role of externalizing disorders in the generation of stress. However, Rudolph et al. (2000) and Rudolph (2008) explored the topic in separate samples of children and adolescents. Rudolph et al. (2000) studied clinic-referred youth aged 8–18. The expected patterns of stress generation were observed for depression, but also externalizing disorders (controlling for comorbid depression) predicted dependent *noninterpersonal* (but not interpersonal) stress, with somewhat different patterns for boys and girls—boys more likely displaying associations between externalizing symptoms and dependent noninterpersonal life events such as school problems. Rudolph (2008), in a community sample of youth in the transition to puberty, found that externalizing psychopathology was not predictive of dependent interpersonal stress, but it did predict

dependent noninterpersonal stress. Thus, stress generation occurs with externalizing disorder symptomatology but specifically only with noninterpersonal stress, such as school-related events.

As previously noted, Conway et al. (2012) examined stress generation in a large sample of youth at risk due to maternal depression, using latent variable modeling to test the association of both individual diagnoses and transdiagnostic internalizing and externalizing factors with dependent stress. They found evidence that both of the broad transdiagnostic variables predicted stress generation (e.g., externalizing predicted noninterpersonal but not interpersonal dependent stress). The critical test of whether depression has a unique stress generation effect determined that major depression was an incremental predictor of dependent interpersonal events (but not dependent noninterpersonal events) once the broad factors and all individual diagnoses were partialled out. Thus, it does appear that while stress generation may be common across diverse disorders, history of depression is uniquely linked to dependent interpersonal events.

Predictors of Stress Generation

In recent years most research has been directed less to the evidence of stress generation than to the question of *predictors* of stress generation, particularly among depressed individuals. What is it that depressed people or those at risk for depression "do" that contributes to the occurrence of stressors, especially those with interpersonal content? In this section, three general topics are discussed: how individuals' cognitions about themselves and others influence maladaptive perceptions likely leading to dysfunctional emotional and behavioral reactions; the individual dispositions, experiences, and characteristics that influence the nature and magnitude of emotions and behavioral patterns; and the resources and coping styles available for solving interpersonal problems to prevent them from turning into major stressful life events. These three domains are not distinct, and their grouping herein is somewhat arbitrary. Furthermore, it is likely that the predictors of stress generation are the same or overlap with what we consider to be risk factors for depression. To put it another way, the traditional diathesis (vulnerability)-stress model of depression is essentially a moderation model in which the effects of stressors on depression depend on level of the moderating vulnerability factor, whereas stress generation is in part a mediation model in which vulnerabilities associated with previous depression predict dependent stress occurrence, which in turn triggers further depression. These are not mutually exclusive processes, to be sure.

Cognitive Predictors of Stress Generation

It is generally understood that the ways in which individuals interpret the self, others, and the environment determine emotions and behaviors. The cognitive model of depression has a long history of elaborating on the dysfunctional processes that constitute risk for depression: negatively biased thoughts, expectations, and interpretations of events and experiences that are based on selective attention to, and exaggeration of, the magnitude and meaning of experiences that "confirm" acquired negative schemas about the self, others, and the world. Thus, as an example, a person who is vulnerable to depression is hypothesized to expect herself or himself to be thwarted and inadequate at succeeding at desired goals, or rejected or abandoned or harmed in relationships with others. Consequently, even objectively minor happenings relevant to views of the self may be misconstrued as significant and threatening, and they may promote a cascade of emotional and behavioral responses culminating in a negative life event that triggers depression. Safford, Alloy, Abramson, and Crossfield (2007) compared undergraduate participants selected for high and low levels of negative cognitive style (a composite based on dysfunctional attitudes and negative attribution style) and assessed life events over the following 6 months. They found that those with high levels of negative cognitive styles generated more dependent and interpersonal life events, and results were significant for women but not men. Shih, Abela, and Starrs (2009) also found negative attributional style predicted dependent interpersonal events over a 1-year period in children of depressed parents, but they did not observe gender differences. Kercher and Rapee (2009) studied seventh graders and found evidence that prior depression predicted subsequent depression, partly mediated by dependent events (without distinction made between interpersonal or noninterpersonal) and a cognitive composite composed of negative attribution style and rumination. Cognitive vulnerability interacted with dependent events such that experiencing dependent stressors predicted greater depression for the high cognitively vulnerable youth compared to the low vulnerability group. Hamilton and colleagues (2013) found evidence that negative cognitive style but not rumination predicted the genera-

tion of interpersonal dependent events and also relational aggression; girls were particularly likely, compared to boys, to experience increased depression in the context of relational aggression. Dependent interpersonal events mediated the association between negative cognitive style and depression at follow-up. Notably, Shapero et al. (2013) found that cognitive vulnerability variables no longer predicted stress generation after accounting for correlated social functioning and demographic factors such as age and gender. Overall, there is some evidence for a role of negative cognitive style in the generation of stress. However, it is likely that it works in complex ways with other variables, some of which we discuss further later.

Dispositions, Experiences, and Characteristics That Predict Stress Generation

In this section we discuss the role of formative environmental experiences, traits and dispositions, and characteristic ways in which individuals view and interact with the social world (interpersonal styles). This disparate group of variables is incomplete (omitting, for example, genetic influences), with relatively inadequate knowledge of mechanisms and their interrelationships with each other. Nevertheless, selected relevant studies represent a starting point for fuller understanding of stress generation.

Among formative environmental factors are adverse childhood experiences, including abuse; attachment security based on early parent–child interactions; and evidence of dysfunction in social relationships presumably accumulating from childhood. Childhood abuse and adversity experiences are strongly predictive of a variety of disorders, including depression (e.g., Green et al., 2010; Kessler et al., 2010). There is a body of research indicating that childhood adversity and abuse experiences contribute to social maladjustment and inadequate coping and social problem-solving skills (e.g., Bolger & Patterson, 2001; Hammen et al., 2012; Kim & Cicchetti, 2010). Some evidence has supported the association between childhood abuse and negative cognitive style, and child abuse and stress generation (e.g., Hankin, 2005; Uhrlass & Gibb, 2007), but these studies did not distinguish between dependent and independent stressors. Harkness et al. (2008) showed a significant effect of past childhood abuse in predicting stress generation (dependent interpersonal event onset after depression onset) compared to occurrence of events prior to depression onset, and the effect was strongest for those youth who experienced a first onset. Liu, Choi, Boland, Mastin, and Alloy (2013) studied associations between several forms of child abuse and stress generation in college students with histories of depression, and they hypothesized that links between abuse and stress generation of dependent events would be mediated by negative cognitive style. They found that emotional abuse but not sexual or physical abuse predicted stress generation, and the association was mediated by negative cognitive style.

Another type of adverse early experience that may affect individuals' functioning in social relationships is attachment security. Insecure attachment representations are considered a risk factor for depression (Bowlby, 1969, 1980), commonly viewed as emotional-cognitive-behavioral patterns about self-worth, and self in relation to others and the world, that are acquired in the context of quality of parenting behaviors during infancy. We position research on attachment and stress generation in the category of dispositions and experiences, but arguably they could also be described as dysfunctional cognitions about the self and the relationship between self and others. Several studies have examined associations among checklist measures of attachment representations and stress generation. A study by Hankin, Kassel, and Abela (2005) examined stress generation as a function of insecure attachment, and they found that interpersonal negative events mediated the association between attachment and Time 2 anxiety and depressive symptoms 2 years later in a sample of undergraduates. Hankin et al. (2005) also found that negative cognitive style mediated the relationship between insecure attachment beliefs and later depressive symptoms (see also Shapero et al., 2013, who found links between avoidant attachment beliefs and dependent interpersonal events over 5 months in a sample of adolescents).

Other investigators have pursued the hypothesis that certain interpersonal styles and behaviors may create stressful situations in relationships. An example is *excessive reassurance-seeking*, derived from Coyne's model of the depressive spiral in which depressed individuals seek reassurance to address their doubts that others really care about them, provoking negative reactions from others. Excessive efforts to verify and elicit reassurance may be annoying to others, eventuating in rejection prompting further depression. A series of studies has shown that measures of excessive reassurance-seeking behaviors are psychometrically sound, and they reliably predict and are specific to depressive symptoms (e.g., Joiner & Metalsky, 2001; Starr & Davila, 2008). Several studies have demonstrated that excessive reassurance-seeking tendencies predict the generation of dependent interpersonal life events (Shih et al., 2009; Shih & Auerbach, 2010; Shih & Eberhart, 2008). Stewart and Harkness (2015) found that excessive reassurance-seeking predicted higher rates of partner-initiated romantic breakups during a 1-year follow-up. Stroud, Sosoo, and Wilson (2018) demonstrated that excessive reassurance-seeking mediated the association between rumination and dependent interpersonal events.

Eberhart and Hammen (2009) asked the question, how do women in close relationships who are at risk for depression behave on a daily basis that may generate stress? Undergraduate women in committed relationships were assessed for attachment insecurity and reassurance-seeking tendencies, and they were asked to keep daily records of relationship behaviors that included examples of those constructs (e.g., "I worried that my partner will not want to stay with me," "I found myself asking my romantic partner how he or she truly feels about me") as well as records of daily conflict events. Also, interviews of negative life event occurrence were conducted 4 weeks after initial testing. As predicted, attachment insecurity behaviors and reassurance-seeking behaviors were significantly related to romantic relationship strains on a daily basis and to romantic conflict life events over 4 weeks, controlling for initial depression (and women who currently met diagnostic criteria for current depression were omitted from the study). Further analyses also showed that the link between interpersonal style and depression level 4 weeks later was mediated by romantic conflict stress generation (Eberhart & Hammen, 2010).

Taken together, several studies have implicated interpersonal styles that enact attachment insecurity and excessive reassurance-seeking as predictors of stress generation. The Eberhart study suggested that even minor, daily instances of dysfunctional interpersonal behaviors may contribute to the occurrence of negative life events in the romantic domain. It should be noted that other studies of interpersonal styles and depression have focused on related constructs such as dependency, sociotropy, and rejection sensitivity, which are similarly predictive of (but not necessarily specific to) depression (e.g., Joiner & Metalsky, 2001; see review in Hammen & Shih, 2014).

An additional contributor to the occurrence of dependent interpersonal events is the trait or disposition of neuroticism, also termed high negative/emotionality (NE). Its counterpart is positive emotionality/extraversion (PE). Neuroticism is characterized by experiences of heightened distress including anxiety, anger, and dysphoria, and excessive reactions to perceived stress, and is associated with a variety of mental health conditions, negative medical health outcomes, and relatively poor functioning in close relationships (e.g., Lahey 2009). Lahey's review (2009; see also Klein, Kotov, & Bufferd, 2011) indicates an association or predictive relationship between high neuroticism scores and occurrence of diverse acute and chronic stressors, such as marital, family, work, and health difficulties—and heightened depression and other emotional reactions to stress. In a specific test of stress generation as a function of neuroticism, Kercher, Rapee, and Schniering (2009) tested a large sample of young adolescent girls for depression and neuroticism at Time 1 with a Time 2 follow-up 12 months later assessing depression and recent stressful life events. They found that higher neuroticism predicted dependent negative events, and the link between neuroticism and later depression was fully mediated by negative events. Stroud, Sosoo, and Wilson (2015) also demonstrated that high NE predicted interpersonal chronic and acute stress generation.

Resources and Coping Styles That Predict Stress Generation

Stress generation is a construct that was never intended to "blame" the individual for the stresses that triggered his or her depression, but rather to characterize a more inclusive perspective on risk factors and mechanisms of depression. Accordingly, no discussion of contributors to stress generation would be complete without also considering negative environmental factors that represent not only stress exposure but also affect coping resources and behaviors available for responding to or reducing the magnitude and consequences of stressors. The topic of "coping" is far too broad and complex for comprehensive coverage in this chapter (see Compas, Vreeland, & Henry chapter, this volume). Instead, a few illustrative considerations are noted.

Disadvantaged social status confers elevated exposure to stressors, limited options and opportunities for developing flourishing lives, and diminished resources for coping with challenges. Epidemiological studies clearly indicate that, at least within middle- and high-income nations, low income is correlated

with and likely predictive of depression, as is low educational attainment, being female, being divorced or widowed, and ethnic minority status and discrimination (e.g., Bromet et al., 2011; Hasin, Goodwin, Stinson, & Grant, 2005). As an example, being a young single mother with low economic resources is strongly associated with depression (e.g., Wang, Wu, Anderson, & Florence, 2011). Sociodemographic factors associated with depression doubtless contribute to the symptoms because living in disadvantaged conditions is stressful via both chronic and acute stress experiences, and also because such conditions provide fewer resources with which to manage and deal with stressful challenges (e.g., Baum, Garofalo, & Yali, 1999; Lorant et al., 2003). Thus, some individuals are born into highly stressful conditions with features over which they have little control, and which provide minimal socioemotional resources to manage such stressors. Such environments continue to exert limitations on opportunities to develop and surpass limitations—a process that is especially pernicious in childhood and adolescence.

In terms of intraindividual resources and coping skills, disadvantaged individuals commonly have (or had) parents or caregivers struggling with burdens that exceed their coping capabilities and impair effective functioning as models of successful problem-solvers and skillful interpersonal processes. Thus, a child born into highly stressful conditions may learn maladaptive coping skills for managing emotional difficulties and resolving interpersonal difficulties and conflicts.

With respect to coping behaviors and stress generation, Davila and colleagues were the first to demonstrate that a measure developed to quantify interpersonal problem-solving skills showed that lower quality of social problem-solving significantly predicted the generation of interpersonal life events in a sample of high school women (Davila et al., 1995). In view of research showing that certain types of coping strategies are associated with higher rates of depression than others, Holahan and colleagues predicted that avoidance coping, marked by cognitive and behavioral strategies such as denial, minimization, and resisting dealing directly with problematic issues, would predict generation of stress (Holahan, Moos, Holahan, Brennan, & Schutte, 2005). Their large longitudinal study of older adults showed that avoidance coping style predicted more chronic and acute stress 4 years later, and greater depression when assessed at 10 years (although the study did not distinguish between dependent and independent events and chronic stressors).

Another form of passive coping is rumination, defined as a repetitive effort to think about emotional distress and its causes and consequences instead of taking active steps to solve the problems causing the distress. As McLaughlin and Nolen-Hoeksema (2012) noted, such a passive and maladaptive coping strategy typically exacerbates or prolongs the dysphoric symptoms. Their study of rumination among young adolescents showed that higher levels of ruminative responses predicted having higher levels of peer conflict (being the target of peer victimization and rejection), which in turn predicted increases in depressive symptoms (see also Michl, McLaughlin, Shepherd, & Nolen-Hoeksema, 2013, although their studies used self-report checklist measures of stress and did not determine dependent/independent event content). Flynn, Kecmanovic, and Alloy (2010) demonstrated that ruminative response style predicted generation of dependent interpersonal stress and subsequent elevations in depression.

The research on the topic of predictors and mechanisms of stress generation is obviously incomplete, and an area of continuing development. The chapter ends with some thoughts about preliminary conclusions and future directions.

Unresolved Conceptual, Empirical, and Methodological Issues in Stress Generation: Future Directions

It has been more than 25 years since the Hammen (1991a) stress generation paper. The importance of stress in understanding the triggers and mechanisms of depression has grown substantially during this time, prompted in part by developments in genetics and neural and neuroendocrine processes, but also in recognition of the dynamic and bidirectional relationships between stress and depression. As the current chapter has shown, it is now well established that depressive individuals contribute to the occurrence of stressors and may create ongoing or recurrent stressful life conditions. The impact of stress takes an enormous toll on the individual and the course of depression. Stress generation also contributes to distress and dysfunction in spouses, offspring, and other associates.

It further seems likely that it is largely stressors with interpersonal content that are the most problematic, and that are most likely to promote depressive reactions in susceptible individuals. Indeed, a conceptual and empirical priority for further advances, therefore, is the issue of whether and how depression may be—for many but not certainly not all—a disorder of vulnerability in relational functioning. Are the processes that account for depressive reactions the same as, or overlap with, the processes that lead to stress generation? An example of a risk factor that might cause both depression and stress generation is neuroticism, or its related constructs. Neuroticism refers both to biobehavioral mechanisms that are expressed as negative cognitive and emotional reactions to life events and perceived undesirable situations, and to interactional styles and characteristic behaviors that others might find difficult and frustrating, potentially leading to ruptures in the relationship (e.g., Lahey, 2009). Is insecure attachment also both an aspect of the mechanisms of depressive reactions in the face of loss and rejection? Other constructs, however, might be more clearly distinctly related to mechanisms of depression but are unrelated to social behaviors, or the reverse.

Stress generation is also relevant to nondepressive disorders, in which it may similarly represent a contributory factor in course and consequences. More research is needed, for example, to explore externalizing disorders and noninterpersonal types of stressors, and to learn more about potential mechanisms and predictors of the role of stress generation in different disorders.

What are the challenges that need to be addressed in the next phase of stress generation research? In some ways this is a global issue for all psychopathology research: how to more fully characterize and integrate environmental and interactional factors into models that are necessarily complex, and that include a developmental perspective on the origins, progression, and expression of manifestations of vulnerability and disorder. For research on depression involving stress generation, an important question that has emerged in recent years and needs further clarification concerns the causes and predictors of stress generation. Given the centrality of interpersonal difficulties for many cases of depression, the focus is likely to be both the innate and acquired affiliative needs, beliefs, expectations, skills, and strategies that organize what individuals seek in relationships and enact in social interactions. This focus includes response patterns that guide the monitoring and managing of getting and keeping relational bonds that are viewed by the person as essential to self-worth and well-being. What are the essential elements of healthy social functioning, and how do they develop normally—or go awry in depressogenic ways? Although significant leads have emerged, as this review has suggested, there is room for considerably more extensive conceptualization and research effort. Hammen and Shih (2014) noted the gaps in basic knowledge of fundamental processes of intimate relationships from a multiple levels of analysis perspective. Conceptualizing relational bonds is beyond the scope of the current chapter, but it would seem that while attachment theory is a major organizing model, further big questions arise about how to identify and characterize key elements of relating that are central to depressive reactions in the face of social threat, rejection, and loss of close relationships. As one example of an expansive perspective, Slavich and Irwin's (2014) social signal transduction theory of depression focuses on multiple interacting processes, in which perceptions of social threat upregulate components of the immune system related to inflammatory processes. Other broad models of depression and interpersonal processes would be welcome that build on current neurobiological and genetic processes of stress reactivity, and that further elaborate on all the levels of analysis relevant to the generation of interpersonal stress.

Another big question at the other end of the complexity spectrum is whether there are depression-relevant interpersonal vulnerability endophenotypes that could help to bring greater precision to research questions and strategies, in view of the enormous heterogeneity of depression. Relevant endophenotypes for reward processing and stress reactivity (e.g., Bogdan, Nikolova, & Pizzagalli, 2013), or facets of neuroticism or similar dispositions (e.g., Goldstein & Klein, 2014), for example, might be refined for relevance to relational stimuli involving fear of abandonment or threat of or oversensitivity to rejection.

There are numerous *methods* for defining elements of interpersonal vulnerability, such as fear of abandonment or insecure attachment that may be risk factors for depression. These measures may include not only questionnaires and interviews but also potentially neural and genetic constructs that are pertinent indicators and mechanisms of interpersonal processes (e.g., amygdala responses to angry faces). A further step is to determine the extent and processes by which relevant constructs are related to behavior and to each other, and that lead to stress generation and to depression. Eberhart and Hammen (2009) approached this issue through assessment of daily self-reported romantic relationship behaviors, but additional longitudinal fine-grained studies are needed to shed light on how maladaptive interpersonal styles such as rejection

sensitivity, excessive reassurance-seeking, and insecure attachment representations end up provoking negative events that are depression inducing.

There are also intriguing questions about relationship choices that could be pursued to learn more about propensities for stress generation. One such issue is assortative or nonrandom mating, a well-known phenomenon in psychopathology (e.g., Mathews & Reus, 2001), and it is to be anticipated that marriages between spouses with depression and other disorders could have troubled courses. Marital distress and stressful events pertaining to threats to a marriage are highly depressogenic (e.g., Cano & O'Leary, 2000; Whisman, Uebelacker, & Weinstock, 2004). Although there is clear evidence of concordance for depression in spouses, there is very little empirical information to guide research that would help clarify problematic romantic relationship choices among adolescents. Whether choosing partners with dysfunction reflects complementarity or some other processes, partner (and friend) selection research could reveal strategies that inform opportunities for prevention of unwise choices. Along these lines, it would be especially useful to learn more about depressed young women's selection into relationships that are eventually abusive (including their own perpetration as well as victimization). Of course, this issue is relevant to a broad public health issue beyond depression, but further study might identify choice points and predictors that would be informative for treatment interventions potentially aimed at preventing or reducing depression in youth at risk for depression due to problematic romantic relationship choices and ensuing difficulties beyond the vulnerable youths' ability to manage successfully (e.g., Davila, 2008).

In addition to exploring particularly risky situations into which interpersonally vulnerable individuals select themselves, there are numerous interesting questions about the origins and developmental pathways of relationship vulnerabilities. There are bodies of research on interpersonal and social problems in children and adults that stem from adverse family situations such as early childhood adversity (abuse, marital disruption, parental disorder, and substance abuse), as well as low socioeconomic status and its associated stressors, and intergenerational transmission of marital violence, conflict, and divorce (e.g., Bolger & Patterson, 2001; Conger, Conger, & Martin, 2010; Cui & Fincham, 2010; Diekmann & Schmidheiny, 2013; Franklin & Kercher, 2012; Kim & Cicchetti, 2010).

However, further research is needed on the specific types of interactional dysfunction and relevant moderators and mediators that predict depressive outcomes.

Methodologically, future research gains depend on sound *measurement of stressors*; in stress generation studies it is essential to be able to distinguish the degree of dependence/independence on the person. Accordingly—and also for a variety of issues pertaining to validity and objectivity of stressor severity indicators—contextual threat interview methods are strongly recommended, as well as assessment of chronic stressful conditions (Hammen, 2016; Harkness & Monroe, 2016). Also, longitudinal designs are important as a means of ensuring that the depression or hypothesized risk for depression was present before the stressor so that it can validly be claimed that the negative event was not entirely due to depressive symptomatology. Furthermore, such longitudinal designs permit more compelling tests of mediators than do cross-sectional designs. Good measurement and design practices seem obvious and essential, and yet vast numbers of studies in the depression field, just as an example, suffer from inadequacies of various kinds, including lack of validation and standardization of measures and procedures, small and heterogeneous samples that cannot easily be compared, and designs inadequate to clarify causal directions, to name but a few shortcomings.

Treatment Implications

Stress generation in depression has treatment implications that include targets of treatment, outcome measures, and preventive interventions. Given the history of treatment of depression and the complexity of changing dysfunctional behaviors, developing novel interventions, or effecting long-term change, the following ideas are offered as matters of *emphasis* in established interventions, rather than as brave new treatment methods. Attention to stress generation would not be a "new" kind of therapy as much as a perspective to be included in a comprehensive approach to recurrent or chronic depression. Although a modest proposal, consideration of stress generation, especially given its interpersonal context, seems like a long-overdue target.

Targeting stress generation in a currently depressed patient would serve the goal of attempting to alter the course of depressive disorders, contrasting with interventions that primarily address symptom reduction. Although all therapies include strategies to maintain symptom reduction, relapses and recurrences are nonetheless common and problematic. Strategies aimed at reduction of stress generation would be most appropriate for depressed individuals who have patterns of chronic or recurrent depression triggered by repeated stressors; likely even relatively "mild" stressors serve to promote dysphoria. Stress generation interventions would serve as an extension to symptom reduction techniques such as medication management (psychopharmacology), behavioral activation (cognitive-behavioral therapy), or targeting a specific interpersonal problem (interpersonal therapy). For individuals for whom assessment and case formulation reveal particular interpersonal sources of stress, therapists need to assess relevant interpersonal skills and relational response styles and cognitions. On the assumption that dysfunctional styles commonly translate into disruptive daily behaviors, programs for identifying common problem cognitions and behaviors, and learning more effective strategies for problem solving would need to be developed. To some extent, most empirically supported psychotherapies include at least implicit "subroutines" for dealing with problematic romantic/marital and parenting issues, but such programs could be expanded and fine-tuned to deal more specifically with prevention or reduction of interpersonal stressful life events and daily stressors. Two discussions of potential applications of depression therapies to directly address stress-generating interpersonal contexts targeting their behavioral and cognitive contributors represent useful efforts in this direction (Beach, Whisman, & Bodenmann, 2014; Dobson, Quigley, & Dozois, 2014).

Measurement of treatment outcomes should go beyond assessment of symptom and syndrome status, and many have called for increased attention to changes in functional outcomes, such as successful employment, and more stable and effective marital and parenting roles. In the case of stress generation in depression, the goal is to reduce the amount or frequency of stressful encounters with others, and possibly to measurably improve interpersonal problem-solving skills as well as promote more adaptive beliefs and expectations about the self in relation to close others.

Finally, the stress generation perspective has particular implications for preventive interventions. It is not difficult to marshal evidence for the early identification of youth at risk for depression, and cutting across the boundaries of many forms of disorder are risk factors that affect interpersonal adjustment and social functioning. Moreover, adolescence is a time of particular importance for many disorders, including depression, as youth encounter increasingly challenging developmental tasks and make more choices that affect their adult life courses. We can predict that some youth are at ultra-high risk for recurrent depression, for example, in the context of exposure to adverse conditions in childhood, including family discord and parental depression, and youths' own early-onset depression typically occurring in the face of high levels of personal and family stressors (Hammen & Brennan, 2016; Weissman et al., 2016). These are the youth at greatest risk not only for recurrent stress and depression but also continuing intergenerational transmission of depression.

No discussion of preventive intervention is complete without acknowledging the importance of social policies and institutional resources that are essential for creating communities that build prosperity, safety, and opportunity for all, and that support the efforts of individuals and families to pursue paths to healthy development. Stress generation occurs at the civic level, to be sure, and those who are dedicated to the improvement of mental health and well-being are well aware that there is much to be done outside the clinic or consultation room.

References

Bandura, A. (1982). Self-efficacy mechanism in human agency. *American Psychologist, 37*, 122–147.

Bandura, A. (1986). *Social foundations of thought and action: A social cognitive perspective.* Englewood Cliffs, NJ: Prentice Hall.

Baum, A., Garofalo, J. P., & Yali, A. (1999). Socioeconomic status and chronic stress: Does stress account for SES effects on health? *Annals of the New York Academy of Sciences, 896*(1), 131–144.

Beach, S., Whisman, M., & Bodenmann, G. (2014). Couple, parenting, and interpersonal therapies for depression in adults: Toward common clinical guidelines within a stress-generation framework. In I. Gotlib and C. Hammen (Eds.), *Handbook of depression*, 3rd ed. (pp. 552–570). New York, NY: Guilford Press.

Bogdan, R., Nikolova, Y. S., & Pizzagalli, D. A. (2013). Neurogenetics of depression: A focus on reward processing and stress sensitivity. *Neurobiology of Disease, 52*, 12–23.

Bolger, K. E., & Patterson, C. J. (2001). Developmental pathways from child maltreatment to peer rejection. *Child Development, 72*(2), 549–568.

Bowlby, J. (1969). *Attachment and loss: Attachment* (Vol. 1). New York, NY: Basic Books.

Bowlby, J. (1980). *Attachment and loss: Sadness and depression* (Vol. 3). New York, NY: Basic Books.

Brennan, P., Hammen, C., Katz, A., & Le Brocque, R. (2002). Maternal depression, paternal psychopathology, and adolescent diagnostic outcomes. *Journal of Consulting and Clinical Psychology, 70*, 1075–1085.

Bromet, E., Andrade, L., Hwang, I., Sampson, N., Alonso, J., de Girolamo, G., ... Kessler, R. C. (2011). Cross-national epidemiology of DSM-IV major depressive episode. *BMC Medicine 9*, (90). doi:10.1186/1741-7015-9-90

Buss, D. M. (1987). Selection, evocation, and manipulation. *Journal of Personality and Social Psychology, 53*(6), 1214–1221.

Cano, A., & O'Leary, K. D. (2000). Infidelity and separations precipitate major depressive episodes and symptoms of nonspecific depression and anxiety. *Journal of Consulting and Clinical Psychology, 68*, 774–781.

Capaldi, D. M., Knoble, N. B., Shortt, J. W., & Kim, H. K. (2012). A systematic review of risk factors for intimate partner violence. *Partner Abuse, 3*(2), 231–280.

Chun, C. A., Cronkite, R. C., & Moos, R. H. (2004). Stress generation in depressed patients and community controls. *Journal of Social and Clinical Psychology, 23*(3), 390–412.

Conger, R. D., Conger, K. J., & Martin, M. J. (2010). Socioeconomic status, family processes, and individual development. *Journal of Marriage and Family, 72*(3), 685–704.

Connolly, N., Eberhart, N., Hammen, C., & Brennan, P. (2010). Specificity of stress generation: A comparison of adolescents with depressive, anxiety, and comorbid diagnoses. *International Journal of Cognitive Therapy, 3*, 368–379.

Conway, C., Hammen, C., & Brennan, P. (2012). Expanding stress generation theory: Test of a transdiagnostic model. *Journal of Abnormal Psychology, 121*, 754–766.

Coyne, J. C. (1976a). Depression and the response of others. *Journal of Abnormal Psychology, 85*(2), 186–193.

Coyne, J. C. (1976b). Toward an interactional description of depression. *Psychiatry, 39*(1), 28–40.

Coyne, J. C., Kessler, R. C., Tal, M., Turnbull, J., Wortman, C. B., & Greden, J. F. (1987). Living with a depressed person. *Journal of Consulting and Clinical Psychology, 55*(3), 347–352.

Cui, M., & Fincham, F. D. (2010). The differential effects of parental divorce and marital conflict on young adult romantic relationships. *Personal Relationships, 17*(3), 331–343.

Cui, X. J., & Vaillant, G. E. (1997). Does depression generate negative life events? *The Journal of Nervous and Mental Disease, 185*(3), 145–150.

Cummings, E. M., & Davies, P. T. (2002). Effects of marital conflict on children: Recent advances and emerging themes in process-oriented research. *Journal of Child Psychology and Psychiatry, 43*(1), 31–63.

Daley, S. & Hammen, C. (2002). Depressive symptoms and close relationships in late adolescence: Perspectives from dysphoric young women, their best friends, and their romantic partners. *Journal of Consulting and Clinical Psychology, 70*, 129–141.

Daley, S., Hammen, C., Burge, D., Davila, J., Paley, B., Lindberg, N., & Herzberg, D. (1997). Predictors of the generation of episodic stress: A longitudinal study of late adolescent women. *Journal of Abnormal Psychology, 106*, 251–259.

Daley, S., Hammen, C., Davila, J., & Burge, D. (1998). Axis II symptomatology, depression, and life stress during the transition from adolescence to adulthood. *Journal of Consulting and Clinical Psychology, 66*, 595–603.

Daley, S. E., Rizzo, C. J., & Gunderson, B. H. (2006). The longitudinal relation between personality disorder symptoms and depression in adolescence: The mediating role of interpersonal stress. *Journal of Personality Disorders, 20*(4), 352–368.

Danese, A., & McEwen, B. S. (2012). Adverse childhood experiences, allostasis, allostatic load, and age-related disease. *Physiology & Behavior*, *106*(1), 29–39.

Davila, J. (2008). Depressive symptoms and adolescent romance: Theory, research, and implications. *Child Development Perspectives*, *2*, 26–31.

Davila, J., Hammen, C., Burge, D., & Paley, B., & Daley, S. (1995). Poor interpersonal problem solving as a mechanism of stress generation in depression among adolescent women. *Journal of Abnormal Psychology*, *104*(4), 592–600.

Davila, J., Stroud, C. B., & Starr, L. R. (2014). Depression in couples and families. In I. Gotlib and C. Hammen (Eds.), *Handbook of depression*, 3rd ed. (pp. 410–428). New York, NY: Guilford Press.

Diekmann, A., & Schmidheiny, K. (2013). The intergenerational transmission of divorce: A fifteen-country study with the fertility and family survey. *Comparative Sociology*, *12*(2), 211–235.

Dobson, K., Quigley, L., & Dozois, D. (2014). Toward an integration of interpersonal risk models of depression and cognitive-behavioural therapy. *Australian Psychologist*, *49*, 328–336.

Eberhart, N., & Hammen, C. (2009). Interpersonal predictors of stress generation. *Personality and Social Psychology Bulletin*, *35*, 544–556.

Eberhart, N., & Hammen, C. (2010). Interpersonal style, stress, and depression: An examination of transactional and diathesis-stress models. *Journal of Social and Clinical Psychology*, *29*, 23–38.

Flynn, M., Kecmanovic, J., & Alloy, L. B. (2010). An examination of integrated cognitive-interpersonal vulnerability to depression: The role of rumination, perceived social support, and interpersonal stress generation. *Cognitive Therapy and Research*, *34*(5), 456–466.

Franklin, C. A., & Kercher, G. A. (2012). The intergenerational transmission of intimate partner violence: Differentiating correlates in a random community sample. *Journal of Family Violence*, *27*(3), 187–199.

Goldstein, B. L., & Klein, D. N. (2014). A review of selected candidate endophenotypes for depression. *Clinical Psychology Review*, *34*(5), 417–427.

Goodman, S. (2007). Depression in mothers. *Annual Review of Clinical Psychology*, *3*, 107–135.

Goodman, S. H., Rouse, M. H., Connell, A. M., Broth, M. R., Hall, C. M., & Heyward, D. (2011). Maternal depression and child psychopathology: a meta-analytic review. *Clinical Child and Family Psychology Review*, *14*(1), 1–27.

Gotlib, I. H., Lewinsohn, P. M., & Seeley, J. R. (1998). Consequences of depression during adolescence: Marital status and marital functioning in early adulthood. *Journal of Abnormal Psychology*, *107*, 686–690.

Green, J. G., McLaughlin, K. A., Berglund, P. A., Gruber, M. J., Sampson, N. A., Zaslavsky, A. M., & Kessler, R. C. (2010). Childhood adversities and adult psychiatric disorders in the national comorbidity survey replication I: Associations with first onset of DSM-IV disorders. *Archives of General Psychiatry*, *67*(2), 113–123.

Hames, J. L., Hagan, C. R., & Joiner, T. E. (2013). Interpersonal processes in depression. *Annual Review of Clinical Psychology*, *9*, 355–377.

Hammen, C. (1991a). The generation of stress in the course of unipolar depression. *Journal of Abnormal Psychology*, *100*, 555–561.

Hammen, C. (1991b). *Depression runs in families: The social context of risk and resilience in children of depressed mothers.* New York, NY: Springer Verlag.

Hammen, C. (2005). Stress and depression. *Annual Review of Clinical Psychology*, *1*, 293–319.

Hammen, C. (2006). Stress generation in depression: Reflections on origins, research, and future directions. *Journal of Clinical Psychology*, *62*, 1065–1082.

Hammen, C. (2016). Depression and stressful environments: Identifying gaps in conceptualization and measurement. *Anxiety, Stress, & Coping*, *29*, 335–351.

Hammen, C. (2017). Maternal depression and the intergenerational transmission of depression. In N. Cohen (Ed.), *Public health perspectives on depressive disorders* (pp. 147–170). Baltimore, MD: Johns Hopkins University Press.

Hammen, C., Adrian, C., Gordon, D., Burge, D., Jaenicke, C., & Hiroto, D. (1987). Children of depressed mothers: Maternal strain and symptom predictors of dysfunction. *Journal of Abnormal Psychology*, *96*, 190–198.

Hammen, C., & Brennan, P. (2002). Interpersonal dysfunction in depressed women: Impairments independent of depressive symptoms. *Journal of Affective Disorders*, *72*, 145–156.

Hammen, C., & Brennan, P. (2016). *Continuity of stress and depression in 30 years of follow-up.* Paper presented at the Association for Behavioral and Cognitive Therapies, New York, NY.

Hammen, C., Brennan, P., & Le Brocque, R. (2011). Youth depression and early childrearing: Stress generation and intergenerational transmission of depression. *Journal of Consulting and Clinical Psychology*, *79*, 353–363.

Hammen, C., Brennan, P., & Shih, J. (2004). Family discord and stress predictors of depression and other disorders in adolescent children of depressed and nondepressed women. *Journal of the American Academy of Child and Adolescent Psychiatry*, *43*, 994–1002.

Hammen, C., Gordon, D., Burge, D., Adrian, C., Jaenicke, C., & Hiroto, D. (1987). Maternal affective disorders, illness, and stress: Risk for children's psychopathology. *American Journal of Psychiatry*, *144*, 736–741.

Hammen, C., Hazel, N., Brennan, P., & Najman, J. (2012). Intergenerational transmission and continuity of stress and depression: Depressed women and their offspring in 20 years of follow-up. *Psychological Medicine*, *42*, 931–942.

Hammen, C., Marks, T., Mayol, A., & deMayo, R. (1985). Depressive self schemas, life stress, and vulnerability to depression. *Journal of Abnormal Psychology*, *94*, 308–319.

Hammen, C., Rudolph, K., Weisz, J., Rao, U., & Burge, D. (1999). The context of depression in clinic-referred youth: Neglected areas in treatment. *Journal of the American Academy of Child and Adolescent Psychiatry*, *38*, 64–71.

Hammen, C., & Shih, J. (2008). Stress generation and depression. In K. S. Dobson & D. J. A. Dozois (Eds.), *Risk factors in depression* (pp. 409–428). London, UK: Elsevier.

Hammen, C., & Shih, J. (2014). Depression and interpersonal processes. In I. Gotlib and C. Hammen (Eds.), *Handbook of depression*, 3rd ed. (pp. 277–295). New York, NY: Guilford Press.

Hammen, C., Shih, J., & Brennan, P. (2004). Intergenerational transmission of depression: Test of an interpersonal stress model in a community sample. *Journal of Consulting and Clinical Psychology*, *72*, 511–522.

Hamilton, J. L., Stange, J. P., Shapero, B. G., Connolly, S. L., Abramson, L. Y., & Alloy, L. B. (2013). Cognitive vulnerabilities as predictors of stress generation in early adolescence: pathway to depressive symptoms. *Journal of Abnormal Child Psychology*, *41*(7), 1027–1039.

Hanington, L., Heron, J., Stein, A., & Ramchandani, P. (2012). Parental depression and child outcomes–is marital conflict the missing link? *Child: Care, Health and Development*, *38*(4), 520–529.

Hankin, B. L. (2005). Childhood maltreatment and psychopathology: Prospective tests of attachment, cognitive vulnerability, and stress as mediating processes. *Cognitive Therapy and Research*, *29*(6), 645–671.

Hankin, B. L., Kassel, J. D., & Abela, J. R. (2005). Adult attachment dimensions and specificity of emotional distress symptoms: Prospective investigations of cognitive risk and interpersonal stress generation as mediating mechanisms. *Personality and Social Psychology Bulletin*, *31*(1), 136–151.

Harkness, K. L., Lumley, M. N., & Truss, A. E. (2008). Stress generation in adolescent depression: The moderating role of child abuse and neglect. *Journal of Abnormal Child Psychology*, *36*(3), 421–432.

Harkness, K. L., & Luther, J. (2001). Clinical risk factors for the generation of life events in major depression. *Journal of Abnormal Psychology*, *110*(4), 564–572.

Harkness, K. L., & Monroe, S. M. (2016). The assessment and measurement of adult life stress: Basic premises, operational principles, and design requirements. *Journal of Abnormal Psychology*, *125*(5), 727–745.

Harkness, K. L., & Stewart, J. G. (2009). Symptom specificity and the prospective generation of life events in adolescence. *Journal of Abnormal Psychology*, *118*(2), 278.

Hasin, D. S., Goodwin, R. D., Stinson, F. S., & Grant, B. F. (2005). Epidemiology of major depressive disorder: Results from the National Epidemiologic Survey on Alcoholism and Related Conditions. *Archives of General Psychiatry*, *62*(10), 1097–1106.

Hazel, N., Hammen, C., Brennan, P., & Najman, J. (2008). Early childhood adversity and adolescent depression: Mediating role of continued stress. *Psychological Medicine*, *38*, 581–589.

Holahan, C. J., Moos, R. H., Holahan, C. K., Brennan, P. L., & Schutte, K. K. (2005). Stress generation, avoidance coping, and depressive symptoms: A 10-year model. *Journal of Consulting and Clinical Psychology*, *73*(4), 658–666.

Joiner, T. E., & Katz, J. (1999). Contagion of depressive symptoms and mood: meta-analytic review and explanations from cognitive, behavioral, and interpersonal viewpoints. *Clinical Psychology: Science and Practice*, *6*(2), 149–164.

Joiner, T. E., Jr & Metalsky, G. I. (2001). Excessive reassurance seeking: Delineating a risk factor involved in the development of depressive symptoms. *Psychological Science*, *12*(5), 371–378.

Katz, S., Hammen, C., & Brennan, P. (2013). Maternal depression and the intergenerational transmission of relational impairment. *Journal of Family Psychology*, *27*, 86–95.

Keenan-Miller, D., Hammen, C., & Brennan, P. (2007). Adolescent psychosocial risk factors for severe intimate partner violence in young adulthood. *Journal of Consulting and Clinical Psychology*, *75*, 456–463.

Kendler, K. S., Karkowski, L. M., & Prescott, C. A. (1999). Causal relationship between stressful life events and the onset of major depression. *American Journal of Psychiatry*, *156*(6), 837–841.

Kercher, A., & Rapee, R. M. (2009). A test of a cognitive diathesis—stress generation pathway in early adolescent depression. *Journal of Abnormal Child Psychology*, *37*(6), 845–855.

Kercher, A. J., Rapee, R. M., & Schniering, C. A. (2009). Neuroticism, life events and negative thoughts in the development of depression in adolescent girls. *Journal of Abnormal Child Psychology*, *37*(7), 903–915.

Kessler, R. C., McLaughlin, K. A., Green, J. G., Gruber, M. J., Sampson, N. A., Zaslavsky, A. M.,...Williams, D. (2010). Childhood adversities and adult psychopathology in the WHO World Mental Health Surveys. *The British Journal of Psychiatry*, *197*(5), 378–385.

Kim, J., & Cicchetti, D. (2010). Longitudinal pathways linking child maltreatment, emotion regulation, peer relations, and psychopathology. *Journal of Child Psychology and Psychiatry*, *51*(6), 706–716.

Klein, D. N., Kotov, R., & Bufferd, S. J. (2011). Personality and depression: Explanatory models and review of the evidence. *Annual Review of Clinical Psychology*, *7*, 269–295.

Lahey, B. B. (2009). Public health significance of neuroticism. *American Psychologist*, *64*(4), 241–256.

Liu, R. T. (2013). Stress generation: Future directions and clinical implications. *Clinical Psychology Review*, *33*(3), 406–416.

Liu, R. T., & Alloy, L. B. (2010). Stress generation in depression: A systematic review of the empirical literature and recommendations for future study. *Clinical Psychology Review*, *30*(5), 582–593.

Liu, R. T., Choi, J. Y., Boland, E. M., Mastin, B. M., & Alloy, L. B. (2013). Childhood abuse and stress generation: The mediational effect of depressogenic cognitive styles. *Psychiatry Research*, *206*(2), 217–222.

Lorant, V., Deliège, D., Eaton, W., Robert, A., Philippot, P., & Ansseau, M. (2003). Socioeconomic inequalities in depression: A meta-analysis. *American Journal of Epidemiology*, *157*, 98–112.

Mahoney, M. (1974). *Cognition and behavior modification*. Oxford, UK: Ballinger.

Mathews, C. A., & Reus, V. I. (2001). Assortative mating in the affective disorders: A systematic review and meta-analysis. *Comprehensive Psychiatry*, *42*(4), 257–262.

McEwen, B. S. (1998). Stress, adaptation, and disease: Allostasis and allostatic load. *Annals of the New York Academy of Sciences*, *840*(1), 33–44.

McEwen, B. S., & Morrison, J. H. (2013). The brain on stress: Vulnerability and plasticity of the prefrontal cortex over the life course. *Neuron*, *79*(1), 16–29.

McLaughlin, K. A., & Nolen-Hoeksema, S. (2012). Interpersonal stress generation as a mechanism linking rumination to internalizing symptoms in early adolescents. *Journal of Clinical Child & Adolescent Psychology*, *41*(5), 584–597.

Michl, L. C., McLaughlin, K. A., Shepherd, K., & Nolen-Hoeksema, S. (2013). Rumination as a mechanism linking stressful life events to symptoms of depression and anxiety: Longitudinal evidence in early adolescents and adults. *Journal of Abnormal Psychology*, *122*(2), 339–352.

Mischel, W. (1968). *Personality and assessment*. New York, NY: Wiley.

Mischel, W. (1973). Toward a cognitive social learning reconceptualization of personality. *Psychological Review*, *80*, 252–283.

Mischel, W., & Shoda, Y. (1995). A cognitive-affective system theory of personality: Reconceptualizing situations, dispositions, dynamics, and invariance in personality structure. *Psychological Review*, *102*, 246–268.

Phillips, A. C., Carroll, D., & Der, G. (2015). Negative life events and symptoms of depression and anxiety: Stress causation and/or stress generation. *Anxiety, Stress, & Coping*, *28*(4), 357–371.

Plomin, R., DeFries, J. C., & Loehlin, J. C. (1977). Genotype-environment interaction and correlation in the analysis of human behavior. *Psychological Bulletin*, *84*(2), 309–322.

Powers, A. D., Gleason, M. E., & Oltmanns, T. F. (2013). Symptoms of borderline personality disorder predict interpersonal (but not independent) stressful life events in a community sample of older adults. *Journal of Abnormal Psychology*, *122*(2), 469–474.

Rao, U., Hammen, C., & Daley, S. (1999). Continuity of depression during the transition to adulthood: A 5-year longitudinal study of young women. *Journal of the American Academy of Child and Adolescent Psychiatry*, *38*, 908–915.

Raposa, E., Hammen, C., & Brennan, P. (2011). Effects of child psychopathology on maternal depression: The mediating role of child-related acute and chronic stressors. *Journal of Abnormal Child Psychology*, *39*(8), 1177–1186.

Raposa, E., Hammen, C., & Brennan, P. (2015). Close friends' psychopathology as a pathway from early adversity to young adulthood depressive symptoms. *Journal of Clinical Child and Adolescent Psychology*, *44*, 742–750.

Rudolph, K. D. (2008). Developmental influences on interpersonal stress generation in depressed youth. *Journal of Abnormal Psychology*, *117*(3), 673–679.

Rudolph, K. D., Flynn, M., Abaied, J. L., Groot, A., & Thompson, R. (2009). Why is past depression the best predictor of future depression? Stress generation as a mechanism of depression continuity in girls. *Journal of Clinical Child & Adolescent Psychology*, *38*(4), 473–485.

Rudolph, K. D., Hammen, C., Burge, D., Lindberg, N., Herzberg, D., & Daley, S. E. (2000). Toward an interpersonal life-stress model of depression: The developmental context of stress generation. *Development and Psychopathology*, *12*(02), 215–234.

Safford, S. M., Alloy, L. B., Abramson, L. Y., & Crossfield, A. G. (2007). Negative cognitive style as a predictor of negative life events in depression-prone individuals: A test of the stress generation hypothesis. *Journal of Affective Disorders*, *99*(1), 147–154.

Scarr, S., & McCartney, K. (1983). How people make their own environments: A theory of genotype → environment effects. *Child Development*, *54*, 424–435.

Shapero, B. G., Hankin, B. L., & Barrocas, A. L. (2013). Stress generation and exposure in a multi-wave study of adolescents: Transactional processes and sex differences. *Journal of Social and Clinical Psychology*, *32*(9), 989–1012.

Shih, J. H., Abela, J. R., & Starrs, C. (2009). Cognitive and interpersonal predictors of stress generation in children of affectively ill parents. *Journal of Abnormal Child Psychology*, *37*(2), 195. doi:10.1007/s10802-008-9267-z

Shih, J. H., & Auerbach, R. P. (2010). Gender and stress generation: An examination of interpersonal predictors. *International Journal of Cognitive Therapy*, *3*(4), 332–344.

Shih, J. H., & Eberhart, N. K. (2008). Understanding the impact of prior depression on stress generation: Examining the roles of current depressive symptoms and interpersonal behaviours. *British Journal of Psychology*, *99*(3), 413–426.

Shih, J. H., & Eberhart, N. K. (2010). Gender differences in the associations between interpersonal behaviors and stress generation. *Journal of Social and Clinical Psychology*, *29*(3), 243–255.

Shih, J. H., Eberhart, N., Hammen, C., & Brennan, P. A. (2006). Differential exposure and reactivity to interpersonal stress predict sex differences in adolescent depression. *Journal of Clinical Child and Adolescent Psychology*, *35*, 103–115.

Slavich, G. M., & Irwin, M. R. (2014). From stress to inflammation and major depressive disorder: A social signal transduction theory of depression. *Psychological Bulletin*, *140*(3), 774–815.

Starr, L. R., & Davila, J. (2008). Excessive reassurance seeking, depression, and interpersonal rejection: A meta-analytic review. *Journal of Abnormal Psychology*, *117*, 762–775.

Stein, A., Pearson, R., Goodman, S., Rapa, E., Rahman, A., McCallum, M.,...Pariante, C. (2014). Effects of perinatal mental disorders on the fetus and child. *The Lancet*, *384*, 1800–1819.

Stewart, J., & Harkness, K. (2015). The interpersonal toxicity of excessive reassurance-seeking: Evidence from a longitudinal study of romantic relationships. *Journal of Social and Clinical Psychology*, *34*, 392–410.

Stroud, C. B., Sosoo, E. E., & Wilson, S. (2015). Normal personality traits, rumination and stress generation among early adolescent girls. *Journal of Research in Personality*, *57*, 131–142.

Stroud, C. B., Sosoo, E. E., & Wilson, S. (2018). Rumination, excessive reassurance seeking, and stress generation among early adolescent girls. *The Journal of Early Adolescence*. doi:, *38*(2), 139–163.

Uhrlass, D. J., & Gibb, B. E. (2007). Childhood emotional maltreatment and the stress generation model of depression. *Journal of Social and Clinical Psychology*, *26*(1), 119–130.

Uliaszek, A. A., Zinbarg, R. E., Mineka, S., Craske, M. G., Griffith, J. W., Sutton, J. M.,...Hammen, C. (2012). A longitudinal examination of stress generation in depressive and anxiety disorders. *Journal of Abnormal Psychology*, *121*(1), 4–15.

Wang, L., Wu, T., Anderson, J. L., & Florence, J. E. (2011). Prevalence and risk factors of maternal depression during the first three years of child rearing. *Journal of Women's Health*, *20*(5), 711–718.

Weissman, M. M., Wickramaratne, P., Gameroff, M. J., Warner, V., Pilowsky, D., Kohad, R. G.,...Talati, A. (2016). Offspring of depressed parents: 30 years later. *American Journal of Psychiatry*, *173*(10), 1024–1032.

Whisman, M. A., Uebelacker, L. A., & Weinstock, L. M. (2004). Psychopathology and marital satisfaction: The importance of evaluating both partners. *Journal of Consulting and Clinical Psychology*, *72*, 830–838.

Zlotnick, C., Kohn, R., Keitner, G., & Della Grotta, S. A. (2000). The relationship between quality of interpersonal relationships and major depressive disorder: Findings from the National Comorbidity Survey. *Journal of Affective Disorders*, *59*(3), 205–215.

The Stress Sensitization Model

Catherine B. Stroud

Abstract

The stress sensitization model was developed to explain the mechanism through which the relationship between stress and affective disorder onsets changes across the course of the disorder. The model posits that individuals become sensitized to stress over time, such that the level of stress needed to trigger episode onsets becomes increasingly lower with successive episodes. The stress sensitization model has accrued empirical support in the context of major depression and to a lesser extent in bipolar spectrum disorders. Furthermore, expanding upon the original stress sensitization model, research also indicates that early adversity (i.e., early childhood experiences) sensitizes individuals to subsequent proximal stress, increasing risk for psychopathology. In this chapter, the theoretical background underlying the stress sensitization model is reviewed, and research evidence investigating stress sensitization is evaluated. In addition, moderators and mechanisms of stress sensitization effects are reviewed, and recommendations for future research are provided.

Keywords: stress sensitization, kindling, early adversity, childhood maltreatment, life events

The nature of the relationship between stress and psychopathology has received considerable research attention. Central to this work is the observation that the relationship between stress and affective disorders changes across the course of the disorder. The stress sensitization model was formulated to explain the process through which this relationship changes: The model posits that in response to repeated exposure to affective episodes as well as external stress, individuals become sensitized to stress, such that minor (i.e., nonsevere) stressors become increasingly relevant with successive episodes (e.g., Harkness, Hayden, & Lopez-Duran, 2015; Monroe & Harkness, 2005). The stress sensitization model has accumulated support as a mechanism of the changing relationship between stress and episode onset in major depression and to a lesser extent in bipolar spectrum disorders. Expanding upon the original stress sensitization model, research also suggests that early adversity (i.e., early childhood experiences) sensitizes individuals to subsequent proximal stress, increasing risk for psychopathology.

Importantly, stress-related forms of psychopathology, such as major depression and bipolar disorder, are often chronic, highly recurrent conditions, and are associated with significant impairment in work and in relationships, as well as high rates of morbidity and mortality (e.g., Kessler, 2012; Murray & Lopez, 1996). Thus, research evaluating the stress sensitization model has the potential to inform prevention and intervention efforts, with the goal of improving the course of illness and reducing the burdens associated with these conditions. Moreover, early adversity accounts for 30% of psychiatric disorder first onsets among US adolescents and adults (e.g., McLaughlin et al., 2012). As such, research focused on increasing our understanding of stress sensitization processes among those with a history of early adversity may inform efforts designed to prevent first onsets of stress-related forms of psychopathology.

In this chapter, I will review the theoretical background underlying the stress sensitization model, examine research evidence investigating stress sensitization, review potential mechanisms underlying stress sensitization effects, and provide recommendations for future research.

Theoretical Background
Post's Kindling Hypothesis

Post's (1992) kindling hypothesis (herein called Post's model) is the theoretical origin of the stress sensitization model (as applied to psychopathology). The core tenet of Post's model (1992) is that the first episode of an affective disorder is more likely to be preceded by major psychological stressors than are subsequent episodes (Post, 1992). Post drew upon two distinct models to formulate the potential mechanisms underlying this observation: electrophysiological kindling and behavioral sensitization (e.g., Post, 1992; Post & Weiss, 1998). In the animal model of kindling, levels of electrical stimulation that were initially below the threshold needed to elicit seizures in brain tissue develop the capacity to elicit seizures after repeated applications due to progressive increases in behavioral and physiological reactivity (Goddard, McIntyre, & Leech, 1969). If electrical stimulation is repeated, seizures begin to occur autonomously of stimulation. The analog process in humans is the observation that after an initial period of sensitization to stressors, recurrences begin to occur autonomously, in the absence of stressors (e.g., Post & Weiss, 1998). In the animal model of stimulant-induced behavioral sensitization, when the same dose of a stimulant (e.g., cocaine) is repeatedly administered, animals begin to show *increased* behavioral responses (e.g., motor reactivity), with more robust increases observed when the stimulant is given in the same environmental context as prior doses (Post, 1992). The analog process in humans is the observation that repeated stressors may elicit increasingly stronger affective and behavioral responses over time (Post, 1992).

Post (1992) drew upon research elucidating the neurobiological processes associated with kindling and sensitization to propose that changes in "gene expression," which occur in response to electrical and chemical stimulation, as well as in response to psychosocial stressors, have long-term effects on the organism (e.g., changes in neurotransmitter and neuronal transmission), which serve to increase reactivity to future stressors as well as vulnerability to future affective episodes (p. 999). One long-term consequence of kindling and sensitization is the induction of transcription factors, including for example, the proto-oncogene c-fos, which binds at DNA sites and induces mRNAs for other substances, thereby altering gene expression (e.g., Post, 1992). Post proposed that the induction of c-fos and related transcription factors might result in long-term changes in neurotransmitters, neuropeptides, and receptors, which may lead to "long-term synaptic adaptations and memory that could last indefinitely" (p. 1002). Thus, in Post's model, vulnerability to future stressors and affective episodes with successive recurrences was posited to occur because of "memory-like mechanisms" produced via environmentally induced changes in gene transcription (Post, 2016, p. 315). New research supporting epigenetic changes in response to the environment provides a framework for understanding these "memory-like mechanisms"—most relevant here is the assertion that epigenetic mechanisms "are likely the basis for long-term alterations in behavioral responsivity to recurrent events in sensitization" (p. 316).

Although an in-depth review of Post's model and its mechanisms is beyond the scope of this chapter, a number of his assertions have particular relevance for understanding the stress sensitization model. First, expansions of Post's model have implicated early adversity (i.e., early life experiences) as a mechanism through which individuals become sensitized to future proximal stressors in varied forms of psychopathology (e.g., Post, 2007, 2016; Post, Weiss, & Leverich, 1994). Specifically, given that many of the proposed changes that occur in kindling and sensitization correspond to those involved in the development of the nervous system, Post and colleagues (1994) proposed that the model could be used to understand "how early developmental experience could leave behind long-lasting residues and vulnerabilities to depression, post-traumatic stress disorder (PTSD), and other psychiatric disorders" (p. 782). Central to this formulation was the notion that long-term memory of early adversity was encoded in changes in "gene transcription," which served to increase sensitization to subsequent stress and increase vulnerability to psychopathology. Indeed, using new research documenting the phenomenon of epigenetics and more specifically, how early adversity can give rise to epigenetic modifications, Post (2016) has refined his original formulation, positing that early adversity leads to epigenetic modifications (e.g., methylation of the gene for the glucocorticoid receptor) that serve to increase sensitivity to later stress.

Second, Post (e.g., Post, 1992; Post et al., 2003; Post et al., 1994) distinguished between two types of sensitization: (1) episode sensitization and (2) stress sensitization. Episode sensitization refers to the process through which the experience of episodes and their associated neurobiological changes result in trait vulnerabilities that predispose individuals to subsequent episodes, such that recurrences begin to emerge in the face of lower levels of stress. In stress sensitization, early life stress and stress occurring in adulthood can each serve to trigger episodes or leave behind neurobiological vulnerabilities that increase sensitivity to future stress. Importantly, in this process, each form of stress may or may not reach the threshold needed to trigger an episode, but nonetheless they can leave lasting vulnerabilities that engender stress sensitivity (e.g., Post, 2016). Thus, it is postulated that both episode sensitization and stress sensitization render individuals increasingly sensitive to lower levels of stress over time.

Third, although originally developed to explain the course of affective disorders, Post's model has been applied to anxiety disorders, including for example, panic disorder, PTSD, and obsessive-compulsive disorder, though the relevance of sensitization versus kindling processes varies across the disorders (e.g., Post & Weiss, 1998; Post, Weiss, Smith, & Li, 1997). For example, in PTSD, both kindling and stress sensitization processes may be useful in understanding the onset and progression of the disorder. Kindling processes may be used to explain the progression from flashbacks initially triggered by cues associated with the trauma to the emergence of flashbacks occurring in the absence of such cues. Stress sensitization processes may be used to explain the clinical observation that individuals who have experienced prior traumatic events tend to be more sensitive to subsequent trauma (Post & Weiss, 1998), consistent with emerging evidence (e.g., Shao et al., 2015) reviewed later in this chapter.

Fourth, Post postulated that qualities of the stressor (i.e., type, severity, and frequency) would likely shape its long-term effects (e.g., Post, 1992). For example, drawing upon the behavioral sensitization model, he proposed differences in sensitization effects as a function of the frequency of the stressor (single versus repeated); intermittent versus chronic course of the stressor; the interaction between magnitude and the frequency (repetition) of the stressor; and stressor type. Regarding the latter, Post (1992) posited that losses, particularly interpersonal ones, might have different consequences (i.e., behavioral, cognitive, neurobiological) than stressors involving threat of bodily harm, with the former most relevant for depression and the latter most relevant for PTSD. Consistent with this, research suggests that some of the stressor qualities Post proposed (e.g., type, severity, interpersonal nature) shape stress sensitization effects (see later), whereas others (e.g., repetition) remain to be investigated.

Monroe and Harkness's Critical Review of Research Supporting Post's Model

Post's model is perhaps the most influential theoretical framework guiding research on the course of affective disorders (Monroe & Harkness, 2005), as highlighted by the impressive body of empirical research evaluating it (reviewed later). In a critical examination of the research supporting the model, Monroe and Harkness (2005) called attention to the tendency for researchers in the field to misinterpret Post's model, which the authors postulated was in part due to the failure (with some exceptions) to distinguish between the two models underlying Post's model: stress sensitization and stress autonomy (see also Hlastala et al., 2000, for a similar argument). The stress sensitization model asserts that events of lower and lower severity develop the capacity to trigger episodes with successive recurrences (what Post, 1992, referred to as *sensitization*; e.g., Post & Weiss, 1998). The stress autonomy model asserts that episodes of depression occur autonomously of stress with repeated episodes (what Post, 1992, referred to as *kindling*).

To distinguish between the models, Monroe and Harkness (2005) argued that research needed to move beyond examining *whether* (or not) the relationship changes across successive episodes, but instead to examine *how* the role of stress changes. The authors distinguished between the *impact* of events, which refers to the likelihood an event will be followed by an episode (i.e., potency), versus the frequency of events, which refers to the likelihood an event will be present prior to an episode. Importantly, the stress sensitization and stress autonomy models provide a different set of predictions for how the impact and occurrence of major (i.e., severe) and minor (i.e., nonsevere) events change across the course of the disorder. The stress sensitization model predicts that the impact of major and minor events increases with successive episodes as individuals become sensitized to stress. Furthermore, the model predicts the frequency of major events decreases, whereas the frequency of minor events increases, as minor events begin to prevent major events from having the opportunity to affect episode onset due to their increasing impact along with their generally high base rate. In contrast, the stress autonomy model predicts that the impact of major and minor events decreases over the course of depression as stress loses the capacity to trigger episodes. In addition, the model predicts that the frequency of both major and minor events prior to episodes decreases as episodes become increasingly independent of events.

Thus, perhaps most important here, in defining stress sensitization in this manner and distinguishing it from the stress autonomy model, Monroe and Harkness (2005) refined the theory of stress sensitization. In doing so, the authors highlighted that although most of the extant literature supported Post's model, it could not distinguish between the stress sensitization and the stress autonomy models, suggesting a major gap in our understanding of the extent to which research supported the stress sensitization model. Moreover, Monroe and Harkness (2005) provided a lens through which to evaluate existing research investigating the stress sensitization model, which will be adopted in the literature review presented later. Importantly, although their review focused exclusively on major depression, the concepts have been investigated in the context of other disorders (e.g., Weiss et al., 2015) and apply transdiagnostically.

Evidence for Stress Sensitization: Effect of Prior Episodes

Support for the stress sensitization model is emerging in the context of depression and bipolar spectrum disorders. In this section, research investigating the sensitizing effect of progressive episodes, as well as moderators of these effects, will be reviewed.

Depression

Early research examined Post's model using two main strategies. First, early studies focused on investigating "differences in the *proportion* [italics added]" (Monroe & Harkness, 2005, p. 424) of individuals experiencing a prior major life event in first onsets versus recurrences. Supporting Post's model, this work suggested that a greater proportion of individuals experiencing first onsets had a prior major life event, as compared to the proportion of individuals experiencing a recurrence (for reviews, see Mazure, 1998; Monroe & Harkness, 2005). Second, later studies investigated the "differential *prediction* [italics added] by [major] life stress of a first onset versus a recurrence" (Monroe & Harkness, 2005, p. 424) using the odds ratio and

other statistical indices of strength. Also supporting the model, this work suggested that there was a decline in the strength of the relationship between major life stress and major depression with successive recurrences (Mazure, 1998; Monroe & Harkness, 2005).

In one of the most methodologically sophisticated and informative studies using the latter approach, Kendler and colleagues (2000) showed that the strength of the major stress–major depression association declined over the course of the first nine episodes, with the strength declining approximately 13% per episode. Interestingly, after nine episodes, the strength of the association continued to decline, but at a much slower rate of approximately 1% per episode. Importantly, follow-up analyses suggested that the decline in the association (a) reflected within-person changes rather than systematic differences between individuals with few versus many episodes; and (b) held when accounting for genetic risk and when examining exclusively major independent (i.e., uncontrollable) events.

In their critical review of the literature, Monroe and Harkness (2005) called attention to two major limitations in this field of research. First, the authors argued that as a consequence of testing Post's model using these two different strategies (i.e., differences in proportion versus differential strength), earlier and later lines of research were testing two different questions. Specifically, the authors highlighted concerns with the manner in which the odds-ratio was used and interpreted, arguing that the first-onset odds-ratio would always be larger than the recurrence odds-ratio, regardless of real changes in the relationship between major stress and major depression in first onsets versus recurrences (for details, see Monroe & Harkness, 2005). Thus, to unify the literature, Stroud and colleagues (2008) conducted a meta-analysis using a proportion difference effect size, converting the results of studies using the odds-ratio (and other indices of strength) to differences in the proportion of individuals with a prior major life event in first onsets versus recurrences. Overall, the meta-analysis provided support for Post's model (1992) model, with 11% more individuals in the first-onset group reporting a prior major life event than in the recurrence group. Of course, the 11% difference was significant, but small, leaving questions of its clinical significance. Moreover, support for the model was most evident among certain groups or under certain conditions (discussed later).

Second, Monroe and Harkness (2005) argued that few studies could distinguish between the two models underlying Post's model (1992): the stress autonomy model and the stress sensitization model (see also Hlastala et al., 2000). Thus, although Stroud and colleagues' (2008) meta-analysis unified the literature examining Post's model, the findings did not explicitly support the stress sensitization model, as both models predict that the proportion is greater in first onsets versus recurrences, but for different reasons. For the stress autonomy model, the smaller proportion for recurrences, as well as the decline in strength of the association with successive recurrences, is evidence that episodes begin to occur in the absence of stress. In contrast, for the stress sensitization model, both findings are evidence that individuals become sensitized to stress with successive recurrences, such that minor stress develops the capacity to trigger recurrences (resulting in a smaller role for major stress with successive recurrences). Thus, at the time of Monroe and Harkness's (2005) review, although the existing literature supported Post's (1992) model, most research was equivocal with regard to whether it supported stress sensitization (see also Hlastala et al., 2000).

Following Monroe and Harkness's (2005) seminal review, results supporting the stress sensitization model (over the stress autonomy model) began to emerge (Morris, Ciesla, & Garber, 2010; Stroud, Davila, Hammen, & Vrshek-Schallhorn, 2011). For example, in a 5-year longitudinal study of young adult women, Stroud and colleagues (2011) separately investigated the impact (i.e., likelihood of a major depressive episode given an event; Monroe & Harkness, 2005) and frequency (i.e., likelihood of an event given a major depressive episode; Monroe & Harkness, 2005) of major and minor events. As predicted by both models, major events were less likely to present in the 3 months prior to recurrences (versus first onsets), but there was no change in the impact of major events or the frequency of minor events (contradicting both models). Importantly, however, the impact of minor events was greater for recurrences than first onsets, providing robust support for the stress sensitization model. Notably, follow-up analyses indicated the increased impact of minor events held when accounting for the presence of a major event in the past 3 months, and when excluding months in which major events had occurred in the past 3 months from analyses (Stroud, Davila, Vrshek-Schallhorn, & Hammen, 2017), ruling out the possibility that this effect was due to the presence of recent major events (S. M. Monroe, personal communication, March 17, 2017). Thus, the increased impact of minor events observed in those with a history of depression provides robust support for the stress sensitization model.

Other evidence for the stress sensitization model comes from research demonstrating that minor events predict recurrences of major depression (Lenze, Cyranowski, Thompson, Anderson, & Frank, 2008; Monroe et al., 2006; Ormel, Oldehinkel, & Brilman, 2001). For example, Lenze and colleagues (2008) showed that the accumulation of minor events significantly predicted time to recurrence, with each additional minor event experienced increasing risk by approximately 37%. In addition, Ormel and colleagues (2001) found that minor life events were associated with increased risk of recurrences, but not first onsets (but this difference only approached significance). Thus, consistent with the stress sensitization model, this work suggests that minor events become increasingly important with successive recurrences (Monroe & Harkness, 2005). This work, however, cannot ascertain whether this reflects an increase in the impact of minor events (i.e., as individuals become sensitized to stress, the threshold needed to trigger a recurrence is lowered), an increase in the frequency of minor events (i.e., as individuals become sensitized to stress, minor events become more likely to be present prior to episodes), or both (e.g., Stroud et al., 2011). Thus, additional research investigating changes in the impact and frequency of minor events is needed.

Few studies have investigated whether the stress sensitization model is relevant for understanding the link between chronic stress and major depression in first onsets versus recurrences. In a notable exception, Monroe and colleagues (2007) found that chronic stress was more likely to occur among individuals with many prior episodes of depression than among those experiencing first onsets. Importantly, such findings emerged when accounting for the presence of major events (which were less likely to occur prior to recurrences versus first onsets), with major events and chronic stress each independently predicting depression history. Collectively, such findings suggest that chronic stress might play a greater etiological role with successive episodes, consistent with the stress sensitization model. In contrast, however, in a sample of young adult women, chronic stress significantly predicted first onsets, but not recurrences of major depression, suggesting a diminished role for chronic stress with successive recurrences (Daley, Hammen, & Rao, 2000). Thus, research evaluating how the role of chronic stress changes with the course of depression is limited and mixed, underscoring the need for further research (e.g., Hammen, 2005).

In sum, although over a decade has passed since Monroe and Harkness's (2005) seminal review, one of their central conclusions continues to reflect the extant literature: Most research examining how the stress-depression association changes with successive recurrences is equivocal with regards to whether the findings support stress sensitization or stress autonomy interpretations. Importantly, however, of those studies that can distinguish between the stress sensitization and stress autonomy models, findings have predominately supported the stress sensitization model (e.g., Morris et al., 2010; Stroud et al., 2011). Moreover, there are hints of support from research demonstrating that minor events predict recurrences of depression (e.g., Monroe et al., 2006). These promising findings underscore the need to continue to test the stress sensitization model using prospective longitudinal studies wherein individuals are followed across first onsets and recurrences so that within-person changes in the impact and frequency of stressful life events can be examined over the course of the disorder. Given that 50% of people who have a first onset of depression will never develop a recurrence (Monroe & Harkness, 2011), conducting this type of within-person investigation with individuals who experience first onsets *and* at least one recurrence will also permit the evaluation of whether observed changes in the stress-depression association do indeed reflect stress sensitization, as opposed to spurious differences that emerge as a result of comparing individuals experiencing first onsets to those experiencing recurrences, and including individuals in the first-onset group who will never go on to experience a recurrence (K. L. Harkness, personal communication, July 10, 2017).

Moderators of Stress Sensitization Effects

Surprisingly, few studies have investigated factors that moderate stress sensitization effects, and most of the existing studies cannot speak to whether the factors identified moderate stress sensitization or stress autonomy mechanisms (exceptions are highlighted).

CHARACTERISTICS OF THE SAMPLE

In a meta-analytic review that tested Post's model by comparing the proportion of individuals experiencing first onsets who experienced a severe life event prior to episode onset to the proportion of individuals experiencing recurrences who experienced a severe life event prior to episode onset (i.e., the first onset/recurrence differential), three sample characteristics—age, gender, and sample type (clinical versus community sample)—were identified as moderators (Stroud et al., 2008). First, Post's model was supported to a greater extent as the mean age of the sample increased, suggesting that perhaps developmental stage or age moderates changes in the stress-depression association across successive episodes. However, this finding may have been an artifact of comparing a group of individuals experiencing a first onset to a group of individuals experiencing any number of recurrences: given that episode number likely increases with age, Post's model would predict that the first onset/recurrence differential would be larger in older samples simply because the recurrence group will have experienced a greater mean number of episodes. Second, as the percentage of women in the sample increased, support for Post's model weakened. This may indicate that Post's model is less applicable to women than men, thereby suggesting that the mechanisms through which the stress-depression association changes across successive episodes varies according to gender. Alternatively, women may have experienced higher rates of severe life events prior to episode onsets (versus men; a hypothesis supported by prior work; e.g., Kendler, Thornton, & Prescott, 2001). As a result, if severe events retained their capacity to trigger episodes, consistent with the stress sensitization model, the first onset/recurrence differential would be smaller in women than in men, not because of gender differences in the underlying mechanisms, but due to gender differences in rates of precipitating events. Third, support for Post's model was found in patient, but not community samples, an effect that may have been driven by patient samples experiencing a higher mean number of recurrences or more severe depression, as compared to community samples, or biases associated with treatment seeking. Thus, it will be important for future work to investigate whether age, gender, and sample type moderate Post's model, or whether such moderators reflect methodological concerns. In addition, the meta-analytic findings do not distinguish between the stress sensitization and stress autonomy models, and thus, whether such factors moderate stress sensitization effects remains an important question for future research (see Stroud et al., 2008).

Two studies have examined whether genetic risk/family history affects the stress–depression relationship across successive episodes. Although both studies have found that changes in the relationship occur as a function of genetic risk/family history (defined differently in each study), the results conflict with regards to whether stress sensitization and stress autonomy mechanisms are most relevant to those at high versus low risk. Kendler et al. (2001) found that strength of the stress-depression association declined with successive recurrences among all women, with the exception of those at highest genetic risk (defined as having a monozygotic co-twin with a lifetime history of major depression), suggesting that individuals with high genetic risk may be "prekindled" even prior to a first onset. However, given that a decline in the strength of the major stress-major depression association could reflect a stress sensitization or stress autonomy pattern (Monroe & Harkness, 2005), whether those with highest genetic risk are "prekindled" (episodes occur independently of stress even in the absence of a prior history of depression) or "presensitized" (episodes occur at low levels of stress even in the absence of a prior history of depression) remains an important question for future research. Contradicting these findings, a cross-sectional study found that individuals with major depression who had a *positive* family history of major depression (i.e., immediate family member with major depression) and who did not have a major preonset life event had experienced significantly more lifetime episodes than depressed individuals with a *positive* family history and *with* a major preonset life event (Monroe, Slavich, & Gotlib, 2014). Interestingly, however, among individuals with a *negative* family history, those with and without a major preonset event did not differ in number of lifetime episodes. This suggests that kindling (stress autonomy) and stress sensitization mechanisms may be most relevant for those with a positive family history of depression (and as discussed by the authors, perhaps, but not necessarily among those at higher genetic risk). Thus, although the extant literature does not provide a consistent picture of how genetic risk/family history shapes stress sensitization effects, and does not distinguish between the stress sensitization and stress autonomy models, there are hints that genetic risk/family history may modify stress sensitization effects.

CHARACTERISTICS OF THE EVENTS

In accord with Post's (1992) model, most research has focused on whether the relationship between stress and depression in first onsets versus recurrences varies according to event type, including severity level, independence (i.e., controllability), focus, and interpersonal nature. In terms of event independence, two studies have examined whether the etiological significance of major events for first onsets versus recurrences varies for independent (i.e., uncontrollable) versus dependent (i.e., caused in part by the person's actions or behaviors) events. First, Monroe et al. (2007) showed that the frequency of major dependent events decreased with a history of depression (supporting the stress sensitization and stress autonomy models), but the frequency of major independent events was unrelated to a history of depression. Second, Stroud et al. (2011) showed that the impact of major independent events was greater than the impact of major dependent events, regardless of history of depression (contradicting both models). In addition, although all major events were less likely to be present prior to first onsets than recurrences (consistent with both models), the frequency of major independent events *increased* relative to the frequency of dependent major events (for recurrences versus to first onsets). Rather than indicating that the frequency of independent major events increased with a history of depression, this finding suggests that the frequency of major independent events declined less from first onsets to recurrences, as compared to the frequency of major dependent events. Taken together, findings from both studies indicate that major independent events may be particularly relevant for recurrences (Monroe et al., 2006; Stroud et al., 2011), but they do not provide evidence that individuals may be especially sensitized to independent events.

For minor events, results are also mixed and limited with regard to whether stress sensitization effects are stronger for independent or dependent events. Supporting the stress sensitization model, results of a longitudinal study of young adult women showed that the impact of minor independent events increased significantly more strongly than the impact of minor dependent events with a history of depression (Stroud et al., 2011). Such findings suggest that as individuals become sensitized to stress, events of lower severity develop the capacity to trigger episodes, with the threshold lowered more substantially for independent relative to dependent events. In addition, findings from two studies suggest that independence may shape the relevance of minor events for recurrences, but such studies did not directly test whether independence moderated stress sensitization effects (i.e., whether changes in the impact of minor events across successive recurrences were modified by independence). Monroe et al. (2006) found that minor independent, but not dependent, events predicted recurrences of depression (effects were also modified by focus [see later] and medication status). In contrast, other evidence suggests that sensitization effects may be stronger for minor dependent events, with one investigation showing that minor dependent, but not independent, events predicted time to recurrence in psychotherapy patients (Lenze et al., 2008).

Two other dimensions of events may affect sensitization effects. First, for minor events, evidence suggests that minor subject-focused (i.e., events that directly occur to the participant or jointly to the participant and someone else), but not other-focused, events predict recurrences (effects were further modified by independence in both studies and medication status in one study; Lenze et al., 2008; Monroe et al., 2006). Although such findings suggest that subject-focused events may have implications for recurrences, because changes in the impact and occurrence of events across successive episodes were not examined, whether individuals may be particularly sensitized to subject-focused events remains a question for future work (e.g., Monroe et al., 2006). Second, the interpersonal nature of events, including specifically whether the event is a relationship loss (or not), may influence sensitization effects. For example, Slavich and colleagues (2011) showed that individuals with a history of depression may be *selectively sensitized* to events involving interpersonal loss (e.g., death of a close other or relationship dissolution): Individuals with a greater number of prior depressive episodes developed a recurrence following lower levels of stress involving interpersonal loss (but not following lower levels of nonloss stress). In contrast, however, a second study showed that the impact and frequency of major and minor interpersonal events, and relationship loss events specifically, did not vary as a function of depression history (Stroud et al., 2011).

SUMMARY

In sum, given the mixed and limited evidence, it is clear that research designed to elucidate moderators of stress sensitization effects is needed. In terms of sample characteristics, although potential moderators have been identified, including age, gender, sample type, and family history/genetic risk, the extant literature cannot distinguish between the stress autonomy versus stress sensitization models,

and thus, whether such characteristics moderate stress sensitization effects is unknown. In terms of event characteristics, for major events, limited, but converging, evidence suggests that although independent events may be etiologically relevant for recurrences, individuals do not appear to be especially sensitized to independent events (Monroe et al., 2007; Stroud et al., 2011). For minor events, however, individuals appear to be particularly sensitized to independent events (Stroud et al., 2011). In addition, although minor subject-focused (versus other-focused; Monroe et al., 2006) events appear to predict recurrences, whether event focus shapes sensitization effects remains to be examined. Finally, for both major and minor events, findings are mixed regarding whether interpersonal status, and relationship loss, specifically, shape sensitization effects, as some evidence suggests that individuals may be particularly sensitized to such events (Slavich et al., 2011), whereas other work suggests that such events retain their etiological significance with a history of depression (Stroud et al., 2011). It will be important for future work to continue to identify who is most vulnerable to stress sensitization, and under what circumstances, with the goal of informing efforts to prevent recurrences of depression.

Bipolar Spectrum Disorders

Overall, the literature examining whether and how the stress–episode relationship changes across successive episodes among individuals with bipolar disorder has produced mixed findings and is relatively small (Bender & Alloy, 2011; Hlastala et al., 2000). In the most recent critical review of the literature, Bender & Alloy (2011) noted that only 8 of 14 studies supported Post's model. Furthermore, among the four studies that were the strongest methodologically, three did not support Post's model (Dienes, Hammen, Henry, Cohen, & Daley, 2006; Hammen & Gitlin, 1997; Hlastala et al., 2000; Swendsen, Hammen, Heller, & Gitlin, 1995). Findings from two of those studies, however, are relevant for understanding the potential role of stress sensitization in bipolar disorders. First, in a 2-year longitudinal study of outpatients with bipolar 1 disorder, among those with a higher number of lifetime episodes (9 or more), 76% had a major life event in the 6 months prior to onset, compared to 45% among those with a lower number of lifetime episodes (0–8 episodes), contradicting Post's model (Hammen & Gitlin, 1997). However, the impact of major events (defined as time between the occurrence a major event and episode onset) was also *greater* among individuals with a *greater* number of lifetime episodes than among those with fewer lifetime episodes. Consistent with the stress sensitization hypothesis, this suggests that major events may have become more potent with successive episodes (for a similar interpretation, see Hlastala et al., 2000). Second, in a cross-sectional study of patients with bipolar 1 disorder unique in its examination of major and minor stressors, and consequently particularly informative with regards to testing stress sensitization (versus stress autonomy), lifetime episode number did not predict stress levels (defined as high [presence of at least one major event], moderate [presence of at least one minor event, no major events], low [no major or minor events]) prior to episodes, contradicting both the stress sensitization and stress autonomy models (Hlastala et al., 2000).

Importantly, however, in their review, Bender and Alloy (2011) argued that it was too early to draw conclusions from this body of work, because most of the "literature suffers from serious methodological limitations," such as using self-report checklist measures of stress, relying on long retrospective recall intervals, and examining unipolar and bipolar patients within the same analyses (p. 393). Furthermore, the authors noted that existing research had not examined depressive and (hypo) manic episodes separately, and as a result, it was unclear whether effects were specific to episode type and/or specific types of events (i.e., positive versus negative events). Finally, at the time of the review, because only one study had examined the role of minor events (Hlastala et al., 2000), few findings could differentiate between the stress autonomy and stress sensitization models.

Weiss and colleagues (2015) addressed many of these concerns in a prospective longitudinal study of young adults with bipolar spectrum disorders. Consistent with the stress sensitization model, more lifetime depressive episodes predicted a higher level of minor *negative* events prior to depressive episodes (accounting for the number of events in the within-person control period). Similarly, more lifetime hypomanic episodes predicted a higher level of minor *positive* events prior to hypomanic episodes (accounting for the number of events in the within-person control period). Contradicting both the stress sensitization and stress autonomy models, however, the impact of major and minor events did not change across successive episodes. Thus, the findings were partially consistent with the stress sensitization model, and they suggested that effects varied according to event type and episode polarity.

Research on additional moderators of stress sensitization effects in the context of bipolar disorder is scarce. Bender and Alloy (2011) identified three potential moderators that merit investigation based upon preliminary evidence: age, age of initial bipolar disorder onset, and genetic risk for bipolar disorder. Regarding the latter, one study found that patients with bipolar disorder who had a family history of affective disorder had significantly lower levels of stress in the year prior to initial onset, as compared to patients with bipolar disorder who did not have this history (Johnson, Andersson-Lundman, Aberg-Wistedt, & Mathe, 2000). Clearly, research examining factors that modify stress sensitization effects in the context of bipolar disorder is an important question for future work.

In sum, although support for the stress sensitization model is emerging (Weiss et al., 2015), few studies (a) can distinguish between the stress sensitization and stress autonomy models; (b) can speak to how the role of stress changes across successive episodes (i.e., changes in impact, frequency, or both); (c) can address whether effects differ according to episode polarity (depressive versus hypo[manic] episodes) and event type (e.g., positive versus negative events); and (d) can elucidate moderators of stress sensitization effects (e.g., genetic risk; see Bender & Alloy, 2011). A priority for future research will be to conduct studies that evaluate each of these questions with the goal of rigorously testing the stress sensitization model in the context of bipolar disorder (e.g., Bender & Alloy, 2011).

Evidence for Stress Sensitization in Different Forms of Psychopathology: Effect of Early Adversity

Consistent with the stress sensitization model, research suggests that early adversity (i.e., early childhood experiences; e.g., childhood abuse and neglect, parental loss) increases individuals' sensitivity to later proximal stress, thereby increasing risk for depression, bipolar disorder, anxiety disorders, and substance-related outcomes, as well as the broad dimensions of internalizing and externalizing psychopathology. In this section, research exploring the sensitizing effect of early adversity, and factors that shape this effect, will be reviewed.

Depression

Supporting the stress sensitization model, research indicates that, as compared to individuals without a history of early adversity, those who have experienced early adversity are more likely to develop depression in the face of recent stress (e.g., Harkness & Lumley, 2008). For example, in a large epidemiological national sample of adults, the association between past-year major stressors and major depression was stronger among those who had experienced early adversity, such that major stressors were associated with a two-fold increase in the 12-month risk of depression onset among those who had experienced three or more early adversities as compared to those who not experienced early adversity (McLaughlin, Conron, Koenen, & Gilman, 2010). Although examined in fewer investigations, early adversity also appears to render individuals more sensitive to recent chronic stress. For instance, one study showed that the association between past-year chronic stress and depressive symptoms at age 20 was stronger among adults who had experienced higher levels early adversity, as compared to those who had experienced lower levels of early adversity (Starr, Hammen, Conway, Raposa, & Brennan, 2014). Similar findings for the sensitizing effect of early adversity have been obtained in the context of depressive symptoms (Shapero et al., 2014) and dysthymic disorder (Dougherty, Klein, & Davila, 2004).

Importantly, research also indicates that adolescents and adults who have experienced early adversity are more likely to develop depression in the face of lower levels of recent stress (e.g., Hammen, Henry, & Daley, 2000; Harkness, Bruce, & Lumley, 2006; La Rocque, Harkness, & Bagby, 2014; Rudolph & Flynn, 2007), providing robust support for the stress sensitization model. For example, Hammen and colleagues (2000) demonstrated that young women with a history of early adversity were more likely to experience a subsequent onset of major depression in the context of low levels of recent acute stress, as compared to women without such a history. In contrast, under high levels of recent stress, individuals had an increased likelihood of a major depressive episode onset, regardless of level of early adversity. This suggests that, in accord with the stress sensitization model, low levels of recent stress were sufficient to trigger depression among those with a history of early adversity, but severe stress retained the capacity to do so when it occurred (Monroe & Harkness, 2005). Notably, evidence for the relation between lower levels of stress and depression has emerged (a) in the context of varied types of early adversity, including for example, childhood maltreatment (e.g., Harkness et al., 2006; La Rocque et al., 2014) and family disruption (e.g., Rudolph & Flynn, 2007); (b) when conceptu-

alizing recent acute stress continuously (sum of severity scores; e.g., Hammen et al., 2000; Harkness et al., 2006; La Rocque et al., 2014) and categorically (i.e., presence or absence of event; e.g., La Rocque et al., 2014); and (c) when accounting for the effects of recent chronic stress (e.g., Hammen et al., 2000; Harkness et al., 2006) and history of prior depressive episodes (e.g., Hammen et al., 2000; La Rocque et al., 2014), ruling out the possibility that the observed stress sensitization effects were due to depression history or high levels of recent chronic stress.

Interestingly, the sensitizing effect of early adversity may vary according to several factors, including, for example, developmental stage (La Rocque et al., 2014; Rudolph & Flynn, 2007) and gender (Rudolph & Flynn, 2007). In one study, evidence for sensitization effects were observed among depressed adolescents (aged 12–17), but not among depressed emerging adults (aged 18–29), with a history of emotional maltreatment (La Rocque et al., 2014). In a second study, stress sensitization effects were evident in pubertal girls (but not pubertal boys) and prepubertal boys (but not prepubertal girls) who had experienced family disruption, suggesting that during adolescence, developmental stage and gender may shape sensitization effects.

Early adversity also appears to sensitize individuals to certain types of recent stress. Notably, results of two studies indicated that early adversity might sensitize individuals to independent, but not dependent, events. Harkness and colleagues (2006) found that adolescents with a history of childhood maltreatment (i.e., childhood abuse or neglect) reported lower levels of independent, but not dependent, recent acute stress, prior to first onsets of depression, as compared to those without such a history. Similarly, La Rocque et al. (2014) demonstrated that adolescents with a history of emotional abuse reported a lower severity level of recent independent acute stress, prior to depression onset, and were less likely to have experienced an independent event prior to onset, as compared to adolescents without a history of emotional abuse. In contrast, there was not evidence that emotional abuse sensitized adolescents to the effects of recent dependent stress. Importantly, however, such findings may be unique to the developmental period of adolescence given that adolescents report significantly higher levels of independent events than adults (Harkness et al., 2010), and that many of the major events faced by adolescents occur to their parents (e.g., parental divorce), independent of adolescents' behavior (e.g., Harkness et al., 2006). Thus, whether early adversity sensitizes older adults to independent, but not dependent, stress is an important question for future research.

Sensitization effects have also been found to be unique to recent interpersonal acute stress, such that pubertal girls and prepubertal boys with a history of family disruption were more likely to experience depression in the face of low levels of recent interpersonal, but not noninterpersonal, acute stress. Of interest, given that the early adverse experience (i.e., family disruption) was interpersonal, such findings fit with the notion that individuals may be *selectively sensitized* to recent stress (Slavich et al., 2011), with sensitization effects limited to recent stressors that match the early adverse experience. Consistent with this, Slavich and colleagues (2011) demonstrated that individuals who experienced early parental loss or prolonged separation became depressed following lower levels of stress prior to onset, but sensitization effects were unique to stressors involving interpersonal loss. In light of such findings, it is tempting to speculate that selective sensitization effects may provide an additional explanation for why adolescents who experience early adversity are sensitized to independent (Harkness et al., 2006; La Rocque et al., 2014) and interpersonal stress (Rudolph & Flynn, 2007), given early adversity is also often interpersonal and independent.

Findings also suggest that the sensitizing effect of childhood maltreatment may vary according to the type of maltreatment. Indeed, two separate investigations provide converging evidence that emotional, but not physical or sexual, abuse sensitizes individuals to recent acute stress (LaRocque et al., 2014; Shapero et al., 2014). Whether the sensitizing effect of early adversity varies for other types of early adversity (e.g., parental loss, parental divorce) beyond childhood maltreatment remains a question for future research.

The sensitizing effect of early adversity has also been found to vary as a function of the presence of a history of anxiety disorder (Espejo et al., 2007), depression history (Harkness et al., 2006), and neuroticism (Kendler et al., 2004). Although existing research has largely focused on whether early adversity increases vulnerability to subsequent acute stress, one investigation showed that the sensitizing effect of early adversity on recent chronic stress was moderated by genetic variation, such that the association between past-year chronic stress and depressive symptoms was stronger among those with a history of high levels of early adversity (versus low levels),

but only among those who were A homozygotes on the CRHR1 genotype or short-allele homozygotes on 5-HTTLPR genotype (Starr et al., 2014). More research is needed to understand whether early adversity sensitizes individuals to recent chronic stress and to elucidate factors that modify this effect.

Bipolar Spectrum Disorders

Surprisingly, only two studies have examined the sensitizing effect of early adversity (after accounting for the number of prior episodes) using objective contextual stress interviews. In one investigation, adults with a diagnosis of bipolar 1 disorder who had experienced early adversity reported lower levels of acute stress prior to recurrence, as compared to those without this history (Dienes et al., 2006). In a second investigation of adults who predominately had a diagnosis of bipolar II disorder, early adversity did not accelerate time to onset following recent major and minor events, but those who had experienced more early adverse events had fewer negative events prior to a depressive episode (when considering all events regardless of severity), suggesting that greater early adversity was associated with developing depression in the context of fewer events (Shapero et al., 2017). However, when the frequency of major and minor events was examined separately, those who had experienced more early adverse experiences had fewer minor (but not major) events prior to depressive episode onset, contradicting the stress sensitization model. Interestingly, there was not evidence for an association between early adverse events and the frequency of positive events prior to hypomanic episodes. Thus, there is some limited support for stress sensitization, though the effects appear to vary according to the type of recent stress, episode polarity, and the role of stress investigated.

Anxiety Disorders

Little research has addressed whether early adversity sensitizes individuals to recent stress in the context of anxiety disorders. In a notable exception, one investigation found support for the sensitizing effect of early adversity, though effects varied for men and women. For men and women, the association between past-year major stressors and 12-month risk for PTSD and other anxiety disorders (e.g., social phobia, panic disorder) onset was stronger among those who had experienced early adversity, supporting stress sensitization; however, early adversity was associated with increased risk of onset following recent minor events among men, but not women (McLaughlin, Conron, et al., 2010). Early adversity may also sensitize individuals to subsequent traumatic events (i.e., pipeline explosion), with greater PTSD symptoms following the event among those with a history of adversity, as compared to those without this history (Shao et al., 2015).

Substance-Related Outcomes

Limited evidence suggests that stress sensitization processes may be relevant to understanding the role of recent stress in substance-related outcomes. For example, one investigation showed that childhood maltreatment may render individuals more sensitive to chronic stressors, such as neighborhood physical disorder (i.e., presence of vacant and damaged buildings), with the presence of neighborhood disorder associated with greater risk for at-risk alcohol use, but only among those with greater exposure to childhood maltreatment (Keyes, McLaughlin, et al., 2012). In addition, research indicates that childhood maltreatment may have implications for the relation of stress to other substance-related outcomes, including at-risk alcohol use (Young-Wolff, Kendler, & Prescott, 2012), likelihood of smoking cessation (Smith, Oberleitner, Smith, & McKee, 2016), and disordered drug use (Myers, McLaughlin, Wang, Blanco, & Stein, 2014), particularly among women (Myers et al., 2014; Smith et al., 2016; Young-Wolff et al., 2012). An important question for future research in this area will be to examine whether childhood adversity is associated with higher risk in the context of *lower* levels of stress, consistent with the stress sensitization model.

Internalizing and Externalizing Psychopathology

Recent work has implicated stress sensitization as a mechanism through which early adversity contributes to the broad dimensions of externalizing and internalizing psychopathology. Meyers and colleagues (2015) demonstrated that childhood maltreatment potentiated the effect of subsequent exposure to 9/11 during adulthood on risk for developing internalizing and externalizing psychopathology. Although research on moderators is scarce, results of one investigation showed that two genetic polymorphisms (the CRHR1 genotype and 5-HTTLPR genotype) moderated the sensitizing effect of early adversity on internalizing symptoms (Starr et al., 2014). Stress sensitization effects may also have relevance for intimate partner violence, with results from a large epidemiological study suggesting that early adversity increased the potency of past-year stressful life events on risk of perpetrating

among adult men and women (Roberts, McLaughlin, Conron, & Koenen, 2011).

Summary

In sum, the sensitizing effect of early adversity has received support in the context of several disorders. Despite this, there are significant gaps in our understanding of the ways in which early adversity impacts the stress-depression association. First, akin to the literature addressing the changes in the stress-depression association with successive episodes (e.g., Monroe & Harkness, 2005), with few exceptions, the extant literature cannot ascertain whether early adversity increases the impact of stress, the likelihood that stress is present prior to episodes (i.e., frequency), or both. For example, research demonstrating that there is a stronger association of stress and depression among those with versus without a history of early adversity does not reveal whether this reflects increases in impact, frequency, or both. Second, most existing research demonstrating that individuals with early adversity develop psychopathology in the face of lower levels of stress has collapsed major and minor events into one score reflecting total stress either by summing the severity ratings of events (e.g., Dienes et al., 2006; Hammen et al., 2000; La Rocque et al., 2014; Rudolph & Flynn, 2007) or by taking the average threat rating (e.g., Harkness et al., 2006; Slavich et al., 2011). Thus, although we have evidence that individuals with a history of early adversity develop psychopathology in the face of lower *cumulative* and *average* levels of stress (as compared to those without this history), we know little about whether those with a history of early adversity develop psychopathology in the face of exclusively *minor* stressful life events (for an exception, see McLaughlin, Conron, et al., 2010). Future research investigating whether individuals with early adversity develop psychopathology in the face of even minor events (accounting for the presence of major events; S. M. Monroe, personal communication, March 17, 2017) would complement existing evidence for stress sensitization.

In addition, as noted by others (e.g., Harkness et al., 2006), with few exceptions, the literature demonstrating that individuals with early adversity develop psychopathology in the face of lower levels of stress (as compared to individuals without such history) cannot ascertain whether the findings reflect stress sensitization or stress autonomy processes (for an exception, see Harkness et al., 2006). That is, it could be the case that individuals with early adversity develop depression in the face of lower levels of stress (consistent with the stress sensitization model) or in the absence of stress (consistent with the stress autonomy model; Harkness et al., 2006). Thus, one challenging next step is to investigate whether the findings which appear to suggest that those with early adversity develop psychopathology in the face of lower levels of stress indeed reflects a stress sensitization process.

Neurobiological and Psychosocial Mechanisms Underlying Stress Sensitization Effects

Surprisingly, relatively little is known about the underlying mechanisms of stress sensitization. Existing research and theory have focused on (a) neuroendocrine reactivity and other neurobiological mechanisms (e.g., neural structure and function, genetics) and (b) cognitive and other psychological mechanisms (e.g., personality, rumination). Importantly, however, although research and theory have implicated mechanisms in an array of domains, prior work has not explicitly tested whether such mechanisms *mediate* stress sensitization effects. That is, although prior episodes and early adversity have each been shown to be related to several potential mechanisms, it is not known whether such mechanisms are in turn related to a decrease in the threshold of stress needed to trigger episode onset (i.e., stress sensitization). In addition, most work has focused on depression, and thus, research is needed to evaluate the mechanisms underlying stress sensitization in the context of other forms of psychopathology. In this section, potential mechanisms underlying the sensitizing effects of prior episodes and early adversity will be reviewed separately, but given overlap in the proposed mechanisms for each type of sensitization, an important question for future research is to investigate the extent to which the underlying mechanisms are shared versus distinct.

Mechanisms Underlying the Sensitizing Effect of Prior Episodes

One potential neurobiological mechanism of stress sensitization is alterations in hypothalamic-pituitary-adrenal (HPA) axis regulation. Although HPA dysregulation has not been directly examined as an underlying mechanism, several studies support its potential role. First, currently depressed individuals with a history of two or more prior episodes of depression show greater cortisol reactivity to pharmacological challenges than depressed individuals experiencing fewer episodes (e.g., Gervasoni et al., 2004). Second, HPA axis responses to laboratory-based stressor tasks, such as the Trier Social Stress Task (TSST), appear to vary as a function of depression history. For example, in one study of young adults, greater cortisol reactivity predicted increases in depressive symptoms more strongly among those with more prior episodes of depression (Morris, Rao, & Garber, 2012). Notably, results from this study also suggested that the HPA axis might become increasingly sensitized to low levels of stress with successive episodes. Specifically, higher levels of cortisol in the anticipatory period prior to the beginning of TSST predicted increases in subsequent depressive symptoms, with a stronger link observed among those with more prior episodes. Moreover, individuals with high levels of cortisol in the anticipatory period and more prior episodes had the greatest risk for recurrence during the follow-up. This suggests that cortisol reactivity in response to relatively low levels of acute stress (i.e., anticipating an upcoming stressor) may be a mechanism through which individuals become sensitized to stress with repeated episodes (Morris et al., 2012). Interestingly, other evidence suggests that changes in the HPA axis response to stress as a function of depression history may only occur among individuals who experience a stressful life event prior to depressive episode onset. Mazurka and colleagues (2015) showed that among youth experiencing their first depressive episode, those who experienced a life event (of any severity) prior to episode onset exhibited blunted cortisol reactivity in response to the TSST (in comparison to youth without a history of depression), whereas youth experiencing a recurrent episode who experienced a prior life event exhibited steeper cortisol recovery (in comparison to youth without a history of depression or youth experiencing a first onset). In contrast, among those without precipitating life events, there were no differences in cortisol reactivity or recovery as a function of depression history. This suggests the neuroendocrine mechanisms underlying stress sensitization may vary according to depression history, and whether (or not) episodes are precipitated by life events.

Finally, there is evidence that heightened cortisol reactivity to low stress may be associated with increases in depressive symptoms over time, regardless of depression history. Morris and colleagues (2012) showed that accounting for depression history, young adults who exhibited higher cortisol reactivity to a low stress control TSST (which involved performing the task without being evaluated) experienced increases in depressive symptoms over the 6-month follow-up, whereas cortisol reactivity in the high-stress TSST (which contained a social evaluative component) was not associated with subsequent depressive symptoms. In accord with the stress sensitization model, these intriguing findings suggest that heightened cortisol reactivity to minor stress may be a mechanism through which low levels of stress contribute to depression.

Given their role in regulation of behavioral and neuroendocrine responses to stress, and their potential to be damaged by stress exposure (via high levels of glucocorticoids; e.g., McEwen, 2007), structural abnormalities in the medial prefrontal cortex (mPFC) and the hippocampus have also been proposed as potential mechanisms of stress sensitization. Indeed, research indicates that the volume of the hippocampus is smaller in recurrently depressed patients, as compared to both never-depressed individuals (MacQueen et al., 2003; Sheline, Sanghavi, Mintun, & Gado, 1999) and individuals experiencing a first onset (e.g., MacQueen et al., 2003). Interestingly, hippocampal volume is negatively correlated with total time depressed, but not age, suggesting that hippocampal volume loss may occur as a function of depression, rather than increasing age (Sheline et al., 1999). Importantly, some research suggests progressive changes in these regions with successive episodes. For example, in a cross-sectional study of currently depressed and never-depressed adults, reduced volume in the hippocampus, and in particular the dentate gyrus, as well as cortical thinning of the left mPFC, were related to a greater number of past depressive episodes (Treadway et al., 2015). Future longitudinal research is needed to examine whether progressive changes in these areas over the course of depression mediate increasing sensitivity to stress with successive episodes, or whether individual differences in hippocampal volume and cortical thickness in the mPFC represent biological markers of risk for recurrent depression, present prior to first onsets (e.g., Treadway et al., 2015).

Cognitive mechanisms have also been identified. For example, Segal and colleagues (1996) proposed a model in which stress and depressive episodes lead to changes in information processing, thereby reducing the level of stress needed to trigger a recurrence. Specifically, the model posits that stress and depressive episodes strengthen the connections between the nodes of a depressogenic associative network, containing events, emotions, and memories that have been linked with depression. As a result, the accessibility of elements in the network (i.e., depressogenic patterns of thinking and information processing) progressively increases, and the threshold for activating the patterns progressively decreases, such that an increasingly minor level of dysphoria and stress develop the capacity to trigger recurrences. Consistent with the notion that the link between negative cognitions and depressive symptoms increases with successive episodes, findings from a recent study revealed that high levels of dysfunctional attitudes predicted increases in depressive symptoms among individuals with a history of depression, but not among never-depressed individuals (Morris, Kouros, Fox, Rao, & Garber, 2014). An important question to address in future work is whether changes in the accessibility of depressogenic patterns of information processing, and in the activation threshold of such patterns, contribute to stress sensitization effects.

In a recently developed cognitive model, the two-factor sensitization model, Farb and colleagues (2015) posited that sensitization occurs because dysphoric attention (i.e., fixation on negative life events) and dysphoric elaboration (i.e., via rumination) become increasingly "coupled" with each episode, such that minor stress develops the capacity to trigger dysphoric elaborations, thereby increasing risk for relapse/recurrence. In this model, fixation on the negative aspects of stressful events leads to dysphoric elaboration, a process driven by rumination; through rumination the negative aspects of events are integrated into negative schema. With each episode of depression, fixation leads to increases in rumination, further solidifying global negative schema. Increases in rumination, in turn, serve to enhance fixation, reinforce negative schema, and amplify the perceived implications of increasingly more minor stressful life events. Though not designed to explicitly test this model, results from a recent study provided support for rumination as a mechanism of stress sensitization (Ruscio et al., 2015). Specifically, rumination in response to daily stressful life events mediated the link between perceived stressfulness and symptoms of anxiety and depression. Interestingly, this meditational pathway was stronger among those diagnosed with major depression and generalized anxiety disorder (GAD), as compared to healthy controls, and most events were minor. This suggests that increased rumination following even minor events may increase vulnerability to depressive and anxiety symptoms, particularly in those experiencing major depression and GAD. Future research is needed to evaluate whether this link strengthens with successive episodes and whether fixation plays a role in this process, in accord with the central thesis of the two-factor model.

Personality changes, which occur as a result of depressive episodes, may also lead to stress sensitization. Specifically, progressive increases in neuroticism (with successive episodes) are theorized to render individuals increasingly sensitive to lower and lower levels of stress, thereby increasing risk for recurrences (e.g., Ormel et al., 2001). Supporting this, results of one study indicated that neuroticism and minor stressful life events were each more strongly associated with recurrences than first onsets (Ormel et al., 2001). In addition, Kendler and colleagues (1993) demonstrated that even after accounting for levels of neuroticism prior to first onsets, at the 1-year follow-up, neuroticism was higher among those who had experienced an episode of depression during the follow-up period, as compared to those who did not. Thus, depressive episodes may lead to increases in neuroticism, which in turn may increase daily stress reactivity (Bolger & Zuckerman, 1995). The next step is to examine whether increases in neuroticism with successive episodes serves a pathway through which individuals become progressively sensitized to stress.

Mechanisms Underlying the Sensitizing Effect of Early Adversity

Substantial evidence indicates that early adversity leads to lasting alterations in stress-responsive physiological and neuroendocrine systems among children, adolescents, and adults (e.g., Cicchetti & Rogosch, 2012; Tarullo & Gunnar, 2006); in turn, such disruptions result in the inability of such systems to adaptively respond to subsequent stress, permitting lower levels of stress to trigger episode onsets (i.e., stress sensitization; e.g., Heim & Nemeroff, 2001; Heim, Newport, Mletzko, Miller, & Nemeroff, 2008). Consistent with this, prior work has shown that early adversity leads to disruptions in HPA axis regulation, with individuals who experienced early adversity exhibiting different patterns of HPA axis functioning, including both hyper- and hypocortisolism (e.g., Cicchetti & Rogosch, 2012; Tarullo & Gunnar, 2006). For instance, one study of adults found that those with a history of moderate to severe childhood maltreatment exhibited diminished cortisol reactivity to a laboratory-based stressor task, as compared to those without such history (Carpenter et al., 2007).

The second line of research that supports alterations in stress response systems as a mechanism of stress sensitization is abundant evidence indicating

that such alterations are concurrently and longitudinally associated with internalizing psychopathology among children, adolescents, and adults (e.g., Cicchetti & Rogosch, 2001; Lopez-Duran, Kovacs, & George, 2009). Stronger evidence, however, comes from a limited number of prospective studies showing that alterations in stress response systems mediate the prospective relation between early adversity and internalizing psychopathology. For example, findings from one study demonstrated that greater early adversity within the family environment (e.g., low levels of family cohesion, poor parent relationship quality) and low socioeconomic status each predicted greater stress reactivity (assessed via apprehension to venipuncture and ear puncture) in young adulthood, which in turn predicted the subsequent onsets of major depression and anxiety disorders (McLaughlin, Kubzansky, et al., 2010). Given this initial support for disruptions in stress response systems as a mechanism of stress sensitization, a critical next step will be to examine whether such disruptions engender increased sensitivity to low levels of stress among those with a history of early adversity.

Cognitive vulnerabilities have also been proposed. Segal and colleagues (1999) posited that exposure to early adversity strengthens the connections between a network of thoughts, events, and emotions associated with depression, which serves to increase the accessibility of depressogenic patterns of thinking, and lower the threshold for activating such patterns, resulting in stress sensitization. Cognitive models also implicate early adversity in the development and consolidation of cognitive vulnerabilities (e.g., schema, cognitive styles, dysfunctional beliefs), which are posited to shape the interpretation of subsequent stressors, thereby increasing vulnerability in the face of stress (e.g., Beck, 1967; Rose & Abramson, 1992). Indeed, considerable evidence has shown that early adversity (particularly childhood maltreatment) contributes to the development of negative cognitive schemas and dysfunctional attitudes (for reviews, see Alloy, Abramson, Smith, Gibb, & Neeren, 2006; Gibb, 2002). Furthermore, cross-sectional as well as a handful of prospective longitudinal studies show that cognitive vulnerabilities mediate the relation between early adversity and the development of depression (for a review, see Alloy et al., 2006). Interestingly, there is some evidence that certain types of childhood maltreatment, such as childhood emotional abuse, may be more strongly related to negative cognitive vulnerabilities (Gibb et al., 2002), perhaps because the negative cognitions are directly provided to the child by the perpetrator (Rose & Abramson, 1992). Notably, this aligns with some prior work indicating that childhood emotional abuse, but not other types of maltreatment, leads to stress sensitization (e.g., La Rocque et al., 2014). These promising findings, as well as the substantial research and theory linking early adversity, cognitive vulnerabilities, and depression, underscore the need to directly examine whether cognitive vulnerabilities act as a pathway through which early adversity contributes to stress sensitization.

Notably, Harkness and Lumley (2008) developed an integrated psychobiological developmental model, which theorizes that early adversity (specifically childhood maltreatment) contributes to stress sensitization via increasing cognitive schema consolidation and by altering the HPA axis response to stress. The model posits that these two processes interact during adolescence, particularly in the context of high levels of ongoing chronic stress, and stabilize as a result of neurobiological, cognitive, and emotional development. Consequently, the depressogenic schema and HPA axis are "kindled" to respond to subsequent stress, rendering those with a history of early adversity more vulnerable to depression in the face of stress (as compared to those without such history). Future longitudinal research that simultaneously investigates multiple mechanisms (e.g., Harkness et al., 2006), such as those proposed in this model, will shed light on the ways in which early adversity influences stress sensitization on multiple levels of analysis.

Genetic variation in susceptibility to depression may also be a mechanism (e.g., Harkness et al., 2006). Specifically, it has been suggested that individuals with a history of early adversity may have a genetic susceptibility to depression that renders them more sensitive to stress (e.g., Harkness et al., 2006). Supporting this, one prior investigation showed that shared genetic factors contributed to both risk for major depression and increased likelihood of experiencing proximal stressful life events, suggesting that genetic factors may increase risk for depression via increasing exposure to environmental adversities (Kendler & Karkowski-Shuman, 1997). Moreover, research indicates that women with the highest genetic risk for major depression may be "prekindled" (or presensitized) prior to the first onset of depression, suggesting that genetic variation may contribute to stress sensitization (or stress autonomy) prior to the first episode of depression (Kendler et al., 2001). The findings underscore the need for future research investigating whether genetic variation is a mechanism of stress sensitization.

Future Directions of Research
Providing Robust Support for Stress Sensitization

In brief, additional evidence providing *unequivocal* support for the stress sensitization model in the context of prior episodes, as well as early adversity, is clearly needed. Indeed, in line with earlier reviews (Bender & Alloy, 2011; Hlastala et al., 2000; Monroe & Harkness, 2005), much of the literature remains ambiguous regarding whether the findings support the stress sensitization or stress autonomy models. Relatedly, even when the stress sensitization model is supported, few studies have addressed whether the observed effects reflect changes in the impact or frequency of stress, or both (Monroe & Harkness, 2005). To provide robust support for stress sensitization, prospective longitudinal studies that (a) recruit individuals experiencing first onsets and follow them across recurrences; (b) include individuals with and without a history of early adversity; and (c) investigate within-person changes in the impact and frequency of different forms of stressful life events across successive episodes are needed (e.g., Bender & Alloy, 2011; Hammen, 2005; Monroe & Harkness, 2005). Moreover, such investigations should examine how the role of chronic stress changes with successive episodes and as a function of early adversity—a critical question that has been rarely pursued in the literature (e.g., Monroe & Harkness, 2005). This work could further advance the field by elucidating how the stress sensitization process unfolds across development (e.g., La Rocque et al., 2014; Rudolph & Flynn, 2007), as well as by identifying additional factors that moderate stress sensitization effects (e.g., Hammen, 2015).

Investigating Mechanisms of Stress Sensitization

Although many promising mechanisms have been identified (e.g., alterations in HPA axis regulation), research has not yet tested whether these mechanisms *mediate* stress sensitization effects in the context of prior episodes and early adversity, representing a critical direction for future research (e.g., Hammen, 2015; Harkness et al., 2015). Moreover, as highlighted by others (e.g., Harkness et al., 2006), multivariate models should be used to examine multiple mechanisms simultaneously (Hammen, 2015; Harkness et al., 2015), given theoretical models suggest that the underlying mechanisms may complement one another and/or interact throughout development (e.g., Farb et al., 2015; Harkness & Lumley, 2008; Post, 1992; Segal et al.,

1996). Additional mechanisms should also be evaluated in future work. For instance, there are hints that inflammatory activation (e.g., Smid et al., 2015), emotion regulation difficulties (Heleniak, Jenness, Van der Stoep, McCauley, & McLaughlin, 2016), and insecure attachment (Rudolph & Flynn, 2007) might be potential mechanisms of the sensitizing effect of early adversity. In addition, an interesting question to explore in future work will be whether the mechanisms are disorder-specific or apply transdiagnostically (e.g., Hammen, 2015; Harkness et al., 2015). Finally, research has not yet evaluated whether the mechanisms underlying stress sensitization effects vary according to other factors, such as gender, developmental stage, event type, and genetic variation. For example, genetic variation in each CRHR1 and 5-HTTPLR (both of which have connections to stress-responsive systems, including the HPA axis; Heim & Nemeroff, 2001) may moderate the mechanisms (e.g., alterations in HPA axis regulation) underlying the sensitizing effect of early adversity (Starr et al., 2014). Pursuing research that strives to elucidate the underlying mechanisms is critical given the potential that such mechanisms could be targeted by intervention and prevention efforts (e.g., Hammen, 2015).

Testing and Refining the Conceptualization of Different Forms of Stress

A priority for future research will be to test and refine different methods of conceptualizing both recent and early stress (e.g., Hammen, 2015; Monroe & Harkness, 2005). One challenge will be to reliably measure even more minor levels of stress, such as daily hassles, to determine whether those who appear to succumb to psychopathology in the absence of stress (perhaps reflecting stress autonomy) might actually be developing psychopathology in the face of even lower levels of stress (reflecting stress sensitization; e.g., Harkness et al., 2006; Monroe & Harkness, 2005). A second interesting question is how to define recent stress. Curiously, studies examining stress sensitization as a function of successive episodes have largely operationalized stress as the presence (versus absence) of events, whereas studies examining stress sensitization as a function of early adversity have largely operationalized stress as total or mean level. It will be important to consider the rationale for, and implications of, each operationalization for the stress sensitization model. Research examining the role of recent chronic stress (e.g., Monroe & Harkness, 2005) and continued exploration of the facets of different

types of stress that influence stress sensitization effects are additional areas to pursue. For research examining early adversity, it will be critical to examine whether sensitization effects, as well as the mechanisms underlying those effects, vary according to type (e.g., childhood maltreatment, parental divorce; e.g. La Rocque et al., 2014), severity, duration, and timing of the early adversity (e.g., early childhood versus adolescence; e.g., Rudolph & Flynn, 2007), and the timing of the early adversity relative to disorder onset (e.g., Harkness et al., 2006; La Rocque et al., 2014).

Investigating Different Ways of Conceptualizing Psychopathology

Given research indicating that transdiagnostic factors underlie the major psychiatric disorders (e.g., Krueger, 1999) as well as evidence that the effect of childhood maltreatment on psychiatric disorder onset is fully explained by underlying vulnerabilities to experience internalizing and externalizing psychopathology (versus risk for developing specific disorders; Keyes, Eaton, et al., 2012), future research should consider the implications of adopting transdiagnostic models (e.g., Hammen, 2015). Indeed, such an approach would also permit the evaluation of mechanisms and moderators of stress sensitization that cut across various disorders, which may be particularly informative for intervention and prevention efforts. Another compelling question is whether sensitization processes have similar implications and mechanisms depending on whether the development of symptoms (e.g., Shapero et al., 2014) or diagnosable disorders (e.g., Harkness et al., 2006) is explored. This too would be informative for prevention efforts: If indeed the model applies to symptoms (as some research suggests), then the underlying mechanisms could be targeted even prior to the development of diagnosable disorders.

Exploring Complementary and Alternative Theoretical Models

One important question for future work will be to explore theoretical models that may complement the stress sensitization model. For example, stress generation (Hammen, 1991) and stress sensitization may reciprocally influence one another, progressively increasing the rate of recurrences (Monroe & Harkness, 2005). That is, individuals with a history of depression may not only be more likely to generate stress, but also may be more sensitive to that stress when it occurs, setting up a vicious cycle wherein stress and depression continue to reciprocally influence one another over time (see also Monroe et al., 2007). Moreover, early adversity has been identified as a predictor of both stress generation (e.g., Liu, Choi, Boland, Mastin, & Alloy, 2013) and stress sensitization (e.g., Harkness et al., 2006), raising the possibility that individuals with a history of early adversity not only tend to generate higher levels of stress but, in turn, are also more vulnerable to that stress when it occurs, further increasing risk of first onsets and recurrences. In the context of bipolar disorder, Bender and Alloy (2011) have recently explored the possibility that the behavioral approach system (BAS) dysregulation theory and the social rhythm disruption theory might complement and inform research investigating the stress sensitization model in bipolar spectrum disorders.

Alternative theoretical models should also be tested and developed. For example, in depression research, distinctions have been made between the stress sensitization and stress amplification models (e.g., Morris et al., 2010; Oldehinkel, Ormel, Verhulst, & Nederhof, 2014; Rudolph & Flynn, 2007), the latter of which predicts that early adversity and prior episodes of depression amplify depressive reactions to severe, but not nonsevere, stress. In the context of early adversity, an intriguing model for future pursuit is the stress inoculation model (also called the steeling effect), which proposes that exposure to moderate levels of early adversity protects individuals from risk for psychopathology in the face of subsequent stress (for a review, see Liu, 2015; e.g., Oldehinkel et al., 2014; Rudolph & Flynn, 2007). In this model, individuals with a history of *low* levels of early adversity would be expected to be *more* vulnerable to subsequent stress, as compared to those exposed to *moderate* levels of early adversity. Finally, recent critiques have called into question research supporting stress sensitization as a function of prior episodes (Anderson, Monroe, Rohde, & Lewinsohn, 2016), arguing that the association between major stress and successive episodes only seems to weaken as a result of Slater's fallacy—highly recurrent individuals with lower levels of stress needed to trigger recurrences become a larger portion of the sample with each recurrence. In other words, rather than reflecting within-person changes in the stress-depression association over time as proposed by the stress sensitization model, the weakening association observed in prior work reflects between-person differences: As compared to less recurrent individuals, highly recurrent individuals would be expected to develop depression in the

face of lower levels of stress even prior to the first onset (Anderson et al., 2016).

Thus, a challenge for future research will be to conduct research (a) investigating the integration of multiple models, with the goal of understanding how such models might complement and refine the theory of stress sensitization; (b) test alternative approaches for understanding how early adversity and disorder history shape the relationship between stress and psychopathology; and (c) continue to develop new explanations for how this relation changes.

Conclusion

The importance of pursuing research to enhance our understanding of the relation between stress and psychopathology is inherent in the stress sensitization model: Stress becomes even more etiologically important as people become more vulnerable. Consequently, this suggests that prevention efforts must equip those with a history of psychopathology and/or early adversity with strategies for increasing their resiliency in the face of stress, consistent with evidence-based interventions that incorporate strategies designed to manage stress (e.g., cognitive-behavioral therapy, interpersonal psychotherapy). As I hope is evident, we need to design studies that will provide robust evidence for the stress sensitization model, determine how the role of stress changes, elucidate the underlying mechanisms and moderators, and advance theory and measurement. This work will refine our intervention efforts, by, for example, helping individuals develop coping strategies for specific types of events, targeting those individuals who are most likely to be sensitized to stress, and focusing on the mechanisms underlying sensitization effects. In doing so, our intervention and prevention efforts will become more effective in promoting resiliency in those most vulnerable to stress.

References

Alloy, L. B., Abramson, L. Y., Smith, J. M., Gibb, B. E., & Neeren, A. M. (2006). Role of parenting and maltreatment histories in unipolar and bipolar mood disorders: Mediation by cognitive vulnerability to depression. *Clinical Child and Family Psychology Review, 9*(1), 23–64. doi:10.1007/s10567-006-0002-4

Anderson, S. F., Monroe, S. M., Rohde, P., & Lewinsohn, P. M. (2016). Questioning kindling: An analysis of cycle acceleration in unipolar depression. *Clinical Psychological Science, 4*(2), 229–238. doi:10.1177/2167702615591951

Beck, A. T. (1967). *Depression: Clinical, experimental, and theoretical aspects.* New York, NY: Harper & Row.

Bender, R. E., & Alloy, L. B. (2011). Life stress and kindling in bipolar disorder: Review of the evidence and integration with emerging biopsychosocial theories. *Clinical Psychology Review*, *31*(3), 383–398. doi:10.1016/j.cpr.2011.01.004

Bolger, N., & Zuckerman, A. (1995). A framework for studying personality in the stress process. *Journal of Personality and Social Psychology*, *69*(5), 890–902. doi:10.1037/0022-3514.69.5.890

Carpenter, L. L., Carvalho, J. P., Tyrka, A. R., Wier, L. M., Mello, A. F., Mello, M. F., ... Price, L. H. (2007). Decreased adrenocorticotropic hormone and cortisol responses to stress in healthy adults reporting significant childhood maltreatment. *Biological Psychiatry*, *62*(10), 1080–1087. doi:10.1016/j.biopsych.2007.05.002

Cicchetti, D., & Rogosch, F. A. (2001). The impact of child maltreatment and psychopathology on neuroendocrine functioning. *Development and Psychopathology*, *13*(4), 783–804.

Cicchetti, D., & Rogosch, F. A. (2012). Physiological measures of emotion from a developmental perspective: State of the science: Neuroendocrine regulation and emotional adaptation in the context of child maltreatment. *Monographs of the Society for Research in Child Development*, *77*(2), 87–95. doi:10.1111/j.1540-5834.2011.00666.x

Daley, S. E., Hammen, C., & Rao, U. (2000). Predictors of first onset and recurrence of major depression in young women during the 5 years following high school graduation. *Journal of Abnormal Psychology*, *109*, 525–533.

Dienes, K. A., Hammen, C., Henry, R. M., Cohen, A. N., & Daley, S. E. (2006). The stress sensitization hypothesis: Understanding the course of bipolar disorder. *Journal of Affective Disorders*, *95*(1–3), 43–49. doi:10.1016/j.jad.2006.04.009

Dougherty, L. R., Klein, D. N., & Davila, J. (2004). A growth curve analysis of the course of dysthymic disorder: The effects of chronic stress and moderation by adverse parent-child relationships and family history. *Journal of Consulting and Clinical Psychology*, *72*(6), 1012–1021. doi:10.1037/0022-006X.72.6.1012

Espejo, E. P., Hammen, C. L., Connolly, N. P., Brennan, P. A., Najman, J. M., & Bor, W. (2007). Stress sensitization and adolescent depressive severity as a function of childhood adversity: A link to anxiety disorders. *Journal of Abnormal Child Psychology*, *35*(2), 287–299. doi:10.1007/s10802-006-9090-3

Farb, N. A. S., Irving, J. A., Anderson, A. K., & Segal, Z. V. (2015). A two-factor model of relapse/recurrence vulnerability in unipolar depression. *Journal of Abnormal Psychology*, *124*(1), 38–53. doi:10.1037/abn0000031

Gervasoni, N., Bertschy, G., Osiek, C., Perret, G., Denis, R., Golaz, J, ... Aubry, J.-M. (2004). Cortisol responses to combined dexamethasone/CRH test in outpatients with a major depressive episode. *Journal of Psychiatric Research*, *38*(6), 553–557. doi:10.1016/j.jpsychires.2004.04.008

Gibb, B. E. (2002). Childhood maltreatment and negative cognitive styles: A quantitative and qualitative review. *Clinical Psychology Review*, *22*(2), 223–246. doi:10.1016/S0272-7358(01)00088-5

Goddard, G. V., McIntyre, D., & Leech, C. (1969). A permanent change in brain function resulting from daily electrical stimulation. *Experimental Neurology*, *25*, 295–330.

Hammen, C. (1991). Generation of stress in the course of unipolar depression. *Journal of Abnormal Psychology*, *100*, 555–561.

Hammen, C. (2005). Stress and depression. *Annual Review of Clinical Psychology*, *1*(1), 293–319. doi:10.1146/annurev.clinpsy.1.102803.143938

Hammen, C. (2015). Stress sensitivity in psychopathology: Mechanisms and consequences. *Journal of Abnormal Psychology*, *124*(1), 152–154. doi:10.1037/abn0000040

Hammen, C., & Gitlin, M. (1997). Stress reactivity in bipolar patients and its relation to prior history of disorder. *American Journal of Psychiatry*, *154*, 856–857.

Hammen, C., Henry, R., & Daley, S. E. (2000). Depression and sensitization to stressors among young women as a function of childhood adversity. *Journal of Consulting and Clinical Psychology*, *68*(5), 782–787. doi:10.1037/0022-006X.68.5.782

Harkness, K. L., Alavi, N., Monroe, S. M., Slavich, G. M., Gotlib, I. H., & Bagby, R. M. (2010). Gender differences in life events prior to onset of major depressive disorder: The moderating effect of age. *Journal of Abnormal Psychology*, *119*, 791–803.

Harkness, K. L., Bruce, A. E., & Lumley, M. N. (2006). The role of childhood abuse and neglect in the sensitization to stressful life events in adolescent depression. *Journal of Abnormal Psychology*, *115*(4), 730–741. doi:10.1037/0021-843X.115.4.730

Harkness, K. L., Hayden, E. P., & Lopez-Duran, N. L. (2015). Stress sensitivity and stress sensitization in psychopathology: An introduction to the special section. *Journal of Abnormal Psychology*, *124*(1), 1–3. doi:10.1037/abn0000041

Harkness, K. L., & Lumley, M. N. (2008). Child abuse and neglect and the development of depression in children and adolescents. In J. R. Z. Abela, B. L. Hankin, J. R. Z. Abela, & B. L. Hankin (Eds.), *Handbook of depression in children and adolescents*. (pp. 466–488). New York, NY: Guilford Press.

Heim, C., & Nemeroff, C. B. (2001). The role of childhood trauma in the neurobiology of mood and anxiety disorders: Preclinical and clinical studies. *Biological Psychiatry*, *49*(12), 1023–1039. doi:10.1016/S0006-3223(01)01157-X

Heim, C., Newport, D. J., Mletzko, T., Miller, A. H., & Nemeroff, C. B. (2008). The link between childhood trauma and depression: Insights from HPA axis studies in humans. *Psychoneuroendocrinology*, *33*(6), 693–710. doi:10.1016/j.psyneuen.2008.03.008

Heleniak, C., Jenness, J., Van der Stoep, A., McCauley, E., & McLaughlin, K. A. (2016). Childhood maltreatment exposure and disruptions in emotion regulation: A transdiagnostic pathway to adolescent internalizing and externalizing psychopathology. *Cognitive Therapy and Research*, *40*, 394–415.

Hlastala, S. A., Frank, E., Kowalski, J., Sherrill, J. T., Tu, X. M., Anderson, B., & Kupfer, D. J. (2000). Stressful life events, bipolar disorder, and the "kindling model." *Journal of Abnormal Psychology*, *109*(4), 777–786. doi:10.1037/0021-843X.109.4.777

Johnson, L., Andersson-Lundman, G., Aberg-Wistedt, A., & Mathe, A. A. (2000). Age of onset in affective disorder: Its correlation with hereditary and psychosocial factors. *Journal of Affective Disorders*, *59*, 139–148.

Kendler, K. S., & Karkowski-Shuman, L. (1997). Stressful life events and genetic liability to major depression: Genetic control of exposure to the environment? *Psychological Medicine*, *27*, 539–547.

Kendler, K. S., Neale, M. C., Kessler, R. C., Heath, A. C., & Eaves, L. J. (1993). A longitudinal twin study of personality and major depression in women. *Archives of General Psychiatry*, *50*, 853–862.

Kendler, K. S., Thornton, L. M., & Prescott, C. (2001). Gender differences in the rates of exposure to stressful life events and sensitivity to their depressogenic effects. *American Journal of Psychiatry, 158,* 587–593.

Kendler, K. S., Thornton, L. M., & Gardner, C. O. (2000). Stressful life events and previous episodes in the etiology of major depression in women: An evaluation of the "kindling" hypothesis. *The American Journal of Psychiatry, 157*(8), 1243–1251. doi:10.1176/appi.ajp.157.8.1243

Kendler, K. S., Thornton, L. M., & Gardner, C. O. (2001). Genetic risk, number of previous depressive episodes, and stressful life events in predicting onset of major depression. *The American Journal of Psychiatry, 158*(4), 582–586. doi:10.1176/appi.ajp.158.4.582

Kessler, R. C. (2012). The costs of depression. *Psychiatric Clinics of North America, 35,* 1–14. doi:10.1016/j.psc.2011.11.005

Keyes, K. M., Eaton, N. R., Krueger, R. F., McLaughlin, K. A., Wall, M. M., Grant, B. F., & Hasin, D. S. (2012). Childhood maltreatment and the structure of common psychiatric disorders. *British Journal of Psychiatry, 200,* 107–115.

Keyes, K. M., McLaughlin, K. A., Koenen, K. C., Goldmann, E., Uddin, M., & Galea, S. (2012). Child maltreatment increases sensitivity to adverse social contexts: Neighborhood physical disorder and incident binge drinking in Detroit. *Drug and Alcohol Dependence, 122*(1–2), 77–85. doi:10.1016/j.drugalcdep.2011.09.013

Krueger, R. E. (1999). The structure of common mental disorders. *Archives of General Psychiatry, 56,* 921–926.

La Rocque, C. L., Harkness, K. L., & Bagby, R. M. (2014). The differential relation of childhood maltreatment to stress sensitization in adolescent and young adult depression. *Journal of Adolescence, 37*(6), 871–882. doi:10.1016/j.adolescence.2014.05.012

Lenze, S. N., Cyranowski, J. M., Thompson, W. K., Anderson, B., & Frank, E. (2008). The cumulative impact of nonsevere life events predicts depression recurrence during maintenance treatment with interpersonal psychotherapy. *Journal of Consulting and Clinical Psychology, 76,* 979–987.

Liu, R. T. (2015). A developmentally informed perspective on the relation between stress and psychopathology: When the problem with stress is that there is not enough. *Journal of Abnormal Psychology, 124*(1), 80–92. doi:10.1037/abn0000043

Liu, R. T., Choi, J. Y., Boland, E. M., Mastin, B. M., & Alloy, L. B. (2013). Childhood abuse and stress generation: The mediational effect of depressogenic cognitive styles. *Psychiatry Research, 206,* 217–222. doi:10.1016/j.psychres.2012.12.001.

Lopez-Duran, N. L., Kovacs, M., & George, C. J. (2009). Hypothalamic-pituitary-adrenal axis dysregulation in depressed children and adolescents: A meta-analysis. *Psychoneuroendocrinology, 34*(9), 1272–1283. doi:10.1016/j.psyneuen.2009.03.016

MacQueen, G. M., Campell, S., McEwen, B. S., Macdonald, K., Amano, S., Joffe, R. T.,...Young, L. T. (2003). Course of illness, hippocampal function, and hippocampal volume in major depression. *Proceedings of the National Academy of Sciences, 100,* 1387–1392. doi:10.1073/pnas.0337481100

Mazure, C. M. (1998). Life stressors as risk factors for depression. *Clinical Psychology: Science and Practice, 5,* 291–314.

Mazurka, R., Wynne-Edwards, K. E., & Harkness, K. L. (2015). Stressful life events prior to depression onset and the cortisol response to stress in youth with first onset versus recurrent depression. *Journal of Abnormal Child Psychology.* doi:10.1007/s10802-015-0103-y

McEwen, B. S. (2007). Physiology and neurobiology of stress and adaptation: Central role of the brain. *Physiological Reviews, 87,* 873–904.

McLaughlin, K. A., Conron, K. J., Koenen, K. C., & Gilman, S. E. (2010). Childhood adversity, adult stressful life events, and risk of past-year psychiatric disorder: A test of the stress sensitization hypothesis in a population-based sample of adults. *Psychological Medicine, 40*(10), 1647–1658. doi:10.1017/S0033291709992121

McLaughlin, K. A., Green, J. G., Gruber, M. J., Sampson, N. A., Zaslavsky, A. M., & Kessler, R. C. (2012). Childhood adversities and first onset psychiatric disorders in a national sample of adolescents. *Archives of General Psychiatry, 69,* 1151–1160.

McLaughlin, K. A., Kubzansky, L. D., Dunn, E. C., Waldinger, R., Vaillant, G., & Koenen, K. C. (2010). Childhood social environment, emotional reactivity to stress, and mood and anxiety disorders across the life course. *Depression and Anxiety, 27,* 1087–1094.

Meyers, J. L., Lowe, S. R., Eaton, N. R., Krueger, R., Grant, B. F., & Hasin, D. (2015). Childhood maltreatment, 9/11 exposure, and latent dimensions of psychopathology: A test of stress sensitization. *Journal of Psychiatric Research, 68,* 337–345. doi:10.1016/j.jpsychires.2015.05.005

Monroe, S. M., & Harkness, K. L. (2005). Life stress, the "kindling" hypothesis, and the recurrence of depression: Considerations from a life stress perspective. *Psychological Review, 112,* 417–445.

Monroe, S. M., & Harkness, K. L. (2011). Recurrence in major depression: A conceptual analysis. *Psychological Review, 118,* 655–674.

Monroe, S. M., Slavich, G. M., Torres, L. D., & Gotlib, I. H. (2007). Major life events and major difficulties are differentially associated with history of major depressive episodes. *Journal of Abnormal Psychology, 116,* 116–124. doi:10.1037/0021-843X.116.1.116.

Monroe, S. M., Slavich, G. M., & Gotlib, I. H. (2014). Life stress and family history for depression: The moderating role of past depressive episodes. *Journal of Psychiatric Research, 49,* 90–95. doi:10.1016/j.jpsychires.2013.11.005

Monroe, S. M., Torres, L. D., Guillaumot, J., Harkness, K. L., Roberts, J. E., Frank, E., & Kupfer, D. (2006). Life stress and the long-term treatment course of recurrent depression: III. Nonsevere life events predict recurrence for medicated patients over 3 years. *Journal of Consulting and Clinical Psychology, 74,* 112–120.

Morris, M. C., Ciesla, J. A., & Garber, J. (2010). A prospective study of stress autonomy versus stress sensitization in adolescents at varied risk for depression. *Journal of Abnormal Psychology, 119*(2), 341–354. doi:10.1037/a0019036

Morris, M. C., Kouros, C. D., Fox, K. R., Rao, U., & Garber, J. (2014). Interactive models of depression vulnerability: The role of childhood trauma, dysfunctional attitudes, and coping. *British Journal of Clinical Psychology, 53*(2), 245–263. doi:10.1111/bjc.12038

Morris, M. C., Rao, U., & Garber, J. (2012). Cortisol responses to psychosocial stress predict depression trajectories: Social-evaluative threat and prior depressive episodes as moderators. *Journal of Affective Disorders, 143*(1–3), 223–230. doi:10.1016/j.jad.2012.05.059

Murray, C. J. L., & Lopez, A. D. (1996). *The global burden of disease: A comprehensive assessment of mortality and disability from diseases, injuries, and risk factors in 1990 and projected to 2020.* Cambridge, MA: Harvard University Press.

Myers, B., McLaughlin, K. A., Wang, S., Blanco, C., & Stein, D. J. (2014). Associations between childhood adversity, adult stressful life events, and past-year drug use disorders in the National Epidemiological Study of Alcohol and Related Conditions (NESARC). *Psychology of Addictive Behaviors, 28*(4), 1117–1126. doi:10.1037/a0037459

Oldehinkel, A. J., Ormel, J., Verhulst, F. C., & Nederhof, E. (2014). Childhood adversities and adolescent depression: A matter of both risk and resilience. *Development and Psychopathology, 26*(4), 1067–1075. doi:10.1017/s0954579414000534

Ormel, J., Oldehinkel, A. J., & Brilman, E. I. (2001). The interplay and etiological continuity of neuroticism, difficulties, and life events in the etiology of major and subsyndromal, first and recurrent depressive episodes in later life. *American Journal of Psychiatry, 158*, 885–891.

Post, R. M. (1992). Transduction of psychosocial stress into the neurobiology of recurrent affective disorder. *American Journal of Psychiatry, 149*, 999–1010.

Post, R. M. (2007). Kindling and sensitization as models for affective episode recurrence, cyclicity, and tolerance phenomena. *Neuroscience and Biobehavioral Reviews, 31*(6), 858–873. doi:10.1016/j.neubiorev.2007.04.003

Post, R. M. (2016). Epigenetic basis of sensitization to stress, affective episodes, and stimulants: Implications for illness progression and prevention. *Bipolar Disorders, 18*(4), 315–324. doi:10.1111/bdi.12401

Post, R. M., Leverich, G. S., Weiss, S. R. B., Zhang, L.-X., Xing, G., Li, H., & Smith, M. (2003). Psychosocial stressors as predisposing factors to affective illness and PTSD: Potential neurobiological mechanisms and theoretical implications. In D. Cicchetti, E. Walker, D. Cicchetti, & E. Walker (Eds.), *Neurodevelopmental mechanisms in psychopathology* (pp. 491–525). New York, NY: Cambridge University Press.

Post, R. M., & Weiss, S. R. (1998). Sensitization and kindling phenomena in mood, anxiety, and obsessive-compulsive disorders. *Biological Psychiatry, 44*, 193–206.

Post, R. M., Weiss, S. R. B., & Leverich, G. S. (1994). Recurrent affective disorder: Roots in developmental neurobiology and illness progression based on changes in gene expression. *Development and Psychopathology, 6*(4), 781–813. doi:10.1017/S0954579400004788

Post, R. M., Weiss, S. R. B., Smith, M., & Li, H. (1997). Kindling versus quenching. Implications for the evolution and treatment of posttraumatic stress disorder. In R. Yehuda, A. C. McFarlane, R. Yehuda, & A. C. McFarlane (Eds.), *Psychobiology of posttraumatic stress disorder* (Vol. 821, pp. 285–295). New York, NY: New York Academy of Sciences.

Roberts, A. L., McLaughlin, K. A., Conron, K. J., & Koenen, K. C. (2011). Adulthood stressors, history of childhood adversity, and risk of perpetration of intimate partner violence. *American Journal of Preventive Medicine, 40*(2), 128–138. doi:10.1016/j.amepre.2010.10.016

Rose, D. T., & Abramson, L. Y. (1992). Developmental predictors of depressive cognitive style: Research and theory. In D. Cicchetti, S. L. Toth, D. Cicchetti, & S. L. Toth (Eds.), *Developmental perspectives on depression* (pp. 323–349). Rochester, NY: University of Rochester Press.

Rudolph, K. D., & Flynn, M. (2007). Childhood adversity and youth depression: Influence of gender and pubertal status. *Development and Psychopathology, 19*(2), 497–521. doi:10.1017/s0954579407070241

Ruscio, A. M., Gentes, E. L., Jones, J. D., Hallion, L. S., Coleman, E. S., & Swendsen, J. (2015). Rumination predicts heightened responding to stressful life events in major depressive disorder and generalized anxiety disorder. *Journal of Abnormal Psychology, 124*, 17–26.

Segal, Z. V., Williams, J. M., Teasdale, J. D., & Gemar, M. (1996). A cognitive science perspective on kindling and episode sensitization in recurrent affective disorder. *Psychological Medicine, 26*(2), 371–380. doi:10.1017/S0033291700034760

Shao, D., Gao, Q.-L., Li, J., Xue, J.-M., Guo, W., Long, Z.-T., & Cao, F.-L. (2015). Test of the stress sensitization model in adolescents following the pipeline explosion. *Comprehensive Psychiatry, 62*, 178–186. doi:10.1016/j.comppsych.2015.07.017

Shapero, B. G., Black, S. K., Liu, R. T., Klugman, J., Bender, R. E., Abramson, L. Y., & Alloy, L. B. (2014). Stressful life events and depression symptoms: The effect of childhood emotional abuse on stress reactivity. *Journal of Clinical Psychology, 70*(3), 209–223. doi:10.1002/jclp.22011

Shapero, B. G., Weiss, R. B., Burke, T. A., Boland, E. M., Abramson, L. Y., & Alloy, L. B. (2017). Kindling of life stress in bipolar disorder: Effects of early adversity. *Behavior Therapy, 48*(3), 322–334. doi:10.1016/j.beth.2016.12.003

Sheline, Y. I., Sanghavi, M., Mintun, M. A., & Gado, M. H. (1999). Depression duration but not age predicts hippocampal volume loss in medically healthy women with recurrent major depression. *Journal of Neuroscience, 19*, 5034–5043.

Slavich, G. M., Monroe, S. M., & Gotlib, I. H. (2011). Early parental loss and depression history: Associations with recent life stress in major depressive disorder. *Journal of Psychiatric Research, 45*(9), 1146–1152. doi:10.1016/j.jpsychires.2011.03.004

Smid, G. E., van Zuiden, M., Geuze, E., Kavelaars, A., Heijnen, C. J., & Vermetten, E. (2015). Cytokine production as a putative biological mechanism underlying stress sensitization in high combat exposed soldiers. *Psychoneuroendocrinology, 51*, 534–546. doi:10.1016/j.psyneuen.2014.07.010

Smith, P. H., Oberleitner, L. M. S., Smith, K. M. Z., & McKee, S. A. (2016). Childhood adversity interacts with adult stressful events to predict reduced likelihood of smoking cessation among women but not men. *Clinical Psychological Science, 4*(2), 183–193. doi:10.1177/2167702615584589

Starr, L. R., Hammen, C., Conway, C. C., Raposa, E., & Brennan, P. A. (2014). Sensitizing effect of early adversity on depressive reactions to later proximal stress: Moderation by polymorphisms in serotonin transporter and corticotropin releasing hormone receptor genes in a 20-year longitudinal study. *Development and Psychopathology, 26*(4, Pt 2), 1241–1254. doi:10.1017/S0954579414000996

Stroud, C. B., Davila, J., Vrshek-Schallhorn, S., & Hammen, C. (2017). *Testing stress sensitization: Is the enhanced impact of minor events with a history of depression due to the presence of major events?* Unpublished manuscript.

Stroud, C. B., Davila, J., Hammen, C., & Vrshek-Schallhorn, S. (2011). Severe and nonsevere events in first onsets versus recurrences of depression: Evidence for stress sensitization. *Journal of Abnormal Psychology, 120*(1), 142–154. doi:10.1037/a0021659

Stroud, C. B., Davila, J., & Moyer, A. (2008). The relationship between stress and depression in first onsets versus recurrences: A meta-analytic review. *Journal of Abnormal Psychology, 117*(1), 206–213. doi:10.1037/0021-843X.117.1.206

Swendsen, J., Hammen, C., Heller, T., & Gitlin, M. (1995). Correlates of stress reactivity in patients with bipolar disorder. *The American Journal of Psychiatry, 152*, 795–797.

Tarullo, A. R., & Gunnar, M. R. (2006). Child maltreatment and the developing HPA axis. *Hormones and Behavior, 50*(4), 632–639. doi:10.1016/j.yhbeh.2006.06.010

Treadway, M. T., Waskom, M. L., Dillon, D. G., Holmes, A. J., Park, M. T. M., Chakravarty, M. M, ... Pizzagalli, D. A. (2015). Illness progression, recent stress, and morphometry of hippocampal subfields and medial prefrontal cortex in major depression. *Biological Psychiatry, 77*(3), 285–294. doi:10.1016/j.biopsych.2014.06.018

Weiss, R. B., Stange, J. P., Boland, E. M., Black, S. K., LaBelle, D. R., Abramson, L. Y., & Alloy, L. B. (2015). Kindling of life stress in bipolar disorder: Comparison of sensitization and autonomy models. *Journal of Abnormal Psychology, 124*(1), 4–16. doi:10.1037/abn0000014 10.1037/abn0000014.supp (Supplemental)

Young-Wolff, K. C., Kendler, K. S., & Prescott, C. A. (2012). Interactive effects of childhood maltreatment and recent stressful life events on alcohol consumption in adulthood. *Journal of Studies on Alcohol and Drugs, 73*(4), 559–569. doi:10.15288/jsad.2012.73.559

Cognitive Risks

Translating Stress Into Psychopathology

Tina H. Schweizer *and* Benjamin L. Hankin

Abstract

This chapter focuses on how several prominent cognitive risk processes (attention bias, overgeneral autobiographical memory, executive functioning difficulties) and products (negative inferential style, dysfunctional attitudes, depressive rumination) may translate stress into different forms of prevalent psychopathologies, including internalizing (e.g., depression, anxiety) and externalizing disorders (e.g., conduct disorder). First, prominent conceptual models are presented that explain how cognitive risks relate to psychopathology and the interplay between stress and cognition in contributing to psychopathology. Second, the chapter describes how cognitive risks have typically been conceptualized and measured, and it reviews evidence on associations between each cognitive risk and different psychopathologies. Third, three conceptual models are presented that can be used to organize and understand the relations among stress, cognition, and psychopathology—(1) vulnerability-stress, (2) mechanism, and (3) transactional/bidirectional. Last, key future research directions are highlighted, including integrating cognitive risks across multiple units of analysis and establishing a taxonomy of cognitive risk.

Keywords: cognitive risk, stress, psychopathology, attention bias, overgeneral memory, executive functioning, rumination, negative inferential style, dysfunctional attitudes

This chapter centers on maladaptive cognitions that translate stress into different forms of psychopathology. We focus on six prominent cognitive risk *processes* and *products* (see R. E. Ingram, Miranda, & Segal, 1998 for discussion of differentiating cognitive processes and products as risks for psychopathology). Cognitive processes include attention bias, overgeneral autobiographical memory, and executive functioning difficulties. Cognitive products include negative inferential style, dysfunctional attitudes, and depressive rumination. First, we articulate prominent logical conceptual models that can be used as organizing frameworks to explain how cognitive products and processes relate to psychopathology and the interplay between stress and cognition in contributing to psychopathology. Second, we describe how well-studied cognitive risks have been typically conceptualized and measured, and

we review evidence that each of these cognitive risks is associated (concurrently or prospectively) with different forms of prevalent psychopathologies, including internalizing disorders (i.e., depression, bipolar disorder [BD], anxiety disorders), externalizing disorders (i.e., conduct disorder [CD], oppositional defiant disorder [ODD]), attention-deficit/hyperactivity disorder (ADHD), and schizophrenia. We introduce these cognitive risks and review the relevant evidence that they are related to multiple psychopathologies to provide necessary and relevant theoretical and empirical background before discussing the various ways in which cognition can translate stress into psychopathology. In the third section, we describe three conceptual models that can be used to organize and understand the relations among stress, cognition, and psychopathology. Last, we provide two key future research directions, including integrating cognitive risks across multiple units of analysis and the importance of establishing a taxonomy of cognitive risk.

Logical Conceptual Models of the Relationship Between Cognition and Psychopathology

It is important to consider different logical possibilities for how cognition relates to psychopathology, including acting as a correlate, consequence, risk factor/vulnerability, and causal risk factor (e.g., Kazdin, Kraemer, Kessler, Kupfer, & Offord, 1997; Kraemer, Stice, Kazdin, Offord, & Kupfer, 2001). A cognitive factor may be a *correlate* of psychopathology when the two variables are associated (Kazdin et al., 1997). This relationship is identified with cross-sectional or retrospective study designs. A cognitive factor may also be a *consequence* of psychopathology. Or it may be a *risk factor/vulnerability* when it is related to elevations in the probability of psychopathology as compared to the population base rate (Kazdin et al., 1997). Because consequence and risk/vulnerability conceptualizations include specific temporal relationships with psychopathology, prospective longitudinal designs are necessary to test these relationships. Lastly, a cognitive risk factor may act as a *causal risk factor* when the manipulation of the cognitive risk factor leads to changes in the probability of the outcome (psychopathology) (Kazdin et al., 1997). A causal risk factor relationship can be identified using naturalistic or laboratory experiments. Cognitive factors have largely been theorized as risk/vulnerability or causal risk factors; however, broadly speaking, there is variance across studies in the extent to which these relationships are examined with the appropriate designs.

Cognitive Risk Conceptualizations, Measurement, and Associations With Psychopathology

The following sections review evidence for each cognitive risk for psychopathology and relationships with some of the most prevalent, well-studied psychopathologies—depression, BD, PTSD, anxiety (mainly generalized anxiety disorder [GAD], social anxiety disorder [SAD], panic disorder [PD], obsessive-compulsive disorder [OCD]), externalizing disorders (CD, ODD), ADHD, and schizophrenia. We emphasize prior reviews, meta-analyses, and key empirical papers that have investigated associations between the cognitive factors and psychopathologies that are the focus of this chapter, and for which

there is a sufficient knowledge base upon which to draw conclusions.

Attentional Biases

Attentional bias occurs when attention is allocated to specific forms of affective stimuli in a way that is not adaptive (e.g., Beck & Clark, 1997; Mogg, Mathews, & Weinman, 1987; Mogg & Bradley, 2005). Most evidence for attentional biases is for depression and anxiety disorders (see Gibb et al., 2016; Hankin, Snyder, & Gulley, 2016a, for reviews). Three common aspects across most theoretical models of attentional bias are (1) *vigilance* or *orienting toward*, (2) *maintenance on* or *difficulty with disengagement from*, and (3) *avoidance of* affective stimuli (see Cisler & Koster, 2010, for review). Aspects of attentional bias are thought to occur along different time courses and can vary in the degree to which they occur automatically or voluntarily (Cisler & Koster, 2010; Gibb et al., 2016). *Vigilance* or *orienting toward* a specific form of affective stimuli refers to the ease with which attention is pulled toward an affective stimulus. This orienting bias is generally thought to occur at early, automatic stages of processing and is posited to reflect an evolutionarily adaptive early threat or saliency detection system. *Difficulty with disengagement* refers to the extent to which attention is "captured" by an affective stimulus such that the ability to shift attention to other stimuli is impeded. *Attentional avoidance* refers to the tendency for individuals to avoid attending to a certain form of affective stimulus by looking away from it (Williams et al., 1988). Difficulties with disengagement and attentional avoidance are both posited to occur during later stages of processing. Whereas disengagement difficulties may reflect top-down control difficulties (e.g., Eysenck et al., 2007), attentional avoidance is thought to be a strategic response in order to meet an emotion regulation goal of reducing distress (Gross & Thompson, 2007). These aspects of attentional bias are not mutually exclusive and may occur simultaneously, although they may function to maintain and exacerbate psychopathology in different ways (Cisler & Koster, 2010; Gibb et al., 2016).

Common Measures of Attentional Bias

Experimental psychopathologists have used various laboratory measures to assess attention bias, most often in cross-sectional case-control designs. Commonly used behavioral measures include the dot-probe task (MacLeod et al., 1986; Mogg et al., 1995) and an emotional variant of the Stroop task

(Williams, Mathews, & MacLeod, 1996), which both utilize response/reaction time (RT) as indicators of attention bias. In the dot-probe task, individuals respond as quickly as possible to a target cue (probe) that appears in place of either an emotional (e.g., sad, angry, happy face) or neutral (e.g., neutral face) stimulus. Quicker RT when the probe appears in the location of emotional as compared to neutral stimuli suggests *vigilance/orienting toward* emotional stimuli. In contrast, quicker RT for neutral relative to emotional stimuli is an indicator of *attentional avoidance* of emotional stimuli. In the emotional Stroop, individuals are asked to read aloud the color in which nonaffective (e.g., clock) and affective words (e.g., sad) are printed in and ignore the meaning of the words. Slower RT for naming the color of affective words indicates attention bias for emotional stimuli. Though both the dot-probe and emotional Stroop are widely used, they have poor reliability (e.g., Brown et al., 2014; Kappenman et al., 2014; Price et al., 2015; Schmukle, 2005), and attentional biases are *inferred from RT* as opposed to being directly measured. More recently, eye-tracking paradigms have been utilized because they track eye movements continuously (see Armstrong & Olatunji, 2012) and show higher reliability than RT measures (Price et al., 2015). Eye tracking is commonly used either with free-viewing tasks or by supplementing RT tasks with eye tracking (e.g., Price et al., 2015).

Threat Stimuli Bias

There is solid evidence for an *orienting or vigilance* bias to threat (e.g., angry, fearful faces; threat words) across studies of youth and adults with anxiety symptoms and diagnoses as compared to nonanxious individuals based on RT and eye-tracking tasks (Armstrong & Olatunji, 2012; Bar-Haim et al., 2007; Cisler & Koster, 2010; Dudeney, Sharpe, & Hunt, 2015; Gibb et al., 2016; Goodwin et al., 2017; Gotlib & Joormann, 2010; Arditte & Joormann, 2014; Peckham et al., 2010). Biased attention toward threat is seen across GAD, OCD, SAD, PD, and specific phobia in youth and adults (Armstrong & Olatunji, 2012; Bar-Haim et al., 2007; Goodwin et al., 2017; Puliafico & Kendall, 2006). Some research supports attention bias to threat as a risk and causal risk to anxiety. Attention bias to threat longitudinally predicts anxiety symptoms among youth and adults (e.g., Beevers & Carver, 2003; Pérez-Edgar et al., 2011; see Van Bockstaele et al., 2014, for review). Experimental inductions of threat bias increase stress reactivity in nondisordered youth and

adults (Eldar, Ricon & Bar-Haim, 2008; Mathews & MacLeod, 2002), and modification of attention biases using altered dot-probe tasks may be an effective treatment for anxiety disorders (see Kuckertz & Amir, 2015, for review). A relatively smaller body of findings in adults and youth has found *vigilance-avoidance* (Calvo & Avero, 2005; In-Albon et al., 2010; Monk et al., 2006; Schofield et al., 2013) and *avoidance* (e.g., Monk et al., 2006; Pflugshaupt et al., 2005; Salum et al., 2013; Waters, Bradley, & Mogg, 2014) patterns in response to threat (e.g., fear, anger) stimuli for different forms of anxiety, including GAD, separation anxiety, and specific phobia.

Most work on attention bias and threat has focused on anxiety; however, there is some evidence indicating that threat bias is related to other forms of psychopathology, including depression. Threat bias in depression has shown both an *avoidance* and *orienting* pattern. For instance, longitudinal studies of adolescents showed that youth at genetic risk (homozygous short allele of 5-HTTLPR) who avoided angry faces exhibited greater MDD onset over prospective follow-up (Jenness, Young, & Hankin, 2017), and adolescents with clinical anxiety who avoided fearful faces developed greater depression symptoms across 2 years (Price et al., 2016). In contrast, other work found that children and adolescents with higher distress-related disorders (including depression) exhibited vigilance toward angry faces (Salum et al., 2013). Similarly, adult women with remitted MDD demonstrated preferential attention for angry faces, and those who looked at angry faces longer experienced shorter latency to MDD onset (Woody, Owens, Burkhouse, & Gibb, 2016). Taken together, these findings could suggest that attentional avoidance of threat-related emotion confers risk to depression given that behavioral avoidance and disengagement predicts worse adjustment and psychological functioning (Seiffge-Krenke & Klessinger, 2000). However, once an individual develops a current negative mood state (or depression), biases may turn toward self-referential negative emotional stimuli (Mogg & Bradley, 2005).

Dysphoric Stimuli Bias

Most work focused on attention bias for dysphoric stimuli (e.g., sad faces) has been conducted in individuals with depression and suggests *difficulties with disengagement* from dysphoric stimuli (e.g., Mogg & Bradley, 2005). Currently depressed, as well as remitted individuals, tend to exhibit preferential attention for and stare longer at sad stimuli (see Armstrong & Olatunji, 2012, for review). Studies conducted with clinical as well as general community participants across the life span, and using both emotional words and faces as stimuli, find that depression is also associated with an *orienting* bias for dysphoric stimuli (Peckham, McHugh, & Otto, 2010). Attention biases for dysphoric stimuli do not appear to be state dependent. Attention bias to negative stimuli (e.g., sad faces) has been obtained in adults (Peckham et al., 2010) and youth (Hankin, Gibb et al., 2010) with remitted depression. In addition, adults with depression show comparable levels of attentional interference regardless of sad mood induction (Epp, Dobson, Dozois, & Frewen, 2012).

Attention biases for dysphoric stimuli appear to be a risk factor for depression, though the specific pattern of attention bias among youth follows both an *orienting* and *avoidance* pattern.[1] Orienting toward dysphoric stimuli (sad faces) has been found in youth with clinical depression (and no comorbid anxiety) (Hankin, Gibb, Abela, & Flory, 2010). Similarly, greater orienting toward dysphoric stimuli is positively correlated with depression symptoms in youth regardless of psychiatric history (i.e., depression or anxiety history, or no psychiatric history) (Sylvester, Hudziak, Gaffrey, Barch, & Luby, 2016). Some work suggests that youth at risk for depression exhibit orienting bias. Research shows that never-disordered children and adolescents of mothers with depression history displayed bias toward sad faces (Joormann, Talbot, & Gotlib, 2007; Kujawa et al., 2011). In contrast, other work found *avoidance* of sad faces in youth. Children with current depression have exhibited attentional avoidance of sad faces as compared to never-depressed children (Harrison & Gibb, 2015). In addition, youth at risk for depression have also exhibited attentional avoidance. For instance, infants of depressed mothers spend less time looking at their mothers than infants of nondepressed mothers (Boyd, Zayas, & McKee, 2006). Similarly, two studies focused on youth of depressed mothers found attentional avoidance of sad faces (Connell et al., 2013; Gibb, et al., 2009), though these effects arose in interaction with other vulnerability factors, including child's level of trait suppression (Connell et al., 2013) and genotype (Gibb et al., 2009). Overall, results are mixed for patterns of attention bias in youth, which may, in part, be due to methodological differences across studies (e.g., the use of dot probe vs. eye tracking, or the inclusion of sad mood induction or not).

Positive Attentional Bias

Depressed adults tend to exhibit attentional *avoidance* or lack attention toward happy and positive emotional stimuli (Armstrong & Olatunji, 2012; Duque & Vazquez, 2015; Peckham et al., 2010; Winer & Salem, 2016). There is also some evidence for positive stimuli attentional biases in BD and SAD. Some work indicates that adults with BD exhibit a bias *toward* positive stimuli during current manic states (Murphy et al., 1999) and after positive mood induction (Roiser et al., 2009; Trevisani, Johnson, & Carver, 2008), but not in the absence of a positive mood induction (García-Blanco, Salmerón, Perea, & Livianos, 2014; Jabben et al., 2012). Individuals with BD also have been found to demonstrate *avoidance* of positive stimuli while they are currently experiencing depression (García-Blanco et al., 2014; Jabben et al., 2012; Jongen et al., 2007). Similarly, several studies of individuals with SAD have found evidence for avoidance of positive stimuli, including faces (Byrow, Chen, & Peters, 2016; Chen, Clarke, MacLeod, & Guastella, 2012; Schofield et al., 2013; Liang, Tsai, & Hsu, 2017).

Comorbidity

Comorbidity among disorders is highly prevalent (Merikangas et al., 2010), but research is limited on how attentional biases present for individuals with comorbid disorders. Most of the work has focused on the co-occurrence of depression with different forms of anxiety. For instance, one study of adults indicated that those with SAD only, but not those with comorbid SAD and depression, exhibited attentional bias *toward* social threat words (Musa et al., 2003), whereas other work of adults with comorbid SAD and depression, but not those with SAD only, exhibited attentional *avoidance* of angry faces (LeMoult & Joormann, 2012). Adolescents with a "pure" anxiety disorder (i.e., separation, SAD, GAD, panic, PTSD), and no comorbid depression, demonstrated attentional bias *toward* angry faces; those with pure depression exhibited bias *toward sad* faces; and those with comorbid depression and anxiety demonstrated biases *toward both* angry and sad faces (Hankin et al., 2010).

In sum, different patterns of attentional biases (i.e., orienting, difficulty with disengagement, avoidance) for different forms of emotional stimuli (i.e., threat, dysphoric, positive) show specificity and overlap in relation to psychopathological outcomes. For instance, whereas attentional biases in anxiety appear to be specific to threat or fear stimuli (e.g., fearful faces), attentional biases in depression have been centered on sadness or themes of loss (e.g., sad faces). At the same time, however, research also suggests that some attentional bias patterns are present for multiple forms of psychopathology (e.g., attention bias toward angry faces in both anxiety and depression). This suggests that some attentional bias patterns may be transdiagnostic, related to broad dimensions of psychopathology (e.g., internalizing spectrum), and could reflect symptom clusters or emotional dysregulation that cuts across disorders.

Overgeneral Autobiographical Memory

Autobiographical memories contain knowledge about specific past life events (i.e., episodic memories) as well as more abstract, conceptual knowledge about facts or ideas about the self (i.e., semantic memories) (Conway & Pleydell-Pearce, 2000; Renoult, Davidson, Palombo, Moscovitch, & Levine, 2012). *Overgeneral autobiographical memory* (OGM) is considered an autobiographical memory problem in which some individuals tend to recall personal memories that are less specific, elaborate, and detailed (Williams & Broadbent, 1986). One prominent model (CaR-FA-X; Williams, 2006) posits that OGM arises from three main processes that can work independently or in interaction with one another—capture of attention and rumination (CaR), functional avoidance (FA), and executive functioning difficulties (X). According to this model, self-related memories are hypothesized to be organized hierarchically with more abstract, conceptual information organized at the highest level, while more detailed, specific information is located at the lowest level (Conway, 2001; Conway & Fthenaki, 2000; Conway, Pleydell-Pearce, & Whitecross, 2001). When self-relevant information is activated, attention is "captured" at the higher, abstract echelon of memory, which contributes to rumination and impedes the retrieval of lower level, specific memories. Functional avoidance (FA) of specific memories is thought to initially occur in response to early traumatic experiences as a means to regulate emotion (Williams et al., 1996). Over time through negative reinforcement, avoidance of specific negative memories becomes generalized to other memories (i.e., neutral and positive) as a stable memory style. Executive function (X) impairments are thought to hinder retrieval and search processes for specific memories. Thus, although OGM retrieval may initially help an individual to avoid distressing emotions linked to aversive memories (Ganly, Salmon, & McDowall, 2016; Williams

et al. 2007), this pattern may become rigid, harmful, and contribute to psychopathology (Hermans et al. 2008).

Assessment of Overgeneral Autobiographical Memory

OGM is most commonly assessed with cue-word paradigms. In particular, in the Autobiographical Memory Test (AMT; Williams & Broadbent, 1986) individuals are asked to recall a memory of a specific time and place in response to positive (e.g., happy), negative (e.g., failure), or neutral (e.g., bread) cue words that are then scored for degree of specificity. Specific memories are those that happened at a particular time and place and lasted for less than one day (e.g., "The day I adopted my cat"), whereas general memories encompass repeated events (categoric memories; e.g., "When I'm at school"), or events lasting longer than one day (extended memories; e.g., "My trip to Hawaii"). More overgeneral and fewer specific memories both reflect OGM, which has been considered a vulnerability for psychopathology (Williams et al., 2007).

Overgeneral Autobiographical Memory and Psychopathology

Research has primarily focused on the relations between OGM and PTSD or depression. This corpus of work shows concurrent and predictive relationships across time using prospective designs. In addition, OGM persists during depression remission and does not appear to be due to trauma exposure alone. There is a large effect of OGM in individuals with PTSD (Moore & Zoellner, 2007; Ono et al., 2016; Williams et al., 2007) and among adults and youth with depression (Hitchcock et al., 2014; Liu et al., 2013; Ono et al., 2016). OGM prospectively predicts PTSD symptoms after exposure to trauma (e.g., Bryant et al., 2007; Hauer et al., 2009), and it predicts the onset, recurrence, and severity of depression over time among adults (Sumner, Griffith, & Mineka, 2010; Van Daele et al., 2014). Among youth at risk for depression (i.e., familial risk, elevated depression symptoms), OGM predicts the first onset (Hipwell et al., 2011; Rawal & Rice, 2012) and recurrence of depression (Sumner et al., 2011). Contextual and individual difference factors may influence the OGM-depression link. Prospective studies of community samples of youth have only found OGM effects for depression in conjunction with other risks (e.g., high levels of rumination and stress; Hamlat et al., 2015) or have not found a relationship between OGM and depression in youth

(Crane et al. 2015; Gutenbrunner et al., 2017). Gutenbrunner and colleagues (2017) propose that OGM may elevate risk for already susceptible individuals, whereas it may be more transient and not necessarily maladaptive for low-risk individuals.

OGM remains a retrieval style even after remission from depression (King et al., 2010; Kuyken & Dalgleish, 2011; Rawal & Rice, 2012). In addition, OGM exhibits modest levels of stability across several years in adolescents and young adults, suggesting that OGM may be a trait-like vulnerability (Sumner et al., 2014). Finally, OGM does not appear to be a result of trauma exposure alone. Some meta-analyses of children, adolescents (Hitchcock et al., 2014), and adults (Ono et al., 2016) indicate that individuals exposed to trauma (without clinical levels of psychopathology) exhibit higher OGM as compared to controls. In contrast, other work has not consistently found a link between trauma exposure alone (without psychopathology) and OGM (Moore & Zoellner, 2007; Williams et al., 2007). In addition, when links between trauma and OGM are found, the effect of trauma on OGM is weaker than the effect of psychopathology on OGM (Ono et al., 2016). Inconsistent findings may, in part, be due to low statistical power, given that there can be small sample sizes for certain types of trauma (e.g., sexual abuse, emotional abuse) (Sumner et al., 2011). Taken together, trauma exposure may not be a necessary or sufficient condition for OGM to develop, though it may relate to elevations in OGM and psychopathology for some individuals.

A relatively smaller body of work has investigated OGM in relation to other psychopathologies. There is a large effect for OGM in clinical samples with schizophrenia as compared to controls, and this effect is not explained by premorbid IQ or depressive symptoms (Berna et al., 2015). Individuals with BD in a euthymic state also show greater OGM as compared to controls (Boulanger, Lejeune, & Blairy, 2013; Kim et al., 2014). Individuals with OCD, as compared to controls, had greater OGM, but this effect was related to comorbid depression (Wilhelm, McNally, Baer, & Florin, 1997). Most evidence, predominantly based on clinical samples of adults, suggests that OGM is not related to anxiety (e.g., GAD, PD, SAD, specific phobia, OCD) (Burke & Mathews, 1992; Heidenreich, Junghanns-Royack, Rawal, & Rice, 2012; Wenzel & Cochran, 2006; Wenzel, Jackson, & Holt, 2002; Wessel et al., 2001; Williams et al, 2007; Zlomuzica et al., 2014; but see Gutenbrunner, Salmon, & Jose, 2017; Hallford & Mellor, 2017, for exceptions).

In sum, there is solid evidence for the association of OGM with PTSD and depression, and a growing body of work suggesting that OGM is a risk factor for these psychopathologies. There is emerging evidence for links with schizophrenia, BD, and OCD. Though there have been some inconsistencies, most evidence suggests that OGM is not related to anxiety.

Executive Functioning

Executive functioning (EF) is important for the self-regulation of thoughts, emotions, and behaviors, as well as for decision making, evaluating risks, planning for the future, and adapting to new situations. Executive functioning includes multiple higher level processes that control or regulate lower level responses (e.g., perceptual, motor) in flexible ways in order to attain goals (e.g., Banich, 2009; Miyake & Friedman, 2012). One prominent model of EF is the unity/diversity model (Miyake & Friedman, 2012). According to the unity/diversity model, there are three major components of EF— *shifting, inhibition*, and *updating* working memory. Performance on behavioral measures tapping these abilities tends to correlate with one another, which reflects an underlying common EF ability or "unity" across these dimensions (Miyake & Friedman, 2012). Common EF is hypothesized to be the ability to monitor and maintain goals as well as contextual information (e.g., the goal of finishing reading this chapter) (Miyake & Friedman, 2012). In addition to common EF, shifting and updating also show some separability, or "diversity," as indicated by unique variance in test performance tapping these aspects, which is left over after the common variance across measures has been accounted for (Miyake & Friedman, 2012). Interestingly, there is no inhibition specific variance (i.e., inhibition is fully explained by common EF), though researchers still tend to focus on inhibition as a separable aspect of EF. *Working memory* is also commonly considered as another important aspect of EF (e.g., Repovs & Baddeley, 2006). It is worth noting that EF is commonly measured with neuropsychological tasks, which tend to tap several aspects of EF at once. Though not discussed here, there are other behavioral tasks that are more "pure" measures of particular components of EF (see Snyder, Miyake, & Hankin, 2015).

Executive Functioning Components: Shifting, Inhibition, Updating, and Working Memory

Shifting involves switching between task sets (e.g., switching between reading this chapter, surfing the

Web, and reading again). One widely used traditional neuropsychological measure of shifting is the Wisconsin Card Sorting Task (WCST). Shifting ability is reflected by perseverative errors, or persisting in sorting cards according to a rule after receiving feedback that the rule no longer applies, and the number of switches to a different sorting rule. *Inhibition* entails resisting a prepotent (automatic) response and instead engaging in a less automatic yet task-relevant response (e.g., resisting an automatic urge to frolic in the sunshine outside and instead stay inside and read this chapter). A common neuropsychological measure of inhibition is the Color-Word Stroop. *Updating* includes monitoring and identifying task-relevant information as well as replacing information in working memory that is no longer relevant with newer, pertinent information (e.g., monitoring this chapter and identifying a piece of relevant information, holding it in working memory, and then replacing it with the next piece of information). An experimental task measuring updating includes the Verbal *n*-back task, where individuals indicate if the stimulus (e.g., letter) matches the stimulus that was presented *n* items back. *Working memory* (WM) can be broken down into two capacities—*maintenance* and *manipulation* (Repovs & Baddeley, 2006). Both of these aspects involve actively holding information (e.g., numbers, shapes) in mind across a short delay; however, WM manipulation involves changing the information, whereas WM maintenance does not. A common neuropsychological task for WM maintenance is the Digit Span Forward, where individuals repeat a sequence of numbers in forward order. WM manipulation is commonly assessed via Digit Span Backward, where individuals repeat a sequence of numbers in reverse order.

Executive Functioning Components and Psychopathology

Individuals with schizophrenia show the most consistent and pronounced difficulties across aspects of EF. Large effects exist for impairment across measures of shifting, inhibition, updating, and WM manipulation; and medium effects are seen for WM maintenance (Snyder et al., 2015). Some work supports the possibility that impairment in EF may serve as a risk factor for schizophrenia. Children, adolescents, and young adults having clinical symptoms or familial risk show EF impairments that are intermediate between controls and those who develop the disorder (Agnew-Blais & Seidman, 2013; Bora et al., 2014; Fusar-poli et al., 2012). In addi-

tion, adolescents with psychosis risk syndrome show small impairments in EF relative to controls, which become more severe in those who develop the disorder (Giuliano et al., 2012). Lastly, EF difficulties increase with the first onset of a psychotic episode followed by stabilization over time (Lewandowski et al., 2011).

Individuals with BD and MDD exhibit relatively uniform difficulties across all components of EF, though they are not as severe as those seen in individuals with schizophrenia (Snyder et al., 2015). Moreover, the extant data suggest that certain aspects of EF may have state-like qualities, whereas others may be enduring, trait-like features that exist before disorder onset and persist after disorder remission. Individuals with BD show medium effects for performance on tasks tapping shifting, inhibition, and WM manipulation, and a small effect for verbal WM maintenance. Little work has examined updating in individuals with BD. These results are largely based on studies of individuals with euthymic BD, which suggests that these difficulties persist across mood states in both adult (Snyder et al., 2015) and youth samples (Elias et al., 2017). Furthermore, children and adolescents with BD generally show comparable effect sizes to those in adults (Elias et al., 2017; Walshaw, Alloy, & Sabb, 2010), suggesting that EF difficulties are present early in BD and may be stable over development.

Adults with MDD have consistently shown small to medium effects on tasks tapping shifting, inhibition, updating, and WM (Snyder, 2013; Snyder et al., 2015). However, studies of youth have been equivocal. One meta-analysis indicated that children and adolescents with MDD had moderate impairments in inhibition, WM, and shifting (Wagner, Müller, Helmreich, Huss, & Tadic, 2015), whereas a different review did not find impairments in inhibition or WM (Vilgis et al., 2015). It is also unclear if EF impairments are risks or scars of depressive disorder. Some work indicates that EF impairments persist when individuals are in depression remission, suggesting that difficulties are not dependent on mood (Snyder, 2013). In contrast, other work shows impairment in particular aspects of EF (i.e., WM, inhibition) during the first episode of depression, while shifting normalizes during remission (Ahern & Semkovska, 2017).

Research examining OCD and PTSD has generally shown medium to small effect sizes across all domains of EF. Individuals with OCD show small effects for shifting, inhibition, and WM and a large effect for updating. However, simple WM maintenance is not impacted in individuals with OCD. It is also important to note that although OCD and MDD co-occur, EF difficulties are not explained by depression symptoms as EF difficulties persist at the same level even when there are low levels of depression (Snyder et al., 2015). Though based on a relatively small body of studies, adolescents and children with OCD have comparable performance to that of controls across measures of inhibition, shifting, and WM (Abramovitch et al., 2015). Individuals with PTSD show medium effects for shifting and small effects for WM compared to those who were trauma exposed but who did not develop PTSD (Polak et al., 2012). Some meta-analytic work with individuals with PTSD shows no significant difference on inhibition as measured via the Stroop (Polak et al., 2012); however, another review, including multiple inhibition tasks, found that individuals with PTSD do have inhibition difficulties (Aupperle et al., 2012). Another meta-analysis found that when collapsing across all kinds of EF tasks, there was a relatively moderate effect of EF impairment (Scott et al., 2015). It is important to note that concurrent depression may explain EF impairment; however, more work is needed with individuals who have PTSD without depression (Polak et al., 2012).

Relatively less work has examined EF and other disorders. Extant literature shows inconsistent results for links with anxiety. Regarding shifting, some work has found evidence for difficulties in individuals with SAD, GAD, and PD (Airaksinen et al., 2005; Cohen et al., 1996; Mantella et al., 2007), whereas other work has not found significant differences (Airaksinen et al., 2005; Boldrini et al., 2005; Purcell et al., 1998). As for inhibition, some research shows no impairment for GAD (Price & Mohlman, 2007). In contrast, individuals with trait anxiety (e.g., worry) have difficulties with inhibition of competing responses (Bishop, 2008; Eysenck & Derakshan, 2011; Snyder et al., 2010, 2014). Last, moderate effects of WM underperformance are found in anxious individuals (e.g., worry, arousal symptoms, GAD) (Moran, 2016). ADHD shows small-to-medium effects for shifting, inhibition, and WM manipulation; and a small effect for WM maintenance across studies of children and adults (Snyder et al., 2015). Little research has investigated updating and ADHD (Snyder et al., 2015). EF difficulties are present in ODD and CD; however, these may also be explained by concurrent ADHD (Ogilvie et al., 2011).

In sum, there is strong evidence that there are EF difficulties across most forms of psychopathology, though the magnitude of impairment varies depending on the form of psychopathology and aspect of EF. EF impairment may be a transdiagnostic intermediate phenotypic risk factor for psychological disorders (McTeague, Goodkind, & Etkin, 2016).

Cognitive Products
Negative Inferential Style

Negative inferential style (NIS) is the tendency to interpret the causes of undesirable events as internal (i.e., due to one's self and not external circumstances), stable (i.e., likely to recur), and global (i.e., likely to impact other domains of life) and to make negative inferences about the self (e.g., that one is inept) and the consequences of negative events (i.e., other aversive outcomes will follow) (Abramson et al., 1989). NIS is conceptualized as a cognitive vulnerability that increases risk for psychopathology in response to negative events (i.e., the cognitive vulnerability-stress model), so researchers have most often examined the interaction between stressful life events and NIS predicting later psychopathology. Most work has focused on depression. More recently, NIS has also been related to BD, and there is emerging evidence for links with PTSD, ADHD, and schizophrenia.

NIS in interaction with stress prospectively predicts changes in symptoms, first onset, and recurrence of MDD, as well as symptoms and diagnoses of BD, suggesting that NIS functions as a risk factor for mood disorders (Abela & Hankin, 2008; Alloy, Abramson, Walshaw, & Neeren, 2006). Studies examining whether NIS is a trait-like vulnerability that persists regardless of current mood, or whether it is dependent upon a depressive mood state, have focused on individuals with remitted MDD or BD. Evidence has been mixed, with some studies showing that individuals in remission no longer exhibit NIS, whereas other studies show that individuals in remission still exhibit NIS (see Hankin et al., 2016a for review). NIS shows moderate levels of trait-like stability over time (Hankin, Fraley, & Abela, 2005; Hankin, 2008).

NIS is concurrently and longitudinally associated with PTSD (Elwood, Hahn, et al., 2009; Palker-Corell & Marcus, 2004; Runyon & Kenny, 2002), as well as ADHD in adults (see Rucklidge, Brown, Crawford, & Kaplan, 2007, for review). Individuals with schizophrenia exhibit NIS when they are currently experiencing symptoms (Aakre et al., 2009). Little work has investigated associations with CD/ODD, and findings have been mixed. For instance, one study of early adolescents suggests NIS is concurrently associated with ODD as well as greater lifetime externalizing diagnoses (Alloy et al., 2012). In contrast, other work with youth examining vulnerability-stress models shows that NIS interacts with stress to prospectively predict depression, but not externalizing problems (Hankin, 2008; Robinson, Garber, & Hilsman, 1995).

Most work has not found a concurrent or prospective relationship between NIS, either independently or in interaction with stress, and multiple forms of anxiety (e.g., GAD, symptoms of anxious arousal, phobias, OCD) in adolescents or adults (e.g. Alloy et al., 2006; Alloy & Clements, 1998; Hankin, Abramson, Miller, & Haeffel, 2004; Hankin, 2008). However, one study of early adolescents found concurrent associations between NIS and particular anxiety disorders (e.g., social anxiety disorder) and symptoms (e.g., physical, separation) (Alloy et al., 2012). Mixed results may, in part, be due to the forms of anxiety studied and the age of the sample.

Dysfunctional Attitudes

Dysfunctional attitudes (DAs) reflect relatively stable, maladaptive, depressive self-schemas, or cognitive structures that are composed of beliefs about the self, relationships with others, and the world. When activated (e.g., by stress), they bias information processing (e.g., attention, memory retrieval) toward schema-congruent information rather than positive or neutral information and influence how an individual perceives, encodes, and interprets information (Beck, 1976; Beck & Haigh, 2014). There is solid evidence that DAs function as a risk factor for depression and are associated with schizophrenia. Other forms of dysfunctional beliefs have been found in BD and anxiety disorders. DAs exhibit moderate stability, when assessed repeatedly over time, suggesting they are trait-like (Hankin, 2008).

DAs are associated with depression, both concurrently and prospectively, in children, adolescents, and adults (Abela & Hankin, 2008; Alloy, Abramson, Walshaw, & Neeren, 2006; Hankin et al., 2016a; Jacobs et al., 2008). Thus, DA functions as a risk factor for depression. Some work shows that DAs are more specifically related to depression, and not anxiety, in cross-sectional and longitudinal studies (e.g., Alloy et al., 2006; Hankin, Abramson, Miller, & Haeffel, 2004). Individuals with schizophrenia exhibit DAs (Grant & Beck, 2009; Horan et al., 2010; Rector, 2004).

Depressive Rumination

Depressive rumination entails dwelling on the potential meaning, causes, and consequences of one's problems, concerns, or symptoms of distress (e.g., sad mood) (Nolen-Hoeksema, 1991; Nolen-Hoeksema, Wisco, & Lyubomirsky, 2008; Watkins, 2008). Rumination was originally theorized to explain gender differences in depression (Nolen-Hoeksema, 1991) and has been extended to other psychopathologies, suggesting that it is a transdiagnostic process (Nolen-Hoeksema & Watkins, 2011).

A large body of evidence suggests that rumination is a risk factor for mood disorders, including MDD and BD. Rumination is concurrently and longitudinally associated with depressive symptoms, and it predicts clinical depression onset and recurrence in studies of children, adolescents, and adults (e.g., Abela & Hankin, 2011; Aldao, Nolen-Hoeksema, & Schweizer, 2010; Hankin et al., 2016a; Rood et al., 2009). Depressive rumination is associated with increases in depression, but not mania (Alloy et al., 2009). It may be a risk factor for BD, given that higher levels of rumination were found in those at risk for the disorder (Johnson et al., 2008). Rumination also appears to be trait-like as indicated by moderate levels of stability over time (Hankin, 2008), and cross-sectional work showing that individuals remitted from MDD (Watkins, 2008) and BD (Thomas et al., 2007) exhibit similar levels of rumination as those who are currently diagnosed. Experimental studies show that inductions of rumination exacerbate sad mood, suggesting that it may be a causal risk factor (see Nolen-Hoeksema et al., 2008).

The link between depressive rumination and anxiety is well supported (e.g., Nolen-Hoeksema & Watkins, 2011), though the magnitude of the relationship may not be a strong as with depression (Olatunji et al., 2013). Individuals with anxiety disorders (e.g., GAD, SAD, PD, OCD) exhibit strong effects for rumination relative to controls (Olatunji et al., 2013). Rumination has been concurrently and longitudinally associated with changes in generalized anxiety symptoms in adults and youth (Fresco, Frankel, Mennin, Turk, & Heimberg, 2002; Harrington & Blankenship, 2002; Hong, 2007; McLaughlin & Nolen-Hoeksema, 2011), suggesting that it is a risk factor for anxiety. Experimental inductions of rumination exacerbate anxiety in already-anxious individuals and among individuals focusing on anxious themes (Blagden & Craske, 1996; McLaughlin, Borkovec, & Sibrava, 2007), indicating that it may be a causal risk factor for anxiety. Last, depressive rumination relates to aggression (McLaughlin, Aldao, Wisco, & Hilt, 2014), PTSD (Elwood et al., 2007), substance abuse (Nolen-Hoeksema & Harrell, 2002), and eating pathology (Holm-Denoma & Hankin, 2010; Nolen-Hoeksema et al., 2007; Selby et al., 2008).

Cognitive Risk, Stress, and Psychopathology

The interplay of cognitive risk and stress contributes to the development and maintenance of psychopathology. Research focusing on the dynamics of cognitive risk and stress has conceptualized and measured stress in many different ways (e.g., see Monroe & Slavich, this volume, for a more detailed review of stress conceptualization and measurement). A common conceptualization of stress is in terms of *negative life events*, or *stressors*, that are typically assessed through questionnaires or objective contextual stress interviews. Features of negative life events can be conceptualized and measured along several dimensions, including temporal distance from psychopathology (distal to proximal), severity (minor hassles to major events), chronicity (acute events to chronic stress), domain (e.g., interpersonal, academic), and dependence-independence (i.e., the extent to which a stressor is related to an individual's characteristics or behavior). Other approaches include *experimental manipulations* of stress in lab settings (e.g., social challenge tasks such as public speaking or the Trier Social Stress Test; Kirschbaum, Pirke, & Hellhammer, 1993) or following individuals longitudinally through periods of *naturalistic stress-exposure* (e.g., transition to college, war, natural disaster).

In this section, we focus on three broad conceptual models to describe how cognitive risks can translate stress into psychopathology—*vulnerability-stress, mechanism*, and *transactional/bi-directional models*. Cognitive vulnerability has been conceptualized differently across theoretical models, but some core principles are that cognitive vulnerability is often considered a predisposition that makes individuals susceptible to psychopathology, is trait-like and stable but not immutable, and is typically dormant until activated (Ingram et al., 1998; Monroe & Simons, 1991). In the following sections, we provide an overview of each of these frameworks and describe empirical work that has tested these models. Because prospective or experimental designs, as compared to cross-sectional work, are better suited to examine the temporal relationships among cognitive vulnerabilities, stress, and psycho-

pathology, the evidence reviewed next focuses on these designs whenever possible.

Cognitive Vulnerability-Stress Model

Several types of vulnerability-stress models have been articulated for different forms of psychopathology (e.g., Ingram & Price, 2001). These models generally propose that a combined effect of vulnerability and stress contributes to psychopathology, though the relationship between the vulnerability and the stressor may take different forms (e.g., see Monroe & Simons, 1991; Ingram & Luxton, 2005). Here, we focus on the most commonly studied model—an interactive or *moderation* model. According to this perspective, the moderator (cognitive vulnerability) affects the strength or direction of the relationship between the independent variable (stress exposure) and the outcome (psychopathology) (Kraemer et al., 2001). One of the most commonly studied and well-supported examples of this moderation model postulates that individuals with high cognitive vulnerability may have comparable levels of risk for psychopathology as those who have low cognitive vulnerability under low levels of stress. However, at high levels of stress, those with cognitive vulnerability are hypothesized to exhibit heightened levels of psychopathology relative to those who do not possess equally high cognitive risk. In other words, the relationship between higher stress levels and psychopathology is stronger when individuals possess higher cognitive vulnerability.

This cognitive vulnerability-stress moderation model has been supported extensively in studies of cognitive product interpretation biases, particularly regarding depression. For instance, negative life events interact with negative inferential style, dysfunctional attitudes, and depressive rumination to longitudinally predict depressive symptoms and disorder (see Abramson & Alloy, 2006; Abela & Hankin, 2008; Gibb & Coles, 2005; Hankin et al., 2016a; Ingram, Miranda, & Segal, 2006; Jacobs, Reinecke, Gollan, & Kane, 2008; Lakdawalla, Hankin, & Mermelstein, 2007; Lyubomirsky, Layous, Chancellor, & Nelson, 2015, for reviews).

Relatively fewer studies have examined the cognitive vulnerability-stress moderation hypothesis for other cognitive vulnerabilities, such as attentional bias, EF, and OGM, using longitudinal designs or naturalistic stressors. However, evidence suggests that these cognitive processes also contribute to heightened psychopathology symptoms after stress-exposure. For instance, prospective studies of adults indicate that maladaptive attentional bias predicts greater emotional distress following a medical stressor (i.e., diagnosis, failed treatment) (MacLeod & Hagan, 1992; Verhaak, Smeenk, van Minnen, & Kraaimaat, 2004); higher depressive symptoms following negative life events (Beevers & Carver, 2003); and elevated depression and anxiety symptoms across the transition to college (Osinsky, Losch, Hennig, Alexander, & MacLeod, 2012). Longitudinal evidence suggests that different patterns of attentional bias predispose individuals to various manifestations of psychopathology in response to stress. Soldiers showing attentional avoidance of fearful faces at predeployment later developed higher PTSD symptoms after exposure to war-zone stress, whereas soldiers showing difficulties with disengagement from sad faces at predeployment developed higher depression symptoms after exposure to war-zone stress (Beevers, Lee, Wells, Ellis, & Telch, 2011). Youth with EF difficulties show increased vulnerability to stress. Adolescents with poorer EF prospectively show elevations in depression symptoms when they experience negative life events (Lien, Yang, Kuo, & Chen, 2011), as well as higher depression symptoms in the context of a current episode of parental depression (Davidovich et al., 2016). OGM prospectively predicted elevations in depression symptoms among college students who experienced chronic hassles and high stressful life events (Anderson, Goddard, & Powell, 2009; Gibbs & Rude, 2004); depressive episode recurrence among adolescents who experienced high chronic interpersonal stress (Sumner et al., 2011); and depressive symptoms among adolescents who experienced emotional abuse (Stange et al., 2013).

Mechanism Model

The *mechanism model* is a *mediation* model. Here, the relationship between stress and psychopathology is explained by cognitive vulnerability. In other words, stress affects variability in cognitive risk, which in turn contributes to psychopathology (Kraemer et al., 2001). We focus on two ways that this mediation relationship has been examined. The first pathway occurs over a relatively long period of time whereby early adverse life stress contributes to the formation of cognitive vulnerability and, thereafter, onset of psychopathology later on in life. The second pathway unfolds over a shorter time period, such as within months, weeks, or days, and is concerned with how life stressors activate cognitive vulnerabilities that lead to psychopathology. A helpful theoretical distinction between these two patterns is

that the measurement of stress experience is more *distal* or *proximal* to the assessment of psychopathology. Whereas a distal stressor is temporally further away in time from psychopathology, proximal stressors occur closer in time to psychopathology.

Although we discuss these pathways separately next, we note that they are not mutually exclusive and may function simultaneously. In addition, few studies have included and tested all of the necessary components required in a mediation model, that is, stress (distal, or proximal) leading to cognitive risk, which then predicts subsequent psychopathology. Most of the evidence we review next shows that stress predicts cognitive risk; our earlier review of evidence demonstrated that multiple cognitive risks predict later psychopathology. Based on these separate lines of research, we have conceptualized the extant data in terms of this mechanism model, but more direct tests of mediation are needed that can adjudicate between third-variable confounds and important etiological explanations.

Distal Stress and Cognitive Risk Formation

In this chapter, we conceptualize distal life stressors as childhood adversity (e.g., physical, sexual, or emotional abuse, or neglect). One way in which these early stressors may contribute to the formation of psychopathology is via the development of maladaptive cognitive patterns, which crystalize into trait-like vulnerabilities during childhood and adolescence, eventually leading to the development and recurrence of psychopathology over the life span (Alloy et al., 2006; Hankin, Snyder, & Gulley, 2016a; Hankin et al., 2009). We illustrate how these distal stressors predict individual differences in cognitive risk products and processes.

Maltreatment may contribute to the formation of cognitive risk products. Rose and Abramson (1992) proposed that children try to explain the reasons they are experiencing negative experiences and may initially explain the cause of such stressors as being external, unstable, or specific (e.g., "My mom was just in a bad mood that day"). However, repeated, chronic experiences of maltreatment make it difficult for the child to retain these initial attributions and, instead, the child becomes more likely to make internal, stable, and global attributions to explain and predict the source of the ongoing maltreatment (e.g., "There must be something wrong with me that is making my mother do this"). Importantly, child emotional abuse (CEA) is especially potent in the formation of NIS because the perpetrator explicitly provides the child with negative inferences (e.g., "You deserve what you get because you are stupid and worthless"; "I wish you had never been born."). In contrast, child sexual abuse (CSA) or child physical abuse (CPA) may be less likely to contribute to NIS because the child may have more opportunity to generate her or his own explanations for the cause of the abuse. Often, CSA, and to a lesser extent CPA, occurs in a context of chronic CEA. Thus, associations between CSA, or CPA, and cognitive risk need to be disentangled from the influence of CEA.

In line with Rose and Abramson's theory (1992), multiple studies find associations specifically between CEA and NIS, and relations between CSA, or CPA, and cognitive risk tend to substantially weaker after controlling for CEA (see Gibb, 2002; Liu, Kleiman, Nestor, & Cheek, 2015, for reviews). These results suggest that CEA is particularly powerful for the formation of cognitive risk. In addition, cognitive risks, such as the combination of dysfunctional attitudes and NIS (Gibb et al., 2001), as well as NIS by itself (e.g., Alloy et al., 2006; Hankin, 2005), mediate the relationship between CEA and later depression. Studies of children and adolescents similarly show that CEA and peer victimization are both associated with NIS (Gibb & Abela, 2008; Liu et al., 2015) and that verbal victimization prospectively predicts NIS in children (Gibb et al., 2006).

Maltreatment can also influence the development of depressive rumination. Nolen-Hoeksema (1991) theorized that children who fail to develop a sense of control over their environment or who are not taught active, adaptive coping strategies might develop rumination. Indeed, observed negative parenting during early childhood (e.g., greater expressed negative emotion) prospectively predicted higher rumination in middle childhood (Schweizer, Olino, Dyson, Laptook, & Klein, 2017). Individuals who experience maltreatment may be deprived of opportunities to develop active coping, or abusers may actively thwart children's attempts to exert autonomy or control. Among adults, rumination is associated with a history of CEA and CSA (Spasojević & Alloy, 2002; Watkins, 2009) and mediates the concurrent association between CSA and depressive symptoms (Conway et al., 2004). Prospective studies show rumination mediates the relationship between CEA and CSA, and depressive episodes (Spasojević & Alloy, 2002), as well as between CSA and maladaptive consummatory behaviors such as binge eating and substance abuse (Sarin & Nolen-Hoeksema, 2010).

Maltreatment also contributes to cognitive risk processes. Some theorists have proposed that chronic exposure to a threatening environment could lead to attentional biases to negative information because it would be adaptive to attend to threat in these contexts (e.g., MacLeod, 1999). Over time, this pattern would be reinforced into a trait-like tendency, thus making individuals more likely to attend to threat in future situations and, in turn, contribute to later psychopathology. Cross-sectional evidence indicates that physical abuse history is associated with attentional biases for angry faces (Pine et al., 2005; Pollak & Tolley-Schell, 2003) and PTSD (Pine et al., 2005) among children. Furthermore, attention bias for facial and auditory expressions of anger mediated the association between physical abuse and physiological arousal anxiety symptoms among children (Shackman, Shackman, & Pollak, 2007). Similarly, attention bias for angry faces mediated the relationship between observed negative parenting (e.g., controlling, low warmth) and social anxiety in youth (Gulley, Oppenheimer, & Hankin, 2014).

OGM has been proposed to form as a coping response to early adversity or trauma whereby individuals recall fewer details and more general memories in order to avoid emotional distress (Williams et al., 2007). The majority of cross-sectional studies of children and adolescents show that several forms of trauma exposure (typically occurring months or years in the past) relate to increased OGM as compared to controls with moderate to large effects (Hitchcock et al., 2014, for review; see Orbach, Lamb, Sternberg, Williams, & Dawud-Noursi, 2001; Vrielynck et al., 2007, for exceptions).

Maltreatment and trauma can negatively impact EF development and functioning (e.g., DePrince, Weinzierl, & Combs, 2009; Mezzacappa, Kindlon, & Earls, 2001; Raver, Blair, & Willoughby, 2013; Tibu et al., 2016). Childhood maltreatment is associated with worse WM and inhibitory control (e.g., Cowell, Cicchetti, Rogosch, & Toth, 2015; see Hart & Rubia, 2012; Merz, Harlé, Noble, & McCall, 2016; Pechtel & Pizzagalli, 2011, for reviews). Adults with a history of childhood maltreatment demonstrate worse WM, and more severe abuse relates to greater WM difficulties (Cromheeke et al., 2014; Gould et al., 2012; Majer et al., 2010). Similarly, children with an abuse history (but who do not have PTSD) exhibit WM impairment (Perna & Kiefner, 2013). Last, EF deficits mediated the association between complex trauma (e.g., maltreatment, sexual abuse) and PTSD symptoms among children and adolescents (Op den Kedler, Ensink, Overbeek, Maric, & Lindauer, 2017).

Proximal Stress and Cognitive Risk Activation

Proximal stressors occur closer in time to psychopathology and can include various negative life events, such as acute trauma, interpersonal conflicts, academic or career disappointments, or other aversive events (e.g., illness, discrimination) that may occur across different time frames (e.g., daily hassles, weekly stressors, or more chronic stress over months). These stressors contribute to elevations in cognitive risk and subsequent psychopathology. Next, we review literature showing how proximal stressors contribute to cognitive products, attention bias, and EF difficulties. We are not aware of any studies that have examined the effects of more proximal stressors on OGM.

The cognitive products of NIS and dysfunctional attitudes have primarily been studied according to the cognitive vulnerability-stress moderation model as opposed to investigated as mechanisms of the stress–psychopathology relationship. However, we did find one study that examined NIS as a mechanism linking stress and distress. In the original hopelessness theory of depression (Abramson, Metalsky, & Alloy, 1989), negative inferences about stressful life events were hypothesized to mediate the association between stress exposure and hopelessness, which in turn, contributes to depressive symptoms. This mechanism model was tested using multilevel, lagged meditational analyses in a prospective 35-day diary study in which objectively coded daily negative events, negative inferences, hopelessness, and depression were assessed daily in young adults. Negative event-specific inferences predicted next-day hopelessness, which contributed to depressive symptoms thereafter, although daily stressors did not predict next-day negative event–specific cognitions (Russell, Haeffel, Hankin, Maxwell, & Perera, 2014).

Depressive rumination has garnered much attention as a potential mechanism of the relationship between negative life events and psychopathology. According to control theories (Carver & Scheier, 1982; Martin & Tesser, 1996), adverse events make discrepancies between an individual's current state and desired state more salient. Individuals then focus their attention on this discrepancy and engage in rumination as an attempt to resolve it (e.g., Brewin & Vallance, 1997). In longitudinal work spanning 12 months, rumination explained the relationship between stressful life events and both depression and anxiety symptoms in adults (Michl, McLaughlin, Shepherd, & Nolen-Hoeksema, 2013). In adolescents, a prospective study over 7 months found that rumination mediated the relationship between stressful life events and anxiety (but not depression) (Michl et al., 2013). Another prospective study spanning approximately 21 months found that greater dependent interpersonal stress (e.g., relational conflict) predicted higher rumination and depressive symptoms in girls relative to boys (Hamilton, Stange, Abramson, & Alloy, 2015). Studies using experience sampling methods (ESMs), which capture unfolding processes in real time on a more fine-grained temporal scale (e.g., hours, days), show similar effects. ESM studies of nonclinical adults indicate that rumination explains the link between negative events and negative affect (Moberly & Watkins, 2008), stigma-related stressors and psychological distress (Hatzenbuehler et al., 2009), and stressful events and symptoms of MDD and GAD among clinical adults (Ruscio et al., 2015).

Acute stress influences attentional bias patterns and aspects of EF, including updating, inhibition, shifting, and WM. Greater attentional avoidance during high-stress, real-life situations (i.e., life-threatening rocket attack; combat simulation) was concurrently related with PTSD, depression, and anxiety symptoms among community participants (Bar-Haim et al., 2010), and it was concurrently and prospectively related to PTSD in soldiers (Wald, Lubin, Holoshitz, et al., 2011; Wald, Shechner, Bitton, et al., 2011). Experimental investigations with EF show that individuals who completed a challenging cognitive task exhibited worse inhibition (Starcke, Wiesen, Trotzke, & Brand, 2016). Similarly, individuals observed by a third party while performing EF tasks showed impaired performance in updating and inhibition abilities (Horwitz & McCaffrey, 2008). Comparable results have emerged across additional studies using other types of stress inductions (e.g., Henderson et al., 2012; Scholz et al., 2009; but see Starcke et al., 2008, for exception). For instance, individuals who underwent exposure to social stress (TSST) exhibited impairments in shifting (Plessow, Kiesel, & Kirschbaum, 2012) as well as worse WM (Luethi, Meier, & Sandi, 2008; Schoofs, Preuss, & Wolf, 2008). EF difficulties may contribute to psychopathology by impeding an individual's ability to execute adaptive coping skills. Indeed, a short-term prospective study of a community sample of adolescents found that the relationship between worse

WM and shifting at baseline and later depression symptoms was mediated by less frequent adaptive coping such as problem solving (Evans, Kouros, Samanez-Larkin, & Garber, 2016).

Transactional Model

A more complex *transactional model* (e.g., Sameroff & Mackenzie, 2003) posits that stress, cognitive risks, and psychopathology can be predictors and outcomes of one another in a recurring pattern. For instance, the cognitive vulnerability-transactional stress model of depression (Hankin & Abramson, 2001) extends the traditional cognitive vulnerability-stress model by postulating that relationships among cognitions, psychopathology, stress, and other risks are bidirectional. According to this transactional model, stress initially contributes to elevations in negative mood, which in conjunction with cognitive risk as a moderator (i.e., vulnerability-stress model), leads to the enhancement and maintenance of negative affect and then subsequent depression. Depression then contributes to additional dependent stressors (e.g., interpersonal conflict, achievement failures) that, in turn, renew and perpetuate the cycle (i.e., stress generation). In other words, maladaptive cognitive patterns, stress, and psychopathology can be mutually reinforcing and have a snowballing effect. Moreover, other distal risks (e.g., maltreatment, personality/temperament, etc.) may begin this cycle and predict initial stress exposure as well as the formation of cognitive vulnerabilities.

Various studies provide support for this transactional model. Initial levels of cognitive risk and stress predicted future depressive symptoms, and initial stressors and depressive symptoms predicted later cognitive risk in adolescents; these results provide support for the bidirectional associations among stress, depression, and cognitive vulnerability (Calvete, Orue, & Hankin, 2013). Similarly, multiwave research with adolescents also demonstrated reciprocal patterns among depressive symptoms, rumination, and stress (Calvete, Orue, & Hankin, 2015), as well as with dysfunctional attitudes, stress, and depressive symptoms (Hankin, Wetter, Cheely, & Oppenheimer, 2008). Other research shows that the relationship between initial and later depressive symptoms was partly mediated by the joint, interactive effect of cognitive risk products (i.e., NIS and rumination) and dependent stress (Kercher & Rapee, 2009). Last, the personality trait of neuroticism predicted generation of daily dependent stressors as assessed in a month-long

diary study, and the cognitive risks of NIS and dysfunctional attitudes interacted with these additional stress-generated negative events to predict future increases in daily depressive symptoms (Hankin, 2010).

Other research has focused on the *stress-generation* effect of cognitive vulnerabilities. The stress-generation hypothesis was originally articulated in terms of the bidirectional relationship between stress and depression (Hammen, 1991) whereby depressed individuals generate more dependent stress (e.g., interpersonal conflict, rejection) in their lives, which in turn predicts future depression (see Conway, Hammen, & Brennan, 2012; Hammen, 2006; Liu & Alloy, 2010, for reviews). Several studies of cognitive vulnerability have found a stress-generation pattern (see Liu, 2013, for review). NIS, in particular, has received the most consistent support as a stress generation factor (e.g., Calvete, Orue, & Hankin, 2012; Hamilton et al., 2014; Joiner, Wingate, Gencoz, & Gencoz, 2005; Safford, Alloy, Abramson, & Crossfield, 2007; Shih, Abela, & Starrs, 2009; Simons, Angell, Monroe, & Thase, 1993; but see Gibb et al., 2006, for exception). In examining the role of multiple cognitive vulnerabilities as contributing to stress generation, NIS showed the strongest and most consistent effect for predicting future dependent stressors while dysfunctional attitudes also demonstrated a stress generation effect, albeit with smaller effect sizes (Shapero, Hankin, & Barrocas, 2013); stress generation effects for rumination tend to be limited (Liu & Alloy, 2010). Finally, mediation analyses revealed one process explaining why worse EF is associated with elevated depression and anxiety symptoms: Adolescents with poor EF generated more dependent stressful life events about which they ruminated and, in turn, greater rumination predicted more depression and anxiety symptoms (Snyder & Hankin, 2016).

It is important to note that the three specific conceptual models we discussed are not mutually exclusive and may be combined and integrated in different ways. Different models may apply depending on the particular cognitive risk(s) studied, how stress is conceptualized and measured, the form of or stage of psychopathology (i.e., first onset, recurrence), and when in development the process is studied. Pathways may also be moderated by other factors, including by individual and group differences. For example, some studies find gender differences and moderation effects, such that the results regarding cognitive vulnerability-stress and transactional processes over time were stronger in adolescent girls than boys (e.g., Calvete et al., 2013; Hamilton et al., 2015), although gender differences are not always obtained (Calvete et al., 2015).

Consideration of Gender Differences

Gender may moderate the relationships among stress, cognitive risks, and psychopathology. A large body of work has examined gender differences in cognitive products because rates of internalizing psychopathology are higher in women as compared to men (Zahn-Waxler, Crick, Shirtcliff, & Woods, 2006). Women exhibit higher NIS than men (Hankin & Abramson, 2002; Mezulis, Abramson, Hyde, & Hankin, 2004), whereas men have higher dysfunctional attitudes than women (Haeffel et al., 2003; Hankin, 2009). Women exhibit higher depressive rumination than men (Hankin, 2008; Nolen-Hoeksema, 2012); however, some studies do not find gender differences in children and early adolescents (Abela, Brozina, & Haigh, 2002; Abela & Hankin, 2011; Abela, McGirr, & Skitch, 2007; Abela, Vanderbilt, & Rochon, 2004).

Cognitive processes are thought to be universal. Research examining gender differences in cognitive processes has focused on the association between cognitive processes and psychopathology and results have been inconsistent. Some meta-analyses have not found gender differences for EF and attentional bias in depression (Peckham et al., 2010; Snyder, 2013), or for EF in ADHD (e.g., Lipszyc & Schachar, 2010; van Mourik et al., 2005). In contrast, other meta-analyses have found that samples of individuals with BD that contain more women show worse shifting (Arts et al., 2008; Kurtz & Gerraty, 2009), whereas samples of individuals with ADHD containing more men show worse inhibition (Bálint et al., 2009).

Conclusion and Future Directions

In summary, evidence suggests that several cognitive risk processes and products may function both as transdiagnostic and relatively specific vulnerabilities for different forms of psychopathology. Cognitive risks have reliably been linked with psychopathology; however, research has not consistently centered on identifying or ruling out different logical conceptual models for the interrelationships among stress, cognitive factors, and psychopathology. Researchers have typically followed a "silo" approach (Hankin et al., 2016a) whereby most studies tend to focus on only one cognitive process or product, one type of stress, or psychopathological outcome. In addition, most work examining the interrelationship of stress, cognitive risk, and psychopathology has focused primarily on testing only one broad conceptual model (particularly the cognitive-vulnerability stress moderation model) or one aspect of a broad conceptual model (e.g., stress leading to cognitive risk, as opposed to examining the full causal chain of stress to cognitive risk to psychopathology). Thus, more research is needed that systematically pits different logical conceptual models of relationships among factors against one another. This will help to determine to what extent different cognitive risks are best understood as moderators or mediators (or both) of the stress-psychopathology link and how they contribute to psychopathology. Furthermore, most work has focused on clinical samples of adults and has relied on clinical case-control designs. Researchers need to investigate developmental, gender, racial, ethnic, and other social factors (e.g., socioeconomic status) that likely impact the interrelationships of stress, cognition, and psychopathology. In addition, utilizing prospective and ESM designs will allow for ecologically valid temporal dynamics among these variables to be clarified.

Bridging Multiple Units of Analysis

An important avenue of future work concerns the ongoing integration of neurobiological factors with our understanding of how cognitive risks and stress relate to psychopathology. Some research has investigated genetic factors that precede the development of cognitive risks. Molecular genetics have been associated with cognitive products (e.g., rumination; Beevers, Wells, & McGeary, 2009; Hilt, Sander, Nolen-Hoeksema, & Simen, 2007) and cognitive processes (e.g., attention bias to negative emotion) (Gibb et al., 2013). There is also some evidence suggesting that some EF, memory, and attention difficulties may be a form of genetic risk (endophenotypes; Gottesman & Gould, 2003). Biological and environmental factors influence neurodevelopmental and neurodegenerative processes, which impact cognitive functioning. For instance, exposure to postnatal stress impacts the formation and pruning of synaptic connections and receptor expression (Rapoport, Giedd, & Gogtay, 2012).

In addition, researchers should continue expanding on the synthesis of cognitive and neurobiological findings to formulate integrative psychobiological models that articulate the neural mechanisms relating cognitive risk processes and products. For instance, Disner and colleagues (2011) propose that biased attention, rumination, memory, and dysfunctional attitudes are generally associated with an increased influence of subcortical emotional processing regions (e.g., sustained amygdala activity) combined with weakened top-down cognitive control (e.g., hypoactivity in the prefrontal cortex).

Taxonomy and Structure of Cognitive Risk

In order to clarify to what extent and which cognitive risk processes and products may be transdiagnostic or specific to certain forms of psychopathology, it is essential to organize constructs appropriately (e.g., establish their factor structure). However, to date, there is no theoretical or empirically specified structure for the degree to which cognitive risk products and processes are overlapping or distinct. Though the factor structure of many cognitive processes has been identified, at least in individuals without psychopathology (e.g., EF; Miyake & Friedman, 2012), few factor analytic studies have examined the factor structure of cognitive products. By organizing *both* psychopathology and cognitive risks using latent structural models that parsimoniously capture what is common and unique to risk and psychopathology constructs, progress can be made in understanding how cognition translates stress into psychopathology and uncover pathways that are transdiagnostic (i.e., connect to broad psychopathology dimensions) or more specific to particular symptom clusters (Hankin et al., 2016b).

The utility and construct validity of organizing common emotional, behavioral, and cognitive symptoms of psychopathology via latent psychopathology dimensions is an active, ongoing area that is revealing new and interesting findings (e.g., Lahey, Krueger et al, 2017; Snyder, Hankin, Sandman, Head, & Davis, 2017). Recent structural research has investigated a parsimonious latent organization of dimensional psychopathology and found that a *bifactor* model showed the best fit (e.g., Caspi et al., 2014; Laceulle, Vollebergh, & Ormel, 2015; Snyder, Young, & Hankin, 2017). In the bifactor model of psychopathology, the shared variance across symptom features of common disorders, including anxiety, mood, behavior, and substance use problems, are captured by a common latent factor, or the general psychopathology factor (i.e., "p factor"). After the common variance is accounted for, the remaining unique variance in symptoms is then modeled and organized via independent and specific internalizing (anxiety, mood) and externalizing dimensions (behavioral, substance use).

Similar to how clinical scientists have empirically examined the classification of psychopathology via latent dimensional structural models, emerging evidence suggests that the frequently studied and well-supported cognitive products may also be organized according to a bifactor model (Schweizer, Snyder, & Hankin, 2018). In two separate community samples of youth, we obtained evidence for a common cognitive risk factor (i.e., "c factor") that captured the shared variance across multiple cognitive risks (e.g., dysfunctional attitudes, NIS, rumination) and identified several specific, independent cognitive risk factors that reflect unique variance in these cognitive risks (Schweizer, Snyder, Young, & Hankin, 2018). Examining construct validity of the "c factor" revealed that it was significantly related to the p factor and exhibited strong associations with the internalizing specific dimension.

Thus, this empirical work illustrates how identifying an accurate organization of cognitive risks can provide an avenue to uncover cleaner patterns of relationships between cognitive risk and psychopathology in contrast to the traditional approach in cognitive-clinical psychology, which has generally used case-control designs to attempt to demonstrate that a single, purportedly distinct cognitive risk differs in a *DSM*-defined psychiatric disorder (APA, 2013). Furthermore, examining relationships among dimensional latent models of cognitive risk and different stress domains over the life span may help to elucidate clearer trajectories to different manifestations of psychopathology (Hankin et al., 2016b).

Note

1. Though some earlier work has not found evidence for attention bias in clinically depressed youth (Dalgleish et al., 2003; Neshat-Doost, Moradi, Taghavi, Yule, & Dalgleish, 2000; Neshat-Doost, Taghavi, Moradi, Yule, & Dalgleish, 1997), studies were limited by relatively small sample sizes and two utilized the emotional Stroop (Dalgeish et al., 2003; Neshat-Doost et al., 1997).

References

Aakre, J. M., Seghers, J. P., St-Hilaire, A., & Docherty, N. (2009). Attributional style in delusional patients: A comparison of remitted paranoid, remitted nonparanoid, and current paranoid patients with nonpsychiatric controls. *Schizophrenia Bulletin, 35*, 994–1002. doi:10.1093/schbul/sbn033

Abela, J. R., Brozina, K., & Haigh, E. P. (2002). An examination of the response styles theory of depression in third-and seventh-grade children: A short-term longitudinal study. *Journal of Abnormal Child Psychology, 30*(5), 515–527.

Abela, J. R., McGirr, A., & Skitch, S. A. (2007). Depressogenic inferential styles, negative events, and depressive symptoms in youth: An attempt to reconcile past inconsistent findings. *Behaviour Research and Therapy, 45*(10), 2397–2406.

Abela, J. R., Vanderbilt, E., & Rochon, A. (2004). A test of the integration of the response styles and social support theories of depression in third and seventh grade children. *Journal of Social and Clinical Psychology, 23*(5), 653–674.

Abela, J. R. Z., & Hankin, B. L. (2008). *Handbook of depression in children and adolescents.* New York, NY: Guilford Press.

Abela, J. R. Z., & Hankin, B. L. (2011). Rumination as a vulnerability factor to depression during the transition from early to middle adolescence: A multiwave longitudinal study. *Journal of Abnormal Psychology, 120,* 259–271. doi:10.1037/a0022796

Abramovitch, A., Abramowitz, J. S., Mittelman, A., Stark, A., Ramsey, K., & Geller, D. A. (2015). Research review: Neuropsychological test performance in pediatric obsessive-compulsive disorder—a meta-analysis. *Journal of Child Psychology and Psychiatry, 56*(8), 837–847.

Abramson, L. Y., & Alloy, L. B. (2006). Cognitive vulnerability to depression: Current status and developmental irigins. In T. E. Joiner, J. S. Brown, & J. Kistner (Eds.), *The interpersonal, cognitive, and social nature of depression* (pp. 83–100). Mahwah, NJ: Erlbaum.

Abramson, L. Y., Metalsky, G. I., & Alloy, L. B. (1989). Hopelessness depression: A theory-based subtype of depression. *Psychological Review, 96,* 358–372. doi:10.1037//0033-295X.96.2.358

Agnew-Blais, J., & Seidman, L. J. (2013). Neurocognition in youth and young adults under age 30 at familial risk for schizophrenia: A quantitative and qualitative review. *Cognitive Neuropsychiatry, 18*(1–2), 44–82.

Ahern, E., & Semkovska, M. (2017). Cognitive functioning in the first-episode of major depressive disorder: A systematic review and meta-analysis. *Neuropsychology, 31*(1), 52–72. http://dx.doi.org/10.1037/neu0000319

Airaksinen, E., Larsson, M., & Forsell, Y. (2005). Neuropsychological functions in anxiety disorders in population-based samples: Evidence of episodic memory dysfunction. *Journal of Psychiatric Research, 39,* 207–214. doi:10.1016/j.jpsychires.2004.06.001

Aldao, A., Nolen-Hoeksema, S., & Schweizer, S. (2010). Emotion-regulation strategies across psychopathology: A meta-analytic review. *Clinical Psychology Review, 30,* 217–237. doi:10.1016/j.cpr.2009.11.004

Alloy, L. B., Abramson, L. Y., Flynn, M., Liu, R. T., Grant, D. A., Jager-Hyman, S., & Whitehouse, W. G. (2009). Self-focused cognitive styles and bipolar spectrum disorders: Concurrent and prospective associations. *International Journal of Cognitive Therapy, 2*(4), 354–372. doi.org/10.1521/ijct.2009.2.4.354

Alloy, L. B., Abramson, L. Y., Walshaw, P. D., & Neeren, A. M. (2006). Cognitive vulnerability to unipolar and bipolar mood disorders. *Journal of Social and Clinical Psychology, 25,* 726–754. doi:10.1521/jscp.2006.25.7.726

Alloy, L. B., Abramson, L. Y., Whitehouse, W. G., Hogan, M. E., Panzarella, C., & Rose, D. T. (2006). Prospective incidence of first onsets and recurrences of depression in individuals at high and low cognitive risk for depression. *Journal of Abnormal Psychology, 115*(1), 145.

Alloy, L. B., Black, S. K., Young, M. E., Goldstein, K. E., Shapero, B. G., Stange, J. P.,...Abramson, L. Y. (2012). Cognitive vulnerabilities and depression versus other psychopathology symptoms and diagnoses in early

adolescence. *Journal of Clinical Child and Adolescent Psychology, 41,* 539–560. doi:10.1080/15374416.2012.703123

Alloy, L. B., & Clements, C. M. (1998). Hopelessness theory of depression: Tests of the symptom component. *Cognitive Therapy and Research, 22*(4), 303–335.

American Psychiatric Association (APA). (2013). *Diagnostic and statistical manual of mental disorders (DSM-5°).* Washington, DC: Author.

Anderson, R. J., Goddard, L., & Powell, J. H. (2009). Social problem-solving processes and mood in college students: An examination of self-report and performance-based approaches. *Cognitive Therapy and Research, 33*(2), 175–186.

Arditte, K. A., & Joormann, J. (2014). Rumination moderates the effects of cognitive bias modification of attention. *Cognitive Therapy and Research, 38*(2), 189–199.

Armstrong, T., & Olatunji, B. O. (2012). Eye tracking of attention in the affective disorders: A meta-analytic review and synthesis. *Clinical Psychology Review, 32,* 704–723. doi:10.1016/j.cpr.2012.09.004

Arts, B. M. G., Jabben, N., Krabbendam, L., & Van Os, J. (2008). Meta-analyses of cognitive functioning in euthymic bipolar patients and their first-degree relatives. *Psychological Medicine, 38,* 771–785. doi:10.1017/S0033291707001675

Aupperle, R. L., Melrose, A. J., Stein, M. B., & Paulus, M. P. (2012). Executive function and PTSD: Disengaging from trauma. *Journal of Affective Disorders, 62,* 686–694. doi:10.1016/j.neuropharm.2011.02.008

Bálint, S., Czobor, P., Komlósi, S., Meszaros, A., Simon, V., & Bitter, I. (2009). Attention deficit hyperactivity disorder (ADHD): gender-and age-related differences in neurocognition. *Psychological Medicine, 39*(8), 1337–1345.

Banich, M. T. (2009). Executive function: The search for an integrated account. *Current Directions in Psychological Science, 18*(2), 89–94.

Bar-Haim, Y., Lamy, D., Pergamin, L., Bakermans-Kranenburg, M. J., & Van Ijzendoorn, M. H. (2007). Threat-related attentional bias in anxious and nonanxious individuals: A meta-analytic study. *Psychological Bulletin, 133*(1), 1–24.

Bar-Haim, Y., Holoshitz, Y., Eldar, S., Frenkel, T.I., Muller, D., Charney, D.S., Pine, D.S., Fox, N.A., & Wald, I. (2010). Life-threatening danger and suppression of attention bias to threat. *American Journal of Psychiatry, 167*(6), 694–698.

Beck, A. T. (1976). *Cognitive therapy and the emotional disorders.* Oxford, UK: International Universities Press.

Beck, A. T., & Clark, D. A. (1997). An information processing model of anxiety: Automatic and strategic processes. *Behaviour Research and Therapy, 35*(1), 49–58.

Beck, A. T., & Haigh, E. A. (2014). Advances in cognitive theory and therapy: The generic cognitive model. *Annual Review of Clinical Psychology, 10,* 1–24.

Beevers, C. G., & Carver, C. S. (2003). Attentional bias and mood persistence as prospective predictors of dysphoria. *Cognitive Therapy and Research, 27*(6), 619–637.

Beevers, C. G., Lee, H. J., Wells, T. T., Ellis, A. J., & Telch, M. J. (2011). Association of predeployment gaze bias for emotion stimuli with later symptoms of PTSD and depression in soldiers deployed in Iraq. *American Journal of Psychiatry, 168*(7), 735–741.

Beevers, C. G., Wells, T. T., & McGeary, J. E. (2009). The BDNF Val66Met polymorphism is associated with rumination in healthy adults. *Emotion, 9*(4), 579.

Berna, F., Potheegadoo, J., Aouadi, I., Ricarte, J. J., Allé, M. C., Coutelle, R.,...& Danion, J. M. (2015). A meta-analysis of autobiographical memory studies in schizophrenia spectrum disorder. *Schizophrenia Bulletin, 42*(1), 56–66.

Bishop, S. J. (2008). Trait anxiety and impoverished prefrontal control of attention. *Nature Neuroscience, 12*, 92–98. doi:10.1038/nn.2242

Blagden, J. C., & Craske, M. G. (1996). Effects of active and passive rumination and distraction: A pilot replication with anxious mood. *Journal of Anxiety Disorders, 10*(4), 243–252.

Boldrini, M., Del Pace, L., Placidi, G. P. A., Keilp, J., Ellis, S. P., Signori, S., . . . Cappa, S. F. (2005). Selective cognitive deficits in obsessive-compulsive disorder compared to panic disorder with agoraphobia. *Acta Psychiatrica Scandinavica, 111*, 150–158. doi:10.1111/j.1600-0447.2004.00247.x

Bora, E., Lin, A., Wood, S. J., Yung, A. R., McGorry, P. D., & Pantelis, C. (2014). Cognitive deficits in youth with familial and clinical high risk to psychosis: A systematic review and meta-analysis. *Acta Psychiatrica Scandinavica, 130*(1), 1–15.

Boulanger, M., Lejeune, A., & Blairy, S. (2013). Overgenerality memory style for past and future events and emotions related in bipolar disorder. What are the links with problem solving and interpersonal relationships? *Psychiatry Research, 210*(3), 863–870.

Boyd, R. C., Zayas, L. H., & McKee, M. D. (2006). Mother-infant interaction, life events and prenatal and postpartum depressive symptoms among urban minority women in primary care. *Maternal and Child Health Journal, 10*(2), 139.

Brewin, C. R., & Vallance, H. (1997). Self-discrepancies in young adults and childhood violence. *Journal of Interpersonal Violence, 12*(4), 600–606.

Brown, H. M., Eley, T. C., Broeren, S., MacLeod, C., Rinck, M. H. J. A., Hadwin, J. A., & Lester, K. J. (2014). Psychometric properties of reaction time based experimental paradigms measuring anxiety-related information-processing biases in children. *Journal of Anxiety Disorders, 28*(1), 97–107.

Bryant, R. A., Sutherland, K., & Guthrie, R. M. (2007). Impaired specific autobiographical memory as a risk factor for posttraumatic stress after trauma. *Journal of Abnormal Psychology, 116*, 837. doi:10.1037/0021-843X.116.4.837

Burke, M., & Mathews, A. (1992). Autobiographical memory and clinical anxiety. *Cognition & Emotion, 6*(1), 23–35.

Byrow, Y., Chen, N. T., & Peters, L. (2016). Time course of attention in socially anxious individuals: Investigating the effects of adult attachment style. *Behavior Therapy, 47*(4), 560–571.

Calvete, E., Orue, I., & Hankin, B. (2012). P-271-Depression in adolescents: Reciprocal influences between depression, stress and cognitive vulnerabilities. *European Psychiatry, 27*, 1.

Calvete, E., Orue, I., & Hankin, B. L. (2013). Transactional relationships among cognitive vulnerabilities, stressors, and depressive symptoms in adolescence. *Journal of Abnormal Child Psychology, 41*(3), 399–410.

Calvete, E., Orue, I., & Hankin, B. L. (2015). Cross-lagged associations among ruminative response style, stressors, and depressive symptoms in adolescents. *Journal of Social and Clinical Psychology, 34*(3), 203–220.

Calvo, M. G., & Avero, P. (2005). Time course of attentional bias to emotional scenes in anxiety: Gaze direction and duration. *Cognition & Emotion, 19*(3), 433–451.

Carver, C. S., & Scheier, M. F. (1982). Control theory: A useful conceptual framework for personality—social, clinical, and health psychology. *Psychological Bulletin, 92*(1), 111.

Caspi, A., Houts, R. M., Belsky, D. W., Goldman-Mellor, S. J., Harrington, H., Israel, S., . . . & Moffitt, T. E. (2014). The p factor: One general psychopathology factor in the structure of psychiatric disorders? *Clinical Psychological Science, 2*(2), 119–137.

Chen, N. T., Clarke, P. J., MacLeod, C., & Guastella, A. J. (2012). Biased attentional processing of positive stimuli in social anxiety disorder: An eye movement study. *Cognitive Behaviour Therapy, 41*(2), 96–107.

Cisler, J. M., & Koster, E. H. (2010). Mechanisms of attentional biases towards threat in anxiety disorders: An integrative review. *Clinical Psychology Review, 30*(2), 203–216.

Cohen, L. J., Hollander, E., DeCaria, C. M., Stein, D. J., Simeon, D., Liebowitz, M. R., & Aronowitz, B. R. (1996). Specificity of neuropsychological impairment in obsessive-compulsive disorder: A comparison with social phobic and normal control subjects. *Journal of Neuropsychiatry and Clinical Neurosciences, 8*, 82–85.

Connell, A. M., Patton, E., Klostermann, S., & Hughes-Scalise, A. (2013). Attention bias in youth: Associations with youth and mother's depressive symptoms moderated by emotion regulation and affective dynamics during family interactions. *Cognition & Emotion, 27*(8), 1522–1534.

Conway, C., Hammen, C., & Brennan, P. (2012). A comparison of latent class, latent trait, and factor mixture models of DSM-IV borderline personality disorder criteria in a community setting: Implications for DSM-5. *Journal of Personality Disorders, 26*(5), 793–803.

Conway, M., Mendelson, M., Giannopoulos, C., Csank, P. A., & Holm, S. L. (2004). Childhood and adult sexual abuse, rumination on sadness, and dysphoria. *Child Abuse & Neglect, 28*(4), 393–410.

Conway, M. A. (2001). Sensory–perceptual episodic memory and its context: Autobiographical memory. *Philosophical Transactions of the Royal Society of London B: Biological Sciences, 356*(1413), 1375–1384.

Conway, M. A., & Fthenaki, A. (2000). Disruption and loss of autobiographical memory. In L. S. Cermak (Ed.), *Handbook of neuropsychology: Memory and its disorders* (pp. 281–312). Amsterdam, Netherlands: Elsevier Science Publishers B.V.

Conway, M. A., & Pleydell-Pearce, C. W. (2000). The construction of autobiographical memories in the self-memory system. *Psychological Review, 107*(2), 261.

Conway, M. A., Pleydell-Pearce, C. W., & Whitecross, S. E. (2001). The neuroanatomy of autobiographical memory: A slow cortical potential study of autobiographical memory retrieval. *Journal of Memory and Language, 45*(3), 493–524.

Cowell, R. A., Cicchetti, D., Rogosch, F. A., & Toth, S. L. (2015). Childhood maltreatment and its effect on neurocognitive functioning: Timing and chronicity matter. *Development and Psychopathology, 27*(2), 521–533.

Crane, C., Heron, J., Gunnell, D., Lewis, G., Evans, J., & Williams, J. M. G. (2015). Adolescent over-general memory, life events and mental health outcomes: findings from a UK cohort study. *Memory, 24*, 348–368. doi:10.1080/09658211.2015.1008014.

Cromheeke, S., Herpoel, L. A., & Mueller, S. C. (2014). Childhood abuse is related to working memory impairment for positive emotion in female university students. *Child Maltreatment, 19*(1), 38–48.

Dalgleish T., Taghavi R., Neshat-Doost H., Moradi A., Canterbury R., & Yule W. (2003). Patterns of processing bias for emotional information across clinical disorders: A comparison of attention, memory, and prospective cognition in children and adolescents with depression, generalized anxiety, and posttraumatic stress disorder. *Journal of Clinical Child and Adolescent Psychology 32*, 10–21.

Davidovich, S., Collishaw, S., Thapar, A. K., Harold, G., Thapar, A., & Rice, F. (2016). Do better executive functions buffer the effect of current parental depression on adolescent depressive symptoms? *Journal of Affective Disorders, 199*, 54–64.

DePrince, A. P., Weinzierl, K. M., & Combs, M. D. (2009). Executive function performance and trauma exposure in a community sample of children. *Child Abuse & Neglect, 33*(6), 353–361.

Disner, S. G., Beevers, C. G., Haigh, E. A., & Beck, A. T. (2011). Neural mechanisms of the cognitive model of depression. *Nature Reviews Neuroscience, 12*(8), 467–477.

Dudeney, J., Sharpe, L., & Hunt, C. (2015). Attentional bias towards threatening stimuli in children with anxiety: A meta-analysis. *Clinical Psychology Review, 40*, 66–75.

Duque, A., & Vázquez, C. (2015). Double attention bias for positive and negative emotional faces in clinical depression: Evidence from an eye-tracking study. *Journal of Behavior Therapy and Experimental Psychiatry, 46*, 107–114.

Eldar, S., Ricon, T., & Bar-Haim, Y. (2008). Plasticity in attention: Implications for stress response in children. *Behaviour Research and Therapy, 46*(4), 450–461.

Elias, L. R., Miskowiak, K. W., Vale, A. M., Köhler, C. A., Kjærstad, H. L., Stubbs, B.,…& Carvalho, A. F. (2017). Cognitive impairment in euthymic pediatric bipolar disorder: A systematic review and meta-analysis. *Journal of the American Academy of Child & Adolescent Psychiatry, 56*(4), 286–296.

Elwood, L. S., Hahn, K. S., Olatunji, B. O., & Williams, N. L. (2009). Cognitive vulnerabilities to the development of PTSD: A review of four vulnerabilities and the proposal of an integrative vulnerability model. *Clinical Psychology Review, 29*, 87–100. doi:10.1016/j.cpr.2008.10.002

Elwood, L. S., Williams, N. L., Olatunji, B. O., & Lohr, J. M. (2007). Interpretation biases in victims and non-victims of interpersonal trauma and their relation to symptom development. *Journal of Anxiety Disorders, 21*, 554–567. doi:10.1016/j.janxdis.2006.08.006

Epp, A. M., Dobson, K. S., Dozois, D. J., & Frewen, P. A. (2012). A systematic meta-analysis of the Stroop task in depression. *Clinical Psychology Review, 32*(4), 316–328.

Evans, L. D., Kouros, C. D., Samanez-Larkin, S., & Garber, J. (2016). Concurrent and short-term prospective relations among neurocognitive functioning, coping, and depressive symptoms in youth. *Journal of Clinical Child & Adolescent Psychology, 45*(1), 6–20.

Eysenck, M. W., & Derakshan, N. (2011). New perspectives in attentional control theory. *Personality and Individual Differences, 50*(7), 955–960.

Eysenck, M. W., Derakshan, N., Santos, R., & Calvo, M. G. (2007). Anxiety and cognitive performance: Attentional control theory. *Emotion, 7*(2), 336.

Fresco, D. M., Frankel, A. N., Mennin, D. S., Turk, C. L., & Heimberg, R. G. (2002). Distinct and overlapping features of rumination and worry: The relationship of cognitive production to negative affective states. *Cognitive Therapy and Research, 26*(2), 179–188.

Fusar-Poli, P., Bonoldi, I., Yung, A. R., Borgwardt, S., Kempton, M. J., Valmaggia, L.,…& McGuire, P. (2012). Predicting psychosis: Meta-analysis of transition outcomes in individuals at high clinical risk. *Archives of General Psychiatry, 69*(3), 220–229.

Ganly, T. J., Salmon, K., & McDowall, J. (2016). Is remembering less specifically part of an avoidant coping style? Associations between memory specificity, avoidant coping, and stress. *Cognition and Emotion, 31*, 1–12.

García-Blanco, A., Salmerón, L., Perea, M., & Livianos, L. (2014). Attentional biases toward emotional images in the different episodes of bipolar disorder: An eye-tracking study. *Psychiatry Research, 215*(3), 628–633.

Gibb, B. E. (2002). Childhood maltreatment and negative cognitive styles: A quantitative and qualitative review. *Clinical Psychology Review, 22*(2), 223–246.

Gibb, B. E., & Abela, J. R. (2008). Emotional abuse, verbal victimization, and the development of children's negative inferential styles and depressive symptoms. *Cognitive Therapy and Research, 32*(2), 161–176.

Gibb, B. E., Alloy, L. B., Abramson, L. Y., Rose, D. T., Whitehouse, W. G., Donovan, P.,…& Tierney, S. (2001). History of childhood maltreatment, negative cognitive styles, and episodes of depression in adulthood. *Cognitive Therapy and Research, 25*(4), 425–446.

Gibb, B. E., Alloy, L. B., Walshaw, P. D., Comer, J. S., Shen, G. H. C., & Villari, A. G. (2006). Predictors of attributional style change in children. *Journal of Abnormal Child Psychology, 34*, 425–439. doi:10.1007/s10802-006-9022-2

Gibb, B. E., Beevers, C. G., & McGeary, J. E. (2013). Toward an integration of cognitive and genetic models of risk for depression. *Cognition & Emotion, 27*(2), 193–216.

Gibb, B. E., Benas, J. S., Grassia, M., & McGeary, J. (2009). Children's attentional biases and 5- HTTLPR genotype: potential mechanisms linking mother and child depression. *Journal of Clinical Child & Adolescent Psychology, 38*(3), 415–426.

Gibb, B. E., & Coles, M. E. (2005). Cognitive vulnerabilty-stress models of psychopathology: A developmental perspective. In B. L. Hankin & J. R. Z. Abela (Eds.), *Development of psychopathology: A vulnerability-stress perspective* (pp. 104–135). Thousand Oaks, CA: Sage.

Gibb, B. E., McGeary, J. E., & Beevers, C. G. (2016). Attentional biases to emotional stimuli: Key components of the RDoC constructs of sustained threat and loss. *American Journal of Medical Genetics Part B: Neuropsychiatric Genetics, 171*(1), 65–80.

Gibbs, B. R., & Rude, S. S. (2004). Overgeneral autobiographical memory as depression vulnerability. *Cognitive Therapy and Research, 28*(4), 511–526.

Giuliano, J. A., Li, H., Mesholam-Gately, R., Sorenson, S., Woodberry, K., & Seidman, L. (2012). Neurocognition in the psychosis risk syndrome: a quantitative and qualitative review. *Current Pharmaceutical Design, 18*(4), 399–415.

Goodwin, H., Yiend, J., & Hirsch, C. (2017). Generalized anxiety disorder, worry and attention to threat: A systematic review. *Clinical Psychology Review, 54*, 107–122.

Gotlib, I. H., & Joormann, J. (2010). Cognition and depression: Current status and future directions. *Annual Review of Clinical Psychology, 6*, 285–312.

Gottesman, I. I., & Gould, T. D. (2003). The endophenotype concept in psychiatry: Etymology and strategic intentions. *American Journal of Psychiatry, 160*(4), 636–645.

Gould, F., Clarke, J., Heim, C., Harvey, P. D., Majer, M., & Nemeroff, C. B. (2012). The effects of child abuse and neglect on cognitive functioning in adulthood. *Journal of Psychiatric Research, 46*(4), 500–506.

Grant, P. M., & Beck, A. T. (2009). Defeatist beliefs as a mediator of cognitive impairment, negative symptoms, and functioning in schizophrenia. *Schizophrenia Bulletin*, *35*, 798–806. doi:10.1093/schbul/sbn008

Gross, J. J., & Thompson, R. A. (2007). Emotion regulation: Conceptual foundations (pp. 3–24). In J. J. Gross (Ed.), *Handbook of emotion regulation*. New York, NY: Guilford Press.

Gulley, L. D., Oppenheimer, C. W., & Hankin, B. L. (2014). Associations among negative parenting, attention bias to anger, and social anxiety among youth. *Developmental Psychology*, *50*(2), 577.

Gutenbrunner, C., Salmon, K., & Jose, P. E. (2017). Do overgeneral autobiographical memories predict increased psychopathological symptoms in community youth? A 3-year longitudinal investigation. *Journal of Abnormal Child Psychology*, *46*(2), 1–12.

Haeffel, G. J., Abramson, L. Y., Voelz, Z. R., Metalsky, G. I., Dykman, B. M., Hogan, M. E., & Hankin, B. L. (2003). Cognitive vulnerability to depression and lifetime history of Axis I psychopathology: A comparison of dysfunctional attitudes (DAS). *Journal of Cognitive Psychotherapy*, *17*, 3–23.

Hallford, D. J., & Mellor, D. (2017). Autobiographical memory specificity and general symptoms of anxiety: Indirect associations through rumination. *International Journal of Mental Health*, *46*(2), 74–88.

Hamilton, J. L., Stange, J. P., Abramson, L. Y., & Alloy, L. B. (2015). Stress and the development of cognitive vulnerabilities to depression explain sex differences in depressive symptoms during adolescence. *Clinical Psychological Science*, *3*(5), 702–714.

Hamilton, J. L., Stange, J. P., Kleiman, E. M., Hamlat, E. J., Abramson, L. Y., & Alloy, L. B. (2014). Cognitive vulnerabilities amplify the effect of early pubertal timing on interpersonal stress generation during adolescence. *Journal of Youth and Adolescence*, *43*(5), 824–833.

Hamlat, E. J., Connolly, S. L., Hamilton, J. L., Stange, J. P., Abramson, L. Y., & Alloy, L. B. (2015). Rumination and overgeneral autobiographical memory in adolescents: An integration of cognitive vulnerabilities to depression. *Journal of Youth and Adolescence*, *44*(4), 806–818.

Hammen, C. (1991). Generation of stress in the course of unipolar depression. *Journal of Abnormal Psychology*, *100*(4), 555.

Hammen, C. (2006). Stress generation in depression: Reflections on origins, research, and future directions. *Journal of Clinical Psychology*, *62*(9), 1065–1082.

Hankin, B. L. (2005). Childhood maltreatment and psychopathology: Prospective tests of attachment, cognitive vulnerability, and stress as mediating processes. *Cognitive Therapy and Research*, *29*(6), 645–671.

Hankin, B. L. (2008). Rumination and depression in adolescence: Investigating symptom specificity in a multiwave prospective study. *Journal of Clinical Child and Adolescent Psychology*, *37*, 701–713. doi:10.1080/15374410802359627

Hankin, B. L. (2009). Development of sex differences in depressive and co-occurring anxious symptoms during adolescence: Descriptive trajectories and potential explanations in a multiwave prospective study. *Journal of Clinical Child & Adolescent Psychology*, *38*, 460–472. doi:10.1080/15374410902976288

Hankin, B. L. (2010). Personality and depressive symptoms: Stress generation and cognitive vulnerabilities to depression in a prospective daily diary study. *Journal of Social and Clinical Psychology*, *29*(4), 369–401.

Hankin, B. L., & Abramson, L. Y. (2001). Development of gender differences in depression: An elaborated cognitive vulnerability-transactional stress theory. *Psychological Bulletin*, *127*, 773–796. doi:10.1037/0033-2909.127.6.773

Hankin, B. L., & Abramson, L. Y. (2002). Measuring cognitive vulnerability to depression in adolescence: Reliability, validity, and gender differences. *Journal of Clinical Child & Adolescent Psychology*, *31*, 491–504.

Hankin, B. L., Abramson, L. Y., Miller, N., & Haeffel, G. J. (2004). Cognitive vulnerability-stress theories of depression: Examining affective specificity in the prediction of depression versus anxiety in three prospective studies. *Cognitive Therapy and Research*, *28*, 309–345. doi:10.1023/B:COTR.0000031805.60529.0d

Hankin, B. L., Fraley, R. C., & Abela, J. R. (2005). Daily depression and cognitions about stress: evidence for a traitlike depressogenic cognitive style and the prediction of depressive symptoms in a prospective daily diary study. *Journal of Personality and Social Psychology*, *88*(4), 673.

Hankin, B. L., Gibb, B. E., Abela, J. R., & Flory, K. (2010). Selective attention to affective stimuli and clinical depression among youths: Role of anxiety and specificity of emotion. *Journal of Abnormal Psychology*, *119*(3), 491.

Hankin, B. L., Oppenheimer, C., Jenness, J., Barrocas, A. L., Shapero, B. G., & Goldband, J. (2009). Developmental origins of cognitive vulnerabilities to depression: Review of processes contributing to stability and change across time. *Journal of Clinical Psychology*, *65*, 1327–1338. doi:10.1002/jclp.20625

Hankin, B. L., Snyder, H. R., & Gulley, L. D. (2016a). Cognitive risks in developmental psychopathology. In D. Cicchetti (Ed.), *Developmental psychopathology* (vol. 2). Hoboken, NJ: Wiley.

Hankin, B. L., Snyder, H. R., Gulley, L. D., Schweizer, T. H., Bijttebier, P., Nelis, S.,... & Vasey, M. W. (2016b). Understanding comorbidity among internalizing problems: Integrating latent structural models of psychopathology and risk mechanisms. *Development and Psychopathology*, *28*(4pt1), 987–1012.

Hankin, B. L., Wetter, E., Cheely, C., & Oppenheimer, C. W. (2008). Beck's cognitive theory of depression in adolescence: Specific prediction of depressive symptoms and reciprocal influences in a multi-wave prospective study. *International Journal of Cognitive Therapy*, *1*(4), 313–332.

Harrington, J. A., & Blankenship, V. (2002). Ruminative thoughts and their relation to depression and anxiety. *Journal of Applied Social Psychology*, *32*(3), 465–485.

Harrison, A. J., & Gibb, B. E. (2015). Attentional biases in currently depressed children: An eye-tracking study of biases in sustained attention to emotional stimuli. *Journal of Clinical Child & Adolescent Psychology*, *44*(6), 1008–1014.

Hart, H., & Rubia, K. (2012). Neuroimaging of child abuse: a critical review. *Frontiers in Human Neuroscience*, *6*, 52. doi: 10.3389/fnhum.2012.00052

Hatzenbuehler, M. L., Nolen-Hoeksema, S., & Dovidio, J. (2009). How does stigma "get under the skin"? The mediating role of emotion regulation. *Psychological Science*, *20*(10), 1282–1289.

Hauer, B. J., Wessel, I., Engelhard, I. M., Peeters, L. L., & Dalgleish, T. (2009). Prepartum autobiographical memory specificity predicts post-traumatic stress symptoms following complicated pregnancy. *Memory*, *17*(5), 544–556.

Henderson, R. K., Snyder, H. R., Gupta, T., & Banich, M. T. (2012). When does stress help or harm? The effects of stress controllability and subjective stress response on stroop performance. *Frontiers in Psychology, 3:179.* doi: 10.3389/fpsyg.2012.00179

Hermans, D., Vandromme, H., Debeer, E., Raes, F., Demyttenaere, K., Brunfaut, E., & Williams, J. M. G. (2008). Overgeneral autobiographical memory predicts diagnostic status in depression. *Behaviour Research and Therapy, 46*(5), 668–677.

Hilt, L. M., Sander, L. C., Nolen-Hoeksema, S., & Simen, A. A. (2007). The BDNF Val66Met polymorphism predicts rumination and depression differently in young adolescent girls and their mothers. *Neuroscience Letters, 429*(1), 12–16.

Hipwell, A. E., Sapotichne, B., Klostermann, S., Battista, D., & Keenan, K. (2011). Autobiographical memory as a predictor of depression vulnerability in girls. *Journal of Clinical Child & Adolescent Psychology, 40*(2), 254–265.

Hitchcock, C., Nixon, R. D., & Weber, N. (2014). A review of overgeneral memory in child psychopathology. *British Journal of Clinical Psychology, 53*(2), 170–193.

Holm-Denoma, J. M., & Hankin, B. L. (2010). Perceived physical appearance mediates the rumination and bulimic symptom link in adolescent girls. *Journal of Clinical Child & Adolescent Psychology, 39*(4), 537–544.

Hong, R. Y. (2007). Worry and rumination: Differential associations with anxious and depressive symptoms and coping behavior. *Behaviour Research and Therapy, 45*(2), 277–290.

Horan, W. P., Rassovsky, Y., Kern, R. S., Lee, J., Wynn, J. K., & Green, M. F. (2010). Further support for the role of dysfunctional attitudes in models of real-world functioning in schizophrenia. *Journal of Psychiatric Research, 44*, 499–505. doi:10.1016/j.jpsychires.2009.11.001

Horwitz, J. E., & McCaffrey, R. J. (2008). Effects of a third party observer and anxiety on tests of executive function. *Archives of Clinical Neuropsychology, 23*(4), 409–417.

In-Albon, T., Kossowsky, J., & Schneider, S. (2010). Vigilance and Avoidance of Threat in the Eye Movements of Children with Separation Anxiety Disorder. *Journal of Abnormal Child Psychology, 38*(2), 225–235.

Ingram, R. E., & Luxton, D. D. (2005). Vulnerability-stress models. In *Development of psychopathology: A vulnerability-stress perspective* (pp. 32–46). Thousand Oaks, CA: Sage Publications.

Ingram, R. E., Miranda, J., & Segal, Z. V. (1998). *Cognitive vulnerability to depression.* New York, NY: Guilford Press.

Ingram, R. E., Miranda, J., & Segal, Z. (2006). Cognitive vulnerability to depression. In *Cognitive vulnerability to emotional disorders* (pp. 63–91). New York, NY: Psychology Press.

Ingram, R. E., & Price, J. M. (2001). The role of vulnerability in understanding psychopathology. In R. E. Ingram & J. M. Price (Eds.), *Vulnerability to psychopathology: Risk across the lifespan* (pp. 3–19). New York, NY: Guilford Press.

Jabben, N., Arts, B., Jongen, E. M., Smulders, F. T., van Os, J., & Krabbendam, L. (2012). Cognitive processes and attitudes in bipolar disorder: A study into personality, dysfunctional attitudes and attention bias in patients with bipolar disorder and their relatives. *Journal of Affective Disorders, 143*(1), 265–268.

Jacobs, R. H., Reinecke, M. A., Gollan, J. K., & Kane, P. (2008). Empirical evidence of cognitive vulnerability for depression among children and adolescents: A cognitive science and developmental perspective. *Clinical Psychology Review, 28*(5), 759–782.

Jenness, J. L., Young, J. F., & Hankin, B. L. (2017). 5-HTTLPR moderates the association between attention away from angry faces and prospective depression among youth. *Journal of Psychiatric Research, 91*, 83–89.

Johnson, S. L., McKenzie, G., & McMurrich, S. (2008). Ruminative responses to negative and positive affect among students diagnosed with bipolar disorder and major depressive disorder. *Cognitive Therapy and Research, 32*(5), 702–713.

Joiner, T. E., Wingate, L. R., Gencoz, T., & Gencoz, F. (2005). Stress generation in depression: Three studies on its resilience, possible mechanism, and symptom specificity. *Journal of Social and Clinical Psychology, 24*(2), 236–253.

Jongen, E. M., Smulders, F. T., Ranson, S. M., Arts, B. M., & Krabbendam, L. (2007). Attentional bias and general orienting processes in bipolar disorder. *Journal of Behavior Therapy and Experimental Psychiatry, 38*(2), 168–183.

Joormann, J., Talbot, L., & Gotlib, I. H. (2007). Biased processing of emotional information in girls at risk for depression. *Journal of Abnormal Psychology, 116*(1), 135.

Kappenman, E. S., Farrens, J. L., Luck, S. J., & Proudfit, G. H. (2014). Behavioral and ERP measures of attentional bias to threat in the dot-probe task: Poor reliability and lack of correlation with anxiety. *Frontiers in Psychology, 5*: 1368. doi: 10.3389/fpsyg.2014.01368

Kazdin, A. E., Kraemer, H. C., Kessler, R. C., Kupfer, D. J., & Offord, D. R. (1997). Contributions of risk-factor research to developmental psychopathology. *Clinical Psychology Review, 17*(4), 375–406.

Kercher, A., & Rapee, R. M. (2009). A test of a cognitive diathesis-stress generation pathway in early adolescent depression. *Journal of Abnormal Child Psychology, 37*(6), 845–855.

Kim, W. J., Ha, R. Y., Sun, J. Y., Ryu, V., Lee, S. J., Ha, K., & Cho, H. S. (2014). Autobiographical memory and its association with neuropsychological function in bipolar disorder. *Comprehensive Psychiatry, 55*(2), 290–297.

King, M. J., MacDougall, A. G., Ferris, S. M., Levine, B., MacQueen, G. M., & McKinnon, M. C. (2010). A review of factors that moderate autobiographical memory performance in patients with major depressive disorder. *Journal of Clinical and Experimental Neuropsychology, 32*(10), 1122–1144.

Kirschbaum, C., Pirke, K. M., & Hellhammer, D. H. (1993). The "Trier Social Stress Test"—A tool for investigating psychobiological stress responses in a laboratory setting. *Neuropsychobiology, 28*(1–2), 76–81.

Kraemer, H. C., Stice, E., Kazdin, A., Offord, D., & Kupfer, D. (2001). How do risk factors work together? Mediators, moderators, and independent, overlapping, and proxy risk factors. *American Journal of Psychiatry, 158*(6), 848–856.

Kuckertz, J. M., & Amir, N. (2015). Attention bias modification for anxiety and phobias: Current status and future directions. *Current Psychiatry Reports, 17*(2), 9.

Kujawa, A. J., Torpey, D., Kim, J., Hajcak, G., Rose, S., Gotlib, I. H., & Klein, D. N. (2011). Attentional biases for emotional faces in young children of mothers with chronic or recurrent depression. *Journal of Abnormal Child Psychology, 39*(1), 125–135.

Kurtz, M. M., & Gerraty, R. T. (2009). A meta-analytic investigation of neurocognitive deficits in bipolar illness: Profile and effects of clinical state. *Neuropsychology, 23*(5), 551–562.

Kuyken, W., & Dalgleish, T. (2011). Overgeneral autobiographical memory in adolescents at risk for depression. *Memory, 19*(3), 241–250.

Laceulle, O. M., Vollebergh, W. A., & Ormel, J. (2015). The structure of psychopathology in adolescence: Replication of a general psychopathology factor in the TRAILS study. *Clinical Psychological Science, 3*(6), 850–860.

Lahey, B. B., Krueger, R. F., Rathouz, P. J., Waldman, I. D., & Zald, D. H. (2017). A hierarchical causal taxonomy of psychopathology across the life span. *Psychological Bulletin, 143*(2), 142–186.

Lakdawalla, Z., Hankin, B. L., & Mermelstein, R. (2007). Cognitive theories of depression in children and adolescents: A conceptual and quantitative review. *Clinical Child and Family Psychology review, 10*(1), 1–24.

LeMoult, J., & Joormann, J. (2012). Attention and memory biases in social anxiety disorder: The role of comorbid depression. *Cognitive Therapy and Research, 36*(1), 47–57.

Lewandowski, K. E., Cohen, B. M., & Öngur, D. (2011). Evolution of neuropsychological dysfunction during the course of schizophrenia and bipolar disorder. *Psychological Medicine, 41*(2), 225–241.

Liang, C. W., Tsai, J. L., & Hsu, W. Y. (2017). Sustained visual attention for competing emotional stimuli in social anxiety: An eye tracking study. *Journal of Behavior Therapy and Experimental Psychiatry, 54*, 178–185.

Lien, Y. J., Yang, H. J., Kuo, P. H., & Chen, W. J. (2011). Relation of perseverative tendency and life events to depressive symptoms: Findings from a prospective study in non-referred adolescents in Taiwan. *Behavioral Medicine, 37*(1), 1–7.

Lipszyc, J., & Schachar, R. (2010). Inhibitory control and psychopathology: A meta-analysis of studies using the stop signal task. *Journal of the International Neuropsychological Society, 16*(6), 1064–1076.

Liu, R. T. (2013). Stress generation: Future directions and clinical implications. *Clinical Psychology Review, 33*(3), 406–416.

Liu, R. T., & Alloy, L. B. (2010). Stress generation in depression: A systematic review of the empirical literature and recommendations for future study. *Clinical Psychology Review, 30*(5), 582–593.

Liu, R. T., Kleiman, E. M., Nestor, B. A., & Cheek, S. M. (2015). The hopelessness theory of depression: A quarter-century in review. *Clinical Psychology: Science and Practice, 22*(4), 345–365.

Liu, X., Li, L., Xiao, J., Yang, J., & Jiang, X. (2013). Abnormalities of autobiographical memory of patients with depressive disorders: A meta-analysis. *Psychology and Psychotherapy: Theory, Research and Practice, 86*(4), 353–373.

Luethi, M., Meier, B., & Sandi, C. (2008). Stress effects on working memory, explicit memory, and implicit memory for neutral and emotional stimuli in healthy men. *Frontiers in Behavioral Neuroscience, 2*, 5. doi:10.3389/neuro.08.005.2008

Lyubomirsky, S., Layous, K., Chancellor, J., & Nelson, S. K. (2015). Thinking about rumination: The scholarly contributions and intellectual legacy of Susan Nolen-Hoeksema. *Annual Review of Clinical Psychology, 11*, 1–22.

MacLeod, C. (1999). Anxiety and anxiety disorders. In T. Dalgleish & M. Powers (Eds.), *The handbook of cognition and emotion* (pp. 447–477). Chichester, England: Wiley.

MacLeod, C., & Hagan, R. (1992). Individual differences in the selective processing of threatening information, and emotional responses to a stressful life event. *Behaviour Research and Therapy, 30*(2), 151–161.

MacLeod, C., Mathews, A., & Tata, P. (1986). Attentional bias in emotional disorders. *Journal of Abnormal Psychology, 95*(1), 15.

Majer, M., Nater, U. M., Lin, J. M. S., Capuron, L., & Reeves, W. C. (2010). Association of childhood trauma with cognitive function in healthy adults: A pilot study. *BMC Neurology, 10*(1), 61.

Mantella, R. C., Butters, M. A., Dew, M. A., Mulsant, B. H., Begley, A. E., Tracey, B.,...& Lenze, E. J. (2007). Cognitive impairment in late-life generalized anxiety disorder. *The American Journal of Geriatric Psychiatry, 15*(8), 673–679.

Martin, L. L., & Tesser, A. (1996). Some ruminative thoughts. *Advances in Social Cognition, 9*, 1–47.

Mathews, A., & MacLeod, C. (2002). Induced processing biases have causal effects on anxiety. *Cognition & Emotion, 16*(3), 331–354.

McLaughlin, K. A., Aldao, A., Wisco, B. E., & Hilt, L. M. (2014). Rumination as a transdiagnostic factor underlying transitions between internalizing symptoms and aggressive behavior in early adolescents. *Journal of Abnormal Psychology, 123*(1), 13–23.

McLaughlin, K. A., Borkovec, T. D., & Sibrava, N. J. (2007). The effects of worry and rumination on affect states and cognitive activity. *Behavior Therapy, 38*(1), 23–38.

McLaughlin, K. A., & Nolen-Hoeksema, S. (2011). Rumination as a transdiagnostic factor in depression and anxiety. *Behaviour Research and Therapy, 49*(3), 186–193.

McTeague, L. M., Goodkind, M. S., & Etkin, A. (2016). Transdiagnostic impairment of cognitive control in mental illness. *Journal of Psychiatric Research, 83*, 37–46.

Merikangas, K. R., He, J. P., Burstein, M., Swanson, S. A., Avenevoli, S., Cui, L.,...Swendsen, J. (2010). Lifetime prevalence of mental disorders in US adolescents: Results from the National Comorbidity Survey Replication–Adolescent Supplement (NCS-A). *Journal of the American Academy of Child & Adolescent Psychiatry, 49*(10), 980–989.

Merz, E. C., Harlé, K. M., Noble, K. G., & McCall, R. B. (2016). Executive function in previously institutionalized children. *Child Development Perspectives, 10*(2), 105–110.

Mezulis, A. H., Abramson, L. Y., Hyde, J. S., & Hankin, B. L. (2004). Is there a universal positivity bias in attributions? A meta-analytic review of individual, developmental, and cultural differences in the self-serving attributional bias. *Psychological Bulletin, 130*(5), 711.

Mezzacappa, E., Kindlon, D., & Earls, F. (2001). Child abuse and performance task assessments of executive functions in boys. *The Journal of Child Psychology and Psychiatry and Allied Disciplines, 42*(8), 1041–1048.

Michl, L. C., McLaughlin, K. A., Shepherd, K., & Nolen-Hoeksema, S. (2013). Rumination as a mechanism linking stressful life events to symptoms of depression and anxiety: Longitudinal evidence in early adolescents and adults. *Journal of Abnormal Psychology, 122*(2), 339.

Miyake, A., & Friedman, N. P. (2012). The nature and organization of individual differences in executive functions: Four general conclusions. *Current Directions in Psychological Science, 21*(1), 8–14.

Moberly, N. J., & Watkins, E. R. (2008). Ruminative self-focus and negative affect: An experience sampling study. *Journal of Abnormal Psychology, 117*(2), 314.

Mogg, K., & Bradley, B. P. (2005). Attentional bias in generalized anxiety disorder versus depressive disorder. *Cognitive Therapy and Research, 29*(1), 29–45.

Mogg, K., Bradley, B. P., & Williams, R. (1995). Attentional bias in anxiety and depression: The role of awareness. *British Journal of Clinical Psychology, 34*(1), 17–36.

Mogg, K., Mathews, A., & Weinman, J. (1987). Memory bias in clinical anxiety. *Journal of Abnormal Psychology, 96*(2), 94–98.

Monroe, S. M., & Simons, A. D. (1991). Diathesis-stress theories in the context of life stress research: Implications for the depressive disorders. *Psychological Bulletin, 110*(3), 406.

Moore, S. A., & Zoellner, L. A. (2007). Overgeneral autobiographical memory and traumatic events: An evaluative review. *Psychological Bulletin, 133*(3), 419.

Moran, T. P. (2016). Anxiety and working memory capacity: A meta-analysis and narrative review. *Psychological Bulletin, 142*(8), 831–864.

Murphy, F. C., Sahakian, B. J., Rubinsztein, J. S., Michael, A., Rogers, R. D., Robbins, T. W., & Paykel, E. S. (1999). Emotional bias and inhibitory control processes in mania and depression. *Psychological Medicine, 29*, 1307–1321. doi:10.1017/S00332 91799001233

Musa, C., Lépine, J. P., Clark, D. M., Mansell, W., & Ehlers, A. (2003). Selective attention in social phobia and the moderating effect of a concurrent depressive disorder. *Behaviour Research and Therapy, 41*(9), 1043–1054.

Neshat-Doost, H. T., Moradi, A. R., Taghavi, M. R., Yule, W., & Dalgleish, T. (2000). Lack of attentional bias for emotional information in clinically depressed children and adolescents on the dot probe task. *The Journal of Child Psychology and Psychiatry and Allied Disciplines, 41*(3), 363–368.

Neshat-Doost, H., Taghavi, R., Moradi, A., Yule, W., & Dalgleish, T. (1997). The performance of clinically depressed children and adolescents on the modified Stroop paradigm. *Personality and Individual Differences, 23*, 753–759.

Nolen-Hoeksema, S. (1991). Responses to depression and their effects on the duration of depressive episodes. *Journal of Abnormal Psychology, 100*(4), 569.

Nolen-Hoeksema, S. (2012). Emotion regulation and psychopathology: The role of gender. *Annual Review of Clinical Psychology, 8*, 161–187.

Nolen-Hoeksema, S., & Harrell, Z. A. (2002). Rumination, depression, and alcohol use: Tests of gender differences. *Journal of Cognitive Psychotherapy, 16*(4), 391–403.

Nolen-Hoeksema, S., Stice, E., Wade, E., & Bohon, C. (2007). Reciprocal relations between rumination and bulimic, substance abuse, and depressive symptoms in female adolescents. *Journal of Abnormal Psychology, 116*(1), 198.

Nolen-Hoeksema, S., & Watkins, E. R. (2011). A heuristic for developing transdiagnostic models of psychopathology: Explaining multifinality and divergent trajectories. *Perspectives on Psychological Science, 6*(6), 589–609.

Nolen-Hoeksema, S., Wisco, B. E., & Lyubomirsky, S. (2008). Rethinking rumination. *Perspectives on Psychological Science, 3*(5), 400–424.

Ogilvie, J. M., Stewart, A. L., Chan, R. C., & Shum, D. H. (2011). Neuropsychological measures of executive function and antisocial behavior: A meta-analysis. *Criminology, 49*(4), 1063–1107.

Olatunji, B. O., Naragon-Gainey, K., & Wolitzky-Taylor, K. B. (2013). Specificity of rumination in anxiety and depression: A multimodal meta-analysis. *Clinical Psychology: Science and Practice, 20*(3), 225–257.

Ono, M., Devilly, G. J., & Shum, D. H. (2016). A meta-analytic review of overgeneral memory: The role of trauma history, mood, and the presence of posttraumatic stress disorder. *Psychological Trauma: Theory, Research, Practice, and Policy, 8*(2), 157–164.

Op den Kelder, R., Ensink, J. B. M., Overbeek, J., Maric, M., Lindauer, R. J. L. (2017). Executive function as a mediator in the link between single or complex trauma and posttraumatic stress in children and adolescents. *Quality of Life Research, 26*(7), 1–10.

Orbach, Y., Lamb, M. E., Sternberg, K. J., Williams, J. M. G., & Dawud-Noursi, S. (2001). The effect of being a victim or witness of family violence on the retrieval of autobiographical memories. *Child Abuse & Neglect, 25*(11), 1427–1437.

Osinsky, R., Lösch, A., Hennig, J., Alexander, N., & MacLeod, C. (2012). Attentional bias to negative information and 5-HTTLPR genotype interactively predict students' emotional reactivity to first university semester. *Emotion, 12*(3), 460.

Palker-Corell, A., & Marcus, D. K. (2004). Partner abuse, learned helplessness, and trauma symptoms. *Journal of Social and Clinical Psychology, 23*(4), 445–462.

Pechtel, P., & Pizzagalli, D. A. (2011). Effects of early life stress on cognitive and affective function: An integrated review of human literature. *Psychopharmacology, 214*(1), 55–70.

Peckham, A. D., McHugh, R. K., & Otto, M. W. (2010). A meta-analysis of the magnitude of biased attention in depression. *Depression and Anxiety, 27*(12), 1135–1142.

Pérez-Edgar, K., Reeb-Sutherland, B. C., McDermott, J. M., White, L. K., Henderson, H. A., Degnan, K. A.,...& Fox, N. A. (2011). Attention biases to threat link behavioral inhibition to social withdrawal over time in very young children. *Journal of abnormal Child Psychology, 39*(6), 885-895.

Perna, R. B., & Kiefner, M. (2013). Long-term cognitive sequelae: Abused children without PTSD. *Applied Neuropsychology: Child, 2*(1), 1–5.

Pflugshaupt, T., Mosimann, U. P., von Wartburg, R., Schmitt, W., Nyffeler, T., & Müri, R. M. (2005). Hypervigilance–avoidance pattern in spider phobia. *Journal of Anxiety Disorders, 19*(1), 105–116.

Pine, D. S., Mogg, K., Bradley, B. P., Montgomery, L., Monk, C. S., McClure, E.,...Kaufman, J. (2005). Attention bias to threat in maltreated children: Implications for vulnerability to stress-related psychopathology. *American Journal of Psychiatry, 162*(2), 291–296

Plessow, F., Kiesel, A., & Kirschbaum, C. (2012). The stressed prefrontal cortex and goal- directed behaviour: Acute psychosocial stress impairs the flexible implementation of task goals. *Experimental Brain Research, 216*(3), 397–408.

Polak, A. R., Witteveen, A. B., Reitsma, J. B., & Olff, M. (2012). The role of executive function n posttraumatic stress disorder: A systematic review. *Journal of Affective Disorders, 141*(1), 11–21.

Pollak, S. D., & Tolley-Schell, S. A. (2003). Selective attention to facial emotion in physically abused children. *Journal of Abnormal Psychology, 112*(3), 323.

Price, R. B., Kuckertz, J. M., Siegle, G. J., Ladouceur, C. D., Silk, J. S., Ryan, N. D.,...& Amir, N. (2015). Empirical recommendations for improving the stability of the dot-probe task in clinical research. *Psychological Assessment, 27*(2), 365.

Price, R. B., & Mohlman, J. (2007). Inhibitory control and symptom severity in late life generalized anxiety disorder. *Behaviour Research and Therapy, 45*(11), 2628–2639.

Price, R. B., Rosen, D., Siegle, G. J., Ladouceur, C. D., Tang, K., Allen, K. B.,...Silk, J. S. (2016). From anxious youth to depressed adolescents: Prospective prediction of 2-year depression symptoms via attentional bias measures. *Journal of Abnormal Psychology, 125*(2), 267.

Puliafico, A. C., & Kendall, P. C. (2006). Threat-related attentional bias in anxious youth: A review. *Clinical Child and Family Psychology Review, 9*(3–4), 162–180.

Purcell, R., Maruff, P., Kyrios, M., & Pantelis, C. (1998). Neuropsychological deficits in obsessive-compulsive disorder: A comparison with unipolar depression, panic disorder, and normal controls. *Archives of General Psychiatry, 55*(5), 415–423.

Rapoport, J. L., Giedd, J. N., & Gogtay, N. (2012). Neurodevelopmental model of schizophrenia: Update 2012. *Molecular Psychiatry, 17*(12), 1228.

Raver, C. C., Blair, C., & Willoughby, M. (2013). Poverty as a predictor of 4-year-olds' executive function: New perspectives on models of differential susceptibility. *Developmental Psychology, 49*(2), 292.

Rawal, A., & Rice, F. (2012). Examining overgeneral autobiographical memory as a risk factor for adolescent depression. *Journal of the American Academy of Child & Adolescent Psychiatry, 51*(5), 518–527.

Rector, N. A. (2004). Dysfunctional attitudes and symptom expression in schizophrenia: Differential associations with paranoid delusions and negative symptoms. *Journal of Cognitive Psychotherapy, 18*(2), 163–173.

Renoult, L., Davidson, P. S., Palombo, D. J., Moscovitch, M., & Levine, B. (2012). Personal semantics: At the crossroads of semantic and episodic memory. *Trends in Cognitive Sciences, 16*(11), 550–558.

Repovš, G., & Baddeley, A. (2006). The multi-component model of working memory: Explorations in experimental cognitive psychology. *Neuroscience, 139*(1), 5–21.

Robinson, N. S., Garber, J., & Hilsman, R. (1995). Cognitions and stress: Direct and moderating effects on depressive versus externalizing symptoms during the junior high school transition. *Journal of Abnormal Psychology, 104*(3), 453.

Roiser, J., Farmer, A., Lam, D., Burke, A., O'neill, N., Keating, S.,...& McGuffin, P. (2009). The effect of positive mood induction on emotional processing in euthymic individuals with bipolar disorder and controls. *Psychological Medicine, 39*(5), 785–791.

Rood, L., Roelofs, J., Bögels, S. M., Nolen-Hoeksema, S., & Schouten, E. (2009). The influence of emotion-focused rumination and distraction on depressive symptoms in non-clinical youth: A meta-analytic review. *Clinical Psychology Review, 29*(7), 607–616.

Rose, D. T., & Abramson, L. Y. (1992). Developmental predictors of depressive cognitive style: Research and theory. In D. Cicchetti & S. Toth (Eds.), *Rochester symposium of developmental psychopathology*, vol. IV (pp. 323–349). Rochester, NY: University of Rochester Press.

Rucklidge, J., Brown, D., Crawford, S., & Kaplan, B. (2007). Attributional styles and psychosocial functioning of adults with ADHD: Practice issues and gender differences. *Journal of Attention Disorders, 10*(3), 288–298.

Runyon, M. K., & Kenny, M. C. (2002). Relationship of attributional style, depression, and posttrauma distress among children who suffered physical or sexual abuse. *Child Maltreatment, 7*(3), 254–264.

Ruscio, A. M., Gentes, E. L., Jones, J. D., Hallion, L. S., Coleman, E. S., & Swendsen, J. (2015). Rumination predicts heightened responding to stressful life events in major depressive disorder and generalized anxiety disorder. *Journal of Abnormal Psychology, 124*(1), 17–26.

Russel, A., Haeffel, G. J., Hankin, B. L., Maxwell, S. E., & Perera, R. A. (2014). Moving beyond main effects: A data analytic

strategy for testing complex theories of clinical phenomena. *Clinical Psychology: Science and Practice, 21*, 385–397.

Safford, S. M., Alloy, L. B., Abramson, L. Y., & Crossfield, A. G. (2007). Negative cognitive style as a predictor of negative life events in depression-prone individuals: A test of the stress generation hypothesis. *Journal of Affective Disorders, 99*(1), 147–154.

Salum, G. A., Mogg, K., Bradley, B. P., Gadelha, A., Pan, P., Tamanaha, A. C.,...& do Rosario, M. C. (2013). Threat bias in attention orienting: Evidence of specificity in a large community-based study. *Psychological Medicine, 43*(4), 733–745.

Sameroff, A. J., & Mackenzie, M. J. (2003). Research strategies for capturing transactional models of development: The limits of the possible. *Development and Psychopathology, 15*(3), 613–640.

Sarin, S., & Nolen-Hoeksema, S. (2010). The dangers of dwelling: An examination of the relationship between rumination and consumptive coping in survivors of childhood sexual abuse. *Cognition and Emotion, 24*(1), 71–85.

Schmukle, S. C. (2005). Unreliability of the dot probe task. *European Journal of Personality, 19*(7), 595–605.

Schofield, C. A., Inhoff, A. W., & Coles, M. E. (2013). Time-course of attention biases in social phobia. *Journal of Anxiety Disorders, 27*(7), 661–669.

Scholz, U., La Marca, R., Nater, U. M., Aberle, I., Ehlert, U., Hornung, R.,...& Kliegel, M. (2009). Go no-go performance under psychosocial stress: Beneficial effects of implementation intentions. *Neurobiology of Learning and Memory, 91*(1), 89–92.

Schoofs, D., Preuss, D., & Wolf, O. T. (2008). Psychosocial stress induces working memory impairments in an n-back paradigm. *Psychoneuroendocrinology, 33*(5), 643–653.

Schweizer, T. H., Olino, T. M., Dyson, M. W., Laptook, R. S., & Klein, D. N. (2017). Developmental origins of rumination in middle childhood: The roles of early temperament and positive parenting. *Journal of Clinical Child & Adolescent Psychology*, 1–12.

Schweizer, T. H., Snyder, H. R., & Hankin, B. L. (2018). *A reformulated architecture of cognitive risks: Evidence for common and specific dimensions and links to internalizing outcomes*. Manuscript submitted for publication.

Schweizer, T. H., Snyder, H. R., Young, J. F., & Hankin, B. L. (2018). *The structure of cognitive vulnerabilities in adolescence: Evidence for a common cognitive risk factor*. Manuscript in preparation.

Scott, J. C., Matt, G. E., Wrocklage, K. M., Crnich, C., Jordan, J., Southwick, S. M.,...Schweinsburg, B. C. (2015). A quantitative meta-analysis of neurocognitive functioning in posttraumatic stress disorder. *Psychological Bulletin, 141*(1), 105–140.

Seiffge-Krenke, I., & Klessinger, N. (2000). Long-term effects of avoidant coping on adolescents' depressive symptoms. *Journal of Youth and Adolescence, 29*(6), 617–630.

Selby, E. A., Anestis, M. D., & Joiner, T. E. (2008). Understanding the relationship between emotional and behavioral dysregulation: Emotional cascades. *Behaviour Research and Therapy, 46*(5), 593–611.

Shackman, J. E., Shackman, A. J., & Pollak, S. D. (2007). Physical abuse amplifies attention to t hreat and increases anxiety in children. *Emotion, 7*(4), 838.

Shapero, B. G., Hankin, B. L., & Barrocas, A. L. (2013). Stress generation and exposure in a multi-wave study of adolescents:

Transactional processes and sex differences. *Journal of Social and Clinical Psychology, 32*(9), 989–1012.

Shih, J. H., Abela, J. R., & Starrs, C. (2009). Cognitive and interpersonal predictors of stress generation in children of affectively ill parents. *Journal of Abnormal Child Psychology, 37*(2), 195.

Simons, A. D., Angell, K. L., Monroe, S. M., & Thase, M. E. (1993). Cognition and life stress in depression: Cognitive factors and the definition, rating, and generation of negative life events. *Journal of Abnormal Psychology, 102*(4), 584.

Snyder, H. R. (2013). Major depressive disorder is associated with broad impairments on neuropsychological measures of executive function: A meta-analysis and review. *Psychological Bulletin, 139*(1), 81–132.

Snyder, H. R., & Hankin, B. L. (2016). Spiraling out of control: Stress generation and subsequent rumination mediate the link between poorer cognitive control and internalizing psychopathology. *Clinical Psychological Science, 4*(6), 1047–1064.

Snyder, H. R., Hankin, B. L., Sandman, C. A., Head, K., & Davis, E. P. (2017). Distinct patterns of reduced prefrontal and limbic gray matter volume in childhood general and internalizing psychopathology. *Clinical Psychological Science, 5*(6), 1001–1013.

Snyder, H. R., Hutchison, N., Nyhus, E., Curran, T., Banich, M. T., O'Reilly, R. C., & Munakata, Y. (2010). Neural inhibition enables selection during language processing. *Proceedings of the National Academy of Sciences, 107*(38), 16483–16488.

Snyder, H. R., Kaiser, R. H., Warren, S. L., & Heller, W. (2015). Obsessive-compulsive disorder is associated with broad impairments in executive function: A meta-analysis. *Clinical Psychological Science, 3*(2), 301–330.

Snyder, H. R., Kaiser, R. H., Whisman, M. A., Turner, A. E., Guild, R. M., & Munakata, Y. (2014). Opposite effects of anxiety and depressive symptoms on executive function: The case of selecting among competing options. *Cognition & Emotion, 28*(5), 893–902.

Snyder, H. R., Miyake, A., & Hankin, B. L. (2015). Advancing understanding of executive function impairments and psychopathology: Bridging the gap between clinical and cognitive approaches. *Frontiers in Psychology, 6.*

Snyder, H. R., Young, J. F., & Hankin, B. L. (2017). Strong homotypic continuity in common psychopathology-, internalizing-, and externalizing-specific factors over time in adolescents. *Clinical Psychological Science, 5*(1), 98–110.

Spasojević, J., & Alloy, L. B. (2002). Who becomes a depressive ruminator? Developmental antecedents of ruminative response style. *Journal of Cognitive Psychotherapy, 16*(4), 405–419.

Stange, J. P., Hamlat, E. J., Hamilton, J. L., Abramson, L. Y., & Alloy, L. B. (2013). Overgeneral autobiographical memory, emotional maltreatment, and depressive symptoms in adolescence: Evidence of a cognitive vulnerability–stress interaction. *Journal of Adolescence, 36*(1), 201–208.

Starcke, K., Wiesen, C., Trotzke, P., & Brand, M. (2016). Effects of acute laboratory stress on executive functions. *Frontiers in Psychology, 7.*

Starcke, K., Wolf, O. T., Markowitsch, H. J., & Brand, M. (2008). Anticipatory stress influences decision making under explicit risk conditions. *Behavioral Neuroscience, 122*(6), 1352–1360. doi: 10.1037/a0013281

Sumner, J. A., Griffith, J. W., & Mineka, S. (2010). Overgeneral autobiographical memory as a predictor of the course of depression: A meta-analysis. *Behaviour Research and Therapy, 48*(7), 614–625.

Sumner, J. A., Griffith, J. W., Mineka, S., Rekart, K. N., Zinbarg, R. E., & Craske, M. G. (2011). Overgeneral autobiographical memory and chronic interpersonal stress as predictors of the course of depression in adolescents. *Cognition and Emotion, 25*(1), 183–192.

Sumner, J. A., Mineka, S., Zinbarg, R. E., Craske, M. G., Vrshek-Schallhorn, S., & Epstein, A. (2014). Examining the long-term stability of overgeneral autobiographical memory. *Memory, 22*(3), 163–170.

Sylvester, C. M., Hudziak, J. J., Gaffrey, M. S., Barch, D. M., & Luby, J. L. (2016). Stimulus- driven attention, threat bias, and sad bias in youth with a history of an anxiety disorder or depression. *Journal of Abnormal Child Psychology, 44*(2), 219–231.

Thomas, J., Knowles, R., Tai, S., & Bentall, R. P. (2007). Response styles to depressed mood in bipolar affective disorder. *Journal of Affective Disorders, 100*(1), 249–252.

Tibu, F., Sheridan, M. A., McLaughlin, K. A., Nelson, C. A., Fox, N. A., & Zeanah, C. H. (2016). Disruptions of working memory and inhibition mediate the association between exposure to institutionalization and symptoms of attention deficit hyperactivity disorder. *Psychological Medicine, 46*(3), 529–541.

Trevisani, D. P., Johnson, S. L., & Carver, C. S. (2008). Positive mood induction and facial affect recognition among students at risk for mania. *Cognitive Therapy and Research, 32*(5), 639–650.

Van Bockstaele, B., Verschuere, B., Tibboel, H., De Houwer, J., Crombez, G., & Koster, E. H. (2014). A review of current evidence for the causal impact of attentional bias on fear and anxiety. *Psychological Bulletin, 140*(3), 682.

Van Daele, T., Griffith, J. W., Van den Bergh, O., & Hermans, D. (2014). Overgeneral autobiographical memory predicts changes in depression in a community sample. *Cognition and Emotion, 28*(7), 1303–1312.

Van Mourik, R., Oosterlaan, J., & Sergeant, J. A. (2005). The Stroop revisited: A meta-analysis of interference control in AD/HD. *Journal of Child Psychology and Psychiatry, 46*(2), 150–165.

Verhaak, C. M., Smeenk, J. M., van Minnen, A., & Kraaimaat, F. W. (2004). Neuroticism, preattentive and attentional biases towards threat, and anxiety before and after a severe stressor: A prospective study. *Personality and Individual Differences, 36*(4), 767–778.

Vilgis, V., Silk, T. J., & Vance, A. (2015). Executive function and attention in children and adolescents with depressive disorders: A systematic review. *European Child & Adolescent Psychiatry, 24*(4), 365–384.

Vrielynck, N., Deplus, S., & Philippot, P. (2007). Overgeneral autobiographical memory and depressive disorder in children. *Journal of Clinical Child and Adolescent Psychology, 36*(1), 95–105.

Wagner, S., Müller, C., Helmreich, I., Huss, M., & Tadić, A. (2015). A meta-analysis of cognitive functions in children and adolescents with major depressive disorder. *European Child & Adolescent Psychiatry, 24*(1), 5–19.

Wald, I., Lubin, G., Holoshitz, Y., Muller, D., Fruchter, E., Pine, D. S., . . . Bar-Haim, Y. (2011). Battlefield-like stress following simulated combat and suppression of attention bias to threat. *Psychological Medicine, 41*(4), 699–707.

Wald, I., Shechner, T., Bitton, S., Holoshitz, Y., Charney, D. S., Muller, D.,...Bar-Haim, Y. (2011). Attention bias away from threat during life threatening danger predicts PTSD symptoms at one-year follow-up. *Depression and Anxiety*, *28*(5), 406–411.

Walshaw, P. D., Alloy, L. B., & Sabb, F. W. (2010). Executive function in pediatric bipolar disorder and attention-deficit hyperactivity disorder: In search of distinct phenotypic profiles. *Neuropsychology Review*, *20*(1), 103–120.

Waters, A. M., Bradley, B. P., & Mogg, K. (2014). Biased attention to threat in paediatric anxiety disorders (generalized anxiety disorder, social phobia, specific phobia, separation anxiety disorder) as a function of "distress" versus "fear" diagnostic categorization. *Psychological Medicine*, *44*(3), 607–616.

Watkins, E. R. (2008). Constructive and unconstructive repetitive thought. *Psychological Bulletin*, *134*(2), 163.

Watkins, E. R. (2009). Depressive rumination and co-morbidity: Evidence for brooding as a transdiagnostic process. *Journal of Rational- Emotive & Cognitive-Behavior Therapy*, *27*(3), 160–175.

Wenzel, A., & Cochran, C. K. (2006). Autobiographical memories prompted by automatic thoughts in panic disorder and social phobia. *Cognitive Behaviour Therapy*, *35*(3), 129–137.

Wenzel, A., Jackson, L. C., & Holt, C. S. (2002). Social phobia and the recall of autobiographical memories. *Depression and Anxiety*, *15*(4), 186–189.

Wessel, I., Meeren, M., Peeters, F., Arntz, A., & Merckelbach, H. (2001). Correlates of autobiographical memory specificity: The role of depression, anxiety and childhood trauma. *Behaviour Research and Therapy*, *39*(4), 409–421.

Wilhelm, S., McNally, R. J., Baer, L., & Florin, I. (1997). Autobiographical memory in obsessive-compulsive disorder. *British Journal of Clinical Psychology*, *36*(1), 21–31.

Williams, J. M. G., Barnhofer, T., Crane, C., Hermans, D., Raes, F., Watkins, E., & Dalgleish, T. (2007). Autobiographical memory specificity and emotional disorder. *Psychological Bulletin*, *133*(1), 122–148.

Williams, J. M., & Broadbent, K. (1986). Autobiographical memory in suicide attempters. *Journal of Abnormal Psychology*, *95*(2), 144.

Williams, J. M. G. (2006). Capture and rumination, functional avoidance, and executive control (CaRFAX): Three processes that underlie overgeneral memory. *Cognition and Emotion*, *20*(3–4), 548–568.

Williams, J. M. G., Mathews, A., & MacLeod, C. (1996). The emotional Stroop task and psychopathology. *Psychological Bulletin*, *120*(1), 3.

Williams, J.M.G., Watts, F.N., MacLeod, C., & Mathews, A. (1988). *Cognitive psychology and emotional disorders*. Oxford, England: John Wiley & Sons.

Winer, E. S., & Salem, T. (2016). Reward devaluation: Dot-probe meta-analytic evidence of avoidance of positive information in depressed persons. *Psychological Bulletin*, *142*(1), 18.

Woody, M. L., Owens, M., Burkhouse, K. L., & Gibb, B. E. (2016). Selective attention toward angry faces and risk for major depressive disorder in women: Converging evidence from retrospective and prospective analyses. *Clinical Psychological Science*, *4*(2), 206–215.

Zahn-Waxler, C., Crick, N. R., Shirtcliff, E. A., & Woods, K. E. (2006). The origins and development of psychopathology in females and males. In D. Cicchetti & D. J. Cohen (Eds.), *Developmental psychopathology: Theory and method* (pp. 76–138). Hoboken, NJ: Wiley.

Zlomuzica, A., Dere, D., Machulska, A., Adolph, D., Dere, E., & Margraf, J. (2014). Episodic memories in anxiety disorders: Clinical implications. *Frontiers in Behavioral Neuroscience*, *8*, 131. doi: 10.3389/fnbeh.2014.00131

Personality-Stress Vulnerability Models

Thomas M. Olino, Rebekah J. Mennies, *and* Zuzanna K. Wojcieszak

Abstract

There are multiple models through which stress influences the development and emergence of psychopathology. Likewise, there are multiple models that provide explanations of the associations between personality and psychopathology. Though there has been some integration of these models, focusing on diathesis stress and stress generation models, they have frequently been described in separate literatures. This chapter reviews these models and extends their integration. Throughout the chapter, we draw on studies of children, adolescents, and adults and find strong similarities in the results across development. Further, the literature on how these models operate similarly in and differently across sexes is reviewed. Based on the review, we provide a number of recommendations for future studies.

Keywords: personality, temperament, vulnerability, psychopathology, stress models

Multiple models hypothesize relationships between the experience of stress and psychopathology. Similarly, there are multiple models to explain the relationships between personality and psychopathology. Although these models are often described separately, the concepts embedded within each overlap, and conceptual work integrating these historically distinct fields is critical. The present chapter provides a review of models of the relationships between stress and psychopathology, as well as between personality and internalizing and externalizing psychopathology, focusing on ways in which stress and personality interact or influence psychopathology. We extend discussion of personality-psychopathology models that typically do not address the role of stress in the manifestation, course, outcome, and/or assessment of psychopathology. Finally, we conclude by providing suggestions for future studies in this area of research.

Stress-Psychopathology Models

Models have conceptualized stress as a potential risk and/or concomitant factor for psychopathology. One perspective is that stress has a direct, if not causal, influence on the development of psychopathology. One line of research has pursued different themes of stressors and their influence on depressive and anxiety disorders with events involving loss being associated with depression and threat events being associated with anxiety (G. W. Brown, Harris, & Hepworth, 1995; Finlay-Jones & Brown, 1981; Kendler, Hettema, Butera, Gardner, & Prescott, 2003). This work has continued and recent work has revealed specificity about the nature of stressors associated with individual forms of psychopathology (e.g., Vrshek-Schallhorn et al., 2015). Beyond this direct effect model, additional prominent perspectives link stress and psychopathology in (a) diathesis-stress (Meehl, 1962) and (b) stress generation models (Hammen, 1991).

The diathesis-stress model posits that stress operates as a context in which existing vulnerabilities are associated with or predict psychopathology. Much of the "diathesis" in diathesis-stress models can be understood as trait-like individual differences that can be conceptualized as personality constructs (T. A. Brown & Rosellini, 2011; Kendler, Kuhn, & Prescott, 2004; Ormel, Oldehinkel, &

Brilman, 2001). Therefore, these models have explanatory power for understanding who is at greatest risk for an adverse response to stress based on personality vulnerabilities.

In contrast, stress generation models posit that individual characteristics may elicit stress from the environment. This model was initially developed as a means of understanding the maintenance of depression through evocative processes related to the disorder itself (Hammen, 1991, 2005, 2006). There is now a large literature on stress generation in unipolar mood disorders across adolescents and adults (Liu & Alloy, 2010). However, other investigators (e.g., Hankin, 2010) subsequently extended the model to encompass traits that may elicit stress, including rumination and neuroticism, which in turn may lead to increased symptoms or clinically significant disorder. As the stress generation model posits that individuals with psychopathology elicit stress from their environments, relative to a model positing a causal influence of stress on psychopathology, the direction of association between stress and psychopathology is reversed.

Operational Definition of Personality

Individual differences in personality have been consistently examined as vulnerability markers for psychopathology across development. Yet there are multiple perspectives and models used to operationalize personality in older adolescents and adults and temperament in children (Goldsmith, Buss, Plomin, & Rothbart, 1987; McCrae & Costa, 1987; Roberts, 2009; Shiner et al., 2012). In this chapter, we emphasize personality as conceptualized by the Big Five (Goldberg, 1990; John & Srivastava, 1999) and Big Three (Clark & Watson, 1999; Tellegen, 1985) models, originally derived from studies of adults, as the vast majority of work has relied on these models. However, because there is continuity between child temperament and adult personality (Shiner & Masten, 2008), we also describe studies of child temperament. The Big Five model includes neuroticism, extraversion, conscientiousness, agreeableness, and openness to experience, with this last dimension having the most equivocal standing as a fifth factor which has been frequently identified, but inconsistently conceptualized across models (e.g., intellect, culture; Peabody & Goldberg, 1989). The Big Three model includes isomorphic constructs of neuroticism and extraversion, but it includes constraint as a dimension with elements of both conscientiousness and agreeableness as a single dimension. Neuroticism reflects individual differences in propensity for and

response to negative affect states (e.g., sadness, anger, and fear; Zinbarg et al., 2016). Extraversion reflects individual differences in positive mood, sociability, and reward-seeking behavior (Olino, Klein, Durbin, Hayden, & Buckley, 2005; Watson & Clark, 1997), with some arguing that impulsivity and sensation seeking are also part of the construct (Eysenck & Eysenck, 1975). Temperament reflects individual differences in reactivity and regulation (Rothbart & Bates, 2006). Parallel dimensions are identified in the literature on child temperament (Dyson, Olino, Durbin, Goldsmith, & Klein, 2012; Goldsmith et al., 1987) with negative emotionality resembling neuroticism, surgency resembling extraversion, and effortful control showing conceptual overlap with constraint. Although we focus on broad dimensions, we also attend to narrower dimensions when relevant. Next, we rely on the construct labels from the adult literature to streamline our presentation.

Personality-Psychopathology Models

Multiple models have also been proposed that link personality and psychopathology (Klein, Kotov, & Bufferd, 2011; Ormel et al., 2013). Although much of this work has focused on the relationships between personality and depression, the models can and have been applied to many other forms of psychopathology (Kotov, Gamez, Schmidt, & Watson, 2010), particularly anxiety (Clark, Watson, & Mineka, 1994), externalizing disorders (Bogg & Finn, 2010; Prinzie et al., 2003), and substance use disorders (Sher, Bartholow, & Wood, 2000). Although some personality-psychopathology models incorporate stress as a context in which the associations manifest, or as a mechanism linking the constructs, many models fail to clearly address the role that stress may play in linking individual difference factors and disorders. We later address how stress could be fruitfully integrated into these models.

Some models highlight similarities in etiology of personality and psychopathology; some emphasize personality as a causal risk for psychopathology; and others emphasize the role of psychopathology on personality (Klein et al., 2011; Klein & Riso, 1993). The common cause model specifies that personality and psychopathology are both influenced by the same etiological processes and the shared etiology accounts for the associations. Furthermore, after accounting for the mutual causes, associations between personality and psychopathology are no longer present. The continuum/spectrum model identifies a shared etiology of both personality and psychopathology. Furthermore, within this perspective, there is no clear distinction between these constructs. Thus, psychopathology emerges at more extreme ranges of normative personality dimensions. The precursor model identifies similar etiologies of personality and psychopathology, but it notes that these are distinct. Furthermore, this model presupposes that personality temporally precedes and predicts onset of psychopathology.

In contrast to the previously described models, the predisposition model *does not* suggest that there are shared etiologies of personality and psychopathology. Rather, this model suggests that these constructs are distinct; personality temporally precedes and predicts psychopathology.

Two additional models reverse the direction of influence. Specifically, these models hypothesize that psychopathology influences personality. In the concomitants model, current mood state, particularly during clinically significant manifestations of psychopathology, influences the report of personality. The consequences (or scar) model hypothesizes that, rather than having state-dependent influences, psychopathology has persistent influences on personality beyond the end of an episode.

Although these models are presented as discrete, they may not operate independently. For example, personality may be causally related to the emergence of psychopathology (either the precursor or predisposition models) and may also be influenced by the experience of psychopathology (either the concomitant or consequences models). Furthermore, it is unlikely that personality will be the sole construct that leads to psychopathology (Kendler, Gardner, & Prescott, 2002; King, Iacono, & McGue, 2004; Mineka & Zinbarg, 2006). Thus, it is important to identify factors that may exacerbate or attenuate the associations between personality and psychopathology. Stress has been implicated as a critical factor in these relationships.

Personality-Stress-Psychopathology Models

There are many ways through which personality and stress may influence each other and, in turn, influence the development of psychopathology; here, we focus on the most frequently examined conceptualizations of the interrelationships between these processes. However, the research literature on links between stress, personality, and psychopathology must be evaluated with the limitations of the assessment methods used in mind. Past work has often assessed personality, stress, and psychopathology using questionnaire methods from the same informant, raising the possibility of monomethod

bias, which would overestimate associations between constructs. Neuroticism is a construct that includes aspects of stress reactivity (Bolger & Schilling, 1991). Thus, there may be some inherent overlap between the associations between neuroticism and experience of and responses to stress. As such, there is a need to assess constructs using independent methods. As described elsewhere in this handbook, there are also objective interview-based methods available to assess experience of stressful life events to evaluate the presence and severity of specific events (G. Brown & Harris, 1978; Safford, Alloy, Abramson, & Crossfield, 2007).

Additive Models
Kushner (2015) described three models explaining associations between dispositional traits and life stressors in predicting youth psychopathology with the principles of these applying equally well to adults. These are described as additive models, diathesis-stress models, and social push models. In the first of these, personality and stress each have additive effects on risk for youth psychopathology. Indeed, multiple studies have reported that an array of forms of stress incrementally predict internalizing and externalizing behavior problems beyond the influence of personality, and vice versa, across a variety of study designs (Duffy et al., 2007; Lengua, Long, Smith, & Meltzoff, 2005; McKnight, Huebner, & Suldo, 2002; Melis Yavuz, Selcuk, Corapci, & Aksan, 2017; Yang, Chiu, Soong, & Chen, 2008). However, many of these studies examined, but failed to identify significant interactions between stress and personality to predict psychopathology (Auerbach, Abela, Ho, McWhinnie, & Czajkowska, 2010; Cutrona et al., 2005; Dougherty et al., 2013; Xia, Ding, Hollon, & Wan, 2013; Yang et al., 2008).

Diathesis-Stress Models
Diathesis-stress models are examined as tests of moderation (i.e., interactions). In line with such models Meehl (1962) and Kushner (2015) emphasized two patterns of results in which stress and personality may interact to influence the presence of psychopathology. Within a diathesis-stress perspective, personality traits serve as vulnerabilities for psychopathology when an individual faces stressful life events, or associations between personality and psychopathology may be stronger in the context of greater stress. More specifically, individuals with low personality vulnerability will have lower risk for psychopathology, regardless of the experience of stress, whereas individuals with

greater personality vulnerability will be at greater risk for psychopathology as stress increases. In contrast, a "social push" model (Kushner, 2015; Raine, 1992) suggests that individuals with greater personality vulnerability have greater risk for adverse outcomes, regardless of stress; put differently, the endogenous risk these individuals have vis-à-vis personality heightens risk for disorder, irrespective of the environment. However, individuals with less vulnerability develop greater risk as stress increases. Thus, these models attempt to explain which individuals are at risk in specific contexts.

The diathesis-stress model is the most extensively researched model of the interrelationships between stress, personality, and psychopathology, and it complements multiple existing personality-psychopathology models. As defined earlier, the precursor model identifies personality and psychopathology as being distinct constructs but sharing similar etiologies. The predisposition model also argues that personality and psychopathology are distinct and that there are different etiologies of each. In both of these models, personality temporally precedes and predicts psychopathology. An integrated diathesis-stress-predisposition model suggests that personality predicts the onset of psychopathology under conditions of stress, yet personality and psychopathology arise due to distinct causal factors. Although a diathesis-stress-precursor model posits similar associations between personality, stress, and psychopathology, personality and psychopathology share etiological influences. Such shared factors are distinct from stress, which contributes to psychopathology but not personality under this model. Given that the distinction between these two models centers on the issue of shared versus distinct etiological factors for personality and psychopathology, research testing etiological influences is critical toward determining which model best describes the relationship between personality, stress, and psychopathology in a vulnerability-stress context.

Studies examining the diathesis-stress model have relied on samples across youth and adults and have focused on personality dimensions from the Big Five and Big Three models. Neuroticism is the most frequently studied personality diathesis tested as a stress-vulnerability marker (Fox, Halpern, Ryan, & Lowe, 2010; Hutchinson & Williams, 2007; Kandler & Ostendorf, 2016; Kendler et al., 2004; Kopala-Sibley, Danzig, et al., 2016). These studies have found support for the diathesis-stress model in predicting internalizing problems; specifically, there is consistent evidence for effects of neuroticism on depression at higher levels of experienced stress. Although subjective perceptions of stress are important, reports of stress may be influenced by neuroticism. Studies relying on objective measures of stress (e.g., interview-based) are needed to more clearly differentiate the influence of traits versus experienced life events. There are some exemplar studies relying on independent assessments. Within an ongoing prospective study, Ormel et al. (2001) examined the interaction between neuroticism and experience of past year stressful life events in midlife adults predicting depressive episodes. Stressful life events and psychopathology were assessed using in-person interviews and personality was assessed via self-reports. This study found support for the diathesis-stress model using strong, independent assessment methods.

Despite the merits of relying on interview-based methods to assess objective experiences of stress, as stress generation models (Hammen, 1991, 2005, 2006) posit, the experience of stressful life experiences is often dependent on the behavior of individuals. To address this issue, research has tested the impact of naturalistic stressors (e.g., natural disasters) that are independent of study participants' behavior. For example, in a study conducted following the experience of a natural disaster, Kopala-Sibley et al. (2016) found that temperamental sadness (an aspect of negative emotionality) at age 3 was associated with greater depression in the context of greater hurricane exposure and temperamental fear was associated with greater anxiety when youth faced greater hurricane-related stress.

Studies of anxiety disorders have emphasized the role of temperamental behavioral inhibition (BI), which reflects social reticence and failure to approach novelty (Kagan, 1997). BI is associated with neuroticism, cognitive vulnerabilities for psychopathology (Mezulis, Hyde, & Abramson, 2006), and incidence of anxiety disorders (Broeren, Newall, Dodd, Locker, & Hudson, 2013) when more negative life events are faced. Interestingly, Broeren et al. (2013) also found that youth reports of positive dependent (those that are influenced by the individuals' own behavior) life events diminished the influence of BI on later anxiety.

Other studies have examined multiple dimensions of personality within the same study, but they have often conducted analyses for each dimension separately (van der Veen et al., 2017). Fox et al. (2010) found that higher neuroticism was more strongly associated with both depression and anxiety in the context of higher stress. They also reported that lower positive affect, a facet of extraversion, was more strongly associated with depression with greater stress. However, positive affect was not associated with anxiety, regardless of stress. Within the context of youth peer victimization, Sugimura and Rudolph (2012) found evidence for different stress by temperament interactions for boys and girls. In girls, overt victimization was associated with overt aggression, a manifestation of externalizing problems, among those with low inhibitory control. The authors also found that overt and relational victimization predicted depressive symptoms in combination with high neuroticism in girls. However, in boys, relational victimization was associated with depressive symptoms in the context of low neuroticism. The finding for boys was driven by the strong association between neuroticism and depressive symptoms, regardless of stress. Thus, this pattern was consistent with the social push, rather than the diathesis-stress model. In a fully prospective design with the assessment of personality occurring approximately 3 years before women were exposed to a natural disaster, high neuroticism and low extraversion were each associated with greater depressive symptoms in combination with greater quantity of stressors (Kopala-Sibley, Kotov, et al., 2016). Such prospective designs provide evidence that diatheses (e.g., personality) in conjunction with stressors may precede the onset of psychopathology.

Finally, the role of personality and stress in influencing psychopathology may not depend solely on a single dimension of personality. That is, the interaction between one dimension of personality and stress influencing psychopathology may be further moderated by a second dimension of personality. For example, Gulley, Hankin, and Young (2016) found a three-way interaction between negative affectivity, effortful control, and stress to predict depression and anxiety. The authors found that greater effortful control mitigated the effect of higher negative affectivity on depression and anxiety symptoms when stress was low. However, this buffering effect was not present at high levels of stress.

Stress Generation Models
Relationships between personality, stress, and psychopathology are complex and likely involve reciprocal influences over time. The initial conceptualization of stress generation focused on dependent life stressors serving as a maintenance factor for depressive disorders. More generally, psychopathology leads to increased experience of stress; the experience of life stress may, in turn, lead to the continued experience of psychopathology (Hammen, 2006). This perspective can be expanded to whether specific dimensions of personality lead to experience of stressful life events (Hankin, 2010). As described next, these models may provide a mechanistic understanding of how personality, stress, and psychopathology are linked (Potthoff, Holahan, & Joiner, 1995).

The stress generation perspective may be enveloped within the predisposition and/or precursor models. We propose that in an integrated predisposition-stress generation model, personality and psychopathology have distinct etiologies, personality traits originate prior to the onset of psychopathology, and they are mechanistically linked via stress generation. Thus, personality traits may predispose vulnerability to psychopathology via the increased generation of stress, yet the trait and subsequent psychopathology may arise from separate etiological factors. Similarly, incorporation of stress generation and precursor models suggests that certain personality traits increase exposure to stress, which in turn contributes to the onset of psychopathology. Under this stress generation-precursor model, however, personality and psychopathology have similar yet distinct etiologies. This integrated model indicates that (1) stress plays an etiological role in both personality and psychopathology and, in turn, certain traits increase exposure to stress over time; or, conversely, that (2) personality and psychopathology partly originate from a shared factor distinct from stress, yet stress plays an additional mechanistic role in the pathway from personality to psychopathology. As with integrated vulnerability-stress models described earlier, predisposition-stress generation and precursor-stress generation models cannot truly be distinguished without a better understanding of shared versus unique etiological factors contributing to personality and psychopathology. There is a sizeable line of research examining etiological processes in links between personality and psychopathology using genetically informed designs (Hettema, Neale, Myers, Prescott, & Kendler, 2006; Iacono, Carlson, Taylor, Elkins, & McGue, 1999; Kendler, Neale, Kessler, Heath, & Eaves, 1993). It is possible to integrate stress into these investigations to increase understanding of how stressful events may exacerbate these associations.

Rather than focusing on how personality and stress interact, as expected in the predisposition and precursor models, the stress generation model (Hammen, 1991) may be expanded to focus on the influence of personality on stressful life events that, in turn, influence psychopathology. Thus, these models emphasize a causal role of personality on stress exposure and psychopathology within a mediation framework. A particular challenge in evaluating this model is the need for longitudinal designs, which is necessary for establishing temporal sequencing of the processes (Kazdin, 2007; Kraemer et al., 2002). Specifically, the vulnerability factor (personality) would temporally precede the presence of the mediator (stress), which would precede the outcome (psychopathology). These models are particularly challenging to work with because these factors likely dynamically influence each other throughout development.

Foundational studies identifying links between personality and stress exposure were cross-sectional. Using a multi-informant design, Kendler, Gardner, and Prescott (2003) found that neuroticism is a strong predictor of stressful life events among adults. Moreover, Kim et al. (2016) found that personality influenced depression through perceived stress; neuroticism was positively associated with exposure to stressful events, while extraversion, openness to experience, and conscientiousness were negatively associated with stress exposure. Some evidence also finds that stress generation mechanisms result in increases in behavior problems in offspring (Ellenbogen & Hodgins, 2004).

Prospective longitudinal studies have provided stronger evidence for these stress generation mechanisms. Magnus, Diener, Fujita, and Pavot (1993) conducted seminal work finding that neuroticism was associated with negative life events, whereas extraversion was associated with positive events. Stroud, Sosoo, and Wilson (2015) found more nuanced associations with neuroticism predicting greater acute and chronic interpersonal stressors and extraversion predicting fewer interpersonal chronic stressors in young adolescent girls. Other studies support reciprocal influences between personality and stress over time (Shapero, Hankin, & Barrocas, 2013).

Yang et al. (2008) found that experience of a depressive episode and greater neuroticism each predicted greater exposure to stress over the course of a year in adolescents. Consonant with findings from cross-sectional studies, there is strong evidence that stressful life events, particularly those that are dependent events, mediate the association between neuroticism and depression (Kercher, Rapee, & Schniering, 2009; Lakdawalla & Hankin, 2008). The links between stressful events and symptoms

may also be qualified based on the presence of cognitive vulnerabilities (Kercher et al., 2009; Lakdawalla & Hankin, 2008).

Most studies of stress generation have focused exclusively on neuroticism. A small number of studies have taken a broader view of personality by examining both neuroticism and extraversion (Gramstad, Gjestad, & Haver, 2013; Koffel et al., 2016; Wetter & Hankin, 2009). Wetter and Hankin (2009) found that the association between neuroticism and anhedonic depressive symptoms was partially mediated by dependent life events over the course of 2 years in a sample of undergraduate students. However, there was no evidence that stressful life events mediate the association between extraversion and depressive symptoms.

The aforementioned studies have provided opportunities to evaluate mechanisms linking personality and psychopathology through stressful life events in two-wave longitudinal designs. However, confidence in conclusions supporting stress generation models is tempered, because relatively few studies provide a comprehensive test with clear temporal sequencing of the constructs of interests. In a four-wave longitudinal study, Barrocas and Hankin (2011) found that the association between neuroticism and depression was mediated by stressors and, in turn, anxious arousal. Thus, there may be additional mechanisms that more proximally link the experience of stress with psychopathology. The authors also tested models with constructs in alternative, plausible temporal sequences (e.g., neuroticism → arousal → stress → depression); however, the data were less consistent with these models. This study provided a careful evaluation of these models as assessments were conducted at 5-week intervals. In one of the more intensive longitudinal studies, Hankin (2010) examined the links between neuroticism, stressful life events, and depressive symptoms using daily diary assessments over the course of 35 days. The study found that, consistent with studies of longer time courses, stressful events partially accounted for the relationship between personality and depressive symptoms. Although there is generally consistent evidence for the role of stress as a mediator of the relationship between personality, particularly neuroticism, and symptoms of psychopathology, other work suggests that stress may temporally precede personality. Stress may lead to changes in personality in ways that increase trait-like risk for disorder (Ogle, Rubin, & Siegler, 2014), or it may influence the state assessment of personality (Watson, 1988). In a longitudinal study of adolescent girls, Uliaszek et al. (2012) found that the major direction of influence was that the relationship between stress and depression and anxiety was partially mediated by neuroticism.

Pathoplasticity Models

Similar to the predisposition model, the pathoplasticity model suggests that personality is causally related to psychopathology. However, rather than specifically being associated with disorder onset, personality is hypothesized to be associated with features of psychopathology (e.g., the specific form of psychopathology, course, symptom presentation, treatment response). Although some studies of personality and psychopathology integrate stress, studies rarely fully examine pathoplasticity beyond testing manifestations of disorder. Specifically, stress is often implicated in the development of depression, but not anxiety or externalizing disorders (Spinhoven, Elzinga, Hovens, et al., 2011; Uliaszek et al., 2010, 2012); whether other aspects of pathoplasticity are apparent (e.g., treatment response) is less clear in the context of stress. Some naturalistic longitudinal studies have examined the joint influence of personality and stress on course of disorders. There is reasonably strong evidence that personality, including both extraversion (and related) and neuroticism (and related) traits (T. A. Brown, 2007; Bufferd et al., in press; Jorm et al., 2000; Kasch, Rottenberg, Arnow, & Gotlib, 2002; McFarland, Shankman, Tenke, Bruder, & Klein, 2006), and stress (Dougherty, Klein, & Davila, 2004; Spinhoven et al., 2010) individually predict course of depressive and anxiety disorders. There are also mixed findings regarding whether interactive or stress generation mechanisms are present for specific forms or multiple forms of psychopathology (Gulley et al., 2016). However, positive and negative (Spinhoven, Elzinga, Hovens, et al., 2011; Spinhoven, Elzinga, Roelofs, et al., 2011; Spinhoven et al., 2010) findings have been reported concerning the interactive influence of personality and stress on course. As these reports come from the same sample, it is challenging to reconcile these findings.

In the context of treatment, in a systematic meta-analysis, Roberts et al. (2017) recently reported that psychosocial interventions have moderate-large effects ($d = .57$) on reducing neuroticism and small effects ($d = .23$) on increasing extraversion. There have been complementary findings from pharmacological studies of depression with reductions in neuroticism and increases in extraversion found among treatment responders (e.g., Du, Bakish, Ravindran,

& Hrdina, 2002; Tang et al., 2009). Dimensions of reward seeking, which is relevant to extraversion, are associated with faster time to remission from depression in adults (Uher et al., 2012) and adolescents (McMakin et al., 2012) and anxiety in adults (Taylor et al., 2017). Others have reported poorer treatment response to cognitive-behavioral treatment for depression than pharmacotherapy in individuals with high neuroticism (Bagby et al., 2008). However, there have been very few investigations examining the interaction between personality and stress on treatment response. In one of the few studies that has done so, Bulmash, Harkness, Stewart, and Bagby (2009) found that experience of major life events near the beginning of treatment predicted poorer treatment response for depression. Moreover, this association was stronger among individuals with higher levels of self-criticism.

Thus far, our review has emphasized studies examining internalizing symptoms and disorders. Few studies have reported on the associations and interactions between stressful life events, personality, and externalizing problems. Moreover, this small literature is informed by studies of maltreatment exposure and rarely assesses temperament or personality (Alink, Cicchetti, Kim, & Rogosch, 2009; Goldstein, Flett, Wekerle, & Wall, 2009). Because maltreatment may influence the development of temperament dimensions, there are challenges in placing these findings in the same context of the studies of internalizing problems. Some findings suggest that maltreatment influences ego control and ego resiliency, which may have bearing on the temperamental dimension of effortful control, and, in turn, are associated with externalizing problems, but not internalizing problems (Oshri, Rogosch, Burnette, & Cicchetti, 2011). Alink and colleagues (2009) examined a similar developmental pathway and found that emotion regulation mediated the relationship between childhood maltreatment and both internalizing and externalizing symptoms. This mediated effect was moderated by mother–child relatedness, such that the mediated effect was present when in the presence of insecure mother–child relatedness.

Taken together, there is mixed evidence supporting (a) interactive influences between personality dimensions and stressful life events on psychopathology and (b) stress generation mechanisms linking personality and psychopathology. However, much of the supportive evidence of these models involves neuroticism; other traits have been considered less frequently. Similarly, data are mixed concerning the influence of personality factors and stress on the specific presentation and/or course of psychopathology. However, there is evidence that both neuroticism and extraversion exert pathoplastic effects on the course and treatment of depression and other forms of psychopathology.

Gender, Personality, Stress, and Psychopathology

Notable gender differences exist in rates of psychopathology. Females are at greater risk for internalizing disorders, while males are more vulnerable to externalizing problems (e.g., Angst et al., 2016; Cortese, Faraone, Bernardi, Wang, & Blanco, 2016; Merikangas et al., 2010). To better understand the processes that contribute to these differences, research has examined gender differences in temperament and life stress, among other risk markers. Women report greater exposure to stressful life events than men (Feizi, Keshteli, Nouri, Roohafza, & Adibi, 2014; Gramstad et al., 2013), and this pattern appears generally true of adolescents as well (Bouma, Ormel, Verhulst, & Oldehinkel, 2008; Hamilton et al., 2017; Shapero et al., 2013; Starrs et al., 2010; Tubman & Windle, 1995). In contrast, research has failed to provide evidence for gender differences in reported stress during childhood (Gothelf, Aharonovsky, Horesh, Carty, & Apter, 2004; Mezulis et al., 2006). Together, this literature suggests that these gender differences in exposure to life stress may emerge in adolescence and persist throughout adulthood.

The emergent gender differences in stressful life events parallel those of depression, with females having nearly double the prevalence of the disorder in adolescence and adulthood (e.g., Cyranowski, Frank, Young, & Shear, 2000; Hankin et al., 1998). Further, gender differences in neuroticism mirror such differences in exposure to stressful life events; specifically, there tend to be no differences in neuroticism between males and females in childhood (Kopala-Sibley et al., 2016). Research examining fearfulness specifically has found consistent gender differences during the preschool years across parent-report and laboratory observations (Olino, Durbin, Klein, Hayden, & Dyson, 2013); in older children, these differences are less clear (Bouma et al., 2008; Melis Yavuz et al., 2017). However, adolescent and adult females generally endorse higher neuroticism than males (Auerbach et al., 2010; Feizi et al., 2014; Hamilton et al., 2017; Kim et al., 2016; Starrs et al., 2010; Uliaszek et al., 2010), though there are exceptions (e.g., Howard &

Hughes, 2012). Less attention has been devoted to examination of gender differences in other temperament traits, and extant findings are mixed. For instance, studies have found that females report lower extraversion than males (Feizi et al., 2014; Kim et al., 2016), that females are higher in extraversion (Olino et al., 2013; Uliaszek et al., 2010), or that there are no gender differences in extraversion (Howard & Hughes, 2012). In younger samples, research has yielded preliminary evidence that boys exhibit greater frustration (Bouma et al., 2008) and pleasure sensitivity (Visser, Huizinga, Hoekstra, van der Graaf, & Hoekstra-Weebers, 2007), whereas girls exhibit greater withdrawal negativity in infancy but not early childhood (Mezulis et al., 2006). Further examination of gender differences in these traits remains an important target for future research, because such gender differences may constitute a pathway by which traits and stress interact to predict the development of psychopathology.

Researchers have also examined gender as a moderator of associations between stress, temperament, and psychopathology, typically testing whether gender moderates links between constructs. For example, several studies have found that gender moderates the association between life stress and depression, yet interpretations of these findings vary. Uliaszek and colleagues (2010) and Bouma and colleagues (2008) found that the relationship between life stress and depression is stronger in females than males. In an adolescent sample, the association between neuroticism and depressive symptom severity was stronger in females than males (Calvete, Orue, & Gamez-Guadix, 2016). However, other studies have found that females are at greater risk for depression than males when stress is lower, regardless of neuroticism (Kendler et al., 2004). Studies have also found that gender is not a significant moderator of the association between life stress and depression or anxiety (Auerbach et al., 2010), but that the association between avoidant temperament and anxiety/depression symptom severity is stronger for boys than for girls (Auerbach et al., 2010; Lewis & Olsson, 2011). The relation between temperament traits such as neuroticism, extraversion, and BI and internalizing or externalizing symptoms is generally not significantly moderated by gender (Auerbach et al., 2010; Dougherty et al., 2013; Starrs et al., 2010; Visser et al., 2007; Wetter & Hankin, 2009). Avoidant temperament and internalizing symptoms are more strongly positively associated in males than females in early childhood (Lewis & Olsson, 2011).

More comprehensive studies have investigated gender differences within diathesis-stress, stress-buffering, and stress generation models. Research probing three-way interactions between gender, temperament, and stress as predictors of psychopathology has yielded equivocal results. Hastings and colleagues (2011) found a significant interaction between BI, stress reactivity, and gender as they relate to internalizing symptoms, such that greater BI was positively associated with internalizing symptoms in high cortisol-reactive young females only. In contrast, Gulley et al. (2016) failed to find sex differences in interactions between stress and dimensions of personality. However, the authors found a significant interaction between neuroticism, effortful control, and stress exposure in predicting increases in depressive and anxiety symptoms over time. At low levels of stress, effortful control mitigated the influence of negative affect on depression. At high levels of stress, this influence was absent. Work investigating gender differences in stress generation models have yielded similar null results. Barrocas and Hankin (2011) found that gender was not a significant moderator of longitudinal pathways between neuroticism, life stress, anxious arousal, and depressive symptom severity in adolescents. Although this literature has primarily examined gender as a moderator of associations between temperament, stress, and psychopathology, temperament and stress may also serve as mechanisms of gender differences in rates of psychopathology. Accordingly, Kim et al. (2016) found that greater depressive symptoms among adult females were mediated by greater neuroticism, lower extraversion, and greater stress, respectively, as well as by the associations between extraversion and stress, agreeableness and stress, and conscientiousness and stress. However, it should be noted that this study was cross-sectional and further research is needed to examine these associations longitudinally.

In sum, extant literature has examined (1) gender differences in temperament, stress, and psychopathology; (2) whether temperament-psychopathology and stress-psychopathology associations differ as a function of gender; and (3) gender as a moderator of more complex models of temperament, stress, and psychopathology. Previous work indicates that females report greater neuroticism and exposure to life stress than males, particularly after childhood. Notably, females also begin to report higher rates of depression in adolescence and adulthood. However, studies examining gender as a moderator of associations between temperament, stress, and psychopathology have yielded largely mixed or null results. Instead, gender differences in temperament and stress exposure may be potential mechanisms of gender differences in depression and other forms of psychopathology. As such, longitudinal examination of factors such as temperament and life stress as mediators of gender differences in psychopathology are promising targets for future research.

Conclusions

There is an emerging literature on the complex interplay between personality, stress, and psychopathology that has often been tested within diathesis-stress and stress generation models. There is empirical support for personality by stress (i.e., diathesis-stress) interactions, with neuroticism predicting depression more strongly in the context of stress. However, additive effects of the two are also reported, such that both stress and temperament predict psychopathology. Multiple studies show that stress mediates associations between personality and psychopathology, in support of stress generation models (Hammen, 2006; Hankin, 2010). These mediated effects are most frequently found when examining the associations between neuroticism and psychopathology. However, some of these findings come from cross-sectional studies and require replication in further longitudinal studies (Kim et al., 2016). Moreover, as some studies found that stress prospectively predicted personality (Shapero et al., 2013; Stroud et al., 2015) and, in turn, psychopathology, it is important to consider the direction of influence further to better evaluate whether these influences are uni- or bidirectional (Barrocas & Hankin, 2011). Finally, a smaller number of studies have examined how personality and stress influence specific manifestations and course of psychopathology (i.e., the pathoplastic model; Spinhoven, Elzinga, Roelofs, et al., 2011; Uliaszek et al., 2012). However, relative to other models of the links between stress, personality, and psychopathology, there was stronger evidence for both neuroticism and extraversion to predict specific disorder onset and course (G. W. Brown et al., 1995; Bufferd et al., in press; McFarland et al., 2006). These general conclusions are true irrespective of gender, but they appear to be modestly stronger for females (Auerbach et al., 2010; Feizi et al., 2014; Starrs et al., 2010). Moreover, throughout our review, we included studies of children, adolescents, and adults. Nonetheless, we did not see support for these models differing based on the developmental status of the participants.

Future Directions

The literature on the influences of personality and stress on psychopathology is growing and has many unanswered questions. Although many studies have examined elements of the personality-stress-psychopathology interplay, studies that find direct support for theoretical models of these relationships are scarce. There is general support for the influence of personality and an array of stressful life events influencing psychopathology (e.g., Hammen, 1991, 2006; Vrshek-Schallhorn et al., 2015). However, there are a number of important areas of research to pursue to inform questions of etiology, course, and outcome of psychopathology.

The majority of work examining the relationships between stress, personality, and psychopathology focuses on the precursor, predisposition, and pathoplasticity models that rely on stress being a key factor in mitigating or influencing the magnitude of association between personality and psychopathology. However, there are important areas for work in other conceptual models for these relationships. It is critical to evaluate whether relationships that have been examined using tests of mediation, such that the relationship between personality and psychopathology is mediated by experience of stressful life events, are better explained by the common cause model. This model would posit that the manifestations of personality and psychopathology are both influenced by stress. Thus, complementary models can be examined to test these distinct conceptual possibilities.

Additionally, in order to further distinguish between precursor and predisposition models, more research is needed to understand personality etiology, psychopathology etiology, and similarities among the etiology of both constructs. Evidence for the precursor model would be obtained from studies that identify factors that contribute to development of both personality and psychopathology, while evidence for the predisposition model would come from studies that identify distinct nonoverlapping factors leading to development of personality or psychopathology. There is some evidence for shared genetic vulnerability for neuroticism and major depression (De Moor et al., 2015; Smith et al., 2016). Additionally, neuroticism has nonspecific associations with other types of psychopathology (Kotov et al., 2010). However, less is known about genetic overlap between other dimensions of personality and forms of psychopathology. Moreover, additional work is needed to discern other shared and unshared etiologic mechanisms leading toward personality and psychopathology. Stress can influence both personality and psychopathology or contribute to psychopathology in the presence of underlying personality vulnerability. Regardless of the specific model(s) being examined, future studies should account for the possibility of a dynamic interplay between personality, stress, and psychopathology.

The literature has not addressed the continuum model in the context of life stress. There is substantial evidence of the phenotypic overlap between personality and psychopathology (Clark, 2005; Krueger, Caspi, & Moffitt, 2000). It is possible that under low stress, personality ratings are made within normal ranges. However, in the context of high stress, personality ratings may be more pathological. Thus, stress would influence the measurement of personality and/or psychopathology. This would identify expand the meaning of the continuum model by identifying contexts that the overlap between personality and psychopathology becomes stronger. Analytic tools to test this hypothesis have been newly developed (Bauer, 2017); however, these possibilities have not yet been empirically examined.

A consistent challenge in the field focuses on methodological decisions about studying these relationships. First, there are few truly prospective studies that have examined these models that maintain temporal precedence between assessments of personality, stress, and emergent psychopathology. Studies that are intending to evaluate mechanistic relationships among these constructs need to assess these domains consistently to evaluate the directionality of these associations. Second, there is tremendous heterogeneity in the specific methods and measures employed, particularly with respect to the stress assessments. In the context of gene by environment interactions predicting depression, meta-analytic findings suggest that there are stronger associations between genetic risk and depression when objective and interview methods rather than when self-report methods are used (Karg, Burmeister, Shedden, & Sen, 2011). As outlined in other chapters, assessments of stress can come from self-report checklists or through the use of semistructured interviews. Moreover, stressful events can be classified in a number of ways; most often these include independent, dependent, chronic, episodic, interpersonal, and noninterpersonal dimensions. These refined stress categories are most frequently obtained using interviews. Although some of the literature described here utilized interviews to assess stress (Duffy et al., 2007; Hamilton et al., 2017; Spinhoven et al., 2011; Stroud et al., 2015; Uliaszek et al.,

2010, 2012), many of our reviewed studies relied solely on self-report measures of stress. Thus, we have limited ability to discern whether the results substantially differed depending on the types of stressors experienced. Critically for the work reviewed here, previous work highlights the role of dependent life stress being associated with (i.e., generated from) experience of depression (Hammen, 2006) and neuroticism (e.g., Kercher et al., 2009). Future studies would benefit from using life stress interviews to evaluate whether individual types of stressors have different influences on onset and course or specific presentation of psychopathology.

An additional layer of heterogeneity of stress involves whether the relevant stressor is proximal to or distal from the onset of the disorder. Our review focused on stressors temporally closer to the disorder onset. However, early life adversity, low socioeconomic status, and maltreatment may be important contributors to the development of temperament and personality (Gallo, Bogart, Vranceanu, & Matthews, 2005; Lengua & Wachs, 2012); experience and responsivity to stress (Bradley & Corwyn, 2002); and development of psychopathology (Afifi et al., 2011; Jokela & Keltikangas-Järvinen, 2011; MacMillan et al., 2001). Thus, this is an important area to integrate with the findings on stress experienced later in development. Alternatively, investigations could consider how distal and proximal stressors jointly influence emergence of psychopathology.

The current literature base has extensively attended to the role of neuroticism in examining personality, stress, and psychopathology links. However, attention to extraversion has been more modest and consideration of other dimensions of personality has been virtually absent. The attention to extraversion has focused on mechanisms of attenuating the influence of stress and/or on seeking out positive events. These mechanisms may also be fruitful possibilities to examine with respect to constraint, agreeableness, and conscientiousness. Moreover, the existing literature has primarily focused on the interactive influences of a single dimension of personality with stressors to predict psychopathology. However, studies have reported interactions between dimensions of personality (e.g., extraversion by neuroticism) to predict psychopathology (Dougherty, Klein, Durbin, Hayden, & Olino, 2010; Kotelnikova, Mackrell, Jordan, & Hayden, 2015; Vasey et al., 2013). It is possible that these personality by personality interactions will be further moderated by experience of stressful life events to predict psychopathology.

Although frequently described in models of personality and psychopathology, the pathoplasticity model has been rarely formally tested in the work on personality, stress, and psychopathology. Questions remain about whether these relationships are specific to depression, or whether they extend to anxiety, childhood externalizing, or substance use disorders. Additional work may also offer opportunities to examine additional dimensions of personality such as constraint, which is an important personality dimension with respect to externalizing problems (Krueger, McGue, & Iacono, 2001; Krueger et al., 1994). Furthermore, studies with careful attention to specific dimensions of stress would be important to highlight consistencies and differences in patterns of results.

Diathesis-stress and stress generation models are frequently described separately. However, these models can be meaningfully integrated. Stress generation and diathesis-stress models can act synergistically via the differential exposure-reactivity model. Within this perspective, personality dispositions may increase the likelihood of stress exposure and exacerbate the impact of personality on psychopathology (Bolger & Zuckerman, 1995). This differential exposure-reactivity model then has stress operate as a moderator *and* mediator of the relationship between personality and psychopathology. As such, empirical examination of stress reactivity and exposure indices together, rather than separately, is an important target for future research.

A critical challenge in this area is drawing causal inferences from the data. We surveyed many studies that demonstrated prospective prediction. Longitudinal examination of data may aid in establishing directionality of effects. Several studies theorized that traits (e.g., neuroticism) lead to increased stress generation, yet they infrequently test this association prospectively. Such an association is possible and, indeed, has been supported by multiple prospective studies (Gramstad, Gjestad, & Haver, 2013; Kercher et al., 2009; Koffel et al., 2016; Lakdawalla & Hankin, 2008; Wetter & Hankin, 2009; Yang et al., 2008). However, a reciprocal relationship is also possible, yet rarely tested empirically. More specifically, personality may be shaped by chronic early life stress, such that exposure may lead to greater neuroticism, reduced constraint, and reduced extraversion. Although one study yields preliminary support for this model, as adults who reported experiencing early life stress endorsed greater neuroticism, greater openness to experience, and lower conscientiousness, it should be noted that this was a cross-sectional retrospective design (McFarlane et al., 2005). To advance existing literature, longitudinal studies are vital to support a specific model of associations between stress, personality, and psychopathology. However, this is only one requirement of determining that a causal relationship exists. Nearly all studies had no ability to discern whether individuals elicited events in their lives. An alternative strategy is to identify studies that focused on the experience of fateful events (e.g., natural disasters) (Kopala-Sibley, Danzig, et al., 2016; Kopala-Sibley, Kotov, et al., 2016) or, potentially, military combat experiences (Jackson, Thoemmes, Jonkmann, Lüdtke, & Trautwein, 2012; Koffel & Watson, 2009) that are independent of individuals' own personality.

In light of the ubiquitous role of neuroticism in depression (Cuijpers et al., 2010; Lahey, 2009), with and without the joint influence of stress, there is a strong need for identifying broadly disseminable interventions to minimize the impact of this individual difference dimension. Transdiagnostic approaches to intervention have been suggestive of neuroticism being a ripe target for interventions (Barlow, Sauer-Zavala, Carl, Bullis, & Ellard, 2014) and, regardless of presenting problem and intervention modality, psychotherapy has influences on major dimensions of personality (Roberts et al., 2017). Within transdiagnostic approaches to psychotherapy, there are multiple facets of the intervention, including emotional acceptance and understanding the roles of negative emotions that may serve to reduce aversion to negative emotions (Sauer-Zavala, Wilner, & Barlow, 2017). Moreover, approaches borrowed from mindfulness-based interventions include sessions on environment selection, consequences of stress, responses to stressful events, and re-evaluation of one's reaction to stressful events (Armstrong & Rimes, 2016). These interventions have been developed and are used with individuals or groups in acute interventions. Yet there may be benefits to scale the intervention for broader population catchments. The development of interventions using Internet (Dear et al., 2015; Titov et al., 2015) or mobile platforms may be useful toward impacting larger segments of the population.

References

Afifi, T. O., Mather, A., Boman, J., Fleisher, W., Enns, M. W., MacMillan, H., ... Sareen, J. (2011). Childhood adversity and personality disorders: Results from a nationally representative population-based study. *Journal of Psychiatric Research*, *45*, 814–822.

Alink, L. R., Cicchetti, D., Kim, J., & Rogosch, F. A. (2009). Mediating and moderating processes in the relation between maltreatment and psychopathology: Mother-child relationship quality and emotion regulation. *Journal of Abnormal Child Psychology*, *37*, 831–843.

Angst, J., Paksarian, D., Cui, L., Merikangas, K., Hengartner, M., Ajdacic-Gross, V., ... Rössler, W. (2016). The epidemiology of common mental disorders from age 20 to 50: Results from the prospective Zurich cohort study. *Epidemiology and Psychiatric Sciences*, *25*, 24–32.

Armstrong, L., & Rimes, K. A. (2016). Mindfulness-based cognitive therapy for neuroticism (stress vulnerability): A pilot randomized study. *Behavior Therapy*, *47*, 287–298.

Auerbach, R. P., Abela, J. R. Z., Ho, M.-H. R., McWhinnie, C. M., & Czajkowska, Z. (2010). A prospective examination of depressive symptomology: Understanding the relationship between negative events, self-esteem, and neuroticism. *Journal of Social and Clinical Psychology*, *29*, 438–461.

Bagby, R. M., Quilty, L. C., Segal, Z. V., McBride, C. C., Kennedy, S. H., & Costa, P. T. Jr (2008). Personality and differential treatment response in major depression: A randomized controlled trial comparing cognitive-behavioural therapy and pharmacotherapy. *The Canadian Journal of Psychiatry*, *53*, 361–370.

Barlow, D. H., Sauer-Zavala, S., Carl, J. R., Bullis, J. R., & Ellard, K. K. (2014). The nature, diagnosis, and treatment of neuroticism: Back to the future. *Clinical Psychological Science*, *2*, 344–365.

Barrocas, A. L., & Hankin, B. L. (2011). Developmental pathways to depressive symptoms in adolescence: A multi-wave prospective study of negative emotionality, stressors, and anxiety. *Journal of Abnormal Child Psychology*, *39*, 489–500.

Bauer, D. J. (2017). A more general model for testing measurement invariance and differential item functioning. *Psychological Methods*, *22*, 507–526.

Bogg, T., & Finn, P. R. (2010). A self-regulatory model of behavioral disinhibition in late adolescence: Integrating personality traits, externalizing psychopathology, and cognitive capacity. *Journal of Personality*, *78*, 441–470.

Bolger, N., & Schilling, E. A. (1991). Personality and the problems of everyday life: The role of neuroticism in exposure and reactivity to daily stressors. *Journal of Personality*, *59*, 355–386.

Bolger, N., & Zuckerman, A. (1995). A framework for studying personality in the stress process. *Journal of Personality and Social Psychology*, *69*, 890.

Bouma, E. M. C., Ormel, J., Verhulst, F. C., & Oldehinkel, A. J. (2008). Stressful life events and depressive problems in early adolescent boys and girls: The influence of parental depression, temperament and family environment. *Journal of Affective Disorders*, *105*, 185–193.

Bradley, R. H., & Corwyn, R. F. (2002). Socioeconomic status and child development. *Annual Review of Psychology*, *53*, 371–399.

Broeren, S., Newall, C., Dodd, H. F., Locker, R., & Hudson, J. L. (2013). Longitudinal investigation of the role of temperament and stressful life events in childhood anxiety. *Development and Psychopathology*, *26*, 437–449.

Brown, G., & Harris, T. (1978). *The Bedford College life-events and difficulty schedule: Directory of contextual threat ratings of events*. London, UK: Bedford College, University of London.

Brown, G. W., Harris, T. O., & Hepworth, C. (1995). Loss, humiliation and entrapment among women developing depression: A patient and non-patient comparison. *Psychological Medicine, 25*, 7–21.

Brown, T. A. (2007). Temporal course and structural relationships among dimensions of temperament and DSM-IV anxiety and mood disorder constructs. *Journal of Abnormal Psychology, 116*, 313.

Brown, T. A., & Rosellini, A. J. (2011). The direct and interactive effects of neuroticism and life stress on the severity and longitudinal course of depressive symptoms. *Journal of Abnormal Psychology, 120*, 844.

Bufferd, S. J., Dougherty, L. R., Olino, T. M., Dyson, M. W., Carlson, G. A., & Klein, D. N. (in press). Temperament distinguishes persistent/recurrent from remitting anxiety disorders across early childhood. *Journal of Clinical Child and Adolescent Psychology*. doi:10.1080/15374416.2016.1212362.

Bulmash, E., Harkness, K. L., Stewart, J. G., & Bagby, R. M. (2009). Personality, stressful life events, and treatment response in major depression. *Journal of Consulting and Clinical Psychology, 77*, 1067–1077.

Calvete, E., Orue, I., & Gamez-Guadix, M. (2016). Do extraversion and neuroticism moderate the association between bullying victimization and internalizing symptoms? A three-wave longitudinal study. *Journal of School Psychology, 56*, 1–11.

Clark, L. A. (2005). Temperament as a unifying basis for personality and psychopathology. *Journal of Abnormal Psychology, 114*, 505–521.

Clark, L. A., & Watson, D. (1999). Temperament: A new paradigm for trait psychology. In L. A. Pervin & O. P. John (Eds.), *Handbook of personality: Theory and research* (2nd ed., pp. 399–423). New York, NY: Guilford Press.

Clark, L. A., Watson, D., & Mineka, S. (1994). Temperament, personality, and the mood and anxiety disorders. *Journal of Abnormal Psychology, 103*, 103–116.

Cortese, S., Faraone, S. V., Bernardi, S., Wang, S., & Blanco, C. (2016). Gender differences in adult attention-deficit/hyperactivity disorder: Results from the National Epidemiologic Survey on Alcohol and Related Conditions (NESARC). *The Journal of Clinical Psychiatry, 77*, e421–428.

Cuijpers, P., Smit, F., Penninx, B. W., de Graaf, R., ten Have, M., & Beekman, A. T. (2010). Economic costs of neuroticism: A population-based study. *Archives of General Psychiatry, 67*, 1086–1093.

Cutrona, C. E., Russell, D. W., Brown, P. A., Clark, L. A., Hessling, R. M., & Gardner, K. A. (2005). Neighborhood context, personality, and stressful life events as predictors of depression among African American women. *Journal of Abnormal Psychology, 114*, 3.

Cyranowski, J. M., Frank, E., Young, E., & Shear, M. K. (2000). Adolescent onset of the gender difference in lifetime rates of major depression: A theoretical model. *Archives of General Psychiatry, 57*, 21–27.

Dear, B., Staples, L., Terides, M., Karin, E., Zou, J., Johnston, L., . . . Titov, N. (2015). Transdiagnostic versus disorder-specific and clinician-guided versus self-guided internet-delivered treatment for generalized anxiety disorder and comorbid disorders: A randomized controlled trial. *Journal of Anxiety Disorders, 36*, 63–77.

Dougherty, L. R., Klein, D. N., & Davila, J. (2004). A growth curve analysis of the course of dysthymic disorder: The effects of chronic stress and moderation by adverse parent-child relationships and family history. *Journal of Consulting & Clinical Psychology, 72*, 1012–1021.

Dougherty, L. R., Klein, D. N., Durbin, C. E., Hayden, E. P., & Olino, T. M. (2010). Temperamental positive and negative emotionality and children's depressive symptoms: A longitudinal prospective study from age three to age ten. *Journal of Social and Clinical Psychology, 29*, 462–488.

Dougherty, L. R., Tolep, M. R., Bufferd, S. J., Olino, T. M., Dyson, M., Traditi, J., . . . Klein, D. N. (2013). Preschool anxiety disorders: Comprehensive assessment of clinical, demographic, temperamental, familial, and life stress correlates. *Journal of Clinical Child & Adolescent Psychology, 42*, 577–589.

Du, L., Bakish, D., Ravindran, A. V., & Hrdina, P. D. (2002). Does fluoxetine influence major depression by modifying five-factor personality traits? *Journal of Affective Disorders, 71*, 235–241.

Duffy, A., Alda, M., Trinneer, A., Demidenko, N., Grof, P., & Goodyer, I. M. (2007). Temperament, life events, and psychopathology among the offspring of bipolar parents. *European Child & Adolescent Psychiatry, 16*, 222–228.

Dyson, M. W., Olino, T. M., Durbin, C. E., Goldsmith, H. H., & Klein, D. N. (2012). The structure of temperament in preschoolers: A two-stage factor analytic approach. *Emotion, 12*, 44–57.

Ellenbogen, M. A., & Hodgins, S. (2004). The impact of high neuroticism in parents on children's psychosocial functioning in a population at high risk for major affective disorder: A family–environmental pathway of intergenerational risk. *Development and Psychopathology, 16*, 113–136.

Eysenck, H. J., & Eysenck, S. B. G. (1975). *Manual for the Eysenck Personality Questionnaire*. Kent, UK: Hodder & Stoughton.

Feizi, A., Keshteli, A. H., Nouri, F., Roohafza, H., & Adibi, P. (2014). A cross-sectional population-based study on the association of personality traits with anxiety and psychological stress: Joint modeling of mixed outcomes using shared random effects approach. *Journal of Research in Medical Sciences: The Official Journal of Isfahan University of Medical Sciences, 19*, 834–843.

Finlay-Jones, R., & Brown, G. W. (1981). Types of stressful life event and the onset of anxiety and depressive disorders. *Psychological Medicine, 11*, 803–815.

Fox, J. K., Halpern, L. F., Ryan, J. L., & Lowe, K. A. (2010). Stressful life events and the tripartite model: Relations to anxiety and depression in adolescent females. *Journal of Adolescence, 33*, 43–54.

Gallo, L. C., Bogart, L. M., Vranceanu, A.-M., & Matthews, K. A. (2005). Socioeconomic status, resources, psychological experiences, and emotional responses: a test of the reserve capacity model. *Journal of Personality and Social Psychology, 88*, 386.

Goldberg, L. R. (1990). An alternative "description of personality": The big-five factor structure. *Journal of Personality and Social Psychology, 59*, 1216–1229.

Goldsmith, H. H., Buss, A. H., Plomin, R., & Rothbart, M. K. (1987). What is temperament? Four approaches. *Child Development, 58*, 505–529.

Goldstein, A. L., Flett, G. L., Wekerle, C., & Wall, A.-M. (2009). Personality, child maltreatment, and substance use: Examining correlates of deliberate self-harm among university students. *Canadian Journal of Behavioural Science/Revue canadienne des sciences du comportement, 41*, 241.

Gothelf, D., Aharonovsky, O., Horesh, N., Carty, T., & Apter, A. (2004). Life events and personality factors in children and adolescents with obsessive-compulsive disorder and other anxiety disorders. *Comprehensive Psychiatry, 45*, 192–198.

Gramstad, T. O., Gjestad, R., & Haver, B. (2013). Personality traits predict job stress, depression and anxiety among junior physicians. *BMC Medical Education, 13*, 150.

Gulley, L. D., Hankin, B. L., & Young, J. F. (2016). Risk for depression and anxiety in youth: The interaction between negative affectivity, effortful control, and stressors. *Journal of Abnormal Child Psychology, 44*, 207–218.

Hamilton, J. L., Burke, T. A., Stange, J. P., Kleiman, E. M., Rubenstein, L. M., Scopelliti, K. A., . . . Alloy, L.B. (2017). Trait affect, emotion regulation, and the generation of negative and positive interpersonal events. *Behavior Therapy, 48*, 435–447.

Hammen, C. (1991). Generation of stress in the course of unipolar depression. *Journal of Abnormal Psychology, 100*, 555–561.

Hammen, C. (2005). Stress and depression. *Annual Review of Clinical Psychology, 1*, 293–319.

Hammen, C. (2006). Stress generation in depression: Reflections on origins, research, and future directions. *Journal of Clinical Psychology, 62*, 1065–1082.

Hankin, B. L. (2010). Personality and depressive symptoms: Stress generation and cognitive vulnerabilities to depression in a prospective daily diary study. *Journal of Social and Clinical Psychology, 29*, 369–401.

Hankin, B. L., Abramson, L. Y., Moffitt, T. E., Silva, P. A., McGee, R., & Angell, K. E. (1998). Development of depression from preadolescence to young adulthood: Emerging gender differences in a 10-year longitudinal study. *Journal of Abnormal Psychology, 107*, 128–140.

Hastings, P. D., Ruttle, P. L., Serbin, L. A., Mills, R. S. L., Stack, D. M., & Schwartzman, A. E. (2011). Adrenocortical responses to strangers in preschoolers: Relations with parenting, temperament, and psychopathology. *Developmental Psychobiology, 53*, 694–710.

Hettema, J. M., Neale, M. C., Myers, J. M., Prescott, C. A., & Kendler, K. S. (2006). A population-based twin study of the relationship between neuroticism and internalizing disorders. *American Journal of Psychiatry, 163*, 857–864.

Howard, S., & Hughes, B. M. (2012). Construct, concurrent and discriminant validity of Type D personality in the general population: Associations with anxiety, depression, stress and cardiac output. *Psychology & Health, 27*, 242–258.

Hutchinson, J. G., & Williams, P. G. (2007). Neuroticism, daily hassles, and depressive symptoms: An examination of moderating and mediating effects. *Personality and Individual Differences, 42*, 1367–1378.

Iacono, W. G., Carlson, S. R., Taylor, J., Elkins, I. J., & McGue, M. (1999). Behavioral disinhibition and the development of substance-use disorders: Findings from the Minnesota Twin Family Study. *Development and Psychopathology, 11*, 869–900.

Jackson, J. J., Thoemmes, F., Jonkmann, K., Lüdtke, O., & Trautwein, U. (2012). Military training and personality trait development: Does the military make the man, or does the man make the military? *Psychological Science, 23*, 270–277.

John, O. P., & Srivastava, S. (1999). The Big Five trait taxonomy: History, measurement, and theoretical perspectives *Handbook of personality: Theory and research* (Vol. 2, pp. 102–138). New York, NY: Guilford Press.

Jokela, M., & Keltikangas-Järvinen, L. (2011). The association between low socioeconomic status and depressive symptoms depends on temperament and personality traits. *Personality and Individual Differences, 51*, 302–308.

Jorm, A. F., Christensen, H., Henderson, A. S., Jacomb, P. A., Korten, A. E., & Rodgers, B. (2000). Predicting anxiety and depression from personality: Is there a synergistic effect of neuroticism and extraversion? *Journal of Abnormal Psychology, 109*, 145.

Kagan, J. (1997). Temperament and the reactions to unfamiliarity. *Child Development, 68*.

Kandler, C., & Ostendorf, F. (2016). Additive and synergetic contributions of neuroticism and life events to depression and anxiety in women. *European Journal of Personality, 30*, 390–405.

Karg, K., Burmeister, M., Shedden, K., & Sen, S. (2011). The serotonin transporter promoter variant (5-HTTLPR), stress, and depression meta-analysis revisited: Evidence of genetic moderation. *Archives of General Psychiatry, 68*, 444–454.

Kasch, K. L., Rottenberg, J., Arnow, B. A., & Gotlib, I. H. (2002). Behavioral activation and inhibition systems and the severity and course of depression. *Journal of Abnormal Psychology, 111*, 589–597.

Kazdin, A. E. (2007). Mediators and mechanisms of change in psychotherapy research. *Annual Review of Clinical Psychology, 3*, 1–27.

Kendler, K. S., Gardner, C., & Prescott, C. (2003). Personality and the experience of environmental adversity. *Psychological Medicine, 33*, 1193–1202.

Kendler, K. S., Gardner, C. O., & Prescott, C. A. (2002). Toward a comprehensive developmental model for major depression in women. *American Journal of Psychiatry, 159*, 1133–1145.

Kendler, K. S., Hettema, J. M., Butera, F., Gardner, C. O., & Prescott, C. A. (2003). Life event dimensions of loss, humiliation, entrapment, and danger in the prediction of onsets of major depression and generalized anxiety. *Archives of General Psychiatry, 60*, 789–796.

Kendler, K. S., Kuhn, J., & Prescott, C. A. (2004). The interrelationship of neuroticism, sex, and stressful life events in the prediction of episodes of major depression. *American Journal of Psychiatry, 161*, 631–636.

Kendler, K. S., Neale, M. C., Kessler, R. C., Heath, A. C., & Eaves, L. J. (1993). A longitudinal twin study of personality and major depression in women. *Archives of General Psychiatry, 50*, 853–862.

Kercher, A. J., Rapee, R. M., & Schniering, C. A. (2009). Neuroticism, life events and negative thoughts in the development of depression in adolescent girls. *Journal of Abnormal Child Psychology, 37*, 903–915.

Kim, S. E., Kim, H.-N., Cho, J., Kwon, M.-J., Chang, Y., Ryu, S., . . . Kim, H.-L. (2016). Direct and indirect effects of five factor personality and gender on depressive symptoms mediated by perceived stress. *PloS One, 11*, e0154140.

King, S. M., Iacono, W. G., & McGue, M. (2004). Childhood externalizing and internalizing psychopathology in the prediction of early substance use. *Addiction, 99*, 1548–1559.

Klein, D. N., Kotov, R., & Bufferd, S. J. (2011). Personality and depression: Explanatory models and review of the evidence. *Annual Review of Clinical Psychology, 7*, 269–295.

Klein, D. N., & Riso, L. P. (1993). Psychiatric disorders: Problems of boundaries and comorbidity. In C. G. Costello (Ed.), *Basic issues in psychopathology* (pp. 19–66). New York, NY: Guilford Press.

Koffel, E., Kramer, M. D., Arbisi, P. A., Erbes, C. R., Kaler, M., & Polusny, M. A. (2016). Personality traits and combat exposure as predictors of psychopathology over time. *Psychological Medicine, 46*, 209–220.

Koffel, E., & Watson, D. (2009). The two-factor structure of sleep complaints and its relation to depression and anxiety. *Journal of Abnormal Psychology, 118*, 183–194.

Kopala-Sibley, D. C., Danzig, A. P., Kotov, R., Bromet, E. J., Carlson, G. A., Olino, T. M.,...Klein, D. N. (2016). Negative emotionality and its facets moderate the effects of exposure to Hurricane Sandy on children's postdisaster depression and anxiety symptoms. *Journal of Abnormal Psychology, 125*, 471.

Kopala-Sibley, D. C., Kotov, R., Bromet, E. J., Carlson, G. A., Danzig, A. P., Black, S. R.,...Klein, D. N. (2016). Personality diatheses and Hurricane Sandy: Effects on post-disaster depression. *Psychological Medicine, 46*, 865–875.

Kotelnikova, Y., Mackrell, S. V. M., Jordan, P. L., & Hayden, E. P. (2015). Longitudinal associations between reactive and regulatory temperament traits and depressive symptoms in middle childhood. *Journal of Clinical Child and Adolescent Psychology, 44*, 775–786.

Kotov, R., Gamez, W., Schmidt, F., & Watson, D. (2010). Linking "big" personality traits to anxiety, depressive, and substance use disorders: A meta-analysis. *Psychological Bulletin, 136*, 768–821.

Kraemer, H. C., Wilson, G. T., Fairburn, C. G., & Agras, W. S. (2002). Mediators and moderators of treatment effects in randomized clinical trials. *Archives of General Psychiatry, 59*(10), 877–883.

Krueger, R. F., Caspi, A., & Moffitt, T. E. (2000). Epidemiological personology: The unifying role of personality in population-based research on problem behaviors. *Journal of Personality, 68*, 967–998.

Krueger, R. F., McGue, M., & Iacono, W. G. (2001). The higher-order structure of common DSM mental disorders: Internalization, externalization, and their connections to personality. *Personality and Individual Differences, 30*, 1245–1259.

Krueger, R. F., Schmutte, P. S., Caspi, A., Moffitt, T. E., Campbell, K., & Silva, P. A. (1994). Personality traits are linked to crime among men and women: Evidence from a birth cohort. *Journal of Abnormal Psychology, 103*, 328–338.

Kushner, S. C. (2015). A review of the direct and interactive effects of life stressors and dispositional traits on youth psychopathology. *Child Psychiatry & Human Development, 46*, 810–819.

Lahey, B. B. (2009). Public health significance of neuroticism. *American Psychologist, 64*, 241–256.

Lakdawalla, Z., & Hankin, B. L. (2008). Personality as a prospective vulnerability to dysphoric symptoms among college students: Proposed mechanisms. *Journal of Psychopathology and Behavioral Assessment, 30*, 121–131.

Lengua, L. J., Long, A. C., Smith, K. I., & Meltzoff, A. N. (2005). Pre-attack symptomatology and temperament as predictors of children's responses to the September 11 terrorist attacks. *Journal of Child Psychology and Psychiatry, 46*, 631–645.

Lengua, L. J., & Wachs, T. D. (2012). Temperament and risk: Resilient and vulnerable responses to adversity. In M. Zentner & R. L. Shiner (Eds.), *Handbook of temperament* (pp. 519–540). New York, NY: Guilford.

Lewis, A. J., & Olsson, C. A. (2011). Early life stress and child temperament style as predictors of childhood anxiety and depressive symptoms: Findings from the longitudinal study of Australian children. *Depression Research and Treatment, 2011*, 296026.

Liu, R. T., & Alloy, L. B. (2010). Stress generation in depression: A systematic review of the empirical literature and recommendations for future study. *Clinical psychology review, 30*, 582–593.

MacMillan, H. L., Fleming, J. E., Streiner, D. L., Lin, E., Boyle, M. H., Jamieson, E.,...Beardslee, W.R. (2001). Childhood abuse and lifetime psychopathology in a community sample. *American Journal of Psychiatry, 158*, 1878–1883.

Magnus, K., Diener, E., Fujita, F., & Pavot, W. (1993). Extraversion and neuroticism as predictors of objective life events: A longitudinal analysis. *Journal of personality and social psychology, 65*, 1046–1053.

McCrae, R. R., & Costa, P. T. (1987). Validation of the five-factor model of personality across instruments and observers. *Journal of Personality and Social Psychology, 52*, 81–90.

McFarland, B. R., Shankman, S. A., Tenke, C. E., Bruder, G. E., & Klein, D. N. (2006). Behavioral activation system deficits predict the six-month course of depression. *Journal of Affective Disorders, 91*, 229–234.

McFarlane, A., Clark, C. R., Bryant, R. A., Williams, L. M., Niaura, R., Paul, R. H.,...Gordon, E. (2005). The impact of early life stress on psychophysiological, personality and behavioral measures in 740 non-clinical subjects. *Journal of Integrative Neuroscience, 4*, 27–40.

McKnight, C. G., Huebner, E. S., & Suldo, S. (2002). Relationships among stressful life events, temperament, problem behavior, and global life satisfaction in adolescents. *Psychology in the Schools, 39*, 677–687.

McMakin, D. L., Olino, T. M., Porta, G., Dietz, L. J., Emslie, G., Clarke, G.,...Brent, D.A. (2012). Anhedonia predicts poorer recovery among youth with selective serotonin reuptake inhibitor treatment–resistant depression. *Journal of the American Academy of Child and Adolescent Psychiatry, 51*, 404–411.

Meehl, P. E. (1962). Schizotaxia, schizotypy, schizophrenia. *American Psychologist, 17*, 827–838.

Melis Yavuz, H., Selcuk, B., Corapci, F., & Aksan, N. (2017). Role of temperament, parenting behaviors, and stress on Turkish preschoolers' internalizing symptoms. *Social Development, 26*, 109–128.

Merikangas, K. R., He, J.-P., Burstein, M., Swanson, S. A., Avenevoli, S., Cui, L.,...Swendensen, J. (2010). Lifetime prevalence of mental disorders in US adolescents: Results from the National Comorbidity Survey Replication–Adolescent Supplement (NCS-A). *Journal of the American Academy of Child and Adolescent Psychiatry, 49*, 980–989.

Mezulis, A. H., Hyde, J. S., & Abramson, L. Y. (2006). The developmental origins of cognitive vulnerability to depression: Temperament, parenting, and negative life events in childhood as contributors to negative cognitive style. *Developmental Psychology, 42*, 1012–1025.

Mineka, S., & Zinbarg, R. (2006). A contemporary learning theory perspective on the etiology of anxiety disorders: It's not what you thought it was. *American Psychologist, 61*, 10.

De Moor, M. H., Van Den Berg, S. M., Verweij, K. J., Krueger, R. F., Luciano, M., Vasquez, A. A.,...Amin, N. (2015). Meta-analysis of genome-wide association studies for neuroticism, and the polygenic association with major depressive disorder. *JAMA Psychiatry, 72*, 642–650.

Ogle, C. M., Rubin, D. C., & Siegler, I. C. (2014). Changes in neuroticism following trauma exposure. *Journal of Personality, 82*, 93–102.

Olino, T. M., Durbin, C. E., Klein, D. N., Hayden, E. P., & Dyson, M. W. (2013). Gender differences in young children's temperament traits: Comparisons across observational and parent-report methods. *Journal of Personality, 81*, 119–129.

Olino, T. M., Klein, D. N., Durbin, C., Hayden, E. P., & Buckley, M. E. (2005). The structure of extraversion in preschool aged children. *Personality and Individual Differences, 39*, 481–492.

Ormel, J., Jeronimus, B. F., Kotov, R., Riese, H., Bos, E. H., Hankin, B.,...Oldehinkel, A. J. (2013). Neuroticism and common mental disorders: Meaning and utility of a complex relationship. *Clinical Psychology Review, 33*, 686–697.

Ormel, J., Oldehinkel, A. J., & Brilman, E. I. (2001). The interplay and etiological continuity of neuroticism, difficulties, and life events in the etiology of major and subsyndromal, first and recurrent depressive episodes in later life. *American Journal of Psychiatry, 158*, 885–891.

Oshri, A., Rogosch, F. A., Burnette, M. L., & Cicchetti, D. (2011). Developmental pathways to adolescent cannabis abuse and dependence: Child maltreatment, emerging personality, and internalizing versus externalizing psychopathology. *Psychology of Addictive Behaviors, 25*, 634–644.

Peabody, D., & Goldberg, L. R. (1989). Some determinants of factor structures from personality-trait descriptors. *Journal of Personality and Social Psychology, 57*, 552–567.

Potthoff, J. G., Holahan, C. J., & Joiner, T. E. (1995). Reassurance seeking, stress generation, and depressive symptoms: An integrative model. *Journal of Personality and Social Psychology, 68*, 664.

Prinzie, P., Onghena, P., Hellinckx, W., Grietens, H., Ghesquiere, P., & Colpin, H. (2003). The additive and interactive effects of parenting and children's personality on externalizing behaviour. *European Journal of Personality, 17*, 95–117.

Roberts, B. W. (2009). Back to the future: Personality and assessment and personality development. *Journal of Research in Personality, 43*, 137–145.

Roberts, B. W., Luo, J., Briley, D. A., Chow, P. I., Su, R., & Hill, P. L. (2017). A systematic review of personality trait change through intervention. *Psychological Bulletin, 143*, 117–122.

Rothbart, M. K., & Bates, J. E. (2006). Temperament. In N. Eisenberg, W. Damon & R. M. Lerner (Eds.), *Handbook of child psychology: Vol 3, Social, emotional, and personality development* (6th ed., pp. 99–166). Hoboken, NJ: John Wiley & Sons Inc.

Safford, S. M., Alloy, L. B., Abramson, L. Y., & Crossfield, A. G. (2007). Negative cognitive style as a predictor of negative life events in depression-prone individuals: A test of the stress generation hypothesis. *Journal of Affective Disorders, 99*, 147–154.

Sauer-Zavala, S., Wilner, J. G., & Barlow, D. H. (2017). Addressing neuroticism in psychological treatment. *Personality Disorders: Theory, Research, and Treatment, 8*, 191–198.

Shapero, B. G., Hankin, B. L., & Barrocas, A. L. (2013). Stress generation and exposure in a multi-wave study of adolescents: Transactional processes and sex differences. *Journal of Social and Clinical Psychology, 32*, 989–1012.

Sher, K. J., Bartholow, B. D., & Wood, M. D. (2000). Personality and substance use disorders: A prospective study. *Journal of Consulting and Clinical Psychology, 68*, 818.

Shiner, R. L., Buss, K. A., McClowry, S. G., Putnam, S. P., Saudino, K. J., & Zentner, M. (2012). What is temperament now? Assessing progress in temperament research on the twenty-fifth anniversary of Goldsmith et al. (1987). *Child Development Perspectives, 6*, 436–444.

Shiner, R. L., & Masten, A. S. (2008). Personality in childhood: A bridge from early temperament to adult outcomes. *International Journal of Developmental Science, 2*, 158–175.

Smith, D. J., Escott-Price, V., Davies, G., Bailey, M. E., Colodro-Conde, L., Ward, J.,...Lyall, D. (2016). Genome-wide analysis of over 106, 000 individuals identifies 9 neuroticism-associated loci. *Molecular Psychiatry, 21*, 749–757.

Spinhoven, P., Elzinga, B., Hovens, J., Roelofs, K., Van Oppen, P., Zitman, F.,...Penninx, B. (2011). Positive and negative life events and personality traits in predicting course of depression and anxiety. *Acta Psychiatrica Scandinavica, 124*, 462–473.

Spinhoven, P., Elzinga, B., Roelofs, K., Hovens, J. G., van Oppen, P., Zitman, F. G.,...Penninx, B. (2011). The effects of neuroticism, extraversion, and positive and negative life events on a one-year course of depressive symptoms in euthymic previously depressed patients versus healthy controls. *The Journal of Nervous and Mental Disease, 199*, 684–689.

Spinhoven, P., Elzinga, B. M., Hovens, J. G., Roelofs, K., Zitman, F. G., van Oppen, P.,...Penninx, B. (2010). The specificity of childhood adversities and negative life events across the life span to anxiety and depressive disorders. *Journal of Affective Disorders, 126*, 103–112.

Starrs, C. J., Abela, J. R., Shih, J. H., Cohen, J. R., Yao, S., Zhu, X. Z., & Hammen, C. L. (2010). Stress generation and vulnerability in adolescents in mainland China. *International Journal of Cognitive Therapy, 3*, 345–357.

Stroud, C. B., Sosoo, E. E., & Wilson, S. (2015). Normal personality traits, rumination and stress generation among early adolescent girls. *Journal of Research in Personality, 57*, 131–142.

Sugimura, N., & Rudolph, K. D. (2012). Temperamental differences in children's reactions to peer victimization. *Journal of Clinical Child & Adolescent Psychology, 41*, 314–328.

Tang, T. Z., DeRubeis, R. J., Hollon, S. D., Amsterdam, J., Shelton, R., & Schalet, B. (2009). Personality change during depression treatment: A placebo-controlled trial. *Archives of General Psychiatry, 66*, 1322–1330.

Taylor, C. T., Knapp, S. E., Bomyea, J. A., Ramsawh, H. J., Paulus, M. P., & Stein, M. B. (2017). What good are positive emotions for treatment? Trait positive emotionality predicts response to cognitive behavioral therapy for anxiety. *Behaviour Research and Therapy, 93*, 6–12.

Tellegen, A. (1985). Structures of mood and personality and their relevance to assessing anxiety, with an emphasis on self-report. In T. A. Hussain & J. D. Maser (Eds.), *Anxiety and the anxiety disorders* (pp. 681–706). Hillsdale, NJ, England: Lawrence Erlbaum Associates.

Titov, N., Dear, B., Staples, L., Terides, M., Karin, E., Sheehan, J.,...Wootton, B. (2015). Disorder-specific versus transdiagnostic and clinician-guided versus self-guided treatment for major depressive disorder and comorbid anxiety disorders: A randomized controlled trial. *Journal of Anxiety Disorders, 35*, 88–102.

Tubman, J. G., & Windle, M. (1995). Continuity of difficult temperament in adolescence: Relations with depression, life events, family support, and substance use across a one-year period. *Journal of Youth and Adolescence, 24*, 133–153.

Uher, R., Perlis, R., Henigsberg, N., Zobel, A., Rietschel, M., Mors, O.,...Bajs, M. (2012). Depression symptom dimensions as predictors of antidepressant treatment outcome: Replicable evidence for interest-activity symptoms. *Psychological Medicine*, *42*, 967–980.

Uliaszek, A. A., Zinbarg, R. E., Mineka, S., Craske, M. G., Griffith, J. W., Sutton, J. M.,…Hammen, C. (2012). A longitudinal examination of stress generation in depressive and anxiety disorders. *Journal of Abnormal Psychology*, *121*, 4.

Uliaszek, A. A., Zinbarg, R. E., Mineka, S., Craske, M. G., Sutton, J. M., Griffith, J. W.,…Hammen, C. (2010). The role of neuroticism and extraversion in the stress–anxiety and stress–depression relationships. *Anxiety, Stress, & Coping*, *23*, 363–381.

van der Veen, D. C., van Dijk, S. D. M., Comijs, H. C., van Zelst, W. H., Schoevers, R. A., & Oude Voshaar, R. C. (2017). The importance of personality and life-events in anxious depression: from trait to state anxiety. *Aging & Mental Health*, *21*, 1177–1183.

Vasey, M. W., Harbaugh, C. N., Lonigan, C. J., Phillips, B. M., Hankin, B. L., Willem, L.,…Bijttebier, P. (2013). Dimensions of temperament and depressive symptoms: Replicating a three-way interaction. *Journal of Research in Personality*, *47*, 908–921.

Visser, A., Huizinga, G. A., Hoekstra, H. J., van der Graaf, W. T. A., & Hoekstra-Weebers, J. E. H. M. (2007). Temperament as a predictor of internalising and externalising problems in adolescent children of parents diagnosed with cancer. *Supportive Care in Cancer*, *15*, 395–403.

Vrshek-Schallhorn, S., Stroud, C. B., Mineka, S., Hammen, C., Zinbarg, R. E., Wolitzky-Taylor, K.,…Craske, M. G. (2015). Chronic and episodic interpersonal stress as statistically unique predictors of depression in two samples of emerging adults. *Journal of Abnormal Psychology*, *124*, 918.

Watson, D. (1988). Intraindividual and interindividual analyses of positive and negative affect: Their relation to health complaints, perceived stress, and daily activities. *Journal of Personality and Social Psychology*, *54*, 1020.

Watson, D., & Clark, L. A. (1997). Extraversion and its positive emotional core *Handbook of personality psychology* (pp. 767–793). San Diego, CA: Academic Press.

Wetter, E. K., & Hankin, B. L. (2009). Mediational pathways through which positive and negative emotionality contribute to anhedonic symptoms of depression: A prospective study of adolescents. *Journal of Abnormal Child Psychology*, *37*, 507–520.

Xia, L.-X., Ding, C., Hollon, S. D., & Wan, L. (2013). Self-supporting personality and psychological symptoms: The mediating effects of stress and social support. *Personality and Individual Differences*, *54*, 408–413.

Yang, H.-J., Chiu, Y.-J., Soong, W.-T., & Chen, W. J. (2008). The roles of personality traits and negative life events on the episodes of depressive symptoms in nonreferred adolescents: A 1-year follow-up study. *Journal of Adolescent Health*, *42*, 378–385.

Zinbarg, R. E., Mineka, S., Bobova, L., Craske, M. G., Vrshek-Schallhorn, S., Griffith, J. W.,…Anand, D. (2016). Testing a hierarchical model of neuroticism and its cognitive facets: Latent structure and prospective prediction of first onsets of anxiety and unipolar mood disorders during 3 years in late adolescence. *Clinical Psychological Science*, *4*, 805–824.

Stress and Emotion Regulation

The Dynamic Fit Model

Sarah Myruski, Samantha Denefrio, *and* Tracy A. Dennis-Tiwary

Abstract

Emotion regulation (ER) can buffer against the negative effects of stress, but little is understood about processes and contextual factors that influence how and under what conditions this stress buffering occurs. We review previous research on ER in relation to stress and psychopathology, and note that a significant gap in prior research is that is has focused almost exclusively on a small number of deliberative ER strategies. We then highlight growing evidence that automatic and habitual forms of ER, characterized by low resource demands and low conscious awareness, have an important influence on the stress response and its link to psychopathology and well-being. We propose the Dynamic Fit Model of Stress and ER, which posits that (1) both deliberative and automatic ER contribute to the link between stress and psychopathology; (2) the fit between stress demands and ER strategy selection can be mapped along the dimensions of automaticity and flexibility; and (3) negative effects of stress on well-being and psychological functioning emerge when there is a poor fit between stress demands and ER. We discuss how the model delineates elements defining a "good fit" or "poor fit" and how the model can be used to articulate an agenda for future research and hypothesis generation.

Keywords: automatic emotion regulation, emotion regulation flexibility, stress buffering, psychopathology, Dynamic Fit Model

No one is a stranger to stress. Whole industries have grown up around the goal of stress reduction, touting the benefits of everything from stress-reducing teas to mindfulness-based stress reduction. Indeed, stress is universally recognized as a factor in psychopathology across the life span (Dohrenwend, 2000), including anxiety disorders (e.g., Pynoos, Steinberg, & Piacentini, 1999), major depressive disorder (e.g., Heim & Nemeroff, 2001; Wurtman, 2005), substance use disorders (e.g., Khantzian, 1985), personality disorders (e.g., McLean & Gallop, 2003; Stiglmayr et al., 2008), and posttraumatic stress disorder (PTSD; e.g., Ozer, Best, Lipsey, & Weiss, 2003). Thus, understanding factors that buffer against the negative impact of stress is not only of great human interest but also of great interest to psychological science.

Stress involves a complex pattern of psychological and physiological responses. These responses may be to internal or external stimuli and events that are perceived as harmful or threatening. In the face of such challenges, central and peripheral nervous system mechanisms work to maintain allostasis, or relative stability, in the face of stress (Sterling & Eyer, 1988). Allostatic load refers to the finding that adaptation to stress carries with it a biological cost (McEwen & Stellar, 1993), and high levels of allostatic load can contribute to disease (McEwen & Wingfield, 2003), including psychopathology (McEwen, 2000; McEwen & Seeman, 1999).

Important to this concept is the idea that high levels of objective and subjective stress reflect a mismatch between demands (internal or external) and an individual's resources. These resources are multifaceted and include regulatory capacities such as coping (Lazarus, 1966; Lazarus & Folkman, 1984; Lazarus & Lazarus, 1996), social support (e.g., Cohen & Wills, 1985; Cutrona, 1990; Sarason, Sarason, & Pierce, 1990), and executive function (Mendl, 1999; Sprague, Verona, Kalkhoff, & Kilmer, 2011). If there is a mismatch between demands and resources, there is a "poor fit" such that stress exceeds an individual's regulatory threshold and risk for high distress and psychopathology increases.

In this chapter, we focus on emotion regulation (ER) as a key regulatory capacity that can buffer against the negative effects of stress if, we argue, there is a "good fit" between stress demands and ER resources. While there is a large and rich literature on coping and stress (Boekaerts, 1996; Compas, Connor-Smith, Saltzman, Thomsen, & Wadsworth, 2001; Dewe, Cox, & Ferguson, 1993; Folkman, 2013; Lazarus, 1966, for reviews), including some forms of coping that overlap with ER (Gross, 1998b; Kashdan, Barrios, Forsyth, & Steger, 2006; Worthington & Scherer, 2004), most of this research focuses on deliberative and explicit strategies that require conscious effort and awareness (Berkman & Lieberman, 2009; Creswell & Lindsay, 2014; Etkin, Egner, & Kalisch, 2011; Garnefski, Kraaij, & Spinhoven, 2001; Goldin, McRae, Ramel, & Gross, 2008; Mauss, Cook, Cheng, & Gross, 2007; Nolen-Hoeksema & Aldao, 2011). Recent evidence, however, suggests that in certain high-stress situations, relatively automatic ER strategies represent a healthy default mode (Sheppes & Gross, 2012; Sheppes, Scheibe, Suri, & Gross, 2011). Conversely, deliberative strategies tend to be newly learned or atypical, represent a much smaller proportion of our regulatory repertoire, and are more effortful and conscious. Such novel, high-resource strategies are likely a poor fit for highly stressful contexts in which we must act quickly and effectively (Sheppes, Catran, & Meiran, 2009; Sheppes & Meiran, 2007, 2008; Sheppes et al., 2014).

The literature on stress and ER has also paid short shrift to a key component of ER that is consistently emphasized but rarely studied: the flexibility of strategy use within and across changing situational contexts (e.g., Cole, Martin, & Dennis, 2004; Gross, 1998b, 1999; Gross & Feldman Barrett, 2011; Lazarus & Folkman, 1984). Instead, researchers have emphasized the unitary use of putatively adaptive or maladaptive ER strategies across different contexts. However, recent research has begun to examine context–person interactions that emphasize the role of flexibility in emotion

regulation (Bonanno & Burton, 2013; Bonanno, Papa, Lalande, Westphal, & Coifman, 2004; Cheng, 2001; Kashdan & Rottenberg, 2010), suggesting that regulatory flexibility rather than the use of specific ER strategies may best predict psychological functioning (Bonanno & Burton, 2013).

In this chapter, we first review the research literature on stress and ER and note gaps in empirical research on automaticity and flexibility of ER. We then introduce the concept of dynamic fit between stress and ER and describe a novel framework called the Dynamic Fit Model of Stress and ER (see Figure 19.1), which proposes that the negative effects of stress on well-being and psychological functioning emerge when there is a poor fit between stress demands and ER within the dimensions of automaticity and flexibility. We then use this model to articulate an agenda for future research and hypothesis generation.

Stress and Emotion Regulation: Empirical Evidence and Gaps

ER refers to intrinsic and extrinsic processes by which people influence the experience, expression, intensity, and time course of their immediate and future emotions to meet context-specific goals (Buhle et al., 2014; Gross, 2002, 2015; Thompson, 1994; Zaki & Williams, 2013). Individuals also differ in the threshold and intensity of emotional reactivity to emotional stimuli, and heightened or blunted reactivity is related to psychopathology. For example, individuals with depression are less reactive to positive stimuli (Bylsma, Morris, & Rottenberg, 2008 meta-analysis), while anxiety disorders are related to heightened reactivity to threat-relevant stimuli (Carthy, Horesh, Apter, Edge, & Gross, 2010; Goldin, Manber, & Hakimi, 2009; Hare, Tottenham, Galvan, Voss, Glover, & Casey, 2008;). However, maladaptive patterns of ER responses either preceding or following those emotional reactions are both thought to underlie or exacerbate symptoms of psychopathology (e.g., Tomarken & Keener, 1998; Kring & Werner, 2004), and they are also clinically relevant targets for intervention (Carthy et al., 2010). This suggests that while individual difference in emotional reactivity should be considered, ER represents a distinct factor (Cole, Martin, & Dennis, 2004) contributing to the associations between stress and mental health.

Indeed, many studies have demonstrated that ER plays a prominent role in the management of stress. Modulation of unpleasant emotions buffers against the negative influence of stress to reduce

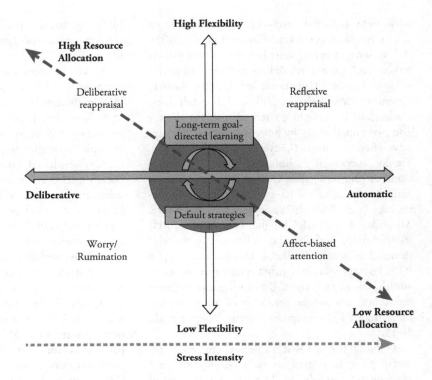

Figure 19.1 The Dynamic Fit Model of Stress and Emotion Regulation.

High Flexibility

High Resource Allocation

Deliberative reappraisal

Reflexive reappraisal

Long-term goal-directed learning

Deliberative

Automatic

Default strategies

Worry/ Rumination

Affect-biased attention

Low Flexibility

Low Resource Allocation

Stress Intensity

symptoms of psychopathology (e.g., Beck, 1979; Sayette, 1993). At the same time, there are bidirectional influences between ER and context (Bonanno & Burton, 2013) suggesting that, while effective ER may buffer the negative effects of stress, stress can also influence the types and flexibility of ER strategies used (Evans & Kim, 2013; Kim et al., 2013). The ability to flexibly modify emotions is a fundamental component of mental health and positive adaptation that, when dysfunctional, corresponds to subjective stress, poor performance, poor health, and mental illness. In this way, ER is a linchpin in the link between stress, risk, and psychopathology.

It is theoretically unassailable and intuitively appealing that ER buffers against stress. The links between stress and ER, however, reflect a complex interplay among biological, social, cognitive, affective, and behavioral factors, and thus significant empirical gaps remain. First, much of the extant research on stress and ER is subsumed under the coping literature. For instance, adaptive coping strategies, including problem-focused and emotion-focused coping, promote resilience following bereavement (e.g., Bonanno & Kaltman, 1999; Stroebe & Schut, 2010). But this coping framework does not address the complexity with respect to the time course of ER. For example, according to several models of ER, including Gross's Process Model

(Gross, 1998a, 1998b; Gross & Thompson, 2006) and Campos's view of the temporal characteristics of ER (Campos, Campos, & Barrett, 1989), ER can occur at any point prior to or following behavioral, experiential, and physiological components of emotion generation. For example, according to Gross (1998a), antecedent-focused ER processes, including situation selection and modification, attentional deployment, and cognitive change, occur prior to emotion generation, while response modulation occurs following emotions. Thus, it is unclear whether the antecedent- or response-focused nature of ER or coping influences its stress-buffering impact.

In addition to the coping literature, there is a significant body of research on stress and ER. The use of deliberative emotion regulation (DER) strategies in the face of stress, such as reappraisal, which emphasizes the positive aspects of a negative stimulus or event, is related to greater resilience and decreased psychopathology (e.g., Garnefski et al., 2001; Nolen-Hoeksema & Aldao, 2011). For example, individuals with greater self-reported resilience tend to use positive emotions to physiologically rebound from negative emotions induced by stress (Garland, Gaylord, & Fredrickson, 2011). In another study, participants instructed to use a positive self-affirmation strategy during a stressful task showed lower cortisol than controls, particularly for those with high reported levels of resources such as self-esteem and optimism (Creswell et al., 2005). Relaxation strategies focused on intentional muscle tension release are related to reduced subjective stress and anxiety (Pawlow & Jones, 2002; Rausch, Gramling, & Auerbach, 2006), and mindfulness meditation is thought to reduce risk for disease and psychopathology by buffering against the negative effects of stress (Creswell & Lindsay, 2014). Finally, successful modulation of negative emotions can buffer against the negative influence of early life stress to reduce symptoms of psychopathology (e.g., Beck, 1979; Sayette, 1993). Cloitre, Miranda, Stovall-McClough, and Han (2005) showed that ER ability plays a key role in the relationship between childhood trauma resulting in PTSD symptoms, and functional impairment in adulthood. In fact, the ability to regulate negative mood was a stronger predictor of adult impairment than PTSD symptom severity (Cloitre et al., 2005).

Habitual use of ER strategies deemed relatively maladaptive is related to reduced physical and psychological well-being. In particular, the use of experiential or expressive suppression of emotions in response to stress has been linked to negative health outcomes, including risk for disease (Barger, Bachen, Marsland, & Manuck, 2000; Jamner, Schwartz, & Leigh, 1988), and stress-induced eating is linked to both reduced emotional distress (Adam & Epel, 2007) but also subsequent disordered eating patterns (Heatherton & Baumeister, 1991). This link between problematic ER strategies and poor well-being translates to therapeutic intervention; for example, cognitive-behavioral therapy approaches emphasizing the use of healthy DER strategies like mindfulness, delay of gratification, and reappraisal have shown to bolster resilience to stress (Benight & Cieslak, 2011; Fava & Tomba, 2009; Southwick & Charney, 2012; Troy & Mauss, 2011). In addition, psychopathology is associated with heightened disruptions in the ability to deliberatively regulate emotions (e.g., Aldao, Nolen-Hoeksema, & Schweizer, 2010; Moore, Zoellner, & Mollenholt, 2008, for review). For example, individuals with a history of depression are more likely to spontaneously use suppression strategies, albeit unsuccessfully, in an attempt to decrease unpleasant emotions (Ehring, Tuschen-Caffier, Schnülle, Fischer, & Gross, 2010), whereas use of reappraisal mitigates the negative impact of stressful life events on depressive symptoms (Troy & Mauss, 2011). This suggests that successful ER is an essential buffer against the detrimental effects of stress and trauma on mental health and illness across the life span.

To complement the behavioral and self-report literature on ER and stress, other researchers aim to identify discrete biobehavioral signatures of ER and show how they predict successful stress buffering and/or contribute to risk for psychopathology. For example, strategies like cognitive reappraisal and mindfulness-based stress reduction techniques bolster prefrontal cortex inhibitory control over subcortical regions involved in the stress response (Creswell & Lindsay, 2014; Etkin et al., 2011; Goldin et al., 2008). In one study, ventrolateral prefrontal cortex mediation of subcortical regions through the nucleus accumbens was related to greater self-reported ER success in explicitly reducing negative emotions to unpleasant pictures (Wager, Davidson, Hughes, Lindquist, & Ochsner, 2008). Successful ER can also modulate the autonomic nervous system (ANS) by either engaging the sympathetic nervous system (SNS) to help cope with a current stressor, as measured by heart rate variability (HRV), or by initiating parasympathetic nervous system (PSNS) activity to induce calm and return to baseline arousal following a stressor, as measured by respiratory sinus arrhythmia (RSA; Appelhans & Luecken, 2006; Porges, 1995, 2007, for reviews). Moreover, individual differences in resting-state ANS activity are related to successful regulation of the stress response in that those with lower PSNS activity during baseline have greater difficulty downregulating negative emotions in response to stress (Fabes & Eisenberg, 1997), while greater baseline SNS activity is related to less subjective distress following a stressor (Fabes, Eisenberg, & Eisenbud, 1993).

Despite substantial evidence that ER strategies are linked to stress and psychopathology, a meta-analytic review revealed that some widely studied strategies, such as reappraisal and acceptance, showed only small to medium effect sizes when considering the relationship with psychopathologies, including anxiety and depression (Aldao et al., 2010). This discrepancy may be at least partially due to methodological approaches that focus solely on DER processes. Specifically, in numerous studies of ER, participants are instructed in the use of these strategies and then deliberatively asked to utilize these strategies during emotion viewing or induction procedures. For example, reappraisal is a cognitive ER strategy reflects the ability to reframe or reinterpret the meaning of an event or stimulus to decrease its emotional impact often through the generation of a neutral or positive appraisal of the event (Gross, 1998b, 2002; Gross & Thompson, 2006; Kumar, Gross, & Ahlskog, 2004). Reappraisal has been the topic of hundreds of research studies (e.g., Buhle et al., 2014; Ochsner & Gross, 2008), but assessment methods invoke deliberative regulatory techniques (e.g., asking participants to intentionally and deliberatively monitor and modify their emotional reactions) rather than those that are relatively automatic because they require little awareness and few resources. Because this methodological approach requires a degree of consciousness and effort, investigations of stress and ER predominantly emphasize deliberative, deliberative processes and inherently lack consideration of AER processes. This same bias toward studying deliberative processes is present in the entire ER literature, whereas more automatic emotion regulation (AER) processes have been relatively neglected until recently (e.g., Mauss, Bunge, & Gross, 2007; Todd & Galinsky, 2012).

Stress and Automatic Emotion Regulation

Only recently have theorists recognized that relatively automatic aspects of ER are used on a constant, moment-to-moment basis and therefore are fundamental to our ability to regulate emotions well or poorly and buffer against the effects of stress (Berkman & Lieberman, 2009; Gyurak, Gross, & Etkin, 2011; Mauss et al., 2007; Todd & Galinsky, 2012). Consistent with research on automatic and unconscious processes (cf. Bargh & Gollwitzer, 1994; Bargh, Gollwitzer, Lee-Chai, Barndollar, & Trötschel, 2001), the idea of unconscious but goal-directed behavior is central to recent theoretical accounts of AER (e.g., Custers & Aarts, 2005; Mauss, et al., 2007; Webb & Sheeran, 2003). This distinction between automatic (nonconscious and implicit) versus deliberative (conscious and deliberative) processes has been discussed using a variety of terms (e.g., Chaiken & Trope, 1999; Devine, 1989; Sloman, 1996; Strack & Deutsch, 2004). For example, the word *automatic* refers to things that are latent and not directly expressed. AER encompasses those aspects of ER that are implicit and latent because they are relatively effortless and automatic (e.g., Mauss, et al., 2007), incidental rather than deliberative (e.g., Berkman & Lieberman, 2009), and reflexive or driven by the object of attention or external information in the environment (Etkin, Egner, Peraza, Kandel, & Hirsch, 2006). In contrast, deliberative aspects of ER are considered relatively controlled, strategic, goal-driven, deliberate, effortful, and intentional.

Existing models fall into two broad categories based on whether emphasis is placed on treating automatic and deliberative as independent ER categories or as opposite ends of a continuous dimension. Here we briefly review definitional issues and several prior models of AER, and we summarize assessment methods and criteria for identifying AER.

Definitions

To formally delineate core components of AER, we draw on the social cognition literature (Bargh, 1989, 1996; Bargh & Ferguson, 2000; Bargh & Gollwitzer, 1994; Bargh et al., 2001; McNally, 1995), which highlights four components of automaticity relevant to ER processes. These components should be thought of as dimensions, ranging from extremely deliberative to extremely automatic, with much room for variation in between. First, in comparison to DER, AER is low in *awareness*, which is the degree to which detection, interpretation, and reactions to a stimulus are amenable to conscious introspection. Importantly, awareness of the processes may be low (e.g., an individual may not know she is shifting attention away from a source of distress), yet awareness of the outcome (e.g., attending to something) is possible. Second, AER is low in *intentionality*, or the driving and instigation of a process by the individual, and thus is difficult to inhibit. Third, and relatedly, AER is lower in *controllability*, or the degree to which the individual person can stop, diminish, or override the target process. Fourth and finally, AER relative to DER is higher in *efficiency*, or the degree to which the process demands attentional resources for its execution.

These dimensions can be further described in terms of stability and in relation to past learning. For example, preconscious automaticity refers to relatively stable processing tendencies that occur when a person merely notices the presence of a stimulus, without goals or intentions (e.g., categorization). Postconscious automaticity refers to a relatively temporary, stimulus-driven aspect of processing that occurs when a person notices the presence of a stimulus and a similar stimulus has recently been consciously attended/processed (e.g., priming). Finally, goal-dependent automaticity refers to relatively stable responses that have become automatic after intentional, conscious learning has occurred. Goal-dependent automaticity, as described later in the model (Figure 19.1), may be a particularly important process underlying the expression of an ER strategy as automatic or deliberative, and the transformations between the two.

Models of Automatic Emotion Regulation

According to Mauss and colleagues (2007), AER is on a continuum with DER. AER is characterized by changes in attentional deployment, appraisal, and cognitive engagement that are initiated in pursuit of a goal without conscious awareness, attention, or control of either the process or goal. Thus, AER is defined as "goal-driven change to any aspect of one's emotions without making a conscious decision to do so" (p. 3). This model encompasses the automatic physiological changes associated with regulating an emotion as well. Mauss and colleagues (2007) make the important point that these automatic processes are different from emotional reactivity because, while reactivity also represents a relatively unconscious process, ER is more malleable in that it can be more readily influenced by contextual factors like sociocultural differences. Like more DER strategies, AER strategies also play an important role in one's emotional health.

This AER model is consistent with Gross's Process Model of ER (Gross, 1998a, 1998b), in identifying that AER strategies are either antecedent focused or response focused, and they can be conceptualized as generally adaptive (e.g., action orientation [Koole & Coenen, 2007], coping and resilience [Bonanno, 2005]) and/or maladaptive (e.g., suppression [Egloff, Schmukle, Burns, & Schwerdtfeger, 2006], avoidant attachment style [Mikulincer, Birnbaum, Woddis, & Nachmias, 2000]), each with distinct neural correlates. Response-focused strategies such as cognitive disengagement and behavioral regulation occur after an emotional response. Because these types of strategies rely upon preceding negative emotional cues, they are more likely to result in maladaptive physiological responses and a failure to adequately reduce negative emotional experiences (Aldao & Nolen-Hoeksema, 2010; Garnefski, Teerds, Kraaij, Legerstee, & van den Kommer, 2004; Mathews & MacLeod, 2005; Silk, Steinberg, & Morris, 2003). In contrast, antecedent-focused strategies, such as selective attentional deployment and reappraisal, occur prior to or very early in the emotional response. When these types of automatic strategies fit with situational cues that dictate how attention and subsequent appraisal should be deployed, they are associated with a greater likelihood of adaptive physiological responses and reduced negative emotions.

Taken together, Mauss and colleagues (2007) note that like deliberative strategies, AER can be both advantageous as well as harmful in regulating negative emotions. This model describes AER in terms of discrete strategies but also places automaticity along a continuum with deliberative processes. There are no specific predictions, however, about potential mobility of strategies along the automatic-deliberative continuum. Furthermore, the adaptiveness of various forms of AER strategies is discussed, but the range of contextual influences on efficacy or efficiency is not fully considered.

Dual-Process Model

According to Gyurak and colleagues (2011), AER and DER are discrete processes with porous boundaries and are thus part of a dual-process system, described as "distinct yet interrelated islands" (p. 401). Both types of ER are posited to contribute to healthy ER capacity. Using the term "implicit ER," they describe AER as a set of processes that take place automatically without monitoring and in the absence of awareness and effort. In contrast, DER requires effort, monitoring, and awareness. This definitional distinction implies that the person is only able to benefit from situational and/or emotional feedback as a deliberative process is employed. Furthermore, an awareness of one's ER strategy use (e.g., deliberative reappraisal) that is constantly being updated can be costly and requires a high degree of resources. Therefore, to meet day-to-day needs, deliberative forms of ER cannot be the only form of regulation as they are too resource heavy or "expensive." For instance, for ER strategies including reappraisal and suppression, recruitment of neurocognitive resources measured via activity of the prefrontal cortex indicate heavy top-down, cognitive demands. The Gyurak and colleagues (2011) model further identifies the existence of cross-over between automatic and deliberative processes and notes this as an important area for future research to explore. For example, the authors suggest that through practice, repetition, and successfully modulating an emotional experience, deliberative processes can become more habitual and implicit. As such, both processes evolve over time and may overlap across situations and depending on the person's needs. Thus, placement of a particular strategy within each category is not fixed.

To better illustrate AER repertoire, the model identifies five specific examples of nondeliberative processes present throughout the literature that range in their level of automaticity: emotional conflict adaptation, habitual emotion regulation, emotion regulatory goals and values, affect labeling, and error-related regulation. For example, emotional conflict adaptation can be measured using an emotional

Stroop task in which reaction times on incongruent (emotional conflict) trials are slower, compared to performance on congruent trials. This behavioral effect is unstructured, effortless, and proceeds without awareness, thus indexing AER.

Extended Model of Emotion Regulation

Todd and Galinsky (2012) build on the dual-process model (Gyurak et al., 2011) by addressing the role of motivation within a changing context in the Extended Model of Emotion Regulation (EMER). This framework singles out affect-biased attention as an understudied form of AER. They define affect-biased attention as an unconscious propensity to attend to one category of salient stimuli over another. They discuss this form of emotion regulation as a preemptive and sensory "tuning filter" that directs attention prior to an emotional experience and continues to guide processing, working at a top-down level subject to the influence of motivational goals. They further argue that this attention filter functions proactively by being repeatedly shaped and updated both over development and within specific emotional events, shaping an individual's emotional experiences.

One of the most widely studied forms of affect-biased attention is threat bias (TB). TB, or selective and exaggerated attention toward threat, is a potential neurocognitive mechanism in anxiety across the life span (Bar-Haim, Lamy, Pergamin, Bakermans-Kranenburg, & Van Ijzendoorn, 2007; Mogg, Mathews, & Eysenck, 1992). As a form of AER, TB functions as an attention filter biased toward negative information, events, and emotions without awareness and requiring little if any conscious effort. TB is thought to promote anxiety by increasing anxious arousal through exaggerated processing of threat, reducing opportunities to disconfirm anxiety-related beliefs. Although TB has been well documented in both clinical and trait-anxious individuals (i.e., Bar-Haim, Lamy, Pergamin, Bakermans-Kranenburg, & Van Ijzendoorn, 2007), emerging evidence has shown that a significant proportion of anxious adults evidence a bias *away* from threat (Cisler & Koster, 2010; Mansell, Clark, Ehlers, & Chen, 1999) or fail to show a bias using traditional reaction-time-based assays. Innovative new research has delved into these empirical challenges, proposing alternate metrics and methods for assessing TB, including trial-level TB variability (Heeren, Mogoaşe, Philippot, & McNally, 2015; Zvielli, Bernstein, & Koster, 2015; Egan & Dennis, 2018), neurophysiological measures of biased attention (Dennis-Tiwary, Denefrio, & Gelber, 2017; Dennis-Tiwary, Egan, Babkirk, & Denefrio, 2016), and eye-tracking methods (Armstrong & Olatunji, 2012). With the hallmark of such recent novel techniques, we are just beginning to understand how mood- and state-related changes in anxiety impact the flexibility of automatic cognitive biases. Thus, TB is a prime candidate for studying the role of AER in anxiety and its potential stress-buffering effects.

The EMER model (Todd & Galinsky, 2012) is further distinguished from other AER models by its rich consideration of development. For example, flexible strategy deployment should gradually develop along with neurocognitive development supporting greater effortful cognitive control. This developmental focus allows for the "evolution" of strategies from relatively reflexive to effortful.

Open Questions About Automatic Emotion Regulation

Several future research questions logically emerge from existing models of AER reviewed earlier (Gyurak et al., 2011; Mauss et al., 2007; Todd & Galinsky, 2012). For example, while it is unclear how strategies dynamically transition from deliberative to automatic over time and vice versa, one likely avenue is habitual use, similar to how procedural tasks are learned and automatized through practice, like driving a car. This process would have implications for therapeutic intervention, such as understanding how cognitive and behavioral strategies for stress management become automatic and more efficient through practice. Further, habitual maladaptive ER could be targeted through interventions that aim to bring those reflexive ER patterns into conscious awareness.

Another topic requiring research attention is how automaticity relates to adaptive or maladaptive ER. For example, repression, a relatively reflexive ER strategy, has been related to both positive and negative mental health outcomes, depending on the context (Bonanno, Znoj, Siddique, & Horowitz, 1999). Frequent use of this strategy has been linked to impaired cognition, reduced social adjustment, and increased physiological reactivity (e.g., Schwartz & Kline, 1995; Weinberger, 1998). However, use of repression following a stressful loss has been associated with greater resilience and reduced psychopathology (Coifman, Bonanno, Ray, & Gross, 2007), suggesting that use of an automatic ER strategy may be adaptive in some contexts and maladaptive in others.

Third, research examining the role of AER in response to both acute and chronic stress is lacking, and the factors contributing to the emergence and trajectories of these automatic processes are not well understood. For instance, AER following relatively acute stress, such as bereavement, is potentially adaptive and promotes resilience (Bonanno, 2005; Bonanno, Keltner, Holen, & Horowitz, 1995). On the other hand, maladaptive or rigid AER may emerge from chronic or severe stress, giving rise to or solidifying automatic patterns of responding that contribute to psychopathologies. Kim and colleagues (2013) found that adults who experienced chronic poverty-related stress throughout childhood showed blunted ventro- and dorsolateral prefrontal cortex activity during a directed ER task. These same prefrontal regions have been implicated in AER processes measured during a startle eye-blink task (Jackson et al., 2003), suggesting that chronic stress may alter patterns of both DER and AER.

In sum, it is crucial for future research to examine both DER and AER in relation to stress. Prior models similarly emphasize the importance of delineating automatic and deliberative processes, often placing them on a single dimension, and specify that effort, awareness, and efficiency are critical factors in distinguishing relatively automatic from deliberative processes. Few models account for contextual effects, developmental change, or processes through which reflexive strategies can become more amendable to top-down, effortful control or become more or less flexible over time.

Assessment Methods and Individual Differences

Several paradigms have been used in recent research to capture AER and related processes. Berkman and Lieberman (2009) argue that, to infer that AER has occurred, some observable process must be measured that differentiates between an outcome that ensues from regulation versus an outcome that ensues in the absence of regulation efforts. Latency to categorize ER-relevant terms is one such method, with faster reactions times indicating a stronger implicit association. For instance, the ER implicit attitudes test (ER-IAT; Mauss, Evers, Wilhelm, & Gross, 2006) assesses whether individuals subconsciously prefer words describing emotional control (e.g., restrains, stable) or expression (e.g., volatile, boiled) with the assumption that this preference will increase the likelihood of automatic implementation of that strategy. Consistent with this, those with emotional control preferences measured by the

ER-IAT reported less negative emotion during a subsequent emotionally provocative task in which emotion control strategies could be enacted.

Other approaches aim to induce the use of AER through experimental manipulation to examine mobility along the automatic-deliberative ER continuum. For example, Mauss and colleagues (2007) showed that priming participants with emotion control words (e.g., "restrains") was associated with decreased self-reported anger following provocation. Williams, Bargh, Nocera, and Gray (2009) used a similar priming method and found that those primed with reappraisal cue words (e.g., reassessed, carefully analyzed) preceding a stressful task showed decreased heart rate change compared to those who did not receive a reappraisal prime. Importantly, individual differences emerged in the extent to which priming of reappraisal cues enhanced ER during the stressor. Participants who reported using deliberative reappraisal more frequently in everyday life also showed greater AER after exposure to the reappraisal prime. This suggests that those who engage in habitual use of DER strategies may have a broader range of mobility between DER and AER approaches and are thus more able to use either approach to fit the contextual demands (Williams et al., 2009).

Several studies (Eder, 2011; Eder, Rothermund, & Proctor, 2010; Gallo, Keil, McCulloch, Rockstroh, & Gollwitzer, 2009; Parks-Stamm, Oettingen, & Gollwitzer, 2010; Webb, Ononaiye, Sheeran, Reidy, & Lavda, 2010) have demonstrated that ER can be automatized through repeated or elaborated implementation of intentional emotional goals during unpleasant emotional situations. Compared to participants prompted with simple goal intentions (i.e., "do not feel disgusted"), participants who internalized more complex if-then plans, or implemented ER intentions (i.e., "if I see blood, then I will feel calm and relaxed"), reported decreased negative emotions and reduced neurophysiological responses to fear and disgust stimuli in an independent assessment (Gallo et al., 2009), suggesting automatizing of these strategies.

Automatic Emotion Regulation and Resource Allocation Efficiency

The automatic/deliberative distinction is also important when considering how a range of factors, like cognitive load, may impact the efficacy and efficiency of ER. As noted earlier, the low effort required for AER, compared to DER, translates into fewer resources recruited and greater regulatory efficiency. For instance, when cognitive load is high and extensive attentional resources are required for task completion, effortful, deliberative processes may suffer, whereas automatic processes do not. Consistent with this, AER may differentially influence subjective versus physiological responses to negative emotional experiences, which has implications for the relative efficiency of ER processes. That is, physiological responses to stress can be downregulated without the resources necessary for conscious awareness of these processes, fewer cognitive resources are needed, and thus ER is more efficient. In support of this notion, in one study (Yuan, Ding, Liu, & Yang, 2015), participants were either primed with reappraisal words (AER) or explicitly instructed to use reappraisal (DER group), and then completed a frustrating task. Both AER and DER groups showed decreased heart rate during emotion induction compared to a control group, suggesting that AER may yield physiological benefits in regulatory contexts without the need for allocation of conscious cognitive resources. Subjective ratings of negative emotion, however, were decreased only in the DER group. Thus, while AER may be cognitively efficient, it may have less of an impact on subjective emotional experiences. Importantly, since the relative effectiveness of ER can be assessed as a combination of biological, behavioral, and experiential measures (Webb, Miles, & Sheeran, 2012), an *efficient* strategy is not always an *effective* one. Furthermore, not all AER is necessarily efficient. For instance, McNally (1995) questioned the capacity-free nature of automatic attention in relation to emotion, such as anxiety, arguing that processing of anxiety-relevant information almost immediately interrupts ongoing processes and takes considerable capacity.

Stress and Emotion Regulation Flexibility

The relative advantages of DER and AER may vary depending on the intensity of stress and negative affect, and an individual's ability to flexibly shift strategies when needed. For instance, while reappraisal may be adaptive when unpleasant emotions are relatively low intensity, suppression may be more appropriate for high-intensity emotions (Sheppes et al., 2011). In some contexts, reappraisal could even be considered maladaptive, if the individual uses this strategy to interpret a stimulus or event in an unrealistic or inflexible way (Gross, 2015). In one study (Bonanno et al., 2004), young adults who reported using *both* suppression and enhancement of their emotions following the September 11th terrorist attack in New York City showed fewer long-term negative effects of the traumatic event. Thus, the adaptiveness of ER may be better described in terms of regulatory flexibility (Bonanno & Burton, 2013) and fit between ER strategies and contextual demands.

Although recent research has presented a more nuanced view of reappraisal in ER (Gross, 2015), this strategy is often characterized as a paradigmatic "adaptive" emotion regulation strategy and is pitted against presumably less adaptive strategies such as expressive suppression. This pitting of adaptive against maladaptive strategies creates not only a false dichotomy between "good" and "bad" emotion regulation but also ignores context of the stressor, individual differences, and the likelihood that these strategies function along a continuum rather than as categorically different types of strategies. In their recent proposal on regulatory flexibility, Bonanno and Burton (2013) argue that these assumptions surrounding assignment of adaptiveness to discrete ER strategies represent a *fallacy of uniform efficacy*. Recent research on the context appropriateness of reappraisal and suppression (Gross, 1998a; Sheppes et al., 2011), and short-term versus long-term strategy efficacy (Cummings, Davies, & Simpson, 1994; Davies, Forman, Rasi, & Stevens, 2002; Thompson, Lewis, & Calkins, 2008), are consistent with the critique of assumptions around uniform efficacy of ER strategies. Bonanno and Burton (2013) highlight three components of flexibility: context sensitivity, repertoire, and feedback response. Each of these interrelated components reflects important dimensions of flexibility that can impact the "goodness of fit" between ER strategy use and the changing demands of stressful contexts.

Context Sensitivity

The first step in the sequence of regulatory flexibility is to attend to important aspects of a potentially stressful context and engage in ER that is an appropriate fit for the demands. Bonanno and Burton (2013) describe this as a probabilistic process, as the individual can only make choices with regard to which ER strategy to use based on the features of the context he or she discerns. Individuals vary in their context sensitivity, as some are more able to attune to essential context cues and filter out unneeded information to inform their ER choices. Another important feature of context sensitivity is the ability to judge which aspects of a stressful situation are controllable and which are not, a capacity called discriminative facility (Cheng, 2001, 2003; Chiu, Hong, Mischel, & Shoda, 1995). Cheng and colleagues showed through a series of studies that individuals with greater ability to judge the controllable aspects of stressful scenarios (e.g., airplane turbulence, health management during cancer treatment) during a laboratory task also reported greater flexibility in the use of coping strategies. Context sensitivity also includes the ability to accurately detect emotional cues in the environment and adjust one's emotional responding in accordance with that context. For example, anger can be an adaptive and appropriate emotion during a protest of injustice (e.g., Lerner, 1997) or maladaptive and damaging in a context of affiliation (e.g., Keltner, Ellsworth, & Edwards, 1993). Taken together, these studies suggest that sensitivity to context is a key aspect of flexibility and determinant of whether ER is adaptive or maladaptive.

Repertoire

Another aspect of regulatory flexibility concerns the breadth of ER repertoire. Individuals differ in the diversity of the ER strategy repertoire at their disposal, the ability to flexibly shift ER approaches over time, and switch between different types of strategies if needed (Gall, Evans, & Bellerose, 2000; Gall, Guirguis-Younger, Charbonneau, & Florack, 2009). This is consistent with a recent study showing that using a greater number of ER strategies is related to lower traumatic stress following a campus mass shooting (Orcutt, Bonanno, Hannan, & Miron, 2014), and more varied use of ER strategies over time is associated with feeling more effective in coping attempts and lower self-reported depression (Cheng, 2001). In addition, greater categorical variability, or the ability to switch among diverse strategy types (e.g., avoidance to reappraisal), is related to better coping with grief following bereavement (Galatzer-Levy, Burton, & Bonanno, 2012; Gupta & Bonanno, 2011) and fewer emotional problems (e.g., Lougheed & Hollenstein, 2012; Southwick, Bonanno, Masten, Panter-Brick, & Yehuda, 2014).

Responsiveness to Feedback

Finally, once an ER strategy has been selected from a repertoire and implemented, one must assess strategy effectiveness and adjust appropriately by maintaining strategy use, shifting to an alternate strategy, or disengaging ER following successful regulation. This responsiveness can be in relation to either external or internal feedback (e.g., Beer, Heerey, Keltner, Scabini, & Knight, 2003; Butler et al., 2003; Füstös, Gramann, Herbert, & Pollatos, 2012). For example, social cues provide feedback on the appropriateness and effectiveness of an ER strategy by

allowing us to see how others are both assessing our emotional expressions and managing their emotions to the same situation (Butler et al., 2003). Also, sensitivity to internal cues, like heart rate, has been shown to be related to more successful directed reappraisal or maintenance of emotional responses (Füstös et al., 2012).

This component of regulatory flexibility overlaps somewhat with context sensitivity and repertoire in that one must be sensitive to emotional context to evaluate whether regulatory attempts remain appropriate for the demands, and one must possess a broad repertoire of ER approaches should shifting to a new strategy be necessary. The responsiveness to feedback component, however, highlights that regulatory flexibility is an ongoing process that must be continuously checked, managed, and updated as stress demands fluctuate and regulatory attempts fail or succeed.

Short-Term Versus Long-Term Efficacy

An advantage of considering regulatory flexibility is that it can account for how an ER approach may be adaptive in the moment but maladaptive in the long run. For example, children developing in a stressful environment, such as one with habitual marital discord, may use hypervigilance to monitor their surroundings for signs of conflict, or avoidance to limit the influence of their surroundings on their internal state (Cummings et al., 1994; Davies et al., 2002; Thompson et al., 2008). Although these strategies may protect the child from negative emotions in the moment, they likely also contribute to long-term rigidity in ER patterns (Thompson & Calkins, 1996) and reduced use of a larger repertoire of potentially more adaptive strategies. In other words, an ER strategy can be simultaneously optimal in the moment but also set the stage for vulnerabilities later.

Gaps in the Research on Stress and Emotion Regulation Flexibility

Although the evidence described earlier indicates that healthy ER may be best thought of in terms of flexibility versus rigidity as opposed to discrete adaptive versus maladaptive strategies, several questions remain to drive avenues for future research. For example, relatively little is known about how flexibility and automaticity interact to contribute to ER adaptiveness. One recent study (Myruski et al., 2017) takes a first step in understanding this relationship, and it illustrates how early, automatic attentional processes relate to emotional flexibility and well-being. Specifically, rapid, automatic appraisal of salient emotional contextual information during an emotional go/no-go task was related to self-reported regulatory flexibility.

In addition, perhaps some aspects of flexibility, such as responsiveness to feedback, must be relatively deliberative, as an individual must consciously and intentionally shift from one strategy to another. In contrast, context sensitivity may be relatively automatic, since it is early, preconscious attentional processes that contribute to detection of important aspects of the emotional context. Furthermore, the elements (e.g., context sensitivity, repertoire) of regulatory flexibility that constitute a good fit between ER approach and stress context should be further explored. Individual differences in flexibility components should also be assessed, as some people may excel at detecting emotional context, but are relatively rigid regarding strategy repertoire, yet little is known about the relative advantages and disadvantages of each aspect of flexibility. In sum, the field is only beginning to explore the relationship between regulatory flexibility, stress, and mental health, and how strengths and weaknesses related to the various components of flexibility can be assessed and targeted for intervention.

Gender, Emotion Regulation, and Stress

A large body of research indicates striking gender differences in emotionality and mental health outcomes (Nolen-Hoeksema, 2012; Tamres, Janicki, & Helgeson, 2002, for reviews) relevant to stress. Studies have shown that, compared to men, women are more aware of their emotions (Ciarrochi, Hynes, & Crittenden, 2005; Joseph & Newman, 2010), show more complexity in conceptualization of emotions (Barrett, Lane, Sechrest, & Schwartz, 2000), and are more analytic of their own emotions (Barrett & Bliss-Moreau, 2009; Gohm, 2003). In addition, the prevalence of depressive and anxiety disorders (Kessler et al., 2007; McLean & Anderson, 2009; Nolen-Hoeksema, 2012) and internalizing symptomatology (Kramer, Kreuger, & Hicks, 2008; Leadbeater, Kuperminc, Blatt, & Hertzog, 1999) is greater in women compared to men. On the other hand, men are more likely than women to reach diagnostic criteria for alcohol-related disorders (Keyes, Grant, & Hasin, 2008) and to exhibit externalizing symptomatology (Kramer, Kreuger, & Hicks, 2008; Leadbeater, Kuperminc, Blatt, & Hertzog, 1999), suggesting that gender differences in regulatory responses to stress may underlie how different patterns of psychopathology may emerge in men and women (Hyde, Mezulis, & Abramson, 2008; Nolen-Hoeksema, 2012; Zahn-Waxler, Shirtcliff, & Marceau, 2008).

Indeed, several studies have provided evidence for consistent gender differences in ER processes (Nolen-Hoeksema, 2012; Tamres et al., 2002, for reviews). For example, women are more likely to use emotion-focused strategies like rumination, the repetitive focus on negative emotions (Butler & Nolen-Hoeksema, 1994; Nolen-Hoeksema & Aldao, 2011), whereas men are more prone to the use of suppression or avoidance (Tamres et al., 2002, for review), and they are particularly more likely to use alcohol to cope with stress (e.g., Cooper, Frone, Russell, & Mudar, 1995; Cooper, Russell, Skinner, Frone, & Mudar, 1992; Nolen-Hoeksema & Harrell, 2002). Although all these strategies can be maladaptive depending on context and chronicity, rumination has been consistently linked with depression and anxiety, and using alcohol to manage stress contributes to substance use disorders (Luce, Engler, & Crowther, 2007; Sher & Grekin, 2007). Nolen-Hoeksema (2012) showed that these gender differences in patterns of maladaptive strategy use statistically accounted for variance in psychopathology symptoms. However, women also report greater use of problem solving, reappraisal, and social support–seeking strategies compared to men, as well as overall more types of ER strategies (Tamres et al., 2002). When use of these potentially more adaptive strategies is considered, only support seeking appears to decrease the gender gap in depression (Nolen-Hoeksema, 2012). Thus, the links between gender, ER, and psychopathology must be explained by more than just discrete adaptive versus maladaptive strategy use. Instead, gender differences regarding ER in response to stress should be examined in terms of fit between ER and stress context, and through the consideration of dimensions of ER such as flexibility-rigidity and automatic-deliberative. For instance, women's greater awareness of emotions may act as both a protective factor against stress (Hilt & Nolen-Hoeksema, 2009) or a greater vulnerability to its negative effects (Barrett et al., 2000), depending on the fit between stress context and strategy use. Specifically, although women report using reappraisal more than men, this strategy could be maladaptive in a context of severe stress such as domestic abuse (Nolen-Hoeksema, 2012). In another study (Nolen-Hoeksema & Aldao, 2011), women reported greater regulatory flexibility compared to men, as indicated by a larger repertoire of ER strategies employed. However, as noted earlier, women are more likely to report ruminating in response to stress compared to men (Tamres et al., 2002; Zlomke & Hahn, 2010), a strategy that inherently suggests a lack of flexibility to disengage and shift strategies. Choices to use this strategy, and difficulties in altering a strategy in response to feedback, may mark regulatory rigidity and serve as a vulnerability factor in the face of stress that exacerbates anxiety and contributes to mental health problems.

Recent research has begun to examine gender differences in automaticity of ER in response to stress. For example, McRae, Ochsner, Mauss, Gabrieli, and Gross (2008) measured brain responses via functional magnetic resonance imaging (fMRI) in men and women during a cognitive reappraisal task. When asked to modulate emotions to unpleasant stimuli, men showed lesser increases in prefrontal activation, but also greater decreases in amygdala activation, in comparison to women. Thus, while emotional responding, as measured by amygdala activity, was reduced, a large degree of deliberative cognitive effort, as measured by prefrontal activity, was not required, suggesting that men are more likely to use AER processes compared to women. If men use AER more frequently, this may account for why women consistently report greater use of ER (Tamres et al., 2002), since widely used methods of ER assessment focus only on deliberative processes.

Finally, there has been a recent theoretical push for researchers to look beyond the traditional gender binary of male/female when examining differences in health-related outcomes (e.g., Bottorff, Oliffe, & Kelly, 2012; Johnson & Repta, 2012). For instance, Lam and McBride-Chang (2007) assessed gender dimensionally as opposed to categorically and showed that individuals low in masculinity but high in femininity reported greater depression, consistent with other findings indicating females are more vulnerable to the negative effects of stress (Barrett & Bliss-Moreau, 2009; Fischer & Manstead, 2000; Kessler et al., 2007; McLean & Anderson, 2009; Nolen-Hoeksema, 2012). However, this study also showed that medium to high levels of masculinity, coupled with high levels of femininity, predicted less depression, indicating that those reporting more androgynous or non-gender-typed characteristics showed less vulnerability to stress. These results indicate that beyond biological sex, individual differences in gender-based personality traits, whether induced biologically or through socialization, may underlie ER processes that represent risks and protective factors against stress. Importantly, this study also showed that greater coping flexibility predicted less depression, regardless of gender, indicating that the ability to be flexible in the face of stress may override or compensate for any potential gender- or personality-based vulnerabilities. These findings highlight the importance of considering dimensionality when it comes not only to psychological constructs like ER automaticity and flexibility, but also regarding gender itself. In sum, further research is needed to understand gender differences in the relative advantages and disadvantages afforded by automaticity, flexibility, and contextual fit of ER in response to stress.

The Dynamic Fit Model of Stress and Emotion Regulation and Directions for Future Research

Taken together, prior research has supported the idea that ER has powerful stress-buffering effects and supports resilience. There are, however, significant gaps in our understanding of how the fit between ER and stress context impacts the efficacy of stress buffering, how the degree to which a given ER process varies along the automatic-deliberative continuum influences this fit, and how ER flexibility must be considered in order to assess the adaptiveness of a given ER strategy, particularly in response to chronic stress. Here we present the Dynamic Fit Model of Stress and ER, which addresses each of these gaps, delineates what comprises a "good fit" between stress and ER, and drives hypothesis generation regarding how a "poor fit" between stress and ER can have negative implications for psychological well-being and mental health.

The Dynamic Fit Model

The model (see Figure 19.1) synthesizes clinical, neuroscience, and life span developmental research within a dynamic person-context interactional framework. We describe emotion regulation strategies along two orthogonal dimensions of *automaticity* and *flexibility*. In contrast to discrete views of emotion regulation, we conceptualize ER as varying continually along the automatic-deliberative and flexibility dimensions, both within people and contexts. The model also shows resource allocation varying along the diagonal because automaticity, as detailed earlier, is a function of resources allocated/control required to enact a given strategy. Finally, stress intensity varies along the X-axis, with greater stress intensity as you move to the right, and the center of the model depicts developmental changes or transformations among strategies, discussed in detail next.

Specific strategies can be plotted within each quadrant in this framework. Here, we plot one per quadrant to illustrate how distinct types of strategies can be characterized as varying along the dimensions of automaticity, flexibility, and resource allocation. The positioning of these dimensions and specific strategies further reflect a "good fit" with the degree of stress intensity. For example, reflexive reappraisal is in the top right quadrant, while deliberative reappraisal is in the top left quadrant. The distinction here is that while the empirical study of reappraisal typically involved conscious and controlled use of reappraisal as a strategy, over time reappraisal might become a habitual reaction to high-stress events, such that it becomes highly automatic, flexible, and efficient, despite the fact that reappraisal is typically considered more "top-down" and therefore conscious and subject to intentional control. Consistent with this view, however, we can also place reappraisal in the top left quadrant when it is used in a more effortful, deliberative, and conscious way in response to low-stress environments. This relative high-resource strategy in the context of low stress carries few costs with it, and thus as posited by the model, represents a good fit with low-stress contexts (see also Sheppes & Gross, 2012).

Turning to the bottom quadrants, these relatively reflexive strategies (rumination and affect-biased attention), while relatively high efficiency (low resource) may be less flexible because they are less amenable to conscious awareness and control. As discussed more later, however, even rumination and worry—typically considered to be forms of distorted cognition that are risk factors in depression, anxiety, and affective disorders—may be adaptive in the context of low and acute stress. In other words, in limited amounts, the relatively automatic use of worry and rumination may require few resources and carry relatively few costs. Indeed, the more flexible the use of these automatic thoughts, the less problematic they are from a psychopathological perspective. Finally, in the bottom right quadrant is affect-biased attention. As a rapid and reflexive evaluative process, such automatic reactions—such as a negativity bias in the context of a high-stress threat—can serve many adaptive functions in terms of triggering an effective fight/flight response, detecting and avoiding danger, and shaping other ER strategy use downstream. If you are caught in a dark alley, and there are shadowy figures lurking, you want an automatic and efficient threat bias to consistently be triggered in order to help you cope with the situation as rapidly and effectively as possible. In the context of an acute, highly stressful context, affect-biased attention may be the optimal, best-fit first responder.

Transformations Among Strategies

The center of the model specifies that long-term goals and learning impact the automaticity of a given ER strategy. That is, with learning and intentionality, strategies can become highly automatic or "default," which are efficient because they require low resource allocation. Strategies that start as relatively resource intensive, conscious, intentional, and effortful can, over time, with practice or development, become automatic and habitual. By the same token, with learning and cognitive development, it is also developmentally appropriate and adaptive for relatively reflexive forms of ER to become more effortful, focused on higher order or distal goals, amenable to regulatory control, and flexible (Todd & Galinsky, 2012). The transformation between default and intentional strategies can go both ways. In moments of stress and high emotional demands, even AER that began as relatively deliberate (reappraisal) can be become explicit or subject to intentionality because conscious monitoring or a change in strategy is required.

The individual differences and contextual factors that influence the transformations between default and intentional ER strategies are poorly understood. This is a topic ripe for empirical inquiry. For example, there may be distinct mechanisms available for flexibly transforming one type of strategy into another (e.g., from the relatively resource heavy to the relatively automatic). One possibility is that there are dual processes responsible, such as top-down, effortful, conscious attempts combined with more bottom-up, implicit learning. In addition, it is unknown whether transformations are context specific or general. Focusing solely on stress intensity here, we do not, in the model, describe how specific characteristics of a stressful context influence the fit between ER and stress. A large body of research on trauma, stress, and psychopathology suggests that these characteristics of trauma context (e.g., is a situation life-threatening, chronic, perpetrator vs. natural disaster, etc.) moderate the impact of stress (Shalev, 1996). In future iterations of the model, these factors will need to be considered. It will be important to draw on future empirical research to inform how context is modeled.

While controllability of ER is not a dimension in the model presented here, it is relevant to understanding the degree of resource allocation a given strategy may require. From a definitional perspective, relatively automatic strategies involve lower intentionality and therefore are less amenable to intentional control. Control in the realm of ER is typically considered desirable, but in terms of resource allocation, it is costly. However, relatively automatic aspects of ER, like affect-biased attention, may be amenable to control and change as in the case of attention and cognitive bias modification techniques (Hakamata et al., 2010; Salum et al., 2017). The relative merits of ER control and efficiency can only be evaluated in relation to context demands. For example, as detailed more later, if you are fleeing for your life, control is less important than rapid efficiency.

What Counts as a "Good Fit" of Emotion Regulation to Stress?

We argue that a more adaptive fit between ER processes and stress intensity reduces the negative impact of stress and promotes emotional well-being and resilience to adversity. Consistent with findings from Sheppes and colleagues (2011), in low-stress contexts, relatively deliberative strategies, despite being resource intensive, are ideal, as awareness, intentionality, and resources are abundant to assess and manage emotions. In contrast, in high-stress contexts, such as in fight/flight situations, more reflexive AER strategies are ideal, as they can be rapidly deployed and are more efficient, allowing for cognitive and physical resources to be used with optimal flexibility and agility. Furthermore, as stress demands fluctuate over time, the ability to flexibly shift from automatic to DER strategies is paramount.

When fit is poor, especially in the context of chronic stress, this can promote maladaptation over time. For example, rumination has been identified as a key cognitive mechanism in depression (Nolen-Hoeksema, 2012). As depicted in our model, rumination used in low-stress circumstances and more deliberatively (and thus in more controllable ways) is unlikely to promote depression. In our model, we propose that it is only its use in chronically stressful circumstances and in inflexible and rigid ways that increases depression risk. Few studies, however, have directly examined the context and flexibility of rumination, assuming that it is consistently maladaptive. Another interesting possibility is that poor fit between ER and stress may represent both pre-existing vulnerabilities for development of psychopathology, as well as emergent patterns in response to chronic stresses that, when engrained, contribute to psychopathology. Thus, the relationship between stress and ER is likely bidirectional, with ER processes acting both as a buffer against and a product of stress context.

Conclusion

In this chapter, we argue that the negative effects of stress on well-being and psychological functioning emerge when there is a poor fit between the intensity of stress demands and ER within the dimensions of automaticity, flexibility, and resource allocation. We present the Dynamic Fit Model of Stress and ER to take a first step toward specifying what constitutes poor and good fit, and to use this model to articulate an agenda for future research and hypothesis generation. Because the model is placed within a person-context interactional framework, it generates a host of questions about contextual factors and individual differences in what comprises a good fit between stress and ER. Individual differences relate to a broad range of person-factors, such as race/ethnicity, gender, age, temperament, personality, and biological mechanisms. We hope future research increasingly addresses contextual factors, such as whether stress is acute or chronic, and individual differences that impact the stress-ER link. We applaud research that examines these processes directly in naturalistic, dynamically changing and clinical contexts, including the development of prevention efforts that aim to optimize the stress-buffering effects of ER.

References

Adam, T. C., & Epel, E. S. (2007). Stress, eating and the reward system. *Physiology & Behavior, 91*(4), 449–458.

Aldao, A., & Nolen-Hoeksema, S. (2010). Specificity of cognitive emotion regulation strategies: A transdiagnostic examination. *Behaviour Research and Therapy, 48*(10), 974–983.

Aldao, A., Nolen-Hoeksema, S., & Schweizer, S. (2010). Emotion-regulation strategies across psychopathology: A meta-analytic review. *Clinical Psychology Review, 30*(2), 217–237.

Appelhans, B. M., & Luecken, L. J. (2006). Heart rate variability as an index of regulated emotional responding. *Review of General Psychology, 10*(3), 229.

Armstrong, T., & Olatunji, B. O. (2012). Eye tracking of attention in the affective disorders: A meta-analytic review and synthesis. *Clinical Psychology Review, 32*(8), 704–723.

Bar-Haim, Y., Lamy, D., Pergamin, L., Bakermans-Kranenburg, M. J., & Van Ijzendoorn, M. H. (2007). *Threat-related attentional bias in anxious and nonanxious individuals: A meta-analytic study. Psychological Bulletin, 133*(1), 1–24.

Barger, S. D., Bachen, E. A., Marsland, A. L., & Manuck, S. B. (2000). Repressive coping and blood measures of disease risk: Lipids and endocrine and immunological responses to a laboratory stressor. *Journal of Applied Social Psychology, 30*(8), 1619–1638.

Bargh, J. A. (1989). Conditional automaticity: Varieties of automatic influence in social perception and cognition. *Unintended Thought, 3*, 51–69.

Bargh, J. A. (1996). Automaticity in social psychology. In E.T. Higgins & A.W. Kruglanski (Eds.), *Social psychology: Handbook of basic principles* (pp. 169–183). New York, NY, US: Guilford Press.

Bargh, J. A., & Ferguson, M. J. (2000). Beyond behaviorism: On the automaticity of higher mental processes. *Psychological Bulletin, 126*(6), 925.

Bargh, J. A., & Gollwitzer, P. M. (1994). Environmental control of goal-directed action: Automatic and strategic contingencies between situations and behavior. In W.D. Spaulding (Ed.), *Nebraska symposium on motivation, Vol. 41. Integrative views of motivation, cognitive, and emotion* (pp. 71–124). Lincoln, NE, US: University of Nebraska Press.

Bargh, J. A., Gollwitzer, P. M., Lee-Chai, A., Barndollar, K., & Trötschel, R. (2001). The automated will: Nonconscious activation and pursuit of behavioral goals. *Journal of Personality and Social Psychology, 81*(6), 1014.

Barrett, L. F., & Bliss-Moreau, E. (2009). She's emotional. He's having a bad day: Attributional explanations for emotion stereotypes. *Emotion, 9*(5), 649.

Barrett, L. F., Lane, R. D., Sechrest, L., & Schwartz, G. E. (2000). Sex differences in emotional awareness. *Personality and Social Psychology Bulletin, 26*(9), 1027–1035.

Beck, A. T. (1979). *Cognitive therapy and the emotional disorders.* New York, NY: Penguin.

Beer, J. S., Heerey, E. A., Keltner, D., Scabini, D., & Knight, R. T. (2003). The regulatory function of self-conscious emotion: Insights from patients with orbitofrontal damage. *Journal of Personality and Social Psychology, 85*(4), 594.

Benight, C. C., & Cieslak, R. (2011). Cognitive factors and resilience: How self-efficacy contributes to coping with adversities. In Steven M. Southwick, Brett T. Litz, Dennis Charney, & Matthew J. Friedman (Eds.), *Resilience and mental health: Challenges across the lifespan* (pp. 45–55). Cambridge, UK: Cambridge University Press.

Berkman, E. T., & Lieberman, M. D. (2009). Using neuroscience to broaden emotion regulation: Theoretical and methodological considerations. *Social and Personality Psychology Compass, 3*(4), 475–493.

Boekaerts, M. (1996). Coping with stress in childhood and adolescence. In M. Zeidner & N.S. Endler (Eds.), *Handbook of coping: Theory, research, applications* (pp. 452–484). Oxford, England: John Wiley & Sons.

Bonanno, G. A. (2005). Resilience in the face of potential trauma. *Current Directions in Psychological Science, 14*(3), 135–138.

Bonanno, G. A., & Burton, C. L. (2013). Regulatory flexibility: An individual differences perspective on coping and emotion regulation. *Perspectives on Psychological Science, 8*(6), 591–612.

Bonanno, G. A., & Kaltman, S. (1999). Toward an integrative perspective on bereavement. *Psychological Bulletin, 125*(6), 760.

Bonanno, G. A., Keltner, D., Holen, A., & Horowitz, M. J. (1995). When avoiding unpleasant emotions might not be such a bad thing: Verbal-autonomic response dissociation and midlife conjugal bereavement. *Journal of Personality and Social Psychology, 69*(5), 975.

Bonanno, G. A., Papa, A., Lalande, K., Westphal, M., & Coifman, K. (2004). The importance of being flexible: The ability to both enhance and suppress emotional expression predicts long-term adjustment. *Psychological Science, 15*(7), 482–487.

Bonanno, G. A., Znoj, H., Siddique, H. I., & Horowitz, M. J. (1999). Verbal-autonomic dissociation and adaptation to midlife conjugal loss: A follow-up at 25 months. *Cognitive Therapy and Research, 23*(6), 605–624.

Bottorff, J. L., Oliffe, J. L., & Kelly, M. (2012). The gender (s) in the room. Thousand Oaks, CA: Sage.

Buhle, J. T., Silvers, J. A., Wager, T. D., Lopez, R., Onyemekwu, C., Kober, H.,…Ochsner, K. N. (2014). Cognitive reappraisal of emotion: A meta-analysis of human neuroimaging studies. *Cerebral Cortex, 24*(11), 2981–2990.

Butler, E. A., Egloff, B., Wlhelm, F. H., Smith, N. C., Erickson, E. A., & Gross, J. J. (2003). The social consequences of expressive suppression. *Emotion, 3*(1), 48.

Butler, L. D., & Nolen-Hoeksema, S. (1994). Gender differences in responses to depressed mood in a college sample. *Sex Roles, 30*(5), 331–346.

Bylsma, L. M., Morris, B. H., & Rottenberg, J. (2008). A meta-analysis of emotional reactivity in major depressive disorder. *Clinical Psychology Review, 28*(4), 676–691.

Campos, J. J., Campos, R. G., & Barrett, K. C. (1989). Emergent themes in the study of emotional development and emotion regulation. *Developmental Psychology, 25*(3), 394–402.

Carthy, T., Horesh, N., Apter, A., Edge, M. D., & Gross, J. J. (2010). Emotional reactivity and cognitive regulation in anxious children. *Behaviour Research and Therapy, Â 48*(5), 384–393.

Chaiken, S., & Trope, Y. (1999). *Dual-process theories in social psychology.* New York, NY: Guilford Press.

Cheng, C. (2001). Assessing coping flexibility in real-life and laboratory settings: A multimethod approach. *Journal of Personality and Social Psychology, 80*(5), 814.

Cheng, C. (2003). Discriminative facility: Cognitive mechanisms of coping. In R. Roth, L.F. Lowenstein, & D.R. Trent (Eds.), *Catching the future: Women and men in global psychology* (pp. 81–89). Lengerich, Germany: Pabst Science Publishers.

Chiu, C.-Y., Hong, Y.-Y., Mischel, W., & Shoda, Y. (1995). Discriminative facility in social competence: Conditional versus dispositional encoding and monitoring-blunting of information. *Social Cognition, 13*(1), 49–70.

Ciarrochi, J., Hynes, K., & Crittenden, N. (2005). Can men do better if they try harder: Sex and motivational effects on emotional awareness. *Cognition & Emotion, 19*(1), 133–141.

Cisler, J. M., & Koster, E. H. (2010). Mechanisms of attentional biases towards threat in anxiety disorders: An integrative review. *Clinical Psychology Review, 30*(2), 203–216.

Cloitre, M., Miranda, R., Stovall-McClough, K. C., & Han, H. (2005). Beyond PTSD: Emotion regulation and interpersonal problems as predictors of functional impairment in survivors of childhood abuse. *Behavior Therapy, 36*(2), 119–124.

Cohen, S., & Wills, T. A. (1985). Stress, social support, and the buffering hypothesis. *Psychological Bulletin, 98*(2), 310.

Coifman, K. G., Bonanno, G. A., Ray, R. D., & Gross, J. J. (2007). Does repressive coping promote resilience? Affective-autonomic response discrepancy during bereavement. *Journal of Personality and Social Psychology, 92*(4), 745.

Cole, P. M., Martin, S. E., & Dennis, T. A. (2004). Emotion regulation as a scientific construct: Methodological challenges and directions for child development research. *Child Development, 75*(2), 317–333.

Compas, B. E., Connor-Smith, J. K., Saltzman, H., Thomsen, A. H., & Wadsworth, M. E. (2001). Coping with stress during childhood and adolescence: Problems, progress, and potential in theory and research. *Psychological Bulletin, 127*(1), 87.

Cooper, M. L., Frone, M. R., Russell, M., & Mudar, P. (1995). Drinking to regulate positive and negative emotions: A motivational model of alcohol use. *Journal of Personality and Social Psychology*, *69*(5), 990.

Cooper, M. L., Russell, M., Skinner, J. B., Frone, M. R., & Mudar, P. (1992). Stress and alcohol use: Moderating effects of gender, coping, and alcohol expectancies. *Journal of Abnormal Psychology*, *101*(1), 139.

Creswell, J. D., & Lindsay, E. K. (2014). How does mindfulness training affect health? A mindfulness stress buffering account. *Current Directions in Psychological Science*, *23*(6), 401–407.

Creswell, J. D., Welch, W. T., Taylor, S. E., Sherman, D. K., Gruenewald, T. L., & Mann, T. (2005). Affirmation of personal values buffers neuroendocrine and psychological stress responses. *Psychological Science*, *16*(11), 846–851.

Cummings, E. M., Davies, P. T., & Simpson, K. S. (1994). Marital conflict, gender, and children's appraisals and coping efficacy as mediators of child adjustment. *Journal of Family Psychology*, *8*(2), 141.

Custers, R., & Aarts, H. (2005). Positive affect as implicit motivator: On the nonconscious operation of behavioral goals. *Journal of Personality and Social Psychology*, *89*(2), 129.

Cutrona, C. E. (1990). Stress and social support—In search of optimal matching. *Journal of Social and Clinical Psychology*, *9*(1), 3–14.

Davies, P. T., Forman, E. M., Rasi, J. A., & Stevens, K. I. (2002). Assessing children's emotional security in the interparental relationship: The security in the interparental subsystem scales. *Child Development*, *73*(2), 544–562.

Dennis-Tiwary, T. A., Denefrio, S., & Gelber, S. (2017). Salutary effects of an attention bias modification mobile application on biobehavioral measures of stress and anxiety during pregnancy. *Biological Psychology*, *127*, 148–156.

Dennis-Tiwary, T. A., Egan, L. J., Babkirk, S., & Denefrio, S. (2016). For whom the bell tolls: Neurocognitive individual differences in the acute stress-reduction effects of an attention bias modification game for anxiety. *Behaviour Research and Therapy*, *77*, 105–117.

Devine, P. G. (1989). Stereotypes and prejudice: Their automatic and controlled components. *Journal of Personality and Social Psychology*, *56*(1), 5.

Dewe, P., Cox, T., & Ferguson, E. (1993). Individual strategies for coping with stress at work: A review. *Work & Stress*, *7*(1), 5–15.

Dohrenwend, B. P. (2000). The role of adversity and stress in psychopathology: Some evidence and its implications for theory and research. *Journal of Health and Social Behavior*, *41*(1), 1–19.

Eder, A. B. (2011). Control of impulsive emotional behaviour through implementation intentions. *Cognition and Emotion*, *25*(3), 478–489.

Eder, A. B., Rothermund, K., & Proctor, R. W. (2010). The prepared emotional reflex: Intentional preparation of automatic approach and avoidance tendencies as a means to regulate emotional responding. *Emotion*, *10*(4), 593.

Egan, L. J., & Dennis-Tiwary, T. A. (2018). Dynamic measures of anxiety-related threat bias: Links to stress reactivity. *Motivation and Emotion*, 1–9.

Egloff, B., Schmukle, S. C., Burns, L. R., & Schwerdtfeger, A. (2006). Spontaneous emotion regulation during evaluated speaking tasks: Associations with negative affect, anxiety expression, memory, and physiological responding. *Emotion*, *6*(3), 356–366.

Ehring, T., Tuschen-Caffier, B., Schnülle, J., Fischer, S., & Gross, J. J. (2010). Emotion regulation and vulnerability to depression: Spontaneous versus instructed use of emotion suppression and reappraisal. *Emotion*, *10*(4), 563.

Etkin, A., Egner, T., & Kalisch, R. (2011). Emotional processing in anterior cingulate and medial prefrontal cortex. *Trends in Cognitive Sciences*, *15*(2), 85–93.

Etkin, A., Egner, T., Peraza, D. M., Kandel, E. R., & Hirsch, J. (2006). Resolving emotional conflict: A role for the rostral anterior cingulate cortex in modulating activity in the amygdala. *Neuron*, *51*(6), 871–882.

Evans, G. W., & Kim, P. (2013). Childhood poverty, chronic stress, self-regulation, and coping. *Child Development Perspectives*, *7*(1), 43–48.

Fabes, R. A., & Eisenberg, N. (1997). Regulatory control and adults' stress-related responses to daily life events. *Journal of Personality and Social Psychology*, *73*, 1107–1117.

Fabes, R. A., Eisenberg, N., & Eisenbud, L. (1993). Behavioral and physiological correlates of children's reactions to others in distress. *Developmental Psychology*, *29*(4), 655.

Fava, G. A., & Tomba, E. (2009). Increasing psychological well-being and resilience by psychotherapeutic methods. *Journal of Personality*, *77*(6), 1903–1934.

Fischer, A. H., & Manstead, A. S. (2000). The relation between gender and emotions in different cultures. *Gender and Emotion: Social Psychological Perspectives*, *1*, 71–94.

Folkman, S. (2013). Stress: Appraisal and coping. In *Encyclopedia of behavioral medicine* (pp. 1913–1915). New York, NY: Springer.

Füstös, J., Gramann, K., Herbert, B. M., & Pollatos, O. (2012). On the embodiment of emotion regulation: Interoceptive awareness facilitates reappraisal. *Social Cognitive and Affective Neuroscience*, *8*(8), 911–917.

Galatzer-Levy, I. R., Burton, C. L., & Bonanno, G. A. (2012). Coping flexibility, potentially traumatic life events, and resilience: A prospective study of college student adjustment. *Journal of Social and Clinical Psychology*, *31*(6), 542–567.

Gall, T. L., Evans, D. R., & Bellerose, S. (2000). Transition to first-year university: Patterns of change in adjustment across life domains and time. *Journal of Social and Clinical Psychology*, *19*(4), 544–567.

Gall, T. L., Guirguis-Younger, M., Charbonneau, C., & Florack, P. (2009). The trajectory of religious coping across time in response to the diagnosis of breast cancer. *Psycho-Oncology*, *18*(11), 1165–1178.

Gallo, I. S., Keil, A., McCulloch, K. C., Rockstroh, B., & Gollwitzer, P. M. (2009). Strategic automation of emotion regulation. *Journal of Personality and Social Psychology*, *96*(1), 11.

Garland, E. L., Gaylord, S. A., & Fredrickson, B. L. (2011). Positive reappraisal mediates the stress-reductive effects of mindfulness: An upward spiral process. *Mindfulness*, *2*(1), 59–67.

Garnefski, N., Kraaij, V., & Spinhoven, P. (2001). Negative life events, cognitive emotion regulation and emotional problems. *Personality and Individual Differences*, *30*(8), 1311–1327.

Garnefski, N., Teerds, J., Kraaij, V., Legerstee, J., & van den Kommer, T. (2004). Cognitive emotion regulation strategies and depressive symptoms: Differences between males and females. *Personality and Individual Differences*, *36*(2), 267–276.

Gohm, C. L. (2003). Mood regulation and emotional intelligence: Individual differences. *Journal of Personality and Social Psychology*, *84*(3), 594.

Goldin, P. R., Manber, T., Hakimi, S., Canli, T., & Gross, J. J. (2009). Neural bases of social anxiety disorder: Emotional reactivity and cognitive regulation during social and physical threat. *Archives of General Psychiatry, 66*(2), 170–180.

Goldin, P. R., McRae, K., Ramel, W., & Gross, J. J. (2008). The neural bases of emotion regulation: Reappraisal and suppression of negative emotion. *Biological Psychiatry, 63*(6), 577–586.

Gross, J. J. (1998a). Antecedent-and response-focused emotion regulation: Divergent consequences for experience, expression, and physiology. *Journal of Personality and Social Psychology, 74*(1), 224.

Gross, J. J. (1998b). The emerging field of emotion regulation: An integrative review. *Review of General Psychology, 2*(3), 271.

Gross, J. J. (1999). Emotion regulation: Past, present, future. *Cognition & Emotion, 13*(5), 551–573.

Gross, J. J. (2002). Emotion regulation: Affective, cognitive, and social consequences. *Psychophysiology, 39*(3), 281–291.

Gross, J. J. (2015). Emotion regulation: Current status and future prospects. *Psychological Inquiry, 26*(1), 1–26.

Gross, J. J., & Feldman Barrett, L. (2011). Emotion generation and emotion regulation: One or two depends on your point of view. *Emotion Review, 3*(1), 8–16.

Gross, J. J., & Thompson, R. A. (2006). Emotion regulation: Conceptual foundations. In J.J. Gross (Ed.), *Handbook of emotion regulation* (pp. 3–26). New York, NY: The Guilford Press.

Gupta, S., & Bonanno, G. A. (2011). Complicated grief and deficits in emotional expressive flexibility. *Journal of Abnormal Psychology, 120*(3), 635.

Gyurak, A., Gross, J. J., & Etkin, A. (2011). Explicit and implicit emotion regulation: A dual-process framework. *Cognition and Emotion, 25*(3), 400–412.

Hare, T. A., Tottenham, N., Galvan, A., Voss, H. U., Glover, G. H., & Casey, B. J. (2008). Biological substrates of emotional reactivity and regulation in adolescence during an emotional go-nogo task. *Biological Psychiatry, 63*(10), 927–934.

Hakamata, Y., Lissek, S., Bar-Haim, Y., Britton, J. C., Fox, N. A., Leibenluft, E.,...Pine, D. S. (2010). Attention bias modification treatment: A meta-analysis toward the establishment of novel treatment for anxiety. *Biological Psychiatry, 68*(11), 982–990.

Heatherton, T. F., & Baumeister, R. F. (1991). Binge eating as escape from self-awareness. *Psychological Bulletin, 110*(1), 86.

Heeren, A., Mogoaşe, C., Philippot, P., & McNally, R. J. (2015). Attention bias modification for social anxiety: A systematic review and meta-analysis. *Clinical Psychology Review, 40*, 76–90.

Heim, C., & Nemeroff, C. B. (2001). The role of childhood trauma in the neurobiology of mood and anxiety disorders: Preclinical and clinical studies. *Biological Psychiatry, 49*(12), 1023–1039.

Hilt, L., & Nolen-Hoeksema, S. (2009). The emergence of gender differences in depression in adolescence. In S. Nolen-Hoeksema & L. M. Hilt (Eds.), *Handbook of Depression in Adolescents*, (pp. 111–135). New York, NY: Routledge.

Hyde, J. S., Mezulis, A. H., & Abramson, L. Y. (2008). The ABCs of depression: Integrating affective, biological, and cognitive models to explain the emergence of the gender difference in depression. *Psychological Review, 115*(2), 291.

Jackson, D. C., Mueller, C. J., Dolski, I., Dalton, K. M., Nitschke, J. B., Urry, H. L.,...Davidson, R. J. (2003). Now you feel it, now you don't: Frontal brain electrical asymmetry and individual differences in emotion regulation. *Psychological Science, 14*(6), 612–617.

Jamner, L., Schwartz, G., & Leigh, H. (1988). Repressive coping predicts monocyte, eosinophile and serum glucose levels: Support for the opioid-peptide hypothesis. *Psychosomatic Medicine, 50*, 567–577.

Johnson, J. L., & Repta, R. (2012). Sex and gender: Beyond binaries. In Oliffe, J.L., Greaves, L. (Eds.), *Designing and conducting gender, sex, and health research* (pp. 17–37). Thousand Oaks, CA: Sage.

Joseph, D. L., & Newman, D. A. (2010). *Emotional intelligence: An integrative meta-analysis and cascading model*, Washington, DC: American Psychological Association.

Kashdan, T. B., Barrios, V., Forsyth, J. P., & Steger, M. F. (2006). Experiential avoidance as a generalized psychological vulnerability: Comparisons with coping and emotion regulation strategies. *Behaviour Research and Therapy, 44*(9), 1301–1320.

Kashdan, T. B., & Rottenberg, J. (2010). Psychological flexibility as a fundamental aspect of health. *Clinical Psychology Review, 30*(7), 865–878.

Keltner, D., Ellsworth, P. C., & Edwards, K. (1993). Beyond simple pessimism: Effects of sadness and anger on social perception. *Journal of Personality and Social Psychology, 64*(5), 740.

Kessler, R. C., Amminger, G. P., Aguilar-Gaxiola, S., Alonso, J., Lee, S., & Ustun, T. B. (2007). Age of onset of mental disorders: A review of recent literature. *Current Opinion in Psychiatry, 20*(4), 359.

Keyes, K. M., Grant, B. F., & Hasin, D. S. (2008). Evidence for a closing gender gap in alcohol use, abuse, and dependence in the United States population. *Drug and Alcohol Dependence, 93*(1), 21–29.

Khantzian, E. (1985). Psychotherapeutic interventions with substance abusers—The clinical context. *Journal of Substance Abuse Treatment, 2*(2), 83–88.

Kim, P., Evans, G. W., Angstadt, M., Ho, S. S., Sripada, C. S., Swain, J. E.,...Phan, K. L. (2013). Effects of childhood poverty and chronic stress on emotion regulatory brain function in adulthood. *Proceedings of the National Academy of Sciences, 110*(46), 18442–18447.

Koole, S. L., & Coenen, L. H. (2007). Implicit self and affect regulation: Effects of action orientation and subliminal self priming in an affective priming task. *Self and Identity, 6*(2–3), 118–136.

Kramer, M. D., Krueger, R. F., & Hicks, B. M. (2008). The role of internalizing and externalizing liability factors in accounting for gender differences in the prevalence of common psychopathological syndromes. *Psychological Medicine, 38*(1), 51–61.

Kring, A. M., & Werner, K. H. (2004). Emotion regulation and psychopathology. In P. Philippot & R. S. Feldman (Eds.), *The Regulation of Emotion* (pp. 359–385). Mahwah, NJ: Lawrence Erlbaum Associates, Inc.

Kumar, N., Gross, J. B., & Ahlskog, J. E. (2004). Copper deficiency myelopathy produces a clinical picture like subacute combined degeneration. *Neurology, 63*(1), 33–39.

Lam, C. B., & McBride-Chang, C. A. (2007). Resilience in young adulthood: The moderating influences of gender-related personality traits and coping flexibility. *Sex Roles, 56*(3–4), 159–172.

Lazarus, R. S. (1966). *Psychological stress and the coping process*. New York: McGraw-Hill.

Lazarus, R. S., & Folkman, S. (1984). Coping and adaptation. In W. D. Gentry (Ed.), *The handbook of behavioral medicine* (pp. 282–325). New York: Guilford.

Lazarus, R. S., & Lazarus, B. N. (1996). *Passion and reason: Making sense of our emotions*: New York, NY: Oxford University Press.

Lerner, M. J. (1997). What does the belief in a just world protect us from: The dread of death or the fear of understanding suffering? *Psychological Inquiry, 8*(1), 29–32.

Leadbeater, B. J., Kuperminc, G. P., Blatt, S. J., & Hertzog, C. (1999). A multivariate model of gender differences in adolescents' internalizing and externalizing problems. *Developmental Psychology, 35*(5), 1268–1282.

Lougheed, J. P., & Hollenstein, T. (2012). A limited repertoire of emotion regulation strategies is associated with internalizing problems in adolescence. *Social Development, 21*(4), 704–721.

Luce, K. H., Engler, P. A., & Crowther, J. H. (2007). Eating disorders and alcohol use: Group differences in consumption rates and drinking motives. *Eating Behaviors, 8*(2), 177–184.

Mansell, W., Clark, D. M., Ehlers, A., & Chen, Y.-P. (1999). Social anxiety and attention away from emotional faces. *Cognition & Emotion, 13*(6), 673–690.

Mathews, A., & MacLeod, C. (2005). Cognitive vulnerability to emotional disorders. *Annual Review of Clinical Psychology, 1*, 167–195.

Mauss, I. B., Bunge, S. A., & Gross, J. J. (2007). Automatic emotion regulation. *Social and Personality Psychology Compass, 1*(1), 146–167.

Mauss, I. B., Cook, C. L., Cheng, J. Y., & Gross, J. J. (2007). Individual differences in cognitive reappraisal: Experiential and physiological responses to an anger provocation. *International Journal of Psychophysiology, 66*(2), 116–124.

Mauss, I. B., Evers, C., Wilhelm, F. H., & Gross, J. J. (2006). How to bite your tongue without blowing your top: Implicit evaluation of emotion regulation predicts affective responding to anger provocation. *Personality and Social Psychology Bulletin, 32*(5), 589–602.

McEwen, B. S. (2000). Allostasis and allostatic load: Implications for neuropsychopharmacology. *Neuropsychopharmacology, 22*(2), 108–124.

McEwen, B. S., & Seeman, T. (1999). Protective and damaging effects of mediators of stress: Elaborating and testing the concepts of allostasis and allostatic load. *Annals of the New York Academy of Sciences, 896*(1), 30–47.

McEwen, B. S., & Stellar, E. (1993). Stress and the individual: Mechanisms leading to disease. *Archives of Internal Medicine, 153*(18), 2093–2101.

McEwen, B. S., & Wingfield, J. C. (2003). The concept of allostasis in biology and biomedicine. *Hormones and Behavior, 43*(1), 2–15.

McLean, C. P., & Anderson, E. R. (2009). Brave men and timid women? A review of the gender differences in fear and anxiety. *Clinical Psychology Review, 29*(6), 496–505.

McLean, L. M., & Gallop, R. (2003). Implications of childhood sexual abuse for adult borderline personality disorder and complex posttraumatic stress disorder. *American Journal of Psychiatry, 160*(2), 369–371. doi:10.1176/appi.ajp.160.2.369

McNally, R. J. (1995). Automaticity and the anxiety disorders. *Behaviour Research and Therapy, 33*(7), 747–754.

McRae, K., Ochsner, K. N., Mauss, I. B., Gabrieli, J. J., & Gross, J. J. (2008). Gender differences in emotion regulation: An fMRI study of cognitive reappraisal. *Group Processes & Intergroup Relations, 11*(2), 143–162.

Mendl, M. (1999). Performing under pressure: Stress and cognitive function. *Applied Animal Behaviour Science, 65*(3), 221–244.

Mikulincer, M., Birnbaum, G., Woddis, D., & Nachmias, O. (2000). Stress and accessibility of proximity-related thoughts: Exploring the normative and intraindividual components of attachment theory. *Journal of Personality and Social Psychology, 78*(3), 509.

Mogg, K., Mathews, A., & Eysenck, M. (1992). Attentional bias to threat in clinical anxiety states. *Cognition & Emotion, 6*(2), 149–159.

Moore, S. A., Zoellner, L. A., & Mollenholt, N. (2008). Are expressive suppression and cognitive reappraisal associated with stress-related symptoms? *Behaviour Research and Therapy, 46*(9), 993–1000.

Myruski, S., Bonanno, G. A., Gulyayeva, O., Egan, L. J., & Dennis-Tiwary, T. A. (2017). Neurocognitive assessment of emotional context sensitivity. *Cognitive, Affective, & Behavioral Neuroscience, 17*(5), 1058–1071.

Nolen-Hoeksema, S. (2012). Emotion regulation and psychopathology: The role of gender. *Annual Review of Clinical Psychology, 8*, 161–187.

Nolen-Hoeksema, S., & Aldao, A. (2011). Gender and age differences in emotion regulation strategies and their relationship to depressive symptoms. *Personality and Individual Differences, 51*(6), 704–708.

Nolen-Hoeksema, S., & Harrell, Z. A. (2002). Rumination, depression, and alcohol use: Tests of gender differences. *Journal of Cognitive Psychotherapy, 16*(4), 391–403.

Ochsner, K. N., & Gross, J. J. (2008). Cognitive emotion regulation: Insights from social cognitive and affective neuroscience. *Current Directions in Psychological Science, 17*(2), 153–158.

Orcutt, H. K., Bonanno, G. A., Hannan, S. M., & Miron, L. R. (2014). Prospective trajectories of posttraumatic stress in college women following a campus mass shooting. *Journal of Traumatic Stress, 27*(3), 249–256.

Ozer, E. J., Best, S. R., Lipsey, T. L., & Weiss, D. S. (2003). Predictors of posttraumatic stress disorder and symptoms in adults: A meta-analysis. *Psychological Bulletin, 129*(1), 52.

Parks-Stamm, E. J., Oettingen, G., & Gollwitzer, P. M. (2010). Making sense of one's actions in an explanatory vacuum: The interpretation of nonconscious goal striving. *Journal of Experimental Social Psychology, 46*(3), 531–542.

Pawlow, L. A., & Jones, G. E. (2002). The impact of abbreviated progressive muscle relaxation on salivary cortisol. *Biological Psychology, 60*(1), 1–16.

Porges, S. W. (1995). Cardiac vagal tone: A physiological index of stress. *Neuroscience & Biobehavioral Reviews, 19*(2), 225–233.

Porges, S. W. (2007). The polyvagal perspective. *Biological Psychology, 74*(2), 116–143.

Pynoos, R. S., Steinberg, A. M., & Piacentini, J. C. (1999). A developmental psychopathology model of childhood traumatic stress and intersection with anxiety disorders. *Biological Psychiatry, 46*(11), 1542–1554.

Rausch, S. M., Gramling, S. E., & Auerbach, S. M. (2006). Effects of a single session of large-group meditation and progressive muscle relaxation training on stress reduction, reactivity, and recovery. *International Journal of Stress Management, 13*(3), 273.

Salum, G. A., Mogg, K., Bradley, B. P., Stringaris, A., Gadelha, A., Pan, P. M., . . . Pine, D. S. (2017). Association between irritability and bias in attention orienting to threat in children and adolescents. *Journal of Child Psychology and Psychiatry, 58*(5), 595–602.

Sarason, B. R., Sarason, I. G., & Pierce, G. R. (1990). *Social support: An interactional view.* Hoboken, NJ: John Wiley & Sons.

Sayette, M. A. (1993). An appraisal-disruption model of alcohol's effects on stress responses in social drinkers. *Psychological Bulletin, 114*(3), 459.

Schwartz, G. E., & Kline, J. P. (1995). Repression, emotional disclosure, and health: Theoretical, empirical, and clinical considerations. In J. W. Pennebaker (Ed.), *Emotion, disclosure, & health* (pp. 177–193). Washington, DC, US: American Psychological Association.

Shalev, A. Y. (1996). Stress versus traumatic stress: From acute homeostatic reactions to chronic psychopathology. In B. A. van der Kolk, A. C. McFarlane, & L. Weisaeth (Eds.), *Traumatic stress: The effects of overwhelming experience on mind, body, and society* (pp. 77–101). New York, NY, US: Guilford Press.

Sheppes, G., Catran, E., & Meiran, N. (2009). Reappraisal (but not distraction) is going to make you sweat: Physiological evidence for self-control effort. *International Journal of Psychophysiology, 71*(2), 91–96.

Sheppes, G., & Gross, J. J. (2012). Emotion regulation effectiveness: What works when. *Handbook of Psychology*, 391–406.

Sheppes, G., & Meiran, N. (2007). Better late than never? On the dynamics of online regulation of sadness using distraction and cognitive reappraisal. *Personality and Social Psychology Bulletin, 33*(11), 1518–1532.

Sheppes, G., & Meiran, N. (2008). Divergent cognitive costs for online forms of reappraisal and distraction. *Emotion, 8*(6), 870.

Sheppes, G., Scheibe, S., Suri, G., & Gross, J. J. (2011). Emotion-regulation choice. *Psychological Science, 22*(11), 1391–1396.

Sheppes, G., Scheibe, S., Suri, G., Radu, P., Blechert, J., & Gross, J. J. (2014). Emotion regulation choice: A conceptual framework and supporting evidence. *Journal of Experimental Psychology: General, 143*(1), 163.

Sher, K. J., & Grekin, E. R. (2007). Alcohol and affect regulation. In J. J. Gross (Ed.), *Handbook of emotion regulation* (pp. 560–580). New York, NY, US: Guilford Press.

Silk, J. S., Steinberg, L., & Morris, A. S. (2003). Adolescents' emotion regulation in daily life: Links to depressive symptoms and problem behavior. *Child Development, 74*(6), 1869–1880.

Sloman, S. A. (1996). The empirical case for two systems of reasoning. *Psychological Bulletin, 119*(1), 3.

Southwick, S. M., Bonanno, G. A., Masten, A. S., Panter-Brick, C., & Yehuda, R. (2014). Resilience definitions, theory, and challenges: Interdisciplinary perspectives. *European Journal of Psychotraumatology, 5*(1), 25338.

Southwick, S. M., & Charney, D. S. (2012). The science of resilience: Implications for the prevention and treatment of depression. *Science, 338*(6103), 79–82.

Sprague, J., Verona, E., Kalkhoff, W., & Kilmer, A. (2011). Moderators and mediators of the stress-aggression relationship: Executive function and state anger. *Emotion, 11*(1), 61.

Sterling, P., & Eyer, J. (1988). Allostasis: A new paradigm to explain arousal pathology. In K. Fisher and J. Reason (Eds.), *Handbook of life stress, cognition and health* (pp. 629–649). New York, NY: Wiley.

Stiglmayr, C., Ebner-Priemer, U., Bretz, J., Behm, R., Mohse, M., Lammers, C. H.,…Kleindienst, N. (2008). Dissociative symptoms are positively related to stress in borderline personality disorder. *Acta Psychiatrica Scandinavica, 117*(2), 139–147.

Strack, F., & Deutsch, R. (2004). Reflective and impulsive determinants of social behavior. *Personality and Social Psychology Review, 8*(3), 220–247.

Stroebe, M., & Schut, H. (2010). The dual process model of coping with bereavement: A decade on. *OMEGA-Journal of Death and Dying, 61*(4), 273–289.

Tamres, L. K., Janicki, D., & Helgeson, V. S. (2002). Sex differences in coping behavior: A meta-analytic review and an examination of relative coping. *Personality and Social Psychology Review, 6*(1), 2–30.

Thompson, R. A. (1994). Emotion regulation: A theme in search of definition. *Monographs of the Society for Research in Child Development, 59*(2–3), 25–52.

Thompson, R. A., & Calkins, S. D. (1996). The double-edged sword: Emotional regulation for children at risk. *Development and Psychopathology, 8*(1), 163–182.

Thompson, R. A., Lewis, M. D., & Calkins, S. D. (2008). Reassessing emotion regulation. *Child Development Perspectives, 2*(3), 124–131.

Todd, A. R., & Galinsky, A. D. (2012). The reciprocal link between multiculturalism and perspective-taking: How ideological and self-regulatory approaches to managing diversity reinforce each other. *Journal of Experimental Social Psychology, 48*(6), 1394–1398.

Tomarkenand, A. J., & Keener, A. D. (1998). Frontal brain asymmetry and depression: A self-regulatory perspective. *Cognition & Emotion, 12*(3), 387–420.

Troy, A. S., & Mauss, I. B. (2011). Resilience in the face of stress: Emotion regulation as a protective factor. *Resilience and Mental Health: Challenges Across the Lifespan, 1*(2), 30–44.

Wager, T. D., Davidson, M. L., Hughes, B. L., Lindquist, M. A., & Ochsner, K. N. (2008). Prefrontal-subcortical pathways mediating successful emotion regulation. *Neuron, 59*(6), 1037–1050.

Webb, T. L., Miles, E., & Sheeran, P. (2012). Dealing with feeling: a meta-analysis of the effectiveness of strategies derived from the process model of emotion regulation. *Psychological Bulletin, 138*(4), 775–808.

Webb, T. L., Ononaiye, M. S., Sheeran, P., Reidy, J. G., & Lavda, A. (2010). Using implementation intentions to overcome the effects of social anxiety on attention and appraisals of performance. *Personality and Social Psychology Bulletin, 36*(5), 612–627.

Webb, T. L., & Sheeran, P. (2003). Can implementation intentions help to overcome ego-depletion? *Journal of Experimental Social Psychology, 39*(3), 279–286.

Weinberger, D. A. (1998). Defenses, personality structure, and development: Integrating psychodynamic theory into a typological approach to personality. *Journal of Personality, 66*(6), 1061–1080.

Williams, L. E., Bargh, J. A., Nocera, C. C., & Gray, J. R. (2009). The unconscious regulation of emotion: Nonconscious reappraisal goals modulate emotional reactivity. *Emotion, 9*(6), 847.

Worthington, E. L., & Scherer, M. (2004). Forgiveness is an emotion-focused coping strategy that can reduce health risks and promote health resilience: Theory, review, and hypotheses. *Psychology & Health, 19*(3), 385–405.

Wurtman, R. J. (2005). Genes, stress, and depression. *Metabolism*, *54*(5), 16–19.

Yuan, J., Ding, N., Liu, Y., & Yang, J. (2015). Unconscious emotion regulation: Nonconscious reappraisal decreases emotion-related physiological reactivity during frustration. *Cognition and Emotion*, *29*(6), 1042–1053.

Zahn-Waxler, C., Shirtcliff, E. A., & Marceau, K. (2008). Disorders of childhood and adolescence: Gender and psychopathology. *Annual Review of Clinical Psychology*, *4*, 275–303.

Zaki, J., & Williams, W. C. (2013). Interpersonal emotion regulation. *Emotion*, *13*(5), 803.

Zlomke, K. R., & Hahn, K. S. (2010). Cognitive emotion regulation strategies: Gender differences and associations to worry. *Personality and Individual Differences*, *48*(4), 408–413.

Zvielli, A., Bernstein, A., & Koster, E. H. (2015). Temporal dynamics of attentional bias. *Clinical Psychological Science*, *3*(5), 772–788.

Stress and the Brain

Structural and Functional Neuroimaging

David Pagliaccio *and* Deanna M. Barch

Abstract

This chapter reviews associations between early life stress and brain structure and function as assessed by structural and functional magnetic resonance imaging. Particularly, this chapter focuses on structural associations in children and adults and the regional overlap with neural alterations observed in major depressive disorder, though we also more briefly cover diffusion imaging, task-based imaging, and resting-state functional connectivity. Major depressive disorder is highlighted given that early life stress is a critical risk factor for depression and the neural alterations observed with stress and depression may serve as key mediating factors of this association. A brief methodological overview is provided for each neuroimaging domain as well as a discussion of limitations and future directions for this field.

Keywords: neuroimaging, MRI, DTI, functional connectivity, stress, depression

Neuroimaging, particularly magnetic resonance imaging (MRI), provides a key methodology for understanding the effects of stress on the brain and for uncovering potential neural mechanisms by which stress can contribute to various mental health conditions. In this chapter, we will focus on studies in children, adolescents, and adults that assess impacts of early life stress (ELS) on the brain. Additionally, we review studies that examine neural differences in major depressive disorder (MDD) as an example of current neuroimaging approaches to studying neural mechanisms of stress in psychopathology. We focus on MDD because ELS has been highlighted as a major risk factor for MDD and because similar subcortical and cortical brain alterations have been noted in relation to both ELS and MDD, making these key potential mechanisms mediating ELS-related risk. We will begin by reviewing common methods for examining brain structure and function and neuroimaging studies relating ELS to brain structure and function. We will then summarize key background regarding early life stress and depression as well as highlighting cortisol and brain structure/function as potential mediators

relating ELS to MDD (see Figure 20.1 for a schematic representation of the mechanisms of interest). Finally, we will review studies of neural alterations in depression and address major limitations and potential future directions for this domain of research.

Relationships Between Early Life Stress and Brain Structure, Function, and Connectivity
Early Life Stress and Brain Structure
A variety of methods are available to examine brain structure. Particularly, as sample sizes have grown, the use of automated methods, like FreeSurfer (https://surfer.nmr.mgh.harvard.edu/), have supplanted manual tracing of individual brain regions participant by participant. Commonly used approaches to quantifying brain morphometry include automated segmentation of subcortical regional volumes and regional parcellation or vertex-wise analysis of cortical areal thickness, surface area, and volume (noting that volume is a composite of thickness and surface area). Importantly, new methods are being developed for more robust analysis of morphometry, for example, face-wise analysis of cortical surface area

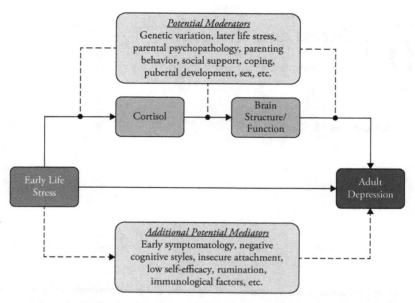

Figure 20.1 Potential mediators and moderators of the relationship between early life stress and depression. This figure displays the proposed mechanism of interest by which alterations in cortisol and brain structure/function mediate effects of early life stress on depression. Although this mechanism is the main focus of this review, we present a variety of other factors that have been suggested to mediate effects of stress on risk for depression. Similarly, while we briefly discuss genetic moderators in this review, we also suggest other potential moderating factors in this schematic diagram.

using mesh-based representations of cortex (Winkler et al., 2012).

These and related methods have been used to link early life stress/adversity to brain structure in child/adolescent and adult populations, respectively (see Tables 20.1 and 20.2). Studies are included here if they examined brain structure, particularly using automated segmentations or hand-tracing to ascertain regional volumes or using voxel-based morphometry (VBM). Study inclusion was not restricted by age at scan, but studies were excluded if ELS was confounded entirely with diagnostic status, for example, comparing individuals with posttraumatic stress disorder (PTSD) secondary to childhood abuse to nonabused individuals. Additionally, we defined ELS broadly here, including childhood abuse, neglect, early institutional/orphanage care, poverty (or low socioeconomic status [SES]), and general adversity/trauma. Although behavioral and clinical work has aimed to identify potentially specific outcomes of these different types of stressors, the neuroimaging literature on outcomes of ELS is relatively young with fewer studies distinguishing among different types of ELS. As such, we include this broad array of potential ELS with the acknowledgment that, for example, experiences like low SES and acute abuse or trauma may function differently as stressors and thus lead to very different neural outcomes. As this field grows, it will be important to directly compare and contrast the effects of different early stressors to explore whether distinct neural outcomes can be identified. Further, it has been suggested that the timing of stress along the developmental trajectory can greatly alter its influence, for example, the same stressor experienced earlier may have a greater impact than if experienced later (Tottenham, 2009). Again, as this field grows, it will be important to continue to test this hypothesis to identify potential developmentally sensitive periods where ELS may have more or less effect on neural development.

The hippocampus is a hub in the neural stress circuitry and has been a focus in animal studies given its vulnerability to the neurotoxic effects of cortisol (Jacobson & Sapolsky, 1991). The hippocampus was the also most examined region among the human imaging studies reviewed here, with 19 studies finding evidence for reduced volumes among individuals with ELS exposure, though 18 other studies reported no significant associations between ELS and hippocampal volume. Importantly, reductions in hippocampal volumes (as well as null results) were observed both in adults and in younger populations and did not appear specific to any particular type of ELS. Interestingly, studies finding significant effects tended to note either bilateral or

Table 20.1. Studies Examining Effects of Early Life Stress on Brain Structure in Children and/or Adolescents

Study	Total N (Exposed N)	Stressor	Analysis	WBV	HC	Amygdala	Other	Notes
Teicher et al., 2004	166(28)	Abuse or neglect	ROI	—	—	—	↓CC	Also includes psychiatric controls
Mehta et al., 2009	25(14)	Institutional care	ROI	↓GMV, ↓WMV	NS	↑ by group, ↓ with time institutionalized	NS CC	—
Rao et al., 2010	87	Early life adversity	ROI	—	→	—	—	Includes MDD and at-risk
Tottenham et al., 2010	78(38)	Institutional care	ROI	NS	NS	↑	NS Caudate	—
Hanson et al., 2010	72(31)	Physical abuse	Voxel-wise, tensor based	↓WBV	—	—	↓ various frontal, parietal, and temporal regions	—
Edmiston et al., 2011	42	CTQ	VBM	—	—	→	↓ dlPFC, sgACC, striatum, temporal cortex, cerebellum, hypothalamus	—
Hanson, Chandra, Wolfe, & Pollak, 2011	317	SES	VBM	NS	→	NS	—	—
Brain Development Cooperative Group, 2012	325	SES	ROI	NS	—	—	NS for various frontal, temporal, parietal and occipital lobe, subcortical, cerebellum, and brainstem regions	Examined changes in longitudinal growth
Sheridan, Fox, Zeanah, McLaughlin, & Nelson, 2012	74(54)	Institutional care	ROI	↓GMV	NS	NS	↓CC, NS basal ganglia	—
Jednoróg et al., 2012	23	SES	VBM/SBM	NS	→	—	↓parahippocampal gyri, middle temporal gyri, insula, left fusiform gyrus, right inferior occipito-temporal region, and left superior/middle frontal gyrus	—
Noble, Houston, Kan, & Sowell, 2012	60	SES	ROI	NS	→	→	↓STG, NS L STG, L MTG, L IFG, left fusiform, ACC	—
Jenkins, Woolley, Hooper, & De Bellis, 2013	102	SES	ROI	↓WBV, ↓GMV	—	—	—	—
Luby et al., 2013	145	SES	ROI	↓GMV, ↓WMV	↓left, NS right	↓left, NS right	—	Mediated by parenting and SLE

(continued)

Table 20.1. Continued

Study	Total N (Exposed N)	Stressor	Analysis	WBV	HC	Amygdala	Other	Notes
De Brito et al., 2013	38(18)	Abuse or neglect	VBM	—	NS	NS	↓mOFC,MTG	—
Ganella et al., 2015	91	CTQ	ROI	—	—	—	↑pituitary (females)	Examined longitudinal growth #
Hair, Hanson, Wolfe, & Pollak, 2015	389	SES	ROI	↓	↓	—	↓ frontal and temporal gray matter	Includes longitudinal imaging
Hanson et al., 2015	128	Physical abuse, orphanage/abandoned, neglect, SES	ROI	—	↓	↓	—	—
Kelly et al., 2015	122(62)	Abuse or neglect	ROI,VBM	NS	NS	NS	↓OFC, middle temporal lobe, supramarginal gyrus; ↑precentral gyrus	—
Gold, Sheridan, et al., 2016	58(21)	Physical and/or sexual abuse	ROI,VBM	—	NS	NS	↓vmPFC,lOFC,rIFG, parahippocampal gyrus, temporal pole, ITG, MTG, STG	partially overlapping sample with Busso et al. (2017)
Kelly et al., 2016	122(62)	Abuse or neglect	VBM	NS	—	—	↓ACC/SFG	Same sample as Kelly et al. (2015)
McLaughlin et al., 2016	94(38)	Abuse or domestic violence	ROI	↓	↓	↓	NS dACC, NS vmPFC	—
Busso et al., 2017	51(19)	CECA/CTQ	ROI	—	NS	NS	↓vmPFC, IFG, parahippocampal gyrus, ITG, MTG	Examined structure as a mediator between maltreatment and psychopathology
Merz, Tottenham, & Noble, 2017	327	SES	ROI	—	NS	↓	—	Effect varied by age
Dahmen et al., 2017	49(25)	Maltreatment and foster placement	ROI	—	↓	—	—	Examined HC subfields as well as total volume
Lim et al., 2017	68(22)	Childhood abuse	ROI/VBM	—	NS	—	↓cerebellum, left insula, right lOFC	Also includes psychiatric controls

Arrows indicate increased or decreased volume or thickness in the group exposed to early life stress or with increasing amount of stress exposure. ACC = anterior cingulate cortex; CC = corpus callosum; CTQ = Childhood Trauma Questionnaire; GMV = gray matter volume; HC = hippocampus; IFG = inferior frontal gyrus; ITG = inferior temporal gyrus; MDD = major depressive disorder; mOFC = medial orbitofrontal cortex; MTG = middle temporal gyrus; NS = nonsignificant effects of early life stress; ROI = region of interest–based analysis; SES = socioeconomic status; STG = superior temporal gyrus; VBM = voxel-based morphometry analysis; WBV = whole brain volume; WMV = white matter volume.
Did not control for WBV.

Table 20.2. Studies examining effects of early life stress on brain structure in adults

Study	Total N (Exposed N)	Stressor	Analysis	WBV	HC	Amygdala	Other	Notes
Stein, Koverola, Hanna, Torchia, & McClarty, 1997	42(21)	CSA	ROI	—	↓Left, NS Right	—	—	Women only
M. Driessen et al., 2000	42	CTQ	ROI	—	→	NS	—	Women only, includes BPD
Vythilingam et al., 2002	46(21)	Early Trauma Inventory (& MDD)	ROI	NS	↓Left in MDD+Abuse vs. MDD and control, NS right	—	—	Women only, includes MDD
Pederson et al., 2004	51(34)	Abuse	ROI	—	NS	—	—	Women only, includes PTSD #
Golier et al, 2005	47(27)	Holocaust Survivors	ROI	NS	NS	NS	↑STG, ↑lateral temporal lobe	Older adults
R. A. Cohen, Grieve, Hoth, Paul, & Sweet, 2006	265	Adverse Childhood Experiences—ELSQ	ROI	↓GMV	NS	NS	↓ACC & caudate, NS when controlling for total brain volume	—
Andersen et al., 2008	42(26)	CSA	ROI	—	→	NS	↓CC, ↓frontal cortex	Women only
Lenze, Xiong, & Sheline, 2008	55	childhood adversity (CECA)	ROI	—	NS	—	—	Women only, includes remitted MDD #
Weniger, Lange, Sachsse, & Irle, 2008	48(23)	Traumatic Antecedent Questionnaire (TAQ)	ROI	NS	NS	NS	—	Women only, includes PTSD and DID
Tomoda, Navalta, Polcari, Sadato, & Teicher, 2009	37(23)	CSA	VBM	—	—	—	↓visual cortex	Women only
Frodl, Reinhold, Koutsouleris, Reiser, & Meisenzahl, 2010	87	CTQ	ROI/VBM	—	→	—	↓ prefrontal volumes in healthy controls with more physical abuse	MDD, MDD x ELS interaction effects
Tomoda, 2011	40(21)	Parental verbal abuse	VBM	—	—	—	↑STG	—
Van Harmelen et al., 2010	181(84)	CEM	VBM	NS	NS	NS	↓medial prefrontal gyrus	Includes unmedicated patients with depression and/or anxiety disorders
Baker et al., 2012	173(97)	Adverse Childhood Experiences—ELSQ	ROI	—	NS	NS	↓ACC, ↓insula; NS caudate	Varied by time of ELS exposure #

(continued)

Table 20.2. Continued

Study	Total N (Exposed N)	Stressor	Analysis	WBV	HC	Amygdala	Other	Notes
Butterworth, Cherbuin, Sachdev, & Anstey, 2012	431	SES—Childhood Poverty	ROI	NS	NS	NS	—	Middle-aged adults
Carballedo et al., 2012	40(20)	CTQ (& MDD Risk)	ROI/VBM	NS	↓	—	↓ mpfc, acc, dlpfc with family history + early abuse	Risk x abuse interaction
Staff et al., 2012	249	SES	ROI	→	→	—	—	Older adults ^
Teicher et al., 2012	193	Adverse Childhood Experiences, CTQ	ROI	→	—	—	—	—
Tomoda, Polcari, Anderson, & Teicher, 2012	52(22)	Witnessing domestic violence	VBM	—	—	—	↓ lingual gyrus	—
Cavanagh et al., 2013	42	SES	ROI	—	—	—	↓cerebellar gray matter	Males only
Chaney et al., 2014	83	CTQ	ROI/VBM	—	→	—	↑left OFC, right dmPFC, NS dlPFC, ACC	Includes MDD
Gorka et al., 2014	818	CTQ	ROI/VBM	—	↓left, NS right	NS	↓mPFC	—
Opel et al., 2014	170	CTQ	ROI	—	→	—	—	Includes MDD
Holz et al., 2015	167(33)	SES	ROI/VBM	NS	—	—	↓OFC ROI and inferior temporal gyrus, superior orbitofrontal gyrus, middle temporal gyrus, precentral gyrus, medial frontal gyrus, and the bilateral insula	—
Grabe et al., 2016	1826(319)	CTQ	ROI/VBM	—	NS	NS	NS	Also examined interactions with FKBP5
Yang et al., 2016	253	SES	VBM	NS	—	—	↑mPFC/ACC	—
Colle et al., 2017	63(35)	Adverse Childhood Experiences	ROI	—	→	—	—	Interaction with sex

Arrows indicate increased or decreased volume or thickness in the group exposed to early life stress or with increasing amount of stress exposure.
ACC = anterior cingulate cortex; CC = corpus callosum; CTQ = Childhood Trauma Questionnaire; GMV = gray matter volume; IFG = inferior frontal gyrus; ITG = inferior temporal gyrus; MDD = major depressive disorder; MTG = middle temporal gyrus; NS = nonsignificant effects of early life stress; ROI = region of interest–based analysis; SES = socioeconomic status; STG = superior temporal gyrus; VBM = voxel-based morphometry analysis; WBV = whole brain volume; WMV = white matter volume. # Did not control for WBV.
^ Do not control for WBV in paper, but results hold when doing so (personal communication).

left-specific reductions in hippocampal volume. Although the mechanisms for this are unclear, there is evidence for differential heritability of the left and right hippocampus with the left being much less heritable (22.3% vs. 77.7%), potentially allowing for a larger environmental effect on volume (Pagliaccio, Barch et al., 2015).

The amygdala is a critical region for the identification and processing of salient and emotional stimuli in one's environment and is implicated in various mental health conditions. The amygdala has also received much attention in the literature on ELS, though the results for this brain region are quite mixed. Two studies noted larger amygdala volumes in children/adolescents adopted out of institutions/orphanages (i.e., youth who likely experienced serious early neglect) compared to controls who were raised at home. One of these studies found larger volumes in children who were adopted later versus early, where later adoption was presumably associated with greater duration of stress/neglect (Tottenham et al., 2010). The other study noted larger volumes in previously institutionalized children compared to controls, but it found a negative relationship between amygdala volumes and time spent in the institution (Mehta et al., 2009), such that less time in the institution was associated with larger amygdala volume. Six other studies have noted *reduced* amygdala volumes in children/adolescents with early life adversity, specifically low SES or physical abuse. This pattern of findings suggests the possibility of unique associations between amygdala and neglect compared to other types of stressors/adversity. Interestingly, studies relating ELS to amygdala volumes in adulthood have typically found nonsignificant results. This may suggest the potential for recovery over development, potentially as a function of continued amygdala development through adolescence (Giedd et al., 1996).

More recently, studies have begun to examine effects of ELS across the rest of the brain, identifying further regions of potential interest. Several studies have identified volumetric reductions in the anterior cingulate cortex (ACC) of adults associated with adverse childhood experiences. The ACC is a large midline brain region and has been implicated in a variety of cognitive, emotional, and regulatory functions. In particular, its central role in conflict monitoring and error detection has been of interest in studying effects of stress and, particularly, anxiety disorders. Volumetric reductions in medial prefrontal cortex (mPFC)/ACC and orbital frontal cortex (OFC) have also been linked to ELS in children and adults. Several other regions have been less consistently associated with ELS or have only been reported in a single study. For example, one study has suggested smaller caudate volume while two others have found nonsignificant relationships between ELS and the caudate. Similarly, evidence for reductions in whole brain or corpus callosum volume has been mixed in the few studies reporting on these outcomes. Importantly, collaborative efforts, such as the enhancing neuroimaging genetics through meta-analysis (ENIGMA) consortium, have begun to collect data from across various sites to perform increasingly large mega-analyses. The ENIGMA MDD network has examined effects of ELS on brain structure in 3,036 participants, also finding smaller caudate volumes associated with childhood adversity exposure (Frodl et al., 2017).

Diagnostic Status Confounds

As noted, we excluded several studies from the table if their examination of ELS was entirely confounded by diagnostic status. Much of this work has focused on individuals with PTSD secondary to childhood trauma. A meta-analysis of these studies has suggested that hippocampal volumes are reduced bilaterally in adults with childhood maltreatment-related PTSD, whereas hippocampal (and amygdala) volumes did not differ in children with maltreatment-related PTSD (Woon & Hedges, 2008). Thus, hippocampal volume reductions after childhood adversity may not be apparent until adulthood, as has been noted in some animal work as well (e.g., Isgor, Kabbaj, Akil, & Watson, 2004). However, there is also work showing reduced hippocampal volumes in women with childhood sexual abuse exposure and PTSD compared to women with childhood sexual abuse exposure but not PTSD, or unexposed women (Bremner et al., 2003); this suggests that hippocampal volume may mark vulnerability to the effects of stress. This hypothesis has been tested more explicitly in a study of twins showing that smaller hippocampal volumes may be a risk factor for developing PTSD after trauma exposure (Gilbertson et al., 2002).

Early Life Stress and White Matter

Work has more recently begun to examine ELS using diffusion tensor imaging (DTI), which characterizes the diffusion of water molecules in the brain to map patterns of white matter connectivity (for a discussion of methodological and interpretation issues, see Alexander, Lee, Lazar, & Field, 2007). DTI involves acquiring several images of the brain in various directions to estimate the magnitude and preferred direction of water flow, represented as an ellipsoid called a tensor, at each voxel. White matter tracts tend to show more diffusion of water along the length of a tract but more restricted flow perpendicular to the tract. This is observed as a more elongated or anisotropic ellipsoid tensor. Gray matter and cerebral spinal fluid, on the other hand, tend to have less restricted water diffusion in all directions. This is observed as a more isotropic or spherical tensor. Fractional anisotropy (FA) is thus a key metric for characterizing DTI, where higher FA values indicate more restricted water flow. Reduced FA has been suggested to indicate reduced white matter integrity or myelination, though FA also typically varies across the brain. Mean diffusivity or the apparent diffusion coefficient is a common metric of the magnitude of diffusion. Various methods have been developed for analyzing DTI, but these mainly fall into two classes. Some methods analyze FA or other metrics at each voxel in the brain. Other methods, called tractography, aim to trace particular known white matter fiber bundles in the brain and isolate these tracts for analysis. For a further discussion of the neuropsychiatric applications of DTI, see Lim and Helpern (2002).

The literature on the relationships between ELS and white matter is quite mixed. There is some evidence for white matter deficits in the corpus callosum, though the localization of this effect has varied (reduced FA in the genu in adult females [Paul et al., 2008] vs. medial and posterior deficits in children with PTSD [Jackowski et al., 2008]). Several other studies have pinpointed white matter deficits in the uncinate fasciculus (Eluvathingal, 2006) and the arcuate fasciculus (Choi, Jeong, Rohan, Polcari, & Teicher, 2009) in individuals exposed to ELS. A study following up on the Bucharest Early Intervention Project also found fairly widespread differences in white matter structure as a function of early neglect evident at age 8, including in the internal and external capsules and corpus callosum (Bick, Fox, Zeanah, & Nelson, 2017). Further, ELS may interact with familial risk for psychopathology, such as MDD. For example, research has found increased FA in the corpus callosum, fornix, inferior fronto-occipital fasciculi, superior longitudinal fasciculus associated with ELS in adults with a family history of MDD, but decreased FA in those without a family history of MDD (Frodl et al., 2012). These tracts provide widespread interhemispherical and anterior-posterior connections, and the authors of this study suggested that these findings may relate to differences in cognitive performance, such as executive functioning, working memory, and attention processing.

Early Life Stress and Brain Function

ELS has been related to alterations in neural responsivity and connectivity. Functional MRI studies examining blood-oxygen-level-dependent (BOLD) signal are a mainstay of cognitive and clinical neuroscience in humans (for a discussion of analysis and interpretation of fMRI, see Lindquist, 2008). Studies of neural responsivity generally contrast changes in regional blood flow induced by different psychological task conditions, for example, when viewing negative versus positive facial expressions, to isolate regions involved in a process or in relation to some relevant aspect of group status (i.e., trauma exposure or not) or continuous covariates (severity of ELS). This work has largely focused on neural responsivity to emotional stimuli. These studies have consistently found that ELS predicts elevated responsivity to negative emotional stimuli, particularly in the amygdala, across a variety of types of ELS (e.g., Bogdan, Williamson, & Hariri, 2012; Dannlowski et al., 2011; Ganzel, Kim, Gilmore, Tottenham, & Temple, 2013; McLaughlin, Peverill, Gold, Alves, & Sheridan, 2015; Pagliaccio, Luby, Bogdan, & Agrawal, 2015; Suzuki, Luby, Botteron, & Dietrich, 2014; Tottenham et al., 2011). It has also been suggested that ELS relates to hypoactivity in the nucleus accumbens, a critical portion of the striatum involved in reward processing, motivation, reinforcement learning and other functions, and to greater depressive symptomatology (Goff et al., 2012; for a review, see Goff & Tottenham, 2015). ELS may also impair regulation of emotion, such that the experience of childhood poverty predicted reduced ventral lateral PFC (vlPFC) and dorsolateral PFC (dlPFC) activity during emotion regulation in adulthood and the effect of childhood poverty was partially mediated by later exposure to stressors across childhood/adolescence (Kim et al., 2013).

Finally, recent work has linked ELS to alterations in functional connectivity. Resting state functional connectivity (rsFC) (Biswal, Yetkin, Haughton, & Hyde, 1995) has been used to examine intrinsic correlations in brain activity at rest rather than during a specific task condition. This method consists of quantifying the correlation between the time-series of activation in two regions or voxels. Given relatively high correlations among homologous regions bilaterally, for example, left and right motor cortex, rsFC is assumed to represent more than monosynaptic connections among regions. Rather, it has been suggested that correlations between spontaneous fluctuations in regional activity may reflect a history of coactivation between regions. Prior rsFC work has generally found alterations in connectivity between the amygdala and mPFC/ACC in children/adolescents exposed to early stress, though the nature of this relationship differed somewhat by sample (Burghy et al., 2012; Gee et al., 2013; Pagliaccio et al., 2015). In addition, recent work has shown a link between poverty as a form of ELS and altered connectivity of the hippocampus and prefrontal cortex (PFC), as well as amygdala and lingual gyrus (Barch et al., 2016). Other work also suggests hyperconnectivity of the thalamus associated with ELS as well in adults (Philip et al., 2016).

Summary of Early Life Stress and Brain Structure/Function

This review of the literature on the relationship between ELS and brain structure/function points to several key findings. There is evidence for reduced hippocampal volume associated with ELS, but more mixed evidence regarding associations between ELS and amygdala, with some studies finding increased volume and some deceased. More recently, the caudate has been highlighted as a potential key region of interest as well. As of yet, there is mixed evidence concerning white matter changes associated with ELS, though alterations in the corpus callosum have been noted with ELS. However, there is consistent evidence for increased amygdala reactivity to negative stimuli associated with ELS. Structural, functional, and connectivity alterations in the mPFC/ACC have also been noted in studies of ELS, as well as alterations in rsFC of both the amygdala and the hippocampus. Overall, this work suggests that ELS may disrupt regions critically underpinning emotion reactivity, stress and emotion regulation, and salience detection with increasing evidence for disruptions in reward processing.

Early Life Stress and Cortisol

Researchers have hypothesized that one of the mechanisms by which ELS influences brain structure, function, and connectivity is via the influence of ELS on cortisol function. Although ELS has been related to various aspects of cortisol function (including baseline and responses to stressors) in many studies, to our knowledge, there has not been a comprehensive meta-analysis examining this relationship. These relationships are reviewed in more detail in Pagliaccio and Barch (2016) and in other chapters in this volume. Briefly, prior work has tended to suggest that ELS is associated with blunted cortisol output in children/adolescents (e.g., Gunnar & Vazquez, 2001; MacMillan et al., 2009; Pagliaccio et al., 2013; but see also Cicchetti, 2009; Cicchetti & Rogosch, 2001; Kaufman et al., 1997). On the other hand, evidence is quite mixed for blunted (e.g., Carpenter et al., 2007; Carpenter, Shattuck, Tyrka, Geracioti, & Price, 2011) versus elevated cortisol (e.g., Heim & Nemeroff, 2001; Heim et al., 2000; Rao, Hammen, Ortiz, Chen, & Poland, 2008) in adults with ELS exposure. More work is needed to fully parse the effects of ELS on the developmental trajectories of normal cortisol function, to examine whether certain types of stressors are differentially associated with elevated/blunted cortisol, and to relate stress-related blunting in cortisol to other outcomes, like brain development and psychopathology.

CORTISOL AND THE BRAIN

As a case example of how cortisol effects might mediate between ELS and brain structure, we will describe the literature linking cortisol to hippocampal volume. Importantly, while the hippocampus is a major source of inhibition on stress circuitry in the brain, the hippocampus is also particularly vulnerable to the neurotoxic effects of cortisol (Jacobson & Sapolsky, 1991). Specifically, animal studies have shown chronic stress and corticosteroid administration to reduce dendritic branching and length of hippocampal CA3 pyramidal neurons (e.g., Conrad, LeDoux, Magariños, & McEwen, 1999; Magariños, McEwen, Flügge, & Fuchs, 1996; McKittrick et al., 2000; Watanabe, Gould, & McEwen, 1992), potentially causing cell death in the CA3 subfield and impairing neurogenesis in the dentate gyrus (Reagan & McEwen, 1997; Sapolsky, 2000). One recent study showed that stress-induced loss of CA1 dendritic spines and decreases in spine length accounted for gray matter volume loss observed by MRI in mice, rather than neuronal or glial loss (Kassem et al., 2012). This may help contextualize changes in brain volume in human MRI studies, in that the volume losses identified in these studies may be due to changes in dendritic morphometry rather than cell death.

A stress-/cortisol-mediated mechanism of change in hippocampal structure is also supported by the human literature. For example, in humans, high endogenous levels of cortisol are associated with smaller hippocampal volumes in older adults (Lupien et al., 2005). Additionally, patients with chronically elevated cortisol levels due to Cushing's syndrome tend to show reductions in hippocampal volume (Andela et al., 2015), with 24-hour mean cortisol levels negatively correlated with hippocampal volumes (Starkman, Gebarski, Berent, & Schteingart, 1992). Importantly, treatment of Cushing's can lead to enlargement of the hippocampus, which is in turn associated with reductions in cortisol (Starkman et al., 1999).

Given the role of the hippocampus in the regulation of the HPA axis (Jacobson & Sapolsky, 1991), it is also important to note that these stress/cortisol effects on the hippocampus may impact responsivity to future stressors. For example, there is some evidence from human studies that smaller hippocampal volumes may be a risk factor for developing PTSD after trauma exposure (Gilbertson et al., 2002). Understanding the role of stress and cortisol in determining brain structure may help explain, at least in part, the underlying neural alterations observed in depression. Importantly, cortisol has been linked to the structure and function of other regions as well. For example, Cushing's syndrome (Andela et al., 2015) and cortisol administration have been related to smaller amygdala volumes (Brown, Woolston, & Frol, 2008) and Cushing's has been linked to increased threat-related activity in the amygdala and hippocampus (Andela et al., 2015).

Depression as a Candidate Early Life Stress–Related Psychiatric Disorder

Depression is among the most common and disabling mental health conditions and one of the forms of psychopathology most strongly linked to early life stress, as detailed next. Recent epidemiological results estimate the lifetime morbid risk for a depressive episode (proportion of people who will eventually experience an episode during their life) at 29.9% (Kessler, Petukhova, & Sampson, 2012). Furthermore, depression leads to a significant decrement in quality of life, loss of work productivity, increases in health care costs (Simon, 2003), and an average loss of over 20 years of life (Colton & Manderscheid, 2006). As of 2007, the national expenditures on care for mood and anxiety disorders were over $36 billion (Soni, 2010). In addition, depression has a relatively early onset, typically prior to or during one's twenties. The lifetime prevalence for a depressive episode among 13- to 17-year-olds is 12.6% (Kessler et al., 2012), but depression can onset even earlier among children/adolescents (see (Costello, Mustillo, Erkanli, Keeler, & Angold, 2003) and has been characterized in children as

young as preschool age (Luby, Heffelfinger et al., 2009; Luby, Si, Belden, Tandon, & Spitznagel, 2009). Yet the efficacy of common treatments for adult MDD is generally quite low. Particularly, remission rates with antidepressant treatment are generally <30%, while dropout rates from such trials are high (Pigott, Leventhal, Alter, & Boren, 2010). Similarly low remission rates are at times observed for cognitive-behavioral therapy and psychodynamic therapies, with 40% of patients seeking additional treatment afterward (E. Driessen et al., 2013). The experience of stressful life events (SLEs) may contribute to ineffective treatment and to treatment resistance (~20%–30% of patients fail to respond to at least one standard course of antidepressants) (Fava & Davidson, 1996). As such, understanding the role of factors such as stress in the neural mechanisms underlying depression may be key to improved treatment and diagnostics.

Linking Stress Exposure and Depression
Genetic Versus Environmental Contributions to Depression

A meta-analysis of genetic epidemiology studies found that the heritability of liability to MDD is ~37% (95% confidence interval [CI] = 31%–42%), which is on the lower end of heritability for psychiatric disorders. Further, although there is minimal contribution of shared environmental factors (95% CI = 0%–5%), there is a large effect of the individual-specific environment of ~63% (95% CI = 58%–67%; Sullivan, Neale, & Kendler, 2000), suggesting that environmental factors are major contributors to depression. The experience of stressful and traumatic life events, particularly early life stress, has been cited as one of the foremost individual environmental factors contributing to MDD risk (Green et al., 2010; Kendler, Karkowski, & Prescott, 1999; Kendler et al., 1995; Kendler, Kuhn, & Prescott, 2004; Kessler & Magee, 2009). It is important to consider these different etiological components when examining brain structure/ function as a mediator of stress effects in depression, as discussed later. Particularly, the substantial variance in depression accounted for by environmental factors may be mediated by stress-related changes in brain structure/function.

Proximal Stress

While this review focuses on the effects of early life stress, there is also a clear and direct effect of more proximal stressors on the onset of MDD. This can also be a difficult issue to separate given potential collinearity between experience of ELS and recent stress; that is, those with higher rates of ELS exposure may also be more likely to experience continued stress later. Nonetheless, a large proportion of first onsets of MDD are preceded by a stressful event (e.g., Stroud, Davila, & Moyer, 2008), and the effects of recent stressors on brain function and connectivity are therefore under study. For example, recent stressors, but not ELS, have been related to brain activity in depressed adults during the presentation of negative words (Hsu, Langenecker, Kennedy, Zubieta, & Heitzeg, 2010). Further, in a large sample of adults, amygdala responses to emotional faces were suggested to moderate the effects of recent stressors on changes internalizing symptoms over time (Swartz, Knodt, Radtke, & Hariri, 2015). More work is needed to fully explore the interacting effects of ELS and proximal stress on brain structure and function as mediators of risk for pathology.

Early Life Stress

In addition to the effect of proximal stressors on the onset of MDD, early life stress has been implicated in increasing risk for MDD. Various types of ELS have been studied in relation to MDD, including physical and sexual abuse, neglect, family discord/disruption, parental divorce, death of friends/family, natural disasters, and low SES, among other stressors. Parental psychopathology, which may mark risk via both genetic and environmental mechanisms, has also been investigated. Epidemiological work by Kessler et al. (1997) has suggested that a large percentage of individuals with MDD have experienced at least some form of significant ELS (74.4% reporting at least one childhood adversity, including loss, parental psychopathology, interpersonal trauma/abuse, accidents/disasters, etc.). This work also noted a decrease in risk over time where the odds of MDD onset decreased for 10 years after the adversity (until reaching an OR of 1) after experience of certain types of ELS (parental divorce, physical attack, or sexual abuse). Thus, risk for onset of mood pathology was highest early after the stress but was apparent for up to ~10 years, though there is also a suggestion that individuals who did not experience pathology by that point might potentially be more resilient to developing later pathology (Kessler, Davis, & Kendler, 1997). This is important to consider again in examining the effects of ELS on the brain and the brain as a mechanism mediating risk for MDD, specifically the timing of ELS and assessments of neural development or alterations. More neuroimaging work examining the course of

brain development following ELS may be critical in parsing the persistence of ELS effects.

A growing body of work has focused on the effects of certain early stressors or traumas, including childhood sexual abuse (CSA). CSA is consistently associated with adult-onset MDD in both men and women, though reports of CSA are much more prevalent among women (for review, see Weiss, Longhurst, & Mazure, 1999). Importantly, research also suggested some degree of temporal decay of effects of abuse, as was also suggested more generally by Kessler et al. (1997). Again, the odds of depression were higher earlier after abuse (minor MDD in adolescents, OR = 15.5) than in adulthood (OR = 2.19 for MDD, 7.80 for recurrent MDD; Collishaw et al., 2007).

Low socioeconomic status (SES) during childhood (generally indexed by household income, parental education attainment, or parental employment) has been also cited as a key risk factor for the development of MDD (hazard ratio = 1.57) as well as for depression recurrence/relapse (rate ratio = 1.61; Gilman, Kawachi, Fitzmaurice, & Buka, 2003). This effect was robust even controlling for a family history of MDD and adult SES, indicating a key role of low SES in childhood (Gilman, Kawachi, Fitzmaurice, & Buka, 2002). It is important to note that low SES is generally coincident with a variety of other specific chronic and acute stressors and thus may serve as a marker of generally elevated stress exposure or of particular stressors of relevance to risk for MDD.

Parental Psychopathology

A parental history of psychopathology, particularly MDD, has often been cited as one of the biggest risk factors for developing depression oneself. Multiple prospective, longitudinal studies have shown that the offspring of depressed parents are at approximately three times greater risk for developing MDD, as well as anxiety and substance use disorders (Lieb, Isensee, Höfler, Pfister, & Wittchen, 2002; Weissman et al., 2006; Williamson, Birmaher, Axelson, Ryan, & Dahl, 2004). Yet it is often difficult to parse the genetic versus environmental mechanisms by which parental MDD increases risk among offspring from these results. Many neuroimaging studies have examined associations with parental history of depression and this has been reviewed previously, for example, examining the influence of family history of depression on neural processing of reward (Luking, Pagliaccio, Luby, & Barch, 2016).

Complexities in the Relationship of Stress to Depression

Stress Generation and Gene–Environment Correlations

The stress-generation hypothesis posits that depressed individuals are likely to behave in ways contributing to the occurrence of negative events in their lives (Hammen, 1991). Thus, it often behooves studies linking stress to depression risk to try to differentiate *dependent* events, those at least partially influenced/created by the individual, from *independent* events, those out of the individual's control. Particularly in retrospective studies, group differences between depressed and nondepressed individuals in stress exposure may capture generated stress rather than causal effects of stress on clinical outcomes. While stress generation appears to be a large factor at work in depression (for a review, see Liu & Alloy, 2010), independent stressors also predict MDD onset (Kendler et al., 1999). Stress generation also has important implications for parental depression as a risk factor for depression; similarly, it may become difficult to parse the mechanisms relating stress to depression as correlations arise between genetic and environmental risk.

Diathesis-Stress Interactions

Diathesis-stress models posit that individual differences in underlying vulnerabilities moderate the effects of stress exposure on later outcomes (Monroe & Simons, 1991). Such vulnerabilities may include genetic moderators, as suggested by, for example, seminal work by Caspi et al. (2003); this finding piqued interest in understanding the role of gene–by–environment interaction in depression by suggesting that carriers of the short allele of the serotonin transporter linked polymorphic region (5-HTTLPR) had increased risk for depression following stress than long allele carriers (Caspi et al., 2003). While it is important to note that replications of this effect have been mixed and often not significant at the meta-analytic level (Risch et al., 2009) and in mega-analyses (Culverhouse et al., 2017), related work has explored genetic moderators of the effects of stress on brain structure and function. For example, several studies have implicated stress system genes as moderating the effects of stress on amygdala and hippocampal structure, function, and connectivity (Di Iorio et al., 2017; Fani et al., 2013; Pagliaccio et al., 2013; Pagliaccio, Luby, Bogdan, & Agrawal, 2015; Pagliaccio et al., 2015; White et al., 2012).

Conceptually, it is interesting to note that while the short allele may sensitize individuals to the depressogenic effect of stress, it may also lead to decreased risk for MDD in those with positive early environments; in contrast, long allele carriers showed little difference in MDD symptomatology based on stress (Taylor et al., 2006). This has been conceptualized as *biological sensitivity to context* (Boyce & Ellis, 2005) or *differential susceptibility* (Belsky & Pluess, 2009), which refers to the potential for genetic and temperamental processes to confer a general sensitivity to one's environment rather than only conferring risk for psychopathology. According to these models, focusing only on negative environmental factors limits our ability to see potentially beneficial effects of genetic variants in those with positive environments.

Additionally, there are several theories as to how early life stress may moderate the effects of later life stress. First, the *stress-amplification* theory posits an overadditive interaction between early and later stress where a history of childhood stress/adversity increases risk for depression among those experiencing later stress. Some evidence for this hypothesis has been found; for example, in prepubertal girls, experience of moderate early adversity amplified effects of later stress on depression risk (Rudolph & Flynn, 2007). Alternatively, the *stress-inoculation* theory suggests that early life stress (though potentially only less severe stress) may buffer against the effects of later life stress on risk for depression, particularly more severe later stress. Finally, the *stress-sensitization* theory posits an underadditive interaction where childhood stress increases risk for depression following more mild stress (but not differentiating effects of severe stress); that is, childhood stress makes individuals more sensitive to the effects of even mild stress (Harkness, Bruce, & Lumley, 2006). This is an additional avenue that calls for further attention in the neuroimaging literature because studies have not generally explored the unique and interacting effects of early and recent life stress on brain structure and function.

Mediators of the Relationship Between Stress and Mood Pathology

As reviewed earlier, there is a robust literature linking stressor exposure and risk for depression. However, despite the strength of these links, it is not yet clear *how* the experience of stressors contributes to risk for depression. Understanding the mechanisms that mediate the influence of stress on later pathology is critical if we are to develop effective preventative or early intervention efforts designed to stave off the deleterious effects of stress. As outlined in

Figure 20.1, a number of important factors have been suggested as potentially critical mediators, including psychological factors, cortisol function, and changes in brain functions and structure. Next we briefly review the literature on each of these potential mediators.

Psychological Mediators

A variety of psychological factors have been suggested to potentially mediate effects of ELS on risk for depression. The hypothesis in this domain is that ELS may alter or confer certain cognitive and emotional factors that in turn increase risk for MDD. Decreases in self-efficacy have been suggested to mediate ~40% of the effect of dependent life events on later MDD (Maciejewski, Prigerson, & Mazure, 2000). Insecure attachment style, negative cognitive style, and later life events have also been suggested as mediators of the effect of childhood maltreatment on later MDD (Hankin, 2005). Ruminative tendencies have also been suggested as a potential mediator between stressful life events and depressive symptomatology in adults (Michl, McLaughlin, Shepherd, & Nolen-Hoeksema, 2013). Finally, early-onset MDD symptoms may mediate effects of childhood trauma on later outcomes as well (Hovens et al., 2012). While there are likely other psychosocial factors that may mediate effects of ELS on risk for depression, it is clear that negative cognitive styles/tendencies and subclinical symptomatology are important constructs to consider in understanding the effects of ELS. These types of psychological factors and traits have been linked to brain structure and function as well, but these links have not been clearly tested in the causal chain from ELS to MDD. For example, a number of studies have linked rumination to neural activity during emotional and cognitive reappraisal tasks (e.g., Cooney, Joormann, Eugène, Dennis, & Gotlib, 2010; Mandell, Siegle, Shutt, Feldmiller, & Thase, 2014; Piguet et al., 2014; Vanderhasselt, Kühn, & Raedt, 2011) as well as many studies linking trait neuroticism to neural responses, particularly to negative emotional stimuli (Servaas et al., 2013). But importantly, this work has yet to test the relationships between ELS, these psychological factors, and the brain concurrently.

Cortisol Function as a Mediator Between Stress and Depression
Cortisol and Depression

One of the major hypothesized biological mechanisms by which stress may contribute to risk for MDD is via impacts on the hypothalamic-pituitary-adrenal (HPA) axis, which mediates the body's response to stress. Particularly, it has been suggested that stress exposure may lead to alterations in the reactivity/regulation of the HPA axis and thus cortisol output, contributing to risk for MDD. MDD and ELS have been robustly linked to alterations in cortisol function, though findings vary based on the outcome of interest, for example, basal cortisol, response to acute psychological stressors, pharmacological challenge, diurnal rhythms, and others. Nonetheless, the importance of cortisol function in depression has been noted in many studies. For example, up to 90% of MDD patients show increased cortisol response to administration of dexamethasone and corticotropin-releasing hormone, where HPA axis dysregulation is most likely due to impaired feedback inhibition (Heuser, Yassouridis, & Holsboer, 1994). Additionally, MDD patients who respond to treatment show a normalization of HPA axis abnormalities thought to mark a decrease in hyperresponsivity to stress (McKay & Zakzanis, 2010). This has led to the idea that HPA normalization may be a common pathway of antidepressant effects (Holsboer & Barden, 1996).

Changes in Brain Structure and Function as a Mediator Between Stress and Depression

As described earlier and highlighted in Figure 20.1, ELS may contribute to alterations in brain structure and function, potentially via its impact on dysregulated HPA axis function and cortisol levels. Here, we first review the literature on brain structure in depression, relating it to findings on ELS. We then review the small literature more directly, testing cortisol and brain structure/function as a mediator of the relationships between ELS and depression.

Depression and Brain Structure

Depression has been related to a variety of alterations in brain structure and function; we will briefly review recent meta-analyses to summarize current findings on these structural and functional alterations in MDD. Particularly, structural studies have noted alterations in gray matter density or volume in a variety of cortical and subcortical regions in MDD, often highlighting the ACC, amygdala, and hippocampus. Cortically, recent meta-analyses of voxel-based morphometric (VBM) studies of gray matter density across participants have noted decreased gray matter in regions of the rostral anterior cingulate cortex, dorsomedial PFC, dorsolateral PFC, and OFC in adults with MDD (Bora, Fornito, Pantelis, & Yücel, 2012; Koolschijn, van Haren, Lensvelt-Mulders, Hulshoff Pol, & Kahn, 2009;

Sacher et al., 2012). A recent study also noted thinner cortex in precentral gyrus, middle frontal gyrus, parahippocampal gyrus, and ACC with increasing numbers of prior depressive episodes reported by adults (Treadway et al., 2015). Additionally, thicker caudal ACC in treatment-resistant MDD patients has been suggested to predict improvement in symptoms over time (Phillips, Batten, Tremblay, Aldosary, & Blier, 2015). As noted earlier, volumetric changes in some of these regions have also been seen associated with ELS.

Subcortically, these meta-analyses have noted volumetric reductions in the hippocampus ($d = -0.41$), the putamen ($d = -0.48$), and caudate ($d = -0.31$) (Koolschijn et al., 2009). Given robust relationships between MDD and hippocampal volumes, two meta-analyses have specifically examined this and confirmed reductions in bilateral hippocampal volumes among depressed patients across measurement techniques (Campbell, Marriott, Nahmias, & MacQueen, 2004; Videbech & Ravnkilde, 2004). A mega-analysis from the ENIGMA group (N = 1,728 MDD patients and N = 7,199 controls) also confirmed decreases in hippocampal volumes present in MDD (Schmaal et al., 2015). Again, as noted earlier, volumetric changes in the hippocampus have been consistently associated with ELS. Further, the number of depressive episodes experienced is negatively correlated with hippocampal volumes (Treadway et al., 2015; Videbech & Ravnkilde, 2004), suggesting that reductions are only observed in individuals experiencing persistent MDD (>2 years). Some of this work has hypothesized that these greater volumetric changes with more persistent MDD implicate a stress-related mechanism in the development of these volumetric alterations, though further longitudinal study is warranted. Importantly, there is evidence that hippocampal volumes are also reduced in children with MDD (McKinnon, Yucel, Nazarov, & MacQueen, 2009). Future work could examine how early these depression-related differences in hippocampal structure appear and to what degree they reflect ELS, depression, or a combination of factors beginning as early as childhood.

Results regarding amygdala volumes in MDD, on the other hand, have been very mixed, even at the meta-analytic level, similar to what has been seen in ELS studies. Studies have suggested that amygdala volumes are decreased in VBM studies of MDD (Sacher et al., 2012), while others point to decreases only in patients with comorbid anxiety disorders or first-episode/drug-free samples (Bora et al., 2012).

And others still, suggesting no difference by diagnostic group (Koolschijn et al., 2009) or even suggested larger left amygdala volumes among inpatients (but not outpatients) as compared to controls (Hajek et al., 2009). Thus, there are likely key differences in sample populations that account for the heterogeneity of findings. Particularly, greater characterization of depression severity, chronicity, treatment, and stress exposure might help to uncover the true causal factors at play linking amygdala volumes to MDD.

Depression and White Matter

A meta-analysis by Murphy and Frodl (2011) of seven studies examining DTI in depressed adults indicated decreased FA in the superior longitudinal fasciculus and increased FA in the fronto-occipital fasciculus (though the latter effect was largely driven by one study; Blood et al., 2010). A more recent meta-analysis found particular decreases in FA in the genu of the corpus callosum in MDD (Wise et al., 2016). Further, risk for MDD based on a parental history has also been linked to lower FA in the corpus callosum, cingulum, superior longitudinal fasciculi, uncinate, and inferior fronto-occipital fasciculi (Huang, Fan, Williamson, & Rao, 2011) with a nonquantitative review implicating reduced FA in the cingulum (Bracht, Linden, & Keedwell, 2015). These findings share some commonalities with the literature on ELS, such as reduced FA in the corpus callous and the uncinate, but both literatures are relatively small and mixed.

Depression and Task-Related Brain Activity

Many studies have examined alterations in neural response to emotional stimuli in depression using fMRI. Meta-analyses have noted decreased responses to positive stimuli in the pregenual ACC, posterior cingulate, putamen, and several other regions, while responses were increased in the subgenual, rectus, inferior, middle, and superior frontal gyrus and other regions in depressed patients compared to healthy controls (Diener et al., 2012; Fitzgerald, Laird, Maller, & Daskalakis, 2008). Meta-analysis has also identified decreased activity in the striatum, thalamus, cerebellum, insula, and ACC, but increased activity in visual and frontal regions, to monetary rewards (W.-N. Zhang, Chang, Guo, Zhang, & Wang, 2013). In response to negative stimuli, depressed patients often showed reduced activity in regions of prefrontal cortex, subgenual, dorsal, and posterior cingulate, and the insula, but they showed increased activity in the amygdala, putamen, insula, and other regions (Diener et al., 2012; Fitzgerald et al., 2008; Hamilton et al., 2012). As described earlier, increased amygdala reactivity to negative stimuli has also been consistently associated with ELS.

Depression and Functional Connectivity

Several studies have attempted to meta-analyze functional connectivity studies in depression, though this work is complicated by the diverse analysis methods used to study resting-state functional connectivity. Many studies examine voxelwise correlations in connectivity with a given seed, seed-to-seed correlations, or more network-based approaches, while others focus on regional homogeneity. Decreased connectivity in MDD has been noted in superior and middle temporal gyrus, the insula, precuneus, superior frontal gyrus, putamen, and thalamus while increased connectivity was noted in the middle and medial frontal gyrus, precuneus, inferior parietal lobule, ACC, hippocampus, posterior cingulate, and cerebellum (Sundermann, 2014). Other meta-analytic work (Kaiser, Andrews-Hanna, & Wager, 2015) and a nonquantitative review (Mulders, van Eijndhoven, & Schene, 2015) also point to important alterations in default mode network connectivity, suggested to implicate self-referential thought and processes. While these results point to important alterations in functional connectivity in MDD, it is difficult to meta-analyze the current literature, which varies greatly in analysis methods, for example, studies utilizing regional homogeneity (ReHo), a data-driven approach

examining local correlations (Zang, Jiang, Lu, He, & Tian, 2004), versus seed/network-based approaches, and thus it is currently unclear at a meta-analytic level whether certain functional networks are particularly altered in MDD. A meta-analysis focused specifically on studies reporting alterations in ReHo in depression found increases in mPFC/dACC ReHo and decreased ReHo in the cerebellum, postcentral gyrus, rolandic operculum, cuneus, and inferior parietal gyrus (Iwabuchi et al., 2015). As with the literature on white matter changes, these findings on rsFC in MDD share some commonalities with the literature on ELS, such as altered connectivity of the amygdala and mPFC/dACC. However, again, both literatures are mixed and further work is needed.

Summary of Neural Changes in Depression

Figure 20.2 highlights some of the main regions of interest relating to both ELS and MDD, including alterations of the amygdala, hippocampus, mPFC, subgenual ACC, and pregenual and rostral ACC. Across modalities, studies implicate alterations in brain structure and function in individuals with depression, particularly the amygdala, hippocampus, regions of the cingulate (mainly dorsal, pregenual, and subgenual), and the PFC (mainly medial). Several of these differences, particularly reduced hippocampal volume, are also found in neuroimaging studies of ELS. However, more work is needed to characterize these relationships, as the participants vary in terms of depression severity and medication

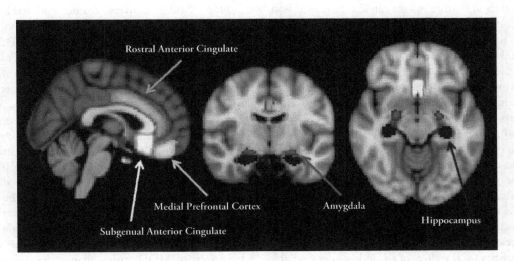

Figure 20.2 Major brain areas showing alterations with early life stress and depression. This figure displays several of the key regions of interest that have shown structural/functional alterations associated with early life stress and depression, including the hippocampus (blue), the amygdala (red), medial prefrontal cortex (pink), the subgenual cingulate (yellow), and the rostral anterior cingulate (green). These regions were extracted from the Harvard-Oxford Cortical and Subcortical Atlases.

status, and the tasks used to assay neural reactivity vary widely as well. Similar to the neuroimaging literature on ELS, while amygdala reactivity is quite consistently elevated in MDD, evidence for differences in amygdala volumes is quite mixed. The nature of white matter changes associated with MDD is unclear, though alterations in the corpus callosum have been noted with both ELS and MDD. Finally, while work examining rsFC in depression has proliferated recently, inconsistent methodologies have largely limited attempts to provide meta-analyses of this growing body of work. There is some indication that alterations in rsFC with amygdala and ACC/mPFC characterize MDD, as in the findings in ELS, but much more work is needed to establish whether these finds are robust. Further, many of these neural changes in MDD have been attributed to stress exposure, though often this is not explicitly tested.

Direct Tests of Early Life Stress–Cortisol–Brain–Depression Mechanisms

Many animal studies have implicated a mechanism by which early life stress increases risk for depression mediated by cortisol and neural alterations, but few human studies have explicitly tested this. Ideally, such tests would involve prospective longitudinal data examining cortisol, neural, and clinical outcomes preceding ELS and following through later development to examine the causal relationships between these factors. Because this is quite difficult and costly, most studies have examined retrospective relationships with longitudinal or cross-sectional data. Further insight can also be gained from intervention studies aimed at treating/alleviating ELS or cortisol effects (Slopen, McLaughlin, & Shonkoff, 2014), for example, studying poverty alleviation interventions (Fernald & Gunnar, 2009), moving children from orphanages to foster care (Zeanah et al., 2003), or pharmacological treatments impacting cortisol function (Zobel et al., 2000). Here, we will review work that has explicitly tested some step of this proposed ELS-cortisol-brain-depression mechanism. Additionally, where prior studies have not tested mediation but have provided the necessary statistics, we have calculated Sobel tests of mediation post hoc (http://quantpsy.org/sobel/sobel.htm). This was only possible when sufficient information was provided to calculate the t-statistics for the effect of the independent variable on the proposed mediator (path a) and for the effect of the mediator on the dependent variable, controlling for the independent variable (path b). While this is not the ideal method for examining mediation (Hayes, 2009, 2012, 2013), this did allow us to further synthesize prior literature that can inform this issue and will hopefully prompt others to explicitly test statistical mediation in their future work relating ELS, cortisol, neural, and/or clinical outcomes.

Early Life Stress, Depression, and Brain Changes

It has been suggested that ELS exposure might account for observed relationships between MDD and neural alterations. While studies have not typically tested mediation models similar to that presented in Figure 20.1, given the temporal ordering of events, these results can likely be conceptualized as showing that ELS is the causal agent predicting neural change as associated MDD outcomes. One important caveat to most current studies is that ELS is most often assessed retrospectively (generally contemporaneous with clinical assessment and/or neuroimaging) rather than being assessed prospectively during early childhood; several related limitations are discussed later. Nonetheless, while hippocampal volume was reduced in a sample of MDD patients, childhood trauma exposure (CTQ scores) was suggested to account for this relationship; that is, MDD patients experience more childhood adversity and this predicted volumes (Opel et al., 2014). Our post-hoc mediation calculations indicated that CTQ scores did in fact mediate the relationship between MDD and volumes of both the left (ta = 5.68, tb = –3.06, Sobel Z = 2.69, p = 0.007) and right hippocampus (ta = 5.68, tb = –3.54, Sobel Z = 3.00, p = 0.002). Conversely, other work has found relationships between ELS and smaller hippocampal volumes that were not mediated by MDD or PTSD experience (Teicher, Anderson, & Polcari, 2012). A similar relationship has been shown where ELS may also account for relationships between MDD and amygdala reactivity (ta = 3.96, tb = 3.55, Sobel Z = 2.64, p = 0.008) (Grant, Cannistraci, Hollon, Gore, & Shelton, 2011). Unfortunately, insufficient information was provided in these studies to test whether neural changes mediated relationships between ELS and MDD, though the directionality of any potential effects would not be distinguishable without longitudinal data. Thus, these mediation effects should be thought of as showing, for example, that CTQ scores share variance with the effects of MDD, rather than addressing more mechanistic mediation hypotheses.

With that said, other work has explicitly tested this type of mediation relationship in a longitudinal study and found that smaller hippocampal volumes partially mediate the effect of early-life adversity on MDD at longitudinal follow-up (Rao et al., 2010). Recent work has also suggested that reduced gray matter in the left hippocampus and mPFC mediate effects of ELS on trait anxiety levels (Gorka, Hanson, Radtke, & Hariri, 2014). These studies are more in line with the proposed mechanism in Figure 20.1.

Cortisol as a Mediator of Early Life Stress Effects on Brain Structure/Function

Recently, other work has linked ELS to neural outcomes via alteration in cortisol function. Work from our lab has suggested that cortisol reactivity at preschool age mediates relationships between ELS experience and both left hippocampal and amygdala volumes, where early cortisol function predicted smaller limbic volumes at school age (Pagliaccio et al., 2013). Interestingly, a composite risk index of several physiological markers, including cortisol (and blood glucose, BMI, blood pressure, triglycerides, etc.) was shown to mediate effects of early SES on cerebellar volumes (Cavanagh et al., 2013). It has also been suggested that cortisol may mediate relationships between ELS and amygdala-mPFC resting-state functional connectivity with early life stress in females (Burghy et al., 2012) and after early institutional care (Gee et al., 2013). Further, it was suggested that more negative amygdala-mPFC connectivity mediated relationships between childhood cortisol levels and adolescent depression severity (Burghy et al., 2012). Recent work from our lab has suggested that greater ELS exposure predicts weaker amygdala-ACC connectivity, where weaker connectivity and elevated concurrent anxiety acted as serial mediators of the effect of ELS on worsening anxiety at a longitudinal follow-up (Pagliaccio et al., 2015). Finally, other work has suggested that childhood poverty predicts reduced default mode network connectivity, which predicts higher anticipatory cortisol, but insufficient information was provided in this paper to test mediated effects (Sripada, Swain, Evans, Welsh, & Liberzon, 2014).

Summary of Tests of Mediated Effects

While much of the work reviewed here helps to inform our understandings of the mechanistic relationships between ELS, cortisol, brain alterations, and risk for depression, few studies have really begun to explicitly test these hypothesized mediation effects. Here, we focused on studies examining neural alterations, but there may be other studies in the literature that inform the degree to which cortisol

alterations mediate relationships between ELS and psychopathology. However, a review of these studies is beyond the scope of this chapter. Despite the power of this mediation approach and the added knowledge to be gained by testing mediation, we should note several caveats. Particularly, the amount of variance accounted for in these relationships is sometimes quite small. Further, much of the interpretation of these mediation effects relies on temporal precedence. That is to say that, while cortisol may serve as a *statistical* mediator of relationships between stress experienced earlier in life and brain volumes assessed later in life, this does not assure that the actual underlying mechanism functions this way. For example, brain volumes could mediate relationships between ELS and cortisol. Alternatively, in this example, cortisol could serve as a marker of another factor that is the actual causal contributor, such as neuroinflammation; that is, ELS could cause increases in both cortisol and inflammation, with inflammation only impacting brain structure. Additionally, it is important to note that there are likely many moderators of mechanisms linking ELS to MDD. For example, as we noted previously, genetic variation may moderate ELS-related risk for MDD; this may be due to a moderation of effects of ELS on the brain. Several studies have begun to examine this—where our work suggests that the additive effect of several SNPs in HPA axis-related genes moderates effects of ELS on hippocampal and amygdala volume (Pagliaccio et al., 2013), amygdala activation (Di Iorio et al., 2017), and amygdala functional connectivity (Pagliaccio et al., 2015). These results suggest that the intrinsic functioning of the HPA axis may be a particularly salient moderator of effects of stress. For a more in-depth review of neuroimaging studies examining gene–environmental interactions, see Bogdan, Pagliaccio, Baranger, and Hariri (2016).

Limitations

There are a variety of common limitations to studying the relationships between early life stress and either neural outcomes or diagnostic outcomes. First, studies examining the effects of early life stress on the brain have only examined one time point of neural data, correlating ELS with putatively later structure or function. While this can be highly informative, this approach does not allow for assessment of whether these neural differences may in fact represent pre-existing vulnerability markers. Without brain imaging early in development, the possibility that stress-related brain differences contribute to vulnerability to stress, rather than result from stress, cannot be precluded. Additionally, most studies are retrospective in their assessment of childhood adversity leading to issues with recall bias. This includes both the potential for inaccurate recall/characterization of childhood adversity by adult reporters and, more important, differentially inaccurate recall as a function of current pathology, for example, if depressed individuals show bias in the reporting or recall of childhood stress (Hardt & Rutter, 2004). Further, if participants are retrospectively reporting on their perception of prior stress rather than more concretely on the actual stressor, this complicates the causal inferences that can be drawn. This may be mitigated somewhat through prospective studies and/or by using interview-based assessments of life stress (S. Cohen, Kessler, & Gordon, 1997), by acquiring information from multiple reporters, or by examining police or government abuse records rather than questionnaire/checklist methods. While these may alleviate some issues with recall bias, they also have their own limitations, for example, collection time and difficulty, dealing with discordance between reporters, biases from other reporters, underreporting to state agencies, and so on. Thus, prospective, multimethod, longitudinal data are needed, which pose unique challenges, for example, attrition, low base rate of severe ELS, ethical imperatives to intervene/report when observing ongoing trauma/abuse, and so on. These costs and benefits must be weighted in future work to best characterize ELS and outcomes of interest. Additionally, it is important to consider the timing of neuroimaging assessment relative to ELS and diagnostic outcomes of interest. Establishing temporal precedence is important in examining neural alterations as potential mediators of ELS on MDD or other mental health outcomes. Thus, imaging the brain in childhood proximal to ELS is important, but challenging. For example, imaging younger children generally leads to larger problems with head motion as well as limiting the length and complexity of task paradigms to be examined. Furthermore, while this literature is expanding, there is generally not a clear consensus as to the time between ELS and when effects on the brain are observable, particularly as this may interact with developmental trajectories during this period. Yet, given the expense of neuroimaging, large-scale but fine-grained assessments of neurodevelopment are challenging.

As mentioned previously, the clustering of early stressors and the independence/dependence of

events also pose challenges to identifying precise mechanisms. While both independent and dependent events have been linked to depression, more care must be given to characterizing the type and impact of ELS. Further, different stressors are often coincident, making it difficult to ascertain specific effects of any given type of stressor, and similarly it is often difficult to ascertain the chronicity and timing of stressors. The confounding of ELS with later pathology has also been an issue in determining the specific effects of stress on outcomes, like cortisol function and the brain. For example, there is a body of literature examining comparing brain structure across individuals with PTSD secondary to childhood trauma and individuals unexposed to trauma. While this can be informative about the neural substrates of PTSD, the confounding of PTSD and ELS limits our ability to make specific claims about effects of ELS.

A variety of limitations also exist specifically regarding neuroimaging analysis. In particular, studies are often inconsistent regarding the use of region-of-interest analyses versus examining whole-brain differences in either structure or function. Future studies should strongly consider reporting whole-brain results in addition to any a priori ROI results, at least in supplementary materials, to further the possibility of larger meta-analyses. These and other problems have begun to be discussed further in the literature as some have tried to catalogue potentially questionable research practices and develop analytic recommendations to address the analytic flexibility that currently characterizes neuroimaging analysis (Poldrack et al., 2017). Additionally, while consistent findings have begun to emerge, the literature still is not unanimous regarding the neural effects of ELS, likely in part due to the small and heterogeneous samples often examined that limit power. Thus, it will be important for future work to assure that sufficiently large samples are being ascertained to clearly establish these relationships as well as to better characterize both ELS exposure and MDD to determine what is accounting for these mixed results.

Summary and Future Directions

Here, we reviewed neuroimaging studies of ELS and MDD, particularly focusing on structural findings. In addition, we examined the role of early life stress in risk for depression and highlight cortisol function and brain structure/function as potential mediating mechanisms. Studies show relatively consistent relationships between MDD and elevated cortisol but mixed association with ELS, though generally pointed toward blunted cortisol after ELS. It will important to further examine the relationship between ELS and cortisol to fully understand this, particularly probing a variety of outcomes, like diurnal rhythms and responsivity to acute stressors, and to examine change in cortisol function over development.

While the literature examining alterations in brain structure and function is still growing, strong parallels are being found between relationships with ELS and with MDD. Particularly, both literatures highlight decreased hippocampal volumes, find mixed evidence related to amygdala volumes, and provide strong evidence for elevated amygdala reactivity. Furthermore, while many studies have focused on the amygdala and hippocampus a priori, recently more whole-brain examinations have been conducted. This is important both for hypothesis generation and to create a more holistic understanding of neural alterations associated with ELS and MDD.

Finally, we addressed data that have explicitly examined some facet of an ELS-cortisol-brain-MDD mechanism. There is a small but growing body of work either that ELS may account for depression-related differences in the brain or that more directly examine cortisol as a mediator between ELS and the brain and/or the brain as a mediator between ELS and pathology. While much of this work relies on temporal precedence to establish directionality, it does begin to provide evidence for aspects of the mechanisms outlined in Figure 20.1. Furthermore, it appears that a variety of studies have the data available but have not examined mediation and moderation effects that can help build our understandings of the causal relationships between ELS, cortisol, brain structure/function, and depression. Given the ease and accessibility of testing a variety of models (e.g., Hayes, 2012, 2013), this should be pursued more frequently, particularly when longitudinal data are available, in order to establish stronger mechanistic understandings linking early life stress to depression.

Future studies of ELS and MDD on brain structure and function should also consider sex as a potential moderator variable, as suggested by the National Institutes of Health for preclinical research (https://orwh.od.nih.gov/resources/pdf/NOT-OD-15-102_Guidance.pdf). While there is evidence for sex differences in MDD risk as well as brain structural development in the current literature (e.g., Giedd, Blumenthal, Jeffries, Castellanos et al., 1999; Giedd, Blumenthal, Jeffries, Rajapakse et al., 1999; Lenroot et al., 2007), sex has not been consistently tested a moderator in studies relating ELS or MDD to the brain and thus may contribute to potential file drawer problems in this field as well as limiting exploration of sex-specific mechanisms for depression risk.

Neuroimaging provides many valuable tools for examining the effects of early life stress and potential neural mechanisms by which stress contributes to risk for mental health disorders. As investigators begin to use larger and more heterogeneous samples and start to contribute to collaborative efforts, such as ENIGMA, the field will be able reduce false positives and negatives in this literature and to detect increasingly nuanced effects. This can similarly be useful in establishing neural signatures that are specific to or common across various types of psychopathology, as has begun to be examined recently for brain structure in children/adolescents (Gold, Brotman, et al., 2016). Further, more heterogeneous samples could aid in parsing potential differential effects of different types of ELS on the brain or in identifying particular developmental periods where the brain is most sensitive to the toxic effects of stress. Further, methodological advances continue to increase the reliability, sensitivity, and specificity of neuroimaging findings in understanding these critical mechanisms. Overall, the neuroimaging field continues to hone in on mechanisms ELS impacts—brain structure, function, and connectivity—and how this contributes to risk for mental illness.

Acknowledgments

Sections of this review have been adapted from Pagliaccio, D., & Barch, D. M. (2016), Early life adversity and risk for depression: Alterations in cortisol and brain structure and function as mediating mechanisms. In *Systems Neuroscience in Depression* (pp. 29–77).

References

Alexander, A. L., Lee, J. E., Lazar, M., & Field, A. S. (2007). Diffusion tensor imaging of the brain. *Neurotherapeutics*, *4*(3), 316–329.

Andela, C. D., van Haalen, F. M., Ragnarsson, O., Papakokkinou, E., Johannsson, G., Santos, A., . . . Pereira, A. M. (2015). Mechanisms in endocrinology: Cushing's syndrome causes irreversible effects on the human brain: A systematic review of structural and functional magnetic resonance imaging studies. *European Journal of Endocrinology*, *173*(1), R1–R14. http://doi.org/10.1530/EJE-14-1101

Andersen, S. L., Tomada, A., Vincow, E. S., Valente, E., Polcari, A., & Teicher, M. H. (2008). Preliminary evidence for sensitive periods in the effect of childhood sexual abuse on regional brain development. *The Journal of Neuropsychiatry and Clinical Neurosciences*, *20*(3), 292–301. http://doi.org/10.1176/jnp.2008.20.3.292

Baker, L. M., Williams, L. M., Korgaonkar, M. S., Cohen, R. A., Heaps, J. M., & Paul, R. H. (2012). Impact of early vs. late childhood early life stress on brain morphometrics. *Brain Imaging and Behavior*. http://doi.org/10.1007/s11682-012-9215-y

Barch, D., Pagliaccio, D., Belden, A., Harms, M. P., Gaffrey, M., Sylvester, C. M.,…Luby, J. (2016). Effect of hippocampal and amygdala connectivity on the relationship between preschool poverty and school-age depression. *American Journal of Psychiatry*, *173*(6), 625–634. http://doi.org/10.1176/appi.ajp.2015.15081014

Belsky, J., & Pluess, M. (2009). Beyond diathesis stress: Differential susceptibility to environmental influences. *Psychological Bulletin*, *135*(6), 885–908.

Bick, J., Fox, N., Zeanah, C., & Nelson, C. A. (2017). Early deprivation, atypical brain development, and internalizing symptoms in late childhood. *Neuroscience*, *342*, 140–153. http://doi.org/10.1016/j.neuroscience.2015.09.026

Biswal, B., Zerrin Yetkin, F., Haughton, V. M., & Hyde, J. S. (1995). Functional connectivity in the motor cortex of resting human brain using echo-planar MRI. *Magnetic resonance in medicine*, *34*(4), 537–541.

Blood, A. J., Iosifescu, D. V., Makris, N., Perlis, R. H., Kennedy, D. N., Dougherty, D. D.,…Calhoun, J. (2010). Microstructural abnormalities in subcortical reward circuitry of subjects with major depressive disorder. *PLoS ONE*, *5*(11), e13945. http://doi.org/10.1371/journal.pone.0013945

Bogdan, R., Pagliaccio, D., Baranger, D. A., & Hariri, A. R. (2016). Genetic moderation of stress effects on corticolimbic circuitry. *Neuropsychopharmacology*, *41*(1), 275–296. http://doi.org/10.1038/npp.2015.216

Bogdan, R., Williamson, D. E., & Hariri, A. R. (2012). Mineralocorticoid receptor iso/val (rs5522) genotype moderates the association between previous childhood emotional neglect and amygdala reactivity. *The American Journal of Psychiatry*, *169*(5), 515–522.

Bora, E., Fornito, A., Pantelis, C., & Yücel, M. (2012). Gray matter abnormalities in major depressive disorder: A meta-analysis of voxel based morphometry studies. *Journal of Affective Disorders*, *138*(1–2), 9–18. http://doi.org/10.1016/j.jad.2011.03.049

Boyce, W. T., & Ellis, B. J. (2005). Biological sensitivity to context: I. An evolutionary-developmental theory of the origins and functions of stress reactivity. *Development and Psychopathology*, *17*(2), 271–301.

Bracht, T., Linden, D., & Keedwell, P. (2015). A review of white matter microstructure alterations of pathways of the reward circuit in depression. *Journal of Affective Disorders*, *187*, 45–53. http://doi.org/10.1016/j.jad.2015.06.041

Brain Development Cooperative Group. (2012). Total and regional brain volumes in a population-based normative sample from 4 to 18 years: The NIH MRI Study of Normal Brain Development. *Cerebral Cortex*, *22*(1), 1–12. http://doi.org/10.1093/cercor/bhr018

Bremner, J. D., Vythilingam, M., Vermetten, E., Southwick, S. M., McGlashan, T., Nazeer, A.,…Ng, C. K. (2003). MRI and PET study of deficits in hippocampal structure and function in women with childhood sexual abuse and posttraumatic stress disorder. *The American Journal of Psychiatry*, *160*(5), 924–932. http://doi.org/10.1176/appi.ajp.160.5.924

Brown, E. S., Woolston, D. J., & Frol, A. B. (2008). Amygdala volume in patients receiving chronic corticosteroid therapy. *Biological Psychiatry*, *63*(7), 705–709. http://doi.org/10.1016/j.biopsych.2007.09.014

Burghy, C. A., Stodola, D. E., Ruttle, P. L., Molloy, E. K., Armstrong, J. M., Oler, J. A.,…Davidson, R. J. (2012). Developmental pathways to amygdala-prefrontal function and internalizing symptoms in adolescence. *Nature Neuroscience*, *15*, 1736–1741. http://doi.org/10.1038/nn.3257

Busso, D. S., McLaughlin, K. A., Brueck, S., Peverill, M., Gold, A. L., & Sheridan, M. A. (2017). Child abuse, neural structure, and adolescent psychopathology: A longitudinal study. *Journal of the American Academy of Child & Adolescent Psychiatry*, *56*(4), 321–328.e1. http://doi.org/10.1016/j.jaac.2017.01.013

Butterworth, P., Cherbuin, N., Sachdev, P., & Anstey, K. J. (2012). The association between financial hardship and amygdala and hippocampal volumes: Results from the PATH through life project. *Social Cognitive and Affective Neuroscience*, *7*(5), 548–556. http://doi.org/10.1093/scan/nsr027

Campbell, S., Marriott, M., Nahmias, C., & MacQueen, G. M. (2004). Lower hippocampal volume in patients suffering from depression: A meta-analysis. *The American Journal of Psychiatry*, *161*(4), 598–607. http://doi.org/10.1176/appi.ajp.161.4.598

Carballedo, A., Lisiecka, D., Fagan, A., Saleh, K., Ferguson, Y., Connolly, G.,…Frodl, T. (2012). Early life adversity is associated with brain changes in subjects at family risk for depression. *The World Journal of Biological Psychiatry: The Official Journal of the World Federation of Societies of Biological Psychiatry*, *13*(8), 569–578. http://doi.org/10.3109/15622975.2012.661079

Carpenter, L. L., Carvalho, J. P., Tyrka, A. R., Wier, L. M., Mello, A. F., Mello, M. F.,…Price, L. H. (2007). Decreased adrenocorticotropic hormone and cortisol responses to stress in healthy adults reporting significant childhood maltreatment. *Biological Psychiatry*, *62*(10), 1080–1087. http://doi.org/10.1016/j.biopsych.2007.05.002

Carpenter, L. L., Shattuck, T. T., Tyrka, A. R., Geracioti, T. D., & Price, L. H. (2011). Effect of childhood physical abuse on cortisol stress response. *Psychopharmacology*, *214*(1), 367–375. http://doi.org/10.1007/s00213-010-2007-4

Caspi, A., Sugden, K., Moffitt, T. E., Taylor, A., Craig, I. W., Harrington, H.,…Poulton, R. (2003). Influence of life stress on depression: Moderation by a polymorphism in the 5-HTT gene. *Science*, *301*(5631), 386–389. http://doi.org/10.1126/science.1083968

Cavanagh, J., Krishnadas, R., Batty, G. D., Burns, H., Deans, K. A., Ford, I.,…Sattar, N. (2013). Socioeconomic status and the cerebellar grey matter volume. Data from a well-characterised population sample. *Cerebellum (London, England)*, *12*(6), 882–891. http://doi.org/10.1007/s12311-013-0497-4

Chaney, A., Carballedo, A., Amico, F., Fagan, A., Skokauskas, N., Meaney, J., & Frodl, T. (2014). Effect of childhood maltreatment on brain structure in adult patients with major depressive disorder and healthy participants. *Journal of Psychiatry & Neuroscience: JPN*, *39*(1), 50–59. http://doi.org/10.1503/jpn.120208

Choi, J., Jeong, B., Rohan, M. L., Polcari, A. M., & Teicher, M. H. (2009). Preliminary evidence for white matter tract abnormalities in young adults exposed to parental verbal abuse. *Biological Psychiatry*, *65*(3), 227–234. http://doi.org/10.1016/j.biopsych.2008.06.022

Cicchetti, D. (2009). Neuroendocrine functioning in maltreated children. In D. Cicchetti & E. F. Walker (Eds.), Neurodevelopmental Mechanisms in Psychopathology (pp. 345–365). Cambridge, UK: Cambridge University Press. http://doi.org/10.1017/CBO9780511546365.016

Cicchetti, D., & Rogosch, F. A. (2001). The impact of child maltreatment and psychopathology on neuroendocrine functioning. *Development and Psychopathology*, 13(4), 783–804. Retrieved from http://eutils.ncbi.nlm.nih.gov/entrez/eutils/elink.fcgi?dbfrom=pubmed&id=11771908&retmode=ref&cmd=prlinks

Cohen, R. A., Grieve, S., Hoth, K. F., Paul, R. H., & Sweet, L. (2006). Early life stress and morphometry of the adult anterior cingulate cortex and caudate nuclei. *Biological Psychiatry*, 59(10), 975-982.

Cohen, S., Kessler, R. C., & Gordon, L. U. (1997). Measuring stress: A guide for health and social scientists. *Oxford, UK*: Oxford University Press.

Colle, R., Segawa, T., Chupin, M., Dong, M. N. T. K. T., Hardy, P., Falissard, B.,...Corruble, E. (2017). Early life adversity is associated with a smaller hippocampus in male but not female depressed in-patients: A case– control study. BMC psychiatry, 17(1), 71. http://doi.org/10.1186/s12888-017-1233-2

Collishaw, S., Pickles, A., Messer, J., Rutter, M., Shearer, C., & Maughan, B. (2007). Resilience to adult psychopathology following childhood maltreatment: Evidence from a community sample. *Child Abuse & Neglect*, 31(3), 211–229. http://doi.org/10.1016/j.chiabu.2007.02.004

Colton, C. W., & Manderscheid, R. W. (2006). Congruencies in increased mortality rates, years of potential life lost, and causes of death among public mental health clients in eight states. *Preventing Chronic Disease*, 3(2), A42.

Conrad, C. D. C., LeDoux, J. E. J., Magariños, A. M. A., & McEwen, B. S. B. (1999). Repeated restraint stress facilitates fear conditioning independently of causing hippocampal CA3 dendritic atrophy. *Behavioral Neuroscience*, 113(5), 902–913.

Cooney, R. E., Joormann, J., Eugène, F., Dennis, E. L., & Gotlib, I. H. (2010). Neural correlates of rumination in depression. *Cognitive, Affective, & Behavioral Neuroscience*, 10(4), 470–478. http://doi.org/10.3758/CABN.10.4.470

Costello, E. J., Mustillo, S., Erkanli, A., Keeler, G., & Angold, A. (2003). Prevalence and development of psychiatric disorders in childhood and adolescence. *Archives of General Psychiatry*, 60(8), 837–844. http://doi.org/10.1001/archpsyc.60.8.837

Culverhouse, R. C., Saccone, N. L., Horton, A. C., Ma, Y., Anstey, K. J., Banaschewski, T., Burmeister, M.,...Goldman, N. (2017). Collaborative meta-analysis finds no evidence of a strong interaction between stress and 5-HTTLPR genotype contributing to the development of depression. *Molecular Psychiatry*. http://doi.org/10.1038/mp.2017.44

Dahmen, B., Puetz, V. B., Scharke, W., Polier, von, G. G., Herpertz-Dahlmann, B., & Konrad, K. (2017). Effects of early-life adversity on hippocampal structures and associated HPA axis functions. *Developmental Neuroscience*. 23(1), 133 http://doi.org/10.1159/000484238

Dannlowski, U., Stuhrmann, A., Beutelmann, V., Zwanzger, P., Lenzen, T., Grotegerd, D.,...Lindner, C. (2011). Limbic scars: Long-term consequences of childhood maltreatment revealed by functional and structural magnetic resonance imaging. *Biological Psychiatry*, 71(4), 286-293. http://doi.org/10.1016/j.biopsych.2011.10.021

De Brito, S. A., Viding, E., Sebastian, C. L., Kelly, P. A., Mechelli, A., Maris, H., & McCrory, E. J. (2013). Reduced orbitofrontal and temporal grey matter in a community sample of maltreated children. *Journal of Child Psychology and Psychiatry*, 54(1), 105–112. http://doi.org/10.1111/j.1469-7610.2012.02597.x

Di Iorio, C., Carey, C. E., Michalski, L. J., Corral-Frias, N. S., Conley, E. D., Hariri, A. R., & Bogdan, R. (2017). Hypothalamic-pituitary-adrenal axis genetic variation and early stress moderates amygdala function. *Psychoneuroendocrinology*, 80, 170–178. http://doi.org/10.1016/j.psyneuen.2017.03.016

Diener, C., Kuehner, C., Brusniak, W., Ubl, B., Wessa, M., & Flor, H. (2012). A meta-analysis of neurofunctional imaging studies of emotion and cognition in major depression. *NeuroImage*, 1–40. http://doi.org/10.1016/j.neuroimage.2012.04.005

Driessen, E., Van, H. L., Don, F. J., Peen, J., Kool, S., Westra, D.,...Dekker, J. J. (2013). The efficacy of cognitive-behavioral therapy and psychodynamic therapy in the outpatient treatment of major depression: A randomized clinical trial. *American Journal of Psychiatry*, 170(9), 1041–1050. http://doi.org/10.1176/appi.ajp.2013.12070899

Driessen, M., Herrmann, J., Stahl, K., Zwaan, M., Meier, S., Hill, A.,...Petersen, D. (2000). Magnetic resonance imaging volumes of the hippocampus and the amygdala in women with borderline personality disorder and early traumatization. *Archives of General Psychiatry*, 57(12), 1115–1122.

Edmiston, E. E., Wang, F., Mazure, C. M., Guiney, J., Sinha, R., Mayes, L. C., & Blumberg, H. P. (2011). Corticostriatal-limbic gray matter morphology in adolescents with self-reported exposure to childhood maltreatment. *Archives of Pediatrics & Adolescent Medicine*, 165(12), 1069–1077. http://doi.org/10.1001/archpediatrics.2011.565

Eluvathingal, T. J., Chugani, H. T., Behen, M. E., Juhász, C., Muzik, O., Maqbool, M.,...Makki, M. (2006). Abnormal brain connectivity in children after early severe socio-emotional deprivation: A diffusion tensor imaging study, Pediatrics. 117(6), 2093–2100. http://doi.org/10.1542/peds.2005-1727

Fani, N., Gutman, D., Tone, E. B., Almli, L., Mercer, K. B., Davis, J.,...Zamanyan, A. (2013). FKBP5 and attention bias for threat associations with hippocampal function and shape: FKBP5 and attention bias for threat. *JAMA Psychiatry*, 70(4), 392–400. http://doi.org/10.1001/2013.jamapsychiatry.210

Fava, M., & Davidson, K. G. (1996). Definition and epidemiology of treatment-resistant depression. *The Psychiatric Clinics of North America*, 19(2), 179–200.

Fernald, L. C. H., & Gunnar, M. R. (2009). Poverty-alleviation program participation and salivary cortisol in very low-income children. *Social Science & Medicine*, 68(12), 2180–2189. http://doi.org/10.1016/j.socscimed.2009.03.032

Fitzgerald, P. B., Laird, A. R., Maller, J., & Daskalakis, Z. J. (2008). A meta-analytic study of changes in brain activation in depression. *Human Brain Mapping*, 29(6), 683–695. http://doi.org/10.1002/hbm.20426

Frodl, T., Carballedo, A., Fagan, A. J., Lisiecka, D., Ferguson, Y., & Meaney, J. F. (2012). Effects of early-life adversity on white matter diffusivity changes in patients at risk for major depression. *Journal of Psychiatry & Neuroscience*, 37(1), 37–45. http://doi.org/10.1503/jpn.110028

Frodl, T., Janowitz, D., Schmaal, L., Tozzi, L., Dobrowolny, H., Stein, D. J.,...Block, A. (2017). Childhood adversity impacts on brain subcortical structures relevant to depression. *Journal of Psychiatric Research, 86*, 58–65. http://doi.org/10.1016/j.jpsychires.2016.11.010

Frodl, T., Reinhold, E., Koutsouleris, N., Reiser, M., & Meisenzahl, E. M. (2010). Interaction of childhood stress with hippocampus and prefrontal cortex volume reduction in major depression. *Journal of Psychiatric Research, 44*(13), 799–807. http://doi.org/10.1016/j.jpsychires.2010.01.006

Ganella, D. E., Allen, N. B., Simmons, J. G., Schwartz, O., Kim, J. H., Sheeber, L., & Whittle, S. (2015). Early life stress alters pituitary growth during adolescence—a longitudinal study. *Psychoneuroendocrinology, 53*, 185–194. http://doi.org/10.1016/j.psyneuen.2015.01.005

Ganzel, B. L., Kim, P., Gilmore, H., Tottenham, N., & Temple, E. (2013). Stress and the healthy adolescent brain: Evidence for the neural embedding of life events. *Development and Psychopathology, 25*(4pt1), 879–889. http://doi.org/10.1017/S0954579413000242

Gee, D. G., Gabard-Durnam, L. J., Flannery, J., Goff, B., Humphreys, K. L., Telzer, E. H.,…Tottenham, N. (2013). Early developmental emergence of human amygdala prefrontal connectivity after maternal deprivation. *Proceedings of the National Academy of Sciences of the United States of America, 110*(39), 15638–15643. http://doi.org/10.2307/42713387?ref=search-gateway:5df458019d31b0bde9c8d33c0962e965

Giedd, J. N., Blumenthal, J., Jeffries, N. O., Castellanos, F. X., Liu, H., Zijdenbos, A.,…Rapoport, J. L. (1999). Brain development during childhood and adolescence: A longitudinal MRI study. *Nature Neuroscience, 2*(10), 861–863. http://doi.org/10.1038/13158

Giedd, J. N., Blumenthal, J., Jeffries, N. O., Rajapakse, J. C., Vaituzis, A. C., Liu, H.,…Castellanos, F. X. (1999). Development of the human corpus callosum during childhood and adolescence: A longitudinal MRI study. *Progress in Neuropsychopharmacology & Biological Psychiatry, 23*(4), 571–588.

Giedd, J. N., Vaituzis, A. C., Hamburger, S. D., Lange, N., Rajapakse, J. C., Kaysen, D.,…Rapoport, J. L. (1996). Quantitative MRI of the temporal lobe, amygdala, and hippocampus in normal human development: Ages 4–18 years. *The Journal of Comparative Neurology, 366*(2), 223–230.

Gilbertson, M. W., Shenton, M. E., Ciszewski, A., Kasai, K., Lasko, N. B., Orr, S. P., & Pitman, R. K. (2002). Smaller hippocampal volume predicts pathologic vulnerability to psychological trauma. *Nature Neuroscience, 5*(11), 1242–1247. http://doi.org/10.1038/nn958

Gilman, S. E., Kawachi, I., Fitzmaurice, G. M., & Buka, L. (2003). Socio-economic status, family disruption and residential stability in childhood: Relation to onset, recurrence and remission of major depression. *Psychological Medicine, 33*(8), 1341–1355.

Gilman, S. E., Kawachi, I., Fitzmaurice, G. M., & Buka, S. L. (2002). Socioeconomic status in childhood and the lifetime risk of major depression. *International Journal of Epidemiology, 31*(2), 359–367. http://doi.org/10.1016/j.appdev.2008.12.029

Goff, B., & Tottenham, N. (2015). Early-life adversity and adolescent depression: Mechanisms involving the ventral striatum. *CNS Spectrums, 20*(4), 337–345. http://doi.org/10.1017/S1092852914000674

Goff, B., Gee, D. G., Telzer, E. H., Humphreys, K. L., Gabard-Durnam, L., Flannery, J., & Tottenham, N. (2012). Reduced nucleus accumbens reactivity and adolescent depression

following early-life stress. *Neuroscience*, 129–138. http://doi.org/10.1016/j.neuroscience.2012.12.010

Gold, A. L., Brotman, M. A., Adleman, N. E., Lever, S. N., Steuber, E. R., Fromm, S. J.,…Leibenluft, E. (2016). Comparing brain morphometry across multiple childhood psychiatric disorders. *Journal of the American Academy of Child & Adolescent Psychiatry, 55*(12), 1027–1037.e3. http://doi.org/10.1016/j.jaac.2016.08.008

Gold, A. L., Sheridan, M. A., Peverill, M., Busso, D. S., Lambert, H. K., Alves, S.,…McLaughlin, K. A. (2016). Childhood abuse and reduced cortical thickness in brain regions involved in emotional processing. *Journal of Child Psychology and Psychiatry, 57*(10), 1154–1164. http://doi.org/10.1371/journal.pone.0093432

Golier, J. A., Yehuda, R., De Santi, S., Segal, S., Dolan, S., & de Leon, M. J. (2005). Absence of hippocampal volume differences in survivors of the Nazi Holocaust with and without posttraumatic stress disorder. *Psychiatry Research, 139*(1), 53–64. http://doi.org/10.1016/j.pscychresns.2005.02.007

Gorka, A. X., Hanson, J. L., Radtke, S. R., & Hariri, A. R. (2014). Reduced hippocampal and medial prefrontal gray matter mediate the association between reported childhood maltreatment and trait anxiety in adulthood and predict sensitivity to future life stress. *Biology of Mood & Anxiety Disorders, 4*, 12. http://doi.org/10.1186/2045-5380-4-12

Grabe, H. J., Wittfeld, K., Van der Auwera, S., Janowitz, D., Hegenscheid, K., Habes, M.,…Völzke, H. (2016). Effect of the interaction between childhood abuse and rs1360780 of the FKBP5 gene on gray matter volume in a general population sample. *Human Brain Mapping, 37*(4), 1602–1613. http://doi.org/10.1002/hbm.23123

Grant, M. M., Cannistraci, C., Hollon, S. D., Gore, J., & Shelton, R. (2011). Childhood trauma history differentiates amygdala response to sad faces within MDD. *Journal of Psychiatric Research, 45*(7), 886–895. http://doi.org/10.1016/j.jpsychires.2010.12.004

Green, J. G., McLaughlin, K. A., Berglund, P. A., Gruber, M. J., Sampson, N. A., Zaslavsky, A. M., & Kessler, R. C. (2010). Childhood adversities and adult psychiatric disorders in the national comorbidity survey replication I: Associations with first onset of DSM-IV disorders. *Archives of General Psychiatry, 67*(2), 113–123. http://doi.org/10.1001/archgenpsychiatry.2009.186

Gunnar, M. R., & Vazquez, D. M. (2001). Low cortisol and a flattening of expected daytime rhythm: Potential indices of risk in human development. *Development and Psychopathology, 13*(3), 515–538. Retrieved from http://eutils.ncbi.nlm.nih.gov/entrez/eutils/elink.fcgi?dbfrom=pubmed&id=11523846&retmode=ref&cmd=prlinks

Hair, N. L., Hanson, J. L., Wolfe, B. L., & Pollak, S. D. (2015). Association of child poverty, brain development, and academic achievement. *JAMA Pediatrics, 169*(9), 822–829. http://doi.org/10.1001/jamapediatrics.2015.1475

Hajek, T., Kopecek, M., Kozeny, J., Gunde, E., Alda, M., & Höschl, C. (2009). Amygdala volumes in mood disorders—meta-analysis of magnetic resonance volumetry studies. *Journal of Affective Disorders, 115*(3), 395–410. http://doi.org/10.1016/j.jad.2008.10.007

Hamilton, J. P., Etkin, A., Furman, D. J., Lemus, M. G., Johnson, R. F., & Gotlib, I. H. (2012). Functional neuroimaging of major depressive disorder: A meta-analysis and new integration of baseline activation and neural response data. *The American Journal of Psychiatry, 169*(7), 693–703.

Hammen, C. (1991). Generation of stress in the course of unipolar depression. *Journal of Abnormal Psychology, 100*(4), 555–561.

Hankin, B. L. (2005). Childhood maltreatment and psychopathology: Prospective tests of attachment, cognitive vulnerability, and stress as mediating processes. *Cognitive Therapy and Research.* 29(6), 645-671.

Hanson, J. L., Chandra, A., Wolfe, B. L., & Pollak, S. D. (2011). Association between income and the hippocampus. *PLoS ONE, 6*(5), e18712. http://doi.org/10.1371/journal.pone.0018712

Hanson, J. L., Chung, M. K., Avants, B. B., Shirtcliff, E. A., Gee, J. C., Davidson, R. J., & Pollak, S. D. (2010). Early stress is associated with alterations in the orbitofrontal cortex: A tensor-based morphometry investigation of brain structure and behavioral risk. *Journal of Neuroscience, 30*(22), 7466–7472. http://doi.org/10.1523/JNEUROSCI.0859-10.2010

Hanson, J. L., Nacewicz, B. M., Sutterer, M. J., Cayo, A. A., Schaefer, S. M., Rudolph, K. D.,...Davidson, R. J. (2015). Behavioral problems after early life stress: contributions of the hippocampus and amygdala. Biological psychiatry. *Biological Psychiatry, 77*(4), 314–323. http://doi.org/10.1016/j.biopsych.2014.04.020

Hardt, J., & Rutter, M. (2004). Validity of adult retrospective reports of adverse childhood experiences: review of the evidence. *Journal of Child Psychology and Psychiatry, and Allied Disciplines, 45*(2), 260–273. Retrieved from http://doi.wiley.com/10.1111/j.1469-7610.2004.00218.x

Harkness, K. L., Bruce, A. E., & Lumley, M. N. (2006). The role of childhood abuse and neglect in the sensitization to stressful life events in adolescent depression. *Journal of Abnormal Psychology* 115(4), 730.

Hayes, A. F. (2009). Beyond Baron and Kenny: Statistical mediation analysis in the new millennium. *Communication Monographs, 76*(4), 408–420. http://doi.org/10.1080/03637750903310360

Hayes, A. F. (2012). PROCESS: A versatile computational tool for observed variable mediation, moderation, and conditional process modeling. *[White paper]. Retrieved from http://www.afhayes.com/public/process2012.pdf.*

Hayes, A. F. (2013). *Introduction to mediation, moderation, and conditional process analysis.* New York, NY: Guilford Press.

Heim, C., & Nemeroff, C. B. (2001). The role of childhood trauma in the neurobiology of mood and anxiety disorders: Preclinical and clinical studies. *Biological Psychiatry, 49*(12), 1023–1039.

Heim, C., Newport, D. J., Heit, S., Graham, Y. P., Wilcox, M., Bonsall, R.,...Nemeroff, C. B. (2000). Pituitary-adrenal and autonomic responses to stress in women after sexual and physical abuse in childhood. *JAMA: The Journal of the American Medical Association, 284*(5), 592–597. Retrieved from http://archneur.jamanetwork.com/article.aspx?articleid=192947

Heuser, I., Yassouridis, A., & Holsboer, F. (1994). The combined dexamethasone/CRH test: A refined laboratory test for psychiatric disorders. *Journal of Psychiatric Research, 28*(4), 341–356. http://doi.org/10.1016/0022-3956(94)90017-5

Holsboer, F., & Barden, N. (1996). Antidepressants and hypothalamic-pituitary-adrenocortical regulation. *Endocrine Reviews, 17*(2), 187–205.

Holz, N. E., Boecker, R., Hohm, E., Zohsel, K., Buchmann, A. F., Blomeyer, D.,...Plichta, M. M. (2015). The long-term impact of early life poverty on orbitofrontal cortex volume in adulthood: Results from a prospective study over 25 years. *Neuropsychopharmacology, 40*(4), 996–1004. http://doi.org/10.1038/npp.2014.277

Hovens, J. G. F. M., Giltay, E. J., Wiersma, J. E., Spinhoven, P., Penninx, B. W. J. H., & Zitman, F. G. (2012). Impact of childhood life events and trauma on the course of depressive and anxiety disorders. *Acta Psychiatrica Scandinavica, 126*(3), 198–207. http://doi.org/10.1111/j.1600-0447.2011.01828.x

Hsu, D. T., Langenecker, S. A., Kennedy, S. E., Zubieta, J.-K., & Heitzeg, M. M. (2010). fMRI BOLD responses to negative stimuli in the prefrontal cortex are dependent on levels of recent negative life stress in major depressive disorder. *Psychiatry Research, 183*(3), 202–208. http://doi.org/10.1016/j.pscychresns.2009.12.002

Huang, H., Fan, X., Williamson, D. E., & Rao, U. (2011). White matter changes in healthy adolescents at familial risk for unipolar depression: A diffusion tensor imaging study. *Neuropsychopharmacology, 36*(3), 684–691. http://doi.org/10.1038/npp.2010.199

Isgor, C., Kabbaj, M., Akil, H., & Watson, S. J. (2004). Delayed effects of chronic variable stress during peripubertal-juvenile period on hippocampal morphology and on cognitive and stress axis functions in rats. *Hippocampus, 14*(5), 636–648. http://doi.org/10.1002/hipo.10207

Iwabuchi, S. J., Krishnadas, R., Li, C., Auer, D. P., Radua, J., & Palaniyappan, L. (2015). Localized connectivity in depression: A meta-analysis of resting state functional imaging studies. *Neuroscience & Biobehavioral Reviews, 51*, 77–86. http://doi.org/10.1016/j.neubiorev.2015.01.006

Jackowski, A. P., Douglas-Palumberi, H., Jackowski, M., Win, L., Schultz, R. T., Staib, L. W.,...Kaufman, J. (2008). Corpus callosum in maltreated children with posttraumatic stress disorder: A diffusion tensor imaging study. *Psychiatry Research, 162*(3), 256–261. http://doi.org/10.1016/j.pscychresns.2007.08.006

Jacobson, L., & Sapolsky, R. (1991). The role of the hippocampus in feedback regulation of the hypothalamic-pituitary-adrenocortical axis. *Endocrine Reviews, 12*(2), 118–134.

Jednoróg, K., Altarelli, I., Monzalvo, K., Fluss, J., Dubois, J., Billard, C.,...Ramus, F. (2012). The influence of socioeconomic status on children's brain structure. *PLoS ONE, 7*(8), e42486. http://doi.org/10.1371/journal.pone.0042486

Jenkins, J. V., Woolley, D. P., Hooper, S. R., & De Bellis, M. D. (2013). Direct and indirect effects of brain volume, socioeconomic status and family stress on child IQ. *Journal of Child and Adolescent Behavior, 1*(2).1000107.

Kaiser, R. H., Andrews-Hanna, J. R., & Wager, T. D. (2015). Large-scale network dysfunction in major depressive disorder: A meta-analysis of resting-state functional connectivity. *JAMA psychiatry, 72*(6), 603-611.

Kassem, M. S., Lagopoulos, J., Stait-Gardner, T., Price, W. S., Chohan, T. W., Arnold, J. C.,...Bennett, M. R. (2012). Stress-induced grey matter loss determined by MRI is primarily due to loss of dendrites and their synapses. *Molecular Neurobiology.* 47(2), 645-661. http://doi.org/10.1007/s12035-012-8365-7

Kaufman, J., Birmaher, B., Perel, J., Dahl, R. E., Moreci, P., Nelson, B., Wells, W., & Ryan, N. D. (1997). The corticotropin-releasing hormone challenge in depressed abused, depressed nonabused, and normal control children. *Biological Psychiatry, 42*(8), 669–679. http://doi.org/10.1016/S0006-3223(96)00470-2

Kelly, P. A., Viding, E., Puetz, V. B., Palmer, A. L., Mechelli, A., Pingault, J. B.,...McCrory, E. J. (2015). Sex differences in socioemotional functioning, attentional bias, and gray matter volume in maltreated children: A multilevel investigation. *Development and Psychopathology*, *27*(4 Pt 2), 1591–1609. http://doi.org/10.1017/S0954579415000966

Kelly, P. A., Viding, E., Puetz, V. B., Palmer, A. L., Samuel, S., & McCrory, E. J. (2016). The sexually dimorphic impact of maltreatment on cortical thickness, surface area and gyrification. *Journal of Neural Transmission*, *123*(9), 1069–1083. http://doi.org/10.1007/s00702-016-1523-8

Kendler, K. S., Karkowski, L. M., & Prescott, C. A. (1999). Causal relationship between stressful life events and the onset of major depression. *The American Journal of Psychiatry*, *156*(6), 837.

Kendler, K. S., Kessler, R. C., Walters, E. E., MacLean, C., Neale, M. C., Heath, A. C., & Eaves, L. J. (1995). Stressful life events, genetic liability, and onset of an episode of major depression in women. *The American Journal of Psychiatry*, *152*(6), 833–842.

Kendler, K. S., Kuhn, J. W., & Prescott, C. A. (2004). Childhood sexual abuse, stressful life events and risk for major depression in women. *Psychological Medicine*, *34*(8), 1475–1482.

Kessler, R. C., Davis, C. G., & Kendler, K. S. (1997). Childhood adversity and adult psychiatric disorder in the US National Comorbidity Survey. *Psychological Medicine*, *27*(5), 1101–1119. http://doi.org/10.1017/S0033291797005588

Kessler, R. C., & Magee, W. J. (2009). Childhood adversities and adult depression: Basic patterns of association in a US national survey. *Psychological Medicine*, *23*(3), 679. http://doi.org/10.1017/S0033291700025460

Kessler, R. C., Petukhova, M., & Sampson, N. A. (2012). Twelve-month and lifetime prevalence and lifetime morbid risk of anxiety and mood disorders in the United States. *Journal of Methods*. http://doi.org/10.1002/mpr.1359

Kim, P., Evans, G. W., Angstadt, M., Ho, S. S., Sripada, C. S., Swain, J. E.,...Phan, K. L. (2013). Effects of childhood poverty and chronic stress on emotion regulatory brain function in adulthood. *Proceedings of the National Academy of Sciences*, *110*(46), 18442–18447. http://doi.org/10.1073/pnas.1308240110

Koolschijn, P. C. M. P., van Haren, N. E. M., Lensvelt-Mulders, G. J. L. M., Hulshoff Pol, H. E., & Kahn, R. S. (2009). Brain volume abnormalities in major depressive disorder: A meta-analysis of magnetic resonance imaging studies. *Human Brain Mapping*, *30*(11), 3719–3735. http://doi.org/10.1002/hbm.20801

Lenroot, R. K., Gogtay, N., Greenstein, D. K., Wells, E. M., Wallace, G. L., Clasen, L. S.,...Thompson, P. M. (2007). Sexual dimorphism of brain developmental trajectories during childhood and adolescence. *NeuroImage*, *36*(4), 1065–1073. http://doi.org/10.1016/j.neuroimage.2007.03.053

Lenze, S. N., Xiong, C., & Sheline, Y. I. (2008). Childhood adversity predicts earlier onset of major depression but not reduced hippocampal volume. *Psychiatry Research*, *162*(1), 39–49. http://doi.org/10.1016/j.pscychresns.2007.04.004

Lieb, R., Isensee, B., Höfler, M., Pfister, H., & Wittchen, H. U. (2002). Parental major depression and the risk of depression and other mental disorders in offspring: A prospective-longitudinal community study. *Archives of General Psychiatry*, *59*(4), 365–374. Retrieved from http://eutils.ncbi.nlm.nih.gov/entrez/eutils/elink.fcgi?dbfrom=pubmed&id=11926937&retmode=ref&cmd=prlinks

Lim, L., Hart, H., Mehta, M., Worker, A., Simmons, A., Mirza, K., & Rubia, K. (2017). Grey matter volume and thickness abnormalities in young people with a history of childhood abuse. *Psychological Medicine*, 1–13. http://doi.org/10.1017/S0033291717002392

Lim, K. O., & Helpern, J. A. (2002). Neuropsychiatric applications of DTI–a review. NMR in Biomedicine: An International Journal Devoted to the Development and Application of Magnetic Resonance In Vivo, 15(7-8), 587–593.

Lindquist, M. A. (2008). The statistical analysis of fMRI data. *Statistical Science*, *23*(4), 439–464. http://doi.org/10.1214/09-STS282

Liu, R. T., & Alloy, L. B. (2010). Stress generation in depression: A systematic review of the empirical literature and recommendations for future study. *Clinical Psychology Review*, *30*(5), 582–593. http://doi.org/10.1016/j.cpr.2010.04.010

Luby, J., Belden, A., Botteron, K., Marrus, N., Harms, M. P., Babb, C.,...Barch, D. (2013). The effects of poverty on childhood brain development: The mediating effect of caregiving and stressful life events. *JAMA Pediatrics*, *167*(12), 1135–1142. http://doi.org/10.1001/jamapediatrics.2013.3139

Luby, J., Si, X., Belden, A., Tandon, M., & Spitznagel, E. (2009). Preschool depression: Homotypic continuity and course over 24 months. *Archives of General Psychiatry*, *66*(8), 897.

Luby, J. L., Heffelfinger, A. K., Mrakotsky, C., Brown, K. M., Hessler, M. J., Wallis, J. M., & Spitznagel, E. L. (2009). The clinical picture of depression in preschool children, Journal of the American Academy of Child & Adolescent Psychiatry 42(3), 340–348. http://doi.org/10.1097/00004583-200303000-00015

Luking, K. R., Pagliaccio, D., Luby, J. L., & Barch, D. M. (2016). Reward processing and risk for depression across development. *Trends in Cognitive Sciences*, *20*(6), 456–468. http://doi.org/10.1016/j.tics.2016.04.002

Lupien, S. J., Fiocco, A., Wan, N., Maheu, F., Lord, C., Schramek, T., & Tu, M. T. (2005). Stress hormones and human memory function across the lifespan. *Psychoneuroendocrinology*, *30*(3), 225–242. http://doi.org/10.1016/j.psyneuen.2004.08.003

Maciejewski, P. K., Prigerson, H. G., & Mazure, C. M. (2000). Self-efficacy as a mediator between stressful life events and depressive symptoms. Differences based on history of prior depression. *The British Journal of Psychiatry*, *176*, 373–378. Retrieved from http://eutils.ncbi.nlm.nih.gov/entrez/eutils/elink.fcgi?dbfrom=pubmed&id=10827887&retmode=ref&cmd=prlinks

MacMillan, H. L., Georgiades, K., Duku, E. K., Shea, A., Steiner, M., Niec, A.,...Walsh, C. A. (2009). Cortisol response to stress in female youths exposed to childhood maltreatment: Results of the youth mood project. *Biological Psychiatry*, *66*(1), 62–68. http://doi.org/10.1016/j.biopsych.2008.12.014

Magariños, A. M., McEwen, B. S., Flügge, G., & Fuchs, E. (1996). Chronic psychosocial stress causes apical dendritic atrophy of hippocampal CA3 pyramidal neurons in subordinate tree shrews. *The Journal of Neuroscience*, *16*(10), 3534–3540.

Mandell, D., Siegle, G. J., Shutt, L., Feldmiller, J., & Thase, M. E. (2014). Neural substrates of trait ruminations in depression. *Journal of Abnormal Psychology*, *123*(1), 35–48. http://doi.org/10.1037/a0035834

McKay, M. S., & Zakzanis, K. K. (2010). The impact of treatment on HPA axis activity in unipolar major depression.

Journal of Psychiatric Research, 44(3), 183–192. http://doi.org/10.1016/j.jpsychires.2009.07.012

McKinnon, M. C., Yucel, K., Nazarov, A., & MacQueen, G. M. (2009). A meta-analysis examining clinical predictors of hippocampal volume in patients with major depressive disorder. *Journal of Psychiatry & Neuroscience*, 34(1), 41–54.

McKittrick, C. R., Magariños, A. M., Blanchard, D. C., Blanchard, R. J., McEwen, B. S., & Sakai, R. R. (2000). Chronic social stress reduces dendritic arbors in CA3 of hippocampus and decreases binding to serotonin transporter sites. *Synapse*, 36(2), 85–94.

McLaughlin, K. A., Peverill, M., Gold, A. L., Alves, S., & Sheridan, M. A. (2015). Child maltreatment and neural systems underlying emotion regulation. *Journal of the American Academy of Child & Adolescent Psychiatry*, 54(9), 753–762. http://doi.org/10.1016/j.jaac.2015.06.010

McLaughlin, K. A., Sheridan, M. A., Gold, A. L., Duys, A., Lambert, H. K., Peverill, M.,…Pine, D. S. (2016). Maltreatment exposure, brain structure, and fear conditioning in children and adolescents, *Neuropsychopharmacology* 41(8), 1956–1964. http://doi.org/10.1038/npp.2015.365

Mehta, M. A., Golembo, N. I., Nosarti, C., Colvert, E., Mota, A., Williams, S. C. R.,…Sonuga-Barke, E. J. (2009). Amygdala, hippocampal and corpus callosum size following severe early institutional deprivation: The English and Romanian Adoptees study pilot. *Journal of Child Psychology and Psychiatry*, 50(8), 943–951. http://doi.org/10.1111/j.1469-7610.2009.02084.x

Merz, E. C., Tottenham, N., & Noble, K. G. (2017). Socioeconomic status, amygdala volume, and internalizing symptoms in children and adolescents. *Journal of Clinical Child & Adolescent Psychology*, 47(2), 312-323. http://doi.org/10.1080/15374416.2017.1326122

Michl, L. C., McLaughlin, K. A., Shepherd, K., & Nolen-Hoeksema, S. (2013). Rumination as a mechanism linking stressful life events to symptoms of depression and anxiety: Longitudinal evidence in early adolescents and adults. *Journal of Abnormal Psychology*, 122(2), 339–352. http://doi.org/10.1037/a0031994

Monroe, S. M., & Simons, A. D. (1991). Diathesis-stress theories in the context of life stress research: implications for the depressive disorders. *Psychological Bulletin*, 110(3), 406–425. Retrieved from http://psycnet.apa.org/journals/bul/110/3/406.html

Mulders, P. C., van Eijndhoven, P. F., & Schene, A. H. (2015). Resting-state functional connectivity in major depressive disorder: A review. *Neuroscience & Biobehavioral Reviews*, 56, 330-344.

Murphy, M. L., & Frodl, T. (2011). Meta-analysis of diffusion tensor imaging studiesshows altered fractional anisotropy occurring indistinct brain areas in association with depression. *Biology of Mood & Anxiety Disorders*, 1(1), 3. http://doi.org/10.1186/2045-5380-1-3

Noble, K. G., Houston, S. M., Kan, E., & Sowell, E. R. (2012). Neural correlates of socioeconomic status in the developing human brain. *Developmental Science*, 15(4), 516–527. http://doi.org/10.1111/j.1467-7687.2012.01147.x

Opel, N., Redlich, R., Zwanzger, P., Grotegerd, D., Arolt, V., Heindel, W.,…Dannlowski, U. (2014). Hippocampal atrophy in major depression: A function of childhood maltreatment rather than diagnosis? *Neuropsychopharmacology*, 39(12), 2723–2731. http://doi.org/10.1038/npp.2014.145

Pagliaccio, D., & Barch, D. M. (2016). Early life adversity and risk for depression: alterations in cortisol and brain structure and function as mediating mechanisms. In *Systems Neuroscience in Depression* (pp. 29–77).

Pagliaccio, D., Barch, D. M., Bogdan, R., Wood, P. K., Lynskey, M. T., Heath, A. C., & Agrawal, A. (2015). Shared predisposition in the association between Cannabis use and subcortical brain structure. *JAMA Psychiatry*, 72(10), 994–1001. http://doi.org/10.1001/jamapsychiatry.2015.1054

Pagliaccio, D., Luby, J. L., Bogdan, R., & Agrawal, A. (2015). HPA axis genetic variation, pubertal status, and sex interact to predict amygdala and hippocampus responses to negative emotional faces in school-age children. *NeuroImage*. 109, 1–11.

Pagliaccio, D., Luby, J. L., Bogdan, R., Agrawal, A., Gaffrey, M. S., Belden, A. C.,…Barch, D. M., (2013). Stress-system genes and life stress predict cortisol levels and amygdala and hippocampal volumes in children. *Neuropsychopharmacology*. http://doi.org/10.1038/npp.2013.327

Pagliaccio, D., Luby, J. L., Bogdan, R., Agrawal, A., Gaffrey, M. S., Belden, A. C.,…Barch, D. M., (2015). Amygdala functional connectivity, HPA axis genetic variation, and life stress in children and relations to anxiety and emotion regulation. *Journal of Abnormal Psychology*, 124(4), 817–833. http://doi.org/10.1037/abn0000094

Paul, R., Henry, L., Grieve, S. M., Guilmette, T. J., Niaura, R., Bryant, R.,…Gordon, E. (2008). The relationship between early life stress and microstructural integrity of the corpus callosum in a non-clinical population. *Neuropsychiatric Disease and Treatment*, 4(1), 193–201. Retrieved from /pmc/articles/PMC2515911/?report=abstract

Pederson, C. L., Maurer, S. H., Kaminski, P. L., Zander, K. A., Peters, C. M., Stokes-Crowe, L. A., & Osborn, R. E. (2004). Hippocampal volume and memory performance in a community-based sample of women with posttraumatic stress disorder secondary to child abuse. *Journal of Traumatic Stress*, 17(1), 37–40. http://doi.org/10.1023/B:JOTS.0000014674.84517.46

Philip, N. S., Tyrka, A. R., Albright, S. E., Sweet, L. H., Almeida, J., Price, L. H., & Carpenter, L. L. (2016). Early life stress predicts thalamic hyperconnectivity: A transdiagnostic study of global connectivity. *Journal of Psychiatric Research*, 79, 93–100. http://doi.org/10.1016/j.jpsychires.2016.05.003

Phillips, J. L., Batten, L. A., Tremblay, P., Aldosary, F., & Blier, P. (2015). A Prospective, longitudinal study of the effect of remission on cortical thickness and hippocampal volume in patients with treatment-resistant depression. *The International Journal of Neuropsychopharmacology*, 18(8). http://doi.org/10.1093/ijnp/pyv037

Pigott, H. E., Leventhal, A. M., Alter, G. S., & Boren, J. J. (2010). Efficacy and effectiveness of antidepressants: Current status of research. *Psychotherapy and Psychosomatics*, 79(5), 267–279. http://doi.org/10.1159/000318293

Piguet, C., Desseilles, M., Sterpenich, V., Cojan, Y., Bertschy, G., & Vuilleumier, P. (2014). *Neural substrates of rumination tendency in non-depressed individuals. Biological psychology*, 103, 195-202.. http://doi.org/10.1016/j.biopsycho.2014.09.005

Poldrack, R. A., Baker, C. I., Durnez, J., Gorgolewski, K. J., Matthews, P. M., Munafò, M. R.,…Yarkoni, T. (2017). Scanning the horizon: Towards transparent and reproducible neuroimaging research. *Nature Reviews Neuroscience*, 18(2), 115–126. http://doi.org/10.1038/nrn.2016.167

Rao, U., Chen, L.-A., Bidesi, A. S., Shad, M. U., Thomas, M. A., & Hammen, C. L. (2010). Hippocampal changes associated with early-life adversity and vulnerability to depression. *Biological Psychiatry*, *67*(4), 357–364. http://doi.org/10.1016/j.biopsych.2009.10.017

Rao, U., Hammen, C., Ortiz, L. R., Chen, L.-A., & Poland, R. E. (2008). Effects of early and recent adverse experiences on adrenal response to psychosocial stress in depressed adolescents. *Biological Psychiatry*, *64*(6), 521–526. http://doi.org/10.1016/j.biopsych.2008.05.012

Reagan, L. P., & McEwen, B. S. (1997). Controversies surrounding glucocorticoid-mediated cell death in the hippocampus. *Journal of Chemical Neuroanatomy*, *13*(3), 149–167.

Risch, N., Herrell, R., Lehner, T., Liang, K.-Y., Eaves, L., Hoh, J.,…Merikangas, K. R. (2009). Interaction between the serotonin transporter gene (5-HTTLPR), stressful life events, and risk of depression. *JAMA: The Journal of the American Medical Association*, *301*(23), 2462–2471.

Rudolph, K. D., & Flynn, M. (2007). Childhood adversity and youth depression: Influence of gender and pubertal status. *Development and Psychopathology*. 19(2) 497-521.

Sacher, J., Neumann, J., Fünfstück, T., Soliman, A., Villringer, A., & Schroeter, M. L. (2012). Mapping the depressed brain: A meta-analysis of structural and functional alterations in major depressive disorder. *Journal of Affective Disorders*, *140*(2), 142–148. http://doi.org/10.1016/j.jad.2011.08.001

Sapolsky, R. (2000). Glucocorticoids and hippocampal atrophy in neuropsychiatric disorders. *Archives of General Psychiatry*, *57*(10), 925–935.

Schmaal, L., Veltman, D. J., van Erp, T. G. M., Mann, P. G. S. A., Frodl, T., Jahanshad, N.,…Vernooij, M. W. (2015). Subcortical brain alterations in major depressive disorder. *Molecular Psychiatry* 21(6), 806–812. http://doi.org/10.1038/mp.2015.69

Servaas, M. N., van der Velde, J., Costafreda, S. G., Horton, P., Ormel, J., Riese, H., & Aleman, A. (2013). Neuroticism and the brain: A quantitative meta-analysis of neuroimaging studies investigating emotion processing. *Neuroscience & Biobehavioral Reviews*, *37*(8), 1518–1529. http://doi.org/10.1016/j.neubiorev.2013.05.005

Sheridan, M. A., Fox, N. A., Zeanah, C. H., McLaughlin, K. A., & Nelson, C. A. (2012). Variation in neural development as a result of exposure to institutionalization early in childhood. *Proceedings of the National Academy of Sciences*, *109*(32), 12927–12932. http://doi.org/10.1073/pnas.1200041109

Simon, G. (2003). Social and economic burden of mood disorders. *Biological Psychiatry*, *54*(3), 208–215. http://doi.org/10.1016/S0006-3223(03)00420-7

Slopen, N., McLaughlin, K. A., & Shonkoff, J. P. (2014). Interventions to improve cortisol regulation in children: A systematic review. *Pediatrics*, *133*(2), 312–326. http://doi.org/10.1542/peds.2013-1632

Soni, A. (2010). Statistical brief #303: Anxiety and mood disorders: Use and expenditures for adults 18 and older, U.S. civilian noninstitutionalized population, 2007, Agency for Healthcare Research and Quality. Rockville, MD. http://www.meps.ahrq.gov/mepsweb/data_files/publications/st303/stat303.shtml.

Sripada, R. K., Swain, J. E., Evans, G. W., Welsh, R. C., & Liberzon, I. (2014). Childhood poverty and stress reactivity are associated with aberrant functional connectivity in default mode network. *Neuropsychopharmacology*, *39*(9), 2244–2251. http://doi.org/10.1038/npp.2014.75

Staff, R. T., Murray, A. D., Ahearn, T. S., Mustafa, N., Fox, H. C., & Whalley, L. J. (2012). Childhood socioeconomic status and adult brain size: Childhood socioeconomic status influences adult hippocampal size. *Annals of Neurology*, *71*(5), 653–660. http://doi.org/10.1002/ana.22631

Starkman, M. N., Gebarski, S. S., Berent, S., & Schteingart, D. E. (1992). Hippocampal formation volume, memory dysfunction, and cortisol levels in patients with Cushing's syndrome. *Biological Psychiatry*, *32*(9), 756–765.

Starkman, M. N., Giordani, B., Gebarski, S. S., Berent, S., Schork, M. A., & Schteingart, D. E. (1999). Decrease in cortisol reverses human hippocampal atrophy following treatment of Cushing's disease. *Biological Psychiatry*, *46*(12), 1595–1602.

Stein, M. B., Koverola, C., Hanna, C., Torchia, M. G., & McClarty, B. (1997). Hippocampal volume in women victimized by childhood sexual abuse. *Psychological Medicine*, *27*(4), 951–959.

Stroud, C. B., Davila, J., & Moyer, A. (2008). The relationship between stress and depression in first onsets versus recurrences: A meta-analytic review. *Journal of Abnormal Psychology*, *117*(1), 206–213. http://doi.org/10.1037/0021-843X.117.1.206

Sullivan, P. F., Neale, M. C., & Kendler, K. S. (2000). Genetic epidemiology of major depression: Review and meta-analysis. *The American Journal of Psychiatry*, *157*(10), 1552–1562.

Sundermann, B., Olde lütke Beverborg, M., & Pfleiderer, B. (2014). Toward literature-based feature selection for diagnostic classification: A meta-analysis of resting-state fMRI in depression. *Frontiers in human neuroscience*, 8, 692. http://doi.org/10.3389/fnhum.2014.00692/abstract

Suzuki, H., Luby, J. L., Botteron, K. N., & Dietrich, R. (2014). Early life stress and trauma and enhanced limbic activation to emotionally valenced faces in depressed and healthy children. *Journal of the American Academy of Child & Adolescent Psychiatry*, *53*(7), 800-813.

Swartz, J. R., Knodt, A. R., Radtke, S. R., & Hariri, A. R. (2015). A neural biomarker of psychological vulnerability to future life stress. *Neuron*, *85*(3), 505–511. http://doi.org/10.1016/j.neuron.2014.12.055

Taylor, S. E., Way, B. M., Welch, W. T., Hilmert, C. J., Lehman, B. J., & Eisenberger, N. I. (2006). Early family environment, current adversity, the serotonin transporter promoter polymorphism, and depressive symptomatology. *Biological Psychiatry*, *60*(7), 671–676. http://doi.org/10.1016/j.biopsych.2006.04.019

Teicher, M. H., Anderson, C. M., & Polcari, A. (2012). Childhood maltreatment is associated with reduced volume in the hippocampal subfields CA3, dentate gyrus, and subiculum. *Proceedings of the National Academy of Sciences*, *109*(9), E563–572. http://doi.org/10.1073/pnas.1115396109

Teicher, M. H., Dumont, N. L., Ito, Y., Vaituzis, C., Giedd, J. N., & Andersen, S. L. (2004). Childhood neglect is associated with reduced corpus callosum area. *Biological Psychiatry*, *56*(2), 80–85. http://doi.org/10.1016/j.biopsych.2004.03.016

Tomoda, A., Navalta, C. P., Polcari, A., Sadato, N., & Teicher, M. H. (2009). Childhood sexual abuse is associated with reduced gray matter volume in visual cortex of young women. *Biological Psychiatry*, *66*(7), 642–648. http://doi.org/10.1016/j.biopsych.2009.04.021

Tomoda, A., Polcari, A., Anderson, C. M., & Teicher, M. H. (2012). Reduced visual cortex gray matter volume and thickness in young adults who witnessed domestic violence during childhood. *PLoS ONE, 7*(12), e52528. http://doi.org/10.1371/journal.pone.0052528

Tomoda, A., Sheu, Y.-S., Rabi, K., Suzuki, H., Navalta, C. P., Polcari, A., & Teicher, M. H. (2011). Exposure to parental verbal abuse is associated with increased gray matter volume in superior temporal gyrus. *NeuroImage, 54*(Suppl 1), S280–286. http://doi.org/10.1016/j.neuroimage.2010.05.027

Tottenham, N. (2009). A review of adversity, the amygdala and the hippocampus: A consideration of developmental timing. *Frontiers in Human Neuroscience.* http://doi.org/10.3389/neuro.09.068.2009

Tottenham, N., Hare, T. A., Millner, A., Gilhooly, T., Zevin, J. D., & Casey, B. J. (2011). Elevated amygdala response to faces following early deprivation. *Developmental Science, 14*(2), 190–204. http://doi.org/10.1111/j.1467-7687.2010.00971.x

Tottenham, N., Hare, T. A., Quinn, B. T., McCarry, T. W., Nurse, M., Gilhooly, T., … Thomas, K. M. (2010). Prolonged institutional rearing is associated with atypically large amygdala volume and difficulties in emotion regulation. *Developmental Science, 13*(1), 46–61. http://doi.org/10.1111/j.1467-7687.2009.00852.x

Treadway, M. T., Waskom, M. L., Dillon, D. G., Holmes, A. J., Park, M. T. M., Chakravarty, M. M., … Gabrieli, J. D. (2015). Illness progression, recent stress, and morphometry of hippocampal subfields and medial prefrontal cortex in major depression. *Biological Psychiatry, 77*(3), 285–294. http://doi.org/10.1016/j.biopsych.2014.06.018

Van Harmelen, A.L., van Tol, M.-J., van der Wee, N. J. A., Veltman, D. J., Aleman, A., Spinhoven, P., … Elzinga, B. M. (2010). Reduced medial prefrontal cortex volume in adults reporting childhood emotional maltreatment. *Biological Psychiatry, 68*(9), 832–838. http://doi.org/10.1016/j.biopsych.2010.06.011

Vanderhasselt, M. A., Kühn, S., & Raedt, R. (2011). Healthy brooders employ more attentional resources when disengaging from the negative: An event-related fMRI study. *Cognitive, Affective, & Behavioral Neuroscience,* 1–10. http://doi.org/10.3758/s13415-011-0022-5

Videbech, P., & Ravnkilde, B. (2004). Hippocampal volume and depression: A meta-analysis of MRI studies. *The American Journal of Psychiatry, 161*(11), 1957–1966. http://doi.org/10.1176/appi.ajp.161.11.1957

Vythilingam, M., Heim, C., Newport, J., Miller, A. H., Anderson, E., Bronen, R., … Nemeroff, C. B. (2002). Childhood trauma associated with smaller hippocampal volume in women with major depression. *The American Journal of Psychiatry, 159*(12), 2072–2080.

Watanabe, Y., Gould, E., & McEwen, B. S. (1992). Stress induces atrophy of apical dendrites of hippocampal CA3 pyramidal neurons. *Brain Research, 588*(2), 341–345. http://doi.org/10.1016/0006-8993(92)91597-8

Weiss, E. L., Longhurst, J. G., & Mazure, C. M. (1999). Childhood sexual abuse as a risk factor for depression in women: Psychosocial and neurobiological correlates. *The American Journal of Psychiatry, 156*(6), 816–828. http://doi.org/10.1176/ajp.156.6.816

Weissman, M. M., Wickramaratne, P., Nomura, Y., Warner, V., Pilowsky, D., & Verdeli, H. (2006). Offspring of depressed parents: 20 years later. *The American Journal of Psychiatry, 163*(6), 1001–1008. http://doi.org/10.1176/appi.ajp.163.6.1001

Weniger, G., Lange, C., Sachsse, U., & Irle, E. (2008). Amygdala and hippocampal volumes and cognition in adult survivors of childhood abuse with dissociative disorders. *Acta Psychiatrica Scandinavica, 118*(4), 281–290. http://doi.org/10.1111/j.1600-0447.2008.01246.x

White, M. G., Bogdan, R., Fisher, P. M., Muñoz, K. E., Williamson, D. E., & Hariri, A. R. (2012). FKBP5 and emotional neglect interact to predict individual differences in amygdala reactivity. *Genes, Brain and Behavior, 11*(7), 869–878. http://doi.org/10.1111/j.1601-183X.2012.00837.x

Williamson, D. E., Birmaher, B., Axelson, D. A., Ryan, N. D., & Dahl, R. E. (2004). First episode of depression in children at low and high familial risk for depression. *Journal of the American Academy of Child & Adolescent Psychiatry, 43*(3), 291–297. http://doi.org/10.1097/00004583-200403000-00010

Winkler, A. M., Sabuncu, M. R., Yeo, B. T. T., Fischl, B., Greve, D. N., Kochunov, P., … Glahn, D. C., (2012). Measuring and comparing brain cortical surface area and other areal quantities. *NeuroImage, 61*(4), 1428–1443. http://doi.org/10.1016/j.neuroimage.2012.03.026

Wise, T., Radua, J., Nortje, G., Cleare, A. J., Young, A. H., & Arnone, D. (2016). Voxel-based meta-analytical evidence of structural disconnectivity in major depression and bipolar disorder. *Biological Psychiatry, 79*(4), 293–302. http://doi.org/10.1016/j.biopsych.2015.03.004

Woon, F. L., & Hedges, D. W. (2008). Hippocampal and amygdala volumes in children and adults with childhood maltreatment-related posttraumatic stress disorder: A meta-analysis. *Hippocampus, 18*(8), 729–736. http://doi.org/10.1002/hipo.20437

Yang, J., Liu, H., Wei, D., Liu, W., Meng, J., Wang, K., … Qiu, J. (2016). Regional gray matter volume mediates the relationship between family socioeconomic status and depression-related trait in a young healthy sample. *Cognitive, Affective, & Behavioral Neuroscience, 16*(1), 51–62. http://doi.org/10.3758/s13415-015-0371-6

Zang, Y., Jiang, T., Lu, Y., He, Y., & Tian, L. (2004). Regional homogeneity approach to fMRI data analysis. *NeuroImage, 22*(1), 394–400. http://doi.org/10.1016/j.neuroimage.2003.12.030

Zeanah, C. H., Nelson, C. A., Fox, N. A., Smyke, A. T., Marshall, P., Parker, S. W., & Koga, S. (2003). Designing research to study the effects of institutionalization on brain and behavioral development: The Bucharest Early Intervention Project. *Development and Psychopathology, 15*(4), 885–907.

Zhang, W. N., Chang, S.-H., Guo, L.-Y., Zhang, K. L., & Wang, J. (2013). The neural correlates of reward-related processing in major depressive disorder: A meta-analysis of functional magnetic resonance imaging studies. *Journal of Affective Disorders, 151*(2), 531–539. http://doi.org/10.1016/j.jad.2013.06.039

Zobel, A. W., Nickel, T., Künzel, H. E., Ackl, N., Sonntag, A., Ising, M., & Holsboer, F. (2000). Effects of the high-affinity corticotropin-releasing hormone receptor 1 antagonist R121919 in major depression: The first 20 patients treated. *Journal of Psychiatric Research, 34*(3), 171–181.

Neuroendocrinological Models of Stress and Psychopathology

Nestor L. Lopez-Duran, Valerie J. Micol, *and* Andrea Roberts

Abstract

Neuroendocrine systems play a critical role in modulating biological, cognitive, and affective responses to stress. Not surprisingly, variability in neuroendocrine functioning, and particularly the hypothalamic-pituitary-adrenal axis, has been extensively linked to stress-related mental health disorders. This chapter examines the potential mechanisms that underlie this link and the conceptual challenges that must be addressed in order to advance a more cohesive neuroendocrine model of stress-related psychopathology. To this end, the chapter first explores the various sources of variability in neuroendocrine responses to stress, including individual differences in neural networks and neuroendocrine systems, as well as contextual factors, such as characteristics of the stressors and personality traits. The chapter then examines potential proximal and distal mechanisms that link variability in neuroendocrine functioning to the risk for onset, phenomenology, and course of stress-related disorders, including depression and posttraumatic stress disorder.

Keywords: neuroendocrinology, HPA axis, cortisol, psychopathology, stress, depression, PTSD

The two major physiological stress response systems in the human body, the locus coeruleus noradrenaline/autonomic (sympathetic) nervous system and the hypothalamic-pituitary-adrenal axis (HPA axis), are modulated by the concerted activation of numerous hormonal processes (E. R. De Kloet, 2004). Not surprisingly, these hormonal processes have been the focus of intensive research efforts to pinpoint the biological underpinnings of stress-related mental health problems (E. R. De Kloet, Joëls, & Holsboer, 2005). These efforts have led to the identification of robust links between variability in neuroendocrine functioning and the risk for, onset, and phenomenology of many stress-related disorders. The current chapter focuses on the potential mechanisms that underlie these links as well as the conceptual challenges that must be addressed in order to advance a more cohesive neuroendocrine model of stress-related psychopathology.

Conceptual Foundations

The HPA axis is the body's primary neuroendocrine stress response system (Hellhammer, Wüst, & Kudielka, 2009). In specific stressful conditions, the HPA axis modulates a number of biological, cognitive, and behavioral responses to stress. Thus, variability across indices of HPA axis functioning, such as cortisol or adrenocorticotropic hormone (ACTH), has been the primary focus of investigation in related stress research. In fact, there is an extensive literature framing atypically high or low hormonal responses to stress as indices of neuroendocrine dysregulation and a potential contributor to stress-related psychopathology (see, for example, Lopez-Duran, Kovacs, & George, 2009; Yehuda & Seckl, 2011).

The HPA axis's basic response to stress follows four simple steps: (1) stress activates the paraventricular nucleus (PVN) of the hypothalamus to release corticotropin-releasing hormone (CRH); (2) CRH elicits the release of adrenocorticotropic hormone (ACTH) from the anterior pituitary, (3) ACTH leads to the release of corticoids (cortisol in humans) from the adrenal glands, and (4) cortisol then serves as its own regulator by binding to corticoid receptors in the brain that shuts down CRH release (E. R. De Kloet et al., 2005). This regulatory signaling is controlled by mineralocorticoid receptors (MRs) and glucocorticoid receptors (GRs). MRs have a high sensitivity for glucocorticoids and thus play an important role in regulating low tonic (nonstress) levels of cortisol. GRs, on the other hand, have a lower affinity for glucocorticoids and are activated when cortisol saturates MRs, such as when cortisol increases after a stressor. Therefore, atypical cortisol levels observed in some stress-related disorders are often assumed to reflect dysregulation across one or more of these basic HPA axis processes.

However, the HPA axis does not work in isolation; instead, it is modulated by multiple biological and contextual factors outside the HPA axis itself. This makes interpreting variability in HPA axis indices in isolation potentially misleading and complicates the interpretation of findings linking variability in HPA axis functioning and stress psychopathology. Understanding factors that contribute to such variability is an essential first step toward properly contextualizing individual differences in neuroendocrine activation to stress and the impact that such variability may have on purported mechanisms of risk and resilience.

Sources of HPA Axis Variability
Cortical and Limbic Structures That Regulate HPA Axis Activity
The initial activation of the PVN is under the control of networks outside the HPA axis. Specifically, neurons in the PVN respond to excitatory and inhibitory projections from multiple cortical and deep brain regions (Bains, Cusulin, & Inoue, 2015). Excitatory signals come primarily from the parabrachial nucleus of the cerebellum and the bed nucleus of the stria terminalis, both of which relay information from the central nucleus of the amygdala (CeA), a key structure involved in the identification of threat. The CeA, in turn, is activated by the amygdala basolateral complex (BLA), which plays a critical role in integrating information from cortical (e.g., prefrontal cortex) and subcortical structures (e.g., thalamus, hippocampus) and determining whether a stress response to the threat is necessary (Buijs, Eden, & Van Eden, 2000). This means that initial activation of the HPA axis is largely under the control of projections from cortical and deep brain structures and thus variability in HPA axis may reflect variability in multiple prehypothalamic processes.

Stress Type and Goal Orientation
Not all forms of stress lead to excitatory signals to the PVN. In fact, the activation of the HPA axis seems to be restricted to a narrow set of stressors (or activities), including exercise (Hill et al., 2008), threatening situations with low perceived control, and those involving social evaluation (Dickerson & Kemeny, 2004). A variety of theoretical models have been proposed to account for the specificity of HPA axis stress response to certain stressors. For example, Lazarus (1999) proposed a motivational theory arguing that the HPA axis is activated when the individual's central goals are threatened. For example, the HPA axis responds to threats to our safety (survival goals), such as military combat (Steudte-schmiedgen et al., 2015), chronic pain (Van Uum et al., 2008), and endurance sports (Skoluda et al., 2012), the latter of which, evolutionarily, is likely interpreted by our bodies as a significant threat to our survival. Dickerson and Kemeny (2004) further proposed a self-preservation theory, arguing that the HPA axis is sensitive to threats to one's social esteem and social status. An activation of stress-response systems makes sense given that there are clear survival implications of the loss of social status. In the context of evolution, social rejection and loss of social status would lead to isolation and even removal from the safety of one's social group. As discussed later, engagement of the HPA axis would be expected in order to mobilize short- and long-term responses to the threats associated with such social isolation.

A key implication of both of these theories is that HPA axis activation can depend on an individual's goals or need for self-preservation. There is significant variability in the HPA response to laboratory tasks that are designed to elicit threats to the self, such as the Trier Social Evaluative Test (TSST). On average, about 70% of individuals that undergo this test have an HPA axis response, meaning that a substantial number of individuals do not show a response (i.e., an increase in cortisol; Kudielka, Hellhammer, & Wüst, 2009). Although there are likely multiple factors that contribute to responses to this task, there is evidence that individual differences in how participants interpret the task modulate whether the HPA axis is engaged. Such differences can be manipulated experimentally. For example, in one study, researchers made participants consider how they could help others by completing the TSST, which minimized the HPA axis stress response (Abelson et al., 2014). The authors argued that this manipulation shifted the individual's attention to the needs of others, minimizing the focus on one's self-preservation, thus reducing the HPA axis response.

Stress Intensity

The primary goal of HPA axis activation is to respond adaptively to stressors and limit the negative consequences of stress to the organism (E. R. De Kloet et al., 2005). The intensity and duration of this adaptive response, therefore, are often a function of the intensity of the stressor. For example, the HPA axis response to exercise is a function of the intensity of the activity (Hill et al., 2008). To the extent that HPA axis reactivity is meaningfully correlated with stressor intensity, findings linking high hormonal output with psychopathology may reflect appropriate hormonal responses to the increased stress exposure associated with many disorders (e.g., depression; Kessler, 1997). In this case, psychopathology may emerge despite, not because of, elevation in multiple hormonal systems as the HPA axis is arguably serving its adaptive purpose. To the extent that atypically high hormonal outputs reflect adaptive responses to elevated stress exposure, the role of neuroendocrine function in psychopathology would be peripheral and variability in hormonal output would serve only as a correlate of the key mechanisms that actually modulate the risk for stress-related psychopathology.

In modern times, however, the "protective" goal of hormone mobilization may be detrimental more often than not. Specifically, several of our hormonal stress responses are optimally designed for responding to the type of acute, life-threatening stress experienced by our ancestors. Conversely, stress in contemporary Western societies typically manifests as chronic and non-life-threatening, which can nevertheless activate endocrine systems chronically (E. R. De Kloet et al., 2005). Therefore, chronic activation of the HPA axis increases risk not because the HPA axis is dysregulated but because of a disconnect between its original function and the nature of stressors in Western societies. A challenge for stress researchers, therefore, is to differentiate hormonal responses that reflect protective, relatively benign processes from those that paradoxically increase the risk for psychopathology, despite having been shaped by successful adaptation.

Other Stress Hormones: DHEA and Oxytocin

The HPA axis is interconnected to other hormonal systems that play a key role in the modulation of the human stress response, both in terms of modulating the HPA axis itself, as well as modulating other biological and behavioral responses to stress. Among these, dehydroepiandrosterone (DHEA) and oxytocin (OT) are arguably most closely linked to the stress response and should be considered when interpreting variability in HPA axis indices.

DHEA and its sulfate form, DHEAS, are adrenal steroids involved in the synthesis of testosterone (Kroboth & Salek, 1999). DHEA is synthesized primarily in the adrenal gland and its release is largely under the control of ACTH. Thus, DHEA increases in parallel with cortisol in response to stress (Izawa et al., 2008; Lennartsson et al., 2012), although these two hormones differ in function. DHEA(S) has strong anti-glucocorticoid effects and reduces the impact of the HPA axis on immune function by, for example, limiting inflammatory cytokines, lymphocytes, and thymic involution (Kalimi et al., 1994). Most important, DHEA(S) also downregulates the HPA axis via direct action on corticoid receptors (Kalimi et al., 1994) or, indirectly, through its effects on neurocircuitry important to emotion regulation (e.g., amygdala connectivity) (Sripada et al., 2013).

Oxytocin (OT), a mammalian neuropeptide that is synthesized in the hypothalamus, is abundant in many areas of the brain (Lee et al., 2009) and is associated with reproductive and socially affiliative behaviors (Carter & Altemus, 1997). OT also increases in response to stress (Neumann, Wigger, et al., 2000; Neumann, Torner, & Wigger, 2000) and has been shown to downregulate the HPA stress response in experimental studies using exogenous OT administration (Cardoso et al., 2013; Ditzen et al., 2009; Heinrichs et al., 2003). OT also modulates amygdala responses to threatening nonsocial stimuli (Kirsch et al., 2005) and faces (Domes et al., 2007). Further, OT directly inhibits the release of the cortisol precursor corticotropin-releasing hormone (CRH) by the hypothalamus, via direct action on the paraventricular nucleus (PVN) and by modulating excitatory signaling from the amygdala and the septum (Neumann, Wigger, et al., 2000).

In sum, variability across indices of HPA axis functioning can reflect a myriad of stress-related processes that are outside the HPA axis itself, including stress context (intensity, duration, and type), cortical and limbic involvement, individual differences in goal orientation and other psychosocial factors (e.g., sense of control), and variability within other hormonal systems including DHEA and OT. Therefore, atypical neuroendocrine indices in psychopathology are not necessarily indicative of dysregulation of the HPA axis; indeed, such variability alone does establish whether neuroendocrine functioning is causal in risk for stress-related psychopathology or merely an epiphenomenon.

When the HPA Axis Is Dysregulated

However, in some cases, atypical HPA axis functioning (e.g., atypical ACTH, cortisol) may reflect true dysregulation of the HPA axis. That is, in some cases, the magnitude of the HPA axis response to a stressor is inconsistent with the intensity or nature of the stressor, or the input provided to the axis by cortical, limbic, and deep brain regions. Indeed, dysregulation can occur at any level of the HPA axis network. There is evidence of plasticity in glutamate and GABAergic synapses of the PVN in response to chronic stress, leading to changes in GABA receptors that cause excessive activation of CRH-producing neurons (Bains et al., 2015). Dysregulation can also occur at the level of the pituitary in the form of increased or reduced expression of CRH receptors, resulting in hyper- or hyposensitivity of the pituitary to CRH (Newport et al., 2003). Similarly, dysregulated activity of the adrenal in the form of hyper- or hyposensitivity to ACTH can result in cortisol responses that are inconsistent with the intensity of the initial activation (i.e., intensity of CRH and ACTH release). Finally, there is extensive evidence that chronic stress can result in long-term adaptation of MR and GR function in ways that lead to both hyperactivation (Raison & Miller, 2003) and hypoactivation (Yehuda, 2000) of the axis in response to stress.

In conclusion, atypical HPA axis indices may reflect factors related to the stressor, psychological processes, biological processes that precede the activation of the axis, or atypical functioning of one or many processes within the axis itself. Identifying the source of variability may be important to answer the question of whether such variability plays a role in mitigating or exacerbating of risk for stress psychopathology. However, for the purposes of understanding neuroendocrine influences on stress psychopathology, arguably a more critical task is identifying the potential mechanisms, if any, by which atypical HPA axis indices (e.g., high or low cortisol) contribute to the modulation of risk for stress-related psychopathology.

Distal Versus Proximal Effects of Neuroendocrine Activation

To address this issue, it is important to consider that stress has proximal and distal effects on neuroendocrine systems, and these neuroendocrine systems, in turn, have proximal and distal effects on risk mechanisms. By proximal and distal, we primarily refer to the time course of the impact of stress on neuroendocrine functioning and resulting risk mechanisms. For example, stress exposure has an immediate (proximal) impact on the activation of the HPA axis, as well as DHEA and OT release. These immediate effects have, in turn, an impact on behaviors that are relevant to the regulation of stress. For example, OT increases in response to stress and elicits socially affiliative behaviors, which may facilitate adaptive responses to stress when social support is available (Olff et al., 2013). However, stress exposure also has a delayed (distal) effect on neuroendocrine functioning by facilitating long-term adaptations of the system. For example, the progressive downregulation of specific glucocorticoid receptors in response to chronic stress exposure eventually leads to dysregulation of the underlying physiological mechanisms responsible for facilitating extinction learning, which may play a key role in the development of posttraumatic stress disorder (PTSD) (Yehuda & LeDoux, 2007).

Neuroendocrine processes may also have effects on mental health outcomes by impacting mechanisms that are either proximally or distally related, mechanistically, to the disorder. In this case, the terms "proximal" and "distal" do not refer to the time course of the effect of neuroendocrine functioning on outcomes, but to the distance between the mechanism and the phenomenology of a disorder. We call this *mechanistic proximity*. For example, researchers have identified specific links between cortisol and memory consolidation for emotional information. Specifically, elevated cortisol during stress facilitates encoding of memories of stressful events in controlled laboratory studies (Buchanan & Lovallo, 2001); given that memory biases for negative information are associated with increased risk for depression (Ridout et al., 2003), it may be that some of these biases develop in response to cortisol's modulation of memory processes; if so, the impact of neuroendocrine functioning on memory bias would be a process with moderate mechanistic proximity to depression. However, neuroendocrine processes may influence factors that are more distally related to psychopathology. For example, cortisol facilitates fat storage in abdominal areas and is associated with central obesity (Björntorp & Rosmond, 2000). Obesity is also associated with a variety of factors that increase the risk of depression, including reduced mobility, reduced self-esteem, and greater social stigma and discrimination (Bornstein et al., 2006; McElroy et al., 2004). In this example, cortisol impacts physical health, which impacts appearance, which impacts self-esteem, which then increases risk for depression (i.e., long mechanistic proximity).

We propose that the distal versus proximal heuristic in the identification of mechanistic links between neuroendocrine functioning and stress psychopathology is useful, both in terms of conceptually categorizing the mechanisms and in understanding the relevance of neuroendocrine functioning as a modulator and mediator of risk. Therefore, the second half of this chapter uses this heuristic to categorize the processes that may underlie the impact of neuroendocrine functioning on stress psychopathology.

Neuroendocrine Functioning in Stress-Related Psychopathology

Given the critical role that the neuroendocrine systems play in our response to stressful events, researchers have studied the link between neuroendocrine processes and stress-related psychopathology for many decades. These efforts have focused on conditions that are traditionally associated with stress, namely depression and posttraumatic stress disorder. There have been a number of excellent recent reviews of the links between neuroendocrine functioning of stress-related conditions (Lopez-Duran et al., 2009; Meewissee et al., 2007; Staufenbiel et al., 2013). This literature is also extensively reviewed in other chapters of this book; thus, we will avoid replicating those efforts here, presenting only a very brief overview of the current status of this literature with a focus on how such information can help us understand the role of neuroendocrine functioning in psychopathology.

Depression

Depression has been linked to atypical neuroendocrine functioning since the 1960s (Doig et al., 1966). Individuals with depression tend to have elevated overall cortisol levels (i.e., hypercortisolemia) as indexed by ambulatory measures (Gillespie & Nemeroff, 2005), and poor feedback inhibition as indicated by the dexamethasone suppression test (Lopez-Duran et al., 2009). Additionally, depression is also associated with atypical HPA axis responses

to stress, although findings are heterogeneous, implicating poor recovery of the HPA axis stress response in adults (Burke et al., 2005), delayed shutdown in children (Lopez-Duran et al., 2015), and even blunted activation in some subtypes of depression (Harkness, Stewart, & Wynne-Edwards, 2011). Atypical indices of HPA axis functioning may predict depression onset in teens (E. K. Adam et al., 2010) and adults (Harris et al., 2000), as well as depression course (Morris, Rao, & Garber, 2012), although HPA axis function appears to normalize after remission (Vythilingam et al., 2004).

Posttraumatic Stress Disorder

Like depression, PTSD has been extensively linked to dysregulation of HPA axis functioning. Specifically, patients with PTSD tend to show blunted HPA axis functioning throughout the day (Yehuda & Seckl, 2011), although findings are mixed, and the most comprehensive meta-analysis of basal cortisol levels in PTSD found no overall difference between those with and without PTSD (Meewisse et al., 2007). However, the authors found key moderators of this effect. Specifically, lower basal cortisol was found in PTSD patients in the afternoon, in females, and in survivors of sexual or physical abuse. Surprisingly, war veterans did not exhibit altered basal cortisol. Those with PTSD also show a blunted HPA axis response to laboratory stress (Zaba et al., 2015). This blunted profile does not appear to be just a long-term consequence of trauma (such as in the case of adaptation to chronic exposure) because blunted HPA axis responses predict risk for PTSD. For example, survivors of the 2008 Wenchuan earthquake in China who showed lower overall cortisol production following the disaster were more likely to go on to develop PTSD (Luo et al., 2011). Likewise, several researchers have measured cortisol immediately after a trauma at emergency rooms and found that lower cortisol predicted an increased risk for developing PTSD (McFarlane, Atchison, & Yehuda, 1997; Yehuda, McFarlane, & Shalev, 1998).

These are but a few examples of the extensive literature linking stress-related psychopathology and atypical HPA axis functioning. Prospective evidence suggests a potential role of neuroendocrine functioning in the phenomenology of these disorders. Yet the relevant question for a neuroendocrine model of psychopathology is whether neuroendocrine processes play a *functional role* in the risk for onset, intensity, course, or phenomenology of the disorders. That is, is neuroendocrine functioning mechanistically responsible for modulating the risk or phenomenology of stress-related conditions and, if so, how?

Neuroendocrine Function and Mechanisms of Risk for Psychopathology
Proximal Mechanisms

Neuroendocrine processes have proximal effects on risk mechanisms that are closely related to mental health outcomes. In this section, we will explore some of those potential proximal mechanisms. Specifically, we will examine the evidence for a role of neuroendocrine activation in memory, attention, emotion regulation, as well as more overt behaviors, and the role these processes can play in stress-related psychopathology.

MEMORY

Hormones play a central role in modulating memory processes, primarily through their impact on amygdala and hippocampal functioning. Specifically, there is a high density of GRs in the basolateral nucleus of the amygdala (BLA) and the hippocampus that respond to stress-induced cortisol (Donley, Schulkin, & Rosen, 2005). Activation of these receptors contributes to various aspects of memory and learning processes, from Pavlovian conditioning and extinction learning to memory consolidation and retrieval. It is not surprising, therefore, that dysregulation of memory processes is commonly found in stress-related psychopathology (Wolf, 2008), and that some of this may stem from HPA axis activations during stress.

A review of research using animal models (Sandi & Pinelo-Nava, 2007) of the impact of stress on memory shows that stress is associated with increased Pavlovian fear conditioning, a type of implicit memory process. For example, in mice exposed to shock in the laboratory, as shock intensity increases, the strength of the fear-conditioned memory also increases (Cordero, Merino, & Sandi, 1998). Enhancement of this Pavlovian conditioning effect has been linked to GRs in the basolateral nucleus of the amygdala and ventral hippocampus, as inhibition of long-term fear memory has been associated with microinfusion of GR antagonist in those areas (Donley et al., 2005). For example, corticosterone administration after fear conditioning in mice was associated with greater memory consolidation of the conditioned stimulus (Cordero & Sandi, 1998; Hui et al., 2004; Pugh, Fleshner, & Rudy, 1997). Additionally, inhibition of central antagonism of GRs, but not MRs, was associated with decreased fear-memory formation (Cordero &

Sandi, 1998). Thus, GR activation in the basolateral nucleus of the amygdala and hippocampus contributes to Pavlovian fear conditioning. Dysregulation of this system, in the form of excess activation during a fear-related event, may lead to the generalized fear responses associated with some anxiety disorders, such as fear of social evaluation in social anxiety disorder.

In addition to Pavlovian fear conditioning, fear extinction has clinical implications for anxiety disorders, particularly PTSD. During fear extinction, an organism goes through inhibitory training to relearn new responses to a previously feared stimulus. As in fear conditioning, the extinction process has been related to modulation of the GRs in the amygdala (for a review of mechanisms of fear extinction, see Myers & Davis, 2007). For example, administration of a GR agonist, dexamethasone, enhanced fear extinction learning in rats, while administration of a GR antagonist (metyrapone) impaired extinction learning (Yang, Chao, & Lu, 2006). These findings may have clinical implications for the treatment of PTSD, as the disorder is characterized by impairments in extinction of physiological responses to trauma (Guthrie & Bryant, 2006; Rothbaum & Davis, 2003) as well as potential dysregulation in GR functioning (Yehuda et al., 2004).

In human participants, there is evidence, albeit conflicting (Zoladz et al., 2017), that cortisol can enhance memory encoding and retrieval for emotional information. For example, in a seminal placebo-controlled study (Buchanan & Lovallo, 2001), participants were shown pictures of faces of various emotions after being injected with either placebo or cortisol. Those who received cortisol had enhanced memory for emotionally valenced faces in comparison with neutral ones (Buchanan & Lovallo, 2001). Similarly, prelearning stress, induced by a socially evaluative cold pressor task, was associated with enhanced memory for neutral compared to negative words regardless of cortisol activation (Schwabe et al., 2008). However, in this same study, increased cortisol activation post stressor was related to enhanced memory for negative words. Surprisingly, this word effect was noticeable at 1-hour recall time, but not 24 hours later, suggesting that the cortisol memory-enhancing effect for words may be shorter than for faces. Additionally, in a study of prelearning stress on memory, performance on a memory task was enhanced among participants with a high cortisol response to a socially evaluative stress task (Nater et al., 2007). These findings indicate that stress and cortisol activation before a learning task may enhance learning, especially for emotional information. While most evidence for the biological mechanism of these effects is based on animal models, there seems to be a relationship between memory processes and stress through glucocorticoid facilitated activation of the GRs in the basolateral nucleus of the amygdala. It is unclear, however, whether the effect of cortisol on memory contributes to the type of memory biases seen in some anxiety and depression disorders.

In sum, neuroendocrine processing of stress has an impact on fear conditioning and extinction, as well as memory biases for negative information. Specifically, cortisol-related enhancement of memory for negative information and increased fear learning may have proximal implications for the development of stress-related psychopathology in anxiety and depressive disorders. As such, although neuroendocrine processing of stress facilitates behaviors (fear conditioning and extinction) that are adaptive, it is also implicated in stress psychopathology when these types of behaviors become impairing.

ATTENTION

Attention and memory play important roles in human survival and are closely related given that attention facilitates the encoding of memories. During acute stress, the amygdala becomes relatively sensitive but less specific to threatening stimuli, which facilitates a state of hypervigilance to threat (van Marle et al., 2009). Processes within the HPA axis, and specifically preadrenal activity during stress, may contribute to these attentional biases toward threat. This heightened sensitivity and diminished specificity are adaptive in acutely stressful situations where the potential dangers of a false negative are high but may lead to negative outcomes associated with vigilant attentional bias toward threat once the threat has passed.

Research on cortisol reactivity and attentional biases toward threat has been mixed, with some studies finding that cortisol reactivity is associated with attentional bias to threat (Roelofs, Elzinga, & Rotteveel, 2005) and some finding the opposite (Hakamata et al., 2013). For example, participants who showed heightened cortisol responses to the TSST showed greater vigilance to threat indexed via an emotional Stroop task than low cortisol responders (Roelofs et al., 2007). In another study, using an approach-avoidance behavior to threat task after the TSST, high cortisol responders became more vigilant to threat than low cortisol responders (Roelofs et al., 2005). Conversely, Hakamata and colleagues

found that blunted cortisol awakening response in healthy individuals was related to greater attentional bias toward threat.

The aforementioned studies suggest that HPA axis activation may contribute to greater vigilance to threat. However, it is also possible that individuals who have a strong TSST response due to high sensitivity to social evaluation are also the individuals with greater vigilance to threat. In fact, work by Putman and colleagues using direct manipulation of the axis suggests that cortisol may decrease attention to threat. For example, cortisol administration reduced attention to fear stimuli in anxious men (Putman, Hermans, Koppeschaar, et al., 2007), reduced threat-selective spatial attention in low anxiety healthy men (Putman, Hermans, & Van Honk, 2010), and reduced a natural bias toward threat in working memory task among healthy individuals (Putman, Hermans, & van Honk, 2007). Likewise, Hakamata and colleagues (2013) found that blunted cortisol during the early morning was also associated with greater attentional bias toward threat.

Taken together, the research on attentional bias suggests that cortisol may play an inhibitory role in vigilance toward threat. Exogenously administered cortisol attaches to GRs and downregulates the HPA axis. The association between exogenous cortisol and reduced vigilance might indicate that activity of the HPA axis, at the preadrenal level, may be the mechanism of this attention to threat. This is consistent with what we know about HPA axis function and PTSD in that there are low overall cortisol levels (often interpreted as blunted HPA axis functioning), but increased CRH production (Kasckow, Baker, & Geracioti, 2001). Preadrenal processes that facilitate attention to threat would explain why we see increased attention biases toward threat in PTSD (Fani et al., 2012; Wald et al., 2011), even though cortisol levels are low (Chida & Steptoe, 2009; C. S. de Kloet et al., 2007). Low cortisol doesn't necessarily suggest a blunting of HPA axis functioning, but that the important activation within the axis lies in preadrenal activity. Insofar as increased cortisol secretion serves as a regulatory mechanism of vigilance to threat, low cortisol in PTSD represents a failure of the system to downregulate hypervigilance.

MOOD AND EMOTION

Emotion regulation is important for human survival because it helps maintain self-regulatory and survival behavior by alerting us to environmental threats (fight-or-flight response) and facilitating social functioning (for a review, see Gross, 1998). Additionally, emotion regulation allows humans to maintain homeostasis and to increase goal-directed behavior. There is growing evidence of endocrine involvement in emotion regulation, potentially through attentional processes which may modulate emotion, in the case of HPA axis, and through the facilitation of well-being, in the case of DHEA. Stress-related psychopathology is often characterized by poor emotion regulation and aversive mood states (e.g., depressed mood), and thus neuroendocrine systems may be involved in eliciting and/or maintaining dysregulated emotional functioning that contributes to stress psychopathology.

HPA reactivity may play a crucial role in emotion regulation by calibrating the intensity of emotional responses to stress. While cortisol does not impact subjective mood regardless of dose during a neutral situation (Buchanan et al., 2001; Reuter, 2002; van Peer et al., 2007), cortisol administered before a stressor is related to reduced negative emotional experiences in participants with social anxiety (Soravia et al., 2006) and no disorder (Het & Wolf, 2007). The administration of cortisol before stress helps to downregulate the HPA axis during the stress task, which may facilitate emotion regulation. The results of observational studies of cortisol and affect support this conclusion; for example, self-reported affect seems to consistently be related to greater cortisol secretion throughout the day (Davydov et al., 2005; Hanson et al., 2000; Jacobs et al., 2007), suggesting HPA axis hyperactivation. Likewise, decreased cortisol secretion throughout the day is associated with increased positive affect in middle-aged men and women (Steptoe, Wardle, & Marmot, 2005) as well as working parents of preschool-aged children (Hoppmann & Klumb, 2006).

It is possible that the diurnal cortisol–mood relationship is simply a function of stress exposure. Those with higher stress tend to have higher cortisol and also more negative affect. However, findings from experimental manipulation of cortisol suggest that there is a causal pathway between cortisol and affect. The most likely mechanism that modulates this effect is attention. As previously discussed, HPA axis activation tends to increase vigilance to threat. Downregulation of the axis, such as via exogenous cortisol administration, would reduce vigilance and thus prevent emotional responses to threatening stimuli. This would explain why cortisol administration reduces negative responses to laboratory stressors, but it does not change the subjective experience of mood in nonstressful states.

In contrast to cortisol, DHEA may have more direct effects on emotion regulation. Administration of DHEA has been shown to increase positive affect and decrease depressive symptoms in patients with major depressive disorder (Bloch et al., 1999; Friedland et al., 1999). Additionally, DHEA administration enhanced mood in healthy participants during an episodic memory test (Alhaj, Massey, & McAllister-Williams, 2006). However, DHEA was unrelated to mood and well-being in older adults (Wolf et al., 1998), suggesting developmental influences on ties between DHEA and mood.

While research into neural and biological mechanisms of DHEA influences on emotion regulation is just emerging, there seems to be an influence of the brain regions associated with emotional regulation (amygdala) and areas associated with negative emotion (rostral anterior cingulate cortex). In the first functional magnetic resonance imaging (fMRI) study of its kind, administration of DHEA was shown to exhibit increased connectivity between the hippocampus and amygdala, as well as decreased activity in both of these areas (Sripada et al., 2013). There was also enhanced activity of the rostral anterior cingulate cortex, which was associated with a reduction in negative affect (Sripada et al., 2013).

In sum, neuroendocrine activation and secretion of cortisol and DHEA may play a role in emotion regulation and thus provide adaptive responses to stress processing. In addition, dysregulation of these systems may also be a proximal mechanism for emotion dysregulation symptomatology within stress psychopathology.

BEHAVIOR

Hormones play an important role in modulating behavior, such as social/affiliative behaviors and social withdrawal and freezing, in both stressful and nonstressful situations. Some of these behaviors are at the core of stress-related psychopathology. For example, social inhibition among socially anxious individuals contributes to reduced exposure to the feared stimuli, which maintains the fear response (Biederman et al., 1990; Hirshfeld-Becker et al., 2007). Low affiliative behaviors keep individuals from benefiting from the stress-buffering effects of social interaction, which increase the negative sequelae of stress exposure (DeVries, Glasper, & Detillion, 2003). Thus, neuroendocrine functioning may exert its influence on risk through its modulation of specific functional behaviors that are key to maintaining maladaptive behavior.

The association between HPA axis functioning and social inhibition is complex and seemingly contradictory. A large number of studies have found elevated cortisol in socially inhibited youth (Dettling, Gunnar, & Donzella, 1999; Schmidt et al., 1997); this effect appears in infancy and is maintained relatively stable throughout development (Kagan et al., 1988; Kagan, Reznick, & Snidman, 1987). However, other work shows that extroverted behaviors are associated with elevated cortisol secretion during certain social situations, such as at the beginning of the school year, before friend groups have been established (Davis et al., 1999; Gunnar et al., 1997). These differences may stem from the timing of cortisol collection (stress-induced vs. tonic), which reflects different brain processes. Links between high cortisol and social withdrawal have been found primarily when basal cortisol is the index of cortisol function. In contrast, the work on extroverted behavior and cortisol has focused on assessing HPA axis responses during social situations. The finding of heightened cortisol reactivity in extraverted children during certain social situations is consistent with animal models of social behavior. Highly social and curious rats tend to have high CRH in the PVN, resulting in a normative, or even an exaggerated HPA axis response to stress, but have significantly lower CRH in the central nucleus of the amygdala, reducing fear-related withdrawal behaviors (Kabbaj et al., 2000). These rats also have low GR expression in the hippocampus, which contributes to a reduction in anxiety behavior. For example, in rats that are behaviorally inhibited in novel environments, blocking of GRs via GR antagonists in the hippocampus significantly increases exploratory behavior. GR blocking has the effect of releasing the break of the HPA axis by blocking its inhibitory feedback. Thus, the impact of HPA axis on behavioral withdrawal or exploration appears to be a function of GR activation in the hippocampus and concentration of CRH in the amygdala. It is possible then that the socially inhibited behaviors seen in some anxiety disorders are due to an atypical distribution of GRs in the hippocampus and/or atypically high concentration of CRH in the amygdala. It is unknown, however, if stress exposure, whether acute or chronic, results in the reorganization of GRs and CRH expression that would explain the impact of stress and trauma on anxiety conditions associated with high levels of social withdrawal.

OT also has a significant role in human social behavior and is related to the human capacity for trust, attachment, and social bonding, as well as affiliative and maternal behavior (Heinrichs, von Dawans, & Domes, 2009). The hypothalamus releases OT during stressful situations (Nishioka et al., 1998) as well as during positive social contact. OT then plays a modulating role of the stress response by regulating cardiovascular activity and sympathetic and parasympathetic nervous system activity (Petersson & Uvnäs-Moberg, 2007). In addition, OT increases the need for social affiliation in stressful situations and mediates the buffering effect of social support on stress processing (Heinrichs et al., 2003). For example, in a placebo-controlled study, OT administration increased the blunting effect of social support on the HPA axis (Heinrichs et al., 2003). This suggests that OT has a potent stress regulatory role by both eliciting regulatory behaviors, such as seeking social support, but also by enhancing the benefits of social support.

Taken together, there is growing evidence that neuroendocrine responses to stress directly modulate a variety of cognitive, affective, and behavioral processes. These processes, in turn, have been extensively associated with risk for stress-related psychopathology. Therefore, there is a clear *proximal* pathway by which variability in neuroendocrine functioning may play a causal mechanistic role in the development and maintenance of stress-related disorders.

Distal Mechanisms

Stress also has long-term effects on the HPA axis and other endocrine processes. In turn, these processes have lasting effects on mechanisms underlying health conditions associated with risk for stress-related psychopathology, such as obesity, immunity, and the microbiota-gut-brain axis biome. This section will focus on the long-term consequences of variations in HPA axis activity and the mechanisms by which variability in HPA axis reactivity influences health outcomes.

HPA SENSITIZATION

Although chronic exposure to stress is usually associated with downregulation of the HPA axis, there is evidence of sensitization of the axis in certain stress-related mental health disorders (Raison & Miller, 2003). The glucocorticoid cascade hypothesis states that damage to the neural structures regulating HPA axis activity results in a feed-forward circuit in which ongoing stressors drive overproduction of glucocorticoids indefinitely (Sapolsky, Krey, & McEwen, 1986). For example, overproduction of glucocorticoids due to chronic stress may damage key regulatory brain structures, such as the hippocampus, imperative for HPA axis restraint (McEwen & Seeman, 1999). This damage would lead to a dysregulation in HPA axis feedback mechanisms, resulting in glucocorticoid overproduction that can contribute directly to many of the adverse behavioral and physiological outcomes associated with chronic stress (McEwen & Seeman, 1999; Sapolsky et al., 1986). In animal models, administration of exogenous glucocorticoids produced hippocampal degeneration (McEwen, Weiss, & Schwartz, 1968), and lifetime cumulative exposure to glucocorticoids was associated with the degree of hippocampal cell death (Landfield, Baskin, & Pitler, 1981; Landfield, Waymire, & Lynch, 1978; Landfield et al., 1977). The impact of glucocorticoid exposure on the hippocampus appears to focus on alteration of GRs and MRs. For example, a study by Sapolsky et al. (1986) administered cortisol at levels equivalent to those achieved after stress induction for 3 months. After this administration of cortisol, hippocampal GR and MR binding sites were downregulated by 50%, and this receptor depletion showed no recovery 4 months after exposure, suggesting a long-lasting effect of cortisol on GR and MR density (Sapolsky et al., 1986). This decreased availability of receptors limits their ability to downregulate the axis, resulting in increased activity. Taken together, these studies suggest that cumulative exposure to glucocorticoids can lead to the degenerative loss of glucocorticoid receptor neurons in the hippocampus and that chronic stress intensifies this process (Sapolsky et al., 1986).

The hippocampus plays an important role in negative feedback inhibition of the HPA axis response. In animal models, destruction of the hippocampus results in hypersecretion of corticosterone in response to a stressor (Feldman & Conforti, 2008; Knigge & Hays, 1963; Wilson, Greer, Greer, & Roberts, 1980) and attenuation of the suppressive effects of dexamethasone on the stress response (Feldman & Conforti, 1976). Additionally, corticosterone administration results in both a downregulation of MR and GR in the rat hippocampus as well as reduced sensitivity to feedback inhibition by glucocorticoids, exhibited by cortisol hypersecretion in response to stressors (Sapolsky & McEwen, 1985). Thus, greater exposure to glucocorticoids influences MR and GR expression, resulting in impaired negative feedback of the HPA axis response. This association has also been supported in human models; for example, Marin et al. (2007) assessed life stress in healthy women ages 15–19 and found

that exposure to episodic stressors in the context of high chronic stress led to increased cortisol release, both upon awakening and overall daily output, and reduced GR mRNA. Thus, chronic stress may lead to the sensitization of the HPA axis, resulting in greater cortisol production and impaired negative feedback.

Epigenetic programming may also contribute to reduced GR and MR expression. Early adversity is associated with increased methylation of the GR promoter gene, impairing transcription and thus expression of GR in the brain (Meaney et al., 1996). Reduced expression of GR decreases the ability of glucocorticoids to bind to GR and inhibit the stress response, leading to a prolonged HPA axis activation. Studies of postmortem brains of suicide completers who had been subjected to child abuse showed greater methylation of the GR in hippocampal regions (McGowan et al., 2009). Greater methylation was also associated with an attenuated response to the dexamethasone/CRH test (Baumeister, Lightman, & Pariante, 2014). Greater demethylation of the gene coding for the FKBP5, resulting in increased FKBP5 transcription and reduced GR activity, was found in victims of childhood trauma and associated with greater risk for PTSD, depression, and suicide (Klengel et al., 2012).

Poor negative feedback inhibition of the HPA axis has been associated with major depressive disorder (MDD; Pariante, 2006). Patients with MDD consistently show elevated basal cortisol in saliva, blood, urine, and hair (Nemeroff & Vale, 2005; Staufenbiel et al., 2013) and, to a lesser degree, in response to psychosocial stressors (Pariante & Lightman, 2008). Studies have also shown changes in both the function and the expression of GR in patients with MDD (Baumeister, Lightman, & Pariante, 2014). For instance, depressed patients show decreased suppression of cortisol secretion following dexamethasone administration and reduced neural GR expression postmortem (Pariante, 2006). Depressed patients also demonstrated an increased cortisol response to awakening that remains post remission of depression symptoms (Bhagwagar, Hafizi, & Cowen, 2003, 2005; Vreeburg et al., 2010). Additionally, hyperactivity at the HPA axis in response to stress has been identified in asymptomatic first-degree relatives of individuals diagnosed with MDD (Holsboer et al., 2008; Modell et al., 1998). Finally, antidepressant treatment that results in a reduction of MDD symptomatology has been linked to a normalization of the hyperactive HPA axis (Barden, Reul, & Holsboer, 1995), adrenal hypertrophy (Gillespie & Nemeroff, 2005), and improved balance of MR/GR expression (Brady et al., 1991; Reul et al., 1993; Seckl & Fink, 2008).

In summary, chronic exposure to stress may downregulate MRs and GRs in key regulatory regions of the brain, such as the hippocampus. Decreased MR and GR expression lead to poorer feedback inhibition of the HPA axis, resulting in prolonged activity of the stress response and elevated circulating cortisol levels. As a proximal factor in this etiological chain, elevated basal and stress-induced cortisol may then lead to the development of disorders such as MDD and social phobia.

HPA AXIS DOWNREGULATION
Exposure to stress may also result in long-term downregulation or blunting of the HPA axis through the upregulation of regulatory systems. For example, blunted HPA axis functioning, that is, lower activation relative to non-affected peers, has been found among combat-exposed individuals (Bourne, Rose, & Mason, 1968), sexual abuse survivors (Meewissee et al., 2007), survivors of natural disasters (Goenjian et al., 2001), and survivors of motor vehicle accidents (McFarlane et al., 1997). Thus, this blunting effect may be specific to some types of traumatic events. Likewise, there is evidence that this blunting effect is unique, or more commonly observed among those at risk for, or affected with PTSD, which provides a window to understand both the mechanisms of downregulation and how downregulation impacts the phenomenology of PTSD (Yehuda, 2000).

A plethora of research demonstrates lower cortisol in subjects with PTSD compared to healthy controls (Goenjian et al., 2003; Yehuda, 2000; Yehuda & Seckl, 2011). Such blunted cortisol levels occur as a result of increased negative feedback resulting from increased glucocorticoids receptor sensitivity (Yehuda, 2000). Evidence for these findings comes from studies using metyrapone, which blocks cortisol synthesis and thus stops inhibitory feedback by preventing the binding of cortisol to MRs and GRs. After administration of metyrapone, patients with PTSD showed greater ACTH responses than nonaffected individuals (Yehuda et al., 1996). Thus, when negative feedback is prevented, there is clear evidence for HPA axis activation in PTSD, suggesting that the blunted cortisol levels result from increased inhibitory feedback. In addition, when cortisol is administered after metyrapone treatment, PTSD patients show a faster and more pronounced downregulation of ACTH compared to nonaffected

individuals, suggesting enhanced sensitivity to cortisol (Yehuda et al., 1996).

It is still unclear why some stressors may lead to sensitization of the axis while others may lead to blunting. However, there is evidence that the timing of the stressor may play a role. Researchers utilizing dexamethasone have found enhanced suppression of ACTH and cortisol in PTSD patients, indicative of increased GR expression (Yehuda et al., 2004). Greater rises in leukocyte GR correlated with younger age at trauma exposure, suggesting that increased GR in leukocytes may reflect developmental processes (Yehuda & Seckl, 2011). Likewise, there is evidence that blunting of cortisol in plasma and brain tissue may be a compensatory process for increased cortisol in the kidney and liver due to decreased levels of 11-β-dehydrogenase isozyme 2 (11β-HSD2), an enzyme that converts cortisol to inactive corticosterone in peripheral tissues. PTSD patients show evidence of reduced 11β-HSD2, and this effect is greatest in individuals who were the youngest at the time of exposure (Yehuda et al., 2009). This developmental effect may be related to the role that 11β-HSD2 play in facilitating survival. In the context of early life adversity, particularly lack of access to food or key nutrients, decreases in 11β-HSD2 allows cortisol to persist and activate renal MR, increasing sodium retention to prevent against dietary deficiencies. Increased cortisol levels in the liver and kidney would then be complemented by lower levels of plasma cortisol in the brain and muscles to protect against the deleterious catabolic effects of glucocorticoids, promoting longer term survival (Yehuda & Seckl, 2011).

There is evidence that enhanced negative feedback leading to blunted HPA axis activation can impact both risk and maintenance of PTSD. For example, some research suggests that the immediate response of the HPA axis to trauma may predict risk for PTSD. Higher risk of PTSD has been observed in trauma-exposed individuals with lower cortisol levels in the peritraumatic period and those who display an enhanced cortisol suppression in response to dexamethasone (McFarlane et al., 1997). Also, PTSD-specific HPA functioning in the form of diminished morning but elevated afternoon cortisol levels within a week of exposure have been linked with subsequent development of PTSD (Aardal-Eriksson, Eriksson, & Thorell, 2001). Finally, patients administered stress-level doses of hydrocortisone while in treatment in an intensive care unit (ICU) demonstrate lower rates of ICU-related PTSD symptoms than those that were not treated with hydrocortisone (Schelling et al., 1999). Thus, higher glucocorticoids levels in the context of major stressors may be protective against the development of PTSD (Raison & Miller, 2003). Lower cortisol levels in response to stressors may lead to deficits in fear extinction. Glucocorticoid action in the amygdala promotes fear extinction learning (Yehuda & LeDoux, 2007); thus, decreased glucocorticoid availability may impair extinction learning (Myers & Davis, 2007). Animal studies by Yang, Chao, and Lu (2006) found that extinction training produces increases in corticosterone and the administration of the glucocorticoid antagonist metyrapone impairs fear extinction. In human studies, daily low-dose hydrocortisone administration reduced PTSD symptoms, including re-experiencing, hyperarousal, and avoidance, potentially by promoting fear extinction (Aerni et al., 2004). Thus, lower cortisol levels in response to trauma may interfere with extinction learning and increase risk for PTSD.

In conclusion, exposure to traumatic stressors may result in a downregulation of the HPA axis, evidenced by lower cortisol levels and enhanced negative feedback. Downregulation of the HPA axis may represent a developmental process, as younger age at trauma exposure leads to relative lower cortisol levels and greater negative feedback. Lower cortisol levels in response to stressors increase the risk for PTSD, potentially by impairing the fear extinction process.

HPA AXIS AND IMMUNITY

One of the critical functions of the HPA axis is to inhibit the inflammatory immune response during stressors (McEwen et al., 1997). A central component of the human immune response is inflammation. In response to specific types of injuries, the body elicits an inflammatory response aimed to protect healthy cells from further damage and to initiate tissue repair (Petrillo, Bortner, & Cidlowski, 2016). However, chronic or dysregulated inflammation has significant health consequences, such as contributing to a variety of autoimmune disorders such as arthritis and allergies, and it has been linked to the risk and course of depression. Thus, inflammatory responses that fall outside an adaptive range (i.e., by being too low or too high) are maladaptive and may contribute to either poor recovery or to injury and disease. The HPA axis appears to play a key regulatory role in regulating the inflammatory response, with glucocorticoids both facilitating anti-inflammatory responses and downregulating inflammatory responses (Petrillo et al., 2016). However,

chronic stress may impair the anti-inflammatory capacity of HPA axis activity on immune cells, leading to chronic inflammation and disease (Miller, Cohen, & Ritchey, 2002).

The immune response is associated with the release of pro-inflammatory cytokines such as tumor necrosis factor-α (TNF-α), Interleukin-1a and B (IL-1a and IL-1B), and Interleukin-6 (IL-6) (Raison & Miller, 2003; Sapolsky, Romero, & Munck, 2000), which regulate local and systemic responses to the pathogens or insults (Dantzer et al., 2008). Activation of the inflammatory immune response and resultant stimulation of pain receptors initiates the HPA axis stress response (Petrillo et al., 2016; Sapolsky et al., 2000). Cytokines within activated immune cells stimulate the release of glucocorticoids. In turn, glucocorticoids exhibit immunosuppressive and anti-inflammatory effects by inhibiting the synthesis, release, and efficacy of pro-inflammatory cytokines (Sapolsky et al., 2000). For instance, glucocorticoids have an inhibitory effect on nuclear factor KB signaling pathways, which acts to suppress the production and activity of pro-inflammatory cytokines during stressor exposure and return the organisms back to homeostasis after the cessation of stressors (McEwen et al., 1997; McKay & Cidlowski, 1999; Raison & Miller, 2003; Ruzek et al., 1999). Also, direct binding of GR to GREs in DNA enhances the transcription of anti-inflammatory genes and suppresses transcription of pro-inflammatory cytokines (Petrillo et al., 2016). Exposure to high concentrations of glucocorticoids, such as in the context of chronic stress, spurs white blood cells to downregulate receptors responsible for binding to glucocorticoids (G. E. Miller et al., 2002). Reduced receptor availability results in a decreased capacity for the immune system to respond to the anti-inflammatory effects of glucocorticoids (G. E. Miller et al., 2002). Therefore, immune system activity spurs anti-inflammatory effects by glucocorticoids. However, variations in glucocorticoid availability may result in decreased the sensitivity of the immune cells to the anti-inflammatory effects of glucocorticoids, prolonging inflammatory responses and increasing risk for disease.

Activation of pro-inflammatory cytokines is characterized by drastic changes in subjective experience (e.g., mood, energy levels, cognitive capacity) and behaviors design to improve an individual's capacity to cope with infections (Dantzer et al., 2008). For instance, rats and mice administered IL-1B or TNF-α exhibit behavioral signs of sickness, including lack of interest in their physical environment, decreased motor activity, social withdrawal, reduced food and water intake, fatigue, increased slow-wave sleep, and altered cognition (Dantzer, 2001; Dantzer et al., 2008). This constellation of symptoms associated with activation of pro-inflammatory cytokines has been termed "sickness behavior" (Dantzer, 2001). Anti-inflammatory cytokines inhibit pro-inflammatory cytokine production and signaling, in turn regulating the intensity and duration of the immune response and sickness behavior (Heyen et al., 2000; Strle et al., 2007). In animal models of sickness behavior caused by injection of lipopolysaccharide (LPS), attenuation of sickness behavior results from central administration of anti-inflammatory cytokines IL-10 and insulin-like growth factor I (IGF-I), a growth factor behavior like an anti-inflammatory cytokine (Bluthé et al., 1999; Dantzer et al., 1999). Action of glucocorticoids, particularly GR sensitivity, increased anti-inflammatory and decreased pro-inflammatory signaling, thereby playing a role in the production and cessation of sickness behavior. Heightened immune system activation and MDD show similar behavioral manifestations, suggesting that MDD and inflammatory processes may have bidirectional effects. For example, both involve withdrawal from physical and social environments, pain, malaise, and anhedonia (Dantzer et al., 2008). Additionally, higher rates of MDD are found in patients with conditions resulting in chronic inflammation such as cardiovascular disease, type 2 diabetes, and rheumatoid arthritis (Steptoe, 2007). Smith (1991) proposed that MDD may represent a maladaptive version of cytokine-induced sickness occurring as a result of an exacerbated immune response. For example, individuals with known risk factors for psychopathology, such as hyperactive CRH responsivity or decreased GR expression, may also exhibit prolonged immune activation and sickness behavior (Dantzer et al., 2008). In support of this theory, depressed patients display an increased prevalence of inflammatory biomarkers, such as IL-6, TNF-α, and C-reactive protein (Miller, Maletic, & Raison, 2009). Additional support for a link between immune activation and psychopathology comes from studies of cancer and hepatitis C patients in which immunotherapy involving administration of recombinant cytokines IL-2 and IFN-1, used to boost the immune system and treat these conditions, resulted in severe neuropsychiatric changes in patients, including the onset of MDD in up to half of patients (Capuron, Ravaud, & Dantzer, 2000; Capuron et al., 2003; Denicoff et al., 1987; Renault et al., 1987). In-vitro studies of peripheral immune cells taken from patients with MDD exhibit decreased sensitivity to the immunosuppressive effects of cortisol (Pariante & Miller, 2001). This finding follows from the assertion that immune cells downregulate receptors responsible for binding to glucocorticoids in response to elevated levels of glucocorticoids, resulting in decreased anti-inflammatory effects of cortisol (Miller et al., 2002). In normal subjects, glucocorticoids inhibit natural killer cell activity, lymphocyte proliferation, and cytokine production. In depressed subjects, however, this inhibitory effect of glucocorticoids is attenuated. This attenuation is especially apparent among depressed subjects who show dexamethasone non-suppression, suggesting that impaired GR signaling results in impaired inhibition of the immune response (Bluthé, Kelley, & Dantzer, 2006; Leon, Kozak, Rudolph, & Kluger, 1999; Ye & Johnson, 1999). Taken together, this research suggests that HPA axis hyperactivity in response to stress and decreased GR expression may influence immune system activity and immune cell responsivity, resulting in greater exposure to pro-inflammatory cytokines, and increasing risk for the development of MDD.

HPA AXIS AND OBESITY

Recent studies suggest that HPA axis activity may play an important role in the development of obesity, which is, in turn, associated with risk for depression (Bornstein et al., 2006; McElroy et al., 2004). Individuals exposed to chronic stress, such as lower socioeconomic status and greater job strain (Baum, Garofalo, & Yali, 1999; Eric J. Brunner, Chandola, & Marmot, 2007), also display higher rates of obesity (E. J. Brunner, Chandola, & Marmot, 2007; McLaren, 2007). Furthermore, central obesity, that is, obesity of the abdominal area, has been associated with chronic inflammation (Zambon, Pauletto, & Crepaldi, 2005) and increased HPA axis activity (Björntorp & Rosmond, 2000).

The link between HPA axis activity and central obesity was first suggested on studies of Cushing's syndrome. Cushing's syndrome involves hypercortisolemia, hypertension, insulin resistance, hyperglycemia, and rapid weight gain (Hankin, Theile, & Steinbeck, 1977; Nieuwenhuizen & Rutters, 2008). Weight gain associated with Cushing's syndrome shows commonalities with visceral obesity (e.g., fat that accumulates between the organs within the abdominal cavity; Nieuwenhuizen & Rutters, 2008) and treatment by adrenalectomy decreases obesity and glucose intolerance (Björntorp & Rosmond, 2000; Nieuwenhuizen & Rutters, 2008). This suggests that variations in HPA axis reactivity may play an important role in the pathogenesis of obesity.

Studies of the exogenous administration of glucocorticoids suggest that glucocorticoids can facilitate metabolic changes also seen in obesity, such as hyperinsulinemia and insulin resistance (McMahon, Gerich, & Rizza, 1988). CRH overexpression in mice has been associated with increased food intake, weight gain, and insulin resistance (Coste, Murray, & Stenzel-Poore, 2001; Stenzel-Poore et al., 1992), as well as impaired stress coping and learning potential (Coste et al., 2001; Müller et al., 2004). Adrenalectomy has been shown to normalize or prevent weight gain and decrease the appearance of metabolic changes seen in obesity (Dubuc & Wilden, 1986; Yukimura & Bray, 1978). In turn, exogenous glucocorticoid treatment after adrenalectomy results in the reappearance of these obesity symptoms (Ohshima et al., 1984). In humans, a number of studies have shown associations between central obesity and increased cortisol (Cheek et al., 1981; Murphy & Jachan, 1968; Pasquali et al., 1993; Streeten et al., 1969). Cortisol levels post lunch correlate significantly with BMI, waist-to-hip ratio, insulin, fasting glucose, triglycerides, cholesterol, and blood pressure in men, and morning cortisol levels showed significant correlations with BMI and waist-to-hip ratio (Rosmond, Dallman, & Björntorp, 1998). Compared to lean individuals, obese individuals demonstrate increased levels of cortisol in response to stimulation with intravenous ovine CRH (Vgontzas et al., 2007), ACTH, and mental stress tests (Mårin et al., 1992). Taken together, this research suggests that hypercortisolemia plays an important role in the development of obesity, particularly central obesity, supporting variations in HPA axis reactivity as an important risk factor in the pathogenesis of obesity.

A number of mechanisms may explain the link between HPA axis activity and obesity. First, HPA axis hyperactivation may influence obesity through food intake. Exogenous ovine CRH administration and decreased responsivity to dexamethasone suppression have been linked with increases in appetite, especially for more palatable foods (Cizza & Rother, 2011). Obese individuals with higher cortisol levels in response to stress ate more than less reactive obese participants and controls (Epel et al., 2004; Wansink, Cheney, & Chan, 2003). Indeed, chronic and repeated stress has been linked with increased food intake and preferences for "comfort food" (T. C. Adam & Epel, 2007; Epel et al., 2004). Thus, exposure to stressors and subsequent HPA axis hyperactivity may impact food intake and choices, further increasing the risk for obesity.

Another possible mechanism by which HPA axis activity influences obesity is glucocorticoid metabolism. Within adipose tissue, glucocorticoids promote the differentiation of preadipocytes into mature adipocytes while increasing lipoprotein lipase activity (Nieuwenhuizen & Rutters, 2008). Increased availability of active glucocorticoids results in greater development of adipose tissue and weight gain. A model of transgenic mice designed to overproduce 11B-HSD1 found that these mice displayed symptoms of Cushing's syndrome, including increased food intake, weight gain, and behavioral changes (Masuzaki et al., 2001; Masuzaki & Flier, 2003; Tomlinson, 2005). Overexpression of 11B-HSD1 in adipose tissues resulted in visceral obesity and metabolic syndrome in mice fed a high-fat diet (Masuzaki et al., 2001). Conversely, overproduction of 11B-HSD2 in adipose tissue results in decreased food intake, improved glucose tolerance, and greater insulin sensitivity and protects obesity-prone mice from becoming obese when fed a high-fat diet (Kershaw et al., 2005; Masuzaki & Flier, 2003). Expression of 11B-HSD1 in subcutaneous adipose tissue significantly correlated with waist size, subcutaneous adipose tissue to visceral adipose tissue, and total adipose tissue (Simonyte et al., 2009). Obese women who underwent gastric bypass surgery demonstrated decreased mRNA 11B-HSD1 expression in adipose tissue 2 years later (Rask et al., 2013). These findings support an important function of cortisol in the development and maintenance of adipose tissue, further supporting the link between HPA axis activity and the development of obesity.

Sleep may also contribute to the link between HPA axis activity and obesity. Stress exposure leads to shorter, less restorative sleep (Vgontzas et al., 2008) and increased BMI (Cappuccio et al., 2008; Lucassen, Rother, & Cizza, 2012). Individuals who sleep less than 5–6 hours per night on average demonstrated distinct yet modest weight gain (Cappuccio et al., 2008; Lucassen et al., 2012). Basal cortisol levels are at their lowest during nighttime hours and facilitate the transition to sleep; thus, increases in nighttime cortisol may contribute to sleep difficulties. For example, subjects with insomnia displayed increased levels of 24-hour plasma cortisol and ACTH and urinary free cortisol (Balbo, Leproult, & Van Cauter, 2010). Additionally, the combination of altered HPA axis function and obesity has been frequently observed in patients suffering from insomnia, depression, or obstructive sleep apnea

(Balbo et al., 2010; Vgontzas et al., 2007). In obese patients with sleep apnea, morning levels of ACTH and cortisol positively correlated with the number of sleep apnea events the night prior (de Jonge et al., 2012). Treatment of sleep apnea by continuous positive airway pressure resulted in a normalization of cortisol levels (Vgontzas et al., 2007). Thus, variations in HPA axis reactivity may contribute to the comorbidity of obesity with sleep difficulties and disorders.

In summary, hypercortisolemia increases the risk for central obesity potentially by influencing food intake and preferences, glucocorticoid metabolism in adipose tissue, and by disrupting sleep. Central obesity, in turn, is associated with decreased self-esteem and body satisfaction (especially among adolescents who are at risk for depression; Mond et al., 2011; Wardle & Cooke, 2005), social withdrawal (Erermis et al., 2004), and discrimination (Spahlholz et al., 2016), all known risk factors for depression. Thus, obesity is likely an intermediary mechanism by which the HPA axis impacts the development of depression.

HPA AXIS AND MICROBIOTA-GUT-BRAIN AXIS BIOME

The HPA axis plays an important role in the regulation of the microbiota-gut-brain axis, the gastrointestinal microbiota which regulates basic physiological processes through interactions with the central nervous system (CNS), autonomic nervous system (ANS), neuroendocrine, and neuroimmune systems (Scott, Clarke, & Dinan, 2013). Both the external and internal surfaces of our bodies, particularly the gut, contain many of these microorganisms, which contribute to processes such as immunity, nutrient transportation, and metabolism (Petra et al., 2015). Functioning of the symbiotic relationship between our bodies and gut microbiota has important implications for immunity and psychopathology. HPA axis activity plays a role in the regulation of the immune cells in the gut, affecting gut permeability, motility, secretion, barrier function, and gut microbiota composition (Petra et al., 2015). Impacts of chronic stress exposure on HPA axis functioning may dysregulate biome-gut functioning, contributing to increased inflammation and disease.

Emotional and physical stress influences the composition of gut microbiota (Dinan & Cryan, 2012). For example, exposure to chronic stress in adult mice decreased the abundance of *Bacteroides* species and increased *Clostridium* species and increased interleukin-6 and C-C chemokine ligand 2 production, indicative of immune system activation (Bailey et al., 2011). Acute stress increases GI (Overman et al., 2012) and blood-brain-barrier (Esposito et al., 2002) permeability through activation of mast cells. Activation of mast cells disrupts the intestinal barrier and permits penetration of luminal antigens, microflora metabolites, toxins, and lippolysaccarishin into systemic circulation and the CNS (Santos et al., 2001). Stress-induced mast cell activation and subsequent gut permeability increase inflammation and autoimmunity responses (Kinet, 2007; Rottem & Mekori, 2005; Sismanopoulos et al., 2012; Theoharides et al., 2012). Turnbull and Rivier (1999) propose that components of the bacterial cell wall stimulate immune cells within the gut to release inflammatory cytokines, consequently influencing CNS regulation of HPA axis responsivity. Thus, psychological stress increases permeability of the gut through the activation of mast cells, which in turn spurs production of pro-inflammatory cytokines, leading to activation of the HPA axis to downregulate the immune response (Scott et al., 2013). For instance, Shanks et al. (2000) demonstrated that administration of an endotoxin to neonatal rats had long-term effects on both their immune function and HPA axis activity. Meddings and Swain (2000) found increased intestinal permeability and corticosterone levels as a result of restraint stress in rats. Finally, modulation of gut microbiota, such as administration of probiotics, prevented gut leakiness and led to an attenuated response to acute psychological stress in rats (Ait-Belgnaoui et al., 2012). Together these studies suggest that gut microbiota and HPA axis reactivity are dynamically related and that this interplay, in turn, affects long-term mental and physical health outcomes.

Inflammation resulting from microbiota-gut-brain axis dysfunction leads to a number of health concerns. Stress-induced mast cell activation has been implicated in functional GI diseases (Rijnierse, Nijkamp, & Kraneveld, 2007) such as irritable bowel syndrome (Scott et al., 2013). Additionally, increased expression of inflammatory biomarkers within the microbiota, such as IL-6, TNF-α , and C-reactive protein, has been linked with mood disorders such as depression (Miller et al., 2009). Current research suggests that stress causes intestinal mucosal dysfunction, leading to increased translocation of bacteria (leaky gut), which increases immune system reactivity and subsequent HPA axis activation. Thus, stress-induced "leaky gut" may explain HPA axis hyperactivity in MDD (Scott et al., 2013). Support for this hypothesis comes from a clinical study in which patients who took 30 days of gut-stabilizing probiotics demonstrated reduced urinary free cortisol levels and improved scores on measures of psychological well-being compared to controls (Messaoudi et al., 2011). In conclusion, stress influences gut microbiota permeability and composition, leading to increased inflammatory immune responses and HPA axis activity, which in turn influences health outcomes.

Conclusion

In this chapter, we first highlighted the conceptual challenges involved in examining the role of neuroendocrine function in stress-related psychopathology and then reviewed the potential mechanisms by which neuroendocrine processes may impact the risk, course, or phenomenology of stress-related disorders. We argue that understanding the meaning of variability in indices of hormonal functioning is the most difficult conceptual challenge encountered by neuroendocrine researchers. There has been a tendency to oversimplify the meaning of the observed variability in target hormones (e.g., high cortisol means an overactive HPA, which is likely bad). This is not surprising, given our tendency to oversimply the meaning of the observed variability in target hormones. Yet the solution to this problem is complex because it requires the eventual parsing of the variability into sources within and outside neuroendocrine systems. To this end, we call for greater focus on understanding the factors that contribute to individual differences in hormonal outputs at multiple levels of analysis, from understanding the role of psychological processes (e.g., goals) to the development of new methods that allow us to quantify the adaptive value or maladaptation of an endocrine response to different stressors.

We also propose that greater emphasis should be placed on understanding the mechanisms by which variability in neuroendocrine functioning impacts stress-related psychopathology. Unfortunately, such efforts are constrained by our limited understanding of the basic mechanisms of psychopathology in general and by the likelihood that current diagnostic categories encompass shared, transdiagnostic, processes. The Research Domain Criteria proposed by the National Institute of Mental Health (Insel et al., 2010) can provide a basic starting point to identify potential transdiagnostic mechanisms that are impacted by neuroendocrine functioning.

Finally, neuroendocrine function is integrated into multiple other systems (e.g., sympathetic nervous system, immune system) and its impact on psychopathology is most often not independent of these systems. Unfortunately, neuroendocrine research has been generally conducted in isolation, which limits our understanding of how hormones interact with other biological systems to impact stress-related psychopathology. We could argue that this chapter is guilty of the same sin, for the contributions of neuroendocrine systems to psychopathology can't be fully understood without exploring how neuroendocrine processes interact with other brain systems, which are reviewed in other chapters of this book. There is a great need for research that integrates multiple biological systems and explores how these systems work together to facilitate or mitigate the risk and course of stress psychopathology.

References

Aardal-Eriksson, E., Eriksson, T. E., & Thorell, L.-H. (2001). Salivary cortisol, posttraumatic stress symptoms, and general health in the acute phase and during 9-month follow-up. *Biological Psychiatry, 50*(12), 986–993.

Abelson, J. L., Erickson, T. M., Mayer, S. E., Crocker, J., Briggs, H., Lopez-Duran, N. L., & Liberzon, I. (2014). Brief cognitive intervention can modulate neuroendocrine stress responses to the Trier Social Stress Test: Buffering effects of a compassionate goal orientation. *Psychoneuroendocrinology, 44*, 60–70.

Adam, E. K., Doane, L. D., Zinbarg, R. E., Mineka, S., Craske, M. G., & Griffith, J. W. (2010). Prospective prediction of major depressive disorder from cortisol awakening responses in adolescence. *Psychoneuroendocrinology, 35*(6), 921–931.

Adam, T. C., & Epel, E. S. (2007). Stress, eating and the reward system. *Physiology & Behavior, 91*(4), 449–458.

Aerni, A., Traber, R., Hock, C., Roozendaal, B., Schelling, G., Papassotiropoulos, A., ... de Quervain, D. J.-F. (2004). Low-dose cortisol for symptoms of posttraumatic stress disorder. *American Journal of Psychiatry, 161*(8), 1488–1490.

Ait-Belgnaoui, A., Durand, H., Cartier, C., Chaumaz, G., Eutamene, H., Ferrier, L., ... Theodorou, V. (2012). Prevention of gut leakiness by a probiotic treatment leads to attenuated HPA response to an acute psychological stress in rats. *Psychoneuroendocrinology, 37*(11), 1885–1895.

Alhaj, H. A., Massey, A. E., & McAllister-Williams, R. H. (2006). Effects of DHEA administration on episodic memory, cortisol and mood in healthy young men: A double-blind, placebo-controlled study. *Psychopharmacology, 188*(4), 541–551.

Bailey, M. T., Dowd, S. E., Galley, J. D., Hufnagle, A. R., Allen, R. G., & Lyte, M. (2011). Exposure to a social stressor alters the structure of the intestinal microbiota: Implications for stressor-induced immunomodulation. *Brain, Behavior, and Immunity, 25*(3), 397–407.

Bains, J. S., Cusulin, J. I. W., & Inoue, W. (2015). Stress: Stress-related synaptic plasticity in the hypothalamus. *Nature Publishing Group, 16*(7), 377–388.

Balbo, M., Leproult, R., & Van Cauter, E. (2010). Impact of sleep and its disturbances on hypothalamo-pituitary-adrenal axis activity. *International Journal of Endocrinology, 2010*, 759234.

Barden, N., Reul, J. M. H. M., & Holsboer, F. (1995). Do antidepressants stabilize mood through actions on the hypothalamic-pituitary-adrenocortical system? *Trends in Neurosciences*, *18*(1), 6–11.

Baum, A., Garofalo, J. P., & Yali, A. M. (1999). Socioeconomic status and chronic stress: Does stress account for SES effects on health? *Annals of the New York Academy of Sciences*, *896*(1), 131–144.

Baumeister, D., Lightman, S. L., & Pariante, C. M. (2014). The interface of stress and the HPA axis in behavioural phenotypes of mental illness. In: Pariante C., Lapiz-Bluhm M. (eds) *Behavioral Neurobiology of Stress-Related Disorders. Current Topics in Behavioral Neuroscience*, *vol* 18 (pp. 13–24). Berlin: Springer.

Bhagwagar, Z., Hafizi, S., & Cowen, P. J. (2003). Increase in concentration of waking salivary cortisol in recovered patients with depression. *American Journal of Psychiatry*, *160*(10), 1890–1891.

Bhagwagar, Z., Hafizi, S., & Cowen, P. J. (2005). Increased salivary cortisol after waking in depression. *Psychopharmacology*, *182*(1), 54–57.

Biederman, J., Rosenbaum, J. F., Hirshfeld, D. R., Faraone, S. V., Bolduc, E. A., Gersten, M.,...Reznick, J. S. (1990). Psychiatric correlates of behavioral inhibition in young children of parents with and without psychiatric disorders. *Archives of General Psychiatry*, *47*(1), 21.

Björntorp, P., & Rosmond, R. (2000). Obesity and cortisol. *Nutrition*, *16*(10), 924–936.

Bloch, M., Schmidt, P. J., Danaceau, M. A., Adams, L. F., & Rubinow, D. R. (1999). Dehydroepiandrosterone treatment of midlife dysthymia. *Biological Psychiatry*, *45*, 1533–1541.

Bluthé, R.-M., Kelley, K. W., & Dantzer, R. (2006). Effects of insulin-like growth factor-I on cytokine-induced sickness behavior in mice. *Brain, Behavior, and Immunity*, *20*(1), 57–63.

Bluthé, R. M., Castanon, N., Pousset, F., Bristow, A., Ball, C., Lestage, J.,...Dantzer, R. (1999). Central injection of IL-10 antagonizes the behavioural effects of lipopolysaccharide in rats. *Psychoneuroendocrinology*, *24*(3), 301–311.

Bornstein, S. R., Schuppenies, A., Wong, M., & Licinio, J. (2006). Approaching the shared biology of obesity and depression: The stress axis as the locus of gene-environment interactions. *Molecular Psychiatry*, *11*(10), 892–902.

Bourne, P. G., Rose, R. M., & Mason, J. W. (1968). 17-OHCS levels in combat. *Archives of General Psychiatry*, *19*(2), 135.

Brady, L. S., Whitfield, H. J., Fox, R. J., Gold, P. W., Herkenham, M., & Herkenham, M. (1991). Long-term antidepressant administration alters corticotropin-releasing hormone, tyrosine hydroxylase, and mineralocorticoid receptor gene expression in rat brain: Therapeutic implications. *The Journal of Clinical Investigation*, *87*(3), 831–837.

Brunner, E. J., Chandola, T., & Marmot, M. G. (2007). Prospective effect of job strain on general and central obesity in the Whitehall II Study. *American Journal of Epidemiology*, *165*(7), 828–837.

Buchanan, T. W., Brechtel, A., Sollers, J. J., & Lovallo, W. R. (2001). Exogenous cortisol exerts effects on the startle reflex independent of emotional modulation. *Pharmacology, Biochemistry and Behavior*, *68*, 203–210.

Buchanan, T. W., & Lovallo, W. R. (2001). Enhanced memory for emotional material following stress-level cortisol treatment in humans. *Psychoneuroendocrinology*, *26*(3), 307–317.

Buijs, R. M., Eden, C. G. Van, & Van Eden, C. G. (2000). The integration of stress by the hypothalamus, amygdala and prefrontal cortex: Balance between the autonomic nervous system and the neuroendocrine system. *Progress in Brain Research*, *126*, 117–132.

Burke, H. M., Davis, M. C., Otte, C., & Mohr, D. C. (2005). Depression and cortisol responses to psychological stress: A meta-analysis. *Psychoneuroendocrinology*, *30*(9), 846–856.

Cappuccio, F. P., Taggart, F. M., Kandala, N.-B., Currie, A., Peile, E., Stranges, S., & Miller, M. A. (2008). Meta-analysis of short sleep duration and obesity in children and adults. *Sleep*, *31*(5), 619–626.

Capuron, L., Raison, C. L., Musselman, D. L., Lawson, D. H., Nemeroff, C. B., & Miller, A. H. (2003). Association of exaggerated HPA axis response to the initial injection of interferon-alpha with development of depression during interferon-alpha therapy. *American Journal of Psychiatry*, *160*(7), 1342–1345.

Capuron, L., Ravaud, A., & Dantzer, R. (2000). Early depressive symptoms in cancer patients receiving interleukin 2 and/or interferon alfa-2b therapy. *Journal of Clinical Oncology: Official Journal of the American Society of Clinical Oncology*, *18*(10), 2143–2151.

Cardoso, C., Ellenbogen, M. A., Orlando, M. A., Bacon, S. L., & Joober, R. (2013). Intranasal oxytocin attenuates the cortisol response to physical stress: A dose-response study. *Psychoneuroendocrinology*, *38*(3), 399–407.

Carter, C. S., & Altemus, M. (1997). Integrative functions of lactational hormones in social behavior and stress management. *Annals of the New York Academy of Sciences*, *807*(Hd 16679), 164–174.

Cheek, D. B., Graystone, J. E., Seamark, R. F., McIntosh, J. E., Phillipou, G., & Court, J. M. (1981). Urinary steroid metabolites and the overgrowth of lean and fat tissues in obese girls. *The American Journal of Clinical Nutrition*, *34*(9), 1804–1810.

Chida, Y., & Steptoe, A. (2009). Cortisol awakening response and psychosocial factors: A systematic review and meta-analysis. *Biological Psychology*, *80*(3), 265–278.

Cizza, G., & Rother, K. I. (2011). Was Feuerbach right: Are we what we eat? *The Journal of Clinical Investigation*, *121*(8), 2969–2971.

Cordero, M. I., Merino, J. J., & Sandi, C. (1998). Correlational relationship between shock intensity and corticosterone secretion on the establishment and subsequent expression of contextual fear conditioning. *Behavioral Neuroscience*, *112*(4), 885–891.

Cordero, M. I., & Sandi, C. (1998). A role for brain glucocorticoid receptors in contextual fear conditioning: Dependence upon training intensity. *Brain Research*, *786*, 11–17.

Coste, S. C., Murray, S. E., & Stenzel-Poore, M. P. (2001). Animal models of CRH excess and CRH receptor deficiency display altered adaptations to stress. *Peptides*, *22*(5), 733–741.

Dantzer, R. (2001). Cytokine-induced sickness behavior: Where do we stand? *Brain, Behavior, and Immunity*, *15*(1), 7–24.

Dantzer, R., Gheusi, G., Johnson, R. W., & Kelley, K. W. (1999). Central administration of insulin-like growth factor-1 inhibits lipopolysaccharide-induced sickness behavior in mice. *Neuroreport*, *10*(2), 289–292.

Dantzer, R., O'Connor, J. C., Freund, G. G., Johnson, R. W., & Kelley, K. W. (2008). From inflammation to sickness and depression: When the immune system subjugates the brain. *Nature Reviews Neuroscience*, *9*(1), 46–56.

Davis, E. P., Donzella, B., Krueger, W. K., & Gunnar, M. R. (1999). The start of a new school year: Individual differences in salivary cortisol response in relation to child temperament. *Developmental Psychobiology*, *35*(3), 188–196.

Davydov, D. M., Shapiro, D., Goldstein, I. B., & Chicz-DeMet, A. (2005). Moods in everyday situations: Effects of menstrual cycle, work, and stress hormones. *Journal of Psychosomatic Research, 58*(4), 343–349.

de Jonge, L., Zhao, X., Mattingly, M. S., Zuber, S. M., Piaggi, P., Csako, G., & Cizza, G. (2012). Poor sleep quality and sleep apnea are associated with higher resting energy expenditure in obese individuals with short sleep duration. *The Journal of Clinical Endocrinology & Metabolism, 97*(8), 2881–2889.

de Kloet, C. S., Vermetten, E., Heijnen, C. J., Geuze, E., Lentjes, E. G. W. M., & Westenberg, H. G. M. (2007). Enhanced cortisol suppression in response to dexamethasone administration in traumatized veterans with and without posttraumatic stress disorder. *Psychoneuroendocrinology, 32*(3), 215–226.

De Kloet, E. R. (2004). Hormones and the stressed brain. *Annals of the New York Academy of Sciences, 1018,* 1–15.

De Kloet, E. R., Joëls, M., & Holsboer, F. (2005). Stress and the brain: From adaptation to disease. *Nature Reviews Neuroscience, 6*(6), 463–475.

Denicoff, K. D., Rubinow, D. R., Papa, M. Z., Simpson, C., Seipp, C. A., Lotze, M. T., ... Rosenberg, S. A. (1987). The neuropsychiatric effects of treatment with interleukin-2 and lymphokine-activated killer cells. *Annals of Internal Medicine, 107*(3), 293–300.

Dettling, A. C., Gunnar, M. R., & Donzella, B. (1999). Cortisol levels of young children in full-day childcare centers: Relations with age and temperament. *Psychoneuroendocrinology, 24*(5), 519–536.

DeVries, A. C., Glasper, E. R., & Detillion, C. E. (2003). Social modulation of stress responses. *Physiology & Behavior, 79*(3), 399–407.

Dickerson, S. S., & Kemeny, M. E. (2004). Acute stressors and cortisol responses: A theoretical integration and synthesis of laboratory research. *Psychological Bulletin, 130*(3), 355–391.

Dinan, T. G., & Cryan, J. F. (2012). Regulation of the stress response by the gut microbiota: Implications for psychoneuroendocrinology. *Psychoneuroendocrinology, 37*(9), 1369–1378.

Ditzen, B., Schaer, M., Gabriel, B., Bodenmann, G., Ehlert, U., & Heinrichs, M. (2009). Intranasal oxytocin increases positive communication and reduces cortisol levels during couple conflict. *Biological Psychiatry, 65*(9), 728–731.

Doig, R. J., Mummery, R. V, Willis, M. R., & Elkes, A. (1966). Plasma cortisol levels in depression. *The British Journal of Psychiatry: The Journal of Mental Science, 112*(493), 1263–1267.

Domes, G., Heinrichs, M., Gläscher, J., Büchel, C., Braus, D. F., & Herpertz, S. C. (2007). Oxytocin attenuates amygdala responses to emotional faces regardless of valence. *Biological Psychiatry, 62*(10), 1187–1190.

Donley, M. P., Schulkin, J., & Rosen, J. B. (2005). Glucocorticoid receptor antagonism in the basolateral amygdala and ventral hippocampus interferes with long-term memory of contextual fear. *Behavioural Brain Research, 164*(2), 197–205.

Dubuc, P. U., & Wilden, N. J. (1986). Adrenalectomy reduces but does not reverse obesity in ob/ob mice. *International Journal of Obesity, 10*(2), 91–98.

Epel, E. S., Jimenez, S., Brownell, K., Stroud, L., Stoney, C., & Niaura, R. (2004). Are stress eaters at risk for the metabolic syndrome? In *Annals of the New York Academy of Sciences* (Vol. *1032,* pp. 208–210). Malden, MA: Blackwell.

Erermis, S., Cetin, N., Tamar, M., Bukusoglu, N., Akdeniz, F., & Goksen, D. (2004). Is obesity a risk factor for psychopathology among adolescents? *Pediatrics International, 46*(3), 296–301.

Esposito, P., Chandler, N., Kandere, K., Basu, S., Jacobson, S., Connolly, R., ... Theoharides, T. C. (2002). Corticotropin-releasing hormone and brain mast cells regulate blood-brain-barrier permeability induced by acute stress. *Journal of Pharmacology and Experimental Therapeutics, 303*(3), 1061–1066.

Fani, N., Tone, E. B., Phifer, J., Norrholm, S. D., Bradley, B., Ressler, K. J., ... Jovanovic, T. (2012). Attention bias toward threat is associated with exaggerated fear expression and impaired extinction in PTSD. *Psychological Medicine, 42*(3), 533–543.

Feldman, S., & Conforti, N. (1976). Feedback effects of dexamethasone on adrenocortical responses in rats with fornix section. *Hormone Research, 7*(1), 56–60.

Feldman, S., & Conforti, N. (2008). Participation of the dorsal hippocampus in the glucocorticoid feedback effect on adrenocortical activity. *Neuroendocrinology, 30*(1), 52–55.

Friedland, M., Brizendine, L., Roberts, E., Ph, D., Wolkowitz, O. M., Reus, V. I., ... Nelson, N. (1999). Double-blind treatment of major depression with dehydroepiandrosterone. *The American Journal of Psychiatry, 156,* 646–649.

Gillespie, C. F., & Nemeroff, C. B. (2005). Hypercortisolemia and depression. *Psychosomatic Medicine, 67* (Suppl. 1), S26–S28.

Goenjian, A. K., Molina, L., Steinberg, A. M., Fairbanks, L. A., Alvarez, M. L., Goenjian, H. A., & Pynoos, R. S. (2001). Posttraumatic stress and depressive reactions among Nicaraguan adolescents after Hurricane Mitch. *American Journal of Psychiatry, 158*(5), 788–794.

Goenjian, A. K., Pynoos, R. S., Steinberg, A. M., Endres, D., Abraham, K., Geffner, M. E., & Fairbanks, L. A. (2003). Hypothalamic-pituitary-adrenal activity among Armenian adolescents with PTSD symptoms. *Journal of Traumatic Stress, 16*(4), 319–323.

Gross, J. J. (1998). The emerging field of emotion regulation: An integrative review. *Review of General Psychology, 2*(3), 271–299.

Gunnar, M. R., Tout, K., de Haan, M., Pierce, S., & Stansbury, K. (1997). Temperament, social competence, and adrenocorticol activity in preschoolers. *Developmental Psychobiology, 31*(1), 65–85.

Guthrie, R. M., & Bryant, R. A. (2006). Extinction learning before trauma and subsequent posttraumatic stress. *Psychosomatic Medicine, 68,* 307–311.

Hakamata, Y., Izawa, S., Sato, E., Komi, S., Murayama, N., Moriguchi, Y., ... Tagaya, H. (2013). Higher cortisol levels at diurnal trough predict greater attentional bias towards threat in healthy young adults. *Journal of Affective Disorders, 151*(2), 775–779.

Hankin, M. E., Theile, H. M., & Steinbeck, A. W. (1977). An evaluation of laboratory tests for the detection and differential diagnosis of Cushing's syndrome. *Clinical Endocrinology, 6*(3), 185–196.

Hanson, E. K. S., Maas, C. J. M., Meijman, T. F., & Godaert, G. L. R. (2000). Cortisol secretion throughout the day, perceptions of the work environment, and negative affect. *Annals of Behavioral Medicine, 22*(4), 316–324.

Harkness, K. L., Stewart, J. G., & Wynne-Edwards, K. E. (2011). Cortisol reactivity to social stress in adolescents: role of depression severity and child maltreatment. *Psychoneuroendocrinology, 36*(2), 173–181.

Harris, T. ., Borsanyi, S., Messari, K., Stanford, K., Cleary, S. E., Shiers, H. M., ... Hebert, J. (2000). Morning cortisol as a risk factor for subsequent major depressive disorder in adult women. *British Journal of Psychiatry, 177*(6), 505–510.

Heinrichs, M., Baumgartner, T., Kirschbaum, C., & Ehlert, U. (2003). Social support and oxytocin interact to suppress cortisol and subjective responses to psychosocial stress. *Biological Psychiatry, 54*(12), 1389–1398.

Heinrichs, M., von Dawans, B., & Domes, G. (2009). Oxytocin, vasopressin, and human social behavior. *Frontiers in Neuroendocrinology, 30*, 548–557.

Hellhammer, D. H., Wüst, S., & Kudielka, B. M. (2009). Salivary cortisol as a biomarker in stress research. *Psychoneuroendocrinology, 34*(2), 163–171.

Het, S., & Wolf, O. T. (2007). Mood changes in response to psychosocial stress in healthy young women: Effects of pretreatment with cortisol. *Behavioral Neuroscience, 121*(1), 11–20.

Heyen, J. R., Ye, S., Finck, B. N., & Johnson, R. W. (2000). Interleukin (IL)-10 inhibits IL-6 production in microglia by preventing activation of NF-κB. *Molecular Brain Research, 77*(1), 138–147.

Hill, E. E., Zack, E., Battaglini, C., Viru, M., Viru, A., & Hackney, A. C. (2008). Exercise and circulating cortisol levels. *Journal of Endocrinological Investigation, 31*(7), 587–591.

Hirshfeld-Becker, D. R., Biederman, J., Henin, A., Faraone, S. V, Davis, S., Harrington, K., & Rosenbaum, J. F. (2007). Behavioral inhibition in preschool children at risk is a specific predictor of middle childhood social anxiety: A five-year follow-up. *Journal of Developmental & Behavioral Pediatrics, 28*(3), 225–233.

Holsboer, F., Lauer, C. J., Schreiber, W., & Krieg, J.-C. (2008). Altered hypothalamic-pituitary-adrenocortical regulation in healthy subjects at high familial risk for affective disorders. *Neuroendocrinology, 62*(4), 340–347.

Hoppmann, C. A., & Klumb, P. L. (2006). Daily goal pursuits predict cortisol secretion and mood states in employed parents with preschool children. *Psychosomatic Medicine, 68*(6), 887–894.

Hui, G. K., Figueroa, I. R., Poytress, B. S., Roozendaal, B., McGaugh, J. L., & Weinberger, N. M. (2004). Memory enhancement of classical fear conditioning by post-training injections of corticosterone in rats. *Neurobiology of Learning and Memory, 81*(1), 67–74.

Insel, T., Cuthbert, B., Garvey, M., Heinssen, R., & Pine, D. (2010). Research domain criteria (RDoC): Toward a new classification framework for research on men. *The American Journal of Psychiatry, 167*(7), 748–751.

Izawa, S., Sugaya, N., Shirotsuki, K., Yamada, K. C., Ogawa, N., Ouchi, Y., ... Nomura, S. (2008). Salivary dehydroepiandrosterone secretion in response to acute psychosocial stress and its correlations with biological and psychological changes. *Biological Psychology, 79*(3), 294–298.

Jacobs, N., Myin-Germeys, I., Derom, C., Delespaul, P., Van Os, J., & Nicolson, N. A. (2007). A momentary assessment study of the relationship between affective and adrenocortical stress responses in daily life. *Biological Psychology, 74*, 60–66.

Kabbaj, M., Devine, D. P., Savage, V. R., & Akil, H. (2000). Neurobiological correlates of individual differences in novelty-seeking behavior in the rat: Differential expression of stress-related molecules. *Journal of Neuroscience, 20*(18), 6983–6988.

Kagan, J., Reznick, J. S., & Snidman, N. (1987). The physiology and psychology of behavioral inhibition in children. *Child Development, 58*(6), 1459–1473.

Kagan, J., Reznick, J. S., Snidman, N., Gibbons, J., & Johnson, M. O. (1988). Childhood derivatives of inhibition and lack of inhibition to the unfamiliar. *Child Development, 59*(6), 1580–1589.

Kalimi, M., Shafagoj, Y., Loria, R., Padgett, D., & Regelson, W. (1994). Anti-glucocorticoid effects of dehydroepiandrosterone (DHEA). *Molecular and Cellular Biochemistry, 131*, 99–104.

Kasckow, J. W., Baker, D., & Geracioti, T. D. (2001). Corticotropin-releasing hormone in depression and post-traumatic stress disorder. *Peptides, 22*(5), 845–851.

Kershaw, E. E., Morton, N. M., Dhillon, H., Ramage, L., Seckl, J. R., & Flier, J. S. (2005). Adipocyte-specific glucocorticoid inactivation protects against diet-induced obesity. *Diabetes, 54*(4), 1023–1031.

Kessler, R. C. (1997). The effects of stressful life events on depression. *Annual Review of Psychology, 48*(1), 191–214.

Kinet, J.-P. (2007). The essential role of mast cells in orchestrating inflammation. *Immunological Reviews, 217*(1), 5–7.

Kirsch, P., Esslinger, C., Chen, Q., Mier, D., Lis, S., Siddhanti, S., ... Meyer-Lindenberg, A. (2005). Oxytocin modulates neural circuitry for social cognition and fear in humans. *The Journal of Neuroscience: The Official Journal of the Society for Neuroscience, 25*(49), 11489–11493.

Klengel, T., Mehta, D., Anacker, C., Rex-Haffner, M., Pruessner, J. C., Pariante, C. M., ... Binder, E. B. (2012). Allele-specific FKBP5 DNA demethylation mediates gene–childhood trauma interactions. *Nature Neuroscience, 16*(1), 33–41.

Knigge, K. M., & Hays, M. (1963). Evidence of inhibitive role of hippocampus in neural regulation of ACTH release. *Experimental Biology and Medicine, 114*(1), 67–69.

Kroboth, P., & Salek, F. (1999). DHEA and DHEA-S: A review. *Journal of Clinical Psychopharmacology, 39*, 327–348.

Kudielka, B. M., Hellhammer, D. H., & Wüst, S. (2009). Why do we respond so differently? Reviewing determinants of human salivary cortisol responses to challenge. *Psychoneuroendocrinology, 34*(1), 2–18.

Landfield, P., Baskin, R., & Pitler, T. (1981). Brain aging correlates: Retardation by hormonal-pharmacological treatments. *Science, 214*(4520), 581–584 .

Landfield, P. W., Rose, G., Sandles, L., Wohlstadter, T. C., & Lynch, G. (1977). Patterns of astroglial hypertrophy and neuronal degeneration in the hippocampus of aged, memory-deficient rats. *Journal of Gerontology, 32*(1), 3–12.

Landfield, P., Waymire, J., & Lynch, G. (1978). Hippocampal aging and adrenocorticoids: Quantitative correlations. *Science, 202*(4372), 1098–1102.

Lazarus, R. S. (1999). *Stress and emotion: A new synthesis.* New York, NY: Springer.

Lee, H.-J., Macbeth, A. H., Pagani, J. H., & Young, W. S. (2009). Oxytocin: The great facilitator of life. *Progress in Neurobiology, 88*(2), 127–151.

Lennartsson, A., Kushnir, M. M., Bergquist, J., & Jonsdottir, I. H. (2012). DHEA and DHEA-S response to acute psychosocial stress in healthy men and women. *Biological Psychology, 90*(2), 143–149.

Leon, L. R., Kozak, W., Rudolph, K., & Kluger, M. J. (1999). An antipyretic role for interleukin-10 in LPS fever in mice. *American Journal of Physiology—Regulatory, Integrative and Comparative Physiology, 276*(1), 81–89.

Lopez-Duran, N. L., Kovacs, M., & George, C. J. (2009). Hypothalamic-pituitary-adrenal axis dysregulation in depressed children and adolescents: A meta-analysis. *Psychoneuroendocrinology, 34*(9), 1272–1283.

Lopez-Duran, N. L., McGinnis, E., Kuhlman, K. R., Geiss, E., Vargas, I., & Mayer, S. (2015). HPA-axis stress reactivity in youth depression: evidence of impaired regulatory processes in depressed boys. *Stress, 18*(5), 545–553.

Lucassen, E. A., Rother, K. I., & Cizza, G. (2012). Interacting epidemics? Sleep curtailment, insulin resistance, and obesity. *Annals of the New York Academy of Sciences, 1264*(1), 110–134.

Luo, H., Hu, X., Liu, X., Ma, X., Guo, W., Qiu, C., & Wang, Y. (2011). Hair cortisol level as a biomarker for altered hypothalamic-pituitary-adrenal activity in female adolescents with posttraumatic stress disorder after the 2008 Wenchuan Earthquake. *Biological Psychiatry, 72*(1), 65–69

Mårin, P., Darin, N., Amemiya, T., Andersson, B., Jern, S., & Björntorp, P. (1992). Cortisol secretion in relation to body fat distribution in obese premenopausal women. *Metabolism: Clinical and Experimental, 41*(8), 882–886.

Marin, T. J., Martin, T. M., Blackwell, E., Stetler, C., & Miller, G. E. (2007). Differentiating the impact of episodic and chronic stressors on hypothalamic-pituitary-adrenocortical axis regulation in young women. *Health Psychology, 26*(4), 447–455.

Masuzaki, H., & Flier, J. S. (2003). Tissue-specific glucocorticoid reactivating enzyme, 11β-hydroxysteroid dehydrogenase type 1 (11β-HSD1)—A promising drug target for the treatment of metabolic syndrome. *Current Drug Targets—Immune, Endocrine & Metabolic Disorders, 3*(4), 255–262.

Masuzaki, H., Paterson, J., Shinyama, H., Morton, N. M., Mullins, J. J., Seckl, J. R., & Flier, J. S. (2001). A transgenic model of visceral obesity and the metabolic syndrome. *Science, 294*(5549), 2166–2170.

McElroy, S. L., Kotwal, R., Malhotra, S., Nelson, E. B., Keck, P. E., & Nemeroff, C. B. (2004, May 1). Are mood disorders and obesity related? A review for the mental health professional. *Journal of Clinical Psychiatry, 65*(5), 634–651

McEwen, B. S., Biron, C.A., Brunson, K. W., Bulloch, K., Chambers, W. H., Dhabhar, F.S.,...Spencer R. L. (1997). The role of adrenocorticoids as modulators of immune function. *Brain Research Reviews, 23*, 79–133.

McEwen, B. S., & Seeman, T. (1999). Protective and damaging effects of mediators of stress: Elaborating and testing the concepts of allostasis and allostatic load. *Annals of the New York Academy of Sciences, 896*(1), 30–47.

McEwen, B. S., Weiss, J. M., & Schwartz, L. S. (1968). Selective retention of corticosterone by limbic structures in rat brain. *Nature, 220*(5170), 911–912.

McFarlane, A. C., Atchison, M., & Yehuda, R. (1997). The acute stress response following motor vehicle accidents and its relation to PTSD. *Annals of the New York Academy of Sciences, 821*(1 Psychobiology), 437–441.

McGowan, P. O., Sasaki, A., D'Alessio, A. C., Dymov, S., Labonté, B., Szyf, M.,...Meaney, M. J. (2009). Epigenetic regulation of the glucocorticoid receptor in human brain associates with childhood abuse. *Nature Neuroscience, 12*(3), 342–348.

McKay, L. I., & Cidlowski, J. A. (1999). Molecular control of immune/inflammatory responses: Interactions between nuclear factor-κB and steroid receptor-signaling pathways. *Endocrine Reviews, 20*(4), 435–459.

McLaren, L. (2007). Socioeconomic status and obesity. *Epidemiologic Reviews, 29*(1), 29–48.

McMahon, M., Gerich, J., & Rizza, R. (1988). Effects of glucocorticoids on carbohydrate metabolism. *Diabetes/Metabolism Reviews, 4*(1), 17–30.

Meaney, M. J., Diorio, J., Francis, D., Widdowson, J., LaPlante, P., Caldji, C.,...Plotsky, P. M. (1996). Early environmental regulation of forebrain glucocorticoid receptor gene expression: Implications for adrenocortical responses to stress. *Developmental Neuroscience, 18*(1–2), 61–72.

Meddings, J. B., & Swain, M. G. (2000). Environmental stress-induced gastrointestinal permeability is mediated by endogenous glucocorticoids in the rat. *Gastroenterology, 119*(4), 1019–1028.

Meewissee, M.-L., Reitsma, J. B., De Vries, G.-J., Gersons, B. P. R., & Olff, M. (2007). Cortisol and post-traumatic stress disorder in adults. *British Journal of Psychiatry, 191*(5), 387–392.

Messaoudi, M., Lalonde, R., Violle, N., Javelot, H., Desor, D., Nejdi, A.,...Cazau.biel, J.-M. (2011). Assessment of psychotropic-like properties of a probiotic formulation (Lactobacillus helveticus R0052 and Bifidobacterium longum R0175) in rats and human subjects. *British Journal of Nutrition, 105*(5), 755–764.

Miller, A. H., Maletic, V., & Raison, C. L. (2009). Inflammation and its discontents: The role of cytokines in the pathophysiology of major depression. *Biological Psychiatry, 65*(9), 732–741.

Miller, G. E., Cohen, S., & Ritchey, A. K. (2002). Chronic psychological stress and the regulation of pro-inflammatory-cytokines. *Health Psychology, 21*(6), 531–541.

Modell, M. D. S., Lauer, C. J., Schreiber, W., Huber, J., Krieg, J. C., & Holsboer, F. (1998). Hormonal response pattern in the combined DEX-CRH Test is stable over time in subjects at high familial risk for affective disorders. *Neuropsychopharmacology, 18*(4), 253–262.

Mond, J., Van Den Berg, P., Boutelle, K., Hannan, P., & Neumark-Sztainer, D. (2011). Obesity, body dissatisfaction, and emotional well-being in early and late adolescence: Findings from the project EAT study. *Journal of Adolescent Health, 48*(4), 373–378.

Morris, M. C., Rao, U., & Garber, J. (2012). Cortisol responses to psychosocial stress predict depression trajectories: Social-evaluative threat and prior depressive episodes as moderators. *Journal of Affective Disorders, 143*(1–3), 223–230.

Müller, M. B., Uhr, M., Holsboer, F., & Keck, M. E. (2004). Hypothalamic-pituitary-adrenocortical system and mood disorders: Highlights from mutant mice. *Neuroendocrinology, 79*(1), 1–12.

Murphy, B., & Jachan, C. (1968). Clinical evaluation of urinary cortisol determinations by competitive protein-binding radioassay. *Clinical Endocrinology & Metabolism, 28*(3), 343–348.

Myers, K. M., & Davis, M. (2007). Mechanisms of fear extinction. *Molecular Psychiatry, 12*(2), 120–150.

Nater, U. M., Moor, C., Okere, U., Stallkamp, R., Martin, M., Ehlert, U., & Kliegel, M. (2007). Performance on a declarative memory task is better in high than low cortisol responders to psychosocial stress. *Psychoneuroendocrinology, 32*(6), 758–763.

Nemeroff, C. B., & Vale, W. W. (2005). The neurobiology of depression: Inroads to treatment and new drug discovery. *The Journal of Clinical Psychiatry, 66* (Suppl 7), 5–13.

Neumann, I. D., Torner, L., & Wigger, A. (2000). Brain oxytocin: Differential inhibition of neuroendocrine stress responses and anxiety-related behaviour in virgin, pregnant and lactating rats. *Neuroscience, 95*(2), 567–575.

Neumann, I. D., Wigger, A., Torner, L., Holsboer, F., & Landgraf, R. (2000). Brain oxytocin inhibits basal and stress-induced activity of the hypothalamo-pituitary-adrenal axis in male and female rats: Partial action within the paraventricular nucleus. *Journal of Neuroendocrinology, 12*(3), 235–243.

Newport, D. J., Heim, C., Owens, M. J., Ritchie, J. C., Ramsey, C. H., Miller, A. H., & Nemeroff, C. B. (2003). Cerebrospinal fluid corticotropin-releasing factor (CRF) and vasopressin concentrations predict pituitary response in the CRF stimulation test: A multiple regression analysis. *Neuropsychopharmacology, 28*(3) 569–576.

Nieuwenhuizen, A. G., & Rutters, F. (2008). The hypothalamic-pituitary-adrenal-axis in the regulation of energy balance. *Physiology & Behavior, 94*(2), 169–177.

Nishioka, T., Anselmo-Franci, J. A., Li, P., Callahan, M. F., & Morris, M. (1998). Stress increases oxytocin release within the hypothalamic paraventricular nucleus. *Brain Research, 781*(1), 57–61.

Ohshima, K., Shargill, N. S., Chan, T. M., & Bray, G. A. (1984). Adrenalectomy reverses insulin resistance in muscle from obese (ob/ob) mice. *American Journal of Physiology—Endocrinology and Metabolism, 246*(2), 193–197.

Olff, M., Frijling, J. L., Kubzansky, L. D., Bradley, B., Ellenbogen, M. A., Cardoso, C., ... van Zuiden, M. (2013). The role of oxytocin in social bonding, stress regulation and mental health: An update on the moderating effects of context and interindividual differences. *Psychoneuroendocrinology, 38*(9), 1883–1894.

Overman, E. L., Rivier, J. E., Moeser, A. J., Margioris, A., & Angelakis, E. (2012). CRF induces intestinal epithelial barrier injury via the release of mast cell proteases and TNF-α. *PLoS ONE, 7*(6), e39935.

Pariante, C. M. (2006). The glucocorticoid receptor: Part of the solution or part of the problem? *Journal of Psychopharmacology, 20*(4_Suppl), 79–84.

Pariante, C. M., & Lightman, S. L. (2008). The HPA axis in major depression: Classical theories and new developments. *Trends in Neurosciences, 31*(9), 464–468.

Pariante, C. M., & Miller, A. H. (2001). Glucocorticoid receptors in major depression: Relevance to pathophysiology and treatment. *Biological Psychiatry, 49*(5), 391–404.

Pasquali, R., Cantobelli, S., Casimirri, F., Capelli, M., Bortoluzzi, L., Flamia, R., ... Barbara, L. (1993). The hypothalamic-pituitary-adrenal axis in obese women with different patterns of body fat distribution. *The Journal of Clinical Endocrinology & Metabolism, 77*(2), 341–346.

Petersson, M., & Uvnäs-Moberg, K. (2007). Effects of an acute stressor on blood pressure and heart rate in rats pretreated with intracerebroventricular oxytocin injections. *Psychoneuroendocrinology, 32*, 959–965.

Petra, A. I., Panagiotidou, S., Hatziagelaki, E., Stewart, J. M., Conti, P., & Theoharides, T. C. (2015). Gut-microbiota-brain axis and its effect on neuropsychiatric disorders with suspected immune dysregulation. *Clinical Therapeutics, 37*(5), 984–995.

Petrillo, M. G., Bortner, C. D., & Cidlowski, J. A. (2016). Glucocorticoids: Inflammation and immunity. In *The hypothalamic-pituitary-adrenal axis in health and disease: Cushing's syndrome and beyond* (pp. 43–63). Cham: Springer International.

Pugh, R. C., Fleshner, M., & Rudy, J. W. (1997). Type II glucocorticoid receptor antagonists impair contextual not auditory-cue fear conditioning in juvenile rats. *Neurobiology of Learning and Memory, 67*, 75–79.

Putman, P., Hermans, E. J., Koppeschaar, H., Van Schijndel, A., & Van Honk, J. (2007). A single administration of cortisol acutely reduces preconscious attention for fear in anxious young men. *Psychoneuroendocrinology, 32*, 793–802.

Putman, P., Hermans, E. J., & van Honk, J. (2007). Exogenous cortisol shifts a motivated bias from fear to anger in spatial working memory for facial expressions. *Psychoneuroendocrinology, 32*(1), 14–21.

Putman, P., Hermans, E. J., & Van Honk, J. (2010). Cortisol administration acutely reduces threat-selective spatial attention in healthy young men. *Physiology & Behavior, 99*, 294–300.

Raison, C. L., & Miller, A. H. (2003). When not enough is too much: The role of insufficient glucocorticoid signaling in the pathophysiology of stress-related disorders. *American Journal of Psychiatry, 160*(9), 1554–1565.

Rask, E., Simonyte, K., Lönn, L., & Axelson, M. (2013). Cortisol metabolism after weight loss: Associations with 11 β-HSD type 1 and markers of obesity in women. *Clinical Endocrinology, 78*(5), 700–705.

Renault, P. F., Hoofnagle, J. H., Park, Y., Mullen, K. D., Peters, M., Jones, D. B., ... Jones, E. A. (1987). Psychiatric complications of long-term interferon alfa therapy. *Archives of Internal Medicine, 147*(9), 1577–1580.

Reul, J. M., Stec, I., Söder, M., & Holsboer, F. (1993). Chronic treatment of rats with the antidepressant amitriptyline attenuates the activity of the hypothalamic-pituitary-adrenocortical system. *Endocrinology, 133*(1), 312–320.

Reuter, M. (2002). Impact of cortisol on emotions under stress and nonstress conditions: A pharmacopsychological approach. *Neuropsychobiology, 46*, 41–48.

Ridout, N., Astell, A. J., Reid, I. C., Glen, T., & O'Carroll, R. E. (2003). Memory bias for emotional facial expressions in major depression. *Cognition and Emotion, 17*(1), 101–122.

Rijnierse, A., Nijkamp, F. P., & Kraneveld, A. D. (2007). Mast cells and nerves tickle in the tummy: Implications for inflammatory bowel disease and irritable bowel syndrome. *Pharmacology & Therapeutics , 116*(2), 207–235.

Roelofs, K., Bakvis, P., Hermans, E. J., Van Pelt, J., & Van Honk, J. (2007). The effects of social stress and cortisol responses on the preconscious selective attention to social threat. *Biological Psychiatry, 75*, 1–7.

Roelofs, K., Elzinga, B. M., & Rotteveel, M. (2005). The effects of stress-induced cortisol responses on approach–avoidance behavior. *Psychoneuroendocrinology, 30*, 665–677.

Rosmond, R., Dallman, M. F., & Björntorp, P. (1998). Stress-related cortisol secretion in men: Relationships with abdominal obesity and endocrine, metabolic and hemodynamic abnormalities. *The Journal of Clinical Endocrinology & Metabolism, 83*(6), 1853–1859.

Rothbaum, B. O., & Davis, M. (2003). Applying learning principles to the treatment of post-trauma reactions. *Annals of the New York Academy of Sciences, 1008*(1), 112–121.

Rottem, M., & Mekori, Y. A. (2005). Mast cells and autoimmunity. *Autoimmunity Reviews, 4*(1), 21–27.

Ruzek, M. C., Pearce, B. D., Miller, A. H., & Biron, C. A. (1999). Endogenous glucocorticoids protect against cytokine-mediated lethality during viral infection. *The Journal of Immunology, 162*(6), 3527–3533.

Sandi, C., & Pinelo-Nava, M. T. (2007). Stress and memory: Behavioral effects and neurobiological mechanisms. *Neural Plasticity, 2007*, 1–20.

Santos, J., Yang, P., Sö, J. D., Benjamin, M., & Perdue, M. H. (2001). Role of mast cells in chronic stress induced colonic epithelial barrier dysfunction in the rat. *Gut, 48*(5), 630–636.

Sapolsky, R. M., Krey, L. C., & McEwen, B. S. (1986). The neuroendocrinology of stress and aging: The glucocorticoid cascade hypothesis. *Endocrine Reviews, 7*(3), 284–301.

Sapolsky, R. M., & McEwen, B. S. (1985). Down-regulation of neural corticosterone receptors by corticosterone and dexamethasone. *Brain Research, 339*(1), 161–165.

Sapolsky, R. M., Romero, L. M., & Munck, A. U. (2000). How do glucocorticoids influence stress responses? Integrating permissive, suppressive, stimulatory, and preparative actions. *Endocrine Reviews, 21*(1), 55–89.

Schelling, G., Stoll, C., Kapfhammer, H., Rothenhausler, H., Krauseneck, T., Durst, K.,... Briegel, J. (1999). The effect of stress doses of hydrocortisone during septic shock on posttraumatic stress disorder and health-related quality of life in survivors. *Critical Care Medicine, 27*(12), 2678–2683.

Schmidt, L. A., Fox, N. A., Rubin, K. H., Sternberg, E. M., Gold, P. W., Smith, C. C., & Schulkin, J. (1997). Behavioral and neuroendocrine responses in shy children. *Developmental Psychobiology, 30*(2), 127–140.

Schwabe, L., Bohringer, A., Chatterjee, M., & Schachinger, H. (2008). Effects of pre-learning stress on memory for neutral, positive and negative words: Different roles of cortisol and autonomic arousal. *Neurobiology of Learning and Memory, 90*(1), 44–53.

Scott, L. V, Clarke, G., & Dinan, T. G. (2013). The brain-gut axis: A target for treating stress-related disorders. *Modern Trends in Pharmacopsychiatry 28*, 90–99.

Seckl, J. R., & Fink, G. (2008). Antidepressants increase glucocorticoid and mineralocorticoid receptor mRNA expression in rat hippocampus in vivo. *Neuroendocrinology, 55*(6), 621–626.

Shanks, N., Windle, R. J., Perks, P. A., Harbuz, M. S., Jessop, D. S., Ingram, C. D., & Lightman, S. L. (2000). Early-life exposure to endotoxin alters hypothalamic-pituitary-adrenal function and predisposition to inflammation. *Proceedings of the National Academy of Sciences of the United States of America, 97*(10), 5645–5650.

Simonyte, K., Rask, E., Näslund, I., Angelhed, J.-E., Lönn, L., Olsson, T., & Mattsson, C. (2009). Obesity is accompanied by disturbances in peripheral glucocorticoid metabolism and changes in FA recycling. *Obesity, 17*(11), 1982–1987.

Sismanopoulos, N., Delivanis, D.-A., Alysandratos, K.-D., Angelidou, A., Therianou, A., Kalogeromitros, D., & C. Theoharides, T. (2012). Mast cells in allergic and inflammatory diseases. *Current Pharmaceutical Design, 18*(16), 2261–2277.

Skoluda, N., Dettenborn, L., Stalder, T., & Kirschbaum, C. (2012). Elevated hair cortisol concentrations in endurance athletes. *Psychoneuroendocrinology, 37*(5), 611–617.

Smith, R. S. (1991). The macrophage theory of depression. *Medical Hypotheses, 35*(4), 298–306.

Soravia, L. M., Heinrichs, M., Aerni, A., Maroni, C., Schelling, G., Ehlert, U.,... De Quervain, D. J.-F. (2006). Glucocorticoids reduce phobic fear in humans. *Proceedings of the National Academy of Sciences of the United States of America, 103*(14), 5585–5590.

Spahlholz, J., Baer, N., König, H. H., Riedel-Heller, S. G., & Luck-Sikorski, C. (2016). Obesity and discrimination—a systematic review and meta-analysis of observational studies. *Obesity Reviews, 17*(1), 43–55.

Sripada, R. K., Marx, C. E., King, A. P., Rajaram, N., Garfinkel, S. N., Abelson, J. L., & Liberzon, I. (2013). DHEA enhances emotion regulation neurocircuits and modulates memory for emotional stimuli. *Neuropsychopharmacology: Official Publication of the American College of Neuropsychopharmacology, 38*(9), 1798–1807.

Staufenbiel, S. M., Penninx, B. W. J. H., Spijker, A. T., Elzinga, B. M., & van Rossum, E. F. C. (2013). Hair cortisol, stress exposure, and mental health in humans: A systematic review. *Psychoneuroendocrinology, 38*(8), 1220–1235.

Stenzel-Poore, M. P., Cameron, V. A., Vaughan, J., Sawchenko, P. E., & Vale, W. (1992). Development of Cushing's syndrome in corticotropin-releasing factor transgenic mice. *Endocrinology, 130*(6), 3378–3386.

Steptoe, A. (2007). *Depression and physical illness.* (Andrew Steptoe, Ed.). Cambridge: Cambridge University Press.

Steptoe, A., Wardle, J., & Marmot, M. (2005). Positive affect and health-related neuroendocrine, cardiovascular, and inflammatory processes. *Proceedings of the National Academy of Sciences of the United States of America, 102*(18), 6508–6512.

Steudte-schmiedgen, S., Stalder, T., Schönfeld, S., Wittchen, H., Trautmann, S., Alexander, N.,... Kirschbaum, C. (2015). Hair cortisol concentrations and cortisol stress reactivity predict PTSD symptom increase after trauma exposure during military deployment. *Psychoneuroendocrinology, 59*, 123–133.

Streeten, D. H., Stevenson, C. T., Dalakos, T. G., Nicholas, J. J., Dennick, L. G., & Fellerman, H. (1969). The diagnosis of hypercortisolism. Biochemical criteria differentiating patients from lean and obese normal subjects and from females on oral contraceptives. *Journal of Clinical Endocrinology and Metabolism, 29*(9), 1191–1211.

Strle, K., McCusker, R. H., Tran, L., King, A., Johnson, R. W., Freund, G. G.,... Kelley, K. W. (2007). Novel activity of an anti-inflammatory cytokine: IL-10 prevents TNFα-induced resistance to IGF-I in myoblasts. *Journal of Neuroimmunology, 188*(1), 48–55.

Theoharides, T. C., Alysandratos, K.-D., Angelidou, A., Delivanis, D.-A., Sismanopoulos, N., Zhang, B.,... Kalogeromitros, D. (2012). Mast cells and inflammation. *Biochimica et Biophysica Acta, 1822*(1), 21–33.

Tomlinson, J. W. (2005). 11Beta-hydroxysteroid dehydrogenase type 1 in human disease: a novel therapeutic target. *Minerva Endocrinologica, 30*(1), 37–46.

Turnbull, A. V., & Rivier, C. L. (1999). Regulation of the hypothalamic-pituitary-adrenal axis by cytokines: Actions and mechanisms of action. *Physiological Reviews, 79*(1), 1–71.

van Marle, H. J. F., Hermans, E. J., Qin, S., & Fernández, G. (2009). From specificity to sensitivity: How acute stress affects amygdala processing of biologically salient stimuli. *Biological Psychiatry, 66*(7), 649–655.

van Peer, J. M., Roelofs, K., Rotteveel, M., van Dijk, J. G., Spinhoven, P., & Ridderinkhof, K. R. (2007). The effects of cortisol administration on approach–avoidance behavior: An event-related potential study. *Biological Psychology, 76*, 135–146.

Van Uum, S. H. M., Sauvé, B., Fraser, L. A., Morley-Forster, P., Paul, T. L., & Koren, G. (2008). Elevated content of cortisol in hair of patients with severe chronic pain: A novel biomarker for stress. *Stress (Amsterdam, Netherlands), 11*(6), 483–488.

Vgontzas, A. N., Lin, H.-M., Papaliaga, M., Calhoun, S., Vela-Bueno, A., Chrousos, G. P., & Bixler, E. O. (2008). Short sleep duration and obesity: The role of emotional stress and sleep disturbances. *International Journal of Obesity, 32*(5), 801–809.

Vgontzas, A. N., Pejovic, S., Zoumakis, E., Lin, H.-M., Bentley, C. M., Bixler, E. O., . . . Chrousos, G. P. (2007). Hypothalamic-pituitary-adrenal axis activity in obese men with and without sleep apnea: Effects of continuous positive airway pressure therapy. *The Journal of Clinical Endocrinology & Metabolism*, *92*(11), 4199–4207.

Vreeburg, S. A., Hartman, C. A., Hoogendijk, W. J. G., Van Dyck, R., Zitman, F. G., Ormel, J., & Penninx, B. W. J. H. (2010). Parental history of depression or anxiety and the cortisol awakening response. *British Journal of Psychiatry*, *197*(3), 180–185.

Vythilingam, M., Vermetten, E., Anderson, G. M., Luckenbaugh, D., Anderson, E. R., Snow, J., . . . Bremner, J. D. (2004). Hippocampal volume, memory, and cortisol status in major depressive disorder: Effects of treatment. *Biological Psychiatry*, *56*(2), 101–112.

Wald, I., Shechner, T., Bitton, S., Holoshitz, Y., Charney, D. S., Muller, D., . . . Bar-Haim, Y. (2011). Attention bias away from threat during life threatening danger predicts PTSD symptoms at one-year follow-up. *Depression and Anxiety*, *28*, 406–411.

Wansink, B., Cheney, M. M., & Chan, N. (2003). Exploring comfort food preferences across age and gender. *Physiology and Behavior*, *79*(4–5), 739–747.

Wardle, J., & Cooke, L. (2005). The impact of obesity on psychological well-being. *Best Practice & Research Clinical Endocrinology & Metabolism*, *19*(3), 421–440.

Wilson, M. M., Greer, S. E., Greer, M. A., & Roberts, L. (1980). Hippocampal inhibition of pituitary-adrenocortical function in female rats. *Brain Research*, *197*(2), 433–441.

Wolf, O. T. (2008). The influence of stress hormones on emotional memory: Relevance for psychopathology. *Acta Psychologica*, *127*(3), 513–531.

Wolf, O. T., Kudielka, B. M., Hellhammer, D. H., Hellhammer, J., & Kirschbaum, C. (1998). Opposing effects of DHEA replacement in elderly subjects on declarative memory and attention after exposure to a laboratory stressor. *Psychoneuroendocrinology*, *23*(6), 617–629.

Yang, Y.-L., Chao, P.-K., & Lu, K.-T. (2006). Systemic and intra-amygdala administration of glucocorticoid agonist and antagonist modulate extinction of conditioned fear. *Neuropsychopharmacology*, *31*(5), 912–924.

Ye, S. M., & Johnson, R. W. (1999). Increased interleukin-6 expression by microglia from brain of aged mice. *Journal of Neuroimmunology*, *93*(1–2), 139–148.

Yehuda, R. (2000). Biology of posttraumatic stress disorder. *The Journal of Clinical Psychiatry*, *61*(Suppl 7), 14–21.

Yehuda, R., Bierer, L. M., Andrew, R., Schmeidler, J., & Seckl, J. R. (2009). Enduring effects of severe developmental adversity, including nutritional deprivation, on cortisol metabolism in aging Holocaust survivors. *Journal of Psychiatric Research*, *43*(9), 877–883.

Yehuda, R., Golier, J. A., Halligan, S. L., Meaney, M., & Bierer, L. M. (2004). The ACTH response to dexamethasone in PTSD. *American Journal of Psychiatry*, *161*(8), 1397–1403.

Yehuda, R., & LeDoux, J. (2007, October 4). Response variation following trauma: A translational neuroscience approach to understanding PTSD. *Neuron*, *56*(1), 19–32

Yehuda, R., Levengood, R. A., Schmeidler, J., Wilson, S., Guo, L. S., & Gerber, D. (1996). Increased pituitary activation following metyrapone administration in post-traumatic stress disorder. *Psychoneuroendocrinology*, *21*(1), 1–16.

Yehuda, R., McFarlane, A. C., & Shalev, A. Y. (1998). Predicting the development of posttraumatic stress disorder from the acute response to a traumatic event. *Biological Psychiatry*, *44*(12), 1305–1313.

Yehuda, R., & Seckl, J. (2011). Minireview: Stress-related psychiatric disorders with low cortisol levels: A metabolic hypothesis. *Endocrinology*, *152*(12), 4496–4503.

Yehuda, R., Teicher, M. H., Trestman, R. L., Levengood, R. A., & Siever, L. J. (1996). Cortisol regulation in posttraumatic stress disorder and major depression: A chronobiological analysis. *Biological Psychiatry*, *40*(2), 79–88.

Yukimura, Y., & Bray, G. A. (1978). Effects of adrenalectomy on body weight and the size and number of fat cells in the {Zucker} (fatty) rat. *Endocrine Research Communication*, *5*, 189–198.

Zaba, M., Kirmeier, T., Ionescu, I. A., Wollweber, B., Buell, D. R., Gall-Kleebach, D. J., . . . Schmidt, U. (2015). Identification and characterization of HPA-axis reactivity endophenotypes in a cohort of female PTSD patients. *Psychoneuroendocrinology*, *55*, 102–115.

Zambon, A., Pauletto, P., & Crepaldi, G. (2005). Review article: The metabolic syndrome—a chronic cardiovascular inflammatory condition. *Alimentary Pharmacology & Therapeutics*, *22 Suppl 2*(s2), 20–23.

Zoladz, P. R., Cadle, C. E., Dailey, A. M., Fiely, M. K., Peters, D. M., Nagle, H. E., . . . Payment, K. E. (2017). Blunted cortisol response to acute pre-learning stress prevents misinformation effect in a forced confabulation paradigm. *Hormones and Behavior*, *93*, 1–8.

Psychophysiological Models of Stress

Ellen Zakreski *and* Jens C. Pruessner

Abstract

Psychophysiological models have a long history within stress research of trying to explain the link between stress exposure and psychological and physiological disease. The current chapter tries to offer complementary perspectives on this issue. First, it covers the relevant physiological systems (sympathetic, parasympathetic, enteric nervous system) and their markers (heart rate, heart rate variability, blood pressure), such that the reader receives an overview of the significant factors at play. Second, it provides an overview of the various forms of stress (acute, chronic, and stress during early life periods) that are believed to put the individual at heightened risk to develop stress-related disease. Finally, it presents the theories and models that have emerged over the years that try to explain how the various forms of stress can eventually lead to psychological and physical disease. The chapter ends with a short outlook on some recent work emphasizing the interaction between the various systems at play, and how that by itself can play a role in the origin of stress-related disease.

Keywords: heart rate, heart rate variability, blood pressure, autonomic, sympathetic, parasympathetic, enteric, early life

Introduction

Physiology as a branch of biology generally deals with all the functions and systems within a living organism; thus, it is probably the broadest of all domains. In the context of stress, physiology can refer to stress effects on any biological function or system. Historically, however, psychophysiology has focused on electrical activity of organ function, focusing primarily on the brain and the cardiovascular system. Within the brain, research has focused on spontaneous electrical activity recorded from the scalp (electroencephalogram) and recordings in response to (repeated and averaged) stimulation (event-related potentials). Within the periphery, research has focused on the autonomic nervous system with its sympathetic and parasympathetic branches. This area of research by now has extended over many decades, and various markers have been established to serve as surrogates for the activity and integrity of the au-

tonomic system, including blood pressure (systolic, diastolic, mean arterial), heart rate, heart period, and heart period variability (time domain or frequency-domain-based analyses), plasma catecholamines, and skin conductance. In the context of this chapter, we will cover these traditional markers but will extend to other systems as well, to acknowledge the important interaction among the various stress-reactive systems within the organisms.

The driving question in this context is how stress can lead to acute or chronic changes in the activity of physiological systems, and how these changes are then related to disease. Over the course of this chapter, we will first briefly introduce the various physiological systems that deal with stress—the sympathetic, parasympathetic, and enteric nervous systems—and then provide a more in-depth discussion of the markers of these systems that have been established over the years. Finally, we will discuss the different models that have been proposed to explain the stress–disease link, which include various mechanisms by which stress-related change becomes maladaptive, with the consequence of deteriorating health. One of the core assumptions that the various models share is that maladaptive functioning of the autonomic nervous system (ANS) and other stress response systems increase the likelihood of stress-related illness. As usual, the devil is in the detail, and there is little consensus on what constitutes maladaptation, or even what exactly constitutes stress. Further complicating the matter, stress is a very popular and consequently broad topic that is ill-defined where it is often confused or not clearly delineated what causes it, and what is caused by it in the organism. The topic is also challenging to study because what is perceived as stressful by some might be experienced as merely stimulating by others. Generally accepted definitions for psychological stressors include the notion that it is a situation where the individual feels he or she is missing the resources to adequately deal with the demands of the situation (Lazarus & Folkman, 1984), it consists of stimuli that share specific situational characteristics such as uncontrollability, unpredictability, ego involvement, anticipation of negative consequences and novelty (Mason, 1968), or, within a social situation, the presence of social evaluative threat (Dickerson & Kemeny, 2004; i.e., poor performance in a social context or violation of social norms).

Exposure to these kinds of stressors are normal, and we are all prone to experience these situations frequently, but when the physiological systems that normally help us cope with stressors are overactivated or fail to respond adequately, stress-related illness is believed to occur. Individual differences will lead to variations in the thresholds for falling ill from these stressors, and in the type of illnesses that might arise from them, with stress implicated in a broad array of disorders (e.g., depression, anxieties, schizophrenia, burnout, eating disorders). Within the general pathologies, hypertension, obesity, and metabolic syndrome stand out. The different models that have been proposed over the years are covered in later sections, to separate "classic" approaches from more recent models to explain stress-related disease. The chapter ends with a summary, conclusion, and outlook, including some speculations about where the field might be heading.

Autonomic Nervous System
The ANS controls visceral processes such as heart rate, blood pressure, respiration, perspiration, sexual arousal, digestion, metabolism, and the immune system. Walter Cannon's seminal work showed how the ANS links visceral processes with emotion (Cannon, 1928) and helps adapt the organism's internal environment according to internal and external demands (Cannon, 1929).

Although the ANS is sometimes treated as a unified system, it consists of three structurally and functionally distinct systems: the sympathetic nervous system (SNS), the parasympathetic nervous system (PSNS), and the enteric nervous system (ENS). Understanding the basic physiology of each system is important for understanding the exact role of each of these systems and their relation to stress and health. Thus, we start by providing a brief review of ANS physiology and anatomy. This can only be a short and superficial look, and the interested reader is referred to numerous detailed reviews (Furness, Callaghan, Rivera, & Cho, 2014; Shields, 1993; Wehrwein, Orer, & Barman, 2016).

Sympathetic Nervous System
The sympathetic nervous system (SNS) (Shields, 1993; Wehrwein et al., 2016) regulates a broad range of visceral processes but is perhaps best known for coordinating the fight-or-flight response. Potential threats activate preganglionic nerve fibers in the interomediolateral column of the spine. Some sympathetic preganglionic fibers project to the adrenal medulla, where they stimulate chromaffin cells to release epinephrine into the blood. Most sympathetic preganglionic fibers meet with postganglionic fibers near the spine whose axons project throughout the body. Postganglionic fibers innervating sweat glands release acetylcholine at their axon terminals, stimulating perspiration. Other postganglionic fibers release norepinephrine near the target tissue. Norepinephrine and epinephrine bind to adrenergic receptors to accelerate heart rate, raise blood pressure, dilate the pupils, and contribute to the release of stored energy.

Parasympathetic Nervous System
The parasympathetic nervous system (PSNS; Shields, 1993; Wehrwein et al., 2016) regulates many visceral processes, similar to the role of the SNS. The effects of the PSNS on target organs are generally opposite to the effects of SNS activation. Consequently, while the SNS prepares the body for fight or flight, the PSNS is associated with rest and recovery. The structure of the PSNS is similar to the SNS where information travels from the brain to the periphery by a chain of preganglionic and

postganglionic nerve fibers. While sympathetic preganglionic fibers exhibit a thoracolumbar outflow pattern, exiting the middle of the spine, parasympathetic preganglionic fibers exhibit a craniosacral outflow pattern. Some parasympathetic preganglionic fibers give rise to the splanchnic nerve at the sacral portion of the spine. Other parasympathetic preganglionic fibers flow through the cranial nerves III, VII, IX, and X. Cranial nerve X, the vagus nerve, represents the largest nerve in the ANS and is a major parasympathetic relay, controlling (among other organs) the heart, gut, and lungs. Parasympathetic preganglionic fibers in the vagus and other nerves travel throughout the body, terminating near the target tissue. Axon terminals of these fibers primarily release acetylcholine. PSNS activation induces slower heart rate, pupil constriction, increased salivation, lacrimation, gut motility, and urination.

Enteric Nervous System

The enteric nervous system (ENS) is a complex network of neurons spread throughout the gut that regulates various aspects of gastrointestinal function, including the microbiome (Furness et al., 2014; Yoo & Mazmanian, 2017). Once considered part of the PSNS, the ENS is now recognized as a distinct branch of the ANS. Although the ENS is the most complex division of the peripheral nervous system, it is historically the least explored part of the ANS within the context of stress research, although this is changing in recent years. As others review (Carabotti, Scirocco, Maselli, & Severi, 2015), recent studies have found associations between chronic stress, altered ENS function, and illness, making the ENS an exciting new frontier for stress research. At this point, however, the ENS is not explicitly taken into consideration by many of the major physiological models of stress, which prioritize the SNS and PSNS. For this reason, the current review focuses on the PSNS and SNS.

Markers of the Autonomic Nervous System

There are numerous theories implicating the ANS in stress-related disease. Since theory and measurement develop in parallel, understanding how ANS function is measured is vital to the interpretation and advancement of these theories. Probably one of the most important limitations of studying the ANS is that many aspects of autonomic function cannot be assessed directly in a noninvasive manner. Researchers examining conscious humans must assess ANS activity indirectly by measuring the end product of ANS activity, for example epinephrine or norepinephrine release, or by recording changes in other physiological processes known to be under autonomic control such as heart rate, heart period variability, or blood pressure. This can present significant challenges since these physiological processes are affected by systems other than the ANS, making interpretation difficult. Often data must be preprocessed to remove artifacts and to obtain specific information about the ANS. Furthermore, there is often discordance among researchers regarding which measures are best and how to interpret them. There are many methods available for assessing ANS function. We review these measures briefly, focusing on measures that are common in stress research, then discuss individual differences in how these markers relate to health and stress.

Blood Pressure

Blood pressure is an indirect marker of both SNS and PSNS activity, although it is considered more of a chronic measure of ANS dysregulation. It is typically operationalized as systolic, diastolic, or mean arterial pressure. Systolic and diastolic pressure describe the maximum and minimum pressure the blood is exerting on the arterial walls when flowing through in response to the heart's activity. Mean arterial pressure is a combination measure of the two, but with the diastolic pressure weighted double (twice the diastolic pressure plus the systolic pressure divided by three). Diastolic pressure is considered more accurate when aiming to determine blood supply to body tissues and organs. Blood pressure is considered an important marker of ANS activity in the context of chronic stress and cardiovascular disease, as its acute state is strongly influenced by situational factors. As with other stress markers, repeated assessment over time in the context of acute stress testing does exist but is found less common (Juster et al., 2012).

High blood pressure, also called hypertension, describes excessive systolic, diastolic, or mean arterial pressure. Untreated hypertension for prolonged periods of time is a known and consistent risk factor for cardiovascular disease, stroke, and vascular dementia (Faraco & Iadecola, 2013). As hypertension is typically not associated with any symptoms, the possibility of it arising and manifesting for long periods of time is a serious concern; thus, general physicians will check for it regularly, especially in middle to late adulthood. The cause of hypertension is typically multifactorial, with acute and chronic stressors contributing to it. Other known risk factors are a body mass index (BMI) greater than 25, sedentary lifestyle, bad dietary habits, and excessive alcohol consumption, all of which can also be related to chronic stress (Elliott, 2007).

Heart Rate

Heart rate (HR) is defined as the average number of heart beats per minute and is inversely related to heart period (HP), defined as the average time between beats. HR/HP can be monitored by electrocardiography (EKG). To record EKG, electrodes are placed on the chest and sometimes also on the arms or legs for reference, and the electrical signal of the heart is measured. Spikes in the EKG trace called R-peaks indicate depolarization of the heart's ventricles. One R-peak marks one heartbeat. The time between successive R-peaks is called an R-R interval (see Figure 22.1). HP is the average R-R interval over time, while HR is the average number of R-peaks per minute. HR/HP provides a cheap, straightforward approximation of physiological arousal yet provides limited insight into ANS function. Since HR/HP depends on both SNS and PSNS, it is difficult to pinpoint the physiological origin of differences in HR/HP between individuals, or within an individual. For instance, faster HR (shorter HP) could reflect higher SNS activity, reduced PSNS activity, or both. One approach to overcome this limitation is to pharmacologically block the PSNS or SNS and then measure the resulting change in HR/HP from baseline. As Chapleau and Sabharwal (2011) explain, the increase in HR from baseline after administering a parasympathetic blocker (e.g., atropine) indicates PSNS tone, while SNS tone is indicated by the decrease in HR after administering a sympathetic blocker (e.g., propranolol). However, pharmacological interventions are invasive and limit ecological validity.

Heart Period Variability

The heart's rhythm is not constant but varies. Heart period variability (HPV), often called heart rate var-

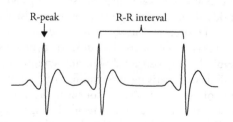

Figure 22.1 Illustration of an EKG recording. A heart beat is marked by a prominent upward deflection called an R-peak. The time between two R-peaks is an R-R interval.

iability, is the amount of variation in R-R intervals over time and reflects the flexibility of the ANS. Total HPV first attracted interest as a prognostic indicator since lower HPV predicts greater morbidity and mortality among heart disease patients (Bigger et al., 1992; Huikuri et al., 1999; Odemuyiwa et al., 1991), making HPV a valuable marker of ANS function. HPV, however, has its limitations. Relations between HPV and ANS function are easily distorted by artifacts such as false heart beats or ectopic beats, so data must be carefully screened for artifacts before further analysis (Camm et al., 1996). Furthermore, HPV can be difficult to interpret because, like HR/HP, total HPV depends on both PSNS and SNS (Camm et al., 1996). Higher HPV could reflect increased PSNS activity, reduced SNS activity, or both. Information about PSNS activity can be extracted by focusing on specific types of HRV, the so-called high-frequency HPV, or respiratory sinus arrhythmia.

HIGH-FREQUENCY HEART PERIOD VARIABILITY OR RESPIRATORY SINUS ARRHYTHMIA

High-frequency HPV, also called respiratory sinus arrhythmia (RSA), is attributable to the PSNS since the PSNS is capable of changing HR faster than the SNS (Warner & Cox, 1962). There are several reasons for this. First, the nerves conveying parasympathetic input to the heart have more myelin than their sympathetic counterparts, enabling them to carry information faster. Second, parasympathetic postganglionic axon terminals are much closer to the heart than sympathetic axon terminals, so parasympathetic signals reach their target regions in the heart faster. Third, the PSNS employs mainly acetylcholine, which binds to fast-acting ionotropic receptors, while norepinephrine released from the SNS binds to slow-acting metabotropic receptors. Acetylcholine is also rapidly broken down by enzymes so the effects of PSNS activation more rapidly dissipate. Consequently, high-frequency HPV can be regarded as a valid marker of PSNS activity.

High-frequency HPV associated with PSNS activity is often called respiratory sinus arrhythmia (RSA), since rapid changes in R-R intervals result from respiratory gating of vagal outflow to the heart. Inhalation speeds up HR, while exhalation slows HR (Eckberg, 1983). RSA is the amount of R-R interval variability arising from respiration. Greater RSA (greater high-frequency HPV) is believed to indicate greater PSNS (vagal) influence over the heart (Berntson, Cacioppo, & Grossman, 2007). The association between RSA and vagal tone is not without controversy, however. Some researchers argue that minor changes in respiratory rate and volume may confound relations between RSA and vagal tone and should be controlled for either statistically or experimentally (Grossman & Taylor, 2007). Others disagree, arguing that controlling for respiratory parameters is unnecessary and may remove important information about PSNS activity (Lewis, Furman, McCool, & Porges, 2012). Potential respiratory confounds are important to stress research because common laboratory stress tasks such as the Trier Social Stress Test (TSST) (Kirschbaum, Pirke, & Hellhammer, 1993) require prolonged speaking, which affects breathing.

THE VARIOUS WAYS OF CALCULATING HEART PERIOD VARIABILITY AND THE LACK OF CONSENSUS

Diverse opinions exist on what should be the exact method of measurement and interpretation of RSA and other forms of HPV (Berntson et al., 2007; Grossman & Taylor, 2007; Lewis et al., 2012). This lack of consensus, coupled with different research goals and theoretical perspectives, has led to a wide range of recommendations for quantifying HPV (Allen, Chambers, & Towers, 2007; Camm et al., 1996; Sassi et al., 2015; Shaffer & Ginsberg, 2017). Some measures capture RSA, so specifically reflect PSNS activity, while others reflect both the PSNS and SNS. HPV measures are generally divided into frequency-domain, geometric, and time-domain measures.

Frequency-domain measures use spectral analysis methods (e.g., Fourier transform) to convert the R-R interval time series into the frequency domain, then calculate the power (variability) within a particular frequency bandwidth (in adults, high-frequency power band is defined as 0.15–0.4 Hz, while low-frequency power band ranges from 0.04 to 0.15 Hz). High-frequency power is R-R interval variability within the bandwidth of normal human respiration (9–24 breaths per minute) and can be used to capture RSA, and thus PSNS activity. Low-frequency HPV was once thought to index SNS activity; however, it is now clear that both PSNS and SNS contribute to low-frequency HPV (Reyes del Paso, Langewitz, Mulder, Van Roon, & Duschek, 2013).

Geometric measures of HPV are also available. Poincaré plots visualize complex correlation patterns within the R-R interval series (Kamen & Tonkin, 1995). These patterns can be quantified by fitting an ellipse to the Poincaré plot and then measuring

dispersion on the SD1 and SD2 planes (Tulppo, Makikallio, Takala, Seppanen, & Huikuri, 1996). SD2 (a measure of long-term variability) depends on the SNS and PSNS, while SD1 (a measure of short-term variability) indexes PSNS activity (Kamen, Krum, & Tonkin, 1996).

Time-domain measures of HPV are simpler to determine. Examples of time-domain measures include standard deviation between normal R-R intervals (SDNN) and root mean square of successive differences (RMSSD). SDNN measures reflect both SNS and PSNS activity (Camm et al., 1996), while RMSSD (Berntson, Lozano, & Chen, 2005) reflects RSA and thus indexes PSNS activity.

Although frequency-domain measures are widely used (Allen et al., 2007), they make statistical assumptions that may not always be accurate in the context of stress research. For instance, frequency-domain measures assume signal stationarity, an assumption that is violated if the ANS is perturbed by external events (e.g., a stressor). Time-domain measures, however, do not assume stationarity, so in this regard they may be advantageous for stress research. For stress researchers who wish to examine how the PSNS responds to speech-based stress tasks such as the TSST, RMSSD and SD1 may also be preferable over frequency-domain measures, since evidence suggests that RMSSD and SD1 are less susceptible to potential respiratory confounds (Penttila et al., 2001; Pitzalis et al., 1996), and so are less likely to be contaminated by speech. Type of HPV measure can therefore interact with aspects of the study design (e.g., violations of stationarity assumptions, potential for respiratory confounds) to influence results obtained by a particular study.

Pre-Ejection Period

The SNS can be noninvasively probed by pre-ejection period (PEP) (Newlin & Levenson, 1979; Sherwood et al., 1990). PEP, an index of beta-adrenergic drive, is the time between contraction of the heart's ventricles and the opening of the aortic valve. Shorter PEP indexes higher SNS activity. PEP can be measured by combining EKG with impedance cardiography. Like HPV, PEP is easily distorted by artifacts such as false heartbeats, so data should be manually screened before analysis. PEP may also be affected by posture (Houtveen, Groot, & De Geus, 2005). This may be relevant for stress research, since common laboratory stress tasks such as the TSST require participants to switch between sitting and standing throughout the task. This can complicate interpretation since it is unclear to what extent a change in PEP during the TSST constitutes a psychological stress response or a posture change response.

Skin Conductance Response
Another noninvasive index of SNS activity is skin conductance response (SCR), also known as galvanic skin conductance. SCR is the change in the electrical properties of the skin resulting from perspiration (Boycsein, 2012). Unlike HR/HP or blood pressure, sweat glands are exclusively under sympathetic control, making SCR a cleaner index of SNS activity (Dawson, Schell & Filion, 2007). SCR is measured by applying low voltage to the skin through electrodes and then examining the change in conductance. Higher skin conductance response indicates greater SNS activity. Similar to PEP and HPV, SCR is vulnerable to distortion. For instance, the amplitude of one skin conductance response can be biased by the amplitude of the previous response unless certain analytical methods are used (Benedek & Kaernbach, 2010). Like PEP and HPV, methods for analyzing SCR and removing artifacts vary between studies, and this variation could contribute to mixed findings.

Plasma Norepinephrine and Epinephrine
The catecholamines norepinephrine and epinephrine can be measured in blood plasma to index SNS activity. As Mills and Dimsdale (1992) review, there are several methodological limitations associated with plasma catecholamines. First, measuring blood is invasive. Second, catecholamines degrade rapidly, so samples must be frozen immediately. Third, norepinephrine and epinephrine can be difficult to interpret since they are not always correlated with one another, although both are believed to indicate SNS activity. A meta-analysis of stress research (Goldstein & Kopin, 2008) found that epinephrine responsivity was strongly associated with adrenocorticotrophin ($r = 0.93$), a hormone of the HPA axis, while the association between epinephrine and norepinephrine responsivity to stress was much weaker ($r = 0.40$); however, the validity of these findings is questionable because of the author's use of subjective ratings to establish these relationships. This could partly reflect the fact that norepinephrine and epinephrine respond to different stimuli. For instance, norepinephrine levels increased more in response to physical exercise, while epinephrine was more responsive to psychosocial stress (Dimsdale & Moss, 1980). Norepinephrine and epinephrine therefore likely reflect distinct components of the SNS

with potentially distinct implications for health and disease. Measuring both catecholamines is therefore not redundant and will likely provide a more comprehensive picture of what the SNS is doing; therefore, it should be the method of choice.

Salivary Alpha-Amylase
Salivary alpha-amylase (Chatterton, Vogelsong, Lu, Ellman, & Hudgens, 1996; Nater et al., 2006; Nater & Rohleder, 2009), an enzyme that breaks down starch and kills bacteria, may index beta-adrenergic sympathetic activity since salivary alpha-amylase has been found to correlate with blood levels of norepinephrine (Thoma, Kirschbaum, Wolf, & Rohleder, 2012), and pharmacologically blocking beta-adrenergic receptors suppresses the salivary alpha-amylase response to stress (van Stegeren, Rohleder, Everaerd, & Wolf, 2006). Salivary alpha-amylase is appealing because it is less invasive to collect and more chemically stable than plasma catecholamines, and it can be measured in the same saliva sample as other stress-related biomarkers such as cortisol. Compared to other SNS markers, such as PEP or SCR, salivary alpha-amylase can facilitate data collection since participants do not need to be connected to electrical monitoring equipment. Nonetheless, alpha-amylase has some drawbacks. Compared to PEP or SCR, alpha-amylase has reduced temporal resolution since saliva can only be sampled every few minutes. Consequently, researchers using alpha-amylase may miss important changes in SNS activity. A more critical issue is that alpha-amylase may not provide a pure indicator of SNS. Alpha-amylase and plasma norepinephrine do not always correlate (Petrakova et al., 2015). Alpha-amylase may further be confounded by PSNS activity (Nagy et al., 2015), salivary flow rate, and posture (Bosch, Veerman, de Geus, & Proctor, 2011). Consequently, studies using alpha-amylase as a marker of SNS activity may sometimes tell a different story than studies using more pure markers of SNS activity like PEP or SCR.

Links With Stress and Stress-Related Disease
Effects of Acute Stress
Normally, the PSNS is more active during rest than the SNS. Individual differences in basal (resting) activity of the PSNS and SNS have been associated with various, typically chronic, stress-related health problems. A review of this literature exceeds the scope of this chapter, but examples include physical disease like metabolic syndrome (Hu, Lamers,

Hiles, Penninx, & de Geus, 2016), cardiovascular disease (Greenwood, Stoker, & Mary, 1999; Odemuyiwa et al., 1991; Thayer & Lane, 2007), and psychological symptoms such as internalizing problems (e.g., anxiety and depression) (Davis, Suveg, Whitehead, Jones, & Shaffer, 2016; Dieleman et al., 2015; Ishitobi et al., 2010; Shinba, 2014), and externalizing problems (e.g., antisocial behavior) (Pine et al., 1996; Snoek, Goozen, Matthy, Buitelaar, & Engeland, 2004).

The PSNS typically deactivates in response to stress, while the SNS activates. The typical stress response thus manifests as increased HR, blood pressure, salivary alpha-amylase, plasma catecholamines and SCR, shorter PEP, and decreased total HPV and RSA. The autonomic stress response is believed to help the organism survive, at least in the short term, by inhibiting nonessential functions, releasing stored energy, and redirecting resources to where they are needed most. Similar to other stress systems, such as the hypothalamic-pituitary-adrenal (HPA) axis, the ANS is responsive to physical stress (Mastorakos, Pavlatou, Diamanti-Kandarakis, & Chrousos, 2005), uncontrollability (Peters et al., 1998), and social evaluative threat (Bosch et al., 2009); however, the ANS responds faster and for a shorter duration when compared to the HPA axis (Ulrich-Lai & Herman, 2009). The ANS also responds to challenges that do not evoke a significant HPA axis response, such as mental effort (Peters et al., 1998). Thus, in a way, the ANS acts like a first responder, while the HPA axis represents the second, more profound and sustained response.

Autonomic reactivity to stress is the magnitude of change from baseline during acute stress. Like baseline activity, reactivity is an important functional parameter of the ANS and is associated with many stress-related disorders such as cardiovascular disease, depression, and anxiety.

A change in ANS basal activity or ANS reactivity to stress may be a correlate or predictor of cardiovascular illness. Earlier studies associated higher autonomic reactivity with current and future cardiovascular illness. For instance, cardiovascular reactivity, as indicated by higher heart rate reactivity or blood pressure reactivity, has been found to predict stroke (Everson et al., 2001) and hypertension (Carroll et al., 2012) and is associated with more carotid plaque and atherosclerosis (Gianaros et al., 2002). Higher plasma norepinephrine reactivity, a marker of SNS reactivity, was also found to predict hypertension (Flaa, Eide, Kjeldsen, & Rostrup, 2008) and is observed in patients with Tako-Tsubo cardiomyopathy

(Smeijers et al., 2015). Higher PSNS reactivity, indexed by a greater decrease in RSA during stress, has also been associated with coronary aortic calcification (Gianaros et al., 2005); however, the majority of studies associate risk of cardiovascular disease with blunted PSNS reactivity (Ginty, Kraynak, Fisher, & Gianaros, 2017). While earlier research suggests that higher reactivity, particularly of the SNS, correlates with current and future cardiovascular problems, a growing number of studies now associate current or future cardiovascular disease with blunted reactivity (less change in activity) of both the SNS and PSNS (Ginty et al., 2017).

Here, blunted ANS reactivity predicted cardiovascular disease-related hospitalization, and even death (Sherwood et al., 2017). By itself, blunted ANS reactivity has been associated with higher central adiposity (a risk factor for cardiovascular disease), particularly among chronically stressed individuals (Singh & Shen, 2013). Blunted cardiovascular reactivity has also been associated with atherosclerosis (Chumaeva et al., 2009; Heponiemi et al., 2007). Atherosclerosis itself again is associated with blunted SNS and PSNS reactivity, respectively indexed by less change in PEP and RSA (Heponiemi et al., 2007). Cardiovascular patients also showed blunted SNS reactivity as indexed by plasma norepinephrine and epinephrine levels (Stanford et al., 1997). Taken together, these findings exemplify how relations between cardiovascular disease and ANS reactivity are complex, with some studies observing a positive association between reactivity and disease, while other studies observe the opposite association. However, there is always the possibility that unknown factors cause both ANS changes and the cardiovascular disease process.

In addition, some authors (Sharpley, 2002; Taylor, 2010) suggest that altered ANS reactivity may be the link between cardiovascular disease and affective disorders, such as depression, since cardiovascular disease and affective disorders tend to co-occur (Hare, Toukhsati, Johansson, & Jaarsma, 2014) and share common antecedents (e.g., chronic stress). The ANS also helps mediate the relationship between emotion (affect) with cardiovascular function (Cannon, 1928). Consequently, many studies have explored associations between affective disorders and ANS reactivity. As with cardiovascular disease, however, the relationship between affective disorders and ANS is complex and varies between studies. Earlier research tended to associate depression with increased cardiovascular and SNS reactivity. A meta-analysis (Kibler & Ma, 2004) found that depression was associated with increased HR and blood pressure reactivity. Similarly, Light, Kothandapani, and Allen (1998) associated depression with greater SNS reactivity as indexed by PEP. However, and similar to the shift in the literature observed with cardiovascular disease, more recent studies tend to associate depression with blunted cardiovascular and SNS reactivity (Brindle, Ginty, & Conklin, 2013; Salomon, Bylsma, White, Panaite, & Rottenberg, 2013; Salomon, Clift, Karlsdottir, & Rottenberg, 2009). With regard to the PSNS, relations with depression are more consistent. According to a recent meta-analysis (Hamilton & Alloy, 2016), depression tends to be associated with blunted RSA.

ANS reactivity has been implicated in numerous other stress-related psychopathologies, including anxiety (Dieleman et al., 2015; Hoehn-Saric, McLeod, & Zimmerli, 1989), posttraumatic stress disorder (Blechert, Michael, Grossman, Lajtman, & Wilhelm, 2007; McFall, Murburg, Ko, & Veith, 1990), internalizing problems (Boyce et al., 2001; Hastings et al., 2008), externalizing problems (Boyce et al., 2001; Snoek et al., 2004; Waters, Boyce, Eskenazi, & Alkon, 2016), and eating disorders (Het et al., 2015; Koo-Loeb, Pedersen, & Girdler, 1998; Messerli-Burgy, Engesser, Lemmenmeier, Steptoe, & Laederach-Hofmann, 2010). Findings on the direction, however, are mixed. Some of these studies associate pathology with higher reactivity (Dieleman et al., 2015; McFall et al., 1990), while others associate the same pathology with blunted reactivity (Blechert et al., 2007; Hoehn-Saric et al., 1989; Koo-Loeb et al., 1998). Reasons for this inconsistency are not entirely clear and could stem from the diversity of measures used to index autonomic activity, the sensitivity of measures to confounds, or different definitions of what "reactivity" constitutes (i.e., some authors define reactivity as the rate of change, while others define it as magnitude of change).

Chronic Stress

"Chronic stress" is a heterogeneous term whose definition often varies by author and methodological approach. Perhaps a more vague but therefore generally accepted definition is a sustained period of ongoing exposure to stimuli which are perceived as threatening or difficult to cope with (Selye, 1978). These stressors can vary in intensity from mild (daily hassles like commuter traffic or a noisy work environment) to severe (bereavement, chronic illness, emotional, sexual or physical abuse).

Chronic stress is believed to lead to an ongoing perturbation of the stress response systems like the ANS or HPA axis geared toward providing the organism with additional energy to adapt to stress. This chronic activation is believed to be associated with an imbalance in energy regulation and can by itself become a possible source of disease. Chronic stress as a possible source of ANS dysregulation and eventual physical or psychological disease has been around as a concept for a long time (e.g., Selye, 1936), and as a consequence, a multitude of studies have examined the link between chronic stress and ANS activity. As so often, the literature is a mixed bag, with some studies showing evidence for an increase in SNS and a decrease in PSNS activity as a consequence of chronic stress, with others observing a decrease in predominantly SNS activity, and yet others showing no effects (Fries et al., 2005; Hellhammer, Meinlschmidt, & Pruessner, 2018; McGirr et al., 2010; Vanitallie, 2002). Despite these inconsistencies, research tends to find that chronic stress can lead to enduring changes in ANS and other stress response systems. Putative models, like the allostatic load model and the theory of general adaptation syndrome, assume that the changes in the stress response systems associated with exposure to chronic stressors, rather than the stressors itself, are to blame for the health state of the individual.

Early Life Adversity

Early life adversity, such as childhood neglect, physical or sexual abuse, or exposure to conflict during critical development periods, appears to have particularly pervasive effects on health across the life span and is believed to precipitate or exacerbate internalizing problems (e.g., depression, anxiety), externalizing problems (e.g., aggression), cardiovascular disease, substance abuse, and other health problems (Dvir, Ford, Hill, & Frazier, 2014; Felitti et al., 1998).

The effects of early life adversity on health may be mediated by enduring alterations of the physiological stress systems, including the ANS (Shonkoff et al., 2012). Research has associated early life adversity with altered ANS function at baseline and under stress. For example, among studies examining baseline activity, early life adversity is associated with greater SNS activity (Esposito, Koss, Donzella, & Gunnar, 2016) and lower PSNS activity (Dale et al., 2017; Gray, Theall, Lipschutz, & Drury, 2017). Findings are more mixed for basal cardiovascular activity. Some studies associate early life adversity with greater cardiovascular activity (Dale et al., 2017), while others observe lower cardiovascular activity (Winzeler et al., 2016). Research on ANS reactivity and early life adversity is particularly heterogeneous. Individuals exposed to early life adversity have been shown to possess greater cardiovascular reactivity (Heim et al., 2000), greater SNS reactivity (Cărnuță, Crișan, Vulturar, Opre, & Miu, 2015; Kuras et al., 2017; Lucas-Thompson & Granger, 2014), and greater PSNS reactivity (Skowron et al., 2011). Contrarily, other studies associate early life adversity with blunted cardiovascular reactivity (Lucas-Thompson & Granger, 2014; Voellmin et al., 2015), blunted SNS reactivity (Busso, McLaughlin, & Sheridan, 2017; McLaughlin et al., 2015; Mielock, Morris, & Rao, 2017), and blunted PSNS reactivity (Calkins, Graziano, Berdan, Keane, & Degnan, 2008). Interestingly, while several studies observe significant associations between SNS reactivity and early life adversity, the effect of early life adversity on PSNS reactivity is often nonsignificant (Busso et al., 2017; Cărnuță et al., 2015; Dale et al., 2017; McLaughlin et al., 2015; Winzeler et al., 2016). Taken together, relations of early life adversity with ANS function are therefore mixed and are likely moderated by numerous factors such as sex (Gray et al., 2017), task (McLaughlin, Sheridan, Alves, & Mendes, 2014), type of adversity (Skowron et al., 2011), and genes (Allegrini, Evans, de Rooij, Greaves-Lord, & Huizink, 2017).

Classical Physiological Models in Stress Research
Selye's General Adaptation Syndrome
Hans Selye is often referred to as the grandfather of stress research, and his seminal work on the effects of acute and chronic stress on especially the adrenal glands is included in most contemporary psychology textbooks that address "stress." In his book *The Stress of Life* (Selye, 1978), he describes how his clumsy handling of laboratory rats led to their frequent escape with subsequent chase and recapture. He later noticed that the rats who had temporarily escaped him had larger adrenal glands than those handled by his colleagues who had apparently not been exposed to the same (clumsy) treatment. This initial observation was followed by a systematic investigation into the causes and meaning of the change of the adrenal glands as a consequence of this special type of environmental stressor (i.e., him losing the rats). Selye ended up spending most of his life investigating the consequences of stress and realized that chronic stress can have profound consequences on health and disease. In the case of the handled rats, the increase in volume and weight of the adrenal glands had to do with the constant stim-

ulation of the HPA axis and the subsequent need for a higher production of stress hormones, to which the glands responded by increasing their size and weight, to satisfy the high demand.

Selye's work culminated in the formulation of the general adaptation syndrome (GAS), a theory which at its core contained the idea that there is a temporal process in the response to chronic stress. In the beginning, when the individual is first exposed to the (chronic) increase in demand, the organism is responding by increasing its ability to defend itself—its stress response systems (i.e., energy systems like the SNS and HPA) become chronically active to maximize the bodily defenses. This, according to Selye, will indeed enable the organism to better deal with the threat at hand, at the price of depleting its surplus resources. Should the period of chronic stress continue to tax the individual, eventually the organism is no longer able to increase its energy availability, and the reactivity of the systems declines even below normal activity. At this point, there is a mismatch between what the environment demands and what the individual can deliver, and the health of the individual is at risk. Selye was not specific as to what disease can occur, and he suggested that it depended on the individual characteristics of the organism as to what exactly happens. This is in line with the various physical and psychological consequences that stress can have—depression, burnout, ulcers, or heart disease were all possible consequences, according to Selye.

Selye's theory is compelling because of its simplicity. It rings true that an overtaxed system eventually will break—the pitcher that goes to the well too often is broken at last. It is rather intuitive that we cannot expect our bodies to perform at 110% for prolonged periods of time without something eventually happening to us. At the same time, that is also the significant weakness of the model—it is blurry on the exact mechanisms, and by leaving the exact consequences undefined it becomes very difficult if not impossible to test empirically. To Selye's credit, neuroscience at the time was not much advanced for many of the systems to be understood in detail, or the endocrine and neural mechanisms to be known yet. So his legacy certainly is to put the term "stress" on the agenda of physiologists, psychologists, and neuroscientists ever since.

Diathesis-Stress Models
The diathesis-stress model (Meehl, 1962) aims to address one of the shortcomings of the general adaptation syndrome theory, namely that chronic

stress does not always precipitate disease. The diathesis-stress model is not so much one model, and there is no single individual that could be clearly associated with the numerous models that were generated over the years in the diathesis stress context (Ingram & Luxton, 2005). At the core, is a straightforward idea: A specific vulnerability exists in the individual that is unrelated with negative outcomes as long as there is no significant stress exposure; once the individual has to endure significant amounts of stress, disease is likely to occur. There have been numerous variations on the initial concept—strict threshold models that assume a constant vulnerability, various models that allow for changing vulnerabilities depending on external or internal circumstances, models that allow for an interaction between the type of stressor and the specific vulnerability, and models that consider static versus dynamic vulnerabilities (e.g., McKeever & Huff, 2003; Monroe & Hadjiyannakis, 2002; Monroe & Simons, 1991; Post, 1992; Zubin & Spring, 1977). Also similar to the general adaption syndrome theory, the empirical testability of the diathesis-stress model is limited—it can explain disease post hoc ("the person fell ill from depression because he or she was vulnerable to it"), but it is much harder to determine what exactly the factors are that define a specific vulnerability.

Allostatic Load Theory

Allostatic load theory is associated with, but also stands in contrast to, the "homeostasis" concept developed by Claude Bernard and elaborated on by Cannon (1929). Chronologically appearing after the work of Selye (1978), allostatic load theory focuses on the long-term cost of the individual to maintain homeostasis. At the core is the assumption that individuals depend on surplus energy (typically from endogenous energy stores in terms of adipose tissue in the long term, glucose and protein in the short term) for emergency responses to occur when experiencing stress. If demands for increased energy are prolonged, an organism would then be in danger of using up these surplus energy stores, and it is likely to react to the danger of depletion. Thus, to maintain the ability of emergency responses, especially during times of chronic demand, in response the organism might increase its energy uptake and storage by first initiating feelings of hunger, and secondly by engaging in mechanisms to increase the storage of energy (e.g., through glucocorticoid signaling) so that the anticipated chronic demand can better be dealt with. This concept has been called

"allostasis" (McEwen, 1998; Sterling & Eyer, 1988), which literally means "stability through change." Similar to Selye who followed in the footsteps of Cannon with homeostasis of physiological systems, allostasis was first described by Sterling and Eyer in 1988, referring to the cardiovascular system and how it adjusts during resting and active states. From there, allostasis was then generalized to other systems, like the HPA axis (McEwen, 1998).

In contrast to homeostasis, allostasis changes physiological parameters so that homeostatic processes can continue. Thus, while homeostasis keeps "set points" and describes the processes to maintain these (such as body temperature), allostasis describes the modification of other parameters to keep these set points. For example, the increase in food intake in response to increased metabolism when exposed to a harsh environment would be the allostatic change that enables the homeostatic process of keeping the body temperature stable when the organism is out in the cold.

This can be further exemplified by looking at various examples in the context of various systems across the body. For example, to maintain necessary amounts of oxygen and nutrient supply to the muscles during exercise, catecholamines have to be released through the SNS to adjust heart rate and blood pressure. The release of catecholamines, and the subsequent increase in heart rate and blood pressure, is an allostatic process. Within the endocrine system, the release of glucocorticoids by the HPA axis, and the subsequent increase in food intake after exposure to a psychological or physical stressor, is an example for an allostatic process to keep energy levels stable, which itself is a homeostatic process. In a sense, allostasis and homeostasis are two sides of the same coin. While homeostasis focuses on the aspects that remain stable, allostasis focuses on the aspects that are changing for the system to remain stable.

Once the focus shifts from the systems that overall remain stable to the parameters that are changing to keep the system stable, it becomes apparent that "stability" might be a costly process: Depending on the demands, it might involve the "wearing out" of those parameters that undergo constant change to ensure this overall stability of the system. This is where the emphasis is with this theory: the concept of allostatic load. What is the price to pay for keeping the organism stable? Being looked into for several decades now, there is a realization that part of the metabolic changes with aging might in fact be allostatic changes (McEwen, 2002; Robertson &

Watts, 2016). Metabolic syndrome, a condition that affects an increasing number of people in developed countries, describes a cluster of risk factors for physical disease, including abdominal obesity, elevated blood pressure, elevated glucose levels, high blood triglyceride levels, and others. It is associated with a reduced life expectancy, and increased risk for disease, mostly diabetes and atherosclerosis. Future research will have to provide further evidence to the idea that in many individuals, these metabolic changes occurring with aging might represent the body's response to accumulated and chronic life stress.

Autonomic Space Model

OVERVIEW

Considering the association between SNS activity and PSNS activity may help resolve inconsistent relationships between autonomic function and health reported in the literature (Berntson & Cacioppo, 2004). Early researchers like Langley (1921) promoted the view that SNS and PSNS activity are reciprocally associated such that when one branch activates, the other deactivates. Autonomic space model (Berntson, Cacioppo, & Quigley, 1991, 1993) argues that other modes of associations between the SNS and PSNS exist and have important implications for health and behavior as well. In addition to reciprocal associations, SNS and PSNS activity can change in the same direction (coactivity) or the PSNS and SNS can uncouple from one another. The mode of association between the PSNS and SNS can be represented as a position on a two-dimensional grid called autonomic space (Figure 22.2), with SNS activity on one dimension and PSNS activity on the other. A person's position in autonomic space can be quantified at rest or during stress using pharmacological or noninvasive methods (Berntson, Cacioppo, Binkley, et al., 1994; Berntson, Cacioppo, & Quigley, 1994; Cacioppo et al., 1994).

Position in autonomic space can vary between or within individuals and is predicted to impact health by affecting the response of target organs that are innervated by both the SNS and PSNS (e.g., heart rate [HR]). Autonomic space model predicts that compared to nonreciprocal modes, reciprocity broadens the response range of the target organ, accelerates the response, and increases directional stability of the response, so that the change goes in one direction rather than fluctuating back and forth. Reciprocal modes therefore facilitate greater reactivity of target organs (e.g., greater HR reactivity) while nonreciprocal modes, particularly coactivity,

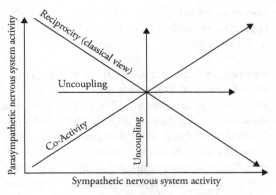

Figure 22.2 Autonomic space is a two-dimensional grid representing the range of possible associations between PSNS activity and SNS activity in standardized units. Associations can vary from reciprocity (high PSNS activity and low SNS activity, or *vice versa*), co-activity (co-activation or co- deactivation), or uncoupling (i.e. uncorrelated) changes in activity.

preserve the baseline state of the target organ, manifesting as blunted cardiovascular reactivity to stress.

The association between the SNS and PSNS may also correlate with health and behavior because different modes of SNS-PSNS coupling have distinct neurological correlates. A shift from one mode to another may therefore reflect the dominance or integrity of a particular neurological system. Reciprocity is largely dependent on baroreflex mechanisms in the brainstem, while nonreciprocal associations can occur when limbic brain regions such as amygdala and hypothalamus inhibit autonomic control centers in the brain stem. As Berntson and colleagues comment, limbic and anterior regions are implicated in emotion and appraisal (Berntson & Cacioppo, 2004; Berntson et al., 1991). Appraising a situation as threatening may therefore modulate the association between the SNS and PSNS. Consistent with this, classical conditioning experiments have observed coactivation during anticipation of electric shock in humans (Obrist, Wood, & Perez-Reyes, 1965) and rats (Iwata & LeDoux, 1988), potentially linking coactivation to certain types of psychological stress. Furthermore, coactivation occurs more often during psychological stress, while physical stressors more often induce reciprocity (Berntson, Cacioppo, Binkley, et al., 1994; Cacioppo et al., 1994).

The exact situational determinants and neurological mechanisms underlying autonomic space have yet to be specified. Nonetheless, position in autonomic space is expected to better discriminate between certain tasks (e.g., physical vs. psychological stress). They may also better predict physiological and psychological function than markers that do not discriminate between the SNS and PSNS (e.g., HR), or markers that reflect only PSNS activity or SNS activity.

EMPIRICAL SUPPORT AND CURRENT STATUS OF AUTONOMIC SPACE MODEL

Evidence of nonreciprocal PSNS-SNS coupling has existed for some time (Cannon, 1939; Gellhorn, Cortell, & Feldman, 1940; Koizumi, Terui, Kollai, & Brooks, 1982; Kollai & Koizumi, 1979). Berntson et al. (1993) review empirical data in humans demonstrating the existence of coactivity, reciprocity, and uncoupling. Subsequent research also shows that different patterns of PSNS-SNS coupling not only exist but have important functional implications. In a study of mental workload, Backs (1995) measured heart period, RSA, and Traube-Hering-Mayer waves (a SNS marker) while participants performed tasks with varying levels of physical and mental demand. As predicted by autonomic space model, nonreciprocal modes were associated with blunted heart period reactivity, supporting the notion that different modes of coupling differentially affect the physiology of target organs like the heart, which are innervated by both the PSNS and SNS. Also consistent with autonomic space theory, Backs (1995) found that position in autonomic space was a better predictor of mental workload than HR, demonstrating that autonomic space conveys unique and important information about function that is not conveyed by other autonomic markers. This is demonstrated in other studies as well. Using PEP and RSA as markers of the SNS and PSNS, respectively, Giuliano et al. (2017) found that position in autonomic space was a better marker of working memory than either SNS activity or PSNS activity alone. Adults exhibiting reciprocal activation showed better working memory capacity during mental challenge compared to coactivators. Similarly, preschoolers showing reciprocal activation (specifically PSNS deactivation and SNS activation) exhibited better emotional and attentional regulation during social challenge (Clark, Skowron, Giuliano, & Fisher, 2016). Reciprocal PSNS-SNS coupling, therefore, appears to correlate with abilities that could help individuals cope with challenging situations such as difficult working memory tasks and emotional and attentional regulation.

The relationship between the PSNS and SNS has been found to be a better predictor of stress-related outcomes than either considered alone. El-Sheikh et al. (2009) found that children exhibiting coactivity (either high RSA and SCR reactivity, or low RSA and SCR reactivity) developed more externalizing problems if they were exposed to marital conflict, while reciprocal activation appeared to reduce risk of externalizing problems in conflict-exposed children. Likewise, in toddlers, prenatal adversity predicted more aggression in children exhibiting coactivation, while toddlers exhibiting reciprocal activation showed less aggression (Suurland, van der Heijden, Huijbregts, van Goozen, & Swaab, 2017). Similarly, in adolescence, coactivation was also found to exacerbate the effect of early life adversity on aggression (Gordis, Feres, Olezeski, Rabkin, & Trickett, 2010). Adults showing coactivation have also shown worse aggression (Wagner & Abaied, 2015) and depression (Holterman, Murray-Close, & Breslend, 2016) following peer victimization compared to those with reciprocal activation. Taken together, these findings suggest that across development, PSNS-SNS coupling moderates the effects of various forms of adversity on different health outcomes. Nonreciprocal coupling is associated with greater vulnerability to stress-related mental health problems, like depression and externalizing problems, while reciprocal coupling indicates resilience against the harmful effects of stress.

In addition to stress-related mental health problems, coactivity may also indicate other stress-related problems like cardiovascular disease. Coactivation alters HR dynamics (Eickholt et al., 2018; Tulppo et al., 2005) and may predispose individuals to atrial fibrillation (Tan et al., 2008), a risk factor for heart attack and stroke (Odutayo et al., 2016). Hypothetically, situations that induce coactivity chronically may precipitate or exacerbate atrial fibrillation, placing individuals at greater risk of heart disease; however, this idea has yet to be explored empirically.

Although data implicate coactivity as a risk factor for disease, there may nonetheless be advantages associated with coactivity. During stress, coactivity is associated with increased secretory immune system function (Bosch, de Geus, Veerman, Hoogstraten, & Amerongen, 2003) and less negative affect (Miller, Kahle, Lopez, & Hastings, 2015). The adaptive function of coactivity should be further examined because it may help explain why and when coactivity occurs.

STRENGTHS AND LIMITATIONS OF THE AUTONOMIC SPACE MODEL

The autonomic space model is among the first models to acknowledge nonreciprocal coupling between PSNS and SNS activity. A significant strength of this model is to highlight the functional significance of nonreciprocal coupling of SNS and PSNS activity (i.e., SNS-PSNS coactivation or uncoupled changes in activity). This model could also improve our capacity to predict health outcomes in individuals exposed to stress. Researching the relationship between health and the activity of a single autonomic branch has so far yielded inconsistent results. Many pathologies are sometimes associated with higher activity and other times lower activity of the same marker. The association between autonomic branches may yield a more consistent and reliable predictor of stress-related health problems than either branch alone, since the functional impact of one branch's activity depends on the activity of the other branch.

On the other hand, the autonomic space model presents some limitations and opportunities for growth. The model excels at predicting important performance and health outcomes but falls short at explaining them. Although coactivity may predict worse stress-related health outcomes, the temporal dimension is unresolved—it is unclear whether coactivity causes, co-occurs, or results from adverse health outcomes. It is also unclear how different modes of coupling develop overtime. Some authors propose that passive cognitive challenge can evoke coactivity while active challenges evoke reciprocity (Berntson, Cacioppo, & Fieldstone, 1996; Bosch et al., 2003). This does not readily explain why the same task elicits coactivity in some individuals yet reciprocity in others (e.g., El-Sheikh et al., 2009). Finally, the autonomic space model only considers associations between the PSNS and SNS. Unlike other physiological models of stress (e.g., adaptive calibration model), it has yet to consider associations between the ANS and other stress systems such as the HPA axis. Neurological mechanisms underlying different modes of coupling are also vague. The developers of the autonomic space model suggest anterior brain regions, particularly those linked to emotion and attention, control the switch between reciprocity and coactivity (Berntson et al., 1991). Specifying these neurological mechanisms, and linking them to specific cognitive, physiological and behavioral processes, may help explain how reciprocity and coactivity develop over time, interact with other systems (e.g., the HPA axis), and contribute to stress-related health problems. Despite the limitations, the autonomic space model is a valuable contribution to stress research because it reveals the importance of investigating the associations between components of the ANS.

Neurovisceral Integration Theory

OVERVIEW

Neurovisceral integration theory (Smith, Thayer, Khalsa, & Lane, 2017; Thayer, Hansen, Saus-Rose, & Johnsen, 2009; Thayer & Lane, 2000, 2009) considers the neurological and cognitive mechanisms underlying the association between health and autonomic function. According to neurovisceral integration theory (NIT), the SNS and PSNS are extensions of the central autonomic network (CAN), a system that regulates homeostasis, attention, and emotion. The CAN integrates diverse information about internal and external conditions, and selects biological and behavioral responses adaptive for the current context. Among the core assumptions of the CAN is that it connects higher order cortical regions (e.g., ventromedial prefrontal, anterior cingulate, insular cortex), midlevel regions (e.g., central amygdala, hypothalamus, periaqueductal gray), and brainstem regions (e.g., nucleus of the solitary tract, ventrolateral medulla, parabrachial nucleus) with the sensory and motor neurons of the ANS (Benarroch, 1993; Thayer & Lane, 2009). The bidirectional flow of information across the CAN forms an integrated representation of internal and external demands and coordinates emotion, attention, and visceral state to respond to these demands.

Internal and external demands change constantly. Health and well-being, therefore, require the CAN to rapidly and accurately detect changes in demands, select appropriate responses, and inhibit inappropriate ones. When the CAN malfunctions, individuals could thus become stuck in a state that no longer fits the current context. Stress-related health problems such as anxiety can arise when individuals become stuck in a defensive mode even when the context is no longer threatening (Brosschot, Gerin, & Thayer, 2006).

The CAN's capacity to dynamically and efficiently integrate information depends significantly on the prefrontal cortex, which provides a more detailed representation of the broader context and enhances the salience of long-term goals (Smith et al., 2017). Among the brain structures forming the CAN, there is also a regulation hierarchy; for example, the prefrontal cortex inhibits subcortical divisions of the CAN such as the central amygdala. These subcortical regions respond to simpler, more immediate cues and promote a defensive mental and physiological state (e.g., fight-or-flight response). Insufficient prefrontal control can lead to overexcitation of the amygdala, prolonging the fight-or-flight response even when the context is no longer threatening. Adequate prefrontal control is therefore assumed to be important for preventing stress-related illness.

NIT asserts that higher RSA is an indicator of adequate prefrontal control over the CAN. Individuals with higher RSA should thus be less vulnerable to stress-related illness for several reasons. First, higher RSA indicates more prefrontal control, and subsequently better executive function, and control over attention and emotion. This capacity is likely to minimize adverse consequences of exposure to stressors by resolving stressful situations efficiently and preventing their occurrence in the future. Control over attention and emotion can further prevent overactivation of the SNS and HPA axis by preventing an exaggerated perception of threat, thereby limiting allostatic load. The prefrontal cortex also directly inhibits brain regions that activate the HPA axis and SNS stress response such as the central amygdala. This could help reduce allostatic load.

EMPIRICAL SUPPORT AND CURRENT STATUS OF NEUROVISCERAL INTEGRATION THEORY

Consistent with NIT, studies suggest that individuals with higher RSA levels at rest experience less stress-related health problems. High basal RSA is also negatively correlated with several stress-related illnesses, including cardiovascular disease (Thayer & Lane, 2007), depression (Agelink, Boz, Ullrich, & Andrich, 2002), and anxiety (Dieleman et al., 2015). RSA also moderates the effects of adversity on health. Higher basal RSA appears to reduce the impact of early life adversity on internalizing problems (El-Sheikh, Harger, & Whitson, 2001; McLaughlin, Alves, & Sheridan, 2014), externalizing problems (El-Sheikh et al., 2001), aggression (Suurland, van der Heijden, Huijbregts, van Goozen, & Swaab, 2018), delinquency (Hinnant, Erath, & El-Sheikh, 2015), and substance use (Hinnant et al., 2015).

According to NIT, higher basal RSA predicts resilience to stress partly because higher RSA reflects greater prefrontal control over emotion and attention. In line with these predictions, numerous studies associate higher basal RSA levels with better regulation of attention (Suess, Porges, & Plude, 1994) and emotion (Appelhans & Luecken, 2006), reduced attention to threatening stimuli (Park, Bavel, Vasey, & Thayer, 2013), and better executive function (Holzman & Bridgett, 2017), all of which

depend on prefrontal control (Heatherton, 2011). Neuroimaging studies associate higher RSA with greater prefrontal activity (Thayer, Åhs, Fredrikson, Sollers, & Wager, 2012) and greater functional connectivity between the medial prefrontal cortex and amygdala (Sakaki et al., 2016). Together these results support the notion that higher basal RSA indexes better prefrontal control over emotion and attention.

Prefrontal control, as indicated by high RSA, may also protect individuals from stress-related illness by inhibiting systems like the SNS or HPA axis that increase allostatic load. Consistent with this claim, women with early life adversity released less cortisol and pro-inflammatory cytokines during stress exposure if they also had high RSA levels (Tell, Mathews, Burr, & Janusek, 2018). Higher baseline RSA is also associated with lower cardiovascular reactivity to stress (Grossman, Watkins, Wilhelm, Manolakis, & Lown, 1996; Souza et al., 2009). RSA also tends to negatively correlate with SNS activity; however, as we discussed in the section on the autonomic space model, PSNS and SNS activation is not always reciprocal (Berntson et al., 1993). Sometimes the SNS and PSNS coactivate or uncouple. It is unclear, however, how these nonreciprocal modes of SNS-PSNS coupling fit within NIT or, in other words, whether the autonomic space model can complement NIT or is in conflict with it.

NIT further predicts that higher SNS activity indicates dysfunctional prefrontal control and greater susceptibility to stress-related illness. Consistent with this, in children with higher SNS reactivity, parental depression led to worse psychosocial adjustment (Abaied, 2016), and more internalizing and externalizing problems (Cummings, El-Sheikh, Kouros, & Keller, 2007). The relationship between health and SNS activity or reactivity may be more complicated than suggested by NIT, however. Some studies associate SNS hyperactivity with anxiety (Dieleman et al., 2015; Lambert et al., 2010; Schoorl, Rijn, Wied, Goozen, & Swaab, 2016) and depression (Ishitobi et al., 2010; Lambert et al., 2010). Contrarily, a few studies associate SNS hypoactivity with the same conditions: anxiety (Hoehn-Saric et al., 1989) and depression (Cubała & Landowski, 2014; Schwerdtfeger & Rosenkaimer, 2011). Similar to the SNS, stress-related problems have been associated with both hyperactivity and hypoactivity of the HPA axis (Boyce & Ellis, 2005). The relationship between blunted SNS/HPA axis activity and stress-related problems does not easily fit within the framework of NIT.

STRENGTHS AND LIMITATIONS OF NEUROVISCERAL INTEGRATION THEORY

NIT reinforces the prognostic value of basal RSA as a predictor of stress-related illness. Individuals with higher RSA appear more resilient against stress-related illness. NIT also articulates neurocognitive processes such as emotional regulation that link high basal RSA with resilience. Furthermore, NIT provides a model of how different neural systems within the CAN interact to control autonomic function, cognition, emotion, and ultimately health. Understanding how chronic adversity and other factors interact to influence the CAN may help us better understand how stress-related illness develops over time. Furthermore, since the CAN consists of brain regions that regulate other stress systems such as the HPA axis, NIT may help us understand how the ANS interacts with these other systems to affect health; however, its predictions about the SNS and HPA axis may need updating to account for inconsistent associations between blunted activity/reactivity and stress-related illness. NIT has a few other limitations. While this theory accounts for the relationship between health and basal RSA, it does not clearly explain the relationship between health and vagal reactivity, or the reactivity of other physiological systems, for that matter. Furthermore, NIT predominantly focuses on RSA. The SNS may receive less attention in NIT because this theory considers reciprocal associations between the SNS and PSNS, and does not consider alternative possible associations, like coactivity, between the SNS and PSNS.

Polyvagal Theory

OVERVIEW

Polyvagal theory (PT) (Porges, 1995, 1997, 1998, 2001, 2003, 2007, 2009) makes predictions about stress-related illness by considering how different parts of the ANS emerged at different points in evolution. PT argues that the ANS consists of three phylogenetically, structurally, and functionally distinct components: the dorsal vagus, the SNS, and the ventral vagus. Prominently, PT argues that these systems evolved to cope with different situations and have different effects on health.

According to PT, the first system to evolve was the dorsal vagus (or unmyelinated vagus), which is a distinct branch of the PSNS originating from the dorsal motor nucleus. The dorsal vagus is a potent suppressor of heart rate and metabolism. In threatening situations, activation of the dorsal vagus allows organisms to avoid detection by predators and to conserve resources. This primitive stress response, often referred to as immobilization or freezing response, is adaptive for primitive organisms (e.g., reptiles), but it can be deadly for more recently evolved organisms like humans, who require a constant energy supply.

The next system to evolve was the SNS, which increases metabolism, counteracting the effects of the dorsal vagus. According to PT, moderate SNS activity inhibits the dorsal vagus, while robust SNS activation, along with activation of the HPA axis, facilitates the fight-or-flight response by mobilizing stored energy and promoting vigilance, aggression, and other defensive behaviors. While the fight-or-flight response is not as harmful as the immobilization response, consistent with allostatic load theory, PT predicts that chronic activation of the SNS or HPA axis damages organs over time. Vigilance, aggression, and other defensive behaviors are also maladaptive for social organisms such as humans, as these behaviors can alienate sources of social support while increasing potential sources of adversity.

The final component of the ANS, according to PT, and the most recent system to have evolved, is the ventral vagus (or myelinated vagus), which is a distinct branch of the PSNS originating from the nucleus ambiguus within the reticular formation. Like the dorsal vagus, the ventral vagus slows heart rate, but not as much or for as long as the dorsal vagus. Since the ventral vagus is myelinated, it exerts more rapid and precise control over heart rate than the dorsal vagus or SNS. Consequently, according to PT, RSA is a marker specifically of ventral vagal activity. PT argues that the ventral vagus evolved to meet the needs of more advanced social organisms and protects their health in four ways. (1) The ventral vagus promotes homeostasis. It supports vegetative functions conducive to growth and recovery, and it conveys information about visceral state back to the brain. (2) The ventral vagus limits allostatic load by inhibiting the SNS and HPA axis. Acute reductions in vagal tone are already sufficient to increase metabolism, so the organism can respond to certain challenges without activating the SNS and HPA axis. (3) The ventral vagus facilitates self-soothing and helps regulate emotion and attention. (4) Finally, the ventral vagus facilitates social engagement, by preventing defensive behaviors, and through anatomical and physiological connections with structures involved in communication. Together, the ventral vagus thus facilitates homeostasis, recovery from stress, minimizes allostatic load, and promotes cognition and behaviors that are known to protect individuals from stress such as emotional and attentional regulation, and social engagement.

Each of the components of the ANS, the ventral vagus, SNS/HPA axis, and dorsal vagus, supports different functions that are incompatible with each other; thus, they are activated at different times. PT predicts that these three systems activate in a hierarchical manner, consistent with the principle of Jacksonian dissolution (Jackson, 1958). Jackson's principle states that evolutionarily more recent systems inhibit older ones. If the recent system is no longer sufficient, the next most recent system takes over, shifting the organism to a more primitive response. Applying Jackson's principle, PT predicts that in safe environments, the ventral vagus inhibits the SNS and HPA axis, supporting social engagement and self-soothing. In response to moderate challenge, the ventral vagus may moderately withdraw to increase metabolism. In more threatening situations, the ventral vagus withdraws more completely, freeing the SNS and HPA axis, switching the organism from social engagement to a fight-or-flight response. If the fight-or-flight response is insufficient to deal with threat, as a last resort the SNS and HPA axis also withdraw, freeing the dorsal vagus to mount an immobilization (freezing) response. This allows organisms to respond to different levels of threat.

PT makes several predictions about stress-related health problems. High ventral vagal activity, as indexed by high levels of RSA, indicates the individual perceives safety and is socially engaged, a situation more likely to emerge in nonstressful environments. Since the ventral vagus promotes growth and recovery and prevents overactivation of the SNS and HPA axis, hypothetically, individuals with higher basal RSA should also be less susceptible to stress-related illness. Both PT and NIT associate higher basal RSA with better health outcomes and resilience against stress. PT further predicts that in addition to high basal RSA, healthy individuals should also exhibit brief decreases in RSA during acute stress. Failure to reduce RSA during stress (i.e., blunted RSA reactivity) is further predicted to correlate with poor health and developmental outcomes. Blunted RSA and SNS reactivity to stress may also indicate an immobilization response, particularly in the presence of life-threatening, traumatic events. Such a reactivity profile is likely to occur in conditions of extreme adversity and also predicts poor health outcomes since prolonged suppression of metabolism would be expected to damage the heart and brain.

EMPIRICAL SUPPORT AND CURRENT STATUS OF POLYVAGAL THEORY

Consistent with PT, basal RSA positively correlates with attention regulation (Suess et al., 1994), emotion regulation (Appelhans & Luecken, 2006), social engagement (Geisler, Kubiak, Siewert, & Weber, 2013), and prosocial behavior (Beauchaine et al., 2013). This is in line with the notion that the ventral vagus, as indexed by RSA, facilitates social engagement, emotional regulation, and attention regulation.

Also consistent with PT, research has found that RSA reliably decreases during challenge (Beauchaine, Gatzke-Kopp, & Mead, 2006), and moderate reduction in RSA during challenge is associated with better executive function (Marcovitch et al., 2010) and cognitive performance (Roos et al., 2018). The relationship between RSA reactivity and cognitive outcomes, however, appears to vary by context. Some studies find that high RSA reactivity predicts better cognitive outcomes in nonstressful environments, but worse outcomes in individuals living in chronically stressful environments (Giuliano, Roos, Farrar, & Skowron, 2018; Obradovic, Bush, Stamperdahl, Adler, & Boyce, 2010). PT does not readily explain why and how the environment would moderate the relationship between RSA reactivity and cognitive outcomes.

Both PT and NIT predict that individuals with higher basal RSA are less vulnerable to the harmful effects of stress. As mentioned in the section on NIT, ample research suggests that individuals with high RSA develop fewer health problems when exposed to adversity (El-Sheikh et al., 2009; Hinnant et al., 2015; McLaughlin, Alves, et al., 2014; Suurland et al., 2017). Studies also find that low basal RSA is associated with various stress-related illnesses such as cardiovascular disease (Thayer & Lane, 2007), depression (Agelink et al., 2002), and anxiety (Dieleman et al., 2015).

Like NIT, PT predicts that the relationship between higher basal RSA and better health outcomes is partly mediated by inhibition of the SNS and HPA axis. As mentioned in the section on NIT, this prediction is inconsistently supported. Some studies associate stress-related illness with greater SNS or HPA axis activity, while others studies associate stress-related illness with lower (not higher) SNS or HPA axis activity. Nonetheless, the relationship between SNS hypoactivity and poor health outcomes may still be consistent with PT. Hypothetically, SNS hypoactivity may indicate that the individual has shifted to the immobilization response, mediated by the dorsal vagus.

STRENGTHS AND LIMITATIONS OF POLYVAGAL THEORY

PT identifies processes such as social engagement and self-regulation that link higher RSA with better resilience against stress-related illness. Inhibition of the HPA axis and SNS may be another mechanism linking high vagal tone to better resilience; however, it is difficult to evaluate this claim given the inconsistent associations between SNS/HPA axis activity and stress-related disease reported in the literature. Nonetheless, PT may potentially explain why SNS activity and reactivity are inconsistently associated with stress-related problems. Individuals with higher SNS activity or reactivity are at increased risk of allostatic load, whereas blunted SNS activity may be a sign the individual has entered the immobilization phase.

PT, like all theories, has a number of limitations. First, the theory assumes inhibitory (i.e., reciprocal) relationships between the SNS and PSNS. Like NIT, PT should be expanded to accommodate coactivation of SNS and PSNS. Another limitation concerns predictions made about reactivity. Consistent with PT, some studies associate higher RSA reactivity to stress with better cognitive outcomes; however, other studies find that the relationship between reactivity and cognitive outcomes is moderated by context. PT does not clearly explain why context moderates effects of RSA reactivity; however, biological sensitivity to context theory does.

Biological Sensitivity to Context Theory
OVERVIEW
The relationship between autonomic function and health may vary between studies because the impact of autonomic function depends on the individual's context. Biological sensitivity to context theory (BSC) (Boyce & Ellis, 2005; Ellis & Boyce, 2008) is an evolutionary developmental theory that emphasizes how the environment interacts with the reactivity of the physiological stress systems in the organism to determine health and developmental outcomes. An intuitive concept in BSC is that high reactivity per se is neither good nor bad. The relationship between reactivity and health depends on what the environment demands. Theories that existed before BSC, such as the diathesis-stress or allostatic load theory, predict that highly reactive individuals are more vulnerable to stress-related illness because they accumulate more allostatic load. As Boyce and Ellis (2005) review, while data certainly exist that associate greater reactivity with worse health and developmental outcomes, a large number of studies associate greater reactivity with better health and developmental outcomes. To explain these inconsistent findings, BSC proposes that whether a particular level of reactivity harms or promotes health depends on the individual's context. Specifically, high reactivity exacerbates health problems in adverse environments but promotes positive health and developmental outcomes in supportive, nonstressful environments. In contrast, less reactive individuals may not fair as poorly in stressful environments, but they do not benefit as much from supportive environments, showing the same moderate outcomes regardless of the environment.

To explain the interaction between environment and physiological reactivity, BSC argues that low reactivity and high reactivity each are advantageous in different environments. In nonstressful environments, high reactivity maximizes long-term growth and survival by enhancing attention and engagement with positive sources of stimulation. In supportive environments, the physiological stress response systems are infrequently and briefly perturbed, preventing excess allostatic load. When stress becomes more frequent or intense, high reactivity leads to excess allostatic load. In moderately stressful conditions, low reactivity is therefore conducive to long-term growth and survival since it limits allostatic load. In highly threatening environments, low reactivity ceases to be advantageous, since activation of the physiological stress response systems is required to survive. High reactivity may be necessary to survive in the short term, but it comes at the expense of undermining long-term growth and survival.

Since high and low reactivity are adaptive in different environments, BSC proposes that humans evolved to shift their reactivity toward a level optimal for the individual's environment. Boyce and Ellis (Boyce & Ellis, 2005; Ellis & Boyce, 2008) predict a U-shaped relationship between increasing levels of adversity and physiological reactivity. Individuals exposed to extremely supportive or extremely stressful environments are predicted to develop higher reactivity, while those exposed to moderately stressful environments develop low reactivity. This process is believed to occur gradually early in development. Consequently, individuals may therefore exhibit a level of reactivity that is no longer adaptive for their current context, if their individual environmental context changes after a critical development period.

EMPIRICAL SUPPORT AND CURRENT STATUS OF BIOLOGICAL SENSITIVITY TO CONTEXT THEORY

An early test of BSC (Ellis, Essex, & Boyce, 2005) observed the expected U-shaped relationship between adversity and reactivity. High SNS reactivity tended to occur among children exposed to extremely low or extremely high adversity; low SNS reactivity was common in environments that were not particularly stressful or supportive. It is nonetheless worth noting that many individuals exposed to extreme adversity early in life, such as Romanian orphans, exhibit blunted (not greater) SNS reactivity (McLaughlin et al., 2015); thus, the relationship between adversity and ANS reactivity may be more complex than the U-shaped relationship initially proposed by BSC.

Ample empirical evidence supports BSC's prediction that adversity and autonomic reactivity interact to determine health outcomes. Consistent with BSC, studies associate greater reactivity with worse health outcomes in adverse environments, but better outcomes in supportive environments. In terms of cardiovascular reactivity, Cook et al. (2012) found that greater cardiovascular reactivity predicted worse interpersonal competence and anger regulation for adolescents experiencing maltreatment, but better interpersonal competence and anger regulation for adolescents in more supportive environments.

Using RSA reactivity as a marker of PSNS reactivity, Conradt and colleagues (2016) found that higher RSA reactivity at 1 month of age predicted more internalizing and externalizing problems at 3 years of age—but only for children with high levels of caregiver stress. Likewise, in preschoolers, Obradovic and colleagues (2010) examined several outcomes, including externalizing behaviors, prosocial behavior, and social engagement. High RSA reactivity predicted worse outcomes in children living in stressful environments, but better outcomes in children living in nonstressful condition. Contexts also moderate the effects of SNS reactivity. For instance, El-Sheikh et al. (2007) found that for girls (but not boys), the combination of high early life adversity and high SCR reactivity increased risk of internalizing and externalizing problems.

Contrary to predictions made by BSC, numerous studies also suggest the opposite association between reactivity and stress-related illness. For example, higher PSNS reactivity to stress appeared to reduce rather than exacerbate the impact of childhood adversity on children's internalizing pathology (McLaughlin, Alves, et al., 2014). Also contrary to BSC, higher SNS reactivity reduced rather than exacerbated the impact of maternal depression on children's externalizing pathology (Waters et al., 2016). Interestingly, a large number of studies examining the interaction between early life adversity and autonomic reactivity observe sex differences, which are not clearly explained by BSC theory (El-Sheikh et al., 2007; Gray et al., 2017; Lorber, Erlanger, & Slep, 2013; Sijtsema, Roon, Groot, & Riese, 2015).

STRENGTHS AND LIMITATIONS OF BIOLOGICAL SENSITIVITY TO CONTEXT THEORY

BSC speaks to how autonomic function might more accurately predict health when the individual's context is also taken into consideration. BSC is one of the few theories that attempt to explain why the relationship between health and autonomic function varies between studies; thus, it could also explain why the relationship between autonomic function and early life adversity varies between studies.

BSC nonetheless has a few limitations. Extreme adversity is not always associated with heightened stress reactivity as predicted by BSC. Furthermore, some studies observe interactions between adversity and reactivity that go against BSC. Sometimes the expected interaction is observed in one sex but not the other. Furthermore, BSC focuses on general physiological reactivity and does not make specific predictions about individual stress systems. This is problematic, since as autonomic space theory reveals, PSNS and SNS activity can change independently of one another. It is unclear how to classify these individuals within BSC theory. From the perspective of polyvagal theory, the PSNS, SNS, and HPA axis response to stress differentially impacts health; thus, it may be unreasonable to predict that individuals with high SNS reactivity will have the same health outcomes as individuals with high PSNS reactivity.

New Developments
Adaptive Calibration Model
OVERVIEW

A new theory, the adaptive calibration model of stress responsivity (ACM) (Del Giudice, Ellis, & Shirtcliff, 2011), aims to explain individual differences in the physiological stress systems, the HPA axis, SNS, and PSNS. To explain how stress systems develop over time and impact health, ACM expands on biological sensitivity to context theory (BSC), incorporating concepts from polyvagal theory (PT), allostatic load theory, and other models in stress research in addition to concepts from evolutionary biology (e.g., life history theory). According to the ACM, the stress response systems evolved to serve three key functions: (1) to help survive acute stressors by implementing allostasis, (2) filter and encode information about threats and opportunities in the environment, and based on this information, (3) affect physiology and behavior in a way that guides development toward a phenotype that is optimal for the given environment. Here, "optimal" means to maximize reproductive fitness. Consequently, alterations in stress system function can lead to characteristics that may be undesirable, but over the course of human evolution, increased the likelihood of passing one's genes on to the next generation.

The ACM also provides a taxonomy that can be used to describe individual differences in stress system function (baseline activity and stress reactivity). As summarized in Table 22.1, there are four patterns of responsivity. Each pattern emerges in a particular environment and predicts specific health and developmental outcomes. Type I, the sensitive type, is similar to the sensitive phenotype described in BSC and develops in very low levels of early life adversity. Sensitive individuals are more susceptible to stress-related illness if they encounter adversity but exhibit better health and developmental outcomes in nonstressful environments. Consistent with PT, the sensitive type, which shows higher PSNS activity and reactivity, is expected to show better social engagement and emotional and attentional regulation in supportive environments. Type II, the buffered type, develops in conditions that are not particularly safe or adverse. When buffered individuals encounter adversity, they are less susceptible to stress-related illness, but they are also less susceptible to positive environmental influences. Type III, the vigilant type, develops in more stressful conditions and is characterized by a robust and persistent fight-or-flight response. These individuals are more susceptible to stress-related illness but are more

likely to survive harsh conditions, at least to the point where they reproduce. Finally, type IV, the unemotional type, emerges in extremely harsh conditions and is characterized by blunted activity and reactivity of the PSNS, SNS, and HPA axis. The unemotional type is expected to show high rates of antisocial behavior and other problems due to a reduced sensitivity to social feedback. Importantly, different types are not discrete categories but are continuous with each other. Individuals thus can transition from one type to another depending on their cumulative exposure to early life adversity at critical periods in development such as prenatal development, early childhood, puberty, and potentially other periods.

EMPIRICAL SUPPORT AND CURRENT STATUS OF THE ADAPTIVE CALIBRATION MODEL

The ACM is a new theory, so empirical support thus far is limited. Nonetheless, a few studies support the basic predictions of ACM. Del Giudice, Hinnant, Ellis and El-Sheikh (2011) examined children exposed to varying levels of early life adversity and measured SCR and RSA basal activity and stress reactivity (no markers of the HPA axis were included). Using finite mixture modeling, the authors reduced the variance in SCR and RSA activity and reactivity into the four patterns predicted by the ACM. Pattern was related to early life adversity as predicted by the ACM. More recently, a study of men (Ellis, Oldehinkel, & Nederhof, 2016) measured PSNS, SNS, and HPA axis markers at rest and during stress. Again, the four-pattern classification was validated, and pattern associated with early life adversity in the expected direction. For the most part, pattern was also associated with the predicted behavioral and developmental outcomes. For instance, as expected, the unemotional type was associated with the highest levels of aggression and rule breaking.

While the ACM predicts four patterns of responsivity, additional patterns might exist. In a large sample of adolescents, Quas et al. (2014) found six distinct responsivity patterns. While the first four

Table 22.1. Four patterns of stress system responsivity predicted by the adaptive calibration model

	Type I. Sensitive	Type II. Buffered	Type III. Vigilant	Type IV. Unemotional
SNS basal activity	Moderate	Low/moderate	High	Low
SNS reactivity	High/moderate	Low/moderate	High	Low
PSNS basal activity	High	Moderate	Low	Low
PSNS reactivity	High	Moderate	Low/moderate	Low
HPA axis basal activity	Moderate	Moderate	High/moderate	Low
HPA axis reactivity	High	Moderate	Moderate	Low

corresponded to the patterns predicted by ACM, two patterns were new. In a separate study, Kolacz et al. (2016) found three types (sensitive, buffered, and vigilant) in addition to a novel type. Kolacz et al. (2016) did not observe the unemotional type, potentially because they did not sufficiently sample individuals with extreme levels of early life adversity.

STRENGTHS AND LIMITATIONS OF THE ADAPTIVE CALIBRATION MODEL

Since the ACM integrates multiple perspectives covered by other theories (BSC, PT, allostatic load), the theory has multiple strengths. Like PT, the ACM acknowledges that reactivity and basal activity predict distinct outcomes. Like BSC, the ACM aims to account for heterogeneous relationships between autonomic function and chronic stress, and autonomic function and health. The ACM provides insights into how individual differences in stress system function develop over time depending on genes and exposure to early life adversity. Since the relationship between early life adversity and stress reactivity is nonlinear, it may partly explain why effects of early life adversity on stress system physiology vary between studies. The ACM improves upon BSC by making specific predictions about PSNS, SNS, and HPA axis reactivity. For instance, both the sensitive and vigilant type show higher reactivity, but the sensitive type shows predominantly higher PSNS reactivity, whereas the SNS shows predominantly higher SNS reactivity; consequently, sensitive and vigilant types are associated with distinct ecological antecedents and distinct health and developmental outcomes.

ACM nonetheless has several limitations and opportunities for growth. First, ACM is a complex model, making it difficult to falsify. Low, moderate, high, and extreme exposure to early life adversity are expected to have different effects on stress function. Since there is no standard operational definition of early life adversity, it is difficult to delineate low, moderate, high, and extreme adversity, particularly when a wide range of events and experiences can be called "adverse." A similar argument can be made regarding reactivity and baseline activity—there is no standardized definition of low, moderate, and high reactivity or activity. This limitation could apply to any theory about ANS function; however, it is particularly relevant to the ACM since it posits nonlinear associations between reactivity, adversity, and health. The absence of quantitative definitions for low, moderate, and high reactivity/activity makes the theory more difficult to falsify. Despite these

limitations, the ACM is a promising new model that encourages researchers to consider relations between the SNS, PSNS, and HPA axis and other neuroendocrine systems as well.

Changes in Physiology as a Result of Interaction With Other Systems—Empirical Findings

Recently, our group has begun to systematically examine the interaction between both the HPA axis and ANS on the psychological, physiological, and endocrine level during an acute stress test. To this end, we looked at the cross-correlation between the SNS and HPA axis stress responses (Engert et al., 2011) and how behavioral variables depend on the ratio of HPA reactivity to autonomic reactivity (Ali & Pruessner, 2012). Further, we combined the dexamethasone suppression test with the Trier Social Stress Test (TSST) to study the effects of stress on the ANS in the absence of a reactive HPA axis. This study (Andrews et al., 2012) was the first attempt to systematically investigate the effect of manipulating these stress systems, and thus deserves a somewhat more detailed description: Here, we exposed 30 healthy young men to a psychosocial stressor and measured salivary cortisol, a hormone of the HPA axis, in addition to salivary alpha-amylase, heart rate, blood pressure, and subjective stress. As the main experimental manipulation, half of the subjects received a standard dose of dexamethasone (DEX; 2 mg) the night before testing, resulting in elevated negative feedback at the level of the pituitary and a central low-cortisol state since DEX cannot cross the blood–brain barrier (de Kloet et al., 1974, 1975), resulting in increased corticotropin-releasing hormone (CRH), but suppresses subsequent secretion of peripheral HPA axis hormones, adrenocorticotropin and cortisol. This can be compared to a state where the HPA axis is dysfunctional and unable to respond to stress, as discussed for states like burnout and chronic fatigue syndrome. As a result of this manipulation, subjects who received DEX demonstrated a higher increase in subjective stress post TSST, and a significantly higher heart rate throughout the protocol, when compared to the placebo group. This suggested an active compensation between the HPA axis and ANS, where SNS activity may be elevated, or PSNS activity may be diminished, in the presence of a suppressed HPA axis response.

Although we were the first group to combine an acute psychosocial stressor with DEX to investigate this cross-talk, others have also reported such an association, and a number of hypotheses have been proposed to explain the increased SNS activity following dexamethasone administration. First, the dexamethasone-induced low-cortisol state in the brain could have elevated heart rate via a CRH surge (due to the lack of negative feedback), by way of a periventricular nucleus and locus coeruleus connection (Yamaguchi & Okada, 2009). Also, Chrousos and Gold (1992) found that norepinephrine potentiates the release of CRH, creating a feedforward mechanism between the systems; thus, a central ANS mechanism could have been initiated to augment the HPA axis response, a mechanism also discussed by Suzuki et al. (2003). Consequently, the increased cardiovascular activity found in a population where cortisol output of the HPA axis is suppressed may be due to these factors individually and/or in combination (Andrews et al., 2012). Since the regulation of the ANS and HPA axis overlaps at several points in the brain (Ulrich-Lai & Herman, 2009), predominantly in the hypothalamus, it can be speculated that this is an active compensatory mechanism, such that the absence of the peripheral HPA response may up-regulate SNS activity or decrease PSNS activity, compensating for the lack of a stress response in one system with altered activity in the other, to keep the organism in an equilibrium, and allow allostasis.

This can be interpreted to have demonstrated a potential pathway for the development of cardiovascular disease, metabolic syndrome, and diabetes (Sabbah, Watt, Sheiham, & Tsakos, 2008; Seeman et al., 2001; Selye, 1970). This further points to a potential disease mechanism where either a blunted HPA axis activity or an increased cardiovascular reactivity might lead to these types of disease.

We also investigated (Andrews & Pruessner, 2013) suppressing the ANS (SNS) by using propranolol (PROP) in combination with the TSST. When administering subjects PROP 1 hour before the TSST, thereby preventing a SNS response, we observed signs of a compensatory increase in HPA axis activity in response to stress (Andrews & Pruessner, 2013). As expected, cardiovascular activation was strongly suppressed in the PROP group. Heart rate, salivary alpha-amylase, and systolic blood pressure levels all showed very small or no increase in response to stress, in the PROP group. In contrast, subjective stress and diastolic blood pressure were not different between the two groups. The main result that indicated significant cross-talk between the HPA axis and SNS was observed for cortisol levels, which were significantly higher in the experimental group.

The finding of higher HPA axis activity after SNS suppression has also been reported by a number of other laboratories (Benschop et al., 1996; Kizildere et al., 2003; Maheu et al., 2005; Oei et al., 2010; Simeckova et al., 2000), suggesting that the absence of SNS response leads to an increase in HPA axis activity, compensating for the lack of a stress response with an increase in another stress response system, to keep the organism in an equilibrium. These results are quite intriguing, as one could have expected a lower cortisol response in the absence of a physiological stress response; after all, no physiological arousal is signaling to the brain a state of stress, as would be expected from past research on emotion and emotion processing (e.g., Dutton & Aron, 1974). The fact that SNS suppression augments the cortisol stress responses strongly suggests that at a central level the lack of a physiological response is answered by a stronger activation of the HPA axis.

This mechanism that results in higher cortisol responses to stress has potential psychopathological effects as well, since central hyperactivity of the HPA axis (i.e., increased CRH secretion) is associated with depression and mood disorders. Some of the most prominent theories on depression suggest that it is the central effect of CRH that is associated with depressive symptomatology and mood dysfunction, through the effects of CRH in core limbic structures related to mood and anxiety, for example, the amygdala and the prefrontal cortex (Binder & Nemeroff, 2010; Hauger et al., 2009; Nemeroff, 1996, 1998). This is in line with the proposed neuroanatomical mechanisms to explain the compensatory effect between the HPA axis and ANS as well. First, there is the possibility of an increase in epinephrine production due to propranolol's blocking noradrenergic binding to beta 2-adrenergic receptors. Epinephrine could then in turn increase CRH release from the hypothalamus, with subsequent increase in cortisol (Viru et al., 2007)—this represents a central mechanism. Second, there is also the possibility of a direct inhibitory effect of SNS activation on the adrenal cortex. In cases where the SNS system is inhibited, a disinhibition of the HPA axis could result (Viru et al., 2007). This represents a compensatory mechanism at the level of the adrenal cortex. These two mechanisms could further complement each other, making the HPA/SNS interaction more potent. While the exact routes of action still await further empirical confirmation, the available evidence points to a negative interaction between the SNS and HPA after they have been triggered by central nervous system components when threat is detected. Taken together, these preliminary pharmacological manipulations point toward mechanisms by which the wear and tear on the stress systems can lead to cardiovascular disease and metabolic syndrome with aging. Especially when combined with a sedentary lifestyle and physical inactivity, increased food consumption, insulin resistance, abdominal obesity, and hypertension could potentially follow from these effects.

Conclusion

As we have seen over the course of this chapter, how the ANS functions at rest and in response to stressors has important implications for stress-related illness. Although research findings are mixed, evidence suggests that autonomic activity and reactivity may mediate and moderate the effects of stress on health and developmental outcomes. Specifically, for accepted markers of the PSNS like RSA, the evidence consistently points to better health with higher levels of basal activity on this particular variable. A diverse range of psychophysiological models attempt to explain how the ANS contributes to stress-related health outcomes. These models vary in key elements of the ANS, how these elements are measured, and whether lack of or excessive activity/reactivity might be a sign of impaired health or constitute a health risk.

Future Directions

It is challenging to integrate and evaluate psychophysiological models of stress since research findings vary considerably between studies, providing conflicting information about the relationship between ANS function and health outcomes. Mixed research findings could partly arise from the considerable variation in how researchers measure ANS function, and how those measures are interpreted. Developing and consistently implementing a clear set of methodological standards specific for stress research may therefore help resolve inconsistent results. Mixed findings also potentially suggest that relationships between ANS function and health outcomes are moderated by various external factors and internal factors. Some of the psychophysiological models discussed here, such as biological sensitivity to context theory, provide insight into potential factors that moderate the relationship between autonomic function and health.

Future research should continue to determine why the relationship between autonomic function and health outcomes varies. Examining the inter-

play between the PSNS, SNS, and other stress response systems, such as the HPA axis, will be an important avenue for future research. Autonomic space model, neurovisceral integration theory, polyvagal theory, and the adaptive calibration model all provide testable hypotheses about how the PSNS, SNS, and other stress systems like HPA axis interact with each other to affect health and well-being. Future research should test these hypotheses and expand current models to include new systems such as the enteric nervous system. Novel methodological approaches should also be considered, like the use of innovative statistical methods such as finite mixture modeling to determine how different patterns of activity or reactivity across multiple stress systems are associated with different health and developmental outcomes. Pharmacological manipulation of the stress response systems such as the propanol and dexamethasone experiments discussed earlier could help introduce systematic experimental manipulation into the field, and help researchers better understand the interaction of the various physiological systems at play in health and disease.

References

Abaied, J. L. (2016). Skin conductance level reactivity as a moderator of the link between parent depressive symptoms and psychosocial adjustment in emerging adults. *Journal of Social and Personal Relationships, 33*(4), 534–556. doi:10.1177/0265407515583170

Agelink, M. W., Boz, C., Ullrich, H., & Andrich, J. (2002). Relationship between major depression and heart rate variability. Clinical consequences and implications for antidepressive treatment. *Psychiatry Research, 113*, 139–149. doi:10.1016/S0165-1781(02)00225-1

Ali, N., & Pruessner, J. C. (2012). The salivary alpha amylase over cortisol ratio as a marker to assess dysregulations of the stress systems. *Physiology & Behavior, 106*(1), 65–72. doi:10.1016/j.physbeh.2011.10.003

Allegrini, A. G., Evans, B. E., de Rooij, S., Greaves-Lord, K., & Huizink, A. C. (2017). Gene × environment contributions to autonomic stress reactivity in youth. *Development and Psychopathology, 31*, 1–15. doi:10.1017/S095457941700181X

Allen, J., Chambers, A. S., & Towers, D. N. (2007). The many metrics of cardiac chronotropy: A pragmatic primer and a brief comparison of metrics. *Biological Psychology, 74*(2), 243–262. doi:10.1016/j.biopsycho.2006.08.005

Andrews, J., D'Aguiar, C., & Pruessner, J. C. (2012). The combined dexamethasone/TSST paradigm—a new method for psychoneuroendocrinology. *PLOS ONE, 7*(6), e38994. doi:10.1371/journal.pone.0038994

Andrews, J., & Pruessner, J. C. (2013). The combined propranolol/TSST paradigm—a new method for psychoneuroendocrinology. *PLOS ONE, 8*(2), e57567. doi:10.1371/journal.pone.0057567

Appelhans, B. M., & Luecken, L. J. (2006). Heart rate variability as an index of regulated emotional responding. *Review of General Psychology, 10*(3), 229. doi:10.1037/1089-2680.10.3.229

Backs, R. W. (1995). Going beyond heart rate: Autonomic space and cardiovascular assessment of mental workload. *The International Journal of Aviation Psychology*, 5(1), 25–48. doi:10.1207/s15327108ijap0501_3

Beauchaine, T. P., Gatzke-Kopp, L., & Mead, H. K. (2006). Polyvagal theory and developmental psychopathology: Emotion dysregulation and conduct problems from preschool to adolescence. *Biological Psychology*, 74(2), 174–184. doi:10.1016/j.biopsycho.2005.08.008

Beauchaine, T. P., Gatzke-Kopp, L., Neuhaus, E., Chipman, J., Reid, J. M., & Webster-Stratton, C. (2013). Sympathetic- and parasympathetic-linked cardiac function and prediction of externalizing behavior, emotion regulation, and prosocial behavior among preschoolers treated for ADHD. *Journal of Consulting and Clinical Psychology*, 81(3), 481. doi:10.1037/a0032302

Benarroch, E. E. (1993). The central autonomic network— Functional-organization, dysfunction, and perspective. *Mayo Clinic Proceedings*, 68(10), 988–1001. doi:10.1016/j.ijpsycho.2015.08.004

Benedek, M., & Kaernbach, C. (2010). A continuous measure of phasic electrodermal activity. *Journal of Neuroscience Methods*, 190(1), 80–91. doi:10.1016/j.jneumeth.2010.04.028

Benschop, R. J., Jacobs, R., Sommer, B., Schurmeyer, T. H., Raab, J. R., Schmidt, R. E., & Schedlowski, M. (1996). Modulation of the immunologic response to acute stress in humans by beta-blockade or benzodiazepines. *FASEB Journal*, 10(4), 517–524. doi:10.1096/fasebj.10.4.8647351

Berntson, G. G., & Cacioppo, J. T. (2004). Heart rate variability: Stress and psychiatric conditions. In M. Malik & A. J. Camm (Eds.), *Dynamic electrocardiography*. Austin, TX: Futura Publishing.

Berntson, G. G., Cacioppo, J. T., Binkley, P. F., Uchino, B. N., Quigley, K. S., & Fieldstone, A. (1994). Autonomic cardiac control. III. Psychological stress and cardiac response in autonomic space as revealed by pharmacological blockades. *Psychophysiology*, 31(6), 599–608. doi:10.1111/j.1469-8986.1994.tb02352.x

Berntson, G. G., Cacioppo, J. T., & Fieldstone, A. (1996). Illusions, arithmetic, and the bidirectional modulation of vagal control of the heart. *Biological Psychology*, 44(1), 1–17. doi:10.1016/S0301-0511(96)05197-6

Berntson, G. G., Cacioppo, J. T., & Grossman, P. (2007). Whither vagal tone. *Biological Psychology*, 74(2), 295–300. doi:10.1016/j.biopsycho.2006.08.006

Berntson, G. G., Cacioppo, J. T., & Quigley, K. S. (1991). Autonomic determinism: The modes of autonomic control, the doctrine of autonomic space, and the laws of autonomic constraint. *Psychological Review*, 98(4), 459–487. doi:10.1037/0033-295X.98.4.459

Berntson, G. G., Cacioppo, J. T., & Quigley, K. S. (1993). Cardiac psychophysiology and autonomic space in humans: Empirical perspectives and conceptual implications. *Psychological Bulletin*, 114(2), 296–322. doi:10.1037/0033-2909.114.2.296

Berntson, G. G., Cacioppo, J. T., & Quigley, K. S. (1994). Autonomic cardiac control. I. Estimation and validation from pharmacological blockades. *Psychophysiology*, 31(6), 572–585. doi:10.1111/j.1469-8986.1994.tb02350.x

Berntson, G. G., Lozano, D. L., & Chen, Y. J. (2005). Filter properties of root mean square successive difference (RMSSD) for heart rate. *Psychophysiology*, 42(2), 246–252. doi:10.1111/j.1469-8986.2005.00277.x

Bigger Jr., J. T., Fleiss, J. L., Steinman, R. C., Rolnitzky, L. M., Kleiger, R. E., & Rottman, J. N. (1992). Frequency domain measures of heart period variability and mortality after myocardial infarction. *Circulation*, 85(1), 164–171. doi:10.1161/circ.85.1.1728446

Binder, E. B., & Nemeroff, C. B. (2010). The CRF system, stress, depression and anxiety-insights from human genetic studies. *Molecular Psychiatry*, 15(6), 574–588. doi:10.1038/mp.2009.141

Blechert, J., Michael, T., Grossman, P., Lajtman, M., & Wilhelm, F. H. (2007). Autonomic and respiratory characteristics of posttraumatic stress disorder and panic disorder. *Psychosomatic Medicine*, 69(9), 935–943. doi:10.1097/PSY.0b013e31815a8f6b

Bosch, J. A., de Geus, E. J. C., Carroll, D., Goedhart, A. D., Anane, L. A., van Zanten, J. J., . . . Edwards, K. M. (2009). A general enhancement of autonomic and cortisol responses during social evaluative threat. *Psychosomatic Medicine*, 71(8), 877–885. doi:10.1097/PSY.0b013e3181baef05

Bosch, J. A., de Geus, E. J. C., Veerman, E. C. I., Hoogstraten, J., & Amerongen, A. V. (2003). Innate secretory immunity in response to laboratory stressors that evoke distinct patterns of cardiac autonomic activity. *Psychosomatic Medicine*, 65(2), 245–258. doi:10.1097/01.PSY.0000058376.50240.2D

Bosch, J. A., Veerman, E. C. I., de Geus, E. J., & Proctor, G. B. (2011). Alpha-amylase as a reliable and convenient measure of sympathetic activity: Don't start salivating just yet! *Psychoneuroendocrinology*, 36(4), 449–453. doi:10.1016/j.psyneuen.2010.12.019

Boyce, T. W. & Ellis, B. J. (2005). Biological sensitivity to context: I. An evolutionary-developmental theory of the origins and functions of stress reactivity. *Development and Psychopathology*, 17, 271–301. doi:10.1017/S0954579405050145

Boyce, T. W., Quas, J., Alkon, A., Smider, N. A., Essex, M. J., Kupfer, D. J., & MacArthur Assessment Battery Working Group of the MacArthur Foundation Research Network on Psychopathology and Development. (2001). Autonomic reactivity and psychopathology in middle childhood. *The British Journal of Psychiatry*, 179(2), 144–150. doi:10.1192/bjp.179.2.144

Boycsein, W. (2012). *Electrodermal activity*. New York, NY: Springer Science+Business Media.

Brindle, R. C., Ginty, A. T. & Conklin, S. M. (2013). Is the association between depression and blunted cardiovascular stress reactions mediated by perceptions of stress? *International Journal of Psychophysiology*, 90, 66–72. doi:10.1016/j.ijpsycho.2013.06.003

Brosschot, J. F., Gerin, W., & Thayer, J. F. (2006). The perseverative cognition hypothesis: A review of worry, prolonged stress-related physiological activation, and health. *Journal of Psychosomatic Research*, 60(2), 113–124. doi:10.1016/j.jpsychores.2005.06.074

Busso, D. S., McLaughlin, K. A., & Sheridan, M. A. (2017). Dimensions of adversity, physiological reactivity, and externalizing psychopathology in adolescence: Deprivation and threat. *Psychosomatic Medicine*, 79(2), 162–171. doi:10.1097/PSY.0000000000000369

Cacioppo, J. T., Berntson, G. G., Binkley, P. F., Quigley, K. S., Uchino, B. N., & Fieldstone, A. (1994). Autonomic cardiac control. II. Noninvasive indices and basal response as revealed by autonomic blockades. *Psychophysiology*, 31(6), 586–598. doi:10.1111/j.1469-8986.1994.tb02351.x

Calkins, S. D., Graziano, P. A., Berdan, L. E., Keane, S. P., & Degnan, K. A. (2008). Predicting cardiac vagal regulation in early childhood from maternal–child relationship quality during toddlerhood. *Developmental Psychobiology*, *50*(8), 751–766. doi:10.1002/dev.20344

Camm, A. J., Malik, M., Bigger, J. T., Breithardt, G., Cerutti, S., Cohen, R. J., Coumel, P., Fallen, E. L., Kennedy, H. L., Kleiger, R. E., Lombardi, F., Malliani, A., Moss, A. J., Rottman, J. N., Schmidt, G., Schwartz, P. J. &...Singer, D. H. (1996). Heart rate variability. Standards of measurement, physiological interpretation, and clinical use. *European Heart Journal*, *17*, 354–381. doi:10.1093/oxfordjournals.eurheartj.a014868.

Cannon, W. B. (1928). The mechanism of emotional disturbance of bodily functions. *New England Journal of Medicine*, *198*, 877–884. doi:10.1056/Nejm192806141981701

Cannon, W. B. (1929). Organization for physiological homeostasis. *Physiological Reviews*, *9(3)*, 399–431. doi:10.1152/physrev.1929.9.3.399

Cannon, W. B. (1939). *The wisdom of the body*. New York, NY: Norton.

Carabotti, M., Scirocco, A., Maselli, M. A., & Severi, C. (2015). The gut-brain axis: Interactions between enteric microbiota, central and enteric nervous systems. *Annals of Gastroenterology*, *28*(2), 203–209. Retrieved from https://www.ncbi.nlm.nih.gov/pmc/articles/PMC4367209/

Cărnuță, M., Crișan, L. G., Vulturar, R., Opre, A., & Miu, A. C. (2015). Emotional non-acceptance links early life stress and blunted cortisol reactivity to social threat. *Psychoneuroendocrinology*, *51*, 176–187. doi:10.1016/j.psyneuen.2014.09.026

Carroll, D., Ginty, A. T., Painter, R. C., Roseboom, T. J., Phillips, A. C., & de Rooij, S. R. (2012). Systolic blood pressure reactions to acute stress are associated with future hypertension status in the Dutch Famine Birth Cohort Study. *International Journal of Psychophysiology*, *85*(2), 270–273. doi:10.1016/j.ijpsycho.2012.04.001

Chapleau, M. W., & Sabharwal, R. (2011). Methods of assessing vagus nerve activity and reflexes. *Heart Failure Reviews*, *16*(2), 109–127. doi:10.1007/s10741-010-9174-6

Chatterton, R. T., Vogelsong, K. M., Lu, Y. C., Ellman, A. B., & Hudgens, G. A. (1996). Salivary alpha-amylase as a measure of endogenous adrenergic activity. *Clinical Physiology*, *16*(4), 433–448. doi:10.1111/j.1475-097X.1996.tb00731.x

Chrousos, G. P., & Gold, P. W. (1992). The concepts of stress and stress system disorders. Overview of physical and behavioral homeostasis. *JAMA*, *267*(9), 1244–1252. doi:10.1001/jama.1992.03480090092034

Chumaeva, N., Hintsanen, M., Ravaja, N., Puttonen, S., Heponiemi, T., Pulkki-Raback, L.,...Keltikangas-Jarvinen, L. (2009). Interactive effect of long-term mental stress and cardiac stress reactivity on carotid intima-media thickness: The Cardiovascular Risk in Young Finns study. *Stress*, *12*(4), 283–293. doi:10.1080/10253890802372406

Clark, C., Skowron, E. A., Giuliano, R. J., & Fisher, P. A. (2016). Intersections between cardiac physiology, emotion regulation and interpersonal warmth in preschoolers: Implications for drug abuse prevention from translational neuroscience. *Drug and Alcohol Dependence*, *163*, S60–S69. doi:10.1016/j.drugalcdep.2016.01.033

Conradt, E., Beauchaine, T., Abar, B., Lagasse, L., Shankaran, S., Bada, H.,...Lester, B. (2016). Early caregiving stress exposure moderates the relation between respiratory sinus arrhythmia reactivity at 1 month and biobehavioral outcomes at age 3. *Psychophysiology*, *53*(1), 83–96. doi:10.1111/psyp.12569

Cook, E. C., Chaplin, T. M., Sinha, R., Tebes, J. K., & Mayes, L. C. (2012). The stress response and adolescents' adjustment: The impact of child maltreatment. *Journal of Youth and Adolescence*, *41*(8), 1067–1077. doi:10.1007/s10964-012-9746-y

Cubała, W., & Landowski, J. (2014). Low baseline salivary alpha-amylase in drug-naïve patients with short-illness-duration first episode major depressive disorder. *Journal of Affective Disorders*, *157*, 14–17. doi:10.1016/j.jad.2013.12.043

Cummings, M. E., El-Sheikh, M., Kouros, C. D., & Keller, P. S. (2007). Children's skin conductance reactivity as a mechanism of risk in the context of parental depressive symptoms. *Journal of Child Psychology and Psychiatry*, *48*(5), 436–445. doi:10.1111/j.1469-7610.2006.01713.x

Dale, L. P., Shaikh, S. K., Fasciano, L. C., Watorek, V. D., Heilman, K. J., & Porges, S. W. (2017). College females with maltreatment histories have atypical autonomic regulation and poor psychological wellbeing. *Psychological Trauma: Theory, Research, Practice, and Policy*, *10*(4), 427–434. doi:10.1037/tra0000342

Davis, M., Suveg, C., Whitehead, M., Jones, A., & Shaffer, A. (2016). Preschoolers' psychophysiological responses to mood induction tasks moderate the intergenerational transmission of internalizing problems. *Biological Psychology*, *117*, 159–169. doi:10.1016/j.biopsycho.2016.03.015

Dawson, M. E., Schell, A. M., & Filion, D. L. (2007). The electrodermal system. In J. T. Cacioppo, L. G. Tassinary, & G. G. Berntson, G. G. (Eds.), *Handbook of pPsychophysiology* (pp. 159–181). Cambridge, UK: Cambridge University Press.

de Kloet, E. R., van der Vies, J., & de Wied, D. (1974). The site of the suppressive action of dexamethasone on pituitary-adrenal activity. *Endocrinology*, *94*(1), 61–73. doi:10.1210/endo-94-1-61

de Kloet, R., Wallach, G., & McEwen, B. S. (1975). Differences in corticosterone and dexamethasone binding to rat brain and pituitary. *Endocrinology*, *96*(3), 598–609. doi:10.1210/endo-96-3-598

Del Giudice, M., Ellis, B., & Shirtcliff, E. (2011). The adaptive calibration model of stress responsivity. *Neuroscience & Biobehavioral Reviews*, *35*(7), 1562–1592. doi:10.1016/j.neubiorev.2010.11.007

Del Giudice, M., Hinnant, B. J., Ellis, B. J., & El-Sheikh, M. (2011). Adaptive patterns of stress responsivity: A preliminary investigation. *Developmental Psychology*, *48*(3), 775–790. doi:10.1037/a0026519

Dickerson, S. S., & Kemeny, M. E. (2004). Acute stressors and cortisol responses: a theoretical integration and synthesis of laboratory research. *Psychological Bulletin*, *130*(3), 355-391. doi:10.1037/0033-2909.130.3.355

Dieleman, G. C., Huizink, A. C., Tulen, J., Utens, E., Creemers, H. E., van der Ende, J., & Verhulst, F. C. (2015). Alterations in HPA-axis and autonomic nervous system functioning in childhood anxiety disorders point to a chronic stress hypothesis. *Psychoneuroendocrinology*, *51*, 135–150. doi:10.1016/j.psyneuen.2014.09.002

Dimsdale, J. E., & Moss, J. (1980). Plasma catecholamines in stress and exercise. *JAMA*, *243*(4), 340–342. doi:10.1001/jama.1980.03300300018017

Dutton, D. G., & Aron, A. P. (1974). Some evidence for heightened sexual attraction under conditions of high anxiety. *Journal of Personality and Social Psychology*, *30*(4), 510–517. doi:10.1037/h0037031

Dvir, Y., Ford, J. D., Hill, M., & Frazier, J. A. (2014). Childhood maltreatment, emotional dysregulation, and psychiatric comorbidities. *Harvard Review of Psychiatry*, 22(3), 149–161. doi:10.1097/HRP.0000000000000014

Eckberg, D. L. (1983). Human sinus arrhythmia as an index of vagal cardiac outflow. *Journal of Applied Physiology*, 54(4), 961–966. doi:10.1152/jappl.1983.54.4.961

Eickholt, C., Jungen, C., Drexel, T., Alken, F., Kuklik, P., Muehlsteff, J., Makimoto, H., Hoffmann, B., Kelm, M., Ziegler, D., Kloecker, N., Willems, S. &...Meyer, C. (2018). Sympathetic and parasympathetic coactivation induces perturbed heart rate dynamics in patients with paroxysmal atrial fibrillation. *Medical Science Monitor: International Medical Journal of Experimental and Clinical Research*, 24, 2164–2172. doi:10.12659/MSM.905209

El-Sheikh, M., Harger, J., & Whitson, S. M. (2001). Exposure to interparental conflict and children's adjustment and physical health: The moderating role of vagal tone. *Child Development*, 72(6), 1617–1636. doi:10.1111/1467-8624.00369

El-Sheikh, M., Keller, P. S., & Erath, S. A. (2007). Marital conflict and risk for child maladjustment over time: Skin conductance level reactivity as a vulnerability factor. *Journal of Abnormal Child Psychology*, 35(5), 715–727. doi:10.1007/s10802-007-9127-2

El-Sheikh, M., Kouros, C. D., Erath, S., Cummings, E. M., Keller, P., Staton, L.,...Collins, W. A. (2009). Marital conflict and children's externalizing behavior: Interactions between parasympathetic and sympathetic nervous system activity. *Monographs of the Society for Research in Child Development*, 74(1), vii–79. doi:10.1111/j.1540-5834.2009.00501.x

El-Sheikh, M., Harger, J., & Whitson, S. M. (2001). Exposure to interparental conflict and children's adjustment and physical health: The moderating role of vagal tone. *Child Development*, 72(6), 1617–1636. doi:10.1111/1467-8624.00369

Elliott, W. J. (2007). Systemic hypertension. *Current Problems in Cardiology*, 32(4), 201–259. doi:10.1016/j.cpcardiol.2007.01.002

Ellis, B. J., & Boyce, T. W. (2008). Biological sensitivity to context. *Current Directions in Psychological Science*, 17(3), 183–187. doi:10.1111/j.1467-8721.2008.00571.x

Ellis, B. J., Essex, M. J., & Boyce, W. T. (2005). Biological sensitivity to context: II. Empirical explorations of an evolutionary developmental theory. *Development and Psychopathology*, 17(2), 303–328. doi:10.1017/S0954579405050157

Ellis, B. J., Oldehinkel, A. J., & Nederhof, E. (2016). The adaptive calibration model of stress responsivity: An empirical test in the Tracking Adolescents and Individual Lives Survey study. *Development and Psychopathology*, 29(3), 1–21. doi:10.1017/S0954579416000985

Engert, V., Vogel, S., Efanov, S. I., Duchesne, A., Corbo, V., Ali, N., & Pruessner, J. C. (2011). Investigation into the cross-correlation of salivary cortisol and alpha-amylase responses to psychological stress. *Psychoneuroendocrinology*, 36(9), 1294–1302. doi:10.1016/j.psyneuen.2011.02.018

Esposito, E. A., Koss, K. J., Donzella, B., & Gunnar, M. R. (2016). Early deprivation and autonomic nervous system functioning in post-institutionalized children. *Developmental Psychobiology*, 58(3), 328–340. doi:10.1002/dev.21373

Everson, S. A., Lynch, J. W., Kaplan, G. A., Lakka, T. A., Sivenius, J., & Salonen, J. T. (2001). Stress-induced blood pressure reactivity and incident stroke in middle-aged men.

Stroke, 32(6), 1263–1270. https://www.ncbi.nlm.nih.gov/pubmed/11387485

Faraco, G., & Iadecola, C. (2013). Hypertension: A harbinger of stroke and dementia. *Hypertension*, 62(5), 810–817. doi:10.1161/HYPERTENSIONAHA.113.01063

Felitti, V. J., Anda, R. F., Nordenberg, D., Williamson, D. F., Spitz, A. M., Edwards, V.,...Marks, J. S. (1998). Relationship of childhood abuse and household dysfunction to many of the leading causes of death in adults. The Adverse Childhood Experiences (ACE) Study. *American Journal of Preventative Medicine*, 14(4), 245–258. doi:10.1016/S0749-3797(98)00017-8

Flaa, A., Eide, I. K., Kjeldsen, S. E., & Rostrup, M. (2008). Sympathoadrenal stress reactivity is a predictor of future blood pressure: An 18-year follow-up study. *Hypertension*, 52(2), 336–341. doi:10.1161/Hypertensionaha.108.111625

Fries, E., Hesse, J., Hellhammer, J., & Hellhammer, D. H. (2005). A new view on hypocortisolism. *Psychoneuroendocrinology*, 30(10), 1010–1016. doi:10.1016/j.psyneuen.2005.04.006

Furness, J. B., Callaghan, B. P., Rivera, L. R., & Cho, H. J. (2014). The enteric nervous system and gastrointestinal innervation: Integrated local and central control. *Advances in Experimental Medicine and Biology*, 817, 39–71. doi:10.1007/978-1-4939-0897-4_3

Geisler, F., Kubiak, T., Siewert, K., & Weber, H. (2013). Cardiac vagal tone is associated with social engagement and self-regulation. *Biological Psychology*, 93(2), 279–286. doi:10.1016/j.biopsycho.2013.02.013

Gellhorn, E., Cortell, R., & Feldman, J. (1940). The autonomic basis of emotion. *Science*, 92, 288–289. doi:10.1126/science.92.2387.288

Gianaros, P. J., Bleil, M. E., Muldoon, M. F., Jennings, R. J., Sutton-Tyrrell, K., McCaffery, J. M., & Manuck, S. B. (2002). Is cardiovascular reactivity associated with atherosclerosis among hypertensives? *Hypertension*, 40(5), 742–747. doi:10.1161/01.HYP.0000035707.57492.EB

Gianaros, P. J., Salomon, K., Zhou, F., Owens, J. F., Edmundowicz, D., Kuller, L. H., & Matthews, K. A. (2005). A greater reduction in high-frequency heart rate variability to a psychological stressor is associated with subclinical coronary and aortic calcification in postmenopausal women. *Psychosomatic Medicine*, 67(4), 553–560. doi:10.1097/01.psy.0000170335.92770.7a

Ginty, A. T., Kraynak, T. E., Fisher, J. P., & Gianaros, P. J. (2017). Cardiovascular and autonomic reactivity to psychological stress: Neurophysiological substrates and links to cardiovascular disease. *Autonomic Neuroscience*, 207, 2–9. doi:10.1016/j.autneu.2017.03.003

Giuliano, R. J., Gatzke-Kopp, L. M., Roos, L. E., & Skowron, E. A. (2017). Resting sympathetic arousal moderates the association between parasympathetic reactivity and working memory performance in adults reporting high levels of life stress. *Psychophysiology*, 54(8), 1195–1208. doi:10.1111/psyp.12872

Giuliano, R. J., Roos, L. E., Farrar, J. D., & Skowron, E. A. (2018). Cumulative risk exposure moderates the association between parasympathetic reactivity and inhibitory control in preschool-age children. *Developmental Psychobiology*, 60(3), 324–332. doi:10.1002/dev.21608

Goldstein, D. S., & Kopin, I. J. (2008). Adrenomedullary, adrenocortical, and sympathoneural responses to stressors: A meta-analysis. *Endocrine Regulations*, 42(4), 111–119. Retrieved from https://www.ncbi.nlm.nih.gov/pubmed/18999898

Gordis, E. B., Feres, N., Olezeski, C. L., Rabkin, A. N., & Trickett, P. K. (2010). Skin conductance reactivity and respiratory sinus arrhythmia Among maltreated and comparison youth: Relations with aggressive behavior. *Journal of Pediatric Psychology*, 35(5), 547–558. doi:10.1093/jpepsy/jsp113

Gray, S. A. O., Theall, K., Lipschutz, R., & Drury, S. (2017). Sex differences in the contribution of respiratory sinus arrhythmia and trauma to children's psychopathology. *Journal of Psychopathology and Behavioral Assessment*, 39(1), 67–78. doi:10.1007/s10862-016-9568-4

Greenwood, J. P., Stoker, J. B., & Mary, D. A. (1999). Single-unit sympathetic discharge: Quantitative assessment in human hypertensive disease. *Circulation*, 100(12), 1305–1310. Retrieved from https://www.ncbi.nlm.nih.gov/pubmed/10491375

Grossman, P., & Taylor, E. W. (2007). Toward understanding respiratory sinus arrhythmia: Relations to cardiac vagal tone, evolution and biobehavioral functions. *Biological Psychology*, 74(2), 263–285. doi:10.1016/j.biopsycho.2005.11.014

Grossman, P., Watkins, L. L., Wilhelm, F. H., Manolakis, D., & Lown, B. (1996). Cardiac vagal control and dynamic responses to psychological stress among patients with coronary artery disease. *The American Journal of Cardiology*, 78(12), 1424–1427. doi:10.1016/S0002-9149(97)89295-8

Hamilton, J. L., & Alloy, L. B. (2016). Atypical reactivity of heart rate variability to stress and depression across development: Systematic review of the literature and directions for future research. *Clinical Psychology Review*, 50, 67–79. doi:10.1016/j.cpr.2016.09.003

Hare, D. L., Toukhsati, S. R., Johansson, P., & Jaarsma, T. (2014). Depression and cardiovascular disease: A clinical review. *European Heart Journal*, 35(21), 1365–1372. doi:10.1093/eurheartj/eht462

Hauger, R. L., Risbrough, V., Oakley, R. H., Olivares-Reyes, J. A., & Dautzenberg, F. M. (2009). Role of CRF receptor signaling in stress vulnerability, anxiety, and depression. *Annals of the New York Academy of Sciences*, 1179, 120–143. doi:10.1111/j.1749-6632.2009.05011.x

Hastings, P. D., Nuselovici, J. N., Utendale, W. T., Coutya, J., McShane, K. E., & Sullivan, C. (2008). Applying the polyvagal theory to children's emotion regulation: Social context, socialization, and adjustment. *Biological Psychology*, 79(3), 299–306. doi:10.1016/j.biopsycho.2008.07.005

Heatherton, T. F. (2011). Neuroscience of self and self-regulation. *Annual Review of Psychology*, 62, 363–390. doi:10.1146/annurev.psych.121208.131616

Heim, C., Newport, J. D., Heit, S., Graham, Y. P., Wilcox, M., Bonsall, R.,...Nemeroff, C. B. (2000). Pituitary-adrenal and autonomic responses to stress in women after sexual and physical abuse in childhood. *JAMA*, 284(5), 592–597. doi:10.1001/jama.284.5.592

Hellhammer, D., Meinlschmidt, G., Pruessner, J. C. (2018). Conceptual endophenotypes: A strategy to advance the impact of psychoneuroendocrinology in precision medicine. *Psychoneuroendocrinology*, 89, 147–160. doi:10.1016/j.psyneuen.2017.12.009.

Heponiemi, T., Elovainio, M., Pulkki, L., Puttonen, S., Raitakari, O., & Keltikangas-Jarvinen, L. (2007). Cardiac autonomic reactivity and recovery in predicting carotid atherosclerosis: The cardiovascular risk in young Finns study. *Health Psychology*, 26(1), 13–21. doi:10.1037/0278-6133.26.1.13

Het, S., Vocks, S., Wolf, J. M., Hammelstein, P., Herpertz, S., & Wolf, O. T. (2015). Blunted neuroendocrine stress reactivity in young women with eating disorders. *Journal of Psychosomatic Research*, 78(3), 260–267. doi:10.1016/j.jpsychores.2014.11.001

Hinnant, B. J., Erath, S. A., & El-Sheikh, M. (2015). Harsh parenting, parasympathetic activity, and development of delinquency and substance use. *Journal of Abnormal Psychology*, 124(1), 137–151. doi:10.1037/abn0000026

Hoehn-Saric, R., McLeod, D. R., & Zimmerli, W. D. (1989). Somatic manifestations in women with generalized anxiety disorder. Psychophysiological responses to psychological stress. *Archives of General Psychiatry*, 46(12), 1113–1119. doi:10.1001/archpsyc.1989.01810120055009

Holterman, L., Murray-Close, D. K., & Breslend, N. L. (2016). Relational victimization and depressive symptoms: The role of autonomic nervous system reactivity in emerging adults. *International Journal of Psychophysiology*, 110, 119–127. doi:10.1016/j.ijpsycho.2016.11.003

Holzman, J. B., & Bridgett, D. J. (2017). Heart rate variability indices as bio-markers of top-down self-regulatory mechanisms: A meta-analytic review. *Neuroscience & Biobehavioral Reviews*, 74, 233–255. doi:10.1016/j.neubiorev.2016.12.032

Houtveen, J. H., Groot, P. F. C., & De Geus, E. J. C. (2005). Effects of variation in posture and respiration on RSA and pre-ejection period. *Psychophysiology*, 42(6), 713–719. doi:10.3109/13651501.2010.500737

Hu, M. X., Lamers, F., Hiles, S. A., Penninx, B., & de Geus, E. (2016). Basal autonomic activity, stress reactivity, and increases in metabolic syndrome components over time. *Psychoneuroendocrinology*, 71, 119–126. doi:10.1016/j.psyneuen.2016.05.018

Huikuri, H. V., Makikallio, T., Airaksinen, K. E., Mitrani, R., Castellanos, A., & Myerburg, R. J. (1999). Measurement of heart rate variability: A clinical tool or a research toy? *Journal of the American College of Cardiology*, 34(7), 1878–1883. doi:10.1016/S0735-1097(99)00468-4

Ingram, R. E., & Luxton, D. D. (2005). Vulnerability-stress models. In B. L. Hankin & J. R. Z. Abela (Eds.), *Development of psychopathology: A vulnerability-stress perspective* (pp. 32–46). Thousand Oaks, CA: Sage.

Ishitobi, Y., Akiyoshi, J., Tanaka, Y., Ando, T., Okamoto, S., Kanehisa, M., Kohno, K., Ninomiya, T., Maruyama, Y., Tsuru, J., Kawano, A., Hanada, H., Isogawa, K. &...Kodama, K. (2010). Elevated salivary α-amylase and cortisol levels in unremitted and remitted depressed patients. *International Journal of Psychiatry in Clinical Practice*, 14, 268–273. doi:10.3109/13651501.2010.500737

Iwata, J., & LeDoux, J. E. (1988). Dissociation of associative and nonassociative concomitants of classical fear conditioning in the freely behaving rat. *Behavioral Neuroscience*, 102(1), 66–76. doi:10.1037/0735-7044.102.1.66

Jackson, J. H. (1958). Evolution and dissolution of the nervous system. In J. Taylor (Ed.), *Selected writings of John Hughlings Jackson* (pp. 45–118). London, UK: Stapes Press.

Juster, R. P., Perna, A., Marin, M. F., Sindi, S., & Lupien, S. J. (2012). Timing is everything: Anticipatory stress dynamics among cortisol and blood pressure reactivity and recovery in healthy adults. *Stress*, 15(6), 569–577. doi:10.3109/10253890.2012.661494

Kamen, P. W., Krum, H., & Tonkin, A. M. (1996). Poincare plot of heart rate variability allows quantitative display of parasympathetic nervous activity in humans. *Clinical Science*, *91*(2), 201–208. doi:10.1042/cs0910201

Kamen, P. W., & Tonkin, A. M. (1995). Application of the Poincare plot to heart-rate-variability—A new measure of functional status in heart-failure. *Australian and New Zealand Journal of Medicine*, *25*(1), 18–26. doi:10.1111/j.1445–5994.1995.tb00573.x

Kibler, J. L., & Ma, M. (2004). Depressive symptoms and cardiovascular reactivity to laboratory behavioral stress. *International Journal of Behavioral Medicine*, *11*(2), 81–87. doi:10.1207/s15327558ijbm1102_3

Kirschbaum, C., Pirke, K. M., & Hellhammer, D. H. (1993). The Trier Social Stress Test—A tool for investigating psychobiological stress responses in a laboratory setting. *Neuropsychobiology*, *28*(1–2), 76–81. doi:10.1159/000119004

Kizildere, S., Gluck, T., Zietz, B., Scholmerich, J., & Straub, R. H. (2003). During a corticotropin-releasing hormone test in healthy subjects, administration of a beta-adrenergic antagonist induced secretion of cortisol and dehydroepiandrosterone sulfate and inhibited secretion of ACTH. *European Journal of Endocrinology*, *148*(1), 45–53. Retrieved from https://www.ncbi.nlm.nih.gov/pubmed/12534357

Koizumi, K., Terui, N., Kollai, M., & Brooks, C. M. (1982). Functional significance of coactivation of vagal and sympathetic cardiac nerves. *Proceedings of the National Academy of Sciences*, *79*(6), 2116–2120. doi:10.1073/pnas.79.6.2116

Kolacz, J., Holochwost, S. J., Gariépy, J., & Mills-Koonce, R. W. (2016). Patterns of joint parasympathetic, sympathetic, and adrenocortical activity and their associations with temperament in early childhood. *Developmental Psychobiology*, *58*(8), 990–1001. doi:10.1002/dev.21429

Kollai, M., & Koizumi, K. (1979). Reciprocal and non-reciprocal action of the vagal and sympathetic nerves innervating the heart. *Journal of the Autonomic Nervous System*, *1*(1), 33–52. doi:10.1016/0165-1838(79)90004-3

Koo-Loeb, J. H., Pedersen, C., & Girdler, S. S. (1998). Blunted cardiovascular and catecholamine stress reactivity in women with bulimia nervosa. *Psychiatry Research*, *80*(1), 13–27. doi:10.1016/S0165-1781(98)00057-2

Kuras, Y. I., McInnis, C. M., Thoma, M. V, Chen, X., Hanlin, L., Gianferante, D., & Rohleder, N. (2017). Increased alpha-amylase response to an acute psychosocial stress challenge in healthy adults with childhood adversity. *Developmental Psychobiology*, *59*(1), 91–98. doi:10.1002/dev.21470

Lambert, E., Dawood, T., Straznicky, N., Sari, C., Schlaich, M., Esler, M., & Lambert, G. (2010). Association between the sympathetic firing pattern and anxiety level in patients with the metabolic syndrome and elevated blood pressure. *Journal of Hypertension*, *28*(3), 543–550. doi:10.1097/HJH.0b013e3283350ea4

Langley, J. N. (1921). *The autonomic nervous system*. Cambridge, UK: Heffler & Sons.

Lazarus, R. S., & Folkman, S. (1984). *Stress, appraisal, and coping*. New York, NY: Springer.

Lewis, G. F., Furman, S. A., McCool, M. F., & Porges, S. W. (2012). Statistical strategies to quantify respiratory sinus arrhythmia: Are commonly used metrics equivalent? *Biological Psychology*, *89*(2), 349–362. doi:10.1016/j.biopsycho.2011.11.009

Light, K. C., Kothandapani, R. V, & Allen, M. T. (1998). Enhanced cardiovascular and catecholamine responses in women with depressive symptoms. *International Journal of Psychophysiology*, *28*(2), 157–166. doi:10.1016/S0167-8760(97)00093-7

Lorber, M. F., Erlanger, A. C., & Slep, A. M. (2013). Biological sensitivity to context in couples: Why partner aggression hurts some more than others. *Journal of Consulting and Clinical Psychology*, *81*(1), 166–176. doi:10.1037/a0030973

Lucas-Thompson, R. G., & Granger, D. A. (2014). Parent–child relationship quality moderates the link between marital conflict and adolescents' physiological responses to social evaluative threat. *Journal of Family Psychology*, *28*(4), 538–548. doi:10.1037/a0037328

Maheu, F. S., Joober, R., & Lupien, S. J. (2005). Declarative memory after stress in humans: differential involvement of the beta-adrenergic and corticosteroid systems. *The Journal of Clinical Endocrinology & Metabolism*, *90*(3), 1697–1704. doi:10.1210/jc.2004–0009

Marcovitch, S., Leigh, J., Calkins, S. D., Leerks, E. M., O'Brien, M., & Blankson, N. A. (2010). Moderate vagal withdrawal in 3.5-year-old children is associated with optimal performance on executive function tasks. *Developmental Psychobiology*, *52*(6), 603–608. doi:10.1002/dev.20462

Mastorakos, G., Pavlatou, M., Diamanti-Kandarakis, E., & Chrousos, G. P. (2005). Exercise and the stress system. *Hormones (Athens)*, *4*(2), 73–89. Retrieved from https://www.ncbi.nlm.nih.gov/pubmed/16613809

Mason, J.W. (1968). The scope of psychoendocrine research. *Psychosomatic Medicine*, *30*(5), 565-575.

McEwen, B. S. (1998). Stress, adaptation, and disease. Allostasis and allostatic load. *Annals of the New York Academy of Sciences*, *840*, 33–44. doi:10.1111/j.1749–6632.1998.tb09546.x

McEwen, B. S. (2002). Sex, stress and the hippocampus: allostasis, allostatic load and the aging process. *Neurobiology of Aging*, *23*(5), 921–939. doi:10.1016/S0197-4580(02)00027-1

McFall, M. E., Murburg, M. M., Ko, G. N., & Veith, R. C. (1990). Autonomic responses to stress in Vietnam combat veterans with posttraumatic-stress-disorder. *Biological Psychiatry*, *27*(10), 1165–1175. doi:10.1016/0006-3223(90)90053-5

McGirr, A., Diaconu, G., Berlim, M. T., Pruessner, J. C., Sablé, R., Cabot, S., & Turecki, G. (2010). Dysregulation of the sympathetic nervous system, hypothalamic–pituitary–adrenal axis and executive function in individuals at risk for suicide. *Journal of Psychiatry & Neuroscience*, *35*(6), 399–408.

McKeever, V. M., & Huff, M. E. (2003). A diathesis-stress model of posttraumatic stress disorder: Ecological, biological, and residual stress pathways. *Review of General Psychology*, *7*(3), 237–250.

McLaughlin, K. A., Alves, S., & Sheridan, M. A. (2014). Vagal regulation and internalizing psychopathology among adolescents exposed to childhood adversity. *Developmental Psychobiology*, *56*(5), 1036–1051. doi:10.1002/dev.21187

McLaughlin, K. A., Sheridan, M. A., Alves, S., & Mendes, W. (2014). Child maltreatment and autonomic nervous system reactivity: Identifying dysregulated stress reactivity patterns by using the biopsychosocial model of challenge and threat. *Psychosomatic Medicine*, *76*(7), 538–546. doi:10.1097/PSY.0000000000000098

McLaughlin, K. A., Sheridan, M. A., Tibu, F., Fox, N. A., Zeanah, C. H., & Nelson, C. A. (2015). Causal effects of the early caregiving environment on development of stress response systems in children. *Proceedings of the National Academy of Sciences*, *112*(18), 5637–5642. doi:10.1073/pnas.1423363112

Meehl, P. E. (1962). Schizotaxia, schizotypy, schizophrenia. *American Psychologist, 17*, 827–838*Schizophrenia (pp. 21–46). Abingdon, UK: Routledge.* doi:10.1037/h0041029

Messerli-Burgy, N., Engesser, C., Lemmenmeier, E., Steptoe, A., & Laederach-Hofmann, K. (2010). Cardiovascular stress reactivity and recovery in bulimia nervosa and binge eating disorder. *International Journal of Psychophysiology, 78*(2), 163–168. doi:10.1016/j.ijpsycho.2010.07.005

Mielock, A. S., Morris, M. C., & Rao, U. (2017). Patterns of cortisol and alpha-amylase reactivity to psychosocial stress in maltreated women. *Journal of Affective Disorders, 209*, 46–52. doi:10.1016/j.jad.2016.11.009

Miller, J. G., Kahle, S., Lopez, M., & Hastings, P. D. (2015). Compassionate love buffers stress-reactive mothers from fight-or-flight parenting. *Developmental Psychology, 51*(1), 36–43. doi:10.1037/a0038236

Mills, P. J., & Dimsdale, J. E. (1992). Sympathetic nervous system responses to psychosocial stressors. In T. J. R. Turner, A. Sherwood, & K. C. Light (Eds.), *Individual differences in cCardiovascular rResponse to sStress.* New York, NY: Plenum Press.

Monroe, S. M., & Hadjiyannakis, H. (2002). The social environment and depression: Focusing on severe life stress. In I. H. Gotlib & C. L. Hammen (Eds.), *Handbook of depression* (pp. 314–340). New York, NY: Guilford Press.

Monroe, S. M., & Simons, A. D. (1991). Diathesis-stress theories in the context of life-stress research: Implications for the depressive disorders. *Psychological Bulletin, 110*, 406–425.

Nagy, T., van Lien, R., Willemsen, G., Proctor, G., Efting, M., Fulop, M.,... Bosch, J. A. (2015). A fluid response: Alpha-amylase reactions to acute laboratory stress are related to sample timing and saliva flow rate. *Biological Psychology, 109*, 111–119. doi:10.1016/j.biopsycho.2015.04.012

Nater, U. M., La Marca, R., Florin, L., Moses, A., Langhans, W., Koller, M. M., & Ehlert, U. (2006). Stress-induced changes in human salivary alpha-amylase activity: Associations with adrenergic activity. *Psychoneuroendocrinology, 31*(1), 49–58. doi:10.1016/j.psyneuen.2005.05.010

Nater, U. M., & Rohleder, N. (2009). Salivary alpha-amylase as a non-invasive biomarker for the sympathetic nervous system: Current state of research. *Psychoneuroendocrinology, 34*(4), 486–496. doi:10.1016/j.psyneuen.2009.01.014

Nemeroff, C. B. (1996). The corticotropin-releasing factor (CRF) hypothesis of depression: New findings and new directions. *Molecular Psychiatry, 1*(4), 336–342. Retrieved from https://www.ncbi.nlm.nih.gov/pubmed/9118360

Nemeroff, C. B. (1998). Psychopharmacology of affective disorders in the 21st century. *Biological Psychiatry, 44*(7), 517–525. doi:10.1016/S0006-3223(98)00068-7

Newlin, D. B., & Levenson, R. W. (1979). Pre-ejection period: Measuring beta-adrenergic influences upon the heart. *Psychophysiology, 16*(6), 546–552. doi:10.1111/j.1469-8986.1979.tb01519.x

Obradovic, J., Bush, N. R., Stamperdahl, J., Adler, N. E., & Boyce, W. T. (2010). Biological sensitivity to context: The interactive effects of stress reactivity and family adversity on socioemotional behavior and school readiness. *Child Development, 81*(1), 270–289. doi:10.1111/j.1467-8624.2009.01394.x

Obrist, P. A., Wood, D. M., & Perez-Reyes, M. (1965). Heart rate during conditioning in humans: Effects of UCS intensity, vagal blockade, and adrenergic block of vasomotor activity. *Journal of Experimental Psychology, 70*(1), 32–42. doi:10.1037/h0022033

Odemuyiwa, O., Malik, M., Farrell, T., Bashir, Y., Poloniecki, J., & Camm, J. (1991). Comparison of the predictive characteristics of heart rate variability index and left ventricular ejection fraction for all-cause mortality, arrhythmic events and sudden death after acute myocardial infarction. *American Journal of Cardiology, 68*(5), 434–439. doi:10.1016/0002-9149(91)90774-F

Odutayo, A., Wong, C. X., Hsiao, A. J., Hopewell, S., Altman, D. G., & Emdin, C. A. (2016). Atrial fibrillation and risks of cardiovascular disease, renal disease, and death: Systematic review and meta-analysis. *British Medical Journal, 354*, i4482. doi:10.1136/bmj.i4482

Oei, N. Y., Tollenaar, M. S., Elzinga, B. M., & Spinhoven, P. (2010). Propranolol reduces emotional distraction in working memory: A partial mediating role of propranolol-induced cortisol increases? *Neurobiology of Learning and Memory, 93*(3), 388–395. doi:10.1016/j.nlm.2009.12.005

Park, G., Van Bavel, J. J., Vasey, M. W., & Thayer, J. F. (2013). Cardiac vagal tone predicts attentional engagement to and disengagement from fearful faces. *Emotion, 13*(4), 645–656. doi:10.1037/a0032971

Penttila, J., Helminen, A., Jartti, T., Kuusela, T., Huikuri, H. V, Tulppo, M. P.,... Scheinin, H. (2001). Time domain, geometrical and frequency domain analysis of cardiac vagal outflow: Effects of various respiratory patterns. *Clinical Physiology, 21*(3), 365–376. doi:10.1046/j.1365-2281.2001.00337.x

Peters, M. L., Godaert, G. L., Ballieux, R. E., van Vliet, M., Willemsen, J. J., Sweep, F. C., & Heijnen, C. J. (1998). Cardiovascular and endocrine responses to experimental stress: Effects of mental effort and controllability. *Psychoneuroendocrinology, 23*(1), 1–17. doi:10.1016/S0306-4530(97)00082-6

Petrakova, L., Doering, B. K., Vits, S., Engler, H., Rief, W., Schedlowski, M., & Grigoleit, J. S. (2015). Psychosocial stress increases salivary alpha-amylase activity independently from plasma noradrenaline levels. *PLoS One, 10*(8), e0134561. doi:10.1371/journal.pone.0134561

Pine, D. S., Wasserman, G., Coplan, J., Staghezza-Jaramillo, B., Davies, M., Fried, J. E.,... Shaffer, D. (1996). Cardiac profile and disruptive behavior in boys at risk for delinquency. *Psychosomatic Medicine, 58*(4), 342–353. doi:10.1097/00006842-199607000-00007

Pitzalis, M. V, Mastropasqua, F., Massari, F., Forleo, C., DiMaggio, M., Passantino, A.,... Rizzon, P. (1996). Short- and long-term reproducibility of time and frequency domain heart rate variability measurements in normal subjects. *Cardiovascular Research, 32*(2), 226–233. doi:10.1016/0008-6363(96)00086-7

Porges, S. W. (1995). Orienting in a defensive world: Mammalian modifications of our evolutionary heritage: A polyvagal theory. *Psychophysiology, 32*(4), 301–318. doi:10.1111/j.1469-8986.1995.tb01213.x

Porges, S. W. (1997). Emotion: An evolutionary by-product of the neural regulation of the autonomic nervous system. *Annals of the New York Academy of Sciences, 807*, 62–77. doi:10.1111/j.1749-6632.1997.tb51913.x

Porges, S. W. (1998). Love: An emergent property of the mammalian autonomic nervous system. *Psychoneuroendocrinology, 23*(8), 837–861. doi:10.1016/S0306-4530(98)00057-2

Porges, S. W. (2001). The polyvagal theory: Phylogenetic substrates of a social nervous system. *International Journal of Psychophysiology*, *42*(2), 123–146. doi:10.1016/S0167-8760(01)00162-3

Porges, S. W. (2003). The polyvagal theory: Phylogenetic contributions to social behavior. *Physiology & Behavior*, *79*(3), 503–513. doi:10.1016/S0031-9384(03)00156-2

Porges, S. W. (2007). The polyvagal perspective. *Biological Psychology*, *74*(2), 116–143. doi:10.1016/j.biopsycho.2006.06.009

Porges, S. W. (2009). The polyvagal theory: New insights into adaptive reactions of the autonomic nervous system. *Cleveland Clinic Journal of Medicine*, *76*(Suppl 2), S86–S90. doi:10.3949/ccjm.76.s2.17

Post, R. M. (1992). Transduction of psychosocial stress into the neurobiology of recurrent affective disorder. *American Journal of Psychiatry*, *149*, 999–1010. doi:10.1176/ajp.149.8.999

Quas, J., Yim, I., Oberlander, T., Nordstokke, D., Essex, M., Armstrong, J.,...Boyce, W. (2014). The symphonic structure of childhood stress reactivity: Patterns of sympathetic, parasympathetic, and adrenocortical responses to psychological challenge. *Development and Psychopathology*, *26*(4), 963–982. doi:10.1017/S0954579414000480

Reyes del Paso, G. A., Langewitz, W., Mulder, L. J. M., Van Roon, A., & Duschek, S. (2013). The utility of low frequency heart rate variability as an index of sympathetic cardiac tone: A review with emphasis on a reanalysis of previous studies. *Psychophysiology*, *50*(5), 477–487. doi:10.1111/psyp.12027

Robertson, T., & Watts, E. (2016). The importance of age, sex and place in understanding socioeconomic inequalities in allostatic load: Evidence from the Scottish Health Survey (2008-2011). *BMC Public Health*, *16*, 126. doi:10.1186/s12889-016-2796-4

Roos, L. E., Beauchamp, K. G., Giuliano, R., Zalewski, M., Kim, H. K., & Fisher, P. A. (2018). Children's biological responsivity to acute stress predicts concurrent cognitive performance. *Stress*, *21*(4), 347–354. doi:10.1080/10253890.2018.1458087

Sabbah, W., Watt, R. G., Sheiham, A., & Tsakos, G. (2008). Effects of allostatic load on the social gradient in ischaemic heart disease and periodontal disease: Evidence from the Third National Health and Nutrition Examination Survey. *Journal of Epidemiology and Community Health*, *62*(5), 415–420. doi:10.1136/jech.2007.064188

Sakaki, M., Yoo, H. J., Nga, L., Lee, T. H., Thayer, J. F., & Mather, M. (2016). Heart rate variability is associated with amygdala functional connectivity with MPFC across younger and older adults. *Neuroimage*, *139*, 44–52. doi:10.1016/j.neuroimage.2016.05.076

Salomon, K., Bylsma, L. M., White, K. E., Panaite, V., & Rottenberg, J. (2013). Is blunted cardiovascular reactivity in depression mood-state dependent? A comparison of major depressive disorder remitted depression and healthy controls. *International Journal of Psychophysiology*, *90*(1), 50–57. doi:10.1016/j.ijpsycho.2013.05.018

Salomon, K., Clift, A., Karlsdottir, M., & Rottenberg, J. (2009). Major depressive disorder is associated with attenuated cardiovascular reactivity and impaired recovery among those free of cardiovascular disease. *Health Psychology*, *28*(2), 157–165. doi:10.1037/a0013001

Sassi, R., Cerutti, S., Lombardi, F., Malik, M., Huikuri, H. V, Peng, C. K., Schmidt, G. & Yamamoto, Y. (2015). Advances in heart rate variability signal analysis: Joint position statement by the e-Cardiology ESC Working Group and the European Heart Rhythm Association co-endorsed by the Asia Pacific Heart Rhythm Society. *Europace*, *17*(9), 1341–1353. doi:10.1093/europace/euv015

Schoorl, J., Rijn, S., Wied, M., Goozen, S. H. M., & Swaab, H. (2016). Variability in emotional/behavioral problems in boys with oppositional defiant disorder or conduct disorder: The role of arousal. *European Child & Adolescent Psychiatry*, *25*(8), 821–830. doi:10.1007/s00787-015-0790-5

Schwerdtfeger, A., & Rosenkaimer, A.-K. (2011). Depressive symptoms and attenuated physiological reactivity to laboratory stressors. *Biological Psychology*, *87*(3), 430–438. doi:10.1016/j.biopsycho.2011.05.009

Seeman, T. E., McEwen, B. S., Rowe, J. W., & Singer, B. H. (2001). Allostatic load as a marker of cumulative biological risk: MacArthur studies of successful aging. *Proceedings of the National Academy of Sciences*, *98*(8), 4770–4775.

Selye, H. (1936). A syndrome produced by diverse nocuous agents. *Nature*, *138*, 32.

Selye, H. (1970). Stress and aging. *Journal of the American Geriatrics Society*, *18*, 669-680. doi:10.1111/j.1532-5415.1970.tb02813.x

Selye, H. (1978). *The stress of life*. New York, NY: McGraw-Hill Education.

Shaffer, F., & Ginsberg, J. P. (2017). An overview of heart rate variability metrics and norms. *Frontiers in Public Health*, *5*, 258. doi:10.3389/fpubh.2017.00258

Sharpley, C. F. (2002). Heart rate reactivity and variability as psychophysiological links between stress, anxiety, depression, and cardiovascular disease: Implications for health psychology Interventions. *Australian Psychologist*, *37*(1), 56–62. doi:10.1080/00050060210001706686

Sherwood, A., Allen, M. T., Fahrenberg, J., Kelsey, R. M., Lovallo, W. R., & Vandoornen, L. J. P. (1990). Methodological guidelines for impedance cardiography. *Psychophysiology*, *27*(1), 1–23. doi:10.1111/j.1469-8986.1990.tb02171.x

Sherwood, A., Hill, L. K., Blumenthal, J. A., Adams, K. F., Paine, N. J., Koch, G. G.,...Hinderliter, A. L. (2017). Blood pressure reactivity to psychological stress is associated with clinical outcomes in patients with heart failure. *American Heart Journal*, *191*, 82–90. doi:10.1016/j.ahj.2017.07.003

Shields, R. W. (1993). Functional anatomy of the autonomic nervous system. *Journal of Clinical Neurophysiology*, *10*(1), 2–13. doi:10.1097/00004691-199301000-00002

Shinba, T. (2014). Altered autonomic activity and reactivity in depression revealed by heart-rate variability measurement during rest and task conditions. *Psychiatry and Clinical Neurosciences*, *68*(3), 225–233. doi:10.1111/pcn.12123

Shonkoff, J. P., Garner, A. S., The Committee on Psychosocial Aspects of Child and Family Health, Committee on Early Childhood, Adoption, and Dependent Care & Section on Developmental and Behavioral Pediatrics. (2012). The lifelong effects of early childhood adversity and toxic stress. *Pediatrics*, *129*(1), E232–E246. doi:10.1542/peds.2011–2663

Sijtsema, J. J., Roon, A. M., Groot, P. F. C., & Riese, H. (2015). Early life adversities and adolescent antisocial behavior: The role of cardiac autonomic nervous system reactivity in the TRAILS study. *Biological Psychology*, *110*, 24–33. doi:10.1016/j.biopsycho.2015.06.012

Simeckova, M., Jansky, L., Lesna, I. I., Vybiral, S., & Sramek, P. (2000). Role of beta adrenoceptors in metabolic and cardiovascular responses of cold exposed humans. *Journal of Thermal Biology*, 25(6), 437–442. doi:10.1016/S0306-4565(00)00007-3

Singh, K., & Shen, B. J. (2013). Abdominal obesity and chronic stress interact to predict blunted cardiovascular reactivity. *International Journal of Psychophysiology*, 90(1), 73–79. doi:10.1016/j.ijpsycho.2013.03.010

Skowron, E. A., Loken, E., Gatzke-Kopp, L. M., Cipriano-Essel, E. A., Woehrle, P. L., Epps, J. J., Gowda, A., & Ammerman, R. T. (2011). Mapping cardiac physiology and parenting processes in maltreating mother–child dyads. *Journal of Family Psychology*, 25(5), 663–674. doi:10.1037/a0024528

Smeijers, L., Szabó, B. M., van Dammen, L., Wonnink, W., Jakobs, B. S., Bosch, J. A., & Kop, W. J. (2015). Emotional, neurohormonal, and hemodynamic responses to mental stress in Tako-Tsubo cardiomyopathy. *The American Journal of Cardiology*, 115(11), 1580–1586. doi:10.1016/j.amjcard.2015.02.064

Smith, R., Thayer, J. F., Khalsa, S. S., & Lane, R. D. (2017). The hierarchical basis of neurovisceral integration. *Neuroscience & Biobehavioral Reviews*, 75, 274–296. doi:10.1016/j.neubiorev.2017.02.003

Snoek, H., Goozen, S., Matthy, W., Buitelaar, J., & Engeland, H. (2004). Stress responsivity in children with externalizing behavior disorders. *Development and Psychopathology*, 16(2), 389–406. doi:10.1017/S0954579404044578

Souza, G. G. L., Mendonça-de-Souza, A. C. F., Barros, E. M., Coutinho, E. F. S., Oliveira, L., Mendlowicz, M. V, … Volchan, E. (2009). Resilience and vagal tone predict cardiac recovery from acute social stress. *Stress*, 10(4), 368–374. doi:10.1080/10253890701419886

Stanford, S. C., Mikhail, G., Salmon, P., Gettins, D., Zielinski, S., & Pepper, J. R. (1997). Psychological stress does not affect plasma catecholamines in subjects with cardiovascular disorder. *Pharmacology Biochemistry and Behavior*, 58(4), 1167–1174. doi:10.1016/S0091-3057(97)00335-3

Sterling, P., & Eyer, J. (1988). Allostasis: A new paradigm to explain arousal pathology. In S. Fisher & J. Reason (Eds.), *Handbook of life stress, cognition and health* (pp. 629–649). New York, NY: John Wiley & Sons.

Suess, P. E., Porges, S. W., & Plude, D. J. (1994). Cardiac vagal tone and sustained attention in school-age children. *Psychophysiology*, 31(1), 17–22. doi:10.1111/j.1469-8986.1994.tb01020.x

Suurland, J., van der Heijden, K. B., Huijbregts, S. C. J., van Goozen, S. H. M., & Swaab, H. (2017). Interaction between prenatal risk and infant parasympathetic and sympathetic stress reactivity predicts early aggression. *Biological Psychology*, 128, 98–104. doi:10.1016/j.biopsycho.2017.07.005

Suurland, J., van der Heijden, K. B., Huijbregts, S. C. J., van Goozen, S. H. M., & Swaab, H. (2018). Infant parasympathetic and sympathetic activity during baseline, stress and recovery: Interactions with prenatal adversity predict physical aggression in toddlerhood. *Journal of Abnormal Child Psychology*, 46(4), 755–768. doi:10.1007/s10802-017-0337-y

Suzuki, T., Nakamura, Y., Moriya, T., Sasano, H. (2003). Effects of steroid hormones on vascular functions. *Microscopy research and technique*, 60. 76–84.

Tan, A. Y., Zhou, S. M., Ogawa, M., Song, J., Chu, M., Li, H. M., … Chen, P. S. (2008). Neural mechanisms of paroxysmal atrial fibrillation and paroxysmal atrial

tachycardia in ambulatory canines. *Circulation*, 118(9), 916–925. doi:10.1161/Circulationaha.108.776203

Taylor, C. B. (2010). Depression, heart rate related variables and cardiovascular disease. *International Journal of Psychophysiology*, 78(1), 80–88. doi:10.1016/j.ijpsycho.2010.04.006

Tell, D., Mathews, H. L., Burr, R. L., & Janusek, L. (2018). During stress, heart rate variability moderates the impact of childhood adversity in women with breast cancer. *Stress*, 21(2), 1–9. doi:10.1080/10253890.2018.1424132

Thayer, J. F., Åhs, F., Fredrikson, M., Sollers, J. J., & Wager, T. D. (2012). A meta-analysis of heart rate variability and neuroimaging studies: Implications for heart rate variability as a marker of stress and health. *Neuroscience & Biobehavioral Reviews*, 36(2), 747–756. doi:10.1016/j.neubiorev.2011.11.009

Thayer, J. F., Hansen, A. L., Saus-Rose, E., & Johnsen, B. (2009). Heart rate variability, prefrontal neural function, and cognitive performance: The neurovisceral integration perspective on self-regulation, adaptation, and health. *Annals of Behavioral Medicine*, 37(2), 141–153. doi:10.1007/s12160-009-9101-z

Thayer, J. F., & Lane, R. D. (2000). A model of neurovisceral integration in emotion regulation and dysregulation. *Journal of Affective Disorders*, 61(3), 201–216. doi:10.1016/S0165-0327(00)00338-4

Thayer, J. F., & Lane, R. D. (2007). The role of vagal function in the risk for cardiovascular disease and mortality. *Biological Psychology*, 74(2), 224–242. doi:10.1016/j.biopsycho.2005.11.013

Thayer, J. F., & Lane, R. D. (2009). Claude Bernard and the heart–brain connection: Further elaboration of a model of neurovisceral integration. *Neuroscience & Biobehavioral Reviews*, 33(2), 81–88. doi:10.1016/j.neubiorev.2008.08.004

Thayer, J. F., Åhs, F., Fredrikson, M., Sollers, J. J., & Wager, T. D. (2012). A meta-analysis of heart rate variability and neuroimaging studies: Implications for heart rate variability as a marker of stress and health. *Neuroscience & Biobehavioral Reviews*, 36(2), 747–756. doi:10.1016/j.neubiorev.2011.11.009

Thayer, J. F., Hansen, A. L., Saus-Rose, E., & Johnsen, B. (2009). Heart rate variability, prefrontal neural function, and cognitive performance: The neurovisceral integration perspective on self-regulation, adaptation, and health. *Annals of Behavioral Medicine*, 37(2), 141–153. doi:10.1007/s12160-009-9101-z

Thoma, M. V., Kirschbaum, C., Wolf, J. M., & Rohleder, N. (2012). Acute stress responses in salivary alpha-amylase predict increases of plasma norepinephrine. *Biological Psychology*, 91(3), 342–348. doi:10.1016/j.biopsycho.2012.07.008

Tulppo, M. P., Kiviniemi, A. M., Hautala, A. J., Kallio, M., Seppanen, T., Makikallio, T. H., & Huikuri, H. V. (2005). Physiological background of the loss of fractal heart rate dynamics. *Circulation*, 112(3), 314–319. doi:10.1161/Circulationaha.104.523712

Tulppo, M. P., Makikallio, T. H., Takala, T. E. S., Seppanen, T., & Huikuri, H. V. (1996). Quantitative beat-to-beat analysis of heart rate dynamics during exercise. *American Journal of Physiology-Heart and Circulatory Physiology*, 271(1), H244–H252. doi:10.1152/ajpheart.1996.271.1.H244

Ulrich-Lai, Y. M., & Herman, J. P. (2009). Neural regulation of endocrine and autonomic stress responses. *Nature Reviews Neuroscience*, 10(6), 397–409. doi:10.1038/nrn2647

van Stegeren, A., Rohleder, N., Everaerd, W., & Wolf, O. T. (2006). Salivary alpha amylase as marker for adrenergic activity during stress: Effect of betablockade. *Psychoneuroendocrinology*, *31*(1), 137–141. doi:10.1016/j. psyneuen.2005.05.012

Vanitallie, T. B. (2002). Stress: A risk factor for serious illness. *Metabolism-Clinical and Experimental*, *51*(6), 40–45. doi:10.1053/meta.2002.33191

Viru, A., Viru, M., Karelson, K., Janson, T., Siim, K., Fischer, K., & Hackney, A. C. (2007). Adrenergic effects on adrenocortical cortisol response to incremental exercise to exhaustion. *European Journal of Applied Physiology*, *100*(2), 241–245. doi:10.1007/s00421-007-0416-9

Voellmin, A., Winzeler, K., Hug, E., Wilhelm, F. H., Schaefer, V., Gaab, J., La Marca, R., Pruessner, J. C. & Bader, K. (2015). Blunted endocrine and cardiovascular reactivity in young healthy women reporting a history of childhood adversity. *Psychoneuroendocrinology*, *51*, 58–67. doi:10.1016/j. psyneuen.2014.09.008

Wagner, C. R., & Abaied, J. L. (2015). Relational victimization and proactive versus reactive relational aggression: The moderating effects of respiratory sinus arrhythmia and skin conductance. *Aggressive Behavior*, *41*(6), 566–579. doi:10.1002/ab.21596

Warner, H. R., & Cox, A. (1962). A mathematical model of heart rate control by sympathetic and vagus efferent information. *Journal of Applied Physiology*, *17*, 349–355. doi:10.1152/jappl.1962.17.2.349

Waters, S. F., Boyce, T. W., Eskenazi, B., & Alkon, A. (2016). The impact of maternal depression and overcrowded housing on associations between autonomic nervous system reactivity and externalizing behavior problems in vulnerable Latino children. *Psychophysiology*, *53*(1), 97–104. doi:10.1111/psyp.12539

Wehrwein, E. A., Orer, H. S., & Barman, S. M. (2016). Overview of the anatomy, physiology, and pharmacology of the autonomic nervous system. *Comprehensive Physiology*, *6*(3), 1239–1278. doi:10.1002/cphy.c150037

Winzeler, K., Voellmin, A., Hug, E., Kirmse, U., Helmig, S., Princip, M., ... Wilhelm, F. H. (2016). Adverse childhood experiences and autonomic regulation in response to acute stress: the role of the sympathetic and parasympathetic nervous systems. *Anxiety, Stress, & Coping*, *30*(2), 145–154. doi:10.1080/10615806.2016.1238076

Yamaguchi, N., & Okada, S. (2009). Cyclooxygenase-1 and -2 in spinally projecting neurons are involved in CRF-induced sympathetic activation. *Auton Neuroscience*, *151*(2), 82–89. doi:10.1016/j.autneu.2009.06.009

Yoo, B. B., & Mazmanian, S. K. (2017). The enteric network: Interactions between the immune and nervous systems of the gut. *Immunity*, *46*(6), 910–926. doi:10.1016/j.immuni.2017.05.011

Zubin, J., & Spring, B. (1977). Vulnerability: A new view of schizophrenia. *Journal of Abnormal Psychology*, *86*(2), 103–126. doi:10.1037/0021-843X.86.2.103

Psychoneuroimmunology of Stress and Mental Health

George M. Slavich

Abstract

Psychoneuroimmunology (PNI) is the study of how psychological, neural, and immunologic processes interact and affect human health and behavior. Although once a relatively small field, some of the most exciting discoveries in psychopathology and mental health research have recently involved ideas and methods from PNI. In reviewing this work, I first summarize the structure and function of the human immune system, focusing primarily on inflammation. Second, I describe neural and physiologic pathways that link the brain and immune system, which give neurocognitive processes the ability to regulate the immune system and immunologic processes the ability to affect neural, cognitive-emotional, and behavioral outcomes. Third, I review studies examining associations between life stress and inflammation, and inflammation and mental health. Finally, I highlight several promising avenues for future research. Overall, despite the notable impact that PNI has already had on our understanding of mental and physical health, many important questions remain unanswered.

Keywords: stress, cytokines, inflammation, anxiety, depression, posttraumatic stress disorder, schizophrenia, suicide, health, disease

The question of how mental health problems originate goes back centuries. In the early days before Christ, the Greeks viewed mental disorders as arising out of imbalances in bodily fluids. Many years later, Plato proposed that imbalances in the mind, body, and sprit could cause emotional distress; and then in the 18th and 19th centuries, the idea emerged that adverse life experiences—especially during childhood—could have negative effects on the human psyche that persist well into adulthood and potentially touch every aspect of a person's social and emotional life (Maddux & Winstead, 2015). Indeed, historical perspectives on the fundamental origins of mental illness have been as varied and as creative as the human imagination itself.

The modern field of psychopathology has made substantial progress in terms of focusing researchers' attention on more biologically plausible mechanisms that may underlie mental illness, but even so, a wide variety of pathways are still considered, including those that involve social, psychological, neural, immunologic, genetic, and genomic processes. Integrating across these different complex systems and levels of analysis to achieve a more sensible and coherent perspective on the underlying pathophysiology of mental illness is no small task. Yet a relatively small group of scientists has been doing just this for decades, having started years before the Research Domain Criteria (RDoC) initiative made interdisciplinary research on psychopathology popular. They call themselves *psychoneuroimmunologists*.

Psychoneuroimmunologists' area of study, called *psychoneuroimmunology* (or *PNI* for short), is a highly integrative field that examines how psychological, neural, and immunologic processes influence each other and shape human health and behavior (Irwin & Slavich, 2017). Using a variety of different in vivo, in situ, and in vitro techniques in both human and animal model systems, PNI has yielded numerous discoveries that have helped to greatly clarify how social, psychological, and behavioral factors influence the activity of the immune system; how the immune system affects cognition, emotion, neural processes, and behavior; and how these bidirectional interactions shape risk for a variety of mental and physical health problems, including anxiety disorders, depression, posttraumatic stress disorder (PTSD), cardiovascular disease, chronic pain, certain cancers, and neurodegeneration. A complete overview of this very large literature is beyond the scope of the present review, but thankfully, many excellent summaries of PNI and the allied field of health psychology have been written over the years (e.g., Ader, Cohen, & Felten, 1995; Cohen & Herbert, 1996; Haroon, Raison, & Miller, 2012; Kiecolt-Glaser, McGuire, Robles, & Glaser, 2002; Maier & Watkins, 1998; Miller, Chen, & Cole, 2009).

One of the most basic and fundamental cornerstones of PNI involves the discovery that components of the immune system involved in inflammation are influenced not just by factors such as viruses and bacteria that are present inside the body, but also by cues, signals, and events occurring in the external social and physical environment (Glaser & Kiecolt-Glaser, 2005). Such effects do not comport with classic models of the immune system, which suggest that inflammation is regulated largely by internal interactions that occur below the shoulders and that do not involve the brain. However, it is now widely recognized that social-environmental processes, including psychological stress, can substantially upregulate inflammatory activity (e.g., Denson, Spanovic, & Miller, 2009; Irwin & Cole, 2011; Segerstrom & Miller, 2004; Steptoe, Hamer, & Chida, 2007), and that inflammation can in turn increase a person's risk for a variety of health problems and related adverse outcomes (Couzin-Frankel, 2010; Fagundes & Way, 2014; Shields, Moons, & Slavich, 2017; Slavich, 2015). As a result, PNI has provided the much-needed empirical basis for several new theories of stress and mental health that are notable in large part because they identify specific mechanisms that have a high likelihood of being directly involved in disease onset, maintenance, and/or progression (e.g., Kinney et al., 2010; O'Donovan, Slavich, Epel, & Neylan, 2013; Raison & Miller, 2013; Slavich & Irwin, 2014).

The purpose of the present review is to provide an overview of recent thinking and research on stress and mental health from the perspective of PNI. First, I briefly summarize the main structure and function of the human immune system, with a primary focus on inflammatory biology. Second, I describe neural and physiologic pathways that link the brain and immune system, which in turn give neurocognitive processes the ability to regulate the immune system and immunologic processes the ability to affect the brain, cognition, emotion, and behavior. Third, I review recent studies examining associations between stress and inflammation, and inflammation and mental health. Finally, I highlight some possible avenues for future research on stress and health from a PNI perspective.

The Immune System

The fundamental goal of the human immune system is to keep the body biologically safe and protected from foreign pathogens. It thus plays a critical role in promoting health and survival, especially during times of physical injury or infection. The system has two interconnected branches that are referred to as *innate immunity* and *adaptive immunity*, and these branches work together to provide humans with short- and long-term protection against pathogens that could enter the body through open body cavities (e.g., the nose or mouth) or through wounds created during fighting or social conflict (Medzhitov, 2007; Takeda, Kaisho, & Akira 2003). The systems are described in greater detail in the following sections.

Innate Immunity

Innate immunity represents the body's highly conserved, rapid, first-line defense against tissue damage and microbial infection. The innate immune system response is mediated by innate immune cells (e.g., monocytes/macrophages and dendritic cells) that circulate throughout the body and use invariant receptors to detect a wide variety of pathogens that have the potential to cause biological harm if left unaddressed. Once these cells identify an injury or infection, they initiate a complex cascade of inflammatory processes that help contain an infection and promote healing and recovery (Medzhitov, 2007).

Activation of the innate immune system frequently begins when receptors located on immune cells recognize highly conserved features of microbes or *pathogen-associated molecular patterns* (PAMPs), such as lipopolysaccharide (LPS), unmethylated cytosine-guanine dinucleotide or CpG sequences in bacterial and viral genomes, and double-stranded RNA viruses. This recognition strategy is termed *pattern recognition*, and innate immune receptors that use this strategy are called *pattern recognition receptors.* One of the most well-characterized families of pattern recognition receptors are *toll-like receptors* (TLRs). TLRs are present on macrophages, neutrophils, and dendritic cells, and they recognize conserved components of a wide variety of microbes, including bacteria, viruses, and fungi (Akira, Takeda, & Kaisho, 2001; Medzhitov, 2001). Examples of this family of TLRs include types that bind to, and become activated by, specific ligands such as LPS (TLR4), double-stranded RNA (TLR3), and single-stranded RNA (TLR7 and TLR8; Barton, 2008).

When any of these TLRs are activated, a conserved signaling cascade is initiated that results in the activation of two principal intracellular transcription factors—namely, nuclear factor-κB (NF-κB) and interferon regulatory factors (Karin, 2006; Kawai & Akira, 2007). These transcription factors in turn drive the expression of pro-inflammatory immune response genes, such as tumor necrosis factor-α (*TNF-α*) and interleukin-1 (*IL-1*), which results in the synthesis and secretion of small, soluble proteins called *cytokines*. As I describe in more detail later, cytokines act mainly on leukocytes and endothelial cells to upregulate and control the body's inflammatory response during times of pathogenic threat, and they are frequently assessed in biobehavioral and clinical studies as indices of individuals' immune-related stress reactivity or disease risk (Karin, 2006; Raison, Capuron, & Miller, 2006). Together, this complex biological reaction is referred to as the *acute-phase response*, and it is characterized by substantial increases in inflammatory activity that can occur both locally (i.e., at the site of a specific injury or infection) or systemically (i.e., throughout the body; Hennessy, Schiml-Webb, & Deak, 2009).

Adaptive Immunity

When innate immune system defenses are insufficient for addressing a biological threat, the second branch of the immune system, *adaptive immunity*, is called into action. In contrast to innate immunity, which is nonspecific and does not confer long-term protection for the host, adaptive immunity involves the proliferation of microbial-specific white blood cells (i.e., *lymphocytes*) that attempt to neutralize or eliminate microbes based on an *immunological memory* of having previously responded to a specific pathogen or antigen (Gruys, Toussaint, Niewold, & Koopmans, 2005; Murphy, 2011). Whereas the innate immune response is rapid, occurring over minutes or hours, the adaptive immune response takes days to develop (Slavich & Irwin, 2014).

In contrast to innate immunity, adaptive immunity is initiated by antigen-presenting cells (APCs), such as macrophages or dendritic cells, which help the immune system differentiate between the host's own cells (i.e., "self") and those of invading bacteria or viruses (i.e., "nonself" or "foreign"). These APCs are attracted to sites in the body where they ingest, or *endocytose*, invading antigen. Once the foreign antigen has been ingested and processed, APCs then migrate from the infection site to local lymph nodes, where they present antigen peptides to T helper (Th) cells, resulting in the release of different cytokines, including interleukin-2 (IL-2), interleukin-4 (IL-4), interleukin-5 (IL-5), and interferon gamma (IFN-γ), which help promote and control the adaptive immune response (Murphy, 2011).

As described later, the cytokines produced during this process can have wide-ranging effects on mood, cognition, and behavior. In addition, on an immunologic level, these inflammatory mediators induce Th cells to become activated, to proliferate, and to then differentiate into one of two cell types. One type of resulting Th B cells become antibody-producing cells (i.e., plasma cells), and another type leaves the lymph node to coordinate cytotoxic cell responses that eliminate foreign pathogens and help return the body to biological safety. What primarily differentiates this response from the innate immune system response is its capacity to remember past threats. It does this by keeping a part of antigen-specific Th cells, cytotoxic T cells, and B cells around after the adaptive immune response has effectively ended, thereby forming an *immunological memory* of the pathogen that enables the adaptive immune system to respond more quickly and more effectively when the same foreign invader returns in the future (Murphy, 2011).

Inflammatory Cytokines

We have already discussed the fact that cytokines are a key mediator of the inflammatory response and briefly reviewed how they coordinate innate and adaptive immune system reactions to pathogens. Given their central role in stress physiology and in shaping mental health, however, cytokines deserve a bit more attention and description. This is especially true because, as alluded to earlier, cytokines are the primary biological endpoint of immune system activity that presently gets assessed in biobehavioral studies of stress and mental health.

Cytokines are released from several different types of immune cells, including monocytes/macrophages, dendritic cells, and neutrophils, and their primary function is to coordinate cell-to-cell communication during times of physical injury or infection. However, they can also alter neurochemical and neuroendocrine processes that have wide-ranging effects on human physiology and behavior (Curfs, Meis, & Hoogkamp-Korstanje, 1997). Cytokines may thus be thought to function in a manner similar to neurotransmitters and hormones insofar as they mediate physiologic responses, rely on receptor-ligand interactions, and have self (autocrine), local (paracrine), and distal (endocrine) effects (Jain & Mills, 2007). Broadly speaking, cytokines can be categorized as those that are primarily involved in innate immunity (e.g., tumor necrosis factor-α [TNF-α], interleukin-1 [IL-1], interleukin-6 [IL-6], interleukin-8 [IL-8], and interleukin-10 [IL-10]) versus adaptive immunity (e.g., IFN-γ, IL-2, IL-4, and IL-5), and those that increase (i.e., *upregulate*) inflammatory activity, which are called *pro-inflammatory cytokines*, versus those that decrease (i.e., *downregulate*) inflammatory activity, which are called *anti-inflammatory* cytokines.

Literally hundreds of cytokines have been identified to date (Dinarello, 2007), some of which have been studied extensively by immunologists and others of which remain relatively unexplored. In the context of psychology and psychiatry, however, the situation is very different. Indeed, as of today, only a small number of cytokines have been consistently examined across studies of stress and mental health. Those cytokines are, primarily, IL-1, IL-6, and TNF-α.

Collectively, these cytokines coordinate a variety of cell functions that stimulate and enhance a complex set of immunologic processes that help to locate, identify, and kill pathogens. One of their main purposes is to orchestrate the deployment of the body's biological "soldiers" (i.e., immune cells) to sites of injury or infection during times of stress. In this model, the stress hormones epinephrine and norepinephrine call immune cells out of the spleen, bone marrow, and lymph nodes (i.e., the "barracks") and into the bloodstream (i.e., the "boulevards"); then, cytokines help promote vascular permeability and cellular adhesion, which allows immune cells to leave the bloodstream and migrate to affected tissue (i.e., "battlefields"), where they can neutralize or eliminate foreign pathogens (Dhabhar, Malarkey, Neri, & McEwen, 2012). Each cytokine plays a slightly different role in this process. For example, IL-1 activates the expression of the endothelial adhesion molecule intercellular adhesion molecule-1 (ICAM-1), which promotes firm adhesion to endothelial cells for eventual extravasation (i.e., migra-

tion of cells from circulation to tissue; Smith, Marlin, Rothlein, Toman, & Anderson, 1989). TNF-α, in turn, stimulates the production of the adhesion molecule E-selectin on the endothelium, which binds to adhesion molecules on neutrophils (Hubbard & Rothlein, 2000). Small polypeptides called *chemokines*, which are activated by TNF-α, IL-6, and IL-1, play an important role in this process, as they continually survey the body to screen for pathogens in a process called *immunosurveillance*. Once a pathogen or infection has been identified, chemokines can act as *chemoattractants* that recruit other immune cells to the site of inflammatory activity (Murphy, 2011). Finally, these cytokines help promote the differentiation of lymphocytes called *cytotoxic T cells*, which ultimately assist in killing pathogens, especially viruses.

In addition to helping coordinate the mobilization and distribution of immune cells throughout the body, cytokines play a critical role in promoting and regulating the most commonly recognized signs of inflammation. These biobehavioral effects are briefly described in Table 23.1. At specific sites of infection, for example, cytokines promote redness, heat, swelling, and pain that combine to accelerate wound healing, limit the spread of infection, and heighten the host's awareness of the injury (Murphy, 2011). At a more systemic level, cytokines induce the production of the acute-phase protein *C-reactive protein* (CRP), which is a robust biomarker of inflammation that is frequently measured in both biomedical research and in clinical settings (e.g., as an indicator of cardiovascular disease risk). CRP, in turn, acts with cytokines to promote increased body temperature, fever, heart rate, and respiratory rate, which combine to help kill off pathogens and conserve vital energy during times of injury (Poon, Ho, Chiu, & Chang, 2013; Ricciotti & FitzGerald, 2011).

Finally, on a neurocognitive and behavioral level, cytokines communicate with the central nervous system to induce a constellation of behaviors known as *sickness behaviors* (Hart, 1988). These behaviors include increased pain and threat sensitivity, anhedonia, fatigue, psychomotor retardation, and social-behavioral withdrawal. These behaviors have several functions and are intended, for example, to draw attention to potential injuries (i.e., pain sensitivity), heighten an individual's awareness of potential threats in the surrounding social and physical environment (i.e., threat sensitivity), help an individual recuperate and recover from possible injury (i.e., anhedonia, fatigue), and reduce the likelihood that an infected individual will spread an infection to

Table 23.1 Inflammatory Cytokines and Their Key Characteristics

Cytokine	Family	Producer Cells	Function
Pro-inflammatory cytokines			
Interleukin-1β (IL-1β)	Unassigned	Macrophages	Key mediator of sickness behavior; promotes fever and pain hypersensitivity; involved in HPA axis activation, lymphocyte activation, macrophage and neutrophil activation, endothelial activation, prostanoid synthesis, and IL-6 synthesis
Interleukin-2 (IL-2)	Hematopoietins	T cells	Facilitates immunoglobulin production by B cells, and differentiation and proliferation of NK cells
Interleukin-6 (IL-6)[a]	Hematopoietins	Macrophages, T cells	Key mediator of acute phase response; promotes fever, and T and B cell differentiation and activation; can downregulate inflammation by inhibiting TNF-α and IL-1 production
Interleukin-8 (IL-8)	Chemokines	Macrophages	Key mediator of inflammation; recruits neutrophils to the site of inflammation and induces chemotaxis in target cells
Tumor Necrosis Factor-α (TNF-α)	TNF family	Macrophages, NK cells	Key mediator of sickness behavior; promotes fever and suppresses appetite; stimulates HPA axis, endothelial activation, and neutrophil activation; induces apoptotic cell death
Anti-inflammatory cytokines			
Interleukin-4 (IL-4)	Hematopoietins	T cells	Inhibits production of the pro-inflammatory cytokines TNF-α and IL-1; stimulates B and T cell proliferation
Interleukin-10 (IL-10)	Unassigned	Macrophages, T cells	Inhibits production of the pro-inflammatory cytokines IL-1, IL-6, and TNF-α; Enhances B cell proliferation and antibody production

Note: [a] Although IL-6 is listed as a pro-inflammatory cytokine, as described, it can also have anti-inflammatory effects. NK cells = natural killer cells; HPA axis = hypothalamic-pituitary-adrenal axis. Reprinted with permission from Slavich, G. M., & Irwin, M. R. (2014). From stress to inflammation and major depressive disorder: A social signal transduction theory of depression. *Psychological Bulletin, 140*, 774–815. Washington, DC: American Psychological Association.

nearby conspecifics (i.e., psychomotor retardation, social-behavioral withdrawal). When combined, these effects help increase an individual's ultimate likelihood of survival during times of physical injury or threat. At the same time, it should be noted that these neurocognitive and behavioral outcomes are very similar—if not identical in some instances—to several symptoms of anxiety and depression, which is what provided some of the first indications that inflammation may play a role in anxiety disorders and depression (Slavich & Irwin, 2014).

Inflammation: A Double-Edged Sword

From this brief description of the immune system, it should be clear that mounting a rapid and effective inflammatory response to physical injury or the first signs of a pathogen is critical for resolving infection, repairing tissue damage, and promoting survival (Kushner, 1982; Medzhitov, 2008). Unfortunately, though, what can save us in the short run can also kill us in the long run. This is because persistent elevations in inflammatory activity can cause *oxidative stress*, driven in part by cytokine-related increases in the production of free radical species derived from oxygen (i.e., ROI), which can directly oxidize DNA and also interfere with mechanisms of DNA repair. For example, whereas the pro-inflammatory cytokine TNF-α enhances the formation of ROI by neutrophils and other cells in the body, TNF-α, IFN-γ, and interleukin-1β (IL-1β) stimulate the expression of inducible nitric oxide synthase in inflammatory and epithelial cells (Federico et al., 2007). These interactions in turn lead to DNA mutations, genomic instability, and ultimately increased risk for numerous health problems that have an inflammatory component. As a result, although inflammation was once thought of as being involved in only a few disorders, such as cardiovascular disease and certain cancers, it is now recognized that chronic inflammation is present in several psychiatric disorders, such as PTSD and depression, and that it plays a role in the development, exacerbation, or progression of numerous physical disease conditions, including asthma, rheumatoid arthritis, diabetes, obesity, atherosclerosis, ovarian and breast cancer, and Alzheimer's disease (Couzin-Frankel, 2010; Slavich, 2015; see also Bower, Crosswell, & Slavich, 2014; Schrepf et al., 2013).

Understanding when inflammation is beneficial for health and when it is harmful largely comes down to the question of how the inflammatory response is regulated (Slavich, 2015). In this context, a beneficial inflammatory response is one that occurs quickly and in response to an actual physical or biological threat, and that then dissipates once the threat has passed. One factor that can substantially alter immune system responding and prolong inflammation is psychological stress (Segerstrom & Miller, 2004; Steptoe et al., 2007). In the next section, therefore, we review the primary neurobiological and physiologic pathways that give experiences of stress the ability to affect inflammatory activity.

Central Regulation of Inflammatory Activity

As alluded to already, the human inflammatory response is a highly complex, tightly regulated process that is influenced by numerous physiologic events occurring throughout the periphery of the body. However, systemic inflammatory activity is also regulated by processes occurring in the brain, including by neurocognitive representations of the surrounding social and physical environment (Irwin & Cole, 2011). This neuro-inflammatory link is critical for survival because it enables the immune system to mobilize and redistribute immune cells not just *after* a physical injury or infection has occurred, but *in advance* of a physical assault that could increase an individual's risk for a pathogen-related infection (Dhabhar et al., 2009; Rosenberger et al., 2009). An anticipatory immunologic response such as this is helpful for wound healing and recovery, but most important, it can be critical for survival in instances where a quick biological response is needed to limit the spread of infection, which likely explains why it was highly conserved.

Several excellent reviews have described the specific mechanisms linking neural and immunologic processes (e.g., Dantzer et al., 2008; Irwin & Cole, 2011; Maier & Watkins, 1998; Pavlov & Tracey, 2004; Radtke, Macdonald, & Tacchini-Cottier, 2013; Rivest, 2009; Sternberg, 2006). For the present discussion, however, it is perhaps most important to understand that immunologic responses to social-environmental adversity represent the body's attempt to deploy its resources to best handle the specific biological threats that are most likely to be present in different environments. Because psychological stressors, such as those involving social conflict or rejection, historically increased a person's risk for physical wounding, the types of psychological stressors that individuals experience in the present-day environment are most likely to upregulate expression of pro-inflammatory immune response genes, which combat bacteria and other extracellular pathogens that an individual could be exposed to during physical injury. This response is accompanied by a reciprocal downregulation of antiviral immune response genes, which target intracellular pathogens such as viruses that are spread in social situations. We have referred to this increased pro-inflammatory/reduced antiviral skewing of the human basal gene expression profile (i.e., the *basal transcriptome*) as the *conserved transcriptional response to adversity* (CTRA; Slavich & Cole, 2013; Slavich & Irwin, 2014), and it is depicted in Figure 23.1.

A fundamental principal of the CTRA involves the ability for the immune system to activate ancestral host defense programs in response to present-day social-environmental adversity. The immune system cannot directly detect social threats in the surrounding environment, though, so it relies on the brain, which can alert the peripheral immune system to the presence of a threat via multiple non–mutually exclusive pathways. Two of the main pathways are the sympathetic nervous system (SNS) and hypothalamic-pituitary-adrenal (HPA) axis (Irwin & Cole, 2011; Slavich & Irwin, 2014). Additionally, a third pathway was recently discovered that involves a direct physical connection between the brain and peripheral immune system via meningeal lymphatic vessels, which were previously not known to exist. We briefly discuss each of these neural-immune pathways next.

Sympathetic Nervous System

The SNS can influence the production of pro-inflammatory cytokines by releasing the neurotransmitter norepinephrine into peripheral tissues, primary

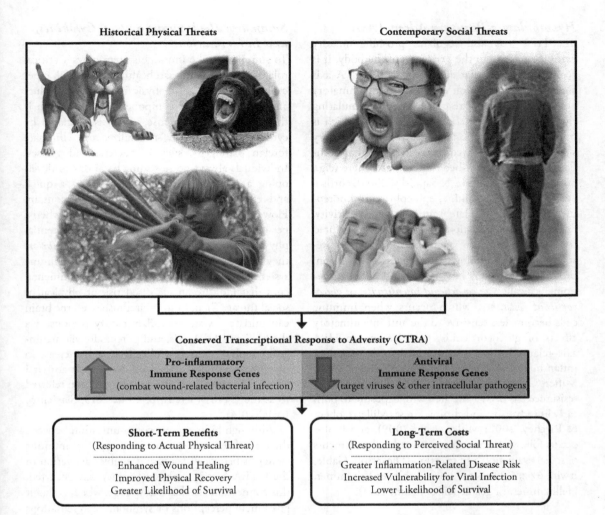

Historical Physical Threats

Contemporary Social Threats

Conserved Transcriptional Response to Adversity (CTRA)

| **Pro-inflammatory** **Immune Response Genes** (combat wound-related bacterial infection) | **Antiviral** **Immune Response Genes** (target viruses & other intracellular pathogens) |

Short-Term Benefits
(Responding to Actual Physical Threat)
....
Enhanced Wound Healing
Improved Physical Recovery
Greater Likelihood of Survival

Long-Term Costs
(Responding to Perceived Social Threat)
....
Greater Inflammation-Related Disease Risk
Increased Vulnerability for Viral Infection
Lower Likelihood of Survival

Figure 23.1 Conserved transcriptional response to adversity (CTRA) (see Slavich & Cole, 2013; Slavich & Irwin, 2014). The innate immune system developed to counter physical threats from predatory animals and hostile conspecifics that dominated our ancestral environment. Exposure to these threats activates a conserved transcriptional response to adversity (CTRA) that involves upregulation of pro-inflammatory immune response genes, which combat extracellular pathogens and wound-related bacterial infections, and downregulation of antiviral immune response genes, which target intracellular pathogens such as viruses. This redeployment of the leukocyte basal transcriptome is adaptive in the context of actual physical threat because it enhances wound healing and recovery from injury and infection. However, the CTRA can also be activated by modern-day social, symbolic, anticipated, and imagined threats, leading to increased risk for several mental and physical health conditions that involve inflammation. Reprinted with permission from Slavich, G. M., & Irwin, M. R. (2014).

From stress to inflammation and major depressive disorder: A social signal transduction theory of depression. *Psychological Bulletin, 140*, 774–815. Washington, DC: American Psychological Association.

and secondary lymphoid organs, and all other major organ systems, including the vasculature and perivascular tissues. Once released, norepinephrine modulates immune response gene transcription via stimulation of β-adrenergic receptors and, possibly, α-adrenergic signaling (Grisanti et al., 2011; Huang et al., 2012; Nance & Sanders, 2007). This adrenergic signaling cascade suppresses transcription of antiviral type I interferon genes (Cole, Korin, Fahey, & Zack,

1998; Lee et al., 2000), and it upregulates transcription of the pro-inflammatory immune response genes *IL1, TNF*, and *IL6*, leading to increased systemic inflammatory activity and decreased antiviral activity (Cole et al., 2010; Grebe et al., 2010). Ultimately, therefore, the SNS plays a central role in coordinating the CTRA, which involves "steering" innate immune system responses between pro-inflammatory and antiviral phenotypes (Slavich & Cole, 2013).

Hypothalamic-Pituitary-Adrenal Axis

The HPA axis also regulates pro-inflammatory cytokine activity in the periphery of the body. It is typically thought that activation of the HPA axis suppresses transcription of both pro-inflammatory and antiviral immune response genes by stimulating the release of the glucocorticoid cortisol, which is one of the body's most potent anti-inflammatory substances. However, cortisol can also enhance inflammation. As described in detail elsewhere (e.g., Sorrells, Caso, Munhoz, & Sapolsky, 2009), cortisol enables the catecholamines epinephrine and norepinephrine to upregulate immune system activity, facilitates the mobilization of immune cells to injured tissues, and can also augment inflammatory responses to immunologic challenges. In addition, prolonged elevations in cortisol can lead to a phenomenon called *glucocorticoid insensitivity*, or *glucocorticoid resistance*, which occurs when immune cells become less sensitive to the anti-inflammatory effects of glucocorticoids, thus leading to HPA axis–related increases (as opposed to decreases) in inflammation (Avitsur, Stark, & Sheridan, 2001; Miller, Cohen, & Ritchey, 2002). Glucocorticoid resistance has been associated with exposure to both early life adversity and chronic stress (Miller, Cohen, & Ritchey, 2002; Miller et al., 2009), and it also occurs following acute stressors that involve elements of social evaluation and rejection (Dickerson, Gable, Irwin, Aziz, & Kemeny, 2009; Rohleder, Schommer, Hellhammer, Engel, & Kirschbaum, 2001).

Meningeal Lymphatic Vessels

Finally, although the brain and immune system have historically been thought of as physically separate systems, which has required researchers to consider *indirect* pathways by which the brain may communicate with the peripheral immune system and vice versa, two landmark studies recently revealed that the brain is directly connected to the periphery via meningeal lymphatic vessels that were previously not known to exist (Aspelund et al., 2015; Louveau et al., 2015). Although these lymphatic vessels are primarily responsible for draining excess fluid from the central nervous system in order to help maintain fluid homeostasis, these vessels also serve as a physical path along which immune cells can travel from the brain to the peripheral immune system and back again. As a result, neural and immunologic signals originating in the central nervous system have the ability to *directly influence* inflammatory activity in the periphery, and vice versa, via immune cell trafficking (Slavich & Auerbach, 2018).

Summary: The Immune System, Cytokines, and Inflammation

To summarize, the immune system plays a critical role in promoting human health and survival, especially during times of physical injury, wounding, and infection. A key component of this system is the inflammatory response, which is mediated by cytokines that identify, neutralize, and eliminate foreign pathogens, such as bacteria and viruses. Individuals always possess some basal risk of developing a bacterial infection that requires a quick and effective inflammatory response to contain. However, this risk is substantially increased when a person is exposed to situations involving potential physical danger. To detect such situations *before* they occur, I have hypothesized that the immune system relies on the brain to identify environmental cues that indicate an increased risk of physical or social threat. Then, in such circumstances, the brain can initiate a systemic inflammatory response via the SNS and HPA axis, and potentially via meningeal lymphatic vessels. Collectively, this increase in pro-inflammatory activity and decrease in antiviral activity in response to social threat has been referred to as the CTRA (Slavich & Cole, 2013; Slavich & Irwin, 2014).

Although bidirectional communication between the central nervous system and peripheral immune system is beneficial because it enables activation of the CTRA before a physical injury has occurred, this connection also has a downside, which is that it gives mere perceptions or symbolic representations of social-environmental threat the ability to activate the CTRA in the absence of actual physical threat. Therefore, threats that are purely imagined—including those that have not yet happened or that may never actually occur—can lead to substantial increases in inflammatory activity when such a response is not necessary to support survival. This reactivity pattern may not be problematic if it occurs infrequently or if increases in inflammation are quickly resolved. As discussed earlier, however, sustained increases in inflammatory activity can occur via several mechanisms, including neuroinflammatory sensitization and glucocorticoid resistance, and prolonged elevations in inflammation in turn increase a person's risk for several mental and physical health problems (Slavich & Irwin, 2014). Psychological stress is a key factor that can induce and sustain inflammatory activity, so we examine links between stress and inflammation next, with a focus on the specific types of stressors that are most strongly associated with inflammatory activity.

Stress and Inflammation

Research on associations between stress and inflammation has been conduced both in the laboratory and in the context of naturalistic cross-sectional and longitudinal studies. Whereas studies conducted in the laboratory have the advantage of being able to standardize and control the stress exposure that participants experience (e.g., using an experimental stress-induction task), the external validity of such studies is limited. On the other hand, studies involving the assessment of naturally occurring stressors in a person's life have the benefit of high external validity, but obtaining a comprehensive assessment of individuals' life stress exposure is both complicated and costly, as has been discussed elsewhere (see Monroe, 2008; Monroe, Slavich, & Georgiades, 2014; Slavich, 2016; Slavich & Auerbach, 2018). An overview of both naturalistic and laboratory-based studies of stress and inflammation is provided next, with a focus on the specific types of stressors that are most strongly associated with elevated inflammatory activity.

Early Adversity and Inflammation

Numerous studies have examined associations between early life adversity (i.e., stressful experiences generally occurring before age 18) and inflammatory activity. These studies have characterized early life stress in several different ways, but they converge to yield remarkably similar findings linking early life stress with heightened inflammatory activity (Fagundes & Way, 2014). In one recent prospective population-based study, for example, investigators followed more than 4,600 children for nearly 10 years and assessed their acute life event exposure at seven time points between 1.5 and 8 years of age. Levels of inflammatory activity were, in turn, assessed at age 10 and at age 15. Consistent with the formulation that stressors involving social and physical threat are strongly associated with heightened inflammatory activity, the investigators found that greater exposure to physical or sexual abuse, being separated from a mother or father, and being taken into foster care prior to age 8 prospectively predicted higher basal levels of IL-6 and CRP at age 10, as well as higher levels of CRP at age 15 (Slopen, Kubzansky, McLaughlin, & Koenen, 2013). In a second study that assessed both prenatal stressors (i.e., family structure, parental education, parental occupation, and family income) and early life stressors (e.g., parental occupation, changes in parental marital status, changes in family environment, death of a sibling, unemployment, housing problems,

financial difficulties, etc.), prenatal stressors were strongly associated with higher CRP levels in adulthood (Mage = 42.2 years old), and these effects were independent of childhood adversity and potential confounding factors, including maternal health problems reported during pregnancy (Slopen et al., 2015). Converging results have been provided by other studies showing that growing up in a risky early environment, characterized in part by chronic unpredictability, harsh discipline, a lack of parental love and/or close supervision, and verbal, physical, and/or sexual abuse, is associated with elevated levels of CRP in young adulthood (Danese, Pariante, Caspi, Taylor, & Poulton, 2007; Taylor, Lehman, Kiefe, & Seeman, 2006), and by studies showing that a socially tumultuous early environment predicts elevated levels of IL-6 in young adulthood (Cho, Bower, Kiefe, Seeman, & Irwin, 2012; Slopen et al., 2010) and higher levels of IL-6 and TNF-α in older adulthood (Kiecolt-Glaser, Gouin et al., 2011; cf. Carpenter, Gawuga, Tyrka, & Price, 2012).

Several studies have also examined associations between socioeconomic status in childhood and levels of inflammatory activity in adulthood. Consistent with the studies described earlier, this literature has provided evidence that lower socioeconomic status in childhood is associated with greater inflammatory activity in adulthood. In a recent multisite, community-based, prospective study of more than 1,000 women, for example, women raised in low socioeconomic status families had higher levels of CRP than their high-status counterparts. These effects were robust to several potential demographic and clinical confounds (e.g., ethnicity, study site, age, health problems, smoking status, medication use, etc.), and they appeared to be mediated by individuals' body mass index (BMI) and education level in adulthood (Matthews et al., 2016). Similar findings have been reported for circulating levels of IL-6 and CRP in mixed samples of adult men and women (e.g., Appleton et al., 2012; Carroll, Cohen, & Marsland, 2011; Taylor et al., 2006), and also in studies of ethnically diverse adolescents (Miller & Chen, 2007). Interestingly, in this latter study, inflammatory activity was measured at the molecular level by assessing levels of mRNA for glucocorticoid receptor and toll-like receptor 4. Results revealed that adolescents who grew up in low socioeconomic status households exhibited increased expression of genes that code for TLR4, which is involved in activating the innate immune system response, and decreased expression of genes that code for the glucocorticoid receptor, which is typically responsible for downregulating inflammation in response to cortisol (Miller & Chen, 2007). These findings are noteworthy because they suggest that early life stress may reach deep inside the body to affect inflammatory activity at the level of gene expression.

Finally, there is substantial evidence that childhood bullying, abuse, and trauma strongly predict levels of inflammatory activity in adulthood. In a large prospective longitudinal cohort study that followed all individuals born in Britain during 1 week in 1958 (N = 7,102), exposure to childhood bullying occurring between 7 and 11 years old was found to predict heightened levels of CRP in midlife, even when controlling for several potential confounding factors, including psychopathology in childhood, childhood BMI, and parental social class during childhood, as well as social class, smoking behavior, diet, and exercise in adulthood (Takizawa, Danese, Maughan, & Arseneault, 2015). In contrast, with respect to childhood abuse and trauma, a recent meta-analytic review of 25 studies revealed that these early life adversities are associated with heightened levels of CRP, IL-6, and TNF-α, and that the effects are not influenced by several potential confounding factors, including individuals' age, BMI, or gender (Baumeister, Akhtar, Ciufolini, Pariante, & Mondelli, 2016). In subgroup analyses that tested for differential effects as a function of type of early life stress experienced, the authors found that physical and sexual abuse occurring during childhood were associated with elevations in TNF-α and IL-6, but not CRP. Conversely, parental absence during childhood was primarily associated with significant elevations in CRP, whereas emotional abuse occurring during childhood was not related to any of the inflammatory markers examined (Baumeister et al., 2016). Considered together, these studies provide substantial evidence that early life stress exposure is associated with elevations in several inflammatory markers, and some evidence that these stress-inflammation effects may differ as a function of the specific type of early adversity experienced.

Adulthood Life Stress and Inflammation

Paralleling results from the studies of childhood adversity described earlier, there is also a relatively large and consistent body of work linking naturally occurring social stressors in adolescence and adulthood with elevated levels of inflammatory activity. Interestingly, these results also seem to be particularly strong for social stressors that involve elements of social devaluation, conflict, threat, isolation, or rejection (for reviews, see Herbert & Cohen, 1993;

Kiecolt-Glaser, Gouin, & Hantsoo, 2010; Segerstrom & Miller, 2004; Slavich & Irwin, 2014). In a recent analysis of more than 1,100 adults in the United States, for example, low socioeconomic status (i.e., indexed as poorer education, income, and occupational prestige) predicted higher levels of CRP, and this effect was partially attenuated for men possessing more psychological resources (e.g., optimism, perceived mastery and control, purpose in life) but not for women possessing such resources (Elliot & Chapman, 2016). At least two other studies have shown similar associations between lower socioeconomic status and elevated levels of CRP in adulthood (Gimeno et al., 2007; Janicki-Deverts, Cohen, Kalrab, & Matthews, 2012), and there is also evidence that IL-6 is elevated in individuals with lower socioeconomic status (Gruenewald, Cohen, Matthews, Tracy, & Seeman, 2009; see also Petersen et al., 2008; Pollitt et al., 2007).

Consistent with the CTRA model presented earlier, there is also evidence that negative interpersonal interactions involving friends, peers, and family members influence systemic inflammatory activity. In one study that assessed daily experiences of negative interpersonal interactions in the domains of family, peers, and school, for example, more daily experiences of social conflict, harassment, and punishment were associated with higher levels of CRP (Fuligni et al., 2009). In a second longitudinal study that assessed levels of acute and chronic stress exposure, as well as inflammatory levels, every 6 months for 2 years, experiencing a recent acute stressful life event was associated with within-person increases in the inflammatory cytokines IL-4, IL-5, and IFN-γ for individuals who were also exposed to high levels of chronic family stress, but not for those exposed to low levels of chronic family stress (Marin, Chen, Munch, & Miller, 2009), thus highlighting potential interactive effects between acute and chronic stress exposure in structuring inflammatory levels (see also Chiang, Eisenberger, Seeman, & Taylor, 2012).

In addition to socioeconomic status and interpersonal relationships, numerous studies have examined how inflammatory levels differ among people reporting various levels of social isolation and connection. Consistent with an abundance of research showing that social isolation substantially increases risk for all-cause mortality (Holt-Lunstad, Robles, & Sbarra, 2017), a community based case-cohort study and a nationally representative cohort study both revealed that individuals who are socially isolated are approximately 2.0–2.5 times more likely to have clinically high levels of CRP as compared to those who are socially well integrated (Ford, Loucks, & Berkman, 2006; Heffner, Waring, Roberts, Eaton, & Gramling, 2011). Again, consistent with the CTRA model presented earlier, high levels of social isolation have also been found to be associated with a systematic upregulation of pro-inflammatory immune response genes and a reciprocal downregulation of genes involved in antibody production (Cole, Hawkley, Arevalo, & Cacioppo, 2011), thus providing evidence that social isolation has relatively broad effects on immunologic processes that are relevant for health (for a review, see Slavich & Cole, 2013).

Collectively, these studies provide evidence that different forms of chronic social stress are associated with elevated inflammatory activity at both the gene expression and protein level. In addition, we have conducted several studies examining how experiencing just one recent, socially stressful major life event is sufficient for upregulating inflammation. To model these effects, we have identified specific major life events that involve a combination of interpersonal loss and social rejection, which we have called *targeted rejection*. These stressors, which we have defined as "social rejection that is directed at, and meant to affect, a single person, and that involves an active and intentional severing of relational ties with that person," occur most frequently in the context of intimate relationships (e.g., getting broken-up with) or work (e.g., getting fired), and they have been found to precipitate the development of depression three times faster than other major life events of the same objectively rated severity (Slavich, Thornton, Torres, Monroe, & Gotlib, 2009). In one study that examined the effects of these acute life events on inflammatory biology, we followed participants at elevated risk for depression for 2.5 years and assessed their recent acute life event exposure and current inflammatory levels every 6 months. Consistent with the CTRA model, individuals exhibited significantly higher levels of inflammatory gene expression at study visits when they had experienced a recent targeted rejection major life event as compared to study visits when no such life event had recently occurred (Murphy, Slavich, Rohleder, & Miller, 2013).

In a second independent longitudinal study in which we assessed participants at elevated risk for asthma every 6 months for 2 years, we found the exact same pattern of effects, but this time for *anti*-inflammatory gene expression. Namely, individuals exhibited significantly lower levels of

anti-inflammatory gene expression during study visits when they had experienced a recent targeted rejection life event as compared to study visits when no such stressor had occurred (Murphy, Slavich, Chen, & Miller, 2015). Importantly, these effects were not found for other types of similarly severe stressors, including other interpersonal and noninterpersonal stressors, and they were especially strong for individuals who self-reported having higher levels of subjective social status, suggesting that perceptions of social standing may moderate the effects of targeted rejection on inflammatory gene expression (Murphy et al., 2015). More broadly, these studies provide evidence that experiencing even one major life event is sufficient for increasing pro-inflammatory gene expression and reducing anti-inflammatory gene expression, so long as the life event involves the seemingly critical "ingredient" of targeted rejection.

Laboratory-Based Social Stressors and Inflammation

Finally, numerous studies have attempted to manipulate experiences of stress in the laboratory to model how social stressors affect inflammatory activity (Marsland, Walsh, Lockwood, & John-Henderson, 2017). These studies have the arguable limitation that they utilize laboratory-based stressors that have differing degrees of external validity, but they possess the notable advantage of being able to standardize the stress exposure and, in addition, assess inflammatory activity in a relatively controlled environment. The main take-away message from this body of work is that even relatively brief laboratory stressors (e.g., lasting 5–15 minutes) can induce increases in inflammatory activity, and this is especially true when the stressors (a) involve elements of social evaluation, conflict, rejection, or exclusion, or (b) trigger emotions that are frequently associated with these experiences, such as shame and humiliation (Slavich & Auerbach, 2018; Slavich & Irwin, 2014; Slavich, O'Donovan, et al., 2010).

In one prototypic laboratory-based study, married couples were asked to take part in a social support interaction during a first study visit and a hostile marital interaction during a subsequent visit. Whereas couples who were independently judged to be low in hostility were relatively unaffected by these tasks, those who were high in hostility exhibited significantly greater increases in plasma IL-6 and TNF-α following the hostile marital interaction than following the social support interaction (Kiecolt-Glaser et al., 2005). In another study, participants were randomly assigned to write about either a traumatic experience in which they blamed themselves or a neutral experience. Writing about the stressful experience involving self-blame led to significant increases in a soluble receptor for TNF-α (i.e., sTNF-RII); in addition, participants who experienced the greatest increases in self-reported shame during this stressor exhibited the greatest stress-induced increases in pro-inflammatory cytokine activity (Dickerson, Kemeny, Aziz, Kim, & Fahey, 2004).

One of the most commonly used tasks for inducing an experience of stress in the laboratory is the Trier Social Stress Test (TSST; Kirschbaum, Pirke, & Hellhammer, 1993; for a review, see Shields & Slavich, 2017). In this social stress-inducing paradigm, participants are first asked to prepare and then give an impromptu speech in front of a panel of nonresponsive, socially rejecting "expert" raters wearing white lab coats. Sometimes they are also audiotaped or videotaped and told that the tapes will be carefully reviewed by another expert who specializes in behavioral coding and analysis. Afterward, participants are asked to perform difficult mental arithmetic out loud in front of the expert raters (e.g., start at 1,022 and count backward by 7s, and then by 13s).

In one prototypic study that used the TSST, participants who completed the TSST in the presence of socially rejecting raters exhibited greater in vitro LPS-stimulated production of TNF-α and greater glucocorticoid resistance than those who performed the TSST in the absence of these raters, thus indicating the importance of social evaluation for inducing an heightened inflammatory response (Dickerson, Gable, et al., 2009). Perhaps most interesting is the fact that although participants judged these two experimental conditions to be equally challenging, controllable, and difficult, those who perceived more social evaluation in both conditions of the TSST exhibited greater increases in TNF-α. Moreover, these effects were robust even while adjusting for participants' perceived levels of TSST-related challenge, controllability, and difficulty.

INDIVIDUAL DIFFERENCES IN INFLAMMATORY REACTIVITY TO LABORATORY-BASED STRESSORS

Although a complete summary of psychological processes and clinical factors that predict differences in inflammatory responding to the TSST and similar laboratory-based stressors is beyond the scope of this discussion (for reviews, see Campbell & Ehlert, 2012; Slavich & Irwin, 2014), a few example studies

are useful for describing the wide variety of factors that have been found to predict stress-induced inflammatory reactivity in the laboratory. For example, in one report of two separate studies, participants reporting higher levels of trait loneliness exhibited greater LPS-stimulated production of TNF-α, IL-1β, and IL-6 in response to the TSST as compared to their less lonely counterparts (Jaremka et al., 2013; see also Hackett, Hamer, Endrighi, Brydon, & Steptoe, 2012). In a second study, individuals reporting greater experiences of fear to the TSST exhibited more pronounced TSST-related increases in sTNF-RII (Moons, Eisenberger, & Taylor, 2010). In a third study, a public speaking task similar to the TSST induced significant feelings of anxiety, depression, and anger, and greater increases in anxiety and anger were, in turn, independently related to greater increases in circulating levels of IL-6 (Carroll, Low, et al., 2011). Finally, a fourth study found that individuals who had more difficulty maintaining a positive cognitive-affective state during the TSST had the greatest TSST-induced IL-1β reactivity, which in turn predicted their levels of depression over the following year (Aschbacher et al., 2012).

Different forms of life stress exposure and perceived stress burden have also been associated with inflammatory reactivity to stress in the laboratory. In one study, for example, greater levels of TSST-induced perceived stress predicted greater increases TSST-induced IL-1β (Yamakawa et al., 2009; see also Prather et al., 2009). In a second study, more moderate-to-severe early life stress was unrelated to baseline levels of IL-6, but strongly related to participants' IL-6 reactivity to the TSST (Carpenter et al., 2010). Finally, in a third study that sampled adolescent girls at elevated risk for psychopathology, greater exposure to peer victimization predicted greater TSST-induced increases in the pro-inflammatory cytokines IL-6 and IL-1β; moreover, these effects were strongest for girls reporting high levels of hopelessness (Giletta et al., 2018).

Finally, given substantial interest in the role of inflammation in depression, several studies have examined how depression levels moderate the effects of acute social stressors on inflammatory reactivity in the laboratory (for a review, see Slavich & Irwin, 2014). In one early study, depressed and nondepressed women completed a variant of the TSST, in which increased levels of anxiety and shame and led to greater LPS-stimulated production of the pro-inflammatory cytokines TNF-α and IL-6 for both depressed and nondepressed women. As compared to nondepressed women, however, depressed women exhibited elevations in CRP that persisted following the TSST (Miller, Rohleder, Stetler, & Kirschbaum, 2005). In a second study that examined associations between stress-induced inflammatory activity and depression in adult males with both depression and early life stress exposure, depressed individuals with early life stress exhibited greater TSST-induced increases in IL-6 and NF-κB, as well as higher levels of IL-6 during the post-TSST recovery period, as compared to nondepressed males; moreover, greater depression severity was an independent predictor of participants' TSST-induced increases in both IL-6 and NF-κB (Pace et al., 2006). Finally, in a more recent study of adult men and women with depression, a variant of the TSST induced relatively greater increases in TNF-α, IL-6, and CRP in depressed versus nondepressed men and women (Weinstein et al., 2010).

Neural Processes Associated With Inflammatory Reactivity to Laboratory-Based Social Stress

One of the more important frontiers in this area of research involves the examination of how neural processes regulate peripheral inflammatory activity and vice versa. Research along these lines is critical for advancing our basic mechanistic understanding of pathways that underlie inflammatory reactivity, but also for shedding light on neurocognitive processes that could potentially be modified to reduce persistent neuroimmune responses to stress and, therefore, disease risk. As a result, my lab has spent considerable time pioneering the integration of ideas and methods from psychology, neuroscience, immunology, genetics, and genomics to elucidate how psychological and neural processes regulate the immune system, and how the immune system in turn affects human behavior and disease risk.

In the first study to ever examine neurocognitive processes underlying inflammatory responding to social stress, for example, we had healthy young adults complete the TSST while we assessed their levels of IL-6 and sTNF-RII. Then, we exposed a subset of these participants to a brief experience of social rejection (i.e., using Cyberball) while we assessed their neural activity using functional magnetic resonance imaging (fMRI). Three findings were noteworthy. First, consistent with the studies described earlier, the TSST triggered significant increases in IL-6 and sTNF-RII, even though participants were relatively young and healthy. Second, the brief experience of social rejection engaged specific brain regions that prior research has shown are implicated in processing the affective component of physical pain—namely, the bilateral anterior insula and dorsal anterior cingulate cortex (dACC). Finally, greater neural activity in these particular brain regions during social rejection (vs. inclusion) was related to greater inflammatory reactivity to the TSST, thus identifying for the first time specific neurocognitive processes that are associated with inflammatory responding to acute social stress (Slavich, Way, Eisenberger, & Taylor, 2010).

We have since explored these dynamics using other types of laboratory-based social stressors. In one study, for example, we interviewed healthy young participants about their upbringing, likes and dislikes, hopes and aspirations, and personal beliefs. Then, in a subsequent study visit, participants were led to believe that another participant (actually a confederate) was watching their video and judging how they were coming across using a grid of characteristics that included words such as "interesting," "friendly," "caring," "insecure," "lazy," and "arrogant." Consistent with the neuroimaging study described above, this relatively brief, 10-minute experience of social evaluation led to significant increases in IL-6; moreover, these effects were strongest for individuals who exhibited the greatest neural activity in the left amygdala in response to negative versus neutral feedback words (Muscatell et al., 2015). In a subsequent analysis of these same participants, we found that individuals who were lower in subjective social status exhibited greater IL-6 responses to the social evaluation task, and that these effects were mediated by neural activity in the dorsomedial prefrontal cortex, which plays a role in *mentalizing*, or thinking about the thoughts and feelings of others (Muscatell et al., 2016; see also Dedovic, Slavich, Muscatell, Irwin, & Eisenberger, 2016).

Likewise, some studies have examined how experimentally induced changes in immune system function affect neural responses to social stress. In one early study, for example, healthy adults were randomized to receive either an inflammatory challenge (i.e., bacterial endotoxin) or placebo (i.e., saline) via intravenous injection. Then, participants had their brains scanned while they were socially excluded (i.e., using Cyberball). Consistent with the basic dynamics of the innate immune system described earlier, administration of bacterial endotoxin triggered significant increases in circulating levels of IL-6, in addition to physical sickness symptoms and depressive mood, and increases in IL-6 were in turn associated with greater neural activity in the anterior insula and dACC. Further confirming the likely relevance of these brain regions for inflammatory responding, activity in these specific brain areas mediated the association between endotoxin-induced increases in IL-6 and depressive mood in female (but not male) participants (Eisenberger, Inagaki, Rameson, Mashal, & Irwin, 2009).

Collectively, these neuroimmune studies provide evidence of a bidirectional link between neural and inflammatory processes that has important implications for understanding the biological bases of mental and physical health problems. Namely, whereas the former studies demonstrated that neural activity in brain regions that process experiences of physical pain is associated with inflammatory responding to acute social stress, the latter study revealed that greater endotoxin-induced increases in inflammatory activity are associated with greater activity in physical pain-related neural circuitry. I have hypothesized that this bidirectional link between neural and inflammatory processes may be critical for survival during times of physical danger to the extent that it heightens threat sensitivity and increases the production of immune factors that help accelerate wound healing and recovery. As illustrated in Figure 23.2, however, if this neural-immune response becomes self-promoting—for example, because of persistent neural responding to actual or perceived threat, or because of an illness or infection that prolongs the inflammatory response—then this neuro-immune dynamic could become engaged in a self-promoting, recursive loop that leads to hypervigilance, threat sensitivity, and anxiety symptoms in the short term, and increases a person's risk for potentially serious mental and physical health problems over the long run (Slavich & Cole, 2013; Slavich & Irwin, 2014).

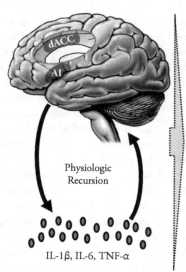

Neuro-Inflammatory Sensitization

dACC

AI

Physiologic Recursion

IL-1β, IL-6, TNF-α

Cognitive-Emotional & Health Effects

Short-term

Hypervigilance
Anticipation of adversity
Sensitivity to pain
Social anxiety

Medium-term

Disrupted sleep
Chronic pain
Depressed mood
Social withdrawal

Long-term

Susceptibility to infection
Inflammatory diseases
Accelerated aging
Early mortality

Figure 23.2 Neuro-inflammatory sensitization to adversity (see Slavich & Cole, 2013; Slavich & Irwin, 2014). Bidirectional links between the brain and periphery allow the brain to regulate inflammatory activity, and inflammatory activity to in turn influence neural processes in the brain. This dynamic is initiated by experiences of early life stress or chronic adversity, which promote a pro-inflammatory skewing of the leukocyte basal transcriptome (i.e., the CTRA) that feeds back on pain-related neural systems to perpetuate subjective perceptions of threat. Brain regions involved in this process include the anterior insula (AI) and dorsal anterior cingulate cortex (dACC, shown in the insert). As a result of this physiologic recursion, experiences of social-environmental adversity can become "biologically embedded" and sustain perceptions of threat for months or years after the original social-environmental impetus has passed. The consequences of these dynamics are multifold and start with increased hypervigilance, chronic anticipation of adversity, sensitivity to pain, and symptoms of social anxiety. As activation of the CTRA persists, somatic and affective symptoms of depression may develop. Finally, after years of sustained engagement, these dynamics may confer increased risk for inflammation-related disorders, infection, accelerated biological aging, and early mortality. Abbreviations: IL-1β = interleukin-1β, IL-6 = interleukin-6, and TNF-α = tumor necrosis factor-α. Reprinted with permission from Slavich, G. M., & Irwin, M. R. (2014). From stress to inflammation and major depressive disorder: A social signal transduction theory of depression. *Psychological Bulletin, 140,* 774–815. Washington, DC: American Psychological Association.

Inflammation and Mental Health

So far, we have reviewed the basic purpose and function of the immune system, as well as some of the key neural and physiologic processes that influence immune system activity. We have also discussed how components of the immune system involved in inflammation are influenced by psychological stress. Now, we turn to the important question of how inflammatory processes are altered in the context of several major psychiatric disorders and related mental health conditions—specifically, major depression, PTSD, schizophrenia, and self-harm and suicide. Finally, we examine a few recent studies that have performed comparative analyses across these disorders. The main take-home message from this body of work is that although there is substantial evidence that mental illness is associated with aberrations in immune system function, there is notable variability in these effects. In addition, we presently know very little about how mental illness–related aberrations in immune system function initially come about and how immunologic processes that are associated with these disorders give rise to specific symptoms.

Major Depression

The most systematic evidence linking aberrant immune system function with psychiatric status is in the context of major depression (Slavich & Auerbach, 2018; Slavich & Irwin, 2014). Early on, Sigmund Freud wrote that "The complex of melancholia behaves like an open wound" (1917/1957, p. 253), but it was not until the 1960s that sickness behaviors were conceptualized as a strategy for conserving energy (Miller, 1964) and not until the 1980s that this biobehavioral response was recognized as a highly conserved, adaptive reaction to physical injury and infection (Hart, 1988). Then in the early 1990s, Ronald Smith (1991) proposed a "Macrophage Theory of Depression," which hypothesized that cytokines might affect neural function to cause depression.

Today, five major lines of research converge to suggest that inflammation plays a prominent role in at least some forms of depression (for a review, see Slavich & Irwin, 2014). First, doctors have long noticed that depression frequently co-occurs with several physical diseases that have an inflammatory basis (Barton, 2008; Calder, 2006). These conditions include rheumatoid arthritis, inflammatory bowel disease, metabolic syndrome, coronary heart disease, and chronic pain. For example, individuals with rheumatoid arthritis and inflammatory bowel disease are two-to-three times more likely to have

major depression than the general population (Graff, Walker, & Bernstein, 2009; Katz & Yelin, 1993; Regier et al., 1988), and the prevalence of depression in individuals experiencing chronic pain is as high as 86% (Poole, White, Blake, Murphy, & Bramwell, 2009; see also Bair et al., 2004). Second, depression is consistently associated with elevations in several markers of inflammatory activity, including IL-1, IL-6, TNF-α, and CRP (Dowlati et al., 2010; Hiles, Baker, de Malmanche, & Attia, 2012; Howren, Lamkin, & Suls, 2009), and elevations in these biomarkers appear to precede the development of depression in many cases (Gimeno et al., 2009; van den Biggelaar et al., 2007).

These lines of research provide data that are largely correlational, but a third line of work has shown that immunologic challenges that upregulate inflammatory activity, such as IFN-α administration, typhoid vaccination, and endotoxin administration, frequently trigger depressive-like behaviors in animal model systems of depression and diagnosable forms of major depressive disorder (MDD) in humans. For example, up to 50% of patients receiving IFN-α for the treatment of hepatitis C and cancer have been observed to subsequently develop MDD (Capuron & Miller, 2004; Raison et al., 2006). Likewise, typhoid vaccination has been found to induce increases in negative mood, confusion, and fatigue, which are mediated by increases in IL-6 (Harrison et al., 2009; Strike, Wardle, & Steptoe, 2004; Wright, Strike, Brydon, & Steptoe, 2005), and bacterial endotoxin has been found to elicit heightened anxiety, as well as sad mood, anhedonia, cognitive impairment, fatigue, reduced food intake, altered sleep, and social-behavioral withdrawal (for a review, see DellaGioia & Hannestad, 2010). Fourth, each of these three inflammatory challenges has been shown to alter metabolic or neural activity in brain regions that have been implicated in depression, including the basal ganglia, cerebellum, ACC, and ventral striatum. In one study, for example, long-term administration of IFN-α was associated with reduced neural responses to a hedonic reward task in the bilateral ventral striatum, which is involved in reward-related responding, and this reduced activity was in turn correlated with greater symptoms of anhedonia, depression, and fatigue (Capuron et al., 2012). Similar neural changes have been reported following bacterial endotoxin administration as well (Eisenberger, Berkman, et al., 2010).

Finally, at least three anti-inflammatory agents have been found to alleviate depressive symptoms in double-blind, randomized, placebo-controlled studies. These agents include celecoxib, which is a cyclooxygenase (COX)-2 inhibitor commonly used for treating excessive inflammation and pain, and the TNF-α antagonists etanercept and infliximab, which are used to treat rheumatoid arthritis, psoriasis, and other inflammatory conditions. In one recent double-blind, placebo-controlled study, for example, 60 outpatients with treatment-resistant depression were randomly assigned to receive either three infusions of the TNF-α antagonist infliximab or placebo at baseline, week 2, and week 6 of a 12-week clinical trial (Raison et al., 2013). Although no overall differences in depression severity were found between the two groups over the trial, 62% of infliximab-treated patients with starting CRP levels above 5 mg/L exhibited a treatment response (i.e., ≥ 50% reduction in depressive symptoms during the trial) as compared to only 33% of placebo-treated patients. Interestingly, clinical improvements were seen across a variety of symptoms, including anxiety and depressive symptoms, psychomotor retardation, suicidal ideation, and behavioral motivation and performance. Consistent with the possibility that these improvements were mediated by changes in inflammatory activity, infliximab-treated responders showed significantly greater decreases in levels of CRP from baseline to week 12 as compared to placebo-treated responders (Raison et al., 2013).

SOCIAL SIGNAL TRANSDUCTION THEORY OF DEPRESSION

Collectively, this research has provided the empirical basis for the first fully integrated, multilevel theory of depression, called *social signal transduction theory of depression*, which describes the full set of social, psychological, and biological mechanisms linking experiences of social stress with risk for depression (see Figure 23.3; Slavich & Irwin, 2014). According to this theory, social stressors that historically increased an organism's risk for physical threat, such as those involving social conflict, isolation, rejection, and exclusion, are represented by neural systems that process the affective and interoceptive aspects of physical and social pain, including the anterior insula and dACC. These regions in turn project to lower level brain regions, including the hypothalamus and brainstem autonomic control nuclei, which modulate the activity of the HPA axis and SNS—and therefore the production of cortisol, epinephrine, norepinephrine, and acetylcholine—which in turn influence systemic inflammatory activity. Whereas cortisol and acetylcholine typically

suppress (but can also increase) inflammatory activity, epinephrine and norepinephrine both promote inflammation by inducing the activation of the intracellular transcription factors NF-κB and AP-1, which upregulate the expression of pro-inflammatory immune response genes, including *IL1B*, *IL6*, *IL8*, and *TNF*. Expression of these genes ultimately leads to the production of pro-inflammatory cytokines that induce depressive symptoms such as sad mood, anhedonia, fatigue, psychomotor retardation, and social-behavioral withdrawal, in addition to other cognitive, affective, and somatic phenomena that often co-occur with depression—namely, increased hypervigilance, anxiety, and pain sensitivity. The central nervous system can also influence peripheral inflammation via efferent vagus nerve activity, which downregulates inflammation by strongly suppressing *TNF* gene transcription.

Ultimately, this highly conserved, biological response to adversity is critical for survival during times of actual physical threat insofar as it prepares the body to deal with physical wounding and infection, should they occur. In the present-day social environment, however, these social signal transduction pathways are most frequently activated not by impending *physical danger*, but by contemporary *social threats*, including those that are purely symbolic, anticipated, or imagined. It is under these social-environmental conditions, therefore, that this biological response can lead to an increasingly pro-inflammatory phenotype that is hypothesized to be a key phenomenon driving depression pathogenesis and recurrence, as well as the overlap of depression with several somatic conditions including asthma, rheumatoid arthritis, chronic pain, metabolic syndrome, cardiovascular disease, obesity, and neurodegeneration (for a complete overview, see Slavich & Irwin, 2014).

Posttraumatic Stress Disorder

The second largest literature on inflammation and mental health involves PTSD. There are several reasons for this, including the fact that (a) life stress exposure, which is known to increase inflammation, is the main psychosocial precipitant of the disorder; (b) cytokines are known to induce hypervigilance, which is a cardinal symptom of PTSD; and (c) many individuals with PTSD develop somatic health problems that have an inflammatory basis, including chronic pain, heart disease, diabetes, and neurodegeneration (O'Donovan & Neylan, 2017). Overall, studies examining associations between inflammation and PTSD have yielded mixed findings. At the

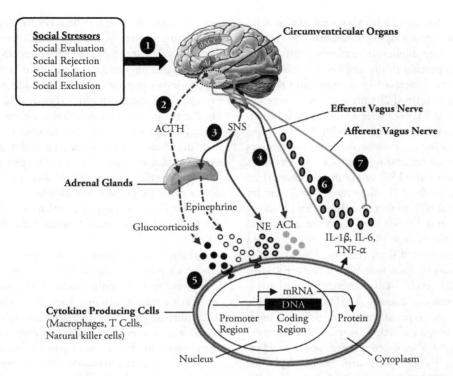

Figure 23.3 Social signal transduction theory of depression (see Slavich & Irwin, 2014). Social signal transduction theory of depression describes mechanisms that convert, or *transduce*, experiences of the external social environment into the internal biological environment of depression pathogenesis. (**1**) Social-environmental experiences indicating possible social threat or adversity (e.g., social conflict, evaluation, rejection, isolation, or exclusion) are represented neurally, especially in brain systems that process experiences of social and physical pain. Key nodes in this neural network include the anterior insula (AI) and dorsal anterior cingulate cortex (dACC, shown in the insert). These regions project to lower level brain areas (e.g., hypothalamus, brainstem autonomic control nuclei) that have the ability to initiate and modulate inflammatory activity via three pathways that involve (**2**) the hypothalamic-pituitary-adrenal axis, (**3**) sympathetic nervous system, and (**4**) efferent vagus nerve. (**5**) Activation of these pathways leads to the production of glucocorticoids, epinephrine, norepinephrine, and acetylcholine, which interact with receptors on cytokine producing cells. Whereas glucocorticoids and acetylcholine have anti-inflammatory effects, epinephrine and norepinephrine activate intracellular transcription factors (e.g., nuclear factor-κB and activator protein 1) that bind to *cis*-regulatory DNA sequences to upregulate inflammatory gene expression. When this occurs and immune response genes are expressed, DNA is transcribed into RNA and then translated into protein. The resulting change in cell function leads to the production of pro-inflammatory cytokines (e.g., interleukin-1β, interleukin-6, tumor necrosis factor-α) that signal the brain to induce cognitive, emotional, and behavioral alterations that include several hallmark symptoms of depression (e.g., sad mood, anhedonia, fatigue, psychomotor retardation, altered appetite and sleep, and social-behavioral withdrawal). Cytokines can exert these effects on the central nervous system by (**6**) passing through "leaky" or incomplete regions of the blood-brain barrier (e.g., circumventricular organs, organum vasculosum of the lamina terminalis) and by (**7**) stimulating primary afferent nerve fibers in the vagus nerve, which relays information to brain systems that regulate mood, motor activity, motivation, sensitivity to social threat, and arousal. Bidirectional communication between the brain and peripheral immune system may also occur via meningeal lymphatic vessels, along which cytokines have been shown to travel (not shown). Although these neurocognitive and behavioral responses are adaptive during times of actual threat, these social signal transduction pathways can also be initiated by purely symbolic, anticipated, or imagined threats—that is, situations that have not yet happened or that may never actually occur. Moreover, activation of these pathways can become self-promoting over time due to neuro-inflammatory sensitization and, as a result, remain engaged long after an actual threat has passed. In such instances, these dynamics can increase risk for depression in the short term, and possibly promote physical disease, accelerate biological aging, and hasten mortality over the long run. Abbreviations: ACTH = adrenocorticotropic hormone, SNS = sympathetic nervous system, NE = norepinephrine, ACh = acetylcholine, mRNA = messenger ribonucleic acid, IL-1β = interleukin-1β, IL-6 = interleukin-6, and TNF-α = tumor necrosis factor-α. Reprinted with permission from Slavich, G. M., & Irwin, M. R. (2014).

From stress to inflammation and major depressive disorder: A social signal transduction theory of depression. *Psychological Bulletin, 140*, 774–815. Washington, DC: American Psychological Association.

same time, recent meta-analyses have found that, on average, concentrations of inflammatory markers are substantially higher in patients with PTSD compared to psychiatrically healthy controls.

In one recent meta-analytic review and metaregression that examined 20 different studies, levels of IL-1β, IL-6, and IFN-γ were found to each be significantly elevated in patients with PTSD versus psychiatrically healthy individuals. Follow-up analyses revealed several interesting findings. For example, longer duration of PTSD symptoms was associated with higher levels of IL-1β; greater PTSD severity was associated with higher IL-6 levels; and levels of IL-1β, IL-6, and TNF-α were significantly elevated in PTSD patients even when those with comorbid MDD were excluded from analyses. Finally, in the metaregression analysis, four factors that are known to influence levels of inflammatory activity—namely, presence of comorbid MDD, psychotropic medication use, type of immunologic assay used, and time of blood collection—explained substantial proportions of the heterogeneity across studies. Impressively, these four factors alone explained 100% of the heterogeneity for studies assessing IL-1β, 100% for studies assessing CRP, and 79.9% for studies assessing IL-6. In sum, therefore, inflammatory activity appears to be elevated in PTSD in a manner that is at least somewhat independent of depression, and the heterogeneity that has been observed in these effects across studies of PTSD (and possibly other disorders) may be attributable to a relatively few clinical and technical factors (Passos et al., 2015).

Schizophrenia

Schizophrenia is a particularly complicated disorder from a pathophysiology standpoint. One of the most widely reported findings, though, is that risk for the disorder is associated with pre- and perinatal exposure to several adverse events that substantially upregulate inflammatory activity, including exposure to infections (Brown, 2006; Mednick, Huttunen, & Machon, 1994) and to prenatal life stressors, such as the loss of a father during pregnancy (Huttunen & Niskanen, 1978; see also Malaspina et al., 2008). Several other findings also argue for a potentially important role of cytokines in risk for schizophrenia. For example, life stressors that are known to trigger increased pro-inflammatory cytokine activity frequently precipitate symptom exacerbation in schizophrenia (Kinney et al., 2010), and prenatal maternal stress is associated with levels of cytokine activity that are equal to those seen in persons expe-

riencing chronic stress (Entringer et al., 2008). Perhaps more directly, genetic studies have shown that alleles that are associated with increased risk for schizophrenia also affect the structure of receptors for pro-inflammatory cytokines in addition to the expression of those cytokines (Lencz et al., 2007). Finally, neurobiological mechanisms have been described that link excessive inflammatory responding with an imbalance of glutamatergic and dopaminergic neurotransmission that may in turn promote both psychotic symptoms (Müller & Schwarz, 2006) and a progressive loss of brain tissue that in turn contributes to cognitive deficits evident in individuals with the disorder (Monji, Kato, & Kanba, 2009).

Finally, evidence from postmortem studies also supports a role for inflammation in schizophrenia. In a recent meta-analytic review of 41 postmortem studies that included brains from 783 patients with schizophrenia and 762 psychiatric controls, for example, analyses revealed significantly higher density of microglia in the brains of patients with schizophrenia as compared to healthy control participants, with these neurobiological alterations most frequently being seen in the temporal cortex. Moreover, patients with schizophrenia were found to exhibit significantly greater pro-inflammatory gene expression and higher pro-inflammatory cytokine levels, as compared to their nonaffected counterparts (Van Kesteren et al., 2017). Ultimately, although we are still far from having a comprehensive, biologically grounded theory of schizophrenia that describes exactly how the immune system is involved in this complex disorder, some promising integrative models have been proposed that help explain several features of the disorder (e.g., Kinney et al., 2010).

Self-Harm and Suicide

Research has also examined associations between inflammation and suicidal behavior. As with all psychiatric conditions other than major depression, the specific inflammatory mechanisms that might give rise to self-harm and suicide remain poorly understood. Nevertheless, in one recent meta-analysis that examined associations between suicidality and cytokine levels in blood, cerebrospinal fluid (CSF), and postmortem tissue across 18 studies (N = 583), levels of IL-1β and IL-6 were elevated in both blood and in the postmortem brain samples of individuals with suicidality as compared with both patients without suicidality and healthy controls. Moreover, individuals' inflammatory levels were able to distinguish psychiatric patients with suicidality from psychiatric patients without suicidality and healthy controls. The meta-analysis also found that CSF levels of IL-8 were lower in individuals exhibiting suicidal behavior (Black & Miller, 2015).

Given these associations between inflammation and suicide, some researchers have recently begun examining pathways underlying these links. In one recent study, investigators quantified levels of TNF-α gene expression and related factors in the dorsolateral prefrontal cortex of the postmortem brains of individuals who died by suicide with depression versus with other psychiatric disorders (cohort 1), and of those with depression who died of suicide versus non-suicide-related causes (cohort 2). Consistent with a potential role for inflammation in suicide, TNF-α expression was greater in the dorsolateral prefrontal cortex of individuals who died by suicide than of those who died of non-suicide-related causes, regardless of their psychiatric diagnosis (i.e., depressed or other psychiatric disorder). Furthermore, in a separate cohort, the authors found that TNF-α expression was elevated in persons diagnosed with MDD regardless of how they died (i.e., suicide or non-suicide-related causes), as compared to nondepressed individuals who passed away. Finally, the authors found that expression of a microRNA involved in pro-inflammatory cytokine regulation (i.e., miR-19a-3p) was specifically upregulated in individuals who died by suicide (Wang, Roy, Turecki, Shelton, & Dwivedi, 2018).

Given the fact that suicide is presently the second leading cause of death in young adults worldwide (WHO, 2012), there is clearly a pressing need to better understand the biological basis of this phenomenon. Several interesting conceptual and integrative reviews have recently attempted to clarify this pathophysiologic picture (e.g., Brundin, Bryleva, & Rajamani, 2017; Serafini et al., 2013; Slavich & Auerbach, 2018). At present, however, the number of studies is relatively limited, the results are somewhat mixed, and it remains unclear to what extent cytokine activity can specifically induce suicidal behavior.

Comparative Reviews

Finally, at least two studies have compared inflammatory marker levels across different psychiatric disorders. The first meta-analysis examined 28 studies that assessed CSF cytokine and tryptophan catabolites in patients with MDD, bipolar disorder, and schizophrenia. CSF levels of IL-1β and kynurenic acid were significantly higher in patients with bipolar disorder and schizophrenia compared to healthy controls. In addition, CSF levels of IL-6 and IL-8 were found to be significantly higher in patients with schizophrenia and MDD compared to healthy controls (Wang & Miller, 2017). The second meta-analysis examined 115 studies that assessed cytokine levels in blood in acutely and chronically ill patients with MDD, bipolar disorder, and schizophrenia. Levels of IL-6, TNF-α, a soluble receptor for IL-2 (sIL-2R), and a cytokine receptor antagonist (IL-1RA) were significantly higher in acutely ill patients with MDD, bipolar mania, and schizophrenia compared to healthy controls. Moreover, treatment was associated with significant reductions in levels of IL-6 in both MDD and schizophrenia, significant reductions in levels of IL-1RA in bipolar mania, and significant increases in levels of sIL-2R in schizophrenia. In chronically ill patients, levels of IL-6 were significantly elevated in patients with MDD, euthymic (but not depressed) bipolar disorder, and schizophrenia as compared with controls, as were levels of IL-1β and sIL-2R in patients with both chronic schizophrenia and euthymic bipolar disorder (Goldsmith, Rapaport, & Miller, 2016).

Although theoretical perspectives on how and why immune markers are altered across different psychiatric disorders is presently limited, one possibility is that it occurs as a result of stress-induced activation of central and peripheral immune cells, which in turn synthesize and release cytokines into circulation (Michopoulos, Powers, Gillespie, Ressler, & Jovanovic, 2017). This possibility is consistent with the social signal transduction theory of depression described earlier, and also with the finding that some disorders—especially those involving anxiety and fear—are associated with increased sympathetic tone and decreased parasympathetic activity, which is known to upregulate inflammation. However, much more research is needed to fully understand these issues.

Future Directions

Considered together, the literatures reviewed here provide substantial evidence that stress alters immune system activity, and that several immune markers are altered in persons with mental health problems. At the same time, numerous issues remain unresolved, thus highlighting several avenues for future research on stress, the immune system, and mental health. I summarize some of the main avenues next.

1. As reviewed here, there is growing evidence that not all stressors have the same impact on

inflammatory biology or health (Monroe, Slavich, Torres, & Gotlib, 2007; Slavich, Monroe, & Gotlib, 2011; Slavich, O'Donovan, et al., 2010; Slavich & Irwin, 2014; Slavich, 2016). Moreover, there is great variability in how "stress" is defined and assessed (Epel et al., 2018; Harkness & Monroe, 2016). One critical avenue for future research, therefore, is to better standardize assessment procedures and to examine what types of stress are most strongly related to different aspects of immune system function and health. Such studies could examine the effects of acute versus chronic stressors, as well as those occurring during different periods of life, across different life domains (e.g., work, finances, intimate relationships), and involving different social-psychological characteristics (e.g., interpersonal loss, physical danger, humiliation, entrapment) (Slavich, in press).

2. Relatedly, although numerous theoretical papers have discussed how lifetime stress exposure might impact biological functioning and health, the number of studies that have actually assessed acute and chronic stress exposure over the entire life course is extremely small (Malat, Jacquez, & Slavich, 2017; Shields & Slavich, 2017). Therefore, much more research is required to understand how stressors occurring over the life course exert a cumulative impact on immune system function. Such work could examine important questions concerning whether there are sensitive or critical periods for damaging effects, as well as whether there are specific periods during which time reversibility is possible. I have developed the Stress and Adversity Inventory (STRAIN) to allow investigators to quickly assess lifetime stress exposure in an efficient and reliable manner in both adolescents (Slavich, Stewart, Esposito, Shields, & Auerbach, in press) and adults (Slavich & Shields, 2018), and the resulting lifetime stress exposure scores have been shown to predict several cognitive, biological, and health-related outcomes (e.g., Cuneo et al., 2017; Goldfarb, Shields, Daw, Slavich, & Phelps, 2017; Toussaint, Shields, Dorn, & Slavich, 2016). However, more work is needed to link these scores to the specific immune markers and disorders describe here.

3. Despite the main finding that levels of inflammation are elevated in the context of psychiatric illness, there is substantial variability in these levels across individuals. Therefore, more research is needed to elucidate factors that are associated with elevated inflammatory activity in both psychiatrically healthy and psychiatrically ill individuals. Given the multitude of biobehavioral factors that can affect immune system function, such work could assess some combination of individuals' life stress exposure and subjective experience, diet, sleep, exercise, pollution exposure, vaccination and illness history, and genetic profile, to name a few. This research will be important for understanding factors that moderate individuals' inflammatory levels, but it will also be critical for shedding light on the extent to which aberrant immune system function is an inherent biological feature of some disorders, or certain disorder subtypes, versus merely a concomitant of those disorders.

4. Given the involvement of stress in increasing inflammatory activity and the role that inflammation plays in several major chronic diseases, additional research is sorely needed to identify neurocognitive processes that influence inflammatory reactivity to stress that could be potentially targeted to reduce inflammation and improve human health. We have identified neural responsivity to social threat and exclusion as one such process (Slavich, Way, et al., 2010), as well as cognitive control of emotional information (Shields, Young Kuchenbecker, Pressman, Sumida, & Slavich, 2016). However, other cognitive-emotional process that are involved in stress reactivity might also play a role, including those involved in attention and memory for social- and stress-related information, as well as negative affective responding and emotion regulation.

5. Finally, despite the possibility that targeting inflammatory processes could help reduce chronic disease risk, relatively little is presently known about different psychosocial and psychopharmacological interventions that could have a salutary effect on immune system function and mental and physical health. As we have reviewed elsewhere (e.g., Black & Slavich, 2016; Slavich & Irwin, 2014), reduced inflammation has been associated with the administration of at least three psychosocial interventions, including cognitive-behavioral stress management, mindfulness-based stress reduction, and Kirtan Kriya meditation, as well as with several psychopharmacological interventions, including the TNF-α antagonists etanercept and infliximab, the COX-2 inhibitor celecoxib, and omega-3 fatty acid supplementation. However, the total number of intervention studies that have been conducted to date is still relatively small, and the findings across these studies are not wholly consistent.

Therefore, several important questions remain unanswered, including, for example, which patients benefit most from targeting inflammatory pathways and which do not see any improvement (and why)? What are the specific multilevel mechanisms of action? And do these interventions have effects on symptom severity, clinical course, or likelihood of recurrence in a manner that is mediated by intervention-related reductions in inflammatory activity?

Conclusion

In conclusion, we are presently experiencing a watershed moment in the search for processes that underlie several major psychiatric disorders, and many of the most exciting discoveries on this topic are employing ideas and methods from PNI. This research has already elucidated entirely new bodily structures that link the brain and peripheral immune system, revealed the broad extent to which stress alters immune system activity, and highlighted the role the immune system plays in promoting certain psychiatric symptoms. This work has also led to the identification of immune mediators that could potentially be targeted to reduce disease burden and improve human health. However, numerous questions remain unanswered, and many of the most important and clinically relevant discoveries still lie ahead. Addressing these issues will not be easy, and it will require individuals who possess the desire and training needed to combine methods from psychology, neuroscience, immunology, genetics, and genomics. However, the upside potential is huge, as this work will undoubtedly contribute greatly to our understanding of the social, psychological, and biological bases of mental and physical health.

References

Ader, R., Cohen, N., & Felten, D. (1995). Psychoneuroimmunology: Interactions between the nervous system and the immune system. *The Lancet*, *345*, 99–103. doi:10.1016/s0140-6736(95)90066-7

Akira, S., Takeda, K., & Kaisho, T. (2001). Toll-like receptors: Critical proteins linking innate and acquired immunity. *Nature Immunology*, *2*, 675–680. doi:10.1038/90609

Appleton, A. A., Buka, S. L., McCormick, M. C., Koenen, K. C., Loucks, E. B., & Kubzansky, L. D. (2012). The association between childhood emotional functioning and adulthood inflammation is modified by early-life socioeconomic status. *Health Psychology*, *31*, 413–422. doi:10.1037/a0027300

Aschbacher, K., Epel, E., Wolkowitz, O. M., Prather, A. A., Puterman, E., & Dhabhar, F. S. (2012). Maintenance of a positive outlook during acute stress protects against proinflammatory reactivity and future depressive symptoms.

Brain, Behavior, and Immunity, *26*, 346–352. doi:10.1016/j.bbi.2011.10.010

Aspelund, A., Antila, S., Proulx, S. T., Karlsen, T. V., Karaman, S., Detmar, M., . . . Alitalo, K. (2015). A dural lymphatic vascular system that drains brain interstitial fluid and macromolecules. *Journal of Experimental Medicine*, *212*, 991–999. doi:10.1084/jem.20142290

Avitsur, R., Stark, J. L., & Sheridan, J. F. (2001). Social stress induces glucocorticoid resistance in subordinate animals. *Hormones and Behavior*, *39*, 247–257. doi:10.1006/hbeh.2001.1653

Bair, M. J., Robinson, R. L., Eckert, G. J., Stang, P. E., Croghan, T. W., & Kroenke, K. (2004). Impact of pain on depression treatment response in primary care. *Psychosomatic Medicine*, *66*, 17–22. doi:10.1097/01.PSY.0000106883.94059.C5

Barton, G. M. (2008). A calculated response: Control of inflammation by the innate immune system. *Journal of Clinical Investigation*, *118*, 413–420. doi:10.1172/JCI34431

Baumeister, D., Akhtar, R., Ciufolini, S., Pariante, C. M., & Mondelli, V. (2016). Childhood trauma and adulthood inflammation: A meta-analysis of peripheral C-reactive protein, interleukin-6 and tumour necrosis factor-α. *Molecular Psychiatry*, *21*, 642–649. doi:10.1038/mp.2015.67

Black, C., & Miller, B. J. (2015). Meta-analysis of cytokines and chemokines in suicidality: Distinguishing suicidal versus nonsuicidal patients. *Biological Psychiatry*, *78*, 28–37. doi:10.1016/j.biopsych.2014.10.014

Black, D. S., & Slavich, G. M. (2016). Mindfulness meditation and the immune system: A systematic review of randomized controlled trials. *Annals of the New York Academy of Sciences*, *1373*, 13–24. doi:10.1111/nyas.12998

Bower, J. E., Crosswell, A. D., & Slavich, G. M. (2014). Childhood adversity and cumulative life stress: Risk factors for cancer-related fatigue. *Clinical Psychological Science*, *2*, 108–115. doi:10.1177/2167702613496243

Brown, A. S. (2006). Prenatal infection as a risk factor for schizophrenia. *Schizophrenia Bulletin*, *32*, 200–202. doi:10.1093/schbul/sbj052

Brundin, L., Bryleva, E. Y., & Rajamani, K. T. (2017). Role of inflammation in suicide: From mechanisms to treatment. *Neuropsychopharmacology*, *42*, 271–283. doi:10.1038/npp.2016.116

Calder, P. C. (2006). n-3 polyunsaturated fatty acids, inflammation, and inflammatory diseases. *American Journal of Clinical Nutrition*, *83*, 1505S–1519S. doi:10.1093/ajcn/83.6.1505s

Campbell, J., & Ehlert, U. (2012). Acute psychosocial stress: Does the emotional stress response correspond with physiological responses? *Psychoneuroendocrinology*, *37*, 1111–1134. doi:10.1016/j.psyneuen.2011.12.010

Caporon, L., & Miller, A. H. (2004). Cytokines and psychopathology: Lessons from interferon-alpha. *Biological Psychiatry*, *56*, 819–824. doi:10.1016/j.biopsych.2004.02.009

Capuron, L., Pagnoni, G., Drake, D. F., Woolwine, B. J., Spivey, J. R., Crowe, R. J., . . . Miller, A. H. (2012). Dopaminergic mechanisms of reduced basal ganglia responses to hedonic reward during interferon alfa administration. *Archives of General Psychiatry*, *69*, 1044–1053. doi:10.1001/archgenpsychiatry.2011.2094

Carpenter, L. L., Gawuga, C. E., Tyrka, A. R., Lee, J. K., Anderson, G. M., & Price, L. H. (2010). Association between plasma IL-6 response to acute stress and early-life adversity in healthy adults. *Neuropsychopharmacology*, *35*, 2617–2623. doi:10.1038/npp.2010.159

Carpenter, L. L., Gawuga, C. E., Tyrka, A. R., & Price, L. H. (2012). C-reactive protein, early life stress, and wellbeing in healthy adults. *Acta Psychiatrica Scandinavica, 126*, 402–410. doi:10.1111/j.1600-0447.2012.01892.x

Carroll, J. E., Cohen, S., & Marsland, A. L. (2011). Early childhood socioeconomic status is associated with circulating interleukin-6 among mid-life adults. *Brain, Behavior, and Immunity, 25*, 1468–1474. doi:10.1016/j.bbi.2011.05.016

Carroll, J. E., Low, C. A., Prather, A. A., Cohen, S., Fury, J. M., Ross, D. C., & Marsland, A. L. (2011). Negative affective responses to a speech task predict changes in interleukin (IL)-6. *Brain, Behavior, and Immunity, 25*, 232–238. doi:10.1016/j.bbi.2010.09.024

Chiang, J. J., Eisenberger, N. I., Seeman, T. E., & Taylor, S. E. (2012). Negative and competitive social interactions are related to heightened proinflammatory cytokine activity. *Proceedings of the National Academy of Sciences of the United States of America, 109*, 1878–1882. doi:10.1073/pnas.1120972109

Cho, H. J., Bower, J. E., Kiefe, C. I., Seeman, T. E., & Irwin, M. R. (2012). Early life stress and inflammatory mechanisms of fatigue in the Coronary Artery Risk Development in Young Adults (CARDIA) study. *Brain, Behavior, and Immunity, 26*, 859–865. doi:10.1016/j.bbi.2012.04.005

Cohen, S., & Herbert, T. B. (1996). Health psychology: Psychological factors and physical disease from the perspective of human psychoneuroimmunology. *Annual Review of Psychology, 47*, 113–142. doi:10.1146/annurev.psych.47.1.113

Cole, S. W., Arevalo, J. M., Takahashi, R., Sloan, E. K., Lutgendorf, S. K., Sood, A. K., Sheridan, J. F., & Seeman, T. E. (2010). Computational identification of gene-social environment interaction at the human IL6 locus. *Proceedings of the National Academy of Sciences of the United States of America, 107*, 5681–5686. doi:10.1073/pnas.0911515107

Cole, S. W., Hawkley, L. C., Arevalo, J. M., & Cacioppo, J. T. (2011). Transcript origin analysis identifies antigen-presenting cells as primary targets of socially regulated gene expression in leukocytes. *Proceedings of the National Academy of Sciences of the United States of America, 108*, 3080–3085. doi:10.1073/pnas.1014218108

Cole, S. W., Korin, Y. D., Fahey, J. L., & Zack, J. A. (1998). Norepinephrine accelerates HIV replication via protein kinase A-dependent effects on cytokine production. *The Journal of Immunology, 161*, 610–616.

Couzin-Frankel, J. (2010). Inflammation bares a dark side. *Science, 330*, 1621. doi:10.1126/science.330.6011.1621

Cuneo, M. G., Schrepf, A., Slavich, G. M., Thaker, P. H., Goodheart, M., Bender, D.,…Lutgendorf, S. K. (2017). Diurnal cortisol rhythms, fatigue and psychosocial factors in five-year survivors of ovarian cancer. *Psychoneuroendocrinology, 84*, 139–142. doi:10.1016/j.psyneuen.2017.06.019

Curfs, J. H., Meis, J. F., & Hoogkamp-Korstanje, J. A. (1997). A primer on cytokines: Sources, receptors, effects, and inducers. *Clinical Microbiology Reviews, 10*, 742–780.

Danese, A., Pariante, C. M., Caspi, A., Taylor, A., & Poulton, R. (2007). Childhood maltreatment predicts adult inflammation in a life-course study. *Proceedings of the National Academy of Sciences of the United States of America, 104*, 1319–1324. doi:10.1073/pnas.0610362104

Dantzer, R., O'Connor, J. C., Freund, G. G., Johnson, R. W., & Kelley, K. W. (2008). From inflammation to sickness and depression: When the immune system subjugates the brain. *Nature Reviews Neuroscience, 9*, 46–56. doi:10.1038/nrn2297

Dedovic, K., Slavich, G. M., Muscatell, K. A., Irwin, M. R., & Eisenberger, N. I. (2016). Dorsal anterior cingulate cortex responses to repeated social evaluative feedback in young women with and without a history of depression. *Frontiers in Behavioral Neuroscience, 10*, 64. doi:10.3389/fnbeh.2016.00064

DellaGioia, N., & Hannestad, J. (2010). A critical review of human endotoxin administration as an experimental paradigm of depression. *Neuroscience and Biobehavioral Reviews, 34*, 130–143. doi:10.1016/j.neubiorev.2009.07.014

Denson, T. F., Spanovic, M., & Miller, N. (2009). Cognitive appraisals and emotions predict cortisol and immune responses: A meta-analysis of acute laboratory social stressors and emotion inductions. *Psychological Bulletin, 135*, 823–853. doi:10.1037/a0016909

Dhabhar, F. S., Burke, H. M., Epel, E. S., Mellon, S. H., Rosser, R., Reus, V. I., & Wolkowitz, O. M. (2009). Low serum IL-10 concentrations and loss of regulatory association between IL-6 and IL-10 in adults with major depression. *Journal of Psychiatric Research, 43*, 962–969. doi:10.1016/j.jpsychires.2009.05.010

Dhabhar, F. S., Malarkey, W. B., Neri, E., & McEwen, B. S. (2012). Stress-induced redistribution of immune cells—From barracks to boulevards to battlefields: A tale of three hormones—Curt Richter Award Winner. *Psychoneuroendocrinology, 37*, 1345–1368. doi:10.1016/j.psyneuen.2012.05.008

Dickerson, S. S., Gable, S. L., Irwin, M. R., Aziz, N., & Kemeny, M. E. (2009). Social-evaluative threat and proinflammatory cytokine regulation: An experimental laboratory investigation. *Psychological Science, 20*, 1237–1244. doi:10.1111/j.1467-9280.2009.02437.x

Dickerson, S. S., Kemeny, M. E., Aziz, N., Kim, K. H., & Fahey, J. L. (2004). Immunological effects of induced shame and guilt. *Psychosomatic Medicine, 66*, 124–131. doi:10.1097/01.PSY.0000097338.75454.29

Dinarello, C. A. (2007). Historical review of cytokines. *European Journal of Immunology, 37*(Suppl 1), S34–S45. doi:10.1002/eji.200737772

Dowlati, Y., Herrmann, N., Swardfager, W., Liu, H., Sham, L., Reim, E. K., & Lanctôt, K. L. (2010). A meta-analysis of cytokines in major depression. *Biological Psychiatry, 67*, 446–457. doi:10.1016/j.biopsych.2009.09.033

Eisenberger, N. I., Berkman, E. T., Inagaki, T. K., Rameson, L. T., Mashal, N. M., & Irwin, M. R. (2010). Inflammation-induced anhedonia: Endotoxin reduces ventral striatum responses to reward. *Biological Psychiatry, 68*, 748–754. doi:10.1016/j.biopsych.2010.06.010

Eisenberger, N. I., Inagaki, T. K., Rameson, L. T., Mashal, N. M., & Irwin, M. R. (2009). An fMRI study of cytokine-induced depressed mood and social pain: The role of sex differences. *Neuroimage, 47*, 881–890. doi:10.1016/j.neuroimage.2009.04.040

Elliot, A. J., & Chapman, B. P. (2016). Socioeconomic status, psychological resources, and inflammatory markers: Results from the MIDUS study. *Health Psychology, 35*, 1205–1213. doi:10.1037/hea0000392

Entringer, S., Kumsta, R., Nelson, E. L., Hellhammer, D. H., Wadhwa, P. D., & Wü, S. (2008). Influence of prenatal psychosocial stress on cytokine production in adult women. *Developmental Psychobiology, 50*, 579–587. doi:10.1002/dev.20316

Epel, E. S., Crosswell, A. D., Mayer, S. E., Prather, A. A., Slavich, G. M., Puterman, E., & Mendes, W. B. (2018). More than a feeling: A unified view of stress measurement for population science. *Frontiers in Neuroendocrinology*, *49*, 146–169. doi:10.1016/j.yfrne.2018.03.001

Fagundes, C. P., & Way, B. (2014). Early-life stress and adult inflammation. *Current Directions in Psychological Science*, *23*, 277–283. doi:10.1177/0963721414535603

Federico, A., Morgillo, F., Tuccillo, C., Ciardiello, F., & Loguercio, C. (2007). Chronic inflammation and oxidative stress in human carcinogenesis. *International Journal of Cancer*, *121*, 2381–2386. doi:10.1002/ijc.23192.

Ford, E. S., Loucks, E. B., & Berkman, L. F. (2006). Social integration and concentrations of C-reactive protein among US adults. *Annals of Epidemiology*, *16*, 78–84. doi:10.1016/j.annepidem.2005.08.005

Freud, S. (1957). Mourning and melancholia. In J. Strachey (Ed. and Trans.), *The standard edition of the complete psychological works of Sigmund Freud* (Vol. 14, pp. 243–258). London, UK: Hogarth Press. (Original work published 1917)

Fuligni, A. J., Telzer, E. H., Bower, J., Cole, S. W., Kiang, L., & Irwin, M. R. (2009). A preliminary study of daily interpersonal stress and C-reactive protein levels among adolescents from Latin American and European backgrounds. *Psychosomatic Medicine*, *71*, 329–333. doi:10.1097/PSY.0b013e3181921b1f

Giletta, M., Slavich G. M., Rudolph, K. D., Hastings, P. D., Nock, M. K., & Prinstein, M. J. (2018). Peer victimization predicts heightened inflammatory reactivity to social stress in cognitively vulnerable adolescents. *Journal of Child Psychology and Psychiatry*, *59*, 129–139. doi:10.1111/jcpp.12804

Gimeno, D., Brunner, E. J., Lowe, G. D., Rumley, A., Marmot, M. G., & Ferrie, J. E. (2007). Adult socioeconomic position, C-reactive protein and interleukin-6 in the Whitehall II prospective study. *European Journal of Epidemiology*, *22*, 675–683. doi:10.1007/s10654-007-9171-9

Gimeno, D., Kivimäki, M., Brunner, E. J., Elovainio, M., De Vogli, R., Steptoe, A., . . . Ferrie, J. E. (2009). Associations of C-reactive protein and interleukin-6 with cognitive symptoms of depression: 12-year follow-up of the Whitehall II study. *Psychological Medicine*, *39*, 413–423. doi:10.1017/S0033291708003723

Glaser, R., & Kiecolt-Glaser, J. K. (2005). Stress-induced immune dysfunction: Implications for health. *Nature Reviews Immunology*, *5*, 243–251. doi:10.1038/nri1571

Goldfarb, E. V., Shields, G. S., Daw, N. D., Slavich, G. M., & Phelps, E. A. (2017). Low lifetime stress exposure is associated with reduced stimulus-response memory. *Learning and Memory*, *24*, 162–168. doi:10.1101/lm.045179.117

Goldsmith, D. R., Rapaport, M. H., & Miller, B. J. (2016). A meta-analysis of blood cytokine network alterations in psychiatric patients: Comparisons between schizophrenia, bipolar disorder and depression. *Molecular Psychiatry*, *21*, 1696–1709. doi:10.1038/mp.2016.3

Graff, L. A., Walker, J. R., & Bernstein, C. N. (2009). Depression and anxiety in inflammatory bowel disease: A review of comorbidity and management. *Inflammatory Bowel Diseases*, *15*, 1105–1118. doi:10.1002/ibd.20873

Grebe, K. M., Takeda, K., Hickman, H. D., Bailey, A. L., Embry, A. C., Bennink, J. R., & Yewdell, J. W. (2010). Cutting edge: Sympathetic nervous system increases proinflammatory cytokines and exacerbates influenza A virus pathogenesis. *The Journal of Immunology*, *184*, 540–544. doi:10.4049/jimmunol.0903395

Grisanti, L. A., Woster, A. P., Dahlman, J., Sauter, E. R., Combs, C. K., & Porter, J. E. (2011). α1-adrenergic receptors positively regulate Toll-like receptor cytokine production from human monocytes and macrophages. *Journal of Pharmacology and Experimental Therapeutics*, *338*, 648–657. doi:10.1124/jpet.110.178012

Gruenewald, T. L., Cohen, S., Matthews, K. A., Tracy, R., & Seeman, T. E. (2009). Association of socioeconomic status with inflammation markers in black and white men and women in the Coronary Artery Risk Development in Young Adults (CARDIA) study. *Social Science and Medicine*, *69*, 451–459. doi:10.1016/j.socscimed.2009.05.018

Gruys, E., Toussaint, M. J., Niewold, T. A., & Koopmans, S. J. (2005). Acute phase reaction and acute phase proteins. *Journal of Zhejiang University Sciences B*, *6*, 1045–1056. doi:10.1631/jzus.2005.B1045

Hackett, R. A., Hamer, M., Endrighi, R., Brydon, L., & Steptoe, A. (2012). Loneliness and stress-related inflammatory and neuroendocrine responses in older men and women. *Psychoneuroendocrinology*, *37*, 1801–1809. doi:10.1016/j.psyneuen.2012.03.016

Harkness, K. L., & Monroe, S. M. (2016). The assessment and measurement of adult life stress: Basic premises, operational principles, and design requirements. *Journal of Abnormal Psychology*, *125*, 727–745. doi:10.1037/abn0000178

Haroon, E., Raison, C. L., & Miller, A. H. (2012). Psychoneuroimmunology meets neuropsychopharmacology: Translational implications of the impact of inflammation on behavior. *Neuropsychopharmacology*, *37*, 137–162. doi:10.1038/npp.2011.205

Harrison, N. A., Brydon, L., Walker, C., Gray, M. A., Steptoe, A., & Critchley, H. D. (2009). Inflammation causes mood changes through alterations in subgenual cingulate activity and mesolimbic connectivity. *Biological Psychiatry*, *66*, 407–414. doi:10.1016/j.biopsych.2009.03.015

Hart, B. L. (1988). Biological basis of the behavior of sick animals. *Neuroscience and Biobehavioral Reviews*, *12*, 123–137. doi:10.1016/S0149-7634(88)80004-6

Heffner, K. L., Waring, M. E., Roberts, M. B., Eaton, C. B., & Gramling, R. (2011). Social isolation, C-reactive protein, and coronary heart disease mortality among community-dwelling adults. *Social Science and Medicine*, *72*, 1482–1488. doi:10.1016/j.socscimed.2011.03.016

Hennessy, M. B., Schiml-Webb, P. A., & Deak, T. (2009). Separation, sickness, and depression: A new perspective on an old animal model. *Current Directions in Psychological Science*, *18*, 227–231. doi:10.1111/j.1467-8721.2009.01641.x

Herbert, T. B., & Cohen, S. (1993). Stress and immunity in humans: A meta-analytic review. *Psychosomatic Medicine*, *55*, 364–379. doi:10.1097/00006842-199307000-00004

Hiles, S. A., Baker, A. L., de Malmanche, T., & Attia, J. (2012). A meta-analysis of differences in IL-6 and IL-10 between people with and without depression: Exploring the causes of heterogeneity. *Brain, Behavior, and Immunity*, *26*, 1180–1188. doi:10.1016/j.bbi.2012.06.001

Holt-Lunstad, J., Robles, T. F., & Sbarra, D. A. (2017). Advancing social connection as a public health priority in the United States. *American Psychologist*, *72*, 517–530. doi:10.1037/amp0000103

Howren, M. B., Lamkin, D. M., & Suls, J. (2009). Associations of depression with C-reactive protein, IL-1, and IL-6: A meta-analysis. *Psychosomatic Medicine*, *71*, 171–186. doi:10.1097/PSY.0b013e3181907c1b

Huang, J. L., Zhang, Y. L., Wang, C. C., Zhou, J. R., Ma, Q., Wang, X., Shen, X. H., & Jiang, C. L. (2012). Enhanced phosphorylation of MAPKs by NE promotes TNF-α production by macrophage through α adrenergic receptor. *Inflammation, 35*, 527–534. doi:10.1007/s10753-011-9342-4

Hubbard, A. K., & Rothlein, R. (2000). Intercellular adhesion molecule-1 (ICAM-1) expression and cell signaling cascades. *Free Radical Biology and Medicine, 28*, 1379–1386. doi:10.1016/S0891-5849(00)00223-9

Huttunen, M. O., & Niskanen, P. (1978). Prenatal loss of father and psychiatric disorders. *Archives of General Psychiatry, 35*, 429–431. doi:10.1001/archpsyc.1978.01770280039004

Irwin, M. R., & Cole, S. W. (2011). Reciprocal regulation of the neural and innate immune systems. *Nature Reviews Immunology, 11*, 625–632. doi:10.1038/nri3042

Irwin, M. R., & Slavich, G. M. (2017). Psychoneuroimmunology. In J. T. Cacioppo, L. G. Tassinary, & G. G. Berntson (Eds.), *Handbook of psychophysiology* (4th ed., pp. 377–398). New York, NY: Cambridge University Press.

Jain, S., & Mills, P. J. (2007). Cytokines, chronic stress, and fatigue. In G. Fink (Ed.), *Encyclopedia of stress* (2nd ed., pp. 698–704). Oxford, UK: Academic Press. doi:10.1016/B978-012373947-6.00727-3

Janicki-Deverts, D., Cohen, S., Kalrab, P., & Matthews, K. A. (2012). The prospective association of socioeconomic status with C-reactive protein levels in the CARDIA study. *Brain, Behavior, and Immunity, 26*, 1128–1135. doi:10.1016/j.bbi.2012.07.017

Jaremka, L. M., Fagundes, C. P., Peng, J., Bennett, J. M., Glaser, R., Malarkey, W. B., & Kiecolt-Glaser, J. K. (2013). Loneliness promotes inflammation during acute stress. *Psychological Science, 24*, 1089–1097. doi:10.1177/0956797612464059

Karin, M. (2006). Nuclear factor-κB in cancer development and progression. *Nature, 441*, 431–436. doi:10.1038/nature04870

Katz, P. P., & Yelin, E. H. (1993). Prevalence and correlates of depressive symptoms among persons with rheumatoid arthritis. *Journal Rheumatology, 20*, 790–796.

Kawai, T., & Akira, S. (2007). Antiviral signaling through pattern recognition receptors. *Journal of Biochemistry, 141*, 137–145. doi:10.1093/jb/mvm032

Kiecolt-Glaser, J. K., Gouin, J. P., & Hantsoo, L. (2010). Close relationships, inflammation, and health. *Neuroscience and Biobehavioral Reviews, 35*, 33–38. doi:10.1016/j.neubiorev.2009.09.003

Kiecolt-Glaser, J. K., Gouin, J. P., Weng, N. P., Malarkey, W. B., Beversdorf, D. Q., & Glaser, R. (2011). Childhood adversity heightens the impact of later-life caregiving stress on telomere length and inflammation. *Psychosomatic Medicine, 73*, 16–22. doi:10.1097/PSY.0b013e31820573b6

Kiecolt-Glaser, J. K., Loving, T. J., Stowell, J. R., Malarkey, W. B., Lemeshow, S., Dickinson, S. L., & Glaser, R. (2005). Hostile marital interactions, proinflammatory cytokine production, and wound healing. *Archives of General Psychiatry, 62*, 1377–1384. doi:10.1001/archpsyc.62.12.1377

Kiecolt-Glaser, J. K., McGuire, L., Robles, T. F., & Glaser, R. (2002). Psychoneuroimmunology: Psychological influences on immune function and health. *Journal of Consulting and Clinical Psychology, 70*, 537–547. doi:10.1037//0022-006x.70.3.537

Kinney, D. K., Hintz, K., Shearer, E. M., Barch, D. H., Riffin, C., Whitley, K., & Butler, R. (2010). A unifying hypothesis of schizophrenia: Abnormal immune system development may help explain roles of prenatal hazards, post-pubertal onset, stress, genes, climate, infections, and brain dysfunction.

Medical Hypotheses, 74, 555–563. doi:10.1016/j.mehy.2009.09.040

Kirschbaum, C., Pirke, K. M., & Hellhammer, D. H. (1993). The "Trier Social Stress Test"—A tool for investigating psychobiological stress responses in a laboratory setting. *Neuropsychobiology, 28*, 76–81. doi:10.1159/000119004

Kushner, I. (1982). The phenomenon of the acute phase response. *Annals of the New York Academy of Sciences, 389*, 39–48. doi:10.1111/j.1749-6632.1982.tb22124.x

Lee, H. J., Takemoto, N., Kurata, H., Kamogawa, Y., Miyatake, S., O'Garra, A., & Arai, N. (2000). GATA-3 induces T helper cell type 2 (Th2) cytokine expression and chromatin remodeling in committed Th1 cells. *The Journal of Experimental Medicine, 192*, 105–115. doi:10.1084/jem.192.1.105

Lencz, T., Morgan, T. V., Athanasiou, M., Dain, B., Reed, C. R., Kane, J. M., Kucherlapati, R., & Malhotra, A. K. (2007). Converging evidence for a pseudoautosomal cytokine receptor gene locus in schizophrenia. *Molecular Psychiatry, 12*, 572–580. doi:10.1038/sj.mp.4001983

Louveau, A., Smirnov, I., Keyes, T. J., Eccles, J. D., Rouhani, S. J., Peske, J. D.,...Harris, T. H. (2015). Structural and functional features of central nervous system lymphatic vessels. *Nature, 523*, 337–341. doi:10.1038/nature14432

Maddux, J. E., & Winstead, B. A. (Eds.). (2015). *Psychopathology: Foundations for a contemporary understanding* (3rd ed.). New York, NY: Routledge.

Maier, S. F., & Watkins, L. R. (1998). Cytokines for psychologists: Implications of bidirectional immune-to-brain communication for understanding behavior, mood, and cognition. *Psychological Review, 105*, 83–107. doi:10.1037/0033-295X.105.1.83

Malaspina, D., Corcoran, C., Kleinhaus, K. R., Perrin, M. C., Fennig, S., & Nahon, D. (2008). Acute maternal stress in pregnancy, schizophrenia in offspring: A cohort prospective study. *BMC Psychiatry, 8*:71. doi:10.1186/1471-244x-8-71

Malat, J., Jacquez, F., & Slavich, G. M. (2017). Measuring lifetime stress exposure and protective factors in life course research on racial inequality and birth outcomes. *Stress, 20*, 379–385. doi:10.1080/10253890.2017.1341871

Marin, T. J., Chen, E., Munch, J. A., & Miller, G. E. (2009). Double-exposure to acute stress and chronic family stress is associated with immune changes in children with asthma. *Psychosomatic Medicine, 71*, 378–384. doi:10.1097/PSY.0b013e318199dbc3

Marsland, A. L., Walsh, C., Lockwood, K., & John-Henderson, N. A. (2017). The effects of acute psychological stress on circulating and stimulated inflammatory markers: A systematic review and meta-analysis. *Brain, Behavior, and Immunity, 64*, 208–219. doi:10.1016/j.bbi.2017.01.011

Matthews, K. A., Chang, Y., Bromberger, J. T., Karvonen-Gutierrez, C. A., Kravitz, H. M., Thurston, R. C., & Montez, J. K. (2016). Childhood socioeconomic circumstances, inflammation, and hemostasis among midlife women: Study of Women's Health across the Nation (SWAN). *Psychosomatic Medicine, 78*, 311–318. doi:10.1097/PSY.0000000000000283

Mednick, S. A., Huttunen, M. O., & Machon, R. A. (1994). Prenatal influenza infections and adult schizophrenia. *Schizophrenia Bulletin, 20*, 263–267. doi:10.1093/schbul/20.2.263

Medzhitov, R. (2001). Toll-like receptors and innate immunity. *Nature Reviews Immunology, 1*, 135–145. doi:10.1038/35100529

Medzhitov, R. (2007). Recognition of microorganisms and activation of the immune response. *Nature, 449*, 819–826. doi:10.1038/nature06246

Medzhitov, R. (2008). Origin and physiological roles of inflammation. *Nature*, *454*, 428–435. doi:10.1038/nature07201

Michopoulos, V., Powers, A., Gillespie, C. F., Ressler, K. J., & Jovanovic, T. (2017). Inflammation in fear- and anxiety-based disorders: PTSD, GAD, and beyond. *Neuropsychopharmacology Reviews*, *42*, 254–270. doi:10.1038/npp.2016.146

Miller, G., & Chen, E. (2007). Unfavorable socioeconomic conditions in early life presage expression of proinflammatory phenotype in adolescence. *Psychosomatic Medicine*, *69*, 402–409. doi:10.1097/PSY.0b013e318068fcf9

Miller, G., Chen, E., & Cole, S. W. (2009). Health psychology: Developing biologically plausible models linking the social world and physical health. *Annual Review of Psychology*, *60*, 501–524. doi:10.1146/annurev.psych.60.110707.163551

Miller, G. E., Chen, E., Fok, A. K., Walker, H. A., Lim, A., Nicholls, E. F., Cole, S.W., & Kobor, M.S. (2009). Low early-life social class leaves a biological residue manifested by decreased glucocorticoid and increased proinflammatory signaling. *Proceedings of the National Academy of Sciences of the United States of America*, *106*, 14716–14721. doi:10.1073/pnas.0902971106

Miller, G. E., Cohen, S., & Ritchey, A. K. (2002). Chronic psychological stress and the regulation of pro-inflammatory cytokines: A glucocorticoid-resistance model. *Health Psychology*, *21*, 531–541. doi:10.1037/0278-6133.21.6.531

Miller, G. E., Rohleder, N., Stetler, C., & Kirschbaum, C. (2005). Clinical depression and regulation of the inflammatory response during acute stress. *Psychosomatic Medicine*, *67*, 679–687. doi:10.1097/01.psy.0000174172.82428.ce

Miller, N. E. (1964). Some psychophysiological studies of the motivation and of the behavioral effects of illness. *Bulletin of the British Psychological Society*, *17*, 1–20.

Monji, A., Kato, T., & Kanba, S. (2009). Cytokines and schizophrenia: Microglia hypothesis of schizophrenia. *Psychiatry Clinical Neuroscience*, *63*, 257–265. doi:10.1111/j.1440-1819.2009.01945.x

Monroe, S. M. (2008). Modern approaches to conceptualizing and measuring human life stress. *Annual Review of Clinical Psychology*, *4*, 33–52. doi:10.1146/annurev.clinpsy.4.022007.141207

Monroe, S. M., Slavich, G. M., & Georgiades, K. (2014). The social environment and depression: The roles of life stress. In I. H. Gotlib & C. L. Hammen (Eds.), *Handbook of depression* (3rd ed., pp. 296–314). New York, NY: The Guilford Press.

Monroe, S. M., Slavich, G. M., Torres, L. D., & Gotlib, I. H. (2007). Major life events and major chronic difficulties are differentially associated with history of major depressive episodes. *Journal of Abnormal Psychology*, *116*, 116–124. doi:10.1037/0021-843X.116.1.116

Moons, W. G., Eisenberger, N. I., & Taylor, S. E. (2010). Anger and fear responses to stress have different biological profiles. *Brain, Behavior, and Immunity*, *24*, 215–219. doi:10.1016/j.bbi.2009.08.009

Müller, N., & Schwarz, M. (2006). Schizophrenia as an inflammation-mediated dysbalance of glutamatergic neurotransmission. *Neurotoxic Research*, *10*, 131–148. doi:10.1007/BF03033242

Murphy, K. (2011). *Janeway's immunobiology*. New York, NY: Garland Science.

Murphy, M. L. M., Slavich, G. M., Chen, E., & Miller, G. E. (2015). Targeted rejection predicts decreased anti-inflammatory gene expression and increased symptom severity in youth with asthma. *Psychological Science*, *26*, 111–121. doi:10.1177/0956797614556320

Murphy, M. L. M., Slavich, G. M., Rohleder, N., & Miller, G. E. (2013). Targeted rejection triggers differential pro- and anti-inflammatory gene expression in adolescents as a function of social status. *Clinical Psychological Science*, *1*, 30–40. doi:10.1177/2167702612455743

Muscatell, K. A., Dedovic, K., Slavich, G. M., Jarcho, M. R., Breen, E. C., Bower, J. E., Irwin, M. R., & Eisenberger, N. I. (2015). Greater amygdala activity and dorsomedial prefrontal-amygdala coupling are associated with enhanced inflammatory responses to stress. *Brain, Behavior, and Immunity*, *43*, 46–53. doi:10.1016/j.bbi.2014.06.201

Muscatell, K. A., Dedovic K., Slavich, G. M., Jarcho M. R., Breen, E. C., Bower, J. E., Irwin, M. R., & Eisenberger, N. I. (2016). Neural mechanisms linking social status and inflammatory responses to social stress. *Social Cognitive and Affective Neuroscience*, *11*, 915–922. doi:10.1093/scan/nsw025

Nance, D. M., & Sanders, V. M. (2007). Autonomic innervation and regulation of the immune system (1987–2007). *Brain, Behavior, and Immunity*, *21*, 736–745. doi:10.1016/j.bbi.2007.03.008

O'Donovan, A., & Neylan, T. C. (2017). Associations of trauma and posttraumatic stress disorder with inflammation and endothelial function: On timing, specificity, and mechanisms. *Biological Psychiatry*, *82*, 861–863. doi:10.1016/j.biopsych.2017.10.002

O'Donovan, A., Slavich, G. M., Epel, E. S., & Neylan, T. C. (2013). Exaggerated neurobiological sensitivity to threat as a mechanism linking anxiety with increased risk for diseases of aging. *Neuroscience and Biobehavioral Reviews*, *37*, 96–108. doi:10.1016/j.neubiorev.2012.10.013

Pace, T. W. W., Mletzko, T. C., Alagbe, O., Musselman, D. L., Nemeroff, C. B., Miller, A. H., & Heim, C. M. (2006). Increased stress-induced inflammatory responses in male patients with major depression and increased early life stress. *American Journal of Psychiatry*, *163*, 1630–1633. doi:10.1176/appi.ajp.163.9.1630

Passos, I. C., Vasconcelos-Moreno, M. P., Costa, L. G., Kunz, M., Brietzke, E., Quevedo, J.,... Kauer-Sant'Anna, M. (2015). Inflammatory markers in post-traumatic stress disorder: A systematic review, meta-analysis, and meta-regression. *Lancet Psychiatry*, *2*, 1002–1012. doi:10.1016/S2215-0366(15)00309-0

Pavlov, V. A., & Tracey, K. J. (2004). Neural regulators of innate immune responses and inflammation. *Cellular and Molecular Life Sciences*, *61*, 2322–2331. doi:10.1007/s00018-004-4102-3

Petersen, K. L., Marsland, A. L., Flory, J., Votruba-Drzal, E., Muldoon, M. F., & Manuck, S. B. (2008). Community socioeconomic status is associated with circulating interleukin-6 and C-reactive protein. *Psychosomatic Medicine*, *70*, 646–652. doi:10.1097/PSY.0b013e31817b8ee4

Pollitt, R. A., Kaufman, J. S., Rose, K. M., Diez-Roux, A. V., Zeng, D., & Heiss, G. (2007) Early-life and adult socioeconomic status and inflammatory risk markers in adulthood. *European Journal of Epidemiology*, *22*, 55–66. doi:10.1007/s10654-006-9082-1

Poole, H., White, S., Blake, C., Murphy, P., & Bramwell, R. (2009). Depression in chronic pain patients: Prevalence and measurement. *Pain Practice*, *9*, 173–180. doi:10.1111/j.1533-2500.2009.00274.x

Poon, D. C., Ho, Y. S., Chiu, K., & Chang, R. C. (2013). Cytokines: How important are they in mediating sickness?

Neuroscience and Biobehavioral Reviews, 37, 1–10. doi:10.1016/j.neubiorev.2012.11.001

Prather, A. A., Carroll, J. E., Fury, J. M., McDade, K. K., Ross, D., & Marsland, A. L. (2009). Gender differences in stimulated cytokine production following acute psychological stress. *Brain, Behavior, and Immunity, 23*, 622–628. doi:10.1016/j.bbi.2008.11.004

Radtke, F., Macdonald, H. R., & Tacchini-Cottier, F. (2013). Regulation of innate and adaptive immunity by Notch. *Nature Reviews Immunology, 13*, 427–437. doi:10.1038/nri3445

Raison, C. L., Capuron, L., & Miller, A. H. (2006). Cytokines sing the blues: Inflammation and the pathogenesis of depression. *Trends in Immunology, 27*, 24–31. doi:10.1016/j.it.2005.11.006

Raison, C. L., & Miller, A. H. (2013). The evolutionary significance of depression in Pathogen Host Defense (PATHOS-D). *Molecular Psychiatry, 18*, 15–37. doi:10.1038/mp.2012.2

Raison, C. L., Rutherford, R. E., Woolwine, B. J., Shuo, C., Schettler, P., Drake, D. F., Haroon, E., & Miller, A. H. (2013). A randomized controlled trial of the tumor necrosis factor antagonist infliximab for treatment-resistant depression: The role of baseline inflammatory biomarkers. *JAMA Psychiatry, 70*, 31–41. doi:10.1001/2013.jamapsychiatry.4

Regier, D. A., Boyd, J. H., Burke, J. D. Jr., Rae, D. S., Myers, J. K., Kramer, M., . . . Locke, B. Z. (1988). One-month prevalence of mental disorders in the United States. Based on five Epidemiologic Catchment Area sites. *Archives of General Psychiatry, 45*, 977–986. doi:10.1001/archpsyc.1988.01800350011002

Ricciotti, E., & FitzGerald, G. A. (2011). Prostaglandins and inflammation. *Arteriosclerosis, Thrombosis, and Vascular Biology, 31*, 986–1000. doi:10.1161/ATVBAHA.110.207449

Rivest, S. (2009). Regulation of innate immune responses in the brain. *Nature Reviews Immunology, 9*, 429–439. doi:10.1038/nri2565

Rohleder, N., Schommer, N. C., Hellhammer, D. H., Engel, R., & Kirschbaum, C. (2001). Sex differences in glucocorticoid sensitivity of proinflammatory cytokine production after psychosocial stress. *Psychosomatic Medicine, 63*, 966–972. doi:10.1097/00006842-200111000-00016

Rosenberger, P. H., Ickovics, J. R., Epel, E., Nadler, E., Jokl, P., Fulkerson, J. P., Tillie, J. M., & Dhabhar, F. S. (2009). Surgical stress-induced immune cell redistribution profiles predict short-term and long-term postsurgical recovery: A prospective study. *The Journal of Bone and Joint Surgery, 91*, 2783–2794. doi:10.2106/JBJS.H.00989

Schrepf, A., Clevenger, L., Christensen, D., DeGeest, K., Bender, D., Ahmed, A., . . . Lutgendorf, S. K. (2013). Cortisol and inflammatory processes in ovarian cancer patients following primary treatment: Relationships with depression, fatigue, and disability. *Brain, Behavior, and Immunity, 30*, S126–S134. doi:10.1016/j.bbi.2012.07.022

Segerstrom, S. C., & Miller, G. E. (2004). Psychological stress and the human immune system: A meta-analytic study of 30 years of inquiry. *Psychological Bulletin, 130*, 601–630. doi:10.1037/0033-2909.130.4.601

Serafinia, G., Pompilia, M., Serettia, M. E., Stefania, H., Palermoa, M., Coryell, W., & Girardia, P. (2013). *European Neuropsychopharmacology, 23*, 1672–1686. doi:10.1016/j.euroneuro.2013.06.002

Shields, G. S., Moons, W. G., & Slavich, G. M. (2017). Inflammation, self-regulation, and health: An immunologic model of self-regulatory failure. *Perspectives on Psychological Science, 12*, 588–612. doi:10.1177/1745691616689091

Shields, G. S., & Slavich, G. M. (2017). Lifetime stress exposure and health: A review of contemporary assessment methods and biological mechanisms. *Social and Personality Psychology Compass, 11*(8):e12335. doi:10.1111/spc3.12335

Shields, G. S., Young Kuchenbecker, S., Pressman, S. D., Sumida, K. D., & Slavich, G. M. (2016). Better cognitive control of emotional information is associated with reduced pro-inflammatory cytokine reactivity to emotional stress. *Stress, 19*, 63–68. doi:10.3109/10253890.2015.1121983

Slavich, G. M. (2015). Understanding inflammation, its regulation, and relevance for health: A top scientific and public priority. *Brain, Behavior, and Immunity, 45*, 13–14. doi:10.1016/j.bbi.2014.10.012

Slavich, G. M. (2016). Life stress and health: A review of conceptual issues and recent findings. *Teaching of Psychology, 43*, 346–355. doi:10.1177/0098628316662768

Slavich, G. M. (in press). Stressnology: The primitive (and problematic) study of life stress exposure and pressing need for better measurement. *Brain, Behavior, and Immunity*. doi:10.1016/j.bbi.2018.08.011

Slavich, G. M., & Auerbach, R. P. (2018). Stress and its sequelae: Depression, suicide, inflammation, and physical illness. In J. N. Butcher & J. M. Hooley (Eds.), *APA handbook of psychopathology: Vol. 1. Psychopathology: Understanding, assessing, and treating adult mental disorders* (pp. 375–402). Washington, DC: American Psychological Association.

Slavich, G. M., & Cole, S. W. (2013). The emerging field of human social genomics. *Clinical Psychological Science, 1*, 331–348. doi:10.1177/2167702613478594

Slavich, G. M., & Irwin, M. R. (2014). From stress to inflammation and major depressive disorder: A social signal transduction theory of depression. *Psychological Bulletin, 140*, 774–815. doi:10.1037/a0035302

Slavich, G. M., Monroe, S. M., & Gotlib, I. H. (2011). Early parental loss and depression history: Associations with recent life stress in major depressive disorder. *Journal of Psychiatric Research, 45*, 1146–1152. doi:10.1016/j.jpsychires.2011.03.004

Slavich, G. M., O'Donovan, A., Epel, E. S., & Kemeny, M. E. (2010). Black sheep get the blues: A psychobiological model of social rejection and depression. *Neuroscience and Biobehavioral Reviews, 35*, 39–45. doi:10.1016/j.neubiorev.2010.01.003

Slavich, G. M., & Shields, G. S. (2018). Assessing lifetime stress exposure using the Stress and Adversity Inventory for Adults (Adult STRAIN): An overview and initial validation. *Psychosomatic Medicine, 80*, 17–27. doi:10.1097/PSY.0000000000000534

Slavich, G. M., Stewart, J. G., Esposito, E. C., Shields, G. S., & Auerbach, R. P. (in press). The Stress and Adversity Inventory for Adolescents: Associations with mental and physical health, risky behaviors, and psychiatric diagnoses in youth seeking treatment. *Journal of Child Psychology and Psychiatry*.

Slavich, G. M., Thornton, T., Torres, L. D., Monroe, S. M., & Gotlib, I. H. (2009). Targeted rejection predicts hastened onset of major depression. *Journal of Social and Clinical Psychology, 28*, 223–243. doi:10.1521/jscp.2009.28.2.223

Slavich, G. M., Way, B. M., Eisenberger, N. I., & Taylor, S. E. (2010). Neural sensitivity to social rejection is associated with inflammatory responses to social stress. *Proceedings of the National Academy of Sciences of the United States of America, 107*, 14817–14822. doi:10.1073/pnas.1009164107

Slopen, N., Kubzansky, L. D., McLaughlin, K. A., & Koenen, K. C. (2013). Childhood adversity and inflammatory processes in youth: A prospective study. *Psychoneuroendocrinology, 38*, 188–200. doi:10.1016/j.psyneuen.2012.05.013

Slopen, N., Lewis, T. T., Gruenewald, T. L., Mujahid, M. S., Ryff, C. D., Albert, M. A., & Williams, D. R. (2010). Early life adversity and inflammation in African Americans and whites in the midlife in the United States survey. *Psychosomatic Medicine, 72*, 694–701. doi:10.1097/PSY.0b013e3181e9c16f

Slopen, N., Loucks, E. B., Appleton, A. A., Kawachi, I., Kubzansky, L. D., Non, A. L., . . . Gilman, S. E. (2015). Early origins of inflammation: An examination of prenatal and childhood social adversity in a prospective cohort study. *Psychoneuroendocrinology, 51*, 403–413. doi:10.1016/j.psyneuen.2014.10.016

Smith, C. W., Marlin, S. D., Rothlein, R., Toman, C., & Anderson, D. C. (1989). Cooperative interactions of LFA-1 and Mac-1 with intercellular adhesion molecule-1 in facilitating adherence and transendothelial migration of human neutrophils in vitro. *Journal of Clinical Investigation, 83*, 2008–2017. doi:10.1172/JCI114111

Smith, R. S. (1991). The macrophage theory of depression. *Medical Hypotheses, 35*, 298–306. doi:10.1016/0306-9877(91)90272-Z

Sorrells, S. F., Caso, J. R., Munhoz, C. D., & Sapolsky, R. M. (2009). The stressed CNS: When glucocorticoids aggravate inflammation. *Neuron, 64*, 33–39. doi:10.1016/j.neuron.2009.09.032

Steptoe, A., Hamer, M., & Chida, Y. (2007). The effects of acute psychological stress on circulating inflammatory factors in humans: A review and meta-analysis. *Brain, Behavior, and Immunity, 21*, 901–912. doi:10.1016/j.bbi.2007.03.011

Sternberg, E. M. (2006). Neural regulation of innate immunity: A coordinated nonspecific host response to pathogens. *Nature Reviews Immunology, 6*, 318–328. doi:10.1038/nri1810

Strike, P. C., Wardle, J., & Steptoe, A. (2004). Mild acute inflammatory stimulation induces transient negative mood. *Journal of Psychosomatic Research, 57*, 189–194. doi:10.1016/S0022-3999(03)00569-5

Takeda, K., Kaisho T., & Akira S. (2003). Toll-like receptors. *Annual Review of Immunology, 21*, 335–376. doi:10.1146/annurev.immunol.21.120601.141126

Takizawa, R., Danese, A., Maughan, B., & Arseneault, L. (2015). Bullying victimization in childhood predicts inflammation and obesity at mid-life: A five-decade birth cohort study. *Psychological Medicine, 45*, 2705–2715. doi:10.1017/S0033291715000653

Taylor, S. E., Lehman, B. J., Kiefe, C. I., & Seeman, T. E. (2006). Relationship of early life stress and psychological functioning to adult C-reactive protein in the coronary artery risk development in young adults study. *Biological Psychiatry, 60*, 819–824. doi:10.1016/j.biopsych.2006.03.016

Toussaint, L., Shields, G. S., Dorn, G., & Slavich, G. M. (2016). Effects of lifetime stress exposure on mental and physical health in young adulthood: How stress degrades and forgiveness protects health. *Journal of Health Psychology, 21*, 1004–1014. doi:10.1177/1359105314544132

van den Biggelaar, A. H., Gussekloo, J., de Craen, A. J., Frölich, M., Stek, M. L., van der Mast, R. C., & Westendorp, R. G. (2007). Inflammation and interleukin-1 signaling network contribute to depressive symptoms but not cognitive decline in old age. *Experimental Gerontology, 42*, 693–701. doi:10.1016/j.exger.2007.01.011

Van Kesteren, C. F. M. G., Gremmels, H., De Witte, L. D., Hol, E. M., Van Gool, A. R., Falkai, P. G., . . . Sommer, I. E. C. (2017). Immune involvement in the pathogenesis of schizophrenia: A meta-analysis on postmortem brain studies. *Translational Psychiatry, 7*, e1075. doi:10.1038/tp.2017.4

Wang, A. K., & Miller, B. J. (2017). Meta-analysis of cerebrospinal fluid cytokine and tryptophan catabolite alterations in psychiatric patients: Comparisons between schizophrenia, bipolar disorder, and depression. *Schizophrenia Bulletin, 44*, 75–83. doi:10.1093/schbul/sbx035

Wang, Q., Roy, B., Turecki, G., Shelton, R. C., & Dwivedi, Y. (2018). Role of complex epigenetic switching in tumor necrosis factor-α upregulation in the prefrontal cortex of suicide subjects. *American Journal of Psychiatry, 175*, 262–274. doi:10.1176/appi.ajp.2017.16070759

Weinstein, A. A., Deuster, P. A., Francis, J. L., Bonsall, R. W., Tracy, R. P., & Kop, W. J. (2010). Neurohormonal and inflammatory hyper-responsiveness to acute mental stress in depression. *Biological Psychology, 84*, 228–234. doi:10.1016/j.biopsycho.2010.01.016

World Health Organization [WHO] (2012). Disease and injury regional mortality estimates, 2000–2012.

Wright, C. E., Strike, P. C., Brydon, L., & Steptoe, A. (2005). Acute inflammation and negative mood: Mediation by cytokine activation. *Brain, Behavior, and Immunity, 19*, 345–350. doi:10.1016/j.bbi.2004.10.003

Yamakawa, K., Matsunaga, M., Isowa, T., Kimura, K., Kasugai, K., Yoneda, M., Kaneko, H., & Ohira, H. (2009). Transient responses of inflammatory cytokines in acute stress. *Biological Psychology, 82*, 25–32. doi:10.1016/j.biopsycho.2009.05.001

Genetic and Epigenetic Models

Rudolf Uher

Abstract

Both genetic variation and environmental exposures play key roles in the development of mental health or psychopathology. Their roles are interdependent: The effects of genetic variants depend on environment, and the impact of environment depends on the genetic variants. This chapter will explain and critically review the most important models of gene–environment interplay, including gene–environment correlation, gene–environment interaction, and epigenetics. Gene–environment correlation describes a mechanism where genetic variants influence the likelihood of environmental exposure. Gene–environment interactions refer to a mechanism where genetic variants influence the impact of an environmental exposure on the individual. Finally, epigenetics provides a molecular mechanism through which environmental exposures affect the function of genes for long periods of time. The chapter concludes with a discussion of the limits of current knowledge, its implications for treatment and prevention, and directions for further research.

Keywords: gene–environment correlation, gene–environment interactions, epigenetics, stress, psychopathology

Genetic Factors, Stress, and Psychopathology

People who experience adversity are more likely to develop most types of mental disorders. Although the universal observation of sequential associations between stress and psychopathology is indisputable, it does not answer important questions about causation and individual differences in the experience and consequences of stress. Why are some individuals more likely to experience and report stress than others? Why do some individuals develop a mental disorder while others remain healthy and resilient after experiencing a similar degree of adversity? How does the effect of early stress persist to influence psychopathology over the life course? Answers to these questions are emerging from research on the intricate interplay between genes and environment. In this chapter, we will learn about the principles of genetic and epigenetic mechanisms that underlie the relationships between environment and psychopathology.

To do this, we will first set the stage by defining key concepts and terminology. We will then examine the reasons why genetic and environmental factors are not independent (including a review of gene–environment correlations), before proceeding to explore the genetic differences in how environment affects individuals (including gene–environment interactions). We will also describe the mechanisms through which environment impacts the functions of genes (including epigenetics).

The Concepts and Terminology of Gene–Environment Interplay

In examining the mechanisms of stress and psychopathology, we will frequently use the adjective *genetic* to refer to any aspect of the information that is carried in the sequence of the deoxyribonucleic acids (or DNA) in the cells of an organism. DNA is composed of two connected strands of base pairs: the sequence of four different base pairs (adenosine, cytosine, guanine, and thymine; abbreviated as A, C, G, and T, respectively) carries all information needed for all cells in an organism to grow and function. DNA is the vehicle for information to be passed from parents to their children. The entire sample of DNA in a cell is the *genome*. The human genome is composed of 3 billion DNA base pairs that are organized into 46 separate long chains of DNA, or chromosomes. These include 22 pairs of autosomes (two copies of the same chromosome, one inherited from the biological mother and the other inherited from the biological mother) and two sex chromosomes that determine biological sex (females carry two copies of the X chromosome; males carry one copy of X chromosome and one copy of the much smaller Y chromosome). *Genes* are sequences of DNA within the genome that encode proteins. There are approximately 19,000 genes in the human genome. Genes are annotated with uppercase alphanumeric abbreviations that are printed in italics (e.g., *BDNF* stands for the brain-derived neurotrophic factor gene). Genes make up approximately 2% of the genome DNA. The rest of the genome is described as *intergenic* and contains a variety of elements that may influence how genes are being used.

Although the sequence of DNA base pairs in the genome of any human closely resembles that of another human, there are on average 2.5 million places where the sequence differs between any two individuals. We use the word *locus* (plural *loci*) to refer to a position in the genome. The loci where the DNA sequence commonly differs from one individual to another are referred to as genetic *variants* or *polymorphisms*. The most common type of polymorphism is a *single-nucleotide polymorphism* (SNP), a difference in just one base pair. SNPs are referred to with codes composed of "rs" followed by 4 to 10 digits (e.g., rs6265 is an SNP within the BDNF gene) or by a chromosome number followed by a position marked as the number of base pairs from the beginning of the chromosome. The actual base pairs that may occupy a polymorphic locus are referred to as alleles. The combination of the two alleles that occupy the same locus on the two chromosomes is referred to as the genotype. For example, a SNP with alleles A and T can have three genotypes: AA (A homozygote), AT (heterozygote), or TT (T homozygote).

We use the adjective *heritable* to describe all properties that are passed from parents to offspring through genetic information. Although *heritable* implies genetic, the two words are not synonymous,

because genetic information may be modified through *mutations* in the process of being passed from parents to offspring. Consequently, a child may carry elements of genetic information not inherited from his or her parents. We call these recent alterations of the DNA de novo mutations. We use the concept *heritability* to quantify the total contribution of all genetic variants to a particular characteristic, or *trait*, of an individual. Heritability is defined as a proportion of variance (the sum of all differences between individuals) of a trait that is due to genetic factors. Heritability ranges from 0 to 1. Heritability of a trait can be indirectly estimated from similarity of monozygotic versus dizygotic twins. The methods that use similarities between individuals with different degree of biological relatedness (twins, families, adoption studies, and assisted conception studies) to infer the genetic and environmental contributions to individual differences are commonly referred to as *quantitative genetics*. This is distinguished from *molecular genetics* that uses genetic variants measured in a laboratory.

Until the end of the 20th century, molecular genetic methods were largely limited to measuring relatively small numbers of polymorphisms. The necessity to focus the molecular genetic study led to researchers selecting variants in genes that they believed might be important for a particular trait, referred to as *candidate genes*. Rapid technological advances in the first decade of the 20th century have enabled systematic measurement of hundreds of thousands or millions of polymorphisms that cover the entire human genome. Because polymorphisms that are located close to each other in the genome are likely to be inherited together, the alleles in nearby loci tend to be linked to each other across the human population. The resulting regional correlation is known as *linkage disequilibrium* (LD). Thanks to LD, we do not need to measure every single polymorphism directly, and the measurement of several hundred thousand SNPs enables estimating the genotypes on all known common polymorphisms through *imputation*. The measurement of a large number of polymorphisms through imputation has enabled *genome-wide association studies* (GWASs) that test variants across the entire genome for association with a given trait or disease. Because of the need to statistically account for multiple testing, GWASs require very large samples (typically tens or hundreds of thousands of individuals) to detect multiple associated variants. Across many human traits and common diseases, GWASs have been successful in identifying associated genetic variants, of which the vast majority would not have been identified through candidate gene approaches. Most human traits and common diseases are influenced by a very large number of genetic variants of which each has a very small effect on its own. A large number of associated variants can be summed up into a *polygenic risk score* (PRS), a continuous variable that can be much more strongly predictive than any individual molecular variant in isolation (Martin, Daly, Robinson, Hyman, & Neale, 2019). *Epigenetics* denotes multiple types of modifications of the genome that can change the function of genes without altering the DNA base pair sequence (Yet, Tsai, Castillo-Fernandez, Carnero-Montoro, & Bell, 2016). Examples of epigenetic modifications include *DNA methylation* (attachment of a methyl group to cytosine residuals) and *histone acetylation* (attachment of acetyl residues to the proteins that help maintain the shape of DNA in chromosomes). Epigenetic changes may occur in response to developmental or environmental stimuli and may determine which genes are transcribed into proteins (Rutter, 2016).

The study of gene–environment interplay also requires an accurate conceptualization of the environmental factors. Although *stress* is a widely used term, it can be ambiguous because it has been used broadly to refer to both adverse environments and the individual's psychological or behavioral response to these. We therefore use the terms *environment* or *environmental factors* to specify the conditions and events external to the individual. We refer to the negative aspects of social and physical environment as *adversity*. We reserve the term *trauma* for major negative events that occur in a short and discrete time. We use the term *childhood maltreatment* to describe relational adversity caused by adults to children and adolescents under age 16 years. Childhood maltreatment includes physical, sexual, and emotional abuse, as well as physical and emotional neglect and exposure to violence. Interpersonal adversity committed on a child by another child of similar age is called *peer victimization* or bullying. Discrete adverse environmental events at any age are referred to as *stressful life events* (SLEs). Examples of SLEs are divorce, loss of employment, mugging, or burglary, but also life-altering news that concerns key individuals or values in one's life (e.g., loss of a cherished idea). Longer lasting adverse conditions can be referred to as *difficulties* or reflected in indicators of socioeconomic status.

We use the term *gene–environment interplay* for all types of models and relationships that include both genetic and environmental factors. Concepts and terminology that relate to specific types of the interplay between genetic and environmental factors, including gene–environment correlations, gene–environment interactions, Mendelian randomization, differential susceptibility, and polygenic susceptibility scores, will be reviewed in detail in the next three sections of this chapter.

Genetic Propensity to Exposure: Gene–Environment Correlations

Some individuals are more likely to be exposed to certain environmental conditions than others. This may often be for genetic reasons, and when it is, we refer to this relationship as a *gene–environment correlation*. Borrowing from statistics, where a lowercase "r" is used as a symbol for correlation, a gene–environment correlation is often abbreviated as *rGE* (Knafo & Jaffee, 2013). A gene–environment correlation can occur for several reasons. First, our genes may be related to our environment because we share a proportion of our genome with our relatives, and our relatives, especially parents, also create a substantial part of our environment. This is referred to as *passive gene–environment correlation*, because the carrier of the gene is not directly involved in shaping or selecting environment. For example, parents with depression may be on average less positive toward their children, and their offspring may experience more negative and stressful life events. Parents with depression also pass their genetic variants, including those related to the risk of depression, to their children. Thus, exposure to less positive parenting and negative life events is linked to heritable factors predisposing to depression in the offspring. Passive gene–environment correlation can easily be mistaken for a causal effect. For example, it has long been thought that maternal smoking during pregnancy played a causal role in attention-deficit/hyperactivity disorder (ADHD) in children. However, the same genetic variants that influence mother smoking also contribute to the causation of ADHD (Thapar et al., 2009). This intricate relationship was discovered using the ingenious assisted conception design that follows children who are either genetically related or genetically unrelated to their birth mother. This is in agreement with the finding that when a mother smoked during one pregnancy and not during another pregnancy, both siblings were at similarly increased risk of ADHD (Skoglund, Chen, D'Onofrio, Lichtenstein, & Larsson, 2014). Together these studies have demonstrated that smoking in pregnancy is associated with, but does not cause, ADHD. Smoking in pregnancy is also associated with low birth weight and in this case an assisted conception study suggests that the effects of smoking are causal, probably reflecting direct deleterious influence on the developing fetus. Thus, the same environmental risk factor can be noncausally correlated with one outcome and causally correlated with another outcome.

A second reason for rGE is because genetic variants may influence behaviors that elicit specific responses from one's environment. This relationship is referred to as *evocative (or reactive) gene–environment correlation*. A typical example is that children who carry genes for antisocial behavior may provoke parents to adopt a harsher approach to parenting. Hence, the association between harsh parenting and antisocial personality may not be entirely causal (Marceau et al., 2013). The ability of genes to evoke behaviors by others extends to peers. Children with a genetic disposition to an outgoing temperament evoked more prosocial behaviors from their 5-year-old peers (DiLalla, Bersted, & John, 2015). A sad example of evocative gene–environment correlation is that lower cognitive ability, strongly influenced by genetic factors, precedes and predicts violent victimization throughout childhood: Children who are less gifted are more likely to become victims of abusers and bullies (Danese et al., 2017). Evocative gene–environment correlations have been seen with specific variants in candidate genes. For example, a variant of the oxytocin receptor gene *OXTR* may help a child elicit more positive emotion and involvement from a caregiver (Kryski, Smith, Sheikh, Singh, & Hayden, 2014). Knowledge of these evocative gene–environment correlations puts into perspective the ubiquitous correlations between interpersonal victimization and psychopathology and suggests that part of what appears to be an environmental effect may in fact be due to one's genetic makeup.

A third reason why some individuals experience more adversity than others is because genetic factors may influence the likelihood of selecting specific environments. We refer to this type of gene–environment relationship as active (or selective) gene–environment correlation. The role of active rGE increases with age, as individuals have progressively more autonomy and choice about the environments in which they live. Its effects are seen in peer groups where individuals choose to spend time with others who are like them. The type of peer group is strongly associated with antisocial and addictive behaviors, including delinquency, alcohol use, and smoking. Twin studies found that peer group related to differences in alcohol use and smoking behaviors between dizygotic

but not monozygotic twins, thus demonstrating that the association between a deviant peer group and substance use behavior is genetic in nature (Wills & Carey, 2013). Knowledge of such active gene–environment correlations allows us to examine complex causal mechanisms that may involve distinct genetic factors in peer group selection and in addictive behavior alongside peer influences on behavior. For example, it appears that smoking initiation is strongly influenced by peer group, but the persistence of smoking is under stronger genetic effect (Wills & Carey, 2013).

In addition to true passive, evocative, and active gene–environment correlations, apparent correlations may occur as artifacts of research methods that rely on self-reported measures of the environment. Specifically, genetic factors may influence the tendency to under- or overreport certain kinds of environmental experiences. For example, individuals with a genetic disposition to anxiety may have attention bias toward threat and as a consequence will remember and report more threatening experiences. In this case, the correlation between genes and environment does not exist in reality because the genetic effect has influence on the *reporting* of rather than the exposure to adverse environment. For example, we have seen definite genetic associations with the experience of independent life events that are extremely unlikely to be either provoked or influenced by the individual (Power et al., 2013). The potential for such *spurious gene–environment correlations* should be considered when interpreting results that depend on self-report in measuring environment. Objective measures of environment are needed to separate real and spurious gene–environment interactions.

Strong correlations between genetic polymorphisms and environmental exposures can be used to test the causal role of environmental factors. *Mendelian randomization* (MR) is a specific application of gene–environment correlation to the study of causal effects of environment. Where a genetic variant exists that is strongly associated with increased likelihood of exposure to a given environmental factor, the association between that variant and an outcome is an indirect test of the causal effect of the environmental factor (Davey Smith & Hemani, 2014). "Randomization" refers to the fact that transmission of specific genetic variants occurs by chance and therefore MR permits stronger causal claims than simple association between exposure and outcome in a population. Causal inference with MR requires three assumptions to be met: (1) a genetic polymorphism is reliably associated with the exposure to an environmental factor, (2) the genetic polymorphism is not associated with confounding factors that are associated with both the environment and the outcome of interest, and (3) the genetic polymorphism is associated with the outcome only through the exposure to the environmental factor. In general, the assumptions have been approximately met for several examples of environmental toxins, and MR studies have helped to confirm or clarify the causal roles of cigarette smoking in lung cancer and mortality (Hallden et al., 2016) and cannabis in schizophrenia (Gage et al., 2017). These studies were possible because of strong associations between specific genes (e.g., muscarinergic/nicotine receptors) and environmental toxins exposure (e.g., cigarette smoking). Comparably strong genetic correlations have not been found for social adversity, which limits the application of MR for the study of stress and psychopathology.

Although the aforementioned MR studies showcase the use of rGE as a powerful research tool, the most important message from rGE research is that association does not necessarily equal causation. The noncausal associations between environmental factors and illness should remind us to always probe an apparently strong association through experimental research before declaring causality.

Genetic Sensitivity to Environment: Gene–Environment Interactions

Individuals vary greatly in their responses to environment. Among individuals who are exposed to the same type of adversity, we typically see a broad range of outcomes, including different types of psychopathology as well as health and resilience. This universal observation led researchers to ask what makes one individual so different from others in his or her sensitivity to the impact of adversity. First, this question was answered in general terms using the methods of quantitative genetics. A large twin study has shown that heritable factors not just increase the likelihood of depression overall, but also amplify the depressogenic effect of stressful life events. Women who were monozygotic twins of someone with major depressive disorder were more than twice as likely to develop a major depressive episode following a severe stressful life event than women whose monozygotic twin was unaffected. These relationships were much weaker among a dizygotic set of twins, suggesting that heritable factors play a role in sensitivity to environment. This set of results was interpreted as suggesting the presence of a gene–environment interaction (Kendler et al., 1995).

The essence of a *gene–environment interaction* is that a combination of genetic and environmental factors has unique effects on individuals that differ from a simple sum of the separate effects of genes and of environment. The exact definition of this concept depends on context. Biologically, a gene–environment interaction is defined as one or more genetic factor and one or more environmental factors being part of the same causal mechanism that leads to an outcome in the same individual. This biological concept is most directly relevant to the understanding of etiology and informing prevention of illness, but it can rarely be directly tested in humans. Instead, the likelihood of a gene–environment interaction is indirectly inferred from statistical models. Statistically, a gene–environment interaction is typically tested in a regression model as a contribution of an interaction term to the prediction of outcome over and above the direct (main) effects of the genetic and the environmental factors. The interaction term is constructed as the product of the genetic and environmental variables. Although the concept of "interaction" is established in statistics, it is important to keep in mind that this statistical construct is not equivalent to a biological interaction (Rothman & Greenland, 2005; Rothman, Greenland, & Walker, 1980). Depending on the size and selection of the sample and the accuracy and scale of measurement of the genetic and environmental factors, the presence or absence of statistical interaction may or may not correspond to the presence or absence of biological gene–environment interaction.

The distinction between biological and statistical interaction may be best illustrated by an example that involves nutrition component as the environmental factor. Phenylketonuria (PKU) is an autosomal recessive genetic disorder that can lead to severe intellectual disability and epilepsy. These serious consequences occur when a genetic factor (two copies of phenylalanine hydroxylase gene with loss of function mutations) is combined with an environmental factor (phenylalanine in the diet). Because both the genetic factor and the environmental factor are necessary to cause the outcome, PKU is an example of a gene–environment interaction. Because phenylalanine is a universal food ingredient, making up approximately 5% of proteins in food, everyone in a general population is exposed and therefore no statistical interaction can be seen. In general, we will only be able to detect a statistical interaction if both the genetic and the environmental factors vary substantially in the population under study. PKU was first discovered in 1934 by Asbjörn Fölling, a Norwegian physician, through chemical analysis of urine of affected individuals, and its genetic nature was inferred from its aggregation in families (Centerwall & Centerwall, 2000). Twenty years later it was discovered that the condition can be prevented. It is thanks to the fact that PKU occurs through a gene–environment interaction that a modification of the environmental factor (a diet low in phenylalanine) completely prevents the serious outcomes in individuals who test positive for the genetic disposition (through the Guthrie test from a neonatal heel prick). Thus, in addition to being an example of mismatch between biological and statistical interactions, PKU illustrates the potential of gene–environment interactions in prevention.

Another problematic feature of using statistical interactions to infer causal mechanisms is that the detection of statistical interactions may depend on the scale of measurement and the specifications of a statistical model. This feature of statistical interaction can be demonstrated on the twin study of vulnerability to the development of depression following stressful life events, mentioned in the introductory paragraph of this section (Kendler et al., 1995). The key findings of this study were as follows: In the absence of stressful life events, the probability of depression onset in women at low and high genetic risk was 0.5% and 1.1%, respectively. In a month following a stressful life, the risk of depression onset increased to 6.2% in women at low genetic risk and to 14.6% in women at high genetic risk. Whether this pattern of data suggests an interaction or not depends on whether we quantify the probability of depression in terms of a sum of cases caused by genetic and environmental factors (linear scale, additive model) or as a product of risk ratios (logarithmic scale, multiplicative model). Under an *additive model*, we take the baseline risk of depression, 0.5%, and add the 0.6% (1.1%–0.5%) increase with genetic vulnerability alone and the 5.7% increase (6.2%–0.5%) with a stressful life event to estimate that in the absence of interaction the combination of genetic vulnerability and a stressful life event should lead to a risk of depression of 6.8%. Since the observed 14.6% rate of depression is substantially higher, Kendler and colleagues concluded that the data indicate a gene–environment interaction. Under a *multiplicative model*, one would calculate that the presence of genetic vulnerability increases the risk of depression 2.2-fold (1.1%/0.5%), and stressful life events increase the risk 12.4-fold (6.2%/0.5%); therefore, in the absence of interaction, the combination of genetic vulnerability and stressful life

events should lead to a risk of depression of 13.64% (0.5% × 2.2 × 12.4). The similarity of this expected rate to the observed rate of 14.6% would suggest absence of interaction between genetic liability to depression and stressful life events under a multiplicative model of depression risk. Had the researchers used logistic regression, as is commonly done for categorical outcomes such as the diagnosis of depression, they would have found no interaction. Such discrepancies will happen in most cases where both the genetic and the environmental factors have a direct effect on depression (the interested reader is invited to recalculate the results in a scenario where genetic vulnerability on its own does not increase the risk of depression). The fact that additive and multiplicative models can lead to very different conclusions highlights the importance of considering our models carefully before testing. Epidemiologists Rothman and Greenland have carried out a theoretical analysis of interactions and have concluded that departures from the additive model are more likely to correspond to biological interactions and also better quantify the value of interactions for public health than departures from multiplicative model (Rothman & Greenland, 2005; Rothman, Greenland, & Walker, 1980). Therefore, for most purposes, the additive model is the preferred framework for testing gene–environment interactions, confirming the interpretation by Kendler and colleagues (Kendler et al., 1995).

Although Kendler and colleagues used family history to quantify the genetic propensity to depression, it is now possible to measure specific molecular genetic variants that may sensitize their carriers to the effects of environmental factors. Gene–environment interactions with specific molecular genetic variants may be more directly applicable to prevention and treatment because such variants can be easily measured with high accuracy and they may give clues to specific biological mechanisms underlying the observed effects. The first gene–environment interaction with a specific molecular genetic variant was reported in 2002. Caspi and colleagues selected the *MAOA* (monoamine oxidase A) gene, which encodes an enzyme that inactivates norepinephrine, dopamine, and serotonin in the brain, as relevant to the development of antisocial behaviors, because individuals with a rare dysfunctional variant of this gene displayed an extraordinary propensity to violence. They hypothesized that individuals who carry a much more common variant that slightly decreases the functionality of this gene may be prone to develop antisocial behaviors if they are also exposed to maltreatment in childhood, a known environmental risk factor for antisocial behavior (Caspi et al., 2002). Since the *MAOA* gene is located on the X chromosome, biological males only carry a single copy of the gene, which simplifies the testing of the genetic effect in men. Men also display antisocial behaviors much more frequently than women. Therefore, Caspi et al. decided to test their hypothesis in male participants of a population cohort with highly complete long-term follow-up data on childhood maltreatment and antisocial behavior. They found that men who carried the less functional *MAOA* variant were more likely to develop antisocial behaviors after being exposed to maltreatment in their childhood compared to carriers of the *MAOA* variant associated with higher gene expression (Caspi et al., 2002). In other words, it appeared that the intact *MAOA* gene capable of high expression of the enzyme protected its carriers from developing antisocial behavior after being exposed to maltreatment. The remarkable sensitizing and protective effects of *MAOA* in moderating the effects of childhood maltreatment on antisocial and violent behaviors were replicated across a number of studies and were confirmed in meta-analyses (Byrd & Manuck, 2014; Taylor & Kim-Cohen, 2007). Because the polymorphism in MAOA was selected based on prior biological knowledge, we refer to this as a candidate gene–environment interaction.

Other candidate gene–environment interactions have had less straightforward replication records. In 2003, Caspi and colleagues reported a second gene–environment interaction involving a length polymorphism in the promotor region of the gene encoding serotonin transporter (this polymorphism is often abbreviated as 5-HTTLPR, standing for 5-hydroxy-tryptamine transporter linked polymorphic region) and interpersonal adversity in the development of major depressive disorder (Caspi et al., 2003). The length polymorphism in the promotor region of the serotonin transporter gene is often abbreviated as 5-HTTLPR, standing for 5-hydroxy-tryptamine transporter linked polymorphic region. 5-HTTLPR has two common variants that differ in the number of repeats of a common 20– to 23–base pair sequence: a long (l) variant with 16 repeats is more active in terms of more readily increasing the transcription of the serotonin transporter in response to cellular signals than the short (s) variant with 14 repeats. Because the serotonin transporter gene is located on chromosome 17, an autosome, each individual carries two alleles and their combination results into three possible genotypes: long allele homozygotes

(ll), heterozygotes (ls), and shared allele homozygotes (ss). The original report suggested that the less active short alleles of 5-HTTLPR sensitize their carriers to the depressogenic effects of either childhood maltreatment or stressful life events, with ss homozygotes being the most sensitive (Caspi et al., 2003). A large number of both replication and nonreplications have been reported and the issue whether this is a real gene–environment interaction continues to be debated to date (Bleys, Luyten, Soenens, & Claes, 2018; Caspi et al., 2010; Culverhouse et al., 2018; Karg, Burmeister, Shedden, & Sen, 2011; Sharpley, Palanisamy, Glyde, Dillingham, & Agnew, 2014). Some authors favor the explanation that the original finding was a false positive and published replication may reflect a bias toward publishing positive findings more readily than negative findings (de Vries, Roest, Franzen, Munafo, & Bastiaansen, 2016). Another feasible explanation is that the gene–environment interaction involving the 5-HTTLPR may specifically involve sensitivity to developing persistent depression following exposure to maltreatment in childhood (Brown & Harris, 2008). The specific hypothesis that increasing the number of s allele increases the likelihood of persistent depression among individuals exposed to childhood maltreatment has been supported and replicated in three independent samples, including a reanalysis of the Dunedin cohort with data from additional follow-ups (Brown et al., 2013; Uher et al., 2011). Other candidate gene polymorphisms, including a common variant in the brain-derived neurotrophic factor gene (*BDNF*), may be involved in sensitizing individuals to new onsets of depression following stressful life events in adulthood (Brown et al., 2014; Hosang et al., 2014).

Psychiatric genetics has demonstrated a large number of genetic effects with small effect sizes, of which the large majority are in genomic regions that were not expected to be involved based on knowledge of specific genes' functions. Although some polymorphisms in candidate genes may play relatively specific and complementary roles in the development of mental disorders following exposures to adversity, it is likely that most genetic variants involved in gene–environment interactions will be outside genes identified as candidate genes. Therefore, to advance our knowledge of gene–environment interactions, it will be necessary to interrogate the entire human genome. Several genome-wide scans for gene–environment interactions, referred to as genome-wide interaction studies (GWISs), have been reported, but their results have been either negative or unreplicated (Dunn et al., 2016; Ikeda et al., 2016;

Otowa et al., 2016; Peterson et al., 2018). The likely reason for the failure of the first wave of GWIS to find replicable gene–environment interactions is their limited statistical power. Our ability to find the multitude of gene–environment interactions is limited by the modest size of human samples with high-quality data on environmental exposure relative to the number of tests that need to be carried out and controlled for (Caspi, Hariri, Holmes, Uher, & Moffitt, 2010). The size of human cohorts with high-quality data on environmental exposures is two orders of magnitude smaller than the size of the case-control samples used in genome-wide association studies (Uher, 2014). In addition, the statistical tests of interactions have less power than tests of direct association, so even larger samples are needed to detect gene–environment interactions (Caspi et al., 2010). These are the reasons why our knowledge of gene–environment interactions is still limited to few candidate genes.

The successful use of polygenic risk scores for quantifying the genetic risk for disorders across many genetic variants has raised hopes that a similar polygenic approach can be applied in the study of gene–environment interactions. There have been several attempts to test interactions between a polygenic risk score for a disorder and environmental adversity, but their results have been inconsistent (Mullins et al., 2016; Peyrot et al., 2014, 2017). This should not be surprising, considering that these studies rely on the untested assumption that the genetic variants that make one sensitive to an environmental exposure are the same as those that directly increase the risk of a disorder. Yet current knowledge and theoretical considerations suggest that genetic variants responsible for sensitivity to environment are likely to be distinct from those that directly increase the risk of mental illness (Uher, 2009). Obtaining a polygenic risk score of environmental sensitivity would require a very large sample of individuals with data on multiple environmental exposures. In the absence of such sample, Keers and colleagues have used the discordant monozygotic twin method to quantify the polygenic contribution to environmental sensitivity indirectly. Because the two members of a monozygotic twin pair are genetically identical, any differences between them can be attributed to environment. The more sensitive to environment a pair of monozygotic twins are, the more will they differ on measures of psychopathology. Keers and colleagues derived a polygenic environmental sensitivity score from a genome-wide association study of within monozygotic twin pair differences in psychopathology

and demonstrated that it predicts response to both negative and positive environmental exposures in new samples (Keers et al., 2016). Specifically, polygenic environmental sensitivity interacted with quality of parenting to predict emotional symptoms in 12-year-olds, and it interacted with intensity of cognitive-behavioral therapy to predict better treatment response in children with anxiety (Keers et al., 2016). These results provide an early indication that a polygenic environmental sensitivity, distinct from a genetic disposition to illness, shapes the impact of both positive and negative aspects of environment, at least in childhood. In the future, this approach may be refined to specifically index sensitivity to various aspects of environment at different stages of individual development.

Although present knowledge converges to suggest that gene–environment interactions are an important part of causation of most mental disorders, the majority of the genetic variants involved in gene–environment interactions remain unknown. The field is waiting for high-quality GWISs to uncover more definite causal mechanisms.

How Environment Impacts on the Genome: Epigenetics

Early life experiences exert a lasting influence on mental health throughout the life course. Maltreatment in the first decade of life increases the risk for most types of mental illness in adulthood (Scott et al., 2012), and its effects persist into old age (Nanni, Uher, & Danese, 2012). The decades-lasting effects of environmental exposures raise the question of how early experiences get engraved in the circuitry of the developing brain to influence long-term physical and mental health. Epigenetics has the potential to provide an answer to this question. The term *epigenetics* refers to modifications to the genetic material that influence the way genes function without changing the DNA sequence. These modifications include the alteration of the DNA supporting histone proteins, as well as modification of the DNA itself through the addition of small chemical attachments to the DNA bases. The best understood epigenetic modification is DNA methylation, which involves addition of a methyl group, a single carbon residue, to a cytosine nucleotide to form a 5-methylcytosine. DNA methylation in gene regulatory sequences, including the promoter region, usually results in gene silencing and reduced gene expression. However, the effects of DNA methylation on gene function depends on the period in development during which the methylation occurs. DNA methylation is a regulatory mechanism which ensures that genes are only expressed when needed.

Studies of experimental animals suggest that DNA methylation in specific genes mediates the long-term effects of adverse early experiences on behavior. For example, low maternal nurturing during the first week of life of rat pups is associated with increased methylation of a neuron-specific promoter of the glucocorticoid receptor gene (Weaver et al., 2004). The expression of this gene is then reduced, the number of glucocorticoid receptors in the brain is decreased, and the animals show a stronger hormonal response to stress throughout their life (Zhang, Labonte, Wen, Turecki, & Meaney, 2013). The effects of maternal care on cortisol response and behavior can be eliminated by pharmacological treatment that erases epigenetic marks, proving that methylation of the glucocorticoid receptor gene promoter is a necessary link in the process leading to the long-term physiological and behavioral consequences of poor maternal care (Weaver et al., 2004; Zhang et al., 2013). The level of care experienced in infancy can permanently shape the stress responses in the brain and affect behaviors throughout the life course.

Although the findings in experimental animals provide a clear picture of how epigenetic modifications encode the long-term memory trace of early life environmental exposures, the potential of this knowledge to improve human health depends on how well these mechanisms generalize to humans. Targeted examination of brain tissue from suicide victims found that the human equivalent of the glucocorticoid receptor gene promoter is also more methylated in the brains of individuals who had experienced maltreatment during childhood (McGowan et al., 2009). This finding suggested that DNA methylation mediated the effects of early environment in rodents and humans in similar ways. But epigenetic measurement of DNA methylation in human brain is not easily accessible, and the results necessarily depend on small and selected samples. The practical applications of epigenetics could be much broader if the relevant epigenetic modification could be measured in an accessible tissue, such as blood or saliva. Some studies suggested the existence of epigenetic trace, in the form of DNA methylation, in the human blood or saliva (Tyrka et al., 2015, 2016). However, the largest and best controlled examination of DNA methylation in human blood showed no relationship between DNA methylation and the experience of early life adversity (Marzi et al., 2018). In fact, it has been shown that some initial promising results may have been confounded

by factors such as cigarette smoking, which is associated with exposure to adverse environment and is also a powerful determinant of DNA methylation (Marzi et al., 2018). Therefore, in the absence of routinely available brain samples, the application of epigenetics to human mental health remains an unrealized potential.

Sex and Gender Issues

In research involving molecular genetic information, biological sex is typically used as an integral part of analysis. Agreement between reported and genotypic sex is often used as one of the initial steps in quality control that helps determine errors in matching genotypes with clinical data. It is therefore important to distinguish between biological sex and self-identified gender, so that individuals with diverse gender identities can be represented in gene–environment research and are not mistakenly excluded because of apparent discrepancy between genetic and phenotypic sex. Yet, to date, it has been rare for gene–environmental studies to separately account for sex and gender. Going forward, it will be important to consistently use "sex" for biological sex determined by the presence of a Y chromosome, and "gender" for self-identified gender identity that is inclusive of nonbinary gender identity.

Most investigations of genetic and epigenetic embedding of environmental adversity have been carried out in mixed-sex samples, with the assumption that the mechanisms are similar in males and females. This assumption may be reasonable in many cases, but it often remains untested. There are notable sex and gender differences in the likelihood of exposure to many environmental factors and in the prevalence of many types of psychopathology. Females are more likely to be exposed to sexual abuse, and males are more often exposed to physical maltreatment in childhood (Moody, Cannings-John, Hood, Kemp, & Robling, 2018). Anxiety and depression are more common in females; ADHD, autism spectrum disorders, and substance use are more common in males. Consequently, spuriously "specific" associations between types of adversity and diagnoses may emerge, if sex is not taken into account in the analyses.

When examining how psychopathology is passed on from parents to offspring, researchers have observed patterns of differential transmission to daughters and sons depending on whether a genetic risk variant originates from the biological mother or the biological father. When a father is affected with severe mental illness, the risk of psychotic symptoms and disorders is elevated in his daughters more than in his sons; when a mother is affected with severe mental illness, the risk is higher in her sons than in her daughters (Aylott et al., 2018; Goldstein et al., 2011). These sex-specific parent-of-origin effects in transmission of psychopathology may suggest involvement of genetic variants located on the X chromosome. Fathers pass the X chromosome to their daughters, but not sons. Male offspring obtain their only X chromosome from their mother and not from their father.

Examination of genetic variants located on the sex chromosomes is complicated by the fact that males and females carry a different number of alleles. To avoid the statistical challenges, many genome-wide association studies have excluded the sex chromosomes from analyses. The Y chromosome is small and contains few genes. However, the X chromosome is one of the largest chromosomes and may contain disproportionately large numbers of genes that are relevant for brain development and nervous function. Indirect evidence from sex-specific parent-of-origin effects also suggests the involvement of X chromosome–linked variants in the etiology of mental illness. Therefore, it will be important to include the X chromosome in future genetic and gene–environment studies.

One example of a gene relevant to brain function and located on the X chromosome is the monoamine oxidase A gene (*MAOA*). MAOA encodes an enzyme that metabolizes neurotransmitters norepinephrine, serotonin, and dopamine. A common variable number tandem repeat in the promotor of MAOA affects the rate of expression of this enzyme. Individuals who carry the less active MAOA variant are more sensitive to the impact of childhood maltreatment and more likely to develop antisocial behavior after being exposed to maltreatment (Caspi et al., 2002). This gene–environment interaction was initially identified in males. The investigators focused on males because they carry only a single copy of the MAOA gene and because antisocial behavior is more common in males than in females. However, when they carried out a separate analysis of female participants within the same birth cohort, they found similar effects, suggestive on a gene–environment interaction existing in both sexes. This gene–environment interaction has been consistently replicated across multiple samples of males (Byrd & Manuck, 2014). Replications in females have been fewer and their results have been less consistent. At the time of writing, we are not aware of any gene–environment interaction that would be entirely sex-specific.

Gene–Environment Mechanisms in the Development of Mental Health and Illness

The exponential increase in knowledge over the last two decades has ruled out simple causal mechanisms for mental illness. What we know today strongly suggests complex multifactorial causation with multiple genetic and multiple environmental factors being involved in most cases of mental illness. The majority of genetic and environmental risk factors are shared by multiple types of mental illness and are not specific to a particular diagnosis. The effects of environmental factors vary between individuals and depend both on genetic disposition and on prior exposures to other environmental factors, resulting in gene–environment and environment–environment interactions (Uher & Zwicker, 2017). Environmental exposures have the potential to modify the functionality of genome through epigenetic modifications, such as DNA methylation, that may mediate interactions between environmental exposures separated by long periods of time.

The Gaps: What We Do Not Know Yet

Although multifactorial gene–environment interactions may be a generic mechanism underlying most cases of mental illness, the vast majority of these mechanisms remain to be identified. The presently known rGE and gene–environment interactions are probably only a few simplified examples of the multitude of causal mechanisms contributing to mental health and illness. Major gaps in knowledge include the identification of genetic variants that sensitize their carriers to a variety of environmental factors, examining effects specific to a developmental stage of the individual, and examining mechanisms involving more than two causal factors. Over the last decade, the knowledge of disease risk variants exploded with the advent of large genome-wide studies and discoveries of hundreds of causal variants for schizophrenia, bipolar disorder, and major depressive disorder (Psychiatric Genetics Consortium, 2014; Wray et al., 2018). Contrasting with the vast samples used in case-control genetic association analyses, there is a dearth of genetic samples with adequate information on environmental exposures and transdiagnostic psychopathology over the life course (Uher & Zwicker, 2017). The genetic variation that underlies individual differences in sensitivity to environment is presently better indexed collectively through polygenic sensitivity scores or stratified analyses. Yet discovery and dissection of the specific molecular genetic variants underlying sensitivity to environment is a key step on the way to applications of causal mechanisms in personalized prevention and treatment. Therefore, building large studies with high-quality repeated assessments of environment and psychopathology is a core direction in bringing in new knowledge on the causation of mental illness.

Applications of Gene–Environment Research: Present and Future

It is common knowledge that mental illness runs in families and can be inherited. Many people, including those living with mental illness, develop the understanding that because mental illness is genetic, we cannot do anything about the risk. This fatalistic interpretation may be harmful as it undermines motivation for health-enhancing behavior and active coping. Yet everything we know suggests that the impact of genes depends on the environment, including modifiable lifestyle factors. Genetic counselors have developed way of communicating the nuanced message of nondeterministic multifactorial contributions to mental health and illness in a way that increases the individual's sense of agency and encourages proactive health-enhancing behaviors (Austin, Semaka, & Hadjipavlou, 2014). These interventions based on the broad concept of multifactorial gene–environment causation are making positive difference at the present time. As the discovery of specific mechanisms and molecular variants progresses, it is possible to develop and test personalized interventions based on genetic testing. For example, communication personal genetic test of variants involved in genetic sensitivity to cannabis in the causation of psychosis may have a place in the prevention of mental illness through helping some vulnerable individuals delay or avoid regular use of cannabis (Zwicker, Denovan-Wright, & Uher, 2018). Personalized choice of medication or psychotherapy based on combined information on genome and environmental exposure history may be a step further away and will require extensive validation of multivariate prediction algorithms (Uher, 2008). Given the present state of knowledge, genetic therapy involving modification of an individual's genetic material may be a distant option, but personalized treatment selection and prevention indication may be realistic within the next decade, and the applications of gene–environment causation as an explanatory framework in genetic counseling is an immediate opportunity.

References

Austin, J., Semaka, A., & Hadjipavlou, G. (2014). Conceptualizing genetic counseling as psychotherapy in the era of genomic medicine. *Journal of Genetic Counseling, 23*(6), 903–909.

Aylott, A., Zwicker, A., MacKenzie, L. E., Cumby, J., Propper, L., Abidi, S.,…Uher, R. (2018). Like father like daughter: Sex-specific parent-of-origin effects in the transmission of liability for psychotic symptoms to offspring. *Journal of Developmental Origins of Health and Disease, xx*, 1–8.

Bleys, D., Luyten, P., Soenens, B., & Claes, S. (2018). Gene-environment interactions between stress and 5-HTTLPR in depression: A meta-analytic update. *Journal of Affective Disorders, 226*, 339–345.

Brown, G. W., Ban, M., Craig, T. K., Harris, T. O., Herbert, J., & Uher, R. (2013). Serotonin transporter length polymorphism, childhood maltreatment, and chronic depression: A specific gene-environment interaction. *Depression & Anxiety, 30*(1), 5–13.

Brown, G. W., Craig, T. K., Harris, T. O., Herbert, J., Hodgson, K., Tansey, K. E., & Uher, R. (2014). Functional polymorphism in the brain-derived neurotrophic factor gene interacts with stressful life events but not childhood maltreatment in the etiology of depression. *Depression & Anxiety, 31*(4), 326–334.

Brown, G. W., & Harris, T. O. (2008). Depression and the serotonin transporter 5-HTTLPR polymorphism: A review and a hypothesis concerning gene-environment interaction. *Journal of Affective Disorders, 111*(1), 1–12.

Byrd, A. L., & Manuck, S. B. (2014). MAOA, childhood maltreatment, and antisocial behavior: Meta-analysis of a gene-environment interaction. *Biological Psychiatry, 75*(1), 9–17.

Caspi, A., Hariri, A. R., Holmes, A., Uher, R., & Moffitt, T. E. (2010). Genetic sensitivity to the environment: The case of the serotonin transporter gene and its implications for studying complex diseases and traits. *American Journal of Psychiatry, 167*(5), 509–527.

Caspi, A., McClay, J., Moffitt, T. E., Mill, J., Martin, J., Craig, I. W., Taylor, A., & Poulton, R. (2002). Role of genotype in the cycle of violence in maltreated children. *Science, 297*(5582), 851–854.

Caspi, A., Sugden, K., Moffitt, T. E., Taylor, A., Craig, I. W., Harrington, H.,…Poulton, R. (2003). Influence of life stress on depression: Moderation by a polymorphism in the 5-HTT gene. *Science, 301*(5631), 386–389.

Centerwall, S. A., & Centerwall, W. R. (2000). The discovery of phenylketonuria: The story of a young couple, two retarded children, and a scientist. *Pediatrics, 105*(1, Pt 1), 89–103.

Culverhouse, R. C., Saccone, N. L., Horton, A. C., Ma, Y., Anstey, K. J., Banaschewski, T.,…Bierut, L. J. (2018). Collaborative meta-analysis finds no evidence of a strong interaction between stress and 5-HTTLPR genotype contributing to the development of depression. *Molecular Psychiatry, 23*(1), 133–142.

Danese, A., Moffitt, T. E., Arseneault, L., Bleiberg, B. A., Dinardo, P. B., Gandelman, S. B.,…Caspi, A. (2017). The origins of cognitive deficits in victimized children: Implications for neuroscientists and clinicians. *American Journal of Psychiatry, 174*(4), 349–361.

Davey Smith, G., & Hemani, G. (2014). Mendelian randomization: Genetic anchors for causal inference in epidemiological studies. *Human Molecular Genetics, 23*(1), R89–R98.

de Vries, Y. A., Roest, A. M., Franzen, M., Munafo, M. R., & Bastiaansen, J. A. (2016). Citation bias and selective focus on positive findings in the literature on the serotonin transporter gene (5-HTTLPR), life stress and depression. *Psychological Medicine, 46*(14), 2971–2979.

DiLalla, L. F., Bersted, K., & John, S. G. (2015). Evidence of reactive gene-environment correlation in preschoolers' prosocial play with unfamiliar peers. *Developmental Psychology, 51*(10), 1464–1475.

Dunn, E. C., Wiste, A., Radmanesh, F., Almli, L. M., Gogarten, S. M., Sofer, T.,...Smoller, J. W. (2016). Genome-wide association study (GWAS) and genome-wide by environment interaction study (GWEIS) of depressive symptoms in African American and Hispanic/Latina women. *Depression & Anxiety, 33*(4), 265–280.

Gage, S. H., Jones, H. J., Burgess, S., Bowden, J., Davey, S. G., Zammit, S., & Munafo, M. R. (2017). Assessing causality in associations between cannabis use and schizophrenia risk: A two-sample Mendelian randomization study. *Psychological Medicine, 47*(5), 971–980.

Goldstein, J. M., Cherkerzian, S., Seidman, L. J., Petryshen, T. L., Fitzmaurice, G., Tsuang, M. T., & Buka, S. L. (2011). Sex-specific rates of transmission of psychosis in the New England high-risk family study. *Schizophrenia Research, 128*(1–3), 150–155.

Hallden, S., Sjogren, M., Hedblad, B., Engstrom, G., Hamrefors, V., Manjer, J., & Melander, O. (2016). Gene variance in the nicotinic receptor cluster (CHRNA5-CHRNA3-CHRNB4) predicts death from cardiopulmonary disease and cancer in smokers. *Journal of Internal Medicine, 279*(4), 388–398.

Hosang, G. M., Shiles, C., Tansey, K. E., McGuffin, P., & Uher, R. (2014). Interaction between stress and the BDNF Val66Met polymorphism in depression: A systematic review and meta-analysis. *BMC Medicine, 12*, 7.

Ikeda, M., Shimasaki, A., Takahashi, A., Kondo, K., Saito, T., Kawase, K.,...Iwata, N. (2016). Genome-wide environment interaction between depressive state and stressful life events. *Journal of Clinical Psychiatry, 77*(1), e29–e30.

Karg, K., Burmeister, M., Shedden, K., & Sen, S. (2011). The serotonin transporter promoter variant (5-HTTLPR), stress, and depression meta-analysis revisited: Evidence of genetic moderation. *Archives of General Psychiatry, 68*(5), 444–454.

Keers, R., Coleman, J. R., Lester, K. J., Roberts, S., Breen, G., Thastum, M.,...Eley, T. C. (2016). A genome-wide test of the differential susceptibility hypothesis reveals a genetic predictor of differential response to psychological treatments for child anxiety disorders. *Psychotherapy and Psychosomatics, 85*(3), 146–158.

Kendler, K. S., Kessler, R. C., Walters, E. E., MacLean, C., Neale, M. C., Heath, A. C., & Eaves, L. J. (1995). Stressful life events, genetic liability, and onset of an episode of major depression in women. *American Journal of Psychiatry, 152*(6), 833–842.

Knafo, A., & Jaffee, S. R. (2013). Gene-environment correlation in developmental psychopathology. Developmental Psychopathology, 25(1), 1–6.

Kryski, K. R., Smith, H. J., Sheikh, H. I., Singh, S. M., & Hayden, E. P. (2014). Evidence for evocative gene–environment correlation between child oxytocin receptor (OXTR) genotype and caregiver behavior. *Personality and Individual Differences, 64*, 107–110.

Marceau, K., Horwitz, B. N., Narusyte, J., Ganiban, J. M., Spotts, E. L., Reiss, D., & Neiderhiser, J. M. (2013). Gene-environment correlation underlying the association between parental negativity and adolescent externalizing problems. *Child Development, 84*(6), 2031–2046.

Martin, A. R., Daly, M. J., Robinson, E. B., Hyman, S. E., & Neale, B. M. (2019). Predicting polygenic risk of psychiatric disorders. *Biological Psychiatry*.

Marzi, S. J., Sugden, K., Arseneault, L., Belsky, D. W., Burrage, J., Corcoran, D. L.,...Caspi, A. (2018). Analysis of DNA methylation in young people: Limited evidence for an association between victimization stress and epigenetic variation in blood. *American Journal of Psychiatry, 175*(6), 517–529.

McGowan, P. O., Sasaki, A., D'Alessio, A. C., Dymov, S., Labonte, B., Szyf, M., Turecki, G., & Meaney, M. J. (2009). Epigenetic regulation of the glucocorticoid receptor in human brain associates with childhood abuse. *Nature Neuroscience, 12*(3), 342–348.

Moody, G., Cannings-John, R., Hood, K., Kemp, A., & Robling, M. (2018). Establishing the international prevalence of self-reported child maltreatment: A systematic review by maltreatment type and gender. *BMC Public Health, 18*(1), 1164.

Mullins, N., Power, R. A., Fisher, H. L., Hanscombe, K. B., Euesden, J., Iniesta, R.,...Lewis, C. M. (2016). Polygenic interactions with environmental adversity in the aetiology of major depressive disorder. *Psychological Medicine, 46*(4), 759–770.

Nanni, V., Uher, R., & Danese, A. (2012). Childhood maltreatment predicts unfavorable course of illness and treatment outcome in depression: A meta-analysis. *American Journal of Psychiatry, 169*(2), 141–151.

Otowa, T., Kawamura, Y., Tsutsumi, A., Kawakami, N., Kan, C., Shimada, T.,...Sasaki, T. (2016). The first pilot genome-wide gene-environment study of depression in the Japanese population. *PLoS One, 11*(8), e0160823.

Peterson, R. E., Cai, N., Dahl, A. W., Bigdeli, T. B., Edwards, A. C., Webb, B. T.,...Kendler, K. S. (2018). Molecular genetic analysis subdivided by adversity exposure suggests etiologic heterogeneity in major depression. *American Journal of Psychiatry, 175*(6), 545–554.

Peyrot, W. J., Milaneschi, Y., Abdellaoui, A., Sullivan, P. F., Hottenga, J. J., Boomsma, D. I., & Penninx, B. W. (2014). Effect of polygenic risk scores on depression in childhood trauma. *British Journal of Psychiatry, 20*(2), 113–119.

Peyrot, W. J., Van der, A. S., Milaneschi, Y., Dolan, C. V., Madden, P. A. F., Sullivan, P. F.,...& Penninx, B. W. J. H. (2017). Does childhood trauma moderate polygenic risk for depression? A meta-analysis of 5765 subjects from the Psychiatric Genomics Consortium. *Biological Psychiatry*.

Power, R. A., Wingenbach, T., Cohen-Woods, S., Uher, R., Ng, M. Y., Butler, A. W.,...McGuffin, P. (2013). Estimating the heritability of reporting stressful life events captured by common genetic variants. *Psychological Medicine, 43*(9), 1965–1971.

Psychiatric Genetics Consortium. (2014). Biological insights from 108 schizophrenia-associated genetic loci. *Nature, 511*(7510), 421–427.

Rothman, K. J., & Greenland, S. (2005). Causation and causal inference in epidemiology. *American Journal of Public Health, 95*(Suppl. 1), S144–S150.

Rothman, K. J., Greenland, S., & Walker, A. M. (1980). Concepts of interaction. *American Journal of Epidemiology, 112*(4), 467–470.

Rutter, M. (2016). Why is the topic of the biological embedding of experiences important for translation? *Developmental Psychopathology, 28*(4, pt2), 1245–1258.

Scott, K. M., McLaughlin, K. A., Smith, D. A., & Ellis, P. M. (2012). Childhood maltreatment and DSM-IV adult mental disorders: Comparison of prospective and retrospective findings. *British Journal of Psychiatry, 200*(6), 469–475.

Sharpley, C. F., Palanisamy, S. K., Glyde, N. S., Dillingham, P. W., & Agnew, L. L. (2014). An update on the interaction between the serotonin transporter promoter variant (5-HTTLPR), stress and depression, plus an exploration of non-confirming findings. *Behavioral Brain Research, 273*, 9–105.

Skoglund, C., Chen, Q., D'Onofrio, B. M., Lichtenstein, P., & Larsson, H. (2014). Familial confounding of the association between maternal smoking during pregnancy and ADHD in offspring. *Journal of Child Psychology and Psychiatry, 55*(1), 61–68.

Taylor, A., & Kim-Cohen, J. (2007). Meta-analysis of gene-environment interactions in developmental psychopathology. *Developmental Psychopathology, 19*(4), 1029–1037.

Thapar, A., Rice, F., Hay, D., Boivin, J., Langley, K., van den, B. M., Rutter, M., & Harold, G. (2009). Prenatal smoking might not cause attention-deficit/hyperactivity disorder: Evidence from a novel design. *Biological Psychiatry, 66*(8), 722–727.

Tyrka, A. R., Parade, S. H., Welch, E. S., Ridout, K. K., Price, L. H., Marsit, C., Philip, N. S., & Carpenter, L. L. (2016). Methylation of the leukocyte glucocorticoid receptor gene promoter in adults: Associations with early adversity and depressive, anxiety and substance-use disorders. *Translational Psychiatry, 6*(7), e848.

Tyrka, A. R., Ridout, K. K., Parade, S. H., Paquette, A., Marsit, C. J., & Seifer, R. (2015). Childhood maltreatment and methylation of FK506 binding protein 5 gene (FKBP5). *Developmental Psychopathology, 27*(4 Pt 2), 1637–1645.

Uher, R. (2008). The implications of gene-environment interactions in depression: Will cause inform cure? *Molecular Psychiatry, 13*(12), 1070–1078.

Uher, R. (2009). The role of genetic variation in the causation of mental illness: An evolution-informed framework. *Molecular Psychiatry, 14*(12), 1072–1082.

Uher, R. (2014). Gene-environment interactions in common mental disorders: An update and strategy for a genome-wide search. *Social Psychiatry* and *Psychiatric Epidemiology, 49*(1), 3–14.

Uher, R., Caspi, A., Houts, R., Sugden, K., Williams, B., Poulton, R., & Moffitt, T. E. (2011). Serotonin transporter gene moderates childhood maltreatment's effects on persistent but not single-episode depression: Replications and implications for resolving inconsistent results. *Journal of Affective Disorders, 135*(1–3), 56–65.

Uher, R., & Zwicker, A. (2017). Etiology in psychiatry: Embracing the reality of poly-gene-environmental causation of mental illness. *World Psychiatry, 16*(2), 121–129.

Weaver, I. C., Cervoni, N., Champagne, F. A., D'Alessio, A. C., Sharma, S., Seckl, J. R., ... Meaney, M. J. (2004). Epigenetic programming by maternal behavior. *Nature Neuroscience, 7*(8), 847–854.

Wills, A. G., & Carey, G. (2013). Adolescent peer choice and cigarette smoking: Evidence of active gene-environment correlation? *Twin Research and Human Genetics, 16*(5), 970–976.

Wray, N. R., Ripke, S., Mattheisen, M., Trzaskowski, M., Byrne, E. M., Abdellaoui, A., ... Sullivan, P. F. (2018). Genome-wide association analyses identify 44 risk variants and refine the genetic architecture of major depression. *Nature Genetics, 50*(5), 668–681.

Yet, I., Tsai, P. C., Castillo-Fernandez, J. E., Carnero-Montoro, E., & Bell, J. T. (2016). Genetic and environmental impacts on DNA methylation levels in twins. *Epigenomics, 8*(1), 105–117.

Zhang, T. Y., Labonte, B., Wen, X. L., Turecki, G., & Meaney, M. J. (2013). Epigenetic mechanisms for the early environmental regulation of hippocampal glucocorticoid receptor gene expression in rodents and humans. *Neuropsychopharmacology, 38*(1), 111–123.

Zwicker, A., Denovan-Wright, E. M., & Uher, R. (2018). Gene-environment interplay in the etiology of psychosis. *Psychological Medicine, 48*(12), 1925–1936.

Developmental Timing of Stress Effects on the Brain

Keira B. Leneman *and* Megan R. Gunnar

Abstract

The physiological stress response integrates endocrine, autonomic, and neural structures and pathways to respond and adapt to an organism's environment. This integration is dynamic throughout development, with certain periods of rapid change for each system. With the introduction of chronic stress, physiological responses that may be adaptive in the immediate context can have long-term consequences for physical and emotional health, influencing systems differently depending upon developmental status at the time of stress exposure. From the nonhuman literature, prenatal, infancy, and adolescence are developmental stages that seem especially sensitive to major stress exposures. Human studies are less conclusive. Although much work has been done on prenatal stress and certain stressors (e.g., deprivation) during infancy and early childhood, more work is needed that addresses the challenges of isolating periods of environmental insults as well as carefully considering how prior developmental and subsequent experiences moderate exposure to major stress conditions at different points in development. Information on the transition from childhood to adolescence is especially sparse. A more comprehensive understanding of these developmental processes will enable a more targeted approach to ameliorating negative consequences of stress with both prevention and intervention.

Keywords: chronic stress, developmental timing, cortisol, stress response, consequences of stress

As reviewed elsewhere in this volume, stress increases the risk of psychopathology. Not only is heightened stress often noted before the first onset of disorder, but individuals who develop psychiatric conditions frequently have a history of stressful experiences, often beginning early in life. Indeed, animal models support the hypothesis that stress during development programs the developing central nervous system (CNS), influencing the subsequent capacity to cope with stressful experiences. Many of these effects can be viewed as adaptive, allowing survival and reproduction, but at a cost of increased risk of pathology. Various mechanisms have been proposed to explain how stress "gets under the skin" to influence lifetime health and disease, but nearly all invoke activity of stress-mediating systems and the brain regions and pathways involved in their regulation. Two systems and their central regulatory pathways have received the most attention: the hypothalamic-pituitary-adrenocortical (HPA) system and central corticotropin-releasing hormone (CRH) system and the sympathetic (SNS) and parasympathetic (PNS) nervous systems and corresponding central autonomic network (Benarroch, 1993; Herman et al., 2016).

Stress-mediating systems are not fully developed at birth, including the ones that we discuss in this chapter. The maturation of these systems likely interacts with stress timing during periods of rapid brain growth and plasticity to influence neurobehavioral development and the risk of later mental health problems. In the human literature, what constitutes a sensitive period for early life stress has not been determined. Early life stress is sometimes defined as prenatal (Entringer, Buss, & Wadhwa, 2015), any time before puberty (Romens, McDonald,

Svaren, & Pollak, 2015), or before 18 years of age (Bernstein, Ahluvalia, Pogge, & Handelsman, 1997). In the animal literature, three periods have received particular attention: prenatal (Cottrell & Seckl, 2009), perinatal (Meaney & Szyf, 2005), and peripubertal (Romeo, 2010).

In this chapter, we will briefly outline what is known about the key stress-mediating systems, with particular attention to the mechanisms through which chronic psychological stress alters their regulation in the brain. We focus on chronic stressors because these are the most likely to influence physiological systems in the long term and because the literature on stress and psychopathology deals with stressors that are of a prolonged or chronic nature, that is, neglect, maltreatment, major natural disasters, and war. Furthermore, the focus on chronic stress falls in line with the concept of stress as a U-shaped or J-shaped curve. The capacity to mount a stress response is necessary for survival, and there is increasing evidence that moderate exposure to stressors is beneficial to functioning (e.g., Lyons & Parker, 2007). It is when stress levels are extremely high, and especially for an extended period of time, that deleterious effects are seen (Boyce & Ellis, 2005; Lyons, Parker, & Schatzberg, 2010; Tronick, 2006).

We will focus our analysis on stressor pathways that involve perception and interpretation of events as threatening to well-being, because these are the likely pathways through which early life stress increases the risk of psychopathology. Numerous other mechanisms are also critical to the biological embedding of early life stress, including epigenetic alterations, oxidative stress, neurotransmitter systems, the microbiome, and the immune system (Heim & Binder, 2012; Meaney & Szyf, 2005). However, covering all these is beyond the scope of this chapter. We describe what is known about the effects of chronic psychological stressors on brain systems associated with threat perception, stress reactivity, and self-regulation, at different points in development, with an eye to what these data can tell us about potentially sensitive periods. Finally, we point to areas that need attention if we are to understand how the timing of major stressful experiences affects the developing brain and the risk for psychopathology.

Anatomy and Physiology in the Response to Chronic Stress

The anatomy and physiology of HPA, SNS, and PNS systems have been described in detail in other chapters in this volume (see Lopez-Duran, Roberts, Foster, and Mayer Chapter 22 and Pruessner, Chapter 23). Here we will summarize key facets of the mature systems, as this context is important for understanding the relevance of these stress-mediating systems. The HPA, SNS, and PNS systems are critical for maintaining homeostatic balance, both under normal conditions and conditions of acute or chronic challenge (Sapolsky, Romero, & Munck, 2000). The concept of allostasis describes how the activation of stress-mediating systems maintains "stability through change," allowing for modification of homeostatic set points in response to changes in the environment (McEwen & Wingfield, 2010). Although critical for survival, the activation of these systems is metabolically costly and, when prolonged, puts growth-promoting processes on hold in order to shift resources to address immediate challenges. If frequently or chronically activated, allostatic processes produce wear-and-tear on the body (allostatic load or overload) that increases the risk of physical and mental health disorders (Danese & McEwen, 2012). The effects of prolonged delays in growth-promoting processes during development can be dramatic, resulting in stunting of physical growth and a general reduction in brain volume (Johnson, Bruce, Tarullo, & Gunnar, 2011).

The Hypothalamic-Pituitary-Adrenocortical Axis: Basic Functioning, Connections to Other Brain Regions, and Effects With Chronic Stress

The HPA axis is one of the two primary stress-mediating systems in mammals. The other is the sympathetic adrenomedullary system (SAM), which is part of the autonomic nervous system (ANS). These systems interact on multiple levels; however, for clarity we will discuss the HPA and ANS systems separately and then describe their interaction. Because models of how early experiences "get under the skin" include the HPA axis as a key mechanism, we begin there.

Activation of the HPA axis begins with the release of corticotropin-releasing hormone (CRH) from the paraventricular nucleus (PVN) of the hypothalamus. CRH then acts to stimulate secretion of adrenocorticotropic hormone (ACTH) from the anterior pituitary, which travels to the cortex of the adrenal glands, interacting with receptors there to cause the synthesis and release of glucocorticoids (cortisol in humans and corticosterone in rodents). CRH-secreting cells in the PVN are under tonic GABAergic inhibition; thus, generally speaking, production of

CRH is a matter of lifting that inhibition. The HPA axis can be activated by homeostatic-threatening changes in the body (e.g., very cold temperatures), even when the person is unconscious; such effects are *somatic stressors*. Signals about the state of the body arrive at the PVN across brainstem pathways, often via parasympathetic afferents to the nucleus tractus solitarus. The PVN also responds to stressors that require processing by higher brain regions in order to be experienced as threatening. Such stressors are often referred to as *processive* or *psychological stressors* and activate the PVN via trans-synaptic pathways in the limbic system of the brain (Ulrich-Lai & Herman, 2009).

The PVN also responds to circulating cortisol levels that, via various mechanisms, inhibit the activity of CRH neurons. Whether, how intense, and how prolonged a PVN-CRH response is depends on all these inputs (Herman et al., 2016). Following release of CRH from the PVN, it takes 20–25 minutes, give or take a few minutes, for cortisol to reach peak levels. Cortisol is lipid soluble and easily enters all cells of the body. Once in the cell, cortisol needs to dock with its receptors in order to produce effects. Although some cortisol actions are rapid, most involve gene transcription and effects can span hours (Herman et al., 2016). However, CRH, the primary releasing factor in the HPA axis, is also produced in other brain regions involved in threat detection and response and is critical in rapidly orchestrating behavioral responses to perceived threats—increasing activity of the immune system (Quintanar & Guzman-Soto, 2013) and activating the SNS (Nijsen et al., 2000).

The HPA axis is regulated by multiple negative feedback mechanisms operating at different levels of the axis and central nervous system on different time scales—mechanisms include membrane-based inhibition of PVN activity, delayed genomic signaling, and long-term influences over RNA stability. Each of these pathways works to return HPA axis activity to baseline once threat responding is no longer needed. Among many other functions, negative feedback regulation is predominantly influenced by glucocorticoid receptors (GRs), low-affinity cortisol receptors that become occupied in multiple brain regions once the high-affinity receptors (mineralocorticoid receptors [MRs]) are occupied (Myers, Scheimann, Franco-Villanueva, & Herman, 2017). This occurs in response to highly stressful stimulation and at the peak of the daily cycle of cortisol. MRs in the brain, occupied at basal levels of cortisol, support many aspects of neuronal health,

including maintaining neuronal sensitivity to neurotransmitters. This enables normal functioning of the brain. Indeed, de Kloet (2014) has argued that critical elements of behavioral health depend on the balance of MR to GR activation (de Kloet, 2014). Relative to MRs, GRs are widely distributed in the brain with the highest numbers found in the hippocampus, amygdala, and medial prefrontal cortex (Ulrich-Lai & Herman, 2009), regions also frequently implicated in psychopathology. However, other regions of the prefrontal cortex also contain GRs and are sensitive to chronic elevations in cortisol.

Sex differences in HPA axis reactivity and regulation have been noted; however, they appear mostly due to associations with gonadal steroid hormones and are therefore predominantly observed following puberty (Herman et al., 2003, 2016), although one paper does note sex differences in early childhood, specifically with regard to the relationship between anxiety symptoms and stress reactivity (Kryski, Smith, Sheikh, Singh, & Hayden, 2013), finding that more anxious girls demonstrated a stronger and more prolonged cortisol response to a lab stressor than less anxious girls or boys, regardless of their current anxiety.

Activity of the HPA axis serves multiple functions, including altering or preparing the body to respond to future stressors (Sapolsky et al., 2000). Many of these preparatory actions operate through GRs. Prolonged activation of GRs alters the structure and function of the amygdala, hippocampus, and prefrontal cortex, brain regions involved in memory, self-regulation, and threat perception (Lupien, McEwen, Gunnar, & Heim, 2009). These physiological changes influence emotion, cognition, and the regulation of the sympathetic and parasympathetic nervous systems. Cortisol effects that increase amygdala reactivity and, conversely, reduce prefrontal cortex regulation of the amygdala appear to bias the organism toward more readily shifting from reflective cognitive functioning (i.e., higher executive functioning) to reflexive, defensive cognitions and actions (e.g., Vyas, Mitra, Shankaranarayana Rao, & Chattarji, 2002). Although this may enhance survival in dangerous contexts, it may impede healthy development and increase risk for affective disorders. Whereas most of the foundational information on biological systems and connectivity as described earlier has been done in rats, where stronger inferences can be made because experimental designs are possible, results are emerging in human studies that are consistent with the animal findings (Pagliaccio et al., 2014).

As in many endocrine systems, chronic elevations in cortisol also result in an altering of the mechanisms that regulate its production. These alterations can occur via many mechanisms at various levels of the HPA axis (Herman et al., 2016). Fast negative feedback does not appear to be altered (Herman et al., 2016). Instead, chronic stress alters pathways that deliver information about processive or psychological threat to the PVN. These pathways include circuits in the ventral hippocampus and ventromedial prefrontal cortex. Because CRH neurons in the PVN are under constant GABAergic (i.e., inhibitory) control, excitatory inputs to PVN GABAergic cells increase inhibition of CRH. This type of input from the ventral hippocampus and ventromedial PFC leads to reduced CRH drive (McEwen, Nasca, & Gray, 2016). Chronic elevations in cortisol can also have positive feedback effects on the central nucleus of the amygdala, where an increase in volume is observed along with an increase in CRH, which is believed to then enhance reactivity to future psychological stressors (McEwen et al., 2016). Furthermore, chronic CRH influence on the pituitary gland is sometimes accompanied by downregulation of pituitary ACTH production, which reduces the capacity of CRH to stimulate increases in cortisol production by the adrenal gland (Sanchez et al., 2010). Chronic activation of the adrenal cortex, however, increases its volume and allows it to respond more to less ACTH stimulation (Sanchez et al., 2010). Thus, the impacts of chronic stress on this system are complex, with multiple regulatory and counterregulatory actions, making it difficult to predict whether hyper- or hypoactivity of cortisol production will develop.

Sympathetic and Parasympathetic Nervous Systems: Basic Functioning, Connections to the Brain, and Effects of Chronic Stress

The other main arm of mammalian stress responding is the sympathetic adrenomedullary (SAM) system, which is part of the autonomic nervous system (ANS). With its sympathetic and parasympathetic subcomponents, the ANS is capable of rapidly activating the visceromotor, skeletal-motor, and cardiovascular systems. As part of the parasympathetic nervous system (PNS), the vagus nerve (10th cranial nerve) innervates the smooth muscle of the trachea, and bronchial and gastrointestinal tracts, as well as serving a major role in regulating cardiac activity. It also provides afferent feedback from all these regions via the NTS to inform the CNS about the state of the body (Thayer, Ahs, Fredrikson,

Sollers, & Wager, 2012). In humans, vagal activity, sometimes referred to as "vagal tone," can be measured using high-frequency (HF) heart rate variability (HRV) or, alternatively, the variability in heart rate surrounding respiration, also termed "respiratory sinus arrhythmia" (RSA). HRV has been interpreted as a measure of how strongly cortical and subcortical areas shape autonomic and brainstem responsivity (Thayer et al., 2012). Sex differences have sometimes been noted in autonomic functioning and regulation, including magnitude and pattern differences (Macey, Ogren, Kumar, & Harper, 2016), but no sex differences across development have been clearly outlined. With regard to HRV specifically, women have demonstrated greater mean heart rate and greater high-frequency HRV (Koenig & Thayer, 2016).

Activation of the sympathetic nervous system (SNS) prepares the body for intense activity, such as that needed in response to immediate threat (i.e., fight/flight). Thus, activation of the SNS results in heart rate increases, increases in blood glucose, and diversion of blood from skin and visceral organs to skeletal muscles. Most actions of the SNS involve postganglionic innervation of end-organs via the release of norepinephrine; however, there is an exception with the SAM system, a system that is critical for stress responding. On the chromaffin cells of the adrenal medulla, preganglionic neurons of the SNS synapse and trigger the release of small amounts of norepinephrine and much more substantial amounts of epinephrine. These are then released into circulation and act as hormones to amplify the SNS stress response. There is good evidence that the SAM systems and the HPA system are more closely aligned in their responses to different types of stressor than are the SAM and SNS system (Goldstein & Kopin, 2008).

The autonomic nervous system is regulated by a complex network in the CNS, sometimes termed the "central autonomic network" (CAN; Benarroch, 1993). The core of this network consists of the amygdala, insula, and cingulate cortex. Recent functional neuroimaging work has illuminated the distributed brain networks associated with sympathetic reactivity, including networks supporting executive functioning and the salience or vigilance systems (Macey et al., 2016). Parasympathetic connectivity has been associated more with default mode network areas (Beissner, Meissner, & Napadow, 2013). Thayer and Lane (2000) proposed a Neurovisceral Integration (NVI) model built upon the CAN model but focused on interactions with vagal activity.

The NVI model identifies cardiac ganglia as the foundational level and works up through multiple levels to the executive control network level. This level is comprised of the dorsolateral PFC and parietal cortex, responsible for top-down, goal-state directed prediction signaling (Smith, Thayer, Khalsa, & Lane, 2017).

Of particular relevance for stress reactivity and alterations in response to chronic stress, is the locus coeruleus–norephinephrine (LC-NE) system. In interaction with amygdalar CRH, the LC-NE system is a critical mediator of anxiety in response to threat (Tsigos & Chrousos, 2002). The LC provides a major source of NE to cortical and limbic regions important for arousal, cognition, attention, and sleep. Direct influences on the two autonomic branches have been demonstrated as well (Wood & Valentino, 2017). Chronic stress exposure has been linked to enhanced sensitivity of the LC to CRH, resulting in increased capacity for NE release (Ulrich-Lai & Herman, 2009).

Hypothalamic-Pituitary-Adrenocortical and Autonomic Nervous System Integration and Changes With Chronic Stress

Interactions between the HPA, SNS, and PNS systems occur on multiple levels and influence how chronic stress alters the functioning of stress-mediating systems. Thus, for example, the enzyme phenylethanolamine N-methyltransferase (PNMT) is needed to convert norepinephrine to epinephrine. Cortisol increases PNMT and thus facilitates the production of epinephrine (E). When chronic stress results in elevated cortisol, this then enhances the capacity of an adrenomedullary response; when chronic stress results in hypocortisolism, this reduces adrenomedullary response capabilities. As noted, chronic elevations in cortisol increase the capacity of the amygdala to activate CRH in response to threat, which in turn enhances central drive of the LC-NE system. This activation helps to coordinate a central NE and vigilance response with peripheral sympathetic fight/flight. Afferent coordination of central and peripheral responding during acute or chronic psychological stressors occurs via feedback from the periphery via the nucleus tractus solitarius, and via cortisol as the brain is a major target organ of this steroid hormone. Notably, Epi and NE are large molecules that do not pass through the blood–brain barrier (Sapolsky et al., 2000). It is these changes that have led researchers to examine the role of stress-mediating systems in increasing the risk for the onset of disorders of negative affect (e.g., anxiety, depression), and/or for maintaining these disorders once they arise (e.g., Strüber, Strüber, & Roth, 2014).

Development of Stress-Responsive Systems

The type of impact that chronic stress has on the HPA and ANS systems and related brain networks will depend on when during development they are experienced. During development, these systems are open to being shaped by experience, especially during periods of rapid change. It is therefore important to review the development of the key stress-mediating systems: the HPA, SNS, and PNS. Although once viewed solely from the perspective of risk, it is currently held that maturing stress systems are being calibrated to the degree of stressfulness or demand the organism is likely to face during its development (Del Giudice, Ellis, & Shirtcliff, 2011). What is not clear is whether the shaping of stress-responsive systems occurs during sensitive periods (i.e., times of heightened sensitivity to change that will then continue forward semipermanently). If so, then we would expect that once set, they would be relatively stable, influencing individual differences in response to stressors later in development. Although animal models tend to support this view, we have relatively little evidence for this phenomenon in human development, and at least one theory posits nearly continuous calibration and recalibration of stress-responsive systems throughout childhood and adolescence (Del Giudice et al., 2011). Nonetheless, while we cannot directly translate from animal models to humans, particularly with regards to timing (Heim & Binder, 2012; Pryce, 2008), animal studies provide evidence that there is a sensitive pre- to perinatal period for these stress-mediating systems.

Development of the Hypothalamic-Pituitary-Adrenocortical Axis From Prenatal to Adolescence

As the target of much research on stress, understanding developmental changes in the HPA axis and each of the three component regions (hypothalamus, pituitary, and adrenal) is of critical importance. This knowledge helps to elucidate when experiences may have the most impact on later functioning. Although the adult adrenal cortex consists of three zones (glomerulosa, fasciculata, and reticularis) that produce aldosterone (a mineralocorticoid), glucocorticoids (i.e., cortisol in humans), and DHEA(s) (androgens), respectively, such differentiation develops over time. In the first trimester, the fetal adrenal cortex consists of a large fetal zone that produces DHEA. This steroid is delivered to the placenta, where it is converted into estrogens to sustain pregnancy (Bronson & Bale, 2016; Ishimoto & Jaffe, 2011). The fetal zone involutes in the months following birth, allowing the adult patterning of the gland to become established. As early as the first trimester, two other zones begin to be observable, permitting the production of cortisol by 7–10 weeks of gestation. Following a brief period of activity, the enzyme necessary for cortisol production is inhibited until about week 22 to 23 of gestation (Ishimoto & Jaffe, 2011). Thus, it is not until late in the second and throughout the third trimester that cortisol produced by the fetus likely affects fetal brain development. During this period and increasingly with gestational age, perturbations to the mother, including threats to her physical well-being, or to the fetus (e.g., eclampsia) provoke a cortisol response of the fetus, most likely stimulated by CRH from the placenta (Gitau, Fisk, & Glover, 2004). There are, however, other routes whereby cortisol and CRH can affect fetal development in the first and early second trimester that will be discussed in the section "Prenatal Stress."

The HPA axis is responsive to stressors in the newborn period and, indeed, mounts a large cortisol response to labor and delivery (Gunnar & Vazquez, 2006). Salivary levels of cortisol in newborns, reflecting the unbound fraction of the hormone, are relatively comparable to adult levels. Plasma levels, however, are low because low binding globulin activity means that less total cortisol needs to be produced in order to achieve efficacious levels of unbound or active hormone. Using salivary cortisol measures, activity of the axis has been shown to vary with the newborn's arousal level, being the lowest during sleep and the highest in response to distress-eliciting events, including such innocuous stimulation as being undressed, weighed, and measured (Gunnar, 1992).

The HPA axis exhibits a rhythm from birth, initially showing two peaks roughly 12 hours apart, which by at least as early as 6 weeks has conformed to one peak early in the day (Gunnar & Vazquez, 2006). Throughout the first several years of life, cortisol levels vary across the day with feeding and napping schedules. Not until children have given up their afternoon nap does the diurnal rhythm appear fully mature (Watamura, Donzella, Kertes, & Gunnar, 2004). The diurnal rhythm provides a source of baseline physiological regulation and is a frequently examined measure of the impact of chronic stress in children and adults.

Maturation of the glucocorticoid receptor system (GR and MR) is also critical for mediating the effects of cortisol. In tissues like the lungs, GRs must be present and functioning by the third trimester to enable cortisol to stimulate surfactant, a substance needed to mature the lungs. In postnatal studies, GRs in the hippocampus, one of the most well-studied regions in this area of scholarship, are stable from birth to adulthood in humans and marmosets (Pryce, 2008). There is some evidence for postnatal increases in GR expression in the prefrontal and visual association cortices when infants and young adults are compared to older adults. To our knowledge, comparable data for MR development in humans is not available. In rhesus monkeys, numbers of CRH receptors were stable between 2 weeks and 12 weeks of age. However, CRH receptors in the dentate gyrus of the hippocampus were absent in 1- and 2-week-old animals, but significantly more abundant by 11–12 weeks of age. The opposite pattern was found in the lateral and medial geniculate nuclei, where high levels were found early in life and were practically nonexistent in 11- to 12-week-old animals (Grigoriadis et al., 1995). Developmental changes in receptors in different regions of the brain and body likely reflect not-yet-understood developmental differences in the role of glucocorticoids in normal growth and development.

For the first 3 months after birth, the human infant's adrenal gland continues to respond to even mild stimulation. During this time, the quality of handling by the caregiver is associated with differential cortisol responses (Gunnar, Talge, & Herrera, 2009a). After about 3 months of age, cortisol responses are not observed to mild perturbations, but they are observed to more invasive stressors, such as inoculations. By about 1 year of age, once the typical infant has formed specific attachments and has begun to use caregivers as sources of security, it becomes difficult to elevate cortisol to many laboratory stressors as long as the parent is present or readily available. Some have questioned whether this is evidence for a human stress hyporesponsive period, like that seen in mice and rats—a period in early development of general blunted responsivity to stressors (Gunnar, Brodersen, Krueger, & Rigatuso, 1996). However, separation is a potent stressor for human infants, as observed when toddlers experience new child care settings (see Gunnar, 2017, for review). Therefore, like nonhuman primates, the human infant does *not* exhibit a stress hyporesponsive period like that seen in rats and mice.

The capacity of caregivers to buffer responses to threat is evident throughout childhood for children who have developed a secure attachment. Separations also continue to provoke elevations in cortisol throughout the preschool years. Thus, even after children have adapted to full days at child care, cortisol increases over baseline by midafternoon, only to decline to typical bedtime levels once children go home (Sumner, Bernard, & Dozier, 2010). However, by the elementary years, children can stay 8 hours or more away from home without demonstrating activation of the HPA axis. They can also begin to use friends as a source of stress buffering, although parents remain powerful stress-buffering agents until puberty (Gunnar, 2017).

Puberty marks a major transition for the HPA axis. Baseline cortisol levels rise and there is some evidence that the stress response also increases, although this may reflect changes from childhood to adolescence in potency of self-evaluative stress (Gunnar, Wewerka, Frenn, Long, & Griggs, 2009b; van den Bos, de Rooij, Miers, Bokhorst, & Westenberg, 2014). Sex differences in regulation of the HPA axis also emerge during adolescence as the hypothalamic-pituitary-gonadal (HPG) axis and HPA axis increasingly influence one another (Shirtcliff et al., 2015). Prior to adolescence, reports of sex differences in activity of the HPA axis are unreliable (van der Voorn, Hollanders, Ket, Rotteveel, & Finken, 2017). Romeo and colleagues (2006, 2016) have provided evidence in rat models for puberty as another sensitive period for the HPA axis, but so far this has not been convincingly demonstrated in humans.

Development of the Autonomic Nervous System

While developmental changes in the HPA axis seem to extend through puberty, the two branches of the ANS are thought to be fairly established early in childhood. The sympathetic system develops as an outward expansion from the neural tube beginning in the first trimester. During the second trimester, fetal chromaffin cells arising from the neural crest migrate through the fetal cortex to increasingly occupy the center of the adrenal gland and form the embryonic adrenal medulla. The adrenal medulla, a component of the SAM system, develops alongside the rest of the sympathetic nervous system (Artal, 1980). The maturation of the medulla involves both the development of splanchic innervation and the development of the adrenal cortex production of cortisol, because, as mentioned earlier, this hormone

is essential for the production of PNMT, the rate-limiting enzyme in epinephrine (E) production. Indeed, in human development, NE predominates over E until after birth when the balance of production from the adrenal medulla shifts. Full development of the adrenal medulla is not achieved in humans until about age 3.

A functioning sympathoadrenal system is essential for survival as the fetus transitions to extrauterine life. This system produces a surge of catecholamines (i.e., E and NE) as the fetus nears term and during the process of labor and delivery that are essential to neonate viability. Catecholamines are necessary for survival in response to hypoxia, temperature changes, and other challenges during the transition from intra- to extrauterine existence. This surge is of fetal origin, as only 10%–20% of maternal catecholamines cross the placenta, although maternal catecholamines that lead to reduced blood flow to the placenta could stimulate large increases in the fetus (Artal, 1980).

The importance of an active sympathoadrenal system for fetal and neonatal survival may also explain the pattern of beta-adrenergic receptor activity in fetal and early postnatal life. Beta-adrenergic receptors appear very early, before a functional sympathetic system. Unlike in the mature organism, where frequent stimulation of the receptor results in down-regulation of its availability and responsiveness, in the fetus, a positive effect of stimulation on receptor number and sensitivity is seen (Slotkin, Auman, & Seidler, 2003). The plasticity of the receptor system is a double-edged sword, allowing the fight/flight system to adapt to harsh intra- and early extrauterine environments but also potentially producing vulnerability particularly to stimulant drugs such as nicotine. The sympathetic system continues to adapt during postnatal development. For example, environmental temperature early in life shapes differential sympathetic responding in sweat glands, such that adults respond differently to heat based on the degree of heat and humidity experienced as infants (Young, 2002). This adaptation also likely includes responses to the psychosocial environment.

As with the sympathoadrenal system, the parasympathetic system also begins its development during the fetal period. However, its development lags behind that of the sympathetic system (Porges & Furman, 2011). This is observed first during fetal development but generally follows during the first year of life. With the development of the PNS, the infant becomes less reactive and more organized. For example, patterns of heart rate variability prior to 32 weeks of gestation are dominated by sympathetic input, whereas after 32 weeks increasingly heart rate patterns reflect better vagal regulation (Schneider et al., 2009) The development of the vagal system also supports the infant's capacity to sustain longer periods of social engagement (Porges & Furman, 2011).

Sex differences in the development of autonomic systems have some supporting evidence. In line with observations demonstrating increased vulnerability of male offspring, female fetuses have shown indicators for more adaptive autonomic responses to acute stress, including faster heart rates. Furthermore, male fetuses show a steeper developmental trajectory between early and mid-late gestation in terms of a transition to more elevated fetal heart rate variability (Dipietro & Voegtline, 2017). Similar sex differences were noted for fetuses of high maternal distress pregnancies, with fetal heart rate variability exhibiting evidence of accelerated development in male fetuses and delayed development in female fetuses (Doyle et al., 2015).

The Timing of Stress During Development
Challenges of Studying Stress Timing Effects in Humans

Although research on humans is the focus of the developmental changes outlined earlier, much of the research on stress and development has been performed using animal models. This has permitted experimental control that enhances causal inference and invasive measurement procedures to better understand mechanisms. Although animal work has implications for the study of human development, translating across species is challenging, particularly when the question is one of stress timing. Rats and mice, the most commonly used laboratory animal, are born less mature than human infants. Indeed, the first week of life in rats, a period when many of the early life stress studies commence, is roughly equivalent to the last trimester of human pregnancy. Furthermore, while the sequence of brain maturation is similar across species, when maturational events occur relative to birth, their time scales are markedly different. As noted by Heim and Binder (2012), this means that animal studies may have "limited validity in elucidating sensitive periods for the effects of early life stress in humans" (p. 104). Thus, while animal studies clearly support the idea that stress early in life alters brain development and we can use these results to help direct human studies, we cannot translate timing effects directly across species.

Another concern is that stressors of childhood (e.g., maltreatment, maternal depression) that are associated with psychopathology occur over prolonged periods of time, making it difficult to isolate sensitive periods for particular neurobehavioral effects. Furthermore, while for some types of adversity (e.g., Hurricane Katrina), the timing of the event relative to the child's age can be determined with some accuracy, for children at the highest risk because of poverty or family dysfunction, a long period of adversity may both precede and follow the acute stressor, again making it difficult to determine stress timing effects. This raises the possibility that the response to a stressor like Hurricane Katrina might reflect more trait-like changes in stress-response systems shaped by chronic exposure to stressors during prior development.

Many human studies rely on retrospective reports of childhood adversity, and this raises questions of reporting accuracy. A recent study of adults with adverse childhood experiences that pitted prospective and retrospective reports using two long-term longitudinal studies found that at the individual item level, only death/loss of a parent was consistent in pro- and retrospective data (Reuben et al., 2016). Other measures, including neglect and abuse, correlated poorly. In addition, different methods (e.g., interviews versus questionnaires) may elicit different memories of prior or even current experiences, leading both to questions of validity of these methods, and also to potentially different brain correlates of early adversity depending on reporting method.

We are also challenged by the types of measures of neurodevelopment and stress-reactivity we can employ at different ages. Neuroimaging of infants is becoming more common, but it must be done when they are asleep, which limits the kinds of functional response questions that can be explored. Young preschoolers are notoriously difficult to study in imaging environments, although neurodevelopmental assessments can be used to explore functional aspects of brain development. Functional imaging becomes easier as children get older and is often employed in studies of adolescents. Despite the problem that the same task may be approached differently by children of different ages, functional imaging studies are among our best techniques for establishing structure–function relations during development (Tottenham & Sheridan, 2010). However, there is the added obstacle that in development, what starts out as an alteration in one neural system may end up cascading into altered development of other neural systems that depend on input from the structures originally impacted (O'Donnell & Meaney, 2017). Thus, stress encountered at an earlier period of development may ultimately end up influencing neural systems whose ontogeny is much later in development. In addition, regarding stress-mediating physiological systems, our measures often do not directly assess the system of interest but rather the activity of end-organs affected by those systems (e.g., cardiac activity used to assess SNS and PNS activity; Herman et al., 2016). Thus, we need to consider the development of the end-organs we are measuring (e.g., the heart) as well as the stress-responsive system that is influencing it (SNS and PNS).

There is also the issue of risk and protective processes, internal or external to the child, that moderate the effects of stress on neurobehavioral development. For example, the same stressor may have greater effects on amygdalar development for a child high in fear-related traits compared to a bolder child. Genetics, temperament, and supportive parental care are all factors that, in addition to timing, may influence stress reactivity and the impact of a stressor on neurobehavioral development (Gee & Casey, 2015; Gunnar & Quevedo, 2007). On a broader level, stress does not just impact the child, but also the family and surrounding environment. These effects are hard to control for and can easily compound, making the impacts of a stressor challenging to discern (Braun et al., 2017).

Additionally, it is likely that different types of adversity are more or less stressful and have differential impacts on the brain at different points in development. There have been several attempts to identify underlying dimensions of adversity so that we can fine-tune our understanding how adverse experiences affect neurodevelopment. For example, McLaughlin and Sheridan (2016) argue that deprivation and threat constitute the two most common underlying dimensions of early life stress, under which specific types of stressors (e.g., abuse, neglect, poverty) can be placed. They argue that quantifying experiences along these two dimensions will help specify how and when adverse experiences influence neurobehavioral development. We argue that a third dimension, development, needs to also be considered, because the same experience may be weighted differently or mark different processes in terms of its impact on neurobehavioral development along the threat and deprivation continua as a function of the child's age. For example, neglect in infancy may not only result in deprivation of developmentally

appropriate stimulation, but because the baby is dependent for survival on the care of adults, it may also be a systemic stressor, resulting in physical threats to the infant. Likewise, physical abuse experienced in the home may lead to disruptive behavior in childhood that results in school suspension and, thus, reduced cognitive stimulation. Thus, where we place a type of adverse care in regard to its underlying dimensions may change with development, complicating our attempts to discern associations between types of adversity and neurobehavioral development.

Finally, especially in the case of domestic abuse and neglect, the question of heritable influences confounds interpretation of stress timing. There is good evidence that heritable emotional problems among parents contribute to their risk of abusing or neglecting their children (Belsky, 1993). Thus, it is always possible that altered stress responding in the offspring of maltreating parents may be explained by genetic similarities between abusing parents and their children (i.e., passive gene–environment correlation), highlighting the importance of considering genetic influences on what may appear to be an environmental effect. Likewise, studies of prenatal stress also face the confound of the mother and her offspring being genetically related; thus, genetics and not experience might be the basis for any findings. Twin and adoption designs are clearly needed in order to disentangle genes and experience effects on stress and its timing. There are some stress studies that do control for genetic similarities between parents and offspring. For example, using children of in vitro fertilization, researchers compared the impact of prenatal stress on those who did and did not share their mother's genes (Rice et al., 2010). Shared genes were not involved in maternal stress during pregnancy influencing gestational age, birthweight, and externalizing problems, but they were involved in associations of prenatal stress with attention-deficit problems. In addition to twin and adoption studies, studies directly examining genotypic variation interactions with stress experiences at different points in development will be helpful in isolating the genotypic patterns that interact with experience to shape altered patterns of stress responding and risk for psychopathology.

With these caveats in mind, we turn to the evidence on the effects of developmental timing of chronic stressors on the development of stress-mediating systems and the neural systems regulating and affected by stress exposure from conception through adolescence.

Fetal Stress and Later Developmental Outcomes

One of the most rapid periods in development occurs before birth. Human brain development begins in the embryonic period, defined as conception through gestational week 8, with the differentiation of some epiblast cells into neural progenitor cells. From these cells come neurons and the neural tube that will eventually become the spinal cord and brain. In the fetal period, gestational week 9 until birth, neural and glial migration occurs allowing for the eventual formation of the six-layered neocortex. The first developments of gyri and sulci also occur during this period (Houston, Herting, & Sowell, 2014; Stiles & Jernigan, 2010). In the third trimester, the fetal brain advances rapidly in complexity and density with neuronal specialization, dendritic arborization, and expansive synaptic formation. Both the hippocampus and amygdala, regions especially important in the stress-sensitive network, are identifiable by around 8 weeks of gestation and continue to develop rapidly throughout the prenatal period (see Gunnar & Davis, 2013, for review). The marked development of the brain during gestation confers a high degree of plasticity and receptivity to influences from the uterine environment.

Stressors such as maternal depression and natural disasters during fetal development increase offspring risk for neurodevelopmental disorders and psychopathologies (e.g., Bronson & Bale, 2016). Although both maternal depression and a stressor independent of maternal psychopathology, such as a natural disaster, may impact the fetus via similar neurobiological pathways, they should be considered distinct phenomena as they often have independent impacts. Heightened cortisol in maternal plasma or in amniotic fluid is associated with lower birthweight, which in turn is associated with poorer neurocognitive development, greater HPA axis reactivity to stressors, and heightened risk for cardiovascular disease (Baibazarova et al., 2013; Braun et al., 2017; O'Donnell & Meaney, 2017). Initial observations of the association between birthweight and cardiovascular disease led to the Barker hypothesis of fetal programming, now known as the developmental origins of health and disease (DOHaD) theory, which argues that health trajectories are initiated in the womb and that adaptations to a harsh intrauterine environment are maladaptive if there is a mismatch between prenatal and postnatal conditions. The fetus preadapted to a harsh prenatal environment will be at risk for obesity, metabolic disorder, and heart disease if born into a benign, high-resourced postnatal environment. Although the original DOHaD argument arose from concerns about the impacts of prenatal nutrition on later biobehavioral development, because nutrition and stress may follow final common pathways in producing effects on fetal growth, tissue programming, and increased risk for physical and mental disorders, current DOHaD perspectives argue that both stress and poor nutrition may have similar effects on the fetus (Monk, Georgieff, & Osterholm, 2013; O'Donnell & Meaney, 2017).

We once thought that the placenta protected the fetus from stressors impinging on the mother. Now the placenta is viewed more as a sensory organ, sampling the maternal milieu and transmitting information to the fetus, allowing fetal adaptation in anticipation of the stressfulness of the postnatal environment (Schulkin, 1999). Elevations in maternal production of catecholamines that reduce blood flow to the fetus are one pathway through which maternal psychological state may influence fetal development (Rakers et al., 2015). Activity of the maternal HPA axis also can influence fetal development, but because the HPA axis plays a role in gestation and parturition, there are multiple regulatory mechanisms centered on the placenta that intervene between maternal cortisol production and fetal impacts. The placenta produces its own CRH that increases in response to maternal cortisol. Cortisol increases during pregnancy as maternal estrogen production stimulates increases in binding globulins, requiring the mother to produce more cortisol to maintain sufficient unbound and biological active levels. By the third trimester, however, increasing unbound cortisol is noted along with rising CRH. This activity likely stimulates the fetal HPA axis to increase its own cortisol production, which is critical to lung maturation and the transition to extrauterine life. The 11ß-HSD2 enzyme, which changes in its activity over the course of pregnancy, plays an important role in regulating the complex dance between maternal cortisol, CRH and fetal HPA activity. In the placenta, the 11ß-HSD2 enzyme converts cortisol to an inert form of the steroid. In pregnancies associated with higher levels of cortisol and near term (i.e., 37+ weeks of gestation), 11ß-HSD2 decreases, allowing more maternal cortisol to cross over to the fetus. There is some evidence that NE and E also reduce 11ß-HSD2 activity (Sarkar et al., 2001, as cited by Baibazarova et al., 2013). Thus, rising CRH levels in response to rising maternal levels of unbound cortisol and decreasing 11ß-HSD2 activity both with increases in catecholamines and cortisol are routes through which maternal stress may be transmitted to the fetus via increased exposure to cortisol. Consequently, fetal growth may be impaired and brain development affected (Ishimoto & Jaffe, 2011; Ong, Chng, Meaney, & Buschdorf, 2013).

Gestational timing of fetal exposure to high cortisol levels may have a large influence on outcomes. Early in pregnancy, when 11ß-HSD2 levels are typically high as an intended barrier against high cortisol levels, damages to this barrier or elevated maternal cortisol levels can expose the fetus to harmful levels of cortisol. However, when this occurs later in gestation, when the fetus is already preparing for elevated cortisol levels, increases in maternal cortisol in the moderate ranges may serve to enhance child outcomes (Gunnar & Davis, 2013). Studies linking gestational timing to postnatal outcomes demonstrate that behavioral outcomes are most directly related to stress in midgestation, but that birthweight and motor functioning seem to be impacted more by earlier perturbations (Charil, Laplante, Vaillancourt, & King, 2010). Some of these connections are mediated by sex—a point that will be discussed at length later.

Epigenetic changes are a potential mechanism through which prenatal stress influences the developing child (Braun et al., 2017; Bronson & Bale, 2016; Marasco, Herzyk, Robinson, & Spencer, 2016). Epigenetic alterations to genes regulating neurodevelopment and stress reactivity and regulation may have a long-term impact on children's adaptation to the environment, although these alterations may not become functionally significant until a postnatal challenge arises (Provencal & Binder, 2015). Regarding neural changes associated with prenatal stress, both impaired and enhanced child functioning have been noted. One effect of elevated maternal stress during pregnancy is a reduction in gestational length, which may be accompanied by accelerated development of systems required for survival outside the womb (as reviewed in Gunnar & Davis, 2013). This has been observed using measures of heart rate and somatic-cardiac coupling (e.g., DiPietro et al., 2010; Doyle et al., 2015). On the other hand, there is also evidence that indices of higher stress, such as placental CRH early in gestation, impair neurodevelopmental maturation, as in a slower development of the fetus's response to vibroacoustic stimulation (Class et al., 2008). Natural disasters experienced during pregnancy have also been shown to impact fetal development (Charil et al., 2010) and impair cognitive development (Li et al., 2015). The Li et al.

study found that the effect of disaster on visuospatial memory reflecting hippocampal development was most salient when the natural disaster was experienced during mid- to late versus early gestation.

There have been several studies using neuroimaging to examine the postnatal correlates of prenatal stress, here defined as symptoms of poor maternal mental health. For example, reduced gray matter among 6- to 9-year-olds has been associated with mid-gestation pregnancy anxiety (Buss, Davis, Muftuler, Head, & Sandman, 2010). A larger cortisol awakening response (CAR) later in pregnancy when the response is typically attenuated is associated with shorter gestation, often within the range considered near-term (Buss et al., 2009), which in turn is associated with reduced gray matter volume in 6- to 10-year old children (Davis et al., 2011). Furthermore, in their review, O'Donnell and Meaney (2017) note that in several different studies, maternal antenatal depression, controlling for postnatal depression, is associated with cortical thinning as well as modified amygdala connectivity measured in late childhood. They also note that these structural brain patterns are consistent with those observed in the brains of adults with depression, and thus may help explain intergenerational transmission of depression risk. The challenge with this interpretation, though, is that genotypic similarity between mother and child may also explain these findings.

Sex differences frequently have also been reported in the correlation between maternal cortisol in pregnancy and infant outcomes, indicating that the sex of the fetus may moderate the impact of prenatal stress (see Zijlmans, Riksen-Walraven, & de Weerth, 2015, for review), in ways similar to those noted in animal studies (e.g., Braun et al., 2017; Weinstock, 2007). Sandman, Glynn, and Davis (2013) proposed a sex-based viability-vulnerability hypothesis in which they argue that male fetuses adapt less to harsh intrauterine conditions, which increases their risk of failing to survive a harsh gestation. For example, whereas the female placenta is more responsive to increased maternal cortisol concentrations, resulting in a slowing of growth when maternal levels are high early in pregnancy, male fetuses do not slow their growth in these circumstances, thus using metabolic resources that might be needed in a stressed pregnancy to maintain viability (Sandman et al., 2013). It is notable in this regard, however, that in both rats and sheep, the male placenta shows greater reductions in 11β-HSD2 in response to maternal glucocorticoids than does the female placenta (Charil et al., 2010). Thus, sex differences may be species specific.

Some neural evidence of female fetal adaptation has been demonstrated through work looking at brain networks. Although boys and girls ages 6–9 years did not differ in global network structure, higher maternal cortisol during pregnancy was associated with an increase in network cost (denser connectivity) in girls only. Furthermore, network connectivity mediated the relationship between maternal cortisol levels in pregnancy and girls' internalizing symptoms (Kim et al., 2016). Brain effects of prenatal stress may depend on a combination of sex and timing. In the study just mentioned, the third trimester was the period more sensitive to producing sex differences in network responsivity to maternal cortisol. In another study, elevated maternal cortisol during earlier, but not later pregnancy was related to larger right amygdala volume in females only. Furthermore, the association between maternal cortisol and girls' affective problems was partially mediated by amygdala volume. There were no relationships found between maternal cortisol in pregnancy and hippocampal volume for either sex (Buss et al., 2012). However, the hippocampus may not exhibit an impact of early life stress until later in development (Heim & Binder, 2012).

The effects of prenatal stress on behavioral, cognitive, and physical health probably depend on the quality of the postnatal environment. In DOHaD, the expectation is that poor outcomes will be manifested if the prenatal environment inaccurately foreshadowed the postnatal environment. Thus, if the body is prepared to survive conditions of relative famine and is born into an environment rich in calories, weight gain will be rapid and the child will be on a trajectory toward obesity, metabolic disorder, and cardiovascular disease. Studies of prenatal stress have often attempted to statistically control for stress in the postnatal environment to establish that prenatal effects were clearly due to prenatal conditions. However, there is evidence that as in the study of prematurity, negative consequences of prenatal stress for cognitive and emotional development are most likely to be observed if the postnatal environment is not supportive (Bergman, Sarkar, Glover, & O'Connor, 2010; Grant, Sandman, Wing, Dmitrieva, & Poggi, 2015). Thus, although the effects of prenatal stress may be sex specific in some ways and modifiable by the postnatal environment, the weight of the evidence indicates that the brain is significantly sensitive to stress during fetal development.

Outcomes of Stress During Infancy and Early Childhood

After birth, infancy continues to be a period of large developmental changes and therefore sensitivity to the environment. Though the majority of neuronal production and migration occurs prenatally, synaptogenesis continues postnatally in the first years of life with both overproliferation and pruning of synapses in neuronal systems supporting foundational skills such as visual perception, word learning, and social orienting (Johnson, 2001). Stress during infancy may affect this development, weakening some connections while strengthening others. Stress and glucocorticoids have significant impacts on oligodendrocytes and myelin, resulting in altered development of white matter integrity in animal models (Kim, Kim, & Chang, 2013). This is particularly important because proliferation and migration of glial cells and the myelination of nerves are critical to healthy brain development. Through postnatal development, there are different trajectories for gray and white matter volume. In general, a linear increase is seen in white matter, with most pronounced changes being in early childhood and adolescence. In contrast, a curvilinear, U-shaped trajectory is seen in gray matter volume, increasing rapidly until about age 10 and then decreasing. Stress influences gray matter volume through apoptosis, and alterations in dendritic arborization, although these effects differ by brain region (Lupien et al., 2009).

There is a burgeoning animal literature supporting the effect of early life stress on the interconnected brain systems regulating the HPA axis, SNS and PNS systems, defensive behavioral responses, and cognitive control systems (e.g., Lupien et al., 2009). A number of recent reviews conclude that there is a sensitive period for stress effects in early life (Heim & Binder, 2012). Broadly, early childhood is thought to exhibit peak sensitivity for the development of the amygdala and hippocampus, two structures directly implicated in stress-responsive neural systems (Teicher, Samson, Anderson, & Ohashi, 2016). Some of the most salient stressors in this early developmental period are related to attachment figures (i.e., low parental sensitivity, death of a caregiver, or abuse perpetrated by a caregiver). On the other hand, attachment security acts as a strong and wide-ranging buffer of stress-mediating systems, reducing elevations in stress physiology even when children are emotionally upset (e.g., Bergman et al., 2010; Gunnar & Quevedo, 2007). In rats and humans, disrupted maternal caregiving and quality has been linked to altered HPA development and responsivity, PFC and amygdala activity and connectivity, and altered gene expression for gluco-corticoid receptors (Herman et al., 2003; Gee & Casey, 2015; Gunnar & Quevedo, 2007).

Some of the most persuasive animal data supporting the postnatal impact of early adversity comes from studies of Rhesus monkeys, whose neurological maturation at birth is similar to humans. At Yerkes Primate Center, there are a significant number of female Rhesus monkeys who maltreat their infants (Maestripieri, McCormack, Lindell, Higley, & Sanchez, 2006), providing the opportunity for study of primate models of maltreatment and the developing brain. Using a cross-fostering design, maltreated infants were found to become juveniles whose left and right amygdala volumes correlated positively with the rate of abuse they received as infants (Howell et al., 2014). This research group has also shown that cortisol levels early in life are elevated in the maltreated infants and predict a reduction in white matter integrity in the corpus callosum and other brain regions in adolescent monkeys (Howell et al., 2013).

One of the reasons the Rhesus data are compelling is that we can rule out prenatal stress and both pre- and postnatal malnutrition as alternative explanations for the observed effects. Neither of these factors can be ruled out in another literature, that on institutionalized infants, which also provides compelling evidence that early adversity, even when followed by rearing in supportive environments, has long-term implications for brain development. When adoption of institutionalized infants (typically orphaned and abandoned children) occurs by 6 months, early institutionalization does not appear to have lasting impacts on brain or behavior (Rutter & Sonuga-Barke, 2010). Furthermore, infants who experience care in institutions with a small number of children assigned to each caregiver, individually responsive care, and good cognitive and social stimulation do not appear to have cognitive deficits (see Gunnar, 2001, for review). In contrast, typical institutional care consisting of high infant-to-caregiver ratios, frequent staff turnover, routinized care, propped bottles, and little responsive contact is associated with blunted activity of the HPA axis and of the SNS when measured in the first years after adoption (Koss, Mliner, Donzella, & Gunnar, 2016) and later in middle childhood (McLaughlin et al., 2015). Hyporesponsiveness of the HPA axis in these children, in turn, predicts problems in attention regulation several years later when children enter formal schooling (Koss et al., 2016). There is some

suggestion that stress reactivity is recalibrated as they enter puberty to match their nonadopted, positively adjusted peers, although more work is needed to verify this (Flannery et al., 2017; Quevedo, Johnson, Loman, Lafavor, & Gunnar, 2012).

Deficits in executive functions, including attention regulation, are the most consistent finding in research on postinstitutionalized (PI) children, even those adopted by a year of age (Gunnar & Davis, 2013). Given this, it is not surprising to find that the prefrontal cortex appears to be reduced in volume in PI adolescents, whether they were adopted before and after their first birthdays (Hodel et al., 2015). Significant reductions in gray matter, but not for white matter volume for the whole cortex, have also been noted among children fostered out of institutional care; in contrast, both white and gray matter volume are reduced for children who remained in the institution (Sheridan, Fox, Zeanah, McLaughlin, & Nelson, 2012). This later finding suggests that when deprivation terminates, white matter integrity can recover. How long this plasticity lasts in development has not been determined.

Whether subcortical structures exhibit volume alterations following institutional care is unclear. The amygdala has been examined in five studies. In one it was found to be smaller, in two larger, and in the others not different from comparison youth (Hanson et al., 2015; Hodel et al., 2015; Mehta et al., 2009; Sheridan et al., 2012; Tottenham et al., 2010). Likewise, in these same studies the hippocampus was examined and in only one was reduced hippocampal volume found (Hodel et al., 2015). None of these studies examined adults with histories of early institutional care, and there is some evidence that hippocampal differences may emerge later, perhaps in response to amygdalar hyperactivity (Tottenham & Sheridan, 2010). In this regard, it is notable that while volumetric differences are inconsistent for the amygdala and hippocampus following early institutional care, reactivity effects for the amygdala are more consistent. For both PI and maltreated children, compared to controls, the amygdala responds more intensely to socially threatening stimuli (Maheu et al., 2010; Tottenham et al., 2010), and this was also noted for the left hippocampus (Maheu et al., 2010). Finally, during aversive conditioning, PI youth activated a broader network of regions, including a tighter coupling of the hippocampus and prefrontal cortex, than did comparison youth (Silvers et al., 2016). Notably, as reported in the same study, this pattern may be protective because the broader pattern of activation negatively predicted anxiety symptoms assessed 2 years later. In sum, for the PI children and youth, although they were removed from adverse care early, typically before 3 years of age, after many years in supportive homes both alterations in stress physiology and in the broad neural networks regulating emotional distress, self-regulation, and defensive responding are observed.

Individuals who experienced maltreatment early in life are the other main group whose experiences provide evidence for the effect of the timing of early life stress on brain development. There are numerous reports of alterations in brain structure and function related to maltreatment (for review, see Teicher et al., 2016). However, there are several problems in using data on maltreated children to understand the timing of early life stress. First, while the age at which maltreatment is identified may demarcate when maltreatment stopped, it is unlikely to demarcate an end to significant stress. Disruption in care arrangements, poverty, parental psychopathology, dangerous neighborhoods, and underperforming schools are all more likely to be experienced in the lives of previously maltreated children than in nonmaltreated children (Cicchetti, 1991). To address this, some studies compare children who may be experiencing similar contextual stress (nonmaltreated peers that are also low socioeconomic status) in order to isolate effects of maltreatment (e.g., Cicchetti, 1991). Others, particularly those using retrospective self-report, are often not as rigorous in defining the comparison group. Second, many studies use patients with psychopathology plus maltreatment histories versus individuals with neither as the comparison group, rendering it difficult to distinguish between correlates of maltreatment versus psychopathology. Third, and critical for this chapter, there are very few studies exploring the timing of maltreatment on brain development and the development of stress-mediating systems. Here we examine studies comparing maltreatment in infancy and early childhood (i.e., up to age 5 years) relative to chronic and/or later maltreatment.

Hanson and colleagues (2015) reported both the amygdala and the hippocampus were smaller in youth maltreated early in life, but the effect was similar to those reared in poverty but not maltreated. Notably, reduced hippocampal volume partially mediated the relationship between early life stress and externalizing behavior problems (Hanson et al., 2015). Two other studies also support the idea that the hippocampus is particularly sensitive to maltreatment in infancy and early childhood (Andersen

et al., 2008; Rao et al., 2010). Andersen and colleagues (2008) found that reduced hippocampal volume was related to maltreatment early in life. Rao and colleagues (2010) noted that, instead of maltreatment, low parental nurturance during early development was associated with smaller hippocampal volume in adolescence and early adulthood. Notably, studying the effects of early adversity on hippocampal volume later in development may be more revealing than studying these effects on the hippocampus earlier in life because this allows cascading effects of early experiences to be observed (see Tottenham & Sheridan, 2010, for review). Although enhanced amygdala volume and modified connectivity to PFC and hippocampal regions have frequently been noted in studies of maltreatment, we know of only one study that examined associations between maltreatment timing and amygdala volume; furthermore, this study only considered maltreatment from ages 6 to 18 years (Pechtel, Lyons-Ruth, Anderson, & Teicher, 2014). Regarding the development of the prefrontal regulatory regions, we know of no study using imaging that has attempted to isolate the effects of early maltreatment. However, one study of 3- to 9-year-olds isolated maltreatment during infancy as the period contributing the most to impaired executive functions (Cowell, Cicchetti, Rogosch, & Toth, 2015), suggesting an impact of maltreatment on prefrontal regions. Similarly, with regard to activity of the HPA axis, only one study has attempted to examine the effects of stress timing and the results were complex (Kuhlman, Vargas, Geiss, & Lopez-Duran, 2015). Children exposed to more traumatic experiences prior to their first birthday recovered from a stressor task more slowly, suggesting an impairment in negative feedback regulation of the HPA axis. The timing of trauma exposure had sex-differentiated effects for the cortisol diurnal rhythm, with a flatter rhythm being observed for males whose first traumatic exposure was earlier in development and for girls whose first exposure was later. It is important to note that none of these studies are longitudinal or experimental, so causality and directionality cannot be concluded. As noted earlier, this is why animal experimental studies are so critical to this area of research.

In summary, several types of life stress during the first years of life are related to long-term outcomes. Early adversity has been correlated with reduced hippocampal volume and increased amygdalar volume and activity later in life. Although these effects harken to the results of animal studies, it is likely that specific effects will ultimately differ by brain region, type of stressor, and whether the stressful conditions in infancy were preceded and/or followed by negative life experiences. In future research, it will be important to pursue longitudinal studies, where changes in neural functioning and behavior can be measured to control for starting point, rather than relying on a one-time assessment later in life. We turn now to the data on late childhood and adolescence.

Outcomes of Stress During Middle Childhood and Adolescence

Initially, early childhood was considered the primary sensitive period, with the most rapid and diverse developmental growth. Recently, adolescence has piqued research curiosities due to the numerous social and biological changes requiring adjustment, adaptation, and accommodation for children that will soon become young adults. We consider middle childhood and adolescence together because studies of the effects of stress, particularly those using imaging, typically include children who vary widely in age, usually from middle childhood through adolescence. As noted earlier, stress-mediating systems, particularly the HPA axis, undergo marked changes during puberty, resulting in increased basal levels and decreased sensitivity to parental social buffering compared to childhood (Gunnar, 2017). The peripubertal period in rats, as noted earlier, appears to be a second sensitive period for shaping activity of the HPA axis (Romeo, 2010). In addition, adolescence is a time of heightened malleability of neural systems and another sensitive period, perhaps, for some systems (Cymerblit-Sabba et al., 2015; Fuhrmann, Knoll, & Blakemore, 2015; Knudsen, 2004). The extent to which neural plasticity reflects pubertal changes independent of the age is not clear, although there is increasing evidence that puberty plays a critical role, above and beyond that of chronological age (Blakemore, Burnett, & Dahl, 2010).

In humans, there is good evidence that the amygdala and hippocampus, along with the striatum, undergo structural volume increases throughout this period (Gee & Casey, 2015; Goddings et al., 2014; Sowell, Thompson, Holmes, Jernigan, & Toga, 1999). Notably, these areas are also some of the most stress responsive, as discussed previously, making this an important period when experience could influence future psychological functioning through neurodevelopmental processes. There is also an increase in stress-related psychopathology during adolescence, along with increased sexual dimorphism in psychopathology during this period (Suleiman & Dahl, 2017). Adolescent onset of psychiatric disorder, however, may reflect processes set into motion earlier in development. Specifically relevant to stress timing is the question of whether pubertal changes (i.e., hormonal elevations) are triggers for expression of earlier stress exposures versus the possibility that stressors in adolescence compound on earlier experiences, a version of the double-hit hypothesis (Eiland & Romeo, 2013; Negriff, Saxbe, & Trickett, 2015; Romeo et al., 2006). Finally, with puberty, social evaluation by peers becomes more salient and stressful (van den Bos, van Duijvenvoorde, & Westenberg, 2016), increasing the likelihood that bullying and social rejection will have even more impact than in childhood (Fisher et al., 2015).

Due to the challenge of studying stress exposures isolated to the adolescent period, much of the work on stress during this time has used rat models. Stress exposure in adolescent rats has been shown to reduce dendritic complexity in the hippocampus and prefrontal cortex while increasing complexity in the amygdala, effects that have been seen in both sexes (Eiland & Romeo, 2013; Romeo, 2017). Stress induces increases in spine density in the amygdala in adult rats, but the opposite is seen in young adolescent rats (Romeo, 2017). Thus, some associations between stress and the amygdala are similar and some different when comparing adolescent and adult animals. Unique changes in behavior, gene expression, and neurogenesis profiles have been demonstrated when rats are exposed to stressors in adolescence versus in adulthood (Eiland & Romeo, 2013). Some of these results are replicated in humans, but others are not. For example, relative to rats, the human hippocampus does not seem to be as affected by adolescent stress (Lupien et al., 2009). However, factors potentially influencing this include general species differences, different stressor paradigms, and differential developmental trajectories for neural regions like the hippocampus (Heim & Binder, 2012; Tottenham & Sheridan, 2010).

In humans, only a handful of studies isolate the impact of adolescent stress exposure relative to that in childhood and adulthood. One study found that adults reporting sexual abuse after the age of 12 were significantly more likely to have symptoms of post-traumatic stress disorder (PTSD) than those reporting the same abuse before the age of 12. The associations with the timing of reported sexual abuse were reversed for depression (Schoedl et al., 2010). Although this study provides some support for differential timing effects, it did not consider associated brain changes. Another study investigating stress timing examined magnetic resonance imaging (MRI) scans in 18- to 22-year-old women reporting childhood sexual abuse at different ages. The volumes of different brain regions were associated with the timing of exposure. The hippocampus was smaller for women with a history of abuse in childhood (3–5 years old) and mid-adolescence (11–13 years old), while the frontal cortex volume was reduced in women experiencing abuse between the ages of 14 and 16 years (Andersen et al., 2008). Unfortunately, we do not have similar studies examining different types of childhood stressors and their timing.

As part of adolescent brain development, sex differences arise in the basal ganglia, hippocampus, and amygdala. Although females reach overall peak volume levels earlier than males, males have a more rapid increase in amygdala volume, a region shown to be more sensitive to testosterone levels, while females demonstrate a quicker growth of the hippocampus, which is more sensitive to estrogen levels (Lenroot & Giedd, 2010). As noted, these areas are associated with disorders such as anxiety and depression, which also demonstrate sex differences. Development of functional connectivity differs as well; for example, left frontal lobe connectivity increases in boys and decreases in girls across adolescence (Lenroot & Giedd, 2010). However, morphological and functional differences do not seem to translate to behavior; females and males show certain different patterns of activation that correspond to similar observable behaviors across the two sexes, potentially reflecting different strategies for achieving similar outcomes (Lenroot & Giedd, 2010). Nonetheless, these sexually dimorphic developmental patterns may interact with the timing of stress to yield different neural consequences for males and females. Because of sexual dimorphism in the hypothalamic-pituitary-gonadal (HPG) axis, bidirectional effects of the HPA and HPG axis would be expected to yield sex differences in the effects of stress experienced postpuberty (see Sisk & Zehr, 2005, for review).

Thus, while research in nonhuman animals suggests that the peripubertal period is a time when significant stress will have unique effects on the neural systems regulating stress physiology, defensive behavior, and self-regulation, this hypothesis has not been adequately tested in human development. However, there are several studies that suggest this will be an important avenue for research.

Conclusions and Future Directions

Although the animal literature provides clear evidence of sensitive periods of development during which stress influences the regulatory set points of stress-mediating systems and the neural systems that regulate threat perception, defensive behavior, and self-regulation, the limitations of analogous work on humans preclude firm conclusions. In particular, more work on the role of stressor timing in the context of human development and maladaptation is needed. This may prove challenging because the stressors that occur in the lives of children are typically not confined to an isolated age period. For example, as noted, the child might be abused during a particular age period, but because abuse correlates with other adversities (e.g., poverty, parental psychopathology, and so on) it is likely preceded and followed by adversities that are themselves stress inducing. Nevertheless, there is evidence in the human literature that significant stressors experienced early in life have long-term impacts on stress physiology and neurodevelopment.

The literature on prenatal stress is the most well developed and clearly points to significant impacts on the development of the fetus and timing of delivery. There is also a rapidly emerging literature examining differences in the structure and functional activity of multiple brain regions in prenatally stressed children. However, in much of this work, the goal has been to prove that the effects are pre- and not postnatal; therefore, we know less about whether postnatal experience moderates the effects of prenatal stress. One can imagine both cascading and compensatory influences. For example, consistent with the DOHaD model, prenatal stress might alter how the body manages calories and increase stress sensitivity, leading to both a risk of obesity and stress-induced eating, which then results in obesity that increases the risk of metabolic disorder. Alternatively, prenatal stress may result in premature birth, smaller size, and increased fearfulness in neonates. This, in turn, may lead some mothers to compensate by being more sensitive and responsive to this child who seems to need more nurturing, and this might support the development of a secure attachment relationship, which will serve as a powerful stress buffer for that child, reducing the potential negative consequences of their prenatal stress exposure. Understanding cascading and compensatory processes following early life stress exposure is an important direction for future research on prenatal stress and, indeed, on stress experienced at any point in development.

There is also growing evidence that adverse care during the first few years of life has long-lasting impacts, even for children who are removed and placed in highly resourced and supportive homes. As in all the human literature about early adversity, however, there are marked individual differences in outcomes in those with similar early experiences (multifinality). This generates a need to identify the factors that explain why some individuals succumb and others thrive following exposure to major and prolonged stressful life experiences. Again, it is time to move beyond proving that stress has long-term effects, to explaining individual differences and the processes that promote resilience and recovery. This has been done in the behavioral literature (Masten, 2007); however, we are only beginning to explore molecular and neurobiological underpinnings of resilience and recovery (e.g., Bowes & Jaffee, 2013).

Regarding the transition from childhood to adolescence, the literature in rats and mice is generating excitement about the possibility that puberty opens another sensitive period when stressors can have long-lasting effects, but protective interventions can as well. So far, however, there are only meager data that speak to this hypothesis in humans. There is a growing body of information on the childhood and adolescent impacts of exposure to traumatic events, most notably physical and sexual abuse. Unfortunately, as we noted, much of it concerns PTSD and compares brain structure and function in individuals with PTSD traumatized in childhood to healthy controls without a history of trauma. This makes it difficult to disentangle the impacts of trauma from neural differences that might have existed before the trauma exposure and made these individuals more susceptible to developing PTSD. Thus, in the future we need more studies contrasting exposure to stressful and/or traumatic events during middle childhood versus in adolescence. We also need these studies to include both individuals with and without psychopathology, and with and without trauma histories.

In addition to these gaps in the literature, there are others that will need to be addressed to understand the role of stress timing in development. First, the cleanest design to assess stress timing would be to find individuals who were exposed to the same type of major stressor, but at different developmental periods. However, that assumes that the same event is composed of the same stressors when experienced during different ages. Take, for example, a natural disaster and a family with an infant and a young teenager. For the infant, if the attachment figure continues to be able to meet the infant's needs responsively and sensitively during and following the disastrous event, then it may not be much of a stressor in the infant's life. However, the teenager in the family likely understands the danger posed by the event resulting in this child fearing for his or her life and the lives of her family members, making this a traumatic event for the teenager. She might also suffer from dislocation following the event, loss of friends and school, and may be privy to parents' worries and anxieties, making this a very prolonged period of stress. If exposure to the natural disaster has greater impacts on the adolescent than the infant, is this because adolescents are more vulnerable to stress or because the natural disaster is experienced as a very different type of stressor for the infant and the teen?

There is yet another reason that cognitive development creates challenges in studying the impact of stress timing. Specifically, events experienced earlier in life may take on different meaning as children's conceptual abilities develop. For example, children's understanding of adoption changes with development, with older children more likely to construe the absence of the biological mother as a loss, which may lead to concerns about future abandonment (Brodzinsky, Singer, & Braff, 1984). For children adopted from adverse conditions, achieving this level of cognitive awareness might constitute the "second hit" that precipitates fears, anxieties, and cascading neurodevelopmental impacts. The capacity of human beings to increasingly, with development, reflect on their own existence, to make meaning, and have that meaning powerfully impact physiology and neurobiology is a major challenge to understanding stress timing.

A well-known problem in stress research is that the subjective experience of events is often more important than the objective nature in determining what is stressful for different individuals (Lazarus & Folkman, 1984). Less well appreciated is that the subjective nature of what makes experiences stressful has considerable ramifications for our understanding of how adverse life conditions translate into stress responses and impacts during different developmental periods. This is a place where some concerted conceptual work would be a boon to the field. The need to consider how the competencies of children at different points in development intersect with the objective nature of the adverse exposures to determine the stress experienced by the child is part of the larger challenge of doing a better job of differentiating types of adversities (Sheridan & McLaughlin, 2014).

Lastly, although problems like the human capacity for reflection and meaning-making cannot be modeled in laboratory animals, we cannot understand the role of stress timing in development without integrating human and animal research. Although there is no species that evolved to be a model of human development, we need the animal work to design experiments that allow the tests of causality and the invasive procedures that uncover mechanisms. But research in animals needs to be done in conjunction with research on human development with much cross-talk among researchers. The barriers between researchers studying human development and those studying animal models are breaking down, as are those between research focused on different levels of analysis. The chapters complied in this volume speak to the greater integration in the field—a hopeful direction for the future of research on stress and development.

Acknowledgments

The writing of this chapter was supported by HD075349 to the second author.

References

Andersen, S. L., Tomada, A., Vincow, E. S., Valente, E., Polcari, A., & Teicher, M. H. (2008). Preliminary evidence for sensitive periods in the effect of childhood sexual abuse on regional brain development. *The Journal of Neuropsychiatry and Clinical Neuroscience*, *20*(3), 292–301. https://doi.org/10.1176/appi.neuropsych.20.3.292

Artal, R. (1980). Fetal adrenal medulla. *Clinical Obstetrics and Gynecology*, *23*(3), 825–836.

Baibazarova, E., Van De Beek, C., Cohen-Kettenis, P. T., Buitelaar, J., Shelton, K. H., & Van Goozen, S. H. M. (2013). Influence of prenatal maternal stress, maternal plasma cortisol and cortisol in the amniotic fluid on birth outcomes and child temperament at 3 months. *Psychoneuroendocrinology*, *38*, 907–915. https://doi.org/10.1016/j.psyneuen.2012.09.015

Beissner, F., Meissner, K., & Napadow, V. (2013). The autonomic brain: An activation likelihood estimation meta-analysis for central processing of autonomic function. *The Journal of Neuroscience*, *33*(25), 10503–10511. https://doi.org/10.1523/JNEUROSCI.1103-13.2013

Belsky, J. (1993). Etiology of child maltreatment: A developmental-ecological analysis. *Psychological Bulletin*, *114*(3), 413–434. https://doi.org/10.1037/0033-2909.114.3.413

Benarroch, E. E. (1993). The central autonomic network: functional organization, dysfunction, and perspective. In *Mayo Clinic Proceedings* (Vol. 68, No. 10, pp. 988–1001). New York, NY: Elsevier.

Bergman, K., Sarkar, P., Glover, V., & O'Connor, T. G. (2010). Maternal prenatal cortisol and infant cognitive development: Moderation by infant-mother attachment. *Biological Psychiatry*, *67*, 1026–1032. https://doi.org/10.1016/j.biopsych.2010.01.002

Bernstein, D. P., Ahluvalia, T., Pogge, D., & Handelsman, L. (1997). Validity of the Childhood Trauma Questionnaire in an adolescent psychiatric population. *Journal of the American Academy of Child & Adolescent Psychiatry*, *36*(3), 340–348. https://doi.org/10.1097/00004583-199703000-00012

Blakemore, S. J., Burnett, S., & Dahl, R. E. (2010). The role of puberty in the developing adolescent brain. *Human Brain Mapping*, *31*, 926–933. https://doi.org/10.1002/hbm.21052

Bowes, L., & Jaffee, S. R. (2013). Biology, genes, and resilience: Toward a multidisciplinary approach. Trauma, Violence, & Abuse, *14*(3), 195–208. https://doi.org/10.1177/1524838013487807

Boyce, W. T., & Ellis, B. J. (2005). Biological sensitivity to context: I. An evolutionary–developmental theory of the origins and functions of stress reactivity. *Development and Psychopathology*, *17*, 271–301. https://doi.org/10.1017/S0954579405050145

Braun, K., Bock, J., Wainstock, T., Matas, E., Gaisler-Salomon, I., Fegert, J.,...Segal, M. (2017). Experience-induced transgenerational (re-)programming of neuronal structure and functions: Impact of stress prior and during pregnancy. *Neuroscience & Biobehavioral Reviews*. https://doi.org/10.1016/j.neubiorev.2017.05.021

Brodzinsky, D. M., Singer, L. M., & Braff, A. M. (1984). Children's understanding of adoption. *Child Development*, *55*(3), 869–878.

Bronson, S. L., & Bale, T. L. (2016). The placenta as a mediator of stress effects on neurodevelopmental reprogramming. *Neuropsychopharmacology*, *41*, 207–218. https://doi.org/10.1038/npp.2015.231

Buss, C., Davis, E. P., Muftuler, L. T., Head, K., & Sandman, C. A. (2010). High pregnancy anxiety during mid-gestation is associated with decreased gray matter density in 6-9-year-old children. *Psychoneuroendocrinology*, *35*, 141–153. https://doi.org/10.1016/j.psyneuen.2009.07.010

Buss, C., Davis, E. P., Shahbaba, B., Pruessner, J. C., Head, K., & Sandman, C. A. (2012). Maternal cortisol over the course of pregnancy and subsequent child amygdala and hippocampus volumes and affective problems. *Proceedings of the National Academy of Sciences*, *109*(20), E1312–E1319. https://doi.org/10.1073/pnas.1201295109

Buss, C., Entringer, S., Reyes, J. F., Chicz-DeMet, A., Sandman, C. A., Waffarn, F., & Wadhwa, P. D. (2009). The maternal cortisol awakening response in human pregnancy is associated with the length of gestation. *American Journal of Obstetrics and Gynecology*, *201*, 398.e1–398.e8. https://doi.org/10.1016/j.ajog.2009.06.063

Charil, A., Laplante, D. P., Vaillancourt, C., & King, S. (2010). Prenatal stress and brain development. *Brain Research Reviews*, *65*, 56–79. https://doi.org/10.1016/j.brainresrev.2010.06.002

Cicchetti, D. (1991). Fractures in the crystal: Developmental psychopathology and the emergence of self. *Developmental Review*, *11*, 271–287.

Class, Q. a, Buss, C., Davis, E. P., Gierczak, M., Pattillo, C., Chicz-DeMet, A., & Sandman, C. A. (2008). Low levels of corticotropin-releasing hormone during early pregnancy are associated with precocious maturation of the human fetus. *Developmental Neuroscience*, *30*, 419–426. https://doi.org/10.1159/000191213

Cottrell, E. C., & Seckl, J. R. (2009). Prenatal stress, glucocorticoids and the programming of adult disease. *Frontiers in Behavioral Neuroscience*, *3*(19), 1–9. https://doi.org/10.3389/neuro.08.019.2009

Cowell, R. A., Cicchetti, D., Rogosch, F. A., & Toth, S. L. (2015). Childhood maltreatment and its effect on neurocognitive functioning: Timing and chronicity matter. *Development and Psychobiology, 27*, 521–533.

Cymerblit-Sabba, A., Zubedat, S., Aga-mizrachi, S., Biady, G., Nakhash, B., Rubin, S.,...Avital, A. (2015). Mapping the developmental trajectory of stress effects: Pubescence as the risk window. *Psychoneuroendocrinology, 52*, 168–175. https://doi.org/10.1016/j.psyneuen.2014.11.012

Danese, A., & McEwen, B. S. (2012). Adverse childhood experiences, allostasis, allostatic load, and age-related disease. *Physiology and Behavior, 106*, 29–39. https://doi.org/10.1016/j.physbeh.2011.08.019

Davis, E. P., Buss, C., Muftuler, L. T., Head, K., Hasso, A., Wing, D. A.,...Sandman, C. A. (2011). Children's brain development benefits from longer gestation. *Frontiers in Psychology, 2*(1), 1–7. https://doi.org/10.3389/fpsyg.2011.00001

de Kloet, E. R. (2014). From receptor balance to rational glucocorticoid therapy. *Endocrinology, 155*(8), 2754–2769. https://doi.org/10.1210/en.2014-1048

Del Giudice, M., Ellis, B. J., & Shirtcliff, E. a. (2011). The Adaptive Calibration Model of stress responsivity. *Neuroscience and Biobehavioral Reviews, 35*(7), 1562–1592. https://doi.org/10.1016/j.neubiorev.2010.11.007

DiPietro, J. A., Kivlighan, K. T., Costigan, K. A., Rubin, S. E., Shiffler, D. E., Henderson, J. L., & Pillion, J. P. (2010). Prenatal antecedents of newborn neurological maturation. *Child Development, 81*(1), 115–130. https://doi.org/10.1111/j.1467-8624.2009.01384.x

DiPietro, J. A., & Voegtline, K. M. (2017). The gestational foundation of sex differences in development and vulnerability. *Neuroscience, 342*, 4–20. https://doi.org/10.1016/j.neuroscience.2015.07.068

Doyle, C., Werner, E., Feng, T., Lee, S., Altemus, M., Isler, J. R., & Monk, C. (2015). Pregnancy distress gets under fetal skin: Maternal ambulatory assessment and sex differences in prenatal development. *Developmental Psychobiology, 57*, 607–625. https://doi.org/10.1002/dev.21317

Eiland, L., & Romeo, R. D. (2013). Stress and the developing adolescent brain. *Neuroscience, 249*, 162–171. https://doi.org/10.1016/j.neuroscience.2012.10.048

Entringer, S., Buss, C., & Wadhwa, P. D. (2015). Prenatal stress, development, health and disease risk: A psychobiological perspective-2015 Curt Richter Award Paper. *Psychoneuroendocrinology, 62*, 366–375. https://doi.org/10.1016/j.psyneuen.2015.08.019

Fisher, H. L., Caspi, A., Moffitt, T. E., Wertz, J., Gray, R., Newbury, J.,...Arseneault, L. (2015). Measuring adolescents' exposure to victimization: The Environmental Risk (E-Risk) Longitudinal Twin Study. *Development and Psychopathology, 27*, 1399–1416. https://doi.org/10.1017/S0954579415000838

Flannery, J. E., Gabard-Durnam, L. J., Shapiro, M., Goff, B., Caldera, C., Louie, J.,...Tottenham, N. (2017). Diurnal cortisol after early institutional care—Age matters. *Developmental Cognitive Neuroscience, 25*, 160–166.

Fuhrmann, D., Knoll, L. J., & Blakemore, S. J. (2015). Adolescence as a sensitive period of brain development. *Trends in Cognitive Sciences, 19*(10), 558–566. https://doi.org/10.1016/j.tics.2015.07.008

Gee, D. G., & Casey, B. J. (2015). The impact of developmental timing for stress and recovery. *Neurobiology of Stress, 1*, 184–194. https://doi.org/10.1016/j.ynstr.2015.02.001

Gitau, A., Fisk, N. M., & Glover, V. (2004). Human fetal and maternal corticotrophin releasing hormone responses to acute stress. *Archives of Disease in Childhood Fetal and Neonatal Edition, 89*, F29–F32. https://doi.org/10.1016/j.psyneuen.2013.09.018.Scn8a

Goddings, A. L., Mills, K. L., Clasen, L. S., Giedd, J. N., Viner, R. M., & Blakemore, S. J. (2014). The influence of puberty on subcortical brain development. *NeuroImage, 88*, 242–251. https://doi.org/10.1016/j.neuroimage.2013.09.073

Goldstein, D. S., & Kopin, I. J. (2008). Adrenomedullary, adrenocortical, and sympathoneural responses to stressors: A meta-analysis. *Endocrine Regulations, 42*, 111–119. https://doi.org/http://dx.doi.org/18999898

Grant, K., Sandman, C. A., Wing, D. A., Dmitrieva, J., & Poggi, E. (2015). Prenatal programming of postnatal susceptibility to memory impairments: A developmental double jeopardy. *Psychological Science, 26*(7), 1054–1062. https://doi.org/10.1177/0956797615580299

Grigoriadis, D. E., Dent, G. W., Turner, J. G., Uno, H., Shelton, S. E., De Souza, E. B., & Kalin, N. H. (1995). Corticotropin-releasing factor (CRF) receptors in infant rhesus monkey brain and pituitary gland: Biochemical characterization and autoradiographic localization. *Developmental Neuroscience, 17*(5–6), 357–367.

Gunnar, M. R. (1992). Reactivity of the hypothalamic-pituitary-adrenocortical system to stressors in normal infants and children. *Pediatrics, 90*(3), 491–497. Retrieved from http://pediatrics.aappublications.org/content/90/3/491.abstract%5Cnpapers3://publication/uuid/AA8A89E4-0E05-4F82-A220-C8820B3B7AB7

Gunnar, M. R. (2001). Effects of early deprivation: Findings from orphanage-reared infants and children. In C. A. Nelson & M. Luciana (Eds.), *Handbook of developmental cognitive neuroscience* (pp. 617–629). Cambridge, MA: MIT Press.

Gunnar, M. R. (2017). Social buffering of stress in development: A career perspective. *Perspectives on Psychological Science, 12*(3), 355–373. https://doi.org/10.1177/1745691616680612

Gunnar, M. R., Brodersen, L., Krueger, K., & Rigatuso, J. (1996). Dampening of adrenocortical responses during infancy: Normative changes and individual differences. *Child Development, 67*(3), 877–889.

Gunnar, M. R., & Davis, E. P. (2013). The effects of stress on early brain and behavioral development. In H. B. Tager-Flusberg (Ed.), *Cognitive development* (pp. 447–466). New York, NY: Elsevier.

Gunnar, M. R., Talge, N. M., & Herrera, A. (2009a). Stressor paradigms in developmental studies: What does and does not work to produce mean increases in salivary cortisol. *Psychoneuroendocrinology, 34*, 953–967. https://doi.org/10.1016/j.psyneuen.2009.02.010

Gunnar, M. R., & Quevedo, K. (2007). The neurobiology of stress and development. *Annual Review of Psychology, 58*, 145–173. https://doi.org/10.1146/annurev.psych.58.110405.085605

Gunnar, M. R., & Vazquez, D. (2006). Stress neurobiology and developmental psychopathology. In D. Cicchetti & D. J. Cohen (Eds.), *Developmental Psychopathology* (2nd ed., pp. 533–577). *Developmental Neuroscience*, Vol. 2. New York, NY: Wiley.

Gunnar, M. R., Wewerka, S., Frenn, K., Long, J. D., & Griggs, C. (2009b). Developmental changes in hypothalamus–pituitary–adrenal activity over the transition to adolescence: Normative changes and associations with puberty. *Developmental*

Psychopathology, *21*(1), 69–85. https://doi.org/10.1017/S0954579409000054.Developmental

Hanson, J. L., Nacewicz, B. M., Sutterer, M. J., Cayo, A. A., Schaefer, S. M., Rudolph, K. D.,...Davidson, R. J. (2015). Behavioral problems after early life stress: Contributions of the hippocampus and amygdala. *Biological Psychiatry*, *77*, 314–323.

Heim, C., & Binder, E. B. (2012). Current research trends in early life stress and depression: Review of human studies on sensitive periods, gene-environment interactions, and epigenetics. *Experimental Neurology*, *233*, 102–111. https://doi.org/10.1016/j.expneurol.2011.10.032

Herman, J. P., Figueiredo, H., Mueller, N. K., Ulrich-Lai, Y., Ostrander, M. M., Choi, D. C., & Cullinan, W. E. (2003). Central mechanisms of stress integration: Hierarchical circuitry controlling hypothalamo-pituitary-adrenocortical responsiveness. *Frontiers in Neuroendocrinology*, *24*, 151–180. https://doi.org/10.1016/j.yfrne.2003.07.001

Herman, J. P., McKlveen, J. M., Ghosal, S., Kopp, B., Wulsin, A., Makinson, R.,...Myers, B. (2016). Regulation of the hypothelamic-pituitary-adrenocortical stress response. *Comparative Physiology*, *6*(2), 603–621. https://doi.org/10.1002/cphy.c150015.

Hodel, A. S., Hunt, R. H., Cowell, R. A., Van Den Heuvel, S. E., Gunnar, M. R., & Thomas, K. M. (2015). Duration of early adversity and structural brain development in post-institutionalized adolescents. *Neuroimage*, *105*, 112–119.

Houston, S. M., Herting, M. M., & Sowell, E. R. (2014). The neurobiology of childhood structural brain development: Conception through adulthood. *Current Topics in Behavioral Neuroscience*, *16*, 3–17. https://doi.org/10.1007/7854

Howell, B. R., Grand, A. P., McCormack, K. M., Sh, i. Y., LaPrarie, J. L., Maestripieri, D.,...Sanchez, M. M. (2014). Early adverse experience increases emotional reactivity in juvenile rhesus macaques: Relation to amygdala volume. *Developmental Psychobiology*, *56*, 1735–1746.

Howell, B. R., McCormack, K. M., Grand, A. P., Sawyer, N. T., Zhang, X., Maestripieri, D.,...Sanchez, M. M. (2013). Brain white matter microstructure alterations in adolescent rhesus monkeys exposed to early life stress: Associations with high cortisol during infancy. *Biology of Mood and Anxiety Disorders*, *3*, 21.

Ishimoto, H., & Jaffe, R. B. (2011). Development and function of the human fetal adrenal cortex: A key component in the feto-placental unit. *Endocrine Reviews*, *32*(3), 317–355. https://doi.org/10.1210/er.2010-0001

Johnson, M. H. (2001). Functional brain development in humans. *Nature Reviews Neuroscience*, *2*, 475–483.

Johnson, A. E., Bruce, J., Tarullo, A. R., & Gunnar, M. R. (2011). Growth delay as an index of allostatic load in young children: Predictions to disinhibited social approach and diurnal cortisol activity. *Development and Psychopathology*, *23*, 859–871. https://doi.org/10.1017/S0954579411000356

Kim, D.-J., Davis, E. P., Sandman, C. A., Sporns, O., O'Donnell, B. F., Buss, C., & Hetrick, W. P. (2016). Prenatal maternal cortisol has sex-specific associations with child brain network properties. *Cerebral Cortex*, *27*, 1–12. https://doi.org/10.1093/cercor/bhw303

Kim, J. W., Kim, Y. J., & Chang, Y. P. (2013). Administration of dexamethasone to neonatal rats induces hypomyelination and changes in the morphology of oligodendrocyte precursors. *Comparative Medicine*, *63*, 48–54.

Knudsen, E. I. (2004). Sensitive periods in the development of the brain and behavior. *Journal of Cognitive Neuroscience*, *16*(8), 1412–1425. https://doi.org/10.1162/0898929042304796

Koenig, J., & Thayer, J. F. (2016). Sex differences in healthy human heart rate variability: A meta-analysis. *Neuroscience and Biobehavioral Reviews*, *64*, 288–310. https://doi.org/10.1016/j.neubiorev.2016.03.007

Koss, K. J., Mliner, S. B., Donzella, B., & Gunnar, M. R. (2016). Early adversity, hypocortisolism, and behavior problems at school entry: A study of internationally adopted children. *Psychoneuroendocrinology*, *66*, 31–38.

Kryski, K. R., Smith, H. J., Sheikh, H. I., Singh, S. M., & Hayden, E. P. (2013). HPA axis reactivity in early childhood: Associations with symptoms and moderation by sex. *Psychoneuroendocrinology*, *38*, 2327–2336. https://doi.org/10.1016/j.psyneuen.2013.05.002

Kuhlman, K. R., Vargas, I., Geiss, E. G., & Lopez-Duran, N. L. (2015). Age of trauma onset and HPA axis dysregulation among trauma-exposed youth. *Journal of Traumatic Stress*, *28*, 572–579.

Lazarus, R. S., & Folkman, S. (1984). Coping and adaptation. In W. D. Gentry (Ed.), *The handbook of behavioral medicine* (pp. 282–325). New York: Guilford.

Lenroot, R. K., & Giedd, J. N. (2010). Sex differences in the adolescent brain. *Brain and Cognition*, *72*(1), 46–55. https://doi.org/10.1016/j.bandc.2009.10.008.

Li, N., Wang, Y., Zhao, X., Gao, Y., Song, M., Yu, L.,...Wang, X. (2015). Long-term effect of early-life stress from earthquake exposure on working memory in adulthood. *Neuropsychiatric Disease and Treatment*, *11*, 2959–2965. https://doi.org/10.2147/NDT.S88770

Lupien, S. J., McEwen, B. S., Gunnar, M. R., & Heim, C. (2009). Effects of stress throughout the lifespan on the brain, behaviour and cognition. *Nature Reviews Neuroscience*, *10*, 434–445.

Lyons, D. M., & Parker, K. J. (2007). Stress inoculation-induced indications of resilience in monkeys. *Journal of Traumatic Stress*, *20*(4), 423–433. https://doi.org/10.1002/jts.

Lyons, D. M., Parker, K. J., & Schatzberg, A. F. (2010). Animal models of early life stress: Implications for understanding resilience. *Developmental Psychobiology*, *52*, 616–624. https://doi.org/10.1002/dev.20500

Maestripieri, D., McCormack, K., Lindell, S. G., Higley, J. D., & Sanchez, M. M. (2006). Influence of parenting style on the offspring's behaviour and CSF monoamine metabolite levels in crossfostered and noncrossfostered female rhesus macaques. *Behavioral Brain Research*, *175*, 90–95.

Macey, P. M., Ogren, J. A., Kumar, R., & Harper, R. M. (2016). Functional imaging of autonomic regulation: Methods and key findings. *Frontiers in Neuroscience*, *9*(513), 1–23. https://doi.org/10.3389/fnins.2015.00513

Maheu, F. S., Dozier, M., Guyer, A. E., Mandell, D., Peloso, E., Poeth, K.,...Ernst, M. (2010). A preliminary study of medial temporal lobe function in youths with a history of caregiver deprivation and emotional neglect. *Cognition, Affect, and Behavioral Neuroscience*, *19*, 34–49.

Marasco, V., Herzyk, P., Robinson, J., & Spencer, K. A. (2016). Pre- and post-natal stress programming: Developmental exposure to glucocorticoids causes long-term brain-region specific changes to transcriptome in the precocial Japanese quail. *Journal of Neuroendocrinology*, *28*, 1–17. https://doi.org/10.1111/jne.12387

Masten, A. S. (2007). Resilience in developing systems: Progress and promise as the fourth wave rises. *Development and Psychopathology*, 19, 921–930. https://doi.org/10.1017/S0954579407000442

McEwen, B. S., Nasca, C., & Gray, J. D. (2016). Stress effects on neuronal structure: Hippocampus, amygdala, and prefrontal cortex. *Neuropsychopharmacology Reviews*, 41, 3–23. https://doi.org/10.1038/npp.2015.171

McEwen, B. S., & Wingfield, J. C. (2010). What is in a name? Integrating homeostasis, allostasis and stress. *Hormones and Behavior*, 57, 105–111. https://doi.org/10.1016/j.yhbeh.2009.09.011

McLaughlin, K. A., & Sheridan, M. A. (2016). Beyond cumulative risk: A dimensional approach to childhood adversity. *Current Directions in Psychological Science*, 25(4), 239–245. https://doi.org/10.1177/0963721416655883

McLaughlin, K. A., Sheridan, M. A., Tibu, F., Fox, N. A., Zeanah, C. H., & Nelson, C. A. (2015). Causal effects of the early caregiving environment on development of stress response systems in children. *Proceedings of the National Academy of Sciences*, 112, 5637–5642.

Meaney, M. J., & Szyf, M. (2005). Environmental programming of stress responses through DNA methylation: Life at the interface between a dynamic environment and a fixed genome. *Dialogues in Clinical Neuroscience*, 7(2), 103–123. https://doi.org/http://dx.doi.org/10.1523/JNEUROSCI.3652-05.2005

Mehta, M. A., Golembo, N. I., Nosarti, C., Colvert, E., Mota, A., Williams, S. C., … Sonuga-Barke, E. J. (2009). Amygdala, hippocampal and corpus callosum size following severe early institutional deprivation: The English and Romanian Adoptees study pilot. *Journal of Child Psychology & Psychiatry*, 50, 943–951.

Monk, C., Georgieff, M. K., & Osterholm, E. A. (2013). Research review: Maternal prenatal distress and poor nutrition—Mutually influencing risk factors affecting infant neurocognitive development. *Journal of Child Psychology and Psychiatry*, 54(2), 115–130. https://doi.org/10.1111/jcpp.12000

Myers, B., Scheimann, J. R., Franco-Villanueva, A., & Herman, J. P. (2017). Ascending mechanisms of stress integration: Implications for brainstem regulation of neuroendocrine and behavioral stress responses. *Neuroscience and Biobehavioral Reviews*, 74, 366–375. https://doi.org/10.1016/j.neubiorev.2016.05.011

Negriff, S., Saxbe, D. E., & Trickett, P. K. (2015). Childhood maltreatment, pubertal development, HPA axis functioning, and psychosocial outcomes: An integrative biopsychosocial model. *Developmental Psychobiology*, 57(8), 984–993. https://doi.org/10.1002/nbm.3369.

Nijsen, M. J., Croiset, G., Stam, R., Bruijnzeel, A., Diamant, M., de Wied, D., & Wiegant, V. M. (2000). The role of the CRH type 1 receptor in autonomic responses to corticotropin-releasing hormone in the rat. *Neuropsychopharmacology*, 22, 388–399. https://doi.org/10.1016/S0893-133X(99)00126-8

O'Donnell, K. J., & Meaney, M. J. (2017). Fetal origins of mental health: The developmental origins of health and disease hypothesis. *American Journal of Psychiatry*, 174(4), 319–328. https://doi.org/10.1176/appi.ajp.2016.16020138

Ong, S. X., Chng, K., Meaney, M. J., & Buschdorf, J. P. (2013). Decreased hippocampal mineralocorticoid: Glucocorticoid receptor ratio is associated with low birth weight in female cynomolgus macaque neonates. *Journal of Molecular Endocrinology*, 51(1), 59–67. https://doi.org/10.1530/JME-12-0218

Pagliaccio, D., Luby, J. L., Bogdan, R., Agrawal, A., Gaffrey, M. S., Belden, A. C., … Barch, D. M. (2014). Stress-system genes and life stress predict cortisol levels and amygdala and hippocampal volumes in children. *Neuropsychopharmacology*, 39, 1245–1253. https://doi.org/10.1038/npp.2013.327

Pechtel, P., Lyons-Ruth, K., Anderson, C. M., & Teicher, M. H. (2014). Sensitive periods of amygdala development: The role of maltreatment in preadolescence. *Neuroimage*, 87, 236–244.

Porges, S.W., & Furman, S. A. (2011). The early development of the autonomic nervous system provides a neural platform for social behavior: A polyvagal perspective. *Infant and Child Development*, 20(1), 106–118. https://doi.org/10.1002/icd.688.

Provençal, N., & Binder, E. B. (2015). The effects of early life stress on the epigenome: From the womb to adulthood and even before. *Experimental Neurology*, 268, 10–20. https://doi.org/10.1016/j.expneurol.2014.09.001

Pryce, C. R. (2008). Postnatal ontogeny of expression of the corticosteroid receptor genes in mammalian brains: Inter-species and intra-species differences. *Brain Research Reviews*, 57(2), 596–605. https://doi.org/10.1016/j.brainresrev.2007.08.005

Quevedo, K., Johnson, A., Loman, M., Lafavor, T., & Gunnar, M. R. (2012). The confluence of early deprivation and puberty on the cortisol awakening response: A study of post-institutionalized children. *International Journal of Behavioral Development*, 36, 19–28.

Quintanar, J. L., & Guzmán-Soto, I. (2013). Hypothalamic neurohormones and immune responses. *Frontiers in Integrative Neuroscience*, 7(56), 1–17. https://doi.org/10.3389/fnint.2013.00056

Rakers, F., Bischoff, S., Schiffner, R., Haase, M., Rupprecht, S., Kiehntopf, M., … Schwab, M. (2015). Role of catecholamines in maternal-fetal stress transfer in sheep. *American Journal of Obstetrics and Gynecology*, 213, 684.e1–684.e9. https://doi.org/10.1016/j.ajog.2015.07.020

Rao, H., Betancourt, L., Giannetta, J. M., Brodsky, N. L., Korczykowski, M., Avants, B. B., … Farah, M. J. (2010). Early parental care is important for hippocampal maturation: Evidence from brain morphology in humans. *Neuroimage*, 49, 1144–1150.

Reuben, A., Moffitt, T. E., Caspi, A., Belsky, D. W., Harrington, H., Schroeder, F., … Danese, A. (2016). Lest we forget: Comparing retrospective and prospective assessments of adverse childhood experiences in the prediction of adult health. *Journal of Child Psychology and Psychiatry and Allied Disciplines*, 57(10), 1103–1112. https://doi.org/10.1111/jcpp.12621

Rice, F., Harold, G. T., Boivin, J., van den Bree, M., Hay, D. F., & Thapar, A. (2010). The links between prenatal stress and offspring development and psychopathology: Disentangling environmental and inherited influences. *Psychological Medicine*, 40, 335–345. https://doi.org/10.1017/S0033291709005911

Romens, S. E., McDonald, J., Svaren, J., & Pollak, S. D. (2015). Associations between early life stress and gene methylation in children. *Child Development*, 86(1), 303–309. https://doi.org/10.1111/cdev.12270

Romeo, R. D. (2010). Pubertal maturation and programming of hypothalamic-pituitary-adrenal reactivity. *Frontiers in*

Neuroendocrinology, 31, 232–240. https://doi.org/10.1016/j.yfrne.2010.02.004

Romeo, R. D. (2017). The impact of stress on the structure of the adolescent brain: Implications for adolescent mental health. *Brain Research, 1654*, 185–191. https://doi.org/10.1016/j.brainres.2016.03.021

Romeo, R. D., Bellani, R., Karatsoreos, I. N., Chhua, N., Vernov, M., Conrad, C. D., & McEwen, B. S. (2006). Stress history and pubertal development interact to shape hypothalamic-pituitary-adrenal axis plasticity. *Endocrinology, 147*(4), 1664–1674. https://doi.org/10.1210/en.2005-1432

Romeo, R. D., Patel, R., Pham, L., & So, V. M. (2016). Adolescence and the ontogeny of the hormonal stress response in male and female rats and mice. *Neuroscience and Biobehavioral Reviews, 70*, 206–216. https://doi.org/10.1016/j.neubiorev.2016.05.020

Rutter, M., & Sonuga-Barke, E. J. (2010). X. Conclusions: overview of findings from the era study, inferences, and research implications. *Monograph Social Research Child Development, 75*, 212–229.

Sanchez, M. M., McCormack, K., Grand, A. P., Fulks, R., Graff, A., & Maestripieri, D. (2010). Effects of sex and early maternal abuse on adrenocorticotropin hormone and cortisol responses to the corticotropin-releasing hormone challenge during the first 3 years of life in group-living rhesus monkeys. *Development and Psychopathology, 22*, 45–53. https://doi.org/10.1017/S0954579409990253

Sandman, C. A., Glynn, L. M., & Davis, E. P. (2013). Is there a viability-vulnerability tradeoff? Sex differences in fetal programming. *Journal of Psychosomatic Research, 75*(4), 327–335. https://doi.org/10.1016/j.jpsychores.2013.07.009.IS

Sapolsky, R. M., Romero, L. M., & Munck, A. U. (2000). How do glucocorticoids influence stress responses? Integrating permissive, suppressive, stimulatory, and preparative actions. *Endocrine Reviews, 21*(1), 55–89. https://doi.org/10.1210/er.21.1.55

Schneider, U., Schleussner, E., Fiedler, A., Jaekel, S., Liehr, M., Haueisen, J., & Hoyer, D. (2009). Fetal heart rate variability reveals differential dynamics in the intrauterine development of the sympathetic and parasympathetic branches of the autonomic nervous system. *Physiological Measurement, 30*, 215–226. https://doi.org/10.1088/0967-3334/30/2/008

Schoedl, A. F., Costa, M. C. P., Mari, J. J., Mello, M. F., Tyrka, A. R., Carpenter, L. L., & Price, L. H. (2010). The clinical correlates of reported childhood sexual abuse: An association between age at trauma onset and severity of depression and PTSD in adults. *Journal of Child Sexual Abuse, 19*(2), 156–170. https://doi.org/10.1080/10538711003615038

Schulkin, J. (1999). Corticotropin-releasing hormone signals adversity in both the placenta and the brain: Regulation by glucocorticoids and allostatic overload. *Journal of Endocrinology, 161*, 349–356. https://doi.org/10.1677/joe.0.1610349

Sheridan, M. A., Fox, N. A., Zeanah, C., McLaughlin, K. A., & Nelson, C. A. (2012). Variation in neural development as a result of exposure to institutionalization early in childhood. *Proceedings of the National Academy of Sciences, 109*, 12927–12932.

Sheridan, M. A., & McLaughlin, K. A. (2014). Dimensions of early experience and neural development: Deprivation and threat. *Trends in Cognitive Sciences, 18*(11), 580–585. https://doi.org/10.1016/j.tics.2014.09.001

Shirtcliff, E. A., Dismukes, A. R., Marceau, K., Ruttle, P. L., Simmons, J. G., & Han, G. (2015). A dual-axis approach to understanding neuroendocrine development. *Developmental Psychobiology, 57*, 643–653. https://doi.org/10.1002/dev.21337

Silvers, J. A., Lumian, D. S., Gabard-Durnam, L., Gee, D. G., Goff, B., Fareri, D. S.,...Tottenham, N. (2016). Previous institutionalization is followed by broader amygdala-hippocampal-PFC network connectivity during aversive learning in human development. *Journal of Neuroscience, 36*, 6420–6430.

Sisk, C. L., & Zehr, J. L. (2005). Pubertal hormones organize the adolescent brain and behavior. *Frontiers in Neuroendocrinology, 26*, 163–174. https://doi.org/10.1016/j.yfrne.2005.10.003

Slotkin, T., Auman, J. T., & Seidler, F. J. (2003). Ontogenesis of beta-adrenoceptor signaling: Implications for perinatal physiology and for fetal effects of tocolytic drugs. *The Journal of Pharmacology and Experimental Therapeutics, 306*, 1–7. https://doi.org/10.1124/jpet.102.048421

Smith, R., Thayer, J. F., Khalsa, S. S., & Lane, R. D. (2017). The hierarchical basis of neurovisceral integration. *Neuroscience and Biobehavioral Reviews, 75*, 274–296. https://doi.org/10.1016/j.neubiorev.2017.02.003

Sowell, E. R., Thompson, P. M., Holmes, C. J., Jernigan, T. L., & Toga, A.W. (1999). In vivo evidence for post-adolescent brain maturation in frontal and striatal regions. *Nature Neuroscience, 2*(10), 859–861. https://doi.org/10.1038/13154

Stiles, J., & Jernigan, T. L. (2010). The basics of brain development. *Neuropsychology Review, 20*, 327–348. https://doi.org/10.1007/s11065-010-9148-4

Strüber, N., Strüber, D., & Roth, G. (2014). Impact of early adversity on glucocorticoid regulation and later mental disorders. *Neuroscience and Biobehavioral Reviews, 38*(1), 17–37. https://doi.org/10.1016/j.neubiorev.2013.10.015

Suleiman, A. B., & Dahl, R. E. (2017). Leveraging neuroscience to inform adolescent health: The need for an innovative transdisciplinary developmental science of adolescence. *Journal of Adolescent Health, 60*, 240–248. https://doi.org/10.1016/j.jadohealth.2016.12.010

Sumner, M. M., Bernard, K., & Dozier, M. (2010). Young children's full-day patterns of cortisol production on child care days. *Archives of Pediatrics & Adolescent Medicine, 164*(6), 567–571. https://doi.org/10.1001/archpediatrics.2010.85

Teicher, M. H., Samson, J. A., Anderson, C. M., & Ohashi, K. (2016). The effects of childhood maltreatment on brain structure, function and connectivity. *Nature Review Neuroscience, 17*, 652–666.

Thayer, J. F., Åhs, F., Fredrikson, M., Sollers, J. J., & Wager, T. D. (2012). A meta-analysis of heart rate variability and neuroimaging studies: Implications for heart rate variability as a marker of stress and health. *Neuroscience and Biobehavioral Reviews, 36*, 747–756. https://doi.org/10.1016/j.neubiorev.2011.11.009

Thayer, J. F., & Lane, R. D. (2000). A model of neurovisceral integration in emotion regulation and dysregulation. *Journal of Affective Disorders, 61*, 201–216. https://doi.org/10.1016/S0165-0327(00)00338-4

Tottenham, N., Hare, T. A., Quinn, B. T., McCarry, K., Nurse, M., Gilhooly, T.,...Casey, B. J. (2010). Prolonged institutional rearing is associated with atypically larger amygdala volume and difficulties in emotion regulation. *Developmental Science, 13*, 46–61.

Tottenham, N., & Sheridan, M. A. (2010). A review of adversity, the amygdala and the hippocampus: A consideration of developmental timing. *Frontiers in Human Neuroscience, 3*, 1–18. https://doi.org/10.3389/neuro.09.068.2009

Tronick, E. (2006). The inherent stress of normal daily life and social interaction leads to the development of coping and resilience, and variation in resilience in infants and young children comments on the papers of Suomi and Klebanov & Brooks-Gunn. *Annals of the New York Academy of Sciences, 1094*, 83–104. https://doi.org/10.1196/annals.1376.008

Tsigos, C., & Chrousos, G. P. (2002). Hypothalamic-pituitary-adrenal axis, neuroendocrine factors and stress. *Journal of Psychosomatic Research, 53*, 865–871. https://doi.org/10.1016/S0022-3999(02)00429-4

Ulrich-Lai, Y. M., & Herman, J. P. (2009). Neural regulation of endocrine and autonomic stress responses. *Nature Reviews Neuroscience, 10*, 397–409. https://doi.org/10.1038/nrn2647

van den Bos, E., de Rooij, M., Miers, A. C., Bokhorst, C. L., & Westenberg, P. M. (2014). Adolescents' increasing stress response to social evaluation: Pubertal effects on cortisol and alpha-amylase during public speaking. *Child Development, 85*(1), 220–236. https://doi.org/10.1111/cdev.12118

van den Bos, E., van Duijvenvoorde, A. C. K., & Westenberg, P. M. (2016). Effects of adolescent sociocognitive development on the cortisol response to social evaluation. *Developmental Psychology, 52*(7), 1151–1163. http://dx.doi.org/10.1037/dev0000133

van der Voorn, B., Hollanders, J. J., Ket, J. C. F., Rotteveel, J., & Finken, M. J. J. (2017). Gender-specific differences in hypothalamus–pituitary–adrenal axis activity during childhood: A systematic review and meta-analysis. *Biology of Sex Differences, 8*(1), 3. https://doi.org/10.1186/s13293-016-0123-5

Vyas, A., Mitra, R., Shankaranarayana Rao, B. S., & Chattarji, S. (2002). Chronic stress induces contrasting patterns of dendritic remodeling in hippocampal and amygdaloid neurons. *The Journal of Neuroscience, 22*(15), 6810–6818. https://doi.org/20026655

Watamura, S. E., Donzella, B., Kertes, D. A., & Gunnar, M. R. (2004). Developmental changes in baseline cortisol activity in early childhood: Relations with napping and effortful control. *Developmental Psychobiology, 45*, 125–133. https://doi.org/10.1002/dev.20026

Weinstock, M. (2007). Gender differences in the effects of prenatal stress on brain development and behaviour. *Neurochemical Research, 32*, 1730–1740. https://doi.org/10.1007/s11064-007-9339-4

Wood, S. K., & Valentino, R. J. (2017). The brain norepinephrine system, stress and cardiovascular vulnerability. *Neuroscience and Biobehavioral Reviews, 74*, 393–400. https://doi.org/10.1016/j.neubiorev.2016.04.018

Young, J. B. (2002). Programming of sympathoadrenal function. *Trends in Endocrinology and Metabolism, 13*(9), 381–385. https://doi.org/10.1016/S1043-2760(02)00661-6

Zijlmans, M. A. C., Riksen-Walraven, J. M., & de Weerth, C. (2015). Associations between maternal prenatal cortisol concentrations and child outcomes: A systematic review. *Neuroscience and Biobehavioral Reviews, 53*, 1–24. https://doi.org/10.1016/j.neubiorev.2015.02.015

Coping Models of Stress and Resilience

Bruce E. Compas, Allison Vreeland, *and* Lauren Henry

Abstract

This chapter provides a review of research on the role of processes of coping as a source of resilience to the adverse effects of stress in childhood, adolescence, and adulthood. Advances in research on models of coping that distinguish responses based on stressor controllability are emphasized. Important similarities between models of coping and emotion regulation are highlighted to encourage integration of research on these two topics. Findings from research on the association between coping and symptoms of psychopathology in adulthood, childhood, and adolescence are reviewed. Directions for future research, including the implications of research on coping for the development of preventive interventions and treatments, are highlighted.

Keywords: coping, emotion regulation, resilience, risk, stress, psychopathology, prevention

Exposure to acute stressful events and chronic adversity is the single most potent risk factor for psychopathology and one of the most powerful sources of risk for physical illness across the life span (Cohen, Murphy, & Prather, 2019; Hammen, 2015; Grant et al., 2003; Harkness & Monroe, 2016). However, there are large individual differences in who is vulnerable as opposed to who is resilient to the deleterious effects of acute and chronic stress. One major source of these individual differences in the effects of stress is the broad set of processes encompassing the ways that individuals respond to stress. These processes involve both automatic and controlled responses to stress and include efforts to act on or change sources of stress, adapt to stressful events and circumstances, and regulate emotions that arise in response to stress. Research on *coping*, including the regulation of emotions in response to stress, has a long history and has undergone significant change since the original conceptualizations of and methods used to study this construct. However, continued improvement in conceptual models, measurement, and study design, as well as focused

research on the cognitive and neurobiological substrates of coping, is necessary for continued progress. This chapter provides an overview of current research on coping as a source of resilience in childhood, adolescence, and adulthood and outlines directions for future research.

We first consider broad issues in the conceptualization, definition, and research methods in the study of processes of coping with stress. Second, we summarize research on coping and psychopathology in adults, drawing on and updating findings from previous reviews (e.g., Aldao, Nolen-Hoeksema, & Schweizer, 2010; Taylor & Stanton, 2007). Third, we provide an overview of findings on the association of coping with psychopathology in children and adolescents, drawing on a recent comprehensive meta-analysis and review (e.g., Compas et al., 2017). Finally, we outline key issues in the field and provide an outline for future research. Our focus is on coping, but throughout this chapter we note important similarities between the closely related concepts of coping and emotion regulation. However, a complete analysis of the relations between these two constructs is beyond the scope of the current chapter, and we refer readers to other more detailed sources (e.g., Compas et al., 2014, 2017).

Conceptualization and Definitions of Coping

Previous reviews have noted a lack of consensus in the definition and conceptualization of coping (and emotion regulation) in children, adolescents, and adults (e.g., Adrian, Zeman, & Veits, 2011; Aldao et al., 2010; Carver & Connor-Smith, 2010; Compas et al., 2001, 2017; Eisenberg, Spinrad, & Eggum, 2010; Skinner, Edge, Altman, & Sherwood, 2003; Taylor & Stanton, 2007). As noted by Compas et al. (2017), clear consensus on the definitions of coping (and emotion regulation) is needed in order to identify the boundaries of what is and is not included within this construct, to shape the identification of the structure and subtypes of coping, and to guide the selection of measures for research on the association of coping with psychopathology. It is encouraging, therefore, that since earlier reviews of coping there have been some signs of convergence on the central features of this construct.

Definitions of Coping

The challenge of establishing consensus regarding definitions of coping is reflected in the vast literature on this topic. A PsychInfo search on January 1, 2019, for the key term "coping" yielded 39,742 citations, and a search for the previous 5 years (January 1, 2014, to January 1, 2019) resulted in 6,290 citations, suggesting that research on coping continues to be an active and robust topic of research and scholarship. The agreement on several of the core features of coping appears across several definitions and conceptualizations. For example, the definitions of coping offered by Lazarus and Folkman (1984), Compas et al. (2001), and Skinner, Zimmer-Gembeck, and colleagues (e.g., Skinner & Wellborn, 1994) highlight the role of coping as a process of responding to stress. Further, these definitions emphasize coping as a controlled, effortful process; that is, responses that require conscious, purposeful, and intentional thoughts and behaviors. However, Lazarus and Folkman (1984) emphasize cognitive appraisals of stress as precipitants of coping responses, whereas Compas et al. (2001) focus on objectively stressful events or circumstances in the environment as precipitants of coping responses. The Lazarus and Folkman model incorporates two broad types of coping that differ based on the focus

and goals of coping efforts: problem-focused coping (i.e., efforts to resolve the source of stress, including problem solving) and emotion-focused coping (i.e., efforts to palliate one's emotions, including seeking social support and escape/avoidance) (e.g., Folkman & Moskowitz, 2004). The Compas et al. (2001) definition is linked to a control-based model of coping that includes primary control coping (i.e., efforts to directly act on the source of stress or one's emotions, including problem solving and emotional modulation), secondary control coping (i.e., efforts to adapt to the source of stress, including acceptance and cognitive reappraisal), and disengagement coping (i.e., efforts to orient away from the source of stress or one's emotions, including avoidance or denial) (e.g., Compas, Jaser, Dunn, & Rodriguez, 2012; Rudolph, Dennig, & Weisz, 1995; Weisz, McCabe, & Dennig, 1994). Skinner, Zimmer-Gembeck, and colleagues (e.g., Skinner & Wellborn, 1994; Skinner & Zimmer-Gembeck, 2007; Zimmer-Gembeck & Skinner, 2011; Zimmer-Gembeck et al., 2014) define coping as action *regulation* under stress, which includes coordination, mobilization, energizing, directing and guiding behavior, emotion, and orientation when responding to stress.

The scope of the construct of coping has broadened since the earlier work of Lazarus and Folkman (1984), with a growing emphasis on coping as the regulation of a wide range of functions, including emotion, behavior, cognitions, physiology, and the environment, in response to stress (e.g., Compas et al., 2001; Eisenberg, Fabes, & Guthrie, 1997; Kopp, 1989; Zimmer-Gembeck & Skinner, 2016). Specifically, a unifying feature of conceptualizations of coping is the central role of *regulatory processes* (e.g., Compas et al., 2014; Zimmer-Gembeck et al., 2014). Regulation involves a broad array of responses, including efforts to initiate, delay, terminate, modify the form/content, or modulate the amount or intensity of a thought, emotion, behavior, or physiological reaction (Compas et al., 2001). Coping includes the regulation of these processes that occur specifically in response to a stressor. The link between coping and emotion regulation is highlighted by Kopp (1989), who argued that "emotion regulation is a term used to characterize the processes and characteristics involved in *coping* with heightened levels of positive and negative emotions" (p. 343; italics added).

Conceptualizations of coping further share a distinction between automatic and controlled processes. A fundamental contrast throughout psychological science is made between dual processes that are characterized as automatic versus controlled, including distinctions between processes that are labeled as regulation versus reactivity, intentional versus incidental, conscious versus nonconscious, and voluntary versus involuntary (e.g., Bargh & Williams, 2007; Connor-Smith, Compas, Wadsworth, Thomsen, & Saltzman, 2000; Eisenberg, Hofer, & Vaughan, 2007; Eisenberg et al., 2010; Gross & Thompson, 2007; Haggard, 2019; Mauss, Bunge, & Gross, 2007). Automatic, incidental, involuntary processes are rooted in temperamental differences in reactivity to the environment that emerge early in development; furthermore, some responses are acquired through processes of associative conditioning that do not involve conscious control (e.g., Compas, Connor-Smith, & Jaser, 2004). In contrast, controlled, intentional, voluntary responses often involve higher order, complex cognitive processes that are thought to develop more fully in middle and late childhood (Zimmer-Gembeck & Skinner, 2016). The distinction between controlled (volitional) and automatic (involuntary) actions and behaviors has a strong basis in neuroscience (Haggard, 2017, 2019) that provides a cornerstone for these two processes as they arise in response to stress. Coping refers specifically to controlled, but excludes automatic, responses to stress; thus, we will focus on individuals' controlled responses to stress.

There are several reasons to focus on coping as controlled as opposed to automatic processes in response to stress. Controlled processes reflect both covert cognitive and overt behavioral strategies that children, adolescents, and adults purposefully use to respond to stress and regulate their emotions. These responses occur in both stressful and emotionally arousing situations and may be more accessible to conscious awareness than nonconscious processes (Rabiner, Lenhart, & Lochman, 1990; see also Haggard, 2019). Consequently, controlled processes, or at least those within conscious awareness, may be more amenable to self-reports and reports by other informants of these efforts (e.g., Compas et al., 2014). In addition, controlled processes are less likely than automatic processes to be confounded with symptoms of internalizing and externalizing psychopathology. For example, an automatic anger response may be highly correlated with symptoms of externalizing psychopathology in part because anger is included as an externalizing symptom (e.g., Achenbach & Rescorla, 2001). Lastly, controlled processes can be more readily changed than automatic processes through interventions that are designed to

enhance resilience by teaching skills for coping with stress and regulating emotions. A growing body of evidence suggests that interventions targeting coping skills are efficacious in the prevention and treatment of psychopathology in children and adolescents (e.g., Compas et al., 2010; Lochman & Wells, 2004; Tein, Sandler, Ayers, & Wolchik, 2006; Tein, Sandler, MacKinnon, & Wolchik, 2004).

Despite the importance of focusing on controlled processes of coping, several aspects of these processes present significant challenges, as they may reflect elements of both automatic and controlled processes. Rather than a simple dichotomy, automatic and controlled processes lie on a continuum (Gross & Thompson, 2007; Hopp, Troy, & Mauss, 2011). Some processes that are initially automatic may be brought under purposeful control, and processes that require effort may become automatized with repeated practice (e.g., Evers et al., 2014; Hankin, Badanes, Smolen, & Young, 2015; Mauss et al., 2007). A noteworthy example of this comes from research on rumination (e.g., Nolen-Hoeksema, Wisco, & Lyubomirksy, 2008). Rumination can occur in the form of uncontrollable, intrusive thoughts or as purposefully dwelling on thoughts about one's emotions, as in the case of depressive rumination. However, the distinction between controlled and automatic processes remains central to understanding coping.

Structure and Subtypes of Coping

Research on the association of coping with symptoms of psychopathology requires the clear delineation of subtypes of coping; however, there has been relatively little agreement regarding the structure of coping. For example, in a seminal review of the structure of coping, Skinner et al. (2003) identified over 400 different subtypes of coping in research across childhood, adolescence, and adulthood. Subtypes include widely studied coping (and emotion regulation) strategies such as problem solving, cognitive reappraisal, cognitive avoidance, emotional expression, and acceptance, as well as less frequently examined strategies such as physical exercise, stoicism, and thought stopping. Given that over 400 subtypes of coping have been presented in research (Skinner et al., 2003), it is not surprising that these subtypes have been organized into numerous different structures. Among the most common are (a) problem-focused versus emotion-focused (Lazarus & Folkman,1984), (b) approach versus avoidance (Roth & Cohen, 1986), (c) active versus passive (Jensen, Turner, Romano, & Karoly, 1991), (d) cognitive versus behavioral (Moos, Brennan, Fondacaro, & Moos, 1990), and (e) primary control engagement versus secondary control engagement versus disengagement (Compas et al., 2001).

Despite repeated calls to reach consensus on the structure and subtypes of coping, recent publications demonstrate sustained disagreement and confusion. For example, Vanucci et al. (2018) analyzed seven subtypes of coping (focusing on and venting emotions; denial; active coping; planning; emotional support seeking; instrumental support seeking; use of humor) in adolescents and young adults. Pereira et al. (2018) examined only two subtypes: avoidance and positive coping in 8- to 12-year-olds. Gudino, Stiles, and Diaz (2018) created composites for active and avoidant coping and included scales for cognitive decision making, direct problem solving, seeking understanding, positive cognitive restructuring, avoidant actions, and cognitive avoidance in young adolescents. Erath, Kaeppler, and Tu (2018) examined scales of cognitive distancing, support seeking, and revenge seeking in 12-year-olds. And Hilpert et al. (2018) examined daily reports of emotion-focused coping in adult marital dyads.

This lack of consensus regarding the structure of coping has slowed progress in the field (Compas et al., 2001, 2014, 2017; Skinner et al., 2003). Most critically, the heterogeneous structure of coping has made it incredibly difficult to compare and accumulate results from different investigations. Further, measures of coping differ in the items that are included within dimensions of coping, making it difficult to aggregate findings relevant to the same stressor or precipitant or to compare results across different stressors or precipitants. The identification of the structure of coping has been approached using either bottom-up models (i.e., derived through exploratory factor analysis [EFA] or through rational grouping of strategies) or top-down models (i.e., theory-driven and tested using confirmatory factor analysis [CFA]) systems). Problems with bottom-up approaches include lack of clarity, limited comprehensiveness of categories, inability to determine hierarchical structures, and difficulty determining whether categories are distinct (Skinner et al., 2003). Skinner et al. (2003) highlighted the merits of three top-down coping structures that have been supported in children and adolescents using CFA (Ayers, Sandler, & Twohey, 1998; Connor-Smith et al., 2000; Walker, Smith, Garber, & Van Slyke, 1997). The strengths of these and other top-down approaches include tests of clear conceptual models of the structure of coping, the development of measures that reflect these models, use of detailed and complex data analytic approaches, and cross-validation with multiple large samples (Skinner et al., 2003). Further, Skinner et al. (2003) noted that although these models are not without problems, they "represent guideposts for empirical efforts to search for the structure of coping" (p. 232).

Example of the Structure of Coping: A Control-Based Model

An example of a theory-based and empirically tested model of coping can be found in the three-factor control-based model of coping represented in the work of Compas and colleagues and Weisz and colleagues (Compas et al., 2001, 2014; Connor-Smith et al., 2000; Rudolph et al., 1995). In this model, responses to stress are first distinguished along the dimension of automatic versus controlled processes; coping responses are considered controlled, volitional efforts to regulate cognition, behavior, emotion, and physiological processes, as well as aspects of the environment in response to stress. Coping responses are further distinguished as primary control engagement (problem solving, emotional modulation, emotional expression), secondary control engagement (acceptance, cognitive reappraisal, positive thinking, distraction), or disengagement (cognitive and behavioral avoidance, denial, wishful thinking). This model is supported by at least nine confirmatory factor analytic studies with children, adolescents, and adults exposed to and coping with a wide range of stressors (peer stressors, family stressors, economic stressors, war-related stressors, cancer, chronic pain), from diverse socioeconomic and cultural backgrounds and international samples (Euro-American, Native American Indian, Spanish, Bosnian, Chinese), using multiple informants (Benson et al., 2011; Compas, Beckjord et al., 2006, Compas, Boyer et al., 2006; Connor-Smith et al., 2000; Connor-Smith & Calvete, 2004; Wadsworth, Reickmann, Benson, & Compas, 2004; Xiao et al., 2010; Yao et al., 2010). These studies provide robust support for this three-factor control-based model of coping. This model represents one way to bring order and structure to understanding how individuals cope with stress and provides a guide for testing alternative models of coping.

Coping Flexibility

An important perspective on the nature of coping that has developed alongside of research on the structure of coping emphasizes the importance of the flexible use of multiple different coping strategies in response to the varying demands of acute and chronic stress. Research focused on coping flexibility (Cheng, Lau, & Chan, 2014) and regulatory or affective flexibility (Bonanno, 2004; Bonanno & Burton, 2013; Zhu & Bonanno, 2018) emphasizes the importance of having a variety of coping skills or strategies that can be implemented depending on the ever-changing demands of a given source of stress. This includes having a broad repertoire of skills, a balanced profile of different types of skills, sensitivity to contexts in which skills might be used, varying coping responses across situations and over time within a given stressful episode, and attending to feedback on the relative success or failure of a strategy to cope with sources of stress (Bonanno & Burton, 2013; Cheng et al., 2014). This research suggests that adaptive or effective coping can only be captured empirically when a wide range of skills and strategies are assessed in response to a wide range of stressors (see later for further discussion of coping flexibility).

Coping and Psychopathology in Adulthood

Several reviews have examined the associations between coping and closely related processes of emotion regulation with symptoms of psychopathology in adults (e.g., Aldao et al., 2010; Nolen-Hoeksema, 2012; Taylor & Stanton, 2007; Webb, Miles, & Sheeran, 2012). Taylor and Stanton (2007) reviewed resources (i.e., optimism, psychological control or mastery, self-esteem, and social support) that support the ability to cope with stress. The authors outlined the ways in which aspects of the early environment (e.g., low socioeconomic status and harsh parenting), genetic predispositions (serotonin and dopamine functioning), and the interface between the two (gene–environment interactions) influence the development of coping resources and processes. Further, Taylor and Stanton (2007) discuss the ways in which coping resources impact physiology and mental health, both as antecedents of specific coping strategies and acting directly to influence outcomes. Research suggests that the use of avoidant strategies predicts increased distress, and approach strategies are associated with psychological and physical health. However, avoidant coping predicts adjustment more consistently than approach strategies in the literature. Taylor and Stanton (2007) suggest that this may be, in part, due to certain strategies only having utility with stressors amenable to change (i.e., controllable stressors).

While acknowledging progress in the coping literature, Taylor and Stanton (2007) underline the importance of further research into origins of coping (both genetic and environmental), the development of coping across the life span, and the mechanisms by which coping relates to mental and physical outcomes, in order to inform interventions and improve mental and physical outcomes under stress. The authors highlight the potential benefits of increased knowledge of the neural mechanisms that reflect coping, in particular, for evaluating psychosocial interventions. Taylor and Stanton (2007) suggest focusing on coping processes and proximal environmental factors as intervention targets, as they may be more malleable than trait-like coping resources or distal environmental factors.

Aldao et al. (2010) reviewed the relationship between six emotion-regulation/coping strategies (acceptance, avoidance, problem solving, reappraisal, rumination, and suppression) and symptoms of four psychopathologies (anxiety, depression, eating disorders, and substance-related disorders). Notably, suppression and avoidance have been widely theorized to be risk factors for psychopathology (Carver, Scheier, & Weintraub, 1989; Folkman & Lazarus, 1980), while problem solving, reappraisal, and acceptance have been hypothesized to be protective against the development of psychopathology (Compas et al., 2017; Gross, 1998). Rumination has been reported to be negatively associated with problem solving and to interfere with decision making (Hong, 2007; Ward, Lyubomirsky, Sousa, & Nolen-Hoeksema, 2003). Aldao et al. (2010) included 114 studies in a meta-analysis and found that each coping/emotion regulation strategy was associated with psychological symptoms in the hypothesized direction: Maladaptive strategies (e.g., suppression, avoidance, and rumination) were associated with more psychological symptoms, while adaptive strategies (e.g., problem solving, acceptance, and reappraisal) were associated with fewer psychological symptoms. However, when looking more closely at the magnitude of the relationships between specific coping/emotion regulation strategies and each psychopathology separately, unique associations emerged.

Maladaptive coping/emotion regulation strategies were more strongly related to overall psychopathology than adaptive coping/emotion regulation strategies. Specifically, the effect size for rumination was large ($r = 0.49$); the effect sizes for avoidance ($r = 0.38$), suppression ($r = 0.34$), and problem solving ($r = -0.31$) were medium to large; the effect size for acceptance ($r = -0.19$) was small to medium; and the effect size for reappraisal was nonsignificant ($r = -0.14$). These findings suggest that psychopathology may be more closely affected by maladaptive strategies than by the use of adaptive strategies. Additionally, some coping/emotion regulation strategies were more closely related to specific psychopathologies than others, with a number of emotion regulation strategies more closely related to depression and anxiety than eating disorders or substance use. For example, acceptance was related to lower symptoms of depression ($r = -0.20$) and anxiety ($r = -0.25$) but was not associated with substance abuse ($r = 0.00$). Reappraisal was related to lower depression ($r = -0.17$) and anxiety ($r = -0.13$) but not eating disorder symptoms ($r = -0.05$).

Finally, Aldao et al. (2010) examined sample age and type as moderators of the relationship between strategies and symptoms of psychopathology. Age significantly moderated the relationship between psychopathology and problem solving and suppression, with adults having stronger associations than children or adolescents. One possible explanation of these findings is that adults are better able to report and/or utilize problem solving and suppression strategies than children or adolescents due to their more developed executive control processes. Sample type was also a significant moderator of avoidance, problem solving, rumination, and suppression, with clinical samples having stronger associations than nonclinical participants, suggesting that the strength of these relations is contingent upon clinical severity. In sum, Aldao et al. (2010) found that maladaptive strategies are more strongly related to symptoms of psychopathology than adaptive strategies. One important limitation of this review is its focus on dispositional coping/emotion regulation. A growing body of research has focused on the use of versatile coping strategies in adjustment to situational characteristics.

A meta-analysis of the effects of coping flexibility on psychological adjustment is provided by Cheng et al. (2014). Cheng and colleagues (2014) reviewed 90 studies examining the associations between flexibility in coping and the broad construct of psychological adjustment. There is a growing interest in coping flexibility. However, despite a large and growing body of research, there is a lack of consensus on the definition and conceptualization of coping flexibility. This seminal review identified five major conceptualizations of coping flexibility reported in literature: broad repertoire, balanced profile, cross-situational variability, strategy-situation fit, and perceived ability. *Broad repertoire* is characterized by the use of a (appropriately named) broad repertoire of coping strategies (Pearlin & Schooler,

1978). Proponents of a broad repertoire argue that effective coping is dependent upon the number of strategies available rather than the type of strategy used. The *balanced profile* definition of coping flexibility is characterized by a moderate range of coping strategies, rather than a wider range as posited by broad repertoire scholars. In this perspective, individuals who cope flexibly do not have a strong preference for any specific coping strategy, resulting in a balanced coping profile with a variety of coping strategies used equally.

Unlike researchers who focus on the structure of a flexible coping profile, another camp contends that flexible coping depends upon an interplay between strategy deployment and the environment. Within this approach, the *cross-situational variability* conceptualization of coping contends that adaptive coping changes in association with the fluctuating nature of contextual features, and individuals should alter their coping strategies to each stressful event as it unfolds. A similar situational perspective is the *strategy-situation fit* conceptualization that proposes that individuals should vary their coping patterns to adapt to environmental changes.

In their meta-analysis, Cheng et al. found cognitive flexibility to be related to psychological adjustment with a small to moderate effect size. More specifically, within the five conceptualization of coping flexibility, studies adopting the *perceived ability* ($r = 0.32$) or *strategy-situation fit* ($r = 0.27$) conceptualizations showed a stronger association between cognitive flexibility and psychological adjustment than studies adopting the *balanced profile* ($r = 0.19$), *broad repertoire* ($r = 0.12$), or *cross-situational variability* conceptualizations ($r = 0.12$). Integrating these findings together shows that although having a broad repertoire of diverse coping strategies and the ability to use diverse strategies to handle distinct stressful demands is associated with better psychological adjustment, both the formulation of strategies that match specific situational demands and the possession of higher order "meta-coping" skills facilitate flexible coping.

Cheng et al. (2014) evaluated individualism (vs. collectivism), socioeconomic status (SES), age, and gender as moderators of the relationships between coping flexibility and psychological adjustment. Individualism and age were significant moderators of coping flexibility, accounting for 10% and 13% of the variance, respectively. Studies including participants with lower levels of individualism showed a stronger association between coping flexibility and psychological adjustment than studies including participants with high levels of individualism. Age also moderated this association, such that studies with older participants showed a stronger association than studies assessing younger participants. No statistically significant effects were found for SES or gender as moderators.

The enhanced understanding of cognitive flexibility provided by Cheng et al. (2014) proposes that cognitive flexibility denotes one's ability to formulate and adjust coping strategies to meet a particular situation as well as the mastery of meta-coping skills that promote the implementation of flexible coping strategies.

Coping and Psychopathology in Childhood and Adolescence

Several narrative reviews have examined the relations between coping (and emotion regulation) and internalizing and externalizing symptoms in children and adolescents. We begin by briefly summarizing several earlier reviews and then consider a recent comprehensive meta-analysis (Compas et al., 2017) in more detail. In one of the earliest reviews of coping and psychopathology in children and adolescents, Compas et al. (2001) provided a narrative summary of findings from 63 published studies that reported on analyses of coping and internalizing and externalizing symptoms of psychopathology in children and adolescents. The authors conducted a narrative review as a function of two broad dimensions of coping: engagement versus disengagement coping and problem-focused versus emotion-focused coping. The general pattern of findings suggested that forms of engagement coping and problem-focused coping were associated with lower internalizing and externalizing symptoms. In contrast, disengagement coping and emotion-focused coping were generally associated with higher levels of internalizing and externalizing symptoms. However, this review did not provide quantitative analyses of these patterns of findings.

Eisenberg et al. (2010) described the association of children's emotion regulation with internalizing and externalizing problems. They reported a general pattern of negative associations between emotion regulation and internalizing and externalizing problems in samples ranging from infancy through childhood and adolescence. More narrowly focused reviews have examined coping with specific samples or subgroups and specific outcomes. Examples include adolescents coping with social stressors (Clarke, 2006), adolescents coping with relationship stressors (Seiffge-Krenke, 2011), children coping with the

chronic stress associated with poverty (Evans & Kim, 2013), and children and adolescents coping with chronic illness (Aldridge & Roesch, 2007; Blount et al., 2008; Compas et al., 2012).

In one of the few meta-analyses of coping and emotion regulation in childhood and adolescence, Clarke (2006) examined the relations between active coping and psychosocial health among youth in 40 studies of coping with interpersonal stress. Four areas of psychosocial functioning were examined: externalizing problems, internalizing problems, social competence, and academic performance. The association between active coping and psychosocial functioning across the four areas examined was small, with correlations ranging from 0.02 to 0.12 (Clarke, 2006). In a second meta-analysis of 26 studies including children and adolescents, Aldridge and Roesch (2007) examined how children cope with cancer-related stress based on two coping taxonomies: approach versus avoidance coping and problem-focused versus emotion-focused coping. In this analysis, approach, avoidance, and emotion-focused coping were unrelated to overall adjustment. A small positive association was found between problem-focused coping and adjustment, indicating greater use of problem-focused coping was associated with poorer adjustment. Finally, Schäfer, Naumann, Holmes, Tuschen-Caffier, and Samson (2017) conducted a meta-analysis of the association between emotion regulation strategies and symptoms of depression and anxiety in adolescence. Results from this review of 35 studies indicated that emotion regulation strategies considered to be "adaptive" (cognitive reappraisal, problem solving, and acceptance) were significantly negatively related to symptoms of anxiety and depression, and those considered to be "maladaptive" (avoidance, suppression, and rumination) were significantly positively related to symptoms of anxiety and depression.

In the most comprehensive meta-analytic review to date, Compas et al. (2017) examined several overarching issues related to the study of coping, emotion regulation, and internalizing and externalizing symptoms of psychopathology in childhood and adolescence, including a quantitative meta-analysis of 212 studies ($N = 80,850$ participants) that measured the associations between coping (and emotion regulation) with symptoms of internalizing and externalizing psychopathology. This meta-analysis addressed the association of broad *domains* of coping and emotion regulation (e.g., total coping, emotion regulation), intermediate *factors* of coping and emotion regulation (e.g., primary control coping, secondary control coping), and specific coping and emotion regulation *strategies* (e.g., emotional expression, cognitive reappraisal) with internalizing and externalizing symptoms. For cross-sectional studies, which made up the majority of studies included, three potential moderators were examined: age, measure quality, and single versus multiple informants. Finally, findings from longitudinal studies were also reviewed because these provide stronger tests of the effects. The primary goal of the Compas et al. (2017) meta-analysis was to determine if there is evidence for an association of domains, factors, and strategies of coping (and emotion regulation) with internalizing and externalizing symptoms of psychopathology. The results led to an answer of a qualified yes. Clear evidence was found for significant associations between coping (and emotion regulation) and symptoms of internalizing and externalizing psychopathology. However, several methodological limitations in the field qualified the strength of these findings and suggest directions for future research. We now summarize the findings from this review.

Cross-Sectional Studies

Compas et al. (2017) found significant effect sizes for the associations between domain-level coping and emotion regulation and psychopathology, ranging from small to medium in magnitude (unadjusted and adjusted ranged from $r = -0.11$ to 0.27). A small significant negative association was found for the broad domain of adaptive coping with externalizing symptoms ($r = -0.11$). Conversely, a significant medium *positive* association was found between maladaptive coping and internalizing symptoms ($r = 0.27$). These findings are important in providing the first quantitative evidence that broad domain-level measures of coping are associated with symptoms of psychopathology in children and adolescents. However, a closer examination of the items included in the broad domains of coping suggests that they provide relatively limited information about what children and adolescents do to regulate their emotions or cope with stress. For example, the emotion regulation coping subscale from the Children's Emotion Management Scales (e.g., Zeman, Shipman, & Penza-Clyve, 2001; Zeman et al., 2010) includes the following items: "I keep myself from losing control of my worried/angry/sad feelings," and "I try to calmly settle the problem when I feel worried/mad/sad." These items reflect descriptions of the degree to which children are *able* to regulate their emotions but do not include information about the strategies

used to achieve regulation. Further, findings on the use of "maladaptive" coping are largely tautological. That is, if types of coping are labeled a priori as maladaptive or dysregulated, then it is circular to show that these strategies are related to higher levels of symptoms of psychopathology. Further, the basis for the distinction between adaptive or maladaptive coping is often not clear. Therefore, Compas et al. (2017) suggested that researchers discontinue the use of measures that label coping (and emotion regulation) as adaptive or maladaptive on an a priori basis in favor of measures that provide more detailed descriptions of factors or strategies that are used to cope with stress.

Compas et al. (2017) found evidence that intermediate factors of coping are associated with both internalizing and externalizing symptoms. The general factor of engagement/approach coping had small but significant negative associations with internalizing symptoms ($r = -0.07$); however, this effect was no longer significant after adjusting for possible publication bias. Disengagement coping had small significant positive associations with both internalizing ($r = 0.18$) and externalizing symptoms ($r = 0.13$). The most consistent factor-level evidence was found for primary control coping and secondary control coping, both of which were significantly negatively associated with both internalizing and externalizing symptoms with the effect sizes ranging from small to medium in magnitude (unadjusted and adjusted effect sizes ranged from $r = -0.14$ to -0.30). These findings suggest that the control-based model that includes primary and secondary control coping has promise for understanding types of coping that are related to lower levels of symptoms (Compas et al., 2012, 2014). It is noteworthy that Compas et al. (2017) found that problem-focused coping had only a small negative association with internalizing symptoms ($r = -0.07$), and neither of the effect sizes for emotion-focused coping was significant. It appears that problem-focused and emotion-focused coping have played a smaller role in research on coping in children and adolescents in more recent research on coping and may have been supplanted at the factor level by primary control and secondary control coping, both in terms of the frequency that they are studied and the magnitude of effects they produce. Finally, social support coping continues to be widely studied, yet, despite having enough studies to calculate effect sizes, Compas et al. (2017) found no significant associations between social support and symptoms of psychopathology. While these findings suggest that using social support may not be an effective means of coping or regulating emotions for children and adolescents, it is also plausible that measures of social support may not be capturing the way that social networks are used by children and adolescents to cope with stress and regulate emotions (see Rueger et al., 2016, for a meta-analysis of available and enacted social support and depressive symptoms in adolescence).

Despite the expectation that measures of specific strategies would yield a more detailed and nuanced picture of the association of coping and symptoms, Compas et al. (2017) found relatively little evidence at the level of strategies. Small but significant positive associations with symptoms were found for emotional suppression, avoidance, and denial ($r = .09$ to 0.17). However, none of the other 11 effect sizes that could be estimated were significant. These findings differ from those reported by Aldao et al. (2010), which found significant associations between specific strategies (e.g., avoidance, acceptance) and symptoms of psychopathology. This discrepancy may be due in part to differences in measurement; while the studies included in the Compas et al. (2017) meta-analysis included reports of how children and adolescents coped with or regulated specific stressors or emotions, the studies included in the reviews by both Aldao et al. (2010) focused on dispositional or "habitual" use of strategies, or how individuals typically respond to stressors.

Overall this pattern of findings found by Compas et al. (2017) presents a challenge for the field. The limited findings for measures assessing specific strategies of coping (and emotion regulation) may reflect problems in the quality of these measures (e.g., a limited number of items in these scales). Alternatively, this may suggest that examining specific strategies in isolation may provide only a partial picture of the ways that individuals use multiple strategies to regulate their emotions and cope with stress. That is, effective coping may require a repertoire of skills that can be used flexibly in response to different emotions or stressors (e.g., Cheng et al., 2014). The most consistent effect sizes in the current meta-analysis were found for measures that aggregate coping and emotion regulation strategies into intermediate-level factors. This level of analysis may capture cohesive factors of coping and emotion regulation strategies that are often used together and provide a more complete picture of how these strategies function in relation to symptoms of psychopathology. For example, the effect sizes for cognitive reappraisal and acceptance were not significant,

but the use of secondary control coping, which includes these two strategies along with distraction, was significantly associated with fewer symptoms.

A limitation of studying coping and emotion regulation processes at the factor level is the lack of information about the relative use of different strategies and specific strategies that may be carrying the effects. An important step for future research is to unpack these factors to examine the associations of more comprehensive measures that include larger samples of items reflecting the specific coping and emotion regulation strategies that comprise them. That is, improvement is needed in the quality of measures of specific strategies that can be used in various combinations to understand which of a given set of strategies may have the strongest effects. For example, the RSQ (Connor-Smith et al., 2000) includes only three items to assess each of four strategies that make up secondary control coping (acceptance, cognitive reappraisal, positive thinking, distraction). Analyses of parcels that include a larger number of items for each strategy could yield more information about how the strategies that comprise secondary control coping are used flexibly in different combinations and how these patterns are related to psychopathology.

Compas et al. (2017) examined possible moderators of the cross-sectional associations between coping and symptoms of psychopathology, with the clearest findings emerging for age. Analyses of age as moderator yielded a significant effect size for the association of engagement/approach coping with internalizing symptoms, with a small but significant negative effect size for adolescents and a nonsignificant effect for children. There was also an effect for age as a moderator of cognitive reappraisal and internalizing symptoms with a small negative association for adolescents and a small positive association for children. Finally, age was a moderator of the association of emotional suppression and internalizing symptoms; there was a significant positive association for adolescents, while the association for children was nonsignificant. Although these findings do not support a clear developmental pattern for the association of coping with symptoms, results are similar to those reported in other reviews. For example, Aldao et al. (2010) found that the association of problem solving and suppression with symptoms of psychopathology was stronger for adults than children and adolescents. Similarly, Cheng et al. (2014) reported a significantly larger effect size for the association of coping flexibility and measures of psychological adjustment for older (over age 30) as compared to younger (under age 30, including a small number of studies with adolescents) participants.

Consistent with developmental models of coping and emotion regulation (e.g., Zimmer-Gembeck & Skinner, 2016), the few significant age effects found by Compas et al. (2017) suggest a stronger association between coping and emotion regulation strategies with internalizing symptoms for adolescents as compared with children. However, the majority of the tests of age as a moderator of effect sizes were nonsignificant. While reviews of the development of coping and emotion regulation suggest more frequent use of cognitively demanding strategies, such as secondary control coping, in adolescents as compared to children (e.g., Skinner & Zimmer-Gembeck, 2007; Zimmer-Gembeck & Skinner, 2011, 2016), it is still unknown whether the use of these strategies is more *adaptive* in adolescents as compared to children. Further, Compas et al. (2017) found few differences in associations among coping and emotion regulation and symptoms related to age. It is important to note, however, that the wide variation in samples made it difficult to conduct clear comparisons by age, as the mean age of the study sample was used to code the sample as child or adolescent. The necessary approximations of age may have obscured findings related to development. Notably, in a meta-analysis by Schäfer et al. (2017), age was not a significant moderator of the association between emotion regulation and symptoms of depression and anxiety in adolescents.

The evidence found by Compas et al. (2017) for the association of coping and emotion regulation with internalizing and externalizing symptoms was considerably weaker in longitudinal studies. Only disengagement coping, social support coping, and avoidance were significantly positively associated with internalizing symptoms in longitudinal analyses (effect sizes ranged from $r = 0.12$ to 0.18). Thus, there is substantially less evidence for the association of coping and emotion regulation with symptoms of psychopathology in longitudinal as compared with cross-sectional studies. Several factors may have contributed to these diminished effect sizes. First, there were only 17 studies with longitudinal data that could be included in the meta-analysis, yielding a smaller body of evidence to evaluate these associations. Second, it is possible that the only longitudinal associations between coping and emotion regulation and symptoms are for those factors or strategies that are related to *higher* levels of symptoms over time. In contrast, factors that are associated with *lower* levels of symptoms (e.g., primary control coping

and secondary control coping) may only be correlates of symptoms when measured at the same point in time, as evidenced by the consistent cross-sectional findings found by Compas et al. (2017) for these factors, and they may not be associated with symptoms longitudinally.

Summary and Future Directions

Research on coping has much to offer for understanding processes of risk and resilience to stress and psychopathology. However, in many ways, coping research has reached a plateau and has stagnated. In their recent review of coping, emotion regulation and psychopathology in children and adolescents, Compas et al. (2017) offered an agenda for future research and we will briefly summarize these directions here.

Improve Conceptual Models

As described earlier, research on coping with stress continues to be hindered by a lack of consensus on the key features and subtypes of coping. Two significant challenges are of greatest importance. First, clear conceptual models of the structure of coping need to be tested using top-down methods such as CFA. The three-factor structure of primary control coping, secondary control coping, and disengagement coping offers a promising direction for such work, as it has been confirmed using CFA in diverse samples of adolescents (e.g., Benson et al., 2011; Xiao et al., 2010) and adults (e.g., Compas, Beckjord et al., 2006; Compas, Boyer et al., 2006). However, this model has not been tested in younger children to determine if these factors are less differentiated earlier in development. Second, research on coping and the closely related construct of emotion regulation needs greater integration and synthesis. The processes of coping and emotion regulation are concerned with the same set of strategies of adaptation. Specifically, all of the strategies identified in the meta-analysis of Compas et al. (2017) have appeared in studies of *both* emotion regulation and coping. The distinction between these constructs and the factors and strategies they encompass has led to an underestimation of our knowledge base of these processes. Based on the findings presented earlier, it appears that many of the distinctions between these two constructs are artificial, and that the synthesis of these two lines of theory and research is long overdue.

Improve Research Designs and Methods

A major limitation of previous research on coping has been the almost exclusive reliance on cross-sectional studies using questionnaires to obtain reports from single informants on both coping and other constructs of interest (e.g., symptoms of psychopathology). Although questionnaires can provide important information on the ways that children, adolescents, and adults cope with stress and regulate their emotions in their daily lives, the limitations of questionnaires to assess coping and emotion regulation are well documented. Some limitations of questionnaire measures of coping and emotion regulation include reliance on retrospective reports and concerns about accuracy of recall (particularly with children and adolescents), confounding of items with their outcomes, and variations in the recall period across different measures (Folkman & Moskowitz, 2004). Rather than simply abandoning the use of questionnaires to assess coping and emotion regulation, questionnaires can be augmented by other methods that can provide more objective evidence for the strategies children and adolescents use to cope with stress and regulate their emotions.

In studies using cross-sectional and single-informant methods, the direction of the associations of coping and emotion regulation with symptoms cannot be determined when both are measured at a single, contemporaneous time point. Although this design remains useful as an initial step in addressing new or novel research questions, it cannot be the focus for advances in this area of research. Further, by relying on a single source of information for both coping and emotion regulation and symptoms (e.g., questionnaire measures of coping and emotion regulation with questionnaire measures of psychopathology symptoms), this level of evidence may be confounded by shared method variance. Further, questionnaires need to be used in concert with other methodologies to improve external validity and generalizability. Ecological momentary assessment (EMA) of coping and emotion regulation offers an important method to understand these processes in real-world contexts and closer to real time. For example, Allen et al. (2016) used EMA with a sample of children and adolescents (9–14 years old) during which they reported on perceived control, emotional reactivity (anxiety and physiological arousal), and emotion regulation strategy use in response to daily negative life events. Children's perceptions of control over negative life events were related to less anxious reactivity and greater use of both problem solving and cognitive restructuring as reported in EMA.

Experimental designs and methods are also needed in which coping and emotion regulation are directly manipulated and causal effects on proxy measures of symptoms can be assessed under controlled conditions. Examples of this approach can be found in the rich tradition of experimental studies of emotion regulation in adults and children (e.g., Eisenberg, Smith, & Spinrad, 2011; Fox, Kirwan, & Reeb-Sutherland, 2012; Gross & Jazaieri, 2014; Penela, Walker, Degnan, Fox, & Henderson, 2015). A recent study by Bettis et al. (2018, in press) extended these methods to study aspects of secondary control coping under controlled conditions in the laboratory. Adolescents (ages 9–15 years old) responded to depictions of mothers displaying anger or sadness and were instructed to either just view the picture, try to think of it in a way that made it less stressful (i.e., cognitive reappraisal), or think of something else to take their mind off of the picture (i.e., distraction). Use of distraction and reappraisal during the laboratory paradigm was associated with lower levels of negative emotion during the task. Youth emotion ratings while implementing distraction, but not reappraisal, during the laboratory task were associated with youth self-reported use of secondary control coping in response to family stress. Youth symptoms of anxiety and depression were also significantly positively associated with negative emotion ratings during the laboratory task, and both laboratory task and self-reported coping and emotion regulation accounted for significant variance in symptoms in youth. Findings from Bettis et al. (2018, in press) suggest that both questionnaire and laboratory methods to assess coping and emotion regulation in youth are important for understanding these processes as possible mechanisms of risk and resilience, and continued integration of these methods is a priority for future research.

Identify Cognitive and Neurobiological Substrates of Coping

Research in psychopathology has been reshaped by an emphasis on underlying processes as reflected in the Research Domain Criteria (RDoC) from the National Institute of Mental Health (Casey et al., 2014; Insel & Cuthbert, 2015). A similar approach is needed to provide a better understanding of the processes that reflect the neurobiological foundations and substrates of coping and emotion regulation (see Etkin, Büchel, & Gross, 2015; Fernandez, Jazaieri, & Gross, 2016). One important avenue for future research involves the examination of neurocognitive correlates of coping and emotion regulation. Several aspects of executive function (e.g., working memory, attentional control) may provide a foundation for the use of coping and emotion regulation, as these processes often require the use of complex cognitive skills (Campbell et al., 2009; Eisenberg & Zhou, 2016; McRae et al., 2010).

Understand Coping in Context

Research on the neurobiological substrates of coping and emotion regulation needs to be balanced by careful attention to the context in which children and adolescents are engaged in the processes of coping. First, coping will be better understood by examining this process in the context in which emotions arise. For example, a child or adolescent who experiences sadness in the context of a peer rejection may be faced with a very different challenge than one who experiences sadness in the context of chronic stress associated with living with a depressed parent. Current questionnaire measures of coping often do not assess the context in which emotions occur and, as a consequence, possible differences in emotions as a function of the context in which they arise. Second, guided by research on coping flexibility (Cheng et al., 2014), it will be important to examine flexibility in coping with different types of stress, including levels of objective and perceived control as important aspects of context (Skinner & Zimmer-Gembeck, 2011). Third, it will be important to give greater attention to the broader social context in which coping and emotion regulation occur, especially poverty and economic hardship. For example, the work of Wadsworth and colleagues has shown that the types of coping that may be adaptive for children and adolescents exposed to chronic economic hardship may differ from youth who live in more economically advantaged environments (e.g., Wadsworth, 2015; Wadsworth & Compas, 2002; Wadsworth et al., 2013).

Translate Research Into Interventions

Finally, one of the primary goals of research on coping with stress is to inform the development and implementation of interventions to prevent or treat the adverse mental and physical health problems that arise as a result of acute and chronic stress (Compas & Bettis, 2019, in press). Studies of the efficacy of interventions that target coping skills represent an important next step for research in this field for several reasons. First, intervention studies using randomized designs can provide true experimental tests of the associations of coping and emotion regulation with psychopathology in real-world contexts. Second, intervention trials, especially preventive interventions, can provide information on the

role of coping and emotion regulation in the etiology of internalizing and externalizing symptoms. And most important, intervention research can clarify the role that coping and emotion regulation can play in alleviating and preventing psychopathology. There is promising evidence that interventions can lead to changes in specific types of coping and that these changes account for the effects of these interventions on changes in symptoms (e.g., Compas et al., 2010; Tein et al., 2004, 2006). A high priority for future research is to develop interventions based on coping theory and research and to test the effects of these interventions using multiple methods to capture changes in coping as a central mediator of the effects of these interventions. The field of coping research will have reached maturity when these goals are met.

References

Achenbach, T. M., & Rescorla, L. A. (2001). *Manual for the Achenbach system of empirically based assessment school-age forms profiles*. Burlington, VT: ASEBA. doi:10.1002/9781118625392.wbecp150

Adrian, M., Zeman, J., & Veits, G. (2011). Methodological implications of the affect revolution: A 35-year review of emotion regulation assessment in children. *Journal of Experimental Child Psychology*, *110*, 171–197. doi:10.1016/j.jecp.2011.03.009

Aldao, A., Nolen-Hoeksema, S., & Schweizer, S. (2010). Emotion-regulation strategies across psychopathology: A meta-analytic review. *Clinical Psychology Review*, *30*(2), 217–237. doi:10.1016/j.cpr.2009.11.004

Aldridge, A. A., & Roesch, S. C. (2007). Coping and adjustment in children with cancer: A meta-analytic study. *Journal of Behavioral Medicine*, *30*(2), 115–129. doi:10.1007/s10865-006-9087-y

Allen, B. K., Silk, J. S., Meller, S., Tan, P. Z., Ladouceur, C. D., Sheeber, L. B., ... Ryan, N. D. (2016). Parental autonomy granting and child perceived control: Effects on the everyday emotional experience of anxious youth. *Journal of Child Psychology and Psychiatry*, *57*(7), 835–842. doi:10.1111/jcpp.12482

Ayers, T. S., Sandler, I. N., & Twohey, J. L. (1998). Conceptualization and measurement of coping in children and adolescents. In *Advances in clinical child psychology*, Vol. 20 (pp. 243–301). New York, NY: Springer. doi:10.1007/978-1-4757-9038-2_8

Bargh, J. A., & Williams, L. E. (2007). The nonconscious regulation of emotion. In J. Gross (Ed.), *Handbook of emotion regulation* (pp. 429–445). New York, NY: Guilford Press.

Benson, M. A., Compas, B. E., Layne, C. M., Vandergrift, N., Pašalić, H., Katalinksi, R., & Pynoos, R. S. (2011). Measurement of post-war coping and stress responses: A study of Bosnian adolescents. *Journal of Applied Developmental Psychology*, *32*, 323–335. doi:10.1016/j.appdev.2011.07.001

Bettis, A. H., Henry, L., Prussien, K. V., Vreeland, A., Smith, M., Adery, L. H., & Compas, B. E. (2018). Laboratory and self-report methods to assess reappraisal and distraction in youth. *Journal of Clinical Child & Adolescent Psychology*, 1–11. doi:10.1080/15374416.2018.1466306.

Blount, R. L., Simons, L. E., Devine, K. A., Jaaniste, T., Psychol, M., Cohen, L. L., . . . Hayutin, L. G. (2008). Evidence-based assessment of coping and stress in pediatric psychology. *Journal of Pediatric Psychology, 33*(9), 1021–1045. doi:10.1093/jpepsy/jsm071

Bonanno, G. A. (2004). Loss, trauma, and human resilience: Have we underestimated the human capacity to thrive after extremely aversive events? *American Psychology, 59*(1), 20–28. doi:10.1037/0003-066X.59.1.20

Bonanno, G. A., & Burton, C. L. (2013). Regulatory flexibility: An individual differences perspective on coping and emotion regulation. *Perspectives on Psychological Science, 8*(6), 591–612. doi:10.1177/1745691613504116

Campbell, L. K., Scaduto, M., Van Slyke, D., Niarhos, F., Whitlock, J. A., & Compas, B. E. (2009). Executive function, coping, and behavior in survivors of childhood acute lymphocytic leukemia. *Journal of Pediatric Psychology, 34*(3), 317–327. doi:10.1093/jpepsy/jsn080

Carver, C. S., & Connor-Smith, J. (2010). Personality and coping. *Annual Review of Psychology, 61*, 679–704. doi:10.1146/annurev.psych.093008.100352

Carver, C. S., Scheier, M. F., & Weintraub, J. K. (1989). Assessing coping strategies: A theoretically based approach. *Journal of Personality and Social Psychology, 56*(2), 267–283. doi:10.1037/0022-3514.56.2.267

Casey, B. J., Oliveri, M. E., & Insel, T. (2014). A neurodevelopmental perspective on the research domain criteria (RDoC) framework. *Biological Psychiatry, 76*(5), 350–353. doi:10.1016/j.biopsych.2014.01.006

Cheng, C., Lau, H. B., & Chan, M. S. (2014). Coping flexibility and psychological adjustment to stressful life changes: A meta-analytic review. *Psychological Bulletin, 140*(6), 1582–1607. doi:10.1037/a0037913

Clarke, A. T. (2006). Coping with interpersonal stress and psychosocial health among children and adolescents: A meta-analysis. *Journal of Youth and Adolescence, 35*(1), 10–23. doi:10.1007/s10964-005-9001-x

Cohen, S., Murphy, M.L.M., & Prather, A.A. (2019). Ten surprising facts about stressful life events and disease risk. *Annual Review of Psychology, 70*, 577–597.

Compas, B. E., Beckjord, E., Agocha, B., Sherman, M. L., Langrock, A., Grossman, C., . . . Luecken, L. (2006). Measurement of coping and stress responses in women with breast cancer. *Psycho-Oncology, 15*, 1038–1054.

Compas, B. E., & Bettis, A. H. (2019). Coping and emotion regulation. In M. J. Prinstein, E. A. Youngstrom, E. J. Mash, & R. A. Barkley (Eds.), *Treatment of childhood disorders* (4th ed.). New York, NY: Guilford Press.

Compas, B. E., Boyer, M. C., Stanger, C., Colletti, R. B., Thomsen, A. H., Dufton, L. M., & Cole, D. A. (2006). Latent variable analysis of coping, anxiety/depression, and somatic symptoms in adolescents with chronic pain. *Journal of Consulting and Clinical Psychology, 74*, 1132–1142. doi:10.1037/0022-006X.74.6.1132

Compas, B. E., Champion, J. E., Forehand, R., Cole, D. A., Reeslund, K. L., Fear, J., . . . Merchant, M. J. (2010). Coping and parenting: Mediators of 12-month outcomes of a family group cognitive-behavioral preventive intervention with families of depressed parents. *Journal of Consulting and Clinical Psychology, 78*, 623–634. doi:10.1037/a0020459

Compas, B. E., Connor-Smith, J. K., & Jaser, S. S. (2004). Temperament, stress reactivity, and coping: Implications for depression in childhood and adolescence. *Journal of Clinical Child and Adolescent Psychology, 33*, 21–31. doi:10.1207/S15374424JCCP3301_3

Compas, B. E., Connor-Smith, J. K., Saltzman, H., Thomsen, A. H., & Wadsworth, M. (2001). Coping with stress during childhood and adolescence: Problems, progress, and potential in theory and research. *Psychological Bulletin, 127*, 87–127. doi:10.1037/0033-2909.127.1.87

Compas, B. E., Jaser, S. S., Bettis, A. H., Watson, K. H., Gruhn, M. A., Dunbar, J. P., . . . Thigpen, J. C. (2017). Coping, emotion regulation, and psychopathology in childhood and adolescence: A meta-analysis and narrative review. *Psychological Bulletin, 143*(9), 939–991. doi:10.1037/bul0000110

Compas, B. E., Jaser, S. S., Dunbar, J. P., Watson, K. H., Bettis, A. H., Gruhn, M. A., & Williams, E. K. (2014). Coping and emotion regulation from childhood to early adulthood: Points of convergence and divergence. *Australian Journal of Psychology, 66*(2), 71–81. doi:10.1111/ajpy.12043

Compas, B. E., Jaser, S. S., Dunn, M. J., & Rodriguez, E. M. (2012). Coping with chronic illness in childhood and adolescence. *Annual Review of Clinical Psychology, 8*, 455–480. doi:10.1146/annurev-clinpsy-032511-143108

Connor-Smith, J. K., & Calvete, E. (2004). Cross-cultural equivalence of coping and involuntary responses to stress in Spain and the United States. *Anxiety, Stress & Coping, 17*, 163–185. doi:10.1080/10615800410001709412

Connor-Smith, J. K., Compas, B. E., Wadsworth, M. E., Thomsen, A. H., & Saltzman, H. (2000). Responses to stress in adolescence: Measurement of coping and involuntary responses to stress. *Journal of Consulting and Clinical Psychology, 68*(6), 976–992. doi:10.1037/0022-006X.68.6.976

Eisenberg, N., Fabes, R. A., & Guthrie, I. K. (1997). Coping with stress: The roles of regulation and development. In S. A. Wolchik & I. N. Sandler (Eds.), *Handbook of children's coping: Linking theory and intervention* (pp. 41–70). New York, NY: Plenum.

Eisenberg, N., Hofer, C., & Vaughan, J. (2007). Effortful control and its socioemotional consequences. In J. J. Gross (Ed.), *Handbook of emotion regulation* (pp. 287–306). New York, NY: Guilford Press.

Eisenberg, N., Smith, C. L., & Spinrad, T. L. (2011). Effortful control: Relations with emotion regulation, adjustment and socialization in childhood. In K. D. Vohs & R. F. Baumsister (Eds.), *Handbook of self-regulation: Research, theory, and applications* (pp. 263–283). New York, NY: Guilford Press.

Eisenberg, N., Spinrad, T. L., & Eggum, N. D. (2010). Emotion related self-regulation and its relation to children's maladjustment. *Annual Review of Clinical Psychology, 6*, 495–525. doi:10.1146/annurev.clinpsy.121208.131208

Eisenberg, N., & Zhou, Q. (2016). Conceptions of executive function and regulation: When and to what degree do they overlap? In J. A. Griffin, P. McCardle, & L. S. Freund (Eds.), *Executive function on preschool-age children: Integrating measurement, neurodevelopment, and translational research* (pp. 115–136). Washington, DC: American Psychological Association. doi:10.1037/14797-006

Erath, S. A., Kaeppler, A. K., & Tu, K. M. (2018). Coping with peer victimization predicts peer outcomes across the transition to middle school. *Social Development*, 1–19. doi:10.1111/sode.12330

Etkin, A., Büchel, C., & Gross, J. J. (2015). The neural bases of emotion regulation. *Nature Reviews: Neuroscience, 16*, 693–700. doi:10.1038/nrn4044

Evans, G. W., & Kim, P. (2013). Childhood poverty, chronic stress, self-regulation, and coping. *Child Development Perspectives*, 7(1), 43–48. doi:10.1111/cdep.12013

Evers, C., Hopp, H., Gross, J. J., Fischer, A. H., Manstead, A. S., & Mauss, I. B. (2014). Emotion response coherence: A dual-process perspective. *Biological Psychology*, 98, 43–49. doi:10.1016/j.biopsycho.2013.11.003

Fernandez, K. C., Jazaieri, H., & Gross, J. J. (2016). Emotion regulation: A transdiagnostic perspective on a new RDoC domain. *Cognitive Therapy and Research*, 40(3), 426–440. doi:10.1007/s10608-016-9772-2

Folkman, S., & Lazarus, R. S. (1980). An analysis of coping in a middle-aged community sample. *Journal of Health and Social Behavior*, 21, 219–239. doi:10.2307/2136617

Folkman, S., & Moskowitz, J. T. (2004). Coping: Pitfalls and promise. *Annual Review of Psychology*, 55, 745–774. doi:10.1146/annurev.psych.55.090902.141456

Fox, N. A., Kirwan, M., & Reeb-Sutherland, B. (2012). Measuring the physiology of emotion and emotion regulation—Timing is everything. *Monographs of the Society for Research in Child Development*, 77(2), 98–108. doi:10.1111/j.1540–5834.2011.00668.x

Grant, K. E., Compas, B. E., Stuhlmacher, A. F., Thurm, A. E., McMahon, S. D., & Halpert, J. A. (2003). Stressors and child and adolescent psychopathology: Moving from markers to mechanisms of risk. *Psychological Bulletin*, 129, 447–466. doi:10.1037/0033-2909.129.3.447

Gross, J. J. (1998). Antecedent-and response-focused emotion regulation: Divergent consequences for experience, expression, and physiology. *Journal of Personality and Social Psychology*, 74, 224. doi:10.1037//0022-3514.74.1.224

Gross, J. J., & Jazaieri, H. (2014). Emotion, emotion regulation, and psychopathology: An affective science perspective. *Clinical Psychological Science*, 2(4), 387–401. doi:10.1177/2167702614536164

Gross, J. J., & Thompson, R. A. (2007). Emotion regulation: Conceptual foundations. In J. J. Gross (Ed.), *Handbook of emotion regulation* (pp. 3–24). New York, NY: Guilford Press.

Gudino, O. G., Stiles, A. A., & Diaz, K. I. (2018). Violence exposure and psychopathology in Latino youth: The moderating role of active and avoidant coping. *Child Psychiatry & Human Development*, 49(3), 468–479. doi:10.1007/s10578-017-0767-3

Haggard, P. (2017). Sense of agency in the human brain. *Nature Reviews Neuroscience*, 18, 196–207.

Haggard, P. (2019). The neurocognitive bases of human volition. *Annual Review of Psychology*, 70, 9–28. doi:10.1146/annurev-psych-010418-103348

Hammen, C. (2015). Stress sensitivity in psychopathology: Mechanisms and consequences. *Journal of Abnormal Psychology*, 124(1), 152–154. doi:10.1037/abn0000040

Hankin, B. L., Badanes, L. S, Smolen, A., & Young, J. F. (2015). Cortisol reactivity to stress among youth: Stability over time and genetic variants for stress sensitivity. *Journal of Personality and Social Psychology*, 124, 54–67. doi:10.1037/abn0000030

Harkness, K. L., & Monroe, S. M. (2016). The assessment and measurement of adult life stress: Basic premises, operational principles, and design requirements. *Journal of Abnormal Psychology*, 125(5), 727–745. doi:10.1037/abn0000178

Hilpert, P., Xu, F., Milek, A., Atkins, D. C., Bodenmann, G., & Bradbury, T. N. (2018). Couples coping with stress: Between-person differences and within-person processes. *Journal of Family Psychology*, 32(3), 366–374. doi:10.1037/fam0000380

Hong, R. Y. (2007). Worry and rumination: Differential associations with anxious and depressive symptoms and coping behavior. *Behaviour Research and Therapy*, 45(2), 277–290. doi:10.1016/j.brat.2006.03.006

Hopp, H., Troy, A. S., & Mauss, I. B. (2011). The unconscious pursuit of emotion regulation: Implications for psychological health. *Cognition and Emotion*, 25, 532–545. doi:10.1080/02699931.2010.532606

Insel, T. R., & Cuthbert, B. N. (2015). Brain disorders? Precisely. *Science*, 348(6234), 499–500. doi:10.1126/science.aab2358

Jensen, M. P., Turner, J. A., Romano, J. M., & Karoly, P. (1991). Coping with chronic pain: A critical review of the literature. *Pain*, 47(3), 249–283. doi:10.1016/0304-3959(91)90216-K

Kopp, C. B. (1989). Regulation of distress and negative emotions: A developmental view. *Developmental Psychology*, 25, 343–354. doi:10.1037/0012-1649.25.3.343

Lazarus, R. S., & Folkman, S. (1984). *Stress, appraisal, and coping*. New York, NY: Springer.

Lochman, J. E., & Wells, K. C. (2004). The Coping Power program for preadolescent aggressive boys and their parents: Outcome effects at one-year follow-up. *Journal of Consulting and Clinical Psychology*, 72, 571–578.

Mauss, I. B., Bunge, S. A., & Gross, J. J. (2007). Automatic emotion regulation. *Social and Personality Psychology Compass*, 1, 146–167. doi:10.1111/j.1751–9004.2007.00005.x

McRae, K., Hughes, B., Chopra, S., Gabrieli, J. D. E., Gross, J. J., & Ochsner, K. N. (2010). The neural bases of distraction and reappraisal. *Journal of Cognitive Neuroscience*, 22(2), 248–262. doi:10.1162/jocn.2009.21243

Moos, R. H., Brennan, P. L., Fondacaro, M. R., & Moos, B. S. (1990). Approach and avoidance coping response among older problem and nonproblem drinkers. *Psychology and Aging*, 5(1), 31–40. doi:10.1037/0882-7974.5.1.31

Nolen-Hoeksema, S. (2012). Emotion regulation and psychopathology: The role of gender. *Annual Review of Clinical Psychology*, 8, 161–187. doi:10.1146/annurev-clinpsy-032511-143109

Nolen-Hoeksema, S., Wisco, B. E., & Lyubomirsky, S. (2008). Rethinking rumination. *Perspectives on Psychological Science*, 3, 400–424. doi:10.1111/j.1745–6924.2008.00088.x

Pearlin, L. I., & Schooler, C. (1978). The structure of coping. *Journal of Health and Social Behavior*, 19(1), 2–21. doi:10.2307/2136319

Penela, E. C., Walker, O. L., Degnan, K. A., Fox, N. A., & Henderson, H. A. (2015). Early behavioral inhibition and emotion regulation: Pathways toward social competence in middle childhood. *Child Development*, 86(4), 1227–1240. doi:10.1111/cdev.12384

Pereira, A. I., Muris, P., Roberto, M. S., Marques, T., Goes, R., & Barros, L. (2018). Examining the mechanisms of therapeutic change in a cognitive-behavioral intervention for anxious children: The role of interpretation bias, perceived control, and coping strategies. *Child Psychiatry & Human Development*, 49(1), 73–85. doi:10.1007/s10578-017-0731-2

Rabiner, D. L., Lenhart, L., & Lochman, J. E. (1990). Automatic versus reflective social problem solving in relation to children's sociometric status. *Developmental Psychology*, 26, 1010–1016.

Roth, S., & Cohen, L. J. (1986). Approach, avoidance, and coping with stress. *American Psychologist*, 47(7), 813–819. doi:10.1037/0003-066X.41.7.813

Rudolph, K. D., Dennig, M. D., & Weisz, J. R. (1995). Determinants and consequences of children's coping in the medical setting: Conceptualization, review, and critique.

Psychological Bulletin, 118(3), 328. doi:10.1037//0033-2909.118.3.328

Rueger, S. Y., Malecki, C. K., Pyun, Y., Aycock, C., & Coyle, S. (2016). A meta-analytic review of the association between perceived social support and depression in childhood and adolescence. *Psychological Bulletin, 142*(10), 1017–1067. doi:10.1037/bul0000058

Schäfer, J. O., Naumann, E., Holmes, E. A., Tuschen-Caffier, B., & Samson, A. C. (2017). Emotion regulation strategies in depressive and anxiety symptoms in youth: A meta-analytic review. *Journal of Youth and Adolescence, 46*(2), 261–276. doi:10.1007/s10964-016-0585-0

Seiffge-Krenke, I. (2011). Coping with relationship stressors: A decade review. *Journal of Research on Adolescence, 21*(1), 196–210. doi:10.1111/j.1532-7795.2010.00723.x

Skinner, E. A., Edge, K., Altman, J., & Sherwood, H. (2003). Searching for the structure of coping: A review and critique of category systems for classifying ways of coping. *Psychological Bulletin, 129*, 216–269. doi:10.1037/0033-2909.129.2.216

Skinner, E. A., & Wellborn, J. G. (1994). Coping during childhood and adolescence: A motivational perspective. In D. L. Featherman, R. M. Lerner, & M. Perlmutter (Eds), *Life-span development and behavior, Vol. 12.* (pp. 91–133). Hillsdale, NJ: Lawrence Erlbaum.

Skinner, E. A., & Zimmer-Gembeck, M. J. (2007). The development of coping. *Annual Review of Psychology, 58*, 119–144. doi:10.1146/annurev.psych.58.110405.085705

Skinner, E. A., & Zimmer-Gembeck, M. J. (2011). Perceived control and the development of coping. In S. Folkman (Ed.), *Oxford library of psychology. The Oxford handbook of stress, health, and coping* (pp. 35–59). New York, NY: Oxford University Press.

Taylor, S. E., & Stanton, A. L. (2007). Coping resources, coping processes, and mental health. *Annual Review of Clinical Psychology, 3*, 377–401. doi:10.1146/annurev.clinpsy.3.022806.091520

Tein, J. Y., Sandler, I. N., Ayers, T. S., & Wolchik, S. A. (2006). Mediation of the effects of the Family Bereavement Program on mental health problems of bereaved children and adolescents. *Prevention Science, 7*, 179–195. doi:10.1007/s11121-006-0037-2

Tein, J. Y., Sandler, I. N., MacKinnon, D. P., & Wolchik, S. A. (2004). How did it work? Who did it work for? Mediation in the context of a moderated prevention effect for children of divorce. *Journal of Consulting and Clinical Psychology, 72*, 617–624. doi:10.1037/0022-006X.72.4.617

Vannucci, A., Flannery, K. M., & Ohannessian, C. M. (2018). Age-varying associationgs between coping and depressive symptoms throughout adolescence and emerging adulthood. *Development and Psychopathology, 30*(2), 665–681. doi:10.1017/S0954579417001183

Wadsworth, M. E. (2015). Development of maladaptive coping: A functional adaptation to chronic, uncontrollable stress. *Child Development Perspectives, 9*(2), 96–100. doi:10.1111/cdep.12112

Wadsworth, M. E., & Compas, B. E. (2002). Coping with family conflict and economic strain: The adolescent perspective. *Journal of Research on Adolescence, 12*(2), 243–274. doi:10.1111/1532-7795.00033

Wadsworth, M. E., Reickmann, T., Benson, M. A., & Compas, B. E. (2004). Coping and responses to stress in Navajo adolescents: Psychometric properties of the Responses to Stress Questionnaire. *Journal of Community Psychology, 32*, 391–411. doi:10.1002/jcop.20008

Wadsworth, M. E., Rindlaub, L., Hurwich-Reiss, E., Rienks, S., Bianco, H., & Markman, H. J. (2013). A longitudinal examination of the adaptation to poverty-related stress model: Predicting child and adolescent adjustment over time. *Journal of Clinical Child & Adolescent Psychology, 42*(5), 713–725. doi:10.1080/15374416.2012.755926

Walker, L. S., Smith, C. A., Garber, J., & Van Slyke, D. A. (1997). Development and validation of the pain response inventory for children. *Psychological Assessment, 9*, 392–405. doi:10.1037/1040-3590.9.4.392

Ward, A., Lyubomirsky, S. Sousa, L., & Nolen-Hoeksema, S. (2003). Can't quite commit: Rumination and uncertainty. *Personality and Social Psychology Bulletin, 29*(1), 96–107. doi:10.1177/0146167202238375

Webb, T. L., Miles, E., & Sheeran, P. (2012). Dealing with feeling: A meta-analysis of the effectiveness of strategies derived from the process model of emotion regulation. *Psychological Bulletin, 138*, 775–808. doi:10.1037/a0027600

Weisz, J. R., McCabe, M. A., & Dennig, M. D. (1994). Primary and secondary control among children undergoing medical procedures: Adjustment as a function of coping style. *Journal of Consulting and Clinical Psychology, 62*, 324–332. doi:10.1037/0022-006X.62.2.324

Xiao, J., Yao, S., Zhu, X., Zhang, C., Auerbach, R. P., Mcwhinnie, C. M., & Abela, J. R. Z. (2010). The responses to stress questionnaire: Construct validity and prediction of depressive and social anxiety symptoms in a sample of Chinese adolescents. *Stress and Health: Journal of the International Society for the Investigation of Stress, 26*, 238–249. doi:10.1002/smi.1291

Yao, S., Xiao, J., Zhu, X., Zhang, C., Auerbach, R. P., Mcwhinnie, C. M.,... Wang, C. (2010). Coping and involuntary responses to stress in Chinese university students: Psychometric properties of the Responses to Stress Questionnaire. *Journal of Personality Assessment, 92*(4), 356–361. doi:10.1080/00223891.2010.482015

Zeman, J., Shipman, K., & Penza-Clyve, S. (2001). Development and initial validation of the children's sadness management scale. *Journal of Nonverbal Behavior, 25*(3), 187–205. doi:10.1023/A:1010623226626

Zeman, J. L., Cassano, M., Suveg, C., & Shipman, K. (2010). Initial validation of the Children's Worry Management Scale. *Journal of Child and Family Studies, 19*(4), 381–392. doi:10.1007/s10826-009-9308-4

Zhu, Z., & Bonanno, G. A. (2018). Affective flexibility: Relations to expressive flexibility, feedback, and depression. *Clinical Psychological Science, 5*(6), 930–942. doi:10.1177/2167702617717337

Zimmer-Gembeck, M. J., Dunbar, M. J., Ferguson, S., Rowe, S. L., Webb, H., & Skinner, E. A. (2014). Guest editorial: Introduction to special issue. *Australian Journal of Psychology, 66*, 65–70. doi:10.1111/ajpy.12056

Zimmer-Gembeck, M. J., & Skinner, E. A. (2011). The development of coping across childhood and adolescence: An integrative review and critique of research. *International Journal of Behavioral Development, 35*(1), 1–17. doi:10.1177/0165025410384923

Zimmer-Gembeck, M. J., & Skinner, E. A. (2016). The development of coping: Implications for psychopathology and resilience. In D. Cicchetti (Ed.), *Developmental psychopathology: Risk, resilience, and intervention* (pp. 485–545). Hoboken, NJ: John Wiley & Sons. doi:10.1002/9781119125556.devpsy410

Biological Sensitivity to Context

A Framework for Understanding Relations Between
Early Life Experiences and Problem Behaviors

Nila Shakiba, Elisabeth Conradt, *and* Bruce J. Ellis

Abstract

It is now well established that early experiences of adversity play a central role in development of many mental health problems in adulthood. However, the effects are more pronounced and detrimental for some individuals compared to others. Informed by the biological sensitivity to context model, an evolutionary-developmental model of individual differences in stress responsivity, the present chapter highlights the role of stress response system as one moderating mechanism in the pathway between early life experiences and development of internalizing and externalizing behaviors. The model posits that the magnitude and integrated patterns of autonomic and adrenocortical responses to psychosocial challenges are indicators of the organisms' level of susceptibility to both positive and negative environmental influences. The final part of the chapter focuses on the role of early life experiences in programming the functioning of stress response systems, development of adaptive stress responsivity patterns, and related behavioral profiles.

Keywords: biological sensitivity to context, adaptive calibration model, differential susceptibility, developmental programming, biological embedding, conditional adaptation, early adversity, HPA axis, autonomic nervous system, stress reactivity

The origins of many mental and physical health problems in adults can be traced back to early life experiences (Danese & McEwen, 2012; Gillman, 2005; Mersky, Topitzes, & Reynolds, 2013; Shonkoff, Boyce, & McEwen, 2009; Shonkoff et al., 2012). Early experiences of adversity such as childhood maltreatment and neglect (Chapman et al., 2004; Horwitz, Widom, McLaughlin, & White, 2001; Nanni, Uher, & Danese, 2011; Spataro, Mullen, Burgess, Wells, & Moss, 2004), socioeconomic disparities (Melchior et al., 2007; Murali & Oyebode, 2004; Reiss, 2013; Yoshikawa, Aber, & Beardslee, 2012), and family disruption (Amato & Sobolewski, 2001; Gilman, Kawachi, Fitzmaurice, & Buka, 2003) have lifelong effects on individuals' mental health and well-being. However, these effects are stronger for some individuals compared to others. This fact raises the important question of why early

life events have varying effects on health. What are the intervening and moderating mechanisms through which these effects unfold?

In an attempt to address these crucial questions, Boyce and Ellis (2005) proposed the theory of biological sensitivity to context (BSC), which highlights the role of physiological systems, such as the stress response system, as one of the central underlying mechanisms linking early stress and later health outcomes. This evolutionary-developmental model of individual differences in stress responsivity centers on two specific ideas that will form the main structure of the present chapter: (1) the significance of early life experiences in programming the functioning of stress response systems and related stress responsivity patterns, and (2) the conceptualization of individual differences in magnitude and patterns of physiological responses to psychosocial stressors as proxies for organisms' levels of susceptibility to environmental influences. Boyce and Ellis (2005) introduced the metaphors of "orchids" and "dandelions" to describe children with varying levels of susceptibility to early rearing experiences. They referred to children with heightened physiological reactivity (i.e., higher levels of physiological arousal to psychosocial challenges relative to the resting state) as "orchid children" to represent their greater susceptibility to both positive and negative early contextual influences, in a "for better and for worse" manner. By contrast, they use the metaphor of "dandelion children" to describe children with low physiological reactivity who seem to be indifferent to the quality of their rearing environments and function comparably across different environmental conditions (Boyce & Ellis, 2005).

Informed by the BSC theory, the focus of this chapter will be on the role of stress response systems—the autonomic nervous system (ANS) and the hypothalamic-pituitary-adrenal (HPA) axis—in the pathway connecting early life experiences to later development of internalizing and externalizing behaviors. In the first section, we will review the BSC theory and present empirical updates on the physiological markers of sensitivity to context. We selectively review the literature examining the interactive effects of different early rearing environments and variations in stress reactivity across both ANS and HPA axis in predicting risk of developing mental health problems (i.e., internalizing and externalizing problems).

The second assumption of the BSC theory, which we will articulate in the second part of the chapter, is related to the developmental origins of variation in sensitivity to context. Boyce and Ellis (2005) argue that biological sensitivity to context is not a fixed property. Rather, it is shaped by developmental experiences. They posit a U-shaped, curvilinear relation between early stress exposures and biological sensitivity to context (indexed by the magnitude of stress reactivity). They proposed that there are two types of "orchid children": (a) those who have been reared under highly supportive conditions, and (b) those exposed to markedly adverse conditions. As a result of adaptation to their rearing environments, these two kinds of orchid children have developed "context-sensitive endophenotypes" (Ellis & Boyce, 2011, p. 1), which enhance their survival and reproductive success in both of these contrasting contexts. In contrast, dandelion children are those who tend to show low physiological reactivity to stressors, and they develop in an environ-

ment that is neither extremely safe and nurturing nor harsh and challenging. Recently, Del Giudice, Ellis, and Shirtcliff (2011) proposed the adaptive calibration model (ACM), which extends the BSC theory and adds another type of dandelion children (to the original BSC model). Unlike the previous group, these dandelion children are reared in extremely stressful and traumatic environments. Through the second part of the chapter, we will provide a recap of the ACM and present updates on its current empirical status with respect to the developmental programming of the autonomic and adrenocortical stress response systems. We will exclusively review literature suggesting how different stress reactivity patterns (i.e., low vs. high reactivity) may develop as a result of organisms' "conditional adaptation" to their developmental environments.

Variability in Susceptibility to Environmental Influences: Stress Response Systems as One Key Marker of Susceptibility or Vulnerability?

Clinical and epidemiological research has documented that exposure to adverse environments early in life places individuals at increased risk of developing a wide range of mental health disorders. However, there is striking evidence suggesting that individuals vary in whether and/or the extent to which they are influenced by their environments (as reviewed in Belsky & Pluess, 2009 and Ellis, Boyce, Belsky, Bakermans-Kranenburg, & Van IJzendoorn, 2011). Some individuals seem to function similarly across different developmental conditions, while others demonstrate distinct behavioral and health outcomes under different developmental conditions with various levels of support and adversity. What causes this variability? The evolutionary-developmental model of differential susceptibility (Belsky, 2005; Belsky, Bakermans-Kranenburg, & van IJzendoorn, 2007; Boyce & Ellis, 2005; Ellis et al., 2011) and the diathesis-stress model (Monroe & Simons, 1991; Zuckerman, 1999) postulate that some individuals have behavioral (difficult temperament, behavioral inhibition or negative emotionality), genetic ("plasticity or susceptibility allele": e.g., *5-HTTLPR, DRD4*; Belsky et al., 2009), or physiological (e.g., high autonomic or cortisol reactivity to stressors) susceptibilities and are more likely than others to function poorly or develop psychopathology under adverse developmental conditions (Belsky & Pluess, 2009).

On the other hand, the differential susceptibility theory, but not the diathesis-stress model, contends that the very same individuals who are most adversely impacted by negative environmental conditions during development (e.g., harsh and insensitive parenting, parental conflict) conversely benefit more than others from highly supportive and nurturing environments. In other words, these differentially responsive individuals are affected by both the negative and positive features of their developmental environments in a "for better and for worse" manner (Belsky et al., 2007; Belsky & Pluess, 2009; Ellis et al., 2011). For instance, in investigating the interactive effects of child temperament traits and maternal discipline in the prediction of children's behavior during early childhood (i.e., the first 3 years of life), van Zeijl and colleagues (2007) found that children with difficult temperaments (i.e., those who become easily upset and inadaptable) demonstrated more susceptibility than others to both positive and negative discipline. Compared to children with easy temperaments, these difficult children showed fewer externalizing behaviors when their mothers practiced more positive discipline strategies (e.g., distraction): "for better." However, they exhibited more externalizing behavior problems in the context of negative discipline (e.g., prohibitions): "for worse." In another investigation by Morgan, Shaw, and Olino (2012), boys characterized as high on negative emotionality (another behavioral marker of susceptibility) who became easily distressed and displayed more intense negative emotional reactions (i.e., fussing and crying) to laboratory tasks (at 18 months) displayed fewer internalizing problems (at age 6), when they had higher positive sibling relationship quality (at age 5). These children, however, demonstrated higher internalizing problems and fewer social skills when the quality of their sibling relationship was more destructive.

The key point to consider here is that children with difficult temperaments tend to show susceptibility to both positive and negative features of their environment, regardless of when they are assessed. However, for children with heightened negative emotionality, their susceptibility to environmental influences is more prominent during infancy than any other time throughout their life (Slagt, Dubas, Dekovic, & van Aken, 2016).

With respect to genetic markers of susceptibility, Hankin et al. (2011) found that genetically susceptible youths (i.e., those who carried short alleles of the serotonin transporter promoter polymorphism; 5-HTTLPR) showed high levels of positive affect under the contexts of supportive/positive parenting ("for better"). The same individuals who carried this

susceptibility allele also exhibited low levels of positive affect when exposed to unsupportive/nonpositive parenting ("for worse"). In contrast, youths who carried the long alleles of 5-HTTLPR (low-susceptible individuals) exhibited equivalent and constant levels of positive affect across different parenting environments. Considering a great body of evidence (e.g., Bakermans-Kranenburg & van IJzendoorn, 2011; Knafo, Israel, & Ebstein, 2011; Kochanska, Kim, Barry, & Philibert, 2011) delineating that individuals carrying these types of alleles are susceptible to both positive and negative features of their environment "for better and for worse," Belsky and colleagues (2009) suggest that these genetic traits should be better conceptualized and referred to as "plasticity genes" than the "vulnerability gene" or "risk alleles." This argument challenges the central assumption of the diathesis-stress model, which exclusively views individuals carrying these genetic alleles as "vulnerable" individuals who are at increased risks of developing psychopathology under adverse conditions.

A large body of empirical work suggests that variations in the functioning of stress response systems may also explain why some people are more influenced than others by the quality of their environments. For instance, Obradović and colleagues (2010) documented that among children who were exposed to family adversity, those with heightened stress reactivity to laboratory challenges demonstrated relatively elevated externalizing symptoms and lower school engagement and prosocial behaviors, compared to their peers with low stress reactivity ("for worse"). However, equally reactive children raised in a family setting with low family adversity (as an indication of positive environment) exhibited the lowest levels of externalizing symptoms and the highest levels of school engagement and prosocial behaviors ("for better").

Brock and colleagues (2017) examined whether the combination of biobehavioral plasticity markers, including negative emotionality (i.e., high inhibition and sadness, low joy), psychophysiology (skin conductance level), and the 5-HTTLPR polymorphism, might serve as "cumulative plasticity" or "susceptibility" factors that moderate the effects of interparental relationship satisfaction at preschool age on the development of internalizing problems from kindergarten until early adolescence. Their findings revealed that children who scored higher on an aggregated biobehavioral plasticity index showed more internalizing problems when their parents reported low relationship satisfaction. However, among these high-plasticity children, the risk of developing internalizing problems was significantly reduced in the context of a positive interparental relationship.

A handful of meta-analyses and research reviews exist in the literature that exclusively and comprehensively review the empirical findings for different behavioral (Slagt, Dubas, Dekovic, & van Aken, 2016) and genetic markers of susceptibility (e.g., Bakermans-Kranenburg & Van IJzendoorn, 2011; Belsky et al., 2009; Nugent, Tyrka, Carpenter, & Price, 2011; Van IJzendoorn, Belsky, & Bakermans-Kranenburg, 2012). However, to our knowledge, there is no review of physiological markers of susceptibility. Therefore, in the present chapter, we limit our discussion to these markers of environmental susceptibility and the role that they play in moderating (i.e., either buffering or augmenting) the effects of different early life experiences on later development of externalizing and internalizing problems.

Early Life Stress and the Development of Internalizing and Externalizing Behaviors: ANS and HPA Axis as Moderators

It is now well established that early adversity alters development in ways that increase vulnerability to psychopathology (Shonkoff, Boyce, & McEwen, 2009) while also potentially fine-tuning social and cognitive abilities to match high-adversity contexts (Ellis, Bianchi, Griskevicius, & Frankenhuis, 2017). In recent years, significant attempts have been made to elucidate the mechanisms underlying these individual differences and to discover the characteristics of highly susceptible individuals (Belsky & Pluess, 2009; Obradović & Boyce, 2009).

In exploring the role of stress response systems as one key physiological mechanism underlying these individual variations (Boyce & Ellis, 2005; Ellis et al., 2011), a rich body of empirical work focuses on variations in the activity of the autonomic nervous system (e.g., Cummings, El-Sheikh, Kouros, & Keller, 2007; El-Sheikh & Hinnant, 2011; Essex, Armstrong, Burk, Goldsmith, & Boyce, 2011; McLaughlin, Rith-Najarian, Dirks, & Sheridan, 2015; Obradović, Bush, & Boyce, 2011; Somers, Ibrahim, & Luecken, 2017) as marked by changes in the activity of the two branches of parasympathetic nervous system (PNS) and sympathetic nervous system (SNS), in exposure to psychosocial challenges. Fewer studies have investigated the moderating effects of HPA activity as indexed by cortisol reactivity in the association between early life stress

and vulnerability to developing internalizing and externalizing problems. Together, these empirical studies suggest that under different environmental conditions variability in both ANS and HPA axis reactivity contribute to organisms' adaptive and maladaptive functioning (Adam, Klimes-Dougan, & Gunnar, 2007; Boyce & Ellis, 2005; Ellis, Jackson, & Boyce, 2006).

We systematically searched the literature for the empirical papers testing for the interactive effects of different indices of early familial and environmental adversity and/or support and variations in activation of (1) the ANS reactivity (hypo- vs. hyperreactivity) within the two branches of the PNS (assessed via respiratory sinus arrhythmia; RSA) and SNS (assessed via skin conductance level, pre-ejection period, or salivary amylase), and (2) the HPA axis (assessed via salivary cortisol concentrations) in predicting internalizing and/or externalizing problems from infancy to later adolescence. We review our findings next.

AUTONOMIC STRESS REACTIVITY AS AN INDICATOR OF DIFFERENTIAL SUSCEPTIBILITY

A large body of work has attempted to delineate how the interactions between various environmental factors (e.g., the quality of caregiving and attachment, caregiver stress) and infants', children's, and adolescents' autonomic functioning may predict early and later internalizing and externalizing behaviors. These studies targeted measures of both sympathetic and parasympathetic branches of the autonomic nervous system in their investigation of the physiological markers of differential susceptibility.

Heart rate is regulated by neural output from the PNS (vagal nerve), which slows heart rate, and the SNS, which accelerates it (see Shaffer, McCraty, & Zerr, 2014 for a review of heart rate regulation). Even at rest, both parasympathetic and sympathetic nerves are active, with vagal effects dominant. In this tonic state, the PNS remains engaged, applying a cardiac brake that inhibits cardiac activity and promotes vegetative functions (i.e., rest and digest). The PNS promotes emotional regulation and social engagement under normal circumstances. When stressors are encountered, the PNS withdraws quickly, promoting rapid and flexible responding to stress and coping with mild to moderate stressors (e.g., solving a difficult puzzle). PNS withdrawal enables the excitatory SNS to operate unopposed. This coupled PNS withdrawal and SNS activation increases cardiac output. Following SNS activation, secretion of epinephrine and norepinephrine by the adrenal medulla supports fight/flight responses (e.g., increased heart rate, respiration, blood supply to skeletal muscles, and glucose release in the bloodstream).

The activity of the ANS is commonly measured during resting states, in response to challenges (reactivity), and during recovery phases. Due to space limitations, we restricted our literature review to empirical studies that examined stress reactivity as defined by changes in the activity of stress response systems from baseline to challenge conditions. We excluded studies that measured differential influences of resting and basal levels and the recovery episodes on mental health outcomes.

PARASYMPATHETIC NERVOUS SYSTEM
REACTIVITY

An extensive body of literature has documented that the activity of the PNS moderates associations between early life experiences and the development of psychopathology. PNS functioning is commonly indexed by respiratory sinus arrhythmia (RSA), which is the naturally occurring variation in heart rate as a function of respiration (Bornstein & Suess, 2000; Calkins, 1997). RSA occurs due to increases in vagal efference during exhalation, which decelerates heart rate, and decreases in vagal efference during inhalation, which accelerates heart rate (Beauchaine, 2001; Porges, 1995, 2007). When no stress or threats are perceived in the environment, RSA increases (i.e., vagal augmentation) and acts as a physiological "brake" to decelerate the heart rate and maintain physiological restoration and social functioning. However, in the face of stress and unexpected events, RSA decreases (i.e., the "brake" is released; vagal withdrawal), which allows sympathetic activation, increases in cardiac outputs, and mobilization of physiological and attentional resources for effective coping with environmental demands. The vagal regulation of cardiac activity plays a key role in emotion regulation and social functioning (polyvagal theory; Porges, 2007, 2011).

A growing body of evidence suggests that the effects of RSA reactivity on health outcomes are highly context-dependent and vary by the type of the environments that children and adolescents experience early in life. However, the literature seems to be very conflicted and unclear for the directions of PNS reactivity effects (low vs. high reactivity) across different environmental conditions. On the one hand, studies reported that early experiences of various forms of adversity, such as maternal psychopathology (Shanahan, Calkins, Keane, Kelleher, & Suffness, 2014; Shannon, Beauchaine, Brenner, Neuhaus, & Gatzke-Kopp, 2007), harsh and intrusive parenting (Dyer, Blocker, Day, & Bean, 2016), caregiving stress (Conradt et al., 2016), and family adversity (i.e., financial stress, parenting overload, marital conflict, maternal depression; Obradović et al, 2010) significantly increase the risk of developing internalizing and externalizing problems among those who showed *high* RSA reactivity to laboratory challenges. Contrary to these studies' findings, other empirical work has suggested that *lower* RSA reactivity may indeed serve as a vulnerability factor for developing pathology under adverse conditions (e.g., Davis, Suveg, Whitehead, Jones, & Shaffer, 2016; El-Sheikh & Whitson, 2006; Keller, Kouros, Erath, Dahl, & El-Sheikh, 2014; McLaughlin, Alves, & Sheridan, 2014).

Some of these divergent findings across the extant literature may be in part explained by the nature of the sample (clinical vs. normal sample, age, and sex), the type of adversity that they were exposed to early in life, and the different features of laboratory challenges employed to measure stress reactivity. For instance, in one study, contrary to researchers' expectations, a mother's lower practice of authoritarian (aversive parenting) and higher practice of authoritative (supportive) parenting style predicted more externalizing problems only in female adolescents who showed high RSA reactivity to laboratory challenges. Conversely, in females with low RSA reactivity, higher levels of authoritative parenting predicted fewer externalizing problems. However, in males with high RSA reactivity (more sensitive males), having a highly authoritarian mother was associated with greater risk of externalizing problems (Dyer et al., 2016).

Likewise, Obradovic and colleagues (2011) suggest that the discrepant moderation findings for the effects of high versus low RSA reactivity levels in the pathways between early adversity and child adjustment problems might be also explained by the nature of the laboratory challenge tasks that are employed to elicit stress in children (e.g., cognitive or interpersonal tasks). They found opposite results for the interactive effects of marital conflict and RSA reactivity to the cognitive tasks on externalizing symptoms than to the interpersonal task. High levels of marital conflict exposure predicted greater levels of externalizing symptoms in children who showed higher RSA reactivity to the cognitive challenge task than those with low RSA reactivity. However, in response to an interpersonal conflict task, no difference was found in levels of externalizing symptoms between the high and low reactive children who experienced high marital conflict.

Common across most of these studies is that the group who were identified as "more biologically sensitive" and highly susceptible to environmental influences (either high- or low-RSA reactive groups) showed elevated psychological symptom levels in the context of high adversity, but lower symptoms in contexts of low adversity, high protection, and nurturance. In other words, in a majority of cases, these individuals appeared to be susceptible to both positive and negative features of their environment in a "for better and for worse" manner. By contrast, the "less biologically sensitive" and low-susceptible group was not as affected by the quality of their environment and showed similar adaptation (they did not differ in their levels of psychological symptoms and problem behaviors) across different contexts. Further empirical studies are needed to illuminate the role of PNS reactivity in the pathway between early life experiences and development of psychopathology.

SYMPATHETIC NERVOUS SYSTEM REACTIVITY

In response to environmental challenges and threats, the activation of SNS fosters "fight-or-flight" response, which increases sweat gland secretion, heart rate, cardiac output, systolic blood pressure, oxygen flow throughout the body, and the release of catecholamines into the bloodstream (Berntson, Cacioppo, & Quigley, 1991). Sympathetic activity is commonly indexed by skin conductance level (SCL), cardiac pre-ejection period (PEP), and salivary alpha-amylase (sAA). SCL refers to electrodermal activity caused by the activity of sweat glands. These glands are solely innervated by the SNS. PEP indexes the contraction time interval (electrical-mechanical delay) in the left ventricle that occurs between the onset of ventricular depolarization and the opening of the aortic valve. sAA is one of the enzymes in saliva that is released by the parotid gland and is involved in digestion of starch in the oral cavity and also has a bacterial interactive function which clears and inhibits the growth of some undesirable bacteria from the oral cavity (Granger, Kivlighan, El-Sheikh, Gordis, & Stroud, 2007; Nater & Rohleder, 2009; Scannapieco, Torres, & Levine, 1993). It also functions as a marker of the adrenergic component of the stress response systems. Activations of both SNS and PNS under stressful conditions stimulate secretion of sAA from salivary glands and significantly augment its concentration levels.

Heightened sensitivity of the three indices of SNS to physiological changes in the body caused by physical and psychological stressors makes them reliable and noninvasive biomarkers in measuring acute and chronic stress. These parameters also serve to index pathological dysregulation of the autonomic system under adverse and clinical conditions (Ali & Pruessner, 2012; Schumacher, Kirschbaum, Fydrich, & Ströhle, 2013). Studies have reported elevated risks of internalizing problems among high-risk individuals with higher levels of SCL (Dawson, Schell, & Filion, 2007; Fowles, 1988), and higher sAA concentration levels (Allwood et al., 2011; Schumacher et al., 2013). Lower levels of SCL and sAA have also been found to be associated with antisocial and externalizing problems (Crowell et al., 2005, 2006; Keller & El-Sheikh, 2009; Spinrad et al., 2009). Similarly, reduced PEP reactivity (lengthened PEP) to laboratory stressors predicted increases in alcohol use and conduct problems in high-risk samples (Beauchaine et al., 2001; Brenner & Beauchaine, 2011; Crowell et al., 2006).

Similar to the parasympathetic branch of the ANS, activity of the SNS seems to be highly influenced by early contextual influences. Further, depending on the magnitude of SNS responses to psychosocial challenges relative to resting state or baseline condition (i.e., low vs. high SNS reactivity), individuals may be at reduced or elevated risks of developing mental health problems under adverse conditions, as per predictions of the diathesis-stress model and differential susceptibility theory. These individuals also vary in their levels of susceptibility to potential benefits and resources in the environment, as per the prediction of the differential susceptibility theory.

A substantial body of work has suggested that the effects of early adversity on children's and adolescents' psychological adjustment may vary depending on the magnitude of SNS responses to psychosocial challenges (i.e., SNS reactivity). However, there are significant inconsistencies across these studies' findings. Some studies reported that *greater* SCL, sAA, and PEP responses to laboratory stress tasks predict more externalizing and internalizing problems particularly in those who experienced higher levels of adversity (e.g., parental depression [Cummings et al., 2007], paternal antisocial personality disorder [Shannon et al., 2007], parental marital conflict [El-Sheikh, 2005; El-Sheikh, Keller, & Erath, 2007; Obradovic et al., 2011], victimization [Rudolph, Troop-Gordon, & Granger, 2010, 2011], single-parent household [Diamond, Fagundes,

& Cribbet, 2012], and maltreatment [Gordis, Feres, Olezeski, Rabkin, & Trickett, 2010]). Conversely, other studies have reported that emotional and behavioral problems are greatest among those with the combination of *lower* SCL, sAA, and PEP reactivity and more experiences of adversity (e.g., harsh parenting [Erath, El-Sheikh, Hinnant, & Cummings, 2011], parental power assertion [Kochanska, Brock, Chen, Aksan, & Anderson, 2015], and peer victimization [Gregson, Tu, & Erath, 2014]). Furthermore, these low-SNS reactive individuals demonstrated fewer behavioral problems and negative emotional traits problems than their high-SNS reactive peers when they experienced more positive and supportive (e.g., warm and positive parent–child relationships; Kochanska et al., 2015).

Further interpretation of these inconsistent and complex findings revealed that the moderating effects of heightened versus lower SNS reactivity to stress might be gender, age, and context specific and vary by the nature and the type of family stressors. In particular, in the majority of studies that we reviewed, higher SCL reactivity was identified as a biological risk factor in one sex, but a protective factor in another sex. For instance, in the context of interparental marital conflict, El-Sheikh and colleagues (2007) reported more externalizing and internalizing problems in girls with higher SCL reactivity. However, for boys, lower (but not higher) SCL reactivity predicted stronger associations between aggressive marital conflict and externalizing problems. Similarly, Diamond et al. (2012) suggested that living in a single-parent household may differentially impact female and male adolescents' mental health and adjustment as a function of their autonomic responses to stressors. They found more externalizing problems among adolescent boys with high SCL reactivity and girls with low SCL reactivity who lived in a single-parent versus two-parent household.

The strength of the association between family stress and subsequent mental health problems may also change by age in individuals with varying levels of sensitivity to context. Erath and colleagues (2011) found that in the context of high harsh parenting, boys (but not girls) with *lower* SCL reactivity initially demonstrated elevated externalizing behavior at age 8 and their behavior remained relatively high through age 10. However, boys with higher SCL showed relatively low levels of externalizing behavior at age 8, but it significantly increased by late childhood, such that at age 10 their behavior was as high as their peers with lower SCL reactivity. In both girls and boys with low experiences of harsh parenting, lower externalizing behavior emerged in early childhood and persisted until late childhood.

Regardless of these mixed findings for the direction of associations for individuals with higher versus lower SNS and PNS reactivity, ANS functioning primarily operated as one biological marker of susceptibility that moderated the effects of environmental factors on children's and adolescents' mental health outcomes. Specifically, those who showed greater biological sensitivity to context (i.e., high-susceptible group; those showed either low or high SNS reactivity) had more adjustment problems under adverse conditions, but more resilient outcomes under less stressful environmental conditions. Low-susceptible individuals, on the other hand, appeared to be less impacted by the quality of their environments. However, it is important to note that ANS functioning does not necessarily and globally serve as a sensitivity factor without considering gender, age, and domain-specific implications.

The patterns that we detected for the moderating effects of ANS functioning across studies are more consistent with the differential susceptibility theory than the diathesis-stress model. According to differential susceptibility theory, children and adolescents who demonstrate elevated susceptibility to environmental influences will show not only poorer outcomes under adverse conditions, but they also show positive outcomes in more positive and supportive environments. In studies that we reviewed, low-stressful environments were operationalized as a "positive environment." In most cases, low- and high-susceptible individuals showed different patterns of outcomes under low- and high-stress conditions. High-susceptible individuals showed the worst health outcomes under very stressful environments, but fewer adjustment problems under less stressful environments than their low-susceptible peers. This suggests that individual differences in biological responses to stress are better implicated as plasticity traits rather than vulnerability factors.

Hypothalamic-Pituitary-Adrenal Axis Reactivity as an Indicator of Differential Susceptibility

Exposure to acute and chronic stressful conditions activates the HPA axis (in addition to ANS) through releasing corticotropin-releasing factor (CRF) from the hypothalamus, which stimulates the secretion of adrenocorticotropic hormone (ACTH) from the pituitary gland. The release of ACTH hormone in turn induces the production and secretion of cortisol from the adrenal cortex into the bloodstream (Gunnar & Vazquez, 2006). This in turn initiates a negative feedback process that serves as a regulatory mechanism for controlling and suppressing the further secretion of cortisol. When the concentration of cortisol in the bloodstream rises to a certain level, the negative feedback circuitry becomes activated and induces the hypothalamus and pituitary gland to shut down the production and release of CRF and ACTH (see Chapter 22 and 26 for further discussion of the activity of HPA axis under stressful situations).

Chronic experiences of adversity may modify the activity of the HPA axis and negative feedback circuitry and lead to alterations in patterns of HPA axis responsivity (lower or higher level of cortisol secretion; Miller, Chen, & Zhou, 2007). A handful of studies have shown that chronic stressors, such as interparental conflict (Davies, Sturge-Apple, Cicchetti, & Cummings, 2007), maternal prenatal stress (Tollenaar, Beijers, Jansen, Riksen-Walraven, & DeWeerth, 2011), and maternal depression (Barry et al., 2015), are associated with elevated cortisol in response to stressors. In contrast, there is some emerging evidence for the dampened activity of the HPA axis and reduced cortisol levels in response to chronic stressors like prenatal substance exposure (Lester et al., 2010), poor maternal care (Engert et al., 2010), and childhood maltreatment (MacMillan et al., 2009).

The variability in direction and magnitude of HPA axis responses to chronic stressors is accounted for (in part) by age, the nature and controllability of stressors, the time since onset, and the emotions they elicit (Fisher & Gunnar, 2010; Miller et al., 2007; Tollenaar et al., 2011). Some of the diverse findings in the literature may also reflect methodological artifacts. A meta-analysis by Miller and colleagues (2007) showed that across studies, exposure to uncontrollable (vs. controllable) stressors, traumatic (vs. nontraumatic) events, social-evaluative threats, and recent onset or ongoing exposure to stressors (vs. distant trauma) were associated with greater activity of the HPA axis (i.e., increases in cortisol output or hypercortisolism). On the other hand, reduced or blunted activity of HPA axis (i.e., hypocortisolism) may develop following an organism's long-term adaptation to chronic stressors and prolonged period of HPA hyperactivity. In other words, individuals experiencing chronic stress may initially exhibit prolonged and elevated activity of HPA axis, and over time, as a result of desensitization to stressors, they may develop blunted cortisol

responsivity pattern (Fries, Hesse, Hellhammer, & Hellhammer, 2005). Although short-term and elevated activity of the HPA axis to acute stressors is protective and promotes adaptation to stress, prolonged and repeated activation of the HPA axis may cause biological "wear and tear," which markedly elevates the risk of health problems (McEwen, 1998, 2000; Shonkoff et al., 2012; Sterling & Eyer, 1988). Downregulation of the HPA axis in chronically stressed individuals serves as a defensive and regulatory mechanism that reduces their risks of developing poor health outcomes (Koss & Gunnar, 2018).

However, as we mentioned earlier in the chapter and consistent with the biological sensitivity to context theory and the differential susceptibility theory, the joint effects of environmental factors (environmental risk vs. support) and individual characteristics predict whether or not a person may develop psychopathology or function adaptively. With respect to individual differences in the activity of HPA axis in response to challenges (i.e., low vs. high cortisol reactivity), a handful of studies examined the moderating effects of HPA axis reactivity to laboratory challenges in the pathway between exposure to various forms of family and environmental adversity/support and children and adolescents' amplified or reduced risks of developing psychopathology. These studies are distinct based on whether they identified high and/or low cortisol reactivity as a risk or protective factor for psychological disorders.

The first group of studies report more internalizing and externalizing problems among children (Barrios, Bufferd, Klein, & Dougherty, 2017) and adolescents who experienced significant adversity early in life and also exhibited *elevated* cortisol responses to laboratory stressors (as compared with their peers who showed reduced cortisol responses). For instance, high levels of family aggression and conflict were associated with posttraumatic stress symptoms and antisocial behavior (Saxbe, Margolin, Spies Shapiro, & Baucom, 2012) and greater internalizing behavior problems (i.e., anxiety and depression; Bergman, Cummings, & Davies, 2014) only among adolescents who showed elevated cortisol reactivity (relative to baseline) to laboratory challenges (e.g., laboratory-based family discussion conflict). On the other hand, dampened cortisol reactivity appeared to attenuate the effects of family conflict on adolescents' psychological and behavioral problems.

Consistent with the differential susceptibility theory, but not the diathesis-stress model, individuals with elevated cortisol reactivity relative to their low-reactive peers were found to be more susceptible to both positive and negative features of their rearing conditions in a "for better and for worse" manner. In a study by Hastings and colleagues (2011), temperamentally inhibited 4-year-olds who had a highly punitive mother and showed greater cortisol reactivity after interacting with adult strangers demonstrated the most behavioral and emotional problems ("for worse"). However, these highly reactive children presented the lowest levels of externalizing problems when their mothers did not practice harsh parenting ("for better"). In another study by Obradović and colleagues (2010), children with elevated cortisol reactivity (but not low cortisol reactivity) showed higher levels of prosocial behaviors in the context of low adversity ("for better"), and lower levels of prosocial behaviors ("for worse") when they were raised in adverse family environments (indexed by high parenting overload, harsh and restrictive parenting, financial stress, martial conflict, negative/anger expressiveness, and maternal depression). No significant difference was found in the levels of prosocial behaviors in low cortisol reactive children across different family conditions. Likewise, in the context of childhood maltreatment, Cook, Chaplin, Sinha, Tebes, and Mayes (2012) reported increased interpersonal competence and anger regulation ("for better") in 15-year-old adolescents who were exposed to low childhood maltreatment and exhibited heightened cortisol, heart rate, and blood pressure reactivity to the Trier Social Stress Task. However, these adolescents showed decreased interpersonal competence and anger regulation when they reported on higher levels of childhood maltreatment ("for worse").

The effects of high physiological reactivity on individuals' behavior and health outcomes appeared to be bidirectional and context-dependent across these studies. That is, high reactivity promoted competence and enhanced adaptive functioning in the context of low adversity and high support, but it also served as a risk factor and significantly enhanced the rates of disease in the context of high adversity (Boyce & Ellis, 2005; Ellis & Boyce, 2008). In other words, heightened stress reactivity reflects organisms' greater openness to environmental influences (both positive and negative influences), rather than a vulnerability and risk-augmenting factor.

In contrast to these aforementioned studies that indicated higher rates of internalizing and externalizing problems among individuals with high cortisol reactivity, some work suggests that *low*-reactive individuals may also develop externalizing or internalizing problems under adverse conditions. For instance, the results of Kushner, Barrios, Smith, and Dougherty (2016) showed that a recent experience of significant stressful events predicts greater externalizing problems and poorer psychosocial functioning in 4-year-old children who showed blunted cortisol reactivity. These researchers found no significant evidence of externalizing symptoms and psychological malfunctioning among preschoolers with high cortisol reactivity.

In addition, some work documents the vulnerability of both *high-* and *low*-reactive individuals to adverse features of their environment. However, they argue that their mental health outcomes (internalizing or externalizing problems) may vary by the type and severity of adversity that they have experienced. For instance, findings of von Klitzing and associates (2012) revealed that the effects of disrupted family environments (indexed by high conflict, low cohesion and expressiveness) and peer victimization (measured at age 5) on children's emotional symptoms (reported at age 6) vary depending on their levels of cortisol responses to stressors. The highest levels of emotional symptoms (i.e., anxiety, depressive mood, shyness) were reported by parents of children who lived in a very negative family environment and showed *elevated* cortisol responses. A disrupted family environment was not related to emotional symptoms among *low*-reactive children. Instead, in these children, high levels of peer victimization at preschool predicted greater emotional symptoms.

Even in response to the same type and levels of adversity, low versus high cortisol reactive groups may show different mental health problems. In a group of young adults (aged 18–22) who experienced high levels of childhood maltreatment, Hagan, Roubinov, Mistler, and Luecken (2014) reported a greater risk of developing internalizing problems among individuals who showed *higher* cortisol reactivity to laboratory challenges (conflict role-play task). On the other hand, they observed the highest levels of externalizing problems among *low*-reactive youths. Equally reactive youths who experienced low maltreatment had the lowest levels of internalizing symptoms.

The research reviewed in this chapter suggests that cortisol reactivity moderates the relations between environmental adversity (early and current) and subsequent mental health outcomes and adaptive functioning. However, some inconsistencies appeared across the studies regarding developmental predictors of internalizing and externalizing behaviors under adverse rearing conditions. Although most differential susceptibility studies have found that the effects of stressful rearing conditions on internalizing and externalizing problems are accentuated by high cortisol reactivity, some studies have found the opposite (e.g., Hagan et al., 2014; Kushner et al., 2016; von Klitzing et al., 2012).

Intervention and Therapeutic Implications of Differential Susceptibility Theory

Differential susceptibility and diathesis-stress models both illustrate that not all individuals who experience adversity will develop psychopathology and some may actually be resilient and function adaptively. Moreover, the first but not the second model stipulates that the same individuals who are deleteriously impacted by environmental risks and adversity might also profit most from the positive and constructive changes in their environment.

In translating these theoretical premises into preventive and therapeutic interventions for at-risk populations, one may speculate that the effects of intervention would not be equivalent across individuals with varying levels of susceptibility to environmental influences. Effects are expected to be largest for highly susceptible individuals and smallest for low-susceptible individuals. In recent years, researchers have attempted to evaluate the effectiveness of interventions—particularly those with the primary goal of making positive changes in child care quality—among children with varying levels of susceptibility (i.e., low- vs. high-susceptible children; Bakermans-Kranenburg, Van IJzendoorn, Pijlman, Mesman, & Juffer, 2008; Belsky & van IJzendoorn, 2015). Much of the research conducted in this area suggests that the efficacy of different intervention programs may vary as a function of individuals' genetic makeup (i.e., whether or not they carry plasticity genes as a marker of susceptibility; van IJzendoorn & Bakermans-Kranenburg; 2015) or their temperament (Klein Velderman, Bakermans-Kranenburg, Juffer, & van IJzendoorn, 2006).

Considering these empirical findings, interventionists, therapists and policy makers may raise the question of whether neurobiological susceptibility to environmental influences should be utilized as a screening tool to identify the subset of individuals who are responsive and benefit most from intervention effects. Moreover, they may wonder whether and how the knowledge of differential susceptibility could optimize the efficacy of intervention prevention programs and maximize their impacts. It is important to note that, even though research has indicated that there are individual variations in openness and responsivity to intervention effects, due to ethical issues, we certainly cannot exclude less susceptible and low-susceptible people (e.g., those who showed low HPA and autonomic reactivity to laboratory challenges) from receiving interventions. Instead, the advocates of the differential susceptibility theory propose that the intervention programs designed and delivered to these individuals should be more intensified and long-lasting than those applied to highly susceptible people. They may also benefit from multiple intervention programs rather than one specific program (Belsky & van IJzendoorn, 2015; Ellis et al., 2011).

The other important point to consider before applying the notions of differential susceptibility to therapeutic and preventive interventions is that there is not enough research indicating that a person who is susceptible to one specific intervention strategy may be also susceptible to other environmental manipulations. In addition, no evidence has supported the notion that children who are susceptible to their environments will remain susceptible throughout their life. Similarly, it is quite possible that at some developmental stages low-susceptible individuals may become more susceptible (Belsky & van IJzendoorn, 2015). Ellis and colleagues (2011) argue that neurobiological susceptibility is a dimensional feature (i.e., there is continuum of susceptibility). Therefore, we should not simply conclude that low-susceptible individuals are not responsive to interventions and should be excluded. Rather, the type and the dosage of intervention employed for them should be adjusted in accordance with their susceptibility levels.

There is a paucity of research testing the differential effectiveness of interventions in children with different levels of physiological reactivity to stressors (i.e., hyper- vs. hypoautonomic and HPA reactivity). It is also not evident whether the same individuals with plasticity genes or difficult temperament who benefit most from intervention effects (van IJzendoorn & Bakermans-Kranenburg, 2015) may be also physiologically reactive to stressors. Future studies should test whether the efficacy of interventions in reducing children and adolescents' internalizing and externalizing problems may vary as function of their autonomic and adrenocortical reactivity levels to stressors. Lastly, future research should consider the role of individual characteristics (e.g., age, gender), in addition to physiological profile, when examining the effects of environmental risks and supports on individuals' mental health outcomes.

Biological Sensitivity to Context: Developmental Origins of Individual Variations in Sensitivity to Context

Individuals vary in how quickly and efficiently they respond to stressful situations. Some respond quickly and strongly to psychosocial challenges, while others may show small changes in their physiological responses following stressful situations and relative to resting states. As we discussed in the previous section, understanding individual differences in stress responsivity is particularly crucial as it functions as one of the key underlying mechanisms of variability in the link between developmental experiences and mental health outcomes. From the evolutionary-developmental model of biological sensitivity context (Boyce & Ellis, 2005; Ellis, Essex, & Boyce, 2005) and the adaptive calibration model (Del Giudice, Ellis, & Shirtcliff, 2011), the origin of such individual variations in the functioning of stress response systems is traced back to early experiences (together with genotypic variation).

The BSC model and the ACM posit that, in response to various environmental conditions over the course of development, organisms have evolved an ability to modify their developmental trajectories and phenotypic features to match the demands of their social and physical environments (i.e., a process known as *conditional adaptation*; Boyce & Ellis, 2005). Thus, individual variations in the magnitude and patterns of stress responsivity result largely from organisms' adaptations to their developmental conditions (ranging from highly adverse to highly supportive) and should be viewed as adaptive responses to these varying conditions, rather than as evidence of dysregulation (Boyce & Ellis, 2005; Del Giudice et al., 2011).

It has been widely accepted in the developmental and clinical literature that chronic or repeated experiences of adversity early in life (prenatal and postnatal stress) become biologically embedded and cause dysregulation of physical systems (Evans & English, 2002; McEwen & Seeman, 2003; McEwen, 2008; Shonkoff, Boyce, & McEwen, 2009). In the long term, these influences could adversely impact organisms' development, behavior, and health (Danese & McEwen, 2012; Shonkoff et al., 2012). Developmental models such as the allostatic load (Lupien et al., 2006; McEwen & Stellar, 1993) and diathesis-stress explain that in the face of environmental stressors and challenges, a cascade of physiological regulatory responses are activated (e.g., secretion and release of catecholamine and cortisol, elevations in heart rate and blood pressure, mobilization of bodily resources) that in the short term promote and maintain organisms' physiological stability (i.e., allostasis; Sterling & Eyer, 1988). The concept of *allostasis* in particular refers to the process by which the parameters of the regulatory systems, including the HPA axis, are modified (i.e., either increasing or decreasing the parameters' value within their normal range of functioning) to adaptively adjust to the demands of the environment, and to maintain internal homeostasis (Lupien et al., 2006; McEwen & Stellar, 1993). However, prolonged and excessive activation of these physiological systems (e.g., greater mobilization of body nutrients, secretion of stress hormones) due to demands of chronic stress causes biological "wear and tear," which markedly elevates the risk of health problems (McEwen, 1998, 2000; Shonkoff et al., 2012; Sterling & Eyer, 1988). *Allostatic load* is indeed viewed in terms of the physiological costs that these stress regulatory systems pay for constant adaptation (i.e., maintaining optimal physiological state) to chronic or cumulative stressors (McEwen, 1998, 2000).

Within these developmental models, an optimal level is defined for the operation of physiological systems in the face of challenge, and deviations from that optimum (i.e., under or over activation) are treated as "dysregulated" or "maladaptive" physiological responses which cause pathology (Evan & English, 2002; Lupien et al., 2006; McEwen, 1998, 2000). Numerous studies provide empirical evidence for *hypocortisolism* (Heim, Ehlert, & Hellhammer, 2000) and *hypercortisolism* as markers of physical "wear and tear" and risks for developing psychopathology. For instance, blunted cortisol responses to laboratory stressors in females who experienced childhood sexual abuse were associated with depressive symptoms and antisocial behaviors (Shenk, Noll, Putnam, & Trickett, 2010). Studies also provide support for the link between increased activity of HPA axis (i.e., hypercortisolism) and vulnerability to mental health disorders. For example, Davies, Sturge-Apple, and Cicchetti (2011) found that interparental conflict predicted increased cortisol reactivity among temperamentally inhibited and vigilant children, and this in turn was associated with greater internalizing symptoms.

Thus, the effects of adversity on maladaptive outcomes (i.e., internalizing and externalizing symptoms) appear partially mediated by biological stress reactivity (either blunted or elevated ANS and HPA axis reactivity). The key assumption of the allostatic load model is that chronic adversity early in life is biologically embedded in parameters of stress response systems and alters their functioning. Dysregulation of stress response systems will in turn increase the risk of developing psychopathology in a positive linear fashion (McEwen, 1998, 2000). However, this argument does not provide any explanation for the variability that is observed in physiological responses and patterns of behavior and health outcomes to environmental challenges. Why do some individuals seem to survive and thrive despite adversity, while others succumb and are negatively impacted in confrontation with similar stressors? Why do not all the individuals who experience the same type and levels of adversity develop similar responsivity patterns, such that some show hyperreactivity while others show hyporeactivity (Boyce & Ellis, 2005; Del Giudice, Ellis, & Shirtcliff, 2011; Ellis et al., 2011)? What is the functional significance of these variations?

Ellis and Del Giudice (2014) argue that the allostatic load model does not fully capture the complicated relations that exist between early life stress, the regulatory effects of stress response systems, and health outcomes. They specifically claim that the model excessively emphasizes the long-term costs (i.e., wear and tear) associated with early adversity and chronic stress and fails to acknowledge the significant role that early life experiences (including both positive and adverse experiences) play in calibrating the functioning of physiological systems in relation to adaptive behavioral strategies that are functional in context (Del Giudice & Ellis, 2016; Ellis & Del Giudice, 2014; Ellis, Del Giudice, & Shirtcliff, 2017).

To fill these gaps and to provide a more balanced and clear picture of the relation between early stress and health, Del Giudice, Ellis, and Shirtcliff (2011) proposed the adaptive calibration model (ACM), an evolutionary-developmental model of individual differences in stress responsivity, as a promising alternative to the allostatic load model. The ACM model centers on the developmental programming of the stress response systems and the different patterns of stress responsivity and associated life history strategies that emerge and develop as a result of organisms' adaptation to various environmental conditions (Del Giudice et al., 2011; Ellis & Del Giudice, 2014; Ellis, Del Giudice, & Shirtcliff, 2017).

According to the ACM, the developing organism collects and encodes information about the key features of its environment through the activation of the regulatory physiological systems, including the HPA axis and ANS systems. Over time, this information is biologically embedded in parameters of these systems and causes structural changes (i.e., resetting the activation threshold and magnitude of responses) in their functioning (i.e., "biological embedding"). This biologically embedded information serves as an informative source for the organisms to forecast the environment that they are likely to inhabit in the future and adjust their development and behaviors accordingly (Bateson, 2001; Boyce & Ellis, 2005; Ellis & Del Giudice, 2014; West-Eberhard, 2003). Furthermore, this encoded information is used by the stress response system (SRS) to calibrate the structure and the activity of the stress response system itself, which results in patterns of stress responsivity and behavioral profiles that are adaptive to organisms' local environments. The SRS also operates as a regulatory system that calibrate organisms' degrees of openness and susceptibility to environmental influences ranging from highly adverse and unpredictable to highly supportive and protected (Del Giudice et al., 2011). We discussed this function of the SRS in more detail in the previous section.

Early Life Experiences and Development of Adaptive Stress Responsivity Patterns and Behavioral Strategies

A great body of work has attempted to investigate the developmental programming of SRS under different developmental conditions. These empirical studies are distinguished by the type of the environment that they targeted and the magnitude and patterns of stress responsivity (i.e., blunted or elevated stress responses) that they identified under those specific environmental conditions, ranging from challenging/threatening to protective/supportive environments. Among them, some work suggests that the experiences of moderate adversity early in life, as experienced by the majority of children raised in middle-class and relatively stable family environments, are associated with the development of relatively dampened physiological reactivity (Macrì`, Zoratto, & Laviola, 2011; Parker, Buckmaster, Schatzberg, & Lyons, 2004; Parker & Maestripieri, 2011). However, under more acutely challenging and stressful childhood environments (e.g., maternal depression and psychological distress [Azar, Paquette, Zoccolillo, Baltzer, & Tremblay, 2007], economic stress [Essex, Klein, Cho, & Kalin, 2002], and overcontrolling parenting [Taylor et al., 2013]), research has found both upregulation (e.g., Conradt et al., 2014; Holochwost et al., 2017; Wilsmer Fries, Shirtcliff, & Pollak, 2008) and downregulation (e.g., Fisher, Kim, Bruce, & Pears, 2012; Koss, Mliner,

Donzella, & Gunnar, 2016; Peckins, Susman, Negriff, Noll, & Trickett, 2015) of the activity of SRS.

Interestingly, an emerging body of research posits that not only early chronic stress "gets under the skin" and calibrates parameters of SRS, but that exposure to disproportionately safe and supportive environment can also become biologically embedded and upregulate the activation of stress response systems (e.g., DePasquale, Raby, Hoye, & Dozier, 2018; Ellis, Essex, & Boyce, 2005; Shirtcliff, Skinner, Obasi, & Haggerty, 2017). Taken these findings together, they all suggest that different developmental experiences calibrate and influence the activity of SRS in a potentially linear fashion. They also report that depending on the severity and chronicity of stressors that individuals encounter early in life, they may show either blunted or heightened stress reactivity.

The conflicting and complex findings in the literature for the associations between early experiences and the magnitude and patterns of stress responsivity can potentially be explained by Boyce and Ellis's biological sensitivity to context theory (2005). According to the theory, early life experiences program the functioning of the SRS in a nonlinear fashion, with hyperactivity of SRS likely to emerge under both highly stressful and highly supportive environmental conditions. Unlike the allostatic load model, which defines a single optimal stress responsivity pattern across different environmental conditions, Boyce and Ellis (2005) proposed three adaptive stress responsivity patterns that each emerge under specific environmental conditions: (a) childhood exposure to excessively safe, predictable, and supportive and/or low-stressful family environments upregulates the activation of SRS and increases susceptibility to potential benefits and resources in the environment (*sensitive* pattern); (b) early life experiences of high adversity, instability, and harshness are also associated with upregulation of SRS and the development of heightened ANS and HPA axis reactivity. These physiological characteristics further increase children's vigilance to dangers and threats in their environments (*vigilant* pattern); and (c) children's exposure to rearing environments that are neither challenging and threatening nor safe and supportive is associated with the development of dampened stress reactivity. Intermittent experiences of moderately stressful and supportive environments in these children protect and buffer them against more adverse experiences in the future and enhance their coping capabilities (*buffered* pattern). Del Giudice and colleagues' (2011) adaptive calibration model of individual differences in stress responsivity builds on the BSC U-shaped curve model by proposing a fourth type of the stress responsivity pattern (i.e., *unemotional* pattern), which is characterized by blunted physiological stress reactivity, and it specifically emerges under traumatic and chronically stressful conditions.

These four prototypical stress responsivity patterns are further distinguished based on the dominant physiological stress profiles (the integrated and joint activity of ANS and HPA axis during a resting state and in response to acute stressors), and the behavioral strategies that individuals classifying under each responsivity pattern are more likely to show. In particular, development of highly responsive SRS under safe, supportive, and low-stress environments enhances individuals' social learning and their engagement with the social world. Individuals with a *sensitive* profile are less likely to engage in risky and aggressive behaviors. In the face of stress, they also show sustainably moderate to high activation of the SNS and HPA axis, and relatively high PNS responsivity. In addition, development of *vigilant* pattern and increased physiological stress responsivity under dangerous, unpredictable, and stressful environment enhances a person's alertness and ability to effectively react to threats and dangers in the environment. At the same time, it may increase the risks of aggressive, antisocial, risk-taking (i.e., externalizing) behaviors particularly in males, and more anxious and depressive (i.e., internalizing) behaviors in females. Under stressful conditions, the vigilant phenotype is characterized by high SNS and HPA axis responsivity and low to moderate PNS responsivity.

The ACM also proposes two blunted/dampened patterns of stress responsivity that develop under two different environmental conditions, each characterized by distinctive behavioral and physiological profiles. First, the *buffered* profile that emerges under environments with moderate levels of adversity and support is typically characterized with average scores on all the parameters of the SRS (i.e., moderate HPA, SNS, PNS responsivity). Individuals showing this phenotype tend to exhibit fewer anxiety and aggressive behaviors, compared to their peers with other responsivity patterns (i.e., vigilant and unemotional). The buffered responsivity pattern is generally viewed as a "protective factor" that inoculates the person against more severe experiences of adversity in the future and reduces the risk of negative health and behavioral outcomes (consistent with the *stress inoculation hypothesis*; Eysenck, 1983; Lyons & Parker, 2007; Rutter, 1987). Second, the *unemotional* pattern that is predicted to develop under severely stressful, dangerous, and traumatic situations is marked by low stress responsivity profiles across HPA, SNS, and PNS systems. Inefficient and lack of physiological responsivity constrains social learning, sensitivity and responsivity to social feedback and environmental threats and dangers (i.e., low anxiety and empathy), and significantly increases the risk of impulsive, risk-taking, and antisocial behaviors, particularly in men (Del Giudice et al., 2011, 2012; Ellis, Oldehinkel, & Nederhof, 2017).

In summary, each of the ACM patterns of stress responsivity may be associated with some costs and negative consequences for individuals' health and well-being (especially the vigilant and the unemotional patterns that emerge at the high-risk end of the environmental spectrum). However, from an evolutionary point of view, they are considered as adaptive responses that have maximized organisms' fitness to their rearing contexts. In addition, the disparate results in the stress literature for the links between early environmental conditions and the magnitude and patterns of stress responsivity may be partially explained by studies' failure to examine the nonlinear associations between them, and also not to consider the full range of environmental influences, instead of targeting only one specific type of environment (i.e., either adverse or positive; Boyce & Ellis, 2005; Del Giudice et al., 2011; Ellis, Oldehinkel, & Nederhof, 2017). However, results of any single study examining the linear statistical associations could provide some empirical support for each of the ACM four stress responsivity patterns and would be best explained by a segment of the BSC U-shaped curve model (Boyce & Ellis, 2005; Del Giudice et al., 2011).

Past Research Testing the Biological Sensitivity to Context Theory and the Adaptive Calibration Model

Few studies have attempted to empirically test the BSC developmental programming hypothesis and the ACM by considering the full range of environmental influences and the related physiological and behavioral profiles; more research is needed to fully validate the core assumptions of these models. Due to the space limitation, we restricted our review to studies that primarily and explicitly tested for the nonlinear relations between childhood psychosocial stressors and the stress responsivity patterns (i.e., stress reactivity to laboratory challenges) as proposed in the BSC theory and the ACM across one

or more of the three SRS subsystems (PNS, SNS, and HPA). These studies are further distinguished based on whether or not they tested the full ACM (i.e., if they tested for the behavioral correlates of each responsivity pattern), and by the analytic approach that they applied to test the models' assumptions (i.e., variable-centered vs. person-centered statistical models). In our review of the stress literature, we therefore intentionally excluded the empirical work that was not explicitly guided by the ACM and BSC theory or used these theoretical models as a framework to interpret their findings (e.g., Berry et al., 2017; Gunnar, Frenn, Wewerka, & Van Ryzin, 2009; Quas et al., 2014). Our exclusion criteria also involve the studies that only examined patterns of baseline physiological activity in testing the models' assumptions (e.g., Bush, Obradović, Adler, & Boyce, 2011; Kolacz, Holochwost, Gariépy, & Mills-Koonce; 2016), especially given that both the ACM and BSC theory center more on individual differences in stress reactivity than baseline activation.

The first empirical test of the BSC U-shaped curve model was conducted by Ellis, Essex, and Boyce (2005), where, through use of exploratory *signal detection analyses* (a form of person-centered analyses), they searched for the contextual factors and the personal characteristics that best distinguished high stress reactivity children (i.e., operationalized as the top 25% of stress reactivity scores) from their less reactive peers (i.e., bottom 75% of stress reactivity scores). They further examined for the curvilinear, U-shaped relations between childhood rearing conditions and the ANS and HPA axis functioning as proposed by BSC U-shaped curve model. Across two independent samples of high-risk children (ranging from 3 to 7 years old), a disproportionate number of children whose parents reported low-stress family environments, high family routines, and high family socioeconomic status demonstrated high autonomic reactivity to laboratory stressors, as per the *sensitive* pattern in the BSC model and the ACM. Likewise, in one of the samples, a significant proportion of children growing up in a very harsh and unpredictable family environment exhibited heightened sympathetic and adrenocortical reactivity, consistent with the *vigilant* pattern. Conversely, in both studies, a group of children with low to moderate experiences of adversity/support exhibited the lowest reactivity levels. Together, their exploratory findings provided some support for the curvilinear U-shaped associations between childhood adversity/support and sympathetic reactivity. Use of signal detection analysis in this study enabled the researchers to identify the unique dimensions of family and ecological environments that singly and interactively regulate the ANS and HPA responsivity. However, their findings only validated the three-pattern classification in the BSC model.

Later other researchers attempted to examine the nonlinear associations between childhood adversity/support and the SRS functioning through use of the traditional variable-centered analyses, such as regression and ANOVA. Guided by the BSC U-shaped curve model, they tested for a curvilinear relationship between a single environmental measure of adversity/support and the functioning of one SRS subsystem (SNS, PNS, or HPA). For instance, Hagan and colleagues (2014) examined the effects of college students' perceptions of interparental conflict (prior to age 16) on the magnitude and patterns of cortisol responses to a challenging role-play task. Ouellet-Morin and associates (2018) also examined the association between adult males' recalled experiences of abuse and neglect (prior to age 18) and their cortisol reactivity to the Trier Social Stress Test. As predicted by the BSC model, across both studies, individuals who reported either relatively low or high childhood adversity demonstrated greater cortisol concentrations pre to post laboratory challenges (i.e., higher cortisol reactivity), compared to their peers who had experienced moderate levels of adversity, and exhibited lower cortisol responses to laboratory challenges.

Although these studies provided confirmatory supports for the three stress responsivity patterns (i.e., sensitive, vigilant, buffered), use of a variable-centered approach dramatically restricted their power to simultaneously test for the effects of multiple familial and the environmental factors and the functioning of all the SRS subsystems. The proponents of the ACM particularly argue that the four prototypical stress responsivity patterns are developed through the interaction among all the main SRS subsystems, and they are well characterized by the combination of subsystems' parameters (Del Giudice et al., 2011, 2012; Ellis et al., 2017). In addition, because of the low-risk nature of these studies' sample (inadequate or lack of participants from very high-risk family background), they were not adequately positioned to examine and find evidence for the *unemotional* pattern in the ACM.

In testing for the nonlinear association between environmental stress, support, and optimal stress responsivity levels, other researchers have employed person-centered analytic approaches (i.e., *latent mixture modeling*). The primary aim of these studies was to identify distinct groups of individuals who show stress responsivity patterns as characterized by multiple parameters of the SRS. They further investigated whether and how the individuals classified under each physiological profile (low vs. high stress responsivity) may vary by their childhood levels of adversity and support exposure.

Del Giudice and colleagues (2012) were among the first who empirically investigated and provided some confirmatory supports for the ACM predictions in a diverse sample of children (8–10 years old) from a wide range of familial and ecological conditions (as defined by high levels of family warmth/predictability to high levels of ecological adversity and negative family relationships). Their findings revealed four classes of individuals who significantly differed in their levels of ANS functioning as indexed by RSA and SCL during resting conditions and in response to star-tracking task. They identified the largest class of children (45%) as the *buffered* class, comprising those who showed high PNS basal activity, low SNS basal activity, and low SNS reactivity. The *sensitive* children (the second largest class) showed relatively high PNS baseline, and high SNS baseline and reactivity. Compared to the sensitive class, children in the *unemotional* class exhibited lower basal PNS and SNS activity and lower than average SNS reactivity. On the other hand, *vigilant* children, who exhibited higher than average basal SNS and SNS reactivity, included the smallest class of children (10%). Further investigation of individual variations in the levels of environmental support and stress exposure among these four classes of children revealed that the highest levels of negative family relationships (+2 SD) and the lowest levels of family warmth/predictability (–2 SD) were reported by children in the *unemotional* and *vigilant* classes, respectively. As expected, children in the *sensitive* and *buffered* classes reported greater experiences of family warmth and predictability.

Although the work of Del Giudice et al. (2012) validated the four-pattern classification of the ACM, the empirical test of the stress responsivity patterns under challenging conditions was limited to ANS functioning. However, as the model posits, the activity of the three SRS subsystems (i.e., SNS, PNS, and HPA axis) is integrated and cross-regulated. In addition, the joint function of the SRS subsystems is central in development and identification of the responsivity patterns. Likewise, to fully assess and validate all the key premises of the ACM, and to better understand and differentiate between the characteristics of the four physiological profiles, researchers need to examine the relations between multisystem physiological profiles and behavioral strategies. To address these limitations, Ellis, Oldehinkel, and Nederhof (2017) examined the calibration of two major stress response systems (ANS and HPA axis) and the emergence of four stress responsivity patterns and correlated behavioral strategies (aggressive/rule-breaking and withdrawn/depressed behaviors) in a sample of adolescent males (11–16 years old) who had experienced a wide range of familial and ecological psychosocial stress and support. To our knowledge, this is the first and only empirical study to date that has investigated all the key predictions of the ACM responsivity patterns by giving a thoughtful consideration of past research limitations.

Through use of the *latent profile analysis*, a form of person-centered analysis, Ellis and colleagues (2017) identified four classes of adolescents who differed meaningfully in their developmental history, physiological functioning, and behavioral outcomes. This type of analysis is typically used when researchers expect that distinct subgroups of individuals may exist within the sample distribution, and individuals within each subgroup share similar characteristics. Their four classes reasonably mapped onto the four patterns of stress responsivity proposed by the ACM. In brief, adolescents classified under the *sensitive* profile demonstrated higher than average stress responsivity across all three SRS and reported growing up in a high-quality family environment as defined by more warmth/support and less stress/rejection in the family environment. This group later obtained lower scores on aggressive/rule-breaking behavior and higher scores on withdrawn/depressed behavior. Consistent with past research (e.g., Del Giudice et al., 2012), the majority of participants in the sample (74%) appeared as the members of the *buffered* class. These individuals displayed moderate basal activity and reactivity across all three SRS subsystems, and they had average levels of behavioral, familial, and ecological stress exposure. By contrast, the latent profile analysis placed the smallest number of participants (6%) into the *vigilant* profile. These individuals demonstrated heightened baseline and PNS reactivity (stronger vagal withdrawal), the highest levels of withdrawn/depressed behaviors, and reported relatively high familial and ecological stress. Finally, authors named the fourth class *unemotional*, because of its similarity with the unemotional pattern in ACM (i.e., stronger vagal withdrawal, below than average HPA reactivity, low-quality family environment, low scores on withdrawal/depressed behavior, and high scores on aggressive/rule-breaking behavior).

Conclusions and Future Directions

The present chapter reviewed and highlighted the role of stress response systems as one major mechanism underlying the association between early adverse life experiences and mental health. It also elucidated how variations in parameters of ANS and HPA axis reactivity levels may function as a biological marker of susceptibility to environmental influences that moderate the deleterious effects of early stress on later development of internalizing and externalizing behaviors. Reviewing the literature for the moderating effects of PNS, SNS, and HPA reactivity in the pathway between early adversity and mental health outcomes, it appeared that the empirical findings best fit with the premises of the evolutionary framework than the disease model (i.e., allostatic load and diathesis-stress models), particularly in relation to the cross-over interactions that are central to the differential susceptibility perspective.

Much of the work we reviewed here viewed chronic childhood adversity from the lens of pathology and notably failed to capture and take into account possible developmental adaptations to stress. There is emerging evidence driven by the evolutionary-developmental perspective that documents and proposes that children from high-risk family settings may have some promising strengths, including cognitive and social skills that have developed as a result of their adaptation to high-adversity context (Ellis, Bianchi, Griskevicius, & Frankenhuis, 2017; Mittal, Griskevicius, Simpson, Sung, & Young, 2015; Young, Griskevicius, Simpson, Waters, & Mittal, 2018). Future work and intervention policies could profit from this perspective to build upon and foster the strengths and specialized skills of these so-called stress-adapted (instead of at-risk) individuals to enhance their resilience and fitness outcome (Ellis et al., 2017).

The present chapter exclusively highlighted the role of SRS as one major intervening mechanism in the pathway between early stress and mental health. An innovative and growing body of research has attempted to uncover additional intervening regulatory systems and processes involved in the biological embedding of prenatal and postnatal adversity, such as immune system functioning (Glaser & Kiecolt-Glaser, 2005; Slavich & Irwin, 2014) and epigenetic processes (Champagne & Curley, 2008; Smearman et al., 2016). These regulatory systems and processes are typically investigated in isolation. Future research should focus on the regulatory influences of early stress on the integrated activity of these systems, and how such alterations over time impact organisms' health and development.

The concept of a "sensitive period" has not been well investigated and agreed upon with regard to the developmental programming of the SRS under adverse conditions and associated variability in pathogenesis of internalizing and externalizing problems throughout the life course. Studies we reviewed in this chapter did not explicitly account for the timing and duration of the exposure to chronic stress in examining HPA axis and ANS reactivity levels (hypoactivity vs. hyperreactivity) and the severity of psychological problems. Bosch and colleagues (2012) showed that exposure to adversity during different developmental timeframes from the prenatal period to adolescence (ages 0–5, 6–11, 12–13, 14–15 years) was associated with different cortisol reactivity patterns. Exposure to adversities during late childhood (ages 6–11 years) was associated with increased cortisol reactivity, whereas the experience of adversity during early and adolescence (ages 12–15) predicted low cortisol reactivity. No significant effects were found for childhood adversity before age 5. Although these results contrast with the findings of studies we reviewed in previous sections, it underscores the importance of accounting for timing of stress exposure in examining the regulation of HPA axis under adverse conditions.

A handful of studies have suggested that sex differences in patterns of cortisol, RSA, and skin conductance level reactivity to stressors may account for variations in mental health outcomes between males and females (Kelly, Tyrka, Anderson, Price, & Carpenter, 2008; Kryski, Smith, Sheikh, Singh, & Hayden, 2013; Seeman, Singer, Wilkinson, & McEwen, 2001). In general, they have documented variations in hormonal levels (e.g., changes in estrogen levels; Bonen et al., 1991; Kirschbaum et al., 1999; Rubinow & Schmidt, 1999; Zahn-Waxler, Shirtcliff, & Marceau, 2008) during puberty and menstrual cycle (Weiss, Longhurst, & Mazure, 1999) as major origins of the sex differences in the levels of cortisol reactivity. Moreover, they reported that boys and girls may show different levels and patterns of physiological responses, depending on the nature and the type of stressors to which they are exposed. In some studies, females were more sensitive and physiologically reactive to social rejection and interpersonal stressors, which significantly increased their vulnerability to depression (Hankin,

Mermelstein, & Roesch, 2007; Stroud, Salovey, & Epel, 2002), whereas males were more reactive to achievement-related challenges (Stroud, Salovey, & Epel, 2002). Notably, the potential moderating influence of sex in the pathway between early adversity and variations in cortisol reactivity levels and development of psychopathology has not been well investigated. On this topic, future research needs to take into account sex differences in physiological responses to different types of stressors as it examines these associations.

In conclusion, the theories and empirical evidence presented in this chapter have advanced our understanding of the contribution of environmental and biological factors and their interactions to the development of internalizing and externalizing behavior. Throughout the chapter, we sought to underscore the crucial and powerful influences of early life experiences on programming the functioning of SRS and development of adaptive patterns of stress responsivity, as proposed by the two evolutionary-developmental models of BSC and ACM. We have illustrated that the impacts of early experiences are not the same for all individuals. The effect of early life stress on internalizing and externalizing behavior appears to be partially explained by, and depends upon, the functioning of the SRS in the face of challenge.

References

Adam, E. K., Klimes-Dougan, B., & Gunnar, M. R. (2007). Social regulation of the adrenocortical response to stress in infants, children and adolescents: Implications for psychopathology and education. In D. Coch, K. W. Fischer, & G. Dawson (Eds.), *Human behavior, learning, and the developing brain: Typical development* (pp. 264–314). New York, NY: Guilford Press.

Ali, N., & Pruessner, J. C. (2012). The salivary alpha amylase over cortisol ratio as a marker to assess dysregulations of the stress systems. *Physiology & Behavior, 106,* 65–72. doi:10.1016/j.physbeh.2011.10.003

Allwood, M. A., Handwerger, K., Kivlighan, K. T., Granger, D. A., & Stroud, L. R. (2011). Direct and moderating links of salivary alpha-amylase and cortisol stress-reactivity to youth behavioral and emotional adjustment. *Biological Psychology, 88,* 57–64. doi:10.1016/j.biopsycho.2011.06.008

Amato, P. R., & Sobolewski, J. M. (2001). The effects of divorce and marital discord on adult children's psychological well-being. *American Sociological Review, 66,* 900–921. doi:10.2307/3088878

Azar, R., Paquette, D., Zoccolillo, M., Baltzer, F., & Tremblay, R. E. (2007). The association of major depression, conduct disorder, and maternal overcontrol with a failure to show a cortisol buffered response in 4-month-old infants of teenage mothers. *Biological Psychiatry, 62,* 573–579. doi:10.1016/j.biopsych.2006.11.009

Bakermans-Kranenburg, M. J., & van IJzendoorn, M. H. (2011). Differential susceptibility to rearing environment depending on dopamine-related genes: New evidence and a meta-analysis. *Development and Psychopathology*, 23, 39–52. doi:10.1017/S0954579410000635

Bakermans-Kranenburg, M. J., van IJzendoorn, M. H., Pijlman, F. T., Mesman, J., & Juffer, F. (2008). Experimental evidence for differential susceptibility: Dopamine D4 receptor polymorphism (DRD4 VNTR) moderates intervention effects on toddlers' externalizing behavior in a randomized controlled trial. *Developmental Psychology*, 44, 293–300. doi:10.1037/0012-1649.44.1.293

Barrios, C. S., Bufferd, S. J., Klein, D. N., & Dougherty, L. R. (2017). The interaction between parenting and children's cortisol reactivity at age 3 predicts increases in children's internalizing and externalizing symptoms at age 6. *Development and Psychopathology*, 29, 1319–1331. doi:10.1017/S0954579417000293

Barry, T. J., Murray, L., Fearon, R. P., Moutsiana, C., Cooper, P., Goodyer, I. M., . . . & Halligan, S. L. (2015). Maternal postnatal depression predicts altered offspring biological stress reactivity in adulthood. *Psychoneuroendocrinology*, 52, 251–260. doi:10.1016/j.psyneuen.2014.12.003

Bateson, P. (2001). Fetal experience and good adult design a. *International Journal of Epidemiology*, 30, 928–934. doi:10.1093/ije/30.5.928

Beauchaine, T. (2001). Vagal tone, development, and Gray's motivational theory: Toward an integrated model of autonomic nervous system functioning in psychopathology. *Development and Psychopathology*, 13, 183–214.

Beauchaine, T. P., Katkin, E. S., Strassberg, Z., & Snarr, J. (2001). Disinhibitory psychopathology in male adolescents: Discriminating conduct disorder from attention-deficit/hyperactivity disorder through concurrent assessment of multiple autonomic states. *Journal of Abnormal Psychology*, 110, 610–624.

Belsky, J. (2005). Differential susceptibility to rearing influence: An evolutionary hypothesis and some evidence. In B. Ellis & D. Bjorklund (Eds.), *Origins of the social mind: Evolutionary psychology and child development* (pp. 139–163). New York, NY: Guilford Press.

Belsky, J., Bakermans-Kranenburg, M. J., & van IJzendoorn, M. H. (2007). For better and for worse: Differential susceptibility to environmental influences. *Current Directions in Psychological Science*, 16, 300–304. doi:10.1111/j.1467-8721.2007.00525.x

Belsky, J., Jonassaint, C., Pluess, M., Stanton, M., Brummett, B., & Williams, R. (2009). Vulnerability genes or plasticity genes?. *Molecular Psychiatry*, 14, 746–754. doi:10.1038/mp.2009.44

Belsky, J., & Pluess, M. (2009). Beyond diathesis stress: Differential susceptibility to environmental influences. *Psychological Bulletin*, 135, 885–908. doi:10.1037/a0017376

Belsky, J., & van IJzendoorn, M. H. (2015). What works for whom? Genetic moderation of intervention efficacy. *Development and Psychopathology*, 27, 1–6. doi:10.1017/S0954579414001254

Bergman, K. N., Cummings, E. M., & Davies, P. T. (2014). Interparental aggression and adolescent adjustment: The role of emotional insecurity and adrenocortical activity. *Journal of Family Violence*, 29, 763–771. doi:10.1007/s10896-014-9632-3

Berntson, G. G., Cacioppo, J. T., & Quigley, K. S. (1991). Autonomic determinism: The modes of autonomic control, the doctrine of autonomic space, and the laws of autonomic constraint. *Psychological Review*, 98, 459–487.

Berry, D., Blair, C., Willoughby, M., Granger, D. A., Mills-Koonce, W. R., & Family Life Project Key Investigators. (2017). Maternal sensitivity and adrenocortical functioning across infancy and toddlerhood: Physiological adaptation to context?. *Development and Psychopathology*, 29, 303–317. doi:10.1017/s0954579416000158

Bonen, A., Haynes, F. W., & Graham, T. E. (1991). Substrate and hormonal responses to exercise in women using oral contraceptives. *Journal of Applied Physiology* 70, 1917–1927. doi:00005768-198101320-00181

Bornstein, M. H., & Suess, P. E. (2000). Physiological self-regulation and information processing in infancy: Cardiac vagal tone and habituation. *Child Development*, 71, 273–287. doi:10.1111/1467-8624.00143

Bosch, N. M., Riese, H., Reijneveld, S. A., Bakker, M. P., Verhulst, F. C., Ormel, J., & Oldehinkel, A. J. (2012). Timing matters: Long term effects of adversities from prenatal period up to adolescence on adolescents' cortisol stress response. The TRAILS study. *Psychoneuroendocrinology*, 37, 1439–1447. doi:10.1016/j.psyneuen.2012.01.013

Boyce, W. T., & Ellis, B. J. (2005). Biological sensitivity to context: I. An evolutionary–developmental theory of the origins and functions of stress reactivity. *Development and Psychopathology*, 17, 271–301. doi:10.1017S0954579405050145

Brenner, S. L., & Beauchaine, T. P. (2011). Pre-ejection period reactivity and psychiatric comorbidity prospectively predict substance use initiation among middle-schoolers: A pilot study. *Psychophysiology*, 48, 1588–1596. doi:10.1111/j.1469-8986.2011.01230.x

Brock, R. L., Kochanska, G., & Boldt, L. J. (2017). Interplay between children's biobehavioral plasticity and interparental relationship in the origins of internalizing problems. *Journal of Family Psychology*, 31, 1040–1050. doi:10.1037/fam0000335

Bush, N. R., Obradović, J., Adler, N., & Boyce, W. T. (2011). Kindergarten stressors and cumulative adrenocortical activation: The "first straws" of allostatic load? *Development and Psychopathology*, 23, 1089–1106. doi:10.1017/s0954579411000514

Calkins, S. D. (1997). Cardiac vagal tone indices of temperamental reactivity and behavioral regulation in young children. *Developmental Psychobiology: The Journal of the International Society for Developmental Psychobiology*, 31, 125–135.

Champagne, F. A., & Curley, J. P. (2008). Maternal regulation of estrogen receptor α methylation. *Current Opinion in Pharmacology*, 8, 735–739. doi:10.1016/j.coph.2008.06.018

Chapman, D. P., Whitfield, C. L., Felitti, V. J., Dube, S. R., Edwards, V. J., & Anda, R. F. (2004). Adverse childhood experiences and the risk of depressive disorders in adulthood. *Journal of Affective Disorders*, 82, 217–225. doi:10.1016/j.jad.2003.12.013

Conradt, E., Abar, B., Lester, B. M., LaGasse, L. L., Shankaran, S., Bada, H., . . . Hammond, J. A. (2014). Cortisol reactivity to social stress as a mediator of early adversity on risk and adaptive outcomes. *Child Development*, 85, 2279–2298. doi:10.1111/cdev.12316

Conradt, E., Beauchaine, T., Abar, B., Lagasse, L., Shankaran, S., Bada, H., . . . Lester, B. (2016). Early caregiving stress exposure moderates the relation between respiratory sinus arrhythmia reactivity at 1 month and biobehavioral outcomes at age 3. *Psychophysiology*, 53, 83–96. doi:10.1111/psyp.12569

Cook, E. C., Chaplin, T. M., Sinha, R., Tebes, J. K., & Mayes, L. C. (2012). The stress response and adolescents' adjustment: The impact of child maltreatment. *Journal of Youth and Adolescence*, 41, 1067–1077. doi:10.1007/s10964-012-9746-y.

Crowell, S. E., Beauchaine, T. P., Gatzke-Kopp, L., Sylvers, P., Mead, H., & Chipman-Chacon, J. (2006). Autonomic correlates of attention-deficit/hyperactivity disorder and oppositional defiant disorder in preschool children. *Journal of Abnormal Psychology*, 115, 174–178. doi:10.1037/0021-843X.115.1.174

Crowell, S. E., Beauchaine, T. P., McCauley, E., Smith, C. J., Stevens, A. L., & Sylvers, P. (2005). Psychological, autonomic, and serotonergic correlates of parasuicide among adolescent girls. *Development and Psychopathology*, 17, 1105–1127. doi:10.1017OS0954579405050522

Cummings, E. M., El-Sheikh, M., Kouros, C. D., & Keller, P. S. (2007). Children's skin conductance reactivity as a mechanism of risk in the context of parental depressive symptoms. *Journal of Child Psychology and Psychiatry*, 48, 436–445. doi:10.1111/j.1469-7610.2006.01713.x

Danese, A., & McEwen, B. S. (2012). Adverse childhood experiences, allostasis, allostatic load, and age-related disease. *Physiology & Behavior*, 106, 29–39. doi:10.1016/j.physbeh.2011.08.019

Davies, P. T., Sturge-Apple, M. L., & Cicchetti, D. (2011). Interparental aggression and children's adrenocortical reactivity: Testing an evolutionary model of allostatic load. *Development and Psychopathology*, 23, 801–814. doi:10.1017/S0954579411000319

Davies, P. T., Sturge-Apple, M. L., Cicchetti, D., & Cummings, E. M. (2007). The role of child adrenocortical functioning in pathways between interparental conflict and child maladjustment. *Developmental Psychology*, 43, 918–930. doi:10.1037/0012-1649.43.4.918

Davis, M., Suveg, C., Whitehead, M., Jones, A., & Shaffer, A. (2016). Preschoolers' psychophysiological responses to mood induction tasks moderate the intergenerational transmission of internalizing problems. *Biological Psychology*, 117, 159–169. doi:10.1016/j.biopsycho.2016.03.015

Dawson, M. E., Schell, A. M., & Filion, D. L. (2007). The electrodermal system. *Handbook of Psychophysiology*, 2, 200–223.

Del Giudice, M., & Ellis, B. J. (2016). Evolutionary foundations of developmental psychopathology. In D. Cicchettit (Ed.), *Developmental neuroscience* (3rd ed.), Vol. 2. (pp. 1–58). New York, NY: John Wiley & Sons.

Del Giudice, M., Ellis, B. J., & Shirtcliff, E. A. (2011). The adaptive calibration model of stress responsivity. *Neuroscience & Biobehavioral Reviews*, 35, 1562–1592. doi:10.1016/j.neubiorev.2010.11.007

Del Giudice, M., Hinnant, J. B., Ellis, B. J., & El-Sheikh, M. (2012). Adaptive patterns of stress responsivity: A preliminary investigation. *Developmental Psychology*, 48, 775–790. doi:10.1037/a0026519

DePasquale, C. E., Raby, K. L., Hoye, J., & Dozier, M. (2018). Parenting predicts strange situation cortisol reactivity among children adopted internationally. *Psychoneuroendocrinology*, 89, 86–91. doi:10.1016/j.psyneuen.2018.01.003

Diamond, L. M., Fagundes, C. P., & Cribbet, M. R. (2012). Individual differences in adolescents' sympathetic and parasympathetic functioning moderate associations between family environment and psychosocial adjustment. *Developmental Psychology*, 48, 918–932. doi:10.1037/a00269011

Dyer, W. J., Blocker, D. J., Day, R. D., & Bean, R. A. (2016). Parenting style and adolescent externalizing behaviors: The moderating role of respiratory sinus arrhythmia. *Journal of Marriage and Family*, 78, 1149–1165. doi:10.1111/jomf.12316

Ellis, B. J., Bianchi, J., Griskevicius, V., & Frankenhuis, W. E. (2017). Beyond risk and protective factors: An adaptation-based approach to resilience. *Perspectives on Psychological Science*, 12, 561–587. doi:10.1177/1745691617693054

Ellis, B. J., & Boyce, W. T. (2008). Biological sensitivity to context. *Current Directions in Psychological Science*, 17, 183–187. doi:10.1111/j.1467-8721.2008.00571.x

Ellis, B. J., & Boyce, W. T. (2011). Differential susceptibility to the environment: Toward an understanding of sensitivity to developmental experiences and context. *Development and Psychopathology*, 23, 1–5. doi:10.1017/S095457941000060X

Ellis, B. J., Boyce, W. T., Belsky, J., Bakermans-Kranenburg, M. J., & van IJzendoorn, M. H. (2011). Differential susceptibility to the environment: An evolutionary–neurodevelopmental theory. *Development and Psychopathology*, 23, 7–28. doi:10.1017/S0954579410000611

Ellis, B. J., & Del Giudice, M. (2014). Beyond allostatic load: Rethinking the role of stress in regulating human development. *Development and Psychopathology*, 26, 1–20. doi:10.1017/S0954579413000849

Ellis, B. J., Del Giudice, M., & Shirtcliff, E. A. (2017). The adaptive calibration model of stress responsivity: Concepts, findings, and implications for developmental psychopathology. In T. P. Beauchaine & S. P. Hinshaw (Eds.), *Child and adolescent psychopathology* (3rd ed., pp. 237–276). New York, NY: Wiley & Sons.

Ellis, B. J., Essex, M. J., & Boyce, W. T. (2005). Biological sensitivity to context: II. Empirical explorations of an evolutionary–developmental theory. *Development and Psychopathology*, 17, 303–328. doi:10.10170S0954579405050157

Ellis, B. J., Jackson, J. J., & Boyce, W. T. (2006). The stress response systems: Universality and adaptive individual differences. *Developmental Review*, 26, 175–212. doi:10.1016/j.dr.2006.02.004

Ellis, B. J., Oldehinkel, A. J., & Nederhof, E. (2017). The adaptive calibration model of stress responsivity: An empirical test in the Tracking Adolescents' Individual Lives Survey study. *Development and Psychopathology*, 29, 1001–1021. doi:10.1017/S0954579416000985

El-Sheikh, M. (2005). The role of emotional responses and physiological reactivity in the marital conflict–child functioning link. *Journal of Child Psychology and Psychiatry*, 46, 1191–1199. doi:10.1111/j.1469-7610.2005.01418.x

El-Sheikh, M., & Hinnant, J. B. (2011). Marital conflict, respiratory sinus arrhythmia, and allostatic load: Interrelations and associations with the development of children's externalizing behavior. *Development and Psychopathology*, 23, 815–829. doi:10.1017/S0954579411000320

El-Sheikh, M., Keller, P. S., & Erath, S. A. (2007). Marital conflict and risk for child maladjustment over time: Skin conductance level reactivity as a vulnerability factor. *Journal of Abnormal Child Psychology*, 35, 715–727. doi:10.1007/s10802-007-9127-2

El-Sheikh, M., & Whitson, S. A. (2006). Longitudinal relations between marital conflict and child adjustment: Vagal regulation as a protective factor. *Journal of Family Psychology*, 20, 30–39. doi:10.1037/0893-3200.20.1.30

Engert, V., Efanov, S. I., Dedovic, K., Duchesne, A., Dagher, A., & Pruessner, J. C. (2010). Perceived early-life maternal care and the cortisol response to repeated psychosocial stress. *Journal of Psychiatry & Neuroscience*, 35, 370–377. doi:10.1503/jpn.100022

Erath, S. A., El-Sheikh, M., Hinnant, J. B., & Cummings, E. M. (2011). Skin conductance level reactivity moderates the association between harsh parenting and growth in child externalizing behavior. *Developmental Psychology, 47*, 693–706. doi:10.1037/a0021909

Essex, M. J., Armstrong, J. M., Burk, L. R., Goldsmith, H. H., & Boyce, W. T. (2011). Biological sensitivity to context moderates the effects of the early teacher–child relationship on the development of mental health by adolescence. *Development and Psychopathology, 23*, 149–161. doi:10.1017/S0954579410000702

Essex, M. J., Klein, M. H., Cho, E., & Kalin, N. H. (2002). Maternal stress beginning in infancy may sensitize children to later stress exposure: Effects on cortisol and behavior. *Biological Psychiatry, 52*, 776–784. doi:10.1016/s0006-3223(02)01553-6

Evans, G. W., & English, K. (2002). The environment of poverty: Multiple stressor exposure, psychophysiological stress, and socioemotional adjustment. *Child Development, 73*, 1238–1248. doi:10.1111/1467-8624.00469

Eysenck, H. J. (1983). Stress, disease, and personality: The inoculation effect. In C.L. Cooper (Ed.), *Stress research* (pp. 121–146). New York, NY: Wiley & Sons.

Fisher, P. A., & Gunnar, M. R. (2010). Early life stress as a risk factor for disease in adulthood. In R. A. Lanius, E. Vermetten, & C. Pain (Eds.), *The impact of early life trauma on health and disease* (pp. 133–141). Cambridge, UK: Cambridge University Press.

Fisher, P. A., Kim, H. K., Bruce, J., & Pears, K. C. (2012). Cumulative effects of prenatal substance exposure and early adversity on foster children's HPA-axis reactivity during a psychosocial stressor. *International Journal of Behavioral Development, 36*, 29–35. doi:10.1177/0165025411406863

Fowles, D. C. (1988). Psychophysiology and psychopathology: A motivational approach. *Psychophysiology, 25*, 373–391.

Fries, E., Hesse, J., Hellhammer, J., & Hellhammer, D. H. (2005). A new view on hypocortisolism. *Psychoneuroendocrinology, 30*, 1010–1016. doi:10.1016/j.psyneuen.2005.04.006

Gillman, M. W. (2005). Developmental origins of health and disease. *The New England Journal of Medicine, 353*, 1848–1850. doi:10.1056/NEJMe058187

Gilman, S. E., Kawachi, I., Fitzmaurice, G. M., & Buka, S. L. (2003). Family disruption in childhood and risk of adult depression. *American Journal of Psychiatry, 160*, 939–946. doi:/10.1176/appi.ajp.160.5.939

Glaser, R., & Kiecolt-Glaser, J. K. (2005). Stress-induced immune dysfunction: implications for health. *Nature Reviews. Immunology, 5*, 243–251. doi:10.1038/nri1571

Gordis, E. B., Feres, N., Olezeski, C. L., Rabkin, A. N., & Trickett, P. K. (2010). Skin conductance reactivity and respiratory sinus arrhythmia among maltreated and comparison youth: Relations with aggressive behavior. *Journal of Pediatric Psychology, 35*, 547–558. doi:10.1093/jpepsy/jsp113

Granger, D. A., Kivlighan, K. T., El-Sheikh, M. O. N. A., Gordis, E. B., & Stroud, L. R. (2007). Salivary α-amylase in biobehavioral research: Recent developments and applications. *Annals of the New York Academy of Sciences, 1098*, 122–144. doi:10.1196/annals.1384.008

Gregson, K. D., Tu, K. M., & Erath, S. A. (2014). Sweating under pressure: Skin conductance level reactivity moderates the association between peer victimization and externalizing behavior. *Journal of Child Psychology and Psychiatry, 55*, 22–30. doi:10.1111/jcpp.12086

Gunnar, M. R., Frenn, K., Wewerka, S. S., & Van Ryzin, M. J. (2009). Moderate versus severe early life stress: Associations with stress reactivity and regulation in 10–12-year-old children. *Psychoneuroendocrinology, 34*, 62–75. doi:10.1016/j.psyneuen.2008.08.013

Gunnar, M. R., & Vazquez, D. M. (2006). Stress neurobiology and developmental psychopathology. In D. Cicchetti & D. J. Cohen (Eds.), *Developmental psychopathology* (Vol. 2, 2nd ed., pp. 533–577). New York, NY: Wiley. doi:10.1002/9780470939390.ch13

Hagan, M. J., Roubinov, D. S., Mistler, A. K., & Luecken, L. J. (2014). Mental health outcomes in emerging adults exposed to childhood maltreatment: The moderating role of stress reactivity. *Child Maltreatment, 19*, 156–167. doi:10.1177/1077559514539753

Hankin, B. L., Mermelstein, R., & Roesch, L. (2007). Sex differences in adolescent depression: Stress exposure and reactivity models. *Child Development, 78*, 279–295. doi:10.1111/j.1467-8624.2007.00997.x

Hankin, B. L., Nederhof, E., Oppenheimer, C. W., Jenness, J., Young, J. F., Abela, J. R. Z.,...Oldehinkel, A. J. (2011). Differential susceptibility in youth: Evidence that 5-HTTLPR x positive parenting is associated with positive affect "for better and worse." *Translational Psychiatry, 1*(10), e44.

Hastings, P. D., Ruttle, P. L., Serbin, L. A., Mills, R. S., Stack, D. M., & Schwartzman, A. E. (2011). Adrenocortical responses to strangers in preschoolers: Relations with parenting, temperament, and psychopathology. *Developmental Psychobiology, 53*, 694–710. doi:10.1002/dev.20545

Heim, C., Ehlert, U., & Hellhammer, D. H. (2000). The potential role of hypocortisolism in the pathophysiology of stress-related bodily disorders. *Psychoneuroendocrinology, 25*, 1–35. doi:10.1016/s0306-4530(99)00035-9

Holochwost, S. J., Gariepy, J. L., Mills-Koonce, W. R., Propper, C. B., Kolacz, J., & Granger, D. A. (2017). Individual differences in the activity of the hypothalamic pituitary adrenal axis: Relations to age and cumulative risk in early childhood. *Psychoneuroendocrinology, 81*, 36–45. doi:10.1016/j.psyneuen.2017.03.023

Horwitz, A. V., Widom, C. S., McLaughlin, J., & White, H. R. (2001). The impact of childhood abuse and neglect on adult mental health: A prospective study. *Journal of Health and Social Behavior, 42*, 184–201. doi:10.2307/3090177

Keller, P. S., & El-Sheikh, M. (2009). Salivary alpha-amylase as a longitudinal predictor of children's externalizing symptoms: Respiratory sinus arrhythmia as a moderator of effects. *Psychoneuroendocrinology, 34*, 633–643. doi:10.1016/j.psyneuen.2008.12.016

Keller, P. S., Kouros, C. D., Erath, S. A., Dahl, R. E., & El-Sheikh, M. (2014). Longitudinal relations between maternal depressive symptoms and child sleep problems: the role of parasympathetic nervous system reactivity. *Journal of Child Psychology and Psychiatry, 55*, 172–179. doi:10.1111/jcpp.12151

Kelly, M. M., Tyrka, A. R., Anderson, G. M., Price, L. H., & Carpenter, L. L. (2008). Sex differences in emotional and physiological responses to the Trier Social Stress Test. *Journal of Behavior Therapy and Experimental Psychiatry, 39*, 87–98. doi:10.1016/j.jbtep.2007.02.003.

Kirschbaum, C., Kudielka, B. M., Gaab, J., Schommer, N. C., & Hellhammer, D. H. (1999). Impact of gender, menstrual cycle phase, and oral contraceptives on the activity of the hypothalamus–pituitary–adrenal axis. *Psychosomatic Medicine, 61*, 154–162. doi:10.1097/00006842-199903000-00006

Klein Velderman, M., Bakermans-Kranenburg, M. J., Juffer, F., & van IJzendoorn, M. H. (2006). Effects of attachment-based interventions on maternal sensitivity and infant attachment: Differential susceptibility of highly reactive infants. *Journal of Family Psychology*, *20*, 266–274. doi:10.1037/0893-3200.20.2.266

Knafo, A., Israel, S., & Ebstein, R. P. (2011). Heritability of children's prosocial behavior and differential susceptibility to parenting by variation in the dopamine receptor D4 gene. *Development and Psychopathology*, *23*, 53–67. doi:10.1017/S0954579410000647

Kochanska, G., Brock, R. L., Chen, K. H., Aksan, N., & Anderson, S. W. (2015). Paths from mother-child and father-child relationships to externalizing behavior problems in children differing in electrodermal reactivity: A longitudinal study from infancy to age 10. *Journal of Abnormal Child Psychology*, *43*, 721–734. doi:10.1007/s10802-014-9938-x

Kochanska, G., Kim, S., Barry, R. A., & Philibert, R. A. (2011). Children's genotypes interact with maternal responsive care in predicting children's competence: Diathesis–stress or differential susceptibility? *Development and Psychopathology*, *23*, 605–616. doi:10.1017/S0954579411000071

Kolacz, J., Holochwost, S. J., Gariépy, J. L., & Mills-Koonce, W. R. (2016). Patterns of joint parasympathetic, sympathetic, and adrenocortical activity and their associations with temperament in early childhood. *Developmental Psychobiology*, *58*, 990–1001. doi:10.1002/dev.21429

Koss, K. J., & Gunnar, M. R. (2018). Annual research review: Early adversity, the hypothalamic–pituitary–adrenocortical axis, and child psychopathology. *Journal of Child Psychology and Psychiatry*, *59*, 327–346. doi:10.1111/jcpp.12784

Koss, K. J., Mliner, S. B., Donzella, B., & Gunnar, M. R. (2016). Early adversity, hypocortisolism, and behavior problems at school entry: A study of internationally adopted children. *Psychoneuroendocrinology*, *66*, 31–38. doi:10.1016/j.psyneuen.2015.12.018.

Kryski, K. R., Smith, H. J., Sheikh, H. I., Singh, S. M., & Hayden, E. P. (2013). HPA axis reactivity in early childhood: Associations with symptoms and moderation by sex. *Psychoneuroendocrinology*, *38*, 2327–2336. doi:10.1016/j.psyneuen.2013.05.002

Kushner, M. R., Barrios, C., Smith, V. C., & Dougherty, L. R. (2016). Physiological and behavioral vulnerability markers increase risk to early life stress in preschool-aged children. *Journal of Abnormal Child Psychology*, *44*, 859–870. doi:10.1007/s10802-015-0087-7

Lester, B. M., LaGasse, L. L., Shankaran, S., Bada, H. S., Bauer, C. R., Lin, R., ... Higgins, R. (2010). Prenatal cocaine exposure related to cortisol stress reactivity in 11-year-old children. *The Journal of Pediatrics*, *157*, 288–295. doi:10.1016/j.jpeds.2010.02.039

Lupien, S. J., Ouellet-Morin, I., Hupbach, A., Tu, M. T., Buss, C., Walker, D., ... McEwen, B. S. (2006). Beyond the stress concept: Allostatic load—a developmental biological and cognitive perspective. In D. Cicchetti & D. J. Cohen (Eds.), *Developmental psychopathology: Vol. 2. Developmental neuroscience* (pp. 578–628). Hoboken, NJ: Wiley.

Lyons, D. M., & Parker, K. J. (2007). Stress inoculation-induced indications of resilience in monkeys. *Journal of Traumatic Stress*, *20*, 423–433. doi:10.1002/jts.20265

MacMillan, H. L., Georgiades, K., Duku, E. K., Shea, A., Steiner, M., Niec, A., ... Walsh, C. A. (2009). Cortisol response to stress in female youths exposed to childhood maltreatment: results of the youth mood project. *Biological Psychiatry*, *66*, 62–68. doi:10.1016/j.biopsych.2008.12.014

Macrì, S., Zoratto, F., & Laviola, G. (2011) Early-stress regulates resilience, vulnerability and experimental validity in laboratory rodents through mother-offspring hormonal transfer. *Neuroscience & Biobehavioral Reviews*, *35*, 1534–1543. doi:10.1016/j.neubiorev.2010.12.014

McEwen, B. S. (1998). Protective and damaging effects of stress mediators. *New England Journal of Medicine*, *338*, 171–179. doi:10.1056/nejm199801153380307

McEwen, B. S. (2000). Allostasis and allostatic load: Implications for neuropsychopharmacology. *Neuropsychopharmacology*, *22*, 108–124. doi:10.1016/s0893-133x(99)00129-3

McEwen, B. S. (2008). Central effects of stress hormones in health and disease: Understanding the protective and damaging effects of stress and stress mediators. *European Journal of Pharmacology*, *583*, 174–185. doi:10.1016/j.ejphar.2007.11.071

McEwen, B. S., & Seeman, T. (2003). Stress and affect: Applicability of the concepts of allostasis and allostatic load. In R. Davidson, S. Scherer, & H. Hill Goldsmith (Eds.), *Handbook of affective sciences* (pp. 1117–1137). Oxford, UK: Oxford University Press.

McEwen, B. S., & Stellar, E. (1993). Stress and the individual: Mechanisms leading to disease. *Archives of Internal Medicine*, *153*, 2093–2101.

McLaughlin, K. A., Alves, S., & Sheridan, M. A. (2014). Vagal regulation and internalizing psychopathology among adolescents exposed to childhood adversity. *Developmental Psychobiology*, *56*, 1036–1051. doi:10.1002/dev.21187.

McLaughlin, K. A., Rith-Najarian, L., Dirks, M. A., & Sheridan, M. A. (2015). Low vagal tone magnifies the association between psychosocial stress exposure and internalizing psychopathology in adolescents. *Journal of Clinical Child & Adolescent Psychology*, *44*, 314–328. doi:10.1080/15374416.2013.843464

Melchior, M., Moffitt, T. E., Milne, B. J., Poulton, R., & Caspi, A. (2007). Why do children from socioeconomically disadvantaged families suffer from poor health when they reach adulthood? A life-course study. *American Journal of Epidemiology*, *166*, 966–974. doi:10.1093/aje/kwm155

Mersky, J. P., Topitzes, J., & Reynolds, A. J. (2013). Impacts of adverse childhood experiences on health, mental health, and substance use in early adulthood: A cohort study of an urban, minority sample in the US. *Child Abuse & Neglect*, *37*, 917–925. doi:10.1016/j.chiabu.2013.07.011

Miller, G. E., Chen, E., & Zhou, E. S. (2007). If it goes up, must it come down? Chronic stress and the hypothalamic-pituitary-adrenocortical axis in humans. *Psychological Bulletin*, *133*, 25–45. doi:10.1037/0033-2909.133.1.25

Mittal, C., Griskevicius, V., Simpson, J. A., Sung, S., & Young, E. S. (2015). Cognitive adaptations to stressful environments: When childhood adversity enhances adult executive function. *Journal of Personality and Social Psychology*, *109*, 604–621. doi:10.1037/pspi0000028

Monroe, S. M., & Simons, A. D. (1991). Diathesis-stress theories in the context of life stress research: Implications for the depressive disorders. *Psychological Bulletin*, *110*, 406–425. 10.1037/0033-2909.110.3.406

Morgan, J. K., Shaw, D. S., & Olino, T. M. (2012). Differential susceptibility effects: The interaction of negative emotionality and sibling relationship quality on childhood internalizing problems and social skills. *Journal of Abnormal Child Psychology*, *40*, 885–899. doi:10.1007/s10802-012-9618-7

Murali, V., & Oyebode, F. (2004). Poverty, social inequality and mental health. *Advances in Psychiatric Treatment, 10*, 216–224. doi:10.1192/apt.10.3.216

Nanni, V., Uher, R., & Danese, A. (2011). Childhood maltreatment predicts unfavorable course of illness and treatment outcome in depression: A meta-analysis. *American Journal of Psychiatry, 169*, 141–151. doi:10.1176/appi.ajp.2011.11020335

Nater, U. M., & Rohleder, N. (2009). Salivary alpha-amylase as a non-invasive biomarker for the sympathetic nervous system: Current state of research. *Psychoneuroendocrinology, 34*, 486–496. doi:10.1016/j.psyneuen.2009.01.014

Nugent, N. R., Tyrka, A. R., Carpenter, L. L., & Price, L. H. (2011). Gene–environment interactions: Early life stress and risk for depressive and anxiety disorders. *Psychopharmacology, 214*, 175–196. doi:10.1007/s00213-010-2151-x

Obradović, J., & Boyce, W. T. (2009). Individual differences in behavioral, physiological, and genetic sensitivities to contexts: Implications for development and adaptation. *Developmental Neuroscience, 31*, 300–308. doi:10.1159/000216541

Obradović, J., Bush, N. R., & Boyce, W. T. (2011). The interactive effect of marital conflict and stress reactivity on externalizing and internalizing symptoms: The role of laboratory stressors. *Development and Psychopathology, 23*, 101–114. doi:10.1017/S0954579410000672

Obradović, J., Bush, N. R., Stamperdahl, J., Adler, N. E., & Boyce, W. T. (2010). Biological sensitivity to context: The interactive effects of stress reactivity and family adversity on socioemotional behavior and school readiness. *Child Development, 81*, 270–289. doi:10.1111/j.1467-8624.2009.01394.x

Ouellet-Morin, I., Robitaille, M. P., Langevin, S., Cantave, C., Brendgen, M., & Lupien, S. J. (2018). Enduring effect of childhood maltreatment on cortisol and heart rate responses to stress: The moderating role of severity of experiences. *Development and Psychopathology*, 1–12. doi:10.1017/s0954579418000123

Parker, K. J., Buckmaster, C. L., Schatzberg, A. F., & Lyons, D. M. (2004). Prospective investigation of stress inoculation in young monkeys. *Archives of General Psychiatry, 61*, 933–941. doi:10.1001/archpsyc.61.9.933

Parker, K. J., & Maestripieri, D. (2011). Identifying key features of early stressful experiences that produce stress vulnerability and resilience in primates. *Neuroscience & Biobehavioral Reviews, 35*, 1466–1483. doi:10.1016/j.neubiorev.2010.09.003

Peckins, M. K., Susman, E. J., Negriff, S., Noll, J., & Trickett, P. K. (2015). Cortisol profiles: A test for adaptive calibration of the stress response system in maltreated and nonmaltreated youth. *Development and Psychopathology, 27*, 1461–1470. doi:10.1017/s0954579415000875

Porges, S. W. (1995). Orienting in a defensive world: Mammalian modifications of our evolutionary heritage. A polyvagal theory. *Psychophysiology, 32*, 301–318.

Porges, S. W. (2007). The polyvagal perspective. *Biological Psychology, 74*, 116–143.

Porges, S. W. (2011). *The polyvagal theory: Neurophysiological foundations of emotions, attachment, communication, and self-regulation* (Norton Series on Interpersonal Neurobiology). New York, NY: W. W. Norton & Company.

Quas, J. A., Yim, I. S., Oberlander, T. F., Nordstokke, D., Essex, M. J., Armstrong, J. M.,...Boyce, W. T. (2014). The symphonic structure of childhood stress reactivity: Patterns of sympathetic, parasympathetic, and adrenocortical responses

to psychological challenge. *Development and Psychopathology, 26*, 963–982. doi:10.1017/s0954579414000480

Reiss, F. (2013). Socioeconomic inequalities and mental health problems in children and adolescents: A systematic review. *Social Science & Medicine, 90*, 24–31. doi:10.1016/j.socscimed.2013.04.026

Rubinow, D. R., & Schmidt, P. J. (1999). The neurobiology of menstrual cycle-related mood disorders. In D. S. Charney, E. J. Nestler, & B. S. Bunney (Eds.), *Neurobiology of mental illness* (pp. 907–914). New York, NY: Oxford University Press.

Rudolph, K. D., Troop-Gordon, W., & Granger, D. A. (2010). Peer victimization and aggression: Moderation by individual differences in salivary cortiol and alpha-amylase. *Journal of Abnormal Child Psychology, 38*, 843–856. doi:10.1007/s10802-010-9412-3

Rudolph, K. D., Troop-Gordon, W., & Granger, D. A. (2011). Individual differences in biological stress responses moderate the contribution of early peer victimization to subsequent depressive symptoms. *Psychopharmacology, 214*, 209–219. doi:10.1007/s00213-010-1879-7

Rutter, M. (1987). Psychosocial resilience and protective mechanisms. *American Journal of Orthopsychiatry, 57*, 316–331. doi:10.1111/j.1939-0025.1987.tb03541.x

Saxbe, D. E., Margolin, G., Spies Shapiro, L. A., & Baucom, B. R. (2012). Does dampened physiological reactivity protect youth in aggressive family environments? *Child Development, 83*, 821–830. doi:10.1111/j.1467-8624.2012.01752.x

Scannapieco, F. A., Torres, G., & Levine, M. J. (1993). Salivary α-amylase: Role in dental plaque and caries formation. *Critical Reviews in Oral Biology & Medicine, 4*, 301–307. doi:10.1177/10454411930040030701

Schumacher, S., Kirschbaum, C., Fydrich, T., & Ströhle, A. (2013). Is salivary alpha-amylase an indicator of autonomic nervous system dysregulations in mental disorders?—A review of preliminary findings and the interactions with cortisol. *Psychoneuroendocrinology, 38*, 729–743. doi:10.1016/j.psyneuen.2013.02.003

Seeman, T. E., Singer, B., Wilkinson, C. W., & McEwen, B. (2001). Gender differences in age-related changes in HPA axis reactivity. *Psychoneuroendocrinology, 26*, 225–240. doi:10.1016/s0306-4530(00)00043-3

Shaffer, F., McCraty, R., & Zerr, C. L. (2014). A healthy heart is not a metronome: An integrative review of the heart's anatomy and heart rate variability. *Frontiers in Psychology, 5*, 1040. doi:10.3389/fpsyg.2014.01040

Shanahan, L., Calkins, S. D., Keane, S. P., Kelleher, R., & Suffness, R. (2014). Trajectories of internalizing symptoms across childhood: The roles of biological self-regulation and maternal psychopathology. *Development and Psychopathology, 26*, 1353–1368. doi:10.1017/S0954579414001072

Shannon, K. E., Beauchaine, T. P., Brenner, S. L., Neuhaus, E., & Gatzke-Kopp, L. (2007). Familial and temperamental predictors of resilience in children at risk for conduct disorder and depression. *Development and Psychopathology, 19*, 701–727. doi:10.1017/S0954579407000351

Shenk, C. E., Noll, J. G., Putnam, F. W., & Trickett, P. K. (2010). A prospective examination of the role of childhood sexual abuse and physiological asymmetry in the development of psychopathology. *Child Abuse & Neglect, 34*, 752–761. doi:10.1016/j.chiabu.2010.02.010

Shirtcliff, E. A., Skinner, M. L., Obasi, E. M., & Haggerty, K. P. (2017). Positive parenting predicts cortisol functioning six years later in young adults. *Developmental Science, 20*, e12461. doi:10.1111/desc.12461

Shonkoff, J. P., Boyce, W. T., & McEwen, B. S. (2009). Neuroscience, molecular biology, and the childhood roots of health disparities: Building a new framework for health promotion and disease prevention. *Jama, 301*, 2252–2259. doi:10.1001/jama.2009.754

Shonkoff, J. P., Garner, A. S., Siegel, B. S., Dobbins, M. I., Earls, M. F., McGuinn, L.,... Committee on Early Childhood, Adoption, and Dependent Care. (2012). The lifelong effects of early childhood adversity and toxic stress. *Pediatrics, 129*, e232–e246. doi:10.1542/peds.2011-2663

Slagt, M., Dubas, J. S., Deković, M., & van Aken, M. A. (2016). Differences in sensitivity to parenting depending on child temperament: A meta-analysis. *Psychological Bulletin, 142*, 1068–1110. doi:10.1037/bul0000061

Slavich, G. M., & Irwin, M. R. (2014). From stress to inflammation and major depressive disorder: A social signal transduction theory of depression. *Psychological Bulletin, 140*, 774–815. doi:10.1037/a0035302

Smearman, E. L., Almli, L. M., Conneely, K. N., Brody, G. H., Sales, J. M., Bradley, B.,... Smith, A. K. (2016). Oxytocin receptor genetic and epigenetic variations: Association with child abuse and adult psychiatric symptoms. *Child Development, 87*, 122–134. doi:10.1111/cdev.12493

Somers, J. A., Ibrahim, M. H., & Luecken, L. J. (2017). Biological sensitivity to the effects of childhood family adversity on psychological well-being in young adulthood. *Child Maltreatment, 22*, 236–264. doi:10.1177/1077559517711041

Spataro, J., Mullen, P. E., Burgess, P. M., Wells, D. L., & Moss, S. A. (2004). Impact of child sexual abuse on mental health. *The British Journal of Psychiatry, 184*, 416–421. doi:10.1192/bjp.184.5.416

Spinrad, T. L., Eisenberg, N., Granger, D. A., Eggum, N. D., Sallquist, J., Haugen, R. G.,... Hofer, C. (2009). Individual differences in preschoolers' salivary cortisol and alpha-amylase reactivity: Relations to temperament and maladjustment. *Hormones and Behavior, 56*, 133–139. doi:10.1016/j.yhbeh.2009.03.020

Sterling, P., & Eyer, J. (1988). Allostasis: A new paradigm to explain arousal pathology. In S. Fisher & J. Reason (Eds.), *Handbook of life stress, cognition and health* (pp. 629–649). New York, NY: Wiley.

Stroud, L. R., Salovey, P., & Epel, E. S. (2002). Sex differences in stress responses: Social rejection versus achievement stress. *Biological Psychiatry, 52*, 318–327. doi:10.1016/s0006-3223(02)01333-1

Taylor, Z. E., Spinrad, T. L., VanSchyndel, S. K., Eisenberg, N., Huynh, J., Sulik, M. J., & Granger, D. A. (2013). Sociodemographic risk, parenting, and effortful control: Relations to salivary alpha-amylase and cortisol in early childhood. *Developmental Psychobiology, 55*, 869–880. doi:10.1002/dev.21079

Tollenaar, M. S., Beijers, R., Jansen, J., Riksen-Walraven, J. M. A., & De Weerth, C. (2011). Maternal prenatal stress and cortisol reactivity to stressors in human infants. *Stress, 14*, 53–65. doi:10.3109/10253890.2010.499485

van IJzendoorn, M. H., & Bakermans-Kranenburg, M. J. (2015). Genetic differential susceptibility on trial: Meta-analytic support from randomized controlled experiments. *Development and Psychopathology, 27*, 151–162. doi:10.1017/S0954579414001369

van IJzendoorn, M. H., Belsky, J., & Bakermans-Kranenburg, M. J. (2012). Serotonin transporter genotype 5HTTLPR as a marker of differential susceptibility? A meta-analysis of child and adolescent gene-by-environment studies. *Translational Psychiatry, 2*, e147. doi:10.1038/tp.2012.73

van Zeijl, J., Mesman, J., Stolk, M. N., Alink, L. R., van IJzendoorn, M. H., Bakermans-Kranenburg, M. J.,... Koot, H. M. (2007). Differential susceptibility to discipline: The moderating effect of child temperament on the association between maternal discipline and early childhood externalizing problems. *Journal of Family Psychology, 21*, 626–636. doi:10.1037/0893-3200.21.4.626

von Klitzing, K., Perren, S., Klein, A. M., Stadelmann, S., White, L. O., Groeben, M.,... Hatzinger, M. (2012). The interaction of social risk factors and HPA axis dysregulation in predicting emotional symptoms of five- and six-year-old children. *Journal of Psychiatric Research, 46*, 290–297. doi:10.1016/j.jpsychires.2011.12.004

Weiss, E. L., Longhurst, J. G., & Mazure, C. M. (1999). Childhood sexual abuse as a risk factor for depression in women: psychosocial and neurobiological correlates. *American Journal of Psychiatry, 156*, 816–828. doi:10.1176/ajp.156.6.816

West-Eberhard, M. J. (2003). *Developmental plasticity and evolution*. New York, NY: Oxford University Press.

Wilsmer Fries, A. B., Shirtcliff, E. A., & Pollak, S. D. (2008). Neuroendocrine dysregulation following early social deprivation in children. *Developmental Psychobiology, 50*, 588–599. doi:10.1002/dev.20319

Yoshikawa, H., Aber, J. L., & Beardslee, W. R. (2012). The effects of poverty on the mental, emotional, and behavioral health of children and youth: Implications for prevention. *American Psychologist, 67*, 272–284. doi:10.1037/a0028015

Young, E. S., Griskevicius, V., Simpson, J. A., Waters, T. E., & Mittal, C. (2018). Can an unpredictable childhood environment enhance working memory? Testing the sensitized-specialization hypothesis. *Journal of Personality and Social Psychology*. doi:10.1037/pspi0000124

Zahn-Waxler, C., Shirtcliff, E. A., & Marceau, K. (2008). Disorders of childhood and adolescence: Gender and psychopathology. *Annual Review of Clinical Psychology, 4*, 275–303. doi:10.1146/annurev.clinpsy.3.022806.091358

Zuckerman, M. (1999). *Vulnerability to psychopathology: A biosocial model*. Washington, DC: American Psychological Association. doi:10.1037/10316-000

The Temporal Elements of Psychological Resilience to Potential Trauma

Kan Long *and* George A. Bonanno

Abstract

Potential trauma is common across the life span. Responses to these highly aversive events vary significantly, yet many individuals will demonstrate psychological resilience and a clear pattern of psychological health and adaptive functioning in the wake of extreme adversity. Amid expanding conceptual diversity and a proliferation of research, we present a novel, unified framework for resilience that consists of four constituent, temporally related elements: baseline or preadversity functioning, the actual aversive circumstances, postadversity resilient outcomes, and predictors of resilient outcomes. The temporal framework integrates and extends several existing lines of research by conceptualizing resilience as a process that unfolds over time with each temporal element playing an essential role.

Keywords: potentially traumatic events, PTE, resilience, trauma, temporal framework

Potentially traumatic events (PTEs) are prevalent across the life span (Copeland et al., 2007; Norris, 1992). While a majority of the population will experience at least one if not several PTEs (Breslau, 2009), responses to these highly aversive events vary significantly between individuals (Bonanno, 2004). Over the past decade, a burgeoning body of research has focused on elucidating the nature of this marked variability in responses to potential trauma. A striking pattern that has consistently emerged is the human capacity for resilience in the face of extreme adversity.

Background

The term "resilience" was first coined during the early 1970s to explain the "absorb[tion] of change and disturbance" in ecological systems (Holling, 1973, p. 14). Although inquiry in the field of developmental psychology during this period was focused predominantly on psychopathology, the notion of psychological resilience also began to appear in the literature on early human development (Garmezy, 1972; Rutter, 1979; Werner et al., 1971; Werner & Smith, 1977). Resilience was originally conceptualized as a descriptor for children who endured highly

aversive circumstances, yet grew into functional, capable individuals. Developmental theory eventually expanded to include positive adaptation and healthy adjustment as research on resilience gained greater traction. In this regard, a prominent line of research has investigated resilience over the life span and examined children and adolescents exposed to recurrent, chronic adversity who nevertheless reached normative developmental milestones and exhibited social competence, professional proficiency, and adaptive functioning across other domains in adulthood (DiRago & Vaillant, 2007; Gralinski-Bakker, Hauser, Stott, Billings, & Allen, 2004; Sampson & Laub, 1992; Vaillant & Davis, 2000).

As researchers and theorists turned their attention toward resilience in trauma-exposed adult populations, the conceptual focus began to shift. Whereas developmental research has tended to emphasize chronic adversity and life course outcomes, research on extreme adversity in adults has generally centered on single PTEs (e.g., loss, trauma, or disaster). Further, these types of PTEs tend to be isolated rather than a product of systemic issues or a deleterious environment. Thus, the increasing interest in trauma exposure and psychological health in adults (Bonanno et al., 1995, 2001, 2002; Ryff & Singer, 2002) contributed to a novel perspective on resilience in which the focus moved from distal psychological outcomes occurring in the extended aftermath of exposure to more proximal patterns of mental health and psychological adjustment (Bonanno et al., 2001, 2011; Bonanno, 2004, 2005).

Though the largest corpus of scientific evidence lies in the literature on psychological resilience in individuals (Bonanno, Romero, & Klein, 2015), the concept has broadened to include families (Hawley & DeHaan, 1996; McCubbin et al., 2002; Patterson, 1988, 2002; Walsh, 1996) and communities (Norris et al., 2008; Sonn & Fisher, 1998). To accommodate the application of resilience beyond individuals, a range of social constructs and group behaviors became integrated into conceptualizations of resilience. For example, psychological resilience in family systems has involved family communication patterns (McCubbin & McCubbin, 1988), family problem solving and flexibility (Walsh, 1996), and family identity (Patterson, 2002). Likewise, prior work has developed a formulation of resilience in communities that incorporates sense of community (Sonn & Fisher, 1998), social capital (Kawachi, 1999), and collective efficacy (Sampson, Raudenbush, & Earls, 1997).

Defining Resilience

As psychological resilience gained increasing prominence, a corresponding proliferation in the research and theory surrounding the construct contributed to widening the scope of both the definition and use of the term (Bonanno et al., 2015; Luthar, Cicchetti, & Becker, 2000). Presently, resilience—as relevant to psychological health and functioning—has taken on myriad meanings in a variety of contexts. For instance, psychological resilience has been defined as the interactive process by which positive adaptation is cultivated and maintained (Egeland, Carlson, & Sroufe, 1993; Norris, Stevens, Pfefferbaum, Wyche, & Pfefferbaum, 2008), a post-PTE outcome characterized by healthy functioning and adjustment (e.g., Bonanno, 2004; Masten, 2007; Norris, Tracy, & Galea, 2009; Rutter, 2002), a personality trait (e.g., a "resilient" type; Smith et al., 2008), or a collection of capacities, characteristics, and resources (Aldrich, 2012; Norris et al., 2008). Additional conceptual diversity arises from application of the term in reference to both acute and chronic life stressors (Bonanno & Diminich, 2013) as well as across populations that include children

(Masten, 2001), adults (Bonanno, 2004), families (Walsh, 2006, 2013), and neighborhoods or communities (Norris et al., 2008).

Given the multiple and overlapping meanings of "resilience," we contend that the use of the term as a descriptor for a single construct leads to a reduction in the conceptual and scientific precision necessary to propel future lines of research. Our aim in recognizing these limitations is not to suggest that continued inquiry is unfeasible; indeed, we believe that research on resilience is at an essential turning point and holds significant promise. We propose that the concept of resilience is best realized as a broad, umbrella phenomenon that encompasses a number of temporally related elements (Bonanno, 2004, 2005; Bonanno & Diminich, 2013; Carver, 1998; Cutter et al., 2008; Masten & Narayan, 2012; Norris et al., 2008). In the following sections, we present a novel, unified framework in order to advance research and theory on psychological resilience.

The Temporal Elements of Resilience

Bonanno and colleagues (2015) recently proposed an integrative framework for examining resilience in individuals, families, and communities that consisted of four basic temporal elements (Figure 28.1). These four elements include (a) baseline or preadversity adjustment that serves as the anchoring reference point, (b) the actual aversive circumstances, (c) postadversity resilient outcomes referenced to both the aversive circumstances and baseline adjustment, and (d) predictors of resilient outcomes measured prior to, during, and after the aversive circumstances. In the context of this framework, psychological resilience is conceptualized as a process that unfolds over time (Bonanno, 2012).

Baseline Adjustment

The first temporal element is baseline or preadversity adjustment. Baseline adjustment refers to the functioning of individuals, families, or communities prior to the onset of aversive circumstances (i.e., baseline or preadversity psychological adjustment). Prospective and longitudinal research on resilience in the face of highly aversive events has illustrated that the inclusion of baseline measures reduces issues of sampling and memory bias, thereby allowing for more reliable and comprehensive conclusions to be drawn. While it is preferable to obtain an index of psychological adjustment at baseline, the task poses notable challenges and many situations arise where pre-event assessments are either not feasible or available. However, postadversity resilient

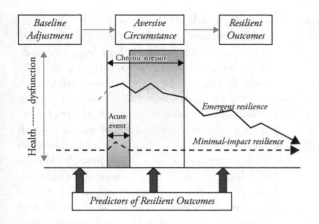

Figure 28.1 Temporal relations between stressful life experiences and the outcomes they produce define unique pharmacotherapeutic approaches for ameliorating stress-related outcomes.

outcomes are nearly always implicitly or explicitly referenced to baseline adjustment. Thus, in the absence of baseline adjustment measures, it becomes increasingly critical to subject measures of post-event resilient outcomes to careful scrutiny.

Aversive Circumstances

The second temporal element is comprised of the aversive circumstances themselves. Although baseline adjustment may be temporally precedent, all instances of psychological resilience must be referenced to an actual real-world event or series of events (Bonanno, 2004, 2012; Luthar et al., 2000).

ACUTE VERSUS CHRONIC

When parsing the differences between aversive circumstances, an essential distinction lies in the contrast between acute and chronic adversity. Generally speaking, acute and chronic events differ with regard to the intensity and duration of impact (Bonanno, 2004; Fergus & Zimmerman, 2004). Acute adversity involves an event that is relatively isolated, demands and / or results in the loss of resources, and exerts its primary impact over a transient period, typically less than 1 month. For example, acute events may include natural disasters (e.g., flood, hurricane), serious transportation accident, physical assault, terrorist attack, explosion, or fire. In turn, chronic adversity refers to an event or series of events that exert a recurrent and cumulative impact on resources and adaptation over the course of many months or years. Chronic events may consist of emotional or physical neglect, prolonged physical or sexual abuse, civil war, and political violence.

LEVEL OF EXPOSURE

Level of exposure is another aspect of aversive circumstances that varies across individuals. Individuals can experience the same highly aversive event over a

comparable period of time; however, each person may contend with varying degrees of exposure to the event's aversive characteristics. For instance, level of exposure may differ with regard to direct experience of life-threatening events (Bonanno et al., 2005; Galatzer-Levy et al., 2013), physical proximity to the aversive circumstances (Galea et al., 2002; Hoven et al., 2005), and loss of family members or friends (Norris et al., 2008). Other common features of exposure include the presence of physical dangers (Norris et al., 2002; Okumura et al., 1998) and injuries (Galea et al., 2007), media consumption (Vasterman et al., 2005), and secondary resource repercussions (e.g., property damage or loss of employment; Hobfoll, 1989, 2002; Norris et al., 2005). Level of exposure has been shown to exert individual and cumulative effects on responses to adversity (Bonanno et al., 2010).

PROXIMAL AND DISTAL EXPOSURE

Aversive circumstances may also be distinguished based on whether the impact of a potentially traumatic event is immediate or long term. Bonanno and colleagues (2010) proposed the terms *proximal* and *distal* exposure to differentiate between these two types of aversive contexts. Proximal exposure refers to events and consequences that occur during the approximate period of adversity. For example, individuals may find themselves in imminent physical danger or witness the death and serious injury of others as an event unfolds. By contrast, distal exposure denotes events and consequences that surface in the time following the period of adversity. Individuals may experience a sudden, acute stressor followed by protracted consequences that may include persistent injuries, displacement or relocation, and repeated repercussive events that interfere with daily functioning. The distinction between proximal and distal exposure serves to demarcate *when* events and consequences occur; however, the constructs may also be observed in more complex combinations.

Resilient Outcomes

The third temporal element consists of postadversity resilient outcomes. Resilient outcomes refer to the functioning of individuals, families, or communities following aversive circumstances in the aftermath of exposure (i.e., postadversity psychological adjustment).

THE DIAGNOSTIC AND AVERAGE-LEVEL APPROACHES

The two most common approaches to studying highly aversive and potentially traumatic life events have employed either a binary focus on psychopathology or average-level measures of psychological adjustment.

The first of these approaches operates under the assumption that diagnostic categories reflecting the presence and absence of psychopathology (i.e., extreme responses) fully capture possible responses to extreme adversity. Research on psychopathology has played a crucial role in chronicling the adverse consequences of exposure to PTEs and the associated public health costs. While the potentially harmful effects of trauma exposure were recognized in the first quarter of the 20th century, significant debate ensued over the presentation, prevalence, and existence of trauma-related disorders (Lamprecht & Sack, 2002). In addition, psychological issues experienced in the wake of PTEs were stigmatized as malingering or personal weakness, and treatment was difficult to obtain (Shepard, 2001). A critical turning point occurred in 1980—PTSD was formally recognized as a diagnostic category, which led to a corresponding expansion in research and treatment (Foa & Kozak 1986; Foa et al., 1991; McNally, 2003). In more recent years, similar advances took place in relation to psychological difficulties following bereavement when diagnostic criteria were proposed for prolonged grief (PG; Boelen, de Keijser, van den Hout, & van den Bout, 2007; Bonanno, Neria et al., 2007; Horowitz, Siegel et al., 1997; Prigerson et al., 2009; Shear, Frank, Houck, & Reynolds, 2005).

Although these developments provided a foundation for understanding adaptation following aversive circumstances, the diagnostic approach is limited in key ways. Per the principles of this approach, dysfunctional or abnormal responses are viewed as synonymous with diagnostic categories, such as posttraumatic stress disorder (PTSD), major

depressive disorder (MDD), or PG. By this logic, normal or resilient responses are by default indicated by the absence of psychopathology (e.g., Krystal & Neumeister, 2009; Rutter, 1985; Sarapas et al., 2011; Yehuda & Flory, 2007). The exclusive reliance on diagnostic categories, however, results in ambiguity regarding the prevalence or course of extreme responses. A historical examination of trauma research indicates significant variability in the manifestation of PTSD symptoms (Jones, 2006; Jones & Wessely, 2005; Jones et al., 2003; Sundin, Fear, Iversen, Rona, & Wessely, 2010) and clear boundaries for the diagnostic category have yet to be established with the endeavor hindered by the ongoing expansion of diagnostic criteria for PTSD (McNally, 2012). As it stands, the current *DSM-5* criteria for PTSD give rise to 636,120 distinct symptom combinations that qualify for the diagnostic label (Galatzer-Levy & Bryant, 2013). This lack of diagnostic precision in combination with selection or response biases has led to considerable variability in the prevalence rates of psychopathology across studies and poses a significant problem for research on highly aversive life events (Bonanno, Brewin, Kaniasty, & La Greca, 2010; Johnson & Thompson, 2008).

Moreover, the binary conceptualization of psychological outcomes offers scant information regarding the plausible heterogeneity of different responses to potential trauma. Put differently, when all individuals who do not develop psychopathology following exposure are placed into a single category of nonpsychopathology, resilient outcomes become conflated with other nonpathological responses, which ultimately masks variation (Bonanno et al., 2011). In this way, the psychopathology approach presumes that the course of postadversity outcomes follows a single *homogenous* pattern over time (Duncan, Duncan, & Strycker, 2006; Muthén, 2004). By contrast, more recent work examining the range of responses to aversive events has consistently demonstrated *heterogeneity* in outcomes and significant variation among individuals (Bonanno, 2004; Bonanno et al., 2011; Galatzer-Levy & Bonanno, 2013).

The second approach employs the use of average-level data on psychological adjustment in order to discern how the average response in a group of exposed individuals differs from a comparison group (e.g., nonexposed individuals or other patient population). As such, the average-level approach is primarily concerned with the impact of an aversive event rather than individual differences in post-event responses. The typical pattern of PTSD symptoms, when averaged at the group level, is characterized by an initial elevation in the weeks immediately following exposure that gradually declines over the course of several years and returns to the assumed baseline (Breslau, 2001). The use of average-level scores has been frequently applied in studies examining predictors of PTSD or PG and in meta-analytic research (Currier, Neimeyer, & Berman, 2008; Norris et al., 2002).

That said, the average-level approach is hampered by the assumption that the statistical mean reflects the normal or modal response to potential trauma. The limitations inherent to the use of averages were first broached more than a century ago (e.g., Johannsen, 1903; Skinner, 1936), and although the approach serves as a descriptive index of the distribution in outcome and allows for an identification of longitudinal trends, the use of average-level data may obscure other interesting effects (Bloembergen & Zewail, 1984; Siegler, 1987). This issue is of particular concern to the study of psychological adjustment in the presence of extreme adversity because the data are often nonnormal and the average may not accurately reflect the full range of responses across the sample. Moreover, the average-level approach fails to capture the variance inherent to longitudinal distributions and is unable to identify resilient trajectories or other patterns in the data that are not represented by the single, average pattern of change (Galatzer-Levy & Bonanno, 2012, 2014; Mancini, Bonanno, & Clark, 2011). Therefore, in order to accurately assess resilient outcomes following exposure and to model heterogeneity in responses to potential trauma over time, it is necessary to obtain repeated and longitudinal measurements (Bonanno, 2012).

THE TRAJECTORY APPROACH

A more recent approach utilizing latent growth modeling has addressed the limits of diagnoses and the problem of averages by identifying trajectories of psychological adjustment to more successfully capture heterogeneity in outcomes. Studies that employed latent growth modeling methods (e.g., latent growth mixture modeling, latent class growth analysis) have identified four prototypical trajectories of psychological adjustment in the context of highly aversive events: chronic dysfunction, recovery, delayed reactions, and resilience (e.g., Bonanno, 2004, 2005; Bonanno et al., 2011). An examination of different age groups and types of aversive circumstances revealed two distinct resilient trajectories— emergent resilience and minimal-impact resilience (Bonanno & Diminich, 2013). These two forms of resilience are associated with separable aversive circumstances. *Emergent resilience* has been observed in the context of chronic adversity and refers to a pattern of initially moderate to elevated levels of psychological symptoms that steadily improve and return to normal range after the chronic potential trauma has abated. *Minimal-impact resilience* has been observed following more acute types of adversity and is defined as a pattern of stable, low-level psychological symptoms evident both before and after the onset of acute potential trauma. It is relevant to note that prior work has predominantly associated emergent resilience with developmental populations and minimal-impact resilience with adult populations. However, the apparent link between type of resilience and age is most likely a product of the focus on chronic aversive events in developmental research and the emphasis on acute aversive events in adult research. We discuss these two forms of resilience in more detail later.

Emergent Resilience

The ongoing, recurrent nature of chronic adversity tends to exert enduring effects on a broad range of psychological and physiological functions (de Kloet, Derijk, & Meijer, 2011; Lupien et al., 2009; Offidani & Ruini, 2012); therefore, emergent resilience often becomes most apparent once the aversive circumstances have subsided. The trajectory of emergent resilience is characterized by a capacity for weathering caustic life circumstances as evidenced by the ability to reach normal developmental milestones and attain psychological health in the aftermath of chronic adversity. While emergent resilience does not reflect a sudden rebound toward health and adaptation, improvements are often evident soon after chronic adversity has abated with this return to normal levels of functioning continuing to unfold over time. For example, a child may experience significant difficulties within a chronically abusive family system. However, if the child were to eventually proceed through normal developmental stages and exhibit adaptive psychological adjustment as well as other relevant competencies in functioning (Elder, 1998; Luthar et al., 2000; Masten & Coatsworth, 1998; Waters & Sroufe, 1983), this pattern would be emblematic of emergent resilience.

To date, the bulk of prior work on emergent resilience comes from developmental research that has examined chronic exposure to poverty or abuse (Garmezy, 1993; Luthar, 1999; Werner, 1993) and civil war, among other aversive circumstances (Betancourt & Khan, 2008; Betancourt et al., 2013).

A classic study of emergent resilient outcomes followed a multiracial cohort of children exposed to perinatal stress, chronic poverty, chronic familial discord, and parental psychopathology from the perinatal period to adulthood (Werner 1993, 1995; Werner & Smith, 1977, 1992). By late adolescence, children who demonstrated emergent resilience were observed to be competent, caring, and motivated as well as successful in several domains, including academic endeavors and social functioning (Werner, 1993). As these resilient individuals reached adulthood, the majority continued to evidence adaptation and healthy psychological adjustment as indicated by scholastic and professional achievements that surpassed their high-risk peers and were comparable to the accomplishments of low-risk peers who had developed in more stable environments (Werner, 1993).

In a more recent applied example, Betancourt and colleagues (2013) examined trajectories of internalizing symptoms and behavioral problems in youth exposed to the civil war in Sierra Leone. The war in Sierra Leone had dragged on for 11 long years, and many of the youths in the study had been commandeered to serve as child soldiers. A significant portion of the youth in their sample exhibited consistently low symptom levels indicative of minimal-impact resilience. However, the most common pattern observed was an emergent resilience trajectory of initially moderate or high level of symptoms that gradually improved to normal levels only after several years had passed.

Although the literature on emergent resilience is most robust in developmental psychology, it is important to note that the study of this type of resilient outcome is not limited to the experience of childhood adversity alone. Emergent resilience has also been reported in a handful of studies from the adult literature that investigated prolonged instances of adversity. Hobfoll and colleagues (2011) examined the impact of the Second Intifada and chronic exposure to extreme war violence and mass casualty in a large sample of Palestinians from the Gaza and West Bank regions. The most common outcome trajectory identified by Hobfoll and colleagues (2011) was suggestive of the established pattern of emergent resilience and consisted of moderately elevated symptoms of PTSD and depression followed by gradual improvement.

Minimal-Impact Resilience
The relatively discrete and isolated nature of acute adversity typically produces transient disruptions in

normal functioning followed by a fairly rapid return to baseline adjustment (e.g., Bisconti, Bergeman, & Boker, 2004; Bonanno 2004). As such, minimal-impact resilience in the face of acute PTEs becomes apparent shortly after the event occurs. The trajectory of minimal-impact resilience is characterized by a pattern of low-level, transient psychological symptoms or distress that remains stable before and after the aversive event (Bonanno, 2004, 2005; Bonanno et al., 2011).

The body of evidence for minimal-impact resilience has arisen predominantly from research on adults (Bonanno & Diminich, 2013; Bonanno et al., 2015), and it is the most commonly observed outcome across many types of PTEs. For instance, the minimal-impact resilience trajectory was identified in the context of exposure to a large-scale terrorist attack (Bonanno, Rennicke, & Dekel, 2005), disease epidemic (Bonanno, Ho et al., 2008), natural disasters (La Greca et al., 2013; Norris et al., 2009; Pietrzak et al., 2013; Tang, 2007), and mass shootings (Mancini, Littleton & Grills, 2015; Orcutt et al., 2014). Similarly, minimal-impact resilience was found following bereavement (Bonanno et al., 2002; Maccallum et al., 2015), divorce (Malgaroli, Galatzer-Levy, & Bonanno, 2017; Mancini et al., 2011), and job loss (Mancini et al., 2011; Stolove, Galatzer-Levy & Bonanno, 2017). The same trajectory of resilience was observed in the wake of traumatic injury (Bombardier et al., 2016; Bonanno et al., 2012; deRoon-Cassini, Mancini, Rusch, & Bonanno, 2010), life-threatening medical events (Morin et al., 2017), cancer diagnosis (Burton, Galatzer-levy & Bonanno, 2015; Deshields, Tibbs, Fan, & Taylor, 2006; Helgeson, Snyder, & Seltman, 2004; Lam et al., 2010), heart attack (Galatzer-Levy & Bonanno, 2014), and chronic pain (Zhu, Galatzer-Levy, & Bonanno, 2014). Finally, the stable trajectory of low-level symptoms characteristic of minimal-impact resilience has been observed in the presence of exposure to multiple PTEs during the course of police service (Galatzer-Levy, Madan, Neylan, Henn-Haase, & Marmar, 2011), acute health events (Morin et al., 2017), and military deployment or active duty (Andersen et al., 2014; Donoho et al., 2017; Porter et al., 2017).

Although the majority of studies have been conducted with adult populations, minimal-impact resilience is equally relevant and noteworthy in children and adolescents. Recent developmental work has documented trajectories of minimal-impact resilience in youth exposed to acute potential trauma (Hong et al., 2014; La Greca et al., 2013; Le Brocque,

Hendrikz, & Kenardy, 2010). Le Brocque et al. (2010) found that the modal response in a large sample of children hospitalized for traumatic injuries was a stable trajectory of low-level posttraumatic stress, comparable to minimal-impact resilience outcomes observed in adults who experienced traumatic injury (e.g., deRoon-Cassini et al., 2010). In a similar study, Self-Brown and colleagues (2013) collected data on PTSD symptoms in a diverse group of children residing in New Orleans who were exposed to Hurricane Katrina at 3, 13, 19, and 25 months post disaster. Across the sample, the majority of children exhibited the minimal-impact resilience trajectory. One benefit of latent growth modeling is that developmental sequelae can be incorporated and minimal-impact resilience trajectories can be adjusted to reflect trends in developing populations (Feldman, Masyn, & Conger, 2009; Galatzer-Levy & Bonanno, 2013).

To date, the vast majority of prior trajectory research has demonstrated resilient outcomes on the basis of psychological symptom severity and chronicity (e.g., PTSD, depression, anxiety). Although psychological symptoms are foundational in the study of how individuals respond to adversity, resilience, by definition, should extend to other relevant psychological, social, and functional areas as well. Previous studies found that outcome trajectories were nearly identical when comparing indices of different types of psychological symptoms (e.g., Bonanno et al., 2012; deRoon-Cassini et al., 2010; Mancini et al., 2015); however, other aspects of psychological adjustment and functioning have rarely been included.

A few studies have begun to examine whether resilience is evident across multiple domains of psychological and functional adaptation. When multiple outcomes spanning a wider range of areas are assessed, the pattern of resilience holds. For example, a previous study of breast cancer illustrated that women who demonstrated a pattern of minimal-impact resilience also exhibited better psychosocial outcomes on other measures (e.g., social adjustment; Lam et al., 2012). Another study of patients with blood disorders found low rates of psychopathology and intact occupational and social functioning (Almahmoud et al., 2016).

In order to advance this avenue of research, a recent study applied a new robust analytical framework to test whether individuals exhibiting the minimal-impact resilience trajectory in relation to psychological symptoms would maintain healthy psychological adjustment in other key domains

following spinal cord injury, spousal loss, and heart attack (Long, Galatzer-Levy, & Bonanno, in preparation). Across all three PTEs, resilient individuals who displayed stable, low trajectories of psychological symptoms simultaneously demonstrated health and adaptation in other areas that included social functioning, quality of life, health, and cognition.

Predictors of Resilient Outcomes

The fourth temporal element includes predictors of resilient outcomes. A multitude of resilience-promoting factors are purportedly associated with "resilience" and referenced as descriptors or measures of the construct. The relationship between these factors and resilient outcomes tends to be a presumption made on the basis of theory or clinical observation rather than empirical study. A corresponding gap in the literature exists in relation to predictors of resilience in families and communities. However, this issue has been mitigated in the literature on individual resilience by a large body of studies that has consistently and even prospectively linked predictors with resilient outcomes.

Prior systematic reviews have aggregated the empirical evidence for key predictors of resilient outcomes in child (Bonanno & Diminich, 2013; Cicchetti & Rogosch, 2012; Fergus & Zimmerman, 2004; Luthar, 2003; Masten & Narayan, 2012; Werner, 1995), adult (Bonanno, 2004; Bonanno et al., 2011; Reich, Zautra, & Hall, 2010), and aging populations (Ong, Bergeman, & Boker, 2009). Across all literatures, several types of variables are often reliably associated with resilient responses to adversity, yet no single predictor emerges as dominant. Instead, a variety of unique factors appear to exert relatively small effects with each independently explaining a modest amount of the overall variance in resilient outcomes (e.g., Bonanno, Galea et al., 2007; Werner, 1985). Although some of the factors linked to resilient outcomes are reasonably stable such as those related to personality traits, others are likely to vary in concert with shifting life circumstances as well as the waxing and waning of available resources (Hobfoll, 1989, 2002). In this way, predictors of resilience are not inert but rather fluid and likely to change over time.

PREDICTORS OF EMERGENT RESILIENCE
Caregiver–Child Relationships
One important aspect of a child's environment that predicts emergent resilience is related to characteristics of the caregiver–child relationship. Previous work has tied a nurturing parent–child relationship,

a stable living situation, and a consistent and constructive parental disciplinary style to emergent resilient outcomes (Conger & Conger, 1992, 2002; DuMont, Widom, & Czaja, 2007; Masten et al., 1999; Werner, 1993; Wyman et al., 1992). Oftentimes, chronic adversity negatively impacts the relationship between parents and children; therefore, the presence of a supportive relationship with a substitute caregiver, including a grandparent, older sibling, or other adults outside of the immediate family, has also been tied to emergent resilience (Conger & Conger, 2002; Flores, Cicchetti, & Rogosch, 2005; Rutter, 1979; Werner, 1995).

Personal Qualities, Cognitive Skills, and Emotion

Several individual characteristics have been implicated as factors relevant to emergent resilient outcomes. Personal qualities including self-esteem and positive self-image have been associated with resilience in the context of childhood adversity (Cicchetti & Rogosch, 1997; DuMont & Provost, 1999; Flores et al., 2005; Werner, 1995; Wyman et al., 1992). With regard to cognitive skills, higher intelligence (Masten et al., 1999), better-developed readings skills (Werner, 1993), and problem-solving abilities (DuMont & Provost, 1999; Werner, 1995) were related to emergent resilience as well. Patterns of emotion have also been linked to adaptation in the presence of chronic aversive events. In one longitudinal study, early child abuse or neglect was associated with greater emotional lability and negativity, which led to emotion regulation difficulties that subsequently contributed to higher levels of internalizing symptoms during middle childhood (Kim-Spoon, Cicchetti, & Rogosch, 2013). Positive emotions play a role as well and are associated with resilient outcomes in instances of exposure to chronic stress and adversity (Curtis & Chicchetti, 2007; Werner & Smith, 1992).

Flexibility

The ability to flexibly engage in cognitive processes and emotion regulation represents another predictor of emergent resilience (Cicchetti & Rogosch, 1997; Flores et al., 2005). For instance, cognitive flexibility was found to be a long-term buffer in a sample of Palestinian children exposed to potential trauma during and after the First Intifada period beginning in 1987 (Qouta, El-Sarraj, & Punamäki, 2001). Specifically, cognitive flexibility was unrelated to psychological adjustment when traumatic exposure was at its highest level. However, 3 years later, high-exposure children with high cognitive flexibility

evinced better psychological adjustment when compared to high-exposure children with low cognitive flexibility. The construct of flexibility will be discussed further in the section on predictors of minimal-impact resilience.

Genes

Recently, an increasing amount of attention has been devoted to gene-by-environment interactions in the presence of chronic adversity (Nugent et al., 2011). In a landmark study, Caspi et al. (2002) demonstrated that "a functional polymorphism in the promoter of the monoamine oxidase A (MAOA) gene" acted as a moderator of the association between childhood maltreatment and antisocial behavior later in life (p. 851). As relevant to resilient outcomes, prior investigations have demonstrated that genetic variation in the serotonin transporter gene (5-HTTLPR), oxytocin (OXTR) and dopamine (DRD4 -521C/T) receptor genes, and corticotropin releasing hormone receptor gene (CRHR1) moderated the effects of maltreatment in children who displayed emergent resilience (Cicchetti & Rogosch, 2012).

PREDICTORS OF MINIMAL-IMPACT RESILIENCE

Demographics

Demographic variables, including age, gender, and race/ethnicity, have been the subject of frequent study as predictors of resilience.

Previous work has found that younger children who experienced a traumatic injury were less likely to exhibit a minimal-impact resilience trajectory than older children (Le Broque et al., 2010). Relatedly, younger children experienced greater psychology difficulty following exposure to disaster than adults (Norris et al., 2002). At the same time, older age has been linked to adaptation following PTEs. For example, older adults may demonstrate higher levels of distress in the presence of disasters; however, they ultimately experience fewer long-term psychological issues than younger adults (Huerta & Horton, 1978; Kato, Asukai et al., 1996; Knight et al., 2000). Older adults exposed to the 9/11 terrorist attacks were more likely to display the minimal-impact resilience trajectory (Bonanno, Galea et al., 2007). The same pattern was found following spousal loss with older adults experiencing better psychological adjustment (Bonanno & Kaltman, 1999; Mancini et al., 2011) and lower mortality rates than their younger bereaved counterparts (Martikainen & Valkonen, 1996; Stroebe & Stroebe, 1993).

Across child and adult populations, male gender appears to exert a small but consistent effect as a predictor of resilient outcomes (Ahern, Galea et al., 2004; Bonanno, Ho et al., 2008; Bonanno, Galea et al., 2007; Carr et al., 1997; Galea et al.,2008; Hoven, et al., 2005; Vernberg, LaGreca, Silverman, & Prinstein, 1996; Weems et al., 2010).

In contrast, the predictive utility of racial and ethnic variation maintains weak support as a result of limitations stemming from a lack of data, racially or ethnically homogenous samples, or the presence of other confounding variables.

Personality
Given the malleability of personality depending on situational or environmental factors (McCrae et al., 2000) as well as issues of directionality when personality is assessed after the onset of PTEs (Bonanno & Mancini, 2008), prospective studies provide the strongest evidence for personality as a predictor of resilient outcomes. When measured prior to PTE exposure, low negative affectivity (Weems et al., 2007), high trait self-enhancement (Gupta & Bonanno, 2010), and a less ruminative response style (Nolen-Hoeksema & Morrow, 1991) predicted better post-PTE psychological adjustment. Similar findings were observed in relation to pre-event perceived control (Ullman & Newcomb, 1999) and trait resilience (Ong et al., 2010). Several studies have also directly linked personality with the minimal-impact resilience trajectory. In one longitudinal study of traumatic injury, low trait negative affectivity and high trait positive affectivity were each associated with a greater probability of displaying the minimal-impact resilience trajectory (Quale & Schanke, 2010). In another prospective study, optimism measured years prior to the onset of a first heart attack was found to predict a minimal-impact resilience trajectory of consistently low depression symptoms (Galatzer-Levy & Bonanno, 2014).

Exposure
The nature of exposure to potential trauma is often referenced as a central factor in determining responses to acute adversity. Across the life span, a higher degree of proximal exposure has been associated with increased posttraumatic stress (Bonanno, Rennicke, & Dekel, 2005; La Greca, Silverman, Vernberg, & Prinstein, 1996; Nolen-Hoeksema & Morrow, 1991) and reduced rates of the minimal-impact resilience trajectory (Bonanno et al., 2005, 2006; Le Brocque et al., 2010). It is noteworthy, however, that the impact of exposure on the

prevalence of resilience was found to be relatively small. For example, prospective studies of PTSD symptoms measured in soldiers before and after combat deployment have reported a prevalence of minimal-impact resilience in upward of 80% of their samples (Berntsen et al., 2012; Bonanno et al., 2012). When trajectories of PTSD symptoms were examined separately for soldiers with and without significant combat exposure, although minimal-impact resilience was reduced for soldiers with significant combat exposure, rates were still over 80% for this group (Donoho et al., 2017).

Past and Present Stress
Prior research that examined prior exposure to potential trauma and present life stress in relation to post-PTE psychological adjustment has offered varying accounts depending on methodology. Among the studies that employed retrospective measures, both past and present stress were associated with greater risk for PTSD (Brewin et al., 2000) and lower odds of exhibiting the minimal-impact resilience trajectory following PTEs (Bonanno, Galea et al., 2007). However, research involving prospective data indicated that prior experiences of potential trauma functioned as predictors of psychological adjustment upon subsequent exposure only in instances when the PTE had led to the development of PTSD (Breslau, Peterson, & Schultz, 2008). Though it may be tempting to infer the converse, it remains unclear whether individuals who display minimal-impact resilience following previous exposure to potential trauma would be more likely to display this trajectory when encountering future PTEs.

Economic Resources
Despite several studies that tie economic resources to post-PTE psychological adjustment, this association has not been identified in relation to trajectories of resilience (Bonanno, Rennicke, & Dekel, 2005; Bonanno, Galea et al., 2007). Critically, the loss of resources is part and parcel of distal exposure (i.e., stressors or consequences occurring after a PTE has occurred). Previous studies have illustrated that enduring the loss of income, livelihood, or personal property increased rates of PTSD and decreased the probability that individuals would demonstrate minimal-impact resilience following natural disasters (Neria, Nandi, & Galea, 2008; van Griensven et al., 2006), terrorist attacks (Bonanno, Galea et al., 2007), and other life events (Mancini et al., 2011).

Social Support

Social support is frequently cast as a protective factor following exposure to loss and potential trauma; however, the findings in the extant literature remain mixed. On one hand, several studies have reported evidence of a relationship between the presence of social support and better post-PTE psychological adjustment (Brewin et al., 2000; Kaniasty & Norris, 2009; La Greca et al., 1996). Similarly, social resources were identified as a predictor of minimal-impact resilience outcomes following disasters (Bonanno, Galea et al., 2007; Bonanno, Ho et al., 2008). On the other hand, prospective bereavement research found that social support did not appear to buffer against loss-related stress; instead, instrumental support from family and friends predicted minimal-impact resilience (Bonanno, Wortman et al., 2002). Interestingly, a recent longitudinal study of perceived social support and PTSD symptoms in traumatic injury patients found an association between PTSD symptom severity and increased negative social support over a 6-year period; however, these perceptions of social support were not related to changes in PTSD symptoms over time (Nickerson et al., 2017).

Positive Emotion

An appreciable number of studies have illustrated that the benefits of positive emotion (Lyubomirsky, King, & Diener, 2005; Seligman & Csikszentmihalyi, 2000) appear to be most pronounced in the context of potential trauma and extreme adversity (Bonanno, 2004, 2005; Moskowitz, Folkman, & Acree, 2003; Ong, Bergeman, & Chow, 2010). One line of evidence comes from prior research on positive emotion and psychological adaptation following 9/11. Papa and Bonanno (2008) found that college students who were exposed to a sadness induction and went on to express genuine smiles during a monologue about their life after the terrorist attacks experienced better psychological adjustment 2 years later. In another study of remote reactions to 9/11, self-reported positive emotions mediated the relationships between pre-event ego resilience and post-event depression among a sample of college students (Fredrickson, Tugade, Waugh, & Larkin, 2003). As a complement to the unique association between trait self-enhancement and the minimal-impact resilience trajectory, self-enhancers were more likely to have experienced positive emotion when discussing the 9/11 attacks (Bonanno et al., 2005). The salutary effects of positive emotions were identified in bereaved individuals as well

(Bonanno & Keltner, 1997). One representative example comes from a prospective bereavement study in which positive emotions mediated the relationship between spousal loss and alterations in diurnal cortisol response (Ong, Fuller-Rowell, Bonanno, & Almeida, 2011). Lastly, recent work on trait emotion found that a greater disposition toward the experience of positive emotions functioned as a prospective buffer of post-PTE distress with the protective effect becoming increasingly robust at the highest levels of exposure (Long & Bonanno, 2017).

Appraisal

Another pertinent predictor is the way that individuals appraise or interpret a highly aversive event (Lazarus & Folkman, 1984), and appraisal models of resilience have become the subject of renewed interest (Kalisch, Müller, & Tüscher, 2015; Mancini & Bonanno, 2009; Troy & Mauss, 2011). By way of example, a given PTE may be appraised as threatening or harmful (i.e., a threat appraisal) or as an opportunity for growth or mastery (i.e., a challenge appraisal; Ferguson, Mathews, & Cox, 1999). Longitudinal studies of spinal cord injury found that patients who made threat appraisals experienced higher anxiety over time (Kennedy, Lude, Efström, & Smithson, 2011). In contrast, spinal cord injury patients who interpreted their injury as a challenge to be met rather than exclusively as a threat demonstrated lower levels of depression. As an extension of these findings, spinal cord injury patients who exhibited the minimal-impact resilience trajectory were also found to have made more challenge appraisals and fewer threat appraisals (Bonanno, Kennedy, et al., 2012).

Flexibility

A growing line of research has begun to emphasize flexibility in self-regulation (Bonanno, 2005; Cheng, 2001; Kashdan & Rottenberg, 2010) in relation to stress and adversity. The concept of regulatory flexibility (Bonanno & Burton, 2013) refers to an individual's ability to adequately assess situational demands, employ many different behaviors or strategies, and make adjustments to optimize self-regulation in accordance with the changing characteristics and features of aversive circumstances.

Coping is one area where the importance of flexibility has routinely emerged. The success of coping efforts is thought to be less a function of a strategy's proscribed adaptiveness, and more a product of whether the coping strategy is the best fit given the nature of a situation (Aspinwall & Taylor, 1997;

Block, 1993; Lazarus & Folkman, 1984). In a sample of Israeli college students, low coping flexibility was associated with higher posttraumatic stress at high levels of exposure to terrorist attacks, whereas high coping flexibility corresponded to relatively minimal changes in posttraumatic stress across levels of exposure (Bonanno et al., 2011). By the same token, a study of PTEs in American college students found that individuals exhibiting the minimal-impact resilience trajectory were more likely to use coping strategies focused on maintaining normal goals and plans rather than strategies centered on the potential trauma (Galatzer-Levy et al., 2012).

Flexibility in processes related to emotion regulation is another notable predictor of resilient outcomes (Bonanno, 2001; Consedine, Magai, & Bonanno, 2002; Gross, 1999; Gupta & Bonanno, 2011). In a sample of New York City undergraduates who had begun college just prior to the 9/11 terrorist attacks, expressive flexibility or the ability to both up-regulate (i.e., enhance) and down-regulate (i.e., suppress) emotional facial expressions based on situational demands predicted lower psychological distress 2 years later (Bonanno et al., 2004). Follow-up studies of this sample over extended periods of time found that expressive flexibility was similarly associated with a trajectory of stable, low distress (Burton, Galatzer-Levy, & Bonanno, 2012) as well as ratings of health and well-being made by the participants' close friends (Westphal, Seivert, & Bonanno, 2010). Among the many facets of regulatory flexibility, choice flexibility defined as the ability to select strategies based on context has also emerged as a promising factor. In a sample of firefighters exposed to PTEs in the line of duty, individuals low in regulatory choice flexibility experienced greater PTSD symptoms as PTE exposure increased as compared to those high in choice flexibility (Levy-Gigi et al., 2015). In sum, prior research highlights the notion that it is not solely whether emotion regulation is successful that predicts resilient outcomes but also whether individuals are able to apply and adjust these strategies flexibly.

Genes

Research on the relationship between genetic variation and resilient outcomes in the presence of acute adversity is nascent. Presently, our lab is working on a new area of research examining single-nucleotide polymorphisms in individuals who demonstrate the minimal-impact resilience trajectory following PTEs and whether genetic variation differentiates resilience from other response trajectories.

Implications and Conclusions

Over the past several decades, psychological resilience in the face of loss, trauma, and other forms of extreme adversity has continued to gain increasing prominence. Amid an ever-expanding set of definitions and conceptualizations, we described a unified framework that operationalizes resilience as an integrative and dynamic process consisting of four temporal elements: baseline or preadversity adjustment, aversive circumstances, postadversity resilient outcomes, and predictors of resilient outcomes (Bonanno et al., 2015). The temporal framework synthesizes the extant literature and establishes the existence of a robust body of support for each element of resilience as it simultaneously highlights future directions for new research on psychological resilience.

The growing momentum behind this new research direction argues for a subtle but important shift in perspective. Historically, the traditional understanding of potential trauma has focused primarily on extreme reactions and categorical mental disorders, most commonly PTSD. The notion that trauma is synonymous with PTSD took root within psychology and psychiatry and their related disciplines as well as in the minds of the broader public. The equation of potential trauma with PTSD became so engrained that as research began to illustrate that most people exposed to PTEs did not develop PTSD or other forms of psychopathology, the evidence was simply assimilated into the existing model. In other words, the focus on psychopathology was transformed into a focus on psychopathology versus resilience. Despite the integration of the term "resilience," this binary distinction between psychopathology and resilience is no different from the traditional psychopathology approach. Indeed, describing resilience as the absence of a disorder is analogous to defining health as the absence of disease (Almedom & Glandon, 2007), which ultimately does little to advance our understanding of the true variation in responses to potential trauma or the nature of genuinely resilient outcomes.

As our work and the research of many others have shown, the resilient trajectory is only one of several possible outcomes following PTEs. Prior work has, nonetheless, converged on the reliable and replicable finding that resilience is the modal and most common response to potential trauma. Together, the evidence indicates that most individuals faced with extreme adversity will persevere and continue to go about their lives more or less as they had before the onset of potential trauma. The robustness of this finding suggests then that rather than trying to understand psychopathology in isolation, as the field has done for decades, we should focus instead on understanding resilience. If resilience is the norm, then we must ask how or why it occurs with such frequency. Thus, the central question shifts to defining and elucidating the mechanisms that underlie resilience.

A common objection to this shift in emphasis is that it ignores those most in need. Critically, the movement of theory and research toward resilience does not ignore psychopathology; rather, it serves to illuminate it. In order to fully understand PTSD and other patterns of dysfunction, we must first understand natural resilience. It is only then that we might consider how resilience breaks down, which is likely to involve complex processes and interactions at genetic, biological, and psychological levels. By gaining a greater understanding of psychological resilience and the deviating pathways that lead to maladjustment and functional difficulties, we will be far better equipped to develop targeted interventions capable of short-circuiting these patterns and minimizing suffering in the aftermath of potential trauma.

References

Ahern, J., Galea, S., Resnick, H., & Vlahov, D. (2004). Television images and probable posttraumatic stress disorder after September 11: The role of background characteristics, event exposures, and perievent panic. *Journal of Nervous and Mental Disease, 192*, 217–226.

Aldrich, D. P. (2012). *Building resilience: Social capital in post-disaster recovery.* Chicago, IL: University of Chicago Press.

Almahmoud, S. Y., Coifman, K. G., Ross, G. S., Kleinert, D., & Giardina, P. (2016). Evidence for multidimensional resilience in adult patients with transfusion-dependent thalassemias: Is it more common than we think? *Transfusion Medicine, 26*(3), 186–194.

Almedom, A. M., & Glandon, D. (2007). Resilience is not the absence of PTSD any more than health is the absence of disease. *Journal of Loss and Trauma, 12*(2), 127–143.

Andersen, S. B., Karstoft, K.-I., Bertelsen, M., & Madsen, T. (2014). Latent trajectories of trauma symptoms and resilience: The 3-year longitudinal prospective USPER study of Danish veterans deployed in Afghanistan. *The Journal of Clinical Psychiatry, 75*(9), 1001–1008.

Aspinwall, L. G., & Taylor, S. E. (1997). A stitch in time: Self-regulation and proactive coping. *Psychological Bulletin, 121*, 417–436.

Berntsen, D., Johannessen, K. B., Thomsen, Y. D., Bertelsen, M., Hoyle, R. H., & Rubin, D. C. (2012). Peace and war: Trajectories of posttraumatic stress disorder symptoms before, during, and after military deployment in Afghanistan. *Psychological Science, 23*, 1557–1565. doi:10.1177/0956797612457389

Betancourt, T. S., & Khan, K. T. (2008). The mental health of children affected by armed conflict: Protective processes and pathways to resilience. *International Review of Psychiatry, 20*(3), 317–328. doi:10.1080/09540260802090363

Betancourt, T. S., McBain, R., Newnham, E. A., & Brennan, R. T. (2013). Trajectories of internalizing problems in war-affected Sierra Leonean youth: Examining conflict and postconflict factors. *Child Development, 84*(2), 455–470.

Bisconti, T. L., Bergeman, C. S., & Boker, S. M. (2004). Emotional well-being in recently bereaved widows: A dynamical systems approach. *Journals of Gerontology: Series B: Psychological Sciences & Social Sciences, 59B*(4), P158–P167.

Block, J. (1993). Studying personality the long way. In D. C. Funder, R. D. Parke, C. Tomlinson-Keasey, & K. Widaman (Eds.), *Studying lives through time: Personality and development* (pp. 9–41). Washington, DC: American Psychological Association.

Bloembergen, N., & Zewail, A. H. (1984). Energy redistribution in isolated molecules and the question of mode-selective laser chemistry revisited. New experiments on the dynamics of collisionless energy redistribution in molecules possibilities for laser-selective chemistry with subpicosecond pu. *The Journal of Physical Chemistry, 88*(23), 5459–5465. doi:10.1021/j150667a004

Boelen, P. A., de Keijser, J., van den Hout, M. A., & van den Bout, J. (2007). Treatment of complicated grief: A comparison between cognitive-behavioral therapy and supportive Counseling. *Journal of Consulting and Clinical Psychology, 75*(2), 277–284.

Bombardier, C. H., Hoekstra, T., Dikmen, S., & Fann, J. R. (2016). Depression trajectories during the first year after traumatic brain injury. *Journal of Neurotrauma, 33*(23), 2115–2124.

Bonanno, G. A. (2001). The self-regulation of emotion. In T. J. Mayne & G. A. Bonanno (Eds.), *Emotions: Current issues and future directions* (pp. 251–285). New York, NY: Guilford Press.

Bonanno, G. A. (2004). Loss, trauma, and human resilience: Have we underestimated the human capacity to thrive after extremely aversive events? *American Psychologist, 59*(1), 20–28.

Bonanno, G. A. (2005). Resilience in the face of loss and potential trauma. *Current Directions in Psychological Science, 14*(3), 135–138.

Bonanno, G. A., Brewin, C. R., Kaniasty, K., & La Greca, A. M. (2010). Weighing the costs of disaster: Consequences, risks, and resilience in individuals, families, and communities. *Psychological Science in the Public Interest, 11*(1), 1–49.

Bonanno, G. A., & Burton, C. L. (2013). Regulatory flexibility: An individual differences perspective on coping and emotion regulation. *Perspectives on Psychological Science, 8*(6), 591–612. doi:10.1177/1745691613504116

Bonanno, G. A., & Diminich, E. D. (2013). Annual research review: Positive adjustment to adversity–Trajectories of minimal–impact resilience and emergent resilience. *Journal of Child Psychology and Psychiatry, 54*(4), 378–3401.

Bonanno, G. A., Galea, S., Bucciarelli, A., & Vlahov, D. (2006). Psychological resilience after disaster: New York City in the aftermath of the September 11th terrorist attack. *Psychological Science, 17*(3), 181–186. doi:10.1111/j.1467–9280.2006.01682.x

Bonanno, G. A., Galea, S., Bucciarelli, A., & Vlahov, D. (2007). What predicts psychological resilience after disaster? The role of demographics, resources, and life stress. *Journal of Consulting and Clinical Psychology, 75*(5), 671–682.

Bonanno, G. A., Ho, S. A. Y., Chan, J. C. K., Kwong, R. S. Y., Cheung, C. K. Y., Wong, C. P. Y., & Wong, V. C. W. (2008).

Psychological resilience and dysfunction among hospitalized survivors of the SARS epidemic in Hong Kong: A latent class approach. *Health Psychology*, *27*(5), 659–667. doi:10.1037/0278-6133.27.5.659

Bonanno, G. A., & Kaltman, S. (1999). Toward an integrative perspective on bereavement. *Psychological Bulletin*, *125*, 760–776.

Bonanno, G. A., Keltner, D., Holen, A., & Horowitz, M. J. (1995). When avoiding unpleasant emotions might not be such a bad thing: Verbal-autonomic response dissociation and midlife conjugal bereavement. *Journal of Personality & Social Psychology*, *69*(5), 975–989.

Bonanno, G. A., Kennedy, P., Galatzer-Levy, I. R., Lude, P., & Elfström, M. L. (2012). Trajectories of resilience, depression, and anxiety following spinal cord injury. *Rehabilitation Psychology*, *57*(3), 236.

Bonanno, G.A., & Mancini, A.D. (2008). The human capacity to thrive in the face of potential trauma. *Pediatrics*, *121*, 369–375.

Bonanno, G. A, Mancini, A. D., Horton, J. L., Powell, T. M., LeardMann, C. A., Boyko, E. J., ... Smith, T. C. (2012). Trajectories of trauma symptoms and resilience in deployed US military service members: prospective cohort study. *The British Journal of Psychiatry*, *200*(4), 317–323. doi:10.1192/bjp.bp.111.096552

Bonanno, G. A., Neria, Y., Mancini, A., Coifman, K. G., Litz, B., & Insel, B. (2007). Is there more to complicated grief than depression and posttraumatic stress disorder? A test of incremental validity. *Journal of Abnormal Psychology*, *116*(2), 342–351.

Bonanno, G. A., Papa, A., & O'Neill, K. (2001). Loss and human resilience. *Applied and Preventive Psychology*, *10*, 193–206.

Bonanno, G. A., Rennicke, C., & Dekel, S. (2005). Self-enhancement among high-exposure survivors of the September 11th terrorist attack: Resilience or social maladjustment? *Journal of Personality and Social Psychology*, *88*(6), 984–998.

Bonanno, G. A., Romero, S. A., & Klein, S. I. (2015). The temporal elements of psychological resilience: An integrative framework for the study of individuals, families, and communities. *Psychological Inquiry*, *26*(2), 139–169.

Bonanno, G. A., Westphal, M., & Mancini, A. D. (2011). Resilience to loss and potential trauma. *Annual Review of Clinical Psychology*, *7*, 511–535. doi:10.1146/annurev-clinpsy-032210-104526

Bonanno, G. A., Wortman, C. B., Lehman, D. R., Tweed, R. G., Haring, M., Sonnega, J.... (2002). Resilience to loss and chronic grief: A prospective study from preloss to 18-months postloss. *Journal of Personality & Social Psychology*, *83*(5), 1150–1164.

Bonanno, G. A., & Keltner, D. (1997). Facial expressions of emotion and the course of conjugal bereavement. *Journal of Abnormal Psychology*, *106*(1), 126.

Breslau, N. (2001). Outcomes of posttraumatic stress disorder. *Journal of Clinical Psychiatry*, *62*, 55–59.

Breslau, N. (2009). The epidemiology of trauma, PTSD, and other posttrauma disorders. *Trauma, Violence, & Abuse*, *10*(3), 198–210.

Breslau, N., Peterson, E. L., & Schultz, L. R. (2008). A second look at prior trauma and the posttraumatic stress disorder effects of subsequent trauma: A prospective epidemiological study. *Archives of General Psychiatry*, *65*, 431–437.

Brewin, C. R., Andrews, B., & Valentine, J. D. (2000). Meta-analysis of risk factors for posttraumatic stress disorder in trauma-exposed adults. *Journal of Consulting and Clinical Psychology*, *68*, 748–766.

Burton, C. L., Galatzer-Levy, I., & Bonanno, G. A. (2012). Expressive flexibility and long-term adjustment: A prospective study. Unpublished manuscript.

Burton, C. L., Galatzer-Levy, I. R., & Bonanno, G. A. (2015). Treatment type and demographic characteristics as predictors for cancer adjustment: Prospective trajectories of depressive symptoms in a population sample. *Health Psychology*, *34*(6), 602.

Carr, V.J., Lewin, T.J., Webster, R.A., Kenardy, J.A., Hazell, P.L., & Carter, G.L. (1997). Psychosocial sequelae of the 1989 Newcastle earthquake: II. Exposure and morbidity profiles during the first 2 years post-disaster. *Psychological Medicine*, *27*, 167–178.

Carver, C. S. (1998). Resilience and thriving: Issues, models, and linkages. *Journal of Social Issues*, *54*(2), 245–266.

Caspi, A., McClay, J., Moffitt, T. E., Mill, J., Martin, J., Craig, I. W., ... Poulton, R. (2002). Role of genotype in the cycle of violence in maltreated children. *Science*, *297*(5582), 851–854.

Cheng, C. (2001). Assessing coping flexibility in real-life and laboratory settings: A multimethod approach. *Journal of Personality and Social Psychology*, *80*, 814–833.

Cicchetti, D., & Curtis, W. J. (2007). Multilevel perspectives on pathways to resilient functioning. *Development and Psychopathology*, *19*(3), 627–629.

Cicchetti, D., & Rogosch, F. A. (1997). The role of self-organization in the promotion of resilience in maltreated children. *Development and Psychopathology*, *9*(4), 797–815.

Cicchetti, D., & Rogosch, F. A. (2012). Gene by environment interaction and resilience: Effects of child maltreatment and serotonin, corticotropin releasing hormone, dopamine, and oxytocin genes. *Development and Psychopathology*, *24*(2), 411.

Conger, R. D., & Conger, K. J. (1992). A family process model of economic hardship and adjustment of early adolescent boys. *Child Development*, *63*(3), 526.

Conger, R. D., & Conger, K. J. (2002). Resilience in Midwestern families: Selected findings from the first decade of a prospective, longitudinal study. *Journal of Marriage and Family*, *64*(2), 361–373. doi:10.1111/j.1741-3737.2002.00361.x

Consedine, N. S., Magai, C., & Bonanno, G. A. (2002). Moderators of the emotion inhibition-health relationship: A review and research agenda. *Review of General Psychology*, *6*, 204–228.

Copeland, W. E., Keeler, G., Angold, A., & Costello, E. J. (2007). Traumatic events and posttraumatic stress in childhood. *Archives of General Psychiatry*, *64*(5), 577–584.

Currier, J. M., Neimeyer, R. A., & Berman, J. S. (2008). The effectiveness of psychotherapeutic interventions for bereaved persons: A comprehensive quantitative review. *Psychological Bulletin*, *134*(5), 648–661.

Cutter, S. L., Barnes, L., Berry, M., Burton, C., Evans, E., Tate, E., & Webb, J. (2008). A place-based model for understanding community resilience to natural disasters. *Global Environmental Change*, *18*(4), 598–606.

De Kloet, E. R., Derijk, R. H., & Meijer, O. C. (2011). Corticosteroid receptor involvement in the stress response. In *The Handbook of Stress* (pp. 47–75). Malden, MA: Wiley-Blackwell.

DeRoon-Cassini, T. A., Mancini, A. D., Bonanno, G. A., & Rusch, M. D. (2010). Psychopathology and resilience following traumatic injury: A latent growth mixture model analysis. *Rehabilitation Psychology, 55*(1), 1–11.

Deshields, T., Tibbs, T., Fan, M. Y., & Taylor, M. (2006). Differences in patterns of depression after treatment for breast cancer. *Psycho-oncology, 15*(5), 398–406.

DiRago, A., & Vaillant, G. (2007). Resilience in inner city youth: Childhood predictors of occupational status across the lifespan. *Journal of Youth and Adolescence, 36*(1), 61–70.

Donoho, C. J., Bonanno, G. A., Porter, B., Kearney, L., & Powell, T. M. (2017). A decade of war: Prospective trajectories of post-traumatic stress disorder symptoms among deployed US military personnel and the influence of combat exposure. *American Journal of Epidemiology, 186*(12), 1310–1318.

Dumont, M., & Provost, M. A. (1999). Resilience in adolescents: Protective role of social support, coping strategies, self-esteem, and social activities on experience of stress and depression. *Journal of Youth and Adolescence, 28*(3), 343–363.

DuMont, K. A., Widom, C. S., & Czaja, S. J. (2007). Predictors of resilience in abused and neglected children grown-up: The role of individual and neighborhood characteristics. *Child Abuse & Neglect, 31*(3), 255–274.

Duncan, T. E., Duncan, S. C., & Strycker, L. A. (2006). *An introduction to latent variable growth curve modeling: Concepts, issues, and applications.* Quantitative methodology series (2nd ed., xii–261). Mahwah, NJ: Lawrence Erlbaum.

Egeland, B., Carlson, E., & Sroufe, L. A. (1993). Resilience as process. *Development and Psychopathology, 5*, 517.

Elder, G. H. (1998). The life course as developmental theory. *Child Development, 69*(1), 1–12. doi:10.1111/j.1467–8624.1998.tb06128.x

Feldman, B. J., Masyn, K. E., & Conger, R. D. (2009). New approaches to studying problem behaviors: A comparison of methods for modeling longitudinal, categorical adolescent drinking data. *Developmental Psychology, 45*(3), 652–676. doi:10.1037/a0014851

Fergus, S., & Zimmerman, M. A. (2004). Adolescent resilience: A framework for understanding healthy development in the face of risk. *Annual Review of Public Health, 26*, 399–419.

Ferguson, E., Matthews, G., & Cox, T. (1999). The Appraisal of Life Events (ALE) scale: Reliability and validity. *British Journal of Health Psychology, 4*, 97–116.

Flores, E., Cicchetti, D., & Rogosch, F. A. (2005). Predictors of resilience in maltreated and nonmaltreated Latino children. *Developmental Psychology, 41*(2), 338–351.

Foa, E. B., & Kozak, M. J. (1986). Emotional processing of fear: Exposure to corrective information. *Psychological Bulletin, 99*(1), 20–35. doi:10.1037/0033-2909.99.1.20

Foa, E. B., Rothbaum, B. O., Riggs, D. S., & Murdock, T. B. (1991). Treatment of posttraumatic stress disorder in rape victims: A comparison between cognitive-behavioral procedures and counseling. *Journal of Consulting and Clinical Psychology, 59*(5), 715–723. doi:10.1037/0022-006X.59.5.715

Fredrickson, B. L., Tugade, M. M., Waugh, C. E., & Larkin, G. R. (2003). What good are positive emotions in crisis? A prospective study of resilience and emotions following the terrorist attacks on the United States on September 11th, 2001. *Journal of Personality and Social Psychology, 84*(2), 365.

Galatzer-Levy, I. R., & Bonanno, G. A. (2012). Beyond normality in the study of bereavement: Heterogeneity in depression outcomes following loss in older adults. *Social Science & Medicine, 74*(12), 1987–1994. doi:10.1016/j.socscimed.2012.02.022

Galatzer-Levy, I. R., & Bonanno, G. A. (2013). Heterogeneous patterns of stress over the four years of college: Associations with anxious attachment and ego-resiliency. *Journal of Personality, 81*(5), 476–486. doi:10.1111/jopy.12010

Galatzer-Levy, I. R., & Bonanno, G. A. (2014). Optimism and death: Predicting the courses and consequences of depression trajectories in response to acute coronary syndrome. *Psychological Science, 25*(12), 2177–2188.

Galatzer-Levy, I. R., Brown, A. D., Henn-Haase, C., Metzler, T. J., Neylan, T. C., & Marmar, C. R. (2013). Positive and negative emotion prospectively predict trajectories of resilience and distress among high-exposure police officers. *Emotion, 13*(3), 545.

Galatzer-Levy, I. R., & Bryant, R. A. (2013). 636,120 ways to have posttraumatic stress disorder. *Perspectives on Psychological Science, 8*(6), 651–662.

Galatzer-Levy, I. R., Burton, C. L., & Bonanno, G. A. (2012). Coping flexibility, potentially traumatic life events, and resilience: A prospective study of college student adjustment. *Journal of Social & Clinical Psychology, 31*, 542–567.

Galatzer-Levy, I. R., Madan, A., Neylan, T. C., Henn-Haase, C., & Marmar, C. R. (2011). Peritraumatic and trait dissociation differentiate police officers with resilient versus symptomatic trajectories of posttraumatic stress symptoms. *Journal of Traumatic Stress, 24*(5), 557–565.

Galea, S., Ahern, J., Resnick, H., Kilpatrick, D., Bucuvalas, M., Gold, J., & Vlahov, D. (2002). Psychological sequelae of the September 11 terrorist attacks in New York City. *New England Journal of Medicine, 346*(13), 982–987.

Galea, S., Tracy, M., Norris, F., & Coffey, S.F. (2008). Financial and social circumstances and the incidence and course of PTSD in Mississippi during the first two years after Hurricane Katrina. *Journal of Traumatic Stress, 21*, 357–368.

Galea, S., Brewin, C. R., Gruber, M., Jones, R. T., King, D. W., King, L. A., . . . Kessler, R. C. (2007). Exposure to hurricane related stressors and mental illness after Hurricane Katrina. *Archives of General Psychiatry, 64*, 1427–1434.

Garmezy, N. (1972). Invulnerable children: The fact and fiction of competence and disadvantage. *American Journal of Orthopsychiatry, 42*, 328.

Garmezy, N. (1993). Children in poverty: Resilience despite risk. *Psychiatry, 56*, 127–136.

Gralinski-Bakker, J. H., Hauser, S. T., Stott, C., Billings, R. L., & Allen, J. P. (2004). Markers of resilience and risk: Adult lives in a vulnerable population. *Research in Human Development, 1*(4), 291–326. doi:10.1207/s15427617rhd0104_4

Gross, J. J. (1999). Emotion regulation: Past, present, future. *Cognition & Emotion, 13*, 551–573.

Gupta, S., & Bonanno, G. A. (2010). Trait self-enhancement as a buffer against potentially traumatic events: A prospective study. *Psychological Trauma: Theory, Research, Practice, and Policy, 2*, 83–92.

Gupta, S., & Bonanno, G. A. (2011). Complicated grief and deficits in emotional expressive flexibility. *Journal of Abnormal Psychology, 120*, 635–643.

Hawley, D. R., & DeHaan, L. (1996). Toward a definition of family resilience: Integrating Life-Span and Family Perspectives. *Family Process, 35*(3), 283–298.

Helgeson, V. S., Snyder, P., & Seltman, H. (2004). Psychological and physical adjustment to breast cancer over 4 years: Identifying distinct trajectories of change. *Health Psychology, 23*(1), 3–15. doi:10.1037/0278-6133.23.1.3

Hobfoll, S. E. (1989). Conservation of resources: A new attempt at conceptualizing stress. *American Psychologist, 44*(3), 513–524.

Hobfoll, S. E. (2002). Social and psychological resources and adaptation. *Review of General Psychology, 6*(4), 307–324.

Hobfoll, S. E., Mancini, A. D., Hall, B. J., Canetti, D., & Bonanno, G. A. (2011). The limits of resilience: Distress following chronic political violence among Palestinians. *Social Science & Medicine, 72*(8), 1400–1408.

Holling, C. S. (1973). Resilience and stability of ecological systems. *Annual Review of Ecology and Systematics, 4*(1), 1–23.

Hong, S.-B., Youssef, G. J., Song, S.-H., Choi, N.-H., Ryu, J., McDermott, B.,... Kim, B.-N. (2014). Different clinical courses of children exposed to a single incident of psychological trauma: a 30-month prospective follow-up study. *Journal of Child Psychology and Psychiatry, 5*(11), 1226–1233. doi:10.1111/jcpp.12241

Horowitz, M. J., Siegel, B., Holen, A., Bonanno, G. A., Milbrath, C., & Stinson, C. H. (1997). Diagnostic criteria for complicated grief disorder. *American Journal of Psychiatry, 154*(7), 904–910.

Hoven, C. W., Duarte, C. S., Lucas, C. P., Wu, P., Mandell, D. J., Goodwin, R. D.,... Susser, E. (2005). Psychopathology among New York City public school children 6 months after September 11. *Archives of General Psychiatry, 62*, 545–552.

Huerta, F., & Horton, R. (1978). Coping behavior of elderly flood victims. *The Gerontologist, 18*(6), 541–546.

Johannsen, W. L. (1903). Concerning heredity in populations and in pure lines. *Trad. Harold Gall Y Elga Putschar. En: Selected Readings in Biology for Natural Sciences, 3*, 172–215.

Johnson, H., & Thompson, A. (2008). The development and maintenance of post-traumatic stress disorder (PTSD) in civilian adult survivors of war trauma and torture: A review. *Clinical Psychology Review, 28*(1), 36–47. doi:http://dx.doi.org/10.1016/j.cpr.2007.01.017

Jones, E. (2006). Historical approaches to post-combat disorders. *Philosophical Transactions of the Royal Society B: Biological Sciences, 361* (1468), 533–542. doi:10.1098/rstb.2006.1814

Jones, E., Vermaas, R. H., McCartney, H., Beech, C., Palmer, I., Hyams, K., & Wessely, S. (2003). Flashbacks and post-traumatic stress disorder: The genesis of a 20th-century diagnosis. *The British Journal of Psychiatry, 182*(2), 158–163. doi:10.1192/bjp.02.231

Jones, E., & Wessely, S. (2005). *Shell shock to PTSD: Military psychiatry from 1900 to the Gulf War*. East Sussex, UK: Psychology Press.

Kalisch, R., Müller, M. B., & Tüscher, O. (2015). A conceptual framework for the neurobiological study of resilience. *Behavioral and Brain Sciences, 38*, E92.

Kaniasty, K., & Norris, G. H. (2009). Distinctions that matter: Received social support, perceived social support, and social embeddedness after disasters. In Y. Neria, S. Galea, & F. N. Norris, (Eds.), *Mental health and disasters* (pp. 175–200). New York, NY: Cambridge University Press.

Kashdan, T. B., & Rottenberg, J. (2010). Psychological flexibility as a fundamental aspect of health. *Clinical Psychology Review, 30*, 865–878.

Kato, H., Asukai, N., Miyake, Y., Minakawa, K., & Nishiyama, A. (1996). Post-traumatic symptoms among younger and elderly evacuees in the early stages following the 1995 Hanshin-Awaji earthquake in Japan. *Acta Psychiatrica Scandinavica, 93*, 477–481.

Kawachi, I. (1999). Social capital and community effects on population and individual health. *Annals of the New York Academy of Sciences, 896*(1), 120–130.

Kennedy, P., Lude, P., Elfstrom, M. L., & Smithson, E. F. (2011). Psychological contributions to functional independence: A longitudinal investigation of spinal cord injury rehabilitation. *Archives of Physical Medicine and Rehabilitation, 92*, 597–602.

Kim-Spoon, J., Cicchetti, D., & Rogosch, F. A. (2013). A longitudinal study of emotion regulation, emotion lability-negativity, and internalizing symptomatology in maltreated and nonmaltreated children. *Child Development, 84*(2), 512–527.

Knight, B. G., Gatz, M., Heller, K., & Bengtson, V. L. (2000). Age and emotional response to the Northridge earthquake: A longitudinal analysis. *Psychology and Aging, 15*, 627–634.

Krystal, J. H., & Neumeister, A. (2009). Noradrenergic and serotonergic mechanisms in the neurobiology of posttraumatic stress disorder and resilience. *Brain Research, 1293*, 13–23. doi:http://dx.doi.org/10.1016/j.brainres.2009.03.044

Lazarus, R. S., & Folkman, S. (1984). *Stress, appraisal, and coping*. New York: Springer.

La Greca, A. M., Lai, B. S., Llabre, M. M., Silverman, W. K., Vernberg, E. M., & Prinstein, M. J. (2013). Children's postdisaster trajectories of PTS symptoms: Predicting chronic distress. In *Child & Youth Care Forum* (pp. 1–19). New York, NY: Springer.

LaGreca, A., Silverman, W., Vernberg, E., & Prinstein, M. J. (1996). Symptoms of posttraumatic stress in children after Hurricane Andrew. A prospective study. *Journal of Consulting and Clinical Psychology, 64*, 712–723.

Lam, W. W., Shing, Y. T., Bonanno, G. A., Mancini, A. D., & Fielding, R. (2012). Distress trajectories at the first year diagnosis of breast cancer in relation to 6 years survivorship. *Psycho-Oncology, 21*(1), 90–99.

Lam, W. W. T., Bonanno, G. A., Mancini, A. D., Ho, S., Chan, M., Hung, W. K.,... Fielding, R. (2010). Trajectories of psychological distress among Chinese women diagnosed with breast cancer. *Psycho-Oncology, 19*(10), 1044–1051. doi:10.1002/pon.1658

Lamprecht, F., & Sack, M. (2002). Posttraumatic stress disorder revisited. *Psychosomatic Medicine, 64*(2), 222–237.

Le Brocque, R. M., Hendrikz, J., & Kenardy, J. A. (2010). The course of posttraumatic stress in children: Examination of recovery trajectories following traumatic injury. *Journal of Pediatric Psychology, 35*(6), 637–645. doi:10.1093/jpepsy/jsp050

Levy-Gigi, E., Bonanno, G. A., Shapiro, A. R., Richter-Levin, G., Kéri, S., & Sheppes, G. (2015). Emotion regulatory flexibility sheds light on the elusive relationship between repeated traumatic exposure and posttraumatic stress disorder symptoms. *Clinical Psychological Science, 4*(1), 28–39.

Long, K., & Bonanno, G. A. (2017). Trait emotion predicts psychological distress following potentially traumatic events: A prospective study. Unpublished manuscript.

Lupien, S. J., McEwen, B. S., Gunnar, M. R., & Heim, C. (2009). Effects of stress throughout the lifespan on the brain, behaviour and cognition. *Nature Reviews Neuroscience, 10*(6), 434–445.

Luthar, S. S. (1999). *Poverty and children's adjustment*. Newbury Park, CA: Sage.

Luthar, S. S. (2003). *Resilience and vulnerability: Adaptation in the context of childhood adversities*. New York, NY: Cambridge University Press.

Luthar, S. S., Cicchetti, D., & Becker, B. (2000). The construct of resilience: A critical evaluation and guidelines for future work. *Child Development*, *71*(3), 543–562.

Lyubomirsky, S., King, L. A., & Diener, E. (2005). The benefits of frequent positive affect. *Psychological Bulletin*, *131*, 803–855.

Maccallum, F., Galatzer-Levy, I. R., & Bonanno, G. A. (2015). Trajectories of depression following spousal and child bereavement: A comparison of the heterogeneity in outcomes. *Journal of Psychiatric Research*, *69*, 72–79.

Malgaroli, M., Galatzer-Levy, I. R., & Bonanno, G. A. (2017). Heterogeneity in trajectories of depression in response to divorce is associated with differential risk for mortality. *Clinical Psychological Science*, *5*(5), 843–850.

Mancini, A. D., & Bonanno, G. A. (2009). Predictors and parameters of resilience to loss: Toward an individual differences model. *Journal of Personality*, *77*(6), 1805–1832.

Mancini, A. D., Bonanno, G. A., & Clark, A. E. (2011). Stepping off the hedonic treadmill: Latent class analyses of individual differences in response to major life events. *Journal of Individual Differences*, *32*(3), 144–1582. doi:10.1027/1614-0001/a000047

Mancini, A. D., Littleton, H. L., & Grills, A. E. (2015). Can people benefit from acute stress? Social support, psychological improvement, and resilience after the Virginia Tech campus shootings. *Clinical Psychological Science*, *4*(3), 401–417.

Martikainen, P., & Valkonen, T. (1996). Mortality after the death of a spouse: Rates and causes of death in a large Finnish cohort. *American Journal of Public Health*, *86*(8 Pt 1), 1087–1093.

Masten, A. S. (2001). Ordinary magic: Resilience processes in development. *American Psychologist*, *56*(3), 227–238.

Masten, A. S. (2007). Resilience in developing systems: Progress and promise as the fourth wave rises. *Development and Psychopathology*, *19*(3), 921–930.

Masten, A. S., & Coatsworth, J. D. (1998). The development of competence in favorable and unfavorable environments: Lessons from research on successful children. *American Psychologist*, *53*(2), 205–220. doi:10.1037/0003-066X.53.2.205

Masten, A. S., Hubbard, J. J., Gest, S. D., Tellegen, A., Garmezy, N., & Ramirez, M. (1999). Competence in the context of adversity: Pathways to resilience and maladaptation from childhood to late adolescence. *Development and Psychopathology*, *11*(1), 143–169.

Masten, A. S., & Narayan, A. J. (2012). Child development in the context of disaster, war, and terrorism: Pathways of risk and resilience. *Annual Review of Psychology*, *63*, 227–257.

McCrae, R. R., Costa, P. T., Ostendorf, F., Angleitner, A., Hrebick- ova, M., Avia, M. D.,...Smith, P. B. (2000). Nature over nurture: Temperament, personality, and life span development. *Journal of Personality and Social Psychology*, *78*, 173–186.

McCubbin, H. I., & McCubbin, M. A. (1988). Typologies of resilient families: Emerging roles of social class and ethnicity. *Family Relations*, *37*(3), 247–254. doi:10.2307/584557

McCubbin, M., Balling, K., Possin, P., Frierdich, S., & Bryne, B. (2002). Family resiliency in childhood cancer. *Family Relations*, 51, 103–111.

McNally, R. J. (2012). The ontology of posttraumatic stress disorder: Natural kind, social construction, or causal system? *Clinical Psychology: Science and Practice*, *19*(3), 220–228. doi:10.1111/cpsp.12001

McNally, R. J. (2003). Progress and controversy in the study of posttraumatic stress disorder. *Annual Review of Psychology*, 54, 229–252.

Morin, R. T., Galatzer-Levy, I. R., Maccallum, F., & Bonanno, G. A. (2017, March 20). Do multiple health events reduce resilience when compared with single events? *Health Psychology*, *36*(8), 721. doi:10.1037/hea0000481

Moskowitz, J. T., Folkman, S., & Acree, M. (2003). Do positive psychological states shed light on recovery from bereavement? Findings from a 3-year longitudinal study. *Death Studies*, 27, 471–500.

Muthén, B. (2004). Latent variable analysis: Growth mixture modeling and related techniques for longitudinal data. In D. Kaplan (Ed.), *Handbook of quantitative methodology for the social sciences* (pp. 345–368). Newbury Park, CA: Sage.

Neria, Y., Nandi, A., & Galea, S. (2008). Post-traumatic stress disorder following disasters: A systematic review. *Psychological Medicine*, *38*(4), 467–480.

Nickerson, A., Creamer, M., Forbes, D., McFarlane, A. C., O'donnell, M. L., Silove, D.,...Bryant, R. A. (2017). The longitudinal relationship between post-traumatic stress disorder and perceived social support in survivors of traumatic injury. *Psychological Medicine*, *47*(1), 115–126.

Nolen-Hoeksema, S., & Morrow, J. (1991). A prospective study of depression and posttraumatic stress symptoms after a natural disaster: The 1989 Loma Prieta earthquake. *Journal of Personality and Social Psychology*, *61*, 115–121.

Norris, F., Stevens, S., Pfefferbaum, B., Wyche, K., & Pfefferbaum, R. (2008). Community resilience as a metaphor, theory, set of capacities, and strategy for disaster readiness. *American Journal of Community Psychology*, *41*(1–2), 127–150.

Norris, F. H. (1992). Epidemiology of trauma: Frequency and impact of different potentially traumatic events on different demographic groups. *Journal of Consulting and Clinical Psychology*, *60*(3), 409.

Norris, F. H., Baker, C. K., Murphy, A. D., & Kaniasty, K. (2005). Social support mobilization and deterioration after Mexico's 1999 flood: Effects of context, gender, and time. *American Journal of Community Psychology*, *36*(1–2), 15–28.

Norris, F. H., Friedman, M. J., Watson, P. J., Byrne, C. M., Diaz, E., & Kaniasty, K. (2002). 60,000 Disaster victims speak: Part I. An empirical review of the empirical literature, 1981–2001. *Psychiatry*, *65*(3), 207–239.

Norris, F. H., Tracy, M., & Galea, S. (2009). Looking for resilience: Understanding the longitudinal trajectories of responses to stress. *Social Science & Medicine*, *68*, 2190–2198.

Nugent, N. R., Tyrka, A. R., Carpenter, L. L., & Price, L. H. (2011). Gene–environment interactions: early life stress and risk for depressive and anxiety disorders. *Psychopharmacology*, *214*(1), 175-196.

Offidani, E., & Ruini, C. (2012). Psychobiological correlates of allostatic overload in a healthy population. *Brain, Behavior, and Immunity*, *26*(2), 284–291. doi:10.1016/j.bbi.2011.09.009

Okumura, T., Suzuki, K., Fukuda, A., Kohama, A., Takasu, N., Ishimatsu, S., & Hinohara, S. (1998). The Tokyo subway sarin attack: Disaster management, Part 1: Community emergency response. *Academic Emergency Medicine*, 5, 613–617.

Ong, A. D., Bergeman, C. S., & Boker, S. M. (2009). Resilience comes of age: Defining features in later adulthood. *Journal of Personality*, *77*(6), 1777–1804.

Ong, A. D., Bergeman, C. S., & Chow, S. M. (2010). Positive emotions as a basic building block of resilience in adulthood.

In Reich, J. W., Zautra, A. J., & Hall, J. S.(Ed.), *Handbook of adult resilience* (pp. 81–93). New York, NY.

Ong, A. D., Fuller-Rowell, T. E., Bonanno, G. A., & Almeida, D. M. (2011). Spousal loss predicts alterations in diurnal cortisol activity through prospective changes in positive emotion. *Health Psychology, 30,* 220–227.

Orcutt, H. K., Bonanno, G. A., Hannan, S. M., & Miron, L. R. (2014). Prospective trajectories of posttraumatic stress in college women following a campus mass shooting. *Journal of Traumatic Stress, 27*(3), 249–256. doi:10.1002/jts.21914

Papa, A., & Bonanno, G. A. (2008). Smiling in the face of adversity: The interpersonal and intrapersonal functions of smiling. *Emotion, 8,* 1–12.

Patterson, J. M. (1988). Families experiencing stress: I. The Family Adjustment and Adaptation Response Model: II. Applying the FAAR Model to health-related issues for intervention and research. *Family Systems Medicine, 6*(2), 202–237. doi:10.1037/h0089739

Patterson, J. M. (2002). Integrating family resilience and family stress theory. *Journal of Marriage and Family, 64*(2), 349–360. doi:10.2307/3600109

Pietrzak, R. H., Van Ness, P. H., Fried, T. R., Galea, S., & Norris, F. H. (2013). Trajectories of posttraumatic stress symptomatology in older persons affected by a large-magnitude disaster. *Journal of Psychiatric Research, 47*(4), 520–526.

Porter, B., Bonanno, G. A., Frasco, M. Dursa, E., Bossarte, R., & Boyko, E. (2017). Prospective post-traumatic stress disorder symptoms trajectories in active duty and separated military personnel. *Journal of Psychiatric Research, 89,* 55–64.

Prigerson, H. G., Horowitz, M. J., Jacobs, S. C., Parkes, C. M., Aslan, M., Goodkin, K.,...Maciejewski, P. K. (2009). Prolonged grief disorder: Psychometric validation of criteria proposed for DSM-V and ICD-11. *PLoS Med, 6*(8), e1000121. Retrieved from http://dx.doi.org/10.1371/journal.pmed.1000121

Qouta, S., El-Sarraj, E., & Punamäki, R.-L. (2001). Mental flexibility as resiliency factor among children exposed to political violence. *International Journal of Psychology, 36*(1), 1–7. Retrieved from 10.1080/00207590042000010

Quale, A. J., & Schanke, A. K. (2010). Resilience in the face of coping with a severe physical injury: A study of trajectories of adjustment in a rehabilitation setting. *Rehabilitation Psychology, 55,* 12–22.

Rutter, M. (1979). Protective factors in children's responses to stress and disadvantage. In M. W. Kent & J. E. Rolf (Eds.), *Primary prevention of psychopathology: Vol. 3: Social competence in children* (Vol. 3, pp. 49–74). Hanover, NH: University Press of New England.

Rutter, M. (1985). Resilience in the face of adversity: Protective factors and resistance to psychiatric disorder. *The British Journal of Psychiatry, 147,* 598–611. doi:10.1192/bjp.147.6.598

Rutter, M. (2002). The interplay of nature, nurture, and developmental influences: The challenge ahead for mental health. *Archives of General Psychiatry, 59,* 996–1000.

Ryff, C. D., & Singer, B. (2002). From social structure to biology: Integrative science in pursuit of human health and well-being. In S. J. Snyder & C. R. Lopez (Eds.), *Handbook of positive psychology* (pp. 541–555). Oxford, UK: Oxford University Press.

Sampson, R. J., & Laub, J. H. (1992). Crime and deviance in the life course. *Annual Review of Sociology, 18,* 63–84. Retrieved from http://www.jstor.org/stable/2083446

Sampson, R. J., Raudenbush, S. W., & Earls, F. (1997). Neighborhoods and violent crime: A multilevel study of collective efficacy. *Science, 277* (5328), 918–924

Sarapas, C., Cai, G., Bierer, L. M., Golier, J. A., Galea, S., Ising, M.,...Uhr, M. (2011). Genetic markers for PTSD risk and resilience among survivors of the World Trade Center attacks. *Disease Markers, 30*(2–3), 101–110.

Self-Brown, S., Lai, B. S., Thompson, J. E., McGill, T., & Kelley, M. L. (2013). Posttraumatic stress disorder symptom trajectories in Hurricane Katrina affected youth. *Journal of Affective Disorders, 147*(1), 198–204.

Seligman, M. E., & Csikszentmihalyi, M. (2000). Special issue on happiness, excellence, and optimal human functioning. *American Psychologist, 55*(1), 5–183.

Shear, K., Frank, E., Houck, P. R., & Reynolds, C. F. (2005). Treatment of complicated grief: A randomized controlled trial. *JAMA: Journal of the American Medical Association, 293*(21), 2601–2608.

Shepard, B. (2001). *A war of nerves: Soldiers and psychiatrists in the twentieth century.* Cambridge, MA: Harvard University Press.

Siegler, R. S. (1987). The perils of averaging data over strategies: An example from children's addition. *Journal of Experimental Psychology: General, 116*(3), 250–264. doi:10.1037/0096-3445.116.3.250

Skinner, B. F. (1936). The effect on the amount of conditioning of an interval of time before reinforcement. *Journal of General Psychology, 14*(2), 279–295.

Smith, B., Dalen, J., Wiggins, K., Tooley, E., Christopher, P., & Bernard, J. (2008). The brief resilience scale: Assessing the ability to bounce back. *International Journal of Behavioral Medicine, 15*(3), 194–200. doi:10.1080/10705500802222972

Sonn, C. C., & Fisher, A. T. (1998). Sense of community: Community resilient responses to oppression and change. *Journal of Community Psychology, 26*(5), 457–472.

Stolove, C. A., Galatzer-Levy, I. R., & Bonanno, G. A. (2017). Emergence of depression following job loss prospectively predicts lower rates of reemployment. *Psychiatry Research, 253,* 79–83.

Stroebe, M. S., & Stroebe, W. (1993). *The mortality of bereavement: Theory, research, and intervention* (pp. 175–195). New York, NY: Cambridge University Press.

Sundin, J., Fear, N., Iversen, A., Rona, R., & Wessely, S. (2010). PTSD after deployment to Iraq: conflicting rates, conflicting claims. *Psychological Medicine, 40*(3), 367–382. doi:10.1017/s0033291709990791

Tang, C. S. (2007). Trajectory of traumatic stress symptoms in the aftermath of extreme natural disaster: A study of adult Thai survivors of the 2004 Southeast Asian earthquake and tsunami. *The Journal of Nervous and Mental Disease, 195*(1), 54–59.

Troy, A. S., & Mauss, I. B. (2011). Resilience in the face of stress: emotion regulation as a protective factor. *Resilience and Mental Health: Challenges Across the Lifespan, 1*(2), 30-44.

Ullman, J., & Newcomb, M. (1999). I felt the earth move: A prospective study of the 1994 Northridge earthquake. In L. Cohen, P. Slomkowski, & C. Robins (Eds.), *Historical and geographical influences on psychopathology* (pp. 217–246). Mahwah, NJ: Lawrence Erlbaum.

Vaillant, G. E., & Davis, J. T. (2000). Social/emotional intelligence and midlife resilience in schoolboys with low tested intelligence. *American Journal of Orthopsychiatry, 70*(2), 215–222. Retrieved from http://dx.doi.org/10.1037/h0087783

Van Griensven, F., Chakkraband, M. S., Thienkrua, W., Pengjuntr, W., Cardozo, B. L., Tantipiwatanaskul, P., ...Sabin, M. (2006). Mental health problems among adults in tsunami-affected areas in southern Thailand. *JAMA*, *296*(5), 537–548.

Vasterman, P., Yzermans, C. J., & Dirkzwager, A. J. E. (2005). The role of the media and media hypes in the aftermath of disasters. *Epidemiologic Reviews*, *27*(1), 107–114.

Vernberg, E. M., La Greca, A. M., Silverman, W. K., & Prinstein, M. J. (1996). Prediction of posttraumatic stress symptoms in children after Hurricane Andrew. *Journal of Abnormal Psychology*, *105*, 237–248.

Walsh, F. (1996). The concept of family resilience: Crisis and challenge. *Family Process*, *35*(3), 261–281. doi:10.1111/j.1545–5300.1996.00261.x

Walsh, F. (2006). *Strengthening family resilience* (2nd ed.). New York, NY: Guilford Press.

Walsh, F. (2013). Community-based practice applications of a family resilience framework. In D. S. Becvar (Ed.), *Handbook of family resilience* (pp. 65–82). New York, NY: Springer.

Waters, E., & Sroufe, L. A. (1983). Social competence as a developmental construct. *Developmental Review*, *3*(1), 79–97. doi:10.1016/0273-2297(83)90010-2

Weems, C. F., Pina, A. A., Costa, N. M., Watts, S. E., Taylor, L. K., & Cannon, M. F. (2007). Predisaster trait anxiety and negative affect predict posttraumatic stress in youths after hurricane Katrina. *Journal of Consulting and Clinical Psychology*, *75*, 154–159.

Weems, C. F., Taylor, L. K., Cannon, M. F., Marino, R. C., Romano, D. M., Scott, B. G., ...Triplett, V. (2010). Posttraumatic stress, context, and the lingering effects of the Hurricane Katrina disaster among ethnic minority youth. *Journal of Abnormal Child Psychology*, *38*, 49–56.

Werner, E. E. (1985). Stress and protective factors in children's lives. In A. R. Nicol (Ed.), *Longitudinal studies in child psychology and psychiatry* (pp. 335–355). New York, NY: Wiley and Sons.

Werner, E. E. (1993). Risk, resilience, and recovery: Perspectives from the Kauai Longitudinal Study. *Development and Psychopathology*, *5*(4), 503–515.

Werner, E. E. (1995). Resilience in development. *Current Directions in Psychological Science*, *4*(3), 81–85.

Werner, E. E., Bierman, J. M., & French, F. E. (1971). *The children of Kauai: A longitudinal study from the prenatal period to age ten*. Honolulu: University of Hawaii Press.

Werner, E. E., & Smith, R. S. (1977). *Kauai's children come of age*. Honolulu: University of Hawaii Press.

Werner, E. E., & Smith, R. S. (1992). *Overcoming the odds: High risk children from birth to adulthood*. Ithaca, NY: Cornell University Press.

Westphal, M., Seivert, N. H., & Bonanno, G. A. (2010). Expressive flexibility. *Emotion*, *10*, 92–100.

Wyman, P. A., Cowen, E. L., Work, W. C., Raoof, A., Gribble, P. A., Parker, G. R., & Wannon, M. (1992). Interviews with children who experienced major life stress: Family and child attributes that predict resilient outcomes. *Journal of the American Academy of Child & Adolescent Psychiatry*, *31*(5), 904–910.

Yehuda, R., & Flory, J. D. (2007). Differentiating biological correlates of risk, PTSD, and resilience following trauma exposure. *Journal of Traumatic Stress*, *20*(4), 435–447. doi:10.1002/jts.20260

Zhu, Z., Galatzer-Levy, I. R., & Bonanno, G. A. (2014). Heterogeneous depression responses to chronic pain onset among middle-aged adults: a prospective study. *Psychiatry Research*, *217*(1), 60–66.

Novel Pharmacotherapeutics for Stress-Related Disorders

Jamie E. Mondello, Jenny E. Pak, Dennis F. Lovelock, *and* Terrence Deak

Abstract

Most mental health problems associated with psychological distress originate with activation of centrally regulated stress pathways, yet a diverse range of central nervous system and somatic disease states can be influenced by exposure to severe or unrelenting stress. The goal of this chapter is to provide a conceptual framework to guide the development of pharmacological intervention strategies. We propose that careful consideration of the relationship between the timing of stressful life experiences, pharmacological intervention, and the ultimate expression of disease symptomatology is critical for the development of pharmacological interventions to treat stress-related disorders. We review a range of physiological systems that are known to be activated by stress, offering potentially new targets for drug development efforts, and argue that participant selection is a key predictor of drug efficacy trials. In doing so, we point toward inflammatory signaling pathways as a potential final common mediator of multiple stress-related disease states.

Keywords: stress, cytokines, inflammation, pharmacotherapy, stress-related disorders, anxiety, depression, hypothalamic-pituitary-adrenal axis, sympathetic nervous system, review

Introduction

The 21st century has witnessed unprecedented growth in the development, use, and cost of pharmacotherapeutic agents in developed countries. Interestingly, the cost of drug development efforts specifically targeting mental health problems has also grown astronomically, underscoring the importance of strategic planning in the development of pharmacotherapeutic interventions for mental health. This issue is particularly challenging within the context of stress-related disorders, where the causal relationship between stressful life experiences and subsequent development and expression of stress-related disorders is often tenuous. The matter is further complicated because a wide range of physiological systems and processes are involved in the initial reaction to stress, which do not necessarily reflect the systems that ultimately display stress-related dysfunction. Indeed, most mental health problems associated with psychological distress

originate with activation of centrally regulated stress pathways, yet a diverse range of central nervous system (CNS) and somatic disease states can be influenced by exposure to severe or unrelenting stress. Thus, identifying the physiological pathways that are mechanistic, and potential treatment targets, is challenging.

To frame a discussion of pharmacotherapeutic strategies in the treatment of stress-related disorders, we must first give careful consideration to the construct at hand. A large number of perspectives on the definition of "stress" have been provided, spanning decades of research into stress-related health outcomes (Cannon, 1935; Mason, 1975; Selye, 1936; Wingfield & Sapolsky, 2003). Although we will not go into depth on these matters here, we will use the term "stress" in the present chapter to refer to threats (internal or external) that activate multiple, stress-responsive systems in the body. Although innumerable disease states are influenced by stress, we focus on major depressive disorder (MDD) due to its prevalence and the progress that has been made in understanding the relation between MDD and stress-related processes. Where feasible, we comment on other stress-related disorders (posttraumatic stress disorder [PTSD], generalized anxiety disorder [GAD], and phobias) as they relate to specific pharmacotherapeutic targets, though our review of these other conditions is by no means comprehensive. Development of PTSD, as with MDD, is linked to a history of traumatic experiences, particularly exposure to combat or sexual assault (Kessler, Sonnega, Bromet, Hughes, & Nelson, 1995; Mueser et al., 1998). While anxiety disorders such as GAD and phobias have not generally been shown to be associated with a history of real-life aversive experiences (although see Newman & Bland, 1994), we construe them as stress-related disorders due to patients' exaggerated stress response to perceived harmful stimuli. Moreover, development of anxiety disorders has been shown to precede depression, indicating similar etiologies between the two (Slavich & Irwin, 2014). Thus, despite the somewhat tenuous nature of the relationship between stressful life events and the onset of major psychiatric illnesses, evidence to support such an association is certainly precedented, as are the involvement of stress-responsive systems and inflammatory signaling pathways.

Additionally, we feel it is imperative to draw attention to several key conceptual issues in order to provide an appropriate lens through which our subsequent literature review should be viewed. First is the issue of the temporal relationships between stressful life events, the stress-responsive systems activated as an immediate result, and the clinically relevant consequences that might emerge days, weeks, months, or years later. Pharmacological *prevention*, prophylaxis, or inoculation (see Figure 29.1 for a schematic model) is particularly difficult to achieve because it would require treatments to be administered in advance of major life stressors. Though difficult to predict for most individuals, there are certainly cases in which prophylactic strategies might be effective, such as prior to deployment of military personnel. *Intervention* is perhaps more readily achievable, but it requires that individuals receive pharmacological intervention within a relatively short time frame after the stressful experience(s) as a means to minimize ongoing distress and prevent the induction of a permanent disease state. The basic premise here is that, in cases of prevention or intervention, the therapeutic goal is to eliminate the prospect of a transient state of distress becoming a permanent or recurring condition across the life span. More often, the influence of major life stressors or the cumulative impact of stress across the life span results in clinically diagnosed disease states that persist for prolonged periods, or during recurrent episodes, throughout life. In these cases, the disease has been fully inculcated and the pharmacotherapeutic strategy must be focused on the pathophysiological processes associated with expression of the disease state, which may or may not relate to the mechanisms by which those changes were induced. In doing so, pharmacotherapy most often achieves the goal of providing *palliative care*, in which chronic administration of drug treatments leads to transient reversal of disease symptomatology during the period of active drug administration. Palliative care has become the gold standard in nearly all clinical trials, with few studies assessing the potential *curative* prospects for drug treatment, which would be defined as a permanent reversal of the disease state that persists even after cessation of pharmacotherapy.

With this conceptual framework in mind, the overarching goal of this chapter is to provide an overview of both classic and contemporary pharmacological targets being investigated in the treatment of stress-related disorders. In doing so, we propose that careful consideration of the relationship between the timing of stressful life experiences and the ultimate expression of disease symptomatology is a critical first step in the development of pharmacological interventions to treat stress-related disorders. Additionally, we critique how well current drugs target stress-related disorders, asserting that appropriate selection of patient subpopulations determines the success of pharmacotherapies. For this reason, we focused our discussion on clinical findings, emphasizing the relationship between regimens of drug administration (dose and frequency) and therapeutic efficacy. We posit that *inflammatory signaling pathways* are the potential final common mediator of multiple stress-related disease states. As such, relevant comorbidities relating to stress-exacerbated inflammation (rheumatoid arthritis, osteoarthritis, cardiovascular disease, psoriasis, cancer, chronic fatigue asthma, chronic obstructive pulmonary disease, muscular dystrophy) are addressed in passing. We recognize that the agents characterized in this chapter may have therapeutic actions that are independent of inflammation, or that represent additive or synergistic effects that are in part contributed by their influence on inflammatory-signaling pathways. Finally, we take the position that understanding

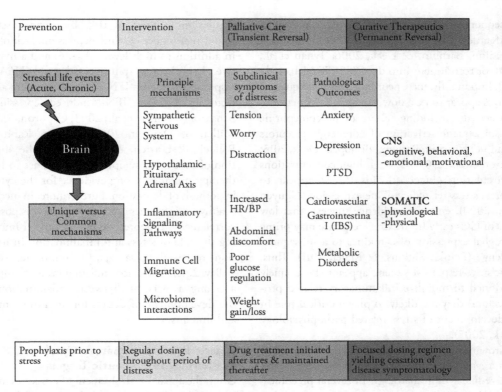

| Prevention | Intervention | Palliative Care (Transient Reversal) | Curative Therapeutics (Permanent Reversal) |

Stressful life events (Acute, Chronic)

Brain

Unique versus Common mechanisms

Principle mechanisms

Sympathetic Nervous System

Hypothalamic-Pituitary-Adrenal Axis

Inflammatory Signaling Pathways

Immune Cell Migration

Microbiome interactions

Subclinical symptoms of distress:

Tension

Worry

Distraction

Increased HR/BP

Abdominal discomfort

Poor glucose regulation

Weight gain/loss

Pathological Outcomes

Anxiety

Depression

PTSD

CNS
-cognitive, behavioral,
-emotional, motivational

Cardiovascular

Gastrointestinal (IBS)

Metabolic Disorders

SOMATIC
-physiological
-physical

| Prophylaxis prior to stress | Regular dosing throughout period of distress | Drug treatment initiated after stres & maintained thereafter | Focused dosing regimen yielding cessation of disease symptomatology |

Figure 29.1 Relationship between type of pharmcotherapy (top) and timing of stressful life events (bottom). Mediating this relationship are stressful life events that activate principle mechanisms to produce subclinical symptoms of distress and ultimately result in pathological outcomes.

stress-related pathophysiology requires a whole-organism, integrated approach to physiology that considers not just CNS manifestations of stress and its consequences but also the interaction between central and peripheral organ systems.

Major Depressive Disorder as a Prototypical Stress-Related Disorder

According to the World Health Organization, depression is an extremely pervasive mental disorder affecting approximately 300 million people, of all ages and genders, worldwide (World Health Organization, 2017). The initial framework used to formulate and explain pharmacotherapeutic treatments for depression was the monoamine hypothesis, which presumed that depression was a result of a monoamine (noradrenaline, serotonin, and/or dopamine) deficiency in the brain (reviewed in Delgado, 2000). The first line of antidepressants consisted of drugs that acted to increase the concentration of monoamines: monoamine oxidase inhibitors (MAOIs) and tricyclic antidepressants (TCAs), later followed by selective serotonin-reuptake inhibitors (SSRIs) and serotonin and norepinephrine reuptake inhibitors (SNRIs) (Hirschfeld, 2000). However,

treatment using these drugs yields a significant number of nonresponders and oftentimes adverse side effects ranging from sexual dysfunction and apathy to lethal overdose (Bschor et al., 2012; Rush et al., 2006; Settle, 1998). These issues, combined with emerging trends in our understanding of the pathophysiology of depression, led investigators toward a different avenue for therapeutic treatment of depression: stress and inflammation.

Exposure to psychological stressors activates two primary systems, including the sympathetic nervous system (SNS) and the hypothalamic-pituitary-adrenal (HPA) axis. We now know that these systems set into motion many downstream effects of stress, including induction of multiple tell-tale signs of neuroinflammation as well, even in the absence of overt infection or tissue damage (reviewed in Deak et al., 2015; Deak, Kudinova, Lovelock, Gibb, & Hennessy, 2017). Acute and chronic stress challenges in rodent models, for instance, have shown significantly increased expression of pro-inflammatory cytokines (e.g., Deak et al., 2005; Jankord et al., 2010; Nguyen et al., 1998) and chemokines (Blandino et al., 2009; Wohleb et al., 2011) in the brain. Evidence suggests that many of these neuroimmune consequences of stress may involve microglial proliferation (Nair & Bonneau, 2006), activation (Blandino, Barnum, & Deak, 2006; Tynan et al., 2010), or recruitment into the CNS (Wohleb et al., 2011). Importantly, these neuroimmune consequences of stress appear to be a downstream consequence of SNS activity, including release of norepinephrine and subsequent activation of adrenergic receptors (Blandino, Hueston, Barnum, Bishop, & Deak, 2013; Johnson et al., 2005). Though high concentrations of circulating glucocorticoids (GCs) appear to suppress stress-related cytokine expression (Nguyen et al., 2000), emerging evidence suggests that low doses of GCs early in the stress response may prime microglial expression of cytokines to a subsequent challenge (Frank, Watkins, & Maier, 2011). Thus, classic stress-responsive systems appear to be uniquely positioned to mobilize inflammatory-related processes, and they are likely to play a critical role in the development of stress-related pathophysiology (Deak, 2007).

Growing evidence suggests that inflammation plays a significant role in the development of depressive-like symptomatology. In several preclinical and clinical studies of depression, lipopolysaccharide (LPS; a component of the cell wall of gram-negative bacteria that is often used to mimic acute illness) increased expression of inflammatory cytokines (proteinaceous signaling molecules that orchestrate communication among immune cells and other physiological systems, including the CNS) that in turn resulted in depressive-like behavior. Interestingly, the depressive-like effects of LPS were ameliorated with treatment by conventional antidepressants, suggesting a key role for immune signaling molecules in the pathophysiology of depression (Tonelli, Holmes, & Postolache, 2008; Yirmiya et al., 2000; Yirmiya, 1996). Administration of pro-inflammatory cytokines alone, such as interleukin (IL)-1β, IL-6, and tumor necrosis factor (TNF)-α, also induced depressive-like behavior in animal models (Dantzer, O'Connor, Freund, Johnson, & Kelley, 2008). Furthermore, patients being treated for cancer, hepatitis C or other infectious diseases that have received interferon-α (IFN-α) treatment, a known inducer of pro-inflammatory cytokines, often consequently displayed behaviors associated with depression (Danzter, O'Connor, Lawson, & Kelley, 2011; Raison, Capuron, & Miller, 2006). An important observation to note is that not all patients receiving IFN-α treatment end up developing depressive symptoms, indicating that there may be predisposing factors that lead to cytokine-induced depression in those at risk. Independent studies found that higher baseline depression, lack of sleep in addition to high levels of IL-6, and a hyperactive hypothalamic-pituitary-adrenal (HPA)-axis response upon first IFN-α treatment were all risk factors in developing IFN-α-induced depression-like behavior (Capuron et al., 2003; Capuron, Ravaud, Miller, & Dantzer, 2004; Prather, Rabinovitz, Pollock, & Lotrich, 2009). To date, the observation of depressive symptoms in response to IFN-α therapy provides strong evidence for the cytokine hypothesis of depression. Furthermore, in medically healthy subjects, increased inflammation is positively correlated with depressive mood, further implicating the role of stress and inflammation in depression (reviewed in Dantzer, O'Connor, Lawson, & Kelley, 2011). Thus, accumulating evidence supports a strong association between inflammation and the development of depression in animal models and humans.

Classic Pro-Inflammatory Cytokines as Pharmacotherapeutic Targets

Given the apparent involvement of cytokines in both stress and depression, the development of drugs that target pro-inflammatory cytokines or their signaling pathways is a major area of interest. These efforts, however, are complicated by the fact that cytokines and their receptors are widely distributed throughout the body and are involved in numerous normal and pathophysiological processes. Additionally, most pro-inflammatory cytokines are large lipophobic proteins that do not readily cross the blood–brain barrier, the interface between the CNS and periphery, which complicates the goal of achieving therapeutic outcomes that are specific to stress-related, CNS-dependent (i.e., psychiatric) ailments. Thus, in order to inhibit the action of cytokines, functional antagonists cannot be made by simply modifying the biochemical structure of the parent molecule/ cytokine, as they will likely not be able to passage into the CNS and effect therapeutic change. Instead, drug development efforts targeting inflammatory signaling pathways frequently strive toward development of lipid-soluble, small-molecule variants that readily gain access to the CNS. Nevertheless, substantial progress has been made in the development of anti-inflammatory drugs in stress-related psychiatric illness generally, and depression specifically. For this reason, our review of novel pharmacotherapeutic targets in the treatment of stress-related disorders will emphasize what is known about MDD as a case example, with ongoing discussion of how those pathways or drugs targeting them have been found to impact other inflammation-associated processes.

Given the large number of cytokines and other inflammatory signaling molecules that exist in the body, many potential pharmacotherapeutic targets are possible. A meta-analysis evaluating cytokine concentrations found that only TNF-α and IL-6 levels were significantly elevated in MDD patients, suggesting them as potential targets (Dowlati et al., 2010). Many clinical trials investigating the efficacy of TNF-α antagonists as monotherapy for depression have already been undertaken (reviewed in Soczynska et al., 2009). Preclinical studies suggest that the role of TNF-α in stress-related disorders may extend to anxiety as well, since 8-week administration of etanercerpt, a TNF-α inhibitor, decreased anxiety-like behavior in rats in the elevated plus maze (Bayramgurler et al., 2013). In humans, studies targeting these pathways often include patients with other comorbid inflammatory diseases and examine depressive symptoms as an additional outcome variable. A small clinical trial found that etanercept coadministered with chemotherapy significantly reduced fatigue compared to patients administered the chemotherapy alone (Monk et al., 2006). A randomized double-blind clinical phase III trial also investigated the effect of etanercept (50 mg twice a week for 12 weeks) or placebo treatment on the depressive symptoms of 597 patients with moderate to severe psoriasis (Tyring et al., 2006). By week 12, the proportion of those showing at least a 50% improvement in depressive symptoms from baseline was significantly greater in those receiving etanercept compared to placebo, independent of improvement of psoriasis symptoms. Decreases in depression were maintained for up to 96 weeks in the second open-label component of the study, during which the same dose of etanercept was used (Krishnan et al., 2007). Another clinical trial administered a single dose of 5 or 10 mg/kg of infliximab, a chimeric monoclonal antibody antagonist to TNF-α, to Crohn's disease patients and followed up on the treatment 4 weeks later (Persoons et al., 2005). At 4 weeks, a significantly smaller percentage of patients showed depressive symptoms compared to baseline (16% vs. 24%). C-reactive protein (CRP) is an acute phase protein often measured as an inflammatory marker in inflammatory-related diseases (Vincent, Donadello, & Schmit, 2011). Of the patients who achieved remission of depressive symptoms, the median CRP levels (mg/L) were higher at baseline compared to both nondepressed

and nonresponder patients. By week 4, there was an overall drop in the median CRP, and CRP levels were not different between those that achieved remission, nonresponders, and nondepressed subjects (Persoons et al., 2005). These findings provide evidence of the beneficial effects of targeting TNF-α signaling, especially in depressed patients in a proinflammatory state.

Factoring in the inflammatory state of patients when utilizing anti-inflammatory treatments like TNF-α antagonists for depression may be critical (Raison et al., 2013). A randomized double-blind clinical trial administered three infusions of infliximab (5 mg/kg) or placebo at 0, 2, and 6 weeks of a 12-week study. In addition to measuring Hamilton Depression Rating Scale (HAM-D) scores at these time points, the investigators also measured proinflammatory biomarkers, including high-sensitivity CRP, TNF, and TNF-soluble receptors I and II. While there was a significant main effect of time, with HAM-D scores significantly decreasing from baseline to the end of the trial, no differences in this decrease were found between the infliximab and placebo group. However, when baseline CRP levels were taken into account, a different picture emerged: Infliximab-treated patients with a high level of inflammation (levels of CRP > 5 mg/L) displayed a greater decrease in HAM-D scores than placebo-treated patients, while infliximab-treated patients with lower levels of inflammation (levels of CRP < 5 mg/L) fared *worse* than placebo-treated patients. Additionally, baseline levels of TNF and its soluble receptors were higher in infliximab-treated responders than in infliximab-treated nonresponders. This clinical trial serves as an important example of the importance of considering underlying inflammatory conditions when using anti-inflammatory treatment to target depression.

IL-6 is another cytokine heavily implicated in depression, and a number of IL-6 inhibitors that are being investigated in clinical trials for inflammatory diseases show therapeutic potential for treating depression (Fonseka, McIntyre, Soczynska, & Kennedy, 2015). Tocilizumab, an anti-IL-6 antibody, has been shown to be effective in normalizing CRP levels and treating a number of inflammatory-related diseases, including rheumatoid arthritis and Crohn's disease (Choy et al., 2002; Ito et al., 2004; Tanaka, Narazaki, & Kishimoto, 2011). There is some evidence that tocilizumab administered to rheumatoid arthritis patients can improve quality of life and mental state, and reduce fatigue (Townes et al., 2012). A small, open-label trial that administered tocilizumab (8 mg/kg) monthly for 6 months to rheumatoid arthritis patients who were resistant to traditional rheumatoid arthritis treatment measured Hospital Anxiety and Depression Scale (HADS) scores across treatment (Traki et al., 2014). Tocilizumab improved quality of life and anxiety symptoms, but it did not significantly reduce depressive symptoms. Thus, it is possible that tocilizumab is more suited for treating anxiety, especially given that clinically diagnosed anxiety is associated with elevated IL-6 levels (O'Donovan et al., 2010). Nevertheless, a phase II open-label clinical trial (ClinicalTrials.gov Identifier: NCT02660528) is currently investigating the effects of tocilizumab (162 mg every 2 weeks x 4 doses) on treatment-resistant depression, although this study will not be examining pro-inflammatory markers in patients. A randomized, double-blind, placebo-controlled clinical trial is also currently being conducted on another IL-6 inhibitor, sirukumab (ClinicalTrials. gov Identifier: NCT02473289). In this study, either sirukumab (50 mg on Day 1, 28, and 56) or placebo is administered as adjunctive treatment in treatment-resistant depressed patients. Baseline differences in CRP levels will also be measured. Notably, after reviewing results from a global phase III clinical trial, the Arthritis Advisory Committee of the Food and Drug Administration did not recommend approval of a similar dose of sirukumab as treatment for rheumatoid arthritis on August 2, 2017, citing significant safety concerns. Moreover, while tocilizumab is considered generally tolerable in humans, it often causes immune-related side effects, such as infection and lowered neutrophil counts (Kim et al., 2015). Thus, the side effects that stem from global inhibition of IL-6 may limit its use as a treatment for depression.

Given concerns that current IL-6 inhibitors may inadvertently block protective effects of IL-6, growing attention is being given to developing drugs that target IL-6 signaling more precisely (Fonseka et al., 2015; Maes, Anderson, Kubera, & Berk, 2014). IL-6 can have pro-inflammatory actions via activation of soluble IL-6 receptors (trans-signaling pathway activation) or anti-inflammatory actions via activation of membrane bound IL-6 receptors (classical signaling pathway activation). Most IL-6 inhibitors are monoclonal antibodies that target either both types of IL-6 receptors, such as tocilizumab, or IL-6 itself, such as sirukumab (Kim et al., 2015). Soluble gp130 is the natural antagonist to specifically IL-6 trans-signaling via inhibition of the IL-6/soluble IL-6 receptor complex, and Sgp130fc

(Sgp130 bound to the Fc portion of IgG) has been shown to inhibit IL-6 induced depressive-like behaviors in a mouse model (Rizzo et al., 2012). More studies are needed to determine whether targeting IL-6 trans-signaling provides an advantage over global IL-6 inhibition in treating depression, but an ongoing challenge will be the development of IL-6 inhibitors that successfully cross the blood–brain barrier.

Signal Transduction Inhibitors Targeting Inflammatory Signaling Pathways

Another way to inhibit the actions of pro-inflammatory cytokines is to inhibit the intracellular signaling pathways activated downstream of cytokine receptors. Conceptually, it should be noted that the action of many cytokines occurs in a feed-forward manner in which cytokine release accelerates further cytokine induction through auto-induction (i.e., IL-1 induces de novo synthesis of more IL-1) and/or induction of secondary cytokines (IL-1 induces expression of IL-6). Consequently, inhibition of pro-inflammatory cytokines can be done through targeting either (1) upstream of cytokines, thereby inducing cytokine expression and subsequent activation of cognate receptors; or (2) downstream of cytokines, due to ligand-dependent receptor activation. Importantly, P38-MAPkinase and NK-kB signaling pathways are involved in both upstream and downstream control of cytokines, positioning signal transduction inhibitors of these families as potential therapeutic targets for tempering inflammation.

p38 MAPK

Many studies have shown that p38 MAPK inhibitors block pro-inflammatory cytokine production such as IL-1, TNF-α, and IL-6, as well as cytokine-induced depressive behavior, via SERT activation (Kumar, Boehm, & Lee, 2003). Various p38 MAPK inhibitors have been investigated preclinically and clinically as treatments for autoimmune and inflammatory disorders, including Crohn's diseases and rheumatoid arthritis (Genovese et al., 2011; Kumar et al., 2003; Schreiber et al., 2006). However, at the time of writing, clinicaltrials.gov indicated that only one clinical trial utilizing a p38 MAPK inhibitor to treat depression has been conducted. Researchers from GlaxoSmithKline investigated p38 MAP kinase inhibitor Losmapimod (GW856553) as a treatment for depression in two randomized, double-blind clinical trials (Inamdar et al., 2014). The study designs consisted of non-treatment-resistant MDD subjects with loss of energy and psychomotor retardation, who received 7.5 mg of Losmapimod twice a day for 6 weeks. While the first study was cut short, at the time of termination, there were indications that Losmapimod was effective in reducing depressive symptoms when compared to placebo treatment by week 6. However, the second fully completed study, which used a significantly larger sample size, showed no difference in reduction of depressive symptoms in the Losmapimod-treated group compared to the placebo-treated group. Interestingly, the depressed subjects did not seem to show an elevated inflammatory state compared to healthy subjects at baseline, as determined with IL-6 and CRP levels. It is possible that recruiting MDD patients based on clinical symptoms rather than inflammatory state inadvertently created a floor effect with respect to inflammation, reducing the ability of Losmapimod to reduce depressive symptoms via anti-inflammatory actions.

NF-κB

NF-κB is another inflammatory signaling pathway crucial to cytokine-related depressive behavior. Binding of IL-1β and TNF-α to their respective receptors activates the NF-κB pathway, which in turn regulates the production of many pro-inflammatory cytokines (Vallabhapurapu & Karin, 2009). Various studies using rodent models have shown that inhibition of NF-κB blocks depressive-like behavior and suppresses neurogenesis (Koo, Russo, Ferguson, Nestler, & Duman, 2010; Nadjar, Bluthé, May, Dantzer, & Parnet, 2005). There has also been growing interest in natural inhibitors of NF-κB, including vitamin D, curcumin, and α-Tocopherol (Haroon, Raison, & Miller, 2012).

Vitamin D may potentially reduce depression through its roles in NF-κB signaling and suppression of inflammation. Inflammatory and immune-related cells transform inactive vitamin D metabolites into the active metabolite, calcitriol. Calcitriol, in turn, suppresses pro-inflammatory cytokine production via inhibition of the NF-κB pathway and has been shown to increase proliferation and activation of anti-inflammatory regulatory T cells (Tregs) (Colotta, Jansson, & Bonelli, 2017). Not only have numerous studies found reduced levels of vitamin D in depressed patients, but severity of depression has also been shown to be negatively correlated with vitamin D (reviewed in Parker, Brotchie, & Graham, 2017). Many clinical trials investigating the efficacy of Vitamin D supplementation in reducing depressive symptoms have been conducted, with mixed results. Li et al. (2014) conducted a meta-analysis evaluating the use of Vitamin D in treating depression and found that it did not significantly reduce depression scores, although there was considerable heterogeneity among studies. However, limitations of extant clinical studies include lack of establishment of vitamin D deficiency at baseline, failure to affirm improved vitamin D levels over the course of treatment, and interventions that did not specifically administer vitamin D. After accounting for these issues by excluding such studies, another meta-analysis found that vitamin D supplementation provided a significant decrease in depressive symptoms and that daily doses of 800 International Unit (IU) or more were the most effective dose (Spedding & Simon, 2014).

Vitamin D supplementation as adjunctive therapy to conventional antidepressants has also shown some encouraging results. An open-label trial found that older depressed patients who took 300,000 IU of cholecalciferol (vitamin D3) with antidepressants had significantly lower HAM-D scores after 4 weeks compared to those only taking antidepressants (Zanetidou et al., 2011). A randomized, double-blind, placebo-controlled clinical trial coadministered fluoxetine with vitamin D3 (1500 IU) or placebo daily for 8 weeks in MDD patients, of which 95% were initially vitamin D deficient (Khoraminya, Tehrani-Doost, Jazayeri, Hosseini, & Djazayery, 2013). Coadministration of vitamin D and fluoxetine significantly improved vitamin D status and was more effective at improving depression status than fluoxetine-placebo treatment from week 4 onward. Therefore, vitamin D has shown effectiveness as either a monotherapy or adjunctive therapy for depression.

Another potential therapeutic is curcumin, derived from the curry spice turmeric, which has shown efficacy in multiple animal models of depression as well as antioxidant and neuroprotective properties (Lopresti, Hood, & Drummond, 2012). Clinical studies have shown curcumin to have anti-inflammatory effects in a number of inflammatory-related diseases, yet therapeutic potential of curcumin as an antidepressant has been inconclusive (Andrade, 2014; Shehzad, Rehman, & Lee, 2013). MDD patients who received a curcumin-piperine combination (1000–10 mg per day) with conventional antidepressant therapy for 6 weeks showed greater reductions in anxious and depressive symptoms than those who received antidepressant therapy alone (Panahi, Badeli, Karami, & Sahebkar, 2015). However, among other issues, the study was not randomized, blinded, or placebo controlled and did not take into account the pro-inflammatory state of patients. A small randomized double-blind trial that administered curcumin (500 mg twice daily) or placebo for 8 weeks did not find any difference between the two groups in reduction of depressive symptoms (Lopresti, Maes, Maker, Hood, & Drummond, 2014). Further examination revealed that, while there was no difference between both groups from baseline to week 4, the curcumin group showed significant reductions in depressive symptoms from week 4 to week 8; the effect was most pronounced in those with atypical depression, defined as mood reactivity to potential or actual positive events and two or more of the following symptoms: significant weight gain or increased appetite, hypersomnia, leaden paralysis, or history of interpersonal rejection sensitivity (American Psychiatric Association, 2013). Atypical depression has been shown to be associated with a higher inflammatory state, including increased CRP, IL-6, and TNF-α levels (Hickman, Khambaty, & Stewart, 2014; Lamers et al., 2013). Therefore, it is possible that the antidepressant effects of curcumin are slower acting than initially thought and only effective in certain subpopulations of depressed patients.

Finally, patients with depression also display lowered circulating levels of vitamin E, unrelated to dietary intake (Maes et al., 2000; Owen, Batterham, Probst, Grenyer, & Tapsell, 2005). In humans, α-Tocopherol is considered the most active form of Vitamin E. α-Tocopherol pretreatment in rodents was shown to suppress LPS-induced pro-inflammatory cytokine production and sickness behavior, effects that occur via actions on the NF-κB pathway (Berg, Godbout, Kelley, & Johnson, 2004; Godbout, Berg, Krzyszton, & Johnson, 2005). α-Tocopherol was also shown to suppress depressive-like behavior induced by TNF-α administration in mice (Manosso et al., 2013). Currently, an ongoing clinical trial is investigating the antidepressant effects of α-Tocopherol (200 mg twice a day) coadministered with ascorbic acid, or Vitamin C (200 mg twice a day), for 12 weeks (ClinicalTrials.gov Identifier: NCT02793648). The second open-label portion of the study will examine the long-term effects of treatment for another 12 weeks.

Chemokines as Emerging Therapeutic Targets

Chemokines, signaling molecules that serve as chemoattractants to immune cells, are another group of inflammatory-related factors being investigated for their role in depression. While interventions designed to reduce biological activity of some chemokines show potential as depression treatments, more studies are necessary to determine which chemokines, if any, are best to investigate for their therapeutic potential in depression. Developing successful chemokine receptor antagonists that are effectively targeted and dosed in humans has historically been difficult and may partially explain why no clinical trials have been undertaken to investigate their therapeutic potential for treating depression (Horuk, 2009; Schall & Proudfoot, 2011). Moreover, even if a chemokine has shown to be associated with depression symptomatology, it is not always clear if reductions or increases of that chemokine's levels would be the most effective treatment. Thus, this section will focus mainly on preclinical and correlative clinical findings regarding the role of chemokines in depression.

One possible therapeutic target is chemokine ligand 2/monocyte chemotactic protein (MCP)-1, which, when bound to its receptor (CCR2) on peripheral immune cells, promotes migration of inflammatory monocytes into the brain (Yamasaki, Liu, Lin, & Ransohoff, 2012). LPS administration, often used as a cytokine-inducing model of depression in animals, elevated MCP-1 messenger RNA and protein levels as well as CCR2+ microglia and inflammatory monocytes in the brain (Cazareth, Guyon, Heurteaux, Chabry, & Petit-Paitel, 2014). A recent study indicated that a peripherally acting drug, ginsenoside Rg1, suppressed LPS- and chronic stress-induced depressive-like behaviors via disrupted proinflammatory (Ly6Chi) monocyte recruitment into the brain and subsequent inhibition of MCP-1 signaling (Zheng et al., 2016). Furthermore, blocking peripheral MCP-1 signaling via administration of a neutralizing MCP-1 monoclonal antibody suppressed LPS-induced depressive symptoms (Zheng et al., 2016). Two meta-analyses examining chemokines in depression found that levels of MCP-1 were significantly higher in depressed patients compared to healthy controls (Eyre et al., 2016; Köhler et al., 2017). Therefore, emerging preclinical studies and descriptive work in patients suggest that MCP-1 may be a key chemokine to target for treatment of depression.

On the other hand, another recent meta-analysis found that, out of all peripheral chemokines examined (eotaxin-1, eotaxin-3, IP-10, MCP-1, MCP-4, MDC, MIP-1α, MIP-1β, and TARC), only macrophage-derived chemokine (MDC) levels were altered in patients who responded to antidepressant treatment. More specifically, these patients showed a significant increase in MDC levels by the end of treatment, indicating that elevations of MDC are associated with reductions in depressive symptoms (Milenkovic et al., 2017). MDC binds to CCR4, which, among other cell types, is primarily found in T-Helper 2 cells and Tregs (Yoshie & Matsushima, 2014). Another chemokine of interest is CX3CL1 (or fractalkine). CX3CL1 is primarily expressed by neurons in the brain and thought to inhibit microglia via binding to its receptor, CX3CR1, that is primarily expressed on microglia (Bacon & Harrison, 2000). CX3CR1-deficient mice exhibited prolonged microglia activation, elevated microglial expression of IL-1β and indoleamine 2,3-dioxygenase (IDO), and prolonged depressive-like behavior following LPS administration (Corona et al., 2010). Alternatively, another study found that CX3CR1-deficient mice were resistant to the depressive behavior and microglial morphology changes that resulted in wild-type mice following a chronic despair model (Hellwig et al., 2016). In sum, futures studies are needed to uncover the role of MCP-1, MDC, CX3CL1, and other chemokines in depression.

Prostaglandins as a Mainstay of Inflammation

Nonsteroidal anti-inflammatory drugs (NSAIDS) and cyclooxygenase (COX) inhibitors are also used as pharmacotherapy for a number of diseases. COX-1 and COX-2 are the rate-limiting enzymes in the metabolism of arachidonic acid to prostaglandins, important lipids that are involved in multiple aspects of inflammation. Cox-1 is constitutively expressed in many, but not all, tissues and cells and is thought to be related to resolution of inflammatory processes (Morita, 2002). In contrast, COX-2 is constitutively expressed in the brain, is normally expressed in low levels in most tissues, and is highly inducible by inflammatory challenges and pro-inflammatory cytokines (Kaufmann, Andreasson, Isakson, & Worley, 1997). Centrally elevated expressions of COX-2 have been found in a rodent model of depression and peripherally in patients with recurrent depression (Cassano, Hidalgo, Burgos, Adris, & Argibay, 2006; Gałecki et al., 2012). Some preclinical studies have shown that inhibition of COX-2, via administration of the drug celecoxib, ameliorates inflammation and improves depressive-like behavior (Guo et al., 2009; Myint et al., 2007). Therefore, of the COX enzymes, COX-2 has been primarily investigated as a possible target to inhibit in the treatment for depression.

Some have examined if aspirin, a nonselective COX inhibitor, can be used as a preventative measure for depression. One study examining 345 women across 10 years found that women who had previously taken aspirin showed a lowered risk for development of MDD (Pasco et al., 2010). On the other hand, another study evaluating the aspirin use and cardiovascular and cognitive state of 5,556 older men (aged 69 to 87 years) found aspirin use may be associated with higher risk of depression in a 5-year follow-up (Almeida, Alfonso, Jamrozik, Hankey, & Flicker, 2010). They found that not only was aspirin not associated with lower rates of depression in older men, but those who had used aspirin in the past and had *stopped* by the time of assessment had a greater chance of showing depressive symptoms. However, higher incidence of depression as a result of past aspirin use may have been due to increased health complications, such as bleeding and cerebrovascular lesions, which may have, in turn, increased risk of depression (Almeida et al., 2010). These findings illustrate the importance of considering off-target health effects of drugs targeting inflammation in the treatment of stress-related diseases. A following study from the same researchers found that older men (aged 69 to 87 years old) with high total plasma homocysteine, which is associated with increased risk of cardiovascular events and depression, showed a lower risk of depression if they took aspirin (Almeida et al., 2012). While findings regarding benefits of aspirin as a preventative measure for depression are tenuous at best, other NSAIDs have yet to be studied.

In contrast, there have been encouraging results in clinical studies examining the therapeutic effects of COX inhibitors as palliative treatment. One study pooled data from five nearly identical randomized and double-blind trials examining male and female subjects with active osteoarthritis that were assessed for depression using the Patient Health Questionnaire-9 (PHQ-9). Subjects were given either COX-2 inhibitor (celecoxib), nonselective COX inhibitors (ibuprofen and naproxen), or placebo (Iyengar et al., 2013). After 6 weeks of treatment, both NSAID groups (receiving celecoxib or ibuprofen/naproxen) showed a reduction in PHQ-9 scores and a trend toward change in classification of depression, indicating resolution of depression. The researchers noted that the group receiving celecoxib was administered half the dose that had previously shown therapeutic benefits (200 mg/day instead of 400 mg/day), which possibly reduced the therapeutic effect of celecoxib on depressive symptoms. Köhler, Benros, Nordentoft, Mors, and Krogh (2015) also conducted a meta-analysis of randomized clinical trials evaluating the use of NSAIDs/cytokine inhibitors as treatments for depression and found that anti-inflammatory treatments, especially COX-2 inhibitors, reduced depressive symptoms.

Perhaps the clearest benefits of COX inhibitors are found in studies when they were concomitantly administered with typical antidepressants, especially in patients who have shown resistance to antidepressants. Abbasi, Hosseini, Modabbernia, Ashrafi, and Akhondzadeh (2012) conducted a randomized and double-blind study on 40 patients diagnosed with MDD, coadministered either sertraline (200 mg/day), an antidepressant, with celecoxib (200 mg/day) or placebo for 6 weeks. By week 4 the response to treatment rate was 95% in the celecoxib-sertraline group, compared to 50% in the placebo-Sertraline group and, by the end of the study, significantly more patients who received celecoxib treatment (35%) were in remission than those who received placebo (5%). It is of note that, while this study used a different measure of depressive symptoms than the Iyengar et al. study (Hamilton Depression Rating Scale vs. PHQ-9, respectively), both studies utilized the same dose of celecoxib for the same duration of time, suggesting the superiority of celecoxib when used in combination with antidepressants. Many more clinical trials have evaluated celecoxib, and a meta-analysis determined that celecoxib is a safe and effective adjunctive therapy option (Faridhosseini, Sadeghi, Farid, & Pourgholami, 2014). Thus, while COX-2 alone may not be effective in treating depression, it may have value as an augmentative strategy.

More recent findings have challenged the notion that COX-2 has a purely pro-inflammatory function in the brain. COX-2 regulates synaptic plasticity, blood flow, and memory consolidation (Minghetti, 2004) but also exhibits anti-inflammatory and neuroprotective effects in response to certain inflammatory challenges. Mice genetically deficient in COX-2 showed an exacerbated response to LPS in the form of increased neuronal damage, microglia and astrocyte activation, and expression of pro-inflammatory cytokines and chemokines. The same study found that chronic administration of celecoxib to wild-type mice also increased LPS-induced levels of IL-1β when compared to wild-type mice only administered LPS (Aid, Langenbach, & Bosetti, 2008). Even though studies utilizing celecoxib have yielded encouraging results, the drug also has confounding off-target effects unrelated to inflammation that complicate interpretation of the results (Miller & Raison, 2015). For instance, celecoxib was shown to affect glucocorticoid receptors and cadherin-11, an adhesion molecule that may be involved in synaptic regulation and fear- and anxiety-related responses (Manabe et al., 2000).

Although once considered to be solely involved in maintenance, Cox-1 is now gaining more recognition for having a pro-inflammatory role. Centrally, Cox-1 is expressed by perivascular cells and microglia, the primary immune cells of the brain (Maes, 2012). Genetic deficiency or pharmacological inhibition of COX-1 has been shown to alleviate the inflammatory and oxidative effects of LPS administration (Choi, Langenbach, & Bosetti, 2008). In a mouse Parkinsonian model, COX-1 was upregulated and an inhibition of COX-1 extended life span (Gu et al., 2010). Therefore, focus has been shifting from COX-2 to COX-1 as a target to attenuate neuroinflammation as a COX-inhibiting treatment for depression (Maes, 2012).

IDO as a Mediator of the Kynurenine Pathway

There is also evidence for the involvement of the kynurenine pathway in inflammation and, consequently, depression. The kynurenine pathway involves the catabolism of tryptophan, an essential amino acid that is a biosynthetic precursor to various neuroactive compounds, most notably serotonin (Davis & Liu, 2015). One particular point of interest in this pathway is indoleamine 2,3-dioxygenase (IDO), a rate-limiting enzyme responsible for degrading tryptophan into kynurenine, an intermediate that is further catabolized into either neuroprotective or neurotoxic metabolites (reviewed in Dantzer, O'Connor, Lawson, & Kelley, 2011). IDO is of interest as it is cytokine activated, possessing anti-inflammatory properties, and implicated as a mediator of depressive-like symptoms in animal models. Although the dysregulation of kynurenine pathway metabolites has been evident in depression, the specific role of IDO is unclear; IDO may reduce tryptophan, resulting in lowered serotonin levels, or it may elevate kynurenine, resulting in the neurotoxic metabolites quinolinic acid and 3-hydroxykynurenine (reviewed in Dantzer, O'Connor, Lawson, & Kelley, 2011). Nevertheless, the inhibition of IDO has produced positive results preclinically and may prove useful clinically. Administration of an IDO inhibitor, 1-methyl tryptophan (1-MT), blocked depressive-like behaviors in inflammatory and chronic stress models of depression (Laugeray et al., 2016; O'Connor, Lawson, Andre, et al., 2009; O'Connor, Lawson, André, et al., 2009). 1-MT and INCB24360, another IDO inhibitor, are currently being clinically investigated as immunotherapy for a number of cancers, but neither has been evaluated for their potential behavioral effects in depressed patients (clinicaltrials.gov). There is great interest in developing more potent and selective IDO inhibitors as cancer treatments, which may indirectly inform its potential application in treating depression (Jiang et al., 2015a).

In addition to IDO inhibitors, other avenues involving the kynurenine pathway and its potential involvement in a pharmocotherapeutic treatment for depression are being explored. The omega-3 polyunsaturated fatty acids eicosapentanoic acid (EPA) and docosahexanoic acid (DHA) are components found in fish oils that have been gathering attention for their anti-inflammatory action and beneficial effect on depressed patients (Maes et al., 2009; Mocking et al., 2016). A recent in vitro study exploring the effects of EPA and DHA and SSRIs (sertraline and venlafaxine) on IL-1β administration indicated that the antidepressive properties of EPA and DHA may be related to altering IDO activity (Borsini et al., 2017). Treatment with EPA, DHA, sertraline, and venlafaxine reversed IL-1β-induced increases in IDO levels, by 36%, 81%, 44%, and 38%, respectively (Borsini et al., 2017). DHA treatment also prevented the usual increase levels of neurotoxic metabolites such as quinolinic acid (Borsini et al., 2017). Although the direct effect of the omega-3 fatty acids on the kynurenine pathway is unclear, these findings suggest that the beneficial effects of EPA and DHA are mediated by actions on the kynurenine pathway and are worthy of further investigation.

In addition to IDO, tryptophan 2,3-dioxygenase (TDO) may also be a target of interest for novel pharmacotherapeutics in depression. TDO acts similarly to IDO by metabolizing tryptophan into kynurenine, but it was previously thought to be expressed solely in the liver. However, recent evidence has shown the presence of TDO in the brain and other regions (Dantzer et al., 2011). Preclinical and clinical studies are needed to determine if TDO is a useful target in treating depression via the kynurenine pathway.

Immune Cell Interactions With the Central Nervous System: A Critical Role for Immune-to-Brain Communication

Recent research has underscored the importance of cell-to-cell interactions within the CNS as critical for CNS function. For instance, we now recognize the importance of astrocytes and microglia in synaptic transmission, an effect that has come to be known as the tripartite synapse (Allen & Barres, 2009; Araque, Parpura, Sanzgiri, & Haydon, 1999). Even more recently, studies have established the role of the brain vasculature in delivery of nutrients and synaptic health, which is now known as the neurovascular unit in the normal functioning brain (reviewed in Barres, 2008; Muoio, Persson, & Sendeski, 2014). In a diseased or otherwise compromised state, immune cells in particular have a tendency to migrate toward sites of damage or infiltrate the CNS from the periphery. Thus, the CNS is a highly dynamic cellular landscape, with glial and other immune cells providing novel cellular targets for development of cell-type-specific pharmacotherapeutics. The evidence for cell-type-specific targets in treating depression is reviewed briefly as follows.

Microglia

Some authors have argued that virtually every hypothesis regarding the pathophysiology underlying MDD can be tied back to microglial-related neuroinflammation (Singhal & Baune, 2017). Therefore, there is great interest in blocking the activation of microglia, which are largely considered to be the resident immune cells of the brain. Minocycline, a tetracycline antibiotic, is frequently described as a putative microglial inhibitor, blocking many aspects of microglia activation and proliferation that results in anti-inflammatory effects (Soczynska et al., 2012). Preclinically, minocycline was shown to inhibit stress-induced cytokine expression (Blandino et al., 2009, 2006) and depressive-like behaviors in various animal models of depression (Arakawa et al., 2012; Henry et al., 2008; O'Connor, Lawson, André, et al., 2009). A small open-label study revealed that patients with psychotic depression showed a significant reduction in depressive symptoms after receiving minocycline (50 mg twice daily for the first week, then three times daily until end of trial at 6 weeks) as adjunctive therapy to antidepressant treatment (Miyaoka et al., 2012). A randomized, double-blind, placebo-controlled phase IV clinical trial (ClinicalTrials.gov Identifier: NCT02263872) also evaluating the use of minocycline as adjunctive therapy was recently completed, but results are not yet available. It is important to keep in mind that minocycline has broad, often nonspecific effects, including actions on astrocytes, neurons, and oligodendrocytes, as well as peripheral immune cells, that contribute to unwanted side effects and may not be relevant to treating depression (Miller & Raison, 2015; Möller et al., 2016).

A growing body of work indicates that altering phosphodiesterase 4 (PDE4) and its hydrolysis of cAMP may limit microglial function. Inhibition of PDE4 is thought to suppress the activation of microglia and astrocytes, due to resulting increased levels of cAMP and cAMP-dependent PKA, CREB, and BDNF that exert anti-inflammatory and antidepressant effects (Wang et al., 2017). Administration of rolipram, a PDE4 inhibitor, results in anti-inflammatory effects in various inflammatory-related rodent models (Atkins et al., 2007; Taguchi et al., 1999; Wang et al., 2012), and clinical studies dating back to the 1980s have shown that it is also effective in ameliorating depressive symptoms (Bertolino et al., 1988; Zeller, Stief, Pflug, & Sastre-y-Hernandez, 1984). However, side effects, including nausea, emesis, and gastrointestinal abnormalities, have limited the therapeutic use of rolipram (Montana & Dyke, 2002). Two other PDE4 inhibitors approved to treat peripheral inflammatory disorders, roflumilast and apremilast, must inhibit PDE4 by no more than 50% as similar side effects are apparent at higher doses (Wang et al., 2017).

The PDE4 inhibitor etazolate hydrochloride (SQ 20,009) has shown promising preclinical results indicating antidepressant, anxiolytic, and anti-inflammatory effects and appears to be safe and well tolerated (Beer, Chasin, Clody, & Vogel, 1972; Guo et al., 2014; Jindal, Mahesh, Bhatt, & Pandey, 2016; Jindal, Mahesh, Gautam, Bhatt, & Pandey, 2012; Vellas et al., 2011). Unfortunately, it seems as though the development of etazolate has been discontinued for reasons unrelated to the efficacy or tolerability of the drug (Wang et al., 2017). Another PDE4 inhibitor, Ibudilast, was shown to inhibit microglial activation and has widespread anti-inflammatory effects, including reduced pro-inflammatory cytokine/chemokine production, increased anti-inflammatory production, and reduced myelin basic protein-induced IL-12, IFN-γ, and T-cell production (Rolan, Hutchinson, & Johnson, 2009). Furthermore, it was shown to have a favorable safety profile and to be well tolerated in humans, although it has not yet been tested as a treatment for depression or anxiety disorders (Rolan et al., 2009; Vesterinen et al., 2015). In addition to investigation of better-tolerated PDE4 inhibitors, increasing attention has been given to more selective targeting of PDE4 subtypes, specifically PDE4A, PDE4B, and PDE4D (Wang et al., 2017). However, their specific roles in mediating behavioral and inflammatory changes related to depression and anxiety have yet to be determined.

Monocyte-Derived Cells

Although there is extensive evidence supporting the role of resident microglia as key participants in stress-related neuroinflammation, chronic stress may also be associated with peripheral immune cells migrating into the CNS. This hypothesis arose from the early demonstration that chemokines, factors known to promote immune cell migration, were increased in the CNS after acute stress, thereby serving as a precipitating stimulus for passage of immune cells into the brain. This has now been shown in mice subjected to chronic stress in the form of social defeat (Hodes et al., 2014; Wohleb et al., 2011), with studies showing that infiltration of peripheral monocytes into the brain is the mechanism that leads to anxiety- and depressive-like behaviors (Wohleb et al., 2011). Thus, understanding the mechanisms by which stressful life experiences alter immune cell function and phenotypes may provide novel pharmacotherapeutic strategies for the treatment of stress-related disorders down the road.

T Cells

Given that depression involves cell-mediated immunity as well as cytokine-related inflammation, targeting T lymphocytes and related pathways could prove beneficial as a treatment (Maes, 2011). T cells have shown to have a protective effect against stress in animal models. Lymphocytes transferred from chronically socially defeated mice to naïve lymphopenic mice conferred antidepressant behavior and increased neurogenesis in the brain (Brachman, Lehmann, Maric, & Herkenham, 2015). Moreover, CD4+ T cells transferred from naïve mice to naive lymphopenic mice also resulted in antidepressant behavior (Clark, Soroka, Song, Li, & Tonelli, 2016). These findings suggest that the inflammatory phenotype encoded in circulating immune cells may be important for determining subsequent mood state, thus supporting the notion that immune-to-brain communication is essential for understanding the role of inflammation in psychiatric disease states.

While more studies are needed to investigate which T-cell subpopulations are best to target, some evidence points to regulatory T cells (Tregs) (Haroon et al., 2012). Tregs are known as suppressors of the immune system, potentially through anti-inflammatory factors IL-10 and transforming growth factor (TGF), with all three shown to be reduced in depression (Grosse et al., 2016; Y. Li et al., 2010).

Additionally, lowered levels of Tregs in MDD patients are negatively correlated with the monocyte proinflammatory gene expression (Grosse et al., 2016). Killed *Mycobacterium vaccae* (*M. vaccae*) generate Treg cells in mice, mediated by IL-10 and TGF-β (Zuany-Amorim et al., 2002). One study showed that administration of heat-killed *M. vaccae* in mice reduced anxiety-like behavior and enhanced proactive coping in a chronic psychosocial stress model, which is associated with resiliency to stress-induced depression (Reber et al., 2016; Wood, Walker, Valentino, & Bhatnagar, 2010). Moreover, *M. vaccae* prevented a stress-induced decline of tryptophan. Anti-CD25 administration, which depletes Tregs, blocked the anxiolytic effects in *M. vaccae*–treated mice, but it did not prevent the proactive coping response (Reber et al., 2016). A randomized open-label, phase III clinical study found that administration of SRL172 (heat-killed *M. vaccae*) improved quality of life but not survival rates in non-small-cell lung cancer patients (O'Brien et al., 2004). More clinical studies are necessary to determine if treatment targeting Treg deficiencies reduces depressive symptoms in patients.

T-helper 17 (Th17) cells and effector T (Teff) cells may also be promising targets. A few studies have seen levels of pro-inflammatory Th17 cells and its primary cytokine IL-17 upregulated in depressed patients, although some have not (reviewed in Slyepchenko et al., 2016). Blocking Th17 cell function by administering anti-IL-17A in mice blocked depressive behavior (Beurel, Harrington, & Jope, 2013). On the other hand, activation of autoreactive Teff cells, through immunization with a weak agonist of myelin-derived peptide, was able to recover decreased neurogenesis and BDNF levels as well as depressive-like behavior following chronic mild stress (Lewitus et al., 2009). While animal studies indicate that antidepressants alter T cell function, more studies are needed to further determine the role of T cells in depression.

Microbiome

The role of the microbiome in general physiology and the development of numerous pathophysiological disease states is a particularly robust area of research, and extensive reviews are available elsewhere (Foster & McVey Neufeld, 2013; Kelly et al., 2016; Sherwin, Dinan, & Cryan, 2017). The central tenet of this work is that bacteria comprising the microbiome establish a steady-state interaction with the host immune system, and that disruptions in the microbiome can thereby influence the tonic activational state of the immune system, thereby impacting multiple disease states. Thus, the use of specific probiotic formulations designed to alter the composition of the microbiome, particularly in the gut, is of interest in treating depression. This approach has been referred to as "psychobiotics," or the use of living organisms to treat psychiatric illnesses (Dinan, Stanton, & Cryan, 2013). Various studies have found that specific bacterial compositions are associated with depression in humans (Aizawa et al., 2016; Jiang et al., 2015b; Lin et al., 2017; Naseribafrouei et al., 2014). For instance, depressive symptom severity may be negatively correlated with levels of genus *Faecalibacterium* (Jiang et al., 2015b). Moreover, fecal microbiota transfer from depressed human patients to microbiota-deficient rats conferred depressive-like and anxiety-like behaviors as well as altered tryptophan metabolism, suggesting that the administration of probiotics may reduce symptoms (Kelly et al., 2016). Of particular note is the association of depression with the underrepresentation of the genus *Bifidobacterium* and *Lactobacillus* (Aizawa et al., 2016). Administration of *Bifidobacteria infantis* 35624 reduced various pro-inflammatory markers in ulcerative colitis, chronic fatigue syndrome, and psoriasis patients in three separate trials (Groeger et al., 2013). One randomized, double-blind, placebo-controlled study found that probiotic treatment containing *Lactobacillus casei* strain Shirota elevated mood in healthy subjects with poorer mood at baseline (Benton, Williams, & Brown, 2007). Another randomized, double-blind study showed that daily administration of probiotics containing *Lactobacillus helveticus* R0052 and *Bifidobacterium longum* R0175 for 30 days was significantly more effective at reducing psychological distress and depression symptoms in healthy volunteers than the placebo treatment (Messaoudi et al., 2011). Utilization of probiotics as antidepressant therapy could provide exciting new opportunities for more individualized treatment in the future.

The Renin-Angiotensin System and Inflammation

Hypertension, or elevated blood pressure, is associated with chronic stress and anxiety, although the exact nature of the relationship is not fully understood (Byrd & Brook, 2014). The renin-angiotensin system is heavily involved in regulating blood pressure, mostly through its key neuropeptide Angiotensin II (Ang II), which shapes vascular constriction, sympathetic nervous system activation, and water and sodium retention, among other processes (Schmieder, 2005). Ang II exerts most of its effects via binding to Ang II type 1 (AT1) receptor, which influences inflammation through a multitude of cellular actions. For instance, AT1 activates NF-κb, nicotinamide adenine dinucleotide phosphate oxidase, microglial RhoA/Rho kinase pathway, COX-2, and inducible nitric oxide synthase, as well as stimulates the release of pro-inflammatory cytokines (Vian et al., 2017). Moreover, the renin-angiotensin system is involved with T cells, which both produce Ang II and express AT1, and HPA axis function (Dinh, Drummond, Sobey, & Chrissobolis, 2014; Vian et al., 2017).

Preliminary evidence indicates that targeting activity of the renin-angiotensin system may be particularly useful for treating depression (Vian et al., 2017). Administration of candesartan, an AT1 receptor blocker, suppressed LPS-induced central iNOS and Cox-2 expression, and microglial production of pro-inflammatory factors, and it reduced anxiety-like behavior in rats (Benicky et al., 2011). Other AT1 receptor blockers (Valsartan and Irbesartan) may lead to hippocampal neurogenesis, increase BDNF, and reverse depressive-like behavior that results from unpredictable mild stress (Ayyub, Najmi, & Akhtar, 2017; Ping, Qian, Song, & Zhaochun, 2014). Likewise, angiotension-converting enzyme inhibitors, which prevent the conversion of Ang I to Ang II, have been shown to have anti-inflammatory and antidepressant effects (Giardina & Ebert, 1989; Torika, Asraf, Roasso, Danon, & Fleisher-Berkovich, 2016). At this time, no clinical trials have been conducted specifically to test the effect of AT1 receptor blockers and angiotensin-converting enzyme inhibitors on neuropsychiatric patients. However, clinical studies investigating other diseases have shown that AT1 receptor blockers and angiotensin-converting enzyme inhibitors can elevate mood and may decrease the risk for depression (reviewed in Vian et al., 2017).

Pharmacotherapeutic Approaches Arising From Classic Stress-Responsive Systems: The HPA Axis and Beyond
Corticotropin-Releasing Hormone
Corticotropin-releasing hormone (CRH) is a peptide hormone secreted from multiple stress-responsive CNS structures, most notably the PVN, and mediates behavioral and physiological changes that occur as a result of stressful experiences

(Grammatopoulos & Chrousos, 2002). In particular, CRH regulates the endocrine, autonomic, and immune responses to stress by activating the HPA axis (Smagin & Dunn, 2000; Smagin, Heinrichs, & Dunn, 2001). CRH in the CNS works to inhibit inflammation, whereas peripheral CRH stimulates inflammation (Tsigos & Chrousos, 2002). Preclinical studies have shown that CRH receptor 1 (CRHR1) antagonists produce anxiolytic and antidepressant effects in animal models (Deak et al., 1999; Waters et al., 2015), generating interest in the therapeutic potential of CRHR1 antagonists in depression. The most promising evidence came from a small open-label study that administered CRHR1 antagonist NBI-30775/R121919 in depressed patients at a low dose (5 mg/d starting dose that was escalated up to 40 mg/d) and a high dose (40 mg/d dose that was escalated up to 80 mg/d) for 30 days (Zobel et al., 2000). Patients administered the low dose experienced a significant reduction in depression and anxiety, and patients administered the higher doses fared even better, with 8 out of 10 patients characterized as responders by the end of treatment. After treatment stopped, depressive symptoms (both doses) and anxiety symptoms (only the higher dose) worsened in as little as 2 days, indicating NBI30775/R121919 served as palliative care. Unfortunately, while no changes of liver enzymes or any other significant side effects were found at the doses used by the investigators, clinical development of NBI30775/R121919 was terminated after hepatic toxicity was found in two healthy controls who received high doses of NBI30775/R121919 in an unpublished safety study (Künzel et al., 2003; Paez-Pereda, Hausch, & Holsboer, 2011).

Since this initial first successful study, no other CRHR1 antagonists have made it past phase II clinical trials. Various drugs, including pexacerfont (BMS-562086), CP316,311, and verucerfont (NBI-77860/GSK561679), showed no effect or performed more poorly than placebos in terms of symptom reductions in studies targeting GAD, MDD, PTSD, and anxiety in the context of alcohol use disorder (Binneman et al., 2008; Coric et al., 2010; Grillon et al., 2015; Kwako et al., 2014; GlaxoSmithKline Results Summary for CRS106139). However, verucerfont was shown to reduce levels of ACTH in women with congenital adrenal hyperplasia and to suppress ACTH/cortisol levels in anxious, alcohol-dependent women following a dexamethasone-CRH challenge, indicating its regulation of HPA function in humans (Schwandt et al., 2016; Turcu et al., 2016).

The apparent failure of virtually all CRHR1 antagonists to influence depressive symptoms raises questions concerning the interpretation of available preclinical data. In particular, concerns have been raised surrounding the targeting and timing of intervention; for example, CRHR1 antagonists may be of better use as treatment for disorders in which stressors play a more "dynamic" role, such as PTSD or panic disorders, rather than for chronic conditions such as in MDD and generalized anxiety disorder (Koob & Zorrilla, 2012; Spierling & Zorrilla, 2017). The initial response to stress is thought to be mediated by CRHR1-CRH interactions, and it has been posited that CRHR1 receptor antagonists may be more appropriately used as preventative or early treatment before CRH activation becomes chronic (Ryabinin et al., 2012; Spierling & Zorrilla, 2017). On the other hand, CRHR2 and urocortin interactions are thought to be more involved in later, adaptive responses to stress, and more attention has been given to these as potential targets in neuropsychiatric diseases (Ryabinin et al., 2012). Additionally, there is some thought that CRHR1 antagonists may be best suited for a subpopulation of patients who show high activation of CRH systems, suggesting a personalized medicine approach may be more effective (Spierling & Zorrilla, 2017). The merits of CRH-CRHR1 activation as prognostic indices of treatment response to CRH-CRHR1 antagonists may therefore be warranted for future clinical trials

Glucocorticoids

Corticosteroids, including cortisol in humans and corticosterone in rodents and other species, are further downstream in the HPA axis (reviewed in Spencer & Deak, 2017). Glucocorticoid (GC) binding to glucocorticoid receptors (GRs) has various anti-inflammatory actions, from inhibition of the expression of pro-inflammatory genes to inhibition of NF-κB and MAP-kinase related activity (Barnes & Adcock, 2009). Moreover, GCs play a crucial role in exerting negative feedback on the HPA axis, including inhibition of its precursor CRH (Pace, Hu, & Miller, 2007). Both MDD and PTSD have been shown to have impaired HPA-axis negative feedback, though the manifestation of the HPA-axis dysfunction is often unclear and may vary across PTSD, MDD, and other stress-related disorders. With that said, the global actions of glucocorticoids across many cell types throughout the body make it difficult to disentangle effects that are mediated by anti-inflammatory actions of the drugs versus those that remain independent of inflammation.

Whether GR agonism, through administration of GC therapy, can relieve PTSD symptoms is currently under investigation. PTSD may be associated with enhanced HPA-axis negative feedback, exhibited by suppressed cortisol levels (Pitman et al., 2012). For instance, lower levels of cortisol immediately following trauma have been linked to greater risk of developing PTSD, and individuals with PTSD showed greater suppression of cortisol following a dexamethasone challenge (Delahanty, Raimonde, & Spoonster, 2000; McFarlane, Atchison, & Yehuda, 1997; Yehuda, Boisoneau, Lowry, & Giller, 1995). Reduced cortisol levels are thought to contribute to enhanced retrieval of traumatic experiences and the re-experiencing symptoms that characterize PTSD (de Quervain, 2007; Steckler & Risbrough, 2012). A small double-blind, placebo-controlled, crossover designed study found that low-dose cortisol treatment (10 mg/day) for a month significantly reduced PTSD symptoms, particularly re-experiencing and avoidance symptoms (Aerni et al., 2004). On the other hand, hydrocortisone treatment (10 mg/day and 30 mg/day) for a week in female patients with PTSD showed no effect in a randomized, double-blind, placebo-controlled crossover study (Ludäscher et al., 2015). Administration of a single dose of GC treatment (4 mg/kg) immediately following traumatic memory reactivation reduced avoidance symptoms in PTSD participants in another double-blind placebo-controlled study; however, these effects were transient as they lasted for less than a month (Surís, North, Adinoff, Powell, & Greene, 2010). Finally, PTSD patients receiving hydrocortisone augmentation to prolonged exposure behavioral therapy had lower PTSD symptoms than those receiving placebo (Yehuda et al., 2015). Responders to hydrocortisone treatment showed a greater GR sensitivity at baseline, suggesting a potential to predict responsiveness of patients to glucocorticoid treatment.

Administration of cortisol may be useful as a preventative measure as well for PTSD. Patients treated in an intensive care unit (ICU) are at risk for developing PTSD symptoms, given the extreme stress they experience (Schelling et al., 1998, 2003). Administration of hydrocortisone was shown to reduce later development of PTSD symptoms in ICU patients (Schelling et al., 1999, 2001, 2004). One recent large follow-up study of a randomized, double-blind, placebo-controlled, clinical trial ($n = 1,244$) found that administration of dexamethasone during cardiac surgery had no effect overall on the development of PTSD 18 months later, but further subgroup analysis revealed that females who received dexamethasone exhibited significantly lower rates of PTSD and depression (Kok et al., 2016). Two separate double-blind, placebo-controlled studies found that hydrocortisone administration within 12 hours of a traumatic event was more effective than placebo at reducing PTSD and depressive symptoms (Delahanty et al., 2013; Zohar et al., 2011). Furthermore, a recent meta-analysis evaluating pharmacological interventions that were initiated within the first month of a traumatic or aversive event showed that hydrocortisone was a more effective treatment than beta-blockers or SSRIs for prevention of PTSD (Sijbrandij, Kleiboer, Bisson, Barbui, & Cuijpers, 2015), further underscoring the importance of timing of drug delivery. However, the authors noted that more studies are needed to fully determine the benefits of GC administration. Currently, there are two ongoing clinical trials investigating cortisol/dexamethasone as preventative treatment for PTSD (ClinicalTrials.gov Identifier: NCT00855270; ClinicalTrials.gov Identifier: NCT02753166), and a phase IV trial investigating the effects of hydrocortisone for fear responses and memory of fear in veterans with PTSD has recently been completed with unavailable results (ClinicalTrials.gov Identifier: NCT00674570).

There is also some preliminary evidence that GC treatment at a range of doses can relieve symptoms in patients with phobias, another fear-related disorder that can originate due to traumatic experience and/or be exacerbated by major life stressors. A single dose of cortisol (25 mg) administered 1 hour before exposure to the Trier Social Stress Test significantly reduced self-report fear in socially phobic individuals as compared to placebo treatment in a double-blind study (Soravia et al., 2006). Additionally, greater change in cortisol levels was associated with lower fear ratings among those who received corticosterone. Similarly, cortisol (10 mg) administered 1 hour before presentation of a photograph of a spider was shown to reduce stimulus-induced fear among individuals with a spider phobia, and this reduction was maintained when subjects were reexposed to the stimulus 2 days later (Soravia et al., 2006). Cortisol augmentation was likewise shown to enhance the efficacy of behavioral exposure therapy for patients with a phobia for heights (de Quervain et al., 2011). Intriguingly, endogenous cortisol levels can affect the response to exposure therapy for patients with phobia of spiders (Lass-Hennemann & Michael, 2014). Patients treated with behavioral therapy in the morning, when basal

cortisol levels are higher, showed less fear of spiders than those treated in the afternoon, when basal cortisol levels are lower, and these effects were still present at the 3-month posttreatment assessment. These findings suggest that glucocorticoid therapy may be a useful adjunct in the treatment of certain anxiety-related disorders.

Given that GC therapy has been shown to have adverse side effects, including inducing an immunocompromised state with prolonged drug treatment, there have been efforts to more selectively target the specific mechanisms of GCs that ameliorate symptoms (Huscher et al., 2009). For instance, delta 9,11 derivatives of steroids are being screened for their potential to exert anti-inflammatory effects of GCs without the unwanted side effects (Baudy et al., 2012). VBP15 is a novel delta 9,11 class drug that was initially developed to treat muscular dystrophy but may show to have some use for treating stress-related disorders (Heier et al., 2013). Structurally similar to GCs, VBP15 was favored due to its high affinity for GR, low affinity for mineralocorticoid receptor, and selective NF-κB inhibition. VBP15 activation of GR blocks NF-κB-mediated inflammation, including expression of TNF-α, IL-6, and Cox-2. Moreover, VBP15 does not appear to exert the same immunotoxic and immunosuppressive properties as prednisolone, a synthetic derivative of cortisol. A phase I clinical trial found VBP15 (vamorolone) to be safe in humans, and other ongoing studies are also evaluating its safety and tolerability (Guglieri et al., 2017; ClinicalTrials.gov Identifier: NCT02760277; ClinicalTrials.gov Identifier: NCT02760264). These findings raise the possibility that VBP15 may prove to be a viable treatment for stress-related disorders as well.

Glucocorticoid Resistance

While GC treatment is a potentially promising anti-inflammatory therapy, portions of patients with inflammatory and immune diseases show an impaired negative feedback response to administration of GCs, an effect that is often described as GC resistance. Depression, in particular, is frequently associated with GC resistance, affecting as many as 80% of MDD patients (Heuser, Yassouridis, & Holsboer, 1994). Unlike PTSD, HPA dysfunction associated with MDD can take multiple forms, including hypercortisolemia (i.e., increased CORT during the trough of circadian rhythms), reduced response to CRH challenge, or ineffective axis "shutoff" in response to dexamethasone. Nevertheless, high levels of cortisol in those that go on to develop depression following a trauma tend to have higher cortisol levels immediately following the trauma (McFarlane et al., 1997). Extended exposure to GCs leads to GC resistance, or impaired GR function resulting in insensitivity to GCs (Barnes & Adcock, 2009). Impaired GR function can manifest as reduced numbers of GRs, reduced affinity of ligands to GRs, and diminished ability of GR to alter transcription (Ramamoorthy & Cidlowski, 2013). This is particularly important to inflammatory-related diseases associated with elevated levels of GCs.

Various targets and treatments have been examined toward the goal of enhancing GR function and thereby reducing GC insensitivity, including NF-κB/MAP-kinase signaling pathways, PDE4, and Tregs—all of which have been discussed previously. For instance, administration of p38 MAPK inhibitor SB203580 was shown to reverse suppression of GR function in steroid-dependent asthma patients who exhibited GC resistance (Irusen et al., 2002). A recent study found that administration of SB203580 ameliorated depressive-like behaviors in a mouse model for Alzheimer's disease (Guo et al., 2017). Currently a phase II trial is investigating another p38 inhibitor, AZD7624, in corticosteroid-resistant asthmatics (ClinicalTrials.gov Identifier: NCT02753764). Moreover, vitamin D was shown to recover dexamethasone-induced reduction in GR expression as well as enhance T cell IL-10 production in GC-resistant asthmatics.

Others are examining ways to selectively enhance the mechanisms by which GCs reduce transcription of inflammatory-related genes. Activation of the GR results in recruitment of histone deacetylease 2 (HDAC2), an enzyme involved in reduction of histone acetylation, limiting the availability of RNA polymerase II to transcribe NF-κB related gene expression (Ito et al., 2006). Theophylline, a bronchodilator commonly prescribed for asthma and COPD reduces GC insensitivity in patients by inhibiting PDE3/PDE4 and also by activating HDAC2 (Barnes, 2013; Cosio et al., 2004). Unfortunately, theophylline is also associated with a high rate of side effects, which some believe is due to PDE inhibition (Barnes, 2013). As the restoration of HDAC2 levels following theophylline administration appears to be due to selective inhibition of phosphoinositide-3-kinase-δ (PI3Kδ), some are investigating the use of PI3Kδ as a more specific means of targeting of GC insensitivity (To et al., 2010). Currently, PI3Kδ inhibitors are being tested in a number of inflammatory-related diseases and more selective inhibitors are being developed (Hoegenauer

et al., 2017; Marone, Cmiljanovic, Giese, & Wymann, 2008). Whether these drugs can reduce depression in patients who experience GC resistance is yet to be seen, but the possibility merits future study.

Endocannabinoids

Endocannabinoids, N-arachidonylethanolamide (anandamide) and 2-arachidonoylglycerol (2-AG), are a class of lipid mediators that make up the endocannabinoid system, in addition to cannabinoid receptors (CBs) and proteins that mediate and metabolize endocannabinoids (Vinod & Hungund, 2006). Components of the endocannabinoid system can be found centrally and peripherally, with the CB_1 receptors located primarily in the brain and CB_2 receptors in the peripheral organs (reviewed in Laurentiis, Araujo, & Rettori, 2014). The EC system has been implicated in modulating stress and HPA axis, with its dysregulation being associated with numerous mental disorders and neuropathies, including depression, schizophrenia, anxiety, and neuroinflammation (Hillard, Weinlander, & Stuhr, 2012). A small double-blind placebo-controlled study revealing the anxiolytic effects of 300 mg of cannabidiol (CBD), one of the active cannabinoids found in the cannabis plant, on a simulated public speaking test (SPST) in healthy subjects (Zuardi, Cosme, Graeff, & Guimarães, 1993) led to the investigation of the anxiolytic properties of CBD on social anxiety disorder (SAD) patients (Bergamaschi et al., 2011). Fear of public speaking is a common symptom of SAD, and SAD patients are more likely to "self-medicate" with cannabis than those with other anxiety disorders (Brunello et al., 2000; Buckner et al., 2008). One preliminary double-blind placebo-controlled cross-over study found that a single 400 mg dose of CBD resulted in a significant reduction of Visual Analogue Mood Scale (VAMS) anxiety scores in SAD patients who experienced a stress-inducing single-photon emission computed tomography imaging procedure (Crippa et al., 2011). A larger double-blind placebo-controlled study found that acute administration of CBD (600 mg) to SAD patients significantly reduced VAMS anxiety scores during SPST compared to a placebo (Bergamaschi et al., 2011).

Studies of natural and synthetic cannabinoids in treating PTSD have found that PTSD patients may "self-medicate," or use cannabinoids as a coping measure (reviewed in Betthauser, Pilz, & Vollmer, 2015). A retrospective chart review study examined 80 psychiatric evaluations of PTSD patients enrolled in the New Mexico Medical Cannabis Program. Cannabis use was associated with 75% reduction of Clinician Administered Posttraumatic Scale for *DSM-IV* (CAP) scores in all three areas of major PTSD symptoms (re-experiencing, avoidance, and hyperarousal), suggesting that cannabis may have a comprehensive role in mitigating PTSD symptoms (Greer, Grob, & Halberstadt, 2014). However, the lack of appropriate controls and other biases limit interpretation of these results. A retrospective study examined the effect of synthetic cannabinoid nabilone administration at varying doses on mentally ill inmates, of which 90% had PTSD (Cameron, Watson, & Robinson, 2014). Nabilone pretreatment and posttreatment measures showed that administration resulted in reduced PTSD-associated insomnia, nightmares, and PTSD symptoms, as well as an improvement in global assessment of functioning. Another small open-label clinical trial found that nabilone administration, starting at 0.5 mg nightly and titrated up or down based on efficacy at a maximum of 6 mg daily, significantly reduced the severity of, or completely terminated, nightmares in PTSD patients who experienced treatment-resistant nightmares (Fraser, 2009). Patients also described subjective improvements regarding sleep time and daytime flashbacks. Lastly, a small randomized, double-blind, placebo-controlled cross-over design study administered nabilone in PTSD patients with treatment-resistant nightmares on a similar dosing schedule for 7 weeks that did not exceed 3 mg (Jetly, Heber, Fraser, & Boisvert, 2015). Nabilolone significantly reduced CAPS Recurring and Distressing Dream scores and Clinical Global Impression of Change scores, and it significantly increased General Well Being Questionnaire scores. Larger clinical trials are needed to further elude the benefits of cannabinoid treatment on PTSD, although this literature suggests that cannabinoids are successful in alleviating at least some symptoms of PTSD.

There is also interest in developing treatments that target the endocannabinoid system more specifically. Of particular interest is the fatty acid amide hydrolase (FAAH) and monoacylglycerol lipase (MAGL) hydrolysis of endocannabinoid ligands anandamide and 2-AG, respectively. MDD patients and PTSD patients have been shown to have lowered basal levels of anandamide and 2-AG (Hill, Miller, Ho, Gorzalka, & Hillard, 2008; Hill et al., 2013; Hill, Miller, Carrier, Gorzalka, & Hillard, 2009; Neumeister et al., 2013). Preclinically, blocking of anandamide and 2-AG degradation via inhibition of FAAH and MAGL has shown to have anti-inflammatory effects, such as suppression of proinflammatory cytokines, iNOS, and Cox-2 expression as well as reduced prostaglandin production and microglial activation (Kerr et al., 2013; Murphy et al., 2012; Nomura et al., 2011; Tchantchou et al., 2014). Moreover, blocking FAAH and MAGL effects has behavioral benefits in animal models. While it has been established for some time that inhibition of FAAH has anxiolytic-like effects, more recently, evidence suggests that FAAH antagonism is particularly effective under highly stressful conditions (Patel, Hill, Cheer, Wotjak, & Holmes, 2017). This anxiolytic effect in aversive environments may be due to concomitant increase of anandamide in areas of the brain highly involved in anxiety, such as the amygdala (Gunduz-Cinar, Hill, McEwen, & Holmes, 2013). No clinical trials have yet tested the efficacy of FAAH inhibitors on treating neuropsychiatric patients, but inhibition of FAAH has been shown to be effective in raising levels of anandamide in humans (Huggins, Smart, Langman, Taylor, & Young, 2012; Ozalp & Barroso, 2009). On the other hand, preclinical behavioral studies regarding MAGL and 2-AG are a little more muddled, but there is evidence to suggest that inhibition of MAGL and subsequent increase in 2-AG signaling have anxiolytic-like effects (reviewed in Patel, Hill, Cheer, Wotjak, & Holmes, 2017). The level of 2-AG inhibition does appear to be crucial, however, as high levels, but not lower levels, of inhibition have been shown to deregulate and desensitize CB1 receptors, acting more as an antagonist rather than an agonist (Kinsey et al., 2013; Schlosburg et al., 2011). Moreover, current popular inhibitors, such as URB602 and JZL184, have off-target effects that warrant development of more selective MAGL inhibitors (Kohnz & Nomura, 2014).

Neuropeptide Y

Neuropeptide Y (NPY) is another potential therapeutic for PTSD (reviewed in Schmeltzer, Herman, & Sah, 2016), with a growing body of evidence implicating it in the stress response and the pathophysiology behind PTSD, as NPY modulates various behavioral and physiological functions, including memory and learning, fear, and circadian rhythms (Redrobe, Dumont, Herzog, & Quirion, 2004; Redrobe, Dumont, St-Pierre, & Quirion, 1999; White, 1993). NPY is modulated in primates via four known G protein–coupled receptors, Y1, Y2, Y4, and Y5 (Dumont, Jacques, Bouchard, & Quirion, 1998). The Y1 receptor (Y1R) has been suggested to regulate the evident anxiolytic effects of NPY (Cohen et al., 2012), with several Y1R agonists having shown anxiolytic effects and antagonists showing anxiogenic effects (reviewed in Schmeltzer, Herman, & Sah, 2016). The Y2 receptor (Y2R), on the other hand, seems to regulate anxiogenic effects, with Y2R agonists exhibiting anxiogenic effects (reviewed in Schmeltzer, Herman, & Sah, 2016). With NPY showing a strong affinity for Y1R, Y2R, and Y5R (Alexander et al., 2013), research in the recent years have focused on these receptors.

Prophylactic treatments that may prevent the development of PTSD after trauma are also being studied, including intranasal NPY as a preventative measure and intervention for PTSD. Serova, Mulhall, and Sabban (2017) studied intranasal NPY and a selective NPY Y1R agonist, [Leu^{31}Pro^{34}]NPY, in a single prolonged stress animal model of PTSD. Delivery through the intranasal route was selected to bypass the blood–brain barrier for direct interaction with the necessary brain regions to maximize treatment efficacy, a common strategy for delivery of drugs (and peptides in particular) with poor CNS penetration. In multiple studies, NPY delivered shortly before or immediately after experience with an extreme stressor blocked induction of typical indications of PTSD symptoms, with relatively long-lasting effects (a week or more) (Serova et al., 2013). Further studies with [Leu^{31}Pro^{34}]NPY found similar results. A higher dose of [Leu^{31}Pro^{34}]NPY, infused immediately after experience with an extreme stressor, was able to prevent depressive-like behavior (Serova, Mulhall, & Sabban, 2017), confirming the effectiveness of agonizing the Y1R; however, it is not known if Y1R agonism plays a role in preventing anxiety-behavior seen following intranasal NPY treatment. Serova, Mulhall, and Sabban (2017) note that [Leu^{31}Pro^{34}]NPY has also been shown to act on the Y5 receptor (Y5R), so additive treatment benefits through use of Y5R may be a possibility. [Leu^{31}Pro^{34}]NPY also prevented an increase in CRF gene expression, potentially preventing the abnormal HPA axis activity associated with PTSD. Thus, these studies and others contribute to a growing body of literature suggesting NPY may be a druggable target to ameliorate stress-related pathophysiology.

Conclusions and Future Directions

Overall, stress is mechanistically positioned to alter the physiological functioning of most systems in the body, potentially leading to physical and psychological maladaptation through enhanced inflammation. Put differently, inflammation may be a final common mediator of multiple, diverse health conditions associated with stress; while unfortunate, understanding this pathway informs numerous pharmacotherapeutic strategies for the amelioration of stress-related health outcomes. Overall, we aimed to highlight three major reasons as to why certain novel treatments may or may not have had effective results: (1) inappropriate *timing* of treatment, (2) inappropriate molecular or pathway *targeting* of treatment, and (3) misidentification of which individuals are poised to benefit from specific treatments. More specifically, the progression of stress-related disorders involves specific windows of time that likely impact whether a given treatment is best suited as prevention, intervention, palliative care, or curative treatment. Secondly, anti-inflammatory treatments, while efficacious, impact diverse and multiple systems in potentially negative ways, necessitating more specific targeting of inflammatory pathways. Furthermore, while some targets have shown to be effective as monotherapy, others may be more suited as adjunctive therapy, such as what was shown for Cox-2 inhibitors. Finally, it is important to take into account the many ways that stress-related disorders can manifest in patients in order to not administer treatment indiscriminately. As Miller and Raison (2015) argue, for instance, a study examining the effects of anti-inflammatory treatments must be conducted on subjects who display increased inflammation in the first place. Indeed, such arguments form the fundamental basis for movements toward "personalized medicine," as we have argued in the past (Deak et al., 2015). Regardless of these considerations, future progress will be dependent upon investigators with a broad, integrative understanding of stress physiology, including interactions between neural, endocrine, and immune systems.

Acknowledgments

Research reported in this publication was supported by the National Institute of Health grants P50AA017823 and RO1AG043467 to T. Deak, and the Center for Development and Behavioral Neuroscience at Binghamton University. Any opinions, findings, and conclusions or recommendations expressed in this material are those of the author(s) and do not necessarily reflect the views of the aforementioned funding agencies. The authors have no conflicts of interest to declare.

References

Abbasi, S.-H., Hosseini, F. F., Modabbernia, A. A., Ashrafi, M. M., & Akhondzadeh, S. S. (2012). Effect of celecoxib add-on treatment on symptoms and serum IL-6 concentrations in patients with major depressive disorder: Randomized double-blind placebo-controlled study. *Journal of Affective Disorders*, *141*(2–3), 308–314. Retrieved from http://eutils.ncbi.nlm.nih.gov/entrez/eutils/elink.fcgi?dbfrom=pubmed&id=22516310&retmode=ref&cmd=prlinks%5Cnpapers2://publication/doi/10.1016/j.jad.2012.03.033

Aerni, A., Traber, R., Hock, C., Roozendaal, B., Schelling, G., Papassotiropoulos, A., … de Quervain, D. J.-F. (2004). Low-dose cortisol for symptoms of posttraumatic stress disorder. *American Journal of Psychiatry*, *161*(8), 1488–1490. doi:10.1176/appi.ajp.161.8.1488

Aid, S., Langenbach, R., & Bosetti, F. (2008). Neuroinflammatory response to lipopolysaccharide is exacerbated in mice genetically deficient in cyclooxygenase-2. *Journal of Neuroinflammation*, *5*, 17. doi:10.1186/1742-2094-5-17

Aizawa, E., Tsuji, H., Asahara, T., Takahashi, T., Teraishi, T., Yoshida, S., … Kunugi, H. (2016). Possible association of Bifidobacterium and Lactobacillus in the gut microbiota of patients with major depressive disorder. *Journal of Affective Disorders*, *202*, 254–257. doi:10.1016/j.jad.2016.05.038

Alexander, S. P. H., Benson, H. E., Faccenda, E., Pawson, A. J., Sharman, J. L., Spedding, M., … Collaborators, C. (2013). The concise guide to pharmacology 2013/14: G protein-coupled receptors. *British Journal of Pharmacology*, *170*(8), 1459–1581. doi:10.1111/bph.12445

Allen, N. J., & Barres, B. A. (2009). Neuroscience: Glia—more than just brain glue. *Nature*, *457*(7230), 675–677. doi:10.1038/457675a

Almeida, O. P., Alfonso, H., Jamrozik, K., Hankey, G. J., & Flicker, L. (2010). Aspirin use, depression, and cognitive impairment in later life: The health in men study. *Journal of the American Geriatrics Society*, *58*(5), 990–999.

Almeida, O. P., Flicker, L., Yeap, B. B., Alfonso, H., McCaul, K., & Hankey, G. J. (2012). Aspirin decreases the risk of depression in older men with high plasma homocysteine. *Translational Psychiatry*, *2*(8), e151. doi:10.1038/tp.2012.79

American Psychiatric Association. (2013). *Diagnostic and statistical manual of mental disorders* (5th ed.). Washington DC: American Psychiatric Association. : Author. doi:10.1176/appi.books.9780890425596.744053

Andrade, C. (2014). A critical examination of studies on curcumin for depression. *The Journal of Clinical Psychiatry*, *75*(10), 1110–1112. . doi:10.4088/JCP.14f09489

Arakawa, S., Shirayama, Y., Fujita, Y., Ishima, T., Horio, M., Muneoka, K., … Hashimoto, K. (2012). Minocycline produced antidepressant-like effects on the learned helplessness rats with alterations in levels of monoamine in the amygdala and no changes in BDNF levels in the hippocampus at baseline. *Pharmacology Biochemistry and Behavior*, *100*(3), 601–606.

Araque, A., Parpura, V., Sanzgiri, R. P., & Haydon, P. G. (1999). Tripartite synapses: Glia, the unacknowledged partner. *Trends in Neurosciences*, *22*(5), 208–215. doi:10.1016/S0166-2236(98)01349-6

Atkins, C. M., Oliva, J., Alonso, O. F., Pearse, D. D., Bramlett, H. M., & Dietrich, W. D. (2007). Modulation of the cAMP signaling pathway after traumatic brain injury. *Experimental Neurology*, *208*(1), 145–158.

Ayyub, M., Najmi, A. K., & Akhtar, M. (2017). Protective effect of irbesartan, an angiotensin (AT1) receptor antagonist, in unpredictable chronic mild stress induced depression in mice. *Drug Research*, *67*(1), 59–64. doi:10.1055/s-0042-118172

Bacon, K. B., & Harrison, J. K. (2000). Chemokines and their receptors in neurobiology: Perspectives in physiology and homeostasis. *Journal of Neuroimmunology*, *104*(1), 92–97. doi:10.1016/S0165-5728(99)00266-0

Barnes, P., & Adcock, I. (2009). Glucocorticoid resistance in inflammatory diseases. *The Lancet*, *373*(9678), 1915–1917. doi:10.1016/S0140-6736(09)60326-3.Glucocorticoid

Barnes, P. J. (2013). Theophylline. *American Journal of Respiratory and Critical Care Medicine*, *188*(8), 901–906. doi:10.1164/rccm.201302-0388PP

Barres, B. A. (2008). The mystery and magic of glia: A perspective on their roles in health and disease. *Neuron*, *60*(3), 430–440. doi:10.1016/j.neuron.2008.10.013

Baudy, A. R., Reeves, E. K. M., Damsker, J. M., Heier, C., Garvin, L. M., Dillingham, B. C., … Hoffman, E. P. (2012). -9,11 modification of glucocorticoids dissociates nuclear factor- B inhibitory efficacy from glucocorticoid response element-associated side effects. *Journal of Pharmacology and Experimental Therapeutics*, *343*(1), 225–232. doi:10.1124/jpet.112.194340

Bayramgurler, D., Karson, A., Yazir, Y., Celikyurt, I. K., Kurnaz, S., & Utkan, T. (2013). The effect of etanercept on aortic nitric oxide-dependent vasorelaxation in an unpredictable chronic, mild stress model of depression in rats. *European Journal of Pharmacology*, *710*(1–3), 67–72. doi:10.1016/j.ejphar.2013.04.007

Beer, B., Chasin, M., Clody, D. E., & Vogel, J. R. (1972). Cyclic adenosine monophosphate phosphodiesterase in brain: effect on anxiety. *Science*, *176*(4033), 428–430. doi:10.1126/science.176.4033.428

Benicky, J., Sánchez-Lemus, E., Honda, M., Pang, T., Orecna, M., Wang, J., … Saavedra, J. M. (2011). Angiotensin II AT1 receptor blockade ameliorates brain inflammation. *Neuropsychopharmacology*, *36*(4), 857–870. doi:10.1038/npp.2010.225

Benton, D., Williams, C., & Brown, A. (2007). Impact of consuming a milk drink containing a probiotic on mood and cognition. *European Journal of Clinical Nutrition*, *61*(3), 355–361. doi:10.1038/sj.ejcn.1602546

Berg, B. M., Godbout, J. P., Kelley, K. W., & Johnson, R. W. (2004). α-Tocopherol attenuates lipopolysaccharide-induced sickness behavior in mice. *Brain, Behavior, and Immunity*, *18*(2), 149–157. doi:10.1016/S0889-1591(03)00113-2

Bergamaschi, M. M., Queiroz, R. H. C., Chagas, M. H. N., de Oliveira, D. C. G., De Martinis, B. S., Kapczinski, F., … Crippa, J. A. S. (2011). Cannabidiol reduces the anxiety induced by simulated public speaking in treatment-naïve social phobia patients. *Neuropsychopharmacology*, *36*(6), 1219–1226. doi:10.1038/npp.2011.6

Bertolino, A., Crippa, D., di Dio, S., Fichte, K., Musmeci, G., Porro, V., … Schratzer, M. (1988). Rolipram versus imipramine in inpatients with major, "minor" or atypical depressive disorder: A double-blind double-dummy study aimed at testing a novel therapeutic approach. *International Clinical Psychopharmacology*, *3*(3), 245–253.

Betthauser, K., Pilz, J., & Vollmer, L. E. (2015). Use and effects of cannabinoids in military veterans with posttraumatic stress disorder. *American Journal of Health-System Pharmacy*, *72*(15), 1279–1284. doi:10.2146/ajhp140523

Beurel, E., Harrington, L. E., & Jope, R. S. (2013). Inflammatory T helper 17 cells promote depression-like behavior in mice. *Biological Psychiatry*, *73*(7), 622–630. doi:10.1016/j.biopsych.2012.09.021

Binneman, B., Feltner, D., Kolluri, S., Shi, Y., Qiu, R., & Stiger, T. (2008). A 6-week randomized, placebo-controlled trial of

CP-316,311 (a selective CRH1 antagonist) in the treatment of major depression. *American Journal of Psychiatry*, *165*(5), 617–620. doi:10.1176/appi.ajp.2008.07071199

Blandino, P., Barnum, C. J., & Deak, T. (2006). The involvement of norepinephrine and microglia in hypothalamic and splenic IL-1β responses to stress. *Journal of Neuroimmunology*, *173*(1–2), 87–95. doi:10.1016/j.jneuroim.2005.11.021

Blandino, P., Barnum, C. J., Solomon, L. G., Larish, Y., Lankow, B. S., & Deak, T. (2009). Gene expression changes in the hypothalamus provide evidence for regionally-selective changes in IL-1 and microglial markers after acute stress. *Brain, Behavior, and Immunity*, *23*(7), 958–968. doi:10.1016/j.bbi.2009.04.013

Blandino, P., Hueston, C. M., Barnum, C. J., Bishop, C., & Deak, T. (2013). The impact of ventral noradrenergic bundle lesions on increased IL-1 in the PVN and hormonal responses to stress in male Sprague Dawley rats. *Endocrinology*, *154*(7), 2489–2500.

Borsini, A., Alboni, S., Horowitz, M. A., Tojo, L. M., Cannazza, G., Su, K.-P., … Zunszain, P. A. (2017). Rescue of IL-1beta-induced reduction of human neurogenesis by omega-3 fatty acids and antidepressants. *Brain, Behavior, and Immunity*, *65*, 230–238.

Brachman, R. A., Lehmann, M. L., Maric, D., & Herkenham, M. (2015). Lymphocytes from chronically stressed mice confer antidepressant-like effects to naive mice. *Journal of Neuroscience*, *35*(4), 1530–1538.

Brunello, N., Den Boer, J. A., Judd, L. L., Kasper, S., Kelsey, J. E., Lader, M., … Wittchen, H. U. (2000). Social phobia: Diagnosis and epidemiology, neurobiology and pharmacology, comorbidity and treatment. *Journal of Affective Disorders*, *60*(1), 61–74. doi:10.1016/S0165-0327(99)00140-8

Bschor, T., Ising, M., Erbe, S., Winkelmann, P., Ritter, D., Uhr, M., & Lewitzka, U. (2012). Impact of citalopram on the HPA system. A study of the combined DEX/CRH test in 30 unipolar depressed patients. *Journal of Psychiatric Research*, *46*(1), 111–117.

Buckner, J. D., Schmidt, N. B., Lang, A. R., Small, J. W., Schlauch, R. C., & Lewinsohn, P. M. (2008). Specificity of social anxiety disorder as a risk factor for alcohol and cannabis dependence. *Journal of Psychiatric Research*, *42*(3), 230–239. doi:10.1016/j.jpsychires.2007.01.002

Byrd, J. B., & Brook, R. D. (2014). Anxiety in the "age of hypertension." *Current Hypertension Reports*, *16*(10), 486. doi:10.1007/s11906-014-0486-0

Cameron, C., Watson, D., & Robinson, J. (2014). Use of a synthetic cannabinoid in a correctional population for posttraumatic stress disorder–related insomnia and nightmares, chronic pain, harm reduction, and other indications. *Journal of Clinical Psychopharmacology*, *34*(5), 559–564. doi:10.1097/JCP.0000000000000180

Cannon, W. B. (1935). Stresses and strains of homeostasis. *The American Journal of the Medical Sciences*, *189*(1), 1–14. doi:10.1097/00000441-193501000-00001

Capuron, L., Raison, C. L., Musselman, D. L., Lawson, D. H., Nemeroff, C. B., & Miller, A. H. (2003). Association of exaggerated HPA axis response to the initial injection of interferon-alpha with development of depression during interferon-alpha therapy. *American Journal of Psychiatry*, *160*(7), 1342–1345. doi:10.1176/appi.ajp.160.7.1342

Capuron, L., Ravaud, A., Miller, A. H., & Dantzer, R. (2004). Baseline mood and psychosocial characteristics of patients developing depressive symptoms during interleukin-2 and/or interferon-alpha cancer therapy. *Brain, Behavior, and Immunity*, *18*(3), 205–213.

Cassano, P., Hidalgo, a, Burgos, V., Adris, S., & Argibay, P. (2006). Hippocampal upregulation of the cyclooxygenase-2 gene following neonatal clomipramine treatment (a model of depression). *The Pharmacogenomics Journal*, *6*(6), 381–387. doi:10.1038/sj.tpj.6500385

Cazareth, J., Guyon, A., Heurteaux, C., Chabry, J., & Petit-Paitel, A. (2014). Molecular and cellular neuroinflammatory status of mouse brain after systemic lipopolysaccharide challenge: Importance of CCR2/CCL2 signaling. *Journal of Neuroinflammation*, *11*(1), 132. doi:10.1186/1742-2094-11-132

Choi, S.-H., Langenbach, R., & Bosetti, F. (2008). Genetic deletion or pharmacological inhibition of cyclooxygenase-1 attenuate lipopolysaccharide-induced inflammatory response and brain injury. *FASEB Journal: Official Publication of the Federation of American Societies for Experimental Biology*, *22*(5), 1491–1501. doi:10.1096/fj.07-9411com

Choy, E. H. S., Isenberg, D. A., Garrood, T., Farrow, S., Ioannou, Y., Bird, H., … Panayi, G. S. (2002). Therapeutic benefit of blocking interleukin-6 activity with an anti-interleukin-6 receptor monoclonal antibody in rheumatoid arthritis: A randomized, double-blind, placebo-controlled, dose-escalation trial. *Arthritis and Rheumatism*, *46*(12), 3143–3150. doi:10.1002/art.10623

Clark, S. M., Soroka, J. A., Song, C., Li, X., & Tonelli, L. H. (2016). CD4+ T cells confer anxiolytic and antidepressant-like effects, but enhance fear memory processes in Rag2−/− mice. *Stress*, *19*(3), 303–311. doi:10.1080/10253890.2016.1191466

Cohen, H., Liu, T., Kozlovsky, N., Kaplan, Z., Zohar, J., & Mathé, A. A. (2012). The neuropeptide Y (NPY)-ergic system is associated with behavioral resilience to stress exposure in an animal model of post-traumatic stress disorder. *Neuropsychopharmacology*, *37*(2), 350–363. doi:10.1038/npp.2011.230

Colotta, F., Jansson, B., & Bonelli, F. (2017). Modulation of inflammatory and immune responses by vitamin D. *Journal of Autoimmunity*, *85*, 78–97 doi:10.1016/j.jaut.2017.07.007

Coric, V., Feldman, H. H., Oren, D. A., Shekhar, A., Pultz, J., Dockens, R. C., … Stock, E. G. (2010). Multicenter, randomized, double-blind, active comparator and placebo-controlled trial of a corticotropin-releasing factor receptor-1 antagonist in generalized anxiety disorder. *Depression and Anxiety*, *27*(5), 417–425. doi:10.1002/da.20695

Corona, A. W., Huang, Y., O'Connor, J. C., Dantzer, R., Kelley, K. W., Popovich, P. G., & Godbout, J. P. (2010). Fractalkine receptor (CX3CR1) deficiency sensitizes mice to the behavioral changes induced by lipopolysaccharide. *Journal of Neuroinflammation*, *7*(1), 93. doi:10.1186/1742-2094-7-93

Cosio, B. G., Tsaprouni, L., Ito, K., Jazrawi, E., Adcock, I. M., & Barnes, P. J. (2004). Theophylline restores histone deacetylase activity and steroid responses in COPD macrophages. *Journal of Experimental Medicine*, *200*(5), 689–695. doi:10.1084/jem.20040416

Crippa, J. A. S., Nogueira Derenusson, G., Borduqui Ferrari, T., Wichert-Ana, L., Duran, F. L., Martin-Santos, R., … Cecilio Hallak, J. E. (2011). Neural basis of anxiolytic effects of cannabidiol (CBD) in generalized social anxiety disorder: a preliminary report. *Journal of Psychopharmacology (Oxford)*, *25*(1), 121–130. doi:10.1177/0269881110379283

Dantzer, R., O'Connor, J. C., Freund, G. G., Johnson, R. W., & Kelley, K. W. (2008). From inflammation to sickness and depression: when the immune system subjugates the brain. *Nature Reviews Neuroscience, 9*(1), 46–56. doi:10.1038/nrn2297

Dantzer, R., O'Connor, J. C., Lawson, M. A., & Kelley, K. W. (2011). Inflammation-associated depression: From serotonin to kynurenine. *Psychoneuroendocrinology, 36*(3), 426–436. doi:10.1016/j.psyneuen.2010.09.012

Davis, I., & Liu, A. (2015). What is the tryptophan kynurenine pathway and why is it important to neurotherapeutics? *Expert Review of Neurotherapeutics, 15*(7), 719–721. doi:10.1586/14737175.2015.1049999

Deak, T. (2007). From classic aspects of the stress response to neuroinflammation and sickness: implications for individuals and offspring. *International Journal of Comparative Psychology, 20*(549987), 96–110. Retrieved from http://escholarship.org/uc/item/6549c9s1.pdf

Deak, T., Bordner, K. A., McElderry, N. K., Barnum, C. J., Blandino, P., Deak, M. M., & Tammariello, S. P. (2005). Stress-induced increases in hypothalamic IL-1: A systematic analysis of multiple stressor paradigms. *Brain Research Bulletin, 64*(6), 541–556. doi:10.1016/j.brainresbull.2004.11.003

Deak, T., Kudinova, A., Lovelock, D. F., Gibb, B. E., & Hennessy, M. B. (2017). A multispecies approach for understanding neuroimmune mechanisms of stress. *Dialogues in Clinical Neuroscience, 19*(1), 37–53.

Deak, T., Nguyen, K. T., Ehrlich, A. L., Watkins, L. R., Spencer, R. L., Maier, S. F.,... Gold, P. W. (1999). The impact of the nonpeptide corticotropin-releasing hormone antagonist antalarmin on behavioral and endocrine responses to stress. *Endocrinology, 140*(1), 79–86. doi:10.1210/en.140.1.79

Deak, T., Quinn, M., Cidlowski, J. A., Victoria, N. C., Murphy, A. Z., & Sheridan, J. F. (2015). Neuroimmune mechanisms of stress: Sex differences, developmental plasticity, and implications for pharmacotherapy of stress-related disease. *Stress, 18*(4), 367–380. doi:10.3109/10253890.2015.1053451

de Quervain, D. J. F. (2007). Glucocorticoid-induced reduction of traumatic memories: implications for the treatment of PTSD. *Progress in Brain Research, 167*, 239–247 doi:10.1016/S0079-6123(07)67017-4

Delahanty, D. L., Gabert-Quillen, C., Ostrowski, S. A., Nugent, N. R., Fischer, B., Morris, A.,... Fallon, W. (2013). The efficacy of initial hydrocortisone administration at preventing posttraumatic distress in adult trauma patients: A randomized trial. *CNS Spectrums, 18*(2), 103–111. doi:10.1017/S1092852913000096

Delahanty, D. L., Raimonde, A. J., & Spoonster, E. (2000). Initial posttraumatic urinary cortisol levels predict subsequent PTSD symptoms in motor vehicle accident victims. *Biological Psychiatry, 48*(9), 940–947. doi:10.1016/S0006-3223(00)00896-9

Delgado, P. L. (2000). Depression: The case for a monoamine deficiency. *Journal of Clinical Psychiatry, 61*, 7–11.

Dinan, T. G., Stanton, C., & Cryan, J. F. (2013). Psychobiotics: A novel class of psychotropic. *Biological Psychiatry, 74*(10), 720–726. doi:10.1016/j.biopsych.2013.05.001

Dinh, Q. N., Drummond, G. R., Sobey, C. G., & Chrissobolis, S. (2014). Roles of inflammation, oxidative stress, and vascular dysfunction in hypertension. *BioMed Research International*. doi:10.1155/2014/406960

Dowlati, Y., Herrmann, N., Swardfager, W., Liu, H., Sham, L., Reim, E. K., & Lanctôt, K. L. (2010). A meta-analysis of cytokines in major depression. *Biological Psychiatry, 67*(5), 446–457. doi:10.1016/j.biopsych.2009.09.033

Dumont, Y., Jacques, D., Bouchard, P., & Quirion, R. (1998). Species differences in the expression and distribution of the neuropeptide Y Y1, Y2, Y4, and Y5 receptors in rodents, guinea pig, and primates brains. *Journal of Comparative Neurology, 402*(3), 372–384.

Eyre, H. A., Air, T., Pradhan, A., Johnston, J., Lavretsky, H., Stuart, M. J., & Baune, B. T. (2016). A meta-analysis of chemokines in major depression. *Progress in Neuro-Psychopharmacology and Biological Psychiatry, 68*, 1–8. doi:10.1016/j.pnpbp.2016.02.006

Faridhosseini, F., Sadeghi, R., Farid, L., & Pourgholami, M. (2014). Celecoxib: A new augmentation strategy for depressive mood episodes. A systematic review and meta-analysis of randomized placebo-controlled trials. *Human Psychopharmacology, 29*(3), 216–223. doi:10.1002/hup.2401

Fonseka, T. M., McIntyre, R. S., Soczynska, J. K., & Kennedy, S. H. (2015). Novel investigational drugs targeting IL-6 signaling for the treatment of depression. *Expert Opinion on Investigational Drugs, 24*(4), 459–475. doi:10.1517/13543784.2014.998334

Foster, J. A., & McVey Neufeld, K.-A. (2013). Gut–brain axis: How the microbiome influences anxiety and depression. *Trends in Neurosciences, 36*(5), 305–312.

Frank, M. G., Watkins, L. R., & Maier, S. F. (2011). Stress- and glucocorticoid-induced priming of neuroinflammatory responses: Potential mechanisms of stress-induced vulnerability to drugs of abuse. *Brain, Behavior, and Immunity, 25*(Suppl. 1), S21–S28. doi:10.1016/j.bbi.2011.01.005

Fraser, G. A. (2009). The use of a synthetic cannabinoid in the management of treatment-resistant nightmares in posttraumatic stress disorder (PTSD). *CNS Neuroscience and Therapeutics, 15*(1), 84–88.

Gałecki, P., Gałecka, E., Maes, M., Chamielec, M., Orzechowska, A., Bobińska, K.,... Szemraj, J. (2012). The expression of genes encoding for COX-2, MPO, iNOS, and sPLA2-IIA in patients with recurrent depressive disorder. *Journal of Affective Disorders, 138*(3), 360–366. doi:10.1016/j.jad.2012.01.016

Genovese, M. C., Cohen, S. B., Wofsy, D., Weinblatt, M. E., Firestein, G. S., Brahn, E.,... Tong, S. E. (2011). A 24-week, randomized, double-blind, placebo-controlled, parallel group study of the efficacy of oral SCIO-469, a p38 mitogen-activated protein kinase inhibitor, in patients with active rheumatoid arthritis. *Journal of Rheumatology, 38*, 846–854. doi:10.3899/jrheum.100602

Giardina, W. J., & Ebert, D. M. (1989). Positive effects of captopril in the behavioral despair swim test. *Biological Psychiatry, 25*(6), 697–702. doi:10.1016/0006-3223(89)90240-0

Godbout, J. P., Berg, B. M., Krzyszton, C., & Johnson, R. W. (2005). α-Tocopherol attenuates NFκB activation and pro-inflammatory cytokine production in brain and improves recovery from lipopolysaccharide-induced sickness behavior. *Journal of Neuroimmunology, 169*(1–2), 97–105. doi:10.1016/j.jneuroim.2005.08.003

Grammatopoulos, D. K., & Chrousos, G. P. (2002). Functional characteristics of CRH receptors and potential clinical applications of CRH-receptor antagonists. *Trends in Endocrinology and Metabolism, 13*(10), 436–444. doi:10.1016/S1043-2760(02)00670-7

Greer, G. R., Grob, C. S., & Halberstadt, A. L. (2014). PTSD symptom reports of patients evaluated for the New Mexico Medical Cannabis Program. *Journal of Psychoactive Drugs, 46*(1), 73–77. doi:10.1080/02791072.2013.873843

Grillon, C., Hale, E., Lieberman, L., Davis, A., Pine, D. S., & Ernst, M. (2015). The CRH1 antagonist GSK561679 increases human fear but not anxiety as assessed by startle. *Neuropsychopharmacology: Official Publication of the American College of Neuropsychopharmacology, 40*(5), 1064–1071. doi:10.1038/npp.2014.316

Groeger, D., O'Mahony, L., Murphy, E. F., Bourke, J. F., Dinan, T. G., Kiely, B.,...Quigley, E. M. M. (2013). Bifidobacterium infantis 35624 modulates host inflammatory processes beyond the gut. *Gut Microbes, 4*(4), 325–339. doi:10.4161/gmic.25487

Grosse, L., Hoogenboezem, T., Ambrée, O., Bellingrath, S., Jörgens, S., de Wit, H. J.,...Drexhage, H. A. (2016). Deficiencies of the T and natural killer cell system in major depressive disorder. T regulatory cell defects are associated with inflammatory monocyte activation. *Brain, Behavior, and Immunity, 54*, 38–44. doi:10.1016/j.bbi.2015.12.003

Gu, X.-L., Long, C.-X., Sun, L., Xie, C., Lin, X., & Cai, H. (2010). Astrocytic expression of Parkinson's disease-related A53T α-synuclein causes neurodegeneration in mice. *Molecular Brain, 3*(1), 12. doi:10.1186/1756-6606-3-12

Guglieri, M., Clemens, P., Cnaan, A., Damsker, J., Gordish-Dressman, H., Morgenroth, L.,...Hoffman, E. (2017). Vision DMD: A drug development program for vamorolone in Duchenne muscular dystrophy. *Acta Myologica, 36*(2), 73. doi:10.1016/j.ejpn.2017.04.1270

Gunduz-Cinar, O., Hill, M. N., McEwen, B. S., & Holmes, A. (2013). Amygdala FAAH and anandamide: Mediating protection and recovery from stress. *Trends in Pharmacological Sciences, 34*(11), 637–644. doi:10.1016/j.tips.2013.08.008

Guo, J., Chang, L., Li, C., Li, M., Yan, P., Guo, Z.,...Wang, Q. (2017). SB203580 reverses memory deficits and depression-like behavior induced by microinjection of Aβ1–42 into hippocampus of mice. *Metabolic Brain Disease, 32*(1), 57–68. doi:10.1007/s11011-016-9880-4

Guo, J., Lin, P., Zhao, X., Zhang, J., Wei, X., Wang, Q., & Wang, C. (2014). Etazolate abrogates the lipopolysaccharide (LPS)-induced downregulation of the cAMP/pCREB/BDNF signaling, neuroinflammatory response and depressive-like behavior in mice. *Neuroscience, 263*, 1–14. doi:10.1016/j.neuroscience.2014.01.008

Guo, J. Y., Li, C. Y., Ruan, Y. P., Sun, M., Qi, X. L., Zhao, B. S., & Luo, F. (2009). Chronic treatment with celecoxib reverses chronic unpredictable stress-induced depressive-like behavior via reducing cyclooxygenase-2 expression in rat brain. *European Journal of Pharmacology, 612*(1–3), 54–60. doi:10.1016/j.ejphar.2009.03.076

Haroon, E., Raison, C. L., & Miller, A. H. (2012). Psychoneuroimmunology meets neuropsychopharmacology: Translational implications of the impact of inflammation on behavior. *Neuropsychopharmacology, 37*(1), 137–162. doi:10.1038/npp.2011.205

Heier, C. R., Damsker, J. M., Yu, Q., Dillingham, B. C., Huynh, T., Van der Meulen, J. H.,...Nagaraju, K. (2013). VBP15, a novel anti-inflammatory and membrane-stabilizer, improves muscular dystrophy without side effects. *EMBO Molecular Medicine, 5*(10), 1569–1585. doi:10.1002/emmm.201302621

Hellwig, S., Brioschi, S., Dieni, S., Frings, L., Masuch, A., Blank, T., & Biber, K. (2016). Altered microglia morphology and higher resilience to stress-induced depression-like behavior in CX3CR1-deficient mice. *Brain, Behavior, and Immunity, 55*, 126–137. doi:10.1016/j.bbi.2015.11.008

Henry, C. J., Huang, Y., Wynne, A., Hanke, M., Himler, J., Bailey, M. T.,...Godbout, J. P. (2008). Minocycline attenuates lipopolysaccharide (LPS)-induced neuro-inflammation, sickness behavior, and anhedonia. *Journal of Neuroinflammation, 5*(1), 15. doi:10.1186/1742-2094-5-15

Heuser, I., Yassouridis, A., & Holsboer, F. (1994). The combined dexamethasone/CRH test: A refined laboratory test for psychiatric disorders. *Journal of Psychiatric Research, 28*(4), 341–356.

Hickman, R. J., Khambaty, T., & Stewart, J. C. (2014). C-reactive protein is elevated in atypical but not nonatypical depression: Data from the National Health and Nutrition Examination Survey (NHANES) 1999–2004. *Journal of Behavioral Medicine, 37*(4), 621–629. doi:10.1007/s10865-013-9510-0

Hill, M. N., Bierer, L. M., Makotkine, I., Golier, J. A., Galea, S., McEwen, B. S.,...Yehuda, R. (2013). Reductions in circulating endocannabinoid levels in individuals with post-traumatic stress disorder following exposure to the World Trade Center attacks. *Psychoneuroendocrinology, 38*(12), 2952–2961. doi:10.1016/j.psyneuen.2013.08.004

Hill, M. N., Miller, G. E., Carrier, E. J., Gorzalka, B. B., & Hillard, C. J. (2009). Circulating endocannabinoids and N-acyl ethanolamines are differentially regulated in major depression and following exposure to social stress. *Psychoneuroendocrinology, 34*(8), 1257–1262.

Hill, M. N., Miller, G. E., Ho, W.-S. V, Gorzalka, B. B., & Hillard, C. J. (2008). Serum endocannabinoid content is altered in females with depressive disorders: A preliminary report. *Pharmacopsychiatry, 41*(2), 48–53. doi:10.1055/s-2007-993211

Hillard, C. J., Weinlander, K. M., & Stuhr, K. L. (2012). Contributions of endocannabinoid signaling to psychiatric disorders in humans: Genetic and biochemical evidence. *Neuroscience, 204*, 207–229. doi:10.1016/j.neuroscience.2011.11.020

Hirschfeld, R. M. A. (2000). History and evolution of the monoamine hypothesis of depression. *Journal of Clinical Psychiatry, 61*(Suppl. 6), 4–6. doi:10.4088/JCP.v61n0201

Hodes, G. E., Pfau, M. L., Leboeuf, M., Golden, S. A., Christoffel, D. J., Bregman, D.,...Russo, S. J. (2014). Individual differences in the peripheral immune system promote resilience versus susceptibility to social stress. *Proceedings of the National Academy of Sciences, 111*(45), 16136–16141. doi:10.1073/pnas.1415191111

Hoegenauer, K., Soldermann, N., Zécri, F., Strang, R. S., Graveleau, N., Wolf, R. M.,...Burkhart, C. (2017). Discovery of CDZ173 (Leniolisib), representing a structurally novel class of PI3K delta-selective inhibitors. *ACS Medicinal Chemistry Letters, 8*(9), 975–980. doi:10.1021/acsmedchemlett.7b00293

Horuk, R. (2009). Chemokine receptor antagonists: Overcoming developmental hurdles. *Nature Reviews. Drug Discovery, 8*(1), 23–33. doi:10.1038/nrd2734

Huggins, J. P., Smart, T. S., Langman, S., Taylor, L., & Young, T. (2012). An efficient randomised, placebo-controlled clinical trial with the irreversible fatty acid amide hydrolase-1 inhibitor PF-04457845, which modulates endocannabinoids but fails to induce effective analgesia in patients with pain due to osteoarthritis of the knee. *Pain, 153*(9), 1837–1846. doi:10.1016/j.pain.2012.04.020

Huscher, D., Thiele, K., Gromnica-Ihle, E., Hein, G., Demary, W., Dreher, R.,...Buttgereit, F. (2009). Dose-related patterns of glucocorticoid-induced side effects. *Annals of the*

Rheumatic Diseases, 68(7), 1119–1124. doi:10.1136/ard.2008.092163

Inamdar, A., Merlo-Pich, E., Gee, M., Makumi, C., Mistry, P., Robertson, J.,…Ratti, E. (2014). Evaluation of antidepressant properties of the p38 MAP kinase inhibitor losmapimod (GW856553) in Major Depressive Disorder: Results from two randomised, placebo-controlled, double-blind, multicentre studies using a Bayesian approach. *Journal of Psychopharmacology, 28*(6), 570–581.

Irusen, E., Matthews, J. G., Takahashi, A., Barnes, P. J., Chung, K. F., & Adcock, I. M. (2002). p38 mitogen-activated protein kinase-induced glucocorticoid receptor phosphorylation reduces its activity: Role in steroid-insensitive asthma. *Journal of Allergy and Clinical Immunology, 109*(4), 649–657. doi:10.1067/mai.2002.122465

Ito, H., Takazoe, M., Fukuda, Y., Hibi, T., Kusugami, K., Andoh, A.,…Kishimoto, T. (2004). A pilot randomized trial of a human anti-interleukin-6 receptor monoclonal antibody in active Crohn's disease. *Gastroenterology, 126*(4), 989–996. doi:10.1053/j.gastro.2004.01.012

Ito, K., Yamamura, S., Essilfie-Quaye, S., Cosio, B., Ito, M., Barnes, P. J., & Adcock, I. M. (2006). Histone deacetylase 2-mediated deacetylation of the glucocorticoid receptor enables NF-kappaB suppression. *The Journal of Experimental Medicine, 203*(1), 7–13. doi:10.1084/jem.20050466

Iyengar, R. L., Gandhi, S., Aneja, A., Thorpe, K., Razzouk, L., Greenberg, J.,…Farkouh, M. E. (2013). NSAIDs are associated with lower depression scores in patients with osteoarthritis. *American Journal of Medicine, 126*(11), 1017.e11–1017.e18. doi:10.1016/j.amjmed.2013.02.037

Jankord, R., Zhang, R., Flak, J. N., Solomon, M. B., Albertz, J., & Herman, J. P. (2010). Stress activation of IL-6 neurons in the hypothalamus. *American Journal of Physiology. Regulatory, Integrative and Comparative Physiology, 299*(1), R343–R351. doi:10.1152/ajpregu.00131.2010

Jetly, R., Heber, A., Fraser, G., & Boisvert, D. (2015). The efficacy of nabilone, a synthetic cannabinoid, in the treatment of PTSD-associated nightmares: A preliminary randomized, double-blind, placebo-controlled cross-over design study. *Psychoneuroendocrinology, 51*(Supplement C), 585–588.

Jiang, H., Ling, Z., Zhang, Y., Mao, H., Ma, Z., Yin, Y.,…Ruan, B. (2015b). Altered fecal microbiota composition in patients with major depressive disorder. *Brain, Behavior, and Immunity, 48*, 186–194. doi:10.1016/j.bbi.2015.03.016

Jiang, T., Sun, Y., Yin, Z., Feng, S., Sun, L., & Li, Z. (2015a). Research progress of indoleamine 2,3-dioxygenase inhibitors. *Future Medicinal Chemistry, 7*(2), 185–201. doi:10.4155/fmc.14.151

Jindal, A., Mahesh, R., Bhatt, S., & Pandey, D. (2016). Molecular modifications by regulating cAMP signaling and oxidant-antioxidant defence mechanisms, produce antidepressant-like effect: A possible mechanism of etazolate aftermaths of impact accelerated traumatic brain injury in rat model. *Neurochemistry International, 111*, 3–11. doi:10.1016/j.neuint.2016.12.004

Jindal, A., Mahesh, R., Gautam, B., Bhatt, S., & Pandey, D. (2012). Antidepressant-like effect of etazolate, a cyclic nucleotide phosphodiesterase 4 inhibitor—An approach using rodent behavioral antidepressant tests battery. *European Journal of Pharmacology, 689*(1–3), 125–131. doi:10.1016/j.ejphar.2012.05.051

Johnson, J. D., Campisi, J., Sharkey, C. M., Kennedy, S. L., Nickerson, M., Greenwood, B. N., & Fleshner, M. (2005).

Catecholamines mediate stress-induced increases in peripheral and central inflammatory cytokines. *Neuroscience, 135*(4), 1295–1307. doi:10.1016/j.neuroscience.2005.06.090

Kaufmann, W. E., Andreasson, K. I., Isakson, P. C., & Worley, P. F. (1997). Cyclooxygenases and the central nervous system. *Prostaglandins, 54*(3), 601–624. doi:10.1016/S0090-6980(97)00128-7

Kelly, J. R., Borre, Y., O' Brien, C., Patterson, E., El Aidy, S., Deane, J.,…Dinan, T. G. (2016). Transferring the blues: Depression-associated gut microbiota induces neurobehavioural changes in the rat. *Journal of Psychiatric Research, 82*, 109–118. doi:10.1016/j.jpsychires.2016.07.019

Kerr, D. M., Harhen, B., Okine, B. N., Egan, L. J., Finn, D. P., & Roche, M. (2013). The monoacylglycerol lipase inhibitor JZL184 attenuates LPS-induced increases in cytokine expression in the rat frontal cortex and plasma: Differential mechanisms of action. *British Journal of Pharmacology, 169*(4), 808–819.

Kessler, R. C., Sonnega, A., Bromet, E., Hughes, M., & Nelson, C. B. (1995). Posttrauumatic stress disorder in the National Comorbidity Survey. *Archives of General Psychiatry, 52*(12), 1048–1060.

Khoraminya, N., Tehrani-Doost, M., Jazayeri, S., Hosseini, A., & Djazayery, A. (2013). Therapeutic effects of vitamin D as adjunctive therapy to fluoxetine in patients with major depressive disorder. *Australian and New Zealand Journal of Psychiatry, 47*(3), 271–275.

Kim, G. W., Lee, N. R., Pi, R. H., Lim, Y. S., Lee, Y. M., Lee, J. M.,…Chung, S. H. (2015). IL-6 inhibitors for treatment of rheumatoid arthritis: Past, present, and future. *Archives of Pharmacal Research, 38*(5), 575–584. doi:10.1007/s12272-015-0569-8

Kinsey, S. G., Wise, L. E., Ramesh, D., Abdullah, R., Selley, D. E., Cravatt, B. F., & Lichtman, A. H. (2013). Repeated low-dose administration of the monoacylglycerol lipase inhibitor JZL184 retains cannabinoid receptor type 1–mediated antinociceptive and gastroprotective effects. *Journal of Pharmacology and Experimental Therapeutics, 345*, 492–501. doi:10.1124/jpet.112.201426

Köhler, C. A., Freitas, T. H., Maes, M., de Andrade, N. Q., Liu, C. S., Fernandes, B. S.,…Carvalho, A. F. (2017). Peripheral cytokine and chemokine alterations in depression: a meta-analysis of 82 studies. *Acta Psychiatrica Scandinavica, 135*(5), 373–387. doi:10.1111/acps.12698

Köhler, O., Benros, M., Nordentoft, M., Mors, P., & Krogh, J. (2015). Effect of anti-inflammatory treatment on depression, depressive symptoms and side effects: A systematic review and meta-analysis of randomized clinical trials. *European Psychiatry, 30*, 342. doi:10.1016/s0924-9338(15)30268-6

Kohnz, R. a, & Nomura, D. K. (2014). Chemical approaches to therapeutically target the metabolism and signaling of the endocannabinoid 2-AG and eicosanoids. *Chemical Society Reviews, 43*(19), 6859–6869. doi:10.1039/c4cs00047a

Kok, L., Hillegers, M. H., Veldhuijzen, D. S., Cornelisse, S., Nierich, A. P., van der Maaten, J. M.,…Dexamethasone for Cardiac Surgery Study Group. (2016). The effect of dexamethasone on symptoms of posttraumatic stress disorder and depression after cardiac surgery and intensive care admission: Longitudinal follow-up of a randomized controlled trial. *Critical Care Medicine, 44*(3), 512–520. doi:10.1097/CCM.0000000000001419

Koo, J. W., Russo, S. J., Ferguson, D., Nestler, E. J., & Duman, R. S. (2010). Nuclear factor- B is a critical mediator of stress-impaired neurogenesis and depressive behavior. *Proceedings of the National Academy of Sciences*, *107*(6), 2669–2674. doi:10.1073/pnas.0910658107

Koob, G. F., & Zorrilla, E. P. (2012). Update on corticotropin-releasing factor pharmacotherapy for psychiatric disorders: A revisionist view. *Neuropsychopharmacology*, *37*(1), 308–309. doi:10.1038/npp.2011.213

Krishnan, R., Cella, D., Leonardi, C., Papp, K., Gottlieb, A. B., Dunn, M.,…Jahreis, A. (2007). Effects of etanercept therapy on fatigue and symptoms of depression in subjects treated for moderate to severe plaque psoriasis for up to 96 weeks. *British Journal of Dermatology*, *157*(6), 1275–1277.

Kumar, S., Boehm, J., & Lee, J. C. (2003). p38 MAP kinases: Key signalling molecules as therapeutic targets for inflammatory diseases. *Nature Reviews Drug Discovery*, *2*(9), 717–726. doi:10.1038/nrd1177

Künzel, H. E., Zobel, A. W., Nickel, T., Ackl, N., Uhr, M., Sonntag, A.,…Holsboer, F. (2003). Treatment of depression with the CRH-1-receptor antagonist R121919: Endocrine changes and side effects. *Journal of Psychiatric Research*, *37*(6), 525–533. doi:10.1016/S0022-3956(03)00070-0

Kwako, L. E., Spagnolo, P. A., Schwandt, M. L., Thorsell, A., George, D. T., Momenan, R.,…Heilig, M. (2014). The corticotropin releasing hormone-1 (CRH1) receptor antagonist pexacerfont in alcohol dependence: A randomized controlled experimental medicine study. *Neuropsychopharmacology*, *40*(5), 1053–1063. doi:10.1038/npp.2014.306

Lamers, F., Vogelzangs, N., Merikangas, K. R., de Jonge, P., Beekman, A. T. F., & Penninx, B. W. J. H. (2013). Evidence for a differential role of HPA-axis function, inflammation and metabolic syndrome in melancholic versus atypical depression. *Molecular Psychiatry*, *18*(6), 692–699. doi:10.1038/mp.2012.144

Lass-Hennemann, J., & Michael, T. (2014). Endogenous cortisol levels influence exposure therapy in spider phobia. *Behaviour Research and Therapy*, *60*, 39–45. doi:10.1016/j.brat.2014.06.009

Laugeray, A., Launay, J. M., Callebert, J., Mutlu, O., Guillemin, G. J., Belzung, C., & Barone, P. R. (2016). Chronic treatment with the IDO1 inhibitor 1-methyl-D-tryptophan minimizes the behavioural and biochemical abnormalities induced by unpredictable chronic mild stress in mice—Comparison with fluoxetine. *PLoS ONE*, *11*(11), e0164337. doi:10.1371/journal.pone.0164337

Laurentiis, A., Araujo, H., & Rettori, V. (2014). Role of the endocannabinoid system in the neuroendocrine responses to inflammation. *Current Pharmaceutical Design*, *20*(29), 4697–4706. doi:10.2174/1381612820666140130212957

Lewitus, G. M., Wilf-Yarkoni, A., Ziv, Y., Shabat-Simon, M., Gersner, R., Zangen, A., & Schwartz, M. (2009). Vaccination as a novel approach for treating depressive behavior. *Biological Psychiatry*, *65*(4), 283–288. doi:10.1016/j.biopsych.2008.07.014

Li, G., Mbuagbaw, L., Samaan, Z., Falavigna, M., Zhang, S., Adachi, J. D.,…Thabane, L. (2014). Efficacy of vitamin D supplementation in depression in adults: A systematic review. *The Journal of Clinical Endocrinology and Metabolism*, *99*(3), 757–767.

Li, Y., Xiao, B., Qiu, W., Yang, L., Hu, B., Tian, X., & Yang, H. (2010). Altered expression of CD4+CD25+ regulatory T cells and its 5-HT1a receptor in patients with major depression disorder. *Journal of Affective Disorders*, *124*(1), 68–75.

Lin, P., Ding, B., Feng, C., Yin, S., Zhang, T., Qi, X.,…Li, Q. (2017). Prevotella and Klebsiella proportions in fecal

microbial communities are potential characteristic parameters for patients with major depressive disorder. *Journal of Affective Disorders*, *207*(October 2016), 300–304. doi:10.1016/j.jad.2016.09.051

Lopresti, A. L., Hood, S. D., & Drummond, P. D. (2012). Multiple antidepressant potential modes of action of curcumin: A review of its anti-inflammatory, monoaminergic, antioxidant, immune-modulating and neuroprotective effects. *Journal of Psychopharmacology*, *26*(12), 1512–1524. doi:10.1177/0269881112458732

Lopresti, A. L., Maes, M., Maker, G. L., Hood, S. D., & Drummond, P. D. (2014). Curcumin for the treatment of major depression: A randomised, double-blind, placebo controlled study. *Journal of Affective Disorders*, *167*, 368–375. doi:10.1016/j.jad.2014.06.001

Ludäscher, P., Schmahl, C., Feldmann, R. E., Kleindienst, N., Schneider, M., & Bohus, M. (2015). No evidence for differential dose effects of hydrocortisone on intrusive memories in female patients with complex post-traumatic stress disorder—a randomized, double-blind, placebo-controlled, crossover study. *Journal of Psychopharmacology*, *29*(10), 1077–1084. doi:10.1177/0269881115592339

Maes, M. (2011). Depression is an inflammatory disease, but cell-mediated immune activation is the key component of depression. *Progress in Neuro-Psychopharmacology and Biological Psychiatry*, *35*(3), 664–675. doi:10.1016/j.pnpbp.2010.06.014

Maes, M. (2012). Targeting cyclooxygenase-2 in depression is not a viable therapeutic approach and may even aggravate the pathophysiology underpinning depression. *Metabolic Brain Disease*, *27*(4), 405–413. doi:10.1007/s11011-012-9326-6

Maes, M., Anderson, G., Kubera, M., & Berk, M. (2014). Targeting classical IL-6 signalling or IL-6 *trans*-signalling in depression? *Expert Opinion on Therapeutic Targets*, *18*(5), 495–512. doi:10.1517/14728222.2014.888417

Maes, M., De Vos, N., Pioli, R., Demedts, P., Wauters, A., Neels, H., & Christophe, A. (2000). Lower serum vitamin E concentrations in major depression: Another marker of lowered antioxidant defenses in that illness. *Journal of Affective Disorders*, *58*(3), 241–246. doi:10.1016/S0165-0327(99)00121-4

Maes, M., Yirmyia, R., Noraberg, J., Brene, S., Hibbeln, J., Perini, G.,…Maj, M. (2009). The inflammatory & neurodegenerative (I&ND) hypothesis of depression: Leads for future research and new drug developments in depression. *Metabolic Brain Disease*, *24*(1), 27–53. doi:10.1007/s11011-008-9118-1

Manabe, T., Togashi, H., Uchida, N., Suzuki, S. C., Hayakawa, Y., Yamamoto, M.,…Chisaka, O. (2000). Loss of cadherin-11 adhesion receptor enhances plastic changes in hippocampal synapses and modifies behavioral responses. *Molecular and Cellular Neurosciences*, *15*(6), 534–546. doi:10.1006/mcne.2000.0849

Manosso, L. M., Neis, V. B., Moretti, M., Daufenbach, J. F., Freitas, A. E., Colla, A. R., & Rodrigues, A. L. (2013). Antidepressant-like effect of alpha-tocopherol in a mouse model of depressive-like behavior induced by TNF-alpha. *Progress in Neuropsychopharmacology and Biological Psychiatry*, *46*, 48–57. doi:10.1016/j.pnpbp.2013.06.012

Marone, R., Cmiljanovic, V., Giese, B., & Wymann, M. (2008). Targeting phosphoinositide 3-kinase—Moving towards therapy. *Biochimica et biophysica acta (BBA)- Proteins and Proteomics*, *1784*(1), 159–185. doi:10.1016/j.bbapap.2007.10.003

Mason, J. W. (1975). A historical view of the stress field. *Journal of Human Stress*, *1*(2), 22–36. doi:10.1080/0097840X.1975.9940405

McFarlane, A. C., Atchison, M., & Yehuda, R. (1997). The acute stress response following motor vehicle accidents and its relation to PTSD. *Annals of the New York Academy of Sciences*, *821*(1), 437–441.

Messaoudi, M., Lalonde, R., Violle, N., Javelot, H., Desor, D., Nejdi, A.,...Cazaubiel, J.-M. (2011). Assessment of psychotropic-like properties of a probiotic formulation (Lactobacillus helveticus R0052 and Bifidobacterium longum R0175) in rats and human subjects. *British Journal of Nutrition*, *105*(5), 755–764.

Milenkovic, V. M., Sarubin, N., Hilbert, S., Baghai, T. C., Stöffler, F., Lima-Ojeda, J. M.,...Nothdurfter, C. (2017). Macrophage-derived chemokine: A putative marker of pharmacological therapy response in major depression. *Neuroimmunomodulation*, *24*(2), 106–112.

Miller, A. H., & Raison, C. L. (2015). Are anti-inflammatory therapies viable treatments for psychiatric disorders?: Where the rubber meets the road. *JAMA Psychiatry*, *72*(6), 527–528. doi:10.1001/jamapsychiatry.2015.22

Minghetti, L. (2004). Cyclooxygenase-2 (COX-2) in inflammatory and degenerative brain diseases. *Journal of Neuropathology and Experimental Neurology*, *63*(9), 901–910. doi:10.1007/1-4020-5688-5_5

Miyaoka, T., Wake, R., Furuya, M., Liaury, K., Ieda, M., Kawakami, K.,...Horiguchi, J. (2012). Minocycline as adjunctive therapy for patients with unipolar psychotic depression: An open-label study. *Progress in Neuro-Psychopharmacology and Biological Psychiatry*, *37*(2), 222–226. doi:10.1016/j.pnpbp.2012.02.002

Mocking, R. J., Harmsen, I., Assies, J., Koeter, M. W., Ruhe, H. G., & Schene, A. H. (2016). Meta-analysis and meta-regression of omega-3 polyunsaturated fatty acid supplementation for major depressive disorder. *Translational Psychiatry*, *6*, e756. Retrieved from http://ovidsp.ovid.com/ovidweb.cgi?T=JS&CSC=Y&NEWS=N&PAGE=fulltext&D=prem&AN=26978738http://sfx.ucl.ac.uk/sfx_local?sid=OVID:medline&id=pmid:26978738&id=doi:10.1038%252Ftp.2016.29&issn=2158-3188&isbn=&volume=6&issue=&spage=e756&pages=e756&date=2016&title=

Möller, T., Bard, F., Bhattacharya, A., Biber, K., Campbell, B., Dale, E.,...Boddeke, H. W. G. M. (2016). Critical data-based re-evaluation of minocycline as a putative specific microglia inhibitor. *Glia*, *64*(10), 1788,1794. doi:10.1002/glia.23007

Monk, J. P., Phillips, G., Waite, R., Kuhn, J., Schaaf, L. J., Otterson, G. A.,...Villalona-Calero, M. A. (2006). Assessment of tumor necrosis factor alpha blockade as an intervention to improve tolerability of dose-intensive chemotherapy in cancer patients. *Journal of Clinical Oncology*, *24*(12), 1852–1859. doi:10.1200/JCO.2005.04.2838

Montana, J. G., & Dyke, H. J. (2002). Update on the therapeutic potential of PDE4 inhibitors. *Expert Opinion on Investigational Drugs*, *11*(1), 1–13. doi:10.1517/13543784.11.1.1

Morita, I. (2002). Distinct functions of COX-1 and COX-2. *Prostaglandins & Other Lipid Mediators*, *68*, 165–175. doi:10.1016/S0090-6980(02)00029-1

Mueser, K. T., Goodman, L. B., Trumbetta, S. L., Rosenberg, S. D., Osher, F. C., Vidaver, R.,...Foy, D. W. (1998). Trauma and posttraumatic stress disorder in severe mental illness. *Journal of Consulting and Clinical Psychology*, *66*(3), 493–499. doi:10.1037/0022-006x.66.3.493

Muoio, V., Persson, P. B., & Sendeski, M. M. (2014). The neurovascular unit—Concept review. *Acta Physiologica*, *210*(4), 790–798. doi:10.1111/apha.12250

Murphy, N., Cowley, T. R., Blau, C. W., Dempsey, C. N., Noonan, J., Gowran, A.,...Lynch, M. A. (2012). The fatty acid amide hydrolase inhibitor URB597 exerts anti-inflammatory effects in hippocampus of aged rats and restores an age-related deficit in long-term potentiation. *Journal of Neuroinflammation*, *9*(1), 79. doi:10.1186/1742-2094-9-79

Myint, A. M., Steinbusch, H. W. M., Goeghegan, L., Luchtman, D., Kim, Y. K., & Leonard, B. E. (2007). Effect of the COX-2 inhibitor celecoxib on behavioural and immune changes in an olfactory bulbectomised rat model of depression. *Neuroimmunomodulation*, *14*(2), 65–71.

Nadjar, A., Bluthé, R.-M., May, M. J., Dantzer, R., & Parnet, P. (2005). Inactivation of the cerebral NFκB pathway inhibits interleukin-1β-induced sickness behavior and c-Fos expression in various brain nuclei. *Neuropsychopharmacology*, *30*(8), 1492–1499. doi:10.1038/sj.npp.1300755

Nair, A., & Bonneau, R. H. (2006). Stress-induced elevation of glucocorticoids increases microglia proliferation through NMDA receptor activation. *Journal of Neuroimmunology*, *171*(1–2), 72–85. doi:10.1016/j.jneuroim.2005.09.012

Naseribafrouei, A., Hestad, K., Avershina, E., Sekelja, M., Linløkken, A., Wilson, R., & Rudi, K. (2014). Correlation between the human fecal microbiota and depression. *Neurogastroenterology and Motility*, *26*(8), 1155–1162. doi:10.1111/nmo.12378

Neumeister, A., Normandin, M. D., Pietrzak, R. H., Piomelli, D., Zheng, M. Q., Gujarro-Anton, A.,...Huang, Y. (2013). Elevated brain cannabinoid CB1 receptor availability in post-traumatic stress disorder: A positron emission tomography study. *Molecular Psychiatry*, *18*(9), 1034–1040. doi:10.1038/mp.2013.61

Newman, S. C., & Bland, R. C. (1994). Life events and the 1-year prevalence of major depressive episode, generalized anxiety disorder, and panic disorder in a community sample. *Comprehensive Psychiatry*, *35*(1), 76–82. doi:10.1016/0010-440X(94)90173-2

Nguyen, K. T., Deak, T., Owens, S. M., Kohno, T., Fleshner, M., Watkins, L. R., & Maier, S. F. (1998). Exposure to acute stress induces brain interleukin-1β protein in the rat. *Journal of Neuroscience*, *18*(6), 2239–2246. Retrieved from http://www.scopus.com/inward/record.url?eid=2-s2.0-0032521115&partnerID=tZOtx3y1

Nguyen, K. T., Deak, T., Will, M. J., Hansen, M. K., Hunsaker, B. N., Fleshner, M.,...Maier, S. F. (2000). Timecourse and corticosterone sensitivity of the brain, pituitary, and serum interleukin-1β protein response to acute stress. *Brain Research*, *859*(2), 193–201. doi:10.1016/S0006-8993(99)02443-9

Nomura, D. K., Morrison, B. E., Blankman, J. L., Long, J. Z., Kinsey, S. G., Marcondes, M. C. G.,...Cravatt, B. F. (2011). Endocannabinoid hydrolysis generates brain prostaglandins that promote neuroinflammation. *Science*, *334*(6057), 809–813. doi:10.1126/science.1209200

O'Brien, M. E. R., Anderson, H., Kaukel, E., O'Byrne, K., Pawlicki, M., von Pawel, J.,...Povey, J. (2004). SRL 172 (killed Mycobacterium vaccae) in addition to standard chemotherapy improves quality of life without affecting survival, in patients with advanced non-small-cell lung cancer: Phase III results. *Annals of Oncology, 15*(6), 906–914. doi:10.1093/annonc/mdh220

O'Connor, J. C., Lawson, M. A., Andre, C., Briley, E. M., Szegedi, S. S., Lestage, J.,...Kelley, K. W. (2009). Induction of IDO by bacille calmette-guerin is responsible for development of murine depressive-like behavior. *The Journal of Immunology, 182*(5), 3202–3212. doi:10.4049/jimmunol.0802722

O'Connor, J. C., Lawson, M. A., André, C., Moreau, M., Lestage, J., Castanon, N.,...Dantzer, R. (2009). Lipopolysaccharide-induced depressive-like behavior is mediated by indoleamine 2,3-dioxygenase activation in mice. *Molecular Psychiatry, 14*(5), 511–522. doi:10.1038/sj.mp.4002148

O'Donovan, A., Hughes, B. M., Slavich, G. M., Lynch, L., Cronin, M. T., O'Farrelly, C., & Malone, K. M. (2010). Clinical anxiety, cortisol and interleukin-6: Evidence for specificity in emotion-biology relationships. *Brain, Behavior, and Immunity, 24*(7), 1074–1077. doi:10.1016/j.bbi.2010.03.003

Owen, A. J., Batterham, M. J., Probst, Y. C., Grenyer, B. F. S., & Tapsell, L. C. (2005). Low plasma vitamin E levels in major depression: Diet or disease? *European Journal of Clinical Nutrition, 59*(2), 304–306. doi:10.1038/sj.ejcn.1602072

Ozalp, A., & Barroso, B. (2009). Simultaneous quantitative analysis of N-acylethanolamides in clinical samples. *Analytical Biochemistry, 395*(1), 68–76. doi:10.1016/j.ab.2009.08.005

Pace, T. W., Hu, F., & Miller, A. H. (2007). Cytokine-effects on glucocorticoid receptor function: Relevance to glucocorticoid resistance and the pathophysiology and treatment of major depression. *Brain, Behavior, and Immunity, 21*(1), 9–19. doi:10.1016/j.bbi.2006.08.009

Paez-Pereda, M., Hausch, F., & Holsboer, F. (2011). Corticotropin releasing factor receptor antagonists for major depressive disorder. *Expert Opinion on Investigational Drugs, 20*(4), 519–535.

Panahi, Y., Badeli, R., Karami, G. R., & Sahebkar, A. (2015). Investigation of the efficacy of adjunctive therapy with bioavailability-boosted curcuminoids in major depressive disorder. *Phytotherapy Research, 29*(1), 17–21. doi:10.1002/ptr.5211

Parker, G. B., Brotchie, H., & Graham, R. K. (2017). Vitamin D and depression. *Journal of Affective Disorders, 208*, 56–61. doi:10.1016/j.jad.2016.08.082

Pasco, J. A., Jacka, F. N., Williams, L. J., Henry, M. J., Nicholson, G. C., Kotowicz, M. A., & Berk, M. (2010). Clinical implications of the cytokine hypothesis of depression: The association between use of statins and aspirin and the risk of major depression. *Psychotherapy and Psychosomatics, 79*(5), 323–325.

Patel, S., Hill, M. N., Cheer, J. F., Wotjak, C. T., & Holmes, A. (2017). The endocannabinoid system as a target for novel anxiolytic drugs. *Neuroscience and Biobehavioral Reviews, 76*, 56–66. doi:10.1016/j.neubiorev.2016.12.033

Persoons, P., Vermeire, S., Demyttenaere, K., Fischler, B., Vandenberghe, J., Van Oudenhove, L.,...Rutgeerts, P. (2005). The impact of major depressive disorder on the short- and long-term outcome of Crohn's disease treatment with infliximab. *Alimentary Pharmacology & Therapeutics, 22*(2), 101–110.

Ping, G., Qian, W., Song, G., & Zhaochun, S. (2014). Valsartan reverses depressive/anxiety-like behavior and induces hippocampal neurogenesis and expression of BDNF protein in unpredictable chronic mild stress mice. *Pharmacology Biochemistry and Behavior, 124*, 5–12. doi:10.1016/j.pbb.2014.05.006

Pitman, R. K., Rasmusson, A. M., Koenen, K. C., Shin, L. M., Orr, S. P., Gilbertson, M. W.,...Liberzon, I. (2012). Biological studies of post-traumatic stress disorder. *Nature Reviews Neuroscience, 13*(11), 769–787. doi:10.1038/nrn3339

Prather, A. A., Rabinovitz, M., Pollock, B. G., & Lotrich, F. E. (2009). Cytokine-induced depression during IFN-alpha treatment: The role of IL-6 and sleep quality. *Brain, Behavior, and Immunity, 23*(8), 1109–1116. doi:10.1016/j.bbi.2009.07.001

Quervain, D. J. De, Bentz, D., Michael, T., Bolt, O. C., Wiederhold, B. K., de Quervain, D. J.-F.,...Wilhelm, F. H. (2011). Glucocorticoids enhance extinction-based psychotherapy. *Proceedings of the National Academy of Sciences of the United States of America, 108*(16), 6621–6625. doi:10.1073/pnas.1018214108

Raison, C. L., Capuron, L., & Miller, A. H. (2006). Cytokines sing the blues: Inflammation and the pathogenesis of depression. *Trends in Immunology, 27*(1), 24–31. doi:10.1016/j.it.2005.11.006

Raison, C. L., Rutherford, R. E., Woolwine, B. J., Shuo, C., Schettler, P., Drake, D. F.,...Miller, A. H. (2013). A randomized controlled trial of the tumor necrosis factor antagonist infliximab for treatment-resistant depression: the role of baseline inflammatory biomarkers. *JAMA Psychiatry, 70*(1), 31–41. doi:10.1001/2013.jamapsychiatry.4

Ramamoorthy, S., & Cidlowski, J. A. (2013). Exploring the molecular mechanisms of glucocorticoid receptor action from sensitivity to resistance. *Endocrine Development, 24*, 41–56. doi:10.1159/000342502

Reber, S. O., Siebler, P. H., Donner, N. C., Morton, J. T., Smith, D. G., Kopelman, J. M.,...Lowry, C. A. (2016). Immunization with a heat-killed preparation of the environmental bacterium *Mycobacterium vaccae* promotes stress resilience in mice. *Proceedings of the National Academy of Sciences, 113*(22), E3130–E3139. doi:10.1073/pnas.1600324113

Redrobe, J. P., Dumont, Y., Herzog, H., & Quirion, R. (2004). Characterization of neuropeptide Y, Y(2) receptor knockout mice in two animal models of learning and memory processing. *Journal of Molecular Neuroscience, 22*(3), 159–166.

Redrobe, J. P., Dumont, Y., St-Pierre, J. A., & Quirion, R. (1999). Multiple receptors for neuropeptide Y in the hippocampus: Putative roles in seizures and cognition. *Brain Research, 848*(1–2), 153–166. doi:10.1016/S0006-8993(99)02119-8

Rolan, P., Hutchinson, M., & Johnson, K. (2009). Ibudilast: A review of its pharmacology, efficacy and safety in respiratory and neurological disease. *Expert Opinion on Pharmacotherapy, 10*(17), 2897–2904. doi:10.1517/14656560903426189

Rush, A. J., Trivedi, M. H., Wisniewski, S. R., Nierenberg, A. A., Stewart, J. W., Warden, D.,...Fava, M. (2006). Acute and longer-term outcomes in depressed outpatients requiring one or several treatment steps: A STAR*D report. *American Journal of Psychiatry, 163*(11), 1905–1917.

Ryabinin, A. E., Tsoory, M. M., Kozicz, T., Thiele, T. E., Neufeld-Cohen, A., Chen, A.,...Kaur, S. (2012). Urocortins: CRF's siblings and their potential role in anxiety, depression and alcohol drinking behavior. *Alcohol, 46*(4), 349–357. doi:10.1016/j.alcohol.2011.10.007

Schall, T. J., & Proudfoot, A. E. I. (2011). Overcoming hurdles in developing successful drugs targeting chemokine receptors.

Nature Reviews Immunology, 11(5), 355–363. doi:10.1038/nri2972

Schelling, G., Briegel, J., Roozendaal, B., Stoll, C., Rothenhäusler, H. B., & Kapfhammer, H. P. (2001). The effect of stress doses of hydrocortisone during septic shock on posttraumatic stress disorder in survivors. *Biological Psychiatry, 50*(12), 978–985. doi:10.1016/S0006-3223(01)01270-7

Schelling, G., Kilger, E., Roozendaal, B., De Quervain, D. J. F., Briegel, J., Dagge, A., . . . Kapfhammer, H. P. (2004). Stress doses of hydrocortisone, traumatic memories, and symptoms of posttraumatic stress disorder in patients after cardiac surgery: A randomized study. *Biological Psychiatry, 55*(6), 627–633. doi:10.1016/j.biopsych.2003.09.014

Schelling, G., Richter, M., Roozendaal, B., Rothenhäusler, H.-B., Krauseneck, T., Stoll, C., . . . Kapfhammer, H.-P. (2003). Exposure to high stress in the intensive care unit may have negative effects on health-related quality-of-life outcomes after cardiac surgery. *Critical Care Medicine, 31*(7), 1971–1980. doi:10.1097/01.CCM.0000069512.10544.40

Schelling, G., Stoll, C., Haller, M., Briegel, J., Manert, W., Hummel, T., . . . Peter, K. (1998). Health-related quality of life and posttraumatic stress disorder in survivors of the acute respiratory distress syndrome. *Critical Care Medicine, 26*(4), 651–659. doi:10.1097/00003246-199804000-00011

Schelling, G., Stoll, C., Kapfhammer, H. P., Rothenhausler, H. B., Krauseneck, T., Durst, K., . . . Briegel, J. (1999). The effect of stress doses of hydrocortisone during septic shock on posttraumatic stress disorder and health-related quality of life in survivors. *Critical Care Medicine, 27*(12), 2678–2683.

Schlosburg, J. E., Blankman, J. L., Long, J. Z., Nomura, D. K., Pan, B., Kinsey, S. G., . . . Cravatt, B. F. (2011). Chronic monoacylglycerol lipase blockade causes functional antagonism of the endocannabinoid system. *Nature neuroscience, 13*(9), 1113–1119.

Schmeltzer, S. N., Herman, J. P., & Sah, R. (2016). Neuropeptide Y (NPY) and posttraumatic stress disorder (PTSD): A translational update. *Experimental Neurology, 284*(July), 196–210. doi:10.1016/j.expneurol.2016.06.020

Schmieder, R. E. (2005). Mechanisms for the clinical benefits of angiotensin II receptor blockers. *American Journal of Hypertension, 18*(5), 720–730. doi:10.1016/j.amjhyper.2004.11.032

Schreiber, S., Feagan, B., D'Haens, G., Colombel, J.-F., Geboes, K., Yurcov, M., . . . Steffgen, J. (2006). Oral p38 mitogen-activated protein kinase inhibition with BIRB 796 for active Crohn's disease: A randomized, double-blind, placebo-controlled trial. *Clinical Gastroenterology and Hepatology, 4*(3), 325–334. doi:10.1016/j.cgh.2005.11.013

Schwandt, M. L., Cortes, C. R., Kwako, L. E., George, D. T., Momenan, R., Sinha, R., . . . Heilig, M. (2016). The CRF1 antagonist verucerfont in anxious alcohol-dependent women: Translation of neuroendocrine, but not of anti-craving effects. *Neuropsychopharmacology, 41*(12), 2818–2829. doi:10.1038/npp.2016.61

Selye, H. (1936). A syndrome produced by diverse nocuous agents. *Nature, 1936*(1), 1936.

Serova, L., Mulhall, H., & Sabban, E. (2017). NPY1 receptor agonist modulates development of depressive-like behavior and gene expression in hypothalamus in SPS rodent PTSD model. *Frontiers in Neuroscience, 11.* doi:10.3389/fnins.2017.00203

Serova, L. I., Tillinger, A., Alaluf, L. G., Laukova, M., Keegan, K., & Sabban, E. L. (2013). Single intranasal neuropeptide Y infusion attenuates development of PTSD-like symptoms to traumatic stress in rats. *Neuroscience, 236*(Suppl. C), 298–312.

Settle, E. C. (1998). Antidepressant drugs: Disturbing and potentially dangerous adverse effects. *Journal of Clinical Psychiatry, 59*(suppl 16), 25–30.

Shehzad, A., Rehman, G., & Lee, Y. S. (2013). Curcumin in inflammatory diseases. *BioFactors, 39*(1), 69–77. doi:10.1002/biof.1066

Sherwin, E., Dinan, T. G., & Cryan, J. F. (2017). Recent developments in understanding the role of the gut microbiota in brain health and disease. *Annals of the New York Academy of Sciences 1420*(1), 5–25. doi:10.1111/nyas.13416

Sijbrandij, M., Kleiboer, A., Bisson, J. I., Barbui, C., & Cuijpers, P. (2015). Pharmacological prevention of post-traumatic stress disorder and acute stress disorder: A systematic review and meta-analysis. *The Lancet Psychiatry, 2*(5), 413–421. doi:10.1016/S2215-0366(14)00121-7

Singhal, G., & Baune, B. T. (2017). Microglia: An interface between the loss of neuroplasticity and depression. *Frontiers in Cellular Neuroscience, 11*(September), 1–16. doi:10.3389/fncel.2017.00270

Slavich, G. M., & Irwin, M. R. (2014). From stress to inflammation and major depressive disorder: A social signal transduction theory of depression. *Psychological Bulletin, 140*(3), 774–815. doi:10.1037/a0035302

Slyepchenko, A., Maes, M., Köhler, C. A., Anderson, G., Quevedo, J., Alves, G. S., . . . Carvalho, A. F. (2016). T helper 17 cells may drive neuroprogression in major depressive disorder: Proposal of an integrative model. *Neuroscience and Biobehavioral Reviews, 64*, 83–100. doi:10.1016/j.neubiorev.2016.02.002

Smagin, G. N., & Dunn, A. J. (2000). The role of CRF receptor subtypes in stress-induced behavioural responses. *European Journal of Pharmacology, 405*, 199–206. doi:10.1016/S0014-2999(00)00553-7

Smagin, G. N., Heinrichs, S. C., & Dunn, A. J. (2001). The role of CRH in behavioral responses to stress. *Peptides, 22*(5), 713–724. doi:10.1016/S0196-9781(01)00384-9

Soczynska, J. K., Kennedy, S. H., Goldstein, B. I., Lachowski, A., Woldeyohannes, H. O., & McIntyre, R. S. (2009). The effect of tumor necrosis factor antagonists on mood and mental health-associated quality of life: Novel hypothesis-driven treatments for bipolar depression? *NeuroToxicology, 30*(4), 497–521. doi:10.1016/j.neuro.2009.03.004

Soczynska, J. K., Mansur, R. B., Brietzke, E., Swardfager, W., Kennedy, S. H., Woldeyohannes, H. O., . . . McIntyre, R. S. (2012). Novel therapeutic targets in depression: Minocycline as a candidate treatment. *Behavioural Brain Research, 235*(2), 302–317. doi:10.1016/j.bbr.2012.07.026

Soravia, L. M., Heinrichs, M., Aerni, A., Maroni, C., Schelling, G., Ehlert, U., . . . de Quervain, D. J.-F. (2006). Glucocorticoids reduce phobic fear in humans. *Proceedings of the National Academy of Sciences, 103*(14), 5585–5590. doi:10.1073/pnas.0509184103

Spedding, S., & Simon. (2014). Vitamin D and depression: A systematic review and meta-analysis comparing studies with and without biological flaws. *Nutrients, 6*(4), 1501–1518. doi:10.3390/nu6041501

Spencer, R. L., & Deak, T. (2017). A users guide to HPA axis research. *Physiology and Behavior, 178*, 43–65. doi:10.1016/j.physbeh.2016.11.014

Spierling, S. R., & Zorrilla, E. P. (2017). Don't stress about CRF: Assessing the translational failures of CRF1antagonists.

Psychopharmacology, *234*(9–10), 1467–1481. doi:10.1007/s00213-017-4556-2

Steckler, T., & Risbrough, V. (2012). Pharmacological treatment of PTSD—established and new approaches. *Neuropharmacology*, *62*(2), 617–627. doi:10.1016/j.neuropharm.2011.06.012

Sukoff Rizzo, S. J., Neal, S. J., Hughes, Z. A., Beyna, M., Rosenzweig-Lipson, S., Moss, S. J., & Brandon, N. J. (2012). Evidence for sustained elevation of IL-6 in the CNS as a key contributor of depressive-like phenotypes. *Translational Psychiatry*, *2*(12), e199. doi:10.1038/tp.2012.120

Surís, A., North, C., Adinoff, B., Powell, C. M., & Greene, R. (2010). Effects of exogenous glucocorticoid on combat-related PTSD symptoms. *Annals of Clinical Psychiatry*, *22*(4), 274–279.

Taguchi, I., Oka, K., Kitamura, K., Sugiura, M., Oku, a, & Matsumoto, M. (1999). Protection by a cyclic AMP-specific phosphodiesterase inhibitor, rolipram, and dibutyryl cyclic AMP against Propionibacterium acnes and lipopolysaccharide-induced mouse hepatitis. *Inflammation Research: Official Journal of the European Histamine Research Society*, *48*(7), 380–385. doi:10.1007/s000110050475

Tanaka, T., Narazaki, M., & Kishimoto, T. (2011). Anti-interleukin-6 receptor antibody, tocilizumab, for the treatment of autoimmune diseases. *FEBS Letters*, *585*(23), 3699–3709. doi:10.1016/j.febslet.2011.03.023

Tchantchou, F., Tucker, L. B., Fu, A. H., Bluett, R. J., Joseph, T., Patel, S., & Zhang, Y. (2014). The fatty acid amide hydrolase inhibitor PF-3845 promotes neuronal survival, attenuates inflammation and improves functional recovery in mice with traumatic brain injury. *Neuropharmacology*, *85*, 427–439.

To, Y., Ito, K., Kizawa, Y., Failla, M., Ito, M., Kusama, T.,... Barnes, P. J. (2010). Targeting phosphoinositide-3-kinase-δ with theophylline reverses corticosteroid insensitivity in chronic obstructive pulmonary disease. *American Journal of Respiratory and Critical Care Medicine*, *182*(7), 897–904. doi:10.1164/rccm.200906-0937OC

Tonelli, L. H., Holmes, A., & Postolache, T. T. (2008). Intranasal immune challenge induces sex-dependent depressive-like behavior and cytokine expression in the brain. *Neuropsychopharmacology*, *33*(5), 1038–1048. doi:10.1038/sj.npp.1301488

Torika, N., Asraf, K., Roasso, E., Danon, A., & Fleisher-Berkovich, S. (2016). Angiotensin converting enzyme inhibitors ameliorate brain inflammation associated with microglial activation: Possible implications for Alzheimer's disease. *Journal of Neuroimmune Pharmacology*, *11*(4), 774–785. doi:10.1007/s11481-016-9703-8

Townes, S. V., Furst, D. E., & Thenkondar, A. (2012). The impact of tocilizumab on physical function and quality of life in patients with rheumatoid arthritis: a systematic literature review and interpretation. *Open Access Rheumatology: Research and Reviews*, *4*, 87–92. Retrieved from http://www.dovepress.com/getfile.php?fileID=13593%0Ahttp://ovidsp.ovid.com/ovidweb.cgi?T=JS&PAGE=reference&D=emed14&NEWS=N&AN=365632068%0Ahttp://ovidsp.ovid.com/ovidweb.cgi?T=JS&PAGE=reference&D=prem&NEWS=N&AN=27790016

Traki, L., Rostom, S., Tahiri, L., Bahiri, R., Harzy, T., Abouqal, R., & Hajjaj-Hassouni, N. (2014). Responsiveness of the EuroQol EQ-5D and Hospital Anxiety and Depression Scale (HADS) in rheumatoid arthritis patients receiving tocilizumab. *Clinical Rheumatology*, *33*(8), 1055–1060. doi:10.1007/s10067-014-2609-z

Tsigos, C., & Chrousos, G. P. (2002). Hypothalamic-pituitary-adrenal axis, neuroendocrine factors and stress. *Journal of Psychosomatic Research*, *53*, 865–871. doi:10.1016/S0022-3999(02)00429-4

Turcu, A. F., Spencer-Segal, J. L., Farber, R. H., Luo, R., Grigoriadis, D. E., Ramm, C. A.,...Auchus, R. J. (2016). Single-dose study of a corticotropin-releasing factor receptor-1 antagonist in women with 21-hydroxylase deficiency. *The Journal of Clinical Endocrinology & Metabolism*, *101*(3), 1174–1180.

Tynan, R. J., Naicker, S., Hinwood, M., Nalivaiko, E., Buller, K. M., Pow, D. V,...Walker, F. R. (2010). Chronic stress alters the density and morphology of microglia in a subset of stress-responsive brain regions. *Brain, Behavior, and Immunity*, *24*(7), 1058–1068.

Tyring, S., Gottlieb, A., Papp, K., Gordon, K., Leonardi, C., Wang, A.,...Krishnan, R. (2006). Etanercept and clinical outcomes, fatigue, and depression in psoriasis: Double-blind placebo-controlled randomised phase III trial. *Lancet*, *367*(9504), 29–35. doi:10.1016/S0140-6736(05)67763-X

Vallabhapurapu, S., & Karin, M. (2009). Regulation and function of NF-κB transcription factors in the immune system. *Annual Review of Immunology*, *27*(1), 693–733. doi:10.1146/annurev.immunol.021908.132641

Vellas, B., Sol, O., Snyder, P. J., Ousset, P.-J., Haddad, R., Maurin, M.,... Pando, M. P. (2011). EHT0202 in Alzheimer's disease: A 3-month, randomized, placebo-controlled, double-blind study. *Current Alzheimer Research*, *8*(2), 203–212.

Vesterinen, H. M., Connick, P., Irvine, C. M. J., Sena, E. S., Egan, K. J., Carmichael, G. G.,...Chandran, S. (2015). Drug repurposing: A systematic approach to evaluate candidate oral neuroprotective interventions for secondary progressive multiple sclerosis. *PLoS ONE*, *10*(4). doi:10.1371/journal.pone.0117705

Vian, J., Pereira, C., Chavarria, V., Köhler, C., Stubbs, B., Quevedo, J.,...Fernandes, B. S. (2017). The renin–angiotensin system: a possible new target for depression. *BMC Medicine*, *15*(1), 144. doi:10.1186/s12916-017-0916-3

Vincent, J. L., Donadello, K., & Schmit, X. (2011). Biomarkers in the critically ill patient: C-reactive protein. *Critical Care Clinics*, *27*(2), 241–251.

Vinod, K. Y., & Hungund, B. L. (2006). Role of the endocannabinoid system in depression and suicide. *Trends in Pharmacological Sciences*, *27*(10), 539–545. doi:10.1016/j.tips.2006.08.006

Wang, C., Wang, Z., Li, M., Li, C., Yu, H., Zhou, D., & Chen, Z. (2017). Reducing neuroinflammation in psychiatric disorders: Novel target of phosphodiesterase 4 (PDE4) and developing of the PDE4 inhibitors. In *Mechanisms of neuroinflammation intech*.

Wang, C., Yang, X. M., Zhuo, Y. Y., Zhou, H., Lin, H. B., Cheng, Y. F.,... Zhang, H. T. (2012). The phosphodiesterase-4 inhibitor rolipram reverses Abeta-induced cognitive impairment and neuroinflammatory and apoptotic responses in rats. *International Journal of Neuropsychopharmacol*, *15*(6), 749–766. doi:10.1017/S1461145711000836

Waters, R. P., Rivalan, M., Bangasser, D. A., Deussing, J. M., Ising, M., Wood, S. K.,...Summers, C. H. (2015). Evidence for the role of corticotropin-releasing factor in major depressive disorder. *Neuroscience and Biobehavioral Reviews*, *58*, 63–78. doi:10.1016/j.neubiorev.2015.07.011

White, J. D. (1993). Neuropeptide Y: a central regulator of energy homeostasis. *Regulatory Peptides*, *49*(2), 93–107. doi:10.1016/0167-0115(93)90431-7

Wingfield, J. C., & Sapolsky, R. M. (2003). Reproduction and resistance to stress: When and how. *Journal of Neuroendocrinology, 15*(8), 711–724.

Wohleb, E. S., Hanke, M. L., Corona, A. W., Powell, N. D., Stiner, L. M., Bailey, M. T.,...Sheridan, J. F. (2011). Adrenergic receptor antagonism prevents Anxiety-Like Behavior and Microglial Reactivity Induced by Repeated Social Defeat. *Journal of Neuroscience, 31*(17), 6277–6288.

Wood, S. K., Walker, H. E., Valentino, R. J., & Bhatnagar, S. (2010). Individual differences in reactivity to social stress predict susceptibility and resilience to a depressive phenotype: Role of corticotropin-releasing factor. *Endocrinology, 151*(4), 1795–1805.

World Health Organization. (2017). Depression. https://www.who.int/en/news-room/fact-sheets/detail/depression

Yamasaki, R., Liu, L., Lin, J., & Ransohoff, R. M. (2012). Role of CCR2 in immunobiology and neurobiology. *Clinical and Experimental Neuroimmunology, 3*(1), 16–29.

Yehuda, R., Bierer, L. M., Pratchett, L. C., Lehrner, A., Koch, E. C., Van Manen, J. A.,...Hildebrandt, T. (2015). Cortisol augmentation of a psychological treatment for warfighters with posttraumatic stress disorder: Randomized trial showing improved treatment retention and outcome. *Psychoneuroendocrinology, 51*, 589–597. doi:10.1016/j.psyneuen.2014.08.004

Yehuda, R., Boisoneau, D., Lowry, M. T., & Giller, E. L. (1995). Dose-response changes in plasma cortisol and lymphocyte glucocorticoid receptors following dexamethasone administration in combat veterans with and without posttraumatic stress disorder. *Archives of General Psychiatry, 52*(7), 583–593. doi:10.1001/archpsyc.1995.03950190065010

Yirmiya, R. (1996). Endotoxin produces a depressive-like episode in rats. *Brain Research, 711*(1–2), 163–174. doi:10.1016/0006-8993(95)01415-2

Yirmiya, R., Pollak, Y., Morag, M., Reichenberg, A., Barak, O., Avitsur, R.,...Pollmächer, T. (2000). Illness, cytokines, and depression. *Annals of the New York Academy of Sciences, 917*, 478–487.

Yoshie, O., & Matsushima, K. (2014). CCR4 and its ligands: From bench to bedside. *International Immunology, 27*(1), 11–20. doi:10.1093/intimm/dxu079

Zanetidou, S., Murri, M. B., Buffa, A., Malavolta, N., Anzivino, F., & Bertakis, K. (2011). Vitamin D supplements in geriatric major depression. *International Journal of Geriatric Psychiatry, 26*(11), 1209–1210. doi:10.1002/gps.2703

Zeller, E., Stief, H.-J., Pflug, B., & Sastre-y-Hernandez, M. (1984). Results of a Phase II study of the antidepressant effect of rolipram. *Pharmacopsychiatry, 17*, 188–190. doi:10.1055/s-2007-1017435

Zheng, X., Ma, S., Kang, A., Wu, M., Wang, L., Wang, Q.,...Hao, H. (2016). Chemical dampening of Ly6Chi monocytes in the periphery produces anti-depressant effects in mice. *Scientific Reports, 6*(1), 19406. doi:10.1038/srep19406

Zobel, A. W., Nickel, T., Künzel, H. E., Ackl, N., Sonntag, A., Ising, M., & Holsboer, F. (2000). Effects of the high-affinity corticotropin-releasing hormone receptor 1 antagonist R121919 in major depression: the first 20 patients treated. *Journal of Psychiatric Research, 34*(3), 171–181. doi:10.1016/S0022-3956(00)00016-9

Zohar, J., Yahalom, H., Kozlovsky, N., Cwikel-Hamzany, S., Matar, M. A., Kaplan, Z.,...Cohen, H. (2011). High dose hydrocortisone immediately after trauma may alter the trajectory of PTSD: Interplay between clinical and animal studies. *European Neuropsychopharmacology, 21*(11), 796–809. doi:10.1016/j.euroneuro.2011.06.001

Zuany-Amorim, C., Sawicka, E., Manlius, C., Le Moine, A., Brunet, L. R., Kemeny, D. M.,...Walker, C. (2002). Suppression of airway eosinophilia by killed Mycobacterium vaccae-induced allergen-specific regulatory T-cells. *Nature Medicine, 8*(6), 625–629. doi:10.1038/nm0602-625

Zuardi, A. W., Cosme, R. A., Graeff, F. G., & Guimarães, F. S. (1993). Effects of ipsapirone and cannabidiol on human experimental anxiety. *Journal of Psychopharmacology, 7*(1 Suppl.), 82–88. doi:10.1177/026988119300700112

Cognitive-Behavioral Interventions for Disorders of Extreme Stress

Posttraumatic Stress Disorder and Acute Stress Disorder

J. Gayle Beck, Allison M. Pickover, Alexandra J. Lipinski, Han N. Tran, *and* Thomas S. Dodson

Abstract

In this chapter, we review the current literature on cognitive-behavioral treatments for posttraumatic stress disorder (PTSD) and acute stress disorder (ASD). Particular attention is paid to treatments for PTSD that have strong empirical support, specifically cognitive processing therapy, prolonged exposure, and eye movement desensitization and reprocessing therapy. Cognitive-behavioral treatments for ASD have evolved differently, with greater emphasis on treatment packages; notably, this literature is less well developed and deserving of considerable more study, relative to the PTSD literature. Throughout the chapter, we have addressed areas for future study, as well issues that are currently salient in the treatment of these two conditions.

Keywords: cognitive-behavioral therapy, PTSD, ASD, intervention, cognitive processing therapy, prolonged exposure, EMDR

Exposure to stress is an expected part of life, often taking the form of rejection, disappointment, or loss. This volume focuses on stress, conceptualized in many different ways. Within the trauma field, extreme stressors, sometimes referred to as traumas, are seen as the proximal "cause" of mental health conditions. By current definition, a trauma involves "exposure to actual or threatened death, serious injury, or sexual violence" (American Psychiatric Association [APA], 2013, p. 271). Epidemiological estimates suggest that 37%–92% of adults in the United States will be exposed to a traumatic event during the course of their lifetime (e.g., Breslau, 2012; Kessler, Chiu, Demler, Merikangas, & Walters, 2005). Although most individuals who experience a traumatic event ultimately will not experience serious mental health problems, a significant minority will report either short- or long-term trauma-related mental health symptoms. In this chapter, we will focus on two specific forms of posttrauma mental health problems, acute stress disorder (ASD) and posttraumatic stress disorder (PTSD). Following a brief description and overview of these two conditions, we will delve into

the literature examining the efficacy and effectiveness of several different forms of cognitive-behavioral treatments (CBT) for ASD and PTSD. As will be noted, impressive progress has been made in treating these conditions in the past several decades, with important implications for alleviating posttrauma mental health problems. Although progress has been made, we will discuss areas where our science is not as well developed, highlighting important directions for future work.

Understanding Acute Stress Disorder and Posttraumatic Stress Disorder

Although many individuals will experience some symptoms in the first few weeks following a trauma (Riggs, Rothbaum, & Foa, 1995; Rothbaum, Foa, Riggs, Murdock, & Walsh, 1992), the defining characteristics of ASD and PTSD differ somewhat from the normative pattern of symptom reduction. According to current nosology, ASD is defined by the presence of intrusion symptoms (e.g., distressing dreams related to the trauma), inability to experience positive emotions, dissociative symptoms (e.g., dissociative amnesia), efforts to avoid thoughts and reminders of the trauma, and arousal symptoms (e.g., sleep disturbance, hypervigilance). These symptoms last anywhere from 3 days to 1 month in the immediate aftermath of the traumatic event. ASD was first introduced into the *Diagnostic and Statistical Manual of Mental Disorders* (*DSM*) in 1994 (APA, 1994), motivated by two objectives: (1) to recognize acute stress reactions that arise in the initial month following trauma exposure, which previously had gone unrecognized or were characterized as adjustment difficulties, and (2) to identify individuals who were at risk for subsequent PTSD (see Bryant, Friedman, Spiegel, Ursano, & Strain, 2011). Recent revisions to the ASD diagnosis (APA, 2013) have de-emphasized dissociative symptoms in ASD, given conflicting research concerning whether these symptoms independently predict PTSD (e.g., Breh & Seidler, 2007; Harvey & Bryant, 2002; for an extended discussion of dissociation in ASD, see Cardeña & Carlson, 2011).

Considering ASD more broadly, there is mixed evidence about the utility of this diagnosis in predicting PTSD. Bryant (2011) provided a systematic analysis of prospective studies published between 1994 and 2009, examining whether a diagnosis of ASD predicts future PTSD. This review suggested moderately good positive predictive power for the ASD diagnosis, indicating that across studies at least half of the participants with ASD subsequently met criteria for PTSD. However, sensitivity was poor, in that most individuals who were diagnosed with PTSD did not meet criteria for ASD previously. Recent data suggest that the *DSM-5* criteria for ASD show comparable positive predictive power and improved sensitivity for PTSD (e.g., Bryant et al., 2015). Importantly, irrespective of whether one used *DSM-IV* or *DSM-5* criteria, over 50% of individuals who were diagnosed with ASD were subsequently diagnosed with an additional psychiatric condition, although not necessarily PTSD. This finding suggests that ASD serves as a marker for additional mental health problems following trauma but lacks specificity in predicting PTSD. When considering the evidence base for current CBT interventions for this condition, this feature of ASD should be kept in mind.

In contrast to ASD, considerably more is known about PTSD. Changes to the diagnostic criteria for PTSD for *DSM-5* resulted in four symptom clusters, reflecting the addition of a cluster describing negative alterations in thoughts and emotions (e.g., distorted sense of responsibility for the trauma,

persistent feelings of fear, shame, guilt, or anger; APA, 2013). This cluster of symptoms was added to the three more traditional components of PTSD: intrusion symptoms, avoidance of reminders of the traumatic event, and arousal symptoms (Wilson, 1994). As noted, these symptom clusters parallel those contained in the criteria for ASD, reflecting conceptualization of the two conditions as similar in symptom presentation and underlying psychopathology. Galatzer-Levy and Bryant (2013) provide a cogent discussion of the evolution of the PTSD diagnosis, noting that each iteration of changes to these criteria has expanded the number and types of symptoms that are included, perhaps leading to a more amorphous definition of the disorder than is optimal.

Despite limitations of current diagnostic criteria, it is well recognized that PTSD is associated with significant disability, including marital difficulties and divorce, increased likelihood of physical health problems, greater likelihood of involvement with the legal system, and less vocational stability and success (e.g., Backhaus, Gholizadeh, Godfrey, Pittman, & Afari, 2016; Birkley, Eckhardt, & Dykstra, 2016; Fang et al., 2015). In addition, PTSD is recognized as a disorder of comorbidity; this disorder is often accompanied by depression, anxiety disorders, substance abuse, and other psychiatric conditions (e.g., Kessler et al., 2005). Despite the apparent presence of a "cause" for PTSD (exposure to a traumatic event), only 8% to 9% of trauma-exposed individuals will develop PTSD during their lifetime. Moreover, the specificity of trauma exposure to PTSD is poor; trauma exposure is often followed by other problems such as generalized anxiety, major depression, social anxiety disorder, and substance abuse. When PTSD does develop, the condition typically follows a chronic and nonremitting course, if not treated (e.g., Bray et al., 2016; Steinert, Hofmann, Leichsenring, & Kruse, 2015).

Fortunately, the past decades have included concentrated efforts to develop, test, and refine specific CBTs for ASD and PTSD, as will be reviewed in the remainder of this chapter. We will begin with a review of CBTs for PTSD, as considerably more progress has occurred in this domain, relative to development and examination of treatments for ASD. As will be noted, several treatments have garnered considerable research attention, specifically cognitive processing therapy, prolonged exposure, and eye movement desensitization and reprocessing therapy. These three approaches to treatment have very different presumed mechanisms of action, although as noted, they may not differ markedly with respect to efficacy or effectiveness. We will close our review with discussion of promising developments in the literature on CBTs of PTSD and ASD, alongside discussion of areas where additional research is sorely needed.

Cognitive-Behavioral Treatments for Posttraumatic Stress Disorder

As noted, there are three specific forms of CBT that are widely regarded as "first-line" interventions for PTSD: cognitive processing therapy (CPT), prolonged exposure (PE), and eye movement desensitization and reprocessing therapy (EMDR). These three treatments have been heavily investigated and received recognition from a variety of national and international organizations. CPT, PE, and EMDR are all considered level I treatments according to VA/DoD Clinical Practice Guidelines (2004), the National Institute for Health and Clinical Excellence (2005), the Australian National Health and Medical Research Council Guidelines (2007), and the International Society for Traumatic Stress Studies (Foa, Keane, Friedman, & Cohen, 2008). CPT and PE are considered level I treatments by the APA (2004), while EMDR is rated as a level II treatment by this group. Most available care guidelines for PTSD list trauma-focused psychological interventions as the first-line treatment for this condition, to be selected over pharmacological treatment. These guidelines consider medication as either an adjunct to trauma-focused psychosocial treatment or a second-line intervention. As we will review in the sections that follow, CPT, PE, and EMDR each have a robust literature supporting their use, although differences exist with respect to the depth of the database undergirding each treatment. Additional questions exist within each literature concerning how the intervention is best disseminated to clinicians and the mechanism of action by which the treatment achieves its outcomes.

Cognitive Processing Therapy

Cognitive processing therapy (CPT; Resick & Schnicke, 1996) aims to teach the patient with PTSD how to use specific skills to address two different types of trauma-related cognitive distortions, termed assimilation (distorting what occurred during the trauma to fit with prior beliefs) and overaccommodation (changing beliefs as a result of the trauma). Within CPT, these distortions produce "stuck points," or specific dysfunctional beliefs that maintain emotional upset and PTSD symptoms.

The intervention is 12 weeks long, when conducted in an outpatient setting. The original CPT protocol included an exposure element, wherein the patient is asked to write a detailed account of her worst traumatic experience. CPT includes the following intervention elements: overview of and rationale for the treatment; psychoeducation about the symptoms of PTSD; discussion about how the patient makes meaning out of the traumatic event; psychoeducation about the relationship between events, thoughts, and feelings; teaching skills to challenge stuck points in order to adopt more balanced beliefs; and addressing self-blame. The last five sessions of CPT focus on applying these skills to five core areas: safety, trust, power/control, esteem, and intimacy. Clients are assigned practice of these skills between sessions as homework.

EFFICACY AND EFFECTIVENESS OF COGNITIVE PROCESSING THERAPY

Existing research has demonstrated the efficacy and effectiveness of CPT for the treatment of PTSD involving patients with PTSD stemming from different types of traumatic events. Numerous randomized clinical trials (RCTs) have been conducted on CPT, some contrasting this therapy with an inactive comparison (e.g., wait list or treatment as usual; e.g., Resick & Schnicke, 1992) and others comparing this treatment with other active interventions (e.g., Resick, Nishith, Weaver, Astin, & Feuer, 2002). As summarized by Cusack et al. (2016) in a recent meta-analysis of studies on the psychological treatment of PTSD, the evidence supporting CPT as an effective intervention for PTSD is moderately strong. Relative to inactive comparison conditions, CPT showed a weighted mean effect size difference of −32.2 (95% confidence interval: −46.3 to −18.05; standardized mean effect size difference of −1.40 [95% confidence interval: −1.95 to −0.85]). In addition to efficacy studies, this literature has a number of effectiveness trials, studies that examine the impact of CPT when studied under "real-world," naturalistic circumstances. For example, Forbes and colleagues (2012) evaluated CPT against a treatment-as-usual condition for veterans presenting with military-related PTSD in Australia. Veterans who received CPT showed significantly greater improvements in PTSD symptoms, anxiety, depression, and social and dyadic relationships, relative to the treatment-as-usual condition. Like many effectiveness trials involving veteran samples (Steenkamp, Litz, Hoge, & Marmar, 2015), patients in the Forbes et al. (2012) study had remaining treatment needs, suggesting that although CPT can be helpful in naturalistic settings, it may need to be augmented when used to assist veterans with PTSD.

Importantly, CPT has been compared with other interventions for PTSD, in an effort to examine comparative efficacy. Resick et al. (2002) compared the outcome of CPT with PE and a minimal attention condition, in the treatment of 171 women experiencing PTSD following a sexual assault. This trial is distinguished by being adequately powered and relying on a sample with polytrauma histories. Results indicated that both CPT and PE were efficacious for these patients, relative to a minimal attention condition, with no notable treatment differences between the two interventions on measures of PTSD and depression. In the completer sample, 76% of the CPT sample and 58% of the PE sample reported good end-state functioning, a difference that was not statistically significant. Patients in the CPT and PE conditions retained their gains during the 9-month follow-up interval. These results support the utility of both CPT and PE in the treatment of PTSD and suggest that both are equally efficacious. In a more recent comparison, Surís, Link-Malcolm, Chard, Ahn, and North (2013) compared the efficacy of CPT with present-centered therapy (PCT), an intervention that focuses exclusively on provision of general support for current issues in the patient's life. In PCT, explicit discussion of trauma-related topics is discouraged. Eighty-six veterans (84.8% female) who had experienced military sexual trauma participated in this trial. Surís et al. (2013) reported no between-group differences between treatment conditions on clinician-based measures, although patients who received CPT reported greater gains in self-reported PTSD symptoms, relative to the PCT condition.

In sum, research evidence clearly supports the efficacy and effectiveness of CPT. Studies on CPT have included patients experiencing PTSD owing to varying types of traumas, who have been treated in a variety of different settings by many different types of clinicians (e.g., therapists with advanced training in CPT versus more general training in CBT), an indicator of CPT's effectiveness. With regard to moderators of treatment response, Resick et al. (2012) examined the impact of dissociation on treatment outcomes across three conditions: CPT, cognitive processing therapy-cognitive (CPT-C), and written trauma account only (WA). These authors found more improvements on PTSD symptoms for individuals with high dissociation, particularly depersonalization, who received CPT

relative to CPT-C. For those with lower levels of dissociation, receiving CPT-C resulted in more improvement compared to CPT. Another study of CPT examined whether past or current diagnoses of alcohol use disorder (AUD) moderated PTSD outcome (Kaysen et al., 2014). They noted a nonsignificant interaction, suggesting that CPT may be equally effective in individuals diagnosed with PTSD both with and without AUDs. As noted by Cusack et al. (2016), however, there is a need for future studies to examine other variables (related to, for example, clinicians, settings) that may moderate treatment efficacy. Importantly, CPT was selected as one of two treatments for widespread dissemination and implementation within the Veterans Administration (VA) care system (Ruzek, Karlin, & Zeiss, 2012).

COGNITIVE PROCESSING THERAPY-COGNITIVE (ONLY)

One aspect of CPT that some clinicians find challenging involves asking patients to write a detailed account of their worst traumatic experience. To dismantle the specific components of CPT, Resick et al. (2008) compared the standard CPT protocol with the cognitive component only (CPT-C) and the written account component only (WA), in a sample of 150 female victims of interpersonal violence. Patients improved across all three treatment conditions, not only on PTSD symptoms but also on depression, anxiety, anger, guilt, shame, and cognitive distortions. Results also showed that CPT-C had a lower dropout rate compared to the CPT and WA conditions (22%, 34%, and 26%, respectively), although these rates were not examined statistically. As a result of this study, the use of CPT-C has increased (relative to CPT), particularly in applied settings. Interest in CPT-C has been bolstered by effectiveness studies. For example, Morland and colleagues (2014) compared CPT-C delivered via videoteleconferencing (VTC) or in-person in a noninferiority RCT; the sample included 120 male veterans living in rural areas of Hawaii. Patients in both conditions showed significant improvements in PTSD symptoms at posttreatment, with treatment gains maintained at 3 and 6 months follow-up. Additionally, no differences between groups were noted for levels of therapeutic alliance, treatment compliance, or satisfaction. In light of effectiveness studies on CPT-C, it is anticipated that this form of CPT will continue to gain in popularity as this intervention becomes more widely disseminated.

GROUP COGNITIVE PROCESSING THERAPY AND COGNITIVE PROCESSING THERAPY-COGNITIVE (ONLY)

Although CPT originally was designed to be delivered as a group therapy (Resick & Schnicke, 1992), the majority of empirical studies on this treatment have used an individual format. Recently, Resick et al. and the STRONG STAR Consortium (2015) compared Group CPT-C with Group PCT in the treatment of 108 active duty military personnel with PTSD (92.5% male). Participants in both Group CPT-C and Group PCT showed significant reductions in PTSD symptom severity, with treatment gains maintained at 1-year follow-up. Group CPT-C resulted in significantly greater symptom reduction in PTSD, relative to Group PCT. Compared with individual format CPT-C, the effects of treatment delivered in a group format on symptoms of depression was more modest. In light of pressing demand for effective PTSD treatments within large health care systems, extension of the literature on CPT to include a group format is an important advancement (Sloan, Beck, & Sawyer, 2017).

COGNITIVE PROCESSING THERAPY IN THE INTERNATIONAL CONTEXT

Several studies have examined CPT in non-US populations. As reviewed, Forbes et al. (2012) reported successful use of CPT for veterans in Australia. Expanding to a non-Western setting, Bass and colleagues (2013) conducted a RCT comparing CPT-C (delivered in a group setting) with individual support for female survivors of sexual violence presenting with high levels of PTSD symptoms in the Democratic Republic of Congo. Both interventions were delivered by community paraprofessionals; those in the CPT condition received 2 weeks of in-person training from experts. Significant gains were noted on measures of anxiety-depression, PTSD, and functional impairments; individuals who received CPT reported significantly larger gains, relative to individuals who received individual support. At the 6-month follow-up time point, 9% of individuals who received CPT and 42% of individuals who received individual support met criteria for probable PTSD. This study represents an important extension of the CPT literature for several reasons. First, the patients were low-income individuals who had experienced sexual trauma in the context of a conflict-affected country, a population that one would expect to be difficult to treat. Second, CPT was delivered by paraprofessionals, in contrast to other studies that utilized mental health professionals who received substantial training and supervision in the conduct of CPT. In this context, the very positive patient outcomes are particularly impressive. Third, group treatments typically yield lower effect sizes, relative to individual format treatments (e.g., Sloan et al., 2017); in this trial, the obtained effect size for the between-condition difference in PTSD at posttreatment was robust ($d = 1.4$), suggesting that with appropriate cultural adaptations, CPT can be transported into non-Western environments with good outcomes. We await additional cross-cultural trials, particularly those involving low-resource counties, as these will help to expand knowledge about how to disseminate and implement CBT internationally. Recognition of ways that various forms of CBT will need to be adapted to non-Western cultures will help expand the reach of these evidence-based therapies; for example, in the Bass et al. (2013) study, handouts needed to be modified to accommodate low literacy levels. Systematic consideration of various adaptations will help to establish the flexibility of specific forms of CBT, as well as limits to that flexibility.

Prolonged Exposure

Prolonged exposure (PE) therapy is a structured intervention with a very long history (Foa, Hembree, & Rothbaum, 2007). Originally introduced over 30 years ago for the treatment of anxiety-based disorders, PE centers on helping the PTSD patient to confront trauma-related cues that evoke excessive, unrealistic fear. PE is founded on emotional processing theory (Foa & Kozak, 1986), which proposes that fear can be conceptualized as stimulus, response, and meaning elements, which form cognitive networks or structures. Pathological fear structures are characterized by excessive response elements, reflecting escape and avoidance of feared stimuli as well as physiological arousal. PE thus places emphasis on helping the patient confront feared stimuli, both imaginally (in session) and in real life (in vivo). Psychoeducation is included to help the patient understand the nature of his or her PTSD symptoms, as well as the rationale for treatment. Slow, paced breathing also is taught as a means for the patient to control autonomic arousal during exposure. PE typically involves 10 to 15, 90-minute sessions which focus on imaginal exposure, followed by discussion with the therapist to encourage further processing of trauma-related thoughts and feelings. Patients are asked to conduct in vivo practice as homework, in addition to listening to the previous audiotaped session. The key element of this therapy is for the

PTSD patient to permit prolonged exposure with feared trauma-related cues, until the anxiety and discomfort reduce (extinction learning).

EFFICACY AND EFFECTIVENESS OF PROLONGED EXPOSURE

Over two dozen RCTs have been conducted to evaluate the efficacy of PE for treating PTSD against other active treatments (e.g., EMDR, CPT) and control conditions (McLean & Foa, 2011). As summarized by Cusack et al. (2016), PE showed a weighted mean effect size difference of −28.9 (95% confidence interval: −35.5 to −22.3; standardized mean effect size difference of −1.27 [95% confidence interval: −1.54 to −1.00]). These authors characterize the strength of evidence supporting PE as an effective treatment for PTSD as high. An earlier meta-analysis that included seven additional RCTs not assessed in the Cusack et al. (2016) report also found that PE performed significantly better than control conditions, indicating a large effect size at posttreatment (Hedge's g = 1.08) and at follow-up (1 to 12 months posttreatment; Hedge's g = 0.68) (Powers, Halpern, Ferenschak, Gillihan, & Foa, 2010). Examining potential moderators of treatment, Powers et al. (2010) found no significant relationship between effect size and a number of moderators, including time since trauma, study publication year, treatment dose (i.e., number of hours and sessions), study quality (e.g., study included description of withdrawals and dropouts), or types of index trauma of the participants (combat/terror, childhood sexual abuse, rape, mixed trauma).

Additionally, the effectiveness of PE in real-world settings has been supported in samples drawn from VA health care centers (e.g., Eftekhari et al., 2013; Goodson, Lefkowitz, Helstrom, & Gawrysiak, 2013; Mouliso, Tuerk, Schnurr, & Rauch, 2016; Tuerk et al., 2011). Eftekhari et al. (2013) evaluated program outcomes for PE (and CPT) across VA health care centers participating in the large-scale training rollout program. Patients included 1,931 veterans of different war eras who had experienced a wide range of traumas; mental health providers included 804 professionals who had all received PE training. The effect size for pre- to posttreatment reduction in self-reported PTSD symptoms was large (d = 0.87); consideration of only veterans who completed at least eight sessions of PE indicated a substantially larger effect (d = 1.21), suggesting that the "dosage" of PE is salient in the effectiveness of this treatment. In a related study, Mouliso et al. (2016) examined whether PE showed differential effectiveness for male versus female veterans receiving PTSD treatment within the VA, noting comparable effect sizes for PE in both male and female patients (d = 1.3 and 1.4, respectively). PE has also been shown to be effective for adolescent trauma survivors with PTSD symptoms. Foa, McLean, Capaldi, and Rosenfield (2013) examined the impact of PE for adolescent girls reporting PTSD following sexual abuse who were treated in a rape crisis center; relative to supportive counseling, girls who received PE showed significantly larger reductions in PTSD.

In sum, a large research base clearly supports the efficacy and effectiveness of PE. Studies on this treatment have included patients experiencing PTSD due to varying types of traumas; these studies have crossed many different settings and included individuals with a range of backgrounds and training. These trials provide evidence to support the efficacy and effectiveness of PE as a treatment for PTSD. As noted, PE was selected as one of two evidence-based treatments to be disseminated to clinicians within the VA care system (Ruzek et al., 2012).

PROLONGED EXPOSURE IN THE INTERNATIONAL CONTEXT

The effectiveness of PE has been extended in recent studies that have translated or adapted the PE protocol for use in various non-Western societies (e.g., Asukai, Saito, Tsuruta, Ogami, & Kishimoto, 2008; Vera et al., 2011). Asukai et al. (2008) translated the PE protocol into Japanese and then conducted a pilot study assessing the tolerability of this protocol with participants from psychiatric outpatient clinics in Japan. The authors noted significant decreases in PTSD symptoms following treatment and at 3- and 6-month follow-ups. Asukai, Saito, Tsuruta, Kishimoto, and Nishikawa (2010) replicated these findings and noted that PE (as utilized in both of these studies) did not seem to require culture-related modifications. In a small feasibility study, Vera et al. (2011) reported that PE seemed to be both effective and feasible for use with Spanish-speaking PTSD patients in an outpatient setting in Puerto Rico. Small modifications were made to the PE protocol to enhance cultural fit. For example, the authors incorporated spouses (or romantic partners) in several sessions, given the saliency of the family within Latino culture. These authors discuss the salient role of training and ongoing supervision/consultation in the successful use of PE in this context.

Several international efforts suggest that PE can be used with patients who report other psychiatric conditions, in addition to PTSD. For example, van den Berg et al. (2015) conducted a single-blind RCT with patients from outpatient treatment centers in Holland; in each case, patients were receiving primary care for psychosis and also received a PTSD diagnosis. Patients were randomized to PE, EMDR, or a waitlist condition. Results revealed that both PE and EMDR produced a significant reduction of PTSD symptoms, relative to the waitlist condition. In a similar vein, Schiff, Nacasch, Levit, Katz, and Foa (2015) explored whether PE could be used to treat sexual assault-related PTSD in women who were seeking help at methadone clinics in Israel. In this report, PE was expanded to range up to 19 sessions and was delivered by social workers who staffed the clinic. Significant reductions in PTSD symptoms were noted, with few instances of relapse in the use of illicit drugs (notably, the authors indicate that relapse among female patients in methadone clinics in Israel is low; as such, it is difficult to interpret this finding). These studies suggest that PE may hold considerable promise as an empirically supported therapy that needs little or no cultural adaptation. Clearly, additional dissemination research is needed to expand the use of PE into non-Western, low-income countries.

Eye Movement Desensitization and Reprocessing Therapy

Eye movement desensitization and reprocessing therapy (EMDR) was introduced as a therapy for PTSD in 1989 (Shapiro, 1989). EMDR conceptualizes posttraumatic stress symptoms as the result of a failure to create a coherent trauma memory. Therefore, a central goal of EMDR is to foster integration of the trauma memory, so that it can be processed accurately (McGuire, Lee, & Drummond, 2014). Main features of EMDR include short periods of imaginal exposure to the trauma memory and associated negative cognitions while engaging in saccadic eye movements directed by the therapist (e.g., tracking the therapist's finger back and forth), followed by a period of disengaging with the trauma memory, and then scanning for changes, thoughts, physical feelings, and emotions. EMDR also aims to replace negative cognitions with adaptive/positive cognitions utilizing practiced imagery.

The use of saccadic eye movements during imaginal exposure is a distinctive feature of EMDR and has been the subject of debate, specifically whether the use of this technique is necessary for treatment gains (e.g., Lohr, Tolin, & Lilienfeld, 1998). Critics of EMDR have claimed that the exposure component of EMDR accounts for improvements

that result from this treatment, positing that eye movements are unnecessary (Davidson & Parker, 2001). In EMDR, the saccadic eye movements are thought to provide affective distance from the trauma exposure, an assertion which conflicts with tenets of traditional extinction theory that undergird PE (McGuire et al., 2014). Reviews of available research regarding the utility of the saccadic eye movements in EMDR have been mixed. A meta-analysis by Davidson and Parker (2001) compared the efficacy of EMDR (with eye movements) with EMDR using an eye-fixed condition; there were no significant differences in outcome between studies where EMDR included eye movements and those which did not. However, a more recent meta-analysis by Lee and Cuijpers (2013) found a significant medium effect size ($d = 0.41$) for the utility of the eye movement in increasing the efficacy of EMDR on PTSD, relative to EMDR conducted without eye movements. These authors note that Davidson and Parker's (2001) meta-analysis did not weigh sample sizes when computing average effect sizes in this analysis.

Despite evidence that supports EMDR as an efficacious treatment for PTSD, the mechanism by which this treatment reduces PTSD symptoms remains poorly understood. There have been several proposed theoretical explanations for EMDR's efficacy, including accounts based on the orienting response hypothesis, the working memory account hypothesis, and an account based on increased interhemispheric interaction (see Jeffries & Davis, 2013, for a review). One proposed mechanism of EMDR is based on adaptive information-processing theory, which conceptualizes PTSD symptoms as a failure to completely process the traumatic memory (Shapiro, 2007) and posits that horizontal eye movement may increase communication between the left and right brain hemispheres, presumably facilitating processing of the trauma memory (Christman, Garvey, Propper, & Phaneuf, 2003). Another proposed mechanism for EMDR's efficacy posits a working memory model, wherein eye movements create a distraction that splits working memory load; the reduced memory load serves to decrease affect and vividness of the trauma memory (Gunter & Bodner, 2008), allowing for reprocessing and integration of the trauma memory. Additionally, some critics of EMDR have posited a fear extinction model, where the exposure elements in the EMDR protocol account for symptom amelioration (Davidson & Parker, 2001; Spates & Koch, 2003). Although recent research has begun to investigate various proposed mechanisms for the impact of eye movements in the context of EMDR (e.g., Herkt et al., 2014; Leer et al., 2017; Thomaes, Engelhard, Sijbrandij, Cath, & Van den Heuvel, 2016), no consensus has been reached in the literature to date. As a result, EMDR has drawn criticism as to whether it adds to existing treatments for PTSD (Herbert et al., 2000). Although EMDR continues to receive empirical support as a useful treatment for PTSD, future research is needed to further understand explanatory mechanisms for this treatment modality.

EFFICACY AND EFFECTIVENESS OF EYE MOVEMENT DESENSITIZATION AND REPROCESSING THERAPY

Efficacy studies have found that EMDR produces good outcomes when used to treat PTSD (Bisson et al., 2007; Bradley, Greene, Russ, Dutra, & Westen, 2005; Chen, Zhang, Hu, & Liang, 2015; Cusack et al., 2016; Ho & Lee, 2012; Van Der Kolk et al., 2007). In a meta-analysis comparing EMDR to exposure-based CBT, Ho and Lee (2012) found no significant differences between the two treatments in reduction of PTSD symptoms. Similarly, Bisson et al. (2007) found that EMDR and exposure-based CBT were both superior treatments for reducing PTSD symptoms compared to other therapies (i.e., stress management, group CBT). Van Der Kolk et al. (2007) found that EMDR was superior to pill placebo and fluoxetine in reducing symptoms of PTSD and depression. Bradley et al. (2005) found that EMDR and exposure did not significantly differ with regard to their efficacy in the treatment of PTSD symptoms, and both were superior to inactive control conditions. In addition to calculating effect sizes for each study that was included, a meta-analysis by Cusack and colleagues (2016) assessed for concerns related to risk of bias, consistency, directness, and precision when determining overall strength of evidence (SOE) for each treatment outcome (i.e., reduction in depressive symptoms, reduction in PTSD symptoms, and loss of PTSD diagnosis). Evidence for EMDR's efficacy was found for reduction of depression symptoms (standardized mean effect size difference of −1.13; 95% confidence interval: −1.52 to −0.74 weighted mean effect size difference data not reported), loss of PTSD diagnosis (standardized mean effect size difference of 0.64, 95% confidence interval: 0.46 to 0.81), and PTSD symptoms (effect size difference of −1.08; 95% confidence interval: −1.83 to −0.33). Questions regarding consistency and precision of methodology were raised by the EMDR studies in this meta-analysis, which weakens the SOE for EMDR's efficacy.

Namely, EMDR's SOE for reduction in depression and loss of PTSD status was found to be moderate, while SOE for reduction in PTSD symptoms was found to be low. As such, the results of this meta-analysis concluded that the overall SOE for EMDR for PTSD as low to moderate. Although medium to large effect sizes have been noted for EMDR in reducing PTSD symptoms across meta-analyses, additional research is needed in light of findings by Cusack and colleagues.

EMDR also has been studied in effectiveness studies among several trauma populations, including survivors of motor vehicle accidents (Boccia, Piccardi, Cordellieri, Guariglia, & Giannini, 2015), Syrian refugees (Acarturk et al., 2016), survivors of serious cardiac events (Arabia, Manca, & Solomon, 2011), survivors of domestic abuse (Tarquinio et al., 2012), active duty service members (McLay et al., 2016), and adult survivors of childhood abuse (Ehring et al., 2014). Although each of these studies documents that EMDR can be helpful for the reduction of PTSD symptoms when used in "real-life" settings, it is important to note that the evidence for EMDR's effectiveness in treating PTSD in combat veterans has been mixed. A review by Albright and Thayer (2010) noted limited evidence for the positive effects of EMDR in this population and cited a need for additional RCTs to further examine the effectiveness of EMDR among veterans. Likewise, Bisson and colleagues (2007) note that combat veterans with PTSD responded to EMDR at a lower rate than civilians with PTSD, relative to waitlist controls. Although available evidence suggests that EMDR is an effective treatment for PTSD symptoms across a number of trauma samples, more research is needed to understand potential moderating factors that contribute to outcomes obtained with this treatment.

Additional Treatments for Posttraumatic Stress Disorder

A number of other structured CBT interventions for PTSD have been developed and examined. For example, stress inoculation training (Kilpatrick, Veronen, & Resick, 1982; Meichenbaum, 1974) is a cognitive-behavioral approach that includes psychoeducation, relaxation training, breathing retraining, guided self-dialog, thought stopping, and imaginal exposure. This package treatment has some empirical support for its efficacy and is regarded as a front-line treatment by the VA/DOD and the International Society for Traumatic Stress Studies (Cusack et al., 2016). Likewise, group present centered therapy (GPCT) has empirical support for its efficacy and effectiveness. GPCT focuses on teaching PTSD patients to manage their symptoms in a group context and discourages focus on revisiting the trauma. The core components of GPCT include psychoeducation, peer support, and the development of peer-facilitated problem solving. GPCT was originally developed as a protocol-based form of supportive therapy, to be used as an active treatment comparison in PTSD treatment trials (Schnurr, Friedman, Lavori, & Hsieh, 2001). As summarized by Bradley et al. (2005), supportive therapy has a medium to large effect size in the treatment of PTSD. GPCT mirrors "treatment as usual" within the VA care system, and it has been shown to rival CBT when used in a group format, in the treatment of veterans with chronic PTSD (Schnurr et al., 2003). A number of additional promising CBT-based interventions have emerged and are being studied, including couple- and family-based approaches, virtual reality-based exposure therapy, dialectical behavior therapy, and interventions designed to address emotion regulation prior to beginning exposure-based work (see Kearns & Rothbaum, 2012). As we will discuss in the final section of this chapter, these promising interventions are both needed and welcome, given that current evidence-based interventions (CPT, PE, and EMDR) are sometimes not tolerated by patients or do not completely reduce their PTSD symptoms. A number of salient issues persist when considering CBT approaches to the treatment of PTSD. The presence of these issues reflects the need for continued refinement and expansion of available treatments, particularly for individuals with chronic PTSD.

Cognitive-Behavioral Therapy for Acute Stress Disorder

In contrast to the PTSD treatment literature, much of the literature on treating individuals with ASD has focused on treatment packages that include a variety of cognitive and behavioral interventions. In this literature, the typical outcome is whether a patient with ASD receives a diagnosis of PTSD following treatment or during follow-up given the abbreviated time frame during which an ASD diagnosis can occur. In one of the early studies in this arena, Bryant, Harvey, Dang, Sackville, and Basten (1998) compared a CBT intervention and supportive counseling (SC) in a sample of motor vehicle accident (MVA) and industrial accident survivors who reported either full or subsyndromal criteria for ASD. The CBT intervention involved five 90-minute

sessions comprised of psychoeducation, progressive muscle relaxation, imaginal exposure, cognitive restructuring, and graded in vivo exposure. Results suggested that CBT outperformed SC, with significantly fewer participants qualifying for a PTSD diagnosis in the CBT condition (relative to the SC condition) at posttreatment and 6-month follow-up. CBT patients also had better outcomes in terms of severity of intrusions, avoidance symptoms, and depressive symptoms, relative to those who received SC.

Subsequent variations of Bryant et al.'s (1998) protocol provide initial support for the generalizability and longevity of CBT's effects on individuals with ASD. Bryant, Moulds, Guthrie, and Nixon (2003) noted that CBT outperformed SC in a group of MVA and nonsexual assault survivors who had sustained a mild traumatic brain injury. Additionally, 4-year follow-up data from the group's CBT-informed interventions for ASD (i.e., Bryant et al., 1998; Bryant, Sackville, Dang, Moulds, & Guthrie, 1999) found that participants who received CBT-based interventions experienced lower intensity of total PTSD symptoms and lower frequency and intensity of avoidance symptoms than survivors who received SC (Bryant, Moulds, & Nixon, 2003). Two studies have examined whether hypnosis might provide added benefit to this CBT package treatment for ASD. Bryant, Moulds, Guthrie, and Nixon (2005) compared CBT (alone), CBT with hypnosis (CBT+H), and SC, in a sample of 87 survivors of nonsexual assault or MVA. CBT+H differed from CBT in that imaginal exposure exercises were preceded by a 15-minute hypnosis induction. Across conditions, participants received treatment for five 90-minute sessions. Among treatment completers, CBT outperformed SC at posttreatment; both CBT and CBT+H led to lower PTSD total symptom severity and intensity scores, and fewer intrusion and avoidance symptoms, relative to SC. Benefits for CBT and CBT+H were found at 6-month follow-up as well. At both assessment periods, treatment completers who received CBT or CBT+H had lower rates of PTSD than treatment completers who received SC. Contrary to expectations, hypnosis did not appear to yield any substantial benefit. At 3-year follow-up (Bryant et al., 2006), CBT again outperformed SC, with no appreciable benefit of hypnosis.

Prolonged Exposure

In addition to the treatment package developed and studied by Bryant and colleagues, several studies have examined the use of PE in the treatment of

ASD. Bryant and colleagues (1999) compared an intervention combining PE and anxiety training management (PE+ATM) with PE and SC in a sample of MVA and nonsexual assault survivors. The PE+ATM intervention included (in addition to PE) breathing retraining, progressive muscle relaxation, and self-talk exercises for anxiety management. The sample included 66 patients with full or subsyndromal ASD. At posttreatment, fewer participants who had received PE or PE+ATM met criteria for PTSD at posttreatment and 6-month follow-up, relative to SC. More participants who received PE or PE+ATM showed clinically significant gains in term of intrusions and avoidance at posttreatment, and in terms of avoidance at follow-up, relative to SC. Depression symptoms were similarly reduced across all three groups. In a secondary data analysis, Bryant, Moulds, and Guthrie (2001) noted that individuals who received PE reported less use of distraction, less reliance on self-punishment, less worry, and greater use of reappraisal to cope with trauma-related cognitions, relative to individuals who received SC. Extending Bryant et al.'s (1999) results, Bryant and colleagues (2008) found superior results for participants with ASD who received five sessions of PE relative to participants who received five sessions of cognitive restructuring and a waitlist comparison group. In contrast to these findings, Freyth, Elsesser, Lohrmann, and Sartory (2010) did not find a difference in clinical outcomes for participants who received three sessions of PE compared with participants who received three sessions of SC. The PE and SC groups did not differ on measures of posttrauma symptoms, trauma-related cognitions, peritraumatic dissociation, persistent dissociation, or depression symptoms across posttreatment and 3-month follow-up assessments. In sum, PE, alone or in conjunction with other CBT treatment elements, may be useful in treating posttrauama symptoms in individuals with symptoms of ASD. However, the potency of this approach may depend on the dosage and duration of treatment, as well as other factors such as symptom severity.

Cognitive Processing Therapy

To date, there has been one report examining CPT as a treatment for ASD. Nixon (2012) compared a modified CPT protocol with SC in a sample of 30 interpersonal assault survivors with ASD. In this report, CPT was shortened to six sessions. Participants in both treatment conditions reported posttreatment reductions in PTSD symptoms, depression symptoms, and trauma-related beliefs, with no notable differences between CPT and SC. The author noted that the small sample size may have limited the ability to detect differences; effect sizes for symptom reduction were larger for the CPT group than the SC group at posttreatment and follow-up in this study. Additional research on the efficacy of this treatment approach may be warranted given this preliminary evidence.

Thoughts About Cognitive-Behavioral Therapy for Acute Stress Disorder

As noted, the literature on CBT for acute stress disorder (ASD) is not as well developed as the literature on CBT for PTSD. Methodological concerns are frequently present, including small sample sizes. Importantly, this literature has been hampered by a somewhat myopic focus on reduction in PTSD symptoms as the primary outcome following successful treatment. As previously discussed, a diagnosis of ASD does not cleanly predict the development of PTSD, as recent data suggest that ASD may be a risk marker for the development of many different forms of psychiatric symptoms (Bryant et al., 2015). As such, it would seem important for outcome studies on ASD to include a broader assessment of psychiatric outcomes. Greater clarification is needed concerning how best to conceptualize treatment targets, which may help to refine current treatments for ASD.

Salient Issues and Future Directions in the Literature on Cognitive-Behavioral Therapy for Posttraumatic Stress Disorder and Acute Stress Disorder

Within the literature on CBT treatment for both PTSD and ASD, a number of common key issues have emerged, specifically dropout from treatment, clinicians' perceptions of CBT, variation of response rates across studies, and cultural adaptations. These are salient issues with important implications for patient care, and they will be discussed in this section.

Treatment dropout is a frequent concern in this literature. As noted by Imel, Laska, Jakupcak, and Simpson (2013), dropout rates are often used as a proxy for patients' tolerance for a specific treatment. A meta-analysis by these authors noted that the aggregate proportion of dropout from therapy across all RCTs (subsuming 1,850 patients with PTSD) was 18.28%. Variability was noted across studies, which did not reveal differences between specific forms of treatment with respect to dropout rates. In contrast with previous reviews (e.g., Swift & Greenberg, 2012), higher rates of dropout were not obtained for CBT, relative to SC, by Imel and colleagues (2013), likely owing to improved meta-analytic methodology. As well, dropout from treatment among individuals with ASD can be relatively high (Koucky, Galovski, & Nixon, 2012). Discussion within this literature involves potential factors that may account for dropout rates. One could speculate that natural (or treatment-related) improvements in posttrauma symptoms could lead patients to conclude that further treatment is not necessary. On the other hand, trauma survivors may find treatment highly aversive and so be unwilling to remain in treatment. Most experts within the trauma field agree that current CBT interventions warrant continued consideration, particularly with respect to enhancing treatment engagement and tolerability.

As summarized by Kehle-Forbes and Kimerling (2017), several interventions designed to improve retention in therapy are currently under study. Motivational enhancement strategies are the best studied of these approaches, which revolve around motivational interviewing (MI; Miller & Rollnick, 2002). MI centers on a respectful stance with the patient, designed to build rapport and help the individual explore and resolve ambivalence concerning behavior change and therapy. Work in this area is in the early stages. Seal et al. (2012) noted that four sessions of MI administered by telephone resulted in higher rates of treatment initiation and retention among veterans within the VA. A second randomized trial compared a four session in-person motivational enhancement group with a control condition (Murphy, Thompson, Murray, Rainey, & Uddo, 2009), reporting that veterans who received MI attended more PTSD program appointments (65% versus 54%) and remained in the PTSD program longer (8.8 months versus 7.4 months), relative to those randomized to the control condition. As noted by Kehle-Forbes and Kimerling (2017), these early studies show that MI potentially can improve patients' willingness to begin PTSD-focused treatment and to stay the course, once treatment is initiated. We await continued work in this area.

A second approach that is garnering attention as a means to improve treatment retention is shared decision making (SDM; President's New Freedom Commission on Mental Health, 2003). SDM is a process wherein patients are provided with up-to-date information concerning specific treatment options, including evidence-based outcomes, potential side effects, and duration of treatment. SDM intends to help a patient arrive at a treatment choice that is based on scientific evidence, knowledgeable expectations, and personal values. The patient works with a care provider to explore each treatment option. Additional approaches that are being explored include use of a mobile phone app that reminds patients about treatment appointments and homework assignments (see Reger et al., 2013). As noted by Kehle-Forbes and Kimerling (2017), these approaches represent areas where current interest is high.

A related concern in this literature involves clinicians' perceptions that treatments with a direct trauma focus will increase distress and anxiety and lead to higher rates of dropout (e.g., Kilpatrick & Best, 1984). Feeny, Hembree, and Zoellner (2003) reviewed the empirical literature that examined clinician concerns about exposure-based forms of CBT; one of the primary clinician concerns discussed in this review was that exposure therapy will lead to symptom exacerbation and dropout from therapy. Time has not eliminated this concern, as it was echoed by clinicians in a recent survey conducted at a VA residential treatment program for PTSD (Cook et al., 2013). Although data have repeatedly documented that (very small) increases in symptoms may be noted during trauma-focused CBT treatment, large exacerbations are not common and, importantly, are not predictive of dropout from treatment (e.g., Larsen, Wiltsey Stirman, Smith, & Resick, 2016; Nishith, Resick, & Griffin, 2002). As such, addressing clinicians' attitudes concerning various forms of CBT for PTSD is needed, particularly as negative attitudes may lead a clinician to discourage a patient from trying an evidence-based form of CBT.

It is notable as well that CBT-based interventions for PTSD and ASD do not work for everyone (Bradley et al., 2005). Despite years of study and refinement of these interventions, the field at present has only just begun to understand patient-driven moderators of outcome. We know, for example, that civilian samples may have better treatment outcomes, compared to military and veteran samples (e.g., Bradley et al., 2005; Steenkamp et al., 2015), although this finding has not consistently been found and so remains an issue for further study. Some have speculated that military and veteran samples tend to be clinically complex, which could account for reduced effectiveness in these populations. Gerger, Munder, and Barth (2014) examined problem complexity as a moderator for treatment outcome. In this report, problem complexity was defined as chronic symptoms (lasting > 6 months), the presence of multiple problems (e.g., comorbid psychiatric disorders, refugee status, involvement in a violent or abusive romantic relationship), the presence of complex traumatization (e.g., intentional trauma, trauma during childhood), and a formal PTSD diagnosis. This meta-analysis suggested that trauma-specific interventions (such as those discussed in this chapter) showed a significantly larger effect, relative to nonspecific interventions (such as PCT) but *only* for studies involving noncomplex clinical samples. In studies that involved complex patient samples, the difference between trauma-specific and nonspecific interventions was notably smaller. These findings suggest that we need to design and test ways to augment effectiveness for those patients with chronic, long-standing problems that are compounded by comorbidity, difficult life circumstances, and/or an extensive trauma history.

Lastly, as noted in this chapter, the field is just beginning to consider ways in which CBT-focused treatments for PTSD and ASD can be used in an international context. The vast majority of the ASD and PTSD treatment literature is anchored in Western countries. At present, studies have addressed the question of whether a given treatment will work in a different culture from the one in which it was developed. Given the large proportion of trauma and violence that occurs outside of Westernized countries, considerably greater attention to cultural considerations in the treatment of ASD and PTSD is warranted. Hinton and Nickerson (2012) provided a thoughtful overview of factors that should be considered when transporting an intervention into the international context. Paying particular attention to the treatment of survivors of persecution, torture, and sexual abuse with trauma-related symptoms, these authors discuss an array of factors such as the presence of current stressors, bereavement, and culturally specific interpretations of symptoms. We anticipate that this will be an area where the literature develops further in the near future.

Summary and Conclusions

As noted throughout this chapter, considerable progress has been made in our understanding of PTSD and ASD and how to treat these conditions. Looking back in time, the field has made extraordinary progress in developing, refining, and testing the efficacy and effectiveness of specific cognitive-behavioral interventions for these conditions (see Monson, Friedman, & LaBash [2014] for a historical overview). And yet, in many respects, our work is just beginning. As advances are made in understanding etiological processes that underlie trauma-related symptoms, we will need to amend and modify intervention efforts. Moreover, as health care becomes more personalized, we anticipate that mental health care will follow suit. It is possible, for example, that interventions for ASD will become personalized once we have more understanding of factors that predict the development of specific mental health conditions (e.g., PTSD versus depression versus generalized anxiety). And concerted efforts need to be made to adapt and disseminate effective treatments for ASD and PTSD into parts of the world where people are most in need of these interventions. As noted in this chapter, CBT holds tremendous promise for reducing suffering and impairment from trauma-related symptoms. With continued efforts, it is likely that CBT-based interventions will impact trauma-related symptoms through larger scale dissemination and implementation.

References

Acarturk, C., Konuk, E., Cetinkaya, M., Senay, I., Sijbrandij, M., Gulen, B., & Cuijpers, P. (2016). The efficacy of eye movement desensitization and reprocessing for post-traumatic stress disorder and depression among Syrian refugees: Results of a randomized controlled trial. *Psychological Medicine, 46*, 2583–2593. doi:10.1017/S0033291716001070

Albright, D. L., & Thayer, B. (2010). Does EMDR reduce post-traumatic stress disorder symptomatology in combat veterans? *Behavioral Interventions, 25*, 1–19. doi:10.1002/bin.295

American Psychiatric Association. (1994). *Diagnostic and statistical manual of mental disorders* (4th ed.). Washington, DC: American Psychiatric Publishing.

American Psychiatric Association. (2004). *Practice guideline for the treatment of patients with acute stress disorder and posttraumatic stress disorder*. Washington, DC: Author. Retrieved from http://www.psychiatryonline.com/pracGuide/pracGuideTopic_11.aspx

American Psychiatric Association. (2013). *Diagnostic and statistical manual of mental disorders* (5th ed.). Arlington, VA: American Psychiatric Publishing.

Arabia, E., Manca, M. L., & Solomon, R. M. (2011). EMDR for survivors of life-threatening cardiac events: Results of a pilot study. *Journal of EMDR Practice and Research, 5*, 2–13. doi:10.1891/1933-3196.5.1.2

Asukai, N. Saito, A., Tsuruta, N., Kishimoto, J., & Nishikawa, T. (2010). Efficacy of exposure therapy for Japanese patients with posttraumatic stress disorder due to mixed traumatic events: A randomized controlled study. *Journal of Traumatic Stress, 23*, 744–750. doi:10.1002/jts.20589

Asukai, N., Saito, A., Tsuruta, N., Ogami, R., & Kishimoto, J. (2008). Pilot study on prolonged exposure of Japanese patients with posttraumatic stress disorder due to mixed traumatic events. *Journal of Traumatic Stress, 21*, 340–343. doi:10.1002/jts.20337

Australian National Health and Medical Research Council (NHMRC) Guidelines & Australian Centre for Posttraumatic

Mental Health. (2007). Australian guidelines for the treatment of adults with acute stress disorder and posttraumatic stress disorder. Retrieved from https://www.psychology.org.au/Assets/Files/ACPMH_FullASDandPTSDGuidelines.pdf

Backhaus, A., Gholizadeh, S., Godfrey, K., Pittman, J., & Afari, N. (2016). The many wounds of war: The association of service-related and clinical characteristics with problems with the law in Iraq and Afghanistan veterans. *International Journal of Law and Psychiatry, 49*, 205–213. doi:10.1016/j.ijlp.2016.10.007

Bass, J. K., Annan, J., McIvor Murray, S., Kaysen, D., Griffiths, S., Cetinoglu, T., . . . Bolton, P. A. (2013). Controlled trial of psychotherapy for Congolese survivors of sexual violence. *New England Journal of Medicine, 368*, 2182–2191. doi:10.1056/nejmoa1211853

Birkley, E. L., Eckhardt, C. I., & Dykstra, R. E. (2016). Posttraumatic stress disorder symptoms, intimate partner violence, and relationship functioning: A meta-analytic review. *Journal of Traumatic Stress, 29*, 397–405. doi:10.1002/jts.22129

Bisson, J. I., Ehlers, A., Matthews, R., Pilling, S., Richards, D., & Turner, S. (2007). Psychological treatments for chronic post-traumatic stress disorder: Systematic review and meta-analysis. *The British Journal of Psychiatry, 190*, 97–104. doi:10.1192/bjp.bp.106.021402

Boccia, M., Piccardi, L., Cordellieri, P., Guariglia, C., & Giannini, A. M. (2015). EMDR therapy for PTSD after motor vehicle accidents: Meta-analytic evidence for specific treatment. *Frontiers in Human Neuroscience, 9*, 2013. doi:10.3389/fnhum.2015.00213

Bradley, R., Greene, J., Russ, E., Dutra, L., & Westen, D. (2005). A multidimensional meta-analysis of psychotherapy for PTSD. *The American Journal of Psychiatry, 162*, 214–227. doi:10.1176/appi.ajp.162.2.214

Bray, R. M., Engel, C. C., Williams, J., Jaycox, L. H., Lane, M. E., Morgan, J. K., & Unützer, J. (2016). Posttraumatic stress disorder in U.S. military primary care: Trajectories and predictors of one-year prognosis. *Journal of Traumatic Stress, 29*, 340–348. doi:10.1002/jts.22119

Breh, D. C., & Seidler, G. H. (2007). Is peritraumatic dissociation a risk factor for PTSD? *Journal of Trauma & Dissociation, 8*, 53–69. doi:10.1300/j229v08n01_04

Breslau, N. (2012). Epidemiology of posttraumatic stress disorder in adults. In J. G. Beck & D. M. Sloan (Eds.), *Handbook of traumatic stress disorders* (pp. 84–97). New York, NY: Oxford University Press.

Bryant, R. A. (2011). Acute stress disorder as a predictor of posttraumatic stress disorder: A systematic review. *Journal of Clinical Psychiatry, 72*, 233–239. doi:10.4088/jcp.09r05072blu

Bryant, R. A., Creamer, M., O'Donnell, M., Silove, D., McFarlane, A. C., & Forbes, D. (2015). A comparison of the capacity of *DSM-IV* and *DSM-5* acute stress disorder definitions to predict posttraumatic stress disorder and related disorders. *Journal of Clinical Psychiatry, 76*, 391–397. doi:10.4088/jcp.13m08731

Bryant, R. A., Friedman, M. J., Spiegel, D., Ursano, R., & Strain, J. (2011). A review of Acute Stress Disorder in *DSM-5*. *Depression and Anxiety, 28*, 802–817. doi:10.1002/da.20737

Bryant, R. A., Harvey, A. G., Dang, S. T., Sackville, T., & Basten, C. (1998). Treatment of acute stress disorder: A comparison of cognitive-behavioral therapy and supportive counseling. *Journal of Consulting and Clinical Psychology, 66*, 862–866. doi:10.1037//0022-006X.66.5.862

Bryant, R. A., Mastrodomenico, J., Felmingham, K. L., Hopwood, S., Kenny, L., Kandris, E. . . . Creamer, M. (2008). Treatment of acute stress disorder: A randomized controlled trial. *Archives of General Psychiatry, 65*, 659–667. doi:10.1001/archpsyc.65.6.659

Bryant, R. A., Moulds, M., & Guthrie, R. M. (2001). Cognitive strategies and the resolution of acute stress disorder. *Journal of Traumatic Stress, 14*, 213–219. doi:10.1023/A:1007856103389

Bryant, R. A., Moulds, M., Guthrie, R., & Nixon, R. D. V. (2003). Treating acute stress disorder following mild traumatic brain injury. *American Journal of Psychiatry, 160*, 585–587. doi:10.1176/ appi.ajp.160.3.585

Bryant, R. A., Moulds, M., Guthrie, R., & Nixon, R. D. V. (2005). The additive benefit of hypnosis and cognitive-behavioral therapy in treating acute stress disorder. *Journal of Consulting and Clinical Psychology, 73*, 334–340. doi:10.1037/0022-006X.73.2.334

Bryant, R. A., Moulds, M. L., & Nixon, R. V. D. (2003). Cognitive behaviour therapy of acute stress disorder: A four-year follow-up. *Behaviour Research and Therapy, 41*, 489–494. doi:10.1016/S0005-7967(02)00179-1

Bryant, R. A., Moulds, M. L., Nixon, R. D. V., Mastrodomenico, J., Flemingham, K., & Hopwood, S. (2006). Hypnotherapy and cognitive behaviour therapy of acute stress disorder: A three year follow-up. *Behaviour Research and Therapy, 44*, 1331–1335. doi:10.1016/j.brat.2005.04.007

Bryant, R. A., Sackville, T., Dang, S. T., Moulds, M., & Guthrie, R. (1999). Treating acute stress disorder: An evaluation of cognitive behavior therapy and supportive counseling techniques. *American Journal of Psychiatry, 156*, 1780–1786.

Cardeña, E., & Carlson, E. (2011). Acute stress disorder revisited. *Annual Review of Clinical Psychology, 7*, 245–267. doi:10.1146/annurev-clinpsy-032210-104502

Chen, L., Zhang, G., Hu, M., & Liang, X. (2015). Eye movement desensitization and reprocessing versus cognitive-behavioral therapy for adult posttraumatic stress disorder: Systematic review and meta-analysis. *Journal of Nervous and Mental Disease, 203*, 443–451. doi:10.1097/nmd.0000000000000306

Christman, S. D., Garvey, K. J., Propper, R. E., & Phaneuf, K. A. (2003). Bilateral eye movements enhance the retrieval of episodic memories. *Neuropsychology, 17*, 221–229. doi:10.1037/0894-4105.17.2.221

Cook, J. M., O'Donnell, C., Dinnen, S., Bernardy, N., Rosenheck, R., & Hoff, R. (2013). A formative evaluation of two evidence-based psychotherapies for PTSD in VA residential treatment programs. *Journal of Traumatic Stress, 26*, 56–63. doi:10.1002/jts.21769

Cusack, K., Jonas, D. E., Forneris, C. A., Wines, C., Sonis, J., Middleton, J. C., . . . Gaynes, B. N. (2016). Psychological treatments for adults with posttraumatic stress disorder: A systematic review and meta-analysis. *Clinical Psychology Review, 43*, 128–141. doi:10.1016/j.cpr.2015.10.003

Davidson, P. R., & Parker, K. H. (2001). Eye movement desensitization and reprocessing (EMDR): A meta-analysis. *Journal of Consulting and Clinical Psychology, 69*, 305–316. doi:10.1037/0022-006X.69.2.305

Eftekhari, A., Ruzek, J. I., Crowley, J. J., Rosen, C. S., Greenbaum, M. A., & Karlin, B. E. (2013). Effectiveness of national implementation of prolonged exposure therapy in veterans affairs care. *Journal of the American Medical Association Psychiatry, 70*, 949–955. doi:10.1001/jamapsychiatry.2013.36

Ehring, T., Welboren, R., Morina, N., Wicherts, J. M., Freitag, J., & Emmelkamp, P. M. (2014). Meta-analysis of psychological treatments for posttraumatic stress disorder in adult survivors of childhood abuse. *Clinical Psychology Review, 34*, 645–657. doi:10.1016/j.cpr.2014.10.004

Fang, S. C., Schnurr, P. P., Kulish, A. L., Holowka, D. W., Marx, B. P., Keane, T. M., & Rosen, R. (2015). Psychosocial functioning and health-related quality of life associated with posttraumatic stress disorder in male and female Iraq and Afghanistan war veterans: The VALOR registry. *Journal of Women's Health, 24*, 1038–1046. doi:10.1089/jwh.2014.5096

Feeny, N. C., Hembree, E. A., & Zoellner, L. A. (2003). Myths regarding exposure therapy for PTSD. *Cognitive and Behavioral Practice, 10*, 85–90. doi:10.1016/S1077-7229(03)80011-1

Foa, E. B., Hembree, E. A., & Rothbaum, B. O. (2007). Treatments that work. *Prolonged exposure therapy for PTSD: Emotional processing of traumatic experiences: Therapist guide*. New York, NY: Oxford University Press.

Foa, E. B., Keane, T. M., Friedman, M. J., & Cohen, J. A. (Eds.). (2008). *Effective treatments for PTSD: Practice guidelines from the International Society for Traumatic Stress Studies*. New York, NY: Guilford Press.

Foa, E. B., & Kozak, M. J. (1986). Emotional processing of fear: Exposure to corrective information. *Psychological Bulletin, 99*, 20–35. doi:10.1037/0033-2909.99.1.20

Foa, E. B., McLean, C. P., Capaldi, S., & Rosenfield, D. (2013). Prolonged exposure vs. supportive counseling for sexual abuse related PTSD in adolescent girls: A randomized clinical trial. *Journal of the American Medical Association, 310*, 2650–2657. doi:10.1001/jama.2013.282829

Forbes, D., Lloyd, D., Nixon, R. D. V., Elliott, P., Varker, T., Perry, D.,... Creamer, M. (2012). A multisite randomized controlled effectiveness trial of cognitive processing therapy for military-related posttraumatic stress disorder. *Journal of Anxiety Disorders, 26*, 442–452. doi.org/10.1016/j.janxdis.2012.01.006

Freyth, C., Elsesser, K., Lohrmann, T., & Sartory, G. (2010). Effects of additional prolonged exposure to psychoeducation and relaxation in acute stress disorder. *Journal of Anxiety Disorders, 24*, 909–917. doi.org/10.1016/j.janxdis.2010.06.016

Galatzer-Levy, I. R., & Bryant, R. A. (2013). 636,120 ways to have posttraumatic stress disorder. *Perspectives on Psychological Science, 8*, 651–662. doi:10.1177/1745691613504115

Gerger, H., Munder, T., & Barth, J. (2014). Specific and nonspecific psychological interventions for PTSD symptoms: A meta-analysis with problem complexity as a moderator. *Journal of Clinical Psychology, 70*, 601–615. doi:10.1002/jclp.22059

Goodson, J. T., Lefkowitz, C. M., Helstrom, A. W., & Gawrysiak, M. J. (2013). Outcomes of prolonged exposure therapy for veterans with posttraumatic stress disorder. *Journal of Traumatic Stress, 26*, 419–425. doi:10.1002/jts.21830

Gunter, R. W., & Bodner, G. E. (2008). How eye movements affect unpleasant memories: Support for a working-memory account. *Behaviour Research and Therapy, 46*, 913–931. doi:10.1016/j.brat.2008.04.006

Harvey, A. G., & Bryant, R. A. (2002). Acute stress disorder: A synthesis and critique. *Psychological Bulletin, 128*, 886–902. doi:10.1037//0033-2909.128.6.886

Herbert, J. D., Lilienfeld, S. O., Lohr, J. M., Montgomery, R. W., O'Donohue, W. T., Rosen, G. M., & Tolin, D. F. (2000). Science and pseudoscience in the development of eye movement desensitization and reprocessing: Implications for clinical psychology. *Clinical Psychology Review, 20*, 945–971. doi:10.1016/S0272-7358(99)00017-3

Herkt, D., Tumani, V., Grön, G., Kammer, T., Hofmann, A., & Abler, B. (2014). Facilitating access to emotions: Neural signature of EMDR stimulation. *PLoS One, 9*(8), e106350. doi:10.1371/journal.pone.0106350

Hinton, D. E., & Nickerson, A. (2012). Treating trauma-related symptoms in special populations. In J. G. Beck & D. M. Sloan (Eds.), *Handbook of traumatic stress disorders* (pp. 504–512). New York, NY: Oxford University Press.

Ho, M. K., & Lee, C. W. (2012). Cognitive behaviour therapy versus eye movement desensitization and reprocessing for post-traumatic disorder—Is it all in the homework then? *European Review of Applied Psychology/Revue Européenne De Psychologie Appliquée, 62*, 253–260. doi:10.1016/j.erap.2012.08.001

Imel, Z. E., Laska, K., Jakupcak, M., & Simpson, T. L. (2013). Meta-analysis of drop-out in treatments for posttraumatic stress disorder. *Journal of Consulting and Clinical Psychology, 81*, 394–404. doi:org/10.1037/a0031474 and org/10.1037/a0031474.supp

Jeffries, F. W., & Davis, P. (2013). What is the role of eye movements in eye movement desensitization and reprocessing (EMDR) for post-traumatic stress disorder (PTSD)? A review. *Behavioural and Cognitive Psychotherapy, 41*(3), 290–300. doi:10.1017/S1352465812000793

Kaysen, D., Schumm, J., Pedersen, E. R., Seim, R. W., Bedard-Gilligan, M., & Chard, K. (2014). Cognitive processing therapy for veterans with comorbid PTSD and alcohol use disorders. *Addictive Behaviors, 39*(2), 420–427.

Kearns, M. C., & Rothbaum, B. O. (2012). Promising psychological treatments. In J. G. Beck & D. M. Sloan (Eds.), *Handbook of traumatic stress disorders* (pp. 463–472). New York, NY: Oxford University Press.

Kehle-Forbes, S., & Kimerling, R. (2017). Patient engagement in PTSD treatment. *PTSD Research Quarterly, 28*. Retrieved from https://www.ptsd.va.gov/professional/newsletters/research-quarterly/V28N3.pdf

Kessler, R. C., Chiu, W. T., Demler, O., Merikangas, K. R., & Walters, E. E. (2005). Prevalence, severity, and co-morbidity of 12-month DSM–IV disorders in the National Comorbidity Survey Replication. *Archives of General Psychiatry, 62*, 617–627. doi:10.1001/archpsyc.62.6.617

Kilpatrick, D. G., & Best, C. L. (1984). Some cautionary remarks on treating sexual assault victims with implosion. *Behavior Therapy, 15*, 421–423.

Kilpatrick, D. G., Veronen, L. J., & Resick, P. A. (1982). Psychological sequelae to rape: Assessment and treatment strategies. In D. M. Dolays and R. L. Meredith (Eds.), *Behavioral medicine: Assessment and treatment strategies* (pp. 473–497). New York, NY: Plenum Press.

Koucky, E. M., Galovski, T. E., & Nixon, R. D. V. (2012). Acute stress disorder: Conceptual issues and treatment outcomes. *Cognitive and Behavioral Practice, 19*, 495–496. doi:10.1016/j.cbpra.2011.07.003

Larsen, S. E., Wiltsey Stirman, S., Smith, B. N., & Resick, P. A. (2016). Symptom exacerbations in trauma-focused treatments: Associations with treatment outcome and non-completions. *Behaviour Research and Therapy, 77*, 68–77. doi:10.1016/j.brat.2015.12.009

Lee, C. W., & Cuijpers, P. (2013). A meta-analysis of the contribution of eye movements in processing emotional memories. *Journal of Behavior Therapy and Experimental Psychiatry, 44*, 231–239. doi:10.1016/j.jbtep.2012.11.001

Leer, A., Engelhard, I. M., Lenaert, B., Struyf, D., Vervliet, B., & Hermans, D. (2017). Eye movement during recall reduces objective memory performance: An extended replication. *Behaviour Research and Therapy, 92*, 94–105. doi:10.1016/j.brat.2017.03.002

Lohr, J. M., Tolin, D. F., & Lilienfeld, S. O. (1998). Efficacy of eye movement desensitization and reprocessing: Implications for behavior therapy. *Behavior Therapy, 29*, 123–156. doi:10.1016/S0005-7894(98)80035-X

McGuire, T. M., Lee, C. W., & Drummond, P. D. (2014). Potential of eye movement desensitization and reprocessing therapy in the treatment of post-traumatic stress disorder. *Psychology Research and Behavior Management, 7*, 273–283. doi:10.1002/(SICI)1099-0879

McLay, R. N., Webb-Murphy, J. A., Fesperman, S. F., Delaney, E. M., Gerard, S. K., Roesch, S. C.,...Johnston, S. L. (2016). Outcomes from eye movement desensitization and reprocessing in active-duty service members with posttraumatic stress disorder. *Psychological Trauma: Theory, Research, Practice, and Policy, 8*, 702–708. doi:10.1037/tra0000120

McLean, C. P., & Foa, E. B. (2011). Prolonged exposure therapy for post-traumatic stress disorder: A review of evidence and dissemination. *Expert Reviews of Neurotherapeutics, 11*, 1151–1163. doi: 10.1586/ERN.11.94

Meichenbaum, D. (1974). Self instructional methods. In F. H. Kanfer and A. P. Goldstein (Eds.), *Helping people change* (pp. 357–391). New York, NY: Pergamon Press.

Miller, W. R., & Rollnick, S. (2002). *Motivational Interviewing: Preparing people for change* (2nd ed.). New York, NY: Guilford Press.

Monson, C. M., Friedman, M. J., & LaBash, H. (2014). A psychological history of PTSD. In M. J. Friedman, T. M. Keane, & P. A. Resick (Eds.) *Handbook of PTSD: Science and practice* (2nd ed.) (pp. 60–78). New York, NY: Guilford Press.

Morland, L. A., Mackintosh, M. A., Greene, C. J., Rosen, C. S., Chard, K. M., Resick, P., & Frueh, B. C. (2014). Cognitive processing therapy for posttraumatic stress disorder delivered to rural veterans via telemental health: A randomized noninferiority clinical trial. *The Journal of Clinical Psychiatry, 75*, 470–476. doi:10.4088/jcp.13m08842

Mouliso, E. R., Tuerk, P. W., Schnurr, P. P., & Rauch, S. A. (2016). Addressing the gender gap: Prolonged exposure for PTSD in veterans. *Psychological Services, 13*, 308–316. doi:10.1037/ser0000040

Murphy, R. T., Thompson, K. E., Murray, M., Rainey, Q., & Uddo, M. M. (2009). Effect of a motivation enhancement intervention on veterans' engagement in PTSD treatment. *Psychological Services, 6*, 264–278. doi:org/10.1037/a0017577

National Institute for Health and Clinical Excellence (2005). *Post-traumatic stress disorder*. Retrieved from https://www.nice.org.uk/guidance/cg26/resources/posttraumatic-stress-disorder-management-pdf-975329451205

Nishith, P., Resick, P. A., & Griffin, M. G. (2002). Pattern of change in prolonged exposure and cognitive-processing therapy for female rape victims with posttraumatic stress disorder. *Journal of Consulting and Clinical Psychology, 70*, 880–886. doi:10.1037//0022-006X.70.4.880

Nixon, R. D. (2012). Cognitive processing therapy versus supportive counseling for acute stress disorder following assault: A randomized pilot trial. *Behavior Therapy, 43*, 825–836. doi:org/10.1016/j.beth.2012.05.001

Powers, M. B., Halpern, J. M., Ferenschak, M. P., Gillihan, S. J., & Foa, E. B. (2010). A meta-analytic review of prolonged exposure for posttraumatic stress disorder. *Clinical Psychology Review, 30*, 635–641. doi:10.1016/j.cpr.2010.04.007

President's New Freedom Commission on Mental Health. (2003). *Achieving the promise: Transforming mental health care in American. Final Report* (DHHS Pub. No. SMA-03-3832). Rockville, MD: Author.

Reger, G. M., Hoffman, J., Riggs, D., Rothbaum, B. O., Ruzek, J., Holloway, K. M., & Kuhn, E. (2013). The "PE Coach" smartphone application: An innovative approach to improving implementation, fidelity, and homework adherence during prolonged exposure. *Psychological Services, 10*, 342–349. doi:org/10.1037/a0032774

Resick, P. A., Galovski, T. E., Uhlmansiek, M. O. B., Scher, C. D., Clum, G. A., & Young-Xu, Y. (2008). A randomized clinical trial to dismantle components of cognitive processing therapy for posttraumatic stress disorder in female victims of interpersonal violence. *Journal of Consulting and Clinical Psychology, 76*, 243–258. doi:10.1037/0022-006x.76.2.243

Resick, P. A., Nishith, P., Weaver, T. L., Astin, M. C., & Feuer, C. A. (2002). A comparison of cognitive processing therapy with prolonged exposure and a waiting condition for the treatment of chronic posttraumatic stress disorder in female rape victims. *Journal of Consulting and Clinical Psychology, 70*, 867–879. doi:10.1037//0022-006x.70.4.867

Resick, P. A., & Schnicke, M. K. (1992). Cognitive processing therapy for sexual assault victims. *Journal of Consulting and Clinical Psychology, 60*, 748–756. doi:10.1037/0022-006x.60.5.748

Resick, P. A., & Schnicke, M. K. (1996). *Cognitive processing therapy for rape victims*. Newbury Park, CA: Sage.

Resick, P. A., Suvak, M. K., Johnides, B. D., Mitchell, K. S., & Iverson, K. M. (2012). The impact of dissociation on PTSD treatment with cognitive processing therapy. *Depression and Anxiety, 229*, 718–730. doi: 10.1002/da.21938

Resick, P. A., Wachen, J. S., Mintz, J., Young-McCaughan, S., Roache, J. D., Borah, A. M.,...Peterson, A. L. (2015). A randomized clinical trial of group cognitive processing therapy compared with group present-centered therapy for PTSD among active duty military personnel. *Journal of Consulting and Clinical Psychology, 83*, 1058–1168. doi:10.1037/ccp0000016

Riggs, D. S., Rothbaum, B. O., & Foa, E. B. (1995). A prospective examination of symptoms of posttraumatic stress disorder in victims of nonsexual assault. *Journal of Interpersonal Violence, 10*, 201–214. doi:10.1177/0886260595010002005

Rothbaum, B. O., Foa, E. B., Riggs, D. S., Murdock, T., & Walsh, W. (1992). A prospective examination of post-traumatic stress disorder in rape victims. *Journal of Traumatic Stress, 5*, 455–475, doi:10.1002/jts.2490050309

Ruzek, J. I., Karlin, B. E., & Zeiss, A. (2012). Implementation of evidence based psychological treatments in the Veterans Health Administration. In R. K. McHugh & D. H. Barlow (Eds.), *The dissemination of evidence based psychological treatments* (pp. 78–96). Oxford, England: Oxford University Press.

Seal, K. H., Abadjian, L., McCamish, N., Shi, Y., Tarasovsky, G., & Weingardt, K., (2012). A randomized controlled trial of telephone motivational interviewing to enhance mental health treatment engagement in Iraq and Afghanistan veterans. *General Hospital Psychiatry, 34*, 450–459. doi:org/10.1016/j.genhosppsych.2012.04.007

Schiff, M., Nacasch, N., Levit, S., Katz, N., & Foa, E. B. (2015). Prolonged Exposure for treating PTSD among female methadone patients who were survivors of sexual abuse in Israel. *Social Work in Health Care, 54*, 687–707. doi:10.1080/00981389.2015.1058311

Schnurr, P. P., Friedman, M. J., Foy, D. W., Shea, M. T., Hsieh, F. Y., Lavori, P. W.,...Bernardy, N. C. (2003). Randomized trial of trauma-focused group therapy for posttraumatic stress disorder: Results from a Department of Veterans Affairs Cooperative study. *Archives of General Psychiatry, 60*, 481–489. doi:10.1001/archpsyc.60.5.481

Schnurr, P. P. Friedman, M. J., Lavori, P. W., & Hsieh, F. Y. (2001). Design of Department of Veterans Affairs Cooperative Study No. 420: Group treatment of posttraumatic stress disorder. *Controlled Clinical Trials, 22*, 74–88. doi:10.1016/s0197-2456(00)00118-5

Shapiro, F. (1989). Eye movement desensitization: A new treatment for post-traumatic stress disorder. *Journal of Behavior Therapy and Experimental Psychiatry, 20*, 211–217. doi:10.1016/0005-7916(89)90025-6

Shapiro, F. (2007). EMDR, adaptive information processing, and case conceptualization. *Journal of EMDR Practice and Research, 1*, 68–87. doi:10.1891/1933-3196.1.2.68

Sloan, D. M., Beck, J. G., & Sawyer, A. T. (2017). Trauma-focused group therapy. In S. Gold, J. Cook, and C. Dalenberg (Eds.), *Handbook of trauma psychology. Volume 2: Trauma practice* (pp. 467–484). Washington, DC: American Psychological Association.

Spates, C. R., & Koch, E. (2003). From eye movement and desensitization and reprocessing to exposure therapy: A review of the evidence for shared mechanisms. *Japanese Journal of Behavior Analysis, 18*, 62–75.

Steenkamp, M. M., Litz, B. T., Hoge, C. W., & Marmar, C. R. (2015). Psychotherapy for military-related PTSD: A review of randomized clinical trials. *Journal of the American Medical Association, 314*, 489–500. doi:10.1001/jama.2015.8370

Steinert, C., Hofmann, M., Leichsenring, F., & Kruse, J. (2015). The course of PTSD in naturalistic long-term studies: High variability of outcomes. A systematic review. *Nordic Journal of Psychiatry, 69*, 483–496. doi:10.3109/08039488.2015.1005023

Swift, J. K., & Greenberg, R. P. (2012). Premature discontinuation in adult psychotherapy: A meta-analysis. *Journal of Consulting and Clinical Psychology, 80*, 547–559. doi:org/10.1037/a0028226

Surís, A., Link-Malcolm, J., Chard, K., Ahn, C., & North, C. (2013). A randomized clinical trial of cognitive processing therapy for veterans with PTSD related to military sexual trauma. *Journal of Traumatic Stress, 26*, 28–37. doi:10.1002/jts.21765

Tarquinio, C., Brennstuhl, M., Rydberg, J. A., Schmitt, A., Mouda, F., Lourel, M., & Tarquinio, P. (2012). Eye movement desensitization and reprocessing (EMDR) therapy in the treatment of victims of domestic violence: A pilot study. *European Review of Applied Psychology, 62*, 205–212. doi:10.1016/j.erap.2012.08.006

Thomaes, K., Engelhard, I. M., Sijbrandij, M., Cath, D. C., & Van den Heuvel, O. A. (2016). Degrading traumatic memories with eye movements: A pilot functional MRI study in PTSD. *European Journal of Psychotraumatology, 7*(1), 31371. doi:10.3402/ejpt.v7.31371

Tuerk, P. W., Yoder, M., Grubaugh, A., Myrick, H., Hamner, M., & Acierno, R. (2011). Prolonged exposure therapy for combat-related posttraumatic stress disorder: An examination of treatment effectiveness for veterans of the wars in Afghanistan and Iraq. *Journal of Anxiety Disorders, 25*, 397–403. doi:10.1016/j.janxdis.2010.11.002

VA/DoD Clinical Practice Guideline Working Group. (2004). *Management of post-traumatic stress.* Washington, DC: VA Office of Quality and Performance.

Van den Berg, D. G., de Bont, P. M., van der Vleugel, B. M., de Roos, C., de Jongh, A., Van Minnen, A., & van der Gaag, M. (2015). Prolonged exposure vs eye movement desensitization and reprocessing vs waiting list for posttraumatic stress disorder in patients with a psychotic disorder: A randomized clinical trial. *Journal of the American Medical Association Psychiatry, 72*, 259–267. doi:10.1001/jamapsychiatry.2014.2637

Van der Kolk, B. A., Spinazzola, J., Blaustein, M. E., Hopper, J. W., Hopper, E. K., Korn, D. L., & Simpson, W. B. (2007). A randomized clinical trial of eye movement desensitization and reprocessing (EMDR), fluoxetine, and pill placebo in the treatment of posttraumatic stress disorder: Treatment effects and long-term maintenance. *Journal of Clinical Psychiatry, 68*, 37–46. doi:10.4088/jcp.v68n0105

Vera, M., Reyes-Rabanillo, M. L., Juarbe, D., Pérez-Pedrogo, C., Olmo, A., Kichic, R., & Chaplin, W. F. (2011). Prolonged exposure for the treatment of Spanish-speaking Puerto Ricans with posttraumatic stress disorder: A feasibility study. *BMC Research Notes, 4*, 415–422. doi:10.1186/1756-0500-4-415

Wilson, J. P. (1994). The historical evolution of PTSD diagnostic criteria: From Freud to *DSM-IV*. *Journal of Traumatic Stress, 7*, 681–698. doi:10.1007/bf02103015

Mindfulness-Based Stress Reduction and Mindfulness-Based Cognitive Therapy

Philip A. Desormeau, Kathleen M. Walsh, *and* Zindel V. Segal

Abstract

Over the past two decades, investigations of mindfulness meditation have demonstrated considerable efficacy in reducing the symptom burden associated with a variety of medical and mental health disorders (Baer, 2003). This chapter reviews the theoretical basis for offering training in mindfulness meditation to these populations, and it outlines the structure of mindfulness-based interventions, as well as their impact on stress and psychological indices of mental and physical health. We first define mindfulness in terms of the core cognitive processes that are engaged through this practice and then review how mindfulness reduces ruminative and elaborative processing, factors known to perpetuate stress reactivity. From there, we describe the dominant theoretical model of mindfulness's impact on stress-related disorders—the mindfulness stress-buffering account (MSBA; Creswell & Lindsay, 2014)—and highlight how using this framework can inform intervention science in the area of stress reactivity.

Keywords: mindfulness meditation, mindfulness-based interventions, mindfulness stress-buffering account, stress-related disorders, MSBA

Interest in mindfulness has increased exponentially over the past two decades, a development spurred by the accumulating data indicating that mindfulness meditation is associated with marked relief from a variety of medical conditions and mental health disorders (Baer, 2003). The typical delivery formats for this work have been via manualized interventions designed for both specific and broad-spectrum clinical populations. Two prominent examples are mindfulness-based stress reduction (MBSR), which was designed to treat chronic pain in the context of a variety of medical disorders (Kabat-Zinn, 2011), and mindfulness-based cognitive therapy (MBCT), which addresses relapse vulnerability in mood disorders (Segal, Williams, & Teasdale, 2013).

The aim of this chapter is to describe the empirical and theoretical foundations of mindfulness in its clinical usage; the types of affect regulation strategies that reduce the effects of stress and that are achieved via the practice of mindfulness meditation; the background, format, and empirical basis for mindfulness-based interventions such as MBSR and MBCT; and the empirical evidence documenting the impact of such mindfulness-based interventions on stress and psychological indices of mental and physical health.

We begin by defining mindfulness and briefly outlining the cognitive processes that are engaged through the practice of mindfulness meditation. We then introduce its benefits in treating a variety of disorders and document its role in managing stress reactivity—a key process proposed to influence stress-sensitive biological and psychological disorders. Although further research on mindfulness-based interventions and stress is needed, existing studies provide some insight into the underlying mechanisms and mediating factors driving the effects of mindfulness as a self-regulation strategy. We then touch on current models of mindfulness and how they contribute to our understanding of stress, as well as noting the limitations of these models, and the fact that these only partially account for the psychological and biological mediating factors paramount to stress processes. We feature the mindfulness stress-buffering account (MSBA; Creswell & Lindsay, 2014) as a model that can explain the impact of mindfulness training on stress reactivity and inform intervention science. Finally, we elucidate the rationale, development, and empirical support for MBSR and MBCT in the context of treating stress-related disorders, and we provide recommendations for future work needed in this area.

Mindfulness

Clinical researchers and Buddhist scholars have proposed numerous conceptualizations and definitions of mindfulness, which vary with regard to presupposed underlying psychological components and the degree of secularization from Buddhist doctrine (Bishop et al., 2004; Gethin, 2011). Perhaps the most cited definition is provided by Kabat-Zinn (2003), who defined mindfulness as "the awareness that emerges through paying attention on purpose, in the present moment, and nonjudgmentally to the unfolding of experience moment to moment" (p. 145). Implied in this definition are the acts of monitoring and bringing acceptance to one's phenomenological experience, regardless of its valence and intensity (Quaglia, Brown, Lindsay, Creswell, & Goodman, 2015). These cognitive processes are purportedly fostered through the regular practice of mindfulness meditation (Lindsay & Creswell, 2017), and they distinguish mindfulness from the automaticity of functioning in daily life, in which one mechanically behaves according to a narrow range of prepotent responses shaped by past events and future concerns (Kabat-Zinn, 1990). By intentionally adopting a mindful stance, one is better able to disengage from an "automatic pilot" mode and behave more flexibly in the present moment to purposefully approach a valued life direction.

Mindfulness is also conceptualized as an adaptive emotion regulation strategy that can supplant the maladaptive strategies that characterize psychiatric conditions (Chambers, Gullone, & Allen, 2009). Emotion regulation (ER) is commonly defined as the effective management of emotional experience to support goal-directed activities (Gross & Thompson, 2007), and according to prevailing ER models (Gross, 2015), psychopathology and functional impairment emerge from ER deficits

(Sheppes, Suri, & Gross, 2015; Werner & Gross, 2010). For instance, individuals with a current or past diagnosis of major depression report greater use of maladaptive strategies such as thought suppression and rumination—that is, repetitive thinking focused on the experience of negative mood (Joormann & Gotlib, 2010). Moreover, greater rumination and avoidance and less cognitive reappraisal—that is, the reinterpretation of emotionally evocative situations—are associated with greater symptom severity in major depression, anxiety and eating disorders, and substance misuse (Aldao, Nolen-Hoeksema, & Schweizer, 2010). Considering that ER deficits appear to be at the core of many psychiatric disorders (Gross & Munoz, 1995), mindfulness presents itself as a potentially valuable alternative to more habitual strategies. From an ER perspective, mindfulness is a blend of metacognitive awareness with top-down (e.g., affect labeling, reappraisal) *and* bottom-up strategies (e.g., sensory perception) that together alleviate negative affect (Guendelman, Medeiros, & Rampes, 2017). This property differentiates mindfulness-based interventions and practices from other psychological therapies that primarily emphasize top-down cognitive strategies (for a review, see Van der Velden, Kuyken, Wattar et al., 2015). More specifically, rather than modifying the content of negative core beliefs, mindfulness training encourages clients to focus on current sensory experiences and detachment from negative automatic thoughts (Farb, Anderson, Irving, & Segal, 2014). Through this deployment of top-down cognitive strategies and bottom-up experiential strategies, mindfulness-based interventions may be best suited for simultaneously addressing emotion-generation *and* emotion-regulation deficits associated with psychopathology (Guendelman, Medeiros, & Rampes, 2017).

Mindfulness-Based Interventions

Mindfulness has become a core element in several treatment protocols targeting a variety of physical and psychological conditions, though it is most prominently featured in MBSR (Kabat-Zinn, 1990) and MBCT (Segal, Williams, & Teasdale, 2013). In light of the fact that a majority of physical and emotional disorders have a chronic and recurrent course, a compelling rationale for featuring mindfulness meditation as an element in the treatment of clinical disorders is that the skills and attitudes that are fostered through practice are applicable not just to periods of symptom acuity, but equally to remission and recovery. Just as homework in more standard cognitive-behavioral therapies is intended to teach patients skills for affect regulation that can be continued beyond the point of recovery, the same is true for the practice of mindfulness. The utilization of skills acquired during treatment need not stop once symptoms have decreased, and in fact, there is good evidence that continuing with these practices can sustain treatment response (Crane, Crane, Eames et al., 2014).

MBSR and MBCT are both group interventions that were designed to address a range of medical and psychological disorders. They provide group participants with a psychological rationale and a structured 8-week format for learning and practicing mindfulness meditation in the context of affect regulation and stress reduction. At their most general level, these programs seek to develop patient skills in metacognitive awareness, as well as curiosity and approach toward negative internal experiences. It is proposed that by being willing to actively expose oneself to, and tolerate, uncomfortable internal states, individuals will be likely to respond to stressful life events by engaging in adaptive behavioral regulatory strategies (e.g., problem solving, behavioral activation) over unhelpful automatic behaviors (e.g., rumination, substance use). Patients suffering from chronic pain were initially targeted by MBSR, whereas prevention of relapse in mood disorders was the primary focus of MBCT. More recently, as the evidence of their clinical effectiveness has mounted, MBSR and MBCT have been tailored to other stress-related conditions.

Mindfulness-Based Stress Reduction

Developed at the University of Massachusetts Medical School in 1979 by Jon Kabat-Zinn, the MBSR curriculum was heavily influenced by Kabat-Zinn's own experience translating Theravada and Mahayana Buddhist philosophies for understanding the nature of suffering (Kabat-Zinn, 2011). The intention was to embody mindfulness-based principles and practices while recontextualizing those components to increase accessibility to clinicians and clients alike (Kabat-Zinn, 2011). Although the MBSR program was originally designed for clients struggling with chronic pain and co-occurring psychological symptoms, it has since garnered support for its efficacy in the treatment of other physical conditions (for example, fibromyalgia and cardiovascular risk; Fjorback, Arendt, Ørnbøl, Fink, & Walach, 2011). In addition, its burgeoning popularity has encouraged clinicians to incorporate mindfulness training into their clinical practices, with a large number of American medical schools devoting segments of their curricula to mindfulness training (Buchholz, 2015).

MBSR is structured as an outpatient group treatment in which 2.5-hour sessions are scheduled on a weekly basis for 8 weeks along with a 1-day silent meditation retreat. Two instructors guide the sessions and embody a curious and nonjudgmental attitude toward experience, the same attitudes that the patients are asked to employ when exploring their own thoughts, feelings, and bodily sensations. Although there is some variance across countries, the size of an MBSR group can range anywhere from 10 to 30 individuals. Over the course of treatment, clients are gradually introduced to and invited to practice multiple forms of mindfulness meditation, including mindful eating, the Body Scan, mindful movement, and sitting meditation. In addition, group time is spent discussing stress reactivity, interpersonal relationships, and basic psychoeducation related to the cumulative effects of stress on the body. Group members are asked to schedule approximately 45 minutes of mindfulness practice each day, which can include both longer, formal meditations as well as briefer informal meditations that can be practiced throughout the day.

Because there is a premium placed on experiential learning in approach, each MBSR session commences with a 30- to 35-minute period of meditation. Following this, patients are invited to discuss the practice, noting how experience can be broken down into patterns of thoughts, feelings, and sensations, and how mindful awareness relates to the psychological or physical condition being treated. In earlier sessions, clients monitor the occurrence of pleasant and unpleasant events, as well as their level of awareness during the events along with the bodily sensations that accompanied the events. In later sessions, negative thoughts about emotionally evocative stimuli are introduced as a focus of awareness. During this mindfulness meditation, participants might observe distressing thoughts such as "I am a failure" or "I am unlovable" in a manner that does not require disputing or challenging the content of the thought, but rather acknowledges that critical thoughts are present in their awareness. Lastly, the group often discusses topics such as stress triggers, how bodily sensations can help return attention to the present moment, the automatic nature of stress reactivity, and how the practice can be brought into everyday life so that it can be a portable skill that patients can access throughout the day.

Based on the current state of evidence, MBSR is effective for healthy individuals in improving low mood, anxiety, and perceived stress, as well as maladaptive emotion regulation strategies such as rumination and worry (Chiesa & Serretti, 2009). Randomized controlled trials examining the effects of MBSR have also established its efficacy for physical conditions, including but not limited to chronic pain, breast cancer, multiple sclerosis, rheumatoid arthritis, and fibromyalgia (Fjorback, Arendt, Ørnbøl, Fink, & Walach, 2011). Finally, clinical researchers have also shown that MBSR significantly alleviates self-reported stress and anxiety, improves caregiver self-efficacy, and normalizes biological markers of stress in primary caregivers (Lengacher et al., 2012; Oken et al., 2010).

Mindfulness-Based Cognitive Therapy

MBCT was developed by Zindel Segal, Mark Williams, and John Teasdale in the 1990s as a relapse prevention program that addressed the unique needs of patients in remission from major depressive disorder (MDD; Segal, Williams, & Teasdale, 2013). The content and structure of MBCT was closely aligned to that of MBSR but also integrated aspects of cognitive-behavioral therapies for depression, viewing the value of mindfulness training from the lens of the interactive cognitive subsystems (ICS) model proposed by Barnard and Teasdale (1991). The ICS model states that information from the internal or external environment can be processed under one of two modes of mind: the "doing" mode and "being" mode. The "doing" mode is goal oriented and focused on problem solving to resolve discrepancies between one's actual and idealized life circumstances. In contrast, the "being" mode is present centred and emphasizes the direct contingencies of the current context. People who are susceptible to depressive relapse or recurrence are primarily dominated by the "doing" mode at the expense of the "being" mode, but they can establish an optimal balance between modes through the cultivation of metacognitive awareness. Through the application of metacognitive awareness, clients are better able to shift between modes based on their needs in the current situation (Barnard & Teasdale, 1991) and thus refrain from maladaptive coping strategies such as rumination, which is a risk factor for depressive relapse and recurrence (Ingram, Atchley, & Segal, 2011). In essence, engaging the "being" mode allows clients to refrain from behaving automatically in response to triggering environmental cues, including stressful life events, and act

in a fashion that more closely aligns with their values, regardless of attendant negative thoughts or emotions. For instance, by being able to observe the ebb and flow of negative thoughts and emotions without the need to correct or dispute them, a person arguing with a romantic partner would be better positioned to identify and disengage from unhelpful habits, such as making hurtful comments, and instead engage in more productive behaviors that might de-escalate the conflict. In MBCT, functioning from the "being" mode is promoted through the regular practice of mindfulness meditation (Segal, Williams, & Teasdale, 2013).

The development of MBCT was fostered by the need to increase the protection against depression's recurrence and was a novel treatment format that could be easily added to either pharmacological or psychological monotherapies. The thinking here was that a sequential approach to treatment, namely treating the depression with one modality and providing a different modality for the prevention of relapse, could be most effective (Guidi, Tomba & Fava, 2016). In addition, despite the empirical support for their efficacy in treating depression, antidepressant medications do not target depressogenic dysfunctional attitudes, which may be a core vulnerability factor that plays an important role in risk for relapse and recurrence (Segal et al., 2010). When triggered by dysphoric environmental cues, individuals vulnerable to depression experience cognitive reactivity—the reactivation of entrenched negative automatic thoughts—the cumulative effect of which may be to reinforce negative core beliefs and reinstate depressive symptoms (Ingram, Atchley, & Segal, 2011). According to the MBCT model, mindfulness practices derive their prophylactic effects by training clients to disengage from "automatic pilot" and employ adaptive emotion regulation strategies, thus preventing the dysphoric cycle from restarting again (Segal, Williams, & Teasdale, 2013). For instance, after losing a job, a patient who has been through MBCT might notice when she has engaged in ruminative thinking (e.g., "I'm such a failure, I can't even hold a job") and, instead of continuing to do this, might instead see that she has a choice about how to proceed. This choice might lead to employing more adaptive strategies such as reappraisal (e.g., reframing the job loss as an opportunity to engage in a different, more fulfilling profession) or problem solving (e.g., searching the Internet for job openings). Similar to MBSR, MBCT is an 8-week outpatient group treatment consisting of weekly 2.5-hour sessions and a one-time silent meditation retreat.

One interesting requirement that relates to the provision of MBCT as well as MBSR is that therapists need to have a personal mindfulness practice (see Segal et al., 2016). The number of clients participating in the group intervention is kept below 15 individuals. Over the course of treatment, clients are invited to practice different types of mindfulness meditation, and they also receive psychoeducation regarding major depressive disorder, dysfunctional attitudes, relapse signatures, and the importance of early intervention when depression looms.

As is the case with MBSR, group members are asked to schedule approximately 45 minutes into their day for home practice, with practices including the Body Scan, mindful movement, and seated meditations utilizing different sensory anchors. Following each practice, clients are invited to reflect on and record what they noticed as a way of consolidating the approach, curiosity, and distress tolerance regulatory frameworks that are taught in the program.

As mentioned earlier, MBCT was originally developed as a relapse prevention program for the treatment of remission-phase depression (Segal, Williams, & Teasdale, 2013). Several randomized controlled trials have evaluated prophylactic outcomes following MBCT, and they have reported that MBCT outperformed treatment as usual (Ma & Teasdale, 2004; Teasdale et al., 2000) and was equivalent to antidepressant treatment (Kuyken et al., 2015; Segal et al., 2010) in reducing the risk of relapse and recurrence in formerly depressed individuals. Most recently, a large individual patient data meta-analysis supported these conclusions (for a review, see Kuyken et al., 2016). Interestingly, the early evidence from a digital version of MBCT that was developed to increase access to this approach has been supportive of its ongoing utilization for the reduction of residual depressive symptoms, an important predictor of later episode return (Dimidjian, Beck, Felder et al., 2014).

Mindfulness and Stress

Although emotion dysregulation may not be central to the pathophysiology of physical disorders such as heart disease and fibromyalgia, the impact of mindfulness-based interventions on the stress-related exacerbations of both illness course and prognosis has been significant (Chiesa & Serretti, 2010). This suggests that patients practicing mindfulness can reduce their reliance on emotion regulatory strategies that exacerbate psychological *and* physical symptoms. Moreover, mindfulness has been linked to several psychological and biological indices of stress reactivity (Brown, Ryan, & Creswell, 2007; Chiesa & Serretti, 2009) that are thought to modulate symptom severity of many psychological and medical conditions (Creswell & Lindsay, 2014).

With regard to psychological indices of stress, Carmody and Baer (2008) examined the effects of MBSR on self-reported trait mindfulness, psychological and physical symptoms, perceived stress, and psychological well-being in highly stressed individuals. MBSR participants demonstrated elevated trait mindfulness and psychological well-being, as well as reductions in perceived stress and psychological and medical symptoms from pretreatment to posttreatment. Importantly, the gains in these constructs were associated with the length of time for home meditation practices between sessions. Trait mindfulness fully mediated the relation between home practices and decreased psychological symptoms and perceived stress, and it partially mediated the relation between home practices and psychological well-being. Similarly, Boyle, Stanton, Ganz, Crespi, and Bower (2017) also compared the effects of a mindfulness-based intervention and a wait-list control condition on emotion regulation strategies that were hypothesized to mediate the relation between mindfulness and stress. Specifically, the authors hypothesized that following mindfulness training, mindfulness and self-kindness (the extension of kindness to oneself following a stressful life event) would increase, whereas rumination (repetitive negative thinking regarding focus on one's negative mood state) would decrease. Their findings revealed that increases in self-kindness indeed mediated the effects of mindfulness training on depressive symptoms from pre- to posttreatment, and both self-kindness and mindfulness mediated the effects of the intervention on perceived stress from pretreatment to 3-month follow-up.

As for biological indices of stress, Creswell, Myers, Cole, and Irwin (2009) examined the impact of MBSR on biological markers of HIV in HIV-infected adults. Citing evidence that psychological stress could accelerate the progression of HIV and compromise the efficacy of antiretroviral treatments, the authors argued that MBSR and similar stress-management interventions could help maintain the integrity of immune system functioning. More specifically, Creswell and colleagues hypothesized that MBSR would steady or elevate levels of CD4+ T lymphocytes, which reflect immune functioning and are depleted in HIV-infected persons. Consistent with their hypothesis, MBSR maintained CD4+ T lymphocyte counts from pretreatment to posttreatment, while participants randomized to the control condition experienced further decline. As similar findings have been reported for other physical conditions such as cancer and diabetes (Lengacher et al., 2013; Tovote et al., 2015), stress management via mindfulness training may produce beneficial shifts in biomarkers of stress-related processes.

Despite these promising findings, many researchers have studied the link between mindfulness and stress without a strong a priori theoretical model, which can sometimes hamper the interpretation of findings that do not support hypothesized relationships. Moreover, while many studies document how mindfulness interacts with stress outcomes, there remain a number of unanswered questions that could be profitably explored using a multimethod approach. For example, assessing both the psychological *and* biological facets of stress reactivity and pertinent mediating factors could improve our understanding of *how* mindfulness operates through mediators to impact health outcomes. However, the mediating pathways behind the aforementioned findings have not been fully explored. Similar limitations also extend to studies on mindfulness-based interventions and stress. That is, although there are numerous studies reporting the effectiveness of mindfulness interventions, investigations into the mechanisms of action of mindfulness have not kept pace (Gu, Strauss, Bond, & Cavanagh, 2015). This general pattern is problematic, as the establishment of factors through which mindfulness produces its salutary effects would benefit clinicians and clients alike. For instance, such knowledge may allow for the enhancement of active therapeutic components and the distinction between unique intervention effects versus those stemming from common treatment factors (Kazdin, 2007).

Currently, the majority of research on the mechanisms of mindfulness has been focused on mediators identified in the theories underlying MBSR and MBCT. As such, analyses have been predominantly constrained to psychological constructs such as decentering, ruminative thinking, well-being, and metacognition (Gu, Strauss, Bond, & Cavanagh, 2015). Other clinical researchers have seen fit to propose their own models of mindfulness, drawing more pointedly on the cognitive and affective elements in the practice itself (Baer, 2003; Brown, Ryan, & Creswell, 2007; Grabovac, Lau, & Willett, 2011; Hölzel et al., 2011; Shapiro, Carlson, Astin, & Freedman, 2006; Vago & Silbersweig, 2012). Several of the models posit some form of self-regulation (Hölzel et al., 2011; Shapiro et al., 2006; Vago & Silbersweig, 2012), attentional reorienting (Grabovac et al., 2011; Hölzel et al., 2011), and exposure (Baer, 2003; Brown et al., 2007; Shapiro et al., 2006) as prospective drivers of mindful awareness. However, the aforementioned models do not explicitly address the link between mindfulness and stress reactivity. As stated earlier, reporting *whether* mindfulness impacts health outcomes and works through particular psychological mediators is important to know; however, these findings rely predominantly on self-report measures that presume self-awareness of such psychological states, and they stop short of explaining *how* mindfulness modifies both psychological and biological indices of stress.

Mindfulness Stress-Buffering Account: A Model of Mindfulness and Stress Reactivity

To fill this research gap, Creswell and Lindsay (2014) have proposed the mindfulness stress-buffering account (MSBA) as an integrative account linking previously disparate findings and levels of analysis. Put simply, they hypothesize that mindfulness meditation derives its therapeutic effects by targeting the underlying psychological and biological markers of stress. Unlike the previously described models that expound on the underlying structure of mindfulness, the MSBA focuses on the causal pathway by which mindfulness and subsumed facets influence stress reactivity. Although the roles of mindfulness, rumination, and other constructs are indeed important for understanding mindfulness meditation, this model postulates that assessment of underlying stress-related processes is required to ascertain whether mindfulness practices and interventions *directly* impact pathogenic processes that are specific to psychological and physical conditions. From this model, two predictions stand out; first, people with high levels of stress are more likely to benefit from mindfulness training than are people with low levels of stress, and second, mindfulness training is likely to yield more pronounced effects in people struggling with psychological or physical conditions that are spurred on or maintained by stress (Creswell & Lindsay, 2014). These predictions were evaluated in numerous empirical investigations that detailed the effects of mindfulness on stress-related biological pathways and disease-specific processes (Brown, Weinstein, & Creswell, 2012; Creswell, Myers, Cole, & Irwin, 2009; Creswell, Pacilio, Lindsay, &

Brown, 2014; Nyklíček, Mommersteeg, Van Beugen, Ramakers, & Van Boxtel, 2013).

Empirical Support for the Mindfulness Stress-Buffering Account

Since its conception, several empirical studies have investigated facets of stress reactivity that directly relate to the MSBA, though few studies have directly referenced and evaluated the model. Nevertheless, the studies described next help to refine the current understanding of the link between mindfulness meditation and stress reactivity, while also highlighting new avenues for future research.

PHYSIOLOGICAL INDICES OF STRESS REACTIVITY

Creswell, Pacilio, Lindsay, and Brown (2014) assessed the impact of mindfulness on stress reactivity in undergraduate students following a stress-induction task. The participants were randomized to either a 3-day mindfulness training or cognitive training workshop, the latter of which was designed to promote analytical problem-solving skills. Both groups provided self-report ratings of perceived stress and biological measures of neuroendocrine responses (i.e., salivary cortisol, blood pressure). Interestingly, the authors' findings indicated that mindfulness training and dispositional mindfulness regardless of treatment condition mitigated perceived stress; however, participants within the mindfulness group demonstrated elevated cortisol levels following a stress-induction task in comparison to the control group. Additional analyses revealed that participants low in trait mindfulness who participated in the mindfulness training showed the highest elevations in cortisol levels following stress induction. The discrepancy in self-reported and neuroendocrine findings underscores the importance of incorporating dispositional measures of mindfulness and other pre-existing factors in studies of mindfulness training, as mindfulness may confer different sets of benefits to practitioners with different dispositions. Moreover, the discrepant findings in this study may be a result of the good health of the participants, as one would expect mindfulness training to produce more pronounced effects on populations with stress-related issues or conditions.

Other findings would suggest that mindfulness training impacts perceived stress and biological indices of stress in both healthy *and* clinical patients with varying degrees of expertise in meditation. Schutte and Malouff (2014) reviewed studies examining the impact of mindfulness training on the enzyme telomerase, which is involved in determining the length of telomeres (Gomez et al., 2012; Zvereva, Shcherbakova, & Dontsova, 2010). Telomeres are cell structures that maintain the integrity of chromosomes and facilitate cell division, and their length is predictive of health outcomes, with longer telomeres predicting better immune system functioning (Gomez et al., 2012; Zvereva, Shcherbakova, & Dontsova, 2010). The authors discovered that mindfulness meditation led to significant increases in telomerase activity in cells implicated in immune functioning. Similarly, Kaliman and colleagues (2014) compared experienced meditators to nonmeditators after engaging in 8 hours of contemplative practices or leisure activities, respectively. The authors measured various biological measures such as salivary cortisol and inflammatory genes in cells important to immune functioning. The gene markers were collected prior to and following the 8-hour interventions, whereas salivary cortisol samples were collected during a stress-induction task. Kaliman and colleagues reported that meditators exhibited reductions in pro-inflammatory and other immunity-related genes relative to nonmeditators, and reductions in activity of these genes predicted better cortisol recovery following stress induction in participants regardless of group.

These studies highlight the importance of incorporating both physiological and psychological indices of stress, as well as taking into account pre-existing factors such as dispositional mindfulness. Understanding these factors may give valuable information on the level of stress reactivity being experienced, elucidating how mindfulness training can make a positive impact on reducing stress reactivity according to the MSBA.

NEURAL INDICES OF STRESS REACTIVITY

Research investigating the neural correlates of stress has also suggested that mindfulness training can modify the neural representation of stress reactivity. Neuroimaging studies have found, for example, that MBSR participants exhibited increased gray-volume volume and density in the left caudate nucleus (Farb, Segal, & Anderson, 2013) and the left hippocampus, posterior cingulum, middle temporal gyrus, and cerebellum (Hölzel et al., 2011), respectively. Moreover, mindfulness practitioners and intervention participants exhibited diverging functional brain patterns in comparison to control groups (Tang, Hölzel, & Posner, 2015), demonstrating differential activation of brain regions implicated in attention (e.g., anterior cingulum and striatum), emotion regulation (e.g., prefrontal cortex, amygdala), and self-awareness (e.g., medial prefrontal cortex, insula). Participants exhibiting higher trait mindfulness demonstrated less resting-state activation of the amygdala—a brain region implicated in the salience of external and internal cues—than did participants lower in trait mindfulness (Tang, Hölzel, & Posner, 2015).

Two interesting observations can be made from these patterns of neuroimaging findings. First, mindful awareness appears to recruit large-scale brain networks broadly classified as "top-down" regulatory pathways (e.g., prefrontal cortices) or "bottom-up" reactivity pathways (Chiesa & Serretti, 2009). Second, the top-down and bottom-up systems correspond to brain regions and neural networks involved in stress reactivity and management (Creswell & Lindsay, 2014). By modifying these cortical pathways in the central nervous system, mindfulness can trigger downstream effects that modify activation of the peripheral nervous subsystems responsible for stress processing, such as the sympathetic-adrenal-medullary (SAM) and hypothalamic-pituitary-adrenal (HPA) axes (Creswell & Lindsay, 2014). The corollary of these alterations in biological functioning would be less output of SAM- and HPA-related neurotransmitters and neurohormones. Furthermore, the exact effect of mindfulness training is specific to the relation between indices of stress and disease pathogenic processes; that is, the way in which mindfulness influences health outcomes for a given psychological or medical condition is contingent on how the stress process triggers or maintains disease processes (Creswell & Lindsay, 2014).

In line with these observations, Creswell and colleagues (2016) directly evaluated aspects of the MSBA model by recruiting highly stressed participants and randomizing them to either 3-day mindfulness training or relaxation training workshops. Prior to and following the intervention program, participants underwent functional magnetic resonance imaging (fMRI) to model resting-state brain-activation patterns and provided blood samples at pretreatment and at 4 months posttreatment to measure Interleukin-6 (IL-6), a cytokine that stimulates the immune response and is reflective of systemic inflammation. Their findings revealed that relative to relaxation training, mindfulness training increased resting-state connectivity between the posterior cingulate cortex, which is implicated in processing information about the self, and the left dorsolateral prefrontal cortex, which is implicated

in executive control. The increases in connectivity seen in the mindfulness group mediated the relation between the intervention and circulating IL-6 at the 4-month follow-up.

Finally, Taren and colleagues (2015) conducted a two-part fMRI study, in which they first recruited healthy individuals to rate their perceived stress in the past month and undergo fMRI scanning. The authors found that participants who reported higher stress over the past month showed activation of brain regions implicated in stress and emotional reactivity, the amygdala and the anterior cingulum. In their second study, Taren and colleagues recruited high-stress individuals to participate in either a 3-day mindfulness training or relaxation training workshop and then underwent fMRI scanning. Their findings revealed that mindfulness training decreased activation of the amygdala and anterior cingulum relative to the relaxation group, signifying that mindfulness participants experienced less stress reactivity following the program.

Altogether, these neuroimaging studies support the notion that mindfulness training modifies functional brain patterns that could in turn cause downstream, stress-relieving effects on the peripheral stress systems. Furthermore, the findings indicate that mindfulness indeed operates through top-down (i.e., the dorsolateral prefrontal cortex) and bottom-up biological pathways (e.g., amygdala) responsible for stress regulation and reactivity, respectively. Finally, as indicated in the previous section, the incorporation of psychological and physiological indices of stress and pre-existing factors may provide a more comprehensive understanding of a person's level of stress reactivity, and, in line with the MSBA, why and how mindfulness training may reduce stress.

Recent Investigations of Mindfulness-Based Interventions and Stress

The studies reviewed in the previous section used brief mindfulness exercises to evaluate the effects of mindfulness meditation on various perceived stress and biomarkers of stress. The MSBA does not make specific predictions about mindfulness-based interventions, but given that mindfulness meditation is the bedrock of these treatments, it is likely that they might yield similar findings. As detailed earlier, MBSR and MBCT are efficacious in many different settings with a variety of different populations. However, seldom have clinical findings addressed Creswell and Lindsay's prediction that the benefits of mindfulness practice—and by extension, mindfulness-based interventions—come through the reduction of stress reactivity (Creswell & Lindsay, 2014). The following studies represent recent investigations of the link between such mindfulness-based interventions and the degree of support for MSBA.

Empirical Support for Mindfulness-Based Stress Reduction

Baer, Carmody, and Hunsinger (2012) recruited participants who were experiencing high stress reactivity related to physical conditions (e.g., chronic illness, chronic pain) or other personal or occupational stressors, and they investigated changes in mindfulness and perceived stress during and after a course of MBSR. Levels of perceived stress and mindfulness were measured both before and after the intervention, as well as every week for the length of the course. Comparing posttreatment to pretreatment, the authors observed increased mindfulness and decreased perceived stress. Additionally, through analysis of the weekly self-reports of stress and mindfulness, Baer and colleagues (2012) found that changes in mindfulness preceded changes in perceived stress, suggesting a causal link between the two. These results suggested that developing mindfulness skills acted as a mediator for the beneficial effects of MBSR; the authors reasoned that these results were in line with the theory that through MBSR people learn to respond mindfully to their environment, teaching them the skills needed to allow them to respond appropriately and adaptively to environmental stress. These findings support predictions from the MSBA, in that mindfulness appears to meaningfully reduce self-reported stress reactivity.

In a similar vein, Snippe, Dziak, Lanza, Nyklíček, and Wichers (2017) were interested in exploring changes in stress reactivity and stress sensitivity throughout the course of MBSR training. The authors found that stress reactivity, defined by an association between external daily events and perceived stress, decreased over the course of the MBSR intervention, while stress sensitivity, defined as an association between perceived stress and negative emotions, did not decrease. Additionally, they found that perceived stress and negative affect decreased in a linear fashion, indicating that stress reactivity and negative affect decreased gradually over the course of MBSR training. This suggests that the regular practice of mindfulness skills is pivotal for reducing negative internal states throughout treatment, and it may be important for maintaining gains post treatment. They also found that symptom improvement

was linked to a greater number of MBSR sessions attended and higher rates of home practice. In sum, the aforementioned findings speak to the utility of MBSR in cultivating skills that aid participants in coping with the subjective experience of stress. Furthermore, mindful awareness and practices appear to be directly related to reductions in perceived stress, presumably allowing clients to react more adaptively to stressors in their environment.

While the two studies mentioned earlier delineate potential mechanisms accounting for the benefits of MBSR, they fall short in applying a multimethod approach that incorporates biological markers along with psychological markers. These types of designs are more in line with MBSA and can provide more direct data on the question of whether the benefits of MBSR (and presumably other mindfulness-based interventions or MBIs) are expressed at biological levels of analysis. Research adopting such an approach would contribute to a more comprehensive understanding of how mindfulness-based interventions address the experiential, behavioral, *and* physiological responses involved in stress reactivity, rather than focusing on any one of these responses alone.

One study that adopted this methodology was conducted by Carlson, Speca, Faris, and Patel (2007) and explored change in a number of stress biomarkers in MBSR. Participants were diagnosed with either breast or prostate cancer, and perceived stress, immune cell counts, cortisol, and blood pressure were measured at multiple time points, including 6-month and 12-month follow-up periods. Participants reported decreased levels of stress following MBSR, and these gains were maintained at the 12-month follow-up period, suggesting long-lasting effects of mindfulness training on perceived stress. With regard to biological indices of stress, cortisol and pro-inflammatory cytokines, which are both associated with perceived stress, decreased from baseline to posttreatment and continued to decrease to the 12-month follow-up period. In contrast, blood pressure and heart rate decreased only at posttreatment. Finally, heart rate and pro-inflammatory cytokine levels were both associated with self-reported stress, indicating that some biological markers (e.g., heart rate) are more closely aligned with perceived stress than others (e.g., cortisol).

By establishing a link between mindfulness training and biomarkers of stress, Carlson and colleagues (2007) set the stage for future studies to further explore this relation via stress-induction paradigms and randomized controlled trials. For instance, Nyklíček, Mommersteeg, Van Beugen, Ramakers, and Van Boxtel (2013) randomly assigned participating community members to MBSR or a wait-list control condition, with participants completing a stress task before and after completing MBSR or the control condition. The lab stressor was modeled after the Trier Social Stress Test, and it consisted of three stages (i.e., baseline rest period, stress period, and recovery period). During the stress period, participants completed a mental arithmetic task and a speech task in which participants prepared a speech on short notice and presented in front of a camera. The stress-induction protocol was conducted at pretreatment and posttreatment, and measures of perceived stress, cortisol levels, blood pressure, and heart rate variability were collected at varying points throughout the stress procedure. MBSR participants reported decreased perceived stress from pretreatment to posttreatment relative to the control participants, but no significant differences existed between the groups with regard to heart rate variability during stress induction. Additionally, there were no differences in cortisol reactivity to the task (Nyklíček et al., 2013), though reductions in blood pressure from pretreatment to posttreatment were greater for the MBSR group relative to the control group, as well as small reductions in blood pressure during the experimental stress procedure. Although not entirely contradictory to Carlson and colleagues (2007), these findings call into question the purportedly unique contribution of mindfulness training for modifying biomarkers of stress, as proposed by the MSBA.

Similarly, Jensen, Vangkilde, Frokjaer, and Hasselbalch (2012) compared MBSR training to inactive and active control conditions, the latter of which was designed to resemble MBSR in structure while replacing meditation practices with relaxation techniques. The majority of the participants were undergraduate students randomly assigned to one of the aforementioned treatments. In addition to a number of cognitive measures of attention and executive functioning, the authors also measured self-reported dispositional mindfulness, perceived stress, and MBSR compliance, as well as saliva cortisol secretion, specifically reporting on the total magnitude and pattern of cortisol release throughout the day. Jensen and colleagues (2012) reported that although perceived stress and cortisol decreased from pretreatment to posttreatment compared to the *inactive* control, these same constructs did not differentiate MBSR from the *active* control condition. The lack of significant differences between MBSR

and the active condition is not surprising, considering the documented effects of relaxation on stress management; nevertheless, it begs the question of whether the construct of mindfulness uniquely contributes to stress management, or whether mindfulness training functions through some common treatment factor. Of note, the MBSR participants exhibited increased levels of self-reported mindfulness, while participants from the active and inactive control conditions did not. In contrast, MBSR compliance was not associated with any of the stress-related constructs, further questioning the role of mindfulness as a mechanism of action underlying the stress-alleviating effects of MBSR.

Finally, Rosenkranz and colleagues (2013) compared MBSR to an active control condition, the Health Enhancement Program (HEP), which closely matched MBSR without the inclusion of mindfulness practices. The experiment was structured to explore whether MBSR could buffer the effects of psychological and physiological representations of stress during a stress-induction protocol. Participants were recruited from the community and were randomly assigned to either MBSR or HEP, after which they completed an experimental stress paradigm called the Trier Social Stress Test (TSST). The TSST is designed to induce psychological stress by asking participants to prepare and present an impromptu speech in front of a camera and two confederates posing as judges, after which the participant must also then complete a mental arithmetic task. The authors also measured self-reported physical and psychological symptoms and amount of out-of-session practice, saliva cortisol collected at several time points throughout the TSST, and stress-sensitive molecular markers of inflammation—tumor necrosis factor alpha (TNF-α) and interleukin-8 (IL-8). In addition, participants collected five saliva samples at home for three consecutive days. Finally, to measure neurogenic inflammation following stress induction, participants were measured for skin inflammation following the application of a topical inflammatory cream at pretreatment and posttreatment. The authors indicated that the extent of inflammation could expand beyond the application of the topical cream if influenced by such factors as stress.

Results indicated that the treatment groups reduced self-reported psychological symptoms, physical symptoms, and stress-induced salivary cortisol in response to the TSST from pretreatment to posttreatment, but they did not significantly differ from one another. However, there were some nonsignificant trends in favor of MBSR with regard to diurnal slope of cortisol release at posttreatment. At a 4-month posttreatment follow-up, the trend reached significance, with MBSR participants exhibiting steeper diurnal slopes than HEP participants. In addition, findings concerning TNF-α and IL-8 revealed no significant main or interaction effects of time or treatment group, though MBSR participants had smaller flare sizes at posttreatment relative to the HEP participants. Finally, the authors reported no significant differences between treatment groups with regard to amount of time spent practicing and its effects on the aforementioned biomarkers of stress.

The empirical support for the benefits of MBSR on stress reactivity suggests that reductions in stress may not be uniquely tied to increases in mindfulness At this relatively early stage in the literature, however, it is not clear that these findings are definitive and further research that is in line with the MSBA. For example, perhaps the reduction of stress reactivity is dependent upon pre-existing trait mindfulness, which may in turn differentially impact physiological factors, psychological factors, or both.

Empirical Support for Mindfulness-Based Cognitive Therapy and Stress

In stark contrast to MBSR, few studies have explored the relation between MBCT and biological indices of stress and stress-related factors, though this is not surprising, because unlike MBSR, MBCT was not designed with the purpose of managing stress. Nevertheless, the reviewed articles that follow provide preliminary evidence for its efficacy on a number of biological indices.

Gex-Fabry and colleagues (2012) investigated the effect of MBCT on diurnal cortisol in patients diagnosed with recurrent MDD who were currently in remission. The participants were randomly assigned to either MBCT and treatment as usual, or treatment as usual alone. Over the course of treatment, saliva samples were collected at different time points throughout the day on six separate occasions occurring at pretreatment, posttreatment, and follow-up sessions scheduled every trimester up until the 12-month period. The diurnal cortisol profile was measured in three different ways: the amount of cortisol present upon awakening, the average amount of cortisol exposure in a given day, and the degree to which cortisol declined throughout the day (i.e., the diurnal slope). The authors reported that the variability within groups exceeded the variability between groups on all cortisol measures, and

no meaningful main or interaction effects accounted for a significant amount of variability in any of the measures.

O'Leary, O'Neill, and Dockray (2016) conducted a systematic review analyzing studies of mindfulness-based interventions on cortisol levels to assess whether measuring cortisol can meaningfully contribute to our understanding of mindfulness training in therapy. Their systematic review revealed that although interventions such as MBSR and MBCT produced within-group effects, comparisons between said interventions and control groups yielded no significant differences between conditions on cortisol levels.

Wheeler and colleagues (2014) conducted a pilot study investigating the effects of MBCT on depressive symptoms and heart-rate variability (HRV). They argued that previous studies have established HRV as a mediator between MDD and cardiac issues and conditions, and that major depression is typically accompanied by abnormalities in heart rate and HRV. As such, the authors hypothesized that MBCT would reduce depressive symptoms *and* increase HRV. Individuals with at least one primary clinical diagnosis were recruited for the study, and they underwent electrocardiogram monitoring to collect resting-state and stress-induced heart rate and HRV at pretreatment and posttreatment. In addition, participants were also assessed for cardiovascular risk factors, quality of life, and depressive symptoms. Findings revealed that MBCT improved self-report quality of life and depressive symptoms, but they did not significantly impact heart rate and HRV at posttreatment. Despite the null findings, the authors note that their study may not have been properly powered to detect significance in heart rate or HRV changes, though one must also question the theoretical and practical utility of assessing biomarkers with small effect sizes.

Gonzalez-Garcia and colleagues (2014) conducted a randomized, controlled trial that compared the effects of MBCT to usual care in HIV-infected participants. The authors assessed perceived stress, quality of life, and depressive and anxiety symptoms, as well as biomarkers from the disease-specific and stress-sensitive pathogenesis implicated in HIV. The biological measures included CD4+ T lymphocyte counts and HIV-RNA viral load, both of which reflect general immune system functioning and are typically reduced in HIV-infected individuals relative to noninfected individuals. These psychological and biological measurements were collected at pretreatment, posttreatment, and a 3-month follow-up assessment. The authors reported that relative to routine follow-up appointments, participants from the MBCT program reported less perceived stress, depressive symptoms, and anxiety, and improved quality of life at posttreatment, all of which were maintained at the 3-month mark. In contrast, no differences were detected between the MBCT and the group in CD4+ T lymphocyte counts at pretreatment or posttreatment, though statistical significance was attained at follow-up, with MBCT participants showing higher concentrations than control participants. Finally, no group differences were detected in HIV-RNA viral loads across all time points. This study provided preliminary support for the link between MBCT and stress factors; however, because the authors did not conduct a mediation analysis, it is unclear whether the stress indices mediated the relation between mindfulness training and health outcomes, and whether a causal relationship existed between the psychological and biological indices of stress.

In sum, the studies discussed earlier provide preliminary evidence for the ability of mindfulness-based interventions to impact stress reactivity and other health outcomes. Although some work has examined mindfulness and related constructs as prospective mediators of change, very seldom have stress indices been submitted to mediation analyses. As suggested by Creswell and Lindsay (2014), such analyses are paramount to the advancement of theoretical and practical understanding of mindfulness training and mindfulness-based interventions. Without a theoretical model, such as the MSBA or some other account of the mindfulness-stress link, it becomes difficult to ascertain the true effects of mindfulness training. It is conceivable that MBSR, MBCT, and other MBIs derive their primary effect from the alleviation of perceived stress versus biomarkers of stress; however, MSBA stipulates a number of antecedent conditions that would minimize the therapeutic benefits of MBIs on health outcomes. For instance, many of the studies reviewed reported few effects of MBSR on stress factors, but they were often testing for effects in normal, healthy individuals. According to the MSBA, the impact of MBIs on psychological and biological facets of stress are expected to be *most* pronounced for those who are experiencing high levels of stress, which calls the former strategy into question. Not only does this potentially explain why the practice of mindfulness may have produced negligible changes, but it also underscores the importance of interpreting such findings from an a priori theoretical framework.

Concluding Remarks

Investigations into mindfulness training have consistently found support for its benefits in improving health outcomes and indices of stress, although the efficacy of manualized mindfulness-based interventions has been less consistently supported. In addition, most studies constrain their designs and analyses to questions of efficacy and effectiveness rather than addressing underlying mechanisms of action or evaluating key assumptions of theoretical models. To this point, few researchers have explored core assumptions of the mindfulness stress-buffering model relating to underlying mechanisms of action, the impact of mindfulness on psychological *and* biological indices of stress, and whether stress markers mediate the relation between mindfulness training on mental and physical health outcomes. Nevertheless, as this line of research is still in its infancy and requires additional outcome studies, grounding subsequent empirical studies in theoretical models of mindfulness and stress could drastically change the trajectory of findings in this area. Not only would such a theory-informed approach direct future research, but it would also allow for a more comprehensive understanding of the relation between mindfulness and stress reactivity. In addition, it may help inform the clinical application of mindfulness-based interventions, especially with regard to selecting appropriate efficacy measures of such interventions (e.g., CD4+ T lymphocytes) for psychological and physical conditions (e.g., HIV-related stress) treated in real-world clinical settings.

Our review of the literature also highlighted a number of methodological concerns that should be addressed in future studies of mindfulness and stress. First, considering several studies have reported few significant differences between mindfulness training and control conditions on stress reactivity, we must question whether the construct of mindfulness is alone sufficient for producing the stress-related effects of mindfulness-based interventions. As such, alternative explanations for these findings should be considered. For instance, the relation between mindfulness-based interventions and stress reactivity could be mediated by several *interacting* constructs that include mindfulness, or that mindfulness itself is actually not a significant driver of stress reduction. To examine these questions, future research should include measures of several psychological constructs from competing models of stress management that could also realistically account for the therapeutic benefits of mindfulness-based interventions. Some candidate variables are relaxation, diaphragmatic breathing, distraction, or, in light of the fact that most of these interventions are group based, the effects of illness normalization and a supportive interpersonal learning environment.

Second, researchers should consider the assumptions and suggestions of prevailing theories of mindfulness, including the MSBA, as they may inform research design and analyses and guide interpretations of findings. For instance, the MSBA predicts more pronounced effects of mindfulness training on highly stressed individuals and selective effects on disease-specific pathogenesis. More specifically, when researching the effects of stress-management therapies on, for example, HIV-infected persons, one should measure compromised physiological systems associated with the condition of interest, which in the case of HIV would be the CD4+ T lymphocytes. As such, some of the null findings reported by the articles reviewed earlier may in fact be consistent with the MSBA, as they may have, for instance, recruited healthy individuals.

Third, the discrepancy between perceived stress and biomarkers of stress needs to be addressed in future studies, as this will go some distance in explaining how psychological and biological stress indices relate to one another and how they can be situated in a multimethod research framework. For instance, whether mindfulness training produces immediate reductions in perceived stress but delayed effects on biomarkers of stress can be examined by implementing a longitudinal design in which psychological and biological indices of stress are collected across several time points. Considering the mixed findings for mindfulness-based interventions on stress reactivity, future research should also examine whether the appropriate stress-sensitive biological mechanisms are being targeted.

To understand how mindfulness operates on stress processes, several biomarkers of stress should be assessed in single studies and regressed onto mindfulness practice and state and trait measures of mindfulness. Finally, regardless of any correspondence or discrepancies in findings, future studies should assess whether biomarkers provide theoretical or practical utility beyond that which can be obtained through self-reports. This objective can be achieved through multimethod approaches of mindfulness and stress that examine the incremental validity of biological measures. Overall, these steps would set the groundwork for deepening our understanding of mindfulness and adapting our clinical practices according to shifts in scientific

knowledge. This chapter has endeavored to provide a comprehensive overview of the prevalent theories, as well as the strengths and limitations of recent studies examining the relationship between mindfulness meditation and stress. Although often supported by anecdotal reference to meditators having a calm or settled temperament, the ability to move beyond these characterizations and provide a scientifically grounded explanation of the effects of mindfulness on stress remains a work in progress. We would recommend that future studies adhere to strong theoretical models such as the MSBA when looking to address gaps in the literature. Exploring the psychological and biological indices of stress and their mediating mechanisms are crucial steps in providing a more accurate and functional model of how mindfulness moderates stress, and it will ultimately inform the design of more effective and targeted mindfulness-based interventions to teach these skills to individuals.

References

Aldao, A., Nolen-Hoeksema, S., & Schweizer, S. (2010). Emotion-regulation strategies across psychopathology: A meta-analytic review. *Clinical Psychology Review, 30*(2), 217–237. doi:10.1016/j.cpr.2009.11.004

Baer, R. A. (2003). Mindfulness training as a clinical intervention: A conceptual and empirical review. *Clinical Psychology: Science and Practice, 10*(2), 125–143. doi:10.1093/clipsy.bpg015

Baer, R. A., Carmody, J., & Hunsinger, M. (2012). Weekly change in mindfulness and perceived stress in a mindfulness-based stress reduction program. *Journal of Clinical Psychology, 68*(7), 755–765. doi:10.1002/jclp.21865

Barnard, P. J., & Teasdale, J. D. (1991). Interacting cognitive subsystems: A systemic approach to cognitive-affective interaction and change. *Cognition and Emotion, 5*(1), 1–39. doi:10.1080/02699939108411021

Bishop, S. R., Lau, M., Shapiro, S., Carlson, L., Anderson, N. D., Carmody, J.,...Devins, G. (2004). Mindfulness: A proposed operational definition. *Clinical Psychology: Science and Practice, 11*(3), 230–241. doi:10.1093/clipsy.bph077

Boyle, C. C., Stanton, A. L., Ganz, P. A., Crespi, C. M., & Bower, J. E. (2017). Improvements in emotion regulation following mindfulness meditation: Effects on depressive symptoms and perceived stress in younger breast cancer survivors. *Journal of Consulting and Clinical Psychology, 85*(4), 397–402. doi:10.1037/ccp0000186

Brown, K. W., Ryan, R. M., & Creswell, J. D. (2007). Mindfulness: Theoretical foundations and evidence for its salutary effects. *Psychological Inquiry, 18*(4), 211–237. doi:10.1080/10478400701598298

Brown, K. W., Weinstein, N., & Creswell, J. D. (2012). Trait mindfulness modulates neuroendocrine and affective responses to social evaluative threat. *Psychoneuroendocrinology, 37*(12), 2037–2041. doi:10.1016/j.psyneuen.2012.04.003

Buchholz, L. (2015). Exploring the promise of mindfulness as medicine. *JAMA: Journal of the American Medical Association, 314*(13), 1327–1329. Retrieved from http://myaccess.library.

utoronto.ca/login?url=http://search.proquest.com.myaccess.
library.utoronto.ca/docview/1732319139?accountid=14771

Carlson, L. E., Speca, M., Faris, P., & Patel, K. D. (2007). One
year pre-post intervention follow-up of psychological,
immune, endocrine and blood pressure outcomes of
mindfulness-based stress reduction (MBSR) in breast and
prostate cancer outpatients. *Brain, Behavior, and Immunity,
21*(8), 1038–1049. doi:10.1016/j.bbi.2007.04.002

Carmody, J., & Baer, R. A. (2008). Relationships between
mindfulness practice and levels of mindfulness, medical and
psychological symptoms and well-being in a mindfulness-
based stress reduction program. *Journal of Behavioral
Medicine, 31*(1), 23–33. doi:10.1007/s10865-007-9130-7

Chambers, R., Gullone, E., & Allen, N. B. (2009). Mindful
emotion regulation: An integrative review. *Clinical Psychology
Review, 29*(6), 560–572. doi:10.1016/j.cpr.2009.06.005

Chiesa, A., & Serretti, A. (2009). Mindfulness-based stress
reduction for stress management in healthy people: A review
and meta-analysis. *The Journal of Alternative and Complementary
Medicine, 15*(5), 593–600. doi:10.1089/acm.2008.0495can

Chiesa, A., & Serretti, A. (2010). A systematic review of neuro-
biological and clinical features of mindfulness meditations.
Psychological Medicine, 40(8), 1239–1252. doi:10.1017/
S0033291709991747

Crane, C., Crane, R. S., Eames, C., Fennell, M. J., Silverton, S.,
Williams, J. M., Barnhofer, T. (2014). The effects of amount
of home meditation practice in mindfulness based cognitive
therapy on hazard of relapse to depression in the Staying Well
After Depression Trial. *Behaviour Research & Therapy, 63*,
17–24. doi:10.1016/j.brat.2014.08.015

Creswell, J. D., & Lindsay, E. K. (2014). How does mindfulness
training affect health? A mindfulness stress buffering account.
Current Directions in Psychological Science, 23(6), 401–407.
doi:10.1177/0963721414547415

Creswell, J. D., Myers, H. F., Cole, S. W., & Irwin, M. R.
(2009). Mindfulness meditation training effects on CD4+ T
lymphocytes in HIV-1 infected adults: A small randomized
controlled trial. *Brain, Behavior, and Immunity, 23*(2),
184–188. doi:10.1016/j.bbi.2008.07.004

Creswell, J. D., Pacilio, L. E., Lindsay, E. K., & Brown, K. W.
(2014). Brief mindfulness meditation training alters
psychological and neuroendocrine responses to social
evaluative stress. *Psychoneuroendocrinology, 44*, 1–12.
doi:10.1016/j.psyneuen.2014.02.007

Creswell, J. D., Taren, A. A., Lindsay, E. K., Greco, C. M.,
Gianaros, P. J., Fairgrieve, A.,…Ferris, J. L. (2016).
Alterations in resting-state functional connectivity link
mindfulness meditation with reduced interleukin-6: A
randomized controlled trial. *Biological Psychiatry, 80*(1),
53–61. doi:10.1016/j.biopsych.2016.01.008

Dimidjian, S., Beck, A., Felder, J. N., Boggs, J. M., Gallop, R.,
& Segal, Z. V. (2014). Web-based mindfulness-based
cognitive therapy for reducing residual depressive symptoms:
An open trial and quasi-experimental comparison to
propensity score matched controls. *Behaviour Research &
Therapy, 63*, 83–89. doi:10.1016/j.brat.2014.09.004

Farb, N. A. S., Anderson, A. K., Irving, J. A., & Segal, Z. V.
(2014). Mindfulness interventions and emotion regulation.
In J. J. Gross (Ed.), *Handbook of emotion regulation* (2nd ed.,
pp. 548–567). New York, NY: Guilford Press. Retrieved
from http://myaccess.library.utoronto.ca/login?url=http://
search.proquest.com.myaccess.library.utoronto.ca/docview/1
617244012?accountid=14771

Farb, N. A. S., Segal, Z. V., & Anderson, A. K. (2013).
Mindfulness meditation training alters cortical representations
of interoceptive attention. *Social Cognitive and Affective
Neuroscience, 8*(1), 15–26. doi:10.1093/scan/nss066

Fjorback, L. O., Arendt, M., Ørnbøl, E., Fink, P., & Walach, H.
(2011). Mindfulness-based stress reduction and mindfulness-
based cognitive therapy—A systematic review of randomized
controlled trials. *Acta Psychiatrica Scandinavica, 124*(2),
102–119. doi:10.1111/j.1600-0447.2011.01704.x

Gethin, R. (2011). On some definitions of mindfulness.
Contemporary Buddhism, 12(1), 263–279. doi:10.1080/14639
947.2011.564843

Gex-Fabry, M., Jermann, F., Kosel, M., Rossier, M. F., Van, d. L.,
Bertschy, G.,…Aubry, J. (2012). Salivary cortisol profiles in
patients remitted from recurrent depression: One-year
follow-up of a mindfulness-based cognitive therapy trial.
Journal of Psychiatric Research, 46(1), 80–86. doi:10.1016/j.
jpsychires.2011.09.011

Gomez, D. E., Armando, R. G., Farina, H. G., Menna, P. L.,
Cerrudo, C. S., Ghiringhelli, P. D., & Alonso, D. F. (2012).
Telomere structure and telomerase in health and disease.
International Journal of Oncology, 41(5), 1561–1569.
doi:10.3892/ijo.2012.1611

Gonzalez-Garcia, M., Ferrer, M. J., Borras, X., Muñoz-Moreno,
J. A., Miranda, C., Puig, J.,…Fumaz, C. R. (2014).
Effectiveness of mindfulness-based cognitive therapy on the
quality of life, emotional status, and CD4 cell count of
patients aging with HIV infection. *AIDS and Behavior,
18*(4), 676–685. doi:10.1007/s10461-013-0612-z

Grabovac, A.D., Lau, M.A. & Willett, B.R. (2011). Mechanisms
of mindfulness: A Buddhist psychological model.
Mindfulness, 2, 154–166. doi:10.1007/s12671-011-0054-5

Gross, J. J. (2015). Emotion regulation: Current status and future
prospects. *Psychological Inquiry, 26*(1), 1–26. doi:10.1080/104
7840X.2014.940781

Gross, J. J., & Muñoz, R. F. (1995). Emotion regulation and
mental health. *Clinical Psychology: Science and Practice, 2*(2),
151–164. doi:10.1111/j.1468-2850.1995.tb00036.x

Gross, J. J., & Thompson, R. A. (2007). Emotion regulation:
Conceptual foundations. In J. J. Gross (Ed.), *Handbook of
emotion regulation* (pp. 3–24). New York, NY: Guilford
Press. Retrieved from http://myaccess.library.utoronto.ca/
login?url=https://search-proquest-com.myaccess.library.
utoronto.ca/docview/621612529?accountid=14771

Gu, J., Strauss, C., Bond, R., & Cavanagh, K. (2015). How do
mindfulness-based cognitive therapy and mindfulness-
based stress reduction improve mental health and well-
being? A systematic review and meta-analysis of mediation
studies. *Clinical Psychology Review, 37*, 1–12. doi:10.1016/j.
cpr.2015.01.006

Guendelman, S., Medeiros, S., & Rampes, H. (2017).
Mindfulness and emotion regulation: Insights from
neurobiological, psychological, and clinical studies. *Frontiers
in Psychology, 8*, 23. Retrieved from http://myaccess.library.
utoronto.ca/login?url=http://search.proquest.com.myaccess.
library.utoronto.ca/docview/1899909476?accountid=14771

Guidi, J., Tomba, E., & Fava, G. A. (2016). The sequential
integration of pharmacotherapy and psychotherapy in the
treatment of major depressive disorder. *American Journal
of Psychiatry. 173*, 128–137. doi:10.1176/appi.ajp.2015.
15040476.

Hölzel, B. K., Lazar, S. W., Gard, T., Schuman-Olivier, Z., Vago,
D. R., & Ott, U. (2011). How does mindfulness meditation

work? Proposing mechanisms of action from a conceptual and neural perspective. *Perspectives on Psychological Science*, *6*(6), 537–559. doi:10.1177/1745691611419671

Ingram, R. E., Atchley, R. A., & Segal, Z. V. (2011). *Vulnerability to depression: From cognitive neuroscience to prevention and treatment*. New York, NY: Guilford Press. Retrieved from http://myaccess.library.utoronto.ca/login?url=http://search.proquest.com.myaccess.library.utoronto.ca/docview/898675724?accountid=14771

Jensen, C. G., Vangkilde, S., Frokjaer, V., & Hasselbalch, S. G. (2012). Mindfulness training affects attention—Or is it attentional effort? *Journal of Experimental Psychology: General*, *141*(1), 106–123. doi:10.1037/a0024931

Joormann, J., & Gotlib, I. H. (2010). Emotion regulation in depression: Relation to cognitive inhibition. *Cognition and Emotion*, *24*(2), 281–298. doi:10.1080/02699930903407948

Kabat-Zinn, J. (1990). *Full catastrophe living*. New York, NY: Delta Publishing.

Kabat-Zinn, J. (2003). Mindfulness-based stress reduction (MBSR). *Constructivism in the Human Sciences*, *8*(2), 73–107. Retrieved from http://myaccess.library.utoronto.ca/login?url=http://search.proquest.com.myaccess.library.utoronto.ca/docview/620535552?accountid=14771

Kabat-Zinn, J. (2011). Some reflections on the origins of MBSR, skillful means, and the trouble with maps. *Contemporary Buddhism*, *12*(1), 281–306. doi:10.1080/14639947.2011.564844

Kaliman, P., Álvarez-López, M. J., Cosín-Tomás, M., Rosenkranz, M. A., Lutz, A., & Davidson, R. J. (2014). Rapid changes in histone deacetylases and inflammatory gene expression in expert meditators. *Psychoneuroendocrinology*, *40*, 96–107. doi:10.1016/j.psyneuen.2013.11.004

Kazdin, A. E. (2007). Mediators and mechanisms of change in psychotherapy research. *Annual Review of Clinical Psychology*, *3*, 1–27. doi:10.1146/annurev.clinpsy.3.022806.091432

Kuyken, W., Hayes, R., Barrett, B., Byng, R., Dalgleish, T., Kessler, D., . . . Byford, S. (2015). Effectiveness and cost-effectiveness of mindfulness-based cognitive therapy compared with maintenance antidepressant treatment in the prevention of depressive relapse or recurrence (PREVENT): A randomised controlled trial. *The Lancet*, *386*(9988), 63–73. doi:10.1016/S0140-6736(14)62222-4

Kuyken, W., Warren, F. C., Taylor, R. S., Whalley, B., Crane, C., Bondolfi, G., . . . Dalgleish, T. (2016). Efficacy of mindfulness-based cognitive therapy in prevention of depressive relapse: An individual patient data meta-analysis from randomized trials. *JAMA Psychiatry*, *73*(6), 565–574. doi:10.1001/jamapsychiatry.2016.0076

Lengacher, C. A., Kip, K. E., Barta, M. K., Post-White, J., Jacobsen, P., Groer, M., . . . Shelton, M. M. (2012). A pilot study evaluating the effect of mindfulness-based stress reduction on psychological status, physical status, salivary cortisol, and Interleukin-6 among advanced-stage cancer patients and their caregivers. *Journal of Holistic Nursing*, *30*(3), 170–185. doi:10.1177/0898010111435949

Lengacher, C. A., Kip, K. E., Post-White, J., Fitzgerald, S., Newton, C., Barta, M., . . . Klein, T. W. (2013). Lymphocyte recovery after breast cancer treatment and mindfulness-based stress reduction (MBSR) therapy. *Biological Research for Nursing*, *15*(1), 37–47.

Lindsay, E. K., & Creswell, J. D. (2017). Mechanisms of mindfulness training: Monitor and acceptance theory (MAT). *Clinical Psychology Review*, *51*, 48–59. doi:10.1016/j.cpr.2016.10.011

Ma, S. H., & Teasdale, J. D. (2004). Mindfulness-based cognitive therapy for depression: Replication and exploration of differential relapse prevention effects. *Journal of Consulting and Clinical Psychology*, *72*(1), 31–40. doi:10.1037/0022-006X.72.1.31

Nyklíček, I., Mommersteeg, P. M. C., Van Beugen, S., Ramakers, C., & Van Boxtel, G. J. (2013). Mindfulness-based stress reduction and physiological activity during acute stress: A randomized controlled trial. *Health Psychology*, *32*(10), 1110–1113. doi:10.1037/a0032200

Oken, B. S., Fonareva, I., Haas, M., Wahbeh, H., Lane, J. B., Zajdel, D., & Amen, A. (2010). Pilot controlled trial of mindfulness meditation and education for dementia caregivers. *The Journal of Alternative and Complementary Medicine*, *16*(10), 1031–1038. doi:10.1089/acm.2009.0733

O'Leary, K., O'Neill, S., & Dockray, S. (2016). A systematic review of the effects of mindfulness interventions on cortisol. *Journal of Health Psychology*, *21*(9), 2108–2121. doi:10.1177/1359105315569095

Quaglia, J. T., Brown, K. W., Lindsay, E. K., Creswell, J. D., & Goodman, R. J. (2015). From conceptualization to operationalization of mindfulness. In K. W. Brown, J. D. Creswell, & R. M. Ryan (Eds.), *Handbook of mindfulness: Theory, research, and practice; handbook of mindfulness: Theory, research, and practice* (pp. 151–170). New York, NY: Guilford Press. Retrieved from http://myaccess.library.utoronto.ca/login?url=http://search.proquest.com.myaccess.library.utoronto.ca/docview/1671637653?accountid=14771

Rosenkranz, M. A., Davidson, R. J., MacCoon, D. G., Sheridan, J. F., Kalin, N. H., & Lutz, A. (2013). A comparison of mindfulness-based stress reduction and an active control in modulation of neurogenic inflammation. *Brain, Behavior, and Immunity*, *27*, 174–184. doi:10.1016/j.bbi.2012.10.013

Schutte, N. S., & Malouff, J. M. (2014). A meta-analytic review of the effects of mindfulness meditation on telomerase activity. *Psychoneuroendocrinology*, *42*, 45–48. doi:10.1016/j.psyneuen.2013.12.017

Segal, Z. V., Bieling, P., Young, T., MacQueen, G., Cooke, R., Martin, L., . . . Levitan, R. D. (2010). Antidepressant monotherapy vs sequential pharmacotherapy and mindfulness-based cognitive therapy, or placebo, for relapse prophylaxis in recurrent depression. *Archives of General Psychiatry*, *67*(12), 1256–1264. doi:10.1001/archgenpsychiatry.2010.168

Segal, Z. V., Williams, J. M., & Teasdale, J. D. (2013). *Mindfulness-based cognitive therapy for depression* (2nd ed.). New York, NY: Guilford Press. Retrieved from http://myaccess.library.utoronto.ca/login?url=http://search.proquest.com.myaccess.library.utoronto.ca/docview/126943 1842?accountid=14771

Segal, Z., Williams, M., Teasdale, J., Crane, R., Dimidjian, S., Ma, H., Woods, S., & Kuyken, W. (2016). *Mindfulness-based cognitive therapy: Training pathway*. Retrieved from http://mbct.com/wp-content/uploads/MBCT-Training-Pathway-Final_Version1.pdf

Shapiro, S. L., Carlson, L. E., Astin, J. A., & Freedman, B. (2006). Mechanisms of mindfulness. *Journal of Clinical Psychology*, *62*(3), 373–386. doi:10.1002/jclp.20237

Sheppes, G., Suri, G., & Gross, J. J. (2015). Emotion regulation and psychopathology. *Annual Review of Clinical Psychology*, *11*, 379–405. doi:10.1146/annurev-clinpsy-032814-112739

Snippe, E., Dziak, J. J., Lanza, S. T., Nyklíček, I., & Wichers, M. (2017). The shape of change in perceived stress, negative affect, and stress sensitivity during mindfulness-based stress reduction. *Mindfulness, 8*(3), 728–736. doi:10.1007/s12671-016-0650-5

Tang, Y., Hölzel, B. K., & Posner, M. I. (2015). The neuroscience of mindfulness meditation. *Nature Reviews Neuroscience, 16*(4), 213–225. doi:10.1038/nrn3916

Taren, A. A., Gianaros, P. J., Greco, C. M., Lindsay, E. K., Fairgrieve, A., Brown, K. W.,...Creswell, J. D. (2015). Mindfulness meditation training alters stress-related amygdala resting state functional connectivity: A randomized controlled trial. *Social Cognitive and Affective Neuroscience, 10*(12), 1758–1768. doi:10.1093/scan/nsv066

Teasdale, J. D., Segal, Z. V., Williams, J. M., Ridgeway, V. A., Soulsby, J. M., & Lau, M. A. (2000). Prevention of relapse/recurrence in major depression by mindfulness-based cognitive therapy. *Journal of Consulting and Clinical Psychology, 68*(4), 615–623. doi:10.1037/0022-006X.68.4.615

Tovote, K. A., Schroevers, M. J., Snippe, E., Sanderman, R., Links, T. P., Emmelkamp, P. M. G., & Fleer, J. (2015). Long-term effects of individual mindfulness-based cognitive therapy and cognitive behavior therapy for depressive symptoms in patients with diabetes: A randomized trial. *Psychotherapy and Psychosomatics, 84*(3), 186–187. doi:10.1159/000375453

Vago, D. R., & Silbersweig, D. A. (2012). Self-awareness, self-regulation, and self-transcendence (S-ART): A framework for understanding the neurobiological mechanisms of mindfulness. *Frontiers in Human Neuroscience, 6*, 30. doi:10.3389/fnhum.2012.00296

van der Velden, A., Kuyken, W., Wattar, U., Crane, C., Pallesen, K., Dahlgaard, J., Fjorback, L., & Piet, J. (2015). A systematic review of mechanisms of change in mindfulness-based cognitive therapy in the treatment of recurrent major depressive disorder. *Clinical Psychology Review, 37*, 26–39. doi:10.1016/j.cpr.2015.02.001

Werner, K., & Gross, J. J. (2010). Emotion regulation and psychopathology: A conceptual framework. In A. M. Kring & D. M. Sloan (Eds.), *Emotion regulation and psychopathology: A transdiagnostic approach to etiology and treatment; emotion regulation and psychopathology: A transdiagnostic approach to etiology and treatment* (pp. 13–37). New York, NY: Guilford Press. Retrieved from http://myaccess.library.utoronto.ca/login?url=https://search-proquest-com.myaccess.library.utoronto.ca/docview/621973873?accountid=14771

Wheeler, A., Denson, L., Neil, C., Tucker, G., Kenny, M., Beltrame, J. F.,...Proeve, M. (2014). Investigating the effect of mindfulness training on heart rate variability in mental health outpatients: A pilot study. *Behaviour Change, 31*(3), 175–188. doi:10.1017/bec.2014.14

Zvereva, M. I., Shcherbakova, D. M., & Dontsova, O. A. (2010). Telomerase: structure, functions, and activity regulation. *Biochemistry (Moscow), 75*(13), 1563–1583.

Expressive Writing and Stress-Related Disorders

Kay Wilhelm *and* Joanna Crawford

Abstract

Expressive writing (EW) was developed in the 1980s by Pennebaker and colleagues, who defined it as "writing focusing on traumatic, stressful or emotional events, and the feelings inspired by these." There have been developments in terms of process, covering a range of instructions, target groups, and writing conditions and, more recently, benefit-finding writing (BFW) about benefits derived from stress or traumatic situations. EW has now been trialed across a broad range of situations, involving mental and physical health domains. Results from meta-analyses find small but significant improvements more related to physical health than mental health parameters. It is thought to be best suited to people with mild-to-moderate psychological distress who are addressing stress-related conditions and situations. The chapter describes common forms of EW and explores the place of BFW. Some mechanisms for expressive writing are discussed, but these are still speculative.

Keywords: expressive writing, emotional disclosure, stress, stress and coping, coping, psychological distress, benefit finding

Writing about one's own personal experiences is a common practice across the general population, and it is recognized for its profound influence on our thoughts and feelings. It takes a number of forms, including journaling, memoirs, and letters. All enable the writer to collect and make sense of her thoughts, express emotions and ideas she may not wish to or cannot verbalize, to record secrets, reflect on experience, and to create a narrative (Pennebaker & Seagal, 1999; Pennebaker & Smyth, 2016).

"Expressive writing" (EW), is the term coined by James Pennebaker in the 1980s to describe a type of writing focusing on traumatic, stressful, or emotional events, and the feelings inspired by these occurrences (Pennebaker, Barger, & Trebout, 1989; Pennebaker & Beall, 1986; Pennebaker, Hughes, & O'Heeron, 1987; Pennebaker, Kiecolt-Glaser, & Glaser, 1988). There is now a significant body of literature showing that EW leads to improvements in physical health and to some extent in psychological

health, across a range of populations (Baikie & Wilhelm, 2005; Frattaroli, 2006; Frisina, Borod, & Lepore, 2004; Harris, 2006; Kállay, 2015; Oh & Kim, 2016; Pennebaker & Smyth, 2016; Smyth, 1998; Travagin, Margola, & Revenson, 2015).

We will describe the development of EW, initial findings and application of EW, and common variations to a range of stress-related disorders, proposed mechanisms for its effects on mental and physical health, and remaining questions and research directions.

Pennebaker's original questions about the effects of disclosure of secrets or private information on health were based on the premise that "holding things in" led to detrimental effects on health which were ameliorated by their disclosure (Pennebaker & Beall, 1986; Pennebaker, Hughes, & O'Heeron, 1987). Pennebaker and Beall's initial expressive writing (EW) study (1986) concerned university freshmen writing about the facts and feelings surrounding their "most traumatic or upsetting experiences" for a minimum of 15 minutes on 4 consecutive days as part of an assignment when starting college (see writing instructions in Box 32.1). The control writing group wrote about superficial topics (such as their room, their shoes, plans for the day) without revealing any emotion. The important issue for both groups was to write for the full time: They were asked to go back and repeat themselves, perhaps writing a little differently, if they ran out of ideas.

Exploring the Types of Expressive Writing

Traditional/Standard Expressive Writing (Also Known as Written Emotional Disclosure)

The term "therapeutic writing" encapsulates all such variants—that is, writing as a form of therapy to improve physical or mental health (Nyssen et al., 2016).

The original paradigm, developed by Pennebaker and colleagues (Pennebaker & Beall, 1986; Pennebaker, Kiecolt-Glaser, & Glaser, 1988; Pennebaker & Seagal, 1999), in Box 32.1, asked participants to write about "the most traumatic or upsetting event of their lives" and they could choose to write about either the same event or different upsetting events each day (Pennebaker & Beall, 1986; Pennebaker, Kiecolt-Glaser, & Glaser, 1988; Pennebaker & Seagal, 1999). The most striking finding was that compared to the control group, the EW group made significantly fewer visits to a doctor in the following 6 months and had a more successful adjustment to

their first year. Although many reported being initially upset by the writing experience, they reported a great sense of meaning in their lives as a result. The authors concluded that "writing about earlier traumatic experience was associated with both short-term increases in physiological arousal and long-term decreases in health problems" (Pennebaker & Beall, 1986, p. 280).

Following the promising results of initial studies using the original EW paradigm (see Box 32.1), many researchers adapted EW for people coping with a particular stressor or difficult life situation, such as job loss (Spera, Buhrfeind, & Pennebaker, 1994), relationship breakup (Lepore & Greenberg, 2002), caregiving (Harvey-Knowles, Sanders, Ko, Manusov, & Yi, 2017; Lovell, Moss, & Wetherall, 2016; Riddle, Smith, & Jones, 2016), bereavement (Lichtenthal & Cruess, 2010), or specific condition (such as chronic pain, asthma, cancer, cystic fibrosis, or arthritis) (Frattaroli, 2006; Nyssen et al., 2016). Participants are usually instructed to write only about their deepest thoughts and feelings on the specified topic. For example, an EW intervention for kidney transplant recipients asked participants to "write about your deepest thoughts and feelings about your experience with kidney failure and transplant" (Possemato et al., 2010, p. 50). However, some EW interventions for people with specific conditions allow participants to write about other stressors, as in sample of participants with Stargardt's disease (a progressive macular degeneration) who reported improved psychological health outcomes 3 weeks postintervention and improved self-reported physical health outcomes at 6 weeks postintervention (Bryan & Lu, 2016).

The variations typically involve participants being instructed to write for 15–30 minutes on 3 or 4 consecutive days (or at weekly intervals) (Nyssen et al., 2016), while the instructions and topics that participants are directed to write about differ between these variants. Researchers have since modified writing instructions to give more specific focus to participants' writing with the aim of increasing benefits gained from the writing task (Guastella & Dadds, 2008; Sloan et al., 2007).

Positive and Benefit-Finding Writing

Other forms of therapeutic writing that focus on *positive* thoughts and feelings include writing about one's "best possible future self" (King, 2001) or positive life experiences (Burton & King, 2009). The instructions in Box 32.2 were used in a study of healthy college students, where the writing group

---

Box 32.1 Writing Instructions From Original Expressive Writing Studies

For the next 4 days, I would like you to write your very deepest thoughts and feelings about the most traumatic experience of your entire life or an extremely important emotional issue that has affected you and your life. In your writing, I'd like you to really let go and explore your deepest emotions and thoughts. You might tie your topic to your relationships with others, including parents, lovers, friends, or relatives; to your past, your present, or your future; or to who you have been, who you would like to be, or who you are now. You may write about the same general issues or experiences on all days of writing or about different topics each day. All of your writing will be completely confidential.

Don't worry about spelling, grammar, or sentence structure. The only rule is that once you begin writing, you continue until the time is up (Pennebaker & Evans, 2014, p. 14).

reported significantly fewer health complaints, relative to a control group, 4–6 weeks later (Burton & King, 2009).

Another variation involves writing any *positive* thoughts and feelings about a stressful experience. Instructions for benefit-finding writing (BFW) for adults with type 1 or type 2 diabetes (Box 32.3, from Crawford et al., 2017) used in our research, were adapted from Stanton and colleagues' (2002) Benefit-Finding Writing (BFW) study for women with breast cancer.

Putting Stress Into Words

Pennebaker described EW as "putting stress into words" (Pennebaker, 1993), and many early EW studies focused on the effects on stress, symptoms of posttraumatic stress disorder (PTSD), physiological markers of stress response (skin conductance, heart rate variability, and cortisol levels), and indicators of physical health, such as health care utilization and self-reported health. Early studies, generally of undergraduate student samples, reported significant improvements in psychological well-being at least 1 month post writing, along with improvements in physiological parameters related to stress and self-reported health according to a meta-analysis examining 13 EW studies (Smyth, 1998).

Later EW studies examined changes in heart rate variability (HRV), a measure of stress reactivity (Seeley, Yanez, Stanton, & Hoyt, 2017). Greater HRV is considered to be a physiological indicator of adaptive emotional regulation (Denson, Grisham, & Moulds, 2011), and chronically lower HRV is associated with worry (Aldao, Mennin, & McLaughlin, 2013), anxiety disorders, chronic inflammation, and cardiovascular disease (Shaffer, McCraty & Zerr, 2014). In adults with hypertension, EW has been thought to buffer increases in a very low frequency wave of HRV (found only in controls) (Beckwith, McGuire, Greenberg, & Gervitz, 2005). Because EW may provide the opportunity for both emotional expression and cognitive change (Niles, Byrne Hamilton, Lieberman, Hur, & Stanton, 2016), this finding is consistent with research demonstrating that cognitive reappraisal of an anger-inducing event is associated with increases in HRV, compared to suppression of emotions or a control condition (Denson et al., 2011). Recent research has reported participants with a higher emotional processing style exhibited higher HRV following EW after a laboratory stressor (Seeley et al., 2017). The authors suggested that those with a preference or ability to process emotions (higher dispositional emotional processing style) may better engage in EW and thus derive greater benefit, in terms of improved emotional regulation indicated by higher HRV.

Some interesting patterns of changes in distress in indicators of autonomic nervous system activity have emerged over the months after a course of EW. A frequently reported pattern is initially heightened arousal (measured by cortisol levels) during EW (Nyssen et al., 2016), followed by improvements in psychological and/or physical health, several months later (Baikie & Wilhelm, 2005; Pennebaker & Smyth, 2016). For example, one study found that the EW group showed significantly higher cortisol levels than the control group for the first writing session, which decreased and were similar to the control group for the remaining writing sessions (Sloan & Marx, 2004a). However, the EW group's greater increases in cortisol levels during the first writing session predicted greater improvement in psychological symptoms 1 month later. Notably, participants' self-reported emotional responses corresponded with their changes in cortisol levels (Sloan & Marx, 2004b). Further, in participants with diagnosed PTSD, EW has been found to attenuate cortisol responses in later exposure to trauma-related memories (Smyth, Hockemeyer, & Tulloch, 2008). This suggests a mechanism whereby EW could improve PTSD symptoms, and there is evidence from several studies that EW can reduce PTSD symptoms (Blasio et al., 2015; Bragdon & Lombardo, 2012; Meston, Lorenz, & Stephenson, 2013; Sloan, Marx, & Epstein, 2005; Sloan, Sawyer, Lawmaster, Warwick, & Marx, 2015). However, the findings are inconsistent as some studies have found that EW was associated with no change (e.g., Smyth, Hockemeyer, & Tulloch, 2008) or worsening of PTSD symptoms (Gidron, Peri, Connolly, & Shalev, 1996).

Overall, evidence from a range of indicators of physiological markers during EW suggests that writing about stressful events has a significant short-term effect on arousal and stress reactivity and that the pattern of physiological responses is linked to the words used and emotions expressed (Hughes, Uhlmann, & Pennebaker, 1994) and may be associated with later psychological benefits of EW (Sloan & Marx, 2004; Smyth, Hockemeyer, & Tulloch, 2008). Also, participants who were "high disclosers"

during EW gained greater benefit, in terms of physiological indicators of improved emotional regulation, than "low disclosers" (Pennebaker, Hughes, & O'Heeron, 1987; Seeley et al., 2017). The findings demonstrating links between the writing process and physiological responses have "implications for considering the mind and body as fluid, dynamic systems" (Pennebaker, 1993, p. 539), which may be relevant to the physical health benefits of EW.

Because EW appeared to have greater effects on physical health than for mental health (Baikie & Wilhelm, 2005; Frattaroli, 2006), there has been interest in adapting EW to assist people in coping with a medical illness or chronic health condition (Nyssen et al., 2016), including chronic pain (Lumley, Sklar, & Carty, 2012), asthma (Smyth, Stone, Hurewitz & Kaell, 1999), cancer (Oh & Kim, 2016; Zachariae & Toole, 2015), or cystic fibrosis (Taylor, Wallander, Anderson, Beasley, & Brown, 2003). Very few studies have investigated EW in populations with a diagnosed mental illness. Several studies have examined the effects of EW on PTSD symptoms, but most samples with diagnosed PTSD included participants who have experienced a trauma or upsetting event, but not necessarily met criteria for PTSD (e.g., Smyth, Hockemeyer, & Tulloch, 2008). Three published trials have examined the effects of EW in adults with current depression (Baikie, Geerligs, & Wilhelm, 2012; Kovac & Range, 2002; Krpan et al., 2013), but only one confirmed diagnoses of major depressive disorder with a structured clinical interview (Krpan et al., 2013). We are not aware of any published EW studies using participants with anxiety disorders.

Moderators of the Effects of Expressive Writing
Dosage of Expressive Writing: Number, Duration, and Spacing of Writing Sessions
Whereas most studies of EW involved participants writing for 15–30 minutes on three or four consecutive occasions, or at weekly intervals (Nyssen et al., 2016), there is some variation in the "dosage" of writing sessions. Two meta-analyses of EW studies found the number of writing sessions as a significant moderator of the impact of EW, with intervention studies involving three or more sessions having a marginally larger effect on overall health and psychological health than those using fewer than three sessions (Frattaroli, 2006). Similarly, a meta-analysis of EW studies for adolescents found that interventions with more than three sessions had a larger mean effect size than those with a maximum

of three sessions (Travagin et al., 2015). In terms of the duration of writing sessions, Frattaroli (2006) reported that EW interventions with sessions lasting at least 15 minutes had significantly larger effect sizes than those with sessions of less than 15 minutes. Spacing writing sessions at least 1 day apart was by two meta-analyses associated with larger effect sizes than interventions with sessions on consecutive days (Smyth, 1998; Travagin et al., 2015), although spacing was not a significant moderator in the meta-analysis by Frattaroli (2006), nor in experimental investigations of its effects (Chung & Pennebaker, 2008; Sheese, Brown, & Graziano, 2004). There have been reports of significant improvements in self-reported physical health from just 2 minutes, on two occasions, of either EW or positive writing (Burton & King, 2008) or from three sessions of EW within 1 hour (Chung & Pennebaker, 2008). Thus, there is some evidence that the benefits of EW may be greater with a larger number of longer writing sessions, and some surprisingly brief EW interventions seem to have benefits as well.

Type of Instructions for Expressive Writing Interventions

The wide variation in instructions for EW and its variants makes it difficult to ascertain which instructions are most likely to maximize the benefits of EW for a given population, and how EW should be timed in relation to a traumatic or upsetting event.

Newer instruction formats such as BFW may provide similar health benefits as traditional EW in students (Lichtenthal & Cruess, 2010; Lu & Stanton, 2010) or people with a medical condition (Danoff-Burg et al., 2006; Stanton et al., 2002) and may even be more helpful than EW for participants with high trait anxiety (Danoff-Burg et al., 2006). However, there is a much larger body of evidence for standard EW in reducing symptoms of PTSD (e.g., Blasio et al., 2015; Horsch et al., 2016; Sayer et al., 2015; Sloan et al., 2015) than for BFW (Lichtenthal & Cruess, 2010). More research is needed to determine when or whether it is most helpful to direct participants to write about a specific event or stressor or to follow the original EW paradigm and allow participants to choose the most upsetting event/s of their lives to write about. In our experience, writers prefer the opportunity to be able to write about stressful situations before they are pointed toward benefit finding.

There is evidence that modifying EW instructions to maximize the participant engagement in writing can enhance psychological or physical health benefits. For example, of 146 EW studies included in the Frattaroli's (2006) meta-analysis, 50% gave participants directed questions or examples of what to disclose, and 4% gave instructions designed to promote cognitive processing or insight. Their findings suggest that EW studies that give participants directed questions or examples have significantly higher effect sizes for psychological health (and overall outcomes), compared to studies without directed questions or examples.

However, providing participants with further guidance during EW sessions, in the form of either real-time instant messaging, or written personalized guidance prior to each session of Internet-based EW, has not been found to enhance the effects of EW on psychological or physical symptoms (Beyer et al., 2014). In fact, participants who received these forms of guidance, provided by trained psychology students, had poorer outcomes than participants who completed standard EW. The authors suggested that the provision of real-time guidance by an unknown person over the Internet may have interfered with the emotional processing of stressful events during EW (Beyer et al., 2014). However, these results cannot be generalized to the provision of psychological support to EW participants by a qualified practitioner with whom the participant has an established therapeutic relationship.

Timing of Expressive Writing in Relation to Stressor

The timing of EW in relation to a trauma or stressful event may also affect the outcomes. It has been suggested that EW is most effective following a traumatic event, rather than during the event (Pennebaker & Chung, 2007). However, EW can benefit some people experiencing ongoing stressful situations, such as caregiving (Riddle, Smith, & Jones, 2016). One meta-analysis found that studies in which participants wrote about a more recent trauma or topic had higher effect sizes for both psychological and reported health outcomes, compared to studies where participants wrote about events further in the past (Frattaroli, 2006). Consistent with this, EW for caregivers has been found to be more effective for those who have been in a caregiving role for less than 5 years (Riddle et al., 2016). There is also evidence suggesting that EW *before* an upcoming stressful event, such as surgery, is ineffective (Koschwanez et al., 2017).

Overall, it appears that EW has the greatest benefits when the instructions are sufficiently detailed for participants to readily engage in EW (e.g., directed questions or examples and without the distraction or interference of real-time guidance during an EW session). Further research is needed to identify the most helpful topics for a person with a given condition to be directed to write about (e.g., a trauma or topic of his or her choice, or a specified stressor), and how long after a traumatic or upsetting event it is best to use EW.

Context and Mode of Expressive Writing

Potential context-related moderators of effects of EW include the mode of expression (writing, typing, or speaking), whether the writing is done at home or in a clinic/laboratory setting, privacy, and whether another person reads the writings resulting from EW.

The successful administration of EW via the Internet (Baikie, Geerligs, & Wilhelm, 2012; Possemato, Ouimette, & Geller, 2010; Sayer et al., 2015; Stockton, Joseph, & Hunt, 2014) raises questions of whether typing or handwriting is more effective in EW. One meta-analysis of EW studies found that mode of disclosure (typing, handwriting, or talking) did not moderate treatment effects (Frattaroli, 2006). This is significant because Internet-based EW has the potential to broaden the dissemination of EW-based interventions to large populations.

Frattaroli's (2006) meta-analysis also examined effects of location of EW and found that studies where EW was conducted at home (in a room alone) had significantly higher psychological effect sizes than EW studies conducted in a clinic or laboratory (in a room with other participants). This may indicate that when participants feel "safer" and less inhibited in expressing their emotions in their setting, they are more likely to fully engage in EW and therefore experience its benefits (Nazarian & Smyth, 2010). However, Nazarian and Smyth (2010) found that students undertaking EW in a controlled laboratory setting reported feeling more comfortable, and had greater improvements in symptoms of depression and physical health, compared to students completing EW at home. Of note, the majority of study participants were college students with roommates and may have actually had greater privacy in the laboratory setting! Further, in a subsequent community sample, Nazarian and Smyth (2013) reported no location effect, possibly because those participants may have had more privacy at home than the students in their first study. Thus, the perception of the degree of privacy and confidence in

safely expressing emotions may be more important than the location per se.

Consistent with this was the finding that EW studies in which the writings were not going to be read by another party had marginally higher effect sizes for psychological outcomes, compared to those where a researcher was going to read the writings (Frattaroli, 2006). Similarly, when participants who knew that their writings were going to be read by a psychology student guide (unknown to participant) selected less private or stressful topics to write about, and experienced less anger and other negative emotions during EW, compared to those completing standard unguided EW. They speculated that those who knew that their writings would be read by another person monitored or censored their disclosures, and inhibited their emotional expression, which in turn may have contributed to the poorer outcomes among the guided EW groups, relative to the standard EW group (Beyer et al., 2014).

Interestingly, Nazarian and Smyth (2010) found that the perceived authority of the researcher facilitating the EW intervention significantly interacted with the location in its effect on depressive symptoms. Their study included experimental manipulation of the apparent authority of the researcher (either "novice" or "expert"). The participants who undertook their EW at home, under instruction by an "expert" researcher, had a significant decrease in depressive symptoms, whereas those in the home-based EW group instructed by a "novice" had increase of their depressive symptoms. They suggested that participants doing EW at home, instructed by a "novice" researcher, of low perceived authority, may have felt less comfortable or safe, resulting in less engagement in EW and only partially processing memories of upsetting events, resulting in a worsening of symptoms. However, it is also possible that the two groups had differing expectations for improvement, and with the group instructed by an "expert" having higher expectations for improvement. This striking finding may also explain some of the inconsistencies in the findings of EW studies, because studies vary widely in the perceived authority of the researchers facilitating EW interventions.

Overall, research to date suggests that EW is more likely to provide greater benefits when conducted in a private location, either handwritten or typed, presented by a researcher of high perceived authority, and not to be read by a researcher (even one unknown to the participant). It has been proposed that such conditions are more likely to enable participants to feel confident and safe in engaging fully, to experience the range of emotions required to process the upsetting event or topic, and not to be distracted or interrupted (Beyer et al., 2014; Nazarian & Smyth, 2010).

Although EW only seems helpful for some (Frattaroli, 2006; Kallay, 2015; Pennebaker & Smyth, 2016), researchers have highlighted that even if EW's benefits are small, it warrants further investigation as a low-cost, noninvasive, easily disseminated and accessible intervention, able to be used independently (Frattaroli, 2006; Nyssen et al., 2016). It is therefore important to understand when and where EW works best. Next we consider some of the variations in EW, because the proposed mechanisms of how EW works may differ depending on the instructions used (Guastella & Dadds, 2008).

Sample/Population Characteristics

Successful EW studies have been reported across multiple countries, languages, and ethnicities (Smyth & Pennebaker, 2008), making it unlikely that the effects of EW are bound to one culture. However, it is possible that different modes of disclosure, for example talking rather than writing, may be more suitable for some cultures or groups.

Although the largest effect sizes reported were those of early EW studies in healthy students (Smyth, 1998), as noted previously, Frattaroli's (2006) meta-analysis of 146 studies reported larger effects of EW in populations with physical health problems, in keeping with findings that the physical health benefits of EW have tended to outweigh the mental health benefits (Baikie & Wilhelm, 2005; Frattaroli, 2006; Frisina et al., 2004). Frattaroli (2006) also found that selection of participants on the basis of psychological health was not a between-studies moderator of the effects of EW. However, his meta-analysis found that for within-study analyses, participants with higher stress showed greater benefits from EW for physical health, but interestingly, not for psychological health. One recent study reported effects of EW on depressive and cancer-related symptoms were greater among participants with elevated depressive symptoms *and* high social support at baseline, but that EW was ineffective for those with elevated depressive symptoms but little social support at baseline (Milbury et al., 2017), suggesting that despite EW being seen as a self-help in nature, social support is required for more depressed participants to benefit.

Frattaroli's (2006) finding that studies involving participants with a history of trauma or serious stressor had greater effect sizes for the subjective impact of EW is in line with a study reporting that the effects of EW tend to be greater when participants write about more severe topics or events (Pachankis & Goldfried, 2010). It appears that EW may be more effective among participants experiencing some PTSD symptoms (but without a PTSD diagnosis), although this remains to be tested.

Individual Characteristics

Initially, researchers suggested that EW may be particularly effective for people who have difficulty experiencing, identifying, or expressing their emotions to others (Paez, Velasco, & Gonzalez, 1999; Pennebaker, 1997). In support of this, students high in emotional suppression were found to have greater reductions in symptoms of depression following EW, compared to "low suppressors" (Gortner, Rude, & Pennebaker, 2006). This is somewhat at odds with a study showing that "high disclosers" during EW gain greater benefit, in terms of physiological indicators of improved emotional regulation than "low disclosers" (Pennebaker, Hughes, & O'Heeron, 1987; Seeley et al., 2017). However, the possibility that some "emotional suppressors" find disclosing more acceptable in a written format could be further explored.

The contextual life stressors of participants are further potential moderators of the effects of EW. It is possible that if a person has several life stressors, writing about one stressor may assist in resolving the emotions associated with that topic, but not other life stressors. Although this has not yet been examined in relation to EW, it has been found that emotional coping and social support seeking specifically in relation to breast cancer only predicted better adjustment up to 1 year later in women when their contextual life stress was low (that is, in the absence of other major life stressors; Stanton, 2012). Hence, contextual life stress should be considered as a potential moderator of EW interventions when participants are directed to write about a particular stressor.

There are no consistent gender differences in responses to EW. Smyth's (1998) meta-analysis reported greater effects for men, but this was not replicated by Frattaroli's (2006) meta-analysis, which found no gender effects on psychological health, self-reported health, or subjective impact. Some studies have reported clearly superior responses to EW for women, such as a report that EW resulted in significant reductions in symptoms of PTSD and depression and HIV-related symptoms solely in women (Ironson et al., 2013), whereas others have reported a superior response by men (Smyth, 1998). As men exhibit higher levels of alexithymia (Levant, Hall, Williams, & Hasan, 2009) and women tend to have greater use of emotional-focussed coping (Stanton, 2012), Levant and colleagues (2009) suggested that gender differences in response to EW may be attributed to gender differences in dispositional emotional expressivity. Consistent with this, men have been found to be less likely than women to disclose more emotionally intense negative events in a diary-based intervention (Garrison & Kahn, 2010).

Outcome Measures Used in Expressive Writing Studies
Linguistic Outcomes
Although first interested in physical parameters of stress, Pennebaker and colleagues went on to consider outcomes related to the writing process itself and developed a linguistic analysis tool (Linguistic Inquiry and Word Count [LIWC]; Pennebaker & Francis, 1996; Pennebaker, Booth, Boyd, & Francis, 2015). Initially, EW was directed at enabling disclosure of thoughts and emotions related to specific stressful events and trauma, with the aim of enabling venting of emotions (e.g., exposure to negative emotions, venting pent-up emotions safely). Their use of LIWC and linguistic analyses soon made it apparent that processes involved in EW promoted finding meaning and creating a narrative when the writing continued over a few days (Pennebaker, 1993; Pennebaker, Mayne, & Francis, 1997; Pennebaker & Seagal, 1999). Continuing writing on the same or related topics also allowed for the issues to be recast and explored in more depth. They reported four linguistic features associated with greater improvement in mental and physical health following trauma:

1. Increasing rates of positive emotion words (such as *happy, love, good*)
2. A moderate number of negative emotion words (such as *angry, hurt, ugly*)
3. Increasing numbers of cognitive words that implied "causal" connections (such as *because, effect, reason*)
4. Increasing numbers of cognitive words that implied "insight" (such as *understand, reason, know*) (Pennebaker, Mayne & Francis, 1997; Pennebaker & Seagal, 1999)

The suggestion (Pennebaker & Smyth, 1999) that the formation of narrative is a key mechanism of the mental and physical health improvements following EW will be discussed later in the section on proposed mediators of EW.

Mental Health Outcomes
The effects of EW on mental and/or physical health have now been examined in a wide range of populations in over 280 studies (Nyssen et al., 2016). Several reviews (Baikie & Wilhelm, 2005; Kallay, 2015; Pennebaker & Smyth, 2016; Smyth & Pennebaker, 2008) and meta-analyses (Frattaroli, 2006; Frisina, Borod, & Lepore, 2004; Nyssen et al., 2016; Smyth, 1998) of EW studies are available, including recent meta-analyses of studies of EW for specific populations, such as caregivers (Riddle et al., 2016), cancer patients (Oh & Kim, 2016; Zachariarae & O'Toole, 2015), adolescents (Travagin, Margola, & Revenson, 2015), or for specific outcomes, such as health utilization (Harris, 2006). Almost all benefits of EW tend to emerge at least 2 weeks post writing (Nyssen et al., 2016), with most studies using follow-up periods of 1–4 months.

However, standard EW often involves an immediate increase in negative mood (Nyssen et al., 2016), and, indeed, reports that many participants wept in the initial sessions (Pennebaker & Seagal, 1999), even when followed by longer term psychological benefits (Baikie & Wilhelm, 2005). More recent research has identified complex patterns of emotional arousal during EW, with a zigzag pattern of negative affect across a 3-day EW intervention formed by increases in negative affect during each writing session, interspersed by decreases in negative affect between sessions (Pascual-Leone et al., 2016).

Mental health benefits of EW include significant decreases in symptoms of depression (e.g., Blasio et al., 2015; Harvey-Knowles, Sanders, Ko, Manusov, & Yi, 2017; Horsch et al., 2016; Krpan et al., 2013), anxiety (e.g., Alparone, Pagliaro, & Rizzo, 2015), PTSD (e.g., Blasio et al., 2015; Horsch et al., 2016; Sayer et al., 2015; Sloan, Sawyer, Lawmaster, Wernick, & Marx, 2015), perceived stress (e.g., Sadovnik, Sumner, Bragger, & Pastor, 2011), and occupational burnout (Tarquini, Trani, & Solano, 2016) and increased posttraumatic growth (Stockton, Joseph, & Hunt, 2014). With a small number of exceptions (Krpan et al., 2013; Smyth, Hockemeyer, & Tulloch, 2008), however, the samples used to examine improvements in these psychological symptoms have been either healthy students or people who have experienced a specific stressor or medical condition, rather than samples of participants with a diagnosed mental illness.

Of the few EW studies conducted in samples of people with a severe psychiatric illness, most have failed to demonstrate significant benefits of EW (Frisina et al., 2004). Among the three published studies of EW in participants with depression, one found significant improvements in depression (Krpan et al., 2013), one found no significant differences between the EW and control groups (Baikie et al., 2012), and one, among severely depressed participants with suicidal ideation, found an increase in health care utilization following EW (Kovac & Range, 2002). The results of EW studies in participants diagnosed with PTSD have also been inconsistent, some reporting improvement (Smyth, Hockemeyer, & Tulloch, 2008) and others, worsening (Gidron et al., 1996) of PTSD symptoms following EW. It has been suggested that the limited effects of EW in psychiatric populations may be due to the disordered thinking inherent in such conditions interfering with the cognitive processing involved in EW (Frisina et al., 2004). Pennebaker and Smyth (2016) have commented on the lack of EW studies for people with major mental disorders, noting that clinicians have expressed concerns about the appropriateness of EW for these populations, and it may be necessary to modify the instructions for depressed participants, such as providing more guidance or focusing on more positive aspects of experiences in writing.

There is limited evidence for behavioral changes following EW, including reduced aggression in adolescents (Kliewer et al., 2011) and improved exam performance (Ramirez & Beilock, 2011). However, EW has not been found to have a significant effect on health-related behaviors such as exercise, cigarette, and alcohol or prescription drug use (Frattaroli, 2006; Frisina et al., 2004; Pennebaker, Kiecolt-Glaser, & Glaser, 1988; Smyth, 1998).

Physical Health Outcomes

As noted, the physical health benefits of EW have tended to outweigh the mental health benefits (Baikie & Wilhelm, 2005; Frattaroli, 2006; Frisina et al., 2004). They include improvements in immune function (Pennebaker, Kiecolt-Glaser, & Glaser, 1988; Petrie, Booth, Pennebaker et al., 1995), including in patients with human immunodeficiency virus (HIV) infection (Petrie, Fontanilla, Thomas, Booth, & Pennebaker, 2004); blood pressure (McGuire, Greenberg, Gervirtz, 2005); liver function (Francis & Pennebaker, 1992); lung function in asthma; disease severity in rheumatoid arthritis (Smyth, Stone, Hurewitz, & Kaell, 1999); and number of days in hospital (Norman, Lumley, Dooley, & Diamond, 2004). In cancer patients, EW has been found to have a small but significant effect on physical symptoms, such as fatigue, pain,

and sleep disturbance, but not on psychological or cognitive symptoms, according to a recent meta-analysis of 14 trials (Oh & Kim, 2016).

Health care utilization is a commonly used outcome measure in EW studies, given the striking results of early EW trials (King & Miner, 2000; Pennebaker & Beall, 1986; Pennebaker & Francis, 1996). A meta-analysis of 30 studies found that EW significantly reduced health care utilization in healthy samples, but not in people with medical diagnoses, exposure to a stressful experience, or elevated psychological symptoms (Harris, 2006), consistent with previous meta-analyses outlined earlier. It could be argued that while in healthy populations, decreased health utilization may be an indicator of overall improved health or reduction in visits to the doctor for trivial or stress-related reasons, in medically ill populations, continued (or increased) health care utilization may be necessary to manage the condition.

Conclusions From Meta-Analyses

A subsequent, larger meta-analysis of 146 randomized controlled trials (RCTs) of EW among a wide range of clinical and healthy samples (Frattaroli, 2006) found significant positive effects of EW, albeit with even smaller effect sizes than the previous meta-analyses. Frattaroli (2006) reported an overall effect size of EW of unweighted $r = .075$ (equivalent to a Cohen's $d = .151$), with small but significant positive effects on psychological health outcomes ($r = .056$), physiological functioning ($r = .059$), and reported health ($r = .072$). He speculated that the smaller effect sizes than in previous meta-analyses were due to the higher proportion (almost half) of unpublished studies included (Frattaroli, 2006). In contrast to Harris (2006), Frattaroli (2006) found that the effects of EW were greater in populations with physical health problems, while Smyth (1998) had reported smaller effects on psychological health among students than in the general population. This is likely to reflect the greater potential for change in psychological health outcome measures between groups.

The most recent meta-analysis (Nyssen et al., 2016) examined 64 studies of all forms of therapeutic writing in populations with long-term conditions such as asthma, insomnia, or depression. The authors found that for studies of unfacilitated therapeutic writing (i.e., without the assistance, feedback, or support of a clinician or researcher), there were almost no significant effects on mental or physical health outcomes for people with long-term conditions, including insignificant effects on symptoms of depression or anxiety, but they did find a significant reduction in disease severity in inflammatory arthropathies, based on four studies (Nyssen et al., 2016). The authors suggested that facilitated therapeutic writing may be beneficial for people with long-term conditions, but this meta-analysis excluded studies conducted among people who had undergone stressful life events (such as bereavement or domestic violence), unless PTSD was clinically diagnosed. Given that greater effect sizes of EW have been found among participants who report a history of trauma or serious stressor (Frattaroli, 2006), it is possible that Nyssen et al. (2016) had excluded the studies likely to show the greatest benefits of EW. Further, this meta-analysis included a wider range of writing interventions, including poetry and diaries as well as EW, adding further heterogeneity. In contrast, studies that adhered to the "optimal conditions" of EW (such as privacy during sessions and specific disclosure instructions) had been found to have a greater mean effect size (Frattaroli, 2006). Other suggested reasons for differences in findings and small effect sizes in these meta-analyses included differing pools of RCT populations for each meta-analysis and heterogeneity in terms of outcomes assessed, number and duration of sessions, setting, and specific instructions (Nyssen et al., 2016). While Frattaroli's meta-analysis (2006) reported a small positive effect of EW on psychological health, "psychological health" was a broad domain including 13 categories, ranging from anger to coping strategies to dissociative experiences, with EW having differing effects on each. Hence, it may be difficult to capture the "true" degree of the impact of EW averaged across so many dimensions.

A meta-analysis of 11 RCT studies of EW specifically in women with breast cancer found a significant effect of EW using either an emotional prompt or a benefit-finding prompt on reducing negative somatic symptoms in patients in the 3-month follow-up group. This effect was short term, but again the writing studies produced greater effects on somatic symptoms rather than psychological ones (Zhou, Wu, An, & Li, 2015).

Adverse Effects of Expressive Writing: When Is Expressive Writing Not Advisable?

In addition to the pattern of short-term distress often associated with standard EW, there have been a small number of reports of longer term negative psychological effects of EW. For example, EW was found to worsen psychological symptoms in adult survivors of childhood abuse (Batten, Follette, Rasmussen, & Palm, 2002) and Vietnam veterans with PTSD (Gidron et al., 1996). A pilot RCT of EW for euthymic adults with type 2 diabetes found that 3 months later, EW was associated with worsening in depressive symptoms, with no change in diabetes distress (Dennick, Bridle, & Sturt, 2015). Of note, the latter EW study involved writing at home about any stressful experience over the past month, rather than a diabetes-specific topic or the original EW paradigm of "the most upsetting event/s of one's life." The authors noted their participants had difficulty engaging in EW due to difficulty in identifying and disclosing stressors, and there was little evidence of continuity in the topics discussed (Dennick et al., 2015).

Benefit-Finding Writing: The Benefits Without the Distress?

Conversely, writing about positive experiences tends to improve mood immediately after writing (Burton & King, 2004, 2009; King, 2001). For example, college students writing about their most positive life experience had significantly higher positive affect and significantly lower negative affect, compared to a control writing group, immediately post writing (Burton & King, 2009). Writing about one's best possible self has also been found to lead to greater increase in positive affect, and no difference in negative affect, compared to controls (Nazarian & Smyth, 2013). The promising results of these preliminary studies examining health effects of writing about *positive* experiences (Burton & King, 2004, 2009; King, 2001) have led researchers to question whether, for some stressors or medical conditions, BFW may have the same longer term health benefits as EW, without the short-term distress associated with EW.

In terms of immediate emotional responses, BFW appears to lie somewhere between EW and writing about positive life experiences. Writing about any positive thoughts and experiences about a specific stressor or illness tends to result in either no mood change (Frederiksen et al., 2017) or less distress than standard EW (Guastella & Dadds, 2006; Nazarian & Smyth, 2013). Two studies in nonclinical populations compared immediate emotional responses in multiple forms of writing interventions. Guastella and Dadds (2006) found that the BF group reported the greatest increase in positive affect, immediately post writing, versus all of the other writing groups, including traditional EW and modified EW. However, there were no differences between benefit-finding (BF) and control groups in levels of negative affect post writing, whereas the EW groups reported significantly increased negative affect post writing. Nazarian & Smyth (2013) reported their BF group showed a slight but significant increase in distress, compared to controls, but this increase in distress was significantly smaller than the increased distress reported by the standard EW group. Further, the BF group had significantly smaller decrease in positive affect than the EW group. Overall, BF writing is associated with less distress and more positive affect, immediately post writing, compared to standard EW.

In nonclinical samples, BFW has been associated with greater increases in posttraumatic growth (Guastella & Dadds, 2008) and greater use of cognitive insight words (Nazarian & Smyth, 2013), compared to EW. A pilot RCT among bereaved students, comparing BFW, "sense-making writing" and EW with a control group, found significant differences between the groups in symptoms of depression, PTSD, and grief, with the most substantial reductions in these symptoms appearing to be among those in the BFW group (Lichtenthal & Cruess, 2010). Whereas the reductions within the BFW group were not statistically significant (probably due to small sample size), the results were promising for BFW (Lichtenthal & Cruess, 2010). They noted that BFW may have been more suited to their sample than other bereaved ones, as their sample had mostly experienced their loss over a year ago and was neither very distressed nor met criteria for prolonged grief disorder.

A study (Lu & Stanton, 2010) comparing multiple forms of writing interventions among students found that a variant similar to BFW (termed "cognitive reappraisal," involving writing about positive thoughts about a stressful event, and related challenges, opportunities, and coping strategies used) significantly reduced physical symptoms 1 and 2 months later, compared to forms of writing not involving cognitive reappraisal. However, EW alone did not reduce physical symptoms. The authors concluded that this was consistent with previous findings that writing about the benefits of a traumatic or upsetting event in the absence of negative emotional disclosure can improve physical health.

In women with early-stage breast cancer, both BFW and EW groups had significantly fewer medical appointments for cancer-related morbidities, relative to the control group (Stanton et al., 2002). In adults with lupus or rheumatoid arthritis, both BFW and EW groups had lower fatigue at 3 months,

relative to a control writing group (Danoff-Burg, Agee, Romanoff, Kremer, & Strosberg, 2006), while BFW appeared more useful in pain reduction associated with high trait anxiety. Thus, the current, limited evidence suggests that BFW may provide similar health benefits to EW but without the associated short-term distress. This warrants further investigation.

Moderators of Positive and Benefit-Finding Writing
Benefit Finding

Given that BF has been associated with adaptive coping (Cavell, Broadbent, Donkin, Gear, & Morton, 2016), and more positive psychological adjustment to stressors (Algoe & Stanton, 2009; Helgeson, Reynolds, & Tomlich, 2006), it is possible that increased levels of BF mediate the mental and physical health effects of BF writing. Posttraumatic growth, a concept closely related to BF (Sears, Stanton, & Danoff-Burg, 2003), has been found to increase following BF writing more than following EW (Guastella & Dadds, 2008). Further, BF has been found to increase following more intensive psychological interventions (Chiba, Miyamoto, & Harada, 2015; Groarke, Curtis, & Kerin, 2013). Somewhat surprisingly, BF is rarely assessed as an outcome or potential moderator in studies of BF writing. One current trial of trial of BF writing for caregivers is assessing BF as an outcome, according to its published protocol (Brand, O'Connell, & Gallagher, 2015). To our knowledge, there are no published trials that indicate whether or not BF, as assessed by self-report measures, actually increases after BF writing.

Global Cognitive Focus

It has been hypothesized that positive mood promotes a broadened scope of attention and more flexible cognitive processing (Fredrickson, 2001; Isen, 1990) and that writing about positive life experiences may promote an ongoing "broadened cognitive focus" through eliciting a more expansive view of the self and world (Burton & King, 2009). There is some evidence to support this, with one study finding that cognitive broadening partially mediated the effect of a positive writing intervention on improved physical health (Burton & King, 2009). However, as noted by the authors of this study, the underlying physiological causes of improved health following positive writing remain unknown. For example, how does a broadened cognitive focus promoted by positive writing translate to improved physical health? Burton and King (2009) suggest that a general decline in heart rate reactivity to stressors experienced following the writing may be a potential moderator.

Structured/Combined Expressive Writing and Benefit-Finding Writing Interventions for Specific Stressors

More recently, researchers have developed therapeutic writing interventions for specific stressors, which involve different instructions for each of the three or four writing sessions. Typically, these involve EW for the initial sessions, followed by BFW and/or writing about the future (in relation to the same stressor) in the later session/s. These interventions are designed to give participants the opportunity to express and explore their negative thoughts and feelings about the stressor before aiming to induce desired cognitive changes by encouraging them to identify any positive thoughts and feelings about that stressor (Frederiksen et al., 2017). For example, a recent study of infertile couples involved EW for the first two sessions (writing their thoughts and feelings about involuntary childlessness), followed by a third BFW session (writing about "positive thoughts and feelings that they experienced in relation to their involuntary childlessness") (Frederiksen et al., 2017, p. 394). Here, participants in the writing intervention group were relative to those in the control writing group. Compared to the control writing group, participants reported higher levels of negative mood, and lower levels of positive emotions, immediately after their EW sessions, with no mood change after their BFW session of BFW, and significantly reduced depressive symptoms 14–16 weeks later,

In another example of structured EW, women who had completed treatment for early-stage breast cancer were provided with different topics on each of 4 days of writing, including their deepest thoughts and feelings about cancer (Day 1), making sense of cancer and its meaning (Day 2), perceived benefits of their experience with cancer and challenges overcome (Day 3), and finally, thoughts about the future, including coping strategies (Gellaitry et al., 2010). Participants who followed these instructions had significantly greater satisfaction with their emotional support, compared to a control group (Gellaitry et al., 2010).

Mechanisms of Expressive Writing

Perhaps more so than for most other psychological interventions, the mechanisms of the effects of EW on mental and physical health remain unclear (Low,

Stanton, & Danoff-Burg, 2006; Nyssen et al., 2016). There are several hypotheses regarding how EW achieves its effects. However, while each of these proposed mechanisms has been tested separately, there have been few studies considering multiple associations simultaneously in order to examine their relative predictive utility (Niles, Byrne Haltom, Lieberman, Hur, & Stanton, 2016). One intriguing question is how the seemingly different interventions of EW and BF writing can both result in positive health outcomes (Low et al., 2006). Evidence suggests multiple pathways for the effects of these writing interventions (Smyth & Pennebaker, 2008), with some specific to EW.

Inhibition

The original theory of EW, relying on the mechanism of emotional inhibition, proposed that active inhibition of emotions, thoughts, and behaviors increases arousal within the autonomic and central nervous systems, and over time leads to stress and ill health, whereas subsequent release (i.e., catharsis) releases stress and later improves health, in terms of autonomic function and health visits (Pennebaker & Beall, 1986; Pennebaker, Hughes, & O'Heeron, 1987). If such release following inhibition of thoughts and feelings is the main mechanism of EW, then it would be expected that the benefits of EW would be greater when participants write about traumas that have not previously been disclosed (Kallay, 2015). Frattaroli's (2006) meta-analysis found that studies that instructed participants to only write about previously undisclosed topics did have marginally higher effect sizes for psychological health, but not for physical health or subjective impact. However, the inhibition theory cannot account for the findings of Greenberg, Wortman, and Stone (1996), who reported that participants who wrote about an imaginary trauma (i.e., one they had not experienced and therefore by definition had not been subject to inhibition) benefited as much as those who wrote about a real trauma in terms of reduced health care utilization. Greenberg and colleagues (1996) suggested that this indicated that expression of previously suppressed memories and related affect was not necessary for the health benefits of EW, and that other mechanisms, such as habituation, catharsis, and cognitive change, may explain the benefits experienced by the "imaginary trauma" group.

Exposure

Several researchers have suggested that some of the benefits of EW may be explained by its similarity to exposure therapy (Lepore, Greenberg, Bruno, & Smyth, 2002; Sloan, Marx, & Epstein, 2005). Exposure therapy is the cornerstone of treatment of anxiety-related disorders and PTSD, and it involves participants approaching feared, but safe, objects, situations, thoughts, sensations, and memories, with the goal of reducing fear reactions to these stimuli (Foa & McLean, 2016). Mowrer's (1960) two-factor learning theory posited that avoidance maintains anxiety by preventing extinction learning (that is, learning that a condition stimulus no longer signals harm), and that exposure to the conditioned stimulus without escape eventually reduces the fear response. This conceptualization of exposure therapy was further developed by Foa and Kozak's (1986) emotional processing theory, which incorporated the role of cognitive structures related to the feared stimuli (Foa & McLlean, 2016). During exposure therapy for PTSD, a patient is asked to recount the traumatic experience in great detail, verbally or in writing (Craske et al., 2008), which clearly overlaps with EW. If repeated exposure to emotional memories of stressful events is a mechanism through which EW works, this would be indicated by both within-session and between-session habituation (reduction) of anxiety or distress (Foa & McClean, 2016), and EW should be more effective for participants who write repeatedly of the same event, in greater detail, and who stay focused on the stressful event in their writing (Niles et al., 2016).

There is substantial evidence for repeated exposure being at least one mechanism of EW. Writing repeatedly about the same trauma over three sessions has been associated with greater improvements in physical health and PTSD symptoms than writing about three different events (Sloan, Marx, & Epstein, 2005). Frattaroli's (2006) meta-analysis revealed that EW leads to reductions in trauma-related stress, and that more sessions and longer session duration produce stronger benefits. Further, between-session habituation of distress in EW has been demonstrated (Pascual-Leone et al., 2016). However, contrary to predictions, neither the similarity of writing content in different sessions nor the extent to which participants stayed on topic during their writing has been found to relate to health improvements (Campbell & Pennebaker, 2003; Pennebaker & Francis, 1996).

Given that EW studies often involve participants writing about a variety of stressful experiences, such as students writing about experiences ranging from loneliness at college to suicide attempts (Pennebaker, Colder, & Sharp, 1990), who may or may not have a trauma history or symptoms of PTSD, it is possible that the mechanism of repeated exposure may apply more for those participants with symptoms of PTSD. This is supported by the findings that EW is more effective for those with a trauma history (Frattaroli, 2006) and those who write about more severe stressors (Pachankis & Goldfried, 2010).

Putting Feelings Into Words

Early "catharsis" theory (Scheff, 1979) proposed that vividly experiencing emotions in the context of present safety is required for healing and health benefits, as it would allow participants to develop perceptions of mastery over distressing feelings (Greenberg et al., 1996; Scheff, 1979). This is supported by the finding that the degree of arousal (indicated by cortisol levels) during the first session of EW predicted greater improvement in psychological symptoms 1 month later (Sloan & Marx, 2004a). However, this overlaps with emotional processing theory for exposure therapy, which postulates that the fear structures must first be activated, in order to be modified (Foa & Kozak, 1986; Foa & McClean, 2016).

Affect labeling or "putting feelings into words" (Lieberman, Inagaki, Tabibnia, & Crockett, 2011) has also been proposed as a mechanism of EW (Sloan & Marx, 2004). Multiple neuroimaging studies have demonstrated that affect labeling can reduce affect-related responses in the amygdala, an area of the brain important in emotional processing (Lieberman et al., 2007, 2011).

Affect labeling while watching negative emotional pictures has been associated with lower distress, compared to passive watching (Lieberman et al., 2011). In EW studies, the potential mechanism of labeling and describing emotions has been investigated by linguistic analyses using the Linguistic Inquiry and Word Count software (LIWC; Pennebaker & Francis, 1996; Pennebaker, Booth, Boyd, & Francis, 2015), to examine whether the rate of "emotional" word use is associated with greater effects of EW on psychological or physical health. As noted previously, early research found that increasing rates of positive emotion words (such as *happy*, *love*) and a moderate number of negative emotion words (such as *angry*, *hurt*) were associated with greater effects of EW (Pennebaker, Mayne, & Francis, 1997; Pennebaker & Seagal, 1999). More recent research has found that the effects of EW are partially mediated by higher use of positive emotion words combined with moderate use of negative emotion words (Williamson et al., 2017), an increase in positive emotion words (Hevey & Wilczkiewicz, 2014; Pulverman, Lorenz, & Meston, 2015), and decrease in negative emotion words (Pulverman et al., 2015). A decrease in use of negative emotion words across EW sessions has also been associated with higher levels of self-distancing when reflecting on stressors following EW (Park, Ayduk, & Kross, 2016). Therefore, while the use of emotion words is related to the effects of EW, it is *changes* in the pattern of emotional word use, and their relationship with emotional regulation processes, that predicts improvement following EW.

One unanswered question is whether participants continue to express emotions to a greater degree in their everyday life following emotional expression during EW. While alexithymia has mainly been examined as a moderator of the effects of EW, one recent study suggests that EW can also reduce alexithymia (Tarquini, Di Trani, & Solano, 2016). An RCT of employees subjected to work relocation found that EW resulted in significantly reduced scores on a self-report measure of alexithymia up to 7 months later, including significant decreases in Difficulty Identifying Feelings, Difficulty Describing Feelings, and Externally Oriented Thinking subscales (Tarquini et al., 2016). The authors suggested that EW may have activated skills necessary to process emotional aspects of a stressful event. However, this study did not examine whether the reduction in alexithymia mediated the improvements in psychological well-being and occupational burnout also found in the EW group (Tarquini et al., 2016). The possible role of reduced alexithymia following EW warrants further investigation, given that alexithymia has been associated with poorer outcomes following stressful experiences (Ziadni et al., 2017).

Creation of a Narrative and Cognitive Processing

Another proposed mechanism involves the formation of a narrative regarding a stressful event (Pennebaker & Smyth, 1999; Smyth et al., 2001). Memories of traumatic events tend to be more disorganized than other memories, and it has been suggested that the creation of narratives of traumatic events can enable the experience to be cognitively organized, stored, and assimilated into memory, thereby reducing the distress associated with the event (Foa & Riggs, 1993). In support of this, narrative writing has been found to result in less illness-related activity restriction (but more avoidant thinking) than a fragmented writing intervention

involving lists (Smyth et al., 2001). Further, other EW studies have found that higher ratings of the degree of narrative structure of the writings (using such criteria as a clear beginning, middle, and end, and a coherent framework of characters with their interrelations explained) has been associated with reduced depressive symptoms and perceived stress (Danoff-Burg, Mosher, Seawall & Agee, 2010), and that greater narrative coherence predicted lower divorce-related distress and depressive symptoms (Bourassa, Manvelian, Boals, Mehl, & Sbarra, 2017).

The role of cognitive reappraisals during EW has also been assessed in relation to improvements following EW. Linguistic analyses using LIWC have found that benefits of EW are associated with increasing numbers of causation words, such as *because* and *effect* (Park et al., 2016; Pennebaker, Mayne, & Francis, 1997; Pennebaker & Seagal, 1999; Warner et al., 2006) and increasing numbers of cognitive insight words, such as *understand* and *reason* (Pennebaker, Mayne, & Francis, 1997; Pennebaker & Seagal, 1999; Warner et al., 2006). Moreover, greater use of insight words has been associated with greater posttraumatic growth following EW (Stockton, Joseph, & Hunt, 2014). However, these results have not always been replicated (Williamson et al., 2017).

As well as examining indicators of cognitive change *during* EW, researchers have suggested that EW may result in more long-lasting cognitive changes by enabling participants to change self-schemas (Pulverman, Boyd, Stanton, & Meston, 2017). Schemas are cognitive frameworks or generalizations, through which one selectively processes and interprets information (Markus, 1977). Thus, schemas can affect people's perceptions and behaviors and be associated with negative psychological consequences when self-schema are negative or unhelpful, such as "I am vulnerable" or "I am defective" (Young, Klosko, & Weshaar, 2003). A recent study of EW for women with a history of childhood sexual abuse compared essays on sexual identity written by participants at pre-EW, post-EW, and up to 6 months later, using a "meaning extraction method" of language analysis (Pulverman, Boyd, Stanton, & Meston, 2017). Following EW, the women showed changes in their use of certain sexual abuse self-schema themes, such as reduced use of the abuse theme and increased use of the existentialism theme (reflecting meaning-making). The authors suggested that EW enabled participants to process their history of abuse, by organizing their memories and emotions about the abuse and/or habituating to thoughts of the abuse, resulting in a reduced salience of the abuse in their later essays of their identity (Pulverman et al., 2017). However, it is not known if such changes in self-schema relate to improvements in physical or mental health following EW. Future research could use this innovative method of examining changes in self-schema following EW in other populations and investigate whether such changes mediate improvements in other outcomes.

Finally, several studies have demonstrated that cognitive processing and other mechanisms, such as habituation from repeated exposure, are related to improvements following EW. For example, Lu and Stanton (2010) compared four types of writing among students: EW alone, "cognitive reappraisal" alone, combined EW and cognitive appraisal, and control writing, and they found the combination of EW and cognitive appraisal to be the most effective in reducing physical symptoms. Niles and colleagues (2016) coded EW essays for indicators of a range of mechanisms and found that greater use of self-affirmation statements (indicating positive reflections on the self) and greater level of detail in describing the event (an indicator of exposure) predicted reduced anxiety following EW.

Thus, as for exposure and emotional expression, there is substantial evidence that formation of a narrative and other cognitive changes during and after EW provides mechanisms of its psychological and physical health benefits.

Physiological Mechanisms

One of the most intriguing questions regarding EW is how this brief psychological intervention results in *physical* health benefits. For example, two studies have reported that EW led to improved wound healing, but not improvements in perceived stress (Koschwanez et al., 2013; Weinman, Ebrecht, Scott, Walburn, & Dyson, 2008). Thus, if wound-healing effects of EW are not operating via reductions in stress (Koschwanez et al., 2017), at least stress as captured by self-report measures, then one of the key challenges is to understand how these psychological processes interact with physiological processes (Lutgendorf & Ullrich, 2002).

As outlined previously, EW has effects on cortisol levels (Sloan & Marx, 2004a; Smyth et al., 2008), heart rate variability (Beckwith McGuire et al., 2005; Seeley et al., 2017), and immune functioning (Pennebaker, Kiecolt-Glaser, & Glaser, 1988; Petrie, Booth, Pennebaker et al., 1995; Petrie et al., 2004). However, pathway models, in which psychological

processes lead to physiological processing, which subsequently lead to physical health changes, require further investigation. For example, Lutgendorf and Ullrich (2002) proposed a model (p. 190) in which EW leads to decreased chronic stress, improved mood, and decreased PTSD symptoms, which then leads to normalized cortisol and immune function, which in turn leads to improvements in physical health.

A small number of studies have examined these interactions. For example, it has been hypothesized that EW reduces stress-related thinking, which in turn reduces the cortisol awakening response and subsequently reduces somatic symptoms. One study investigating this hypothesis (O'Connor et al., 2013) found that higher levels of perseverative cognition (worry and stress-related thinking) during standard EW predicted increased cortisol levels after awakening at 4-week follow-up, and increased upper respiratory infection (URI) symptoms, compared to those who had lower levels of perseverative cognition during the intervention. However, this study found the two writing interventions examined— standard expressive writing and positive writing—did not have a significant effect, compared to a control condition, on cortisol awakening response or URI. Therefore, the study did not provide evidence for this physiological pathway as mediating the effects of expressive writing.

Heart rate variability (HRV) has been examined in relation to psychological processes and physical outcomes. Bourassa and colleagues compared traditional EW, narrative EW, and control writing and found that only narrative EW resulted in increased HRV 7 months later (Bourassa, Allen, Mehl & Sbarra, 2017). However, it could not be examined as a mediator of reduced blood pressure, given that blood pressure did not differ between the groups at follow-up.

Conclusions, Directions for Expressive Writing Research, and Unanswered Critical Issues

EW seems best suited for people with mild-to-moderate psychological distress. Studies of participants with very little distress may find it difficult to demonstrate benefits due to a "floor" effect, whereas participants with a severe distress or mental illness may find EW too distressing or difficult to engage with and require a more intensive therapist-supported psychological treatment. Indeed, the majority of EW studies are conducted among participants experiencing some degree of distress due to a specific stressor or medical condition, but not meeting criteria for a mental illness.

It is recommended that EW be undertaken with therapist support and follow-up in vulnerable populations (with severe trauma history, or difficulty engaging in EW), given the likelihood of immediate short-term distress and possibility of psychological symptoms worsening ensuing months in these groups.

Expressive writing has been trialed across a broad range of situations, involving mental and physical health domains. The trials are of mixed quality and, as noted, cover a range of instructions, target groups, and writing conditions. However, the emerging themes include the small but significant improvements in physical health parameters, more so than in mental health parameters. The interventions are targeted at stress-related conditions and situations, and effects may be greater in people with high trait anxiety and those who are better at disclosing; however, EW has also been found to be useful for people who find it difficult to disclose in face-to-face situations.

The mechanisms for improvement post EW are still unclear. There are recent developments in making writing instructions more specific and exploring writing that involves benefit finding, even in very stressful situations such as potentially life-threatening illness. The writing task does need to take the individual writer in account, the degree of likely stress associated with the writing, location, degree of oversight, degree of privacy and disclosure, and therapist interaction, but this is true of most therapeutic interventions. Some of the remaining questions concerning expressive writing include the following:

1. How do we clarify the pathway of stress reduction, from expressive writing to improvements in physical health?

2. Whom does EW work best for? Given that overall effect sizes are small, is this because most participants are gaining a small benefit from EW, or because some participants have no benefit but others have a significant degree of benefit? If the latter, who is most likely to benefit?

3. Is the best approach to start with EW and follow with BFW?

4. How constrained should the instructions be? Is it better to let the writer determine whether he or she needs to write about distressing events before engaging in BFW?

5. What is the best method of disseminating EW? A major appeal of EW is the potential as a home-based, cost-effective, self-help intervention. However, research to date suggests that screening

and therapist support may be required, particularly in dealing with conditions which involve a great deal of distress.

6. How can EW be disseminated in a cost-effective manner while taking into account these clinical considerations— online programs with limited clinical support involving screening, and monitoring by clinicians who only provide support when needed?

On a more personal note, we have found that using expressive writing in clinical settings has been a rewarding experience. People generally like to try it, and we have had very positive feedback in both settings, which show that people find the experience challenging but rewarding. Some need encouragement, and feedback about the research can be useful in providing motivation. In research settings, we have identified some of the interesting questions still to be answered.

References

Aldao, A., Mennin, D. S., & McLaughlin, K. A. (2013). Differentiating worry and rumination: Evidence from heart rate variability during spontaneous regulation. *Cognitive Therapy and Research, 37*(3), 613–619.

Algoe, S.B., & Stanton, A.L. (2009) Is Benefit Finding Good for Individuals With Chronic Disease? In Park, C. L., Lechner, S.C., Antoni, M.H., & Stanton, A. L. (Eds.) Medical Illness and Positive Life Change: Can Crisis Lead to Personal Transformation? Washington, DC, US: American Psychological Association.

Alparone, F. R., Pagliaro. S., & Rizzo, I. (2015). The words to tell their own pain: linguistic markers of cognitive reappraisal in mediating benefits of expressive writing. *Journal of Social and Clinical Psychology, 34*, 495–507.

Baikie, K. A., Geerligs, L., & Wilhelm, K. (2012). Expressive writing and positive writing for participants with mood disorders: An online randomized controlled trial. *Journal of Affective Disorders, 136*(3), 310–319.

Baikie, K. A., & Wilhelm, K. (2005) Emotional and physical health benefits of expressive writing. *Advances in Psychiatric Treatment, 11*, 338–346.

Batten, S. V., Follette, V. M., Hall, M. L., & Palm, K. M. (2002). Physical and psychological effects of written emotional disclosure among sexual abuse survivors. *Behavior Therapy, 33*, 107–122.

Beckwith McGuire, K. M., Greenberg, M. A., & Gervitz, R. (2005). Autonomic effects of expressive writing in individuals with elevated blood pressure. *Journal of Health Psychology, 10*(2), 197–209.

Beyer, J. A., Lumley, M. A., Latsch, D. V., Oberleitner, L. M. S., Carty, J. N., & Radcliffe, A. M. (2014). Computer-based written emotional disclosure: The effects of advance or real-time guidance and moderation by Big 5 personality traits. *Anxiety, Stress and Coping, 27*, 477–493.

Blasio, P. D., Camisasca, E., Caravita, S. C. S., Ionio, C., Milani, L., & Valtolina, G. G. (2015). The effects of expressive writing on postpartum depression and posttraumatic stress symptoms. *Psychological Reports, 117*, 856–882.

Bourassa, K. J., Allen, J. J. B., Mehl, M. R., & Sbarra, D. A. (2017). The impact of narrative expressive writing on heart rate, heart rate variability, and blood pressure following marital separation. *Psychosomatic Medicine, 79*, 697–705.

Bourassa, K. J., Manvelian, A., Boals, A., Mehl, M, & Sbarra, D. A. (2017). Tell me a story: The creation of narrative as a mechanism of psychological recovery following marital separation. *Journal of Social and Clinical Psychology, 36*, 359–379.

Bragdon, R. S., & Lombardo, W. T. (2012). Written disclosure treatment for posttraumatic stress disorder in substance use disorder inpatient. *Behavior Modification, 36*, 875–896.

Brand, C., O'Connell, B. H., & Gallagher, S. (2015). A randomised controlled trial of benefit finding in caregivers: The Building Resources in Caregivers Study Protocol. *Health Psychology Open*, July–December, 1–7. doi:10.1177/2055102915595019

Bryan, J. L., & Lu, Q. (2016). Vision for improvement: Expressive writing as an intervention for people with Stargardt's disease, a rare eye disease. *Journal of Health Psychology, 21*, 709–719.

Burton, C. M., & King, L. A. (2004). The health benefits of writing about intensely positive experiences. *Journal of Research in Personality, 38*, 150–163.

Burton, C. M., & King, L. A. (2008). Effects of (very) brief writing on health: The two-minute miracle. *British Journal of Health Psychology, 13*, 9–14.

Burton, C. M., & King, L. A. (2009). The health benefits of writing about positive experiences: The role of broadened cognition. *Psychology and Health, 24*, 867–879.

Campbell, R. S., & Pennebaker, J. W. (2003). The secret life of pronouns: Flexibility in writing style and physical health. *Psychological Science, 14*, 60–65.

Cavell, S., Broadbent, E., Donkin, L., Gear, K., Morton, R. P. (2016). Observations of benefit finding in head and neck cancer patients. *European Archives of Oto-Rhino-Laryngology, 273*, 479–485.

Chiba, R., Miyamoto, Y., & Harada, N. (2015). Psychological transformation by an intervention to facilitate benefit finding among people with chronic mental illness in Japan. *Psychiatric Care, 52*, 139–144.

Chung, C. K., & Pennebaker, J. W. (2008). Variations in the spacing of expressive writing sessions. *British Journal of Health Psychology, 13*, 15–21.

Craske, M. G., Kircanski, K., Zelikowsky, M., Mystkowski, J., Chowdhury, N., & Baker, A. (2008). Optimizing inhibitory learning during exposure therapy. *Behaviour Research and Therapy, 46*, 5–27.

Crawford, J., Wilhelm, K., Robins, L., & Proudfoot, J. (2017). Writing for health: Rationale and protocol for a randomized controlled trial of Internet-based benefit-finding writing for adults with type 1 or type 2 diabetes. *JMIR Research Protocols, 6*, e42.

Danoff-Burg, S., Agee, J. D., Romanoff, N. R., Kremer, J. M., & Strosberg, J. M. (2006). Benefit finding and expressive writing in adults with lupus or rheumatoid arthritis. *Psychology and Health, 21*, 651–665.

Danoff-Burg, S., Mosher, C. E., Seawall, A. H., & Agee, J. D. (2010). Does narrative writing instruction enhance the benefits of expressive writing? *Anxiety, Stress and Coping, 23*, 341–352.

Dennick, K., Bridle, C., & Sturt, J. (2015). Written emotional disclosure for adults with type 2 diabetes: A primary care feasibility study. *Primary Health Care Research and Development, 16*, 179–187.

Denson, T. F., Grisham, J. R., & Moulds, M. L. (2011). Cognitive reappraisal increases heart rate variability in response to an anger provocation. *Motivation and Emotion, 35*, 14–22.

Foa, E. B., & Kozak, M. J. (1986). Emotional processing of fear: exposure to corrective information. *Psychological Bulletin, 99*, 20–35.

Foa, E. B., & McLean, C. P. (2016). The efficacy of exposure therapy for anxiety-related disorders and its underlying mechanisms: The case of OCD and PTSD. *Annual Review of Clinical Psychology, 12*, 1–28.

Foa, E. B., & Riggs, D. S. (1993). Posttraumatic stress disorder in rape victims. In H. B. Oldham, A. Tasman, & M. B. Riba (Eds.), *American Psychiatric Press Review of Psychiatry* (vol. 12, pp. 273–303). Washington, DC: American Psychiatric Press.

Francis, M. E., & Pennebaker, J. W. (1992). Putting stress into words: The impact of writing on physiological, absentee, and self-reported emotional well-being measures. *American Journal of Health Promotion, 6*, 280–287.

Frattaroli, J. (2006) Experimental disclosure and its moderators: A meta-analysis. *Psychological Bulletin, 132*, 823–865.

Frederiksen, Y., O'Toole, M. S., Mehlsen, M. Y., Hauge, B., Elbaek, H. O., Zachariae, R., & Ingerslev, H. J. (2017). The effect of expressive writing for infertile couples: A randomized controlled trial. *Psychology and Counselling, 32*, 391–402.

Fredrickson, B. L. (2001). The role of positive emotions in positive psychology: The broaden-and-build theory of positive emotions. *American Psychologist, 56*, 218–226.

Frisina, P. G., Borod, J. C., & Lepore, S. J. (2004). A meta-analysis of the effects of written emotional disclosure on the health outcomes of clinical populations. *Journal of Nervous and Mental Disease, 192*, 629–634.

Garrison, A. M., & Kahn, J. H. (2010). Intraindividual relations between the intensity and disclosure of daily emotional events: The moderating role of depressive symptoms. *Journal of Counselling Psychology, 57*, 187–197.

Gellaitry, G., Peters, K., Bloomfield, D., & Horne, R. (2010). Narrowing the gap: The effects of an expressive writing intervention on perceptions of actual and ideal emotional support in women who have completed treatment for early stage breast cancer. *Psych-Oncology, 19*, 77–84.

Gidron, Y., Peri, T, Connolly, J., & Shalev, A. Y. (1996). Written disclosure in posttraumatic stress disorder: Is it beneficial for the patient? *Journal of Nervous and Mental Disease, 184*, 505–507.

Gortner, E-M., Rude, S. S., & Pennebaker, J. W. (2006). Benefits of expressive writing in lowering rumination and depressive symptoms. *Behavior Therapy, 37*, 292–303.

Greenberg, M. A., Wortman, C. B., & Stone, A. A. (1996). Emotional expression and physical health: Revising traumatic memories or fostering self-regulation. *Journal of Personality and Social Psychology, 71*(3), 588–602.

Groarke, A., Curtis, R., & Kerin, M. (2013). Cognitive-behavioural stress management enhances adjustment in women with breast cancer. *British Journal of Health Psychology, 18*, 623–641.

Guastella, A. J., & Dadds, M. R. (2006). Cognitive-behavioral models of emotional writing: A validation study. *Cognitive Therapy Research, 30*, 397–414

Guastella, A. J., & Dadds, M. R. (2008). Cognitive-behavioural emotion writing tasks: A controlled trial of multiple processes. *Journal of Behaviour Therapy and Experimental Psychiatry, 39*, 558–66.

Harris, A. H. S. (2006). Does expressive writing reduce health care utilization? A meta-analysis of randomized trials. *Journal of Consulting and Clinical Psychology, 74,* 243–252.

Harvey-Knowles, J., Sanders, E., Ko, L., Manusov, V., & Yi, J. (2017). The impact of written emotional disclosure on cancer caregivers' perceptions of burden, stress, and depression: A randomized controlled trial. *Health Communication, 3,* 1–9.

Helgeson, V. S., Reynolds, K. A., & Tomlich, P. L. (2006). A meta-analytic review of benefit-finding and growth. *Journal of Consulting and Clinical Psychology, 74,* 797–816.

Hevey, D., & Wilczkiewicz, E. (2014). Changes in language use mediate expressive writing's benefits on health-related quality of life following myocardial infarction. *Health Psychology and Behavioral Medicine, 2*(1), 1053–1066.

Horsch, A., Tolsa, J. F., Gilbert, L., du Chene, L. J., Muller-Nix, C., & Bickle Graz, M. (2016). Improving maternal health following preterm birth using an expressive writing intervention: A randomized controlled trial. *Child Psychiatry and Human Development, 47,* 780–791.

Hughes, C. F., Uhlmann, C., & Pennebaker, J. W. (1994). The body's response to processing emotional trauma: Linking verbal text with autonomic activity. *Journal of Personality, 62,* 565–585.

Ironson, G., O'Cleirigh, C., Leserman, J., Stuetzle, R., Fordiani, J., Fletcher, M., & Schneiderman, N. (2013). Gender-specific effects of an augmented written emotional disclosure intervention on posttraumatic, depressive, and HIV-disease-related outcomes: A randomized controlled trial. *Journal of Consulting and Clinical Psychology, 81,* 284–298.

Isen, A. M. (1990). The influence of positive and negative affect on cognitive organization: Some implications for development. In N. Stein, B. Leventhal, & T. Trabasso (Eds.), *Psychological and biological approaches to emotion* (pp. 75–94). Hillsdale, NJ: Erlbaum.

Kállay, E. (2015). Physical and psychological benefits of written emotional expression: Review of meta-analyses and recommendations. *European Psychologist, 20,* 242–251.

King, L. A. (2001). The health benefits of writing about life goals. *Personality and Social Psychology Bulletin, 27*(7), 798–807.

King, L. A., & Miner, K. N. (2000). Writing about the perceived benefits of traumatic events: Implications for physical health. *Personality and Social Psychology Bulletin, 47,* 1105–1117.

Kliewer, W., Lepore, S. J., Farrell, A. D., Allison, K. W., Meyer, A. L., Sullivan, T. N., & Greene, A.Y. (2011). A school-based expressive writing intervention for at-risk urban adolescents' aggressive behavior and emotional lability. *Journal of Clinical Child and Adolescent Psychology, 40,* 693–705.

Koschwanez, H. E., Kerse, N., Darragh, M., Jarrett, P., Booth, R. J., & Broadbent, E. (2013). Expressive writing and wound healing in older adults: A randomized controlled trial. *Psychosomatic Medicine, 75,* 581–590.

Koschwanez, H. E., Robinson, H., Beban, G., MacCormick, A., Hill, A., Windsor, J., Booth, R., Jullig, M., & Broadbent, E. (2017). Randomized clinical trial of expressive writing on wound healing following bariatric surgery. *Health Psychology, 36,* 630–640.

Kovac, S. H., & Range L. M. (2002). Does writing about suicidal thoughts and feelings reduce them? *Suicide and Life Threatening Behavior, 32,* 428–440.

Krpan, K. M., Kross, E., Berman, M. G., Deldin, P. J., Askren, M. K., & Jonides, J. (2013). An everyday activity as a treatment for depression: The benefits of expressive writing for people diagnosed with major depressive disorder. *Journal of Affective Disorders, 150*(3), 1148–1151.

Lepore, S. J., & Greenberg, M. A. (2002). Mending broken hearts: Effects of expressive writing on mood, cognitive processing, social adjustment and health following a relationship breakup. *Psychology and Health, 17,* 547–560.

Lepore, S. J., Greenberg, M. A., Bruno, M., & Smyth, J. M. (2002). Expressive writing and health: Self-regulation of emotion-related experience, physiology, and behaviour. In S. J. Lepore & J. M. Smyth (Eds.), *The writing cure: How expressive writing promotes health and emotional well-being* (pp. 99–117). Washington DC: American Psychological Association.

Lichtenthal, W. G., Cruess, D. G. (2010). Effects of directed written disclosure on grief and distress symptoms among bereaved individuals. *Death Studies, 34,* 475–99.

Lieberman, M. D., Eisenberg, N. I., Crockett, M. J., Tom, S., Pfeifer, J. H., & Way, B. M. (2007). Putting feelings into words: Affect labelling disrupts amygdala activity in response to affective stimuli. *Psychological Science, 18,* 421–428.

Lieberman, M. D., Inagaki, T. K., Tabibnia, G., & Crockett, M. J. (2011). Subjective responses to emotional stimuli during labelling, reappraisal, and distraction. *Emotion* 11, 468–480.

Levant, R. F., Hall, R. J., Williams, C. M., & Hasan, N. T. (2009). Gender differences in alexithymia. *Psychology of Men and Masculinity, 10,* 190–203.

Lovell, B., Moss, M., & Wetherall, M. A. (2016). Assessing the feasibility and efficacy of written benefit-finding for caregivers of children with autism: A pilot study. *Journal of Family Studies, 22,* 32–42.

Low, C. A., Stanton, A. L., & Danoff-Burg, S. (2006). Expressive disclosure and benefit finding writing among breast cancer patients: Mechanisms for positive health effects. *Health Psychology, 25,* 181–189.

Lu, Q., & Stanton, A. L. (2010). How benefits of expressive writing vary as a function of writing instructions, ethnicity, and ambivalence over emotional expression. *Psychology and Health, 25,* 669–684.

Lumley, M. A., Sklar, E. R., & Carty, J. N. (2012). Emotional disclosure interventions for chronic pain: From the laboratory to the clinic. *Translational Behavioral Medicine, 2,* 73–81.

Lutgendorf, S. K., & Ullrich, P. (2002). Cognitive processing, disclosure, and health: Psychological and physiological mechanisms. In S. J. Lepore & J. M. Smyth (Eds.), *The writing cure: How expressive writing promotes health and emotional well-being* (pp. 177–196). Washington, DC: American Psychological Association.

Markus, H. (1977). Self-schemata and processing information about the self. *Journal of Personality and Social Psychology, 35,* 63–78.

McGuire, K. M., Greenberg, M. A., & Gervirtz, R. (2005). Autonomic effects of expressive writing in individuals with elevated blood pressure. *Journal of Health Psychology, 10,* 197–209.

Meston, C. M., Lorenz, T. A., & Stephenson, K. R. (2013). Effects of expressive writing on sexual dysfunction, depression, and PTSD in women with a history of childhood sexual abuse: Results from a randomized clinical trial. *The Journal of Sexual Medicine, 10,* 2177–2189.

Milbury, K., Lopez, G., Spelman, A., Wood, C., Matin, S. F., Tannir, N., . . . Cohen, L. (2017). Examination of moderators of expressive writing in patients with renal cell carcinoma:

The role of depression and social support. *Psychooncology*, 26(9), 1361–1368.

Mowrer, O. H. (1960). Learning theory and behavior. Hoboken, NJ, US: John Wiley & Sons Inc.

Nazarian, D., & Smyth, J. M. (2010). Context moderates the effects of an expressive writing intervention: A randomized two-study replication and extension. *Journal of Social and Clinical Psychology*, 29, 903–929.

Nazarian, D., & Smyth, J. M. (2013). An experimental test of instructional manipulations in expressive writing interventions: Examining processes of change. *Journal of Social and Clinical Psychology*, 32, 71–96.

Niles, A. N., Byrne Haltom, K. E., Lieberman, M. D., Hur, C., & Stanton, A. L. (2016). Writing content predicts benefit from written expressive disclosure: Evidence for repeated exposure and self-affirmation. *Cognition and Emotion*, 30, 258–274.

Norman, S. A., Lumley, M. A., Dooley, J. A., & Diamond, M. P. (2004). For whom does it work? Moderators of the effects of written emotional disclosure in women with chronic pelvic pain. *Psychosomatic Medicine*, 66, 174–183.

Nyssen, O. P., Taylor, S. J., Wong, G., Steed, E., Bourke, L., Lord, J.,…Meads, C. (2016). Does therapeutic writing help people with long-term conditions? Systematic review, realist synthesis and economic considerations. *Health Technology Assessment*, 20(27), vii–xxxvii, 1–367.

O'Connor, D. B., Walhker S., Hendrickx H., & Schaefer, A. (2013) Stress-related thinking predicts the cortisol awakening repsonses and somatic symptoms in healthy adults. *Psychoneuroendocrinology*, 38, 438-446.

Pachankis, J. E., & Goldfried, M. R. (2010). Expressive writing for gay-related stress: Psychosocial benefits and mechanisms underlying improvement. *Journal of Consulting and Clinical Psychology*, 78, 98–110.

Paez, D., Velasco, C., Gonzalez, J. L. (1999). Expressive writing and the role of alexythimia as a dispositional deficit in self-disclosure and psychological health. *Journal of Personality and Social Psychology*, 77(3), 630–641.

Pascual-Leone, A. R., & Kramer, U. (2016). Does feeling bad, lead to feeling good? Arousal patterns during expressive writing. *Review of General Psychology*, 20, 336–347.

Oh, P. J., & Kim, S. H. (2016). The effects of expressive writing interventions for cancer: A meta-analysis. *Oncology Nursing Forum*, July 1, Oncology Nursing Society.

Park, J., Ayduk, O., & Kross, E. (2016). Stepping back to move forward: Expressive writing promotes self-distancing. *Emotion*, 16, 249–364.

Pennebaker, J. W. (1993). Putting stress into words: Health, linguistic, and therapeutic implications. *Behaviour Research and Therapy*, 31, 539–548.

Pennebaker, J. W. (1997). *Opening up: The healing power of emotional expression*. New York, NY: Guilford Press.

Pennebaker, J. W., Barger, S. D., & Trebout, J. (1989). Disclosure of traumas and health among Holocaust survivors. *Psychosomatic Medicine*, 51, 577–589.

Pennebaker, J. W., & Beall, S. K. (1986). Confronting a traumatic event: Toward an understanding of inhibition and disease. *Journal of Abnormal Psychology*, 95, 274–81.

Pennebaker, J. W., Booth, R. J., Boyd, R. L., & Francis, M. E. (2015). *Linguistic Inquiry and Word Count: LIWC2015*. Austin, TX: Pennebaker Conglomerates.

Pennebaker, J. W., & Chung, C. K. (2007). Expressive writing, emotional upheavals, and health. In H. F. R. Silver (Ed.), *Handbook of health psychology* (pp. 263–284). New York, NY: Oxford University Press.

Pennebaker, J.W. & Evans, J.F. (2014). *Expressive Writing: Words that Heal*. Enumclaw, WA: Idyll Arbor.

Pennebaker, J. W., & Francis, M. (1996). Cognitive, emotional, and language processes in disclosure. *Cognition and Emotion*, 10, 601–626.

Pennebaker, J. W., Hughes, C. F., & O'Heeron, R. C. (1987). The psychophysiology of confession. Linking inhibitory and psychosomatic processes. *Journal of Personality and Clinical Psychology*, 52, 781–793.

Pennebaker, J. W., Kiecolt-Glaser, J. K., & Glaser, R. (1988). Disclosure of traumas and immune function. *Journal of Consulting and Clinical Psychology*, 56, 239–245.

Pennebaker, J. W., Mayne, T. J., & Francis, M. E. (1997). Linguistic predictors of adaptive bereavement. *Journal of Personality and Social Psychology*, 72, 863–871.

Pennebaker, J. W., Colder, M., & Sharp, L. K. (1990). Accelerating the coping process. *Journal of Personality and Social Psychology*, 58, 528–537.

Pennebaker, K. W., & Seagal, J. D. (1999). Forming a story: The health benefits of narrative. *Journal of Clinical Psychology*, 55, 1243–1254.

Pennebaker, J. W., & Smyth, J. M. (1999).Sharing one's story: Translating emotional experiences into words as a coping tool, In C.R. Snyder (Ed.), Coping : The psychology of what works (pp 70-89). New York: Oxford University Press.

Pennebaker, J. W., & Smyth, J. M. (2016). *Opening up by writing it down: How expressive writing improves health and eases emotional pain* (3rd ed.). New York, NY: Guilford Press.

Petrie, K. J., Booth, R. J., Pennebaker, J. W., Davison, K. P., & Thomas, M. G. (1995). Disclosure of trauma and immune response to a hepatitis B vaccination program. *Journal of Consulting and Clinical Psychology*, 63, 787–792.

Petrie, K. J., Fontanilla, I., Thomas, M. G., Booth, R. J., & Pennebaker, J. W. (2004). Effect of written emotional expression on immune function in patients with human immunodeficiency virus infection: A randomized trial. *Psychosomatic Medicine*, 66, 272–275.

Possemato, K., Ouimette, P., & Geller, P. A. (2010). Internet-based expressive writing for kidney transplant recipients: Effects on posttraumatic stress and quality of life. *Traumatology*, 6, 49–54.

Pulverman, C. S., Boyd, R. L., Stanton, A. M., & Meston, C. M. (2017). Changes in the sexual self-schema of women with a history of childhood sexual abuse following expressive writing treatment. *Psychological Trauma: Theory, Research, Practice and Policy*, 9, 181–188.

Pulverman, C. S., Lorenz, T. A., & Meston, C. M. (2015). Linguistic changes in expressive writing predict psychological outcomes in women with history of childhood sexual abuse and adult sexual dysfunction. *Psychological Trauma*, 7, 50–57.

Ramirez, G., & Beilock, S. L. (2011). Writing about testing worries boosts exam performance in the classroom. *Science*, 331, 211–213.

Riddle, J. P., Smith, H. E., & Jones, C. J. (2016). Does written emotional disclosure improve the psychological and physical health of caregivers? *Behaviour Research and Therapy*, 8, 23–32.

Sadovnik, A., Sumner, K., Bragger, J., & Pastor, S. C. (2011). Effects of expressive writing about workplace events on satisfaction, stress and well-being. *Journal of Academy of Business and Economics*, 11, 231–237.

Sayer, N. A., Noorbaloochi, S., Frazier, P. A., Pennebaker, J. W., Orazem, R. J., Schnurr, P. P., ... Litz, B. T. (2015). Randomized controlled trial of online expressive writing to address readjustment difficulties among U.S. Afghanistan and Iraq war veterans. *Journal of Traumatic Stress, 28*, 381–390.

Scheff, T. J. (1979). *Catharsis in healing, ritual, and drama.* Berkeley: University of California Press.

Sears, S. R., Stanton, A. L., & Danoff-Burg, S. (2003). The yellow brick road and the emerald city: Benefit-finding, positive reappraisal coping and posttraumatic growth in women with early-stage breast cancer. *Health Psychology, 22*, 487–497.

Seeley, S. H., Yanez, B., Stanton, A. L., & Hoyt, M. A. (2017). An emotional processing writing intervention and heart rate variability: The role of emotional approach. *Cognition and Emotion, 31*, 988–994.

Shaffer, F., McCraty, R., & Zerr, C. L. (2014). A healthy heart is not a metronome: An integrative review of the heart's anatomy and heart rate variability. *Frontiers in Psychology, 5*, 1–19.

Sheese, B. E., Brown, E. L., & Graziano, W. G. (2004). Emotional expression in cyberspace: Searching for moderators of the Pennebaker disclosure effect via email. *Health Psychology, 23*, 457–464.

Sloan, D. M., & Marx, B. P. (2004a). A closer examination of the structured written disclosure procedure. *Journal of Consulting and Clinical Psychology, 72*, 165–175.

Sloan, D. M., & Marx, B. P. (2004b). Taking pen to hand: Evaluating theories underlying the written disclosure paradigm. *Clinical Psychology: Science and Practice, 11*, 121–137.

Sloan, D. M., Marx, B. P., & Epstein, E. M. (2005). Further examination of the exposure model underlying the efficacy of written emotional disclosure. *Journal of Consulting and Clinical Psychology, 73*, 549–554.

Sloan, D. M., Marx, B. P., Epstein, E. M., & Lexington, J. M. (2007). Does altering the writing instructions influence outcome associated with written disclosure? *Behaviour Therapy, 38*, 155–168.

Sloan, D. M., Sawyer, A. T., Lawmaster, S. E., Warwick, J., & Marx, B. P. (2015). Efficacy of narrative writing as an intervention for PTSD: Does the evidence support its use? *Journal of Contemporary Psychotherapy, 45*, 215–225.

Smyth, J. M. (1998). Written emotional expression: Effect sizes, outcome types, and moderating variables. *Journal of Consulting and Clinical Psychology, 66*, 174–184.

Smyth, J. M., Hockemeyer, J. R., & Tulloch, H. (2008). Expressive writing and post-traumatic stress disorder: Effects on trauma symptoms, mood states, and cortisol reactivity. *British Journal of Health Psychology, 13*, 85–93.

Smyth, J. M., & Pennebaker, J. W. (2008). Exploring the boundary conditions of expressive writing: In search of the right recipe. *British Journal of Health Psychology, 13*, 1–7.

Smyth, J. M., Stone, A. A., Hurewitz, A., & Kaell, A. (1999). Effects of writing about stressful experiences on symptoms reduction in patients with asthma or rheumatoid arthritis: A randomized controlled trial. *JAMA, 281*(14), 1304–1309.

Smyth, J. M., True, N., & Souto, J. (2001). Effects of writing about traumatic experiences: The necessity for narrative structuring. *Journal of Social and Clinical Psychology, 20*, 161–172.

Spera, S. P., Buhrfeind, E. D., & Pennebaker, J. W. (1994). Expressive writing and coping with job loss. *Academy of Management Journal, 37*, 722–733.

Stanton, A. L. (2012). Regulating emotions during stressful experiences: The adaptive utility of coping through emotional approach. In S. Folkman (Ed.), *The Oxford handbook of stress, health, and coping* (pp. 369–386). New York, NY: Oxford University Press.

Stanton, A. L., Danoff-Burg, S., Sworowski, L. A., Collins, C. A., Branstetter, A. D., Rodriguez-Hanley, ... Austenfeld, J. L. .(2002). Randomized, controlled trial of written emotional expression and Benefit-finding in breast cancer patients. *Journal of Clinical Oncology, 20*, 4160–4168.

Stockton, H., Joseph, S., & Hunt, N. (2014). Expressive writing and posttraumatic growth: An Internet-based study. *Traumatology: An International Journal, 20*, 75–83.

Tarquini, M. Di Trani, M., & Solano, L. (2016). Effects of an expressive writing intervention on a group of public employees subjected to work relocation. *Work, 53*, 793–804.

Taylor, L. A., Wallander, J. L., Anderson, D., Beasley, P., & Brown, R. T. (2003). Improving health care utilization, improving chronic disease utilization, health status, and adjustment in fibrosis: A preliminary report. *Journal of Clinical Psychology in Medical Settings, 10*, 9–16.

Travagin, G., Margola, D., & Revenson, T. S. (2015). How effective are expressive writing interventions for adolescents? A meta-analytic review. *Clinical Psychology Review, 36*, 42–55.

Warner, L. J., Lumley, M. A., Casey, R. J., Pierantoni, W., Salazar, R., Zoratti, E. M., Enberg, R., & Simon, M. R. (2006). Health effects of written emotional disclosure in adolescents with asthma: A randomized, controlled trial. *Journal of Pediatric Psychology, 31*, 557–568.

Weinman, J., Ebrecht, M., Scott, S., Walburn, J., & Dyson, M. (2008). Enhanced wound healing after emotional disclosure intervention. *Journal of Health Psychology, 13*, 95–102.

Williamson, T. J., Stanton, A. L., Austin, J. E., Valdimarsdottir, H. B., Wu, L. M., Krull, J. L., & Rini C. M. (2017). Helping yourself by offering help: Mediators of expressive helping in survivors of hematopoietic stem cell transplant. *Annals of Behavioral Medicine, 33*, 1541–1551.

Young, J. E., Klosko, J. S., & Weshaar, M. E. (2003). *Schema therapy: A practitioner's guide.* New York, NY: Guilford Press.

Zachariae, R., & Toole, M. S. (2015). The effect of expressive writing intervention on psychological and physical health outcomes in cancer patients—a systematic review and meta-analysis. *Psycho-Oncology, 24*, 1349–1359.

Zhou, C., Wu, Y., An, S., & Li, X. (2015). Effect of expressive writing intervention on health outcomes in breast cancer patients: A systematic review and meta-analysis of randomized controlled trials. *PLoS ONE, 10*(7), e0131802. https://doi.org/10.1371/journal.pone.0131802

Ziadni, M. S., Jasinski, M. J., Labouvie-Vief, G., and Lumley, M. A. (2017). Alexithymia, defenses, and ego strength: Cross-sectional and longitudinal relationships with psychological well-being and depression. *Journal of Happiness Studies, 18*, 1799–1813. https://link.springer.com/article/10.1007%2Fs10902-016-9800-7.

Stress and Mental Health: Epilogue

Elizabeth P. Hayden *and* Kate L. Harkness

Abstract

In this epilogue, the editors of this volume provide a synthesis of the preceding chapters. In addition to highlighting the current state of the scientific literature, future directions for the rapidly evolving field of stress and mental health are outlined, with an emphasis on key issues surrounding the development of new methods and levels of analysis, improvements in assessment approaches, and how training and collaboration can evolve toward the goal of facilitating new insights. Prominent conceptual issues requiring consideration and clarification are discussed, with a particular focus on the fundamental principles that underlie models of stress and mental health, as well as resilience.

Keywords: stress, resilience, diathesis-stress, development, gender differences, psychopathology, assessment

Our goal in editing this volume was to provide a comprehensive, current overview of the methods, concepts, and empirical findings that are central to the field of stress and mental health. Despite, or perhaps because of, the vigor, breadth, and depth of the field, this was no small task. As the preceding chapters in this volume attest, research on stress and mental health is cutting edge, extensive, and methodologically diverse. Scientists who identify as stress researchers represent a diversity of vantage points and methods possibly unparalleled in other domains of scientific inquiry. Indeed, the field is replete with opportunities for scientists to apply "multiple levels of analysis" via the use of biological (e.g., molecular and psychophysiological approaches), quantitative, behavioral (e.g., indices of cognitive and affective responses to stress), and many other methods toward understanding the intricate processes by which stress eventuates in a broad array of adaptive and maladaptive outcomes.

In addition to drawing upon diverse scientific disciplines, the outcomes of interest, as well as the methodologies used by stress scientists, vary in scope. With respect to the former, for organizational purposes we have organized this volume in part around specific disorders; nevertheless, the impact of stress and vulnerabilities to it are almost always transdiagnostic, eventuating in different mental health outcomes due to complex interplay with other endogenous and exogenous factors. Having said that, researchers can and often do "work backwards" from diagnostic outcomes with great success, yielding useful insights with respect to how stress and other processes interact to confer risk for a specific mental health outcome (e.g., schizophrenia; Walker et al., Chapter 7). This approach generates knowledge that can be fruitfully integrated with approaches that focus more specifically on transdiagnostic processes (e.g., Dennis-Tiwary et al., Chapter 19). With regard to diverse methodological approaches, exceptionally fine-grained, micro-level methods such as pharmacotherapeutics for stress-related disorders (Deak & Lovelock, Chapter 30) and the role of stress in substance use (Vendruscolo & Koob, Chapter 9) have been fruitfully applied to study stress processes under controlled conditions.

In contrast, other scientists take a broader, macro-level approach to understanding stress with the goal of capturing person–environment interaction, developing and testing models of the dynamic, transactional interplay between individuals and their environments as they unfold across the life span (e.g., Halperin & Goodman, Chapter 13; Shakiba, Conradt, & Ellis, Chapter 28).

These diverse approaches have their own unique strengths; for example, the study of stress processes via animal models typically lends greater experimental control and internal validity, and such methods are oftentimes more amenable to tests of replicability than studies of such processes in humans. In contrast, much of the descriptive, oftentimes correlational work on how stress impacts child development in the "real world" aims to maximize external validity by characterizing the complex pathways through which children's individual difference factors interact with diverse contextual processes to influence an array of outcomes. We feel strongly that the field is strengthened by this richness and diversity of approaches and methods. While the stress response unfolds through specific, fine-grained biological processes that can be dissected in the lab, these processes must ultimately be understood within the context of "real-world" health outcomes. Thus, there is currently no conceptual or empirical grounds by which one approach could be defensibly privileged above others.

However, the richness of methods and vantage points complicates the ability to synthesize what is known about stress and mental health. To date, conclusions concerning the precise mechanisms of stress, and for whom and when these mechanisms are most likely to exert their impact, have often been studied using method- or discipline-specific approaches. For example, as noted by Stroud (Chapter 16), understanding the mechanisms of stress sensitization in depression (i.e., the widely studied phenomenon by which stress exposure results in heightened reactivity to future stressors, and thus depression risk) will benefit from integration of factors such as inflammatory processes, emotion regulation, and a general broadening of scope to explore how these process variables relate to not only depression but other mental health outcomes. We therefore conclude this volume with recommendations for future work on stress and mental health with the specific goal of identifying ways in which greater clarity and integration across diverse perspectives in stress science might be attained.

Practical Considerations in the Study of Stress and Mental Health
Evaluating and Integrating Diverse Levels of Analysis

The probabilistic nature of associations between stress and mental health outcomes is a recurring theme throughout this volume; for example, many chapters in this volume focus on variability in individual differences in personality (Oltmanns & White, Chapter 8; Olino, Wojcieszak, & Mennies, Chapter 18), genetic factors (Uher, Chapter 25), and psychophysiological reactivity (Lopez-Duran, Roberts, Foster, & Mayer, Chapter 22; Zakreski & Pruessner, Chapter 23) as a means of understanding who is most vulnerable to stressful life events. These individual differences in responses to stress can be understood as falling under the rubric of *stress sensitivity*.

It is axiomatic that there are ample individual differences in stress sensitivity; furthermore, that these differences are evinced across multiple systems and levels of analysis is widely accepted. Current consensus calls for a multilevel, multimodel assessment approach, a stance with which we fully agree. Nevertheless, we assert that certain levels are ultimately essential for understanding mental health. For example, basic science focused on altering stress reactivity of specific biological systems necessitates indexing the relevant biological processes; findings from work such as this have important direct (Deak & Lovelock, Chapter 30) and indirect (Desormeau, Walsh, & Segal, Chapter 32) implications for intervention. However, to have practical utility, work demonstrating that a specific biological system relevant to stress can be manipulated must ultimately be supported by the parallel amelioration of negative mental health outcomes. Controlled trials that manipulate change in putative causal mechanisms (biological or otherwise) alongside tests of relevant behavioral outcomes can prove useful for testing theory as well as informing the development of interventions.

It is also possible that certain causal mechanisms of stress have significant main effects on human adaptation; in some cases, these may be only weakly related to other mechanisms that make fairly meager contributions to health outcomes. The low convergence typically found between indices of different aspects of stress reactivity is often interpreted as reflecting both measurement error and the fact that diverse, nonredundant systems come online in the context of the stress response. This may very well be true in many cases, but it may also be true that certain vantage points are limited in terms of yielding meaningful information about stress reactivity. It is premature at this juncture to draw conclusions about which processes are and are not important for particular mental health outcomes; having said that, we encourage the reader not to assume that each and every modality for studying stress reactivity is essential in cases where sufficient data ultimately indicate otherwise. As has been noted for psychopathology in general (Berenbaum, 2013), simply because multiple factors contribute to the stress response does not mean that all are useful, meaningful, or important. Toward the goal of developing parsimonious etiological models of stress sensitivity and health outcomes, scientists will need to evaluate the magnitude of the contribution various factors yield in accounting for how stress sensitivity relates to adaptation.

We also encourage researchers in this field to avoid reifying biological levels of analysis over behavioral or other levels, or generally assuming that such levels are the most fundamental to the stress response (Berenbaum, 2013). All human behavior has biological correlates, but this very ubiquity does not mean that all biological processes yield incremental insights into more specific or complex stress response processes. At minimum, the complex processes that unfold in stress responding cannot be localized to a specific biological substrate (Turkheimer, 1998). As noted by Miller and Keller (2000, p. 213), it is important to remember that "biological information is not inherently more fundamental, more accurate, more representative, or even more objective." In certain cases, biological accounts may indeed be the best lens through which a stress process is viewed, but this assertion is a hypothesis to be rigorously tested, not accepted as an a priori fact.

Assessing Stress Sensitivity

Additionally, the importance of assessing indices of stress sensitivity well, and distinguishing them from stress exposure itself, is not always recognized. With respect to the former point, we encourage stress scientists, particularly those interested in human development, to address the need for standardized and validated indices of stress sensitivity that are suitable for a broad range of developmental stages. Standardized approaches to assessing stress sensitivity, if widely adopted, would play an important role in unifying the field. For example, it is currently challenging to draw broad conclusions about the development of stress responding given the heterogeneity

in paradigms used to index stress sensitivity in childhood (Gunnar, Talge, & Herrera, 2009; Kryski et al., 2011). Undoubtedly, much of the variability in findings across studies of stress sensitivity stems from differences in assessment, rather than veridical differences related to risk processes, age, or other substantive factors. Reducing variability in assessment approaches is therefore essential toward developing a cohesive understanding of stress sensitivity.

Relatedly, standardized approaches to assessing stress sensitivity would inform our understanding of developmental norms in stress responding. In particular, variation in facets of stress responding (e.g., cortisol stress reactivity) is often interpreted as reflecting "hyper-" or "hyporeactivity" to stress, despite the fact that the field typically lacks extensive normative data on how typically developing humans respond to stressors in controlled laboratory settings. As noted, many laboratory paradigms have been used to elicit cortisol stress reactivity in all groups, but especially in young children, where an established paradigm has been lacking (cf. the Trier Social Stress Test, which is widely used with adults; Kirschbaum, Pirke, & Hellhammer, 1993). Unfortunately, many of these tasks have not been thoroughly vetted in terms of their construct validity and psychometric properties. This renders it difficult to (1) choose a specific paradigm based on its established validity, (2) establish what a normatively developing child's cortisol response to a mild stressor is, (3) make informed claims about what might constitute an underreactive or overreactive cortisol stress response, and (4) understand what the key predictors of these are. Thus, in cases where "best practice" in terms of assessment has not yet been determined, we recommend that scientists invest substantial effort in resolving measurement issues rather than prematurely testing causal models that rely on unvalidated indices of central constructs.

Additionally, strict tests of stress exposure and stress sensitivity require rigorous, orthogonal assessment of each construct; indeed, it is essential to avoid confounding stress *exposure* with stress *sensitivity*. Such confounding can occur for a number of reasons. In particular, individuals who show heightened reactivity to stress are often biased in their recollections of stress exposure. Toward developing useful causal models of how stress impacts mental health, studies of relations between stress exposure and sensitivity must disentangle environmental stressors from the responses to those exposures by the use of independent, objective assessment approaches. One of us has written extensively about these issues; we refer the reader to Harkness and Monroe (2016) for a more thorough consideration of this critical topic.

Furthermore, the very same markers that reflect stress sensitivity can play an important role in eliciting life stress via evocative processes such as gene–environment correlation, or specifically, stress generation in the current context (Hammen, Chapter 15). For example, maladaptive personality traits (Hammen, Chapter 15; Oltmanns & White, Chapter 8) contribute to stress exposure via the elicitation of social stressors, while simultaneously rendering individuals with such traits less capable of effectively managing stress in an adaptive manner. In a case such as this, it becomes somewhat misleading to attribute negative outcomes to stress exposure per se when at least some of the causal process should be attributed to pre-existing, within-person traits. This is not an inconsequential consideration given that the implications for intervention and prevention differ significantly with respect to whether stressful life events are random or evoked by the individual. It may also be the case that individuals with maladaptive traits may be less capable of recognizing any role they may have played in eliciting stress. Thus, we once again call for objective assessments of life events by trained interviewers, as checklist measures of stressful life events are ill suited to address potential biases related to personality.

Training and Collaboration

Transdisciplinary training and collaboration are essential toward facilitating scientists' ability to synthesize the mechanisms by which stress exposure influences a broad range of outcomes. Here, as academic clinical psychologists, we speak primarily to training in clinical science. Given psychology's interdisciplinary nature and status as a hub science (Cacioppo, 2007; McFall, Treat, & Simons, in press), clinical scientists are uniquely positioned to play a key role in integrating research on stress processes. Indeed, as cogently articulated by McFall, Treat, and Simons, while clinical scientists must develop expertise in the relevant methodologies and theories from our own field, they cannot afford to focus exclusively on narrowly defined psychological approaches, particularly in a field as broad as stress and adaptation.

Reflecting the wisdom of this assertion, students who train in a psychology department are increasingly likely to acquire expertise in molecular genetics, neuroimaging, computational modeling, and many other tools that a naïve observer might not think of as "psychological approaches" per se. However, because there are practical limitations to the number of domains in which one can develop genuine expertise, collaborative relationships with diverse fields ranging from sociology to immunology are essential. Indeed, we encourage clinical science programs and clinical scientists to choose methodologies and collaborations based on the evidence at hand, rather than on their familiarity or because of assumptions about which methods are the most important or sophisticated (McFall, Treat, & Simons, in press). We also note that testing integrative, interactive models of stress exposure and stress sensitivity necessitates huge samples, which also renders collaboration across labs essential.

Conceptual Recommendations in the Study of Stress and Mental Health
Sex or Gender?

There are many examples of instances in which males and females differ in stress-sensitive processes (e.g., Vrshek-Schallhorn, Ditcheva, & Corneau, Chapter 5). Additionally, ample data from the literature on normative child development indicate that boys and girls differ in sensitivity to specific kinds of environments (e.g., certain parenting behaviors; Amicarelli et al., 2018). However, it is oftentimes unclear whether such differences are best understood in terms of sex, a biological distinction, or genderedness (i.e., the extent to which an individual hews to norms associated with a specific gender). This is especially problematic for research on adolescent development, when gender roles typically become more salient and crystallized, becoming relatively distinct from biological sex. The distinction between the two is not inconsequential for theory, but also because the implications for intervention differ depending on whether the causal mechanism is related to genuine sex differences versus gender. For example, adolescent girls are more likely than boys to report exposure to stressful life events in the interpersonal domain (e.g., conflict with friends or romantic partners), and in some studies these events are stronger prospective predictors of adolescent girls' maladjustment than boys' (e.g., Hamilton, Stange, Abramson, & Alloy, 2014). In this case, if girls' increased vulnerability to interpersonal stress is primarily due to a potentially maladaptive overvaluation of close relationships, an intervention focused on shifting attitudes and cognition toward decatastrophizing interpersonal stress might prove more effective than one focused more specifically on altering a mechanism related to a biologically based sex difference. We therefore urge investigators to avoid conflating gender and sex by assessing gender specifically when relevant.

Resilience

We acknowledge that this volume primarily focuses on the role of stress in negative outcomes, as befitting a volume on stress and mental health. Nevertheless, there is a substantial research literature aimed at developing a better understanding of resilience to stress that is extensively reviewed in this volume by Long and Bonanno (Chapter 28) and Compas, Vreeland, and Henry (Chapter 26). Resilience is generally used to define characteristics of those who manage to avoid negative outcomes despite exposure to factors tied to maladaptation (i.e., stressful life events in the present context; Werner, 1995). As recently articulated by Bonanno, Romero, and Klein (2015), resilience is a multidimensional construct and may be best conceptualized as an umbrella phenomenon that encompasses a number of elements that unfold over time. That is, resilience should be seen as a developmental *process*, not as a generalized and fixed property of individuals. Therefore, they suggest that trajectories of adjustment should be tracked longitudinally, as some negative health outcomes may only emerge during specific, potentially distal periods of development (e.g., onset of schizophrenia in young adulthood in the context of early life trauma; Owen, Sawa, & Mortensen, 2016). Thus, it would be premature to infer resilience in the absence of long-term follow-up.

Furthermore, resilience is oftentimes defined based on positive behavioral outcomes, an approach which fails to speak directly to the causal processes involved and runs the risk of introducing a certain circularity to the construct. As noted elsewhere (Hayden & Durbin, 2018), Long and Bonanno make the important point that resilience must be considered within the overall effect size of a risk factor. For example, in cases where a life stressor is associated with significant impairment for only a minority of those who experience it, it may not be sensible to invoke the concept of resilience to account for the absence of mental health problems given that most exposed emerge unscathed. Additionally, in order for markers of resilience to have incremental validity in predicting outcomes following stress exposure, such markers cannot merely index the absence of risk (e.g., the absence of

neighborhood violence). One of us has also written at length about this topic in another volume in this series, to which we refer the interested reader (Hayden & Durbin, 2018).

Beyond Diathesis-Stress

In addition to refining concepts of resilience, we encourage stress researchers to test models other than the predominant diathesis-stress model (Meehl, 1962), in which negative outcomes following stress exposure are a consequence only for those with a latent vulnerability. Put differently, in this model, vulnerable persons do not develop problems as long as they are not exposed to the relevant environmental precipitants. This model has been a mainstay of explanatory accounts of the development of psychopathology for decades, and it may indeed be the most accurate framework for conceptualizing many pathways to disorder. However, as touched on in this volume, particularly by Shakiba, Conradt, and Ellis (Chapter 28), other models of the relationship between stress and individual differences are not only possible but potentially important. These include differential susceptibility (Boyce & Ellis, 2005), in which an individual difference factor serves to increase sensitivity to an array of positive and negative environmental factors, such that individuals with this "susceptibility" are not only more vulnerable to stress but are also more likely to thrive in enriched environments. Additionally, models of stress inoculation (also referred to as "steeling effects" and "hardiness"; Liu, 2015) posit curvilinear associations between stress exposure and outcomes, such that exposure to mild stressors is in fact adaptive (perhaps because it mobilizes the resources needed to cope with the inevitable stressors of life), and it is when stress is either "too low" or "too high" that individuals become vulnerable.

These models have received far less empirical scrutiny than the diathesis-stress model, so relatively little is known to date about the conditions under which these models might be accurate characterizations of stress-sensitive processes important to mental health. These certainly require further study. However, when testing differential susceptibility, we encourage investigators to be cognizant of the fact that the lack of a negative outcome is not interchangeable with the presence of an exceptionally positive outcome, the latter of which is requisite to support differential susceptibility. Additionally, for those interested in stress inoculation, we note that the thresholds at which (1) stress exposure becomes adaptive, and (2) the point at which additional stress becomes overwhelming and maladaptive must vary across individuals. In other words, the lower and upper bounds of stress exposure needed to promote "hardiness" must vary across individuals, necessitating complex models that go beyond simple tests of nonlinearity associations between stress and adaptation.

Final Conclusions

We have noted but a few outstanding issues in the field of stress and mental health. No single discipline or research method will suffice in resolving these issues. We wish to highlight the fact that some key issues can be at least partially addressed through the use of long-term follow-ups of typically developing and at-risk children and their families; however, such work will benefit from a renewed investment in developing rigorously validated assessment tools that inform our understanding of developmental trajectories of stress responding. Additionally, controlled trials in humans in which putative risk mechanisms are experimentally manipulated are a valuable complement to naturalistic, descriptive work that characterizes developmental pathways.

It is an exciting yet challenging time to work in this field. We hope this volume aids the interested reader in identifying the many areas that require further exploration and clarity, and also provides some useful guidance with respect to the tools that should be brought to bear in order to shed light on this complex field. We look forward to seeing the exciting scientific developments the future holds for understanding stress and mental health.

References

Amicarelli, A. R., Kotelnikova, Y., Smith, H. J., Kryski, K. R., & Hayden, E. P. (2018). Parenting differentially influences the development of boys' and girls' inhibitory control. *The British Journal of Developmental Psychology. 36*, 371–383.

Berenbaum, H. (2013). Classification and psychopathology research. *Journal of Abnormal Psychology, 122*(3), 894–901.

Bonanno, G. A., Romero, S. A., & Klein, S. I. (2015). The temporal elements of psychological resilience: An integrative framework for the study of individuals, families, and communities. *Psychological Inquiry, 26*(2), 139–169.

Boyce, W. T., & Ellis, B. J. (2005). Biological sensitivity to context: I. An evolutionary-developmental theory of the origins and functions of stress reactivity. *Development and Psychopathology, 17*(2), 271–301.

Cacioppo, J. (2007). Psychology is a hub science. *APS Observer, 20*(8). Retrieved from https://www.psychologicalscience.org/observer/psychology-is-a-hub-science

Gunnar, M. R., Talge, N. M., & Herrera, A. (2009). Stressor paradigms in developmental studies: What does and does not work to produce mean increases in salivary cortisol. *Psychoneuroendocrinology, 34*(7), 953–967.

Harkness, K. L., & Monroe, S. M. (2016). The assessment and measurement of adult life stress: Basic premises, operational principles, and design requirements. *Journal of Abnormal Psychology, 125*(5), 727–745.

Hayden, E. P., & Emily Durbin, C. (2018). Development and psychopathology. In T. H. Ollendick, S. W. White, & B. A. White (Eds.), *The Oxford handbook of clinical child and adolescent psychology*, 31–41. New York: Oxford University Press.

Kirschbaum, C., Pirke, K. M., & Hellhammer, D. H. (1993). The "Trier Social Stress Test" – a tool for investigating psychobiological stress responses in a laboratory setting. *Neuropsychobiology, 28*(1-2), 76–81.

Kryski, K. R., Smith, H. J., Sheikh, H. I., Singh, S. M., & Hayden, E. P. (2011). Assessing stress reactivity indexed via salivary cortisol in preschool-aged children. *Psychoneuroendocrinology, 36*(8), 1127–1136.

Liu, R. T. (2015). A developmentally informed perspective on the relation between stress and psychopathology: When the problem with stress is that there is not enough. *Journal of Abnormal Psychology, 124*(1), 80–92.

McFall, R. M., Treat, T. A., & Simons, R. F. (2015). *Clinical science model*. In R. Cautin & S. Lilienfeld (Eds.), *Encyclopedia of clinical psychology*, 1–9. Hoboken: Wiley-Blackwell. https://onlinelibrary.wiley.com/doi/book/10.1002/9781118625392

Meehl, P. E. (1962). Schizotaxia, schizotypy, schizophrenia. *American Psychologist, 17*(12), 827–838. doi:10.1037/h0041029

Miller, G. A., & Keller, J. (2000). Psychology and neuroscience: Making peace. *Current Directions in Psychological Science, 9*(6), 212–215.

Owen, M. J., Sawa, A., & Mortensen, P. B. (2016). Schizophrenia. *The Lancet, 388*(10039), 86–97.

Stange, J. P., Hamilton, J. L., Abramson, L. Y., & Alloy, L. B. (2014). A vulnerability-stress examination of response styles theory in adolescence: stressors, sex differences, and symptom specificity. *Journal of Clinical Child and Adolescent Psychology, 43*(5), 813–827.

Turkheimer, E. (1998). Heritability and biological explanation. *Psychological Review, 105*(4), 782–791.

Werner, E. E. (1995). Resilience in development. *Current Directions in Psychological Science, 4*(3), 81–84.

INDEX

BSDs. *See* bipolar spectrum disorders
Bucharest Early Intervention
    Project 277
Buddhism 690–91
buffered stress response pattern 505,
    505*t*, 613–16
bulimia nervosa (BN)
    childhood maltreatment and sexual
        violation antecedent to 226–27
    definition of 212
    depression and 233
    diagnostic criteria for 225
    negative appearance-related feedback
        antecedent to 232
    occupational stress and 228–29
    prevalence rates 212, 225
    risk factors for 229
bullying 528, 549
butterfly effects 83

C

CAARMS (Comprehensive Assessment of
    At-Risk Mental States) 159
calcitriol 649
calibration, adaptive. *See* adaptive
    calibration model (ACM)
Camberwell Studies 104
CAN. *See* central autonomic network
Canada 222
candesartan 656
candidate genes 548
cannabidiol (CBD) 659
cannabinoids 212, 659–60
cannabis 659–60
capture of attention and rumination
    (CaR) 375
CAR. *See* cortisol awakening response
carbenoxolone 206
cardiovascular conditions
    comorbidity with PTSD 316, 320
    psychophysiology of depression 83
caregiver–child relationships 631–32
Caribbean Blacks 112–13
catechol-O-methyltransferase
    (COMT) 162, 167
catharsis theory 717
CBD. *See* cannabidiol
CBT. *See* cognitive-behavioral therapy
CD. *See* conduct disorder
CECA (Childhood Experiences of Care
    and Abuse) 63*t*, 114–15
celecoxib 534, 651–52
central autonomic network (CAN)
    499–500
central nervous system (CNS)
    development of 561
    immune cell interactions 653–55
CFA. *See* confirmatory factor analysis
c factor 386
chaos 272
checklists 60
    self-report 12, 16, 32
chemoattractants 522

chemokine ligand 2/monocyte chemotactic
    protein (MCP)-1 650–51
chemokines 522, 650–51
Chernobyl nuclear power plant
    explosion 248–49
child abuse. *See* child maltreatment
childhood
    early 572–75
    middle 575–76
childhood adversity. *See* early life stress
    (ELS)
Childhood Experiences of Care and Abuse
    (CECA) 63*t*, 114–15
childhood-onset psychotic
    experiences 165
Childhood Trauma Questionnaire
    (CTQ) 62*t*
child maltreatment
    in bipolar spectrum disorders 142–48
    in cognitive risk formation 381–82
    definition of 549
    developmental effects of 270, 279
    in disordered eating 226–27
    emotional abuse 147, 381–82
    examples 99*t*
    in inflammation 528
    physical abuse 147, 382
    proximal effects 115
    sensitizing effects 359
    sexual abuse 147, 251–52, 382, 445
    timing of 574
children
    acute stress disorder in 252–53, 257–58
    adopted 275
    autonomic functioning 291, 293
    autonomic nervous system
        development 567
    behavioral functioning 290–92
    birth outcomes 290
    brain functioning 291, 293
    caregiver–child relationships 631–32
    coping 591–92
    dandelions 602
    emotional functioning 290–92
    functional assessment of 304
    future directions for research 577
    HPA development 566–67
    interpersonal stressors 110–11
    life events 110
    maternal perinatal depression
        and 289–303
    neuroendocrine functioning 291–94
    orchids 602
    postinstitutionalized 573
    in poverty 276–77
    preschool-aged 242–43
    psychopathology in 591–92
    psychopathology risk in 287–312
    PTSD in 242–43, 246–48, 252–55,
        257–58
    temperament 302–3
Children's Emotion Management
    Scales 592

China 246
cholecalciferol (vitamin D3) 649
chronic adversity. *See* chronic stress
chronic conditions
    benefit-finding writing about 707,
        707*b*
    comorbidity with PTSD 317, 320, 323
chronic pain 317, 320, 323
chronic stress 627
    concept of 562
    definition of 98
    examples 99*t*
    future directions for research 108, 538
    impacts in adulthood 106–8
    interpersonal 99*t*
    noninterpersonal 99*t*
    physiological effects of 494, 562–65
    potency for depression 107–8
    recent 106–8
    research challenges 107
    response to 562–65
    types of 98, 99*t*
chronic stressors 14, 228–32
Cicero 1
civil disturbance 249
classical frequentist modeling 76–77,
    77*t*, 79
Clinical Practice Guidelines (VA/DoD)
    675, 680–81
clinical psychological modeling 76–77, 77*t*
closed-form derivations 78
close-ended approaches 35
clustering 61–66
cognition. *See also* rumination
    in alcohol dependence 201
    collaborative 12
    coping-related 82
    gender differences in 385
    global cognitive focus 715–16
    interactive cognitive subsystems (ICS)
        model 692
    negative inferential style 378–83, 385
    negative thought content in
        depression 87
    predictors of emergent resilience 632
    in psychopathology 85, 372
    in stress generation 338
    in stress sensitization 362–64
cognition-intensive coping 85, 93
cognitive-behavioral therapy (CBT) 343,
    673–88
    for ASD 681–82
    future directions 682–84
    with hypnosis 681
    in international context 684
    motivational enhancement strategies
        for 683
    for PTSD 675–81
    salient issues 682–84
cognitive deficits, compromised 85
cognitive processing therapy
    (CPT) 675–77
    for ASD 682

D

DA. *See* dopamine
daily diaries 34–35
Daily Diary Interview 36
Daily Experiences Survey 36
Daily Hassles Checklist 35
Daily Hassles Scale 31–32, 41n1
Daily Inventory of Stressful Events
    (DISE) 36–37
daily stress and hassles 27–44
    assessment of 33–37
    association with major depressive
        disorder (MDD) 37–38
    clinical literature on 37–39
    concepts 28–31
    cross-sectional inventories of 31–33
    definitions 28–31
    examples 37–39
    generations of 31–40
    measurement of 37–41
    ratings of 28–29
Daily Stress Inventory 35–36
dandelion children 602
danger 105
DAs. *See* dysfunctional attitudes
decisional control (DC) 81, 85
decision making, shared 683
definitional issues 7–26
dehydroepiandrosterone (DHEA)
    465–66, 470
11-β-dehydrogenase isozyme 2 (11β-HSD2)
    294, 473, 476, 570–72
deliberative emotion regulation (DER)
    strategies 417–19
demographic variables
    predictors of minimal-impact
        resilience 632–33
    pretrauma characteristics 245
    in stress–depression relationship 111–14
dependence, alcohol 199–219
dependent events 30, 99t
dependent stress
    in anxiety disorders 337
    in depression history 332–33
depression. *See also* major depressive
    disorder (MDD)
    in adolescents 108–10, 115
    in adults 99–108, 115
    in Alzheimer's disease 659
    with anxiety 337
    bipolar 137
    in borderline personality disorder 337
    brain effects 447–50
    with bulimic symptoms 233
    cardiovascular psychophysiology of 83
    in childhood 110–11
    childhood adversity effects 115
    chronic stress potency for 107–8
    cortisol effects 447
    demographic variables 111–14
    in dependent stress 332–33
    diathesis-stress model of 446
    early adversity effects 115–16, 357–59

early life stress–related 434,
    435f, 444–45, 447, 450–51
    in eating disorders 233
    environmental contributions 444
    ethnicity effects 112–13
    in fathers 299–300
    functional connectivity effects 449
    future directions for research 118–19
    genetic contributions 444
    heritability 294–95
    inflammation effects 533–34
    intergenerational transmission of 336
    interpersonal stress effects 332
    interventions for 119, 343–44
    life stress in 119, 137
    macrophage theory of 533
    major 362–63, 533–34
    maternal 294–96, 336
    mechanisms of action 294–96
    medication for 295–96
    negative thought content in 87
    neural changes in 449–50, 449f
    neuroendocrine functioning in 467
    overgeneral autobiographical memory
        in 375–76
    perinatal 287–312
    postnatal 288, 292–94
    postpartum 287–88, 294
    prenatal 288, 290–92, 294–95
    prenatal stress and 289
    prevention of 119, 343–44
    prior episode effects 352–54
    recent stress effects 99–111
    research considerations 98–99
    risk factors for 335, 447
    sex differences in 163, 279
    social signal transduction theory
        of 534, 535f
    socioeconomic status and 113–14
    stress effects 97–126, 446–50
    stress exposure effects 444–45
    stress generation effects 331–47
    in stress generation models 402
    stress-related 467
    stress response pathways 55–56
    stress sensitization 357–59, 362–63
    youth depressive disorder 334
depressive rumination 379–80, 383, 385
deprivation 51–52
    developmental effects 270
    early 57–59
    institutional 270
    in psychopathology 57–59
DER (deliberative emotion regulation)
    strategies 417–19
descriptive modeling 76–77
desensitization, eye movement 675,
    679–80
determinism, reciprocal 87
deterministic modeling 76–77,
    77t, 78–80
development
    early 116

fetal stress and 570–72
future directions for research 576–77
organizational-developmental
    perspective 268
psychobiological 364
stress timing effects 568–69, 577
developmental origins of health and
    disease (DOHaD) theory 570, 572
developmental plasticity 268
developmental psychopathology 265–85
    early stress and 274–77
    future directions 280–81
    genetics and 273–74
    sex differences in 278–80
    stress and 268–69, 273–77
    tenets 266–68
    theories 268–69
developmental systems theory 268–69
dexamethasone 657–58
DHEA (dehydroepiandrosterone) 465–66,
    470
diabetes mellitus
    comorbidity with PTSD 320
    type 2, 315, 317
*Diagnostic and Statistical Manual of Mental
    Disorders* (*DSM*) 30, 674
*Diagnostic and Statistical Manual of
    Mental Disorders*, fifth edition
    (*DSM-5*) 184, 221
    definition of ASD 243–44
    definition of PTSD 242, 244, 322
    diagnostic criteria for ASD 674
    diagnostic criteria for PTSD 628, 674
    preschool criteria for PTSD 242–43
*Diagnostic and Statistical Manual of
    Mental Disorders*, fourth edition
    (*DSM-IV*) 242
*Diagnostic and Statistical Manual of
    Mental Disorders*, third edition
    (*DSM-III*) 242
diagnostic approaches 628–29
Dialectical Behavior Therapy 119
diaries, daily 34–35
diathesis-stress models 397–401, 495–96
    conceptual recommendations 729–30
    for depression 446
    for eating disorders 222–23, 233–34
    future directions 407
    gender differences 405
    for problem behaviors 602
differential equations
    individual-difference latent stochastic
        dynamical 82–83
    nonlinear unidimensional 88–89, 89f
    Ornstein-Uhlenbeck 81, 83, 92
    simple first-order linear model for
        coping propensity 83–85, 84f
differential susceptibility 446,
    602–3, 610
    autonomic stress reactivity and 604–5
    evolutionary-developmental model
        of 602
    HPA reactivity and 607–10

veterans. *See also* military
PTSD in 246–47, 318
VA/DoD Clinical Practice
Guidelines 675, 680–81
women 227, 247
victimization, peer 549
videoteleconferencing 676
Vietnam War veterans 246–47, 318
vigilance 372
vigilant stress response pattern 505,
505*t*, 613–16
violence
community 249–50, 271
criminal 250
developmental effects 271, 279
family 271
intimate partner violence 251–52
sexual 251
Violence Exposure Scale for
Children - Revised 65*t*
Virginia Tech University shootings 249
vitamin C 650
vitamin D 649, 659
vitamin D3 (cholecalciferol) 649
vitamin E 650
voxel-based morphometry (VBM) 436
VTC. *See* videoteleconferencing
vulnerability 603
cognitive 380–81
genetic 162
personality-stress models 397–413
to psychopathology 372

to psychosis risk 162
shared 323
stress 112
to stress sensitivity 162

W

war-related trauma 246–47
water contamination 248–49
weight-based teasing 231
weight teasing 230
Weiner, Herbert 7
white matter 441–42, 448
Whites 112–13, 169
Wiener-process models 83
withdrawal/negative affect stage of alcohol
addiction 199–200, 200*f*, 212
animal models 202–3, 205
brain stress systems 209–10
glucocorticoid receptor activity
alterations 205
neural circuitry associated with
210–11, 211*f*
WM. *See* working memory
women. *See also* gender differences
in military 227, 256
mothers' parenting 301–2
perinatal depression 287–312
postnatal depression 288
postpartum depression 287–88
prenatal health behaviors 296
PTSD in 247
selection into abusive relationships 334

sexual trauma 227
veterans 227, 247
working memory 376–77
difficulties 377–78
psychopathology 377–78
updating 376–77
World Health Organization
(WHO) 250–51
writing
benefit-finding 706–7,
707*b*, 714–16
emotional disclosure 706
evaluative comments 12–13, 16–17,
19–20
expressive 705–24, 706*b*
number, duration, and spacing of
sessions 708–9
positive 715–16
about positive experiences 706–7,
707*b*
putting feelings into words 717–18
sense-making 715
therapeutic 706

Y

youth. *See also* adolescents
ASD in 250, 254–55
gunshot injuries in 250
prevention of depression
for 343–44
PTSD in 250, 254–55, 257
youth depressive disorder 334